D1627361

The **R&A**

GOLFER'S HANDBOOK 2009

EDITOR RENTON LAIDLAW

The R&A is golf's world rules and development body and organiser of The Open Championship. It operates with the consent of more than 130 national and international, amateur and professional organisations, from over 120 countries and on behalf of an estimated 30 million golfers in Europe, Africa, Asia–Pacific and The Americas (outside the USA and Mexico). The United States Golf Association (USGA) is the game's governing body in the United States and Mexico.

MACMILLAN

First published 1984 by Macmillan
This edition published 2009 by Macmillan
an imprint of Pan Macmillan Ltd
Pan Macmillan, 20 New Wharf Road, London N1 9RR
Basingstoke and Oxford
Associated companies throughout the world
www.panmacmillan.com

ISBN: 978-0-230-7360-23 (Cloth)

ISBN: 978-0-230-7360-47 (Paper laminate case)

Copyright © Macmillan London Limited 1984, 1985, 1986
Macmillan Press Limited 1987, 1988, 1989, 1990, 1991, 1992
Pan Macmillan 1993, 1994
Macmillan General Books 1995, 1996, 1997, 1998, 1999, 2000
Macmillan Publishers Ltd 2001, 2002, 2003, 2004, 2005, 2006, 2007, 2008, 2009

The right of the editor to be identified as the
author of this work has been asserted by him in accordance
with the Copyright, Designs and Patents Act 1988.

All rights reserved. No part of this publication may be
reproduced, stored in or introduced into a retrieval system, or
transmitted, in any form, or by any means (electronic, mechanical,
photocopying, recording or otherwise) without the prior written
permission of the publisher. Any person who does any unauthorized
act in relation to this publication may be liable to criminal
prosecution and civil claims for damages.

Note
Whilst every care has been taken in compiling the information contained in
this book, the Publishers, Editor and Sponsors accept no responsibility for
any errors or omissions.

Correspondence
Letters on editorial matters should be addressed to:
The Editor, The R&A Golfer's Handbook, Pan Macmillan,
20 New Wharf Road, London N1 9RR

The information on golf courses and clubs contained in
this Handbook is available for purchase on disk as
mailing labels. For further information please
e-mail golfmailing@macmillan.co.uk

9 8 7 6 5 4 3 2 1

A CIP catalogue record for this book is available from the British Library

Designed and typeset by Penrose Typography, Maidstone, Kent

Printed and bound in Great Britain by Mackays of Chatham plc, Chatham, Kent

Contents

Part III Women's Professional Events

Part IV Men's Amateur Events

Part V Women's Amateur Events

Part VI Mixed Men's and Women's Amateur Tournaments

Part VII Junior Tournaments and Events

Hamish Ritchie is elected Captain of the Royal and Ancient Golf Club of St Andrews

© GSR Photographic

Retired insurance broker Hamish Ritchie is the Royal and Ancient Golf Club of St Andrews Captain for 2008–2009. Born in Milngavie near Glasgow but now living in Buckinghamshire he has been a member of the club since 1974 and served on the General Committee from 1994 to 1998. Educated at Loretto and at Christ Church, Oxford, he was an Oxford Blue, is a former captain of the Oxford University Golf Club and a member of the Oxford and Cambridge Golfing Society which he captained from 1994 to 1996. A former captain and chairman of Denham he is also a member at Rye, the Duke's Course at St Andrews and the Chechessee Creek Club and plays off 12.

Dedicated Irishman gets a taste for the majors

Renton Laidlaw looks back on a glorious golfing year

There are years when the naming of the Golfer of the Year is a comparatively simple task and 2008 was one of them with Padraig Harrington top of the list with his incredible back-to-back major successes in The Open at wild and windy Royal Birkdale and at Oakmont in the US PGA Championship where he was hunted down by Sergio García and another former Open champion, Ben Curtis

Of course García's rise to No. 2 in the world helped by wins in America, Asia and Europe was highly creditable and there was much to commend the consistency of European No. 1 Robert Karlsson who became the first and, as it turns out, the last person to win the European Money list, renamed The Race to Dubai this year.

Of course we thrilled at the "turn-back-the-clock" performances of Greg Norman in mid-summer, marvelled at the amazing performances of the Korean Ji-Yai Shin, not least in the Ricoh British Women's Open, and were stunned by the courageous and hopefully not foolhardy play by Tiger Woods when winning the US Open on one leg at Torrey Pines, but it is Harrington who wins top spot.

We all know about his dedication – the long hours he spends on the practice ground with coach and friend Bob Torrance – which has enabled him to reach new heights but it was the manner of his wins that stood out in 2008 and the modest way he handled himself afterwards that impressed. He played so relentlessly that he never looked like losing out to Ian Poulter or Greg Norman at Royal Birkdale and at Oakland Hills he broke Sergio García's heart for a second time just as he had at

Carnoustie a year earlier with a polished back nine and a winning last day 66. This was a vintage "Boy's Paper" golfing adventure which enabled Harrington to write his own chapter in the record books.

He became the first European golfer to win The Open and the US PGA back to back – indeed any two majors consecutively for that matter. He was the first European since Tommy Armour in 1933 to win the US PGA and the first Irishman to win two Opens and a US PGA. They were performances that catapulted him to a new level and half-way to a Grand Slam. Why can't he join Gary Player, Gene Sarazen, Ben Hogan, Jack Nicklaus and Tiger Woods as a winner of all four majors? He has only to pick up a Green Jacket at Augusta and win the US Open to achieve what he thought once was the impossible dream. Not any more for the popular Irishman.

While Harrington delighted us with his golf, so too did Sergio García who has not yet won a major but is unlikely to end his career without one. García is a different, a better player these days. He has a more mature attitude and his consistency and overall play are to be admired. In 2008 he won the Players' Championship, often regarded these days as the fifth unofficial major, and took titles in both Europe, where he now has his own event in Spain, and in Asia.

Quietly and effectively, the Spanish live-wire, whose hero has long been Severiano Ballesteros, climbed above Adam Scott, Jim Furyk, Ernie Els and Vijay Singh in the world rankings although the Fijian, helped by two Fedex Cup wins, topped the money list in the United States but did not win the Vardon

Padraig Harrington

Sergio García

Robert Karlsson

© Phil Sheldon/Getty Images

Tiger Woods

Ji-Yai Shin

Greg Norman

Trophy that goes to the player with the lowest scoring average for the season. García won that with 69.65.

In Europe, the Vardon Trophy goes to the golfer who wins most money on Tour and that award went to Robert Karlsson after a year long battle with Miguel Angel Jiménez, Lee Westwood and Harrington, all of whom had the chance to overtake him at the end of the season at the 21st and last Volvo Masters at Valderrama although it is hard to imagine that no tournaments will be played in future on a course which has played such an important part in the fabric of the Tour. Paraphrasing General McArthur, I am sure the Tour will be back there.

Meanwhile Volvo are staying in the south of Spain to sponsor a revamped match-play competition designed to take over from the long-running World Match-play Championship started by Mark McCormack in 1964 but which, sadly, has run its course.

No Swede ever won the Vadon Trophy but the tall stylish Karlsson from the small town of Katrinholm finished No. 1 in Europe. He was helped by 12 top ten finishes (ironically one less than Westwood achieved) and two late season wins. Like García he too has become a much more competent performer now that he has adopted a less self-critical approach.

No doubt inspired, like García, by what Harrington has achieved, Karlsson will be chasing his first major title in 2009 and hoping also that Tiger will be back to further test him. What Tiger manages to achieve this year we shall have to wait and see. Similar knee trouble to that experienced by Woods, caused a dramatic slump in Ernie Els' form although, hopefully now that he is more settled in America, he may come roaring back to become a serious major title contender again.

Of course, many might feel that World No.1 Woods is a worthy Golfer of the Year because of the way he managed on virtually one leg to win his 14th major at Torrey Pines, a course on which he had played and won on since a youngster. What the golf world is hoping is that his determination to play there last year despite medical advice that he could do even further damage to the knee by play-

ing will not prevent his resuming his dominant role and hamper his bid to top Jack Nicklaus' 18 majors record. He needs five more!

If Woods' performance was gutsy then Greg Norman's was quite frankly unbelievable. He played in The Open in order to warm up for the Senior Open at Royal Troon the following week then came within a whisker of winning the main event! He led with nine to play before running out of steam in his bid to become the oldest winner. Recently married to former tennis ace Chris Evert, Norman who went on to finish fourth in the Senior Open and then third the following week in the US Senior Open behind Eduardo Romero, put it all down to being happier than ever with his life. Now more used to deciding whether a new business deal is worth pursuing rather than what line a putt might be, Norman thrilled the older generation as he took on golfers half his age including Chris Wood who, ten years after Justin Rose picked up the Silver Medal as leading amateur and turned professional, did the same.

Shin has had another fantastic year, winning her first major and making history by completing a first ever victory in all three of the Korean LPGA's Grand Slam events. She has become a prolific winner and it will be interesting to see how the youngster, who gave up golf for a year to look after her brother after her mother died, will fare in America where she will not feel homesick because Koreans are doing so well there whether they can speak English or not!

Many others merited consideration in 2008 – Bernhard Langer, one of golf's ultimate professionals taking top spot on the Champions Tour money list, Anthony Kim winning twice and being a star of the winning American Ryder Cup side whose captain Paul Azinger did such a wonderful job in galvanising his team into a winning combination at a time when losing was not an option. Then there was the unheralded Scottish trio who went to Adelaide and came back with the Eisenhower Trophy as World Amateur team champions ... fantastic, but in the end Harrington's winning of two majors was more than outstanding, it was phenomenal.

Double major winner Padraig claims a place at the top table

John Huggan on the Dubliner's inspirational season

There was a time, of course, when American domination (and European humiliation) at the highest level of professional golf was all but complete. As recently as 1979, just before the genius that was Seve Ballesteros broke the mould and won the first of what would be five majors, it was the case that only one European, Tony Jacklin, had been Open Champion in almost 30 years; that only Jacklin had won the US Open in the previous half century; that no European had finished first in a USPGA Championship since 1931; and that no one from the old world had ever been helped into a Green Jacket at the Masters. And the Ryder Cup? Let's not go there.

Things changed quickly, of course. Inspired by the example of the great and charismatic Spaniard, Europe's very best soon learned that the Americans were beatable, both individually and collectively. Since Ballesteros won The Open at Royal Lytham three decades ago, as many as seven Europeans have won at least one of golf's four most important events and Europe has seven times defeated the US in the Ryder Cup.

More recently, the Grand Slam picture has been more evenly balanced. Well, sort of. If one assumes that Tiger Woods is a continent by himself – or that, as rumoured, the world's best golfer is indeed from another planet – then majors in the 21st century have been spread more equitably. Since the beginning of 2000, Woods has picked up 12, the rest of America has 11, the rest of the world ten and Europe only three.

Significantly, those three European victories have all come in the last 18 months and all were recorded by one man, Padraig Harrington. Could it be, as they

were by Ballesteros, that the rest of Europe's best will be inspired by their compatriot's example and step up to the game's top table? One who seems ready to move up a level is Robert Karlsson, who finished top of the last-ever European Tour Order of Merit. The lanky Swede recorded top 20 finishes in all four of 2008's majors – three of those top tens.

Time will tell on that one, but for now the four majors reflect only the fact that golf's sharpest end has never before been more cosmopolitan. In 2008, a South African, Trevor Immelman, a one-legged Woods and Harrington (twice) emerged as the winners. Which, if it proves anything, it is that once Woods is eliminated from the majors equation – as he was through injury from last year's Open and USPGA – then the rest of the world is only too ready and willing to take on and beat America's finest.

Increased representation has much to do with that phenomenon. Take the USPGA Championship, once the most insular of the three American majors. Of the 73 players who made the cut at

Determined Padraig Harrington produced two of the most inspired performances to win back-to-back majors and make European golfing history

© Hugh Routledge/Phil Sheldon Golf Picture Library

Trevor Immelman, who led from start to finish to join Gary Player in the Champions' Locker Room, receives the Green Jacket from Zach Johnson

the 12-foot putt he made on the 72nd green to tie Mediate.

With Woods undergoing season-ending surgery only days after his third US Open win and so temporarily out of the Grand Slam picture, an opportunity arose for those who aspire to similar greatness. And it was Harrington who answered the call. Overcoming an injury of his own – pain in his right elbow had his defence of The Open title in doubt right up until the last minute – the Irishman played Woods-like golf over the second nine holes of the final round to put an end to the

Oakland Hills in 2008, less than half – 35 – were Americans. Eleven years earlier at Winged Foot, 56 of the 77 weekend qualifiers were nephews of Uncle Sam. In 1987 at PGA National only nine of those who played the final two rounds were not US-born. And in 1977, 69 of the 71 who made the cut were American.

Alongside such familiarity has come boldness, with Immelman's '08 Masters victory a perfect, if unexpected, example. With Woods snapping at his heels, the 28-year old Springbok played some superbly consistent golf over the closing 18-holes, his patience and precise ball striking an example to all who aspire to major championship success. Perhaps even more impressive was the fact that, four weeks before making his way to Augusta National, the two-time South African Open champion was in hospital recovering from the removal of what was thankfully a benign tumour.

If that was remarkable enough, it was nothing compared to the performance turned in by Woods two months later, when the US Open made its maiden visit to Torrey Pines. Battling what was eventually revealed to be a chronic injury to the anterior cruciate ligament in his left knee, the now 14-time major champion impressed even himself by first tying Rocco Mediate over 72-holes, then seeing off his compatriot in the 18-hole play-off.

En route to what Woods called "in the circumstances, my greatest ever victory," he was truly inspired. Few will ever forget the brace of eagles he recorded in the last six holes of his third round or

fairytale-like challenge of Greg Norman.

The highlight of that final back nine played in testing blustery condition conditions that only seemed nice in comparison with the Armageddon-like weather preceding it was the 5-wood Harrington struck from a tricky downhill lie to the elusive and controversially re-modelled penultimate green. Already armed with what appeared to be a winning

Tiger Woods won his 14th major on one leg at Torrey Pines

lead, the Irishman was brave enough and talented enough to not only find the putting surface but hit the ball so close to the cup as to guarantee an easy eagle. It was surely one of the top five shots struck by anyone all year.

"I convinced myself, as you can when you are winning tournaments, that the down-slope was a help to me," said the two-time champion. "I said, well this is great. I know it is going to come out low so I cannot get it in the air."

Still, for all Harrington's heroics, the star of the Birkdale show for long enough was Norman.

For the first three and a half days at Royal Birkdale, the 53-year old Australian played like a man half his age. Two shots clear with 18-holes to play, he was still one ahead with nine to go. That the two-time Open winner eventually faded to a closing 77 and a tie for third place six shots behind Harrington did little to diminish the enormity of his accomplishment. In golf's most unforgiving environment – made even more so by the severity of the weather – Norman was good enough to beat all but two of the world's best players and, happily, qualify for what will surely be an emotional and nostalgic return to Augusta National for the 2009 Masters, an event in which he has been runner-up four times.

In the end, Harrington was just too good for the Great White Shark and so it proved again three weeks later in Detroit when the 37-year old Dubliner held off a strong challenge from another old adversary, Sergio García, to become the first European golfer in almost 80 years to lift the enormous Wanamaker Trophy. Again too, Harrington was almost Woods-like in the way he clinched his third major title, holing out resolutely

Europe's Golfer of the Year Padraig Harrington with the USPGA trophy – his second major victory in 2008

© Liz Anthony/Phil Sheldon Golf Picture Library

for a crucial par-birdie-par finish that was, just as at Carnoustie in the 2007 Open, enough to break the Spaniard's heart.

Three majors in 13 months is an impressive haul, but it is perhaps as well to remember that only in one of those did Harrington finish ahead of Woods. The American, hopefully back to full fitness, remains the yardstick by which all contemporary major champions are measured.

Eleven made the cut in all four men's majors

	Masters	US Open	The Open	USPGA
Robert Allenby (AUS)	T42	T18	T7	T31
Stuart Appleby (AUS)	T14	T36	T51	T15
Paul Casey (ENG)	T11	T65	T76	T15
Jim Furyk (USA)	T33	T36	T5	T29
Retief Goosen (RSA)	T17	T14	T32	T24
Padraig Harrington (IRL)	T5	T36	1	1
Robert Karlsson (SWE)	T8	T4	T7	T20
Justin Leonard (USA)	T20	T36	T16	T58
Phil Mickelson (USA)	T5	T18	T19	T7
Andres Romero (ARG)	T8	T36	T32	T7
Mike Weir (CAN)	T17	T18	T39	T42

Harrington wins European Shot of the Year

Padraig Harrington's favourite club in his bag is his 5-wood and he used it great effect at The Open last July en route to the successful defence of his title. The 37-year-old from Dublin used it to hit a glorious second shot at the par 5 71st hole on the final day at Royal Birkdale to set up an eagle.

In fact he hit his 5-wood twice at the hole because he used it off the tee and was left with 220 yards to the green and 249 yards to the flag as he battled with Greg Norman and Ian Poulter for the title.

He knew he could make a birdie if he used the 5-wood a second time. "I was worried if I laid up and made par it was likely to be very close at the finish because I would be giving Greg a great chance to get to within a shot of me and that is not comfortable going down the last," he recalled.

He decided to go for it. With trouble on the right and left he felt a low shot would be an advantage. " It was always a worrying shot but once I hit it I knew it was perfect. It felt good," he says. Even his caddie said "good shot" to him before the ball had hit the green and stopped rolling. That was unusual.

The big bonus was that it finished three feet from the pin. " I would have been happy to have been on the green and taking my chance at two putting for a birdie but the eagle I made was even better. You cannot have too big a lead going down the 18th in a major. In the end Harrington won by four shots!

Although Graeme McDowell's 7-iron second shot at the third extra hole against Jeev Milkha Singh which helped him win the Ballantine's Championship in Korea was deemed the second best shot of the year, Harrington's tee shot at the 71st hole of the US PGA Championship came third. He hit it to eight feet and made a birdie 2 helping him to victory in a tense last day battle with former Open champion Ben Curtis and Sergio García whom he beat in a play-off for The Open in 2007 at Carnoustie.

Top ranked Swedish pair win World Cup of Golf

European No. 1 Robert Karlsson and his Ryder Cup colleague Henrik Stenson were favourites to win the World Cup of Golf at Mission Hills in China and duly took the trophy back to Sweden for only the second time since the event was first played in 1953. They shared a first prize of $1.7 million

The Swedes, the highest ranked pair in the competition – they are sixth and 12th respectively in the world rankings – produced a dramatic last day foursomes performance with a nine-birdie 63 for a winning total of 27-under-par 261 – three better than the Spaniards Miguel Angel Jiménez and Pablo Larrazabal who had led with Australians Brendan Jones and Richard Green going into the final day. The Australians finished third tied with the Japanese pair Ryuji Imaada and Toru Taniguchi.

The only other time the Swedes won was in 1991 when Per-Ulrick Johansson and Anders Forsbrand were successful in Rome. This latest victory gave Karlsson a fitting end to a wonderful season and a first win of the season for his Ryder Cup partner Stenson who went on to win the first prize of $1.2 million in the Nedbank Challenge in South Africa by nine shots with a 21 under par score of 267. Kenny Perry came second and Karlsson third.

Valhalla victory ends America's Ryder Cup nightmare

Mike Aitken on another classic shot making encounter

For an occasion which is years in the planning, delivers three days of the most intense competition in all of sport and demands endless hours of commitment on the course from the players, the Ryder Cup has always been about great moments.

When you look back at the treasured duels between Europe and the USA for Samuel Ryder's trophy, it's the shotmaking skills which live on most vividly in the memory. By way of pertinent examples, just think of that astonishing 3-wood from a fairway bunker on the home hole at Palm Beach Gardens in 1983 which Seve Ballesteros executed to earn a half with Fuzzy Zoeller or Paul Casey's ace with a 4-iron on the 213 yard 14th at the K Club in 2006 that helped the English pair of Casey and David Howell defeat Stewart Cink and Zach Johnson.

In this regard, the 2008 staging of the match at Valhalla in Louisville, Kentucky, echoed the heritage of all the other contests held since 1927, only more so. From the second Padraig Harrington got the match underway on Friday morning by splitting the first fairway to the ebullient denouement on Sunday afternoon when Jim Furyk picked up a conceded putt, the 37th duel between some of the world's most gifted golfers was awash with the bravado generated by thrilling play.

Thanks to Paul Azinger's gritty and thoughtful brand of captaincy, America rediscovered how to enjoy themselves against Europe and hit plenty of great shots along the way. The USA, with a telling blend of youth and experience, won the cup back for the first time since 1999 by the margin of 16½–11½ after learning to trust a sense of adventure.

According to Jim Furyk, a veteran of many sore losses at the hands of Europe, the fresh faces on the American side deserved thanks for restoring the home side's pride. "When you're playing well, when you're ahead, when you're winning, you always have a lot more energy and always have that look of having fun and enjoying yourself," reflected the former US Open champion. "And when you're down, when you lose, when you're trying to come from behind, it's a lot more difficult to have a good time. The

The USA team celebrate their Louisville victory

© Tim Sloan/AFP/Getty Images

[rookies] brought a lot of enthusiasm. They infused just amazing energy into the crowd, into the team and won the majority of the points."

While he might be neither the most subtle nor thoughtful golfer on the planet, in many ways the colossal power of J.B. Holmes, one of three southerners on captain Azinger's team, was at the heart of America's convincing victory. Along with fellow Kentuckian Kenny Perry and Boo Weekley, Holmes galvanised the support of America's 13th man by turning up the volume to take advantage of their underdog status in the absence of the injured Tiger Woods.

Ian Poulter was a controversial captain's pick but he rewarded Nick Faldo's confidence with four and a half points

On Sunday, in his singles match against Søren Hansen, Holmes had already secured the 14th and 16th holes before he unleashed one of those no-holds barred 350 yard drives on the 17th. The Scottish vernacular would bequeath this mighty blow the admiring sobriquet of the full "simmet and drawers". Left with just 80 yards to the pin, Holmes confidently wedged the ball to two feet and clinched the point.

Of all the stunning shots struck by the inspired Weekley, none, perhaps, was finer than the swing from a bunker on the par 4 15th hole on Saturday. His escape from a trap located 153 yards from the green finished two feet from the cup and helped Weekley and Holmes defeat Lee Westwood and Hansen.

Remembering all the cuts and thrusts which the swordsmen threw at one another over five sessions of exhilarating action, surely the turning point arrived later on Saturday afternoon. Sergio García and Paul Casey came to the 18th all square in fourballs with Steve Stricker and Ben Curtis. Although the Spaniard was rarely at his best in Louisville, he

recaptured a spark in this game and made four birdies in six holes between the eighth and the 13th. Just when it seemed as if the advantage lay with Europe on the closing hole after Stricker had pushed his second shot into the nasty rough strewn mounding to the right of the green, the American finessed a delicate chip and run down the bank before holing a breathtaking putt from 15 feet. As García rued: "Every time we did something, they did something on top of us. It was very impressive."

Not that the USA enjoyed a monopoly on exhilarating shotmaking. Graeme McDowell, in the process of defeating Stewart Cink in singles, struck a 3 wood to the tenth green which was as pure as any fairway shot you'll ever see. Casey's long iron to the 18th green, that helped secure a half with Hunter Mahan in a compelling contest, was all the more notable for coming hard on the heels of the jaw-dropping 40 foot putt holed minutes earlier by the American from the front of the 17th green.

And, on Saturday, in the closing fourball match between Robert Karlsson and Henrik Stenson and Mahan and Phil Mickelson, Karlsson reeled off no fewer than six birdies on the back nine. The Swede even gave himself an eagle opportunity on the 18th thanks to a fantastic approach with a long iron to the back of the green, which spun back towards the hole and finished 15 feet from the cup.

Nor will anyone who followed the foursomes tie between Oliver Wilson and Stenson against Mickelson and Anthony Kim, who were four up after six holes, forget the moment on the 17th green when the rookie Englishman holed from 25 feet to bank the most improbable point of the week. As Nick Faldo observed: "The golf was pretty exceptional. We've all experienced something really quite amazing, the level these guys can play now."

In the end, the spoils went to the side which produced the best putting performance, a point which their team captain Azinger hoped would be the case. He was proved so right. The USA were peerless on Valhalla's greens while Europe needed more than Ian Poulter's velvety touch – the English wild card was the leading scorer on either team – rather than the out-of-sorts performances of Westwood, Garcia and Harrington, who didn't win any of their 12 ties.

The result, however, did much to ensure a lively future for the Cup. The Americans, defeated in previous three matches and five of the previous six were getting anxious and corporate America was showing signs that they were beginning to lose interest in the contest. Now, when the Ryder Cup returns to the Celtic Manor Resort in Wales next year, there will be no shortage of excitement as the Americans try to win for the first time in Europe since, believe it or not, 1993 and the home side do their best to win the Cup back.

Why it is important for golf to be part of the Olympics

Andy Farrell finds out the facts from Peter Dawson

There are countries where golf needs to and wants to grow but cannot because of a lack of finance. Yet this could change if the game was to be included in the Olympics. Although the competitors chasing the medals would be the world's top professionals rather than top amateurs what is important to remember is that the money that would become available as a result to golf's national bodies would go only to the amateurs playing at grass roots level. Joining the Olympic Movement is not just a chance worth taking, it is an opportunity not to be missed.

Copenhagen in October may not obviously feature alongside Augusta in April, Bethpage State Park in June, Turnberry in July or Hazeltine in August but the Danish capital will be the setting for one of the most important highlights of the 2009 golf season. This could be the most significant date for the game this year because it is then that the International Olympic Committee will decide not just where the 2016 Games will be held but whether golf will be one of up to two new sports to be included.

Having mounted its most serious, and unified, bid yet, it is entirely possible that golf will be offering gold medals in one of the following cities – Chicago, Madrid, Tokyo or Rio de Janeiro. Golf and the Olympics have not mixed since 1904, although over the last decade or so it has been an animated talking point within the sport. Now Peter Dawson, the chief executive of The R&A, whose role is to develop golf worldwide, says it is "comfortably the biggest grow-the-game opportunity" that currently exists.

To explain, Dawson states: "So many countries that are affiliated to The R&A and are members of the International Golf Federation tell us that government support, specifically financial support, of golf in their respective countries would grow enormously if the game was an Olympic sport. It is a simple fact – governments support Olympic sports far more than they do non-Olympic sports.

"Where golf is already strong the game has plateaued in terms of the number of participants, in fact keeping it at that level is a challenge," says Dawson. "The future growth is going to come in countries where golf is still relatively unimportant and, significantly, many of those countries are exactly

the ones where the government supports only Olympic sports."

More than a century on from the last Olympic golf tournament, the concept sounds perverse about a sport where its major championships, and events such as the Ryder Cup, offer such iconic moments. Yet golf only needs to look at tennis for a model of the benefits that can be derived from returning to the Olympic fold.

Peter Dawson

A decade after the reintroduction of tennis in 1988, Morocco, a country with hardly any tennis pedigree, now have three men in the top 50 in the world and Dawson adds: "My former opposite number at Wimbledon, Chris Gorringe, insists that Russian tennis would not be where it is today had the game not been included in the Olympics". Elena Dementieva, the women's champion in Beijing, says this: "If you ask anyone in the street in Russia what a Grand Slam is they have no idea but they know what winning a Gold Medal means. To be an Olympic champion would be the top of my career." Winning Wimbledon last summer might have been the pinnacle of Rafael Nadal's career but tears of joy flowed in Beijing when he received his Gold Medal and the Spanish national anthem was played. Roger Federer, whose pride in carrying the

Swiss flag at the Opening Ceremony in China was obvious, was equally delighted with a Gold in the doubles. "You could say the competitive golf landscape doesn't need the Olympics," adds Dawson, "but I believe this is a bigger deal to players than people might think."

Golf was first played at the second Olympiad, in Paris in 1900. American Charles Sand won the men's competition while his countrywoman, Margaret Abbott, who was studying art in the city with her novelist mother, took the women's title. She told relatives that her French competitors "apparently misunderstood the nature of the game scheduled for that day and turned up to play in high heels and tight skirts". Legend has it she died in 1955 still unaware she had competed at the Olympics.

Four years later, in St Louis, Canadian George Lyon won the gold and he travelled to London to defend the title in 1908. According to *The Complete Book of the Olympics*, all the British competitors boycotted the event due to an internal dispute leaving Lyon as the only competitor. He was offered the gold medal by default but refused to accept it and golf's Olympic sojourn came to an end ... until, perhaps, now.

Back in 2001 the game applied to be part of the Beijing Games. The bid failed because the International Golf Federation, led by The R&A and the United States Golf Association, was not representative of the professional game. An Olympic event would have been for amateurs only. Working on a seven-year lead-time, the IOC decided not to add any sports for 2012, in fact they dropped baseball and softball. This year seven sports are bidding for up to two slots in 2016 – golf, karate, roller sports, rugby sevens, squash, along with baseball and softballs which are re-applying.

So what has changed since 2001? "For golf to get back into the Olympics, the IOC made it very clear they wanted the top professionals," said Dawson. "They want the top players in any sport. Anyone who says the Olympics is for amateurs is not in touch with what is going on. The only amateur sport left in the Olympics I know about is boxing."

While recognised by the IOC, the International Golf Federation needed to widen its scope. It set up an Olympic Committee featuring representatives from the major championships and the professional tours. Some of these bodies, such as the women's circuits and the European Tour, were always enthusiastic supporters of the idea. "We deal with many different PGAs and National Associations around the world and they have all been urging us to bring golf into the Olympics," said George O'Grady, executive director of the European Tour.

The introduction of drug testing in 2008 was an important step forward but another problem has been the willingness of all the game's leaders to resolve the crucial issue of scheduling an Olympic tournament in an already crowded calendar. "We are through the battle of getting golf organisations interested in the Olympics," Dawson says: "We know everyone in golf is behind it, led by the administrators with the players, who have never had a chance to win a Gold Medal, coming along strongly behind. The women have been behind it for a while, the men increasingly so. We have just been through a filming process where all the top players have stated their support."

What does golf bring to the Olympics? "The ideals that make golf great line up well with the Olympic ideal according to Ty Votaw, a senior executive at the PGA Tour, and former commissioner of the LPGA, who has been seconded to the IGF to lead the bid. He and Dawson met IOC delegates and staff and talked to other sporting federations in Beijing last year.

As for the format of the actual competition, this had not been finalised but it looks like as if there will be individual men's and women's events, in separate weeks over four days at either strokeplay, or match-play, or a mixture of both with a strokeplay qualifying and then a knock-out format.

Bringing golf and the Olympics together is proving a unique challenge for Votaw because the two have existed separately for so long.

He insists: "If golf were to become part of the Olympics it would not. despite what has been said by many, take away from the other major championships. It would be in addition to and not necessarily more important than them. Other sports in the Olympics still have their own pinnacles, tennis with their Grand Slam events, the World Cup in soccer, the Tour de France in cycling. If Lorena Ochoa or KJ Choi were to win a Gold medal at the Olympics the reception they would receive and the headlines they would create in their home countries would be as big, if not bigger, than if they won a major."

Golf could not have two better advocates than Dawson and Votaw. "This is something we can achieve," Dawson said. "There is stiff competition but I think golf has a compelling case. Already this bid has strengthened the game in an organisational sense because getting all these bodies talking together is a great thing.

"If golf does not get in, we will have to take the view that golf is not likely to get in for quite some time. We would have to turn our minds then to persuading national governments that golf is worthy of support whether it is an Olympic sport or not. We will continue emphasising golf's strengths but that is much more difficult."

Tears as Sörenstam retires from the international scene

Lewine Mair highlights Annika's fabulous career

Not too many Carmelite nuns can have gone about their business more quietly and unostentatiously than Annika Sörenstam. The Swede retired at the end of 2008 from a career in which she won a glorious total of 89 championships around the world. These included 72 triumphs on the LPGA Tour and 10 majors.

Having spent long hours practising alongside Tiger Woods at Isleworth, Sörenstam was probably closer to him than she was to any of her sister competitors. Hence the reason that when she realised the time had come to call it a day, she told him before anyone else. Tiger made no attempt to suggest she should wait around to see if her mood changed. Instead, he merely checked that she was at peace with her decision.

For a long time, Sörentstam's career was on a par with Woods'. They used to compare notes on their respective majors and when, in 2005, Woods was the first to arrive at 10 major titles, he sent a text to Sorenstam which consisted of a succinct "10 – 9". Annika made it to ten in 2006 but by then Woods was well on his way to the 14-strong tally on which he signed off after winning the US Open virtually on one leg.

Annika was not long into her career when she came under the influence of Karl Enhager, the Swedish psychologist who, when he first looked in at golf from the outside, wondered what an earth it was that made golfers think that two putts per green were acceptable? "Why think in terms of two putts instead of one?" he asked. With this kind of thinking, he felt that sub-60 scores were by no means out of the question.

When I first saw Annika, she was a student at the University of Arizona and was playing as an amateur at the 1991 Ping tournament at Moon Valley. She opened with a 67 to take the lead and, when I asked what she was aiming for in golf, she replied, "I want to score in the 50s".

On the assumption that I had not heard her properly, I asked if she could repeat what she had said. This time, there was no question of wires being crossed. "I want to score in the 50s," she reiterated, very politely.

She never did achieve that with any regularity but when, back at Moon Valley in 2001, she did hand in a 59, she became known as "Ms 59".

Since Annika's brand of golf was so orderly and unemotional, she was never the right person to lead the singles' line-up in the 1996 Solheim Cup at St Pierre – even if her overall Solheim Cup points haul of 21 is the best yet. Europe were 9–7 ahead overnight and, while Annika defeated Pat Bradley by 2 and 1 in the top game, she did not make the kind of Laura Davies-type waves which would have inspired those in the matches behind.

Yet, to the surprise of many, the golfing occasion on which she shone more brightly than any other was on her one foray into the men's game – the 1993 Colonial tournament on the PGA Tour.

Since this was in the days before Michelle Wie competed in a spate of men's events, there was an extraordinary degree of interest in how she would fare. People poured in to watch and, when she opened with a 71, Aaron Barber, one of her playing companions, was moved to remark, "She's a machine. I've never played with someone who didn't miss a shot." Her second round was a 74

Annika Sorenstam at the Kapalua LPGA Classic in October, 2008

© Donald Miralle/Stringer/Getty Images

but, when she holed a long putt across the last green, she did so to tumultuous applause. Her tears at the end had less to do with disappointment at missing the cut – it came on 141 and she was 145 – than the fact that she had given her all.

Kenny Perry, when he collected the first prize, that week generously conceded, "People will say I won Annika's tournament".

Annika, who had by then turned herself from a relatively short hitter into a long one by dint of some judicious training, learned a lot about her game that week and duly put it into practice. In 2004, she won a remarkable ten of the 20 events she played around the world, with pride of place going to her seventh major, the McDonalds LPGA championship.

In 2005 there were two more majors to spice her 11 world-wide victories, while she picked up her 10th and presumably her final major – the US Open – in 2006. That was the year when she admitted that she sometimes had to pinch herself to believe what she had done. "There are lots of times when I ask myself, 'Why is this happening to me?' but I think you just have to enjoy it and be thankful. If I were to start analysing it too much, it might not go on happening."

Partly down to back problems, she did not win in America in 2007. But she returned with a vengeance to win three times at the start of the 2008 season before suddenly she realised that the magic had dissipated.

Hers was an emotional departure from the Ricoh Women's British Open at Sunningdale last August. As she left the 18th tee, the rain beating down on the umbrellas was louder than the applause but not for long. She hit a second to ten feet at this closing par five and, as she walked towards the green, she noticed a message on the main scoreboard reading "Annika, you will be missed". Having waved to the scoreboard's operators, she wiped away the first of not a few tears.

"There are times," she said, as she signed for her closing 68, "when there's a little opening in the focus and the feelings come out and this was one of them."

As Annika bowed out of the majors at Sunningdale, so there was a seismic shift from West to East as Ji Yai Shin made off with the £160,000 first prize, with 12 other Asian players finishing in the top 20. What is behind the meteoric progress of these Eastern stars?

The answer is pretty straightforward. They work at least twice as hard as everyone else, with eight hours a day being nothing out of the ordinary for your average Korean golfing aspirant.

If hard work is all it takes, this new breed could dominate for the foreseeable future. If, on the other hand, a golfer needs to be fuelled as much by enjoyment as industry, it makes sense to look to Sweden and the generation reared on glorious tales of Annika who continued to win before she finally called it a day as a full time competitor having made history by becoming the first woman professional to earn more than $22 million in prize-money, having won 89 titles including 72 on the LPGA circuit and 10 majors.

Sörenstam has been such a role model and inspiration for the Swedish women that it must have given her great satisfaction that the Swedes swept to success in the 2008 Women's World Amateur Team Championship for the Espirito Santo Trophy at the Grange Club in Adelaide. The Scandinavians – Anna Nordqvist, reigning European amateur champion Caroline Hedwall, and Pernilla Lindvall – led from start to finish overpowering Spain by 12 shots and the Americans by 14! Their winning 19-under-par 561 total was just three more than the lowest ever returned in the competition by the Americans in 1998. Their winning margin was the biggest since the Americans won in 1998.

Sweden, who are the only team to have finished in the top 10 in all 23 Espirito Santo competitions, won the event previously in 2004. Their wire to wire victory was the first since the Americans did so 18 years ago. The Swedish team captain Walter Danevid, who also coached the Swedish Eisenhower team to third place behind Scotland a week later, commented: "The team members are all very good players. They often say that this event features the stars of tomorrow and the team lived up to that."

© James Knowler/Getty Images

Sweden's victorious Espirito Santo team, Caroline Hedwall, Anna Nordqvist and Pernilla Lindvall

There even was a time when Seve was *persona non grata*

Art Spander on today's very different PGA Tour

Seve Ballesteros wasn't allowed. It was 1989, not that long ago, 20 years to be exact, but a distance of forever in golf. The PGA Tour had its rules, ridiculous as they might seem now. In those days the PGA Tour also had a touch of xenophobia.

So Seve Ballesteros, who already had played in five Tour tournaments, the maximum under a philosophy that seemed more protectionist than logical, was kept from entering The Memorial, Jack Nicklaus' famed event in Ohio. That Seve had won five majors had no bearing on the issue.

The incident distressed Tom Watson. "Once he wins five," argued Watson, condemning the regulation, "why the heck do you keep him off our tour? Our sponsors want to have Seve, who should have the right to play anywhere he wants." As golfers now do. Which is the reason the PGA Tour has in effect become the "We don't care where you grew up or learned the game, you're more than welcome" Tour. The World Tour. The best-golf-on-the-planet tour.

Neil Diamond, the singer-composer, had a song about immigration to the United States, with the lyrics, "… they're all coming to America." And that's what the golfers from Britain and South Africa and Australia and Argentina, Columbia and South Korea are doing.

A nation that, according to the inscription on the base of the Statue of Liberty, once opened its arms to the "huddled masses yearning to breathe free," now has opened them to sportsmen and athletes yearning to succeed. Look around. It's not just the PGA Tour, where the Harringtons and Singhs and Immelmans, and seemingly tons of Australians, have become stars. It's in baseball, where a third of the players are from the Caribbean nations. Or pro basketball with Yao Ming of China and Pau Gasol of Spain at the front of the invasion. Or ice hockey, with Russians and Swedes filling rosters.

America, for all its faults, always has been the land of opportunity. Let's see if you can make it. And if you can, then congratulations.

Hasn't golf always been inclusive rather than exclusive? Didn't Vardon and Ray come over figuratively to teach Americans a few things and later,

particularly from Carnoustie, Scottish pros come over to teach them literally? Didn't Ben Hogan, more than a half-century past, travel to Carnoustie for the 1953 Open and enthrall the citizenry with his Championship performance.

America is where the money is. America is where the Tiger is, although he has missed months because of that knee surgery. The PGA Tour is the proving ground, the place where you find out how well you can play and, no denying, how rich you can become.

The exceptions are the Ryder Cup and to a degree the Presidents Cup. Then nationalism becomes prevalent. Otherwise, golf is the most individual of games. Nobody worries about your passport, only your scorecard. If America falls for actors and actresses from the other side of the oceans, why then wouldn't it swoon over athletes

It wasn't easy for Severiano Ballesteros when he first went to America

© Augusta National/Getty Images

from afar? In his own way, Sergio García, is no different from Spanish countryman and Hollywood star Antonio Banderas, even if their occupations are at a variance. They have young women screeching on their behalf.

Greg Norman deserves some of the credit. He attempted to create a so-called World Tour. An Australian who had taken root in the United States, and for a while was the most compelling player on Tour, believed the game should flourish in coun-

Sergio Garcia has won more events in America than Europe

tries other than the United States. It has, although not quite as Norman suspected.

Television took over golf, the way it has taken over every sport in the US. Television meant huge rights fees. Huge rights fees meant enormous purses. Enormous purses meant international attention.

The word 'foreigners' is inappropriate. Something like 80 golfers from nations other than America are on the PGA Tour. Yet, some living in the US at least part of the time if not all of the time, are hardly foreigners. Rather they are golfers.

Tiger Woods won the US Open in 2008. The previous four years it was won by an Argentinian (Angel Cabrera, 2007), an Australian (Geoff Ogilvy,

2006), a New Zealander (Michael Campbell, 2005) and a South African (Retief Goosen, 2004). Nobody had to ask of these champions, "Who's he?"

Golf, someone suggested, is a world game, and Americans don't completely own it, but they do get it. In 2008, Trevor Immelman, a South African, albeit one who plays the US Tour, won the Masters, and Padraig Harrington, the Irishman, won the USPGA Championship after taking his second straight Open.

Tiger technically was the only American winner of a major. Except Immelman has a home in Florida. The way Geoff Ogilvy has a home in Arizona. As Ernie Els and Retief Goosen have homes in Florida. These players aren't strangers and they definitely aren't foreigners. Call them quasi-Americans.

Finchem needs the stars

Fred Couples used to refer to the homeland of the Presidents Cup International Team, invariably featuring Els, Goosen, Vijay Singh and Stuart Appleby, as Florida. Luke Donald went to university – Northwestern – in America, won the intercollegiate championship and now plays the PGA Tour. He's English. To a point. Donald resides in Florida and has an American girl friend. Paul Casey, another Englishman, went to Arizona State University and plays the Tour. Justin Rose and Ian Poulter are quintessentially English but are near neighbours at Lake Nona in Florida.

PGA Tour commissioner Tim Finchem, as his players, has been magnanimous in his approach. He wants stars. He needs them. He wants TV ratings. He wants the best players in the world on the Tour. That's what he has.

The next generation doesn't appear to be changing. Three of the past four US Amateurs, including 2008 when it was taken by the young New Zealander Danny Lee, were won by non-US golfers. The United States is the attraction, the PGA Tour the goal.

Seve Ballesteros must get wistful. The changes came too late for him but not for those who have followed.

It is perhaps symbolic that every PGA Tour tournament from the end of July to the end of September, a total of seven, was won by someone other than an American.

These days, golf doesn't care who you are, only what you shoot.

Fifty years on three Scots make history in Adelaide

Mark Garrod on a well-deserved Eisenhower Trophy win

A notable double was completed when Scotland became men's world amateur team champions for the first time in Adelaide, Australia, just 11 months after Colin Montgomerie and Marc Warren had given the country their maiden victory at the World Cup of Golf in China.

Callum Macaulay, Wallace Booth and Gavin Dear lifted the Eisenhower Trophy with a magnificent nine-stroke victory over the United States and it came 50 years after Australia came to Scotland and won the first Trophy match over the Old Course at St Andrews.

From 1958 to 2000 the four home nations competed as Great Britain and Ireland, winning in 1964, 1976, 1988 and 1998, but after the decision to let them "go it alone" none had managed a top three placing in the following three stagings of the event.

The Scottish trio's captain George Crawford hailed their victory as "an historic occasion", while Macaulay, runner-up in the individual standings to American world number two Rickie Fowler, commented: "We set out to try to win, but to go out and do it is unbelievable."

Tied at halfway, Scotland went four clear when Booth, brother of Curtis Cup player Carly, added a 69 at The Grange to his sparkling six under par 67 at Royal Adelaide and Dear contributed a 71. Two scores out of three count each day and the clinching stretch came when national champion Macaulay had four successive birdies early in the final round. In the windy conditions he finished with a one under 72 and Dear's 75 meant a 20 under par total of 560. Wales came 11th, England 14th and Ireland, home international champions, 22nd.

Danny Lee was part of the New Zealand side which tied with the Welsh, having gone into the final round in fourth spot. The year's outstanding amateur opened with three sub-par rounds, but closed with an 84. That, though, should not detract from a marvellous season for the 18-year-old Korean-born player, who took over from Tiger Woods as the youngest-ever winner of the United States amateur title when he defeated Trip Kuehne in the final and also won the Western Amateur, a double which earned

Wallace Booth, Gavin Dear and Callum Macaulay of Scotland, 2008 winners of the Eisenhower Trophy

© James Knowler/Getty Images

him the Mark H McCormack Medal as world number one.

At Turnberry, Reinier Saxton became only the second Dutchman to win the Amateur Championship, 17-year-old Tommy Fleetwood just failing in his bid to become the youngest-ever holder of the prestigious trophy. For the record, the other golfer from the Netherlands to win the title was Rolf Muntz in 1990.

While Saxton can look forward to competing in The Masters, Germany's Stephan Gross secured himself a place in the 2009 Open Championship by taking the European title, but the pair could not stop Great Britain and Ireland winning the St Andrews Trophy. The Continent of Europe were beaten 13½–10½ at Kingsbarns, with Wallace Booth winning all his four games.

Chris Wood takes the Silver Medal

One of the most immmpressive amateur performances of the year was produced by Chris Wood. As a 10-year-old Wood attended the 1998 Open and marvelled at the achievement of Justin Rose, who just before his 18th birthday, achieved world-wide fame by pitching in at the 72nd hole and finishing joint fourth. No amateur in any major has matched that performance since, but on the championship's return to Royal Birkdale a decade later, Wood came mighty close.

Chris Wood won the Silver Medal at The Open then quickly turned professional

Having qualified with nothing to spare at neighbouring Hillside, no special attention was paid to the 6ft 5in England international when he opened with a five over par 75. But a chip-in birdie completed a second round 70 – and brought back memories of Rose, of course – then, by adding a 73 Wood, who as a teenager was on Bristol City's books until an injury switched his focus from soccer to golf, found himself paired with Ian Poulter on the final day.

After a birdie on the ninth hole he was in third place only three off the lead and, while it was Poulter who finished runner-up to Padraig Harrington, Wood's joint fifth spot put him on the golfing map. "I didn't feel any pressure at all really apart from the first tee," he said of his closing 72. "I was looking at the leaderboards because I was just enjoying it – it's been the best week of my life."

Not that his sister Abi was aware of the enormity of it at first. She was travelling in Europe at the time and sent a text asking: "Are you at that Open thingy yet?"

Wood obviously collected the silver medal as leading amateur – but only by four strokes from Kent's Tom Sherreard, who came through regional and final qualifying for a noteworthy 19th place alongside, amongst others, Phil Mickelson and Masters champion Trevor Immelman.

Illness kills off the dream

Sherreard, who finished in spectacular eagle-birdie fashion, remained amateur, but a week later Wood announced he was turning professional. He even led the SAS Masters in Sweden, before a bout of food poisoning over the weekend crushed his hopes of a dream début.

Yorkshire's Danny Willett made an instant impact on his first European Tour appearance too. World-ranked number one at the time and a member of the 2007 Walker Cup side, Willett eagled his first hole, had another six holes later and was lying second to Lee Westwood after the first round of the Andalucian Open.

He finished 19th there and 10th in the Spanish Open at Seville, displays which prompted him to leave the amateur ranks in mid-season. Two more top 20 finishes quickly followed but playing so few events he had to attend the qualifying school.

Both Wood and Willett earned their cards and, along with Callum Macaulay, a member of Scotland's winning Eisenhower Trophy team who was also successful, were playing on the 2009 European Tour's Race to Dubai.

© Sheldon Golf Picture Library

Danny Lee wins McCormack Medal – see page 252

Nowhere is the game growing faster than in the Far East

Spencer Robinson on Asia's remarkable boom

"The journey of a thousand miles must begin with a single step." So says a famous Chinese proverb. Well, after years of baby steps, there is strong evidence to suggest that Asia is finally set fair for a giant leap that will see the world's most buoyant continent establish itself as a *bona fide* global golfing force.

For so long labelled the exclusive preserve of the region's rich and well-to-do, the Royal and Ancient game is now being embraced across Asia.

While the lack of public facilities means it's premature to describe golf as a sport for the masses, the wide acceptance of the game as a "worthy activity" and its importance as a revenue generator through golf tourism have significantly raised its profile. So, too, have the performances of Asian players on the world stage.

Until "Mr" Lu Liang-huan doffed his pork-pie hat with such *élan* at Royal Birkdale when finishing runner-up to Lee Trevino in the 1972 Open Championship, there was little awareness either of golf in Asia or Asian golfers.

Almost 40 years on, Asian women dominate the US LPGA Tour, the premier playground for the world's pre-eminent female golfers, while their male counterparts are finally establishing a foothold in the upper echelons of the game.

While Choi Kyung-ju, or KJ as he is better known, has been a serial winner in America over the past five years and has contended for The Open Championship, we are now seeing the emergence of a high-quality supporting cast led by Indians Jeev Milkha Singh and Jyoti Randhawa and Thais Prayad Marksaeng and Thongchai Jaidee and Liang Wen-chong of China.

Liang is the pin-up boy of golf in the People's Republic, the world's most populous country. He's already won a European Tour event – the Singapore Masters in 2007 – that helped him to top the Asian Tour Order of Merit standings. That, in turn, earned him starts at the US Masters and The Open Championship in 2008, the first player from his country to appear in the world's oldest golfing event.

"I'm sure he'll be the first of many," says Duncan Weir, The R&A's Director of Golf Develop-ment. The time will come, too, says Weir, when an Asian will win The Open. "My personal view is that it's quite close. You're seeing good players coming out of India, Korea and surely the Chinese to come. It will happen and it will be great to see."

As well as teenage prodigies such as Japan's Ryo Ishikawa and Korean Noh Seung-yul, twentysome-things Ben Leong of Malaysia and Thai Chinnarat Phadungsil, both in their 20's, are names to remem-ber.

Across the length and breadth of Asia, national golfing associations are starting to reap the divi-dends of structured junior programmes set up since the turn of the century. Meanwhile, more Asians are making their way through the acclaimed American college golf system.

Nick Faldo holds a children's clinic during the 2007 Faldo Series Asia final in Mission Hills.

©Getty Images

Consider also the reach of the HSBC China Junior Golf Programme, launched in conjunction with the China Golf Association in 2007. As well as a mini-tour of six regular stops and a final, the programme is part of a strategy that includes a series of summer and winter golf camps aimed at introducing youngsters to the sport and commencing golf training in schools in Beijing, Yunnan, Hefei and Shanghai.

With PE teachers being supplied with equipment and coached in the art of coaching, it is estimated that at least 30,000 children in China touched a golf club for the first time in their school in 2008. Other programmes around Asia are also in place to identify and nurture potential champions.

In the women's game, we've seen a slew of stars following in the footsteps of Se Ri Pak, the lady credited with sparking the remarkable surge in popularity of golf among girls in Asia in general and Korea in particular.

Inbee Park was aged nine when Pak won the US Women's Open in 1998. Ten years on, Park herself savoured success in the prestigious Major championship.

Reflecting on that victory, Park, the youngest winner of the US Women's Open, said: "I thank Se-ri for what she's done for Korean golf. Ten years ago I was watching her winning this event on TV. I didn't know anything about golf then.

"It was very impressive for a little girl and just looking at her I thought I could do it, too. So I picked up a golf club a couple of days after that. Se-ri inspired a lot of girls in Korea and Asia. A lot of them started playing golf because of her."

Now there are literally hundreds queuing up for a shot at fairway fame and fortune. Listen to Annika Sörenstam. "If you watch the Korean LPGA there is tremendous talent – and they all want to be out here (on the LPGA Tour). It's going to be a con-tinuous growth of Asians," insists the Swede.

It's not only Asia's female golfing professionals who set new benchmarks in excellence. Vying with Park and fellow 2008 Major winners Yani Tseng and Ji-Yai Shin (winner of the Ricoh Women's British Open at Sunningdale), for one of the golfing achievements of the year was Moriya Jutanugarn.

The 13-year-old Thai created a notable slice of golfing history when she defied stiff breezes at the Hesketh Golf Club in Southport to win The R&A Junior Open. Bangkok-based Moriya, a scratch handicapper, entered the record books as the first female winner of the tournament that traditionally precedes The Open Championship every two years.

Meanwhile, the men's Asian Tour continues to make steady strides. In 2008 its schedule was made up of 30 tournaments, offering total purses of almost US$40 million.

While the lion's share of those funds came from co-sanctioned events with Europe and Japan, officials are encouraged by the fact that the Tour visited 14 countries or territories – Brunei, Cambodia, China, Chinese Taipei, Hong Kong, India, Indonesia, Korea, Macau, Malaysia, the Philippines, Singapore, Thailand and Vietnam. In 2009 the Tour will break new ground when it co-sanctions the Omega European Masters in Switzerland.

Kyi Hla Han, the Asian Tour's executive chairman, said: "It is a terrific milestone for the Asian Tour. I believe it will pave the way for our Tour and playing members to enjoy greater achievements."

In addition to the Asian Tour, there are also now burgeoning domestic professional circuits in China, India, Korea and Thailand while the 10-leg ASEAN Tour, set up to offer increased playing opportunities for local players starved of tournament exposure, is entering its third season. No wonder optimism in Asian golfing circles is at an all-time high.

Fasten your seat belts as Asia embarks on a new, exciting phase in that journey of a thousand miles.

© Getty Images

The Asian team that beat an International side in the 2007 Lexus Cup. They were not so fortunate last year

How a lad from Scunthorpe inspired a golfing generation

Bill Elliott on Tony Jacklin's pivotal role in Europe

July 1969 was some month. Buzz Aldrin played golf on the Moon while back on Earth Tony Jacklin was, figuratively, over the same Moon when he ended a weary 17 year wait for British fans by winning The Open at Royal Lytham and St Annes.

His seven iron approach after a drive that split the fairway was followed by a 25 foot putt that finished inches from the hole allowing Henry Longhurst to say in hushed tones on BBC Television that "here was the shortest putt ever to win the Championship".

Forty years ago Jacklin was just 25 years old and Britain was a very different place to what it is today. For those of us who were there at Lytham that momentous afternoon it may seem as if it were yesterday or at least last week but truth is it was an age ago. Now here we are striding past the foothills of the 21st Century, lives hitched to computers, a gallon of petrol costing darn close to what many people considered a half-decent weekly wage in 1969.

When The Open begins at Turnberry this summer Jacko will be 65 – he was born on July 7, 1944 – and will be entitled to have his pension sent over to his home in southern Florida. From Scunthorpe, where he grew up, to Florida has been some trip, a journey that has embraced some glorious times and some great sadness as well.

What is beyond doubt, however, is that Jacklin was a pivotal figure in the popularising of golf not just in Britain but throughout Europe. Without his involvement in the embryonic European Tour there would be so much less to savour. He jump-started the whole shebang.

This was not just because he was able to play the game to a sublime level; not just because he won that Open and followed up the following year with victory in the United States Open but because Tony Jacklin brought glamour, excitement and an undiluted personality to the party.

He was a sports star who made news on the front pages of newspapers as well as on the back. He was the first golfer to reach out and touch those people who instinctively regarded the grand, old game as something the others played. The way he dressed and acted fitted the changing times perfectly. His

personal musical preference may have been more Frank Sinatra than Elvis or The Beatles but his public image was on the sharp side of rock'n'roll.

When the European Tour was launched in 1972 it was fired forward on the shoulders of his achievements. John Jacobs, the man charged with this launch, made Jacklin's inclusion the centre of his marketing strategy. To do this an agreement was reached whereby he would be paid appearance money for performing throughout Europe. Subsequently this cash template may have brought its own problems for the Tour but it was understandable it should be officially agreed then.

After all Jacklin, at the time, was a star member of the American circuit guaranteed to earn serious prize-money. Europe, relatively, was offering peanuts. The deal was struck and Tony, as ever, entered into this great, new adventure with unbounded enthusiasm. Between 1972 and 1982 he won eight times in Europe and would have secured

Tony Jacklin was a pivotal figure at the start of the European Tour

© Bob Thomas/Getty Images

© Andrew Redington/Getty Images

Tony Jacklin, here with Sandy Lyle, was fortunate that he took over as captain during a golden period for European golf

another couple of Opens had it not been for a combination of desperate weather and Lee Trevino's uncanny ability to pull off extraordinarily unlikely shots at key moments.

Jacklin was, of course, playing for Great Britain & Ireland in the Ryder Cup through this period but it was when he became captain in 1983 that the old match against the USA changed forever and altered this man's life as well. As a player Jacklin had grown as tired as everyone else with the Americans' routine ability to turn up, yawn and thrash the opposition. His luck as captain was to take charge of an expanded European team and a side that included Seve Ballesteros, Nick Faldo, Sandy Lyle, Bernhard Langer and Ian Woosnam.

Top role for Severiano

Yet while even the greatest general needs decent foot-soldiers in any campaign, Jacklin's brilliance as a leader was in persuading Ballesteros to become his on-course heartbeat and then in making sure everything else around the players was as spot on as was humanly possible.

In 1979 when I travelled with the side to The Greenbrier I had flown in the back of the plane in economy. Nothing unusual there but what might surprise you is that to my right on that BA flight sat the entire Ryder Cup team with the top officials. A clumsy stewardess managed to spill a glass of red wine over Jacklin's very beige team trousers and the same woman then refused to let him past her meals trolley and back to his seat after he had made a trip to the loo to try to clean himself up a bit.

It was at this moment that the momentum for Europe's stunning success in the modern matches was created for when Jacklin was invited to be skipper he insisted that he would only do so if the team travelled right, dressed right and stayed in the best possible accommodation. "This is about the players. Do it my way or find someone else," he told Ken Schofield, executive director of the European Tour who had the job of coaxing him back to captain the Ryder Cup team. After the disappointment of being passed over as a player in 1981 because it was felt he was too old, Tony took some convincing.

The officials almost did try to find someone else but eventually sense prevailed and Jacklin was given his head. Instead of flying economy, the side flew to America on Concorde; instead of cheap shirts inappropriate to the weather they wore the finest materials available; crucially, instead of feeling second-class, they began to believe in their ability to beat the American stars and nearly did in 1983. In Florida that year, America won by a single point at a contest in which the shot of the match was a wonderful, impossible recovery with a 3-wood from a step-faced bunker on the last which finished just a few feet from the pin.

Outstanding leader

In 1985, of course, Jacklin's battle plans did pay off when Europe won so memorably at The Belfry to end a 28 year gap between victories. The day ended with Jacklin leading his chaps out on to the roof of the pro shop from where they sprayed the crowd with champagne while overhead Concorde swooped low over the course and dipped its wings in salute. Off to the side a military band played Land Of Hope And Glory. Naturally, everyone cried.

There will be those who will say that Jacklin's Open and US Open victories take precedence over this, and subsequent, happy Ryder Cup scenes but while it is true that these achievements mark him out historically, the context of his professional life is irretrievably embroidered by the Ryder Cup.

It was in this arena that that boy from Scunthorpe showed himself to be an outstanding leader of men as well as a great European. As a testimony I suspect he will be happy to accept this 40th anniversary salute for his glorious Open success Maybe not 'over the Moon' this time but content enough at having left a a wonderful legacy whatever way you choose to analyse it. Today's players have so much to be grateful to Tony Jacklin for the role he played in helping to create the European Tour as we know it today.

Why Australians are successful on golf's international circuits

Former Tour player Mike Clayton has the answers

The success of the modern, widely travelled Australian professional players has been the subject of some curiosity to outsiders who wonder how a country with a small population can produce players who successfully compete far from home for the majority of the year.

Australians have always been a nation of travellers and our sportsmen well understand that they can never earn the respect of their hard marking countrymen and women unless they have proved their worth against the rest of the world.

Norman Von Nida, the great little champion from Queensland, was the first Australian professional to make his living entirely from the tour and he was a mentor and inspiration to the many generations who followed. Peter Thomson was an early protégé and there was no happier man than the Von when Thomson took his first Open at Birkdale in 1954.

Thomson was, however, a discourager of players heading to America but there was a clear and fundamental change in the psyche of young Australian players in the early 1990s. Prior to that there had been up to 20 players playing in Europe but by 2008 there were only a few regulars including Peter O'Malley, Richard Green, Peter Fowler, Scott Strange and Marcus Fraser still plying their trade in Europe.

There is much to be said for the notion that the success of one group of players inspires others that it is possible to compete successfully all over the world and many have pointed to the inspiration of Greg Norman, the most attention-grabbing player we have ever seen in Australia.

"I think that we have a generation of players inspired to play and do great things by Greg Norman", says the 2006 US Open champion Geoff Ogilvy.

Ogilvy, Adam Scott, Aaron Baddeley and the rest can tell you shot by shot of Greg's torments at Augusta, Troon, Inverness, St Andrews and Shinnecock Hills but despite his disappointments he was the man every kid watched and idolised for two decades.

Ogilvy witnessed first hand Norman's greatest day that came at Royal St George's in 1993 and

there is much of the Norman game to be seen when one watches Ogilvy.

Wayne Grady, who grew up playing at the same Brisbane club as Norman, never cared much for playing golf in Europe and was determined to play his golf in America. He won the German Open in 1984 and that gave him the security of a three-year exemption and the confidence to head to America in 1985 and he won the 1990 USPGA Championship.

Grady was an underrated player and he showed the next generation that it was possible for single-minded players to succeed in America.

Two men from Melbourne, Steven Bann and Dale Lynch, were important parts of the technical improvement of the new generation. Both were unsuccessful on Tour (almost always the recipe for fine teachers because they don't just preach the things that worked for them) despite years of beating balls and their way of staying involved was to teach.

Bann and Lynch were employed in 1990 by the fledgling Melbourne based Victorian Institute of Sport and their goal was to give their players the skills to compete in America on a tour they did not see as the impregnable fortress that many before had done.

Peter Thomson was an early Australian globetrotter

© Chris McGrath/Getty Images

Geoff Ogilvy, a star pupil who went on to win the US Open

old. Within six years of taking up the game, Baddeley stunned the country when he beat Greg Norman, Colin Montgomerie and Nick O'Hern at Royal Sydney in the Australian Open and he won the Open again as a professional at Kingston Heath a year later.

Gary Edwin, a maverick teacher from the Gold Coast of Queensland, has taught a number of players his easily-recognised method including Rod Pampling, Peter Lonard, Gavin Coles and a rejuvenated Peter Senior.

"I would have won much more if I had met Gary when I was 14 instead of as a broken down 40 year old", said Senior.

Edwin deserves credit because, unlike Baddeley, Ogilvy, Appleby and Allenby, his players were not outstanding junior players. Lonard, recovering from Ross River Fever (a debilitating illness leaving sufferers listless for months and even years), was a club pro in Sydney and Pampling could barely make a cut in his first forays onto the local tour.

Adam Scott's father is a golf pro and Adam was an obvious talent from an early age. Lynch took Baddeley to the Australian Junior championship in Alice Springs in the late 1990s and "Aaron played pretty well and finished second ... by 15 shots!"

Another brilliant junior player following Norman, Grady, Ian Baker-Finch and Scott out of Queensland is Jason Day and many have high hopes for him.

Our courses too have helped. The Victorians all grew up playing the famed sandbelt courses including Victoria (the home club of Thomson, Ogilvy and 1954 Amateur Champion Doug Bachli), Yarra Yarra (where Allenby and Appleby were members) Royal Melbourne, Metropolitan, Kingston Heath, Peninsula, Commonwealth and Woodlands. Ogilvy's brilliant pitch off the short grass and up the steep bank fronting the final green at Winged Foot that won him the 2006 US Open was a shot learned on his home course in Melbourne and the preponderance of bunkers on the sandbelt almost guarantees every Melbourne man is a terrific bunker player – Thomson aside who would tell you he wasn't very good because he was never in them!

Ogilvy, one of the star pupils notes that "My generation has benefited from the institutes of sport and a no stone unturned approach to the game by great coaches like Dale Lynch and Steve Bann".

Bann and Lynch were believers in giving the players the technical skills they would need for an enduring career and they were prepared to make significant changes to a player's technique without worrying about the player having to play well in the short term. It was always the long term goals that took precedence.

Bann's first notable student was a skinny 14-year-old named Robert Allenby and he and Stuart Appleby were talented and willing pupils. Bann and Lynch used a logical system that gave them measurable skills and solid techniques as well as an innovative series of golf-specific exercises designed to fine tune their bodies into golfing machines.

Richard Green was a part of the early Victorian Institute programme as was the former German and Australian Open Champion Steve Allan and more recently the most promising player to come out has been Jarrod Lyle who in 2008 played brilliantly on the Nationwide Tour and easily reclaimed his place on the main tour for 2009.

Lynch unearthed another uncommon talent when Aaron Baddeley came knocking as a 13 year

Australians winning around the world

Underlining just how successful Australians are around the world, just check out these facts: Geoff Ogilvy and Adam Scott both won on the PGA Tour in 2008 and six Australians were successful on the US Nationwide Tour – Jarrod Lyle, who won twice, Ewan Porter, Gavin Coles, Aron Price, Greg Chalmers and Marc Leishman. In Europe, Scott Strange won at Celtic Manor and in Asia, where over 20 Australians play, there were Asian Tour victories for Rick Kulacz, Scott Hend and David Gleeson while Andrew McKenzie and Andrew Tchudin won on the Korean circuit.

The Yorkshireman who has influenced the game so much

Ken Schofield meets up with "Dr Golf" John Jacobs

Take a leisurely 90 minutes' drive down the M3 motorway from London and you will arrive at the pretty little New Forest village of Lyndhurst, where a man whose contribution to golf has been immense now lives. John Jacobs' influence on the game for the past 70 years as a coach, teacher and administrator is incalculable … and if you happen to drop by when he is at home and not fishing (his other great love) the chances are that he'll want to have a look at your swing and if necessary, sort things out in the gentlest of ways. He is the ultimate enthusiast whose no gimmicks, no nonsense teaching method has not only stood the test of time but been the blueprint for other teachers around the world.

Very rarely can one man have made such an impact on golf as determined Yorkshireman Jacobs, now in his 80's and as excited about every aspect of the game as when he first started out as an assistant nearly 70 years ago. Yet it is not only as a teacher that he has made his mark. It was his outstanding commitment that helped forge the start of the now burgeoning European International Tour. He can rightly claim to be the father of the Tour even if, modestly, he would play that down.

If golf has dominated his life it is hardly surprising. He was born between the two World Wars into a family steeped in Yorkshire golfing history at the renowned Lindrick Gold Club, venue in 1957 of what at the time, was a rare Ryder Cup triumph over the Americans. John was an accomplished player winning the Dutch Open and South African Match-play Championship at a time when there were no tournament players as such and those who wanted to play in events had to squeeze them in between their duties as club professionals, as he was for many years at Sandy Lodge near London.

He represented Great Britain and Ireland in the Ryder Cup successfully but sadly not as often as he would have liked. He missed selection narrowly in 1953 when the match was played at Wentworth and even more poignantly four years later at Lindrick, but he travelled with the team to the Thunderbird Country Club in Palm Springs, California, in 1955 and was a huge success. Playing with his usual fighting spirit he won both his 36-hole matches on the last green, teaming up with Johnny Fallon to beat Chandler Harper and Jerry Barber in the foursomes, then overcoming Dr. Cary Middlecoff, twice US Open Champion, in the singles.

Today, as international Tours have been developed almost beyond belief, a performance such as Jacobs produced at Thunderbird would have been enough to guarantee him personality status for life, but that was never going to be the case in the 1950's and 60's. Later he played an important part along with Jack Nicklaus in persuading the PGA to include

John Jacobs (centre) receives the Golf Europe Legend Award 2008 from Manfred Wutzlhofer, CEO of Messe München (left) and Ken Schofield

Continental players in the Cup match and was given the honour of captaining the first two European sides in 1979 and again in 1981.

At 40, Jacobs' playing days over, he teamed up with Laddie Lucas, his close friend and mentor from Sandy Lodge days. Together they launched the John

Butch Harmon insists all teachers owe a debt of gratitude to John Jacobs

Jacobs Golf Centres. After initial planning difficulties, the concept became a very viable business. This also satisfied the desire of both to make golf more available to the masses. About this time, Jacobs and Lucas were at the forefront of a move to the larger 1.68 inch ball which has been so instrumental in the huge advance in European playing standards.

Jacobs Golf Schools became very popular in the U.S. Butch Harmon commented at the time, "All of us out here teaching golf today owe a dept of gratitude to John".

Jacobs was inducted into the Teaching Hall of Fame in 1971. That award is just one of the deserved International honours he has received – honours that include his induction into the World Golf Hall of Fame in St Augustine, Florida, an O.B.E. from Her Majesty the Queen and Honorary Membership of the Royal and Ancient Golf Club of St. Andrews, of which he is so proud. In 1996, the then Prime Minister, John Major, presented him with the Lifetime Achievement Award for his contribution to the golf industry. These honours more than underline the massive footprint he has left on the game over the past seven decades but there is another aspect of John's contribution to golf which, in its own way, is just as important a legacy.

In August 1971, Major John Bywaters, the then Secretary of the Professional Golfers' Association,

with the unanimous support of the tournament players of the day, invited John to become their first Director General, with the task of forming an autonomous tournament circuit.

He realised that Britain alone was neither geographically nor economically large enough to sustain a viable round-the-year circuit. Using his enormous network of contacts in Britain's boardrooms and his friendship with the presidents and chief executives of the Golfing Federations in Western Europe who were responsible for running the various Continental Opens, he worked to make the dream a reality. It helped that he was highly respected by the Continental Federations having, at some stage, coached most of their national teams and in some cases still does, although he is about to give up his role of coach to the Spanish teaching professionals and amateur teams after 38 years.

What emerged was a totally independent European Tour, offering a greatly enhanced opportunity for those professionals who preferred playing tournaments to working as club professionals to ply their trade more competitively and eventually much more profitably. The rest is history. The story of the European Tour since 1971 has been one of continued growth and John is rightly proud of the way "his baby" has prospered globally.

Today his peers continue to recognise Jacobs' outstanding contribution to golf. The leading money earner on the PGA Seniors Tour which caters for those professionals 50 years and over is presented with the John Jacobs Trophy annually.

The PGA's of Europe made him their President in 1999 and 2000. He is also a Vice President of the Association of Golf Writers who in 2003 presented him with the Michael Williams Award.

A prolific author of nine golf instruction books, Jacobs was the first to teach golf on television in a long association with Yorkshire TV and he even pioneered giving lessons on radio in a series organised by long-time BBC golf producer John Fenton. Latterly he was a key member of the ITV golf team that covered events in the early years of the European Tour.

In 2002, Sportscoach UK awarded him the Dyson Trophy which relates to all different sports. And still the awards keep coming.

Last year he was the recipient of the 2008 Legend of Golf Award at the Golf Munich Trade show, where he conducted a lively question-and-answer session with an audience who wanted to hear just one more time the "Doctor" tell them the secret – *his* secret of golfing success. In every sense, John Jacobs, never one to suffer fools gladly but generous in spirit, is a truly remarkable man – as remarkable as is his legacy of having introduced the game to millions around the world and making it so much more enjoyable to play.

When Watson and Nicklaus had an Open head-to-head

Keith Mackie remembers the "Duel in the Sun"

As they waited on the tee at the 14th in the final round of their epic confrontation for The Open title at Turnberry in 1977, with the rest of the international field way behind Tom Watson looked Jack Nicklaus in the eye and said: "This is what it's all about, isn't it Jack?"

Nicklaus, never one to waste words, replied cryptically: "You're damn right."

And so they entered the final phase of a championship that still ranks as the best of the best for many of golf's experienced commentators. Identical opening rounds of 68 and 70 meant they were paired together on the third day. A lightning storm forced them to take shelter among the rocks on the shore for half an hour, but they continued to strike sparks off each other when play resumed and shot-for-shot rounds of 65 put them jointly into a three-stroke lead.

Light rough, light winds and perfect high summer sunshine set the scene for the final dramatic day 31 years ago. Nicklaus quickly established a three-shot advantage, but Watson nibbled away at his lead and stood only one behind after booming two drivers to the heart of the long seventh. He was still one shot adrift as they played the 209-yard 15th where he over-compensated for the drop into trouble on the right by pulling his four-iron tee shot wide of the green. Faced with a downhill shot from a bare lie he chose to putt rather than chip the ball from 60 feet. "It was enough downhill to need only the weight of a 30-foot putt," he said later. As if under remote control the ball slid down and across the slope into the centre of the hole. Nicklaus, perfectly positioned on the green, two putted for a solid par but now they were level with three to play.

Cautiously played pars at the tricky 16th were followed by perfect tee shots at the par-five 17th. Playing first, Watson hit a superb three-iron to 25 feet before Nicklaus came up just short of the green with a four-iron. A delicate pitch-and-run left him within five feet and he watched Watson's putt like a hawk as it turned in towards the hole and finished stone dead for a birdie 4. Nicklaus allowed for the slight break he had seen on Watson's putt,

but his ball went straight on past the cup. He took 5 and Watson was ahead for the first time,

Tom found the middle of the 18th fairway with a one-iron tee shot. Jack went for broke. He had not been on the best of terms with his driver all week, suffering from an intermittent pull-hook that would have put him into serious trouble if Turnberry's rough had been as thick and savage as usual. This time he came off the ball a fraction and blocked it to the right where the fairway was fringed with heavy gorse bushes. His ball came to rest inches from oblivion, but partly obscured by spikey overhanging branches. From further back in the fairway Watson got his blow in first – a superlative seven-iron from 172 yards that finished no more than two feet from the hole.

As Nicklaus lashed into his recovery shot the ball flicked against one of the branches, but it still

Jack Nicklaus and Tom Watson by the commemorative plaque on the 18th tee of the Ailsa Course at Turnberry renamed in honour of their "Duel in the Sun" in the 1977 Open Championship

© David Cannon/Getty Images

Nick Price, along with Greg Norman and Tom Watson, has won The Open at Turnberry

The other winner that day was Turnberry itself. Built in 1903 as an exclusive resort with its golf course laid out beneath the gaze of a massive red-roofed, white-walled hotel, with its own station on the Glasgow-Girvan line the course was drummed into service as an airfield during both world wars. The massive expanse of concrete runway and taxi-ways laid out across its lovely acres for the 1939-1945 conflict almost ended its existence, but, at vast expense, the concrete was ripped up and 30,000 cubic yards of topsoil brought in to re-create the fine course designed by renowned architect Mackenzie Ross. The entire course, tees, greens and fairways, was turfed at incredible expense in the straightened times of postwar Britain but the result was that in 1951 Turnberry rose majestically again from the ashes of war.

An unbelievable 63

The Watson–Nicklaus spectacular marked Turnberry's debut as an Open venue and when the championship returned nine years later, conditions could not have been more different. Gone was the light rough and brilliant sunshine to be replaced with strong winds, cold rain, narrow fairways and deep, clinging rough. The average score in the opening round was 78.19 with the high-class field collectively 1,251 shots over par. The following day, in conditions still tough enough to allow only 15 sub-par rounds, Greg Norman shot an unbelievable open record-equalling 63 that enabled him, by the end of the week, to claim his first major title by five shots.

When Turnberry staged its third Open, in 1994, Tom Watson rolled back the years with opening rounds of 68-65 to hold the championship lead. A decade after his fifth Open title he could not maintain the magic of 1977 and finished 69-74 to share 11th place. Nick Price of Zimbabwe and Jesper Parnevik of Sweden battled to the final hole, both completing all four rounds in the 60s. Parnevik, refusing to look at the leader boards, and hearing a roar from the crowds around the 17th green when Price holed a 60-foot eagle putt, believed he needed a birdie at the last to win. He attacked the pin with a wedge, came up fractionally short and took three more to get down, leaving Price the luxury of a comfortably played for par and victory.

reached the front of the green. Now he had to make a 35-foot putt to have any chance of forcing a play-off. Of the thousands of people massed around that final green, only two expected the putt to drop. One of them was Nicklaus, whose concentration and confidence was never more acute than at moments like this. The other was Watson. "I told my caddie to expect Jack to make the putt," he said later. "I train myself to expect these things to happen and then it doesn't come as a shock and affect my own play."

Nicklaus duly obliged, but Watson made light of his short putt for a round of 65 to claim the second of his five Open titles, putting the finishing touch to perhaps the greatest and most sporting contest in the long history of the championship. For the record, American Hubert Green finished in third place, 11 shots behind, followed by another impressive quarter from across the Atlantic – Lee Trevino, Ben Crenshaw, Arnold Palmer and Ray Floyd.

The Three Turnberry Golfing Musketeers

With The Open having been played only three times at the Ayrshire Championship venue, the role of honour is a short one – Tom Watson in 1977, Greg Norman in 1986 and Nick Price in 1994.

1977	Tom Watson (USA)	68-70-65-65—268	£10,000
1986	Greg Norman (AUS)	74-63-74-69—280	£70,000
1994	Nick Price (ZIM)	69-66-68-67—269	£110,000

© Bom Thomas/Getty Images

Championship dates

	The Masters	US Open	The Open	US PGA Championship
2009	April 9–12 Augusta National, Augusta, GA	June 18-21 Bethpage State Park (Black Course), Farmingdale, NY	July 16-19 Ailsa Course, Turnberry, Ayrshire	August 13–16 Hazeltine National GC, Chaska, MN
2010	April 8–11 Augusta National, Augusta, GA	June 17-20 Pebble Beach Golf Links, CA	July 15–18 St Andrews (Old Course), Fife	August Whistling Straits (Straits Course), Sheboygan, WI
2011	April 7–10 Augusta National, Augusta, GA	June 16-19 Congressional (Md) CC (Blue Course), Bethesda, MD	July 14–17 Royal St George's GC, Sandwich, Kent	August 12–15 Atlanta Athletic Club, Deluth, GA
2012	April 5–8 Augusta National, Augusta, GA	June 14-17 The Olympic Club, San Francisco, CA	July 19–22 Royal Lytham & St Annes, Lancashire	August Kiawah Island (Ocean Course), John's Island, SC
2013	April 11–13 Augusta National, Augusta, GA	June 13-16 Merion GC, Ardmore, PA		August Oak Hill CC (East Course), Pittsford, NY
2014	TBC Augusta National, Augusta, GA	June 12–15 Pinehurst Resort, NC		
2015		TBC Chambers Bay, Puget Sound, WA		

Ryder Cup
2010 Celtic Manor Resort, Newport, Wales
2012 Medinah Country Club, IL
2014 Gleneagles Hotel, Perthshire, Scotland
2016 Hazeltine National GC, Chaska, MN
2018 TBC
2020 Whistling Straits, Kohler, WI
2022 TBC

Solheim Cup
2009 at Rich Harvest Farms, Super Grove, IL – August 17–23
2011 at Killeen Castle, Ireland – date TBA

Presidents Cup
(USA v Rest of the World except Europe)
2009 Harding Park GC, San Francisco, CA
2011 Royal Melbourne GC, Victoria, Australia

The Senior Open Championship
2009 Sunningdale GC – July 23–26
2010 Carnoustie – July 22–25

R&A Contacts
Up-to-date news of The R&A and its activities can be found at
www.randa.org
The R&A can be contacted on: Tel 01334 460000 Fax 01334 460001
Chief Executive: Peter Dawson
Director: Michael Tate
Director of Championships: David Hill
Director of Rules and Equipment Standards: David Rickman
Director – Research and Testing: Steve Otto   Director – Rules of Golf: Grant Moir
Director of Golf Development: Duncan Weir
Director – Golf Course Management: Steve Isaac
Commercial Director: Angus Farquhar   Financial Director: Mark Dobell
Heritage & Museum Director: Peter Lewis   Asia Pacific Director: Dominic Wall
Assistant Director and Head of Communications: Malcolm Booth

R&A dates, 2009–2011

	2009	2010	2011
The Open Championship	July 16–19 Turnberry	July 15–18 St Andrews	July 14–17 Royal St George's
The Open Championship Final Qualifying (local)	July 6–7 Glasgow–Gailes Links Western Gailes Kilmarnock (Barassie)	July 5–6 Kingsbarns Ladybank The Fairmont, St Andrews	July 4–5 Littlestone Prince's Royal Cinque Ports
The Senior Open Championship	July 23–26 Sunningdale	July 22–25 Carnoustie	July 21–24 TBA
The Amateur Championship	June 15–20 Formby West Lancashire	June 14–19 Muirfield North Berwick	June 13–18 Hillside Hesketh
The Senior Open Amateur Championship	August 5–7 Prestwick	August 11–13 Walton Heath	August 3–5 Royal Portrush
The Junior Open Championship	—	July 12–14 Lundin GC	—
The Boys' Amateur Championship	August 10–15 Royal St George's	August 10–15 Kilmarnock Barassie	August 9–14 Burnham & Berrow
The Boys' Home Internationals	August 4–6 Hankley Common	August 3–5 Southerness	August 2–4 Royal St David's
The Jacques Léglise Trophy	August 28–29 Ganton	August 27–28 Italy	August 26–27 Neguri, Spain
The Walker Cup	September 12–13 Merion, USA	—	September 10–11 Royal Aberdeen
The St Andrews Trophy	—	August 27–28 Italy	—
The Eisenhower Trophy	—	October 28–31 Olivos GC/Buenos Aires GC	—
Espirito Santo Trophy	—	October 20–23 Olivos GC/Buenos Aires GC	—

Other fixtures and tour schedules can be found on pages 408–415

Abbreviations

ALB	Albania	INA	Indonesia	PHI	Philippines
ARG	Argentina	IND	India	POL	Poland
AUS	Australia	IOM	Isle of Man	POR	Portugal
AUT	Austria	IRL	Ireland	PUR	Puerto Rico
BEL	Belgium	ISL	Iceland	QAT	Qatar
BER	Bermuda	ISR	Israel	RUS	Russia
BHR	Bahrain	ITA	Italy	LCA	Saint Lucia
BRA	Brazil	JAM	Jamaica	SIN	Singapore
BUL	Bulgaria	JPN	Japan	RSA	South Africa
CAN	Canada	KEN	Kenya	SCO	Scotland
CHN	China	KOR	Korea (South)	SVK	Slovakia
CIV	Côte d'Ivoire	LAT	Latvia	SLO	Slovenia
CHI	Chile	LIB	Lebanon	SRI	Sri Lanka
COL	Colombia	LBA	Libya	SWE	Sweden
CRC	Costa Rica	MAS	Malaysia	SWZ	Swaziland
CZE	Czech Republic	MEX	Mexico	SUI	Switzerland
DEN	Denmark	MON	Monaco	TPE	Taiwan
EGY	Egypt	MYA	Myanmar		(Chinese Taipei)
ENG	England	NAM	Namibia	THA	Thailand
ESA	El Salvador	NED	Netherlands	TRI	Trinidad and
ESP	Spain	NCA	Nicaragua		Tobago
FIJ	Fiji	NIR	Northern Ireland	TUN	Tunisia
FIN	Finland	NOR	Norway	TUR	Turkey
FRA	France	NZL	New Zealand	UGA	Uganda
GER	Germany	PAK	Pakistan	USA	United States
GUA	Guatemala	PAN	Panama	VEN	Venezuela
HKG	Hong Kong	PAR	Paraguay	WAL	Wales
HUN	Hungary	PER	Peru	ZIM	Zimbabwe

GBI   Great Britain and Ireland

(am)	Amateur	(M)	Match play	Jr	Junior
(D)	Defending champion	(S)	Stroke play	Sr	Senior

Where available, total course yardage and the par for a course are displayed in square brackets, i.e. [6686–70]

* indicates winner after play-off

Karlsson makes history on European Tour

Tall Swede Robert Karlsson became the first Scandinavian to win the European Tour Order of Merit when he amassed €2,732,748 to edge Padraig Harrington and Lee Westwood into second and third places in the 2008 season's table.

With nine career victories to his name, including the Mercedez-Benz Championship and Alfred Dunhill Links Championship last season, the popular 39-year-old is the most prolific Swedish winner on Tour. Son of a greenkeeper from St Malm, Karlsson works closely with Annchristine Lundström and during the 2008 season, in addition to his two wins, he had ten other top 10 finishes including top 10's at The Masters, the US Open and The Open. He was one of 11 players to make the cut in all four majors.

The 39-year-old Ryder Cup player, who is married with two children, now lives in Monaco.

Nicklaus and Sörenstam join Olympic bid

Two of golf's greatest golfers – Jack Nicklaus, winner of 18 major titles, and Annika Sörenstam, who retired last year after a career in which she scored 89 victories, have been appointed Global Ambassadors to help the International Golf Federation's bid to re-instate golf into the Olympic Games.

"Golf truly embodies the Olympic spirit with its foundation of honour, integrity, dignity and sportsmanship", said Nicklaus. "The inclusion of golf in the Games would strengthen the Olympic movement around the world."

Sörenstam added: "Now that I have stepped aside from competitive golf, I want to grow the game around the world and what better way to do that than through the Olympic movement?".

Golf growing in South America

The number of people playing golf in South America is rising by 10 per cent each year according to the latest KPMG Benchmark report but the number involved remains a very small percentage of the total population.

Of the 380 million population only 120,000 play the game which represents three in every 10,000. Fuelled by high growth economies and the extensive media exposure given to golfers such as former US Open champion Angel Cabrera and Colombia's Camillo Villegas, over 130 courses are being built at the moment.

Of the 550 courses in South America, the greatest number, 264, are in Argentina where there are 48,300 registered golfers with next best Brazil where over 25,000 play on that country's 107 courses.

PART I

The Major Championships

The Open Championship

July 17–20, 2008

Padraig Harrington gains legendary status by gloriously winning his second Open at stormy Royal Birkdale

Most recently Arnold Palmer did it in 1961, Lee Trevino in 1972, Tom Watson in 1983, Tiger Woods in 2006 and in 2008 Padraig Harrington defended The Open title brilliantly in some of the most difficult weather conditions ever experienced in the Championship. To realise the magnitude of his achievement, he was the first European golfer to win successive Opens since James Braid in 1906! Yet in the days leading up to the event, Harrington's right wrist injury threatened to keep him out of the Championship. Had it not been for the remedial work of physio Dale Richardson and the fact that it was The Open, Harrington might not

© Dave Shopland/Phil Sheldon Golf Picture Library

Padraig Harrington

have teed it up at all! For most of the final day it was Harrington and Greg Norman, rolling back the years, who battled it out. At the ninth the Australian was ahead by one but it was the Irishman who played best under pressure over the closing holes, moving into a two shot lead after the 16th as Norman lost ground. The Dubliner, who covered the last six holes in four-under-par, clinched his success at the 17th when hitting a 5-wood 249 yards to three feet – the shot of the Championship and the year – and then holing the putt for an eagle and the comfort of a four-shot lead on the final tee. He knew he had taken his golf game to a new level as he walked proudly down the last to a standing ovation for a finishing round of 69 and a winning total of three-over-par 283. He was the first European to win at Royal Birkdale since the event was first staged at the Lancashire links in 1954.

It was so different from Carnoustie the previous year when he needed extra holes to edge out Sergio García. The scoring may have been higher than normal this time but the golf produced was magnificent in the cruel weather conditions which buffeted the players for most of the week although the sun came out on the final day as Europe produced the first two in Harrington and Ian Poulter, who came home in two under par 34 for 69 and 287. Missed chances for birdies at three of the last six holes ended his title dream. For Norman, who finished joint third with Sweden's Henrik Stenson, it was a remarkable week, too, because the 53-year-old who, after an absence of three years, had only entered the event as a warm up for the Senior Open being played the following week at Royal Troon. His dream of a third Open victory evaporated as he managed only one birdie but ran up eight bogeys in a closing 77.

Twenty-five-year-old Chris Wood from Long Ashton, who fired a closing 72, finished a magnificent joint fifth with former US Open champion Jim Furyk, and took the silver medal which goes to the leading amateur by four from Thomas Sherreard. Within days Wood had turned professional.

Australians have a habit of doing well at Royal Birkdale and after a wind and rain-lashed first day there were three on the leader board! Robert Allenby, Adam Scott and former double Open champion Norman were in the top six tied on level par with American Bart Bryant. Only US Open runner-up Rocco Mediate helped by phenomenal putting, Barclays Scottish Open champion Graham McDowell and Scott managed to beat par with rounds of 69 and significantly all were off after 12.00 on the first day by which time the weather had eased a bit from the early morning horrors. Royal Birkdale has always been

First Round	Second Round	Third Round	Fourth Round
–1 McDowell	–1 Choi	+2 Norman	+3 Harrington
–1 Mediate	£ Norman	+4 Harrington	+7 Poulter
–1 Allenby	+1 Villegas	+4 Choi	+9 Norman
£ Norman	+2 Harrington	+5 Wakefield	+9 Stenson
£ Scptt	+2 McDowell	+7 Curtis	+10 Furyk
£ Bryant	+2 Mediate	+7 Kim	+10 Wood (am)
	+2 Allenby	+7 Noren	
	+2 Furyk	+7 Fisher	
	+2 Duval		
	+2 Noren		

a tough par 70 even more so in the cruel crosswinds and heavy rain. Average score among the morning starters was 79 and for the later starters 76. The toughest hole – the 499 yards par 4 sixth into the wind, averaged 4.89 on the day. Some out early could not reach the green with a driver and 3-wood. Conditions were so difficult in the morning that Ernie Els, who ran up three successive 6's on the back nine, stumbled to an 80, his highest score in The Open. Phil Mickelson, who lost a ball and took 7 at the sixth, had 79. Early starter Simon Dyson, who had a 9 in his 82, declared the course unplayable. Both Rich Beem and, surprisingly, Sandy Lyle retired. Retief Goosen, on what he called one of the most brutal days at The Open, managed four birdies in his 71, but Norman had only two bogeys on his card and just missed a putt on the final green for 69. McDowell had only one bogey on the card and finished birdie, birdie to share the lead. Scott, too, had only one bogey when he three putted the 16th while Allenby, playing in his 16th Open, came home in a brilliant 32 for his 69. Defending champion Padraig Harrington, helped by anti-inflamatory pills and early morning physio on his damaged wrist, shot a creditable 74 – a score matched by, among others, five times champion Tom Watson, 1998 Royal Birkdale winner Mark O'Meara and Justin Rose.

Conditions were easier and more pleasant on the second day but Royal Birkdale still provided a tough test with only ten players shooting rounds in the 60's. For most of the day it was 53-year-old Norman, attempting to become the oldest winner of the Championship (Old Tom Morris holds that record being 46 when he took the title in 1867), who headed the leader board with his second successive 70 but later Korean golfer KJ Choi handed in a 67 to edge him off the top and become the only player under par at the end of the second day on one-under. Nobody finished better than Colombian Camillo Villegas who birdied the last five holes – 2, 4, 3, 4, 3 – for a 65, the best round of the week. He was in third place on one-over par, a shot clear of a group of golfers including defending champion Harrington who put in a finish almost as good as Villegas. He birdied the 15th, made the only eagle of the day at the par 5 17th. and made 3 at the par 4 last for a 68 and 142.

Former champions miss out

Kent amateur Thomas Sherreard was among those who beat 70, his 69, putting him on 146 one behind another amateur, Chris Wood, who holed a pitch at the last. Only these two of the five amateurs who started made the cut in the chase for the Silver Medal. With the likely cut coming at plus 9 (three shots lower than the highest half-way cut which was at Carnoustie in 1999) things did not look good for Colin Montgomerie who had a triple bogey and two double bogeys in the early holes but the Scot fought back well to make it as did Ernie Els, who has never missed a cut in The Open, and Phil Mickelson, who was round in 68. Among those who missed out, however, were Tom Watson, Paul Lawrie, Mark O'Meara, Mark Calcavecchia and John Daly. In all 83 players made it through to the weekend.

The average score on day one had been 76, just under 74 on day two but on the third day with the gusting wind causing so much trouble, the average was 75.76. Balls moving on the green at the 10th caused a mid afternoon delay that upset the momentum of some of the competitors. Nobody managed a score in the 60's and only four players – England's Simon Wakefield, former champion Ben Curtis, who holed his second shot at the 451 yards third, another American, Davis Love III, and Swede Stenson managed to match the par of 70. When he finished, Wakefield said that he felt he had run a marathon but Harrington, round in 72, admitted he had enjoyed the tough conditions because it had helped him focus although it had been the most difficult putting day he had ever known. Few enjoyed it.

David Duval was out in 44 for 83, Nick Dougherty in 43 for 79 and there were high scores on the back nine as well. Jim Furyk stumbled home in 43 for 77, Stuart Appleby in 43 for 79 and both Graeme McDowell and Justin Rose took 42 on the back nine for 80 and 82 respectively. At one stage KJ Choi, a seven times winner in America and a winner once on the European Tour, was three ahead but on a day when double-bogeys and triple bogeys were commonplace, the Korean ended the day one behind the 1986 and 1993 winner Norman. Cheered on at every hole by the hugely supportive crowd and, looking remarkably comfortable on a day which was physically and mentally demanding Norman, watched by new wife tennis star Chris Evert, fired a five hour third round 72 to take a two shot lead into the final day.

It still blew on the final day and players found the conditions again testing. Norman quickly lost ground but on six-over-par was still one ahead of Harrington at the turn, with Ian Poulter and Simon Wakefield two behind and Curtis, Stenson and Anthony Kim a stroke further back. While Poulter, Norman and Stenson maintained their challenge Wakefield, nephew of former England cricket wicketkeeper Bob Taylor, came home in 43 for 79. With his father Richard on the bag it was Wood who took the silver medal as leading amateur but as the event drew to a close, it was Harrington who took control. From his point of view, of course, Tiger's injury which prevented his being at Birkdale was immaterial. He had, after all, won the Claret Jug with Tiger in the field the previous year. Helped by his coach Bob Torrance and his psychologist Bob Rotella a week that had begun with uncertainty and anxiety about his fitness had ended in glorious fashion. The Claret Jug remained on his sideboard for another year.

2008 Open Championship (137th) *Royal Birkdale*   [7421–71]

Total Prize Money: £4.26 million. Entries: 2,418. 16 Regional Qualifying Courses: Ashridge, Berwick upon Tweed (Goswick), Coventry, Effingham, Enville, Ferndown, Gog Magog, Lindrick, Musselburgh, Old Fold Manor, Pannal, Pleasington, Prestbury, Rochester & Cobham Park, Royal Ashdown Forest, Royal Dublin.

International Final Qualifying:

Africa (Royal Johannesburg & Kensington)

Josh Cunliffe (RSA)	65-65—130
Darren Fichardt (RSA)	68-63—131
Douglas McGuigan (SCO)	67-67—134
Hennie Otto (RSA)	69-65—134

America (Dearborn, MI)

Paul Goydos (USA)	65-66—131
Michael Letzig (USA)	67-66—133
Doug Labelle II (USA)	68-66—134
Craig Barlow (USA)	66-69—135
Rich Beem (USA)	67-68—135
Davis Love III (USA)	67-68—135
Kevin Stadler (USA)	69-66—135

America (TPC Michigan)

Jeff Overton (USA)	63-67—130
John Rollins (USA)	67-69—136
Alex Cejka (GER)	68-69—137
Matt Kuchar (USA)	69-68—137
Tim Petrovic (USA)	67-70—137
Scott McCarron (USA)	71-67—138
Thom Gillis (USA)	71-68—139

Asia (Sentosa, Singapore)

Danny Chia (MAS)	69-69—138
Adam Blyth (AUS)	73-66—139
Chih-Bing Lam (SIN)	72-68—140
Angelo Que (PHI)	69-71—140

Australasia (The Lakes, Sydney)

Andrew Tampion (AUS)	67-71—138
Peter Fowler (AUS))	71-70—141
Bradley Lamb (AUS))	71-70—141
Ewan Porter (AUS))	72-69—141

Europe (Sunningdale, Old & New, England)

Ariel Canete (ARG)	67-66—133
Simon Wakefield (ENG)	65-68—133
Gregory Bourdy (FRA)	66-68—134
Johan Edfors (SWE)	67-67—134
Ross Fisher (ENG)	66-68—134
Jean-Baptiste Gonnet (FRA)	66-68—134
Thomas Aiken (RSA)	68-67—135
Philip Archer (SWE)	68-67—135
David Horsey (ENG)	68-67—135
Jose-Filipe Lima (POR)	66-69—135
Alexander Noren (SWE)	72-63—135
Anthony Wall (ENG)	66-69—135
Paul Waring (ENG)	68-67—135
Steve Webster (ENG)	68-67—135
Martin Wiegele (AUT)	69-66—135
Peter Baker (ENG)	70-66—136
Simon Dyson (ENG)	65-71—136

Local Final Qualifying:

Hillside

Jamie Elson (ENG)	67-73—140
Rohan Blizard (AUS) (am)	71-72—143
Jean Van de Velde (FRA)	70-73—143
Chris Wood (ENG) (am)	71-72—143

Southport & Ainsdale

Jon Bevan (ENG)	70-71—141
Thomas Sherreard (ENG) (am)	72-69—141
Gary Boyd (ENG)	71-72—143
Jamie Howarth (ENG)	70-73—143

West Lancashire

Philip Walton (ENG)	72-70—142
Barry Hume (ENG)	70-75—145
Jonathan Lomas (ENG)	75-72—147
Peter Appleyard (ENG)	72-75—147

The final field of 156 players included 5 amateurs. 83 players (including 2 amateurs) qualified for the last two rounds with scores of 149 and better.

1	Padraig Harrington (IRL)	74-68-72-69—283	£750000	€938565
2	Ian Poulter (ENG)	72-71-75-69—287	450000	563139
3	Greg Norman (AUS)	70-70-72-77—289	255000	319112
	Henrik Stenson (SWE)	76-72-70-71—289	255000	319112
5	Jim Furyk (USA)	71-71-77-71—290	180000	225255
	Chris Wood (ENG) (am)	75-70-73-72—290		
7	Robert Allenby (AUS)	69-73-76-74—292	96944	121318
	Stephen Ames (CAN)	73-70-78-71—292	96944	121318
	Paul Casey (ENG)	78-71-73-70—292	96944	121318
	Ben Curtis (USA)	78-69-70-75—292	96944	121318
	Ernie Els (RSA)	80-69-74-69—292	96944	121318
	David Howell (ENG)	76-71-78-67—292	96944	121318
	Robert Karlsson (SWE)	75-73-75-69—292	96944	121318
	Anthony Kim (USA)	72-74-71-75—292	96944	121318
	Steve Stricker (USA)	77-71-71-73—292	96944	121318
16	K J Choi (KOR)	72-67-75-79—293	53166	66533
	Justin Leonard (USA)	77-70-73-73—293	53166	66533
	Adam Scott (AUS)	70-74-77-72—293	53166	66533
19	Anders Hansen (DEN)	78-68-74-74—294	37770	47267
	Grégory Havret (FRA)	71-75-77-71—294	37770	47267
	Trevor Immelman (RSA)	74-74-73-73—294	37770	47267
	Fredrik Jacobson (SWE)	71-72-79-72—294	37770	47267
	Davis Love III (USA)	75-74-70-75—294	37770	47267
	Graeme McDowell (NIR)	69-73-80-72—294	37770	47267
	Rocco Mediate (USA)	69-73-76-76—294	37770	47267
	Phil Mickelson (USA)	79-68-76-71—294	37770	47267
	Alexander Noren (SWE)	72-70-75-77—294	37770	47267
	Thomas Sherreard (ENG) (am)	77-69-76-72—294		
	Jean Van de Velde (FRA)	73-71-80-70—294	37770	47267
	Simon Wakefield (ENG)	71-74-70-79—294	37770	47267
	Paul Waring (ENG)	73-74-76-71—294	37770	47267
32	Retief Goosen (RSA)	71-75-73-76—295	25035	31330
	Richard Green (AUS)	76-72-76-71—295	25035	31330
	Todd Hamilton (USA)	74-74-72-75—295	25035	31330
	Tom Lehman (USA)	74-73-73-75—295	25035	31330
	Nick O'Hern (AUS)	74-75-74-72—295	25035	31330
	Andres Romero (ARG)	77-72-74-72—295	25035	31330
	Heath Slocum (USA)	73-76-74-72—295	25035	31330
39	Thomas Aiken (RSA)	75-71-82-68—296	16645	20830
	Woody Austin (USA)	76-72-74-74—296	16645	20830
	Grégory Bourdy (FRA)	74-74-75-73—296	16645	20830
	Bart Bryant (USA)	70-78-74-74—296	16645	20830
	Ariel Canete (ARG)	78-71-76-71—296	16645	20830
	David Duval (USA)	73-69-83-71—296	16645	20830
	Ross Fisher (ENG)	72-74-71-79—296	16645	20830
	Simon Khan (ENG)	77-72-71-76—296	16645	20830
	Graeme Storm (ENG)	76-70-72-78—296	16645	20830
	Camilo Villegas (COL)	76-65-79-76—296	16645	20830
	Mike Weir (CAN)	71-76-74-75—296	16645	20830
	Jay Williamson (USA)	73-72-77-74—296	16645	20830
51	Stuart Appleby (AUS)	72-71-79-75—297	11785	14748
	Michael Campbell (NZL)	75-74-74-74—297	11785	14748
	David Frost (RSA)	75-73-73-76—297	11785	14748
	Sergio García (ESP)	72-73-74-78—297	11785	14748
	Zach Johnson (USA)	73-72-76-76—297	11785	14748
	Doug Labelle II (USA)	78-70-74-75—297	11785	14748
	Anthony Wall (ENG)	71-73-81-72—297	11785	14748
58	Richard Finch (ENG)	75-73-78-72—298	10650	13327
	Tom Gillis (USA)	74-72-79-73—298	10650	13327

137th Open Championship *continued*

58T	Peter Hanson (SWE)	71-72-78-77—298	10650	13327
	Colin Montgomerie (SCO)	73-75-74-76—298	10650	13327
	Kevin Stadler (USA)	72-75-78-73—298	10650	13327
	Scott Verplank (USA)	77-67-78-76—298	10650	13327
64	Søren Hansen (DEN)	75-69-77-78—299	10200	12764
	Wen Chong Liang (CHN)	77-71-77-74—299	10200	12764
	Jonathan Lomas (ENG)	75-73-76-75—299	10200	12764
67	Jean-Baptiste Gonnet (FRA)	75-72-73-80—300	9900	12389
	David Horsey (ENG)	74-70-79-77—300	9900	12389
	Lee Westwood (ENG)	75-74-78-73—300	9900	12389
70	Brendan Jones (AUS)	74-73-83-71—301	9350	11700
	Pablo Larrazabal (ESP)	75-74-73-79—301	9350	11700
	Jose-Filipe Lima (POR)	73-76-75-77—301	9350	11700
	Jeff Overton (USA)	72-75-75-79—301	9350	11700
	Craig Parry (AUS)	77-70-77-77—301	9350	11700
	John Rollins (USA)	73-75-77-76—301	9350	11700
	Justin Rose (ENG)	74-72-82-73—301	9350	11700
	Martin Wiegele (AUT)	75-74-78-74—301	9350	11700
78	Nick Dougherty (ENG)	75-71-79-77—302	8850	11075
	Lucas Glover (USA)	78-71-77-76—302	8850	11075
80	Martin Kaymer (GER)	75-72-79-77—303	8700	10887
81	Philip Archer (ENG)	75-74-78-77—304	8600	10762
82	Sean O'Hair (USA)	75-73-80-78—306	8500	10637
83	Chih Bing Lam (SIN)	72-75-83-81—311	8400	10511

The following players missed the cut:

84	Peter Appleyard (ENG)	74-76—150	£3200
	Aaron Baddeley (AUS)	75-75—150	3200
	Peter Baker (ENG)	75-75—150	3200
	Jon Bevan (ENG)	78-72—150	3200
	Alex Cejka (GER)	76-74—150	3200
	Stewart Cink (USA)	75-75—150	3200
	Joshua Cunliffe (RSA)	79-71—150	3200
	Pelle Edberg (SWE)	76-74—150	3200
	James Kingston (RSA)	77-73—150	3200
	Paul Lawrie (SCO)	77-73—150	3200
	Scott McCarron (USA)	75-75—150	3200
	Damien McGrane (IRL)	79-71—150	3200
	Prayad Marksaeng (THA)	77-73—150	3200
	Pat Perez (USA)	82-68—150	3200
	Richard Sterne (RSA)	78-72—150	3200
	Yoshinobu Tsukada (JPN)	75-75—150	3200
	Tom Watson (USA)	74-76—150	3200
	Azuma Yano (JPN)	74-76—150	3200
102	Craig Barlow (USA)	79-72—151	2650
	Mark Calcavecchia (USA)	76-75—151	2650
	Charles Howell III (USA)	76-75—151	2650
	Ryuji Imada (JPN)	77-74—151	2650
	Søren Kjeldsen (DEN)	81-70—151	2650
	Mark O'Meara (USA)	74-77—151	2650
	Geoff Ogilvy (AUS)	77-74—151	2650
	Vijay Singh (FIJ)	80-71—151	2650
	Brandt Snedeker (USA)	72-79—151	2650
	Andrew Tampion (AUS)	78-73—151	2650
	Hideto Tanihara (JPN)	76-75—151	2650
	Oliver Wilson (ENG)	77-74—151	2650
114	Simon Dyson (ENG)	82-70—152	2650
	Johan Edfors (SWE)	78-74—152	2650
	Niclas Fasth (SWE)	79-73—152	2650

114T	Paul Goydos (USA)	77-75—152	2650
	Benjamin Hebert (FRA) (am)	79-73—152	
	Barry Hume (SCO)	76-76—152	2650
	Matt Kuchar (USA)	79-73—152	2650
	Michael Letzig (USA)	78-74—152	2650
	Hunter Mahan (USA)	80-72—152	2650
	David Smail (NZL)	76-76—152	2650
124	Gary Boyd (ENG)	77-76—153	2375
	Tim Clark (USA)	76-77—153	2375
	Boo Weekley (USA)	80-73—153	2375
127	Angel Cabrera (ARG)	77-77—154	2375
	Miguel Angel Jiménez (ESP)	72-82—154	2375
	Douglas McGuigan (SCO)	79-75—154	2375
	Rod Pampling (AUS)	77-77—154	2375
	Angelo Que (PHI)	76-78—154	2375
	Jeff Quinney (USA)	79-75—154	2375
	Rory Sabbatini (RSA)	79-75—154	2375
134	Rohan Blizard (AUS) (am)	78-77—155	
	Ewan Porter (AUS)	76-79—155	2375
136	Jamie Elson (ENG)	78-78—156	2375
	J B Holmes (USA)	79-77—156	2375
	Hennie Otto (RSA)	79-77—156	2375
	Scott Strange (AUS)	84-72—156	2375
140	Hiroshi Iwata (JPN)	73-84—157	2375
	Reinier Saxton (NED) (am)	80-77—157	
142	Adam Blyth (AUS)	81-77—158	2375
	Michio Matsumura (JPN)	82-76—158	2375
	Tim Petrovic (USA)	82-76—158	2375
145	Bradley Lamb (AUS)	85-74—159	2375
	Philip Walton (IRL)	77-82—159	2375
	Steve Webster (ENG)	79-80—159	2375

148	Darren Fichardt (RSA)	82-78—160	2100	153	John Daly (USA)	80-89—169	2100
	Jerry Kelly (USA)	83-77—160	2100		Jamie Howarth (ENG)	85-74—169	2100
150	Shuntaro Kai (JPN)	80-81—161	2100		Sandy Lyle (SCO)	RTD	
151	Danny Chia (MAS)	76-87—163	2100		Rich Beem (USA)	RTD	
152	Peter Fowler (AUS)	82-82—164	2100				

2007 Open Championship *Carnoustie* July 19–22 [7421–71]

Total Prize Money: £4.2 million. Entries: 2,443. 16 Regional Qualifying Courses: Ashridge, Effingham, Enville, Gog Magog, Minchinhampton, Musselburgh, Notts, Old Fold Manor, Pannal, Pleasington, Prestbury, Rochester & Cobham Park, Royal Ashdown Forest, Royal Dublin, Silloth-on-Solway, Trentham. Final field: 156 players included 6 amateurs of whom 70 players (including 1 amateur) made the half-way cut with scores of 146 and better

1	Padraig Harrington (IRL)*	69-73-68-67—277	£750000	20T	Zach Johnson (USA)	73-73-68-70—284	42000
2	Sergio García (ESP)	65-71-68-73—277	450000		Pat Perez (USA)	73-70-71-70—284	42000
	Four-hole play-off – Harrington 3-3-4-5; García 5-3-4-4			23	Jonathan Byrd (USA)	73-72-70-70—285	35562
3	Andres Romero (ARG)	71-70-70-67—278	290000		Mark Calcavecchia		
4	Ernie Els (RSA)	72-70-68-69—279	200000		(USA)	74-70-72-69—285	35562
	Richard Green (AUS)	72-73-70-64—279	200000		Chris DiMarco (USA)	74-70-66-75—285	35562
6	Stewart Cink (USA)	69-73-68-70—280	145500		Retief Goosen (RSA)	70-71-73-71—285	35562
	Hunter Mahan (USA)	73-73-69-65—280	145500	27	Paul Casey (ENG)	72-73-69-72—286	28178
8	K J Choi (KOR)	69-69-72-71—281	94750		Lucas Glover (USA)	71-72-70-73—286	28178
	Ben Curtis (USA)	72-74-70-65—281	94750		J J Henry (USA)	70-71-71-74—286	28178
	Steve Stricker (USA)	71-72-64-74—281	94750		Rodney Pampling (AUS)	70-72-72-72—286	28178
	Mike Weir (CAN)	71-68-72-70—281	94750		Ian Poulter (ENG)	73-73-70-70—286	28178
12	Markus Brier (AUT)	68-75-70-69—282	58571		Adam Scott (AUS)	73-70-72-71—286	28178
	Paul Broadhurst ENG	71-71-68-72—282	58571		Vijay Singh (FIJ)	72-71-68-75—286	28178
	Telle Edberg (SWE)	72-73-67-70—282	58571	34	Angel Cabrera (ARG)	68-73-72-74—287	24000
	Jim Furyk (USA)	70-70-71-71—282	58571	35	Niclas Fasth (SWE)	75-69-73-71—288	20107
	Miguel Angel Jiménez				Mark Foster (ENG)	76-70-73-69—288	20107
	(ESP)	69-70-72-71—282	58571		Charley Hoffman (USA)	75-69-72-72—288	20107
	Justin Rose (ENG)	75-70-67-70—282	58571		Shaun Micheel (USA)	70-76-70-72—288	20107
	Tiger Woods (USA)	69-74-69-70—282	58571		Nick Watney (USA)	72-71-70-75—288	20107
19	Paul McGinley (IRL)	67-75-68-73—283	46000		Boo Weekley (USA)	68-72-75-73—288	20107
20	Rich Beem (USA)	70-73-69-72—284	42000		Lee Westwood (ENG)	71-70-73-74—288	20107

Other players who made the cut: Nick Dougherty (ENG), Rory McIlroy (NIR) (am), Ryan Moore (USA), 289; Ross Bain (SCO), Arron Oberholser (USA), Carl Pettersson (SWE), John Senden (AUS), 290; Jerry Kelly (USA), Won Joon Lee (KOR), 291; Tom Lehman (USA), Kevin Stadler (USA), 293; Thomas Bjørn (DEN), Grégory Bourdy (FRA), Brian Davis (ENG), David Howell (ENG), 294; Michael Campbell (NZL), Anders Hansen (DEN), Scott Verplank (USA), 295; Trevor Immelman (RSA), Mark O'Meara (USA), Toru Taniguchi (JPN), 296; John Bevan (ENG), Luke Donald (ENG), 297; Raphaël Jacquelin (FRA), Sandy Lyle (SCO), 298; Alastair Forsyth (SCO), Sean O'Hair (USA), 299; Fredrik Andersson Hed (SWE), Peter Hanson (SWE), 300

R&A engraver Alex Harvey dies

Alex Harvey, who engraved the name of the winner of The Open Championship on the Claret Jug before it was handed over to the champion for 32 years died in 2008 aged 83.

The Perth-based craftsman took over the job in 1973 and retired in 2005 – the same year Jack Nicklaus played in his last Open. The decision to do the job on the day was taken to avoid the embarrassment of a champion returning with the trophy the following year having forgotten to have his name engraved on it.

The job remains in the Harvey family. Alex's son Garry took over from him in 2006.

2006 Open Championship Royal Liverpool, Hoylake July 20–23 [7528–72]

Total Prize Money: £3,898,000. Entries: 2,434. 16 Regional Qualifying Courses: Ashridge, County Louth, Effingham, Little Aston, Minchinhampton, Musselburgh, Notts, Old Fold Manor, Orsett, Pannal, Pleasington, Prestbury, Rochester & Cobham Park, Royal Ashdown Forest, Silloth-on-Solway, Trentham. Final field: 156 players (4 amateurs) or whom 71 (2 amateurs) made the half-way cut on 143 or less.

1	Tiger Woods (USA)	67-65-71-67—270	£720000	16T	Brett Rumford (AUS)	68-71-72-71—282	45000
2	Chris DiMarco (USA)	70-65-69-68—272	430000	22	Mark Hensby (AUS)	68-72-74-69—283	35375
3	Ernie Els (RSA)	68-65-71-71—275	275000		Phil Mickelson (USA)	69-71-73-70—283	35375
4	Jim Furyk (USA)	68-71-66-71—276	210000		Greg Owen (ENG)	67-73-68-75—283	35375
5	Sergio García (ESP)	68-71-65-73—277	159500		Charl Schwartzel (RSA)	74-66-72-71—283	35375
	Hideto Tanihara (JPN)	72-68-66-71—277	159500	26	Paul Broadhurst (ENG)	71-71-73-69—284	29100
7	Angel Cabrera (ARG)	71-68-66-73—278	128000		Jerry Kelly (USA)	72-67-69-76—284	29100
8	Carl Pettersson (SWE)	68-72-70-69—279	95333		Hunter Mahan (USA)	73-70-68-73—284	29100
	Andres Romero (ARG)	70-70-68-71—279	95333		Rory Sabbatini (RSA)	69-70-73-72—284	29100
	Adam Scott (AUS)	68-69-70-72—279	95333		Lee Slattery (ENG)	69-72-71-72—284	29100
11	Ben Crane (USA)	68-71-71-70—280	69333	31	Simon Khan (ENG)	70-72-68-75—285	24500
	S K Ho (KOR)	68-73-69-70—280	69333		Scott Verplank (USA)	70-73-67-75—285	24500
	Anthony Wall (ENG)	67-73-71-69—280	69333		Lee Westwood (ENG)	69-72-75-69—285	24500
14	Retief Goosen (RSA)	70-66-72-73—281	56500		Thaworn Wiratchant (THA)	71-68-74-72—285	35591
	Sean O'Hair (USA)	69-73-72-67—281	56500	35	Michael Campbell (NZL)	70-71-75-70—286	19625
16	Robert Allenby (AUS)	69-70-69-74—282	45000		Luke Donald (ENG)	74-68-73-71—286	19625
	Mikko Ilonen (FIN)	68-69-73-72—282	45000		Marcus Fraser (AUS)	68-71-72-75—286	19625
	Peter Lonard (AUS)	71-69-68-74—282	45000		Robert Karlsson (SWE)	70-71-71-74—286	19625
	Geoff Ogilvy (AUS)	71-69-70-72—282	45000		Rod Pampling (AUS)	69-71-74-72—286	19625
	Robert Rock (ENG)	69-69-73-71—282	45000		John Senden (AUS)	70-73-73-70—286	19625

Other players who made the cut: Stephen Ames (CAN), Thomas Bjørn (DEN), Mark Calcavecchia (USA), Miguel Angel Jiménez (ESP), Brandt Jobe (USA), Søren Kjeldsen (DEN), Jeff Sluman (USA), 287; John Bickerton (ENG), Simon Dyson (ENG), Gonzalo Fernandez Castano (ESP), Andrew Marshall (ENG), Henrik Stenson (SWE), Marius Thorp (NOR) (am), Tom Watson (USA), Simon Wakefield (ENG), 288; Tim Clark (RSA), David Duval (USA), Keiichiro Fukabori (JPN), José-María Olazábal (ESP), Mike Weir (CAN), 289; Andrew Buckle (AUS), Graeme McDowell (NIR), 290; Mark O'Meara (USA), Marco Ruiz (PAR), 291; Chad Campbell (USA), 292; Fred Funk (USA), Vaughn Taylor (USA), 294; Todd Hamilton (USA), Edoardo Molinari (ITA) (am), 295; Bart Bryant (USA), 296; Paul Casey (ENG), 298

2005 Open Championship St Andrews (Old Course) June 14–17 [7279–72]

Total Prize Money: £3,854,900. Entries: 2,499 (record). 16 Regional Qualifying Courses: Alwoodley, Ashridge, Hadley Wood, Hindhead, The Island, Little Aston, Minchinhampton, Notts, Orsett, Pleasington, Prestbury, Renfrew, Rochester & Cobham Park, Royal Ashdown Forest, Silloth-on-Solway, Trentham. Final Field: 156 (7 amateurs), of whom 80 (4 amateurs) made the half-way cut on 145 or less.

1	Tiger Woods (USA)	66-67-71-70—274	£720000	15T	Nick O'Hern (AUS)	73-69-71-70—283	46286
2	Colin Montgomerie (SCO)	71-66-70-72—279	430000		Lloyd Saltman (SCO) (am)	73-71-68-71—283	
3	Fred Couples (USA)	68-71-73-68—280	242500	23	Bart Bryant (USA)	69-70-71-74—284	32500
	José-María Olazábal (ESP)	68-70-68-74—280	242500		Tim Clark (RSA)	71-69-70-74—284	32500
5	Michael Campbell (NZL)	69-72-68-72—281	122167		Scott Drummond (SCO)	74-71-69-70—284	32500
	Sergio García (ESP)	70-69-69-73—281	122167		Brad Faxon (USA)	72-66-70-76—284	32500
	Retief Goosen (RSA)	68-73-66-74—281	122167		Nicholas Flanagan (AUS)	73-71-69-71—284	32500
	Bernhard Langer (GER)	71-69-70-71—281	122167		Tom Lehman (USA)	75-69-70-70—284	32500
	Geoff Ogilvy (AUS)	71-74-67-69—281	122167		Eric Ramsay (SCO) (am)	68-74-74-68—284	
	Vijay Singh (FIJ)	69-69-71-72—281	122167		Tadahiro Takayama (JPN)	72-72-70-70—284	32500
11	Nick Faldo (ENG)	74-69-70-69—282	66750		Scott Verplank (USA)	68-70-72-74—284	32500
	Graeme McDowell (NIR)	69-72-74-67—282	66750	32	Richard Green (AUS)	72-68-72-73—285	26500
	Kenny Perry (USA)	71-71-68-72—282	66750		Sandy Lyle (SCO)	74-67-69-75—285	26500
	Ian Poulter (ENG)	70-72-71-69—282	66750	34	Simon Dyson (ENG)	70-71-72-73—286	22000
15	Darren Clarke (NIR)	73-70-67-73—283	46286		Ernie Els (RSA)	74-67-75-70—286	22000
	John Daly (USA)	71-69-70-73—283	46286		Peter Hanson (SWE)	72-72-71-71—286	22000
	David Frost (RSA)	77-65-72-69—283	46286		Thomas Levet (FRA)	69-71-75-71—286	22000
	Mark Hensby (AUS)	67-77-69-70—283	46286		Joe Ogilvie (USA)	74-70-73-69—286	22000
	Trevor Immelman (RSA)	68-70-73-72—283	46286		Adam Scott (AUS)	70-71-70-75—286	22000
	Sean O'Hair (USA)	73-67-70-73—283	46286		Henrik Stenson (SWE)	74-67-73-72—286	22000

Other players who made the cut: Stuart Appleby (AUS), K J Choi (KOR), Hiroyuki Fujita (JPN), Søren Hansen (DEN), Tim Herron (USA), Simon Khan (ENG), Maarten Lafeber (NED), Paul McGinley (IRL), Bob Tway (USA), Tom Watson (USA), Steve Webster (ENG), 287; Robert Allenby (AUS), Luke Donald (ENG), Fredrik Jacobson (SWE), Thongchai Jaidee (THA), Miguel Angel Jiménez (ESP), Paul Lawrie (SCO), Justin Leonard (USA), Bo Van Pelt (USA), 288; John Bickerton (ENG), Mark Calcavecchia (USA), Phil Mickelson (USA), Eduardo Molinari (ITA) (am), Greg Norman (AUS), Tino Schuster (GER), 289; Peter Lonard (AUS), 290; Chris DiMarco (USA), Pat Perez (USA), Chris Riley (USA), Robert Rock (ENG), David Smail (NZL), Duffy Waldorf (USA), 291; Patrik Sjöland (SWE), 292; Scott Gutschewski (USA), S K Ho (KOR), Ted Purdy (USA), 293; Steve Flesch (USA), 294; Rodney Pampling (AUS), Graeme Storm (ENG), 296; Matthew Richardson (ENG) (am), 297

2004 Open Championship Royal Troon July 15–18 [7175–71]

Total Prize Money: £4,064,000. Entries: 2221 Regional Qualifying Courses: Alwoodley, Ashridge, Co.Louth, Hadley Wood, Hindhead, Little Aston, Minchinhampton, Notts, Orsett, Pleasington, Prestbury, Renfrew, Rochester & Cobham Park, Royal Ashdown Forest, Silloth-on-Solway, Trentham. Final qualifying courses: Glasgow (Gailes), Irvine, Turnberry Kintyre, Western Gailes. Final Field: 156 (5 amateurs), of whom 73 (1 amateur) made the half-way cut on 145 or less.

1	Todd Hamilton (USA)*	71-67-67-69—274	£720000	20T	Paul Casey (ENG)	66-77-70-72—285	38100
2	Ernie Els (RSA)	69-69-68-68—274	430000		Bob Estes (USA)	73-72-69-71—285	38100
Four-hole play-off: Hamilton 4-4-3-4; Els 4-4-4-4					Gary Evans (ENG)	68-73-73-71—285	38100
3	Phil Mickelson (USA)	73-66-68-68—275	275000		Vijay Singh (FIJ)	68-70-76-71—285	38100
4	Lee Westwood (ENG)	72-71-68-67—278	210000	25	Colin Montgomerie (SCO)	69-69-72-76—286	32250
5	Thomas Levet (FRA)	66-70-71-72—279	159500		Ian Poulter (ENG)	71-72-71-72—286	32250
	Davis Love III (USA)	72-69-71-67—279	159500	27	Takashi Kamiyama (JPN)	70-73-71-73—287	29000
7	Retief Goosen (RSA)	69-70-68-73—280	117500		Rodney Pampling (AUS)	72-68-74-73—287	29000
	Scott Verplank (USA)	69-70-70-71—280	117500		Jyoti Randhawa (IND)	73-72-70-72—287	29000
9	Mike Weir (CAN)	71-68-71-71—281	89500	30	Kelichiro Fukabori (JPN)	73-71-70-74—288	24500
	Tiger Woods (USA)	70-71-68-72—281	89500		Shigeki Maruyama (JPN)	71-72-74-71—288	24500
11	Mark Calcavecchia (USA)	72-73-69-68—282	69333		Mark O'Meara (USA)	71-74-68-75—288	24500
	Darren Clarke (NIR)	69-72-73-68—282	69333		Nick Price (ZIM)	71-71-69-77—288	24500
	Skip Kendall (USA)	69-66-75-72—282	69333		David Toms (USA)	71-71-74-72—288	24500
14	Stewart Fink (USA)	72-71-71-69—283	56500		Bo Van Pelt (USA)	72-71-71-74—288	24500
	Barry Lane (ENG)	69-68-71-75—283	56500	36	Stuart Appleby (AUS)	71-70-73-75—289	18750
16	K J Choi (KOR)	68-69-74-73—284	47000		Kim Felton (AUS)	73-67-72-77—289	18750
	Joakim Haeggman (SWE)	69-73-72-70—284	47000		Tetsuji Hiratsuka (JPN)	70-74-70-75—289	18750
	Justin Leonard (USA)	70-72-71-71—284	47000		Steve Lowery (USA)	69-73-75-72—289	18750
	Kenny Perry (USA)	69-70-73-72—284	47000		Hunter Mahan (USA)	74-69-71-75—289	18750
20	Michael Campbell (NZL)	67-71-74-73—285	38100		Tjaart Van Der Walt (RSA)	70-73-72-74—289	18750

Other players who made the cut: Kenneth Ferrie (ENG), Charles Howell III (USA), Trevor Immelman (RSA), Andrew Oldcorn (SCO), Adam Scott (AUS) 290; Paul Bradshaw (ENG), Alastair Forsyth (SCO), Mathias Grönberg (SWE), Migel Angel Jiménez (ESP), Jerry Kelly (USA), Shaun Micheel (USA), Sean Whiffin (ENG) 291; Steve Flesch (USA), Ignaçio Garrido (ESP), Rafaël Jacquelin (FRA) 292; James Kingston (RSA), Paul McGinley (IRL), Carl Pettersson (SWE) 293; Paul Broadhurst (ENG), Gary Emerson (ENG), Brad Faxon (USA) 294; Chris DiMarco (USA), Mark Foster (ENG), Stuart Wilson (SCO) (am) 296; Mårten Olander (SWE), Rory Sabbatini (RSA) 297; Martin Erlandsson (SWE), Paul Wesselingh (ENG) 298; Bob Tway (USA) 299; Rich Beem (USA), Christian Cévaër (FRA) 300; Sandy Lyle (SCO) 303

2003 Open Championship Royal St George's July 17–20 [7034–71]

Prize Money £3.9 million. Entries: 2152. Regional qualifying courses: Alwoodley, Ashridge, Blackmoor, Co.Louth, Hadley Wood, Hindhead, Little Aston, Minchinhampton, Notts, Ormskirk, Orsett, Renfrew, Silloth-on-Solway, Stockport, Trentham, Wildernesse. Final qualifying courses: Littlestone, North Foreland, Prince's, Royal Cinque Ports. Final Field: 156 (3 amateurs), of whom 75 (no amateurs) made the half-way cut on 150 or less.

1	Ben Curtis (USA)	72-72-70-69—283	£700000	22T	Padraig Harrington (IRL)	75-73-74-69—297	32917
2	Thomas Bjørn (DEN)	73-70-69-72—284	345000		Thomas Levet (FRA)	71-73-74-73—291	32917
	Vijay Singh (FIJ)	75-70-69-70—284	345000		JL Lewis (USA)	78-70-72-71—291	32917
4	Davis Love III (USA)	69-72-72-72—285	185000	28	Mark Foster (ENG)	73-73-72-74—292	26000
	Tiger Woods (USA)	73-72-69-71—285	185000		SK Ho (KOR)	70-73-72-77—292	26000
6	Brian Davis (ENG)	77-73-68-68—286	134500		Paul McGinley (IRL)	77-73-69-73—292	26000
	Fredrik Jacobson (SWE)	70-76-70-70—286	134500		Andrew Oldcorn (SCO)	72-74-73-73—292	26000
8	Nick Faldo (ENG)	76-74-67-70—287	97750		Nick Price (ZIM)	74-72-72-74—292	26000
	Kenny Perry (USA)	74-70-70-73—287	97750		Mike Weir (CAN)	74-76-71-71—292	26000
10	Gary Evans (ENG)	71-75-70-72—288	68000	34	Stewart Cink (USA)	75-75-75-68—293	18778
	Sergio García (ESP)	73-71-70-74—288	68000		José Coceres (ARG)	77-70-72-74—293	18778
	Retief Goosen (RSA)	73-75-71-69—288	68000		Bob Estes (USA)	77-71-76-69—293	18778
	Hennie Otto (RSA)	68-76-75-69—288	68000		Shingo Katayama (JPN)	76-73-73-71—293	18778
	Phillip Price (WAL)	74-72-69-73—288	68000		Scott McCarron (USA)	71-74-73-75—293	18778
15	Stuart Appleby (AUS)	75-71-71-72—289	49333		Adam Mednick (SWE)	76-72-76-69—293	18778
	Chad Campbell (USA)	74-71-72-72—289	49333		Gary Murphy (IRL)	73-74-73-73—293	18778
	Pierre Fulke (SWE)	77-72-67-73—289	49333		Marco Ruiz (PAR)	73-71-75-74—293	18778
18	Ernie Els (RSA)	78-68-72-72—290	42000		Duffy Waldorf (USA)	76-73-71-73—293	18778
	Mathias Grönberg (SWE)	71-74-73-72—290	42000	43	Robert Allenby (AUS)	73-75-74-72—294	14250
	Greg Norman (AUS)	69-79-74-68—290	42000		Rich Beem (USA)	76-74-75-69—294	14250
	Tom Watson (USA)	71-77-73-69—290	42000		Tom Byrum (USA)	77-72-71-74—294	14250
22	Angel Cabrera (ARG)	75-73-70-73—291	32917	46	Markus Brier (AUT)	76-71-74-74—295	11864
	K J Choi (KOR)	77-72-72-70—291	32917		Fred Couples (USA)	71-75-71-78—295	11864
	Peter Fowler (AUS)	77-73-70-71—291	32917		Brad Faxon (USA)	77-73-70-75—295	11864

2003 Open Championship continued

46T	Mathew Goggin (AUS)	76-72-70-77—295	11864	53T	Trevor Immelman (RSA)	77-73-72-74—296	10200
	Tom Lehman (USA)	77-73-72-73—295	11864		Raphaël Jacquelin (FRA)	77-71-72-76—296	10200
	Ian Poulter (ENG)	78-72-70-75—295	11864		David Lynn (ENG)	73-76-71-76—296	10200
	Anthony Wall (ENG)	75-74-71-75—295	11864		Mark McNulty (ZIM)	79-71-77-69—296	10200
53	Michael Campbell (NZL)	78-72-74-72—296	10200		Rory Sabbatini (RSA)	79-71-75-71—296	10200

Other players who made the cut: Darren Clarke (NIR), Alastair Forsyth (SCO), Skip Kendall (USA), Peter Lonard (AUS), Phil Mickelson (USA), Craig Parry (AUS) 297; Charles Howell III (USA), Stephen Leaney (AUS), Len Mattiace (USA), Mark O'Meara (USA) 298; Katsuyoshi Tomori (JPN) 300; John Rollins (USA) 301; Chris Smith (USA) 302; John Daly (USA), Ian Woosnam (WAL) 303; Jesper Parnevik (SWE), Mark Roe (ENG) DQ

2002 Open Championship Muirfield July 18–21   [7034–71]

Prize Money £3.885 million. Entries: 2260. Regional qualifying courses: Alwoodley, Blackmoor, Co.Louth, Hadley Wood, Hindhead, Little Aston, Minchinhampton, Northamptonshire County, Notts, Ormskirk, Orsett, Renfrew, Silloth-on-Solway, Stockport, Trentham, Wildernesse. Final qualifying courses: Dunbar, Gullane No.1, Luffness New, North Berwick. Final Field: 156 (3 amateurs), of whom 83 (no amateurs) made the half-way cut on 144 or less.

1	Ernie Els (RSA)*	70-66-72-70—278	£700000	28	Bradley Dredge (WAL)	70-72-74-68—284	24000
2	Stuart Appleby (AUS)	73-70-70-65—278	286667		Niclas Fasth (SWE)	70-73-71-70—284	24000
	Steve Elkington (AUS)	71-73-68-66—278	286667		Pierre Fulke (SWE)	72-69-78-65—284	24000
	Thomas Levet (FRA)	72-66-74-66—278	286667		Jerry Kelly (USA)	73-71-70-70—284	24000
					Bernhard Langer (GER)	72-72-71-69—284	24000
Four-hole play-off: Appleby, Elkington, Els and Levet. Sudden death: Els and Levet					Jesper Parnevik (SWE)	72-72-70-70—284	24000
					Loren Roberts (USA)	74-69-70-71—284	24000
5	Gary Evans (ENG)	72-68-74-65—279	140000		Des Smyth (IRL)	68-69-74-73—284	24000
	Padraig Harrington (IRL)	69-67-76-67—279	140000		Tiger Woods (USA)	70-68-81-65—284	24000
	Shigeki Maruyama (JPN)	68-68-75-68—279	140000	37	Darren Clarke (NIR)	72-67-77-69—285	16917
8	Thomas Bjørn (DEN)	68-70-73-69—280	77500		Andrew Coltart (SCO)	71-69-74-71—285	16917
	Sergio García (ESP)	71-69-71-69—280	77500		Neal Lancaster (USA)	71-71-76-67—285	16917
	Retief Goosen (RSA)	71-68-74-67—280	77500		Stephen Leaney (AUS)	71-70-75-69—285	16917
	Søren Hansen (DEN)	68-69-73-70—280	77500		Scott Verplank (USA)	72-68-74-71—285	16917
	Scott Hoch (USA)	74-69-71-66—280	77500		Ian Woosnam (WAL)	72-72-73-68—285	16917
	Peter O'Malley (AUS)	72-68-75-65—280	77500	43	Trevor Immelman (RSA)	72-72-71-71—286	13750
14	Justin Leonard (USA)	71-72-68-70—281	49750		Steve Jones (USA)	68-75-73-70—286	13750
	Peter Lonard (AUS)	72-72-68-69—281	49750		Carl Pettersson (SWE)	67-70-76-73—286	13750
	Davis Love III (USA)	71-72-71-67—281	49750		Esteban Toledo (MEX)	73-70-75-68—286	13750
	Nick Price (ZIM)	68-70-75-68—281	49750	47	Paul Eales (ENG)	73-71-76-67—287	12000
18	Bob Estes (USA)	71-70-73-68—282	41000		Jeff Maggert (USA)	71-68-80-68—287	12000
	Scott McCarron (USA)	71-68-72-71—282	41000		Rocco Mediate (USA)	71-72-74-70—287	12000
	Greg Norman (AUS)	71-72-71-68—282	41000	50	Fredrik Andersson (SWE)	74-70-74-70—288	10267
	Duffy Waldorf (USA)	67-69-77-69—282	41000		Warren Bennett (ENG)	71-68-82-67—288	10267
22	David Duval (USA)	72-71-70-70—283	32000		Ian Garbutt (ENG)	69-70-74-75—288	10267
	Toshimitsu Izawa (JPN)	76-68-72-67—283	32000		Mikko Ilonen (FIN)	71-70-77-70—288	10267
	Mark O'Meara (USA)	69-69-77-68—283	32000		Shingo Katayama (JPN)	72-68-74-74—288	10267
	Corey Pavin (USA)	69-70-75-69—283	32000		Barry Lane (ENG)	74-68-72-74—288	10267
	Chris Riley (USA)	70-71-76-66—283	32000		Ian Poulter (ENG)	69-69-78-72—288	10267
	Justin Rose (ENG)	68-75-68-72—283	32000		Bob Tway (USA)	70-66-78-74—288	10267

Other players who made the cut: Stewart Cink (USA), Joe Durant (USA), Nick Faldo (ENG), Richard Green (AUS), Kuboya Kenichi (JPN), Paul Lawrie (SCO), Steve Stricker (USA) 289; Chris DiMarco (USA), Phil Mickelson (USA), Jarrod Moseley (AUS) 290; Stephen Ames (TRI), Jim Carter (USA), Matthew Cort (ENG), Len Mattiace (USA), Toru Taniguchi (JPN), Mike Weir (CAN) 291; Sandy Lyle (SCO), Chris Smith (USA) 292; Anders Hansen (DEN), Roger Wessels (RSA) 293; David Park (WAL) 294; Mark Calcavecchia (USA), Lee Janzen (USA) 295; Colin Montgomerie (SCO) 297; David Toms (USA) 298

2001 Open Championship Royal Lytham & St Annes July 19–22 [6905–71]

Prize Money £3,229,748. Entries 2255. Regional qualifying courses: Alwoodley, Blackmoor, Burnham & Berrow, Carlisle, County Louth, Copt Heath, Coxmoor, Hadley Wood, Hindhead, Little Aston, Northamptonshire County, Orsett, Renfrew, Stockport, Wildernesse, Wilmslow. Final qualifying courses: Fairhaven, Hillside, St Anne's Old Links, Southport & Ainsdale. Final field comprised 156 players, of whom 70 (including one amateur) made the half-way cut on 144 or better.

1	David Duval (USA)	69-73-65-67—274	£600000	21	Davis Love III (USA)	73-67-74-67—281	32500
2	Niclas Fasth (SWE)	69-69-72-67—277	360000		Nick Price (ZIM)	73-67-68-73—281	32500
3	Darren Clarke (NIR)	70-69-69-70—278	141667	23	Michael Campbell (NZL)	71-72-71-68—282	30500
	Ernie Els (RSA)	71-71-67-69—278	141667		Greg Owen (ENG)	69-68-72-73—282	30500
	Miguel Angel Jiménez (ESP)	69-72-67-70—278	141667	25	Bob Estes (USA)	74-70-73-66—283	27500
	Bernhard Langer (GER)	71-69-67-71—278	141667		Joe Ogilvie (USA)	69-68-71-75—283	27500
	Billy Mayfair (USA)	69-72-67-70—278	141667		Eduardo Romero (ARG)	70-68-72-73—283	27500
	Ian Woosnam (WAL)	72-68-67-71—278	141667		Tiger Woods (USA)	71-68-73-71—283	27500
9	Sergio García (ESP)	70-72-67-70—279	63750	29	Barry Lane (ENG)	70-72-72-70—284	25000
	Mikko Ilonen (FIN)	68-75-70-66—279	63750	30	Stewart Cink (USA)	71-72-72-70—285	21500
	Jesper Parnevik (SWE)	69-68-71-71—279	63750		David Dixon (ENG) (am)	70-71-70-74—285	
	Kevin Sutherland (USA)	75-69-68-67—279	63750		Phil Mickelson (USA)	70-72-72-71—285	21500
13	Billy Andrade (USA)	69-70-70-71—280	40036		Justin Rose (ENG)	69-72-74-70—285	21500
	Alex Cejka (GER)	69-69-69-73—280	40036		Phillip Price (WAL)	74-69-71-71—285	21500
	Retief Goosen (RSA)	74-68-67-71—280	40036		Nicolas Vanhootegem (BEL)	72-68-70-75—285	21500
	Raphaël Jacquelin (FRA)	71-68-69-72—280	40036		Scott Verplank (USA)	71-72-70-72—285	21500
	Colin Montgomerie (SCO)	65-70-73-72—280	40036	37	Andrew Coltart (SCO)	75-68-70-73—286	16300
	Loren Roberts (USA)	70-70-70-70—280	40036		Padraig Harrington (IRL)	75-66-74-71—286	16300
	Vijay Singh (FIJ)	70-70-71-69—280	40036		Dudley Hart (USA)	74-69-69-74—286	16300
	Des Smyth (IRL)	74-65-70-71—280	40036		Frank Lickliter (USA)	71-71-73-71—286	16300
					Toru Taniguchi (JPN)	72-69-72-73—286	16300

Other players who made the cut: Richard Green (AUS), JP Hayes (USA), Paul Lawrie (SCO), Mark O'Meara (USA), Steve Stricker (USA) 287; Robert Allenby (AUS), Chris DiMarco (USA), Brad Faxon (USA), Matt Gogel (USA), Peter Lonard (AUS), Adam Scott (AUS), Lee Westwood (ENG) 288; Mark Calcavecchia (USA), Paul Curry (ENG), Carlos Franco (PAR), Paul McGinley (IRL), José María Olazábal (ESP), Rory Sabbatini (RSA), Duffy Waldorf (USA) 289; Stuart Appleby (AUS) 290; Gordon Brand Jr (SCO), Brandel Chamblee (USA), Pierre Fulke (SWE) 291; Neil Cheetham (ENG) 295; Alexandre Balicki (FRA), Thomas Levet (FRA) 296; David Smail (NZL) 298; Scott Henderson (SCO), Sandy Lyle (SCO) 301.

2000 Open Championship St Andrews Old Course. Fife July 20–23 [7115–72]

Prize Money £2,722,150. Entries 2477. Regional qualifying courses: Alwoodley, Beau Desert, Blackmoor, Burnham & Berrow, Camberley Heath, Carlisle, Copt Heath, County Louth, Coxmoor, Hadley Wood, Hindhead, Northamptonshire County, Ormskirk, Renfrew, Romford, Stockport, Wildernesse. Final qualifying courses: Ladybank, Leven, Lundin, Scotscraig. Final field comprised 156 players, of whom 74 (none amateur) made the half-way cut on 144 or better.

1	Tiger Woods (USA)	67-66-67-69—269	£500000	11T	Phil Mickelson (USA)	72-66-71-72—281	37111
2	Ernie Els (RSA)	66-72-70-69—277	245000		Bob May (USA)	72-72-66-71—281	37111
	Thomas Bjørn (DEN)	69-69-68-71—277	245000		Dennis Paulson (USA)	68-71-69-73—281	37111
4	Tom Lehman (USA)	68-70-70-70—278	130000	20	Steve Flesch (USA)	67-70-71-74—282	25500
	David Toms (USA)	69-67-71-71—278	130000		Padraig Harrington (IRL)	68-72-70-72—282	25500
6	Fred Couples (USA)	70-68-72-69—279	100000		Steve Pate (USA)	73-70-71-68—282	25500
7	Loren Roberts (USA)	69-68-70-73—280	66250		Bob Estes (USA)	72-69-70-71—282	25500
	Paul Azinger (USA)	69-72-72-67—280	66250		Paul McGinley (IRL)	69-72-71-70—282	25500
	Pierre Fulke (SWE)	69-72-70-69—280	66250		Notah Begay III (USA)	69-73-69-71—282	25500
	Darren Clarke (NIR)	70-69-68-73—280	66250	26	Mark O'Meara (USA)	70-73-69-71—283	20000
11	Bernhard Langer (GER)	74-70-66-71—281	37111		Colin Montgomerie (SCO)	71-70-72-70—283	20000
	Mark McNulty (ZIM)	69-72-70-70—281	37111		Miguel Angel Jiménez (ESP)	73-71-71-68—283	20000
	David Duval (USA)	70-70-66-75—281	37111		Mark Calcavecchia (USA)	73-70-71-69—283	20000
	Stuart Appleby (AUS)	73-70-68-70—281	37111		Dean Robertson (SCO)	73-70-68-72—283	20000
	Davis Love III (USA)	74-66-74-67—281	37111				
	Vijay Singh (FIJ)	70-70-73-68—281	37111				

Other players who made the cut: José Maria Olazábal (ESP), Jean Van de Velde (FRA), Steve Jones (USA), Jarmo Sandelin (SWE), 284; Eduardo Romero (ARG), Sergio García (ESP), Jesper Parnevik (SWE), Craig Parry (AUS), José Coceres (ARG), Robert Allenby (AUS) 286; Nick Faldo (ENG), Justin Leonard (USA), Stewart Cink (USA), Jim Furyk (USA), Nick O'Hern (AUS), Jarrod Moseley (AUS), Gary Orr (SCO), Jeff Maggert (USA), Retief Goosen (RSA), Lucas Parsons (AUS), Tsuyoshi Yoneyama (JPN) 287; Mike Weir (CAN), Ian Garbutt (ENG), Rocco Mediate (USA), 288; David Frost (RSA), Tom Watson (USA), Shigeki Maruyama (JPN), Greg Owen (ENG), Andrew Coltart (SCO) 289; Christy O'Connor Jr (IRL), Jeff Sluman (USA), Steve Elkington (AUS), Kirk Triplett (USA) 290; Desvonde Botes (RSA), Ian Poulter (ENG), Per-Ulrik Johansson (SWE), Lee Westwood (ENG) 291; Gordon Brand Jr (SCO), Ian Woosnam (WAL), 292; Tom Kite (USA), Kazuhiko Hosokawa (JPN) 294; Peter Senior (AUS), Lionel Alexandre (FRA) 295; Dudley Hart (USA) Retd.

1999 Open Championship *Carnoustie, Angus* July 15–18 [7361–71]

Prize Money £2,009,550. Entries 2222. Regional qualifying courses: Beau Desert, Blackmoor, Burnham & Berrow, Carlisle, Copt Heath, County Louth, Coxmoor, Glenbervie, Hankley Common, Moortown, Northamptonshire County, Ormskirk, Romford, South Herts, Stockport, Wildernesse. Final qualifying courses: Downfield, Monifieth Links, Montrose Links, Panmure. Final field comprised 156 players, of whom 73 (none amateurs) made the half-way cut on 154 or better.

1	P Lawrie* (SCO)	73-74-76-67—290	£350000		18	B Langer (GER)	72-77-73-75—297	20500
2	J Leonard (USA)	73-74-71-72—290	185000			A Coltart (SCO)	74-74-72-77—297	20500
	J Van de Velde (FRA)	75-68-70-77—290	185000			F Nobilo (NZL)	76-76-70-75—297	20500
Four-hole play-off (15th–18th): Lawrie 5-4-3-3-; Leonard						P Sjöland (SWE)	74-72-77-74—297	20500
5-4-4-5; Van de Velde 6-4-3-5						L Westwood (ENG)	76-75-74-72—297	20500
4	C Parry (AUS)	76-75-67-73—291	100000			C Rocca (ITA)	81-69-74-73—297	20500
	A Cabrera (ARG)	75-69-77-70—291	100000		24	P O'Malley (AUS)	76-75-74-73—298	15300
6	G Norman (AUS)	76-70-75-72—293	70000			E Els (RSA)	74-76-76-72—298	15300
7	D Frost (RSA)	80-69-71-74—294	50000			B Watts (USA)	74-73-77-74—298	15300
	D Love III (USA)	74-74-77-69—294	50000			I Woosnam (WAL)	76-74-74-74—298	15300
	T Woods (USA)	74-72-74-74—294	50000			MA Martin (ESP)	74-76-72-76—298	15300
10	J Parnevik (SWE)	74-71-78-72—295	34800		29	P Harrington (IRL)	77-74-74-74—299	13500
	S Dunlap (USA)	72-77-76-70—295	34800		30	J Maggert (USA)	75-77-75-73—300	11557
	R Goosen (RSA)	76-75-73-71—295	34800			D Clarke (NIR)	76-75-76-73—300	11557
	H Sutton (USA)	73-78-72-72—295	34800			P Stewart (USA)	79-73-74-74—300	11557
	J Furyk (USA)	78-71-76-70—295	34800			P Fulke (SWE)	75-75-77-73—300	11557
15	T Yoneyama (JPN)	77-74-73-72—296	26000			T Bjørn (DEN)	79-73-75-73—300	11557
	C Montgomerie (SCO)	74-76-72-74—296	26000			T Herron (USA)	81-70-74-75—300	11557
	S Verplank (USA)	80-74-73-69—296	26000			L Mattiace (USA)	73-74-75-78—300	11557

Other players who made the cut: M McNulty (ZIM), D Hart (USA), P Baker (ENG), N Price (ZIM), M Weir (CAN), P Affleck (WAL) 301; D Waldorf (USA), M James (ENG) 302; S Pate (USA), N Ozaki (JPN), J Sluman (USA), D Howell (ENG) 303; N Price (ENG), T Levet (FRA), K Tomori (JPN), K J Choi (KOR), B Hughes (AUS), D Robertson (SCO), B Estes (USA), S Allan (AUS), P Lonard (AUS) 304; D Paulson (USA), J Robinson (ENG), S Luna (ESP), P Price (WAL) 305; J Ryström (SWE), D Duval (USA), M Brooks (USA) 306; J Sandelin (SWE) 307; S Strüver (GER) 308; L Thompson (ENG) 309; B Davis (ENG), J Huston (USA) 310; L Janzen (USA) 311; K Shingo (JPN) 312; M Thompson (ENG), D Cooper (ENG) 313.

Royal Birkdale's sixth hole the toughest in 2008

Writing in the official programme for the 2008 Open Championship at Royal; Birkdale, club professional Brian Hodgkinson suggested that the 499 yards par 4 sixth hole could be the most difficult. He pointed out there were three options off the tee – play up short of the cross bunker leaving yourself with a blind shot to the tee but with a good angle to the green; drive left of the bunker which would require a longer second shot or take on a 280 yards carry to clear the bunker. The exposed green sloped from back to front which could mean some of the quickest putts on the course ... but he never mentioned the hidden danger – the wind. It blew so strongly at Birkdale that the sixth hole emerged as the most difficult of all Championship holes in 2008. During a stormy week when players were forced because of the wind to play much longer clubs than normal for their approaches, the statistics tell the story of the cruel sixth perfectly. Of all the Championship holes played during 2008, this was the one that caused the biggest headache. It averaged 4.764.

Eagles 0   Birdies 10   Pars 160   Bogeys 244   Double bogeys 53   Others 7

Plaque commemorates unsung Open Champion

It has taken 140 years but the 1865 Open champion Andrew Strath has now been recognised by the Prestwick Golf Club, where he served as a professional, and by the South Ayrshire Council.

After intense research, much of it undertaken by St Andrews-based historian Dr David Malcolm it was discovered that Strath, who died from tuberculosis at the age of 32 not too long after taking over from Tom Morris as the club professional, was buried in a pauper's grave in the St Nicholas' churchyard that overlooks the first green.

Now at last a plaque has been unveiled to a man who finished in the top four five times in The Open and who gave his family name to the famous bunker in front of the 11th green at St Andrews.

Interestingly, Young Tom Morris played as a 14-year-old in the Championship won by Strath and went on himself to make golfing history before he died at the early age of just 25.

Open Championship History

The Belt

Date		Winner	Score	Venue	Entrants	Prize money £
1860	Oct 17	W Park, Musselburgh	174	Prestwick	8	—
1861	Sept 26	T Morris Sr, Prestwick	163	Prestwick	12	—
1862	Sept 11	T Morris Sr, Prestwick	163	Prestwick	6	—
1863	Sept 18	W Park, Musselburgh	168	Prestwick	14	10
1864	Sept 16	T Morris Sr, Prestwick	167	Prestwick	6	15
1865	Sept 14	A Strath, St Andrews	162	Prestwick	10	20
1866	Sept 13	W Park, Musselburgh	169	Prestwick	12	11
1867	Sept 26	T Morris Sr, St Andrews	170	Prestwick	10	16
1868	Sept 23	T Morris Jr, St Andrews	154	Prestwick	12	12
1869	Sept 16	T Morris Jr, St Andrews	157	Prestwick	14	12
1870	Sept 15	T Morris Jr, St Andrews	149	Prestwick	17	12

Having won it three times in succession, the Belt became the property of Young Tom Morris and the Championship was held in abeyance for a year. In 1872 the Claret Jug was, and still is, offered for annual competition but it was not available to present at the time to Tom Morris Jr in 1872.

The Claret Jug

Date		Winner	Score	Venue	Entrants	Prize money £
1872	Sept 13	T Morris Jr, St Andrews	166	Prestwick	8	20
1873	Oct 4	T Kidd, St Andrews	179	St Andrews	26	20
1874	April 10	M Park, Musselburgh	159	Musselburgh	32	29
1875	Sept 10	W Park, Musselburgh	166	Prestwick	18	20
1876	Sept 30	B Martin, St Andrews	176	St Andrews	34	27
(D Strath tied but refused to play off)						
1877	April 6	J Anderson, St Andrews	160	Musselburgh	24	20
1878	Oct 4	J Anderson, St Andrews	157	Prestwick	26	20
1879	Sept 27	J Anderson, St Andrews	169	St Andrews	46	45
1880	April 9	B Ferguson, Musselburgh	162	Musselburgh	30	†
1881	Oct 14	B Ferguson, Musselburgh	170	Prestwick	22	21
1882	Sept 30	B Ferguson, Musselburgh	171	St Andrews	40	45
1883	Nov 16	W Fernie*, Dumfries	158	Musselburgh	41	20
After a play-off with B Ferguson, Musselburgh: Fernie 158; Ferguson 159						
1884	Oct 3	J Simpson, Carnoustie	160	Prestwick	30	23
1885	Oct 3	B Martin, St Andrews	171	St Andrews	51	34
1886	Nov 5	D Brown, Musselburgh	157	Musselburgh	46	20
1887	Sept 16	W Park Jr, Musselburgh	161	Prestwick	36	20
1888	Oct 6	J Burns, Warwick	171	St Andrews	53	24
1889	Nov 8	W Park Jr*, Musselburgh	155	Musselburgh	42	22
After a play-off with A Kirkaldy: Park Jr 158; Kirkaldy 163						
1890	Sept 11	J Ball, Royal Liverpool (am)	164	Prestwick	40	29.50
1891	Oct 6	H Kirkaldy, St Andrews	166	St Andrews	82	30.50

After 1891 the competition was extended to 72 holes and for the first time entry money was imposed

Date		Winner	Score	Venue	Entrants	Prize money £
1892	Sept 22–23	H Hilton, Royal Liverpool (am)	305	Muirfield	66	100
1893	Aug 31–Sept 1	W Auchterlonie, St Andrews	322	Prestwick	72	100
1894	June 11–12	J Taylor, Winchester	326	Sandwich, R St George's	94	100
1895	June 12–13	J Taylor, Winchester	322	St Andrews	73	100
1896	June 10–11	H Vardon*, Ganton	316	Muirfield	64	100
After a 36-hole play-off with JH Taylor: Vardon 157; Taylor 161						
1897	May 19–20	H Hilton, Royal Liverpool (am)	314	Hoylake, R Liverpool	86	100
1898	June 8–9	H Vardon, Ganton	307	Prestwick	78	100
1899	June 7–8	H Vardon, Ganton	310	Sandwich, R St George's	98	100
1900	June 6–7	J Taylor, Mid-Surrey	309	St Andrews	81	125
1901	June 5–6	J Braid, Romford	309	Muirfield	101	125
1902	June 4–5	A Herd, Huddersfield	307	Hoylake, R Liverpool	112	125
1903	June 9–10	H Vardon, Totteridge	300	Prestwick	127	125

† prize money not known

Open Championship Claret Jug winners history *continued*

Date	Winner	Score	Venue	Entrants	Qualifiers	Prize-money £
1904 June 8–10	J White, Sunningdale	296	Sandwich, R St George's	144		125
1905 June 7–9	J Braid, Walton Heath	318	St Andrews	152		125
1906 June 13–15	J Braid, Walton Heath	300	Muirfield	183		125
1907 June 20–21	A Massy, La Boulie	312	Hoylake, R Liverpool	193		125
1908 June 18–19	J Braid, Walton Heath	291	Prestwick	180		125
1909 June 10–11	J Taylor, Mid-Surrey	295	Deal, R Cinque Ports	204		125
1910 June 22–24	J Braid, Walton Heath	299	St Andrews	210		135
1911 June 26–29	H Vardon*, Totteridge	303	Sandwich, R St George's	226		135

After a play-off with A Massy. The play-off was over 36 holes, but Massy picked up at the 35th before holing out. He had taken 148 for 34 holes, and when Vardon holed out at the 35th hole his score was 143

Date	Winner	Score	Venue	Entrants	Qualifiers	Prize-money £
1912 June 24–25	E Ray, Oxhey	295	Muirfield	215		135
1913 June 23–24	J Taylor, Mid-Surrey	304	Hoylake, R Liverpool	269		135
1914 June 18–19	H Vardon, Totteridge	306	Prestwick	194		135
1915–19 No Championship						
1920 June 30–July 1	G Duncan, Hanger Hill	303	Deal, R Cinque Ports	190	81	225
1921 June 23–25	J Hutchison*, Glenview, Chicago	296	St Andrews	158	85	225

After a play-off with R Wethered (am): Hutchison 150; Wethered 159

Date	Winner	Score	Venue	Entrants	Qualifiers	Prize-money £
1922 June 22–23	W Hagen, Detroit, USA	300	Sandwich, R St George's	225	80	225
1923 June 14–15	A Havers, Coombe Hill	295	Troon	222	88	225
1924 June 26–27	W Hagen, Detroit, USA	301	Hoylake, R Liverpool	277	86	225
1925 June 25–26	J Barnes, USA	300	Prestwick	200	83	225
1926 June 22–24	R Jones, USA (am)	291	R Lytham and St Annes	293	117	225
1927 July 13–15	R Jones, USA (am)	285	St Andrews	207	108	275
1928 May 9–11	W Hagen, USA	292	Sandwich, R St George's	271	113	275
1929 May 8–10	W Hagen, USA	292	Muirfield	242	109	275
1930 June 18–20	R Jones, USA (am)	291	Hoylake, R Liverpool	296	112	400
1931 June 3–5	T Armour, USA	296	Carnoustie	215	109	500
1932 June 8–10	G Sarazen, USA	283	Sandwich, Prince's	224	110	500
1933 July 5–7	D Shute*, USA	292	St Andrews	287	117	500

After a play-off with C Wood, USA: Shute 149; Wood 154

Date	Winner	Score	Venue	Entrants	Qualifiers	Prize-money £
1934 June 27–29	T Cotton, Waterloo, Belgium	283	Sandwich, R St George's	312	101	500
1935 June 26–28	A Perry, Leatherhead	283	Muirfield	264	109	500
1936 June 24–26	A Padgham, Sundridge Park	287	Hoylake, R Liverpool	286	107	500
1937 July 7–9	T Cotton, Ashridge	290	Carnoustie	258	141	500
1938 July 6–8	R Whitcombe, Parkstone	295	Sandwich, R St George's	268	120	500
1939 July 5–7	R Burton, Sale	290	St Andrews	254	129	500
1940–45 No Championship						
1946 July 3–5	S Snead, USA	290	St Andrews	225	100	1,000
1947 July 2–4	F Daly, Balmoral	293	Hoylake, R Liverpool	263	100	1,000
1948 June 30–July 2	T Cotton, Royal Mid-Surrey	284	Muirfield	272	97	1,000
1949 July 6–8	A Locke*, RSA	283	Sandwich, R St George's	224	96	1,500

After a play-off with H Bradshaw: Locke 135; Bradshaw 147

Date	Winner	Score	Venue	Entrants	Qualifiers	Prize-money £
1950 July 5–7	A Locke, RSA	279	Troon	262	93	1,500
1951 July 4–6	M Faulkner, England	285	R Portrush	180	98	1,700
1952 July 9–11	A Locke, RSA	287	R Lytham and St Annes	275	96	1,700
1953 July 8–10	B Hogan, USA	282	Carnoustie	196	91	2,500
1954 July 7–9	P Thomson, Australia	283	Birkdale	349	97	3,500
1955 July 6–8	P Thomson, Australia	281	St Andrews	301	94	3,750
1956 July 4–6	P Thomson, Australia	286	Hoylake, R Liverpool	360	96	3,750
1957 July 3–5	A Locke, RSA	279	St Andrews	282	96	3,750
1958 July 2–4	P Thomson*, Australia	278	R Lytham and St Annes	362	96	4,850

After a play-off with D Thomas: Thomson 139; Thomas 143

Date	Winner	Score	Venue	Entrants	Qualifiers	Prize-money £
1959 July 1–3	G Player, RSA	284	Muirfield	285	90	5,000
1960 July 6–8	K Nagle, Australia	278	St Andrews	410	74	7,000
1961 July 12–14	A Palmer, USA	284	Birkdale	364	101	8,500
1962 July 11–13	A Palmer, USA	276	Troon	379	119	8,500
1963 July 10–12	R Charles*, New Zealand	277	R Lytham and St Annes	261	119	8,500

After a play-off with P Rodgers, USA: Charles 140; Rodgers 148

Date	Winner	Score	Venue	Entrants	Qualifiers	Prize-money £
1964 July 8–10	T Lema, USA	279	St Andrews	327	119	8,500
1965 July 7–9	P Thomson, Australia	285	R Birkdale	372	130	10,000
1966 July 6–9	J Nicklaus, USA	282	Muirfield	310	130	15,000
1967 July 12–15	R De Vicenzo, Argentina	278	Hoylake, R Liverpool	326	130	15,000
1968 July 10–13	G Player, RSA	289	Carnoustie	309	130	20,000
1969 July 9–12	A Jacklin, England	280	R Lytham and St Annes	424	129	30,334
1970 July 8–11	J Nicklaus*, USA	283	St Andrews	468	134	40,000

After a play-off with Doug Sanders, USA: Nicklaus 72; Sanders 73

Date	Winner	Score	Venue	Entrants	Qualifiers	Prize-money £
1971 July 7–10	L Trevino, USA	278	R Birkdale	528	150	45,000

Date	Winner	Score	Venue	Entrants	Qualifiers	Prize-money £
1972 July 12–15	L Trevino, USA	278	Muirfield	570	150	50,000
1973 July 11–14	T Weiskopf, USA	276	Troon	569	150	50,000
1974 July 10–13	G Player, RSA	282	R Lytham and St Annes	679	150	50,000
1975 July 9–12	T Watson*, USA	279	Carnoustie	629	150	50,000

After a play-off with J Newton, Australia: Watson 71; Newton 72

Date	Winner	Score	Venue	Entrants	Qualifiers	Prize-money £
1976 July 7–10	J Miller, USA	279	R Birkdale	719	150	75,000
1977 July 6–9	T Watson, USA	268	Turnberry	730	150	100,000
1978 July 12–15	J Nicklaus, USA	281	St Andrews	788	150	125,000
1979 July 18–21	S Ballesteros, Spain	283	R Lytham and St Annes	885	150	155,000
1980 July 17–20	T Watson, USA	271	Muirfield	994	151	200,000
1981 July 16–19	B Rogers, USA	276	Sandwich, R St George's	971	153	200,000
1982 July 15–18	T Watson, USA	284	R Troon	1121	150	250,000
1983 July 14–17	T Watson, USA	275	R Birkdale	1107	151	310,000
1984 July 19–22	S Ballesteros, Spain	276	St Andrews	1413	156	445,000
1985 July 18–21	A Lyle, Scotland	282	Sandwich, R St George's	1361	149	530,000
1986 July 17–20	G Norman, Australia	280	Turnberry	1347	152	634,000
1987 July 16–19	N Faldo, England	279	Muirfield	1407	153	650,000
1988 July 14–18	S Ballesteros, Spain	273	R Lytham and St Annes	1393	153	700,000
1989 July 20–23	M Calcavecchia*, USA	275	R Troon	1481	156	750,000

Four-hole play-off (1st, 2nd, 17th and 18th): Calcavecchia 4-3-3-3, W Grady (AUS) 4-4-4-4, G Norman (AUS) 3-4-4-X

Date	Winner	Score	Venue	Entrants	Qualifiers	Prize-money £
1990 July 19–22	N Faldo, England	270	St Andrews	1707	152	825,000
1991 July 18–21	I Baker-Finch, Australia	272	R Birkdale	1496	156	900,000
1992 July 16–19	N Faldo, England	272	Muirfield	1666	156	950,000
1993 July 15–18	G Norman, Australia	267	Sandwich, R St George's	1827	156	1,000,000
1994 July 14–17	N Price, Zimbabwe	268	Turnberry	1701	156	1,100,000
1995 July 20–23	J Daly*, USA	282	St Andrews	1836	159	1,250,000

Four-hole play-off (1st, 2nd, 17th and 18th): Daly 4-3-4-4, C Rocca (ITA) 5-4-7-3

Date	Winner	Score	Venue	Entrants	Qualifiers	Prize-money £
1996 July 18–21	T Lehman, USA	271	R Lytham and St Annes	1918	156	1,400,000
1997 July 17–20	J Leonard, USA	272	R Troon	2133	156	1,586,300
1998 July 16–19	M O'Meara*, USA	280	R Birkdale	2336	152	1,800,000

Four-hole play-off (15th–18th): O'Meara 4-4-5-4, B Watts (AUS) 5-4-5-5

Date	Winner	Score	Venue	Entrants	Qualifiers	Prize-money £
1999 July 15–18	P Lawrie*, Scotland	290	Carnoustie	2222	156	2,000,000

Four-hole play-off: Lawrie 5-4-3-3, J Leonard (USA), V de Velde (FRA) 5-4-4-5

Date	Winner	Score	Venue	Entrants	Qualifiers	Prize-money £
2000 July 20–23	T Woods, USA	269	St Andrews	2477	156	2,750,000
2001 July 19–22	D Duval, USA	274	R Lytham and St Annes	2255	156	3,300,000
2002 July 18–21	E Els*, RSA	278	Muirfield	2260	156	3,800,000

Four hole play-off: Els 4-3-5-4–16, T Levet (FRA) 4-2-5-5, S Appleby (AUS) 4-4-4-5, S Elkington (AUS) 5-3-4-5. Sudden death:: Els 4, Levet 5

Date	Winner	Score	Venue	Entrants	Qualifiers	Prize-money £
2003 July 17–20	B Curtis, USA	283	Sandwich, R St George's	2152	156	3,898,000
2004 July 15–18	T Hamilton*, USA	274	Royal Troon	2221	156	4,064,000

Four-hole play-off: Hamilton 4-4-3-4, Els (RSA) 4-4-4-4

Date	Winner	Score	Venue	Entrants	Qualifiers	Prize-money £
2005 July 14–17	T Woods, USA	274	St Andrews	2499	156	4,000,000
2006 July 20–23	T Woods, USA	270	R Liverpool	2434	156	4,000,000
2007 July 19–22	P Harrington, Ireland*	277	Carnoustie	2443	156	4,200,000

Four-hole play-off: Harrington 3-3-4-5, S Garcia (ESP) 5-3-4-4

Date	Winner	Score	Venue	Entrants	Qualifiers	Prize-money £
2008 July 17–20	P Harrington, Ireland	283	R Birkdale	2418	156	4,260,000

The Open Silver Medal winners 1949–2008

Year	Name	Venue	Final Position	Final Score
1949	Frank Stranahan (USA)	Sandwich	13	290
1950	Frank Stranahan (USA)	Troon	9	286
1951	Frank Stranahan (USA)	Portrush	12	295
1952	J.W. Jones (ENG)	Lytham & St Annes	27	304
1953	Frank Stranahan (USA)	Carnoustie	2	286
1954	Peter Toogood (AUS)	Birkdale	15	291
1955	Joe Conrad (USA)	St Andrews	22	293
1956	Joe Carr (IRL)	Hoylake	36	306
1957	W.D. Smith (SCO)	St Andrews	5	286
1958	Joe Carr (IRL)	Lytham & St Annes	37	298
1959	Reid Jack (SCO)	Muirfield	5	288
1960	Guy Wolstenholme (ENG)	St Andrews	6	283
1961	Ronald White (ENG)	Birkdale	38	306
1962	Charles Green (SCO)	Troon	37	308
1965	Michael Burgess (ENG)	Birkdale	29	299

Open Championship Silver Medal winners *continued*

Year	Name	Venue	Final Position	Final Score
1966	Ronnie Shade (SCO)	Muirfield	16	293
1968	Michael Bonallack (ENG)	Carnoustie	21	300
1969	Peter Tupling (ENG)	Lytham & St Annes	28	294
1970	Steve Melnyk (USA)	St Andrews	41	298
1971	Michael Bonallack (ENG)	Birkdale	22	291
1973	Danny Edwards (USA)	Troon	39	296
1978	Peter McEvoy (ENG)	Carnoustie	39	293
1979	Peter McEvoy (ENG)	Lytham & St Annes	17	294
1980	Jay Sigel (USA)	Muirfield	38	291
1981	Hal Sutton (USA)	Sandwich	47	295
1982	Malcolm Lewis (ENG)	Royal Troon	42	300
1985	José-María Olazábal (ESP)	Sandwich	24	289
1987	Paul Mayo (IRL)	Muirfield	57	297
1988	Paul Broadhurst (ENG)	Lytham & St Annes	57	296
1989	Russell Claydon (ENG)	Troon	69	293
1991	Jim Payne (ENG)	Birkdale	38	284
1992	Daren Lee (ENG)	Muirfield	68	293
1993	Iain Pyman (ENG)	Sandwich	27	281
1994	Warren Bennett (ENG)	Turnberry	70	286
1995	Steve Webster (ENG)	St Andrews	24	289
1996	Tiger Woods (USA)	Lytham & St Annes	21	281
1997	Barclay Howard (SCO)	Troon	59	293
1998	Justin Rose (ENG)	Birkdale	4	282
2001	David Dixon (ENG)	Lytham & St Annes	30	285
2004	Stuart Wilson (SCO)	Troon	63	296
2005	Lloyd Saltman (SCO)	St Andrews	15	283
2006	Marius Thorp (NOR)	Hoylake	48	288
2007	Rory McIlroy (NIR)	Carnoustie	42	289
2008	Chris Wood (ENG)	Birkdale	5	290

1,238 bunkers raked by volunteer greenkeepers

The best golfers in the world were in 1,238 bunkers during last year's Open at Royal Birkdale but none of them had to rake them after they had played out. Members of the British and International Golf Greenkeepers Association (BIGGA) did it for them as they have been doing since 1984.

Last year's 60-strong team from places as far apart as Hawaii and Australia not only raked the bunkers, they also helped course manager Chris Whittle and his team keep the course in great condition throughout the Championship.

Records on the numbers of bunkers raked have been kept since 1995 and last year the players were in 10 per cent more bunkers than in 1008 when the event was last played at Royal Birkdale – a statistic that suggests the the moving and improving of bunkers presented an increased challenge last year. Of course, the 30–50 mph winds and driving rain did not help the competitors avoid them! Records show that competitors in The Open are in the fewest bunkers when playing the Old Course at St Andrews (701 in 1995, a remarkably low 448 in 2000 and 676 in 2005). Lytham and Carnoustie are where there is the greatest amount of bunker play. In 1996 at Lytham, 1,618 bunkers were raked and at the same venue in 2001 the number was 1,585. Carnoustie's total in 1999 was 1,474 and in 2007 the figure was 1,311.

US Open Championship

June 12–16, 2008

Tiger Woods plays through the pain to win Major number 14 at Torrey Pines and calls it the greatest of them all

He had not played for ten weeks prior to coming to Torrey Pines, the venue of the 108th US Open, but despite the pain he often felt from a left knee not fully recovered from surgery, Tiger Woods managed to play 91 holes before he saw off the gallant Rocco Mediate. He had won his 14th major but his bravery came at a cost. Having aggravated the injury, he needed further urgent knee surgery which kept him out of golf for the rest of the year and into 2009. The pair had tied on one-under-par 283 (usually over par wins this event), and were still locked after both shot 71 in the 18-hole play-off. It was only when 45-year-old Mediate, attempting to become the oldest winner of the title, bunkered his tee shot at the first extra hole, hit his second into the crowd and failed to make par that Woods won. It was a hard-fought third US Open victory for Woods, one which enabled him to equal Jack Nicklaus' record of three Grand Slams (victory in all four majors at least three times). Woods now needs to win five more majors to beat Jack's 18- major record which many believed would never be surpassed.

© Dave Shopland/Phil Sheldon Golf Picture Library

Tiger Woods

Only the USGA persevere with an 18-hole play-off the following day which is usually anti-climatic but on this occasion the play-off, watched by 25,000 fans, maintained the drama that had been shown throughout an entertaining week. Woods had the early advantage and out in level par 35 led Mediate by two. When the older player dropped a shot on the 10th it was assumed that the World No 1 would cruise home but he dropped shots at the next two holes and then never-say-die Mediate birdied three in a row to take an improbable one-shot lead which he held to the 18th. While Woods hit the green in two and birdied. Mediate could only par after driving into a fairway bunker and the two went into sudden death starting at the 18th. Another bunkered tee shot was the final undoing of underdog Mediate and his failure to match his rival's par allowed Woods to collected his 14th major.

When it was over, Woods praised Mediate for his "gutsy performance" and admitted that having played with the handicap of a knee injury his latest major triumph was, in the circumstances, the greatest of them all. The way it finished was somewhat anti-climatic for a Championship that had had everything. At times Tiger had winced with obvious pain when playing tee shots but insisted: "I would never have pulled out of this one. Not in front of these fans. They have always been great." He should know! His first win at Torrey Pines came in the World Junior Championship when he was just nine years old.

For some the first day ended unhappily. Top British amateur Gary Wolstenholme, who secured a place in the event for the first time as a late replacement for the injured Sean O'Hair, stumbled to an 83. Two former winners fared badly – the defending champion Angel Cabrera going round in 79 and the 2002

First Round	Second Round	Third Round	Fourth Round
–3 Hicks	–3 Appleby	–3 Woods	–1 Mediate
–3 Streelman	–2 Karlsson	–2 Westwood	–1 Woods
–2 Mediate	–2 Woods	–1 Mediate	£ Westwood
–2 Appleby	–2 Mediate	+1 Trahan	+1 Karlsson
–2 Axley	–1 Jiménez	+1 Ogilvy	+2 Trahan
–2 Ogilvy	–1 Westwood	+2 Jiménez	+2 Jiménez
–1 Fowler	–1 Love III	+2 Karlsson	+3 Merrick
–1 Karlsson	–1 Trahan	+2 Allenby	+3 Pettersson
–1 Westwood	£ Pettersson	+2 Villegas	+4 Axley
–1 Els	£ Els	+2 Mahan	+4 Ogilvy
£ Mickelson	£ Ogilvy	+3 Els	+4 Slocum
+1 Woods	£ Allenby	+3 Merrick	+4 Snedeker
	£ Donald	+3 García	+4 Villegas
		+3 Weir	

winner Michael Campbell in only one shot better. Justin Rose and Colin Montgomerie, battling to rediscover his best form, struggled to 79 and Open champion Padraig Harrington was another on the seven-over-par 78 mark.

Wolstenholme, Cabrera, Campbell, Rose and Montgomerie all missed the cut but Harrington improved 11 shots on the second day with a 67 in which he said he played less well than in his 78! First round leaders Justin Hicks and Kevin Streelman fired 80 and 77 on the second day and survived the cut among the 80 who made it on seven-over-par or better. When second round leader Stuart Appleby holed a birdie putt on the last to finish on three under-par, he put out nine players on eight-over who had been hoping to survive on the "anyone within 10 shots of the lead" rule. Ian Poulter pulled out after 15 holes of the second round with a wrist injury.

The second day belonged to Woods who despite his knee problems fired a 30 on his back nine (the front nine at Torrey Pines) to move menacingly into a share of second place with in-form Swede Robert Karlsson and Rocco Mediate on two under-par, one behind Appleby.

It was the third time that Woods had shot 30 in a major – the previous occasions being on the back nine in the 1997 Masters and on the front nine of the 1998 Open Championship at Royal Birkdale. While he was moving up the leader board he left his two big name first two rounds partners six behind. Adam Scott and Phil Mickelson were both on four-over-par. At half-way, 35 of the players who made the cut were non-American and of the top 13 on the leaderboard nine were international players with only Woods, Mediate, Davis Love and DJ Trahan representing America in a major that had been won for the last four years by non-Americans.

The third day also belonged to Tiger, winner of six PGA Tour events at Torrey Pines including the last four Buick Championships. It did not start well for him, however, when he double- bogeyed the first hole for the second time in the Championship. It was his third double bogey of the week and of the season! After four holes the World No 1 was three over for the day and was still two behind when he came to the monster 614 yards par 5 13th. That is where the fireworks began.

Taking inspiration from his playing partner Karlsson, who had holed from 60 feet for a birdie at the 11th, Woods went one better two holes later rolling in a 66 footer downhill for an eagle. It is a putt that many believed was even more dramatic than the tram-liner he holed for a birdie at the 17th at Sawgrass in the 2000 Players' Championship. Although he bogeyed the 14th and only made pars at the next two, Woods put in a barnstorming grandstand finish pitching in for an unlikely birdie from the rough at the 17th when it seemed certain he would drop a shot and then making eagle again at the last after his 227 yards 5-wood finished 40 feet from the hole. The putt for 3 edged him past England's Lee Westwood.

Tiger's dramatic tramliner

Woods had played little golf leading up to the Championship and Westwood, paired with him on the final day, had not been busy competitively either having missed the cut in the Players' Championship and pulling out of the BMW Championship suffering from tonsillitis. With 29 wins to his credit, Westwood knows how to win but was well aware of Tiger's record when leading or tied for the lead in a major after 54 holes – on 13 occasions he had never lost! Still, the consistent Westwood, who had dropped only four shots to par in 54 holes, knew there was still the chance for him to become the first English golfer since Tony Jacklin in 1970 to win the US Open.

With a round to go only Woods, Westwood and third-placed Mediate were under par with Trahan and Geoff Ogilvy one over. There were, however, four Europeans in the top 11. Joining Westwood were Miguel Angel Jiménez and Karlsson lying joint fifth tied with Robert Allenby, Camilo Villegas and Hunter Mahan all five behind Woods with Sergio García one shot further back in the same group as Ernie Els, former Masters champion Mike Weir and John Merrick. Spare a thought for Phil Mickelson, however, who at the 13th, where Tiger made one of his 3's, ran up a 9!

The decision of the USGA to set up the course in a fair but more adventurous way had paid off over three rounds and the final round again provided the 50,000 crowd with plenty of exciting golf on the longest course (7643 yards) in US Open history. Heath Slocum fired a 65, the best round of the week, to finish ninth and for a time it looked as if Ernie Els might be in the mix after he chipped in for a birdie at the 10th. A triple bogey at the 15th dashed his hopes, however, and the battle for the title boiled down to a race for the line between Westwood, Mediate and Woods. With nine to go, Westwood led on two under par, one ahead of Mediate and two ahead of Tiger but he made bogeys at three out of four holes after the turn and in the end needed to birdie the last (as did Woods) to tie Mediate who, with a level-par closing 71, had posted a one-under-par 283 total. In the end, Westwood missed from 20 feet at the 18th for the birdie but Woods, with a final flourish, holed from 15 feet to force the 12th play-off for the title in the past 50 years. Trahan, playing in only his fifth major (he had missed the half-way cut in the previous four), took fourth place. For Woods and Mediate there was one more day to go and even then a further 18 could not separate them. Woods needed one more hole to finally clinch the most courageous victory of the season.

2008 US Open Championship (108th) Torrey Pines, La Jolla, CA [7643–71]

Prize Money: $7.5 million. Entries: 8,390   June 12–15

Players are of American nationality unless stated

Final Qualifying

Osaka, Japan

Artemio Murakami (PHI)	69-69—138
Craig Parry (AUS)	70-68—138

Daly City, CA

John Ellis	69-71—140
Jason Gore	67-73—140
Michael Allen	70-70—140
Jeff Wilson (am)	70-71—141
Garrett Chaussard	68-73—141
Craig Barlow	71-70—141
Jordan Cox (am)	70-71—141

Littleton, CO

Brian Kortan	70-68—138
Jay Choi (KOR)	69-71—140

Walton Heath, UK

Ross Fisher (ENG)	67-70—137
Alastair Forsyth (SCO)	69-68—137
Ross McGowan (ENG)	67-71—138
Robert Dinwiddie (ENG)	71-67—138
Philip Archer (ENG)	69-69—138
Thomas Levet (FRA)	69-70—139
Johan Edfors (SWE)	69-70—139

Tequesta, FL

Bobby Collins	69-69—138
Philippe Gasnier (BRA)	69-71—140
Joey Lamille	73-68—141

Roswell, GA

Jason Bohn	62-67—129
Matt Kuchar	64-65—129
D J Trahan	67-67—134

Lake Forest, IL

Hunter Haas	68-68—136
Chris Kirk	68-71—139
Ian Leggatt (CAN)	69-70—139
D A Points	69-70—139
Mark O'Meara	70-70—140
Jonathan Purcott	72-69—141

Beallsville, MD

David Hearn (CAN)	71-66—137
Brian Bergstol	71-68—139

Augusta, MO

Bob Gaus	76-66—142

Purchase, NY

Kevin Silva	70-69—139
Yohann Benson (CAN)	75-67—142
Jeffrey Bors	72-70—142
Mike Gilmore	70-73—143

Columbus, OH #1

Carl Pettersen (SWE)	64-67—131
Bart Bryant	69-65—134
Ben Crane	69-66—135
Derek Fathauer (am)	67-68—135
Robert Garrigus	63-72—135
Joe Ogilvie	66-69—135
Kevin Tway (am)	68-68—136
Fredrik Jacobson (SWE)	71-66—137
Jarrod Lyle (AUS)	69-68—137
John Malinger	67-70—137
Kyle Stanley (am)	71-66—137
Nick Watney	66-71—137
Dean Wilson	69-68—137
Davis Love III	72-66—138
Jesper Parnevik (SWE)	69-69—138
Pat Perez	71-67—138
Eric Axley	70-69—139
Justiin Hicks	69-70—139
Dustin Johnson	70-69—139
Steve Marino	69-70—139
Rocco Mediate	72-67—139
Jonathan Mills (CAN)	73-66—139

Cresswell, OR

Nick Taylor (CAN)	70-68—138
Rob Rashell	69-71—140

Cordova, TN

John Merrick	65-65—130
Scott Piercy	64-68—132
Michael Quagliano	64-68—132
Brett Quigley	66-66—132
Kevin Streelman	64-69—133
Travis Bertoni	67-67—134
D J Brigman	64-70—134
Patrick Sheehan	66-68—134
Chris Stroud	65-69—134
Michael Letzig	68-68—136
Scott Sterling (AUS)	66-70—136
Brandt Jobe	65-71—136
Casey Wittenberg	69-68—137
Mathew Goggin (AUS)	67-70—137

Richmond, VA

Rich Beem	67-70—137
Charlie Beljan	69-70—139

Columbus, OH #2

Peter Tomasulo	63-35—128
Andrew Dresser	67-66—133
Fernando Figueroa (ESA)	67-67—134
Chris Devlin (NIR)	68-67—135
Sean English	64-71—135
Jimmy Henderson	71-65—136

Final Field: 156 (11 amateurs), of whom 80 (including 3 amateurs) made the cut on 149 or less.

1	Tiger Woods*	72-68-70-73—283	$1350000
2	Rocco Mediate	69-71-72-71—283	810000

Tiger Woods won at the 19th hole of the extra round

3	Lee Westwood (ENG)	70-71-70-73—284	491995
4	Robert Karlsson (SWE)	70-70-75-71—286	307303
	D J Trahan	72-69-73-72--286	307303
6	Miguel Angel Jiménez (ESP)	75-66-74-72—287	220686
	John Merrick	73-72-71-71—287	220686
	Carl Pettersson (SWE)	71-71-77-68—287	220686
9	Eric Axley	69-79-71-69—288	160769
	Geoff Ogilvy (AUS)	69-73-72-74—288	160769
	Heath Slocum	75-74-74-65—288	160769
	Brandt Snedeker	76-73-68-71—288	160769
	Camilo Villegas (COL)	73-71-71-73—288	160769
14	Stewart Cink	72-73-77-67—289	122159
	Ernie Els (RSA)	70-72-74-73—289	122159
	Retief Goosen (RSA)	76-69-77-67—289	122159
	Rod Pampling (AUS)	74-70-75-70—289	122159
18	Robert Allenby (AUS)	70-72-73-75—290	87230
	Chad Campbell	77-72-71-70—290	87230
	Sergio García (ESP)	76-70-70-74—290	87230
	Ryuji Imada (JPN)	74-75-70-71—290	87230
	Brandt Jobe	73-75-69-73—290	87230
	Hunter Mahan	72-74-69-75—290	87230
	Phil Mickelson	71-75-76-68—290	87230
	Mike Weir (CAN)	73-74-69-74—290	87230
26	Anthony Kim	74-75-70-72—291	61252
	Adam Scott (AUS)	73-73-75-70—291	61252
	Boo Weekley	73-76-70-72—291	61252
29	Aaron Baddeley (AUS)	74-73-71-74—292	48482
	Bart Bryant	75-70-78-69—292	48482
	Jeff Quinney	79-70-70-73—292	48482
	Patrick Sheehan	71-74-74-73—292	48482
	Steve Stricker	73-76-71-72—292	48482
	Michael Thompson (am)	74-73-73-72—292	
	Scott Verplank	72-72-74-74—292	48482
36	Stuart Appleby (AUS)	69-70-79-75—293	35709
	Daniel Chopra (SWE)	73-75-75-70—293	35709
	Robert Dinwiddie (ENG)	73-71-75-74—293	35709
	Jim Furyk	74-71-73-75—293	35709
	Todd Hamilton	74-74-73-72—293	35709
	Padraig Harrington (IRL)	78-67-77-71—293	35709
	Justin Leonard	75-72-75-71—293	35709
	Jonathan Mills	72-75-75-71—293	35709
	Joe Ogilvie	71-76-73-73—293	35709
	Pat Perez	75-73-75-70—293	35709
	Andres Romero (ARG)	71-73-77-72—293	35709
	Oliver Wilson (ENG)	72-71-74-76—293	35709
48	Tim Clark (RSA)	73-72-74-75—294	23985
	Dustin Johnson	74-72-75-73—294	23985
	Matt Kuchar	73-73-76-72—294	23985
	Jarrod Lyle (AUS)	75-74-74-71—294	23985
	John Rollins	75-68-79-72—294	23985
53	Ben Crane	75-72-77-71—295	20251
	Søren Hansen (DEN)	78-70-76-71—295	20251
	Martin Kaymer (GER)	75-70-73-77—295	20251
	Davis Love III	72-69-76-78—295	20251
	Kevin Streelman	68-77-78-72—295	20251
58	Stephen Ames (CAN)	74-74-77-71—296	18664
	Rory Sabbatini (RSA)	73-72-75-76—296	18664

60	Alastair Forsyth (SCO)	76-73-74-74—297	17691
	Rickie Fowler (am)	70-79-76-72—297	
	Brett Quigley	73-72-77-75—297	17691
	David Toms	76-72-72-77—297	17691
	Nick Watney	73-75-77-72—297	17691
65	Paul Casey (ENG)	79-70-76-73—298	16514
	Trevor Immelman (RSA)	75-73-72-78—298	16514
	John Malinger	73-75-78-72—298	16514
	Vijay Singh (FIJ)	71-78-76-73—298	16514
69	Derek Fathauer (am)	73-73-78-75—299	
	D A Points	74-71-77-77—299	15778
71	Woody Austin	72-72-77-79—300	15189
	Andrew Dresser	76-73-79-72—300	15189
	Andrew Svoboda	77-71-74-78—300	15189
74	Justin Hicks	68-80-75-78—301	14306
	Ian Leggatt (CAN)	72-76-76-77—301	14306
	Jesper Parnevik (SWE)	77-72-77-75—301	14306
77	Ross McGowan (ENG)	76-72-78-77—303	13718
78	Rich Beem	74-74-80-76—304	13276
	Chris Kirk	75-74-78-77—304	13276
80	Luke Donald (ENG)	71-71-77 WD	2000

The following players missed the half-way cut. All professionals received $2000 each:

81	Robert Garrigus	77-73—150	107T	Fredrik Jacobson	74-79—153	134T	Jay Choi	79-80—159
	Mathew Goggin (AUS)	77-73—150		(SWE)			Steve Flesch	78-81—159
	Hunter Haas	80-70—150		Lee Janzen	75-78—153		Jeff Wilson (am)	78-81—159
	J B Holmes	75-75—150		Shingo Katayama	77-76—153	138	Jeffrey Bors	81-79—160
	Zach Johnson	76-74—150		(JPN)		139	Yohann Benson	83-78—161
	Thomas Levet (FRA)	74-76—150		Kevin Tway (am)	75-78—153		Michael Campbell	78-83—161
	Scott Sterling (AUS)	80-70—150	114	D J Brigman	79-75—154		(NZL)	
	Kyle Stanley (am)	72-78—150		Henrik Stenson	78-76—154		Philippe Gasnier	86-75—161
	Toru Taniguchi (JPN)	74-76—150		(SWE)			(BRA)	
	Jon Turcott	77-73—150		Bubba Watson	77-77—154		Chris Stroud	84-77—161
	Casey Wittenberg	72-78—150	117	Charlie Beljan	76-79—155	143	Garrett Chaussard	80-82—162
92	K J Choi (KOR)	74-77—151		Travis Bertoni	82-73—155		Bobby Collins	84-78—162
	Ben Curtis	75-76—151		Angel Cabrera (ARG)	79-76—155		Brian Kortan	78-84—162
	John Ellis	77-74—151		Nick Dougherty	78-77—155		Artemio Murakami	79-83—162
	Ross Fisher	73-78—151		(ENG)			(PHI)	
	David Hearn (CAN)	76-75—151		Jason Gore	79-76—155	147	Fernando Figueroa	78-85—163
	Steve Marino	73-78—151		Joey Lamielle	76-79—155		(ESA)	
	Mark O'Meara	75-76—151		Dean Wilson	76-79—155		Jimmy Henderson	81-82—163
	Scott Piercy	78-73—151	124	Craig Barlow	80-76—156		(am)	
	Rob Rashell	81-70—151		Brad Bryant	77-79—156	149	Niclas Fasth (SWE)	78-86—164
	Justin Rose (ENG)	79-72—151		Johan Edfors (SWE)	79-77—156	150	Gary Wolstenholme	83-82—165
	Richard Sterne (RSA)	76-75—151		Bob Gaus	80-76—156		(ENG) (am)	
	Peter Tomasulo	76-75—151		Colin Montgomerie	79-77—156	151	Brian Bergstol	86-81—167
104	Jonathan Byrd	75-77—152		(SCO)			Chris Devlin	84-83—167
	Michael Letzig	77-75—152		Craig Parry (AUS)	75-81—156		Mike Gilmore	86-81—167
	Nick Taylor (CAN)	77-75—152		Kevin Silva	80-76—156		Michael Quagliano	86-81—167
	(am)		131	Jordan Cox (am)	80-77—157		(am)	
107	Michael Allen	78-75—153		Sean English	75-82—157	155	Ian Poulter (ENG)	78- WD
	Jason Bohn	76-77—153		Jerry Kelly	75-82—157	156	Mark Calcavecchia	WD
	Charles Howell III	75-78—153	134	Phil Archer (ENG)	78-81—159			

2007 US Open *Oakmont, PA* June 14–17   [7230–70]

Prize money: $6.8 million. Entries: 8,544

1	Angel Cabrera (ARG)	69-71-76-69—285	$1260000	20T	Mike Weir (CAN)	74-72-73-75—294	86200
2	Jim Furyk	71-75-70-70—286	611336	23	Ken Duke	74-75-73-73—295	71905
	Tiger Woods	71-74-69-72—286	611336		Nick O'Hern (AUS)	76-74-71-74—295	71905
4	Niclas Fasth (SWE)	71-71-75-70—287	325923		Brandt Snedeker	71-73-77-74—295	71905
5	David Toms	72-72-73-72—289	248948	26	Stuart Appleby (AUS)	74-72-71-79—296	57026
	Bubba Watson	70-71-74-74—289	248948		J J Henry	71-78-75-72—296	57026
7	Nick Dougherty (ENG)	68-77-74-71—290	194245		Camilo Villegas (COL)	73-77-75-71—296	57026
	Jerry Kelly	74-71-73-72—290	194245		Boo Weekley	72-75-77-72—296	57026
	Scott Verplank	73-71-74-72—290	194245	30	D J Brigman	74-74-74-75—297	45313
10	Stephen Ames (CAN)	73-69-73-76—291	154093		Fred Funk	71-78-74-74—297	45313
	Paul Casey (ENG)	77-66-72-76—291	154093		Peter Hanson (SWE)	71-74-78-74—297	45313
	Justin Rose (ENG)	71-71-73-76—291	154093		Pablo Martin (ESP)	71-76-77-73—297	45313
13	Aaron Baddeley (AUS)	72-70-70-80—292	124706		Graeme McDowell	73-72-75-77—297	45313
	Lee Janzen	73-73-73-73—292	124706		(NIR)		
	Hunter Mahan	73-74-72-73—292	124706		Charl Schwartzel (RSA)	75-73-73-76—297	45313
	Steve Stricker	75-73-68-76—292	124706	36	Mathew Goggin (AUS)	77-73-74-74—298	37159
17	Jeff Brehaut	73-75-70-75—293	102536		Shingo Katayama (JPN)	72-74-79-73—298	37159
	Jim Clark (RSA)	72-76-71-74—293	102536		Jeev Milkha Singh (IND)	75-75-73-75—298	37159
	Carl Pettersson (SWE)	72-72-75-74—293	102536		Tom Pernice	72-72-75-79—298	37159
20	Anthony Kim	74-73-80-67—294	86200		Ian Poulter (ENG)	72-77-72-77—298	37159
	Vijay Singh (FIJ)	71-77-70-76—294	86200		Lee Westwood (ENG)	72-75-79-72—298	37159

Other players who made the cut: Kenneth Ferrie (ENG), Geoff Ogilvy (AUS), John Rollins, 299; Olin Browne, Ben Curtis, Chris DiMarco, Marcus Fraser (AUS), Zach Johnson, José-María Olazábal (ESP), 300; Ernie Els (RSA), Charles Howell III, Rory Sabbatini (RSA), Dean Wilson, 301; Anders Hansen (DEN), Michael Putnam, 302; Chad Campbell, 303; Michael Campbell (NZL), Bob Estes, Harrison Frazar, Kevin Sutherland, 304; Jason Dufner, 305; George McNeill, 306

2006 US Open *Winged Foot, Mamaroneck, NY* June 15–18   [7264–70]

Prize money: $6.25 million. Entries: 8,584

1	Geoff Ogilvy (AUS)	71-70-72-72—285	$1225000	16T	Arron Oberholser	75-68-74-74—291	99417
2	Jim Furyk	70-72-74-70—286	501249	21	Peter Hedblom (SWE)	72-74-71-75—292	74252
	Phil Mickelson	70-73-69-74—286	501249		Trevor Immelman (RSA)	76-71-70-75—292	74252
	Colin Montgomerie	69-71-75-71—286	501249		José-María Olazábal	75-73-73-71—292	74252
	(SCO)				(ESP)		
5	Padraig Harrington	73-69-74-71—287	255642		Tom Pernice Jr	79-70-72-71—292	74252
	(IRL)				Adam Scott (AUS)	72-76-70-74—292	74252
6	Kenneth Ferrie (ENG)	71-70-71-76—288	183255	26	Craig Barlow	72-75-72-74—293	52314
	Nick O'Hern (AUS)	75-70-74-69—288	183255		Angel Cabrera (ARG)	74-73-74-72—293	52314
	Vijay Singh (FIJ)	71-74-70-73—288	183255		Ernie Els (RSA)	74-73-74-72—293	52314
	Jeff Sluman	74-73-72-69—288	183255		Sean O'Hair	76-72-74-71—293	52314
	Steve Stricker	70-69-76-73—288	183255		Ted Purdy	78-71-71-73—293	52314
	Mike Weir (CAN)	71-74-71-72—288	183255		Henrik Stenson (SWE)	75-71-73-74—293	52314
12	Luke Donald (ENG)	78-69-70-72—289	131670	32	Woody Austin	72-76-72-74—294	41912
	Ryuji Imada (JPN)	76-73-69-71—289	131670		Bart Bryant	72-72-73-77—294	41912
	Ian Poulter (ENG)	74-71-70-74—289	131670		Scott Hend (AUS)	72-72-75-75—294	41912
15	Paul Casey (ENG)	77-72-72-69—290	116735		Steve Jones	74-74-71-75—294	41912
16	Robert Allenby (AUS)	73-74-72-72—291	99417		Rodney Pampling (AUS)	73-75-75-71—294	41912
	David Duval	77-68-75-71—291	99417	37	Stewart Cink	75-71-77-72—295	36647
	David Howell (ENG)	70-78-74-69—291	99417		Jay Haas	75-72-74-74—295	36647
	Miguel Angel Jiménez	70-75-74-72—291	99417		Charles Howell III	77-71-73-74—295	36647
	(ESP)						

Other players who made the cut: Tommy Armour III, Chad Collins, John Cook, Jason Dufner, Fred Funk, Stephen Gangluff (CAN), Bo Van Pelt, Lee Williams, 296; Phillip Archer (ENG), Thomas Bjørn (DEN), Fred Couples, Charley Hoffman, J B Holmes, Kent Jones, Graeme McDowell (NIR), Charl Schwartzel (RSA), 297; Darren Clarke (NIR), 298; Ben Curtis, 299; Kenny Perry, 301; Skip Kendal, Jeev Milkha Singh (IND), Camilo Villegas (COL), 302; Ben Crane, 303; Tim Herron, 305

2005 US Open Pinehurst No.2, NC June 16–19

Prize money: $6.25 million. Entries: 9,048

[7214–70]

1	Michael Campbell (NZL)	71-69-71-69—280	$1170000	15T	Peter Jacobsen	72-73-69-75—289	88120
2	Tiger Woods	70-71-72-69—282	700000		David Toms	70-72-70-77—289	88120
3	Tim Clark (RSA)	76-69-70-70—285	320039	23	Olin Browne	67-71-72-80—290	59633
	Sergio García (ESP)	71-69-75-70—285	320039		Paul Claxton	72-72-72-74—290	59633
	Mark Hensby (AUS)	71-68-72-74—285	320039		Fred Funk	73-71-76-70—290	59633
6	Davis Love III	77-70-70-69—286	187813		Justin Leonard	76-71-70-73—290	59633
	Rocco Mediate	67-74-74-71—286	187813		Kenny Perry	75-70-71-74—290	59633
	Vijay Singh (FIJ)	70-70-74-72—286	187813	28	Stephen Allan (AUS)	72-69-73-77—291	44486
9	Arron Oberholser	76-67-71-73—287	150834		Matt Every (am)	75-73-73-70—291	44486
	Nick Price (ZIM)	72-71-72-72—287	150834		Jim Furyk	71-70-75-75—291	44486
11	Bob Estes	70-73-75-70—288	123857		Geoff Ogilvy (AUS)	72-74-71-74—291	44486
	Retief Goosen (RSA)	68-70-69-81—288	123857		Adam Scott (AUS)	70-71-74-76—291	44486
	Peter Hedblom (SWE)	77-66-70-75—288	123857	33	Angel Cabrera (ARG)	71-73-73-75—292	35759
	Corey Pavin	73-72-70-73—288	123857		Steve Elkington (AUS)	74-69-79-70—292	35759
15	K J Choi (KOR)	69-70-74-76—289	88120		Tim Herron	74-73-70-75—292	35759
	Stewart Cink	73-74-73-69—289	88120		Brandt Jobe	68-73-79-72—292	35759
	John Cook	71-76-70-72—289	88120		Bernhard Langer (GER)	74-73-71-74—292	35759
	Fred Couples	71-74-74-70—289	88120		Shigeki Maruyama (JPN)	71-74-72-75—292	35759
	Ernie Els (RSA)	71-76-72-70—289	88120		Phil Mickelson	69-77-72-74—292	35759
	Ryuji Imada (JPN)	77-68-73-71—289	88120		Ted Purdy	73-71-73-75—292	35759
					Lee Westwood (ENG)	68-72-73-79—292	35759

Other players who made the cut: Chad Campbell, Peter Lonard (AUS), Paul McGinley (IRL), Colin Montgomerie (SCO), Tom Pernice, Rob Rashell, Mike Weir (CAN), 293; Jason Gore, J L Lewis, Nick O'Hern (AUS), 294; Thomas Bjørn (DEN), Nick Dougherty (ENG), Richard Green (AUS), Søren Kjeldsen (DEN), Thomas Levet (FRA), 295; Tommy Armour III, Luke Donald (ENG), Keiichiro Fukabori (JPN), J J Henry, Lee Janzen, Steve Jones, Frank Lickliter, Jonathan Lomas (ENG), Ryan Moore (am), Ian Poulter (ENG), 296; Michael Allen, Steve Flesch, Bill Glasson, John Mallinger, 297; Stephen Ames (TRI), D J Brigman, J Hayes, Rory Sabbatini (RSA), 298; John Daly, Charles Howell III, Omar Uresti, 299; Jeff Maggert, Bob Tway, 300; Graeme McDowell (NIR), Chris Nallen, 301; Craig Barlow. 303; Jerry Kelly, 305

2004 US Open Shinnecock Hills, Southampton, NY June 17–20

Prize money: $6.25 million. Entries: 8,726

[6996–70]

1	Retief Goosen (RSA)	70-66-69-71—276	$1125000	20T	David Toms	73-72-70-76—291	80644
2	Phil Mickelson	68-66-73-71—278	675000		Kirk Triplett	71-70-73-77—291	80644
3	Jeff Maggert	68-67-74-72—281	424604	24	Daniel Chopra (SWE)	73-68-76-75—292	63328
4	Shigeki Maruyama (JPN)	66-68-74-76—284	267756		Lee Janzen	72-70-71-79—292	63328
	Mike Weir (CAN)	69-70-71-74—284	267756		Tim Petrovic	69-75-72-76—292	63328
6	Fred Funk	70-66-72-77—285	212444		Nick Price (ZIM)	73-70-72-77—292	63328
7	Robert Allenby (AUS)	70-72-74-70—286	183828	28	Shaun Micheel	71-72-70-80—293	51774
	Steve Flesch	68-74-70-74—286	183828		Vijay Singh (FIJ)	68-70-77-78—293	51774
9	Stephen Ames (TRI)	74-66-73-74—287	145282	30	Ben Curtis	68-75-72-79—294	46089
	Ernie Els (RSA)	70-67-70-80—287	145282	31	K J Choi (KOR)	76-68-76-75—295	41759
	Chris DiMarco	71-71-70-75—287	145282		Padraig Harrington (IRL)	73-71-76-75—295	41759
	Jay Haas	66-74-76-71—287	145282		Peter Lonard (AUS)	71-73-77-74—295	41759
13	Tim Clark (RSA)	73-70-66-79—288	119770		David Roesch	68-73-74-80—295	41759
	Tim Herron	75-66-73-74—288	119770		Bo Van Pelt	69-73-73-80—295	41759
	Spencer Levin (am)	69-73-71-75—288		36	Charles Howell III	75-70-68-83—296	36813
16	Angel Cabrera (ARG)	66-71-77-75—289	109410		Hidemichi Tanaka (JPN)	70-74-73-79—296	36813
17	Skip Kendall	68-75-74-73—290	98477		Lee Westwood (ENG)	73-71-73-79—296	36813
	Corey Pavin	67-71-73-79—290	98477		Casey Wittenberg (am)	71-71-75-79—296	
	Tiger Woods	72-69-73-76—290	98477				
20	Mark Calcavecchia	71-71-74-75—291	80644				
	Sergio García (ESP)	72-68-71-80—291	80644				

Other players who made the cut: Bill Haas (am), Jerry Kelly, Stephen Leaney (AUS), Spike McRoy, Joe Ogilvie, Pat Perez, Geoffrey Sisk, Scott Verplank 297; Kristopher Cox, Jim Furyk, Zachary Johnson, Chris Riley, John Rollins 298; Dudley Hart, Scott Hoch 299; Tom Carter, Trevor Immelman (RSA) 300; Joakim Haeggman (SWE), Tom Kite, Phillip Price (WAL) 302; Alex Cejka (GER), Craig Parry (AUS) 303; Cliff Kresge, Chez Reavie (am) 304; J J Henry 306; Kevin Stadler 307; Billy Mayfair 310

2003 US Open Olympia Fields CC (North Course), IL June 12–15 [7190–70]

Prize money: $6 million. Entries: 7,820

1	Jim Furyk	67-66-67-72—272	$1080000	20	Mark Calcavecchia	68-72-67-76—283	64170
2	Stephen Leaney (AUS)	67-68-68-72—275	650000		Robert Damron	69-68-73-73—283	64170
3	Kenny Perry	72-71-69-67—279	341367		Ian Leggatt (RSA)	68-70-68-77—283	64170
	Mike Weir (CAN)	73-67-68-71—279	341367		Justin Leonard	66-70-72-75—283	64170
5	Ernie Els (RSA)	69-70-69-72—280	185934		Peter Lonard (AUS)	72-69-74-68—283	64170
	Fredrik Jacobson (SWE)	69-67-73-71—280	185934		Vijay Singh (FIJ)	70-63-72-78—283	64170
	Nick Price (ZIM)	71-65-69-75—280	185934		Jay Williamson	72-69-69-73—283	64170
	Justin Rose (ENG)	70-71-70-69—280	185934		Tiger Woods	70-66-75-72—283	64170
	David Toms	72-67-70-71—280	185934	28	Stewart Cink	70-68-72-74—284	41254
10	Padraig Harrington (IRL)	69-72-72-68—281	124936		John Maginnes	72-70-72-70—284	41254
	Jonathan Kaye	70-70-72-69—281	124936		Dicky Pride	71-69-66-78—284	41254
	Cliff Kresge	69-70-72-70—281	124936		Brett Quigley	65-74-71-74—284	41254
	Billy Mayfair	69-71-67-74—281	124936		Kevin Sutherland	71-71-72-70—284	41254
	Scott Verplank	76-67-68-70—281	124936		Kirk Triplett	71-68-73-72—284	41254
15	Jonathan Byrd	69-66-71-76—282	93359		Tom Watson	65-72-75-72—284	41254
	Tom Byrum	69-69-71-73—282	93359	35	Angel Cabrera (ARG)	72-68-73-72—285	32552
	Tim Petrovic	69-70-70-73—282	93359		Chad Campbell	70-70-69-76—285	32552
	Eduardo Romero (ARG)	70-66-70-76—282	93359		Chris DiMarco	72-71-71-71—285	32552
	Higemichi Tamaka (JPN)	69-71-71-71—282	93359		Fred Funk	70-73-71-71—285	32552
					Sergio García (ESP)	69-74-71-71—285	32552
					Brandt Jobe	70-68-76-71—285	32552
					Mark O'Meara	72-68-67-78—285	32552

Other players who made the cut: Darren Clarke (NIR), Retief Goosen (RSA), Bernhard Langer (GER), Steve Lowery, Colin Montgomerie (SCO), Loren Roberts 286; Woody Austin, Marco Dawson, Niclas Fasth (SWE), Dan Forsman, Darron Stiles 287; Charles Howell III, John Rollins 288; Lee Janzen, Phil Mickelson 289; Trip Kuehne (am), Len Mattiace 290; Ricky Barnes (am), Olin Browne 291; Chris Anderson, Alexander Cejka (GER), Brian Davis (ENG) 292; Jay Don Blake, JP Hayes 293; Fred Couples, Brian Henninger 295; Ryan Dillon 301

2002 US Open Bethpage State Park, Black Course, Farmingdale, NY August 13–16 [7214–70]

Prize money: $5.5 million. Entries: 8,468

1	Tiger Woods	67-68-70-72—277	$1000000	24	Jim Carter	77-73-70-71—291	47439
2	Phil Mickelson	70-73-67-70—280	585000		Darren Clarke (NIR)	74-74-72-71—291	47439
3	Jeff Maggert	69-73-68-72—282	362356		Chris DiMarco	74-74-72-71—291	47439
4	Sergio García (ESP)	68-74-67-74—283	252546		Ernie Els (RSA)	73-74-70-74—291	47439
5	Nick Faldo (ENG)	70-76-66-73—285	182882		Davis Love III	71-71-72-77—291	47439
	Scott Hoch	71-75-70-69—285	182882		Jeff Sluman	73-73-72-73—291	47439
	Billy Mayfair	69-74-68-74—285	182882	30	Jason Caron	75-72-72-73—292	35639
8	Tom Byrum	72-72-70-72—286	138669		K J Choi (KOR)	69-73-73-77—292	35639
	Padraig Harrington (IRL)	70-68-73-75—286	138669		Paul Lawrie (SCO)	73-73-73-73—292	35639
	Nick Price (ZIM)	72-75-69-70—286	138669		Scott McCarron	72-72-70-78—292	35639
11	Peter Lonard (AUS)	73-74-73-67—287	119357		Vijay Singh (FIJ)	75-75-67-75—292	35639
12	Robert Allenby (AUS)	74-70-67-77—288	102338	35	Shingo Katayama (JPN)	74-72-74-73—293	31945
	Jay Haas	73-73-70-72—288	102338		Bernhard Langer (GER)	72-76-70-75—293	31945
	Dudley Hart	69-76-70-73—288	102338	37	Stuart Appleby (AUS)	77-73-75-69—294	26783
	Justin Leonard	73-71-68-76—288	102338		Thomas Bjørn (DEN)	71-79-73-71—294	26783
16	Shigeki Maruyama (JPN)	76-67-73-73—289	86372		Niclas Fasth (SWE)	72-72-74-76—294	26783
	Steve Stricker	72-77-69-71—289	86372		Donnie Hammond	73-77-71-73—294	26783
18	Luke Donald (ENG)	71-76-70-72—290	68995		Franklin Langham	70-76-74-74—294	26783
	Charles Howell III	71-74-70-75—290	68995		Rocco Mediate	72-72-74-76—294	26783
	Steve Flesch	72-72-75-71—290	68995		Kevin Sutherland	74-75-70-75—294	26783
	Thomas Levet (FRA)	71-77-70-72—290	68995		Hidemichi Tanaka (JPN)	73-73-72-76—294	26783
	Mark O'Meara	76-70-69-75—290	68995				
	Craig Stadler	74-72-70-74—290	68995				

Other players who made the cut: Tom Lehman, Frank Lickliter, Kenny Perry, David Toms, Jean Van de Velde (FRA) 295; Craig Bowden, Tim Herron, Robert Karlsson (SWE), José María Olazábal (ESP) 296; Harrison Frazar, Ian Leggatt (CAN), Jesper Parnevik (SWE), Corey Pavin 297; Brad Lardon 298; John Maginnes, Greg Norman (AUS), Bob Tway 299; Andy Miller, Jeev Milkha Singh (IND), Paul Stankowski 300; Spike McRoy 301; Angel Cabrera (ARG), Brad Faxon 302; Kent Jones, Len Mattiace 303; John Daly, Tom Gillis 304; Kevin Warrick (am) 307

2001 US Open Southern Hills CC, Tulsa, OK June 14–18 [6973–70]
Prize money: $5,000,000. Entries: 8,300

1	Retief Goosen* (RSA)	66-70-69-71—276	$900000	22	Scott Verplank	71-71-73-71—286	54813	
2	Mark Brooks	72-64-70-70—276	530000		Thomas Bjørn (DEN)	72-69-73-72—286	54813	
*Play-off: Goosen 70, Brooks 72				24	Mark Calcavecchia	70-74-73-70—287	42523	
3	Stewart Cink	69-69-67-72—277	325310		Hal Sutton	70-75-71-71—287	42523	
4	Rocco Mediate	71-68-67-72—278	226777		Tom Lehman	76-68-69-74—287	42523	
5	Tom Kite	73-72-72-64—281	172912		Olin Browne	71-74-71-71—287	42523	
	Paul Azinger	74-67-69-71—281	172912		Steve Lowery	71-73-72-71—287	42523	
7	Davis Love III	72-69-71-70—282	125172		Joe Durant	71-74-70-72—287	42523	
	Vijay Singh (FIJ)	74-70-74-64—282	125172	30	Dean Wilson	71-74-72-71—288	30055	
	Angel Cabrera (ARG)	70-71-72-69—282	125172		Bob Estes	70-72-75-71—288	30055	
	Phil Mickelson	70-69-68-75—282	125172		Steve Jones	73-73-72-70—288	30055	
	Kirk Triplett	72-69-71-70—282	125172		Gabriel Hjertstedt (SWE)	72-74-70-72—288	30055	
12	Tiger Woods	74-71-69-69—283	91734		Padraig Harrington (IRL)	73-70-71-74—288	30055	
	Sergio García (ESP)	70-68-68-77—283	91734		Jesper Parnevik (SWE)	73-73-74-68—288	30055	
	Michael Allen	77-68-67-71—283	91734		Darren Clarke (NIR)	74-71-71-72—288	30055	
	Matt Gogel	70-69-74-70—283	91734		Bob May	72-72-69-75—288	30055	
16	David Duval	70-69-71-74—284	75337		Bryce Molder (am)	75-71-68-74—288		
	Scott Hoch	73-73-69-69—284	75337		JL Lewis	68-68-77-75—288	30055	
	Chris DiMarco	69-73-70-72—284	75337	40	Bernhard Langer (GER)	71-73-71-74—289	23933	
19	Corey Pavin	70-75-68-72—285	63426		Tim Herron	71-74-73-71—289	23933	
	Chris Perry	72-71-73-69—285	63426		Briny Baird	71-72-70-76—289	23933	
	Mike Weir (CAN)	67-76-68-74—285	63426		Shaun Micheel	73-70-75-71—289	23933	

Other players who made the cut: Fred Funk, Toshimitsu Izawa (JPN), Brandel Chamblee, Jeff Maggert, Duffy Waldorf, Kevin Sutherland, Tom Byrum 290; Eduardo Romero (ARG) 291; Loren Roberts, Colin Montgomerie (SCO), Mark Wiebe, Bob Tway, Hale Irwin, José Coceres (ARG), Scott Dunlap, Brandt Jobe, Frank Lickliter, Jimmy Walker 292; Jim Furyk, Dudley Hart, Richard Zokol (CAN), Tim Petrovic 293; Ernie Els (RSA), Peter Lonard (AUS), Dan Forsman, David Toms, Harrison Frazer, David Peoples 294; Nick Faldo (ENG), Franklin Langham 295; Anthony Kang (KOR), Mathias Grönberg (SWE), Gary Orr (SCO), Thongchai Jaidee (THA) 296; Jim McGovern 297; Stephen Gangluff 301.

2000 US Open Pebble Beach, CA June 15–18 [6846–71]
Prize money: $4,500,000. Entries: 8,457

1	Tiger Woods	65-69-71-67—272	$800000	22	Notah Begay III	74-75-72-73—294	53105	
2	Miguel Angel Jiménez (ESP)	66-74-76-71—287	391150	23	Hal Sutton	69-73-83-70—295	45537	
	Ernie Els (RSA)	74-73-68-72—287	391150		Bob May	72-76-75-72—295	45537	
4	John Huston	67-75-76-70—288	212779		Tom Lehman	71-73-78-73—295	45537	
5	Padraig Harrington (IRL)	73-71-72-73—289	162526		Mike Brisky	71-73-79-72—295	45537	
	Lee Westwood (ENG)	71-71-76-71—289	162526	27	Tom Watson	71-74-78-73—296	34066	
7	Nick Faldo (ENG)	69-74-76-71—290	137203		Nick Price (ZIM)	77-70-78-71—296	34066	
8	Loren Roberts	68-78-73-72—291	112766		Steve Stricker	75-74-75-72—296	34066	
	David Duval	75-71-74-71—291	112766		Steve Jones	75-73-75-73—296	34066	
	Stewart Cink	77-72-72-70—291	112766		Hale Irwin	68-78-81-69—296	34066	
	Vijay Singh (FIJ)	70-73-80-68—291	112766	32	Tom Kite	72-77-77-71—297	28247	
12	José María Olazábal (ESP)	70-71-76-75—292	86223		Chris Perry	75-72-78-72—297	28247	
	Paul Azinger	71-73-79-69—292	86223		Richard Zokol (CAN)	74-74-80-69—297	28247	
	Retief Goosen (RSA)	77-72-72-71—292	86223		Rocco Mediate	69-76-75-77—297	28247	
	Michael Campbell (NZL)	71-77-71-73—292	86223		Lee Porter	74-70-83-70—297	28247	
16	Justin Leonard	73-73-75-72—293	65214	37	Woody Austin	77-70-78-73—298	22056	
	Mike Weir (CAN)	76-72-76-79—293	65214		Jerry Kelly	73-73-81-71—298	22056	
	Fred Couples	70-75-75-73—293	65214		Larry Mize	73-72-76-77—298	22056	
	Scott Hoch	73-76-75-69—293	65214		Craig Parry (AUS)	73-74-76-75—298	22056	
	Phil Mickelson	71-73-73-76—293	65214		Bobby Clampett	68-77-76-77—298	22056	
	David Toms	73-76-72-72—293	65214		Angel Cabrera (ARG)	69-76-79-74—298	22056	
					Lee Janzen	71-73-79-75—298	22056	
					Ted Tryba	71-73-79-75—298	22056	
					Charles Warren	75-74-75-74—298	22056	

Other players who made the cut: Rick Hartmann, Sergio García (ESP), Colin Montgomerie (SCO), Scott Verplank, Thomas Bjørn (DEN) 299; Warren Schutte (SA), Mark O'Meara 300; Darren Clarke (NIR), Keith Clearwater, Jeff Coston 301; Kirk Triplett 302; Dave Eichelberger, Jimmy Green 303; Jeffrey Wilson (am) 304; Jim Furyk; Brandel Chamblee, Carlos Daniel Franco (PAR) 306; Robert Damron 313.

1999 US Open Pinehurst No. 2, NC June 17–20   [7175–70]

Prize money: $3,500,000. Entries: 7,889

1	P Stewart	68-69-72-70—279	$625000	17T	S Verplank	72-73-72-74—291	46756
2	P Mickelson	67-70-73-70—280	370000	23	MA Jiménez (ESP)	73-70-72-77—292	33505
3	V Singh (FIJ)	69-70-73-69—281	196791		N Price (ZIM)	71-74-74-73—292	33505
	T Woods	68-71-72-70—281	196791		T Scherrer	72-72-74-74—292	33505
5	S Stricker	70-73-69-73—285	130655		B Watts	69-73-77-73—292	33505
6	T Herron	69-72-70-75—286	116935		DA Weibring	69-74-74-75—292	33505
7	D Duval	67-70-75-75—287	96260	28	D Berganio Jr	68-77-76-72—293	26185
	J Maggert	71-69-74-73—287	96260		T Lehman	73-74-73-73—293	26185
	H Sutton	69-70-76-72—287	96260	30	B Estes	70-71-77-76—294	23804
10	D Clarke (NIR)	73-70-74-71—288	78862		G Sisk	71-72-76-75—294	23804
	B Mayfair	67-72-74-75—288	78862	32	S Cink	72-74-78-71—295	22448
12	P Azinger	72-72-75-70—289	67347		S Strüver (GER)	70-76-75-74—295	22448
	P Goydos	67-74-74-74—289	67347	34	B Fabel	69-75-78-74—296	19083
	D Love III	70-73-74-72—289	67347		C Franco (PAR)	69-77-73-77—296	19083
15	J Leonard	69-75-73-73—290	58214		G Hjertstedt (SWE)	75-72-79-70—296	19083
	C Montgomerie (SCO)	72-72-74-72—290	58214		R Mediate	69-72-76-79—296	19083
17	J Furyk	69-73-77-72—291	46756		C Parry (AUS)	69-73-79-75—296	19083
	J Haas	74-72-73-72—291	46756		S Pate	70-75-75-76—296	19083
	D Hart	73-73-76-69—291	46756		C Pavin	74-71-78-73—296	19083
	J Huston	71-69-75-76—291	46756		E Toledo (MEX)	70-72-76-78—296	19083
	J Parnevik (SWE)	71-71-76-73—291	46756				

Other players who made the cut: S Allan (AUS), G Hallberg, L Mattiace, C Perry 297; R Allenby (AUS), B Chamblee, L Janzen, D Lebeck, 298; S Elkington (AUS), C Tidland 299; G Kraft, S McRoy, P Price (WAL), J Tyska 300; J Kelly, T Watson, K Yokoo (JPN) 301; J Cook, T Kite 302; C Smith, B Tway 303; L Mize 304; H Kuehne (am) 306; B Burns, T Tryba 308; J Daly 309.

US Open Championship History

Year	Winner	Runner-up	Venue	Score
1894	W Dunn	W Campbell	St Andrews, NY	2 holes

After 1894 decided by stroke-play. From 1895–1897. 36-holes From 1898 72-holes

Year	Winner	Venue	Score	Year	Winner	Venue	Score
1895	HJ Rawlins	Newport	173	1915	J Travers (am)	Baltusrol	290
1896	J Foulis	Southampton	152	1916	C Evans (am)	Minneapolis	286
1897	J Lloyd	Wheaton, IL	162	1917-18	No Championship		
1898	F Herd	South Hamilton, MA	328	1919	W Hagen*	Braeburn	301
1899	W Smith	Baltimore	315	*After a play-off with M Brady: Hagen 77, Brady 78			
1900	H Vardon (ENG)	Wheaton, IL	313	1920	E Ray (ENG)	Inverness	295
1901	W Anderson*	Myopia, MA	315	1921	J Barnes	Washington	289
*After a play-off with A Smith: Anderson 85, Smith 86				1922	G Sarazen	Glencoe	288
1902	L Auchterlonie	Garden City	305	1923	R Jones Jr* (am)	Inwood, LI	295
1903	W Anderson*	Baltusrol	307	*After a play-off with R Cruikshank: Jones 76,			
*After a play-off with D Brown: Anderson 82, Brown 84				Cruikshank 78			
1904	W Anderson	Glenview	304	1924	C Walker	Oakland Hills	297
1905	W Anderson	Myopia, MA	335	1925	W MacFarlane*	Worcester	291
1906	A Smith	Onwentsia	291	*After a play-off with R Jones Jr: MacFarlane 147, Jones 148			
1907	A Ross	Chestnut Hill, PA	302	1926	R Jones Jr (am)	Scioto	293
1908	F McLeod*	Myopia, MA	322	1927	T Armour*	Oakmont	301
*After a play-off with W Smith: McLeod 77, Smith 83				*After a play-off with H Cooper: Armour 76, Cooper 79			
1909	G Sargent	Englewood, NJ	290	1928	J Farrell*	Olympia Fields	294
1910	A Smith*	Philadelphia	289	*After a play-off with R Jones Jr (am): Farrell 143, Jones 144			
*After a play-off with J McDermott and M Smith: A Smith 71,				1929	R Jones Jr* (am)	Winged Foot, NY	294
McDermott 75, M Smith 77				*After a play-off with A Espinosa: Jones 141, Espinosa 164			
1911	J McDermott*	Wheaton, IL	307	1930	R Jones Jr (am)	Interlachen	287
*After a play-off with M Brady and G Simpson: McDermott 80,				1931	B Burke*	Inverness	292
Brady 82, Simpson 85				*After a play-off with G von Elm: Burke 149-148,			
1912	J McDermott	Buffalo, NY	294	von Elm 149-149			
1913	F Ouimet* (am)	Brookline, MA	304	1932	G Sarazen	Fresh Meadow	286
*After a play-off with Harry Vardon and Ted Ray: Ouimet 72,				1933	J Goodman (am)	North Shore	287
Vardon 77, Ray 78)				1934	O Dutra	Merion	293
1914	W Hagen	Midlothian	297	1935	S Parks	Oakmont	299

Year	Winner	Venue	Score
1936	T Manero	Springfield	282
1937	R Guldahl	Oakland Hills	281
1938	R Guldahl	Cherry Hills	284
1939	B Nelson*	Philadelphia	284

After a play-off with C Wood and D Shute: Nelson 138, Wood 141, Shute 76

Year	Winner	Venue	Score
1940	W Lawson Little*	Canterbury, OH	287

After a play-off with G Sarazen: Little 70, Sarazen 73

Year	Winner	Venue	Score
1941	C Wood	Fort Worth, TX	284
1942–45	No Championship		
1946	L Mangrum*	Canterbury	284

After a play-off with Byron Nelson and Vic Ghezzi: Mangrum 144, Nelson 145, Ghezzi 145

Year	Winner	Venue	Score
1947	L Worsham*	St Louis	282

After a play-off with S Snead: Worsham 69, Snead 70

Year	Winner	Venue	Score
1948	B Hogan	Los Angeles	276
1949	Dr C Middlecoff	Medinah, IL	286
1950	B Hogan*	Merion, PA	287

After a play-off with L Mangrum and G Fazio: Hogan 69, Mangrum 73, Fazio 75

Year	Winner	Venue	Score
1951	B Hogan	Oakland Hills, MI	287
1952	J Boros	Dallas, TX	281
1953	B Hogan	Oakmont	283
1954	E Furgol	Baltusrol	284
1955	J Fleck*	San Francisco	287

After a play-off with B Hogan: Fleck 69, Hogan 72

Year	Winner	Venue	Score
1956	Dr C Middlecoff	Rochester, NY	281
1957	D Mayer*	Inverness	282

After a play-off with Dr C Middlecoff: Mayer 72, Middlecoff 79

Year	Winner	Venue	Score
1958	T Bolt	Tulsa, OK	283
1959	W Casper	Winged Foot, NY	282
1960	A Palmer	Denver, CO	280
1961	G Littler	Birmingham, MI	281
1962	J Nicklaus*	Oakmont	283

After a play-off with A Palmer: Nicklaus 71, Palmer 74

Year	Winner	Venue	Score
1963	J Boros	Brookline, MA	293

(After a play-off with J Boros and J Cupit: J Boros 70, J Cupit 73, A Palmer 76

Year	Winner	Venue	Score
1964	K Venturi	Washington	278
1965	G Player* (RSA)	St Louis, MO	282

After a play-off with K Nagle: Player 71, Nagle 74

Year	Winner	Venue	Score
1966	W Casper*	San Francisco	278

After a play-off with A Palmer: Casper 69, Palmer 73

Year	Winner	Venue	Score
1967	J Nicklaus	Baltusrol	275
1968	L Trevino	Rochester, NY	275
1969	O Moody	Houston, TX	281
1970	A Jacklin (ENG)	Hazeltine, MN	281
1971	L Trevino*	Merion, PA	280

After a play-off with J Nicklaus: Trevino 68, Nicklaus 71

Year	Winner	Venue	Score
1972	J Nicklaus	Pebble Beach	290
1973	J Miller	Oakmont, PA	279
1974	H Irwin	Winged Foot, NY	287
1975	L Graham*	Medinah, IL	287

After a play-off with J Mahaffey: Graham 71, Mahaffey 73

Year	Winner	Venue	Score
1976	J Pate	Atlanta, GA	277
1977	H Green	Southern Hills, Tulsa	278
1978	A North	Cherry Hills	285
1979	H Irwin	Inverness, OH	284
1980	J Nicklaus	Baltusrol	272
1981	D Graham (AUS)	Merion, PA	273
1982	T Watson	Pebble Beach	282
1983	L Nelson	Oakmont, PA	280
1984	F Zoeller*	Winged Foot	276

After a play-off with G Norman: Zoeller 67, Norman 75

Year	Winner	Venue	Score
1985	A North	Oakland Hills, MI	279
1986	R Floyd	Shinnecock Hills, NY	279
1987	S Simpson	Olympic, San Francisco	277
1988	C Strange*	Brookline, MA	278

After a play-off with N Faldo: Strange 71, Faldo 75

Year	Winner	Venue	Score
1989	C Strange	Rochester, NY	278
1990	H Irwin*	Medinah	280

After a play-off with M Donald: Irwin 74, Donald 74; Irwin won sudden death play-off with 3 to 4 at first extra hole

Year	Winner	Venue	Score
1991	P Stewart*	Hazeltine, MN	282

After a play-off with S Simpson: Stewart 75, Simpson 77

Year	Winner	Venue	Score
1992	T Kite	Pebble Beach, FL	285
1993	L Janzen	Baltusrol	272
1994	E Els* (RSA)	Oakmont, PA	279

After a play-off with L Roberts and C Montgomerie: Els 74, Roberts 74, Montgomerie 78. Els won sudden death playoff: Els 4,4, Roberts 4,5

Year	Winner	Venue	Score
1995	C Pavin	Shinnecock Hills, NY	280
1996	S Jones	Oakland Hills, MI	278
1997	E Els (RSA)	Congressional, Bethesda	276
1998	L Janzen	Olympic, San Francisco	280
1999	P Stewart	Pinehurst No. 2, NC	279
2000	T Woods	Pebble Beach, CA	272
2001	R Goosen* (RSA)	Southern Hills CC, OK	276

After a play-off with M Brooks: Goosen 70, Brooks 72

Year	Winner	Venue	Score
2002	T Woods	Farmingdale, NY	277
2003	J Furyk	Olympia Fields, IL	272
2004	R Goosen (RSA)	Shinnecock Hills, NY	276
2005	M Campbell (NZL)	Pinehurst No.2, NC	280
2006	G Ogilvy (AUS)	Winged Foot, NY	285
2007	A Cabrera (ARG)	Oakmont, PA	285
2008	T Woods*	Torrey Pines, CA	283

Beat R Mediate at 19th hole of extra round

Longest par 4 at Torrey Pines was toughest

It may have a generous fairway inviting players to be aggressive off the tee according to the local professional but the 504 yards uphill straightaway par 4 at Torrey Pines was the most difficult during the 2008 US Open won by Tiger Woods. It averaged 4.581. Only the longest hitters have a realistic chance to make the green in two but if you miss the putting surface best to leave it short. Why? – because the green is perched up above the fairway and if you finish right, left or through the back the recovery shot is very difficult. Only 15 birdies were scored during the week but the total of bogeys was a massive 210!

Eagles 0   Birdies 15   Pars 208   Bogeys 210   Double bogeys 29   Other 6   Average 4.581

The Masters Tournament

April 10–13, 2008

South African star Immelman stylishly booked his place in the Champions' locker room at Augusta

Twenty-nine-year-old South African Trevor Immelman deservedly won a curiously low-key Masters at Augusta. He kept his nerve while many around him were losing theirs on the final day to end up posting a winning eight-under-par 280 for the first wire-to-wire victory since Ben Crenshaw did the same in 1984.

Taking the famed Green Jacket at the event which is an annual memorial to the great golfing sportsman Bobby Jones is one thing but handling the pressure of leading from day one (jointly with Justin Rose) to the end was a fantastic achievement for the 29-year-old who, just weeks before, had undergone an operation for the removal of a tumour (happily benign) behind his rib cage.

© Don Emmett/AFP/Getty Images

Trevor Immelman

That operation and the anxiety surrounding it had come just a week after he had edged out Rose for victory in the Million Dollar event in his native South Africa. Surgeons had to cut through the rib and muscle in his chest to get the tumour out and for a time Immelman could not walk, far less swing a club.

His fight back to full fitness included a string of missed cuts before Augusta but this was because his brother Mark, coach at Georgia State University said that not all the parts of the swing were working. They all came together, however, at The Masters to give him a victory Immelman described as "a hell of an achievement when you are playing at a time on Tour when Tiger is at his peak."

Only Tiger was not at his best at Augusta in 2008. His putter kept letting him down. He averaged 30 a round yet still managed to finish second! His disappointment was not only his failure to close in on Jack Nicklaus' record 18 professional major wins but also losing his chance this year of a Grand Slam in the same calendar year. Tiger has held all four major titles at the same time before but only three in the same season.

Immelman's roller coaster ride from hospital bed and the threat of his having developed cancer to a Green Jacket was helped at Augusta by a pre-final round telephone message from Gary Player, the only other South African to have made it into the Champion's locker room in the attractive southern style clubhouse.

Immelman, who was just five-years-old when he first met Player, has had a wonderful relationship with the veteran star who was playing in a record 51st major himself and plans to be back this year. "I think he spotted that even then I had a passion for the game", said Immelman. He kept in touch and was always there offering support and advice. He told me that he believed in me and believed I could and would win

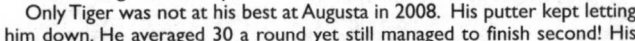

First Round	Second Round	Third Round	Fourth Round
–4 Rose	–8 Immenman	–11 Immelman	–8 Immelman
–4 Immenman	–7 Snedeker	–9 Snedeker	–5 Woods
–3 Bateman	–5 Flesch	–8 Flesch	–4 Cink
–3 Snedeker	–5 Mickelson	–7 Casey	–4 Snedeker
–2 Poulter	–5 Poulter	–5 Woods	–2 Mickelson
–2 Karlsson	–4 Ames	–4 Cink	–2 Harrington
–2 Johnson	–4 Casey	–2 Johnson	–2 Flesch
–2 Ames	–3 Cink	–2 Weekley	–1 Jiménez
–1 Slocum	–3 Oberholser	–2 Harrington	–1 Karlsson
–1 O'Meara	–3 Weir	–2 Romero	–1 Romero
–1 Singh	–2 Goosen	–2 Karlsson	–1 Watney
–1 Lonard	–2 Westwood	–2 O'Hair	–1 Westwood
–1 Oberholser		–2 Goosen	–1 Casey
		–2 Poulter	
		–2 Mickelson	

if I believed I could do it myself. He told me to stay strong through the adversity I would have to handle on the final day."

Player must be extra-specially proud of Immelman who, after a lengthy early morning delay because of fog, shot a four-under-par 68 to tie with Justin Rose on an opening day when defending champion Zach Johnson shot 70, Tiger 72 and those out last finished in the dark! Arnold Palmer, no longer a competitor in the event but now official starter, had got the proceedings under way hitting a drive out of sight, literally into the fog

Immelman added another 68 on the second day as Rose tumbled back down the leader board, slipping from first equal to 29th with a round that included an 8 at the 15th. At half way the South African held a one shot advantage over Nashville-based Brandt Snedeker, the Nationwide Tour Rookie of the year in 2007 with left-handers Steve Flesch and Phil Mickleson and Englishman Ian Poulter two strokes further back. While Poulter celebrated a 16th hole ace and was looking forward to a weekend charge that did not in fact materialise, there were plenty of big names packing their cases and heading home including former winners Player, Fuzzy Zoeller, Larry Mize, Ray Floyd, Ben Crenshaw, José María Olazábal, Bernhard Langer, Tom Watson, Mark O'Meara, Craig Stadler and Fred Couples, who narrowly missed a putt on the last that would have given him a new record of having played in 24 consecutive Masters without missing a cut. Other half-way casualties were Ernie Els, Sergio García and Luke Donald.

Tiger made a move on Saturday with a best-of-the-day 68. On five-under par that still left him six behind the relentlessly efficient Immelman, who birdied three of the last five holes for his 69. Woods knew that after 54 holes there were only four players ahead of him in his quest for another major title and his fifth Masters Green Jacket. Fair-haired Snedeker, a refreshingly quick player in a tournament where rounds in two-balls were taking what many considered an unacceptable five hours, stayed with the South African and was lying second on nine-under-par two off the pace. Flesch was a further shot back and Casey was on seven-under-par coming to the last day but dropped quickly out of contention on Sunday. Despite a closing 79 he still finished joint eighth with, among others, Open champion Padraig Harrington and Miguel Angel Jiménez whose 68, the best of the day and one of only two rounds in the 60's on Sunday, moved him up from 33rd overnight.

The chance of a last-round Tiger charge over the closing holes was given a boost when he rolled in a 25 yarder for a birdie at the 11th (where minutes later Immelman holed from off the green for par) but Tiger's putter was too cold on the week and when he failed to make birdies at the par 5 13th and 15th his chance had disappeared with the South African in such steady form.

Tiger's second place finish did move him through the $5 million in prize-money from The Masters alone. For him it was as much a disappointment not to win as it was a delight for Immelman to collect his first major and join Player in the Champions' locker room.

Month by month in 2008

Swede Daniel Chopra makes it two wins in his last three starts on the PGA Tour by taking the Mercedes Championship in Hawaii. German Martin Kaymer impresses with his first European Tour victory in Abu Dhabi. Dorothy Delasin and Jennifer Rosales lift the Women's World Cup for the Philippines. Adam Scott's stunning closing 61 gives him the Qatar Masters title. Tiger Woods opens up his year with an eight-shot success at the Buick Invitational, his fourth straight win in the event.

2008 Masters (72nd) *Augusta National GC, GA*   April 10–13   [7445–72]

Prize money: $7m. Final field of 93 players (three amateurs) of whom 45 (including no amateurs) made the final half-way cut on 147 or less.

Players are of American nationality unless stated.

1	Trevor Immelman (RSA)	68-68-69-75—280	$1350000
2	Tiger Woods	72-71-68-72—283	810000
3	Stewart Cink	72-69-71-72—284	435000
	Brandt Snedeker	69-68-70-77—284	435000
5	Steve Flesch	72-67-69-78—286	273750
	Padraig Harrington (IRL)	74-71-69-72—286	273750
	Phil Mikelson	71-68-75-72—286	273750
8	Miguel Angel Jiménez (ESP)	77-70-72-68—287	217500
	Robert Karlsson (SWE)	70-73-71-73—287	217500
	Andres Romero (ARG)	72-72-70-73—287	217500
11	Paul Casey (ENG)	71-69-69-79—288	172500
	Nick Watney	75-70-72-71—288	172500
	Lee Westwood (ENG)	69-73-73-73—288	172500
14	Stuart Appleby (AUS)	76-70-72-71—289	135000
	Sean O'Hair	72-71-71-75—289	135000
	Vijay Singh (FIJ)	72-71-72-74—289	135000
17	Retief Goosen (RSA)	71-71-72-76—290	112500
	Henrik Stenson (SWE)	74-72-72-72—290	112500
	Mike Weir (CAN)	73-68-75-74—290	112500
20	Brian Bateman	69-76-72-74—291	84300
	Zach Johnson	70-76-68-77—291	84300
	Justin Leonard	72-74-72-73—291	84300
	Bubba Watson	74-71-73-73—291	84300
	Boo Weekley	72-74-68-77—291	84300
25	Stephen Ames (CAN)	70-70-77-75—292	54844
	Angel Cabrera (ARG)	73-72-73-74—292	54844
	J B Holmes	73-70-73-76—292	54844
	Arron Oberholser	71-70-74-77—292	54844
	Ian Poulter (ENG)	70-69-75-78—292	54844
	Adam Scott (AUS)	75-71-70-76—292	54844
	Jeev Milkha Singh (IND)	71-74-72-75—292	54844
	Richard Sterne (RSA)	73-72-73-74—292	54844
33	Nick Dougherty (ENG)	74-69-74-76—293	42375
	Jim Furyk	70-73-73-77—293	42375
	Heath Slocum	71-76-77-69—293	42375
36	Todd Hamilton	74-73-75-73—295	36875
	Justin Rose (ENG)	68-78-73-76—295	36875
	Johnson Wagner	72-74-74-75—295	36875
39	Niclas Fasth (SWE)	75-70-76-75—296	33000
	Geoff Ogilvy (AUS)	75-71-76-74—296	33000
41	K J Choi (KOR)	72-75-78-73—298	30750
42	Robert Allenby (AUS)	72-74-72-81—299	28500
	David Toms	73-74-72-80—299	28500
44	Ian Woonam (WAL)	75-71-76-78—300	26250
45	Sandy Lyle (SCO)	72-75-78-77—302	24750

The following players missed the half-way cut. Each professional player received $5000:

46	Aaron Baddeley (AUS)	75-73—148	46T	Martin Kaymer (GER)	76-72—148	56T	Rory Sabbatini (RSA)	75-74—149
	Michael Campbell (NZL)	77-71—148		Toru Taniguchi (JPN)	75-73—148		Craig Stadler	77-72—149
				Brett Wetterich	73-75—148	63	Daniel Chopra (SWE)	72-78—150
	Fred Couples	76-72—148	56	Jonathan Byrd	75-74—149		Ben Curtis	75-75—150
	Luke Donald (ENG)	73-75—148		Jerry Kelly	72-77—149		Trip Kuehne (am)	78-72—150
	Ernie Els (RSA)	74-74—148		Hunter Mahan	77-72—149		Shaun Micheel	76-74—150
	Sergio García (ESP)	76-72—148		Nick O'Hern (AUS)	74-75—149		John Rollins	77-73—150
	Charles Howell III	78-70—148		Mark O'Meara	71-78—149		Steve Stricker	73-77—150

63T	Camilo Villegas (COL)	73-77—150	76	Woody Austin	79-73—152	82T	Scott Verplank	77-76—153
	Tom Watson	75-75—150		Tim Clark (RSA)	77-75—152	86	Raymond Floyd	80-74—154
71	Bernhard Langer (GER)	74-77—151		Ben Crenshaw	75-77—152		Wen-chong Liang (CHN)	76-78—154
	José-María Olazábal (ESP)	76-75—151		Richard Green (AUS)	77-75—152	88	Anders Hansen (DEN)	80-75—155
	John Senden (AUS)	80-71—151		Shingo Katayama (JPN)	79-73—152	89	Drew Weaver (am)	76-80—156
	Vaughn Taylor	75-76—151		Peter Lonard (aus)	71-81—152	90	Steve Lowery	81-76—157
	Michael Thompson (am)	73-78—151	82	Mark Calcavecchia	73-80—153	91	Larry Mize	77-81—158
				Søren Hansen (DEN)	75-78—153	92	Fuzzy Zoeller	81-79—160
				D J Trahan	76-77—153	93	Gary Player (RSA)	83-78—161

2007 Masters April 5–8 [7445–72]

Prize money: $7.4 million. Field of 96 players, of whom 60 (no amateurs) made the half-way cut.

1	Zach Johnson	71-73-76-69—289	$1305000	30T	Robert Karlsson (SWE)	77-73-79-72—301	43085
2	Retief Goosen (RSA)	76-76-70-69—291	541333		Scott Verplank	73-77-76-75—301	43085
	Rory Sabbatini (RSA)	73-76-73-69—291	541333		Lee Westwood (ENG)	79-73-72-77—301	43085
	Tiger Woods	73-74-72-72—291	541333		Dean Wilson	75-72-76-78—301	43085
5	Jerry Kelly	75-69-78-70—292	275500		Yong-Eun Yang (KOR)	75-74-78-74—301	43085
	Justin Rose (ENG)	69-75-75-73—292	275500	37	Angel Cabrera (ARG)	77-75-79-71—302	31900
7	Stuart Appleby (AUS)	75-70-73-75—293	233812		J J Henry	71-78-77-76—302	31900
	Padraig Harrington (IRL)	77-68-75-73—293	233812		Tim Herron	72-75-83-72—302	31900
9	David Toms	70-78-74-72—294	210250		Rod Pampling (AUS)	77-75-74-76—302	31900
10	Paul Casey (ENG)	79-68-77-71—295	181250		Jeev Milkha Singh (IND)	72-75-76-79—302	31900
	Luke Donald (ENG)	73-74-75-73—295	181250		Brett Wetterich	69-73-83-77—302	31900
	Vaughn Taylor	71-72-77-75—295	181250	43	Sandy Lyle (SCO)	79-73-80-71—303	26825
13	Tim Clark (RSA)	71-71-80-74—296	135937	44	Bradley Dredge (WAL)	75-70-76-83—304	22533
	Jim Furyk	75-71-76-74—296	135937		David Howell (ENG)	70-75-82-77—304	22533
	Ian Poulter (ENG)	75-75-76-70—296	135937		Miguel Angel Jiménez (ESP)	79-73-76-76—304	22533
	Vijay Singh (FIJ)	73-71-79-73—296	135937		Shingo Katayama (JPN)	79-72-80-73—304	22533
17	Stewart Cink	77-75-75-70—297	108750		José-María Olazábal (ESP)	74-75-78-77—304	22533
	Tom Pernice Jr	75-72-79-71—297	108750	49	Jeff Sluman	76-75-79-75—305	18560
	Henrik Stenson (SWE)	72-76-77-72—297	108750		Craig Stadler	74-73-79-79—305	18560
20	Mark Calcavecchia	76-71-78-73—298	84462	51	Brett Quigley	76-76-79-75—306	17835
	Lucas Glover	74-71-79-74—298	84462	52	Aaron Baddeley (AUS)	79-72-76-80—307	17255
	John Rollins	77-74-76-71—298	84462		Carl Pettersson (SWE)	76-76-79-76—307	17255
	Mike Weir (CAN)	75-72-80-71—298	84462	54	Rich Beem	71-81-75-81—308	16820
24	Stephen Ames (CAN)	76-74-77-72—299	63000	55	Ben Crenshaw	76-74-84-75—309	16530
	Phil Mickelson	76-73-73-77—299	63000		Niclas Fasth (SWE)	77-75-77-80—309	16530
	Geoff Ogilvy (AUS)	75-70-81-73—299	63000	55T	Trevor Immelman (RSA)	74-77-81-77—309	16530
27	K J Choi (KOR)	75-75-74-76—300	53650	58	Arron Oberholser	74-76-84-76—310	16240
	Davis Love III	72-77-77-74—300	53650	59	Billy Mayfair	76-75-83-77—311	16095
	Adam Scott (AUS)	74-78-76-72—300	53650	60	Fuzzy Zoeller	74-78-79-82—313	15950
30	Fred Couples	75-74-78-74—301	43085				
	Charles Howell III	75-77-75-74—301	43085				

Masters starter Phil Harison dies at 81

Phil Harison, the Masters starter, was almost as well known as the European Tour starter Ivor Robson but he outdid Robson in one respect. Ivor could not claim to have been doing the job as long as 82-year-old Mr Harison who died last year. The Augustan had been working the first tee for 60 years! He had visited every Masters, watching the first one as an eight-year-old. He could play a bit, too. In the mid-1980's he played a round with six-times Masters champion Jack Nicklaus and out-did him at the famous short 12th. Nicklaus hit his tee shot close and jokingly said to Mr Harison that he would love to see him hole-in-one. He did just that and he also had an ace when playing with President Eisenhower!

Billy Payne, chairman of The Masters Tournament said: "Phil was a cherished member who made significant contributions to The Masters. He was the face of the Masters to many patrons and did a wonderful job. We are all deeply saddened at his death."

2006 Masters April 6–9 [7445–72]

Prize money: $7 million. Field of 90 players, of whom 47 (no amateurs) made the half-way cut.

1	Phil Mickelson	70-72-70-69—281	$1260000	22T	Jim Furyk	73-75-68-75—291	67200
2	Tim Clark (RSA)	70-72-72-69—283	758000		Mark Hensby (AUS)	80-67-70-74—291	67200
3	Chad Campbell	71-67-75-71—284	315700		Davis Love III	74-71-74-72—291	67200
	Fred Couples	71-70-72-71—284	315700	27	Ernie Els (RSA)	71-71-74-76—292	49700
	Retief Goosen (RSA)	70-73-72-69—284	315700		Padraig Harrington (IRL)	73-70-75-74—292	49700
	José-María Olazábal (ESP)	76-71-71-66—284	315700		Shingo Katayama (JPN)	75-70-73-74—292	49700
	Tiger Woods	72-71-71-70—284	315700		Carl Pettersson (SWE)	72-74-73-73—292	49700
8	Angel Cabrera (ARG)	73-74-70-68—285	210000		Adam Scott (AUS)	72-74-75-71—292	49700
	Vijay Singh (FIJ)	67-74-73-71—285	210000	32	Thomas Bjørn (DEN)	73-75-76-69—293	40512
10	Stewart Cink	72-73-71-70—286	189000		Brandt Jobe	72-76-77-68—293	40512
11	Stephen Ames (CAN)	74-70-70-73—287	161000		Zach Johnson	74-72-77-70—293	40512
	Miguel Angel Jiménez (ESP)	72-74-69-72—287	161000		Ted Purdy	72-76-74-71—293	40512
	Mike Weir (CAN)	71-73-73-70—287	161000	36	Tim Herron	76-71-71-76—294	34416
14	Billy Mayfair	71-72-73-72—288	129500		Rocco Mediate	68-73-73-80—294	34416
	Arron Oberholser	69-75-73-71—288	129500		Rory Sabbatini (RSA)	76-70-74-74—294	34416
16	Geoff Ogilvy (AUS)	70-75-73-71—289	112000	39	Jason Bohn	73-71-77-74—295	30100
	Rod Pampling (AUS)	72-73-72-72—289	112000		Ben Curtis	71-74-77-73—295	30100
	Scott Verplank	74-70-74-71—289	112000		Justin Leonard	75-70-79-71—295	30100
19	Stuart Appleby (AUS)	71-75-73-71—290	91000	42	Rich Beem	71-73-73-79—296	25900
	David Howell (ENG)	71-71-76-72—290	91000		Luke Donald (ENG)	74-72-76-74—296	25900
	Nick O'Hern (AUS)	71-72-76-71—290	91000		Larry Mize	75-72-77-72—296	25900
22	Robert Allenby (AUS)	73-73-74-71—291	67200	45	Olin Browne	74-69-80-74—297	23100
	Darren Clarke (NIR)	72-70-72-77—291	67200	46	Sergio García (ESP)	72-74-79-73—298	21700
				47	Ben Crenshaw	71-72-78-79—300	20300

2005 Masters April 7–10 [7290–72]

Prize money: $7 million. Field of 93 players, of whom 50 (including two amateurs) made the half-way cut.

1	Tiger Woods*	74-66-65-71—276	$1260000	25T	Joe Ogilvie	74-73-73-70—290	61600
2	Chris DiMarco	67-67-74-68—276	756000		Craig Parry (AUS)	72-75-69-74—290	61600
*Play-off: Woods 3, DiMarco 4				28	Jim Furyk	76-67-74-74—291	53900
3	Luke Donald (ENG)	68-77-69-69—283	406000	29	Steve Flesch	76-70-70-76—292	50750
	Retief Goosen (RSA)	71-75-70-67—283	406000		Kenny Perry	76-68-71-77—292	50750
5	Mark Hensby (AUS)	69-73-70-72—284	237300	31	Miguel Angel Jiménez (ESP)	74-74-73-72—293	46550
	Trevor Immelman (RSA)	73-73-65-73—284	237300		Mark O'Meara	72-74-72-75—293	46550
	Rodney Pampling (AUS)	73-71-70-70—284	237300	33	K J Choi (KOR)	73-72-76-73—294	39620
	Vijay Singh (FIJ)	68-73-71-72—284	237300		Shingo Katayama (JPN)	72-74-73-75—294	39620
	Mike Weir (CAN)	74-71-68-71—284	237300		Luke List (am)	77-69-78-70—294	
10	Phil Mickelson	70-72-69-74—285	189000		Ian Poulter (ENG)	72-74-72-76—294	39620
11	Tim Herron	76-68-70-72—286	168000		Adam Scott (AUS)	71-76-72-75—294	39620
	David Howell (ENG)	72-69-76-69—286	168000		Casey Wittenberg	72-72-74-76—294	39620
13	Tom Lehman	74-74-70-69—287	135333	39	Tim Clark (RSA)	74-74-72-75—295	32200
	Justin Leonard	75-71-70-71—287	135333		Fred Couples	75-71-77-72—295	32200
	Thomas Levet (FRA)	71-75-68-73—287	135333		Todd Hamilton	77-70-71-77—295	32200
	Ryan Moore (am)	71-71-75-70—287			Ryan Palmer	70-74-74-77—295	32200
17	Chad Campbell	73-73-67-75—288	112000	43	Stuart Appleby (AUS)	69-76-72-79—296	28000
	Darren Clarke (NIR)	72-76-69-71—288	112000		Jonathan Kaye	72-74-76-74—296	28000
	Kirk Triplett	75-68-72-73—288	112000	45	Stephen Ames (CAN)	73-74-75-75—297	25200
20	Stewart Cink	72-72-74-71—289	84840		Nick O'Hern (AUS)	72-72-76-77—297	25200
	Jerry Kelly	75-70-73-71—289	84840	47	Ernie Els (RSA)	75-73-78-72—298	23100
	Bernhard Langer (GER)	74-74-70-71—289	84840	48	Jay Haas	76-71-76-78—301	21700
	Jeff Maggert	74-74-72-69—289	84840	49	Chris Riley	71-77-78-78—304	20300
	Scott Verplank	72-75-69-73—289	84840	50	Craig Stadler	75-73-79-79—306	19180
25	Thomas Bjørn (DEN)	71-67-71-81—290	61600				

2004 Masters April 8–11 [7290–72]

Prize money: $6 million. Field of 93, of whom 44 (including two amateurs) made the half-way cut.

1	Phil Mickelson	72-69-69-69—279	$1170000	22T	Shaun Micheel	72-76-72-70—290	70200
2	Ernie Els (RSA)	70-72-71-67—280	702000		Justin Rose (ENG)	67-71-81-71—290	70200
3	K J Choi (KOR)	71-70-72-69—282	442000		Tiger Woods	75-69-75-71—290	70200
4	Sergio García (ESP)	72-72-75-66—285	286000	26	Alex Cejka (GER)	70-70-78-73—291	57200
	Bernhard Langer (GER)	71-73-69-72—285	286000	27	Mark O'Meara	73-70-75-74—292	51025
6	Paul Casey (ENG)	75-69-68-74—286	189893		Bob Tway	75-71-74-72—292	51025
	Fred Couples	73-69-74-70—286	189893	29	Scott Verplank	74-71-76-72—293	48100
	Chris DiMarco	69-73-68-76—286	189893	30	José María Olazábal	71-69-79-75—294	46150
	Davis Love III	75-67-74-70—286	189893		(ESP)		
	Nick Price (ZIM)	72-73-71-70—286	189893	31	Bob Estes	76-72-73-74—295	41275
	Vijay Singh (FIJ)	75-73-69-69—286	189893		Brad Faxon	72-76-76-71—295	41275
	Kirk Triplett	71-74-69-72—286	189893		Jerry Kelly	74-72-73-76—295	41275
13	Retief Goosen (RSA)	75-73-70-70—288	125667		Ian Poulter (ENG)	75-73-74-73—295	41275
	Padraig Harrington	74-74-68-72—288	125667	35	Justin Leonard	76-72-72-76—296	35913
	(IRL)				Phillip Price (WAL)	71-76-73-76—296	35913
	Charles Howell III	71-71-76-70—288	125667	37	Paul Lawrie (SCO)	77-70-73-77—297	32663
	Casey Wittenberg (am)	76-72-71-69—288			Sandy Lyle (SCO)	72-74-75-76—297	32663
17	Stewart Cink	74-73-69-73—289	97500	39	Eduardo Romero (ARG)	74-73-74-77—298	30550
	Steve Flesch	76-67-77-69—289	97500	40	Todd Hamilton	77-71-76-75—299	29250
	Jay Haas	69-75-72-73—289	97500	41	Tim Petrovic	72-75-75-78—300	27950
	Fredrik Jacobson (SWE)	74-74-67-74—289	97500		Brandt Snedeker (am)	73-75-75-77—300	
	Stephen Leaney (AUS)	76-71-73-69—289	97500	43	Jeff Sluman	73-70-82-77—302	26650
22	Stuart Appleby (AUS)	73-74-73-70—290	70200	44	Chris Riley	70-78-78-78—304	25350

2003 Masters April 10–13 [7290–72]

Prize money: $6 million. Field of 93, of whom 49 (including three amateurs) made the half-way cut.

1	Mike Weir (CAN)*	70-68-75-68—281	$1080000	23T	Nick Price (ZIM)	70-75-72-76—293	57600
2	Len Mattiace	73-74-69-65—281	648000		Chris Riley	76-72-70-75—293	57600
*Play-off: Weir 4, Mattiace 6					Adam Scott (AUS)	77-72-74-70—293	57600
3	Phil Mickelson	73-70-72-68—283	408000	28	Darren Clarke (NIR)	66-76-78-74—294	43500
4	Jim Furyk	73-72-71-68—284	288000		Fred Couples	73-75-69-77—294	43500
5	Jeff Maggert	72-73-66-75—286	240000		Sergio García (ESP)	69-78-74-73—294	43500
6	Ernie Els (RSA)	79-66-72-70—287	208500		Charles Howell III	73-72-76-73—294	43500
	Vijay Singh (FIJ)	73-71-70-73—287	208500		Hunter Mahan (am)	73-72-73-76—294	
8	Jonathan Byrd	74-71-71-72—288	162000	33	Nick Faldo (ENG)	74-73-75-73—295	36375
	José María Olazábal	73-71-71-73—288	162000		Rocco Mediate	73-74-73-75—295	36375
	(ESP)				Loren Roberts	74-72-76-73—295	36375
	Mark O'Meara	76-71-70-71—288	162000		Kevin Sutherland	77-72-76-70—295	36375
	David Toms	71-73-70-74—288	162000	37	Shingo Katayama (JPN)	74-72-76-74—296	31650
	Scott Verplank	76-73-70-69—288	162000		Billy Mayfair	75-70-77-74—296	31650
13	Tim Clark (RSA)	72-75-71-71—289	120000	39	Robert Allenby (AUS)	76-73-74-74—297	27000
	Retief Goosen (RSA)	73-74-72-70—289	120000		Craig Parry (AUS)	74-73-75-75—297	27000
15	Rich Beem	74-72-71-73—290	93000		Kenny Perry	76-72-78-71—297	27000
	Angel Cabrera (ARG)	76-71-71-72—290	93000		Justin Rose (ENG)	73-76-71-77—297	27000
	K J Choi (KOR)	76-69-72-73—290	93000		Philip Tataurangi (NZL)	75-70-74-78—297	27000
	Paul Lawrie (SCO)	72-72-73-73—290	93000	44	Jeff Sluman	75-72-76-75—298	23400
	Davis Love III	77-71-71-71—290	93000	45	Ryan Moore (am)	73-74-75-79—301	
	Tiger Woods	76-73-66-75—290	93000		Pat Perez	74-73-79-75—301	22200
21	Ricky Barnes (am)	69-74-75-73—291		47	John Rollins	74-71-80-77—302	21000
22	Bob Estes	76-71-74-71—292	72000	48	Jerry Kelly	72-76-77-79—304	19800
23	Brad Faxon	73-71-79-70—293	57600	49	Craig Stadler	76-73-79-77—305	18600
	Scott McCarron	77-71-72-73—293	57600				

2002 Masters April 10–13 [7270–72]

Prize money: $5.6 million. Field of 89, of whom two withdrew and 45 (with no amateurs) made the half-way cut.

1	Tiger Woods	70-69-66-71—276	$1008000	20T	Justin Leonard	70-75-74-70—289	65240
2	Retief Goosen (RSA)	69-67-69-74—279	604800		Nick Price (ZIM)	70-76-70-73—289	65240
3	Phil Mickelson	69-72-68-71—280	380800	24	Mark Brooks	74-72-71-73—290	46480
4	José María Olazábal (ESP)	70-69-71-71—281	268800		Stewart Cink	74-70-72-74—290	46480
					Tom Pernice	74-72-71-73—290	46480
5	Ernie Els (RSA)	70-67-72-73—282	212800		Jeff Sluman	73-72-71-74—290	46480
	Padraig Harrington (IRL)	69-70-72-71—282	212800		Mike Weir (CAN)	72-71-71-76—290	46480
7	Vijay Singh (FIJ)	70-65-72-76—283	187600	29	Robert Allenby (AUS)	73-70-76-72—291	38080
8	Sergio García (ESP)	68-71-70-75—284	173600		Charles Howell III	74-73-71-73—291	38080
9	Angel Cabrera (ARG)	68-71-73-73—285	151200		Jesper Parnevik (SWE)	70-72-77-72—291	38080
	Miguel Angel Jiménez (ESP)	70-71-74-70—285	151200	32	John Daly	74-73-70-75—292	32410
	Adam Scott (AUS)	71-72-72-70—285	151200		Bernhard Langer (GER)	73-72-73-74—292	32410
12	Chris DiMarco	70-71-72-73—286	123200		Billy Mayfair	74-71-72-75—292	32410
	Brad Faxon	71-75-69-71—286	123200		Craig Stadler	73-72-76-71—292	32410
14	Nick Faldo (ENG)	75-67-73-72—287	98000	36	Fred Couples	73-73-76-72—294	26950
	Davis Love III	67-75-74-71—287	98000		Rocco Mediate	75-68-77-74—294	26950
	Shigeki Maruyama (JPN)	75-72-73-67—287	98000		Greg Norman (AUS)	71-76-72-75—294	26950
	Colin Montgomerie (SCO)	75-71-70-71—287	98000		David Toms	73-74-76-71—294	26950
				40	Steve Lowery	75-71-76-73—295	22960
18	Thomas Bjørn (DEN)	74-67-70-77—288	81200		Kirk Triplett	74-70-74-77—295	22960
	Paul McGinley (IRL)	72-74-71-71—288	81200		Tom Watson	71-76-76-72—295	22960
20	Darren Clarke (NIR)	70-74-73-72—289	65240	43	Scott Verplank	70-75-76-75—296	20720
	Jerry Kelly	72-74-71-72—289	65240	44	Lee Westwood (ENG)	75-72-74-76—297	19600
				45	Bob Estes	73-72-75-78—298	18480

2001 Masters April 11–14 [6985–72]

Prize money: $5,574,920. Field of 93, of whom 47 (with no amateurs) made the half-way cut.

1	Tiger Woods	70-66-68-68—272	$1008000	20T	Jeff Maggert	72-70-70-71—283	65240
2	David Duval	71-66-70-67—274	604800	24	Darren Clarke (NIR)	72-67-72-73—284	53760
3	Phil Mickelson	67-69-69-70—275	380800	25	Tom Scherrer	71-71-70-73—285	49280
4	Toshimitsu Izawa (JPN)	71-66-74-67—278	246400	26	Fred Couples	74-71-73-68—286	44800
	Mark Calcavecchia	72-66-68-72—278	246400	27	Padraig Harrington (IRL)	75-69-72-71—287	40600
6	Bernhard Langer (GER)	73-69-68-69—279	181300		Justin Leonard	73-71-72-71—287	40600
	Jim Furyk	69-71-70-69—279	181300		Mike Weir (CAN)	74-69-72-72—287	40600
	Ernie Els (RSA)	71-68-68-72—279	181300		Steve Jones	74-70-72-71—287	40600
	Kirk Triplett	68-70-70-71—279	181300	31	Stuart Appleby (AUS)	72-70-70-76—288	33208
10	Brad Faxon	73-68-68-71—280	128800		Mark Brooks	70-71-77-70—288	33208
	Steve Stricker	66-71-72-71—280	128800		Duffy Waldorf	72-70-71-75—288	33208
	Miguel Angel Jiménez (ESP)	68-72-71-69—280	128800		Lee Janzen	67-70-72-79—288	33208
	Angel Cabrera (ARG)	66-71-70-73—280	128800		David Toms	72-72-71-73—288	33208
	Chris DiMarco	65-69-72-74—280	128800	36	Hal Sutton	74-69-71-75—289	28840
15	José María Olazábal (ESP)	70-68-71-72—281	95200	37	Loren Roberts	71-74-73-72—290	26320
	Paul Azinger	70-71-71-69—281	95200		Chris Perry	68-74-74-74—290	26320
	Rocco Mediate	72-70-66-73—281	95200		Scott Hoch	74-70-72-74—290	26320
18	Vijay Singh (FIJ)	69-71-73-69—282	81200	40	Steve Lowery	72-72-78-70—292	22960
	Tom Lehman	75-68-71-68—282	81200		Shingo Katayama (JPN)	75-70-73-74—292	22960
20	Mark O'Meara	69-74-72-68—283	65240		Franklin Langham	72-73-75-72—292	22960
	Jesper Parnevik (SWE)	71-71-72-69—283	65240	43	Dudley Hart	74-70-78-71—293	19600
	John Huston	67-75-72-69—283	65240		Bob May	71-74-73-75—293	19600
					Jonathan Kaye	74-71-74-74—293	19600
				46	Carlos Franco (PAR)	71-71-77-75—294	17360
				47	Robert Allenby (AUS)	71-74-75-75—295	16240

2000 Masters April 5–8 [6985–72]

Prize money: $4,61 million. Field of 95, of whom 57 (with no amateurs) made the half-way cut.

1	Vijay Singh (FIJ)	72-67-70-69—278	$828000	28T	Justin Leonard	72-71-77-73—293	28673
2	Ernie Els (RSA)	72-67-74-68—281	496800		Stewart Cink	75-72-72-74—293	28673
3	Loren Roberts	73-69-71-69—282	266800		Mike Weir (CAN)	75-70-70-78—293	28673
	David Duval	73-65-74-70—282	266800		Dudley Hart	75-71-72-75—293	28673
5	Tiger Woods	75-72-68-69—284	184000		Paul Azinger	72-72-77-72—293	28673
6	Tom Lehman	69-72-75-69—285	165600		Masashi Ozaki (JPN)	72-72-74-75—293	28673
7	Davis Love III	75-72-68-71—286	143367		Thomas Bjørn (DEN)	71-77-73-72—293	28673
	Carlos Franco (PAR)	79-68-70-69—286	143367	37	Fred Funk	75-68-78-73—294	21620
	Phil Mickelson	71-68-76-71—286	143367		Jay Haas	75-71-75-73—294	21620
10	Hal Sutton	72-75-71-69—287	124200		Notah Begay III	74-74-73-73—294	21620
11	Greg Norman (AUS)	80-68-70-70—288	105800	40	Ian Woosnam (WAL)	74-70-76-75—295	17480
	Nick Price (ZIM)	74-69-73-72—288	105800		Sergio García (ESP)	70-72-75-78—295	17480
	Fred Couples	76-72-70-70—288	105800		Jesper Parnevik (SWE)	77-71-70-77—295	17480
14	Chris Perry	73-75-72-69—289	80500		Darren Clarke (NIR)	72-71-78-74—295	17480
	Jim Furyk	73-74-71-71—289	80500		Mark Brooks	72-76-73-74—295	17480
	John Huston	77-69-72-71—289	80500		Retief Goosen (RSA)	73-69-79-74—295	17480
	Dennis Paulson	68-76-73-72—289	80500	46	Shigeki Maruyama (JPN)	76-71-74-75—296	13800
18	Jeff Sluman	73-69-77-71—290	69000		Scott Gump	75-70-78-73—296	13800
19	Padraig Harrington (IRL)	76-69-75-71—291	53820	48	Brandt Jobe	73-74-76-74—297	12604
	Steve Stricker	70-73-75-73—291	53820	49	Miguel Angel Jiménez (ESP)	76-71-79-72—298	11623
	Jean Van de Velde (FRA)	76-70-75-70—291	53820		Steve Pate	78-69-77-74—298	11623
	Colin Montgomerie (SCO)	76-69-77-69—291	53820		David Toms	74-72-73-79—298	11623
	Bob Estes	72-71-77-71—291	53820	52	Steve Elkington (AUS)	74-74-78-73—299	10948
	Glen Day	79-67-74-71—291	53820		Rocco Mediate	71-74-75-79—299	10948
25	Larry Mize	78-67-73-74—292	37567	54	Jack Nicklaus	74-70-81-78—303	10672
	Craig Parry (AUS)	75-71-72-74—292	37567		David Gossett (am)	75-71-79-78—303	10672
	Steve Jones	71-70-76-75—292	37567	56	Skip Kendall	76-72-77-83—308	10580
28	Nick Faldo (ENG)	72-72-74-75—293	28673	57	Tommy Aaron	72-74-86-81—313	10488
	Bernhard Langer (GER)	71-71-75-76—293	28673				

1999 Masters April 8–11 [6985–72]

Prize money: $3.2 million. Field of 96, of whom 56 (including four amateurs) made the half-way cut.

1	JM Olazábal (ESP)	70-66-73-71—280	$720000	27T	E Els (RSA)	71-72-69-80—292	29000
2	D Love III	69-72-70-71—282	432000		R Mediate	73-74-69-76—292	29000
3	G Norman (AUS)	71-68-71-73—283	272000	31	T Lehman	73-72-73-75—293	23720
4	B Estes	71-72-69-72—284	176000		S Maruyama (JPN)	78-70-71-74—293	23720
	S Pate	71-75-65-73—284	176000		M O'Meara	70-76-69-78—293	23720
6	D Duval	71-74-70-70—285	125200		J Sluman	70-75-70-78—293	23720
	C Franco (PAR)	72-72-68-73—285	125200		B Watts	73-73-70-77—293	23720
	P Mickelson	74-69-71-71—285	125200	36	J Huston	74-72-71-77—294	20100
	N Price (ZIM)	69-72-72-72—285	125200		A Magee	70-77-72-75—294	20100
	L Westwood (ENG)	75-71-68-71—285	125200	38	B Andrade	76-72-72-75—295	18800
11	S Elkington (AUS)	72-70-71-74—287	92000		M Brooks	76-72-75-72—295	18800
	B Langer (GER)	76-66-72-73—287	92000		R Floyd	74-73-72-76—295	18800
	C Montgomerie (SCO)	70-72-71-74—287	92000		C Stadler	72-76-70-77—295	18800
14	J Furyk	72-73-70-73—288	70000		S Stricker	75-72-69-79—295	18800
	L Janzen	70-69-73-76—288	70000		S García (ESP) (am)	72-75-75-73—295	
	B Jobe	72-71-74-71—288	70000	44	J Haas	74-69-79-75—297	14000
	I Woosnam (WAL)	71-74-71-72—288	70000		T Herron	75-69-74-79—297	14000
18	B Chamblee	69-73-75-72—289	52160		S Hoch	75-73-70-79—297	14000
	B Glasson	72-70-73-74—289	52160		T McKnight (am)	73-74-73-77—297	
	J Leonard	70-72-73-74—289	52160	48	S Lyle (SCO)	71-77-70-80—298	12000
	S McCarron	69-68-76-76—289	52160		C Parry (AUS)	75-73-73-77—298	12000
	T Woods	72-72-70-75—289	52160	50	C Perry	73-72-74-80—299	10960
23	L Mize	76-70-72-72—290	41600		M Kuchar (am)	77-71-73-78—299	
24	B Faxon	74-73-68-76—291	35200	52	O Browne	74-74-72-80—300	9980
	P-U Johansson (SWE)	75-72-71-73—291	35200		J Daly	72-76-71-81—300	9980
	V Singh (FIJ)	72-76-71-72—291	35200		P Stewart	73-75-77-75—300	9980
27	S Cink	74-70-71-77—292	29000		B Tway	75-73-78-74—300	9980
	F Couples	74-71-76-71—292	29000	56	T Immelman (RSA) (am)	72-76-78-79—305	

The Masters History (players are of American nationality unless stated)

Date	Winner	Score	Date	Winner	Score
1934 Mar 22–25	H Smith	284	1974 Apr 11–14	G Player (RSA)	278
1935 Apr 4–8	G Sarazen*	282	1975 Apr 10–13	J Nicklaus	276
After a play-off with Craig Wood: Sarazen 144, Wood 149			1976 Apr 8–11	R Floyd	271
			1977 Apr 7–10	T Watson	276
1936 Apr 2–6	H Smith	285	1978 Apr 6–9	G Player (RSA)	277
1937 Apr 1–4	B Nelson	283	1979 Apr 12–15	F Zoeller*	280
1938 Apr 1–4	H Picard	285	*After a play-off with Ed Sneed and Tom Watson:*		
1939 Mar 30–Apr 2	R Guldahl	279	*Zoeller 4,3; Watson 4,4; Sneed 4,4*		
1940 Apr 4–7	J Demaret	280	1980 Apr 10–13	S Ballesteros (ESP)	275
1941 Apr 3–6	C Wood	280	1981 Apr 9–12	T Watson	280
1942 Apr 9–12	B Nelson*	280	1982 Apr 8–11	C Stadler*	284
After a play-off with Ben Hogan: Nelson 69, Hogan 70			*After a play-off with Dan Pohl: Stadler 4, Pohl 5*		
1946 Apr 4–7	H Keiser	282	1983 Apr 7–11	S Ballesteros (ESP)	280
1947 Apr 3–6	J Demaret	281	1984 Apr 12–15	B Crenshaw	277
1948 Apr 8–11	C Harmon	279	1985 Apr 11–14	B Langer (GER)	282
1949 Apr 7–10	S Snead	283	1986 Apr 10–13	J Nicklaus	279
1950 Apr 6–9	J Demaret	282	1987 Apr 9–12	L Mize*	285
1951 Apr 5–8	B Hogan	280	*After a play-off with Severiano Ballesteros and*		
1952 Apr 3–6	S Snead	286	*Greg Norman: Mize 4, 3; Norman 4, 4;*		
1953 Apr 9–12	B Hogan	274	*Ballesteros 5*		
1954 Apr 8–12	S Snead*	289	1988 Apr 7–10	A Lyle (SCO)	281
After a play-off with Ben Hogan: Snead 69, Hogan 70			1989 Apr 6–9	N Faldo (ENG)*	283
			After a play-off with Scott: Faldo 5,3; Hoch 5, 4		
1955 Apr 7–10	C Middlecoff	279	1990 Apr 5–8	N Faldo (ENG)*	278
1956 Apr 5–8	J Burke	289	*After a play-off with Raymond Floyd: Faldo 4, 4;*		
1957 Apr 4–7	D Ford	283	*Floyd 4, 5*		
1958 Apr 3–6	A Palmer	284	1991 Apr 11–14	I Woosnam (WAL)	277
1959 Apr 2–5	A Wall	284	1992 Apr 9–12	F Couples	275
1960 Apr 7–10	A Palmer	282	1993 Apr 8–11	B Langer (GER)	277
1961 Apr 6–10	G Player (RSA)	280	1994 Apr 7–10	JM Olazábal (ESP)	279
1962 Apr 5–9	A Palmer*	280	1995 Apr 6–9	B Crenshaw	274
After a play-off with Gary Player and Dow Finsterwald: Palmer 68, Player 71, Finsterwald 77			1996 Apr 11–14	N Faldo (ENG)	276
			1997 Apr 10–13	T Woods	270
1963 Apr 4–10	J Nicklaus	286	1998 Apr 9–12	M O'Meara	279
1964 Apr 9–12	A Palmer	276	1999 Apr 8–11	JM Olazábal (ESP)	280
1965 Apr 8–11	J Nicklaus	271	2000 Apr 6–9	V Singh (FIJ)	278
1966 Apr 7–11	J Nicklaus*	288	2001 Apr 5–8	T Woods	272
After a play-off with Tommy Jacobs and Gay Brewer Jr: Nicklaus 70, Jacobs 72, Brewer Jr 78			2002 Apr 11–14	T Woods	276
			2003 Apr 10–13	M Weir (CAN)*	281
1967 Apr 6–9	G Brewer	280	*After a play-off with Len Mattiace: Weir 4,*		
1968 Apr 11–14	R Goalby	277	*Mattiace 6*		
1969 Apr 10–13	G Archer	281	2004 Apr 8–11	P Mickelson	279
1970 Apr 9–13	W Casper*	279	2005 Apr 7–10	T Woods*	276
After a play-off with Gene Littler: Casper 69, Littler 74			*After a play-off with Chris DiMarco: Woods 3, DiMarco 4*		
			2006 Apr 6–9	P Mickelson	281
1971 Apr 8–11	C Coody	279	2007 Apr 5–8	Z Johnson	289
1972 Apr 6–9	J Nicklaus	286	2008 Apr 10–13	T Immelman (RSA)	280
1973 Apr 5–9	T Aaron	283			

US PGA Championship

August 7–10, 2008

History is made as Harrington edges out García in a dramatic last day duel at Oakland Hills

Padraig Harrington admits he loves the back nine of a major on the final day. He powered his way in the last two hours to victory at The Open in 2007 and did so again at the 90th US PGA Championship at Oakland Hills – the course they call "The Monster". Yet eschewing the course's dreaded nickname Harrington, coming from six back at half way – just as he did at Carnoustie – fired an impressive 66-66 over the final 36 holes for a three-under-par winning total of 277 to edge out by two shots Sergio García for the second time and former Open champion Ben Curtis. Only these three finished under par. Curtis summed up Harrington's outstanding performance best when he said: "Padraig knows how to and isn't afraid to win".

© Liz Anthony/Phil Sheldon Golf Picture Library

Padraig Harrington

With his victory the Irishman became only the fourth European to win the title and the first since the Silver Scot Tommy Armour in 1930. What delighted him most was that he is the first European golfer to win two majors in one season. His victory was his third major success in 13 months and if the dedicated Padraig, coached by Bob Torrance, had one regret it was that he had to wait seven months before the next major – the 2009 Masters at Augusta! In addition, Harrington became only the fourth player to win The Open and the US PGA Championships in the same year. Walter Hagen did it in 1924, Nick Price in 1994 and Tiger Woods in 2000 and 2006.

Harrington's victory, which moved him into No.3 spot in the world rankings, insisted there is still much to improve in his game. "I cannot control Phil or Tiger who are ahead of me in the rankings. I can only focus on controlling what I do," said Harrington. Coach Torrance has always described him as the most dedicated of his pupils and now the Irishman is reaping a rich reward for his long hours and hard work on the range.

At half-way Harrington was lying 24th. He moved to tied fourth with his third round 66 which included four birdies in a row from the 13th and went on to clinch victory after an engrossing duel with García, with whom he was playing, and with Curtis who was playing in the last group.

The American led by a shot going into the final round but an outward half of 32 saw García lead into the back nine only for the Dubliner to overpower both of them with a glorious inward 32 in which he single-putted eight greens notably at the 16th and 18th for pars and the 17th for the birdie that gave him the lead on his own for the first time. "In a major nobody goes without making a mistake and I knew if I could hang in there I would get my opportunity and, if it was going to be my day, I'd take it", said Padraig, whose opportunity came when García hit his second into the water at the 16th. With the half-way leaders having to play 36 holes on the last day because of storms on Saturday which thankfully softened

First Round	Second Round	Third Round	Fourth Round
–2 Karlsson	–1 Holmes	–2 Curtis	–3 Harrington
–2 Singh	£ Curtis	–1 Holmes	–1 García
–1 Romero	£ Rose	–1 Stenson	–1 Curtis
–1 Duke	£ Wi	+1 Harrington	+1 Villegas
–1 García	+1 Toms	+1 García	+1 Stenson
–1 Mayfair	+1 Stenson	+1 Wi	+4 Mickleson
–1 O'Hair	+2 Cabrera	+2 Romero	+4 Romero
£ Kim	+2 Snedeker	+2 Singh	+5 Forsyth
£ Moore	+2 Jingh	+3 Villegas	+5 Rose
£ Mickelson	+2 Baddeley	+3 Flesch	+5 Singh
£ Pampling	+2 García	+3 Baddeley	+5 Wi
£ Wi	+2 Duke	+3 Toms	
£ Gay	+2 O'Hair		
£ Allen			
£ Cabrera			

up the course, the Championship provided a fittingly dramatic end to the majors season. Interestingly, 14 of the top 19 on the leaderboard at the end were overseas players.

For Sweden's Robert Karlsson the majors in 2008 had provided rich pickings with top ten finishes in The Masters, the US Open and The Open but his start in the fourth major of the year was unpromising. His approach to the first green hit the back edge of the putting surface, then bounced on to a cart path. He ran up a double-bogey but eight holes later he was three-under par having shot five birdies and ended up sharing the first day lead with Jeev Milkha Singh on two-under-par 68.

After a long day marred by an 85 minute storm delay which meant 18 players were unable to complete their opening rounds, only seven golfers had beaten par with Andres Romero, who had to complete his round on Friday, Ken Duke, Billy Mayfair, Sean O'Hair and Sergio García on 69, one behind the leaders. Open champion Harrington birdied the first three holes hitting the stick with his tee shot at the short third but felt he should have done better than 71. Too many putts lipped out for the Irishman to be happy! Less delighted was Lee Westwood who had no birdies in a 77.

Conditions were even more difficult on the second day with the course drying out and the wind fresher but it did not prevent England's Justin Rose from producing what he described as his best round of the year – a 67 that moved him into second spot on the leader board with Korean Charlie Wi and former Open champion Ben Curtis one behind leader JB Holmes who, at the 36-hole stage, was the only man under par on one-under.

Brilliant Romero equals record

The secret of Rose's success was two-fold – how well he controlled his emotions on a course that is so mentally demanding and his hot putter. He required only 25 putts in his round with just 11 on the back nine. On the second day the 15th, 16th, 17th, and 18th holes gave up only 18 birdies between them! At Oakland Hills, birdies were hard to come by!

Although admitting he had so far "lacked focus", Open champion Padraig Harrington on 145 with Ian Poulter and Paul Casey on 146 made the cut but several European notables missed out including Lee Westwood, Ross Fisher, Nick Dougherty, Darren Clarke and Colin Montgomerie who followed up an opening 76 with an 84 matching his worst round in a major.

Seventy-three players on eight-over-par made the half-way cut after another day when the way the course had been set up provided plenty of negative observations including this from CBS commentator and European Ryder Cup captain Nick Faldo: "Why, when you have got the toughest set of greens and such a great lay-out, do you need rough like this?"

Romero's 65, which equalled the course record and moved him up from 48th and into contention for the title and, sadly, the weather were the main stories on the third day. Heavy rain, thunder and lightning which hit the course on three separate occasions, caused a frustrating four hour delay. When play was finally called off six players had still not started their third rounds.

As an early starter, Romero was fortunate to have completed his round, which included seven birdies, before the storms. The Argentinian, who finished third at Carnoustie in The Open in 2008, improved 13 shots on his second round 78 and became only the ninth player to have shot 65 on the classic Donald Ross designed course. The delays meant that in order to complete on schedule the leaders were faced with having to play two rounds on Sunday.

After the one and a half inches of rain that had fallen on Saturday the course was playing two shots easier when the third round was completed on Sunday with Open champion Harrington one of the biggest upward movers with his four-under-par 66. This left him on one over par with García, who had bogeyed the last in his 69, and Wi. Behind them came Romero tied on three over with Steve Flesch, Aaron Baddeley and David Toms. Ahead of them were only three players – Henrik Stenson and Holmes on one under par both one behind the leader, former Open champion 26-year-old Ben Curtis. A double and a triple bogey on the back nine had dented Justin Rose's chance of success but on four over he was in the group only six back along with Angel Cabrera, Phil Mickelson, Graeme McDowell and Prayed Marksaeng. With 18 holes to play 17 players were within six shots of the lead.

Curtis started the final round well with a birdie but García did better with a birdie, eagle start. After eight Curtis and García were tied for the lead with Harrington three back and Stenson still well in contention. After the Swede dropped back the title race developed into a three-man challenge over the closing holes.

It was Harrington who did best at the death, however, holing from 10 feet for a birdie to take the lead on his own for the first time at the short 17th where García missed from a shorter distance. The Irishman, although bunkered off the tee at the 18th and still in the rough in two, hit a 7-iron to 20 feet and holed the double-breaker down the hill for a par-winning putt. García, bunkered by the green, took 5 as Curtis, coming behind, ran up a 4 at the short 17th. It was all over.

Harrington, had found his lost focus over the last two rounds and had moved his golfing career brilliantly to an even higher level.

2008 US PGA Championship (90th) *Oakland Hills (South Course), Bloomfield, MI*

August 7–10   [7395–70]

Prize money: $7.5 million. Entries: Field of 156 players, of whom 73 made the half-way cut on 148 or less.

Players are of American nationality unless stated

1	Padraig Harrington (IRL)	71-74-66-66—277	$1350000
2	Ben Curtis	73-67-68-71—279	660000
	Sergio García (ESP)	69-73-69-68—279	660000
4	Henrik Stenson (SWE)	71-70-68-72—281	330000
	Camilo Villegas (COL)	74-72-67-68—281	330000
6	Steve Flesch	73-70-70-69—282	270000
7	Phil Mickelson	70-73-71-70—284	231250
	Andres Romero (ARG)	69-78-65-72—284	231250
9	Alastair Forsyth (SCO)	73-72-70-70—285	176725
	Justin Rose (ENG)	73-67-74-71—285	176725
	Jeev Milkha Singh (IND)	68-74-70-73—285	176725
	Charlie Wi	70-70-71-74—285	176725
13	Aaron Baddeley (AUS)	71-71-71-73—286	137250
	Ken Duke	69-73-73-71—286	137250
15	Stuart Appleby (AUS)	76-70-69-72—287	107060
	Paul Casey (ENG)	72-74-72-69—287	107060
	Graeme McDowell (NIR)	74-72-68-73—287	107060
	Prayad Marksaeng (THA)	76-70-68-73—287	107060
	David Toms	72-69-72-74—287	107060
20	Angel Cabrera (ARG)	70-72-72-74—288	78900
	Brian Gay	70-74-72-72—288	78900
	Robert Karlsson (SWE)	68-77-71-72—288	78900
	Boo Weekley	72-71-79-66—288	78900
24	Mark Brown (NZL)	77-69-74-69—289	57000
	Retief Goosen (RSA)	72-74-69-74—289	57000
	Fredrik Jacobson (SWE)	75-71-70-73—289	57000
	Brandt Snedeker	71-71-74-73—289	57000
	Nicholas Thompson	71-72-73-73—289	57000
29	Jim Furyk	71-77-70-72—290	47550
	J B Holmes	71-68-70-81—290	47550
31	Robert Allenby (AUS)	76-72-72-71—291	38825
	Chris DiMarco	75-72-72-72—291	38825
	Ernie Els (RSA)	71-75-70-75—291	38825
	Paul Goydos	74-69-73-75—291	38825
	Geoff Ogilvy (AUS)	73-74-74-70—291	38825
	Sean O'Hair	69-73-76-73—291	38825
	Ian Poulter (ENG)	74-71-73-73—291	38825
	D J Trahan	72-71-76-72—291	38825
39	Steve Elkington (AUS)	71-73-73-75—292	30200
	Rory Sabbatini (RSA)	72-73-73-74—292	30200
	Steve Stricker	71-75-77-69—292	30200
42	Briny Baird	71-72-73-77—293	24500
	Michael Campbell (NZL)	73-71-75-74—293	24500
	Tom Lehman	74-70-75-74—293	24500
	John Senden (AUS)	76-72-72-73—293	24500
	Mike Weir (CAN)	73-75-71-74—293	24500
47	Michael Allen	70-75-71-78—294	18070
	Charles Howell III	72-76-77-69—294	18070
	Billy Mayfair	69-78-75-72—294	18070
	Carl Petterson (SWE)	71-74-76-73—294	18070
	Dean Wilson	73-73-77-71—294	18070
52	Peter Hanson (SWE)	71-73-75-76—295	16250
	John Merrick	73-75-70-77—295	16250
	Charl Schwartzel (RSA)	77-70-73-75—295	16250
55	Tim Clark (RSA)	76-72-73-75—296	15750

2008 US PGA Championship *continued*

55T	Anthony Kim	70-75-74-77—296	15750
	James Kingston (RSA)	72-76-74-74—296	15750
58	Justin Leonard	74-71-72-80—297	15375
	Pat Perez	73-73-79-72—297	15375
60	John Malinger	72-75-77-74—298	15000
	Steve Marino	73-74-75-76—298	15000
	Chez Reavie	78-70-78-72—298	15000
63	Paul Azinger	72-76-76-75—299	14500
	Mark Calcavecchia	71-76-76-76—299	14500
	Niclas Fasth (SWE)	73-73-75-78—299	14500
	Corey Pavin	75-73-73-78—299	14500
	Kevin Sutherland	76-71-77-75—299	14500
68	Hiroyuki Fujita (JPN)	77-70-76-77—300	14150
	Peter Lonard (AUS)	74-74-74-78—300	14150
70	Bubba Watson	75-73-77-76—301	14000
71	Richard Green (AUS)	71-77-79-76—303	13900
72	Rocco Mediate	73-74-72-85—304	13800
73	Louis Oosthuizen (RSA)	76-72-81-77—306	13700

The following players missed the half-way cut. Each player received $2500:

74	Rich Beem	73-76—149
	Fred Couples	76-73—149
	John Daly	74-75—149
	Simon Dyson (ENG)	73-76—149
	Frank Esposito Jr	71-78—149
	Todd Hamilton	76-73—149
	Zach Johnson	76-73—149
	Brendan Jones (AUS)	71-78—149
	Søren Kjeldsen (DEN)	75-74—149
	Ryan Moore	70-79—149
	Tom Pernice Jr	75-74—149
	Bob Tway	75-74—149
	Johnson Wagner	78-71—149
87	Mark Brooks	74-76—150
	Daniel Chopra (SWE)	74-76—150
	Jay Haas	73-77—150
	J J Henry	76-74—150
	Richard S Johnson (SWE)	75-75—150
	Nick O'Hern (AUS)	74-76—150
	Adan Scott (AUS)	77-73—150
	Vaughn Taylor	78-72—150
95	KJ Choi (KOR)	78-73—151
	Stewart Cink	75-76—151
	Darren Clarke (NIR)	75-76—151
	Anders Hansen (DEN)	75-76—151
	Miguel Angel Jiménez (ESP)	73-78—151
	Steve Lowery	74-77—151
	Rod Pampling (AUS)	70-81—151
	Heath Slocum	74-77—151

95T	Scott Strange (AUS)	73-78—151
	Don Yrene	75-76—151
105	Stephen Ames (CAN)	77-75—152
	Tommy Armour III	79-73—152
	Chad Campbell	76-76—152
	Davis Love III	77-75—152
	Alan Morin	76-76—152
	Hennie Otto (RSA)	76-76—152
	Jyoti Randhawa (IND)	77-75—152
	Vijay Singh (FIJ)	76-76—152
113	Ross Fisher (ENG)	77-76—153
	Søren Hansen (DEN)	77-76—153
	Trevor Immelman (RSA)	76-77—153
	Jerry Kelly	79-74—153
	Parker McLachlin	76-77—153
	Sonny Skinner	78-75—153
	Tim Weinhart	74-79—153
120	Sam Arnold	80-74—154
	Bart Bryant	77-77—154
	Martin Kaymer (GER)	75-79—154
	Toru Taniguchi (JPN)	79-75—154
	Steve Webster (ENG)	78-76—154
125	Ryan Benzel	77-78—155
	Ben Crane	75-80—155
	Jim Estes	79-76—155
	Cliff Kresge	83-72—155
	George McNeill	78-77—155
	Scott Verplank	77-78—155
	Lee Westwood (ENG)	77-78—155

125T	Oliver Wilson (ENG)	78-77—155
133	Matthew Goggin (AUS)	81-75—156
	Scott Hebert	80-76—156
	Peter Hedblom (SWE)	76-80—156
	Rick Leibovich	78-78—156
	Jeff Quinney	81-75—156
138	Jonathan Byrd	75-82—157
	Ryuji Imada (JPN)	80-77—157
	Greg Kraft	78-79--157
	Jeff Martin	78-79—157
	Tim Thelen	81-76—157
143	Woody Austin	79-79—158
	Kyle Flinton	79-79—158
	Pablo Larrazábal (ESP)	80-78—158
	Brad Martin	77-81—158
	Kirk Sanders	78-80—158
148	Nick Dougherty (ENG)	77-82—159
149	Hunter Mahan	81-79—160
	Colin Montgomerie (SCO)	76-84—160
151	Eric Gugas	87-74—161
152	David Long	80-82—162
153	Vince Jewell	85-78—163
154	Eric Manning	81-88—169
155	Brad Dean	86-74—170
156	Kenny Perry	79 WD

2007 US PGA Championship *Southern Hills, Tulsa, OK* August 9–12 [7131–70]

Prize money: $7 million. Field of 156, of whom 72 made the half-way cut.

1	Tiger Woods	71-63-69-69—272	$1260000	23T	Peter Hanson (SWE)	72-71-69-73—285	51000
2	Woody Austin	68-70-69-67—274	756000		Kenny Perry	72-72-71-70—285	51000
3	Ernie Els (RSA)	72-68-69-66—275	476000		Ian Poulter (ENG)	71-73-70-71—285	51000
4	Arron Oberholser	68-72-70-69—279	308000		Heath Slocum	72-70-72-71—285	51000
	John Senden (AUS)	69-70-69-71—279	308000		Steve Stricker	77-68-69-71—285	51000
6	Simon Dyson (ENG)	73-71-72-64—280	227500		Camilo Villegas (COL)	69-71-74-71—285	51000
	Trevor Immelman (RSA)	75-70-66-69—280	227500	32	Brad Bryant	74-70-72-70—286	34750
	Geoff Ogilvy (AUS)	69-68-74-69—280	227500		Stewart Cink	72-70-72-72—286	34750
9	Kevin Sutherland	73-69-68-71—281	170333		John Daly	67-73-73-73—286	34750
	Scott Verplank	70-66-74-71—281	170333		Luke Donald (ENG)	72-71-70-73—286	34750
	Boo Weekley	76-69-65-71—281	170333		Shaun Micheel	73-71-70-72—286	34750
12	Stephen Ames (CAN)	68-69-69-76—282	119833		Phil Mickelson	73-69-75-69—286	34750
	Stuart Appleby (AUS)	73-68-72-69—282	119833		Lee Westwood (ENG)	69-74-75-68—286	34750
	K J Choi (KOR)	71-71-68-72—282	119833		Brett Wetterich	74-71-70-71—286	34750
	Anders Hansen (DEN)	71-71-71-69—282	119833	40	Paul Casey (ENG)	72-70-74-71—287	27350
	Justin Rose (ENG)	70-73-70-69—282	119833		Richard Green (AUS)	72-73-70-72—287	27350
	Adam Scott (AUS)	72-68-70-72—282	119833	42	Darren Clarke (NIR)	77-66-71-74—288	20850
18	Ken Duke	73-71-69-71—284	81600		Niclas Fasth (SWE)	71-68-79-70—288	20850
	Joe Durant	71-73-70-70—284	81600		Padraig Harrington (IRL)	69-73-72-74—288	20850
	Hunter Mahan	71-73-72-68—284	81600		Charles Howell III	75-70-72-71—288	20850
	Pat Perez	70-69-77-68—284	81600		Colin Montgomerie (SCO)	72-73-73-70—288	20850
	Brandt Snedeker	74-71-69-70—284	81600		Sean O'Hair	70-72-70-76—288	20850
23	Steve Flesch	72-73-68-72—285	51000		Rod Pampling (AUS)	70-74-72-72—288	20850
	Retief Goosen (RSA)	70-71-74-70—285	51000		David Toms	71-74-71-72—288	20850
	Nathan Green (AUS)	75-68-67-75—285	51000				

Other players who made the cut: Brian Bateman, Lucas Glover, Frank Lickliter II, Shingo Katayama (JPN), Anthony Kim, Nick O'Hern, Bob Tway, 289; Chad Campbell, Robert Karlsson (SWE), Will MacKenzie, 290; Billy Mayfair, Paul McGinley (IRL), 291; Thomas Bjørn (DEN), Corey Pavin , Brett Quigley, Graeme Storm (ENG), 293; Todd Hamilton, Tim Herron, Troy Matteson, 294; Tom Lehman, Mike Small, 296; Ryan Benzel, 297; Sergio García (ESP), DQ

2006 US PGA Championship *Medinah, Il* August 16–20 [7561–72]

Prize money: $6.5 million. Field of 156, of whom 70 made the half-way cut.

1	Tiger Woods	69-68-65-68—270	$1224000	24	Chad Campbell	71-72-75-66—284	53100
2	Shaun Micheel	69-70-67-69—275	734400		Stewart Cink	68-74-73-69—284	53100
3	Luke Donald (ENG)	68-68-66-74—276	353600		Tim Clark (RSA)	70-69-75-70—284	53100
	Sergio García (ESP)	69-70-67-70—276	353600		Steve Flesch	72-71-69-72—284	53100
	Adam Scott (AUS)	71-69-69-67—276	353600		Anders Hansen (DEN)	72-71-70-71—284	53100
6	Mike Weir (CAN)	72-67-65-73—277	244800	29	Jim Furyk	70-72-69-74—285	41100
7	K J Choi (KOR)	73-67-67-71—278	207787		Robert Karlsson (SWE)	71-73-69-72—285	41100
	Steve Stricker	72-67-70-69—278	207787		Heath Slocum	73-70-72-70—285	41100
9	Ryan Moore	71-72-67-69—279	165000		Lee Westwood (ENG)	69-72-71-73—285	41100
	Geoff Ogilvy (AUS)	69-68-68-74—279	165000		Dean Wilson	74-70-74-67—285	41100
	Ian Poulter (ENG)	70-70-68-71—279	165000	34	Retief Goosen (RSA)	70-73-68-75—286	34500
12	Chris DiMarco	71-70-67-72—280	134500		Trevor Immelman (RSA)	73-71-70-72—286	34500
	Sean O'Hair	72-70-70-68—280	134500		Davis Love III	68-69-73-76—286	34500
14	Tim Herron	69-67-72-73—281	115000	37	Richard Green (AUS)	73-69-73-72—287	29250
	Henrik Stenson (SWE)	68-68-73-72—281	115000		J B Holmes	71-70-68-78—287	29250
16	Woody Austin	71-69-69-73—282	94000		Graeme McDowell (NIR)	75-68-72-72—287	29250
	Ernie Els (RSA)	71-70-72-69—282	94000		Billy Mayfair	69-69-73-76—287	29250
	Phil Mickelson	69-71-68-74—282	94000	41	Billy Andrade	67-69-78-74—288	23080
	David Toms	71-67-71-73—282	94000		Daniel Chopra (SWE)	72-67-76-73—288	23080
20	Robert Allenby (AUS)	68-74-71-70—283	71250		J J Henry	68-73-73-74—288	23080
	Jonathan Byrd	69-72-74-68—283	71250		Chris Riley	66-72-73-77—288	23080
	Harrison Fraser	69-72-69-73—283	71250		Justin Rose (ENG)	73-70-70-75—288	23080
	Fred Funk	69-69-74-71—283	71250				

Other players who made the cut: Olin Browne, Lucas Glover, 289; Jerry Kelly, 290; Rich Beem, Nathan Green (AUS), Ryan Palmer, Corey Pavin, Kenny Perry, Joey Sindelar, 291; Stephen Ames (CAN), Stuart Appleby (AUS), Aaron Baddeley (AUS), José-María Olazábal (ESP), Hideto Tanihara (JPN), 292; Ben Curtis, Steve Lowery, 293; Jason Gore, Jeff Maggert, Charles Warren, 295; Miguel Angel Jiménez (ESP), Bob Tway, 296; David Howell (ENG), 297; Jay Haas, Don Yrene, 300; Jim Kane, 301

2005 US PGA Championship Baltusrol, NJ August 11–15   [7392–70]

Prize money: $6.25 million. Field of 156, of whom 79 made the half-way cut.

1	Phil Mickelson	67-65-72-72—276	$1170000	23T	Shingo Katayama (JPN)	71-66-74-72—283	56400
2	Thomas Bjørn (DEN)	71-71-63-72—277	572000		Paul McGinley (IRL)	72-70-72-69—283	56400
	Steve Elkington (AUS)	68-70-68-71—277	572000		Tom Pernice Jr	69-73-69-72—283	56400
4	Davis Love III	68-68-68-74—278	286000		Kenny Perry	69-70-70-74—283	56400
	Tiger Woods	75-69-66-68—278	286000	28	Chad Campbell	71-71-70-72—284	41500
6	Michael Campbell	73-68-69-69—279	201500		Stewart Cink	71-72-66-75—284	41500
	(NZL)				Bob Estes	71-72-73-68—284	41500
	Retief Goosen (RSA)	68-70-69-72—279	201500		Arron Oberholser	74-68-69-73—284	41500
	Geoff Ogilvy (AUS)	69-69-72-69—279	201500		Jesper Parnevik (SWE)	68-69-72-75—284	41500
	Pat Perez	68-71-67-73—279	201500		Vaughn Taylor	75-69-71-69—284	41500
10	Steve Flesch	70-71-69-70—280	131800	34	Jason Bohn	71-68-68-78—285	31917
	Dudley Hart	70-73-66-71—280	131800		Ben Curtis	67-73-67-78—285	31917
	Ted Purdy	69-75-70-66—280	131800		Jim Furyk	72-71-69-73—285	31917
	Vijay Singh (FIJ)	70-67-69-74—280	131800		Fredrik Jacobson (SWE)	72-69-73-71—285	31917
	David Toms	71-72-69-68—280	131800		Jerry Kelly	70-65-74-76—285	31917
15	Stuart Appleby (AUS)	67-70-69-75—281	102500		Scott Verplank	71-72-71-71—285	31917
	Charles Howell III	70-71-68-72—281	102500	40	K J Choi (KOR)	71-70-73-72—286	22300
17	Tim Clark (RSA)	71-73-70-68—282	82500		Ben Crane	68-76-72-70—286	22300
	Trevor Immelman (RSA)	67-72-72-71—282	82500		Miguel Angel Jiménez	72-72-69-73—286	22300
	Jack Johnson	70-70-73-69—282	82500		(ESP)		
	Joe Ogilvie	74-68-69-71—282	82500		John Rollins	68-71-73-74—286	22300
	Bo Van Pelt	70-70-68-74—282	82500		Steve Schneiter (CAN)	72-72-72-70—286	22300
	Lee Westwood (ENG)	68-68-71-75—282	82500		Adam Scott (AUS)	74-69-72-71—286	22300
23	Sergio García (ESP)	72-70-71-70—283	56400		Patrick Sheehan	73-71-71-71—286	22300

Other players who made the cut: Fred Funk, Todd Hamilton, Bernhard Langer (GER), JL Lewis, José María Olazábal (ESP), Greg Owen (ENG), Ryan Palmer, Ian Poulter (ENG), Heath Slocum, Henrik Stenson (SWE). Mike Wier (CAN), Yong-Eun Yang (KOR) 287; Paul Casey (ENG), Carlos Franco (PAR), Peter Hanson (SWE), Mark Hensby (AUS), Scott McCarron, Sean O'Hair, Steve Webster (ENG) 288; Woody Austin, Luke Donald (ENG), Ron Philo Jr, Chris Riley 289; Mark Calcavecchia, Fred Couples 290; Stephen Ames (CAN), Joe Durant 291; John Daly, Rory Sabbatini (RSA) 292; Mike Small 295; Kevin Sutherland 296; Darrell Kestner 299; Hal Sutton 300

2004 US PGA Championship Whistling Straits, Kohler, WI August 12–15   [7514–72]

Prize money: $6.25 million. Field of 155, of whom 73 made the half-way cut.

1	Vijay Singh (FIJ)*	67-68-69-76—280	$1125000	17T	David Toms	72-72-69-72—285	76857
2	Justin Leonard	66-69-70-75—280	550000	24	Tom Byrum	72-73-71-70—286	46714
	Chris DiMarco	68-70-71-71—280	550000		Chad Campbell	73-70-71-72—286	46714
*Three hole play-off: Singh 3-3-4; Leonard 4-3-4; DiMarco 4-3-4					Luke Donald (ENG)	67-73-71-75—286	46714
4	Ernie Els (RSA)	66-70-72-73—281	267500		JL Lewis	73-69-72-72—286	46714
	Chris Riley	69-70-69-73—281	267500		Shaun Micheel	77-68-70-71—286	46714
6	K J Choi (KOR)	68-71-73-70—282	196000		Geoff Ogilvy (AUS)	68-73-71-74—286	46714
	Paul McGinley (IRL)	69-74-70-69—282	196000		Tiger Woods	75-69-69-73—286	46714
	Phil Mickelson	69-72-67-74—282	196000	31	Carlos Daniel Franco	69-75-72-71—287	34250
9	Robert Allenby (AUS)	71-70-72-70—283	152000		(PAR)		
	Stephen Ames (CAN)	68-71-69-75—283	152000		Charles Howell III	70-71-72-74—287	34250
	Ben Crane	70-74-69-70—283	152000		Miguel Angel Jiménez	76-65-75-71—287	34250
	Adam Scott (AUS)	71-71-69-72—283	152000		(ESP)		
13	Darren Clarke (NIR)	65-71-72-76—284	110250		Nick O'Hern (AUS)	73-71-68-75—287	34250
	Brian Davis (ENG)	70-71-69-74—284	110250		Chip Sullivan	72-71-73-71—287	34250
	Brad Faxon	71-71-70-72—284	110250		Bo Van Pelt	74-71-70-72—287	34250
	Arron Oberholser	73-71-70-70—284	110250	37	Briny Baird	67-69-75-77—288	24687
17	Stuart Appleby (AUS)	68-75-72-70—285	76857		Steve Flesch	73-72-67-76—288	24687
	Stewart Cink	73-70-70-72—285	76857		Jay Haas	68-72-71-77—288	24687
	Matt Gogel	71-71-69-74—285	76857		Todd Hamilton	72-73-75-68—288	24687
	Fredrik Jacobson (SWE)	72-70-70-73—285	76857		Trevor Immelman (RSA)	75-69-72-72—288	24687
	Jean-François Remesy	72-71-70-72—285	76857		Zach Johnson	75-70-69-74—288	24687
	(FRA)				Ian Poulter (ENG)	73-72-70-73—288	24687
	Loren Roberts	68-72-70-75—285	76857		Brett Quigley	74-69-73-72—288	24687

Other players who made the cut: Tommy Armour III, Niclas Fasth (SWE), Padraig Harrington (IRL), David Howell (ENG) 289; Michael Campbell (NZL), Nick Faldo (ENG), Joe Ogilvie, Patrick Sheehan, Duffy Waldorf 290; Carl Pettersson (SWE) 291; Paul Azinger, S K Ho (KOR), Rod Pampling (AUS), Craig Parry (AUS), Eduardo Romero (ARG), Hidemichi Tanaka (JPN), Bob Tway 292; Woody Austin, Shingo Katayama (JPN), Jeff Sluman, Scott Verplank 293; Scott Drummond (SCO), Bernhard Langer (GER) 294; Robert Gamez, Mark Hensby (AUS) 296; Colin Montgomerie (SCO) 297; Roy Biancalana 299; Jeff Coston 301; Skip Kendall 304.

2003 US PGA Championship Oak Hill CC, Rochester, NY August 14–17 [7134–70]

Prize money: $6 million. Field of 156, of whom 70 made the half-way cut.

1	Shaun Micheel	69-68-69-70—276	$1080000	23	Stuart Appleby (AUS)	74-73-71-70—288	52000
2	Chad Campbell	69-72-65-72—278	648000		Luke Donald (ENG)	73-72-71-72—288	52000
3	Tim Clark (RSA)	72-70-68-69—279	408000		Phil Mickelson	66-75-72-75—288	52000
4	Alex Cejka (GER)	74-69-68-69—280	288000		Adam Scott (AUS)	72-69-72-75—288	52000
5	Ernie Els (RSA)	71-70-70-71—282	214000	27	Woody Austin	72-73-69-75—289	43000
	Jay Haas	70-74-69-69—282	214000		Geoff Ogilvy (AUS)	71-71-77-70—289	43000
7	Fred Funk	69-73-70-72—284	175667	29	Todd Hamilton	70-74-73-73—290	36600
	Loren Roberts	70-73-70-71—284	175667		Padraig Harrington (IRL)	72-76-69-73—290	36600
	Mike Weir (CAN)	68-71-70-75—284	175667		Frank Lickliter II	71-72-71-76—290	36600
10	Billy Andrade	67-72-72-74—285	135500		Peter Lonard (AUS)	74-74-69-73—290	36600
	Niclas Fasth (SWE)	76-70-71-68—285	135500		David Toms	75-72-71-72—290	36600
	Charles Howell III	70-72-70-73—285	135500	34	Fred Couples	74-71-72-74—291	29000
	Kenny Perry	75-72-70-68—285	135500		Lee Janzen	68-74-72-77—291	29000
14	Robert Gamez	70-73-70-73—286	98250		JL Lewis	71-75-71-74—291	29000
	Tim Herron	69-72-74-71—286	98250		Jesper Parnevik (SWE)	73-72-72-74—291	29000
	Scott McCarron	74-70-71-71—286	98250		Vijay Singh (FIJ)	69-73-70-79—291	29000
	Rod Pampling (AUS)	66-74-73-73—286	98250	39	Robert Allenby (AUS)	70-77-73-72—292	22000
18	Carlos Franco (PAR)	73-73-69-72—287	73000		Briny Baird	73-71-67-81—292	22000
	Jim Furyk	72-74-69-72—287	73000		Mark Calcavecchia	73-71-76-72—292	22000
	Toshimitsu Izawa (JPN)	71-72-71-73—287	73000		Joe Durant	71-76-75-70—292	22000
	Rocco Mediate	72-74-71-70—287	73000		Hal Sutton	75-71-67-79—292	22000
	Kevin Sutherland	69-74-71-73—287	73000				

Other players who made the cut: Angel Cabrera (ARG), Tom Pernice Jr, Duffy Waldorf 293; Ben Crane, Trevor Immelman (RSA), Shigeki Maruyama (JPN) 294; José Coceres (ARG), Gary Evans (ENG), Brian Gay, Len Mattiace, José María Olazábal (ESP), 295; Chris DiMarco 296; Aaron Baddeley (AUS), Bob Estes, Scott Hoch, Bernhard Langer (GER) 297; Jonathan Kaye, Billy Mayfair, Ian Poulter (ENG), Eduardo Romero (ARG), Philip Tataurangi (NZL) 298; Paul Casey (ENG) 299; Bob Burns 300; Rory Sabbatini (RSA) 302; Michael Campbell (NZL), K J Choi (KOR) 304

2002 US PGA Championship Hazeltine National, Chaska, MN August 15–18 [7360–72]

Prize money: $5.5 million. Field of 156 (one amateur), of whom 72 made the half-way cut.

1	Rich Beem	72-66-72-68—278	$990000	22	Heath Slocum	73-74-75-69—291	57000
2	Tiger Woods	71-69-72-67—279	594000	23	Michael Campbell (NZL)	73-70-77-72—292	44250
3	Chris Riley	71-70-72-70—283	374000		Retief Goosen (RSA)	69-69-79-75—292	44250
4	Fred Funk	68-70-73-73—284	235000		Bernhard Langer (GER)	70-72-77-73—292	44250
	Justin Leonard	72-66-69-77—284	235000		Justin Rose (ENG)	69-73-76-74—292	44250
6	Rocco Mediate	72-73-70-70—285	185000		Adam Scott (AUS)	71-71-76-74—292	44250
7	Mark Calcavecchia	70-68-74-74—286	172000		Jeff Sluman	70-75-74-73—292	44250
8	Vijay Singh (FIJ)	71-74-74-68—287	159000	29	Brad Faxon	74-72-75-72—293	33500
9	Jim Furyk	68-73-76-71—288	149000		Tom Lehman	71-72-77-73—293	33500
10	Robert Allenby (AUS)	76-66-77-70—289	110714		Craig Perks (NZL)	72-76-74-71—293	33500
	Stewart Cink	74-74-72-69—289	110714		Kenny Perry	73-68-78-74—293	33500
	José Coceres (ARG)	72-71-72-74—289	110714		Kirk Triplett	75-69-79-70—293	33500
	Pierre Fulke (SWE)	72-68-78-71—289	110714	34	David Duval	71-77-76-70—294	26300
	Sergio García (ESP)	75-73-73-68—289	110714		Ernie Els (RSA)	72-71-75-76—294	26300
	Ricardo Gonzalez (ARG)	72-71-73-71—289	110714		Neal Lancaster	72-73-75-74—294	26300
	Steve Lowery	71-71-73-74—289	110714		Phil Mickelson	76-72-78-68—294	26300
17	Stuart Appleby (AUS)	73-74-74-69—290	72000		Mike Weir (CAN)	73-74-77-70—294	26300
	Steve Flesch	72-74-73-71—290	72000	39	Chris DiMarco	76-69-77-73—295	21500
	Padraig Harrington (IRL)	71-73-74-72—290	72000		Joel Edwards	73-74-77-71—295	21500
	Charles Howell III	72-69-80-69—290	72000		John Huston	74-74-75-72—295	21500
	Peter Lonard (AUS)	69-73-75-73—290	72000		Scott McCarron	73-71-79-72—295	21500

Other players who made the cut: Briny Baird, Søren Hansen (DEN), Shigeki Maruyama (JPN), Loren Roberts, Kevin Sutherland 296; Angel Cabrera (ARG), Steve Elkington (AUS), Davis Love III, Len Mattiace, Tom Watson 297; Cameron Beckman, Tim Clark (RSA), Brian Gay, Toshimitsu Izawa (JPN), Lee Janzen, Greg Norman (AUS), Chris Smith 298; Joe Durant, Nick Faldo (ENG), Hal Sutton 299, JJ Henry 301; Don Berry, Matt Gogel, JP Hayes, Joey Sindelar 302; Dave Tentis 304; José María Olazábal (ESP) 305; Pat Perez 309; Thomas Levet (FRA) 310; Stephen Ames (TRI) W/D

2001 US PGA Championship *Atlanta Athletic Club, Duluth, GA* August 16–19   [7213–70]

Prize money: $5.205 million. Field of 150, of whom 76 made the half-way cut.

1	David Toms	66-65-65-69—265	$936000	16T	Chris DiMarco	68-67-71-71—277	70666
2	Phil Mickelson	66-66-66-68—266	562000	22	Mark O'Meara	72-63-70-73—278	44285
3	Steve Lowery	67-67-66-68—268	354000		Shigeki Maruyama	68-72-71-67—278	44285
4	Mark Calcavecchia	71-68-66-65—270	222500		(JPN)		
	Shingo Katayama (JPN)	67-64-69-70—270	222500		Paul Azinger	68-67-69-74—278	44285
6	Billy Andrade	68-70-68-66—272	175000		Paul McGinley (IRL)	68-72-71-67—278	44285
7	Jim Furyk	70-64-71-69—274	152333		Briny Baird	70-69-72-67—278	44285
	Scott Verplank	69-68-70-67—274	152333		J Brian Gay	70-68-69-71—278	44285
	Scott Hoch	68-70-69-67—274	152333		Charles Howell III	71-67-69-71—278	44285
10	David Duval	66-68-67-74—275	122000	29	Greg Norman (AUS)	70-68-71-70—279	29437
	Justin Leonard	70-69-67-69—275	122000		Tiger Woods	73-67-69-70—279	29437
	Kirk Triplett	68-70-71-66—275	122000		Nick Price (ZIM)	71-67-71-70—279	29437
13	Steve Flesch	73-67-70-66—276	94666		K J Choi (KOR)	66-68-72-73—279	29437
	Jesper Parnevik (SWE)	70-68-70-68—276	94666		Bob Tway	69-69-71-70—279	29437
	Ernie Els (RSA)	67-67-70-72—276	94666		Carlos Franco (PAR)	67-72-71-69—279	29437
16	Stuart Appleby (AUS)	66-70-68-73—277	70666		Niclas Fasth (SWE)	66-69-72-72—279	29437
	Mike Weir (CAN)	69-72-66-70—277	70666		Christopher Smith	69-71-68-71—279	29437
	Dudley Hart	66-68-73-70—277	70666		José María Olazábal	70-70-68-71—279	29437
	José Coceres (ARG)	69-68-73-67—277	70666		(ESP)		
	Robert Allenby (AUS)	69-67-73-68—277	70666				

Other players who made the cut: Fred Couples, Davis Love III, Bob Estes, Angel Cabrera (ARG), Andrew Coltart (SCO), Retief Goosen (RSA) 280; Andrew Oldcorn (SCO), Greg Chalmers (AUS), Jerry Kelly, Hal Sutton, Kenny Perry, Lee Westwood (ENG), Rick Schuller 281; Nick Faldo (ENG), Ian Woosnam (WAL), Joe Durant, Vijay Singh (FIJ), Scott Dunlap, Tom Pernice, Chris Riley, Frank Lickliter 282; Brad Faxon, Stewart Cink, Phillip Price (WAL), Grant Waite (NZL) 283; Skip Kendall, Thomas Bjørn (DEN), Jonathan Kaye, Rocco Mediate 284; Tom Watson, Steve Stricker, Robert Damron 285; Fred Funk, Scott McCarron 286; John Huston 287; Bob May 291; Paul Stankowski 293; Steve Pate 294; Colin Montgomerie (SCO) DQ

2000 US PGA Championship *Valhalla GC, Louisville, KY* August 17–20   [7167–72]

Prize money: $5 million. Field of 150, of whom 80 made the half-way cut.

1	Tiger Woods*	66-67-70-67—270	$900000	19T	JP Hayes	69-68-68-86—281	56200
2	Bob May	72-66-66-66—270	540000		Angel Cabrera (ARG)	72-71-71-67—281	56200
After a three hole play-off: Woods 3-4-5–12; May 4-4-5–13					Robert Allenby (AUS)	73-71-68-69—281	56200
3	Thomas Bjørn (DEN)	72-68-67-68—275	340000		Lee Janzen	76-70-70-65—281	56200
4	Greg Chalmers (AUS)	71-69-66-70—276	198667	24	Paul Azinger	72-71-66-73—282	41000
	José María Olazábal				Steve Jones	72-71-70-69—282	41000
	(ESP)	76-68-63-69—276	198667		Jarmo Sandelin (SWE)	74-72-68-68—282	41000
	Stuart Appleby (AUS)	70-69-68-69—276	198667	27	Brad Faxon	71-74-70-68—283	34167
7	Franklin Langham	72-71-65-69—277	157000		Skip Kendall	72-72-69-70—283	34167
8	Notah Begay III	72-66-70-70—278	145000		Tom Pernice	74-69-70-70—283	34167
9	Tom Watson	76-70-65-68—279	112500	30	Mike Weir (CAN)	76-69-68-71—284	28875
	Fred Funk	69-68-74-68—279	112500		Jean Van de Velde	70-74-69-71—284	28875
	Davis Love III	68-69-72-70—279	112500		(FRA)		
	Darren Clarke (NIR)	68-72-72-67—279	112500		Stephen Ames (TRI)	69-71-71-73—284	28875
	Scott Dunlap	66-68-70-75—279	112500		Kenny Perry	78-68-70-68—284	28875
	Phil Mickelson	70-70-69-70—279	112500	34	Sergio García (ESP)	74-69-73-69—285	24000
15	Stewart Cink	72-71-70-67—280	77500		Chris Perry	72-74-70-69—285	24000
	Lee Westwood (ENG)	72-72-69-67—280	77500		Mark Calcavecchia	73-74-71-67—285	24000
	Chris DiMarco	73-70-69-68—280	77500		Ernie Els (RSA)	74-68-72-71—285	24000
	Michael Clark II	73-70-67-70—280	77500		Blaine McCallister	73-71-70-71—285	24000
19	Tom Kite	70-72-69-70—281	56200				

Other players who made the cut: Toshimitsu Izawa (JPN), Colin Montgomerie (SCO) 286; Jeff Sluman, Justin Leonard, Paul Stankowski, Steve Pate, David Toms 287; Bernhard Langer (GER), Mark O'Meara, Shigeki Maruyama (JPN), Duffy Waldorf, Brian Henninger 288; Nick Faldo (ENG), Jesper Parnevik (SWE), Steve Lowery, Brian Watts, Glen Day, Andrew Coltart (SCO), Jonathan Kaye 289; Padraig Harrington (IRL), Loren Roberts, Curtis Strange, Carlos Franco (PAR), Dennis Paulson, Joe Ogilvie 290; Wayne Grady (AUS), Craig Stadler, Bill Glasson, Miguel Angel Jiménez (ESP), Jay Haas 291; Greg Kraft, Kirk Triplett 292; John Huston 293; Jim Furyk, Paul Lawrie (SCO) 294; Robert Damron, Billy Mayfair, Scott Hoch 297; Masashi Ozaki (JPN), Rory Sabbatini 299; Hidemichi Tanaka (JPN) 301; Frank Dobbs 313

1999 US PGA Championship *Medinah, IL* August 12–15   [7401–72]

Prize money: $3 million. Field of 149, of whom 74 made the half-way cut.

1	T Woods	70-67-68-72—277	$630000	21	D Frost (RSA)	75-68-74-71—288	33200
2	S García (ESP)	66-73-68-71—278	378000		S Hoch	71-71-75-71—288	33200
3	S Cink	69-70-68-73—280	203000		S Kendall	74-65-71-78—288	33200
	J Haas	68-67-75-70—280	203000		JL Lewis	73-70-74-71—288	33200
5	N Price (ZIM)	70-71-69-71—281	129000		K Wentworth	72-70-72-74—288	33200
6	B Estes	71-70-72-69—282	112000	26	F Couples	73-69-75-72—289	24000
	C Montgomerie (SCO)	72-70-70-70—282	112000		C Franco (PAR)	72-71-71-75—289	24000
8	J Furyk	71-70-69-74—284	96500		J Kelly	69-74-71-75—289	24000
	S Pate	72-70-73-69—284	96500		H Sutton	72-73-73-71—289	24000
10	D Duval	70-71-72-72—285	72166		J Van de Velde (FRA)	74-70-75-70—289	24000
	MA Jiménez (ESP)	70-70-75-70—285	72166	31	P Goydos	73-70-71-76—290	20000
	J Parnevik (SWE)	72-70-73-70—285	72166		M James (ENG)	70-74-79-67—290	20000
	C Pavin	69-74-71-71—285	72166		T Tryba	70-72-76-72—290	20000
	C Perry	70-73-71-71—285	72166	34	S Flesch	73-71-72-75—291	15428
	M Weir (CAN)	68-68-69-80—285	72166		P Lawrie (SCO)	73-72-72-74—291	15428
16	M Brooks	70-73-70-74—287	48600		T Lehman	70-74-76-71—291	15428
	G Hjertstedt (SWE)	72-70-73-72—287	48600		B Mayfair	75-69-75-72—291	15428
	B Jobe	69-74-69-75—287	48600		K Perry	74-69-72-76—291	15428
	G Turner (NZL)	73-69-70-75—287	48600		S Verplank	73-72-73-73—291	15428
	L Westwood (ENG)	70-68-74-75—287	48600		L Wadkins	72-69-74-76—291	15428

Other players who made the cut: P Azinger, Angel Cabrera (ARG), C DiMarco, N Faldo (ENG), H Irwin, R Karlsson (SWE), D Waldorf, B Watts 292; O Browne, D Love III, R Mediate, V Singh (FIJ), K Triplett 293; JP Hayes, A Magee, J Sluman 294; P Mickelson, M O'Meara, P Stewart, B Tway 295; M Calcavecchia, B Faxon, G Kraft, B Langer (GER) 296; A Cejka (GER), A Coltart (SCO), M Reid 297; S Dunlap, B Zabriski 298; R Beem, T Bjørn (DEN), N Ozaki (JPN) 299; F Funk 300

US PGA Championship History

Date	Winner	Runner-up	Venue	By
1916 Oct 8–14	J Barnes	J Hutchison	Siwanoy, NY	1 hole
1919 Sept 15–20	J Barnes	F McLeod	Engineers' Club, NY	6 and 5
1920 Aug 17–21	J Hutchison	D Edgar	Flossmoor, IL	1 hole
1921 Sept 26–Oct 1	W Hagen	J Barnes	Inwood Club, NY	3 and 2
1922 Aug 12–18	G Sarazen	E French	Oakmont, PA	4 and 3
1923 Sept 23–29	G Sarazen	W Hagen	Pelham, NY	38th hole
1924 Sept 15–20	W Hagen	J Barnes	French Lick, IN	2 holes
1925 Sept 21–26	W Hagen	W Mehlhorn	Olympic Fields, IL	6 and 4
1926 Sept 20–25	W Hagen	L Diegel	Salisbury, NY	4 and 3
1927 Oct 31–Nov 5	W Hagen	J Turnesa	Dallas, TX	1 hole
1928 Oct 1–6	L Diegel	A Espinosa	Five Farms, MD	6 and 5
1929 Dec 2–7	L Diegel	J Farrell	Hill Crest, CA	6 and 4
1930 Sept 8–13	T Armour	G Sarazen	Fresh Meadows, NY	1 hole
1931 Sept 7–14	T Creavy	D Shute	Wannamoisett, RI	2 and 1
1932 Aug 31–Sept 4	O Dutra	F Walsh	St Paul, MN	4 and 3
1933 Aug 8–13	G Sarazen	W Goggin	Milwaukee, WI	5 and 4
1934 July 24–29	P Runyan	C Wood	Buffalo, NY	38th hole
1935 Oct 18–23	J Revolta	T Armour	Oklahoma, OK	5 and 4
1936 Nov 17–22	D Shute	J Thomson	Pinehurst, NC	3 and 2
1937 May 26–30	D Shute	H McSpaden	Pittsburgh, PA	37th hole
1938 July 10–16	P Runyan	S Snead	Shawnee, PA	8 and 7
1939 July 9–15	H Picard	B Nelson	Pomonok, NY	37th hole
1940 Aug 26–Sept 2	B Nelson	S Snead	Hershey, PA	1 hole
1941 July 7–13	V Ghezzie	B Nelson	Denver, CO	38th hole
1942 May 23–31	S Snead	J Turnesa	Atlantic City, NJ	2 and 1
1943 *No Championship*				
1944 Aug 14–20	B Hamilton	B Nelson	Spokane, WA	1 hole
1945 July 9–15	B Nelson	S Byrd	Dayton, OH	4 and 3
1946 Aug 19–25	B Hogan	E Oliver	Portland, OR	6 and 4
1947 June 18–24	J Ferrier	C Harbert	Detroit, MI	2 and 1
1948 May 19–25	B Hogan	M Turnesa	Norwood Hills, MO	7 and 6
1949 May 25–31	S Snead	J Palmer	Richmond, VA	3 and 2
1950 June 21–27	C Harper	H Williams	Scioto, OH	4 and 3

US PGA Championship History *continued*

Date	Winner	Runner-up	Venue	By
1951 June 27–July 3	S Snead	W Burkemo	Oakmont, PA	7 and 6
1952 June 18–25	J Turnesa	C Harbert	Louisville, KY	1 hole
1953 July 1–7	W Burkemo	F Lorza	Birmingham, MI	2 and 1
1954 July 21–27	C Harbert	W Burkemo	St Paul, MN	4 and 3
1955 July 20–26	D Ford	C Middlecoff	Meadowbrook, MI	4 and 3
1956 July 20–24	J Burke	T Kroll	Canton, MA	3 and 2
1957 July 17–21	L Hebert	D Finsterwald	Dayton, OH	3 and 1

Changed to stroke play in 1958

Date	Winner	Venue	Score
1958 July 17–20	D Finsterwald	Llanerch, PA	276
1959 July 30–Aug 2	B Rosburg	Minneapolis, MN	277
1960 July 21–24	J Hebert	Firestone, Akron, OH	281
1961 July 27–31	J Barber*	Olympia Fields, IL	277

*After a play-off with Don January: Barber 67, January 68

Date	Winner	Venue	Score
1962 July 19–22	G Player (RSA)	Aronimink, PA	278
1963 July 18–21	J Nicklaus	Dallas, TX	279
1964 July 16–19	B Nichols	Columbus, OH	271
1965 Aug 12–15	D Marr	Laurel Valley, PA	280
1966 July 21–24	A Geiberger	Firestone, Akron, OH	280
1967 July 20–24	D January*	Columbine, CO	281

*After a play-off with Don Massengale: January 69, Massengale 71

Date	Winner	Venue	Score
1968 July 18–21	J Boros	Pecan Valley, TX	281
1969 Aug 14–17	R Floyd	Dayton, OH	276
1970 Aug 13–16	D Stockton	Southern Hills, OK	279
1971 Feb 25–28	J Nicklaus	PGA national, FL	281
1972 Aug 3–6	G Player (RSA)	Oakland Hills, MI	281
1973 Aug 9–12	J Nicklaus	Canterbury, OH	277
1974 Aug 8–11	L Trevino	Tanglewood, NC	276
1975 Aug 7–10	J Nicklaus	Firestone, Akron, OH	276
1976 Aug 12–16	D Stockton	Congressional, MD	281
1977 Aug 11–14	L Wadkins*	Pebble Beach, CA	287

*After a sudden death play-off with Gene Littler: Wadkins 4-4-3; Littler 4-4-4

Date	Winner	Venue	Score
1978 Aug 3–6	J Mahaffey*	Oakmont, PA	276

*After a sudden death play-off with Jerry Pate and Tom Watson: Mahaffey 4-3; Pate 4,4; Watson 4-4

Date	Winner	Venue	Score
1979 Aug 2–5	D Graham (AUS)*	Oakland Hills, MI	272

*After a sudden death play-off with Ben Crenshaw: Graham 4-4-2; Crenshaw 4-4-4

Date	Winner	Venue	Score
1980 Aug 7–10	J Nicklaus	Oak Hill, NY	274
1981 Aug 6–9	L Nelson	Atlanta, GA	273
1982 Aug 5–8	R Floyd	Southern Hills, OK	272
1983 Aug 4–7	H Sutton	Pacific Palisades, CA	274
1984 Aug 16–19	L Trevino	Shoal Creek, AL	273
1985 Aug 8–11	H Green	Cherry Hills, Denver, CO	278

Date	Winner	Venue	Score
1986 Aug 7–10	R Tway	Inverness, Toledo, OH	276
1987 Aug 6–9	L Nelson*	PGA National, FL	287

*After a sudden death play-off with Lanny Wadkins: Nelson 4, Wadkins 5

Date	Winner	Venue	Score
1988 Aug 11–14	J Sluman	Oaktree, OK	272
1989 Aug 10–13	P Stewart	Kemper Lakes, IL	276
1990 Aug 9–12	W Grady (AUS)	Shoal Creek, AL	282
1991 Aug 8–11	J Daly	Crooked Stick, IN	276
1992 Aug 13–16	N Price (ZIM)	Bellerive, MS	278
1993 Aug 12–15	P Azinger*	Inverness, Toledo, OH	272

*After a sudden death play-off with Greg Norman: Azinger 4-4, Norman 4-5

Date	Winner	Venue	Score
1994 Aug 11–14	N Price (ZIM)	Southern Hills, OK	269
1995 Aug 10–13	S Elkington (AUS)*	Riviera, LA	267

*After a sudden death play-off against Colin Montgomerie: Elkington 3, Montgomerie 4

Date	Winner	Venue	Score
1996 Aug 8–11	M Brooks*	Valhalla, Kentucky	277

*After a play-off against Kenny Perry: Brooks 4, Perry 5

Date	Winner	Venue	Score
1997 Aug 14–17	D Love III	Winged Foot, NY	269
1998 Aug 13–16	V Singh (FIJ)	Sahalee, Seattle, WA	271
1999 Aug 12–15	T Woods	Medinah, IL	277
2000 Aug 17–20	T Woods*	Valhalla, Louisville KY	270

*After a three-hole play-off with Bob May: Woods 3-4-5, May 4-4-5

Date	Winner	Venue	Score
2001 Aug 16–19	D Toms	Atlanta Athletic Club, GA	265
2002 Aug 15–18	R Beem	Hazeltine National, MN	278
2003 Aug 14–17	S Micheel	Oak Hill, NY	276
2004 Aug 12–15	V Singh (FIJ)*	Whistling Straits, WI	280

*After a three hole play-off with Chris DiMarco and Justin Leonard.: Singh 3-3-4, DiMarco 4-3-4, Leonard 4-3-4

Date	Winner	Venue	Score
2005 Aug 11–15	P Mickelson	Baltusrol, NJ	276
2006 Aug 16–20	T Woods	Medinah, IL	270
2007 Aug 9–12	T Woods	Southern Hills, OK	272
2008 Aug 7–10	P Harrington	Oakland Hills, MI	277

Eighteenth hole lives up to its reputation

The most difficult hole in the Championship history of Oakland Hills has always been the 18th and it maintained its reputation at the 2008 US PGA Championship last year. Designer Rees Jones had toughened it up even more for the event by adding two more bunkers giving the hole a grand total of seven – four of them around the green. The 498 yards dog-leg par 4 with a fairway that slopes from right to left averaged 4.661 over the four days. The drive is not so difficult as the long-iron second shot uphill to the shallowest of greens with a mound in the middle of it. Padraig Harrington, the winner of the title parred it in three of the four rounds but did not manage to make one of only 14 birdies.

Eagles 0   Birdies 14   Pars 181   Bogeys 220   Double bogeys 32   Others 10   Average 4.661

Men's Grand Slam Titles

Jack Nicklaus   Tiger Woods   Walter Hagen

Photographs © Phil Sheldon Golf Picture Library

The modern Grand Slam comprises four events – the British and US Open Championships, the US PGA Championship and The Masters Tournament at Augusta.

	Open	US Open	Masters	US PGA	Total Titles
Jack Nicklaus (USA)	3	4	6	5	18
Tiger Woods (USA)	3	3	4	4	14
Walter Hagen (USA)	4	2	0	5	11
Ben Hogan (USA)	1	4	2	2	9
Gary Player (RSA)	3	1	3	2	9
Tom Watson (USA)	5	1	2	0	8
Arnold Palmer (USA)	2	1	4	0	7
Gene Sarazen (USA)	1	2	1	3	7
Sam Snead (USA)	1	0	3	3	7
Lee Trevino (USA)	2	2	0	2	6
Nick Faldo (ENG)	3	0	3	0	6

The original Grand Slam comprised the British and US Open Championships and the British and US Amateur Championships.

	Open	US Open	Amateur	US Amateur	Total Titles
Bobby Jones (USA)	3	4	1	5	13
John Ball (ENG)	1	0	8	0	9
Harold Hilton (ENG)	2	0	4	1	7
Harry Vardon (ENG)	6	1	0	0	7

Note: Tiger Woods won three consecutive US Amateur Championships in 1994, 1995 and 1996. Only Bobby Jones has won all four recognised Grand Slam events in the same year – 1930.

Ricoh Women's British Open Championship

Talented Korean star Ji-Yai Shin shines to land her first major title at Sunningdale

Not many of the spectators who turned up at Sunningdale for the Ricoh Women's British Open knew much about the 20-year-old who played so well to win the title. Her name was Ji-Yai Shin but if she was not known in Europe she had certainly made her mark in her own country. She was Korea's Player of the Year in 2007 when she won nine times and was out of the top five only twice in 18 starts – once finishing second and on the other occasions 10th. She averaged 70.68 in 2007 and her 2008 record had been equally impressive. In six starts in Korea she had won three times and had also won, come second three times (twice in play-offs), fifth and twice seventh in international events.

© Hugh Routledge/Phil Sheldon Golf Picture Library

Ji-Yai Shin

Capable of turning on her special brand of golfing magic wherever she played, Shin had always had a realistic chance of winning at Sunningdale even if her name was not on everyone's lips. Making only four bogeys all week she swept to a three-shot victory over Taiwanese golfer Yani Tseng, winner earlier in the year of the McDonald's LPGA Championship. Just a shot further back sharing third spot was prolific winner Yuri Fudoh from Japan and Eun-Hee Ji, another Korean who had been fifth in this event in 2007.

Shin's success meant that Korean golfers had ended the 2008 majors season having won two of the four titles. Lorena Ochoa, the defending champion at Sunningdale who would finish joint seventh this time, had taken the Kraft Nabisco title at Mission Hills in California and Tseng had triumphed in the LPGA Championship.

For Shin, victory at Sunningdale was a life changing experience. It ensured she had invitations to the next ten Ricoh Women's British Opens and earned her the right to accept a card to play the LPGA Tour. Initially her thoughts were to stick with her plan and play the Japanese Tour in 2009 before trying America a year later. That could change but what was sure in Shin's mind was the fact that she had achieved one of her greatest golfing goals. "My whole life I have been waiting for this time", said Shin who gave up archery at 13 to turn to golf and was a scratch player within three years, "Now my dream has come true."

She had not dreamt too much the night before the final round which she went into trailing Fudoh by a shot. "I was very nervous and did not sleep well," she said. Once at the course, however, she was the personification of calmness and control firing a closing bogey free 66 to blow away the opposition. She

First Round	Second Round	Third Round	Fourth Round
−7 Inkster	−10 Fudoh	−13 Fudoh	−18 Shin
−6 Ueda	−10 Shin	−12 Shin	−15 Tseng
−6 Fudoh	−9 Inkster	−11 Miyazato	−14 Ji
−6 Oh	−8 Kerr	−10 Kerr	−14 Fudoh
−6 Diaz	−8 Song	−10 Inkster	−13 Miyazato
−6 Prammanasudh	−7 Ochoa	−9 Kim	−12 Kerr
−6 Head	−7 Gulbis	−9 Tseng	−11 Ochoa
−5 Hudson	−6 Diaz	−9 Ji	−11 Ueda
−5 McPherson	−6 Ueda	−9 Choi	−10 Kim
−5 Steinhauer	−6 Ji	−8 Ochoa	−10 Han
		−8 Ueda	−10 Creamer
			−10 Webb
			−10 Gulbis

played like a veteran yet became the fifth youngest winner of a major behind Morgan Pressel who was 18 when she won the 2007 Kraft Nabisco, Yani Tseng, the 2008 McDonald's PGA champion and Inbee Park the 2008 US Open champion both of whom were 19 when they won and Sandra Post who was a slightly younger 20-year-old than Shin when she landed the 1968 LPGA Championship. Shin was also the first golfer to win a major without being a member of the LPGA Tour since Laura Davies finished first in the 1987 US Women's Open.

If it was a special week for Shin it was special as well for Annika Sörenstam, playing in her 57th and final major in her last season on Tour. The Swedish golfer's career figures to date were impressive. She had won 85 times worldwide including 10 majors and was cheered up the last hole where the huge scoreboard echoed the thoughts of everyone with the message "Annika you will be missed." She ended her last British Open in style hitting the 6-iron she had used a few weeks earlier to hole her second shot for an eagle at her last US Open to 20 feet for a closing birdie.

She had finished tied second and tied third in the first two majors of the season but after announcing her retirement from competitive golf she could not quite find the intensity of competition which had been a hallmark of her play for over 15 years. She may have hit every green in regulation in that final round at Sunningdale but the desire, the motivation, the drive was somewhat missing. Even she could not quite understand why that had happened but the girl who claimed she was born to compete had no regrets at quitting to think about doing other things and starting a family. Walking up to the last green in the rain she called over her caddie of nine years Terry Macnamara to come under her umbrella and share the moment with her – a gesture not lost on those who were watching.

Julie Inkster, thirty-one times an LPGA Tour winner including seven majors, was the first round leader with a bogey-free 67. Travelling from Switzerland to London Inkster, who had been struggling with her swing, found herself on the same plane as Karrie Webb and her coach Ian Triggs. She asked Triggs if he could have a look at her on the range and he seemed to have put her right as she chased the honour of become the oldest winner of an LPGA event and emulate Webb, Se Ri Pak and Karen Stupples, all former winners of the title at the exquisitely prepared Surrey course.

Three eagles for Diaz

Inkster led from a group of seven players which included Momoka Ueda and Fudoh but lost the lead on a blustery second day to Fudoh and Shin, both of whom shot 68 and moved to 10-under-par one ahead of Inkster.   Defending champion Ochoa was on seven under lying joint sixth and Laura Diaz was on the leaderboard at six-under-par after becoming only the third player in LPGA history to score three eagles in one round with 3's at the par 5 1st and 10th, and a 2 at the 11th where she holed a 65 yards wedge shot.   Seventy–eight players made the cut on one-over-par but Pressel, and Se Ri Pak, the first Korean to win the title in 2001 were among the half-way casualties. Another Korean Jeong Jang, winner in 2005, withdrew with a wrist injury.

At the end of the third day Fudoh, already a double winner on the 2008 Japanese circuit, had edged in front of Shin with another Japanese golfer Ai Miyazato in third spot after a near flawless 68. Inkster was still a challenger sharing fourth spot with fellow American Cristie Kerr.

The final round developed into a battle between Fudoh and Shin. The Korean drew level with a birdie at the fifth and gradually pulled away from her Japanese rival who finally finished in a tie for fourth with Eun-Hee Ji. Yani Tseng, with a final round 66, grabbed second place after a Championship that had not lacked drama and emotion and had provided in Ji-Yai Shin the third first time major winner of the year. The fact that 13 Asian golfers, all with a dedicated work ethic, finished in the top 20 at Sunningdale underlined the competitive strength from that part of the world The hungry winner's first priority at the end was to enjoy a good meal before heading back home to Korea to celebrate her outstanding success.

2008 Ricoh Women's British Open Championship

Sunningdale [6408–72]

Prize money: €1.55 million. Final field of 144 (6 amateurs), of whom 78 (1 amateur) made the half-way cut on 145 or under.

Final Qualifying at The Berkshire:

Stefania Croce (ITA)	Anja Monke (GER)	Lee-Anne Pace (RSA)
Martina Gillen (IRL)	Eric Blaberg (USA)	Claire Coughlan-Ryan (IRL)
Lydia Hall (WAL)	Krystle Caithness (SCO) (am)	Leah Hart (AUS)
Marjet van der Graaf (NED)	Tania Elosegui Mayor (ESP)	Kiran Matharu (ENG)
Naomi Edwards (ENG) (am)	Margherita Rigon (ITA)	Iben Tinning (DEN)
Lora Fairclough (ENG)	Elizabeth Bennett (ENG) (am)	
Samantha Head (ENG)	Rebecca Coakley (IRL)	

1	Ji-Yai Shin (KOR)	66-68-70-66—270	€202336
2	Ya-Ni Tseng (TPE)	70-69-68-66—273	126460
3	Eun Hee Ji (KOR)	68-70-69-67—274	79037
	Yuri Fudoh (JPN)	66-68-69-71—274	79037
5	Ai Miyazato (JPN)	68-69-68-70—275	56907
6	Cristie Kerr (USA)	71-65-70-70—276	49319
7	Lorena Ochoa (MEX)	69-68-71-69—277	42464
	Momoko Ueda (JPN)	66-72-70-69—277	42464
9	Paula Creamer (USA)	72-69-70-67—278	30603
	Natalie Gulbis (USA)	69-68-70-71—278	30603
	Hee Won Han (KOR)	71-69-71-67—278	30603
	In Kyung Kim (KOR)	71-68-72-67—278	30603
	Karrie Webb (AUS)	72-69-69-68—278	30603
14	Juli Inkster (USA)	65-70-71-73—279	21709
	Seon Hwa Lee (KOR)	71-68-70-70—279	21709
	Hee Young Park (KOR)	69-71-69-70—279	21709
17	Shi Hyun Ahn (KOR)	68-72-71-69—280	17625
	Minea Blomqvist (FIN)	68-73-72-67—280	17625
	Jee Yound Lee (KOR)	71-72-71-66—280	17625
	Ji Young Oh (KOR)	66-73-71-70—280	17625
21	Nicole Castrale (USA)	69-72-72-68—281	15175
	Na Yeon Choi (KOR)	69-71-68-73—281	15175
	Kristy McPherson (USA)	67-75-74-65—281	15175
24	Meredith Duncan (USA)	71-73-71-67—282	11786
	Sophie Gustafson (SWE)	69-69-74-70—282	11786
	Mi Hyun Kim (KOR)	70-70-67-75—282	11786
	Eun-A Lin (KOR)	74-71-72-65—282	11786
	Jane Park (USA)	69-70-73-70—282	11786
	Suzann Pettersen (NOR)	70-70-71-71—282	11786
	Stacy Prammanasudh (USA)	66-74-72-70—282	11786
	Annika Sörenstam (SWE)	72-72-70-68—282	11786
	Karen Stupples (ENG)	67-73-72-70—282	11786
	Sakura Yokomine (JPN)	71-72-69-70—282	11786
34	Laura Diaz (USA)	66-72-75-70—283	9010
	Anja Monke (GER)	73-67-70-73—283	9010
	Angela Park (BRA)	71-74-71-37—283	9010
	Bo Bae Song (KOR)	68-68-74-73—283	9010
38	Ji-Hee Lee (KOR)	68-75-68-73—284	7745
	Leta Lindley (USA)	71-71-72-70—284	7745
	Paula Marti (ESP)	68-72-72-72—284	7745
	Catriona Matthew (SCO)	68-75-72-69—284	7745
42	Candie Kung (TPE)	72-67-74-72—285	6797
	Anna Nordqvist (SWE) (am)	70-73-69-73—285	
	Reilley Rankin (USA)	69-73-72-71—285	6797
45	Lora Fairclough (ENG)	70-74-73-69—286	6006
	Janice Moodie (SCO)	69-76-70-71—286	6006
	Sun Young Yoo (KOR)	73-72-69-72—286	6006

48	Hye Jung Choi (KOR)	72-70-73-72—287	4552
	Jin Joo Hong (KOR)	75-70-69-73—287	4552
	Katherine Hull (AUS)	69-73-69-76—287	4552
	Jill McGill (USA)	75-68-72-72—287	4552
	Joanne Mills (AUS)	70-73-72-72—287	4552
	Gloria Park (KOR)	73-72-74-68—287	4552
	Karin Sjodin (SWE)	72-73-71-71—287	4552
	Lotta Wahlin (SWE)	69-76-71-71—287	4552
56	Helen Alfredsson (SWE)	69-76-72-71—288	3224
	Il-Mi Chung (KOR)	73-72-71-72—288	3224
	Rebecca Hudson (ENG)	67-76-72-73—288	3224
59	Jimin Kang (KOR)	69-76-74-70—289	2541
	Teresa Lu (TPE)	70-72-73-74—289	2541
	Becky Morgan (WAL)	72-72-74-71—289	2541
	Kris Camulis (USA)	73-70-74-72—289	2541
	Wendy Ward (USA)	71-71-74-73—289	2541
64	Erica Blasberg (USA)	75-70-73-72—290	1972
	Christina Kim (USA)	71-73-72-74—290	1972
	Gwladys Nocera (FRA)	73-69-75-73—290	1972
	Marianne Skarpnord (NOR)	68-72-72-78—290	1972
	Sherri Steinhauer (USA)	67-75-76-72—290	1972
69	Tania Elosegui (ESP)	70-73-75-73—291	1643
	Johanna Head (ENG)	66-76-73-76—291	1643
	Rachel Hetherington (AUS)	70-72-74-75—291	1643
	Maria Hjörth (SWE)	69-74-72-76—291	1643
	Trish Johnson (ENG)	72-70-76-73—291	1643
74	Becky Brewerton (WAL)	70-73-76-73—292	1454
75	Moira Dunn (USA)	74-69-77-74—294	1359
	Maria Jose Uribe (COL) (am)	71-73-74-76—294	
77	Laura Davies (ENG)	70-75-75-75—295	1264
78	Mhairi McKay (SCO)	71-74-73-78—296	1201

The following players missed the cut.

79	Rebecca Coakley (IRL)	74-78—152		111T	Na On Min (KOR)	77-72—149
	Elizabeth Bennett (ENG) (am)	74-72—146			In-Bee Park (KOR)	74-75—149
	Shanshan Feng (CHN)	77-69—146			Miki Saiki (JPN)	76-73—149
	Lisa Hall (ENG)	72-74—146		115	Yukari Baba (JPN)	77-73—150
	Pat Hurst (USA)	74-72—146			Se Ri Pak (KOR)	74-76—150
	Karine Icher (FRA)	74-72—146			Louise Stahle (SWE)	77-73—150
	Felicity Johnson (ENG)	69-77—146			Iben Tinning (DEN)	76-74—150
	Soo Yun Kang (KOR)	72-74—146			Linda Wessberg (SWE)	74-76—150
	Meena Lee (KOR)	72-74—146			Amy Yang (KOR)	71-79—150
	Angela Stanford (USA)	70-76—146		121	Martina Eberl (GER)	74-77—151
88	Stacy Lee Bregman (RSA)	73-74—147			Melissa Reid (ENG)	75-76—151
	Louise Friberg (SWE)	75-72—147			Marjet van der Graaf (NED)	75-76—151
	Katie Futcher (USA)	74-73—147		124	Kyeong Bae (KOR)	79-73—152
	Sandra Gal (GER) (am)	72-75—147			Lydia Hall (WAL)	73-79—152
	Brittany Lang (USA)	70-77—147			Kelli Kuehne (USA)	75-77—152
	Diana Luna (ITA)	74-73—147			Alena Sharp (CAN)	77-75—152
	Paige Mackenzie (USA)	74-73—147		128	Claire Coughlan-Ryan (IRL)	77-76—153
	Marta Prieto (ESP)	74-73—147			Veronica Zorzi (ITA)	77-76—153
	Maria Verchenova (RUS)	69-78—147		130	Johanna Westerberg (SWE)	80-74—154
97	Maria Boden (SWE)	76-72—148		131	Krystle Caithness (SCO) (am)	76-79—155
	Anne-Lise Caudal (FRA)	74-74—148			Diana D'Alessio (USA)	80-75—155
	Irene Cho (USA)	75-73—148			Allison Fouch (USA)	77-78—155
	Stefania Croce (ITA)	74-74—148			Caroline Hedwall (SWE) (am)	76-79—155
	Naomi Edwards (ENG) (am)	75-73—148			Ludivine Kreutz (FRA)	81-74—155
	Nikki Garrett (AUS)	72-76—148			Lisa Holm Sorensen (DEN)	76-79—155
	Song-Hee Kim (KOR)	73-75—148		137	Rebecca Coakley (IRL)	79-77—156
	Carin Koch (SWE)	75-73—148			Leah Hart (AUS)	79-77—156
	Brittany Lincicome (USA)	75-73—148			Margherita Rigon (ITA)	75-81—156
	Lee-Anne Pace (RSA)	73-75—148			Emma Zackrisson (SWE)	76-80—156
	Grace Park (KOR)	72-76—148		141	Kiran Matharu (ENG)	79-78—157
	Morgan Pressel (USA)	74-74—148				
	Lindsey Wright (AUS)	74-74—148			Jeong Jang (KOR)	70 RTD
	Heather Young (USA)	73-75—148			Young Kim (KOR)	81 RTD
111	Martina Gillen (IRL)	74-75—149			Samantha Head (ENG)	WD

2007 Weetabix Women's British Open   *St Andrews Old Course*   [6638–73]

Prize money: £2.5 million

1	Lorena Ochoa (MEX)	67-73-73-74—287	£160000	16T	Melissa Reid (ENG) (am)	73-75-76-72—296		
2	Maria Hjörth (SWE)	75-73-72-71—291	85000		Annika Sörenstam (SWE)	72-71-77-76—296	14041	
	Jee Young Lee (KOR)	72-73-75-71—291	85000	23	Beth Bader (USA)	73-77-75-72—297	11060	
4	Reilley Rankin (USA)	73-74-74-71—292	55000		Natalia Gulbis (USA)	73-76-76-72—297	11060	
5	Eun Hee Ji (KOR)	73-71-77-72—293	42000		Alena Sharp (CAN)	77-70-79-71—297	11060	
	Se Ri Pak (KOR)	73-73-75-72—293	42000		Sherri Steinhauer (USA)	72-71-80-74—297	11060	
7	Paula Creamer (USA)	73-75-74-72—294	30500		Wendy Ward (USA)	71-70-80-76—297	11060	
	Catriona Matthew (SCO)	73-68-80-73—294	30500	28	Jimin Kang (KOR)	77-72-75-75—299	9100	
	Miki Saiki (JPN)	76-70-81-67—294	30500		Sarah Lee (KOR)	72-76-79-72—299	9100	
	Linda Wessberg (SWE)	74-73-72-75—294	30500		Suzann Pettersen (NOR)	74-76-78-71—299	9100	
11	Yuri Fudoh (JPN)	74-69-81-71—295	20300		Ji-Yai Shin (KOR)	76-74-77-72—299	9100	
	Brittany Lincicome (USA)	71-76-75-73—295	20300		Karrie Webb (AUS)	77-73-74-75—299	9100	
	Mhairi McKay (SCO)	75-74-79-67—295	20300	33	Louise Friberg (SWE)	69-76-80-75—300	7062	
	Na On Min (KOR)	72-75-75-73—295	20300		Sophie Gustafson (SWE)	73-72-81-74—300	7062	
	In-Bee Park (KOR)	69-79-76-71—295	20300		Kim Hall (USA)	74-74-79-73—300	7062	
16	Becky Brewerton (WAL)	74-75-74-73—296	14041		Juli Inkster (USA)	79-68-82-71—300	7062	
	Karine Icher (FRA)	72-71-77-76—296	14041		Trish Johnson (ENG)	75-75-77-73—300	7062	
	Virginie Lagoutte-Clement (FRA)	72-73-78-73—296	14041		Cristie Kerr (USA)	77-71-79-73—300	7062	
	Gloria Park (KOR)	74-75-76-71—296	14041		Candie Kung (TPE)	72-74-79-75—300	7062	
	Stacy Prammanasudh (USA)	74-76-72-74—296	14041		Meena Lee (KOR)	71-76-79-74—300	7062	
					Gwladys Nocera (FRA)	78-72-75-75—300	7062	

Other players who made the cut: Rebecca Hudson (ENG), In Kyung Kim (KOR), Michele Redman (USA), Kerry Smith (ENG) (am), Karen Stupples (ENG), Lotta Wahlin (SWE), 301; Hye Yong Choi (KOR) (am), Catrin Nilsmark (SWE), 303; Dina Ammaccapane (USA), Rachel Bell (ENG), Beth Daniel (USA), Grace Park (KOR), Sally Watson (SCO) (am), 304; Rachel Hetherington (AUS), Belen Mozo (ESP) (am), Momoko Ueda (JPN), 305; Lisa Hall (ENG), Jin Joo Hong (KOR), Christina Kim (USA), Ai Miyazato (JPN), Anna Nordquist (SWE) (am), Iben Tinning (DEN), 306; Joanne Mills (AUS), 308; Diana D'Alessio (USA), Martina Eberl (GER), 309; Nicole Castrale (USA), 310; Meg Mallon (USA), 311; Naomi Edwards (ENG) (am), 312

2006 Weetabix Women's British Open   *Royal Lytham & St Annes*   [6308–72]

Prize money: £1.05 million

1	Sherri Steinhauer (USA)	73-70-66-72—281	£160000	22T	Jee Young Lee (KOR)	72-77-69-74—292	11500	
2	Sophie Gustafson (SWE)	76-67-69-72—284	85000	25	Shi Hyun Ahn (KOR)	75-73-69-76—293	10600	
	Cristie Kerr (USA)	71-76-66-71—284	85000	26	Jackie Gallagher-Smith (USA)	77-74-71-72—294	9460	
4	Juli Inkster (USA)	66-72-74-73—285	50000		Tracy Hanson (USA)	74-77-70-73—294	9460	
	Lorena Ochoa (MEX)	74-73-65-73—285	50000		Jeong Jang (KOR)	78-73-68-75—294	9460	
6	Beth Daniel (USA)	73-70-71-72—286	37000		Michelle Wie (USA)	74-74-72-74—294	9460	
	Lorie Kane (CAN)	73-69-74-70—286	37000		Young-A Yang (KOR)	72-75-68-79—294	9460	
8	Julieta Granada (PAR)	71-73-70-73—287	32000	31	Nicole Castrale (USA)	73-75-71-76—295	7810	
9	Ai Miyazato (JPN)	71-75-75-67—288	29000		Anja Monke (GER)	75-76-70-74—295	7810	
10	Hee Won Han (KOR)	80-71-69-70—290	21250		Liselotte Neumann (SWE)	76-72-70-77—295	7810	
	Karine Icher (FRA)	72-73-71-74—290	21250		Annika Sörenstam (SWE)	72-71-73-79—295	7810	
	Joo Mi Kim (KOR)	73-73-73-71—290	21250		Lindsey Wright (USA)	71-71-74-79—295	7810	
	Candie Kung (TPE)	72-70-71-77—290	21250	36	Becky Brewerton (WAL)	76-73-73-74—296	6375	
	Nina Reis (SWE)	70-76-69-75—290	21250		Vicki Goetze-Ackerman (USA)	75-72-71-78—296	6375	
	Karen Stupples (ENG)	73-69-70-78—290	21250		Young Jo (KOR)	80-70-74-72—296	6375	
16	Il-Mi Chung (KOR)	72-71-75-73—291	14041		Angela Stanford (USA)	76-69-80-71—296	6375	
	Laura Davies (ENG)	72-72-73-74—291	14041		Sun Young Yoo (KOR)	76-74-71-75—296	6375	
	Natalie Gulbis (USA)	72-74-67-78—291	14041		Veronica Zorzi (ITA)	74-76-78-68—296	6375	
	Gwladys Nocera (FRA)	70-73-71-77—291	14041					
	Sukura Yokomine (JPN)	72-73-75-71—291	14041					
	Heather Young (USA)	72-74-70-75—291	14041					
22	Kyeong Bae (KOR)	73-73-75-71—292	11500					
	Paula Creamer (USA)	72-71-73-76—292	11500					

Other players who made the cut: Yuri Fudoh (JPN), Nikki Garrett (AUS), Patricia Meunier-Lebouc (FRA), 297; Chieko Amanuma (JPN), Silvia Cavalleri (ITA), Maria Hjörth (SWE), Christina Kim (USA), Sarah Lee (KOR), 298; Marisa Baena (COL), Rita Hakkarainen (FIN), Allison Hanna (USA), Teresa Lu (TPE), Joanne Morley (ENG), Lee Ann Walker-Cooper (USA), 299; Brittany Lincicome (USA), Becky Morgan (WAL), Morgan Pressel (USA), Kris Tamulis (USA), 300; Amy Yang (KOR) (am), 301; Lynnette Brooky (NZL), Seon Hwa Lee (KOR), Elisa Serramia (ESP), Ursula Wikstrom (FIN), 302; Laura Diaz (USA), 303; Marta Prieto (ESP), 304; Helena Alterby (SWE), Wendy Ward (USA), 305; Rachel Hetherington (AUS), 306; Belen Mozo (ESP) (am), 307; Iben Tinning (DEN), 311

2005 Weetabix Women's British Open Royal Birkdale, Southport, Lancashire [6463–72]

Prize money: £1.05 million

1	Jeong Jang (KOR)	68-66-69-69—272	£160000	21	Catriona Matthew (SCO)	73-72-72-67—284	13500
2	Sophie Gustafson (SWE)	69-73-67-67—276	100000	22	Brandie Burton (USA)	74-75-71-65—285	11767
3	Young Kim (KOR)	74-68-67-69—278	70000		Cecilia Ekelundh (SWE)	77-69-71-68—285	11767
	Michelle Wie (USA) (am)	75-67-67-69—278			Candie Kung (TAI)	76-71-67-71—285	11767
5	Cristie Kerr (USA)	73-66-69-71—279	46333		Nicole Perrot (CHI)	70-72-69-74—285	11767
	Liselotte Neumann (SWE)	71-70-68-70—279	46333		Sophie Sandolo (ITA)	71-73-73-68—285	11767
	Annika Sörenstam (SWE)	73-69-66-71—279	46333		Linda Wessberg (SWE)	72-71-73-69—285	11767
8	Natalie Gulbis (USA)	76-70-68-66—280	33500	28	Shi Hyun Ahn (KOR)	78-68-67-73—286	9283
	Grace Park (KOR)	77-68-67-68—280	33500		Becky Brewerton (WAL)	75-71-65-75—286	9283
	Louise Stahle (SWE) (am)	73-65-73-69—280			Laura Davies (ENG)	76-70-66-74—286	9283
11	Ai Miyazato (JPN)	72-73-69-67—281	25250		Christina Kim (USA)	79-70-71-66—286	9283
	Michele Redman (USA)	75-71-67-68—281	25250		Anja Monke (GER)	73-73-70-70—286	9283
	Karen Stupples (ENG)	74-71-65-71—281	25250		Miriam Nagl (GER)	74-75-69-68—286	9283
	Karrie Webb (AUS)	75-66-69-71—281	25250	34	Heather Bowie (USA)	74-69-72-72—287	7530
15	Paula Creamer (USA)	75-69-65-73—282	17300		Marty Hart (USA)	79-70-71-67—287	7530
	Yuri Fudoh (JPN)	75-69-68-70—282	17300		Rebecca Hudson (ENG)	78-70-71-68—287	7530
	Juli Inkster (USA)	74-68-68-72—282	17300		Emilee Klein (USA)	71-73-70-73—287	7530
	Carin Koch (SWE)	76-68-66-72—282	17300		Jill McGill (USA)	76-70-72-69—287	7530
	Becky Morgan (WAL)	79-66-67-70—282	17300	39	Minea Blomquist (SWE)	78-68-72-70—288	6500
20	Pat Hurst (USA)	75-65-70-73—283	14250		Wendy Doolan (AUS)	77-72-67-72—288	6500
					Sherri Steinhauer (USA)	74-73-70-71—288	6500

Other players who made the cut: Helen Alfredsson (SWE), Michelle Ellis (AUS), Riikka Hakkarainen (FIN), Rachel Hetherington (AUS), Riko Higashio (JPN), Amanda Moltke-Leth (DEN), Gwladys Nocera (FRA), Kim Saiki (USA), Iben Tinning (DEN), Kris Tschetter (USA), 289; Carlota Ciganda (ESP) (am), Moira Dunn (USA), Kris Lindstrom (USA), Kimberley Williams (USA), 290; Catherine Cartwright (USA), Beth Daniel (USA), 291; Young Jo (KOR), Lorie Kane (CAN), Aree Song (KOR), Bo Bae Song (KOR). 292; Judith Van Hagen (NED), Shani Waugh (AUS), 293; Laura Diaz (USA), Sung Ah Yim (KOR), 294; Amy Hung (TAI), Paula Marti (ESP), 295; Siew-Ai Lim (MAS), Yu Ping Lin (TAI), 296; Karen Lunn (AUS), 301

2004 Weetabix Women's British Open Sunningdale (Old Course) [6392–72]

Prize money: £1.05 million

1	Karen Stupples (ENG)	65-70-70-64—269	£160000	21T	Se Ri Pak (KOR)	73-70-69-69—281	12250
2	Rachel Teske (AUS)	70-69-65-70—274	100000	23	Jeong Jang (KOR)	70-68-73-71—282	11250
3	Heather Bowie (USA)	70-69-65-71—275	70000		Aree Song (KOR)	72-70-70-70—282	11250
4	Lorena Ochoa (MEX)	69-71-66-70—276	55000	25	Juli Inkster (USA)	71-75-69-68—283	10200
5	Beth Daniel (USA)	69-69-71-68—277	39667		Seol-An Jeon (KOR)	69-69-70-75—283	10200
	Michele Redman (USA)	70-71-70-66—277	39667		Toshimi Kimura (JPN)	70-75-68-70—283	10200
	Guilia Sergas (ITA)	72-71-67-67—277	39667	28	Alison Nicholas (ENG)	75-71-70-69—285	9450
8	Minea Blomqvist (FIN)	68-78-62-70—278	29000	29	Candie Kung (TPE)	73-69-71-73—286	8925
	Laura Davies (ENG)	76-69-69-70—278	29000		Catriona Matthew (SCO)	68-74-68-76—286	8925
	Jung Yeon Lee (KOR)	67-72-70-69—278	29000	31	Wendy Doolan (AUS)	71-72-74-70—287	7950
11	Pat Hurst (USA)	72-72-66-69—279	23000		Natascha Fink (AUT)	74-70-70-73—287	7950
	Cristie Kerr (USA)	69-73-63-74—279	23000		Gloria Park (KOR)	72-73-75-67—287	7950
13	Laura Diaz (USA)	70-69-70-71—280	15906		Kirsty Taylor (ENG)	72-74-72-69—287	7950
	Natalie Gulbis (USA)	68-71-70-71—280	15906	35	Soo-Yun Kang (KOR)	71-74-74-69—288	7000
	Hee Won Han (KOR)	72-68-70-70—280	15906		Becky Morgan (WAL)	74-72-69-73—288	7000
	Christina Kim (USA)	73-68-68-71—280	15906		Jennifer Rosales (PHI)	75-70-70-73—288	7000
	Carin Koch (SWE)	70-70-70-70—280	15906	38	Denise Killeen (USA)	72-72-70-75—289	6125
	Paula Marti (ESP)	73-66-68-73—280	15906		Jill McGill (USA)	71-72-71-75—289	6125
	Grace Park (KOR)	71-70-69-70—280	15906		Patricia Meunier-Lebouc (FRA)	70-75-71-73—289	6125
	Annika Sörenstam (SWE)	68-71-70-71—280	15906		Nadina Taylor (AUS)	69-74-72-74—289	6125
21	Michelle Estill (USA)	70-72-68-71—281	12250				

Other players who made the cut: Hiromi Mogi (JPN), Shiho Ohyama (JPN), Ana B Sanchez (ESP), Louise Stahle (SWE) (am), Sherri Steinhauer (USA) 290; Bettina Hauert (GER), Angela Jerman (USA), Pamela Kerrigan 291; Ashli Bunch (USA), Audra Burks (USA), Johanna Head (ENG), Katherine Hull (AUS), Kelli Kuehne (USA), Gwladys Nocera (FRA) 292; Lynnette Brooky (NZL), A J Eathorne (CAN), Wendy Ward (USA) 293; Emilee Klein (USA) 294; Helen Alfredsson (SWE), Hsiao Chuan Lu (CHN), Betsy King (USA), Janice Moodie (SCO) 295; Raquel Carriedo (ESP), Ana Larraneta (ESP) 296; Vicki Goetze-Ackerman (USA), Laurette Maritz (RSA) 297; Samantha Head (ENG) 298; Maria Hjörth (SWE) 305

2003 Weetabix Women's British Open *Royal Lytham and St Annes, Lancashire* [6308–72]

Prize money: £1.05 million

1	Annika Sörenstam (SWE)	68-72-68-70—278	£160000	19T	Laura Davies (ENG)	75-70-70-74—289	12500
					Hee Won Han (KOR)	75-71-70-73—289	12500
2	Se Ri Pak (KOR)	69-69-69-72—279	100000		Lorie Kane (CAN)	69-75-70-75—289	12500
3	Grace Park (KOR)	74-65-71-70—280	62500		Becky Morgan (WAL)	72-70-71-76—289	12500
	Karrie Webb (AUS)	67-72-70-71—280	62500	24	Brandie Burton (USA)	76-69-69-76—290	8996
5	Patricia Meunier-	70-69-67-76—282	45000		Moira Dunn (USA)	70-74-74-72—290	8996
	Lebouc (FRA)				Michiko Hattori (JPN)	78-69-71-72—290	8996
6	Vicki Goetze-Ackerman	73-71-68-71—283	37000		Pat Hurst (USA)	73-71-74-72—290	8996
	(USA)				Soo-Yun Kang (KOR)	70-75-72-73—290	8996
	Wendy Ward (USA)	67-71-69-76—283	37000		Emilee Klein (USA)	72-70-74-74—290	8996
8	Sophie Gustafson (SWE)	73-69-71-71—284	32000		Lorena Ochoa (MEX)	74-65-77-74—290	8996
9	Young Kim (KOR)	73-70-72-70—285	29000		Dottie Pepper (USA)	71-75-71-73—290	8996
10	Candie Kung (TPE)	73-71-69-73—286	25000		Jennifer Rosales (PHI)	69-72-76-73—290	8996
	Gloria Park (KOR)	70-75-69-72—286	25000		Iben Tinning (DEN)	71-73-73-73—290	8996
12	Paula Marti (ESP)	71-70-70-76—287	21000		Hiroko Yamaguchi (JPN)	72-71-75-72—290	8996
	Karen Stupples (ENG)	69-74-70-74—287	21000		Young-A Yang (KOR)	71-75-71-73—290	8996
14	Lynnette Brooky (NZL)	70-74-75-69—288	16150	36	Georgina Simpson	69-73-74-75—291	7000
	Beth Daniel (USA)	74-71-67-76—288	16150		(ENG)		
	Laura Diaz (USA)	73-74-71-70—288	16150	37	Christine Kuld (DEN)	69-76-75-72—292	6375
	Jeong Jang (KOR)	76-69-72-71—288	16150		Meg Mallon (USA)	71-72-71-78—292	6375
	Cristie Kerr (USA)	74-71-71-72—288	16150		Michele Redman (USA)	71-69-76-76—292	6375
19	Heather Bowie (USA)	70-66-74-79—289	12500		Nadina Taylor (AUS)	71-74-72-75—292	6375

Other players who made the cut: Elisabeth Esterl (GER), Akiko Fukushima (JPN), Johanna Head (ENG), Juli Inkster (USA), Catrin Nilsmark (SWE) 293; Kelli Kuehne (USA), Elisa Serramia (ESP) (am), Rachel Teske (AUS), Karen Weiss (USA), 294; Kasumi Fujii (JPN), Angela Jerman (USA), Carin Koch (SWE), Kelly Robbins (USA) 295; Cherie Byrnes (AUS), Michelle Ellis (AUS), Woo-Soon Ko (KOR), Shani Waugh (AUS) 296; Heather Daly-Donofrio (USA), Susan Parry (USA), Kirsty Taylor (ENG) 297; Helen Alfredsson (SWE), Alison Nicholas (ENG) 298; Beth Bauer (USA) 299; Silvia Cavalleri (ITA), Sophie Sandolo (ITA), Angela Stanford (USA) 300; Suzanne Strudwick (ENG) 303; Marnie McGuire (NZL) 308

2002 Weetabix Women's British Open *Turnberry, Ayrshire* [6407–72]

Prize money: £1,000,000

1	Karrie Webb (AUS)	66-71-70-66—273	£154982	24	Patricia Meunier	69-71-69-76—285	10249
2	Michelle Ellis (AUS)	69-70-68-68—275	84990		Lebouc (FRA)		
	Paula Marti (ESP)	69-68-69-69—275	84990		Suzann Pettersen (NOR)	72-71-72-70—285	10249
4	Jeong Jang (KOR)	73-69-66-69—277	42308	26	Dorothy Delasin (PHI)	70-71-70-75—286	9366
	Candie Kung (TPE)	65-71-71-70—277	42308		Elisabeth Esterl (GER)	67-71-72-76—286	9366
	Catrin Nilsmark (SWE)	70-69-69-69—277	42308		Emilee Klein (USA)	68-71-72-75—286	9366
	Jennifer Rosales (PHI)	69-70-65-73—277	42308	29	Brandie Burton (USA)	71-70-71-75—287	7949
8	Beth Bauer (USA)	70-67-70-71—278	25164		Cristie Kerr (USA)	72-71-69-75—287	7949
	Carin Koch (SWE)	68-68-68-74—278	25164		Kelli Kuehne (USA)	75-67-71-74—287	7949
	Meg Mallon (USA)	69-71-68-70—278	25164		Yu Ping Lin (TPE)	73-69-74-71—287	7949
11	Sophie Gustafson (SWE)	69-73-69-68—279	19748		Iben Tinning (DEN)	71-69-71-76—287	7949
	Se Ri Pak (KOR)	67-72-69-71—279	19748	34	Toshimi Kimura (JPN)	74-70-70-74—288	7249
13	Natalie Gulbis (USA)	69-70-67-74—280	16581	35	Kathryn Marshall (SCO)	70-71-76-72—289	6499
	Pat Hurst (USA)	69-70-69-72—280	16581		Catriona Matthew (SCO)	73-71-70-75—289	6499
	Angela Stanford (USA)	69-70-69-72—280	16581		Liselotte Neumann	70-71-71-77—289	6499
16	Tina Barrett (USA)	67-70-70-76—283	14348		(SWE)		
	Beth Daniel (USA)	73-68-68-74—283	14348		Kelly Robbins (USA)	70-75-68-76—289	6499
18	Jean Bartholomew	71-72-72-69—284	12099		Shani Waugh (AUS)	70-73-74-72—289	6499
	(USA)			40	Helen Alfredsson (SWE)	70-75-71-74—290	5249
	Wendy Doolan (AUS)	70-69-71-74—284	12099		Lora Fairclough (ENG)	71-69-73-77—290	5249
	Jane Geddes (USA)	71-69-70-74—284	12099		Becky Iverson (USA)	69-76-72-73—290	5249
	Marine Monnet (FRA)	71-70-70-73—284	12099		Karen Lunn (AUS)	73-71-72-74—290	5249
	Fiona Pike (AUS)	72-73-67-72—284	12099		Sophie Sandolo (ITA)	71-74-68-77—290	5249
	Rachel Teske (AUS)	67-74-68-75—284	12099				

Other players who made the cut: Asa Gottmo (SWE), Mhairi McKay (SCO) 291; Heather Daly-Donofrio (USA), Federica Dassu (ITA), Tracy Hanson (USA), Johanna Head (ENG), Becky Morgan (WAL), Giulia Sergas (ITA) 292; Heather Bowie (USA), Grace Park (KOR), Suzanne Strudwick (ENG) 293; Raquel Carriedo (ESP), Karen Stupples (ENG), Wendy Ward (USA) 294; Betsy King (USA) 295; Vicki Goetze-Ackerman (USA) 296; Mi Hyun Kim (KOR), Charlotta Sörenstam (SWE) 297; Tonya Gill (USA) 298; Riikka Hakkarainen (FIN) 299; Marina Arruti (ESP) 301; Ana Larraneta (ESP) 302

2001 Weetabix Women's British Open *Sunningdale, Berkshire* [6245–72]

Prize money: £730,000

1	Se Ri Pak (KOR)	71-70-70-66—277	£155000	21T	Emilee Klein (USA)	71-70-71-73—285	11125
2	Mi Hyun Kim (KOR)	72-65-71-71—279	100000		Lora Fairclough (ENG)	71-70-67-77—285	11125
3	Laura Diaz (USA)	74-70-69-67—280	51813	25	Danielle Ammaccapane	75-68-74-69—286	9071
	Iben Tinning (DEN)	71-69-72-68—280	51813		(USA)		
	Janice Moodie (SCO)	67-70-71-72—280	51813		Dina Ammaccapane	72-71-74-69—286	9071
	Catriona Matthew (SCO)	70-65-72-73—280	51813		(USA)		
7	Kristal Parker (USA)	72-71-71-67—281	25600		Silvia Cavalleri (ITA)	71-73-72-70—286	9071
	Marina Arruti (ESP)	71-73-70-67—281	25600		Maria Hjörth (SWE)	72-73-71-70—286	9071
	Kathryn Marshall (SCO)	75-71-68-67—281	25600		Gloria Park (KOR)	71-73-71-71—286	9071
	Kelli Kuehne (USA)	71-70-71-69—281	25600		Lee Ji Hee (KOR)	75-71-69-71—286	9071
	Kasumi Fujii (JPN)	71-71-69-70—281	25600		Laura Davies (ENG)	68-73-69-76—286	9071
12	Raquel Carriedo (ESP)	73-70-70-69—282	17750	32	Annika Sörenstam (SWE)	70-74-74-69—287	6767
	Tracy Hanson (USA)	72-69-70-71—282	17750		Marisa Baena (COL)	72-74-72-69—287	6767
	Rosie Jones (USA)	70-69-71-72—282	17750		Suzann Pettersen (NOR)	78-64-74-71—287	6767
15	Brandie Burton (USA)	72-71-73-67—283	14400		Wendy Doolan (AUS)	72-68-75-72—287	6767
	Pearl Sinn (USA)	74-70-72-67—283	14400		Grace Park (KOR)	70-71-74-72—287	6767
	Jill McGill (USA)	70-70-72-71—283	14400		Kelly Robbins (USA)	69-72-73-73—287	6767
	Karrie Webb (AUS)	74-67-68-74—283	14400		Mhairi McKay (SCO)	70-72-72-73—287	6767
19	Becky Morgan (WAL)	73-68-71-72—284	12575		Hee Won Han (KOR)	72-73-69-73—287	6767
	Trish Johnson (ENG)	70-67-72-75—284	12575		Hiromi Kobayashi (JPN)	72-70-71-74—287	6767
21	Johanna Head (ENG)	68-70-75-72—285	11125		Rebecca Hudson (ENG)	71-70-70-76—287	
	Marlene Hedblom (SWE)	70-74-69-72—285	11125		(am)		

Other players who made the cut: Sophie Gustafson (SWE), Kellee Booth (USA), Joanne Morley (ENG), Vicki Goetze-Ackerman (USA) 288; Lorie Kane (CAN), Suzanne Strudwick (ENG), Tina Barrett (USA), Cindy Schreyer (USA), Elisabeth Esterl (GER), Riikka Hakkarainen (FIN) 289; Joanne Mills (AUS) 290; Becky Iverson (USA), Yu Ping Lin (TPE) 291; Liselotte Neumann (SWE) 292; Carin Koch (SWE), Jenny Lidback (PER), Marine Monnet (FRA), Diane Barnard (ENG) 293; Kaori Harada (JPN), Laurette Maritz (RSA), Karin Icher (FRA), Lisa Hed (SWE) 294; Nicola Moult (ENG), Helen Alfredsson (SWE), Patricia Meunier-Lebouc (FRA) 295; Kirsty Taylor (ENG) 296; Judith Van Hagen (NED), Claire Duffy (ENG) 297; Dorothy Delasin (PHI) 298.

2000 Women's British Open Championship *Royal Birkdale* [6285–73]

Prize money: £730,000

1	Sophie Gustafson (SWE)	70-66-71-75—282	£120000	20	Kelly Robbins (USA)	73-74-73-70—290	8475
2	Kirsty Taylor (ENG)	71-74-72-67—284	50713		Karen Weiss (USA)	73-70-75-72—290	8475
	Becky Iverson (USA)	70-70-75-69—284	50713		Rachel Hetherington	71-74-73-72—290	8475
	Liselotte Neumann (SWE)	71-73-71-69—284	50713		(AUS)		
	Meg Mallon (USA)	74-69-71-70—284	50713		Brandie Burton (USA)	72-74-71-73—290	8475
6	Laura Philo (USA)	72-73-72-68—285	27500	24	Michele Redman (USA)	74-73-73-71—291	7275
7	Karrie Webb (AUS)	68-75-72-71—286	23250		Alicia Dibos (PER)	72-73-74-72—291	7275
8	Janice Moody (SCO)	73-74-73-67—287	19500		Marine Monnet (FRA)	72-73-74-72—291	7275
	Vicki Goetze-Ackerman	77-69-73-68—287	19500		Raquel Carriedo (ESP)	76-71-72-72—291	7275
	(USA)			28	Riko Higashio (JPN)	74-72-76-70—292	6313
10	Maggie Will (USA)	74-72-76-66—288	13250		Susan Redman (USA)	70-78-71-73—292	6313
	Michelle McGann (USA)	72-76-69-71—288	13250		Jill McGill (USA)	71-71-76-74—292	6313
	Juli Inkster (USA)	70-69-77-72—288	13250		Mhairi McKay (SCO)	74-71-71-76—292	6313
	Jenny Lidback (PER)	71-71-73-73—288	13250	32	Shani Waugh (AUS)	73-74-76-70—293	5400
	Trish Johnson (ENG)	71-72-72-73—288	13250		Michelle Estill (USA)	72-75-75-71—293	5400
	Kellee Booth (USA)	73-71-71-73—288	13250		Sofia Grönberg	80-69-73-71—293	5400
	Kathryn Marshall (SCO)	72-69-73-74—288	13250		Whitmore (SWE)		
17	Pat Bradley (USA)	74-71-74-70—289	9850		Gail Graham (CAN)	79-71-71-72—293	5400
	Rosie Jones (USA)	72-72-73-72—289	9850		Betsy King (USA)	74-73-73-73—293	5400
	Annika Sörenstam (SWE)	70-76-71-72—289	9850				

Other players who made the cut: Giulia Sergas (ITA), Maria Hjörth (SWE), Tina Barrett (USA), Leigh Ann Mills (USA), Julie Forbes (SCO), Wendy Daden (ENG), Pernilla Sterner (SWE), Laura Davies (ENG) 294; Anna Berg (SWE), Yu Ping Lin (TPE), Aki Takamura (JPN), Karen Pearce (AUS) 295; Silvia Cavalleri (ITA), Stephanie Arricau (FRA), Sara Eklund (SWE), Karen Stupples (ENG), Sandrine Mendiburu (FRA), Jenifer Feldott (USA), Helen Alfredsson (SWE), Anne-Marie Knight (AUS) 296; Federica Dassu (ITA) 297; Kristal Parker-Gregory (USA), Elizabeth Esterl (GER) 298; Catrin Nilsmark (SWE), Smriti Mehra (IND), Johanna Head (ENG) 299; Mardi Lunn (AUS), Mandy Adamson (RSA), Dale Reid (SCO) 300; Hiromi Kobayashi (JPN), Lisa De Paulo (USA) 301; Hsui Feng Tseng (CHN), Nina Karlsson (SWE), Judith Van Hagen (NED) 303; Emilee Klein (USA), Gina Marie Scott (NZL), Laurette Maritz (RSA) 304; Lora Fairclough (ENG) 306.

1999 Weetabix Women's British Open Woburn G&CC, Bedfordshire   [6463–73]

Prize money: £575,000

1	S Steinhauer (USA)	71-71-68-73—283	£100000	17T	C Figg-Currier (USA)	69-76-72-73—290	6614
2	A Sörenstam (SWE)	69-71-72-72—284	60000		V Van	72-75-70-73—290	6614
3	H Dobson (ENG)	71-72-72-70—285	31666		Ryckeghem (BEL)		
	C Flom (USA)	71-74-69-71—285	31666		K Taylor (ENG)	73-71-72-74—290	6614
	F Pike (AUS)	70-70-71-74—285	31666	24	G Sergas (ITA) (am)	71-73-74-73—291	
6	E Klein (USA)	72-70-73-71—286	16000		J Morley (ENG)	70-75-73-73—291	5300
	S Gustafson (SWE)	73-69-72-72—286	16000		A Nicholas (ENG)	73-71-73-74—291	5300
	M Lunn (AUS)	71-72-70-73—286	16000		M Hjörth (SWE)	71-68-77-75—291	5300
	I Tinning (DEN)	68-69-75-74—286	16000		S Lowe (ENG)	72-74-70-75—291	5300
	C McCurdy (USA)	73-70-68-75—286	16000		P Meunier-	73-70-72-76—291	5300
11	S Mehra (IND)	70-70-76-71—287	11000		Lebouc (FRA)		
12	C Koch (SWE)	74-72-72-70—288	9625		M Yoneyama (JPN)	73-70-72-76—291	5300
	S Strudwick (ENG)	71-70-76-71—288	9625	31	C Nilsmark (SWE)	72-71-76-73—292	4150
14	R Jones (USA)	73-71-73-72—289	8033		M Hirase (JPN)	73-72-74-73—292	4150
	L Philo (USA)	69-71-75-74—289	8033		D Barnard (ENG)	73-72-74-73—292	4150
	L Neumann (SWE)	72-70-72-75—289	8033		K Marshall (SCO)	72-75-72-73—292	4150
17	D Richard (USA)	72-73-73-72—290	6614		S Cavalleri (ITA)	73-72-73-74—292	4150
	L Navarro (ESP)	70-70-77-73—290	6614		Yu Chen Huang (TPE)	71-75-72-74—292	4150
	M McNamara (AUS)	72-70-75-73—290	6614		R Hudson (ENG) (am)	72-69-75-76—292	
	T Kimura (JPN)	69-74-74-73—290	6614				

Other players who made the cut: L Davies (ENG), T Barrett (USA), M McKay (SCO), C Dibnah (AUS), K Webb (AUS) J Head (ENG), R Higashio (JPN) 293; C Sörenstam (SWE), J Moodie (SCO), L Hackney (ENG), J Forbes (SCO), J McGill (USA), K Orum (DEN), F Dassu (ITA), A Belen Sanchez (ESP) 294; N Scranton (USA), M Baena (COL), H Kobayashi (JPN), L Lambert (AUS), T Johnson (ENG), A Takamura (JPN), E Poburski (GER), M Dunn (USA), B Pestana (RSA) 297; J Mills (AUS), M Sutton (ENG), B Morgan (WAL) (am), C Schmitt (FRA) 299; P Wright (SCO), S Croce (ITA) 300; N Nijenhuis (NED) (am), C Matthew (SCO) 301; M Hageman (NED) 302; Le Kreutz (FRA), V Stensrud (NOR) 303.

Women's British Open History

Year	Winner	Country	Venue	Score
1976	J Lee Smith	England	Fulford	299
1977	V Saunders	England	Lindrick	306
1978	J Melville	England	Foxhills	310
1979	A Sheard	South Africa	Southport and Ainsdale	301
1980	D Massey	USA	Wentworth (East)	294
1981	D Massey	USA	Northumberland	295
1982	M Figueras-Dotti	Spain	Royal Birkdale	296
1983	Not played			
1984	A Okamoto	Japan	Woburn	289
1985	B King	USA	Moor Park	300
1986	L Davies	England	Royal Birkdale	283
1987	A Nicholas	England	St Mellion	296
1988	C Dibnah*	Australia	Lindrick	296
*Won play-off after a tie with S Little				
1989	J Geddes	USA	Ferndown	274
1990	H Alfredsson*	Sweden	Woburn	288
*Won play-off at fourth extra hole after a tie with J Hill				
1991	P Grice-Whittaker	England	Woburn	284
1992	P Sheehan	USA	Woburn	207
Reduced to 54 holes by rain				
1993	K Lunn	Australia	Woburn	275
1994	L Neumann	Sweden	Woburn	280
1995	K Webb	Australia	Woburn	278
1996	E Klein	USA	Woburn	277
1997	K Webb	Australia	Sunningdale	269
1998	S Steinhauer	USA	Royal Lytham & St Annes	292
1999	S Steinhauer	USA	Woburn	283
2000	S Gustafson	Sweden	Royal Birkdale	282
2001	SR Pak	Korea	Sunningdale	277
2002	K Webb	Australia	Turnberry	273

Year	Winner	Country	Venue	Score
2003	A Sörenstam	Sweden	Royal Lytham & St Annes	278
2004	Karen Stupples	England	Sunningdale (Old Course)	269
2005	Jeong Jang	Korea	Royal Birkdale	272
2006	Sherri Steinhauer	USA	Royal Lytham & St Annes	281
2007	Lorena Ochoa	Mexico	St Andrews Old Course	287
2008	Ji-Yai Shin	Korea	Sunningdale	270

Twenty-one made the cut in all four women's majors

	Kraft Nabisco	US PGA	US Open	British Open
Lorena Ochoa (MEX)	1	T3	T31	T7
Suzann Pettersen (SWE)	T2	T34	T13	T24
Annika Sörenstam (SWE)	T2	T3	T24	T24
Maria Hjorth (SWE)	4	2	T51	T69
Mi Hyun Kim (KOR)	T6	T10	T6	T24
Na Yeon Choi (KOR)	T6	T18	T19	T21
Karen Stupples (ENG)	12	T58	T31	T24
Karrie Webb (AUS)	T13	T29	T38	T9
Angela Park (BRA)	T21	70	T3	T34
Paula Creamer (USA)	T21	T10	T6	T9
Yani Tseng (KOR)	T21	1	T42	2
Ji-Young Oh (KOR)	T31	T29	T31	T17
Rachel Hetherington (AUS)	T31	T46	T42	T69
Shi Hyun Ahn (KOR)	T42	T6	T64	T17
Momoka Ueda (JPN)	T47	T25	T13	7
Il Mi Chung (KOR)	T58	T40	T71	T56
Hee-Won Han (KOR)	T6	T40	T71	T9
Cristie Kerr (USA)	T21	T10	T13	6
Candie Kung (USA)	T21	T10	T19	T42
Jee Young Lee (KOR)	T21	T18	T13	T17
Seon Hwa Lee (KOR)	5	T10	T27	T14

Month by month in 2008

Six birdies in the final nine holes, the last of them a 25-foot putt, sweep Tiger Woods to the Dubai Desert Classic crown. He then takes his run to eight wins in nine tournaments by capturing the Accenture World Match Play – after almost going out in the first round to JB Holmes, who had begun the month by beating Phil Mickelson in a play-off to retain the FBR Open. Annika Sörenstam registers her 70th LPGA title, her first for 15 months. The European Tour visits India for the first time.

US Women's Open Championship

Korean teenager Inbee Park tames Interlachen to become the youngest winner of US Women's Open

Former US Girl's Junior champion Inbee Park from Korea became the youngest winner of the US Women's Open when she swept to an impressive four shot victory over Sweden's Helen Alfredsson with a nine-under-par total of 293 at the historic Interlachen Country Club in Minnesota. The 19-year-old beat the previous youngest record set by inspirational Se Ri Pak who was 20 when she won the event in 1998 after an 18-hole play-off followed by a further two holes of sudden death against Jenny Chuasiriporn. It was getting up in the middle of the night at her home just outside Seoul to watch Pak's victory on TV with her parents that inspired Inbee to take up golf in the first place.

Her success, coming in her second year on Tour, was her first just as victory in the US Open had been a first break-through for, among others, Annika Sörenstam and Britain's Laura Davies, who disappointingly crashed out at half way this time shooting a second round 81 after her first round 70 had put her close to the top of the leaderboard.

Inbee's triumph enabled her to match Mickey Wright, Amy Alcott, Joanne Gunderson Carner and Hollis Stacey all of whom have won the Junior Girls' and the Open titles in the past. "I am so honoured to win this Championship," said Park adding: "I really would like to thank Se Ri for what she has done for Korean golf. Two days after watching her win this title I picked up a club for the first time. All the family play and my mother was here to watch me this week. My father wanted to come but I told him he would be better to watch the golf on TV back home!"

Inbee Park

© Mike Erhmann/Sports Illustrated/Getty Images

Inbee also told reporters that she wanted to share her win with Annika Sörenstam who was playing in what she said would be her last US Open although she hinted that if she decided in a few years time to play a few events again the US Championship, which she won three times, would be high on her list. Although disappointed to finish no higher than tied 24th, Sörenstam, who retired at the end of the season, did finish off in style holing a 199 yards 6-iron for an eagle 3 at the last.

Inbee was not favourite to land the title with a round to go. Six-time Tour winner Paula Creamer was the most fancied to win her first major. She was on eight-under-par at the 54-hole stage while Stacey Lewis, a former US Women's amateur champion playing in her first event as a professional, was the leader on nine-under but the day belonged to Park.

First Round	Second Round	Third Round	Fourth Round
−6 Hurst	−6 A Park	−9 Lewis	−9 I Park
−6 Oh	−5 Blomqvist	−8 Creamer	−5 Alfredsson
−5 S-H Kim	−5 I Park	−7 Alfredsson	−4 A Park
−4 Creamer	−5 Alfredsson	−6 I Park	−4 Lewis
−4 Shin	−4 Creamer	−5 IK Kim	−4 IK Kim
−4 MJ Uribe	−4 Jangl	−4 MH Kim	−3 Sergas
−3 Freiberg	−4 Kerr	−4 MJ Uribe	−3 Castrale
−3 Blomqvist	−4 Kung	−4 A Park	−3 MH Kim
−3 I Park	−4 Shin	−3 Y Kim	−3 Creamer
−3 Weissberg	−3 MJ Uribe	−3 Ueda	−2 Lu
−3 Matthew	−3 Lu	−3 Lu	−2 JM Uribe
−3 Davies	−3 Lewis	−3 Jang	−2 Prammanasudh
−3 Alfredsson	−3 Ueda		
	−3 Miyazato		

While Park took the ultimate prize there was an impressive start to her professional career for Lewis, who played in the winning US Curtis Cup side at St Andrews earlier in the year. She suffers from scoliosis and had to wear a hard plastic brace for seven and a half years before she was informed that the treatment to straighten her spine had not worked and that after all she would require surgery. After graduating from Arizona State University with two degrees in finance and accounting she had a steel rod with five screws attached to her vertebrae implanted in her back – an operation so dangerous that had it not worked she would have been paralyzed. It worked and the brave Lewis continued her golfing career, finishing joint third with In-Kyung Kim, also from Korea, and Brazilian Angela Park, all three a shot behind runner-up Helen Alfredsson.

The par 73 course stretched to 6789 yards was the longest in US Women's Open history and the second longest on the LPGA Tour but two scores of six-under-par 67 led at the end of the first day. Pat Hurst, who lost a play-off for the 2006 US Women's Open title to Annika Sörenstam, and second year pro Ji Young Oh, who insisted it was the "best round of her life", led by one from Song-Hee Kim. Hurst was one of seven Americans plus seven Europeans in the Championship who had competed at the course in the 2002 Solheim Cup.

Reigning US Women's amateur champion Maria Jose Uribe from Colombia opened with a 69 and the group on 70 included Laura Davies with defending champion Cristie Kerr tied 21st on 72. Michelle Wie, not helped by a 9 at the difficult ninth, fired an 81 and would go on to miss the half-way cut.

Thunder storms caused a delay of close to two and a half hours on the second day and play could not be completed but as darkness fell Angela Park, the 2007 Rolex Rookie of the Year, grabbed the lead with a 67 for six under – a stroke clear of Inbee Park, Sweden's Minea Blomqvist and 2007 European Solheim Cup captain and 1993 Nabisco Dinah Shore Championship winner Helen Alfredsson. Kerr, adding a second round 72 was only two back in defence of her title. Patricia Meunier-Lebouc had her second hole in one of the season when she aced the 164 yards 12th hole with a 7-iron but still missed the halfway cut. After her opening 67, Hurst fired 78 and Oh 76 but both made it through to weekend action.

There was a further shorter weather delay because of thunder and lightning on Saturday morning but the round was completed on schedule with Lewis, who had won the qualifying competition for the event, played shortly after she had turned professional taking the lead with a 67 but Creamer, who along with In-Kyung Kim fired second best of the day rounds of 69, was just one shot back with a round to go. Forty-three-year-old Alfredsson was a further shot back with amateur Uribe tied seventh. Conditions on the final day were cool and blustery causing the average score to be three strokes above par on 76.162. Winner Park, helped by rationing her putts to just 26 in her closing 71, was the only golfer in the last nine groups to better par as she collected the first prize cheque of $585,000 and was showered with beer by her Korean golfing chums. Her caddie Brad Beecher was tossed into the lake!

Alfredsson had cause to rue five three-putts in her closing 75 but still finished a shot ahead of the disappointed Creamer who fired a closing 78 and said "It simply was not my day," adding "but Inbee's score was a heck of a round".

Inbee's first name apparently translates into "Queen" in English. At Interlachen in 2008 she certainly produced a regal performance.

Winner Inbee Park had stellar junior career

Before turning professional, Inbee Park – who started playing golf when she was 10-years-old – made her name on the American Junior Golf Association circuit, winning nine titles. She was five-times Rolex Junior All-American and in 2002, when she won the US Girls' Junior Championship, she was named AJGA Rolex Junior Player of the Year. She reached the semi-final of the US Amateur Championship in 2003 and, having turned professional in 2006, had 11 top ten finishes on the Duramed Futures Tour. On the LPGA Tour in 2008 she had seven top 10's: and won $1,138,370 in prize-money.

Safeway International	73-66-65-73—277	9th	$28,158
KRAFT NABISCO	73-70-70-73—286	9th	$45,289
Corona Championship	69-64-72-74—279	3rd	$77,323
Ginn Tribute	67-68-73-70—278	6th	$75,183
Wegmans LPGA	68-68-69-74—279	6th	$54,899
US OPEN	72-69-71-71—283	1st	$585,000
P and G Beauty	70-65-70—205	10th	$34,344

2007 US Women's Open Championship (63rd)

Interlachen CC, Edina MN   [6789–73]

Prize Money: $3.1 million. Entries 1,251. Field of 156 (including 26 amateurs), of whom 74 (including 7 amateurs) made the cut on 150 or less.

Players are of American nationality unless stated

1	Inbee Park (KOR)	72-69-71-71—283	$585000
2	Helen Alfredsson (SWE)	70-71-71-75—287	350000
3	In-Kyung Kim (KOR)	71-73-69-75—288	162487
	Stacy Lewis	73-70-67-78—288	162487
	Angela Park (BRA)	73-67-75-73—288	162487
6	Nicole Castrale	74-70-74-71—289	94117
	Paula Creamer	70-72-69-78—289	94117
	Mi Hyun Kim (KOR)	72-72-70-75—289	94117
	Giulia Sergas (ITA)	73-74-72-70—289	94117
10	Teresa Lu (TPE)	71-72-73-74—290	75734
	Maria Jose Uribe (COL) (am)	69-74-72-75—290	
12	Stacy Prammanasudh	75-72-71-73—291	71002
13	Cristie Kerr	72-70-75-75—292	60878
	Jee Young Lee (KOR)	71-75-74-72—292	60878
	Suzann Pettersen (NOR)	77-71-73-71—292	60878
	Momoko Ueda (JPN)	72-71-73-76—292	60878
17	Catriona Matthew (SCO)	70-77-73-73—293	51380
	Morgan Pressel	74-74-72-73—293	51380
19	Na Yeon Choi (KOR)	76-71-71-76—294	43376
	Jeong Jang (KOR)	73-69-74-78—294	43376
	Jessica Korda (CZE) (am)	72-78-75-69—294	
	Candy Kung (TPE)	72-70-79-73—294	43376
	Ji-Yai Shin (KOR)	69-74-79-72—294	43376
24	Pat Hurst	67-78-77-73—295	35276
	Song-Hee Kim (KOR)	68-76-75-76—295	35276
	Annika Sörenstam (SWE)	75-70-72-78—295	35276
27	Minea Blomqvist (FIN)	72-69-76-79—296	28210
	Laura Diaz	77-70-73-76—296	28210
	Seon Hwa Lee (KOR)	75-70-73-78—296	28210
	Ai Miyazato (JPN)	71-72-76-77—296	28210
31	Sun-Ju Ahn (KOR)	76-71-78-72—297	21567
	Young Kim (KOR)	74-71-71-81—297	21567
	Brittany Lang	71-75-74-77—297	21567
	Lorena Ochoa (MEX)	73-74-76-74—297	21567
	Ji Young Oh (KOR)	67-76-76-78—297	21567
	Karen Stupples (ENG)	74-73-75-75—297	21567
	Alison Walshe (am)	73-74-73-77—297	
38	Amanda Blumenherst (am)	72-78-71-77—298	
	Jennifer Rosales (PHI)	74-72-77-75—298	18690
	Sherri Steinhauer	75-75-71-77—298	18690
	Karrie Webb (AUS)	75-75-72-76—298	18690
42	Rachel Hetherington (AUS)	71-75-78-75—299	15261
	Katherine Hull (AUS)	72-72-77-78—299	15261
	Eun-Hee Ji (KOR)	76-72-77-74—299	15261
	Ma On Min (KOR)	77-73-73-76—299	15261
	Paola Moreno (COL) (am)	73-76-75-75—299	
	Jane Park	78-71-75-75—299	15261
	Reilley Rankin	72-75-79-73—299	15261
	Yani Tseng (TPE)	71-74-75-79—299	15261
	Lindsey Wright (AUS)	78-72-74-75—299	15261
51	Maria Hjörth (SWE)	76-74-73-77—300	12153
	Sakura Yokamine (JPN)	71-75-77-77—300	12153
53	Louise Friberg (SWE)	69-74-79-79—301	10376
	Christina Kim	73-76-75-77—301	10376
	Leta Lindley	77-73-76-75—301	10376

53T	Sherri Turner	76-70-81-74—301	10376
57	Linda Wessberg (SWE)	70-79-79-74—302	9463
58	Marcy Hart	78-72-78-75—303	8697
	Brittany Lincicome	74-73-78-78—303	8697
	Meg Mallon	75-72-82-74—303	8697
	Karin Sjodin (SWE)	74-76-74-79—303	8697
	Angela Stanford	76-73-73-81—303	8697
	Whitney Wade	77-73-74-79—303	8697
64	Shi Hyun Ahn (KOR)	73-73-77-81—304	7935
	Na Ri Kim (KOR)	76-71-79-78—304	7935
	Sydnee Michaels (am)	71-76-76-81—304	
	Janice Moodie (SCO)	78-71-80-75—304	7935
68	Jimin Kang (KOR)	73-72-77-83—305	7673
69	Kim Hall	74-76-76-80—306	7542
70	Michele Redman	74-76-80-77—307	7411
71	Il Mi Chung (KOR)	76-74-75-83—308	7215
	Hee-Won Han (KOR)	74-76-74-84—308	7215
	Tiffany Lua (am)	72-75-80-81—308	
74	Meena Lee (KOR)	75-74-80-82—311	7019

The following players missed the cut.

75	Laura Davies (ENG)	70-81—151
	Moira Dunn	74-77—151
	Mina Harigae (am)	72-79—151
	Julieta Granada (PAR)	74-77—151
	Carin Koch (SWE)	76-75—151
	Hee Youn Park	76-75—151
	Jenny Shin (am)	73-78—151
	Amy Yang	73-78—151
	Sun Young Yoo	76-75—151
	Aiko Yoshiba (JPN)	79-72—151
85	Cydney Clanton	77-75—152
	Kelli Kuehne	76-76—152
	Hilary Lunke	74-78—152
	Miriam Nagl (GER)	76-76—152
	Grace Park (KOR)	75-77—152
	Alexis Thompson (am)	75-77—152
	Carri Wood	76-76—152
	Heather Young	76-76—152
93	Laurie Brower	81-72—153
	Diana D'Alessio	79-74—153
	Anna Grzebien	76-77—153
	Natalie Gulbis	73-80—153
	Ha-Na Jang (KOR)	73-80—153
	Mi-Jeong Jeon (KOR)	73-80—153
	Erynne Lee	77-76—153
	Martha Nause	78-75—153
	Sunny Oh (KOR)	79-74—153
102	Jeanne Cho-Hunick (KOR)	81-73—154
	Danah Ford	78-76—154
	Allison Fouch	79-75—154
	Sophie Gustafson (SWE)	77-77—154

102T	Candy Hannemann (BRA)	78-76—154
	Janell Howland	78-76—154
	Amy Hung (TPE)	77-77—154
	Sarah Lee (KOR)	78-76—154
	Jill McGill	78-76—154
	Gwladys Nocera (FRA)	81-73—154
	Se Ri Pak (KOR)	76-78—154
	Bomi Suh (KOR)	75-79—154
	Gina Umeck	77-77—154
115	Heather Daly-Donofrio	74-81—155
	Wendy Doolan (AUS)	79-76—155
	Shanshan Feng (CHN)	77-78—155
	Juli Inkster	74-81—155
	Jennie Lee (KOR) (am)	74-81—155
	Joanne Lee (am)	78-77—155
	Jennifer Song (am)	79-76—155
	Victoria Tanco (ARG) (am)	74-81—155
	Leah Wigger	74-81—155
124	Chieko Amanuma (JPN)	80-76—156
	Eva Dahllof (SWE)	77-79—156
	Birdie Kim (KOR)	79-77—156
	Kimberley Kim (am)	77-79—156
	Liselotte Neumann (SWE)	78-78—156
	Cyd Okino (am)	79-77—156
	Michelle Wie	81-75—156
131	Patricia Meunier-Lebouc (FRA)	77-80—157

131T	Jean Reynolds	75-82—157
	Alena Sharp (CAN)	77-80—157
134	Silvia Cavalleri (ITA)	76-82—158
	Courtney Ellenbogen (am)	79-79—158
	Jamie Fischer	80-78—158
	Meaghan Francella	79-79—158
	Nicole Hage	79-79—158
	Sin Ham (KOR)	78-80—158
	Charlotte Mayorkas	83-75—158
	Kristen Park (am)	80-78—158
	Ashleigh Simon (RSA)	79-79—158
143	Rachel Bailey (AUS)	80-79—159
	Bettina Hauert (GER)	79-80—159
	Kristen Samp	79-80—159
146	Kyeong Bae (KOR)	79-81—160
	Kathleen Ekey	80-80—160
	Virada Nirapathpongporn (THA)	81-79—160
149	Katrina Leckovic (CAN)	81-80—161
150	Lynn Valentine	80-82—162
151	Tara Goedeken	80-83—163
152	Angela Oh	87-77—164
153	Lauren Doughtie (am)	78-87—165
	Emily Powers (am)	81-84—165
155	Sarah Almond (am)	87-79—166
156	Vanessa Brockett	87-80—167

2007 US Women's Open Championship Southern Pines, SC   [6664–71]

Prize money: $3.1 million

1	Cristie Kerr	71-72-66-70—279	$560000	25T	Il Mi Chung (KOR)	73-72-74-72—291	24767
2	Lorena Ochoa (MEX)	71-71-68-71—281	271022		Katherine Hull (AUS)	72-74-71-74—291	24767
	Angela Park (BRA)	68-69-74-70—281	271022		Mi-Jeong Jeon (KOR)	76-72-73-70—291	24767
4	Se Ri Pak (KOR)	74-72-68-68—282	130549		Young Kim (KOR)	75-71-72-73—291	24767
	In-Bee Park (KOR)	69-73-71-69—282	130549		Seon Hwa Lee (KOR)	72-73-71-75—291	24767
6	Ji-Yai Shin (KOR)	70-69-71-74—284	103581		Sherri Steinhauer	75-72-72-72—291	24767
7	Jee Young Lee (KOR)	72-71-71-71—285	93031	32	Laura Davies (ENG)	72-75-72-73—292	19754
8	Jeong Jang (KOR)	72-71-70-73—286	82464		Moire Dunn	73-71-74-74—292	19754
	Mi Hyun Kim (KOR)	71-75-70-70—286	82464		Annika Sörenstam (SWE)	70-77-72-73—292	19754
10	Kyeong Bae (KOR)	74-71-72-70—287	66177	35	Nicole Castrale	75-73-70-75—293	17648
	Julieta Granada (PAR)	70-69-75-73—287	66177		Natalie Gulbis	74-72-74-73—293	17648
	Ai Miyazato (JPN)	73-73-72-69—287	66177		Charlotte Mayorkas	70-73-78-72—293	17648
	Morgan Pressel	71-70-69-77—287	66177		Kris Tamulis	72-71-74-76—293	17648
14	Joo Mi Kim (KOR)	70-73-70-75—288	55032	39	Shi Hyun Ahn (KOR)	70-72-76-76—294	14954
	Brittany Lincicome	71-74-71-72—288	55032		Erica Blasberg	74-69-75-76—294	14954
16	Paula Creamer	72-74-71-72—289	44219		Laura Diaz	74-72-73-75—294	14954
	Amy Hung (TPE)	70-69-75-75—289	44219		Jennie Lee (am)	71-74-75-74—294	
	Jimin Kang	73-73-73-70—289	44219		Janice Moodie (SCO)	71-76-74-73—294	14954
	Birdie Kim (KOR)	73-70-71-75—289	44219		Becky Morgan (WAL)	75-72-73-74—294	14954
	Catriona Matthew (SCO)	75-67-74-73—289	44219		Jennifer Song (KOR) (am)	72-73-73-76—294	
	Angela Stanford	72-71-73-73—289	44219	46	Diana D'Alessio	73-70-77-75—295	12268
22	Dina Ammaccapane	72-72-70-73—290	33878		Wendy Doolan (AUS)	73-70-75-77—295	12268
	Shiho Ohyama (JPN)	69-73-73-75—290	33878		Meena Lee (KOR)	71-75-74-75—295	12268
	Sakura Yokomine (JPN)	72-71-74-73—290	33878		Sherri Turner	73-74-73-75—295	12268
25	Hye Jung Choi (KOR)	77-68-70-76—291	24767				

Other players who made the cut: Amanda Blumenherst (am), Jimin Jeong (KOR), Song-Hee Kim (KOR), Su A Kim (KOR), Leta Lindley, Teresa Lu (TPE), Amy Yang (KOR), Sung Ah Yim (KOR), 296; Katie Futcher, Candie Kung (TPE), Jane Park, 297; Pat Hurst, In-Kyung Kim (KOR), 298; Allison Fouch, Karin Sjodin (SWE), 300; Aree Song (KOR), 301; Mina Harigae (am), Karine Icher (FRA), 305

2006 US Women's Open Championship Newport CC, Newport, RI   [6564–71]

Prize money: $3.1 million

1	Annika Sörenstam (SWE)*	69-71-73-71—284	$560000	20T	Kristina Tucker (SWE)	72-74-74-76—296	41654
2	Pat Hurst	69-71-75-69—284	335000	24	Amy Hung (TPE)	76-72-77-72—297	32873
*Play off: 18 holes: Sörenstam 70, Hurst 74					Lorie Kane (CAN)	73-72-75-77—297	32873
3	Se Ri Pak (KOR)	69-74-74-69—286	156038		Sherri Steinhauer	72-75-72-78—297	32873
	Stacy Prammanasudh	72-71-71-72—286	156038		Shani Waugh (AUS)	77-72-73-75—297	32873
	Michelle Wie	70-72-71-73—286	156038	28	Tracy Hanson	75-71-78-74—298	22529
6	Juli Inkster	73-70-71-73—287	103575		Jeong Jang (KOR)	72-71-75-80—298	22529
7	Brittany Lincicome	72-72-69-78—291	93026		Cristie Kerr	73-74-75-76—298	22529
10	Amanda Blumenherst (am)	70-77-73-73—293			Carin Koch (SWE)	74-73-73-78—298	22529
	Sophie Gustafson (SWE)	72-72-71-78—293	66174		Candie Kung (TPE)	74-70-77-77—298	22529
	Young Kim (KOR)	75-69-75-74—293	66174		Ai Miyazato (JPN)	74-75-70-79—298	22529
	Jee Young Lee (KOR)	71-75-70-77—293	66174		Becky Morgan (WAL)	70-74-77-77—298	22529
	Patricia Meunier-Lebouc (FRA)	72-73-73-75—293	66174		Suzann Pettersen (NOR)	73-74-75-76—298	22529
	Jane Park (am)	69-73-75-76—293			Morgan Pressel	74-75-75-73—298	22529
16	Paula Creamer	71-72-76-75—294	53577	37	Dawn Coe-Jones (CAN)	74-75-77-73—299	17647
	Natalie Gulbis	76-71-74-73—294	53577		Karrie Webb (AUS)	73-76-74-76—299	17647
	Sherri Turner	72-74-76-72—294	53577		Lindsey Wright (AUS)	74-73-76-76—299	17647
19	Catriona Matthew (SCO)	74-76-72-74—295	48007		Heather Young	76-71-77-75—299	17647
20	Lorena Ochoa (MEX)	71-73-77-75—296	41654	41	Maria Hjörth (SWE)	74-75-73-78—300	14954
	Gloria Park (KOR)	70-78-76-72—296	41654		Mi Hyun Kim (KOR)	75-72-75-78—300	14954
	Karen Stupples (ENG)	78-72-70-76—296	41654		Yu Ping Lin (TPE)	76-74-75-75—300	14954
					Aree Song (KOR)	77-72-79-72—300	14954
					Wendy Ward	77-73-77-73—300	14954

Other players who made the cut: Yuri Fudoh (JPN), Julieta Granada (PAR), Nancy Scranton, 301; Dana Dormann, Seon Hwa Lee (KOR), Siew-Ai Lin (MAS), Alena Sharp (CAN), Karin Sjodin (SWE), Angela Stanford, 302; Moira Dunn, Karine Icher (FRA), 303; Nicole Castrale, Silvia Cavalleri (ITA), Rosie Jones, Ashley Knoll (am), Diana Luna (MON), 304; Beth Bader, 305; Dana Ammaccapane, 306; Denise Munzlinger, Sung Ah Yin (KOR), 307; Kimberly Kim (am), Kim Saiki, 309; Lynnette Brooky (NZL), 311

2005 US Women's Open Championship *Cherry Hill, CO*   [6749–71]

Prize money: $1.5 million

1	Birdie Kim (KOR)	74-72-69-72—287	$560000	23T	Sarah Huarte	74-76-73-73—296	34556
2	Brittany Lang (am)	69-77-72-71—289			Gloria Park (KOR)	74-75-74-73—296	34556
	Morgan Pressel (am)	71-73-70-75—289			Nicole Perrot (CHI)	70-70-78-78—296	34556
4	Natalie Gulbis	70-75-74-71—290	272723		Jennifer Rosales (PHI)	72-76-73-75—296	34556
	Lorie Kane (CAN)	74-71-76-69—290	272723		Annika Sörenstam		
6	Karine Icher (FRA)	69-75-75-72—291	116310		(SWE)	71-75-73-77—296	34556
	Young Jo (KOR)	74-71-70-76—291	116310		Michelle Wie (am)	69-73-72-82—296	
	Candie Kung (TPE)	73-73-71-74—291	116310	31	Rachel Hetherington		
	Lorena Ochoa (MEX)	74-68-77-72—291	116310		(AUS)	74-69-76-78—297	23479
10	Cristie Kerr	74-71-72-75—292	80523		Mi Hyun Kim (KOR)	72-73-76-76—297	23479
	Angela Stanford	69-74-73-76—292	80523		Brittany Lincicome	74-74-78-71—297	23479
	Karen Stupples (ENG)	75-70-69-78—292	80523		Catriona Matthew		
13	Tina Barrett	73-74-71-75—293	61402		(SCO)	73-72-75-77—297	23479
	Heather Bowie	77-73-69-74—293	61402		Karrie Webb (AUS)	76-73-73-75—297	23479
	Jamie Hullett	75-72-70-76—293	61402	36	Kim Saiki	74-73-74-77—298	20386
	Soo Yun Kang (KOR)	74-74-74-71—293	61402		Wendy Ward	74-74-75-75—298	20386
	Paige MacKenzie (am)	75-75-69-74—293		38	Il Mi Chung (KOR)	75-71-76-77—299	17939
	Meg Mallon	71-74-75-73—293	61402		Johanna Head (ENG)	74-73-75-77—299	17939
19	Paula Creamer	74-69-72-79—294	47480		Juli Inkster	77-71-75-76—299	17939
	Rosie Jones	73-72-74-75—294	47480		Young Kim (KOR)	73-73-70-83—299	17939
	Leta Lindley	73-76-73-72—294	47480		Sarah Lee (KOR)	79-70-75-75—299	17939
	Liselotte Neumann	70-75-73-76—294	47480		Amanda McCurdy		
	(SWE)				(am)	75-75-71-78—299	17939
23	Helen Alfredsson (SWE)	72-73-74-77—296	34556		Aree Song (KOR)	77-70-72-80—299	17939
	Laura Diaz	75-73-72-76—296	34556				

Other players who made the cut: Se Ri Pak (KOR), Nancy Scranton, 300; Beth Bader, Dorothy Delasin (PHI), Hee Won Han (KOR), 301; Arnie Cochran (am), Jeong Janh (KOR), 302; Katie Allison, Eva Dahllof (SWE), Stephanie Louden, Grace Park (KOR), Suzann Pettersen (NOR), Kris Tschetter, 303; Katie Futcher, Sophie Gustafson (SWE), Kaori Higo (JPN), Carri Wood, 304; Candy Hannemann (BRA), 307; Jean Bartholomew, 309.

2004 US Women's Open Championship *The Orchards, South Hadley, MA*   [6473–71]

Prize money: $3.1 million

1	Meg Mallon	73-69-67-65—274	$560000	20T	Kate Golden	74-71-72-71—288	38660
2	Annika Sörenstam	71-68-70-67—276	335000		Johanna Head (ENG)	76-69-70-73—288	38660
	(SWE)				Rosie Jones	74-72-72-70—288	38660
3	Kelly Robbins	74-67-68-69—278	208863		Young Kim (KOR)	71-73-76-68—288	38660
4	Jennifer Rosales (PHI)	70-67-69-75—281	145547		Kim Saiki	70-68-74-76—288	38660
5	Candie Kung (TPE)	70-68-74-70—282	111173		Liselotte Neumann	72-72-72-72—288	38660
	Michele Redman	70-72-73-67—282	111173		(SWE)		
7	Moira Dunn	73-67-72-71—283	86744	27	Beth Daniel	69-74-71-75—289	29195
	Pat Hurst	70-71-71-71—283	86744		Cristie Kerr	73-71-74-71—289	29195
	Jeong Jang (KOR)	72-74-71-66—283	86744	29	Shi Hyun Ahn (KOR)	73-71-72-74—290	24533
10	Michelle Ellis (Aus)	70-69-72-73—284	68813		Lorie Kane (CAN)	75-70-72-73—290	24533
	Carin Koch (SWE)	72-67-75-70—284	68813		Deb Richard	71-73-72-74—290	24533
	Rachel Teske (AUS)	71-69-70-74—284	68813	32	Allison Hanna	71-75-74-71—291	20539
13	Paula Creamer (am)	72-69-72-72—285			Becky Morgan (WAL)	71-74-73-73—291	20539
	Patricia Meunier–	67-75-74-69—285	60602		Se Ri Pak (KOR)	70-76-71-74—291	20539
	Labouc (FRA)				Sherri Steinhauer	74-71-73-73—291	20539
	Michelle Wie (am)	71-70-71-73—285			Karen Stupples (ENG)	72-72-77-71—291	20539
16	Mi Hyun Kim (KOR)	76-68-71-71—286	54052	37	Jenna Daniels	76-71-72-73—292	16897
	Suzann Pettersen	74-72-71-69—286	54052		AJ Easthorne (CAN)	73-72-75-72—292	16897
	(NOR)				Natalie Gulbis	73-71-75-73—292	16897
	Karrie Webb (AUS)	72-71-71-72—286	54052		Jamie Hullett	72-74-74-72—292	16897
19	Catriona Matthew	73-71-72-71—287	48432		Christina Kim	74-71-76-71—292	16897
	(SCO)				Jill McGill	71-75-71-75—292	16897
20	Dawn Coe-Jones (CAN)	71-73-72-72—288	38660		Gloria Park (KOR)	76-71-73-72—292	16897

Other players who made the cut: Donna Andrews, Laura Diaz, Jennifer Greggain, Ji-Hee Lee, Mhairi McKay (SCO), Lorena Ochoa (MEX) 293; Jennie Lee (am) 294; Katherine Hull 295; Tina Barrett, Catherine Cartwright, Hee-Won Han (KOR) 296; Brittany Lincicome (am) 297; Loraine Lambert, Aree Song (KOR) 298; Liz Earley, Allison Finney, Juli Inkster 299; Mee Lee (KOR), Seol-An Jeon (KOR), Courtney Swaim 300; Hilary Lunke, Grace Park (KOR) 301; Li Ying Ye 304.

2003 US Women's Open Championship Pumpkin Ridge GC, North Plains, OR [6509–71]

Prize money: $3.1 million

1	Hilary Lunke*	71-69-68-75—283	$560000	20	Beth Daniel	73-69-77-74—293	43491
2	Kelly Robbins	74-69-71-69—283	272004		Yuri Fudoh (JPN)	74-72-75-72—293	43491
	Angela Stanford	70-70-69-74—283	272004	22	Lorie Kane (CAN)	73-75-73-73—294	36575
*Play-off rounds: Hilary Lunke 70, Angela Stanford 71,					Christina Kim	74-74-72-74—294	36575
Kelly Robbins 73					Leta Lindley	73-69-77-75—294	36575
4	Annika Sörenstam	72-72-67-73—284	150994		Catriona Matthew	74-70-76-74—294	36575
	(SWE)				(SCO)		
5	Aree Song (am)	70-73-68-74—285		26	Danielle Ammaccapane	74-74-73-74—295	28354
6	Jeong Jang (KOR)	73-69-69-75—286	115333		Dorothy Delasin (PHI)	79-70-76-70—295	28354
	Mhairi McKay (SCO)	66-70-75-75—286	115333		Kelli Kuehne	72-74-75-74—295	28354
8	Juli Inkster	69-71-74-73—287	97363		Paula Marti (ESP)	71-76-76-72—295	28354
9	Rosie Jones	70-72-73-73—288	90241	30	Ashli Bunch	71-73-77-75—296	22678
10	Grace Park (KOR)	72-76-73-68—289	79243		Annette DeLuca	71-73-78-74—296	22678
	Suzann Pettersen (NOR)	76-69-69-75—289	79243		Elizabeth Janangelo	75-73-73-75—296	
12	Donna Andrews	69-72-72-77—290	71362		(am)		
13	Laura Diaz	71-71-74-76—292	56500		Mi-Hyun Kim (KOR)	73-73-73-77—296	22678
	Natalie Gulbis	73-69-72-78—292	56500		Jane Park (am)	76-73-74-73—296	
	Cristie Kerr	72-73-73-74—292	56500	35	Candy Hannemann	75-69-73-80—297	20360
	Patricia Meunier-	73-69-74-76—292	56500		(BRA)		
	Lebouc (FRA)				Stephanie Louden	71-74-77-75—297	20360
	Lorena Ochoa (MEX)	71-75-72-74—292	56500		Guilia Sergas (ITA)	70-74-79-74—297	20360
	Jennifer Rosales (PHI)	74-69-76-73—292	56500		Kirsty Taylor (ENG)	71-75-73-78—297	20360
	Rachel Teske (AUS)	71-73-72-76—292	56500	39	Michele Redman	71-74-74-79—298	18783

Other players who made the cut: Heather Bowie, Karen Stupples (ENG) 299; Beth Bauer, Hee-Won Han (KOR), Jamie Hullett, Emilee Klein, Becky Morgan (WAL), Karen Weiss 300; Sherri Turner 301; Se Ri Pak (KOR) 302; Leigh Ann Hardin (am) 303; Morgan Pressel (am) 304; Alison Nicholas (ENG), Suzanne Strudwick (ENG), Michelle Vinieratos 305; Yu Ping Lin (TPE) 306; Mollie Fankhauser (am) 307; Irene Cho (am) 308; Mardi Lunn (AUS) 309

2002 US Women's Open Championship Prairie Dunes, Hutchinson, KS [6253–70]

Prize money: $3 million.

1	Juli Inkster	67-72-71-66—276	$535000	22T	Susan Ginter-Brooker	74-72-70-74—290	26894
2	Annika Sörenstam	70-69-69-70—278	315000		Jeong Jang (KOR)	73-73-74-70—290	26894
	(SWE)				Rosie Jones	71-77-69-73—290	26894
3	Shani Waugh (AUS)	67-73-71-72—283	202568		Mi Hyun Kim (KOR)	74-72-70-74—290	26894
4	Raquel Carriedo (ESP)	75-71-72-66—284	141219		Meg Mallon	73-75-73-69—290	26894
5	Se Ri Pak (KOR)	74-75-68-68—285	114370		Catriona Matthew		
6	Mhairi McKay (SCO)	70-75-71-70—286	101421		(SCO)	69-80-72-69—290	26894
7	Beth Daniel	71-76-71-69—287	78016		Stacy Prammanasudh	75-74-72-69—290	26894
	Laura Diaz	67-72-77-71—287	78016		Michele Redman	71-69-73-77—290	26894
	Kelli Kuehne	70-76-72-69—287	78016	32	Brandie Burton	70-74-76-71—291	18730
	Janice Moodie (SCO)	71-72-71-73—287	78016		Laura Davies (ENG)	75-73-68-75—291	18730
	Jennifer Rosales (PHI)	73-72-74-68—287	78016		Hee-Won Han (KOR)	72-77-70-72—291	18730
12	Lynnette Brooky (NZL)	73-73-69-73—288	54201		Cristie Kerr	74-71-72-74—291	18730
	Stephanie Keever	72-71-73-72—288	54201		Charlotta Sörenstam	73-70-77-71—291	18730
	Jill McGill	71-70-69-78—288	54201		(SWE)		
	Joanne Morley (ENG)	78-68-73-69—288	54201	37	Jenna Daniels	72-70-77-73—292	15209
	Kelly Robbins	71-74-74-69—288	54201		Wendy Doolan (AUS)	73-76-75-68—292	15209
	Rachel Teske (AUS)	75-71-72-70—288	54201		Jackie Gallagher-Smith	70-76-73-73—292	15209
18	Donna Andrews	74-74-70-71—289	40738		Carin Koch (SWE)	73-72-70-77—292	15209
	Beth Bauer	74-72-71-72—289	40738		Liselotte Neumann	72-74-70-76—292	15209
	Lorie Kane (CAN)	69-77-69-74—289	40738		(SWE)		
	Grace Park (KOR)	71-77-71-70—289	40738		Karen Stupples (ENG)	80-68-72-72—292	15209
22	Danielle Ammaccapane	74-71-73-72—290	26894		Kris Tschetter	72-77-72-71—292	15209
	Michelle Ellis (AUS)	71-71-75-73—290	26894				

Other players who made the cut: Jean Bartholomew, Audra Burke, Mitzi Edge, Jung Yeon Lee (KOR), Gloria Park (KOR), Cindy Schreyer, Leslie Spalding 293; Alicia Dibos (PER), Vicki Goetze-Ackerman, Angela Jerman (am), Ara Koh (KOR), Sherri Steinhauer, Karen Weiss, Aree Song Wongluekiet (THA) 294; Amy Fruhwirth, Kim Saiki; Sherri Turner 295; Heather Bowie, Soo Young Moon (KOR) 296; Patricia Meunier-Lebouc (FRA) 297; Dawn Coe-Jones (CAN), Dorothy Delasin (PHI), Pearl Sin (KOR) 298; Allison Finney 299; Tracy Hanson 300; Michele Vinieratos 301.

2001 US Women's Open Championship Southern Pines, NC [6256–70]

Prize money: $2.7 million.

Pos	Player	Scores	Prize
1	Karrie Webb (AUS)	70-65-69-69—273	$520000
2	Se Ri Pak (KOR)	69-70-70-72—281	310000
3	Dottie Pepper	74-69-70-69—282	202580
4	Cristie Kerr	69-73-71-70—283	118697
	Sherri Turner	72-70-71-70—283	118697
	Catriona Matthew (SCO)	72-68-70-73—283	118697
7	Lorie Kane (CAN)	75-68-72-69—284	80726
	Kristi Albers	71-69-74-70—284	80726
	Kelli Kuehne	70-71-72-71—284	80726
	Wendy Doolan	71-70-70-73—284	80726
11	Sophie Gustafson (SWE)	74-66-74-71—285	66581
12	Kelly Robbins	72-68-76-70—286	57088
	AJ Eathorne (CAN)	67-71-75-73—286	57088
	Juli Inkster	68-72-71-75—286	57088
	Yuri Fudoh (JPN)	73-68-70-75—286	57088
16	Emilee Klein	72-69-75-71—287	46885
	Michele Redman	70-72-73-72—287	46885
	Annika Sörenstam (SWE)	70-72-73-72—287	46885
19	Maria Hjörth (SWE)	70-71-77-70—288	37327
	Marisa Baena (COL)	71-72-75-70—288	37327
	Jill McGill	68-76-72-72—288	37327
	Wendy Ward	70-71-74-73—288	37327
19T	Dorothy Delasin (PHI)	75-70-70-73—288	37327
24	Beth Daniel	73-70-71-75—289	30091
	Audra Burks	70-72-72-75—289	30091
26	Brandie Burton	73-70-77-70—290	24649
	Helen Alfredsson (SWE)	71-73 74-72—290	24649
	Mi Hyun Kim (KOR)	68-76-72-74—290	24649
	Janice Moodie (SCO)	71-70-73-76—290	24649
30	Kris Tschetter	72-74-77-68—291	20472
	Michelle Ellis	75-69-75-72—291	20472
	Candy Hannemann (BRA) (am)	73-73-72-73—291	
	Meg Mallon	72-70-76-73—291	20472
34	Pat Hurst	73-71-76-72—292	18408
	Natalie Gulbis (am)	73-71-75-73—292	
	Catrin Nilsmark (SWE)	70-76-72-74—292	18408
	Dina Ammaccapane	69-73-75-75—292	18408
	Karen Weiss	74-71-71-76—292	18408
39	Marcy Newton	74-72-74-73—293	16061
	Liselotte Neumann (SWE)	70-73-76-74—293	16064
	Rosie Jones	73-68-75-77—293	16061
	Grace Park (KOR)	76-70-69-78—293	16061

Other players who made the cut: Leta Lindley, Paula Marti (ESP), Amy Fruhwirth, Aki Nakano, Cindy Figg-Currier, Alison Nicholas (ENG) 294; Pearl Sinn (KOR) 295; Stephanie Keever (am), Christina Kim (am), Sherri Steinhauer 296; Smriti Mehra (IND), Jean Bartholamew, Raquel Carriedo (ESP) 297; Terry-Jo Myers; Yu Ping Lin (TPE), Jamie Hullett 299, Lynnette Brooky, Lisa Strom 299

2000 US Women's Open Championship Merit Club, Libertyville, IL [6540–72]

Prize money: $2.7 million.

Pos	Player	Scores	Prize
1	Karrie Webb (AUS)	69-72-68-73—282	$500000
2	Cristie Kerr	72-71-74-70—287	240228
	Meg Mallon	68-72-73-74—287	240228
4	Rosie Jones	73-71-72-72—288	120119
	Mi Hyun Kim (KOR)	74-72-70-72—288	120119
6	Grace Park (KOR)	74-72-73-70—289	90458
	Kelli Kuehne	71-74-73-71—289	90458
8	Beth Daniel	71-74-72-73—290	79345
9	Annika Sörenstam (SWE)	73-75-73-70—291	67369
	Kelly Robbins	74-73-71-73—291	67369
	Laura Davies (ENG)	73-71-72-75—291	67369
12	Jennifer Rosales (PHI)	75-75-69-73—292	55355
	Pat Hurst	73-72-72-75—292	55355
	Dorothy Delasin (PHI)	76-68-72-76—292	55355
15	Se Ri Pak (KOR)	74-75-75-69—293	47846
	Kellee Booth	70-78-75-70—293	47846
17	Janice Moodie (SCO)	73-77-75-69—294	40586
	Kathryn Marshall (SCO)	72-72-77-73—294	40586
	Shani Waugh (AUS)	69-75-73-77—294	40586
	Lorie Kane (CAN)	71-74-72-77—294	40586
21	Jackie Gallagher Smith	71-77-73-74—295	34113
	Wendy Doolan (AUS)	77-69-74-75—295	34113
23	Donna Andrews	73-75-79-70—297	28404
	Kristi Albers	71-77-73-76—297	28404
	Michele Redman	74-74-73-76—297	28404
	Juli Inkster	70-74-73-80—297	28404
27	Charlotta Sörenstam (SWE)	75-74-76-73—298	21740
	AJ Eathorne (CAN)	73-77-73-75—298	21740
	Silvia Cavalleri (ITA)	72-73-75-78—298	21740
	Joanne Morley (ENG)	73-72-74-79—298	21740
31	Tina Barrett	72-78-75-74—299	17067
	Danielle Ammaccapane	72-73-79-75—299	17067
	Emilee Klein	77-72-75-75—299	17067
	Fiona Pike (AUS)	72-74-77-76—299	17067
	Kate Golden	72-75-76-76—299	17067
	Jenny Lidback (PER)	73-74-76-76—299	17067
	Carin Koch (SWE)	75-73-73-78—299	17067
	Sophie Gustafson (SWE)	72-78-71-78—299	17067
	Hiromi Kobayashi (JPN)	77-72-70-80—299	17067

Other players who made the cut: Michelle Ellis (AUS), Valerie Skinner, Mary Beth Zimmerman, Naree Wongluekiet (am) 300; Catriona Matthew (SCO), Jill McGill 301; Leta Lindley, Nancy Scranton, Nancy Lopez, Jan Stephenson (AUS) 302; Jae Jean Ro (am), Betsy King, Sara Sanders 302; Jean Zedlitz 304; Marisa Baena (COL), Anna Macosko 305; Hilary Homeyer (am) 306; Carri Wood 307; Barb Mucha 308; Pearl Sinn (KOR) 310; Michelle McGann 311

1999 US Women's Open Championship Old Waverley, West Point, MS   [6421–72]

Prize money: $1.75 million.

I	J Inkster	65-69-67-71—272	$315000	20T	L Lindley	72-72-73-70—287	21832
2	S Turner	69-69-68-71—277	185000		S Gustafson (SWE)	72-72-70-73—287	21832
3	K Kuehne	64-71-70-74—279	118227		D Andrews	69-71-72-75—287	21832
4	L Kane (CAN)	70-64-71-75—280	82399		H Fukushima (JPN)	69-70-71-77—287	21832
5	C Koch (SWE)	72-69-68-72—281	62938	25	K Saiki	70-71-73-74—288	16006
	M Mallon	70-70-69-72—281	62938		S Croce (ITA)	71-71-71-75—288	16006
7	K Webb (AUS)	70-70-68-74—282	53132		R Jones	71-70-72-75—288	16006
8	H Dobson (ENG)	71-70-73-69—283	45244		L Kiggens	71-67-73-77—288	16006
	M Hjörth (SWE)	73-69-70-71—283	45244		S Steinhauer	68-69-73-78—288	16006
	C Matthew (SCO)	69-68-74-72—283	45244	30	M Lunn (AUS)	72-71-74-72—289	11652
	G Park (KOR) (am)	70-67-73-73—283			J Zedlitz	75-67-75-72—289	11652
12	H Alfredsson (SWE)	72-68-70-74—284	37666		M McKay (SCO)	73-68-76-72—289	11652
	B Iverson	72-64-73-75—284	37666		N Scranton	69-72-75-73—289	11652
14	M Redman	72-71-75-67—285	32389		D Coe Jones	73-71-71-74—289	11652
	Se Ri Pak (KOR)	68-70-74-73—285	32389		A Acker Macosko	73-71-71-74—289	11652
	D Pepper	68-69-72-76—285	32389		K Robbins	70-70-74-75—289	11652
17	L Neumann (SWE)	73-71-69-73—286	27422	37	H Kobayashi (JPN)	74-70-76-70—290	10078
	AJ Eathorne (CAN)	69-71-71-75—286	27422		D Dormann	74-70-73-73—290	10078
	C Nilsmark (SWE)	69-71-70-76—286	27422		K Booth (am)	71-73-70-76—290	
20	C McCurdy	72-72-74-69—287	21832				

Other players who made the cut: M Estill, M Berteotti, K Tschetter, W Ward, M Dunn 291; P Kerrigan, S Strudwick (ENG) 292; B King, B Daniel, B Mucha, A Munt, W Doolan, V Odegard 293; M Will, R Hetherington (AUS) 294; J Lidback, L Hackney, C Figg-Currier, A Nicholas (ENG) 295; P Rizzo 296; J Feldott, P Hammel 297; K Millies 298; T Green 299

US Women's Open History

Year	Winner	Runner-up		Venue	Score
1946	P Berg	B Jamieson		Spokane	5 and 4

Changed to strokeplay

Year	Winner		Venue	Score
1947	B Jamieson		Greensboro	300
1948	B Zaharias		Atlantic City	300
1949	L Suggs		Maryland	291
1950	B Zaharias		Wichita	291
1951	B Rawls		Atlanta	294
1952	L Suggs		Bala, PA	284
1953	B Rawls*		Rochester, NY	302

*Won play-off after a tie with J Pung 71-77

1954	B Zaharias		Peabody, MA	291
1955	F Crocker		Wichita	299
1956	K Cornelius*		Duluth	302

*Won play-off after a tie with B McIntire (am) 75-82

1957	B Rawls		Mamaroneck	299
1958	M Wright		Bloomfield Hills, MI	290
1959	M Wright		Pittsburgh, PA	287
1960	B Rawls		Worchester, MA	292
1961	M Wright		Springfield, NJ	293
1962	M Lindstrom		Myrtle Beach	301
1963	M Mills		Kenwood	289
1964	M Wright*		San Diego	290

*Won play-off after a tie with R Jessen, Seattle 70-72

1965	C Mann		Northfield, NJ	290
1966	S Spuzich		Hazeltine National, MN	297
1967	C Lacoste (FRA) (am)		Hot Springs, VA	294

Year	Winner	Venue	Score
1968	S Berning	Moselem Springs, PA	289
1969	D Caponi	Scenic-Hills	294
1970	D Caponi	Muskogee, OK	287
1971	J Gunderson-Carner	Erie, PA	288
1972	S Berning	Mamaroneck, NY	299
1973	S Berning	Rochester, NY	290
1974	S Haynie	La Grange, IL	295
1975	S Palmer	Northfield, NJ	295
1976	J Carner*	Springfield, PA	292

*Won play-off after a tie with S Palmer – Carner 76, Palmer 78

1977	H Stacy	Hazeltine, MN	292
1978	H Stacy	Indianapolis	299
1979	J Britz	Brooklawn, CN	284
1980	A Alcott	Richland, TN	280
1981	P Bradley	La Grange, IL	279
1982	J Alex	Del Paso, Sacramento, CA	283
1983	J Stephenson (AUS)	Broken Arrow, OK	290
1984	H Stacy	Salem, MA	290
1985	K Baker	Baltusrol, NJ	280
1986	J Geddes*	NCR	287

*Won play-off after a tie with J Carner and A Okamoto – Davies 71, Okamoto 73, Carner 74

1987	L Davies (ENG)*	Plainfield	285

*Won play-off after a tie with J Carner and A Okamoto – Davies 71, Okamoto 73, Carner 74

1988	L Neumann (SWE)	Baltimore	277
1989	B King	Indianwood, MI	278
1990	B King	Atlanta Athletic Club, GA	284
1991	M Mallon	Colonial, TX	283
1992	P Sheehan*	Oakmont, PA	280

*Won play-off after a tie with J Inkster – Sheehan 72, Inkster 74

1993	L Merton	Crooked Stick	280
1994	P Sheehan	Indianwood, MI	277
1995	A Sörenstam (SWE)	The Broadmore, CO	278
1996	A Sörenstam (SWE)	Pine Needles Lodge, NC	272
1997	A Nicholas (ENG)	Pumpkin Ridge, OR	274
1998	SR Pak (KOR)*	Blackwolf Run, WI	290

*Won play-off after a tie with J Chausiriporn (am) – both shot 73 then in sudden death Pak 5,3; Chausiriporn 5,4

1999	J Inkster	Old Waverley, West Point, MS	272
2000	K Webb (AUS)	Merit Club, Libertyville, IL	282
2001	K Webb (AUS)	Pine Needles Lodge & GC, NC	273
2002	J Inkster	Prairie Dunes, KS	276
2003	H Lunke*	Pumpkin Ridge GC, OR	283

*Won play-off after a tie with Kelly Robins and Angela Stanford – Lunke 70, Stanford 71, Robins 73

2004	M Mallon	The Orchards, S Hadley, MA	274
2005	B Kim (KOR)	Cherry Hills CC, CO	287
2006	A Sörenstam (SWE)*	Newport CC, RI	284

*Won play-off after a tie with Pat Hurst – Sörenstam 70, Hurst 74

2007	C Kerr	Southern Pines, NC	279
2008	I Park (KOR)	Interlachen, MN	283

McDonald's LPGA Championship

Taiwan Rookie Pro Yani Tseng takes LPGA title and ends Lorena Ochoa's Grand Slam hopes

World No 1 Lorena Ochoa's hopes of winning a third major title in a row and of achieving a Grand Slam of titles in 2008 were shattered by the rookie pro Yani Tseng from Taiwan with whom she was paired on the final day of the McDonald's LPGA Championship at the Bulle Rock golf course in Havre de Grace in Maryland. The course was the longest in LPGA Championship history at 6641 yards and it included the longest par 5 in history – the 596 yards 11th.

Nineteen-year-old Tseng from Taoyuan near Taipei, became the first Taiwanese golfer to win an LPGA major when she holed a five-foot putt at the fourth extra hole to defeat Swede Maria Hjorth for the title after both had tied on 12-under-par 276, a shot clear of Ochoa and former No 1 Annika Sörenstam.

Tseng is not the youngest winner of an LPGA major. That honour is held by Morgan Pressel who was just 18 when she won the Kraft Nabisco title in 2007. Tseng, a former US Women's Public Links champion – she beat Michelle Wie in the 2004 final – is only the fourth first-year player to win an LPGA major and the first since Se Ri Pak took the 1998 LPGA Championship.

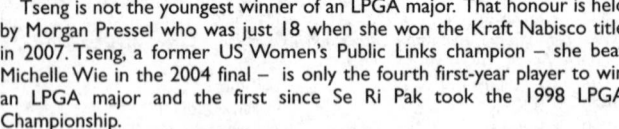

Yani Tseng

On receiving the $300,000 cheque Tseng said: "I feel very excited at becoming the first Taiwanese to win a major. Before on the course I have only heard the crowd shouting 'Lorena, Lorena' but this time it was 'Yani, Yani'".

Tseng took up golf when she was six. Coached initially by Tony Kao in Taiwan and latterly Ernie Huang, her mentor, in the United States, she had string of top amateur victories including the North and South Women's Championship in which she beat Pressel in the final. In addition to her US Public Links title she was also twice Asia Pacific Junior champion before turning professional in 2007 and playing (and winning) on the Asian and Canadian Women's circuits. She qualified for the LPGA Tour at her first attempt.

Tseng, who has also received help from fellow Taiwanese professional TC Chen with whom she practices from time to time, had not made a particularly bright start to the Championship with an opening 73 but she followed this up with a 70, a 65 and a closing 68 to finished tied with Hjorth who paid the penalty on the last day for a double bogey at the 13th where she lost a ball off the tee.

"The ball was always going left, hit someone on the arm and kicked into the really high stuff but I think it would have ended in that anyway. Apart from that I played solid golf and I am very proud of myself".

Hjorth did have a huge piece of good fortune on the par 5 15th where she took a gamble and attempted to play across the marshlands and a creek. The ball landed in the creek but ricocheted off a rock onto and across the green from where she made a birdie! Although she chipped in at the 16th, she made a bogey at the second last hole, losing the lead and dropping her back into a tie for the lead and the play-off that could easily have involved Lorena Ochoa Women and Annika Sörenstam, the world's two top players, as well.

First Round	Second Round	Third Round	Fourth Round
–6 Kane	–10 Ochoa	–12 Lee	–12 Tseng
–6 Bastel	–9 Wright	–11 Hjorth	–12 Hjorth
–5 Hetherington	–8 Kane	–10 Sörenstam	–11 Sörenstam
–5 Wright	–7 Hetherington	–10 Ochoa	–11 Ochoa
–4 Doolan	–7 Lang	–8 Tseng	–10 Diaz
–4 Castrale	–7 Oh	–8 Diaz	–8 Ahn
–4 Hong	–6 Hong	–8 Lang	–8 Pressel
–4 Hjorth	–6 Sörenstam	–8 Wright	–8 Kuehne
–4 Baena	–6 Ellis	–7 Cho	–8 Cho
	–6 Baena	–7 Baena	
		–7 Oh	

Ochoa, who said she had not felt the pressure of trying to keep her major titles run going and was relaxed at all times, pin-pointed her third round 72 as the day she lost her chance. "In the conditions my final round 71 was not so bad. I played well especially with my irons but I could not hole any putts when I needed to. I never give up and always felt something might happen but it never did. It wasn't my time."

Lorena, who had led at half-way by a shot from Australian Lindsey Wright, almost made the play-off but her sand wedge shot from just 10 yards off the green at the 16th which she described as "just perfect" failed to drop. "The ball was not even going fast and was right on it. I could not believe it did not go in," she said.

The Mexican had plenty of praise for the winner. "She is a great player ... very impressive. She is a rookie but handles herself well. I really like her. She is a great competitor and I wish her well."

Tied with Ochoa just one off the play-off was former No 1 Sörenstam, playing her last season on the LPGA Tour. She admitted that, like Ochoa, she had played really well but didn't "convert" when she came to the greens. "I gave it my all but got nothing out of the round," she said adding: "I just thought this was going to be my week.. I like it here and I am going to miss it all."

The Swede left a putt which would have got her into the play-off short at the 18th, effectively ending her opportunity to tie Mickey Wright's four LPGA title wins before leaving the competitive scene.

Four-time Tour winner Lorie Kane from Canada and Emily Bastel, who was leading money earner on the Duramed Futures Tour in 2007, fired opening rounds of 66 to lead on the first day from Rachel Hetherington and Lindsey Wright. Kane would eventually finish in a tie for 40th while Ms Bastel missed the cut by one after adding a 76 on the second day.

Defending champion Suzann Pettersen opened with a 71 but finished in a tie for 34th. after adding further rounds of 68, 74 and 72. Ochoa moved into the lead on the second day when 77 players made the half-way cut at a new low record even par The previous low cuts had been one-over par in 1987 and 1999. It was Korean golfer Jee Young Lee who led after 54 holes by one from Hjorth who moved up with a third round 65 which matched winner Tseng's and Lee's Saturday scores but while Tseng went on to beat Horth in the play-off Lee finished joint 18th after closing with a 78.

McDonald's winner Yani Tseng takes Rookie title

Nineteen-year-old Yani Tseng, winner of the McDonald's LPGA title, was the LPGA Rookie of the Year. With 10 Top Tens she edged out Na-Yeon Choi who had nine Top Tens in a battle that was not decided until the last event of the season. Tseng, whose 388 birdies earned her top spot in that category, made a total of $1,752,086 in prize-money in her first year on Tour. She played in 27 events and had a scoring average of 70.77 to finish fourth in this category for the season. She missed only one half-way cut and in addition to her victory she posted five second-place finishes and two thirds. Her Top Ten finishes were:

SBS Open	70-72-69—211	8th	$23,432
Mastercard Classic	68-69-74—211	2nd	$118,722
Ginn Open	68-64-69-71—272	2nd	$233,732
McDONALD'S LPGA	73-70-65-68—276	1st	$300,000
State Farm Classic	66-66-66-72—270	2nd	$156,002
RICOH BRITISH OPEN	70-69-68-66—273	2nd	$196,540
CN Canadian	70-64-68-77—279	3rd	$147,046
Navistar Classic	71-66-68-70—275	6th	$35,624
Longs Drugs	68-72-70-72—282	3rd	$78,948
Grand China Air	72-67-68—207	2nd	$171,913

2008 McDonald's LPGA Championship

Bulle Rock, Havre de Grace, MD [6596–72]

Prize Money: $2 million. Field of 150 players, of whom 81 made the half-way cut on 144 or less.

Players are of American nationality unless stated

1	Yani Tseng (TPE)*	73-70-65-68—276	$300000
2	Maria Hjörth (SWE)	68-72-65-71—276	180180
Tseng won at the fourth extra hole			
3	Lorena Ochoa (MEX)	69-65-72-71—277	115911
	Annika Sörenstam (SWE)	70-68-68-71—277	115911
5	Laura Diaz	71-68-69-70—278	81385
6	Shi Hyun Ahn (KOR)	73-69-69-69—280	53763
	Irene Cho (KOR)	72-68-69-71—280	53763
	Kelli Kuehne	69-70-71-70—280	53763
	Morgan Pressel	73-69-70-68—280	53673
10	Nicole Castrale	68-72-71-70—281	31938
	Paula Creamer	71-70-71-69—281	31938
	Jimin Jeong (KOR)	73-68-69-71—281	31938
	Cristie Kerr	71-70-71-69—281	31938
	Mi Hyun Kim (KOR)	72-70-71-68—281	31938
	Candie Kung (TPE)	70-72-70-69—281	31938
	Seon Hwa Lee (KOR)	73-71-70-67—281	31938
	Giulia Sergas (ITA)	71-71-69-70—281	31938
18	Marisa Baena (COL)	68-70-71-73—282	21929
	Na Yeon Choi (KOR)	75-67-69-71—282	21929
	Jeong Jang (KOR)	72-72-68-70—282	21929
	Brittany Lang	70-67-71-74—282	21929
	Jee Young Lee (KOR)	70-69-65-78—282	21929
	Jill McGill	72-70-72-68—282	21929
	Lindsey Wright (AUS)	67-68-73-74—282	21929
25	Jimin Kang (KOR)	72-68-70-73—283	17806
	Kristy McPherson	73-70-72-68—283	17806
	Angela Stanford	72-71-67-73—283	17806
	Momoko Ueda (JPN)	72-67-71-73—283	17806
29	H J Choi (KOR)	69-74-71-70—284	14896
	Eun-Hee Ji (KOR)	72-70-72-70—284	14896
	Liselotte Neumann (SWE)	70-72-71-71—284	14896
	Ji Young Oh (KOR)	69-68-72-75—284	14896
	Karrie Webb (AUS)	71-71-69-73—284	14896
34	Louise Friberg (SWE)	70-73-73-69—285	11887
	Sophie Gituel (FRA)	70-72-72-71—285	11887
	Young Kim (KOR)	69-73-69-74—285	11887
	Brittany Lincicome	75-68-70-72—285	11887
	Jane Park	72-69-70-74—285	11887
	Suzann Pettersen (NOR)	71-68-74-72—285	11887
40	Il Mi Chung (KOR)	71-71-72-72—286	9289
	Michelle Ellis (AUS)	71-67-76-72—286	9289
	Hee-Won Han (KOR)	69-71-73-73—286	9289
	Amy Hung (TPE)	71-71-75-69—286	9289
	Lorie Kane (CAN)	66-70-76-74—286	9289
	Gloria Park (KOR)	70-69-71-76—286	9289
46	Kyeong Bae (KOR)	71-71-70-75—287	6905
	Karine Icher (FRA)	70-74-69-74—287	6905
	Rachek Hethetrington (AUS)	68-69-75-75—287	6905
	Su A Kim (KOR)	70-70-71-76—287	6905
	Carolina Llano (COL)	75-67-68-77—287	6905
	Se Ri Pak (KOR)	70-72-73-72—287	6905
	Inbee Park (KOR)	69-74-74-70—287	6905
	Stacy Prammanasudh	75-69-73-70—287	6905
	Jennifer Rosales (PHI)	70-74-70-73—287	6905

46T	Sherri Steinhauer	73-71-73-70—287	6905
56	Wendy Doolan (AUS)	69-75-70-74—288	5623
	Sandra Gal (GER)	70-70-75-73—288	5623
58	Silvia Cavelleri (ITA)	72-72-73-72—289	4876
	Shanshan Feng (CHN)	72-72-73-72—289	4876
	Candy Hannemann (BRA)	75-68-76-70—289	4876
	Jin Joo Hong (KOR)	68-70-76-75—289	4876
	Michele Redman	71-69-73-76—289	4876
	Nancy Scranton	71-69-74-75—289	4876
	Karen Stupples (ENG)	71-71-76-71—289	4876
65	Julieta Granada (PAR)	70-69-77-74—290	4242
	Leta Lindley	72-72-73-73—290	4242
	Becky Lucidi	73-71-71-75—290	4242
	Mhairi McKay (SCO)	75-69-77-69—290	4242
	Linda Wessberg (SWE)	72-72-71-75—290	4242
70	Angela Park (BRA)	74-70-69-78—291	3946
71	Charlotte Mayorkas	73-71-76-72—292	3872
	Young-A Yang (KOR)	74-68-77-73—292	3872
73	Moira Dunn	72-72-72-77—293	3725
	Tracy Hanson	70-73-75-75—293	3725
	Soo-Yun Kang (KOR)	69-74-72-78—293	3725
	Alena Sharp (CAN)	74-70-73-76—293	3725
77	Meaghan Francella	70-72-77-75—294	3584
	Sun Young Yoo (KOR)	71-73-73-77—294	3584
79	Danielle Downey	71-73-73-78—295	3514
80	Jamie Hullett	70-74-79-74—297	3469
81	Allison Fouch	72-72-79-76—299	3425

The following players missed the cut.

82	Diana D'Alessio	71-74—145
	Katie Futtcher	74-71—145
	Natalie Gulbis	73-72—145
	Kim Hall	71-74—145
	Christina Kim	71-74—145
	Song-Hee-Kim (KOR)	70-75—145
	Carin Koch (SWE)	76-69—145
	Meena Lee (KOR)	71-74—145
	Seo-Jae Lee (KOR)	71-74—145
	Catriona Matthew (SCO)	72-73—145
	Maria Jose Uribe (COL) (am)	71-74—145
	Eunjung Yi (KOR)	70-75—145
94	Meredith Duncan	74-72—146
	Liz Janangelo	73-73—146
	In-Kyung Kim (KOR)	74-72—146
	Ai Miyazato (JPN)	77-69—146
	Reilley Rankin	74-72—146
	Carri Wood	75-71—146
100	Jenny Park-Choi	77-70—147
	Dorothy Delasin	75-72—147
	Katherine Hull (AUS)	73-74—147
	Pat Hurst	72-75—147
	Sarah Jane Kenyon (AUS)	74-73—147
	Paige Mackenzie	73-74—147
	Sherri Turner	77-70—147

100T	Wendy Ward	74-73—147
108	Erica Blasberg	71-77—148
	Audra Burks	75-73—148
	Heather Daly-Donofrio	73-75—148
	Sophie Gustafson (SWE)	77-71—148
	Sarah Lee (KOR)	75-73—148
	Sung Ah Yim	73-75—148
114	Helen Alfredsson (SWE)	75-74—149
	Laura Davies (ENG)	75-74—149
	Birdie Kim (KOR)	75-74—149
	Teresa Lu (TPE)	76-73—149
	Miriam Nagl (BRA)	72-77—149
	Mikaela Parmlid (SWE)	77-72—149
	Hee Young Park (KOR)	73-76—149
	Nicole Perrot (CHI)	74-75—149
122	Minea Blomqvist (FIN)	75-75—150
	Eva Dahllof (SWE)	77-73—150
	Annette DeLuca	74-76—150
	Sarah Kemp (AUS)	77-73—150
	Meg Mallon	76-74—150
	Patricia Meunier-Lebouc (FRA)	78-72—150
	Nina Reis (SWE)	76-74—150
	Kris Tamulis	74-76—150

122T	Heather Young	74-76—150
131	Dina Ammaccapane	73-78—151
	Mollie Fankhauser	73-78—151
	Taylor Leon	76-75—151
	Karin Sjodin (SWE)	74-77—151
135	Allison Hanna-Williams	78-74—152
	Seol-An Jeon (KOR)	78-74—152
137	Jamie Fischer	79-75--154
	Russy Gulyanamitta (THA)	78-76—154
	Na On Min (KOR)	77-77--154
	Virada Nirapathpongporn (THA)	79-75—154
	Anna Rawson	75-79—154
142	Jackie Gallagher-Smith	80-76—156
143	Beth Bader	83-75—158
144	Wendy Modic	82-78—160
145	Violeta Recamoza (MEX)	84-77—161
146	Marci Bozarth	83-82—165
	Emily Bastel	66-76 WD
	Johanna Head (ENG)	72-72 WD
	Becky Iverson	73-73 WD
	Lisa Depaulo	86-86 WD

2007 McDonald's LPGA Championship Bulle Rock, Havre de Grace, MD [6596–72]

Prize money: $2 million

1	Suzann Pettersen (NOR)	69-67-71-67—274	$300000	21T	In-Kyung Kim (KOR)	73-70-71-71—285	20585
2	Karrie Webb (AUS)	68-69-71-67—275	179038	25	Wendy Doolan (AUS)	76-70-70-70—286	17350
3	Ma On Min (KOR)	71-70-65-70—276	129880		Pat Hurst	69-75-76-66—286	17350
4	Lindsey Wright (AUS)	71-70-71-66—278	100473		Jeong Jang (KOR)	73-71-71-71—286	17350
5	Angela Park (BRA)	67-73-68-71—279	80869		Birdie Kim (KOR)	67-71-73-75—286	17350
6	Paula Creamer	71-68-73-68—280	53422		Kim Saiki-Maloney	67-73-70-76—286	17350
	Sophie Gustafson (SWE)	70-71-71-68—280	53422	30	Laura Davies (ENG)	68-75-71-73—287	14801
	Brittany Lincicome	69-69-73-69—280	53422		Leta Lindley	76-69-72-70—287	14801
	Lorena Ochoa (MEX)	71-71-69-69—280	53422		Teresa Lu (TPE)	70-72-72-73—287	14801
10	Nicole Castrale	70-73-68-70—281	35730	33	Maria Hjörth (SWE)	69-75-74-70—288	13069
	Jee Young Lee (KOR)	71-72-68-70—281	35730		Se Ri Pak (KOR)	73-70-74-71—288	13069
	Sarah Lee (KOR)	71-69-72-69—281	35730		Angela Stanford	73-71-72-72—288	13069
	Catriona Matthew (SCO)	71-69-74-67—281	35730	36	Kate Golden	74-73-74-68—289	11096
14	Morgan Pressel	68-71-70-73—282	30192		Jimin Kang (KOR)	73-72-74-70—289	11096
15	Mi Hyun Kim (KOR)	70-73-71-69—283	26925		Seon Hwa Lee (KOR)	71-74-71-73—289	11096
	Stacy Prammanasudh (AUS)	68-74-71-70—283	26925		Nancy Scranton	73-73-74-69—289	11096
	Annika Sörenstam (SWE)	70-69-73-71—283	26925		Giulia Sergas (ITA)	69-74-74-72—289	11096
18	Cristie Kerr	75-70-73-66—284	23396	41	Irene Cho	72-72-76-70—290	9037
	Siew-Ai Lim (MAS)	72-69-70-73—284	23396		Johanna Head (ENG)	75-72-75-68—290	9037
	Mhairi McKay (SCO)	71-69-74-70—284	23396		Becky Morgan (WAL)	73-72-75-70—290	9037
21	Shi Hyun Ahn (KOR)	71-73-71-70—285	20585		Reilley Rankin	71-71-74-74—290	9037
	Meaghan Francella	72-75-68-70—285	20585		Sherri Turner	71-73-74-72—290	9037
	Juli Inkster	73-73-73-66—285	20585				

Other players who made the cut: Kyeong Bae (KOR), Dorothy Delasin, Kimberly Hall, Marcy Hart, Joo Mi Kim (KOR), Mena Lee (KOR), Ji-Young Oh (KOR), Gloria Park (KOR), Michele Redman, Linda Wessberg (SWE), 291; Christina Kim, Charlotte Mayorkas, Sherri Steinhauer, 292; Rachel Hetherington (AUS), Karin Sjodin (SWE), Heather Young, 293; Silvia Cavalleri (ITA), Katherine Hull (AUS), Lorie Kane (CAN), Yu Ping Lin (TPE), In-Bee Park (KOE), Young-A Yang (KOR), 294; Liselotte Neumann (SWE); 295; Maria Baena (COL), Il Mi Chung (KOR), Moira Dunn, Jackie Gallagher-Smith, Brittany Lang, 296; Virada Nirapathpongporn (THA), Jane Park, 297; Erica Blasberg, Eva Dahllof (SWE), Karen Davies, Vicki Goetze-Ackerman, Sung Ah Yim (KOR), 298; Laura Diaz, 299; Meredith Duncan, Patricia

2006 McDonald's LPGA Championship Bulle Rock, Havre de Grace, MD [6596–72]

Prize money: $1.8 million

1	Se Ri Pak (KOR)*	71-69-71-69—280	$270000	25T	Hee-Won Han (KOR)	68-73-75-71—287	16207
2	Karrie Webb (AUS)	70-70-72-68—280	163998		Heather Young	71-75-70-71—287	16207
*Play-off: 1st extra hole: Pak 3, Webb 4				29	Il-Ne Chung (KOR)	71-72-75-70—288	13558
3	Mi Hyun Kim (KOR)	68-71-71-71—281	105501		Liselotte Neumann (SWE)	69-74-75-70—288	13558
	Ai Miyazato (JPN)	68-72-69-72—281	105501		Nancy Scranton	73-73-73-69—288	13558
5	Shi Hyun Ahn (KOR)	69-70-71-72—282	57464		Angela Stanford	70-76-72-70—288	13558
9	Young Kim (KOR)	69-72-73-69—283	34174		Kris Tamulis	73-71-75-69—288	13558
	Lorena Ochoa (MEX)	68-72-71-72—283	34174	34	Marisa Baena (COL)	72-72-74-71—289	11044
	Reilley Rankin	68-73-74-68—283	34174		Nicole Castrale	64-75-74-76—289	11044
	Annika Sörenstam (SWE)	71-69-75-68—283	34174		Rachel Hetherington	70-72-74-73—289	11044
	Sung Ah Yim (KOR)	72-68-74-69—283	34174		(AUS)		
14	Jee Young Lee (KOR)	70-71-70-73—284	26847		Juli Inkster	70-74-73-72—289	11044
	Meena Lee (KOR)	71-72-69-72—284	26847		Nina Reis (SWE)	70-73-73-73—289	11044
16	Silvia Cavalleri (ITA)	69-71-72-73—285	22896	39	Beth Daniel	71-71-73-75—290	8979
	Seon Hwa Lee (KOR)	67-74-75-69—285	22896		Allison Hanna	74-69-78-69—290	8979
	Sherri Steinhauer	70-71-71-73—285	22896		Maria Hjörth (SWE)	68-77-73-72—290	8979
	Wendy Ward	69-74-70-72—285	22896		Nicole Perrot (CHI)	70-71-76-73—290	8979
20	Yuri Fudoh (JPN)	69-74-71-72—286	19215		Michele Redman	73-72-73-72—290	8979
	Natalie Gulbis	72-73-72-69—286	19215	44	Julieta Grenada (PAR)	71-73-71-76—291	7363
	Young Jo (KOR)	72-72-70-72—286	19215		Sophie Gustafson (SWE)	72-72-75-72—291	7363
	Suzann Pettersen (NOR)	70-72-74-70—286	19215		Candie Kung (TPE)	68-78-71-74—291	7363
	Lindsey Wright (AUS)	72-73-68-73—286	19215		Yu Ping Lin (TPE)	74-72-72-73—291	7363
25	Minea Blomqvist (FIN)	71-71-70-75—287	16207		Jessica Reese-Quayle	73-73-72-73—291	7363
	Laura Diaz	71-74-72-70—287	16207				

Other players who made the cut: Paula Creamer, Rosie Jones, Carin Koch (SWE), Brittany Lincicome, Kim Saiki, 292; Michelle Ellis (AUS), Jill McGill, Miriam Nagl (GER), Mikaela Parmlid (SWE), 293; Jackie Gallagher-Smith, Jeong Jang (KOR), Teresa Lu (TPE), 294; Christina Kim, Siew-Ai Lim (MAS), Gloria Park (KOR), Karin Sjodin (SWE), 295; Laura Davies (ENG), Wendy Doolan (AUS), Birdie Kim (KOR), Sarah Lee (KOR), 296; Ashli Bunch, Dorothy Delasin, Morgan Pressel, Karen Stupples (ENG), 297; Kristi Albers, 299; Moira Dunn, 300; Jamie Fischer, Becky Iverson, 302.

2005 McDonald's LPGA Championship *Bulle Rock, Havre de Grace, MD* [6486–72]
Prize money: $1.8 million

1	Annika Sörenstam (SWE)	68-67-69-73—277	$270000	20T	Laura Diaz	67-72-76-73—288	19797
2	Michelle Wie (am)	69-71-71-69—280			Meena Lee (KOR)	70-71-72-75—288	19797
3	Paula Creamer	68-73-74-67—282	140517		Karrie Webb (AUS)	74-75-72-67—288	19797
	Laura Davies (ENG)	67-70-74-71—282	140517	25	Shi Hyun Ahn (KOR)	78-71-72-68—289	16096
5	Natalie Gulbis	67-71-73-73—284	82486		Kirsti Albers	70-72-73-74—289	16096
	Lorena Ochoa (MEX)	72-72-68-72—284	82486		Il Mi Chung (KOR)	71-68-79-71—289	16096
7	Moira Dunn	71-68-72-74—285	43993		Hee-Won Han (KOR)	73-74-72-70—289	16096
	Pat Hurst	72-73-71-69—285	43993		Leta Lindley	72-72-75-70—289	16096
	Mi Hyun Kim (KOR)	69-75-74-67—285	43993		Karen Stupples (ENG)	72-71-71-75—289	16096
	Young Kim (KOR)	73-68-68-76—285	43993	31	Rosie Jones	72-69-74-75—290	13733
	Carin Koch (SWE)	74-70-69-72—285	43993		Liselotte Neumann		
	Gloria Park (KOR)	71-71-72-71—285	43993		(SWE)	70-71-74-75—290	13733
13	Juli Inkster	75-71-71-69—286	29309	33	Jamie Hullett	70-75-71-75—291	11225
	Jeong Jang (KOR)	71-71-69-75—286	29309		Jimin Kang (KOR)	73-74-72-72—291	11225
	Candie Kung (TAI)	72-73-73-68—286	29309		Cristie Kerr	74-72-67-78—291	11225
16	Marisa Baena (COL)	70-69-73-75—287	23899		Christina Kim	73-72-78-68—291	11225
	Jennifer Rosales (PHI)	71-73-69-74—287	23899		Brittany Lincicome	72-72-75-72—291	11225
	Angela Stanford	69-73-73-72—287	23899		Meg Mallon	74-69-76-72—291	11225
	Lindsey Wright (AUS)	71-72-72-72—287	23899		Janice Moodie (SCO)	73-74-72-72—291	11225
20	Beth Bader	72-72-72-72—288	19797		Stacy Prammanasudh	72-76-72-71—291	11225
	Heather Bowie	72-71-71-74—288	19797				

Other players who made the cut: Birdie Kim (KOR), 292, Rachel Hetherington (AUS), Hilary Lunke, Paula Marti (ESP), Joanne Morley (ENG), 293; Johanna Head (ENG), Lorie Kane (CAN), Aree Song (KOR), 294; Heather Daly-Donofrio, Catriona Matthew (SCO), Suzann Pettersen (NOR), Michele Redman, Kim Saiki, 295; Dawn Coe-Jones (CAN), Beth Daniel, Wendy Doolan (AUS), Yu Ping Lin (TAI), Stephanie Louden, Jill McGill, Nicole Perrot (CHI), Nancy Scranton, Sung Ah Yim (KOR), 296; Tina Barrett, Patricia Baxter-Johnson, Tina Fischer (GER), Laurel Kean, Emilee Klein, Bernadette Luse, Sae-Hee Son (KOR), Kris Tschetter, 297; Maria Hjörth (SWE), 298; Katie Allison, Catherine Cartwright, A J Eathorne (CAN), Katherine Hull (AUS), Reilley Rankin, 299; Laurie Rinker, Nadina Taylor (AUS), 300; Candy Hannemann (BRA), 302; Barb Mucha, 305.

2004 McDonald's LPGA Championship *Du Pont CC, DE* [6408–71]
Prize money: $1.6 million

1	Annika Sörenstam	68-67-64-72—271	$240000	17T	Betsy King	76-70-70-68—284	18654
	(SWE)				Se Ri Pak (KOR)	69-73-70-72—284	18654
2	Shi Hyun Ahn (KOR)	69-70-69-66—274	144780	23	Tina Barrett	75-71-68-71—285	14596
3	Grace Park (KOR)	68-70-70-68—276	105028		Jeong Jang	71-71-71-72—285	14596
4	Gloria Park (KOR)	67-72-68-71—278	73322		Siew-Ai Lim (MAS)	72-70-71-72—285	14596
	Angela Stanford	69-71-67-71—278	73322		Stacy Prammanasudh	73-71-69-72—285	14596
6	Juli Inkster	70-66-70-73—279	49145		Kim Saiki	69-72-72-72—285	14596
	Christina Kim	74-69-64-72—279	49145		Sherri Steinhauer	69-72-74-70—285	14596
8	Wendy Doolan (AUS)	73-70-65-72—280	35538		Chiharu Yamaguchi	67-73-70-75—285	
	Soo-Yun Kang	69-68-71-72—280	35538		(JPN)		14596
	Lorena Ochoa (MEX)	71-67-67-75—280	35538	30	Moira Dunn	68-74-72-72—286	10631
11	Carin Koch (SWE)	69-71-68-73—281	28734		Mi-Hyun Kim (KOR)	72-70-74-70—286	10631
	Reilley Rankin	70-67-71-73—281	28734		Young Kim (KOR)	70-73-74-69—286	10631
13	Pat Hurst	69-69-75-69—282	24466		Patricia Meunier-	71-70-76-69—286	
	Mhairi McKay (SCO)	72-69-69-72—282	24466		Labouc (FRA)		10631
	Jennifer Rosales (PHI)	66-70-74-72—282	24466		Janice Moodie (SCO)	72-71-73-70—286	10631
16	Meg Mallon	69-73-70-71—283	21718		Aree Song (KOR)	71-72-69-74—286	10631
17	Kristi Albers	70-74-69-71—284	18654		Charlotta Sörenstam	74-70-70-72—286	
	Dawn Coe-Jones (CAN)	72-72-70-70—284	18654		(SWE)		10631
	Michelle Ellis (AUS)	72-70-69-73—284	18654		Karen Stupples (ENG)	67-73-73-73—286	10631
	Cristie Kerr	69-73-71-71—284	18654		Wendy Ward	72-72-71-71—286	10631

Other players who made the cut: Beth Daniel, Stephanie Louden (AUS), Karrie Webb (AUS) 287; Jean Bartholomew, Ashli Bunch, Laura Davies (ENG), Becky Iverson, Becky Morgan (WAL), Deb Richard, Karen Pearce (AUS) 289; Heather Daly-Donofrio, Hee-Won Han (KOR), Lorie Kane (CAN), Yu Ping Lin (TPE), Kelly Robbins, Giulia Sergas (ITA), Rachel Teske (AUS) 290; Pat Bradley, Diana D'Alessio, Kate Golden, Jamie Hullett, Emilee Klein 291; Helen Alfredsson (SWE), Natalie Gulbis, Catriona Matthew (SCO) 292; Amy Fruhwirth, Tammy Green, Seol-An Jeon (KOR), Angela Jerman, Candie Kung (TPE), Soo Young Moon (KOR) 293; Isabelle Beisiegel (CAN), Vicki Goetz-Ackerman, Jill McGill, Dotty Pepper 294; Jenna Daniels, Sophie Gustafson (SWE), Kim Williams 295; Candy Hannemann (BRA) 296; Jackie Gallagher-Smith 297; Heather Bowie 299.

2003 McDonald's LPGA Championship *Du Pont CC, DE*   [6408–71]

Prize money: $1.6 million

1	Annika Sörenstam (SWE)*	70-64-72-72—278	$240000	20	Donna Andrews	73-70-70-74—287	16719
					Tina Barrett	76-69-71-71—287	16719
*Sörenstam winner at first extra hole of play-off with Grace Park					Michelle Ellis (AUS)	73-70-71-73—287	16719
2	Grace Park (KOR)	69-72-70-67—278	147934		Natalie Gulbis	71-69-78-69—287	16719
3	Beth Daniel	71-71-70-72—284	85718		Kelli Kuehne	73-73-65-76—287	16719
	Rosie Jones	73-68-72-71—284	85718		Lorena Ochoa (MEX)	72-72-71-72—287	16719
	Rachel Teske (AUS)	69-70-74-71—284	85718		Karen Stupples (ENG)	73-73-71-70—287	16719
6	Kate Golden	72-70-68-75—285	41873	27	Danielle Ammaccapane	74-72-74-68—288	13769
	Young Kim (KOR)	70-73-72-70—285	41873		Meg Mallon	74-69-70-75—288	13769
	JoAnne Mills (AUS)	68-73-75-69—285	41873		Angela Stanford	72-73-71-72—288	13769
	Becky Morgan (WAL)	73-70-70-72—285	41873	30	Laura Diaz	73-70-75-71—289	11987
	Young-A Yang (KOR)	73-74-69-69—285	41873		Tracy Hanson	71-77-70-71—289	11987
11	Akiko Fukushima (JPN)	72-68-74-72—286	24037		Mi-Hyun Kim (KOR)	72-72-71-74—289	11987
	Hee-Wan Han (KOR)	67-69-74-76—286	24037		Deb Richard	75-71-74-69—289	11987
	Jeong Jang (KOR)	72-73-69-72—286	24037	34	Moira Dunn	78-70-72-70—290	10367
	Angela Jerman	73-72-69-72—286	24037		Lorie Kane (CAN)	72-75-70-73—290	10367
	Patricia Meunier-Lebouc (FRA)	75-69-72-70—286	24037		Cristie Kerr	74-69-75-72—290	10367
	Suzann Pettersen (NOR)	70-71-75-70—286	24037	37	Juli Inkster	71-72-71-77—291	8970
	Michele Redman	74-70-69-73—286	24037		Hilary Lunke	72-70-75-74—291	8970
	Jennifer Rosales (PHI)	74-68-74-70—286	24037		Catriona Matthew (SCO)	72-73-75-71—291	8970
	Wendy Ward	68-69-75-74—286	24037		Jan Stephenson (AUS)	74-72-69-76—291	8970

Other players who made the cut: Jill McGill,Terry-Jo Myers 292; Vicki Goetze-Ackerman, Pat Hurst, Giulia Sergas (ITA) 293; Marisa Baena (COL), Brandie Burton, Jung Yeon Lee (KOR), Se Ri Pak (KOR), Leslie Spalding 294;Yu Ping Lin (TPE), Kathryn Marshall (SCO), Joanne Morley (ENG) 295; Dorothy Delasin (PHI), Kim Saiki 296; Dawn Coe-Jones (CAN), Jane Crafter (AUS), Wendy Doolan (AUS), Jackie Gallagher-Smith, Karrie Webb (AUS) 297; Fiona Pike (AUS) 298; Heather Bowie 299; Marnie McGuire (NZL) 300; Mitzi Edge, Marcy Hart, Michelle McGann 301; Marilyn Lovander, Liselotte Neumann (SWE), Dottie Pepper 304; Kim Williams 306.

2002 McDonald's LPGA Championship *Du Pont CC, DE*   [6408–71]

Prize money: $1.4 million

1	Se Ri Pak (KOR)	71-70-68-70—279	$225000	20T	Barb Mucha	70-73-75-75—293	16950
2	Beth Daniel	67-70-68-77—282	136987	22	Silvia Cavalleri (ITA)	72-73-73-76—294	15450
3	Annika Sörenstam (SWE)	70-76-73-65—284	99375		Maria Hjörth (SWE)	78-70-75-71—294	15450
					Kelly Robbins	70-75-74-75—294	15450
4	Juli Inkster	69-75-70-71—285	69375	25	Danielle Ammaccapane	73-76-73-73—295	12543
	Karrie Webb (AUS)	68-71-72-74—285	69375		Brandie Burton	74-76-74-71—295	12543
6	Carin Koch (SWE)	68-73-73-72—286	46500		Vicki Goetze-Ackerman	72-72-74-77—295	12543
	Michele Redman	74-69-70-73—286	46500		Tammie Green	70-78-73-74—295	12543
8	Catriona Matthew (SCO)	70-73-75-70—288	37125		Leta Lindley	72-77-71-75—295	12543
					Kathryn Marshall (SCO)	73-73-72-77—295	12543
9	Kristi Albers	74-73-73-70—290	30625		Gloria Park (KOR)	75-72-73-75—295	12543
	Michelle McGann	71-72-72-75—290	30625		Kris Tschetter	74-75-75-71—295	12543
	Karen Stupples (ENG)	75-70-70-75—290	30625	33	Eva Dahllof (SWE)	75-73-75-73—296	9056
12	Meg Mallon	73-72-76-70—291	24650		Dorothy Delasin (PHI)	79-68-73-76—296	9056
	Kim Saiki	71-71-69-80—291	24650		Moira Dunn	74-75-75-72—296	9056
	Karen Weiss	70-74-75-72—291	24650		Michelle Ellis (AUS)	72-77-74-73—296	9056
15	Akiki Fukushima (JPN)	71-71-76-74—292	19650		Lorie Kane (CAN)	70-74-76-76—296	9056
	Natalie Gulbis	72-72-75-73—292	19650		Mi Hyun Kim (KOR)	77-71-72-76—296	9056
	Kelli Kuehne	71-75-74-72—292	19650		Charlotta Sörenstam (SWE)	75-73-74-74—296	9056
	Grace Park (KOR)	72-73-73-74—292	19650				
	Rachel Teske (AUS)	72-71-77-72—292	19650		Sherri Turner	74-73-76-73—296	9056
20	Laura Diaz	73-71-71-78—293	16950				

Other players who made the cut: Jane Crafter (AUS), Heather Daly-Donofrio, Tracy Hanson, Pat Hurst, Cristie Kerr, Mhairi McKay (SCO) 297; Angela Buzminski, Jackie Gallagher-Smith, Betsy King, Joanne Morley (ENG), Jennifer Rosales (PHI) 298; Beth Bauer, Jenna Daniels, Michelle Estill, Liselotte Neumann (SWE), Susie Parry 299; Hee-Won Han (KOR), Jeong Jang (KOR) 300; Stephanie Keever, Angela Stanford 301; Denise Killeen, Marnie McGuire (NZL), Patricia Meunier-Lebouc 302; Emilee Klein 303; Becky Iverson, Val Skinner 304; Chris Johnson 305; A J Eathorne (CAN) 307; Karen Pearce 308; Alicia Dibos (PER), Shiho Katano (JPN) 309.

2001 McDonald's LPGA Championship Du Pont CC, DE   [6408–71]

Prize money: $1.5 million

1	Karrie Webb (AUS)	67-64-70-69—270	$225000	17T	Dottie Pepper	71-72-71-68—282	16819
2	Laura Diaz	67-71-66-68—272	139639		Kelly Robbins	69-74-71-68—282	16819
3	Maria Hjörth (SWE)	71-67-66-70—274	90577		Rachel Teske (AUS)	68-72-70-72—282	16819
	Wendy Ward	65-69-71-69—274	90577	26	Heather Daly-Donofrio	75-68-71-69—283	13162
5	Annika Sörenstam (SWE)	68-69-71-67—275	64157		Beth Daniel	71-71-70-71—283	13162
6	Laura Davies (ENG)	67-68-70-71—276	48684		Akiko Fukushima (JPN)	66-72-73-72—283	13162
	Becky Iverson	66-73-67-70—276	48684		Nancy Scranton	73-68-70-72—283	13162
8	Mi Hyun Kim (KOR)	70-70-68-69—277	39250	30	Dawn Coe-Jones	72-69-71-72—284	11603
9	Helen Alfredsson (SWE)	68-66-74-70—278	35476		Catriona Matthew (SCO)	71-72-72-69—284	1 603
10	Michele Redman	69-66-73-71—279	30245		Grace Park (KOR)	71 72-71-70—284	11633
	Maggie Will	68-74-67-70—279	30245	33	Danielle Ammaccapane	69-71-71-74—285	10257
12	Rosie Jones	71-69-71-69—280	25013		Jane Crafter (AUS)	71-71-69-74—285	10257
	Lorie Kane (CAN)	69-71-71-69—280	25013		Patricia Meunier-Lebouc	70-73-71-71—285	10257
	Liselotte Neumann (SWE)	69-72-68-71—280	25013		(FRA)		
15	Wendy Doolan (AUS)	70-71-72-68—281	21239		Sherri Turner	71-72-72-70—285	10257
	Juli Inkster	71-71-69-70—281	21239	37	Brandie Burton	69-74-68-75—286	9125
17	Pat Hurst	72-68-72-70—282	16819		Hee Won Han (KOR)	70-75-72-69—286	9125
	Carin Koch (SWE)	69-73-71-69—282	16819	39	Kathryn Marshall (SCO)	71-73-71-72—287	8011
	Leta Lindley	71-71-70-70—282	16819		Se Ri Pak (KOR)	71-73-69-74—287	8011
	Meg Mallon	71-74-67-70—282	16819		Deb Richard	72-71-73-71—287	8011
	Mhairi McKay (SCO)	68-72-70-72—282	16819		Kris Tschetter	71-74-69-73—287	8011
	Terry-Jo Myers	70-71-69-72—282	16819				

Other players who made the cut: Alicia Dibos, Vicki Goetze-Ackerman, Gloria Park (KOR), Kristal Parker 288; Suzy Green, Jenny Lidback (PER), Marnie McGuire 289; Mitzi Edge, Jackie Gallagher-Smith, Emilee Klein, Sara Sanders 290; Amy Alcott, Donna Andrews, Marisa Baena (COL), Susan Ginter, Betsy King, Charlotta Sörenstam (SWE), Leslie Spalding 291; Dorothy Delasin (PHI), Alison Nicholas (ENG) 292; Jean Bartholomew, Gail Graham (CAN), Joanne Morley (ENG) 293; Janice Moodie (SCO), Barb Mucha, Joan Pitcock 294; Annette DeLuca 296; Michelle McGann 299.

2000 McDonald's LPGA Championship Du Pont CC, DE   [6386–71]

Prize money: $1.4 million

1	Juli Inkster*	72-69-65-75—281	$210000	23	Pat Bradley	68-76-67-76—287	13304
	Inkster winner at second hole of play-off with Croce				Betsy King	68-78-67-74—287	13304
2	Stefania Croce (ITA)	72-67-74-68—281	130330		Janice Moodie (SCO)	72-73-71-71—287	13304
3	Se Ri Pak (KOR)	73-69-69-71—282	76319		Alison Nicholas (ENG)	72-72-71-72—287	13304
	Nancy Scranton	72-70-67-73—282	76319		Dottie Pepper	71-73-69-74—287	13304
	Wendy Ward	69-69-68-76—282	76319	28	Rosie Jones	70-74-74-70—288	11191
6	Heather Bowie	74-70-70-69—283	42503		Jenny Lidback (PER)	75-71-71-71—288	11191
	Jane Crafter (AUS)	72-69-69-73—283	42503		Gloria Park (KOR)	68-75-75-70—288	11191
	Laura Davies (ENG)	70-66-75-72—283	42503		Karen Weiss	73-71-70-74—288	11191
9	Akiko Fukushima (JPN)	71-72-71-70—284	29839		Barb Whitehead	73-72-70-73—288	11191
	Jan Stephenson (AUS)	70-69-69-76—284	29839	33	Beth Daniel	72-72-70-75—289	9698
	Karrie Webb (AUS)	72-70-69-73—284	29839		Emilee Klein	74-71-71-73—289	9698
12	Amy Fruhwirth	74-71-70-70—285	21885		Kim Saiki	77-69-71-72—289	9698
	Mi Hyun Kim (KOR)	70-73-70-72—285	21885	36	Jean Bartholomew	71-71-74-74—290	8464
	Leta Lindley	71-73-71-70—285	21885		Alicia Dibos (PER)	72-74-74-70—290	8464
	Kelly Robbins	72-72-73-68—285	21885		Cindy McCurdy	73-74-71-72—290	8464
	Annika Sörenstam (SWE)	70-73-70-72—285	21885		Maggie Will	74-72-67-77—290	8464
17	Dawn Coe-Jones	71-73-72-70—286	16602	40	Sophie Gustafson (SWE)	76-70-69-76—291	6820
	Wendy Doolan (AUS)	69-71-71-75—286	16602		Carin Koch (SWE)	74-70-73-74—291	6820
	Jane Geddes	66-74-73-73—286	16602		Barb Mucha	72-72-70-77—291	6820
	Pat Hurst	71-70-71-74—286	16602		Laura Philo	72-74-73-72—291	6820
	Meg Mallon	72-73-69-72—286	16602		Jennifer Rosales (PHI)	71-73-74-73—291	6820
	Michele Redman	70-70-70-76—286	16602		Sherri Steinhauer	70-75-68-78—291	6820

Other players who made the cut: Cindy Flom, Kathryn Marshall (SCO), Leigh Ann Mills, Patty Sheehan, Kris Tschetter, Mary Beth Zimmerman 292; Cindy Figg-Currier, Yu Ping Lin (TPE), 293; Jill McGill, Joanne Morley (ENG) 293; Marisa Baena (COL), AJ Eathorne (CAN), Vicki Goetze-Ackerman, Kate Golden, Tracy Hanson, Catrin Nilsmark (SWE) 294; Ashli Bunch, Val Skinner, Leslie Spalding 295; Pamela Kerrigan, Nancy Lopez, Shani Waugh (AUS) 296; Danielle Ammaccapane, Debbi Koyama (JPN) 298; Moira Dunn 299; Carmen Hajjar 300; Julie Piers 301; Dina Ammaccapane 305

1999 McDonald's LPGA Championship *Du Pont CC, DE*   [6376–71]

Prize money: $1.4 million

1	J Inkster	68-66-69-65—268	$210000	22	L Kiggens	68-74-69-68—279	14063
2	L Neumann (SWE)	67-67-70-68—272	130330		A Fukushima (JPN)	70-70-69-70—279	14063
3	M Lunn (AUS)	68-74-65-66—273	84538		V Odegard	69-70-70-70—279	14063
	N Scranton	69-68-66-70—273	84538		A Finney	67-69-71-72—279	14063
5	R Jones	64-72-68-70—274	54596	26	P Sinn	71-71-70-68—280	11087
	C Kerr	70-64-69-71—274	54596		Mi Hyun Kim (KOR)	70-70-71-69—280	11087
7	E Klein	72-68-67-68—275	35224		V Fergon	67-73-70-70—280	11087
	J McGill	70-69-68-68—275	35224		J Crafter	70-69-71-70—280	11087
	L Davies (ENG)	65-71-71-68—275	35224		L Lindley	70-72-67-71—280	11087
	Se Ri Pak (KOR)	68-69-67-71—275	35224		B Mucha	70-70-69-71—280	11087
11	M Hirase	70-73-68-65—276	23487		K Kuehne	68-67-72-73—280	11087
	S Sanders	70-68-68-70—276	23487		A Nicholas (ENG)	67-73-66-74—280	11087
	T Green	68-70-68-70—276	23487		T Johnson (ENG)	67-70-69-74—280	11087
	J Lidback	67-67-72-70—276	23487		L Kane	70-66-70-74—280	11087
	M Mallon	70-71-63-72—276	23487	36	T Tombs	71-71-69-70—281	8164
16	A Sörenstam (SWE)	73-68-68-68—277	18415		H Stacy	73-68-70-70—281	8164
	S Redman	70-68-70-69—277	18415		C Koch	68-73-70-70—281	8164
	J Stephenson	69-69-69-70—277	18415		N Bowen	70-72-68-71—281	8164
19	D Pepper	71-72-68-67—278	16301		S Waugh	70-69-71-71—281	8164
	S Steinhauer	74-69-65-70—278	16301		C Figg-Currier	71-70-67-73—281	8164
	H Kobayashi (JPN)	70-67-71-70—278	16301				

Other players who made the cut: Dana Dormann, W Doolan, J Moodie (SCO), R Hetherington (AUS), M Spencer-Devlin 282; C Flom, M Nause, B Iverson, M McGann, D Eggeling, S Croce (ITA), T Barrett 283; K Coats, K Tschetter, P Hammel, C Nilsmark (SWE), K Saiki, D Richard, S Little, C Johnson, S Gustafson (SWE) 284; M Hjörth (SWE), M Will 285; P Bradley 286; K Robbins 287; D Barnard 288; M McGeorge 289; B King, D Killeen 290; K Lunn (AUS) 299

LPGA Championship History

The Championship was known simply as the LPGA Championship from its inauguration in 1955 until 1987. It was sponsored by Mazda from 1988 until 1993 when the sponsorship was taken over by McDonald's. Only in the first year was it decided by match-play when Beverly Hanson beat Louise Suggs in the final.

Year	Winner	Venue	Score
1955	B Hanson	Orchard Ridge	4 and 3
1956	M Hagge*	Forest Lake	291
After a play-off with Patty Berg			
1957	L Suggs	Churchill Valley	285
1958	M Wright	Churchill CC	288
1959	B Rawls	Churchill CC	288
1960	M Wright	French Lick	292
1961	M Wright	Stardust	287
1962	J Kimball	Stardust	282
1963	M Wright	Stardust	294
1964	M Mills	Stardust	278
1965	S Haynie	Stardust	279
1966	G Ehret	Stardust	282
1967	K Whitworth	Pleasant Valley	284
1968	S Post*	Pleasant Valley	294
After a play-off with K Whitworth			
1969	B Rawls	Concord	293
1970	S Englehorn*	Pleasant Valley	285
After a play-off with K Whitworth			
1971	K Whitworth	Pleasant Valley	288
1972	K Ahern	Pleasant Valley	293
1973	M Mills	Pleasant Valley	288
1974	S Haynie	Pleasant Valley	288

Year	Winner	Venue	Score
1975	K Whitworth	Pine Ridge	288
1976	B Burfeindt	Pine Ridge	287
1977	C Higuchi (JPN)	Bay Tree	279
1978	N Lopez	Kings Island	275
1979	D Caponi	Kings Island	279
1980	S Little (SA)	Kings Island	285
1981	D Caponi	Kings Island	280
1982	J Stephenson (AUS)	Kings Island	279
1983	P Sheehan	Kings Island	279
1984	P Sheehan	Kings Island	272
1985	N Lopez	Kings Island	273
1986	P Bradley	Kings Island	277
1987	J Geddes	Kings Island	275
1988	S Turner	Kings Island	281
1989	N Lopez	King's Island	274
1990	B Daniel	Bethesda	280
1991	M Mallon	Bethesda	274
1992	B King	Bethesda	267
1993	P Sheehan	Bethesda	275
1994	L Davies (ENG)	Wilmington, Delaware	275
1995	K Robbins	Wilmington, Delaware	274
1996	L Davies (ENG)	Wilmington, Delaware	213

Reduced to 54 holes – bad weather

Year	Winner	Venue	Score
1997	C Johnson	Wilmington, Delaware	281
1998	Se Ri Pak (KOR)	Wilmington, Delaware	273
1999	J Inkster	Wilmington, Delaware	268
2000	J Inkster*	Wilmington, Delaware	281

*Inkster beat Stefania Croce (ITA) at the second extra hole

Year	Winner	Venue	Score
2001	K Webb (AUS)	Wilmington, Delaware	270
2002	Se Ri Pak (KOR)	Wilmington, Delaware	279
2003	A Sörenstam (SWE)*	Wilmington, Delaware	271

*Sörenstam beat Grace Park (KOR) at the first extra hole

Year	Winner	Venue	Score
2004	A Sörenstam (SWE)	Wilmington, Delaware	271
2005	A Sörenstam (SWE)	Bulle Rock, MD	277
2006	Se Ri Pak (KOR)*	Bulle Rock, MD	280

*Pak beat Karrie Webb (AUS) at first extra hole

Year	Winner	Venue	Score
2007	S Pettersen (NOR)	Bulle Rock, MD	274
2008	Y Tseng (TPE)*	Bulle Rock, MD	278

*Tseng beat M Hjörth (SWE) at the fourth extra hole

Kraft Nabisco Championship

formerly known as the Nabisco Dinah Shore

Big splash at Mission Hills as brilliant Lorena Ochoa wins the first major of the year by five shots

It was back in 1988 that Amy Alcott, who played her last competitive round in the 2008 edition of the Kraft Nabisco Championship, began the tradition of the winner diving into Poppy's Pond beside the 18th green at Mission Hills as an unconventional way to celebrate her success. The post-round splash-around at the end of the first major of the year is surely the most unusual of golfing traditions.

© Stephen Dunn/Getty Images

Lorena Ochoa

Back in 1988, Alcott's caddie Bill Kurre joined her in the lake but Mexican Lorena Ochoa, the 2008 winner went much further. Her caddie jumped in with her, of course. but so too did her mum, dad, brother, sister-in-law and 15 other friends and family!

This was a mass celebration as Ochoa, the so-called Tiger Woods of ladies professional golf, gave herself the chance to win all four majors in the same year with an 11-under-par 277 total for a five shot advantage over the field and a $300,000 cheque. In the end it was the late-charging former winner Annika Sörenstam, despite being unwell throughout the weekend, and Norwegian Suzann Pettersen who filled the runner-up spot. For Pettersen it was the second successive year she had come second.

As for Ochoa, she was asked whether a Grand Slam victory of all four majors in the same season was a realistic possibility. Her answer was short and to the point – Yes! No one even queried her confidence!

Ochoa did not quite lead from start to finish. She ended the first round one shot behind leader Karen Stupples, the former British Open champion, but the talented Mexican had moved out in front with Heather Young at half way, led on her own by one from Korean Hee-Won Han after 54-holes and helped by a closing bogey-free 67 swept to a comfortable second successive major win. Ochoa had ended the 2007 majors season with an equally impressive victory at St Andrews in the Ricoh Women's British Open.

With her success, Ochoa has 26 of the 27 points she needs to gain entrance to the LPGA and World Golf Halls of Fame but she will not be inducted into them until 2012 when she will have completed her regulation tenth season on Tour. With her win at Mission Hills she had notched up 20 wins, twice led the scoring averages and been twice top money earner since joining the Tour in 2003. Following the Kraft Nabisco event she had moved into fourth place behind Sörenstam, Karrie Webb and Julie Inkster in the career money list with $11,289,776. Although Sörenstam passed the $11 million mark in 163 starts Ochoa achieved the feat in 128 – a new record.

In her post-victory press conference Ochoa, playing in her eighth Kraft Nabisco event having first played as an amateur, told reporters: "I woke up this morning feeling great … and could not stop thinking about jumping in the lake! I always had good momentum, on the course. I never thought about this being a major. I just enjoyed it. It just seemed easy, just like it was at St Andrews last August."

Asked who or what can stop her she replied: "I hope nobody and nothing. I know it is just the beginning of the year but I have set myself high goals this year and I'll try to keep going with the flow."

First Round	Second Round	Third Round	Fourth Round
–5 Stupples	–5 Ochoa	–6 Ochoa	–11 Ochoa
–4 Ochoa	–5 Young	–5 Han	–6 Pettersen
–4 Miyazato	–4 Hjorth	–4 Kerr	–6 Sörenstam
–2 Uribe (am)	–4 Kim	–4 Lee	–5 Hjorth
–2 Kim	–3 Han	–4 Hjorth	–4 Lee
–2 Neumann	–3 Sörenstam	–3 Park	–3 Han
–2 Hjorth	–2 Neumann	–3 Neumann	–3 Kim
	–2 Miyazato	–3 Young	–3 Choi
	–2 Pak	–2 Pettersen	–2 Park
	–2 Stupples	–2 Sörenstam	–1 Pak
			–1 Young

Sörenstam, who had visited the hospital on Saturday and been diagnosed as suffering from a stomach virus and dehydration, was glad to have managed to finish, especially with her best of the week 68. Asked whether she thought it possible for a player to win all four majors in one year she said: "I think it is and Lorena is playing great golf but she will have to peak at the right times and need a little bit of luck."

Pettersen, who had rounds of 65 and 68 to gallop through the field at the weekend, was delighted with her strong finish and overall performance. "When it is windy the way it was this course plays very difficult. There are so many really tough shots and putting is not easy on the firm greens so 11-under at the weekend made me very happy." With justification because she had moved up to joint runner-up from 62nd at the 36-hole stage.

On Thursday the Tour's newest mum Stupples had a bogey-free 67 to lead by one from Ochoa and the Japanese golfer Ai Miyazato, who had seven birdies in her 68. Reigning USGA Amateur champion Maria Jose Uribe, who attends UCLA, had a 70 and Mallory Blackwelder from the University of Kentucky shot 71. Defending champion Morgan Pressel, who became the youngest winner of a Tour major when taking the title in 2007 at age 18 years, 10 months and nine days, was also on 71.

Seventy one players, including six of the nine former winners in the field, made the half-way cut with scores of five-over-par or better and three of the six amateurs made it too.

On Saturday Ochoa, with a 71, joined Heather Young in the lead on five-under par 139 just a shot clear of Swede Maria Hjorth and Mi Hyun Kim from Korea, back in action after knee surgery four months earlier. Sörenstam was just two behind and Pettersen 10 back after rounds of 74 and 75. First round pace-setter Stupples tumbled to a 75.

A third round of 71 again gave Ochoa a one shot lead over Hee-Won Han and a two shot advantage over Seon Hwa Lee and Hjorth. Karrie Webb scored her third LPGA ace with a 6-iron at the 163 yards eighth. It was the 21st ace in the history of the event but the former winner was five shots behind with a round to go. Defending champion Pressel was ten back.

The leading amateur prize went to Duke University junior Amanda Blumenherst who finished joint 30th but it was the lively Ochoa who dominated the final day. At the end only 10 of the 71 who had made the halfway cut finished under par.

Lorena Ochoa's fabulous season ... again!

Mexican golfer Lorena Ochoa completed her fifth season on the LPGA Tour without missing a half-way cut. In fact she has missed only three cuts in the five years she has been on Tour. Named in *Time Magazine*'s Influential Top 100 for her passion and dedication to those in need – she has created a Foundation to improve education and reduce drop-outs and funded the building of a school in her home town of La Barranca – Miss Ochoa has chalked up 24 career wins and had 96 Top Ten finishes from 122 starts! Her 2008 season in detail:

HSBC Champions	66-65-69-68—268	1st	$300,000
Mastercard Classic	76-70-68—214	8th	$30,550
Safeway International	65-67-68-66—266	1st	$225,000
KRAFT NABISCO	68-71-71-67—277	1st	$300,000
Corona Championship	66-66-66-69—267	1st	$195,000
Ginn Open	68-67-65-69—269	1st	$390,000
SenGroup Champs.	73-74-71-69—287	5th	$62,719
Michelob Ultra	65-68-74-70—277	12th	$35,347
Sybase Classic	68-67-71—206	1st	$300,000
McDONALDS LPGA	69-65-72-71—277	3rd	$115,911
Wegman's LPGA	72-70-68-69—279	6th	$54,899
US OPEN	73-74-76-74—297	31st	$21,567
Evian Masters	65-73-70-68—276	5th	$146,966
RICOH BRITISH	69-68-71-69—277	7th	$65,841
CN Canadian	66-68-74-73—281	4th	$93,406
Safeway Classic	69-70-70—209	6th	$43,482
Navistar Classic	67-67-69-70—273	1st	$210,000
Samsung World	69-73-70-69—281	3rd	$64,063
Long Drugs	70-68-74-72—284	4th	$61,073
Kapalua Classic	74-69-73-71—87	14th	$22,704
Lorena Ochoa Inv.	73-71-70-70—284	14th	$15,772
ADT Championship	75-74	17th	$8533

2008 Kraft Nabisco Championship

Mission Hills CC, (Dinah Shore Tournament Course), Rancho Mirage, CA   [6673–72]

Prize money: $2m. Final field of 110 players (including five amateurs), of whom 71 (including three amateurs) made the final half-way cut on 149 or less. *(Players are of American nationality unless stated)*

1	Lorena Ochoa (MEX)	68-71-71-67—277	$300000
2	Suzann Pettersen (NOR)	74-75-65-68—282	160369
	Annika Sörenstam (SWE)	71-70-73-68—282	160369
4	Maria Hjörth (SWE)	70-70-72-71—283	104317
5	Seon Hwa Lee (KOR)	73-71-68-72—284	83963
6	Na Yeon Choi (KOR)	74-72-69-70—285	58859
	Hee-Won Han (KOR)	72-69-70-74—285	58859
	Mi Hyun Kim (KOR)	70-70-76-69—285	58859
9	Inbee Park (KOR)	73-70-70-73—286	45289
10	Se Ri Pak (KOR)	72-70-73-72—287	39692
	Heather Young	69-70-74-74—287	39692
12	Karen Stupples (ENG)	67-75-74-72—288	35621
13	Natalie Gulbis	69-74-73-73—289	32364
	Karrie Webb (AUS)	76-70-69-74—289	32364
15	Diana D'Alessio	74-69-72-75—290	27275
	Meg Mallon	73-73-72-72—290	27275
	Liselotte Neumann (SWE)	70-72-71-77—290	27275
	Angela Stanford	75-73-71-71—290	27275
19	Janice Moodie (SCO)	73-73-74-71—291	23815
	Sakura Yokomini (JPN)	76-73-72-70—291	23815
21	Helen Alfredsson (SWE)	75-72-73-72—292	19506
	Paula Creamer	71-74-73-74—292	19506
	Cristie Kerr	74-72-66-80—292	19506
	Candie Kung (TPE)	73-74-75-70—292	19506
	Brittany Lang	75-70-72-75—292	19506
	Jee Young Lee (KOR)	73-71-75-73—292	19506
	Angela Park (BRA)	77-71-73-71—292	19506
	Michele Redman	71-72-76-73—292	19506
	Yani Tseng (TPE)	72-71-75-74—292	19506
30	Amanda Blumenhurst (am)	73-73-73-74—293	
31	Heather Daly-Donofrio	75-71-73-75—294	14190
	Rachel Hetherington (AUS)	76-69-74-75—294	14190
	Jeong Jang (KOR)	73-73-74-74—294	14190
	Ai Miyazato (JPN)	68-74-77-75—294	14190
	Ji-Young Oh (KOR)	77-72-71-74—294	14190
	Shiho Oyama (JPN)	72-72-76-74—294	14190
	Ji-Yai Shin (KOR)	73-71-76-74—294	14190
38	Katherine Hull (AUS)	76-70-74-75—295	11271
	Hee Young Park (KOR)	75-72-74-74—295	11271
	Morgan Pressel	71-74-75-75—295	11271
	Giulia Sergas ITA)	74-75-77-69—295	11271
42	Shi Hyun Ahn (KOR)	74-72-74-76—296	9383
	H J Choi (KOR)	72-74-74-76—296	9383
	Sophie Gustafson (SWE)	74-71-76-75—296	9383
	Mhairi McKay (SCO)	78-71-72-75—296	9383
	Lindsey Wright (AUS)	73-73-76-74—296	9383
47	Beth Bader	76-71-75-75—297	7887
	Marisa Baena (COL)	73-72-76-76—297	7887
	Minea Blomqvist (FIN)	75-74-76-72—297	7887
	Momoko Ueda (JPN)	71-75-76-75—297	7887
51	Silvia Cavalleri (ITA)	76-72-71-79—298	6819
	Russy Gulyanamitta (THA)	78-70-74-76—298	6819
	Soo-Yun Kang (KOR)	72-76-74-76—298	6819
	Becky Morgan (WAL)	72-77-72-77—298	6819
55	Laura Davies (ENG)	76-71-75-77—299	6106
	Pat Hurst	73-72-77-77—299	6106

55T	Reilley Rankin	72-77-70-80—299	6106
58	Il Mi Chung (KOR)	71-77-75-77—300	5394
	Juli Inkster	74-75-76-75—300	6394
	Teresa Lu (TPE)	72-76-75-77—300	6394
	Maria Jose Uribe (am)	70-74-78-78—300	
	Wendy Ward	75-71-78-76—300	6394
63	Moira Dunn	76-68-78-79—301	4783
	Julieta Granada (PAR)	74-73-74-80—301	4783
	Carin Koch (SWE)	72-76-75-78—301	4783
	Meena Lee (KOR)	71-75-75-80—301	4783
	Sarah Lee (KOR)	74-74-72-81—301	4783
68	Mallory Blackwelder (am)	71-76-76-79—302	
	Alena Sharp (CAN)	75-72-78-77—302	4478
70	Meaghan Francella	75-73-79-76—303	4376
71	Sung Ah Yim (KOR)	76-73-80-83—312	4274

The following players missed the cut.

72	Kyeong Bae (KOR)	74-76—150
	Becky Brewerson (WAL)	74-76—150
	Nicole Castrales	75-75—150
	Eun-Hee Ji (KOR)	78-72—150
	Young Kim (KOR)	73-77—150
	Karin Sjodin (SWE)	76-74—150
	Linda Wessberg (SWE)	76-74—150
79	Sun-Ju Ahn (KOR)	74-77—151
	Louise Friberg (SWE)	76-75—151
	Jin Joo Hong (KOR)	76-75—151
	Catriona Matthew (SCO)	77-74—151
	Charlotte Mayorkas	77-74—151
	Jane Park	73-78—151
	Alison Walshe (am)	78-73—151
86	Karine Icher (FRA)	76-76—152
	Hilary Lunke	77-75—152
	Jennifer Rosales (PHI)	76-76—152
89	Grace Park (KOR)	76-77—153
	Sherri Steinhauer	78-75—153
	Carri Wood	78-75—153

92	Laura Diaz	79-75—154
	Jimin Kang (KOR)	76-78—154
	Christina Kim	77-77—154
	Na On Min (KOR)	79-75—154
96	Amy Hung (TPE)	72-83—155
	Birdie Kim (KOR)	80-75—155
	In-Kyung Kim (KOR)	77-78—155
	Brittany Lincicome	75-80—155
	Jill McGill	78-77—155
	Gloria Park (KOR)	77-78—155
	Stacy Prammanasudh	77-78—155
103	Amy Alcott	79-77—156
	Gwladys Nocera (FRA)	77-79—156
105	Mina Harigae (am)	82-76—158
	Bettina Hauert (GER)	77-81—158
107	Kim Saiki-Maloney	82-78—160
	Patricia Meunier-Lebouc (FRA)	83 W/D
	Nicole Perrot (CHI)	W/D
	Dorothy Delasin	disqualified

2007 Kraft Nabisco Championship

[6673–72]

Prize money: $1.8 million

1	Karrie Webb* (AUS)	70-68-76-65—279	$270000	20T	Sherri Steinhauer	71-78-70-74—293	22881
1	Morgan Pressel	74-72-70-69—285	$300000		Karrie Webb (AUS)	70-77-73-73—293	22881
2	Brittany Lincicome	72-71-71-72—286	140945	24	Juli Inkster	75-75-72-72—294	20451
	Catriona Matthew (SCO)	70-73-72-71—286	140945		Christina Kim	72-77-71-74—294	20451
	Suzann Pettersen (NOR)	72-69-71-74—286	140945	26	Jimin Kang (KOR)	76-73-73-73—295	19337
5	Shi Hyun Ahn (KOR)	68-73-74-72—287	69688	27	Nicole Castrale	76-71-74-75—296	17565
	Meaghan Francella	72-72-69-74—287	69688		Julieta Granada (PAR)	74-77-72-73—296	17565
	Stacy Lewis (am)	71-73-73-70—287			Angela Park (BRA)	73-74-75-74—296	17565
	Stacy Prammanasudh	76-70-70-71—287	69688		Lindsey Wright (AUS)	74-69-77-76—296	17565
9	Maria Hjörth (SWE)	70-73-72-73—288	50114	31	Laura Diaz	73-79-71-74—297	14116
10	Lorena Ochoa (MEX)	69-71-77-72—289	41340		Young Jo (KOR)	74-76-72-75—297	14116
	Se Ri Pak (KOR)	72-70-70-77—289	41340		Mi Hyun Kim (KOR)	74-72-74-77—297	14116
	Angela Stanford	72-75-73-69—289	41340		Leta Lindley	73-75-73-76—297	14116
13	Jee Young Lee (KOR)	70-77-71-72—290	34321		Hee-Young Park (KOR)	73-74-77-73—297	14116
	Sarah Lee (KOR)	72-74-70-74—290	34321		Annika Sörenstam (SWE)	75-76-71-75—297	14116
15	Paula Creamer	73-67-73-78—291	28651		Heather Young	74-75-76-72—297	14116
	Brittany Lang	71-73-75-72—291	28651	38	Helen Alfredsson (SWE)	78-69-74-77—298	10782
	Ai Miyazato (JPN)	76-73-69-73—291	28651		Marisa Baena (COL)	73-75-73-77—298	10782
	Ji-Yai Shin (KOR)	76-72-71-72—291	28651		Dorothy Delasin	73-76-76-75—298	10782
19	Moira Dunn	76-73-72-71—292	25108		Yuri Fudoh (JPN)	73-76-75-74—298	10782
20	Laura Davies (ENG)	74-73-73-73—293	22881		Pat Hurst	71-76-74-77—298	10782
	Cristie Kerr	75-73-72-73—293	22881		Gwladys Nocera (FRA)	72-77-72-77—298	10782

Other players who made the cut: Sophie Gustafson (SWE), Kim Saiki-Maloney, Sakura Yokomine (JPN), 299; Wendy Doolan, Shiho Oyama (JPN), Gloria Park (KOR), 300; Tina Barrett, Hee-Won Han (KOR), Young Kim (KOR), Becky MorgaN (WAL), 301; Karine Icher (FRA), Jeong Jang (KOR), Reilley Rankin, Veronica Zorzi (ITA), 302; Diana D'Alessio, Soo-Yun Kang (KOR), Aree Song (KOR), 303; Carin Koch (SWE). Candie Kung (TPE), Liselotte Neumann (SWE), Nicole Perrot (CHI), 304; Mi-Jeong Jeon (KOR), 305; Tracy Hanson, Taylor Leon (am), Michele Redman, 306; Esther Choe (am); Joo Mi Kim (KOR), Grace Park (KOR), 307; Jin Joo Hong (KOR), 310; Meg Mallon, 311

2006 Kraft Nabisco Championship

[6569–72]

Prize money: $1.8 million

1	Karrie Webb* (AUS)	70-68-76-65—279	$270000	19T	Veronica Zorzi (ITA)	74-72-75-71—292	21221
2	Lorena Ochoa (MEX)	62-71-74-72—279	168226	24	Paula Creamer	69-71-79-74—293	17610
*Webb won sudden death play-off:: Webb 5, Ochoa 6					Dorothy Delasin	72-72-74-75—293	17610
3	Natalie Gulbis	73-71-68-68—280	108222		Karine Icher (FRA)	73-73-77-70—293	17610
	Michelle Wie	66-71-73-70—280	108222		Carin Koch (SWE)	70-72-76-75—293	17610
5	Juli Inkster	69-73-74-68—284	75985		Candie King (TAI)	72-75-72-74—293	17610
6	Hee-Won Han (KOR)	75-72-68-71—286	57104	29	Young Jo (KOR)	72-73-75-74—294	14199
	Annika Sörenstam (SWE)	71-72-73-70—286	57104		Meena Lee (KOR)	72-76-72-74—294	14199
8	Shi Hyun Ahn (KOR)	70-71-71-75—287	41293		Patricia Meunier-Lebouc	77-67-77-73—294	14199
	Helen Alfredsson (SWE)	70-72-72-73—287	41293		(FRA)		
	Brittany Lang	70-74-72-71—287	41293		Ai Miyazato (JPN)	70-77-72-75—294	14199
11	Stacy Prammanasudh	67-73-76-72—288	33388		Becky Morgan (WAL)	76-70-75-73—294	14199
	Michele Redman	72-72-72-72—288	33388		Jennifer Rosales (PHI)	72-76-73-73—294	14199
13	Beth Daniel	72-72-72-73—289	29289	35	Il Mi Chung (KOR)	72-77-73-73—295	11329
	Morgan Pressel	69-76-70-74—289	29289		Cristie Kerr	71-76-75-73—295	11329
15	Yuri Fudoh (JPN)	75-73-69-73—290	26710		Grace Park (KOR)	74-72-78-71—295	11329
	Angela Park (am)	68-73-75-74—290			Sherri Steinhauer	72-77-75-71—295	11329
17	Pat Hurst	73-73-73-72—291	24592		Wendy Ward	71-75-76-73—295	11329
	Karen Stupples (ENG)	69-74-72-76—291	24592	40	Suzann Pettersen (NOR)	75-75-75-74—296	9763
19	Tina Barrett	72-75-74-71—292	21221		Aree Song (KOR)	74-76-72-74—296	9763
	Jeong Jang (KOR)	71-75-76-70—292	21221	42	Marisa Baena (COL)	75-72-71-79—297	8842
	Young Kim (KOR)	74-73-70-75—292	21221		Mi Hyun Kim (KOR)	75-74-75-73—297	8842
	Seon Hwa Lee (KOR)	69-69-74-80—292	21221		Rachel Hetherington (AUS)	74-75-76-72—297	8842

Other players who made the cut: Kyeong Bae (KOR), Jimin Kang (KOR), Birdie Kim (KOR), Sarah Lee (KOR), Janice Moodie (SCO), Liselotte Neumann (SWE), Se Ri Pak (KOR), 298; Johanna Head (ENG), Christine Kim, Gwladys Nocera (FRA), Kim Saiki, 299; Jee Young Lee (KOR), Sung Ah Yim (KOR), 300; Lorie Kane (CAN), Soo Young Moon (KOR), Reilley Rankin, 301; Brandie Burton, 302; Maru Martinez (am), In-Bee Park (am), 304; Joo Mi Kim (KOR), 305; Nicole Perrot (CHI), 306; Katherine Hull (AUS), Meg Mallon, 307; Kate Golden, Sydnee Michaels (am), 308; A J Eathorne (CAN), 314

2005 Kraft Nabisco Championship   [6460–72]

Prize money: $1.8 million

1	Annika Sörenstam (SWE)	70-69-66-68—273	$270000
2	Rosie Jones	69-70-71-71—281	166003
3	Laura Diaz	75-69-71-68—283	106791
	Cristie Kerr	72-70-70-71—283	106791
5	Mi Hyun Kim (KOR)	69-71-72-72—284	68165
	Grace Park (KOR)	73-68-76-67—284	68165
7	Juli Inkster	70-74-72-69—285	51350
8	Lorie Kane (CAN)	71-76-69-70—286	44988
9	Beth Daniel	74-72-69-72—287	34591
	Dorothy Delasin (PHI)	71-72-73-71—287	34591
	Wendy Doolan (AUS)	74-69-73-71—287	34591
	Candie Kung (TPE)	72-73-71-71—287	34591
	Reilley Rankin	73-68-74-72—287	34591
14	Brandie Burton	72-71-72-73—288	27175
	Kim Saiki	74-71-70-73—288	27175
	Michelle Wie (am)	70-74-73-71—288	
17	Natalie Gulbis	73-71-72-73—289	24267
	Hee-Won Han (KOR)	76-71-69-73—289	24267
19	Shi Hyun Ahn (KOR)	77-76-71-66—290	21692
	Paula Creamer	74-72-72-72—290	21692
	Young Kim (KOR)	76-70-70-74—290	21692
	Morgan Pressel (am)	70-73-72-75—290	
23	Laura Davies (ENG)	73-71-71-77—292	19086
	Pat Hurst	71-74-74-73—292	19086
	Sherri Steinhauer	71-72-75-74—292	19086
	Karen Stupples (ENG)	69-80-70-73—292	19086
27	Dawn Coe-Jones (CAN)	74-73-74-72—293	16723
	Jeong Jang (KOR)	77-74-71-71—293	16723
	Se Ri Pak (KOR)	77-70-70-76—293	16723
30	Michelle Estill	71-79-71-73—294	14565
	Julieta Granada (PAR) (am)	75-71-70-78—294	
	Carin Koch (SWE)	70-73-75-76—294	14565
	Jill McGill	73-72-77-72—294	14565
	Stacy Prammanasudh	75-74-74-71—294	14565
35	Helen Alfredsson (SWE)	76-72-74-73—295	12383
	Leta Lindley	74-77-73-71—295	12383
	Lorena Ochoa (MEX)	76-75-73-71—295	12383
	Jennifer Rosales (PHI)	71-79-74-71—295	12383
39	Tina Barrett	73-77-71-75—296	10288
	Yuri Fudoh (JPN)	75-75-75-71—296	10288
	Rachel Hetherington (AUS)	77-73-72-74—296	10288
	Christina Kim	76-71-73-76—296	10288
	Janice Moodie (SCO)	74-77-74-71—296	10288

Other players who made the cut: Joo Mi Kim (KOR), Catriona Matthew (SCO), Ai Miyazato (JPN), Gloria Park (KOR), Charlotta Sörenstam (SWE), Karrie Webb (AUS), 297; Heather Bowie, Tina Fischer (GER), Meg Mallon, Jane Park (am), Wendy Ward, 298; Liselotte Neumann (SWE), Giulia Sergas (ITA), Bo Bae Song (KOR), 299; Katherine Hull (AUS), Kelli Kuehne, Michele Redman, Angela Stanford, 300; Donna Andrews, Betsy King, 301; Trish Johnson (ENG), Aree Song (KOR), 302; Sophie Gustafson (SWE), Emilee Klein, 303; Stephanie Arricau (FRA), Hilary Lunke, 304; Heather Daly-Donofrio, Candy Hannemann (BRA), 305; Nancy Scranton, 306; Catrin Nilsmark (SWE), 310; Jamie Hullett, 311; Laurel Kean, 316

2004 Nabisco Dinah Shore   [6673–72]

Prize money: $1.6 million

1	Grace Park (KOR)	72-69-67-69—277	$240000
2	Aree Song (KOR)	66-73-69-70—278	146826
3	Karrie Webb (AUS)	68-71-71-69—279	106512
4	Michelle Wie (am)	69-72-69-71—281	
5	Cristie Kerr	71-71-71-69—282	74358
	Catriona Matthew (SCO)	67-75-70-70—282	74358
7	Mi-Hyun Kim (KOR)	71-70-71-71—283	54261
8	Rosie Jones	67-73-71-73—284	36737
	Christina Kim	72-72-70-70—284	36737
	Candie Kung (TPE)	69-75-71-69—284	36737
	Jung Yeon Lee (KOR)	69-69-71-75—284	36737
	Lorena Ochoa (MEX)	67-76-74-67—284	36737
13	Hee-Won Han (KOR)	72-71-71-71—285	26420
	Stacy Prammanasudh	71-71-69-74—285	26420
	Annika Sörenstam (SWE)	71-76-69-69—285	26420
16	Laura Davies (ENG)	71-77-70-68—286	20633
	Wendy Doolan (AUS)	70-69-72-75—286	20633
	Young Kim (KOR)	74-72-67-73—286	20633
	Carin Koch (SWE)	70-72-71-73—286	20633
	Se Ri Pak (KOR)	72-73-72-69—286	20633
	Karen Stupples (ENG)	70-76-68-72—286	20633
22	Michele Redman	73-73-70-71—287	17846
23	Jeong Jang (KOR)	76-71-70-72—289	17203
24	Brandie Burton	70-76-71-73—290	15944
	Tammie Green	71-78-71-70—290	15944
	Jane Park (am)	71-74-73-72—290	
	Dottie Pepper	68-70-74-78—290	15944
28	Danielle Ammaccapane	75-77-73-66—291	13682
	Donna Andrews	70-74-73-74—291	13682
	Tina Barrett	75-70-73-73—291	13682
	Juli Inkster	74-74-73-70—291	13682
	Wendy Ward	72-74-70-75—291	13682
33	Vicki Goetze-Ackerman	73-79-71-69—292	11897
	Kelly Robbins	69-74-78-71—292	11897
35	Dorothy Delasin (PHI)	76-71-71-75—293	10306
	Pat Hurst	72-76-69-76—293	10306
	Lorie Kane (CAN)	74-76-72-71—293	10306
	Rachel Teske (AUS)	75-71-71-76—293	10306
	Iben Tinning (DEN)	70-75-77-71—293	10306
40	Helen Alfredsson (SWE)	75-72-71-76—294	8541
	Beth Daniel	72-74-74-74—294	8541
	Kate Golden	73-78-74-69—294	8541
	Elizabeth Janangelo (am)	71-78-70-75—294	
	Emilee Klein	71-73-76-74—294	8541

Other players who made the cut: Beth Bauer, Paula Creamer (am), Jill McGill 295; Sophie Gustafson (SWE), Stephanie Louden, Meg Mallon, Sherri Steinhauer 296; Michelle Ellis (AUS), Laurel Kean, Becky Morgan (WAL) 297; Jackie Gallagher-Smith, Ji-Hee Lee (KOR), Charlotta Sörenstam (SWE) 298; Moira Dunn, Natalie Gulbis, Betsy King, Jennifer Rosales (PHI) 300; Marisa Baena (COL), Heather Bowie, Heather Daly-Donofrio, Soo-Yun Kang (KOR), Miho Koga (JPN), Yu Ping Lin (TPE), Janice Moodie (SCO) 301; Hilary Lunke 302; JoAnne Carner, Dawn Coe-Jones, Joanne Mills (AUS) 303; Mhairi McKay (SCO), Shani Waugh (AUS) 304; Mardi Lunn (AUS) 305; Kelli Kuehne 306; Amy Alcott 308; Nancy Lopez WD

2003 Nabisco Dinah Shore

Prize money: $1.6 million

[6520–72]

1	Patricia Meunier Lebouc (FRA)	70-68-70-73—281	$240000	21T	Jeong Jang (KOR)	75-73-76-69—293	17440
2	Annika Sörenstam (SWE)	68-72-71-71—282	146120		Virada Nirapathpongporn (am)	76-72-72-73—293	
3	Lorena Ochoa (MEX)	71-70-74-68—283	106000		Michele Redman	70-72-76-75—293	17440
4	Laura Davies (ENG)	70-75-69-70—284	82000		Aree Song (am)	72-77-73-71—293	
5	Beth Daniel	75-74-68-70—287	51200		Karrie Webb (AUS)	70-79-71-73—293	17440
	Laura Diaz	76-71-69-71—287	51200	27	Leta Lindley	76-70-75-73—294	15840
	Maria Hjörth (SWE)	72-72-73-70—287	51200	28	Tammie Green	77-71-73-74—295	14160
	Catriona Matthew (SCO)	71-74-72-70—287	51200		Christina Kim	72-76-71-76—295	14160
9	Jennifer Rosales (PHI)	74-70-72-72—288	35600		Betsy King	75-74-70-76—295	14160
	Michelle Wie (am)	72-74-66-76—288			Candie Kung (TPE)	74-75-74-72—295	14160
11	Juli Inkster	75-74-66-75—290	29160		Charlotta Sörenstam (SWE)	73-74-71-77—295	14160
	Cristie Kerr	74-71-74-71—290	29160	33	Heather Bowie	72-78-72-74—296	11373
	Woo-Soon Ko (KOR)	74-73-70-73—290	29160		Heather Daly-Donofrio	74-77-72-73—296	11373
	Rosie Jones	71-75-72-72—290	29160		Moira Dunn	74-80-73-69—296	11373
15	Dawn Coe-Jones (CAN)	72-74-72-73—291	22080		Amy Fruhwirth	73-75-75-73—296	11373
	Dorothy Delasin (PHI)	71-71-76-73—291	22080		Vicki Goetze-Ackerman	75-74-74-73—296	11373
	Catrin Nilsmark (SWE)	71-78-73-69—291	22080		Meg Mallon	72-76-73-75—296	11373
	Se Ri Pak (KOR)	71-72-71-77—291	22080	39	Beth Bauer	74-76-70-77—297	9440
	Karen Stupples (ENG)	71-71-76-73—291	22080		Jackie Gallagher-Smith	75-74-74-74—297	9440
20	Hee-Won Han (KOR)	73-74-75-70—292	19040		Lorie Kane (CAN)	72-72-78-75—297	9440
21	Danielle Ammaccapane	75-68-78-72—293	17440				

Other players who made the cut: Brandie Burton, Raquel Carriedo (ESP), Michelle Ellis (AUS), Liselotte Neumann (SWE), Gloria Park (KOR), Kelly Robbins 298; Natalie Gulbis, Rachel Teske (AUS), Wendy Ward 299; Sophie Gustafson (SWE), Pat Hurst, Kelli Kuehne, Barb Mucha, Dottie Pepper, Angela Stanford 300; Nanci Bowen, Akiko Fukushima (JPN), Laurel Kean, Mi-Hyun Kim (KOR), Joanne Morley (ENG), Kim Saiki, Lindsey Wright (AUS) (am) 301; Helen Alfredsson (SWE), Donna Andrews, Emilee Klein, Stephanie Louden, Janice Moodie (SCO), Shani Waugh (AUS) 302; Mhairi McKay (SCO), Patty Sheehan 303; Suzanne Strudwick (ENG) 304; Tina Fischer (GER) 305; Tracy Hanson 306; Kasumi Fujii (JPN), Yu Ping Lin (TPE) 307; Pat Bradley 308; Dale Eggeling 310; Mardi Lunn (AUS) 311

2002 Nabisco Dinah Shore

Prize money: $1.5 million

[6460–72]

1	Annika Sörenstam (SWE)	70-71-71-68—280	$225000	21T	Janice Moodie (SCO)	73-73-73-70—289	16350
2	Liselotte Neuman (SWE)	69-70-73-69—281	136987	25	Sophie Gustafson (SWE)	77-69-71-73—290	13800
3	Rosie Jones	72-69-72-69—282	88125		Hee-Won Han (KOR)	74-74-73-69—290	13800
	Cristie Kerr	74-70-70-68—282	88125		Laurel Kean	79-74-71-66—290	13800
5	Akiko Fukushima (JPN)	73-76-68-66—283	56250		Suzann Pettersen (NOR)	74-71-73-72—290	13800
	Carin Koch (SWE)	73-73-71-66—283	56250		Michele Redman	75-70-72-73—290	13800
7	Karrie Webb (AUS)	75-70-67-72—284	42375	30	Laura Diaz	74-73-73-71—291	12225
8	Lorena Ochoa (am)	75-69-71-70—285			Aree Song Wongluekiet (am)	71-74-73-73—291	
9	Becky Iverson	71-74-68-73—286	31050	32	Heather Daly-Donofrio	74-73-72-73—292	11100
	Lorie Kane (CAN)	73-72-70-71—286	31050		Kathryn Marshall (SCO)	75-72-73-72—292	11100
	Leta Lindley	72-72-72-70—286	31050		Alison Nicholas (ENG)	76-71-70-75—292	11100
	Se Ri Pak (KOR)	74-71-71-70—286	31050		Gloria Park (KOR)	70-76-75-71—292	11100
	Grace Park (KOR)	75-73-70-68—286	31050	36	Marisa Baena (COL)	79-74-68-72—293	8524
14	Vicki Goetze-Ackerman	74-73-68-72—287	21900		Maria Hjörth (SWE)	76-73-69-75—293	8524
	Heather Bowie	75-71-72-69—287	21900		Pat Hurst	78-72-71-72—293	8524
	Beth Daniel	71-70-75-71—287	21900		Chris Johnson	75-71-76-71—293	8524
	Dorothy Delasin (PHI)	72-73-69-73—287	21900		Betsy King	71-75-73-74—293	8524
	Kris Tschetter	74-69-73-71—287	21900		Kelli Kuehne	74-73-73-73—293	8524
19	Juli Inkster	73-76-71-68—288	18225		Meg Mallon	75-73-74-71—293	8524
	Mhairi McKay (SCO)	73-72-73-70—288	18225		Sherri Steinhauer	73-78-70-72—293	8524
21	Laura Davies (ENG)	75-75-69-70—289	16350		Wendy Ward	77-74-73-69—293	8524
	Wendy Doolan (AUS)	78-70-72-69—289	16350				
	Mi Hyun Kim (KOR)	74-75-69-71—289	16350				

Other players who made the cut: Helen Alfredsson (SWE), Yuri Fudoh (JPN), Jeong Jang (KOR), Yu Ping Lin (TPE) 294; Donna Andrews, Barb Mucha 295; Penny Hammel, Karin Icher (FRA), Catriona Matthew (SCO), Deb Richard 296; Tina Barrett, Amy Fruhwirth, Jill McGill 298; Moira Dunn, Kelly Robbins, Pearl Sinn (KOR), Naree Song Wongluekiet (am) 299; Brandie Burton, Charlotta Sörenstam (SWE), Sherri Turner 300; Dina Ammaccapane, Rachel Teske (AUS), Karen Weiss 301; Amy Alcott, Kate Golden 302; Emilee Klein 303; Patty Sheehan 305; Tammie Green 306; Meredith Duncan (am) 307; Hiromi Kobayashi (JPN) 312

2001 Nabisco Dinah Shore

[6520–72]

Prize money: $1.25 million

1	Annika Sörenstam (SWE)	72-70-70-69—281	$225000	21T	Loreno Ochoa (MEX) (am)	72 71-74-73—290	
2	Karrie Webb (AUS)	73-72-70-69—284	87557	23	Becky Iverson	75-70-72-74—291	15955
	Janice Moodie (SCO)	72-72-70-70—284	87557	24	Maria Hjörth	73-72-75-72—292	14540
	Dottie Pepper	71-71-71-71—284	87557		Tammie Green	72-73-75-72—292	14540
	Akiko Fukushima (JPN)	74-68-70-72—284	87557		Kelly Robbins	75-72-72-73—292	14540
	Rachel Teske (AUS)	72-73-66-73—284	87557		Penny Hammel	70-75-72-75—292	14540
7	Sophie Gustafson (SWE)	72-74-70-69—285	41891	28	Meg Mallon	74-71-78-70—293	12063
	Brandie Burton	74-69-72-70—285	41891		Grace Park (KOR)	75-75-72-71—293	12063
9	Laura Diaz	71-74-69-72—286	33589		Dina Ammaccapane	74-74-73-72—293	12063
	Pat Hurst	70-68-74-74—286	33589		Rosie Jones	73-73-75-72—293	12063
11	Laura Davies (ENG)	71-73-75-68—287	25957		Alison Nicholas (ENG)	71-75-75-72—293	12063
	Dorothy Delasin (PHI)	73-70-74-70—287	25957		Stefania Croce (ITA)	74-72-73-74—293	12063
	Se Ri Pak (KOR)	73-69-73-72—287	25957		Emilee Klein	72-74-72-75—293	12063
	Tina Barrett	71-73-70-73—287	25957	35	Kelli Kuehne	75-70-75-74—294	10446
15	Mi Hyun Kim (KOR)	74-71-70-73—288	20736	36	Jan Crafter (AUS)	78-73-74-70—295	9124
	Carin Koch (SWE)	70-69-75-74—288	20736		Heather Bowie	77-73-73-71—295	9124
	Juli Inkster	70-75-68-75—288	20736		Charlotte Sörenstam	78-71-75-71—295	9124
18	Liselotte Neumann (SWE)	70-74-74-71—289	18220		(SWE)		
	Jeong Jang (KOR)	74-71-71-73—289	18220		Nancy Scranton	72-75-75-73—295	9124
	Michele Redman	71-72-71-75—289	18220		Moira Dunn	78-73-70-74—295	9124
21	Jill McGill	75-71-70-74—290	16711		Wendy Ward	76-73-70-76—295	9124

Other players who made the cut: Amy Fruhwirth, Joanne Morley (ENG), Danielle Ammaccapane, Lorie Kane (CAN) 296; Helen Alfredsson (SWE), Aree Wongluekiet (am) 297; Jenny Lidback (PER), Cindy Figg Currier, Nanci Bowen, Leta Lindley, Chris Johnson, Cathy Johnston Forbes, Donna Andrews 298; Beth Daniel, Laurie Kean, Pearl Sinn (KOR) 299; Jackie Gallagher-Smith, Vickie Goetze Ackerman, Caroline McMillan, Vicki Fergon, Naree Wongluekiet (am) 300; Wendy Doolan (AUS), Nancy Lopez, Hiromi Kobayashi (JPN) 301; Cristie Kerr, Susie Redman 302; Joan Pitcock, Catrin Nilsmark (SWE), Kellee Booth 303; Ok Hee Ku (JPN) 305; Dawn Coe-Jones, Marine Monnet (FRA) 306; Betsy King 309

2000 Nabisco Dinah Shore

[6520–72]

Prize money: $1.25 million

1	Karrie Webb (AUS)	67-70-67-70—274	$187500	17T	Kaori Higo (JPN)	76-72-73-71—292	14321
2	Dottie Pepper	68-72-72-72—284	116366		Sherri Steinhauer	73-71-77-71—292	14321
3	Meg Mallon	75-70-73-67—285	84916		Charlotta Sörenstam	75-75-70-72—292	14321
4	Cathy Johnston-	74-71-71-70—286	59755		(SWE)		
	Forbes				Juli Inkster	76-71-73-72—292	14321
5	Michele Redman	73-73-69-71—286	59755		Nancy Bowen	75-72-73-72—292	14321
6	Helen Dobson (ENG)	73-74-72-68—287	40750		Carin Koch (SWE)	79-70-70-73—292	14321
	Chris Johnson	73-68-73-73—287	40750		Nancy Scranton	78-70-71-73—292	14321
8	Rosie Jones	74-71-74-69—288	31135		Barb Mucha	77-71-70-74—292	14321
	Kim Saiki	72-77-68-71—288	31135	27	Jane Geddes	74-72-78-69—293	10969
10	Jenny Lidback (PER)	75-72-74-68—289	24170		Leta Lindley	73-76-73-71—293	10969
	Wendy Doolan (AUS)	73-73-69-74—289	24170		Catriona Matthew	72-77-73-71—293	10969
	Pat Hurst	72-72-70-75—289	24170		(SCO)		
	Aree Song	75-71-68-75—289			Alison Nicholas (ENG)	71-74-74-74—293	10969
	Wongluekiet (am)			31	Susie Redman	73-75-74-72—294	9507
14	Kristi Albers	77-71-72-70—290	20845		Caroline McMillan	73-74-74-73—294	9507
	Se Ri Pak (KOR)	73-71-77-70—291	18957		(ENG)		
	Janice Moodie (SCO)	74-72-70-75—291	18957		Gail Graham (CAN)	71-75-75-73—294	9507
17	Kelly Robbins	79-69-73-71—292	14321		Brandie Burton	74-75-71-74—294	9507
	Annika Sörenstam	76-72-73-71—292	14321				
	(SWE)						

Other players who made the cut: Akiko Fukushima (JPN), Tina Barrett, Dawn Coe Jones, Laura Davies (ENG), Cristie Kerr, Fumiko Muraguchi (JPN), Lorie Kane (CAN), Beth Bauer (am) 295; Pearl Sinn (KOR), Nancy Lopez, Wendy Ward, Barb Whitehead 296; Cindy McCurdy, Becky Iverson, Mi Hyun Kim (KOR), Jill McGill, Patty Sheehan, Beth Daniel 297; Kris Tschetter, Donna Andrews, Mary Beth Zimmerman, Jan Stephenson (AUS) 298; Helen Alfredsson (SWE), Eva Dahlloff (SWE), Jackie Gallagher-Smith, Catrin Nilsmark (SWE), Amy Fruhwirth 299; Mayumi Hirase (JPN), Penny Hammel, Tammie Green, Sherri Turner, Rachel Hetherington (AUS) 300; Maggie Will, Ayako Okamoto (JPN), Julie Piers, Kathryn Marshall (SCO) 301; Marnie McGuire (NZL) 302; Liselotte Neumann (SWE) 306; Dale Eggeling 309

1999 Nabisco Dinah Shore

[6460–72]

Prize money: $1 million

1	D Pepper	70-66-67-66—269	$150000	13T	K Tschetter	68-70-73-75—286	13712
2	M Mallon	66-69-71-69—275	93093	21	M Spencer-Devlin	72-69-77-69—287	9692
3	K Webb (AUS)	73-71-70-66—280	67933		H Stacy	74-74-69-70—287	9692
4	K Robbins	69-73-67-72—281	52837		M Estill	70-76-71-70—287	9692
5	C Sörenstam (SWE)	72-68-76-66—282	42772		R Hetherington (AUS)	70-74-71-72—287	9692
6	J Inkster	72-66-71-74—283	35224		N Lopez	72-73-69-73—287	9692
7	C Matthew (SCO)	72-73-69-70—284	26502		D Eggeling	73-70-70-74—287	9692
	A Sörenstam (SWE)	70-73-71-70—284	26502		H Kobayashi (JPN)	70-69-74-74—287	9692
	J Moodie (SCO)	69-68-75-72—284	26502		D Andrews	70-69-74-74—287	9692
10	S Steinhauer	70-72-72-71—285	19289	29	H Dobson (ENG)	74-72-74-68—288	7812
	M Hjörth (SWE)	77-68-68-72—285	19289		D Dormann	74-73-71-70—288	7812
	H Alfredsson (SWE)	69-71-73-72—285	19289		L Kane (CAN)	73-74-71-70—288	7812
13	R Jones	73-70-73-70—286	13712		J Pitcock	77-68-73-70—288	7812
	M Will	72-71-73-70—286	13712	33	W Ward	74-73-72-70—289	6516
	M Redman	71-74-69-72—286	13712		A Alcott	74-71-71-73—289	6516
	P Bradley	73-69-72-72—286	13712		J Geddes	73-72-71-73—289	6516
	C McCurdy	70-74-69-73—286	13712		T Green	70-75-71-73—289	6516
	Se Ri Pak (KOR)	73-69-69-75—286	13712		B Mucha	73-75-67-74—289	6516
	M Hirase	70-72-69-75—286	13712		J Crafter (AUS)	70-74-71-74—289	6516

Other players who made the cut: K Saiki, T Tombs, N Bowen, G Park (am) 290; K Marshall (SCO), E Klein, M Nause, P Hurst, B Daniel 291; G Graham, T Johnson, C Figg-Currier 292; T Barrett, C Johnson, M McGeorge, D Coe-Jones, K Albers, S Turner, A Nicholas (ENG) 293; L Neumann (SWE), M McGann, T Hanson, M Hattori 294; C Johnston-Forbes, P Sinn, L Kiggens 295; V Fergon, Dina Ammaccapane 296; D Richard, J Piers, J Chuasiriporn (am) 297; E Crosby, C Flom, L Davies (ENG) 298; P Sheehan, TJ Myers, Dani Ammaccapane, K Harada 299; B King 300; B Iverson 301; V Skinner, S Gustafson 302

Kraft Nabisco History

This event was inaugurated in 1972 as the Colgate Dinah Shore and continued to be sponsored by Colgate until 1981. Nabisco took over the sponsorship in 1982; and the Nabisco Dinah Shore was designated a Major Championship in 1983. The Championship became the Kraft Nabisco in 2005. Mission Hills CC, Rancho Mirage, California, is the event's permanent venue.

Year	Winner	Score	Year	Winner	Score
1972	J Blalock	213	1990	B King	283
1973	M Wright	284	1991	A Alcott	273
1974	J Prentice*	289	1992	D Mochrie*	279
After a play-off with Jane Blalock and Sandra Haynie			*After a play-off with J Inkster*		
1975	S Palmer	283	1993	H Alfredsson (SWE)	284
1976	J Rankin	285	1994	D Andrews	276
1977	K Whitworth	289	1995	N Bowen	285
1978	S Post*	283	1996	P Sheehan	281
After a play-off with Penny Pulz			1997	B King	276
1979	S Post*	276	1998	P Hurst	281
After a play-off with Nancy Lopez			1999	D Pepper	269
1980	D Caponi	275	2000	K Webb (AUS)	274
1981	N Lopez	277	2001	A Sörenstam (SWE)	281
1982	S Little	278	2002	A Sörenstam (SWE)	280
1983	A Alcott	282	2003	P Meunier-Lebouc (FRA)	281
1984	J Inkster*	280	2004	G Park (KOR)	277
After a play-off with P Bradley			2005	A Sörenstam (SWE)	273
1985	A Miller	278	2006	K Webb (AUS)*	279
1986	P Bradley	280	*After a play-off with L Ochoa*		
1987	B King*	283	2007	M Pressel	285
After a play-off with P Sheehan			2008	L Ochoa (MEX)	277
1988	A Alcott	274			
1989	J Inkster	279			

du Maurier Classic History

The du Maurier Classic was inaugurated in 1973 and designated a Major Championship in 1979.
It was discontinued after 2000 and was replaced as a major on the US LPGA schedule by the Weetabix Women's British Open.

Players are of American nationality unless stated

Year	Winner	Venue	Score
1973	J Bourassa*	Montreal GC, Montreal	214
After a play-off with S Haynie and J Rankin			
1974	CJ Callison	Candiac GC, Montreal	208
1975	J Carner*	St George's CC, Toronto	214
After a play-off with C Mann			
1976	D Caponi*	Cedar Brae G&CC, Toronto	212
After a play-off with J Rankin			
1977	J Rankin	Lachute G&CC, Montreal	214
1978	J Carner	St George's CC, Toronto	278
1979	A Alcott	Richelieu Valley CC, Montreal	285
1980	P Bradley	St George's CC, Toronto	277
1981	J Stephenson (AUS)	Summerlea CC, Dorian, Quebec	278
1982	S Haynie	St George's CC, Toronto	280
1983	H Stacy	Beaconsfield CC, Montreal	277
1984	J Inkster	St George's CC, Toronto	279
1985	P Bradley	Beaconsfield CC, Montreal	278
1986	P Bradley*	Board of Trade CC, Toronto	276
After a play-off with A Okamoto			
1987	J Rosenthal	Islesmere GC, Laval, Quebec	272
1988	S Little (RSA)	Vancouver GC, Coquitlam, BC	279
1989	T Green	Beaconsfield GC, Montreal	279
1990	C Johnston	Westmount G&CC, Kitchener, Ontario	276
1991	N Scranton	Vancouver GC, Coquitlam, BC	279
1992	S Steinhauer	St Charles CC, Winnipeg, Manitoba	277
1993	B Burton*	London H&CC, Ontario	277
After a play-off with B King			
1994	M Nause	Ottawa Hunt Club, Ontario	279
1995	J Lidback	Beaconsfield CC, Montreal	280
1996	L Davies (ENG)	Edmonton CC, Edmonton, Alberta	277
1997	C Walker	Glen Abbey GC, Toronto	278
1998	B Burton	Essex G&CC, Ontario	270
1999	K Webb (AUS)	Priddis Greens G&CC, Calgary, Alberta	277
2000	M Mallon	Royal Ottawa GC, Aylmer, Quebec	282

Month by month in 2008

Another 25-foot closing birdie putt at the Arnold Palmer Invitational gives Tiger Woods his ninth win in 10 starts. Lorena Ochoa is proving almost as dominant in the women's game. Wins by 11 and seven strokes mean the Mexican has triumphed in seven of her last 12 events. Woods, however, suffers his first defeat of 2008 when he is "only" fifth in the WGC–CA Championship won by Australian Geoff Ogilvy. Graeme McDowell wins in South Korea to boost his Ryder Cup bid.

Women's Grand Slam Titles

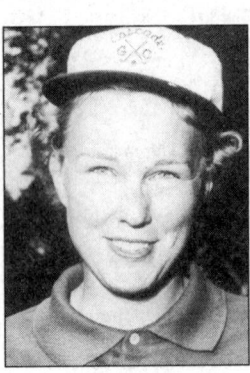

Patty Berg *Mickey Wright* *Louise Suggs*

Photographs © Phil Sheldon and Empics

	British Open[1]	US Open[2]	McDonald's LPGA[3]	Kraft Nabisco[4]	du Maurier[5]	Title-holders[6]	Western[7]	*Total Titles*
Patty Berg (USA)	0	1	0	—	—	7	7	15
Mickey Wright (USA)	0	4	4	—	—	2	3	13
Louise Suggs (USA)	0	2	1	—	—	4	4	11
Annika Sörenstam (SWE)	1	3	3	3	0	—	—	10
'Babe' Zaharias (USA)	0	3	—	—	—	3	4	10
Karrie Webb (AUS)	3	2	1	2	1	—	—	9
Betsy Rawls (USA)	0	4	2	—	—	0	2	8
Juli Inkster (USA)	0	2	2	2	1	—	—	7

[1] The Weetabix Women's British Open was designated a major on the LPGA Tour in 2001
[2] The US Open became an LPGA major in 1950
[3] The McDonald's LPGA Championship was designated a major in 1955
[4] The Kraft Nabisco event was designated a major in 1983
[5] The du Maurier event was designated a major in 1979 but discontinued after 2000
[6] The Titleholders Championship was a major from 1937–1966 and in 1972
[7] The Western event was a major from 1937 to 1967

Super Career Grand Slam: Only Karrie Webb has won five of the qualifying majors – the Women's British Open, the US Open, the LPGA Championship, the Kraft Nabisco and du Maurier. She completed her Super Grand Slam in 2002.

Career Grand Slam: Only Louise Suggs (1957), Mickey Wright (1962), Pat Bradley (1986), Julie Inkster (1999), Karrie Webb (2001) and Annika Sörenstam (2003) have won all the designated majors at the time they were playing.

Grand Slam: Only Babe Zaharias in 1950 (three majors) and Sandra Haynie (USA) in 1964 (two majors) have won all the majors available that season.

Note: Glenna Collett Vare (USA) won six US Amateurs between 1922 and 1935 including three in a row in 1928, 1929 and 1930. Jo Anne Carner (USA) won five US Amateurs between 1957 and 1968. Julie Inkster won three US Amateurs in 1980, 1981 and 1982.

PART II

Men's Professional Tournaments

World Golf Rankings 2008

Eight of the top 10 in the official World Rankings at the end of 2008 were international players and five of them – Sergio García, Padraig Harrington, Robert Karlsson, Henrik Stenson and Lee Westwood were European golfers. The only two Americans in the top 10 were Tiger Woods who retained his No 1 spot and Phil Mickelson in third place in the rankings. In all there were 38 international players in the top 50 of whom 17 were European.

Ranking		Name	Country	Points Average	Total Points	No. of Events	2006/2007 Pts Lost	2008 Pts Gained
1	(1)	Tiger Woods,	USA	12.27	490.82	40	−720.03	+426.24
2	(12)	Sergio García	ESP	8.21	427.11	52	−224.73	+408.10
3	(2)	Phil Mickelson	USA	7.19	352.09	49	−344.05	+312.68
4	(8)	Padraig Harrington	IRL	7.07	360.42	51	−287.69	+330.64
5	(10)	Vijay Singh	FIJ	6.78	372.91	55	−294.20	+357.24
6	(41)	Robert Karlsson	SWE	5.15	272.76	53	−142.58	+269.91
7	(56)	Camilo Villegas	COL	4.97	248.46	50	−99.53	+235.14
8	(4)	Ernie Els	RSA	4.87	262.85	54	−310.88	+196.19
9	(16)	Henrik Stenson	SWE	4.86	247.69	51	−227.76	+256.12
10	(23)	Lee Westwood	ENG	4.80	259.41	54	−161.76	+238.05
11	(13)	Geoff Ogilvy	AUS	4.52	217.01	48	−213.51	+212.05
12	(75)	Anthony Kim	USA	4.52	230.44	51	−92.49	+254.94
13	(3)	Jim Furyk	USA	4.40	215.37	49	−305.95	+193.77
14	(5)	Steve Stricker	USA	3.97	178.51	45	−211.09	+131.66
15	(92)	Kenny Perry	USA	3.94	201.19	51	−86.47	+218.01
16	(24)	Stewart Cink	USA	3.93	192.55	49	−181.75	+207.47
17	(7)	Adam Scott	AUS	3.89	175.12	45	−268.81	+159.40
18	(9)	KJ Choi	KOR	3.84	203.36	53	−253.50	+158.42
19	(6)	Justin Rose	ENG	3.67	168.74	46	−224.21	+81.11
20	(19)	Trevor Immelman	RSA	3.46	183.64	53	−195.38	+174.76
21	(38)	Miguel A Jiménez	ESP	3.41	183.97	54	−122.84	+169.69
22	(35)	Mike Weir,	CAN	3.41	173.69	51	−116.71	+157.63
23 ·	(89)	Justin Leonard	USA	3.30	178.13	54	−95.71	+188.71
24	(119)	Ben Curtis	USA	3.17	149.04	47	−78.01	+157.61
25	(76)	Martin Kaymer	GER	3.16	173.56	55	−86.69	+192.72
26	(22)	Ian Poulter	ENG	3.14	169.79	54	−163.18	+131.70
27	(51)	Robert Allenby	AUS	3.11	189.83	61	−133.35	+195.67
28	(29)	Tim Clark	RSA	3.03	157.78	52	−108.64	+128.82
29	(84)	Ross Fisher	ENG	2.95	153.14	52	−65.89	+132.98
30	(28)	Andres Romero	ARG	2.92	151.86	52	−122.93	+130.49
31	(17)	Luke Donald	ENG	2.89	118.35	41	−195.87	+112.95
32	(11)	Rory Sabbatini	RSA	2.83	153.04	54	−201.64	+101.58
33	(39)	Shingo Katayama	JPN	2.83	158.62	56	−112.96	+129.38
34	(106)	Graeme McDowell	NIR	2.81	160.32	57	−84.18	+164.64
35	(18)	Aaron Baddeley	AUS	2.79	133.96	48	−169.66	+94.84
36	(77)	Jeev Milkha Singh	IND	2.78	206.03	74	−135.23	+212.57
37	(33)	Stephen Ames	CAN	2.76	129.58	47	−110.52	+122.08
38	(36)	Stuart Appleby	AUS	2.67	152.34	57	−141.11	+146.59
39	(101)	Oliver Wilson	ENG	2.61	140.85	54	−68.64	+130.61
40	(232)	Rory McIlroy	NIR	2.59	103.79	40	−23.04	+96.42
41	(14)	Angel Cabrera	ARG	2.57	128.57	50	−165.60	+66.88
42	(21)	Paul Casey	ENG	2.57	125.71	49	−160.12	+112.16
43	(44)	Richard Sterne	RSA	2.50	130.13	52	−98.70	+110.65
44	(34)	Hunter Mahan	USA	2.50	137.31	55	−123.41	+108.70
45	(26)	Retief Goosen	RSA	2.49	134.71	54	−186.23	+129.25
46	(15)	Zach Johnson	USA	2.44	117.05	48	−167.03	+ 75.76
47	(45)	Boo Weekley	USA	2.42	130.55	54	−131.06	+129.06
48	(46)	Soren Hansen	DEN	2.41	127.90	53	−96.23	+98.85
49	(171)	Lin Wen–Tang	TPE	2.36	94.56	40	−36.40	+91.86
50	(69)	Søren Kjeldsen	DEN	2.30	133.42	58	−79.33	+113.91

Ranking in brackets indicates position at 31st December 2007

European Tour 2008 (at end of 2008 season)

www.europeantour.com

Final Order of Merit (Top 118 keep their cards for the 2009 season)

#	Player	Earnings
1	Robert Karlsson (SWE)	€2732748
2	Padraig Harrington (IRL)	2459109
3	Lee Westwood (ENG)	2424642
4	Miguel Angel Jiménez (ESP)	2066596
5	Graeme McDowell (NIR)	1859346
6	Ross Fisher (ENG)	1836530
7	Henrik Stenson (SWE)	1798617
8	Martin Kaymer (GER)	1794500
9	Sergio García (ESP)	1591917
10	Søren Kjeldsen (DEN)	1440979
11	Oliver Wilson (ENG)	1270705
12	Jeev Milkha Singh (IND)	1218209
13	Darren Clarke (NIR)	1151038
14	Søren Hansen (DEN)	1123897
15	Retief Goosen (RSA)	1051335
16	Peter Hanson (SWE)	992622
17	James Kingston (RSA)	973594
18	Pablo Larrazábal (ESP)	960858
19	Ian Poulter (ENG)	946806
20	Richard Finch (ENG)	937438
21	Paul Casey (ENG)	930347
22	Anthony Wall (ENG)	914779
23	Richard Green (AUS)	888793
24	Francesco Molinari (ITA)	880241
25	Alvaro Quiros (ESP)	833800
26	Paul McGinley (IRL)	824726
27	Colin Montgomerie (SCO)	815153
28	Charl Schwartzel (RSA)	797225
29	Peter Hedblom (SWE)	796220
30	Damien McGrane (IRL)	748289
31	Alexander Noren (SWE)	742091
32	Scott Strange (AUS)	739368
33	Grégory Havret (FRA)	725271
34	Gonzalo Fdez-Castaño (ESP)	711546
35	David Lynn (ENG)	705767
36	Rory McIlroy (NIR)	696335
37	Hennie Otto (RSA)	683369
38	Peter Lawrie (IRL)	682181
39	Andres Romero (ARG)	680601
40	Paul Lawrie (SCO)	679530
41	Felipe Aguilar (CHI)	676182
42	Ernie Els (RSA)	674098
43	Adam Scott (AUS)	671437
44	Nick Dougherty (ENG)	658974
45	David Howell (ENG)	652491
46	Grégory Bourdy (FRA)	648924
47	Anders Hansen (DEN)	644154
48	John Bickerton (ENG)	627816
49	Steve Webster (ENG)	604181
50	Graeme Storm (ENG)	597121
51	Oliver Fisher (ENG)	594587
52	Jean-François Lucquin (FRA)	592104
53	Mark Brown (NZL)	585671
54	Robert-Jan Derksen (NED)	577074
55	Simon Dyson (ENG)	570949
56	José Manuel Lara (ESP)	564408
57	Angel Cabrera (ARG)	559625
58	Markus Brier (AUT)	553961
59	Ignacio Garrido (ESP)	545822
60	Thomas Levet (FRA)	539391
61	Alastair Forsyth (SCO)	489359
62	Louis Oosthuizen (RSA)	485036
63	Mikael Lundberg (SWE)	476930
64	Gary Orr (SCO)	472033
65	Johan Edfors (SWE)	456696
66	Maarten Lafeber (NRF)	451975
67	Jyoti Randhawa (IND)	449402
68	Thongchai Jaidee (THA)	446505
69	Michael Campbell (NZL)	430147
70	Ross McGowan (ENG)	429173
71	Raphaël Jacquelin (FRA)	427576
72	Robert Dinwiddie (ENG)	426811
73	Martin Erlandsson (SWE)	416897
74	Bradley Dredge (WAL)	416720
75	Richard Sterne (RSA)	415040
76	David Frost (RSA)	413795
77	Stephen Gallacher (SCO)	413367
78	Andrew McLardy (RSA)	411416
79	Magnus A Carlsson (SWE)	405998
80	Jarmo Sandelin (SWE)	395255
81	Justin Rose (ENG)	392562
82	Mark Foster (ENG)	377430
83	Ricardo Gonzalez (ARG)	369737
84	Simon Khan (ENG)	368038
85	Pelle Edberg (SWE)	366001
86	Greg Norman (AUS)	363976
87	Robert Allenby (AUS)	359992
88	Simon Wakefield (ENG)	359428
89	Jamie Donaldson (WAL)	350286
90	Rafa Echenique (ARG)	346344
91	Mikko Ilonen (FIN)	329916
92	Daniel Chopra (SWE)	329319
93	SSP Chowrasia (IND)	327283
94	Niclas Fasth (SWE)	322369
95	Christian Cévaër (FRA)	318231
96	Marcel Siem (GER)	309839
97	Marc Warren (SCO)	307396
98	Gary Murphy (IRL)	301792
99	Paul Broadhurst (ENG)	290416
100	Alvaro Velasco (ESP)	286888
101	Thomas Björn (DEN)	285252
102	Marcus Fraser (AUS)	282452
103	Miles Tunnicliff (ENG)	282333
104	Michael Jonzon (SWE)	280465
105	Paul Waring (ENG)	279872
106	Phillip Archer (ENG)	275495
107	Lee Slattery (ENG)	275242
108	Michael Lorenzo-Vera (FRA)	269091
109	Alejandro Cañizares (ESP)	265000
110	Benn Barham (ENG)	262222
111	Robert Rock (ENG)	258149
112	Sam Little (ENG)	253975
113	Daniel Vancsik (ARG)	246896
114	David Dixon (ENG)	240032
115	Peter O'Malley (AUS)	239024
116	Shiv Kapur (IND)	233532
117	Jean-Baptiste Gonnet (FRA)	231077
118	François Delamontagne (FRA)	223746
119	Patrik Sjöland (SWE)	223413
120	Garry Houston (WAL)	219447

Career Money List (at end of 2008 season)

Colin Montgomerie still ahead in European career earnings

Colin Montgomerie kept his No 1 spot on the European Tour Career Earnings list at the end of 2008. The Scot has made €23,585,716 in prize-money, just under €2 million more than second placed Ernie Els. Padraig Harrington, helped by his two major wins, is in third spot with just under €20 million with Retief Goosen and Darren Clarke completing the top five. Twenty of the golfers in the top 50 have made €9 million or more and 49 of the top 50 €5 million or more. Anders Forsbrand, now retired from competitive golf, is in 100th spot having made just over €3 million.

1	Colin Montgomerie (SCO)	€ 23,585,716	51	Steve Webster (ENG)	4,934,385
2	Ernie Els (RSA)	21,851,420	52	David Lynn (ENG)	4,859,745
3	Padraig Harrington (IRL)	19,482,981	53	Ignacio Garrido (ESP)	4,776,951
4	Retief Goosen (RSA)	18,419,527	54	Peter Hanson (SWE)	4,495,491
5	Darren Clarke (NIR)	16,709,804	55	Ricardo Gonzalez (ARG)	4,378,717
6	Lee Westwood (ENG)	16,512,812	56	Costantino Rocca (ITA)	4,368,165
7	Miguel Angel Jiménez (ESP)	14,169,628	57	Jarmo Sandelin (SWE)	4,367,393
8	Vijay Singh (FIJ)	13,299,221	58	Jean Van De Velde (FRA)	4,325,421
9	Sergio García (ESP)	12,709,588	59	Pierre Fulke (SWE)	4,310,837
10	Thomas Björn (DEN)	12,582,672	60	Alastair Forsyth (SCO)	4,297,122
11	Bernhard Langer (GER)	12,575,729	61	Joakim Haeggman (SWE)	4,289,116
12	Angel Cabrera (ARG)	11,691,431	62	Brian Davis (ENG)	4,252,771
13	José Maria Olazábal (ESP)	11,510,011	63	Simon Dyson (ENG)	4,192,622
14	Michael Campbell (NZL)	11,384,644	64	Fredrik Jacobson (SWE)	4,138,959
15	Robert Karlsson (SWE)	10,977,667	65	Stephen Gallacher (SCO)	4,132,986
16	Paul Mcginley (IRL)	10,102,687	66	Gordon Brand Jr (SCO)	4,084,502
17	David Howell (ENG)	9,947,269	67	Peter Hedblom (SWE)	4,004,548
18	Ian Poulter (ENG)	9,670,890	68	Peter Baker (ENG)	3,988,148
19	Ian Woosnam (WAL)	9,570,678	69	Jean-François Remesy (FRA)	3,918,722
20	Paul Casey (ENG)	9,225,955	70	Charl Schwartzel (RSA)	3,861,244
21	Niclas Fasth (SWE)	8,847,243	71	Maarten Lafeber (NED)	3,816,130
22	Henrik Stenson (SWE)	8,839,603	72	Jamie Spence (ENG)	3,811,210
23	Nick Faldo (ENG)	7,996,254	73	David Gilford (ENG)	3,756,909
24	Paul Lawrie (SCO)	7,578,769	74	Mathias Grönberg (SWE)	3,733,994
25	Eduardo Romero (ARG)	7,518,085	75	Sandy Lyle (SCO)	3,717,808
26	Adam Scott (AUS)	7,346,598	76	Grégory Havret (FRA)	3,657,161
27	Trevor Immelman (RSA)	6,686,450	77	Patrik Sjöland (SWE)	3,628,379
28	Barry Lane (ENG)	6,652,180	78	Simon Khan (ENG)	3,616,853
29	Søren Hansen (DEN)	6,637,775	79	Richard Sterne (RSA)	3,611,661
30	Peter O'Malley (AUS)	6,616,130	80	Per-Ulrik Johansson (SWE)	3,585,449
31	Justin Rose (ENG)	6,414,678	81	Jesper Parnevik (SWE)	3,559,745
32	Phillip Price (WAL)	6,405,562	82	Fred Couples (USA)	3,506,121
33	Richard Green (AUS)	6,349,645	83	Mark Roe (ENG)	3,454,502
34	Paul Broadhurst (ENG)	6,297,076	84	Gary Evans (ENG)	3,433,122
35	Anders Hansen (DEN)	6,254,786	85	Roger Chapman (ENG)	3,387,795
36	Søren Kjeldsen (DEN)	6,203,537	86	Miguel Angel Martin (ESP)	3,364,172
37	Nick O'Hern (AUS)	6,175,792	87	José Manuel Lara (ESP)	3,301,833
38	Graeme McDowell (NIR)	6,043,148	88	Peter Fowler (AUS)	3,261,420
39	Bradley Dredge (WAL)	5,918,995	89	Markus Brier (AUT)	3,254,290
40	Thomas Levet (FRA)	5,698,018	90	Jeev Milkha Singh (IND)	3,249,820
41	Raphaël Jacquelin (FRA)	5,583,115	91	Emanuele Canonica (ITA)	3,248,613
42	Luke Donald (ENG)	5,518,713	92	Tom Lehman (USA)	3,224,568
43	Sam Torrance (SCO)	5,491,084	93	Oliver Wilson (ENG)	3,221,891
44	Andrew Coltart (SCO)	5,383,739	94	Graeme Storm (ENG)	3,175,311
45	Mark McNulty (IRL)	5,366,794	95	Santiago Luna (ESP)	3,171,988
46	Seve Ballesteros (ESP)	5,334,860	96	Ronan Rafferty (NIR)	3,165,250
47	Gary Orr (SCO)	5,167,805	97	Stephen Dodd (WAL)	3,154,367
48	John Bickerton (ENG)	5,154,473	98	Andres Romero (ARG)	3,136,383
49	Nick Dougherty (ENG)	5,010,979	99	Robert-Jan Derksen (NED)	3,088,689
50	Anthony Wall (ENG)	4,995,803	100	Anders Forsbrand (SWE)	3,086,484

Tour Statistics (Reuters Performance Data)

Stroke average

Pos	Name	Total Rounds	Stroke Avg,
1	Robert Karlsson (SWE)	86	70.08
2	Lee Westwood (ENG)	75	70.44
3	Sergio García (ESP)	46	70.63
4	Jeev Milkha Singh (IND)	89	70.73
5	Gary Orr (SCO)	78	70.74
6	David Lynn (ENG)	97	70.79
	Graeme McDowell (NIR)	99	70.79

Driving accuracy

Pos	Name	Rounds	%
1	Pedro Linhart (ESP)	52	76.5
2	Peter O'Malley (AUS)	70	72.8
3	Henrik Nyström (SWE)	74	71.3
4	John Bickerton (ENG)	82	70.3
5	Ian Garbutt (ENG)	25	70.2
6	Francesco Molinari (ITA)	97	69.0
	Andrew Coltart (SCO)	32	69.0

Driving distance

Pos	Name	Rounds	Avg. yards
1	Alvaro Quiros (ESP)	77	309.7
2	Rafael Cabrera Bello (ESP)	35	303.2
3	Christian Nilsson (SWE)	27	302.9
4	Emanuele Canonica (ITA)	75	301.9
5	Joakim Bäckström (SWE)	55	301.3
6	Paul Waring (ENG)	60	300.6
	Paolo Terreni (ITA)	41	300.6

Greens in regulation

Pos	Name	Rounds	%
1	Steven O'Hara (SCO)	29	75.3
2	Johan Edfors (SWE)	79	75.2
	Lee Westwood (ENG)	48	75.2
4	Thomas Levet (FRA)	82	75.1
	Rafael Cabrera Bello (ESP)	35	75.1
6	Søren Hansen (DEN)	64	73.4
7	Peter O'Malley (AUS)	70	73.2

Putts per greens in regulation

Pos	Name	Rounds	Putts per GIR
1	Danny Willett (ENG)	30	1.719
2	David Howell (ENG)	82	1.723
3	SSP Chowrasia (IND)	32	1.730
4	Rafa Echenique (ARG)	81	1.734
5	Miguel Angel Jiménez (ESP)	64	1.736
6	Padraig Harrington (IRL)	26	1.744
7	Sergio García (ESP)	24	1.745

Robert Karlsson – the first and last Swede to top the European Tour Money List, now renamed "The Race to Dubai"

© Getty Images

Average putts per round

Pos	Name	Rounds	Putts per round
1	SSP Chowrasia (IND)	32	27.4
2	David Howell (ENG)	82	28.1
3	Paul Broadhurst (ENG)	78	28.3
4	Padraig Harrington (IRL)	26	28.4
5	Christian Cévaër (FRA)	76	28.6
	Rafa Echenique (ARG)	81	28.6
	Kyron Sullivan (WAL)	51	28.6

Sand saves

Pos	Name	Rounds	%
1	James Kingston (RSA)	54	77.8
2	Danny Willett (ENG)	30	72.7
3	Jeev Milkha Singh (IND)	72	70.9
4	Ernie Els (RSA)	26	68.4
5	Robert Karlsson (SWE)	58	67.8
6	Francesco Molinari (ITA)	97	67.2
7	Retief Goosen (RSA)	27	66.7
	Steve Alker (NZL)	34	66.7

Scrambles[1]

Pos	Name	Rounds	%
1	Paul Casey (ENG)	24	64.0
2	Robert Karlsson (SWE)	58	63.7
3	Sergio García (ESP)	24	63.1
4	Richard Green (AUS)	52	62.5
5	David Lynn (ENG)	94	62.0
	Wen-chong Liang (CHN)	24	62.0
7	Paul Broadhurst (ENG)	78	61.4

[1]Where player makes par after missing green in regulation

PGA European Tour statistics 2008

Twenty-nine holes-in-one

Anthony Painter	5th hole, MasterCard Masters	Miguel A Jiménez	5th hole, BMW PGA Ch.
Justin Maker	12th hole, MasterCard Masters	Chapchai Nirat	2nd hole, Open de France
Martin Doyle	7th hole, NZ Open	Robert-J Derksen	16th hole, Open de France
Joost Luiten	12th hole, Alfred Dunhill Ch.	Pelle Edberg	17th hole, The Barclays Scottish Open
Oliver Wilson	16th hole, Alfred Dunhill Ch.	Phil Mickelson	5th hole, The Barclays Scottish Open
Gary Boyd	12th hole, Joburg Open	Fredrik Jacobson	13th hole, USPGA Champ.
Miguel A Jiménez	7th hole, Dubai Desert Classic	Marcus Fraser	3rd hole, KLM Open
C Muniyappa	12the hole, Indian Masters	Phillip Archer	7th hole, Quinn Insurance British Masters
AH Murakami	17th hole, Indonesia Open	Jeev Milkha Singh	7th hole, Quinn Insurance British Masters
Darren Clarke	4th hole, Indonesia Open	Alvaro Quiros	12th hole, Quinn Insurance British Masters
Jason Knutzon	4th hole, Indonesia Open		
Francesco Molinari	14th hole, Malaysian Open	Unho Park	8th hole, Alfred Dunhill Links Championship
Gareth Paddison	15th hole, Maderia Is. Open		
Ian Poulter	16th hole, Masters Tourn.	Jean-F Lucquin	8th hole, Portugal Masters
Adam Groom	3rd hole, Volvo China Open	Camilo Villegas	12th hole, Castelló Masters
Steven Jeppesen	6th hole, The Irish Open		

Biggest catch-up in last round by a winner

7 shots   Arjun Atwal, Maybank Malaysian Open

Four albatrosses

Steven Jeffress	15th hole, NZ Open
Joakim Backstrom	15th hole, Russian Open
Thongachai Jaidee	14th hole, KLM Open
Mads Vibe-Hastrup	1st hole, European Masters

Largest winning margin

9 shots   Damien McGrane   Volvo China Open

High finish by a winner

76 (+4)   Phil Mickelson   HSBC Champions

Wire-to-wire winners (no ties)

Martin Kaymer	Abu Dhabi Golf Ch.
Scott Strange	Wales Open
Ross Fisher	European Open
Gregory Havret	Johnnie Walker Ch.
Soren Kjeldsen	Volvo Masters

Most birdies in one round

Adam Scott 11 Qatar Masters (round 4)
Hennie Otto 11 Italian Open (round 3)

Fourteen course records

Kevin Stadler	64 (-8)	HSBC Champions
Peter Fowler	62 (-10)	NZ Open
Garth Mulroy	64 (-8)	SA Airways Open
Adam Scott	61 (-11)	Qatar Masters
Jyoti Randhawa	65 (-7)	Indian Masters
Graeme McDowell	64 (-8)	Ballantine's Ch.
Pablo Martin	63 (-8)	Open de Portugal
Oliver Wilson	66 (-6)	Volvo China Open
Ignacio Garrido	63 (-9)	Open de Espana
Robert Karlsson	61 (-11)	Italian Open
Lee Westwood	64 (-8)	Irish Open
Robert Dinwiddie	63 (-9)	BMW PGA Ch.
Ross Fisher	63 (-9)	European Open
Camillo Villegas	65 (-5)	The Open Ch.

Wire-to-wire winners (with ties)

Geoff Ogilvy	Accenture Match-play Ch.
Gregory Bourdy	Open de Portugal
Trevor Immelman	The Masters
Jeev Milkha Singh	Austria Golf Open
Padblo Larrazabal	Open de France Alstom
Peter Hanson	SAS Scandinavian Masters

Most consecutive eagles

Kane Webber 2   Ballantine's Championship
(round 2, holes 9–10)

Eight multiple winners

Tiger Woods – Dubai Desert Classic, WGC– Accenture Match Play, US Open Championship

Richard Finch – New Zealand Open, Irish Open

Miguel Angel Jiménez – UBS Hong Kong Open, BMW PGA Championship

Martin Kaymer – Abu Dhabi Golf Championship, BMW International Open

Graeme McDowell – Ballantine's Championship, The Barclays Scottish Open

Padraig Harrington – The Open Championship, USPGA Championship

Darren Clarke – BMW Asian Open, The KLM Open

Robert Karlsson – Mercedes-Benz Championship, Alfred Dunhill Links Championship

First-time winners on the European Tour

Richard Finch (ENG)	Michael Hill New Zealand Open
James Kingston (RSA)	South African Airways Open
Martin Kaymer (GER)	Abu Dhabi Golf Championship
SSP Chowrasia (THI)	EMAAR-MGF Indian Masters
Filepe Aguilar (ARG)	Enjoy Jakarta Astro Indonesian Open
Mark Brown (NZL)	Johnnie Walker Classic
Damien McGrane (IRL)	Volvo China Open
Peter Lawrie (IRL)	Open de Espana
Hennie Otto (RSA)	Methorios Capital Italian Open
Scott Strange (AUS)	The Celtic Manor Wales Open
David Dixon (ENG)	St Omer Open
Pablo Larrazabal (ESP)	Open de France Alstom
Jean-François Lucquin (FRA)	Omega European Masters

Top 20 on the European Tour 2008

	Name	Played	Wins	Top 3	Top 10	MC	Stroke Av.
1	Robert Karlssson	23	2	8	12	1	70.08
2	Padraig Harrington	14	2	2	4	1	70.90
3	Lee Westwood	22	0	7	13	1	70.44
4	MA Jiménez	26	2	5	9	4	70.87
5	Graeme McDowall	28	2	3	8	6	70.79
6	Ross Fisher	27	1	3	9	4	71.34
7	Henrik Stenson	25	0	5	10	3	71.03
8	Martin Kaymer	25	2	5	8	4	71.05
9	Sergio García	13	1	3	6	0	70.63
10	Soren Kjeldsen	29	1	1	5	6	70.95
11	Oliver Wilson	26	0	4	7	0	71.52
12	Jeev M Singh	25	1	3	8	4	70.73
13	Darren Clarke	28	2	3	7	7	70.84
14	Søren Hansen	25	0	2	10	3	71.17
15	Retief Goosen	15	0	1	3	0	71.52
16	Peter Hanson	28	1	2	6	5	71.27
17	James Kingston	22	1	2	5	6	72.13
18	Pablo Larrazabal	28	1	2	3	10	72.20
19	Ian Poulter	16	0	1	2	2	71.96
20	Richard Finch	29	2	2	7	13	72.24

Dai Davies – an appreciation of his work

Last year was a sad one for *The Golfer's Handbook* which lost one of its best known and most loyal contributors, Dai Davies. He had been writing his overview of the majors for several years but had suggested before the end of 2007 that he might not be able to continue last year because he had been diagnosed with cancer.

He should have been on assignment last April at The Masters but by then he was too ill to travel and died a few weeks later survived by his wife Patricia, herself a golf journalist. For over 20 years he was the golf writer for *The Guardian* until he retired in 2004 but then continued to write for the paper and for *The Observer* and the *Sunday Telegraph*.

A life-long fan of Jack Nicklaus and of Sandy Lyle, he admitted that professionally he had "had a ball" visiting almost every place he had wanted to covering golf – a game he loved, respected and did so much to enhance. A colleague wrote later that while many sportswriters know their subject, few did to the depth that Dai did and even fewer with his passion. He was 69.

PGA European Tour top 20

MC Missed cut   — Did not play   * Involved in play-off

#	Player	HSBC Champions To (2007)	USB Hong Kong Open	MasterCard Masters	Michael Hill NZ Open	Alfred Dunhill C/ship	S. African Airways Open	Joburg Open (2008)	Abu Dhabi Championship	Qatar Masters	Dubai Desert Classic	Indian Masters	Indonesian Open	WGC-Accenture MP	Johnnie Walker Classic	Malaysian Open	Ballantines C/ship	WGC-CA Championship	Madeira Island Open	Open de Andalucia	Open de Portugal	The Masters
1	Robert Karlsson (SWE)	—	2T	—	—	—	—	—	11T	60T	19T	—	—	33T	34T	—	—	30T	—	—	—	8T
2	Padraig Harrington (IRL)	5T	—	—	—	—	—	—	11T	—	—	—	17T	—	—	14T	—	—	—	—	—	5T
3	Lee Westwood (ENG)	2T	—	—	—	—	—	2T	5	10T	—	—	17T	—	—	—	—	34T	—	3	—	11T
4	Miguel A Jiménez (ESP)	—	—	1	—	—	—	—	43T	67T	54T	—	—	33T	25T	—	—	26T	—	—	19T	—
5	Graeme McDowell (NIR)	—	6	—	—	—	—	MC	20T	5	12T	—	—	MC	—	17T	1*	48T	—	—	—	—
6	Ross Fisher (ENG)	2T	—	—	—	33T	MC	—	MC	25T	10T	—	—	—	—	—	—	34T	—	—	—	—
7	Henrik Stenson (SWE)	—	9T	—	—	—	—	—	2T	2	6T	—	—	3	—	—	—	57T	—	—	—	17T
8	Martin Kaymer (GER)	—	—	—	—	—	—	—	1	MC	2	—	—	33T	—	—	—	57T	—	39T	—	46T
9	Sergio García (ESP)	46T	—	—	—	—	—	—	7T	19T	—	—	17T	—	—	15T	—	—	—	—	—	46T
10	Søren Kjeldsen (DEN)	—	15T	29T	—	—	—	—	MC	20T	33T	11	—	—	—	21T	—	11	—	—	—	15T
11	Oliver Wilson (ENG)	—	—	—	25T	2	—	MC	20T	MC	MC	—	—	—	48T	52T	8	—	—	—	—	—
12	Jeev Milkha Singh (IND)	—	—	—	—	—	—	MC	56T	19T	MC	2	—	11T	MC	2	26T	—	—	—	—	25T
13	Darren Clarke (NIR)	—	—	—	33T	3T	4	61T	—	MC	63	21T	—	—	10T	—	—	—	—	MC	24T	—
14	Søren Hansen (DEN)	58T	—	—	—	—	—	—	34T	42T	6T	—	—	33T	14T	—	—	70T	—	—	—	MC
15	Retief Goosen (RSA)	18T	20T	—	—	—	16T	—	—	—	—	—	—	33T	—	—	—	2T	—	—	—	17T
16	Peter Hanson (SWE)	33T	5	—	—	—	—	—	43T	51T	MC	—	—	33T	—	—	—	61T	—	54T	MC	—
17	James Kingston (RSA)	—	MC	—	52T	1	41T	7T	—	44T	—	—	MC	—	—	—	—	70T	—	—	—	—
18	Pablo Larrazabal (ESP)	—	—	—	40T	60T	21T	—	—	—	—	MC	MC	—	—	—	—	—	15T	32T	MC	—
19	Ian Poulter (ENG)	38T	—	—	—	—	—	—	9T	MC	39T	—	—	17T	MC	—	—	57T	—	—	—	25T
20	Richard Finch (ENG)	—	MC	10T	1	—	—	—	4T	42T	MC	64T	—	—	48T	—	—	—	MC	—	—	—

2008 performances at a glance

RT Retired   WD Withdrew   FQ Failed to qualify   DQ Disqualified

Volvo China Open	BMW Asian Open	Open de España	Italian Open	Irish Open	BMW Championship	Celtic Manor Wales Open	BA-CA Austria Open	US Open Championship	Aa St Omer Open	BMW International Open	Open de France	European Open	Barclays Scottish Open	137th Open Championship	Russian Open	WGC–Bridgestone Inv.	US PGA Championship	Scandinavian Masters	KLM Open	Johnnie Walker Champ.	Omega European Masters	Mercedes–Benz Champ.	Quinn Direcct Masters	dunhill links championship	Open de Madrid	Portugal Masters	Castelló Masters	Volvo Masters
—	—	3	3T	3T	2	—	4T	—	—	13T	6T	—	7T	—	—	20T	20T	MC	—	—	1	—	—	1*	—	3T	—	32T
—	—	—	31T	—	MC	—	36T	—	—	17T	—	1	—	20T	1	—	—	—	—	—	—	—	—	13T	—	—	—	13T
—	—	—	3T	RT	—	—	3	—	—	5T	—	19T	67T	—	2T	MC	—	10T	—	—	—	—	2	8T	—	16T	—	4T
8T	—	MC	4T	—	—	1*	RT	—	6T	—	MC	66T	—	3T	MC	—	10T	MC	—	—	—	3T	3T	—	RT	29T	38T	—
5T	MC	—	—	MC	57	39T	8T	—	—	MC	13T	3	1	19T	—	56T	15T	—	—	MC	—	16T	39T	31T	—	42T	—	8T
56T	42T	—	—	24T	68T	10T	—	MC	—	12	64T	1	25T	39T	—	56T	MC	—	20T	10T	—	3T	7T	2T	—	3T	—	11T
—	6	—	—	—	40T	—	—	MC	—	6T	—	—	33T	3T	—	16T	4T	—	3	—	—	—	—	MC	—	—	MC	45
—	7T	—	—	10T	16T	21T	—	53T	—	1*	MC	—	—	80	—	68T	MC	14T	55T	MC	—	8T	—	2T	16T	30T	—	2T
—	—	—	—	—	—	—	18T	—	—	—	2	—	51T	—	36T	2T	—	—	—	—	—	—	—	—	—	—	1	4T
—	56T	18T	—	38T	35T	10T	61T	—	—	13T	7T	—	38T	MC	—	—	MC	7	MC	MC	—	16T	30T	MC	—	16T	—	4T
2T	11T	—	2	35T	2	MC	—	36T	—	—	MC	—	9T	MC	—	27T	MC	—	20T	10T	—	—	—	40T	—	RT	—	46
—	23T	—	—	40T	MC	10T	1	—	—	MC	21T	10T	9T	FQ	—	—	9T	—	—	—	11T	5T	24T	—	—	13T	—	54T
—	1	22T	—	16T	MC	4T	19T	—	—	MC	DQ	MC	FQ	—	6T	MC	—	1	44T	—	25T	MC	48T	—	23T	—	—	11T
—	—	3	—	—	34T	35T	8T	53T	—	3	5	MC	64T	—	73T	MC	—	6T	10T	—	8T	—	8T	—	7T	—	—	13T
—	11T	—	—	—	6T	—	—	14T	13T	—	—	—	32T	—	4T	24T	—	—	—	—	69T	—	52T	—	—	—	—	—
—	—	8T	—	58T	16T	MC	—	—	—	30T	42T	6T	MC	58T	—	—	52T	1	MC	3T	—	14T	30T	52T	—	45T	7T	13T
—	—	—	—	10T	25T	—	—	—	—	MC	MC	27T	2	MC	—	78	55T	—	—	—	—	35T	MC	36T	—	6	—	50T
—	MC	MC	16T	—	15T	38T	—	RT	61T	1	—	MC	70T	—	76	MC	—	—	—	MC	MC	65T	10T	MC	3	—	51T	39T
—	—	—	—	—	—	—	—	RT	—	—	30T	48T	25T	2	—	16T	31T	—	—	—	—	—	—	—	—	—	—	29T
12T	62T	7	—	1	MC	MC	—	—	—	55T	MC	MC	MC	58T	—	36T	—	—	—	MC	MC	6T	MC	MC	—	MC	7T	52

2008 European Tour and Past Results

(in chronological order)

Note: The HSBC Champions Tournament, the UBS Hong Kong Open, the MasterCard Masters, the Blue Chip New Zealand Open, the dunhill championship and the South African Airways Open, which were all played in 2007 were included in the 2008 European international schedule

HSBC Champions Tournament *Sheshan International. Shanghai, China*   [7199–72]

1	Phil Mickelson (USA)*	68-66-68-76—278	€575455
2	Ross Fisher (ENG)	68-68-68-74—278	299893
	Lee Westwood (ENG)	70-74-67-67—278	299893

Mickelson won at the second extra hole

2005 David Howell (ENG)   2007 Yang-Eun Yang (KOR)

UBS Hong Kong Open *Hong Kong GC, Fanling*   [6703–70]

1	Miguel Angel Jiménez (ESP)	65-67-66-67—265	€255710
2	K J Choi (KOR)	62-72-65-67—266	114410
	Thongchai Jaidee (THA)	66-67-68-65—266	114410
	Robert Karlsson (SWE)	64-64-66-72—266	114410

1959 Lu Liang-Huan (TPE)	1972 W Godfrey (NZL)	1985 M Aebi (USA)	1997 F Nobilo (NZL)
1960 P Thomson (AUS)	1973 F Phillips (AUS)	1986 S Kanai (JPN)	1998 Kang Wook-soon
1961 K Nagle (AUS)	1974 Lu Liang-huan (TPE)	1987 I Woosnam (WAL)	(KOR)
1962 L Woodward (AUS)	1976 Hsieh Yung-yo (TPE)	1988 Hsieh Chin-sheng	1999 P Sjoland (SWE)
1963 Hsieh Yung-yo (TPE)	1976 Ho Ming-Chung (TPE)	(TPE)	2000 S Dyson (ENG)
1964 Hsieh Yung-yo (TPE)	1977 Hsieh Min-Nan (TPE)	1989 B Claar (USA)	2001 JM Olazabal (ESP)
1965 P Thomson (AUS)	1978 Hsieh Yung-yo (TPE)	1990 K Green (USA)	2002 F Jacobson (SWE)
1966 F Phillips (AUS)	1979 G Norman (AUS)	1991 B Langer (GER)	2003 P Harrington (IRE)
1967 P Thomson (AUS)	1980 Kuo Chie-hsiung (TPE)	1992 T Watson (USA)	2004 MA Jiménez (ESP)
1968 R Vines (AUS)	1981 Chen Tse-Ming (TPE)	1993 B Watts (USA)	2005 C Montgomerie (SCO)
1969 T uguhara (JPN)	1982 K Cox (AUS)	1994 D Frost (USA)	2007 José Manuel Lara (ESP)
1970 I Katsumatu (JPN)	1983 G Norman (AUS)	1995 G Webb (USA)	
1971 O Moody (USA)	1984 B Brask (USA)	1996 R Cuello (PHI)	

MasterCard Masters *Huntingdale, Melbourne, Australia* (Australian unless stated)   [6980–72]

1	Aaron Baddeley*	70-66-69-70—275	€164170
2	Daniel Chopra (SWE)	69-70-65-71—275	93029

Baddeley won at the fourth extra hole

3	Stuart Appleby	69-71-68-69—277	61563

1979 B Vivien (NZL)	289	1987 G Norman	273	1995 P Senior	280	2002 P Lonard	279
1980 G Littler (USA)	288	1988 I Baker-Finch	283	1996 C Parry	279	2003 R Allenby	277
1981 G Norman	289	1989 G Norman	280	1997 P Lonard	276	2004 R Green	271
1982 G Marsh	289	1990 G Norman	273	1998 B Hughes	268	2005 R Allenby	271
1983 G Norman	288	1991 P Senior	278	1999 C Spence	276	2007 J Rose (ENG)	276
1984 G Norman	285	1992 C Parry	283	2000 M Campbell (NZL) 282			
1985 B Langer (GER)	281	1993 B Hughes	281	2001 C Montgomerie	278		
1986 M O'Meara (USA)	284	1994 C Parry	282	(SCO)			

Michael Hill New Zealand Open *The Hills, Queenstown* (New Zealand unless stated)

[7243–72]

1	Richard Finch (ENG)	73-65-64-72—274	€144895
2	Steven Bowditch (AUS)	69-65-71-72—277	68221
	Paul Sheehan (AUS)	68-67-73-69—277	68221

1907 A Duncan (am)	159	1913 E Douglas	303	1922 A Brooks	308	1928 S Morpeth (am)	303
1908 J Clements	353	1914 E Douglas	313	1923 A Brooks	312	1929 A Shaw	299
1909 J Clements	324	1915–1918 Not played		1924 E Moss	301	1930 A Shaw	284
1910 A Duncan (am)	295	1919 E Douglas	327	1925 E Macfarlane (am) 308		1931 A Shaw	287
1911 A Duncan (am)	319	1920 J Kirkwood (AUS)	304	1926 A Shaw	307	1932 A Shaw	289
1912 J Clements	321	1921 E Douglas	302	1927 E Moss	300	1933 E Moss	300

1934	A Shaw	288	1956	H Berwick (am)	292	
1935	A Murray	286	1957	K Nagle (AUS)	294	
1936	A Shaw	292	1958	K Nagle (AUS)	278	
1937	J Hornabrook (am)	299	1959	P Thomson (AUS)	287	

1934 A Shaw 288
1935 A Murray 286
1936 A Shaw 292
1937 J Hornabrook (am) 299
1938 AD Locke (RSA) 299
1939 J Hornabrook (am) 291
1940–1945 Not played
1946 R Glading (am) 306
1947 R Glading (am) 291
1948 A Murray 294
1949 J Galloway 283
1950 P Thomson (AUS) 280
1951 P Thomson (AUS) 288
1952 A Murray 293
1953 P Thomson (AUS) 295
1954 R Charles (am) 280
1955 P Thomson (AUS) 280

1956 H Berwick (am) 292
1957 K Nagle (AUS) 294
1958 K Nagle (AUS) 278
1959 P Thomson (AUS) 287
1960 P Thomson (AUS) 281
1961 P Thomson (AUS) 267
1962 K Nagle (AUS) 281
1963 B Devlin (AUS) 273
1964 K Nagle (AUS) 266
1965 P Thomson (AUS) 278
1966 R Charles 273
1967 K Nagle (AUS) 275
1968 K Nagle (AUS) 272
1969 K Nagle (AUS) 273
1970 R Charles 271
1971 P Thomson (AUS) 276
1972 B Dunk (AUS) 279
1973 R Charles 283
1974 R Gilder (USA) 283

1975 B Dunk (AUS) 272
1976 S Owen 284
1977 B Byman (USA) 290
1978 R Shearer (AUS) 277
1979 S Ginn (AUS) 278
1980 B Allin (USA) 274
1981 R Shearer (AUS) 285
1982 T Gale (AUS) 284
1983 I Baker-Finch (AUS) 280
1984 C Pavin (USA) 269
1985 C Pavin (USA) 277
1986 R Davis (AUS) 262
1987 R Rafferty (NIR) 279
1988 I Stanley (AUS) 273
1989 R Shearer (AUS) 277
1990 Not Played
1991 R Davis (AUS) 273
1992 G Waite 268

1993 P Fowler (AUS) 273
1994 C Jones (AUS) 273
1995 (Jan) L Parsons (AUS) 282
1995 (Dec) P O Malley (AUS) 272
1996 M Long 275
1997 G Turner 278
1998 M Lane 279
1999 Not played
2000 M Campbell 269
2001 D Smail 273
2002 C Parry (AUS) 273
2003 M Pearce 278
2004 G Coles (ENG) 282
2005 N Fasth (SWE) 266
2006 N Green (AUS) 279
2007 N Green (AUS) 279

Alfred Dunhill Championship   *Leopard Creek, Mpumalanga, RSA*   [7249–72]
(1959–99 combined with South African PGA Championship)

1	John Bickerton (ENG)	70-69-68-68—275	€158500
2	Ernie Els (RSA)	70-69-64-73—276	92100
	Lee Slattery (ENG)	73-65-67-71—276	92100

1995 E Els (RSA) Wanderers Club 271
1996 S Strüver (GER) Houghton GC 202 (54)
1997 N Price* (ZIM) Houghton GC 269
*Price beat D Frost at 1st extra hole
1998 T Johnstone (ZIM) Houghton GC 271
1999 E Els (RSA) Houghton GC 273
2000 A Wall (ENG) Houghton GC 204
2001 A Scott (AUS) Houghton GC 267
2002 J Rose (ENG) Houghton GC 268

2003 M Foster* (ENG) Houghton GC 273
* Foster beat Paul Lawrie, T Immelman, B Vaughan, A Hansen and D McGuigan at 2nd extra hole
2004 M Siem* (GER) Houghton GC 266
*Siem beat G Havret and R Jacquelin at 3rd extra hole
2005 C Schwartzel* (RSA) Leopard Creek 281
*Schwartzel beat N Cheetham at 1st extra hole
2006 E Els (RSA) Leopard Creek 274
2007 A Quiros (ESP) Leopard Creek 275

South African Airways Open   *Pearl Valley, Paarl, Western Cape* (South African unless stated)
[7438–72]

1	James Kingston	73-69-71-71—284	€158500
2	Oliver Wilson (ENG)	76-69-67-73—285	115000
3	Darren Clarke (NIR)	72-73-74-68—287	48750
	Garth Mulroy	80-70-64-73—287	48750
	Louis Oosthuizen	78-72-66-71—287	48750
	Kyron Sullivan (WAL)	72-71-73-71—287	48750

1903 LB Waters
1904 LB Waters
1905 AG Gray
1906 AG Gray
1907 LB Waters
1908 G Fotheringham
1909 J Fotheringham
1910 G Fotheringham
1911 G Fotheringham
1912 G Fotheringham
1913 JAW Prentice (am)
1914 G Fotheringham
1919 WH Horne
1920 LB Waters
1921 J Brews
1922 F Jangle
1923 J Brews
1924 BH Elkin
1925 SF Brews
1926 J Brews
1927 SF Brews
1928 J Brews
1929 A Tosh

1930 SF Brews
1931 SF Brews
1932 C McIlvenny
1933 SF Brews
1934 SF Brews
1935 AD Locke (am)
1936 CE Olander
1937 AD Locke (am)
1938 AD Locke
1939 AD Locke
1940 AD Locke
1946 AD Locke
1947 RW Glennie (am)
1948 JM Janks (am)*
1949 SF Brews
1950 AD Locke
1951 AD Locke
1952 SF Brews
1953 JR Boyd (am)
1954 RC Taylor (am)
1955 AD Locke
1956 G Player
1957 HR Henning*

1958 AA Stewart (am)
1959 D Hutchinson (am)
1960 G Player
1961 R Waltman
1962 HR Henning
1963 R Waltman
1964 A Henning
1965 G Player
1966 G Player
1967 G Player
1968 G Player
1969 G Player
1970 T Horton (ENG)
1971 S Hobday
1972 G Player
1973 RJ Charles (NZL)
1974 R Cole
1975 G Player
1976 D Hayes
1976 G Player
1977 G Player
1978 H Baiocchi
1979 G Player

1980 R Cole
1981 G Player
1982 Not played
1983 C Bolling (USA)
1984 T Johnstone (ZIM)
1985 G Levenson
1986 D Frost
1987 M McNulty
1988 W Westner
1989 S Wadsworth
1990 T Dodds
1991 W Westner
1992 E Els
1993 C Whitelaw
1994 T Johnstone (ZIM)
1995 R Goosen
1996 E Els
1997 V Singh (Fij)
1998 E Els
1999 D Frost
2000 M Grönberg (SWE)
2001 M McNulty (ZIM)
2002 T Clark

South African Airways Open continued

2003 T Immelman*	2004 T Immelman	2007 E Els
*Beat T Clark at 1st extra	2005 T Clark	
hole	2006 R Goosen	

Joburg Open   Royal Johannesburg and Kensington, RSA   [7990–71 7119–72]

1	Richard Sterne (RSA)	71-68-67-65—271	€174350
2	Magnus A Carlsson (SWE)	70-66-69-66—271	101310
	Garth Mulroy (RSA)	67-72-66-66—271	101310

*Sterne won at the second extra hole

2007 A Canete (ARG)

The Royal Trophy   Amata Spring, Bangkok, Thailand   [7381–72]

Cancelled

Abu Dhabi Championship   Abu Dhabi, UAE   [7500–72]

1	Martin Kaymer (GER)	66-65-68-74—273	€225421
2	Henrik Stenson (SWE)	67-70-69-71—277	117475
	Lee Westwood (ENG)	69-73-65-70—277	117475

2006 C DiMarco (USA)   2007 P Casey (ENG)

Qatar Masters   Abu Dhabi   [7388–72]

1	Adam Scott (AUS)	69-73-65-61—268	€285071
2	Henrik Stenson (SWE)	69-70-67-65—271	190045
3	Charl Schwartzel (RSA)	70-67-69-67—273	107074

1998	A Coltart (SCO)	270	2002 A Scott (AUS) 269	2004 J Haeggman	
1999	P Lawrie (SCO)	268	2003 D Fichardt (RSA)* 275	(SWE)	272
2000	R Muntz (NED)	280	*Beat J Kingston at 1st extra	2005 E Els (RSA)	276
2001	T Johnstone		hole	2006 H Stenson (SWE) 273	
	(ZIM)	274		2007 R Goosen (RSA) 273	

Dubai Desert Classic   Emirates GC, Dubai   [7301–72]

1	Henrik Stenson (SWE)	68-64-69-68—269	€309862
2	Ernie Els (RSA)	66-65-68-71—270	206569
3	Niclas Fasth (SWE)	69-69-65-68—271	104671
	Tiger Woods (USA)	68-67-67-69—271	104671

1989 M James* (ENG)	Emirates	277	1998 JM Olazábal (ESP)	Emirates	269
*James beat P O'Malley at first extra hole			1999 D Howell (ENG)	Dubai Creek	275
1990 E Darcy (IRE)	Emirates	276	2000 J Coceres (ARG)	Dubai Creek	274
1991 Not played			2001 T Bjørn (DEN)	Emirates	266
1992 S Ballesteros (ESP)*	Emirates	272	2002 E Els (RSA)	Emirates	272
*Ballesteros beat R Rafferty at second extra hole			2003 R-J Derksen (NED)	Emirates	271
1993 W Westner (RSA)	Emirates	274	2004 M O'Meara (USA)	Emirates	271
1994 E Els (RSA)	Emirates	268	2005 E Els (RSA)	Emirates	269
1995 F Couples (USA)	Emirates	268	2006 T Woods (USA)*	Emirates	269
1996 C Montgomerie (SCO)	Emirates	270	*Woods beat E Els at first extra hole		
1997 R Green (AUS)*	Emirates	272	2007 H Stenson (SWE)	Emirates	269
*Green beat I Woosnam & G Norman at first extra hole					

EMAAR-MGF Indian Masters   Delhi   [7041–72]

1	SSP Chowrasia (IND)	70-71-71-67—279	€280561
2	Damien McGrane (IRL)	67-69-75-70—281	187038
3	José-Manuel Lara (ESP)	68-72-71-72—283	105380

Enjoy Jakarta Astro Indonesian Open *Cengkareng, Jakarta* [6899–70]

1	Felipe Aguilar (CHI)	65-62-67-68—262	€127883
2	Jeev Milkha Singh (IND)	65-66-65-67—263	91919
3	James Kamte (RSA)	62-67-68-67—264	46576
	Prom Meesawat (THA)	66-63-68-67—264	46576

2005	T Wiratchant (THA)	255	2006	S Dyson (ENG)	268
			2007	M Ilonen (FIN)	275

WGC – Accenture Match Play Championship *Gallery, Tucson, AZ, USA*

Winner: Tiger Woods (USA)   €919992
Runner-up: Stewart Cink (USA)   545181
Third place: Henrik Stenson (SWE)   391849

Full details of this event can be found on page 188

Johnnie Walker Classic *DFL, New Delhi, India* [7156–72]

1	Mark Brown (NZL)	71-68-64-67—270	€276387
2	Greg Chalmers (AUS)	68-69-68-68—273	123659
	Taichiro Kiyota (JPN)	68-67-67-71—273	123659
	Scott Strange (AUS)	71-67-68-67—273	123659

1992	I Palmer (RSA)	Bangkok, Thailand	268	2000	M Campbell (NZL)	Ta Shee, Taiwan	276
1993	N Faldo (ENG)	Singapore Island	269	2001	T Woods (USA)	Bangkok, Thailand	263
1994	G Norman (AUS)	Blue Canyon, Phuket	277	2002	R Goosen (RSA)	Perth, Australia	274
1995	F Couples (USA)	Orchard GC, Manila	277	2003	E Els (RSA)	Perth, Australia	259
1996	I Woosnam (WAL)*	Tanah Merah, Singapore	272	2004	MA Jiménez (ESP)	Bangkok, Thailand	271
*Woosnam beat A Coltart at 3rd extra hole				2005	A Scott (AUS)	Beijing, China	270
1997	E Els (RSA)	Hope Island, Queensland	278	2006	K Stadler (USA)	Perth, Australia	268
1998	T Woods (USA)*	Blue Canyon CC, Phuket	279	2007	A Haig (RSA)*	Phuket, Thailand	275
*Woods beat E Els at 2nd extra hole				*Beat at R Sterne at 1st extra hole			
1999	Not played						

Maybank Malaysian Open *Kota Permai, Kuala Lumpur, Malaysia* [6979–72]

1	Arjun Atwal (IND)*	70-68-68-64—270	€219483
2	Peter Hedblom (SWE)	66-68-65-71—270	146322
*Atwal won at the second extra hole			
3	Simon Dyson (ENG)	64-71-67-69—271	74142
	Kane Webber (aus)	67-71-68-65—271	74142

1992	V Singh (FIJ)		1997	L Westwood (ENG)	*Beat Harrington at 3rd	2003	A Atwal (IND)
1993	G Norquist (USA)		1998	E Fryatt	extra hole	2004	T Jaidee (THA)
1994	J Haegmann (SWE)		1999	G Norquist (USA)	2002 A Forsyth (SCO)*	2005	T Jaidee (THA)
1995	C Devers (USA)		2000	Y Wei Tze (TPE)	*Beat S Leaney at 2nd extra	2006	C Wi (KOR)
1996	S Fiesch (USA)		2001	V Singh (FIJ)*	hole	2007	P Hedblom (SWE)

Ballantine's Championship *Pinx, Jeju Island, Korea* [7345–72]

1	Graeme McDowell (NIR)*	68-64-66-66—264	€333330
2	Jeev Milkha Singh (IND)	68-66-64-66—264	222220
*McDowell won at the third extra hole			
3	Paul McGinley (IRL)	68-67-67-69—271	125200

WGC – CA Championship *Doral, Orlando, FL, USA* [7266–72]

1	Geoff Ogilvy (AUS)	65-67-68-71—271	€865160
2	Jim Furyk (USA)	69-71-64-68—272	339655
	Retief Goosen (RSA)	71-69-64-68—272	339655
	Vijay Singh (FIJ)	73-68-63-68—272	339655

Full details of this event can be found on page 189

Madeira Island Open   *Santo da Serra, Madeira*   [6826–72]

1	Alastair Forsyth (SCO)*	70-70-66-67—273	€116660	
2	Hennie Otto (RSA)	67-67-67-72—273	77770	

Forsyth won at the first extra hole

3	Gary Clark (ENG)	72-71-64-70—277	43820	

1993	M James (ENG)	Campo de Golf da Madeira	281	2000	N Fasth (SWE)	Santo da Serra GC	279
				2001	D Smyth (IRL)	Santo da Serra GC	270
1994	M Lanner (SWE)	Campo de Golf da Madeira	206 (54)	2002	D Borrego (ESP)	Santo da Serra GC	281
				2003	B Dredge (WAL)	Santo da Serra GC	272
1995	S Luna (ESP)	Campo de Golf da Madeira	272	2004	C Hanell (SWE)	Santo da Serra GC	284
				2005	R-J Derksen (NED)	Santo da Serra GC	275
1996	J Sandelin (SWE)	Campo de Golf da Madeira	279	2006	J Van de Velde (FRA)	Santo da Serra GC	273
1997	P Mitchell (ENG)	Santo de Serra GC	204 (54)	2007	D Vancsik (ARG)	Santo da Serra GC	270
1998	M Lanner (SWE)	Santo de Serra GC	277				
1999	P Linhart (SWE)	Santo da Serra GC	276				

Open de Andalucia   *Aloha, Spain*   [6881–72]

1	Thomas Levet (FRA)*	69-68-68-67—272	€166660	
2	Oliver Fisher (ENG)	70-68-67-67—272	111110	

Levet won at the first extra hole

3	Lee Westwood (ENG)	65-73-66-71—275	62600	

2007	L Westwood (ENG)	268

Open de Portugal   *Oitavos Dunes, Estoril*   [6893–71]

1	Grégory Bourdy (FRA)*	63-65-68-70—266	€208330	
2	Alastair Forsyth (SCO)	65-69-66-66—266	108565	
	David Howell (ENG)	67-68-67-64—266	108565	

Bourdy won at the third extra hole

1953	EC Brown (SCO)	Estoril	260		1985	W Humphreys (ENG)	Quinta do Lago	279
1954	A Miguel (ESP)	Estoril	263		1986	M McNulty (NIR)	Quinta do Lago	270
1955	F van Donck (BEL)	Estoril	267		1987	R Lee (ENG)	Estoril	195 (54)
1956	A Miguel (ESP)	Estoril	268		1988	M Harwood (AUS)	Quinta do Lago	280
1958	P Alliss (ENG)	Estoril	264		1989	C Montgomerie (SCO)	Quinta do Lago	264
1959	S Miguel (ESP)	Estoril	265		1990	M McLean (ENG)	Quinta do Lago	274
1960	K Bousfield (ENG)	Estoril	268		1991	S Richardson (ENG)	Estela	283
1961	K Bousfield (ENG)	Estoril	263		1992	R Rafferty (NIR)	Vila Sol	273
1962	A Angelini (ITA)	Estoril	269		1993	D Gilford (ENG)*	Vila Sol	275
1963	R Sota (ESP)	Estoril	204 (54)		*Gilford beat J Berendt at first extra hole*			
1964	A Miguel (ESP)	Estoril	279		1994	P Price (WAL)	Penha Longa	278
1966	A Angelini (ITA)	Estoril	273		1995	A Hunter (SCO)*	Penha Longa	277
1967	A Gallardo (ESP)	Estoril	214 (54)		*Hunter beat D Clarke at first extra hole*			
1968	M Faulkner (ENG)	Estoril	273		1996	W Riley (AUS)	Aroeira	271
1969	R Sota (ESP)	Estoril	270		1997	M Jonzon (SWE)	Aroeira	269
1970	R Sota (ESP)	Estoril	274		1998	P Mitchell (ENG)	Algarve	274
1971	L Platts (ENG)	Estoril	277		1999	V Phillips (ENG)*	Penina	276
1972	G Garrido (ESP)	Estoril	196 (54)		*Phillips beat J Bickerton at first extra hole*			
1973	J Benito (ESP)*	Penina	294		2000	G Orr (SCO)	Penina	275
Benito beat B Gallacher at first extra hole					2001	P Price (WAL)	Algarve	273
1974	BGC Huggett (WAL)	Estoril	272		2002	C Pettersson (SWE)*	Vale do Lobo	142 (36)
1975	H Underwood (USA)	Penina	292		*Pettersson beat D Gilford at first extra hole*			
1976	S Balbuena (ESP)	Quinta do Lago	283		2003	F Jacobson (SWE)	Vale do Lobo	283
1977	M Ramos (ESP)	Penina	287		2004	MA Jiménez (ESP)	Vale do Lobo	272
1978	H Clark (ENG)	Penina	291		2005	P Broadhurst (ENG)	Quinta de Marinha	271
1979	B Barnes (SCO)	Vilamoura	287		2006	P Broadhurst (ENG)	Le Meridien Penina	271
1982	S Torrance (SCO)	Penina	207 (54)		2007	P Martin-Benavides (ESP) (am)	Quinta de Marinha	278
1983	S Torrance (SCO)	Troia	286					
1984	A Johnstone (ZIM)	Quinta do Lago	274					

The MASTERS TOURNAMENT *Augusta National, GA, USA* [7445–72]

1	Trevor Immelman (RSA)	68-68-69-75—280	€857957
2	Tiger Woods (USA)	72-71-68-72—283	514774
3	Stewart Cink (USA)	72-69-71-72—284	276453
	Brandt Snedeker (USA)	69-68-70-77—284	276453

Full details of this event can be found on page 64

Volvo China Open *Beijing International* [7321–72]

1	Damien McGrane (IRL)	68-69-68-73—278	€232121
2	Simon Griffiths (ENG)	68-72-73-74—287	103857
	Michael Lorenzo-Vera (FRA)	67-69-72-79—287	103857
	Oliver Wilson (ENG)	72-66-70-79—287	103857
	Andrew McLardy (AUS)	72-70-67-70—279	111464

1995 Raul Fretes (PAR)
1996 Prayed Marksaeng (THA)
1997 Cheng Jun (CHI)
1998 Ed Fryatt (ENG)
1999 Kyi Hla Han (MYA)
2000 Simon Dyson (ENG)
2001 Charlie Wi (KOR)
2002 David Gleeson (AUS)
2003 Zhang Lian-Wei (CHI)
2004 Stephen Dodd (WAL)
2005 Paul Casey (ENG)
2006 Jeev Milkha Singh (IND)
2007 M Brier (AUT)

BMW Asian Open *Tomson, Shanghai Pudong, China* [7326-72]

1	Darren Clarke (NIR)	71-69-67-73—280	€243507
2	Robert-Jan Derksen (NED)	70-69-69-73—281	162336
3	Robert Dinwiddie (ENG)	70-73-66-74—283	75487
	Wen-tang Lin (TPE)	71-71-69-72—283	75487
	Francesco Molinari (ITA)	71-75-68-69—283	75487

2002 J Sandelin (SWE) 278
2003 P Harrington (IRL) 273
2004 MA Jiménez (ESP) 274
2005 E Els (RSA) 262
2006 G Fernandez-Castaño (ESP) 281
2007 R Jacquelin (FRA) 278

Open de España *Real, Sevilla* (Spanish unless stated)

1	Peter Lawrie (IRL)*	68-70-68-67—273	€333330
2	Ignacio Garrido (ESP)	66-63-72-72—273	222220

Lawrie won at the second extra hole

3	Søren Hansen (DEN)	68-70-67-69—274	125200

1912 A Massy (FRA)
1913–15 Not played
1916 A de la Torre
1917 A de la Torre
1918 Not played
1919 A de la Torre
1921 E Lafitte (FRA)
1923 A de la Torre
1925 A de la Torre
1926 J Bernardino
1927 A Massy (FRA)
1928 A Massy (FRA)
1929 E Lafitte (FRA)
1930 J Bernardino
1932 G Gonzalez
1933 G Gonzalez
1934 J Bernardino
1935 A de la Torre
1936–40 Not played
1941 M Provencio
1942 G Gonzalez
1943 M Provencio
1944 N Sagardia

1945 C Celles
1946 M Morcillo
1947 M Gonzalez (am)
1948 M Morcillo
1949 M Morcillo
1950 A Cerda (ARG)
1951 M Provencio
1952 M Faulkner (ENG)
1953 M Faulkner (ENG)
1954 S Miguel
1955 H de Lamaze (FRA) (am)
1956 P Alliss (ENG)
1957 M Faulkner (ENG)
1958 P Alliss (ENG)
1959 PW Thomson (AUS)
1960 S Miguel
1961 A Miguel

1963 R Sota
1964 A Miguel
1966 R de Vicenzo (ARG)
1967 S Miguel
1968 R Shaw (AUS)
1969 J Garaialde (FRA)
1970 A Gallardo
1971 D Hayes (RSA)
1972 A Garrido*
*Beat V Barrias at 3rd extra hole
1973 NC Coles (ENG)
1974 J Heard (USA)
1975 A Palmer (USA)
1976 E Polland (NIR)
1977 B Gallacher (SCO)
1978 B Barnes (SCO)
1979 D Hayes (RSA)
1980 E Polland (NIR)
1981 S Ballesteros

1982 S Torrance (SCO)
1983 E Darcy (IRL)
1984 B Langer (GER)
1985 S Ballesteros
1986 H Clark (ENG)
1987 N Faldo (ENG)
1988 M James (ENG)
1989 B Langer (GER)
1990 R Davis (AUS)
1991 E Romero*
*Beat S Ballesteros at 7th extra hole
1992 A Sherborne (ENG)
1993 J Haeggman (SWE)
1994 C Montgomerie (SCO)
1995 S Ballesteros
1996 P Harrington (IRL)

1997 M James (ENG)*
*Beat G Norman at 3rd extra hole
1998 T Bjørn (DEN)
1999 J Sandelin (SWE)
2000 B Davis (ENG)
2001 R Karlsson (SWE)
2002 S García
2003 K Ferrie (ENG)*
*Beat P Hedblom & P Lawrie at 2nd extra hole
2004 C Cévaër (FRA)
2005 P Hanson (SWE)*
*Beat P Gustafsson at 1st extra hole
2006 N Fasth (SWE)
2007 C Schwartzel (RSA)

Methorios Capital Italian Open   Castello di Tolcinasco, Milan   (Italian unless stated)   [7283–72]

(Formerly the Telecom Italia Open)

1	Hennie Otto (RSA)		65-66-63-69—263		€283330
2	Oliver Wilson (ENG)		66-69-65-64—264		188880
3	Robert Karlsson (SWE)		68-61-69-67—265		106420

1925	F Pasquali	Stresa	154	1980	M Mannelli	Rome	276
1926	A Boyer (FRA)	Stresa	147	1981	J M Canizares (ESP)*	Milan	280
1927	P Alliss (ENG)	Stresa	145	*Canizares beat B Clampett at first extra hole			
1928	A Boyer (FRA)	Villa d'Este	145	1982	M James (ENG)	Is Molas	280
1929	R Golias (FRA)	Villa d'Este	143	1983	B Langer (GER)*	Ugolino	271
1930	A Boyer (FRA)	Villa d'Este	140	*Langer beat S Ballesteros and K Brown at second extra hole			
1931	A Boyer (FRA)	Villa d'Este	141	1984	A Lyle (SCO)	Milan	277
1932	A Boomer (ENG)	Villa d'Este	143	1985	M Piñero (ESP)	Molinetto	267
1934	N Nutley (ENG)	San Remo	132	1986	D Feherty (NIR)*	Albarella, Venice	270
1935	P Alliss (ENG)	San Remo	262	*Feherty beat R Rafferty at second extra hole			
1936	H Cotton (ENG)	Sestriere	268	1987	S Torrance (SCO)*	Monticello	271
1937	M Dallemagne (FRA)	San Remo	276	*Torrance beat J Rivero at sixth extra hole			
1938	F van Donck (BEL)	Villa d'Este	276	1988	G Norman (AUS)	Monticello	270
1947	F van Donck (BEL)	San Remo	263	1989	R Rafferty (NIR)	Monticello	273
1948	A Casera	San Remo	267	1990	R Boxall (ENG)	Milan	267
1949	H Hassanein (EGY)	Villa d'Este	263	1991	C Parry (AUS)	Castelconturbia	279
1950	U Grappasonni	Rome	281	1992	A Lyle (SCO)	Monticello	270
1951	J Adams (SCO)	Milan	289	1993	G Turner (NZL)	Modena	267
1952	E Brown (SCO)	Milan	273	1994	E Romero (ARG)	Marco Simone	272
1953	F van Donck (BEL)	Villa d'Este	267	1995	S Torrance (SCO)	Le Rovedine	269
1954	U Grappasonni	Villa d'Este	272	1996	J Payne (ENG)	Bergamo GC	275
1955	F van Donck (BEL)	Venice	287	1997	B Langer (GER)	Gardagolf	273
1956	A Cerda (ARG)	Milan	284	1998	JM Olazábal (ESP)	Castelconturbia	195 (54)
1957	H Henning (RSA)	Villa d'Este	273	1999	D Robertson (SCO)	Circolo GC, Torino	271
1958	P Alliss (ENG)	Varese	282	2000	I Poulter (ENG)	Is Molas	267
1959	P Thomson (AUS)	Villa d'Este	269	2001	G Havret (SWE)	Is Molas	268
1960	B Wilkes (RSA)	Venice	285	2002	I Poulter (ENG)	Olgiata GC	197 (54)
1961	R Sota (ESP)	Garlenda	282	2003	M Grönberg (SWE)	Gardagolf, Brescia	271
1962–1971 Not played				2004	G McDowell (NIR)*	Castello di	197 (54)
1972	N Wood (SCO)	Villa d'Este	271			Tolcinasco	
1973	A Jacklin (ENG)	Rome	284	*McDowell beat T Levet at fourth extra hole			
1974	P Oosterhuis (ENG)	Venice	249 (63)	2005	S Webster (ENG)	Castello di Tolcinasco	270
1975	W Casper (USA)	Monticello	286	2006	F Molinari (ITA)	Castello di Tolcinasco	265
1976	B Dassu	Is Molas	280	2007	G Fernandez-	Castello di Tolcinasco	200
1977	A Gallardo (ESP)*	Monticello	286		Castaño (ESP)*		
*Gallardo beat B Barnes at fourth extra hole				*Fernandez-Costaño beat M Brier (AUT) at second extra hole			
1978	D Hayes (RSA)	Pevero	293				
1979	B Barnes (SCO)*	Monticello	281				
*Barnes beat D Hayes at fourth extra hole							

Irish Open   Adare Manor, Co.Limerick   [7453–72]

1	Richard Finch (ENG)	71-72-65-70—278		€416660
2	Felipe Aguilar (CHI)	71-72-67-70—280		277770
3	Robert Karlsson (SWE)	71-70-69-71—281		118750
	Maarten Lafeber (NED)	71-71-72-67—281		118750
	Gary Murphy (IRL)	74-70-68-69—281		118750
	Lee Westwood (ENG)	75-70-64-72—281		118750

1927	G Duncan (ENG)	Portmarnock	312	1949	H Bradshaw (IRL)	Belvoir Park	286
1928	E Whitcombe (ENG)	Newcastle	288	1950	H Pickworth (ENG)	Royal Dublin	287
1929	A Mitchell (ENG)	Portmarnock	309	1953	E Brown (SCO)	Belvoir Park	272
1930	C Whitcombe (ENG)	Portrush	289	1975	C O'Connor Jr (IRL)	Woodbrook	275
1931	E Kenyon (ENG)	Royal Dublin	291	1976	B Crenshaw (USA)	Portmarnock	284
1932	A Padgham (ENG)	Cork	283	1977	H Green (USA)	Portmarnock	283
1933	E Kenyon (ENG)	Malone	286	1978	K Brown (SCO)	Portmarnock	281
1934	S Easterbrook (ENG)	Portmarnock	284	1979	M James (ENG)	Portmarnock	282
1935	E Whitcombe (ENG)	Newcastle	292	1980	M James (ENG)	Portmarnock	284
1936	R Whitcombe (ENG)	Royal Dublin	281	1981	S Torrance (SCO)	Portmarnock	276
1937	B Gadd (ENG)	Portrush	284	1982	J O'Leary (IRL)	Portmarnock	287
1938	A Locke (RSA)	Portmarnock	292	1983	S Ballesteros (ESP)	Royal Dublin	271
1939	A Lees (ENG)	Newcastle	287	1984	B Langer (GER)	Royal Dublin	267
1946	F Daly (NIR)	Portmarnock	288	1985	S Ballesteros (ESP)*	Royal Dublin	278
1947	H Bradshaw (IRL)	Portrush	290	*Ballesteros beat B Langer at second extra hole			
1948	D Rees (WAL)	Portmarnock	295	1986	S Ballesteros (ESP)	Portmarnock	285

1987	B Langer (GER)	Portmarnock	269
1988	I Woosnam (WAL)	Portmarnock	278
1989	I Woosnam (WAL)*	Portmarnock	278

*Woosnam beat P Walton at first extra hole

1990	JM Olazábal (ESP)	Portmarnock	282
1991	N Faldo (ENG)	Killarney	283
1992	N Faldo* (ENG)	Killarney	274

*Faldo beat W Westner at fourth extra hole

1993	N Faldo (ENG)*	Mount Juliet	276

*Faldo beat JM Olazábal at first extra hole

1994	B Langer (GER)	Mount Juliet	275
1995	S Torrance (SCO)*	Mount Juliet	277

*Torrance beat S Cage and H Clonk at second extra hole

1996	C Montgomerie (SCO)	Druid's Glen	279
1997	C Montgomerie (SCO)	Druid's Glen	269
1998	D Carter (ENG)*	Druid's Glen	278

*Carter beat C Montgomerie at first extra hole

1999	S García (ESP)	Druid's Glen	268
2000	P Sjöland (SWE)	Ballybunion	270
2001	C Montgomerie (SCO)	Fota Island	266
2002	S Hansen (DEN)*	Fota Island	270

*Hansen beat N Fasth, D Fichardt & R Bland at 4th extra hole

2003	M Campbell (NZL)*	Portmarnock	277

*Campbell beat T Bjørn and P Hedblom at first extra hole

2004	B Rumford (AUS)	Portmarnock	274
2005	S Dodd (WAL)	Maynooth	279
2006	T Bjørn (DEN)	Maynooth	283
2007	P Harrington (IRL)*	Adare Manor	283

*Harrington beat B Dredge (WAL) at first extra hole

BMW PGA Championship Wentworth Club, Surrey, England   [7320–70]

1	Miguel Angel Jiménez (ESP)*	70-67-72-68—277	€750000
2	Oliver Wilson (ENG)	70-66-73-68—277	500000

*Jiménez won at the second extra hole

3	Luke Donald (ENG)	72-69-73-65—279	253350
	Robert Karlsson (SWE)	66-69-70-74—279	253350
5	Jyoti Randhawa (IND)	73-68-69-70—280	190800
6	Retief Goosen (RSA)	76-69-70-66—281	126450
	Richard Green (AUS)	70-69-73-69—281	126450
	Alexander Noren (SWE)	75-68-71-67—281	126450
	Andres Romero (ARG)	72-69-73-67—281	126450
10	Alejandro Cañizares (ESP)	72-66-74-70—282	76275
	Paul Casey (ENG)	71-68-73-70—282	76275
	Simon Khan (ENG)	71-71-71-69—282	76275
	Søren Kjeldsen (DEN)	71-65-76-70—282	76275
	Paul McGinley (IRL)	65-66-79-72—282	76275
	Steve Webster (ENG)	71-70-72-69—282	76275
16	Felipe Aguilar (CHI)	71-67-74-71—283	57375
	Oliver Fisher (ENG)	71-73-69-70—283	57375
	Peter Hanson (SWE)	72-71-70-70—283	57375
	Martin Kaymer (GER)	71-70-71-71—283	57375
	Gary Orr (SCO)	70-68-73-72—283	57375
	Daniel Vancsik (ARG)	68-70-72-73—283	57375
22	Paul Lawrie (SCO)	72-73-70-69—284	49500
	Charl Schwartzel (RSA)	68-71-73-72—284	49500
	Marc Warren (SCO)	69-70-75-70—284	49500
25	Robert-Jan Derksen (NED)	70-70-76-69—285	44100
	Simon Dyson (ENG)	75-67-73-70—285	44100
	Jean-Baptiste Gonnet (FRA)	75-69-73-68—285	44100
	James Kingston (RSA)	72-71-71-71—285	44100
	Carlos Rodiles (ESP)	72-71-70-72—285	44100
30	Alastair Forsyth (SCO)	72-70-72-72—286	38025
	Thongchai Jaidee (THA)	72-69-74-71—286	38025
	Sam Little (ENG)	74-68-73-71—286	38025
	Miles Tunnicliff (ENG)	70-65-77-74—286	38025
34	Rafa Echenique (ARG)	70-73-68-76—287	33300
	Marcus Fraser (AUS)	67-69-76-75—287	33300
	Søren Hansen (DEN)	76-66-73-72—287	33300
	Peter Lawrie (IRL)	73-72-70-72—287	33300
38	Grégory Bourdy (FRA)	72-71-71-74—288	30600
	Grégory Havret (FRA)	70-74-73-71—288	30600
40	Anders Hansen (DEN)	75-69-77-68—289	27000
	Damien McGrane (IRL)	72-66-77-74—289	27000
	Louis Oosthuizen (RSA)	67-76-74-72—289	27000
	Hennie Otto (RSA)	71-69-75-74—289	27000
	Henrik Stenson (SWE)	74-70-74-71—289	27000
	Simon Wakefield (ENG)	68-71-77-73—289	27000

BMW PGA Championship *continued*

46	Angel Cabrera (ARG)	73-72-72-73—290	21150
	Ricardo Gonzales (ARG)	73-70-74-73—290	21150
	Gary Houston (WAL)	68-74-75-73—290	21150
	Henrik Nyström (SWE)	72-72-70-76—290	21150
	Peter O'Malley (AUS)	71-72-74-73—290	21150
	Alvaro Velasco (ESP)	69-76-71-74—290	21150
	Sam Walker (ENG)	75-68-72-75—290	21150
53	Paul Broadhurst (ENG)	72-71-74-74—291	16200
	Ariel Canete (ARG)	74-71-71-75—291	16200
	Jamie Donaldson (WAL)	72-72-74-73—291	16200
	Nick Dougherty (ENG)	70-73-76-72—291	16200
57	Graeme McDowell (NIR)	70-73-75-74—292	13950
58	Johan Edfors (SWE)	71-74-73-75—293	12825
	Mark Foster (ENG)	72-70-73-78—293	12825
	Thomas Levet (FRA)	74-71-73-75—293	12825
	Michael Lorenzo-Vera (FRA)	69-76-75-73—293	12825
62	Anton Haig (RSA)	70-75-75-74—294	11700
63	Ignacio Garrido (ESP)	73-68-74-82—297	11025
	David Howell (ENG)	70-71-77-79—297	11025
65	Magnus A Carlsson (SWE)	70-72-79-77—298	10125
	Marcel Siem (GER)	71-73-78-76—298	10125
67	Robert Dinwiddie (ENG)	78-63-79-79—299	9450
68	Ross Fisher (ENG)	72-73-80-75—300	8775
	Matthew Morris (ENG)	71-74-76-79—300	8775
70	Ross McGowan (ENG)	73-72-74-83—302	8200

1955	K Bousfield (ENG)	Pannal	277		1983	S Ballesteros (ESP)	R St George's	278	
1956	CH Ward (ENG)	Maesdu	282		1984	H Clark (ENG)	Wentworth Club	204	(54)
1957	P Alliss (ENG)	Maesdu	286		1985	P Way (ENG)*	Wentworth Club	282	
1958	H Bradshaw (IRL)	Llandudno	287		*Way beat AWB Lyle at third extra hole				
1959	DJ Rees (WAL)	Ashburnham	283		1986	R Davis (AUS)*	Wentworth Club	281	
1960	AF Stickley (ENG)	Coventry	247	(63)	*Davis beat D Smyth at third extra hole				
1961	BJ Bamford (ENG)	R Mid-Surrey	266		1987	B Langer (GER)	Wentworth Club	270	
1962	P Alliss (ENG)	Little Aston	287		1988	I Woosnam (WAL)	Wentworth Club	274	
1963	PJ Butler (ENG)	R Birkdale	306		1989	N Faldo (ENG)	Wentworth Club	272	
1964	AG Grubb (ENG)	Western Gailes	287		1990	M Harwood (AUS)	Wentworth Club	271	
1965	P Alliss (ENG)	Prince's	286		1991	S Ballesteros (ESP)*	Wentworth Club	271	
1966	GB Wolstenholme (ENG)	Saunton	278		*Ballesteros beat C Montgomerie at first extra hole				
					1992	T Johnstone (ZIM)	Wentworth Club	272	
1967	BGC Huggett (WAL)	Thorndon Park	271		1993	B Langer (GER)	Wentworth Club	274	
					1994	JM Olazábal (ESP)	Wentworth Club	271	
1967	ME Gregson (ENG)	Hunstanton	275		1995	B Langer (GER)	Wentworth Club	279	
1968	PM Townsend (ENG)	R Mid-Surrey	275		1996	C Rocca (ITA)	Wentworth Club	274	
					1997	I Woosnam (WAL)	Wentworth Club	275	
1968	D Talbot (ENG)	Dunbar	276		1998	C Montgomerie (SCO)	Wentworth Club	274	
1969	B Gallacher (SCO)	Ashburnham	293						
1972	A Jacklin (ENG)	Wentworth Club	279		1999	C Montgomerie (SCO)	Wentworth Club	270	
1973	P Oosterhuis (ENG)	Wentworth Club	280						
1974	M Bembridge (ENG)	Wentworth Club	278		2000	C Montgomerie (SCO)	Wentworth Club	271	
1975	A Palmer (USA)	R St George's	285						
1976	NC Coles (ENG)*	R St George's	280		2001	A Oldcorn (ENG)	Wentworth Club	272	
*Coles beat E Darcy and G Player at third extra hole					2002	A Hansen (DEN)	Wentworth Club	269	
1977	M Piñero (ESP)	R St George's	283		2003	I Garrido (ESP)*	Wentworth Club	270	
1978	N Faldo (ENG)	R Birkdale	278		*Garrido beat T Immelman at extra hole of play-off				
1979	V Fernandez (ARG)	St Andrews	288		2004	S Drummond (SCO)	Wentworth Club	269	
1980	N Faldo (ENG)	R St George's	283		2005	A Cabrera (ARG)	Wentworth Club	273	
1981	N Faldo (ENG)	Ganton	274		2006	D Howell (ENG)	Wentworth Club	271	
1982	A Jacklin (ENG)*	Hillside	284		2007	A Hansen (DEN)*	Adare Manor	280	
*Jacklin beat B Langer at first extra hole					*Beat J Rose at first extra hole				

Wales Open *Celtic Manor Resort, Newport, Wales*   [7352–71]

1	Scott Strange (AUS)	63-66-69-64—262	€376671
2	Robert Karlsson (SWE)	67-67-68-64—266	251114
3	Raphaël Jacquelin (FRA)	66-68-68-68—270	141477

2000	S Tinning (DEN)	Newport	273	2004	S Khan* (ENG)	Newport	267
2001	P McGinley* (IRL)	Newport	138	*Khan beat P Casey at second extra hole			
*McGinley beat D Lee and P Lawrie at fifth extra hole				2005	MA Jiménez (ESP)	Newport	262
2002	P Lawrie (SCO)	Newport	272	2006	R Karlsson (SWE)	Newport	260
2003	I Poulter (ENG)	Newport	270	2007	R Sterne (RSA)	Newport	263

Bank Austria Open Fontana, Vienna   [7066–71]

1	Jeev Milkha Singh (IND)	64-63-71—198	€216660	
2	Simon Wakefield (ENG)	66-65-68—199	144440	
3	Pelle Edberg (SWE)	64-72-65—201	57200	No play on first day –
	Martin Erlandsson (SWE)	67-69-65—201	57200	Heavy rain.
	Peter Fowler (AUS)	65-67-69—201	57200	
	Michael Jonzon (SWE)	70-64-67—201	57200	
	Iain Pyman (ENG)	69-67-65—201	57200	

1997	E Simsek (GER)	266	2001	C Gane (ENG)	270	2005	M Hoey (IRL)	265	2007 R Green (AUS)* 268
1998	K Karissimi	269	2002	M Brier (AUT)	267	2006	M Brier (AUT)	266	*Beat J-F Remesey (FRA) at
1999	J Ciola	263	2003	R Coles (ENG)	275				1st extra hole
2000	Not played		2004	M Brier (AUT)	261				

US OPEN CHAMPIONSHIP Torrey Pines, La Jolla, CA,, USA   [7643–71]

1	Tiger Woods (USA)*	72-68-70-73—283	€858180
2	Rocco Mediate (USA)	69-71-72-71—283	514908
*Woods won at the 19th hole of the extra round			
3	Lee Westwood (ENG)	70-71-70-73—284	312755

Full details of this event can be found on page 53

St Omer Open St Omer, Lumbres, France   [6845–71]

1	David Dixon (ENG)	77-67-69-66—279	€100000
2	Christian Nilsson (SWE)	75-64-70-71—280	66660
3	Steven O'Hara (SCO)	74-69-70-68—281	37560

2000	P Edmond	274	2003	B Rumford (AUS)	269	2005	J Bäckström	280	2006 C Monasterio 274
2001	S Delagrange	272	2004	P Lima (POR)	279		(SWE)		(ARG)
2002	N Vanhootagem	277							2007 C Suneson (ESP) 276

BMW International Munich, Germany   [6957–72]

1	Martin Kaymer (GER)*	68-63-67-75—273	€333330	
2	Anders Hansen (DEN)	69-70-67-67—273	222220	
*Kaymer won at the first extra hole				
3	John Bickerton (ENG)	70-70-68-67—275	103333	
	Paul Casey (ENG)	70-68-67-70—275	103333	
	Mark Foster (ENG)	67-72-68-68—275	103333	

1989	D Feherty (NIR)	Golfplatz, Munich	269	1998	R Claydon (ENG)	GC München	270
1990	P Azinger* (USA)	Golfplatz, Munich	277	1999	C Montgomerie	GC München	268
*Azinger beat D Feherty at first extra hole					(SCO)		
1991	A Lyle (SCO)	Golfplatz, Munich	268	2000	T Bjørn (DEN)	GC München	368
1992	P Azinger* (USA)	Golfplatz, Munich	266	2001	J Daly (USA)	GC München	261
*Azinger beat G Day, B Langer, A Forsbrand and M James at first				2002	T Bjørn (DEN)	GC München	264
extra hole				2003	L Westwood (ENG)	GC München	269
1993	P Fowler (AUS)	Golfplatz, Munich	267	2004	M A Jiménez (ESP)	GC München	267
1994	M McNulty (ZIM)	St Eurach L&GC	274	2005	D Howell (ENG)	GC München	265
1995	F Nobilo (NZL)	St Eurach L&GC	272	2006	H Stenson (SWE)	GC München	273
1996	M Farry (FRA)	St Eurach L&GC	132 (36)	2007	N Fasth (SWE)	GC München	275
1997	R Karlsson (SWE)	GC München	264				

Open de France ALSTOM Le Golf National, Paris, France   [7225–71]

1	Pablo Larazabal (ESP)	65-70-67-67—269	€666660
2	Colin Montgomerie (SCO)	69-68-68-68—273	444440
3	Søren Hansen (DEN)	69-69-67-69—274	250400

Open de France ALSTOM *continued*

Year	Winner	Venue	Score		Year	Winner	Venue	Score
1906	A Massy (FRA)	La Boulie	292		1966	DJ Hutchinson (RSA)	La Boulie	274
1907	A Massy (FRA)	La Boulie	294		1967	BJ Hunt (ENG)	St Germain	271
1908	JH Taylor (ENG)	La Boulie	300		1968	PJ Butler (ENG)	St Cloud	272
1909	JH Taylor (ENG)	La Boulie	290		1969	J Garaialde (FRA)	St Nom-la-Bretêche	277
1910	J Braid (SCO)	La Boulie	298		1970	D Graham (AUS)	Chantaco	268
1911	A Massy (FRA)	La Boulie	284		1971	Lu Liang Huan	Biarritz	262
1912	J Gassiat (FRA)	La Boulie	284		1972	B Jaeckel* (USA)	Biarritz & La Nivelle	265
1913	G Duncan (ENG)	Chantilly	304		*Jaeckel beat C Clark at first extra hole			
1914	JD Edgar (ENG)	Le Touquet	284		1973	P Oosterhuis (ENG)	La Boulie	280
1920	W Hagen (USA)	La Boulie	298		1974	P Oosterhuis (ENG)	Chantilly	284
1921	A Boomer (ENG)	Le Touquet	284		1975	B Barnes (SCO)	La Boulie	281
1922	A Boomer (ENG)	La Boulie	284		1976	V Tshabalaia (RSA)	Le Touquet	272
1923	J Ockenden	Dieppe	284		1977	S Ballesteros (ESP)	Le Touquet	282
1924	CJH Tolley (am) (ENG)	La Boulie	290		1978	D Hayes (RSA)	La Baule	269
1925	A Massy (FRA)	Chantilly	291		1979	B Gallacher (SCO)	Lyons	284
1926	A Boomer (ENG)	St Cloud	280		1980	G Norman (AUS)	St Cloud	268
1927	G Duncan (ENG)	St Germain	290		1981	A Lyle (SCO)	St Germain	270
1928	CJH Tolley (am) (ENG)	La Boulie	283		1982	S Ballesteros (ESP)	St Nom-la-Bretêche	278
1929	A Boomer (ENG)	Fourqueux	283		1983	N Faldo* (ENG)	La Boulie	277
1930	ER Whitcombe (ENG)	Dieppe	282		*Faldo beat DJ Russell and JM Canizares at third extra hole			
1931	A Boomer (ENG)	Deauville	291		1984	B Langer (GER)	St Cloud	270
1932	AJ Lacey (ENG)	St Cloud	296		1985	S Ballesteros (ESP)	St Germain	263
1933	B Gadd (ENG)	Chantilly	283		1986	S Ballesteros (ESP)	La Boulie	269
1934	SF Brews	Dieppe	284		1987	J Rivero (ESP)	St Cloud	269
1935	SF Brews	Le Touquet	292		1988	N Faldo (ENG)	Chantilly	274
1936	M Dallemagne (FRA)	St Germain	277		1989	N Faldo (ENG)	Chantilly	273
1937	M Dallemagne (FRA)	St Cloud	278		1990	P Walton* (IRL)	Chantilly	275
1938	M Dallemagne (FRA)	Fourqueux	282		*Walton beat B Langer at second extra hole			
1939	M Pose	Le Touquet	285		1991	E Romero (ARG)	National GC	281
1946	TH Cotton (ENG)	St Cloud	269		1992	MA Martin (ESP)	National GC	276
1947	TH Cotton (ENG)	Chantilly	285		1993	C Rocca* (ITA)	National GC	273
1948	F Cavalo	St Cloud	287		*Rocca beat P McGinley at first extra hole			
1949	U Grappasonni (ITA)	St Germain	275		1994	M Roe (ENG)	National GC	274
1950	R De Vicenzo (ARG)	Chantilly	279		1995	P Broadhurst (ENG)	National GC	274
1951	H Hassanein (EGY)	St Cloud	278		1996	R Allenby* (AUS)	National GC	272
1952	AD Locke (RSA)	St Germain	268		*Allenby beat B Langer at first extra hole			
1953	AD Locke (RSA)	La Boulie	276		1997	R Goosen (RSA)	National GC	271
1954	F van Donck (BEL)	St Cloud	275		1998	S Torrance (SCO)	National GC	276
1955	B Nelson (USA)	La Boulie	271		1999	R Goosen* (RSA)	Golf du Médoc	272
1956	A Miguel (ESP)	Deauville	277		*Goosen beat G Turner at second extra hole of play-off			
1957	F van Donck (BEL)	St Cloud	266		2000	C Montgomerie (SCO)	Le Golf National	272
1958	F van Donck (BEL)	St Germain	276		2001	JM Olazábal (ESP)	Lyon GC	268
1959	DC Thomas (WAL)	La Boulie	276		2002	M Mackenzie (ENG)	Le Golf National	279
1960	R De Vicenzo (ARG)	St Cloud	275		2003	P Golding (ENG)	Le Golf National	273
1961	KDG Nagle (AUS)	La Boulie	271		2004	J-F Remesy (FRA)	Le Golf National	272
1962	A Murray (AUS)	St Germain	274		2005	J-F Remesy* (FRA)	Le Golf National	273
1963	B Devlin (AUS)	St Cloud	273		*Remesy beat J Van de Velde at first extra hole			
1964	R de Vicenzo (ARG)	Chantilly	272		2006	J Bickerton (ENG)	Le Golf National	273
1965	R Sota (ESP)	St Nom-la-Bretêche	268		2007	G Storme (ENG)	Le Golf National	277

European Open *London GC, England*   [7257–72]

1	Ross Fisher (ENG)	63-68-69-68—268		€506392
2	Sergio García (ESP)	71-64-74-66—275		337586
3	Graeme McDowell (NIR)	65-67-71-73—276		190200

Year	Winner	Venue	Score		Year	Winner	Venue	Score
1978	B Wadkins* (USA)	Walton Heath	283		1990	P Senior (AUS)	Sunningdale	267
*Wadkins beat B Gallacher and G Morgan at first extra hole					1991	M Harwood (AUS)	Walton Heath	277
1979	A Lyle (SCO)	Turnberry	275		1992	N Faldo (ENG)	Sunningdale	262
1980	T Kite (USA)	Walton Heath	284		1993	G Brand Jr (SCO)	E. Sussex National	275
1981	G Marsh (AUS)	Royal Liverpool	275		1994	D Gilford (ENG)	E. Sussex National	275
1982	M Piñero (ESP)	Sunningdale	266		1995	B Langer* (GER)	The K Club	280
1983	L Aoki (JPN)	Sunningdale	274		*Langer beat B Lane at second extra hole			
1984	G Brand Jr (SCO)	Sunningdale	270		1996	P-U Johansson (SWE)	The K Club	277
1985	B Langer (GER)	Sunningdale	269		1997	P-U Johansson (SWE)	The K Club	267
1986	G Norman* (AUS)	Sunningdale	269		1998	M Grönberg (SWE)	The K Club	275
*Norman beat K Brown at first extra hole					1999	L Westwood (ENG)	The K Club	271
1987	P Way (ENG)	Walton Heath	279		2000	L Westwood (ENG)	The K Club	276
1988	I Woosnam (WAL)	Sunningdale	260		2001	D Clarke (IRL)	The K Club	273
1989	A Murray (AUS)	Walton Heath	277		2002	M Campbell (NZL)	The K Club	282

2003	P Price (WAL)	The K Club	272	2006	S Dodd (WAL)	The K Club	279
2004	R Goosen (RSA)	The K Club	275	2007	C Montgomerie (SCO)	The K Club	269
2005	K Ferrie (ENG)	The K Club	285				

The Barclay's Scottish Open Loch Lomond, Glasgow, Scotland [7149–71]

1	Graeme McDowell (NIR)	67-70-66-68—271	€631044
2	James Kingston (RSA)	70-70-67-66—273	420692
3	Richard Green (AUS)	67-68-70-69—274	213167
	Miguel Angel Jiménez (ESP)	68-69-68-69—274	213167

1986	D Feherty* (NIR)	Haggs Castle	270	1997	T Lehman (USA)	Loch Lomond	265
*Feherty beat C O'Connor Jr & I Baker-Finch at 2nd extra hole				1998	L Westwood (ENG)	Loch Lomond	276
1987	I Woosnam (WAL)	Gleneagles	264	1999	C Montgomerie (SCO)	Loch Lomond	268
1988	B Lane (ENG)	Gleneagles	271	2000	E Els (RSA)	Loch Lomond	273
1989	M Allen (USA)	Gleneagles	272	2001	R Goosen (RSA)	Loch Lomond	268
1990	I Woosnam (WAL)	Gleneagles	269	2002	E Romero* (ARG)	Loch Lomond	273
1991	C Parry (AUS)	Gleneagles	268	*Romero beat F Jacobsen at 1st extra hole of play-off			
1992	P O'Malley (AUS)	Gleneagles	262	2003	E Els (RSA)	Loch Lomond	267
1993	J Parnevik (SWE)	Gleneagles	271	2004	T Levet (FRA)	Loch Lomond	269
1994	C Mason (ENG)	Gleneagles	265	2005	T Clark (RSA)	Loch Lomond	265
1995	W Riley (AUS)	Carnoustie	276	2006	J Edfors (SWE)	Loch Lomond	271
1996	I Woosnam (WAL)	Carnoustie	289	2007	G Havret (FRA)*	Loch Lomond	270
1996	T Bjørn (DEN)	Loch Lomond	277	*Havret beat P Mickelson (USA) at first extra hole			

The 137th OPEN CHAMPIONSHIP Royal Birkdale [7173–70]

1	Padraig Harrington (IRL)	74-68-72-69—283	€938565
2	Ian Poulter (ENG)	72-71-75-69—287	563139
3	Greg Norman (AUS)	70-70-72-77—289	319112
	Henrik Stenson (SWE)	76-72-70-71—289	319112

Full details of this events can be found on page 38

Inteco Russian Open Le Meridien, Moscow, Russia [7154–72]

1	Mikael Lundberg (SWE)	67-64-68-68—267	€210237
2	José-Manuel Lara (ESP)	67-68-70-64—269	140158
3	Benn Barham (ENG)	69-68-65-68—270	78965

1996	C Watts (ENG)	2000	M Bernardini (ITA)	*Beat M Wiegele at 2nd	*Lundberg won at 4th extra
1997	M Reale (ESP)	2001	J Donaldson (WAL)	extra hole	hole
1998	W Bennett (ENG)	2002	I Pyman (ENG)	2004 G Emerson (ENG)	2006 A Cañizares (ESP)
1999	I Pyman (ENG)	2003	M Fraser* (AUS)	2005 M Lundberg* (SWE)	

WGC – Bridgestone Invitational Firestone CC, Akron, OH, USA [7400–70]

1	Vijay Singh (FIJ)	67-66-69-68—270	€860584
2	Stuart Appleby (AUS)	70-66-67-68—271	404793
	Lee Westwood (ENG)	70-65-67-69—271	404793

Full details of this event can be found on page 191

US PGA CHAMPIONSHIP Oakland Hills, Bloomfield, MI [7395–70]

1	Padraig Harrington (IRL)	71-74-66-66—277	€867219
2	Ben Curtis (USA)	73-67-68-71—279	423973
	Sergio García (ESP)	69-73-69-68—279	432973

Full details of this event can be found on page 73

SAS Masters (formerly Scandinavian Masters) Arlandastad, Stockholm, Sweden [6845–70]

1	Peter Hanson (SWE)	66-66-68-71—271	€266660
2	Nick Dougherty (ENG)	66-66-70-70—272	138965
	Pelle Edberg (SWE)	69-67-66-70—272	138965

1977	N Coles (ENG)	Foxhills	288	1980	B Gallacher (SCO)	Moortown	268
1978	B Waites (ENG)	Foxhills	286	1981	B Barnes* (SCO)	Dalmahoy	276
1979	M King (ENG)	Moor Park	281	*Barnes beat B Waites at fourth extra hole			

SAS Masters continued

1982	N Faldo (ENG)	Notts	270	1996	F Nobilo (NZL)	Gut Kaden	270
1983	B Langer (GER)	St Mellion	269	1997	R McFarlane (ENG)	Gut Kaden	282
1984	J Gonzalez* (BRA)	St Mellion	265	1998	L Westwood (ENG)	Gut Kaden	265

*Gonzalez beat M James at second extra hole

1985	Not played			1999	T Woods (USA)	St Leon-Rot	273
1986	I Woosnam (WAL)	The Belfry	277	2000	L Westwood (ENG)	Gut Kaden, Hamburg	273
1987	Not played			2001	T Woods (USA)	St Leon-Rot	266
1988	Not played			2002	T Woods* (USA)	St Leon-Rot	268

*Woods beat C Montgomerie at third extra hole of play-off

1989	C Montgomerie (SCO)	Quinta do Lago	264	2003	P Harrington* (IRL)	Gut Kaden	269

*Harrington beat T Bjørn at first extra hole

1990	M McLean (ENG)	Quinta do Lago	274	2004	T Immelman (RSA)	Gut Kaden	271
1991	Not played			2005	N Fasth* (SWE)	Gut Kaden	274

*Fasth won at third extra hole

1992	Not played			2006	R Karlsson (SWE)	Gut Kaden	263
1993	Not played			2007	A Romero (ARG)	Gut Kaden	269
1994	Not played						
1995	B Langer (GER)	Gut Kaden	270				

The KLM Open (formerly Dutch Open) Kennemer, Zandvoort, The Netherlands   [6626–70]

1	Darren Clarke (NIR)	68-64-66-66—264	€300000
2	Paul McGinley (IRL)	69-68-67-64—268	200000
3	Henrik Stenson (SWE)	68-65-68-68—269	112680

1919	D Oosterveer (NED)	The Hague	158	1969	G Wolstenholme (ENG)	Utrecht	277
1920	H Burrows	Kennemer	155	1970	V Fernandez (ARG)	Eindhoven	279
1921	H Burrows	Domburg	151	1971	R Sota (ESP)	Kennemer	277
1922	G Pannell	Noordwijk	160	1972	J Newton (AUS)	The Hague	277
1923	H Burrows	Hilversumsche	153	1973	D McClelland (ENG)	The Hague	279
1924	A Boomer	The Hague	138	1974	B Barnes (SCO)	Hilversumsche	211(54)
1925	A Boomer	The Hague	144	1975	H Baiocchi (RSA)	Hilversumsche	279
1926	A Boomer	The Hague	151	1976	S Ballesteros (ESP)	Kennemer	275
1927	P Boomer	The Hague	147	1977	R Byman (USA)	Kennemer	278
1928	ER Whitcombe	The Hague	141	1978	R Byman (USA)	Noordwijkse	211(54)
1929	JJ Taylor	Hilversumsche	153	1979	G Marsh (AUS)	Noordwijkse	285
1930	J Oosterveer (NED)	The Hague	152	1980	S Ballesteros (ESP)	Hilversumsche	280
1931	F Dyer	Kennemer	145	1981	H Henning (RSA)	The Hague	280
1932	A Boyer	The Hague	137	1982	P Way (ENG)	Utrecht	276
1933	M Dallemagne	Kennemer	143	1983	K Brown (SCO)	Kennemer	274
1934	SF Brews	Utrecht	286	1984	B Langer (GER)	Rosendaelsche	275
1935	SF Brews	Kennemer	275	1985	G Marsh (AUS)	Noordwijkse	282
1936	F van Donck (BEL)	Hilversumsche	285	1986	S Ballesteros (ESP)	Noordwijkse	271(70)
1937	F van Donck (BEL)	Utrecht	286	1987	G Brand Jr (SCO)	Hilversumsche	272
1938	AH Padgham (ENG)	The Hague	281	1988	M Mouland (WAL)	Hilversumsche	274
1939	AD Locke (RSA)	Kennemer	281	1989	JM Olazábal* (ESP)	Kennemer	277

*Olazábal beat R Chapman and R Rafferty at ninth extra hole

1946	F van Donck (BEL)	Hilversumsche	290	1990	S McAllister (SCO)	Kennemer	274
1947	G Ruhl	Eindhoven	290	1991	P Stewart (USA)	Noordwijkse	267
1948	C Denny	Hilversumsche	290	1992	B Langer* (GER)	Noordwijkse	277

*Langer beat G Brand Jr at second extra hole

1949	J Adams (ENG)	The Hague	294	1993	C Montgomerie (SCO)	Noordwijkse	281
1950	R De Vicenzo (ARG)	Breda	269	1994	MA Jiménez (ESP)	Hilversumsche	270
1951	F van Donck (BEL)	Kennemer	281	1995	S Hoch (USA)	Hilversumsche	269
1952	C Denny	Hilversumsche	284	1996	M McNulty (ZIM)	Hilversumsche	266
1953	F van Donck (BEL)	Eindhoven	286	1997	S Strüver (GER)	Hilversumsche	266
1954	U Grappasonni (ITA)	The Hague	295	1998	S Leaney (AUS)	Hilversumsche	266
1955	A Angelini (ITA)	Kennemer	280	1999	L Westwood (ENG)	Hilversumsche	269
1956	A Cerda	Eindhoven	277	2000	S Leaney (AUS)	Nordwijkse	269
1957	J Jacobs (ENG)	Hilversumsche	284	2001	B Langer* (GER)	Nordwijkse	269

*Langer beat W Bennett at first extra hole

1958	D Thomas (WAL)	Kennemer	277	2002	T Dier (GER)	Hilversum	263
1959	S Sewgolum (RSA)	The Hague	283	2003	M Lafeber (NED)	Hilversum	267
1960	S Sewgolum (RSA)	Eindhoven	280	2004	D Lynn (ENG)	Hilversum	264
1961	BBS Wilkes (RSA)	Kennemer	279	2005	G F Castano (ESP)	Hilversum	269
1962	BGC Huggett (WAL)	Hilversumsche	274	2006	S Dyson* (ENG)	Kennemer	270

*Dyson beat R Green at first extra hole

1963	R Waltman (RSA)	Wassenaar	279	2007	R Fisher (ENG)	Kennemer	268
1964	S Sewgolum (RSA)	Eindhoven	275				
1965	A Miguel (ESP)	Breda	278				
1966	R Sota (ESP)	Kennemer	276				
1967	P Townsend (ENG)	The Hague	282				
1968	J Cockin (ENG)	Hilversumsche	292				

Johnnie Walker Championship *Gleneagles, Scotland* [7374–73]

1	Grégory Havret (FRA)	68-71-69-70—278	€292355	
2	Graeme Storm (ENG)	74-69-68-68—279	194899	
3	Peter Hanson (SWE)	74-72-66-69—281	98759	
	David Howell (ENG)	75-67-68-71—281	98759	

1999	W Bennett (ENG)	282	2003	S Kjeldsen (DEN)	279	2007	M Warren (SCO)*	280
2000	P Fulke (SWE)	271	2004	M Tunnicliffe (ENG)	275	*Beat S Wakefield (ENG) at 2nd extra		
2001	P Casey (ENG)	274	2005	E Canonica (ITA)	281	hole		
2002	A Scott (AUS)	262	2006	P Casey (ENG)	276			

Omega European Masters *Crans-sur-Sierre, Switzerland since 1939* [6857–71]

1	Jean-François Lucquin (FRA)*	68-67-69-67—271	€333330	
2	Rory McIlroy (NIR)	63-71-66-71—271	222220	

Lucquin won at the second extra hole

3	Christian Cévaër (FRA)	68-69-68-67—272	95000	
	Julien Clément (SUI)	69-68-67-68—272	95000	
	Miguel Angel Jiménez (ESP)	68-69-68-67—272	95000	
	Gary Orr (SCO)	67-71-67-67—272	95000	

Year	Player	Venue	Score		Year	Player	Score
1923	A Ross	Engen	149		1973	H Baiocchi (RSA)	278
1924	P Boomer (ENG)	Engen	150		1974	RJ Charles (NZL)	275
1925	A Ross	Engen	148		1975	D Hayes (RSA)	273
1926	A Ross	Lucerne	145		1976	M Piñero (ESP)	274
1929	A Wilson	Lucerne	142		1977	S Ballesteros (ESP)	273
1930	A Boyer	Samedan	150		1978	S Ballesteros (ESP)	272
1931	M Dallemagne (FRA)	Lucerne	145		1979	H Baiocchi (RSA)	275
1934	A Boyer	Lausanne	133		1980	N Price (ZIM)	267
1935	A Boyer	Lausanne	137		1981	M Piñero* (ESP)	277
1936	F Francis (am)	Lausanne	134		*Piñero beat T Johnstone and A Garrido at first extra hole		
1937	M Dallemagne (FRA)	Samedan	138		1982	I Woosnam* (WAL)	272
1938	J Saubaber	Zumikon	139		*Woosnam beat W Longmuir at third extra hole		
1939	F Cavalo (ITA)	Crans-sur-Sierre	273		1983	N Faldo* (ENG)	268
1948	U Grappasonni (ITA)		285		1984	J Anderson (CAN)	261
1949	M Dallemagne (FRA)		270		1985	C Stadler (USA)	267
1950	A Casera (ITA)		276		1986	JM Olazábal (ESP)	262
1951	EC Brown (SCO)		267		1987	A Forsbraneng	268
1952	U Grappasonni (ITA)		267		1989	S Ballesteros (ESP)	266
1953	F van Donck (BEL)		267		1990	R Rafferty (NIR)	267
1954	AD Locke (RSA)		276		1991	J Hawkes (RSA)	268
1955	F van Donck (BEL)		277		1992	J Spence* (ENG)	271
1956	DJ Rees (WAS)		278		*Spence beat A Forsbrand at second extra hole		
1957	A Angelini (ITA)		270		1993	B Lane (ENG)	270
1958	K Bousfield (ENG)		272		1994	E Romero (ARG)	266
1959	DJ Rees (WAL)		274		1995	M Grönberg (SWE)	270
1960	H Henning (RSA)		270		1996	C Montgomerie (SCO)	260
1961	KDG Nagle (AUS)		268		1997	C Rocca (ITA)	266
1962	RJ Charles* (NZL)		272		1998	S Strüver* (GER)	263
*after play-off with PJ Butler (ENG) and F van Donck (BEL)					*Strüver beat P Sjoland at first extra hole		
1963	DJ Rees* (WAL)		278		1999	L Westwood (ENG)	270
*after play-off with HR Henning (RSA)					2000	E Romero (ARG)	261
1964	HR Henning (RSA)		276		2001	R Gonzalez (ARG)	268
1965	HR Henning (RSA)		208 (54)		2002	R Karlsson (SWE)	270
1966	A Angelini (ITA)		271		2003	E Els (RSA)	267
1967	R Vines (AUS)		272		2004	L Donald (ENG)	265
1968	R Bernardini (ITA)		272		2005	S García (ESP)	270
1969	R Bernardini (ITA)		277		2006	B Dredge (WAL)	267
1970	G Marsh (AUS)		274		2007	B Rumford (AUS)*	268
1971	PM Townsend (ENG)		270		*Beat P Archer (ENG) at 1st extra hole		
1972	G Marsh (AUS)		270				

Mercedes-Benz Championship (formerly German Masters) *Gut Lärchenhof, Cologne* [7289–72]

1	Robert Karlsson (SWE)	67-69-68-71—275	€320000
2	Francesco Molinari (ITA)	71-71-65-70—277	220000
3	Michael Campbell (NZL)	71-70-68-70—279	101516
	Ross Fisher (ENG)	68-73-68-70—279	101516
	Miguel Angel Jiménez (ESP)	72-73-68-66—279	101516

1987	AWB Lyle (SCO)	278	1994	S Ballesteros (ESP)	270	
1988	JM Olazábal (ESP)	279	1995	A Forsbrand (SWE)	264	
1989	B Langer (GER)	276	1996	D Clarke (IRL)	264	
1990	S Torrance (SCO)	272	1997	B Langer (GER)	267	
1991	B Langer* (GER)	275	1998	C Montgomerie (SCO)	266	
*Beat R David at 1st extra hole			1999	S García* (ESP)	277	
1992	B Lane	272	2000	M Campbell (NZL)	197(54)	
1993	S Richardson (ENG)	271				

2001	B Langer (GER)	266
2002	S Leaney (AUS)	266
2003	KJ Choi (KOR)	262
2004	P Harrington (IRL)	275
2005	R Goosen (RSA)	268
2006	Not played	
*Beat P Harrington at 2nd extra hole		
2007	S Hansen (DEN)	271

Ryder Cup *Valhalla, Louiseville, KY, USA*   [7496–71]
Result: USA 16½ Europe 11½
Fuller details of this event can be found in International Team Events on page 194

Quinn Direct British Masters   *The Belfry, Sutton Coldfield*   [7230–72]

1	Gonzalo Fernandez-Castaño (ESP)*	71-70-68-67—276	€381612
2	Lee Westwood (ENG)	68-70-68-70—276	254408
*Fernandez-Castaño won at the third extra hole			
3	Michael Campbell (NZL)	69-72-65-72—278	143333

1946T	AD Locke (RSA)	Stoneham	286				
	J Adams (ENG)			*Hunt beat B Barnes at third extra hole			
1947	A Lees (ENG)	Little Aston	283	1978	T Horton (ENG)	St Pierre	279
1948	N Von Nida (AUS)	Sunningdale	272	1979	G Marsh (AUS)	Woburn	283
1949	C Ward (ENG)	St Andrews	290	1980	B Langer (GER)	St Pierre	270
1950	D Rees (WAL)	Hoylake	281	1981	G Norman (AUS)	Woburn	273
1951	M Faulkner (ENG)	Wentworth Club	281	1982	G Norman (AUS)	St Pierre	267
1952	H Weetman (ENG)	Mere	281	1983	L Woosnam (WAL)	St Pierre	269
1953	H Bradshaw (IRL)	Sunningdale	272	1985	L Trevino (USA)	Woburn	278
1954	AD Locke (RSA)	Prince's	291	1986	S Ballesteros (ESP)	Woburn	275
1955	H Bradshaw (IRL)	Little Aston	277	1987	M McNulty (ZIM)	Woburn	274
1956	C O'Connor (IRL)	Prestwick	277	1988	A Lyle (SCO)	Woburn	273
1957	E Brown (SCO)	Hollinwell	275	1989	N Faldo (ENG)	Woburn	267
1958	H Weetman (ENG)	Little Aston	276	1990	M James (ENG)	Woburn	270
1959	C O'Connor (IRL)	Portmarnock	276	1991	S Ballesteros (ESP)	Woburn	275
1960	J Hitchcock (ENG)	Sunningdale	275	1992	C O'Connor Jr* (IRL)	Woburn	270
1961	P Thomson (AUS)	Porthcawl	284	*O'Connor beat T Johnstone at first extra hole			
1962	D Rees (WAL)	Wentworth Club	278	1993	P Baker (ENG)	Woburn	266
1963	B Hunt (ENG)	Little Aston	282	1994	I Woosnam (WAL)	Woburn	271
1964	C Legrange (RSA)	Royal Birkdale	288	1995	S Torrance (SCO)	Collingtree Park	270
1965	B Hunt (ENG)	Portmarnock	283	1996	R Allenby* (AUS)	Collingtree Park	284
1966	N Coles (ENG)	Lindrick	278	*Allenby beat MA Martin at first extra hole			
1967	A Jacklin (ENG)	R St George's	274	1997	G Turner (NZL)	Forest of Arden	275
1968	P Thomson (AUS)	Sunningdale	274	1998	C Montgomerie (SCO)	Forest of Arden	281
1969	C Legrange (RSA)	Little Aston	281	1999	B May (USA)	Woburn	269
1970	B Huggett (WAL)	R Lytham & St Annes	293	2000	G Orr (SCO)	Woburn	267
1971	M Bembridge (ENG)	St Pierre	273	2001	T Levet* (FRA)	Woburn	274
1972	RJ Charles (NZL)	Northumberland	277	*Beat M Gronberg, D Howell & R Karlsson at 3rd extra hole			
1973	A Jacklin (ENG)	St Pierre	272	2002	J Rose (ENG)	Woburn	269
1974	B Gallacher* (SCO)	St Pierre	282	2003	G Owen (ENG)	Forest of Arden	274
*Gallacher beat G Player at first extra hole				2004	B Lane (ENG)	Forest of Arden	272
1975	B Gallacher (SCO)	Ganton	289	2005	T Bjørn (DEN)	Forest of Arden	282
1976	B Dassu (ITA)	St Pierre	271	2006	J Edfors (SWE)	The Belfry	277
1977	G Hunt* (ENG)	Lindrick	291	2007	L Westwood (ENG)	The Belfry	273

Alfred Dunhill Links Championship *St Andrews (Old Course), Kingsbarns and Carnoustie* [all 72]

1	Robert Karlsson (SWE)	67-70-76-65—278	€545811
2	Ross Fisher (ENG)	64-76-73-65—278	284439
	Martin Kaymer (GER)	65-72-73-68—278	284439
*Karlsson won at the first extra hole			

2001	P Lawrie (SCO)	270	2003	L Westwood (ENG)	267	2005	C Montgomerie (SCO)	279
2002	P Harrington* (IRL)	269	2004	S Gallacher* (SCO)	269	2006	P Harrington (IRL)	271
*Beat E Romero at 2nd extra hole			*Beat G McDowell at 1st extra hole			2007	N Dougherty (ENG)	270

Madrid Masters Club de Campo Villa, Madrid   [6950–71]

1	Charl Schwartzel (RSA)	69-64-66-66—265	€166660
2	Ricardo Gonzalez (ARG)	69-69-62-68—268	111110
3	Pablo Larrazabal (ESP)	68-72-62-67—269	62600

Portugal Masters Oceânico Victoria, Vilamoura   [7231–72]

1	Alvaro Quiros (ESP)	66-68-67-68—269	€500000
2	Paul Lawrie (SCO)	70-65-70-67—272	333330
3	Ross Fisher (ENG)	67-70-65-71—273	155000
	Robert Karlsson (SWE)	69-67-66-71—273	155000
	Steven Webster (ENG)	72-67-66-68—273	155000
2007	S Webster (ENG)	263	

Castelló Masters Club de Campo del Mediterráneo, Castellón   [7111–72]

1	Sergio García (ESP)	66-65-66-67—264	€333330
2	Peter Hedblom (SWE)	68-65-68-66—267	222220
3	Alexader Noren (SWE)	68-68-68-65—269	125200

Volvo Masters Club de Golf Valderrama, Cadiz, Spain   [6988–71]

1	Søren Kjeldsen (DEN)	65-71-69-71—276	€708000
2	Martin Kaymer (GER)	73-70-67-68—278	369000
2	Anthony Wall (ENG)	69-69-71-69—278	369000

1988	N Faldo (ENG)	Valderrama	284	2001	P Harrington (IRL)	Montecastillo	204(54)
1989	R Rafferty (NIR)	Valderrama	282	2002	B Langer* (GER)	Valderrama	281
1990	M Harwood (AUS)	Valderrama	286		C Montgomerie* (SCO)		281
1991	R Davis (AUS)	Valderrama	280	*declared a tie after bad light stopped play after two holes of			
1992	A Lyle* (SCO)	Valderrama	287	their sudden-death play-off			
*Lyle beat C Montgomerie at first extra hole				2003	F Jacobsen (SWE)	Valderrama	276
1993	C Montgomerie (SCO)	Valderrama	274	2004	I Poulter* (ENG)	Valderrama	277
1994	B Langer (GER)	Valderrama	276	*Poulter beat S Garcia at first extra hole of play-off			
1995	A Cejka (GER)	Valderrama	282	2005	P McGinley (IRL)	Valderrama	274
1996	M McNulty (ZIM)	Valderrama	276	2006	J Milkha Singh (IND)	Valderrama	282
1997	L Westwood (ENG)	Montecastillo	200(54)	2007	J Rose (ENG)*	Valderrama	283
1998	D Clarke (NIR)	Montecastillo	271	*Rose beat S Dyson (ENG) at 2nd hole of sudden-death			
1999	MA Jiménez (ESP)	Montecastillo	269	play-off			
2000	P Fulke (SWE)	Montecastillo	272				

Omega Mission Hills World Cup Mission Hills GC, China   [7069–71]

1	Sweden (Robert Karlsson and Henrik Stenson)	65-67-66-63—261	€1336760 shared
2	Spain (Miguel Angel Jiménez and Pablo Larrazabal)	64-63-67-70—264	707696
3	Australia (Richard Green and Brendan Jones)	63-68-63-76—270	432481
	Japan (Ryuji Imada and Toru Tamiguchi)	66-68-68-68—270	432481

Fuller details can be found in World Championship Events, page 211

Top amateurs earn European Tour cards – see page 187 for list of qualifiers

2009 season

HSBC Champions Tournament   *Sheshan GC, Shanghai*   [7191-72]

1	Sergio García (ESP)	66-68-72-68—274	€650382
2	Oliver Wilson (ENG)	67-68-69-70—274	433601
3	Peter Hanson (SWE)	69-70-70-66—275	219708
3	Geoff Ogilvy (AUS)	70-65-70-70—275	219708

UBS Hong Kong Open   *Hong Kong GC, Fanling*   [6734–70]

1	Wen-tang Lin (TPE)	65-69-64-67—265	€327383
2	Rory McIlroy (NIR)	70-64-66-65—265	170610
	Francesco Molinari (ITA)	66-67-67-65—265	170610

Sportsbet Australian Masters   *Huntingdale, Melbourne*   [6980–72]

1	Rod Pampling (AUS)	71-68-70-67—276	€140193
2	Marcus Fraser (AUS)	73-67-71-65—276	79442
3	Robert Allenby (AUS)	73-66-67-73—279	52572

Alfred Dunhill Championship   *Leopard Creek, Mpumalanga, RSA*   [6631m–72]

1	Richard Sterne (RSA)	68-66-68-69—271	€158,500
2	Johan Edfors (SWE)	66-69-71-66—272	92,100
	Robert Rock (ENG)	66-67-69-70—272	92,100

South African Open Championship   *Pearl Valley Golf Estates*   [7319–72]

1	Richard Sterne* (RSA)	72-69-67-66—274	€158,500
2	Gareth Maybin (NIR)	66-69-69-70—274	115,000

Sterne won at first extra hole

3	Ernie Els (RSA)	67-67-77-64—275	53,200
	Lee Westwood (ENG)	66-68-68-73—275	53,200
	Rory McIlroy (NIR)	70-68-67-70—275	53,200

García leads The Race to Dubai going into 2009

After five of the 53 events on The Race to Dubai's 2009 schedule Sergio García leads the way. The Spaniard, making a fast start, had already collected €650,383 by the end of 2008. Remember the 2009 European season began in November 2008 for the last time. From 2010 the season will begin in January and end in November each year.

Ryder Cup golfer Oliver Wilson, Richard Sterne, Wen-Tang Lin, Peter Hanson, Rory McIlroy, Geoff Ogilvy, Henrik Stenson, Francisco Molinari and Charl Schwartzel fill the remaining top 10 spots in the race to secure a place in the end of season big money bonanza in Dubai.

Spectator initiative marks Open's landmark year

Any spectator born in 1959 will be admitted free to next week's UBS Hong Kong Open as the tournament celebrates its 50th edition. The offer is one of a string of initiatives to mark the US$2.5 million showpiece's historic milestone.

The inaugural Hong Kong Open was staged at the Hong Kong Golf Club in Fanling in 1959 – it has been held every year since and always at the same venue.

The 50th tournament takes place from November 20–23 and to underline the unique nature of the occasion, anyone with a Hong Kong ID card or passport showing they were born in 1959 will be granted free entry each day.

Major winners Nick Faldo, Bernhard Langer and José María Olazábal, past Hong Kong champions Miguel Ángel Jiménez and José Manuel Lara and top Chinese players Liang Wenchong and Zhang Lianwei will be guests at the "Chater Garden Public Launch" at 19:15 on Tuesday (November 18).

1,127 victories on the European Tour
between season 1971 and 2008

English golfers have scored 239 victories on the European Tour, the Spaniards 147, the Scots 125 and the Americans 111 and in all four cases one man in particular has taken the bulk of the titles. Nick Faldo with 30 wins is the main title-holder for England while Seve's 50 victories makes up a third of the Spanish successes. It will come as no surprise that Colin Montgomerie's 31 wins was best for Scotland and Tiger Woods' 36 easily outscored the other 110 Americans who have won titles on the European Tour.

When it comes to one-man bands, Bernhard Langer takes a bow. He has won 42 of the 54 German victories with Ian Woosnam not far behind having scored 29 of his country's 43. Vijay Singh can claim the best average, however, having scored all 13 wins for Fiji. The statistics do not include American majors before 1999 because they were not then part of the European Tour. The full list includes representatives from 35 different countries. In all there have been 358 different winners on Tour.

	Country	Victories	Different winners	Best winner (No. of wins)
1	England	239	77	Nick Faldo (30)
2	Spain	147	27	Severiano Ballesteros (50)
3	Scotland	125	20	Colin Montgomerie (31)
4	United States	111	49	Tiger Woods (36)
5	Australia	99	34	Greg Norman (14)
6	South Africa	86	26	Ernie Els (24)
7	Sweden	78	24	Robert Karlsson (9)
8	Germany	54	6	Bernhard Langer (42)
9	Ireland	45	13	Padraig Harrington (14)
10	Wales	43	8	Ian Woosnam (29)
11	Northern Ireland	32	5	Darren Clarke (12)
12	Zimbabwe	29	3	Mark McNulty (16)
13	Argentina	6	10	Eduardo Romero (8)
14	New Zealand	24	6	Michael Campbell (8)
15	France	20	10	Thomas Levet (4)
16	Denmark	18	6	Thomas Bjørn (9)
17	Fiji	13	1	Vijah Singh (13)
18	Italy	11	6	Costantino Rocca (5)
19	India	7	3	Arjun Atwal (3)
				Jeev Milkha Singh (3)
20	Thailand	4	3	Thongchai Jaidee (3)
21	The Netherlands	4	3	Robert Jan Derksen (2)
22	Canada	3	2	Mike Weir (2)
23	South Korea	3	3	KJ Choi, Charlie Wi, YE Yang
24	Austria	2	1	Markus Brier (2)
25	China	2	2	Lian Wei-Zhang
				Liang Wen Chong
26	Finland	2	1	Mikko Ilonen
27	Trinidad and Tobago	2	1	Stephen Ames
28	Belgium	1	1	Philippe Toussaint
29	Brazil	1	1	Jaime Gonzales
30	Chile	1	1	Felipe Aguilar
31	Japan	1	1	Isao Aoki
32	Portugal	1	1	Daniel Silva
33	Singapore	1	1	Mardan Mammet
34	Switzerland	1	1	André Bossert
35	Taiwan	1	1	Yeh Wei-Tee
	Total	1,127	358	

European Seniors Tour 2008

Final Ranking (Top 30 earn full Tour card for 2009)

1	Ian Woosnam (WAL)	€320,120		52	Bob Larratt (ENG)	26,965
2	Gordon J Brand (ENG)	257,744		53	Manuel Piñero (ESP)	26,791
3	Peter Mitchell (ENG)	217,488		54	Noel Ratcliffe (AUS)	25,752
4	Juan Quiros (ESP)	190,164		55	Martin Poxon (ENG)	24,866
5	Bill Longmuir (SCO)	177,033		56	Bertus Smit (RSA)	23,813
6	Nick Job (ENG)	162,683		57	Matt Briggs (ENG)	23,366
7	Carl Mason (ENG)	156,414		58	John Hoskison (ENG)	23,229
8	Sam Torrance (SCO)	152,753		59	Mike Miller (SCO)	23,204
9	Costantino Rocca (ITA)	140,532		60	Jimmy Heggarty (NIR)	23,020
10	Domingo Hospital (ESP)	124,660		61	Sandy Lyle(SCO)	21,700
11	Angel Franco (PAR)	121,252		62	Steve Stull (USA)	20,953
12	Tony Johnstone (ZIM)	118,910		63	Terry Gale (AUS)	20,360
13	Jerry Bruner (USA)	118,543		64	Jim Lapsley (NZL)	20,177
14	Katsuyoshi Tomori (JPN)	113,252		65	Maurice Bembridge (ENG)	19,909
15	Luis Carbonetti (ARG)	110,251		66	John Mashego (RSA)	16,661
16	Bob Cameron (ENG)	106,700		67	Philip Harrison (ENG)	16,465
17	Ross Drummond (SCO)	106,343		68	Denis Durnian (ENG)	15,976
18	Eamonn Darcy (IRL)	105,632		69	Eddie Polland (NIR)	15,403
19	José Rivero (ESP)	103,852		70	Graham Banister (AUS)	15,399
20	Stewart Ginn (AUS)	102,223		71	John Benda (USA)	14,533
21	Des Smyth (IRL)	98,589		72	Jean Pierre Sallat (FRA)	13,970
22	David Merriman (AUS)	93,429		73	Tommy Horton (ENG)	12,394
23	Bob Boyd (USA)	91,312		74	Ian Mosey (ENG)	11,935
24	Angel Fernandez (CHI)	81,595		75	Torsten Giedeon (GER)	11,916
25	John Chillas (SCO)	81,400		76	Tim Rastall (ENG)	11,755
26	Denis O'Sullivan (IRL)	76,875		77	Tony Price (WAL)	11,397
27	Giuseppe Cali (ITA)	74,406		78	Alfonso Barrera (ARG)	11,390
28	Simon Owen (NZL)	72,814		79	Antonio Garrido (ESP)	10,056
29	Pete Oakley (USA)	69,893		80	Tony Charnley (ENG)	9,368
30	Martin Gray (SCO)	65,538		81	Ian Palmer (RSA)	8,906
				82	Bill McColl (SCO)	8,569
31	Delroy Cambridge (JAM)	60,308		83	Victor Garcia (ESP)	7,736
32	Guillermo Encina (CHI)	56,681		84	Liam Higgins (IRL)	7,057
33	Horacio Carbonetti (ARG)	56,200		85	Ronald Stelten (USA)	6,930
34	Emilio Rodriquez (ESP)	55,458		86	Gavan Levenson (RSA)	6,402
35	Andrew Murray (ENG)	55,043		87	Steve Martin (SCO)	5,672
36	David Good (AUS)	54,038		88	Alberto Croce (ITA)	4,854
37	John Bland (RSA)	52,127		89	Peter Teravainen (USA)	4,699
38	Bobby Lincoln (RSA)	49,880		90	Martin Galway (ENG)	4,616
39	Gery Watine (FRA)	49,389		91	Bill Hardwicj (CAN)	4,076
40	David J Russell (ENG)	49,342		92	Bob Lendzion (USA)	3,437
41	Jeff Hall (ENG)	48,923		93	Ray Carrasco (USA)	3,134
42	Gordon Brand Jr (SCO)	47,602		94	Gordon Townhill (ENG)	2,669
43	Jim Rhodes (ENG)	44,929		95	Mike Gallacher (ENG)	2,508
44	Bob Charles(NZL)	40,092		96	Mitch Kierstenson (ENG)	2,495
45	Tony Allen (ENG)	36,190		97	Greg Hopkins (USA)	1,450
46	Kevin Spurgeon (ENG)	34,669		98	Baldovino Dassu (ITA)	1,444
47	Philippe Dugeny (FRA)	33,462		99	Andy Bownes(ENG)	839
48	Adan Sowa (ARG)	31,567		100	Robin Mann (ENG)	835
49	Seiji Ebihara (JPN)	31,127		101	Peter Dahkberg (SWE)	757
50	Bruce Heuchan (CAN)	30,479		102	Helmuth Schumacher (SUI)	306
51	Mark James (ENG)	29,508				

Career Money List

1	Carl Mason (ENG)	€1,799,375	51	Bob Lendzion (USA)	460,492
2	Tommy Horton (ENG)	1,525,210	52	Bob Shearer (AUS)	459,657
3	Noel Ratbliffe (AUS)	1,263,694	53	Mike Miller (SCO)	434,265
4	Nick Job (ENG)	1,232,452	54	Christy O'Connor Jr (IRL)	421,266
5	Jim Rhodes (ENG)	1,096,112	55	Costantino Rocca (ITA)	418,314
6	Denis O'Sullivan (IRL)	1,078,545	56	Ian Mosey (ENG)	417,224
7	Sam Torrance (SCO)	1,059,609	57	Paul Leonard (NIR)	414,918
8	Terry Gale (AUS)	1,013,279	58	Bill Hardwick (CAN)	407,971
9	Seiji Ebihara (JPN)	1,004,417	59	Gery Watine (FRA)	404,199
10	Jerry Bruner (USA)	998,782	60	Bernard Gallagher (SCO)	390,573
11	Bill Longmuir (SCO)	989,776	61	Priscillo Diniz (BRA)	388,580
12	John Chillas (SCO)	984,801	62	Gary Player (RSA)	384,284
13	Neil Coles (ENG)	928,968	63	David Jones (NIR)	374,369
14	David Good (AUS)	922,633	64	Loren Roberts (USA)	372,829
15	Denis Durnian (ENG)	907,326	65	John Fourie (RSA)	370,647
16	Delroy Cambridge (JAM)	885,063	66	Jay Haas (USA)	369,869
17	Malcolm Gregson (ENG)	833,972	67	Bruce Heuchan (CAN)	353,002
18	Bob Cameron (ENG)	789,245	68	Tony Johnstone (ZIM)	327,883
19	Tom Watson (USA)	788,294	69	Braig Defoy (WAL)	326,196
20	Maurice Bembridge (ENG)	758,219	70	Tom Kite (USA)	325,596
21	Luis Carbonetti (ARG)	756,708	71	Ian Woosnam (WAL)	320,120
22	Eduardo Romero (ARG)	752,153	72	Denis Watson (ZIM)	307,391
23	Giuseppe Cali (ITA)	736,152	73	Bobby Lincoln (RSA)	299,274
24	Bob Charles (NZL)	708,712	74	Bernhard Langer (GER)	288,270
25	Simon Owen (NZL)	697,993	75	Barry Vivian (NZL)	287,062
26	Gordon J Brand (ENG)	675,032	76	Ross Drummond (SCO)	278,345
27	Guillermo Encina (CHI)	664,711	77	Jeff Van Wagenen (USA)	278,344
28	David Creamer (ENG)	662,658	78	Steve Stull (USA)	270,536
29	Brian Huggett (WAL)	638,783	79	Gavan Levenson (RSA)	262,848
30	Eddie Polland (NIR)	638,283	80	Ross Metherell (AUS)	255,539
31	Horacio Carbonetti (ARG)	610,059	81	Manuel Piñero (ESP)	255,503
32	Ian Stanley (AUS)	607,584	82	Kevin Spurgeon (ENG)	251,851
33	Antonio Garrido (ESP)	589,605	83	John Irwin (CAN)	250,934
34	Juan Quiros (ESP)	585,158	84	Brian Jones (AUS)	245,918
35	Eamonn Darby (IRL)	574,705	85	John Mashego (RSA)	242,873
36	Alan Tapie (USA)	574,238	86	Tony Allen (ENG)	238,584
37	José Rivero (ESP)	571,473	87	Martin Poxon (ENG)	236,117
38	Des Smyth (IRL)	558,671	88	Katsuyoshi Tomori (JPN)	235,895
39	Stewart Ginn (AUS)	549,083	89	Brian Barnes (SCO)	234,975
40	John Grace (USA)	539,694	90	Peter Townsend (ENG)	230,974
41	David J Russell (ENG)	514,912	91	Emilio Rodriguez (ESP)	230,483
42	David Huish (SCO)	512,325	92	Craig Stadler (USA)	229,731
43	Ray Barrasco (USA)	501,711	93	John McTear (SCO)	228,055
44	Martin Gray (SCO)	498,245	94	Peter Dawson (ENG)	225,353
45	Bobby Verwey (RSA)	496,778	95	Mark James (ENG)	225,250
46	John Bland (RSA)	492,865	96	Bill Brask (USA)	221,902
47	Pete Oakley (USA)	488,456	97	Jay Horton (USA)	219,067
48	Brian Waites (ENG)	482,280	98	Peter Mitchell (ENG)	217,488
49	Alberto Croce (ITA)	469,717	99	Hank Woodrome (USA)	211,049
50	Liam Higgins (IRL)	467,706	100	Bruce Vaughan (USA)	206,591

Tour Results

DGM Barbados Open	Royal Westmoreland, Barbados	Bill Longmuir (SCO)	206 (-10)
Azores Senior Open	Batalha, Ponta Del Gada, Azores	Stewart Ginn (AUS)	211 (-5)
US Senior PGA Championship	Oak Hill, USA		

1 Jay Haas (USA)	69-72-72-74—287	
2 Bernhard Langer (GER)	71-71-70-76—288	
3 Scott Hoch (USA)	71-74-72-72—289	
Scott Simpson (USA)	76-71-69-73—289	
Joey Sindelar (USA)	76-69-72-72—289	

Parkridge Polish Seniors Chp.	Krakow Valley, Poland	Ian Woosnam (WAL)	202 (-14)
Jersey Seniors Classic	La Moye, Jersey	Tony Johnstone (ZIM)	213 (-3)
Ryder Cup Wales Seniors Open	Conwy, Wales	Peter Mitchell (ENG)	213 (-3)
Irish Seniors Open	Ballyliffin, Co. Donegal	Juan Quiros (ESP)	212 (-1)
Russian Seniors Open	Pestovo, Moscow	Ian Woosnam (WAL)	204 (-12)
Senior Open Championship	Royal Troon, Scotland		

1 Bruce Vaughan (USA)*	68-71-69-70—278
2 John Cook (USA)	69-71-67-71—278

Vaughan won at the first extra hole

3 Eduardo Romero (ARG)	68-73-68-70—279

US Senior Open	Broadmoor Springs, CO, USA
1 Eduardo Romero (ARG)	67-69-65-73—274
2 Fred Funk (USA)	65-69-69-75—278
3 Mark McNulty (IRL)	68-70-73-68—279

Bad Ragaz PGA Seniors Open	Bad Ragaz, Switzerland	Carl Mason (ENG)	195 (-15)
52nd PGA Seniors Championship	Slaley Hall, England		

1 Gordon J Brand (ENG)*	72-77-68-75—292
2 Gordon Brand Jr (SCO)	73-75-74-70—292

GJ Brand won at the sixth extra hole

3 Eamonn Darcy (IRL)	74-74-74-71—293
Sam Torrance (SCO)	76-75-75-67—293
Juan Quiros (ESP)	73-71-76-73—293

Travis Perkins Group Senior Masters	Dukes, Woburn, England	Gordon J Brand (ENG)	207 (-9)
Casa Serena Open	Casa Serena, Prague, Czech Rep	Bernhard Langer (GER)	201 (-12)
Weston Homes PGA International Seniors	Stoke-by-Nayland, Suiffolk, England	Nick Job (ENG)	202 (-14)
Scottish Seniors Open	Dalmahoy, Edinburgh	Peter Mitchell (ENG)	207 (-9)
Italian Seniors Open	Palazzo Arraga, Lake Garda, Italy	Peter Mitchell (ENG)	203 (-13)
OKI Castellón Open España	Club de Campo Mediterráneo, Spain	Sam Torrance (SCO)	203 (-13)

Seniors Tour Records 2008

Low 9 holes

27 (-8)	Ricardo Gonzalez (ARG)	Madrid Masters

Low 18 holes

61 (-11)	Adam Scott (AUS)	Commericalbank Qatar Masters
61 (-11)	Robert Karlsson (SWE)	Methorios Capital Italian Open

Low first 36 holes

127 (-15)	Jeev Milkha Singh (IND)	Bank Austria GolfOpen
127 (-13)	Felipe Aguilar (CHI)	Enjoy Jakarta Astro Indonesia Open

Low first 54 holes

194 (-22)	Hennie Otto (RSA)	Methorios Capital Italian Open
194 (-16)	Robert Karlsson (SWE)	UBS Hong Kong Open
194 (-16)	Felipe Aguilar (CHI)	Enjoy Jakarta Astro Indonesia Open

Seniors Tour Records 2008

Multiple Winners

3	Tiger Woods (USA)	Dubai Desert Classic, WGC–Accenture Match Play, US Open Championship
2	Richard Finch (ENG)	Michael Hill New Zealand Open, The Irish Open
	Miguel Angel Jiménez (ESP)	UBS Hong Kong Open, BMW PGA Ch.
	Martin Kaymer (GER)	Abu Dhabi Golf Ch., BMW International Open
	Graeme McDowell (NIR)	Ballantine's Ch., The Barclays Scottish Open
	Padraig Harrington (IRL)	The 137th Open Ch., USPGA Ch.
	Darren Clarke (NIR)	BMW Asian Open, The KLM Open
	Robert Karlsson (SWE)	Mercedes-Benz Ch., Alfred Dunhill Links Ch.

First time winners

Richard Finch (ENG)	Michael Hill New Zealand Open
James Kingston (RSA)	South African Airways Open
Martin Kaymer (GER)	Abu Dhabi Golf Championship
SSP Chowrasia (IND)	EMAAR-MGF Indian Masters
Felipe Aguilar (CHI)	Enjoy Jakarta Astro Indonesia Open
Mark Brown (NZL)	Johnnie Walker Classic
Damien McGrane (IRL)	Volvo China Open
Peter Lawrie (IRL)	Open de Espana
Hennie Otto (RSA)	Methorios Capital Italian Open
Scott Strange (AUS)	The Celtic Manor Wales Open
David Dixon (ENG)	Saint-Omer Open
Pablo Larrazabal (ESP)	Open de France ALSTOM
Jean-François Lucquin (FRA)	Omega European Masters

Woosnam puts illness behind him to land top Senior spot

For former Ryder Cup captain Ian Woosnam, 2008 was a very important year. After suffering from debilitating ME, he not only resumed his competitive career on the European Senior Tour, he won two titles and ended up in No. 1 spot.

Topping the earnings table was particularly pleasing because he was writing another chapter in European golfing history by doing so. He is now the first player to have topped the main money list and won the Vardon Trophy and to have landed the John Jacobs Trophy for being most successful senior of the year.

"Others will do it in the future but it is nice to be the first to complete the double," said Woosnam, who added that there was extra special delight in winning the trophy named after top teacher and Father of the European Tour John Jacobs because he had had a few lessons from him in his younger days. "Fortunately he didn't mess about with my swing," he added with a smile.   Woosnam has one of the smoothest, most envied swings in golf.

The Welshman, who topped the main Tour money list in 1987 and 1990, ended his first season on the Senior Tour with €320,120 in prize-money – €62,376 ahead of second-placed Gordon J Brand in the table. In Poland, "Woosie" closed with a record 63 at the Krakow Valley Golf and Country Club to win the Polish Senors Championship sponsored by Parkridge, who also happen to sponsor him.

Winning in Poland was huge for Woosnam, who had taken the World Match-play Championship in 2002 but had not won a stroke-play event since being successful in the PGA Championship at Wentworth in 1997. His other 2008 Senior Tour victory came in the Russian Seniors Open at the Pestovo Golf and Yacht Club and he was second behind US Champions Tour No. 1 Bernhard Langer in the Casa Serena Open in the Czech Republic.

To be so successful when he admits he is still only 75 per cent fit says much for the Welshman's courage and determination. "I still don't feel too well in the mornings and get tired easily," he says, "and going away for two weeks is really draining."

His next goal is to win the Senior Open and add a senior major to the Masters Green Jacket he earned at Augusta in 1991. For the moment the John Jacobs Trophy takes up its place alongside the two Vardon Trophies, his Masters and 2006 Ryder Cup mementoes and, of course, the OBE he received for his services to the game.

European Challenge Tour 2008

www.europeantour.com

Final Order of Merit (top 20 earn card for PGA European Tour)

1	David Horsey (ENG)	€144,118		51	Björn Pettersson (SWE)	34,536
2	Gary Lockerbie (ENG)	138,509		52	Joel Sjoholm (SWE)	32,811
3	Taco Remkes (NED)	137,331		53	Anders Schmidt Hansen (DEN)	32,781
4	Gareth Maybin (NIR)	117,719		54	Gregory Molteni (ITA)	32,168
5	Estanislao Goya (ARG)	113,336		55	Colm Moriarty (IRL)	31,527
6	Seve Benson (ENG)	111,529		56	George Murray (SCO)	30,518
7	Alessandro Tadini (ITA)	106,893		57	André Bossert (SUI)	30,142
8	Richie Ramsay (SCO)	106,656		58	Benjamin Miarka (GER)	29,575
9	Steven O'Hara (SCO)	103,212		59	Eirik Tage Johansen (NOR)	28,772
10	Jeppe Huldahl (DEN)	96,818		60	Nicolas Vanhootegem (BEL)	28,680
11	Klas Eriksson (SWE)	96,514		61	Richard Treis (GER)	27,862
12	Alexandre Rocha (BRA)	93,684		62	Lorenzo Gagli (ITA)	27,454
13	Richard Bland (ENG)	92,645		63	Adam Gee (ENG)	27,328
14	Rafael Cabrera Bello (ESP)	89,847		64	Jan-Are Larsen (NOR)	25,477
15	Wil Besseling (NED)	89,358		65	Miguel Rodriguez (ARG)	25,065
16	Marcus Higley (ENG)	85,946		66	Eric Ramsay (SCO)	24,480
17	John E Morgan (ENG)	77,254		67	Matthew Cort (ENG)	23,970
18	Christian Nilsson (SWE)	75,200		68	James Morrison (ENG)	23,924
19	Antti Ahokas (FIN)	74,867		69	Andreas Högberg (SWE)	23,443
20	Stuart Davis (ENG)	67,105		70	Julien Clément (SUI)	23,313
				71	Christophe Brazillier (FRA)	23,090
21	Marco Ruiz (PAR)	66,845		72	Anthony Snobeck	23,089
22	Andrew McArthur (SCO)	64,560		73	Edward Rush (ENG)	22,854
23	Raphaël De Sousa (SUI)	63,133		74	Lars Brovold (NOR)	22,798
24	Gary Clark (ENG)	62,161		75	François Calmels (FRA)	22,259
25	Chris Gane (ENG)	61,769		76	Andrew Marshall (ENG)	21,465
26	Mark F Haastrup (DEN)	61,625		77	Kasper Linnet Jorgensen (DEN)	20,711
27	Roope Kakko (FIN)	57,319		78	Ian Garbutt (ENG)	20,544
28	Michael Hoey (NIR)	52,424		79	Adrien Bernadet (FRA)	20,533
29	Gary Boyd (ENG)	51,296		80	Jaakko Makitalo (FIN)	19,874
30	Andrew T Aampion (AUS)	51,021		81	Johan Sköld (SWE)	19,459
31	Richard McEvoy (ENG)	49,265		82	Marco Soffietti (ITA)	19,444
32	Mikko Korhonen (FIN)	48,288		83	Michele Reale (ITA)	19,322
33	David Drysdale (SCO)	46,846		84	Soren Juul (DEN)	19,064
34	Inder Van Weerelt (NED)	46,671		85	Steven Jeppesen (SWE)	18,501
35	Branden Grace (RSA)	46,540		86	Andrew Butterfield (ENG)	18,310
36	Greig Hutcheon (SCO)	46,293		87	Cesar Monasterio (ARG)	17,979
37	Julien Quesne (FRA)	46,144		88	Matthew Zions (AUS)	17,460
38	Bernd Wiesberger (AUT)	45,452		89	Jamie Little (ENG)	17,444
39	Joakim Haeggman (SWE)	44,899		90	Tiago Crux (POR)	17,156
40	Robert Coles (ENG)	44,590		91	Sébastien Delegrange (FRA)	16,744
41	Roland Steiner (AUT)	44,221		92	Ben Mason (ENG)	16,292
42	Michael McGeady (IRL)	42,945		93	Tyrone Ferreira (RSA)	16,029
43	Liam Bond (WAL)	41,611		94	Lloyd Saltman (SCO)	5,708
44	Thomas Feyrsinger (AUT)	41,005		95	James Heath (ENG)	15,386
45	Matthew Morris (ENG)	40,563		96	Sebastian L Saavwdra (ARG)	15,381
46	Simon Robinson (ENG)	38,550		97	Gustavo Rojas (ARG)	15,220
47	Andrew Willey (ENG)	38,504		98	Martin Monguzzi (ARG)	15,168
48	Carlos Del Moral (ESP)	35,947		99	Peter Kaensche (NOR)	14,973
49	Mark Tullo (CHI)	35,251		100	Rikard Karlberg (SWE)	14,938
50	Ricardo Santos (POR)	35,001				

Results

Abierto del Litoral Personal 2007	Rosario, Argentina	Miguel Rodriguez (ARG)	271 (-9)
102nd Abierto Visa de la Republica	Buenos Aires	Marco Ruiz (PAR)	275 (-5)
Tusker Kenya Open	Karen GC, Nairobi	Iain Pyman (ENG)	272 (-12)
Abierto del Centro	Cordoba, Argentina	Estanislao Goya (ARG)*	272 (-12)

*Goya beat Gary Boyd (ENG) at fist extra hole

103rd Abierto Visa de la Republica	Hurlingham Club, Argentina	Antti Ahokas (FIN)	270 (-10)
II Club Colombia Masters	Bogotá	Wil Besseling (NED)	268 (-16)
AGF-Allianz Open Cotes d'Armour Bretagne	Golf Blue Green de Pléneuf Val André	Joakim Haeggman (SWE)	275 (-5)
Banque Populaire Moroccan Classic	El Jadida Sofitel, Morocco	Michael Hoey (NIR)	276 (-12)
Piemonte Open	Turin	Seve Benson (ENG)	269 (-19)
Wroclaw Open	Toya, Poland	Gary Clark (ENG)	262 (-18)
Oceânico Dev. Pro-Am Challenge	Worsley Park, Manchester	Alessandro Tadini (ITA)	264 (-16)
Reale Challenge de España	Retamares, Madrid	Andrew McArthur (SCO)	280 (-8)
Aa St Omer Open	St Omer, Lumbres	David Dixon (ENG)	279 (-5)
SK Golf Challenge	St Laurence, Lohja, Finland	Simon Robinson (ENG)	271 (-13)
Telenet Trophy	Limburg, Belgium	David Horsey (ENG)	269 (-19)
Scottish Challenge	Cardrona, Peebles	Taco Remkes (NED)	271 (-13)
AGF-Allianz EurOpen de Lyon	Monthieux	David Horsey (ENG)	266 (-22)
Credit Suisse Challenge	Wylihof, Luterbach	Rafael Cabrera Bello (ESP)	267 (-25)
MAN Nö Open	Adamstal, Ramsal, Austria	André Bossert (SUI)*	265 (-15)

*Bossert beat M Brier (AUT) at the first extra hole

SWALEC Wales Challenge	Vale, Wales	Michael McGeady (IRL)*	284 (-4)

*McGeady beat J Sjoholm (SWE) at the second extra hole

Challenge of Ireland	Glasson, Athlone	Andrew Tampion (AUS)	280 (-8)
Lexus Open	Dilling, Norway	Jeppe Huldahl (DEN)	271 (-17)
Trophee de Genève	Geneva, Switzerland	Klas Eriksson (SWE)*	274 (-14)

*Eriksson beat W Besseling (NED), and A Rocha (BRA) at the fourth extra hole

Vodaphone Challenge	Elfrather Möhle, Germany	Richie Ramsay (SCO)	272 (-16)
Ypsilon Challenge	Ypsilon, Liberec, Czech Rep	Sev Benson (ENG)*	268 (-16)

*Benson beat Rafael Cabrera Bello (ESP) and Branden Grace (RSA) at third extra hole

ECCO Tour Championship	Kokkedal, Copenhagen, Denmark	Antti Ahokas (FIN)	271 (-17)
Dubliner Challenge	The Hills, Gothenburg, Sweden	Mark S Haastrup (DEN)	206 (-7)
Qingdao Open	Qingdao Huashan, China	Gareth Maybin (NIR)	269 (-19)
Kazakhstan Open	Nurtau, Almaty	Gary Lockerbie (ENG)	273 (-15)
Dutch Futures	Houtrak, Amsterdam	Taco Remkes (NED)*	275 (-13)

*Remkes beat Jeppe Huldahl (DEN) at the first extra hole

AGF-Allianz Open de Toulouse	Golf de Toulouse-Seilh, Toulouse	Richie Ramsay (SCO)	269 (-19)
Margara Diehl-Ako Platinum Open	Margara, Italy	Taco Remkes (NED)*	270 (-18)

*Remkes beat Roop Kakko (FIN) at the first extra hole

Apulia San Domenico Grand Final	San Domenico Golf, Puglia, Italy	Estanislao Goya (ARG)	267 (-17)

US PGA Tour 2008

Players are of US nationality unless stated   **www.pgatour.com**

Final Ranking

The top 125 on the money list retained their cards for the 2009 season. The top 40 earned a spot at The Masters.

#	Player	Money	#	Player	Money	#	Player	Money
1	Vijay Singh (FIJ)	$6,601,094	43	Pat Perez	1,756,038	90	Greg Kraft	1,204,559
2	Tiger Woods	5,775,000	44	Billy Mayfair	1,750,683	91	John Mallinger	1,201,433
3	Phil Mickelson	5,188,875	45	Tim Clark (RSA)	1,722,030	92	Tim Wilkinson	1,167,607
4	Sergio García (ESP)	4,858,224	46	Bart Bryant	1,719,153	93	Michael Letzig	1,166,977
5	Kenny Perry	4,663,794	47	Rod Pampling (AUS)	1,702,952	94	Tim Herron	1,164,999
6	Anthony Kim	4,656,265	48	Davis Love III	1,695,237	95	Paul Casey (ENG)	1,156,414
7	Camilo Villegas (COL)	4,422,641	49	Aaron Baddeley (AUS)	1,665,587	96	Brian Davis (ENG)	1,151,558
8	Padraig Harrington (IRL)	4,313,551	50	Jerry Kelly	1,652,400	97	Cliff Kresge	1,068,207
9	Stewart Cink	3,979,301	51	Paul Goydos	1,640,737	98	Vaughn Taylor	1,053,423
10	Justin Leonard	3,943,542	52	Daniel Chopra (SWE)	1,630,690	99	Justin Rose (ENG)	1,047,854
11	Robert Allenby (AUS)	3,606,700	53	Zach Johnson	1,615,123	100	Kevin Na	1,041,059
12	Jim Furyk	3,455,714	54	Fredrik Jacobson (SWE)	1,597,423	101	Jonathan Byrd	1,039,584
13	Ryuji Imada (JPN)	3,029,363	55	Mark Wilson	1,578,337	102	Joe Ogilvie	1,035,831
14	Mike Weir (CAN)	3,020,135	56	Rory Sabbatini (RSA)	1,559,277	103	John Rollins	1,016,032
15	Geoff Ogilvy (AUS)	2,880,099	57	Lee Westwood (ENG)	1,550,880	104	Bill Haas	1,000,939
16	KJ Choi (KOR)	2,683,442	58	Bubba Watson	1,533,523	105	Lucas Glover	998,491
17	Ben Curtis	2,615,798	59	Brandt Snedeker	1,531,442	106	Michael Allen	981,263
18	Kevin Sutherland	2,581,311	60	Steve Lowery	1,524,275	107	Tim Petrovic	958,577
19	Trevor Immelman (RSA)	2,566,199	61	Charlie Wi (KOR)	1,515,395	108	Scott McCarron	952,070
20	Ernie Els (RSA)	2,537,290	62	Tommy Armour III	1,501,256	109	Fred Couples	949,281
21	Carl Pettersson (SWE)	2,512,538	63	Heath Slocum	1,491,916	110	Charley Hoffman	945,702
22	Stuart Appleby (AUS)	2,484,630	64	Ben Crane	1,488,505	111	JJ Henry	931,162
23	Steve Stricker	2,438,304	65	Ian Poulter (ENG)	1,488,214	112	Corey Pavin	924,282
24	Chad Campbell	2,404,770	66	Peter Lonard (AUS)	1,462,894	113	Nathan Green (AUS)	912,867
25	Boo Weekley	2,398,751	67	Luke Donald (ENG)	1,456,650	114	Will MacKenzie	911,194
26	DJ Trahan	2,304,368	68	Ryan Palmer	1,453,183	115	Bo Van Pelt	903,967
27	Stephen Ames (CAN)	2,285,707	69	Charles Howell III	1,449,232	116	Eric Axley	899,215
28	Ken Duke	2,238,885	70	Matt Kuchar	1,447,638	117	Alex Cejka (GER)	893,998
29	Dudley Hart	2,218,817	71	Chez Reavie	1,444,102	118	Jeff Overton	890,489
30	Hunter Mahan	2,208,855	72	Retief Goosen (RSA)	1,431,965	119	Richard S. Johnson	884,367
31	Brian Gay	2,205,513	73	Johnson Wagner	1,431,001	120	Brett Quigley	878,216
32	JB Holmes	2,166,131	74	Rocco Mediate	1,420,875	121	Nick Watney	878,173
33	Woody Austin	2,146,431	75	Nick O'Hern	1,370,771	122	Angel Cabrera (ARG)	868,182
34	Steve Marino	2,094,267	76	George McNeill	1,361,532	123	Jason Bohn	866,786
35	Sean O'Hair	2,089,857	77	Scott Verplank	1,359,620	124	Brad Adamonis	862,413
36	Andres Romero (ARG)	2,064,612	78	Kevin Streelman	1,352,705	125	Martin Laird	852,752
37	Briny Baird	2,039,808	79	Dean Wilson	1,350,002			
38	Jeff Quinney	1,999,371	80	Tom Pernice Jr	1,336,277	126	Shane Bertsch	841,248
39	Adam Scott (AUS)	1,979,160	81	Marc Turnesa	1,329,920	127	Bob Estes	829,395
40	Mathew Goggin (AUS)	1,969,962	82	Cameron Beckman	1,312,837	128	Patrick Sheehan	805,897
			83	John Merrick	1,312,005	129	Joe Durant	802,568
41	Nicholas Thompson	1,869,329	84	Parker McLachlin	1,311,839	130	Charles Warren	800,694
42	Dustin Johnson	1,789,895	85	Steve Elkington (AUS)	1,291,114	131	David Toms	799,114
			86	John Senden (AUS)	1,269,083	132	Bob Tway	785,641
			87	Steve Flesch	1,265,059	133	Mark Calcavecchia	784,810
			88	Ryan Moore	1,214,900	134	Jason Gore	779,664
			89	Troy Matteson	1,212,018	135	Matt Jones	775,889
						136	Jason Day	767,393
						137	Jay Williamson	758,862
						138	Robert Garrigus	756,732
						139	Steve Allan	743,970

Career Money List (at end of 2008 season)

1	Tiger Woods	$82,354,376	51	Paul Azinger	14,447,210
2	Vijay Singh (FIJ)	60,709,312	52	Jay Haas	14,440,317
3	Phil Mickelson	50,522,901	53	Mark O'Meara	14,136,017
4	Jim Furyk	38,809,826	54	Steve Elkington (AUS)	14,130,705
5	Davis Love III	37,325,550	55	Lee Janzen	13,957,747
6	Ernie Els (RSA)	33,663,401	56	Kirk Triplett	13,564,082
7	David Toms	28,711,065	57	Shigeki Maruyama (JPN)	13,353,024
8	Justin Leonard	27,109,459	58	Woody Austin	13,349,536
9	Kenny Perry	26,196,442	59	Kevin Sutherland	13,085,208
10	Stewart Cink	25,055,994	60	Tom Pernice Jr	12,866,379
11	Sergio García (ESP)	24,399,000	61	Luke Donald (ENG)	12,825,014
12	Mike Weir (CAN)	23,860,124	62	John Cook	12,433,599
13	Stuart Appleby (AUS)	23,194,485	63	Dudley Hart	12,408,096
14	Mark Calcavecchia	23,081,228	64	Billy Andrade	12,361,151
15	Scott Verplank	22,430,292	65	Zach Johnson	12,260,837
16	Fred Funk	20,925,849	66	José María Olazábal (ESP)	12,002,594
17	Nick Price (ZIM)	20,563,108	67	Joe Durant	11,954,193
18	Tom Lehman	20,378,513	68	Payne Stewart	11,737,008
19	Chris DiMarco	20,251,008	69	Tim Clark (RSA)	11,638,389
20	Fred Couples	20,121,480	70	Duffy Waldorf	11,638,275
21	Retief Goosen (RSA)	19,707,369	71	Carl Pettersson (SWE)	11,562,074
22	Robert Allenby (AUS)	19,281,384	72	Frank Lickliter II	11,278,816
23	KJ Choi (KOR)	18,801,639	73	Joey Sindelar	11,196,462
24	Scott Hoch	18,498,499	74	Rod Pampling (AUS)	11,054,489
25	Adam Scott (AUS)	18,369,560	75	Tom Kite	11,041,042
26	Jeff Sluman	18,114,866	76	Scott McCarron	10,552,162
27	Jerry Kelly	18,048,119	77	John Rollins	10,332,303
28	Brad Faxon	17,656,554	78	Jonathan Kaye	10,207,704
29	Billy Mayfair	17,653,397	79	Bernhard Langer (GER)	10,111,921
30	Rory Sabbatini (RSA)	17,616,264	80	Craig Stadler	10,021,897
31	Bob Estes	17,225,501	81	Tom Watson	10,004,299
32	Steve Stricker	17,143,884	82	Briny Baird	9,597,907
33	David Duval	16,869,175	83	Aaron Baddeley (AUS)	9,287,083
34	Charles Howell III	16,668,108	84	Chris Riley	9,286,680
35	Chad Campbell	16,585,604	85	Heath Slocum	9,256,094
36	Steve Flesch	16,327,302	86	Carlos Franco (PAR)	9,247,875
37	Geoff Ogilvy (AUS)	16,306,625	87	David Frost (RSA)	9,178,775
38	Jeff Maggert	15,745,293	88	Mark Brooks	9,131,304
39	Bob Tway	15,731,456	89	John Daly	9,109,268
40	Tim Herron	15,685,381	90	Ben Crane	9,090,282
41	Stephen Ames (CAN)	15,591,077	91	Trevor Immelman (RSA)	9,084,340
42	Padraig Harrington (IRL)	15,286,873	92	Jonathan Byrd	9,077,876
43	Hal Sutton	15,267,685	93	Brett Quigley	9,049,674
44	Jesper Parnevik (SWE)	15,149,185	94	Peter Lonard	9,009,671
45	Loren Roberts	15,103,510	95	Bart Bryant	8,962,989
46	Rocco Mediate	14,791,140	96	Tommy Armour III	8,943,812
47	John Huston	14,762,421	97	Brian Gay	8,922,840
48	Steve Lowery	14,643,503	98	Justin Rose (ENG)	8,710,418
49	Corey Pavin	14,606,155	99	Dan Forsman	8,687,983
50	Greg Norman (AUS)	14,473,229	100	Paul Goydos	8,554,942

International golfers make their presence felt

Twenty-four of the top 60 money earners on the PGA Tour Money List at the end of the 2008 were from countries outside America – from Fiji, Spain, Colombia, Ireland, Australia, Japan, Canada, South Korea, South Africa, Sweden. Argentina and England. The American circuit has never been more international than it is today,

2008 Tour Statistics

Driving accuracy
(Percentage of fairways hit in regulation)

Pos	Name	Rds	%
1	Olin Browne	77	80.42
2	Omar Uresti	74	74.85
3	Heath Slocum	104	73.95
4	Bart Bryant	81	73.87
5	Zach Johnson	85	73.73
6	Scott Verplank	82	73.57
7	Robert Gamez	79	73.36
8	Joe Durant	92	73.05
9	Chez Reavie	102	72.56
10	Brian Davis (ENG)	108	72.47

Greens in regulation

Pos	Name	Rds	%
1	Joe Durant	92	71.10
2	Robert Allenby (AUS)	108	70.40
3	Harrison Frazar	73	70.34
4	John Huston	56	70.30
5	Briny Baird	113	70.00
6	Kent Jones	68	69.71
7	Hunter Mahan	87	69.61
8	John Riegger	73	69.49
9	JJ Henry	108	69.19
10	John Senden (AUS)	93	69.08

Driving distance (Average yards per drive)

Pos	Name	Rds	Yds
1	Bubba Watson	97	315.1
2	Robert Garrigus	90	311.0
3	JB Holmes	86	310.3
4	Justin Johnson	92	309.7
5	Steve Allan	58	303.2
6	Tag Ridings	88	303.0
7	Nick Watney	96	302.9
8	Adam Scott (AUS)	51	302.1
9	Davis Love III	78	301.3
10	Charles Warren	79	301.1

Putting averages (Average per round)

Pos	Name	Rds	Avg
1	Corey Pavin	65	27.92
2	Padraig Harrington (IRL)	50	28.04
3	Daniel Chopra (SWE)	83	28.06
4	John Mallinger	95	28.14
5	Bob Tway	64	28.23
6	Nathan Green (AUS)	95	28.24
7	Brian Gay	94	28.34
8	Aaron Baddeley (AUS)	73	28.38
9	Jeff Quinney	87	28.39
10	Ryuji Imada (JPN)	80	28.43

Sand saves

Pos	Name	Rds	%	Pos	Name	Rds	%
1	Dudley Hart	74	63.71	6	Mark Wilson	107	60.14
2	Corey Pavin	69	63.11	7	Gavin Coles	54	59.42
3	Phil Mickelson	80	62.50	8	Craig Knada	65	59.43
4	Mike Weir (CAN)	88	62.09	9	Padraig Harrington (IRL)	52	59.06
5	Daniel Copra (SWE)	84	61.64		Ian Poulter (ENG)	51	58.06

Scoring averages

Pos	Name	Rds	Avg	Pos	Name	Rds	Avg
1	Sergio García (ESP)	72	69.12	11	Kenny Perry	97	69.83
2	Phil Mickelson	80	69.17	12	Ernie Els (RSA)	51	69.90
3	Padraig Harrington (IRL)	52	69.28	13	Ben Curtis	80	69.98
	Anthony Kim	81	69.28		Steve Stricker	75	69.98
5	Camilo Villegas (COL)	79	69.49	15	Stephen Ames (CAN)	83	69.99
6	Vijay Singh (FIJ)	82	69.58	16	Stewart Cink	87	70.02
7	Jim Furyk	95	69.69		Brian Gay	102	70.02
8	Robert Allenby (AUS)	108	69.73	18	Chad Campbell	94	70.04
	Stuart Appleby (AUS)	87	69.73	19	Adam Scott (AUS)	51	70.06
10	Justin Leonard	101	69.77	20	Steve Marino	119	70.07
					Kevin Sutherland	98	70.07

Top 20 on the US Tour 2008

	Name	Played	Wins	Top 3	Top 10	MC	Stroke Av.
1	Vijay Singh	3	3	4	8	5	69.58
2	Tiger Woods	6	4	5	6	0	*
3	Phil Mickelson	21	2	3	8	1	69.17
4	Sergio García	19	1	4	7	1	69.12
5	Kenny Perry	26	3	4	7	1	69.83
6	Anthony Kim	22	2	5	8	3	69.28
7	Camilo Villegas	22	2	3	7	3	69.49
8	Padraig Harrington	15	2	2	6	2	69.28
9	Stewart Cink	22	1	3	7	1	69.95
10	Justin Leonard	25	1	2	8	1	69.77
11	Jim Furyk	26	0	2	9	3	69.69
12	Robert Allenby	26	0	3	9	1	69.67
13	Ryuji Imada	25	1	3	5	8	70.56
14	Mike Weir	26	0	1	8	5	70.14
15	Geoff Ogilvy	20	1	2	6	6	70.25
16	KJ Choi	21	1	1	5	6	70.26
17	Ben Curtis	22	0	2	5	4	69.98
18	Kevin Sutherland	26	0	2	6	4	70.07
19	Trevor Immelman	22	1	2	3	8	70.52
20	Ernie Els	16	1	2	5	5	69.90

*Woods did not play enough rounds to be given an official stroke average. Unofficially he averaged 69.15 for his 20 stroke-play rounds (not including the play-off for the US Open).

Twelve first-time winners on the PGA Tour

Brian Gay, Mayakoba Golf Classic
Greg Kraft, Puerto Rico Open
Andres Romero (ARG), Zurich Classic
Johnson Wagner, Shell Houston Open
Anthony Kim, Wachovia Championship, AT&T National
Ryuji Imada (JPN), AT&T Classic

Richard S. Johnson, US Bank in Milwaukee
Chez Reavie, RBC Canadian Open
Parker McLachlin, Legends Reno-Tahoe Open
Camilo Villegas (COL), BMW Championship, The Tour Championship
Dustin Johnson, Turning Stone Champ.
Marc Turnesa, JTS Hospitals for Children Open

Vijay Singh tops $18 million in a season

Fiji's Vijay Singh came off a three month break from golf to hole a 10 foot winning birdie putt worth $1.35 million on the final hole of the Chevron Woods World Challenge at Sherwood Country Club in California. It rounded off his 2008 season – easily the most lucrative of his career – in spectacular fashion

In 2008 Singh, who finished the US Tour's No 1 money-earner for the third time in six years, made $6.6million in regular Tour play, picked up a $10 million bonus for his victory in the Fedex Cup and then added the Chevron Woods prize-money to prove he had not lost his touch after his lengthy break to get rid of some niggling injuries including tendonitis. He went one whole month without hitting a ball but there was no rustiness when he returned.

The birdie putt edged out Steve Stricker and underlined that Singh, who will be 46 this year, is still a worthy and dangerous competitor. "When I turn up at a tournament and feel I cannot win it I will quit but as long as I feel I can win I shall keep on playing," he said.

US PGA Tour top 20

MC Missed cut   — Did not play

Players are of US nationality unless stated otherwise

Player	Mercedes-Benz C/ship	Sony Open	Bob Hope Chrysler Classic	Buick Invitational	FBR Open	AT&T Pebble Beach	Northern Trust Open	WGC–Accenture MatchPlay	Mayakoba Classic	Honda Classic	PODS Championship	Arnold Palmer Invitational	WGC-CA Championship	Puerto Rico Open	Zurich Classic	Shell Houston Open	The Masters	Verizon Heritage	EDS Byron Nelson C/ship
1 Vijay Singh (FIJ)	12	45	—	23	MC	2	36	5	—	—	—	3	2	—	—	—	14	—	—
2 Tiger Woods	—	—	—	1	—	—	—	1	—	—	—	1	5	—	—	—	2	—	—
3 Phil Mickelson	—	—	—	6	2	MC	1	17	—	—	—	21	20	—	—	23	5	—	—
4 Sergio García (ESP)	—	—	—	—	—	—	46	17	—	43	—	31	15	—	—	—	MC	—	19
5 Kenny Perry	—	MC	3	67	17	—	62	—	—	20	30	48	—	—	23	—	—	—	50
6 Anthony Kim	—	—	3	67	30	—	MC	—	—	49	—	—	—	—	MC	MC	—	2	19
7 Camilo Villegas (COL)	—	—	13	34	—	MC	33	—	24	—	44	26	—	—	—	MC	7	—	—
8 Padraig Harrington (IRL)	—	—	—	—	14	3	17	—	—	—	—	—	—	—	4	26	5	—	—
9 Stewart Cink	—	—	26	3	MC	—	—	2	—	—	2	—	20	—	DQ	—	3	7	—
10 Justin Leonard	8	—	2	5	43	43	—	4	—	30	—	—	34	—	—	39	20	17	19
11 Jim Furyk	5	20	—	37	—	14	MC	33	—	—	—	31	2	—	MC	—	33	4	—
12 Robert Allenby (AUS)	—	MC	12	35	25	—	7	33	—	4	14	—	20	—	—	35	42	14	—
13 Ryuji Imada (JPN)	—	69	16	2	WD	—	5	—	—	—	2	—	34	—	MC	—	—	MC	MC
14 Mike Weir (CAN)	4	—	56	WD	43	14	MC	33	—	MC	—	—	20	—	MC	—	17	—	—
15 Geoff Ogilvy (AUS)	—	—	—	MC	MC	—	MC	33	—	—	10	14	1	—	—	2	39	—	—
16 KJ Choi (KOR)	28	1	—	MC	20	—	7	5	—	—	—	—	—	—	—	11	41	—	—
17 Ben Curtis	—	—	—	MC	65	—	62	—	—	65	—	MC	—	15	—	47	MC	41	—
18 Kevin Sutherland	—	—	56	13	4	MC	22	—	—	38	14	—	—	—	42	8	—	—	7
19 Trevor Immelman (RSA)	—	—	—	—	MC	—	MC	17	—	MC	65	48	40	—	—	MC	1	—	MC
20 Ernie Els (RSA)	—	—	—	—	—	—	—	33	—	1	MC	—	75	—	—	—	MC	MC	—

2008 performances at a glance

* Involved in play-off   WD Withdrew   DQ Disqualified

Wachovia Cup	Players Championship	AT&T Classic	Crowne Plaza Invitational	Memorial Tournament	Stanford St Jude C/ship	US Open Championship	Travelers Championship	Buick Open	AT&T National	John Deere Classic	The Open Championship	US Bank Championship	RBC Canadian Open	WGC–Bridgestone Inv.	Legends Reno-Tahoe Open	USPGA Championship	Wyndham Championship	Barclays Classic	Deutsche Bank C/ship	BMW Championship	Viking Classic	Tour Championship	Turning Stone C/ship	Valero Texas Open	Justin Timberlake Open	Frys.com Open	Ginn sur Mer Classic	Children's Miracle Classic
17	MC	—	—	11	65	5	—	—	—	MC	—	1	—	MC	MC	1*	1	44	—	22	—	—	—	—	—	—	—	—
—	—	—	—	—	1*	—	—	—	—	—	—	—	—	—	—	—	—	—	—	—	—	—	—	—	—	—	—	—
12	21	—	1	20	—	18	—	—	—	—	19	—	—	4	—	7	—	19	73	17	—	3	—	—	—	—	—	—
34	1*	—	—	5	4	18	—	—	—	—	51	—	—	36	—	2	—	2	5	20	—	2	—	—	—	—	—	—
49	15	2	46	1	24	—	6	1	—	1*	—	6	—	66	—	WD	—	48	80	44	—	24	—	—	—	—	—	—
1	42	—	40	—	—	26	—	—	1	—	7	—	8	36	—	55	—	12	27	3	—	3	—	—	—	—	—	—
55	66	3	—	18	9	—	—	36	—	39	—	53	—	—	4	—	MC	3	1	—	1*	—	—	—	—	—	—	—
—	MC	—	—	4	36	—	—	—	1	—	—	20	—	1	—	MC	87	55	—	—	—	—	—	—	—	—	—	—
8	21	11	—	30	—	14	1	—	—	—	MC	—	—	43	—	MC	38	33	60	—	24	—	—	—	—	—	—	—
—	MC	—	33	—	1*	36	—	55	—	—	16	—	—	20	—	58	7	7	17	—	10	—	11	—	—	—	—	—
7	27	—	MC	39	—	36	—	36	3	—	5	—	14	27	—	29	—	12	7	3	—	—	—	—	—	—	—	—
4	42	—	—	10	2	18	—	—	3	—	7	—	—	20	—	31	—	38	44	38	—	16	2	—	—	—	—	—
17	MC	1*	—	39	—	18	—	MC	—	MC	—	—	—	—	—	MC	69	MC	13	67	—	17	3	—	15	—	—	—
MC	32	—	15	2	—	18	—	MC	—	39	5	—	—	42	—	7	2	67	—	6	—	—	10	4	—	—	—	—
22	MC	—	7	9	—	9	—	—	MC	—	—	—	68	—	31	—	MC	72	28	—	—	—	—	—	—	—	—	—
—	MC	—	MC	53	—	MC	—	49	—	16	—	—	16	—	MC	—	12	21	5	—	9	—	—	—	—	—	—	—
2	42	—	33	46	—	MC	13	—	—	7	—	48	—	—	2	—	4	27	13	—	5	—	—	—	—	—	—	—
MC	MC	34	15	—	—	—	27	—	27	8	—	—	30	—	42	63	MC	2	50	55	—	15	—	—	24	2	—	—
MC	—	—	—	30	2	65	—	—	MC	—	19	—	—	36	—	MC	—	70	50	13	—	10	—	—	—	—	—	—
—	6	—	—	MC	—	14	—	—	—	7	—	—	27	—	31	—	MC	3	17	—	6	—	—	—	—	—	—	—

Tour Results 2008 (in chronological order)

Players are of American nationality unless stated

Mercedes-Benz Championship *Plantation Course, Kapalua, HI* [7411–73]

1	Daniel Chopra (SWE)*	69-72-67-66—274	$1100000
2	Steve Stricker	73-69-68-64—274	630000

*Chopra won at the fourth extra hole

3	Stephen Ames (CAN)	72-67-70-66—275	410000

Sony Open *Waialae CC, Honolulu, HI* [7060–70]

1	K J Choi (KOR)	64-65-66-71—266	$954000
2	Rory Sabbatini (RSA)	66-69-66-68—269	572400
3	Jerry Kelly	67-67-69-67—270	360400

Bob Hope Chrysler Classic *The Classic Club, La Quinta, CA* [7305–72]

1	D J Trahan	67-64-68-70-65—334	$918000
2	Justin Leonard	68-64-67-66-72—337	550800
3	Anthony Kim	69-67-67-66-69—338	295800
	Kenny Perry	66-72-65-66-69—338	295800

Buick Invitational *Torrey Pines (South), San Diego, CA* [6874–72]

1	Tiger Woods	67-65-66-71—269	$936000
2	Ryuji Imada (JPN)	69-72-69-67—277	561600
3	Stewart Cink	68-69-69-73—279	301600
	Rory Sabbatini (RSA)	67-75-70-67—279	301600

FBR Open *TPC Scottsdale, AZ* [7216–71]

1	J B Holmes*	68-65-66-71—270	$1080000
2	Phil Mickelson	68-68-67-67—270	648000

*Holmes won at the first extra hole

3	Charles Warren	65-69-67-70—271	408000

AT&T Pebble Beach National Pro-Am *Pebble Beach* [6816–72]

1	Steve Lowery*	69-71-70-68—278	$1080000
2	Vijay Singh (FIJ)	70-70-67-71—278	648000

*Lowery won at first extra hole

3	Dudley Hart	69-70-68-72—279	312000
	John Malinger	67-74-73-65—279	312000
	Corey Pavin	73-69-71-66—279	312000

Northern Trust Open (formerly the Nissan Open)
Riviera CC, Pacific Palisades, CA [7279–71]

1	Phil Mickelson	68-64-70-70—272	$1116000
2	Jess Quinney	69-67-67-71—274	669600
3 .	Luke Donald (ENG)	68-71-70-68—277	359600
	Padraig Harrington (IRL)	69-69-71-68—277	359600

WGC – Accenture Match Play Championship *Gallery, Tucson, AZ*

Winner:	Tiger Woods	$1350000
Runner-up:	Stewart Cink	8690000
third place:	Henrik Stenson (SWE)	575000

Full details of this event can be found on page 188

Mayakoba Classic *El Camaleon, Riviera Maya, MX* [6923–70]

1	Brian Gay	66-67-62-69—264	$630000
2	Steve Marino	67-69-64-66—266	378000
3	Matt Kuchar	68-69-64-67—268	203000
	John Merrick	64-68-69-67—268	203000

Honda Classic *PGA National Championship, Palm Beach FL* [7241–70]

1	Ernie Els (RSA)	67-70-70-67—274	$990000
2	Luke Donald (ENG)	64-74-66-71—275	594000
3	Nathan Green (AUS)	71-70-68-67—276	374000

PODS Championship *Tampa Bay, FL* [7240-71]

1	Sean O'Hair	69-71-71-69—280	$954000
2	Stewart Cink	66-73-69-74—282	294591
	Ryuji Imada (JPN)	72-70-72-68—282	294591
	Troy Matteson	70-72-71-69—282	294591
	Billy Mayfair	68-71-71-72—282	294591
	George McNeill	70-72-71-69—282	294591
	John Senden (AUS)	67-74-74-67—282	294591

Arnold Palmer Invitational *Bay Hill, Orlando, FL* [7239–70]

1	Tiger Woods	70-68-66-66—270	$1044000
2	Bart Bryant	68-68-68-67—271	626400
3	Cliff Kresge	67-68-71-67—273	301600
	Sean O'Hair	72-69-63-69—273	301600
	Vijay Singh (FIJ)	66-65-73-69—273	301600

WGC – CA Championship *Doral, Orlando, FL* [7266–72]

1	Geoff Ogilvy (AUS)	65-67-68-71—271	$1350000
2	Jim Furyk	69-71-64-68—272	530000
	Retief Goosen (RSA)	71-69-64-68—272	530000
	Vijay Singh (FIJ)	73-68-63-68—272	53000

Full details of this event can be found on page 189

Puerto Rico Open *Rio Grande, Puerto Rico* [7569–72]

1	Greg Kraft	69-66-69-70—274	$630000
2	Jerry Kelly	67-66-72-70—275	308000
	Bo Van Pelt	64-68-71-72—275	308000

Zurich Classic of New Orleans *TPC Avondale, New Orleans, LA*

[7341–72]

1	Andres Romero (ARG)	73-69-65-68—275	$1116000
2	Peter Lonard (AUS)	67-70-70-69—276	669600
3	Tim Wilkinson (NZL)	71-68-71-67—277	421600

Shell Houston Open *Redstone, Humble, TX* [7457–72]

1	Johnson Wagner	63-69-69-71—272	$1008000
2	Chad Campbell	73-64-65-72—274	492800
	Geoff Ogilvy (AUS)	67-73-66-68—274	492800

THE MASTERS *Augusta National, GA*   [7445–72]

1	Trevor Immelman (RSA)	68-68-69-75—280	$1350000
2	Tiger Woods	72-71-68-72—283	810000
3	Stewart Cink	72-69-71-72—284	435000
	Brandt Snedeker	69-68-70-77—284	435000

Full details of this event are to be found on page 64

Verizon Heritage *Harbour Town, Hilton Head Island, SC*   [6973–71]

1	Boo Weekley	69-64-65-71—271	$990000
2	Aaron Baddeley (AUS)	69-67-67-69—272	484000
	Anthony Kim	67-67-67-71—272	484000

EDS Byron Nelson Championship *TPC Four Seasons, Irving, TX*

[7022–70]

1	Adam Scott (AUS)*	68-67-67-71—273	$1152000
2	Ryan Moore	67-70-68-68—273	691200

*Scott won at the third extra hole

3	Bart Bryant	72-66-67-72—277	435200

Wachovia Championship *Quail Hollow, Charlotte, NC*   [7442–72]

1	Anthony Kim	70-67-66-69—272	$1152000
2	Ben Curtis	69-71-72-65—277	691200
3	Jason Bohn	68-67-72-71—278	435200

The Players Championship *TPC, Sawgrass, Ponte Vedra Beach, FL*

[7215–72]

1	Sergio García (ESP)*	66-73-73-71—283	$1710000
2	Paul Goydos	68-71-70-74—283	1026000

*García won at the first extra hole

3	Jeff Quinney	71-73-77-70—284	646000

AT&T Classic *TPC Sugarloaf, Duluth, GA*   [7259–72]

1	Ryuji Imada (JPN)*	71-69-66-67—273	$990000
2	Kenny Perry	66-69-69-69—273	594000

*Imada won at the first extra hole

3	Camilo Villegas (COL)	68-69-71-66—274	374000

Crowne Plaza Invitational *Colonial, Forth Worth, TX*   [7054–70]

1	Phil Mickelson	65-68-65-68—266	$1098000
2	Tim Clark (RSA)	68-69-64-66—267	536800
	Rod Pampling (AUS)	69-67-63-68—267	536800

Memorial Tournament *Muirfield Village, Columbus, OH*   [7265–72]

1	Kenny Perry	66-71-74-69—280	$1080000
2	Mathew Goggin (AUS)	65-72-71-74—282	396000
	Jerry Kelly	66-72-73-71—282	396000
	Justin Rose (ENG)	68-73-70-71—282	396000
	Mike Weir (CAN)	71-72-68-71—282	396000

Stanford St Jude Championship *TPC Southwind, Memphis, TN*

[7244–70]

1	Justin Leonard*	68-73-67-68—276	$1080000
2	Robert Allenby (AUS)	71-71-69-65—276	528000
	Trevor Immelman (RSA)	74-66-67-69—276	528000

*Leonard won at the second extra hole

US OPEN Championship *Torrey Pines, La Jolla, CA* [7643–71]

1	Tiger Woods*	72-68-70-73—283	$1350000
2	Rocco Mediate	69-71-72-71—283	810000

Woods won at the 19th hole of the extra round

3	Lee Westwood (ENG)	70-71-70-73—284	491995

Full details of this event can be found on page 53

Travelers Championship *River Highlands, Cromwell, CN* [6820–70]

1	Stewart Cink	66-64-65-67—262	$1080000
2	Tommy Armour III	69-64-65-65—263	528000
	Hunter Mahan	68-63-67-65—263	528000

Buick Open *Warwick Hills, Grand Blanc, MI* [7127–72]

1	Kenny Perry	69-67-67-66—269	$900000
2	Woody Austin	66-67-69-68—270	440000
	Bubba Watson	67-67-68-68—270	440000

AT&T National *Congressional , Bethesda, MD* [7255–70]

1	Anthony Kim	67-67-69-65—268	$1080000
2	Fredrik Jacobson (SWE)	67-72-66-65—270	648000
3	Robert Allenby (AUS)	68-69-67-67—271	256500
	Tommy Armour III	67-69-66-69—271	256500
	Jim Furyk	70-68-67-66—271	256500
	Nick O'Hern (AUS)	70-65-67-69—271	256500
	Rod Pampling (AUS)	66-69-71-65—271	256500
	Dean Wilson	69-70-65-67—271	256500

John Deere Classic *Deere Run, Silvis, IL* [7257–71]

1	Kenny Perry*	65-66-67-70—268	$756000
2	Brad Adamonis	66-66-66-70—268	369600
	Jay Williamson	69-68-62-69—268	369600

Perry won at the first extra hole

137th OPEN CHAMPIONSHIP *Royal Birkdale, England* [7173–70]

1	Padraig Harrington (IRL)	74-68-72-69—283	$1498875
2	Ian Poulter (ENG)	72-71-75-69—287	899325
3	Greg Norman (AUS)	70-70-72-77—289	509618
	Henrik Stenson (SWE)	76-72-70-71—289	509618

Full details of this event can be found on page 38

US Bank Championship *Brown Deer Park, Milwaukee, WI* [6759–70]

1	Richard S Johnson	63-67-70-64—264	$720000
2	Ken Duke	67-65-68-65—265	432000
3	Chad Campbell	67-67-68-65—267	208000
	Chris Riley	68-66-67-66—267	208000
	Dean Wilson	65-73-64-65—267	208000

RBC Canadian Open *Glen Abbey, Oakville, ON* [7222–71]

1	Chez Reavie	65-64-68-70—267	$900000
2	Billy Mayfair	68-66-68-68—270	540000
3	Steve Marino	67-67-67-70—271	290000
	Sean O'Hair	65-71-67-68—271	290000

WGC – Bridgestone Invitational Firestone CC, Akron, OH   [7400–70]

1	Vijay Singh (FIJ)	67-66-69-68—270	$1350000
2	Stuart Appleby (AUS)	70-66-67-68—271	635000
	Lee Westwood (ENG)	70-65-67-69—271	635000

Full details of this event can be found on page 191

Legends Reno-Tahoe Open Montreux GCC, Reno, NV   [7472–72]

1	Parker McLachlin	68-62-66-74—270	$540000
2	Brian Davis	67-67-68-75—277	264000
	John Rollins	70-66-70-71—277	264000

US PGA CHAMPIONSHIP Oakland Hills, Bloomfield, MI   [7395–70]

1	Padraig Harrington (IRL)	71-74-66-66—277	1350000
2	Ben Curtis	73-67-68-71—279	660000
	Sergio García (ESP)	69-73-69-68—279	660000

Full details of this event can be found on page 73

Wyndham Championship Sedgefield, Greensboro', NC   [7117–70]

1	Carl Pettersson (SWE)	64-61-66-68—259	$918000
2	Scott McCarron	65-64-64-68—261	550800
3	Rich Beem	70-67-63-63—263	346800

The Barclays Ridgewood, Westchester, Harrison, NY   [7304–71]

1	Vijay Singh (FIJ)*	70-70-66-70—276	$1260000
2	Sergio García (ESP)	70-67-69-70—276	616000
	Kevin Sutherland	70-69-69-68—276	616000

*Singh won at the second extra hole

Deutsche Bank Championship TPC Boston, Norton, MA   [7207–71]

1	Vijay Singh (FIJ)	64-66-69-63—262	$1260000
2	Mike Weir (CAN)	61-68-67-71—267	756000
3	Ernie Els (RSA)	66-65-69-70—270	406000
	Camilo Villegas (COL)	68-66-63-73—270	406000

BMW Championship Bellerive, St Louis, MO   [7326–71]

1	Camilo Villegas (COL)	65-66-66-68—265	$1260000
2	Dudley Hart	67-69-66-65—267	756000
3	Jim Furyk	70-62-66-70—268	406000
	Anthony Kim	68-67-66-67—268	406000

Ryder Cup Valhalla, Louisville, KY   [7496–71]

USA 16½, Europe 11½

Full details of this event can be found on page 194

Viking Classic Annandale, Madison MS   [7199–72]

1	Will MacKenzie*	70-64-67-68—269	$648000
2	Brian Gay	66-68-67-68—269	316800
	Marc Turnesa	65-68-66-70—269	316800

*MacKenzie won at the second extra hole

Tour Championship *East Lake GC, Atlanta, GA* [7154–70]

1	Camilo Villegas (COL)*	72-66-69-66—273	$1260000
2	Sergio García (ESP)	70-65-67-71—273	756000

Villegas won at the first extra hole

3	Anthony Kim	64-69-72-69—274	409500
	Phil Mickelson	68-68-69-69—274	409500

Turning Stone *Atunyote, Verona, NY* [7482–72]

1	Dustin Johnson	72-68-70-69—279	$1080000
2	Robert Allenby (AUS)	71-68-71-70—280	648000
3	Steve Allan	68-74-70-69—281	244714
	Woody Austin	74-69-69-69—281	244714
	Mathew Goggin	71-70-71-69—281	244714
	Ryuji Imada (JPN)	72-71-69-69—281	244714
	Robert Garrigus	72-72-68-69—281	244714
	Charles Howell III	71-68-69-73—281	244714
	Davis Love III	75-70-66-70—281	244714

Valero Texas Open *La Cantera, San Antonio, TX* [6896–70]

1	Zach Johnson	69-66-62-64—261	$810000
2	Charlie Wi	67-68-67-61—263	336000
	Tim Wilkinson	67-69-63-64—263	336000
	Mark Wilson	68-66-66-63—263	336000

JTS Hospitals for Children Open *TPC Summerlin. Las Vegas, NV* [7243–72]

1	Marc Turnesa	62-64-65-68—263	$738000
2	JMatt Kuchar	63-63-71-67—264	442800
3	Chad Campbell	65-67-67-67—266	213200
	John Mullinger	64-64-70-68—226	213200
	Michael Allen	63-69-64-70—266	213200

Frys.com Open *Grayhawk, Scottsdale, AZ* [7125–70]

1	Cameron Beckman*	69-66-64-63—262	$900000
2	Kevin Sutherland	67-66-63-66—262	540000

Beckman won at the second extra hole

3	Mathew Goggin (AUS)	69-63-68-63—263	340000

Ginn sur Mer Classic *The Conservatory, Palm Coast, FL* [7663–72]

1	Ryan Palmer	67-71-72-71—281	$828000
2	Ken Duke	70-69-72-71—282	276000
	Michael Letzig	65-74-70-73—282	276000
	George McNeill	71-71-71-69—282	276000
	Vaughn Taylor	69-74-69-70—282	276000
	Nicholas Thompson	71-70-72-69—282	276000

Children's Miracle Network Classic
Magnolia and Palm Courses, Lake, Buena Vista, FL [7516–72, 6957–72]

1	Davis Love III	66-69-64-64—263	$828000
2	Tommy Gainey	68-66-66-64—264	496800
3	Steve Marino	65-66-66-71—268	266800
	Scott Verplank	64-64-69-70—268	266800

Del Webb Father-Son Challenge   *Champions Gate, Orlando, FL*

I	Larry Nelson and Drew Nelson	61-62—123	$210,000
2	Davis Love III and Dru Love	63-62—125	120,000
3	Tom Kite and David Kite	61-65—126	90,000

4 Raymond Floyd and Raymond Floyd Jr, Bernhard Langer and Stefan Langer, Hale Irwin and Steven Irwin 127; 7 Nick Faldo and Matthew Faldo, Mark O'Meara and Shaun O'Meara, Arnold Palmer and Sam Saunders 128; 10 Greg Norman and Greg Norman Jr 129; 11 Vijay Singh and Qass Singh 131; 12 Paul Azinger and Aaron Stewart, Fuzzy Zoeller and Gretchen Zoeller 133; 14 Curtis Strange and David Strange 134; 15 Jack Nicklaus and Jack Nicklaus II 138; 16 Billy Casper and Bob Casper 139; 17 Craig Stadler and Chris Stadler 140; 18 Lee Trevino and Daniel Trevino 142

Wendy's 3-Tour Challenge   *Rio Secco GC, NA*

I	Champions Tour (Nick Price (ZIM) 65, Jay Haas 66, Fred Funk 68)	199	$500,000
2	PGA Tour (Kenny Perry 66, Stewart Cink 67, Rocco Mediate 69)	202	$1,750,000
3	LPGA (Natalie Gulbis 67, Cristie Kerr 67, Helen Alfredsson (SWE) 78)	212	$1,750,000

Merrill Lynch Shoot-out   *Tiburon GC, Naples, FL*   [7288–72]

I	Scott Hoch and Kenny Perry	65-60-60—185	$365,000 each
2	JB Holes and Boo Weekley	67-62-60—189	230,000
3	Greg Norman and Camillo Villegas	69-65-57—191	132.500

Chevron World Challenge   *Sherwood Country Club, Thousand Oaks, CA*

I	Vijay Singh (FIJ)	71-72-67-67—277	$1,350,000
2	Steve Stricker	71-71-68-68—278	84,000
3	Anthony Kim	71-70-67-73—281	49,500
	Hunter Mahan	71-72-70-68—281	49,500

New arrangement is good news for Gordon J Brand

British PGA Seniors champion Gordon J Brand has the chance to play this year in the US PGA Seniors Championship following a decision by the British PGA and the PGA of America for reciprocal exemption.

The American Championship is being played from May 14–17 at the Canterbury Club in Cleveland, Ohio, while the British PGA Seniors, sponsored by the De Vere Collection, is scheduled for June 25–28 at Slaley Hall in Northumberland.

Few Changes to Augusta National for 2009

Despite criticism that the added length put on Augusta National for The Masters has reduced the excitement experienced each year on the back nine on the final day, the club are making few changes for the 2009 tournament. Chairman Billy Payne has trimmed only 10 yards off the scorecard but has the facility to reduce the length further in the case of bad weather.

"As we have done every year since the inception of The Masters, we evaluate the golf course and make what refinements we think is necessary. What we have done this year is make minor changes in order to provide greater flexibility in the event of adverse weather."

Trevor Immelman, the South African winner of the 2008 tournament, shot a closing 75 – the highest last round score since Arnold Palmer was successful in 1962. The previous year, Zach Johnston's one-over-par 289 winning total was the highest in the history of the event which started in 1934.

In addition, a new practice facility will be completed in time for the 2009 edition of the event.

The R&A announces new golf club rules

The R&A has announced revisions to golf's equipment Rules, which are designed to enhance the benefits of accuracy by making playing from the rough a more challenging prospect. The new Rules, which relate to club face grooves, are the culmination of an extensive collaboration research project between The R&A and the United States Golf Association. This research shows that modern groove configurations can allow players to generate almost as much spin from the rough as is available from the fairway, resulting in a reduction in the value of accuracy. The Rules will apply to all clubs manufactured after January 1, 2010. Clubs manufactured before this will remain legal until at least 2024 if they conform to the regulations prior to 2010.

The revised Rules, which will significantly increase the spin differential between shots from the fairway and shots from the rough, augment the existing limitation on grooves and will affect all clubs (with the exception of drivers and putters). The new regulations limit groove volume and groove edge sharpness. Essentially, larger volume grooves have the ability to channel away more material, such as water or grass, similar to the tread on car tyres. At the same time, sharper groove edges facilitate a better contact between club and ball, even in the presence of debris.

Both new regulations will apply to golf clubs with lofts greater than or equal to 25 degrees (generally a standard 5-iron and above) with only the rule limiting groove volume applying to clubs of lesser loft.

It is intended that the new Rules will be introduced as a Condition of Competition at top professional level from January 1, 2010, and at top amateur level and in other professional events from January 1, 2014. The R&A and the USGA will introduce such a Condition of Competiion at their resective championships in accordance with this schedule.

Norman and Norman top Golf Skills Challenge

Twenty-three-year-old Greg Norman Jr and his father won the $800,000 ADT Golf Skills Challenge at the Fairmont Turnberry Isle Resort last year. The competition for golfers and their caddies (Greg Jr carried the bag for his father at The 2008 Open), tests eight skills – long driving, mid-iron play, greenside bunker recovery, pitching over a hazard, trouble shots, chip shots, pitching and short iron play with the last category worth $250,000.

In addition to the Norman family pairing Fred Couples, who won the long driving section with a hit of 311 yards, played with Joe LaCava, Peter Jacobsen with Mike Cowan and Rocco Mediate with Matthew Achatz.

Norman Jr, who is currently at the University of Miami, won the short iron play category when his 111yards pitch finished an inch from the hole. Mediate's effort lipped out. The Normans also won the pitching over a hazard category and the putting with Greg Sr holing out both times.

Month by month in 2008

Trevor Immelman, in hospital in December for the removal of a benign tumour on his diaphragm, becomes South Africa's first Masters champion since Gary Player in 1978. He beats Tiger Woods by three even with a closing 75. Lorena Ochoa wins her second major title, the Kraft Nabisco, by five and follows up with further victories by 11 and three. That's 10 wins in 15. Darren Clarke holes a 40-footer in China for his first European Tour victory in nearly five years.

US Champions Tour 2008

www.pgatour.com

Final Ranking *Players are of American nationality unless stated*

1	Bernhard Langer (GER)	$2,035,073	26	Tim Simpson	782,641
2	Jay Haas	1,991,726	27	Craig Stadler	752,732
3	Fred Funk	1,825,931	28	David Eger	749,087
4	Jeff Sluman	1,728,443	29	Mike Goodes	676,084
5	John Cook	1,721,038	30	Bob Gilder	657,283
6	Loren Roberts	1,674,939	31	Joe Ozaki (JPN)	609,363
7	Eduardo Romero (ARG)	1,615,099	32	Gil Morgan	580,406
8	Andy Bean	1,506,789	33	Tom Purtzer	576,752
9	Scott Hoch	1,497,530	34	Fulton Allem	546,242
10	Tom Kite	1,284,592	35	Jim Thorpe	508,332
11	Lonnie Nielsen	1,224,012	36	Ben Crenshaw	503,362
12	Nick Price	1,195,264	37	Morris Hatalsky	493,542
13	Brad Bryant	1,128,413	38	Jerry Pate	481,879
14	Scott Simpson	1,127,626	39	Bruce Fleisher	477,256
15	Denis Watson	1,112,580	40	Bobby Wadkins	473,499
16	Mark McNulty (IRL)	1,078,272	41	Dana Quigley	450,195
17	Mark Wiebe	1,061,949	42	Allen Doyle	441,235
18	DA Weibring	1,059,197	43	Don Pooley	439,866
19	Gene Jones	1,022,061	44	David Edwards	430,974
20	Tom Watson	972,343	45	Vicente Fernandez (ARG)	424,075
21	RW Eaks	942,316	46	Fuzzy Zoeller	415,519
22	Tom Jenkins	900,932	47	Phil Blackmar	383,547
23	Bruce Vaughan	832,595	48	Gary Hallberg	378,738
24	Keith Fergus	822,151	49	Tom McKnight	375,379
25	Joey Sindelar	783,333	50	Mark James	335,286

Career Money List

1	Hale Irwin	$24,920,665	26	Tom Wargo	7,809,846
2	Gil Morgan	18,964,141	27	Doug Tewell	7,707,695
3	Dana Quigley	14,406,269	28	John Bland	7,511,059
4	Bruce Fleisher	13,990,386	29	JC Snead	7,375,981
5	Larry Nelson	13,262,808	30	Mike McCullough	7,323,749
6	Allen Doyle	13,031,711	31	Bob Murphy	7,211,001
7	Jim Thorpe	12,985,193	32	José Maria Canizares (ESP)	7,180,392
8	Tom Kite	12,878,502	33	Loren Roberts	7,170,842
9	Tom Jenkins	12,126,298	34	Bruce Lietzke	7,155,498
10	Jim Colbert	11,684,239	35	DA Weibring	7,094,391
11	Dave Stockton	11,159,503	36	Craig Stadler	7,030,999
12	Tom Watson	11,023,827	37	Dale Douglass	7,019,089
13	Lee Trevino	9,853,603	38	Walter Hall	6,930,162
14	Raymond Floyd	9,472,853	39	Morris Hatalsky	6,899,559
15	Bob Gilder	9,443,293	40	Tom Purtzer	6,793,471
16	Jay Sigel	9,392,812	41	Chi Chi Rodriguez (PUR)	6,642,834
17	Isao Aoki (JPN)	9,343,160	42	Jim Albus	6,398,450
18	Graham Marsh (AUS)	9,149,600	43	Dave Eichelberger	6,390,330
19	Bob Charles (NZL)	9,044,003	44	Bobby Wadkins	6,224,681
20	Jim Dent	8,992,119	45	Gary Player (RSA)	6,005,261
21	Bruce Summerhays	8,943,420	46	Ed Dougherty	5,929,735
22	Vicente Fernandez (ARG)	8,694,146	47	Mark McNulty (IRL)	5,917,968
23	Jay Haas	8,533,527	48	Leonard Thompson	5,630,524
24	John Jacobs	8,489,965	49	Hugh Baiocchi	5,532,612
25	Mike Hill	8,383,104	50	Hubert Green	5,510,127

Tour Statistics

Driving accuracy

Pos	Name	Rounds	%
1	David Edwards	74	80.00
2	Mark McNulty (IRL)	80	78.84
3	Fred Funk	58	78.39
4	Bruce Fleisher	73	78.23
5	Hale Irwin	65	77.50
6	John Cook	83	76.10
7	Larry Nelson	49	76.03
8	Scott Simpson	84	75.97
9	Tom McKnight	70	75.93
10	Dave Eichelberger	80	75.84

Driving distance

(Average yards per drive)

Pos	Name	Rounds	Yds
1	Tom Purtzer	79	295.5
2	Eduardo Romero (ARG)	60	293.0
3	Sandy Lyle (SCO)	49	289.7
4	Joey Sindelar	63	288.7
5	Gil Morgan	76	287.1
6	Lonnie Nielsen	86	286.9
7	RW Eaks	77	286.7
	Keith Fergus	89	286.7
9	John Harris	84	282.3
10	Bernhard Langer (GER)	66	282.1

Greens in regulation

Pos	Name	Rounds	%
1	Joey Sindelar	63	75.47
2	John Cook	83	73.90
3	Fred Funk	58	73.82
4	Tom Purtzer	79	73.74
5	Brad Bryant	73	73.47
6	Scott Simpson	84	73.27
7	Jeff Sluman	84	73.20
8	Nick Price (ZIM)	54	73.03
9	Loren Roberts	80	72.58
10	Fulton Allem	53	72.22

Sand saves

Pos	Name	Rounds	%
1	Ron Streck	50	69.64
2	Wayne Grady	62	62.96
3	Jeff Sluman	84	59.76
4	Curtis Strange	50	59.62
5	Massy Kuramoto (JPN)	57	57.89
6	Fred Funk	58	56.45
7	Denis Watson	85	56.38
8	Dave Stockton	41	55.56
9	Phil Blackmaar	61	55.26
10	Bernhard Langer (GER)	66	54.84

Scrambling

(Made par after missing greens in regulation)

Pos	Name	Rounds	%
1	Jeff Sluman	84	68.63
2	Jay Haas	68	67.09
3	Ron Streck	50	66.24
4	Mark McNulty (IRL)	80	63.81
5	Fulton Allem	53	63.20
6	Nick Price (ZIM)	54	63.09
7	Bernhard Langer (GER)	66	62.99
8	Bruce Fleisher	73	62.66
9	Scott Simpson	84	62.36
10	Bob Gilder	91	62.14

Putts per round

Pos	Name	Rounds	%
1	Joe Ozaki (JPN)	84	68.63
2	Phil Blackmar	68	67.09
3	Massy Kuramoto (JPN)	50	66.24
4	Gary Hallberg	80	63.81
5	Mark O'Meara	53	63.20
6	Ben Crenshaw	54	63.09
7	Wayne Grady	66	62.99
8	Morris Hatalsky	73	62.66
9	Craig Stadler	84	62.36
10	Tom Kite	91	62.14

Multiple winners

Scott Hoch, Allianz Championship, The ACE Group Classic

Bernhard Langer (GER), Toshiba Classic, Ginn Championship, Administaff Small Business Classic

Tom Watson, Outback Steakhouse Pro-Am, Liberty Mutual Legends of Golf

Denis Watson, AT&T Champions Classic, FedEx Kinko's Classic

Jay Haas, Senior PGA Championship, Principal Charity Classic

Eduardo Romero (ARG), Dick's Sporting Goods Open, U.S. Senior Open, SAS Championship

Fred Funk, MasterCard Championship, JELD-WEN Tradition

Jeff Sluman, Bank of America Championship, Walmart First Tee Open

RW Eaks, 3M Championship, Greater Hickory Classic

Course records

Joe Ozaki, 65, The Cap Cana Championship (2nd round)

Dana Quigley, 62, 3M Championship (1st round)

Tom Watson, 64, JELD-WEN Tradition (2nd round)

RW Eaks, 61, Greater Hickory Classic (3rd round)

Tour Results

MasterCard Championship	Hualalai, Ka'upulehu-Kona, HI	Fred Funk	195 (-21)
Turtle Bay Championship	Kahuku, HI	Jerry Pate	211 (-5)
Allianz Championship	Broken Sound, Boca Raton FL	Scott Hoch	202 (-14)
The ACE Group Classic	Quail West, Naples FL	Scott Hoch*	202 (-14)

Hoch won a four-way play-off at the first extra hole

Wendy's Champions Skins Game	Royal Kaanapaii, Lahaina HI	Fuzzy Zoeller and Peter Jacobsen	6 skins
Toshiba Classic	Newport Beach, CA	Bernhard Langer* (GER)	199 (-11)

Langer beat J Haas at the seventh extra hole

AT&T Classic	Valencia CA	Denis Watson*	209 (-7)

Watson beat B Bryant and L Roberts at the third extra hole

Ginn Championship	Ocean Hammock, Palm Coast, FL	Bernhard Langer (GER)	204 (-12)
The Cap Cana	Punta Espada, Cap Cana, Dominican R	Mark Wiede	202 (-14)
Outback Steakhouse Pro-Am	TPC Tampa Bay, Lutz, FL	Tom Watson	204 (-9)
Liberty Mutual Legends of Golf	Savannah Harbor, GA	Andy North and Tom Watson	185 (-31)
FedEx Kinko's Classic	The Hills, Austin, TX	Denis Watson	206 (-10)
Regions Charity Classic	RT Jones Trail, Hoover, AL	Andy Bean	203 (-13)

Senior PGA Championship   Oak Hill, Rochester, NY

1	Jay Haas	69-72-72-74—287
2	Bernhard Langer (GER)	71-71-70-76—288
3	Scott Hoch	71-74-72-72—289
	Scott Simpson	76-71-69-73—289
	Joey Sindelar	76-69-72-72—289

Principal Charity Classic	Glen Oaks, West Des Moines, IA	Jay Haas	203 (-10)
Bank of America Championship	Nashawtuc, Concord, MA	Jeff Sluman	199 (-17)
Commerce Bank Championship	Eisenhower Park East, Meadow, NY	Loren Roberts	201 (-12)
Dick's Sporting Goods Open	En-Joie Endicott, NY	Eduardo Romero (ARG)	199 (-17)

European Senior Open   Royal Troon

1	Bruce Vaughan*	68-71-69-70—278
2	John Cook (USA)	69-71-67-71—278

Vaughan won at the first extra hole

3	Eduardo Romero (ARG)	68-73-68-70—279

US Senior Open   Broad Moor, Colorado Springs, CO

1	Eduardo Romero (ARG)	67-69-65-73—274
2	Fred Funk	65-69-69-75—278
3	Mark McNulty (IRL)	68-70-73-68—279

JELD-WEN Tradition	Crosswater, Sunriver, OR	Fred Funk	269 (-19)
Boeing Classic	TPC Snoqualmie, WA	Tom Kite	202 (-14)
Wal-Mart First Tee Open	Pebble Beach, CA	Jeff Sluman	202 (-14)
Greater Hickory Classic	Rock Barn, Conover, NC	R W Eaks	200 (-16)
SAS Championship	Prestonwood, Cary, NC	Eduardo Romero (ARG)	201 (-15)
Constellation Energy Senior TPC	Baltimore CC, Timonium, MD	D A Weibring	271 (-9)
Administaff Small Business Classic	Augusta Pines, Spring, TX	Bernhard Langer (GER)	204 (-12)
AT&T Championship	Oak Hills, San Antonio, TX	John Cook	197 (-16)
Charles Schwab Cup Championship	Sonoma, CA	Andy Bean	268 (-20)
Del Webb Father-Son Challenge	Champions Gate, Orlando, FL	Larry Nelson and Drew Nelson	

Bernhard Langer tops US prize-money list

Bernhard Langer, who was top prize-money earner in Europe in 1981 and 1984, ended his first full season on the US Champions Tour by grabbing the No. 1 spot from Jay Haas, Fred Funk and Eduardo Romero.

In 20 starts he won three times and was out of the top 10 only six times in amassing earnings o f$2,035,073. He averaged 282 yards off the tee and although he finished 22nd in the Putts Per Round category he still topped the average score table with 69.65. He was pipped, however, by Haas for the Charles Schwab Cup competition which guarantees the winner in a points table a $1 million annuity.

Now based in Orlando, the former European Ryder Cup captain has not taken long to settle down on the Champions circuit. "When I turned 50 and came to play out here I thought it would be a bitter sweet experience but after playing four or five events I knew that this was the Tour I wanted to play on for the next few years."

Langer added that he was not missing the other Tours on which he was playing before turning 50, adding: "I've played against the young guys long enough. I've done my time out there. Now I can spend more time with the family and even the tee times are better!"

Latterly Langer, a double winner of a Green Jacket, admitted that on the main Tours he had been getting tee-off times between 6.45 and 7.15 which meant getting up at 4.00 and warming up in the dark. It was not much fun.

Another advantage, Langer say,s about playing in America now is the fact that all the players on the Champions Tour are the same age. "We have known each other and can relate to each other. Most of us have kids or even grandchildren unlike the 20-year-olds you play with on the main Tour. They don't know anything about being married and having children so don't relate the same way as we do on the Champions Tour. After all, our main topic of conversation is 'which part of the body hurts today?'"

Another reason why Langer enjoys playing in America – he will only return to Europe in future for his own event and The Open – is the fact that the seniors play courses more adjusted to their lengths of golf rather than the young fellows who hit the ball 40–50 yards further.

How golf's new Race to Dubai works

The key points of The Race to Dubai which replaces the old Order of Merit are:

Players will be ranked during the season according to their earnings from all events on The European Tour International Schedule including the Major Championships and World Golf Championships.

The players ranked 1 to 60 will qualify to compete in the season's finale, the Dubai World Championship, on the Greg Norman designed Earth course at Jumeirah Golf Estates. Norman has described the last four holes as among the most demanding mile of play in golf.

On conclusion of the Dubai World Championship, the players ranked 1 to 15 in The Race to Dubai will share a Bonus Pool of US$10 million.

The number one player will receive US$2 million, the runner-up US$1.5 million and the third-placed player US$1 million with prizes down to the 15th player, who will earn US$250,000.

With a $10 million purse for the Dubai World Championship, there is real opportunity for the leading Race to Dubai positions to change over the course of this tournament.

If the winner of the Dubai World Championship is also the leader of The Race to Dubai at the end of the season he will claim a total prize of US$3.6 million.

Players must play a minimum of 12 tournaments in The Race to Dubai (the Dubai World Championship counts as a tournament) – at least two of these tournaments must be played in Europe.

The winner of The Race to Dubai earns a seven-year exemption on The European Tour.

US Nationwide Tour 2008

www.pgatour.com

Players are of American nationality unless stated

Final Ranking (Top 20 earned US Tour Card)

1	Matt Bettencourt	$447,863	51	Vance Veazey	136,486
2	Brendon de Jonge	437,035	52	Michael Putnam	130,981
3	Jeff Klauk	407,418	53	Fran Quinn	122,756
4	Jarrod Lyle	382,738	54	Chad Ginn	120,966
5	Bill Lunde	341,446	55	Garth Mulroy	119,353
6	Colt Knost	329,509	56	JJ Killeen	117,264
7	Darron Stiles	324,627	57	Chris Smith	115,482
8	Greg Chalmers (AUS)	321,930	58	Chris Nallen	114,021
9	Scott Piercy	320,187	59	Joe Daley	113,597
10	Greg Owen	309,805	60	Tee McCabe	111,543
11	Peter Tomasulo	296,704	61	Henrik Bjornstad (NOR)	110,388
12	Rick Price	284,922	62	Cameron Percy	110,293
13	Kris Blanks	280,588	63	Gary Christian (ENG)	107,021
14	David Mathis	276,412	64	David Hearn	106,860
15	Casey Wittenberg	271,919	65	Robert Damron	101,505
16	DA Points	266,696	66	Rich Barcelo	100,468
17	Arjun Atwal (IND)	259,186	67	Matt Hansen	99,828
18	Aron Price (AUS)	249,144	68	Scott Gardiner (AUS)	99,473
19	Marc Leishman	244,224	69	Dustin Bray	98,755
20	Brendon Todd	244,224	70	Fabian Gomez	96,482
21	Scott Gutschewski	238,215	71	Esteban Toledo (MEX)	96,083
22	Spencer Levin	236,185	72	David McKenzie	96,049
23	Bryce Molder	234,651	73	Sebastian Fernandez	93,971
24	Matt Weibring	228,155	74	Brad Fritsch	93,478
25	Ricky Barnes	218,902	75	Tom Johnson	90,270
26	David Branshaw	215,320	76	Brian Smock	89,056
27	Hunter Haas	209,461	77	Chris Kirk	88,441
28	Chris Tidland	203,255	78	Keoke Cotner	87,467
29	Ryan Hietala	198,476	79	Kyle Thompson	87,271
30	DJ Brigman	197,513	80	BJ Staten	86,498
31	Roger Tambellini	194,227	81	Scott Parel	86,484
32	Bubba Dickerson	189,734	82	Brendan Steele	84,281
33	Justin Hicks	184,861	83	Tommy Tolles	82,490
34	Matt Every	178,239	84	Bret Guetz	82,232
35	Daniel Summerhays	177,845	85	Dave Schultz	82,125
36	Josh Broadaway	172,881	86	Geoffrey Sisk	81,775
37	Scott Dunlap	170,081	87	Jason Schultz	79,192
38	Garrett Osborn	165,309	88	Craig Bowden	78,607
39	Bob May	165,113	89	Tom Gillis	72,968
40	Bryan DeCorso	163,471	90	Keith Nolan	72,812
41	Ewan Porter	159,124	91	Bradley Iles	70,733
42	Jeff Brehaut	155,029	92	Jim Herman	67,532
43	Chris Anderson	152,263	93	Jonathan Fricke	66,140
44	Oskar Bergman	152,098	94	Blake Adams	63,071
45	Webb Simpson	148,991	95	Miguel A Carballo (ARG)	62,049
46	Alex Prugh	144,790	96	Jeff Gallagher	61,850
47	Kyle Reifers	142,438	97	Dicky Pride	59,626
48	Gavin Coles	142,000	98	Wade Ormsby	58,602
49	Skip Kendall	140,027	99	Steve Wheatcroft	57,329
50	Won Joon Lee (KOR)	137,694	100	Todd Fischer	56,004

Tour Results

Moviestar Panama Championship	Panama City	Scott Dunlap	277 (-3)
Mexico Open	Tres Morias, Morelia, MX	Jarrod Lyle (AUS)	267 (-17)
HSBC NZ PGA Championship	Clearwater, Christchurch, NZ	Darron Stiles	134 (-10)
The Moonah Classic	Moonah, Mornington Peninsula	Ewan Porter (AUS)	275 (-13)
Chitimacha Louisiana Open	Le Triomphe, Broussard, LA	Gavin Coles	272 (-12)
Livermore Valley Wine Country Championship	Wente Vineyards, Livermore, CA	Aron Price* (AUS)	283 (-5)

Price beat JJ Killeen at the second extra hole

Athens Regional Foundation Classic	Jennings Mill, Athens, GA	Robert Damron*	277 (-11)

Damron beat Greg Owen (ENG) at the first extra hole

Henrico County Open	Dominion Club, Richmond, VA	Greg Chalmers* (AUS)	274 (-14)

Chalbers beat H Bjornstad (NOR) at the second extra hole

South Georgia Classic	Kinderlou Forest, Valdosta, GA	Bryan DeCorso	274 (-14)
Fort Smith Classic	Hardscrabble, Fort Smith, AR	Colt Knost	268 (-12)
BMW Charity Pro-Am	Bright's Creek, NC; Thornblade SC; SCCC	David Mathis	266 (-22)
Melwood Prince George's County Open	Mitchellville, MD	Jeff Klauk	276 (-12)
Bank of America Open	Glen Club, Glenview, IL	Kris Blanks	272 (-16)
Rex Hospital Open	Wakefield Plantation, Raleigh, NC	Scott Gutschewski	270 (-14)
Knoxville Open	Fox Den, Knoxville, TN	Jarrod Lyle (AUS)*	269 (-19)

Lyle beat Chris Kirk at the first extra hole

Fort Wayne Gretzky Classic	Georgian Bay, Raven GC, ON, Canada	Justin Hicks	269 (-15)
Nationwide Tour Players Cup	Pete Dye, Bridgeport, WV	Rick Price*	273 (-15)

Price beat Chris Anderson at first extra hole

Price Cutter Charity Championship	Highland Springs, Springfield, MO	Colt Knost	262 (-26)
Nationwide Children's Invitational	OSU Scarlet, Columbus, OH	Bill Lunde	279 (-5)
Cox Classic	Champions Run, Omaha, NE	Ryan Hietala	265 (-19)
Preferred Health Systems Wichita Open	Crestview, Wichita, KS	Scott Piercy	262 (-22)
Xerox Classic	Irondequoit, Rochester, NY	Brendon De Jonge	267 (-13)
Northeast Pennsylvania Classic	Glenmaura, Scranton, PA	Scott Piercy	267 (-13)
Utah Championship	Willow Creek, Sandy, UT	Brendon Todd	262 (-22)
Albertson's Boise Open	Hillcrest, Boise, ID	Chris Tidland	264 (-20)
Oregon Classic	Shadow Hills, Junction City, OR	Matt Bettencourt	269 (-19)
WNB Classic	Midland, TX	Marc Leishman (AUS)	267 (-21)
Chattanooga Classic	Black Creek, Chattanooga, TB	Arjun Atwal (IND)*	264 (-24)

Atwal beat Webb Simpson at first extra hole

Miccosukee Championship	Miccosukee G&CC, Miami, FL	DA Points*	272 (-12)

Points beat Matt Bettancourt at first extra hole

Nationwide Tour Championship	TPC Craig Ranch, McKinney, TX	Matt Bettencourt	367 (-17)

US Nationwide Tour statistics leaders

Driving distance – Won Joon Lee (84 rounds), 315.7 yards average

Driving accuracy – Geoffrey Sisk (75 rounds), 79.48%

Greens in regulation – Bob May (68 rounds), 75.59%

Putts per round – David Mathis (82 rounds) – 28.81 average

Sand saves – Greg Owen (ENG) (62 rounds), 61.33%

Scrambling – Jeff Klauk (88 rounds), 64.69%

Top Ten finishes – Greg Chalmers (AUS) (10)

Japan PGA Tour 2008

Players are of Japanese nationality unless stated

www.jgto.org/jgto/WG02000000Init.do

Token Homemate Cup	Token Tado, Nagoya, Mie	Katsumasa Miyamoto	276 (-8)
Tsuruya Open	Yamanohara, Hyogo	SK Ho (KOR)	272 (-12)
THE CROWNS	Nagoya, Aichi	Tomohiro Kondo*	271 (-9)

* Kondo beat Hiroyuki Fujita at the second extra hole

Pine Valley Beijing Open	Beijing, China	Hiroyuki Fujita	276 (-12)
JPGA Championship	Press, Gunma	Shingo Katayama	265 (-23)
Munsingwear Open KSB Cup	Tojigaoka Marine Hills, Okayama	Hideto Tanihara	270 (-18)
Mitsubishi Diamond Cup	Higashi hirono, Hyogo	Prayad Marksaeng (THA)	274 (-10)
Mizuno Open Yomiuri Classic	Yomiuri, Hyogo	Prayad Marksaeng (THA)	269 (-15)
UBS Japan Golf Tour Championship	Shishido Hills, Ibaraki	Hidemasa Hoshino	272 (-12)
Sega Sammy Cup	North Country CC, Hokkaido	Jeev Milkha Singh (IND)	275 (-13)
Sun-Chorella Classic	Otaru, Hokkaido	Takuya Taniguchi	284 (-4)
Vana H Cup KBC AUGUSTA	Keya, Fukuoka	Shintaro Kai	278 (-10)
Fujisankei Classic	Fujizakura, Yamanashi	Toyokazu Fujishima	271 (-13)
ANA Open	Sapporo, Hokkaido	Azuma Yano	273 (-15)
Asia-Pacific Panasonic Open	Ibaraki, Osaka	Hideto Tanihara	264 (-16)
Coca-Cola Tokai Classic	Miyoshi, Aichi	Toshinori Muto	277 (-11)
Canon Open	Totsuka, Kanagawa	Makoto Inque	275 (-13)
Japan Open	Koga, Fukuoka	Shingo Katayama	283 (-1)
Bridgestone Open	Sodegaura, Chiba	Azuma Yano	267 (-21)
ABC Championship	ABC, Hyogo	Ryo Ishikawa	279 (-3)
Championship by Lexus	Otone, Ibaraki	SK Ho (KOR)	269 (-15)
Mitsui Sumitomo VISA Taiheiyo Masters	Taiheiyo Club, Gotemba Course	Shingo Katayama	272 (-3)
Dunlop Phoenix	Phoenix CC	Prayad Marksaeng (THA)	276 (-8)
Casio World Open	Kochi Kuroshio CC	Koumei Oda	277 (-11)
Golf Nippon Series JT Cup	Tokyo Yomiuri CC	Jeev Milkha Singh (IND)	268 (-12)

Final Money List

1	Shingo Katayama	¥186,094,895	6	SK Ho (KOR)	98,009,498
2	Azuma Yano	137,064,052	7	Brendan Jones (AUS)	93,613,324
3	Prayad Marksaeng (THA)	126,430,825	8	Shintaro Kai	89,110,256
4	Hideto Tanihara	110,414,719	9	Hiroyuki Fujita	82,420,197
5	Ryo Ishikawa	106,318,166	10	Toshinori Mutu	78,382,804

Month by month in 2008

Sergio García beat Paul Goydos in a play-off to capture the Players Championship, his seventh and biggest PGA Tour victory. Compatriot Miguel Angel Jiménez wins the BMW PGA at Wentworth after a play-off with Oliver Wilson. Richard Finch is Irish Open champion, but only after falling into the river playing his third shot on the final hole. Annika Sörenstam has her third victory of the season, then announces she is to retire from tournament golf at the end of the year.

Japan Challenge Tour 2008

Players are of Japanese nationality unless stated

PRGR Cup	Oakvillage, Chiba	Tatsunori Nukaga	209 (-4)
Arita Tokyu Challenge	Arita Tokyu, Wakayama	Masamichi Uehira*	139 (-5)
Uehira won at the third play-off hole			
Mochizuki Tokyu JGTO Challenge III3	Mochizuko, Nagano	Shigeru Nonaka	133 (-11)
Novil Cup	Tokushima	Taichiro Kiyota	198 (-18)
Everlife Cup Challenge	Queen's Hill, Fukuoka	Yuta Ikeda	133 (-9)
Shizu Hills Tommy Cup	Shizu Hills, Ibaraki	Hirotaro Naito	199 (-11)
Sunroyal Cup	Sunroyal, Hyogo	Masamichi Uehira	130 (-14)
SRIXON Challenge	Arima Royal, Hyogo	Shigeru Nonaka	137 (-7)
Toshin Challenge	Lake Wood, Toshin, Mie	Hiro Aoyama	136 (-8)
PRGR Cup	Narita Hightree, Chiba	Ihiroaki Ijima	278 (-10)

Korean PGA Tour 2008

Players are of Korean nationality unless stated

Korea-China Tour KEB Invitational	Bae-Sang Moon
SBS Emerson Pacific Tottori Pref. Open	Seung Ho Lee
SK Telekom Open	Kyung Ju (KJ) Choi
SBS Tomato Open	Hyung Sung Kim
Caltex Maekyung Open	Seoul Inn Choon Hwang*
Hwang beat Seung Yul Noh at first extra hole	
SBS Lake Hills Open	Andrew Tschudin (AUS)
SBS Kunho Asiana Open	Inn Choon Hwang
Philos Open	In Hoi Hur
SBS Ace Bank Montvert	Hyung Sung Kim
SBS Johnnie Walker Blue Open	Wook Soon Kang
SBS Yonwoo Heavenland Open	Wi Joong Kim
Korea-China Tour KEB Invitational	Dae Sub Kim
Sansung Benest Open	Andrew McKenzie (AUS)
51st Korean Open	Sang Moon Bae
Shinhan Donghae Open	Kyung Ju (KJ) Choi
SBS Meritz Solmoro Open	Hyung Tae Kim
Dongby Promi Cup Match-play	Kyung Sool Kang
SBS Hang Tour	Ho Sung Choi
NH Nonghyup Korean PGA Championship	Andrew McKenzie* (AUS)

McKenzie beat Sang Hyun Park and Jong Yul Suk at first extra hole

Final Money List

1	Sang-Moon Bae	KW470,654,286	6	Kyung-Nam Kang	243,576,667
2	Hyung-Sung Kim	356,158,000	7	Andrew Mackenzie (AUS)	241,919,286
3	Dae-Sub Kim	270,824,190	8	Fung-Hoon Kang	207,988,167
4	Kyung-Ju Choi	270,000,000	9	Hyung-Dae Kim	197,481,333
5	Inn-Choon Hwang	265,200,100	10	Wi-Joong Kim	194,933,400

Asian Tour 2008

www.asiantour.com

Emaar-MGF Indian Masters	Delhi	SSP Chowrasia (IND)	279 (-9)
Enjoy Jacarta Astro Indonesian Open	Cengkareng	Felipe Aguilar (CHI)	262 (-18)
SAIL Open	Jaypee, Noida, India	Mark Brown (NZL)	274 (-14)
WGC – Accenture Match Play	The Gallery at Dove Mt, Tucson, AZ	Tiger Woods (USA)	
Johnnie Walker Classic	DLF CC, India	Mark Brown (NZL)	270 (-18)
Maybank Malaysian Open	Kota Permai	Arjun Atwal* (IND)	270 (-18)

Atwal beat Peter Hedblom (SWE) at 2nd play-off hole

Ballantines Championship	Pinx GC, Korea	Graeme McDowell* (NIR)	264 (-24)

McDowell beat Jeev Milkha Singh (IND) at the third extra hole

WGC – CA Championship	Doral, FL	Geoff Ogilvy (AUS)	271 (-17)
Asian Tour International	Pattana, Chonduri, Thailand	Lin Wen-tang (TPE)	265 (-23)
International Final Qualifier (137th Open)	Sentosa, Singapore	Danny Chia (MAS)	138 (-6)
Philippine Open	Wack Wack, Manila	Angelo Que (PHI)	283 (-5)
The MASTERS	Augusta National	Trevor Immelman (RSA)	280 (-8)
Volvo China Open	Beijing CBD International	Damien McGrane (IRL)	278 (-10)
BMW Asian Open	Tomson, Shanghai Pudong	Darren Clarke (NIR)	280 (-8)
GS Caltex Maekyung Open	Nam Seoul, Korea	Hwang Inn-choon (KOR)	279 (-9)
Pine Valley Beijing Open	Beijing, China	Hiroyuki Fujita (JPN)	276 (-12)
Bangkok Airways Open	Santiburi Samui CC, Koh Samui, Thailand	Thaworn Wiratchant (THA)	271 (-13)
Worldwide Selangor Masters	Seri Selangor, Kuala Lumpur	Ben Leong (MAS)	269 (-15)
Brunei Open	Bandar Serl Begawan, Brunei	Rick Kulacz (AUS)*	271 (-13)

Kulacz beat Lu Wen-teh (TPE) at first extra hole

Pertamina Indonesian President Invitational	Damai Indah, Indonesia	Scott Hend (AUS)	272 (-16)
Mercuries Taiwan Masters	Taiwan GCC, Taipei	Lu Wen-the (TPE)	277 (-11)
Asia-Pacific Panasonic Open	Ibaraki, Osaka	Hideto Tanihara (JPN)	264 (-16)
Kolon-Hana Bank 51st Korean Open	Woo Jeong, Hills, Cheonan, Korea	Bae Sang-Moon (KOR)	273 (-11)
Hero Honda Indian Open	Delhi, New Delhi	Liang Wen-chang (CHN)	272 (-16)
Midea China Classic	Royal Orchid, Guangzhou	Noh Seung-yul (KOR)	267 (-17)
Macau Open	Macau	David Gleeson (AUS)	266 (-18)
Iskandar Johor Open	Royal Johor, Malaysia	Retief Goosen (RSA)	276 (-12)
HSBC Champions	Sheshan International GC, Shanghai, China	Sergio García (ESP)	274 (-14)
Barclays Singapore Open	Sentosa GC	Jeev Milkha Singh (IND)	277 (-11)
UBS Hong Kong Open	Fanling GC	Wen-tang Lin (TPE)	265 (-15)
World Cup of Golf	Mission Hills, Shenzhen	Sweden (Robert Karlsson and Hendrik Stenson)	261 (-27)
Hana Bank Vietnam Masters	Vietnam GCC, Ho Chi Minh	Thongchai Jaidee* (THA)	273 (-15)

Jaidee beat Rhys Davies (WAL) and Andrew Dodt (AUS) at the third extra hole

Johnnie Walker Cambodian Open	Phokeethra CC, Siem Reap City	Thongchai Jaidee (THA)	264 (-24)
Volvo Masters of Asia	Thai Country Club, Bangkok	Lam Chih Bing (SIN)	274 (-14)

Asian Tour Order of Merit 2008

1	Jeev Milkha Singh (IND)	$1,452,701	6	SSP Chowrasia (IND)	482,293
2	Lin Wen Tang (TPE)	844,734	7	Sang-Moon Bae (KOR)	419,952
3	Mark Brown (AUS)	778.037	8	Thawaorn Wirachant (THA)	404,555
4	Wen-Chong Liang (CHN)	521,428	9	Scott Strange (AUS)	380,678
5	David Gleeson (AUS)	483,120	10	Seung-Yul Noh (KOR)	345,823

Norman Von Nida Tour 2008

Players are of Australian nationality unless stated   **www.pga.org.au**

Nab Victorian Championship	Sanctuary Lakes Resort	Marc Leishman	269 (-19)
OG Roberts South Australian PGA	Blue Lake GC	Heath Reed	248 (-20)
Oceanic 75th. WA PGA Championship	The Cut, Bouvard	Michael Long (NZL)	275 (-13)
NSW PGA Championship	The Vintage Resort, Hunter Valley	Aaron Townsend	267 (-17)

Final Money List

1	Michael Long (NZL)	Aus$27,650	6	Steven M Jones	13,693
2	Aaron Townsend	26,890	7	Tristan Lambert	13,687
3	Timothy Wood	24,972	8	Kurt Barnes	13,484
4	Peter Senior	19,731	9	Peter Wilson	12,639
5	Heath Reed	17,550	10	Ryan Hammond	10,102

Omega China Tour 2008

Players are of Chinese nationality unless stated   **www.worldsportgroup.com**

Guangzhou Championship	Dragon Lake GC	Zhang Lianwei	285 (-3)
Dell Championship	Orient (Xiamen) GCC	Li Chao	274 (-6)
Kunming Championship	Lakeview GC	Lu Wen-teh	283 (-5)
Shanghai Championship	Orient (Singapore) GCC	Hsu Mong-nan	285 (-3)
Sofitel Championship	Zhongshan International Nanjing	Liao Guiming*	278(-10)
*beat Zhang Lianwei at first extra hole of play-off			
Luxehills Championship	Luxehills International	Tsai Chi-huang (TPE)	270 (-18)
Tianjin Championship	Tianjin Yangliuqing GC	Tsa Chi huang (TPE)	289 (+1)
Omega Championship	Beijing Lonxi Hotspring GC	Zhou Jun	282 (-6)

Final Money List

1	Liao Guiming	KMB375,125	6	Chen Xiaoma	155,983
2	Zhang Lianwei	330,000	7	Yuan Hao	132,755
3	Zhou Jun	263,300	8	Wu Weihuang	119,105
4	Li Chao	243,000	9	He Shaocai	101,817
5	Wu Kangchun	184,717	10	Jim Johnson (USA)	100,500

First-time winners on the Asian Tour in 2008

Players from India, Chile, New Zealand, Ireland, Northern Ireland, Korea, Japan, Malaysia, Australia and Singapore were first time winners on the US$ 39 million Asian circuit in 2008 The full list is:

SSP Chowrasia (IND)	Indian Masters	Darren Clarke (NIR)	BMW Asian Open
Felipe Aguilar (CHI)	Indonesian Open	Inn-Choon Hwang (KOR)	Caltex Maekyung Open
Mark Brown (NZL)	Johnnie Walker Classic	Ben Leong (MAS)	Selangor Masters
Graeme McDowell (NIR)	Ballantine's C/ship	Scott Hend (AUS)	Indonesian P/dential Inv.
Damien McGrane (IRL)	Volvo China Open	Hideto Tanihara (JPN)	Asia Pac. Panasonic Open
Hiroyuki Fujita (JPN)	Pine Valley Beijing Open	Seung-yul Noh (KOR)	Midea China Classic
		Lam Chih Bing (SIN)	Volvo Masters of Asia

Australasian Tour 2008   www.pgatour.com.au

Players are of Australian nationality unless stated

IFQ Australasia	The Lakes, Sydney	Andrew Tampion	138 (-8)
HSBC NZ PGA Championship[1]	Clearwater, Christchurch, NZ	Darron Stiles (USA)	134 (-10)
The Moonah Classic[1]	Moonah, Mornington	Ewan Porter	275 (-13)
Johnnie Walker Classic[2]	New Delhi	Mark Brown (NZL)	270 (-18)
HSBC Champions[1]	Sheshan International GC, Shanghai	Sergio Garcia* (ESP)	274 (-14)

Garcia beat Oliver Wilson at second extra hole

Sportsbet Australian Masters[3]	Huntingdale	Rod Pampling	276 (-12)
Cadbury Schweppes Australian PGA Championship	Hyatt Regency Resort, Coolum	Geoff Ogilvy	274 (-14)
Australian Open	Royal Sydney GC	Tim Clark* (RSA)	279 (-9)

Clark beat Matthew Goggin at first extra hole

1904	Hon Michael Scott (am)	1932	Mick Ryan (am)	1962	Gary Player (RSA)	1986	Rodger Davis
1905	Dan Soutar	1933	M Kelly	1963	Gary Player (RSA)	1987	Greg Norman
1906	Carnegie Clark (am)	1934	Bill Bolger	1964	Jack Nicklaus (USA)	1988	Mark Calcavecchia
1907	Hon Michael Scott (am)	1935	F McMahon	1965	Gary Player (RSA)		(USA)
		1936	Gene Sarazen (USA)	1966	Arnold Palmer	1989	Peter Senior
		1937	George Naismith		(USA)	1990	John Morse (USA)
1908	Clyde Pearce (am)	1938	Jim Ferrier (am)	1967	Peter Thomson	1991	Wayne Riley
1909	C Felstead (am)	1939	Jim Ferrier (am)	1968	Jack Nicklaus (USA)	1992	Steve Elkington
1910	Carnegie Clark (am)	1940–1945 not played		1969	Gary Player (RSA)	1993	Brad Faxon (USA)
1911	Carnegie Clark (am)	1946	Ossie Pickworth	1970	Gary Player (RSA)	1994	Robert Allenby
1912	Ivo Whitton (am)	1947	Ossie Pickworth	1971	Jack Nicklaus (USA)	1995	Greg Norman
1913	Ivo Whitton (am)	1948	Ossie Pickworth	1972	Peter Thomson	1996	Greg Norman
1914–1919 not played		1949	Eric Cremin	1973	J C Snead (USA)	1997	Lee Westwood
1920	Joe Kirkwood	1950	Norman Von Nida	1974	Gary Player (RSA)		(ENG)
1921	A Le Fevre	1951	Peter Thomson	1975	Jack Nicklaus (USA)	1998	Greg Chalmers
1922	C Campbell	1952	Norman Von Nida	1976	Jack Nicklaus (USA)	1999	Aaron Baddeley
1923	T Howard	1953	Norman Von Nida	1977	David Graham		(am)
1924	A Russell (am)	1954	Ossie Pickworth	1978	Jack Nicklaus (USA)	2000	Aaron Baddeley
1925	Fred Popplewell	1955	Bobby Locke (RSA)	1979	Jack Newton	2001	Stuart Appleby
1926	Ivo Whitton (am)	1956	Bruce Crampton	1980	Greg Norman	2002	Steve Allan
1927	R Stewart	1957	Frank Phillips	1981	Bill Rogers (USA)	2003	Peter Lonard
1928	Fred Popplewell	1958	Gary Player (RSA)	1982	Bob Shearer	2004	Peter Lonard
1929	Ivo Whitton (am)	1959	Kel Nagle	1983	Peter Fowler	2005	Robert Allenby
1930	F Eyre	1960	Bruce Devlin (am)	1984	Tom Watson (USA)	2006	John Senden
1931	Ivo Whitton (am)	1961	Frank Phillips	1985	Greg Norman		

[1]co-sanctioned event with the Nationwide Tour   [2]co-sanctioned with the Asian and European Tours
[3]co-sanctioned with European Tour

2008 Order of Merit   (Figures in brackets indicate number of tournaments played)

1	Mark Brown (NZL)	(4)	Aus$440,027	11	Peter Senior	(10)	107,896
2	Rod Pampling	(3)	368,300	12	Chris Gaunt	(4)	91,200
3	Geoff Ogilvy	(3)	316,500	13	Shiv Kapur (IND)	(3)	90,587
4	Scott Strange	(5)	268,644	14	Stephen Dartnall	(4)	80,795
5	Greg Chalmers	(6)	204,039	15	Wade Ormsby	(6)	80,045
6	Robert Allenby	(3)	194,300	16	Nathan Green	(3)	79,025
7	Marcus Fraser	(4)	190,196	17	DJ Brigman (USA)	(2)	72,037
8	Ewan Porter	(7)	185,823	18	David McKenzie	(5)	69,835
9	David Smail (NZL)	(4)	150,741	19	Ashley Hall	(6)	68,722
10	Darron Stiles (USA)	(4)	145,157	20	Anthony Summers	(8)	65,094

Canadian Tour 2008

www.cantour.com

Players are of Canadian nationality unless stated

California Spring International	Modesto, CA	Spencer Levin (USA)*	279 (-9)
Levin beat Andrew Parr at second extra hole			
Stockton Sports Commission	Brookside, Stockton, CA	John Ellis (USA)*	272 (-16)
Ellis beat Tommy Barber at second extra hole			
Corona Mazatlan Mexican PGA Championship	El Cid, Mazatlan, MX	John Ellis (USA)	273 (-15)
Iberostar Riviera Maya Open	Riviera Maya, MX	Daniel Im (USA)	277 (-11)
San Luis Potosi Open	La Loma, San Luis Potosi, MX	Russell Surber (USA)	282 (-6)
Times Colonist Open	Uplands, Victoria, BC	Daniel Im (USA)*	268 (-12)
Im beat James Lepp at first extra hole			
Greater Vancouver Charity Classic	Hazelmere, South Surrey, BC	Adam Speirs	275 (-13)
ATB Financial Classic	Cottonwood, Calgary, AB	Dustin Risdon*	264 (-20)
Risdon beat George Bradford (USA) at first extra hole			
Saskatchewan Open	Dakota Dunes, Saskatoon	Josh Geary (NZL)	271 (-17)
TELUS Edmonton Open	Windermere, Edmonton, AB	John Ellis (USA)	266 (-18)
Tour Players Cup	Pine Ridge Winnipeg, MB	Wes Heffernan	270 (-14)
RBC Canadian Open	Glen Abbey, Oakville, ON	Chez Reavie (USA)	267 (-17)

1904	J H Oke	1933	J Kirkwood	1959	D Ford (USA)	1985	C Strange (USA)
1905	G Cumming	1934	T Armour	1960	A Wall Jr (USA)	1986	B Murphy (USA)
1906	C Murray	1935	G Kunes	1961	J Cupit (USA)	1987	C Strange (USA)
1907	P Barrett	1936	L Little	1962	T Kroll (USA)	1988	K Green (USA)
1908	A Murray	1937	H Cooper	1963	D Ford (USA)	1989	S Jones (USA)
1909	K Keffer	1938	S Snead (USA)	1964	KDG Nagle (AUS)	1990	W Levi (USA)
1910	D Kenny	1939	H McSpaden (USA)	1965	G Littler (USA)	1991	N Price (ZIM)
1911	C Murray	1940	S Snead (USA)	1966	D Massengale (USA)	1992	G Norman (AUS)
1912	G Sargent	1941	S Snead (USA)	1967	W Casper (USA)	1993	D Frost (RSA)
1913	A Murray	1942	C Wood (USA)	1968	RJ Charles (NZL)	1994	N Price (ZIM)
1914	K Kesser	1943-1944	*not played*	1969	T Aaron (USA)	1995	M O'Meara (USA)
1915-1918	*not played*	1945	B Nelson (USA)	1970	D Zarley (USA)	1996	D Hart (USA)
1919	J D Edgar	1946	G Fazio (USA)	1971	L Trevino (USA)	1997	S Jones (USA)
1920	J D Edgar	1947	AD Locke (RSA)	1972	G Brewer Jr (USA)	1998	B Andrade (USA)
1921	W H Trovinger	1948	CW Congdon	1973	T Weiskopf (USA)	1999	H Sutton (USA)
1922	A Watrous	1949	E J Harrison	1974	B Nichols (USA)	2000	T Woods (USA)
1923	C W Hackney	1950	J Ferrier	1975	T Weiskopf (USA)	2001	S Verplank (USA)
1924	L Diegel	1951	J Ferrier	1976	J Pate (USA)	2002	J Rollins (USA)
1925	L Diegel	1952	J Palmer (USA)	1977	L Trevino (USA)	2003	R Tway (USA)
1926	M Smith	1953	D Douglas (USA)	1978	B Lietzke (USA)	2004	V Singh (FIJ)
1927	T Armour	1954	P Fletcher	1979	L Trevino (USA)	2005	Mark Calcavecchia (USA)
1928	L Diegel	1955	A Palmer (USA)	1980	B Gilder (USA)		
1929	L Diegel	1956	D Sanders (am) (USA)	1981	P Oosterhuis (ENG)	2006	Jim Furyk (USA)
1930	T Armour			1982	B Lietzke (USA)	2007	Jim Furyk (USA)
1931	W Hagen	1957	G Bayer (USA)	1983	J Cook (USA)		
1932	H Cooper	1958	W Ellis Jr (USA)	1984	G Norman (AUS)		

Desjardins Montreal Open	Saint Raphael, Ile Bizard, QUE	Graham DeLaet	274 (-10)
Jane Rogers Championship	Lake View, Mississauga, ON	Alex Coe (USA)	265 (-15)
Seaforth Country Classic	Seaforth, ON	Kent Eger	258 (-26)
Canadian Tour Championship	National Pines, Barrie, ON	Tom Stankowski (USA)	272 (-16)
Sport Frances Open	Sports Frances GC, Santiago, Chile	Rafael Gomez (ARG)	277 (-7)
Torneo de Maestros	Olives GC, Buenos Aires	Fabian Gomez (ARG)	271 (-13)
Costa Rica Golf Classic	Reserva Conchal, Guanacaste	Mauricio Molina (ARG)	275 (-9)

Final Order of Merit

1	John Ellis (USA)	$113,315	6 Dustin Risdon	60,406
2	Wes Heffernan	96,154	7 Tom Stankowski (USA)	50,517
3	Daniel Im (USA)	82,954	8 Adam Bland (AUS)	47,225
4	Graham DeLaet	66,065	9 Andrew Parr	44,295
5	George Bradford (USA)	62,405	10 Wil Collins (USA)	39,915

South African Sunshine Tour

www.sunshinetour.com

Players are of South African nationality unless stated

2007–2008

Joburg Open[1]	R Johannesburg & Kensington	Richard Sterne	271 (-13)
IFQ Africa	R Johannesburg & Kensington	Josh Cunliffe	130 (-12)
Dimension Data Pro-Am	Sun City	James Kamte	277 (-11)
Nashua Masters	Wild Coast Sun	Marc Cayeux (ZIM)	268 (-12)
Africa Open	Fish River Sun	Shaun Norris	275 (-13)
Vodacom Championship	Pretoria	James Kingston	271 (-17)
Telcom PGA Chp	Jo'burg CC	Louis Oosthuizen	260 (-28)
Mount Edgecombe Trophy	Mount Edgecombe	Mark Murless	275 (-13)
Finance Bank Zambia Open	Chinama Hills	Tyrone Ferreira	208 (-8)
Vodacom Origins of Golf (Bloemfontein)	Bloemfontein	Dion Fourie	201 (-15)
Samsung Royal Swazi Sun Open	Royal Swazi Sun CC	Jean Hugo	56 pts
Nashua Challenge	Sun City	Keith Horne*	210 (-6)
Horne beat Nic Henning at second extra hole			
Vodacom Origins of Golf (KwaZulu)	Selborne House	Jean Hugo	203 (-13)
Lombard Insurance Classic	Royal Swazi Sun CC	Merrick Bremner	198 (-18)
SAA Pro-Am	Paarl	George Coetzee	207 (-9)
Vodacom Origins of Golf (Western Cape)	Arabella CC	Garth Mulroy	210 (-6)
Telkom PGA Pro-Am	Centurion CC	Merrick Bremner	200 (-16)
Suncoast Classic	Durban	Jake Roos*	210 (-6)
Roos beat Omar Sandys in the play-off			
Vodacom Origins of Golf	Humewood	George Coetzee	212 (-4)
Seekers Travel Pro-Am	Dainfern	Trevor Fisher Jr	206 (-10)
BMG Classic	Johannesburg	Doug McGuigan	206 (-10)
Mitmar Highveld Classic	Witbank	James Kamte	196 (-20)
Platinum Classic	Mooinooi GC	Thomas Aiken	197 (-19)
MTB Namibia PGA Championship	Windhoek CC	TC Charamba (ZIM)	270 (-14)
Coca Cola Championship	Fancourt CC	Garth Mulroy	197 (-19)
Nedbank Affinity Cup	Lost City	Tyrone van Aswegen	204 -12)
Nedbank Golf Challenge	Sun City	Henrik Stenson (SWE)	267 (-21)
Alfred Dunhill Championship[1]	Leopard Creek, Mpumalanga	Richard Sterne	271 (-18)
SA Open Championship[1]	Pearl Valley Golf Estates	Richard Sterne*	274 (-14)

Sterne beat Gareth Maybin (NIR) at first extra hole of play-off

1903	Laurie Waters	1927	Sid Brews
1904	Laurie Waters	1928	Jock Brews
1905	AGGray	1929	Archie Tosh
1906	AGGray	1930	Sid Brews
1907	Laurie Waters	1931	Sid Brews
1908	George Fotheringham	1932	Charles McIlveny
1909	John Fotheringham	1933	Sid Brews
1910	George Fotheringham	1934	Sid Brews
1911	George Fotheringham	1935	Bobby Locke
1912	George Fotheringham	1936	Clarence Olander
1913	James Prentice	1937	Bobby Locke
1914	George Fotheringham	1938	Bobby Locke
1915–1918	Not played	1939	Bobby Locke
1919	WH Horne	1940	Bobby Locke
1920	Laurie Waters	1941–1945	Not played
1921	Jock Brews	1946	Bobby Locke
1922	F Jangle	1947	Ronnie Glennie (a)
1923	Jock Brews	1948	Mickey Janks
1924	Bertie Elkin	1949	Sid Brews
1925	Sid Brews	1950	Bobby Locke
1926	Jock Brews	1951	Bobby Locke

1952	Sid Brews	1971	Simon Hobday
1953	Jimmy Boyd	1972	Gary Player
1954	Reg Taylor (a)	1973	Bob Charles (NZL)
1955	Bobby Locke	1974	Bobby Cole
1956	Gary Player	1975	Gary Player
1957	Harold Henning	1976	Dale Hayes
1958	Arthur Stewart (a)	1976	Gary Player
1959	Denis Hutchinson (a)	1977	Gary Player
1960	Gary Player	1978	Hugh Baiocchi
1961	Retief Waltman	1979	Gary Player
1962	Harold Henning	1980	Bobby Cole
1963	Retief Waltman	1981	Gary Player
1963	Allan Henning	1982	No tournament (two played in 1976)
1964	No tournament (two played in 1963)	1983	Charlie Bolling
1965	Gary Player	1984	Tony Johnstone
1966	Gary Player	1985	Gavin Levenson
1967	Gary Player	1986	David Frost
1968	Gary Player	1987	Mark McNulty (IRL)
1969	Gary Player	1988	Wayne Westner
1970	Tommy Horton	1989	Fred Wadsworth

1990 Trevor Dodds	1994/1995 Retief Goosen	2000/2001 Mark McNulty	2004/2005 Tim Clark
1991 Wayne Westner	1995/1996 Ernie Els	(IRL)	2005/2006 Retief Goosen
1990/1991 Wayne Westner	1996/1997 Vijay Singh (FIJ)	2001/2002 Tim Clark	2006/2007 Ernie Els
1991/1992 Ernie Els	1997/1998 Ernie Els	2002/2003 Trevor	2007/2008 James Kingston
1992/1993 Clinton	1988/1999 David Frost	Immelman	
Whitelaw	1999/2000 Matthias	2003/2004 Trevor	
1993/1994 Tony Johnstone	Grönberg (SWE)	Immelman	

¹joint venture with European Tour

2008 Order or Merit (South African unless stated)

1	Richard Sterne	SAR5,999,264	6	Jean Hugo	761,529
2	Garth Mulroy	1,442,350	7	Chris Williams	741,447
	Robert Rock* (ENG)	1,280,632	8	Keith Horne	714,743
3	Thomas Aiken	967,378	9	Charl Schwartzel	666,347
4	Mark Murless	885,055	10	Adilson da Silva (BRA)	654,471
5	James Kingston	775,903			

*Robert Rock did not play enough events to be included on the official money list

Double win takes Sterne to No 1 spot

South African Richard Sterne raced to the No 1 spot on the Sunshine Tour with wins in the last two events – the Alfred Dunhill Championship at Leopard Creek and the South African Open at the Pearl Valley Golf Estates. He finished over 4.5 million South African Rand ahead of second placed Garth Mulroy. He had started the season in South Africa with victory in the Jo'burg Open,

What delighted the 27-year-old most was his victory in his national Open. "It has long been a goal of mine to get my name on the trophy and at last my dream has came true," said the former South African Amateur champion, adding: "The event is so prestigious and the names on it are unbelievable." It was the eighth successive year that a South African had won the title.

KJ Choi is honoured by the Asian Tour

Korean golfer KJ Choi, who has won titles all over the world, has accepted honorary membership of the Asian Tour.

Kyi Hla Han, Executive Chairman of the Tour announcing the award said: "Choi has been an inspiration to many of our players because he honed his game on the Asian Tour."

The Korean star, who joins Vijay Singh as an honorary member, has won seven times on the US PGA Tour, three times on the Asian Tour and once in Europe. He is Asia's most successful golfer to date and is rated as a possible major winner in the near future.

Son of a rice farmer, he was brought up on Wando Island where there are no golf courses. As a youngster he was concentrating on power-lifting when his schoolteachers suggested he might prefer to switch to golf. He decided to give the game a go and learned how to play by studying Jack Nicklaus' instructional book *Golf My Way!*

He joined the Asian Tour in the mid 1990's, then played in Japan before gaining his US Tour Card in 1999.

"The Asian Tour provided the foundation for my career," says Choi. "I learned how to play in different conditions, I learned about different cultures and most importantly I learned to be patient. The growth potential of the Tour today is tremendous – more than for any other region and I am optimistic, too, about the talent coming out of it."

However, Choi still has one regret. He has not won in Asia outside Korea. That is something he says needs to be rectified sooner rather than later.

Tour de las Americas 2008

www.tourdelasamericas.com

Abierto del Centro	Cordoba GC	Estanislao Goya* (ARG)	272 (-12)
Goya beat Gary Boyd in play-off			
Abierto AAG[1]	Hurlingham Club	Antti Ahokas (FIN)	270 (-10
II Club Columbia Masters[1]	Bogota CC	Wil Besseling (NED)	268 (-16)
82 Abierto de Chile	Hacienda de Chicure	Felipe Aguilar (CHI)	265 (-23)
Abiertio Tres Diamantes	Barquisimeto GC	Sebastian Saavedra (ARG)	206 (-7)
TLA Players' Championship	Fairmont Acapulco Princess	Rafael Gomez (ARG)	200 (-10)
Venezuela Open	Lagunita CC	Angel Romero (COL)	273 (-7)
Taurus Peru Open	Los Incas GC	Alan Wagner (ARG)	275 (-13)
Marriott Venezuela Nations Cup	Caracas GC	P Acuna and A Villavicensio (GUA)	262 (-22)
Carlos Franco Invitational	Carlos Franco GC	Clodomiro Carranza*	280 (-8)
Carranza beat Cesar Monasterio in play-off			
Abierto San Luis	Villa Mercedes GC	Rafael Gomez* (ARG)	276 (-8)
Gomez beat Walter Rodriguez in play-off			
Abierto del Literal	Rosario GC	Andres Romero (ARG)	268 (-12)
De Vicenzo Classic	San Eliseo GC, Buenos Aires	Paulo Pinto (ARG)	284 (-4)
Sports Frances Open 50th Aniversary[2]	Sports Frances, Santiago, Chile	Rafael Gomez (ARG)	277 (-7)
Torneo de Maestros[2]	Olivos Golf Club, Buenos Aires	Fabian Gomez (ARG)	271 (-13)
Costa Rica Golf Classic[2]	Reserva Conchal, Guanacaste	Mauricio Molina (ARG)	275 (-9)

[1]Co-sanctioned event with the European Challenge Tour   [2]Co-sanctioned event with the Canadian Tour

Final Money List 2008

1	Estanislao Goya (ARG)	US$58,104	6	Jesus Amaya (COL)	24,281
2	Rafael Gomez (ARG)	57,582	7	Martin Monguzzi (ARG)	23,750
3	Mauricio Molina (ARG)	34,963	8	Paulo Pinto (ARG)	21,052
4	Clodomiro Carranza (ARG)	34,498	9	Rodolfo Gonzalez (ARG)	21,051
5	Sebastian Saavedra (ARG)	28,371	10	Alan Wagner (ARG)	20,549

Mercedes-Benz Asean Circuit

MB Masters Indonesia	Emeralda G and CC	Lam Chi Bing (SIN)	271 (-17)
MB Masters Phillipines	Tagatay Midlands GC	Wisut Artjanawat (THA)	269 (-19)
ICTSI Mount Malarayat Ch.	Philippines	Angelo Que (OHI)	268 (-20)
MB Masters Malaysia	Saujana GC, Bunga Raya	Ben Leong (MAS)	280 (-8)
B-ING Championship	Pattana G and SR, Chonburi	Felix Casas (PHI)	271 (-17)
International Championship	Imperial Klub, Lippo Karawaki Tangerang	Rory Hie (INA)	278 (-10)
MB Masters Singapore	Laguna National	Paraja Junhasavasdikul (THA)	277 (-11)
MB Masters Vietnam	Van Tri GC	Wisut Artjanawat (THA)	280 (-8)
MB Masters Thailand	The Vintage Club	Danny Chia (MAS)	291 (+3)

Top amateurs earn European Tour cards

Chris Wood, silver medallist in the 2008 Open at Royal Birkdale, and Danny Willett, who for a time was World No.1, both earned their Tour cards at the European Tour's Qualifying School over the Red and Green courses at the PGA Golf de Catalunya in Spain. Over 900 hopefuls were involved in the battle for the 32 cards on offer. Former Ryder Cup golfer Andrew Coltart successfully retained his card. The qualifiers were:

1	Oskar Henningsson (SWE)	66-66-65-74-69-69—409	−21	€18,595
2	Wade Ormsby (AUS)	66-75-64-71-69-68—413	−17	12,087
3	Carlos Del Moral (ESP)	72-67-66-70-67-71—413	−17	12,087
4	Danny Willett (ENG)	70-67-63-70-74-70—414	−16	8,206
5	Chris Wood (ENG)	72-66-69-71-69-68—415	−15	6,719
6	Joakim Haeggman (SWE)	70-67-70-71-69-68—415	−15	6,719
7	Eirik Tage Johansen(NOR)	69-66-67-71-74-69—416	−14	5,851
8	Michael Hoey (NIR)	68-69-71-72-70-67—417	−13	5,479
9	Ake Nilsson (SWE)	71-67-68-66-76-70—418	−12	5,026
10	Bernd Wiesberger (AUT)	71-67-66-69-72-73—418	−12	5,026
11	Gary Clark (ENG)	70-70-70-68-72-69—419	−11	4,624
12	Chinnarat Phadungsil (THA)	78-67-72-67-67-69—420	−10	4,144
13	Anthony Snobeck (FRA)	71-71-66-72-69-71—420	−10	4,144
14	Andrew Coltart (SCO)	71-69-67-71-69-73—420	−10	4,144
15	Fabrizio Zanotti (PAR)	71-72-68-69-71-70—421	−9	3,334
16	Chris Doak (SCO)	75-72-71-62-71-70—421	−9	3,334
17	Lorenzo Gagli (ITA)	73-66-69-70-73-70—421	−9	3,334
18	David Drysdale (SCO)	68-71-67-70-72-73—421	−9	3,334
19	Matthew Millar (AUS)	74-69-69-65-70-74—421	−9	3,334
20	Michael Curtain (AUS)	67-77-71-69-69-69—422	−8	2,706
21	Inder Van Weerelt (NED)	66-71-69-73-74-69—422	−8	2,706
22	Marco Ruiz (PAR)	66-75-65-75-71-70—422	−8	2,706
23	Callum Macauley (am) (SCO)	71-67-72-69-71-72—422	−8	
24	John Mellor (ENG)	68-75-69-72-71-68—423	−7	2,293
25	Marc Cayeux (ZIM)	68-72-68-74-70-71—423	−7	2,293
26	Henrik Nyström (SWE)	68-70-72-71-71-71—423	−7	2,293
27	Stuart Manley (WAL)	67-73-67-72-73-71—423	−7	2,293
28	Branden Grace (RSA)	66-69-70-72-73-73—423	−7	2,293
29	Federico Colombo (ITA)	68-67-76-70-73-70—424	−6	1,769
30	Santiago Luna (ESP)	70-74-73-66-70-71—424	−6	1,769
31	Jonathan CaldwellL (NIR)	67-70-69-74-70-74—424	−6	1,769
32	Alfredo Garcia-Heredia (ESP)	69-69-68-70-72-76—424	−6	1,769

Hak makes European and Asian Tour history

Jason Hak, a Hong Kong youngster now living in Florida, made history last year at the UBS Hong Kong Open, a joint venture between the European and Asian Tours.

Hak shot 70, 70 to make the half-way cut and become the youngest player to make the cut on either Tour. Hak was 107 days younger than Sergio García when he made the cut in the 1985 Turespana Open Mediterranea in Valencia.

The six footer whose hero is Tiger Woods is the youngest to have played in a European Tour event but not the youngest to have teed up in an Asian event. That honour went to Jian-fe Ye who was just 13 yers and 20 days when he played in the 2004 Sanyo Open.

World Championship Events

WGC – Accenture Match Play Championship
(formerly Anderson Consulting Match Play Championship)

Gallery, Tucson, AZ, USA   [7833–72]

First Round
Tiger Woods (USA) beat J B Holmes (USA) 1 hole
Arron Oberholser (USA) beat Mike Weir (CAN) 3 and 1
David Toms (USA) beat Zach Johnson (USA) 2 and 1
Aaron Baddeley (AUS) beat Mark Calcavecchia (USA) 4 and 2
Bradley Dredge (WAL) beat Rory Sabbatini (RSA) 4 and 3
Paul Casey (ENG) beat Robert Karlsson (SWE) 2 holes
K J Choi (KOR) beat Camilo Villegas (COL) 3 and 2
Ian Poulter (ENG) beat Søren Hansen (DEN) 2 and 1

Jonathan Byrd (USA) beat Ernie Els (RSA) 6 and 5
Andres Romero (ARG) beat Retief Goosen (RSA) 2 and 1
Henrik Stenson (SWE) beat Robert Allenby (AUS) 1 hole
Trevor Immelman (RSA) beat Shingo Katayama (JPN) 1 hole
Adam Scott (AUS) beat Brendan Jones (AUS) 2 and 1
Woody Austin (USA) beat Toru Taniguchi (JPN) 6 and 5
Sergio García (ESP) beat John Senden (AUS) 3 and 2
Boo Weekley (USA) beat Martin Kaymer (GER) 2 and 1

Phil Mickelson (USA) beat Pat Perez (USA) 1 hole
Stuart Appleby (AUS) beat Tim Clark (RSA) 3 and 2
Justin Leonard (USA) beat Geoff Ogilvy (AUS) 2 and 1
Lee Westwood (ENG) beat Brandt Snedeker (USA) 3 and 2
Rod Pampling (AUS) beat Justin Rose (ENG) 2 and 1
Nick O'Hern (AUS) beat Scott Verplank (USA) 3 and 2
Vijay Singh (FIJ) beat Peter Hanson (SWE) at 19th
Niklas Fasth (SWE) beat Richard Green (AUS) 6 and 5

Steve Stricker (USA) beat Daniel Chopra (SWE) at 20th
Hunter Mahan (USA) beat Richard Sterne (RSA) 4 and 3
Angel Cabrera (ARG) beat Anders Hansen (DEN) 3 and 2
Luke Donald (ENG) beat Nick Dougherty (ENG) 2 and 1
Colin Montgomerie (SCO) beat Jim Furyk (USA) 3 and 2
Charles Howell III (USA) beat Stephen Ames (CAN) at 19th
Padraig Harrington (IRL) beat Jerry Kelly (USA) 4 and 3
Stewart Cink (USA) beat Miguel Angel Jiménez (ESP) 4 and 3

Second Round

Woods beat Oberholser 3 and 2	Appleby beat Mickelson 2 and 1
Baddeley w.o. Toms	Leonard beat Westwood 2 and 1
Casey beat Dredge 2 and 1	Pampling beat O'Hern 5 and 4
Choi beat Poulter at 19th	Singh beat Fasth 1 hole
Byrd beat Romero 6 and 4	Stricker beat Mahan at 20th
Stenson beat Immelman at 25th	Abrera beat Donald 2 and 1
Austin beat Scott at 19th	Montgomerie beat Howell 1 hole
Weekley beat García 3 and 1	Cink beat Harrington 2 holes

Third Round
Woods beat Baddeley at 20th
Choi beat Casey 2 holes
Stenson beat Byrd 1 hole
Austin beat Weekley 3 and 2
Leonard beat Appleby 3 and 2
Singh beat Pampling at 25th
Cabrera beat Stricker 4 and 3
Cink beat Montgomerie 4 and 2

Semi-finals
Woods beat Stenson 2 and 1
Cink beat Leonard 4 and 2

Final
Tiger Woods beat Stewart Cink 8 and 7

Third Place Match
Henrik Stenson beat Justin Leonard 3 and 2

Quarter-finals
Woods beat Choi 3 and 2
Stenson beat Austin 2 holes
Leonard beat Singh 1 hole
Cink beat Cabrera 3 and 2

Winner	$1350000
Runner-up	800000
Third Place	575000
Fourth Place	475000
Quarter Finals	260000
Third Round	130000
Second Round	90000
First Round	40000

2000   Darren Clarke (NIR) beat Tiger Woods (USA) 4 and 3 at La Costa, Carlsbad, CA, USA
2001   Steve Stricker (USA) beat Pierre Fulke (SWE) 4 and 3 at Metropolitan GC, Melbourne, Australia
2002   Kevin Sutherland (USA) beat Scott McCarron (USA) 1 hole at La Costa, Carlsbad, CA, USA
2003   Tiger Woods (USA) beat David Toms (USA) 2 and 1 at La Costa, Carlsbad, CA, USA
2004   Tiger Woods (USA) beat Davis Love III (USA) 3 and 2 at La Costa, Carlsbad, CA, USA
2005   David Toms (USA) beat Chris DiMarco (USA) 6 and 5 at La Costa, Carlsbad, CA, USA
2006   Geoff Ogilvy (AUS) beat Davis Love III (USA) 3 and 2 at La Costa, Carlsbad, CA, USA
2007   Henrik Stenson (SWE) beat Geoff Ogilvy (AUS) 2 and 1 at Gallery, Tucson, AZ, USA

WGC – CA Championship
(formerly WGC – American Express Championship)

Doral, Orlando, FL, USA   [7266–72]

1	Geoff Ogilvy (AUS)	65-67-68-71—271	$1350000
2	Jim Furyk (USA)	69-71-64-68—272	530000
	Retief Goosen (RSA)	71-69-64-68—272	530000
	Vijay Singh (FIJ)	73-68-63-68—272	530000
5	Tiger Woods (USA)	67-66-72-68—273	285000
6	Nick O'Hern (AUS)	67-75-67-66—275	198333
	Graeme Storm (ENG)	71-70-63-71—275	198333
	Steve Stricker (USA)	71-68-73-63—275	198333
9	Zach Johnson (USA)	69-72-67-68—276	147500
	Adam Scott (AUS)	67-68-69-72—276	147500
11	Søren Kjeldsen (DEN)	69-71-71-66—277	125000
12	K J Choi (KOR)	70-70-67-71—278	106166
	Tim Clark (RSA)	71-69-66-72—278	106166
	Anders Hansen (DEN)	67-71-67-73—278	106166
15	Stephen Ames (CAN)	73-68-68-70—279	86700
	Aaron Baddeley (AUS)	69-74-70-66—279	86700
	Sergio García (ESP)	69-73-69-68—279	86700
	Grégory Havret (FRA)	68-74-68-69—279	86700
	Justin Rose (ENG)	70-71-70-68—279	86700
20	Robert Allenby (AUS)	69-75-66-70—280	75000
	Stewart Cink (USA)	66-74-71-69—280	75000
	Luke Donald (ENG)	68-72-70-70—280	75000
	Phil Mickelson (USA)	67-74-70-69—280	75000
	John Rollins (USA)	74-71-67-68—280	75000
	Mike Weir (CAN)	73-69-67-71—280	75000
26	Miguel Angel Jiménez (ESP)	65-74-71-71—281	66500
	Jeev Milkha Singh (IND)	68-70-70-73—281	66500
	Toru Taniguchi (JPN)	68-73-72-68—281	66500
	Camilo Villegas (COL)	71-72-68-70—281	66500
30	Mark Calcavecchia (USA)	68-71-71-72—282	62500

WGC – CA Championship   *continued*

30T	Robert Karlsson (SWE)	68-70-70-74—282	62500
	Andres Romero (ARG)	68-72-73-69—282	62500
	Boo Weekley (USA)	72-73-69-68—282	62500
34	Stuart Appleby (AUS)	73-71-68-71—283	57500
	Daniel Chopra (SWE)	72-70-69-72—283	57500
	Ross Fisher (ENG)	68-73-70-72—283	57500
	Ryuji Imada (JPN)	68-73-73-69—283	57500
	Justin Leonard (USA)	69-74-70-70—283	57500
	Lee Westwood (ENG)	71-72-72-68—283	57500
40	J B Holmes (USA)	69-72-75-68—284	52500
	Trevor Immelman (RA)	70-74-70-70—284	52500
	Brendan Jones (AUS)	76-75-66-67—284	52500
	Scott Verplank (USA)	71-70-74-69—284	52500
44	Woody Austin (USA)	70-70-74-71—285	48875
	Niclas Fasth (SWE)	72-69-70-74—285	48875
	Hunter Mahan (USA)	72-72-71-70—285	48875
	Richard Sterne (RSA)	71-77-67-70—285	48875
48	Graeme McDowell (NIR)	72-71-70-73—286	47000
	Andrew McLardy (RSA)	74-74-70-68—286	47000
	Brandt Snedeker (USA)	74-70-72-70—286	47000
51	Paul Casey (ENG)	72-75-67-73—287	44750
	S S P Chowrasia (IND)	74-73-68-72—287	44750
	Nick Dougherty (ENG)	70-73-71-73—287	44750
	Richard Green (AUS)	74-72-71-70—287	44750
	Charles Howell III (USA)	69-76-72-70—287	44750
	Arron Oberholser (USA)	72-70-72-73—287	44750
57	Martin Kaymer (GER)	68-74-73-73—288	42250
	Ian Poulter (ENG)	71-72-72-73—288	42250
	Henrik Stenson (SWE)	72-72-76-68—288	42250
	D J Trahan (USA)	74-73-75-66—288	42250
61	Peter Hanson (SWE)	71-74-73-73—291	40250
	Chapchai Nirat (THA)	70-70-74-77—291	40250
	Paul Sheehan (AUS)	72-73-72-74—291	40250
	Brett Wetterich (USA)	70-74-76-71—291	40250
65	Jonathan Byrd (USA)	74-74-72-72—292	38500
	Anton Haig (RSA)	72-80-73-67—292	38500
	Colin Montgomerie (SCO)	75-74-70-73—292	38500
68	Louis Oosthuizen (RSA)	74-72-70-77—293	37625
	Wen-chong Liang (CHN)	74-74-71-74—293	37625
70	Søren Hanson (DEN)	77-77-68-72—294	37000
	James Kingston (RSA)	74-75-68-77—294	37000
	Rory Sabbatini (RSA)	72-74-69-79—294	37000
73	Shingo Katayama (JPN)	75-76-72-72—295	36375
	Craig Parry (AUS)	73-75-72-75—295	36375
75	Ernie Els (RSA)	74-75-73-74—296	36000
76	Mark Brown (NZL)	73-74-76-74—297	35750
77	Heath Slocum (USA)	74-72-78-74—298	35500
WD	Angel Cabrera (ARG)	75-74-68	
WD	Sean O'Hair (USA)	73-75	

1999	Tiger Woods* (USA)	71-69-70-68—278	at Valderrama GC, Cadiz, Spain

Woods beat Miguel Angel Jiménez (ESP) at first extra hole

2000	Mike Weir (CAN)	68-75-65-69—277	at Valderrama GC, Cadiz, Spain
2001	*Cancelled*		
2002	Tiger Woods (USA)	65-65-67-66—263	at Mount Juliet, Kilkenny, Ireland
2003	Tiger Woods (USA)	67-66-69-72—274	at Capital City, Atlanta, GA
2004	Ernie Els (RSA)	69-64-68-69—270	at Mount Juliet, Kilkenny, Ireland
2005	Tiger Woods* (USA)	67-68-68-67—270	at Harding Park, San Francisco, CA

Woods beat John Daly at second extra hole

2006	Tiger Woods (USA)	63-64-67-67—261	at The Grove, Chandlers Cross, Herts
20067	Tiger Woods (USA)	71-66-68-73—278	at Doral, Orlando, FL, USA

WGC – Bridgestone Invitational
Firestone CC, Akron, OH [7400–70]

1	Vijay Singh (FIJ)	67-66-69-68—270	$1350000
2	Stuart Appleby (AUS)	70-66-67-68—271	635000
	Lee Westwood (ENG)	70-65-67-69—271	635000
4	Retief Goosen (RSA)	66-71-68-67—272	310000
	Phil Mickelson (USA)	68-66-68-70—272	310000
6	Darren Clarke (NIR)	70-71-65-67—273	220000
	Peter Lonard (AUS)	69-66-72-66—273	220000
8	Paul Casey (ENG)	70-71-68-65—274	162500
	D J Trahan (USA)	69-67-70-68—274	162500
10	Miguel Angel Jiménez (ESP)	70-66-70-69—275	133000
	Hunter Mahan (USA)	71-66-70-68—275	133000
12	Chris DiMarco (USA)	68-70-68-70—276	111000
	Sean O'Hair (USA)	68-67-73-68—276	111000
14	Chad Campbell (USA)	68-71-68-70—277	95500
	Daniel Chopra (SWE)	67-74-66-70—277	95500
16	K J Choi (KOR)	73-67-70-68—278	82625
	Zach Johnson (USA)	67-68-72-71—278	82625
	Ian Poulter (ENG)	70-68-69-71—278	82625
	Henrik Stenson (SWE)	73-70-68-67—278	82625
20	Robert Allenby (AUS)	71-70-70-68—279	71000
	Tim Clark (RSA)	67-71-71-70—279	71000
	Padraig Harrington (IRL)	69-75-68-67—279	71000
	Robert Karlsson (SWE)	71-67-71-70—279	71000
	Justin Leonard (USA)	68-70-70-71—279	71000
	Steve Lowery (USA)	75-67-70-67—279	71000
	Scott Verplank (USA)	71-70-70-68—279	71000
27	Ernie Els (RSA)	69-74-69-68—280	60000
	Jim Furyk (USA)	68-69-71-72—280	60000
	Charles Howell III (USA)	68-70-70-72—280	60000
	Paul McGinley (IRL)	70-67-72-71—280	60000
	Nick O'Hern (AUS)	70-68-71-71—280	60000
	Justin Rose (ENG)	71-70-68-71—280	60000
	Rory Sabbatini (RSA)	69-67-70-74—280	60000
	Vaughn Taylor (USA)	72-67-69-72—280	60000
	Oliver Wilson (ENG)	71-69-72-68—280	60000
36	Angel Cabrera (ARG)	72-73-68-68—281	52000
	Richard Finch (ENG)	69-75-70-67—281	52000
	Sergio García (ESP)	69-72-68-72—281	52000
	J B Holmes (USA)	69-68-72-72—281	52000
	Trevor Immelman (RSA)	75-64-68-74—281	52000
	Brendan Jones (AUS)	69-73-69-70—281	52000
	Anthony Kim (USA)	71-72-70-68—281	52000
43	Aaron Baddeley (AUS)	79-69-66-68—282	46600
	Stewart Cink (USA)	68-68-74-72—282	46600
	Richard Green (AUS)	72-73-70-67—282	46600
	Brandt Snedeker (USA)	68-76-69-69—282	46600
	Steve Stricker (USA)	68-69-75-70—282	46600
48	Stephen Ames (CAN)	69-71-71-72—283	44250
	Steve Flesch (USA)	70-70-73-70—283	44250
	Hidemasa Hoshino (JPN)	75-73-65-70—283	44250
	David Toms (USA)	72-72-70-69—283	44250
52	Woody Austin (USA)	71-70-72-71—284	42250
	Niclas Fasth (SWE)	71-71-72-70—284	42250
	Rocco Mediate (USA)	68-73-71-72—284	42250
	Chez Reavie (USA)	68-74-70-72—284	42250
56	Ross Fisher (ENG)	69-73-70-73—285	40000
	Fredrik Jacobson (SWE)	71-71-70-73—285	40000
	Graeme McDowell (NIR)	70-71-73-71—285	40000
	Rod Pampling (AUS)	69-71-75-70—285	40000

WGC – Bridgestone Invitational *continued*

56T	Adam Scott (AUS)	69-76-72-68—285	40000
61	Nick Dougherty (ENG)	72-76-69-69—286	38250
	Steve Webster (ENG)	68-72-72-74—286	38250
63	Lucas Glover (USA)	70-75-72-70—287	37000
	Andres Romero (ARG)	73-71-73-70—287	37000
	Scott Strange (AUS)	68-74-73-72—287	37000
66	Kenny Perry (USA)	74-69-73-72—288	35750
	Boo Weekley (USA)	72-73-71-72—288	35750
68	Martin Kaymer (GER)	72-79-68-70—289	34500
	Prayad Marksaeng (THA)	70-73-73-73—289	34500
	Geoff Ogilvy (AUS)	71-67-79-72—289	34500
71	Brett Rumford (AUS)	75-70-76-69—290	33250
	Johnson Wagner (USA)	70-74-75-71—290	33250
73	Søren Hansen (DEN)	75-73-70-74—292	32500
	J J Henry (USA)	69-73-73-77—292	32500
	David Howell (ENG)	70-75-70-77—292	32500
76	Pablo Larrazabal (ESP)	72-75-71-76—294	32000
77	Colin Montgomerie (SCO)	72-71-76-76—295	31750
78	James Kingston (RSA)	73-72-71-80—296	31500
79	Craig Parry (AUS)	70-75-75-77—297	31250
80	Mark Brown (NZL)	80-75-76-70—301	31000

1999	T Woods (USA)	66-71-62-71—270	at Firestone CC, Akron, OH
2000	T Woods (USA)	64-61-67-67—259	at Firestone CC, Akron, OH
2001	T Woods (USA)	66-67-66-69—268	at Firestone CC, Akron, OH
2002	C Parry (AUS)	72-65-66-65—268	at Sahalee, Redmond, WA
2003	D Clarke (NIR)	65-70-66-67—268	at Firestone CC, Akron, OH
2004	S Cink (USA)	63-68-68-70—269	at Firestone CC, Akron, OH
2005	T Woods (USA)	66-70-67-71—274	at Firestone CC, Akron, OH
2006	T Woods (USA)	67-64-71-68—270	at Firestone CC, Akron, OH
2007	V Singh (FIJ)	67-66-69-68—270	at Firestone CC, Akron, OH

Pavin to lead America at Celtic Manor

Former US Open Champion Corey Pavin, who beat Greg Norman to the title at Shinnecock Hills in 1995, is the PGA of America's choice to lead their Ryder Cup side in defence of the Trophy at Celtic Manor Resort next year.

Pavin, who played in three Ryder Cups at Kiawah Island in 1991, at The Belfry in 1993 and at Oak Hill two years, later won eight out of 13 points and was a vice-captain to Tom Lehman in Ireland in 2006

Marrakech to become a golfing Mecca

Marrakech is braced to become one of the most sought-after golf destinations, challenging more traitional markets such as Spain and Portugal. With ten new courses planned for opening there by 2012, there can be little doubt that golf is high on the tourism agenda. The long-awaited opening of The Assoufid Golf Club delivers the city's most compelling and conclusive golf proposition, setting the standard for the competitive set.

Laura and Ernie win in Morocco

Laura Davies led from start to finish to take the Lalla Meryem Cup in Rabat last year. She shot a 13-under-par total of 206 to score her 71st career success while Ernie Els was the winner at Royal Golf Dar Es Salam of the Hassan II Trophy – the men's equivalent which has been an annual event since 1971. Els shot a 17-under-par score to edge out Simon Dyson and Johan Edfors.

Other International Events

Hassan II Trophy *Dar-es-Salaam, Rabat, Morocco*

1971 O Moody (USA)	1981 B Eastwood (USA)	1995 N Price (ZIM)	2004 S Luna (ESP)
1972 R Cerrudo (USA)	1982 F Connor (USA)	1996 I Garrido (ESP)	2005 E Compton (USA)
1973 W Casper (USA)	1983 R Streck (USA)	1997 C Montgomerie	2006 S Torrance (SCO)*
1974 L Ziegler (USA)	1984 R Maltbie (USA)	(SCO)	*Torrance beat Raphael
1975 W Casper (USA)	1985 K Green (USA)	1998 S Luna (ESP)	Jacquelin (FRA) at first extra
1976 S Balbuena (USA)	1986–90 Not played	1999 D Toms (USA)*	hole
1977 L Trevino (USA)	1991 V Singh (FIJ)	2000 R Chapman (ENG)	2007 P Harrington (IRL)
1978 P Townsend (ENG)	1992 P Stewart (USA)	2001 J Haegmann (SWE)	2008 E Els (RSA)
1979 M Brannan (USA)	1993 P Stewart (USA)	2002 S Luna (ESP)	
1980 E Sneed (USA)	1994 M Gates (ENG)	2003 S Luna (ESP)	

Nedbank Golf Challenge *always at Gary Player course, Sun City, South Africa* [7162–72]

1982 (Jan) J Miller (USA)	277	1993	N Price (ZIM)	264	2002	E Els (ESP)	267
1982 (Dec) R Floyd* (USA)	280	1994	N Faldo (ENG)	272	2003	S García* (ESP)	274
*Floyd beat Craig Stadler (USA) in play-off		1995	C Pavin (USA)	276	*García beat R Goosen (RSA) in play-off		
1983 S Ballesteros (ESP)	274	1996	C Montgomerie* (SCO)	274	2004	R Goosen (RSA)	281
1984 S Ballesteros (ESP)	279	*Montgomerie beat E Els (RSA) in play-off			2005	J Furyk* (USA)	282
1985 B Langer (GER)	278	1997	N Price (ZIM)	275	*Furyk beat D Clarke (NIR), R Goosen		
1986 M McNulty (ZIM)	282	1998	N Price* (ZIM)	273	(RSA) and A Scott (AUS) at second extra		
1987 I Woosnam (WAL)	274	*Price beat T Woods (USA) in play-off			hole		
1988 F Allem (RSA)	278	1999	E Els (RSA)	263	2006	J Furyk (USA)	276
1989 D Frost (RSA)	276	2000	E Els* (RSA)	268	2007	T Immelman (RSA)	272
1990 D Frost (RSA)	284	*Els beat L Westwood (ENG) in play-off			2008	H Stenson (SWE)	267
1991 B Langer (GER)	272	2001	S García* (ESP)	268			
1992 D Frost (RSA)	276	*García beat E Els (RSA) in play-off					

Mauritius Open *Belle Mare Plage, Mauritius*

1994 Michael McLean (ENG)	2002 Mark Mouland (WAL)	2007 Peter Baker (ENG) (men)
1995 Marcello Santi (ITA)	2003 Mark Mouland (WAL)	Lara Tadiotto (ITA) (women)
1996 Philip Golding (ENG)	2004 Miles Tunnicliffe (ENG)	2008 Jamie Donaldson (WAL) (men)
1997 Gordon Sherry (SCO)	2005 Miles Tunnicliffe (ENG)	Karen Margrethe Juul (DEN)
1998 Roger Davis (AUS)	2006 Van Philips (ENG) (men)	(women)
1999 Jonathan Lomas (ENG)	Lora Fairclough (ENG)	
2000 Michael McLean (ENG)	(women)	
2001 Sebastian Delagrange (FRA)		

Chevron World Challenge (formerly Target World Challenge) *Sherwood Thousand Oaks, California*

1999 Tom Lehman (USA)	2002 Padraig Harrington	2004 Tiger Woods (USA)	2007 Tiger Woods (USA)
2000 Davis Love III (USA)	(IRE)	2005 Luke Donald (ENG)	2008 Vijay Singh (FIJ)
2001 Tiger Woods (USA)	2003 Davis Love III (USA)	2006 Tiger Woods (USA)	

Nelson Mandela Invitational

2002 Hugh Baiocchi and Deane Pappas (RSA)	2007 Not played
2003 Lee Westwood (ENG) and Simon Hobday (RSA)	This event is no longer held
2004 Ernie Els and Vincent Tshabalala (RSA)	
2005 Tim Clark and Vincent Tshabalala (RSA)	
2006 Bobby Lincoln and Retief Goosen* (RSA)	
*Lincoln and Goosen beat John Bland and Alan Michell (RSA)	
at second extra hole	

International Team Events 2008

37th Ryder Cup *Valhalla, Louisville, KY*   September 18–20   [7496–71]

Non-playing captains: Paul Azinger (USA), Nick Faldo (Europe)

USA		**Europe**	
First Day – Foursomes			
Mickelson & Kim (halved)	½	Harrington & Karlsson (halved)	½
Leonard & Mahan (3 and 2)	1	Stenson & Casey	0
Cink & Campbell (1 hole)	1	Poulter & Rose	0
Perry & Furyk (halved)	½	Westwood & García (halved)	½
	2		1
Fourballs			
Mickelson & Kim (2 holes)	1	Harrington & McDowell	0
Stricker & Curtis	0	Poulter & Rose (4 and 2)	1
Leonard & Mahan (4 and 3)	1	García & Jiménez	0
Holmes & Weekley (halved)	½	Westwood & Hansen (halved)	½
	2½		1½

First day match position: USA 5½, Europe 2½

Second Day – Foursomes			
Cink & Campbell	0	Poulter & Rose (4 and 3)	1
Leonard & Mahan (halved)	½	Jiménez & McDowell (halved)	½
Mickelson & Kim	0	Stenson & Wilson (2 and 1)	1
Perry & Furyk (3 and 1)	1	Harrington & Karlsson	0
	1½		2½
Foursomes			
Holmes & Weekley (2 and 1)	1	Westwood & Hansen	0
Stricker & Curtis (halved)	½	García & Casey (halved)	½
Perry & Furyk	0	Poulter & McDowell (1 hole)	1
Mickelson & Mahan (halved)	½	Stenson & Karlsson (halved)	½
	2		2

Second day match position: USA 9, Europe 7

Third Day – Singles			
Anthony Kim (5 and 4)	1	Sergio García (ESP)	0
Hunter Mahan (halved)	½	Paul Casey (ENG) (halved)	½
Justin Leonard	0	Robert Karlsson (SWE) (5 and 3)	1
Phil Mickelson	0	Justin Rose (ENG) (3 and 2)	1
Kenny Perry (3 and 3)	1	Henrik Stenson (SWE)	0
Boo Weekley (4 and 2)	1	Oliver Wilson (ENG)	0
J B Holmes (2 and 1)	1	Søren Hansen (DEN)	0
Jim Furyk (2 and 1)	1	Miguel Angel Jiménez (ESP)	0
Stewart Cink	0	Graeme McDowell (NIR) (2 and 1)	1
Steve Stricker	0	Ian Poulter (ENG) (3 and 2)	1
Ben Curtis (2 and 1)	1	Lee Westwood (ENG)	0
Chad Campbell (2 and 1)	1	Padraig Harrington (IRL)	0
	7½		4½

Result: USA 16½, Europe 11½

Ryder Cup – Inaugurated 1927

2006 *K Club, Straffan, Ireland* September 22–24
Result: Europe 18½, USA 9½
Captains: Ian Woosnam (Eur), Tom Lehman (USA)
First Day, Morning – Fourballs
Harrington & Montgomerie lost to Woods & Furyk 1 hole
Casey & Karlsson halved with Cink & Henry
García & Olazábal beat Toms & Wetterich 3 and 2
Clarke & Westwood beat Mickelson & DiMarco 1 hole

Afternoon – Foursomes
Harrington & McGinley halved with Campbell & Johnson
Howell & Stenson halved with Cink & Toms
Westwood & Montgomerie halved with Mickelson &
  DiMarco
Donald & García beat Woods & Furyk 2 holes

Second Day, Morning – Fourballs
Casey & Karlsson halved with Cink & Henry
García & Olazábal beat Mickelson & DiMarco 3 and 2
Clarke & Westwood beat Woods & Furyk 3 and 2
Stenson & Harrington lost to Verplank & Johnson 2 and 1

Afternoon – Foursomes
García & Donald beat Mickelson & Toms 2 and 1
Montgomerie & Westwood halved with Campbell & Taylor
Casey & Howell beat Cink & Johnson 5 and 4
Harrington & McGinley lost to Woods & Furyk 3 and 2

Third Day – Singles
Colin Montgomerie (sco) beat David Toms 1 hole
Sergio García (ESP) lost to Stewart Cink 4 and 3
Paul Casey (ENG) beat Jim Furyk 2 and 1
Robert Karlsson (SWE) lost to Tiger Woods 3 and 2
Luke Donald (ENG) beat Chad Campbell 2 and 1
Paul McGinley (IRL) halved with JJ Henry
Darren Clarke (NIR) beat Zach Johnson 3 and 2
Henrik Stenson (SWE) beat Vaughn Taylor 4 and 3
David Howell (ENG) beat Brett Wetterich 5 and 4
José María Olazábal (ESP) beat Phil Mickelson 2 and 1
Lee Westwood (ENG) beat Chris DiMarco 2 holes
Padraig Harrington (IRL) lost to Scott Verplank 4 and 3

2004 *Oakland Hills Country Club, Bloomfield,*
        Detroit, MI, USA Sept 17–19
Result: USA 9½, Europe 18½
Captains: Hal Sutton (USA),
  Bernhard Langer (Eur)
First Day, Morning – Fourball
Woods & Mickelson lost to Montgomerie & Harrington
  2 and 1
Love & Campbell lost to Clarke & Jiménez 5 and 4
Riley & Cink halved with McGinley & Donald
Toms & Furyk lost to García & Westwood 5 and 3

Afternoon – Foursomes
DiMarco & Haas beat Jiménez & Levet 3 and 2
Love & Funk lost to Montgomerie & Harrington 4 and 2
Mickelson & Woods lost to Clarke & Westwood 1 hole
Perry & Cink lost to García & Donald 2 and 1

Second Day, Morning – Fourball
Haas & DiMarco halved with García & Westwood
Woods & Riley beat Clarke & Poulter 4 and 3
Furyk & Campbell lost to Casey & Howell 1 hole
Cink & Love beat Montgomerie & Harrington 3 and 2

Afternoon – Foursomes
DiMarco & Haas lost to Clarke & Westwood 5 and 4
Mickelson & Toms beat Jiménez & Levet 4 and 3
Funk & Furyk lost to Donald & García 1 hole
Love & Woods lost to Harrington & McGinley 4 and 3

Third Day – Singles
Tiger Woods beat Paul Casey (Eng) 3 and 2
Phil Mickelson lost to Sergio García (Esp) 3 and 2
Davis Love III halved with Darren Clarke (NI)
Jim Furyk beat David Howell (Eng) 6 and 4
Kenny Perry lost to Lee Westwood (Eng) 1 hole
David Toms lost to Colin Montgomerie (Sco) 1 hole
Chad Campbell beat Luke Donald (Eng) 5 and 3
Chris DiMarco beat Miguel Angel Jiménez (Esp)
  1 hole
Fred Funk lost to Thomas Levet (Fra) 1 hole
Chris Riley lost to Ian Poulter (Eng) 3 and 2
Jay Haas lost to Padraig Harrington (Irl) 1 hole
Stewart Cink lost to Paul McGinley (Irl) 3 and 2

2002 *The Brabazon Course, The De Vere Belfry,*
        Sutton Coldfield, West Midlands, England
        September
Result: Europe 13½, USA 12½
Captains: Sam Torrance (Eur), Curtis Strange (USA)

First Day, Morning – Fourball
Bjørn & Clarke beat Azinger & Woods 1 hole
García & Westwood beat Duval & Love 4 and 3
Langer & Montgomerie beat Furyk & Hoch 4 and 3
Fasth & Harrington lost to Mickelson & Toms 1 hole

Afternoon – Foursomes
Bjørn & Clarke lost to Sutton & Verplank 2 and 1
García & Westwood beat Calcavecchia & Woods
  2 and 1
Langer & Montgomerie halved with Mickelson & Toms
Harrington & McGinley lost to Cink & Furyk 3 and 2

Second Day, Morning – Foursomes
Fulke & Price lost to Mickelson & Toms 2 and 1
García & Westwood beat Cink & Furyk 2 and 1
Langer & Montgomerie beat Hoch & Verplank 1 hole
Bjørn & Clarke lost to Love & Woods 4 and 3

Afternoon – Fourball
Fasth & Parnevik lost to Calcavecchia & Duval 1 hole
García & Westwood lost to Love & Woods 1 hole
Harrington & Montgomerie beat Mickelson & Toms
  2 and 1
Clarke & McGinley halved with Furyk & Hoch

Third Day – Singles
Colin Montgomerie (Sco) beat Scott Hoch 5 and 4
Sergio García (Esp) lost to David Toms 1 hole
Darren Clarke (NI) halved with David Duval
Bernhard Langer (Ger) beat Hal Sutton 4 and 3
Padraig Harrington (Irl) beat Mark Calcavecchia 5 and 4
Thomas Bjørn (Den) beat Stewart Cink 2 and 1
Lee Westwood (Eng) lost to Scott Verplank 2 and 1
Niclas Fasth (Swe) halved with Paul Azinger
Paul McGinley (Irl) halved with Jim Furyk
Pierre Fulke (Swe) halved with Davis Love III
Phillip Price (Wal) beat Phil Mickelson 3 and 2
Jesper Parnevik (Swe) halved with Tiger Woods

1999 *The Country Club, Brookline, MA., USA*
        Sept 24–26
Result: USA 14½, Europe 13½
Captains: Ben Crenshaw (USA), Mark James (Eur)
First Day: Morning – Foursomes
Montgomerie & Lawrie beat Duval & Mickelson 3 and 2
Parnevik & García beat Lehman & Woods 2 and 1
Jiménez & Harrington halved halved with Love &
  Stewart
Clarke & Westwood lost to Sutton & Maggert 3 and 2

1999 *continued*

Afternoon – Fourball
Montgomerie & Lawrie halved with Love & Leonard
Parnevik & García beat Mickelson & Furyk 1 hole
Jiménez & Olazábal beat Sutton & Maggert 2 and 1
Clarke & Westwood beat Duval & Woods 1 hole

Second Day: Morning – Foursomes
Montgomerie & Lawrie lost to Sutton & Maggert 1 hole
Clarke & Westwood beat Furyk & O'Meara 3 and 2
Jiménez & Harrington lost to Pate & Woods 1 hole
Parnevik & García beat Stewart & Leonard 3 and 2

Afternoon – Fourball
Clarke & Westwood lost to Mickelson & Lehman 2 and 1
Parnevik & García halved with Love & Duval
Jiménez & Olazábal halved with Leonard & Sutton
Montgomerie & Lawrie beat Pate & Woods 2 and 1

Third Day – Singles
Lee Westwood lost to Tom Lehman 3 and 2
Darren Clarke lost to Hal Sutton 4 and 2
Jarmo Sandelin lost to Phil Mickelson 4 and 3
Jean Van de Velde lost to Davis Love III 6 and 5
Andrew Coltart lost to Tiger Woods 3 and 2
Jesper Parnevik lost to David Duval 5 and 4
Padraig Harrington beat Mark O'Meara 1 hole
Miguel Angel Jiménez lost to Steve Pate 2 and 1
José Maria Olazábal halved with Justin Leonard
Colin Montgomerie beat Payne Stewart 1 hole
Sergio García lost to Jim Furyk 4 and 3
Paul Lawrie beat Jeff Maggert 4 and 3

1997 *Valderrama Golf Club, Sotogrande, Cadiz,*
Spain Sept 26–28

Result: Europe 14½, USA 13½
Captains: Seve Ballesteros (Eur), Tom Kite (USA)

First Day: Morning – Fourball
Olazábal & Rocca beat Love & Mickelson 1 hole
Faldo & Westwood lost to Couples & Faxon 1 hole
Parnevik & Johansson beat Lehman & Furyk 1 hole
Montgomerie & Langer lost to Woods & O'Meara 3 and 2

Afternoon – Foursomes
Rocca & Olazábal lost to Hoch & Janzen 1 hole
Langer & Montgomerie beat O'Meara & Woods 5 and 3
Faldo & Westwood beat Leonard & Maggert 3 and 2
Parnevik & Garrido halved with Lehman & Mickelson

Second Day: Morning – Fourball
Montgomerie & Clarke beat Couples & Love 1 hole
Woosnam & Bjørn beat Leonard & Faxon 2 and 1
Faldo & Westwood beat Woods & O'Meara 2 and 1
Olazábal & Garrido halved with Mickelson & Lehman

Afternoon – Foursomes
Montgomerie & Langer beat Janzen & Furyk 1 hole
Faldo & Westwood lost to Hoch & Maggert 2 and 1
Parnevik & Garrido halved with Leonard & Woods
Olazábal & Rocca beat Love & Couples 5 and 4

Third Day – Singles
Ian Woosnam lost to Fred Couples 8 and 7
Per-Ulrik Johansson beat Davis Love III 3 and 2
Costantino Rocca beat Tiger Woods 4 and 2
Thomas Bjørn halved with Justin Leonard
Darren Clarke lost to Phil Mickelson 2 and 1
Jesper Parnevik lost to Mark O'Meara 5 and 4
José Maria Olazábal lost to Lee Janzen 1 hole
Bernhard Langer beat Brad Faxon 2 and 1
Lee Westwood lost to Jeff Maggert 3 and 2
Colin Montgomerie halved with Scott Hoch
Nick Faldo lost to Jim Furyk 3 and 2
Ignacio Garrido lost to Tom Lehman 7 and 6

1995 *Oak Hill Country Club, Rochester, NY, USA*
Sept 22–24

Result: USA 13½, Europe 14½
Captains: Lanny Wadkins (USA),
Bernard Gallacher (Eur)

First Day: Morning – Foursomes
Faldo & Montgomerie lost to Pavin & Lehman 1 hole
Torrance & Rocca beat Haas & Couples 3 and 2
Clark & James lost to Love & Maggert 4 and 3
Langer & Johansson beat Crenshaw & Strange 1 hole

Afternoon – Fourball
Gilford & Ballesteros beat Faxon & Jacobsen 4 and 3
Torrance & Rocca lost to Maggert & Roberts 6 and 5
Faldo & Montgomerie lost to Couples & Love 3 and 2
Langer & Johansson lost to Pavin & Mickelson 6 and 4

Second Day: Morning – Foursomes
Faldo & Montgomerie beat Haas & Strange 4 and 2
Torrance & Rocca beat Love & Maggert 6 and 5
Woosnam & Walton lost to Roberts & Jacobsen 1 hole
Langer & Gilford beat Pavin & Lehman 4 and 3

Afternoon – Fourball
Torrance & Montgomerie lost to Faxon & Couples
  4 and 2
Woosnam & Rocca beat Love & Crenshaw 3 and 2
Ballesteros & Gilford lost to Haas & Mickelson
  3 and 2
Faldo & Langer lost to Pavin & Roberts 1 hole

Third Day – Singles
Seve Ballesteros lost to Tom Lehman 4 and 3
Howard Clark beat Peter Jacobsen 1 hole
Mark James beat Jeff Maggert 4 and 3
Ian Woosnam halved with Fred Couples
Costantino Rocca lost to Davis Love III 3 and 2
David Gilford beat Brad Faxon 1 hole
Colin Montgomerie beat Ben Crenshaw 3 and 1
Nick Faldo beat Curtis Strange 1 hole
Sam Torrance beat Loren Roberts 2 and 1
Bernhard Langer lost to Corey Pavin 3 and 2
Philip Walton beat Jay Haas 1 hole
Per-Ulrik Johansson lost to Phil Mickelson 2 and 1

1993 *The Brabazon Course, The De Vere Belfry,*
Sutton Coldfield, West Midlands, England
Sept 24–26

Result: Europe 13, USA 15
Captains: Bernard Gallacher (Eur), Tom Watson (USA)

First Day: Morning – Foursomes
Torrance & James lost to Wadkins & Pavin 4 and 3
Woosnam & Langer beat Azinger & Stewart 7 and 5
Ballesteros & Olazábal lost to Kite & Love 2 and 1
Faldo & Montgomerie beat Floyd & Couples 4 and 3

Afternoon – Fourball
Woosnam & Baker beat Gallagher & Janzen 1 hole
Lane & Langer lost to Wadkins & Pavin 4 and 2
Faldo & Montgomerie halved with Azinger & Couples
Ballesteros & Olazábal beat Kite & Love 4 and 3

Second Day: Morning – Foursomes
Faldo & Montgomerie beat Wadkins & Pavin 3 and 2
Langer & Woosnam beat Couples & Azinger 2 and 1
Baker & Lane lost to Floyd & Stewart 3 and 2
Ballesteros & Olazábal beat Kite & Love 2 and 1

Afternoon – Fourball
Faldo & Montgomerie lost to Beck & Cook 2 holes
James & Rocca lost to Pavin & Gallagher 5 and 4
Woosnam & Baker beat Couples & Azinger 6 and 5
Olazábal & Haeggman lost to Floyd & Stewart 2 and 1

Third Day - Singles
Ian Woosnam halved with Fred Couples
Barry Lane lost to Chip Beck 1 hole
Colin Montgomerie beat Lee Janzen 1 hole
Peter Baker beat Corey Pavin 2 holes
Joakim Haeggman beat J Cook 1 hole
Sam Torrance (withdrawn at start of day) halved with
  Lanny Wadkins (withdrawn at start of day)
Mark James lost to Payne Stewart 3 and 2
Constantino Rocca lost to Davis Love III 1 hole
Seve Ballesteros lost to Jim Gallagher Jr 3 and 2
José Maria Olazábal lost to Ray Floyd 2 holes
Bernhard Langer lost to Tom Kite 5 and 3
Nick Faldo halved with Paul Azinger

1991 *The Ocean Course, Kiawah Island, SC, USA*
   Sept 26–29
Result: USA 14½, Europe 13½
Captains: Dave Stockton (USA),
  Bernard Gallacher (Eur)

First Day: Morning - Foursomes
Ballesteros & Olazábal beat Azinger & Beck 2 and 1
Langer & James lost to Floyd & Couples 2 and 1
Gilford & Montgomerie lost to Wadkins & Irwin 4 and 2
Faldo & Woosnam lost to Stewart & Calcavecchia
  1 hole

Afternoon - Fourball
Torrance & Feherty halved with Wadkins & O'Meara
Ballesteros & Olazábal beat Azinger & Beck 2 and 1
Richardson & James beat Pavin & Calcavecchia 5 and 4
Faldo & Woosnam lost to Floyd & Couples 5 and 3

Second Day: Morning - Foursomes
Torrance & Feherty lost to Irwin & Wadkins 4 and 2
James & Richardson lost to Calcavecchia & Stewart
  1 hole
Faldo & Gilford lost to Azinger & O'Meara 7 and 6
Ballesteros & Olazábal beat Couples & Floyd 3 and 2

Afternoon - Fourball
Woosnam & Broadhurst beat Azinger & Irwin 2 and 1
Langer & Montgomerie beat Pate & Pavin 2 and 1
James & Richardson beat Wadkins & Levi 3 and 1
Ballesteros & Olazábal halved with Couples & Stewart

Third Day - Singles
Nick Faldo beat Ray Floyd 2 holes
David Feherty beat Payne Stewart 2 and 1
Colin Montgomerie halved with Mark Calcavecchia
José Maria Olazábal lost to Paul Azinger 2 holes
Steven Richardson lost to Corey Pavin 2 and 1
Seve Ballesteros beat Wayne Levi 3 and 2
Ian Woosnam lost to Chip Beck 3 and 1
Paul Broadhurst bat Mark O'Meara 3 and 1
Sam Torrance lost to Fred Couples 3 and 2
Mark James lost to Lanny Wadkins 3 and 2
Bernhard Langer halved with Hale Irwin
David Gilford (withdrawn) halved with Steve Pate
  (withdrawn – injured)

1989 *The Brabazon Course, The De Vere Belfry,*
  Sutton Coldfield, West Midlands, England
  Sept 22–24
Result: Europe 14, USA 14
Captains: Tony Jacklin (Eur), Ray Floyd (USA)

First Day: Foursomes - Morning
Faldo & Woosnam halved with Kite & Strange
Clark & James lost to Stewart & Wadkins 1 hole
Ballesteros & Olazábal halved with Beck & Watson
Langer & Rafferty lost to Calcavecchia & Green 2 and 1

Fourball - Afternoon
Brand & Torrance beat Azinger & Strange 1 hole
Clark & James beat Couples & Wadkins 3 and 2
Faldo & Woosnam beat Calcavecchia & McCumber 1 hole
Ballesteros & Olazábal beat O'Meara & Watson 6 and 5

Second Day: Foursomes - Morning
Faldo & Woosnam beat Stewart & Wadkins 3 and 2
Brand & Torrance lost to Azinger & Beck 4 and 3
O'Connor & Rafferty lost to Calcavecchia & Green 3 and 2
Ballesteros & Olazábal beat Kite & Strange 1 hole

Fourball - Afternoon
Faldo & Woosnam lost to Azinger & Beck 2 and 1
Canizares & Langer lost to Kite & McCumber 2 and 1
Clark & James beat Stewart & Strange 1 hole
Ballesteros & Olazábal beat Calcavecchia & Green 4 and 2

Third Day: Singles
Seve Ballesteros lost to Paul Azinger 1 hole
Bernhard Langer lost to Chip Beck 3 and 1
José Maria Olazábal beat Payne Stewart 1 hole
Ronan Rafferty beat Mark Calvecchia 1 hole
Howard Clark lost to Tom Kite 8 and 7
Mark James beat Mark O'Meara 3 and 2
Christy O'Connor Jr beat Fred Couples 1 hole
José Maria Canizares beat Ken Green 1 hole
Gordon Brand Jr lost to Mark McCumber 1 hole
Sam Torrance lost to Tom Watson 3 and 1
Nick Faldo lost to Lanny Wadkins 1 hole
Ian Woosnam lost to Curtis Strange 1 hole

1987 *Muirfield Village Golf Club, Dublin, OH, USA*
   Sept 25–27
Result: Europe 15, USA 13
Captains: Jack Nicklaus (USA), Tony Jacklin (Eur)
First Day: Foursomes - Morning
Kite & Strange beat Clark & Torrance 4 and 2
Pohl & Sutton beat Brown & Langer 2 and 1
Mize & Wadkins lost to Faldo & Woosnam 2 holes
Nelson & Stewart lost to Ballesteros & Olazábal 1 hole

Fourball - Afternoon
Crenshaw & Simpson lost to Brand & Rivero 3 and 2
Bean & Calcavecchia lost to Langer & Lyle 1 hole
Pohl & Sutton lost to Faldo & Woosnam 2 and 1
Kite & Strange lost to Ballesteros & Olazábal 2 and 1

Second Day: Foursomes - Morning
Kite & Strange beat Brand & Rivero 3 and 1
Mize & Sutton halved with Faldo & Woosnam
Nelson & Wadkins lost to Langer & Lyle 2 and 1
Crenshaw & Stewart lost to Ballesteros & Olazábal 1 hole

Fourball - Afternoon
Kite & Strange lost to Faldo & Woosnam 5 and 4
Bean & Stewart beat Brand & Darcy 3 and 2
Mize & Sutton beat Ballesteros & Olazábal 2 and 1
Nelson & Wadkins lost to Langer & Lyle 1 hole

Third Day: Singles
Andy Bean beat Ian Woosnam 1 hole
Dan Pohl lost to Howard Clark 1 hole
Larry Mize halved with Sam Torrance
Mark Calcavecchia beat Nick Faldo 1 hole
Payne Stewart beat José Maria Olazábal 2 holes
Scott Simpson beat José Rivero 2 and 1
Tom Kite beat Sandy Lyle 3 and 2
Ben Crenshaw lost to Eamonn Darcy 1 hole
Larry Nelson halved with Bernhard Langer
Curtis Strange lost to Seve Ballesteros 2 and 1
Lanny Wadkins beat Ken Brown 3 and 2
Hal Sutton halved with Gordon Brand Jr

1985 *The Brabazon Course, The De Vere Belfry, Sutton Coldfield, West Midlands, England* Sept 13–15

Result: Europe 16½, USA 11½
Captains: Tony Jacklin (Eur), Lee Trevino (USA)

First Day: Foursomes – Morning
Ballesteros & Pinero beat Strange & O'Meara 2 and 1
Faldo & Langer lost to Kite & Peete 3 and 2
Brown & Lyle lost to Floyd & Wadkins 4 and 3
Clark & Torrance lost to Stadler & Sutton 3 and 2

Fourball – Afternoon
Way & Woosnam beat Green & Zoeller 1 hole
Ballesteros & Pinero beat Jacobsen & North 2 and 1
Canizares & Langer halved with Stadler & Sutton
Clark & Torrance lost to Floyd & Wadkins 1 hole

Second Day: Fourball – Morning
Clark & Torrance beat Kite & North 2 and 1
Way & Woosnam beat Green & Zoeller 4 and 3
Ballesteros & Pinero lost to O'Meara & Wadkins 3 and 2
Langer & Lyle halved with Stadler & Strange

Foursomes – Afternoon
Canizares & Rivero beat Kite & Peete 7 and 5
Ballesteros & Pinero beat Stadler & Sutton 5 and 4
Way & Woosnam lost to Jacobsen & Strange 4 and 3
Brown & Langer beat Floyd & Wadkins 3 and 2

Third Day: Singles
Manuel Pinero beat Lanny Wadkins 3 and 1
Ian Woosnam lost to Craig Stadler 2 and 1
Paul Way beat Ray Floyd 2 holes
Seve Ballesteros halved with Tom Kite
Sandy Lyle beat Peter Jacobsen 3 and 2
Bernhard Langer beat Hal Sutton 5 and 4
Sam Torrance beat Andy North 1 hole
Howard Clark beat Mark O'Meara 1 hole
Nick Faldo lost to Hubert Green 3 and 1
José Rivero lost to Calvin Peete 1 hole
José Maria Canizares beat Fuzzy Zoeller 2 holes
Ken Brown lost to Curtis Strange 4 and 2

1983 *PGA National Golf Club, Palm Beach Gardens, FL, USA* Oct 14–16

Result: USA 14½, Europe 13½
Captains: Jack Nicklaus (USA), Tony Jacklin (Eur)

First Day: Foursomes – Morning
Watson & Crenshaw beat Gallacher & Lyle 5 and 4
Wadkins & Stadler lost to Faldo & Langer 4 and 2
Floyd & Gilder lost to Canizares & Torrance 4 and 3
Kite & Peete beat Ballesteros & Way 2 and 1

Fourball – Afternoon
Morgan & Zoeller lost to Waites & Brown 2 and 1
Watson & Haas beat Faldo & Langer 2 and 1
Floyd & Strange lost to Ballesteros & Way 1 hole
Crenshaw & Peete halved with Torrance & Woosnam

Second Day: Foursomes – Morning
Floyd & Kite lost to Faldo & Langer 3 and 2
Wadkins & Morgan beat Canizares & Torrance 7 and 5
Gilder & Watson lost to Ballesteros & Way 2 and 1
Haas & Strange beat Waites & Brown 3 and 2

Fourball – Afternoon
Wadkins & Stadler beat Waites & Brown 1 hole
Crenshaw & Peete lost to Faldo & Langer 2 and 1
Haas & Morgan halved with Ballesteros & Way
Gilder & Watson beat Torrance & Woosnam 5 and 4

Third Day: Singles
Fuzzy Zoeller halved with Seve Ballesteros
Jay Haas lost to Nick Faldo 2 and 1
Gil Morgan lost to Bernhard Langer 2 holes

Bob Gilder beat Gordon J Brand 2 holes
Ben Crenshaw beat Sandy Lyle 3 and 1
Calvin Peete beat Brian Waites 1 hole
Curtis Strange lost to Paul Way 2 and 1
Tom Kite halved with Sam Torrance
Craig Stadler beat Ian Woosnam 3 and 2
Lanny Wadkins halved with José Maria Canizares
Ray Floyd lost to Ken Brown 4 and 3
Tom Watson beat Bernard Gallacher 2 and 1

1981 *Walton Heath GC, Tadworth, Surrey, England* Sept 18–20

Result: USA 18½, Europe 9½
Captains: John Jacobs (Eur), Dave Marr (USA)

First Day: Foursomes – Morning
Langer & Pinero lost to Trevino & Nelson 1 hole
Lyle & James beat Rogers & Lietzke 2 and 1
Gallacher & Smyth beat Irwin & Floyd 3 and 2
Oosterhuis & Faldo lost to Watson & Nicklaus 4 and 3

Fourball – Afternoon
Torrance & Clark halved with Kite & Miller
Lyle & James beat Crenshaw & Pate 3 and 2
Smyth & Canizares beat Rogers & Lietzke 6 and 5
Gallacher & Darcy lost to Irwin & Floyd 2 and 1

Second Day: Fourball – Morning
Faldo & Torrance lost to Trevino & Pate 7 and 5
Lyle & James lost to Nelson & Kite 1 hole
Langer & Pinero beat Irwin & Floyd 2 and 1
Smyth & Canizares lost to Watson & Nicklaus 3 and 2

Foursomes – Afternoon
Oosterhuis & Torrance lost to Trevino & Pate 2 and 1
Langer & Pinero lost to Watson & Nicklaus 3 and 2
Lyle & James lost to Rogers & Floyd 3 and 2
Gallacher & Smyth lost to Nelson & Kite 3 and 2

Third Day: Singles
Sam Torrance lost to Lee Trevino 5 and 3
Sandy Lyle lost to Tom Kite 3 and 2
Bernard Gallacher halved with Bill Rogers
Mark James lost to Larry Nelson 2 holes
Des Smyth lost to Ben Crenshaw 6 and 4
Bernhard Langer halved with Bruce Lietzke
Manuel Pinero beat Jerry Pate 4 and 2
José Maria Canizares lost to Hale Irwin 1 hole
Nick Faldo beat Johnny Miller 2 and 1
Howard Clark beat Tom Watson 4 and 3
Peter Oosterhuis lost to Ray Floyd 2 holes
Eamonn Darcy lost to Jack Nicklaus 5 and 3

From 1979 GBI became a European team

1979 *The Greenbrier, White Sulphur Springs, WV, USA* Sept 14–16

Result: USA 17, Europe 11
Captains: Billy Casper (USA), John Jacobs (Eur)

First Day: Fourball – Morning
Wadkins & Nelson beat Garrido & Ballesteros 2 and 1
Trevino & Zoeller beat Brown & James 3 and 2
Bean & Elder beat Oosterhuis & Faldo 2 and 1
Irwin & Mahaffey lost to Gallacher & Barnes 2 and 1

Foursomes – Afternoon
Irwin & Kite beat Brown & Smyth 7 and 6
Zoeller & Green lost to Garrido & Ballesteros 3 and 2
Trevino & Morgan halved with Lyle & Jacklin
Wadkins & Nelson beat Gallacher & Barnes 4 and 3

Second Day: Foursomes – Morning
Elder & Mahaffey lost to Lyle & Jacklin 5 and 4
Bean & Kite lost to Oosterhuis & Faldo 6 and 5
Zoeller & Hayes halved with Gallacher & Barnes
Wadkins & Nelson beat Garrido & Ballesteros 3 and 2

Fourball – Afternoon
Wadkins & Nelson beat Garrido & Ballesteros
5 and 4
Irwin & Kite beat Lyle & Jacklin 1 hole
Trevino & Zoeller lost to Gallacher & Barnes 3 and 2
Elder & Hayes lost to Oosterhuis & Faldo 1 hole
Third Day: **Singles**
Lanny Wadkins lost to Bernard Gallacher 3 and 2
Larry Nelson beat Seve Ballesteros 3 and 2
Tom Kite beat Tony Jacklin 1 hole
Mark Hayes beat Antonio Garrido 1 hole
Andy Bean beat Michael King 4 and 3
John Mahaffey beat Brian Barnes 1 hole
Lee Elder lost to Nick Faldo 3 and 2
Hale Irwin beat Des Smyth 5 and 3
Hubert Green beat Peter Oosterhuis 2 holes
Fuzzy Zoeller lost to Ken Brown 1 hole
Lee Trevino beat Sandy Lyle 2 and 1
Gil Morgan, Mark James: injury; match a half

1977 *Royal Lytham & St Annes GC, St Annes,*
Lancs, England Sept 15–17
Result: USA 12½, GBI 7½
Captains: Brian Huggett (GBI),
Dow Finsterwald (USA)

First Day: **Foursomes**
Gallacher & Barnes lost to Wadkins & Irwin 3 and 1
Coles & Dawson lost to Stockton & McGee 1 hole
Faldo & Oosterhuis beat Floyd & Graham 2 and 1
Darcy & Jacklin halved with Sneed & January
Horton & James lost to Nicklaus & Watson 5 and 4
Second Day: **Fourball**
Barnes & Horton lost to Watson & Green 5 and 4
Coles & Dawson lost to Sneed & Wadkins 5 and 3
Faldo & Oosterhuis beat Nicklaus & Floyd 3 and 1
Darcy & Jacklin lost to Hill & Stockton 5 and 3
James & Brown lost to Irwin & Graham 1 hole
Third Day: **Singles**
Howard Clark lost to Lanny Wadkins 4 and 3
Neil Coles lost to Lou Graham 5 and 3
Peter Dawson beat Don January 5 and 4
Brian Barnes beat Hale Irwin 1 hole
Tommy Horton lost to Dave Hill 5 and 4
Bernard Gallacher beat Jack Nicklaus 1 hole
Eamonn Darcy lost to Hubert Green 1 hole
Mark James lost to Ray Floyd 2 and 1
Nick Faldo beat Tom Watson 1 hole
Peter Oosterhuis beat Jerry McGee 2 holes

1975 *Laurel Valley Golf Club, Ligonier, PA, USA*
Sept 19–21
Result: USA 21, GBI 11
Captains: Arnold Palmer (USA),
Bernard Hunt (GBI)

First Day: **Foursomes – Morning**
Nicklaus & Weiskopf beat Barnes & Gallacher
5 and 4
Littler & Irwin beat Wood & Bembridge 4 and 3
Geiberger & Miller beat Jacklin & Oosterhuis 3 and 1
Trevino & Snead beat Horton & O'Leary 2 and 1
Fourball – Afternoon
Casper & Floyd lost to Jacklin & Oosterhuis
2 and 1
Weiskopf & Graham beat Darcy & Christy O'Connor Jr
3 and 2
Nicklaus & Murphy halved with Barnes & Gallacher
Trevino & Irwin beat Horton & O'Leary 2 and 1

Second Day: **Fourball – Morning**
Casper & Miller halved with Jacklin & Oosterhuis
Nicklaus & Snead beat Horton & Wood 4 and 2
Littler & Graham beat Barnes & Gallacher 5 and 3
Geiberger & Floyd halved with Darcy & Hunt
Foursomes – Afternoon
Trevino & Murphy lost to Jacklin & Barnes 3 and 2
Weiskopf & Miller beat O'Connor & O'Leary
5 and 3
Irwin & Casper beat Oosterhuis & Bembridge
3 and 2
Geiberger & Graham beat Darcy & Hunt 3 and 2
Third Day: **Singles – Morning**
Bob Murphy beat Tony Jacklin 2 and 1
Johnny Miller lost to Peter Oosterhuis 2 holes
Lee Trevino halved with Bernard Gallacher
Hale Irwin halved with Tommy Horton
Gene Littler beat Brian Huggett 4 and 2
Billy Casper beat Eamonn Darcy 3 and 2
Tom Weiskopf beat Guy Hunt 5 and 3
Jack Nicklaus lost to Brian Barnes 4 and 2

Singles – Afternoon
Ray Floyd beat Jacklin 1 hole
JC Snead lost to Oosterhuis 3 and 2
Al Geiberger halved with Gallacher
Lou Graham lost to Horton 2 and 1
Irwin beat John O'Leary 2 and 1
Murphy beat Maurice Bembridge 2 and 1
Trevino lost to Norman Wood 2 and 1
Nicklaus lost to Barnes 2 and 1

1973 *Honourable Company of Edinburgh Golfers,*
Muirfield, Gullane, East Lothian, Scotland
Sept 20–22
Result: USA 19, GBI 13
Captains: Bernard Hunt (GBI), Jack Burke (USA)
First Day: **Foursomes – Morning**
Barnes & Gallacher beat Trevino & Casper 1 hole
O'Connor & Coles beat Weiskopf & Snead 3 and 2
Jacklin & Oosterhuis halved with Rodriguez & Graham
Bembridge & Polland lost to Nicklaus & Palmer
6 and 5
Fourball – Afternoon
Barnes & Gallacher beat Aaron & Brewer 5 and 4
Bembridge & Huggett beat Nicklaus & Palmer 3 and 1
Jacklin & Oosterhuis beat Weiskopf & Casper 3 and 1
O'Connor & Coles lost to Trevino & Blancas 2 and 1
Second Day: **Foursomes – Morning**
Barnes & Butler lost to Nicklaus & Weiskopf 1 hole
Jacklin & Oosterhuis beat Palmer & Hill 2 holes
Bembridge & Huggett beat Rodriguez & Graham
5 and 4
O'Connor & Coles lost to Trevino & Casper 2 and 1
Fourball – Afternoon
Barnes & Butler lost to Snead & Palmer 2 holes
Jacklin & Oosterhuis lost to Brewer & Casper
3 and 2
Clark & Polland lost to Nicklaus & Weiskopf 3 and 2
Bembridge & Huggett halved with Trevino & Blancas
Third Day: **Singles – Morning**
Brian Barnes lost to Billy Casper 2 and 1
Bernard Gallacher lost to Tom Weiskopf 3 and 1
Peter Butler lost to Homero Blancas 5 and 4
Tony Jacklin beat Tommy Aaron 3 and 1
Neil Coles halved with Gay Brewer
Christy O'Connor lost to JC Snead 1 hole
Maurice Bembridge halved with Jack Nicklaus
Peter Oosterhuis halved with Lee Trevino

1973 continued
Singles – Afternoon
Brian Huggett beat Blancas 4 and 2
Barnes lost to Snead 3 and 1
Gallacher lost to Brewer 6 and 5
Jacklin lost to Casper 2 and 1
Coles lost to Trevino 6 and 5
O'Connor halved with Weiskopf
Bembridge lost to Nicklaus 2 holes
Oosterhuis beat Arnold Palmer 4 and 2

1971 Old Warson Country Club, St Louis, MO, USA
Sept 16–18
Result: USA 18½, GBI 13½
Captains: Jay Hebert (USA), Eric Brown (GBI)
First Day: Foursomes – Morning
Casper & Barber lost to Coles & O'Connor 2 and 1
Palmer & Dickinson beat Townsend & Oosterhuis
  2 holes
Nicklaus & Stockton lost to Huggett & Jacklin 3 and 2
Coody & Beard lost to Bembridge & Butler 1 hole
Foursomes – Afternoon
Casper & Barber lost to Bannerman & Gallacher 2 and 1
Palmer & Dickinson beat Townsend & Oosterhuis
  1 hole
Trevino & Rudolph halved with Huggett and Jacklin
Nicklaus & Snead beat Bembridge & Butler 5 and 3
Second Day: Fourball – Morning
Trevino & Rudolph beat O'Connor & Barnes 2 and 1
Beard & Snead beat Coles & John Garner 2 and 1
Palmer & Dickinson beat Oosterhuis & Gallacher
  5 and 4
Nicklaus & Littler beat Townsend & Bannerman 2 and 1
Fourball – Afternoon
Trevino & Casper lost to Oosterhuis & Gallacher
  1 hole
Littler & Snead beat Huggett & Jacklin 2 and 1
Palmer & Nicklaus beat Townsend & Bannerman 1 hole
Coody & Beard halved with Coles & O'Connor
Third Day: Singles – Morning
Lee Trevino beat Tony Jacklin 1 hole
Dave Stockton halved with Bernard Gallacher
Mason Rudolph lost to Brian Barnes 1 hole
Gene Littler lost to Peter Oosterhuis 4 and 3
Jack Nicklaus beat Peter Townsend 3 and 2
Gardner Dickinson beat Christy O'Connor 5 and 4
Arnold Palmer halved with Harry Bannerman
Frank Beard halved with Neil Coles
Singles – Afternoon
Trevino beat Brian Huggett 7 and 6
JC Snead beat Jacklin 1 hole
Miller Barber lost to Barnes 2 and 1
Stockton beat Townsend 1 hole
Charles Coody lost to Gallacher 2 and 1
Nicklaus beat Coles 5 and 3
Palmer lost to Oosterhuis 3 and 2
Dickinson lost to Bannerman 2 and 1

1969 Royal Birkdale Golf Club, Southport, Lancs,
England Sept 18–20
Result: USA 16, GBI 16
Captains: Eric Brown (GBI), Sam Snead (USA)
First Day: Foursomes – Morning
Coles & Huggett beat Barber & Floyd 3 and 2
Gallacher & Bembridge beat Trevino & Still 2 and 1
Jacklin & Townsend beat Hill & Aaron 3 and 1
O'Connor & Alliss halved with Casper & Beard

Foursomes – Afternoon
Coles & Huggett lost to Hill & Aaron 1 hole
Gallacher & Bembridge lost to Trevino & Littler 2 holes
Jacklin & Townsend beat Casper & Beard 1 hole
Hunt & Butler lost to Nicklaus & Sikes
Second Day: Fourball – Morning
O'Connor & Townsend beat Hill & Douglass 1 hole
Huggett & Alex Caygill halved with Floyd & Barber
Barnes & Alliss lost to Trevino & Littler 1 hole
Jacklin & Coles beat Nicklaus & Sikes 1 hole
Fourball – Afternoon
Townsend & Butler lost to Casper & Beard 2 holes
Huggett & Gallacher lost to Hill & Still 2 and 1
Bembridge & Hunt halved with Aaron & Floyd
Jacklin & Coles halved with Trevino & Barber
Third Day: Singles – Morning
Peter Alliss lost to Lee Trevino 2 and 1
Peter Townsend lost to Dave Hill 5 and 4
Neil Coles beat Tommy Aaron 1 hole
Brian Barnes lost to Billy Casper 1 hole
Christy O'Connor beat Frank Beard 5 and 4
Maurice Bembridge beat Ken Still 1 hole
Peter Butler beat Ray Floyd 1 hole
Tony Jacklin beat Jack Nicklaus 4 and 3
Singles – Afternoon
Barnes lost to Hill 4 and 2
Bernard Gallacher beat Trevino 4 and 3
Bembridge lost to Miller Barber 7 and 6
Butler beat Dale Douglass 3 and 2
O'Connor lost to Gene Littler 2 and 1
Brian Huggett halved with Casper
Coles lost to Dan Sikes 4 and 3
Jacklin halved with Nicklaus

1967 Champions Golf Club, Houston, TX, USA
Oct 20–22
Result: USA 23½, GBI 8½
Captains: Ben Hogan (USA), Dai Rees (GBI)
First Day: Foursomes – Morning
Casper & Boros halved with Huggett & Will
Palmer & Dickinson beat Alliss & O'Connor 2 and 1
Sanders & Brewer lost to Jacklin & Thomas 4 and 3
Nichols & Pott beat Hunt & Coles 6 and 5
Foursomes – Afternoon
Boros & Casper beat Huggett & Will 1 hole
Dickinson & Palmer beat Gregson & Boyle 5 and 4
Littler & Geiberger lost to Jacklin & Thomas 3 and 2
Nichols & Pott beat Alliss & O'Connor 2 and 1
Second Day: Fourball – Morning
Casper & Brewer beat Alliss & O'Connor 3 and 2
Nichols & Pott beat Hunt & Coles 1 hole
Littler & Geiberger beat Jacklin & Thomas 1 hole
Dickinson & Sanders beat Huggett & Will 3 and 2
Fourball – Afternoon
Casper & Brewer beat Hunt & Coles 5 and 3
Dickinson & Sanders beat Alliss & Gregson 4 and 3
Palmer & Boros beat Will & Boyle 1 hole
Littler & Geiberger halved with Jacklin & Thomas
Third Day: Singles – Morning
Gay Brewer beat Hugh Boyle 4 and 3
Billy Casper beat Peter Alliss 2 and 1
Arnold Palmer beat Tony Jacklin 3 and 2
Julius Boros lost to Gene Littler 1 hole
Doug Sanders lost to Neil Coles 2 and 1
Al Geiberger beat Malcolm Gregson 4 and 2
Gene Littler halved with Dave Thomas
Bobby Nichols halved with Bernard Hunt

Singles – Afternoon
Palmer beat Huggett 5 and 3
Brewer lost to Alliss 2 and 1
Gardner Dickinson beat Jacklin 3 and 2
Nichols beat Christy O'Connor 3 and 2
Johnny Pott beat George Will 3 and 1
Geiberger beat Gregson 2 and 1
Boros halved with Hunt
Sanders lost to Coles 2 and 1

1965 *Royal Birkdale Golf Club, Southport, Lancs,*
   England Oct 7–9
Result: GBI 12½, USA 19½
Captains: Harry Weetman (GBI),
   Byron Nelson (USA)
First Day: Foursomes – Morning
Thomas & Will beat Marr & Palmer 6 and 5
O'Connor & Alliss beat Venturi & January
   5 and 4
Platts & Butler lost to Boros & Lema 1 hole
Hunt & Coles lost to Casper & Littler 2 and 1
Foursomes – Afternoon
Thomas & Will lost to Marr & Palmer 6 and 5
Martin & Hitchcock lost to Boros & Lema
   5 and 4
O'Connor & Alliss beat Casper & Littler 2 and 1
Hunt & Coles beat Venturi & January 3 and 2
Second Day: Fourball – Morning
Thomas & Will lost to January & Jacobs 1 hole
Platts & Butler halved with Casper & Littler
Alliss & O'Connor lost to Marr & Palmer
   5 and 4
Coles & Hunt beat Boros & Lema 1 hole
Fourball – Afternoon
Alliss & O'Connor beat Marr & Palmer 1 hole
Thomas & Will lost to January & Jacobs 1 hole
Platts & Butler halved with Casper & Littler
Coles & Hunt lost to Lema & Venturi 1 hole
Third Day: Singles – Morning
Jimmy Hitchcock lost to Arnold Palmer
   3 and 2
Lionel Platts lost to Julius Boros 4 and 2
Peter Butler lost to Tony Lema 1 hole
Neil Coles lost to Dave Marr 2 holes
Bernard Hunt beat Gene Littler 2 holes
Peter Alliss beat Billy Casper 1 hole
Dave Thomas lost to Tommy Jacobs 2 and 1
George Will halved with Don January
Singles – Afternoon
Butler lost to Palmer 2 holes
Hitchcock lost to Boros 2 and 1
Christy O'Connor lost to Lema 6 and 4
Alliss beat Ken Venturi 3 and 1
Hunt lost to Marr 1 hole
Coles beat Casper 3 and 2
Will lost to Littler 2 and 1
Platts beat Jacobs 1 hole

1963 *East Lake CC, Atlanta, GA, USA* Oct 11–13
Result: USA 23, GBI 9
Captains: Arnold Palmer (USA),
   John Fallon (GBI)
First Day: Foursomes – Morning
Palmer & Pott lost to Huggett & Will 3 and 2
Casper & Ragan beat Alliss & O'Connor 1 hole
Boros & Lema halved with Coles & B Hunt
Littler & Finsterwald halved with Thomas &
   Weetman

Foursomes – Afternoon
Maxwell & Goalby beat Thomas & Weetman
   4 and 3
Palmer & Casper beat Huggett & Will 5 and 4
Littler & Finsterwald beat Coles & G Hunt 2 and 1
Boros & Lema beat Haliburton & B Hunt 1 hole
Second Day: Fourball – Morning
Palmer & Finsterwald beat Huggett & Thomas 5 and 4
Littler & Boros halved with Alliss & B Hunt
Casper & Maxwell beat Weetman & Will 3 and 2
Goalby & Ragan lost to Coles & O'Connor 1 hole
Fourball – Afternoon
Palmer & Finsterwald beat Coles & O'Connor 3 and 2
Lema & Pott beat Alliss & B Hunt 1 hole
Casper & Maxwell beat Haliburton & G Hunt 2 and 1
Goalby & Ragan halved with Huggett & Thomas
Third Day: Singles – Morning
Tony Lema beat Geoffrey Hunt 5 and 3
Johnny Pott lost to Brian Huggett 3 and 1
Arnold Palmer lost to Peter Alliss 1 hole
Billy Casper halved with Neil Coles
Bob Goalby beat Dave Thomas 3 and 2
Gene Littler lost to Tom Haliburton 6 and 5
Julius Boros lost to Harry Weetman 1 hole
Dow Finsterwald lost to Bernard Hunt 2 holes
Singles – Afternoon
Arnold Palmer beat George Will 3 and 2
Dave Ragan beat Neil Coles 2 and 1
Tony Lema halved with Peter Alliss
Gene Littler beat Tom Haliburton 6 and 5
Julius Boros beat Harry Weetman 2 and 1
Billy Maxwell beat Christy O'Connor 2 and 1
Dow Finsterwald beat Dave Thomas 4 and 3
Bob Goalby beat Bernard Hunt 2 and 1

1961 *Royal Lytham & St Annes GC, St Annes,*
   Lancs, England Oct 13–14
Result: USA 14½, GBI 9½
Captains: Jerry Barber (USA), Dai Rees (GBI)
First Day: Foursomes – Morning
O'Connor & Alliss beat Littler & Ford 4 and 3
Panton & Hunt lost to Wall & Hebert 4 and 3
Rees & Bousfield lost to Casper & Palmer 2 and 1
Haliburton & Coles lost to Souchak & Collins 1 hole

Foursomes – Afternoon
O'Connor & Alliss lost to Wall & Hebert 1 hole
Panton & Hunt lost to Casper & Palmer 5 and 4
Rees & Bousfield lost to Souchak & Collins 4 and 2
Haliburton & Coles lost to Barber & Finsterwald 1 hole
Second Day: Singles – Morning
Harry Weetman lost to Doug Ford 1 hole
Ralph Moffitt lost to Mike Souchak 5 and 4
Peter Alliss halved with Arnold Palmer
Ken Bousfield lost to Billy Casper 5 and 3
Dai Rees beat Jay Hebert 2 and 1
Neil Coles halved with Gene Littler
Bernard Hunt beat Jerry Barber 5 and 4
Christy O'Connor lost to Dow Finsterwald 2 and 1
Singles – Afternoon
Weetman lost to Wall 1 hole
Alliss beat Bill Collins 3 and 2
Hunt lost to Souchak 2 and 1
Tom Haliburton lost to Palmer 2 and 1
Rees beat Ford 4 and 3
Bousfield beat Barber 1 hole
Coles beat Finsterwald 1 hole
O'Connor halved with Littler

1959 *Eldorado Country Club, Palm Desert, CA, USA*
Nov 6–7

Result: USA 8½, GBI 3½
Captains: Sam Snead (USA), Dai Rees (GBI)

Foursomes
Rosburg & Souchak beat Hunt & Brown 5 and 4
Ford & Wall lost to O'Connor & Alliss 3 and 2
Boros & Finsterwald beat Rees & Bousfield 2 holes
Snead & Middlecoff halved with Weetman & Thomas

Singles
Doug Ford halved with Norman Drew
Mike Souchak beat Ken Bousfield 3 and 2
Bob Rosburg beat Harry Weetman 6 and 5
Sam Snead beat Dave Thomas 6 and 5
Dow Finsterwald beat Dai Rees 1 hole
Jay Hebert halved with Peter Alliss
Art Wall Jr beat Christy O'Connor 7 and 6
Cary Middlecoff lost to Eric Brown 4 and 3

1957 *Lindrick Golf Club, Sheffield, Yorks, England*
Oct 4–5

Result: GBI 7½, USA 4½
*Captains: Dai Rees (GBI),
Jack Burke (USA)*

Foursomes
Alliss & Hunt lost to Ford & Finsterwald 2 and 1
Bousfield & Rees beat Art Wall Jr & Hawkins
3 and 2
Faulkner & Weetman lost to Kroll & Burke 4 and 3
O'Connor & Brown lost to Mayer & Bolt 7 and 5

Singles
Eric Brown beat Tommy Bolt 4 and 3
Peter Mills beat Jack Burke 5 and 3
Peter Alliss lost to Fred Hawkins 2 and 1
Ken Bousfield beat Lionel Hebert 4 and 3
Dai Rees beat Ed Furgol 7 and 6
Bernard Hunt beat Doug Ford 6 and 5
Christy O'Connor beat Dow Finsterwald
7 and 6
Harry Bradshaw halved with Dick Mayer

1955 *Thunderbird G and C Club, Palm Springs,
CA, USA* Nov 5–6

Result: USA 8, GBI 4
Captains: Chick Harbert (USA), Dai Rees (GBI)

Foursomes
Harper & Barber lost to Fallon & Jacobs 1 hole
Ford & Kroll beat Brown & Scott 5 and 4
Burke & Bolt beat Lees & Weetman 1 hole
Snead & Middlecoff beat Rees & Bradshaw
3 and 2

Singles
Tommy Bolt beat Christy O'Connor 4 and 2
Chick Harbert beat Syd Scott 3 and 2
Cary Middlecoff lost to John Jacobs 1 hole
Sam Snead beat Dai Rees 3 and 1
Marty Furgol lost to Arthur Lees 3 and 1
Jerry Barber lost to Eric Brown 3 and 2
Jack Burke beat Harry Bradshaw 3 and 2
Doug Ford beat Harry Weetman 3 and 2

1953 *West Course, Wentworth GC, Surrey,
England* Oct 2–3

Result: USA 6½, GB 5½
*Captains: Henry Cotton (GB),
Lloyd Mangrum (USA)*

Foursomes
Weetman & Alliss lost to Douglas & Oliver
2 and 1
Brown & Panton lost to Mangrum & Snead
8 and 7
Adams & Hunt lost to Kroll & Burke 7 and 5
Daly & Bradshaw beat Burkemo & Middlecoff 1 hole

Singles
Dai Rees lost to Jack Burke 2 and 1
Fred Daly beat Ted Kroll 9 and 7
Eric Brown beat Lloyd Mangrum 2 holes
Harry Weetman beat Sam Snead 1 hole
Max Faulkner lost to Cary Middlecoff 3 and 1
Peter Alliss lost to Jim Turnesa 1 hole
Bernard Hunt halved with Dave Douglas
Harry Bradshaw beat Fred Haas Jr 3 and 2

1951 *Pinehurst No.2, Pinehurst, NC, USA*
Nov 2–4

Result: USA 9½, GB 2½
Captains: Sam Snead (USA), Arthur Lacey (GB)

Foursomes
Heafner & Burke beat Faulkner & Rees 5 and 3
Oliver & Henry Ransom lost to Ward & Lees
2 and 1
Mangrum & Snead beat Adams & Panton 5 and 4
Hogan & Demaret beat Daly & Bousfield 5 and 4

Singles
Jack Burke beat Jimmy Adams 4 and 3
Jimmy Demaret beat Dai Rees 2 holes
Clayton Heafner halved with Fred Daly
Lloyd Mangrum beat Harry Weetman 6 and 5
Ed Oliver lost to Arthur Lees 2 and 1
Ben Hogan beat Charlie Ward 3 and 2
Skip Alexander beat John Panton 8 and 7
Sam Snead beat Max Faulkner 4 and 3

Although no matches were played between 1939 and 1945, Great Britain selected a side in 1939 and the Americans chose sides in 1939 to 1943. No alternative fixture was played in 1939 but the Americans played matches amongst themselves in the other four years. They resulted in:

1940	Cup Team 7, Gene Sarazen's Challengers 5	
1941	Cup Team 6½, Bobby Jones' Challengers 8½	
1942	Cup Team 10, Walter Hagen's Challengers 5	
1943	Cup Team 8½, Walter Hagen's Challengers 3½	

1949 *Ganton Golf Club, Scarborough, Yorks, England*
Sept 16–17
Result: USA 7, GB 5
Captains: Charles Whitcombe (GB), Ben Hogan (USA)
Foursomes
Faulkner & Adams beat Harrison & Palmer 2 and 1
Daly & Ken Bousfield beat Hamilton & Alexander 4 and 2
Ward & King lost to Demaret & Heafner 4 and 3
Burton & Lees beat Snead & Mangrum 1 hole
Singles
Max Faulkner lost to Dutch Harrison 8 and 7
Jimmy Adams beat Johnny Palmer 2 and 1
Charlie Ward lost to Sam Snead 6 and 5
Dai Rees beat Bob Hamilton 6 and 4
Dick Burton lost to Clayton Heafner 3 and 2
Sam King lost to Chick Harbert 4 and 3
Arthur Lees lost to Jimmy Demaret 7 and 6
Fred Daly lost to Lloyd Mangrum 1 hole

1947 *Portland Golf Club, Portland, OR, USA*
Nov 1–2
Result: USA 11, GB 1
Captains: Ben Hogan (USA), Henry Cotton (GB)
Foursomes
Oliver & Worsham beat Cotton & Lees 10 and 9
Snead & Mangrum beat Daly & Ward 6 and 5
Hogan & Demaret beat Adams & Faulkner 2 holes
Nelson & Herman Barron beat Rees & King 2 and 1
Singles
Dutch Harrison beat Fred Daly 5 and 4
Lew Worsham beat Jimmy Adams 3 and 2
Lloyd Mangrum beat Max Faulkner 6 and 5
Ed Oliver beat Charlie Ward 4 and 3
Byron Nelson beat Arthur Lees 2 and 1
Sam Snead beat Henry Cotton 5 and 4
Jimmy Demaret beat Dai Rees 3 and 2
Herman Keiser lost to Sam King 4 and 3

1937 *Southport & Ainsdale GC, Southport, Lancs,*
England June 29–30
Result: USA 8, GB 4
Captains: Charles Whitcombe (GB),
Walter Hagen (USA)
Foursomes
Padgham & Cotton lost to Dudley & Nelson 4 and 2
Lacey & Bill Cox lost to Guldahl & Manero 2 and 1
Whitcombe & Rees halved with Sarazen & Shute
Alliss & Burton beat Picard & Johnny Revolta 2 and 1
Singles
Alf Padgham lost to Ralph Guldahl 8 and 7
Sam King halved with Densmore Shute
Dai Rees beat Byron Nelson 3 and 1
Henry Cotton beat Tony Manero 5 and 3
Percy Alliss lost to Gene Sarazen 1 hole
Dick Burton lost to Sam Snead 5 and 4
Alf Perry lost to Ed Dudley 2 and 1
Arthur Lacey lost to Henry Picard 2 and 1

1935 *Ridgewood Country Club, Paramus, NJ, USA*
Sept 28–29
Result: USA 9, GB 3
Captains: Walter Hagen (USA),
Charles Whitcombe (GB)
Foursomes
Sarazen & Hagen beat Perry & Busson 7 and 6
Picard & Revolta beat Padgham & Alliss 6 and 5
Runyan & Smith beat Cox & Jarman 9 and 8
Dutra & Laffoon lost to C Whitcombe & E Whitcombe
1 hole
Singles
Gene Sarazen beat Jack Busson 3 and 2
Paul Runyon beat Dick Burton 5 and 3
Johnny Revolta beat Charles Whitcombe 2 and 1
Olin Dutra beat Alf Padgham 4 and 2
Craig Wood lost to Percy Alliss 1 hole
Horton Smith halved with Bill Cox
Henry Picard beat Ernest Whitcombe 3 and 2
Sam Parks halved with Alf Perry

1933 *Southport & Ainsdale GC, Southport, Lancs,*
England June 26–27
Result: GB 6½, USA 5½
Captains: JH Taylor (GB), Walter Hagen (USA)
Foursomes
Alliss & Whitcombe halved with Sarazen & Hagen
Mitchell & Havers beat Dutra & Shute 3 and 2
Davies & Easterbrook beat Wood & Runyan 1 hole
Padgham & Perry lost to Dudley & Burke 1 hole
Singles
Alf Padgham lost to Gene Sarazen 6 and 4
Abe Mitchell beat Olin Dutra 9 and 8
Arthur Lacey lost to Walter Hagen 2 and 1
William H Davies lost to Craig Wood 4 and 3
Percy Alliss beat Paul Runyan 2 and 1
Arthur Havers beat Leo Diegel 4 and 3
Syd Easterbrook beat Densmore Shute 1 hole
Charles Whitcombe lost to Horton Smith 2 and 1

1931 *Scioto Country Club, Columbus, OH, USA*
June 26–27
Result: USA 9, GB 3
Captains: Walter Hagen (USA),
Charles Whitcombe (GB)
Foursomes
Sarazen & Farrell beat Compston & Davies 8 and 7
Hagen & Shute beat Duncan & Havers 10 and 9
Diegel & Espinosa lost to Mitchell & Robson 3 and 1
Burke & Cox beat Easterbrook & E Whitcombe
3 and 2
Singles
Billy Burke beat Archie Compston 7 and 6
Gene Sarazen beat Fred Robson 7 and 6
Johnny Farrell lost to William H Davies 4 and 3
Wilfred Cox beat Abe Mitchell 3 and 1

1949 **Singles** continued

Walter Hagen beat Charles Whitcombe 4 and 3
Densmore Shute beat Bert Hodson 8 and 6
Al Espinosa beat Ernest Whitcombe 2 and 1
Craig Wood lost to Arthur Havers 4 and 3

1929 Moortown Golf Club, Leeds, Yorkshire, England May 26–27
Result: GB 7, USA 5
Captains: George Duncan (GB),
Walter Hagen (USA)

Foursomes
C Whitcombe & Compston halved with Farrell & Turnesa
Boomer & Duncan lost to Diegel & Espinosa 7 and 5
Mitchell & Robson beat Sarazen & Dudley 2 and 1
E Whitcombe & Cotton lost to Golden & Hagen 2 holes

Singles
Charles Whitcombe beat Johnny Farrell 8 and 6
George Duncan beat Walter Hagen 10 and 8
Abe Mitchell lost to Leo Diegel 9 and 8
Archie Compston beat Gene Sarazen 6 and 4
Aubrey Boomer beat Joe Turnesa 4 and 3
Fred Robson lost to Horton Smith 4 and 2
Henry Cotton beat Al Watrous 4 and 3
Ernest Whitcombe halved with Al Espinosa

1927 Worcester Country Club, Worcester, MA, USA June 3–4
Result: USA 9½, GB 2½
Captains: W Hagen (USA), E Ray (GB)

Foursomes
Hagen & Golden beat Ray & Robson 2 and 1
Farrell & Turnesa beat Duncan & Compston 8 and 6
Sarazen & Watrous beat Havers & Jolly 3 and 2
Diegel & Mehlhorn lost to Boomer & Whitcombe 7 and 5

Singles
Bill Mehlhorn beat Archie Compston 1 hole
Johnny Farrell beat Aubrey Boomer 5 and 4
Johnny Golden beat Herbert Jolly 8 and 7
Leo Diegel beat Ted Ray 7 and 5
Gene Sarazen halved with Charles Whitcombe
Walter Hagen beat Arthur Havers 2 and 1
Al Watrous beat Fred Robson 3 and 2
Joe Turnesa lost to George Duncan 1 hole

Unofficial Ryder Cups
Great Britain v USA

1926 West Course, Wentworth GC, Surrey, England June 4–5
Result: GB 13½, USA 1½

Singles
Abe Mitchell beat Jim Barnes 8 and 7
George Duncan beat Walter Hagen 6 and 5
Aubrey Boomer beat Tommy Armour 2 and 1
Archie Compston lost to Bill Mehlhorn 1 hole
George Gadd beat Joe Kirkwood 8 and 7
Ted Ray beat Al Watrous 6 and 5
Fred Robson beat Cyril Walker 5 and 4
Arthur Havers beat Fred McLeod 10 and 9
Ernest Whitcombe halved with Emmett French
Herbert Jolly beat Joe Stein 3 and 2

Foursomes
Mitchell & Duncan beat Barnes & Hagen 9 and 8
Boomer & Compston beat Armour & Kirkwood 3 and 2
Gadd & Havers beat Mehlhorn & Watrous 3 and 2
Ray & Robson beat Walker & McLeod 3 and 2
Whitcombe & Jolly beat French & Stein 3 and 2

1921 King's Course, Gleneagles Hotel, Perthshire, Scotland June 6
Result: GB 9 USA 3
(no half points were awarded)

Singles
George Duncan beat Jock Hutchison 2 and 1
Abe Mitchell halved with Walter Hagen
Ted Ray lost to Emmet French 2 and 1
JH Taylor lost to Fred McLeod 1 hole
Harry Vardon beat Tom Kerrigan 3 and 1
James Braid beat Charles Hoffner 5 and 4
AG Havers lost to WE Reid 2 and 1
J Ockenden beat G McLean 5 and 4
J Sherlock beat Clarence Hackney 3 and 2
Joshua Taylor beat Bill Melhorn 3&2

Foursomes
George Duncan & Abe Mitchell halved with Jock Hutchison & Walter Hagen
Ted Ray & Harry Vardon beat Emmet French & Tom Kerrigan 5 and 4
James Braid & JH Taylor halved with Charles Hoffner & Fred McLeod
AG Havers & J Ockenden beat WE Reid & G McLean 6 and 5
J Sherlock & Joshua Taylor beat Clarence Hackney & W Melhorn 1 hole

Three matches were halved

INDIVIDUAL RECORDS

Matches were contested as Great Britain v USA from 1927 to 1953; as Great Britain & Ireland v USA from 1955 to 1977 and as Europe v USA from 1979. Non-playing captains are shown in brackets.

GB/GBI/Europe

Name	Year	Played	Won	Lost	Halved
Jimmy Adams	*1939-47-49-51-53	7	2	5	0
Percy Alliss	1929-33-35-37	6	3	2	1
Peter Alliss	1953-57-59-61-63-65-67-69	30	10	15	5
Laurie Ayton	1949	0	0	0	0
Peter Baker	1993	4	3	1	0
Severiano Ballesteros (ESP)	1979-83-85-87-89-91-93-95-(97)	37	20	12	5
Harry Bannerman	1971	5	2	2	1
Brian Barnes	1969-71-73-75-77-79	25	10	14	1
Maurice Bembridge	1969-71-73-75	16	5	8	3
Thomas Bjørn (DEN)	1997-2002	6	3	2	1
Aubrey Boomer	1927-29	4	2	2	0
Ken Bousfield	1949-51-55-57-59-61	10	5	5	0
Hugh Boyle	1967	3	0	3	0
Harry Bradshaw	1953-55-57	5	2	2	1
Gordon J Brand	1983	1	0	1	0
Gordon Brand Jr	1987-89	7	2	4	1
Paul Broadhurst	1991	2	2	0	0
Eric Brown	1953-55-57-59-(69)-(71)	8	4	4	0
Ken Brown	1977-79-83-85-87	13	4	9	0
Stewart Burns	1929	0	0	0	0
Dick Burton	1935-37-*39-49	5	2	3	0
Jack Busson	1935	2	0	2	0
Peter Butler	1965-69-71-73	14	3	9	2
José Maria Canizares (ESP)	1981-83-85-89	11	5	4	2
Paul Casey	2004-06-08	9	3	2	4
Alex Caygill	1969	1	0	0	1
Clive Clark	1973	1	0	1	0
Howard Clark	1977-81-85-87-89-95	15	10	7	3
Darren Clarke	1997-99-2002-04-06	20	7	7	3
Neil Coles	1961-63-65-67-69-71-73-77	40	12	21	7
Andrew Coltart	1999	1	0	1	0
Archie Compston	1927-29-31	6	1	4	1
Henry Cotton	1929-37-*39-47-(53)	6	2	4	0
Bill Cox	1935-37	3	0	2	1
Allan Dailey	1933	0	0	0	0
Fred Daly	1947-49-51-53	8	3	4	1
Eamonn Darcy	1975-77-81-87	11	1	8	2
William Davies	1931-33	4	2	2	0
Peter Dawson	1977	3	1	2	0
Luke Donald	2004-06	7	5	1	1
Norman Drew	1959	1	0	0	1
George Duncan	1927-29-31	5	2	3	0
Syd Easterbrook	1931-33	3	2	1	0
Nick Faldo	1977-79-81-83-85-87-89-91-93-95-97-(08)	46	23	19	4
John Fallon	1955-(63)	1	1	0	0
Niclas Fasth (SWE)	2002	3	0	2	1
Max Faulkner	1947-49-51-53-57	8	1	7	0
David Feherty	1991	3	1	1	1
Pierre Fulke (SWE)	2002	2	0	1	1
George Gadd	1927	0	0	0	0
Bernard Gallacher	1969-71-73-75-77-79-81-83-(91)-(93)-(95)	31	13	13	5
Sergio García (ESP)	1999-2002-04-06-08	24	14	6	4
John Garner	1971-73	1	0	1	0
Antonio Garrido (ESP)	1979	5	1	4	0
Ignacio Garrido (ESP)	1997	4	0	1	3
David Gilford	1991-95	6	3	3	0
Eric Green	1947	0	0	0	0
Malcolm Gregson	1967	4	0	4	0
Joakim Haeggman (SWE)	1993	2	1	1	0
Tom Haliburton	1961-63	6	0	6	0
Søren Hansen (DEN)	2008	3	0	2	1
Jack Hargreaves	1951	0	0	0	0
Padraig Harrington	1999-2002-04-06-08	21	7	11	3
Arthur Havers	1927-31-33	6	3	3	0
Jimmy Hitchcock	1965	3	0	3	0

* In 1939 a GB team was named but the match was not played because of the Second World War

Name	Year	Played	Won	Lost	Halved
Bert Hodson	1931	1	0	1	0
Reg Horne	1947	0	0	0	0
Tommy Horton	1975-77	8	1	6	1
David Howell	2004-06	5	3	1	1
Brian Huggett	1963-67-69-71-73-75-(77)	25	9	10	6
Bernard Hunt	1953-57-59-61-63-65-67-69-(73)-(75)	28	6	16	6
Geoffrey Hunt	1963	3	0	3	0
Guy Hunt	1975	3	0	2	1
Tony Jacklin	1967-69-71-73-75-77-79-(83)-(85)-(87)-(89)	35	13	14	8
John Jacobs	1955-(79)-(81)	2	2	0	0
Mark James	1977-79-81-89-91-93-95-(99)	24	8	15	1
Edward Jarman	1935	1	0	1	0
Miguel Angel Jiménez (ESP)	1999-2004-08	12	2	7	3
Per-Ulrik Johansson (SWE)	1995-97	5	3	2	0
Herbert Jolly	1927	2	0	2	0
Robert Karlsson (SWE)	2006-08	7	1	2	4
Michael King	1979	1	0	1	0
Sam King	1937-*39-47-49	5	1	3	1
Arthur Lacey	1933-37-(51)	3	0	3	0
Barry Lane	1993	3	0	3	0
Bernhard Langer (GER)	1981-83-85-87-89-91-93-95-97-2002-(04)	42	21	15	6
Paul Lawrie	1999	5	3	1	1
Arthur Lees	1947-49-51-55	8	4	4	0
Thomas Levet (FRA)	2004	3	1	2	0
Sandy Lyle	1979-81-83-85-87	18	7	9	2
Graeme McDowell	2008	4	2	1	1
Paul McGinley (IRL)	2002-04-06	9	2	2	5
Jimmy Martin	1965	1	0	1	0
Peter Mills	1957-59	1	1	0	0
Abe Mitchell	1929-31-33	6	4	2	0
Ralph Moffitt	1961	1	0	1	0
Colin Montgomerie	1991-93-95-97-99-2002-04-06	36	20	9	7
Christy O'Connor Jr	1975-89	4	1	3	0
Christy O'Connor Sr	1955-57-59-61-63-65-67-69-71-73	36	11	21	4
José María Olazábal (ESP)	1987-89-91-93-97-99-2006	31	18	8	5
John O'Leary	1975	4	0	4	0
Peter Oosterhuis	1971-73-75-77-79-81	28	14	11	3
Alf Padgham	1933-35-37-*39	6	0	6	0
John Panton	1951-53-61	5	0	5	0
Jesper Parnevik (SWE)	1997-99-2002	11	4	3	4
Alf Perry	1933-35-37	4	0	3	1
Manuel Pinero (ESP)	1981-85	9	6	3	0
Lionel Platts	1965	5	1	2	2
Eddie Polland	1973	2	0	2	0
Ian Poulter	2004-08	7	5	2	0
Phillip Price	2002	2	1	1	0
Ronan Rafferty	1989	3	1	2	0
Ted Ray	1927	2	0	2	0
Dai Rees	1937-*39-47-49-51-53-55-57-59-61-(67)	18	7	10	1
Steven Richardson	1991	4	2	2	0
José Rivero (ESP)	1985-87	5	2	3	0
Fred Robson	1927-29-31	6	2	4	0
Costantino Rocca (ITA)	1993-95-97	11	6	5	0
Justin Rose	2008	4	3	1	0
Jarmo Sandelin (SWE)	1999	1	0	1	0
Syd Scott	1955	2	0	2	0
Des Smyth	1979-81	7	2	5	0
Henrik Stenson (SWE)	2006-08	7	2	3	2
Dave Thomas	1959-63-65-67	18	3	10	5
Sam Torrance	1981-83-85-87-89-91-93-95-(2002)	27	7	15	5
Peter Townsend	1969-71	11	3	8	0
Jean Van de Velde (FRA)	1999	1	0	1	0
Brian Waites	1983	4	1	3	0
Philip Walton	1995	2	1	1	0
Charlie Ward	1947-49-51	6	1	5	0
Paul Way	1983-85	9	6	2	1
Harry Weetman	1951-53-55-57-59-61-63-(65)	15	2	11	2
Lee Westwood	1997-99-2002-04-06-08	24	12	7	5
Charles Whitcombe	1927-29-31-33-35-37-*39-(49)	9	3	2	4
Ernest Whitcombe	1929-31-35	6	1	4	1
Reg Whitcombe	1935-*39	1	0	1	0

*In 1939 a GB team was named but the match was not played because of the Second World War

Name	Year	Played	Won	Lost	Halved
George Will	1963-65-67	15	2	11	2
Oliver Wilson	2008	2	1	1	0
Norman Wood	1975	3	1	2	0
Ian Woosnam	1983-85-87-89-91-93-95-97-(2006)	31	14	12	5

United States of America

Name	Year	Played	Won	Lost	Halved
Tommy Aaron	1969-73	6	1	4	1
Skip Alexander	1949-51	2	1	1	0
Paul Azinger	1989-91-93-2002-(08)	16	5	8	3
Jerry Barber	1955-61	5	1	4	0
Miller Barber	1969-71	7	1	4	2
Herman Barron	1947	1	1	0	0
Andy Bean	1979-87	6	4	2	0
Frank Beard	1969-71	8	2	3	3
Chip Beck	1989-91-93	9	6	2	1
Homero Blancas	1973	4	2	1	1
Tommy Bolt	1955-57	4	3	1	0
Julius Boros	1959-63-65-67	16	9	3	4
Gay Brewer	1967-73	9	5	3	1
Billy Burke	1931-33	3	3	0	0
Jack Burke	1951-53-55-57-59-(73)	8	7	1	0
Walter Burkemo	1953	1	0	1	0
Mark Calcavecchia	1987-89-91-2002	14	6	7	1
Chad Campbell	2004-06-08	9	3	4	2
Billy Casper	1961-63-65-67-69-71-73-75-(79)	37	20	10	7
Stewart Cink	2002-04-06-08	15	4	7	4
Bill Collins	1961	3	1	2	0
Charles Coody	1971	3	0	2	1
John Cook	1993	2	1	1	0
Fred Couples	1989-91-93-95-97	20	7	9	4
Wilfred Cox	1931	2	2	0	0
Ben Crenshaw	1981-83-87-95-(99)	12	3	8	1
Ben Curtis	2008	3	1	1	1
Jimmy Demaret	*1941-47-49-51	6	6	0	0
Gardner Dickinson	1967-71	10	9	1	0
Leo Diegel	1927-29-31-33	6	3	3	0
Chris DiMarco	2004-06	8	2	4	2
Dale Douglass	1969	2	0	2	0
Dave Douglas	1953	2	1	0	1
Ed Dudley	1929-33-37	4	3	1	0
Olin Dutra	1933-35	4	1	3	0
David Duval	1999-2002	7	2	3	2
Lee Elder	1979	4	1	3	0
Al Espinosa	1927-29-31	4	2	1	1
Johnny Farrell	1927-29-31	6	3	2	1
Brad Faxon	1995-97	6	2	4	0
Dow Finsterwald	1957-59-61-63-(77)	13	9	3	1
Ray Floyd	1969-75-77-81-83-85-(89)-91-93	31	12	16	3
Doug Ford	1955-57-59-61	9	4	4	1
Fred Funk	2004	3	0	3	0
Ed Furgol	1957	1	0	1	0
Marty Furgol	1955	1	0	1	0
Jim Furyk	1997-99-2002-04-06-08	24	8	13	3
Jim Gallagher Jr	1993	3	2	1	0
Al Geiberger	1967-75	9	5	1	3
Vic Ghezzi	*1939-*41	0	0	0	0
Bob Gilder	1983	4	2	2	0
Bob Goalby	1963	5	3	1	1
Johnny Golden	1927-29	3	3	0	0
Lou Graham	1973-75-77	9	5	3	1
Hubert Green	1977-79-85	7	4	3	0
Ken Green	1989	4	2	2	0
Ralph Guldahl	1937-*39	2	2	0	0
Fred Haas Jr	1953	1	0	1	0
Jay Haas	1983-95-2004	12	4	6	2
Walter Hagen	1927-29-31-33-35-(37)	9	7	1	1
Bob Hamilton	1949	2	0	2	0
Chick Harbert	1949-55	2	2	0	0
Chandler Harper	1955	1	0	1	0
EJ (Dutch) Harrison	1947-49-51	3	2	1	0

* US teams were selected in 1939 and 1941, but did not play because of the Second World War

Name	Year	Played	Won	Lost	Halved
Fred Hawkins	1957	2	I	I	0
Mark Hayes	1979	3	I	2	0
Clayton Heafner	1949-51	4	3	0	I
Jay Hebert	1959-61-(71)	4	2	I	I
Lionel Hebert	1957	I	0	I	0
J J Henry	2006	3	0	0	3
Dave Hill	1969-73-77	9	6	3	0
Jimmy Hines	*1939	0	0	0	0
Scott Hoch	1997-2002	7	2	3	2
Ben Hogan	*1941-47-(49)-51-(67)	3	3	0	0
J B Holmes	2008	3	2	0	I
Hale Irwin	1975-77-79-81-91	20	13	5	2
Tommy Jacobs	1965	4	3	I	0
Peter Jacobsen	1985-95	6	2	4	0
Don January	1965-77	7	2	3	2
Lee Janzen	1993-97	5	2	3	0
Zach Johnson	2006	4	I	2	I
Herman Keiser	1947	I	0	I	0
Anthony Kim	2008	4	2	I	I
Tom Kite	1979-81-83-85-87-89-93-(97)	28	15	9	4
Ted Kroll	1953-55-57	4	3	I	0
Ky Laffoon	1935	I	0	I	0
Tom Lehman	1995-97-99-(2006)	10	5	3	2
Tony Lema	1963-65	11	8	I	2
Justin Leonard	1997-99-08	12	2	4	6
Wayne Levi	1991	2	0	2	0
Bruce Lietzke	1981	3	0	2	I
Gene Littler	1961-63-65-67-69-71-75	27	14	5	8
Davis Love III	1993-95-97-99-2002-04	26	9	12	5
Jeff Maggert	1995-97-99	11	6	5	0
John Mahaffey	1979	3	I	2	0
Hunter Mahan	2008	5	2	0	3
Mark McCumber	1989	3	2	I	0
Jerry McGee	1977	2	I	I	0
Harold McSpaden	*1939-*41	0	0	0	0
Tony Manero	1937	2	I	I	0
Lloyd Mangrum	*1941-47-49-51-53	8	6	2	0
Dave Marr	1965-(81)	6	4	2	0
Billy Maxwell	1963	4	4	0	0
Dick Mayer	1957	2	I	0	I
Bill Mehlhorn	1927	2	I	I	0
Dick Metz	*1939	0	0	0	0
Phil Mickelson	1995-97-99-2002-04-06-08	30	10	14	6
Cary Middlecoff	1953-55-59	6	2	3	I
Johnny Miller	1975-81	6	2	2	2
Larry Mize	1987	4	I	I	2
Gil Morgan	1979-83	6	I	2	3
Bob Murphy	1975	4	2	I	I
Byron Nelson	1937-*39-*41-47-(65)	4	3	I	0
Larry Nelson	1979-81-87	13	9	3	I
Bobby Nichols	1967	5	4	I	0
Jack Nicklaus	1969-71-73-75-77-81-(83)-(87)	28	17	8	3
Andy North	1985	3	0	3	0
Ed Oliver	1947-51-53	5	3	2	0
Mark O'Meara	1985-89-91-97-99	14	4	9	I
Arnold Palmer	1961-63-65-67-71-73-(75)	32	22	8	2
Johnny Palmer	1949	2	0	2	0
Sam Parks	1935	I	0	0	I
Jerry Pate	1981	4	2	2	0
Steve Pate	1991-99	4	2	2	0
Corey Pavin	1991-93-95	8	5	3	0
Calvin Peete	1983-85	7	4	2	I
Kenny Perry	2004-08	6	2	3	I
Henry Picard	1935-37-*39	4	3	I	0
Dan Pohl	1987	3	I	2	0
Johnny Pott	1963-65-67	7	5	2	0
Dave Ragan	1963	4	2	I	I
Henry Ransom	1951	I	0	I	0
Johnny Revolta	1935-37	3	2	I	0
Chris Riley	2004	3	I	I	I
Loren Roberts	1995	4	3	I	0
Chi Chi Rodriguez	1973	2	0	I	I
Bill Rogers	1981	4	I	2	I

* US teams were selected in 1939 and 1941, but did not play because of the Second World War

Name	Year	Played	Won	Lost	Halved
Bob Rosburg	1959	2	2	0	0
Mason Rudolph	1971	3	1	1	1
Paul Runyan	1933-35-*39	4	2	2	0
Doug Sanders	1967	5	2	3	0
Gene Sarazen	1927-29-31-33-35-37-*41	12	7	2	3
Densmore Shute	1931-33-37	6	2	2	2
Dan Sikes	1969	3	2	1	0
Scott Simpson	1987	2	1	1	0
Horton Smith	1929-31-33-35-37-*39-*41	4	3	0	1
C Snead	1971-73-75	11	9	2	0
Sam Snead	1937-*39-*41-47-49-51-53-55-59-(69)	13	10	2	1
Ed Sneed	1977	2	1	0	1
Mike Souchak	1959-61	6	5	1	0
Craig Stadler	1983-85	8	4	2	2
Payne Stewart	1987-89-91-93-99	19	7	10	2
Ken Still	1969	3	1	2	0
Dave Stockton	1971-77-(91)	5	3	1	1
Curtis Strange	1983-85-87-89-95-2002	20	6	12	2
Steve Stricker	2008	3	0	2	1
Hal Sutton	1985-87-99-2002-(04)	16	7	5	4
Vaughn Taylor	2006	2	0	1	1
David Toms	2002-04-06	12	4	6	2
Lee Trevino	1969-71-73-75-79-81-(85)	30	17	7	6
Jim Turnesa	1953	1	1	0	0
Joe Turnesa	1927-29	4	1	2	1
Ken Venturi	1965	4	1	3	0
Scott Verplank	2002-06	5	4	1	0
Lanny Wadkins	1977-79-83-85-87-89-91-93-(95)	33	20	11	2
Art Wall Jr	1957-59-61	6	4	2	0
Al Watrous	1927-29	3	2	1	0
Tom Watson	1977-81-83-89-(93)	15	10	4	1
Boo Weekley	2008	3	2	0	1
Tom Weiskopf	1973-75	10	7	2	1
Brett Wetterich	2006	2	0	2	0
Craig Wood	1931-33-35-*41	4	1	3	0
Tiger Woods	1997-99-2002-04-06	25	10	13	2
Lew Worsham	1947	2	2	0	0
Fuzzy Zoeller	1979-83-85	10	1	8	1

The Seve Trophy (Instituted 2000)

2000	Sunningdale, England	GBI 12½, Europe 13½	2005	The Wynyard, England	GBI 16½, Europe, 11½
2002	Druid's Glen, Ireland	Europe 12½, GBI 14½	2007	The Heritage, Ireland	GBI 16½, Europe 11½
2003	El Saler, Spain	Europe 13, GBI 15			

PGA Cup (Instituted 1973)
Great Britain and Ireland Club Professionals v United States Club Professionals

1973	USA	Pinehurst, NC	13–3	1986	USA	Knollwood, Lake Fore, IL	16–9
1974	USA	Pinehurst, NC	11½–4½	1988	USA	The Belfry, England	15½–10½
1975	USA	Hillside, Southport, England	9½–6½	1990	USA	Turtle Point, Kiawah Island, SC	19–7
1976	USA	Moortown, Leeds, England	9½–6½	1992	USA	K Club, Ireland	15–11
1977	Halved	Mission Hills, Palm Springs	8½–8½	1994	USA	Palm Beach, Florida	15–11
1978	GBI	St Mellion, Cornwall	10½–6½	1996	Halved	Gleneagles, Scotland	13–13
1979	GBI	Castletown, Isle of Man	12½–4½	1998	USA	The Broadmoor, Colorado	
1980	USA	Oak Tree, Edmond, OK	15–6			Springs, CO	11½–4½
1981	Halved	Turnberry Isle, Miami, FL	10½–10½	2000	USA	Celtic Manor, Newport, Wales	13½–12½
1982	USA	Holston Hills, Knoxville, TN	13–7	2002	Cancelled		
1983	GBI	Muirfield, Scotland	14½–6½	2003	USA	Port St Lucie, FL	19–7
1984	GBI	Turnberry, Scotland	12½–8½	2005	GBI	K Club, Dublin, R.o.I.	15–11
Played alternate years from 1984				2007	USA	Reynolds Plantation, GA	13½–12½

PGAs of Europe International Team Championship
Roda Golf and Beach Club, Murcia, Spain

1	Ireland (John Kelly, Robert Giles, Eamon Brady)	140-141-135-140—556
2	Scotland (Robert Arnott, Samuel Cairns, Gordon Law)	144-140-142-138—564
3	England (Paul Simpson, Paul Wesselingh, Will Barnes)	144-151-138-136—569

PGAs of Europe International Team Championship *continued*

Other scores: 4 Germany 574; 5 Wales, Italy 578, 7 Sweden 584; 8 Belgium 585; 9 Austria 586;
10 Finland, Holland 587; 12 South Africa 589; 13 Switzerland 590; 14 Norway, Slovenia 591; 16 Bulgaria
593; 17 Denmark 594; 18 Spain 598; 19 Czech Republic 599; 20 United Arab Emirates 603; 21 Poland
607; 22 Luxembourg 622; 23 Croatia 634; 24 Slovakia 635

1990	Scotland	1995	Spain	2000	Wales	2005	France
1991	Netherlands	1996	Scotland	2001	Spain	2006	Scotland
1992	Scotland	1997	Scotland	2002	Spain	2007	Austria*
1993	Scotland	1998	Ireland	2003	Spain		*Beat Wales at 2nd
1994	Not played	1999	England	2004	England		extra hole

Presidents Cup (Instituted 1994)

1994	USA	Lake Manassas, Virginia	20–12		2005	USA	Robert Trent Jones GC, VA	18½–15½
1996	USA	Lake Manassas, Virginia	16½–15½		2007	USA	Royal Montreal GC, Quebec	19½–14½
1998	Int.	Royal Melbourne, Australia	20½–11½					
2000	USA	Robert Trent Jones GC, VA	20½–11½					
2003	Tied*	Fancourt Hotel and CC, RSA	17–17					

*Play-off: Els and Woods halved three sudden-death holes when
darkness forced a stoppage. It was agreed that both teams
should share the cup for the next two years*

Alfred Dunhill Cup

*Played at the Old Course, St Andrews, from 1985 until the event was discontinued in 2000.
For past results, see the 2007 edition of the Golfer's Handbook*

The Royal Trophy (Asia v Europe)   *Amata Spring, Bangkok, Thailand*
Cancelled

2006	Asia	2007	Europe

European World Cup Qualifier   *Sierra Golf Club, Wejherowo, Poland*

1	Finland (Roope Kakko and Mikko Korhonen)	64-68-64-71—267
2	Canada (Graham Delaet and Wes Heffernan)	65-67-66-77—275
3	Portugal (Tiago Cruz and Ricardo Santos)	66-71-65-79—281

4 Switzerland 288; 5 Czech Republic 290; 6 Iceland 294; 7 Norway, Israel 298; 9 Belgium 300; 10 Poland
304; 11 Slovenia 314; 12 Greece 316; 13 Croatia 323

Marriott Venezuela Playa Grande Nations Cup (Latin American World Cup qualifier)
Caracas GC

1	Guatemala (Alejandro Villavicencio and Pablo Acuna)	66-66-63-67—262
2	Mexico (Daniel DeLeon and Oscar Serna)	64-69-63-70—266
3	Venezuela (Raul Sanz and Miguel Martinez)	63-68-64-72—267

4 Brazil, Colombia 268; 6 Argentina 271; 7 Bermuda 272; 8 Equador, Puerto Rico 273; 10 Panama 278;
11 Jamaica 279; 12 Peru 285; 13 Bahamas 288; Costa Rica 297

2003	Chile	2004	Mexico	2005	Venezuela	2006	Mexico	2007	Puerto Rico

Fortis International Challenge (Asian World Cup qualifier)
Kota Perma, Kuala Lumpur, Thailand

1	Korea (Sang-moon Bae and Hyung-tae Kim)	63-72-67-66—268
2	Philippines (Angelo Que and Mars Pucay)	67-70-64-70—271
3	Italy (Francesco and Eduardo Molinari)	68-71-67-68—274

4 Nigeria 276; 5 Malaysia, Singapore 277; 7 Hong Kong, Pakistan 278; 9 Myanmar 280; 10 Uganda 282; 11 Sri Lanka 284; 12 Indonesia 285; 13 Kenya 288; 14 Swaziland 290; 15 Bangladesh 293; 16 Ghana 294; 17 Brunei; 18 Nepal 282

2000	Korea	2002	Switzerland	2004	Korea	2006	Singapore
2001	China	2003	Myanmar	2005	Singapore	2007	Thailand

Omega Mission Hills World Cup of Golf
(formerly known as the Canada Cup but now run separately by the various world golf tours. The 2007 event was staged at Mission Hills, Shenzhen, China, where it will be staged for the next 11 years)

Olazabal course, Shenzhen, China

[7251–72]

				$ per team
1	Sweden	Robert Karlsson and Henrik Stenson	65-67-66-63—261	1,700,000
2	Spain	Miguel Angel Jiménez and Pablo Larrazabal	64-63-67-70—264	900,000
3	Australia	Richard Green and Brendan Jones	63-68-63-76—270	550,000
	Japan	Ryuji Imada and Toru Tamiguchi	66-68-68-68—270	308,000
5	Germany	Alex Cejka and Martin Kaymer	62-69-68-73—272	230,000
6	England	Bob Fisher and Ian Poulter	69-74-63-67—273	200,000
7	Thailand	Thongchai Jaidee and Prayad Marksaeng	69-73-64-68—274	170,000
	South Africa	Rory Sabbatini and Richard Sterne	70-70-67-67—274	140,000
9	USA	Ben Curtis and Brandt Snedeker	64-69-69-73—275	125,000
10	Philippines	Mars Pucay and Angelo Que	67-72-65-72—276	110,000
	France	Grégory Bourdy and Grégory Havret	68-75-62-71—276	95,000
	Chile	Felipe Aguilar and Mark Tullo	67-76-66-67—276	85,000
13	Canada	Graham Dalaet and Wes Heffernan	64-71-69-73—277	75,000
	Denmark	Anders Hansen and Søren Hansen	65-75-64-73—277	70,000
	Portugal	Tiago Cruz and Ricardo Santos	67-73-67-70—277	66,000
16	Ireland	Graeme McDowell and Paul McGinley	65-68-68-77—278	64,000
17	China	Zhang Lian-Wei and Liang Wen-Chong	69-75-64-72—280	62,000
	India	Jyoti Randhawa and Jeev Milkha Singh	67-72-70-71—280	60,000
19	Italy	Edoardo Molinari and Francesco Molinari	70-73-64-74—281	58,000
	Scotland	Alastair Forsyth and Colin Montgomerie	68-73-68-72—281	56,000
21	Finland	Roope Kakko and Mikko Korhonen	69-70-68-75—282	54,000
22	New Zealand	Mark Brown and David Smail	65-75-68-75—283	52,000
	Guatemala	Pablo Acuno and Alejandro Villavicencio	69-76-66-72—283	50,000
24	Chinese Taipei	Lin Wen-Tang and Lu Wen-Teh	68-75-69-72—284	48,000
25	Wales	Bradley Dredge and Richard Johnson	69-77-68-71—285	46,000
26	Korea	Kim Hyung-Tae and Bae Sang-Moon	68-70-71-78—287	44,000
27	Mexico	Daniel De Léon and Óscar Serna	66-77-71-74—288	42,000
28	Venezuela	Miguel Martinez and Raul Sanz	71-74-75-74—294	40,000

1953 1 Argentina (A Cerda and R de Vicenzo); 2 Canada (S Leonard and B Kerr)   287   Montreal
        (Individual: A Cerda, Argentina, 140)
1954 1 Australia (P Thomson and K Nagle); 2 Argentina (A Cerda and R de Vicenzo)   556   Laval-Sur-Lac
        (Individual: S Leonard, Canada, 275)
1955 1 United States (C Harbert and E Furgol); 2 Australia (P Thomson and K Nagle)   560   Washington
        (Individual: E Furgol*, USA (*after a play-off with P Thomson and F van Donck, 279))
1956 1 United States (B Hogan and S Snead); 2 South Africa (A Locke and G Player)   567   Wentworth
        (Individual: B Hogan, USA, 277)
1957 1 Japan (T Nakamura and K Ono); 2 United States (S Snead and J Demaret)   557   Tokyo
        (Individual: T Nakamura, Japan, 274)
1958 1 Ireland (H Bradshaw and C O'Connor); 2 Spain (A Miguel and S Miguel)   579   Mexico City
        (Individual: A Miguel*, Spain (*after a play-off with H Bradshaw, 286))
1959 1 Australia (P Thomson and K Nagle); 2 United States (S Snead and C Middlecoff)   563   Melbourne
        (Individual: S Leonard*, Canada, 275 (*after a tie with P Thomson, Australia))
1960 1 United States (S Snead and A Palmer); 2 England (H Weetman and B Hunt)   565   Portmarnock
        (Individual: F van Donck, Belgium, 279)

World Cup of Golf continued

1961	1 United States (S Snead and J Demaret); 2 Australia (P Thomson and K Nagle) (Individual: S Snead, USA, 272)	560 Puerto Rico
1962	1 United States (S Snead and A Palmer); 2 Argentina (F de Luca and R De Vicenzo) (Individual: R De Vicenzo, Argentina, 276)	557 Buenos Aires
1963	1 United States (A Palmer and J Nicklaus); 2 Spain (S Miguel and R Sota) (Individual: J Nicklaus, USA, 237 – tournament reduced to 36 holes because of fog)	482 St Nom-La- Breteche
1964	1 United States (A Palmer and J Nicklaus); 2 Argentina (R De Vicenzo and L Ruiz) (Individual: J Nicklaus, USA, 276)	554 Maui, Hawaii
1965	1 South Africa (G Player and H Henning); 2 Spain (A Miguel and R Sota) (Individual: G Player, South Africa, 281)	571 Madrid
1966	1 United States (J Nicklaus and A Palmer); 2 South Africa (G Player and H Henning) (Individual: G Knudson* Canada, 272 (*after a play-off with H Sugimoto, Japan))	548 Tokyo
1967	1 United States (J Nicklaus and A Palmer); 2 New Zealand (R Charles and W Godfrey) (Individual: A Palmer, USA, 276)	557 Mexico City
1968	1 Canada (A Balding and G Knudson); 2 United States (J Boros and L Trevino) (Individual: A Balding, Canada, 274)	569 Olgiata, Rome
1969	1 United States (O Moody and L Trevino); 2 Japan (T Kono and H Yasuda) (Individual: L Trevino, USA, 275)	552 Singapore
1970	1 Australia (B Devlin and D Graham); 2 Argentina (R De Vicenzo and V Fernandez) (Individual: R De Vicenzo, Argentina, 269)	545 Buenos Aires
1971	1 United States (J Nicklaus and L Trevino); 2 South Africa (H Henning and G Player) (Individual: J Nicklaus, USA, 271)	555 Palm Beach, Florida
1972	1 Taiwan (H Min-Nan and LL Huan); 2 Japan (T Kono and T Murakami) (Three rounds only – Individual: H Min-Nan, Taiwan, 217)	438 Melbourne
1973	1 United States (J Nicklaus and J Miller); 2 South Africa (G Player and H Baiocchi) (Individual: J Miller, USA, 277)	558 Marbella, Spain
1974	1 South Africa (R Cole and D Hayes); 2 Japan (I Aoki and M Ozaki) (Individual: R Cole, South Africa, 271)	554 Caracas
1975	1 United States (J Miller and L Graham); 2 Taiwan (H Min-Nan and KC Hsiung) (Individual: J Miller, USA, 275)	554 Bangkok
1976	1 Spain (S Ballesteros and M Pinero); 2 United States (J Pate and D Stockton) (Individual: EP Acosta, Mexico, 282)	574 Palm Springs
1977	1 Spain (S Ballesteros and A Garrido); 2 Philippines (R Lavares and B Arda) (Individual: G Player, South Africa, 289)	591 Manilla, Philippines
1978	1 United States (J Mahaffey and A North); 2 Australia (G Norman and W Grady) (Individual: J Mahaffey, USA, 281)	564 Hawaii
1979	1 United States (J Mahaffey and H Irwin); 2 Scotland (A Lyle and K Brown) (Individual: H Irwin, USA, 285)	575 Glyfada, Greece
1980	1 Canada (D Halldorson and J Nelford); 2 Scotland (A Lyle and S Martin) (Individual: A Lyle, Scotland, 282)	572 Bogota
1981	Not played	
1982	1 Spain (M Pinero and JM Canizares); 2 United States (B Gilder and B Clampett) (Individual: M Pinero, Spain, 281)	563 Acapulco
1983	1 United States (R Caldwell and J Cook); 2 Canada (D Barr and J Anderson) (Individual: D Barr, Canada, 276)	565 Pondok Inah, Jakarta
1984	1 Spain (JM Canizares and J Rivero); 2 Scotland (S Torrance and G Brand Jr) (Played over 54 holes because of storms – Individual: JM Canizares, Spain, 205)	414 Olgiata, Rome
1985	1 Canada (D Halidorson and D Barr); 2 England (H Clark and P Way) (Individual: H Clark, England, 272)	559 La Quinta, Calif.
1986	Not played	
1987	1 Wales* (I Woosnam and D Llewelyn); 2 Scotland (S Torrance and A Lyle) (*Wales won play-off – Individual: I Woosnam, Wales, 274)	574 Kapalua, Hawaii
1988	1 United States (B Crenshaw and M McCumber); 2 Japan (T Ozaki and M Ozaki) (Individual: B Crenshaw, USA, 275)	560 Royal Melbourne, Australia
1989	1 Australia (P Fowler and W Grady); 2 Spain (JM Olazábal and JM Canizares) (Played over 36 holes because of storms – Individual: P Fowler)	278 Las Brisas, Spain
1990	1 Germany (B Langer and T Giedeon); 2 England (M James and R Boxall) tied Ireland (R Rafferty and D Feherty) (Individual: P Stewart, USA, 271)	556 Grand Cypress Resort, Orlando, Florida
1991	1 Sweden (A Forsbrand and P-U Johansson); 2 Wales (I Woosnam and P Price) (Individual: I Woosnam, Wales, 273)	563 La Querce, Rome
1992	1 USA (F Couples and D Love III); 2 Sweden (A Forsbrand and P-U Johansson) (Individual: B Ogle*, Australia, 270 (*after a tie with Ian Woosnam, Wales))	548 La Moraleja II, Madrid, Spain
1993	1 USA (F Couples and D Love III); 2 Zimbabwe (N Price and M McNulty) (Individual: B Langer, Germany, 272)	556 Lake Nona, Orlando, Forida
1994	1 USA(F Couples and D Love III); 2 Zimbabwe (M McNulty and T Johnstone) (Individual: F Couples, USA, 265)	536 Dorado Beach, Puerto Rico
1995	1 USA (F Couples and D Love III); 2 Australia (B Ogle and R Allenby) (Individual: D Love III, USA, 267)	543 Mission Hills, Shenzhen, China

1996	1 South Africa (E Els and W Westner); 2 USA (T Lehman and S Jones) (Individual: E Els, S. Africa, 272)	547	Erinvale, Cape Town South Africa
1997	1 Ireland (P Harrington and P McGinley); 2 Scotland (C Montgomerie and R Russell) (Individual: C Montgomerie, Scotland, 266)	545	Kiawah Island, SC
1998	1 England (N Faldo and D Carter); 2 Italy (C Rocca and M Florioli) (Individual: Scott Verplank, USA, 279)	568	Auckland, New Zealand
1999	1 USA (T Woods and M O'Meara); 2 Spain (S Luna and MA Martin) (Individual: Tiger Woods, USA, 263)	545	The Mines Resort, K Lumpur, Malaysia
2000	1 USA (T Woods and D Duval); 2 Argentina (A Cabrera & E Romero)	254	Buenos Aires GC Argentina
2001	1 South Africa* (E Els and R Goosen); 2 New Zealand (M Campbell and D Smail)		The Taiheiyo Club,
	USA (D Duval and T Woods) tied	254	Japan
	Denmark (T Bjørn and S Hansen)		

*South Africa won at second extra hole

2002	1 Japan (S Maruyama and T Izawa); 2 USA (P Mickelson and D Toms)	252	Puerto Vallarta, Mexico
2003	1 South Africa (T Immelman and R Sabbatini); 2 England (J Rose and P Casey)	275	Kiawah Island, SC
2004	1 England (L Donald and P Casey); 2 Spain (MA Jiménez and S García)	257	Real Club de Sevilla, Spain

Reduced to 54 holes because of rain

2005	1 Wales (B Dredge and S Dodd); 2 Sweden (N Fasth and H Stenson)	189	Vilamoura, Portugal

Reduced to 54 holes because of bad weather

2006	1 Germany* (B Langer and M Siem); 2 Scotland (C Montgomerie and M Warren)	268	Sandy Lane Resort, Barbados

*Germany beat Scotland at first extra hole

2007	1 Scotland* (C Montgomerie and M Warren); 2 Germany (B Weekley and H Slocum)	263	Shenzhen, China

*Scotland beat USA at third extra hole

Golf economy worth €53 million in Europe, Middle East and Africa

Golf is a multi-billion euro enterprise worth €53 billion a year in Europe, the Middle East and Africa according to a pioneering study by the KPMG Golf Advisory Practice.

Nine leading golf bodies teamed up with KPMG to publish the report which also reveals the the game supported half-a-million jobs in the area and pays nearly €10 million in wages.

In GDP terms (the value of the industry once its costs have been subtracted), golf has contributed €14.5 billion to the economy, as much in a single year as the six Olympics before Beijing have done.

Although golf in Europe, the Middle East and Africa is a third of the size of the US golf industry, tourism revenue and golf real estate, the no.1 money earner in the region covered by the survey, now account for almost half the game's total revenue.

The Royal Trophy returns

The Royal Trophy, a Ryder Cup-style matchplay tournament, cancelled in 2008 to respect the death of the King of Thailand's sister, returned in 2009. The tournament, played annually between teams from Europe and Asia, returned to Bangkok, Thailand, in January. The European team captain, Seve Ballesteros, who founded the tournament in 2006, was unavailable as he struggled to regain fitness following surgery to remove a brain tumour.

The composition of the European team had not been announced at the end of 2008 but the captain of the Asian team, Japan's Joe Ozaki, announced that his squad would include Hideto Tanihara (JPN), Liang Wen-chong (CHN), Charlie Wi (KOR) and Prayad Marksaeng (THA).

Sir Bob Charles inducted in the Hall of Fame

Sir Bob Charles, whose victory in the 1963 Open Championship was the first by a left-hander, was one of six golfers inducted into the World Golf Hall of Fame in 2008. Those accepted for membership represent those who have had a positive impact on the game and comprise professional and amateur golfers, architects, journalists, innovators and teachers.

Sir Bob, the first New Zealander to have been honoured, won his first event oin the PGA Tour in 1963 and went on to win 23 times on the Champions Tour in the United States. Although now partially retired, the 72-year-old beat his age on the US Champions Tour in 11 of the 12 rounds he played.

He was joined in the Hall of Fame by Carole Semple Thompson, who won her first event when beating her mother in the Pennsylvanian Championship and went on to compete in more than 100 US Championships, winning seven of them. She played on 12 Curtis Cups and captained two more including the side that beat Great Britain and Ireland at St Andrews last year. She is the sixth female amateur to be inducted after Judy Bell, Dorothy Campbell from North Berwick in Scotland who won three US Women's amateur titles, two British, three Scottish and three Candians Championships as well, Glenna Collett Vare, Dinah Shore and Joyce Wethered.

Pete Dye, designer of over 120 courses with risk and reward options was also indicted along with three others posthumously – writer and journalist Herbert Warren Wind, who wrote for the *New Yorker* magazine and, along with Ben Hogan, the book *The Modern Fundamentals of Golf*, Craig Wood the professional often described as the Greg Norman of his day, and Denny Shute a quiet, shy winner of three majors.

There are currently 126 members in the World Golf Hall of Fame and for the record they are:

Amy Alcott	Leo Diegel	Alister MacKenzie	Thompson
Willie Anderson	Pete Dye	Charles Blair	Patty Sheehan
Isao Aoki	Chick Evans	Macdonald	Dinah Shore
Tommy Armour	Nick Faldo	Lloyd Mangrum	Denny Shute
John Ball Jr	Raymond Floyd	Carol Mann	Charlie Sifford
Seve Balleteros	Herb Graffis	Mark McCormack	Vijay Singh
Jim Barnes	Hubert Green	Cary Middlecoff	Horton Smith
Judy Bell	Ralph Guldahl	Johnny Miller	Marilynn Smith
Deane Beman	Walter Hagen	Tom Morris Jr	Sam Snead
Patty Berg	Marlene Bauer Hagge	Tom Morris Sr	Karsten Solheim
Tommy Bolt	Bob Marlow	Kel Nagle	Annika Sorenstam
Sir Michael Bonallack	Sandra Haynie	Byron Nelson	Payne Stewart
Julius Boros	Hisako "Chako"	Larry Nelson	Curtis Strange
Pat Bradley	Higuchi	Jack Nicklaus	Marlene Stewart
James Braid	Harold Hilton	Greg Norman.	Streit
Jack Burke Jr	Ben Hogan	Ayako Okamoto	Louise Suggs
Bill Campbell	Bob Hope	Francis Ouimet	JH Taylor
Donna Caponi	Dorothy Campbell	Se Ri Pak	Peter Thomson
JoAnne Carner	Hurd Howe	Arnold Palmer	Jerry Travers
Hoe Carr	Juli Inkster	Willie Park Sr	Walter Trvis
Billy Casper	Hale Irwin	Harvey Penick	Lee Trevino
Sir Bob Charles	Tony Jacklin	Henry Pickrd	Richard Tufts.
Neil Coles	John Jacobs	Gary Player	Harry Vardon
Harry Cooper	Betty Jameson	Nick Price	Glenna Collett Vare
Fred Corcoran	Bobby Jones	Judy Rankin	Tom Watson
Sir Henry Cotton	Robert Trent Jones Sr	Betsy Rawls	Karrie Webb
Ben Crenshaw	Betsy King	Clifford Roberts	Johyce Wethered
Bing Crosby.	Tom Kite	Allan Robertson	Kathy Whitworth
Beth Daniel	Bernhard Langer	Chi Chi Rodriguez	Herbert Warren Wind
Bernard Darwin	Lawson Little	Donald Ross and Paul	Craig Wood
Roberto de Vicenzo	Gene Littler	Runyan	Mickey Wright.
Jimmy Demret	Bobby Lock	Gene Sarazen	Babe Zaharias
Joe Dey	Nancy Lopez	Carole Semple	

National and Regional Championships 2008

National Championships

Glenmuir Club Professionals' Championship *Moortown*

1	Paul Simpson (West Berkshire)*		73-67-67-76—283
2	Andrew Barnett (North Wales GR)		71-68-69-75—283

Simpson won at second extra hole

3	Paul Wesselingh (Kedleston Park)		71-70-73-70—284

Year	Winner	Venue	Score
1973	DN Sewell	Calcot Park	276
1974	WB Murray	Calcot Park	275
1975	DN Sewell	Calcot Park	276
1976	WJ Ferguson	Moortown	283
1977	D Huish	Notts	284
1978	D Jones	Pannal	281
1979	D Jones	Pannal	278
1980	D Jagger	Turnberry	286
1981	M Steadman	Woburn	289
1982	D Durnian	Hill Valley	285
1983	J Farmer	Heaton Park	270
1984	D Durnian	Bolton Old Links	278
1985	R Mann	The Belfry	291
1986	D Huish	R Birkdale	278
1987	R Weir	Sandiway	273
1988	R Weir	Harlech	269
1989	B Barnes	Sandwich, Prince's	280
1990	A Webster	Carnoustie	292
1991	W McGill	King's Lynn	285
1992	J Hoskison	St Pierre	275
1993	C Hall	Coventry	274
1994	D Jones	North Berwick	278
1995	P Carman	West Hill	269
1996	B Longmuir	Co Louth	280
1997	B Rimmer	Northop	268
1998	M Jones	Royal St David's	280
1999	S Bebb*	Kings Lynn	283

Bebb beat Chris Hall and Paul Wesselingh at first extra hole

Year	Winner	Venue	Score
2000	R Cameron*	St Andrews	295

Cameron beat Russell Weir at second extra hole

Year	Winner	Venue	Score
2001	S Edwards	County Louth	275
2002	B Cameron	Saunton	280
2003	G Law	St Andrews Bay	280
2004	T Nash	Southport & Ainsdale	270
2005	M Ellis	Woodhall Spa	285
2006	P Wesselingh	Princes	279
2007	J Dwyer*	Royal Porthcawl	282

Beat A Barnett at 3rd extra hole

PGA Seniors' Championship *Slaley Hall*

1	Gordon J Brand (ENG)*		72-77-68-75—292
2	Gordon Brand Jr (SCO)		73-75-74-70—292

G J Brand won at the sixth extra hole

3	Eamonn Darcy (IRL)		74-74-74-71—293
	Sam Torrance (SCO)		76-75-75-67—293
	Juan Quiros (ESP)		73-71-76-73—293

Year	Winner	Venue	Score
1970	M Faulkner	Longniddry	288
1971	K Nagle	Elie	269
1972	K Bousfield	Longniddry	291
1973	K Nagle	Elie	270
1974	E Lester	Lundin	282
1975	K Nagle	Longniddry	268
1976	C O'Connor	Cambridgeshire Hotel	284
1977	C O'Connor	Cambridgeshire Hotel	288
1978	P Skerritt	Cambridgeshire Hotel	288
1979	C O'Connor	Cambridgeshire Hotel	280
1980	P Skerritt	Gleneagles Hotel	286
1981	C O'Connor	North Berwick	287
1982	C O'Connor	Longniddry	285
1983	C O'Connor	Burnham and Berrow	277
1984	E Jones	Stratford-upon-Avon	280
1985	N Coles	Pannal, Harrogate	284
1986	N Coles	Mere, Cheshire	276
1987	N Coles	Turnberry	279
1988	P Thomson	North Berwick	287
1989	N Coles	West Hill	277
1990	B Waites	Brough	269
1991	B Waites	Wollaton Park	277
1992	T Horton	Royal Dublin	290
1993	B Huggett	Sunningdale	204 (54)
1994	J Morgan	Sunningdale	203
1995	J Morgan	Sunningdale	204
1996	T Gale	The Belfry	284
1997	W Hall	The Belfry	277
1998	T Horton	The Belfry	277
1999	R Metherall	The Belfry	276
2000	J Grace	The Belfry	282
2001	I Stanley	Carden Park	278
2002	S Ebihara	Carden Park	267
2003	W Longmuir	Carden Park	271
2004	C Mason*	Carden Park	275

Mason beat Jim Rhodes and Seiji Ebihara after two extra holes

Year	Winner	Venue	Score
2005	S Torrance	Carden Park	271
2006	S Torrance	Stoke by Nayland	268
2007	C Mason	Stole by Nayland	268

Senior PGA Pros Championship *Northants County*

1	Bill Lockie (North Gailes)	72-71-68—211
2	Mike Gallagher (Farthingstone)	69-72-71—212
	Donald Stirling (Wien-Sussenbrunn)	69-72-71—212

| 2005 | S Graham | King's Lynn | 213 | 2007 | D Stirling | Northamptonshire | 211 |

PGA Assistants Championship *The London Club, Kent*

1	Guy Woodman (East Berkshire)	77-66-67—210
2	Jonathan Lupton (Middlesbrough)	73-71-70—214
3	Michael Mulryan (Athenry)	78-67-70—215

1984	G Weir	Coombe Hill	286	1997	P Sefton	De Vere, Blackpool	273
1985	G Coles	Coombe Hill	284	1998	A Raitt	Bearwood Lakes	280
1986	J Brennand	Sand Moor	280	1999	I Harrison	Bearwood Lakes	274
1987	J Hawksworth	Coombe Hill	282	2000	T Anderson	St Annes Old Links	273
1988	J Oates	Coventry	284	2001	C Goodfellow	St Annes Old Links	207
1989	C Brooks	Hillside	291	2002	D Orr	St Annes Old Links	271
1990	A Ashton	Hillside	213 (54)	2003	M Tottey*	St Annes Old Links	204
1991	S Wood	Wentworth	288	*Tottey beat Neil Ridewood at first extra hole			
1992	P Mayo	E Sussex National	285	2004	M Ford	Coventry	208
1993	C Everett	Oaklands	280	2005	M Tottey	The London Club	211
1994	M Plummer	Burnham & Berrow	278	2006	B Taylor	The London Club	206
1995	I Sparkes	The Warwickshire	285	2007	J Lupton	The London Club	213
1996	S Purves	Moor Allerton	281				

Southern Open *The Drift*

1	Matthew Ford (Tudor Park)	66-70-69-69—274
2	Steven Cowie (Hoebridge Centre)	69-70-66-71—276
3	Gary Marks (World of Golf)	74-67-71-66—278

| 2006 | G Marks | 2007 | J Ablett |

Irish PGA Championship *The European Club*

1	Padraig Harrington (unattached)	75-68-70-72—285
2	Philip Walton (unattached)	73-73-73-70—289
3	David Higgins (Waterville)	80-72-69-70—291

1944	H Bradshaw	Hermitage	291	1972	J Kinsella	Bundoran	289
1945	J McKenna	Newlands	283	1973	J Kinsella	Limerick	284
1946	F Daly	Clandeboye	285	1974	E Polland	Portstewart	277
1947	H Bradshaw	County Louth	291	1975	C O'Connor	Carlow	275
1948	J McKenna	Galway	285	1976	P McGuirk	Waterville	291
1949	C Kane	Portrush	301	1977	P Skerritt	Woodbrook	281
1950	H Bradshaw	Grange	277	1978	C O'Connor	Dollymount	286
1951	H Bradshaw	Balmoral	280	1979	D Smyth	Dollymount	215 (54)
1952	F Daly	Mullingar	284	1980	D Feherty	Dollymount	283
1953	H Bradshaw	Dundalk	272	1981	D Jones	Woodbrook	283
1954	H Bradshaw	Newcastle	300	1982	D Feherty	Woodbrook	287
1955	E Jones	Castleroy	276	1983	L Higgins	Woodbrook	275
1956	C Greene	Clandeboye	281	1984	M Sludds	Skerries	277
1957	H Bradshaw	Ballybunion	286	1985	D Smyth	Co Louth	204 (54)
1958	C O'Connor	Royal Belfast	279	1986	D Smyth	Waterville	282
1959	NV Drew	Mullingar	282	1987	P Walton	Co Louth	144 (36)
1960	C O'Connor	Warrenpoint	271	1988	E Darcy	Castle, Dublin	269
1961	C O'Connor	Lahinch	280	1989	P Walton	Castle, Dublin	266
1962	C O'Connor	Bangor	264	1990	D Smyth	Woodbrook	271
1963	C O'Connor	Little Island	271	1991	P Walton	Woodbrook	277
1964	E Jones	Knock	279	1992	E Darcy	K Club	285
1965	C O'Connor	Mullingar	283	1993	M Sludds	K Club	285
1966	C O'Connor	Warrenpoint	269	1994	D Clarke	Galway Bay	285
1967	H Boyle	Tullamore	214 (54)	1995	P Walton	Belvoir Park	273
1968	C Greene	Knock	282	1996	D Smyth	Slieve Russell GC	281
1969	J Martin	Dundalk	268	1997	P McGinley	Fota Island	285
1970	H Jackson	Massareene	283	1998	P Harrington*	Powerscourt	216 (54)
1971	C O'Connor	Galway	278	*Harrington won at first extra hole			

1999	N Manchip	The Island	271
2000	P McGinley	Co Louth	270
2001	D Smyth	Castle Rock	273
2002	P McGinley	Westport	213
2003	P McGinley	Adare Manor	280
2004	P Harrington	St Margaret's	287

2005	P Harrington*	Palmerston House	285
*Harrington won at first extra hole			
2006	D Mortimer	Druids Heath	286
2007	P Harrington*	The European Club	279
*Beat B McGovern at 1st extra hole			

Irish Club Professionals Tournament *Dundalk*

1	John Kelly (St Margaret's)	68-72—140
2	Eamonn Brady (Clontarf)	73-68—141
	Darren McWilliams (unattached)	71-70—141

1993	D Mooney	Royal Tara	208
1994	K O'Donnell	Knockanally	216
1995	D Jones	Fota Island	145
1996	B McGovern	Headfort	140
1997	N Manchip	Mount Wolseley	141
1998	L Robinson	Nuremore	140
1999	N Manchip	Nuremore	139
2000	L Walker	Nuremore	134
2001	M Allen*	Nuremore	142
*Allen won at second extra hole			

2002	N Manchip	Nuremore	135
2003	D Mooney*	Tulfarris	142
*Mooney wn at first extra hole			
2004	C Mallon*	Enniscrone	144
*Mallon won at second extra hole			
2005	S Thornton*	Lisburn	138
*Thornton won at fourth extra hole			
2006	P O'Hagan	Rathsallagh	138
2007	L Walker*	Dundalk	140
*Beat P Martin at 2nd extra hole			

Gleneagles SPGA Championship *PGA Centenary GC*

1	Jason McCreadie (Buchanan Castle)	73-69-71-72—285
2	Graeme Lornie (Kings Links)	69-74-74-70—287
3	Chris Doak (unattached)	74-76-67-71—288

1907	J Hunter	1929	D McCulloch	1953	H Thomson	1971	BJ Gallacher	1990	R Drummond
1908	R Thomson	1930	D McCulloch	1954	J Panton	1972	H Bannerman	1991	S Torrance
1909	TR Fernie	1931	M Seymour	1955	J Panton	1973	BJ Gallacher	1992	P Lawrie
1910	TR Fernie	1932	R Dornan	1956	EC Brown	1974	BJ Gallacher	1993	S Torrance
1911	E Sinclair	1933	M Seymour	1957	EC Brown	1975	D Huish	1994	A Coltart
1912	WM Watt	1934	M Seymour	1958	EC Brown	1976	John Chillas	1995	C Gillies
1913	A Marling	1935	M McDowall	1959	J Panton	1977	BJ Gallacher	1996	B Marchbank
1914	DP Watt	1936	J Forrester	1960	EC Brown	1978	S Torrance	1997	G Law
1915–18	Not played	1937	WM Hastings	1961	RT Walker	1979	AWB Lyle	1998	C Gillies
1919	TR Fernie	1938	JH Ballingall	1962	EC Brown	1980	S Torrance	1999	G Hutcheon
1920	TR Fernie	1939	W Davis	1963	WM Miller	1981	B Barnes	2000	A Forsyth
1921	P Robertson	1940–45	Not played	1964	RT Walker	1982	B Barnes	2001	J Chillas
1922	GE Smith	1946	W Anderson	1965	EC Brown	1983	BJ Gallacher	2002	F Mann
1923	AW Butchart	1947	J McCondichie	1966	EC Brown	1984	I Young	2003	C Kelly
1924	P Robertson	1948	J Panton		J Panton	1985	S Torrance	2004	C Ronald
1925	S Burns	1949	J Panton	1967	H Bannerman	1986	R Drummond	2005	P Lawrie
1926	T Wilson	1950	J Panton	1968	EC Brown	1987	R Drummond	2006	D Robertson
1927	S Burns	1951	J Panton	1969	G Cunningham	1988	S Stephen	2007	M Loftus
1928	S Burns	1952	J Campbell	1970	RDBM Shade	1989	R Drummond		

Scottish Young Professionals Championship *Muckhart GC*

1	Greg McBain (Royal Dornoch)	67-70-67—204
2	David Orr (East Renfrewshire)	69-69-67—205
3	Craig Matheson (Falkirk Tryst)	66-69-71—206

1958	J Carter	1972	TC Maltman		
1959	W Mcondichie	1973	R Fyfe		
1960	RT Walker	1974	J Noon		
1961	RT Walker	1975	TC Maltman		
1962	RT Walker	1976	TC Maltman		
1963	RT Walker	1977	Not played		
1964	L Taylor	1978	J McCallum		
1965	D Huish	1979	S Kelly		
1966	J Steven	1980	N Cameron		
1967	H McCorquodale	1980	F Mann	Dunbar	294
1968	N Wood	*Played twice in 1980*			
1969	D Ross	1981	M Brown	West Kilbride	290
1970	WR Lockie	1982	R Collinson	West Kilbride	294
1971	J Hamilton	1983	A Webster	Stirling	285

1984	C Elliott	Stirling	285	1996	S Thompson	Newmacher	278
1985	C Elliott	Falkirk Tryst	284	1997	M Hastie	Balbirnie Park	275
1986	P Helsby	Erskine	295	1998	D Orr	Balbirnie Park	272
1987	C Innes	Hilton Park	284	1999	A Forsyth	Balbirnie Park	269
1988	G Collinson	Turnberry	289	2000	C Lee	Balbirnie Park	275
1989	C Brooks	Windyhill	282	2001	C Kelly	Spey Bay	275
1990	P Lawrie	Cruden Bay	279	2002	C Kelly	Spey Bay	277
1991	G Hume	Kilmarnock Barassie	299	2003	G Dingwall	Balbirnie Park	281
1992	E McIntosh	Turnberry Hotel	266	2004	G Duncan	Forres	269
1993	J Wither	Alloa	280	2005	A Lockhart	Forres	275
1994	S Henderson	Newmacher	283	2006	C Nicholl	Forres	266
1995	A Tait	Newmacher	276	2007	K Glen	Muckhart	279

Paul Lawrie Young Professionals Matchplay Championship   Newburgh on Ythan

Semi-finals:
Greg McBain (Royal Dornoch) beat James McGhee (Turnhouse) 5 and 4
Graeme Lornie (Kings Links) beat Jamie Wales (Kings Acre) 6 and 4

Final:
Greg McBain beat Graeme Lornie 6 and 4

2005	Chris Campbell (Carnegie Club)	2006	Tom Buchanan (Duddingston)	2007	Stephen Lamb (Broomieknowe)

Northern Open   Spey Valle

1	Chris Doak (unattached)	68-70-70-66—274
2	Lee Harper (Archerfield Links)	70-69-69-69—277
3	Euan Little (Co.Tipperary)	70-73-67-71—281
	Paul McKechnie (Braid Hills)	73-71-66-71—281

1931	J McDowell	1952	J Panton	1966	R Liddle	1981	AP Thomson	1995	J Higgins
1931	JT Henderson	1953	EC Brown	1967	H Bannerman	1982	AR Marshall	1996	S Henderson
1932	J McLean	1954	EC Brown	1968	DK Webster	1983	DA Cooper	1997	D Thomson
1933	J Forrester	1955	EC Brown	1969	H Bannerman		(ENG)	1998	L James
1934	RS Walker	1956	J Panton	1970	AK Pirie	1984	D Huish	1999	A Forsyth
1935	RS Walker	1957	EC Brown	1971	F Rennie	1985	B Barnes	2000	J Payne (ENG)
1936	Jack McLean	1958	G Will	1972	H Bannerman	1986	RD Weir	2001	G Rankin
1937	TB Haliburton	1959	J Panton	1973	D Huish	1987	AJ Hunter	2002	F Mann
1938	Jack McLean	1960	J Panton	1974	WTG Milne	1988	D Huish	2003	G Law
1939–46	Not played	1961	H Weetman	1975	WTG Milne	1989	C Brooks	2004	J McCreadie
1947	JH Ballingall		(ENG)	1976	D Chillas	1990	C Brooks	2005	C Doak
1948	J Panton	1962	J Panton	1977	JE Murray	1991	C Cassells	2006	J McCreadie*
1949	JH Ballingall	1963	G Will	1978	B Barnes	1992	P Smith		*Beat C Doak at 1st
1950	EC Brown	1964	LR Taylor	1979	JC Farmer	1993	K Stables		extra hole
1951	J Panton	1965	JT Brown	1980	D Huish	1994	K Stables	2007	M Urquhart

RCW Welsh National Championship   Cardiff

1	Trevor Jones (Hambrook GR)	70-70-69—209
2	Richard Dinsdale (Parc Golf Academy)	70-73-68—211
3	James Lee (Caerphilly)	73-71-69—213
	Lee Rooke (Vale of Llangollen)	75-69-69—213

1960	RH Kemp Jr	Llandudno	288	1975	C DeFoy	Whitchurch	285
1961	S Mouland	Southerndown	286	1976	S Cox	Radyr	284
1962	S Mouland	Porthcawl	302	1977	C DeFoy	Glamorganshire	135
1963	H Gould	Wrexham	291	1978	BCC Huggett	Whitchurch	145
1964	B Bielby	Tenby	297	1979	Cancelled		
1965	S Mouland	Penarth	281	1980	A Griffiths	Cardiff	139
1966	S Mouland	Conway	281	1981	C DeFoy	Cardiff	139
1967	S Mouland	Pyle and Kenfig	219 (54)	1982	C DeFoy	Cardiff	137
1968	RJ Davies	Southerndown	292	1983	S Cox	Cardiff	136
1969	S Mouland	Llandudno	277	1984	K Jones	Cardiff	135
1970	W Evans	Tredegar Park	289	1985	D Llewellyn	Whitchurch	132
1971	J Buckley	St Pierre	291	1986	P Parkin	Whitchurch	142
1972	J Buckley	Porthcawl	298	1987	A Dodman	Cardiff	132
1973	A Griffiths	Newport	289	1988	I Woosnam	Cardiff	137
1974	M Hughes	Cardiff	284	1989	K Jones	Royal Porthcawl	140

1990	P Mayo	Fairwood Park	136	1999	R Dinsdale	Vale of Glamorgan	134
1991	P Mayo	Fairwood Park	138	2000	M Plummer	Newport	136
1992	C Evans	Asburnham	142	2001	S Dodd	Ashburnham	214
1993	P Price	Caerphilly	138	2002	S Edwards	Pyle & Kenfig	210
1994	M Plummer	Northop	133	2003	S Edwards	Porthmadog	196
1995	S Dodd	Northop	139	2004	M Plummer	Vale of Llangollen	203
1996	M Stanford	Northop	137	2005	S Bebb	Vale of Glamorgan	199
1997	M Ellis	Vale of Glamorgan	139	2006	S Bebb	Tenby	203
1998	L Bond	Vale of Glamorgan	69 (18)	2007	S Dodd	Cardiff	200

Welsh Open PGA Championship *Royal St David's*

1	Chris Doak (unattached)	68-70-70-66—274
2	Lee Harper (Archerfield Links)	70-69-69-69—277
3	Euan Little (Co.Tipperary)	70-73-67-71—281
	Paul McKechnie (Braid Hills)	73-71-66-71—281

2006	L Bond	St Pierre	209
2007	S Dodd*	St Pierre	208

Beat I Walley at 3rd extra hole

The R&A increases its support of the Paul Lawrie Foundation

The R&A has increased its financial backing of the Paul Lawrie Foundation in response to the continued success of the programme. The foundation, which supports junior golf in the north-east of Scotland, was been awarded £25,000 to cover both 2008 and 2009.

Lawrie, a native Aberdonian who spends much time and effort on junior golf, was pleased to accept the grant. "I'm extremely grateful for the increased support of this programme," said Lawrie, "It's a big boost knowing that The R&A are as dedicated as I am to the development of the junior game in Scotland."

The scheme encourages golf through fun games and competitions throughout the year, the largest of which is the Paul Lawrie Flag Finals and U16/U18 Open. This year the event was held at Deeside Golf Club in September with 160 youngsters aged between nine and eighteen turning up to compete.

The 1999 Open Champion aims to encourage the youngsters to develop a work ethic that will improve both their golf and their academic achievement. "I would never have won The Open at Carnoustie without putting in countless hours of practice," he noted, "and I hope that the Foundation will instill in these juniors a similar level of commitment in all aspects of their lives."

On the day, Lawrie also treated players and spectators alike to a fine display of shot-making on the driving range and all present were thrilled with the opportunity to interact so closely with a former Open Champion.

The R&A also supports junior golf programmes in Carnoustie and St Andrews, which like the Paul Lawrie Foundation, are aimed at encouraging local children to try the game. Director of Golf Development at The R&A, Duncan Weir, believes that it is important to provide golfing opportunities to children in Scotland.

"Supporting junior golf here in Scotland, where we are based, is a key aspect of The R&A's work," said Weir, "and we're glad to be able to provide funding for schemes that are increasing participation and enjoyment in the junior game."

Regional Championships

Bedford & Cambridge PGA

2005	D Charlton	2007	P Simpson
2006	D Charlton	2008	D Charlton

Berks, Bucks & Oxon

Professionals		Players	
2005	N Rowlands	2005	P Simpson
2006	G Laird	2006	J Hoskinson
2007	P Simpson	2007	P Simpson
2008	L Jackson	2008	L Jackson

Cheshire & North Wales Open

2005	C Hodges	2007	L Harpin
2006	I Keenan	2008	A Barnett

Cornish Festival

2008	David Dixon

Derbyshire Professionals

2005	P Wesselingh	2007	J Whatley
2006	D Bartlett	2008	M Smith

Devon Open

2005	B Austin	2007	S Mason
2006	B Austin	2008	C Gil

East Anglian Open

2005	I Ellis	2007	D Poulter
2006	D Charlton	2008	D Charlton

East Region PGA

2005	S Standing	2007	R Coles
2006	J Bevitt	2008	P Curry

Essex Open

2005	M Davis	2007	S Cipa
2006	S Khan	2008	J Fryatt

Essex PGA

2005	S Cipa	2007	R Gray
2006	D Turner	2008	B Taylor

Gloucestershire & Somerset

2007	G Ryall	2008	T Jones

Hampshire PGA

2005	R Edwards	2007	B Parker
2006	D Porter	2008	E Rawlings

Hampshire Match Play

2005	D Porter	2007	G Stubbington
2006	A Mew	2008	JBarnes

Hampshire, Isle of Wight and Channel Islands Open

2005	N Smith	2007	J Barnes
2006	M Blackey	2008	D Porter

Herts Professionals

2005	A Clapp	2007	A Clapp (S)
2006	M Bird	2008	R Leonard

Kent Open

2005	M Belsham	2007	F McGuirk
2006	R McGuirk	2008	R Wallis

Lancashire Open

2005	D Shacklady	2007	B Taylor
2006	S Walsh	2008	J Cheetham

Lancashire PGA

2007	D Shacklady	2008	D Smith

Leeds Cup (Stroke Play)

2005	S Edwards (WAL)	2007	J Wells
2006	N Price	2008	S Barber

Leicestershire & Rutland Open

2005	J Palmer (am)	2007	I Lyner
2006	J Herbert	2008	C Fromont

Lincolnshire Open

2005	P Streeter	2007	A Keogh (am)
2006	P Streeter	2008	N Bark

Lincolnshire Professionals

2005	D Drake (M)	2007	J Fulton (S)
	M Evans (S)	2008	D Greenwood (M)
2006	S Bennett (M)		S Bennett (S)
	N Evans (S)		

Manchester Open (Stroke Play)

2005	R Bean	2007	D Smith
2006	R Wragg	2008	Cancelled

Middlesex PGA (Stroke Play)

2005	N Wichelow	2007	Not played
2006	L Clarke	2008	Not played

Midland Professionals

2005	A Carey	2007	S Whiffen
2006	P Streeter	2008	I Walley

Midland Open

2005	D Prosser	2007	G Woolgar
2006	P Streeter (S)	2008	C Clark

Norfolk Open

2005	N Lythgoe	2007	N Lythgoe
2006	S Ballingale (am)	2008	S Ballinhall

Northamptonshire PGA

2007	S Lilly (S)	2008	S Lilly (M+S)

North East Masters (Stroke Play)

2005	K Ferrie	2007	C Paisley (am)
2006	A Wainwright	2008	J Graham

North East/North West

2008	V Guest

North Region PGA

2005	C Corrigan	2007	J Harrison
2006	M Bradley	2008	A Bell

Northumberland & Durham Open

2005	G Bell	2007	D Clark
2006	T Henderson	2008	G Bell

Notts PGA

2005	M Foulkes	2007	J Lines (M)
2006	K Crossland (M)		L Clarke (S)
	P Edwards (S)	2008	P Bagshaw (M)
			P Edwards (S)

Shropshire & Hereford Open

2005	B Ruddick	2007	J Griffiths
2006	D Harris (am)	2008	M Harrison (am)

Shropshire & Hereford PGA

2005	S Russell	2007	N Dulson
2006	S Russell	2008	K Preece

Southern Assistants

2005	G Willman (M)	2007	I Campbell
	J Ablett (S)		
2006	N Clark (M)		
	M Freeland (S)		

Southern Masters

2008	M McLean	2008	M McLean

Southern Professionals

2005	P Sherman	2007	C Roake
2006	G Shoesmith	2008	M Ford

Staffordshire Open

2005	B Rimmer	2007	R O'Hanlon
2006	B Rimmer	2008	D Prosser

Staffordshire PGA

2008	B Rimmer

South Wales Festival

2008	A Smith	2008	A Smith

Suffolk Open

2005	J Abbott (am)	2008	A Collison (M)
2006	S Dainty		A Meredith (S)
2007	A Meredith (am)		

Suffolk PGA

2005	S Harrison (M)	2007	S Warren (M)
	R Mann (S)		A Collison (S)
2006	P Bate (M)	2008	R Beades (M)
	R Mann (S)		A Collison (S)

Surrey Open

2005	I Golding	2007	M McLean
2006	L Atkinson	2008	G Marks

Sussex Open

2005	P Jones	2007	B Newsome (am)
2006	R Fenwick	2008	B Martin

Ulster PGA

2005	S Thornton	2007	M Staunton
2006	D Mooney	2008	E Brady

Warwickshire Open

2005	A Carey	2007	R Kirwan (am)
2006	A Sullivan (am)	2008	A Sullivan (am)

Warwickshire Professionals

2005	A Bownes (S)	2007	C Clark (M+S)
2006	C Clark*	2008	C Clark

*after 6-hole play-off

West Region PGA

2005	M Plummer	2007	C Gill
2006	G Brand Jr	2008	L Thompson

Hills Wiltshire Professionals

2005	M Griffin	2007	S Armor
2006	M Butler	2008	D Hutton

Worcestershire Open

2005	J Jones	2007	S Lane
2006	M Butler	2008	*Cancelled*

Worcestershire PGA

2005	M Sandry	2008	M Butler
2006	D Hutton		
2007	D Prosser*		

*beat L Jones at 4th extra
hole

Yorkshire Open

2005	J Wells	2007	*Not played*
2006	*Not played*	2008	D Dennison

Yorkshire Professionals

2005	G Brand	2007	A Ambler
2006	J Wells	2008	J King

Alliss reappointed PGA Cup captain

Gary Alliss has been given the chance to avenge defeat by the Americans after being reappointed captain of the Great Britain and Ireland PGA Cup team.

The Belfry head professional will lead the team for the 24th staging of the matches against the United States which are being held The Carrick course at The De Vere Deluxe Resort Cameron House on the banks of Loch Lomond in September.

Alliss, whose side came within half a point of making history with a first ever victory in the United States last September, is only the fourth man to captain the team twice since the tournament's inception in 1973.

The 53-year-old, who received a PGA Master Professional award at Royal Birkdale on the eve of last year's Open, is delighted to have been given the opportunity to lead the team for a second tine in what is the equivalent of the club professionals' Ryder Cup.

Alliss will be in charge of a 10-man team whose make-up will be decided via qualification from the 2008 and 2009 Glenmuir PGA Professional Championship.

Having come so close to being the first man to lead a GB&I team to victory in America following the 13½ to 12½ defeat, Alliss is eager to retain the trophy, which had been won by his grandfather Percy and was donated to the PGA by his father Peter.

Month by month in 2008

Tiger Woods, out of action since knee surgery straight after The Masters, returns at the US Open and despite being in real pain birdies the final hole to get into a play-off with Rocco Mediate and plays another 19 holes before winning his 14th and most incredible major title. Two days later he announces he is out for the year and will undergo cruciate ligament reconstruction. It also emerges he played at Torrey Pines with a double stress fracture in his leg.

PART III

Women's Professional Tournaments

Rolex Women's World Golf

Rankings at the end of the European, American and Japanese Tour seasons

Rank	Name	Country	Events	Total	Average
1	Lorena Ochoa	MEX	47	16.15	759.07
2	Yani Tseng	TPE	35	9.50	332.42
3	Annika Sörenstam	SWE	41	9.13	374.28
4	Paula Creamer	USA	53	8.16	432.32
5	Suzann Pettersen	NOR	52	7.79	405.04
6	Ji-Yai Shin	KOR	59	7.25	427.88
7	Cristie Kerr	USA	50	6.01	300.63
8	Helen Alfredsson	SWE	39	5.83	227.21
9	Angela Stanford	USA	51	5.38	274.51
10	Karrie Webb	AUS	46	5.04	231.61
11	Seon-Hwa Lee	KOR	58	4.69	271.88
12	Yuri Fudoh	JPN	45	4.54	204.29
13	Jeong Jang	KOR	55	4.38	241.02
14	Momoko Ueda	JPN	63	4.20	264.47
15	Jee Young Lee	KOR	54	4.19	226.28
16	Maria Hjorth	SWE	55	4.16	228.69
17	Eun-Hee Ji	KOR	57	4.12	234.63
18	Hee-Won Han	KOR	36	4.02	144.88
19	Morgan Pressel	USA	53	3.94	208.69
20	Karen Stupples	ENG	34	3.74	130.93
21	Inbee Park	KOR	57	3.68	209.99
22	Angela Park	BRA	56	3.64	204.09
23	Laura Diaz	USA	51	3.63	185.25
24	Candie Kung	TPE	44	3.53	155.43
25	In Kyung Kim	KOR	53	3.52	186.37
26	Juli Inkster	USA	39	3.46	134.99
27	Sakura Yokomine	JPN	67	3.42	229.16
28	Na Yeon Choi	KOR	51	3.41	173.85
29	Katherine Hull	AUS	58	3.34	193.88
30	Mi Hyun Kim	KOR	49	3.29	161.19
31	Se Ri Pak	KOR	43	3.16	135.83
32	Nicole Castrale	USA	50	3.04	151.92
33	Sophie Gustafson	SWE	53	2.98	158.07
34	Miho Koga	JPN	70	2.83	198.26
35	Song-Hee Kim	KOR	48	2.83	135.83
36	Stacy Prammanasudh	USA	48	2.77	132.81
37	Ai Miyazato	JPN	54	2.76	149.17
38	Catriona Matthew	SCO	46	2.73	125.76
39	Christina Kim	USA	58	2.67	154.86
40	Mi-Jeong Jeon	KOR	64	2.65	169.32
41	Shiho Oyama	JPN	58	2.62	152.04
42	Natalie Gulbis	USA	46	2.61	119.93
43	Ji-Hee Lee	KOR	57	2.55	145.55
44	Akiko Fukushima	JPN	56	2.52	141.03
45	Shi-Hyun Ahn	KOR	37	2.51	92.76
46	Brittany Lang	USA	54	2.46	133.06
47	Jane Park	USA	41	2.33	95.37
48	Shanshan Feng	CHN	31	2.16	75.48
49	Hyun-Ju Shin	KOR	53	2.16	114.23
50	Yuko Mitsuka	JPN	62	2.14	132.80

Ladies' European Tour

www.ladieseuropeantour.com

Final New Star Money List

(figures in brackets show number of tournaments played)

1	Gwladys Nocera (FRA)	(23)	€391,839
2	Helen Alfredsson (SWE)	(3)	320,099
3	Martina Eberl (GER)	(20)	227,296
4	Amy Yang (KOR)	(17)	227,179
5	Anja Monke (GER)	(21)	184,778
6	Suzann Pettersen (NOR)	(4)	183,278
7	Lotta Wahlin (SWE)	(19)	181,114
8	Paula Marti (ESP)	(19)	162,698
9	Lisa Hall (ENG)	(22)	157,288
10	Rebecca Hudson (ENG)	(18)	145,275
11	Laura Davies (ENG)	(13)	139,013
12	Melissa Reid (ENG)	(16)	136,606
13	Anne-Lise Caudal (FRA)	(20)	134,170
14	Tania Elosegui (ESP)	(20)	126,958
15	Becky Brewerton (WAL)	(20)	126,754
16	Marianne Skarpnord (NOR)	(21)	125,753
17	Veronica Zorzi (ITA)	(18)	112,358
18	Annika Sorenstam (SWE)	(6)	102,159
19	Joanne Mills (AUS)	(20)	99,924
20	Emma Zackrisson (SWE)	(20)	99,178
21	Iben Tinning (DEN)	(16)	95,617
22	Nina Reis (SWE)	(16)	92,156
23	Georgina Simpson (ENG)	(22)	91,650
24	Samantha Head (ENG)	(21)	91,014
25	Felicity Johnson (ENG)	(23)	90,360
26	Carmen Alonso (ESP)	(18)	89,736
27	Lisa Holm Sorensen (DEN)	(21)	89,210
28	Louise Stahle (SWE)	(11)	81,028
29	Diana Luna (ITA)	(18)	78,839
30	Ursula Wikstrom (FIN)	(22)	77,323
31	Lynn Brooky (NZL)	(21)	74,436
32	Maria Boden (SWE)	(19)	72,613
33	Minea Blomqvist (FIN)	(6)	71,386
34	Trish Johnson (ENG)	(18)	67,782
35	Maria Hjorth (SWE)	(5)	62,335
36	Johanna Westerberg (SWE)	(19)	58,615
37	Lora Fairclough (ENG)	(17)	55,351
38	Nikki Garrett (AUS)	(21)	55,065
39	Kirsty S Taylor (ENG)	(24)	54,431
40	Marta Prieto (ESP)	(19)	54,194
41	Karen Lunn (AUS)	(23)	51,837
42	Emma Cabrera-Bello (ESP)	(18)	51,325
43	Stacy Lee Bregman (RSA)	(17)	50,937
44	Federica Piovano (ITA)	(17)	50,616
45	Stefania Croce (ITA)	(17)	49,145
46	Sophie Gustafson (SWE)	(7)	48,796
47	Caroline Afonso (FRA)	(18)	47,673
48	Clare Queen (SCO)	(22)	46,321
49	Catriona Matthew (SCO)	(4)	43,862
50	Martina Gillen (IRL)	(20)	43,058
51	Sophie Giquel (FRA)	(5)	41,055
52	Cecilia Ekelundh (SWE)	(14)	39,837
53	Dana Lacey (AUS)	(21)	39,687
54	Anna Rawson (AUS)	(8)	39,295
55	Maria Verchenova (RUS)	(14)	38,262
56	Melodie Bourdy (FRA)	(19)	38,207
57	Marina Arruti (ESP)	(20)	38,010
58	Jade Schaeffer (FRA)	(19)	37,548
59	Beatriz Recari (ESP)	(15)	37,251
60	Leah Hart (AUS)	(19)	36,841
61	Julie Tvede (DEN)	(19)	35,343
62	Denise-Charlotte Becker (GER)	(18)	35,004
63	Lill Kristin Saether (NOR)	(16)	34,356
64	Lee-Anne Pace (RSA)	(20)	34,343
65	Titiya Plucksataporn (THA)	(22)	33,188
66	Ludivine Kreutz (FRA)	(20)	32,704
67	Christine Hallstrom (SWE)	(18)	32,357
68	Laura Cabanillas (ESP)	(16)	31,286
69	Ashleigh Simon (RSA)	(7)	30,485
70	Rebecca Coakley (IRL)	(21)	27,502
71	Kiran Matharu (ENG)	(17)	27,314
72	Johanna Head (ENG)	(8)	27,274
73	Eva Steinberger (AUT)	(23)	26,770
74	Anna Knutsson (SWE)	(18)	26,709
75	Ana B Sanchez (ESP)	(14)	25,102
76	Laurette Maritz (RSA)	(23)	24,957
77	Nicole Gergely (AUT)	(17)	24,952
78	Julie Greciet (FRA)	(17)	24,589
79	Katharina Schallenberg (GER)	(17)	24,074
80	Anna Tybring (SWE)	(20)	22,982
81	Sophie Walker (ENG)	(24)	22,962
82	Laura Terebey (USA)	(17)	22,936
83	Marjet van der Graaff (NED)	(21)	22,908
84	Lydia Hall (WAL)	(21)	22,896
85	Mianne Bagger (DEN)	(19)	22,195
86	Virginie Lagoutte-Clement (FRA)	(8)	21,944
87	Cassandra Kirkland (FRA)	(22)	21,690
88	Yuki Sakurai (JPN)	(7)	21,676
89	Amanda Moltke-Leth (DEN)	(19)	21,431
90	Ellen Smets (BEL)	(21)	21,370
91	Lynn Kenny (SCO)	(24)	21,017
92	Stefanie Michl (AUT)	(19)	20,603
93	Frances Bondad (AUS)	(21)	20,300
94	Carin Koch (SWE)	(5)	20,271
95	Margherita Rigon (ITA)	(23)	19,717
96	Linda Wessberg (SWE)	(8)	19,201
97	Lara Tadiotto (BEL)	(19)	19,005
98	Stephanie Arricau (FRA)	(17)	18,687
99	Natalie Claire Booth (ENG)	(17)	18,484
100	Anna Rossi (ITA)	(24)	17,843

2008 Tour Statistics

Stroke average

		Rnds.	Pts Av.			Rnds.	Pts Av.
1	Suzann Pettersen (NOR)	15	68.60	6 Karen Stupples (ENG)		5	70.80
2	Annika Sörenstam (SWE)	18	69.50	7 Maria Hjorth (SWE)		19	70.89
3	Gwladys Nocera (FRA)	75	70.52	8 Amy Yang (KOR)		53	71.04
4	Sophie Gustafson (SWE)	21	70.71	9 Helen Alfredsson (SWE)		10	71.10
5	Liselotte Neumann (SWE)	4	70.75	10 Louise Stahle (SWE)		30	71.30

Driving accuracy

		Holes	%			Holes	%
1	Dale Reid (SCO)	54	100.00	6 Corinne Dibnah (AUS)		54	85.19
2	Caroline Grady (ENG)	82	92.68	7 Sophie Sandolo (ITA)		598	83.66
3	Rebecca Hudson (ENG)	627	86.44	8 Lynn Brooky (NZL)		741	82.73
4	Georgina Simpson (ENG)	774	86.05	9 Laura Cabanillas (ESP)		607	81.88
5	Suzanne O'Brien (IRL)	28	85.71	10 Frederique Seeholzer (SUI)		447	81.43

Driving distance

		Holes	Av.			Holes	Av.
1	Carmen Alonso (ESP)	36	289.42	6 Jade Schaeffer (FRA)		50	271.88
2	Sandra Carlborg (SWE)	3	287.67	7 Caroline Afonso (FRA)		40	271.65
3	Sophie Gustafson (SWE)	11	276.09	8 Lisa Holm Sorensen (DEN)		53	267.92
4	Suzann Pettersen (NOR)	3	275.00	9 Maria Hjorth (SWE)		9	267.78
5	Ana B Sanchez (ESP)	20	272.60	10 Veronica Zorzi (ITA)		41	266.54

Greens in regulation

		Holes	%			Holes	%
1	Louise Friberg (SWE)	36	86.11	6 Gwladys Nocera (FRA)		152	79.25
2	Suzann Pettersen (NOR)	90	84.44	7 Annika Sörenstam (SWE)		72	79.17
3	Liselotte Neumann (SWE)	36	83.33	8 Laura Davies (ENG)		612	77.94
4	Sophie Gustafson (SWE)	198	81.82	9 Helena A Nordstrom (SWE)		72	77.78
5	Charlotta Sörenstam (SWE)	36	80.56	10 Tania Elosegui (ESP)		864	77.31

Average putts per round

		Rnds	Av.			Rnds	Av.
1	Catriona Matthew (SCO)	3	28.00	7 Yuki Sakurai (JPN)		21	29.24
2	Suzann Pettersen (NOR)	5	28.20	8 Katy Jarochowicz (AUS)		4	29.25
3	Sofia Johansson (SWE)	4	28.50	9 Maria Boden (SWE)		49	29.29
	Liselotte Neumann (SWE)	2	28.50	10 Tamara Hyett (AUS)		4	29.50
5	Minea Blomqvist (FIN)	12	29.00	Maria Ohlsson (SWE)		4	29.50
6	Carlie Butler (AUS)	5	29.20	Melanie Holmes-Smith (AUS)		2	29.50

Sand saves

		Holes	%			Holes	%
1	Jo Pritchard (WAL)	5	100.00	6 Lynn Brooky (NZL)		13	84.62
	Tamara Hyett (AUS)	4	100.00	7 Carin Koch (SWE)		6	83.33
	Maria Ohlsson (SWE)	3	100.00	8 Kirsty J Fisher (ENG)		18	77.78
	Catriona Matthew (SCO)	2	100.00	Denise Simon (GER)		9	77.78
	Antonella Cvitan (SWE)	1	100.00	10 Beth Allen (USA)		33	75.76

2008 Tour Results (in chronological order)

Women's World Cup Sun City, RSA [6376–72]

1	Philippines	65-68-65—198	(Jennifer Rosales, Dorothy Delasin)
2	South Korea	61-72-67—200	(Ji Yai Shin, Eun-Hee)
3	Japan	66-72-65—203	(Shinobu Moromizato, Miki Saiki)
	Taiwan	66-69-68—203	(Yun-Jye Wei, Amy Hung)

Other scores: 205 France; 206 Canada, South Africa, Wales; 207 Paraguay; 208 Scotland; USA; 210 Brazil, China; 212 Sweden; 213 England; 217 Italy, Spain; 218 Australia, Germany; 229 India

For full results and list of past winners, see page 248

MFS Women's Australian Open Kingston Heath, Melbourne, Victoria, Australia [6650–72]

1	Karrie Webb (AUS)*	72-72-73-67—284	€44819
2	Ji-Yai Shin (KOR)	72-71-74-67—284	29879
*Webb won at the second extra hole			
3	Melissa Reid (ENG)	73-76-69-70—288	20915

1994	A Sörenstam (SWE)	286	1998	M McGuire (NZL)	280	*Beat S Pettersen at first extra hole			
1995	L Neumann* (SWE)	283	1999	K Webb (AUS)	270	2003	M McKay (SCO)		277
*Beat A Sörenstam & J Geddes in play-off			2000	K Webb (AUS)	270	2004	L Davis (ENG)		283
1996	C Matthew (SCO)	283	2001	S Gustafson (SWE)	276	2005–2006 Not played			
1997	J Crafter (AUS)	279	2002	K Webb* (AUS)	278	2007	K Webb (AUS)		269

ANZ Ladies' Masters Royal Pines, Gold Coast, Queensland, Australia [6443–72]

1	Lisa Hall (ENG)	68-69-66—203	€53808
2	Hyun Ju Shin (KOR)	68-68-68—204	35872
3	Felicity Johnson (ENG)	70-70-65—205	31523
	Louise Stahle (SWE)	71-67-67—205	31523

1990	J Geddes (USA)	209	1997	G Graham (CAN)	273	2003	L Davies (ENG)	203 (54)
1991	J Geddes (USA)	209	1998	K Webb (AUS)	272	2004	A Sörenstam (SWE)	269
1992	J Crafter (AUS)	207	1999	K Webb (AUS)	262	2005	K Webb (AUS)	272
1993	L Davies (ENG)	211	2000	K Webb (AUS)	274	2006	A Yang (KOR) (am)*	275
1994	L Davies (ENG)	272	2001	K Webb (AUS)	271	*Beat C Cartwright at 1st extra hole		
1995	A Sörenstam (SWE)	270	2002	A Sörenstam* (SWE)	278	2007	K Webb (AUS)	269
1996	J Crafter (AUS)	273	*Beat K Webb in sudden death play-off					

VCI European Ladies Cup La Sella, Alicante, Spain [6283–72]

1	Rebecca Hudson, Trish Johnson (ENG)	64-70-65-71—270	€35000
2	Ellen Smets, Lara Tadiotto (BEL)	65-70-69-71—275	15000
	Martina Eberl, Anja Monke (GER)	66-73-71-65—275	15000

Catalonia Ladies Emporda [6211–71]

1	Lotta Wahlin (SWE)	68-65—133	€9480
2	Tania Elosegui (ESP)	67-72—139	4040
	Rebecca Hudson (ENG)	73-66—139	4040
	Paula Marti (ESP)	72-67—139	4040

2004	Karine Icher (FRA)	190	2006	Gwladys Nocera (FRA)	207
2005	Karine Icher (FRA)	207	2007	Ashleigh Simon (RSA)	208

Open de España Femenino Panorámica, Castellón [6252–72]

1	Emma Zackrisson (SWE)	72-67-71-71—281	€41250
2	Nikki Garrett (AUS)	75-70-71-69—285	20670
	Diana Luna (ITA)	75-72-69-69—285	20670
	Joanne Mills (AUS)	74-73-67-71—285	20670

1982	R Jones (USA)	Sotogrande	224	1985	A Sheard (ENG)	La Manga	285
1983	Not played			1986	L Davies (ENG)	La Manga	286
1984	M Burtons (ENG)	La Manga	286	1987	C Dibnah (AUS)	La Manga	210

Open de España Femenino *continued*

1988	M-L de Taya (FRA)	La Manga	207	2004	S Arricau (FRA)	Coruna	279
1989–2001	*Not played*			2005	I Tinning (DEN)	Panorámica	273
2002	K Icher (FRA)	Salamanca	277	2006	L Brooky (NZL)	Panorámica	275
2003	F Dassu (ITA)	Coruna	279	2007	N Garrett (AUS)	Panorámica	275

Ladies Scottish Open   *The Carrick Cameron House*   [6141–71]

I	Gwladys Nocera (FRA)	69-70-69—208	€30000
2	Maria Boden (SWE)	69-72-69—210	20300
3	Nicole Gergely (AUT)	70-72-69—211	12400
	Rebecca Hudson (ENG)	72-71-68—211	12400

2007   S Gustafson (SWE)   210

Turkish Ladies Open   *National, Antalya*   [6423–73]

I	Lotta Wahlin (SWE)	71-71-73-70—285	€37500
2	Stacy Lee Bregman (RSA)	74-80-71-72—297	18791
	Paula Marti (ESP)	73-77-73-74—297	18791
	Johanna Westerberg (SWE)	80-72-74-71—297	18791

Deutsche Bank Ladies Swiss Open   *Golf Gerre Losone*   [6185–72]

I	Suzann Pettersen (NOR)	67-63-64—194	€78750
2	Amy Yang (KOR)	67-68-65—200	53287
3	Gwladys Nocera (FRA)	70-69-62—201	36750

2006   G Nocera (FRA)   273   2007   B Hauert* (GER)   285
*Beat P Marti (ESP) and A Rawson (AUS) at
4th extra hole

Ladies German Open   *Gut Häusern, Munich*   [6204–72]

I	Amy Yang (KOR)	71-66-63-67—267	€37500
2	Louise Stahle (SWE)	68-69-69-65—271	25375
3	Gwladys Nocera (FRA)	68-70-69-65—272	17500

ABN AMRO Open   (formerly KLM Open)   *Eindhovensche, Netherlands*   [6228–72]

I	Gwladys Nocera (FRA)	67-65-71—203	€37500
2	Melissa Reid (ENG)	68-68-68—204	25375
3	Anne-Lise Caudal (FRA)	68-69-68—205	17500

2004   Elisabeth Esterl (GER)   214   2006   Stephanie Arricau (FRA)   206
2005   Virginie Lagoutte (FRA)   215   2007   G Nocera (FRA)   201

Ladies Open de Portugal   *Quinta de Cima, Portugal*   [6301–73]

I	Anne-Lise Caudal (FRA)	64-69-70—203	€30000
2	Gwladys Nocera (FRA)	67-71-66—204	17150
	Georgina Simpson (ENG)	69-67-68—204	17150

1998   P Conley (AUS)   291   2003   A Munt* (AUS)   209   2005   *Not played*
1999–2001 *Not played*   *Beat E Esterl at 1st extra hole   2006   S Arricau (FRA)   207
2002   K Takanashi (JPN)   139   2004   C Ekelundh (SWE)   206   2007   S Giquel (FRA)   206

Tenerife Ladies Open   *Costa Adeje*   [6080–72]

I	Rebecca Hudson (ENG)*	70-68-71-69—278	€45000
2	Anne-Lise Caudal (FRA)	70-69-69-70—278	30450

*Hudson won at the third extra hole

3	Carlota Ciganda (ESP) (am)	69-66-75-71—281	
	Gwladys Nocera (FRA)	69-71-73-68—281	21000

2002   Raquel Carriedo (ESP)   292   2004   Diana Luna (ITA)   279   2006   Riikka Hakkaainen (FIN)   288
2003   Elisabeth Esterl (GER)   276   2005   Ludivine Kreutz (FRA)   277   2007   N Garrett (AUS)   287

English Open   Oxfordshire, Thame   [6123-72]

1	Rebecca Hudson (ENG)	72-70-64—206	€24750
2	Melissa Reid (ENG)	68-70-69—207	16747
3	Joanne Mills (AUS)	68-76-66—210	11550

1992	L Davies (Tyherington GC)	281	1997–2003	Not played		
1993	L Davies (Tyherington GC)	277	2004	Maria Hjorth (SWE)		197
1994	P Meunier (Tyherington GC)	288	2005	Not Played		
1995	L Davies (The Oxfordshire)	279	2006	Cecelia Ekelundh (SWE)		210
1996	L Davies (The Oxfordshire)	273	2007	B Brewerton (WAL)		209

AIB Irish Open   Portmarnock   [6332-72]

1	Suzann Pettersen (NOR)	69-69-67—205	€67500
2	Marianne Skarpnord (NOR)	71-69-70—210	45675
3	Lynn Brooky (NZL)	73-66-73—212	31500

BMW Ladies Italian Open   Argentario   [5669-71]

1	Martina Eberl (GER)	65-74-67-69—275	€60000
2	Carmen Alonso (ESP)	67-70-77-66—280	40600
3	Becky Brewerton (WAL)	66-71-72-72—281	22186
	Maria Hjörth (SWE)	64-73-72-72—281	22186
	Lisa Holm Sørensen (DEN)	68-70-70-73—281	22186

1987	L Davies (ENG)	Croara	285	1998	not played		
1988	L Davies (ENG)	Ca'Della Nave	269	1999	S Head (ENG)	Poggio dei Medici	214
1989	X Wunsch-Ruiz (ESP)	Carimate	278	2000	S Gustafson (SWE)	Poggio dei Medici	284
1990	F Descampe (BEL)	Lake Garda	282	2001	P Marti (ESP)*	Poggio dei Medici	283
1991	C Dibnah (AUS)	Albarella	272	*Beat R Carriedo at 1st extra hole			
1992	L Davies (ENG)	Frasanelle	274	2002	I Tinning (DEN)	Poggio dei Medici	278
1993	A Arruti (ESP)	GC Lignano	270	2003	L Kreutz (FRA)	Poggio dei Medici	282
1994	C Dibnah (AUS)	GC Lignano	277	2004	AB Sanchez (ESP)	Parco di Roma GC	281
1995	D Booker (AUS)	Il Picciolo GC	284	2005	I Tinning (DEN)	Parco de' Medici	271
1996	L Davies (ENG)	Il Picciolo GC	282	2006	G Nocera (FRA)	Parco de' Medici	274
1997	V van Ryckeghem (NED)	Il Picciolo GC	288	2007	T Johnson (ENG)	Parco de' Medici	273

Evian Masters   Evian-les Bains, France   [6347-72]

1	Helen Alfredsson (SWE)*	72-63-71-67—273	€316875
2	Na Yeon Choi (KOR)	71-67-69-66—273	182457
	Angela Park (BRA)	66-68-68-71—273	182457

*Alfredsson won at the third extra hole

1998	H Alfredsson (SWE)	Royal GC Evian	277	2003	J Inkster (USA)	Evian Masters GC	267
1999	C Nilsmark (SWE)	Evian Masters GC	279	2004	W Doolan (AUS)	Evian Masters GC	270
2000	A Sörenstam (SWE)	Royal GC Evian	276	2005	P Creamer (USA)	Evian Masters GC	273
2001	R Teske (AUS)	Evian Masters GC	273	2006	K Webb (AUS)	Evian Masters GC	272
2002	A Sörenstam (SWE)*	Evian Masters GC	269	2007	N Gulbis (USA)	Evian-les-Bains	284
*Beat K Webb at 1st extra hole				*Beat J Jang (KOR) at 1st extra hole			

RICOH WOMEN'S BRITISH OPEN   Sunningdale   [7408-72]

1	Ji-Yai Shin (KOR)	66-68-70-66—270	€202336
2	Ya-Ni Tseng (TPE)	70-69-68-66—273	126460
3	Eun Hee Ji (KOR)	68-70-69-67—274	79037
	Yuri Fudoh (JPN)	66-68-69-71—274	79037

Full details of this event and former winners are included in Part 1 The Majors page 83

Scandinavian TPC   Frosaker, Sweden   [6264-72]

1	Amy Yang (KOR)	70-69-63—202	€30000
2	Minea Blomqvist (FIN)	74-71-63—208	13395
	Melodie Bourdy (FRA)	71-71-66—208	13395
	Maria Hjörth (SWE)	72-64-72—208	13395
	Lill Kristin Saether (NOR)	71-64-73—208	13395

2005	Annika Sörenstam (SWE)	284	2006	Annika Sörenstam (SWE)	271	2007 C Matthew (SCO) 279

Wales Ladies Championship of Europe *Machynys Peninsula, Llanelli, Wales* [6126–72]

1	Lotta Wahlin (SWE)*	71-67-71—209	€66737
2	Martina Eberl (GER)	65-71-73—209	45158

Wahlin won at the second extra hole

3	Georgina Simpson (ENG)	66-74-70—210	27584
	Henrietta Zuel (ENG)	66-71-73—210	27584
2007	J Mills (AUS) Machynys Peninsula	282	

SAS Ladies Masters *Haga, Oslo, Norway* [6169–72]

1	Gwladys Nocera (FRA)	69-66-68—203	€30000
2	Tania Elosegui (ESP)	70-69-67—206	17150
	Samantha Head (ENG)	70-68-68—206	17150
2007	S Pettersen (NOR) Losby, Norway	204	

Finnair Masters *Helsinki, Finland* [5916–71]

1	Minea Blomqvist (FIN)	69-68-65—202	€30000
2	Ursula Wikstrom (FIN)	68-69-66—203	20300
3	MARTINA EBERL (GER)	71-67-68—206	12400
	Beatriz Recari (ESP)	67-72-67—206	12400
2007	B Hauert (GER) Helsinki, Finland	207	

Nykredit Masters *Simons, Zealand, Denmark* [7043–73]

1	Martina Eberl (GER)	66-73-66—205	€30000
2	Melissa Reid (ENG)	67-66-73—206	20300
3	Annika Sörenstam (SWE)	71-68-71—210	14000
2007	L Hall (ENG)* Helsingor, Denmark	275	

Beat K Matharu (ENG) at 1st extra hole

UNIQA Austrian Open *Föhrenwald, Wiener Neustadt, Austria* [6179–72]

1	Laura Davies (ENG)	71-67-67-68—273	€37500
2	Lisa Hall (ENG)	69-69-70-68—276	25375
3	Diana Luna (ITA)	68-70-70-69—277	17500
2007	L Davis (ENG) Föhrenwald, Austria	200	

Göteborg Masters *Lycke, Sweden* [6662–72]

1	Gwladys Nocera (FRA)	66-62-65-66—259	€37500
2	Nina Reis (SWE)	69-67-73-61—270	25375
3	Felicity Johnson (ENG)	62-70-71-68—271	17500

Vediorbis Open de France *Golf d'Arras, Nord-Pas de Calais* [6195–72]

1	Anja Monke (GER)	67-78-65-68—278	€52500
2	Tania Elosegui (ESP)	74-70-67-69—280	30012
	Nina Reis (SWE)	67-69-72-72—280	30012

1987	L Neumann (SWE)	Fourqueux	293	1998	Not played		
1988	M-L de Lorenzi-Taya			1999	T Johnson (ENG)	Paris International	282
	(FRA)	Fourqueux	290	2000	P Meunier Lebouc (FRA)	Le Golf d'Arras	272
1989	S Strudwick (ENG)	Fourqueux	285	2001	S Pettersen (SWE)	Le Golf d'Arras	289
1990–1992	Not played			2002	L Brooky (NZL)	Le Golf d'Arras	272
1993	M-L de Lorenzi (FRA)	The Var	220	2003	L Brooky (NZL)	Le Golf d'Arras	274
1994	J Forbes (SCO)	Saint-Endreol	283	2004	S Arricau (FRA)	Le Golf d'Arras	281
1995	M-L de Lorenzi (FRA)	Saint-Endreol	210	2005	V Zorzi (ITA)	Le Golf d'Arras	276
1996	T Johnson (ENG)	Le Golf d'Arras	300	2006	V Zorzi (ITA)	Le Golf d'Arras	281
1997	K Lunn (AUS)	Paris International	281	2007	L Wessberg (SWE)	Le Golf d'Arras	277

Madrid Ladies Masters *Casino Club, Retamares, Spain* [6338–73]

1	Gwladys Nocera (FRA)	72-69-67—208	€100000
2	Paula Marti (ESP)	68-74-70—212	42440
3	Catriona Matthew (SCO)	68-75-70—213	28000
2007	M Ebert (GER)	Casino Club	206

Suzhou Taihu Open *Suzhou Taihu, China* [6299–72]

1	Annika Sörenstam (SWE)*	69-69-65—203	€30000
2	Li Ying Ye (CHN)	65-68-70—203	20300

*Sörenstam won at the second extra hole

3	Karen Lunn (AUS)	72-67-71—210	11093
	Amanda Moltke-Leth (DEN)	68-74-68—210	11093
	Chutichai Porani (THA)	72-70-68—210	11093

Saint Four Masters *Saint Four, Jeju, South Korea* [6303–72]

1	Hee Kyung Seo (KOR)	69-67-66—202	€47592
2	Sun Ju Ahn (KOR)	65-70-69—204	21416
3	So Yeon Ryu (KOR)	69-71-65—205	14277

EMAAR-MGF Ladies Masters *Eagleton Resort, Bangalore, India* [6632–72]

Cancelled

2007	G Nocera (FRA)	Bangalore, India	281

Dubai Ladies Masters *Emirates GC, Dubai, UAE*

1	Anja Monke (GER)	68-71-68-68—275	€75,000
2	Veronica Zorzi (ITA)	69-69-71-69—278	50,750
3	Laura Davies (ENG)	70-69-71-69—279	35,000
2007	A Sörenstam (SWE)	Emirates GC, Dubai	278

Nocera is No. 1 on the Ladies' European Tour

Thirty-three-year-old Gwladys Nocera, the former French and German Amateur champion who has been playing on the Ladies European Tour for six years, ended the 2009 season in No. 1 spot having been fourth, second and third in the previous three seasons.

Gwladys, from Moulins, has won ten times, come second on eight occasions and had nine third place finishes since turning professional in late 2002 but 2008 was easily her best season with five wins – the Aberdeen Asset Management Scottish Open, the ABN-AMRO Open, the SAS Masters, the Goteborg Masters and the Madrid Masters.

From her 23 events she made €391,839, beating Helen Alfredsson into second place on the New Star money list. Her career earnings are €1,242,007.

© Jeremy Campion/Phil Sheldon Golf Picture Library

LPGA Tour

www.lpga.com

Players are of American nationality unless stated

Money List

1	Lorena Ochoa (MEX)	$2,763,193	33	Nicole Castrale	540,644	69	Alena Sharp	180,958
2	Paula Creamer	1,823,992	34	Teresa Lu (TPE)	507,618	70	Katie Futcher	176,792
3	Yani Tseng (TPE)	1,752,086	35	Hee Young Park (KOR)	474,744	71	Irene Cho	176,787
4	Annika Sörenstam (SWE)	1,735,912	36	Shanshan Feng (CHN)	472,758	72	Karine Icher (FRA)	176,419
5	Helen Alfredsson (SWE)	1,431,408	37	Stacy Prammanasudh	470,612	73	Kim Hall	175,235
			38	Juli Inkster	441,484	74	Kyeong Bae (KOR)	166,095
6	Seon Hwa Lee (KOR)	1,187,294	39	Leta Lindley	439,213	75	Linda Wessberg (SWE)	165,111
			40	Mi Hyun Kim (KOR)	438,571			
7	Suzann Pettersen (NOR)	1,177,809	41	Catriona Matthew (SCO)	433,726	76	Na On Min (KOR)	146,643
8	Inbee Park (KOR)	1,138,370	42	Lindsey Wright (AUS)	424,937	77	Soo-Yun Kang (KOR)	145,665
9	Angela Stanford	1,134,753	43	Giulia Sergas (ITA)	417,554	78	Moira Dunn	144,656
10	Cristie Kerr	1,108,839	44	Minea Blomqvist (FIN)	417,011	79	Russy Gulyanamitta (THA)	139,402
11	Na Yeon Choi (KOR)	1,095,759	45	Momoko Ueda (JPN)	413,592	80	Wendy Doolan (AUS)	137,542
12	Jeong Jang (KOR)	1,080,097	46	Ai Miyazato (JPN)	410,833			
13	Katherine Hull (AUS)	1,045,619	47	Kristy McPherson	407,237	81	Gloria Park (KOR)	132,336
14	Song-Hee Kim (KOR)	980,883	48	Louise Friberg (SWE)	395,051	82	Jennifer Rosales (PHI)	128,185
15	Eun-Hee Ji (KOR)	913,968	49	Young Kim (KOR)	393,468	83	Meredith Duncan	125,884
16	Candie Kung (TPE)	876,202	50	Allison Fouch	375,345	84	Jamie Hullett	123,868
17	Angela Park (BRA)	869,918	51	Jimin Kang (KOR)	373,365	85	Mikaela Parmlid (SWE)	122,851
18	Karrie Webb (AUS)	854,562	52	Se Ri Pak (KOR)	366,143	86	Dorothy Delasin (PHI)	120,710
19	Hee-Won Han (KOR)	826,679	53	Jin Joo Hong (KOR)	339,534			
20	Laura Diaz	809,541	54	Carin Koch (SWE)	313,468	87	Marisa Baena (COL)	118,646
21	Jee Young Lee (KOR)	795,991	55	Shi Hyun Ahn (KOR)	303,126	88	Meaghan Francella	117,682
22	In-Kyung Kim (KOR)	773,956	56	Natalie Gulbis	266,237	89	Danielle Downey	117,312
23	Karen Stupples (ENG)	726,436	57	HJ Choi (KOR)	253,283	90	Kris Tamulis	117,139
24	Morgan Pressel	711,261	58	Pat Hurst	252,173	91	Reilley Rankin	116,754
25	Sun Young Yoo (KOR)	688,983	59	Diana D'Alessio	235,465	92	Brittany Lincicome	114,963
26	Ji Young Oh (KOR)	680,225	60	Michele Redman	234,907	93	Johanna Head (ENG)	114,927
27	Christina Kim	678,598	61	Wendy Ward	229,092	94	Erica Blasberg	113,428
28	Sophie Gustafson (SWE)	646,303	62	Jill McGill	227,183	95	Laura Davies (ENG)	112,914
			63	Il Mi Chung (KOR)	220,513	96	Kelli Kuehne	110,230
29	Jane Park	631,357	64	Janice Moodie (SCO)	213,074	97	Charlotte Mayorkas	107,556
30	Brittany Lang	630,294	65	Becky Morgan (WAL)	205,838	98	Mollie Fankhauser-Cavanaugh	105,370
31	Maria Hjorth (SWE)	588,396	66	Rachel Hetherington (AUS)	191,169			
32	Meena Lee (KOR)	553,090	67	Heather Young	188,218	99	Eva Dahllof (SWE)	103,260
			68	Sandra Gal	181,162	100	Julieta Granada (PAR)	101,140

Three victories on the LPGA Tour for Ji-Yai Shin

The success story that is Ji-Yai Shin, the 20 year-old Korean golfer, continues. After winning 10 events in 2007 she improved on that in 2008 scoring 11 victories from 35 starts comprising seven on the Korean circuit where she became the first golfer to win the three Korean Ladies Grand Slam events, three on the LPGA circuit where she picked up the $1 million dollar prize at the ADT Championship, and one in Japan. In addition the young Asian golfer, who won her first major – the Ricoh Women's British Open at Sunningdale last summer, lost two play-offs! She is the first non-member of the LPGA Tour – she joined only this year – to win three events in a season. In all she played 10 LPGA events as a non-member in 2008, won the British Open, the Mizuno Classic and the ADT event, had three more top 10's and ended up pocketing $1.77 million in prize-money. Although having scored 21 wins in two years she says that her first goal is to finish Rookie of the Year in 2009 in America and thereafter she will be after taking the No.1 spot from Lorena Ochoa.

2008 Tour Results (in chronological order)

Women's World Cup Sun City, RSA   [6376–72]

1	Philippines	65-68-65—198	(Jennifer Rosales, Dorothy Delasin)
2	South Korea	61-72-67—200	(Ji Yai Shin, Eun-Hee)
3	Japan	66-72-65—203	(Shinobu Moromizato, Miki Saiki)
	Taiwan	66-69-68—203	(Yun-Jye Wei, Amy Hung)

Other scores: 205 France; 206 Canada, South Africa, Wales; 207 Paraguay;
208 Scotland; USA; 210 Brazil, China; 212 Sweden; 213 England; 217 Italy,
Spain; 218 Australia, Germany; 229 India

For full results and list of past winners, see page 248

SBS Open Turtle Bay, Kahuku, HI   [6578–72]

1	Annika Sörenstam (SWE)	70-67-69—206 [-10]	$165000
2	Laura Diaz	70-68-70—208	75867
	Russy Gulyanamitta (THA)	71-69-68—208	75867
	Jane Park	70-68-70—208	75867

Fields Open Ko Olina, Honolulu, HI   [6519–72]

1	Paula Creamer	66-68-66—200	$195000
2	Jeong Jang (KOR)	64-68-69—201	119590
3	Lindsey Wright (AUS)	69-66-67—202	86755

HSBC Women's Champions Tanah Merah, Singapore   [6547–72]

1	Lorena Ochoa (MEX)	66-65-69-68—268	~$300000
2	Annika Sörenstam (SWE)	71-67-70-71—279	183533
3	Paula Creamer	67-71-70-73—281	133140

MasterCard Classic Boisque Real, Mexico City   [6911–72]

1	Louise Friberg (SWE)	72-73-65—210	$195000
2	Yani Tseng (TPE)	68-69-74—211	118722
3	Jill McGill	67-73-72—212	76375
	Jane Park	72-70-70—212	76375

Safeway International Superstition Mountain, AZ   [6662–72]

1	Lorena Ochoa (MEX)	65-67-68-66—266	$225000
2	Jee Young Lee (KOR)	67-67-67-72—273	135135
3	Minea Blomqvist (FIN)	70-68-69-67—274	98031

KRAFT NABISCO CHAMPIONSHIP
Mission Hills, Rancho Mirage, CA   [6673–72]

1	Lorena Ochoa (MEX)	68-71-71-67—277	$300000
2	Suzann Pettersen (NOR)	74-75-65-68—282	160369
	Annika Sörenstam (SWE)	71-70-73-68—282	160369

Fuller details of this event are included in Part 1 The Majors page 113

Corona Championship Tres Marias Morelia, Mexico   [6539–73]

1	Lorena Ochoa (MEX)	66-66-66-69—267	$195000
2	Song-Hee Kim (KOR)	66-69-71-72—278	120196
3	Karine Icher (FRA)	75-66-66-72—279	77323
	Inbee Park (KOR)	69-64-72-74—279	77323

Ginn Open *Orlando, FL* [6505–72]

I	Lorena Ochoa (MEX)	68-67-65-69—269	$390000
2	Yani Tseng (TPE)	68-64-69-71—272	233732
3	Teresa Lu (TPE)	67-69-69-72—277	150362
	Suzann Pettersen (NOR)	68-66-72-71—277	150362

Stanford International Pro-Am *Aventura, FL* [6244/6132–71/70]

I	Annika Sörenstam* (SWE)	68-67-70-70—275	$300000
2	Paula Creamer	68-71-67-69—275	182220
*	*Sörenstam won at the first extra hole*		
3	Young Kim (KOR)	67-67-73-69—276	117224
	Karrie Webb (AUS)	73-69-70-64—276	117224

SemGroup Championship *Cedar Ridge, Broken Arrow, OK* [6602–71]

I	Paula Creamer*	70-71-69-72—282	$270000
2	Juli Inkster	72-73-67-70—282	166426
*	*Creamer won at the second extra hole*		
3	Jeong Jang (KOR)	73-72-73-68—286	107063
	Angela Stanford	73-71-71-71—286	107063

Michelob ULTRA Open *Kingsmill, Williamsburg, VA* [6315–71]

I	Annika Sörenstam (SWE)	64-66-69-66—265	$330000
2	Allison Fouch	69-71-68-64—272	138548
	Jeong Jang (KOR)	67-66-69-70—272	138548
	Christina Kim	70-67-66-69—272	138548
	Karen Stupples (ENG)	67-69-70-66—272	138548

Sybase Classic *Upper Montclair, Clifton, NJ* [6413–72]

I	Lorena Ochoa (MEX)	68-67-71—206	$300000
2	Na Yeon Choi (KOR)	70-68-69—207	114360
	Catriona Matthew (SCO)	68-72-67—207	114360
	Morgan Pressel	70-71-66—207	114360

Corning Classic *Corning CC, NY* [6223–72]

I	Leta Lindley*	73-67-70-67—277	$225000
2	Jeong Jang (KOR)	71-69-69-68—277	138335
*	*Lindley won at the first extra hole*		
3	Mi Hyun Kim (KOR)	71-73-68-66—278	88992
	Sun Young Yoo (KOR)	74-67-71-66—278	88992

Ginn Tribute *Mount Pleasant, SC* [6459–72]

I	Seon Hwa Lee (KOR)*	68-70-69-67—274	$390000
2	Karrie Webb (AUS)	65-66-73-70—274	237445
	Lee won at the first extra hole		
3	Song-Hee Kim (KOR)	68-71-67-69—275	172250

McDONALD'S LPGA CHAMPIONSHIP
Bulle Rock, Havre de Grace, MD [6596–72]

I	Yani Tseng (TPE)*	73-70-65-68—276	$300000
2	Maria Hjörth (SWE)	68-72-65-71—276	180180
	Tseng won at the fourth extra hole		
3	Lorena Ochoa (MEX)	69-65-72-71—277	115911

Fuller details of this event are included in Part I The Majors page 103

Wegman's LPGA *Locust Hill, Pittsford, NY* [6328–72]

1	Eun-Hee Ji (KOR)	70-71-64-67—272	$300000
2	Suzann Pettersen (NOR)	70-65-67-72—274	183986
3	Hee-Won Han (KOR)	69-74-64-69—276	118360
	Jeong Jang (KOR)	68-71-69-68—276	118360

US WOMEN'S OPEN CHAMPIONSHIP
Interlachen CC, Edina, MN [6789–73]

1	Inbee Park (KOR)	72-69-71-71—283	$585000
2	Helen Alfredsson (SWE)	70-71-71-75—287	350000
3	In-Kyung Kim (KOR)	71-73-69-75—288	162487
	Stacy Lewis	73-70-67-78—288	162487
	Angela Park (BRA)	73-67-75-73—288	162487

Jamie Farr Owens Corning Classic
Highland Meadows, Sylvania, OH [6428–71]

1	Paula Creamer	60-65-70-73—268	$195000
2	Nicole Castrale	70-69-67-64—270	118169
3	Eun-Hee Ji (KOR)	65-66-68-72—271	85723

State Farm Classic *Panther Creek, Springfield, IL* [6608–72]

1	Ji Young Oh (KOR)*	66-66-69-69—270	$255000
2	Yani Tseng (TPE)	66-66-66-72—270	156002

*Ji Young Oh won at the first extra hole

3	Na Yeon Choi (KOR)	67-67-69-68—271	113169

Evian Masters *Evian-les-Bains, France* [6347–72]

1	Helen Alfredsson (SWE)*	72-63-71-67—273	$487500
2	Na Yeon Choi (KOR)	71-67-69-66—273	280704
	Angela Park (BRA)	66-68-68-71—273	280704

*Alfredsson won at the third extra hole

For list of past winners, see page 229

RICOH WOMEN'S BRITISH OPEN

Sunnningdale [6408–72]

1	Ji-Yai Shin (KOR)	66-68-70-66—270	$202336
2	Ya-Ni Tseng (TPE)	70-69-68-66—273	126460
3	Eun Hee Ji (KOR)	68-70-69-67—274	79037
	Yuri Fudoh (JPN)	66-68-69-71—274	79037

Full details of this event are included in Part I The Majors page 83

CN Canadian Women's Open *Ottawa, ON* [6510–72]

1	Katherine Hull (AUS)	71-65-72-69—277	$337500
2	Se Ri Pak (KOR)	68-70-68-72—278	202703
3	Yani Tseng (TPE)	70-64-68-77—279	147046

Safeway Classic *Columbia Edgewater, Portland, OR* [6397–72]

1	Cristie Kerr*	71-67-65—203	255000
2	Helen Alfredsson (SWE)	67-67-69—203	133624
	Sophie Gustafson (SWE)	67-68-68—203	133624

*Kerr won at the first extra hole

Bell Micro LPGA Classic *Magnolia Grove, Mobile, AL*   [6253–72]

I	Angela Stanford	70-67-67-73—277	$210000
2	Shanshan Feng (CHN)	67-73-70-68—278	127855
3	Kim Hall	70-74-67-69—280	92750

Navistar LPGA Classic *Prattville, AL*   [6571–72]

I	Lorena Ochoa (MEX)*	67-67-69-70—273	$210000
2	Cristie Kerr	66-71-70-66—273	108577
	Candie Kung (TPE)	69-72-65-67—273	108577

*Ochoa won at the second extra hole

Samsung World Championship *Half Moon Bay, CA*   [6450–72]

I	Paula Creamer	68-74-68-69—279	$250000
2	Song-Hee Kim (KOR)	69-73-70-68—280	156250
3	Juli Inkster	73-72-68-68—281	64063
	Lorena Ochoa (MEX)	69-73-70-69—281	64063
	Suzann Pettersen (NOR)	74-70-69-68—281	64063
	Angela Stanford	69-73-69-70—281	64063

Longs Drugs Challenge *Blackhawk CC, Danville, CA*   [6185–72]

I	In-Kyung Kim (KOR)	67-69-69-73—278	$180000
2	Angela Stanford	70-69-67-75—281	108830
3	Yani Tseng (TPE)	68-72-70-72—282	78948

Kapalua LPGA Classic *Kapalua, Maui, HI*   [6273–72]

I	Morgan Pressel	72-72-67-69—280	$225000
2	Suzann Pettersen (NOR)	68-72-72-69—281	138687
3	Laura Diaz	70-71-71-70—282	100608

Grand China Air LPGA *Haikou, Hainan Island, China*   [6422–72]

I	Helen Alfredsson (SWE)	70-69-65—204	$270000
2	Yani Tseng (TPE)	72-67-68—207	171913
3	Laura Diaz	63-73-72—208	124711

KOLON Championship *Incheon, South Korea*   [6468–72]

I	Candie Kung (TPE)	70-71-69—210	$240000
2	Katherine Hull	66-76-69—211	149117
3	Sophie Gustafson (SWE)	72-70-70—212	78579
	Hee-Won Han (KOR)	71-69-72—212	78579
	Jeong Jang (KOR)	70-71-71—212	78579
	Jee Young Lee (KOR)	74-69-69—212	78579

Mizuno Classic *Kintetsu Kashikojima, Shima Mie, Japan*   [6506–72]

I	Ji-Yai Shin (KOR)	68-66-67—201	$210000
2	Mayu Hattori (JPN)	67-69-71—207	126968
3	Eun-A Lim (KOR)	68-70-70—208	92107

Lorena Ochoa Invitational *Guadalajara, Mexico*   [6644–72]

I	Angela Stanford	68-66-72-69—275	$200000
2	Brittany Lang	68-74-69-65—276	87818
	Annika Sörenstam (SWE)	68-72-67-69—276	87818

ADT Championship
Trump International GC, West Palm Beach, FL   [6523–72]

The field of 29 was cut to 16 after two rounds and to eight after three but then all previous scores were eliminated. The remaining eight played one round for the $1 million first prize. Figures in brackets are the players' scores for the first three rounds.

1	Ji-Yai Shin (KOR)	(215)	70	$1,000,000
2	Karrie Webb (AUS)	(219)	71	100,000
3	Paula Creamer	(212	74	19,875
	Seon Hwa Lee (KOR)	(212)	74	19,875
5	Eun-Hee Ji (KOR)	(217)	75	18,500
6	Angela Stanford	(209)	78	17,750
7	Jeong Jang (KOR	(214)	79	16,625
	Suzann Pettersen (NOR)	(213)	79	16,625

The following failed to make the third round cut: Sun Young Yoo (KOR) 217; Helen Alfredsson (SWE) 219; Angela Park (BRA) 217; Jee Young Lee (KOR) 222; Karen Stupples (AUS) 223; Katherine Hull (AUS) 288; Christina Kim (221); In-Kyung Kim (KOR) 222 – all received $14,000

The following missed the half-way cut: Na Yeon Choi (KOR) 148; Laura Diaz 149; Hee-Won Han (KOR) 149; Maria Hjorth (SWE) 149; Cristie Kerr 49; Candie Kung (TPE) 149; Lorena Ochoa (MEX) 149; Annika Sörenstam (SWE) 149; Nicole Castrale 150; Song-Hee Kim (KOR) 150; Morgan Pressel 150; Yani Tseng (TPE) 151; Meena Lee (KOR) 153; Shanshan Feng (CHN) 156; Ji Young Oh (KOR) 147 – all received $8000

Wendy's 3-Tour Challenge   *Rio Secco GC, NA*

1	Champions Tour (Nick Price (ZIM) 65, Jay Haas 66, Fred Funk 68)	199	
			$500,000
2	PGA Tour (Kenny Perry 66, Stewart Cink 67, Rocco Mediate 69)	202	
			$1,750,000
3	LPGA (Natalie Gulbis 67, Cristie Kerr 67, Helen Alfredsson (SWE) 78)	212	
			$1,750,000

Five Asians are first time winners on the LPGA Tour

Far East golfers dominated the first time winners table on the LPGA Tour in 2008. Asia provided five of the eight winners – two of which were major successes. Australian Katherine Hull, American Leta Lindley and Sweden's Louise Friberg were the only non-Asian first timers. The list is:

In-Kyung Kim (KOR)	Longs Drugs Challenge
Katherine Hull (AUS)	CN Canadian Women's Open
Ji Young Ho (KOR)	LPGA State Farm Classic
Inbee Park (KOR)	US Women's Open
Eun-Hee Ji (KOR)	Wegmans LPGA
Yani Tseng (TAI)	McDonald's LPGA Championship
Leta Lindley (USA)	LPGA Corning Classic
Louise Friberg (SWE)	Mastercard Classic

CN Canadian Women's Tour

Players are of Canadian nationality unless stated   www.cncanadianwomenstour.ca

Sue Kim (a)	Richmond CC, Richmond, BC	72-23—145
Sue Kim (a)	Sunningdale Golf & C, London, ON	71-70—141
Stephanie Sherlock (a)*	Glendale Golf & CC, Winnipeg, MB	68-75—143

*Sherlock beat Kira Meixner and Seema Sadekar at the fourth play-off hole

Kirby Dreher (a)	Camelot Golf & CC, Cumberland, ON	67-76—143

Final Money List

1	Seema Sadekar	$12,670.00	6	Adrienne White	7,508.00
2	Corina Kelepouris	11,821.50		Jennifer Greggain	7,492.50
3	Samantha Richdale	9,775.50	8	Susan Choi	7,492.50
	Jessica Carafiello	9,706.67	9	Katrina Leckovic	7,095.83
5	Walailak Satarak (THA)	8,542.00	10	Marie-Josee Rouleau	6,717.00

Teenager is first amateur to win on Canadian Tour

Sue Kim, a 17-year-old from Langley in British Columbia, made history on the CN Canadian Women's Professional Tour when she won an event at the Richmond Club after a three-hole play-off with Americans Susan Choi and Sarah Tiller. Kim, a member of the Canadian National Amateur team, proved that was no fluke when she again beat the professionals at the Sunningdale Club in London, Ontario. At season's end she was named the Jocelyne Bourassa Player of the Year and won the top amateur award as well.

Sörenstam appointed a USGA Ambassador

Annika Sörenstam, winner of ten majors including three US Open Championships, has been appointed a golfing ambassador for the United States Golf Association. The World Golf and LPGA Hall of Fame inductee has eight times been the Rolex Player of the Year in America, been top money earner on the US Tour a record eight times, has six times had the lowest scoring average on the LPGA Tour and has eight times been named the Golf Writers of America Player of the Year. She is the first golfer to have topped $22 million in prize-money in the United States.

"Annika has earned a rare place in golfing history," says USGA President Jim Vernon. "She will help us make the game more accessible and more relevant to players of all skills."

Korean LPGA Tour

www.klpga.com

Players are of Korean nationality unless stated

2007 China Ladies Sports Seoul Kim Young Joo Open	Orient GC Zephyros	Ji-Yai Shin So Yeon Ruy	203 (-13) 211 (-5)
Woori Investment and Securities Tournament	Ildong Lakes	Ji –Yai Shin	203 (-13)
MBC Tour MC Square Cup	Crown CC	Chae A Oh	219 (-3)
Phoenix Park Classic	Phoenix Park	Ha-Neul Kim	204 (-12)
KB Star Tour in Jeollanam-do	Hamyeong Dynasty GC	Cho Aram*	209 (-7)

*Cho Aram won at first extra hole after play-off with Young RaJo Jo and Sun Ju Ahn

Taeyong Cup Korean Open	Taeyong GC	Ji-Yai Shin*	213 (-3)

*Shin won after a play-off with So Yeon Ryu

Doosan Match-play Championship Final	Ladena GC	Bo-Kyung Kim beat He-yong Choi I hole	
HillState Seokyung Open	Lakeside GC	Ha-Neul Kim	211 (5)
BC Card Classic	Teddy Valley, Jeju Island	Ji-Yai Shin*	211

*Shin won at third extra hole of play-off with Min-Sun Kim, Hyun-Ji Kim and Ni-Hyun Jo

KB Star Tour in Busan	Haeundae GC	Ran Hong	213 (-3)
MBC Tour LOTTE Mart Open	Sky Hill GC	Hye-Yong Choi	203 (-13)
Lakeside Open	Lakeside GC (West course)	Ran Hong	204 (-12)
High I Cup SBS Charity Open	High I GC	Hee Kyung Seo	208 (-8)
KB Star Tour in Chungcheong	Silk River GC	Hee Kyung Seo	209 (-7)
Binhai Open	Binhai GC	Hee Kyung Seo	207 (-9)
SK Energy Invitational		Ha-Neul Kim	135 (-9)

¹reduced to two round because of flooding

Shinsegye Cup KLPGA Ch.	Jayu GC	Ji-Yai Shin	209 (-7)
Samsung Finance Ladies Ch.	Phoenix Park GC	Sun-Ju Ahn	206 (-10)
Interburgo Masters	Interburgo GC, Kyungsan	Hee-Kyung Seo	208 (-11)
Hite Cup	Blue Heron GC	Ji-Yai Shin	203 (-13)
KB Star in Incheon	Sky 72 GC	Ji-Yai Shin*	285 (-3)

*Ji-Yai Shin won at second hole of play-off with Sun-ju Ahn and He-Yong Cho

Hana Bank Kolon Ch.	Sky 72 GC	Candy Kung (TPE)	
MBC Tour S-OIL Champions Inv.	Lord Land GC	Hae-Yoon Kim	206 (-10)
Saint Four Ladies Masters	Saint Four GC	Hee Kyung Seo	202 (-14)
ADT CAPS Championship	Sky Hill, Jeju	Hee Kyung Seo	214 (-8)
Kyoraku Cup (Korea v Japan)	Fukuoka Century GC	Japan 24, South Korea 24*	

*Japan won play-off – Miho Koga beat Jang Jeong at third extra hole

Seo Hee Kyung wins three-in a row to equal record

Korean Seo Hee Kyung equalled the record of Mi-hyun Kim's set 11 years ago when she won three events in a row on the Korean LPGA Tour in 2008. Seo was eight-under-par for her victory in the High ICup, seven-under for her first place finish in the KB Star event at the Silk River course in Chungcheong and nine-under-par for her win in the Binhai Open. She made history, too, by leading wire-to-wire in the first two events she won.

FUTURES Tour

www.duramedfuturestour.com

Players are of American nationality unless stated

Bright House NETWORKS Open	Cleveland Heights, Lakeland, FL	Sunny Oh*	211 (-5)
Oh beat Chella Choi (KOR) and Kim Welch at the first extra hole			
American Systems Invitational	Daytona Beach, FL	Leah Wigger	212 (-4)
Louisiana Pelican Classic	The Wetlands, Lafayette, LA	M J Hur (KOR)*	206 (-10)
Hur beat Vicky Hurst at the first extra hole			
Jalapeno FGC	Palm View Municipal, McAllen, TX	Vicky Hurst	198 (-18)
El Paso Classic	Underwood, El Paso, TX	Kristina Tucker (SWE)	205 (-11)
Mercedes-Benz of Kansas C/ship	Leawood, KS	Mindy Kim	210 (-3)
Aurora Health Care C/ship	Geneva National, WI	Mindy Kim	213 (-3)
Michelob ULTRA F Players C/ship	Hickory Point, Forsyth, IL	Vicky Hurst	272 (-8)
Duramed Championship	Kings Island, Mason, OH	Stephanie Otteson	204 (-9)
Horseshoe Casino FC	Lost Marsh, Hammond, IN	Vicky Hurst	213 (-3)
CIGNA Classic	Gillette Ridge, Bloomfield, CT	Vicky Hurst	209 (-7)
Alliance Bank FGC	Erie Village, Syracuse, NY	Kim Welch*	204 (-9)
Welch beat Jin Young Pak (KOR) at the fourth extra hole			
USI Championship	Beaver Meadow, Concord, NH	Mo Martin	204 (-12)
Falls Auto Group Classic	Crooked Creek, London, KY	Mindy Kim	206 (-10)
Greater Richmond Duramed FUTURES Classic	Richmond, VA	Haeji Kang (KOR)	205 (-11)
The Gettysburg Championship	Gettysburg, PA	Samantha Richdale (CAN)	211 (-5)
ILOVENY Championship	Capital Hills, Albany, NY	Sarah-Jane Kenyon (AUS)	204 (-9)
Duramed Invitational	Chateau Élan, Braselton, GA	Vicky Hurst	211 (-2)

Final Money List

1	Vicky Hurst	$93,107	6	Song Yi Choi (KOR)	38,349
2	Mindy Kim	79,270	7	Jessica Shepley (CAN)	37,705
3	Sarah-Jane Kenyon (AUS)	48,637	8	Leah Wigger	36,719
4	M.J Hur (KOR)	45,137	9	Sophia Sheridan (MEX)	34,397
5	Jin Young Pak (KOR)	42,368	10	Kim Welch	33,768

Legends of Golf Tour

www.thelegendstour.com

Players are of American nationality unless stated

Duane Reade Charity Classic	Ridgewood CC, Paramus, NJ	Patty Sheehan's team	
BJ's Charity Championship	Granite Links GC, Quincy, MA	Cindy Figg-Currier & Sherri Turner	123 (-21)
Wendy's Charity Challenge	Jackson, MI	Cindy Figg-Currier	132 (-6)
Horseshoe Bend Invitational	Horseshoe Bend, AR	Cindy Rarick's team	
Handa Cup	St Augustine, FL	USA beat Rest of World	31–17

Japan LPGA Tour

www.lpga.or.jp (Japanese only)

Players are of Japanese nationality unless stated

Daikin Orchid Ladies Golf Tournament	Okinawa	Bo-Bae Song (KOR)	202 (-14)
Accordia Ladies	Aoshima, Miyazaki	Yuri Fudoh*	205 (-11)
Fudoh beat Yun-Jye Wei (TPE) at third extra hole			
Yokohama PRGR Open		Ji-Yai Shin* (KOR)	212 (-4)
**Shin beat Sakura Yokomine at fourth extra hole*			
Yamaha Ladies Open	Katsuragi, Shizuoka	Hiroko Yamaguchi	217 (+1)
Studio-Alice Open	Hanayashiki, Yokawa, Hyogo	Hyun-Ju Shin (KOR)	210 (-6)
Life Card Ladies Golf Tournament	Kumamoto Airport, Kumamoto	Yukari Baba	207 (-9)
Fujisankei Ladies Classic	Kawana Hotel, Shizuoka	Ayako Uehara	208 (-8)
Crystal Geyser Ladies Golf Tournament	Keiyo CC, Chiba	Miho Koga*	206 (-10)
Koga beat Maiko Wakabayashi at second extra hole			
Salonpas World Tournament	Tokyo Yomiuri Tokyo	Akiko Fukushima*	284 (-4)
Fukushima beat Ji-Yai Shin (KOR) at first extra hole			
Vernal Ladies	Fukuoka Century	Eun-A Lim (KOR)	209 (-7)
Bridgestone Ladies Open	Chukyo, Aichi	Ji-Hee Lee* (KOR)	208 (-8)
Lee beat Miho Koga and Miki Saiki in play-off			
Kosaido Cup	Kosaido GC, Chiba	Akane Iijima	203 (-13)
Resort Trust Ladies Open	The Country Club, Shiga	Mi-Jeong Jeon (KOR)	204 (-12)
Suntory Ladies Open	Rokko International CC, Hyogo	Momoko Ueda	281 (-7)
Nichirei PGM Ladies	Miho GC, Ibaraki	Yuko Mitsuka	200 (-16)
Promise Ladies Golf Tournament	Madame J. GC, Hyogo	Chie Arimura	202 (-14)
Belluna Ladies Cup	Obatago GC, Gunma	Hiromi Mogi	203 (-13)
Meiji Chocolate Cup	Sapporo International (Island Pine Course, Hokkaido	Yuri Fudoh	207 (-9)
Stanley Ladies Golf Tournament	Tomei, Shizuoka	Akiko Fukushima	203 (-13)
Kagome Philanthrophy JLPGA Players Championship	Narashino CC, Chiba	Mi-Jeong Jeon (KOR)	76 (-12)
Axa Ladies Golf Tournament	Tomakomai Resort, Hokkaido	Shinobu Moromizato	210 (-6)
NEC Karuizawa 72 Golf Tournament	Karuizawa 72 GC	Erin Hara	195 (-21)
CAT Ladies	Daihakone CC	Miho Koga	210 (9)
Yonex Ladies Golf Tournament	Tonex CC	Rui Kitada	207 (-9)
Golf 5 Ladies	Mizunami GC, Gifu	Saiki Fujita	203 (-13)
JLPGA Championship Konica Minolta Cup	Katayamazu GC, Ishikawa	Hyun-Ju Shin (KOR)	283 (-5)
Munsingwear Ladies Tokai Classic	Minami Aichi CC	Yuro Fudoh*	208 (-8)
Fudoh beat Momoko Ueda and Yayoi Arasaki in play-off			
Miyagi TV Cup Dunlop Ladies Open Golf Tournament		Momoko Ueda	211 (-5)
Japan Women's Open	Shiun GC, Niigata	Ji Hee Li (KOR)	284 (-4)
Sankyo Ladies Open	Akagi GC	Maiko Wakabayashi	208 (-8)
Fujitsu Ladies	Tokyu 700 GC	Yuri Fudoh	203 (-13)
Masters GC Ladies Open	Masters GC, Hyogo	Shiho Oyama	209 (-7)
Hisako Higuchi IDC Otsuka Kagu Ladies, Musashi Gaoka CC			
Mizuno Classic	Kintetsu Kashikojina CC	Ji-Yai Shin (KOR)	201 (-5)
Ito-En Ladies Golf Tournament	Great Island Club, Chiba	Miho Koga	03 (-13)

Japan LPGA Tour *continued*

Daio Paper Elleair Ladies Open	Elleair GC, Matsuyama	Sakura Yokomine	205 (-11)
JLPGA Tour Championship Ricoh Cup	Miyazaki	Miho Koga	282 (-6)

Money List 2008

1	Miho Koga	¥120,854,137	6	Jeon Mi-Jeong (KOR)	90.850,678
2	Princess Tomo Ri	119,652,786	7	Masaka Mitsusaka	83,555,964
3	Sakura Yokomine	103,192,169	8	Shiko Ohgama	75,039,535
4	Akiko Fukushima	96.500,696	9	Eun-A Lim (KOR)	73,412,062
5	Yuri Fudoh	91,857,367	10	Kou Hara (KOR)	65,867,760

Ladies' African Tour

www.wpga.co.za

WPGA Masters	Parkview, Joburg	Rebecca Hudson (ENG)	204 (-12)
ACER South African Women's Open	Durban	Julie Tvede (DEN)	209 (-10)
Pam Golding Lowveld International	Nelspruit	Stacy Bregman	209 (-7)
Telkom Classic	Zwartkop, Pretoria	Lisa Holm Sorensen (DEN)	203 (-13)

Order of Merit 2008

1	Lisa Holm Sorensen (DEN)	SAR99738	6	Maria Boden (SWE)	60885
2	Stacy Bergman	95673	7	Anne-Lise Caudal (FRA)	52922
3	Julie Tvede (DEN)	87990	8	Morgana Robbertze	48707
4	Rebecca Hudson (ENG)	76490	9	Anna Temple (USA)	46273
5	Marianne Skarpnord (NOR)	66260	10	Lill Kristin Saether (NOR)	35791

1	Stacy Bergman	287 pts	6	Maria Boden (swe)	171
2	Lisa Holm Sorensen (DEN)	264	7	Morgana Robbertze	159.5
3	Marianne Skarpnord (NOR)	245.5	8	Anne-Lise Caudal (FRA)	154
4	Rebecca Hudson (ENG)	242.5	9	Lee-Anne Pace	141
5	Julie Tvede (DEN)	233.5	10	Anna Temple (USA)	137.5

Month by month in 2008

In the first Tiger-less major for over a decade Padraig Harrington, doubtful before the start with a wrist injury, eagles the 17th and becomes the first European to make a successful defence of The Open since James Braid in 1906. Greg Norman, 53 and less than a month into his marriage to former tennis great Chris Evert, leads with a round to go, but with a 77 drops to third behind Harrington and Ian Poulter.

Asian LPGA Tour 2008

www.lagt.org

Thailand Ladies Open	Vintage Club, Samutprakarn	Pornanong Phatlum (THA)	208 (-8)
DLF Women's Indian Open	DFL GCC Phase V, Gurgaon	Pornanong Phatlum (THA)	212 (-4)
Binhai Open	Binhai GC, Shanghai	Seo Hee Kyung (KOR)	207 (-9)
Suzhou Taihu Open	Suzhong Taihu GC	Annika Sörenestam* (SWE)	203 (-13)

Sorenstam, beat Ye Li Ying at second hole of play-off

Final Order of Merit 2008

1 Seo Hee Kyung (KOR)	US$45,000	6 Danielle Montgomery (ENG)	32,162
2 Pornanong Phatlum (THA)	43,620	7 Smriti Mehra (IND)	23,208
3 Annika Sörenstam, (SWE)	38,100	8 Porani Churichai (THA)	20,292
4 Yang Tao Li (KOR)	36,120	9 Hae Kim Jung (KOR)	18,000
5 Ye Li Ying (KOR)	34,873	10 Kim Min Sung (KOR)	16,500

Australian LPG Tour 2007–2008

Players are of Australian nationality unless stated

www.alpgtour.com

Aristocrat Sapphire Coast Classic	Tura Beach	Dana Lacey	138 (-8)
Butler & Pollock Cup	Russell Vale	Bree Turnbull	157 (-2)
St George's Basin Pro-Am	St George's Basin	Sarah Nicholson (NZL)	134 (-10)
Aristocrat Mollymook Classic	Mollymook Hilltops	Vicky Thomas	147 (+1)
Peter Donnelly Classic	Moss Vale	Shani Waugh	138 (-8)
Angostura Lemon Lime & Bitters Pro-Am	Castle Hill	Nikki McConnell	142 (-6)
St Michael's ALPG Classic	St Michaels	Helen Oh	134 (-14)
Peugeot Kangaroo Valley ALPG Classic	Kangaroo Valley	Sunny Park*	140 (4)

Park beat B Turnbull at first extra hole

Xstrata Coal Pro-Am	Branxton	Sarah Oh*	138 (-6)

Oh beat L Brooky at third extra hole

LG Bing Lee NSW Open	Oatlands, Sydney	Laura Davies (ENG)	207 (-9)
MFS Australian Open[1]	Kingston Heath	Karrie Webb*	284 (-8)

Webb beat Ji-Yai Shin (KOR) at second extra hole

ANZ Ladies Masters[1]	Royal Pines, Queensland	Lisa Hall (ENG)	203 (-13)

[1]Joint venture with Ladies European Tour

Final 2007–2008 Money List

1 Karrie Webb	A$99600	6 Felicity Johnson (ENG)	38605
2 Lisa Hall (ENG)	96166	7 Louise Stahle (SWE)	36000
3 Ji Yai Shin (KOR)	68150	8 Amy Yang (KOR)	35680
4 Hyun Ju Shin (KOR)	60000	9 Laura Davies (ENG)	35450
5 Melissa Reid (ENG)	41303	10 Joanne Mills	28144

Order of Merit 2007–2008

1 Karrie Webb	A$99600	6 Vicky Thomas	17776
2 Joanne Mills	28144	7 Frances Bondad	16790
3 Sarah Oh	23775	8 Lindsey Wright	15812
4 Katherine Hull	19408	9 Tamara Beckett	13054
5 Shani Waugh	18921	10 Sarah Nicholson (NZLL)	12487

International Team Events

Solheim Cup

2007 *Halmstad, Tylosand, Sweden*   Sept 14–16
Result: USA 16, Europe 12
Captains: Helen Alfredsson (Europe),
  Betsy King (USA)
First Day – Foursomes
Pettersen & Gustafson halved with Hurst & Kerr
Sörenstam & Matthew lost to Steinhauer & Diaz
4 and 2
Davies & Brewerton lost to Inkster & Creamer 2 and 1
Nocera & Hjörth beat Gulbis & Pressel 3 and 2

Fourballs
Matthew & Iben Tinning beat Hurst & Lincicome
4 and 2
Sörenstam & Hjörth halved with Stanford &
Prammanasudh
Gustafson & Nocera lost to Castrale & Kerr 3 and 2
Johnson & Davies halved with Creamer & Pressel

Second Day – Foursomes
Hjörth & Nocera halved with Steinhauer & Diaz
Gustafson & Pettersen halved with Inkster & Creamer
Tinning & Hauert lost to Hurst & Stanford 4 and 2
Sörenstam & Matthew beat Castrale & Kerr 1 hole

Fourballs
Wessberg & Hjörth halved with Creamer & Lincicome
Johnson & Tinning halved with Inkster & Prammanasudh
Brewerton & Davies beat Gulbis & Castrale 1 hole
Sörenstam & Pettersen beat Kerr & Pressel 3 and 2

Third Day – Singles
Catriona Matthew (SCO) beat Laura Diaz 3 and 2
Sophie Gustafson (SWE) lost to Pat Hurst 2 and 1
Suzann Pettersen (NOR) lost to Stacy Prammanasudh
2 holes
Iben Tinning (DEN) lost to Juli Inkster 4 and 3
Becky Brewerton (WAL) halved with Sherri Steinhauer
Trish Johnson (ENG) lost to Angela Stanford 3 and 2
Annika Sörenstam (SWE) lost to Morgan Pressel 2 and 1
Laura Davies (ENG) beat Brittany Lincicome 4 and 3
Bettina Hauert (GER) lost to Nicole Castrale 3 and 2
Maria Hjörth (SWE) lost to Paula Creamer 2 and 1
Linda Wessberg (SWE) beat Cristie Kerr 1 hole
Gwladys Nocera (FRA) lost to Natalie Gulbis 4 and 3

2005 *Crooked Stick GC, Carmel, IN, USA* Sept 9–11
Result: USA 15½, Europe 12½
Captains: Nancy Lopez (USA),
  Catrin Nilsmark (Europe)
First Day – Foursomes
Daniel & Creamer halved with Koch & Matthew
Kerr & Gulbis lost to Davies & Hjörth 2 and 1
Kim & Hurst halved with Gustafson & Johnson
Redman & Diaz lost to Sörenstam & Pettersen 1 hole

Fourballs
Jones & Mallon beat Hjörth & Tinning 3 and 2
Hurst & Ward beat Sörenstam & Matthew 2 and 1
Kerr & Gulbis lost to Gustafson & Stupples 2 and 1
Creamer & Inkster lost to Davies & Pettersen 4 and 3

Second Day – Foursomes
Kim & Gulbis beat Nocera & Kreutz 4 and 2
Creamer & Inkster beat Davies & Hjörth 3 and 2
Diaz & Ward lost to Gustafson & Koch 5 and 3
Redman & Hurst beat Sörenstam & Matthew 2 holes

Fourballs
Hurst & Kim lost to Davies & Sörenstam 4 and 2
Daniel & Inkster halved with Tinning & Johnson
Kerr & Creamer beat Koch & Matthew 1 hole
Jones & Mallon halved with Gustafson & Pettersen

Third Day – Singles
Juli Inkster beat Sophie Gustafson (SWE) 2 and 1
Paula Creamer beat Laura Davies (ENG) 7 and 5
Pat Hurst beat Trish Johnson (ENG) 2 and 1
Laura Diaz beat Iben Tinning (DEN) 6 and 5
Christina Kim beat Ludivine Kreutz (FRA) 5 and 4
Beth Daniel lost to Annika Sörenstam (SWE) 4 and 3
Natalie Gulbis beat Maria Hjörth (SWE) 2 and 1
Wendy Ward lost to Catriona Matthew (SCO) 3 and 2
Michele Redman lost to Carin Koch (SWE) 2 and 1
Cristie Kerr lost to Gwladys Nocera (FRA) 2 and 1
Meg Mallon beat Karen Stupples (ENG) 3 and 1
Rosie Jones halved with Suzann Pettersen (NOR)

2003 *Barsebäck, Sweden* Sept 12–14
Result: Europe 17½, USA 10½
Captains: Catrin Nilsmark (Europe),
  Patty Sheehan (USA)
First Day – Foursomes
Koch & Davies halved with Daniel & Robbins
Moodie & Matthew beat Inkster & Ward 5 and 3
Sörenstam & Pettersen beat Diaz & Bowie 4 and 3
Gustafson & Esterl beat Mallon & Jones 3 and 2

Fourball
Davies & Matthew lost to Kuehne & Kerr 2 and 1
Sörenstam & Koch lost to Inkster & Daniel 1 hole
Pettersen & Meunier-Labouc beat Stanford & Mallon
3 and 2
Tinning & Gustafson lost to Redman & Jones 2 holes

Second Day – Foursomes
Gustafson & Pettersen beat Kuehne & Kerr 3 and 1
Esterl & Tinning halved with Stanford & Redman
Sörenstam & Koch beat Ward and Bowie 3 and 4
Moodie & Matthew halved with Mallon & Robbins

Fourball
Sanchez & McKay lost to Daniel & Inkster 5 and 4
Gustafson & Davies lost to Kerr & Kuehne 2 and 1
Matthew & Moodie beat Ward & Jones 4 and 3
Sörenstam & Pettersen beat Robbins & Diaz 1 hole

Third Day – Singles
Janice Moodie (SCO) beat Kelli Kuehne 3 and 2
Carin Koch (SWE) lost to Juli Inkster 5 and 4
Sophie Gustafson (SWE) beat Heather Bowie 5 and 4
Iben Tinning (DEN) beat Wendy Ward 2 and 1
Ana Belen Sanchez (ESP) lost to Michele Redman 3 and 1
Catriona Matthew (SCO) beat Rosie Jones 2 and 1

Annika Sörenstam (SWE) beat Angela Stanford 3 and 2
Suzann Pettersen (NOR) lost to Cristie Kerr conceded
Laura Davies (ENG) beat Meg Mallon conceded
Elisabeth Esterl (GER) lost to Laura Diaz 5 and 4
Mhairi McKay (SCO) beat Beth Daniel conceded
Patricia Meunier-Labouc (FRA) beat Kelly Robbins
  conceded

2002 *Interlachen CC, Madina, MN* Sept 20–22
Result: USA 15½, Europe 12½
Captains: Patty Sheehan (USA),
  Dale Reid (Europe)

First Day – Foursomes
Inkster & Diaz lost to Davies & Marti 2 holes
Daniel & Ward beat Carriedo & Tinning 1 hole
Hurst & Robbins lost to Alfredsson & Pettersen 4 and 2
Kuehne & Mallon lost to Koch & Sörenstam 3 and 2

Fourball
Jones & Kerr beat Davies & Marti 1 hole
Diaz & Klein beat Gustafson & Icher 4 and 3
Mallon & Redman beat Hjörth & Sörenstam 3 and 1
Inkster & Kuehne lost to Koch & McKay 3 and 2

Second Day – Foursomes
Kerr & Redman lost to Koch & Sörenstam 4 and 3
Klein & Ward beat McKay & Tinning 3 and 2
Inkster & Mallon beat Davies & Marti 2 and 1
Diaz & Robbins beat Alfredsson & Pettersen 3 and 1

Fourball
Daniel & Ward lost to Koch & Sörenstam 4 and 3
Hurst & Kuehne lost to Hjörth & Tinning 1 hole
Jones & Kerr lost to Carriedo & Icher 1 hole
Klein & Robbins lost to Davies & Gustafson 1 hole

Third Day – Singles
Juli Inkster beat Raquel Carriedo (ESP) 4 and 3
Laura Diaz beat Paula Marti (ESP) 5 and 3
Emilee Klein beat Helen Alfredsson (SWE) 2 and 1
Kelli Kuehne lost to Iben Tinning (DEN) 3 and 2
Michele Redman halved with Suzann Pettersen (NOR)
Wendy Ward halved with Annika Sörenstam (SWE)
Kelly Robbins beat Maria Hjörth (SWE) 5 and 3
Cristie Kerr lost to Sophie Gustafson (SWE) 3 and 2
Meg Mallon beat Laura Davies (ENG) 3 and 2
Pat Hurst beat Mhairi McKay (SCO) 4 and 2
Beth Daniel halved with Carin Koch (SWE)
Rosie Jones beat Karine Icher (FRA) 3 and 2

2000 *Loch Lomond* Oct 6–8
Result: Europe 14½, USA 11½
Captains: Dale Reid (Europe), Pat Bradley (USA)

First Day – Foursomes
Davies & Nicholas beat Pepper & Inkster 4 and 3
Johnson & Gustafson beat Robbins & Hurst 3 and 2
Nilsmark & Koch beat Burton & Iverson 2 and 1
Sörenstam & Moodie beat Mallon & Daniel 1 hole

First Day – Foursomes
Davies & Nicholas lost to Iverson & Jones 6 and 5
Johnson & Gustafson halved with Inkster & Steinhauer
Neumann & Alfredsson lost to Robbins & Hurst 2 holes
Moodie & Sörenstam beat Mallon & Daniel 1 hole

Second Day – Fourball
Nilsmark & Koch beat Scranton & Redman 2 and 1
Neumann & Meunier Labouc halved with Pepper & Burton
Davies & Carriedo halved with Mallon & Daniel
Sörenstam & Moodie lost to Hurst & Robbins 2 and 1
Johnson & Gustafson beat Jones & Iverson 3 and 2
Nicholas & Alfredsson beat Inkster & Steinhauer 3 and 2

Third Day – Singles
Annika Sörenstam lost to Juli Inkster 5 and 4
Sophie Gustafson lost to Brandie Burton 4 and 3
Helen Alfredsson beat Beth Daniel 4 and 3
Trish Johnson lost to Dottie Pepper 2 and 1
Laura Davies lost to Kelly Robbins 3 and 2
Liselotte Neumann halved with Pat Hurst
Alison Nicholas halved with Sherri Steinhauer
Patricia Meunier Labouc lost to Meg Mallon 1 hole
Catrin Nilsmark beat Rosie Jones 1 hole
Raquel Carriedo lost to Becky Iverson 3 and 2
Carin Koch beat Michele Redman 2 and 1
Janice Moodie beat Nancy Scranton 1 hole

1998 *Muirfield Village, Dublin, OH* Sept 18–20
Result: USA 16, Europe 12
Captains: Judy Rankin (USA), Pia Nilsson (Europe)
First Day – Foursomes
Pepper & Inkster beat Davies & Johnson 3 and 1
Mallon & Burton beat Alfredsson & Nicholas 3 and 1
Robbins & Hurst beat Hackney & Neumann 1 hole
Andrews & Green beat A Sörenstam & Matthew 3 and 2

Fourball
King & Johnson halved with Davies & C Sörenstam
Hurst & Jones beat Hackney & Gustafson 7 and 5
Robbins & Steinhauer lost to Alfredsson & de Lorenzi
  2 and 1
Pepper & Burton beat A Sörenstam & Nilsmark 2 holes

Second Day – Foursomes
Andrews & Steinhauer beat A Sörenstam & Matthew
  3 and 2
Mallon & Burton lost to Davies & C Sörenstam 3 and 2
Pepper & Inkster beat Alfredsson & de Lorenzi 1 hole
Robbins & Hurst beat Neumann & Nilsmark 1 hole

Fourball
King & Jones lost to A Sörenstam & Nilsmark 5 and 3
Johnson & Green lost to Davies & Hackney 2 holes
Andrews & Steinhauer beat Alfredsson & de Lorenzi
  4 and 3
Mallon & Inkster beat Neumann & C Sörenstam
  2 and 1

Third Day – Singles
Pat Hurst lost to Laura Davies 1 hole
Juli Inkster lost to Helen Alfredsson 2 and 1
Donna Andrews lost to Annika Sörenstam 2 and 1
Brandie Burton lost to Liselotte Neumann 1 hole
Dottie Pepper beat Trish Johnson 3 and 2
Kelly Robbins beat Charlotta Sörenstam 2 and 1
Chris Johnson lost to Marie Laure de Lorenzi 1 hole
Rosie Jones beat Catrin Nilsmark 6 and 4
Tammie Green beat Alison Nicholas 1 hole
Sherri Steinhauer beat Catriona Matthew 3 and 2
Betsy King lost to Lisa Hackney 6 and 5
Meg Mallon halved with Sophie Gustafson

1996 *St Pierre, Chepstow* Sept 20–22
Result: USA 17, Europe 11
Captains: Judy Rankin (USA), Mickey Walker (Europe)
First Day – Foursomes
Sörenstam & Nilsmark halved with Robbins & McGann
Davies & Nicholas lost to Sheehan & Jones 1 hole
de Lorenzi & Reid lost to Daniel & Skinner 1 hole
Alfredsson & Neumann lost to Pepper & Burton
  2 and 1

Fourball
Davies & Johnson beat Robbins & Bradley 6 and 5
Sörenstam & Marshall beat Skinner & Geddes 1 hole
Neumann & Nilsmark lost to Pepper & King 1 hole
Alfredsson & Nicholas halved with Mallon & Daniel

1996 continued

Second Day – Foursomes
Davies & Johnson beat Daniel & Skinner 4 and 3
Sörenstam & Nilsmark beat Pepper & Burton 1 hole
Neumann & Marshall halved with Mallon & Geddes
de Lorenzi & Alfredsson beat Robbins & McGann 4 and 3

Fourball
Davies & Hackney beat Daniel & Skinner 6 and 5
Sörenstam & Johnson halved with McGann & Mallon
de Lorenzi & Morley lost to Robbins & King 2 and 1
Nilsmark & Neumann beat Sheehan & Geddes 2 and 1

Third Day – Singles
Annika Sörenstam beat Pat Bradley 2 and 1
Kathryn Marshall lost to Val Skinner 2 and 1
Laura Davies lost to Michelle McGann 3 and 2
Liselotte Neumann halved with Beth Daniel
Lisa Hackney lost to Brandie Burton 1 hole
Trish Johnson lost to Dottie Pepper 3 and 2
Alison Nicholas halved with Kelly Robbins
Marie Laure de Lorenzi lost to Betsy King 6 and 4
Joanne Morley lost to Rosie Jones 5 and 4
Dale Reid lost to Jane Geddes 2 holes
Catrin Nilsmark lost to Patty Sheehan 2 and 1
Helen Alfredsson lost to Meg Mallon 4 and 2

1994 The Greenbrier, WA Oct 21–23

Result: USA 13, Europe 7
Captains: JoAnne Carner (USA),
  Mickey Walker (Europe)

First Day – Foursomes
Burton & Mochrie beat Alfredsson & Neuman 3 and 2
Daniel & Mallon lost to Nilsmark & Sörenstam 1 hole
Green & Robbins lost to Fairclough & Reid 2 and 1
Andrews & King lost to Davies & Nicholas 2 holes
Sheehan & Steinhauer beat Johnson & Wright 2 holes

Second Day – Fourball
Burton & Mochrie beat Davies & Nicholas 2 and 1
Daniel & Mallon beat Nilsmark & Sörenstam 6 and 5
Green & Robbins beat Fairclough & Reid 4 and 3
Andrews & King beat Johnson & Wright 3 and 2
Sheehan & Steinhauer lost to Alfredsson & Neumann
  1 hole

Third Day – Singles
Betsy King lost to Helen Alfredsson 2 and 1
Dottie Pepper Mochrie beat Catrin Nilsmark 6 and 5
Beth Daniel beat Trish Johnson 1 hole
Kelly Robbins beat Lora Fairclough 4 and 2
Meg Mallon beat Pam Wright 1 hole
Patty Sheehan lost to Alison Nicholas 3 and 2
Brandie Burton beat Laura Davies 1 hole
Tammie Green beat Annika Sörenstam 3 and 2
Sherri Steinhauer beat Dale Reid 2 holes
Donna Andrews beat Liselotte Neumann 3 and 2

1992 Dalmahoy, Edinburgh Oct 2–4

Result: Europe 11½, USA 6½
Captains: Mickey Walker (Europe),
  Kathy Whitworth (USA)

First Day – Foursomes
Davies & Nicholas beat King & Daniel 1 hole
Neumann & Alfredsson beat Bradley & Mochrie 2 and 1
Descampe & Johnson lost to Ammaccapane & Mallon
  1 hole
Reid & Wright halved with Sheehan & Inkster

Second Day – Fourball
Davies & Nicholas beat Sheehan & Inkster 1 hole
Johnson & Descampe halved with Burton & Richard
Wright & Reid lost to Mallon & King 1 hole
Alfredsson & Neumann halved with Bradley & Mochrie

Third Day – Singles
Laura Davies beat Brandie Burton 4 and 2
Helen Alfredsson beat Danielle Ammaccapane
  4 and 3
Trish Johnson beat Patty Sheehan 2 and 1
Alison Nicholas lost to Juli Inkster 3 and 2
Florence Descampe lost to Beth Daniel 2 and 1
Pam Wright beat Pat Bradley 4 and 3
Catrin Nilsmark beat Meg Mallon 3 and 2
Kitrina Douglas lost to Deb Richard 7 and 6
Liselotte Neumann beat Betsy King 2 and 1
Dale Reid beat Dottie Pepper Mochrie 3 and 2

1990 Lake Nona, FL Nov 16–18

Result: USA 11½, Europe 4½
Captains: Kathy Whitworth (USA),
  Mickey Walker (Europe)

First Day – Foursomes
Bradley & Lopez lost to Davies & Nicholas 2 and 1
Gerring & Mochrie beat Wright & Neumann 6 and 5
Sheehan & Jones beat Reid & Alfredsson 6 and 5
Daniel & King beat Johnson & de Lorenzi 5 and 4

Second Day – Fourball
Sheehan & Jones beat Johnson & de Lorenzi
  2 and 1
Bradley & Lopez beat Reid & Alfredsson 2 and 1
King & Daniel beat Davies & Nicholas 4 and 3
Gerring & Mochrie lost to Neumann & Wright
  4 and 2

Third Day – Singles
Cathy Gerring beat Helen Alfredsson 4 and 3
Rosie Jones lost to Laura Davies 3 and 2
Nancy Lopez beat Alison Nicholas 6 and 4
Betsy King halved with Pam Wright
Beth Daniel beat Liselotte Neumann 7 and 6
Patty Sheehan lost to Dale Reid 2 and 1
Dottie Mochrie beat Marie Laure de Lorenzi
  4 and 2
Pat Bradley beat Trish Johnson 8 and 7

Solheim Cup – Individual Records   Brackets indicate non-playing captain
Europe

Name		Year	Played	Won	Lost	Halved
Helen Alfredsson	SWE	1990-92-94-96-98-2000-02-(07)	24	10	12	2
Becky Brewerton	WAL	2007	3	1	1	1
Raquel Carriedo	ESP	2000-02	5	1	3	1
Laura Davies	ENG	1990-92-94-96-98-2000-02-03-05-07	41	21	16	4
Florence Descampe	BEL	1992	3	0	2	1
Kitrina Douglas	ENG	1992	1	0	1	0
Elisabeth Esterl	GER	2003	3	1	1	1
Lora Fairclough	ENG	1994	3	2	1	0
Sophie Gustafson	SWE	1998-2000-02-03-05-07	23	9	8	6
Lisa Hackney	ENG	1996-98	6	3	3	0
Bettina Hauert	GER	2007	2	0	2	0
Maria Hjörth	SWE	2000-04-05-07	12	3	6	3
Karine Icher	FRA	2002	3	1	2	0
Trish Johnson	ENG	1990-92-94-96-98-2000-05-07	25	5	13	7
Carin Koch	SWE	2000-02-03-05	16	10	3	3
Ludivine Kreutz	FRA	2005	2	0	2	0
Laure de Lorenzi	FRA	1990-96-98	11	3	8	0
Mhairi McKay	SCO	2002-03	5	2	3	0
Kathryn Marshall	SCO	1996	3	1	1	1
Paula Marti	ESP	2002	4	1	3	0
Catriona Matthew	SCO	1998-03-05-07	17	8	7	2
Patricia Meunier Labouc	FRA	2000-03	4	2	1	1
Janice Moodie	SCO	2000-03	8	6	1	1
Joanne Morley	ENG	1996	2	0	2	0
Liselotte Neumann	SWE	1990-92-94-96-98-2000	21	6	10	5
Alison Nicholas	ENG	1990-92-94-96-98-2000	18	7	8	3
Catrin Nilsmark	SWE	1992-94-96-98-2000-(03)-(05)	16	8	7	1
Pia Nilsson	SWE	(1998)	0	0	0	0
Gwladys Nocera	FRA	2005-07	6	2	3	1
Suzann Pettersen	NOR	2002-03-05-07	16	8	3	5
Dale Reid	SCO	1990-92-94-96-(2000-02)	11	4	6	1
Ana Belen Sanchez	ESP	2003	2	0	2	0
Annika Sörenstam	SWE	1994-96-98-2000-02-03-05-07	37	21	12	4
Charlotta Sörenstam	SWE	1998	4	1	2	1
Karen Stupples	ENG	2005	2	1	1	0
Iben Tinning	DEN	2002-03-05-07	14	4	7	3
Mickey Walker	ENG	(1990)-(92)-(94)-(96)	0	0	0	0
Linda Wessberg	SWE	2007	2	1	0	1
Pam Wright	SCO	1990-92-94	6	1	4	1

United States

Name	Year	Played	Won	Lost	Halved
Danielle Ammaccapane	1992	2	1	1	0
Donna Andrews	1994-98	7	4	3	0
Heather Bowie	2003	3	0	3	0
Pat Bradley	1990-92-96-(2000)	8	2	5	1
Brandie Burton	1992-94-96-98-2000	14	8	4	2
Jo Anne Carner	(1994)	0	0	0	0
Nicole Castrale	2007	4	2	2	0
Paula Creamer	2005-07	10	5	4	1
Beth Daniel	1990-92-94-96-2000-02-03-05	29	10	9	7
Laura Diaz	2002-03-05-07	13	6	6	1
Jane Geddes	1996	4	1	2	1
Cathy Gerring	1990	3	2	1	0
Tammie Green	1994-98	6	2	4	0
Natalie Gulbis	2005-07	7	3	4	0
Pat Hurst	1998-2000-02-05-07	20	11	6	3
Juli Inkster	1992-98-2000-02-03-05-07	27	14	10	3
Becky Iverson	2000	4	2	2	0
Chris Johnson	1998	3	0	2	1
Rosie Jones	1990-96-98-2000-02-03-05	22	11	9	2
Cristie Kerr	2002-03-05-07	17	6	10	1
Christina Kim	2005	4	2	1	1
Betsy King	1990-92-94-96-98-(07)	15	7	6	2
Emilee Klein	2002	4	3	1	0

Solheim Cup *continued*

Name	Year	Played	Won	Lost	Halved
Kelli Kuehne	2002-03	8	2	6	0
Brittany Linicombe	2007	3	1	2	0
Nancy Lopez	1990-(2005)	3	2	1	0
Michelle McGann	1996	4	1	1	2
Meg Mallon	1992-94-96-98-2000-02-03-05	29	13	9	7
Alice Miller	(1992)*	0	0	0	0
Dottie Pepper	1990-92-94-96-98-2000	20	13	5	2
Stacy Prammanasudh	2007	3	1	1	1
Morgan Pressel	2007	4	1	2	1
Judy Rankin	(1996)-(98)	0	0	0	0
Michele Redman	2000-02-03-05	11	4	5	2
Deb Richard	1992	2	1	0	1
Kelly Robbins	1994-96-98-2000-02-03	24	10	10	4
Nancy Scranton	2000	2	0	2	0
Patty Sheehan	1990-92-94-96-(2002)-(03)	13	5	7	1
Val Skinner	1996	4	2	2	0
Angela Stanford	2003-07	3	0	2	1
Sherri Steinhauer	1994-98-2000-07	13	6	5	2
Wendy Ward	2002-03-05	11	3	7	1
Kathy Whitworth	(1990)-(92)*	0	0	0	0

Women's World Cup *Sun City, RSA* [6466–72]

1	Philippines	65-68-65—198	(Jennifer Rosales, Dorothy Delasin)
2	South Korea	61-72-67—200	(Ji Yai Shin, Eun-Hee)
3	Japan	66-72-65—203	(Shinobu Moromizato, Miki Saiki)
	Taiwan	66-69-68—203	(Yun-Jye Wei, Amy Hung)
5	France	62-76-67—205	(Gwladys Nocera, Virginie Lagoutte-Clement)
6	Canada	64-73-69—206	(Lorie Kane, Alena Sharp)
	South Africa	68-72-66—206	(Laurette Maritz, Ashleigh Simon)
	Wales	67-71-68—206	(Becky Morgan, Becky Brewerton)
9	Paraguay	66-73-68—207	(Julieta Granada, Celeste Troche])
10	Scotland	68-73-67—208	(Catriona Matthew, Mhairi McKay)
	United States	65-76-67—208	(Pat Hurst, Juli Inkster)
12	Brazil	68-73-69—210	(Candy Hannemann, Angela Park)
	China	67-75-68—210	(Na Zhang, Chun Wang)
14	Sweden	65-77-70—212	(Sophie Gustafson, Maria Hjörth)
15	England	67-76-70—203	(Trish Johnson, Danielle Masters)
16	Italy	73-76-68—217	(Silvia Cavalleri, Diana Luna)
	Spain	69-79-69—217	(Paula Marti Zambrano, Tania Elosegui)
18	Australia	68-78-72—218	(Nikki Garrett, Lindsey Wright)
	Germany	69-78-71—218	(Bettina Hauert, Martina Eberl)
20	India	70-84-75—229	(Simi Mehra, Irina Brar)

2000	Sweden (K Koch and S Gustafson)	425	2006 Sweden (A Sörenstam and L Neumann)	281
2001–2004 *Not played*			2007 Paraguay (J Granada and C Troche)	279
2005	Japan (A Miyazato and R Kitada)	289		

Lexus Cup (Team Asia v Team International)   (inaugurated 2005)
Singapore Island Golf Club (Bukit course) [5265m–72]

Captains: Si Ri Pak (Team Asia), Annika Sörenstam (Team International)

First Day – *Foursomes*
Song-Hee Kim (KOR) and Inbee Park (KOR) beat Helen Alfredsson (SWE) and Christina Kim (USA) 3 and 2
Seon-Hwa Lee (KOR) and Na-Yeon Choi (KOR) lost to Cristie Kerr (USA) and Karen Stupples (ENG)
   2 and 1
Yani Tseng (TPE) and Sarah Lee (KOR) beat Suzann Pettersen (NOR) and Natalie Gulbis (USA) 2 and 1
Se Ri Pak (KOR) and Eun-Hee Ji (KOR) lost to Paula Creamer (USA) and Nicole Castrale (USA) 1 hole
Jeong Jang (KOR) and Candice Kung (TPE) beat Angela Stanford (USA) and Annika Sörenstam (SWE)
   3 and 2

Namika Omata (JPN) and Mayumi Shimomura (JPN) lost to Katherine Hull (AUS) and Nikki Campbell (AUS) 3 and 1

Match position: Asia 3, International 3

Second Day – *Fourballs*
EH Ji and I Park lost to S Pettersen and A Sörenstam 1 hole
SR Pak and SH Lee lost to C Kerr and H Alfredsson 2 holes
J Jang and NY Choi beat P Creamer and N Castrale 1 hole
S Lee and SH Kim beat K Stupples and S Kim 4 and 2
C Kung and M Shimomura beat N Gulbis and A Stanford 4 and 3
Y Tseng and N Omata lost to K Hull and N Campbell 1 hole

Match position: Asia 6, International 6

Third Day – *Singles*

SR Pak lost to A Sörenstam 3 and 2
S Lee beat N Castrale 1 hole
Y Tseng halved with S Pettersen
I Park lost to H Alfredsson 3 and 2
NY Choi beat P Creamer 3 and 2
SH Kim beat C Kerr 1 hole

EH Ji halved with K Stupples
J Jang lost to K Hull
M Shimomura lost to N Gulbis 2 and 1
N Omata halved with S Kim
C Kung beat N Campbell 3 and 2
SH Lee lost to A Stanford 4 and 3

Result: Asia 11½, International 12½

2005 Asia 8, International 16   Tanah Merah GC,   2007 Asia 15, International 8   The Vines, Perth,
                                                          Singapore   Australia
2006 Asia 12½, International 113½ Tanah Merah GC,
                                                          Singapore

---

Only one European golfer in the LPGA Hall of Fame

Although there are 22 members of the LPGA Hall of Fame there is only one European included. It will come as no surprise that that is Annika Sörenstam who was elected in 2003. Membership is accomplished by a strict set of rules including a necessity to have been 10 years on Tour and to have amassed 27 points in a scheme in which a point is given for every LPGA win, two for any major success and points for either winning the Vare Trophy for the lowest scoring average or the Rolex Trophy which is awarded each year to the Player of the Year.

England's Laura Davies is still short of the required number of points despite having won 20 events on the LPGA Tour including four majors, having been a Rolex Player of the Year and having been named as one of the Tour's Top 50 players and teachers. Laura has scored victories in 12 seasons since 1987 and in the years she didn't she was at least second seven times and third twice. She has won 49 times outside America.

The full list of the 22 members of is in order of induction (the figure in brackets is the number of their LPGA Tour wins):

1957 Louise Suggs (58), Betty Jameson (13),
          Patty Berg (60), Babe Didrikson Zaharias
          (41)
1960 Betsy Rawls (55)
1964 Mickey Wright (82)
1975 Kathy Whitworth (88)
1977 Carol Mann (38), Sandra Haynie (42)
1982 JoAnne Carner (43)
1987 Nancy Lopez (48)
1991 Pat Bradley (31)
1993 Patty Sheehan (35)

1994 Dinah Shore (honorary)
1995 Betsy King (34)
1999 Juli Inkster (30), Beth Daniel (33).
          Amy Alcott (29)
2000 Judy Rankin (26)
2001 Donna Caponi (24)
2002 Marlene Hagge (26)
2003 Annika Sörenstam (49)
2005 Karrie Webb (30)
2006 Marilyn Smith (Lifetime Achievement)
2007 Se Ri Pak (24)

PART IV

Men's Amateur Tournaments

World Amateur Golf Ranking

Danny Lee wins the McCormack Medal

Eighteen-year-old Danny Lee, the Korean-born naturalised New Zealander, powered his way to the top of The R&A's World Amateur Golf Ranking with a late burst of point-winning performances that enabled him to overtake long-time leader American Rickie Fowler.

In the closing weeks of the 12 month points-counting period, Lee won the prestigious Western Open, came 20th in the Wyndham Championship at Greensboro on the PGA Tour where he shot four rounds in the 60's and then scored an impressive 5 & 4 success over 19-year-old Florida State golfer Drew Kittleson in the final of the US Amateur Championship at Pinehurst No 2.

"This course seems to like New Zealanders," quipped Lee, having birdied 13 of the 32 holes played in the final. It was at the same course in 2005 that another New Zealander, Michael Campbell, beat Tiger Woods in a head-to-head for the US Open Championship title.

On ending the season as the world's top amateur, Lee said: "It is very rewarding. I have worked hard over the past years and it is fantastic that it has paid off so well. I am extremely honoured."

Lee, who became the youngest winner and the fourth international golfer in the past five years to win the title (Tiger Woods had previously been the youngest), earns invitations to play in The Open, the US Open and The Masters where traditionally he will be paired in the first round with the US Open champion who just happens to be Woods. Lee is hopeful that Tiger will have recovered sufficiently from his knee surgery to tee it up at Augusta.

Yet he might not have taken over the No 1 spot had he listened to a close family friend, Rambert Sim, who advised him to pull out of the US Amateur after injuring a shoulder in his warm up on the range before his quarter-final tie against Morgan Hoffman.

Sim, who is like an uncle to Lee, was concerned that the teenager might do more permanent damage to the injury but Lee was determined to play and did, helped by massage, rubbing ointment and later a hospital x-ray. "He used to listen to me when he was a boy but now he is grown up," said Sim, who was happy at the end that Danny had not taken his advice.

Lee's season had started "Down Under" where he was semi-finalist in the Australian Amateur Championship and won several titles including the Lake Macquarie Amateur Championship and the North Island Stroke Play Championship before heading to America last summer. He was in the top 10 in the world most of the time and after impressive performances in the Southern Amateur and Porter Cup competitions, he won the Western and the US Amateur where he played the 16th hole only once on the morning of the 36 hole final!

In winning the Western and US Amateur titles in the same year, he joins an exclusive list of golfers including Jack Nicklaus, Lanny Wadkins, Justin Leonard and Tiger, the golfer Lee admires most.

He did suffer one disappointment during his record-breaking season. Although hopeful that he might help New Zealand to victory in the World Amateur Team Championship for the Eisenhower Trophy in Adelaide late last year, he played well for three rounds then shot a closing 84. The team slipped from fourth to 11th behind winners Scotland.

Lee, a former New Zealand Amateur title holder, began playing golf at the age of eight after watching his mum play. "I just wanted to have a go," says the teenager who also hit the headlines on the Asian Tour when he came third in the GS Caltex Mae Keoung Open in Seoul behind Kim Kyung-tae. He practises 40 hours a week and his aspiration is to win The Masters. His best non-competitive score is an 11 under par 59 at the Springfield Club.

Lee is the second golfer to receive the McCormack Medal which was first awarded to Colt Knost who had won all four games in the US Walker Cup victory over Great Britain & Ireland at Royal County Down in 2007 and since turning professional has already won twice on the US Nationwide Tour to guarantee himself a place on the PGA Tour in 2009.

The medal, which measures an inch and a half in diameter, is made from sterling silver and features the crest of the Royal and Ancient Golf Club of St Andrews.

© Getty Images

R&A WAGR Top 100

The World Amateur Golf Ranking (WAGR) is compiled by The R&A as the global entry standard for The Amateur Championship and as a service to golf. Coverage currently exceeds 2400 players from 70 countries in 1000 ranking tournaments in 70 countries. WAGR is based on counting every stroke reported to The R&A in stroke play events and on matches won in match play events throughout a 52 week rolling period. The highest ranked player immediately following the US Amateur or the European Amateur, whichever event is staged later in the year, is awarded the Mark H McCormack Medal.

#	Player	Pts. av.
1	Danny Lee (NZL)	1236.78
2	Jorge Campillo (ESP)	1175.76
3	Rickie Fowler (USA)	1159.42
4	Zack Sucher (USA)	1046.25
5	Adam Mitchell (USA)	1038.00
6	Callum Macaulay (SCO)	1034.72
7	Stephan Gross (GER)	1033.82
8	Anders Kristiansen (NOR)	1024.49
9	Kyle Stanley (USA)	1023.81
10	Sihwan Kim (KOR)	1015.87
11	Erik Flores (USA)	1009.84
12	Russell Henley (USA)	1006.12
13	Leighton Lyle (AUS)	1005.00
14	Mike Van Sickle (USA)	1000.00
15	Sam Hutsby (ENG)	995.92
16	Shane Lowry (IRL)	995.16
17	Bi-o Kim (KOR)	993.62
18	Cameron Johnston (RSA)	992.59
19	Dustin Garza (USA)	978.43
20	Morgan Hoffmann (USA)	966.67
21	Cameron Tringale (USA)	964.71
22	Andrea Pavan (ITA)	964.15
23	Tom Sherreard (ENG)	960.42
24	Hudson Swafford (USA)	959.18
25	Nick Taylor (CAN)	955.56
26	Matt Hill (CAN)	950.98
27	Andrew Landry (USA)	947.17
28	Billy Horschel (USA)	945.28
29	Adrian Ford (RSA)	944.62
30	Reinier Saxton (NED)	941.67
31	Matt Savage (USA)	938.46
32	Chris Paisley (ENG)	937.93
33	Jack Newman (USA)	937.50
34	Todd Adcock (ENG)	937.50
35	Cristian Espinoza (CHI)	933.33
36	Robin Wingardh (SWE)	929.27
37	Jesper Kennegard (SWE)	926.67
38	Richard Lee (USA)	925.00
39	Charlie Holland (USA)	923.44
40	Judson Eustaquio (PHI)	921.05
41	Wesley Bryan (USA)	917.14
42	David Lingmerth (SWE)	911.11
43	Jamie Lovemark (USA)	908.33
44	Kevin Tway (USA)	904.48
45	Jon Curran (USA)	902.22
46	Derek Tolan (USA)	896.15
47	Eddie Olson (USA)	895.83
48	David Markle (CAN)	893.62
49	Mark Anderson (USA)	889.36
50	Victor Dubuisson (FRA)	886.49
51	Bobby Hudson (USA)	886.36
52	Benjamin Hebert (FRA)	886.11
53	Brian Harman (USA)	881.40
54	Trent Leon (USA)	880.00
55	Wallace Booth (SCO)	879.17
56	Are Friestad (NOR)	878.79
57	Michael Foster (AUS)	877.78
58	Drew Kittleson (USA)	877.36
59	Matthew Giles (AUS)	875.00
60	Jared Pender (NZL)	874.51
61	Dylan Frittelli (RSA)	872.15
62	Matt Hoffenberg (USA)	871.93
63	Gavin Dear (SCO)	870.15
64	Pedro Figueiredo (POR)	870.00
65	John Chin (USA)	867.92
65	Philip Francis (USA)	867.92
67	Tim Sluiter (NED)	864.71
68	Jason Kang (KOR)	863.64
69	Peter Spearman-Burn (NZL)	862.96
70	Jonathan Hodge (USA)	861.67
71	Henrik Norlander (SWE)	860.42
72	Jurrian van der Vaart (NED)	856.86
73	Jay Moseley (USA)	855.81
74	Brendan Smith (AUS)	853.19
75	Bjorn Akesson (SWE)	852.38
76	Matt Jager (AUS)	849.28
77	Bud Cauley (USA)	847.83
78	George Bryan (USA)	846.38
79	Bronson Burgoon (USA)	845.00
79	Ben Rickett (ENG)	845.00
81	Matthew Swan (USA)	844.07
82	Chris Baker (USA)	843.75
83	Trent Whitekiller (USA)	843.59
84	Dale Whitnell (ENG)	843.24
85	James Allenby (CAN)	841.86
86	Luke Goddard (ENG)	841.54
87	Garrett Merrell (USA)	837.50
88	Tommy Fleetwood (ENG)	834.69
89	Steve Ziegler (USA)	834.15
90	David May (USA)	834.09
91	Andrew Putnam (USA)	833.96
92	David Johnson (USA)	833.33
93	Seung-Su Han (KOR)	831.67
94	Aaron Russell (RSA)	831.25
95	Kevin O'Connell (USA)	830.00
96	Andrew Green (NZL)	830.00
97	Harris English (USA)	828.57
98	Jorge Fernandez (ARG)	828.21
99	Ryan Fox (NZL)	828.13
100	Andy Winings (USA)	827.66

For the full list of qualifying amateurs, visit www.randa.org/wagr

WAGR Counting Events – Europe

* indicates new WAGRanked Player

January
Copa Nacional Puerta de Hierro	Alicante	Moises Cobo (ESP)

February
Campeonato de Barcelona	Barcelona	Borja Etchart (ESP)
Portuguese Amateur	Estela	Pedro Figueiredo (POR)

March
Spanish Amateur	Platja de Pals	Daniel Willett (ENG)
Spanish Youths & Boys	El Bosque	Jordi Garcia Pinto (ESP)
French Boys Championship	Toulouse Seilh	Sebastian Schwind* (GER)
West of Ireland	Co Sligo	Shane Lowry (IRL)

April
Sotogrande Cup – European Nations	Sotogrande	Benjamin Hebert (FRA)/Shane Lowry (IRL)
Scottish Champion of Champions	Leven	Paul Betty (SCO)
Italian Match Play	Bologna	Nino Bertasio* (ITA)
R&A Bursars Championship	Eden/Old, St Andrews	Scott Borrowman (SCO)
Scottish Boys	Southerness	Michael Stewart* (SCO)
Craigmillar Park	Edinburgh	Craig Elliott* (SCO)
Duncan Putter	Southerndown	Nigel Edwards (WAL)
Peter McEvoy Trophy	Copt Heath	Stiggy Hodgson/ Eddie Pepperell (ENG)
Hampshire Salver	Blackmoor/ North Hants	Stiggy Hodgson (ENG)
Cyprus Amateur	Secret Valley	Robert Carson* (SCO)
Trofeo Umberto Agnelli	Royal Park	Nunzio Lombardi (ITA)
Edward Trophy	Glasgow (Gailes)	Scott Henry (SCO)
West of England	Royal North Devon	Andrew Cooley (ENG)
Ticino Championship	Ascona	Edouard Amacher* (SUI)
Trubshaw Cup	Tenby/ Ashburnham	Ben Westgate (WAL)
Coupe Fraysinneau-Mouchy	Fontainebleau	Romain Wattel (FRA)
German Match Play Trophy	Bad Neuenahr	Allen John (GER)

May
Lytham Trophy	Royal Lytham & St Annes	Matthew Haines (ENG)
Royal Tour I	Trelleborg	Morten Madsen (DEN)
Copa Andalucia	Golf Bellavista	Jordi Garcia Pinto/ Carlos Pigem* (ESP)
Irish Amateur Stroke Play	Royal Dublin	Pedro Figueiredo (POR)
Clwyd Open	Prestatyn/ Wrexham	Ben Enoch (WAL)
Leman Championship	Lausanne/ Montreux	Ken Benz* (SUI)

Netherlands Junior Stroke Play		Reiner Saxton (NED)
Trofeo Glauco Lolli Ghetti	Margara	Matteo Manassero* (ITA)
Brabazon Trophy	Trevose	Steven Uzzell (ENG)
Romande Championship	Bonmont	Richard Heath* (AUS)
French Amateur (Coupe Ganay)	St Germain	Stanislas Gautier* (FRA)
Skandia Junior Open	Delsjo	Gary King* (ENG)
Welsh Stroke Play	Conwy (Caernarvon-shire)	Chris Wood (ENG)
Lagonda Trophy	Gog Magog	Dale Whitnell (ENG)
FGT Opening	Meri-Teijo	Mikael Salminen* (FIN)
Royal Tour II	Gyldensteen	Andreas Harto* (DEN)
NGF National Open	Rosendaelsche	Floris de Vries (NED)

June
Swiss Match Play	Interlaken	Marc Dobias (SUI)
Scottish Stroke Play	The Dukes	Wallace Booth (SCO)
Welsh Open Youths	Vale of Llangollen	Jonathan Gidney (ENG)
French Stroke Play (Coupe Murat)	Chantilly GC	David Antonelli (FRA)
Spanish International Youths	Izki	Borja Etchart/ Juan Sarasti (ESP)
East of Ireland	Co Louth	Eoin Arthurs* (IRL)
Italian Boys – Trofeo Andrea Brotto	Margherita	Matteo Manassero (ITA)
Campeonato de Canarias	Buenavista	Carlos Pigem (ESP)
European Mid-Amateur	Postolowo	Michael Flindt* (POL)
Gran Premio citta di Milano	Milan	Matteo Manassero (ITA)
Orientale Championship	Alvaneu Bad	Ken Benz (SUI)
St Andrews Links Trophy	Old/Jubilee	Keir McNicoll (SCO)
German Boys	St Leon Rot	Max Kraemer (GER)
Irish Closed	Belvoir Park	Paul O'Hanlon (IRL)
Basel Championship	Basel	Oliver Gilmartin* (SUI)
Slovenian Amateur	Moravske Toplice	Philippo Okan* (GER)
Scottish Mid-Amateur	Dundonald	Ross Coull* (SCO)
The Amateur	Turnberry	Reinier Saxton (NED)
Scottish Youths Stroke Play	The Roxburghe	David Booth (ENG)
Tennant Cup	Glasgow (Gailes)/ Killermont	Callum Macaulay (SCO)
Berkshire Trophy	The Berkshire	Farren Keenan (ENG)
Peugeot Classic	Prunevelle	Guillaume Cambis (FRA)
Irish Open Youths	Lisburn	Seamus Power (IRL)
Midland Amateur	Worksop/ Retford/ Sherwood Forest	Jason Palmer (ENG)
East of Scotland Aberconwy Cup	Lundin Conwy/ Llandudno (Maesdu)	Rohan Blizard (AUS) Oliver Farr* (WAL)

July

Event	Venue	Winner
European Men's Team (Individual)	Turin	Wallace Booth (SCO)
Cameron Corbett Vase	Haggs Castle	David Addison* (SCO)
Faldo Series Russia	Le Meridien	Mikhail Morozov* (RUS)
Boyd Quaich	St Andrews	Sung-yong Park* (KOR)
Slovak Amateur	Brezno	Stanislav Matus (SLO)
European Boys Team (Individual)	Bled	Anders Kristiansen (DEN)
Luxembourg Amateur	Clervaux	Christopher Mivis (BEL)
Grand Prix d'Anglrt Chiberta	Chiberta	Guillaume Cambis (FRA)
Tucker Trophy	Newport/ Whitchurch	Ben Westgate (WAL)
Sutherland Chalice	Dumfries & Galloway	Scott Henry (SCO)
R&A Junior Open	Hesketh	Steven Lam* (HKG)/ Jordan Spieth* (USA)
Tillman Trophy	East Sussex National	Dale Whitnell (ENG)
North of Ireland	Royal Portrush	Shane Lowry (IRL)
Riverswoods Junior	Toxandria	Kevin Hesbois* (BEL)
Danish Amateur	Silkeborg	Lucas Bjerregaard (DEN)
Omnium Suisse	Lausanne	Ken Benz (SUI)
St David's Gold Cross	Royal St David's	Zac Gould (WAL)
Russian Amateur	Pestovo	Steven Uzzell (ENG)
Biarritz Cup	Biarritz	Sebastien Gros* (FRA)
South of England	Walton Heath	Luke Goddard (ENG)
Danish Youths	Smorum	Filippo Bergamaschi* (ITA)
Carris Trophy	Wallasey	Stiggy Hodgson (ENG)
Scottish Boys Stroke Play	Blairgowrie	Mark Bookless* (SCO)
European Young Masters	Chantilly	Stanislas Gautier (FRA)
Estonian Amateur	Estonian	Claas-Eric Borges* (GER)
Grand Prix des Landes	Golf d'Hossegor	Matthieu Bey (FRA)
Spanish National	Laukariz	Jorge Campillo (ESP)
South of Ireland	Lahinch	Niall Kearney (IRL)

August

Event	Venue	Winner
English Amateur	Woodhall Spa	Todd Adcock (ENG)
Scottish Amateur	Carnoustie	Callum Macaulay (SCO)
Welsh Amateur	Royal Porthcawl	Ben Westgate (WAL)
Swiss International	Brutto-Ergebnisse	Moritz Lampert (GER)
Royal Tour III	Sempachersee	Morten Madsen (DEN)
Zomerwedstrijd	Pan	Reinier Saxton (NED)
Mullingar Trophy	Mullingar	Shane Lowry (IRL)
Parman Cup	Trethorne	Sam Matton* (ENG)
North of England Youths	Middlesbrough	Dale Whitnell (ENG)
Latvian Amateur	Ozo	Karlis Broders (LAT)
Czech Amateur	Austerlitz	Chris Paisley (ENG)
Finnish Amateur	Helsinki	Kalle Samooja (FIN)
Netherlands Stroke Play	De Lage Vuursche	Tim Sluiter (NED)
German Amateur	Seddiner See	Stephan Gross (GER)
Leven Gold Medal	Leven	Keir McNicoll (SCO)
The Boys Amateur Championship	Little Aston	Pedro Figueiredo (POR)
Norwegian Open	Vestfold	Espen Kofstad (NOR)
North East Open	Newburgh-on-Ythan	James Byrne (SCO)
European Amateur Zurich Championship	Esbjerg Hittnau/ Breitenloo/ Schonenberg	Stephan Gross (GER) Mark Casutt* (SUI)
North of Scotland	Nairn	Kris Nicol (SCO)
Lee Westwood Trophy	Rotherham	Gary Wolstenholme (ENG)
Belgian International Junior	Ravenstein	Joachim Hansen (DEN)
South East District Open	Duddingston	Scott Borrowman (SCO)

September

Event	Venue	Winner
Hungarian Amateur	Polus Palace	Gergi Bondicz* (HUN)
Austrian Amateur	Tulin	Stephan Wolters (GER)
Newlands Trophy	Lanark	Wallace Booth (SCO)
Turkish Amateur	Antalya	Jose Maria Joia (POR)
Trophee Jean Lignel Individual	Saint Nom la Breteche	Kevin Turlan (FRA)
Hellenic Amateur	Corfu	Hamza Sayin (TUR)
French Match Play	Fontainebleau	Gary Stal* (FRA)
German National	Hubbelrath	Maximilian Glauert (GER)
Italian National Stroke Play	Castle-conturbia	Nino Bertasio (ITA)
Polish Amateur	Mazury	Michael Flindt (POL)
Duke of York Young Champions	Dundonald	Stiggy Hodgson (ENG)
Portugal Nations Cup – Individual	Valle do Lobo	Luke Goddard (ENG)
Italian International Centrale Championship	Villa d'Este Limpachtal	Nino Bertasio (ITA) Sandro Viglino* (SUI)
Portuguese Federation Cup	Quinta do Peru	Manuel Violas* (POR)
Bulgarian Amateur	Balchik	Richard Heath (AUS)

October

Event	Venue	Winner
European Club Trophy – Individual	Klassis, Istanbul	Victor Dubuisson (FRA)

November

Event	Venue	Winner
Israel Amateur	Caesarea	Asaf Cohen* (ISR)

For the full list of counting events, visit www.randa.org/wagr

European Ranking 2007–2008

English players dominated the European Amateur Ranking in 2007–2008 with 23 places in the top 100. Scotland and Sweden tied for second place with 12 entrants apiece while the third place honours went to Germany with nine players in the top half of the table. Other tallies are: Ireland 7, France 5, Spain and Netherlands 5, Norway and Wales 4 places. The European Rankings are extracted from WAGR and are finalised at the same time.

		Points			Points			Points
1	Jorge Campillo (ESP)	1175.76	34	Farren Keenan (ENG)	812.00	69	Miles Mackman (ENG)	721.43
2	Callum Macaulay (SCO)	1034.72	35	Rudy Thuillier (FRA)	809.43	70	Stefan Wiedergruen (GER)	719.05
3	Stephan Gross (GER)	1033.82	36	Nigel Edwards (WAL)	808.16	71	Eddie Pepperell (ENG)	715.38
4	Anders Kristiansen (NOR)	1024.49	37	Matt Haines (ENG)	804.26	72	Simon Ward (IRL)	711.76
			38	Floris De Vries (NED)	803.39	73	Jamie Abbott (ENG)	711.29
5	Sam Hutsby (ENG)	995.92	39	Seamus Power (IRL)	800.00	74	Ben Westgate (WAL)	704.69
6	Shane Lowry (IRL)	995.16	40	Steven Uzzell (ENG)	792.00	75	Hugues Joannes (BEL)	701.61
7	Andrea Pavan (ITA)	964.15	41	Tobias Rosendahl (SWE)	788.00	76	Billy Hemstock (ENG)	700.00
8	Tom Sherreard (ENG)	960.42				77	Ross Kellett (SCO)	700.00
9	Reinier Saxton (NED)	941.67	42	Paul O'Hara (SCO)	787.72	78	Cristiano Terragni (ITA)	697.73
10	Chris Paisley (ENG)	937.93	43	Victor Almstrom (SWE)	781.40			
11	Todd Adcock (ENG)	937.50	44	Toni Hakula (FIN)	780.00	79	Mark Hillson (SCO)	693.75
12	Robin Wingardh (SWE)	929.27	45	Maximilian Kieffer (GER)	778.85	80	Paul O'Hanlon (IRL)	691.30
13	Jesper Kennegard (SWE)	926.67	46	Charles Ford (ENG)	770.37	81	Lucas Bjerregaard (DEN)	684.38
14	David Lingmerth (SWE)	911.11	47	Niall Kearney (IRL)	766.00	82	Jake Amos (ENG)	682.93
15	Victor Dubuisson (FRA)	886.49	48	Knut Borsheim (NOR)	765.91	83	Markus Larsson (SWE)	678.12
			49	Pontus Widegren (SWE)	765.62	84	Matthew Nixon (ENG)	676.19
16	Benjamin Hebert (FRA)	886.11	50	Allen John (GER)	763.41	85	Maximilian Glauert (GER)	675.00
17	Wallace Booth (SCO)	879.17	51	Fredrik Qvicker (SWE)	761.36	86	Philipp Westermann (GER)	671.88
18	Are Friestad (NOR)	878.79	52	Alexandre Kaleka (FRA)	759.62	87	Tristan Bierenbroodspot (NED)	671.79
19	Gavin Dear (SCO)	870.15	53	Keir McNicoll (SCO)	758.18			
20	Pedro Figueiredo (POR)	870.00	54	Pedro Oriol (ESP)	753.19	88	Jason Palmer (ENG)	671.43
21	Tim Sluiter (NED)	864.71	55	Edouard Dubois (FRA)	749.25	89	Edward Richardson (ENG)	671.43
22	Henrik Norlander (SWE)	860.42	56	Espen Kofstad (NOR)	745.95	90	Sean Einhaus (GER)	670.91
23	Jurrian van der Vaart (NED)	856.86	57	James Byrne (SCO)	744.00	91	Andres Cuenca (ESP)	669.39
24	Bjorn Akesson (SWE)	852.38	58	Alexander Knappe (GER)	741.51	92	Romain Schneider (FRA)	668.29
25	Ben Rickett (ENG)	845.00	59	Michael Stewart (SCO)	738.30	93	Gencer Ozcan (TUR)	666.67
26	Dale Whitnell (ENG)	843.24	60	Ignacio Elvira (ESP)	735.56	94	Tuomas Pollari (FIN)	665.96
27	Luke Goddard (ENG)	841.54	61	Stiggy Hodgson (ENG)	734.15	95	Glenn Campbell (SCO)	664.71
28	Tommy Fleetwood (ENG)	834.69	62	Andrew Cooley (ENG)	733.96	96	Hans-Peter Bacher (AUT)	664.58
			63	Peter Baunsoe (DEN)	733.33			
29	Rhys Enoch (WAL)	826.67	64	Borja Etchart (ESP)	732.79	97	Jason Barnes (ENG)	662.96
30	Paul Cutler (IRL)	820.00	65	Rasmus Nielsen (DEN)	732.65	98	Peter Svajlen (SVK)	660.00
31	Florian Fritsch (GER)	816.22	66	Scott Henry (SCO)	732.31	99	Craig Evans (WAL)	659.38
32	Steven McEwan (SCO)	814.49	67	Dara Lernihan (IRL)	728.12	100	David Palm (SWE)	655.10
33	Kalle Samooja (FIN)	812.82	68	Johan Carlsson (SWE)	725.53			

For the full European Amateur Rankings, visit www.ega-golf.ch

National and International Championships 2008

113th Amateur Championship (inaugurated 1885)   *Turnberry (Ailsa & Kintyre)*
(British or Irish unless stated)

288 entries from 32 countries played in the 36-hole qualifying competition, 64 of whom qualified on 150 or better for the matchplay stage.

Leading Qualifier: Sam Hutsby (Liphook) 68-71—139

First Round

T J Bordeaux (USA) beat Sam Hutsby (Liphook) 3 and 2

Jason Barnes (Chart Hills) beat David Antonelli (FRA) 4 and 2

Reinier Saxton (NED) beat Zachariah Gould (Vale of Glamorgan) 4 and 2

Tom Prowse (AUS) beat Federico Colombo (ITA) 3 and 1

Scott Arnold (AUS) beat Benjamin Hebert (FRA) 3 and 1

Dale Whitnell (Five Lakes) beat David Corsby (Royal Lytham & St Annes) 2 and 1

Pedro Figueiredo (POR) beat Lewis Kirton (Newmachar) 2 and 1

Jamie Abbott (Fynn Valley) beat Edward Richardson (Rye) 2 holes

Callum Macaulay (Tulliallan) beat Neil Henderson (Glen) 4 and 3

John Carroll (Huyton & Prescot) beat Lindsay Renolds (CAN) 3 and 2

James Frazer (Pennard) beat Niall Kearney (Royal Dublin) at 19th

Ignacio Elvira (ESP) beat Andrew Hogan (Newlands) 2 and 1

Kevin McAlpine (Alyth) beat Joon Kim (ITA) 3 and 1

David Markle (CAN) beat Allen John (GER) 2 and 1

Joe Vickery (Newport) beat Maximilian Glauert (GER) 1 hole

Ben Westgate (Trevose) beat Nino Bertasio (ITA) 3 and 1

Andrew Sullivan (Nuneaton) beat Adam Mitchell (USA) 4 and 3

Nigel Edwards (Whitchurch) beat Mark Thistleton (Hayling) 4 and 3

Maximilian Kieffer (GER) beat David Coupland (Boston) 2 and 1

Bill Rankin (USA) beat James Gill (NZL) 2 and 1

Steven McEwan (Caprington) beat Matthew Nixon (Ashton-under-Lyne) 3 and 2

Jake Amos (Kilworth Springs) beat Joel Stalter (FRA) 1 hole

Rhein Gibson (AUS) beat Jonas Blixt (SWE) 1 hole

Andrea Pavan (ITA) beat Derik Ferreira (RSA) 2 and 1

Jorge Campillo (ESP) beat Steven Uzzell (Hornsea) 1 hole

Gareth Shaw (Lurgan) beat Jacques Blaauw (RSA) 4 and 3

Christopher Paisley (Stocksfield) beat Farren Keenan (Sunningdale) 1 hole

Chris Wood (Long Ashton) beat Tim Stewart (AUS) 3 and 2

Jacques Guillet (RSA) w/o Matthew Cryer (Coventry)

Tommy Fleetwood (Formby Hall) beat Jurrian Van Der Vaart (NED) 3 and 1

Floris De Vries (NED) beat Charles Ford (Kirby Muxloe) 1 hole

Jonathan Caldwell (Clandeboye) beat Alexander Culverwell (Dunbar) 4 and 3

Second Round

Barnes beat Bordeaux 4 and 2
Saxton beat Prowse 1 hole
Whitnell beat Arnold 5 and 3
Figueiredo beat Abbott 1 hole
Carroll beat Macaulay at 21st
Frazer beat Elvira at 19th
Markle beat McAlpine at 19th
Vickery beat Westgate 1 hole

Sullivan beat Edwards at 19th
Kieffer beat Rankin 2 holes
McEwan beat Amos 4 and 3
Pavan beat Gibson 1 hole
Campillo beat Shaw 3 and 2
Wood beat Paislet at 23rd
Fleetwood beat Guillet 5 and 4
Caldwell beat De Vries 5 and 3

Third Round
Saxton beat Barnes 3 and 1
Figueiredo beat Whitnell 3 and 2
Frazer beat Carroll 5 and 4
Vickery beat Markle 2 and 1
Sullivan beat Kieffer 5 and 3

Amateur Championship *continued*

Pavan beat McEwan 2 and 1
Campillo beat Wood 5 and 4
Fleetwood beat Caldwell at 20th

Semi-Finals
Saxton beat Vickery 1 hole
Fleetwood beat Sullivan 3 and 2

Quarter Finals
Saxton beat Figueiredo 3 and 2
Vickery beat Frazer at 22nd
Sullivan beat Pavan 2 and 1
Fleetwood beat Campillo 1 hole

Final
Reinier Saxton (NED) beat Tommy Fleetwood
(Formby Hall) 3 and 2

Year	Result	Margin	Venue	Entrants
1885	A MacFie beat H Hutchinson	7 and 6	Hoylake, Royal Liverpool	entrants 44
1886	H Hutchinson beat H Lamb	7 and 6	St Andrews	42
1887	H Hutchinson beat J Ball	1 hole	Hoylake, Royal Liverpool	33
1888	J Ball beat J Laidlay	5 and 4	Prestwick	38
1889	J Laidlay beat L Melville	2 and 1	St Andrews	40
1890	J Ball beat J Laidlay	4 and 3	Hoylake, Royal Liverpool	44
1891	J Laidlay beat H Hilton	at 20th	St Andrews	50
1892	J Ball beat H Hilton	3 and 1	Sandwich, Royal St George's	45
1893	P Anderson beat J Laidlay	1 hole	Prestwick	44
1894	J Ball beat S Fergusson	1 hole	Hoylake, Royal Liverpool	64
1895	L Melville beat J Ball	at 19th	St Andrews	68
From 1896 final played over 36 holes				
1896	F Tait beat H Hilton	8 and 7	Sandwich, Royal St George's	64
1897	A Allan beat J Robb	4 and 2	Muirfield	74
1898	F Tait beat S Fergusson	7 and 5	Hoylake, Royal Liverpool	77
1899	J Ball beat F Tait	at 37th	Prestwick	101
1900	H Hilton beat J Robb	8 and 7	Sandwich, Royal St George's	68
1901	H Hilton beat J Low	1 hole	St Andrews	116
1902	C Hutchings beat S Fry	1 hole	Hoylake, Royal Liverpool	114
1903	R Maxwell beat H Hutchinson	7 and 5	Muirfield	142
1904	W Travis (USA) beat E Blackwell	4 and 3	Sandwich, Royal St George's	104
1905	A Barry beat Hon O Scott	3 and 2	Prestwick	148
1906	J Robb beat C Lingen	4 and 3	Hoylake, Royal Liverpool	166
1907	J Ball beat C Palmer	6 and 4	St Andrews	200
1908	E Lassen beat H Taylor	7 and 6	Sandwich, Royal St George's	197
1909	R Maxwell beat Capt C Hutchison	1 hole	Muirfield	170
1910	J Ball beat C Aylmer	10 and 9	Hoylake, Royal Liverpool	160
1911	H Hilton beat E Lassen	4 and 3	Prestwick	146
1912	J Ball beat A Mitchell	at 38th	Westward Ho!, Royal North Devon	134
1913	H Hilton beat R Harris	6 and 5	St Andrews	198
1914	J Jenkins beat C Hezlet	3 and 2	Sandwich, Royal St George's	232
1915–19	*Not played*			
1920	C Tolley beat R Gardner (USA)	37th hole	Muirfield	165
1921	W Hunter beat A Graham	12 and 11	Hoylake, Royal Liverpool	223
1922	E Holderness beat J Caven	1 hole	Prestwick	252
1923	R Wethered beat R Harris	7 and 6	Deal, Royal Cinque Ports	209
1924	E Holderness beat E Storey	3 and 2	St Andrews	201
1925	R Harris beat K Fradgley	13 and 12	Westward Ho!, Royal North Devon	151
1926	J Sweetser (USA) beat A Simpson	6 and 5	Muirfield	216
1927	Dr W Tweddell beat D Landale	7 and 6	Hoylake, Royal Liverpool	197
1928	T Perkins beat R Wethered	6 and 4	Prestwick	220
1929	C Tolley beat J Smith	4 and 3	Sandwich, Royal St George's	253
1930	R Jones (USA) beat R Wethered	7 and 6	St Andrews	271
1931	E Smith beat J De Forest	1 hole	Westward Ho!, Royal North Devon	171
1932	J De Forest beat E Fiddian	3 and 1	Muirfield	235
1933	Hon M Scott beat T Bourn	4 and 3	Hoylake, Royal Liverpool	269
1934	W Lawson Little (USA) beat J Wallace	14 and 13	Prestwick	225
1935	W Lawson Little (USA) beat Dr W Tweddell	1 hole	R Lytham and St Annes	232
1936	H Thomson beat J Ferrier (AUS)	2 holes	St Andrews	283
1937	R Sweeney jr (USA) beat L Munn	3 and 2	Sandwich, Royal St George's	223
1938	C Yates (USA) beat R Ewing	3 and 2	Troon	241
1939	A Kyle beat A Duncan	2 and 1	Hoylake, Royal Liverpool	167
1940–45	*Not played*			
1946	J Bruen beat R Sweeny (USA)	4 and 3	Birkdale	263
1947	W Turnesa (USA) beat R Chapman (USA)	3 and 2	Carnoustie	200
1948	F Stranahan (USA) beat C Stowe	5 and 4	Sandwich, Royal St George's	168
1949	S McCready beat W Turnesa (USA)	2 and 1	Portmarnock	204
1950	F Stranahan (USA) beat R Chapman (USA)	8 and 6	St Andrews	324
1951	R Chapman (USA) beat C Coe (USA)	5 and 4	Royal Porthcawl	192
1952	E Ward (USA) beat F Stranahan (USA)	6 and 5	Prestwick	286
1953	J Carr beat E Harvie Ward (USA)	2 holes	Hoylake, Royal Liverpool	279

1954	D Bachli (AUS) beat W Campbell (USA)	2 and 1	Muirfield	286
1955	J Conrad (USA) beat A Slater	3 and 2	Royal Lytham and St Annes	240
1956	J Beharrell beat L Taylor	5 and 4	Troon	200
1957	R Reid Jack beat H Ridgley (USA)	2 and 1	Formby	200

In 1956 and 1957 the Quarter Finals, Semi-Finals and Final were played over 36 holes

1958	J Carr beat A Thirlwell	3 and 2	St Andrews	488

In 1958, Semi-Finals and Final only were played over 36 holes

1959	D Beman (USA) beat W Hyndman (USA)	3 and 2	Sandwich, Royal St George's	362
1960	J Carr beat R Cochran (USA)	8 and 7	Royal Portrush	183
1961	MF Bonallack beat J Walker	6 and 4	Turnberry	250
1962	R Davies (USA) beat J Povall	1 hole	Hoylake, Royal Liverpool	256
1963	M Lunt beat J Blackwell	2 and 1	St Andrews	256
1964	G Clark beat M Lunt	at 39th	Ganton	220
1965	MF Bonallack beat C Clark	2 and 1	Royal Porthcawl	176
1966	R Cole (RSA) beat R Shade	3 and 2	Carnoustie (18 holes)	206

Final played over 18 holes because of sea mist

1967	R Dickson (USA) beat R Cerrudo (USA)	2 and 1	Formby	
1968	MF Bonallack beat J Carr	7 and 6	Royal Troon	249
1969	MF Bonallack beat W Hyndman (USA)	3 and 2	Hoylake, Royal Liverpool	245
1970	MF Bonallack beat W Hyndman (USA)	8 and 7	Newcastle, Royal Co Down	256
1971	S Melnyk (USA) beat J Simons (USA)	3 and 2	Carnoustie	256
1972	T Homer beat A Thirlwell	4 and 3	andwich, Royal St George's	253
1973	R Siderowf (USA) beat P Moody	5 and 3	oyal Porthcawl	222
1974	T Homer beat J Gabrielsen (USA)	2 holes	Muirfield	330
1975	M Giles (USA) beat M James	8 and 7	Hoylake, Royal Liverpool	206
1976	R Siderowf (USA) beat J Davies	at 37th	St Andrews	289
1977	P McEvoy beat H Campbell	5 and 4	Ganton	235
1978	P McEvoy beat P McKellar	4 and 3	Royal Troon	353
1979	J Sigel (USA) beat S Hoch (USA)	3 and 2	Hillside	285
1980	D Evans beat D Suddards (RSA)	4 and 3	Royal Porthcawl	265
1981	P Ploujoux (FRA) beat J Hirsch (USA)	4 and 2	St Andrews	256
1982	M Thompson beat A Stubbs	4 and 3	Deal, Royal Cinque Ports	245

Qualifying round introduced

1983	P Parkin beat J Holtgrieve (USA)	5 and 4	Turnberry	288
1984	JM Olazábal (ESP) beat C Montgomerie	5 and 4	Formby	291
1985	G McGimpsey beat G Homewood	8 and 7	Royal Dornoch	457
1986	D Curry beat G Birtwell	11 and 9	Royal Lytham and St Annes	427
1987	P Mayo beat P McEvoy	3 and 1	Prestwick	373
1988	C Hardin (SWE) beat B Fouchee (RSA)	1 hole	Royal Porthcawl	391
1989	S Dodd beat C Cassells	5 and 3	Royal Birkdale	378
1990	R Muntz (NED) beat A Macara	7 and 6	Muirfield	510
1991	G Wolstenholme beat B May (USA)	8 and 6	Ganton	345
1992	S Dundas beat B Dredge	7 and 6	Carnoustie	364
1993	I Pyman beat P Page	at 37th	Royal Portrush	279
1994	L James beat G Sherry	2 and 1	Nairn	288
1995	G Sherry beat M Reynard	7 and 6	Hoylake, Royal Liverpool	288
1996	W Bladon beat R Beames	1 hole	Turnberry	288
1997	C Watson beat T Immelman (RSA)	3 and 2	Royal St Georges, Royal Cinque Ports	369
1998	S García (ESP) beat C Williams	7 and 6	Muirfield	537
1999	G Storm beat A Wainwright	7 and 6	Royal County Down, Kilkeel	433
2000	M Ilonen (FIN) beat C Reimbold	2 and 1	Royal Liverpool and Wallasey	376
2001	M Hoey beat I Campbell	1 hole	Prestwick & Kilmarnock	288
2002	A Larrazábal (ESP) beat M Sell	1 hole	Royal Porthcawl and Pyle & Kenfig	286
2003	G Wolstenholme beat R De Sousa (SUI)	6 and 5	Royal Troon and Irvine	289
2004	S Wilson beat L Corfield	4 and 3	St Andrews, Old and Jubilee Courses	288
2005	B McElhinney beat J Gallagher	5 and 4	Royal Birkdale and Southport & Ainsdale	406
2006	J Guerrier (FRA) beat A Gee	4 and 3	Royal St George's and Prince's	284
2007	D Weaver (USA) beat T Stewart (AUS)	2 and 1	Royal Lytham & St Annes and St Annes Old Links	284

British Seniors' Open Amateur Championship (inaugurated 1969)

Royal Cinque Ports/Prince's

1	Paul Simson (USA)		75-71-70—216
2	Chris Reynolds (Littlestone)		72-77-69—218
3	Graham Cooke (CAN)		71-72-77—220

1969	R Pattinson	Formby	154	1975	HJ Roberts	Turnberry	138
1970	K Bamber	Prestwick	150	1976	WM Crichton	Berkshire	149
1971	GH Pickard	Royal Cinque Ports;		1977	Dr TE Donaldson	Panmure	228
		Royal St George's	150	1978	RJ White	Formby	225
1972	TC Hartley	St Andrews	147	1979	RJ White	Harlech, R St David's	226
1973	JT Jones	Longniddry	142	1980	JM Cannon	Prestwick St Nicholas	218
1974	MA Ivor-Jones	Moortown	149	1981	T Branton	Hoylake, R Liverpool	227

British Seniors' Open Amateur Championship *continued*

1982	RL Glading	Blairgowrie	218	1996	J Hirsch	Blairgowrie	210
1983	AJ Swann (USA)	Walton Heath	222	1997	G Bradley (USA)	Sherwood Forest	216
1984	JC Owens (USA)	Western Gailes	222	1998	D Lane	Western Gailes/	
1985	D Morey (USA)	Hesketh	223			Glasgow Gailes	221
1986	AN Sturrock	Panmure	229	1999	W Shean (USA)	Frilford Heath	219
1987	B Soyars (USA)	Royal Cinque Ports	226	2000	J Hirsch (USA)	Gullane	218
1988	CW Green	Royal Burgess	221	2001	K Richardson (USA)	Royal Portrush	217
1989	CW Green	Moortown, Alwoodley	226	2002	J Baldwin (USA)	Woodhall Spa	216
1990	CW Green	The Berkshire	207	2003	R Smethurst	Blairgowrie	215
1991	CW Green	Prestwick	219	2004	K Richardson (USA)	The Berkshire	213
1992	C Hartland	Purdis Heath	221	2005	A Foster (USA)	Woburn	222
1993	CW Green	Royal Aberdeen	150	2006	P Simson (USA)	Saunton	223
1994	CW Green	Formby, Southport &		2007	A Pierse*	Nairn and Nairn Dunbar	211
		Ainsdale	223	*Beat G Cooke (CAN) at 1st extra hole			
1995	G Steel	Hankley Common	218				

British Mid-Amateur Championship (inaugurated 1995)

This event has been discontinued. For past results see the 2008 edition of the *Golfer's Handbook*.

English Amateur Championship (inaugurated 1925)   *Woodhall Spa*

Leading Qualifier: Jason Barnes (Chart Hills)   68-70—138

Quarter Finals
Adam Keogh (Boston West) beat Luke Goddard (Hendon) at 21st

Chris Paisley (Stocksfield) beat Matthew Nixon (Ashton-under-Lyne) 2 and 1

Thomas Sherreard (Chart Hills) beat Kevin Freeman (Stoke Park) 1 hole

Todd Adcock (Nevill) beat Neil Raymond (Corhampton) 3 and 1

Semi-Finals
Paisley beat Keogh 4 and 2

Adcock beat Sherreard 3 and 1

Final
Todd Adcock beat Chris Paisley 2 and 1

1925	TF Ellison beat S Robinson 1 hole	1965	MF Bonallack beat CA Clark 3 and 2
1926	TF Ellison beat Sq Ldr CH Hayward 6 and 4	1966	MSR Lunt beat DJ Millensted 3 and 2
1927	TP Perkins beat JB Beddard 2 and 1	1967	MF Bonallack beat GE Hyde 4 and 2
1928	JA Stout beat TP Perkins 3 and 2	1968	MF Bonallack beat PD Kelley 12 and 11
1929	W Sutton beat EB Tipping 3 and 2	1969	JH Cook beat P Dawson 6 and 4
1930	TA Bourn beat CE Hardman 3 and 2	1970	Dr D Marsh beat SG Birtwell 6 and 4
1931	LG Crawley beat W Sutton 1 hole	1971	W Humphreys beat JC Davies 9 and 8
1932	EW Fiddian beat AS Bradshaw 1 hole	1972	H Ashby beat R Revell 5 and 4
1933	J Woollam beat TA Bourn 4 and 3	1973	H Ashby beat SC Mason 5 and 4
1934	S Lunt beat LG Crawley at 37th	1974	M James beat JA Watts 6 and 5
1935	J Woollam beat EW Fiddian 2 and 1	1975	N Faldo beat D Eccleston 6 and 4
1936	HG Bentley beat JDA Langley 5 and 4	1976	P Deeble beat JC Davies 3 and 1
1937	JJ Pennink beat LG Crawley 6 and 5	1977	TR Shingler beat J Mayell 4 and 3
1938	JJ Pennink beat SE Banks 2 and 1	1978	P Downes beat P Hoad 1 hole
1939	AL Bentley beat W Sutton 5 and 4	1979	R Chapman beat A Carman 6 and 5
1946	IR Patey beat K Thom 5 and 4	1980	P Deeble beat P McEvoy 4 and 3
1947	GH Micklem beat C Stow 1 hole	1981	D Blakeman beat A Stubbs 3 and 1
1948	AGB Helm beat HJR Roberts 2 and 1	1982	A Oldcorn beat I Bradshaw 4 and 3
1949	RJ White beat C Stowe 5 and 4	1983	G Laurence beat A Brewer 7 and 6
1950	JDA Langley beat IR Patey 1 hole	1984	D Gilford beat M Gerrard 4 and 3
1951	GP Roberts beat H Bennett at 39th	1985	R Winchester beat P Robinson 1 hole
1952	E Millward beat TJ Shorrock 2 holes	1986	J Langmead beat B White 2 and 1
1953	GH Micklem beat RJ White 2 and 1	1987	K Weeks beat R Eggo at 37th
1954	A Thirlwell beat HG Bentley 2 and 1	1988	R Claydon beat D Curry at 38th
1955	A Thirlwell beat M Burgess 7 and 6	1989	S Richardson beat R Eggo 2 and 1
1956	GB Wolstenholme beat H Bennett 1 hole	1990	I Garbutt beat G Evans 8 and 7
1957	A Walker beat G Whitehead 4 and 3	1991	R Willison beat M Pullan 10 and 8
1958	DN Sewell beat DA Procter 8 and 7	1992	S Cage beat R Hutt 3 and 2
1959	GB Wolstenholme beat MF Bonallack 1 hole	1993	D Fisher beat R Bland 3 and 1
1960	DN Sewell beat MJ Christmas at 41st	1994	M Foster beat A Johnson 8 and 7
1961	I Caldwell beat GJ Clark at 37th	1995	M Foster beat S Jarman 6 and 5
1962	MF Bonallack beat MSR Lunt 2 and 1	1996	S Webster beat D Lucas 6 and 4
1963	MF Bonallack beat A Thirlwell 4 and 3	1997	A Wainwright beat P Rowe 2 and 1
1964	Dr D Marsh beat R Foster 1 hole	1998	M Sanders beat S Gorry 6 and 5

1999	P Casey beat S Dyson 2 and 1		2004	J Heath beat D Horsey 3 and 2
2000	P Casey beat G Wolstenholme 4 and 2		2005	P Waring beat S Capper 3 and 2
2001	S Godfrey beat S Robinson 4 and 3		2006	R McGowan beat O Fisher 5 and 4
2002	R Finch beat G Legg 6 and 5		2007	D Willett beat M Cryer 3 and 2
2003	G Lockerbie beat M Skelton 6 and 5			

English Open Amateur Stroke Play Championship (Brabazon Trophy)

Trevose (inaugurated 1947)

1	Steven Uzzell (Hornsea)	66-64-67—197
2	Benjamin Hebert (FRA)	66-67-68—201
3	Paul Cutler (Portstewart)	67-70-67—204
	Tom Lewis (Welwyn Garden City)	67-68-69—204

1947	DMG Sutherland	1965T	CA Clark	1980T	R Rafferty	1993	D Fisher
1948	C Stowe		DJ Millensted		P McEvoy	1994	G Harris
1949	PB Hine		MJ Burgess	1981	P Way	1995T	M Foster
1950	RJ White	1966	PM Townsend	1982	P Downes		CS Edwards
1951	RJ White	1967	RDBM Shade	1983	C Banks	1996	P Fenton
1952	PF Scrutton	1968	MF Bonallack	1984	M Davis	1997	D Park
1953	C Stowe	1969T	R Foster	1985T	R Roper	1998	P Hanson (SWE)
1954	PF Scrutton		MF Bonallack		P Baker	1999	M Side
1955	PF Scrutton	1970	R Foster	1986	R Kaplan	2000	J Lupprien (GER)
1956	SJ Fox	1971	MF Bonallack	1987	JG Robinson	2001	R Walker
1957	D Sewell	1972	PH Moody	1988	R Eggo	2002	C Schwartzel (RSA)
1958	AH Perowne	1973	R Revell	1989T	C Rivett	2003	J Lupton
1959	D Sewell	1974	N Sundelson		RN Roderick	2004	M Richardson
1960	GB Wolstenholme	1975	A Lyle	1990T	O Edmond	2005	L Saltman (SCO)
1961	RDBM Shade	1976	P Hedges		G Evans	2006	R Dinwiddie
1962	A Slater	1977	A Lyle	1991T	G Evans	2007T	R Bechu (FRA)
1963	RDBM Shade	1978	G Brand Jr		M Pullan		J Moul
1964	MF Bonallack	1979	D Long	1992	I Garrido		

English Seniors' Amateur Championship (inaugurated 1981) *Wildernesse*

1	John Jermine (Sunningdale)	73-73-74—220
2	Donald McCart (Sherwood Forest)	74-76-71—221
3	Douglas Arnold (Copthorne)	73-73-76—222
	David Lane (Goring & Streatley)	71-76-75—222
	Chris Reynolds (Littlestone)	74-73-75—222

1981	CR Spalding	1989	G Clark	1996T	G Edwards	2003	D Arnold
1982	JL Whitworth	1990	N Paul		B Berney	2004	R Smethurst
1983	B Cawthray	1991	W Williams	1997	D Lane	2005	R Smethurst
1984	RL Glading	1992	B Cawthray	1998	J Marks	2006	D Arnold
1985	JR Marriott	1993	G Edwards	1999	D Lane	2007	D Lane
1986	R Hiatt	1994T	G Steel	2000	R Smethurst		
1987	I Caldwell		F Jones	2001	R Smethurst		
1988	G Edwards	1995	H Hopkinson	2002	D Arnold		

English Open Mid-Amateur Championship (Logan Trophy) (inaugurated 1988)

Shifnal

1	John Longcake (Silloth on Solway)	67-69-66—202
2	John Kemp (John O'Gaunt)	67-71-65—203
3	James Murphy (Shrigley Hall)	71-64-71—206

1988	P McEvoy		Southport & Ainsdale	1999	S East	2004	S Sansome
1989	A Mew	1994T	I Richardson	2000	B Downing	2005	N Chesters
1990	A Mew		A McLure	2001	S East	2006	M Young
1991	I Richardson	1995	C Banks	2002T	F Illouz	2007	C Edwards
1992	A Mew	1997	C Banks		S Crosby		
1993	R Godley	1998	S East	2003	J Longcake		

English County Champions' Tournament (formerly President's Bowl)   (inaugurated 1962)

always at Woodhall Spa

1	Tommy Fleetwood* (Lancashire)	72-72—144
2	John Longcake (Cumbria)	69-75—144

Fleetwood won at the fifth extra hole

3	Andrew Sullivan (Warwickshire)	72-73—145

1962T	G Edwards	1974T	G Hyde	1986	A Gelsthorpe	1997	J Herbert
	A Thirwell		A Lyle	1987T	F George	1998	GP Wolstenholme
1963T	M Burgess	1975	N Faldo		D Fay	1999	D Griffiths
	R Foster	1976	R Brown	1988	R Claydon	2000	P Bradshaw
1964	M Attenborough	1977	M Walls	1989	R Willison	2001	G Wolstenholme
1965	M Lees	1978	I Simpson	1990T	P Streeter	2002	G Evans
1966	R Stephenson	1979	N Burch		R Sloman	2003	J Crampton
1967	P Benka	1980	D Lane	1991	T Allen	2004	J Phelps
1968	G Hyde	1981	M Kelly	1992	L Westwood	2005	D Horsey
1969	A Holmes	1982	P Deeble	1993	R Walker		*(David Horsey's second round*
1970	M King	1983	N Chesses	1994	GP Wolstenholme		*64 was a record)*
1971	M Lee	1984T	N Briggs	1995	S Webster	2006	G Evans
1972	P Berry		P McEvoy	1996T	J Herbert	2007	J Kemp
1973	A Chandler	1985	P Robinson		G Wolstenholme		

Irish Amateur Open Championship (inaugurated 1892)   *Royal Dublin*

1	Pedro Figueiredo (Portugal)	73-67-70-68—278
2	Connor Doran (Banbridge)	71-71-70-73—285
	Billy Hemstock (Teignmouth)	70-75-69-71—285
	Keir McNicoll (Carnoustie)	73-72-69-71—285

1892	A Stuart beat JH Andrew 1 hole
1893	John Ball beat LS Anderson 8 and 7
1894	John Ball beat DL Low 9 and 7
1895	WB Taylor beat JM Williamson 13 and 11
1896	WB Taylor beat D Anderson 9 and 8
1897	HH Hilton beat LS Anderson 5 and 4
1898	WB Taylor beat ROJ Dallmyer at 37th
1899	John Ball beat JM Williamson 13 and 11
1900	HH Hilton beat SH Fry 11 and 9
1901	HH Hilton beat P Dowie 6 and 5
1902	HH Hilton beat WH Hamilton 5 and 4
1903	G Wilkie beat HA Boyd 1 hole
1904	JS Worthington beat JF Mitchell 6 and 4
1905	HA Boyd beat JF Mitchell 3 and 2
1906	HH Barker beat JS Worthington 5 and 4
1907	JD Brown beat SH Fry 2 and 1
1908	JF Mitchell beat HM Cairnes 3 and 2
1909	LO Munn beat R Garson 2 holes
1910	LO Munn beat G Lockhart 9 and 7
1911	LO Munn beat Hon. Michael Scott 7 and 6
1912	G Lockhart beat P Jenkins 11 and 9
1913	CA Palmer beat LA Phillips 4 and 3
1914–1918	*Not played*
1919	C Bretherton beat TD Armour 5 and 3
1920	GNC Martin beat CW Robertson 6 and 5
1921	D Smyth beat J Gorry 2 holes
1922	A Lowe beat J Henderson 6 and 4
1923	GNC Martin beat CO Hezlet 1 hole

1924	EF Spiller beat JDA McCormack 3 and 1
1925	TA Torrance beat CO Hezlet 4 and 3
1926	CO Hezlet beat RM McConnell 7 and 6
1927	RM McConnell beat DEB Soulby 5 and 3
1928	GS Moon beat EF Spiller 1 hole
1929	CO Hezlet beat JA Lang 1 hole
1930	W Sutton beat DA Fiddian 4 and 2
1931	EA McRuvie beat DEB Soulby 7 and 5
1932	J McLean beat JC Brown 9 and 8
1933	J McLean beat E Fiddian 3 and 2
1934	H Thomson beat HG Bentley 3 and 2
1935	H Thomson beat J McLean 5 and 4
1936	JC Brown beat WM O'Sullivan at 39th
1937	J Fitzsimmons beat RA McKinna 4 and 3
1938	J Bruen jr beat JR Mahon 9 and 8
1939–1945	*Not played*
1946	JB Carr beat AT Kyle 3 and 1
1947	J Burke beat JB Carr 1 hole
1948	RC Ewing beat JB Carr 1 hole
1949	WM O'Sullivan beat BJ Scannell 2 holes
1950	JB Carr beat RC Ewing at 40th
1951	RC Ewing beat JB Carr 2 and 1
1952	NV Drew beat CH Beamish 5 and 4
1953	NV Drew beat WM O'Sullivan 3 and 2
1954	JB Carr beat RC Ewing 6 and 4
1955	JF Fitzgibbon beat JW Hulme 1 hole
1956	JB Carr beat JR Mahon 1 hole
1957	JL Bamford beat W Meharg at 37th

From 1958 decided by Stroke Play

1958	T Craddock	1996	K Nolan
1959	J Duncan	1997	K Nolan
From 1960–1994 not played		1998	M Hoey
1995	P Harrington	1999	G Cullen

2000	N Fox	2004	C Smith
2001	R McEvoy	2005	R Ramsay
2002	L Oosthuizen (RSA)	2006	A Ahokas (FIN)
2003	N Fox	2007	L Saltman

Irish Amateur Close Championship (inaugurated 1893) *Belvoir Park, Belfast*

Leading Qualifier: Alex McCloy (Ballymena) 72-65—137

Quarter Finals
Paul O'Hanlon (Curragh) beat Niall Kearney (Royal Dublin) 4 and 2

Andrew McCormick (Scrabo) beat Rory McNamara (Headfort) 4 and 3

Cian Curley (Newlands) beat Michael Sinclair (Knock) 5 and 4

Dara Lernihan (Castle) beat David Rawluk (Island) at 19th

Semi-Finals
O'Hanlon beat McCormick 2 holes

Lernihan beat Curley 4 and 2

Final
Paul O'Hanlon beat Dara Lernihan at 20th

1893	T Dickson beat G Combe 2 holes	1954	JB Carr beat I Forsythe 4 and 3
1894	R Magill jr beat T Dickson 3 and 1	1955	JR Mahon beat G Crosbie 3 and 2
1895	WH Webb beat J Stevenson 10 and 9	1956	AGH Love beat G Crosbie at 37th
1896	J Stewart-Moore jr beat HAS Upton 8 and 7	1957	JB Carr beat G Crosbie 2 holes
1897	HE Reade beat WH Webb 2 and 1	1958	RC Ewing beat GA Young 5 and 3
1898	WH Webb beat J Stewart-Moore jr 9 and 8	1959	T Craddock beat JB Carr at 38th
1899	HE Reade beat JP Todd 3 and 2	1960	M Edwards beat N Fogarty 6 and 5
1900	RGN Henry beat J McAvoy 4 and 3	1961	D Sheahan beat J Brown 5 and 4
1901	WH Boyd beat HE Reade 7 and 5	1962	M Edwards beat J Harrington at 42nd
1902	FB Newett beat R Shaw 1 hole	1963	JB Carr beat EC O'Brien 2 and 1
1903	HE Reade beat DRA Campbell 5 and 4	1964	JB Carr beat A McDade 6 and 5
1904	HA Boyd beat JP Todd 4 and 2	1965	JB Carr beat T Craddock 3 and 2
1905	FB Newett beat B O'Brien 6 and 5	1966	D Sheahan beat J Faith 3 and 2
1906	HA Boyd beat HM Cairnes at 38th	1967	JB Carr beat PD Flaherty 1 hole
1907	HM Cairnes beat HA Boyd 7 and 6	1968	M O'Brien beat F McCarroll 2 and 1
1908	LO Munn beat A Babbington 10 and 9	1969	V Nevin beat J O'Leary 1 hole
1909	AH Patterson beat EF Spiller at 37th	1970	D Sheahan beat M Bloom 2 holes
1910	JF Jameson beat LO Munn 2 and 1	1971	P Kane beat M O'Brien 3 and 2
1911	LO Munn beat HA Boyd 7 and 6	1972	K Stevenson beat B Hoey 2 and 1
1912	AH Craig beat P Halligan 13 and 11	1973	RKM Pollin beat RM Staunton 1 hole
1913	LO Munn beat HA Boyd 6 and 5	1974	R Kane beat M Gannon 5 and 4
1914	LO Munn beat Earl Annesley 0 and 8	1975	MD O'Brien beat JA Bryan 5 and 4
1915–1918	*Not played*	1976	D Brannigan beat D O'Sullivan 2 holes
1919	E Carter beat WG McConnell 9 and 7	1977	M Gannon beat A Hayes at 19th
1920	CO Hezlet beat CL Crawford 12 and 11	1978	M Morris beat T Cleary 1 hole
1921	E Carter beat G Moore 9 and 8	1979	J Harrington beat MA Gannon 2 and 1
1922	EM Munn beat WK Tillie 3 and 1	1980	R Rafferty beat MJ Bannon 8 and 7
1923	JD McCormack beat LE Werner 2 and 1	1981	D Brannigan beat E McMenamin at 19th
1924	JD McCormack beat DEB Soulby 4 and 2	1982	P Walton beat B Smyth 7 and 6
1925	CW Robertson beat HM Cairnes 4 and 3	1983	T Corridan beat E Power 2 holes
1926	AC Allison beat OW Madden 7 and 6	1984	CB Hoey beat L McNamara at 20th
1927	JD McCormack beat HM Cairnes at 37th	1985	D O'Sullivan beat D Branigan 1 hole
1928	DEB Soulby beat JO Wisdom 7 and 5	1986	J McHenry beat P Rayfus 4 and 3
1929	DEB Soulby beat FP McConnell 4 and 3	1987	E Power beat JP Fitzgerald 2 holes
1930	J Burke beat FP McConnell 6 and 5	1988	G McGimpsey beat D Mulholland 2 and 1
1931	J Burke beat FP McConnell 6 and 4	1989	P McGinley beat N Goulding 3 and 2
1932	J Burke beat M Crowley 6 and 5	1990	D Clarke beat P Harrington 3 and 2
1933	J Burke beat GT McMullan 3 and 2	1991	G McNeill beat N Goulding 3 and 1
1934	JC Brown beat RM McConnell 6 and 5	1992	G Murphy beat JP Fitzgerald 2 and 1
1935	RM McConnell beat J Burke 2 and 1	1993	E Power beat D Higgins 3 and 2
1936	J Burke beat RM McConnell 7 and 6	1994	D Higgins beat P Harrington at 20th
1937	J Bruen jr beat J Burke 3 and 2	1995	P Harrington beat D Coughlan 3 and 2
1938	J Bruen jr beat R Simcox 3 and 2	1996	P Lawrie beat G McGimpsey 3 and 2
1939	GH Owens beat RM McConnell 6 and 5	1997	K Kearney beat P Lawrie 5 and 4
1940	J Burke beat WM O'Sullivan 4 and 3	1998	E Power beat B Omelia 1 hole
1941–1945	*Not played*	1999	C McMonagle beat M Sinclair 2 and 1
1946	J Burke beat RC Ewing 2 and 1	2000	G McDowell beat A McCormick 7 and 6
1947	J Burke beat J Fitzsimmons 2 holes	2001	G McNeill beat S Browne at 20th
1948	RC Ewing beat BJ Scannell 3 and 2	2002	J McGinn beat K Kearney 3 and 1
1949	J Carroll beat P Murphy 4 and 3	2003	M O'Sullivan beat D Carroll 1 hole
1950	B Herlihy beat BC McManus 4 and 3	2004	B McElhinney beat M McGeady 1 hole
1951	M Power beat JB Carr 3 and 2	2005	R McIlroy beat A McCormack 3 and 2
1952	TW Egan beat JC Brown at 41st	2006	R McIlroy beat S Ward 3 and 2
1953	J Malone beat M Power 2 and 1	2007	S Lowry beat N Turner 4 and 3

Irish Seniors' Open Amateur Championship (inaugurated 1970) *Westport*

1	Adrian Morrow (Portmarnock)	72-73-67—212
2	Jimmy Clynch (Laytown & Bettystown)	70-71-77—218
3	John Carroll (Bandon)	74-71-76—221

1970	RC Ewing	1980	GN Fogarty	1990	C Hartland	2000	D Jackson
1971	J O'Sullivan	1981	GN Fogarty	1991	C Hartland	2001	D Jackson
1972	BJ Scannell	1982	J Murray	1992	C Hartland	2002	T Fox
1973	JW Hulme	1983	F Sharpe	1993	P Breen	2003	P Jones
1974	P Walsh	1984	J Boston	1994	B Buckley	2004	MF Morris
1975	SA O'Connor	1985	J Boston	1995	B Hoey	2005	J Baldwin (USA)
1976	BJ Scannell	1986	J Coey	1996	E Condren	2006	J Baldwin (USA)
1977	DB Somers	1987	J Murray	1997	B Wilson	2007	V Smyth
1978	DP Herlihy	1988	WB Buckley	1998	J Harrington		
1979	P Kelly	1989	B McCrea	1999	A Lee		

Scottish Amateur Championship (inaugurated 1922) *Carnoustie*

Quarter Finals

Callum Macaulay (Tulliallan) beat Paul Betty (Hayston) 4 and 2

Greg Paterson (St Andrews New) beat Scott Stewart-Cation (Balbirnie Park) 3 and 2

Steven McEwan (Caprington) beat Scott Borrowman (Dollar) 1 hole

Gordon Yates (Hilton Park) beat Russell Thornton (USA) 2 and 1

Semi-Finals

Macaulay beat Paterson 1 hole

McEwan beat Yates 3 and 2

Final

Callum Macaulay beat Steven McEwan 5 and 3

1922	J Wilson beat E Blackwell at 19th		1968	GB Cosh beat R Renfrew 4 and 3
1923	TM Burrell beat Dr A McCallum 1 hole		1969	JM Cannon beat A Hall 6 and 4
1924	WW Mackenzie beat W Tulloch 3 and 2		1970	CW Green beat H Stuart 1 hole
1925	JT Dobson beat W Mackenzie 3 and 2		1971	S Stephen beat C Green 3 and 2
1926	WJ Guild beat SO Shepherd 2 and 1		1972	HB Stuart beat A Pirie 3 and 1
1927	A Jamieson jr beat Rev D Rutherford at 22nd		1973	IC Hutcheon beat A Brodie 3 and 2
1928	WW Mackenzie beat W Dodds 5 and 3		1974	GH Murray beat A Pirie 2 and 1
1929	JT Bookless beat J Dawson 5 and 4		1975	D Greig beat G Murray 7 and 6
1930	K Greig beat T Wallace 9 and 8		1976	GH Murray beat H Stuart 6 and 5
1931	J Wilson beat A Jamieson Jr 2 and 1		1977	A Brodie beat P McKellar 1 hole
1932	J McLean beat K Greig 5 and 4		1978	IA Carslaw beat J Cuddihy 7 and 6
1933	J McLean beat KC Forbes 6 and 4		1979	K Macintosh beat P McKellar 5 and 4
1934	J McLean beat W Campbell 3 and 1		1980	D Jamieson beat C Green 2 and 1 (18)
1935	H Thomson beat J McLean 2 and 1		1981	C Dalgleish beat A Thomson 7 and 6
1936	ED Hamilton beat R Neill 1 hole		1982	CW Green beat G Macgregor 1 hole
1937	H McInally beat K Patrick 6 and 5		1983	CW Green beat J Huggan 1 hole
1938	ED Hamilton beat R Rutherford 4 and 2		1984	A Moir beat K Buchan 3 and 3
1939	H McInally beat H Thomson 6 and 5		1985	D Carrick beat D James 4 and 2
1940–1945	*Not played*		1986	C Brooks beat A Thomson 3 and 2
1946	EC Brown beat R Rutherford 3 and 2		1987	C Montgomerie beat A Watt 9 and 8
1947	H McInally beat J Pressley 10 and 8		1988	J Milligan beat A Coltart 1 hole
1948	AS Flockhart beat G Taylor 7 and 6		1989	A Thomson beat A Tait 1 hole
1949	R Wright beat H McInally 1 hole		1990	C Everett beat M Thomson 7 and 5
1950	WC Gibson beat D Blair 2 and 1		1991	G Lowson beat L Salariya 4 and 3
1951	JM Dykes beat J Wilson 4 and 2		1992	S Gallacher beat D Kirkpatrick at 37th
1952	FG Dewar beat J Wilson 4 and 3		1993	D Robertson beat R Russell 2 holes
1953	DA Blair beat J McKay 3 and 1		1994	H McKibben beat A Reid at 39th
1954	JW Draper beat W Gray 4 and 3		1995	S Mackenzie beat H McKibben 8 and 7
1955	RR Jack beat AC Miller 2 and 1		1996	M Brooks beat A Turnbull 7 and 6
1956	Dr FWG Deighton beat A MacGregor 8 and 7		1997	C Hislop beat S Cairns 5 and 3
1957	JS Montgomerie beat J Burnside 2 and 1		1998	G Rankin beat M Donaldson 6 and 5
1958	WD Smith beat I Harris 6 and 5		1999	C Heap beat M Loftus 7 and 5
1959	Dr FWG Deighton beat R Murray 6 and 5		2000	S O'Hara beat C Heap 1 hole
1960	JR Young beat S Saddler 5 and 3		2001	B Hume beat C Watson 4 and 3
1961	J Walker beat ST Murray 4 and 3		2002	A McArthur beat S Jamieson 2 and 1
1962	SWT Murray beat RDBM Shade 2 and 1		2003	G Gordon beat S Wilson 4 and 3
1963	RDBM Shade beat N Henderson 4 and 3		2004	G Murray beat P O'Hara 1 hole
1964	RDBM Shade beat J McBeath 8 and 7		2005	G Campbell beat B Shamash at 37th
1965	RDBM Shade beat G Cosh 4 and 2		2006	K McAlpine beat P O'Hara 8 and 7
1966	RDBM Shade beat C Strachan 9 and 8		2007	J Gallagher beat K McNicoll 4 and 3
1967	RDBM Shade beat A Murphy 5 and 4			

Scottish Open Amateur Stroke Play Championship (inaugurated 1967)

Duke's Course, St Andrews

1	Wallace Booth (Comrie)	69-73-68—210
2	Edouard Dubois (FRA)	69-72-73—214
3	Matthew Cryer (Coventry)	73-71-72—216
	Mark Halliday (Royal Aberdeen)	73-73-70—216

1967	B Gallacher	1977	PJ McKellar	1988	S Easingwood	1999	G Rankin
1968	RDBM Shade	1978	AR Taylor	1989	F Illouz	2000	S McKenzie
1969	JS Macdonald	1979	IC Hutcheon	1990	G Hay	2001	J Sutherland
1970	D Hayes	1980	G Brand jr	1991	A Coltart	2002	B Hume
1971	IC Hutcheon	1981	F Walton	1992	D Robertson	2003	G Wolstenholme
1972	BN Nicholas	1982	C Macgregor	1993	A Reid	2004	R Ramsay
1973T	DM Robertson/	1983	C Murray	1994	D Downie	2005	R Dinwiddie
	GJ Clark	1984	CW Green	1995	S Gallacher	2006	S Henry
1974	IC Hutcheon	1985	C Montgomerie	1996	A Forsyth	2007	K McAlpine
1975	CW Green	1986	KH Walker	1997	DB Howard		
1976	S Martin	1987	D Carrick	1998	L Kelly		

Scottish Senior Open Amateur StrokePlay (inaugurated 1978) *Elgin*

1	Bob Stewart (Tulliallan)*	77-70-69—216
2	Iain Stewart (IRL)	73-72-71—216

*Stewart won at the first extra hole

3	Ian Hutcheon (Monifieth) [65+]	76-70-73—219
	David Lane (Goring & Streatley) [65+]	72-71-76—219

1978T	JM Cannon	1983	WD Smith	1992	G Clark	2001	D Lane
	GR Carmichael	1984	A Sinclair	1993	J Maclean	2002	D Lane
1979	A Sinclair	1985	AN Sturrock	1994	DM Lawrie	2003	I Hutcheon
1980	JM Cannon	1986	RL Glading	1995	CW Green	2004	I Hutcheon
1981T	IR Harris	1987	I Hornsby	1996	CW Green	2005	G MacDonald
	Dr J Hastings	1988	J Hayes	1997	CW Green	2006	S Ellis
	AN Sturrock	1989	AS Mayer	1998	CW Green	2007	I Hutcheon
1982T	JM Cannon	1990	C Hartland	1999	G Steel		
	J Niven	1991	CW Green	2000	N Grant		

Scottish Champion of Champions (inaugurated 1970) *always at Leven*

1	Paul Betty (Hayston)	68-70—138
2	Gavin Dear (Murrayshall)	74-65—139
3	Kevin McAlpine (Alyth)	72-70—142
	Gordon Yates (Hilton Park)	74-68—142

Play abandoned after two rounds due to snow

1970	A Horne	1980	I Hutcheon	1990	J Milligan	2000	G Fox
1971	D Black	1981	I Hutcheon	1991	G Hay	2001	M Loftus
1972	R Strachan	1982	G Macgregor	1992	D Robertson	2002	S Carmichael
1973	*Not held*	1983	D Carrick	1993	R Russell	2003	S Wilson
1974	M Niven	1984	S Stephen	1994	G Sherry	2004	A McArthur
1975	A Brodie	1985	I Brotherston	1995	S Gallacher	2005	C Watson
1976	A Brodie	1986	I Hutcheon	1996	M Brooks	2006	G Murray
1977	V Reid	1987	G Shaw	1997	G Rankin	2007	L Saltman*
1978	D Greig	1988	I Hutcheon	1998	G Rankin		*Beat J Gallagher at 1st extra
1979	B Marchbank	1989	J Milligan	1999	D Patrick		hole

Scottish Mid-Amateur Championship (inaugurated 1994) *Dundonald*

Leading Qualifier: Terry Mathieson (Kings Acre) 77-74—151

Quarter Finals

Terry Mathieson (Kings Acre) beat George Robertson (Ravenspark) 5 and 4

John Mitchell (Fraserburgh) beat Andrew Farmer (Kilmacolm) 2 and 1

Steven Robertson (Sandyhills) beat Gordon Landsburgh (Scotscraig) at 19th

Ross Coull (Edzell) beat Nicky Bell (Carlisle) 4 and 3

Semi-Finals

Mitchell beat Mathieson 1 hole

Coull beat S Robertson 1 hole

Final

Ross Coull beat John Mitchell 2 holes

Scottish Mid-Amateur Championship *continued*

1994	C Watson	1998	G Campbell	2002	C Elliot	2006	A Dick
1995	M Thomson	1999	G Crawford	2003	C Gordon	2007	M Clark
1996	B Smith	2000	J Cameron	2004	R Roper		
1997	H McDonald	2001	M Thomson	2005	A Dick		

Welsh Amateur Championship (inaugurated 1895) *Royal Porthcawl*

Quarter Finals
Ben Westgate (Trevose) beat John Jermine (Sunningdale)
1 hole
Adam Runcie (Abergele) beat Ross McLister (Cardiff)
3 and 2
Ben Enoch (Truro) beat Jamie Howie (Royal st David's)
2 holes
Craig Evans (West Monmouthshire) beat Jason
Shufflebotham (Prestatyn) 2 holes

Semi-Finals
Westgate beat Runcie at 21st
Enoch beat Evans 2 and 1

Final
Ben Westgate beat Ben Enoch 5 and 3

1895	J Hunter beat TM Barlow 2 holes	1957	ES Mills beat H Griffiths 2 and 1
1896	J Hunter beat P Plunkett 1 hole	1958	HC Squirrell beat AD Lake 4 and 3
1897	FE Woodhead beat J Hunter 4 and 3	1959	HC Squirrell beat N Rees 8 and 7
1898	FE Woodhead beat Dr E Reid 5 and 4	1960	HC Squirrell beat P Richards 2 and 1
1899	FE Woodhead beat TD Cummins 6 and 5Conway	1961	AD Evans beat J Toye 3 and 2
1900	TM Barlow beat H Ludlow 2 and 1	1962	J Povall beat HC Squirrell 3 and 2
1901	Major Green beat P Plunkett 8 and 7	1963	WI Tucker beat J Povall 4 and 3
1902	J Hunter beat H Ludlow 5 and 4	1964	HC Squirrell beat WI Tucker 1 hole
1903	J Hunter beat TM Barlow 2 holes	1965	HC Squirrell beat G Clay 6 and 4
1904	H Ludlow beat RM Brown 13 and 11	1966	WI Tucker beat EN Davies 6 and 5
1905	J Duncan jr beat AP Cary Thomas 6 and 5	1967	JK Povall beat WI Tucker 3 and 2
1906	G Renwick beat WT Davies 9 and 7	1968	J Buckley beat J Povall 8 and 7
1907	LA Phillips beat LH Gottwaltz 3 and 1	1969	JL Toye beat EN Davies 1 hole
1908	G Renwick beat LA Phillips 7 and 5	1970	EN Davies beat J Povall 1 hole
1909	J Duncan jr beat EJ Byrne 9 and 8	1971	CT Brown beat HC Squirrell 6 and 5
1910	G Renwick beat RM Brown 2 holes	1972	EN Davies beat JL Toye 40th hole
1911	HM Lloyd beat TC Mellor 4 and 2	1973	D McLean beat T Holder 6 and 4
1912	LA Phillips beat CH Turnbull 4 and 3	1974	S Cox beat EN Davies 3 and 2
1913	HN Atkinson beat CJ Hamilton at 38th	1975	JL Toye beat WI Tucker 5 and 4
1914–1919	*Not played*	1976	MPD Adams beat WI Tucker 4 and 5
1920	HR Howell beat J Duncan jr 2 holes	1977	D Stevens beat JKD Povall 3 and 2
1921	CEL Fairchild beat E Rowe 1 hole	1978	D McLean beat A Ingram 11 and 10
1922	HR Howell beat EDSN Carne 12 and 11	1979	TJ Melia beat MS Roper 5 and 4
1923	HR Howell beat CEL Fairchild 3 and 1	1980	DL Stevens beat G Clement 10 and 9
1924	HR Howell beat CH Turnbull 2 and 1	1981	S Jones beat C Davies 5 and 3
1925	CEL Fairchild beat GS Emery 10 and 8	1982	D Wood beat C Davies 8 and 7
1926	DR Lewis beat K Stoker 1 hole	1983	JR Jones beat AP Parkin 2 holes
1927	DR Lewis beat JL Jones 4 and 3	1984	JR Jones beat A Llyr 1 hole
1928	CC Marston beat DR Lewis at 37th	1985	ED Jones beat MA Macara 2 and 1
1929	HR Howell beat R Chapman 4 and 3	1986	C Rees beat B Knight 1 hole
1930	HR Howell beat DR Lewis 2 and 1	1987	PM Mayo beat DK Wood 2 holes
1931	HR Howell beat WG Morgan 7 and 6	1988	K Jones beat RN Roderick at 40th
1932	HR Howell beat HE Davies 7 and 6	1989	S Dodd beat K Jones 2 and 1
1933	JL Black beat AA Duncan 2 and 1	1990	A Barnett beat A Jones 1 hole
1934	SB Roberts beat GS Noon 4 and 3	1991	S Pardoe beat S Jones 7 and 5
1935	R Chapman beat GS Noon 1 hole	1992	H Roberts beat R Johnson 3 and 2
1936	RM de Lloyd beat G Wallis 1 hole	1993	B Dredge beat M Ellis 3 and 1
1937	DH Lewis beat R Glossop 2 holes	1994	C Evans beat M Smith 5 and 4
1938	AA Duncan beat SB Roberts 2 and 1	1995	G Houston beat C Evans 3 and 2
1939–1945	*Not played*	1996	Y Taylor beat DH Park 3 and 2
1946	JV Moody beat A Marshman 9 and 8	1997	JR Donaldson beat M Pilkington 5 and 4
1947	SB Roberts beat G Breen Turner 8 and 7	1998	M Pilkington beat K Sullivan 2 and 1
1948	AA Duncan beat SB Roberts 2 and 1	1999	M Griffiths beat R Brookman 7 and 6
1949	AD Evans beat MA Jones 2 and 1	2000	JG Jermine beat R Brookman 1 hole
1950	JL Morgan beat DJ Bonnell 9 and 7	2001	C Williams beat L Harpin 1 hole
1951	JL Morgan beat WI Tucker 3 and 2	2002	D Price beat L Harpin at 20th
1952	AA Duncan beat JL Morgan 4 and 3	2003	S Manley beat R Davies 8 and 7
1953	SB Roberts beat D Pearson 5 and 3	2004	R Thomas beat J Williams at 41st
1954	AA Duncan beat K Thomas 6 and 5	2005	C Wakeley beat C Mills 7 and 6
1955	TJ Davies beat P Dunn at 38th	2006	L Matthews beat R Davies 1 hole
1956	A Lockley beat WI Tucker 2 and 1	2007	L Matthews beat B Westgate 2 and 1

Welsh Open Amateur Stroke Play Championship (inaugurated 1967) *Conwy*

1	Chris Wood (Long Ashton)	74-75-69-71—289
2	Sam Hutsby (Liphook)	67-75-76-77—295
3	Jamie Abbott (Fynn Valley)	70-80-74-73—297

1967	EN Davies	1977	JA Buckley	1988	RN Roderick	1998	DAJ Patrick
1968	JA Buckley	1978	HJ Evans	1989	SC Dodd	1999	C Williams
1969	DL Stevens	1979	D McLean		*Open event since 1990*	2000	J Donaldson
1970	JK Povall	1980	TJ Melia	1990	G Houston	2001	J Lupton
1971T	EN Davies	1981	D Evans	1991	A Jones	2002	J Doherty
	JL Toye	1982	JR Jones	1992	AJ Barnett	2003	M Skelton
1972	JR Jones	1983	G Davies	1993	M Macara	2004	H Bragason (ISL)
1973	JR Jones	1984	RN Roderick	1994	N Van Hootegem	2005	R Dinwiddie
1974	JL Toye	1985	MA Macara	1995	M Peet	2006	*Event cancelled due*
1975	D McLean	1986	M Calvert	1996	M Blackey		*to bad weather*
1976	WI Tucker	1987	MA Macara	1997	G Wolstenholme	2007	R Parry

Welsh Seniors' Amateur Championship (inaugurated 1975) *always at Aberdovey*

1	Glyn Rees (Fleetwood)	73-73-71—217
2	George Stowe (Aberdovey)	80-71-78—229
3	Keith Stimpson (Wenvoe Castle)	75-80-75—230

1975	A Marshman	1983	WS Gronow	1990	I Hughes	1996	G Isaac	2004	P Jones
1976	AD Evans	1984	WI Tucker	1991	RO Ward	1997	I Hughes	2005	P Jones
1977	AE Lockley	1985	NA Lycett	1992	I Hughes	1998	D Reidford	2006	K Stimpson
1978	AE Lockley	1986T	E Mills/NA	1993	G Perks	1999	G Isaac	2007	K Stimpson
1979	CR Morgan		Lycett	1994T	G Perks/	2000	JR Jones		
1980	ES Mills	1987	WS Gronow		I Hughes/	2001	W Stowe		
1981	T Branton	1988	NA Lycett		A Prytherch	2002	B Cramb		
1982	WI Tucker	1989	WI Tucker	1995	I Hughes	2003	P Jones		

Welsh Seniors' Open Championship Llanddudno (Maesdu)

1	John Jermine (Sunnindale)	69-72-74—215
2	Douglas Arnold (Copthorne)	70-76-72—218
3	Phil Jones (Bromborough)	73-76-74—223

2007	J Baldwin	Llandudno (Maesdu)	222

Welsh Tournament of Champions (inaugurated 1979) *always at Cradoc*

This tournament was postponed because of extremely inclement weather.
It is to be played in April 2009 (and will count as the 2008 event)

1979	J L Toye	1987	J R Jones	1995	G Houston	2003	L James
1980	J M Morrow	1988	S C Dodd	1996	M H Peat	2004	P Grimley
1981	A P Vicary	1989	P Sykes	1997	M Pilkington	2005	I Flower
1982	P M Mayo	1990	G Houston	1998	M Gwyther	2006	J Zanotti
1983	P M Mayo	1991	G Houston	1999	R Williams	2007	J Brute
1984	M Bearcroft	1992	B Dredge	2000	J Davidson		
1985	S C Dodd	1993	B Dredge	2001	N Oakley		
1986	S C Dodd	1994	B Dredge	2002	T Hayward		

European Amateur Championship (inaugurated 1986) *Esbjerg, Denmark*

1	Stephan Gross (GER)	73-68-69-70—280
2	Richard Kind (NED)	69-74-70-68—281
3	Morten Madsen (DEN)	72-74-68-68—282
	Luke Goddard (ENG)	68-72-70-72—282

1986	A Haglund (SWE)		*Beat L Westwood in play-off*	2000	C Pettersson (SWE)	2007	B Herbert (FRA)*
1988	D Ecob (AUS)	1994	S Gallacher (SCO)	2001	S Browne (IRL)		*Beat J Sjoholm (SWE) in 3-*
1990	K Erikson (SWE)	1995	S García (ESP)	2002	R Pellicioli (FRA)		*hole play-off*
1991	J Payne (ENG)	1996	D Olsson (SWE)	2003	B McElhinney (IRL)		
1992	M Scarpa (ITA)	1997	D de Vooght (BEL)	2004	M Richardson (ENG)		
1993	M Backhausen*	1998	P Gribben (IRL)	2005	M Thorp (NOR)		
	(DEN)	1999	G Havret (FRA)	2006	R McIlroy (IRL)		

European Seniors' Championship (inaugurated 1999)   *Oceanico, Portugal*

1	Adrian Morrow (IRL)	69-73-69—211
2	Arthur Pierse (IRL)	71-71-72—214
3	Maurice Kelly (IRL)	74-70-75—219

1999	H-J Ecklebe (GER)	*Beat LJ Trenor (ESP) and D	2005	R Smethurst (ENG)	2007 N Swenson (USA)
2000	HH Giesen (GER)	Arnold (ENG) at 6th extra hole	2006	M Preysler de la	
2001	G Steel (ENG)	2004 DJ Smith (SCO)*		Riva (ESP)	
2002	A Morrison (ENG)	*Beat R Smethurst at 5th		One round cancelled due to	
2003	DJ Smith (SCO)	extra hole		bad weather	

European Mid-Amateur Championship (inaugurated 1999)   *Postowolo, Poland*

1	Michael Flindt (DEN)	73-70-75—218
2	Niklas Rosenkvist (SWE)	76-72-73—221
3	Roger Roper (ENG)	76-73-75—224

1999	H-G Reiter (GER)	2005	JM Zamora (ESP)	2007	G Wolstenholme
2000	F Illouz (FRA)	2006	G Wolstenholme*		(ENG)
2001	B Downing (ENG)		(ENG)		
2002	H-G Reiter (GER)		*Beat J Thomsen at 1st extra		
2003	H-G Reiter (GER)		hole		
2004	F Clerici (ITA)				

Adcock surprises the favourite at Woodhall Spa

The winners of the Scottish and English National Championships both staged fight backs to take their respective titles in 2008

After being two down with six to play, Todd Adcock from The Nevill club beat Chris Paisley from Stocksfield 2 and 1 in the final of the English Amateur Championship at Woodhall Spa. Paisley had been installed favourite because of his good play in American College golf.

Top seeded Callum Macaulay from Tulliallan was a 5 and 3 winner over Steven McEwan (Caprington) in the Scottish final at Carnoustie after losing four of the first five holes and still being one down after the sixth.in the afternoon. Macaulay then won six of the next nine holes.

In Wales Trevose golfer Ben Westgate, seeded No. 1, beat Ben Enoch 5 and 3 at Royal Porthcawl and in the Irish final Paul O'Hanlon (Curragh) was a winner at the 20th hole over Dara Lernihan from the Castle club.

National Orders of Merit

England – PING/EGU Order of Merit 2008

1	Chris Wood (Long Ashton)	1213	6	Christopher Paisley (Stocksfield)	626
2	Dale Whitnell (Five Lakes)	1116	7	Jamie Abbott (Fynn Valley)	612
3	Luke Goddard (Hendon)	894	8	Andrew Sullivan (Nuneaton)	608
4	Sam Hutsby (Liphook)	841	9	Gary Wolstenholme (Carus Green)	602
5	Tommy Fleetwood (Formby Hall)	750	10	Matt Haines (Rochester & Cobham Park)	579

English Golf Ranking 2008

1	Sam Hutsby (Liphook)	977.0	6	Ben Rickett (Surbiton)	845.0
2	Tom Sherreard (Chart Hills)	960.0	7	Luke Goddard (Hendon)	841.0
3	Christopher Paisley (Stocksfield)	937.9	8	Tommy Fleetwood (Formby Hall)	828.0
4	Todd Adcock (Nevill)	937.2	9	Farren Keenan (Sunningdale)	812.0
5	Dale Whitnell (Five Lakes)	857.0	10	Matt Haines (Rochester & Cobham Park)	804.0

Ireland – Willie Gill Award 2008

1	Paul O'Hanlon (Curragh)	175	6	Eoin Arthurs (Forrest Little)	80
2	Shane Lowry (Esker Hills)	165	7	Andrew Hogan (Newlands)	55
3	Niall Kearney (Royal Dublin)	120	8	Pat Murray (Limerick)	55
4	Dara Lernihan (Castle)	110	9	Niall Gorey (Lee Valley)	55
5	Connor Doran (Banbridge)	95	10	Des Morgan (Mullingar)	50

Irish Golf Ranking 2008

1	Shane Lowry (Esker Hills)	995	6	Simon Ward (Co.Louth)	711
2	Paul Cutler (Portstewart)	820	7	Paul O'Hanlon (Curragh)	691
3	Seamus Power (West Waterford)	800	8	Andrew Hogan (Newlands)	638
4	Niall Kearney (Royal Dublin)	766	9	Sergal Rafferty (Dungannon)	588
5	Dara Lernihan (Castle)	728	10	Aaron O'Callaghan (Douglas)	463

Scotland – Order of Merit 2008

1	Steven McEwan (Caprington)	781	6	Gordon Yates (Hilton Park)	457
2	Wallace Booth (Comrie)	692	7	Keir McNicoll (Carnoustie)	450
3	Callum Macaulay (Tulliallan)	525	8	Kris Nicol (Fraserburgh)	381
4	Scott Henry (Cardross)	522	9	Michael Stewart (Troon Wellbeck)	362
5	Scott Borrowman (Dollar)	476	10	Paul O'Hara (Colville Park)	355

Scottish Golf Ranking 2008

1	Callum Macaulay (Tulliallan)	1031	6	Keir McNicoll (Carnoustie)	758
2	Wallace Booth (Comrie)	879	7	Scott Henry (Cardross)	757
3	Gavin Dear (Murrayshall)	870	8	James Byrne (Banchory)	744
4	Steven McEwan (Caprington)	814	9	Michael Stewart (Troon Wellbeck)	738
5	Paul O'Hara (Colville Park)	787	10	Ross Kellett (Colville Park)	700

Wales – Pinnacle Order of Merit 2008

1	Ben Westgate (Trevose)	822.0	6	James Frazer (Pennard)	289.5
2	Nigel Edwards (Whitchurch)	475.0	7	Craig Evans (West Monmouthshire)	289.0
3	Ben Enoch (Truro)	451.0	8	Oliver Farr (Ludlow)	263.0
4	Zac Gould (Vale of Glamorgan)	447.0	9	Adam Runcie (Abergele)	163.0
5	Joe Vickery (Newport)	365.0	10	Jason Shufflebotham (Prestatyn)	145.0

Welsh Golf Ranking 2008

1	Rhys Enoch (Truro)	826	6	James Frazer (Pennard)	587
2	Nigel Edwards (Whitchurch)	808	7	Ben Enoch (Truro)	562
3	Ben Westgate (Trevose)	704	8	Adam Runcie (Abergele)	528
4	Craig Evans (West Monmouthshire)	659	9	Zac Gould (Vale of Glamorgan)	519
5	Joe Vickery (Newport)	623	10	Oliver Farr (Ludlow)	450

Team Events

Walker Cup (Instituted 1922)
Great Britain & Ireland v USA (home team names first)

2007 *Royal County Down* Sept 8–9
Result: USA 12½, GBI 11½
Captains: Colin Dalgliesh (GBI), Buddy Marucci (USA)

First Day – Foursomes
L Saltman & R Davies lost to B Horschel & R Fowler
4 and 3
R McIlroy & J Caldwell halved with C Knost & D Johnson
J Parry & D Horsey beat T Kuehne & K Stanley 2 and 1
J Moul & D Willett halved with W Simpson & J Moore

Singles
R McIlroy lost to B Horschel 1 hole
L Saltman lost to R Fowler 5 and 4
R Davies beat D Johnson 5 and 4
D Willett lost to C Knost 2 holes
L Matthews lost to J Lovemark 5 and 4
N Edwards beat K Stanley 1 hole
J Moul beat C Kirk 1 hole
D Horsey beat W Simpson 1 hole

Second Day – Foursomes
Caldwell & McIlroy lost to Horschel & Fowler
2 and 1
Davies & Edwards lost to Knost & Johnson 1 hole
Moul & Willett lost to Kuehne & Moore 4 and 2
Horsey & Parry lost to Kirk & Lovemark 1 hole

Singles
McIlroy beat Horschel 4 and 2
Davies beat Fowler 3 and 2
Willett halved with Knost
Saltman beat Kuehne 2 and 1
Caldwell beat Stanley 2 holes
Edwards lost to Moore 1 hole
Moul lost to Lovemark 4 and 3
Horsey beat Simpson 1 hole

2005 *Chicago GC, Wheaton, IL* Aug 13–14
Result: USA 12½, GBI 11½
Captains: Bob Lewis (USA),
Garth McGimpsey (GBI)

First Day – Foursomes
A Kim & B Harman halved with NB Edwards &
R Davies
L Williams & M Every beat G Lockerbie & R Dinwiddie
1 hole
J Overton & M Putnam beat O Fisher & M Richardson
2 and 1
K Reifers & B Hurley lost to R Ramsay & L Saltman
4 and 3

Singles
M Every lost to R Davies 4 and 3
A Kim beat G Lockerbie 6 and 5
L Overton beat NB Edwards 5 and 4
M Putnam lost to O Fisher 2 holes
N Thompson lost to M Richardson 5 and 4
B Hurley lost to L Saltman 1 hole
J Holmes beat G Wolstenholme 1 hole
L Williams beat B McElhinney 2 and 1

Second Day – Foursomes
Kim & Harman beat Ramsay & Saltman 4 and 2
Every & Williams lost to Davies & Edwards 2 and 1
Thompson & Holmes beat Fisher & Richardson
2 and 1
Putnam & Overton lost to Lockerbie & Dinwiddie
5 and 3

Singles
Kim lost to Wolstenholme 1 hole
Harman beat Davies 6 and 5
Putnam halved with Fisher
Every halved with Dinwiddie
Holmes lost to Richardson 5 and 4
Reifers lost to Saltman 1 hole
Overton beat Edwards 1 hole
Williams beat Lockerbie 4 and 3

2003 *Ganton, Yorkshire* Sept 6–7
Result: GBI 12½, USA 11½
Captains: Garth McGimpsey (GBI),
Bob Lewis (USA)

First Day – Foursomes
GP Wolstenholme & M Skelton lost to W Haas
& T Kuehne 2 and 1
S Wilson & D Inglis beat L Williams & G Zahringer
2 holes
NB Edwards & S Manley beat C Nallen & R Moore
3 and 2
N Fox & C Moriarty beat A Rubinson & C Wittenberg
4 and 2

Singles
GP Wolstenholme lost to W Haas 1 hole
O Wilson halved with T Kuehne
D Inglis lost to B Mackenzie 3 and 2
S Wilson halved with M Hendrix
NB Edwards beat G Zahringer 3 and 2
C Moriarty lost to C Nallen 1 hole
N Fox lost to A Rubinson 3 and 2
G Gordon lost to C Wittenberg 5 and 4

Second Day – Foursomes
GP Wolstenholme & O Wilson beat W Haas & T Kuehne
5 and 4
N Fox & C Moriarty lost to B Mackenzie & M Hendrix
6 and 5
S Wilson & D Inglis halved with C Wittenberg &
A Rubinson
NB Edwards & S Manley halved with L Williams &
G Zahringer

Singles
O Wilson beat W Haas 1 hole
GP Wolstenholme beat C Wittenberg 3 and 2
M Skelton beat A Rubinson 3 and 2
C Moriarty lost to B Mackenzie 3 and 1
S Wilson lost to M Hendrix 5 and 4
D Inglis beat R Moore 4 and 3
NB Edwards halved with L Williams
S Manley beat T Kuehne 3 and 2

2001 *Ocean Forest, Sea Island, GA* Aug 11–12
Result: GBI 15, USA 9
Captains: D Yates jr (USA), P McEvoy (GBI)
First Day – Foursomes
D Green & DJ Trahan lost to S O'Hara &
GP Wolstenholme 5 and 3
N Cassini & L Glover beat L Donald & N Dougherty
4 and 3
D Eger & B Molder halved with J Elson & R McEvoy
J Driscoll & J Quinney lost to G McDowell & M Hoey
3 and 1
Singles
E Compton beat G Wolstenholme 3 and 2
DJ Trahan beat S O'Hara 2 and 1
J Driscoll lost to N Dougherty 2 and 1
N Cassini beat N Edwards 5 and 4
J Harris lost to M Warren 5 and 4
J Quinney lost to L Donald 3 and 2
B Molder beat G McDowell 2 and 1
L Glover beat M Hoey 1 hole
Second Day – Foursomes
E Compton & J Harris lost to L Donald & N Dougherty
3 and 2
N Cassini & L Glover lost to G McDowell & M Hoey
2 and 1
D Eger & B Molder beat S O'Hara & M Warren 7 and 6
D Green & DJ Trahan lost to J Elson & R McEvoy 1 hole
Singles
L Glover lost to L Donald 3 and 2
J Harris lost to S O'Hara 4 and 3
DJ Trahan lost to N Dougherty 1 hole
J Driscoll lost to M Warren 2 and 1
B Molder beat G McDowell 1 hole
D Green lost to M Hoey 1 hole
E Compton halved with J Elson
N Cassini lost to GP Wolstenholme 4 and 3

1999 *Nairn, Scotland* Sept 11–12
Result: GBI 15, USA 9
Captains: P McEvoy (GBI), D Yates jr (USA)
First Day – Foursomes
Rankin & Storm lost to Haas & Miller 1 hole
Casey & Donald beat Byrd & Scott 5 and 3
Gribben & Kelly lost to Gossett & Jackson 3 and 1
Rowe & Wolstenholme beat Kuchar & Molder 1 hole
Singles
G Rankin lost to E Loar 4 and 3
L Donald beat T McKnight 4 and 3
G Storm lost to H Haas 5 and 4
P Casey beat S Scott 4 and 3
D Patrick lost to J Byrd 6 and 5
S Dyson halved with D Gossett
P Gribben halved with B Molder
L Kelly lost to T Jackson 3 and 1
Second Day – Foursomes
Rankin & Storm beat Loar & McKnight 4 and 3
Dyson & Gribben lost to Haas & Miller 1 hole
Casey & Donald beat Gossett & Jackson 1 hole
Rowe & Wolstenholme beat Kuchar & Molder 4 and 3
Singles
Rankin beat Scott 1 hole
Dyson lost to Loar 5 and 4
Casey beat Miller 3 and 2
Storm beat Byrd 1 hole
Donald beat Molder 3 and 2
Rowe beat Kuchar 1 hole
Gribben beat Haas 3 and 2
Wolstenholme beat Gossett 1 hole

1997 *Quaker Ridge, NY* Aug 9–10
Result: USA 18, GBI 6
Captains: AD Gray jr (USA), C Brown (GBI)
First Day – Foursomes
Howard & Young lost to Elder & Kribel 4 and 3
Rose & Brooks lost to Courville & Marucci 5 and 4
Wolstenholme & Nolan lost to Gore & Harris 6 and 4
Coughlan & Park lost to Leen & Wollman 1 hole
Singles
S Young beat D Delcher 5 and 4
C Watson beat S Scott 1 hole
B Howard lost to B Elder 5 and 4
J Rose beat J Kribel 1 hole
K Nolan lost to R Leen 3 and 2
G Rankin lost to J Gore 3 and 2
R Coughlan halved with C Wollman
GP Wolstenholme lost to J Harris 1 hole
Second Day – Foursomes
Young & Watson lost to Harris & Elder 3 and 2
Howard & Rankin lost to Courville & Marucci 5 and 4
Coughlan & Park lost to Delcher & Scott 1 hole
Wolstenholme & Rose beat Leen & Wollman 2 and 1
Singles
Young beat Kribel 2 and 1
Watson halved with Gore
Rose lost to Courville 3 and 2
Nolan lost to Elder 2 and 1
Brooks lost to Harris 6 and 5
Park lost to Marucci 4 and 3
Wolstenholme lost to Delcher 2 and 1
Coughlan lost to Scott 2 and 1

1995 *Royal Porthcawl, Wales* Sept 9–10
Result: GBI 14, USA 10
Captains: C Brown (GBI),
  AD Gray jr (USA)
First Day – Foursomes
Sherry & Gallacher lost to Harris & Woods 4 and 3
Foster & Howell halved with Bratton & Riley
Rankin & Howard lost to Begay & Jackson 4 and 3
Harrington & Fanagan beat Cox & Kuehne 5 and 3
Singles
G Sherry beat N Begay 3 and 2
L James lost to K Cox 1 hole
M Foster beat B Marucci 4 and 3
S Gallacher beat T Jackson 4 and 3
P Harrington beat J Courville jr 2 holes
B Howard halved with A Bratton
G Rankin lost to J Harris 1 hole
GP Wolstenholme beat T Woods 1 hole
Second Day – Foursomes
Sherry & Gallacher lost to Bratton & Riley 4 and 2
Howell & Foster beat Cox & Kuehne 3 and 2
Wolstenholme & James lost to Marucci & Courville
  6 and 5
Harrington & Fanagan beat Harris & Woods 2 and 1
Singles
Sherry beat Riley 2 holes
Howell beat Begay 2 and 1
Gallacher beat Kuehne 3 and 2
Fanagan beat Courville 3 and 2
Howard halved with Jackson
Foster halved with Marucci
Harrington lost to Harris 3 and 2
Wolstenholme lost to Woods 4 and 3

1993 *Interlachen, Edina, MN* Aug 18–19
Result: USA 19, GBI 5
Captains: M Giles III (USA), G Macgregor (GBI)
First Day – Foursomes
Abandoned – rain & flooding
Singles
A Doyle beat I Pyman I hole
D Berganio lost to M Stanford 3 and 2
J Sigel lost to D Robertson 3 and 2
K Mitchum halved with S Cage
T Herron beat P Harrington I hole
D Yates beat P Page 2 and I
T Demsey beat R Russell 2 and I
J Leonard beat R Burns 4 and 3
B Gay lost to V Phillips 2 and I
J Harris beat B Dredge 4 and 3
Second Day – Foursomes
Doyle & Leonard beat Pyman & Cage 4 and 3
Berganio & Demsey beat Stanford & Harrington 3 and 2
Sigel & Mitchum beat Dredge & Phillips 3 and 2
Harris & Herron beat Russell & Robertson I hole
Singles
Doyle beat Robertson 4 and 3
Harris beat Pyman 3 and 2
Yates beat Cage 2 and I
Gay halved with Harrington
Sigel beat Page 5 and 4
Herron beat Phillips 3 and 2
Mitchum beat Russell 4 and 2
Berganio lost to Burns I hole
Demsey beat Dredge 3 and 2
Leonard beat Stanford 5 and 4

1991 *Portmarnock, Dublin, Ireland* Sept 5–6
Result: USA 14, GBI 10
Captains: G Macgregor (GBI),
*   JR Gabrielsen (USA)*
First Day – Foursomes
Milligan & Hay lost to Mickelson & May 5 and 3
Payne & Evans lost to Duval & Sposa I hole
McGimpsey & Willison lost to Voges & Eger I hole
McGinley & Harrington lost to Sigel & Doyle
   2 and I
Singles
A Coltart lost to P Mickelson 4 and 3
J Payne beat F Langham 2 and I
G Evans beat D Duval 2 and I
R Willison lost to B May 2 and I
G McGimpsey beat M Sposa I hole
P McGinley lost to A Doyle 6 and 4
G Hay beat T Scherrer I hole
L White lost to J Sigel 4 and 3
Second Day – Foursomes
Milligan & McGimpsey beat Voges & Eger 2 and I
Payne & Willison lost to Duval & Sposa I hole
Evans & Coltart beat Langham & Scherrer 4 and 3
White & McGinley beat Mickelson & May I hole
Singles
Milligan lost to Mickelson I hole
Payne beat Doyle 3 and I
Evans lost to Langham 4 and 2
Coltart beat Sigel I hole
Willison beat Scherrer 3 and 2
Harrington lost to Eger 3 and 2
McGimpsey lost to May 4 and 3
Hay lost to Voges 3 and I

1989 *Peachtree, GA* Aug 16–17
Result: GBI 12½, USA 11½
Captains: F Ridley (USA), GC Marks (GBI)
First Day – Foursomes
Gamez & Martin beat Claydon & Prosser 3 and 2
Yates & Mickelson halved with Dodd & McGimpsey
Lesher & Sigel lost to McEvoy & O'Connell 6 and 5
Eger & Johnson lost to Milligan & Hare 2 and I
Singles
R Gamez beat JW Milligan 7 and 6
D Martin lost to R Claydon 5 and 4
E Meeks halved with SC Dodd
R Howe lost to E O'Connell 5 and 4
D Yates lost to P McEvoy 2 and I
P Mickelson beat G McGimpsey 4 and 2
G Lesher lost to C Cassells I hole
J Sigel halved with RN Roderick
Second Day – Foursomes
Gamez & Martin halved with McEvoy & O'Connell
Sigel & Lesher lost to Claydon & Cassells 3 and 2
Eger & Johnson lost to Milligan & Hare 2 and I
Mickelson & Yates lost to McGimpsey & Dodd 2 and I
Singles
Gamez beat Dodd I hole
Martin halved with Hare
Lesher beat Claydon 3 and 2
Yates beat McEvoy 4 and 3
Mickelson halved with O'Connell
Eger beat Roderick 4 and 2
Johnson beat Cassells 4 and 2
Sigel halved with Milligan

1987 *Sunningdale Old* May 27–28
Result: USA 16½, GBI 7½
Captains: GC Marks (GBI), F Ridley (USA)
First Day – Foursomes
Montgomerie & Shaw lost to Alexander & Mayfair
   5 and 4
Currey & Mayo lost to Kite & Mattice 2 and I
Macgregor & Robinson lost to Lewis & Loeffler
   2 and I
McHenry & Girvan lost to Sigel & Andrade 3 and 2
Singles
D Currey beat B Alexander 2 holes
J Robinson lost to B Andrade 7 and 5
CS Montgomerie beat J Sorenson 3 and 2
R Eggo lost to J Sigel 3 and 2
J McHenry lost to B Montgomery I hole
P Girvan lost to B Lewis 3 and 2
DG Carrick lost to B Mayfair 2 holes
G Shaw beat C Kite I hole
Second Day – Foursomes
Currey & Carrick lost to Lewis & Loeffler 4 and 3
Montgomerie & Shaw lost to Kite & Mattice 5 and 3
Mayo & Macgregor lost to Sorenson & Montgomery
   4 and 3
McHenry & Robinson beat Sigel & Andrade 4 and 2
Singles
Currey lost to Alexander 5 and 4
Montgomerie beat Andrade 4 and 2
McHenry beat Loeffler 3 and 2
Shaw halved with Sorenson
Robinson beat Mattice I hole
Carrick lost to Lewis 3 and 2
Eggo lost to Mayfair I hole
Girvan lost to Sigel 6 and 5

1985 *Pine Valley, NJ* Aug 21–22
Result: USA 13, GBI 11
Captains: J Sigel (USA), CW Green (GBI)

First Day – Foursomes
Verplank & Sigel beat Montgomerie & Macgregor
 1 hole
Waldorf & Randolph lost to Hawksworth & McGimpsey
 4 and 3
Sonnier & Haas lost to Baker & McEvoy 6 and 5
Podolak & Love halved with Bloice & Stephen

Singles
S Verplank beat G McGimpsey 2 and 1
S Randolph beat P Mayo 5 and 4
R Sonnier halved with J Hawksworth
J Sigel beat CS Montgomerie 5 and 4
B Lewis lost to P McEvoy 2 and 1
C Burroughs lost to G Macgregor 2 holes
D Waldorf beat D Gilford 4 and 2
J Haas lost to AR Stephen 2 and 1

Second Day – Foursomes
Verplank & Sigel halved with Mayo & Montgomerie
Randolph & Haas beat Hawksworth & McGimpsey
 3 and 2
Lewis & Burroughs beat Baker & McEvoy 2 and 1
Podolak & Love beat Bloice & Stephen 3 and 2

Singles
Randolph halved with McGimpsey
Verplank beat Montgomerie 1 hole
Sigel lost to Hawksworth 4 and 3
Love beat McEvoy 5 and 3
Sonnier lost to Baker 5 and 4
Burroughs lost to Macgregor 3 and 2
Lewis beat Bloice 4 and 3
Waldorf lost to Stephen 2 and 1

1983 *Royal Liverpool, Hoylake* May 25–26
Result: USA 13½, GBI 10½
Captains: CW Green (GBI), J Sigel (USA)

First Day – Foursomes
Macgregor & Walton beat Sigel & Fehr 3 and 2
Keppler & Pierse lost to Wood & Faxon 3 and 1
Lewis & Thompson lost to Lewis & Holtgrieve
 7 and 6
Mann & Oldcorn beat Hoffer & Tentis 5 and 4

Singles
P Walton beat J Sigel 1 hole
SD Keppler lost to R Fehr 1 hole
G Macgregor halved with W Wood
DG Carrick lost to B Faxon 3 and 1
A Oldcorn beat B Tuten 4 and 3
P Parkin beat N Crosby 5 and 4
AD Pierse lost to B Lewis jr 3 and 1
LS Mann lost to J Holtgrieve 6 and 5

Second Day – Foursomes
Macgregor & Walton lost to Crosby & Hoffer 2 holes
Parkin & Thompson beat Faxon & Wood 1 hole
Mann & Oldcorn beat Lewis & Holtgrieve 1 hole
Keppler & Pierse halved with Sigel & Fehr

Singles
Walton beat Wood 2 and 1
Parkin lost to Faxon 3 and 2
Macgregor lost to Fehr 2 and 1
Thompson lost to Tuten 3 and 2
Mann halved with Tentis
Keppler lost to Lewis 6 and 5
Oldcorn beat Holtgrieve 3 and 2
Carrick lost to Sigel 3 and 2

1981 *Cypress Point, CA* Aug 28–29
Result: USA 15, GBI 9
Captains: J Gabrielsen (USA), R Foster (GBI)

First Day – Foursomes
Sutton & Sigel lost to Walton & Rafferty 4 and 2
Holtgrieve & Fuhrer beat Chapman & McEvoy 1 hole
Lewis & von Tacky beat Deeble & Hutcheon 2 and 1
Commans & Pavin beat Evans & Way 5 and 4

Singles
H Sutton beat R Rafferty 3 and 1
J Rassett beat CR Dalgleish 1 hole
R Commans lost to P Walton 1 hole
B Lewis lost to R Chapman 2 and 1
J Mudd beat G Godwin 1 hole
C Pavin beat IC Hutcheon 4 and 3
D von Tacky lost to P Way 3 and 1
J Sigel beat P McEvoy 4 and 2

Second Day – Foursomes
Sutton & Sigel lost to Chapman & Way 1 hole
Holtgrieve & Fuhrer lost to Walton & Rafferty 6 and 4
Lewis & von Tacky lost to Evans & Dalgleish 3 and 2
Rassett & Mudd beat Hutcheon & Godwin 5 and 4

Singles
Sutton lost to Chapman 1 hole
Holtgrieve beat Rafferty 2 and 1
Fuhrer beat Walton 4 and 3
Sigel beat Way 6 and 5
Mudd beat Dalgleish 7 and 5
Commans halved with Godwin
Rassett beat Deeble 4 and 3
Pavin halved with Evans

1979 *Muirfield, Gullane* May 30–31
Result: USA 15½, GBI 8½
Captains: R Foster (GBI), RL Siderowf (USA)

First Day – Foursomes
McEvoy & Marchbank lost to Hoch & Sigel 1 hole
Godwin & Hutcheon beat West & Sutton
 2 holes
Brand jr & Kelley lost to Fischesser & Holtgrieve
 1 hole
Brodie & Carslaw beat Moody & Gove 2 and 1

Singles
P McEvoy halved with J Sigel
JC Davies lost to D Clarke 8 and 7
J Buckley lost to S Hoch 9 and 7
IC Hutcheon lost to J Holtgrieve 6 and 4
B Marchbank beat M Peck 1 hole
G Godwin beat G Moody 3 and 2
MJ Kelley beat D Fischesser 3 and 2
A Brodie lost to M Gove 3 and 2

Second Day – Foursomes
Godwin & Brand lost to Hoch & Sigel 4 and 3
McEvoy & Marchbank beat Fischesser & Holtgrieve
 2 and 1
Kelley & Hutcheon halved with West & Sutton
Carslaw & Brodie halved with Clarke & Peck

Singles
McEvoy lost to Hoch 3 and 1
Brand lost to Clarke 2 and 1
Godwin lost to Gove 3 and 2
Hutcheon lost to Peck 2 and 1
Brodie beat West 3 and 2
Kelley lost to Moody 3 and 2
Marchbank lost to Sutton 3 and 1
Carslaw lost to Sigel 2 and 1

1977 *Shinnecock Hills, NY* Aug 26–27
Result: USA 16, GBI 8
Captains: LW Oehmig(USA),
 AC Saddler (GBI)

First Day – Foursomes
Fought & Heafner beat Lyle & McEvoy 4 and 3
Simpson & Miller beat Davies & Kelley 5 and 4
Siderowf & Hallberg lost to Hutcheon & Deeble 1 hole
Sigel & Brannan beat Brodie & Martin 1 hole

Singles
L Miller beat P McEvoy 2 holes
J Fought beat IC Hutcheon 4 and 3
S Simpson beat GH Murray 7 and 6
V Heafner beat JC Davies 4 and 3
B Sander lost to A Brodie 4 and 3
G Hallberg lost to S Martin 3 and 2
F Ridley beat AWB Lyle 2 holes
J Sigel beat P McKellar 5 and 3

Second Day – Foursomes
Fought & Heafner beat Hutcheon & Deeble 4 and 3
Miller & Simpson beat McEvoy & Davies 2 holes
Siderowf & Sander lost to Brodie & Martin 6 and 4
Ridley & Brannan beat Murray & Kelley 4 and 3

Singles
Miller beat Martin 1 hole
Fought beat Davies 2 and 1
Sander lost to Brodie 2 and 1
Hallberg beat McEvoy 4 and 3
Siderowf lost to Kelley 2 and 1
Brannan lost to Hutcheon 2 holes
Ridley beat Lyle 5 and 3
Sigel beat Deeble 1 hole

1975 *Old Course, St Andrews* May 28–29
Result: USA 15½, GBI 8½
Captains: DM Marsh (GBI), ER Updegraff (USA)

First Day – Foursomes
James & Eyles beat Pate & Siderowf 1 hole
Davies & Poxon lost to Burns & Stadler 5 and 4
Green & Stuart lost to Haas & Strange 2 and 1
Macgregor & Hutcheon lost to Giles & Koch
 5 and 4

Singles
M James beat J Pate 2 and 1
JC Davies halved with C Strange
P Mulcare beat RL Siderowf 1 hole
HB Stuart lost to G Koch 3 and 2
MA Poxon lost to J Grace 3 and 1
IC Hutcheon halved with WC Campbell
GRD Eyles lost to J Haas 2 and 1
G Macgregor lost to M Giles III 5 and 4

Second Day – Foursomes
Mulcare & Hutcheon beat Pate & Siderowf 1 hole
Green & Stuart lost to Burns & Stadler 1 hole
James & Eyles beat Campbell & Grace 5 and 3
Hedges & Davies lost to Haas & Strange 3 and 2

Singles
Hutcheon beat Pate 3 and 2
Mulcare lost to Strange 4 and 3
James lost to Koch 5 and 4
Davies beat Burns 2 and 1
Green lost to Grace 2 and 1
Macgregor lost to Stadler 3 and 2
Eyles lost to Campbell 2 and 1
Hedges halved with Giles

1973 *Brookline, MA* Aug 24–25
Result: USA 14, GBI 10
Captains: JW Sweetser (USA), DM Marsh (GBI)

First Day – Foursomes
Giles & Koch halved with King & Hedges
Siderowf & Pfeil beat Stuart & Davies 5 and 4
Edwards & Ellis beat Green & Milne 2 and 1
West & Ballenger beat Foster & Homer 2 and 1

Singles
M Giles III beat HB Stuart 5 and 4
RL Siderowf beat MF Bonallack 4 and 2
G Koch lost to JC Davies 1 hole
M West lost to HK Clark 2 and 1
D Edwards beat R Foster 2 holes
M Killian lost to MG King 1 hole
W Rodgers lost to CW Green 1 hole
M Pfeil lost to WT Milne 4 and 3

Second Day – Foursomes
Giles & Koch & Homer & Foster 7 and 5
Siderowf & Pfeil halved with Clark & Davies
Edwards & Ellis beat Hedges & King 2 and 1
Rodgers & Killian beat Stuart & Milne 1 hole

Singles
Ellis lost to Stuart 5 and 4
Siderowf lost to Davies 3 and 2
Edwards beat Homer 2 and 1
Giles halved with Green
West beat King 1 hole
Killian lost to Milne 2 and 1
Koch halved with Hedges
Pfeil beat Clark 1 hole

1971 *Old Course, St Andrews* May 26–27
Result: GBI 13, USA 11
Captains: MF Bonallack (GBI),
 JM Winters jr (USA)

First Day – Foursomes
Bonallack & Humphreys beat Wadkins & Simons
 1 hole
Green & Carr beat Melnyk & Giles 1 hole
Marsh & Macgregor beat Miller & Farquhar 2 and 1
Macdonald & Foster beat Campbell & Kite 2 and 1

Singles
CW Green lost to L Wadkins 1 hole
MF Bonallack lost to M Giles III 1 hole
GC Marks lost to AL Miller III 1 hole
JS Macdonald lost to S Melnyk 3 and 2
RJ Carr halved with W Hyndman III
W Humphreys lost to JR Gabrielsen 1 hole
HB Stuart beat J Farquhar 3 and 2
R Foster lost to T Kite 3 and 2

Second Day – Foursomes
Marks & Green lost to Melnyk & Giles 1 hole
Stuart & Carr beat Wadkins & Gabrielsen 1 hole
Marsh & Bonallack lost to Miller & Farquhar 5 and 4
Macdonald & Foster halved with Campbell & Kite

Singles
Bonallack lost to Wadkins 3 and 1
Stuart beat Giles 2 and 1
Humphreys beat Melnyk 2 and 1
Green beat Miller 1 hole
Carr beat Simons 2 holes
Macgregor beat Gabrielsen 1 hole
Marsh beat Hyndman 1 hole
Marks lost to Kite 3 and 2

1969 *Milwaukee, WI* Aug 22–23
Result: USA 10, GBI 8[†]
Captains: WJ Patton (USA), MF Bonallack (GBI)

First Day – Foursomes
Giles & Melnyk beat Bonallack & Craddock 3 and 2
Fleisher & Miller halved with Benka & Critchley
Wadkins & Siderowf lost to Green & A Brooks
W Hyndman III & Inman jr beat Foster & Marks 2 and 1

Singles
B Fleisher halved with MF Bonallack
M Giles III beat CW Green 1 hole
AL Miller jr lost to B Critchley 1 hole
RL Siderowf beat LP Tupling 6 and 5
S Melnyk lost to PJ Benka 3 and 1
L Wadkins lost to GC Marks 1 hole
J Bohmann beat MG King 2 and 1
ER Updegraff beat R Foster 6 and 5

Second Day – Foursomes
Giles & Melnyk halved with Green & Brooks
Fleisher & Miller lost to Benka & Critchley 2 and 1
Siderowf & Wadkins beat Foster & King 6 and 5
Updegraff & Bohmann lost to Bonallack & Tupling 4 and 3

Singles
Fleisher lost to Bonallack 5 and 4
Siderowf halved with Critchley
Miller beat King 1 hole
Giles halved with Craddock
Inman beat Benka 2 and 1
Bohmann lost to Brooks 4 and 3
Hyndman halved with Green
Updegraff lost to Marks 3 and 2

1967 *Royal St George's, Sandwich* May 19–20
Result: USA 13, GBI 7[†]
Captains: JB Carr (GBI), JW Sweetser (USA)

First Day – Foursomes
Shade & Oosterhuis halved with Murphy & Cerrudo
Foster & Saddler lost to Campbell & Lewis 1 hole
Bonallack & Attenborough lost to Gray & Tutwiler 4 and 2
Carr & Craddock lost to Dickson & Grant 3 and 1

Singles
RDBM Shade lost to WC Campbell 2 and 1
R Foster lost to RJ Murphy jr 2 and 1
MF Bonallack halved with AD Gray jr
MF Attenborough lost to RJ Cerrudo 4 and 3
P Oosterhuis lost to RB Dickson 6 and 4
T Craddock lost to JW Lewis jr 2 and 1
AK Pirie halved with DC Allen
AC Saddler beat MA Fleckman 3 and 2

Second Day – Foursomes
Bonallack & Craddock beat Murphy & Cerrudo 2 holes
Saddler & Pirie lost to Campbell & Lewis 1 hole
Shade & Oosterhuis beat Gray & Tutwiler 3 and 1
Foster & Millensted beat Allen & Fleckman 2 and 1

Singles
Shade lost to Campbell 3 and 2
Bonallack beat Murphy 4 and 2
Saddler beat Gray 3 and 2
Foster halved with Cerrudo
Pirie lost to Dickson 4 and 3
Craddock beat Lewis 5 and 4
Oosterhuis lost to Grant 1 hole
Millensted lost to Tutwiler 3 and 1

1965 *Five Farms, MD* Sept 3–4
Result: USA 11, GBI 11[†]
Captains: JW Fischer (USA), JB Carr (GBI)

First Day – Foursomes
Campbell & Gray lost to Lunt & Cosh 1 hole
Beman & Allen halved with Bonallack & Clark
Patton & Tutwiler beat Foster & Clark 5 and 4
Hopkins & Eichelberger lost to Townsend & Shade 2 and 1

Singles
WC Campbell beat MF Bonallack 6 and 5
DR Beman beat R Foster 2 holes
AD Gray jr lost to RDBM Shade 3 and 1
JM Hopkins lost to CA Clark 5 and 3
WJ Patton lost to P Townsend 3 and 2
D Morey lost to AC Saddler 2 and 1
DC Allen lost to GB Cosh 2 holes
ER Updegraff lost to MSR Lunt 2 and 1

Second Day – Foursomes
Campbell & Gray beat Saddler & Foster 4 and 3
Beman & Eichelberger lost to Townsend & Shade 2 and 1
Tutwiler & Patton beat Cosh & Lunt 2 and 1
Allen & Morey lost to CA Clark & Bonallack 2 and 1

Singles
Campbell beat Foster 3 and 2
Beman beat Saddler 1 hole
Tutwiler beat Shade 5 and 3
Allen lost to Cosh 4 and 3
Gray beat Townsend 1 hole
Hopkins halved with CA Clark
Eichelberger beat Bonallack 5 and 3
Patton beat Lunt 4 and 2

1963 *Ailsa Course, Turnberry* May 24–25
Result: USA 14, GBI 10
Captains: CD Lawrie (GBI), RS Tufts (USA)

First Day – Foursomes
Bonallack & Murray beat Patton & Sikes 4 and 3
Carr & Green lost to Gray & Harris 2 holes
Lunt & Sheahan lost to Beman & Coe 5 and 3
Madeley & Shade halved with Gardner & Updegraff

Singles
SWT Murray beat DR Beman 3 and 1
MJ Christmas lost to WJ Patton 3 and 2
JB Carr beat RH Sikes 7 and 5
DB Sheahan beat LE Harris 1 hole
MF Bonallack beat RD Davies 1 hole
AC Saddler halved with CR Coe
RDBM Shade beat AD Gray jr 4 and 3
MSR Lunt halved with CB Smith

Second Day – Foursomes
Bonallack & Murray lost to Patton & Sikes 1 hole
Lunt & Sheahan lost to Gray & Harris 3 and 2
Green & Saddler lost to Gardner & Updegraff 3 and 1
Madeley & Shade lost to Beman & Coe 3 and 2

Singles
Murray lost to Patton 3 and 2
Sheahan beat Davies 1 hole
Carr lost to Updegraff 4 and 3
Bonallack lost to Harris 3 and 2
Lunt lost to Gardner 3 and 2
Saddler halved with Beman
Shade beat Gray 2 and 1
Green lost to Coe 4 and 3

---

† *Some matches were halved but no half points were awarded. From 1971, halved matches were counted with a half point being awarded to each side.*

1961 Seattle, WA Sept 1–2
Result: USA 11, GBI 1
Captains: J Westland (USA), CD Lawrie (GBI)

Foursomes
Beman & Nicklaus beat Walker & Chapman 6 and 5
Coe & Cherry beat Blair & Christmas 1 hole
Hyndman & Gardner beat Carr & G Huddy
 4 and 3
Cochran & Andrews beat Bonallack & Shade 4 and 3

Singles
DR Beman beat MF Bonallack 3 and 2
CR Coe beat MSR Lunt 5 and 4
FM Taylor jr beat J Walker 3 and 2
W Hyndman III beat DW Frame 7 and 6
JW Nicklaus beat JB Carr 6 and 4
CB Smith lost to MJ Christmas 3 and 2
RW Gardner beat RDBM Shade 1 hole
DR Cherry beat DA Blair 5 and 4

1959 Muirfield, Gullane May 15–16
Result: USA 9, GBI 3
Captains: GH Micklem (GBI), CR Coe (USA)

Foursomes
Jack & Sewell lost to Ward & Taylor 1 hole
Carr & Wolstenholme lost to Hyndman & Aaron 1 hole
Bonallack & Perowne lost to Patton & Coe 9 and 8
Lunt & Shepperson lost to Wettlander & Nicklaus
 2 and 1

Singles
JB Carr beat CR Coe 3 and 1
GB Wolstenholme lost to EH Ward jr 9 and 8
RR Jack beat WJ Patton 5 and 3
DN Sewell lost to W Hyndman III 4 and 3
AE Shepperson beat TD Aaron 2 and 1
MF Bonallack lost to DR Beman 2 holes
MSR Lunt lost to HW Wettlander 6 and 5
WD Smith lost to JW Nicklaus 5 and 4

1957 Minikahda, MN Aug 30–31
Result: USA 8, GBI 3[†]
Captains: CR Coe (USA), GH Micklem (GBI)

Foursomes
Baxter & Patton beat Carr & Deighton 2 and 1
Campbell & Taylor beat Bussell & Scrutton 4 and 3
Blum & Kocsis lost to Jack & Sewell 1 hole
Robbins & Rudolph halved with Shepperson &
 Wolstenholme

Singles
WJ Patton beat RR Jack 1 hole
WC Campbell beat JB Carr 3 and 2
R Baxter jr beat A Thirlwell 4 and 3
W Hyndman III beat FWG Deighton 7 and 6
JE Campbell lost to AF Bussell 2 and 1
FM Taylor jr beat D Sewell 1 hole
EM Rudolph beat PF Scrutton 3 and 2
H Robbins jr lost to GB Wolstenholme 2 and 1

1955 Old Course, St Andrews May 20–21
Result: USA 10, GBI 2
Captains: GA Hill (GBI), WC Campbell (USA)

Foursomes
Carr & White lost to Ward & Cherry 1 hole
Micklem & Morgan lost to Patton & Yost 2 and 1
Caldwell & Millward lost to Conrad & Morey 3 and 2
Blair & Cater lost to Cudd & Jackson 5 and 4

Singles
RJ White lost to EH Ward jr 6 and 5
PF Scrutton lost to WJ Patton 2 and 1
I Caldwell beat D Morey 1 hole
JB Carr lost to DR Cherry 5 and 4
DA Blair beat JW Conrad 1 hole
EB Millward lost to BH Cudd 2 holes
RC Ewing lost to JG Jackson 6 and 4
JL Morgan lost to RL Yost 8 and 7

1953 Kittansett, MA Sept 4–5
Result: USA 9, GBI 3
Captains: CR Yates (USA), AA Duncan (GBI)

Foursomes
Urzetta & Venturi beat Carr & White 6 and 4
Ward & Westland beat Langley & AH Perowne 9 and 8
Jackson & Littler beat Wilson & MacGregor 3 and 2
Campbell & Coe lost to Micklem & Morgan 4 and 3

Singles
EH Ward jr beat JB Carr 4 and 3
RD Chapman lost to RJ White 1 hole
GA Littler beat GH Micklem 5 and 3
J Westland beat RC MacGregor 7 and 5
DR Cherry beat NV Drew 9 and 7
K Venturi beat JC Wilson 9 and 8
CR Coe lost to JL Morgan 3 and 2
S Urzetta beat JDA Langley 3 and 2

1951 Royal Birkdale, Southport May 11–12
Result: USA 7, GBI 4[†]
*Captains: RH Oppenheimer (GBI),
 WP Turnesa (USA)*

Foursomes
White & Carr halved with Stranahan & Campbell
Ewing & Langley halved with Coe & McHale
Kyle & Caldwell lost to Chapman & Knowles jr
 1 hole
Bruen jr & Morgan lost to Turnesa & Urzetta 5 and 4

Singles
SM McCready lost to S Urzetta 4 and 3
JB Carr beat FR Stranahan 2 and 1
RJ White beat CR Coe 2 and 1
JDA Langley lost to JB McHale jr 2 holes
RC Ewing lost to WC Campbell 5 and 4
AT Kyle beat WP Turnesa 2 holes
I Caldwell halved with HD Paddock jr
JL Morgan lost to RD Chapman 7 and 6

1949 Winged Foot, New York Aug 19–20
Result: USA 10, GBI 2
Captains: FD Ouimet (USA), PB Lucas (GBI)

Foursomes
Billows & Turnesa lost to Carr & White 3 and 2
Kocsis & Stranahan beat Bruen & McCready 2 and 1
Bishop & Riegel beat Ewing & Micklem 9 and 7
Dawson & McCormick beat Thom & Perowne
 8 and 7

Singles
WP Turnesa lost to RJ White 4 and 3
FR Stranahan beat SM McCready 6 and 5
RH Riegel beat J Bruen jr 5 and 4
JW Dawson beat JB Carr 5 and 3
CR Coe beat RC Ewing 1 hole
RE Billows beat KG Thom 2 and 1
CR Kocsis beat AH Perowne 4 and 2
JB McHale jr beat GH Micklem 5 and 4

---

† Some matches were halved but no half points were awarded. From 1971, halved matches were counted with a half point being awarded to each side.

1947 *Old Course, St Andrews* May 16–17
Result: USA 8, GBI 4
Captains: JB Beck (GBI), FD Ouimet (USA)
Foursomes
Carr & Ewing lost to Bishop & Riegel 3 and 2
Crawley & Lucas beat Ward & Quick 5 and 4
Kyle & Wilson lost to Turnesa & Kammer 5 and 4
White & Stowe beat Stranahan & Chapman 4 and 3
Singles
LG Crawley lost to MH Ward 5 and 3
JB Carr beat SE Bishop 5 and 3
GH Micklem lost to RH Riegel 6 and 5
RC Ewing lost to WP Turnesa 6 and 5
C Stowe lost to FR Stranahan 2 and 1
RJ White beat AF Kammer jr 4 and 3
JC Wilson lost to SL Quick 8 and 6
PB Lucas lost to RD Chapman 4 and 3

1938 *St Andrews* June 3–4
Result: GBI 7, USA 4[†]
Captains: JB Beck (GBI), FD Ouimet (USA)
Foursomes
Bentley & Bruen halved with Fischer & Kocsis
Peters & Thomson beat Goodman & Ward 4 and 2
Kyle & Stowe lost to Yates & Billows 3 and 2
Pennink & Crawley beat Smith & Haas 3 and 1
Singles
J Bruen jr lost to CR Yates 2 and 1
H Thomson beat JG Goodman 6 and 4
LG Crawley lost to JW Fischer 3 and 2
C Stowe beat CR Kocsis 2 and 1
JJF Pennink lost to MH Ward 12 and 11
RC Ewing beat RE Billows 1 hole
GB Peters beat R Smith 9 and 8
AT Kyle beat F Haas jr 5 and 4

1936 *Pine Valley, NJ* Sept 2–3
Result: USA 10, GBI 1[†]
Captains: FD Ouimet (USA),
* W Tweddell (GBI)*
Foursomes
Goodman & Campbell beat Thomson & Bentley
  7 and 5
Smith & White beat McLean & Langley 8 and 7
Yates & Emery halved with Peters & Dykes
Givan & Voigt halved with Hill & Ewing
Singles
JG Goodman beat H Thomson 3 and 2
AE Campbell beat J McLean 5 and 4
JW Fischer beat RC Ewing 8 and 7
R Smith beat GA Hill 11 and 9
W Emery beat GB Peters 1 hole
CR Yates beat JM Dykes 8 and 7
GT Dunlap jr halved with HG Bentley
E White beat JDA Langley 6 and 5

1934 *Old Course, St Andrews* May 11–12
Result: USA 9, GBI 2[†]
Captains: Hon M Scott (GBI), FD Ouimet (USA)
Foursomes
Wethered & Tolley lost to Goodman & Little 8 and 6
Bentley & Fiddian lost to Moreland & Westland
  6 and 5
Scott & McKinlay lost to Egan & Marston 3 and 2
McRuvie & McLean beat Ouimet & Dunlap 4 and 2

Singles
Hon M Scott lost to JG Goodman 7 and 6
CJH Tolley lost to WL Little jr 6 and 5
LG Crawley lost to FD Ouimet 5 and 4
J McLean lost to GT Dunlap jr 4 and 3
EW Fiddian lost to JW Fischer 5 and 4
SL McKinlay lost to GT Moreland 3 and 1
EA McRuvie halved with J Westland
TA Torrance beat MR Marston 4 and 3

1932 *Brookline, MA* Sept 1–2
Result: USA 9, GBI 2[†]
Captains: FD Ouimet (USA), TA Torrance (GBI)
Foursomes
Sweetser & Voigt beat Hartley & Hartley 7 and 6
Seaver & Moreland beat Torrance & de Forest 6 and 5
Ouimet & Dunlap beat Stout & Burke 7 and 6
Moe & Howell beat Fiddian & McRuvie 5 and 4
Singles
FD Ouimet halved with TA Torrance
JW Sweetser halved with JA Stout
GT Moreland beat RW Hartley 2 and 1
J Westland halved with J Burke
GJ Voigt lost to LG Crawley 1 hole
MJ McCarthy jr beat WL Hartley 3 and 2
CH Seaver beat EW Fiddian 7 and 6
GT Dunlap jr beat EA McRuvie 10 and 9

1930 *St George's, Sandwich* May 15–16
Result: USA 10, GBI 2
Captains: RH Wethered (GBI), RT Jones jr (USA)
Foursomes
Tolley & Wethered beat Von Elm & Voigt 2 holes
Hartley & Torrance lost to Jones & Willing 8 and 7
Holderness & Stout lost to MacKenzie & Moe
  2 and 1
Campbell & Smith lost to Johnston & Ouimet 2 and 1
Singles
CJH Tolley lost to HR Johnston 5 and 4
RH Wethered lost to RT Jones jr 9 and 8
RW Hartley lost to G Von Elm 3 and 2
EWE Holderness lost to GJ Voigt 10 and 9
JN Smith lost to OF Willing 2 and 1
TA Torrance beat FD Ouimet 7 and 6
JA Stout lost to DK Moe 1 hole
W Campbell lost to RR MacKenzie 6 and 5

1928 *Wheaton, Chicago, IL* Aug 30–31
Result: USA 11, GBI 1
Captains: RT Jones jr (USA), W Tweddell (GBI)
Foursomes
Sweetser & Von Elm beat Perkins & Tweddell 7 and 6
Jones & Evans beat Hezlet & Hope 5 and 3
Ouimet & Johnston beat Torrance & Storey 4 and 2
Gunn & MacKenzie beat Beck & Martin 7 and 5
Singles
RT Jones jr beat TP Perkins 13 and 12
G Von Elm beat W Tweddell 3 and 2
FD Ouimet beat CO Hezlet 8 and 7
JW Sweetser beat WL Hope 5 and 4
HR Johnston beat EF Storey 4 and 2
C Evans jr lost to TA Torrance 1 hole
W Gunn beat RH Hardman 11 and 10
RR MacKenzie beat GNC Martin 2 and 1

---

† *Some matches were halved but no half points were awarded. From 1971, halved matches were counted with a half point being awarded to each side.*

1926 *Old Course, St Andrews* June 2–3
Result: USA 6, GBI 5[†]
Captains: R Harris (GBI), RA Gardner (USA)
Foursomes
Wethered & Holderness beat Ouimet & Guilford 5 and 4
Tolley & Jamieson lost to Jones & Gunn 4 and 3
Harris & Hezlet lost to Von Elm & Sweetser 8 and 7
Storey & Brownlow lost to Gardner & MacKenzie 1 hole
Singles
CJH Tolley lost to RT Jones jr 12 and 11
EWE Holderness lost to JW Sweetser 4 and 3
RH Wethered beat FD Ouimet 5 and 4
CO Hezlet halved with G Von Elm
R Harris beat JP Guilford 2 and 1
Hon WGE Brownlow lost to W Gunn 9 and 8
EF Storey beat RR MacKenzie 2 and 1
A Jamieson jr beat RA Gardner 5 and 4

1924 *Garden City, New York* Sept 12–13
Result: USA 9, GBI 3
Captains: RA Gardner (USA), CJH Tolley (GBI)
Foursomes
Marston & Gardner beat Storey & Murray 3 and 1
Guilford & Ouimet beat Tolley & Hezlet 2 and 1
Jones & Fownes jr lost to Scott & Scott jr 1 hole
Sweetser & Johnston beat Torrance & Bristowe 4 and 3
Singles
MR Marston lost to CJH Tolley 1 hole
RT Jones jr beat CO Hezlet 4 and 3
C Evans jr beat WA Murray 2 and 1
FD Ouimet beat EF Storey 1 hole
JW Sweetser lost to Hon M Scott 7 and 6
RA Gardner beat WL Hope 3 and 2
JP Guilford beat TA Torrance 2 and 1
OF Willing beat DH Kyle 3 and 2

1922 *National Golf Links, New York* Aug 28–29
Result: USA 8, GBI 4
Captains: WC Fownes (USA), R Harris (GBI)
Foursomes
Guilford & Ouimet beat Tolley & Darwin 8 and 7
Evans & Gardner lost to Wethered & Aylmer 5 and 4
Jones & Sweetser beat Torrance & Hooman 3 and 2
Marston & Fownes beat Caven & Mackenzie 2 and 1

Singles
JP Guilford beat CJH Tolley 2 and 1
RT Jones jr beat RH Wethered 3 and 2
C Evans jr beat J Caven 5 and 4
FD Ouimet beat CC Aylmer 8 and 7
RA Gardner beat WB Torrance 7 and 5
MR Marston lost to WW Mackenzie 6 and 5
WC Fownes jr lost to B Darwin 3 and 1
JW Sweetser lost to CVL Hooman at 37th

1923 *Old Course, St Andrews* May 18–19
Result: USA 6, GBI 5[†]
Captains: R Harris (GBI), RA Gardner (USA)
Foursomes
Tolley & Wethered beat Ouimet & Sweetser 6 and 5
Harris & Hooman lost to Gardner & Marston 7 and 6
Holderness & Hope beat Rotan & Herron 1 hole
Wilson & Murray beat Johnston & Neville 4 and 3
Singles
RH Wethered halved with FD Ouimet
CJH Tolley beat JW Sweetser 4 and 3
R Harris lost to RA Gardner 1 hole
WW Mackenzie lost to GV Rotan 5 and 4
WL Hope lost to MR Marston 6 and 5
EWE Holderness lost to FJ Wright jr 1 hole
J Wilson beat SD Herron 1 hole
WA Murray lost to OF Willing 2 and 1

Unofficial match
1921 *Hoylake* 21 May
Result: USA 9, GBI 3
Foursomes
Simpson & Jenkins lost to Evans & Jones 5 and 3
Tolley & Holderness lost to Ouimet & Guilford 3 and 2
de Montmorency & Wethered lost to Hunter & Platt 1 hole
Aylmer & Armour lost to Wright & Fownes 4 and 2
Singles
CJH Tolley beat C Evans jr 4 and 3
JLC Jenkins lost to FD Ouimet 6 and 5
RH de Montmorency lost to RT Jones jr 4 and 3
JG Simpson lost to JP Guilford 2 and 1
CC Aylmer beat P Hunter 2 and 1
TD Armour beat JW Platt 2 and 1
EWE Holderness lost to F Wright 2 holes
RH Wethered lost to WC Fownes jr 3 and 1

† *Some matches were halved but no half points were awarded. From 1971, halved matches were counted with a half point being awarded to each side.*

Walker Cup – INDIVIDUAL RECORDS
Notes: Bold type indicates captain; in brackets, did not play
† indicates players who have also played in the Ryder Cup

Great Britain and Ireland

Name		Year	Played	Won	Lost	Halved
MF Attenborough	ENG	1967	2	0	2	0
CC Aylmer	ENG	1922	2	1	1	0
†P Baker	ENG	1985	3	2	1	0
JB Beck	ENG	1928-(38)-(47)	1	0	1	0
PJ Benka	ENG	1969	4	2	1	1
HG Bentley	ENG	1934-36-38	4	0	2	2
DA Blair	SCO	1955-61	4	1	3	0
C Bloice	SCO	1985	3	0	2	1

Name		Year	Played	Won	Lost	Halved
MF Bonallack	ENG	1957-59-61-63-65-67-**69-71-73**	25	8	14	3
†G Brand jr	SCO	1979	3	0	3	0
OC Bristowe	ENG	(1923)-24	1	0	1	0
A Brodie	SCO	1977-79	8	5	2	1
A Brooks	SCO	1969	3	2	0	1
M Brooks	SCO	1997	2	0	2	0
C Brown	WAL	**1995**-(97)	0	0	0	0
Hon WGE Brownlow	ENG	1926	2	0	2	0
J Bruen	IRL	1938-49-51	5	0	4	1
JA Buckley	WAL	1979	1	0	1	0
J Burke	IRL	1932	2	0	1	1
R Burns	IRL	1993	2	1	1	0
AF Bussell	SCO	1957	2	1	1	0
S Cage	ENG	1993	3	0	2	1
I Caldwell	ENG	1951-55	4	1	2	1
J Caldwell	IRL	2007	3	1	1	1
W Campbell	SCO	1930	2	0	2	0
JB Carr	IRL	1947-49-51-53-55-57-59-61-63-(**65**)-67	20	5	14	1
RJ Carr	IRL	1971	4	3	0	1
DG Carrick	SCO	1983-87	5	0	5	0
IA Carslaw	SCO	1979	3	1	1	1
†P Casey	ENG	1999	4	4	0	0
C Cassells	ENG	1989	3	2	1	0
JR Cater	SCO	1955	1	0	1	0
J Caven	SCO	1922	2	0	2	0
BHG Chapman	ENG	1961	1	0	1	0
R Chapman	ENG	1981	4	3	1	0
MJ Christmas	ENG	1961-63	3	1	2	0
†CA Clark	ENG	1965	4	2	0	2
GJ Clark	ENG	1965	1	0	1	0
†HK Clark	ENG	1973	3	1	1	1
R Claydon	ENG	1989	4	2	2	0
†A Coltart	SCO	1991	3	2	1	0
GB Cosh	SCO	1965	4	3	1	0
R Coughlan	IRL	1997	4	0	3	1
T Craddock	IRL	1967-69	6	2	3	1
LG Crawley	ENG	1932-34-38-47	6	3	3	0
B Critchley	ENG	1969	4	1	1	2
D Curry	ENG	1987	4	1	3	0
CR Dalgleish	SCO	1981-(07)	3	1	2	0
B Darwin	ENG	1922	2	1	1	0
JC Davies	ENG	1973-75-77-79	13	3	8	2
R Davies	WAL	2005-07	8	4	3	1
P Deeble	ENG	1977-81	5	1	4	0
FWG Deighton	SCO	(1951)-57	2	0	2	0
R Dinwiddie	ENG	2005	2	1	1	0
SC Dodd	WAL	1989	4	1	1	2
†L Donald	ENG	1999-01	8	7	1	0
N Dougherty	ENG	2001	4	3	1	0
B Dredge	WAL	1993	3	0	3	0
†NV Drew	IRL	1953	1	0	1	0
AA Duncan	WAL	(**1953**)	0	0	0	0
JM Dykes	SCO	1936	2	0	1	1
S Dyson	ENG	1999	3	0	2	1
NB Edwards	WAL	2001-03-05-07	12	4	5	3
R Eggo	ENG	1987	2	0	2	0
J Elson	ENG	2001	3	1	0	2
D Evans	WAL	1981	3	1	1	1
G Evans	ENG	1991	4	2	2	0
RC Ewing	IRL	1936-38-47-49-51-55	10	1	7	2
GRD Eyles	ENG	1975	4	2	2	0
J Fanagan	IRL	1995	3	3	0	0
EW Fiddian	ENG	1932-34	4	0	4	0
O Fisher	ENG	2005	4	1	2	1
J de Forest	ENG	1932	1	0	1	0
M Foster	ENG	1995	4	2	0	2
R Foster	ENG	1965-67-69-71-73-(**79**)-(**81**)	17	2	13	2
N Fox	IRL	2003	3	1	2	0
DW Frame	ENG	1961	1	0	1	0
S Gallacher	SCO	1995	4	2	2	0

Walker Cup Individual Records *continued*

Name		Year	Played	Won	Lost	Halved
†D Gilford	ENG	1985	1	0	1	0
P Girvan	SCO	1987	3	0	3	0
G Godwin	ENG	1979-81	7	2	4	1
G Gordon	SCO	2003	1	0	1	0
CW Green	SCO	1963-69-71-73-75-(83)-(85)	17	4	10	3
P Gribben	IRL	1999	4	1	2	1
RH Hardman	ENG	1928	1	0	1	0
A Hare	ENG	1989	3	2	2	0
†P Harrington	IRL	1991-93-95	9	3	5	1
R Harris	SCO	**(1922)-23-26**	4	1	3	0
RW Hartley	ENG	1930-32	4	0	4	0
WL Hartley	ENG	1932	2	0	2	0
J Hawksworth	ENG	1985	4	2	1	1
G Hay	SCO	1991	3	1	2	0
P Hedges	ENG	1973-75	5	0	2	3
CO Hezlet	IRL	1924-26-28	6	0	5	1
GA Hill	ENG	1936-(**55**)	2	0	1	1
M Hoey	IRL	2001	4	3	1	0
Sir EWE Holderness	ENG	1923-26-30	6	2	4	0
TWB Homer	ENG	1973	3	0	3	0
‡CVL Hooman	ENG	1922-23	3	†1	2	†0
WL Hope	SCO	1923-24-28	5	1	4	0
D Horsey	ENG	2007	4	3	1	0
DB Howard	SCO	1995-97	6	0	4	2
†D Howell	ENG	1995	3	2	0	1
G Huddy	ENG	1961	1	0	1	0
W Humphreys	ENG	1971	3	2	1	0
IC Hutcheon	SCO	1975-77-79-81	15	5	8	2
D Inglis	SCO	2003	4	2	1	1
RR Jack	SCO	1957-59	4	2	2	0
L James	ENG	1995	2	0	2	0
†M James	ENG	1975	4	3	1	0
A Jamieson jr	SCO	1926	2	1	1	0
MJ Kelley	ENG	1977-79	7	3	3	1
L Kelly	SCO	1999	2	0	2	0
SD Keppler	ENG	1983	4	0	3	1
†MG King	ENG	1969-73	7	1	5	1
AT Kyle	SCO	1938-47-51	5	2	3	0
DH Kyle	SCO	1924	1	0	1	0
JA Lang	SCO	(1930)	0	0	0	0
JDA Langley	ENG	1936-51-53	6	0	5	1
CD Lawrie	SCO	**(1961)-(63)**	0	0	0	0
ME Lewis	ENG	1983	1	0	1	0
G Lockerbie	ENG	2005	4	1	1	0
PB Lucas	ENG	(1936)-47-(**49**)	2	1	1	0
MSR Lunt	ENG	1959-61-63-65	11	2	8	1
†AWB Lyle	SCO	1977	3	0	3	0
AR McCallum	SCO	1928	1	0	1	0
SM McCready	IRL	1949-51	3	0	3	0
JS Macdonald	SCO	1971	3	1	1	1
G McDowell	IRL	2001	4	2	2	0
B McElhinney	IRL	2005	1	0	1	0
P McEvoy	ENG	1977-79-81-85-89-(**99**)-(**01**)	18	5	11	2
R McEvoy	ENG	2001	2	1	0	1
G McGimpsey	IRL	1985-89-91-(**03**)-(**05**)	11	4	5	2
†P McGinley	IRL	1991	3	1	2	0
G Macgregor	SCO	1971-75-83-85-87-(**91**)-(**93**)	14	5	8	1
RC MacGregor	SCO	1953	2	0	2	0
J McHenry	IRL	1987	4	2	2	0
R McIlroy	IRL	2007	4	1	2	1
P McKellar	SCO	1977	1	0	1	0
WW Mackenzie	SCO	1922-23	3	1	2	0
SL McKinlay	SCO	1934	2	0	2	0
J McLean	SCO	1934-36	4	1	3	0
EA McRuvie	SCO	1932-34	4	1	2	1
JFD Madeley	IRL	1963	2	0	1	1
S Manley	WAL	2003	3	2	0	1
LS Mann	SCO	1983	4	2	1	1

‡In 1922 Hooman beat Sweetser at the 37th – on all other occasions halved matches have counted as such.

Name		Year	Played	Won	Lost	Halved
B Marchbank	SCO	1979	4	2	2	0
GC Marks	ENG	1969-71-**(87)**-**(89)**	6	2	4	0
DM Marsh	ENG	71-**(73)**-**(75)**	3	2	1	0
GNC Martin	IRL	1928	1	0	1	0
S Martin	SCO	1977	4	2	2	0
L Matthews	WAL	2007	1	0	1	0
P Mayo	WAL	1985-87	4	0	3	1
GH Micklem	ENG	1947-49-53-55-**(57)**-**(59)**	6	1	5	0
DJ Millensted	ENG	1967	2	1	1	0
JW Milligan	SCO	1989-91	7	3	3	1
EB Millward	ENG	(1949)-55	2	0	2	0
WTG Milne	SCO	1973	4	2	2	0
†CS Montgomerie	SCO	1985-87	8	2	5	1
JL Morgan	WAL	1951-53-55	6	2	4	0
C Moriarty	IRL	2003	4	1	3	0
J Moul	ENG	2007	4	2	1	1
P Mulcare	IRL	1975	3	2	1	0
GH Murray	SCO	1977	2	1	1	0
SWT Murray	SCO	1963	4	2	2	0
WA Murray	SCO	1923-24-(26)	4	1	3	0
K Nolan	IRL	1997	3	0	3	0
E O'Connell	IRL	1989	4	2	0	2
S O'Hara	SCO	2001	4	2	2	0
A Oldcorn	ENG	1983	4	4	0	0
†PA Oosterhuis	ENG	1967	4	1	2	1
R Oppenheimer	ENG	**(1951)**	0	0	0	1
P Page	ENG	1993	2	0	2	0
D Park	WAL	1997	3	0	3	0
P Parkin	WAL	1983	3	2	1	0
J Parry	ENG	2007	2	1	1	0
D Patrick	SCO	1999	1	0	1	0
J Payne	ENG	1991	4	2	2	0
JJF Pennink	ENG	1938	2	1	1	0
TP Perkins	ENG	1928	2	0	2	0
GB Peters	SCO	1936-38	4	2	1	1
V Phillips	ENG	1993	3	1	2	0
AD Pierse	IRL	1983	3	0	2	1
AH Perowne	ENG	1949-53-59	4	0	4	0
AK Pirie	SCO	1967	3	0	2	1
MA Poxon	ENG	1975	2	0	2	0
D Prosser	ENG	1989	1	0	1	2
I Pyman	ENG	1993	3	0	3	0
†R Rafferty	IRL	1981	4	2	2	0
R Ramsay	SCO	2005	2	1	1	0
G Rankin	SCO	1995-97-99	8	2	6	0
M Richardson	ENG	2005	4	2	2	0
D Robertson	SCO	1993	3	1	2	0
J Robinson	ENG	1987	4	2	2	0
RN Roderick	WAL	1989	2	0	1	1
J Rose	ENG	1997	4	2	2	0
P Rowe	ENG	1999	3	3	0	0
R Russell	SCO	1993	3	0	3	0
AC Saddler	SCO	1963-65-67-**(77)**	10	3	5	2
L Saltman	SCO	2005-07	7	4	3	0
Hon M Scott	ENG	1924-**34**	4	2	2	0
R Scott, jr	SCO	1924	1	1	0	0
PF Scrutton	ENG	1955-57	3	0	3	0
DN Sewell	ENG	1957-59	4	1	3	0
RDBM Shade	SCO	1961-63-65-67	14	6	6	2
G Shaw	SCO	1987	4	1	2	1
DB Sheahan	IRL	1963	4	2	2	0
AE Shepperson	ENG	1957-59	3	1	1	1
G Sherry	SCO	1995	4	2	2	0
AF Simpson	SCO	(1926)	0	0	0	0
M Skelton	ENG	2003	2	1	1	0
JN Smith	SCO	1930	2	0	2	0
WD Smith	SCO	1959	1	0	1	0
M Stanford	ENG	1993	3	1	2	0
AR Stephen	SCO	1985	4	2	1	1
EF Storey	ENG	1924-26-28	6	1	5	0

Walker Cup Individual Records *continued*

Name		Year	Played	Won	Lost	Halved
G Storm	ENG	1999	4	2	2	0
JA Stout	ENG	1930-32	4	0	3	1
C Stowe	ENG	1938-47	4	2	2	0
HB Stuart	SCO	1971-73-75	10	4	6	0
A Thirlwell	ENG	1957	1	0	1	0
KG Thom	ENG	1949	2	0	2	0
MS Thompson	ENG	1983	3	1	2	0
H Thomson	SCO	1936-38	4	2	2	0
CJH Tolley	ENG	1922-23-**24**-26-30-34	12	4	8	0
TA Torrance	SCO	1924-28-30-**32**-34	9	3	5	1
WB Torrance	SCO	1922	2	0	2	0
†PM Townsend	ENG	1965	4	3	1	0
LP Tupling	ENG	1969	2	1	1	0
W Tweddell	ENG	**1928**-(36)	2	0	2	0
J Walker	SCO	1961	2	0	2	0
†P Walton	IRL	1981-83	8	6	2	0
M Warren	SCO	2001	3	2	1	0
C Watson	SCO	1997	3	1	1	1
†P Way	ENG	1981	4	2	2	0
RH Wethered	ENG	1922-23-26-**30**-34	9	5	3	1
L White	ENG	1991	2	1	1	0
RJ White	ENG	1947-49-51-53-55	10	6	3	1
D Willett	ENG	2007	4	0	2	2
R Willison	ENG	1991	4	1	3	0
J Wilson	SCO	1923	2	2	0	0
JC Wilson	SCO	1947-53	4	0	4	0
O Wilson	ENG	2003	3	2	0	1
S Wilson	SCO	2003	4	1	1	2
GB Wolstenholme	ENG	1957-59	4	1	2	1
GP Wolstenholme	ENG	1995-97-99-01-03-05	19	10	9	0
S Young	SCO	1997	4	2	2	0

United States of America

Name	Year	Played	Won	Lost	Halved
†TD Aaron	1959	2	1	1	0
B Alexander	1987	3	2	1	0
DC Allen	1965-67	6	0	4	2
B Andrade	1987	4	2	2	0
ES Andrews	1961	1	1	0	0
D Ballenger	1973	1	1	0	0
R Baxter, jr	1957	2	2	0	0
N Begay III	1995	3	1	2	0
DR Beman	1959-61-63-65	11	7	2	2
D Berganio	1993	3	1	2	0
RE Billows	1938-49	4	2	2	0
SE Bishop	1947-49	3	2	1	0
AS Blum	1957	1	0	1	0
J Bohmann	1969	3	1	2	0
M Brannan	1977	3	1	2	0
A Bratton	1995	3	1	0	2
GF Burns	1975	3	2	1	0
C Burroughs	1985	3	1	2	0
J Byrd	1999	3	1	2	0
AE Campbell	1936	2	2	0	0
JE Campbell	1957	1	0	1	0
WC Campbell	1951-53-(**55**)-57-65-67-71-75	18	11	4	3
N Cassini	2001	4	2	2	0
RJ Cerrudo	1967	4	1	1	2
RD Chapman	1947-51-53	5	3	2	0
D Cherry	1953-55-61	5	5	0	0
D Clarke	1979	3	2	0	1
RE Cochran	1961	1	1	0	0
CR Coe	1949-51-53-(**57**)-**59**-61-63	13	7	4	2
R Commans	1981	3	1	1	1
E Compton	2001	3	1	1	1
JW Conrad	1955	2	1	1	0
J Courville jr	1995-97	6	4	2	0

Name	Year	Played	Won	Lost	Halved
K Cox	1995	3	1	2	0
N Crosby	1983	2	1	1	0
BH Cudd	1955	2	2	0	0
RD Davies	1963	2	0	2	0
JW Dawson	1949	2	2	0	0
D Delcher	1997	3	2	1	0
T Demsey	1993	3	3	0	0
RB Dickson	1967	3	3	0	0
A Doyle	1991-93	6	5	1	0
J Driscoll	2001	3	0	3	0
GT Dunlap jr	1932-34-36	5	3	1	1
†D Duval	1991	3	2	1	0
D Edwards	1973	4	4	0	0
HC Egan	1934	1	1	0	0
D Eger	1991-01	5	3	1	1
HC Eger	1989	3	1	2	0
D Eichelberger	1965	3	1	2	0
B Elder	1997	4	4	0	0
J Ellis	1973	3	2	1	0
W Emery	1936	2	1	0	1
C Evans jr	1922-24-28	5	3	2	0
M Every	2005	4	1	2	1
J Farquhar	1971	3	1	2	0
†B Faxon	1983	4	3	1	0
R Fehr	1983	4	2	1	1
JW Fischer	1934-36-38-(65)	4	3	0	1
D Fischesser	1979	3	1	2	0
MA Fleckman	1967	2	0	2	0
B Fleisher	1969	4	0	2	2
J Fought	1977	4	4	0	0
R Fowler	2007	4	3	1	0
WC Fownes jr	**1922-24**	3	1	2	0
F Fuhrer	1981	3	2	1	0
JR Gabrielsen	1977-(**81**)-(**91**)	3	1	2	0
R Gamez	1989	4	3	0	1
RA Gardner	1922-**23-24-26**	8	6	2	0
RW Gardner	1961-63	5	4	0	1
B Gay	1993	2	0	1	1
M Giles	1969-71-73-75	15	8	2	5
HL Givan	1936	1	0	0	1
L Glover	2001	4	2	2	0
JG Goodman	1934-36-38	6	4	2	0
J Gore	1997	3	2	0	1
D Gossett	1999	4	1	2	1
M Gove	1979	3	2	1	0
J Grace	1975	3	2	1	0
JA Grant	1967	2	2	0	0
AD Gray jr	1963-65-67-(**95**)-(**97**)	12	5	6	1
D Green	2001	3	0	3	0
JP Guilford	1922-24-26	6	4	2	0
W Gunn	1926-28	4	4	0	0
†F Haas jr	1938	2	0	2	0
H Haas	1999	4	3	1	0
†J Haas	1975	3	3	0	0
J Haas	1985	3	1	2	0
W Haas	2003	4	2	2	0
G Hallberg	1977	3	1	2	0
GS Hamer jr	(1947)	0	0	0	0
B Harman	2005	3	2	0	1
J Harris	1993-95-97-01	14	10	4	0
LE Harris jr	1963	4	3	1	0
V Heafner	1977	3	3	0	0
M Hendrix	2003	3	2	0	1
SD Herron	1923	2	0	2	0
T Herron	1993	3	3	0	0
†S Hoch	1979	4	4	0	0
W Hoffer	1983	2	1	1	0
J Holmes	2005	3	2	1	0
J Holtgrieve	1979-81-83	10	6	4	0
JM Hopkins	1965	3	0	2	1

Walker Cup Individual Records *continued*

Name	Year	Played	Won	Lost	Halved
B Horschel	2007	4	3	1	0
R Howe	1989	1	0	1	0
W Howell	1932	1	1	0	0
B Hurley	2005	2	0	2	0
W Hyndman	1957-59-61-69-71	9	6	1	2
J Inman	1969	2	2	0	0
JG Jackson	1953-55	3	3	0	0
T Jackson	1995-99	6	3	2	1
D Johnson	2007	3	1	1	1
K Johnson	1989	3	1	2	0
HR Johnston	1923-24-28-30	6	5	1	0
RT Jones jr	1922-24-26-**28-30**	10	9	1	0
AF Kammer	1947	2	1	1	0
M Killian	1973	3	1	2	0
A Kim	2005	4	2	1	1
C Kirk	2007	2	1	1	0
C Kite	1987	3	2	1	0
†TO Kite	1971	4	2	1	1
RE Knepper	(1922)	0	0	0	0
C Knost	2007	4	2	0	2
RW Knowles	1951	1	1	0	0
G Koch	1973-75	7	4	1	2
CR Kocsis	1938-49-57	5	2	2	1
J Kribel	1997	3	1	2	0
M Kuchar	1999	3	0	3	0
T Kuehne	1995-03-07	10	2	7	1
F Langham	1991	3	1	2	0
R Leen	1997	3	2	1	0
†J Leonard	1993	3	3	0	0
G Lesher	1989	4	1	3	0
B Lewis jr	1981-83-85-87-**(03)**-**(05)**	14	10	4	0
JW Lewis	1967	4	3	1	0
WL Little jr	1934	2	2	0	0
†GA Littler	1953	2	2	0	0
E Loar	1999	3	2	1	0
B Loeffler	1987	3	2	1	0
†D Love III	1985	3	2	0	1
J Lovemark	2007	3	2	1	0
B Mackenzie	2003	3	3	0	0
RR Mackenzie	1926-28-30	6	5	1	0
MJ McCarthy jr	(1928)-32	1	1	0	0
BN McCormick	1949	1	1	0	0
T McKnight	1999	2	0	2	0
JB McHale	1949-51	3	2	0	1
MR Marston	1922-23-24-34	8	5	3	0
D Martin	1989	4	1	1	2
B Marucci	1995-97-**(07)**	6	4	1	1
L Mattiace	1987	3	2	1	0
R May	1991	4	3	1	0
B Mayfair	1987	3	3	0	0
E Meeks	1989	1	0	0	1
SN Melnyk	1969-71	7	3	3	1
†P Mickelson	1989-91	8	4	2	2
AL Miller	1969-71	8	4	3	1
†J Miller	1999	3	2	1	0
L Miller	1977	4	4	0	0
K Mitchum	1993	3	2	0	1
DK Moe	1930-32	3	3	0	0
B Molder	1999-01	8	3	3	2
B Montgomery	1987	2	2	0	0
G Moody	1979	3	1	2	0
J Moore	2007	3	2	0	1
R Moore	2003	2	0	2	0
GT Moreland	1932-34	4	4	0	0
D Morey	1955-65	4	1	3	0
J Mudd	1981	3	3	0	0
†RJ Murphy	1967	4	1	2	1
C Nallen	2003	2	1	1	0

Name	Year	Played	Won	Lost	Halved
JF Neville	1923	1	0	1	0
†JW Nicklaus	1959-61	4	4	0	0
LW Oehmig	(1977)	0	0	0	0
FD Ouimet	1922-23-24-26-30-**32-34-(36)-(38)-(47)-(49)**	16	9	5	2
J Overton	2005	4	3	1	0
HD Paddock jr	1951	1	0	0	1
†J Pate	1975	4	0	4	0
WJ Patton	1955-57-59-63-65-**(69)**	14	11	3	0
†C Pavin	1981	3	2	0	1
M Peck	1979	3	1	1	1
M Pfeil	1973	4	2	1	1
M Podolak	1985	2	1	0	1
M Putnam	2005	4	1	2	1
SL Quick	1947	2	1	1	0
J Quinney	2001	2	0	2	0
S Randolph	1985	4	2	1	1
J Rassett	1981	3	3	0	0
K Reifers	2005	2	0	2	0
F Ridley	1977-**(87)-(89)**	3	2	1	0
RH Riegel	1947-49	4	4	0	0
C Riley	1995	3	1	1	1
H Robbins jr	1957	2	0	1	1
†W Rogers	1973	2	1	1	0
GV Rotan	1923	2	1	1	0
A Rubinson	2003	4	1	3	0
†EM Rudolph	1957	2	1	0	1
B Sander	1977	3	0	3	0
T Scherrer	1991	3	0	3	0
S Scott	1997-99	6	2	4	0
CH Seaver	1932	2	2	0	0
RL Siderowf	1969-73-75-77-**(79)**	14	4	8	2
J Sigel	1977-79-81-**83**-85-87-89-91-93	33	18	10	5
RH Sikes	1963	3	1	2	0
JB Simons	1971	2	0	2	0
†S Simpson	1977	3	3	0	0
W Simpson	2007	3	0	2	1
CB Smith	1961-63	2	0	1	1
R Smith	1936-38	4	2	2	0
R Sonnier	1985	3	0	2	1
J Sorensen	1987	3	1	1	1
M Sposa	1991	3	2	1	0
†C Stadler	1975	3	3	0	0
K Stanley	2007	3	0	3	0
FR Stranahan	1947-49-51	6	3	2	1
†C Strange	1975	4	3	0	1
†H Sutton	1979-81	7	2	4	1
‡JW Sweetser	1922-23-24-26-28-32-**(67)**-(73)	12	7	†4	†1
FM Taylor	1957-59-61	4	4	0	0
D Tentis	1983	2	0	1	1
N Thompson	2005	2	1	1	0
DJ Trahan	2001	4	1	3	0
RS Tufts	**(1963)**	0	0	0	0
WP Turnesa	1947-49-**51**	6	3	3	0
B Tuten	1983	2	1	1	0
EM Tutweiler	1965-67	6	5	1	0
ER Updegraff	1963-65-69-**(75)**	7	3	3	1
S Urzetta	1951-53	4	4	0	0
K Venturi	1953	2	2	0	0
†S Verplank	1985	4	3	0	1
M Voges	1991	3	2	1	0
GJ Voigt	1930-32-36	5	2	2	1
G Von Elm	1926-28-30	6	4	1	1
D von Tacky	1981	3	1	2	0
†JL Wadkins	1969-71	7	3	4	0
D Waldorf	1985	3	1	2	0
EH Ward	1953-55-59	6	6	0	0
MH Ward	1938-47	4	2	2	0
M West	1973-79	6	2	3	1
J Westland	1932-34-53-**(61)**	5	3	0	2
HW Wettlaufer	1959	2	2	0	0
E White	1936	2	2	0	0

‡In 1922 Hooman beat Sweetser at the 37th – on all other occasions halved matches have counted as such.

Walker Cup Individual Records *continued*

Name	Year	Played	Won	Lost	Halved
L Williams	2003-05	7	3	2	2
OF Willing	1923-24-30	4	4	0	0
JM Winters jr	(1971)	0	0	0	0
C Wittenberg	2003	4	1	3	0
C Wollman	1997	3	1	1	1
W Wood	1983	4	1	2	1
†T Woods	1995	4	2	2	0
FJ Wright	1923	1	1	0	0
CR Yates	1936-38-(53)	4	3	0	1
D Yates jr	1989-93-(99)-01	6	3	2	1
RL Yost	1955	2	2	0	0
G Zahringer	2003	3	0	2	1

World Amateur Team Championship (Eisenhower Trophy)   (Instituted 1958)

Royal Adelaide & Grange GC   [7153–73; 6858–72]

1	Scotland	560	(Wallace Booth, Gavin Dear, Callum Macaulay)
2	USA	569	(Rickie Fowler, Jamie Lovemark, Billy Horschel)
3	Sweden	574	(Henrik, Norlander, Pontus Widegoth, Jesper Kennegard)
4	France	575	(Victor Dubuisson, Benjamin Hebert, Alexandre Kaleka)
	Italy		(Federico Colombo, Andrea Pavan, Nino Bertasio)
6	Australia	578	(Matthew Griffin, Tim Stewart, Rohan Blizard)
7	Spain	579	(Borja Etchart, Pedro Oriol, Jorge Campillo)
	Netherlands		(Richard Kind, Floris de Vries, Reinier Saxton)
9	Canada	580	(Nick Taylor, Jordan Irwin, Davide Maride)
	Argentina		(Julian Etulain, Jorge Fernandez Valdes, Emiliano Grillo)
11	Wales	581	(Nigel Edwards, Rhys Enoch, Ben Westgate)
	New Zealand		(Jared Pender, James Gill, Danny Lee)
	South Africa		(Jacques Blaaw, Cameron Johnston, Dylan Frittelli)
14	England	582	(Sam Hutsby, Luke Goddard, Dale Whitnell)

65 teams took part

Individual:

1	Rickie Fowler (USA)	68-67-70-75—280
2	Callum Macaulay (SCO)	67-70-73-72—282
	Nick Taylor (CAN)	73-71-68-70—282
4	Wallace Booth (SCO)	70-67-69-79—285

1958	1 Australia*; 2 United States	1982	1 United States; 2 Sweden
Australia beat United States 224–224 in play-off		1984	1 Japan; 2 United States
1960	1 United States; 2 Australia	1986	1 Canada; 2 United States
1962	1 United States; 2 Canada	1988	1 Great Britain & Ireland; 2 United States
1964	1 Great Britain & Ireland; 2 Canada	1990	1 Sweden; 2 New Zealand
1966	1 Australia; 2 United States	1992	1 New Zealand; 2 United States
1968	1 United States; 2 Great Britain & Ireland	1994	1 United States; 2 Great Britain & Ireland
1970	1 United States; 2 New Zealand	1996	1 Australia; 2 Sweden
1972	1 United States; 2 Australia	1998	1 Great Britain and Ireland; 2 Australia
1974	1 United States; 2 Japan	2000	1 United States; 2 Great Britain & Ireland
1976	1 Great Britain & Ireland; 2 Japan	2002	1 United States; 2 France
1978	1 United States; 2 Canada	2004	1 United States; 2 Spain
1980	1 United States; 2 South Africa	2006	1 Netherlands; 2 Canada

---

PGA Sultan to host 2012 Eisenhower Trophy

The Sultan course at the PGA branded Antalya Club in Turkey has been chosen to host the 2012 World Amateur Team Championship for the Eisenhower Trophy. Scotland, who won the event for the first time in Adelaide last year, will be defending at Antalya which joins a long list of notable venues including the Old.Course at St Andrews, Royal Melbourne and Pinehurst No 2 since the event was started in 1958.

Other courses that are PGA branded include the Centenary Course at Gleneagles Hotel, Palmerston House and the Belfry while overseas there are PGA branded courses in India, Russia, Spain, China and Tunisia.

Europe v Asia–Pacific (Sir Michael Bonallack Trophy) *Valderrama*

Captains: Europe – Gonzaga Escauriaza (ESP); Asia–Pacific – Roger Brennand (NZL)

Europe		Asia–Pacific	
First Day: **Morning – Fourballs**			
Macaulay & Booth	0	Gill & Lee	1
Sjoholm & Akesson	1	Chen & Quek	0
Edwards & Lowry	½	Chomchalam & Fernando	½
Wood & Willett	0	Blizzard & Stewart	1
Oriol & Einhaus	1	B-O Kim & Y-S Kim	0
Afternoon – Foursomes			
Macaulay & Booth	1	Ito & Tamura	0
Sjoholm & Akesson	1	Gill & Lee	0
Hebert & Taleka	1	Chomchalam & Fernando	0
Edwards & Lowry	0	Blizzard & Stewart	1
Wood & Willett	½	B-O Kim & Y-S Kim	½

Match positions: Europe 6, Asia–Pacific 4

Second Day: **Morning – Fourballs**			
Sjoholm & Akesson	1	Gill & Lee	0
Hebert & Taleka	½	Quek & Ito	½
Wood & Willett	1	Chomchalam & Fernando	0
Edwards & Lowry	0	B-O Kim & Y-S Kim	1
Oriol & Einhaus	1	Blizzard & Stewart	0
Afternoon – Foursomes			
Macaulay & Booth	1	Gill & Lee	0
Sjoholm & Akesson	1	Chomchalam & Tamura	0
Hebert & Taleka	1	Quek & Chen	0
Wood & Willett	0	B-O Kim & Y-S Kim	1
Edwards & Lowry	1	Blizzard & Stewart	0

Match position: Europe 13½, Asia–Pacific 6½

Third Day: **Singles**			
Callum Macaulay (SCO)	0	Yuki Ito (JPN)	1
Wallace Booth (SCO)	1	Quincy Quek (SIN)	0
Bjorn Akesson (SWE)	1	Naoyuki Tamura (JPN)	0
Joel Sjoholm (SWE)	1	Anthony Fernando (PHI)	0
Pedro Oriol (ESP)	0	Varut Chomchalam (THA)	1
Chris Wood (ENG)	½	James Gill (NZL)	½
Nigel Edwards (WAL)	0	Ming-Chuan Chen (TPE)	1
Benjamin Hebert (FRA)	0	Tim Stewart (AUS)	1
Sean Einhaus (GER)	1	Yeong-Su Kim (KOR)	0
Alexandre Kaleka (FRA)	1	Danny Lee (NZL)	0
Shane Lowry (IRL)	0	Bi-O Kim (KOR)	1
Daniel Willett (ENG)	1	Rohan Blizzard (AUS)	0

Result: Europe 20, Asia–Pacific 12

2000 Europe	2002 Asia–Pacific	2004 Asia–Pacific	2006 Asia–Pacific

EGA Challenge Trophy *Crete GC*

1 Czech Republic 1096 points; 2 Greece 1130 points; 3 Turkey 1132 points; 4 Hungary 1167 points; 5 Slovakia 1169 points

Winning team: Stanislav Matus, Jiri Korda, Lukas Tintera, Marek Novy, Jan Prokop, Jan Ryba

2006 Belgium

European Amateur Team Championship   *Royal Park, Turin, Italy*

Final placings: 1 Ireland; 2 England; 3 Germany; 4 France; 5 Scotland; 6 Spain; 7 Sweden; 8 Italy
20 countries took part

Winning team: Jonathan Caldwell (Clandeboye), Paul Cutler (Portstewart), Niall Kearney (Royal Dublin), Shane Lowry (Esker Hills), Paul O'Hanlon (Curragh), Gareth Shaw (Lurgan)

1959	1 Sweden, 2 France	1977	1 Scotland, 2 Sweden	1995	1 Scotland, 2 England
1961	1 Sweden, 2 England	1979	1 England, 2 Wales	1997	1 Spain, 2 Scotland
1963	1 England, 2 Sweden	1981	1 England, 2 Scotland	1999	1 Italy, 2 Germany
1965	1 Ireland, 2 Scotland	1983	1 Ireland, 2 Spain	2001	1 Scotland, 2 Ireland
1967	1 Ireland, 2 France	1985	1 Scotland, 2 Sweden	2003	1 Spain, 2 Sweden
1969	1 England, 2 Germany	1987	1 Ireland, 2 England	2005	1 England, 2 Germany
1971	1 England, 2 Scotland	1989	1 England, 2 Scotland	2007	1 Ireland, 2 France
1973	1 England, Scotland	1991	1 England, 2 Italy		
1975	1 Scotland, 2 Italy	1993	1 Wales, 2 England		

European Seniors Mens Championship   *Shannon, Ireland*

1 Ireland; 2 Scotland; 3 Germany; 4 England; 5 Spain; 6 France; 7 Portugal; 8 Sweden
20 countries took part

Winning team: Tommie Basquille (Team Captain). John Carroll, Maurice Kelly, Liam MacNamara, Adrian Morrow, Arthur Pierse, Hugh Smyth

2006	Scotland	2007	Ireland

European Club Cup (Albacom Trophy)   *Club Parco de' Medici, Rome*

1	Saint Nom-La-Bretèche (FRA)	423	(Jean Jacque Wolff, Kevin Turlan, Victor Dubuisson)
2	Racing Club de France (FRA)	426	
3	Raimat GC (ESP)	429	

24 teams took part

1975	Club de Campo, Spain	1987	Puerto de Hierro, Spain	1998	Aalborg, Denmark
1976	Växjö Golfklub, Sweden	1988	Brokenhurst Manor, England	1999	Aalborg, Denmark
1977	Chantilly, France	1989	Ealing, England	2000	Shandon Park,
1978	Hamburger, Germany	1990	Ealing, England		Northern Ireland
1979	Hamburger, Germany	1991	Club de Golf Terramar, Spain	2001	Shandon Park
1980	Limerick, Ireland	1992	Hillerod, Denmark	2002	Bordelais, France
1981	El Prat, Spain	1993	Lahden, Finland	2003	Deauville, France
1982	El Prat, Spain	1994	Kilmarnock (Barassie),	2004	De Houtrak
1983	Rapallo, Italy		Scotland	2005	Klassis, Turkey
1984	Hamburger, Germany	1995	Racing C de France, France	2006	St Leon-Rot, Germany
1985	El Prat, Spain	1996	Racing C de France, France	2007	Golf de la Boulie, France
1986	Hamburger, Germany	1997	Racing C de France, France		

St Andrews Trophy (Great Britain & Ireland v Continent of Europe)

Match instituted 1956, trophy presented 1964

Kingsbarns, by St Andrews

Non-playing Captains: GBI: Colin Dalgleish (SCO); Eur: Alexis Godillot (FRA)

First Day – **Foursomes**
J Caldwell & C Macaulay beat R Saxton & T Sluiter 3 and 1
M Haines & C Paisley beat S Gross & J Kennegard 4 and 3
W Booth & S Lowry beat A Kaleka & B Hebert 4 and 3
S Hutsby & D Whitnell beat A Pavan & J Campillo 1 hole

Singles
Callum Macaulay (SCO) beat Reinier Saxton (NED) 2 and 1
Shane Lowry (IRL) halved with Stephan Gross (GER)
Sam Hutsby (ENG) beat Björn Akesson (SWE) 6 and 4
Steven Uzzell (ENG) lost to Benjamin Hebert (FRA) 1 hole
Wallace Booth (SCO) beat Jorge Campillo (ESP) 5 and 4

First Day – **Singles** *(continued)*
Chris Paisley (ENG) lost to Andrea Pavan (ITA) 3 and 2
Dale Whitnell (ENG) lost to Jesper Kennegard (SWE) 3 and 2
Jonathan Caldwell (IRL) lost to Alexandre Kaleka (FRA) 3 and 1

Match position: GBI 7½ Europe 4½

Second Day – **Foursomes**
S Hutsby & D Whitnell beat S Gross & J Kennegard 3 and 2
J Caldwell & C Macaulay halved with R Saxton & T Sluiter
M Haines & C Paisley halved with A Pavan & J Campillo
W Booth & S Lowry beat A Kaleka & B Hebert 3 and 2

Singles
C Macaulay beat S Gross 3 and 1
S Hutsby halved with J Campillo
W Booth beat Tim Sluiter (NED) 5 and 3
Matthew Haines (ENG) lost to B Akesson 1 hole
D Whitnell lost to B Hebert 6 and 5
C Paisley lost to J Kennegard 3 and 2
S Uzzell lost to A Pavan 4 and 3
S Lowry halved with A Kaleka

Match Result: GBI 13½, Europe 10½

1956	Great Britain & Ireland beat Continent of Europe	12½–2½
1958	Great Britain & Ireland beat Continent of Europe	10–5
1960	Great Britain & Ireland beat Continent of Europe	13–5
1962	Great Britain & Ireland beat Continent of Europe	18–12
1964	Great Britain & Ireland beat Continent of Europe	23–7
1966	Great Britain & Ireland beat Continent of Europe	19½–10½
1968	Great Britain & Ireland beat Continent of Europe	20–10
1970	Great Britain & Ireland beat Continent of Europe	17½–12½
1972	Great Britain & Ireland beat Continent of Europe	19½–10½
1974	Continent of Europe beat Great Britain & Ireland	16–14
1976	Great Britain & Ireland beat Continent of Europe	18½–11½
1978	Great Britain & Ireland beat Continent of Europe	20½–9½
1980	Great Britain & Ireland beat Continent of Europe	19½–10½
1982	Continent of Europe beat Great Britain & Ireland	14–10
1984	Great Britain & Ireland beat Continent of Europe	13–11
1986	Great Britain & Ireland beat Continent of Europe	14½–9½
1988	Great Britain & Ireland beat Continent of Europe	15½–8½
1990	Great Britain & Ireland beat Continent of Europe	13–11
1992	Great Britain & Ireland beat Continent of Europe	14–10
1994	Great Britain & Ireland beat Continent of Europe	14–10
1996	Great Britain & Ireland beat Continent of Europe	16–8
1998	Continent of Europe beat Great Britain & Ireland	14–10
2000	Great Britain & Ireland beat Continent of Europe	13–11
2002	Great Britain & Ireland beat Continent of Europe	14–10
2004	Great Britain & Ireland beat Continent of Europe	17–7
2006	Continent of Europe beat Great Britain & Ireland	15–9

Zone VI African Team Championship *Ndola, Zambia*

1 South Africa 22.5; 2 Zimbabwe 16; 3 Kenya 15.5; 4 Malawi, Swaziland 11.5;

Zambia 11, Namibia 10.5, Botswana 9.5, Uganda 9, Lesotho 3

10 countries took part

Winning Team: Jacques Blaauw, Ryan Clarke, Johan du Buisson, Derik Ferreira, Adrian Ford, Dylan Frittelli, Altheus Kelapile, Dean O'Riley

2007	South Africa

Pan Arab Championship   *Dirab, Riyadh, Saudi Arabia*

Men's competition:

1	Lebanon	920	(Rashid Aqoul, Adnan Hammoud, Ali Hammoud, Ramadan Mehdi)
2	Bahrain	923	
3	Egypt	924	

4 Tunisia 941, 5 Saudi Arabia 942   13 teams played

Best individual: Amr Abouelela (EGY) 73-77-74-74—298

Home Internationals (Raymond Trophy)   *Muirfield*

Ireland 9½, Scotland 5½   Wales 3½, Ireland 11½
England 8½, Wales 6½   Scotland 9½, Wales 5½
England 5, Scotland 10   Ireland 10, England 5

Result: 1 Ireland 3 [31]; 2 Scotland 2 [25]; 3 England 1 [18½]; 4 Wales 0 [15½]

Winning team: Michael Burns (Captain), Eoin Arthurs, Jonathan Caldwell, Cian Curley, Paul Cutler, Alan Dunbar, Niall Kearney, Dara Lernihan, Shane Lowry, Paul O'Hanlon, Cathal O'Malley, Simon Ward

1932	Scotland	1956	Scotland	1972T	Scotland/England	1990	Ireland
1933	Scotland	1957	England	1973	England	1991	Ireland
1934	Scotland	1958	England	1974	England	1992T	England/Ireland
1935T	England/Ireland/	1959T	England/Ireland/	1975	Scotland	1993	England
	Scotland		Scotland	1976	Scotland	1994	England
1936	Scotland	1960	England	1977	England	1995	England
1937	Scotland	1961	Scotland	1978	England	1996	England
1938	England	1962T	England/Ireland/	1979	*No Internationals*	1997	England
1939–46	*No Internationals*		Scotland		*held*	1998	England
	held	1963T	England/Ireland/	1980	England	1999	England
1947	England		Scotland	1981	Scotland	2000	Scotland
1948	England	1964	England	1982	Scotland	2001	England
1949	England	1965	England	1983	Ireland	2002	Wales
1950	Ireland	1966	England	1984	England	2003	Ireland
1951T	Ireland/Scotland	1967	Scotland	1985	England	2004	England
1952	Scotland	1968	England	1986	Scotland	2005	Scotland
1953	Scotland	1969	England	1987	Ireland	2006	Scotland
1954	England	1970	Scotland	1988	England	2007	England
1955	Ireland	1971	Scotland	1989	England		

Senior Home Internationals   *Tenby*

England 5, Wales 4   Ireland 7, Wales 2
Ireland 4½, Scotland 4½   Scotland 4½, Wales 4½
England 4½, Scotland 4½   Ireland 6, England 3

Result: 1 Ireland 2½ [17½]; 2 Scotland 1½ [13½]; 3 England 1½ [12½]; 4 Wales ½ [10½]

Winning team: John Carroll, Michael Coote, Nigel Duke, Maurice Kelly, Liam MacNamara, Adrian Morrow, Hugh Smyth

2002	England	2004	England	2006	Scotland
2003	Ireland & Wales	2005	Ireland	2007	England

English County Championship   *Notts*

Wiltshire 4, Leicester & Rutland 5   Lancashire 5, Wiltshire 4
Hampshire, Isle of Wight & Channel Islands 2,   Hampshire, Isle of Wight & Channel Islands 4½,
   Lancashire 7   Wiltshire 4½
Leicester & Rutland 3½, Hampshire, Isle of Wight &   Lancashire 6, Leicester & Rutland 3
   Channel Islands 5½

Result: 1 Lancashire 3 [18]; 2 Hampshire, Isle of Wight, & Channel Islands 1½ [12]; 3 Leicester & Rutland 1 [11½]; 4 Wiltshire ½ [12½]

Winning team: John Carroll, Jon Hurst, Matthew Nixon, James Robinson, Jack Senior, Sam Stuart, Mark Young

1928	Warwickshire	1954	Cheshire	1974	Lincolnshire	1992	Dorset
1929	Lancashire	1955	Yorkshire	1975	Staffordshire	1993	Yorkshire
1930	Lancashire	1956	Staffordshire	1976	Warwickshire	1994	Middlesex
1931	Yorkshire	1957	Surrey	1977	Warwickshire	1995	Lancashire
1932	Surrey	1958	Surrey	1978	Kent	1996	Hampshire
1933	Yorkshire	1959	Northumberland	1979	Gloucestershire	1997	Yorkshire
1934	Worcestershire	1961	Lancashire	1980	Surrey	1998	Yorkshire
1935	Worcestershire	1962	Northumberland	1981	Surrey	1999	Yorkshire
1936	Surrey	1963	Yorkshire	1982	Yorkshire	2000	Surrey
1937	Lancashire	1964	Northumberland	1983	Berks, Bucks, Oxon	2001	Yorkshire
1938	Staffordshire	1965	Northumberland	1984	Yorkshire	2002	Yorkshire
1939	Worcestershire	1966	Surrey	1985T	Devon	2003	Devon
1947	Staffordshire	1967	Lancashire		Hertfordshire	2004	Surrey
1948	Staffordshire	1968	Surrey	1986	Hertfordshire	2005	Yorkshire
1949	Lancashire	1969	Berks, Bucks, Oxon	1987	Yorkshire	2006	Yorkshire
1950	Not played	1970	Gloucestershire	1988	Warwickshire	2007	Yorkshire
1951	Lancashire	1971	Staffordshire	1989	Middlesex		
1952	Yorkshire	1972	Berks, Bucks, Oxon	1990	Warwickshire		
1953	Yorkshire	1973	Yorkshire	1991	Middlesex		

English Club Championship   (inaugurated 1984)   *Royal North Devon*

1	Hallowes (Yorkshire)	431 (Adam Hodkinson, James Smedley, James Maw)
2	Workington	435 (best second round)
3	Stoke Park	435
4	Sundridge Park	435

1984	Ealing	1990	Ealing	1997	Royal Mid-Surrey	2004	Tavistock
1985	Porters Park	1991	Trentham	1998	Moor Park	2005	Rotherham
1986	Ealing	1992	Bristol & Clifton	1999	Royal Mid-Surrey	2006	Kilworth Springs*
1987	Swindon	1993	Worksop	2000	Coxmoor	*Kilworth Springs beat Stoke
1988	Brokenhurst	1994	Sandmoor	2001	St Mellion	Park with a lower total for the
	Manor	1995	Sandmoor	2002	Woodcote Park	last 18 holes
1989	Ealing	1996	Hartlepool	2003	Southern Valley	2007	Brockenhurst

Scottish Area Team Championship   *Tain*

Semi-finals

Renfrew beat Lanark	5 matches to 4
Ayr beat South	5 matches to 4

Final

Ayrshire beat Renfrewshire	5 matches to 4

Winning team: Ronnie Potts (non-playing captain); John Cairney, Steven McEwan, Tommy McInally, Brian Moore, George Robertson, John Shanks

1990	North East	1995	North	2000	North	2005	Renfrewshire
1991	Glasgow	1996	Renfrewshire	2001	Perth and Kinross	2006	Lothians
1992	North East	1997	Lothians	2002	Perth and Kinross	2007	Lothians
1993	Lothians	1998	Lanarkshire	2003	Lothians		
1994	Lothians	1999	Lothians	2004	Lothians		

Scottish Club Championship   *Windyhill*

1	Thornton	292	(Scott Michie, David Imrie, Michael Main)
2	Cowglen	293	(countback)
3	Hamilton	293	

1985	Cochrane Castle	1993	Troon Wellbeck	2001	Blairgowrie
1986	Thornhill	1994	Kilmarnock Barassie	2002	Tulliallan
1987	Alloa	1995	Kelso	2003	Dumfries & Galloway
1988	Cowglen	1996	Cochrane Castle	2004	Cruden Bay
1989	Cowglen	1997	Blairgowrie	2005	Cardrona
1990	Haggs Castle	1998	Turvill	2006	Cruden Bay
1991	Cochrane Castle	1999	Tulliallan	2007	Ranfurly Castle
1992	Kilmarnock Barassie	2000	Cowglen		

Scottish Club Handicap Championship   *Spey Valley*

1	Whitekirk	67	(John Trotter, David Brodie)
2	Broughty	68	
3	Gifford, Dunfermline,	69	
	Ratho Park		

2001	Dunbar	2003	Galashields	2005	Downfield	2007	Harrison
2002	Newmachar	2004	Braehead	2006	Balmore		

Scottish Foursomes Tournament – *Glasgow Evening Times* Trophy

For results from 1923 when the event was first played to 2003 when it was discontinued, see the 2007 edition of the Golfer's Handbook

109th *Edinburgh Evening News Dispatch* Trophy (inaugurated 1890)   *always at Braid Hills*

Semi-finals:
Carrickvale beat Crammond   8 and 7
Third beat Temple   6 and 5

Winning team: David Ewen, Allyn Dick, Darren Coyle, Craig Elliot

Final:
Carrickvale beat Third   8 and 7

1980	Scottish Universities	1987	Whitehill	1994	Lochend	2001	Barnton Hotel
1981	Royal Bank	1988	Edinburgh Thistle	1995	Harrison	2002	Westermont
1982	Royal Bank	1989	Westermont	1996	Observers	2003	Rhodes
1983	Torphin 20	1990	Edinburgh Thistle	1997	Crags	2004	Carrick Knowe
1984	Silverknowes	1991	Scottish Life	1998	Silverknowes	2005	Riccarton
1985	Bank of Scotland	1992	Harrison	1999	Carrick Knowe	2006	Silverknowes
1986	Bank of Scotland	1993	Crags	2000	Harrison	2007	Carrickvale

Welsh Inter-Counties Championship   *Borth & Ynyslas*

1	Glamorgan	717
2	Caernarfon	736
	Gwent	
4	Flint	738

5 Anglesey 744, 6 Brecon & Radnor 746, 7 Dyfed 755, 8 Denbigh 764

Winning team: Richard Evans, Ian Flower, Richard Hooper, Brent O'Neill, Chris O'Neill, Luke Thomas

Best individuals: 139 Richard Hooper (Glamorgan) 67-72; Mark Parry (Anglesey) 70-69

2003	Gwent	2005	Glamorgan	2007	Caernarfonshire
2004	Caernarvon	2006	Glamorgan		

Welsh Team Championship   *Northop*

Semi-Finals:
Celtic Manor beat Cardiff   3 and 1
Haverfordwest beat Holywell   2 holes

Winning team: Richard Bentham, Robert Naduzzo

Final:
Celtic Manor beat Haverfordwest   at 19th

2003	Pontnewydd	2006	Llandudno
2004	Monmouthshire		(Maesedu)
2005	Whitchurch	2007	Wenvoe Castle

Principal 72 hole Tournaments

Including the National District Championships

Aberconwy Trophy (inaugurated 1976) *always at Conwy and Llandudno (Maesdu), Gwynedd*

1	Oliver Farr (Ludlow)		73-77-70-68—288
2	Richard Hooper (Neath)		71-75-72-72—290
3	Luke Thomas (Vale of Glamorgan)		75-79-72-74—300

1976	JR Jones	1984	D McLean	1992	MJ Ellis	2000	J Donaldson
1977	EN Davies	1985	MA Macara	1993	S Wilkinson	2001	L Harpin
1978	MG Mouland	1986	JR Berry	1994	G Marsden	2002	R Scott
1979	JM Morrow	1987	M Sheppard	1995	S Andrew	2003	R Scott
1980	JM Morrow	1988	MG Hughes	1996	R Williams	2004	B Briscoe
1981	D Evans	1989	JN Lee	1997	I Campbell	2005	T Dykes
1982	G Tuttle	1990	S Wilkinson	1998	J Donaldson	2006	C Evans
1983	GH Brown	1991	S Wilkinson	1999	J Donaldson	2007	J Shufflebottom

Berkshire Trophy (inaugurated 1946) *always at The Berkshire*

1	Farren Keenan (Sunningdale)		71-70-67-71—279
2	Jack Bartlett (Worthing)		66-73-69-73—281
	Jake Shepherd (The Wisley)		72-69-75-65—281

1946	R Sweeney	1960	GB Wolstenholme	1976	PJ Hedges	1993	V Phillips
1947	PB Lucas	1961	MF Bonallack	1977	A Lyle	1994T	J Knight
1948	LG Crawley	1962	SC Saddler	1978	PJ Hedges		A Marshall
1949	PB Lucas	1963	DW Frame	1979	D Williams	1995	G Harris
1950	PF Scrutton	1964	R Foster	1980	P Downes	1996	GP Wolstenholme
1951	PF Scrutton	1965	MF Bonallack	1981	D Blakeman	1997	GP Wolstenholme
1952	PF Scrutton	1966	P Oosterhuis	1982	SD Keppler	1998	M Hilton
1953	JL Morgan	1967	DJ Millensted	1983	S Hamer	1999	D Henley
1954T	Ft Lt K Hall	1968	MF Bonallack	1984	JL Plaxton	2000	C Edwards
	E Bromley-	1969	JC Davies	1985	P McEvoy	2001	G Evans
	Davenport	1970	MF Bonallack	1986	R Muscroft	2002	G Wolstenholme
1955	GH Micklem	1971T	MF Bonallack	1987	J Robinson	2003	R Fisher
1956	GB Wolstenholme		J Davies	1988	R Claydon	2004	S Osborne
1957	MF Bonallack	1972	DP Davidson	1989	J Metcalfe	2005	A Gee
1958T	GB Wolstenholme	1973	PJ Hedges	1990	J O'Shea	2006	D Shewan (RSA)
	AH Perowne	1974	J Downie	1991	J Bickerton	2007	L Collins
1959	JB Carr	1975	N Faldo	1992	V Phillips		

Cameron Corbett Vase (inaugurated 1897) *always at Haggs Castle, Glasgow*

1	David Addison (Kilmarnock [Barassie])		69-71-68-69—277
2	Scott Henry (Cardross)		71-73-68-68—280
3	Scott Borrowman (Dollar)		73-70-71-68—282
	Glenn Campbell (Blairgowrie)		72-69-71-70—282
	Kris Nicol (Fraserburgh)		68-75-69-70—282

1897	AF Duncan	1912	R Scott jr	1929	D McBride	1947	W Maclaren
1898	AF Duncan	1913	R Scott jr	1930	HM Dickson	1948	J Pressley
1899	W Laidlaw	1914	D Martin	1931	HM Dickson	1949	GB Peters
1900	GH Hutcheson	1915–18	No competition	1932	W Stringer	1950	J Gray
1901	G Fox jr	1919	HR Orr	1933	W Tulloch	1951	GB Peters
1902	AF Duncan	1920	DJ Murray	1934	JM Dykes	1952	J Stewart Thomson
1903	G Fox jr		Campbell	1935	H Thomson	1953	J Orr
1904	R Bone	1921	HM Dickson	1936	J Gray	1954	JR Cater
1905	R Bone	1922	WS Macfarlane	1937	TI Craig jr	1955	RC Macgregor
1906	W Gemmill	1923	JO Stevenson	1938	JS Logan	1956	RC Macgregor
1907	G Wilkie	1924	JO Stevenson	1939	A Steel	1957	I Rennie
1908	AF Duncan	1925	A Jamieson jr	1940–41	No competition	1958	DH Reid
1909	EB Tipping	1926	G Chapple	1942	AC Taylor	1959	AS Kerr
1910	JH Irons	1927	RS Rodger	1943–45	No competition	1960	J Mackenzie
1911	G Morris	1928	SL McKinlay	1946	JS Montgomerie	1961	GB Cosh

Cameron Corbett Vase *continued*

1962	JH Richmond	1973	MJ Miller	1985	J McDonald	1997	C Watson
1963	JA Davidson	1974	M Rae	1986	JW Milligan	1998	E Wilson
1964	IA MacCaskill	1975	D Barclay Howard	1987	J Semple	1999	W Bryson
1965	H Frazer	1976	GH Murray	1988	C Everett	2000	P McKechnie
1966	D Black	1977	MJ Miller	1989	AG Tait	2001	P Gault
1967	JRW Walkinshaw	1978	GH Murray	1990	D Robertson	2002	B Hume
1968	CW Green	1979	KW Macintosh	1991	K Gallacher	2003	J McLeary
1969	A Brooks	1980	IA Carslaw	1992	D Kirkpatrick	2004	J McGhee
1970T	J McTear	1981	GH Murray	1993	R Russell	2005	G Campbell
	D Hayes	1982	GH Murray	1994	J Hodson	2006	G Campbell
1971	G Macgregor	1983	AS Oldcorn	1995	D Barclay Howard	2007	W Booth
1972	HB Stuart	1984	D Barclay Howard	1996	C Watson		

Clwyd Open (inaugurated 1991) *always at Prestatyn and Wrexham*

1	Ben Enoch (Truro)	71-69-70-68—278
2	Jason Shufflebotham (Prestatyn)	70-70-75-65—280
	Joe Vickery (Newport)	77-67-71-65—280

1991	G Houston	1996	M Ellis	2001	A Campbell	2006	S Runcie
1992	C O'Carrol	1997	D Park	2002	G Wright	2007	R Pugh
1993	M Ellis	1998	R Donovan	2003	T Dykes		
1994	G Houston	1999	L Harpin	2004	B Westgate		
1995	M Ellis	2000	K Sullivan	2005	M Trow		

Craigmillar Park Open (inaugurated 1961) *always at Craigmillar Park, Edinburgh*

1	Craig Elliot (Carrickvale)	70-65-64—199	Reduced to 54 holes due to
2	Gavin Dear (Murrayshall)	69-69-62—200	bad weather
3	Gary Tough (Letham Grange)	72-62-67—201	

1961	RDBM Shade	1973	DF Campbell	1985	C Bloice	1997	CD Hislop
1962	A Sinclair	1974	GH Murray	1986	SR Easingwood	1998	G Rankin
1963	HM Campbell	1975	IC Hutcheon	1987	RM Roper	1999	S Mackenzie
1964	RDBM Shade	1976	NA Faldo	1988	B Shields	2000	M Warren
1965	GB Cosh	1977	CW Green	1989	RM Roper	2001	S O'Hara
1966	RDBM Shade	1978	DM McCart	1990	SJ Bannerman	2002	M Warren
1967	RDBM Shade	1979	IC Hutcheon	1991	N Walton	2003	G Gordon
1968	RDBM Shade	1980	JB Dunlop	1992	SJ Knowles	2004	J McLeary
1969	GB Cosh	1981	GK MacDonald	1993	R Russell	2005	J Gallagher
1970	PJ Smith	1982	AS Oldcorn	1994	BW Collier	2006	S Jamieson
1971	CW Green	1983	G Macgregor	1995	C Watson	2007	L Saltman
1972	CW Green	1984	G Macgregor	1996	GW Tough		

Duncan Putter (inaugurated 1959) *always at Southerndown, Bridgend, Glamorgan*

1	Nigel Edwards (Whitchurch)	70-74-66-70—280
2	Billy Hemstock (Teignmouth)	70-71-72-74—287
3	Ben Enoch (Truro)	76-73-71-68—288

1959	G Huddy	1972	P Berry (3 rounds)	1984	JP Price	1998	M King
1960	WI Tucker	1973	JKD Povall	1985	P McEvoy	1999	GP Wolstenholme
1961T	G Huddy	1974	S Cox	1986	D Wood	2000	J Donaldson
	WI Tucker	1975	JG Jermine	1987	P McEvoy	2001	N Edwards
1962	EN Davies	1976T	WI Tucker	1988	S Dodd	2002T	S Manley
1963	WI Tucker		H Stott	1989	RN Roderick		N Oakley
1964	JL Toye	1977	H Stott	1990	R Willison	2003	S Manley
1965	P Townsend	1978	P McEvoy	1991	R Willison	2004	N Edwards
1966	MF Attenborough	1979	HJ Evans	1992	R Dinsdale	2005	G Wright
1967	D Millensted	1980	P McEvoy	1993	M Thomson		
1968	JL Morgan	1981T	R Chapman	1994	GP Wolstenholme	2006T	N Chaudhuri
1969	WI Tucker		PG Way	1995	B Dredge		B Akesson (DEN)
1970	JL Toye	1982	D McLean	1996	GP Wolstenholme	2007	N Edwards
1971	W Humphreys	1983	JG Jermine	1997	M Pilkington		

Edward Trophy (inaugurated 1892)   *always at Glasgow GC*

1	Scott Henry (Cardross)	70-68-67-73—278
2	Steven McEwan (Caprington)	72-72-69-67—280
3	Gavin Dear (Murrayshall)	73-71-70-69—283

1976	DM McCart	1984	KH Walker	1992	JA Thomson	200	L Rhind
1977	R Blackwood	1985	GK MacDonald	1993	GC Sherry	2001	M Loftus
1978	R Blackwood	1986	JM Noon	1994	GC Sherry	2002	EJ Ramsay
1979	J Cuddihy	198	S Easingwood	1995	D Blair	2003	J McLeany
1980	D Murdoch	1988	R Blair	1996	A Forsyth	200	EJ Ramsay
1981	DJ Liddle	198	AJ Elliott	199	LW Kelly	200	G Bolton
1982	AF Dunsmore	1990	A Gourlay	1998	DA Patrick	2006	C Watson
1983	S Morrison	199	W Bryson	199	M Loftus	2007	M Clark

Hampshire Salver (inaugurated 1979)   *always at North Hants/Blackmoor*

1	Stiggy Hodgson (Sunningdale)*	68-65-74-68—275
2	Luke Goddard (Hendon)	65-70-72-68—275

*Hodgson won on a last-9 countback

3	Adam Wainwright (Gainsborough)	66-71-71-69—277

1979	P McEvoy	1987	A Rogers	1995	M Treleaven	2003	M Sell
1980	J Morrow	1988	NE Holman	1996	J Knight	2004	R Fisher
1981	AP Sherbourne	1989	P Dougan	1997	JP Rose	2005	R Henley
1982	I Gray	1990	J Metcalfe	1998	SJ Dyson	2006	J Crampton
1983	DG Lane	1991	G Evans	1999	B Mason	2007	R Jones
1984	DH Currie	1992	SR Cage	2000	M Young		
1985	AJ Clapp	1993	DJ Hamilton	2001	G Wolstenholme		
1986	D Gilford	1994	W Bennett	2002	J Moul		

Lagonda Trophy   *1975–1989 at Camberley and from 1990 at The Gog Magog*

1	Dale Whitnell (Five Lakes)	67-68-63-71—269
2	Luke Goddard (Hendon)	68-72-67-65—272
3	Lee Yearn (Ely City)	68-67-67-71—273

1975	WJ Reid	1984	MS Davis	1993	L James	2002	G Wolstenholme
1976	JC Davies	1985	J Robinson	1994	S Webster	2003	S Tiley
1977	WS Gronow	1986	D Gilford	1995	P Nelson	2004	O Fisher
1978	JC Davies	1987	DG Lane	1996	S Collingwood	2005	L Allen
1979	JG Bennett	1988	R Claydon	1997	L Donald	2006	M Thistleton
1980	P McEvoy	1989	T Spence	1998	K Ferrie	2007	M Mackman
1981	N Mitchell	1990	L Parsons	1999	Z Scotland		
1982	A Sherborne	1991	J Cook	2000	M Young		
1983	I Sparkes	1992	L Westwood	2001	D Skinns		

Standard Life Leven Gold Medal (inaugurated 1870)   *always at Leven Links, Fife*

1	Keir McNicoll (Carnoustie)*	67-69-70-67—273
2	Wallace Booth (Comrie)	71-67-66-69—273
	Scott Borrowman (Dollar)	71-68-68-66—273

*McNicoll won at the second extra hole

1870	J Elder	1887	J Foggo	1903	W Henderson	1923	GV Donaldson
1871	R Wallace	1888	DA Leitch	1904	W Henderson	1924	JN Smith
1872	P Anderson	1889	R Adam	1905	G Wilkie	1925	A Robertson
1873	R Armit	1890	W Marshall	1906	G Wilkie	1926	T Ainslie
1874	D Campbell	1891	DM Jackson	1907	M Goodwillie	1927	EA McRuvie
1875	AM Ross	1892	Col DW	1908	W Henderson	1928	EA McRuvie
1876	AM Ross		Mackinnon	1909	W Henderson	1929	EA McRuvie
1877	J Wilkie	1893	HS Colt	1910	W Whyte	1930	EA McRuvie
1878	R Wallace	1894	J Bell jr	1911	G Wilkie	1931	A Dunsire
1879	C Anderson	1895	C Wilkie jr	1912	G Wilkie	1932	J Ballingall
1880	C Anderson	1896	J Bell jr	1913	W Whyte	1933	CA Danks
1881	J Foggo	1897	J Bell jr	1914	GB Rattray	1934	EA McRuvie
1882	J Wilkie	1898	G Wilkie jr	1915–18	No competition	1935	EG Stoddart
1883	J Foggo	1899	G Wilkie jr	1919	G Wilkie	1936	GA Buist
1884	C Anderson	1900	W Henderson	1920	JJ Smith	1937	JY Strachan
1885	R Adam	1901	R Simpson	1921	GV Donaldson	1938	S Macdonald
1886	R Adam	1902	J Bell	1922	SO Shepperd	1939	D Jamieson

Standard Life Leven Gold Medal *continued*

1940–45	*No competition*	1963	W Moyes	1977	IC Hutcheon	1993	L Westwood
1946	EA McRuvie	1961	A Cunningham	1978	R Wallace	1994	B Howard
1947	JE Young	1962	W Moyes	1979	B Marchbank	1995	S Mackenzie
1948	J Imrie	1964	A Cunningham	1980	J Huggan	1996	M Eliasson
1949	WM Ogg	1965	PG Buchanan	1981	IC Hutcheon	1997	S Carmichael
1950	E McRuvie	1966	GM Rutherford	1982	IC Hutcheon	1998	G Rankin
1951	J Imrie	1967	AO Maxwell	1983	J Huggan	1999	J Mathers
1952	HVS Thomson	1968	A Cunningham	1984	S Stephen	2000	G Gordon
1953	O Rolland	1969	P Smith	1985	AD Turnbull	2001	P Whiteford
1954	JW Draper	1970	JC Farmer	1986	P-U Johansson	2002	J Doherty
1955	JW Draper	1971	J Scott Macdonald	1987	G Macgregor	2003	J White
1956	R Dishart	1972	J Rankine	1988	CE Everett	2004	J King
1957	I Pearson	1973	S Stephen	1989	AJ Coltart	2005	G Murray
1958	W McIntyre	1974	P Smith	1990	CE Everett	2006	G Murray
1959	W Moyes	1975	HB Stuart	1991	GA Lowson	2007	B Soutar
1960	T Taylor	1976	IC Hutcheon	1992	D Robertson		

Lytham Trophy (inaugurated 1965) *always at Royal Lytham & St Annes and Fairhaven*

1	Matt Haines (Rochester & Cobham Park)	68-72-74-70—284
2	Dale Whitnell (Five Lakes)	70-72-73-70—285
3	Shane Lowry (Esker Hills)	72-73-72-69—286

1965T	MF Bonallack	1973T	MG King	1984	J Hawksworth	1996	M Carver
	CA Clark		SG Birtwell	1985	MPD Walls	1997	G Rankin
1966	PM Townsend	1974	CW Green	1986	S McKenna	1998	L Kelly
1967	R Foster	1975	G Macgregor	1987	D Wood	1999	T Schuster
1968	R Foster	1976	MJ Kelley	1988	P Broadhurst	2000	D Dixon
1969T	T Craddock	1977	P Deeble	1989	N Williamson	2001	R McEvoy
	SG Birtwell	1978	B Marchbank	1990	G Evans	2002	L Corfield
	JC Farmer	1979	P McEvoy	1991	G Evans	2003	S Wilson
1970T	CW Green	1980	IC Hutcheon	1992	S Cage	2004	J Heath
	GC Marks	1981	R Chapman	1993	T McLure	2005	G Lockerbie
1971	W Humphreys	1982	MF Sludds	1994	W Bennett	2006	J Moul
1972	MF Bonallack	1983	S McAllister	1995	S Gallacher	2007	L Saltman

Newlands Trophy *Lanark*

1	Wallace Booth (Comrie)	72-74-71-68—285
2	Paul O'Hara (Colville Park)	73-74-69-70—286
3	Stewart Henderson (Hamilton)	74-69-72-73—288

2006	J Byrne	2007	C Macaulay

St Andrews Links Trophy (inaugurated 1989) *always at St Andrews (Old and New)*

1	Keir McNicoll (Carnoustie)	67-71-77-68—283
2	Michael Stewart (Troon Welbeck)	68-71-76-69—284
	Rudy Thuillier (FRA)	71-72-68-73—284

1989	R Claydon	1994	DB Howard	1999	D Patrick	2004	J McLeary
1990	S Bouvier (AUS)	1995	G Rankin	2000	M King	2005	L Saltman
1991	R Willison	1996	DB Howard	2001	S O'Hara	2006	O Fisher
1992	C Watson	1997	J Rose	2002	S Mackenzie	2007	L Matthews
1993	G Hay	1998	C Watson	2003	R Finch		

St David's Gold Cross (inaugurated 1930) *always at Royal St David's, Gwynedd*

1	Zac Gould (Vale of Glamorgan)	67-72-70-71—280
2	Craig Evans (West Monmouthshire)	71-73-71-70—285
	Nigel Edwards (Whitchurch)	67-76-71-71—285

1930	GC Stokoe	1936	RMW Pritchard	1947	G Mills	1953	S Lunt
1931	EW Fiddian	1937	IS Thomas	1948	CH Eaves	1954	GB Turner
1932	Dr W Tweddell	1938	SB Roberts	1949	SB Roberts	1955	JL Morgan
1933	IS Thomas	1939	IS Thomas	1950	DMG Sutherland	1956	W Cdr CH
1934	SB Roberts	1940–45	*No competition*	1951	JL Morgan		Beamish
1935	IS Thomas	1946	SB Roberts	1952	SB Roberts	1957	CD Lawrie

1958	GB Turner	1971	A Smith	1984	RJ Green	1997	M Pilkington
1959	MSR Lunt	1972	EN Davies	1985	KH Williams	1998	L Harpin
1960	LJ Ranells	1973	RD James	1986	RN Roderick	1999	D Jones
1961	MSR Lunt	1974	GC Marks	1987	SR Andrew	2000	D Price
1962	PD Kelley	1975	CP Hodgkinson	1988	MW Calvert	2001	C Williams
1963	JKD Povall	1976	JR Jones	1989	AJ Barnett	2002	A Smith
1964	MSR Lunt	1977	JA Fagan	1990	MA Macara	2003	S Manley
1965	MSR Lunt	1978	S Wild	1991	RJ Dinsdale	2004	Z Gould
1966	MSR Lunt	1979	MA Smith	1992	B Dredge	2005	T Dykes
1967	MSR Lunt	1980	CP Hodgkinson	1993	B Dredge	2006	R Thomas
1968	AW Holmes	1981	G Broadbent	1994	C Evans	2007	C Evans
1969	AJ Thomson	1982	MW Calvert	1995	M Skinner		
1970	AJ Thomson	1983	RD James	1996	L Harpin		

Sutherland Chalice (inaugurated 2000)   *Dumfries & Galloway*

1	Scott Henry (Cardross)	67-66-66-69—268
2	Wallace Booth (Comrie)	66-67-67-69—269
3	Steven McEwan (Caprington)	67-67-66-70—270

2000	G Gordon	2003	D Sutton	2006	G Murray
2001	S Carmichael	2004	J King	2007	G Paterson
2002	G Gordon	2005	B Scott		

Tennant Cup (inaugurated 1880)   *always at Glasgow GC*

1	Callum Macaulay (Tulliallan)	68-73-67-64—272
2	Gavin Deer (Murrayshall)	71-72-64-69—276
	Ross Kellet (Colville Park)	71-69-71-65—276
	Steven McEwan (Caprington)	70-68-66-72—276

1880	AW Smith	1910	R Andrew	1949	W Irvine	1979	G Hay
1881	AW Smith	1911	WS Colville	1950	JW Mill	1980	Allan Brodie
1882	AM Ross	1912	R Scott jr	1951	WS McCleod	1981	G MacDonald
1883	J Kirk	1913	SO Shepherd	1952	GT Black	1982	LS Mann
1884	W Doleman	1914	John Caven	1953	AD Gray	1983	C Dalgleish
1885	TR Lamb	1915–19	*No competition*	1954	H McInally	1984	E Wilson
1886	D Bone	1920	G Lockhart	1955	LG Taylor	1985	CJ Brooks
1887	JR Motion	1921	R Scott jr	1956	JM Dykes	1986	PG Girvan
1888	D Bone	1922	WD Macleod	1957	LG Taylor	1987	J Rasmussen
1889	W Milne	1923	FW Baldie	1958	Dr FWG Deighton	1988	C Dalgleish
1890	W Marshall	1924	J Barrie Cooper	1959	JF Milligan	1989	DG Carrick
1891	D Bone	1925	R Scott jr	1960	Dr FWG Deighton	1990	C Everett
1892	D Bone	1926	W Tulloch	1961	R Reid Jack	1991	C Everett
1893	W Doleman	1927	W Tulloch	1962	WS Jack	1992	D Robertson
1894	W Doleman	1928	A Jamieson jr	1963	SWT Murray	1993	D Robertson
1895	JA Shaw	1929	R Scott jr	1964	Dr FWG Deighton	1994	G Rankin
1896	J Thomson	1930	JE Dawson	1965	J Scott Cochran	1995	S Gallacher
1897	D Bone	1931	GNS Tweedale	1966	AH Hall	1996	G Rankin
1898	R Bone	1932	SL McInlay	1967	BJ Gallacher	1997	C Hislop
1899	W Hunter	1933	H Thomson	1968	CW Green	1998	G Rankin
1900	JG Macfarlane	1934	K Lindsay jr	1969	J Scott Cochran	1999	G Fox
1901	R Bone	1935	JM Dykes jr	1970	CW Green	2000	G Fox
1902	CB Macfarlane	1936	JNW Dall	1971	Andrew Brodie	2001	C Watson
1903	CB Macfarlane	1937	WS McCleod	1972	Allan Brodie	2002	B Hume
1904	WS Colville	1938	A Jamieson jr	1973	PJ Smith	2003	G Gordon
1905	TW Robb	1939	GB Peters	1974	D McCart	2004	M Leishman
1906	JG Macfarlane	1940–45	*No competition*	1975	CW Green	2005	A Hall (AUS)
1907	R Andrew	1946	JB Stevenson	1976	IC Hutcheon	2006	J Gallagher
1908	R Carson	1947	JC Wilson	1977	S Martin	2007	W Booth
1909	WS Colville	1948	J Wallace	1978	IA Carslaw		

Tillman Trophy (inaugurated 1980)   *East Sussex*

1	Dale Whitnell (Five Lakes)	72-69-72-68—281
2	Chris Paisley (Stocksfield)	74-70-67-74—285
3	Andrew Cooley (Chobham)	75-70-68-73—286

Tillman Trophy *continued*

1980	J Kelly (AUS)	1987	R Morris	1994	*Not played*	2001	R Fisher
1981	M McLean	1988	E Els (RSA)	1995	P Stuart	2002	A Gee
1982	P Parkin (WAL)	1989	J Cook	1996	S Wakefield	2003	J Smith
1983	P Mayo	1990	M Wiggett	1997	M Searle	2004	D Belch
1984	P Cherry	1991	A Tillman	1998	R Blaxill	2005	J Mason
1985	P Baker	1992	D Probert	1999	J Conteh	2006	R Dinwiddie
1986	P Baker	1993	C Nowicki	2000	B Welch	2007	S Benson

Trubshaw Cup (inaugurated 1989) *always at Ashburnham and Tenby*

1	Ben Westgate (Trevose)	71-67-69-70—277
2	Zac Gould (Vale of Glamorgan)	69-68-75-71—283
3	Oliver Farr (Ludlow)	70-71-70-73—284
	James Frazer (Pennard)	77-73-67-67—284

1989	MA Macara	1996	M Ellis	1999	N Matthews	2004	J Williams
1990	TSM Wilkinson	1994	C Evans	2000	N Edwards	2005	C Smith
1991	S Pardoe	1995	B Dredge	2001	N Edwards	2006	R Enoch
1992	B Dredge	1997	M Pilkington	2002	J Doherty	2007	L Matthews
1993	B Dredge	1998	M Pilkington	2003	N Edwards		

Tucker Trophy (inaugurated 1991) *Whitchurch and Newport*

1	Ben Westgate (Trevose)	71-69-72-69—281
2	Craig Evans (West Monmouthshire)	68-70-71-73—282
3	Joe Vickery (Newport)	72-71-70-71—284

1991	C Evans	1996	M Searle	2001	N Edwards	2006	N Edwards
1992	R Dinsdale	1997	J Donaldson	2002	N Edwards	2007	Z Gould
1993	B Dredge	1998	N Edwards	2003	N Edwards		
1994	D Park	1999	J Donaldson	2004	N Edwards		
1995	M Ellis	2000	I Campbell	2005	J Williams		

Lake Macquarie Tournament (inaugurated 1958) *always at Belmont GC, NSW, Australia*

(Australian unless stated)

1	Danny Lee (NZL)	66-67-66-69—268
2	Matthew Griffin (Victoria)	71-68-71-68—278
3	Michael Smyth (The Australian)	71-68-70-70—279
	Kyu Ha Sim (Oatlands)	74-69-67-69—279

1958	B Devlin	1973	R Davis	1988	D Ecob	2001	N Docherty (ENG)*
1959	P Billings	1974	P Billings	1989	R Claydon (ENG)		*Beat L Hickmott in play-off
1960	P Billings	1975	C Kaye	1990	R Willison (ENG)	2002	C Campbell
1961	P Billings	1976	C Kaye	1991	S Tait	2003	J Lyle
1962	K Johnstone	1977	D Sharpe	1992	S Leaney	2004	J Lyle
1963	K Donohue	1978	R Carlin	1993	S Collins	2005	M Leishman
1964	P Billings	1979	C Kaye	1994	M Wheelhouse (NZL)	2006	A Gee (ENG)
1965	P Billings	1980	G Power	1995	L Peterson	2007	M McGrory*
1966	P Billings	1981	R Chapman (ENG)	1996	S Allan		*Beat J Roach at 3rd extra
1967	T Jones	1982	C Byrum (USA)	1997	G Ogilvy		hole
1968	J Bennett	1983	C Dalgleish (SCO)	1998	B Rumford*		
1969	J Newton	1984	J Crowe (USA)		*Beat G Wolstenholme (ENG)		
1970	D Sharpe	1985	R Picker		in play-off		
1971	D Sharpe	1986	P O'Malley	1999	J Sutherland		
1972	B Boyle	1987	S Robinson	2000	S Strange		

National District Championships

Midland Open (inaugurated 1976) *Worksop, Retford and Sherwood Forest*

1	Jason Palmer (Kirby Muxloe)	69-71-70-71—281
2	Jamie Abbott (Fynn Valley)	72-72-73-66—283
3	Rhys Black (Sherwood Forest)	73-69-73-72—287

1976	P Downes	1984	K Valentine	1992	M McGuire	2000	D Dixon
1977	P Downes	1985	MC Hassall	1993	N Williamson	2001	M Lock
1978	P McEvoy	1986	G Wolstenholme	1994	D Howell	2002	G Wolstenholme
1979	M Tomlinson	1987	C Suneson	1995	G Harris	2003	J Kemp
1980	P Downes	1988	R Winchester	1996	M Carver	2004	R Steele
1981	P Baxter	1989	J Cook	1997	P Streeter	2005	M Cryer
1982	NJ Chesses	1990	J Bickerton	1998	L Donald	2006	E Richardson
1983	CA Banks	1991	P Sefton	1999	G Davies	2007	G Woolgar

South of England Open Amateur *Walton Heath*

1	Luke Goddard (Hendon)	67-71-68-74—280
2	Chris Paisley (Stocksfield)	69-71-70-71—281
	Gary Wolstenholme (Carus Green)	69-71-70-71—281

2005	R McGowan	2007	D Willett
2006	G Wolstenholme*		

Beat R McGowan at 2nd extra hole

West of England Open Amateur Match Play (inaugurated 1912)

always at Burnham & Berrow

Semi-Finals
Miles Mackman (Broome Manor) beat Max Burrow (Exeter) 2 and 1
Laurie Canter (Bath) beat Adam Carson (Long Ashton) 3 and 1

Final
Miles Mackman beat Laurie Canter 2 and 1

1912	RA Riddell	1937	O Austreng	1964	DC Allen	1986	J Bennett
1913	Hon M Scott	1938	HJ Roberts	1965	DE Jones	1987	D Rosier
1914–18	No competition	1939–45	No competition	1966	A Forrester	1988	N Holman
1919	Hon M Scott	1946	JH Neal	1967	A Forrester	1989	N Holman
1920	Hon D Scott	1947	WF Wise	1968	SR Warrin	1990	I West
1921	CVL Hooman	1948	WF Wise	1969	SR Warrin	1991	S Amor
1922	Hon M Scott	1949	J Payne	1970	C Ball	1992	K Baker
1923	D Grant	1950	EB Millward	1971	G Irlam	1993	D Haines
1924	D Grant	1951	J Payne	1972	JA Bloxham	1994	A Emery
1925	D Grant	1952	EB Millward	1973	SC Mason	1995	A March
1926	K Whetstone	1953	F Griffin	1974	CS Mitchell	1996	M Carver
1927	GC Brooks	1954	EB Millward	1975	MR Lovett	1997	SJ Martin
1928	JA Pierson	1955	SJ Fox	1976	No competition	1998	D Dixon
1929	DE Landale	1956	SJ Fox	1977	AR Dunlop	1999	D Dixon
1930	RH de Montmorency	1957	D Gardner	1978	R Broad	2000	J Morgan
		1958	AJN Young	1979	N Burch	2001	L Corfield
1931	DR Howard	1959	DM Woolmer	1980	JM Durbin	2002	J Donaldson
1932	R Straker	1960	AW Holmes	1981	M Mouland	2003	E Butler
1933	DM Anderson	1961	JM Leach	1982	M Higgins	2004	T Burley
1934	Hon M Scott	1962	Sq Ldr WE McCrea	1983	C Peacock	2005	M Mackman
1935	JJF Pennink			1984	GB Hickman	2006	P Godfrey
1936	PH White	1963	KT Warren	1985	AC Nash	2007	M Mackman

West of England Open Amateur Stroke Play (inaugurated 1968) *Royal North Devon*

1	Andrew Cooley (Chobham)	71-76-68-69—284
2	Ryan Newman (Brookmans Park)	75-73-69-68—285
3	Sam Dodds (Coventry)	73-70-71-72—286

1968	PJ Yeo	1979	R Kane	1989	AD Hare	2001	R Finch
1969	A Forrester	1980	PE McEvoy	1990	J Payne	2002	D Barnes
1970	PJ Yeo	1981	N Taee	1991	D Lee	2003	E Butler
1971	P Berry	1982	MP Higgins	1992	M Stanford	2004	L Corfield
1972	P Berry	1983	PE McEvoy	1993	PR Trew	2005	E Richardson
1973	SC Mason	1984	A Sherborne	1994	CP Nowicki	2006	D Horsey
1974	R Abbott	1985	PE McEvoy	1995	G Clark	2007T	D Horsey
1975	BG Steer	1986	P Baker*	1996	R Wiggins		C Wood
1976	R Abbott	*Won at 2nd extra hole after	1997	M Reynard		
1977	PE McEvoy	play-off with PE McEvoy	1998	C Edwards		
1978	JG Bennett*	1987	G Wolstenholme	1999	D Griffiths		
*After play-off with PE McEvoy		1988	MC Evans	2000	S Grewal		

East of Ireland Open Amateur   *Co. Louth*

1	Eoin Arthurs (Forrest Little)	66-76-69-71—282
2	Darra Lernihan (Castle)	68-71-73-74—286
	Cathal O'Malley (Westport)	71-71-71-73—286

1989	D Clarke	1996	N Fox	2001	K Kearney
1990	D O'Sullivan	1997	S Quinlivan	2002	N Fox
1991	P Peppean	1998	G McGimpsey	2003	M Sinclair
1992	R Burns	1999	K Kearney	2004	M Campbell
1993	R Burns	2000	N Fox*	2005	J Carvill
1994	G McGimpsey	*Fox beat M Murphy (better	2006	B McCarroll
1995	D Brannigan	last round)	2007	R Kilpatrick

North of Ireland Open Amateur   *always at Royal Portrush*

Leading Qualifiers: 136 Conor Doran 71-65, Jonathan Caldwell (Clandeboye), 71-65, Dara Lernihan 68-68

Quarter-Finals
Shane Lowry (Esker Hills) beat Fergal Rafferty (Dungannon) 4 and 3
Simon Ward (Co.Louth) beat Paul Buckley (Kanturk) 5 and 3
Alastair Kerr (Clandeboye) beat Gary McDermott (Co.Sligo) 2 and 1
Andrew Morris (Belvoir Park) beat Aaron O'Callaghan (Douglas) 3 and 2

Semi-Finals
Lowry beat Ward at 20th
Morris beat Kerr 2 and 1

Final: Shane Lowry beat Andrew Morris 1 hole

1989	N Anderson	1994	N Ludwell	1999	P Gribben	2004	T Coulter
1990	D Clarke	1995	F Nolan	2000	M Hoey	2005	G Shaw
1991	G McGimpsey	1996	M McGinley	2001	S Paul	2006	D Crowe
1992	G McGimpsey	1997	M Sinclair	2002	G Maybin	2007	G Shaw
1993	G McGimpsey	1998	P Gribben	2003	B McElhinney		

South of Ireland Open Amateur *Lahinch*

Quarter-Finals
Niall Gorey (Lee Valley) beat Kelan McDonagh (Athlone/NUIM) 2 and 1
Paul O'Hanlon (The Curragh) beat Eddie Power (Kilkenny) at 21st
Niall Kearney (The Royal Dublin) beat Nick Grant (Knock) 1 hole
Aaron O'Callaghan (Douglas) bt Austin Graham (Pacific G & C Club) 1 Hole

Semi-Finals
O'Hanlon beat Gorey 3 and 2
Kearney beat O'Callaghan 3 and 2

Final: Niall Kearney beat Paul O'Hanlon 4 and 3

1989	S Keenan	1994	D Higgins	1999	M Campbell	2004	C McNamara
1990	D Clarke	1995	J Fanagan	2000	G McDowell	2005	J Carvill
1991	P McGinley	1996	A Morrow	2001	J Kehoe	2006	S Ward
1992	L MacNamara	1997	P Collier	2002	C Moriarty	2007	D Crowe
1993	P Sheehan	1998	J Foster	2003	M Owens		

West of Ireland Open *Co Sligo (Rosses Point)*

Leading Qualifier: Andrew Hogan (Newlands)   76-67—143

Quarter-Finals	Semi-Finals
Eddie McCormack (Galway) beat Michael Lavelle (K Club) 4 and 3	Lowry beat McCormack 4 and 3
	Morgan beat O'Hanlon 3 and 2
Shane Lowry (Esker Hills) beat Ryan Boal (Castle) at 20th	
Paul O'Hanlon (The Curragh) beat Jonathan Hurst (Shawhill) 2 and 1	**Final**
Desmond Morgan (Mullingar) beat Michael Sinclair (Knock) 3 and 2	Shane Lowry beat Desmond Morgan 2 and 1

1989	P McInerney	1994	P Harrington	1999	M Ilonen (FIN)	2004	P McDonald
1990	N Goulding	1995	E Brady	2000	E Brady	2005	R McIlroy
1991	N Goulding	1996	G McGimpsey	2001	M McDermott	2006	R McIlroy
1992	K Kearney	1997	J Fanagan	2002	S Paul	2007	J Lyons
1993	G McGimpsey	1998	N Fox	2003	M Ryan		

East of Scotland Open Amateur Stroke Play *Lundin*

1	Rohan Blizard (AUS)*	72-72-67-72—283
2	Craig Watson (East Renfrewshire)	74-70-70-69—283
	Peter Latimer (New)	73-72-69-69—283

Blizard won at the second extra hole

1989	K Hird	1994	A Reid	1999	R Beames	2004	R Ramsay
1990	G Lawrie	1995	G Davidson	2000	C Watson	2005	W Booth
1991	R Clark	1996	C Hislop	2001	J King	2006	K McNicoll
1992	ST Knowles	1997	S Meiklejohn	2002	D Inglis	2007	D Stewart
1993	S Meiklejohn	1998	B Lamb (Aus)	2003	J King		

North of Scotland Open Amateur Stroke Play *Nairn*

1	Kris Nicol (Fraserburgh)*	73-74-71-70—288
2	Fraser Fotheringham (Nairn)	72-75-72-69—288
	Mark Lamb (Haddington)	71-73-75-69—288

Nicol won at the third extra hole

1989	G Hickman	1994	E Forbes	1999	N Steven	2004	B Fotheringham
1990	S McIntosh	1995	R Beames	2000	C Watson	2005	E Saltman
1991	S Henderson	1996	C Dunan	2001	G Thomson	2006	K McAlpine
1992	K Buchan	1997	G Crawford	2002	W Booth	2007	M Buchan
1993	D Downie	1998	C Taylor	2003	G Murray		

North-East Scotland District Championship *Newburgh-on-Ythan*

1	James Byrne (Banchory)	72-61-75-69—277
2	Lewis Kirton (Newmachar)	71-70-72-72—285
3	Philip McLean (Peterhead)	73-70-72-71—286

1999	BA Innes	2005	M Kerr*	2002	B Innes	2007	D Stewart
2001	G Gordon		*at 4th extra hole	2004	G Campbell		
2003	J McLeary	2000	E Forbes	2006	M Halliday		

South-East Scotland District Championship *Duddingston*

1	Scott Borrowman (Dollar)	70-67-72—209
2	John Gallagher (Swanston New)	70-70-70—210
3	Philip McLean (Peterhead)	70-69-72—211

Rain washed out the fourth round

1999	S Carmichael	2003	S Wilson	2007	C Macaulay*
2000	J King	2004	E Ramsay		*Beat G Campbell at 1st
2001	J Doherty	2005	S Smith		extra hole
2002	S Armstrong	2006	G Campbell		

West of Scotland Open Amateur   *Cawder*

Not played

1989 A Elliot	1994 J Hodgson	1999 L Kelly	2004 *Not played*
1990 S Knowles	1995 G Rankin	2000 S O'Hara	2005 A Dick
1991 A Coltart	1996 C Hislop	2001 B Fitzsimmons	2006 C Macaulay
1992 S Henderson	1997 C Hislop	2002 G Gordon	2007 J King
1993 B Howard	1998 L Kelly	2003 G Gordon	

Barclay Howard

© Dave Cannon/Allsport/Getty Images

Barclay Howard was a very fine amateur golfer, good enough to represent Great Britain & Ireland in two Walker Cup matches, three St. Andrews Trophies against the Continent of Europe and an Eisenhower Trophy. He was also a very fine, if flawed, human being.

When he died at the tragically premature age of 55 having bravely battled leukemia for more than a decade, a huge crowd turned out for his funeral in his hometown of Johnstone near Glasgow. It was a fitting tribute to an endlessly cheery and good-natured soul who had seen both the best and worst that life has to offer.

First capped for Scotland in 1979, Barclay found himself dropped from the national side five years later as a result of the alcoholism that had all but taken over every minute of his every day. Almost a decade on though, he was back. Cleansed of the demon drink, the wee man from Cochrane Castle proceeded to dedicate himself to the game and, second time around, his golf was even better than before. Make that much better.

A prolific winner of one-day 36-hole events – he garnered well over 100 – Barclay's greatest moment came in the 1997 Open Championship at Royal Troon, where he won the silver medal as the leading amateur. He finished in a tie for 60th place alongside one Jack Nicklaus. Only one month later, just after he had played in his second Walker Cup, the disease that was eventually to end his life was diagnosed.

Other Men's Amateur Tournaments 2008

Berkhamsted Trophy (inaugurated 1960) *always at Berkhamsted*

1	Andrew Sullivan (Purley Chase)		67-71—138
2	Stiggy Hodgson (Sunningdale)		70-70—140
3	Luke Goddard (Hendon)		72-72—144

1960	HC Squirrell	1972	C Cieslewicz	1984	R Willison	1996	L Donald
1961	DW Frame	1973	SC Mason	1985	F George	1997	P Streeter
1962	DG Neech	1974	P Fisher	1986	P McEvoy	1998	G Storm
1963	HC Squirrell	1975	PG Deeble	1987	F George	1999	GP Wolstenholme
1964	PD Flaherty	1976	JC Davie	1988	J Cowgill	2000	J Wormald
1965	LF Millar	1977	AWB Lyle	1989	J Payne	2001	S Godfrey
1966	P Townsend	1978	JC Davies	1990	J Barnes	2002	G Wolstenholme
1967	DJ Millensted	1979	JC Davies	1991	G Homewood	2003	J Knight
1968	PD Flaherty	1980	R Knott	1992	P Page	2004	J Ruth
1969	MM Niven	1981	P Dennett	1993	S Burnell	2005	I Parnaby
1970	R Hunter	1982	DG Lane	1994	M Treleaven	2006	A Norman
1971	A Millar	1983	J Hawksworth	1995	J Crampton	2007	G Blainey

John Cross Bowl (inaugurated 1957) *always at Worplesdon, Surrey*

1	B Taylor (Worplesdon)*		70-70—140
2	D Waite (The Wisley)		72-68—140

Taylor won at the first extra hole

3	M Booker (Royal Wimbledon)		74-67—141
	C Bank (Stanton on the Wolds)		72-69—141

1957	DW Frame	1971	PBQ Drayson	1985	M Devetta	1999	M Galway
1958	G Evans	1972	AR Kerr	1986	C Rotheroe	2000	R Mann
1959	G Evans	1973	DW Frame	1987	B White	2001	J Bint
1960	DW Frame	1974	RPF Brown	1988	B White	2002	D Holmes
1961	DW Frame	1975	BJ Winteridge	1989	KG Jones	2003	D Curtis
1962	DW Frame	1976	DW Frame	1990	D Lee	2004	J Brown
1963	PO Green	1977	DW Frame	1991	P Sefton	2005	M Galway
1964	RL Glading	1978	RPF Brown	1992	R Watts	2006	A Shields
1965	P Townsend	1979	JG Bennett	1993	J Collier	2007	M Booker*
1966	P Townsend	1980	JG Bennett	1994	P Benka		*Beat M Williams at 1st extra
1967	MJ Burgess	1981	ME Johnson	1995	M Galway		hole
1968	PJ Benka	1982	R Boxall	1996	B Barham		
1969	DW Frame	1983	DG Lane	1997	C Banks		
1970	P Dawson	1984	I Gray	1998	J Wormald		

Frame Trophy (inaugurated 1986 for players aged 50+) *always at Worplesdon, Surrey*

1	D Arnold (Copthorne)		73-71-78—222
2	P Bax (Mid Herts)		75-75-74—224
3	N Rogers (Brokenhurst Manor)		76-75-76—227

1988	DW Frame	1993	DW Frame	1998	DG Lane	2003	BK Turner
1989	JRW Walkinshaw	1994	DG Lane	1999	NH Barnes	2004	DG Lane
1990	WJ Williams	1995	M Christmas	2000	DW Frame	2005	ND Coleman
1991	DB Sheahan	1996	DG Lane	2001	DW Frame	2006	NH Barnes
1992	DW Frame	1997	B Turner	2002	BK Turner	2007	AP Stracey

Golf Illustrated Gold Vase (inaugurated 1909, discontinued 2003)
For results see 2007 edition of the Golfer's Handbook

Hampshire Hog (inaugurated 1957) *always at North Hants*

1	Gary King (Tyrrells Wood)*	68-69—137
2	Steven Barwick (Stoke Park)	67-70—137

King won at the first extra hole

3	Luke Goddard (Hendon)	72-68—140
	Darren Renwick (Worthing)	69-71—140
	Adam Wainwright (Gainsborough)	69-71—140

1957	MF Bonallack	1970	Major DA Blair	1984	J Hawksworth	1998	P Rowe
1958	PF Scrutton	1971	DW Frame	1985	A Clapp	1999	C Rodgers
1959	Col AA Duncan	1972	R Revell	1986	R Eggo	2000	M Booker
1960	MF Attenborough	1973	SC Mason	1987	A Rogers	2001	J Lupton
1961	HC Squirrell	1974	TJ Giles	1988	S Richardson	2002	G Wolstenholme
1962	FD Physick	1975	HAN Stott	1989	P McEvoy	2003	M Sell
1963	Sqn Ldr WE McCrea	1976	MC Hughesdon	1990	J Metcalfe	2004	L Kennedy
1964	DF Wilkie	1977	AWB Lyle	1991	M Welch	2005	L Dodd
1965	T Koch de	1978	GF Godwin	1992	S Graham	2006	J Crampton
	Gooreynd	1979	MF Bonallack	1993	D Hamilton	2007	J Barnes
1966	Major DA Blair	1980	RA Durrant	1994	B Ingleby		*Beat R Harrison and E
1967	Major DA Blair	1981	G Brand jr	1995	J Rose		Pepperell at 3rd extra hole
1968	MJ Burgess	1982	A Sherborne	1996	R Tate		
1969	B Critchley	1983	I Gray	1997	GP Wolstenholme		

King George V Coronation Cup *always at Porters Park, Herts*

1	Alan Glynn (Porters Park)	73-66—139
2	Nick Pateman (Porters Park)	71-71—142 countback
3	Graham Povey (Brickendon Manor)	71-71—142

1990	C Boal	1995	S Jarvis	2000	R Chattaway	2005	A Bravant
1991	S Hoffman	1996	N Swaffield	2001	M Payne	2006	A Glynn
1992	R Watts	1997	J Knight	2002	G Evans	2007	L Goddard
1993	D Hamilton	1998	M King	2003	L Gauthier		
1994	S Webster	1999	J Field	2004	J Ruebotham		

Prince of Wales Challenge Cup (inaugurated 1928) *always at Royal Cinque Ports*

1	Billy Britton (Pedham Place)	73-69—142
2	Jack Hiluta (Chelmsford)	76-67—143
	Adam Best (Cleveland)	73-70—143
	Adam Wootton (Oxford City)	72-71—143
	Matthew Evans (Rotherham)	71-72—143
	Michael Swan (Stoke-by-Nayland)	69-74—143

1928	D Grant	1955T	GT Duncan	1973	PJ Hedges	1990T	BS Ingleby
1929	NR Reeves	1956	PF Scrutton	1974	PJ Hedges	1991	S Pardoe
1930	R Harris	1957	No competition	1975	JC Davies	1992	L Westwood
1931	RW Hartley	1958T	KR Mackenzie	1976	MJ Inglis	1993	ML Welch
1932	EN Layton		BAF Belmore	1977	PJ Hedges	1994	I Hardy
1933	JB Nash	1959	D Johnstone	1978	ER Dexter	1995	L Ferris
1934	R Sweeney	1960	CG Moore	1979	GF Godwin	1996	J Maddock
1935	HG Bentley	1961	RH Bazell	1980T	GM Dunsire	1997	J Carter
1936	LOM Munn	1962	Dr J Pittar		B Nicholson	1998	G Woodman
1937	DHR Martin	1963	Sq Ldr WE McCrea	1981	JM Baldwin	1999	A Webster (AUS)
1938	EA Head	1964	NA Paul	1982	SG Homewood	2000	JM Bint
1939–46	No competition	1965T	NA Paul	1983	M Davis	2001	A Webster
1947	PB Lucas		VE Barton	1984T	F Wood	2002	G Homewood
1948	Capt DA Blair	1966	P Townsend		DH Niven	2003	S Tiley
1949	C Stowe	1967	MF Bonallack	1985	RJ Tickner	2004	A Tampion (AUS)
1950	I Caldwell	1968T	NA Paul	1986	JM Baldwin	2005	D Pike*
1951	I Caldwell		GC Marks	1987	S Finch		*Beat D Harris at 1st extra
1952	I Caldwell	1969	MF Attenborough	1988	MP Palmer		hole
1953	JG Blackwell	1970	J Butterworth	1989T	T Lloyd	2006	J Barnes
1954	DLW Woon	1971	VE Barton		NA Farrell	2007	J Jannkowski
1955T	C Taylor	1972	PJ Hedges	1990T	G Homewood		

Rosebery Challenge Cup (inaugurated 1933) *always at Ashridge*

1	Nick Pateman (Porters Park)	67-66—133
2	Luke Goddard (Hendon)	66-68—134
3	John Kemp (John O'Gaunt)	67-69—136

1962	PR Johnston	1974	G Stradling	1986	JE Ambridge	1998	S Vinnicombe
1963	CA Murray	1975	JA Watts	1987	HA Wilkerson	1999	J Kemp
1964	A Millar	1976	G Stradling	1988	N Leconte	2000	J Kemp
1965	EJ Wiggs	1977	J Ambridge	1989	C Slattery	2001	J Ruebotham
1966	A Holmes	1978	RJ Bevan	1990	C Tingey	2002	R Leonard
1967	A Holmes	1979	JB Berney	1991	M Thompson	2003	D Stockwell
1968	A Holmes	1980	JA Watts	1992	R Harris	2004	K Freeman
1969	A Holmes	1981	RY Mitchell	1993	M Hooper	2005	J York
1970	PW Bent	1982	DG Lane	1994	P Wilkins	2006	G Schmidt
1971	AW Holmes	1983	N Briggs	1995	P Wilkins	2007	M Moore
1972	AW Holmes	1984	DG Lane	1996	J Kemp		
1973	AJ Mason	1985	P Wharton	1997	L Watcham		

St George's Grand Challenge Cup (inaugurated 1888)

always at Royal St George's, Sandwich, Kent

1	Adam Wooton (Oxford City)	71-69—140
2	Sam Matton (Bowood)	70-74—144
3	Darren Wright (Rowlands Castle)	75-71—146

1888	J Ball	1920	R Harris	1954	H Berwick (Aus)	1982	SJ Wood
1889	J Ball	1921	WB Torrance	1955	PF Scrutton	1983	R Willison
1890	J Ball	1922	WI Hunter	1956	DAC Marr	1984	SJ Wood
1891	J Ball	1923	F Ouimet (USA)	1957	PF Scrutton	1985	SJ Wood
1892	FA Fairlie	1924	RH Wethered	1958	PF Scrutton	1986	RC Claydon
1893	HH Hilton	1925	D Grant	1959	J Nicklaus (USA)	1987	MR Coodwin
1894	HH Hilton	1926	Maj CO Hezlet	1960	JG Blackwell	1988	T Ryan
1895	E Blackwell	1927	WL Hartley	1961	Sq Ldr WE McCrea	1989	S Green
1896	FG Tait	1928	D Grant	1962	Sq Ldr WE McCrea	1990	P Sullivan
1897	CE Hambro	1929	TA Torrance	1963	Sq Ldr WE McCrea	1991	D Fisher
1898	FG Tait	1930	RW Hartley	1964	Major DA Blair	1992	L Westwood
1899	FG Tait	1931	WL Hartley	1965	MF Bonallack	1993	P Sefton
1900	R Maxwell	1932	HG Bentley	1966	P Townsend	1994	M Welch
1901	SH Fry	1933	JB Beck	1967	Major DA Blair	1995	J Harris
1902	H Castle	1934	AGS Penman	1968	MF Bonallack	1996	M Brooks
1903	CK Hutchison	1935	Maj WHH Aitken	1969	PJ Benka	1997	*Abandoned due to rain*
1904	J Graham jr	1936	DHR Martin	1970	PJ Hedges	1998	C Gold
1905	R Harris	1937	DHR Martin	1971	EJS Garrett	1999	M Williamson (AUS)
1906	S Mure Fergusson	1938	JJF Pennink	1972	JC Davies	2000	P Appleyard
1907	CE Dick	1939	AA McNair	1973	JC Davies	2001	A Gee
1908	AC Lincoln	1940–46	*No competition*	1974	JC Davies	2002	B St John
1909	SH Fry	1947	PB Lucas	1975	JC Davies	2003	N Olsen
1910	Capt CK Hutchison	1948	M Gonzalez	1976	JC Davies	2004	D Crompton
1911	E Martin Smith	1949	PF Scrutton	1977	JC Davies	2005	W Hayter
1912	Hon Michael Scott	1950	E Bromley-Davenport	1978	C Phillips	2006	J Moul
1913	HD Gillies	1951	PF Scrutton	1979	CF Godwin	2007	L Burns*
1914	J Graham jr	1952	GH Micklem	1980	J Simmance		*Beat A Hodkinson at 2nd
1915–19	*No competition*	1953	Major DA Blair	1981	MF Bonallack		extra hole*

Selborne Salver (inaugurated 1976) *always at Blackmoor*

1	Stiggy Hodgson (Sunningdale)	68-65—133
2	Luke Goddard (Hendon)	65-70—135
3	Miles Mackman (Broome Park)	70-67—137
	Adam Wainwright (Gainsborough)	66-71—137

1976	A Miller	1985	SM Bottomley	1994	W Bennett	2003	Z Scotland
1977	CS Mitchell	1986	TE Clarke	1995	S Drummond	2004	R Fisher
1978	GM Brand	1987	A Clapp	1996	J Knight	2005	R Henley
1979	P McEvoy	1988	NE Holman	1997	R Binney	2006	J Moul*
1980	P McEvoy	1989	M Stamford	1998	M Side		*Beat L Dodd at first extra
1981	A Sherborne	1990	J Metcalfe	1999	B Mason		hole*
1982	IA Cray	1991	J Payne	2000	J Franks	2007	M Thistleton*
1983	DG Lane	1992	M Treleaven	2001	G Wolstenholme		*Beat M Cryer at 1st extra
1984	D Curry	1993	M Welch	2002	G Clark		hole*

Foursomes Events 2008

The Antlers (inaugurated 1933) *always at Royal Mid-Surrey*

1	Ajay Patel (Wentworth) & Richard Caldwell (Sunningdale)	143
2	David Clarkson & Alex Gems (Malden)	144 countback
3	Warren Harmston & Steven Brown (Wentworth)	144

1933	TFB Law and PWL Risdon	1962	AW Holmes and JM Leach	1982	IA Carslaw and J Huggan
1934	GA Hill and HS Malik	1963	RC Pickering and MJ Cooper	1983	N Fox and G Lashford
1935	EF Storey and Sir WS Worthington Evans	1964	MF Bonallack and Dr DM Marsh	1984	M Palmer and M Belsham
				1985	S Blight and R Wilkins
1936	HG Bentley and F Francis	1965	MSR Lunt and DE Rodway	1986	M Gerrard and B White
1937	LG Crawley and C Stowe	1966	PD Kelley and Dr DM Marsh	1987	IA Carslaw and J Huggan
1938	RW Hartley and PWL Risdon	1967	*Play abandoned*	1988	A Raitt and P Thornley
1939	LG Crawley and H Thomson	1968	H Broadbent and G Birtwell	1989	A Howard and R Hunter
1940–47	*Not played*	1969T	SR Warrin and JH Cook	1990	AC Livesey and RG Payne
1948	RC Quilter and E Bromley-Davenport		J Povall and K Dabson	1991	WM Hopkinson and MR Cook
			JC Davies and W Humphreys	1992	J C Davies and P J Davies
1949	LG Crawley and JC Wilson		RD Watson-Jones and LOM Smith	1993	M Benka and S Seman
1950	L Gracey and I Caldwell			1994	D Cowap and J Brant
1951	LG Crawley and JC Wilson	1970	JB Carr and R Carr	1995	R Neill and G Evans
1952T	Major DA Blair and GH Micklem	1971	I Mosey and I Gradwell	1996	I Tottingham and R Harris
		1972	MJ Kelley and W Smith	1997	S Kay and R Peacock
	LG Crawley and JC Wilson	1973	DOJ Albutt and P Flaherty	1998	G Willman and B Willman
1953	D Wilson and G Simmons	1974	BF Critchley and MC Hughesdon	1999	D Lomas and K Staunton
1954	JR Thornhill and PF Scrutton			2000	MA Booker and RET Rea
1955	G Evans and D Sewell	1975	JC Davies and PJ Davies	2001	MA Booker and RET Rea
1956	GH Micklem and AF Bussell	1976	JK Tate and P Deeble	2002	MA Booker and RET Rea
1957	Major DA Blair and CD Lawrie	1977	JC Davies and PJ Davies	2003	*Not played*
1958	D Sewell and G Evans	1978	R Chapman and R Fish	2004	MA Booker and RET Rea
1959	HC Squirrell and P Dunn	1979	N Roche and D Williams	2005	C and W Harmston
1960	MSR Lunt and JC Beharrell	1980	G Coles and M Johnson	2006	J Poulton and M Lowe
1961	HC Squirrell and P Dunn	1981	R Boxall and R Chapman	2007	W Harmston and S Brown

Burhill Family Foursomes (inaugurated 1937) *always at Burhill, Surrey*

Semi-Finals:

M & L Prior (Burhill) beat A & S Russell (Burhill) 4 and 2

A & A Gems (New Malden) beat K & H Vincent (Burhill) 4 and 3

Final:

Mike & Lizzie Prior beat Ann & Alexander Gems 6 and 5

1937	Captain JR Stroyan and Miss S Stroyan		Winckley	1972	Mrs S Grant and NJ Grant
1938	W Price and Miss E Price	1959	Jack and Anna van Zwanenberg	1973	MV Blake and Miss B Blake
1939–1946	*Not played*	1960	Mrs M Kippax and JM Kippax	1974	Mrs NR Bailhache and WJ Bailhache
1947	Mrs GH Brooks and PJ Brooks	1961	Mrs R Sutherland Pilch and J Sutherland Pilch	1975	Mrs PR Williams and PM Williams
1948	W Price and Miss E Price				
1949	Mrs EC Pepper and W Pepper	1962	JC Hubbard and Miss Trudi Hubbard	1976	Mrs D Gotla and C Gotla
1950	A Forbes Ilsley and Miss J Ilsley	1963T	GA Rowan-Robinson and Miss 'Pooh' Rowan Robinson	1977	Mrs J Maudsley and C Maudsley
1951	Major E Loxley Land and Miss J Land	1964	Mrs P Todhunter and T Todhunter	1978	Mrs H Calderwood and WR Calderwood
1952	CHV Elliot and Miss S Elliott	1965	Mrs WT Warrin and SR Warrin	1979	Dr AG Wells and Miss E Wells
1953	JC Hubbard and Miss A Hubbard	1966	Mrs WT Warrin and SR Warrin	1980	JL Hall and Miss Cynthia Hall
		1967	Mrs WT Warrin and SR Warrin	1981	Mrs J Fox and N Fox
1954	JC Hubbard and Miss A Hubbard	1968	Mrs CHP Trollope and Nigel Trollope	1982	Mrs J Fox and N Fox
1955	Mrs HP Thornhill and JR Thornhill	1969	Mrs EPP D'A Walton and JF Walton	1983	Mrs J Rowe and D Rowe
				1984	Mrs JS Gilbert and AS Gilbert
1956	Mrs HP Thornhill and JR Thornhill	1970	JF Young and Miss EJ Young	1985	Mrs MM Pollitt and R Pollitt
		1971	PHA Brownrigg and Miss D Brownrigg	1986	Mrs J Maudesley and C Maudesley
1957	CH Young and Mrs PBK Gracey			1987	Mrs A Croft and M Croft
1958	Mrs HM Winckley and JB				

1988	Mrs V Hargreaves and R Hargreaves	1994	MJ Toole and Miss SJ Toole	2002	CH Tilling and Miss A Gadney
1989	Mrs J Lawson and P Lawson	1995	Mrs G Warner and R Warner	2003	M and R-L Hall
1990	Mrs M Maisey and S Maisey	1996	Mrs AP Croft and MC Croft	2004	J and S Burrage
1991	Mrs M Pollitt and R Pollitt	1997	Mrs J Clink and T Clink	2005	S and A Russell
1992	R Stocks and Miss Joanna Stocks	1998	MJ Toole and Miss SJ Toole	2006	A and A Gems
1993	Mrs M Bartlett and Jerome Bartlett	1999	MJ Toole and Miss SJ Toole	2007	A and A Gems
		2000	Mrs V Marchbanks and R Marchbanks		
		2001	Mrs C Warren and R Warren		

Fathers and Sons Foursomes *always at West Hill, Surrey*

Semi-Finals:
JS Cunliffe (Lingfield Park) & EJ Cunliffe (Heron Bay) beat JH & MJ Watts (West Hill) 2 holes
T & J Rowland Clark (Royal Wimbledon) beat AC & JA Stapleton (Gerrards Cross) 3 and 2

Final:
JS & EJ Cunliffe beat T&J Rowland Clark at 20th

1991	DM and WK Laing	1996	MJ and J Hickey	2001	J and D Niven	2006	RA and SA Briars
1992	JA and R Piggott	1997	DR and M Baxter	2002	GR and TG Clark	2007	HD and AH Maurice
1993	B and R Groce	1998	SF and P Brown	2003	R and T Stocks		
1994	RJ and P Hill	1999	R and K Boxall	2004	CEG and JC Kemp		
1995	J and D Niven	2000	G and M Steele	2005	CEG and JC Kemp		

Sunningdale Foursomes (inaugurated 1934)   *always at Sunningdale*

Semi-Finals:
C Cowper (World of Golf) & N Reilly (Surbiton) beat R Black (Sherwood) & R Brown (Worksop)
2 and 1
R Drummond (Beaconsfield) & M Haines (Rochester & Cobham Park) beat N Edwards (Ganton) &
K Smith (Waterlooville) 3 and 1

Final:
Craig Cowper & Neil Reilly beat Rachel Drummond & Matt Haines 1 hole

1934	Miss D Fishwick and EN Layton	1961	Mrs J Anderson and Peter Alliss	1986	R Rafferty and R Chapman
1935	Miss J Wethered and JSF Morrison	1962	ER Whitehead and NC Coles	1987	I Mosey and W Humphreys
1936	Miss J Wethered and JSF Morrison	1963	L Platts and D Snell	1988	SC Mason and A Chandler
1937	AS Anderson and Dai Rees	1964	B Critchley and R Hunter	1989	AD Hare and R Claydon
1938	Miss P Barton and Alf Padgham	1965	Mrs AD Spearman and T Fisher	1990	Miss D Reid and Miss C Dibnah
1939	C Rissik and EWH Kenyon	1966	RRW Davenport and A Walker		
1940–47	*Not played*	1967	NC Coles and K Warren	1991	J Robinson and W Henry
1948	Miss Wanda Morgan and Sam King	1968	JC Davies and W Humphreys	1992	R Boxall and D Cooper
1949	RG French and SS Field	1969	P Oosterhuis and PJ Benka	1993	A Beal and L James
1950	M Faulkner and J Knipe	1970	R Barrell and Miss A Willard	1994	S Webster and A Wall
1951	Miss J Donald and TB Haliburton	1971	A Bird and H Flatman	1995	D Cooper and R Boxall
1952	PF Scrutton and Alan Waters	1972	JC Davies and MG King	1996	L Donald and M O'Connor
1953	Miss J Donald and TB Haliburton	1973	J Putt and Miss M Everard	1997	Mrs J Hall and Miss H Wadsworth
1954	PF Scrutton and Alan Waters	1974	PJ Butler and CA Clark		
1955	W Sharp and SS Scott	1975	*Cancelled due to snow*	1998	D Fisher and W Bennett
1956	G Knipe and DC Smalldon	1976	CA Clark and M Hughesdon	1999	Miss L Walters and R McEvoy
1957	BGC Huggett and R Whitehead	1977	GN Hunt and D Matthew	2000	Mrs C Caldwell and R Caldwell
		1978	GA Caygill and Miss J Greenhalgh	2001	Miss C Lipscombe and S Little
1958	Miss J Donald and Peter Alliss			2002	J Kemp and S Griffiths
1959	MF Bonallack and D Sewell	1979	G Will and R Chapman	2004	R Fisher and S Griffiths
1960	Miss B McCorkindale and MJ Moir	1980	NC Coles and D McClelland	2005	G Lockerbie and P Jenkinson
		1981	A Lyddon and G Brand jr	2006	D Masters and B Evans
		1982	Miss M Walker and Miss C Langford	2007	J Mason and N Walker
		1983	J Davies and M Devetta		
		1984	Miss M McKenna and Miss M Madill		
		1985	J O'Leary and S Torrance		

Worplesdon Mixed Foursomes (inaugurated 1921) *always at Worplesdon, Surrey*

Semi-Finals:
Mrs C Bushell & M Farrant (West Sussex) beat Miss H Ralph (Cowdray Park) & J Harridge
(Worplesdon) I hole
Miss A Coffey & D A Waltham (Worplesdon) beat Miss T Watters & P Milligan (Muswell Hill) I hole

Final:
Miss A Coffey & D A Waltham beat Mrs C Bushell & M Farrant 3 and 2

1921 Miss Helme and TA Torrance	1950 Miss F Stephens and LG	1978 Miss T Perkins and R Thomas
1922 Miss Joyce Wethered and R	Crawley	1979 Miss J Melville and A Melville
Wethered	1951 Mrs AC Barclay and G Evans	1980 Mrs L Bayman and I Boyd
1923 Miss Joyce Wethered and CJ	1952 Mrs RT Peel and GW Mackie	1981 Mrs J Nicholsen and MN Stern
Tolley	1953 Miss J Gordon and G Knipe	1982 Miss B New and K Dobson
1924 Miss SR Fowler and EN Layton	1954 Miss F Stephens and WA Slark	1983 Miss B New and K Dobson
1925 Miss Cecil Leitch and E	1955 Miss P Garvey and PF Scrutton	1984 Mrs L Bayman and MC
Esmond	1956 Mrs L Abrahams and Maj WD	Hughesdon
1926 Mlle de la Chaume and R	Henderson	1985 Mrs H Kaye and D Longmuir
Wethered	1957 Mrs B Singleton and WD Smith	1986 Miss P Johnson and RN
1927 Miss Joyce Wethered and CJH	1958 Mr and Mrs M Bonallack	Roderick
Tolley	1959 Miss J Robertson and I Wright	1987 Miss J Nicholson and B White
1928 Miss Joyce Wethered and JSF	1960 Miss B Jackson and MJ Burgess	1988 Mme A Larrezac and JJ Caplan
Morrison	1961 Mrs R Smith and B Critchley	1989 Miss J Kershaw and M Kershaw
1929 Miss M Gourlay and Maj CO	1962 Viscomtesse de Saint Sauveur	1990 Miss S Keogh and A Rodgers
Hezlet	and DW Frame	1991 J Rhodes and C Banks
1930 Miss M Gourlay and Maj CO	1963 Mrs G Valentine and JE	1992 D Henson and B Turner
Hezlet	Behrend	1993 A Macdonald and S Skeldon
1931 Miss J Wethered and Hon M	1964 Mrs G Valentine and JE	1994 Mr and Mrs K Quinn
Scott	Behrend	1995 Mrs C Caldwell and P Carr
1932 Miss J Wethered and RH	1965 Mrs G Valentine and JE	1996 Miss L Walters and M Naylor
Oppenheimer	Behrend	1997 Miss K Burton and G
1933 Miss J Wethered and B Darwin	1966 Mrs C Barclay and DJ Miller	Wolstenholme
1934 Miss M Gourlay and TA	1967 JF Gancedo and Mlle C Lacoste	1998 Miss K Burton and J Smith
Torrance	1968 JD van Heel and Miss Dinah	1999 Miss AM Boatman and RG
1935 Miss G and J Craddock-	Oxley	Hodgkinson
Hartopp	1969 Mrs R Ferguson and Alistair	2000 Mr and Mrs Galway
1936 Miss J Wethered and Hon T	Wilson	2001 Miss K Fisher and J Harper
Coke	1970 Miss R Roberts and RL Glading	2002 C Court and J Donaldson
1937 Mrs Heppel and LG Crawley	1971 Mrs D Frearson and A Smith	2003 A Downer and L Boxall
1938 Mrs MR Garon and EF Storey	1972 Miss B Le Garreres and CA	2004 Miss L Webb and G O'Connor
1939–45 *Not played*	Strang	2005 Miss A Coffey and A Shields
1946 Miss J Gordon and AA Duncan	1973 Miss T Perkins and RJ Evans	2006 Miss A Coffey and A Shields
1947 Miss J Gordon and AA Duncan	1974 Mrs S Birley and RL Glading	2007 Miss S Lovell and S Stam
1948 Miss W Morgan and EF Storey	1975 Mr and Mrs JR Thornhill	
1949 Miss F Stephens and LG	1976 Mrs B Lewis and J Caplan	
Crawley	1977 Mrs D Henson and J Caplan	

Month by month in 2008

A year on from their duel at Carnoustie Padraig Harrington and Sergio García are at it again in the US PGA at Oakland Hills. Once again it is Harrington who prevails and that makes it back-to-back majors and three of the last six. Ben Curtis's joint second place earns him a Ryder Cup début, but in Europe there is real controversy when Ian Poulter decides not to play the final qualifying event. Despite Darren Clarke winning the penultimate event, captain Nick Faldo picks Poulter and Paul Casey.

University and School Events

Halford-Hewitt Cup (inaugurated 1924)

always at Royal Cinque Ports, Deal, and Royal. St George's

Semi-Finals:
Tonbridge beat Eton 3½–1½
Malvern beat Harrow 4–1

Final:
Tonbridge beat Malvern 4–1

Winning team: AG Clay, J Horn,
JC Hubbard jr, BSE Ingleby, CWA Jones,
CRE Lloyd, RJ Partridge, EJ Richardson,
JC Spurling

1924	Eton	1950	Rugby	1970	Merchiston	1990	Tonbridge
1925	Eton	1951	Rugby	1971	Charterhouse	1991	Shrewsbury
1926	Eton	1952	Harrow	1972	Marlborough	1992	Tonbridge
1927	Harrow	1953	Harrow	1973	Rossall	1993	Shrewsbury
1928	Eton	1954	Rugby	1974	Charterhouse	1994	Tonbridge
1929	Harrow	1955	Eton	1975	Harrow	1995	Harrow
1930	Charterhouse	1956	Eton	1976	Merchiston	1996	Radley
1931	Harrow	1957	George Watson's	1977	George Watson's	1997	Oundle
1932	Charterhouse	1958	Harrow	1978	Harrow	1998	Charterhouse
1933	Rugby	1959	Wellington	1979	Stowe	1999	George Watson's
1934	Charterhouse	1960	Rossall	1980	Shrewsbury	2000	Epsom
1935	Charterhouse	1961	Rossall	1981	George Watson's	2001	Tonbridge
1936	Charterhouse	1962	Oundle	1982	Charterhouse	2002	Charterhouse
1937	Charterhouse	1963	Repton	1983	Charterhouse	2003	Edinburgh Academy
1938	Marlborough	1964	Fettes	1984	Charterhouse	2004	Tonbridge
1939	Charterhouse	1965	Rugby	1985	Harrow	2005	Tonbridge
1940–46	No competition	1966	Charterhouse	1986	Repton	2006	Malvern
1947	Harrow	1967	Eton	1987	Merchiston	2007	George Watson's
1948	Winchester	1968	Eton	1988	Stowe		
1949	Charterhouse	1969	Eton	1989	Eton		

Senior Halford-Hewitt Competitions (inaugurated 2000)

Bernard Darwin Trophy (Original 16) *always at Woking GC*

2000	Wellington	2003	Tonbridge	2006	Tonbridge
2001	Malvern	2004	Charterhouse	2007	Tonbridge
2002	Wellington	2005	Rugby	2008	Tonbridge

GL Mellin Salver (Second 16) *always at West Hill GC*

2000	Lancing	2003	Haileybury	2006	Cranleigh
2001	Cheltenham	2004	Shrewsbury	2007	Oundle
2002	Shrewsbury	2005	Shrewsbury	2008	Haileybury

Cyril Gray Trophy (Remaining 32) *always at Worplesdon*

2000	Stoneyhurst	2003	Stowe	2006	Canford
2001	Canford	2004	Edinburgh Academy	2007	Fettes
2002	George Watson's	2005	Fettes	2008	Canford

Senior Halford-Hewitt Trophy (Play-off between winners of Darwin, Mellin and Gray Trophies)

2000	Wellington	2003	Haileybury	2006	Cranleigh
2001	Canford	2004	Charterhouse	2007	*Not played*
2002	George Watson's	2005	Shrewsbury	2008	*Not played*

Grafton Morrish Trophy (inaugurated 1963)　*Hunstanton and Brancaster*

Semi-Finals
Birkenhead beat Haileybury　2–1
Solihull beat Merchant Taylors　2–1

Winning team: B Dowding,
D Fleet, J Hetherington,　L Meryon,
R Turner, H Westall

Final
Solihull beat Birkenhead　2–1

1963	Tonbridge	1975	Oundle	1987	Harrow	1999	George Heriot's
1964	Tonbridge	1976	Charterhouse	1988	Robert Gordon's	2000	Lancing
1965	Charterhouse	1977	Haileybury	1989	Tonbridge	2001	King's College
1966	Charterhouse	1978	Charterhouse	1990	Clifton		School
1967	Charterhouse	1979	Harrow	1991	Repton	2002	George Heriot's
1968	Wellington	1980	Charterhouse	1992	Charterhouse	2003	Glasgow Academy
1969	Sedbergh	1981	Charterhouse	1993	Malvern	2004	KCS, Wimbledon
1970	Sedbergh	1982	Marlborough	1994	George Heriot's	2005	Malvern
1971	Dulwich	1983	Wellington	1995	Repton	2006	Malvern
1972	Sedbergh	1984	Sedbergh	1996	Coventry	2007	Berkhamsted
1973	Pangbourne	1985	Warwick	1997	George Heriot's		
1974	Millfield	1986	Tonbridge	1998	Solihull		

119th Oxford v Cambridge Varsity Match (inaugurated 1878)　*Hoylake*

Captains: Oxford: Michael Canty; Cambridge: Thomas Woolsey
Foursomes (Cambridge names first):
E Oddy & C Consul beat A Habibi & R Stewart　2 holes
M Canty & W McPhail beat T Woolsey & D Chapman　3 and 2
D Elfant & S Chambers lost to　J Hickmore & C Robinson　10 and 9
J Gibbons & N Kruger lost to D Normoyle & J Whittington　5 and 4
T Smith & O Stephen beat J Valley & B Ramsay　5 and 4

Singles:
Michael Canty (Waterpark & Worcester) lost to Tom Woolsey (St Peter's, York & Queens')　8 and 7
Simon Chambers (Old Swinford & Wadham) lost to Amir Habibi (The Judd & Queens')　7 and 6
David Elfant {Runnymede, Madrid & Lincoln) lost to David Chapman {John Leggott & Trinity)　3 and 2
Claudio Consul (Winchester & Worcester) beat David Normoyle (ThomasDowney & Caius)　1 hole
Edward Oddy (BradfordGS & St EdHall) lost to Jack Hickmore (King's, Grantham & St Catharine's)
　5 and 4
William McPhail (Eton & Somerville) beat James Whittington (Winchester & St John's)　9 and 8
John Gibbons (Warwick & Mansfield) beat Chris Robinson (Wilson's & Robinson)　10 and 8
Neil Kruger (SACollege HS & Green) beat Ruaridh Stewart (Glenalmond & Peterhouse)　4 and 3
Thomas Smith (Ludlow & Worcester)} lost to　JohnValley (Oakville, Canada & Caius)　3 and 2
Oliver Stephen (Merchiston & St Benet's Hall) beat Benoit Ramsay (Alleyn's & Girton)　6 and 5

Result: Oxford beat Cambridge by 8 matches to 7

1878	Oxford	1900	Oxford	1926	Cambridge	1953	Cambridge
1879	Cambridge	1901	Oxford	1927	Cambridge	1954	Cambridge
1880	Oxford	1902	Oxford	1928	Cambridge	1955	Cambridge
1881	Not played	1903	Oxford	1929	Cambridge	1956	Oxford
1882	Cambridge	1904	Oxford	1930	Oxford	1957	Oxford
1883	Oxford	1905	Cambridge	1931	Oxford	1958	Cambridge
1884	Oxford	1906	Cambridge	1932	Oxford	1959	Cambridge
1885	Oxford	1907	Cambridge	1933	Cambridge	1960	Cambridge
1886	Oxford	1908	Cambridge	1934	Oxford	1961	Tie
1887	Cambridge	1909	Oxford	1935	Cambridge	1963	Cambridge
1888	Cambridge	1910	Cambridge	1936	Cambridge	1964	Oxford
1889	Oxford	1911	Oxford	1937	Cambridge	1965	Cambridge
1890	Cambridge	1912	Halved	1938	Cambridge	1966	Cambridge
1891	Cambridge	1913	Halved	1939	Cambridge	1967	Cambridge
1892	Cambridge	1914	Oxford	1940–45	Not played	1968	Cambridge
1893	Cambridge	1915–19	Not played	1946	Cambridge	1969	Cambridge
1894	Oxford	1920	Cambridge	1947	Oxford	1970	Halved
1895	Cambridge	1921	Oxford	1948	Oxford	1971	Oxford
1896	Halved	1922	Cambridge	1949	Cambridge	1972	Cambridge
1897	Cambridge	1923	Oxford	1950	Oxford	1973	Oxford
1898	Cambridge	1924	Cambridge	1951	Cambridge	1974	Cambridge
1899	Oxford	1925	Oxford	1952	Cambridge	1975	Cambridge

1976	Cambridge	1984	Cambridge	1992	Oxford	2000	Cambridge
1977	Cambridge	1985	Oxford	1993	Oxford	2001	Oxford
1978	Oxford	1986	Oxford	1994	Oxford	2002	Cambridge
1979	Oxford	1987	Cambridge	1995	Oxford	2003	Oxford
1980	Oxford	1988	Cambridge	1996	Oxford	2004	Tie
1981	Cambridge	1989	Cambridge	1997	Oxford	2005	Oxford
1982	Cambridge	1990	Cambridge	1998	Cambridge	2006	Tie
1983	Cambridge	1991	Cambridge	1999	Oxford	2007	Cambridge

Oxford and Cambridge Golfing Society for the President's Putter

(inaugurated 1920) *Littlestone and Rye*

Quarter-Finals

Ben Keogh (New College, Oxford) beat
  Peter Pentecost (Pembroke, Cambridge) 4 and 3
John Hudson (Christ's, Cambridge) beat
  Mark Williamson (Fitzwilliam, Cambridge) 2 and 1
Edward Oddy (St Edmund Hall, Oxford) beat
  Richard Marett (St Anne's, Oxford) 7 and 6
Charlie Rotheroe (Keble, Oxford) beat
  Edward Greenhalgh (Brasenose, Oxford) 3 and 2

Semi-Finals

Keogh beat Hudson 2 and 1
Rotheroe beat Oddy 1 hole

Final

Charlie Rotheroe beat Ben Keogh 2 and 1

1920	EWE Holderness	1940–46	*Not played*	1967	JR Midgley	1988	G Woollett
1921	EWE Holderness	1947	LG Crawley	1968	AWJ Holmes	1989	M Froggatt
1922	EWE Holderness	1948	Major AA Duncan	1969	P Moody	1990	G Woollett
1923	EWE Holderness	1949	PB Lucas	1970	DMA Steel	1991	B Ingleby
1924	B Darwin	1950	DHR Martin	1971	GT Duncan	1992	M Cox
1925	HD Gillies	1951	LG Crawley	1972	P Moody	1993	C Weight
1926T	EF Storey	1952	LG Crawley	1973	AD Swanston	1994	S Seman
	RH Wethered	1953	GH Micklem	1974	R Biggs	1995	A Woolnough
1927	RH Wethered	1954	G Huddy	1975	CJ Weight	1996	C Rotheroe
1928	RH Wethered	1955	G Huddy	1976	MJ Reece	1997	C Rotheroe
1929	Sir EWE Holderness	1956	GT Duncan	1977	AWJ Holmes	1998	N Pabari
1930	TA Bourn	1957	AE Shepperson	1978	MJ Reece	1999	C Dale
1931	AG Pearson	1958	Lt-Col AA Duncan	1979	*Cancelled – snow*	2000	C Dale
1932	LG Crawley	1959	ID Wheater	1980	S Melville	2001	B Streather
1933	AJ Peech	1960	JME Anderson	1981	AWJ Holmes	2002	T Etridge
1934	DHR Martin	1961	ID Wheater	1982	DMA Steel	2003	D Hayes
1935	RH Wethered	1962	MF Attenborough	1983	ER Dexter	2004	I Henderson
1936	RH Wethered	1963	JG Blackwell	1984	A Edmond	2005	O Lindsay
1937	JB Beck	1964	DMA Steel	1985	ER Dexter	2006	D Hayes
1938	CJH Tolley	1965	WJ Uzielli	1986	J Caplan	2007	I Henderson
1939	JOH Greenly	1966	MF Attenborough	1987	CD Meacher		

Palmer Cup (Europe university students v USA university students) *Glasgow Gailes*

First Day – Fourball:

Blixt & Hedin beat Hadley & Mitchell 1 hole
Caldwell & Shaw halved with Chappell & Goldberg
Borrowman & Ford lost to Fathauer & Thompson
  2 and 1
Campillo & Sluiter beat Fowler & Horschel 4 and 2

Singles:

Jonas Enander Hedin (SWE) lost to Aaron
  Goldberg 2 holes
Jonas Blixt (SWE) beat Adam Mitchell 5 and 4
Johnnie Caldwell (IRL) lost to Chesson Hadley
  2 and 1
Gareth Shaw (NIR) lost to Derek Fathauer
  1 hole
Scott Borrowman (SCO) beat Billy Horschel
  1 hole
Charlie Ford (ENG) lost to Rickie Fowler 4 and 3
Jorge Campillo (ESP) lost to Kevin Chappell
  4 and 3
Tim Sluiter (NED) beat Michael Thompson
  1 hole

Palmer Cup *continued*

Second Day – Foursomes:
Blixt & Hedin beat Goldberg & Thompson
4 and 3
Borrowman & Ford beat Horschel & Mitchell
3 and 1
Caldwell & Shaw beat Fathauer & Hadley
1 hole
Campillo & Sluiter beat Chappell & Fowler
3 and 2

Singles:
Campillo halved with
Fowler
Blixt beat Thompson
2 and 1
Ford halved with
Horschel
Shaw lost to Hadley
1 hole

Borrowman halved with
Chappell
Hedin beat Mitchell
3 and 2
Caldwell beat Goldberg
3 and 2
Sluiter lost to Fathauer
3 and 1

Result: Europe 14, USA 10

1997	USA	2000	GB&I	2003	Europe	2006	Europe
1998	USA	2001	USA	2004	Europe	2007	USA
1999	USA	2002	USA	2005	USA		

Boyd Quaich (University Championship)   *always at St Andrews (Old and New)*

1	Kevin Park (Griffith)	73(N)-66(O)-74(N)-78(O)—291
	Daniel Sommerville (Clayton State)	73(N)-70(O)-73(N)-78(O)—294
	Gerry Kelly (UCD)	70(N)-72(O)-76(N)-77(O)—295
	Bobby Rushford (Stirling)	73(N)-72(O)-73(N)-77(O)—295

1946	AS Mayer	1963	S MacDonald	1979	D McLeary	1995	C Sanderson
1947T	H Brews	1964	AJ Low	1980	ME Lewis	1996	B Templeton
	FWG Deighton	1965	S MacDonald	1981	P Gallagher	1997	G Maly
1948	JL Lindsay	1966	FE McCarroll	1982	ME Lewis	1998	D Simpson
1949	FD Tatum	1967	B Nicholson	1983	R Risan	1999	O Lindsay
1950	GP Roberts	1968	JW Johnston	1984	J Huggan	2000	G Greer
1951	H Dooley	1969	PH Moody	1985	S Elgie	2001	P Botha*
1952	G Parker	1970	JT Moffat	1986	A Roberts	2002	G Duncan
1953	JL Bamford	1971	JW Johnston	1987	M Pask	2003	R Hooper
1954	I Caldwell	1972	D Greig	1988	A Mathers	2004	G Blainey
1955	HC Squirrll	1973	J Rube	1989	A Mathers	2005	B Westgate
1956	JL Bamford	1974	G Cairns	1990	A Mathers	2006	N O'Connor
1957	DM Marsh	1975	S Dunlop	1991	C Somner	2007	C O'Hagan*
1958	R Mummery	1976	R Watson	1992	L Walker		*Beat R Dixon on better
1959–61	Not played	1977	R Watson	1993	G Sherry		last round
1962	DB Sheahan	1978	R Watson	1994	C Sanderson		

56th Queen Elizabeth Coronation Schools Trophy (inaugurated 1953)

always at Royal Burgess, Barnton

Semi-Finals:
George Heriot's FP beat Lenzie Academicals 2–1
Edinburgh Academicals beat Watsonians 2–1

Winning team: J Archibald,
R Bradly, D Campbell, I Christie,
J Liddel, S McCulloch

Final:
George Heriot's FP beat Edinburgh Academicals 2½–½

1953	Watsonians	1970	Dollar Academicals	1987	Daniel Stewart's/Melville FP
1954	Daniel Stewart's FP	1971	Merchistonians	1988	Watsonians
1955	Watsonians	1972	Merchistonians	1989	Kelvinside Academicals
1956	Watsonians	1973	Merchistonians	1990	Hutchesons' Grammar School
1957	Hillhead High School FP	1974	Old Carthusians		FP
1958	Watsonians	1975	Old Lorettonians	1991	Glasgow High School FP
1959	Glasgow High School FP	1976	Watsonians	1992	Daniel Stewart's/Melville FP
1960	Glasgow High School FP	1977	Glasgow High School FP	1993	Merchistonians
1961	Watsonians	1978	Old Lorettonians	1994	Perth Academy FP
1962	Glasgow High School FP	1979	Gordonians	1995	Glasgow High School FP
1963	Glasgow High School FP	1980	George Heriot's FP	1996	Glasgow High School FP
1964	Dollar Academicals	1981	Ayr Academicals	1997	Old Uppinghamians
1965	Old Lorettonians	1982	George Heriot's FP	1998	Watsonians
1966	Merchistonians	1983	Perth Academy FP	1999	Morrisonians
1967	Merchistonians	1984	Glasgow High School FP	2000	Breadalbane Academicals
1968	Hillhead High School FP	1985	Glasgow High School FP	2001	Old Carthusians
1969	Kelvinside Academicals	1986	Watsonians	2002	Old Campbellians

2003	Breadalbane Academicals	2005	Watsonians	2007	Daniel Stewart's/Melville FP
2004	Glasgow Academicals	2006	Fettesians		

Scottish Universities Championships *Moray GC, Lossiemouth*

1	Mathew Dargie (Stirling)	70-72-72-75—289
2	Paul Betty (Stirling)	76-66-75-73—290
	James Gill (St Andrews)	73-71-72-74—290
	Andrew McLaren (St Andrews)	71-71-74-74—290

2007   C Colraine

Callaway Handicapping

It frequently occurs in social competitions such as office or business association outings that many of the competitors do not have official handicaps. In such cases the best solution is to use the Callaway handicapping system, so called after the name of its inventor, as it is simple to use yet has proved equitable.

Competitors complete their round marking in their gross figures at every hole and their handicaps are awarded and deducted at the end of the 18 holes using the following table:

Competitor's Gross Score	Handicap Deduction
par or less	none
one over par – 75	½ worst hole
76–80	worst hole
81–85	worst hole plus ½ next worse
86–90	two worst holes
91–95	two worst holes plus ½ next
96–100	three worst holes
101–105	three worst holes plus ½ next
106–110	four worst holes
111–115	four worst holes plus ½ next
116–120	five worst holes
121–125	five worst holes plus ½ next
126–130	six worst holes

Note 1: Worst hole equals highest score at any hole regardless of the par of the hole except that the maximum score allowed for any one hole is twice the par of the hole.

Note 2: The 17th and 18th holes are not allowed to be deducted.

Example: Competitor scores 104. From the table he should deduct as his handicap the total of his three worst (i.e. highest) individual hole scores plus half of his fourth worst hole. If he scored one 9, one 8 and several 7's he would therefore deduct a total of 27½ from his gross score of 104 to give a net score of 76½.

County and Other Regional Championships 2008

England

Bedfordshire   G Benson

Berks, Bucks & Oxon   A Walton

Cambridgeshire   L Yearns

Channel Islands   G McFarlane

Cheshire   C Lewis)

Cornwall   J Coleman

Cumbria   J Longcake

Derbyshire   JP Feeney

Devon   D Gee

Dorset   T Adams

Durham   S Dance

Essex   A Winwood

Gloucestershire   O Glaze

Hampshire, Isle of Wight and
  Channel Islands   J Watt

Hertfordshire   P Amess

Isle of Man   J Corke

Kent   L Burns

Lancashire   T Fleetwood

Leicestershire and Rutland   J Palmer

Lincolnshire   D Keddie

Middlesex   S Fallon

Norfolk   S Clarke

Northamptonshire   R Evans

Northumberland   M Penny

Nottinghamshire   M Betteridge

Shropshire and Herefordshire
  J Devereux

Somerset   M Kippen

Staffordshire   M Pearson

Suffolk   O Pearl

Surrey   W Harmston

Sussex   J Doherty

Warwickshire   A Sullivan

Wiltshire   B Stow

Worcestershire   C Bromley

Yorkshire   R Law

Scotland

Angus C Donaldson (M), G Finlay (S)

Argyll and Bute G Bolton (M), L Pirie (S)

Ayrshire C Hamilton (M), S Wallace (S)

Borders Golfers' Association
A Ballantyne (M), I Walker (S)

Clackmannanshire RG Lyons (M),
S Borrowman (S)

Dunbartonshire R Graham (M), C Checkley (S)

Fife D Gould (M), C Martin (S)

Glasgow G Sangster (M), G McDougall (S)

Lanarkshire A Dick (M), S Rennis (S)

Lothians C Orr (M), S Armstrong (S)

North B Fotheringham (S)

North-East (Scotland) A Bews (M),
J Byrne (S)

Perth and Kinross S Graham (M+S)

Renfrewshire M Campbell (M), M Clark (S)

South C Robinson (M), S Kennedy (S)

Stirlingshire N Cunningham (M), J Donaldson (S)

Wales

Anglesey S Parry

Brecon & Radnor G Jones

Caernarfon and District P Roberts

Caernarfonshire Cup M Ellison

Denbigh A Griffiths

Dyfed A Jones

Flintshire J Williams

Glamorgan R Hooper

Gwent (Formerly Monmouthshire Amateur)
N Povall (M), P Rees (S)

Overseas Amateur Championships 2008

Australian (inaugurated 1894)   (Australian unless stated)

1894	LA Whyte	1925	H Sinclair	1956	H Berwick	1983	WJ Smith
1895	RAA Balfour	1926	Len Nettlefold	1957	BH Warren	1984	BP King
	Melville	1927	WS Nankivell	1958	K Hartley	1985	B Ruangkit (THA)
1896	HA Howden	1928	Len Nettlefold	1959	BW Devlin	1986	DJ Ecob
1897	HA Howden	1929	MJ Ryan	1960	Ted Ball	1987	B Johns
1898	HA Howden	1930	HW Hattersley	1961	T Crow	1988	S Bouvier
1899	CES Gillies	1931	HL William	1962	D Bachli	1989	SJ Conran
1900	LA Whyte	1932	Dr RH Bettington	1963	J Hayes (RSA)	1990	CD Gray
1901	HA Howden	1933	WL Hope	1964	B Baker	1991	LKJ Parsons
1902	H Macneil	1934	TS McKay	1965	K Donohoe	1992	MS Campbell (NZL)
1903	DG Soutar	1935	J Ferrier	1966	W Britten	1993	GJ Chalmers
1904	JD Howden	1936	J Ferrier	1967	J Muller	1994	W Bennett (ENG)
1905	Hon. Michael Scott	1937	HL Williams	1968	R Stott	1995	MC Goggin
1906	EA Gill	1938	J Ferrier	1969	RA Shearer	1996	DC Gleeson
1907	Hon. Michael Scott	1939	J Ferrier	1970	PA Bennett	1997	K Felton
1908	Clyde Pearce	1940–45	Not played	1971	GR Hicks	1998	B Rumford
1909	Hon. Michael Scott	1946	AN Waterson	1972	CR Kaye	1999	BM Jones
1910	Hon. Michael Scott	1947	HW Hattersley	1973	RJ Jenner	2000	BP Lamb
1911	JD Howden	1948	D Bachli	1974	TR Gale	2001	S Bowditch
1912	Hector Morrison	1949	WD Ackland-	1975	C Bonython	2002	K Barnes
1913	AR Lempriere		Horman	1976	P Sweeney	2003	J Doherty (SCO)
1914–19	Not played	1950	H Berwick	1977	AY Gresham	2004	A Martin
1920	EL Apperley	1951	Peter Heard	1978	MA Clayton	2005	E Ramsay (SCO)
1921	CL Winser	1952	R Stevens	1979	J Kelly	2006	T Stewart
1922	Ivo Witton	1953	Peter Heard	1980	R Mackay	2007	R Blizard
1923	Ivo Witton	1954	P Toogood	1981	O Moore	2008	A Kristiansen (NOR)
1924	H Sinclair	1955	J Rayner	1982	EM Couper		

Canadian (inaugurated 1895)   (Canadian unless stated)

1895	TH Harley	1926	CR Somerville	1958	B Castator	1985	B Franklin (USA)
1896	JS Gillespie	1927	DD Carrick	1959	J Johnston	1986	B Franklin (USA)
1897	WAH Kerr	1928	CR Somerville	1960	RK Alexander	1987	B Franklin (USA)
1898	GS Lyon	1929	E Held	1961	G Cowan	1988	D Roxburgh
1899	Vere C Brown	1930	CR Somerville	1962	R Taylor	1989	P Major
1900	GS Lyon	1931	CR Somerville	1963	N Weslock	1990	W Sye
1901	WAH Kerr	1932	GB Taylor	1964	N Weslock	1991	J Kraemer
1902	FR Martin	1933	A Campbell	1965	G Henry	1992	D Ritchie
1903	GS Lyon	1934	A Campbell	1966	N Weslock	1993	G Simpson
1904	J Percy Taylor	1935	CR Somerville	1967	S Jones	1994	W Sye
1905	GS Lyon	1936	F Haas jr	1968	J Doyle	1995	G Willis (USA)
1906	GS Lyon	1937	CR Somerville	1969	Wayne McDonald	1996	R McMillan
1907	GS Lyon	1938	T Adams	1970	A Miller	1997	D Goehring
1908	Alex Wilson	1939	K Black	1971	R Siderowf (USA)	1998	C Matthew
1909	E Legge	1940–44	Not played	1972	D Roxburgh	1999	Han Lee (USA)
1910	F Martin	1946	H Martell	1973	G Burns (USA)	2000	Han Lee (USA)
1911	GH Hutton	1947	FR Stranahan (USA)	1974	D Roxburgh	2001	G Paddison (NZL)
1912	George S Lyon	1948	FR Stranahan (USA)	1975	J Nelford	2002	D Pruitt (USA)
1913	GH Turpin	1949	RD Chapman (USA)	1976	J Nelford	2003	R Scott
1914	George S Lyon	1950	W Mawhinney	1977	R Spittle	2004	D Wallace
1915–19	Not played	1951	W McElroy	1978	R Spittle	2005	R Scott
1920	CB Grier	1952	L Bouchey	1979	R Alarcon (MEX)	2006	R Scott
1921	F Thompson	1953	D Cherry	1980	G Olson	2007	N Taylor
1922	CC Fraser	1954	E Harvie Ward (USA)	1981	R Zokol	2008	C Burke
1923	WJ Thompson	1955	M Norman	1982	D Roxburgh		
1924	F Thompson	1956	M Norman	1983	D Milovic		
1925	DD Carrick	1957	N Weslock	1984	W Swartz		

New Zealand (inaugurated 1893)   (New Zealand unless stated)

1893	JA Somerville	1923	J Goss jr	1955	SG Jones	1982	J Peters
1894	H Macneil	1924	L Quin	1956	PA Toogood	1983	C Taylor
1895	G Gosset	1925	TH Horton	1957	EJ McDougall	1984	J Wagner
1896	MS Todd	1926	ADS Duncan	1958	WJ Godfrey	1985	G Power
1897	D Pryde	1927	S Morpeth	1959	SG Jones	1986	P O'Malley (AUS)
1898	W Pryde	1928	TH Horton	1960	R Newdick	1987	O. Kendall
1899	ADS Duncan	1929	S Morpeth	1961	SG Jones	1988	B Hughes (AUS)
1900	ADS Duncan	1930	HA Black	1962	SG Jones	1989	L Peterson
1901	ADS Duncan	1931	R Wagg	1963	J Durry	1990	M Long
1902	SH Gollan	1932	R Wagg	1964	SG Jones	1991	L Parsons (AUS)
1903	K Tareha	1933	BV Wright	1965	J Durry	1992	R Lee
1904	AH Fisher	1934	BM Silk	1966	SG Jones	1993	P Tatamaugi
1905	ADS Duncan	1935	JP Hornabrook	1967	J Durry	1994	P Fitzgibbon
1906	SH Gollan	1936	JP Hornabrook	1968	BA Stevens	1995	S Bittle
1907	ADS Duncan	1937	BM Silk	1969	G Stevenson	1996	D Somerville
1908	HC Smith	1938	PGF Smith	1970	EJ McDougall	1997	C Johns
1909	ADS Duncan	1939	JP Hornabrook	1971	SG Jones	1998	B MacDonald
1910	HB Lusk	1940–45	*Not played*	1972	RC Murray	1999	A Duffin
1911	ADS Duncan	1946	WG Horne	1973	MN Nicholson	2000	E Burgess
1912	BB Wood	1947	BM Silk	1974	RM Barltrop	2001	B Gallie
1913	BB Wood	1948	A Gibbs	1975	SF Reese	2002	M Fraser (AUS)
1914	ADS Duncan	1949	J Holden	1976	TR Pulman	2003	J Nitties (AUS)
1915–18	*Not played*	1950	DL Woon	1977	TR Pulman	2004	G Flint (AUS)
1919	H Crosse	1951	DL Woon	1978	F Nobilo	2005	MI Brown (AUS)
1920	S Morpeth	1952	H Berwick	1979	J Durry	2006	A Green
1921	AG Syme	1953	DL Woon	1980	PE Hartstone	2007	D Lee
1922	ADS Duncan	1954	DL Woon	1981	T Cochrane	2008	T Spearman-Burn

South African (inaugurated 1892)   (South African unless stated)

1892	D Walker	1924	AL Forster	1956	RC Taylor	1984	M Wiltshire
1893	DG Proudfoot	1925	TG McLelland	1957	A Stewart	1985	N Clarke
1894	DG Proudfoot	1926	WS Bryant	1958	JR Boyd	1986	E Els
1895	DG Proudfoot	1927	GJ Chantler	1959	A Walker	1987	B Fouche
1896	DG Proudfoot	1928	B Wynne	1960	WM Grinrod	1988	N Clarke
1897	DG Proudfoot	1929	C Hunter	1961	JG Le Roux	1989	C Rivett
1898	DG Proudfoot	1930	B Wynne	1962	J Hayes	1990	R Goosen
1899	DG Proudfoot	1931	C Coetzer	1963	D Symons	1991	D Botes
1900–01	*Not played*	1932	CE Olander	1964	JR Langridge	1992	B Davidson
1902	DG Proudfoot	1933	B Wynne	1965	P Vorster	1993	L Chitengwa (ZIM)
1903	R Law	1934	CE Olander	1966	Comrie du Toit	1994	B Vaughan
1904	JR Southey	1935	AD Locke	1967	Derek Kemp	1995	W Abery
1905	HCV Nicholson	1936	CE Olander	1968	R Williams	1996	T Moore
1906	Lt. HM Ballinghall	1937	AD Locke	1969	D Thornton	1997	T Immelman
1907	Lt. HM Ballinghall	1938	B Wynne	1970	H Baiocchi	1998	J Hugo
1908	JAW Prentice	1939	O Hayes	1971	C Dreyer	1999	R Sterne
1909	JAW Prentice	1940	HEP Watermeyer	1972	N Dundelson	2000	J Van Zyl
1910	Dr EL Steyn	1941–45	*Not played*	1973	A. Oosthuizen	2001	D Dixon (ENG)
1911	JAW Prentice	1946	JR Boyd	1974	T Lagerwey	2002	R Loubser
1912	HG Stewart	1947	C de G Watermeyer	1975	P Vorster	2003	A Haig
1913	JAW Prentice	1948	RR Ryan	1976	R Kotzen	2004	H Rootman
1914	SM McPherson	1949	RW Glennie	1977	EA Webber (ZIM)	2005	G Coetzee
1915–18	*Not played*	1950	EA Dalton	1978	EA Webber (ZIM)	2006	N Edwards (WAL)
1919	HG Stewart	1951	ES Irwin	1979	L Norval	2007	L de Jager
1920	HG Stewart	1952	M Janks	1980	E Grienewald	2008	J Blaauw
1921	AL Forster	1953	R Brews	1981	D Suddards		
1922	WCE Stent	1954	A Jackson	1982	N James		
1923	WCE Stent	1955	B Keyter	1983	C-C Yuan (CHN)		

South African Stroke Play (inaugurated 1969)   (South African unless stated)

1969 D van der Walt	1980 E Groenewald	1991 N Henning	2002 G Wolstenholme
1970 D Hayes	1981 C-C Yuan (CHN)	1992 J Nelson	(ENG)
1971 K Suddards	1982 Li Wen-sheng (TPE)	1993 D Kinnear	2003 A Kruger
1972 P Dunne	1983 Peter van der Riet	1994 N Homann	2004 H Rootman
1973 G Harvey (ZIM)	1984 D James	1995 M Murless	2005 J Cunliffe
1974 N Sundelson	1985 D van Steden	1996 T Moore	2006 B Grace
1975 G Levenson	1986 C-S Hsieh	1997 U van den Berg	2007 L de Jager
1976 G Harvey (ZIM)	1987 B Fouchee	1998 T Immelman	2008 J Blaauw
1977 M McNulty (ZIM)	1988 N Clarke	1999 J Hugo	
1978 D Suddards	1989 E Els	2000 C McMonagle (IRL)	
1979 D Suddards	1990 P Pascoe	2001 R Sterne	

108th United States Amateur Championship *Pinehurst, NC*

Leading Qualifier: Robbie Fillmore (Provo, UT)   69-65—134

Quarter Finals:
Drew Kittleson (Scottdale, AZ) beat Derek Fathauer (Jensen Beach FL) 3 and 2
Adam Mitchell (Chattanooga, TN) beat Charlie Holland (Dallas, TX) 2 and 1
Danny Lee (NZL) beat Morgan Hoffmann (Saddle Brook, NJ) 4 and 3
Patrick Reed (Augusta, GA) beat Graham Hill (CAN) 4 and 3

Semi-Finals:
Kittleson beat Mitchell 4 and 2
Lee beat Reed 3 and 2

Final: Danny Lee beat Drew Kittleson 5 and 4

1895 CB Macdonald beat C Sands	1938 WP Turnesa beat BP Abbott
1896 HJ Whigham beat JG Thorp	1939 MH Ward beat RE Billows
1897 HJ Whigham beat WR Betts	1940 RD Chapman beat WB McCullough
1898 FS Douglas beat WB Smith	1941 MH Ward beat BP Abbott
1899 HM Harriman beat FS Douglas	*1942–45 Not played*
1900 WJ Travis beat FS Douglas	1946 SE Bishop beat S Quick
1901 WJ Travis beat WE Egan	1947 RH Riegel beat JW Dawson
1902 LN James beat EM Byers	1948 WP Turnesa beat RE Billows
1903 WJ Travis beat EM Byers	1949 CR Coe beat R King
1904 HC Egan beat F Herreshof	1950 S Urzetta beat FR Stranahan
1905 HC Egan beat DE Sawyer	1951 WJ Maxwell beat J Gagliardi
1906 EM Byers beat GS Lyon	1952 J Westland beat A Mengert
1907 JD Travers beat A Graham	1953 G Littler beat D Morey
1908 JD Travers beat MH Behr	1954 A Palmer beat R Sweeney
1909 RA Gardner beat HC Egan	1955 E Harvie Ward beat W Hyndman
1910 WC Fownes jr beat WK Wood	1956 E Harvie Ward beat C Kocsis
1911 HH Hilton (ENG) beat F Herreshof	1957 H Robbins beat FM Taylor
1912 JD Travers beat C Evans jr	1958 CR Coe beat TD Aaron
1913 JD Travers beat JG Anderson	1959 JW Nicklaus beat CR Coe
1914 F Ouimet beat JD Travers	1960 DR Beman beat RW Gardner
1915 RA Gardner beat JG Anderson	1961 JW Nicklaus beat HD Wysong
1916 C Evans jr beat RA Gardner	1962 LE Harris jr beat D Gray
1917–18 Not played	1963 DR Beman beat RH Sikes
1919 SD Herron beat RT Jones jr	1964 WC Campbell beat EM Tutweiler
1920 C Evans jr beat F Ouimet	
1921 JP Guildford beat RA Gardner	*Changed to stroke play*
1922 JW Sweetser beat C Evans jr	
1923 MR Marston beat JW Sweetser	1965 RJ Murphy
1924 RT Jones jr beat G Von Elm	1966 G Cowan (CAN)
1925 RT Jones jr beat W Gunn	1967 RB Dickson
1926 G Von Elm beat RT Jones jr	1968 B Fleisher
1927 RT Jones jr beat C Evans jr	1969 S Melnyk
1928 RT Jones jr beat TP Perkins	1970 L Wadkins
1929 HR Johnston beat OF Willing	1971 G Cowan (CAN)
1930 RT Jones jr beat EV Homans	
1931 F Ouimet beat J Westland	*Reverted to match play*
1932 CR Somerville beat J Goodman	
1933 GT Dunlap jr beat MR Marston	1973 C Stadler beat D Strawn
1934 W Lawson Little jr beat D Goldman	1974 J Pate beat J Grace
1935 W Lawson Little jr beat W Emery	1975 F Ridley beat K Fergus
1936 JW Fischer beat J McLean	1976 B Sander beat CP Moore
1937 J Goodman beat RE Billows	1977 J Fought beat D Fischesser
	1978 J Cook beat S Hoch
	1979 M O'Meara beat J Cook

1980	H Sutton beat B Lewis
1981	N Crosby beat B Lindley
1982	J Sigel beat D Tolley
1983	J Sigel beat C Perry
1984	S Verplank beat S Randolph
1985	S Randolph beat P Persons
1986	S Alexander beat C Kite
1987	W Mayfair beat E Rebmann
1988	E Meeks beat D Yates
1989	C Patton beat D Green
1990	P Mickelson beat M Zerman
1991	M Voges beat M Zerman
1992	J Leonard beat T Scherrer
1993	J Harris beat D Ellis
1994	T Woods beat T Kuehne
1995	T Woods beat G Marucci
1996	T Woods beat S Scott
1997	M Kuchar beat J Kribel
1998	H Kuehne beat T McKnight
1999	D Gossett beat Sung Yoon Kim
2000	J Quinney beat J Driscoll
2001	B Dickerson beat R Hamilton
2002	R Barnes beat H Mahon
2003	N Flanagan (AUS) beat C Wittenberg
2004	R Moore beat L List
2005	E Molinari (ITA) beat D Dougherty
2006	R Ramsay (SCO) beat J Kelly
2007	C Knost beat M Thompson

Other 2008 National Amateur Championship winners

Australia SP	Daniel Willett (ENG)	Israel	Asaf Cohen
South Africa SP	Jacques Blaauw	Italy	Nino Bertsio
Argentine	Luke Goddard (ENG)	Italian MP	Nino Bertasio
Austria	Stephan Wolters (GER)	Japan	Bi-o Kim (KOR)
Brazil	Felipe Lessa	Korea	Bi-o Kim
Bulgaria	Richard Heath (AUS)	Latvia	Karlis Broders
Caribbean	Mauricio Muniz (PUR)	Luxembourg	Christopher Mivis (BEL)
[Hoerman Cup]		Malaysia	Koh Dengshan (SIN)
Central America	Alvaro Ortiz (CRC)	Mexico	Victor Dubuisson (FRA)
China Nationa	Jian-feng Ye	Netherlands	Floris de Vries
Cyprus	Robert Carson (SCO)	Netherlands SP	Tim Sluiter
Czech	Chris Paisley (ENG)	Philippines	Rufino Bayron
Denmark	Lucas Bjerregaard	Poland	Michael Flindt
Estonia	Claas-Eric Borges (GER)	Portugal	Ferdinand Auzo
Finland	Kalle Samooja	Russia	Steven Uzzell (ENG)
France Close	Stanislas Gautier	Singapore	Vasin Sripattranosorn
(Coupe Ganay)		Slovak	Stanislav Matus
France Open SP	David Antonelli	Slovenia	Philippo Okan (GER)
(Coupe Murat)		South America	Cristian Espinoza (CHI)
Germany	Steven Gross	Spain	Daniel Willett (ENG)
Hellenic	Hamsa Sayin (TUR)	Spain (Close)	Jorge Campillo
Hong Kong	Matthew McBain (AUS)	Switzerland	Moritz Lampert (GER)
Hungary	Gergi Bondicz	Swiss MP	Marc Dobias
India	Rahul Bakshi	Taiwan	Tao Huang
Indonesia	Andik Mauludin	Turkey	Jose Maria Joia (POR)

Month by month in 2008

The United States win back the Ryder Cup 16½–11½. Top-scorer, to his huge credit, is controversial selection Ian Poulter with four wins out of five. Europe's top three, Padraig Harrington, Sergio García and Lee Westwood do not win a game between them, but captain Nick Faldo comes in for stick over his singles order and some other decisions. America's six rookies, most notably Anthony Kim, Boo Weekley and Hunter Mahan, rise to the occasion and the week goes like a dream for their captain Paul Azinger.

USA State Championships 2008

US Nationality unless stated

Alabama State Am.	Alexander City	Will Wilcox	Minnesota MP	Duluth	Trent Peterson
Arizona SP	Scottsdale	Chan Kim	Minnesota State Am.	Independence	Trent Peterson
Arizona State Am.	Scottsdale	Jin Song (KOR)	Mississippi State Am.	Tunica	Trey Denton
Arkansas MP	Pine Bluff	Wes McNulty	Missouri State Am.	O'Fallon	Justin Bardgett
Arkansas State Am.	Jonesboro	Wes McNulty	Montana State Am.	Bozeman	Gordon Webb
California State Am.	Toluca Lake	Nick Delio	NCGA Am.	Pebble Beach, CA	Matthew Marshall
Carolinas Am.	Wilmington, NC	Ben Kohles	NCGA SP	Pebble Beach, CA	Matthew Hollinsead
Colorado MP	Castle Rock	Luke Symons	Nebraska MP	Nebraska City	Brandon Crick
Colorado State Am.	Lakewood	Jonathan Marsico	Nebraska State Am.	Lincoln	Jayson Brueggemann
Connecticut State Am.	Ellington	Will Strickler	Nevada MP	Reno	Matt Edwards
Delaware State Am.	Newarg	Eric Onesi	Nevada State Am.	Las Vegas	Brady Exber
Florida MP	Vero Beach	David Johnson	New England Am.	Newton Centre, MA	Matt Broome
Florida State Am.	Tequista	Judson Eustaquio (PHI)	New Hampshire SP	Hudson	Craig Cyr
GAM (Michigan) Ch.	Orchard Lake	Jimmy Chestnut	New Mexico/ West Texas Am.	Tanoan	Tim Madigan
Georgia State Am.	Macon	Russell Henley	New Jersey State Am.	Marlton	Tom Gramigna
Hawaii State Am.	Aiea	Travis Toyama	New York State Am.	Guilderland	Jeff Wolniewicz
Idaho MP	Donnelly	Mike Deboard	N. Carolina Am.	Raleigh	Jack Fields
Idaho State Am.	Blackfoot	Quinn Carbol	N. Dakota State Am.	Jamestown	Tom Hoge
Illinois State Am.	Wheaton	Zach Barlow	Ohio State Am.	Findlay	Vaughn Snyder
Indiana MP	Noblesville	Randy Nichols	Oklahoma SP	Broken Arrow	Trent Whitekiller
Iowa MP	Panora	Mike Ketcham	Oklahoma State Am.	Oklahoma City	Rhein Gibson (AUS)
Iowa State Am.	Pleasant Valley	Mike Oimoen	Oregon State Am.	Bend	Blake Seabaugh
Louisiana State Am.	Lake Charles	Jarrod Barsamian	Oregon SP	Creswell	Andrew Vijarro
Kansas State Am.	Wichita	Cameron Bishop	Pennsylvania State Am.	Bethlehem	Mike Van Sickle
Kentucky State Am.	Paducah	Tyler Sharpe	Rhode Island State Am.	Rumford	David McAndrew
Maine State Am.	Saco	Ryan Gay	Rhode Island SP	East Greenwich	Charlie Blanchard
Maryland State Am.	Pikesville	Michael Mulieri	SCGA Match Play	Goleta, CA	Matt Hoffenberg
Massachusetts State Am.	Marion	John Hadges	SDGA Am.	Rapid City, SD	Geoff Mead
Met Am.	Baiting Hollow, NY	Tommy McDonaugh			
Metropolitan Am.	Norwood Hill, NY	Adam Long			
Metropolitan SP	West Caldwell, NJ	Kevin Foley			
Michigan State Am.	Portage	Jimmy Chestnut			

Southern California Am.	Salticoy	Kevin Marsh	Washington State Am.	Moses Lake	Richard Lee
S. Carolina Am.	Clinton	Lee Palms	W. Virginia State Am.	White Sulphur Springs	Tim Fisher
S. Carolina MP	Columbia	Tripp McAllister			
Tennessee MP	Louden	John Fox	Wisconsin MP	Green Lake	Dustin Schwab
Texas State Am.	Houston	Kelly Kraft	Wisconsin State Am.	Beaver Dam	Ben Bendtsen
Utah State Am.	Heber	Dan Horner			
Vermont State Am.	Rutland	Brian Albertazzi	Wyoming MP	Saratoga	Gabe Maier
			Wyoming State Am.	Jackson Hole	Steve White
Virginia State Am.	Williamsburg	Brinson Paolini			

Canadian Provincial Championships 2008

Atlantic	Bathurst, NB	Eric Locke	Prairie	Saskatoon, SK	Richard Jung*
Ontario	Stratford, ON	Mathieu Rivard	*beat Alvin Choi in play-off		
Pacific	Courtenay, BC	Riley Wheeldon*	Quebec	Hemmingford, QC	Mitch Sutton
*beat Alvin Choi in play-off			Western	Ponoka, AB	Shane O'Neill

Australian State Championships 2008

New South Wales	Michael Raseta	Tasmania	Tim Stewart
Queensland	Jared Consoli	Victoria	Leighton Lyle
South Australia	Chris Austin	Western Australia	Michael Foster

PART V

Women's Amateur Tournaments

Ladies' European Amateur Ranking 2008

The honours were evenly spread among the qualifying nations in the top 100 of the 2008 Ladies' European Ranking. Swedish players notched up the most entrants at 17 with England (12), Spain (10) and France (9) close on their heels. Five German players made it into the top 100, there were six from Austria and Denmark, Scotland and Wales provided five each.

		Points
1	Carlota Ciganda (ESP)	267.50
2	Maria Hernandez (ESP)	242.50
3	Anna Nordqvist (SWE)	205.00
4	Christel Boeljon (NED)	182.60
5	Caroline Masson (GER)	180.50
6	Barbara Genuini (FRA)	180.00
7	Caroline Hedwall (SWE)	168.00
8	Roseanne Niven (SCO)	153.17
9	Azahara Munoz (ESP)	150.00
10	Stephanie Kirchmayr (GER)	148.50
11	Therese Koelbaek (DEN)	135.00
12	Valentine Derrey (FRA)	127.50
13	Breanne Loucks (WAL)	125.50
14	Tara Delaney (IRL)	122.50
15	Benedicte Toumpsin (BEL)	121.50
16	Jacqueline Hedwall (SWE)	116.63
17	Kylie Walker (SCO)	114.63
18	Sahra Hassan (WAL)	114.40
19	Caroline Westrup (SWE)	110.00
20	Pia Halbig (GER)	108.75
21	Dewi Claire Schreefel (NED)	107.60
22	Thea Hoffmeister (GER)	105.50
23	Lucie Andre (FRA)	103.10
24	Charlotte Lorentzen (DEN)	102.50
25	Adriana Zwanck (ESP)	99.50
26	Pamela Prestwell (SCO)	99.10
27	Linda Henriksson (FIN)	98.50
28	Cristina Gugler (AUT)	98.00
29	Laura Gourdraine (FRA)	97.50
	Laura Lansone (LAT)	97.50
31	Carmen Perez-Narbon (ESP)	95.00
32	Jodi Ewart (ENG)	94.50
33	Belen Mozo (ESP)	94.13
34	Christine Wolf (AUT)	92.50
35	Stefanie Endstrasser (AUT)	92.00
36	Elin Andersson (SWE)	90.00
37	Karin Kinnerud (SWE)	87.50
38	Linn Gustafsson (SWE)	87.40
39	Martina Hochwimmer (AUT)	84.00
40	Pernilla Lindberg (SWE)	82.50
41	Marianna Causin (ITA)	82.00
42	Naomi Edwards (ENG)	81.63
43	Tara Davies (WAL)	80.50
44	Sara Wikstrom (SWE)	80.00
45	Giulia Molinaro (ITA)	78.13
46	Teresa Puga (ESP)	77.50
47	Marion Ricordeau (FRA)	76.63
48	Kym Larratt (ENG)	75.00
49	Rachel Jennings (ENG)	74.70
50	Michele Thomson (SCO)	74.63
51	Audrey Goumard (FRA)	74.50
52	Valerie Sternebeck (GER)	73.50
53	Marieke Nivard (NED)	72.00
54	Emilie Lind (SWE)	71.50
55	Danielle McVeigh (IRL)	68.50
56	Isabelle Boineau (FRA)	67.50
	Krystle Caithness (SCO)	67.50
58	Laura Cutler (ENG)	67.25
59	Rhian Wyn Thomas (WAL)	67.13
60	Jutta Degerman (FIN)	65.00
61	Camilla Lennarth (SWE)	64.13
62	Stephanie Derrey (FRA)	62.75
63	Florentyna Parker (ENG)	62.60
64	Valeria Tandrina (ITA)	62.00
65	Rosa Svahn (FIN)	61.34
66	Therese Nilsson (SWE)	61.30
67	Marina Kotnik (AUT)	60.13
68	Kerry Smith (ENG)	60.10
69	Veronika Holisova (CZE)	60.00
	Galina Rotmistrova (RUS)	60.00
	Rachel Connor (ENG)	60.00
	Malene Jorgensen (DEN)	60.00
	Mireia Prat (ESP)	60.00
74	Linda Persson (SWE)	59.00
75	Valentine Gevers (BEL)	58.67
76	Anna Scott (ENG)	58.00
77	Trine Mortensen (DEN)	56.00
78	Holly Aitchinson (ENG)	55.03
79	Nicola Roessler (GER)	55.00
80	Camilla Patussi (ITA)	54.13
81	Lara Katzy (GER)	53.18
82	Ane Urchegui (ESP)	52.00
83	Araceli Felgueroso (ESP)	51.50
84	Sarah Schober (AUT)	50.00
	Teresa Vavruskova (CZE)	50.00
	Nikulina Elizaveta (RUS)	50.00
	Line Vedel Hansen (DEN)	50.00
88	Niamh Kitching (IRL)	49.50
89	Kim Ulander (SWE)	48.50
90	Klara Spilkova (CZE)	48.33
91	Hannah Barwood (ENG)	47.50
92	Hannah Burke (ENG)	47.16
93	Rebecca Sorensen (SWE)	47.00
94	Lucy Gould (WAL)	46.50
95	Emilie Alonso (FRA)	45.00
	Silvie Dittertova (CZE)	45.00
	Malin Enarsson (SWE)	45.00
	Michele Holzwarth (GER)	45.00
99	Desiree Karlsson (SWE)	44.50
100	Laurence Herman (BEL)	44.00

For the full EGA Ladies' European Amateur Rankings, visit www.ega-golf.ch

National and International Tournaments 2008

Ladies British Amateur Championship (inaugurated 1893)

North Berwick   [6242–72]

Leading Qualifier: Caroline Hedwall (SWE) 68-72—140

First Round
Caroline Hedwall (SWE) beat Niamh Kitching (Claremorris) 2 and 1
Emily Ogilvy (Auchterarder) beat Hannah Jenkins (Cradoc) 2 and 1
Marina Kotnik (AUT) beat Kerry Smith (Waterlooville) 2 and 1
Jodi Ewart (Catterick) beat Valerie Sternebeck (GER) 2 and 1
Breanne Loucks (Wrexham) beat Lesley Nicholson (Haddington) 1 hole
Christel Boeljon (NED) beat Florentyna Parker (Royal Birkdale) 1 hole
Maude-Aimee Leblanc (CAN) beat Jenny Pease (Braintree) 2 and 1
Carly Booth (Comrie) beat Stephanie Kirchmayr (GER) 4 and 2

Nina Holleder (GER) beat Tara Davies (Holyhead) 3 and 2
Isabelle Boineau (FRA) beat Holly Aitchison (Bedfordshire) 2 and 1
Jennifer Kirby (CAN) beat Tandi Cuningham (RSA) 4 and 2
Valentine Derrey (FRA) beat Marion Ricordeau (FRA) 5 and 3
Kira Meixner (CAN) beat Marta Silva (ESP) 2 and 1
Michele Thomson (McDonald Ellon) beat Deirdre Smith (Co. Louth) 2 and 1
Jacqueline Hedwall (SWE) beat Kelsey MacDonald (Nairn Dunbar) 1 hole
Rhian Wyn Thomas (Vale of Glamorgan) beat Taylore Karle (USA) 2 and 1

Camilla Lenarth (SWE) beat Ellie Givens (Blackwell Grange) 6 and 4
Pamela Pretswell (Bothwell Castle) beat Pia Halbig (GER) 2 and 1
Sahra Hassan (Vale of Glamorgan) beat Marieke Nivard (NED) 1 hole
Roseanne Niven (Crieff) beat Andre Lucie (FRA) 2 and 1
Barbara Genuini (FRA) beat Hannah Burke (Mid-Herts) 4 and 3
Stefanie Endstrasser (AUT) beat Pemilla Lindberg (SWE) 3 and 2
Allison Goodman (USA) beat Rachel Connor (Manchester) 1 hole
Azahara Muñoz (ESP) beat Mireia Prat (ESP) 3 and 2

Anna Nordqvist (SWE) beat Claire Aitken (Mid Kent) 5 and 3
Kylie Walker (Buchanan Castle) beat Sara Juneau (CAN) 5 and 4
Hannah Ralph (Cowdray Park) beat Cristina Gugler (AUT) 2 and 1
Belen Mozo (ESP) beat Rachel Jennings (Izaak Walton) at 19th
Giulia Molinaro (ITA) beat Audrey Decharne (FRA) 1 hole
Caroline Masson (GER) beat Kristie Smith (AUS) 1 hole
Naomi Edwards (Ganton) beat Krystle Caithness (St Regulus) 3 and 1
Maria Hernandez (ESP) beat Laura Stempfle (GER) at 19th

Second Round
C Hedwall beat Ogilvy 2 and 1
Ewart beat Kotnik 3 and 2
Loucks beat Boeljon 1 hole
Leblanc beat Booth 1 hole
Boineau beat Holleder 1 hole
Derrey beat Kirby 2 and 1
Meixner beat Thomson 1 hole
J Hedwall beat Wyn Thomas 2 holes
Pretswell beat Lennarth 1 hole
Niven beat Hassan 2 and 1
Endstrasser beat Genuini 3 and 1

Muñoz beat Goodman 2 and 1
Nordqvist beat Walker 3 and 2
Ralph beat Mozo 3 and 2
Masson beat Molinaro 4 and 3
Hernandez beat Edwards 5 and 4

Third Round
C Hedwall beat Ewart 4 and 2
Leblanc beat Loucks 1 hole
Derrey beat Boineau 4 and 3
J Hedwall beat Meixner 1 hole
Niven beat Pretswell 2 and 1

Ladies British Amateur Championship *continued*

Third Round *continued*
Muñoz beat Endstrasser 2 holes
Nordqvist beat Ralph 4 and 3
Hernandez beat Masson 5 and 3

Quarter Finals
C Hedwall beat Leblanc 2 holes
J Hedwall beat Derrey I hole
Niven beat Muñoz I hole
Nordqvist beat Hernandez 4 and 2

Semi-Finals
C Hedwall beat J Hedwall 4 and 3
Nordqvist beat Niven 2 and I

Final
Anna Nordqvist (SWE) beat Caroline Hedwall (SWE) 3 and 2

1893	M Scott beat I Pearson 7 and 5	1954	F Stephens beat E Price 4 and 3
1894	M Scott beat I Pearson 2 and 2	1955	J Valentine beat B Romack (USA) 7 and 6
1895	M Scott beat E Lythgoe 5 and 4	1956	M Smith (USA) beat M Janssen (USA) 8 and 7
1896	Miss Pascoe beat L Thomson 2 and 2	1957	P Garvey beat J Valentine 4 and 3
1897	EC Orr beat Miss Orr 4 and 2	1958	J Valentine beat E Price I hole
1898	L Thomson beat EC Neville 7 and 5	1959	E Price beat B McCorkindale at 37th
1899	M Hezlet beat Magill 2 and I	1960	B McIntyre (USA) beat P Garvey 4 and 2
1900	Adair beat Neville 6 and 5	1961	M Spearman beat DJ Robb 7 and 6
1901	Graham beat Adair 2 and I	1962	M Spearman beat A Bonallack I hole
1902	M Hezlet beat E Neville at 19th	1963	B Varangot (FRA) beat P Garvey 2 and I
1903	Adair beat F Walker-Leigh 4 and 3	1964	C Sorenson (USA) beat BAB Jackson at 37th
1904	L Dod beat M Hezlet I hole	1965	B Varangot (FRA) beat IC Robertson 4 and 3
1905	B Thompson beat ME Stuart 2 and 2	1966	E Chadwick beat V Saunders 2 and 2
1906	Kennon beat B Thompson 4 and 3	1967	E Chadwick beat M Everard I hole
1907	M Hezlet beat F Hezlet 2 and I	1968	B Varangot (FRA) beat C Rubin (FRA) at 20th
1908	M Titterton beat D Campbell at 19th	1969	C Lacoste (FRA) beat A Irvin I hole
1909	D Campbell beat F Hezlet 4 and 3	1970	D Oxley beat IC Robertson I hole
1910	Miss Grant Suttie beat L Moore 6 and 4	1971	M Walker beat B Huke 2 and I
1911	D Campbell beat V Hezlet 2 and 2	1972	M Walker beat C Rubin (FRA) 2 holes
1912	G Ravenscroft beat S Temple 2 and 2	1973	A Irvin beat M Walker 2 and 2
1913	M Dodd beat Miss Chubb 8 and 6	1974	C Semple (USA) beat A Bonallack 2 and I
1914	C Leitch beat G Ravenscroft 2 and I	1975	N Syms (USA) beat S Cadden 2 and 2
1915–18	*Not played*	1976	C Panton beat A Sheard I hole
1919	*Abandoned because of railway strike*	1977	A Uzielli beat V Marvin 6 and 5
1920	C Leitch beat M Griffiths 7 and 6	1978	E Kennedy (AUS) beat J Greenhalgh I hole
1921	C Leitch beat J Wethered 4 and 3	1979	M Madill beat J Lock (AUS) 2 and I
1922	J Wethered beat C Leitch 9 and 7	1980	A Quast (USA) beat L Wollin (SWE) 2 and I
1923	D Chambers beat A Macbeth 2 holes	1981	IC Robertson beat W Aitken at 20th
1924	J Wethered beat Mrs Cautley 7 and 6	1982	K Douglas beat G Stewart 4 and 2
1925	J Wethered beat C Leitch at 37th	1983	J Thornhill beat R Lautens (SUI) 4 and 2
1926	C Leitch beat Mrs Garon 8 and 7	1984	J Rosenthal (USA) beat J Brown 4 and 3
1927	T de la Chaume (FRA) beat Miss Pearson 5 and 4	1985	L Beman (IRL) beat C Waite I hole
1928	N Le Blan (FRA) beat S Marshall 2 and 2	1986	M McGuire (NZL) beat L Briars (AUS) 2 and I
1929	J Wethered beat G Collett (USA) 2 and I	1987	J Collingham beat S Shapcott at 19th
1930	D Fishwick beat G Collett (USA) 4 and 3	1988	J Furby beat J Wade 4 and 3
1931	E Wilson beat W Morgan 7 and 6	1989	H Dobson beat E Farquharson 6 and 5
1932	E Wilson beat CPR Montgomery 7 and 6	1990	J Hall beat H Wadsworth 2 and 2
1933	E Wilson beat D Plumpton 5 and 4	1991	V Michaud (FRA) beat W Doolan (AUS) 2 and 2
1934	AM Holm beat P Barton 6 and 5	1992	P Pedersen (DEN) beat J Morley I hole
1935	W Morgan beat P Barton 2 and 2	1993	C Lambert beat K Speak 2 and 2
1936	P Barton beat B Newell 5 and 3	1994	E Duggleby beat C Mourgue d'Algue 2 and I
1937	J Anderson beat D Park 6 and 4	1995	K Hall beat K Mourgue d'Algue 2 and 2
1938	AM Holm beat E Corlett 4 and 3	1996	K Kuehne (USA) beat B Morgan 5 and 3
1939	P Barton beat T Marks 2 and I	1997	A Rose beat M McKay 4 and 3
1940–45	*Not played*	1998	K Rostron beat G Nocera (FRA) 2 and 2
1946	GW Hetherington beat P Garvey I hole	1999	M Monnet (FRA) beat R Hudson I hole
1947	B Zaharias (USA) beat J Gordon 5 and 4	2000	R Hudson beat E Duggleby 5 and 4
1948	L Suggs (USA) beat J Donald I hole	2001	M Prieto (ESP) beat E Duggleby 4 and 3
1949	F Stephens beat V Reddan 5 and 4	2002	R Hudson beat L Wright 5 and 4
1950	Vicomtesse de St Sauveur (FRA) beat J Valentine 3 and 2	2003	E Serramia (ESP) beat P Odefey (GER) 2 holes
		2004	L Stahle (SWE) beat A Highgate 4 and 2
1951	PJ MacCann beat F Stephens 4 and 3	2005	L Stahle (SWE) beat C Coughlan 2 and 2
1952	M Paterson beat F Stephens at 39th	2006	B Mozo (ESP) beat A Nordqvist (SWE) 2 and I
1953	M Stewart (CAN) beat P Garvey 7 and 6	2007	C Ciganda (ESP) beat A Nordqvist (SWE) 4 and 3

Ladies British Open Amateur Stroke Play Championship (inaugurated 1969)

Malone

1	Roseanne Niven (Crieff)*	75-74-71-68—288
2	Kylie Walker (Buchanan Castle)	71-75-73-69—288

Niven won at the first extra hole

3	Tara Delaney (Carlow)	77-69-72-72—290
	Sahra Hassan (Vale of Glamorgan)	72-71-74-73—290

1969	A Irvin	1980	M Mahill	1991	J Morley	2002	B Brewerton
1970	M Everard	1981	J Soulsby	1992	J Hockley	2003	S McKevitt
1971	IC Robertson	1982	J Connachan	1993	J Hall	2004	C Queen*
1972	IC Robertson	1983	A Nicholas	1994	K Speak		*Beat S Evans and S McKevitt
1973	A Stant	1984	C Waite	1995	MJ Pons (ESP)		in sudden-death play-off
1974	J Greenhalgh	1985	IC Robertson	1996	C Kuld (DEN)	2005	H Macrae*
1975	J Greenhalgh	1986	C Hourihane	1997	KM Juul (DEN)		*Beat N Gergely (AUT) at 1st
1976	J Lee Smith	1987	L Bayman	1998	N Nijenhuis		extra hole
1977	M Everard	1988	K Mitchell	1999	B Brewerton	2006	A Rossi (ITA)
1978	J Melville	1989	H Dobson	2000	R Hudson	2007	M Reid
1979	M McKenna	1990	V Thomas	2001	R Hudson		

Ladies British Open Mid-Amateur Championship (inaugurated 2002)

Frilford Heath

Cancelled

2002	A Laing	2004	J Nicolson	2006	M Pow
2003	S Walton	2005	L McGowan	2007	E Duggleby

Senior Ladies British Open Amateur Championship Hilton Templepatrick

1	Chris Utermarck (GER)*	79-76-76—231
2	Susan Dye (Delamere Forest)	76-75-80—231

Utermarck won at the first extra hole

3	Janet Collingham (Sherwood Forest)	80-77-75—232
	Lorna Bennett (Ladybank)	79-77-76—232
	Jane Rees (Hendon)	78-75-79—232

1981	BM King	1988	C Bailey	1995	A Uzielli	2002	R Page
1982	P Riddiford	1989	C Bailey	1996	V Hassett	2003	C Burke (SWE)
1983	M Birtwistle	1990	A Uzielli	1997	T Wiesner (USA)	2004	E Ansgarius (SWE)
1984	O Semelaigne	1991	A Uzielli	1998	A Uzielli	2005	E Ansgarius (SWE)
1985	Dr G Costello	1992	A Uzielli	1999	A Uzielli	2006	C Quinn
1986	P Riddiford	1993	J Thornhill	2000	B Mogensen (DEN)	2007	A Murdoch
1987	O Semelaigne	1994	D Williams	2001	M McKenna		

English Ladies Close Amateur Championship (inaugurated 1912) Ganton

Leading Qualifier: 149   Rachel Jennings (Izaak Walton)

Quarter Finals

Charlotte Ellis (Minchinhampton) beat Sarah Walton (Clitheroe) 4 and 2
Hannah Barwood (Knowle) beat Liz Bennett (Brokenhurst Manor) 4 and 3
Emma Brown (Malton & Norton) beat Rachel Connor (Manchester) 6 and 5
Florentyna Parker (Royal Birkdale) beat Jenny Pease (Braintree) 2 and 1

Semi-Finals

Barwood beat Ellis 3 and 1
Parker beat Brown 1 hole

Final

Hannah Barwood beat Florentyna Parker 2 and 1

1912	M Gardner beat Mrs Cautley at 20th	1920	Joyce Wethered beat Cecil Leitch 2 and 1
1913	FW Brown beat Mrs McNair 1 hole	1921	Joyce Wethered beat Mrs Mudford 12 and 11
1914	Cecil Leitch beat Miss Bastin 2 and 1	1922	Joyce Wethered beat J Stocker 7 and 6
1915–1918	Not played	1923	Joyce Wethered beat Mrs TA Lodge 8 and 7
1919	Cecil Leitch beat Mrs Temple Dobell 10 and 8	1924	Joyce Wethered beat DR Fowler 8 and 7

English Ladies Close Amateur Championship *continued*

1925	DR Fowler beat J Winn 9 and 7
1926	Molly Gourlay beat Elsie Corlett 6 and 4
1927	Mrs H Guedalla beat Enid Wilson 1 hole
1928	Enid Wilson beat Dorothy Pearson 9 and 8
1929	Molly Gourlay beat Diana Fishwick 6 and 5
1930	Enid Wilson beat Mrs RO Porter 12 and 11
1931	Wanda Morgan beat Molly Gourlay 3 and 1
1932	Diana Fishwick beat Miss B Brown 5 and 4
1933	Dorothy Pearson beat M Johnson 5 and 3
1934	P Wade beat M Johnson 4 and 3
1935	Mrs M Garon beat Elsie Corlett at 38th
1936	Wanda Morgan beat P Wade 2 and 1
1937	Wanda Morgan beat M Fyshe 4 and 2
1938	Elsie Corlett beat J Winn 2 and 1
1939–1946	*Not played*
1947	M Wallis beat Elizabeth Price 3 and 1
1948	Frances Stephens beat Zara Bolton 1 hole
1949	Diana Critchley beat Lady Katharine Cairns 3 and 2
1950	Hon Mrs A Gee beat Pamela Davies 8 and 6
1951	Jeanne Bisgood beat A Keiller 2 and 1
1952	Pamela Davies beat Jacqueline Gordon 6 and 5
1953	Jeanne Bisgood beat J McIntyre 6 and 5
1954	Frances Stephens beat Elizabeth Price at 37th
1955	Frances Smith beat Elizabeth Price 4 and 3
1956	Bridget Jackson beat Ruth Ferguson 2 and 1
1957	Jeanne Bisgood beat Margaret Nichol 10 and 8
1958	Angela Bonallack beat Bridget Jackson 3 and 2
1959	Ruth Porter beat Frances Smith 5 and 4
1960	Margaret Nichol beat Angela Bonallack 3 and 1
1961	Ruth Porter beat Peggy Reece 2 holes
1962	Jean Roberts beat Angela Bonallack 3 and 1
1963	Angela Bonallack beat Elizabeth Chadwick 7 and 6
1964	Marley Spearman beat Mary Everard 6 and 5
1965	Ruth Porter beat G Cheetham 6 and 5
1966	Julia Greenhalgh beat Jean Holmes 3 and 1
1967	Ann Irvin beat Margaret Pickard 3 and 2
1968	Sally Barber beat Dinah Oxley 5 and 4
1969	Barbara Dixon beat M Wenyon 6 and 4

1970	Dinah Oxley beat Sally Barber 3 and 2
1971	Dinah Oxley beat Sally Barber 5 and 4
1972	Mary Everard beat Angela Bonallack 2 and 1
1973	Mickey Walker beat Carol Le Feuvre 6 and 5
1974	Ann Irvin beat Jill Thornhill 1 hole
1975	Beverly Huke beat Lynne Harrold 2 and 1
1976	Lynne Harrold beat Angela Uzielli 3 and 2
1977	Vanessa Marvin beat Mary Everard 1 hole
1978	Vanessa Marvin beat Ruth Porter 2 and 1
1979	Julia Greenhalgh beat Susan Hedges 2 and 1
1980	Beverley New beat Julie Walker 3 and 2
1981	Diane Christison beat S Cohen 2 holes
1982	Julie Walker beat C Nelson 4 and 3
1983	Linda Bayman beat C Macintosh 4 and 3
1984	Claire Waite beat Linda Bayman 3 and 2
1985	Patricia Johnson beat Linda Bayman 1 hole
1986	Jill Thornhill beat Susan Shapcott 3 and 1
1987	Joanne Furby beat Maria King 4 and 3
1988	Julie Wade beat Susan Shapcott at 19th
1989	Helen Dobson beat Simone Morgan 4 and 3
1990	Angela Uzielli beat Linzi Fletcher 2 and 1
1991	Nicola Buxton beat Karen Stupples 2 holes
1992	Caroline Hall beat Joanne Hockley 1 hole
1993	Nicola Buxton beat Sarah Burnell 2 and 1
1994	Julie Wade beat S Sharpe 1 hole
1995	Julie Wade beat Elaine Ratcliffe 2 and 1
1996	Joanne Hockley beat Lisa Educate 4 and 3
1997	Kim Rostron beat K Burton 4 and 2
1998	Elaine Ratcliffe beat Lisa Walters at 19th
1999	Fiona Brown beat Kerry Smith 2 and 1
2000	Emma Duggleby beat Rebecca Hudson 4 and 3
2001	Rebecca Hudson beat Emma Duggleby at 20th
2002	Kerry Knowles beat C Court 6 and 5
2003	Emma Duggleby beat N Edwards 2 and 1
2004	Kerry Smith beat S McKevitt 4 and 3
2005	Felicity Johnson beat S Walker at 20th
2006	Kiran Matharu beat Naomi Edwards 5 and 4
2007	Naomi Edwards beat Melissa Reid 2 and 1

English Ladies Close Amateur Stroke Play Championship (inaugurated 1984)

The Berkshire

1	Jodi Ewart (Catterick)*	70-69-76-70—285
2	Liz Bennett (Brokenhurst Manor)	71-73-71-70—285

Ewart won at the fourth extra hole

3	Ellie Gibbons (Blackwell Grange)	73-74-72-69—288
	Florentyna Parker (Royal Birkdale)	69-68-71-80—288
	Kerry Smith (Waterlooville)	72-70-73-73—288

1984	P Grice	1990	K Tebbet	1996	S Gallagher	2002	S Garbutt
1985	P Johnson	1991	J Morley	1997	L Tupholme	2003	S Walker*
1986	S Shapcott	1992	J Morley	1998	E Duggleby	2004	S Reddick
1987	J Wade	1993	J Hall	1999	C Lipscombe	2005	L Eastwood
1988	S Prosser	1994	F Brown	2000	R Hudson	2006	E Bennett
1989	S Robinson	1995	L Walton	2001	C Marron*	2007	J Ewart

English Senior Ladies Stroke Play Championship (inaugurated 1986)   *Beau Desert*

1	Janet Collingham (Sherwood Forest)	81-81-79—241
2	Carolyn Kirk (Ganton)	77-87-78—242
3	Rozalyn Adams (Addington Court)	77-82-85—244

1988	A Thompson	1993	A Uzielli	1998	E Boatman	2003	C Caldwell*
1989	C Bailey	1994	S Bassindale	1999	S Westall	2004	V Saunders
1990	A Thompson	1995	V Morgan	2000	E McCombe	2005	C Stirling
1991	C Bailey	1996	A Uzielli	2001	R Page	2006	G Bray
1992	A Thompson	1997	A Thompson	2002	C Caldwell	2007	S Dye

English Senior Women's Close Match Play Championship (inaugurated 1994)

Stoneham

Leading Qualifier: 153 Christine Quinn (Hockley)

Semi-Finals:
Barbara Laird (Sandiway) beat Janet Collingham (Sherwood Forest) 1 hole
Susan Dye (Delamere Forest) beat Carolyn Kirk (Ganton) 1 hole

Final:
Susan Dye beat Barbara Laird 3 and 2

1994	E Annison	1998	E McCombe	2002	C Stirling	2006	C Watson
1995	A Thompson	1999	E McCombe	2003	C Watson	2007	S Ellis
1996	R Farrow	2000	E McCombe	2004	C Stirling		
1997	G Palmer	2001	A Vine	2005	G Bray		

English Ladies Open Mid-Amateur Championship (inaugurated 1982)   *Wallasey*

Leading Qualifier: Emma Fairnie (Dunbar Ladies) 70-78—148

Quarter Finals:
Nicole Whitmore (Woburn) beat Natalie Lowe (Prestbury)
1 hole
Lucy Williams (Mid-Herts) beat Hermione FitzGerald (Links)
3 and 2
Charlotte Dalton (Ladbrook Park) beat Holly Aitchison
(The Bedfordshire) 3 and 2
Alex Bushby (Strathmore) beat Kate Whitmore (Sandiway)
1 hole

Semi-Finals:
Williams beat N Whitmore 3 and 2
Dalton beat Bushby 4 and 3

Final:
Lucy Williams beat Charlotte Dalton

1982	J Rhodes	1989	L Fairclough	1996	R Bailey	2003	N Timmins
1983	L Davies	1990	L Fletcher	1997	K Smith	2004	F More
1984	P Grice	1991	J Morley	1998	J Lamb	2005	N Edwards
1985	S Lowe	1992	K Speak	1999	K Fisher	2006	C Ellis
1986	S Moorcroft	1993	K Speak	2000	K Keogh	2007	C Aitken
1987	J Wade	1994	J Oliver	2001	A Keighley		
1988	S Morgan	1995	K Smith	2002	*Not played*		

Irish Ladies Close Amateur Championship (inaugurated 1894)   *Westport*

Leading Qualifier: 143 Lisa Maguire (Slieve Russell) 69-74

Quarter Finals:
Lisa Maguire (Slieve Russell) beat Mary Dowling (New Ross)
3 and 1
Gemma Hegarty (Greencastle) beat Jennifer Gannon
(Co. Louth) 5 and 4
Leona Maguire (Slieve Russell) beat Darragh McGowan
(Ballybofey & Stranorlar) 1 hole
Dawn Marie Conaty (Ashbourne) beat Una Marsden
(Tullamore) 8 and 7

Semi-Finals:
Lisa Maguire beat Hegarty 3 and 2
Leona Maguire beat Conaty 4 and 3

Final
Leona Maguire beat Lisa Maguire
3 and 2

1894	Miss Mulligan beat N Graham 3 and 2	1909	Miss Ormsby beat V Hezlet 4 and 2
1895	Miss Cox beat Miss MacLaine 3 and 2	1910	M Harrison beat Miss Magill 5 and 4
1896	N Graham beat N Brownrigg 4 and 3	1911	M Harrison beat F Walker-Leigh 6 and 4
1897	N Graham beat Miss Magill 4 and 3	1912	M Harrison beat Mrs Cramsie 5 and 3
1898	Miss Magill beat M Hezlet 1 hole	1913	J Jackson beat M Harrison 4 and 3
1899	M Hezlet beat Miss Adair 5 and 4	1914	J Jackson beat Miss Meldon 3 and 2
1900	Miss Adair beat V Hezlet 9 and 7	1915–1918	*Not played*
1901	Miss Adair beat F Walker-Leigh 4 and 2	1919	J Jackson beat M Alexander 5 and 4
1902	Miss Adair beat ME Stuart 9 and 7	1920	J Jackson beat Mrs Cramsie 5 and 4
1903	Miss Adair beat V Hezlet 7 and 5	1921	Miss Stuart French beat M Fitzgibbon 4 and 3
1904	M Hezlet beat F Walker-Leigh 3 and 2	1922	Mrs Claude Gotto beat MR Hirsch 2 holes
1905	M Hezlet beat F Hezlet 2 and 1	1923	J Jackson beat Mrs Babington 5 and 4
1906	M Hezlet beat F Hezlet 2 and 1	1924	CG Thornton beat Miss Hewitt 4 and 3
1907	F Walker-Leigh beat Mrs Fitzgibbon 4 and 3	1925	J Jackson beat JF Jameson 2 and 1
1908	M Hezlet beat F Hezlet 5 and 4	1926	P Jameson beat CH Murland 5 and 3

Irish Ladies Close Amateur Championship – *continued*

1927	Miss McLoughlin beat F Blake 2 holes	1970	P Garvey beat M Earner 2 and 1
1928	Mrs Dwyer beat H Clarke 3 and 2	1971	E Bradshaw beat M Mooney 3 and 1
1929	MA Hall beat I Taylor 1 hole	1972	M McKenna beat I Butler 5 and 4
1930	JB Walker beat JF Jameson 2 and 1	1973	M Mooney beat M McKenna 2 and 1
1931	Miss Pentony beat JH Todd 2 and 1	1974	M McKenna beat V Singleton 3 and 2
1932	B Latchford beat D Ferguson 7 and 5	1975	M Gorry beat E Bradshaw 1 hole
1933	Miss Pentony beat F Blacke 3 and 2	1976	C Nesbitt beat M McKenna at 20th
1934	P Sherlock Fletcher beat JB Walker 3 and 2	1977	M McKenna beat R Hegarty 2 holes
1935	D Ferguson beat Miss Ellis 2 and 1	1978	M Gorry beat I Butler 4 and 3
1936	C Tiernan beat S Moore 7 and 6	1979	M McKenna beat C Nesbitt 6 and 5
1937	HV Glendinning beat EL Kidd at 37th	1980	C Nesbitt beat C Hourihane 1 hole
1938	J Beck beat B Jackson 5 and 4	1981	M McKenna beat M Kenny 1 hole
1939	C MacGeagh beat E Gikdea 1 hole	1982	M McKenna beat M Madill 2 and 1
1940–1945 *Not played*		1983	C Hourihane beat V Hassett 6 and 4
1946	P Garvey beat V Reddan at 39th	1984	C Hourihane beat M Madill at 19th
1947	P Garvey beat C Syme 5 and 4	1985	C Hourihane beat M McKenna 4 and 3
1948	P Garvey beat V Reddan 9 and 7	1986	T O'Reilly beat E Higgins 4 and 3
1949	C Syme beat J Beck 9 and 7	1987	C Hourihane beat C Hickey 5 and 4
1950	P Garvey beat T Marks 6 and 4	1988	L Bolton beat E Higgins 2 and 1
1951	P Garvey beat D Forster 12 and 10	1989	M McKenna beat C Wickham at 19th
1952	DM Forster beat PG McCann 3 and 2	1990	ER McDaid beat L Callan 2 and 1
1953	P Garvey beat Mrs Hegarty 8 and 7	1991	C Hourihane beat E McDaid 1 hole
1954	P Garvey beat HV Glendinning 13 and 12	1992	ER Power beat C Hourihane 1 hole
1955	P Garvey beat A O'Donohoe 10 and 9	1993	E Higgins beat A Rogers 2 and 1
1956	P O'Sullivan beat JF Hegarty 14 and 12	1994	L Webb beat H Kavanagh at 20th
1957	P Garvey beat K McCann 3 and 2	1995	ER Power beat S O'Brien-Kenney 1 hole
1958	P Garvey beat Z Fallon 7 and 6	1996	B Hackett beat L Behan 3 and 2
1959	P Garvey beat H Colhoun 12 and 10	1997	S Fanagan beat ER Power 4 and 3
1960	P Garvey beat PG McCann 5 and 3	1998	L Behan beat O Purfield at 19th
1961	K McCann beat A Sweeney 5 and 3	1999	C Coughlan beat ER Power 4 and 3
1962	P Garvey beat M Earner 7 and 6	2000	A Coffey beat C Coughlan 3 and 2
1963	P Garvey beat E Barnett 9 and 7	2001	A Coffey beat C Coughlan 4 and 3
1964	Z Fallon beat P O'Sullivan at 37th	2002	R Coakley beat A Coffey 4 and 3
1965	E Purcell beat P O'Sullivan 3 and 2	2003	M Gillen beat M Dunne 2 holes
1966	E Bradshaw beat P O'Sullivan 3 and 2	2004	D Smith beat T Delaney at 20th
1967	G Brandom beat P O'Sullivan 3 and 2	2005	T Mangan beat C Tucker 3 and 2
1968	E Bradshaw beat M McKenna 3 and 2	2006	T Mangan beat M Gillen 2 and 1
1969	M McKenna beat C Hickey 3 and 2	2007	K Delaney beat M Riordan 3 and 2

Irish Ladies Open Amateur Stroke Play Championship   (inaugurated 1993)

Elm Park

1	Breanne Loucks (Wrexham)	69-72-73—214
2	Roseanne Niven (Crieff)	73-74-70—217
3	Lisa Maguire (Slieve Russell)	72-74-72—218
	Charlotte Wild (Mere)	76-73-69—218

1993	T Eakin	1998	S O'Brien	2003	C Coughlan	2006	M Gillen
1994	H Kavanagh	1999	H Kavanagh	2004	T Delaney*	2007	S Keating (AUS)
1995	N Quigg	2000	R Cookley	*Beat N Gillen at 8th extra			
1996	ER Power	2001	A Laing	*hole*			
1997	Y Cassidy	2002	R Coakley	2005	T Delaney		

Irish Senior Ladies Close Championship   *Hollystown*

Quarter Finals:

Valerie Hassett (Ennis) beat Carmel Cahill (Hermitage)
  2 holes

Sheena O'Brien-Kenney (Grange) beat Mary Madden
  (Ballinasloe) 1 hole

Mary McKenna (Donabate) beat Pauline Walsh (Headfort)
  4 and 3

Violet McBride (Belvoir Park) beat Helen Jones (Strabane)
  2 and 1

Semi-Finals:

O'Brien-Kenney beat Hassett 1 hole
McKenna beat McBride 5 and 4

Final:

Sheena O'Brien-Kenney beat Mary
  McKenna 1 hole

1988	M Magan	1993	G Costello	1998	M Moran	2003	P Williamson
1989	Dr G Costello	1994	G Costello	1999	R Fanagan	2004	A Murdoch (CAN)
1990	A Hesketh	1995	A Gaynor	2000	S Kearney	2005	A Murdoch (CAN)
1991	C Hickey	1996	M Stuart	2001	M McKenna*	2006	T O'Reilly
1992	C Hickey	1997	M O'Donnell	2002	P Williamson	2007	M Madden

Irish Senior Ladies Open Stroke Play Championship *Lisburn*

1	Vikki Thomas (WAL)	82-78-78—238
2	Helen Jones (Strabane)	78-84-77—239
3	Diane Williams (CAN)	79-85-79—243

2007	A Murdoch (CAN)

Scottish Ladies Close Amateur Championship (inaugurated 1903) *Moray (Old)*

Leading Qualifier: 149   Kelsey MacDonald (Nairn Dunbar) 75-74

Quarter Finals:
Jocelyn Carthew (Ladybank) beat Sammy Vass (Tain) 2 and 1
Kylie Walker (Buchanan Castle) beat Jane Turner (Mortonhall) at 22nd
Laura Murray (Alford) beat Clare-Marie Carlton (Fereneze) 2 and 1
Michele Thomson (McDonald Ellon) beat Louise Kenney (Pitreavie) 3 and 2

Semi-Finals:
Carthew beat Walker 3 and 1
Thomson beat Murray at 20th

Final:
Michele Thomson beat Jocelyn Carthew 2 and 1

1903	AM Glover beat MA Graham 1 hole
1904	MA Graham beat M Bishop 6 and 5
1905	D Campbell beat MA Graham at 19th
1906	D Campbell beat AM Glover 3 and 1
1907	FS Teacher beat D Campbell at 21st
1908	D Campbell beat MA Cairns 7 and 6
1909	EL Kyle beat D Campbell 1 hole
1910	EL Kyle beat AM Glover 4 and 3
1911	E Grant-Suttie beat EL Kyle 1 hole
1912	DM Jenkins beat M Neil Fraser 4 and 2
1913	JW McCulloch beat R Mackintosh 4 and 3
1914	ER Anderson beat FS Teacher at 20th
1915–1919	*Not played*
1920	Mrs JB Watson beat L Scroggie 5 and 3
1921	Mrs JB Watson beat Mrs M Martin 1 hole
1922	Mrs JB Watson beat A Kyle 2 and 1
1923	Mrs WH Nicholson beat Mrs JB Watson 2 and 1
1924	CPR Montgomery beat H Cameron 5 and 4
1925	J Percy beat E Grant-Suttie 2 and 1
1926	MJ Wood beat Mrs J Cochrane 2 and 1
1927	B Inglis beat H Cameron 1 hole
1928	JW McCulloch beat P Ramsay 3 and 1
1929	Mrs JB Watson beat Doris Park 3 and 1
1930	Helen Holm beat Doris Park 1 hole
1931	JW McCulloch beat Doris Park at 19th
1932	Helen Holm beat Mrs G Coates at 23rd
1933	MJ Couper beat Helen Holm at 22nd
1934	Nan Baird beat J Anderson 1 hole
1935	M Robertson-Durham beat Nan Baird at 20th
1936	Doris Park beat CPR Montgomery at 19th
1937	Helen Holm beat Mrs I Bowhill 3 and 2
1938	Jessie Anderson beat Helen Holm 2 holes
1939	Jessie Anderson beat Catherine Park at 19th
1939–1946	*Not played*
1947	Jean Donald beat J Kerr 5 and 3
1948	Helen Holm beat Vivien Falconer 5 and 4
1949	Jean Donald beat Helen Holm 6 and 4
1950	Helen Holm beat Charlotte Beddows 6 and 5
1951	Mrs G Valentine beat Moira Paterson 3 and 2
1952	Jean Donald beat Mrs RT Peel 13 and 11

1953	Mrs G Valentine beat Jean Donald 8 and 7
1954	Mrs RT Peel beat Mrs G Valentine 7 and 6
1955	Mrs G Valentine beat Millicent Couper 8 and 6
1956	Mrs G Valentine beat Helen Holm 8 and 7
1957	Marigold Speir beat Helen Holm 7 and 5
1958	Dorothea Sommerville beat Janette Robertson 1 hole
1959	Janette Robertson beat Belle McCorkindale 6 and 5
1960	Janette Robertson beat Dorothea Sommerville 2 and 1
1961	JS Wright (née Robertson) beat AM Lurie 1 hole
1962	JB Lawrence beat C Draper 5 and 4
1963	JB Lawrence beat IC Robertson 2 and 1
1964	JB Lawrence beat SM Reid 5 and 3
1965	IC Robertson beat JB Lawrence 5 and 4
1966	IC Robertson beat M Fowler 2 and 1
1967	J Hastings beat A Laing 5 and 3
1968	Joan Smith beat J Rennie 10 and 9
1969	JH Anderson beat K Lackie 5 and 4
1970	A Laing beat IC Robertson 1 hole
1971	IC Robertson beat A Ferguson 3 and 2
1972	IC Robertson beat CJ Lugton 5 and 3
1973	I Wright beat Dr AJ Wilson 2 holes
1974	Dr AJ Wilson beat K Lackie at 22nd
1975	LA Hope beat JW Smith 1 hole
1976	S Needham beat T Walker 3 and 2
1977	CJ Lugton beat M Thomson 1 hole
1978	IC Robertson beat JW Smith 2 holes
1979	G Stewart beat LA Hope 2 and 1
1980	IC Robertson beat F Anderson 1 hole
1981	A Gemmill beat W Aitken 2 and 1
1982	J Connachan beat P Wright at 19th
1983	G Stewart beat F Anderson 3 and 1
1984	G Stewart beat A Gemmill 3 and 2
1985	A Gemmill beat D Thomson 2 and 1
1986	IC Robertson beat L Hope 3 and 2
1987	F Anderson beat C Middleton 4 and 3
1988	S Lawson beat F Anderson 3 and 1
1989	J Huggon beat L Anderson 5 and 4
1990	E Farquharson beat S Huggan 3 and 2

Scottish Ladies Close Amateur Championship *continued*

1991	C Lambert beat F Anderson 3 and 2		2000	L Kenny beat H Stirling 1 hole	
1992	J Moody beat E Farquharson 2 and 1		2001	L Morton beat L Mackay 6 and 4	
1993	C Lambert beat M McKay 5 and 4		2002	H Stirling beat A Laing 3 and 1	
1994	C Matthew beat V Melvin 1 hole		2003	A Laing beat C Hargan 4 and 2	
1995	H Monaghan beat S McMaster at 21st		2004	A Laing beat C Queen 2 holes	
1996	A Laing beat A Rose 1 hole		2005	F Lockhart beat A Laing 3 and 2	
1997	A Rose beat H Monaghan 3 and 2		2006	M Pow beat A Laing 2 and 1	
1998	E Moffat beat C Agnew 4 and 3		2007	J Wilson beat E Ogilvy 2 and 1	
1999	J Smith beat A Laing 2 and 1 Dunbar				

Scottish Ladies Open Stroke Play Championship (Helen Holm Trophy)
(inaugurated 1973)   *Royal Troon and Troon Portland*

1	Barbara Genuini (FRA)	74-70-70—214
2	Jacqueline Hedwall (SWE)	75-74-67—216
3	Malin Enarsson (SWE)	71-74-72—217

1973	Belle Robertson	1983	Jane Connachan	1993	Julie Wade (ENG)	2002	Heather Stirling
1974	Sandra Needham	1984	Gillian Stewart	1994	K Tebbet	2003	Nathalie David
1975	Muriel Thomson	1985	Pamela Wright	1995	Maria Hjörth (SWE)	2004	Emma Duggleby
1976	Muriel Thomson	1986	Belle Robertson	1996	J Hockley		(ENG)
1977	Beverly Huke (ENG)	1987	Elaine Farquharson	1997	Kim Rostron	2005	Martina Gillen (IRL)
1978	Wilma Aitken	1988	Elaine Farquharson	1998	K-M Juul Esbjerg	2006	Melissa Reid
1979	Belle Robertson	1989	Sara Robinson		(SWE)	2007	Melissa Reid
1980	Wilma Aitken	1990	Catriona Lambert	1999	L Nicholson		
1981	Gillian Stewart	1991	Julie Wade (ENG)	2000	Rebecca Hudson		
1982	Wilma Aitken	1992	Mhairi McKay	2001	Fiona Brown		

Scottish Senior Ladies (Close) Amateur Championship   (inaugurated 1997)

Deeside

Stroke Play

1	Mary Smith (Tain)	79-79—158
2	Moira Thomson (North Berwick)	82-77—159
3	Fiona De Vries (St Rule)	81-79—160
	Margaret Tough (Falkirk)	77-83—160

1997	A Wilson	2000	P Hutton	2003	K Ballantyne	2006	F De Vries
1998	I McIntosh	2001	F Liddle	2004	K Sutherland	2007	K Sutherland
1999	P Williamson	2002	P Williamson	2005	P Williamson		

Match Play

Semi-Finals:
Lorna Bennett (Ladybank) beat Mary Smith (Tain) 2 holes
Fiona De Vries (St Rule) beat Jill Harrison (Cruden Bay) 4 and 3

Final:
Lorna Bennett beat Fiona De Vries at 20th

2006	F De Vries beat H Faulds 4 and 3		2007	L Bennett beat M Tough 2 and 1

Scottish Veteran Ladies Championship *Blairgowrie*

Semi-Finals:
Fiona de Vries (East) beat Sheila Cuthbertson (Borders)
  at 20th
Vivien Welsh (Highland) beatKathleen Sutherland (Northern)
  1 hole

Final:
Fiona de Vries beat Vivien Welsh
  1 hole

2006	K Sutherland beat N Fenton 4 and 3		2007	H Anderson beat C McAndrew 1 hole

Welsh Ladies Close Amateur Championship (inaugurated 1905) *Monmouthshire*

Leading Qualifier: 146   Breanne Loucks (Wrexham) 77-69

Quarter Finals
Rhian Wyn Thomas (Vale of Glamorgan) beat Breanne Loucks (Wrexham) 1 hole

Stephanie Evans (Vale of Llangollen) beat Hannah Jenkins (Cradoc) 3 and 2

Sahra Hassan (Vale of Glamorgan) beat Kelly Miller (Penrhos) 7 and 6

Kirsty O'Connor (Nelson) beat Sarah Morgan (Mountain Ash) 1 hole

Semi-Finals
Evans beat Wyn Thomas 4 and 3

O'Connor beat Hassan 1 hole

Final
Kirsty O'Connor beat Stephanie Evans 2 holes

1905	E Young beat B Duncan 2 and 1	1962	M Oliver beat P Roberts 4 and 2
1906	B Duncan beat Mrs Storry 5 and 4	1963	P Roberts beat N Sneddon 7 and 5
1907	B Duncan beat Mrs Wenham 5 and 4	1964	M Oliver beat M Wright 1 hole
1908	B Duncan beat Miss Lloyd Williams 4 and 2	1965	M Wright beat E Brown 3 and 2
1909	B Duncan beat Mrs Ellis Griffiths 4 and 3	1966	A Hughes beat P Roberts 5 and 4
1910	Miss Lloyd Roberts beat Miss Leaver 4 and 3	1967	M Wright beat C Phipps at 21st
1911	Miss Clay beat Miss Allington-Hughes 2 and 1	1968	S Hales beat M Wright 3 and 2
1912	B Duncan beat P Williams 4 and 2	1969	P Roberts beat A Hughes 3 and 2
1913	Miss Brooke beat Miss Shaw at 19th	1970	A Briggs beat J Morris at 19th
1914	Mrs Vivian Phillips beat Miss Morgan 4 and 3	1971	A Briggs beat EN Davies 2 and 1
1915–1919	*Not played*	1972	A Hughes beat J Rogers 3 and 2
1920	Mrs Rupert Phillips beat M Marley 8 and 6	1973	A Briggs beat J John 3 and 2
1921	M Marley beat I Rieben 7 and 5	1974	A Briggs beat Dr H Lyall 3 and 2
1922	J Duncan beat H Franklyn Thomas 9 and 8	1975	A Johnson (née Hughes) beat K Rawlings 1 hole
1923	MR Cox beat M Marley at 39th	1976	T Perkins beat A Johnson 4 and 2
1924	MR Cox beat B Pyman 11 and 10	1977	T Perkins beat P Whitley 5 and 4
1925	MR Cox beat J Rhys 9 and 7	1978	P Light beat A Briggs 2 and 1
1926	MC Justice beat A Smalley 4 and 3	1979	V Rawlings beat A Briggs 2 holes
1927	J Duncan beat Mrs Blake 1 hole	1980	M Rawlings beat A Briggs 2 and 1
1928	J Duncan beat I Rieben 2 and 1	1981	M Rawlings beat A Briggs 5 and 3
1929	I Rieben beat B Pyman 2 and 1	1982	V Thomas (née Rawlings) beat M Rawlings 7 and 6
1930	MJ Jeffreys beat I Rieben 2 holes	1983	V Thomas beat T Thomas (née Perkins) 1 hole
1931	MJ Jeffreys beat B Pyman 4 and 2	1984	S Roberts beat K Davies 5 and 4
1932	I Rieben beat MJ Jeffreys 2 and 1	1985	V Thomas beat S Jump 1 hole
1933	MJ Jeffreys beat Mrs Bridge 2 and 1	1986	V Thomas beat L Isherwood 7 and 6
1934	I Rieben beat MJ Jeffreys 3 and 2	1987	V Thomas beat S Roberts 3 and 1
1935	*Abandoned*	1988	S Roberts beat F Connor 4 and 2
1936	I Rieben beat M Thompson 2 and 1	1989	H Lawson beat V Thomas 2 and 1
1937	GS Emery beat Dr P Whitaker 10 and 9	1990	S Roberts beat H Wadsworth 3 and 2
1938	B Pyman beat GS Emery 1 hole	1991	V Thomas beat H Lawson 4 and 3
1939	B Burrell beat H Reynolds 2 and 1	1992	J Foster beat S Boyes 4 and 3
1940–1946	*Not played*	1993	A Donne beat V Thomas at 19th
1947	M Barron beat E Jones 1 hole	1994	V Thomas beat L Dermott at 19th
1948	N Seely beat M Barron 12 and 11	1995	L Dermott beat K Stark at 19th
1949	S Bryan Smith beat E Brown 3 and 2	1996	L Dermott beat V Thomas 4 and 3
1950	Dr Garfield Evans beat Nancy Cook 2 and 1	1997	E Pilgrim beat L Davis 4 and 2
1951	E Bromley-Davenport beat Nancy Cook 1 hole	1998	L Davis beat R Morgan 1 hole
1952	Elsie Lever beat Pat Roberts 6 and 5	1999	R Brewerton beat R Morgan at 19th
1953	Nancy Cook beat Elsie Lever 3 and 2	2000	K Evans beat K Phillips at 19th
1954	Nancy Cook beat ED Brown 1 hole	2001	B Brewerton beat S Jones 2 and 1
1955	Nancy Cook beat Pat Roberts 2 holes	2002	E Pilgrim beat A Highgate 1 hole
1956	Pat Roberts beat M Barron 2 and 1	2003	K Phillips beat K Walls 2 and 1
1957	M Barron beat Pat Roberts 6 and 4	2004	S Jones beat A Highgate 1 hole
1958	Nancy Cook Wright beat Pat Roberts 1 hole	2005	S Jones beat S Evans 5 and 4
1959	Pat Roberts beat A Gwyther 6 and 4	2006	S Evans beat B Harries 3 and 2
1960	M Barron beat E Brown 8 and 6	2007	B Loucks beat T Davies 1 hole
1961	M Oliver beat N Sneddon 5 and 4		

Scottish Champion of Champions *Glasgow Gailes*

1	Alexandra Bushby (Northern Division)*	76
2	Carly Booth (Scottish Girls)	76

Bushby won at the first extra hole

3	Cara Gruber (Northern Counties)	78
	Rachael Livingstone (Midlothian)	78

2004	Clare Queen	2005	Krystle Caithness	2006	Elaine Moffat	2007	Claire Hargan

Welsh Senior Ladies Match Play Championship (inaugurated 1990) *Monmouthshire*

Semi-Finals
Vicki Thomas (Carmarthen) beat Denise Richards (Bargoed) 5 and 4
Janet Doleman (Rushcliffe) beat Trudy Carradice (Pyle & Kenfig) 4 and 3

Final
Vicki Thomas beat Janet Doleman 3 and 2

1990	E Higgs	1995	C Thomas	2000	F Shehan	2005	V Thomas
1991	H Lyall	1996	C Thomas	2001	F Shehan	2006	V Thomas
1992	P Morgan	1997	C Thomas	2002	C Thomas	2007	A Lewis
1993	P Morgan	1998	C Thomas	2003	C Thomas		
1994	C Thomas	1999	V Mackenzie	2004	C Thomas		

Welsh Ladies Open Amateur Strokeplay Championship (inaugurated 1976)

Pyle & Kenfig

1	Rhian Wyn Thomas (Vale of Glamorgan)	80-77-71—228
2	Hannah Barwood (Knowle)	78-81-73—232
	Niamh Kitching (Claremorris)	77-73-82—232

1976	P Light	1985	C Swallow	1994	A Rose	2003	V Laing
1977	J Greenhalgh	1986	H Wadsworth	1995	F Brown	2004	D Masters
1978	S Hedges	1987	S Shapcott	1996	E Duggleby	2005	H Brockway*
1979	S Crowcroft	1988	S Shapcott	1997	K Edwards		*Beat K Matharu at 3rd
1980	T Thomas	1989	V Thomas	1998	G Simpson		extra hole
1981	V Thomas	1990	L Hackney	1999	A Walker	2006	N Edwards
1982	V Thomas	1991	M Sutton	2000	R Prout	2007	H MacRae
1983	J Thornhill	1992	C Lambert	2001	V Laing		
1984	L Davies	1993	J Hall	2002	V Laing		

Welsh Senior Ladies Championship *Rolls of Monmouth*

1	Jane Rees (Hendon)*	80-77—157
2	Vicki Thomas (Carmarthen)	78-79—¡57

Rees won at the first extra hole

3	Janet Doleman (Rushcliffe)	80-80—160

2006	V Thomas	2007	V Thomas

Ladies European Open Amateur Championship (inaugurated 1986)

Schloss Schönborn, Austria

1	Carlotta Ciganda (ESP)*	70-73-71-75—289
2	Maria Hernandez (ESP)	70-73-70-76—289

Ciganda won after a three-hole play-off

3	Christel Boelion (NED)	69-73-73-75—290

1986	M Koch (GER)	1994	M Fischer (GER)	2000	E Duggleby (ENG)	2006	B Mozo (ESP)
1988	F Descampe (BEL)	1995	M Hjörth (SWE)	2001	M Eberl (GER)	2007	C Hedwall* (SWE)
1990	M Koch (GER)	1996	S Cavalleri (ITA)	2002	B Brewerton (WAL)		*Beat C Ciganda (ESP) at 3rd
1991	D Bourson (FRA)	1997	S Cavalleri (ITA)	2003	V Beauchet (FRA)		extra hole
1992	J Morley (ENG)	1998	G Sergas (ITA)	2004	C Ciganda (ESP)		
1993	V Steinsrud (NOR)	1999	S Sandolo (ITA)	2005	J Schaeffer (FRA)		

European Senior Ladies Championship (inaugurated 2000) *Oceanico, Portugal*

1	Virginie Burrus (FRA)	75-74-76—225
2	Vicky Pertierra (ESP)	79-77-75—231
3	Cecilia Mourgue D'Algue (FRA)	77-81-75—233

2000	C Mourgue d'Algue (FRA)	2002	C Mourgue d'Algue (FRA)	2004	M-B Heden (SWE)	2007	V Burrus (FRA)
				2005	C Mourgue d'Algue (FRA)		
2001	C Mourgue d'Algue (FRA)	2003	C Cros Chatrier (FRA)	2006	G Ekman (SWE)		

National Orders of Merit 2008

EWGA Order of Merit

1	Elizabeth Bennett (Brokenhurst Manor)	1679
2	Rachel Jennings (Izaak Walton)	1321
3	Naomi Edwards 1 (Ganton)	1254
4	Kerry Smith (Waterlooville)	1121
5	Florentyna Parker (Royal Birkdale)	1090
6	Jodi Ewart (Catterick)	1060
7	Charlotte Ellis (Minchinhampton)	626
8	Hannah Barwood (Knowle)	601
9	Holly Aitchison (Bedfordshire)	555
10	Rachel Connor (Manchester)	500

ILGU Order of Merit

1	Tara Delaney (Carlow)	945
2	Niamh Kitching (Claremorris)	796
3	Lisa Maguire (Slieve Russell)	722
4	Leona Maguire (Slieve Russell)	666
5	Deirdre Smith (Co.Louth)	350
6	Aedin Murphy (Carlow)	345
7	Danielle McVeigh (RCDL)	343
8	Karen Delaney (Carlow)	316
9	Dawn Marie Conaty (Ashbourne)	252
10	Gemma Hegarty (Greencastle)	242

SLGA Order of Merit

1	Kylie Walker (Buchanan Castle)	3250
2	Roseanne Niven (Crieff)	2187
3	Laura Murray (Alford)	2030
4	Louise Kenney (Pitreavie)	1905
5	Megan Briggs (Kilmacolm)	1477
6	Michele Thomson (McDonald Ellon)	1460
7	Pamela Pretswell (Bothwell Castle)	1269
8	Jane Turner (Mortonhall)	1203
9	Kelsey MacDonald (Nairn Dunbar)	1155
10	Lesley Hendry (Routenburn)	1107

WGU Order of Merit

1	Breanne Loucks (Wrexham)	788
2	Sahra Hassan (Vale of Glamorgan)	665
3	Rhian Wyn Thomas (Vale of Glamorgan)	556
4	Tara Davies (Holyhead)	264
5	Kirsty O'Connor (Nelson)	250
6	Stephanie Evans (Vale of Llangollen)	199
7	Hannah Jenkins (Cradoc)	183
8	Samantha Birks (Wolstanton)	125
9	Becky Harries (Haverfordwest)	69
10	Lucy Gould (Bargoed)	67

Teenagers' success in the Home Counties Championships

Teenagers won three of the four Home Countries Championships and the other was won by a 20-year-old! The youngest winner was 13-year-old Leona Maguire from Slieve Russell who beat her twin sister Lisa 3 and 2 in the Lancome-sponsored Irish final played in wet weather at Westport. Lisa did not go away empty handed from the Championship, however, as she had taken the Leitrim Cup as leading qualifier.

Seventeen-year-old Hannah Barwood from the Knowle Club in Gloucestershire became one of the youngest winners of the English Championship when she beat Curtis Cup golfer Florentyna Parker 2 and 1 in the final at Ganton. Hannah, the English Schools champion, had beaten another Curtis Cup player Liz Bennett in the quarter-finals. Hannah is the third teenager to win the title in the past four years. Felicity Johnson was 18 when she won in 2005 and Kiran Mathuru was 17 when she was successful in 2006. In Scotland 19-year-old Michele Thomson, the former Scottish Girl's champion from the McDonald GC in Aberdeenshire, beat Jocelyn Carthew by 2 and 1 in the final at Moray GC. The oldest of the Home Nation winners was Kirsty O'Connor, a 20-year-old student at Ball State University in Indiana who comes from Burnley and became Welsh champion with a two holes victory over Steph Evans at the Monmouthshire Club.

British Golf Museum

Award winning museum at the heart of the Home of Golf

The five star British Golf Museum sits at the heart of the Home of Golf, directly opposite The Royal and Ancient Golf Clubhouse and a mere 67½ yards from the 1st tee of the Old Course.

With exhibits spanning more than three centuries, the Museum highlights key moments in golf's diverse past and brings to life the people who have shaped its history and helped popularise the game.

Marvel at the oldest known set of golf clubs in the world, which date from the early 18th century. Compare the design and materials of these play clubs, long spoons and rut irons with the lightweight materials such as graphite, titanium and tungsten used today.

Alternatively, visitors can trace developments in the manufacture of the golf ball – from the featheries made by Allan Robertson in the mid 19th century to the surlyn covered, four-piece balls of the 21st century.

Bets, challenge matches, amateur tournaments and The Open Championship all feature in the displays. Search for items relating to your golfing hero, whether it is The Open Championship medal won by Tom Morris Jr. in 1872 or the cap worn by Tiger Woods at St Andrews in 2005.

A gallery dedicated to *The Open Championships since 1946* provides a tour of the venues which host golf's oldest major, giving a unique opportunity to admire at close range a full-scale replica of the Claret Jug, the most coveted prize in the professional game. The excitement of The Open can be re-lived in short films which capture the drama from 1923, when Arthur Havers won at Troon, until 2008, when Padraig Harrington successfully defended his title at Birkdale.

Recently an exhibition entitled *Winning in Style: The Ladies' Game Since 1976* was unveiled. Focusing on the growth of ladies' golf since 1976, the first year of the Women's British Open, it covers both the professional and amateur game. Stylish displays showcase some of the most sought-after trophies in women's golf, including the Ladies' British Open Amateur Championship trophy and the Ricoh Women's British Open trophy, which was introduced in 2007.

The Museum continually strives to improve displays and set high standards of interpretation. Interactive displays provide alternative ways of engaging with the history of the game. In *Pages of History*, early documents from the archive of The Royal and Ancient Golf Club can be viewed digitally. Rare moving image, which has been restored and digitised, captures the Great Triumvirate of Braid, Taylor and Vardon in action, while the oldest known golf match, played in 1898 between Willie Park Jr. and Willie Fernie, is a special viewing treat for golf enthusiasts.

As a grand finale, visitors are invited to practice putting using replica clubs and balls from the last 175 years.

A visit to the British Golf Museum is the perfect break from playing golf.

www.britishgolfmuseum.co.uk

Team Events

Curtis Cup (Instituted 1932)
Great Britain & Ireland v USA (home team names first)

Old Course, St Andrews May 30–June 1   [6638–72]

Captains: Mary McKenna (GB!), Carol Semple Thompson (USA)

Great Britain and Ireland		**USA**	
First Day – Foursomes			
E Bennett & J Ewart	0	S Lewis & A Walshe (3 and 1)	1
S Watson &M Thomson (1 hole)	1	M Harigae & J Lee	0
B Loucks & F Parker	0	A Blumenherst & T Joh (1 hole)	1
	1		2
First Day – Fourballs			
C Booth & M Thomson	0	K Kim & M Harigae (3 and 2)	1
S Watson & K Caithness (3 and 2)	1	T Joh & M Bolger	0
F Parker & E Bennett	0	A Blumenherst & S Lewis (3 and 1)	1
	2		4
Second Day – Foursomes			
C Booth & B Loucks (3 and 2)	1	K Kim & J Lee	0
S Watson & M Thomson	0	A Walshe & S Lewis (5 and 4)	1
E Bennett & J Ewart	½	A Blumenherst & T Joh	½
	3½		5½
Second Day – Fourballs			
C Booth & B Loucks	0	K Kim & M Harigae (2 and 1)	1
S Watson & K Caithness (3 and 2)	1	A Blumenherst & M Bolger	0
E Bennett & F Parker	0	A Walshe & S Lewis (1 hole)	1
	4½		7½
Third Day – Singles			
Breanne Loucks (WAL)	0	Kimberly Kim (3 and 1)	1
Jodi Ewart (ENG)	0	Amanda Blumenherst (2 and 1)	1
Elizabeth Bennett (ENG)	0	Stacy Lewis (3 and 2)	1
Carly Booth (SCO)	0	Tiffany Joh (6 and 5)	1
Michele Thomson (SCO)	½	Jennie Lee	½
Florentyna Parker (ENG) (6 and 4)	1	Meghan Bolger	0
Krystle Caithness (SCO) (2 and 1)	1	Mina Harigae	0
Sally Watson (SCO)	0	Alison Walshe (hole)	1

Result: Great Britain & Ireland 7, United States of America 13

2006 *Bandon Dunes, OR* July 29–30
Result: USA 11½, GBI 6½
Captains: Carol Semple Thompson (USA);
Ada O'Sullivan (Monkstown) (GBI)

First Day: Foursomes
P Mackenzie & A Blumenherst beat T Mangan &
  K Matharu 5 and 4
D Grimes & A McCurdy beat M Gillen & N Edwards
  2 holes
J Park & T Leon beat C Coughlan & M Reid 1 hole

Singles
Jenny Suh lost to Kiran Matharu (Cookridge Park)
  2 and 1
Jennie Lee beat Martina Gillen (Beaverstown) 4 and 3
Amanda Blumenherst lost to Breanne Loucks (Wrexham)
  5 and 4

Paige Mackenzie beat Melissa Reid (Chevin)
  5 and 4
Jane Park beat Tara Delaney (Carlow) 3 and 2
Taylor Leon beat Claire Coughlan (Cork) 5 and 4

Second Day: Foursomes
J Park & T Leon halved with T Mangan & T Delaney
J Lee & J Suh lost to M Reid & B Loucks 7 and 5
P Mackenzie & A Blumenherst lost to M Gillen &
  N Edwards 1 hole

Singles
Virginia Grimes lost to M Gillen 3 and 2
Amanda McCurdy lost to B Loucks 3 and 2
P Mackenzie beat Tricia Mangan (Ennis) 1 hole
T Leon beat Naomi Edwards (Ganton) 5 and 4
J Lee beat M Reid 3 and 2
J Park beat T Delaney 3 and 2

2004 *Formby* June 12–13
Result: GBI 8, USA 10
Captains: Ada O'Sullivan (Monkstown) (GBI);
   Martha Kironac (USA)

First Day: Foursomes
S McKevitt & E Duggleby beat P Creamer & J Park
   3 and 2
N Timmins & D Masters beat S Huarte & A Thurman
   I hole
A Laing & C Coughlan beat B Lang & M Wie I hole

Singles
Emma Duggleby beat Elizabeth Janangelo 3 and 2
Danielle Masters lost to Erica Blasberg I hole
Fame More lost to Paula Creamer I hole
Anna Highgate lost to Michelle Wie 5 and 4
Shelley McKevitt lost to Jane Park 4 and 3
Anne Laing lost to Anne Thurman 4 and 3

Second Day: Foursomes
E Duggleby & S McKevitt beat E Blasberg & Sarah Huarte
   2 and I
A Laing & C Coughlan beat E Janangelo & M Wie 3 and 2
N Timmins & D Masters lost to B Lang & A Thurman
   5 and 4

Singles
E Duggleby lost to P Creamer 3 and 2
A Laing beat J Park 3 and I
S McKevitt lost to E Janangelo I hole
Nicola Timmins lost to M Wie 6 and 5
Claire Coughlan beat Brittany Lang 2 holes
D Masters lost to A Thurman I hole

2002 *Fox Chapel, PA* Aug 3–4
Result: USA 11, GBI 7
Captains: Mary Budke (USA), Pam Benka (GBI)

First Day: Foursomes
Duncan & Jerman beat Duggleby & Hudson 4 and 3
Fankhauser & Semple Thompson beat Laing & Stirling
   I hole
Myerscough & Swaim beat Coffey & Smith 3 and 2

Singles
Emily Bastel lost to Rebecca Hudson 2 holes
Leigh Anne Hardin beat Emma Duggleby 2 and I
Meredith Duncan beat Fame More 5 and 4
Angela Jerman beat Sarah Jones 6 and 5
Courtney Swaim beat Heather Stirling 4 and 2
Mollie Fankhauser lost to Vikki Laing I hole

Second Day: Foursomes
Hardin & Bastel lost to Laing & Stirling 3 and I
Myerscough & Swaim beat Hudson & Smith 4 and 2
Duncan & Jerman lost to Coffey & Dugglesby 4 and 2

Singles
Mollie Fankhauser beat Rebecca Hudson 3 and I
Carol Semple Thompson Beat Vikki Laing I hole
Leigh Anne Hardin lost to Emma Duggleby 4 and 3
Laura Myerscough beat Heather Stirling 2 holes
Meredith Duncan beat Akison Coffey 3 and I
Courtney Swaim lost to Sarah Jones 5 and 3

2000 *Ganton* June 24–25
Result: USA 10, GBI 8
Captains: Claire Hourihane Dowling (GBI),
   Jane Bastanchury Booth (USA)

First Day: Foursomes
Andrew & Morgan lost to Bauer & Carol Semple
Thompson I hole

Brewerton & Hudson lost to Keever & Stanford I hole
Duggleby & O'Brien halved with Derby Grimes &
   Homeyer

Singles
Kim Rostron Andrew lost to Beth Bauer 3 and 2
Fiona Brown lost to Robin Weiss I hole
Rebecca Hudson lost to Stephanie Keever 4 and 2
Lesley Nicholson halved with Angela Stanford
Suzanne O'Brien beat Leland Beckel 3 and I
Emma Duggleby lost to Hilary Homeyer I hole

Second Day: Foursomes
Brewerton & Hudson beat Bauer & Thompson 2 and I
Duggleby & O'Brien beat Keever & Stanford 7 and 6
Andrew & Morgan lost to Derby Grimes & Homeyer
   3 and I

Singles
Hudson lost to Bauer I hole
O'Brien beat Weiss 3 and 2
Duggleby beat Keever 4 and 2
Becky Brewerton lost to Homeyer 3 and 2
Becky Morgan beat Stanford 5 and 4
Andrew beat Virginia Derby Grimes 6 and 5

1998 *Minikahda, Minneapolis, MN* Aug 1–2
Result: USA 10, GBI 8
Captains: Barbara McIntire (USA),
   Ita Burke Butler (GBI)

First Day: Foursomes
Bauer & Chuasiriporn lost to Ratcliffe & Rostron I hole
Booth & Corrie Kuehn beat Brown & Stupples 2 and I
Burke & Derby Grimes beat Morgan & Rose 3 and 2

Singles
Kellee Booth beat Kim Rostron 2 and I
Brenda Corrie Kuehn beat Alison Rose 3 and 2
Jenny Chuasiriporn halved with Rebecca Hudson
Beth Bauer beat Hilary Monaghan 5 and 3
Jo Jo Robertson lost to Becky Morgan 2 and I
Carol Semple Thompson lost to Elaine Ratcliffe 3 and 2

Second Day: Foursomes
Booth & Corrie Kuehn beat Morgan & Rose 6 and 5
Bauer & Chuasiriporn lost to Brown & Hudson 2 holes
Burke & Derby Grimes beat Ratcliffe & Rostron
   2 and I

Singles
Booth beat Rostron 2 and I
Corrie Kuehn beat Morgan 2 and I
Thompson lost to Karen Stupples I hole
Robin Burke lost to Hudson 2 and I
Robertson lost to Fiona Brown I hole
Virginia Derby Grimes halved with Ratcliffe

1996 *Killarney* June 21–22
Result: GBI 11½, USA 6½
Captains: Ita Burke Butler (GBI),
   Martha Lang (USA)

First Day: Foursomes
Lisa Walton Educate & Wade lost to K Kuehne & Port
   2 and I
Lisa Dermott & Rose beat B Corrie Kuehn & Jemsek
   3 and I
McKay & Moodie halved with Kerr & Thompson

Singles
Julie Wade lost to Sarah LeBrun Ingram 4 and 2
Karen Stupples beat Kellee Booth 3 and 2
Alison Rose beat Brenda Corrie Kuehn 5 and 4
Elaine Ratcliffe halved with Marla Jemsek
Mhairi McKay beat Cristie Kerr I hole
Janice Moodie beat Carol Semple Thompson 3 and I

Second Day: Foursomes
McKay & Moodie beat Booth & Ingram 3 and 2
Dermott & Rose beat B Corrie Kuehn & Jemsek 2 and 1
Educate & Wade lost to K Kuehne & Port 1 hole

Singles
Wade lost to Kerr 1 hole
Ratcliffe beat Ingram 3 and 1
Stupples lost to Booth 3 and 2
Rose beat Ellen Port 6 and 5
McKay halved with Thompson
Moodie beat Kelli Kuehne 2 and 1

1994 *Chattanooga, TN* July 30–31
Result: GBI 9, USA 9
Captains: Lancy Smith (USA),
Elizabeth Boatman (GBI)

First Day: Foursomes
Sarah LeBrun Ingram & McGill halved with Matthew
  & Moodie
Klein & Thompson beat McKay & Kirsty Speak 7 and 5
Kaupp & Port lost to Wade & Walton 6 and 5

Singles
Jill McGill halved with Julie Wade
Emilee Klein beat Janice Moodie 3 and 2
Wendy Ward lost to Lisa Walton 1 hole
Carol Semple Thompson beat Myra McKinlay 2 and 1
Ellen Port beat Mhairi McKay 2 and 1
Stephanie Sparks lost to Catriona Lambert Matthew
  1 hole

Second Day: Foursomes
Ingram & McGill lost to Wade & Walton 2 and 1
Klein & Thompson beat McKinlay & Eileen Rose
  Power 4 and 2
Sparks & Ward lost to Matthew & Moodie 3 and 2

Singles
McGill beat Wade 4 and 3
Klein lost to Matthew 2 and 1
Port beat McKay 7 and 5
Wendy Kaupp lost to McKinlay 3 and 2
Ward beat Walton 4 and 3
Thompson lost to Moodie 2 holes

1992 *Hoylake* June 5–6
Result: GBI 10, USA 8
Captains: Elizabeth Boatman (GBI), Judy Oliver (USA)

First Day: Foursomes
Hall & Wade halved with Fruhwirth & Goetze
Lambert & Thomas beat Ingram & Shannon 2 and 1
Hourihane & Morley beat Hanson & Thompson 2 and 1

Singles
Joanne Morley halved with Amy Fruhwirth
Julie Wade lost to Vicki Goetze 3 and 2
Elaine Farquharson beat Robin Weiss 2 and 1
Nicola Buxton lost to Martha Lang 2 holes
Catriona Lambert beat Carol Semple Thompson 3 and 2
Caroline Hall beat Leslie Shannon 6 and 5

Second Day: Foursomes
Hall & Wade halved with Fruhwirth & Goetze
Hourihane & Morley halved with Lang & Weiss
Lambert & Thomas lost to Hanson & Thompson
  3 and 2

Singles
Morley beat Fruhwirth 2 and 1
Lambert beat Tracy Hanson 6 and 5
Farquharson lost to Sarah LeBrun Ingram 2 and 1
Vicki Thomas lost to Shannon 2 and 1
Claire Hourihane lost to Lang 2 and 1
Hall beat Goetze 1 hole

1990 *Somerset Hills, NJ* July 28–29
Result: USA 14, GBI 4
Captains: Leslie Shannon (USA), Jill Thornhill (GBI)

First Day: Foursomes
Goetze & Anne Quast Sander beat Dobson & Lambert
  4 and 3
Noble & Margaret Platt lost to Wade & Imrie 2 and 1
Thompson & Weiss beat Farquharson & Helen
  Wadsworth 3 and 1

Singles
Vicki Goetze lost to Julie Wade 2 and 1
Katie Peterson beat Kathryn Imrie 3 and 2
Brandie Burton beat Linzi Fletcher 3 and 1
Robin Weiss beat Elaine Farquharson 4 and 3
Karen Noble beat Catriona Lambert 1 hole
Carol Semple Thompson lost to Vicki Thomas 1 hole

Second Day: Foursomes
Goetze & Sander beat Wade & Imrie 3 and 1
Noble & Platt lost to Dobson & Lambert 1 hole
Burton & Peterson beat Farquharson & Wadsworth
  5 and 4

Singles
Goetze beat Helen Dobson 4 and 3
Burton beat Lambert 4 and 3
Peterson beat Imrie 1 hole
Noble beat Wade 2 holes
Weiss beat Farquharson 2 and 1
Thompson beat Thomas 3 and 1

1988 *Royal St George's* June 10–11
Result: GBI 11, USA 7
Captains: Diane Robb Bailey (GBI), Judy Bell (USA)

First Day: Foursomes
Bayman & Wade beat Kerdyk & Scrivner 2 and 1
Davies & Shapcott beat Scholefield & Thompson
  5 and 4
Thomas & Thornhill halved with Keggi & Shannon

Singles
Linda Bayman halved with Tracy Kerdyk
Julie Wade beat Cindy Scholefield 2 holes
Susan Shapcott lost to Carol Semple Thompson
  1 hole
Karen Davies lost to Pearl Sinn 4 and 3
Shirley Lawson beat Pat Cornett-Iker 1 hole
Jill Thornhill beat Leslie Shannon 3 and 2

Second Day: Foursomes
Bayman & Wade lost to Kerdyk & Scrivner 1 hole
Davies & Shapcott beat Keggi & Shannon 2 holes
Thomas & Thornhill beat Scholefield & Thompson
  6 and 5

Singles
Wade lost to Kerdyk 2 and 1
Shapcott beat Caroline Keggi 3 and 2
Lawson lost to Kathleen McCarthy Scrivner 4 and 3
Vicki Thomas beat Cornett-Iker 5 and 3
Bayman beat Sinn 1 hole
Thornhill lost to Thompson 3 and 2

1986 *Prairie Dunes, KS* Aug 1–2
Result: GBI 13, USA 5
Captains: Judy Bell (USA), Diane Robb Bailey (GBI)

First Day: Foursomes
Kessler & Schreyer lost to Behan & Thornhill 7 and 6
Ammaccapane & Mochrie lost to Davies & Johnson
  2 and 1
Gardner & Scrivner lost to McKenna & Robertson 1 hole

1986 continued

Singles
Leslie Shannon lost to Patricia (Trish) Johnson
  1 hole
Kim Williams lost to Jill Thornhill 4 and 3
Danielle Ammaccapane lost to Lillian Behan 4 and 3
Kandi Kessler beat Vicki Thomas 3 and 2
Dottie Pepper Mochrie halved with Karen Davies
Cindy Schreyer beat Claire Hourihane 2 and 1

Second Day: Foursomes
Ammaccapane & Mochrie lost to Davies & Johnson
  1 hole
Shannon & Williams lost to Behan & Thornhill 5 and 3
Gardner & Scrivner halved with McKenna & Belle
  McCorkindale Robertson

Singles
Shannon halved with Thornhill
Kathleen McCarthy Scrivner lost to Trish Johnson 5 and 3
Kim Gardner beat Behan 1 hole
Williams lost to Thomas 4 and 3
Kessler halved with Davies
Schreyer lost to Hourihane 5 and 4

1984 Muirfield June 8–9

Result: USA 9½, GBI 8½

*Captains: Diane Robb Bailey (GBI),
  Phyllis Preuss (USA)*

First Day: Foursomes
New & Waite beat Pacillo & Sander 2 holes
Grice & Thornhill halved with Rosenthal & Smith
Davies & McKenna lost to Farr & Widman 1 hole

Singles
Jill Thornhill halved with Joanne Pacillo
Claire Waite lost to Penny Hammel 4 and 2
Claire Hourihane lost to Jody Rosenthal 3 and 1
Vicki Thomas beat Dana Howe 2 and 1
Penny Grice beat Anne Quast Sander 2 holes
Beverley New lost to Mary Anne Widman 4 and 3

Second Day: Foursomes
New & Waite lost to Rosenthal & Smith 3 and 1
Grice & Thornhill beat Farr & Widman 2 and 1
Hourihane & Thomas halved with Hammel & Howe

Singles
Thornhill lost to Pacillo 3 and 2
Laura Davies beat Sander 1 hole
Waite beat Lancy Smith 5 and 4
Grice lost to Howe 2 holes
New lost to Heather Farr 6 and 5
Hourihane beat Hammel 2 and 1

1982 Denver, CO Aug 5–6

Result: USA 14½, GBI 3½

*Captains: Betty Probasco (USA),
  Maire O'Donnell (GBI)*

First Day: Foursomes
Inkster & Semple beat McKenna & Robertson 5 and 4
Baker & Smith halved with Douglas & Soulsby
Benz & Hanlon beat Connachan & Stewart 2 and 1

Singles
Amy Benz beat Mary McKenna 2 and 1
Cathy Hanlon beat Jane Connachan 5 and 4
Mari McDougall beat Wilma Aitken 2 holes
Kathy Baker beat Belle McCorkindale Robertson
  7 and 6
Judy Oliver lost to Janet Soulsby 2 holes
Juli Inkster beat Kitrina Douglas 7 and 6

Second Day: Foursomes
Inkster & Semple beat Aitken & Connachan 3 and 2
Baker & Smith beat Douglas & Soulsby 1 hole
Benz & Hanlon lost to McKenna & Robertson 1 hole

Singles
Inkster beat Douglas 7 and 6
Baker beat Gillian Stewart 4 and 3
Oliver beat Vicki Thomas 5 and 4
McDougall beat Soulsby 2 and 1
Carol Semple beat McKenna 1 hole
Lancy Smith lost to Robertson 5 and 4

1980 St Pierre, Chepstow June 6–7

Result: USA 13, GBI 5

*Captains: Carol Comboy (GBI), Nancy Roth
  Syms (USA)*

First Day: Foursomes
McKenna & Nesbitt halved with Terri Moody & Smith
Stewart & Thomas lost to Castillo & Sheehan 5 and 3
Caldwell & Madill halved with Oliver & Semple

Singles
Mary McKenna lost to Patty Sheehan 3 and 2
Claire Nesbitt halved with Lancy Smith
Jane Connachan lost to Brenda Goldsmith 2 holes
Maureen Madill lost to Carol Semple 4 and 3
Linda Moore halved with Mary Hafeman
Carole Caldwell lost to Judy Oliver 1 hole

Second Day: Foursomes
Caldwell & Madill lost to Castillo & Sheehan 3 and 2
McKenna & Nesbitt lost to Moody & Smith 6 and 5
Moore & Thomas lost to Oliver & Semple 1 hole

Singles
Madill lost to Sheehan 5 and 4
McKenna beat Lori Castillo 5 and 4
Connachan lost to Hafeman 6 and 5
Gillian Stewart beat Smith 5 and 4
Moore beat Goldsmith 1 hole
Tegwen Perkins Thomas lost to Semple 4 and 3

1978 Apawamis, NY Aug 4–5

Result: USA 12, GBI 6

Captains: Helen Wilson (USA), Carol Comboy (GBI)

First Day: Foursomes
Daniel & Brenda Goldsmith lost to Greenhalgh &
  Marvin 3 and 2
Cindy Hill & Smith lost to Everard & Thomson 2 and 1
Cornett & Carolyn Hill halved with McKenna &
  Perkins

Singles
Beth Daniel beat Vanessa Marvin 5 and 4
Noreen Uihlein lost to Mary Everard 7 and 6
Lancy Smith beat Angela Uzielli 4 and 3
Cindy Hill beat Julia Greenhalgh 2 and 1
Carolyn Hill halved with Carole Caldwell
Judy Oliver beat Tegwen Perkins 2 and 1

Second Day: Foursomes
Cindy Hill & Smith beat Everard & Thomson 1 hole
Daniel & Goldsmith beat McKenna & Perkins 1 hole
Oliver & Uihlein beat Greenhalgh & Marvin 4 and 3

Singles
Daniel beat Mary McKenna 2 and 1
Patricia Cornett beat Caldwell 3 and 2
Cindy Hill lost to Muriel Thomson 2 and 1
Lancy Smith beat Perkins 2 holes
Oliver halved with Greenhalgh
Uihlein halved with Everard

1976 Royal Lytham & St Annes June 11–12
Result: USA 11½, GBI 6½
Captains: Belle McCorkindale Robertson (GBI),
Barbara McIntyre (USA)

First Day: Foursomes
Greenhalgh & McKenna lost to Daniel & Hill 3 and 2
Cadden & Henson lost to Horton & Massey 6 and 5
Irvin & Perkins beat Semple & Syms 3 and 2

Singles
Ann Irvin lost to Beth Daniel 4 and 3
Dinah Oxley Henson beat Cindy Hill 1 hole
Suzanne Cadden lost to Nancy Lopez 3 and 1
Mary McKenna lost to Nancy Roth Syms 1 hole
Tegwen Perkins lost to Debbie Massey 1 hole
Julia Greenhalgh halved with Barbara Barrow

Second Day: Foursomes
Cadden & Irvin lost to Daniel & Hill 4 and 3
Henson & Perkins beat Semple & Syms 2 and 1
McKenna & Anne Stant lost to Barrow & Lopez 4 and 3

Singles
Henson lost to Daniel 3 and 2
Greenhalgh beat Syms 2 and 1
Cadden lost to Donna Horton 6 and 5
Jennie Lee-Smith lost to Massey 3 and 2
Perkins beat Hill 1 hole
McKenna beat Carol Semple 1 hole

1974 San Francisco, CA Aug 2–3
Result: USA 13, GBI 5
Captains: Sis Choate (USA),
Belle McCorkindale Robertson (GBI)

First Day: Foursomes
Hill & Semple halved with Greenhalgh & McKenna
Booth & Sander beat Lee-Smith & LeFeuvre 6 and 5
Budke & Lauer lost to Everard & Walker 5 and 4

Singles
Carol Semple lost to Mickey Walker 2 and 1
Jane Bastanchury Booth beat Mary McKenna 5 and 3
Debbie Massey beat Mary Everard 1 hole
Bonnie Lauer beat Jennie Lee-Smith 6 and 5
Beth Barry beat Julia Greenhalgh 1 hole
Cindy Hill halved with Tegwen Perkins

Second Day: Foursomes
Booth & Sander beat McKenna & Walker 5 and 4
Budke & Lauer beat Everard & LeFeuvre 5 and 3
Hill & Semple lost to Greenhalgh & Perkins 3 and 2

Singles
Anne Quast Sander beat Everard 4 and 3
Booth beat Greenhalgh 7 and 5
Massey beat Carol LeFeuvre 6 and 5
Semple beat Walker 2 and 1
Mary Budke beat Perkins 5 and 4
Lauer lost to McKenna 2 and 1

1972 Western Gailes June 9–10
Result: USA 10, GBI 8
Captains: Frances Stephens Smith (GBI),
Jean Ashley Crawford (USA)

First Day: Foursomes
Everard & Beverly Huke lost to Baugh & Kirouac 2 and 1
Frearson & Robertson beat Booth & McIntyre 2 and 1
McKenna & Walker beat Barry & Hollis Stacy 1 hole

Singles
Mickey Walker halved with Laura Baugh
Belle McCorkindale Robertson lost to Jane Bastanchury Booth 3 and 1
Mary Everard lost to Martha Wilkinson Kirouac 4 and 3
Dinah Oxley lost to Barbara McIntire 4 and 3
Kathryn Phillips beat Lancy Smith 2 holes
Mary McKenna lost to Beth Barry 2 and 1

Second Day: Foursomes
McKenna & Walker beat Baugh & Kirouac 3 and 2
Everard & Huke lost to Booth & McIntyre 5 and 4
Frearson & Robertson halved with Barry & Stacy

Singles
Robertson lost to Baugh 6 and 5
Everard beat McIntyre 6 and 5
Walker beat Booth 1 hole
McKenna beat Kirouac 3 and 1
Diane Frearson lost to Smith 3 and 1
Phillips lost to Barry 3 and 1

1970 Brae Burn, MA Aug 7–8
Result: USA 11½, GBI 6½
Captains: Carolyn Cudone (USA), Jeanne Bisgood (GBI)

First Day: Foursomes
Bastanchury & Hamlin lost to McKenna & Oxley 4 and 3
Preuss & Wilkinson beat Irvin & Robertson 4 and 3
Jane Fassinger & Hill lost to Everard & Greenhalgh 5 and 3

Singles
Jane Bastanchury beat Dinah Oxley 5 and 3
Martha Wilkinson beat Ann Irvin 1 hole
Shelley Hamlin halved with Belle McCorkindale Robertson
Phyllis Preuss lost to Mary McKenna 4 and 2
Nancy Hager beat Margaret Pickard 5 and 4
Alice Dye beat Julia Greenhalgh 1 hole

Second Day: Foursomes
Preuss & Wilkinson beat McKenna & Oxley 6 and 4
Dye & Hill halved with Everard & Greenhalgh
Bastanchury & Hamlin beat Irvin & Robertson 1 hole

Singles
Bastanchury beat Irvin 4 and 3
Hamlin halved with Oxley
Preuss beat Robertson 1 hole
Wilkinson lost to Greenhalgh 6 and 4
Hager lost to Mary Everard 4 and 3
Cindy Hill beat McKenna 2 and 1

1968 Newcastle, Co Down June 14–15
Result: USA 10½, GBI 7½
Captains: Zara Bolton (GBI), Evelyn Monsted (USA)

First Day: Foursomes
Irvin & Robertson beat Hamlin & Welts 6 and 5
Pickard & Saunders beat Conley & Dill 3 and 2
Howard & Pam Tredinnick lost to Ashley & Preuss 1 hole

Singles
Ann Irvin beat Anne Quast Welts 3 and 2
Vivien Saunders lost to Shelley Hamlin 1 hole
Belle McCorkindale Robertson lost to Roberta Albers 1 hole
Bridget Jackson halved with Peggy Conley
Dinah Oxley halved with Phyllis Preuss
Margaret Pickard beat Jean Ashley 2 holes

Second Day: Foursomes
Oxley & Tredinnick lost to Ashley & Preuss 5 and 4
Irvin & Robertson halved with Conley & Dill
Pickard & Saunders lost to Hamlin & Welts 2 and 1

1968 continued

Singles

Irvin beat Hamlin 3 and 2
Robertson halved with Welts
Saunders halved with Albers
Ann Howard lost to Mary Lou Dill 4 and 2
Pickard lost to Conley I hole
Jackson lost to Preuss 2 and I

1966 Hot Springs, VA July 29–30

Result: USA 13, GBI 5

*Captains: Dorothy Germain Porter (USA),
  Zara Bolton (GBI)*

First Day: Foursomes

Ashley & Preuss beat Armitage & Bonallack I hole
Barbara McIntire & Welts halved with Joan Hastings &
  Robertson
Boddie & Flenniken beat Chadwick & Tredinnick I hole

Singles

Jean Ashley beat Belle McCorkindale Robertson I hole
Anne Quast Welts halved with Susan Armitage
Barbara White Boddie beat Angela Ward Bonallack
  3 and 2
Nancy Roth Syms beat Elizabeth Chadwick 2 holes
Helen Wilson lost to Ita Burke 3 and I
Carol Sorenson Flenniken beat Marjory Fowler 3 and I

Second Day: Foursomes

Ashley & Preuss beat Armitage & Bonallack 2 and I
McIntire & Welts lost to Burke & Chadwick I hole
Boddie & Flenniken beat Hastings & Robertson 2 and I

Singles

Ashley lost to Bonallack 2 and I
Welts halved with Robertson
Boddie beat Armitage 3 and 2
Syms halved with Pam Tredinnick
Phyllis Preuss beat Chadwick 3 and 2
Flenniken beat Burke 2 and I

1964 Porthcawl Sept 11–12

Result: USA 10½, GBI 1½

Captains: Elsie Corlett (GBI), Helen Hawes (USA)

First Day: Foursomes

Spearman & Bonallack beat McIntyre & Preuss 2 and I
Sheila Vaughan & Porter beat Gunderson & Roth 3 and 2
Jackson & Susan Armitage lost to Sorenson & White
  8 and 6

Singles

Angela Ward Bonallack lost to JoAnne Gunderson 6 and 5
Marley Spearman halved with Barbara McIntire
Julia Greenhalgh lost to Barbara White 3 and 2
Bridget Jackson beat Carol Sorenson 4 and 3
Joan Lawrence lost to Peggy Conley I hole
Ruth Porter beat Nancy Roth I hole

Second Day: Foursomes

Spearman & Bonallack beat McIntyre & Preuss 6 and 5
Armitage & Jackson lost to Gunderson & Roth 2 holes
Porter & Vaughan halved with Sorenson & White

Singles

Spearman halved with Gunderson
Lawrence lost to McIntyre 4 and 2
Greenhalgh beat Phyllis Preuss 5 and 3
Bonallack lost to White 3 and 2
Porter lost to Sorenson 3 and 2
Jackson lost to Conley I hole

1962 Broadmoor, CO Aug 17–18

Result: USA 8, GBI 1

*Captains: Polly Riley (USA),
  Frances Stephens Smith (GBI)*

Foursomes

Decker & McIntyre beat Spearman & Bonallack 7 and 5
Jean Ashley & Anna Johnstone beat Ruth Porter &
  Frearson 8 and 7
Creed & Gunderson beat Vaughan & Ann Irvin 4 and 3

Singles

Judy Bell lost to Diane Frearson 8 and 7
JoAnne Gunderson beat Angela Ward Bonallack 2 and I
Clifford Ann Creed beat Sally Bonallack 6 and 5
Anne Quast Decker beat Marley Spearman 7 and 5
Phyllis Preuss beat Jean Roberts I hole
Barbara McIntyre beat Sheila Vaughan 5 and 4

1960 Lindrick May 20–21

Result: USA 6½, GBI 2½

*Captains: Maureen Garrett (GBI),
  Mildred Prunaret (USA)*

Foursomes

Price & Bonallack beat Gunderson & McIntire I hole
Robertson & McCorkindale lost to Eller & Quast 4 and 2
Frances Smith & Porter lost to Goodwin & Anna
  Johnstone 3 and 2

Singles

Elizabeth Price halved with Barbara McIntire
Angela Ward Bonallack lost to JoAnne Gunderson 2 and I
Janette Robertson lost to Anne Quast 2 holes
Philomena Garvey lost to Judy Eller 4 and 3
Belle McCorkindale lost to Judy Bell 8 and 7
Ruth Porter beat Joanne Goodwin I hole

1958 Brae Burn, MA Aug 8–9

Result: GBI 4½, USA 4½

*Captains: Virginia Dennehy (USA),
  Daisy Ferguson (GBI)*

Foursomes

Riley & Romack lost to Bonallack & Price 2 and I
Gunderson & Quast lost to Robertson & Smith 3 and 2
Johnstone & McIntire beat Jackson & Valentine 6 and 5

Singles

JoAnne Gunderson beat Jessie Anderson Valentine 2 holes
Barbara McIntire halved with Angela Ward Bonallack
Anne Quast beat Elizabeth Price 4 and 2
Anna Johnstone lost to Janette Robertson 3 and 2
Barbara Romack beat Bridget Jackson 3 and 2
Polly Riley lost to Frances Stephens Smith 2 holes

1956 Prince's, Sandwich June 8–9

Result: GBI 5, USA 4

Captains: Zara Davis Bolton (GBI), Edith Flippin (USA)

Foursomes

Valentine & Garvey lost to Lesser & Smith 2 and I
Smith & Price beat Riley & Romack 5 and 3
Robertson & Veronica Anstey lost to Downey &
  Carolyn Cudone 6 and 4

Singles

Jessie Anderson Valentine beat Patricia Lesser 6 and 4
Philomena Garvey lost to Margaret Smith 9 and 8
Frances Stephens Smith beat Polly Riley I hole
Janette Robertson lost to Barbara Romack 6 and 4
Angela Ward beat Mary Ann Downey 6 and 4
Elizabeth Price beat Jane Nelson 7 and 6

1954 Merion, PA Sept 2–3
Result: USA 6, GBI 3
Captains: Edith Flippin (USA), Mrs JB Beck (GBI)

Foursomes
Faulk & Riley beat Stephens & Price 6 and 4
Doran & Patricia Lesser beat Garvey & Valentine 6 and 5
Kirby & Barbara Romack beat Marjorie Peel &
   Robertson 6 and 5

Singles
Mary Lena Faulk lost to Frances Stephens 1 hole
Claire Doran beat Jeanne Bisgood 4 and 3
Polly Riley beat Elizabeth Price 9 and 8
Dorothy Kirby lost to Philomena Garvey 3 and 1
Grace DeMoss Smith beat Jessie Anderson Valentine
   4 and 3
Joyce Ziske lost to Janette Robertson 3 and 1

1952 Muirfield June 6–7
Result: GBI 5, USA 4
*Captains: Lady Katherine Cairns (GBI),
   Aniela Goldthwaite (USA)*

Foursomes
Donald & Price beat Kirby & DeMoss 3 and 2
Stephens & JA Valentine lost to Doran & Lindsay 6 and 4
Paterson & Garvey beat Riley & Patricia O'Sullivan 2 and 1

Singles
Jean Donald lost to Dorothy Kirby 1 hole
Frances Stephens beat Marjorie Lindsay 2 and 1
Moira Paterson lost to Polly Riley 6 and 4
Jeanne Bisgood beat Mae Murray 4 and 5
Philomena Garvey lost to Claire Doran 3 and 2
Elizabeth Price beat Grace DeMoss 3 and 2

1950 Buffalo, NY Sept 4–5
Result: USA 7½, GBI 1½
*Captains: Glenna Collett Vare (USA),
   Diana Fishwick Critchley (GBI)*

Foursomes
Hanson & Porter beat Valentine & Donald 3 and 2
Helen Sigel & Kirk lost to Stephens & Price 1 hole
Dorothy Kirby & Kielty beat Garvey & Bisgood 6 and 5

Singles
Dorothy Porter halved with Frances Stephens
Polly Riley beat Jessie Anderson Valentine 7 and 6
Beverly Hanson beat Jean Donald 6 and 5
Dorothy Kielty beat Philomena Garvey 2 and 1
Peggy Kirk beat Jeanne Bisgood 1 hole
Grace Lenczyk beat Elizabeth Price 5 and 4

1948 Birkdale May 21–22
Result: USA 6½, GBI 2½
*Captains: Doris Chambers (GBI),
   Glenna Collett Vare (USA)*

Foursomes
Donald & Gordon beat Suggs & Lenczyk 3 and 2
Garvey & Bolton lost to Kirby & Vare 4 and 3
Ruttle & Val Reddan lost to Page & Kielty 5 and 4

Singles
Philomena Garvey halved with Louise Suggs
Jean Donald beat Dorothy Kirby 2 holes
Jacqueline Gordon lost to Grace Lenczyk 5 and 3
Helen Holm lost to Estelle Lawson Page 3 and 2
Maureen Ruttle lost to Polly Riley 3 and 2
Zara Bolton lost to Dorothy Kielty 2 and 1

1938 Essex, MA Sept 7–8
Result: USA 5½, GBI 3½
*Captains: Frances Stebbins (USA),
   Mrs RH Wallace-Williamson (GBI)*

Foursomes
Page & Orcutt lost to Holm & Tiernan 2 holes
Vare & Berg lost to Anderson & Corlett 1 hole
Miley & Kathryn Hemphill halved with Walker &
   Phyllis Wade

Singles
Estelle Lawson Page beat Helen Holm 6 and 5
Patty Berg beat Jessie Anderson 1 hole
Marion Miley beat Elsie Corlett 2 and 1
Glenna Collett Vare beat Charlotte Walker 2 and 1
Maureen Orcutt lost to Clarrie Tiernan 2 and 1
Charlotte Glutting beat Nan Baird 1 hole

1936 Gleneagles May 6
Result: USA 4½, GBI 4½
*Captains: Doris Chambers (GBI),
   Glenna Collett Vare (USA)*

Foursomes
Morgan & Garon halved with Vare & Berg
Barton & Walker lost to Orcutt & Cheney 2 and 1
Anderson & Holm beat Hill & Glutting 3 and 2

Singles
Wanda Morgan lost to Glenna Collett Vare 3 and 2
Helen Holm beat Patty Berg 4 and 3
Pamela Barton lost to Charlotte Glutting 1 hole
Charlotte Walker lost to Maureen Orcutt 1 hole
Jessie Anderson beat Leona Pressley Cheney 1 hole
Marjorie Garon beat Opal Hill 7 and 5

1934 Chevy Chase, MD Sept 27–28
Result: USA 6½, GBI 2½
*Captains: Glenna Collett Vare (USA),
   Doris Chambers (GBI)*

Foursomes
Van Wie & Glutting halved with Gourlay & Barton
Orcutt & Cheney beat Fishwick & Morgan 2 holes
Hill & Lucille Robinson lost to Plumpton & Walker 2 and 1

Singles
Virginia Van Wie beat Diana Fishwick 2 and 1
Maureen Orcutt beat Molly Gourlay 4 and 2
Leona Pressley Cheney beat Pamela Barton 7 and 5
Charlotte Glutting beat Wanda Morgan
Opal Hill beat Diana Plumpton 3 and 2
Aniela Goldthwaite lost to Charlotte Walker
   3 and 2

1932 Wentworth May 21
Result: USA 5½, GBI 3½
Captains: J Wethered (GBI), M Hollins (USA)

Foursomes
Wethered & Morgan lost to Vare & Hill 1 hole
Wilson & JB Watson lost to Van Wie & Hicks 2 and 1
Gourlay & Doris Park lost to Orcutt & Cheney
   1 hole

Singles
Joyce Wethered beat Glenna Collett Vare 6 and 4
Enid Wilson beat Helen Hicks 2 and 1
Wanda Morgan lost to Virginia Van Wie 2 and 1
Diana Fishwick beat Maureen Orcutt 4 and 3
Molly Gourlay halved with Opal Hill
Elsie Corlett lost to Leona Pressley Cheney 4 and 3

Curtis Cup INDIVIDUAL RECORDS

Bold print: captain; bold print in brackets: non-playing captain
Maiden name in parentheses, former surname in square brackets

Great Britain and Ireland

Name		Year	Played	Won	Lost	Halved
Jean Anderson (Donald)	SCO	1948	6	3	3	0
Kim Andrew (Rostron)	ENG	1998-2000	8	2	6	0
Diane Bailey [Frearson] (Robb)	ENG	1962-72-(84)-(86)-(88)	5	2	2	1
Sally Barber (Bonallack)	ENG	1962	1	0	1	0
Pam Barton	ENG	1934-36	4	0	3	1
Linda Bayman	ENG	1988	4	2	1	1
Baba Beck (Pym)	IRL	(1954)	0	0	0	0
Charlotte Beddows [Watson] (Stevenson)	SCO	1932	1	0	1	0
Lilian Behan	IRL	1986	4	3	1	0
Veronica Beharrell (Anstey)	ENG	1956	1	0	1	0
Pam Benka (Tredinnick)	ENG	1966-68 (2002)	4	0	3	1
Elizabeth Bennett	ENG	2008	5	0	4	1
Jeanne Bisgood	ENG	1950-52-54-(70)	4	1	3	0
Elizabeth Boatman (Collis)	ENG	(1992)-(94)	0	0	0	0
Zara Bolton (Davis)	ENG	1948-(56)-(66)-(68)	2	0	2	0
Angela Bonallack (Ward)	ENG	1956-58-60-62-64-66	15	6	8	1
Carly Booth	SCO	2008	4	1	3	0
Becky Brewerton	WAL	2000	3	1	2	0
Fiona Brown	ENG	1998-2000	4	2	2	0
Ita Butler (Burke)	IRL	1966-(96)	3	2	1	0
Lady Katherine Cairns	ENG	(1952)	0	0	0	0
Krystle Caithness	SCO	2008	3	3	0	0
Carole Caldwell (Redford)	ENG	1978-80	5	0	3	2
Doris Chambers	ENG	(1934)-(36)-(48)	0	0	0	0
Alison Coffey	IRL	2002	3	1	2	0
Carol Comboy (Grott)	ENG	(1978)-(80)	0	0	0	0
Jane Connachan	SCO	1980-82	5	0	5	0
Elsie Corlett	ENG	1932-38-(64)	3	1	2	0
Claire Coughlan	IRL	2004-06	5	3	2	0
Diana Critchley (Fishwick)	ENG	1932-34-(50)	3	1	2	0
Alison Davidson (Rose)	SCO	1996-98	7	4	3	0
Karen Davies	WAL	1986-88	7	4	1	2
Laura Davies	ENG	1984	2	1	1	0
Tara Delanbey	ENG	2006	3	0	2	1
Lisa Dermott	WAL	1996	2	2	0	0
Helen Dobson	ENG	1990	3	1	2	0
Kitrina Douglas	ENG	1982	4	0	3	1
Claire Dowling (Hourihane)	IRL	1984-86-88-90-92-(2000)	8	3	3	2
Marjorie Draper [Peel] (Thomas)	SCO	1954	1	0	1	0
Emma Duggleby	ENG	2000-04	8	5	2	1
Lisa Educate (Walton)	ENG	1994-96	6	3	3	0
Naomi Edwards	ENG	2006	3	1	2	0
Mary Everard	ENG	1970-72-74-78	15	6	7	2
Jodi Ewart	ENG	2008	3	0	2	1
Elaine Farquharson	SCO	1990-92	6	1	5	0
Daisy Ferguson	IRL	(1958)	0	0	0	0
Marjory Ferguson (Fowler)	SCO	1966	1	0	1	0
Elizabeth Price Fisher (Price)	ENG	1950-52-54-56-58-60	12	7	4	1
Linzi Fletcher	ENG	1990	1	0	1	0
Maureen Garner (Madill)	IRL	1980	4	0	3	1
Marjorie Ross Garon	ENG	1936	2	1	0	1
Maureen Garrett (Ruttle)	ENG	1948-(60)	2	0	2	0
Philomena Garvey	IRL	1948-50-52-54-56-60	11	2	8	1
Carol Gibbs (Le Feuvre)	ENG	1974	3	0	3	0
Martine Gillen	IRL	2006	4	2	2	0
Jacqueline Gordon	ENG	1948	2	1	1	0
Molly Gourlay	ENG	1932-34	4	0	2	2
Julia Greenhalgh	ENG	1964-70-74-76-78	17	6	7	4
Penny Grice-Whittaker (Grice)	ENG	1984	4	2	1	1
Caroline Hall	ENG	1992	4	2	0	2
Marley Harris [Spearman] (Baker)	ENG	1962-64	6	2	2	2
Dorothea Hastings (Sommerville)	SCO	1958	0	0	0	0

Name		Year	Played	Won	Lost	Halved
Lady Heathcoat-Amory (Joyce Wethered)	ENG	**1932**	2	1	1	0
Dinah Henson (Oxley)	ENG	1968-70-72-76	11	3	6	2
Anna Highgate	WAL	2004	1	0	1	0
Helen Holm (Gray)	SCO	1936-38-48	5	3	2	0
Ann Howard (Phillips)	ENG	1956-68	2	0	2	0
Rebecca Hudson	ENG	1998-2000-02	11	5	5	1
Shirley Huggan (Lawson)	SCO	1988	2	1	1	0
Beverley Huke	ENG	1972	2	0	2	0
Ann Irvin	ENG	1962-68-70-76	12	4	7	1
Bridget Jackson	ENG	1958-64-68	8	1	6	1
Patricia Johnson	ENG	1986	4	4	0	0
Sarah Jones	WAL	2002	2	1	1	0
Anne Laing	SCO	2004	4	3	1	0
Vikki Laing	SCO	2002	4	2	2	0
Susan Langridge (Armitage)	ENG	1964-66	6	0	5	1
Joan Lawrence	SCO	1964	2	0	2	0
Wilma Leburn (Aitken)	SCO	1982	2	0	2	0
Jenny Lee Smith	ENG	1974-76	3	0	3	0
Breanne Loucks	WAL	2006-08	7	4	3	0
Kathryn Lumb (Phillips)	ENG	1970-72	2	1	1	0
Mhairi McKay	SCO	1994-96	7	2	3	2
Mary McKenna	IRL	1970-72-74-76-78-80-82-84-86- **(2008)**	30	10	16	4
Shelley McKevitt	ENG	2004	4	2	2	0
Myra McKinlay	SCO	1994	3	1	2	0
Suzanne McMahon (Cadden)	SCO	1976	4	0	4	0
Sheila Maher (Vaughan)	ENG	1962-64	4	1	2	1
Tricia Mangan	IRL	2006	3	0	2	1
Kathryn Marshall (Imrie)	SCO	1990	4	1	3	0
Vanessa Marvin	ENG	1978	4	1	3	0
Danielle Masters	ENG	2004	3	1	2	0
Kiran Matharu	ENG	2006	2	1	1	0
Catriona Matthew (Lambert)	SCO	1990-92-94	12	7	4	1
Tegwen Matthews [Thomas] (Perkins)	WAL	1974-76-78-80	14	4	8	2
Moira Milton (Paterson)	SCO	1952	2	1	1	0
Hilary Monaghan	SCO	1998	1	0	1	0
Janice Moodie	SCO	1994-96	8	5	1	2
Fame More	ENG	2002-04	2	0	2	0
Becky Morgan	WAL	1998-2000	7	2	5	0
Wanda Morgan	ENG	1932-34-36	6	0	5	1
Joanne Morley	ENG	1992	4	2	0	2
Nicola Murray (Buxton)	ENG	1992	1	0	1	0
Beverley New	ENG	1984	4	1	3	0
Lesley Nicholson	SCO	2000	1	0	0	1
Suzanne O'Brien	IRL	2000	4	3	0	1
Maire O'Donnell	IRL	**(1982)**	0	0	0	0
Ada O'Sullivan	IRL	**(2004-06)**	0	0	0	0
Florentyna Parker	ENG	2008	4	1	3	0
Margaret Pickard (Nichol)	ENG	1968-70	5	2	3	0
Diana Plumpton	ENG	1934	2	1	1	0
Elizabeth Pook (Chadwick)	ENG	1966	4	1	3	0
Doris Porter (Park)	SCO	1932	1	0	1	0
Eileen Rose Power (McDaid)	IRL	1994	1	0	1	0
Elaine Ratcliffe	ENG	1996-98	6	3	1	2
Clarrie Reddan (Tiernan)	IRL	1938-48	3	2	1	0
Joan Rennie (Hastings)	SCO	1966	2	0	1	1
Melissa Reid	ENG	2006	4	1	3	0
Maureen Richmond (Walker)	SCO	1974	4	2	2	0
Jean Roberts	ENG	1962	1	0	1	0
Belle Robertson (McCorkindale)	SCO	1960-66-68-70-72-**(74)**-**(76)**-82-86	24	5	12	7
Claire Robinson (Nesbitt)	IRL	1980	3	0	1	2
Vivien Saunders	ENG	1968	4	1	2	1
Susan Shapcott	ENG	1988	4	3	1	0
Linda Simpson (Moore)	ENG	1980	3	1	1	1
Ruth Slark (Porter)	ENG	1960-62-64	7	3	3	1
Anne Smith [Stant] (Willard)	ENG	1976	1	0	1	0
Frances Smith (Stephens)	ENG	1950-52-54-56-58-60-**(62)**-**(72)**	11	7	3	1
Kerry Smith	ENG	2002	2	0	2	0
Janet Soulsby	ENG	1982	4	1	2	1

Curtis Cup Individual Records *continued*

Name		Year	Played	Won	Lost	Halved
Kirsty Speak	ENG	1994	1	0	1	0
Gillian Stewart	SCO	1980-82	4	1	3	0
Heather Stirling	SCO	2002	4	1	3	0
Karen Stupples	ENG	1996-98	4	2	2	0
Vicki Thomas (Rawlings)	WAL	1982-84-86-88-90-92	13	6	5	2
Michele Thomson	SCO	2008	4	1	2	1
Muriel Thomson	SCO	1978	3	2	1	0
Jill Thornhill	ENG	1984-86-88	12	6	2	4
Nicola Timmins	ENG	2004	3	1	2	0
Angela Uzielli (Carrick)	ENG	1978	1	0	1	0
Jessie Valentine (Anderson)	SCO	1936-38-50-52-54-56-58	13	4	9	0
Julie Wade	ENG	1988-90-92-94-96	19	6	10	3
Helen Wadsworth	WAL	1990	2	0	2	0
Claire Waite	ENG	1984	4	2	2	0
Mickey Walker	ENG	1972-74	4	3	0	1
Pat Walker	IRL	1934-36-38	6	2	3	1
Verona Wallace-Williamson	SCO	(1938)	0	0	0	0
Nan Wardlaw (Baird)	SCO	1938	1	0	1	0
Sally Watson	SCO	2008	5	3	2	0
Enid Wilson	ENG	1932	2	1	1	0
Janette Wright (Robertson)	SCO	1954-56-58-60	8	3	5	0
Phyllis Wylie (Wade)	ENG	1938	1	0	0	1

United States of America

Name	Year	Played	Won	Lost	Halved
Roberta Albers	1968	2	1	0	1
Danielle Ammaccapane	1986	3	0	3	0
Kathy Baker	1982	4	3	0	1
Barbara Barrow	1976	2	1	0	1
Beth Barry	1972-74	5	3	1	1
Emily Bastel	2002	2	0	2	0
Beth Bauer	1998-2000	7	4	3	0
Laura Baugh	1972	4	2	1	1
Leland Beckel	2000	1	0	1	0
Judy Bell	1960-62-(86)-(88)	2	1	1	0
Peggy Kirk Bell (Kirk)	1950	2	1	1	0
Amy Benz	1982	3	2	1	0
Patty Berg	1936-38	4	1	2	1
Erica Blasberg	2004	2	1	2	1
Amanda Blumenherst	2006-08	8	4	3	1
Barbara Fay Boddie (White)	1964-66	8	7	0	1
Meghan Bolger	2008	3	0	3	0
Jane Booth (Bastanchury)	1970-72-74-(2000)	12	9	3	0
Kellee Booth	1996-98	7	5	2	0
Mary Budke	1974-(2002)	3	2	1	0
Robin Burke	1998	3	2	1	0
Brandie Burton	1990	3	3	0	0
Jo Anne Carner (Gunderson)	1958-60-62-64	10	6	3	1
Lori Castillo	1980	3	2	1	0
Leona Cheney (Pressler)	1932-34-36	6	5	1	0
Sis Choate	(1974)	0	0	0	0
Jenny Chuasiriporn	1998	3	0	2	1
Peggy Conley	1964-68	6	3	1	2
Mary Ann Cook (Downey)	1956	2	1	1	0
Patricia Cornett	1978-88	4	1	2	1
Brenda Corrie Kuehn	1996-98	7	4	3	0
Jean Crawford (Ashley)	1962-66-68-(72)	8	6	2	0
Paula Creamer	2004	3	2	1	0
Clifford Ann Creed	1962	2	2	0	0
Grace Cronin (Lenczyk)	1948-50	3	2	1	0
Carolyn Cudone	1956-(70)	1	1	0	0
Beth Daniel	1976-78	8	7	1	0
Virginia Dennehy	(1958)	0	0	0	0
Virginia Derby Grimes	1998-2000	6	3	1	2
Mary Lou Dill	1968	3	1	1	1
Meredith Duncan	2002	4	3	1	0
Alice Dye	1970	2	1	0	1

Name	Year	Played	Won	Lost	Halved
Mollie Fankhauser	2002	3	1	2	0
Heather Farr	1984	3	2	1	0
Jane Fassinger	1970	1	0	1	0
Mary Lena Faulk	1954	2	1	1	0
Carol Sorensen Flenniken (Sorensen)	1964-66	8	6	1	1
Edith Flippin (Quier)	(1954)-(56)	0	0	0	0
Amy Fruhwirth	1992	4	0	1	3
Kim Gardner	1986	3	1	1	1
Charlotte Glutting	1934-36-38	5	3	1	1
Vicki Goetze	1990-92	8	4	2	2
Brenda Goldsmith	1978-80	4	2	2	0
Aniela Goldthwaite	1934-(52)	1	0	1	0
Joanne Goodwin	1960	2	1	1	0
Virginia Grimes	2006	2	1	1	0
Mary Hafeman	1980	2	1	0	1
Shelley Hamkin	1968-70	8	3	3	2
Penny Hammel	1984	3	1	1	1
Nancy Hammer (Hager)	1970	2	1	1	0
Cathy Hanlon	1982	3	2	1	0
Beverley Hanson	1950	2	2	0	0
Tracy Hanson	1992	3	1	2	0
Patricia Harbottle (Lesser)	1954-56	3	2	1	0
Leigh Anne Hardin	2002	3	1	2	0
Mina Harigae	2008	4	2	2	0
Helen Hawes	(1964)	0	0	0	0
Kathryn Hemphill	1938	1	0	0	1
Helen Hicks	1932	2	1	1	0
Carolyn Hill	1978	2	0	0	2
Cindy Hill	1970-74-76-78	14	5	6	3
Opel Hill	1932-34-36	6	2	3	1
Marion Hollins	(1932)	0	0	0	0
Hilary Homeyer	2000	4	3	0	1
Dana Howe	1984	3	1	1	1
Sarah Huarte	2004	2	0	2	0
Juli Inkster	1982	4	4	0	0
Elizabeth Janangelo	2004	3	1	2	0
Maria Jemsek	1996	3	0	2	1
Angela Jerman	2002	3	2	1	0
Tiffany Joh	2008	4	2	1	1
Ann Casey Johnstone	1958-60-62	4	3	1	0
Mae Murray Jones (Murray)	1952	1	0	1	0
Wendy Kaupp	1994	2	0	2	0
Stephanie Keever	2000	4	2	2	0
Caroline Keggi	1988	3	0	2	1
Tracy Kerdyk	1988	4	2	1	1
Cristie Kerr	1996	3	1	1	1
Kandi Kessler	1986	3	1	1	1
Dorothy Kielty	1948-50	4	4	0	0
Kimberly Kim	2008	4	3	1	0
Dorothy Kirby	1948-50-52-54	7	4	3	0
Martha Kirouac (Wilkinson)	1970-72-(2004)	8	5	3	0
Emilee Klein	1994	4	3	1	0
Nancy Knight (Lopez)	1976	2	2	0	0
Kelli Kuehne	1996	3	2	1	0
Brittany Lang	2004	3	1	2	0
Martha Lang	1992-(96)	3	2	0	1
Bonnie Lauer	1974	4	2	2	0
Sarah Le Brun Ingram	1992-94-96	7	2	4	1
Jennie Lee	2006-08	6	2	3	1
Taylor Leon	2006	4	3	0	1
Stacy Lewis	2008	5	5	0	0
Marjorie Lindsay	1952	2	1	1	0
Patricia Lucey (O'Sullivan)	1952	1	0	1	0
Paige Mackenzie	2006	4	3	1	0
Amanda McCurdy	2006	2	1	1	0
Mari McDougall	1982	2	2	0	0
Jill McGill	1994	4	1	1	2
Barbara McIntire	1958-60-62-64-66-72-(76)	16	6	6	4
Lucile Mann (Robinson)	1934	1	0	1	0
Debbie Massey	1974-76	5	5	0	0

Curtis Cup Individual Records *continued*

Name	Year	Played	Won	Lost	Halved
Marion Miley	1938	2	1	0	1
Dottie Mochrie (Pepper)	1986	3	0	2	1
Evelyn Monsted	(1968)	0	0	0	0
Terri Moody	1980	2	1	0	1
Laura Myerscough	2002	3	3	0	0
Karen Noble	1990	4	2	2	0
Judith Oliver	1978-80-82-(92)	8	5	1	2
Maureen Orcutt	1932-34-36-38	8	5	3	0
Joanne Pacillo	1984	3	1	1	1
Estelle Page (Lawson)	1938-48	4	3	1	0
Jane Park	2004-06	7	4	2	1
Katie Peterson	1990	3	3	0	0
Margaret Platt	1990	2	0	2	0
Frances Pond (Stebbins)	(1938)	0	0	0	0
Ellen Port	1994-96	6	4	2	0
Dorothy Germain Porter	1950-(66)	2	1	0	1
Phyllis Preuss	1962-64-66-68-70-(84)	15	10	4	1
Betty Probasco	(1982)	0	0	0	0
Mildred Prunaret	(1960)	0	0	0	0
Polly Riley	1948-50-52-54-56-58-(62)	10	5	5	0
Jo Jo Robertson	1998	2	0	2	0
Barbara Romack	1954-56-58	5	3	2	0
Jody Rosenthal	1984	3	2	0	1
Anne Sander [Welts] [Decker] (Quast)	1958-60-62-66-68-74-84-90	22	11	7	4
Cindy Scholefield	1988	3	0	3	0
Cindy Schreyer	1986	3	1	2	0
Kathleen McCarthy Scrivner (McCarthy)	1986-88	6	2	3	1
Carol Semple Thompson	1974-76-80-82-90-92-94-96-(98)-2000-02-(06)-(08)	33	16	13	4
Leslie Shannon	1986-88-90-92	9	1	6	2
Patty Sheehan	1980	4	4	0	0
Pearl Sinn	1988	2	1	1	0
Grace De Moss Smith (De Moss)	1952-54	3	1	2	0
Lancy Smith	1972-78-80-82-84-(94)	16	7	5	4
Margaret Smith	1956	2	2	0	0
Stephanie Sparks	1994	2	0	2	0
Hollis Stacy	1972	2	0	1	1
Claire Stancik (Doran)	1952-54	4	4	0	0
Angela Stanford	2000	4	1	2	1
Judy Street (Eller)	1960	2	2	0	0
Louise Suggs	1948	2	0	1	1
Jenny Suh	2006	2	0	2	0
Courtney Swaim	2002	4	3	1	0
Nancy Roth Syms (Roth)	1964-66-76-(80)	9	3	5	1
Anne Thurman	2004	4	3	1	0
Noreen Uihlein	1978	3	1	1	1
Virginia Van Wie	1932-34	4	3	0	1
Glenna Collett Vare (Collett)	1932-(34)-36-38-48-(50)	7	4	2	1
Alison Walshe	2008	4	4	0	0
Wendy Ward	1994	3	1	2	0
Jane Weiss (Nelson)	1956	1	0	1	0
Robin Weiss	1990-92-2000	7	4	2	1
Donna White (Horton)	1976	2	2	0	0
Mary Anne Widman	1984	3	2	1	0
Michelle Wie	2004	4	2	2	0
Kimberley Williams	1986	3	0	3	0
Helen Sigel Wilson (Sigel)	1950-66-(78)	2	0	2	0
Joyce Ziske	1954	1	0	1	0

Women's World Amateur Team Championship for the Espirito Santo Trophy

Grange (East & West), Adelaide, Australia   [6097–74; 5995–74]

1	Sweden	561	(Caroline Hedwall, Anna Nordqvist, Penilla Lindberg)
2	Spain	573	(Azahara Muñoz. Carlota Ciganda, Belen Mozo)
3	USA	575	(Alison Walshe, Amanda Blumenhurst, Tiffany Joh)
4	Canada	583	
5	Japan	584	

6	Germany	585
7	England	586
8	Denmark	587
	Netherlands	
10	South Africa	588
11	Korea	592
	Scotland	

Individual:

1	Caroline Hedwall (SWE)	67-70-73-70—280
2	Anna Nordqvist (SWE)	70-68-74-69—281
3	Azahara Muñoz (ESP)	71-72-74-70—287

48 Teams took part

1964	1 France; 2 United States
1966	1 United States; 2 Canada
1968	1 United States; 2 Australia
1970	1 United States; 2 France
1972	1 United States; 2 France
1974	1 United States; 2 GBI/South § Africa
1976	1 United States; 2 France
1978	1 Australia; 2 Canada

1980	1 United States; 2 Australia
1982	1 United States; 2 New Zealand
1984	1 United States; 2 France
1986	1 Spain; 2 France
1988	1 United States; 2 Sweden
1990	1 United States; 2 New Zealand
1992	1 Spain; 2 GBI

1994	1 United States; 2 Korea
1996	1 Korea; 2 Italy
1998	1 United States; 2 Italy
2000	1 France; 2 Korea
2002	1 Australia; 2 Thailand
2004	1 Sweden; 2 Canada
2006	1 South Africa*; 2 Sweden

*South Africa won on a countback

Commonwealth Tournament (Instituted 1959)

1959	Great Britain	1975	Great Britain	1991	Great Britain	2007	Great Britain
1963	Great Britain	1979	Canada	1995	Australia		
1967	Great Britain	1983	Australia	1999	Australia		
1971	Great Britain	1987	Canada	2003	Australia		

European Ladies Team Championship *Stenungsund, Sweden*

1 Sweden, 2 Netherlands, 3 Spain, 4 England, 5 Denmark, 6 France, 7 Scotland, 8 Austria

16 teams took part

Winning team: Caroline Hedwall, Jacqueline Hedwall, Camilla Lennarth, Pernilla Lindberg, Anna Nordqvist, Caroline Westrup

1959	1 France; 2 Italy
1961	1 France; 2 Italy
1963	1 Belgium; 2 France
1965	1 England; 2 Sccotland
1967	1 England; 2 France
1969	1 France; 2 England
1971	1 England; 2 France
1973	1 England; 2 France

1975	1 France; 2 Spain
1977	1 England; 2 Spain
1979	1 Ireland; 2 Germany
1981	1 Sweden; 2 France
1983	1 Ireland; 2 England
1985	1 England; 2 Italy
1987	1 Sweden; 2 Wales
1989	1 France; 2 England

1991	1 England; 2 Sweden
1993	1 England; 2 Spain
1995	1 Spain; 2 Scotland
1999	1 France; 2 England
2001	1 Sweden; 2 Spain
2003	1 Spain; 2 Sweden
2005	1 Spain; 2 England
2007	1 Spain; 2 Sweden

European Senior Ladies Team Championship *Wouwse Plantage, Netherlands*

1 Sweden, 2 Spain, 3 France, 4 England, 5 Ireland, 6 Belgium, 7 Germany, 8 Italy

14 teams took part

Winning Team: Viveca Hoff, Christine Birke, Gunilla Ekman, Birgitta Ljung; Ann-Kristin Hermansson; Monica Andersson

2006	France	2007	France

Vagliano Trophy – Great Britain & Ireland v Continent of Europe

1959	GBI	1973	GBI	1987	GBI	2001	Europe
1961	GBI	1975	GBI	1989	GBI	2003	GBI
1963	GBI	1977	GBI	1991	GBI	2005	GBI
1965	Europe	1979	Halved	1993	GBI	2007	Europe
1967	Europe	1981	Europe	1995	Europe		
1969	Europe	1983	GBI	1997	Europe		
1971	GBI	1985	GBI	1999	Europe		

European Club Cup (2001–2003 La Boulie, France) *GC Bergischland, Wuppertal, Germany*

1	Germany (Leon Rot)	442	(Sophie Popov, Anne-Katrin Schmitt, Nicole Langelbach)
2	Austria (Gut Murstatten)	452	
3	Spain (Real, Puerta de Hierra)	453	

15 teams took part

Best individual score: Sophie Popov 71-73-74--218

2001	Spain (Jarama Race GC)	2004	Germany (St Leon Rot GC)	2007	Germany I (GC Hubbelrath)
2002	Germany (Bergisch-Land GC)	2005	France (RCF La Boulie)		
2003	Germany (Bergisch-Land GC)	2006	Italy (Asolo GC)		

All-Africa Challenge (inaugurated 1992) *Katantya Heights, Egypt*

1	431	RSA (Monique Smit, Tandi Cuningham, Gina Switala)
2	469	Egypt
3	476	Zambia, Zimbabwe
5	478	Kenya

Best Individual: Monique Smit—212

1992	Team: South Africa Individual: Gillian Tebbutt (RSA)	2000	Team: South Africa Individual: Natu Soro (CIV)* *Beat Nora Mbabazi (UGA) in play-off	2006	Team: Egypt Individual: Naela El Attar (EGY)
1994	Team: South Africa Individual: Wendy Warrington (RSA)	2002	Team: South Africa Individual: Rose Naliaka (KEN)		
1996	Team: South Africa Individual: Michelle Burmester (ZIM)	2004	Team: South Africa Individual: Lumien Lausberg (RSA)		
1998	Team: South Africa Individual: Joanne Norton (RSA)				

Women's Home Internationals *Wrexham*

Wales 5½, Scotland 3½   Ireland ½, Wales 5½
Ireland 5½, England 3½   Scotland 6½, Ireland 2½
England 5, Scotland 4   Wales 3½, England 5½

Result: 1 Wales 2 (14½); 2 Scotland 1 (14, 11 wins); 3 England 2 (14, 9 wins); 4 Ireland 1 (11½)

Winning Team: Amy Boulden (Maesdu), Tara Davies (Holyhead), Stephanie Evans (Valeof Llangollen), Sahra Hassan (Vale of Glamorgan), Hannah Jenkins (Cradoc), Breanne Loucks (Wrexham), Rhian Wyn Thomas (Vale of Glamorgan)

1948	England	1964	England	1978	England	1993	England
1949	Scotland	1965	England	1979T	Scotland	1994	England
1950	Scotland	1966	England		Ireland	1995	England
1951	Scotland	1967	England	1980	Ireland	1996	England
1952	Scotland	1968	England	1981	Scotland	1997	England
1953	England	1969T	England	1982	England	1998	England
1954T	England		Scotland	1983	Matches abandoned	1999	Wales
	Scotland	1970	England		due to weather	2000	England
1955	England	1971	England	1984	England	2001	England
1956	Scotland	1972	England	1985	England	2002	England
1957	Scotland	1973	England	1986	Ireland	2003	Ireland
1958	England	1974T	England/	1987	England	2004	Ireland
1959	England		Scotland	1988	Scotland	2005	England
1960	England		Ireland	1989	England	2006	England
1961	Scotland	1975	England	1990	Scotland	2007	England
1962	Scotland	1976	England	1991	Scotland		
1963	England	1977	England	1992	England		

Senior Home Internationals *Little Aston*

Scotland 3, Wales 5	England 6, Scotland 2,
England 7½, Ireland ½	Wales 5, England 3
Ireland 1, Wales 7	Scotland 5½, Ireland 2½

Result: 1 Wales 3 (17); 2 England 2(16½); 3 Scotland 1 (10½); 4 Ireland 0 (4)

Winning team: Janet Doleman (Rushcliffe), Helen Joyce ( ), Ann Lewis (Royal St David's), Jean O'Connor (Coffs Harbour), Jane Rees (Hendon), Denise Richards (Bargoed), Vicki Thomas (Carmarthen)

2003	England; Ireland; Wales; Scotland	2005	England; Scotland, Wales, Ireland	2007	England; Scotland; Wales; Ireland
2004	England; Scotland; Wales; Ireland	2006	England; Scotland; Wales; Ireland		

England and Wales Ladies County Championship *Long Ashton*

First day: Yorkshire (North) 6, Sussex (South) 3; Leicestershire & Rutland (Midlands North) 6, Dorset (South West) 3; Hertfordshire (East) 6, Warwickshire (Midlands South) 3

Second day: Leicestershire & Rutland 4½, Hertfordshire 4½; Sussex 7, Dorset 2; Warwickshire ½, Yorkshire 8½

Third day: Dorset 4, Warwickshire 5; Yorkshire 5½, Hertfordshire 3½; Leicestershire & Rutland 5½, Sussex 3½

Fourth day: Yorkshire 6, Leicestershire & Rutland 3; Sussex 2½, Warwickshire 6½; Hertfordshire 6½, Dorset 2½

Fifth day: Hertfordshire 6, Sussex 3; Warwickshire 5, Leicestershire & Rutland 4; Dorset 1½, Yorkshire 7½

Result: 1 Yorkshire [5-33½]; 2 Hertfordshire [3½-26½]; 3 Warwickshire [3-20]; 4 Leicestershire & Rutland [2½-23]; 5 Sussex [1-19]; 6 Dorset [0-13]

Winning team: Winifred Varley (captain); Emma Brown, Kim Crooks, Nikki Dunn, Naomi Edwards, Sara Garbutt, Laura Harvey, Ellie Robinson, Helen Searle

1908	Lancashire	1936	Surrey	1966	Lancashire	1988	Surrey
1909	Surrey	1937	Surrey	1967	Lancashire	1989	Cheshire
1910	Cheshire	1938	Lancashire	1968	Surrey	1990	Cheshire
1911	Cheshire	1947	Surrey	1969	Lancashire	1991	Glamorgan
1912	Cheshire	1948	Yorkshire	1970	Yorkshire	1992	Hampshire
1913	Surrey	1949	Surrey	1971	Kent	1993	Lancashire
1920	Middlesex	1950	Yorkshire	1972	Kent	1994	Staffordshire
1921	Surrey	1951	Lancashire	1973	Northumberland	1995	Hampshire
1922	Surrey	1952	Lancashire	1974	Surrey	1996	Cheshire
1923	Surrey	1953	Surrey	1975	Glamorgan	1997	Surrey
1924	Surrey	1954	Warwickshire	1976	Staffordshire	1998	Yorkshire
1925	Surrey	1955	Surrey	1977	Essex	1999	Yorkshire
1926	Surrey	1956	Kent	1978	Glamorgan	2000	Yorkshire
1927	Yorkshire	1957	Middlesex	1979	Essex	2001	Yorkshire
1928	Cheshire	1958	Lancashire	1980	Lancashire	2002	Lancashire
1929	Yorkshire	1959	Middlesex	1981	Glamorgan	2003	Kent
1930	Surrey	1960	Lancashire	1982	Surrey	2004	Yorkshire
1931	Middlesex	1961	Middlesex	1983	Surrey	2005	Yorkshire
1932	Cheshire	1962	Staffordshire	1984	Surrey/Yorkshire	2006	Yorkshire
1933	Yorkshire	1963	Warwickshire	1985	Surrey	2007	Yorkshire
1934	Surrey	1964	Lancashire	1986	Glamorgan		
1935	Essex	1965	Staffordshire	1987	Lancashire		

Scottish Ladies County Championship   *Inchmarlo*

Perth & Kinross 2, Renfrewshire 7

Fife 7, Borders 2

Borders 1, Perth & Kinross 8

Renfrewshire 3, Fife 6

Renfrewshire 7, Borders 2

Perth & Kinross 4, Fife 5

Result: 1 Fife 3 [18]; 2 Renfrewshire 2 [17]; 3 Perth & Kinross 1 [14]; 4 Borders 0 [5]

Winning team: Lorna Bennett, Jocelyn Carthew, Lorna Fury, Fiona Hastie, Susan Jackson, Louise Kenney, Elaine Moffat, Karin Sharp

1992	Dunbartonshire & Argyll	1999	East Lothian	2004	Northern Counties
1993	East Lothian	2000	Northern Counties	2005	Midlothian
1994	East Lothian	2001	Stirlingshire &	2006	Fife
1995	Fife		Clackmannanshire	2007	Midlothian
1996	East Lothian	2002	Stirlingshire &		
1997	Dunbartonshire & Argyll		Clackmannanshire		
1998	East Lothian	2003	Northern Counties		

Welsh Ladies County Championship   *Clyne*

Northern   **Southern**

1	Caernarfon & Anglesey 1½		1	Glamorgan 2
2	Denbigh & Flint 1		2	Monmouth 1
3	Mid Wales ½		3	Carmarthen & Pembroke 0

Final: Glamorgan beat Caernarfon & Anglesey 7½–1½

Winning team: Gemma Bradbury, Katie Bradbury, Natasha Gobey, Miriam Hassan, Sahra Hassan, Rachel C Lewis, Rhian Wyn Thomas, Katie Westphal

Welsh Ladies Team Championship   *Nefyn*

Semi-Finals:

Cradoc beat Holyhead

Vale of Glamorgan beat Newport

Final: Vale of Glamorgan beat Cradoc 3–2

Winning team: Mary Burke, Sahra Hassan, Rita Howells, Zena Jackson, Kelly Miller, Rhian Wyn Thomas

1992	Whitchurch	1996	R. St Davids	2000	Pennard	2004	Rhuddlan
1993	Pennard	1997	St Pierre	2001	Whitchurch	2005	St Pierre
1994	St Pierre	1998	Wrexham	2002	Abergele	2006	Llandudno (Maedsu)
1995	R. St Davids	1999	Pennard	2003	Pennard	2007	Vale of Glamorgan

Asia-Pacific Women's Team Championship: Queen Sirikit Cup   (inaugurated 1979)

Sodegaura, Chiba, Japan

1	410	Korea (Han Jung-Eun, Yang Soo-Jin, Heo Yoon-Kyung)
2	413	Japan
3	427	Chinese Taipei

Other scores: Australia 433, New Zealand 437, Philippines 439, Indonesia 446, Thailand 448

1979	Japan	1987	Japan	1995	Korea	2003	Korea
1980	Japan	1988	Australia	1996	Korea	2004	Korea
1981	Australia	1989	Korea	1997	Japan	2005	Chinese Tapei
1982	Australia	1990	New Zealand	1998	Korea	2006	Chinese Tapei*
1983	Australia	1991	Korea	1999	New Zealand		*Beat New Zealand at first
1984	New Zealand	1992	Korea	2000	Australia		extra hole
1985	Australia	1993	Japan	2001	Australia	2007	Korea
1986	Australia	1994	Korea	2002	Japan		

Mary McKenna to captain two more teams

Mary McKenna has accepted an invitation to captain the Great Britain and Ireland teams for the 2009 Vagliano Trophy and the 2010 Curtis Cup. Mary, who captained the teams in 2007 and 2008, will again be supported by Tegwen Matthews as team manager.

One of Ireland's leading players, Mary won eight Irish Championships between 1969 and 1989 and participated in nine successive Curtis Cup matches and ten Vagliano Trophies. Tegwen was the first Welsh player to be picked for a Curtis Cup team, ultimately playing in four Curtis Cup matches and five Vagliano Trophies.

Trish Wilson, chaiman of the LGU, said: "With these golfing pedigrees, the team could not be in better hands. I firmly believe that a number of the memebrs of the current team will form a core part of both the 2009 Vagliano and 2010 Curtis Cup teams and the rapport already in place between the players, the captain and the manager will be invaluable going into the next series of matches."

The Vagliano Trophy will be played at Hamburger Golf Club, Falkenstein, Germany, on July 24 and 25 while the 2010 Curtis Cup returns to Essex Coutry Club in Manchester, Massachusetts, on June 10 to 13.

Captain McKenna said she was honoured to accept the role of captain again and looks forward to working with the LGU, the girls and her right-hand woman Tegwen for the next two years. "Without doubt, the Curtis Cup at St Andrews will always rank as one of my favourite experiences and I very much hope that I will be able to bring back the Cup and the Vagliano Troophy to Great Britain and Ireland."

Month by month in 2008

Seve Ballesteros is diagnosed with a brain tumour. Surgeons operate three times and every bulletin is eagerly awaited by the 51-year-old star's fans all around the globe. Scotland and Sweden win the men's and women's world amateur team titles in Australia, stand-in Jim Furyk takes the PGA Grand Slam in Bermuda – Padraig Harrington is beaten in a play-off there for the second year running – and Robert Karlsson's victory at the Dunhill Links sees him go top of the European Order of Merit.

Women's Foursomes Events 2008

London Ladies Foursomes   *Camberley Heath*
Final: Chelmsford (Trish Wilson, Fiona Smith) beat Guildford (Kate Shepherd, Sally Peters) 4 and 3

1992	Chelmsford	1996	The Berkshire	2000	Worplesdon	2004	Worplesdon
1993	Knebworth	1997	The Berkshire	2001	Porter's Park	2005	Chelmsford
1994	Knebworth	1998	The Berkshire	2002	Porter's Park	2006	Cowdray Park
1995	The Berkshire	1999	The Berkshire	2003	Chelmsford	2007	Chelmsford

Mothers and Daughters Foursomes   27-hole event   *Royal Mid-Surrey*

1	Ann & Alexandra Peters (Notts Ladies)	77-41—118
2	Charlotte & Christine Griffith (Walton Heath)	80-39—119
3	Elizabeth Boatman (Royal Worlington) & Alex Howe (Royal County Down)	77-43—120

1992	Mrs P Carrick and Mrs A Uzielli		1999	Mrs E Boatman and Miss A Boatman
1993	Mrs P Carrick and Mrs A Uzielli		2000	Lady Bonallack and Mrs G Beasley
1994	Mrs P Carrick and Mrs A Uzielli		2001	Mrs and Miss Gay
1995T	Mrs P Carrick and Mrs A Uzielli		2002	Mrs J Thornhill and Mrs C Weeks
	Mrs P Huntley and Miss J Huntley		2003	A Laughland and R Jenner
1996T	Mrs A Uzielli and Miss C Uzielli		2004	E Proven and S Saggers tied with W and K Laud
	Mrs E Boatman and Miss A Boatman		2005	L and A Boatman
	Mrs S Lines and Miss K Lines		2006	E Boatman and A Howe
1997	Mrs S Lines and Miss K Lines		2007	E Boatman and A Howe
1998	Mrs H Joyce and Miss C Joyce			

Scottish Ladies Foursomes   *Brunston Castle*
Cancelled

1992	Haggs Castle	1997	Stirling	2002	Ladies Panmure,	2006	St Regulus
1993	North Berwick	1998	Prestonfield		Barry	2007	St Regulus
1994	Turnberry	1999	Dunblane New	2003	Drumpellier		
1995	Gullane	2000	Windyhill	2004	Dunblane New		
1996	Hilton Park	2001	Stirling	2005	Stirling		

LGU Coronation Foursomes   *St Andrews (Eden)*

1	Jayne Coles & Claire Pettitt (Burhill)	42 pts
2	Katie Massie & Eileen Preston (Duns)	40
3	Lesley Turner & Jo White (Trent Lock)	33 bih

LGU Australian Spoons

England:	*at Long Ashton*	Bury St Edmunds (Theresa Haslam-Wise, Jane Watson)
Ireland:	*at Mountrath*	Killarney (Muireann O'Farrell, Bernie Nolan)
Scotland:	*at Torwoodlee*	Midlothian (Suzanne Ireland, Diane Moncrieff)
Wales:	*at Borth & Ynyslas*	Newport Links (Maria Ferguson, Sue Younger)

Other Women's Amateur Tournaments 2008

Lady Astor Salver (inaugurated 1951)   *always at The Berkshire*

1	Emma Brown [Duggleby] (Malton & Norton)	73-69—142
2	Sahra Hassan (Vale of Glamorgan)	69-74—143
3	Sarah Attwood (Gog Magog)	72-72--144

1951	J Bisgood	1963	R Porter	1975	J Thornhill	1988	JThornhill
1952	J Bisgood	1964	M Spearman	1976	H Clifford	1989	S Sutton
1953	J Bisgood	1965	M Spearman	1977	A Uzielli	1990T	J Morley
1954	J Donald	1966	A Bonallack	1978	M Everard		J Wade
1955	E Price	1967	M Everard	1979	J Greenhalgh	1991	EJ Smith
1956T	J Barton/	1968	M Everard	1980	J Lock	1992	L Walton
	E Price	1969	J Greenhalgh	1981	A Uzielli	1993	S Lambert
1957	A Ward	1970	B Whitehead	1982	*Abandoned*	1994	S Lambert
1958	A Bonallack	1971	A Uzielli	1983	L Denison-	1995	J Oliver
	nee Ward	1972	J Thornhill		Pender	1996	S Gallagher
1959	E Price	1973 T	L Denison-	1984	L Bayman	1997	J Lamb
1960	A Bonallack		Pender	1985	H Wadsworth	1998	R Morgan
1961	A Bonallack		A Uzielli	1986	C Pierce	1999	*Not played*
1962	R Porter	1974	C Barclay	1987	V Thomas		

2000T	C Court	
	K Taylor	
2001	E Pilgrim	
2002	*Abandoned*	
2003	K Smith	
2004	F Johnston	
2005	C Court	
2006	E Duggleby	
2007	E Bennett	
	(AUS)	

Bridget Jackson Bowl (inaugurated 1982)   *always at Handsworth*

1	Ellis Keenan (Sunningdale)	68-70—138
2	Holly Clyburn (Woodhall Spa)	72-72—144
	Tilly Holder (Woburn)	72-72—144

1982	J Brown	1988	V Thomas	1994	K Speak	2000	R Hudson	2006	S Stubbs
1983	J Brown	1989	H Dobson	1995	K Stupples	2001	L Wright	2007	E Bennett*
1984	T Johnson	1990	S Elliott	1996	R Hudson	2002	C Dowling		(AUS)
1985	T Johnson	1991	F Edmund	1997	K MacIntosh	2003	S McKevitt		*Beat S Hassan at 1st
1986	J Hill	1992	F Brown	1998	C Dowling	2004	F Johnston		extra hole
1987	V Thomas	1993	S Morgan	1999	S McKevitt	2005	A Scott		

Critchley Salver (inaugurated 1982)   *always at Sunningdale*

1	Laura Collin (John O'Gaunt)	71-74—145 } tied
	Kerry Smith (Waterlooville)	74-71—145
3	Holly Aitchison (The Bedfordshire)	76-72—148
	Lucy Gould (Bargoed)	68-80—148
	Sahra Hassan (Vale of Glamorgan)	68-80—148
	Claire Starkie (Silsden)	76-72—148

1982	H Reid	1988T	L Bayman	1993	CG Watson	1997	L Waters	2003	A Highgate
1983	K Douglas		J Wade	1994T	S Lambert	1998	L Waters	2004	N Cruse
1984	L Bayman	1989	L Fletcher		K Speak	1999	LC Tupholme	2005	K Smith
1985	L Bayman	1990	S Hourihane	1995T	K Tebbet	2000	C Court	2006	F Johnson
1986	W Wooldridge	1991	NL Buxton		A Uzielli	2001	E Duggleby	2007	C Aitken
1987	S Moorcraft	1992	C Caldwell	1996	S Gallagher	2002	E Pilgrim		

Hampshire Rose (inaugurated 1973)   *always at North Hants*

1	Ellis Keenan (Sunningdale)	75-67—142
2	Raffi Dyer (Hayling)	75-72—147
3	Kirsty Rands (Burhill)	72-76—148

1973	C Redford	1979	C Larkin	1987	J Thornhill	1995	J Oliver	2004	E Sheffield
1974	P Riddiford	1980	B New	1988	J Thornhill	1996	K Stupples	2005	H Burke
1975	V Marvin	1981	J Nicolson	1989	A MacDonald	1997	S Sanderson	2006	C Aitken
1976T	H Clifford	1982	J Thornhill	1990	S Keogh	1998	C Court	2007	C Aitken
	W Pithers	1983	J Pool	1991	K Egford	1999	C Court		
1977	J Greenhalgh	1984	C Redford	1992	A Uzielli	2000	K Fisher		
1978T	H Clifford		Caldwell	1993	C Hourihane	2001	K Smith		
	Glyn-Jones	1985	A Uzielli	1994T	K Shepherd	2002	K Smith		
	V Marvin	1986	C Hourihane		K Egford	2003	F More		

Liphook Scratch Cup (inaugurated 1992)   *always at Liphook*

1	Holly Aitchison (The Bedfordshire)	70-71—141
2	Liz Bennett (Brokenhurst Manor)	70-72—142
3	Kerry [Smith] Cripps (Waterlooville)	75-70—145

1992T	T Kernan,	1998	K Knowles	2005T	E Bennett	2007	H Aitchison*
	K Shepherd	1999	R Prout		F Smith		*Aitchison's 2nd round
1993	K Egford	2000	K Smith	2006	H Brockway*		65 equals the course
1994	S Sharpe	2001	N Timmins	*set record 65 in 2nd			record; her 134 total
1995	K Shepherd	2002	F More	round			is an event record
1996	K Shepherd	2003	S McKEvitt				
1997	E Weeks	2004	M Allen				

Roehampton Gold Cup (inaugurated 1926)   *always at Roehampton*

(This event has included women professionals since 1982 and has been an Open event since 1987)

1	Danielle Montgomery (The Lambourne)	71-75—146
2	Laura Eastwood (Tavistock)	77-73—150
	Sarah Heath (Telford)	73-77—150
4	Emilee Taylor (Gainsborough) (am)	79-72—151

1926	WM McNair	1951	J Bisgood	1969	A Irvin	1983T	B New	1997T	J Forbes
1927	M Gourlay	1952	J Bisgood	1970	M Everard		V Thomas		J Oliver
1928	C Leitch	1953	J Bisgood	1971	B Huke	1984	B New	1998T	K Lunn
1929	I Doxford	1954	I Bromley	1972	A Irvin	1985	V Thomas		J Head
1930	E Wilson		Davenport	1973T	A Irvin	1986T	K Harridge	1999	K Taylor
1931	V Lamb	1955	L Abrahams		C Redford		P Johnson	2000	S Forster
1932	A Gold	1956	S Allom	1974	L Harrold	1987	D Barnard	2001	T Loveys
1933	A Ramsden	1957	M Roberts	1975T	W Pithers	1988	A Johns	2002	F More
1934	J Hamilton	1958	P Moore		C Redford	1989T	C Lambert	2003	T Loveys
1935	P Barton	1959	MG Lidewell	1976T	A Irvin		C Panton	2004	A Coffey
1936	B Newell	1960	E Price		V Marvin	1990	K Imrie	2005	S Heath
1937	P Barton	1961	L Abrahams	1977	A Uzielli	1991	K Hurley	2006	J Oliver
1938	P Barton	1962	L Abrahams	1978T	C Redford	1992	K Marshall		T Loveys
1939	P Barton	1963	R Porter		Caldwell	1993	B New	2007T	K Taylor
1940–47	*Not played*	1964	RC Archer		B Robertson	1994	C Hall		C Aitken
1948	M Ruttle	1965	M Spearman	1979	B Robertson	1995	S Gallagher		
1949	F Stephens	1966	G Brandon	1980	A Bonallack	1996T	J Morley		
1950	M Ruttle	1967	A Irvin	1981	B Robertson		J Soulsby		
	Garrett	1968	A Irvin	1982	B Robertson				

St Rule Trophy (inaugurated 1984)   *always at St Andrews*

1	Kylie Walker (Buchanan Castle)	75-73—148
2	Audrey Goumard (FRA)	76-73—149
3	Isabelle Boineau (FRA)	76-74—150

1984	P Hammel	1990	A Sörenstam	1996	A Laing	2000	V Laing*	2004	L Stahle
1985	K Imrie	1991	A Rose	1997	K Rostron	*at 16, youngest ever		2005	N Edwards
1986	T Hammond	1992	M Wright	1998	N Clau	winner		2006	K Caithness
1987	J Morley	1993	C Lambert	1999	L Nicholson	2001	A Coffey	2007	M Reid
1988	C Middleton	1994	C Matthew			2002	H Stirling		
1989	C Middleton	1995	M Hjörth			2003	K Borjeskog		

The Leveret (inaugurated 1986)   *always at Formby*

1	Rachel Connor (Manchester)	73-75—148
2	Hannah Barwood (Knowle)	75-74—149
3	Samantha Round (Tadmarton Heath)	72-77—149

1986	P Smillie	1991	H Wilson	1998	J Bell	2003	J Davidson	2006 C Lee*
1987	D Glenn	1992	L Taylor	1999	R Morgan	2004	S Walker	*beat H Barwood on
1988	T Craik	1993	R Millington	2000	K Hutcherson	2005	K Mathuru	countback
1989	K Mitchell	1994	S Gallagher	2001	K Keogh			2007 L Jones
1990	L Walton	1997	E Ratcliffe	2002	J Davidson			

Tenby Ladies Open (inaugurated 1994)   *always at Tenby*

1	Breanne Loucks (Wrexham)	72-72—144
2	Sahra Hassan (Vale of Glamorgan)	73-77—150
3	Amy Boulden (Maesdu)	74-78—152

1994	V Thomas	1998	B Jones	2002	A Highgate	2004	S Evans	
1995	N Lawrenson	1999	B Morgan	2003	K Phillips*	2005	E Holland	
1996	V Thomas	2000	K Hutcherson	*after a play-off with J	2006	S James	
1997	V Thomas	2001	A Waller	Nicholson	2007	S Hassan	

Pleasington Putter (inaugurated 1995)   *always at Pleasington*

1	Tilly Holder (Woburn)	71-73—144
2	Catherine Roberts (Pleasington)	73-73—146
3	Sarah Walton (Clitheroe)	73-74—147

1995	E Clark	1999	D Rushworth	2003	J Ross	2006	K Combes*	
1996	K Egford	2000	C Firth	2004	N Haywood	*set record 141 winning	
1997	K Edwards	2001	L Gibson	2005	S Evans	total	
1998	S Beardsall	2002	S Hunter			2007	S Keating	

Royal Birkdale Scratch Trophy (inaugurated 1984)   *always at Royal Birkdale*

1	Emma [Duggleby] Brown (Malton & Norton)	70-73—143
2	Kelly Tidy (Royal Birkdale)	72-72—144
3	Laura Collin (John o'Gaunt)	72-75—147
	Charlotte Wild (Mere)	74-73—147

1984	J Melville	1989	LD Fairclough	1994	B Jones	1999	F Brown	2004 F Sanderson
1985	K Davies	1990	J Morley	1995	J Oliver	2000	K Fisher	2005 J Ross
1986	J Collingham	1991	Not played	1996	L Tupholme	2001	K Keogh	2006 J Wilson
1987	K Davies	1992	J Collingham	1997	F Brown	2002	K Heywood	2007 R Connor
1988	S Roberts	1993	S Burnell	1998	K Egford	2003	J Nicolson	

Wentworth Scratch Trophy   *always at Wentworth*

(This event included women professionals since 1982 and was an Open event since 1987)

Discontinued – for past results see the 2007 edition of the *Golfer's Handbook*

Munross Trophy (inaugurated 1986)   *always at Montrose*

1	Michele Thomson (McDonald Ellon)	71-71—142
2	Laura Murray (Alford)	76-67—143
3	Megan Briggs (Kilmacolm)	71-73—144

1986	E Farquharson	1991	M Wright*	1996	S Simpson	2000	L Kenny*	2005 J Wilson
1987	S Lawson	1992	C Lambert	1997	V Laing	2001	A Davidson	2006 J Wilson
1988	C Lambert	1993	J Moodie	1998	E Farquharson-	2002	H MacRae	2007 M Briggs
1989	C Lambert	1994	L Nicholson		Black	2003	A Laing	
1990	C Lambert	1995	L Nicholson	1999	A Laing	2004	L Jean	

Mackie Bowl (inaugurated 1974) *always at Gullane No 1*

1	Pamela Pretswell (Bothwell Castle)	67-66—133
2	Kylie Walker (Buchanan Castle)	74-68—142
3	Lesley Atkins (Minto)	75-70—145
	Louise Kenney (Pitreavie)	74-71—145

1974	TM Walker	1981	M Richmond	1988	D Thomson	1995	L Nicholson	2002 C Queen
1975	C Needham	1982	B Robertson	1989	MA Ferguson	1996	J Moodie	2003 L Wells
1976	VML McAlister	1983	B Robertson	1990	K Imrie	1997	H Monaghan	2004 C Queen
1977	LA Hope	1984	G Stewart	1991	M McKay	1998	A Laing	2005 K Walker
1978	B Huke	1985	B Robertson	1992	F McKay	1999	A Rose	2006 J Wilson
1979	J Connachan	1986	LA Hope	1993	M McKay	2000	V Melvin	2007 J Wilson
1980	FC Anderson	1987	F Anderson	1994	V Melvin	2001	L Kenny	

Riccarton Rose Bowl (inaugurated 1970) *always at Hamilton*

1	Kylie Walker (Buchanan Castle)	73-70—143
2	Laura Murray (Alford)	71-73—144
3	Megan Briggs (Kilmacolm)	71-75—146

Before trophy		1975	VM McAllister	1984	G Stewart	1993	M McKay	2002 *Not played*
presented		1976	L Bennett	1985	K Imrie	1994	A Gemmill	2003 A Laing
1970	J Norris	1977	L Bennett	1986	A Shannon	1995	A Laing	2004 C Hargan
1971	I Robertson	1978	L Hope	1987	A Gemmill	1996	M McKay	2005 J Wilson
Rosebowl presented		1979	W Aitken	1988	J Forbes	1997	M McKay	2006 J Wilson
by Mrs Jan Smellie		1980	S Gallacher	1989	L Lundie	1998	A Laing	2007 V Melvin
1972	IH Wylie	1981	W Aitken	1990	F McKay	1999	A Rose	
1973	G Cadden	1982	A Campbell	1991	F McKay	2000	A Davidson	
1974	KL Lackie	1983	L Bennet	1992	C Lambert	2001	L Kenny	

Mary McCallay Trophy (inaugurated 1978)
first year at Southerness, thereafter always at Dumfries & Galloway

Cancelled

1978	J Norris	1984	G Stewart	1990	K Fitzgerald	1996	A Laing	2002 A Laing
1979	W Aitken	1985	J Currie	1991	D Beaty	1997	H Monaghan	2003 L Kenny
1980	J Melville	1986	L Bennett	1992	J Moodie	1998	K Burns	2004 J Carthew
1981	B Robertson	1987	K Imrie	1993	J Moodie	1999	H Stirling	2005 J Wilson
1982	F Anderson	1988	M Wright	1994	C Blackshaw	2000	S Bishop	2006 E Ogilvie
1983	S Gallagher	1989	*Cancelled – rain*	1995	A Rose	2001	L McKay	2007 E Ogilvie

Ness Open (inaugurated 1986) *always at Inverness*

1	Laura Murray (Alford)	76-69—145
2	Megan Briggs (Kilmacolm)	75-72—147
	Lesley Hendry (Routenburn)	72-75—147
	Kylie Walker (Buchanan Castle)	74-73—147

1986	L Anderson	1991	J Jenkins	1996	H Stirling	2001	A Davidson	2006 L Murray
1987	L Phimister	1992	F McKay	1997	C Hargan	2002	*Cancelled*	2007 M Thomson
1988	S Alexander	1993	C Lambert	1998	C Hargan	2003	J Carthew	
1989	M Vass	1994	J Ford	1999	C Hargan	2004	*Cancelled*	
1990	M Vass	1995	H Monaghan	2000	H Stirling	2005	K MacDonald	

Scottish Universities Championships *Moray GC, Lossiemouth*

1	Pamela Pretswell (Glasgow)	80-73-74-76—303
2	Megan Briggs (Strathclyde)	80-77-75-76—308
3	Laura Murray (Robert Gordon)	79-76-74-80—309

2007   K Harper

Women's Regional Amateur Championships 2008

England

Bedfordshire   Holly Aitchison

Berkshire   Laura Webb

Buckinghamshire   Rachel Drummond

Cambridgeshire and
Huntingdonshire   Jackie Gregg

Cheshire   Rachael Goodall

Cornwall   Lynda Simpson

Cumbria   Hester Wallace

Derbyshire   Rebecca Wood

Devon   Charlotte Dommett

Dorset   Melissa McMahon

Durham   P Dobson

Essex   Jenny Pease

Gloucestershire   Cancelled (weather)

Hampshire   Elizabeth Bennett

Hertfordshire   Lucy Williams

Kent   Anne Wheble

Lancashire   Kelly Tidy

Leicestershire and Rutland
Jamie Leigh Voss

Lincolnshire   Holly Clyburn

Middlesex   Tara Watters

Midland Division   Harriet Owers-Bradley

Norfolk   Tracey Williamson

Northamptonshire   Christina Hancock

Northern Division   Faye Sanderson

Northumberland   Julie Ross

Nottinghamshire   Alexandra Peters

Oxfordshire   Samantha Round

Shropshire   Isabel Green

Somerset   Beverley New

South-Eastern Division   Charlotte Ellis

South-Western Division   Ellis Keenan

Staffordshire   Debbie Warren

Suffolk   Vicki Inglis

Surrey   Lisa McGowan

Sussex   Hannah Ralph

Warwickshire   Abbey Gittings

Wiltshire   Hannah Turland

Yorkshire   Naomi Edwards

Ireland

Munster   Niamh Kitching (Claremorris)

Ulster Open   Nikki Moore (Clandeboye)

Connacht   Anne McCormack (Roscommon)

Leinster   Tara Delaney (Carlow)

Midland   Tara Delaney (Carlow)

Scotland

Aberdeenshire   Donna Pocock

Angus   Rebecca Wilson

Ayrshire   Morag MacPherson

Border Counties   Judith Anderson

Dumfriesshire   Lindsey Kirkwood

Dunbartonshire and Argyll
Kylie Walker

East Lothian   Ruth Carroll

Eastern Division   Louise Kenney

Fife County   Fiona [Lockhart] Hastie

Galloway   Christina Meldrum

Lanarkshire   Susan Wood

Midlothian   Rachael Livingstone

Northern Counties   Cara Gruber

Northern Division Ladies
Alexandra Bushby

Perth and Kinross   Laura Walker

Renfrewshire   Megan Briggs

Southern Division   Not played

Stirling and Clackmannan
Alison [Rose] Davidson

Western Division   Megan Briggs

Wales

Caernarfonshire and Anglesey
Tara Davies (Holyhead)

Denbighshire and Flintshire
Beth Davies (Mold)

Glamorgan County
Sahra Hassan (Vale of Glamorgan)

Mid-Wales   Sharon Roberts

Monmouthshire   Hannah Jenkins (Cradoc)

Overseas Amateur Championships 2008

108th United States Women's Amateur Championship (inaugurated 1895)
Eugene, OR

Leading Qualifiers: Stephanie Na (AUS)   69-71—140
Amanda Blumenherst (Scottsdale, AZ) 66-74—140

Quarter Finals:
Azahara Muñoz (ESP) beat Stephanie Na (AUS)   7 and 6
Belen Mozo (ESP) beat Whitney Neuhauser (Barboursville, VA) 6 and 5
Amanda Blumenherst (Scottsdale, AZ) beat Carlota Ciganda (ESP)   4 and 3
Erynne Lee (Silverdale, WA) beat Chelsea Stetzmiller (Placerville, CA)   4 and 3

Semi-Finals:
Muñoz beat Mozo   4 and 3
Blumenherst beat Lee   3 and 2

Final:
Amanda Blumenherst beat Azahara Muñoz   2 and 1

1895	CS Brown beat N Sargent 132
Changed to match play	
1896	B Hoyt beat A Tunure 2 and 1
1897	B Hoyt beat N Sargent 5 and 4
1898	B Hoyt beat M Wetmore 5 and 3
1899	R Underhill beat M Fox 2 and 1
1900	FC Griscom beat M Curtis 6 and 5
1901	G Hecker beat L Herron 5 and 3
1902	G Hecker beat LA Wells 4 and 3
1903	B Anthony beat JA Carpenter 7 and 6
1904	GM Bishop beat EF Sanford 5 and 3
1905	P Mackay beat M Curtis 1 hole
1906	HS Curtis beat MB Adams 2 and 1
1907	M Curtis beat HS Curtis 7 and 6
1908	KC Harley beat TH Polhemus 6 and 5
1909	D Campbell beat N Barlow 3 and 2
1910	D Campbell beat GM Martin 2 and 1
1911	M Curtis beat LB Hyde 5 and 4
1912	M Curtis beat N Barlow 3 and 2
1913	G Ravenscroft beat M Hollins 2 holes
1914	KC Harley beat EV Rosenthal 1 hole
1915	F Vanderbeck beat M Gavin (ENG) 3 and 2
1916	A Stirling beat M Caverly 2 and 1
1917–1918 *Not played*	
1919	A Stirling beat M Gavin (ENG) 6 and 5
1920	A Stirling beat D Campbell Hurd 5 and 4
1921	M Hollins beat A Stirling 5 and 4
1922	G Collett beat M Gavin (ENG) 5 and 4
1923	E Cummings beat A Stirling 3 and 2
1924	D Campbell Hurd beat MK Browne 7 and 6
1925	G Collett beat A Stirling Fraser 9 and 8
1926	H Stetson beat E Goss 2 and 1
1927	MB Horn beat M Orcutt 5 and 4
1928	G Collett beat V Van Wie 13 and 12
1929	G Collett beat L Pressler 4 and 3
1930	G Collett beat V Van Wie 6 and 5

1931	H Hicks beat G Collett Vare 2 and 1
1932	V Van Wie beat G Collett Vare 10 and 8
1933	V Van Wie beat H Hicks 4 and 3
1934	V Van Wie beat D Traung 2 and 1
1935	G Collett Vare beat P Berg 3 and 2
1936	P Barton (ENG) beat M Orcutt 4 and 3
1937	EL Page beat P Berg 7 and 6
1938	P Berg beat EL Page 6 and 5
1939	B Jameson beat D Kirby 3 and 2
1940	B Jameson beat J Cochran 6 and 5
1941	E Hicks Newell beat H Sigel 5 and 3
1942–1945 *Not played*	
1946	B Zaharias beat C Sherman 11 and 9
1947	L Suggs beat D Kirby 2 holes
1948	G Lenczyk beat H Sigel 4 and 3
1949	D Porter beat D Kielty 3 and 2
1950	B Hanson beat M Murray 6 and 4
1951	D Kirby beat C Doran 2 and 1
1952	J Pung beat S McFedters 2 and 1
1953	ML Faulk beat P Riley 3 and 2
1954	B Romack beat M Wright 4 and 2
1955	P Lesser beat J Nelson 7 and 6
1956	M Stewart beat J Gunderson 2 and 1
1957	J Gunderson beat AC Johnstone 8 and 6
1958	A Quast beat B Romack 3 and 2
1959	B McIntyre beat J Goodwin 4 and 3
1960	J Gunderson beat J Ashley 6 and 5
1961	A Quast beat P Preuss 14 and 13
1962	J Gunderson beat A Baker 9 and 8
1963	A Quast beat P Conley 2 and 1
1964	B McIntyre beat J Gunderson 3 and 2
1965	J Ashley beat A Quast 5 and 4
1966	J Gunderson Carner beat JD Stewart Streit at 41st
1967	ML Dill beat J Ashley 5 and 4
1968	J Gunderson Carner beat A Quast 5 and 4

United States Women's Amateur Championship *continued*

1969	C Lacoste (FRA) beat S Hamlin 3 and 2	1989	V Goetze beat B Burton 4 and 3
1970	M Wilkinson beat C Hill 3 and 2	1990	P Hurst beat S Davis at 37th
1971	L Baugh beat B Barry 1 hole	1991	A Fruhwirth beat H Voorhees 5 and 4
1972	M Budke beat C Hill 5 and 4	1992	V Goetze beat A Sörenstam (SWE) 1 hole
1973	C Semple beat A Quast 1 hole	1993	J McGill beat S Ingram 1 hole
1974	C Hill beat C Semple 5 and 4	1994	W Ward beat J McGill 2 and 1
1975	B Daniel beat D Horton 3 and 2	1995	K Kuehne beat A-M Knight 4 and 2
1976	D Horton beat M Bretton 2 and 1	1996	K Kuehne beat M Baena 2 and 1
1977	B Daniel beat C Sherk 3 and 1	1997	S Cavalleri (ITA) beat R Burke 5 and 4
1978	C Sherk beat J Oliver 4 and 3	1998	G Park (KOR) beat J Chuasiriporn 7 and 6
1979	C Hill beat P Sheehan 7 and 6	1999	D Delasin beat J Kang 4 and 3
1980	J Inkster beat P Rizzo 2 holes	2000	N Newton beat L Myerscough 8 and 7
1981	J Inkster beat L Goggin (AUS) 1 hole	2001	M Duncan beat N Perrot at 37th
1982	J Inkster beat C Hanlon 4 and 3	2002	B Lucidi beat B Jackson 3 and 2
1983	J Pacillo beat S Quinlan 2 and 1	2003	V Nirapathpongporn beat J Park 2 and 1
1984	D Richard beat K Williams at 37th	2004	J Park beat A McCurdy
1985	M Hattori (JPN) beat C Stacy 5 and 4	2005	M Pressel beat M Martinez
1986	K Cockerill beat K McCarthy 9 and 7	2006	K Kim* beat K Schallenberg
1987	K Cockerill beat T Kerdyk 3 and 2		*at 14, the youngest-ever winner
1988	P Sinn beat K Noble 6 and 5	2007	MJ Uribe beat A Blumenherst 1 hole

Other 2008 Overseas Amateur Championships

Australia	Kristie Smith	Hellenic	Christina Laoudikou
Australian SP	Stephanie Na	Italy	Valeria Tandrini
Austrian	Martina Hochwimmer	Latvia	Galina Rotmistrove (RUS)
Canada	Stacey Keating (AUS)	Latvia (Close)	Krista Puisite
Cyprus	Veronika Thors Jonsdottir (ISL)	Mexico	Carmen Perez-Narbon (ESP)
		New Zealand	Dana Kim
Czech Republic	Veronika Holisova	Portugal	Carlota Ciganda (ESP)
Denmark	Malene Jorgensen	Russia	Galina Rotmistrove
Estonia	Lil Kuuli	Slovakia	Victoria Tomko
Estonie (Close)	Satu Harju	Slovenia	Martina Hochwimmer (AUT)
Finland	Mireia Prat (ESP)	South Africa	Breanne Loucks (WAL)
France SP (Trophée Cécile Rothschild)	Carlota Ciganda (ESP)	South Africa SP	Breanne Loucks (WAL)
		Spain	Caroline Masson (GER)
France Close		Switzerland	Pamela Pretswell (SCO)
Germany	Caroline Masson	Turkey	Ashleigh Holmes (RSA)
Germany Close	Nicola Roessler		

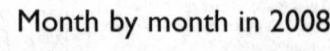

Month by month in 2008

Robert Karlsson becomes the first Swede to be crowned European number one as Søren Kjeldsen takes the last-ever Volvo Masters, but a mere four days later the new season is already under way. Sergio García wins the HSBC Champions, but Karlsson is back to the fore when he and Henrik Stenson combine for World Cup glory. Also in China, compatriot Annika Sörenstam achieves her 89th professional win and, in her second last event, captains the International team to victory over Asia in the Lexus Cup

PART VI

Mixed Men's and Women's Amateur Tournaments

European Nations Cup (formerly the Sherry Cup)   *Sotogrande, Spain*

Men:

1	Shane Lowry (IRL)*	73-67-69-71—280
2	Benjamin Hebert (FRA)	67-72-71-70—280

Lowry won at the first extra hole

3	Moises Cobo Arrayas (ESP)	71-71-69-72—283
	Sean Einhaus (GER)	73-69-73-68—283
	Callum Macaulay (SCO)	69-72-70-72—283

1970 Henric Adam (ENG)	1983 José L de Bernardo	1996 Alvaro Salto (ESP)	2006 N Edwards (WAL)*
1971 Alberto Croze (ITA)	(ESP)	1997 Sergio García (ESP)	*Beat JL Adarraga at 2nd
1972 E de la Riva,	1984 John Marks (ENG)	1998 Sergio García (ESP)	extra hole
J Gancedo (ESP)	1985 José L Padilla (ESP)	1999 Marcel Siem (GER)	2007 R McIlroy* (NIR)
1973 Alberto Croze (ITA)	1986 Borja Queipo de	2000 Gary Wolstenholme	*Beat M Thorp (NOR) at 1st
1974 Veit Pagel (GER)	Llano (ESP)	(ENG)	extra hole
1975 Veit Pagel (GER)	1987 Yago Beamonte (ESP)	2001 Gary Wolstenholme	
1976 Alberto Croze (ITA)	1988 Yago Beamonte (ESP)	(ENG)	
1977 F Jiménez (ESP)	1989 Diego Borrego (ESP)	2002 Lee Harpin (WAL)	
1978 José L de Bernardo	1990 Alvaro Prat (ESP)	2003 Gary Wolstenholme	
(ESP)	1991 Padraig Harrington	(ENG)	
1979 Veit Pagel (GER)	(IRL)	2004 Francesco Molinari	
1980 Jesús López (ESP)	1992 Frederic Cupillar (FRA)	(ITA)	
1981 Veit Pagel (GER)	1993 Francisco Valera (ESP)	2005 Gary Wolstenholme	
1982 Borja Queipo de	1994 Francisco Cea (ESP)	(ENG)	
Llano (ESP),	1995 José María Zamora		
Veit Pagel (GER)	(ESP)		

Team event:
1 Scotland 852; 2 Ireland 857; 3 Sweden, Germany 861

Remaining teams in finishing order: France, Spain, Wales, Norway, England , Italy, Finland, Czech Republic, Denmark, Portugal, Austria, Belgium, Iceland, Netherlands, Slovenia, Russia

Winning Team: Wallace Booth, Callum Macaulay, Keir McNicoll, Scott Henry

2001 England	2003 England	2005 Spain	2007 Denmark
2002 Wales	2004 England	2006 Spain	

Women:

1	Carlota Ciganda (ESP)	73-70-73-70—286
2	Caroline Hedwall (SWE)	73-74-69-75—291
3	Sahra Hassan (WAL)	77-72-73-73—295

1970 Catherine Lacoste (FRA)	1981 Cristina Marsans (ESP)	1991 Caterina Quintanelli	2001 Carmen Alonso (ESP)
1971 Emma Villacieros (ESP)	1982 Marta Figueras Dotti	(ITA)	2002 Kathryn Evans (WAL)
1972 Cristina Marsans (ESP)	(ESP)	1992 Estefania Knut (ESP)	2003 Bettina Hauert (GER)
1973 Emma Villacieros (ESP)	1983 María Orueta (ESP)	1993 Carin Ann Jonasson	2004 Tania Elósegui (ESP)
1974 Emma Villacieros (ESP)	1984 Ursula Beers (SUI)	(SWE)	2005 Stefanie Endstrasser
1975 Cristina Marsans (ESP)	1985 María Orueta (ESP)	1994 Ada O'Sullivan (IRL)	(AUT)
1976 Silvia Marlio (USA)	1986 María C Navarro (ESP)	1995 Maria Hjörth (SWE)	2006 Katharina Schallenberg
1977 Carmen Maestre (ESP)	1987 Lourdes Barbeito (ESP)	1996 Maria Hjörth (SWE)	(GER)*
1978 Carmen Maestre (ESP)	1988 Macarena	1997 Marieke Zelsman (NED)	*Beat S Walker at 2nd extra
1979 Marta Figueras Dotti	Campomanes (ESP)	1998 Nicole Stillig (GER)	hole
(ESP)	1989 Eva Vilagut (ESP)	1999 Martina Eberl (GER)	2007 K Schallenberg (GER)
1980 C de Albox (ESP)	1990 Esther Valera (ESP)	2000 Martina Eberl (GER)	

Team event:
1 Spain 577; 2 Wales 595; 3 Italy 596

Remaining teams in finishing order: Sweden, Germany, Austria, Netherlands, Finland, Denmark, Belgium, Iceland

Winning Team: Carlota Ciganda, Adriana Zwanck Saez, Ane Urchegui

Copa de las Americas

2003 Canada   2005   Canada   2007   USA

Spirit International

Whispering Pines, Houston, TX   [Men's course 7480–72; Women's course 6300–72]

The competition comprises the best 24 teams who qualified from their final positions in the previous year's Eisenhower and Espirito Santo Trophy competitions. The format is four-ball better ball over 72 holes.

Mixed competition:

2001 Mexico	2005 England
2003 USA	2007 England

Men's competition

2007 England

Women's competition:

2007 Korea

Chiberta Grand Prix *Chiberta d'Anglet*

Men:

1	Guillaume Cambis (FRA)	63-65-65-67—260
2	Robert McKnight (SCO)	65-68-67-69—269
	Jason Palmer (ENG)	68-68-66-67—269

2005 J Campillo (ESP)   2006   D Stewart (SCO)   2007   L Goddard (ENG)

Women:

1	Linn Gustafsson (SWE)	68-73-68-66—275
2	Stéphanie Derrey (FRA)	70-73-72-71—286
3	Fanny Bernard (FRA)	71-72-73-72—288
	Marion Ricordeau (FRA)	68-68-71-81—288

Copa los Andes *Cantegril CC, Punta del Este*

Men's competition

1 Argentina 15 pts; 2 Colombia 13 pts; 3 Peru 10 pts; 4 Uruguay 9 pts; 5 Brazil 8 pts; 6 Equador 6 pts; 7 Venezuela 5 pts; 8 Chile 4 pts; 9 Bolivia 2 pts

Argentina beat Bolivia 8–4, Brazil 10–2, Chile 9–3, Colombia 9–3, Equador 10–2, Peru 10–2, Uruguay 9–3 and drew with Venezuela 6–6

Winning team: E Grillo, A Rodriguez; J Etulain, I Fernandez and T Cocha

2006 Columbia   2007   Argentina

Women's competition

1 Argentina 14 pts; 2 Chile 14 pts; 3 Colombia 13 pts; 4 Peru 9 pts; 5 Paraguay 7 pts; 6 Brazil 5 pts; 7 Uruguay 5 pts; 8 Equador 4 pts; 9 Bolivia 1 pt

Argentina beat Bolivia 9–3, Brazil 11–1, Chile 10–2, Equador 12–0; Peru 10–2; Uruguay 11–1 and drew with Colombia 6–6 and Paraguay 6–6

Winning team: J Queen, M Gavi, V Tanc, A Parmigiani and M Olviero

2006 Argentina   2007   Bolivia

Red Sea Open Amateur Championship   *Soma Bay, Egypt*

Men (Gold):
1 Taymour Scarello (EGY)
2 Bensouda Moorri Kamal (MAR)
3 Taymour Aboul Kheir (EGY)

Women (Gold):
1 Maha Haddioui (MAR)
2 Donia Scarello (EGY)

Men (Silver):
1 MY El Kawy (LBA)
2 Ali Mufleh (QAT)

Women (Silver):
1 Helene Guillou (FRA)
2 Dina Abou El Ela (EGY)
3 Maha El Senousy (EGY)

Men (Bronze):
1 Aly M El Shakshouky (LBA)
2 Essam Badawi (EGY)
3 Amir Abdulla (LBA)

Women (Bronze):
1 Paula Martin (IRL)
2 Lamisse Kassar (LIB)
3 Sylvie Lhomer (FRA)

Newark "Ryder Cup"

Nottinghamshire club Newark has been holding its own Ryder Cup-style event since 1995, played alternatively in England and the USA against the Moundbuilders Club of Newark, Ohio. The tournament, for mixed men's and women's teams, is the creation of the then professionals Tony Bennett (Notts) and Larry McIntyre (Ohio). Although last year's match, the eighth staging of the event, was an 8–8 draw the English team, as the holders, retained the Newark Advertiser Cup. Prior to the 2008 event, the Nottinghamshire team had won all the events since the tournament's creation.

PART VII

Junior Tournaments and Events

Boys' and Youths' Tournaments

Boys Amateur Championship   *Little Aston*

Quarter Finals
Fraser McKenna (Balmore) beat Charles Durnian (Fairhaven) 1 hole

Victor Honauer (SUI) beat Moritz Lampert (GER) 1 hole

Levi Johnson (Canterbury) beat Matt Kippen (Enmore Park) 3 and 2

Pedro Figueiredo (POR) beat Cristiano Terragni (ITA) 3 and 2

Semi-Finals
McKenna beat Honauer 1 hole

Figueiredo beat Johnson 2 and 1

Final
Pedro Figueiredo beat
 Fraser McKenna at the 39th

1921	ADD Mathieson beat GH Lintott 37th hole	
1922	HS Mitchell beat W Greenfield 4 and 2	
1923	ADD Mathieson beat HS Mitchell 3 and 2	
1924	RW Peattie beat P Manuevrier (FRA) 2 holes	
1925	RW Peattie beat A McNair 4 and 3	
1926	EA McRuvie beat CW Timmis 1 hole	
1927	EW Fiddian beat K Forbes 4 and 2	
1928	S Scheftel beat A Dobbie 6 and 5	
1929	J Lindsay beat J Scott-Riddell 6 and 4	
1930	J Lindsay beat J Todd 5 and 4	
1931	H Thomson beat F McGloin 9 and 8	
1932	IS MacDonald beat LA Hardie 2 and 1	
1933	PB Lucas beat W McLachlan 3 and 2	
1934	RS Burles beat FB Allpass 12 and 10	
1935	JDA Langley beat R Norris 6 and 5	
1936	J Bruen beat W Innes 11 and 9	
1937	IM Roberts beat J Stewart 8 and 7	
1938	W Smeaton beat T Snowball 3 and 2	
1939	SB Williamson beat KG Thom 4 and 2	
1940–45	*Not played*	
1946	AFD Macgregor beat DF Dunstan 7 and 5	
1947	J Armour beat I Caldwell 5 and 4	
1948	JD Pritchett beat DH Reid 37th hole	
1949	H MacAnespie beat NV Drew 3 and 2	
1950	J Glover beat I Young 2 and 1	
1951	N Dunn beat MSR Lunt 6 and 5	
1952	M Bonallack beat AE Shepperson 37th hole	
1953	AE Shepperson beat AT Booth 6 and 4	
1954	AF Bussell beat K Warren 38th hole	
1955	SC Wilson beat BJK Aitken 39th hole	
1956	JF Ferguson beat CW Cole 2 and 1	
1957	D Ball beat J Wilson 2 and 1	
1958	R Braddon beat IM Stungo 4 and 3	
1959	AR Murphy beat EM Shamash 3 and 1	
1960	P Cros (FRA) beat PO Green 5 and 3	
1961	FS Morris beat C Clark 3 and 2	
1962	PM Townsend beat DC Penman 1 hole	
1963	AHC Soutar beat DI Rigby 2 and 1	
1964	PM Townsend beat RD Gray 9 and 8	
1965	GR Milne beat DK Midgley 4 and 2	
1966	A Phillips beat A Muller 12 and 11	
1967	LP Tupling beat SC Evans 4 and 2	
1968	SC Evans beat K Dabson 3 and 2	
1969	M Foster beat M Gray 37th hole	
1970	ID Gradwell beat JE Murray 1 hole	
1971	H Clark beat G Harvey 6 and 5	
1972	G Harvey beat R Newsome 7 and 5	
1973	DM Robertson beat S Betti (ITA) 5 and 3	
1974	TR Shannon beat A Lyle 10 and 9	
1975	B Marchbank beat A Lyle 1 hole	
1976	M Mouland beat G Hargreaves 6 and 5	
1977	I Ford beat CR Dalgleish 1 hole	
1978	S Keppler beat M Stokes 3 and 2	
1979	R Rafferty beat D Ray 6 and 5	
1980	D Muscroft beat A Llyr 7 and 6	
1981	J Lopez (ESP) beat R Weedon 4 and 3	
1982	M Grieve beat G Hickman 37th hole	
1983	JM Olazábal (ESP) beat M Pendaries (FRA) 6 and 5	
1984	L Vannet beat A Mednick (SWE) 2 and 1	
1985	J Cook beat W Henry 5 and 4	
1986	L Walker beat G King 5 and 4	
1987	C O'Carrol beat P Olsson (SWE) 3 and 1	
1988	S Pardoe beat D Haines 3 and 2	
1989	C Watts beat C Fraser 5 and 3	
1990	M Welch beat M Ellis 3 and 1	
1991	F Valera (ESP) beat R Walton 4 and 3	
1992	L Westerberg (SWE) beat F Jacobson (SWE) 3 and 2	
1993	D Howell beat V Gustavsson (SWE) 3 and 1	
1994	C Smith beat C Rodgers 2 and 1	
1995	S Young beat S Walker 7 and 6	
1996	K Ferrie beat M Pilkington 2 and 1	
1997	S García (ESP) beat R Jones 6 and 5	
1998	S O'Hara beat S Reale (ITA) 1 hole	
1999	A Gutierrez (ESP) beat M Skelton 1 hole	
2000	D Inglis beat D Skinns 1 hole	
2001	P Martin (ESP) beat R Cabrera (ESP) 3 and 2	
2002	M Pilling beat R Davies at 37th	
2003	R Davies beat P Martin (ESP) 1 hole	
2004	J Findlay beat T Sherreard 2 and 1	
2005	B Neumann (GER) beat J Findlay 3 and 2	
2006	M Nixon beat Björn Akesson (SWE) at 38th	
2007	E Cuartero (ESP) beat F Fotheringham 1 hole	

British Youths Open Amateur Championship

This championship bridged the gap between the Boys and the Men's tournaments from 1954 until 1994, when it was discontinued because it was no longer needed. The date on the schedule was used to introduce the Mid Amateur Championship for players over 25 but this event was discontinued after 2007.

For results see 2007 edition of the Golfer's Handbook

English Boys Under-18 Championship (Carris Trophy) *Wallasey*

1	Stiggy Hodgson (Sunningdale)*	75-70-69-74—288
2	Frederick Kollevold (NOR)	73-72-74-69—288

Hodgson won at the fifth extra hole

3	Gary King (Tyrrells Wood)	72-72-74-71—289

1935	R Upex	1955	ID Wheater	1969	ID Gradwell	1983	P Baker	1997	D Griffiths
1936	JDA Langley	1956	G Maisey	1970	MF Foster	1984	J Coe	1998	Y Ali
1937	RJ White	1957	G Maisey	1971	RJ Evans	1985	P Baker	1999	D Porter
1938	IP Garrow	1958	J Hamilton	1972	L Donovan	1986	G Evans	2000	G Lockerbie
1939	CW Warren	1959	RT Walker	1973	S Hadfield	1987	D Bathgate	2001	M Richardson
1946	AH Perowne	1960	PM Baxter	1974	KJ Brown	1988	P Page	2002	C Del Moral
1947	I Caldwell	1961	DJ Miller	1975	A Lyle	1989	I Garbutt	2003	D Denison
1948	I Caldwell	1962	FS Morris	1976	H Stott	1990	M Welch	2004	P Martin (ESP)
1949	PB Hine	1963	EJ Threlfall	1977	R Mugglestone	1991	I Pyman	2005	T Haylock
1950	J Glover	1964	PM Townsend	1978	J Plaxton	1992	M Foster	2006	D Wright
1951	I Young	1965	G McKay	1979	P Hammond	1993	J Harris	2007	M Haines
1952	N Thygesen	1966	A Black	1980	MP McLean	1994	R Duck		
1953	N Johnson	1967	RF Brown	1981	D Gilford	1995	J Rose		
1954	K Warren	1968	P Dawson	1982	M Jarvis	1996	G Storm		

English Boys Under-16 Championship (McGregor Trophy) *High Post*

1	Seb Crookall-Nixon (Workington)	70-69-71-68—278
2	Jamie Carney (Shirley)	71-67-72-70—280
3	James Brockington (Henley)	69-70-71-72—282

1994	G Storm	1997	R Paolillo	2000	M Skelton	2003	W De Vries	2006	O Sharpe
1995	J Rose	1998	MY Ali	2001	P Waring	2004	O Fisher	2007	A Carson
1996	E Molinari	1999	J Heath	2002	M Baldwin	2005	A Myers		

Irish Boys Close Championship (formerly IMSL Irish Boys Championship)

(inaugurated 1983) *Portumna*

1	Paul Dunne (Greystones)	76-70-69-75—290
2	Ian O'Rourke (Cork)	72-74-76-72—294
3	Michael Durcan (Co.Sligo)	76-71-74-74—295
	Garth Boyd (Donaghadee)	74-74-75-72—295

1983	J Carvill	1988	D McGrane	1993	H Armstrong	1998	D Jones	2003	B McCarroll
1984	E O'Connell	1989	D Higgins	1994	P Byrne	1999	M McTernan	2004	R McIlroy
1985	K Kearney	1990	R Burns	1995	L Dalton	2000	D McNamara	2005	N Kearney
1986	D Errity	1991	R Coughlan	1996	M Campbell	2001	M McHugh	2006	S Heal
1987	G McNeill	1992	J O'Sullivan	1997	M Hoey	2002	M McNamara	2007	G McGrane

Irish Youths Open Amateur Championship (inaugurated 1969) *Lisburn*

1	Seamus Power (West Waterford)	69-67-70-71—277
2	Liam Burns (ENG)	71-70-77-70—288
3	Andrew Hogan (Newlands)	75-68-72-75—290

1969	D Branigan	1977	B McDaid	1985	J McHenry	1993	CD Hislop	2001	M Ryan
1970	LA Owens	1978	T Corridan	1986	JC Morris	1994	B O'Melia	2002	G Wright
1971	MA Gannon	1979	R Rafferty	1987	C Everett	1995	S Young	2003	C Mills
1972	MA Gannon	1980	J McHenry	1988	P McGinley	1996	S Young	2004	R McIlroy
1973	J Purcell	1981	J McHenry	1989	A Mathers	1997	N Howley	2005	S Power
1974	S Dunlop	1982	K O'Donnell	1990	D Errity	1998	A Murray	2006	G Shaw
1975	P McNally	1983	P Murphy	1991	R Coughlan	1999	G McDowall	2007	S Power
1976	R McCormack	1984	JC Morris	1992	K Nolan	2000	G McDowall		

Irish Boys Under-15 *Massereene*

1	D McElroy (Ballymena)	74-71—145
2	W Chambers (ENG)	75-73—148
3	J Galbraith (Whitehead)	72-77—149

2007   G Collins

Scottish Boys Championship *Southerness*

Quarter Finals

Michael Stewart (Troon Welbeck) beat
  Mark Bookless (Sandyhills) 3 and 2
David Law (Hazlehead) beat Graeme McDougall
  (Bishopbriggs) 2 and 1
Paul Shields (Kirkhill) beat Colin Baird
  (Bothwell Castle) 5 and 3
Oliver Huish (North Berwick) beat James Ross
  (Royal Burgess) 1 hole

Semi-Finals

Stewart beat Law 2 holes
Shields beat Huish 5 and 4

Final

Michael Stewart beat Paul Shields 8 and 7

1960	L Carver beat S Wilson 6 and 5		1984	K Buchan beat L Vannet 2 and 1
1961	K Thomson beat G Wilson 10 and 8		1985	AD McQueen beat FJ McCulloch 1 hole
1962	HF Urquhart beat S MacDonald 3 and 2		1986	AG Tait beat EA McIntosh 6 and 5
1963	FS Morris beat I Clark 9 and 8		1987	AJ Coltart beat SJ Bannerman 37th hole
1964	WR Lockie beat MD Cleghorn 1 hole		1988	CA Fraser beat F Clark 9 and 8
1965	RL Penman beat J Wood 9 and 8		1989	M King beat D Brolls 8 and 7
1966	J McTear beat DG Greig 4 and 3		1990	B Collier beat D Keeney 2 and 1
1967	DG Greig beat I Cannon 2 and 1		1991	C Hislop beat R Thorton 11 and 9
1968	RD Weir beat M Grubb 4 and 2		1992	A Reid beat A Forsyth 2 and 1
1969	RP Fyfe beat IP Doig 4 and 2		1993	S Young beat A Campbell 4 and 2
1970	S Stephen beat M Henry 38th hole		1994	S Young beat E Little 2 and 1
1971	JE Murray beat AA Mackay 4 and 3		1995	S Young beat M Donaldson 7 and 6
1972	DM Robertson beat G Cairns 9 and 8		1996	S Whiteford beat I McLaughlin 3 and 2
1973	R Watson beat H Alexander 8 and 7		1997	M Donaldson beat L Rhind 1 hole
1974	DM Robertson beat J Cuddihy 6 and 5		1998	S O'Hara beat D Sutton 2 holes
1975	A Brown beat J Cuddihy 6 and 4		1999	L Harper beat M Syme 6 and 5
1976	B Marchbank beat J Cuddihy 2 and 1		2000	S Buckley beat M Risbridger 7 and 6
1977	JS Taylor beat GJ Webster 3 and 2		2001	S Brown beat R Gill 6 and 4
1978	J Huggan beat KW Stables 2 and 1		2002	J Hempstock beat R Taylor 4 and 2
1979	DR Weir beat S Morrison 5 and 3		2003	P Doherty beat G Wood 7 and 5
1980	R Gregan beat AJ Currie 2 and 1		2004	S Henry beat D Yeats 12 and 11
1981	C Stewart beat G Mellon 3 and 2		2005	S Henry beat E Polson 6 and 5
1982	A Smith beat J White 39th hole		2006	J White beat M Main 4 and 3
1983	C Gillies beat C Innes 38th hole		2007	P Ferrier beat W Bremner 1 hole

Scottish Boys Stroke Play Championship (inaugurated 1970)   *Blairgowrie (Lansdowne)*

1	Mark Bookless (Sandyhills)	67-70-75-70—282
2	Sam Binning (Ranfurly Castle)	68-75-71-69—283
3	Michael Stewart (Troon Welbeck)	70-73-70-74—287

1970	D Chillas	1978	R Fraser	1987	C Ronald	1996	M Brown	2005 S McEwan
1971	JE Murray	1979	L Mann	1988	M Urquhart	1997	L Rhind	2006 S McAllister
1972	S Martin	1980	ASK Glen	1989	C Fraser	1998	G Holland	2007 J Byrne*
1973	S Martin	1981	J Gullen	1990	N Archibald	1999	B Hume	*Beat M Stewart at
1974	PW Gallacher	1982	D Purdie	1991	S Gallacher	2000	C Ries (RSA)	3rd extra hole
1975	A Webster	1983	L Vannet	1992	S Gallacher	2001	S Jamieson	
1976	A Webster	1984	K Walker	1993	J Bunch	2002	M Lamb	
1977T	J Huggan	1985	G Matthew	1994	S Young	2003	L Saltman	
	L Mann	1986	G Cassells	1995	C Lee	2004	S Henry	

Scottish Boys Under-16 Stroke Play Championship (inaugurated 1990)   *The Glen*

1	Mikhail Ishaq (Bondhay)	65-70—135
2	Ben Taylor (Walton Heath)	67-71—138
3	Matthias Kaufmann (AUT)	69-70—139

1990	G Davidson	1994	S Fraser	1998	D Inglis	2002	S Borrowman	2006	S McLaren
1991	D Patrick	1995	C Campbell	1999	G Murray	2003	D Addison	2007	I Redford
1992	*Not played*	1996	P Whiteford	2000	W Booth	2004	G Stevenson		
1993	S Lamond	1997	D Inglis	2001	C Johnston	2005	D Renwick		

Scottish Youths Stroke Play Championship   (inaugurated 1979)   *The Roxburghe*

1	David Booth (Rotherham)	67-67-80-73—287
2	James Robinson (Southport & Ainsdale)	73-72-75-69—289
3	Matt Evans (Rotherham)	67-72-73-78—290

1979	A Oldcorn	1985	H Kemp	1991	D Robertson	1997	S Young	2003	M Laird
1980	G Brand jr	1986	A Mednick	1992	R Russell	1998	T Rice	2004	W Booth
1981	S Campbell	1987	K Walker	1993	CD Hislop	1999	J Hendry	2005	P McLachlan
1982	LS Mann	1988	P McGinley	1994	S Gallacher	2000	J Hendry	2006	F Pintor (ESP)
1983	A Moir	1989	J Mackenzie	1995	E Little	2001	J McLeary	2007	S Borrowman
1984	B Shields	1990	S Bannerman	1996	E Little	2002	G Bourdy		

Welsh Boys Championship (inaugurated 1954)   *Newport*

Leading Qualifier: Christopher Nugent (Fulford Heath) 69-72—141

Quarter Finals

Mike Hearne (Southerndown) beat Christopher Nugent (Fulford Heath) at 20th

Ross McLister (Cardiff) beat Dale Parry (Pontypridd) 1 hole

Matthew Moseley (Carmarthen) beat Richard Bentham (Celtic Manor) 1 hole

Patrick Mullins (Whitchurch) beat Matthew Phythian (Rhondda) 6 and 5

Semi-Finals

McLister beat Hearne 4 and 2

Moseley beat Mullins 1 hole

Final

Ross McLister beat Matthew Moseley 2 and 1

1954	JWH Mitchell beat DA Rees 8 and 6	1981	M Evans beat P Webborn 5 and 4
1955	EW Griffith beat DA Rees 3 and 2	1982	CM Rees beat KH Williams 2 holes
1956	DA Rees beat JP Hales 2 and 1	1983	MA Macara beat RN Roderick 1 hole
1957	P Waddilove beat JG Jones 2 and 1	1984	GA Macara beat D Bagg 1 hole
1958	P Waddilove beat J Williams 1 hole	1985	B Macfarlane beat R Herbert 1 hole
1959	C Gilford beat JG Jones 6 and 4	1986	C O'Carroll beat A Salmon 1 hole
1960	C Gilford beat JL Toye 5 and 4	1987	SJ Edwards beat A Herbert 19th hole
1961	AR Porter beat JL Toye 3 and 2	1988	C Platt beat P Murphy 2 and 1
1962	RC Waddilove beat W Wadrup 20th hole	1989	R Johnson beat RL Evans 2 holes
1963	G Matthews beat R Witchell 6 and 5	1990	M Ellis beat C Sheppard 3 and 2
1964	D Lloyd beat M Walters 2 and 1	1991	B Dredge beat A Cooper 2 and 1
1965	G Matthews beat DG Lloyd 7 and 6	1992	Y Taylor beat J Pugh 1 hole
1966	J Buckley beat DP Owen 4 and 2	1993	R Davies beat S Raybould 3 and 2
1967	J Buckley beat DL Stevens 2 and 1	1994	R Peet beat K Sullivan 7 and 6
1968	J Buckley beat C Brown 1 hole	1995	M Palmer beat O Pughe 4 and 3
1969	K Dabson beat P Light 5 and 3	1996	A Smith beat M Griffiths 19th hole
1970	P Tadman beat A Morgan 2 and 1	1997	A Lee beat I Campbell 4 and 3
1971	R Jenkins beat TJ Melia 3 and 2	1998	M Setterfield beat D Price 3 and 2
1972	MG Chugg beat RM Jones 3 and 2	1999	C Mills beat D Price 3 and 2
1973	R Tate beat N Duncan 2 and 1	2000	R Narduzzo beat G Dobson-Jones 1 hole
1974	D Williams beat S Lewis 5 and 4	2001	J Morgan beat B Briscoe St Mellons 3 and 2
1975	G Davies beat PG Garrett 20th hole	2002	C Cole beat J Morgan 4 and 3
1976	JM Morrow beat MG Mouland 1 hole	2003	T Light beat R Young 7 and 6
1977	JM Morrow beat MG Mouland 2 and 1	2004	M Jones beat L Lewis 3 and 2
1978	JM Morrow beat A Laking 2 and 1	2005	A Runcie beat R Merchant 2 and 1
1979	P Mayo beat M Hayward 24th hole	2006	R Merchant beat Z Gould 3 and 1
1980	A Llyr beat DK Wood 2 and 1	2007	J Vickery beat B Enoch 2 and 1

Welsh Boys Stroke Play Championship (inaugurated 1995) *Newport*

1	Christopher Nugent (Fulford Heath)	69-72—141
2	Gareth Blease (Coombe Hill)	69-73—142
3	Michael Evans (Clays)	70-73—143

1995	M Pillangton	1998	G Bennett	2001	J Morgan	2004	L Jones	2007 J Vickery
1996	A Lee	1999	G Bennett	2002	C Cole	2005	J Frazer	
1997	GM James	2000	C Mills	2003	C Wakely	2006	R Merchant	

Welsh Boys Under-15 Championship (inaugurated 1985) *Raglan Parc*

1	Patrick Mullins (Whitchurch)	75-70—145
2	Ryan Davies (Vale of Glamorgan)	71-75—146
3	Jack Bush (Morlais Castle)	74-73—147

1985	A Wesson	1991	M Lucas	1997	RW Johnson	2003	T Smith	2007 M Parry*
1986	A Wesson	1992	MC Gordon	1998	BM Briscoe	2004	Cancelled (bad	*Beat O Baker with
1987	J Grundy	1993	G Jones	1999	L James		weather)	better 2nd round
1988	S Rees	1994	AGL Smith	2000	M Jones	2005	B Enoch	
1989	Y Taylor	1995	C Thomas	2001	P Smith	2006	R Harston	
1990	R Morgan	1996	J Lloyd	2002	Z Gould			

Welsh Open Youths Championship (inaugurated 1993) *Vale of Llangollen*

1	Jonathan Gidney (Church Stretton)	71-70-66-67—274
2	Nick James (Wenvoe Castle)	69-68-71-73—281
3	Adam Sagar (Keighley)	69-71-74-70—284
	Joe Vickery (Newport)	70-76-69-69—284

1993	A McKenna	1996	D Harris	1999	D Price	2002	J Ruth	2005 D Lake
1994	D Quinney	1997	N Matthews	2000	B Welch	2003	M Laskey	2006 J Favata
1995	R Warner	1998	M Hearne	2001	T Dykes	2004	G Slater	2007 S Matton

Peter McEvoy Trophy (inaugurated 1988) *always at Copt Heath*

1	Stiggy Hodgson (Sunningdale)*	71-38-73-68—250
2	Eddie Pepperell (Drayton Park)	69-34-74-73—250

Hodgson won at the first extra hole

3	Jamie Brittain (Shifnal)	72-35-75-69—251
	Gary King (Tyrrells Wood)	71-34-76-70—251

1988	P Sefton	1992	B Davis	1996	M Pilkington	2000	Z Scotland	2004 J Parry
1989	D Bathgate	1993	S Webster	1997	P Rowe	2001	B Harvey	2005 T Sherreard
1990	P Sherman	1994	J Harris	1998	J Rose	2002	M Richardson	2006 L Goddard
1991	L Westwood	1995	C Duke	1999	D Porter	2003	T Hunter	2007 M Haines

Midland Boys Amateur Championship *Erewash*

1	Jamie Cantelo (Whittington Heath)*	72-71—143
2	James Billingham (Cosby)	72-71—143

Cantelo won at the first extra hole

3	Danny Tomlinson (Chevin)	71-73—144

1989	M Wilson	1993	S Webster		K Cliffe	2000	J Prince	2004 R Harris
1990	ML Welch	1994	R Duck	1997	K Hale	2001	O West	2005 A Chesters
1991	S Drummond	1995	C Richardson	1998	E Vernon	2002	B Stafford	2006 D Roland
1992	S Drummond	1996T	S Walker	1999	C Stevenson	2003	C Evans	2007 S Dodds

Midland Youths Championship *Stoke Rochford*

1	Jonathan Gidney (Church Stretton)	65-72-69-66—272
2	Ben Loughrey (Wrag Barn)	70-71-68-65—274
3	Robert Browning (Maxstoke Park)	72-71-67-70—280

Team Events

European Youths Team Championship *Bled, Slovenia*

Final Ranking: 1 Sweden, 2 Norway, 3 England, 4 Portugal, 5 Denmark, 6 Italy, 7 Ireland, 8 Germany (20 teams took part)

Winning Team: Eric Blom, Niclas Carlsson, Pontus Gad, Daniel Jennevret, Mattias Nordqvist, Sebastian Soderberg

1990	1 Italy; 2 Sweden	1996	1 Scotland; 2 Spain	2002	1 Sweden; 2 England
1992	1 Sweden; 2 England	1998	1 Wales; 2 Sweden	2004	1 Scotland; 2 England
1994	1 Ireland; 2 Sweden	2000	1 England; 2 Scotland	2006	1 Spain; 2 Italy

European Boys Team Championship *Bled, Slovenia*

1 Sweden, 2 Norway, 3 England, 4 Portugal, 5 Denmark, 6 Italy, 7 Ireland, 8 Germany (20 teams took part)

Winning Team: Eric Blom, Niclas Carlsson, Pontus Gad, Daniel Jennevret, Mattias Nordqvist, Sebastian Soderberg

1980	Spain	1986	England	1992	Scotland	1998	Ireland	2004	England
1981	England	1987	Scotland	1993	Sweden	1999	England	2005	Netherlands
1982	Italy	1988	France	1994	England	2000	Scotland	2006	Norway
1983	Sweden	1989	England	1995	England	2001	Sweden	2007	Denmark
1984	Scotland	1990	Spain	1996	Spain	2002	Spain		
1985	England	1991	Sweden	1997	Spain	2003	Italy		

Great Britain & Ireland v Continent of Europe (Jacques Léglise Trophy)

Kingsbarns, by St Andrews

Captains: GBI: Michael Stewart (SCO); Eur: Non-Playing Captain: Andreas Pallauf (AUT)

GBI names first:

First Day – **Foursomes**

M Stewart & B Enoch lost to M Manassero & C Terragni 2 and 1

T Fleetwood & S Hodgson beat F Kollevold & D Jennevret 3 and 2

L Lennox & A Dunbar beat E Cuartero & C Pigem 5 and 3

E Pepperell & G King lost to R Wattel & M Kieffer 1 hole

Singles

Michael Stewart (SCO) lost to Kasper Sørensen (DEN) 2 and 1

Tommy Fleetwood (ENG) lost to Matteo Manassero (ITA) 2 holes

Tom Lewis (ENG) halved with Cristiano Terragni (ITA)

Ben Enoch (WAL) beat Carlos Pigem (ESP) 1 hole

Stiggy Hodgson (ENG) lost to Daniel Jennevret (SWE) 2 holes

Gary King (ENG) lost to Emilio Cuartero (ESP) 2 and 1

Alan Dunbar (IRL) halved with Maximilian Kieffer (GER)

Eddie Pepperell (ENG) beat Romain Wattel (FRA) 1 hole

Second Day – **Foursomes**

E Pepperell & G King beat E Cuartero & C Pigem 3 and 2

M Stewart & B Enoch beat M Manassero & C Terragni 1 hole

T Fleetwood & S Hodgson lost to F Kollevold & D Jennevret 1 hole

L Lennox & A Dunbar beat R Wattel & M Kieffer 4 and 3

Singles

E Pepperell halved with K Sørensen

M Stewart beat C Pigem 3 and 1

B Enoch lost to E Cuartero 2 and 1

T Fleetwood beat C Terragni 3 and 2

A Dunbar beat M Manassero 3 and 1

Luke Lennox (IRL) beat R Wattel 3 and 2

T Lewis halved with Fredrik Kollevold (NOR)

S Hodgson beat M Kieffer 1 hole

Match result: GBI 14, Europe 10

Jacques Léglise Trophy *continued*

1958 GBI	1967–76 *Not played*	1984 GBI	1993 GBI	2002 Europe
1959 GBI		1985 GBI	1994 GBI	2003 GBI
1960 GBI	1977 Europe	1986 Europe	1995 GBI	2004 GBI
1961 GBI	1978 Europe	1987 GBI	1996 Europe	2005 Europe
1962 GBI	1979 GBI	1988 GBI	1997 Europe	2006 Europe
1963 GBI	1980 GBI	1989 GBI	1998 GBI	2007 GBI
1964 GBI	1981 GBI	1990 GBI	1999 GBI	
1965 GBI	1982 GBI	1991 GBI	2000 GBI	
1966 GBI	1983 GBI	1992 GBI	2001 Europe	

European Boys Challenge Trophy   *Black Stork, Slovakia*

1 Czech Republic 1082; 2 Hungary 1158; 3 Poland 1171; 4 Slovakia 1181

2006 Austria   2007 *Not played*

Boys' Home Internationals (R&A Trophy)   (inaugurated 1985)   *Royal County Down*

Ireland 8½, Scotland 6½
England 8½, Wales 6½
Ireland 10, Wales 5
England 10, Scotland 5
Scotland 6, Wales 9
England 7, Ireland 8

Result: 1 reland 3 [26½]; 2 England 2 [25½];
3 Wales 1 [20½]; 4 Scotland 0 [17½]

Winning Team: Richard Cusack (Non-playing Captain; Barry Anderson (Co. Sligo), Garth Boyd (Donaghadee), Chris Drumm (Rosslare), Alan Dunbar (Rathmore), Paul Dunne (Greystones), Michael Durcan (Co.Sligo), Luke Lennox (Moyola Park), Garth McGee (Malone), Richard O'Donovan (Lucan), Chris Selfridge (Moyola Park), Reeve Whitson (Mourne)

1985T England	1989 England	1993 England	1998 England	2003 England
Ireland	1990 Scotland	1994 England	1999 England	2004 England
1986 Ireland	1991 England	1995 Scotland	2000 England	2005 England
1987 Scotland	1992T Wales	1996 England	2001 England	2006 Scotland
1988 England	Scotland	1997 Ireland	2002 England	2007 England

English Boys County Championships   *Royal North Devon*

1 Surrey 3 (22½); 2 Warwickshire 2 (12); 3 Lancashire 1 (12); 4 Cornwall 0 (7½)

Winning Team: Tom Berry, Matthew Chapman, Stiggy Hodgson, Gary King, Jake Shepherd, Josh White, Max Williams

1986	Worcestershire	1993	Hertfordshire	2000	Surrey
1987	Cheshire	1994	Sussex	2001	Lancashire
1988	Sussex	1995	Yorkshire	2002	Yorkshire
1989	Yorkshire	1996	Cornwall	2003	Yorkshire
1990	Lancashire	1997	Essex	2004T	Essex
1991	Nottinghamshire	1998	Cheshire		Yorkshire
1992	Shropshire & Herefordshire	1999	Berks, Bucks and Oxon	2005	Yorkshire

2006	Lancashire
2007	Somerset

Scottish Boys Area Team Championship   *Kingsknowe*

1 Lothians 354; 2 Renfrewshire 357; 3 Perth & Kinross 358 (16 teams took part)

Winning Team: Oliver Huish (North Berwick), Mark Dickson (Gullane), Tom Blennerhassett (Dalmahoy), Stuart Boyle (Harburn).

Individual (Niagara Cup): Fraser Moore (Falkirk Tryst)* 67

2000	Lothians	2002	Lothians	2004	Dunbartonshire	2006	Fife
2001	Dunbartonshire	2003	Lothians	2005	Lothians	2007	Ayrshire

Toyota World Junior Team Championship *Chukyo, Japan*

1	825	Norway (Elias Bertheussen, Anders Kristiansen, Are Friestad, Frederik Kollevold)
2	828	Sweden (Niclas Carlsson, Pontus Gad, Daniel Jennevret, Pontus Widegren)
3	831	Australia (Aiden Bae, Daniel Nisbet, Bryden Macpherson, Brendan Smith)

16 teams took part

Individual:

1	Bud Cauley (USA)	68-67-67-70—272
	Anders Kristiansen (NOR)	69-69-68-66—272
3	Pontus Gad (SWE)	71-70-70-64—275

1995	USA	1998	England	2001	South Africa	2004	USA	2007	Sweden
1996	Japan	1999	England	2002	*Not played*	2005	USA		
1997	USA	2000	USA	2003	Korea	2006	Norway		

Month by month in 2008

A week after his World Cup win with Robert Karlsson in China, Henrik Stenson leaves the rest for dead at the Nedbank Challenge in South Africa. After an opening 63 put him five clear, he went on to triumph by nine. Richard Sterne strikes twice in eight days as well, in his case at the Alfred Dunhill Championship and then the South African Open, while in California Vijay Singh puts the icing on his fabulous season – barring the majors, that is – with victory at the Chevron World Challenge. Annika Sörenstam, though, had to settle for seventh place in her final event, the Dubai Masters.

Girls' and Junior Ladies' Tournaments

Girls British Open Championship *Monifieth*

Leading Qualifiers: Laura Gonzalez-Escallon (BEL) 70-73—143
Ana Fernandez de Mesa (ESP) 70-73—143

Quarter-Finals
Laura Gonzalez-Escallon (BEL) beat Louise Larsson (SWE) at 20th
Laetitia Beck (ISR) beat Johanna Tillstrom (SWE) 3 and 2
Kelly Tidy (Royal Birkdale) beat Sophia Popov (GER) 1 hole
Mandy Goyos (ESP) beat Charlotte Lorentzen (DEN) 7 and 6

Semi-Finals
Gonzalez-Escallon beat Beck
  4 and 3
Tidy beat Goyos 5 and 3

Final
Laura Gonzalez-Escallon beat
  Kelly Tidy 2 and 1

1960	S Clarke beat AL Irvin 2 and 1	1985	S Shapcott beat E Farquharson 3 and 1
1961	D Robb beat J Roberts 3 and 2	1986	S Croce beat S Bennett 5 and 4
1962	S McLaren-Smith beat A Murphy 2 and 1	1987	H Dobson beat S Croce 19th hole
1963	D Oxley beat B Whitehead 2 and 1	1988	A Macdonald beat J Posener 3 and 2
1964	P Tredinnick beat K Cumming 2 and 1	1989	M McKinlay beat S Eriksson 19th hole
1965	A Willard beat A Ward 3 and 2	1990	S Cavalleri (ITA) beat E Valera 5 and 4
1966	J Hutton beat D Oxley 20th hole	1991	M Hjorth (SWE) beat J Moodie 3 and 2
1967	P Burrows beat J Hutton 2 and 1	1992	M McKay beat L Navarro 2 holes
1968	C Wallace beat C Reybroeck 4 and 3	1993	M McKay beat A Vincent 4 and 3
1969	J de Witt Puyt beat C Reybroeck 2 and 1	1994	A Vincent beat R Hudson 1 up
1970	C Le Feuvre beat Michelle Walker 2 and 1	1995	A Lemoine beat J Krantz 3 and 2
1971	J Mark beat Maureen Walker 4 and 3	1996	M Monnet beat C Laurens 4 and 3
1972	Maureen Walker beat S Cadden 2 and 1	1997	C Laurens beat M Nagl (GER) 2 and 1
1973	AM Palli beat N Jeanson 2 and 1	1998	M Beautell (ESP) beat M Nagl (GER) 4 and 3
1974	R Barry beat T Perkins 1 hole	1999	S Pettersen (NOR) beat M Nagl (GER) 3 and 1
1975	S Cadden beat L Isherwood 4 and 3	2000	T Calzavara (ITA) beat R Bell 1 hole
1976	G Stewart beat S Rowlands 5 and 4	2001	C Queen beat C Alonso (ESP) 1 hole
1977	W Aitken beat S Bamford 2 and 1	2002	*Rain washed out this tournament in its later stages.*
1978	M L de Lorenzi beat D Glenn 2 and 1		*Awards were made to the top qualifiers:*
1979	S Lapaire beat P Smilie 19th hole		E Cabrera (ESP) beat L Stable (SWE)
1980	J Connachan beat L Bolton 2 holes	2003	M Skarpnord (NOR) beat R Eransus (ESP) 2 and 1
1981	J Connachan beat P Grice 20th hole	2004	A Muñoz (ESP) beat V Derrey (FRA) 4 and 2
1982	C Waite beat M Mackie 6 and 5	2005	A Nordquist (SWE) beat A Muñoz (ESP) 2 and 1
1983	E Orley beat A Walters 7 and 6	2006	B Mozo (ESP) beat S Watson 1 hole
1984	C Swallow beat E Farquharson 1 hole	2007	H Brockway beat K Tidy 4 and 3

English Girls Close Championship *Durham City*

Leading Qualifiers: Jessica Wilson (Blankney) 77-70—147
Abbey Gittings (Walmley) 77-70—147

Quarter Finals
Charlotte Wild (Mere) beat Sian Evans (Faversham) 4 and 2
Rachael Goodall (Heswall) beat Nikki Dunn (Harrogate)
  4 and 2
Sarah Tyson (Redlibbets) beat Giorgina Brown (Mere)
  5 and 4
Heidi Baek (Felixstowe Ferry) beat Abbey Gittings (Walmley)
  2 holes

Semi-Finals
Wild beat Goodall 4 and 3
Tyson beat Baek 4 and 3

Final
Sarah Tyson beat Charlotte Wild
  6 and 5

1964	S Ward beat P Tredinnick 2 and 1		1986	S Shapcott beat N Way 7 and 6
1965	D Oxley beat A Payne 2 holes		1987	S Shapcott beat S Morgan 1 hole
1966	B Whitehead beat D Oxley 1 hole		1988	H Dobson beat S Shapcott 1 hole
1967	A Willard beat G Holloway 1 hole		1989	H Dobson beat A MacDonald 3 and 1
1968	K Phillips beat C le Feuvre 6 and 5		1990	C Hall beat J Hockley 20th hole
1969	C le Feuvre beat K Phillips 2 and 1		1991	N Buxton beat C Hall 2 and 1
1970	C le Feuvre beat M Walker 2 and 1		1992	F Brown beat L Nicholson 2 and 1
1971	C Eckersley beat J Stevens 4 and 3		1993	G Simpson beat L Wixon 7 and 5
1972	C Barker beat R Kelly 4 and 3		1994	K Hamilton beat S Forster 3 and 2
1973	S Parker beat S Thurston 19th hole		1995	R Hudson beat G Nutter 2 and 1
1974	C Langford beat L Harrold 2 and 1		1996	R Hudson beat D Rushworth 8 and 6
1975	M Burton beat R Barry 6 and 5		1997	S McKevitt beat C Ritson 3 and 2
1976	H Latham beat D Park 3 and 2		1998	L Walters beat K Lawton 5 and 4
1977	S Bamford beat S Jolly 21st hole		1999	S Heath beat A Cook 6 and 4
1978	P Smillie beat J Smith 3 and 2		2000	S Walker beat R Wood 1 hole
1979	L Moore beat P Barry 1 hole		2001	A Marshall beat S Walker 3 and 2
1980	P Smillie beat J Soulsby 3 and 2		2002	L Eastwood beat N Haywood 1 hole
1981	J Soulsby beat C Waite 7 and 5		2003	K-A Haskell beat J Hodge 4 and 3
1982	C Waite beat P Grice 3 and 2		2004	M Reid beat K Matharu 3 and 2
1983	P Grice beat K Mitchell 2 and 1		2005	M Reid beat J Hodge 3 and 2
1984	C Swallow beat S Duhig 3 and 1		2006	R Jennings beat C Douglass 1 hole
1985	L Fairclough beat K Mitchell 6 and 5		2007	E Givens beat K Best 2 and 1

Irish Girls' Championship (Blake Cup) (inaugurated 1951) *Mullingar*

Quarter Finals

Leona Maguire (Slieve Russell) beat Victoria Bradshaw (Bangor) 3 and 2

Sarah Crowe (Tipperary) beat Ciara Pender (Ennis) 5 and 4

Emma O'Driscoll (Ballybunion) beat Tara Gribben (Warrenpoint) 2 and 1

Lisa Maguire (Slieve Russell) beat Julie Coyne (Youghal) 6 and 5

Semi-Finals

Leona Maguire beat Crowe 8 and 6

Lisa Maguire beat O'Driscoll at 19th

Final

Lisa Maguire beat Leona Maguire 4 and 3

1951	J Davies beat I Hurst 3 and 2		1983	E McDaid beat S Lynn 20th hole
1952	J Redgate beat A Phillips at 22nd		1984	S Sheehan beat L Tormey 6 and 4
1953	J Redgate beat I Hurst 4 and 3		1985	S Sheehan beat D Hanna 5 and 4
1954–60	*Suspended*		1986	D Mahon beat T Eakin 4 and 3
1961	M Coburn beat C McAuley 6 and 5		1987	V Greevy beat B Ryan 8 and 7
1962	P Boyd beat P Atkinson 4 and 3		1988	L McCool beat P Gorman 3 and 2
1963	P Atkinson beat C Scarlett 8 and 7		1989	A Rogers beat R MacGuigan 2 and 1
1964	C Scarlett beat A Maher 6 and 5		1990	G Doran beat L McCool 3 and 1
1965	V Singleton beat P McKenzie 7 and 6		1991	A Rogers beat D Powell 2 and 1
1966	M McConnell beat D Hulme 3 and 2		1992	M McGreevy beat N Gorman 2 and 1
1967	M McConnell beat C Wallace 6 and 5		1993	M McGreevy beat E Dowdall 2 and 1
1968	C Wallace beat A McCoy 3 and 1		1994	A O'Leary beat D Doyle 23rd hole
1969	EA Mc beat M Sheenan 6 and 5		1995	P Murphy beat G Hegarty 5 and 4
1970	EA Mc beat J Mark 3 and 2		1996	P Murphy beat C Smyth 2 holes
1971	J Mark beat C Nesbitt 3 and 2		1997	J Gannon beat C Coughlan 3 and 2
1972	P Smyth beat M Governey 1 hole		1998	P Murphy beat C Coughlan 5 and 4
1973	M Governey beat R Hegarty 3 and 1		1999	P Murphy beat M Gillen 20th hole
1974	R Hegarty beat M Irvine 2 holes		2000	M Gillen beat N Mullooly 6 and 5
1975	M Irvine beat P Wickham 2 and 1		2001	DM Conaty beat H Nolan 3 and 2
1976	P Wickham beat R Hegarty 5 and 3		2002	K Delaney beat H Nolan 4 and 3
1977	A Ferguson beat R Walsh 3 and 2		2003	K Delaney beat T Delaney 4 and 3
1978	C Wickham beat B Gleeson 1 hole		2004	T Delaney beat S Meadow 8 and 6
1979	L Bolton beat B Gleeson 3 and 2		2005	D McVeigh beat L Toomey 4 and 3
1980	B Gleeson beat L Bolton 3 and 3		2006	S Meadow beat V Bradshaw 5 and 4
1981	B Gleeson beat E Lynn 1 hole		2007	K Gallagher beat S Meadow 2 holes
1982	D Langan beat S Lynn 5 and 4			

Scottish Ladies Junior Open Stroke Play Championship (inaugurated 1955)
(formerly Scottish Under-21 Girls Open Stroke Play Championship)   *Powfoot*

1	Kelsey MacDonald (Nairn Dunbar)	70-70-71—211	
2	Pamela Pretswell (Bothwell Castle)	71-67-74—212	
3	Krystle Caithness (St Regulus)	74-66-73—213	

1955	M Fowler	1969	K Phillips	1983	S Lawson	1997	L Nicholson
1956	B McCorkindale	1970	B Huke	1984	S Lawson	1998	V Laing
1957	M Fowler	1971	B Huke	1985	K Imrie	1999	L Kenny
1958	R Porter	1972	L Hope	1986	K Imrie	2000	L Morton
1959	D Robb	1973	G Cadden	1987	K Imrie	2001	L Kenny
1960	J Greenhalgh	1974	S Lambie	1988	C Lambert	2002	K Brotherton
1961	D Robb	1975	S Cadden	1989	C Lambert	2003	J Wilson
1962	S Armitage	1976	S Cadden	1990	J Moodie	2004	C Queen
1963	A Irvin	1977	S Cadden	1991	C Macdonald	2005	L Fleming
1964	M Nuttall	1978	J Connachan	1992	L McCool	2006	K Caithness
1965	I Wylie	1979	A Gemmill	1993	J Moodie	2007	C Booth
1966	J Smith	1980	J Connachan	1994	C Agnew		
1967	J Bourassa	1981	K Douglas	1995	R Hakkarainen (Fin)		
1968	K Phillips	1982	J Rhodes	1996	L Moffat		

Scottish Girls Close Championship (inaugurated 1960)   *Alyth*
Leading Qualifier: Kelsey MacDonald (Nairn Dunbar) 74-74—148

Quarter Finals
Kelsey MacDonald (Nairn Dunbar) beat Rebecca Wilson
(Monifieth) at 24th

Gillian Scanlan (Hamilton) beat Jill Meldrum (Dullatur)
at 19th

Mhairi Johnstone (Northern) beat Lesley Atkins (Minto)
2 holes

Carly Booth (Comrie) beat Rachael McQueen
(Troon Ladies) 7 and 5

Semi-Finals
MacDonald beat Scanlan 1 hole
Booth beat Johnstone 7 and 6

Final
Carly Booth beat Kelsey MacDonald
4 and 3

1960	J Hastings beat A Lurie 6 and 4	1984	T Craik beat D Jackson 3 and 2
1961	I Wylie beat W Clark 3 and 1	1985	E Farquharson beat E Moffat 2 holes
1962	I Wylie beat U Burnet 3 and 1	1986	C Lambert beat F McKay 4 and 3
1963	M Norval beat S MacDonald 6 and 4	1987	S Little beat L Moretti 3 and 2
1964	JW Smith beat C Workman 2 and 1	1988	J Jenkins beat F McKay 4 and 3
1965	JW Smith beat I Walker 7 and 5	1989	J Moodie beat V Melvin 19th hole
1966	J Hutton beat F Jamieson 2 holes	1990	M McKay beat J Moodie 3 and 2
1967	J Hutton beat K Lackie 4 and 2	1991	J Moodie beat M McKay 5 and 4 Links
1968	M Dewar beat J Crawford 2 holes	1992	M McKay beat L Nicholson 2 and 1
1969	C Panton beat A Coutts 23rd hole	1993	C Agnew beat H Stirling 19th hole
1970	M Walker beat L Bennett 3 and 2	1994	C Nicholson beat L Moffat 3 and 1
1971	M Walker beat S Kennedy 1 hole	1995	L Moffat beat F Lockhart 2 and 1
1972	G Cadden beat C Panton 3 and 2	1996	V Laing beat C Hunter 5 and 4
1973	M Walker beat M Thomson 1 hole	1997	V Laing beat A Walker 5 and 4
1974	S Cadden beat D Reid 3 and 1	1998	V Laing beat L Moffat at 21st hole
1975	W Aitken beat S Cadden 1 hole	1999	V Laing beat L Wells 3 and 2
1976	S Cadden beat D Mitchell 4 and 2	2000	L Kenney beat F Gilbert 3 and 2
1977	W Aitken beat G Wilson 2 holes	2001	H MacRea beat L Kenney 1 hole
1978	J Connachan beat D Mitchell 7 and 5	2002	L Walker beat G Webster 2 and 1
1979	J Connachan beat G Wilson 3 and 1	2003	K Brotherton beat K Caithness 3 and 2
1980	J Connachan beat P Wright 21st hole	2004	K Caithness beat K Brotherton 2 holes
1981	D Thomson beat P Wright 2 and 1	2005	S Watson beat C Booth 2 and 1
1982	S Lawson beat D Thomson 1 hole	2006	R Niven beat R Livingstone 3 and 2
1983	K Imrie beat D Martin 2 and 1	2007	C Booth beat M Briggs 2 and 1

SLGA Under-16 Stroke Play Championship *Craigielaw*

1	Laura Sedda (ITA)	69-76—145
2	Amy Boulden (Maesdu)	73-73—146
	Heidi Baek (Felixstowe Ferry)	70-76—146
	Hannah Turland (Tidworth Garrison)	70-76—146

2006	C Booth	2007	L Maguire

Welsh Girls Championship (inaugurated 1957) *Pennard*

Leading Qualifier: Katherine O'Connor (Tadmarton Heath) 150

Quarter Finals

Katherine O'Connor (Tadmarton Heath) beat Laura Watkins (Bicester) 5 and 4

Kelly Miller (Penrhos) beat Katie Bradbury (Cottrell Park) 2 and 1

Gemma Bradbury (Cottrell Park) beat Sophie Rees (Milford Haven) at 19th

Amy Boulden (Maesdu) beat Emma Davies (Eaton) 7 and 5

Semi-Finals

O'Connor beat Miller 2 and 1

Boulden beat G Bradbury 2 and 1

Final

Amy Boulden beat Katherine O'Connor 2 holes

1957	A Coulman beat S Wynne-Jones 1 hole	1983	N Wesley beat J Foster 4 and 2
1958	S Wynne-Jones beat A Coulman 3 and 1	1984	J Foster beat J Evans 6 and 5
1959	C Mason beat T Williams 3 and 2	1985	J Foster beat S Caley 6 and 5
1960	A Hughes beat D Wilson 6 and 4	1986	J Foster beat L Dermott 3 and 2
1961	J Morris beat S Kelly 3 and 2	1987	J Lloyd beat S Bibbs 2 and 1
1962	J Morris beat P Morgan 4 and 3	1988	L Dermott beat A Perriam 2 holes
1963	A Hughes beat A Brown 8 and 7	1989	L Dermott beat N Stroud 4 and 2
1964	A Hughes beat M Leigh 5 and 3	1990	L Dermott beat N Stroud 6 and 4
1965	A Hughes beat A Reardon-Hughes 19th hole	1991	S Boyes beat R Morgan 3 and 1
1966	S Hales beat J Rogers 1 hole	1992	B Jones beat S Musto 2 and 1
1967	E Wilkie beat L Humphreys 1 hole	1993	K Stark beat S Tudor-Jones 3 and 2
1968	L Morris beat J Rogers 1 hole	1994	K Stark beat J Evans 4 and 3
1969	L Morris beat L Humphreys 5 and 3	1995	E Pilgrim beat L Davis 2 holes
1970	T Perkins beat P Light 2 and 1	1996	K Stark beat S Bourne 4 and 3
1971	P Light beat P Whitley 4 and 3	1997	R Brewerton beat K Stark 19th hole
1972	P Whitley beat P Light 2 and 1	1998	B Brewerton beat L Archer 3 and 1
1973	V Rawlings beat T Perkins 19th hole	1999	K Phillips beat R Last 6 and 5
1974	L Isherwood beat S Rowlands 4 and 3	2000	K Phillips beat J Pritchard 1 hole
1975	L Isherwood beat S Rowlands 1 hole	2001	S Jones beat J Dyer 3 and 2
1976	K Rawlings beat C Parry 5 and 4	2002	L Gould beat R Vaughan-Jones 4 and 3
1977	S Rowlands beat D Taylor 7 and 5	2003	L Gould beat B Loucks 4 and 2
1978	S Rowlands beat G Rees 3 and 2	2004	T Davies beat B Loucks 2 and 1
1979	M Rawlings beat J Richards 19th hole	2005	S Hassan beat L Hall 1 hole
1980	K Davies beat M Rawlings 19th hole	2006	T Davies beat K O'Connor 7 and 6
1981	M Rawlings beat F Connor 4 and 3	2007	B Davies beat A Carling at 22nd
1982	K Davies beat K Beckett 6 and 5		

St Andrews Links Junior Ladies *St Andrews (Strathtyrum)*

Katy McNicoll (Carnoustie) 68

2007	H Aitchison

Team Events

European Lady Juniors Team Championship
This event has been discontinued. For past results see the 2008 edition of the Golfer's Handbook

European Girls Team Championship   *Murcar, Scotland*
Final Ranking: 1 Sweden, 2 England, 3 Netherlands, 4 Switzerland, 5 Denmark, 6 Germany, 7 Czech Republic, 8 Ireland (19 countries played)
Winning team: Josephine Janson, Louise Larsson, Amanda Strang, Johanna Tillstrom

1991	Spain	1997	Spain	2003	Spain	2006	Germany
1993	Spain	1999	Germany	2004	Sweden	2007	Sweden
1995	Sweden	2001	Spain	2005	England		

Girls Home Internationals (Stroyan Cup)   *Panmure*

Wales 4, Scotland 5   Ireland 4½, Wales 4½
Ireland 3, England 6   Scotland 4, Ireland 5
England 6½, Scotland 2½   Wales 2, England 7

Result: 1 England 19½; 2 Ireland 12½; 3 Scotland 11½; 4 Wales 10½

Winning team: Heidi Baek (Felixstowe Ferry), Hannah Barwood (Knowle), Holly Clyburn (Woodhall Spa), Rachel Connor (Manchester), Katie Mundy (Dunwood Manor), Alexandra Peters (Notts Ladies), Helen Searle (West End), Kelly Tidy (Royal Birkdale)

1966	Scotland	1975	England	1984	Scotland	1993	Scotland	2002	England
1967	England	1976	Scotland	1985	England	1994	Scotland	2003	England
1968	England	1977	England	1986	England	1995	England	2004	England
1969	England	1978	England	1987	England	1996	England	2005	England
1970	England	1979	England	1988	England	1997	England	2006	Scotland
1971	England	1980	England	1989	England	1998	England	2007	Scotland
1972	Scotland	1981	England	1990	England	1999	Wales		
1973	Scotland	1982	England	1991	England	2000	England		
1974	England	1983	England	1992	Scotland	2001	England		

Junior Solheim Cup

2002	USA	2003	Europe	2005	USA	2007	Europe

13-year-old Jutanugarn first girl to win The Junior Open

Moriya Jutanugarn, a 13-year-old from Thailand, is the first girl to win The Junior Open, The R&A's biennial 54-hole championship for under-16s, held at the Hesketh GC in Southport. Moriya added a round of 78 in extremely difficult conditions to her opening 75–75 to finish on a nine-over-par total of 225. Moriya, from Bangkok, a scratch golfer, is the Girls' Champion of Thailand. She had never played golf in Europe before and had not set fot on a links course prior to the week of the Championship.

Overnight leader Steven Lam of Hong Kong retained the lead with nine holes to play, but had a triple bogey on the 13th to fall behind and Jordan Speith of Texas tied for second with Lam after a birdie at the last.

Mixed Boys' and Girls' Events

R&A Junior Open Championhips   *Hesketh*

Junior Open Champion:	Moriya Jutanugarn (THA)	72-75-78—225
Runner-Up:	Jordan Spieth (USA)	72-76-78—226
Silver:	Laura Christiaens (BEL)	73-79—152
Bronze:	Huang Zhiying (CHN)	85-81—166
Young Lady Golfer:	Mami Fukda (JPN)	70-80—150
Under 14:	Frederik Hammer (DEN)	76-77—153

Regional Trophies: African: Ali Hichri (TUN) 180; Asia-Pacific: Hwa-Sing Wang (TPE) 167; Nordic & Central European: Annabelle Niven (SCO) 153; Eastern European & Middle East: Laetitia Beck (ISR) 154; North America & Caribbean: Danielle Ortiz (MEX)156; Central & South American: Andrea Novoa (ESA) 179; Southern European: Federica Maria Costantini (ITA) 158; Special Invitation Category: Ignacio Rodriguez (ESP) 142 (14 countries were represented)

Next event: 2010 at Lundin

2006   Gold: Patrick Reed (USA); Silver: Amanjyot (IND); Bronze: Saber Sahli (TUN)

European Young Masters   *Chantilly, France*

European Young Masters Nations Cup

1	648 France (Emilie Alonso, Alexandra Bonetti, Julien Brun, Stanislaus Gautier)	
2	656 Ireland	
3	664 Spain	(26 teams took part)

Boys Individual

1	Stanislaus Gautier (FRA)	211
2	Julien Brun (FRA)	213
3	Moritz Lampert (GER)	216

Girls Individual

1	Lisa Maguire (IRL)	214
2	Leona Maguire (IRL)	218
3	Anna Arrese (ESP)	218

1995	Spain	1998	Italy	2001	France	2004	Spain	2007	Italy
1996	*Not played*	1999	Spain	2002	Spain	2005	Spain		
1997	Italy	2000	Spain	2003	Spain	2006	Germany		

Faldo Series: Grand Final   *Costa Do Sauipe, Brazil*

Boys

Under 21:	Steven Brown (Wentworth, England)	72-69-72—213
Under 18:	Rahul Bakshi (Handigash, India)	73-69-76—218
Under 17:	Rafael Becker (San Fernando, South America)	76-70-73—219
Under 16:	Adrian Otaegui (San Sebastian, Spain)	76-72-77—225
Under 15:	Thomas Clements (Royal Norwich, England)	75-73-76—224

1998:		Under 15	J Cundy		Under 16	S Benson		Under 17	T Sherrard
Under 15	C Stevenson	2001:			Under 15	M Evans		Under 16	O Fisher
1999:		Under 21	B Mackay	2003:				Under 15	R McIlroy
Under 18	S Osborne	Under 18	S Clarke	Under 21	M Pilling	2005:			
Under 17	N Dougherty	Under 17	G Bondarenko	Under 18	L Collins		Under 21	J Parry	
Under 16	J Heath	Under 16	J Cundy	Under 17	N Grant		Under 18	S Capper	
Under 15	M McTernan	Under 15	R Laino	Under 16	J Smith		Under 17	O Fisher	
2000:		2002:		Under 15	O Fisher		Under 16	J Hiluta	
Under 18	N Dougherty	Under 21	J Heath	2004:				Under 15	E Pepperell
Under 17	D Wardrop	Under 18	A Murrell	Under 21	J Heath				
Under 16	P Richardson	Under 17	P Doherty	Under 18	B Evans				

Faldo Series *continued*

2006:		2007:	
Under 21	B Evans	Under 21	B Evans
Under 18	S Doherty	Under 18	J Clarke
Under 17	R McIlroy	Under 17	D Renwick
Under 16	D Renwick	Under 16	J Beisser
Under 15	E Pepperell	Under 15	C Selfridge

Girls

Hannah Barwood (Knowle, England)   78-74-78—230

1998	K Phillips	2000	A Highgate	2002	F Parker	2004	K Matharu	2006	S Meadow
1999	A Highgate	2001	O Rotmistrova	2003	T Delaney	2005	K Matharu	2007	E Goddard

Junior Masters   *Gleneagles (Queen's Course)*

Boys

1	Rory McKinnon (Ranfurly Castle)				31 points				
2	Callum Paterson (Dunblane New)				30				
3	Luke Sutherland (Duff House Royal)				29				
1998	S Noon	2000	P White	2002	L Henderson	2004	R MacNab	2006	J Gibson
1999	E Sneddon	2001	M Frew	2003	L Pirie	2005	L Pirie	2007	L Reid

Girls

1	Jorden Ferrie (Kirkintilloch)				33 pts				
2	Nicole Underhill (Falkirk Tryst)				28 (better inward half)				
3	Rachel Irvine (Ayrshire Ladies)				28				
1998	A Ramsey	2000	D Skinner	2002	N MacNeil	2004	R Livingstone	2006	J Sinclair
1999	E Mathie	2001	M Barbour	2003	M Thomson	2005	M Thomson	2007	C Tait

The Junior Ryder Cup   *Olde Stone, Bowling Green, KY*

Non-Playing Captains: USA: Ken Lindsay; Europe: Gerald Stangl (AUT)

First Day – Foursomes
C Peck & C Whitsett halved with J Brun & A Otaegui
D Frasier & J Johnson beat K Tidy & Leona Maguire 3 and 2
J Kang & A Yun beat C Lloyd & M Lampert 7 and 5
A Thompson & S Brown beat D Nielsen & Lisa Maguire 7 and 6
A Paolucci & J Spieth beat S Gautier & M Manassero 2 holes
E Lee & T Lua beat C Booth & A Arrese 5 and 3

Fourballs
C Whitsett & J Johnson beat M Lampert & K Tidy 2 and 1
C Peck & S Brown beat C Lloyd & Leona Maguire 3 and 1
A Yun & E Lee lost to M Manassero & D Nielsen 1 hole
J Spieth & A Thompson beat S Gautier & Lisa Maguire 6 and 5
A Paolucci & D Frasier beat A Otaegui & A Arrese 5 and 3
J Kang & T Lua beat J Brun & C Booth 5 and 4

Second Day – Singles
Tiffany Lua beat Kelly Tidy (ENG) 1 hole
Cory Whitsett beat Matteo Manassero (ITA) 6 and 5
Jennifer Johnson halved with Carly Booth (SCO)
Jeffrey Kang beat Moritz Lampert (GER) 4 and 3
Erynne Lee beat Daisy Nielsen (DEN) 3 and 1
Jordan Spieth beat Chris Lloyd (ENG) 5 and 4
Sarah Brown beat Leona Maguire (IRL) 4 and 3
Anthony Paolucci beat Adruan Otaegui (ESP) 5 and 4
Alexis Thompson beat Lisa Maguire 1 hole
Cameron Peck beat Stanislas Gautier (FRA) 5 and 4
Danielle Frasier beat Anna Arrese (ESP) 5 and 3
Andrew Yun beat Julien Brun (FRA) 3 and 2

Match result: USA 22, Europe 2

1995	Exhibition Match won by Europe	1997 1999	United States Europe	2002 2004	Europe Europe	2006	Europe

Duke of York Trophy   *Dundonald Links, Ayrshire, Scotland*

1	Stiggy Hodgson (ENG)	69-71-72—212
2	Arnaud Abbas (FRA)	77-70-76—223
3	Carlos Pigem (ESP)	71-75-80—226

Leading Girls:

1	Marieka Nivard (NED)	78-72-77—227
2	Hannah Barwood (ENG)	74-79-75—228
3	Laura Gonzalez-Escallion (ESP)	76-76-77—229
	Laetitia Beck (ISR)	76-73-80—229

2007	C Vigano (ITA)

Faldo Series announces new format for 2009

Nick Faldo has announced a new format for the Faldo Series in 2009, which will make the six-time Major winner's initiative more accessible to an even greater number of young golfers across the UK, Europe and South America.

Now moving into its 13th season, the Faldo Series is changing its format in the UK to include nine Faldo Series UK Championships across the region. These Championships will offer up to 80 players, boys and girls aged 11 to 21, the chance to compete over 36 holes at some of the best tournament venues in the country. The entry fee has been reduced and at the end of each tournament five winners (one from each of the five age-categories) will qualify directly for the Faldo Series Grand Final in Brazil. Furthermore, the leading players from the annual Grand Final in Brazil will be personally invited by Nick to play in the Faldo Series Asia Grand Final at Mission Hills in China.

The intention is to align the UK more closely with the Faldo Series format in other golfing nations throughout the world. With support from The R&A, the European Tour and the PGA, there are now Faldo Series Championships in Iceland, Ireland, Turkey, Russia, Poland and South America – as well as a full season of events on the Faldo Series Asia. The initiative has grown into a genuinely international endeavour, offering its combination of competition and education to more than 4,000 players across the world.

Faldo commented: "Since launching the Faldo Series in the UK in 1996 we have expanded from helping 400 players a year in the UK to over 4,000 annual players world-wide in over 20 countries across Europe, South America and Asia. It's my goal to more than double those numbers in the next few years and the new format in the UK is part of that continued growth. It allows more players from the UK to take part, at a lower cost, all of whom will be just one win away from qualifying for the Grand Final and the chance to join me in Brazil."

PART VIII

Tournaments for the Disabled

Tournaments for the Disabled

North America wins inaugural Fightmaster Cup

The world of international golf witnessed an important event in 2008 with the inaugural tournament of the Fightmaster Cup, described by its promoters as "the alternative Ryder Cup". Sponsored by the Humana Corporation, this event for one-armed golfers was named for Don Fightmaster who lost an arm at the age of 22 but never gave up the quest for sporting excellence, helping many along the way through his charitable foundation.

Played between teams representing North America and Europe, the 12-man American squad was led by Don Fightmaster as its non-playing captain and consisted of eight players from the USA and four from Canada. The European team, captained by Malcolm Guy, consisted of six players from England, two from Ireland and four from Scotland and included six-times International One-Armed Champion Nick Champness.

In the style of the Ryder Cup, the bulk of each team was selected by merit, having earned their places via earlier victories. The remaining players were the personal pick of each team captain.

Played at Simpsonsville, Kentucky, one week before the Ryder Cup, the event formed part of "The Cup Experience", a community-wide celebration staged by the Louisville Host Committee.

The victorious North American squad led by their non-playing captain, the legendary Don Fightmaster

In extremely difficult conditions which included 75-miles-per-hour winds (the remnants of Hurricane Ike) – conditions which might have deterred lesser men – the teams, representing NAOAGA (the North American One-Arm Golfer Association) and SOAG (the UK-based Society of One-Arm Golfers), provided three days of top-quality tournament golf which did not disappoint those who had braved the weather to watch. As Don Fightmaster stated following the singles events on the tournament's third day: "Both teams played exceptional golf in weather in which most people wouldn't even leave the house. We played as a team for the whole tournament and that spirit and camaraderie was evident again in today's singles. We are looking forward to defending the cup in Wales in 2010".

Team Europe captain Malcolm Guy stated that the tournament was "an outstanding success", adding: "We were outplayed over the first two days and left ourselves with too much to do in the singles, but we congratulate Team North America and, like Don, can't wait for another chance to play for the Fightmaster Cup in Wales in two years' time".

Although the North Americans dominated and led through the first two days, leading by 11 to 5 as the teams met to contest the singles events on the third day, the outcome was not decided until almost six hours had elapsed when Canadian John Getchell won his match with Ireland's Michael O'Grady.

Although the contest had already been decided, Englishman Norman Kelly, the oldest player in the tournament, scored a consolation point against Louisville native Bill Frey.

Among many outstanding performances, Team Europe's Darren Grey finished the tournament as the only player to have won each of the matches he played in.

It is intended that the Fightmaster Cup competition will be staged every two years, with venues at or near those hosting that year's Ryder Cup.

British Blind Open *Massereene GC, Antrim, Northern Ireland*

Overall Gross Champion: Ron Plath (USA) 78   **Overall Nett Champion:**

B1	Zohar Sharon (ISR)	104	Mike Mayo (SCO) 64
B2	Bill Davis (USA)	98	
B3	Mike Mayo (SCO)	79	

British Blind Masters *Patshull Park, Shropshire*

1	Peter Hodgkinson	68-82-68-64—282
2	Malcolm Elrick	81-67-72-70—290 (on better last nine)
3	Neil Baxter	76-71-70-73—290

English MatchPlay Championships (for blind golfers) *Guadet Luce GC, Worcestershire*

Quarter Finals:
Paul Appleyard beat Andy Sellars 1 up
Jay Cookson beat Malcolm Elrick 2 and 1
Simon Cookson beat Rory McKnight 4 and 3
Rob Parrot beat Mike Loten 2 and 1

Semi-Finals:
Paul Appleyard beat Jay Cookson 4 and 2
Rob Parrot beat Simon Cookson 2 and 1

Final:
Paul Appleyard beat Rob Parrot 4 and 3

English StrokePlay Championships (for blind golfers) *Stockwood Park Golf Club*

1	Ron Tomlinson	72-65—137
2	Jay Cookson	74-66—140
3	Neil Baxter	75-66—141

Scottish MatchPlay Championships (for blind golfers) *Wishsaw GC & Falkirk Tryst GC*

Quarter Finals:
Myles Clark beat Allan Morgan 7 and 5
Mike Mayo beat Charlie Forbes 2 up
Ally Reid beat Darren Healey 4 and 3
Cameron McDiarmid beat Stuart Wilkie walkover

Semi-Finals:
Ally Reid beat Myles Clark 4 and 3
Cameron McDiarmid beat Mike Mayo 2 and 1

Final:
Cameron McDiarmid beat Ally Reid 2 up

Scottish StrokePlay Championships (for blind golfers) *Gullane Golf Club*

1	Ian Moncrieff*	83-77—160
2	Cameron McDiarmid	78-82—160

Moncrieff won on better last nine

3	Ally Reid	80-81—161

Scotland v England Blind Golf Competition for the Auld Enemies Cup
China Fleet GC (England team names first)

Day 1 – Foursomes
Steve Cook & Andy Sellars lost to Iain Prime & Stuart Wilkie 4 and 3
Simon Cookson & Ron Tomlinson beat Cameron McDiarmid & Peter Philip 8 and 7
Steve Beevers & Derek Field halved with Myles Clark & Ally Reid
Jay Cookson & Brian Richards lost to Mike Mayo & Allan Morgan 2 and 1
Malcolm Elrick & Derrick Sheridan lost to David Paterson & Sam Sloan 4 and 2
Neil Baxter & Mike Loten lost to John Imrie & Gerry Kelly 6 and 5

Day 2 – Four balls
Jay Cookson & Mike Loten beat Allan Morgan & Sam Sloan 2 and 1
Steve Cook & Andy Sellars lost to Charlie Forbes & Stuart Wilkie 3 and 2
Steve Beevers & Derek Field lost to John Imrie & Gerry Kelly 6 and 5
Simon Cookson & Ron Tomlinson lost to David Paterson & Ally Reid 6 and 5
Malcolm Elrick & Derrick Sheridan halved with Mike Mayo & Cameron McDiarmid
Peter Hodgkinson & Bryan Richards lost to Myles Clark & Iain Prime 6 and 5

Auld Enemies Cup *continued*

Day 3 – Singles

Steve Beevers beat Cameron McDiarmid 1 up
Mike Loten halved with John Imrie
Andy Sellars lost to Sam Sloan 4 and 2
Steve Cook lost to Ally Reid 5 and 4
Simon Cookson halved with Gerry Kelly
Jay Cookson beat Myles Clark 2 and 1

Iain Prime conceded to Malcolm Elrick at 16th
Neil Baxter halved with Allan Morgan
Derrick Sheridan lost to Mike Mayo 7 and 6
Derek Field lost to Stuart Wilkie 8 and 6
Bryan Richards halved with David Paterson
Peter Hodgkinson halved with Peter Philip

Match result: England 8½ Scotland 15½

World Blind Golf Championships *Belvoir Park, Belfast*

Men:
Overall Nett Champion: Mike Loten (ENG) 75
Gross winners:

B1	Zohar Sharon (ISR)	85
B2	Peter La Roux (RSA)	77
B3	Ron Plath (USA)	79

Ladies:
Overall Gross and Nett Champion:
Jenny McCallum (AUS) 100/75

Scottish Blind Golf Society

Bendall Trophy	Cameron McDiarmid
East Classic	Cameron McDiarmid
Fife Classic	Bennett Ward &
	Peter Conway
Grampian Classic	Sam Sloan

Greater Glasgow Classic	Cameron McDiarmid
	& Jim McDiarmid
Tayside Classic	Jim Eadie
West Classic	Peter Philip

75th One Arm Golf Society World Championships (inaugurated 1932)

Dunmurry GC, Belfast

Quarter Finals:
Marcus Malo (SWE) beat David Bailey (ENG) 4 and 3
Darren Grey (ENG) beat Robert Paul (ENG) 1 hole
Michael O'Grady (IRL) beat Stuart Griffin (SCO) 5 and 3
Nicholas Champness (ENG) beat David Waterhouse
(ENG) 5 and 6

Semi-Finals:
Robert Paul beat Marcus Malo at 19th
Nicholas Champness beat Michael O'Grady
3 and 2

Final:
Nicholas Champness beat Robert Paul 7 and 6

1933	WR Thomson	1952	H Nicholson	1967	A Wilmott	1980	RP Reid
1934	FW Berridge	1953	AH Barclay	1968	DR Lawrie	1981	A Robinson
1935	R McKarrel	1954	RP Reid	1969	AS Eggo	1982	MJ O'Grady
1936	FW Berridge	1955	R McKarrel	1970	T Atkinson	1983	A Robinson
1937	AW Hanson	1956	RP Reid	1971	A Wilmott	1984	A Robinson
1938	A Burns	1957	JE Lithgo	1972	GC Kerr	1985	A Robinson
1939	A Burns	1958	A Wilmott	1973	DC	1986	MJ O'Grady
1940	J Sharples	1959	CW Gardner		Fightmaster	1987	J Cann
1941–45	Not played	1960	JE Watt	1974	A Wilmott	1988	Q Talbot
1946	R McKarrel	1961	RG Sandler	1975	DC	1989	A Robinson
1947	J Buckley	1962	A Wilmott		Fightmaster	1990	D Parsons
1948	JE Lithgo	1963	RP Reid	1976	DR Lawrie	1991	Q Talbot
1949	G Jackson	1964	RP Reid	1977	A Wilmott	1992	B Crombie
1950	J Buckley	1965	DR Lawrie	1978	A Wilmott	1993	M Benning
1951	RC Graham	1966	RG Sandler	1979	A Robinson	1994	M Benning

1995	D Parsons
1996	D Parsons
1997	B Crombie
1998	N Champness
1999	A Robinson
2000	N Champness
2001	B Swan
2002	N Champness
2003	B Crombie
2004	M Malo
2005	M Malo
2006	N Champness
2007	N Champness

Cattenach Cup (non-qualifiers): John Condie (NIR) 40 pts

Bob Hughes Cup: John O'Callaghan (IRL) 44 pts

President's Prize: Darren Grey (ENG) 39 pts

Society of One-Armed Golfers Stableford Competitions

Scottish *Camperdown Park* (18 holes)
  Malcolm Guy (Old Meldrum) 34 points
Irish *Knightsbrook Hotel and GC* (18 holes)
  Andy Fagan (Castlebarna GC) 28 points

English and Welsh *Badgemore Park* (27 holes)
Nick Champness (Royal Ashdown Forest)
53 points

Humana Fightmaster Cup North America v Europe *Cardinal Club, Simpsonville, KY*

Non-playing captains: Don Fightmaster (North America), Malcolm Guy (Europe)

First Day, Morning – Fourball
John Getchell & Klaus Schaloske lost to Nick Champness & Darren Grey 2 up
Alan Gentry & Scott Lusk beat Michael O'Grady & David Bailey 5 and 4
Laurent Hurtubise & David Hensley beat Robert Paul & David Waterhouse 6 and 5
Mike Benning & Dennis Ithal beat Douglas Jopp & Brendan Swan 5 and 4

Afternoon – Foursomes
Laurent Hurtubise & Scott Lusk beat Hugh Ross and Michael O'Grady 2 and 1
Alan Gentry & Steve Day halved with Stuart Griffin and Norman Kelly
Mike Benning & Bill Frey lost to Robert Paul & Darren Grey 4 and 3
Bobby Baca & Steve Quevillon beat Nick Champness & David Bailey 6 and 4

First day match position: North America 5½, Europe 2½

Second Day, Morning – Fourball
John Getchell & Bill Frey beat Brendan Swan & Michael O'Grady 5 and 4
Mike Benning & David Hensley beat Stuart Griffin & Douglas Jopp 7 and 6
Alan Gentry & Klaus Schaloske lost to Darren Grey & Robert Paul 3 and 1
Laurent Hurtubise & Bobby Baca beat Nick Champness & Brian Crombie 1 up

Afternoon – Foursomes
Seve Day & Scott Lusk beat Michael O'Grady & Brendan Swan 3 and 2
Mike Benning & John Getchell halved with Norman Kelly & Hugh Ross
David Hensley & Bobby Baca lost to Darren Grey & Robert Paul 6 and 5
Steve Quevillon & Dennis Ithal beat David Bailey & Nick Champness 1 up

Second day match position: North America 11, Europe 5

Third Day – Singles
Scott Lusk (USA) halved with Nick Champness (ENG)
Mike Benning (USA) beat Brian Crombie (SCO) 4 and 3
David Hensley (USA) halved with David Waterhouse (ENG)
Bobby Baca (USA) lost to Darren Grey (ENG) 2 up
Steve Day (USA) lost to Stuart Griffin (SCO) 3 and 2
Laurent Hurtubise (CAN) beat Robert Paul (ENG) 3 and 1
John Getchell (CAN) beat Michael O'Grady (IRL) 1 up
Klaus Schaloske (CAN) beat David Bailey (ENG) 1 up
Steve Quevillon (CAN) beat Douglas Jopp (SCO) 1 up
Alan Gentry (USA) beat Brendan Swan (IRL) 3 and 2
Dennis Ithal (USA) beat Hugh Ross (SCO) 3 and 2
Bill Frey (USA) halved with Norman Kelly (ENG)

Result: North America 19½, Europe 8½

Scottish Disability Golf Partnership

Elmwood Coll (Stableford)	Div. 1 (9)	J Pringle & P Fox	48
	Div. 1 (18)	S Thornton & S Buist	56
	Div. 2 (18)	E Auld & R Nicol	67
	Div. 3 (18)	J Gales & P Shepherd	48
Murrayfield GC	J Gales	71	
Elie GC	R Mitchell	54	
Inverness GC	R Drysdale	71	
Inverness GC	Div. 1 (9)	S Thornton	48
Highland Open	Div. 1 (18)	G McNicol	67
	Div. 2 (9)	J Simpson	48
Strathpeffer Spa	J Gibb	72	
Lundin GC	S Fyfe	82	
	Ed Hodge	82	
	M Smith	82	
	D Leggat	82	
Cupar GC	V Shepherd	95	
	S Haxton	95	
	G Dickson	95	

Cupar GC	V Shepherd	95	
	S Haxton	95	
	G Dickson	95	
Bellshill GC	B Drysdale	42	
	A Semple	42	
	J Gray	42	
Scottish Open Cel-am Team	A Vicari (ITA)		
	A Mandich (ITA)		
	D Stewart (ENG)		
Scottish Open C/ship	1 J Gales (SCO)	137	
	2 M Horsley (ENG)	141	
	3 R Singh (RSA)	142	
Scotscraig GC	G Andrew	35	
Thornton GC	J Gales	105	
	F Paterson	105	
	B Drysdale	105	
	A Hughes	105	
Elmwood GS	D Barker	71	
	I Maxwell	71	
	D Todd	71	

20th British Amputee Open Championship *Bryn Meadows Golf, Hotel and Spa*

Nett Champion	Richard Willis (WAL)	147 nett
Senior Champion	John Novak (USA)	163 gross
Overall Champion	Duncan Hamilton-Martin (ENG)	157 gross

Handigolf

National Championship	Terry Kirby	Southern Open	Keith Robinson
North Lincs Open	Terry Kirby	Bolton Metro Unity	*Not played*
Handigolf MK Masters	Tucker Chance	Most Improved Player	Tony Toefeld
Southport Links	Andy Gore		

College Park Cup (formerly the Robinson Cup) *Plum Creek G&CC, Castle Rock, CO*

USA v International (USA names first)

Morning – foursomes:
Dennis Ithal & Kevin Valentine lost to Dan Hewett & Michael Wraight 1 up
Bill Harding & Kellie Valentine halved with Hitoshi Hatakubo & Ken Furuta
John Novak & Mike Hudson beat Mike Carve & Bob MacDermott 1 up
Kim Moore, & Alan Gentry beat Dallas Smith & John McNaughton 6 and 5
Lucian Newman & Dan Hodess beat Steve Wilson Pat Lott 5 and 4
Toby Placencio & Marty Ebel halved with Gwen Davies & Pete Fajt
Corbin Cherry & Ric Backman beat Yoshi Asano & "Mac" Akiyama 3 and 1
Tim Vincent & Dale Perkins beat Ron Versteegen & Vic McClelland 6 and 5

Afternoon – singles:

Dan Cox beat Dan Hewett (CAN) 6 and 5
Kellie Valentine lost to Steve Wilson (GER) 4 and 3
Ric Backman beat Hitoshi Hatakubo (JPN) 2 and 1
Mike Hudson halved with Ken Furuta (JPN)
Dennis Ithal lost to Michael Wraight (ENG) 5 and 3
John Novak beat Yoshio Asano (JPN) 2 and 1
Kim Moore lost to Pat Lott (MEX) 8 and 7

Alan Gentry halved with Vic McClelland (CAN)
Tim Vincent beat Bob MacDermott (CAN) 2 up
Marty Ebel beat Ron Versteegen (CAN) 4 and 2
Dan Hodess lost to "Mac" Akiyama (JPN) 4 and 3
Dale Perkins beat Gwen Davies (CAN) 1 up
Toby Placencio lost to John McNaughton (CAN) 3 and 2
Lucian Newman beat Dallas Smith (CAN) 3 and 2
Kevin Valentine lost to Mike Carve (IRL) 4 and 3
Corbin Cheey halved with Peter Fajt (NOR)

Result: USA 14½, International 9½

1999 International	2001 USA	2003 International	2005 USA	2007 USA
2000 International	2002 International	2004 International	2006 USA	

Special Olympics Triple Crown *The Belfry*

1	Ireland	42-49—91 points
2	England	30-50—80
3	Scotland	23-42—65
4	Wales	24-30—54

Winning team: Rita Dunne (Eastern Region), Kevin O'Callaghan (Munster), Joe Fulton (Leinster), Sarah Hyland (Munster), Frank Hynes (Eastern Region), Ruth O'Mahony (Munster), Oliver Doherty (Ulster) and Robert Slevin (Eastern Region).

Overseas Events

Canadian Blind Open
B1 David Blyth (AUS) 154; B2 Bruce Hooper (USA) 144; B3 Charles Adams (USA) 140
USBGA National Championship
B1 Phil Blackwell (USA) 191; B2 Bruce Hooper (USA) 164; B3 Ron Plath (USA) 167
Australian Blind Golf Open
B1 David Blyth (AUS) 229; B2 Jenny Abela (AUS) 233; B3 Doug Burrows (AUS) 164
Canadian Amputee National Open
Men's Overall Champion: John McNaughton (CAN); Ladies Overall Champion: Gwen Davies (CAN)
USA National Amputee Championship
Men's Overall Champion: Kevin Valentine (USA); Ladies Overall Champion: Kimberly Moore (USA)

Blind Golf Categories: B1 Totally Blind; B2 From the ability to recognise the shape of a hand up to visual acuity of 20/600; B3 From the visual acuity above 20/600 up to visual acuity of less than 20/200

Golf organisations for the disabled

International Blind Golf Association	www.internationalblindgolf.org
English Blind Golf Association	www.blindgolf.co.uk
Scottish Blind Golf Association	www.scottishblindgolf.com
Scottish Disability Golf Partnership (SDGP)	01334 650963
British Amputee & les Autres Sports Association (BALASA)	01206 298610
British Amputee Golf Association	www.baga.org.uk
The Society of One Armed Golfers	01360 622476
	www.soags.co.uk
Handigolf	www.handigolf.org
European Disabled Golf Association	www.edgagolf.com
Physically Challenged Golf Association	www.townusa.com/pcga
Special Olympics Great Britain	www.specialolympicsgb.org
Deaf Golf Association	www.deafgolf.com
Sportability	www.sportability.org

Donations to special needs groups

The R&A supports several organisations which run golf events for players with special needs. In 2008, £25,000 was set aside for this purpose. In addition, The R&A does, on occasion, send referees and other representatives to events run for disabled golfers.

PART IX

Record Scoring

Record Scoring

In the Major Championships nobody has shot lower than 63. There have been seven 63s in the Open, four 63s in the US Open, two 63s in The Masters and ten 63s in the USPGA Championship. The lowest first 36 holes is 130 by Nick Faldo in the 1992 Open at Muirfield and the lowest 72 hole total is 265 by David Toms in the 2001 USPGA Championship at the Atlanta Athletic Club.

The Open Championship

Most times champions
6 Harry Vardon, 1896–98–99–1903–11–14
5 James Braid, 1901–05–06–08–10; JH Taylor, 1894–95–1900–09–13; Peter Thomson, 1954–55–56–58–65; Tom Watson, 1975–77–80–82–83

Most times runner-up
7 Jack Nicklaus, 1964–67–68–72–76–77–79
6 JH Taylor, 1896–1904–05–06–07–14

Oldest winner
Old Tom Morris, 46 years 99 days, 1867
Roberto De Vicenzo, 44 years 93 days, 1967

Youngest winner
Young Tom Morris, 17 years 5 months 8 days, 1868
Willie Auchterlonie, 21 years 24 days, 1893
Severiano Ballesteros, 22 years 3 months 12 days, 1979

Youngest and oldest competitor
Young Tom Morris, 15 years, 4 months, 29 days, 1866
Gene Sarazen, 71 years 4 months 13 days, 1973

Widest margin of victory
13 strokes Old Tom Morris, 1862
12 strokes Young Tom Morris, 1870
8 strokes JH Taylor, 1900 and 1913; James Braid, 1908; Tiger Woods, 2000
6 strokes Harry Vardon, 1903; JH Taylor, 1909; Bobby Jones, 1927; Walter Hagen, 1929; Arnold Palmer, 1962; Johnny Miller, 1976

Lowest winning aggregates
267 Greg Norman, 66-68-69-64, Sandwich, 1993
268 Tom Watson, 68-70-65-65, Turnberry, 1977; Nick Price, 69-66-67-66, Turnberry, 1994
269 Tiger Woods, 67-66-67-69, St Andrews, 2000
270 Nick Faldo, 67-65-67-71, St Andrews, 1990; Tiger Woods 67-65-71-67, Hoylake, 2006

Lowest in relation to par
19 under Tiger Woods, St Andrews, 2000
18 under Nick Faldo, St Andrews, 1990; Tiger Woods, Hoylake, 2006

Lowest aggregate by runner-up
269 (68-70-65-66), Jack Nicklaus, Turnberry, 1977; (69-63-70-67) Nick Faldo, Sandwich, 1993; (68-66-68-67) Jesper Parnevik, Turnberry, 1994

Lowest aggregate by an amateur
281 (68-72-70-71), Iain Pyman, Sandwich, 1993; (75-66-70-70), Tiger Woods, Royal Lytham, 1996

Lowest round
63 Mark Hayes, second round, Turnberry, 1977; Isao Aoki, third round, Muirfield, 1980; Greg Norman, second round, Turnberry, 1986; Paul Broadhurst, third round, St Andrews, 1990; Jodie Mudd, fourth round, Royal Birkdale, 1991; Nick Faldo, second round, Payne Stewart, fourth round, Sandwich, 1993

Lowest round by an amateur
66 Frank Stranahan, fourth round, Troon, 1950; Tiger Woods, second round, Royal Lytham, 1996; Justin Rose, second round, Royal Birkdale, 1998

Lowest first round
64 Craig Stadler, Royal Birkdale, 1983; Christy O'Connor Jr, Royal St George's, 1985; Rodger Davis, Muirfield, 1987; Steve Pate, Ray Floyd, Muirfield, 1992

Lowest second round
63 Mark Hayes, Turnberry, 1977; Greg Norman, Turnberry, 1986; Nick Faldo, Sandwich, 1993

Lowest third round
63 Isao Aoki, Muirfield, 1980; Paul Broadhurst, St Andrews, 1990

Lowest fourth round
63 Jodie Mudd, Royal Birkdale, 1991; Payne Stewart, Sandwich, 1993

Lowest first 36 holes
130 (66-64), Nick Faldo, Muirfield, 1992
132 (67-65), Henry Cotton, Sandwich, 1934; Nick Faldo (67-65) and Greg Norman (66-66), St Andrews, 1990; Nick Faldo (69-63), Sandwich, 1993; Tiger Woods (67-65), Hoylake, 2006

Lowest second 36 holes
130 (65-65), Tom Watson, Turnberry, 1977; (64-66) Ian Baker-Finch, Royal Birkdale, 1991; (66-64) Anders Forsbrand, Turnberry, 1994

Lowest first 54 holes
198 (67-67-64) Tom Lehman, Royal Lytham, 1996
199 (67-65-67), Nick Faldo, St Andrews, 1990; (66-64-69) Nick Faldo, Muirfield, 1992

Lowest final 54 holes
199 (66-67-66) Nick Price, Turnberry, 1994
200 (70-65-65), Tom Watson, Turnberry, 1977; (63-70-67), Nick Faldo, Sandwich, 1993; (66-64-70), Fuzzy Zoeller, Turnberry, 1994; (66-70-64), Nick Faldo, Turnberry 1994

Lowest 9 holes
28 Denis Durnian, first 9, Royal Birkdale, 1983

Champions in three decades
Harry Vardon, 1986, 1903, 1911; JH Taylor, 1894, 1900, 1913; Gary Player, 1959, 1968, 1974

Biggest span between first and last victories
19 years, J.H. Taylor, 1894–1913
18 years, Harry Vardon, 1896–1914
15 years, Willie Park, 1860–75

15 years, Gary Player, 1959–74
14 years, Henry Cotton, 1934–48

Successive victories
4 Young Tom Morris, 1868–72 (no championship 1871)
3 Jamie Anderson, 1877–79; Bob Ferguson, 1880–82, Peter Thomson, 1954–56
2 Old Tom Morris, 1861–62; JH Taylor, 1894–95; Harry Vardon, 1898–99; James Braid, 1905–06; Bobby Jones, 1926–27; Walter Hagen, 1928–29; Bobby Locke, 1949–50; Arnold Palmer, 1961–62; Lee Trevino, 1971–72; Tom Watson, 1982–83; Tiger Woods, 2005–06; Padraig Harrington, 2007–08

Amateur champions
John Ball, 1890, Prestwick; Harold Hilton, 1892, Muirfield; 1897, Royal Liverpool; Bobby Jones, 1926, Royal Lytham; 1927, St Andrews; 1930 Royal Liverpool

Highest number of top five finishes
16 JH Taylor and Jack Nicklaus
15 Harry Vardon and James Braid

Players with four rounds under 70
Ernie Els (68-69-69-68), Sandwich, 1993; Greg Norman (66-68-69-64), Sandwich, 1993; Jesper Parnevik (68-66-68-67), Turnberry, 1994; Nick Price (69-66-67-66), Turnberry, 1994; Tiger Woods (67-66-67-69), St Andrews, 2000; Ernie Els (69-69-68-68), Royal Troon, 2004

Highest number of rounds under 70
37	Nick Faldo	**28**	Tom Watson
33	Jack Nicklaus	**26**	Greg Norman
	Ernie Els	**25**	Nick Price
31	Ernie Els	**22**	Bernhard Langer

Outright leader after every round (since Championship became 72 holes in 1892)
James Braid, 1908; Ted Ray, 1912; Bobby Jones, 1927; Gene Sarazen, 1932; Henry Cotton, 1934; Tom Weiskopf, 1973; Tiger Woods, 2005

Record leads (since 1892)
After 18 holes: 4 strokes, Bobby Jones, 1927; Henry Cotton, 1934; Christy O'Connor jr, 1985
After 36 holes: 9 strokes, Henry Cotton, 1934
After 54 holes: 10 strokes, Henry Cotton, 1934; 7 strokes, Tony Lema, 1964; 6 strokes, James Braid, 1908; Tom Lehman, 1996; Tiger Woods, 2000

Champions with each round lower than previous one
Jack White, 1904, Sandwich, 80-75-72-69; James Braid, 1906, Muirfield, 77-76-74-73; Ben Hogan, 1953, Carnoustie, 73-71-70-68; Gary Player, 1959, Muirfield, 75-71-70-68

Champion with four rounds the same
Densmore Shute, 1933, St Andrews, 73-73-73-73 (excluding the play-off)

Biggest variation between rounds of a champion
14 strokes, Henry Cotton, 1934, second round 65, fourth round 79; 11 strokes, Jack White, 1904, first round 80, fourth round 69; Greg Norman, 1986, first round 74, second round 63, third round 74

Biggest variation between two rounds
20 strokes: R.G. French, 1938, second round 71, third round 91; Colin Montgomerie, 2002, second round 64, third round 84; 18 strokes: A Tingey Jr, 1923, first round 94, second round 76; 17 strokes, Jack Nicklaus, 1981,

first round 83, second round 66; Ian Baker-Finch, 1986, first round 86, second round 69

Best comeback by champions
After 18 holes: Harry Vardon, 1896, 11 strokes behind the leader
After 36 holes: George Duncan, 1920, 13 strokes behind leader
After 54 holes: Paul Lawrie, 1999, 10 strokes behind the leader (won four-hole play-off)

Best comeback by non-champions
Of non-champions, Greg Norman, 1989, seven strokes behind the leader and lost in a play-off

Best finishing round by a champion
64 Greg Norman, Sandwich, 1993
65 Tom Watson, Turnberry, 1977; Severiano Ballesteros, Royal Lytham, 1988; Justin Leonard, Royal Troon, 1997

Worst finishing round by a champion since 1920
79 Henry Cotton, Sandwich, 1934
78 Reg Whitcombe, Sandwich, 1938
77 Walter Hagen, Hoylake, 1924

Best opening round by a champion
66 Peter Thomson, Royal Lytham, 1958; NickFaldo, Muirfield, 1992; Greg Norman, Sandwich, 1993
67 Henry Cotton, Sandwich, 1934; Tom Watson, Royal Birkdale, 1983; Severiano Ballesteros, Royal Lytham, 1988; Nick Faldo, St Andrews, 1990; John Daly, St Andrews, 1995; Tom Lehman, Royal Lytham, 1996; Tiger Woods, St Andrews, 2000; Tiger Woods, St Andrews, 2005; Tiger Woods, Hoylake, 2006

Worst opening round by a champion since 1919
80 George Duncan, Deal, 1920 (he also had a second round of 80)
77 Walter Hagen, Hoylake, 1924

Biggest recovery in 18 holes by a champion
George Duncan, Deal, 1920, was 13 strokes behind the leader, Abe Mitchell, after 36 holes and level after 54

Most consecutive appearances
47 Gary Player, 1955–2001

Championship since 1946 with the fewest rounds under 70
St Andrews, 1946; Hoylake, 1947; Portrush, 1951; Hoylake, 1956; Carnoustie, 1968. All had only two rounds under 70

Longest course
Carnoustie, 2007, 7,421 yards (par 71)

Largest entries
2,499 in 2005, St Andrews

Courses most often used
St Andrews, 27; Prestwick, 24 (but not since 1925); Muirfield, 15; Sandwich, 12; Hoylake, 11; Royal Lytham and St Annes, 10; Royal Birkdale, 8; Royal Troon 8; Carnoustie, 7; Musselburgh, 6; Turnberry, 3; Deal, 2; Royal Portrush and Prince's, 1

Albatrosses
Both Jeff Maggert (6th hole, 2nd round) and Greg Owen (11th hole, 3rd round) made albatrosses during the 2001 Open Championship at Royal Lytham and St Annes. No complete record of albatrosses in the

Prize Money

Year	Total	First Prize £
1860	nil	nil
1863	10	nil
1864	16	6
1876	20	20
1889	22	8
1891	28.50	10
1892	110	(am)
1893	100	30
1910	125	50
1920	225	75
1927	275	100
1930	400	100
1931	500	100
1946	1000	150
1949	1700	300
1953	2450	500
1954	3500	750
1955	3750	1,000
1958	4850	1,000
1959	5000	1,000

Year	Total	First Prize £
1960	7000	1,250
1961	8500	1,400
1963	8500	1,500
1965	10,000	1,750
1966	15,000	2,100
1968	20,000	3,000
1969	30,000	4,250
1970	40,000	5,250
1971	45,000	5,500
1972	50,000	5,500
1975	75,000	7,500
1977	100,000	10,000
1978	125,000	12,500
1979	155,000	15,500
1980	200,000	25,000
1982	250,000	32,000
1983	300,000	40,000
1984	451,000	55,000
1985	530,000	65,000
1986	600,000	70,000
1987	650,000	75,000

Year	Total	First Prize £
1988	700,000	80,000
1989	750,000	80,000
1990	815,000	85,000
1991	900,000	90,000
1992	950,000	95,000
1993	1,000,000	100,000
1994	1,100,000	110,000
1995	1,250,000	125,000
1996	1,400,000	200,000
1997	1,586,300	250,000
1998	1,774,150	300,000
1999	2,029,950	350,000
2000	2,722,150	500,000
2001	3,229,748	600,000
2002	3,880,998	700,000
2003	3,931,000	700,000
2004	4,006,950	720,000
2005	3,854,900	720,000
2006	3,990,916	720,000
2007	4,185,400	750,000
2008	4,260,000	750,000

history of the event is available but since 1979 there have been only four others – by Johnny Miller (Muirfield 5th hole) in 1980, Bill Rogers (Royal Birkdale 17th hole) 1983, Manny Zerman (St Andrews) 2000 and Gary Evans (Royal Troon 4th hole) 2004.

US Open

Most times champion
4 Willie Anderson, 1901–03–04–05; Bobby Jones, 1923–26–29–30; Ben Hogan, 1948–50–51–53; Jack Nicklaus, 1962–67–72–80

Most times runner-up
4 Bobby Jones, 1922–24–25–28; Sam Snead, 1937–47–49–53; Arnold Palmer, 1962–63–66–67; Jack Nicklaus, 1960 (am)–68–71–82

Oldest winner
Hale Irwin, 45 years, 15 days, Medinah, 1990

Youngest winner
Johnny McDermott, 19 years, 10 months, 12 days, Chicago, 1911

Biggest winning margin
15 strokes Tiger Woods, Pebble Beach, 2000

Lowest winning aggregate
272 Jack Nicklaus, Baltusrol, 1980; Lee Janzen, Baltusrol, 1993; Tiger Woods, Pebble Beach, 2000

Lowest in relation to par
12 under Tiger Woods, Pebble Beach, 2000

Lowest round
63 Johnny Miller, fourth round, Oakmont, 1973; Jack Nicklaus, first round, Baltusrol, 1980; Tom Weiskopf, first round, Baltusrol, 1980; Vijay Singh, second round, Olympia Fields, 2003

Lowest 9 holes
29 Neal Lancaster, Shinnecock Hills, 1995, and Oakland Hills, 1996

Lowest first 36 holes
133 Jim Furyk, Vijay Singh, Olympia Fields, 2003

Lowest final 36 holes
132 Larry Nelson, Oakmont, 1983

Lowest first 54 holes
200 Jim Furyk, Olympia Fields, 2003

Lowest final 54 holes
204 Jack Nicklaus, Baltusrol, 1967; Raymond Floyd, Shinnecock Hills, 1986; Steve Jones, Oaklands Hills, 1996

Open attendances

Year	Attendance	Year	Attendance	Year	Attendance	Year	Attendance
1962	37,098	1974	92,796	1986	134,261	1998	180,000
1963	24,585	1975	85,258	1987	139,189	1999	158,000
1964	35,954	1976	92,021	1988	191,334	2000	230,000
1965	32,927	1977	87,615	1989	160,639	2001	178,000
1966	40,182	1978	125,271	1990	207,000	2002	161,000
1967	29,880	1979	134,501	1991	192,154	2003	182,585
1968	51,819	1980	131,610	1992	150,100	2004	176,000
1969	46,001	1981	111,987	1993	140,100	2005	223,000
1970	82,593	1982	133,299	1994	128,000	2006	230,000
1971	70,076	1983	142,892	1995	180,000	2007	153,000
1972	84,746	1984	193,126	1996	170,000	2008	201,500
1973	78,810	1985	141,619	1997	176,797		

Most consecutive appearances
44 Jack Nicklaus 1957 to 2000

Successive victories
3 Willie Anderson, 1903–04–05

Players with four rounds under 70
Lee Trevino, 69-68-69-69, Oak Hill, 1968; Lee Janzen, 67-67-69-69, Baltusrol, 1993

Outright leader after every round
Walter Hagen, Midlothian, 1914; Jim Barnes, Columbia, 1921; Ben Hogan, Oakmont, 1953; Tony Jacklin, Hazeltine, 1970; Tiger Woods, Pebble Beach, 2000; Tiger Woods, Bethpage, 2002

Best opening round by a champion
63 Jack Nicklaus, Baltusrol, 1980

Worst opening round by a champion
91 Horace Rawlins, Newport, RI, 1895
Since World War II: 76 Ben Hogan, Oakland Hills, 1951; Jack Fleck, Olympic, 1955

Amateur champions
Francis Ouimet, Brookline, 1913; Jerome Travers, Baltusrol, 1915; Chick Evans, Minikahda, 1916; Bobby Jones, Inwood, 1923, Scioto, 1926, Winged Foot, 1929, Interlachen, 1930; Johnny Goodman, North Shore, 1933

The Masters

Most times champion
6 Jack Nicklaus, 1963–65–66–72–75–86
4 Arnold Palmer, 1958–60–62–64
4 Tiger Woods, 1997–2001–02–05

Most times runner-up
4 Ben Hogan, 1942–46–54–55; Jack Nicklaus, 1964–71–77–81

Oldest winner
Jack Nicklaus, 46 years, 2 months, 23 days, 1986

Youngest winner
Tiger Woods, 21 years, 3 months, 15 days, 1997

Biggest winning margin
12 strokes Tiger Woods, 1997

Lowest winning aggregate
270 Tiger Woods, 1997

Lowest in relation to par
18 under Tiger Woods, Augusta, 1997

Lowest aggregate by an amateur
281 Charles Coe, 1961 (joint second)

Lowest round
63 Nick Price, 1986; Greg Norman, 1996

Lowest 9 holes
29 Mark Calcavecchia, 1992; David Toms, 1998

Lowest first 36 holes
131 Raymond Floyd, 1976

Lowest final 36 holes
131 Johnny Miller, 1975

Lowest first 54 holes
201 Raymond Floyd, 1976; Tiger Woods, 1997

Lowest final 54 holes
200 Tiger Woods, 1997

Most appearances
51 **Gary Player** 1957–2008
50 Arnold Palmer 1955–2004
49 Doug Ford 1952 to 2001; Gary Player 1957 to 2006

Successive victories
2 Jack Nicklaus, 1965–66; Nick Faldo, 1989–90; Tiger Woods, 2001–02

Players with four rounds under 70
None

Outright leader after every round
Craig Wood, 1941; Arnold Palmer, 1960; Jack Nicklaus, 1972; Raymond Floyd, 1976

Best opening round by a champion
65 Raymond Floyd, 1976

Worst opening round by a champion
75 Craig Stadler, 1982

Worst closing round by a champion
75 Trevor Immelman, 2008

Albatrosses
There have been three albatross twos in the Masters at Augusta National: by Gene Sarazen at the 15th, 1935; by Bruce Devlin at the eighth, 1967; and by Jeff Maggert at the 13th, 1994.

USPGA Championship

Most times champion
5 Walter Hagen, 1921–24–25–26–27; Jack Nicklaus 1963–71–73–75–80

Most times runner-up
4 Jack Nicklaus, 1964–65–74–83

Oldest winner
Julius Boros, 48 years 4 months 18 days, Pecan Valley, 1968

Youngest winner
Gene Sarazen, 20 years 5 months 22 days, Oakmont, 1922

Biggest winning margin
7 strokes Jack Nicklaus, Oak Hill, 1980

Lowest winning aggregate
265 (−15) David Toms, Atlanta Athletic Club, 2001
267 Steve Elkington and Colin Montgomerie, Riviera, 1995 – Montgomerie lost sudden death play-off

Lowest aggregate by runner-up
266 (−14) Phil Michelson, Atlanta Athletic Club, 2001

Lowest in relation to par
18 under Tiger Woods and Bob May, Valhalla, 2000 (May lost three-hole play-off); Tiger Woods, Medinah, 2006

Lowest round
63 Bruce Crampton, Firestone, 1975; Raymond Floyd, Southern Hills, 1982; Gary Player, Shoal Creek, 1984; Vijay Singh, Inverness, 1993; Michael Bradley and Brad Faxon, Riviera, 1995; José Maria Olazábal, Valhalla, 2000; Mark O'Meara, Atlanta Athletic Club, 2001; Thomas Bjørn, Baltusrol, 2005; Tiger Woods, Southern Hills, 2007

Most successive victories
4 Walter Hagen, 1924–25–26–27

Lowest 9 holes
28 Brad Faxon, Riviera, 1995

Lowest first 36 holes
131 Hal Sutton, Riviera, 1983; Vijay Singh, Inverness, 1993; Ernie Els and Mark O'Meara, Riviera, 1995; Shingo Katayama and David Toms, Atlanta Athletic Club, 2001

Lowest final 36 holes
131 Mark Calcavecchia, Atlanta Athletic Club, 2001
132 Miller Barber, Dayton, 1969; Steve Elkington and Colin Montgomerie, Riviera, 1995; Padraig Harrington, Oakland Hills, 2008

Lowest first 54 holes
196 David Toms, Atlanta Athletic Club, 2001

Lowest final 54 holes
199 Steve Elkington, Colin Montgomerie, Riviera, 1995; Mark Calcavecchia, David Toms, Atlanta Athletic Club, 2001

Most appearances
37 Arnold Palmer; Jack Nicklaus

Outright leader after every round
Bobby Nichols, Columbus, 1964; Jack Nicklaus, PGA National, 1971; Raymond Floyd, Southern Hills, 1982; Hal Sutton, Riviera, 1983

Best opening round by a champion
63 Raymond Floyd, Southern Hills, 1982

Worst opening round by a champion
75 John Mahaffey, Oakmont, 1978

Worst closing round by a champion
76 Vijay Singh, Whistling Straits, 2004 (worst in any major since Reg Whitcombe's 78 in 1938 Open)

Albatrosses
Joey Sindelar had an albatross at the fifth hole at Medinah Country Club during the third round of the 2006 PGA Championship

PGA European Tour

Lowest 72-hole aggregate
258 (–14) David Llewellyn (WAL), AGF Biarritz Open, 1988; (18 under par) Ian Woosnam (WAL), Monte Carlo Open, 1990.
259 (–29) Ernie Els (RSA), Johnnie Walker Classic, Lake Karrinyup, 2003; (25 under par) Mark McNulty (ZIM), German Open, Frankfurt, 1987; (21 under par) Tiger Woods (USA), NEC Invitational, 2000

Lowest 9 holes
27 (–9) José María Canizares (ESP), Swiss Open at Crans-sur-Sierre, 1978; (–7) Robert Lee (ENG), Johnnie Walker Monte Carlo Open at Mont Agel, 1985; (–6) Robert Lee, Portuguese Open at Estoril, 1987; (–9) Joakim Haeggman (SWE), Alfred Dunhill Cup at St Andrews, 1997; (–9) Simon Khan, Wales Open at Celtic Manor, 2004; (–9) Andrew Coltart, KLM Open, Kennemer

Lowest 18 holes
60 (–12) Jamie Spence, Canon European Masters at Crans-sur-Sierre, 1992; Bernhard Langer (GER), Linde German Masters at Motzener See, 1997; Darren Clarke, Smurfit European Open at K Club, 1999;

Fredrik Jacobson, Linde German Masters, Gut Larchenhof, 2003; Ernie Els, Heineken Classic, Royal Melbourne, 2004; (–11) Baldovino Dassu (ITA), Swiss Open at Crans-sur-Sierre, 1971; David Llewellyn (WAL), AGF Biarritz Open, 1988; (–10) Paul Curry, Bell's Scottish Open at Gleneagles, 1992; Tobias Dier, TNT Open, Hilversum, 2002; (–9) Ian Woosnam (WAL), Torras Monte Carlo Open at Mont Agel, 1990; (–9) both Darren Clarke and Johan Rystrom, Monte Carlo Open at Mont Agel, 1992; Phillip Archer (ENG), Celtic Manor Wales Open, Celtic Manor, 2006

Lowest 36 holes
124 (–18) Colin Montgomerie (SCO), Canon European Masters at Crans-sur-Sierre, 1996 (3rd and 4th rounds); (–14) Robert Karlsson (SWE), Celtic Manor Wales Open at Celtic Manor, 2006 (1st and 2nd rounds)

Lowest 54 holes
189 (–18) Robert Karlsson (SWE), Celtic Manor Wales Open, Celtic Manor, 2006 (rounds 1-2-3)
192 (–24) Anders Forsbrand (SWE), Ebel European Masters Swiss Open, Crans-sur-Sierre, 1987 (rounds 2-3-4)
192 (–18) Tiger Woods, NEC Invitational, Firestone, Akron, Ohio, 2000 (first 3 rounds)

Lowest first 36 holes
125 (–17 Frankie Minoza, Caltex Singapore Masters, Singapore Island, 2001
125 (–15) Tiger Woods, NEC Invitational World Championship, Firestone, Akron, Ohio, 2000

Largest winning margin
15 strokes Tiger Woods, United States Open, Pebble Beach, 2000 (Note: Bernhard Langer's 17-stroke victory in 1979 at Cacharel Under-25's Championship in Nîmes is not considered a full European Tour event)

Highest winning score
306 Peter Butler (ENG), Schweppes PGA Close Championship at Royal Birkdale, 1963

Youngest winner
Dale Hayes, 18 years 290 days, Spanish Open, 1971

Youngest to make cut
Sergio García, 15 years 46 days, Turespana Open Mediterrania, 1985

Oldest to make cut
Bob Charles 71 years 8 months, 2007 Michael Hill New Zealand Open, The Hills Golf Club, Queenstown

Oldest winner
Des Smyth (IRL), 48 years 34 days, Madeira Island Open, 2001

Most wins in one season
7 Norman von Nida (AUS), 1947

US PGA Tour

Lowest 72-hole aggregate
254 (–26) Tommy Armour III, Valero Texas Open, 2003 (Note: Ernie Els' 261 at the 2003 Mercedes Championship was a record 31 under par)

Lowest 54 holes
189 (–24) Chandler Harper, Texas Open (last three rounds), 1954; John Cook, St Jude Classic (first three rounds), 1996; Mark Calcavecchia, Phoenix Open (first three rounds), 2001; (–21) Tommy Armour III, Valero Texas Open (first three rounds), 2003 (Note: Tim

Herron's 190 at the 2003 Bob Hope Chrysler Classic (rounds 2-4) was a record 26 under par)

Lowest 36 holes
124 (−18) Mark Calcavecchia (USA), Phoenix Open, 2001 (2nd and 3rd rounds) (*Note:* Gay Brewer's 125 at the 1967 Pensacola Open (2nd and 3rd rounds), John Cook's 125 at the 1997 Bob Hope Chrysler Classic (last two rounds), Tom Lehman's 125 at the 2001 Invensys Classic (1st and 2nd rounds) and Tim Herron's 125 at the 2003 Bob Hope Chrysler Classic (2nd and 3rd rounds) were a record 19 under par)

Lowest 18 holes
59 Sam Snead, 3rd round, Greenbrier Open (Sam Snead Festival), White Sulphur Springs, West Virginia, 1959; Al Geiberger, 2nd round, Danny Thomas Memphis Classic, Colonial CC, 1977 (when preferred lies were in operation); (−13) Chip Beck on the 6,914 yards Sunrise GC course, Las Vegas, Las Vegas Invitational, 1991 (finished third but won a bonus prize of $500,000 and another $500,000 for charities; David Duval on 6,940 yards PGA West Arnold Palmer course, CA, final round, Bob Hope Chrysler Classic, 1999 (won tournament with last hole eagle)

Lowest 9 holes
26 (−8) Corey Pavin, US Bank Championship, 2006
27 (−9) Billy Mayfair, Buick Open, 2001; Robert Gamez, Bob Hope Chrysler Classic, 2004; (−8) Mike Souchak, Texas Open, 1955; (−7) Andy North, BC Open, 1975; (−9) Brandt Snedeker, Buick Invitational, 2007

Lowest first 36 holes
125 (−19) Tom Lehman (USA), Invensys Classic 2001; (−17) Mark Calcavecchia (USA), Phoenix Open, 2001; (−15) Tiger Woods, NEC Invitational World Championship, Firestone, Akron, Ohio, 2000; (−15) Corey Pavin, US Bank Championship, 2006; (−15) Carl Pettersson, Wyndham Championship, 2008

Largest winning margin
16 strokes J. Douglas Edgar, Canadian Open Championship, 1919; Joe Kirkwood, Corpus Christi Open 1924; Bobby Locke, Chicago Victory National Championship, 1948

Youngest winner
Johnny McDermott, 19 years 10 months, US Open, 1911

Youngest to make cut
Bob Panasik, 15 years 8 months 20 days, Canadian Open, 1957

Oldest winner
Sam Snead, 52 years 10 months, Greater Greensboro Open, 1965

Most wins in one season
18 Byron Nelson, 1945

National opens – excluding Europe and USA

Lowest 72-hole aggregate
255 Peter Tupling, Nigerian Open, Lagos, 1981

Lowest 36-hole aggregate
124 (18 under par) Sandy Lyle, Nigerian Open, Ikoyi GC, Lagos, 1978 (his first year as a professional)

Lowest 18 holes
59 Gary Player, second round, Brazilian Open, Gavea GC (6,185 yards), Rio de Janeiro, 1974.

Amateur winners
Pablo Martin, 2007 Estoril Open de Portugal, Oitavos

Professional events – excluding Europe and USA

Lowest 72-hole aggregate
260 Bob Charles, Spalding Masters at Tauranga, New Zealand, 1969; Jason Bohn, Bayer Classic, Huron Oaks, Canada, 2001; Brian Kontak, Alberta Open, Canada, 1998.

Lowest 18-hole aggregate
58 (13 under par) Jason Bohn (USA), Bayer Classic, Huron Oaks, Canada, 2001 (*Note:* Miguel Angel Martin had round of 59 at South Argentine Open, 1987)

Lowest 9-hole aggregate
27 Bill Brask (USA) at Tauranga in the New Zealand PGA in 1976

Amateur winners
Charles Evans, 1910 Western Open, Beverly, Illinois; John Dawson, 1942 Bing Crosby, Rancho Santa Fe, California; Gene Littler, 1954 San Diego Open, Rancho Santa Fe, California; Doug Sanders, 1956 Canadian Open, Beaconsfield, Quebec; Scott Verplank 1985 Western Open, Butler National, Illinois; Phil Mickelson 1991 Northern Telecom Open, Tucson, Arizona; Brett Rumford, 1999 ANZ Players Championship, Royal Queensland; Aaron Baddeley, 1999 Australian Open, Royal Sydney

Asian PGA Tour

Lowest 72 holes
259 (−29) Ernie Els, 2003 Johnnie Walker Classic
262 (−26) Jeev Milkha Singh, 1996 Philip Morris Asia Cup (Limited Field); (−26) Ernie Els, 2005 BMW Asian Open (*Note:* Thaworn Wiratchant achieved a 25 under par total of 255 in the 2005 Enjoy Jakarta Standard Chartered Indonesian Open, but preferred lies were in use)

Only players to shoot 20-under par or better more than once
Tiger Woods, 2000 Johnnie Walker Classic; 1997 Asian Honda Classic; Ernie Els, 2003 Johnnie Walker Classic and 2005 BMW Asian Open; Simon Dyson, 2000; Omega Hong Kong Open, 2006 Enjoy Jakarta HSBC Indonesia Open; Retief Goosen, 2005 and 2006 Volkswagen Masters-China; Jeev Milkha Singh, 1996 Philip Morris Asia Cup and 2008 Ballantine's Championship

Highest winning score
293 (+5) Boonchu Ruangkit, 1996 Myanmar Open

Lowest 54 holes
193 (−23) Ernie Els, 2003 Johnnie Walker Classic; David Howell, 2006 TCL Classic (*Note:* Thaworn

Wiratchant achieved an 18 under par total of 192 in the 2005 Enjoy Jakarta Standard Chartered Indonesia Open, but preferred lies were in use)

Lowest 36 holes
125   (−17) Frankie Minoza, 2001 Caltex Singapore Masters (*Note:* David Howell's 127 in the 2006 TCL Classic was also 17 under par)   (*Note:* David Howell's 127 at the 2006 TCL Classic and Chapchai Nirat's 127 at the 2007 TCL Classic were also 17 under par)

Lowest 18 holes
60   (−12) Liang Wen-chong, 2008 Hero Honda Indian Open (*Note:* Kim Felton and Colin Montgomerie had rounds of 60 in the 2000 Omega Hong Kong Open and 2005 Enjoy Jakarta Standard Chartered Indonesian Open respectively, but preferred lies were in operation. Felton's round was 11 under par, Montgomerie's 10 under)

Lowest 9 holes
28   (−8) Chung Chun-hsing, 2001 Maekyung LG Fashion Open; (−7) Chinarat Phadungsil, 2007 Midea China Classic; (−7) Henrik Bjornstad, 2001 Omega Hong Kong Open; (−6) Darren Griff, 2005 Standard Chartered Indonesian Open; (−7) Maarten Lafeber, 2005 UBS Hong Kong Open

Biggest margin of victory
13 strokes   Ernie Els, 2005 BMW Asian Open
12 strokes   Bradley Hughes, 1996 Players Championship

Youngest winners
Chinarat Phadungsil (am), 17 years 5 days, 2005 Double A International Open; Kim Dae-sub (am), 17 years 83 days, 1998 Korean Open; Eddie Lee (am) 18 years and 170 days, 2002 Maekyung LG Fashion Open;

Youngest to play in an Asian event
Ye Jian-fe, 13 years and 20 days, 2004 Sanya Open

Oldest winner
Choi Sang-ho, 50 years and 145 days, 2005 Maekyung Open; Boonchu Ruangkit, 47 years and 258 days, 2004 Thailand Open

Most wins in a season
4   Thaworn Wiratchant, 2005
3   Lin Keng-chi 1995 (Tournament Players Championship, Singapore PGA Championship, Samsung Masters); Simon Dyson 2000 (Omega Hong Kong Open, Macau Open, Volvo China Open)

Most wins on Tour
9   Thaworn Wiratchant
8   Thongchai Jaidee
7   Kang Wook-soon; Thongchai Jaidee, Thaworn Wiratchant

Youngest player to make the cut
Lo Shih-kai, 14 years and 275 days, 2003 Acer Taiwan Open

Oldest player to make the cut
Gary Player, 66 years and 323 days, 2002 Acer Taiwan Open

Holes in one at same hole
Chen Chung-cheng, 2004 Thailand Open, fourth hole, days 1 and 3

Japan Golf Tour

Lowest 72 holes
260   (−20) Masashi 'Jumbo' Ozaki, 1995 Chunichi Crowns, Nagoya Wago
262   (−26) Masashi Ozaki, 1996 Japan Series, Tokyo Yomiuri
266   (−26) Brandt Jobe, 1995 Mitsubishi Gallant, Aso Prince Hotel

Lowest 54 holes
193   (−23) Masahiro Kuramoto, 1987 Maruman Open, Higashi Matsuyama; (−17) Masashi Ozaki, 1995 Chunichi Crowns, Nagoya Wago

Lowest 36 holes
126   (−18) Masahiro Kuramoto, 1987 Maruman Open, Higashi Matsuyama

Lowest 18 holes
59   (−12) Masahiro Kuramoto, 2003 Acom International

Lowest 9 holes
28   (−8) Isao Aoki, 1972 Kanto Pro, Isogo; Takashi Murakami, 1972 Kanto Pro, Isogo; Yoshinori Kaneko, 1994 Nikkei Cup, Mitsui-kanko Tomakomai; Masayuki Kawamura, 1995 Gene Sarazen Jun Classic; Tsuyoshi Yoneyama, 1998 Sapporo Tokyu, Sapporo Kokusai; Toshimitsu Izawa, 2000 TPC Iiyama Cup, Horai

Largest winning margin
15   Masashi Ozaki, 1994 Daiwa International Hatoyama (pre-1973 tour formation: 19 Akira Muraki, 1930 Japan PGA Championship, Takarazuka)

Youngest winner
Seve Ballesteros, 20 years 5 months, 1977 Japan Open, Narashino (pre-1973 tour formation: Toichiro Toda, 18 years 6 months, 1933 Kansai Open)

Oldest winner
Masashi Ozaki, 55 years 8 months, 2002 ANA Open, Sapporo Wattsu

Most wins in a season
9   Tsuneyuki 'Tommy' Nakajima, 1983; Masashi 'Jumbo' Ozaki, 1972

South African Sunshine Tour

Lowest 9-hole score
28   Simon Hobday, 2nd round of the 1987 Royal Swazi Sun Pro Am at Royal Swazi Sun Country Club; Mark McNulty (IRL), 2nd round of 1996 Zimbabwe Open at Chapman Golf Club; David Frost, 2nd round of the 1997 Alfred Dunhill PGA Championship at Houghton Golf Club; Tertius Claassens, 1st round of the 1982 SAB Masters at Milnerton; Brenden Pappas, 2nd round of the 1996 Dimension Data Pro-Am at Gary Player Country Club; Murray Urquhart, 2nd round of the 2001 Royal Swazi Sun Open at Royal Swazi Sun Country Club

Lowest 18-hole score
60   Shane Pringle (ZIM) 30-30, 2002 Botswana Open, Gabarone Golf Club

Lowest first 36 holes
127   Barry Painting (ZIM) 62-65, 2004 FNB Botswana Open, Gabarone Golf Club

Lowest last 36 holes
126 Mark McNulty (IRL) 64-62, 1987 Royal Swazi Sun Pro-Am, Royal Swazi Sun Country Club

Lowest 54 holes
195 Nick Price (ZIM) 61-69-65, 1994 ICL International; Barry Painting (ZIM) 62-65-68, 2004 FNB Botswana Open, Gaberone GC

Lowest 72-hole score
259 Mark McNulty (IRL) 68-65-64-62, 1987 Royal Swazi Sun Pro-Am, Royal Swazi Sun Country Club; David Frost 64-67-65-63, 1994 Lexington PGA, Wanderers Golf Club

Largest winning margin
12 strokes Nick Price (ZIM), 1993 Nedbank Million Dollar, Sun City (non-order of merit event)
11 strokes Nico van Rensburg, 2000 Vodacom Series Gauteng, Silver Lakes

Most wins in a season
Seven wins in 11 tournaments by Mark McNulty (IRL), 1986-87 season – Southern Suns SA Open, AECI Charity Classic, Royal Swazi Sun Pro-Am, Trust Bank Tournament of Champions, Germiston Centenary Golf Tournament, Safmarine Masters, Helix Wild Coast Sun Classic

Most wins in succession
Four Gary Player, 1979-80 – Lexington PGA, Krönenbrau SA Masters, B.A. / Yellow Pages SA Open, Sun City Classic; Mark McNulty (IRL), 1986-87 – Southern Suns SA Open, AECI Charity Classic, Royal Swazi Sun Pro-Am, Trust Bank Tournament of Champions

Most birdies in one round
11 Allan Henning, 1st round of the 1975 Rolux Toro Classic, Glendower Golf Club; John Bland, 1st round of the 1993 SA Open Championship, Durban Country Club; Mark McNulty (IRL), 2nd round of the 1996 Zimbabwe Open, Royal Harare Golf Club; Alan McLean, 3rd round of the 2005 Telkom PGA Championship at Woodhill Country Club (*Note:* Shane Pringle had 10 birdies and an eagle in the 2nd round of the 2002 FNB Botswana Open at Gaborone Golf Club; Marc Cayeux had nine birdies and an eagle in the final round of the 2004 Vodacom Players Championship at Country Club Johannesburg)

Most birdies in a row
9 Alan McLean, from the seventh to the 15th in the 3rd round of the 2005 Telkom PGA Championship at Woodhill Country Club
8 Bobby Lincoln, from the eighth to the 15th in the final round of the AECI Classic, Randpark Golf Club; Mark McNulty (IRL), from the ninth to the 16th in the 2nd round of the 1996 Zimbabwe Open, Royal Harare Golf Club

Lowest finish by a winner
62 Gavan Levenson, last round of the 1983 Vaal Reefs Open, Orkney Golf Club; Mark McNulty (IRL), 1987 Royal Swazi Sun Pro-Am, Royal Swazi Sun Country Club

Most Order of Merit victories
Eight Mark McNulty (IRL), 1981, 82, 85, 86, 87, 93, 98

Youngest winners
Anton Haig, 19 years 4 months, 2005 Seekers Travel Pro-Am, Dainfern; Dale Hayes, 19 years 5 months, Bert Hagerman Invitational, Zwartkops, Dec 1971; Charl Schwartzel, 20 years 3 months, 2004 dunhill championship at Leopard Creek (*Note:* Dale Hayes was 18 years 6 months when he won the unofficial Newcastle Open at Newcastle Golf Club in 1971); Mark Murless, 20 years 5 months, 1996 Platinum Classic, Mooinooi Golf Club; Adam Scott (AUS), 20 years 6 months, 2001 Alfred Dunhill Championship, Houghton Golf Club; Marc Cayeux (ZIM), 20 years 9 months, 1998 Zambia Open, Lusaka Golf Club; Trevor Immelman, 20 years 11 months, Vodacom Players Championship, Royal Cape Golf Club

Oldest winner
Mark McNulty (IRL), 49 years 44 days, 2003 Vodacom Players Championship, Royal Cape Golf Club

Australasian Tour

Most wins
31 Greg Norman

Youngest winner
A Baddeley (19 years), 1999 Australian Open

Oldest winner
Kel Nagle (54 years), 1975 Clearwater Classic (now the New Zealand PGA Championship)

Lowest round
60 (−12) Paul Gow, 2001 Canon Challenge, Castle Hill; (−12) Ernie Els, 2004 Heineken Classic, Royal Melbourne

Canadian Tour

Lowest 72 holes
258 (−26) Kent Eger, 2008 Seaforth Country Classic (*Note:* Tim Clark's 261 at 1998 Royal Oaks New Brunswick Open was a record 27 under par)

Lowest 54 holes
194 (−19) Adam Bland and Kent Eger, 2008 Seaforth Country Classic; (−16) Brian Kontak, 1999 Telus Henry Singer Alberta Open

Lowest 36 holes
126 Matt Cole, 1988 Windsor Charity Classic (first two rounds)

Lowest 18 holes
58 (−13) Jason Bohn, 2001 Bayer Championship

Lowest 9 holes
26 (−9) Jason Bohn, 2001 Bayer Championship

Largest winning margin
11 Arron Oberholser, 1999 Ontario Open Heritage Classic

Most wins in one season
13 Moe Norman

Oldest winner
Moe Norman, 46 years 11 months, 1976 Alberta Open

Youngest winner
James Lepp, 19 years 7 months, 2003 Greater Vancouver Charity Classic

Tour de las Americas

Youngest winner
Andres Romero, 21 years, 2003 Cable and Wireless Masters, Panama City, Panama

Oldest winner
Vicente Fernandez, 54 years, Argentina Open, Jockey Club, Buenos Aires, 2002

Lowest winning aggregate
260 (–20) Rafael Ponce, Acapulco Fest, Fairmont Princess, Acapulco, Mexico, 2004

Biggest comeback to win
9 strokes Venezuela, Copa de Naciones, El Tigre, Nueva Vallarta, Mexico 2004; Rafael Ponce, Acapulco Fest, Fairmont Princess, Acapulco, Mexico, 2004 LPGA Tour

LPGA TOUR

Lowest 72 holes
258 (–22) Karen Stupples, Welch's/Fry's Championship, Dell Urich, Arizona, 2004 (Note: Annika Sörenstam's 261 at 2001 Standard Register Ping, Moon Valley, Arizona, was a record 27 under par)

Lowest 54 holes
192 (–24) Annika Sörenstam, Mizuno Classic, Shiga, Japan, 2003

Lowest 36 holes
124 (–20) Annika Sörenstam, Standard Register Ping, Moon Valley, Arizona, 2001; (–16 Meg Mallon, Welch's/Fry Championship, Dell Urich, Arizona, 2003

Lowest 18 holes
59 (–13) Annika Sörenstam, Standard Register Ping, Moon Valley, Arizona, 2001

Lowest 9 holes
27 (–8) Jimin Kang, ShopRite Classic, Seaview, New Jersey, 2005; (–7) In-Kyung Kim, Jamie Farr Owens Corning Classic, Highland Meadows, Ohio, 2007 (Note: the 28s by Mary Beth Zimmerman, Rail Charity Classic, Springfield, Illinois, 1984, by Annika Sörenstam, Standard Register Ping, Moon Valley, Arizona, 2001, Candie Kung, Wendy's Championship, Tartan Field, Ohio, 2006 and Sarah Lee, Corona Championship, Tres Marias, Mexico, 2007 were also 8 under par, as were the 29s by Nicky Le Roux, Rochester International, Locust Hill, New York, 1990, and Kris Tschetter, Weetabix Women's British Open, Royal Birkdale, England, 2005)

Largest winning margin
14 strokes Cindy Mackey, MasterCard International Pro-am, Knollwood, New York, 1986

Youngest winner
Marlene Hagge, 18 years 14 days, Sarasota Open, 1952

Oldest winner
Beth Daniel, 46 years 8 months 29 days, Canadian Open, 2003

Most wins in a season
13 Mickey Wright, 1963

Most wins
88 Kathy Whitworth

Most majors
15 Patty Berg

Youngest major winner
Morgan Pressel, 18 years 10 months 9 days, Kraft Nabisco Championship, 2007

Oldst major winner
Fay Crocker, 4 5years 7 months 11 days, Titleholders Championship, 1960

Ladies European Tour

Lowest 72 holes
259 (–29) Gwladys Nocera, 2008 Goteborg Masters, Lycke, Sweden

Lowest 54 holes
190 Karine Icher, 2004 Catalonia Masters, Sant Cugat

Most under-par 54 holes
193 (–23) Gwladys Nocera, 2008 Goteborg Masters, Lycke, Sweden

Lowest 36 holes
128 (–16) Gwladys Nocera, 2008 Goteborg Masters, Lycke, Sweden (Note: Sophie Gustafson's 129 at the 2003 Ladies Irish Open, Killarney, was a record 17 under)

Lowest 18 holes
61 (–11) Kirsty Taylor, 2005 Wales Ladies Championship, Machynys Peninsula; (-11) Nina Reis, 2008 Goteborg Masters, Lycke, Sweden (Note: Trish Johnson's 62 in the 1996 Ladies French Open was also 11 under par)

Lowest 9 holes
29 Kitrina Douglas, 1988 Italian Ladies Open, Cá Della Nave; Regine Lautens, 1988 Godiva European Masters, Royal Antwerp; Laura Davies, 1987 First Open de France, Feminin, Fourqueux; Anne Jones, 1990 Trophée International Coconut Skol, Fourqueux; Trish Johnson, 1999 Cantor Fitzgerald, Laura Davies Invitational, Brocket Hall; Trish Johnson, 1999 Marrakech Palmeraie Open, Palmeraie Golf Palace; Rachel Hetherington, 2000 AAMI Women's Australian Open, Yarra Yarra; Federica Dassu, 2000 Chrysler Open, Halmstad; Susan Redman, 2000 Evian Masters, Evian; Minea Blomqvist, 2004 OTP Bank Central European Masters, Old Lake, Hungary; Karine Icher, 2004 Catalonia Masters, Sant Cugat; Paula Marti,2004 Catalonia Masters, Sant Cugat; Veronica Zorzi, 2005 Arras Open de France Dames, Le Golf d'Arras; Nina Karlsson, 2005 OTP Bank Ladies Central European Open, Old Lake; Sophie Gustafson, 2006 Siemens Austrian Ladies Open presented by Uniqa, Golfclub Fohrenwald-Wiener; Stephanie Arricau, 2006 Ladies Open of Portugal, Quinta da Marinha Oitavos; Ludivine Kreutz, 2006 ANZ Ladies Masters, Royal Pines; Nikki Campbell, 2007 MFS Women's Australian Open, Royal Sydney; Michelle Ellis, 2007 ANZ Ladies Masters, Royal Pines; Gwladys Nocera, 2007 Deutsche Bank Ladies Swiss Open, Gerre Losone; Bettina Hauert, 2007 BMW Ladies Italian Open, Parco de Medici; Sophie Giquel, 2007 BMW Ladies Italian Open, Parco de Medici; Carlota Ciganda, 2008 Tenerife Ladies Open, Costa Adeje; Carmen Alonso, 2008 BMW Ladies Italian Open, Argentario; Nina Reis, Gwladys Nocera, Julie Tvede, Paula Marti, Lena Tornevall, all at 2008 Goteborg Masters, Lycke

Largest winning margin
16 strokes Laura Davies, 1995 Guardian Irish Holidays Open, St Margaret's

Youngest winner
Amy Yang (amateur), 16 years 191 days, 2006 ANZ Ladies Masters, Royal Pines

Oldest winner
Federica Dassu, 46 years 105 days, 2003 Open de España Femenino, Campo De Golf De Salamanca

Most wins in a year
7 Marie-Laure de Lorenzi, 1988 (French Open, Volmac Open, Hennessy Cup, Gothenburg Open, Laing Charity Classic, Woolmark Matchplay, Qualitair Spanish Open)

Miscellaneous British

72-hole aggregate
Andrew Brooks recorded a 72-hole aggregate of 259 in winning the Skol (Scotland) tournament at Williamwood in 1974.

Lowest rounds
Playing on the ladies' course (4,020 yards) at Sunningdale on 26th September, 1961, Arthur Lees, the professional there, went round in 52, 10 under par. He went out in 26 (2, 3, 3, 4, 3, 3, 3, 3, 2) and came back in 26 (2, 3, 3, 3, 2, 3, 4, 3, 3).

On 1st January, 1936, A.E. Smith, Woolacombe Bay professional, recorded a score of 55 in a game there with a club member. The course measured 4,248 yards. Smith went out in 29 and came back in 26 finishing with a hole-in-one at the 18th.

Other low scores recorded in Britain are by CC Aylmer, an English International who went round Ranelagh in 56; George Duncan, Axenfels in 56; Harry Bannerman, Banchory in 56 in 1971; Ian Connelly, Welwyn Garden City in 56 in 1972; James Braid, Hedderwick near Dunbar in 57; H. Hardman, Wirral in 58; Norman Quigley, Windermere in 58 in 1937; Robert Webster, Eaglescliffe in 58, in 1970. Harry Weetman scored 58 in a round at the 6171 yards Croham Hurst on 30th January, 1956.

D. Sewell had a round of 60 in an Alliance Meeting at Ferndown, Bournemouth, a full-size course. He scored 30 for each half and had a total of 26 putts. In September 1986, Jeffrey Burn, handicap 1, of Shrewsbury GC, scored 60 in a club competition, made up of 8 birdies, an eagle and 9 pars. He was 30 out and 30 home and no. 5 on his card. Andrew Sherborne, as a 20-year-old amateur, went round Cirencester in 60 strokes. Dennis Gray completed a round at Broome Manor, Swindon (6906 yards, SSS 73) in the summer of 1976 in 60 (28 out, 32 in).

Playing over Aberdour on 13th June, 1936, Hector Thomson, British Amateur champion, 1936, and Jack McLean, former Scottish Amateur champion, each did 61 in the second round of an exhibition. McLean in his first round had a 63, which gave him an aggregate 124 for 36 holes.

Steve Tredinnick in a friendly match against business tycoon Joe Hyman scored a 61 over West Sussex (6211 yards) in 1970. It included a hole-in-one at the 12th (198 yards) and a 2 at the 17th (445 yards).

Another round of 61 on a full-size course was achieved by 18-year-old Michael Jones on his home

course, Worthing GC (6274 yards), in the first round of the President's Cup in May, 1974.

In the Second City Pro-Am tournament in 1970, at Handsworth, Simon Fogarty did the second 9 holes in 27 against the par of 36.

Miscellaneous USA

Lowest rounds
The lowest known scores recorded for 18 holes in America are 55 by E.F. Staugaard in 1935 over the 6419 yards Montebello Park, California, and 55 by Homero Blancas in 1962 over the 5002 yards Premier course in Longview, Texas. Staugaard in his round had 2 eagles, 13 birdies and 3 pars.

Equally outstanding is a round of 58 (13 under par) achieved by a 13-year-old boy, Douglas Beecher, on 6th July, 1976, at Pitman CC, New Jersey. The course measured 6180 yards from the back tees, and the middle tees, off which Douglas played, were estimated by the club professional to reduce the yardage by under 180 yards.

In 1941 at a 6100 yards course in Portsmouth, Virginia, Chandler Harper scored 58.

Jack Nicklaus in an exhibition match at Breakers Club, Palm Beach, California, in 1973 scored 59 over the 6200-yard course.

The lowest 9-hole score in America is 25, held jointly by Bill Burke over the second half of the 6384 yards Normandie CC, St Louis in May, 1970 at the age of 29; by Daniel Cavin, who had seven 3s and two 2s on the par 36 Bill Brewer Course, Texas, in September, 1959; and by Douglas Beecher over the second half of Pitman CC, New Jersey, on 6th July, 1976, at the amazingly young age of 13. The back 9 holes of the Pitman course measured 3150 yards (par 35) from the back tees, but even though Douglas played off the middle tees, the yardage was still over 3000 yards for the 9 holes. He scored 8 birdies and 1 eagle.

Horton Smith scored 119 for two consecutive rounds in winning the Catalina Open in California in December, 1928. The course, however, measured only 4700 yards.

Miscellaneous – excluding GB and USA

Tony Jacklin won the 1973 Los Lagartos Open with an aggregate of 261, 27 under par.

Henry Cotton in 1950 had a round of 56 at Monte Carlo (29 out, 27 in).

In a Pro-Am tournament prior to the 1973 Nigerian Open, British professional David Jagger went round in 59.

Max Banbury recorded a 9-hole score of 26 at Woodstock, Ontario, playing in a competition in 1952.

Women
The lowest score recorded on a full-size course by a woman is 59 by Sweden's Annika Sörenstam on the 6459 yards, par 72 Moon Valley course in Phoenix, Arizona. It broke by two the previous record of 61 by South Korean Se Ri Pak. Sörenstam had begun the tournament with a 65 and by adding rounds of 69 and 68 she equalled the LPGA record of 261 set by Pak

(71-61-63-66) at Highland Meadows in Ohio in 1998. Sörenstam's score represents 27 under par, Pak's 23 under.

The lowest 9-hole score on the US Ladies' PGA circuit is 28, first achieved by Mary Beth Zimmerman in the 1984 Rail Charity Classic and since equalled by Pat Bradley, Muffin Spencer-Devlin, Peggy Kirsch, Renee Heiken, Anika Sörenstam and Danielle Ammaccapane.

The Lowest 36-hole score is the 124 (20 under par) by Sörenstam at Moon Valley and the lowest 54-hole score 193 (23 under par) by Karrie Webb at Walnut Hills, Michigan, in the 2000 Oldsmobile Classic and equalled by Sörenstam at Moon Valley.

Patty Berg holds the record for the most number of women's majors with 15; Kathy Whitworth achieved a record number of tournament wins with 88; Mickey Wright's 13 wins in 1963 was the most in one season and the youngest and oldest winners of LPGA events were Marlene Hagge, 18 years and 14 days when she won the 1952 Sarasota Open and JoAnne Carner, 46 years 5 months 11 days when she won the 1985 Safeco Classic.

The lowest round on the European LPGA is 62 (11 under par) by Trish Johnson in the 1996 French Open. A 62 was also achieved by New Zealand's Janice Arnold at Coventry in 1990 during a Women's Professional Golfers' Association tournament.

The lowest 9-hole score on the European LPGA circuit is 29 by Kitrina Douglas, Regine Lautens, Laura Davies, Anne Jones and Trish Johnson.

In the Women's World Team Championship in Mexico in 1966, Mrs Belle Robertson, playing for the British team, was the only player to break 70. She scored 69 in the third round.

At Westgate-on-Sea GC (measuring 5002 yards), Wanda Morgan scored 60 in an open tournament in 1929.

Since scores cannot properly be taken in matchplay no stroke records can be made in matchplay events. Nevertheless we record here two outstanding examples of low scoring in the finals of national championships. Mrs Catherine Lacoste de Prado is credited with a score of 62 in the first round of the 36-hole final of the 1972 French Ladies' Open Championship at Morfontaine. She went out in 29 and came back in 33 on a course measuring 5933 yards. In the final of the English Ladies' Championship at Woodhall Spa in 1954, Frances Stephens (later Mrs Smith) did the first nine holes against Elizabeth Price (later Mrs Fisher) in 30. It included a hole-in-one at the 5th. The nine holes measured 3280 yards.

Amateurs

National championships

The following examples of low scoring cannot be regarded as genuine stroke play records since they took place in match play. Nevertheless they are recorded here as being worthy of note.

Michael Bonallack in beating David Kelley in the final of the English championship in 1968 at Ganton did the first 18 holes in 61 with only one putt under two feet conceded. He was out in 32 and home in 29. The par of the course was 71.

Charles McFarlane, playing in the fourth round of the Amateur Championship at Sandwich in 1914 against Charles Evans did the first nine holes in 31, winning by 6 and 5.

This score of 31 at Sandwich was equalled on several occasions in later years there. Then, in 1948, Richard Chapman of America went out in 29 in the fourth round eventually beating Hamilton McInally, Scottish Champion in 1937, 1939 and 1947, by 9 and 7.

Francis Ouimet in the first round of the American Amateur Championship in 1932 against George Voigt did the first nine holes in 30. Ouimet won by 6 and 5.

Open competitions

The 1970 South African Dunlop Masters Tournament was won by an amateur, John Fourie, with a score of 266, 14 under par. He led from start to finish with rounds of 65, 68, 65, 68, finally winning by six shots from Gary Player.

Jim Ferrier, Manly, won the New South Wales championship at Sydney in 1935 with 266. His rounds were: 67, 65, 70, 64, giving an aggregate 16 strokes better than that of the runner-up. At the time he did this amazing score Ferrier was 20 years old and an amateur.

Aaron Baddeley became the first amateur to win the Australian Open since Bruce Devlin in 1960 when he took the title at Royal Sydney in 1999. After turning pro he successfully defended the title the following year at Kingston Heath.

Holes below par

Most holes below par

E.F. Staugaard in a round of 55 over the 6419 yards Montbello Park, California, in 1935, had two eagles, 13 birdies and three pars.

American Jim Clouette scored 14 birdies in a round at Longhills GC, Arkansas, in 1974. The course measured 6257 yards.

Jimmy Martin in his round of 63 in the Swallow-Penfold at Stoneham in 1961 had one eagle and 11 birdies.

In the Ricarton Rose Bowl at Hamilton, Scotland, in August, 1981, Wilma Aitken, a women's amateur internationalist, had 11 birdies in a round of 64, including nine consecutive birdies from the 3rd to the 11th.

Mrs Donna Young scored nine birdies and one eagle in one round in the 1975 Colgate European Women's Open.

Jason Bohn had two eagles and 10 birdies in his closing 58 at the 2001 Bayer Classic on the Canadian Tour at the par 71 Huron Oaks.

Consecutive holes below par

Lionel Platts had ten consecutive birdies from the 8th to 17th holes at Blairgowrie GC during a practice round for the 1973 Sumrie Better-Ball tournament.

Roberto De Vicenzo in the Argentine Centre of the Republic Championship in April, 1974 at the Cordoba GC, Villa Allende, broke par at each of the first nine holes. (By starting his round at the 10th hole they were in fact the second nine holes played by Vicenzo.) He had one eagle (at the 7th hole) and eight birdies. The par for the 3,602 yards half was 37, completed by Vicenzo in 27.

Nine consecutive holes under par have been recorded by Claude Harmon in a friendly match over Winged Foot GC, Mamaroneck, NY, in 1931; by Les Hardie at Eastern GC, Melbourne, in April, 1934; by Jimmy Smith at McCabe GC, Nashville, Tenn, in 1969; by 13-year-old Douglas Beecher, in 1976, at Pitman CC, New Jersey; by

Rick Sigda at Greenfield CC, Mass, in 1979; and by Ian Jelley at Brookman Park in 1994.

TW Egan in winning the East of Ireland Championship in 1962 at Baltray had eight consecutive birdies (2nd to 9th) in the third round.

On the United States PGA tour, eight consecutive holes below par have been achieved by six players – Bob Goalby (1961 St Petersburg Open), Fuzzy Zoeller (1976 Quad Cities Open), Dewey Arnette (1987 Buick Open), Edward Fryatt (2000 Doral-Ryder Open), JP Hayes (2002 Bob Hope Chrysler Classic) and Jerry Kelly (2003 Las Vegas Invitational).

Fred Couples set a PGA European Tour record with 12 birdies in a round of 61 during the 1991 Scandinavian Masters on the 72-par Drottningholm course. This has since been equalled by Ernie Els (1994 Dubai Desert Classic), Russell Claydon (1995 German Masters) and Darren Clarke (1999 European Open). Ian Woosnam, Tony Johnstone, Severiano Ballesteros, John Bickerton, Mark O'Meara, Raymond Russell, Darren Clarke, Marcello Santi, Mårten Olander and Craig Spence share another record with eight successive birdies.

The United States Ladies' PGA record is seven consecutive holes below par achieved by Carol Mann in the Borden Classic at Columbus, Ohio in 1975.

Miss Wilma Aitken recorded nine successive birdies (from the 3rd to the 11th) in the 1981 Ricarton Rose Bowl.

This has since been equalled by Ernie Els (1994 Dubai Desert Classic), Russell Claydon and Fredrik Lindgren (1995 Mercedes German Masters) and Darreb Clarke (1999 Smurfit European Open). Ian Woosnam, Tony Johnstone, Severiano Ballesteros, John Bickerton, Mark O'Meara, Raymond Russell, Darren Clarke and Marcello Santi and Marten Olander share another record with eight successive birdies.

Low scoring rarities

At Standerton GC, South Africa, in May 1937, F.F. Bennett, playing for Standerton against Witwatersrand University, did the 2nd hole, 110 yards, in three 2s and a 1. Standerton is a 9-hole course, and in the match Bennett had to play four rounds.

In 1957 a fourball comprising HJ Marr, E Stevenson, C Bennett and WS May completed the 2nd hole (160 yards) in the grand total of six strokes. Marr and Stevenson both holed in one while Bennett and May both made 2.

The old Meadow Brook Club of Long Island, USA, had five par 3 holes and George Low in a round there in the 1950s scored two at each of them.

In a friendly match on a course near Chicago in 1971, assistant professional Tom Doty (23 years) had a remarkable low run over four consecutive holes: 4th (500 yards) 2; 5th (360 yards, dogleg) 1; 6th (175 yards) 1; 7th (375 yards) 2.

RW Bishop, playing in the Oxley Park, July medal competition in 1966, scored three consecutive 2s. They occurred at the 12th, 13th and 14th holes which measured 151, 500 and 136 yards respectively.

In the 1959 PGA Close Championship at Ashburnham, Bob Boobyer scored five 2s in one of the rounds. American Art Wall scored three consecutive 2s in the first round of the US Masters in 1974. They were at the

4th, 5th and 6th holes, the par of which was 3, 4 and 3.

Nine consecutive 3s have been recorded by RH Corbett in 1916 in the semi-final of the Tangye Cup; by Dr James Stothers of Ralston GC over the 2056 yards 9-hole course at Carradale, Argyll, during the summer of 1971; by Irish internationalist Brian Kissock in the Homebright Open at Carnalea GC, Bangor, in June, 1975; and by American club professional Ben Toski.

The most consecutive 3s in a British PGA event is seven by Eric Brown in the Dunlop at Gleneagles (Queen's Course) in 1960.

Hubert Green scored eight consecutive 3s in a round in the 1980 US Open.

The greatest number of 3s in one round in a British PGA event is 11 by Brian Barnes in the 1977 Skol Lager tournament at Gleneagles.

Fewest putts

The lowest known number of putts in one round is 14, achieved by Colin Collen-Smith in a round at Betchworth Park, Dorking, in June, 1947. He single-putted 14 greens and chipped into the hole on four occasions.

Professional Richard Stanwood in a round at Riverside GC, Pocatello, Idaho on 17th May, 1976 took 15 putts, chipping into the hole on five occasions.

Several instances of 16 putts in one round have been recorded in friendly games.

For 9 holes, the fewest putts is five by Ron Stutesman for the first 9 holes at Orchard Hills G&CC, Washington, USA in 1978.

Walter Hagen in nine consecutive holes on one occasion took only seven putts. He holed long putts on seven greens and chips at the other two holes.

In competitive stroke rounds in Britain and Ireland, the lowest known number of putts in one round is 18, in a medal round at Portpatrick Dunskey GC, Wilmslow GC professional Fred Taggart is reported to have taken 20 putts in one round of the 1934 Open Championship. Padraigh Hogan (Elm Park), when competing in the Junior Scratch Cup at Carlow in 1976, took only 20 putts in a round of 67.

The fewest putts in a British PGA event is believed to be 22 by Bill Large in a qualifying round over Moor Park High Course for the 1972 Benson and Hedges Match Play.

Overseas, outside the United States of America, the fewest putts is 19 achieved by Robert Wynn (ENG) in a round in the 1973 Nigerian Open and by Mary Bohen (USA) in the final round of the 1977 South Australian Open at Adelaide.

The USPGA record for fewest putts in one round is 18, achieved by Andy North (1990); Kenny Knox (1989); Mike McGee (1987) and Sam Trehan (1979). For 9 holes the record is eight putts by Kenny Knox (1989), Jim Colbert (1987) and Sam Trehan (1979).

The fewest putts recorded for a 72-hole US PGA Tour event is 93 by Kenny Knox in the 1989 Heritage Classic at Harbour Town Golf Links.

The fewest putts recorded by a woman is 17, by Joan Joyce in the Lady Michelob tournament, Georgia, in May, 1982.

PART X

Fixtures 2009

European Tour Race to Dubai

Early results 2009 season

HSBC Champions	Sheshan International GC, Shanghai	Sergio García (ESP)	274
UBS Hong Kong Open	Hong Kong GC, Fanling, Hong Kong	Wen-tang Lin (TPE)	265
Sportsbet Australian Masters	Huntingdale GC, Melbourne, Australia	Rod Pampling (AUS)	276
Alfred Dunhill Championship	Leopard Creek, Mpumalanga, S Africa	Richard Sterne (RSA)	271
South African Open Championship	Pearl Valley Golf Estates, Paarl, Western Cape, South Africa	Richard Sterne (RSA)*	274

*Sterne beat Gareth Maybin (NIR) at first extra hole

Jan 8–11	Joburg Open, Royal Johannesburg and Kensington Golf Club, Johannesburg, South Africa
Jan 9–11	The Royal Trophy, Amata Spring CC, Bangkok
Jan 15–18	The Abu Dhabi Golf Championship, Abu Dhabi Golf Club, Abu Dhabi, United Arab Emirates
Jan 22–25	Commercialbank Qatar Masters, Doha GC, Doha, Qatar
Jan 29–Feb 1	Dubai Desert Classic, Emirates GC, Dubai, United Arab Emirates
Feb 12–15	Maybank Malaysian Open, Saujanas G and CC, Kuala Lumpur
Feb 19–22	Johnnie Walker Classic, The Vines Resort & Country Club, Perth, Australia
Feb 25–Mar 1	WGC–Accenture Match Play, Ritz-Carlton GC, Dove Mountain, Marana, USA
Feb 26–Mar 1	Indonesia Open, New Kuta GC, Bali, Indonesia
Mar 12–15	WGC–CA Championship, Doral Golf Resort & Spa, Doral, Florida, USA
Mar 19–22	Madeira Islands Open BPI, Porto Santo Golfe, Portugal
Mar 26–29	Open de Andalucia, Real Club de Golf, Seville, Spain
Apr 2–5	Estoril Open de Portugal, Oitavos Dunes, Estoril, Portugal
Apr 9–12	**Masters Tournament**, Augusta National, Augusta, Georgia, USA
Apr 16–19	Volvo China Open, Beijing CBD International GC, Beijing, China
Apr 23–26	Ballantine's Championship, Pinx GC, Jeju Island, South Korea
Apr 30–May 3	Open de España, The Stadium Course, PGA Golf de Cataluña, Gerona, Spain
May 7–10	Italian Open, venue to be decided
May 14–17	The Irish Open, venue to be decided
May 21–24	BMW PGA Championship, Wentworth Club, Surrey, England
May 28–31	The European Open, London Golf Club, Ash, Kent, Englnd
Jun 4–7	The Celtic Manor Wales Open, The Celtic Manor Resort, Newport, Wales
Jun 11–14	Austrian Golf Open, Fontana GC, Vienna, Austria
Jun 18–21	**US Open Championship**, Bethpage State Park (Black Course), Farmingdale, New York, USA
Jun 18–21	Saint-Omer Open, Aa Saint Omer GC, Lumbres, France
Jun 25–28	BMW International Open, Golfclub München Eichenried, Munich, Germany
Jul 2–5	Open de France ALSTOM, Le Golf National, Paris, France
Jul 9–12	The Barclays Scottish Open, Loch Lomond GC, Glasgow, Scotland
Jul 16–19	**138th Open Championship**, Ailsa Course, Turnberry, Ayrshire, Scotland
Jul 23–26	SAS Masters, Barsebäck G & CC, Malmö, Sweden
Jul 30–Aug 2	Czech Golf Open, Prosper Golf Resort, Čeladná, Czech Republic
Aug 6–9	WGC–Bridgestone Invitational, Firestone CC, Akron, Ohio, USA
Aug 13–16	**US PGA Championship**, Hazeltine National GC, Chaska, MN, USA
Aug 13–16	The English Open, St Mellion International Resort, Cornwall, England
Aug 20–23	The KLM Open, Kennemer G&CC, Zandvoort, Netherlands
Aug 27–30	Johnnie Walker Championships,The Gleneagles Hotel, Perthshire, Scotland
Sep 3–6	Omega European Masters, Crans-sur-Sierre, Crans, Switzerland
Sep 10–13	Mercedes-Benz Championship, Golf Club Gut Lärchenhof, Cologne, Germany
Sep 17–20	British Masters, venue to be decided
Sep 24–27	Trophee by Canal+, St Nom La Breteche, Paris, France
Sep 24–27	Volvo World Match Play Championship, Finca Cortesin GC, Malaga, Spain
Oct 1–4	Alfred Dunhill Links Championship, Old Course, St Andrews, Carnoustie & Kingsbarns, Fife, Scotland
Oct 8–11	Madrid Masters, Club de Campo Villa de Madrid, Madrid, Spain
Oct 8–11	Seve Trophy, venue to be decided
Oct 15–18	Portugal Masters, Oceânico Victoria Golf Course, Vilamoura, Portugal
Oct 22–5	CASTELLÓ MASTERS Costa Azahar, Club de Campo del Mediterráneo, Castellón, Spain

Oct 29–Nov 1   TBC
Nov 5–8   HSBC Champions, Sheshan International GC, Shanghai, China
Nov 12–15   UBS Hong Kong Open, Hong Kong GC, Fanling, Hong Kong
Nov 19–2   THE DUBAI WORLD CHAMPIONSHIP, Earth Course, Jumeirah Golf Estates, Dubai,
               United Arab Emirates
Nov 26–29   Omega Mission Hills World Cup, Mission Hills GC, China

US PGA Tour

Jan 5–11   Mercedes-Benz Championship, Plantation Course at Kapalua, HI
Jan 12–18   Sony Open, Waialae CC, HI
Jan 19–25   Bob Hope Chrysler Classic, PGA West, Bermuda Dunes, CA
Jan 26–Feb 1   FBR Open, TPC Scottsdale, AZ
Feb 2–8   Buick Invitational, Torrey Pines GC, San Diego, CA
Feb 9–15   AT&T Pebble Beach National Pro-Am, Pebble Beach, CA
Feb 16–22   Northern Trust Open, Riviera CC, Palisades, CA
Feb 23–Mar 1   **WGC–Accenture Match Play Championship**, Dove Mountain, Tucson, AZ
Feb 23–Mar 1   Mayakoba Golf Classic at Riviera Maya, El Camaleon, Mexico
Mar 2–8   The Honda Classic, PGA National, Palm Beach, FL
Mar 9–15   **WGC–CA Championship**, Doral Golf Resort and Spa, Doral, FL
Mar 9–15   Puerto Rico Open, Trump International, Rio Grande, Puerto Rico
Mar 16–22   Transitions Championship, Innisbrook/Copperhead, Tampa Bay, FL
Mar 23–29   Arnold Palmer Invitational, Bay Hill GC and Lodge, Orlando, FL
Mar 30–Apr 5   Shell Houston Open, Redstone GC, Houston, TX
Apr 6–12   **The Masters**, Augusta National, Augusta, GA
Apr 13–19   Verizon Heritage, Harbour Town Golf Links, Hilton Head Island, SC
Apr 20–26   Zurich Classic of New Orleans, TPC Louisiana, New Orleans, LA
Apr 27–May 3   Wachovia Championshipm Quail Hollow Club, Charlotte, NC
May 4–10   THE PLAYERS Championshipm TPC Sawgrass, Ponte Vedra Beach, FL
May 11–17   Valero Texas Open, La Cantera GC, San Antonio, TX
May 18–24   HP Byron Nelson Championship, TPC Four Seasons Resort, Irving, TX
May 25–31   Crowne Plaza Invitational, Colonial CC, Fort Worth, TX
Jun 1–7   The Memorial, Muirfield Village GC, Dublin, OH
Jun 8–14   Stanford St. Jude Championship, TPC Southwind, Memphis, TB
Jun 15–21   **US Open**, Bethpage Black, Farmingdale, NY
Jun 22–28   Travelers Championship, TPC River Highlands, Cromwell, CT
Jun 29–Jul 5   AT&T National, Congressional CC, Bethesda, MD
Jul 6–12   John Deere Classic, TPC Deere Run, Silvis, IL
Jul 13–19   **The Open Championship**, Turnberry, Scotland
Jul 13–19   US Bank Championship, Brown Deer Park, Milwaukee, MI
Jul 20–26   RBC Canadian Open, Glen Abbey GC, Oakville, Ontario, Canada
Jul 27–Aug 2   Buick Open, Warwick Hills, Grand Blanc, MI
Aug 3–9   **WGC-Bridgestone Invitational**, Firestone South, Akron, OH
Aug 3–9   Legends Reno Tahoe Open, Montreux G&CC, Reno, NV
Aug 10–16   PGA Championship, Hazeltine National, Chaska, MN
Aug 17–23   Wyndham Championship, Sedgefield CC, Greensboro, NC
Aug 24–30   The Barclays, Liberty National, Jersey City, NJ
Aug 31–Sep 7   Deutsche Bank Championship, TPC Boston, Norton, MA
Sept 7–13   BMW Championship, Cog Hill GC, Lemont, IL
Sep 21–27   **The Tour Championship**, East Lake GC, Atlanta, GA

European Golf Association Championships

Jan 29–Feb 1	Portuguese International Ladies' Amateur Championship, Quinta do Peru
Feb 19–22	Portuguese International Amateur Championship, Troia Golf
Feb 25–Mar 1	Spanish International Ladies' Amateur Championship, Real Club de Golf Las Palmas
Feb 25–Mar 1	Spanish International Amateur Championship, R.G. Sevilla
Apr 9–13	French International Lady Juniors' Championship (Esmond Trophy), Saint Cloud
Apr 9–13	French International Boys' Championship (Michel Carlhian Trophy), Toulouse Seilh
Apr 24–26	Scottish Ladies' Open Stroke Play Championship, Troon
Apr 28–30	Cyprus Ladies' Amateur Open, Secret Valley GC
Apr 30–Jun 3	Cyprus Men's Amateur Open, Aphrodite Hills GC
May 1–3	Lytham Trophy, Royal Lytham & St Annes
May 1–3	Welsh Ladies' Amateur Open Stroke Play Championship, Royal Porthcawl
May 6–10	Spanish International Lady Junior Championship, Montanya
May 8–10	Irish Amateur Open Stroke Play Championship, Royal Dublin
May 14–17	German International Ladies' Amateur Championship, Düsseldorfer GC
May 15–17	English Men's Open Stroke Play Championship (Brabazon Trophy), Moortown
May 19–21	Scottish Seniors' Open Amateur Stroke Play Championship, Panmure
May 20–24	French International Match Play (James Gordon Bennett Trophy), TBA
May 22–24	Skandia Lady Junior Open (Youth), Albatross GC
May 22–24	Skandia Junior Open (Youth), Albatross GC
May 22–24	Welsh Amateur Open Stroke Play Championship, Ashburnham GC
May 28–30	Slovenian Ladies' Amateur Championship, Bled GC
May 29–31	Scottish Open Amateur Stroke Play Championship, Murcar Links
May 29–31	French Men Amateur Stroke Play Championship (Murat Cup), Chantilly
May 30–31	Welsh Open Youths' Championship, Radyr GC
May 29–Jun 1	Austrian Ladies' Amateur Championship, TBA
May 29–Jun 1	Austrian Amateur Championship, TBA
Jun 5–7	German Girls' Open, GC St. Leon-Rot (Heidelberg)
Jun 5–7	German Boys' Open, GC St. Leon-Rot (Heidelberg)
Jun 9–13	Ladies' British Open Amateur Championship, Royal St. Davids GC
Jun 13–15	Scottish Mid-Amateur (over 25's) Open Championship, Royal Burgess
Jun 15–20	The Amateur Championship, Formby & West Lancashire
Jun 19–21	Scottish Youths Open Amateur Stroke Play Championship, Renfrew
Jun 20–21	Irish Ladies' Open Stroke Play Championship, Douglas
Jun 22–24	Polish Junior Championship, TBA
Jun 25–28	Croatian Amateur Championship, TBA
Jul 8–10	Slovak Ladies' Amateur Championship, Black Stork
Jul 8–10	Slovak Amateur Championship, Black Stork
Jul 9–11	Luxembourg Ladies' Amateur Championship, Golf de Luxembourg-Belenhaff
Jul 9–11	Luxembourg Mens' Amateur Championship, Golf de Luxembourg-Belenhaff
Jul 14–16	Czech International Lady Junior Championship, Park GCM Ostrava (Silherovice)
Jul 14–16	Czech International Junior Championship, Park GCM Ostrava (Silherovice)
Jul 15–18	Dutch Lady Junior International, Toxandria GC
Jul 15–18	Dutch Junior International, Toxandria GC
Jul 15–19	Russian Ladies' Amateur Open Championship, GYC Pestovo
Jul 15–19	Russian Amateur Open Championship, GYC Pestovo
Jul 17–19	Danish International Ladies' Amateur Championship, Silkeborg GC
Jul 17–19	Danish International Amateur Championship, Silkeborg GC
Jul 21–23	English Boys' (under 18) Open Amateur Stroke Play Ch. (Carris Trophy), Moor Park
Jul 21–23	Scottish Boys' Open Amateur Stroke Play Championship, Ladybank
Jul 21–23	Danish International Lady Junior Championship, Smörum GC
Jul 21–23	Danish International Youth Championship, Smörum GC
Jul 23–24	Scottish Ladies' Junior Open Stroke Play Championship, Nairn Dunbar
Jul 24–26	Estonian Open Ladies' Amateur Championship, Estonian G&CC
Jul 24–26	Estonian Open Amateur Championship, Estonian G&CC
Jul 31–Aug 2	Polish Ladies' Open Amateur Championship, TBA
Aug 4–6	English Ladies' Open Stroke Play, Enmore Park
Aug 5–7	British Senior Championship, Prestwick
Aug 5–8	Czech International Ladies' Amateur Championship, Karlovy Vary GC

Aug 5–8	Czech International Amateur Championship, Karlovy Vary GC
Aug 6–9	German International Amateur Championship, GC Gut Kaden
Aug 7–9	Swiss Ladies' Amateur Championship, Domaine Impérial
Aug 7–9	Swiss Amateur Championship, Domaine Impérial
Aug 7–9	Latvian Ladies' Amateur Open Championship, Ozo GC
Aug 7–9	Latvian Amateur Open Championship, Ozo GC
Aug 10–14	Girls' British Open Amateur Championship, West Lancashire GC
Aug 10–15	British Boys' Championship, Royal St George's
Aug 11–14	English Ladies' Open Mid Amateur Championship, Denham GC
Aug 13–15	Finnish Ladies' Amateur Championship, Tali, Helsinki GC
Aug 13–15	Finnish Amateur Championship, Tali, Helsinki GC
Aug 19–21	Ladies' British Open Amateur Stroke Play Championship, Royal Aberdeen GC
Aug 22–23	Hungarian Junior Amateur Open Championship, TBA
Aug 26–29	Belgian International Lady Junior Championship, Royal GC of Belgium (Ravenstein)
Aug 26–29	Belgian International Junior Championship, Royal GC of Belgium (Ravenstein)
Aug 26–29	Slovenian Amateur Championship, Grad Otocec GC
Sep 1–3	Italian International Individual (Under 16) Championship, Biella GC
Sep 3–5	Hungarian Open Ladies Amateur Championship, TBA
Sep 3–5	Hungarian Open Amateur Championship, TBA
Sep 3–6	Turkish Open Amateur Championship (Ladies) Klassis G&CC (Istanbul)
Sep 3–6	Turkish Open Amateur Championship (Men) Klassis G&CC (Istanbul) 4
Sep 8–10	Irish Senior Ladies' Open Amateur Stroke Play Championship, Laytown & Bettystown
Sep 9–12	Hellenic Ladies' Amateur Championship, TBA
Sep 9–12	Hellenic Amateur Championship, TBA
Sep 9–13	Spanish International Junior Championship, Meis GC
Sep 11–13	Bulgarian Amateur Championship, Blacksearama & Lighthouse, Balchik
Sep 11–13	French International Ladies' Amateur Stroke Play Ch. (Cécile de Rothschild Trophy), TBA
Sep 11–13	Polish Open Amateur Championship, TBA
Sep 15–17	Senior Ladies' British Open Amateur Championship, Pyle & Kenfig GC
Sep 16–20	Italian International Ladies' Amateur Championship, Le Fonti GC
Sep 16–20	Italian International Amateur Championship, Villa d'Este GC
Sep 18–20	Romanian Open Amateur Championship, Lac de Verde
Sep 25–27	Transilvanian Amateur Championship, Paul Tomita GC
Oct 5–6	Israel Juniors Boys' and Girls' Championship, Caesarea GC
Oct 5–8	Israel Amateur Open Championship, Caesarea GC
Oct 6–8	Israel Ladies' Amateur Open Championship, Caesarea GC

European Team Championships

Jun 30–Jul 4	European Amateur Team Championship, Conwy GC, Wales
Jul 2–4	EGA Challenge Trophy – Men, Trophy Toya GC, Poland
Jul 7–11	European Ladies' Team Championship, Bled GC, Slovenia
Jul 7–11	European Girls' Team Championship, Kokkola GC, Finland
Jul 7–11	European Boys' Team Championship, GC de Pan, Netherlands
Jul 30–Aug 1	EGA Challenge Trophy – Boys, TBA
Aug 12–15	European Senior Men's Team Championship, Ascona, Switzerland
Sep 1–4	European Senior Ladies' Team Championship, Dun Laoghaire, Ireland

International European Championships

Jun 4–6	European Mid-Amateur Championship, Rio Real (Marbella), Spain
Jun 11–13	European Seniors Championship, Porto Carras GC, Greece
Jul 23–25	European Young Masters, TBA
Aug 19–22	European Amateur Championship, Chantilly, France
Aug 26–29	European Ladies' Championship, Falsterbo GC, Sweden
Sep 24–26	European Club Trophy – Ladies, GC Bergisch Land, Wuppertal, Germany
Oct 22–24	European Club Trophy – Men, TBA

International Matches

Jul 24–25	Vagliano Trophy, Hamburger GC, Falkenstein, Germany
Sep-4–5	Jacques Léglise Trophy, Kingsbarns, Ganton, England

United States Golf Association Championships

Jan 8–11   Copa de las americas, Buenos Aires GC, Buenos Aires, Argentina
Jun 18–21   **US Open**, Bethpage State Park (Black Course), Farmingdale, NY
Jun 22–27   US Women's Amateur Public Links, Red Tail GC, Devens, MA
Jul 9–12   **US Women's Open**, Saucon Valley CC, Bethlehem, PA
Jul 13–18   US Amateur Public Links, Jimmie Austin OU GC, Norman, OK
Jul 20–25   US Girls' Junior, Trump National GC, Bedminster, NJ
Jul 20–25   US Junior Amateur, Trump National GC, Bedminster, NJ
Jul 30–Aug 2 US Senior Open, Crooked Stick GC, Carmel, IN
Aug 3–9   US Women's Amateur, Old Warson CC St Louis, MO
Aug 24–30   US Amateur, Southern Hills CC, Tulsa, OK
Sep 12–17   USGA Senior Women's Amateur, The Homestead (Cascades Course), Hot Springs, VA
Sep 12–17   USGA Senior Amateur, Beverly CC, Chicago, IL
Sep 12–13   **Walker Cup**, Merion GC, Ardmore, PA
Oct 3–8   US Mid-Amateur, Kiawah Island Club (Cassique Course), Kiawah Island, SC
Oct 3–8   US Women's Mid-Amateur, Golden Hills Golf and Turf Club, Ocala, FL

Asian Tour

Jan 9–11   The Royal Trophy, Amata Spring Country Club, Bangkok, Thailand
Jan 22–25   Asian Tour International, Thailand (venue to be decided)
Feb 5–8   Emaar MGF Indian Masters[1], Delhi Golf Club, New Delhi, India
Feb 12–15   Maybank Malaysian Open[1], Malaysia (venue to be decided)
Feb 19–22   Johnnie Walker Classic[2], The Vines Resort & Country Club, Perth, Australia
Feb 26–Mar 1 **WGC–Accenture Match Play Championship**, Ritz-Carlton GC, Arizona, USA
Feb 26–Mar 1 Indonesia Open[1], Dream Land – New Kuta Golf Resort, Bali, Indonesia
Mar 5–8   Thailand Open, Thailand (venue to be decided)
Mar 12–15   **WGC–CA Championship**, Doral Golf Resort & Spa, Florida, USA
Mar 19–22   SAIL Open, Jaypee Greens, Noida, India
Mar 26–29   Black Mountain Masters, Black Mountain Golf Club, Hua Hin, Thailand
Mar 31–Apr 1 The Open Championship International Final Qualifying, Sentosa Golf Club, Singapore
Apr 9–12   **The Masters**, Augusta National Golf Club, Georgia, USA
Apr 16–19   Volvo China Open[1], Beijing CBD International Golf Club, China
Apr 23–26   Ballantine's Championship[1], Pinx Golf Club, Jeju Island, South Korea
Apr 30–May 3 The Jaidee Invitational, Siam Country Club, Pattaya, Thailand
May 7–10   Pine Valley Beijing Open[3], Pine Valley Golf Club, Beijing, China
May 14–17   GS Caltex Maekyung Open, Nam Seoul Country Club, Seoul, South Korea
May 21–24   SK Telecom Open, South Korea (venue to be decided)
Jun 18–21   **US Open**, Bethpage State Park, Black Course, New York, USA
Jul 16–19   **The Open Championship**, Turnberry, Scotland
Jul 23–26   Pertamina Indonesia President Invitational, Indonesia (venue to be decided)
Jul 30–Aug 2 Selangor Masters, Malaysia (venue to be decided)
Aug 6–9   **WGC–Bridgestone Invitational**, Firestone Country Club, Ohio, USA
Aug 6–9   Brunei Open, Empire Hotel & Country Club, Bandar Seri Begawan, Brunei
Aug 13–16   **US PGA Championship**, Hazeltine National GC, Chaska, USA
Aug 20–23   Mercuries Taiwan Masters, Taiwan GCC, Chinese Taipei
Sept 3–6   Omega European Masters[1], Crans-sur-Sierre, Crans Montana, Switzerland
Oct 1–4   Kolon-Hana Bank Korea Open, Woo Jeong Hills CC, Cheonan, South Korea
Oct 8–11   Hero Honda Indian Open, Delhi Golf Club, New Delhi, India
Oct 15–18   Midea China Classic, Royal Orchid International Golf Club, Guangzhou, China
Oct 22–25   Iskandar Johor Open, Malaysia (venue to be decided)
Oct 29–Nov 1 Barclays Singapore Open, Sentosa Golf Club, Singapore
Nov 5–8   Cambodian Open, Phokeethra Country Club, Siem Reap, Cambodia
Nov 5–8   HSBC Champions[4], Sheshan International Golf Club, Shanghai, China
Nov 12–15   UBS Hong Kong Open[1], Hong Kong Golf Club, Hong Kong
Nov 26–29   Omega Mission Hills World Cup, Mission Hills Golf Club, Shenzhen, China
Dec 10–1   Volvo Masters of Asia, Thai Country Club, Bangkok, Thailand

[1] Joint-sanctioned event with Asian and European Tours   [2] Tri-sanctioned event with Asian, European, and Australasian Tours
[3] Joint-sanctioned event with Asian and Japan Tours   [4] Joint-sanctioned with Asian, European, Australasian and Sunshine Tours

LPGA Tour

Feb 12–14	SBS OPEN, Turtle Bay Resort, Palmer Course, Kahuku, Oahu, HI
Feb 26–Mar 1	Honda LPGA Thailand, Siam CC, Plantation Course, Chonburi, Thailand
Mar 5–8	HSBC Women's Champions, Tanah Merah CC, Garden Course, Singapore
Mar 20–22	MasterCard Classic Honoring Alejo Peralta, BosqueReal CC, Huixquilucan, Mexico
Mar 26–29	Phoenix LPGA International, venue to be decided
Apr 2–5	**Kraft Nabisco Championship**, Mission Hills CC, Dinah Shore Tournament Course. Rancho Mirage, CA
Apr 16–19	Ginn OPEN, venue to be decided
Apr 23–26	Corona Championship, Tres Marias Residential CC, Morelia, Michoacan, Mexico
May 7–10	Michelob ULTRA Open, Kingsmill Resort & Spa, River Course, Williamsburg, VA
May 14–17	Sybase Classic, Upper Montclair CC, Clifton, NJ
May 21–24	LPGA Corning Classic, Corning CC, Corning, NY
Jun 4–7	LPGA State Farm Classic, Panther Creek CC, Springfield, IL
Jun 11–14	**McDonald's LPGA Championship**, Bulle Rock Golf Course, Havre de Grace, MD
Jun 25–28	Wegmans LPGA, Locust Hill CC, Pittsford, NY
Jul 2–5	Jamie Farr Owens Corning Classic, Highland Meadows GC, Sylvania, OH
Jul 9–12	**US Women's Open**[1], Saucon Valley CC, The Old Course, Bethlehem, PA
Jul 23–26	Evian Masters, Evian Masters GC, Evian-les-Bains, France
Jul 30–Aug 2	**RICOH Women's British Open**, Royal Lytham & St. Annes GC, Lytham St. Annes, Lancashire, England
Aug 21–23	**The Solheim Cup**, Rich Harvest Farms, Sugar Grove, IL
Aug 28–30	Safeway Classic, Pumpkin Ridge GC, Ghost Creek Golf Course, North Plains, OR
Sep 3–6	CN Canadian Women's Open, Priddis Greens Golf & CC, Calgary, Alberta, Canada
Sep 11–13	P&G Beauty NW Arkansas Championship, Pinnacle CC, Rogers, AR
Sep 17–20	Samsung World Championship, venue to be decided
Sep 24–27	Longs Drugs Challenge, Blackhawk CC, Danville, CA
Oct 1–4	Navistar LPGA Classic, RTJ Golf Trail, Capitol Hill, The Senator, Prattville, AL
Oct 8–11	Bell Micro LPGA Classic, RTJ Golf Trail, Magnolia Grove, The Crossings, Mobile, AL
Oct 15–18	Kapalua LPGA Classic, Kapalua Resort, The Bay Course, Lahaina, Maui, HI
Oct 23–25	China LPGA, venue to be decided
Oct 30–Nov 1	Hana Bank KOLON Championship, SKY 72 Golf Club, Ocean Course, Incheon, S. Korea
Nov 6–8	Mizuno Classic, Kintetsu Kashikojima CC, Shima-shi, Mie, Japan
Nov 12–15	Lorena Ochoa Invitational, Guadalajara CC, Guadalajara, Mexico
Nov 19–22	Stanford Financial Tour Championship, venue to be decided

[1]not LPGA Tour co-sponsored

Japan PGA Tour

Apr 16–19	Token Homemate Cup, Token Tado Country Club Nagoya, Mie
Apr 23–26	Tsuruya Open, Yamanohara Golf Club Yamanohara Course, Hyogo
Apr 30–May 3	The Crowns, Nagoya Golf Club Wago Course, Aichi
May 5–10	Pine Valley Beijin Open, Pine Valley Golf Resort & CC Jack Nicklaus Course, China
May 28–31	Mitsubishi Diamond Cup Golf, Oarai Golf Club, Ibaraki
Jun 4–7	UBS Japan Golf Tour Championship, Shishido Hills Country Club, Ibaraki
Jun 11–14	Japan PGA Championship, Eniwa Country Club, Hokkaido
Jun 25–28	Mizuno Open Yomiuri Classic, Yomiuri Country Club, Hyogo
Jul 23–26	Nagashima Shigeo Invitational, The North Country Golf Club, Hokkaido
Jul 30–Aug 2	Sun Chlorella Classic, Otaru Country Club, Hokkaido
Aug 20–23	Kansai Open Golf Championship, Takarazuka Golf Club New Course, Hyogo
Aug 27–30	Vana H Cup KBC Augusta, Keya Golf Club, Fukuoka
Sep 3–6	Fujisankei Classic, Fujizakura Country Club, Yamanashi
Sep 17–20	ANA Open, Sapporo Golf Club Wattsu Course, Hokkaido
Sep 24–27	Asia-Pacific Panasonic Open, Jyoyo Country Club East & West Course, Kyoto
Oct 1–4	Coca-Cola Tokai Classic, Miyoshi Country Club West Course, Aichi
Oct 8–11	Canon Open, Totsuka Country Club, Kanagawa

Japan PGA Tour *continued*

Oct 15–18	Japan Open Golf Championship, Musashi Country Club Toyooka Course, Saitama
Oct 22–25	Bridgestone Open, Country Club Sodegaura Course, Chiba
Oct 20–Nov 1	Mynavi ABC Championship, ABC Golf Club, Hyogo
Nov 5–8	The Championship by LEXUS, Otone Country Club, Ibaraki
Nov 12–15	Mitsui Sumitomo VISA Taiheiyo Masters, Taiheiyo Club Gotemba Course, Shizuoka
Nov 19–22	Dunlop Phoenix, Phoenix Country Club, Miyazaki
Nov 26–29	Casio World Open, Kochi Kuroshio Country Club, Kochi
Dec 3–6	Golf Nippon Series JT Cup, Tokyo Yomiuri Country Club, Tokyo

Ladies European Tour

Feb 5–8	ANZ Ladies Masters[1], Royal Pines Resort, Gold Coast, Queensland, Australia
Feb 12–15	Women's Australian Open[1], Metropolitan GC, Melbourne, Australia
Apr 23–26	Comunitat Valenciana European Nations Cup, La Sella Golf Resort, Alicante, Spain
May 7–10	Turkish Ladies Open, National GC, Belek, Antalya, Turkey
May 14–17	Deutsche Bank Ladies Swiss Open, Golf Gerre Losone, Ticino, Switzerland
May 21–24	HypoVereinsbank Ladies German Open, Golfpark Gut Häusern, Nr. Munich, Germany
TBC	Ladies Italian Open, TBC
Jun 5–7	ABN AMRO Ladies Open, Eidhovensche Golf, Valkenswaard, The Netherlands
Jun 12–14	Ladies Open of Portugal, Golden Eagle GC, Rio Maior, Portugal
Jun 26–28	AIB Ladies Irish Open, Portmarnock Hotel & Golf Links, Portmarnock, Co. Dublin, Ireland
Jul 2–4	SAS Masters, Larvik GC, Larvik, Norway
Jul 16–19	Open de España Femenino, TBC
Jul 23–26	**Evian Masters**[1], Evian Masters GC, Evian-Les-Bains, France
Jul 30–Aug 2	**Ricoh Women's British Open**[1], Royal Lytham and St Annes GC, Lancashire, England
Aug 6–9	S4C Wales Ladies Championship of Europe , Royal St.David GC, Harlech, Wales
Aug 13–16	Göteborg Masters, Lycke GC, Gothenburg, Sweden
Aug 21–23	**Solheim Cup**, Rich Harvest Farms, Sugar Grove, Illinois, USA
Aug 28–30	Finnair Masters, Helsinki GC, Tali, Finland
Sept 11–14	UNIQA Ladies Golf Open, Golfclub Föhrenwald, Wiener Neustadt, Austria
Sept 17–20	Vediorbis/Randstad Open de France Dames, Golf d'Arras, Nord-Pas de Calais, France
Sept 24–27	Tenerife Ladies Open, Golf Costa Adeje, Adeje, Tenerife, Spain
Oct 2–4	Madrid Ladies Masters, Casino Club de Golf Retamares, Madrid, Spain
Oct 28–Nov 1	Suzhou Taihu Ladies Open[1], Suzhou Taihu International GC, Shanghai
TBC	Korean Ladies Masters[1], TBC
TBC	Indian Ladies Masters, TBC
Dec 10–13	Dubai Ladies Masters, Emirates Golf Course, (Majlis Course), Dubai, UAE
Dec 18–20	Women's World Cup of Golf[1], TBC

[1] Joint sanction event

Champions Tour

Jan 17–18	Wendy's Champions Skins Game, Ka'anapali Golf Course, Lahaina-Maui, HI
Jan 19–25	Mitsubishi Electric Championship, Hualalai Golf Course, Ka'upulehu-Kona, HI
Feb 9–15	Allianz Championship, Old Course, Broken Sound Club, Boca Raton, FL
Feb 16–22	ACE Group Classic, venue to be decided
Mar 2–8	Toshiba Classic, Newport Beach CC, Newport Beach, CA
Mar 9–15	AT&T Champions Classic, Valencia CC, Valencia, CA
Mar 23–29	Cap Cana Championship, Punta Espada Golf Club, Cap Cana, Dominican Republic
Mar 30–Apr 5	Ginn Championship, Ocean Course, Hammock Beach, Palm Coast, FL
Apr 13–19	Outback Steakhouse Pro-Am, Tampa Bay, Lutz, FL
Apr 20–26	Liberty Mutual Legends of Golf, Westin Savannah Harbor Golf Resort & Spa, Savannah, GA
May 11–17	Regions Charity Classic, Robert Trent Jones Golf Trail, Ross Bridge, Hoover, AL
May 18–24	Senior PGA Championship, Canterbury GC, Beachwood, OH
May 25–31	Principal Charity Classic, Glen Oaks CC, West Des Moines, IA
Jun 1–7	Triton Financial Classic, The Hills CC, Austin, TX
Jun 22–28	Dick's Sporting Goods Open, En-Joie Golf Course, Endicott, NY
Jul 6–12	3M Championship, TPC Twin Cities, Blaine, MN
Jul 20–26	**Senior Open Championship**, Sunningdale Golf Club (Old), Berkshire, England
Jul 27–Aug 2	**US Senior Open Championship**, Crooked Stick GC, Carmel, IN
Aug 17–23	JELD-WEN Tradition, Crosswater Club, Sunriver Resort, Sunriver, OR
Aug 24–30	Boeing Classic, TPC Snoqualmie Ridge, Snoqualmie, WA
Aug 31–Sep 6	Walmart First Tee Open, Pebble Beach Golf Links and Del Monte GolfCourse, Pebble Beach, CA
Sep 14–20	Greater Hickory Classic, Rock Barn Golf & Spa, Conover, NC
Sep 21–27	SAS Championship, Prestonwood CC, Cary, NC
Sep 28–Oct4	Constellation Energy Senior Players, Baltimore CC, Five Farms (East Course), Championship (Baltimore), Timonium, MD
Oct 12–18	Administaff Small Business Classic, The Woodlands CC (Tournament Course), The Woodlands, TX
Oct 19–25	AT&T Championship, Oak Hills CC, San Antonio, TX
Oct 26–Nov 1	Charles Schwab Cup Championship, Sonoma Golf Club, Sonoma, CA
Nov 18–21	Champions Tour National Qualifying Tournament – Finals, venue to be decided
Dec 5–6	Del Webb Father/Son Challenge, ChampionsGate GC (International Course), ChampionsGate, FL

Bob Torrance gets Master Professional honour

Bob Torrance, who is three time major winner Padraig Harrington's coach and father of Ryder Cup captain Sam Torrance, was one of four teachers granted the PGA's highest award of Master Professional last year.

Torrance was honoured along with two other men – Ian Rae, the Scottish national coach and Colin Clingan, a long-time servant of the PGA based at Windmill Hill Golf Club in Milton Keynes.

The fourth recipient of a Masters honour was Essex-based Mickey Walker from the Warren who, in a distinguished career, captained both the Curtis Cup and Solheim Cup sides. She earned an OBE for her services to golf back in 1993.

"These four golfers have clearly advanced the standards in their own particular area of expertise and set targets and markers to which others can aspire," said PGA Chief Executive Sandy Jones.

Immelman Honoured by the European Tour

Twenty-nine year-old Trevor Immelman, winner of The Masters in 2008, is now an honorary member of the PGA European Tour – the 32nd player to achieve that status and the fourth South African. Gary Player, Ernie Els and Retief Goosen are also honorary members.

The award was made in recognition not only of his outstanding achievement in leading from start to finish at Augusta when winning his first major but also for his strong support of the European Tour over the past few years.

"I grew up in South Africa watching the European Tour on television and started my professional career in Europe so being made an honorary member is something I shall cherish for the rest of my life."

Immelman is excited to be part of the Race to Dubai which he considers a fantastic concept. "It's an exciting time for the Tour and it is great that I am part of it," he said when receiving his honorary life membership card from Keith Waters, the Tour's Director of International Policy.

George O'Grady, chief executive of The European Tour, said: "Trevor has always been a great ambassador for the Tour and we are delighted to honour him in this way. Trevor has not only played marvellous golf but showed considerable fortitude and skill when fending off the challenge of many of the world's greatest players to win at Augusta."

Jeev Milkha Singh chases new goals

Asian No. 1 Jeev Milkha Singh, who made history in 2008 by becoming the first player to win over $1 million in a season on the Asian Tour – he earned $1,452,701 – has set his sights on winning a major title.

"I think I have got the game to win a major," the 37-year-old Indian said after his best season so far in which he won four times including victory against a star studded field in the Barclays Singapore Open. He also won twice in Japan and once in Europe (in Austria) and also posted his first top 10 in a major when he finished joint ninth behind Padraig Harrington in the US PGA Championship. In 2008 he moved into the top 40 in the world rankings.

Singh, son of the decorated Olympic runner "The Flying Sikh", has still to measure up to his father's achievements despite his performances over the past three seasons on the golf course.

Coming from a sporting family – his mother captained the Indian national volleyball side – Singh has always had a positive feedback from his parents. "My father always emphasised discipline, work ethic and honesty as the key to success and following that philosophy has got me to where I am today," says Singh, who plans not only to cut down his schedule in 2009 from the 35 events he played last year but also to get fitter.

"My dad is still a bigger name than me in India but if I can get a major under my belt then I can sit at the same table as him," says Singh, who first joined the Asian Tour in 1995.

PART XI

Annual Awards

Annual Awards

European

European Tour Player of the Year

1985	Bernhard Langer (GER)	1993	Bernhard Langer (GER)	2001	Retief Goosen (RSA)
1986	Severiano Ballesteros (ESP)	1994	Ernie Els (RSA)	2002	Ernie Els (RSA)
1987	Ian Woosnam (WAL)	1995	Colin Montgomerie (SCO)	2003	Ernie Els (RSA)
1988	Severiano Ballesteros (ESP)	1996	Colin Montgomerie (SCO)	2004	Vijay Singh (FIJ)
1989	Nick Faldo (ENG)	1997	Colin Montgomerie (SCO)	2005	Michael Campbell (NZL)
1990	Nick Faldo (ENG)	1998	Lee Westwood (ENG)	2006	Paul Casey (ENG)
1991	Severiano Ballesteros (ESP)	1999	Colin Montgomerie (SCO)	2007	Padraig Harrington (IRL)
1992	Nick Faldo (ENG)	2000	Lee Westwood (ENG)	2008	Padraig Harrington (IRL)

Association of Golf Writers' Trophy   (Awarded to the man or woman who, in the opinion of golf writers, has done most for European golf during the year)

1951	Max Faulkner (ENG)	1972	Miss Michelle Walker (ENG)	1992	European Solheim Cup Team
1952	Miss Elizabeth Price (ENG)	1973	Peter Oosterhuis (ENG)		(Mickey Walker capt.)
1953	Joe Carr (IRL)	1974	Peter Oosterhuis (ENG)	1993	Bernhard Langer (GER)
1954	Mrs Roy Smith (Miss Frances	1975	Golf Foundation	1994	Laura Davies (ENG)
	Stephens) (ENG)	1976	GB&I Eisenhower Trophy Team	1995	European Ryder Cup Team
1955	LGU's Touring Team		(Sandy Saddler capt.)		(Bernard Gallacher capt.)
	(Mrs BR Bostock capt.)	1977	Christy O'Connor (IRL)	1996	Colin Montgomerie (SCO)
1956	John Beharrell (ENG)	1978	Peter McEvoy (ENG)	1997	Alison Nicholas (ENG)
1957	Dai Rees (WAL)	1979	Severiano Ballesteros (ESP)	1998	Lee Westwood (ENG)
1958	Harry Bradshaw (IRL)	1980	Sandy Lyle (SCO)	1999	Sergio García (ESP)
1959	Eric Brown (SCO)	1981	Bernhard Langer (GER)	2000	Lee Westwood (ENG)
1960	Sir Stuart Goodwin	1982	Gordon Brand Jr (SCO)	2001	GB&I WalkerCup Team
1961	Commander Charles Roe	1983	Nick Faldo (ENG)		(Peter McEvoy capt.)
1962	Marley Spearman (ENG)	1984	Severiano Ballesteros (ESP)	2002	Ernie Els (RSA)
1963	Michael Lunt (ENG)	1985	European Ryder Cup Team	2003	Annika Sörenstam (SWE)
1964	GB&I Eisenhower Trophy Team		(Tony Jacklin capt.)	2004	European Ryder Cup team
	(Joe Carr capt.)	1986	GB&I Curtis Cup Team		(Bernhard Langer capt.)
1965	Gerald Micklem (ENG)		(Diane Bailey capt.)	2005	Annika Sörenstam (SWE)
1966	Ronnie Shade (SCO)	1987	European Ryder Cup Team	2006	European Ryder Cup team
1967	John Panton (SCO)		(Tony Jacklin capt.)		(Ian Woosnam capt.)
1968	Michael Bonallack (ENG)	1988	Sandy Lyle (SCO)	2007	Padraig Harrington (IRL)
1969	Tony Jacklin (ENG)	1989	GB&I Walker Cup Team	2008	Padraig Harrington (IRL)
1970	Tony Jacklin (ENG)		(Peter McEvoy capt.)		
1971	GB&I Walker Cup Team	1990	Nick Faldo (ENG)		
	(Michael Bonallack capt.)	1991	Severiano Ballesteros (ESP)		

Journalists make it a double triumph for Padraig

Ireland's Padraig Harrington, who has been showered with awards following his victories in The Open and the US PGA Championship in 2008, has come top of two golf journalists polls on both sides of the Atlantic.

In Europe, Harrington polled 90 per cent of the votes in the annual Association of Golf Writers' Trophy ballot leaving stylish Swede Robert Karlsson, the 2008 European money list No. 1, in second place with another, Swede Annika Sörenstam, who retired from regular top-line competition last year, taking third place.

Others who received votes in this poll were top Ryder Cup points scorer Ian Poulter, World No. 2 Sergio García and the winning Scottish trio in the World Amateur Team Championship.

Harrington is only the third golfer since the award was first made in 1951 to have won in successive years. Tony Jacklin won in 1969 and 1970 when he was winner of The Open and the US Open respectively and Peter Oosterhuis took the title in 1973 and in 1974 during his run of four European No. 1 spots in the money list.

European Tour Harry Vardon Trophy

(Awarded to the PGA member heading the Order of Merit at the end of the season)

1937	Charles Whitcombe	1959	Dai Rees	1976	Severiano Ballesteros	1993	Colin Montgomerie
1938	Henry Cotton	1960	Bernard Hunt	1977	Severiano Ballesteros	1994	Colin Montgomerie
1939	Roger Whitcombe	1961	Christy O'Connor	1978	Severiano Ballesteros	1995	Colin Montgomerie
1940–45	In abeyance	1962	Christy O'Connor	1979	Sandy Lyle	1996	Colin Montgomerie
1946	Bobby Locke	1963	Neil Coles	1980	Sandy Lyle	1997	Colin Montgomerie
1947	Norman Von Nida	1964	Peter Alliss	1981	Bernhard Langer	1998	Colin Montgomerie
1948	Charlie Ward	1965	Bernard Hunt	1982	Greg Norman	1999	Colin Montgomerie
1949	Charlie Ward	1966	Peter Alliss	1983	Nick Faldo	2000	Lee Westwood
1950	Bobby Locke	1967	Malcolm Gregson	1984	Bernhard Langer	2001	Retief Goosen
1951	John Panton	1968	Brian Huggett	1985	Sandy Lyle	2002	Retief Goosen
1952	Harry Weetman	1969	Bernard Gallacher	1986	Severiano Ballesteros	2003	Ernie Els
1953	Flory van Donck	1970	Neil Coles	1987	Ian Woosnam	2004	Ernie Els
1954	Bobby Locke	1971	Peter Oosterhuis	1988	Severiano Ballesteros	2005	Colin Montgomerie
1955	Dai Rees	1972	Peter Oosterhuis	1989	Ronan Rafferty	2006	Padraig Harrington
1956	Harry Weetman	1973	Peter Oosterhuis	1990	Ian Woosnam	2007	Justin Rose
1957	Eric Brown	1974	Peter Oosterhuis	1991	Severiano Ballesteros	2008	Robert Karlsson
1958	Bernard Hunt	1975	Dale Hayes	1992	Nick Faldo		(SWE)

Sir Henry Cotton European Rookie of the Year

1960	Tommy Goodwin	1975	No Award	1988	Colin Montgomerie	2000	Ian Poulter (ENG)
1961	Alex Caygill (ENG)	1976	Mark James (ENG)		(SCO)	2001	Paul Casey (ENG)
1962	No Award	1977	Nick Faldo (ENG)	1989	Paul Broadhurst (ENG)	2002	Nick Dougherty (ENG)
1963	Tony Jacklin (ENG)	1978	Sandy Lyle (SCO)	1990	Russell Claydon (ENG)	2003	Peter Lawrie (IRL)
1964	No Award	1979	Mike Miller (SCO)	1991	Per-Ulrik Johansson	2004	Scott Drummond
1966	Robin Liddle (SCO)	1980	Paul Hoad (ENG)		(SWE)		(SCO)
1967	No Award	1981	Jeremy Bennett (ENG)	1992	Jim Payne (ENG)	2005	Gonzolo Fernandez-
1968	Bernard Gallacher (SCO)	1982	Gordon Brand Jr (SCO)	1993	Gary Orr (SCO)		Castano (ESP)
1969	Peter Oosterhuis (ENG)	1983	Grant Turner (NZL)	1994	Jonathan Lomas (ENG)	2006	Marc Warren (SCO)
1970	Stuart Brown (ENG)	1984	Philip Parkin (WAL)	1995	Jarmo Sandelin (SWE)	2007	Martin Kaymer (GER)
1971	David Llewellyn (WAL)	1985	Paul Thomas (WAL)	1996	Thomas Bjørn (DEN)	2008	Pablo Larrazabal (ESP)
1972	Sam Torrance (SCO)	1986	José Maria Olazàbal	1997	Scott Henderson (SCO)		
1973	Philip Elson (ENG)		(ESP)	1998	Olivier Edmond (FRA)		
1974	Carl Mason (ENG)	1987	Peter Baker (ENG)	1999	Sergio García (ESP)		

Pablo Larrazabal is 2008 Sir Henry Cotton Rookie

Twenty-five-year-old Pablo Larrazabal, who scored his maiden victory last year when taking the Open de France Alstom, has become the fourth Spaniard to be named the Sir Henry Cotton Rookie of the Year on the PGA European Tour.

José María Olazábal in 1986, Sergio García in 1999 and Gonzalo Fernandez-Castono in 2005 have also received the award and, like Larrazabal, they all won in their first full year on Tour. What Larrazabal did, however, that the others did not was earn his place in the French event by playing in the 36-hole qualifying tournament!

Born in Barcelona, Larrazabal dived into the lake in front of the 18th green after his victory by four shots over former winner Colin Montgomerie and with Lee Westwood in close attendance.

"This is an amazing honour," he said, "because there are so many great young players on Tour today." Helped by his French success, Larrazabal finished 18th on the European Money List making €40,000 short of €1 million.

Others considered for the award by a selection panel comprising representatives from the European Tour, The R&A and the Association of Golf Writers were Ulsterman Rory McIlroy and the English duo of Robert Dinwiddie and Ross McGowan.

Ladies European Tour New Star Money List

1979	Catherine Panton-Lewis (SCO)	1989	Marie-Laure de Laurenzi (FRA)	1999	Laura Davies (ENG)
1980	Muriel Thomson (SCO)	1990	Trish Johnson (ENG)	2000	Sophie Gustafson (SWE)
1981	Jenny Lee-Smith (ENG)	1991	Corinne Dibnah (AUS)	2001	Raquel Carriedo (ESP)
1982	Jenny Lee-Smith (ENG)	1992	Laura Davies (ENG)	2002	Paula Marti (ESP)
1983	Muriel Thomson (SCO)	1993	Karen Lunn (AUS)	2003	Sophie Gustafson (SWE)
1984	Dale Reid (SCO)	1994	Liselotte Neumann (SWE)	2004	Laura Davies (ENG)
1985	Laura Davies (ENG)	1995	Annika Sörenstam (SWE)	2005	Iben Tinning (DEN)
1986	Laura Davies (ENG)	1996	Laura Davies (ENG)	2006	Laura Davies (ENG)
1987	Dale Reid (SCO)	1997	Alison Nicholas (ENG)	2007	Sophie Gustafson (SWE)
1988	Marie-Laure Taud (FRA)	1998	Helen Alfredsson (SWE)	2008	Gwladys Nocera (FRA)

Ladies European Tour Players' Player of the Year

1995	Annika Sörenstam (SWE)	2000	Sophie Gustafson (SWE)	2005	Iben Tinning (DEN)
1996	Laura Davies (ENG)	2001	Raquel Carriedo (ESP)	2006	Gwladys Nocera (FRA)
1997	Alison Nicholas (ENG)	2002	Annika Sörenstam (SWE)	2007	Sophie Gustafson (SWE)
1998	Sophie Gustafson (SWE)	2003	Sophie Gustafson (SWE)	2008	Gwladys Nocera (FRA)
1999	Laura Davies (ENG)	2004	Stephanie Arricau (FRA)		

Ladies European Tour Ryder Cup Wales Rookie of the Year

1984	Katrina Douglas (ENG)	1993	Annika Sörenstam (SWE)	2002	Kirsty S Taylor (ENG)
1985	Laura Davies (ENG)	1994	Tracy Hansen (USA)	2003	Rebecca Stevenson (AUS)
1986	Patricia Gonzales (COL)	1995	Karrie Webb (AUS)	2004	Minea Blomqvist (FIN)
1987	Trish Johnson (ENG)	1996	Anne-Marie Knight (AUS)	2005	Elisa Serramia (ESP)
1988	Laurette Maritz (USA)	1997	Anna Berg (SWE)	2006	Nikki Garrett (AUS)
1989	Helen Alfredsson (SWE)	1998	Laura Philo (USA)	2007	Louise Stahle (SWE)
1990	Pearl Sinn (KOR)	1999	Elaine Ratcliffe (ENG)	2008	Melissa Reid (ENG)
1991	Helen Wadsworth (WAL)	2000	Guila Sergas (ITA)		
1992	Sandrine Mendiburu (FRA)	2001	Suzann Pettersen (NOR)		

Daily Telegraph Amateur Woman Golfer of the Year

1982	Jane Connachan (SCO)	1992	GBI Curtis Cup Team (Liz Boatman capt.)	1999	Welsh International Team (Olwen Davies capt.)
1983	Jill Thornhill (ENG)	1993	Catriona Lambert and Julie Hall	2000	Rebecca Hudson (ENG)
1984	Gillian Stewart and Claire Waite (ENG)	1994	GBI Curtis Cup Team (Liz Boatman capt.)	2001	Rebecca Hudson (ENG)
1985	Belle Robertson (SCO)	1995	Julie Hall (ENG)	2002	Becky Brewerton (WAL)
1986	GBI Curtis Cup Team (Diane Bailey capt.)	1996	GBI Curtis Cup Team (Ita Butler capt.)	2003	Becky Brewerton (WAL)
1987	Linda Bayman (ENG)	1997	Alison Rose (ENG)	2004	Emma Duggleby (ENG)
1988	GBI Curtis Cup Team	1998	Kim Andrew	2005	Felicity Johnson (ENG)
1989	Helen Dobson (ENG)			2006	*Not awarded*
1990	Angela Uzielli (ENG)			2007	Melissa Reid (ENG)
1991	Joanne Morley (ENG)			2008	*Discontinued*

Joyce Wethered Trophy (Awarded to the outstanding amateur under 25)

1994	Janice Moodie (SCO)	1998	Liza Walters (ENG)	2003	Sophie Walker (ENG)	2007	Henrietta Brockway (ENG)
1995	Rebecca Hudson (ENG)	1999	Becky Brewerton (WAL)	2004	Melissa Reid (ENG)	2008	*Discontinued*
1996	Mhairi McKay (SCO)	2000	Sophie Walker (ENG)	2005	Becky Harries (ENG)		
1997	Rebecca Hudson (ENG)	2001	Clare Queen (ENG)	2006	Sally Little (sco) and Carly Booth (sco)		
		2002	Sarah Jones (ENG)				

Former Curtis Cup Star is top 2008 European Rookie

Former Curtis Cup star Melissa Reid won the Ryder Cup Wales Rookie of the Year award for 2008 on the Ladies European Tour. Twenty-one-year-old Melissa from Derby failed to win her Tour card for the season but played initially by invitation. Although she did not win, she had seven top 10 finishes and made €136,606 to finish 12th on the money list.

American

Winners American unless stated

Arnold Palmer Award (Awarded to the Tour's leading money winner)

1981	Tom Kite	1988	Curtis Strange	1995	Greg Norman (AUS)	2002	Tiger Woods
1982	Craig Stadler	1989	Tom Kite	1996	Tom Lehman	2003	Tiger Woods
1983	Hal Sutton	1990	Greg Norman (AUS)	1997	Tiger Woods	2004	Vijay Singh (FIJ)
1984	Tom Watson	1991	Corey Pavin	1998	David Duval	2005	Tiger Woods
1985	Curtis Strange	1992	Fred Couples	1999	Tiger Woods	2006	Tiger Woods
1986	Greg Norman (AUS)	1993	Nick Price (ZIM)	2000	Tiger Woods	2007	Tiger Woods
1987	Paul Azinger	1994	Nick Price (ZIM)	2001	Tiger Woods	2008	Vijay Singh (FIJ)

Jack Nicklaus Award (Player of the Year decided by player ballot)

1990	Wayne Levi	1995	Greg Norman (AUS)	2000	Tiger Woods	2005	Tiger Woods
1991	Fred Couples	1996	Tom Lehman	2001	Tiger Woods	2006	Tiger Woods
1992	Fred Couples	1997	Tiger Woods	2002	Tiger Woods	2007	Tiger Woods
1993	Nick Price (ZIM)	1998	Mark O'Meara	2003	Tiger Woods	2008	Padraig Harrington
1994	Nick Price (ZIM)	1999	Tiger Woods	2004	Vijay Singh (FIJ)		(IRL)

PGA Tour Rookie of the Year (Decided by player ballot)

1990	Robert Gamez	1996	Tiger Woods	2002	Jonathan Byrd	2007	Brandt Snedeker
1991	John Daly	1997	Stewart Cink	2003	Ben Curtis	2008	Andres Romero
1992	Mark Carnevale	1998	Steve Flesch	2004	Todd Hamilton		(ARG)
1993	Vijay Singh (FIJ)	1999	Carlos Franco (PAR)	2005	Sean O'Hair		
1994	Ernie Els (RSA)	2000	Michael Clark II	2006	Trevor Immelman		
1995	Woody Austin	2001	Charles Howell III		(RSA)		

PGA of America Player of the Year (Decided on merit points)

1948	Ben Hogan	1964	Ken Venturi	1980	Tom Watson	1996	Tom Lehman
1949	Sam Snead	1965	Dave Marr	1981	Bill Rogers	1997	Tiger Woods
1950	Ben Hogan	1966	Billy Casper	1982	Tom Watson	1998	Mark O'Meara
1951	Ben Hogan	1967	Jack Nicklaus	1983	Hal Sutton	1999	Tiger Woods
1952	Julius Boros	1968	not awarded	1984	Tom Watson	2000	Tiger Woods
1953	Ben Hogan	1969	Orville Moody	1985	Lanny Wadkins	2001	Tiger Woods
1954	Ed Furgol	1970	Billy Casper	1986	Bob Tway	2002	Tiger Woods
1955	Doug Ford	1971	Lee Trevino	1987	Paul Azinger	2003	Tiger Woods
1956	Jack Burke	1972	Jack Nicklaus	1988	Curtis Strange	2004	Vijay Singh (FIJ)
1957	Dick Mayer	1973	Jack Nicklaus	1989	Tom Kite	2005	Tiger Woods
1958	Dow Finsterwald	1974	Johnny Miller	1990	Nick Faldo (ENG)	2006	Tiger Woods
1959	Art Wall	1975	Jack Nicklaus	1991	Corey Pavin	2007	Tiger Woods
1960	Arnold Palmer	1976	Jack Nicklaus	1992	Fred Couples	2008	Padraig Harrington
1961	Jerry Barber	1977	Tom Watson	1993	Nick Price (ZIM)		(IRL)
1962	Arnold Palmer	1978	Tom Watson	1994	Nick Price (ZIM)		
1963	Julius Boros	1979	Tom Watson	1995	Greg Norman (AUS)		

Argentinian Andres Romero is 2008 US Rookie

Argentinian Andres Romero, who played on the European Tour in 2006 and 2007 before moving to the US PGA Tour in 2008, celebrated his first season in America by being named Rookie of the Year.

Romero, who led The Open at Carnoustie in 2006 only to see his second shot at the 17th hit the bank of the Barry Burn and ricochet out of bounds, finished sixth that year behind Padraig Harrington.

A winner on the PGA Tour last year – he took the Zurich Classic title – Romero has delighted fans with his aggressive style of play. "If I see a shot I have to go for it and the fans seem to like that," he says.

PGA of America Vardon Trophy (For lowest scoring average over 60 PGA Tour rounds or more)

1937	Harry Cooper		1964	Arnold Palmer	70.01	1987	Dan Pohl	70.25
1938	Sam Snead		1965	Billy Casper	70.85	1988	Chip Beck	69.46
1939	Byron Nelson		1966	Billy Casper	70.27	1989	Greg Norman (AUS)	69.49
1940	Ben Hogan		1967	Arnold Palmer	70.18	1990	Greg Norman (AUS)	69.10
1941	Ben Hogan		1968	Billy Casper	69.82	1991	Fred Couples	69.59
1942–46	No Awards		1969	Dave Hill	70.34	1992	Fred Couples	69.38
1947	Jimmy Demaret	69.90	1970	Lee Trevino	70.64	1993	Nick Price (ZIM)	69.11
1948	Ben Hogan	69.30	1971	Lee Trevino	70.27	1994	Greg Norman (AUS)	69.81
1949	Sam Snead	69.37	1972	Lee Trevino	70.89	1995	Steve Elkington (AUS)	69.82
1950	Sam Snead	69.23	1973	Bruce Crampton (AUS)	70.57	1996	Tom Lehman	69.32
1951	Lloyd Mangrum	70.05	1974	Lee Trevino	70.53	1997	Nick Price (ZIM)	68.98
1952	Jack Burke	70.54	1975	Bruce Crampton (AUS)	70.51	1998	David Duval	69.13
1953	Lloyd Mangrum	70.22	1976	Don January	70.56	1999	Tiger Woods	68.43
1954	Ed Harrison	70.41	1977	Tom Watson	70.32	2000	Tiger Woods	67.79
1955	Sam Snead	69.86	1978	Tom Watson	70.16	2001	Tiger Woods	68.81
1956	Cary Middlecoff	70.35	1979	Tom Watson	70.27	2002	Tiger Woods	68.56
1957	Dow Finsterwald	70.30	1980	Lee Trevino	69.73	2003	Tiger Woods	68.41
1958	Bob Rosburg	70.11	1981	Tom Kite	69.80	2004	Vijay Singh (FIJ)	68.84
1959	Art Wall	70.35	1982	Tom Kite	70.21	2005	Tiger Woods	68.66
1960	Billy Casper	69.95	1983	Ray Floyd	70.61	2006	Jim Furyk	68.66
1961	Arnold Palmer	69.85	1984	Calvin Peete	70.56	2007	Tiger Woods	67.79
1962	Arnold Palmer	70.27	1985	Don Pooley	70.36	2008	Phil Mickelson	69.17
1963	Billy Casper	70.58	1986	Scott Hoch	70.08			

Payne Stewart Award (Presented for respecting and upholding the traditions of the game)

2000	Byron Nelson, Jack Nicklaus, Arnold Palmer	2001	Ben Crenshaw	2004	Jay Haas	2007	Hal Sutton
		2002	Nick Price	2005	Brad Faxon	2008	Davis Love III
		2003	Tom Watson	2006	Gary Player (RSA)		

PGA of America Distinguished Service Award

1988	Herb Graffis	1994	Arnold Palmer	2000	Jack Nicklaus	2006	Fred Ridley
1989	Bob Hope	1995	Patty Berg	2001	Mark McCormack	2007	Jack Burke Jr
1990	No award	1996	Frank Chirkinian	2002	Tim Finchem	2008	Dennis Walters
1991	Gerald Ford	1997	George Bush	2003	Vince Gill		
1992	Gene Sarazen	1998	Paul Runyan	2004	Pete Dye		
1993	Byron Nelson	1999	Bill Dickey	2005	Wally Uihlein		

American Tour players honour Harrington

Ireland's double major winner Padraig Harrington won the Jack Nicklaus Trophy in 2008 having been voted the Player of the Year by his fellow competitors on the US PGA Tour. The Open and the US PGA champion was a comfortable votes winner over Tiger Woods who took the US Open despite playing with an injured knee. Woods had been Player of the Year for eight of the previous nine years. Fijian Vijay Singh, who finished top of the US money list for the second time in five years, was a distant third in the poll.

Harrington is the first European to have won the award and only the fourth non-American. Nick Price of Zimbabwe won in 1993 and 1994, Australian Greg Norman in 1995 and Singh in 2004. Harrington had already been voted PGA of America Player of the Year which is decided on merit points. The only other European to have won this award was Nick Faldo in 1990. Harrington was also named Player of the Year by both the European and American golf writers.

In America last year, Harrington earned $4,313,551 – a substantial increase, as a result of his two major wins, to the $2.7 he earned in 2007. His statistics apart from Greens In Regulation where he was 186th were impressive. He was 32nd in driving distance with 296.3 yards; 5th in putting average with 1.742 putts and in putts per round he was 2nd with a total of 28.04. He had a 58.06% rating in sand saves and with a scoring average of 69.28 only two players bettered him.

Bob Jones Award (Awarded by USGA for distinguished sportsmanship in golf)

1955 Francis Ouimet	1970 Roberto De Vicenzo (ARG)	1983 Maureen Garrett (ENG)	1996 Betsy Rawls
1956 Bill Campbell			1997 Fred Brand
1957 Babe Zaharias	1971 Arnold Palmer	1984 Jay Sigel	1998 Nancy Lopez
1958 Margaret Curtis	1972 Michael Bonallack (ENG)	1985 Fuzzy Zoeller	1999 Ed Updegraff
1959 Findlay Douglas		1986 Jess W Sweetser	2000 Barbara McIntyre
1960 Charles Evans Jr	1973 Gene Littler	1987 Tom Watson	2001 Thomas Cousins
1961 Joe Carr (IRL)	1974 Byron Nelson	1988 Isaac B Grainger	2002 Judy Rankin
1962 Horton-Smith	1975 Jack Nicklaus	1989 Chi-Chi Rodriquez (PUR)	2003 Carol Semple Thompson
1963 Patty Berg	1976 Ben Hogan		
1964 Charles Coe	1977 Joseph C Dey	1990 Peggy Kirk Bell	2004 Jackie Burke
1965 Mrs Edwin Vare	1978 Bob Hope and Bing Crosby	1991 Ben Crenshaw	2005 Nick Price (ZIM)
1966 Gary Player (RSA)		1992 Gene Sarazen	2006 Jay Haas
1967 Richard Tufts	1979 Tom Kite	1993 PJ Boatwright Jr	2007 Louise Suggs
1968 Robert Dickson	1980 Charles Yates	1994 Lewis Oehmig	2008 Gordon Brewer
1969 Gerald Micklem (ENG)	1981 JoAnne Carner	1995 Herbert Warren Wind	
	1982 Billy Joe Patton		

US LPGA Rolex Player of the Year

1966 Kathy Whitworth	1977 Judy Rankin	1988 Nancy Lopez	1999 Karrie Webb (AUS)
1967 Kathy Whitworth	1978 Nancy Lopez	1989 Betsy King	2000 Karrie Webb (AUS)
1968 Kathy Whitworth	1979 Nancy Lopez	1990 Beth Daniel	2001 Annika Sörenstam (SWE)
1969 Kathy Whitworth	1980 Beth Daniel	1991 Pat Bradley	2002 Annika Sörenstam (SWE)
1970 Sandra Haynie	1981 Jo Anne Carner	1992 Dottie Mochrie	2003 Annika Sörenstam (SWE)
1971 Kathy Whitworth	1982 Jo Anne Carner	1993 Betsy King	2004 Annika Sörenstam (SWE)
1972 Kathy Whitworth	1983 Patty Sheehan	1994 Beth Daniel	2005 Annika Sörenstam (SWE)
1973 Kathy Whitworth	1984 Betsy King	1995 Annika Sörenstam (SWE)	2006 Lorena Ochoa (MEX)
1974 JoAnne Carner	1985 Nancy Lopez	1996 Laura Davies (ENG)	2007 Lorena Ochoa (MEX)
1975 Sandra Palmer	1986 Pat Bradley	1997 Annika Sörenstam (SWE)	2008 Lorena Ochoa (MEX)
1976 Judy Rankin	1987 Ayako Okamoto (JPN)	1998 Annika Sörenstam (SWE)	

US LPGA Louise Suggs Rookie of the Year

1962 Mary Mills	1976 Bonnie Lauer	1989 Pamela Wright (SCO)	1998 Se Ri Pak (KOR)
1963 Clifford Ann Creed	1977 Debbie Massey		1999 Mi Hyun Kim (KOR)
1964 Susie Berning	1978 Nancy Lopez	1990 Hiromi Kobayashi (JPN)	2000 Dorothy Delasin (PHI)
1965 Margie Masters	1979 Beth Daniel		
1966 Jan Ferraris	1980 Myra Van Hoose	1991 Brandie Burton	2001 Hee Won Han (KOR)
1967 Sharron Moran	1981 Patty Sheehan	1992 Helen Alfredsson (SWE)	2002 Beth Bauer
1968 Sandra Post	1982 Patti Rizzo		2003 Lorena Ochoa (MEX)
1969 Jane Blalock	1983 Stephanie Farwig	1993 Suzanne Strudwick (ENG)	2004 Shi Hyun Ahn (KOR)
1970 JoAnne Carner	1984 Juli Inkster		2005 Paula Creamer
1971 Sally Little (RSA)	1985 Penny Hammel	1994 Annika Sörenstam (SWE)	2006 Seon-Hua Lee (KOR)
1972 Jocelyne Bourassa	1986 Jody Rosenthal		2007 Angela Park (KOR)
1973 Laura Baugh	1987 Tammi Green	1995 Pat Hurst	2008 Yani Tseng (KOR)
1974 Jan Stephenson	1988 Liselotte Neumann (SWE)	1996 Karrie Webb (AUS)	
1975 Amy Alcott		1997 Lisa Hackney (ENG)	

Zimbabwean wins Nationwide Tour honour

Brendan de Jonge, a 27-year old Zimbabwean who was born in Harare but now lives in Charlotte, North Carolina, was named Golfer of the Year on America's Nationwide Tour.

Brendan, whose hero has long been Nick Price, played in 28 of the 30 Nationwide Tour events and finished second on the money list with $437,035 – just $10,000 behind Matt Bettancourt who passed him for the No. 1 spot at the last tournament of the year.

A graduate of the Virginia Tech the 6ft tall de Jonge, the Tour's "iron man" whose only win was in the Xerox Classic, finished 3rd in the stroke averages with a 69.78 rating for his 101 rounds.

LPGA Vare Trophy

		Scoring av.			Scoring av.			Scoring av.
1953	Patty Berg	75.00	1974	JoAnne Carner	72.87	1995	Annika Sörenstam	
1954	Babe Zaharias	75.48	1975	JoAnne Carner	72.40		(SWE)	71.00
1955	Patty Berg	74.47	1976	Judy Rankin	72.25	1996	Annika Sörenstam	
1956	Patty Berg	74.57	1977	Judy Rankin	72.16		(SWE)	70.47
1957	Louise Suggs	74.64	1978	Nancy Lopez	71.76	1997	Karrie Webb (AUS)	70.01
1958	Beverly Hanson	74.92	1979	Nancy Lopez	71.20	1998	Annika Sörenstam	
1959	Betsy Rawls	74.03	1980	Amy Alcott	71.51		(SWE)	69.99
1960	Mickey Wright	73.25	1981	Jo Anne Carner	71.75	1999	Karrie Webb (AUS)	69.43
1961	Mickey Wright	73.55	1982	Jo Anne Carner	71.49	2000	Karrie Webb (AUS)	70.05
1962	Mickey Wright	73.67	1983	Jo Anne Carner	71.41	2001	Annika Sörenstam	
1963	Mickey Wright	72.81	1984	Patty Sheehan	71.40		(SWE)	69.42
1964	Mickey Wright	72.46	1985	Nancy Lopez	70.73	2002	Annika Sörenstam	
1965	Kathy Whitworth	72.61	1986	Pat Bradley	71.10		(SWE)	68.70
1966	Kathy Whitworth	72.60	1987	Betsy King	71.14	2003	Se Ri Pak (KOR)	70.03
1967	Kathy Whitworth	72.74	1988	Colleen Walker	71.26	2004	Grace Park (KOR)	69.99
1968	Carol Mann	72.04	1989	Beth Daniel	70.38	2005	Annika Sörenstam	
1969	Kathy Whitworth	72.38	1990	Beth Daniel	70.54		(SWE)	69.25
1970	Kathy Whitworth	72.26	1991	Pat Bradley	70.66	2006	Lorena Ochoa (MEX)	69.23
1971	Kathy Whitworth	72.88	1992	Dottie Mochrie	70.80	2007	Lorena Ochoa (MEX)	69.68
1972	Kathy Whitworth	72.38	1993	Nancy Lopez	70.83	2008	Lorena Ochoa (MEX)	69.58
1973	Judy Rankin	73.08	1994	Beth Daniel	70.90			

First Lady of Golf Award

(PGA of America award for women who have made a significant contribution to the game)

1998	Barbara Nicklaus	2002	Nancy Lopez	2006	Kathy Whitworth
1999	Judy Rankin	2003	Renee Powell	2007	Peggy Kirk Bell
2000	*No award given*	2004	Alice Dye	2008	Carol Mann
2001	Judy Bell	2005	Carole Semple-Thompson		

Carol Mann is America's First Lady of Golf

Carol Mann, President of the LPGA from 1973 to 1976, was awarded the First Lady of Golf honour in 2008 by the PGA of America. It is given annually to someone who has made a significant contribution to the promotion of the game.

Now 67, Carol Mann turned professional in 1960 and went on to win 38 titles on the LPGA Tour including the 1965 US Open. In 1977 she was inducted into the LPGA Hall of Fame and the World Golf Hall of Fame in 1998.

Inspired by the legendary Patty Berg, she played a key role in the formation of the modern LPGA Tour heightening its focus on marketing, increased prize purses and extended television coverage.

She is one of America's most respected golf coaches having conducted over 700 clinics. She works extensively for charity and has been a golf analyst for NBC, ABC and ESPN. For a time she wrote an award winning column for the *Houston Post*.

"Receiving this award is very humbling," she said on hearing the news. "Those who have won before me are all my heroes. What those who have guided me in golf instilled in me was one common message – leave it better than you found it."

PART XII

Who's Who in Golf

Who's Who in Golf – Men

Aaron, T.
Allenby, R.
Alliss, P.
Aoki, I.
Atwal, A.
Azinger, P.
Bäckström, J.
Baddeley, A.
Baker, P.
Baker-Finch, I.
Baiocchi, H.
Ballesteros, S.
Barnes, B.
Beem, R.
Beharrell, J.C.
Bennett, W.
Bickerton, J.
Bjørn, T.
Bonallack, M.
Brier, M.
Brooks, M.
Brown, K.
Bryant, B.
Calcavecchia, M.
Campbell, C.
Campbell, W.C.
Canete, A.
Canizares, A.
Canizares, J.M.
Canonica, E.
Casey, P.
Casper, B.
Céveär, C.
Cink, S.
Chapman, R.
Charles, B.
Choi, K.-J.
Chopra, D.
Clark, C.
Clark, H.
Clarke, D.
Cole, B.
Coles, N.
Coltart, A.
Cook, J.
Couples, F.
Crenshaw, B.
Curtis, B.
Daly, J.
Darcy, E.
Davis, R.
De Vicenzo, R.
DiMarco, C.
Dickson, B.

Dodd, S.
Donald, L.
Dougherty, N.
Dredge, B.
Drew, N.
Drummond, S.
Duval, D.
Dyson, S.
Edfors, J.
Edwards, N.
Elkington, S.
Els, E.
Emerson, G.
Faldo, N.
Fasth, N.
Faxon, B.
Feherty, D.
Fernandez, V.
Fernandez-
    Castano, G.
Finsterwald, D.
Fisher, O.
Fisher, R.
Floyd, R.
Ford, D.
Foster, R.
Franco, C.
Frost, D.
Fulke, P.
Funk, F.
Furyk, J.
Gallacher, B.
García, S.
Garrido, I.
Goosen, R.
Grady, W.
Graham, D.
Graham, L.
Green, C.
Green, H.
Green, N.
Haas, J.
Haeggman, J.
Haig, A.
Hamilton, T.
Hansen, A.
Hansen, S.
Hanson, P.
Hayes, D.
Harrington, P.
Henry, J.J.
Hensby, M.
Hoch, H.
Holmes, J.B.

Horton, T.
Howell, D.
Howard, B.
Huggett, B.
Hunt, B.
Ilonen, M.
Immelman, T.
Irwin, H.
Jacklin, T.
Jacobs, J.
Jacobson, F.
Jacquelin, R.
James, M.
Jiminéz, M.A.
Jaidee, T.
January, D.
Janzen, L.
Johansson, P.-U.
Johnson, Z.
Jones, S.
Kim, A.
Kite, T.
Khan, S.
Karlsson, R.
Kuchar, M.
Lane, B.
Langer, B.
Lara, J.M.
Lawrie, P.
Lee, D.
Lehman, T.
Levet, T.
Leonard, J.
Liang W.-C.
Lima, J.-F.
Littler, G.
Love III, D.
Lundberg, M.
Lyle, S.
Lynn, D.
McDowell, G.
McEvoy, P.
McGimpsey, G.
McGinley, P.
Macgregor, G.
McIlroy, R.
McNulty, M.
Maggert, J.
Mahan, H.
Mamat, M.
Marks, G.
Marsh, D.
Marsh, G.
Martin, P.

Mason, C.
Melnyk, S.
Micheel, S.
Mickelson, P.
Miller, J.
Milligan, J.
Mize, L.
Molinari, E.
Molinari, F.
Monasterio, C.
Montgomerie, C.
Nagle, K.
Nelson, L.
Newton, J.
Nicklaus, J.
Nirat, C.
Nobilo, F.
Norman, G.
North, A.
O'Connor, C., Sr
O'Connor, C., Jr
Ogilvy, G.
O'Meara, M.
Olazábal, J.M.
O'Leary, J.
Oosterhuis, P.
Ozaki, M.
Palmer, A.
Pampling, R.
Panton, J.
Parnevik, J.
Parry, C.
Pate, J.
Pavin, C.
Perry, K.
Phadungsil, C.
Player, G.
Poulter, I.
Price, N.
Price, P.
Quigley, D.
Quiros, A.
Rafferty, R.
Ramsay, R.
Randhawa, J.
Remsey, J.-F.
Rivero, J.
Roberts, L.
Rocca, C.
Rogers, B.
Romero, E.
Rose, J.
Saltman, L.
Sandelin, J.

Schwartzel, C.
Scott, A.
Senden, J.
Senior, P.
Sheehan, P.
Siderowf, D.
Siem, M.
Sigel, J.
Simpson, S.
Singh, J.M.
Singh, V.
Smyth, D.
Stadler, C.
Stadler, K.
Stenson, H.
Sterne, R.
Stockton, D.
Storm, G.
Stranahan, F.R.
Strange, C.
Stricker, S.
Suneson, C.
Sutton, H.
Taylor, V.
Thomas, D.
Thomson, P.
Toms, D.
Torrance, S.
Trevino, L.
Van de Velde, J.
Vancsik, D.
Verplank, S.
Wadkins, L.
Walton, P.
Watson, T.
Warren, M.
Webster, S.
Weekley, B.
Weir, M.
Weiskopf, T.
Westwood, L.
Wetterich, B.
Wi, C.
Wilson, O.
Wirachant, T.
Wolstenholme, G.
Woods, E.
Woosnam, I.
Yang, Y-e
Yeh, W.-t.
Zhang, L.-W.
Zoeller, F.

Aaron, Tommy (USA)
Born Gainesville, Georgia, 22 February 1937
Turned professional 1961
After finishing runner-up in the 1972 US PGA Championship he won the 1973 Masters. He was a member of the 1969 and 1973 Ryder Cup teams. Inadvertently marked down a 4 on Roberto de Vicenzo's card for the 17th hole in the 1968 Masters when the Argentinian took 3. De Vicenzo signed for the 4 and lost out by one shot on a play-off for the Green Jacket.

Allenby, Robert (AUS)
Born Melbourne, 12 July 1971
Turned professional 1992
Pipped by a shot from winning the Australian Open as an amateur in 1991 by Wayne Riley's birdie, birdie, birdie finish at Royal Melbourne, he won the title three years later as a professional. After competing on the European Tour and winning four times, he now plays on the US Tour. He has played in four Presidents Cup matches in 1996, 2000, 2003 and 2005. In 2005 returned to Australia to win the Australian Open for a second time. He had won it in 1994.

Alliss, Peter (ENG)
Born Berlin, 28 February 1931
Turned professional 1946
Following a distinguished career as a tournament golfer in which he won 18 titles between 1954 and 1966 and played eight times in the Ryder Cup between 1953 and 1969, he turned to golf commentating. In Britain he works for the BBC and at The Open also for the ABC network. Twice captain of the PGA in 1962 and 1987 he won the Spanish, Italian and Portuguese Opens in 1958. Author or co-author of several golf books and a novel with a golfing background, he has also designed several courses including the Brabazon course at The Belfry in association with Dave Thomas. In 2003 he was awarded Life Membership of the PGA in honour of his lifelong contribution and commitment to the game. In 2005 he received an honorary degree from St Andrews University.

Aoki, Isao (JPN)
Born Abiko, Chiba, 31 August 1942
Turned professional 1964
Successful international performer whose only victory on the PGA Tour came dramatically in Hawaii in 1983 when he holed a 128 yards pitch for an eagle 3 at the last to beat Jack Renner. Only Japanese golfer to win on the European Tour taking the European Open in 1983. He also won the World Match Play in 1978 beating Simon Owen and was runner up the following year. He holed in one at Wentworth in that event to win a condominium at Gleneagles. He was top earner five times in his own country and is the Japanese golfer who has come closest to winning a major title finishing runner-up two shots behind Jack Nicklaus in the 1980 US Open at Baltusrol. Inducted into the World Golf Hall of Fame in 2004.

Atwal, Arjun (IND)
Born Asansol, India, 20 March 1973
Turned professional 1995
Learned the game at Royal Calcutta and became the first Indian to win on the European Tour when he won

the Caltex Singapore Masters in 2002. He won again in 2003 when he won the Carlsberg Malaysian Open. Only the second Indian to earn a card – the first was Jeev Milka Singh. He was top putter on the US Tour in 2005 but is still chasing his first win there.

Azinger, Paul (USA)
Born Holyoke, Massachusetts, 6 January 1960
Turned professional 1981
Joint runner-up with Rodger Davis to Nick Faldo in the 1987 Open at Muirfield he won the US PGA Championship in 1993 beating Greg Norman at the second hole of a play-off at Inverness. That year he finished second on the US money list to Nick Price. In 1994 he played only four events after having been diagnosed with lymphoma in his right shoulder blade. Happily he made a good recovery and scored his 12th US Tour victory in 2000 and his first since his 1993 US PGA win when he opened with a 63 and led from start to finish in the Sony Open in Hawaii. He played in three Ryder Cup matches in 1989, 1991 and 1993 and was on the 2001 team making headlines by holing a bunker shot at the last to halve with Niclas Fasth. An occasional commentator on US television he successfully captained the US Ryder Cup side that won the trophy back at Valhalla in 2008.

Bäckström, Johan (SWE)
Born Umea, 16 March 1978
Turned professional 1998
Despite having a problem with his back, he played boys, youths and senior golf for Sweden as an amateur. Inspired by his golfing hero Fred Couples he won his first title when taking the 2005 Aa St Omer Championship – a joint venture between the Challenge and main European Tour.

Baddeley, Aaron (AUS)
Born New Hampshire, USA, 17 March 1981
Turned professional 2000
Became the first amateur to win the Australian Open since Bruce Devlin in 1969 and the youngest when he took the title at Royal Sydney in 2000. Then, having turned professional he successfully defended it at Kingston Heath. He had shown considerable promise when at age 15, he qualified for the Victorian Open. Represented Australia in the Eisenhower Trophy and holds both Australian and American passports. Now plays on the PGA Tour in America and scored his first victory in 2006 when he took the Verizon Heritage at Harbour Town. He led going into the last round at the US Open at Oakmont in 2007 but finished joint 13th. He beat Swede Daniel Chopra in a play-off for the 2007 MasterCard Australian Masters at Huntingdale in Melbourne.

Baker, Peter (ENG)
Born Shifnal, Shropshire, 7 October 1967
Turned professional 1986
Rookie of the year in 1987, Peter was hailed as the best young newcomer by Nick Faldo when he beat Faldo in a play-off for the Benson and Hedges International in 1988. Several times a winner since then he played in the 1993 Ryder Cup scoring three points out of four. In the

singles he beat Corey Pavin. He was a vice-captain to Ian Woosnam in the 2006 Ryder Cup. Having lost his Tour card, he won it back on the Challenge Tour in 2007.

Baiocchi, Hugh (RSA)

Born Johannesburg, 17 August 1946
Turned professional 1971

A scratch golfer when he was 15, he joined the Champions Tour after playing with distinction for 23 years on the European Tour. He has played in 31 different countries around the world winning in many of them. He gained an extra special delight at winning the 1978 South African Open emulating his long-time golfing hero Gary Player.

Baker-Finch, Ian (AUS)

Born Namour, Queensland, 24 October 1960
Turned professional 1979

Impressive winner of The Open Championship in 1991 at Royal Birkdale he lost his game completely when teeing up in Tour events and was forced, after an agonising spell, to retire prematurely. He commentated originally for Channel Seven in Australia then for ABC and now for CBS in America.

Ballesteros, Severiano (ESP)

Born Pedrena, 9 April 1957
Turned professional 1974

The Charismatic Spaniard who won 52 titles between 1976 and 1999 including three Opens (1979, 1984 at St Andrews and 1988) and The Masters at Augusta in 1980 and again in 1983 survived an operation to remove a brain tumour in 2008. One of four brothers all of whom played golf, Seve was introduced to the game by his big brother Manuel and first hit the headlines when he and Jack Nicklaus finished second to Johnny Miller at Royal Birkdale in 1976. He played in eight Ryder Cups and captained the side to victory at Valderrama in 1977. Never one of golf's straightest hitters his powers of recovery from seemingly impossible positions have been legendary throughout his career. He was the driving force in getting a match started between the British and Irish golfers and the Continentals in 2000. Dogged by long-term back trouble he returned to competitive action in 2005 at the Open de Madrid. And planned to play throughout 2006 but his appearances were few and far between. He did play in The Open when his son caddied for him but missed the cut. Although only a shadow of his former self on the course, he remains popular with the public who remember with great affection his charismatic performances which drew similarities with Arnold Palmer. After playing two events on the American Champions Tour in 2007 he retired from tournament golf but still captained the European side that year against Great Britain and Ireland for the Seve Trophy – an event he created in 2000. Sadly, Seve's side lost to the GB&I team captained by Nick Faldo. He was diagnosed with a brain tumour after collapsing with an epileptic fit at Madrid Airport. His illness touched the hearts of millions around the world who enjoyed over the years his swashbuckling style.

Barnes, Brian (SCO)

Born Addington, Surrey, 3 June 1945
Turned professional 1964

Extrovert Scottish professional whose father-in-law was the late former Open champion Max Faulkner. He was a ten times winner on the European Tour between 1972 and 1981 and was twice British Seniors champion successfully defending the title in 1996. He played in six Ryder Cup matches most notably at Laurel Valley in 1975 when, having beaten Jack Nicklaus in the morning, he beat him again in the afternoon. Although he retired early because of ill-health caused by rheumatoid arthritis he now commentates for Sky Television. More recently he has started to play and fish again after his rheumatic problem was re-diagnosed as caused by eating meat.

Beem, Rich (USA)

Born Phoenix Arizona 24 August 1974
Turned professional 1994.

Playing in only his fourth major championship he hit the headlines in 2002 when he held off the spirited challenge of Tiger Woods to win the US PGA Championship at Hazeltine. Rich, who now lives in Texas, admitted he was 'flabbergasted to have won' having arrived with no expectations, although a winner of two US Tour titles – the 1999 Kemper Open and the 2002 International event at Castle Pines just a few weeks before the US PGA title. Just a year after turning professional Beem had given up the game to sell car stereos and mobile phones before becoming an assistant club professional and returning once again to tournament play in 1999. On the final day at Hazeltine, Beem hit two great shots – a fairway wood to to seven feet for an eagle at the at the 587 yards 11th and a 40 foot putt for a birdie at the 16th which helped him hold off Woods who finished with four birdies in a row. Beem prevented Woods from winning three majors in a year for the second time.

Beharrell, John Charles (ENG)

Born Birmingham, 2 May 1938

Youngest winner of the Amateur Championship when he took the title at Troon (now Royal Troon) in 1956. Held the post of captain of the Royal and Ancient Golf Club of St Andrews in 1998/99. Married Veronica Anstey, former Curtis Cup player, Australian and New Zealand Ladies champion.

Bennett, Warren (ENG)

Born Ruislip, 20 August 1971
Turned professional 1994

Leading amateur in the 1994 Open Championship and winner of the Australian Centennial Amateur Championship the same year. A former British Youths' champion, Bennett won the 1999 Scottish PGA Championship but his professional career has been badly affected by injury.

Bickerton, John (ENG)

Born Redditch, 23 December 1969
Turned professional 1991

Five seconds was his frustrating record on Tour until he came through to win the Abama Canaries Open in

2005. His break through success, which guaranteed him his card for 2006, came as he teed up for the 287th event. He proved the exception to the rule when he was hit twice by lightening while playing as an amateur. Fortunately he was not injured. He won for the second time on the European Tour when he landed the French Open at Golf National. In 2007 he was the surprise winner of the dunhill championship at Leopard Creek when Ernie Els, who was leading, went into the water twice at the final hole.

Bjørn, Thomas (DEN)
Born Silkeborg, 18 February 1971
Turned professional 1993

A former Danish Amateur champion in 1990 and 1991, he became the first Dane to play in the Ryder Cup when he made the team in 1997. Four down after four holes against Justin Leonard in the last day singles at Valderrama he fought back to halve the match and gain a valuable half-point in the European victory. He missed out on the 1999 match because of injury but was in the 2002 side and beat Stewart Cink in the singles. He made the side again in 2004 but narrowly missed out in 2006 despite having won the Nissan Irish Open. He won four times on the Challenge Tour before gaining his full European card. He came joint second to Tiger Woods in the 2000 Open at St Andrews just a few weeks after finishing third behind Woods in the US Open at Pebble Beach. In Japan in 1999 he beat Sergio García at the fourth hole of a play-off for the Dunlop Phoenix title. In 2001 he beat Tiger Woods in the Dubai Desert Classic and looked set to win the 2003 Open at Royal St George's when three shots clear with four to play but took 3 to get out of a bunker at the short 16th. and lost to Ben Curtis, the American playing in his first Open. A week later Bjørn lost a play-off to Michael Campbell in the Nissan Irish Open at Portmarnock. One of Europe's most talented golfers he came close to winning a major again in 2005 when he finished third behind Phil Mickelson in the US PGA Championship at Baltusrol. In the third round he equalled the low round in a major when he shot a 63. During the 2005 European season he had eight top 10 finishes winning the Daily Telegraph Dunlop Masters in a play-off at Forest of Arden. In 2007 he became chairman of the European Tour's Players' committee.

Bonallack KT, OBE, Sir Michael (ENG)
Born Chigwell, Essex, 31 December 1934

One of only three golfing knights (the others are the late Sir Henry Cotton and Sir Bob Charles) he won the Amateur Championship five times between 1961 and 1970 and was five times English champion between 1962 and 1968. He also won the English stroke play title four times and was twice leading amateur in The Open in 1968 and 1971. In his hugely impressive career he played in nine Walker Cup matches captaining the side on two occasions. He participated in five Eisenhower Trophy matches and five Commonwealth team competitions. He scored his first national title win in the 1952 British Boys' Championship and took his Essex County title 11 times between 1954 and 1972. After serving as secretary of The R&A from 1983

Sir Michael Bonallack

© Phil Sheldon Golf Picture Library

to 1999 he was elected captain for 1999/2000. Twice winner of the Association of Golf Writers' award in 1968 and 1999, he also received the Bobby Jones award in 1972, the Donald Ross and Gerald Micklem awards in 1991 and the Ambassador of Golf award in 1995. In 2000 he was inducted into the World Hall Golf of Fame. A former chairman of The R&A selection committee, he served as chairman of the PGA from 1976 to 1981 and is now a non-executive director of the PGA European Tour. He was chairman of the Golf Foundation in 1977 and president of the English Golf Union in 1982. His wife is the former English champion Angela Ward.

Brier, Markus (AUT)
Born Vienna, Austria, 5 July 1968
Turned professional 1995

Scored his first European Tour win "at home" when he won the BA/CA Austrian Open in 2006 and was again a winner in 2007, taking the Volvo China Open at Shanghai Silport. He played for the Continent of Europe in the Seve Trophy match at The Heritage course in Killenard, Ireland, in 2007.

Brooks, Mark (USA)
Born Fort Worth, Texas, 25 March 1961
Turned professional 1983

A seven-time winner on the US Tour between 1988 and 1996 he took the US PGA Championship title in 1996 after a play-off with Kenny Perry at Valhalla. On that occasion he birdied the 72nd hole and the first extra hole to win but he was beaten by South African Retief Goosen in the 18-hole play-off for the 2000 US Open at Southern Hills in Tulsa. Goosen shot 70, Brooks 72.

Brown, Ken (SCO)
Born Harpenden, Hertfordshire, 9 January 1957
Turned professional 1974
Renowned as a great short game exponent, especially with his hickory-shafted putter, he won four times in Europe between 1978 and 85, and took the Southern Open on the US tour in 1987. He played in two winning Ryder Cup sides in 1985 and 1987 having previously played in the 1977, 1979 and 1983 matches. Latterly he has carved out a new career for himself as a television commentator working closely with Peter Alliss on the BBC team and providing the insight for Setanta Television in the satellite company's coverage of the PGA Tour in America. He also works for The Golf Channel.

Bryant, Bart (USA)
Born Gatesville, Texas, 18 November 1962
Turned professional 1986
Won The Memorial Tournament and the Tour Championship in 2005 to finish ninth in the US money list.

Calcavecchia, Mark (USA)
Born Laurel, Nebraska, 12 June 1960
Turned professional 1981
Winner of the 1989 Open Championship at Royal Troon after the first four-hole play-off against Australians Greg Norman and Wayne Grady. He was runner-up in the 1987 Masters at Augusta to Sandy Lyle and came second to Jodie Mudd in the 1990 Players' Championship. He played in the 1987, 1989, 1991 and 2002 Ryder Cup sides.

Campbell, Chad (USA)
Born Andrews, Texas, 31 May 1974
Turned professional 1996
Winner of the Tour Championship in 2003 he was beaten into second place in the 2003 USPGA Championship by Shaun Micheel who hit a wonder approach shot at the last hole at Oak Hill. His seven iron from 175 yards out finished inches from the cup. In 2004, Campbell made his Ryder Cup début and made the team again in 2006 and again in 2008 as a captain's pick.

Campbell, Bill (USA)
Born West Virginia, 5 May 1923
One of America's most distinguished players and administrators. He won the US Amateur Championship in 1964 ten years after finishing runner-up in the Amateur Championship in Britain to Australian Doug Bachli at Muirfield. One of a select group who have been both President of the United States Golf Association (in 1983) and captain of the Royal and Ancient Golf Club of St Andrews (in 1987/88). He played in eight Walker Cup matches between 1951 and 1975 as was captain in 1955.

Canete, Ariel (ARG)
Born Santa Teresita, Argentina, 7 February 1975
Turned professional 1995
After performing consistently well on the European Challenge Tour he won the 2007 Joburg Open in South Africa to gain a two year exemption. As an amateur he played for his country in the Eisenhower Trophy.

Canizares, Alejandro (ESP)
Born Manilva, Malaga, 9 January 1983
Turned professional 2006
A four-time All-American golfer when studying at Arizona State University, he is the son of José Maria Canizares the European and US Champions Tour golfer. When he turned professional in July 2006 he won his third event – the Imperial Collection Russian Open in Moscow.

Canizares, José Maria (ESP)
Born Madrid, 18 February 1947
Turned professional 1967
A seven-time winner on the European Tour between 1972 and 1992 the popular Spaniard now plays full time on the US Champions Tour. A former caddie, he played in four Ryder Cup matches in the 1980s winning five and halving two of his 11 games.

Canonica, Emanuele (ITA)
Born Turin, 7 January 1971
Turned professional 1991
He had been a professional for 14 years before he won his first European title – the 2005 Johnnie Walker Championship at Gleneagles Hotel. Despite being only 5ft 2in tall he is a prodigious hitter of the golf ball. With his win he became only the fifth Italian to win on Tour – the others being Baldovino Dassu, Massimo Mannelli, Massimo Scarpa and Costantino Rocca.

Casey, Paul (ENG)
Born Cheltenham, 21 July 1977
Turned professional 2001
Winner of the English Amateur Championship in 1999 and 2000, he attended Arizona State University where he was a three time All-American and broke records set by Phil Mickelson and Tiger Woods. In the 1999 Walker Cup match, which the Great Britain and Ireland side won at Nairn, he won all of his four games. After turning professional he earned his European Tour card after just five events helped by a second-equal finish in the Great North Open 2001 and 12th place finishes in the Compass English Open and Benson and Hedges International. He became a winner in his 11th event when taking the Gleneagles Scottish PGA title over the PGA Centenary course. His coach is Peter Kostis. In 2002 he shot a course record 62 at Gut Lärchenhof in the Linde German Masters won by Stephen Leaney. In the early part of the 2003 European season he won the ANZ Championship in Sydney and the Benson and Hedges International at The Belfry and played with distinction in the 2004 Ryder Cup at Oakland Hills, Detroit, teaming up with David Howell for a vital foursomes point on the second morning. He played again in the Ryder Cup in 2006 at the K Club. After mis-reported remarks he made about how he geared himself up for the Ryder Cup which some Americans found upsetting he had a quieter 2005 but did win the TCL Classic in China. His place in the England World Cup side, however, was taken by David Howell. He again played with distinction in the Ryder Cup at the K Club in 2006 and was a captain's pick for the 2008 match at Valhalla in Kentucky. He won three more events on the European Tour in 2006 – the

Volvo China Open (played in 2005 but on the 2006 fixture list), the Johnnie Walker Championship at Gleneagles and he landed the £1m first prize by beating Shaun Micheel in the final of the HSBC World Match Play Championship at Wentworth. Leading the 2006 money list with only the Volvo Masters to come, he was pipped for the No.1 spot by Ireland's Padraig Harrington. Casey lost out when Sergio García bogeyed the last to let Harrington finish joint second with two others which was just enough for the Irishman to edge out Casey by €35,252. In 2007 Casey won the Abu Dhabi Open but went winless in 2008.

Casper, Billy (USA)
Born San Diego, California, 24 June 1931
Turned professional 1954
A three-time major title winner he took the US Open in 1959 and 1966 and the US Masters in 1970. In 1966 he came back from seven strokes behind Arnold Palmer with nine to play to force a play-off which he then won. Between 1956 and 1975 he picked up 51 first prize cheques on the US Tour. His European victories were the 1974 Trophée Lancôme and Lancia D'Oro and the 1975 Italian Open. As a senior golfer he won nine times between 1982 and 1989 including the US Senior Open in 1983. Played in eight Ryder Cups and captained the American side in 1979 at The Greenbrier. He and wife Shirley have 11 children several of them adopted. He was named Father of the Year in 1966. Started playing golf aged 5 and rates Ben Hogan, Byron Nelson and Sam Snead as his heroes. Five times Vardon Trophy winner (for low season stroke-average) and twice top money earner he was US PGA Player of the Year in 1966 and 1970. He was inducted into the World Golf Hall of Fame in 1978 and the US PGA Hall of Fame in 1982. Encouraged by his family to play in The Masters for one last time in 2005 he shot 106 but was disqualified for not handing in his card.

Céveär, Christian (FRA)
Born New Caledonia, 10 April 1970
Turned professional 1993
A former world junior champion and Stanford graduate, Christian scored his first victory on the European Tour in 2005 when taking top spot in the Canarias Open de España. He had previously been second in the 1995 Madeira Island Open and 2003 British Masters.

Chapman, Roger (ENG)
Born Nakuru, Kenya, 1 May 1959
Turned professional 1981
After playing on the European Tour for 18 years without success, he lost his card and had to return to the qualifying school in 1999. Regaining his playing privileges with a 12th place finish in the six round competition, he made his breakthrough win by beating Padraig Harrington at the second hole of a play-off in the Brazil Rio de Janeiro Five Hundred Years Open. Later that year he won the Hassan II Trophy at Dar-Es-Salaam in Morocco. A former English Amateur Champion in 1981 he played in the Walker Cup the same year beating Hal Sutton twice in a day at Cypress Point.

Sir Bob Charles

© Phil Sheldon Golf Picture Library

Charles, Sir Bob (NZL)
Born Auckland, 14 March 1936
Turned professional 1960
Three years after turning professional he became the first and still the only New Zealander to win The Open Championship. He defeated Phil Rodgers in the last 36-hole play-off for the title at Royal Lytham and St Annes then was runner-up in 1968 to Gary Player at Carnoustie and in 1969 to Tony Jacklin again at Lytham. Earlier in 1954 he had won the first of his four New Zealand Opens as an amateur. Between 1954 and 1960 he worked in a bank before embarking on a golf career which has seen him win extensively around the world on golf's main Tours and the US Senior Tour. He won seven times on the US Tour, nine times in Europe, 24 times in New Zealand and has also won in Canada, Japan and South Africa. He does everything right-handed except games requiring two hands. In 1972 received the OBE from Her Majesty the Queen, the CBE in 1992 and was knighted in 1999 for his services to golf. He is one of only three left-handers to have won majors – the others being Phil Mickleson and Mike Weir. He has announced his retirement but continues to play a very limited schedule on the European Senior and US Champions Tours and regularly beats his age! At 71 he became the oldest player to make the cut on any of the world's Tours when he shot a second round 68 in the Michael Hill New Zealand Open in 2007.

Choi, K-J (KOR)
Born Wando, South Korea, 19 May 1970
Turned professional 1994
When his high school teacher suggested he take up golf, he studied all Jack Nicklaus' videos. Son of a rice

farmer he was the first Korean to earn a PGA Tour card and won twice in 2002. In 2003 he became the first Korean to win on the Euopean Tour when he won the Linde German Masters. Better known as KJ he won the Chrysler Championship in America in 2006. In 2007 he finished fifth behind Tiger Woods on the American money list having earned over $4.5 million.

Chopra, Daniel (SWE)
Born Stockholm, 23 December 1973
Turned professional 1992
After playing on the Asian and European Tours he turned his attention to the US circuits and won twice on the Nationwide Tour before making his breakthrough on the main tour with victory in the Ginn-sur-Mer Classic at Tesoro. Later he lost a play-off to Aaron Baddeley in the Mastercard Masters at Huntingdale in Melbourne.

Cink, Stewart (USA)
Born Huntsville, Alabama, 21 May 1973
Turned professional 1995
The Rookie of the Year on the US Tour in 1997 when he won the Canon Greater Hartford Classic. The year before he had been top rookie on the Buy.com tour. He missed a two foot putt on the last and, as a result, a place in the play-off for the 2002 US Open with Mark Brooks and eventual winner Retief Goosen. He played in the 2002 Ryder Cup and received a captain's pick from Hal Sutton for the 2004 team and immediately after celebrated by leading from start to finish to win the World Championship NEC Invitational. In 2006, he was again a captain's pick for a place in the Ryder Cup and finished second to Woods in the Bridgestone Invitational the following week. In the 2006 Cup match at the K Club, he beat Sergio García in the singles to prevent the Spaniard winning five points out of five. He again was a captain's pick for the 2008 match.

Clark, Clive (ENG)
Born Winchester, 27 June 1945
Turned professional 1965
In the 1965 Walker Cup at Five Farms East in Maryland, he holed a 35-foot putt to earn a half point against Mark Hopkins and ensure a drawn match against the Americans. After turning professional he played in the 1973 Ryder Cup and was a four time winner of titles between 1966 and 1974. Following a career as commentator with the BBC he continued his golf course architecture work in America, and has received awards for his innovative designs.

Clark, Howard (ENG)
Born Leeds, 26 August 1954
Turned professional 1973
A scratch player by the age of 16 he turned professional after playing in the 1973 Walker Cup. An eleven-time winner on the European tour he played in six Ryder Cups and was in the winning team three times – in 1985 at The Belfry, 1987 at Muirfield Village, when the Europeans won for the first time on American soil, and in 1995 when he gained a vital point

helped by a hole in one in the last day singles against Peter Jacobsen. In the 1985 World Cup played at La Quinta in Palm Springs he was the individual champion. He played 494 tournaments before giving up full-time competition to concentrate on his job as a highly respected golf analyst for Sky television.

Clarke, Darren (NIR)
Born Dungannon, Northern Ireland, 14 August 1968
Turned professional 1990
He became the first European Tour player to shoot 60 twice when he returned that record low score at the European Open at the K Club in 1999. Seven years earlier he had shot a nine under par 60 at Mont Agel in the Monte Carlo Open, but his 60 in Dublin was 12 under par. With his second 60 he also equalled two other records. With 12 birdies on the card he matched the best birdie total in a round and he also scored a record-equalling eight birdies in a row. Tied second in the 1997 Open behind Justin Leonard and third equal in 2001 at Lytham, cigar-smoking Clarke played particularly well in the 2000 Andersen Consulting Match Play Championship at La Costa in California beating Paul Azinger, Mark O'Meara, Thomas Bjørn, Hal Sutton and David Duval to reach the final against Tiger Woods. He became the first European to win a World Golf Championship event when he beat Woods 4 and 3 and picked up the million dollar first prize. He took a second World Championship event in 2003 when he was an impressive winner of the NEC Invitational at Firestone. He played in the 1997, 1999, 2002 and 2004 Ryder Cup matches making a vital half point on the final day with David Duval in the 2002 match and halving with Davis Love III in 2004 at Detroit. Clarke's 2005 season was much reduced because of the illness of his wife Heather but he still managed a second place finish in the Barclays Scottish Open, a third place in the Open de Madrid and a fourth in the Smurfit European Open. Before the end of the year he won the Visa Taiheiyo Masters in Japan. In 2006, is wife lost her battle with cancer but Clarke still managed to win a wild card for the Ryder Cup, winning twice in partnership with good friend Lee Westwood and taking his singles against Zach Johnson. He battled to find his lost form in 2007 but after a winless gap of five years he returned to the winner's circle twice in 2008 taking the BMW Asian Open in Shanghai and the KLM Open in Holland. Despite his two victories he was not offered a captain's pick from Nick Faldo for the 2008 match.

Cole, Bobby (RSA)
Born Springs, 11 May 1948
Turned professional 1966
Winner of the Amateur Championship in 1966 when he beat Ronnie Shade in the final which because of haar (fog) was reduced to 18 holes. Among his victories when he turned professional were two South African Opens in 1974 and 1980.

Coles MBE, Neil (ENG)
Born 26 September 1934   Turned professional 1950
Remarkably he has won golf tournaments in six decades and who is to say he will not win in seven

decades. In 2003 he did not win but in the Travis Perkins event over Wentworth's Edinburgh Course (which he helped design) he shot a 64 – great golf for a man who has been a pro at that time for 54 years. He scored his first victory at the Gor-Ray tournament and made golfing history when he took the Microlease Jersey Seniors Open at La Moye in 2000. Aged 65 and 10 months, he won again the following year when he took the Lawrence Batley Seniors Open at Huddersfield. From 1973 to 1979 he played in 68 events on the main European Tour without missing a half-way cut and became the then oldest winner when he won the Sanyo Open in Barcelona in 1982 at the age of 48 years and 14 days. (Des Smyth has since become an even older winner.) A member of eight Ryder Cup teams, he has represented his country 19 times since turning professional at the age of 16 with a handicap of 14. He has been chairman of the PGA European Tour's Board of Directors since its inception in 1971 and in 2000 was inducted into the World Golf Hall of Fame. Internationally respected he might well have won more in America but for an aversion to flying caused by a bad experience on an internal flight from Edinburgh to London.

Coltart, Andrew (SCO)
Born Dumfries, 12 May 1970
Turned professional 1991
Twice Australian PGA champion in 1994 and 1997 he was the Australasian circuit's top money earner for the 1997/98 season. He made his Ryder Cup début at Brookline in 1999 as a captain's pick and, having not been used in the foursomes and fourballs he lost in the singles on the final day to Tiger Woods. A former Walker Cup and Eisenhower Trophy player he was a member of the only Scottish team to win the Alfred Dunhill Cup at St Andrews in 1995. His European Tour successes include the 1998 Qatar Masters and 2001 Great North Open. His sister Laurae is married to fellow professional Lee Westwood. He lost his Tour card in 2007 but still plays by invitation although starting to carve out a new career as a radio and television commentator.

Cook, John (USA)
Born Toledo, Ohio, 2 October 1957
Turned professional 1979
Given much help in his early years by Jack Nicklaus and Tom Weiskopf he was a regular winner on the US Tour who gave Nick Faldo a fright in the 1992 Open at Muirfield. Three strokes behind with eight to play Cook had moved out in front by a shot after 16 holes on the final day but finished 5,5 to Faldo's 4,4. He was also tied second that year in the US PGA Championship. From a winning position in 2008 he lost the Senior British Open to Bruce Vaughan at Royal Troon.

Couples, Fred (USA)
Born Seattle, Washington, 3 October 1959
Turned professional 1980
Troubled continually with a back problem he has managed to win only one major – the 1992 US Masters but is one of the most popular of all American players. He has always been willing to travel and his overseas victories include two Johnnie Walker World Championships, the Johnnie Walker Classic, the Dubai Desert Classic and the Tournoi Perrier de Paris. On the US Tour he won 14 times between 1983 and 1998 and later won the Shell Houston Open. He played in five Ryder Cup matches and has teed up four times for the US in the Presidents Cup. In 2006, he challenged for The Masters title at Augusta but lost out to Phil Mickelson.

Crenshaw, Ben (USA)
Born Austin, Texas, 11 January 1952
Turned professional 1973
One of golf's great putters who followed up his victory in the 1984 Masters with an emotional repeat success in 1995 just a short time after the death of his long-time coach and mentor Harvey Pennick. He played in four Ryder Cup matches between 1981 and 1995 before captaining the side in 1999 when the Americans came from four points back to win with a scintillating last day singles performance. Winner of the Byron Nelson award in 1976 he was also named Bobby Jones award winner in 1991. Now combines playing with an equally successful career as a golf course designer and is an acknowledged authority on every aspect of the history of the game. In 2002 he was named the Payne Stewart Award winner – an award that recognises a player's respect for and upholding of the traditions of the game.

Curtis, Ben (USA)
Born Columbus, Ohio, 26 May 1977
Turned professional 2000
Shock 750–1 outsider who played superbly at Royal St George's to get his name engraved with all the other golfing greats on the famous Claret Jug. His victory in the 2003 Open, while well deserved, was one of golf's biggest shocks in years. It was his first major appearance. He only qualified for the Championship with a 14th place finish in the Western Open in Chicago – a designated qualifying event. He had never played in Britain nor had he any experience of links golf but he outplayed Tiger Woods, Thomas Bjørn, David Love III and Vijay Singh to take the title with a score of 283. He learned the game in Ohio at the golf course his grandfather built at Ostrander. He was a double winner on the US Tour in 2006 taking the Booz Allen Classic and the 84 Lumber Classic titles and chased Padraig Harrington home to finish second behind the Irishman in the US PGA Championship in 2008 when he also made his début in Paul Azinger's Ryder Cup side at Valhalla.

Daly, John (USA)
Born Sacramento, California, 28 April 1966
Turned professional 1987
Winner of two majors – the 1991 US PGA Championship and the 1995 Open Championship at St Andrews after a play-off with Costantino Rocca, his career has not been without its ups and downs. He admits he has battled alcoholism and, on occasions, has been his own worst enemy when having run-ins with officialdom but he remains popular because of his long hitting. His average drive

is over 300 yards. When he won the US PGA Championship at Crooked Stick he got in as ninth alternate, drove through the night to tee it up without a practice round and shot 69, 67, 69, 71 to beat Bruce Lietzke by three. Given invaluable help at times by Fuzzy Zoeller he writes his own songs and is a mean performer on the guitar. In 2001 took the BMW International Open title at Munich. In 2002 was a member of both the US and European Tours. Curiously, despite winning two majors, he has never played in the Ryder Cup. In 2003 he won the Korean Open and in 2004 beat Luke Donald in a play-off at San Diego to take the Buick Invitational. He no longer holds a PGA Tour card.

Darcy, Eamonn (IRL)
Born Dalgeny, 7 August 1952
Turned professional 1969
One of Ireland's best known players who played more than 600 tournaments on the European Tour despite suffering for many years with back trouble. First played when he was 10 years old and is renowned for his very distinctive swing incorporating a flying right elbow. He played in four Ryder Cups including the memorable one at Muirfield Village in 1987 when Europe won for the first time in America. He scored a vital point in the last day singles holing a tricky left to right downhill seven footer for a valuable point against Ben Crenshaw. Now plays on the European Senior Tour.

Davis, Rodger (AUS)
Born Sydney, 18 May 1951
Turned professional 1974
Experienced Australian who came joint second in the 1987 Open Championship behind Nick Faldo at Muirfield. A regular on the European Tour and for a time the US Champions Tour he has won 27 titles – 19 of them on the Australasian circuit where, in 1988, he picked up an Aus$1 million first prize in the Bicentennial event at Royal Melbourne. Gave up golf for a while but lost all his money in a hotel venture that went wrong and took up tournament play again. Usually played in trademark 'plus twos' but has now retired competitively.

De Vicenzo, Roberto (ARG)
Born Buenos Aires, 14 April 1923
Turned professional 1938
Although he won The Open in 1967 at Royal Liverpool this impressive South American is perhaps best known for the Major title he might have won. In 1968 he finished tied with Bob Goalby at Augusta or he thought he had. He had finished birdie, bogey to do so but sadly signed for the par 4 that had been inadvertently and carelessly put down for the 17th by Tommy Aaron who was marking his card. Although everyone watching on television and at the course saw the Argentinian make 3 the fact that he signed for 4 was indisputable and he had to accept that there would be no play-off. It remains one of the saddest incidents in golf with the emotion heightened by the fact that that Sunday was de Vicenzo's 45th birthday. The gracious manner in which he accepted the disappointments was remarkable. What a contrast to the scenes at Hoylake nine months earlier when, after years of trying, he finally won The

Open beating Jack Nicklaus and Clive Clark in the process thanks to a pressure-packed brilliant last round 70. In fact he was runner-up in the event in 1950 and came third six times. The father of South American golf he was a magnificent driver and is credited with having won over 200 titles in his extraordinary career including nine Argentinian Opens between 1944 and 1974 plus the 1957 Jamaican, 1950 Belgian, 1950 Dutch, 1950, 1960 and 1964 French, 1964 German Open and 1966 Spanish Open titles. He played 15 times for Argentina in the World Cup and four times for Mexico. Inducted into the World Golf Hall of Fame in 1989 he is an honorary member of the Royal and Ancient Golf Club of St Andrews. Planned to return to Britain for the 2006 Open Championship at Hoylake were he won in 1967 but could not make it.

DiMarco, Chris (USA)
Born Huntingdon, New York, 23 August 1968
Turned professional 1990
He made his début in the Presidents Cup in 2003 and the Ryder Cup in 2004 when he also lost a play-off to Vijay Singh in the US PGA Championship at Whistling Straits. In 2005 he was beaten at the first extra hole by Tiger Woods in The Masters at Augusta and later in the year holed the winning putt when making his second appearance in the Presidents Cup. In 2006 he won the Abu Dhabi event on the European Tour. Finished runner-up to Tiger Woods in The Open at Hoylake and again made the Ryder Cup.

Dickson, Bob (USA)
Born McAlester, Oklahoma, 25 January 1944
Turned professional 1968
Best remembered for being one of only four players to complete a Transatlantic amateur double. In 1967 he won the US Amateur Championship at Broadmoor with a total of 285 (the Championship was played over 72 holes from 1965 to 1972) and the British Amateur title with a 2 and 1 win over fellow American Ron Cerrudo at Formby. After turning professional scored two wins on the US Tour.

Dodd, Stephen (WAL)
Born Cardiff, 15 July 1966   Turned professional 1990
Winner of the Amateur Championship at Royal Birkdale in 1989 when he was also a member of the winning Walker Cup team at Peachtree, in Atlanta when Great Britain and Ireland won that event for the first time on American soil. He turned professional the following year but had to wait until the 2005 season for his first victory in Shanghai in the Volvo China Open. Later he added the Nissan Irish Open winning that in a play-off at Carton House against Australian Brett Rumford. With Bradley Dredge gave Wales their second win in the World Cup of Golf over 54 holes at Vilamoura in Portugal. Rainy weather caused cancellation of the last round. In 2007 he won the Smurfit European Open.

Donald, Luke (ENG)
Born Hemel Hempstead, Herts., 7 December 1977
Turned professional 2001
A member of the winning Great Britain and Ireland team against the Americans in the 1999 Walker Cup at

Nairn and again in 2001 before turning professional. In 1999 while attending the North-Western University in Chicago he won the NCAA Championship and was named NCAA Player of the Year. He has played most of his golf in America and scored his first and to date only win on the US Tour when he took the rain-shortened Southern Farms Bureau title, becoming the 18th first-time winner of the season. He has continued to make steady progress and in 2004 lost a play-off to John Daly in the Buick Invitational on the US Tour and won the Scandinavian Masters and Omega European Masters of Europe. He was one of five rookies in the winning 2004 European Ryder Cup team in Detroit having been a captain's pick. Donald continued to play well in 2005 without managing to win any more titles on either side of the Atlantic. In the end he finished 12th on the European Money list and easily kept his US Tour card. In Europe he topped the "Putts per greens in regulation" stats with 1.684 average. He made the 2006 Ryder Cup by right and won his last day singles against Chad Campbell. Donald played on both sides of the Atlantic in 2006 and finished seventh on the European money list with €1,658,059 and ninth on the US PGA Tour with $3,177,408. In 2007 Luke finished 29th on the US Tour money list with a total of $2,190,053 and 38th in Europe but his 2008 season was marred by a wrist injury which he suffered in mid summer, required surgery and kept him out of a probable place in the 2008 Ryder Cup side.

Dougherty, Nick (ENG)
Born Liverpool, 24 May 1982
Turned professional 2001
He was playing off plus 4 and had won the Australian Amateur Championship in 2001 when he turned professional. Started golfing at age 4 and won his first event at six years old. Sir Henry Cotton Rookie of the Year in 2002, Dougherty's career was hindered by a bout of glandular fever in 2003 but he made his break through win when holding off Colin Montgomerie to win the Caltex Masters, a joint venture between the Asian and European Tours in Singapore in 2005. In 2006, he nearly won in Singapore but had a miserable run when he lost form, failing to make 10 cuts in a row.but he did end the season well by winning the Dunhill Links Championship. He had a quiet 2008 during which following the death of his mother he missed several events and lost his chance of a Ryder Cup place.

Dredge, Bradley (WAL)
Born Tredegar, Wales, 6 July 1973
Turned professional 1996
Winner of the Madeira Island Open in 2003, he had his biggest win when sharing the $1,400,000 first prize with Stephen Dodd in the 2005 World Cup of Golf played over 54 holes because of storms in Vilamoura in Portugal. The Welsh pair shot 61 twice in better-ball play and 67 in foursomes for a winning 27-under-par total. In 2007 he won a place in the GB&I side for the Seve Trophy match and although he did not win he came second in the Irish Open and Celtic Manor Wales Open. It was something of a surprise that he did not challenge for a Ryder Cup place in 2008

Drew, Norman (NIR)
Born Belfast, 25 May 1932   Turned professional 1958
Twice Irish Open Amateur champion in 1952 and 1953 he played in the 1953 Walker Cup and six years later represented Great Britain and Ireland in the Ryder Cup.

Drummond, Scott (SCO)
Born Shrewsbury, 29 May 1974
Turned professional 1996
Like Sandy Lyle he is Scottish although born in Shropshire. Graduated from the Challenge Tour in 2004 and spectacularly won the Volvo PGA Championship at Wentworth from a star-studded field but has struggled to find his best form since then.

Duval, David (USA)
Born Jacksonville, Florida, 19 November 1971
Turned professional 1993
A regular winner on the US Tour who wears dark glasses because of an eye stigmatism which is sensitive to light, he won his first major at Royal Lytham and St Annes in 2001 when he became only the second American professional to win The Open over that course. He was the first player in US Tour history to win titles by play-off in consecutive weeks. Played 86 events and had seven second-place finishes and four thirds before making his break-through win in the Michelob Championship then won the following week as well. His father Bob played the US Senior Tour. He was a winner of the US Tour Championship in 1997 and the Players' Championship in 1999. In the 1998 and 2001 Masters he came second and was third in that event in 2000. He played in the 1991 Walker Cup and was a member of the winning Ryder Cup side on his début in 1999 and was also a member of the 2002 Cup side halving his match with Darren Clarke in the singles. Injury and illness have restricted his golf in recent years.

Dyson, Simon (ENG)
Born York, 21 December 1977
Turned professional 1999
Although a three-time winner on the Asian Tour where he was top earner in 2000, he scored his first European Tour success in the joint Asian–European venture in Indonesia in 2006 and later in the season he beat Australian Richard Green in a play-off for the KLM Open at Zandvoort. He finished the year in 21st spot on the money list. In 2007 he shot 64 in the final round of the USPGA Championship to finish in joint sixth place. He was a wild card selection for Nick Faldo's GB&I side in the Seve Trophy.

Edfors, Johan (SWE)
Born Varberg, Sweden, 10 October 1975
Turned professional 1997
The number one player on the 2003 Challenge Tour but lost his card in 2004. Won back his card at the 2005 school and had a brilliant year in 2006, winning three events – the TCL Classic in China, the Quinn Direct British Masters and the Barclays Scottish Open at Loch Lomond.

Edwards, Nigel (WAL)

Born Caerphilly, 9 August 1968

Top scoring member of the winning Walker Cup sides in 2001 and again in 2003 at Ganton when he teamed up with fellow countryman Nigel Manley to score 1½ points in the fourballs, beat George Zahringer in the first day singles and halved with Lee Williams on day two holing from 30 yards from off the green with the putter at the 17th to ensure overall victory. He was again involved in a dramatic finish to the 2005 Walker Cup but one down with one to play and needing to win the last against Jeff Overton his putt narrowly missed. Edwards also played in the 2007 Walker Cup won by America at Royal County Down.

Elkington, Steve (AUS)

Born Inverell, 8 December 1962
Turned professional 1985

A former Australian (1990 and 1991) and New Zealand (1990) champion he is a regular winner on the US Tour despite an allergy to grass. Helped by a closing string of birdies at the Riviera CC in Los Angeles in 1995 he beat Colin Montgomerie in a play-off for the US PGA Championship, the only major he has won to date. Winner of the 1992 Australian Open he has one of the finest swings in golf and is also an accomplished artist in his spare time. He has played four times since 1994 in the Presidents Cup. In 2002 after pre-qualifying for The Open at Dunbar he played off for title at Muirfield with Thomas Levet, Stuart Appleby and eventual winner Ernie Els. He nearly won the US PGA Championship in 2005 finishing second tied with Thomas Bjørn behind Phil Mickelson at Baltusrol.

Els, Ernie (RSA)

Born Johannesburg, 17 October 1969
Turned professional 1989

Teenage winner of the South African Amateur Championship in 1986 he is renowned as one of the game's big hitters. His short game can be deadly too and when on song he is one of the most impressive international performers. He has won two US Opens – in 1994 at Oakmont after a play-off against Loren Roberts and Colin Montgomerie and at Congressional where he beat Montgomerie into second place. Although proficient at Rugby Union and cricket he decided to concentrate on golf when he played off scratch at age 14. He has matched Gary Player's record of winning three successive South African Opens and has collected the South African PGA and Masters titles as well. In 1994 he equalled the European Tour record of 12 birdies in the 61 he fired en route to victory in the Dubai Desert Classic. He was made an honorary member of the PGA European Tour in recognition of his two US Open wins and his three successive World Match Play title successes round the famous West Course. Going for a fourth successive win in 1997 he lost on the last green to Vijay Singh. In 2002 Els won the Heineken Classic at Royal Melbourne, the Dubai Desert Classic and the Genuity Championship on the US Tour before realising his life-long dream by winning The Open Championship at Muirfield 43 years after Gary Player had won at the same venue. He beat Frenchman Thomas Levet in a sudden-death play-off at the first extra hole after tying with him in a four hole play-off which also involved Australians Stuart Appleby and Steve Elkington. All had finished on six-under-par 268. Els played a brilliant recovery from an awkward lie in a greenside trap at the 18th to make the par that earned him his third major title victory. By winning he ended Tiger Woods' hopes of taking all four majors in the same year. Woods had won the Masters and US Open earlier. Els made a whirlwind start to 2003 winning twice in America at the Mercedes Championship where he won with a record 31 under total and the Sony Open in Hawaii and twice on the European Tour taking the Heineken Classic at Royal Melbourne and the Johnnie Walker Classic for the second time. At the Johnnie Walker at Lake Karinyup he was at his blistering best, powering 315 yards plus drives and shooting a remarkable 29-under-par. By the start of September he had added the Barclay's Scottish Open and the Omega European Masters and the HSBC World Match Play Championship and ended up top money earner on the European Tour. At the start of 2004 he shot a record 60 in the first round of the Heineken Classic at Royal Melbourne, eventually winning that event for a third successive year. It proved to be a frustrating year for him in the majors. He lost The Masters by a shot to Phil Mickelson, was beaten in a play-off for The Open at Royal Troon by Todd Hamilton and missed the play-off for the USPGA Championship by a shot. His wins included the American Express Championship at Mount Juliet. He won the HSBC World Matchplay title for a record sixth time and for the second year running was European No 1 becoming the first player to earn more than 4 million euro in a season. During his 2004 European season he was out of the top ten just once in 15 starts. He made a fast start to 2005 winning the Dubai Desert Classic and Qatar Masters in successive weeks and later the BMW Asian Open by 13 shots in Shanghai. He played poorly at The Masters finishing 47th, was 15th in the US Open and 34th at St Andrews in The Open – his last event for six months following a cruciate ligament injury sustained while on holiday. He only returned to action at Sun City late in the year then won the dunhill at Leopard Creek and came second to Retief Goosen in the SAA Open at Fancourt. In 2006, he took time to get back to his best but was still one of ten golfers who played four rounds in all four majors. In 2006 he finished 5th on the European money list and 28th in America. Still battling to find his best form, he finished second to Tiger Woods in the 2007 USPGA Championship but then went on to win the now defunct HSBC World Match Play at Wentworth for a seventh time. By comparison he had a quiet 2008 although he did win once on the US PGA Tour. Has a home at Wentworth but is now based full-time in America in order to ensure the best possible medical help for his autistic son.

Emerson, Gary (ENG)

Born Salisbury, 26 September 1963
Turned professional 1982

Lost his card after finishing 128th in the 2003 Volvo Order of Merit but then gained a two year extension after winning the BMW Russian Open – a joint venture between the main Tour and the Challenge Tour.

Faldo MBE, Nick (ENG)

Born Welwyn Garden City, 18 July 1957
Turned professional 1976

Decided to turn professional after watching the US Masters on television and being impressed by Jack Nicklaus's performance. Europe's most successful major title winner having won three Open Championships in 1987 and 1992 at Muirfield and in 1990 at St Andrews along with three Masters titles in 1989, 1990 and 1996. Of current day players only Tiger Woods with 14 majors and Tom Watson with eight have won more majors. When he successfully defended the Masters in 1990 he became only the second man (after Nicklaus) to win in successive years. Staged a dramatic last day revival to win the 1996 Masters having started the last round six behind Greg Norman. When he realised his swing was not good enough to win majors he completely revamped it with the help of coach David Leadbetter. His 31 European Tour victories include a record three Irish Open victories in a row. In 1992 became the first player to win over £1 million in prize-money during a season. He played with distinction in 11 Ryder Cup matches including the winning teams in 1985, 1987, 1995 and 1997. He holds the record for most games played in the Cup – 46 – and most points won – 25. In 1995 at Oak Hill came from behind to score a vital last day point against Curtis Strange, the American who had beaten him in a play-off for the US Open title in 1988 at The Country Club in Boston. He captained the Ryder Cup side at Valhalla in 2008 when Europe failed to win four in a row. He became the first international player to be named USPGA Player of the Year in 1990 and led the official World Golf Rankings for 81 weeks in 1993–1994. After having teamed up with Swedish caddie Fanny Sunesson for ten years they split only to be reunited as one of golf's best-known partnerships in 2001. Later they split again. His Faldo Junior Series, designed to encourage the best young players to improve, continues to expand. In 2006, he continued with his commentating career with the BBC, Sky, the Golf Channel and CBS with whom he signed an $8m eight-year contract. In 2007 he captained Great Britain and Ireland to victory in the Seve Trophy against the Europeans.

Fasth, Niclas (SWE)

Born Gothenburg, Sweden, 29 April 1972
Turned professional 1989

The studious-looking Swede tried to play both US and European tours in 1998 but found it too difficult. He made the headlines in 2001 when finishing second to David Duval in The Open. In the 2002 Ryder Cup he made a half point against Paul Azinger on the final day. He was a double winner in 2005 taking the New Zealand Open and the prestigious Deutsche Bank Tournament Players' Championship of Europe. In 2007 he came a creditable fourth in the US Open at Oakmont and a week later won the BMW International title in Munich. In 2008 he split with his long-time coach Graham Crisp who was working with him revamping his swing. The changes took time to settle and he missed out on a Ryder Cup place.

Faxon, Brad (USA)

Born Oceanport, New Jersey, 1 August 1961
Turned professional 1983

A former Walker Cup player who competed in the 1983 match he has played twice in the Ryder Cup (1995 and 1997). A seven-time winner on the US Tour he also putted superbly to win the Australian Open at Metropolitan in 1993. In 2005 was named recipient of the Payne Stewart award for respecting and upholding the traditions of the game. Is a member of the PGA Tour Committee.

Feherty, David (NIR)

Born Bangor, Northern Ireland, 13 August 1958
Turned professional 1976

Quick-witted Ulsterman who gave up his competitive golfing career to become a hugely successful commentator for CBS in America where his one-liners are legendary. Had five European title wins and three victories on the South African circuit before switching his golf clubs for a more lucrative career with a microphone.

Fernandez, Vicente (ARG)

Born Corrientes, 5 May 1946
Turned professional 1964

After playing on the European Tour where he won five times between 1975 and 1992 he joined the US Champions Tour competing with considerable success. In this respect he was following in the footsteps of fellow Argentinian Roberto de Vicenzo. Born with one leg shorter than the other which is why he limps, he is remembered in Europe for the 87 foot putt he holed up three tiers on the final green at The Belfry in 1992 to win the Murphy's English Open. His nickname is 'Chino'.

Fernandez-Castano, Gonzalo (ESP)

Born Madrid, 13 October 1980
Turned professional 2004

Twice Spanish amateur champion he began playing golf as a five-year-old and turned professional in 2004 when he was playing off plus 4. He represented Spain in the 2002 Eisenhower Trophy and played for the Continent of Europe against Great Britain and Ireland in 2004. He played twice in the Palmer Cup leading the European students to success against the Americans at Ballybunion in 2004. He picked up the fifth card in the European qualifying School later that year and won for the first time in Holland when he took the 2005 KLM Dutch Open title at Hilversum and was named Sir Henry Cotton Rookie of the Year. In 2006, he came second in the Volvo China Open in Beijing and the following week won the BMW Asian Open after a play-off with Henrik Stenson. In 2007 he won the Telecom Italia Open at Castello di Tolcinasco and in 2008 took the Quinn Direct British Masters in an early evening play-off with Lee Westwood.

Finsterwald, Dow (USA)

Born Athens, Ohio, 6 September 1929
Turned professional 1951

Winner of the 1958 US PGA Championship he won 11 other competitions between 1955 and 1963. He played in four Ryder Cup matches in a row from 1957 and captained the side in 1977. He was US PGA Player of the Year in 1958.

Fisher, Oliver (ENG)
Born Chingford, Essex, 19 August 1988
Turned professional 2006
Became the youngest ever Walker Cup player when he made the 2005 Great Britain and Ireland side. He won the 2006 St Andrews Links Trophy, was runner-up in the 2006 English Amateur and reached the quarter-finals of the US Amateur Championship at Hazeltine. In 2006 he played in the Eisenhower and Bonallack Trophy matches and when he turned professional later that year he was playing off plus 4.

Fisher, Ross (ENG)
Born Ascot, Berkshire, 22 November 1980
Turned professional 2004
Attached to the Wentworth Club, he has been playing since he was three. In 2007 he won his first European Tour title at the KLM Open and started his 2008 European Tour campaign by finishing joint second to Phil Mickelson after a play-off at the HSBC Champions event in Shanghai. Later in the season he won the European Open at the London Club leading from start to finish and ending up six clear of his nearest rival. He lost a play-off again this time to Robert Karlsson when he, Martin Kaymer and the Swede played off for the Alfred Dunhill Links Championship at St Andrews. Fisher drove into the Swilcan Burn at the first extra hole.

Floyd, Raymond (USA)
Born Fort Bragg, North Carolina, 4 September 1942
Turned professional 1961
A four time major winner whose failure to win an Open Championship title prevented his completing a Slam of Majors. He won the US Open in 1986, the Masters in 1976 when he matched the then 72-hole record set by Jack Nicklaus to win by eight strokes and took the US PGA title in 1969 and 1982. In addition to coming second and third in The Open he was also runner-up three times in the Masters and in the US PGA once. After scoring 22 victories on the main US Tour he has continued to win as a senior. Inducted into the World Golf Hall of Fame in 1989 he is an avid Chicago Cubs baseball fan. Played in eight Ryder Cup matches between 1969 and 1993 making history with his last appearance by being the oldest player to take part in the match. He was 49. He was non-playing captain in 1989 when the match was drawn at The Belfry and was a valuable assistant along with Olin Browne and Dave Stockton for Paul Azinger at the 2008 match at Valhalla.

Ford, Doug (USA)
Born West Haven, Connecticut, 6 August 1922
Turned professional 1949
His 25 wins on the US Tour between 1955 and 1963 included the 1975 US Masters. US PGA Player of the Year in 1955, he competed in four Ryder Cup matches in succession from 1955.

Foster, Rodney (ENG)
Born Ascot, Berkshire, 22 November 1941
Played in the Walker Cup five times between 1965 and 1973 and captained the side in 1979. He also captained the Eisenhower Trophy team in 1980.

Franco, Carlos (PAR)
Born Asunción, 24 May 1965
Turned professional 1986
Emerged on to the international stage from humble beginnings. He was one of a family of nine who shared a one-room home at the course where his father was greens superintendent and caddie. All five of his brothers play golf and he was appointed Paraguayan Minister of Sport in 1999. Won twice in his rookie year on the US Tour and became the first player to make more than $1 million in each of his first two seasons. Has scored three wins on the US circuit, five times in Japan where he had 11 top 10 finishes in 1997, once in the Philippines and 19 times in South America. First made headlines at St Andrews when he beat Sam Torrance in the Alfred Dunhill Cup.

Frost, David (RSA)
Born Cape Town, 11 September 1959
Turned professional 1981
He has won as many titles overseas as on the US Tour and still plays regularly on the European Tour The 1993 season was his best in America when he made over $1 million and finished fifth on the money list. He has established a vineyard in South Africa growing 100 acres of vines on the 300-acre estate. He has very quickly earned a reputation for producing quality wines.

Fulke, Pierre (SWE)
Born Nyköping, Sweden, 21 February 1971
Turned professional 1993
Son of a Swedish swimming champion he finished runner-up to Steve Stricker in the 2001 Accenture Matchplay Championship a few weeks after winning the Volvo Masters. Played on the 2002 winning Ryder Cup side. He has now retired from tournament golf but commentates with Goran Zachrisson on Swedish television and designs courses.

Funk, Fred (USA)
Born Tacoma Park, Missouri, 14 June 1956
Turned professional 1981
One of five rookies in the 2004 US Ryder Cup side, he scored his sixth US Tour success a few weeks later when he won the Southern Farm Bureau Classic. In 2005 he won the Tournament Players' Championship at Sawgrass and now plays on the Champions Tour where he has already been a winner.

Furyk, Jim (USA)
Born West Chester, Pennsylvania, 12 May 1970
Turned professional 1992
Considered one of the best players not to have won a major, Furyk put that right when he won the US Open at Olympia Fields, Chicago. He was one of four first-time major winners in 2003. He clearly enjoys playing

in Las Vegas where he has won three Invitational events in 1995, 1999 and 1998. He has teed it up in five Presidents Cups and six Ryder Cups beating Nick Faldo in the singles at Valderrama in 1997. He was also in the 1999, 2002, 2004, 2006 and 2008 sides. Has one of the most easily recognisable if idiosyncratic swings in top line golf. His father Mike has been his only coach. In 2005 he finished fourth top money earner in the United States and was winner of the Cialis Western Open. In 2006 he came second to Tiger Woods in the US Tour money list earning $7,213,316 but won the Harry Vardon Trophy for the best scoring average of 68.66 for golfers who played 60 rounds or more. Furyk had made over $31 million in prize-money on the US Tour by the end of 2006. In 2007, he won the Canadian Open.

Gallacher CBE, Bernard (SCO)
Born Bathgate, Scotland, 9 February 1949
Turned professional 1967

For many years combined tournament golf with the club professional's post at Wentworth where he was honoured in 2000 by being appointed captain. He took up golf at the age of 11 and nine years later was European No.1. He has scored 30 victories worldwide. Gallacher was the youngest Ryder Cup player when he made his début in the 1969 match in which he beat Lee Trevino in the singles. He played in eight Cup matches and captained the side three times losing narrowly in 1991 at Kiawah Island and 1993 at The Belfry before leading the team to success at Oak Hill in 1995. A former member of the European Tour's Board of Directors, he now plays occasionally on the European Senior Tour making his break-through win in 2002 when he took first prize in the Mobile Cup at Stoke Park. In 2003 he was granted honorary membership of the European Tour.

García, Sergio (ESP)
Born Castellon, 9 January 1980
Turned professional 1999

The extrovert Spaniard lost his chance of winning a first major when he was beaten by Ireland's Padraig Harrington in a four-hole play-off at Carnoustie, having led for most of the four days and was again pipped by Harrington in the 2008 USPGA Championship at Oakland Hills. In 2008 he also played host at his own event on the European Tour at Castellon. Having won the French and Amateur Championships in 1997, he took the British title in 1998 and in both years was European Amateur Masters champion. Son of a greenkeeper/professional who now plays on the European Senior Tour, Sergio's future was always going to be in professional golf but he waited until after the 1999 Masters in which he was leading amateur before joining the paid ranks at the Spanish Open. Although only just starting to collect Ryder Cup points he easily made the 1999 team and formed an invaluable partnership with Jesper Parnevik at Brookline scoring three and a half points out of four on the first two days. Victories in the Murphy's Irish Open and Linde German Masters helped him to the 1999 Rookie of the Year title in Europe but arguably an even better performance was finishing runner-up to Tiger Woods in the US PGA Championship at Medinah outside Chicago. Although he

did not win in 2000 he won the Mastercard Colonial and Buick Classic on the US Tour in 2001 and the Mercedes Championship, the Canaries Open de España and the Kolon Cup in Korea. He was in the 2002 Ryder Cup team and formed a useful partnership with Lee Westwood winning three out of four points on the first two days. They teamed up again in the winning 2004 side at Oakland Hills. He himself was unbeaten, winning 4½ out of five points including victory over Phil Mickelson in the singles. In the 2006 Ryder Cup at the K Club he again played well with José María Olazábal in the fourballs and Luke Donald in the foursomes. He scored four out of five points losing only his single to Stewart Cink but he was less successful in Nick Faldo's beaten team that defended the Cup at Valhalla in 2008. He continues to play on both sides of the Atlantic and in 2004 won the EDS Byron Nelson event and the Buick Classic through September. Later in the year he won the Mallorcan Open and lost a play-off to Ian Poulter in the Volvo Masters Andalusia at Valderrama. In 2005, García finished sixth on the European Tour money list and 10th on the US Order of Merit, winning on both sides of the Atlantic. In Europe he won the Omega European Masters and in America was successful in the Booz Allen Classic. One of his biggest regrets is the way he putted on the final day of the 2007 Open at Carnoustie when he made some costly slips with his long handled putter, missed a par putt at the last that would have won him the title then lost the four-hole play-off to Harrington. Sergio became the first European-born players since 1937 to win the Vardon Trophy on the PGA Tour for the lowest score average of 69.12. He ended 2008 as No. 2 in the World Rankings.

Garrido, Ignacio (ESP)
Born Madrid, 27 March 1972
Turned professional 1993

Eldest son of Antonio Garrido who played in the 1979 Ryder Cup, Ignacio emulated his father when he made the team at the 1997 match at Valderrama having earlier that year won the Volvo German Open. In 2003 he had his most impressive win when beating Trevor Immelman in a play-off for the Volvo PGA Championship at Wentworth. In 2008 he lost a play-off at Seville to Peter Lawrie of Ireland for the Open de España. Before turning professional with a handicap of 4 he won the English Amateur Stroke Play title (the Brabazon Trophy) in 1992. In the 80s used to caddie for his father who has since caddied for him on occasion.

Goosen, Retief (RSA)
Born Pietersburg, 3 February 1969
Turned professional 1990

Introduced to golf at the age of 11 he scored his first major success when leading from start to finish at the 2001 US Open at Tulsa and then beating Mark Brooks in the 18-hole play-off by two shots. Although he suffered health problems after being hit by lightning as a teenager he has enjoyed a friendly rivalry with South Africa's other talented player Ernie Els. Winner of the 1990 South African Amateur title, he scored his first professional victory in the Iscor Newcastle Classic a year later. In Europe where he has been helped by Belgian psychologist Jos Vanstiphout, golf's quiet achiever enjoys playing in France where he has won two

French Championships (1997 and 1999) and the Trophée Lancôme in 2000. Just weeks after his US Open win in 2001 he led again from start to finish to win the Scottish Open at Loch Lomond. In 2002 he was a runaway eight shot winner in the Johnnie Walker Classic at Lake Karynup in Perth, Australia. In 2004 he again won the US Open, this time at Shinnecock Hills GC on Long Island producing in the process not only superb control from tee to green but also on the lightning fast greens to prevent Phil Mickelson winning his second major of the year. Goosen single-putted 11 of the first 17 holes of his final round of 71. A week later he returned to Europe to win the Smurfit European Open at the K Club. In 2005 after finishing tied third at The Masters, he was leading going into the last round of the US Open but shot a closing 81 to miss out on a successful defence of his title. He finished 11th behind Michael Campbell but was fifth at The Open and sixth at the US PGA that same year. In 2005 he played again in the Presidents Cup and beat Tiger Woods in the singles at Lake Mannassas. Playing on both sides of the Atlantic he finished fourth on the European money list and eighth on the US list in 2005. Late in the year he beat Ernie Els for the SAA Open at Fancourt. He continued to play steadily throughout 2006, 2007 and 2008.

Grady, Wayne (AUS)
Born Brisbane, 26 July 1957
Turned professional 1973 and again in 1978
One of Australia's most popular players he won the US PGA Championship at Shoal Creek by three shots over Fred Couples. A year earlier he had tied with Greg Norman and eventual winner Mark Calcavecchia for The Open Championship losing out in the first ever four-hole play-off for the title. As chairman of the Australasian Tour from Jack Newton he was the architect of a tie up between the Australasian Tour and the US Nationwide Tour for two joint events a year. With a reduced playing schedule on the US Champions Tour he now commentates regularly for the BBC.

Graham, David (AUS)
Born Windsor, Tasmania, 23 May 1946
Turned professional 1962
Played superbly for a closing 67 round Merion to win the 1981 US Open Championship from George Burns and Bill Rogers. That day he hit every green in regulation. Two years earlier he had beaten Ben Crenshaw at the third extra hole at Oakland Hills to win the US PGA Championship. When he took up the game at age 14 he played with left-handed clubs before making the switch to a right-handed set. Awarded the Order of Australia for his services to golf he is a member of the Cup and Tee committee that sets up Augusta each year for the Masters. A regular winner around the world in the 70s and 80s he won eight times on the US Tour between 1972 and 1983. Now plays on the US Champions Tour but also has gained a considerable reputation as a course designer.

Graham, Lou (USA)
Born Nashville, Tennessee, 7 January 1938
Turned professional 1962
Won the US Open at Medinah in 1975 after a play-off against John Mahaffey

Green OBE, Charlie (SCO)
Born Dumbarton, 2 August 1932
One of Scotland's most successful amateur golfers who was leading amateur in the 1962 Open Championship. A prolific winner he took the Scottish Amateur title three times in 1970, 1982 and 1983. He played in five and was non-playing captain in two more Walker Cups and was awarded the Frank Moran Trophy for his services to Scottish sport in 1974.

Green, Hubert (USA)
Born Birmingham, Alabama, 18 December 1946
Turned professional 1970
Beat Lou Graham for the 1977 US Open at Southern Hills despite being told with four holes to play that he had received a death threat. Three times a Ryder Cup player he also won the 1985 US PGA Championship. His only European Tour victory was the 1977 Irish Open. Best known for his unorthodox swing and distinctive crouching putting style. He is successfully beating throat cancer – an illness that has meant he has been unable to compete in the US Senior Tour. He was inducted into the World Golf Hall of Fame in 2007.

Green, Nathan (AUS)
Born Newcastle, NSW, 13 May 1975
Turned professional 1998
A regular competitor on the US PGA Tour, he played and won the Blue Chip New Zealand Open at Gulf Harbour on his 20th European start.

Haas, Jay (USA)
Born St Louis, Missouri, 2 December 1953
Turned professional 1976
Winner of nine events on the USPGA Tour, he played in his third Ryder Cup as an invitee of the US captain Hal Sutton. He had played in 1983 and 1995. He has played in three Presidents Cups and was a Walker Cup player in 1975. His uncle is former Masters champion Bob Goalby. In 2004 he was named recipient of the Payne Stewart award for respecting and upholding the traditions of the game and received the Bob Jones award for outstanding sportsmanship in 2005. In 2006 he edged out Loren Roberts for the No.1 spot on the US Champions Tour winning five times in the season. In 2007 he won four times and again edged out Roberts in the race for top spot on the money list.

Haeggman, Joakim (SWE)
Born Kalmar, 28 August 1969
Turned professional 1989
Became the first Swedish player to play in the Ryder Cup when he made the side which lost to the Americans at The Belfry in 1993. He received one of team captain Bernard Gallacher's 'wild cards' and beat John Cook in his last day singles. Gave up ice hockey after dislocating his shoulder and breaking ribs in 1994. Realised then that ice hockey and golf do not mix but has become an enthusiastic angler when not on the links. Equalled the world record of 27 for the first nine holes in the Alfred Dunhill Cup over the Old course at St Andrews in 1997. Occasionally acts as commentator

for Swedish TV and was a member of Sam Torrance's Ryder Cup backroom team at The Belfry in 2002 and Bernhard Langer's vice-captain at Oakland Hills in 2004. Returned to the winner's circle in 2004 at Qatar. It was only his second win on the European Tour and his first since 1993.

Haig, Anton (RSA)
Born Johannesburg, 8 May 1986
Turned professional 2004
Became the youngest winner on the European Tour when he beat Richard Sterne and Oliver Wilson in a play-off for the 2007 Johnnie Walker Classic in Phuket but has struggled to find his best form since.

Hamilton, Todd (USA)
Born Galesburg, Illinois, 18 October 1965
Turned professional 1997
Winner of the 2004 Open Championship at Royal Troon beating Ernie Els in a four-hole play-off after both had tied on ten-under-par 274. Having learned his craft on the Asian Tour and Japanese circuit where he won four times in 2003, he earned his US Tour card in 2004 and won the Honda Classic. His performance in The Open was flawless as he kept his nerve to win against Els, Phil Mickelson and World No.1 Tiger Woods among others. He was American Rookie of the Year in 2004.

Hansen, Anders (DEN)
Born Sonderborg, 16 September 1970
Turned professional 1995
Made up eight shots over the last 36 holes to win the BMW PGA Championship at Wentworth in 2007. He had also won the event in 2002.

Hansen, Søren (DEN)
Copenhagen, 21 March 1974   Turned professional 1997
Winner of the Murphy's Irish Open in 2002 and the Mercedes-Benz Championship in 2007, he made his début successfully in the 2008 Ryder Cup at Valhalla.

Hanson, Peter (SWE)
Born Svedala, 4 October 1977
Turned professional 1998
Former winner of the English Strokeplay Championship (the Brabazon Trophy) in 1998 when he was also a member of the winning Swedish Eisenhower Trophy team. He won his first European professional title at the 2005 Jazztel Open de España and partnered Robert Karlsson for Sweden in the 2007 Mission Hills World Cup of Golf. In 2008 he ended a ten year wait for a home winner when he won the SAS Scandinavian Masters in poor weather at Arlandastat.

Harrington, Padraig (IRL)
Born Dublin, Ireland, 31 August 1971
Turned professional 1995
Dubliner Padraig Harrington become only the second Irishman to win The Open when he beat Sergio García of Spain in a four-hole play-off at Carnoustie in 2007, 50 years after Belfast-based Fred Daly had won the title at Hoylake. Harrington praised coach Bob Torrance for his help and Torrance praised the Irishman's work ethic. He did even better in 2008 when he became the first European to win The Open and USPGA Championship in the same year and the first European to win the USPGA Championship since Tommy Armour in 1930. At Royal Birkdale in The Open he held off the challenge posed by Ian Poulter and Greg Norman with a closing 66 highlighted by a 5-wood second shot to two feet at the par 5 17th for a title-clinching eagle. At Oakland Hills just three weeks later his main challengers were Garcia again and Ben Curtis, the 2003 Open champion. Again a closing 66 did the trick for the talented Irishman. A qualified accountant, Harrington was Irish Open and Close Amateur champion (1995) and played three times in the Walker Cup before turning professional. Played in the 1999 Ryder Cup at Brookline and beat Mark O'Meara in the singles. He was a member of the victorious European team for the 2002 match beating Mark Calcavecchia in the final day singles and was a key member of the winning Ryder Cup side at Oakland Hills in 2004 when he teamed up well with Colin Montgomerie and beat Jay Haas in the singles. In 2006, he was one of three Irishmen in Ian Woosnam's team that beat the Americans 18½–9½ at the K Club and again made the side in 2008 but played less well and for the second match made only a half-point. Remembered in 2000 for being disqualified on the final day of the Benson and Hedges International at The Belfry after having moved into a five shot lead at the 54-hole stage. It was only then discovered that one of his playing partners had signed Harrington's card on the first day and not Harrington himself. The manner in which he accepted this disappointment greatly impressed observers. In the autumn of 2002 he won the US$800,000 first prize in the Dunhill Links Championship beating Eduardo Romero at the 2nd play-off hole at St Andrews. Won the BMW Asian Open in Taiwan and the Deutsche Bank SAP Open TPC of Europe in the early part of the 2003 European season. Continued to play well in 2004 and in 2005 won two events on the US Tour. Late in 2006, he took the Dunhill Links championship for the second time at St Andrews which helped him clinch the No.1 spot on the European money list for the first time. Harrington, who finished €35,252 ahead of Paul Casey, had twice come second and twice third in previous years' races for the No.1 spot. Harrington's European winnings amounted to €2,489,336. He finished 68th on the US PGA Tour money list. After finishing fifth in The Masters in 2007, he became the first Irishman since John O'Leary in 1982 to win the Irish Open at Adare Manor and was only pipped for No.1 spot in Europe for a second year running by Justin Rose who won the Volvo Masters, the last event of the season. Named 2007 and 2008 European Golfer of the Year. At the end of his marvellous year Harrington was named PGA of America's Player of the Year. He is only the second European to be honoured since it was first awarded in 1948. Nick Faldo was Player of the Year in 1990.

Hayes, Dale (RSA)
Born Pretoria, 1 July 1952   Turned professional 1970
Former South African amateur stroke play champion who was a regular winner in South Africa and Europe after turning professional. He was Europe's top money earner in 1975 but retired from competitive golf to move into business. He is now a successful television commentator in South Africa with a weekly

programme of his own often working as a double act with veteran Denis Hutchinson.

Henry, J. J. (USA)
Born Fairfield, Connecticut, 2 April 1975
Turned professional 1998
Earned his place in the 2006 Ryder Cup and during the year won the Buick Classic at River Highlands. Made his début in the 2006 Ryder Cup at the K Club.

Hensby, Mark (AUS)
Born Melbourne, 29 June 1972
Turned professional 1995
Played well in three of the four majors in 2005 finishing fifth in The Masters, third in the US Open and just outside the top 10 in The Open. On a rare visit to Europe he landed first prize in the Scandinavian Masters at Kungsangen but only after a play-off with Henrik Stenson.

Hoch, Scott (USA)
Born Raleigh, North Carolina, 24 November 1955
Turned professional 1979
Ryder Cup, Presidents Cup, Walker Cup and Eisenhower Trophy player who was a regular winner on the US Tour. Has scored 10 wins between 1980 and 2001 and has had six more victories worldwide. In 1989 he donated $100,000 of his Las Vegas Invitational winnings to the Arnold Palmer Children's Hospital in Orlando where his son Cameron had been successfully treated for a rare bone infection in his right knee. More unfortunately remembered for missing a short putt at the first extra hole of a play-off that would have won him a Masters Green Jacket.

Holmes, John B. (USA)
Born Campbellsville, Kentucky, 26 April 1982
Turned professional 2005
Big hitter who scored his first win on the US Tour when he won the FBR Open at the TPC at Scottsdale in impressive fashion and made his début in the Ryder Cup in 2008 at Valhalla.

Horton MBE, Tommy (ENG)
Born St Helens, Lancashire, 16 June 1941
Turned professional 1957
A former Ryder Cup player who was No.1 earner on the European Seniors Tour in 1993 and for four successive seasons between 1996 and 1999. Awarded an MBE by Her Majesty the Queen for his services to golf, Tommy is a member of the European Tour Board and is chairman of the European Seniors Tour committee. A distinguished coach, broadcaster, author and golf course architect, Tommy retired as club professional at Royal Jersey in 1999 after 25 years in the post. He continues to play on the Senior Tour.

Howell, David (ENG)
Born Swindon, 23 June 1975
Turned professional 1995
Winner of the 1999 Dubai Desert Classic, he made his Ryder Cup début in 2004 at Oakland Hills where he teamed up with Paul Casey to gain a valuable foursomes point on the second day. He continued to play well in 2005 adding a second victory to his

European Tour CV when winning the BMW International in Munich. Finished seventh in the 2005 European Tour money list making over £1.2 million and in 2006, when his schedule was curtailed by injury, he made over £1.5 million in Europe and finished third in the list. Injury severely restricted his 2007 and 2008 schedules although he did win in 2008.

Huggett MBE, Brian (WAL)
Born Porthcawl, Wales, 18 November 1936
Turned professional 1951
Brian won the first of his 16 European Tour titles in Holland in 1962 and was still winning in 2000 when he landed the Beko Seniors Classic in Turkey after a play-off. A dogged competitor he played in six Ryder Cup matches before being given the honour of captaining the side in 1977 – the last year the Americans took on players from only Great Britain and Ireland. A respected golf course designer, Huggett was awarded the MBE for his services to golf and in particular Welsh golf.

Hunt MBE, Bernard (ENG)
Born Atherstone, Warwickshire, 2 February 1930
Turned professional 1946
One of Britain's most accomplished professionals he won 22 times between 1953 and 1973. He was third in the 1960 Open at the Old Course behind Kel Nagle and fourth in 1964 when Tony Lema took the title at St Andrews. Among his other victories were successes in Egypt and Brazil. Having made eight appearances in the Ryder Cup he captained the side in 1973 and again in 1975. He was PGA captain in 1966 and won the Harry Vardon Trophy as leading player in the Order of Merit on three occasions..

Ilonen, Mikko (FIN)
Born Lahti, 18 December 1979
Turned professional 2001
Became the first Finnish golfer to win the Amateur Championship when he beat Christian Reimbold from Germany 2 and 1 in the 2000 final at Royal Liverpool. He has won both the Finnish match play and stroke play titles. Represented Finland in the 1998 and 2000 Eisenhower Trophy events. Now plays professionally on the European Tour and in 2007 won his first European Tour title when he took the Enjoy Jakarta Astro Indonesian Open, a joint venture with the Asian Tour. Later, he became a double winner on Tour with success in the Scandinavian Masters at Arlandastad. In 2008 he won the Indonesian Open title.

Immelman, Trevor (RSA)
Born Cape Town, South Africa, 16 December 1979
Turned professional 1999
The 2008 Masters champion is son of Johan Immelman, former executive director of the South African Sunshine Tour,. A former South African Match-play and Strokeplay champion and twice South African Open champion Trevor, who had played his early professional golf in Europe before moving to the United States, won his first PGA title when he held off a strong field at the Cialis Western Open at Cog Hill. But his greatest success came at the 2008 Masters Tournament at Augusta where he led from

start to finish to pick up his first major title. He has played in two Presidents Cups.

Irwin, Hale (USA)
Born Joplin, Montana, 3 June 1945
Turned professional 1968
A three time winner of the US Open (1974, 1979 and 1990) he has been a prolific winner on the main US Tour and, since turning 50, on the US Champions Tour. He had 20 wins on the main Tour including the 1990 US Open triumph where he holed a 45-foot putt on the final green at Medinah to force a play-off with Mike Donald then after both were still tied following a further 18 holes became the oldest winner of the Championship at 45 when he sank a 10-foot birdie putt at the first extra hole of sudden death. Joint runner-up to Tom Watson in the 1983 Open at Royal Birkdale where he stubbed the ground and missed a tap-in putt on the final day – a slip that cost him the chance of a play-off. Three times top earner on the Champions Tour where, prior to the start of the 2001 season, he had averaged $90,573 per start in 130 events coming in the top three in 63 of those events and finishing over par in only nine of them, he was inducted into the World Golf Hall of Fame in 2008.

Jacklin CBE, Tony (ENG)
Born Scunthorpe, 7 July 1944   Turned professional 1962
Played an important and often under-rated role in the growth of the PGA European Tour after it became a self-supporting organisation in 1971. Although playing most of his golf in America he was encouraged by John Jacobs, the then executive director of the European Tour, to return to Europe to help build up the circuit. In 1969 he won The Open Championship at Royal Lytham and St Annes – the first British winner of the title since Max Faulkner in 1951. A year later he led from start to finish to win the US Open at Hazeltine – the first British player to win that event since Ted Ray had been successful in 1920 and the only one to have done so to date. He was the first player since Harry Vardon to hold the British and American Open titles simultaneously. He might well have won further Opens but a thunderstorm halted his bid for the title at St Andrews in 1970, he came third in 1971 and in 1972 Lee Trevino chipped in at the 17th at Muirfield and went on to win a title the British player had seemed set to win. He is now one of just 13 honorary members of the Royal and Ancient Golf Club of St Andrews having been elected in 2003 along with Lee Trevino. Played in his last Open in 2005. He has built in Florida with Jack Nicklaus a course known as The Concession, so named because of the putt Jack conceded him in the 1969 Ryder Cup to ensure the overall match was halved. He is now expanding into course design work.

Jaidee, Thongchai (THA)
Born Lop Buri, Thailand, 8 November 1969
Turned professional 1999
The first Thai golfer to win a title on the European Tour when he won the Carlsberg Malaysian Open in 2004. Learned his golf using a bamboo pole with an old 5-iron head and did not play his first nine holes until he was 16. An ex-paratrooper, Jaidee qualified and played all four rounds in the 2001 US Open. An impressive regular on the Asian Tour, he also competes in Europe

Jacobs OBE, John (ENG)
Born Lindrick, Yorkshire, 14 March 1925
The first Executive Director of the independently run PGA European Tour, John Jacobs was awarded the OBE in 2000 for his services to golf as a player, administrator and coach. Known as 'Dr Golf' Jacobs has built up an awesome reputation as a teacher around the world and is held in high esteem by the golfing fraternity. Top American coach Butch Harmon summed up John's contribution in this field of golf when he said: "There is not one teacher who does not owe something to John. He wrote the book on coaching." With 75 per cent of the votes he was inducted into the World Golf Teachers' Hall of Fame and was described at that ceremony as 'the English genius'. Last year he was also welcomed into the World Golf Hall of Fame in America. Having played in the 1955 Ryder Cup match he captained the side in 1979 when Continental players were included for the first time and again in 1981. Ken Schofield who succeeded him as European Tour supremo believes that John changed the face of golf sponsorship. In 2002 he received the Association of Golf Writers' award for outstanding services to golf.

Jacobsen, Frederik (SWE)
Born Moindal, Sweden, 26 September 1974
Turned professional 1994
He made his European Tour winning breakthrough when he took the 2003 Omega Hong Kong Open and then followed that up with victory in the Algarve Open de Portugal. He finished fifth in the US Open, sixth in The Open and became the latest player to shoot 60 when he did so in the first round of the Linde German Masters. He won his third title of the European season when he beat Carlos Rodiles in the end-of-season Volvo Masters at Andalucia. With that win at Valderrama, Jacobsen became the first Swede to win three titles in a season and by doing so moved into the top 20 of the world rankings for the first time. He finished the European season fourth in the Volvo Order of Merit. Played almost exclusively from 2005 in America but is still chasing his first win there.

Jacquelin, Rafaël (FRA)
Born Lyon, 8 May 1974
Turned professional 1995
Ten years after turning professional Rafaël Jacquelin became the latest French golfer to win on Tour when he won the 2005 Madrid Open at Club de Campo. The Frenchman with a most graceful swing had had four second place finishes previously. His success came in his 238th event. As an amateur he won the French title. Originally wanted to be a soccer player but a knee injury thwarted his plans and he turned instead to tennis and later to golf. In 2007 he led wire-to-wire when winning the BMW Asian Open. He and Gregory Havret finished third behind Scotland and the USA in the 2007 World Cup of Golf at Mission Hills in China.

James, Mark (ENG)

Born Manchester, 28 October 1953
Turned professional 1976

Veteran of over 500 European tournaments he was for a time chairman of the European Tour's Tournament committee. A seven-time Ryder Cup player including the 1995 match at Oak Hill when he scored a vital early last day point against Jeff Maggert, he captained the side at Brookline in 1999. Four times a top five finisher in The Open Championship he has won 18 European Tour events and four elsewhere but these days, having successfully battled cancer, he is just as happy working in his Yorkshire garden. Caused some raised eyebrows with some of his comments in his book reviewing the 1999 Ryder Cup entitled 'Into the Bear Pit', then followed that up with a less controversial sequel. Affectionately known as Jesse to his friends. He qualified for the US Champions Tour in 2004 and won one of that Tour's five majors – the Ford Senior Players Championship. Through 2008 continued to play on the US Champions Tour with only infrequent visits back to play in European Senior events and occasionally join Ken Brown and Peter Alliss on the BBC golf commentating team.

January, Don (USA)

Born Plainview, Texas, 20 November 1929
Turned professional 1955

Winner of the US Open in 1967 he followed up his successful main Tour career in which he had 11 wins between 1956 and 1976 with double that success as a Senior winning 22 times. Much admired for his easy rhythmical style.

Janzen, Lee (USA)

Born Austin, Minnesota, 28 August 1964
Turned professional 1986

Twice a winner of the US Open in 1993 and again in 1998 when he staged the best final round comeback since Johnny Miller rallied from six back to win the title 25 years earlier. Five strokes behind the late Payne Stewart after 54 holes at Baltusrol he closed with a 67 to beat Stewart with whom he had also battled for the title in 1993.

Jiménez, Miguel Angel (ESP)

Born Malaga, 4 January 1964
Turned professional 1982

Talented Spaniard who was runner-up to Tiger Woods in the 2000 US Open. This was a year after making his successful début in the Ryder Cup. One of seven brothers he did not take up golf until his mid-teens. He loves cars, drives a Ferrari and has been nicknamed 'The Mechanic' by his friends. His best-remembered shot was the 3-wood he hit into the hole for an albatross 2 at the infamous 17th hole at Valderrama in the Volvo Masters but he was credited with having played the Canon Shot of the Year when he chipped in at the last to win 1998 Trophée Lancôme. In 2000 lost in a play-off at Valderrama in a World Championship to Tiger Woods. He played in the 2002, 2004 and 2008 European Ryder Cup sides and won four times during the 2004 European season, taking the Johnnie Walker Classic title in Bangkok, the Algarve Portuguese Open

at Penina, the BMW Asian Open in Shanghai and the BMW German Open in Munich. He had a quieter 2005 but finished 14th in the money list helped by victories in the Omega Hong Kong Open and the Celtic Manor Resort Wales Open and four other top 10 finishes. In 2006 he finished 23rd on the PGA European Tour money list and was 21st in 2007. He started the 2008 season well, winning the UBS Hong Kong Open for the second time in three years and became BMW PGA champion when he beat Oliver Wilson in a play-off at Wentworth.

Johansson, Per-Ulrik (SWE)

Born Uppsala, 6 December 1966
Turned professional 1990

A former amateur international at both junior and senior level he became the first Swede to play in two Ryder Cups when he made the 1995 and 1997 teams. In 1997 he played Phil Mickelson with whom he had studied at Arizona State University. In 1991 he was winner of the Sir Henry Cotton Rookie of the Year award in Europe. For a time, he played in America but was dogged by injury. In 2007 he was a winner again in Europe, regaining his main Tour card with victory in the Russian Open in Moscow over Robert Jan Derksen of the Netherlands.

Johnson, Zach (USA)

Born Iowa City, 24 February 1976
Turned professional 1998

The winner of the 2004 BellSouth Classic, he made his début in the Ryder Cup at the K Club in 2006 and won The Masters at Augusta in 2007. Later, he won first prize in the AT&T Classic at TPC Sugarloaf and earned a Presidents Cup spot. Surprisingly missed out on Ryder Cup honours in 2008.

Jones, Steve (USA)

Born Artesia, New Mexico, 27 December 1958
Turned professional 1981

First player since Jerry Pate in 1976 to win the US Open after having had to qualify. His 1996 victory was the result of inspiration he received from reading a Ben Hogan book given to him the week before the Championship at Oakland Hills. Uses a reverse overlapping grip as a result of injury. Indeed his career was put on hold for three years after injury to his left index finger following a dirt-bike accident. He dominated the 1997 Phoenix Open shooting 62, 64, 65 and 67 for an 11 shot victory over Jesper Parnevik That week his 258 winning total was just one outside the low US Tour record set by Mike Souchak in 1955. Played in the 1999 Ryder Cup.

Karlsson, Robert (SWE)

Born St Malm, Sweden, 3 September 1969
Turned professional 1989

A regular winner on the European Tour he finished 4th on the money list in 2006 but dropped to 27th in 2007 before topping the earnings table in 2008. The most successful Swede on the European Tour – he has won nine times – he was a member of the winning 2006 Ryder Cup side and the losing 2008 team. He played with Peter Hanson in the 2007 Mission Hills World Cup of Golf in Shenzhen and in 2008 teamed up with

Henrik Stenson to win the trophy for Sweden for a second time. It was a fitting finale to a year in which he made the cut in all four majors and towards the end of the season won the Mercedes-Benz German Masters and the Alfred Dunhill Links Championship to clinch the No. 1 spot. At one point during the summer he was never out of the top four in five consecutive events finishing 3,3,3,2,4.

Kim, Anthony (USA)
Born Los Angeles, California 19 June 1985
Turned professional: 2006
He spent three years at the University of Oklahoma but turned professional after making $338,067 in just two starts on Tour. A three-time All-American he was a member of the successful 2005 US Walker Cup side and made a winning début in the Ryder Cup at Valhalla in 2008 beating Sergio Garcia in the singles.

Kite, Tom (USA)
Born Austin, Texas, 9 December 1949
Turned professional 1972
He won the US Open at Pebble Beach in 1992 in difficult conditions when aged 42 to lose the 'best player around never to have won a Major' tag. With 19 wins on the main Tour he was the first to top $6million, $7 million, $8 million and $9 million dollars in prize money. Has been playing since he was 11 and after a lifetime wearing glasses had laser surgery to correct acute near-sightedness. He played in seven Ryder Cups and was captain at Valderrama in 1997. He now plays the US Senior Tour. He was inducted into the World Golf Hall of Fame in 2004.

Khan, Simon (ENG)
Born Epping, 16 June 1972   Turned professional 1991
Inspired by friend Scott Drummond's victory a week earlier in the Volvo PGA Championship, Simon took first prize by overhauling Paul Casey in the final round of the 2004 Celtic Manor Resort Wales Open.

Kuchar, Matt (USA)
Born Lake Mary, Florida, 21 June 1978
Turned professional 2002
Winner of the US Amateur in 1997 he was leading amateur in the 1998 Masters and US Open Championship. Scored his first win as a professional when he landed the 2002 Honda Classic.

Liang, Wen-Chong (CHN)
Born Zhongshan, China, 2 August 1978
Turned professional 1999
Became the second Chinese winner on Tour when he won the Clariden Leu Singapore Open in 2007. His friend and mentor has been Zhang Lian-wei. Introduced to the game while still at school he played with a most unorthodox swing but one which works for him.

Lane, Barry (ENG)
Born Hayes, Middlesex, 21 June 1960
Turned professional 1976
After winning his way into the 1993 Ryder Cup he hit the headlines when he won the first prize of $1 million in the Andersen Consulting World Championship in beating David Frost in the final at Greyhawk in

Bernhard Langer

© Phil Sheldon Golf Picture Library

Arizona. He has played over 500 European events, winning five times between 1988 and 2008. In 2004, aged 44, he won the British Masters at Marriott Forest of Arden.

Langer, Bernhard (GER)
Born Anhausen, 27 August 1957
Turned professional 1972
One of the game's most respected figures and consistent performers he is best known for having conquered the putting yips on more than one occasion. Twice winner of the US Masters in 1985 and 1993 he has never managed to win The Open despite coming second twice and third on three occasions. Deeply religious he was for many years Germany's only top player. He has been an inspiration to many taking his own National title on 12 occasions and winning 37 titles in Europe between 1980 and 2000. In 1979 he won the Cacherel Under 25s Championship by 17 shots. He played nine times in the Ryder Cup between 1981 and 1997 proving a mainstay in foursomes and fourballs with 11 different partners. He regained his place for the 2002 match after having been overlooked for a captain's pick in 1999 and made 3½ points – 2½ of them partnering Colin Montgomerie. He then captained with considerable success the winning 2004 team at Oakland Hills. Now plays both the US and European Tours. Has won 11 times in Germany including five German Opens. When he turned 50 he won his first event on the US Champions Tour.

Lara, José Manuel (ESP)
Born Valencia, 21 May 1977   Turned professional 1997
Scored his first European Tour victory in the 2007 UBS Hong Kong Open, a joint venture with the Asian Tour. He led from start to finish on his own after the first round.

Lawrie MBE, Paul (SCO)
Born Aberdeen, 1 January 1969
Turned professional 1986
Made golfing history when he came from 10 shots back on the final day to win the 1999 Open Championship at Carnoustie after a play-off against former winner Justin Leonard and Frenchman Jean Van de Velde. With his win he became the first home-based Scot since Willie Auchterlonie in 1893 to take the title. Still based in Aberdeen he hit the opening tee shot in the 1999 Ryder Cup and played well in partnership with Colin Montgomerie in foursomes and four balls and in the singles earned a point against Jeff Maggert. Originally an assistant at Banchory Golf Club on Royal Deeside Lawrie has had a hole named after him at the club. Coached off and on by former Tour player Adam Hunter and Scottish Rugby Union psychologist Dr Richard Cox, Lawrie has been awarded an MBE for his achievements in golf.

Lee, Danny (NZL)
Born 24 July 1990
Helped by his victory in the US Amateur Championship in 2008 he moved to the top of the Royal and Ancient Golf Club of St Andrews amateur rankings and won the McCormack Trophy. Although Korean by birth he has been brought up in New Zealand and America. Late in 2008 he became a naturalised New Zealander and led his country in the Eisenhower Trophy competition won by Scotland in Adelaide. Dannt finished ied 11th in the Australian Masters and made the cut in three of the last four pro events in which he played.

Lehman, Tom (USA)
Born Austin, Minnesota, 7 March 1959
Turned professional 1982
Winner of The Open Championship at Royal Lytham and St Annes in 1996 he was runner-up in the US Open that year and third in 1997. He was runner-up in the 1994 Masters having come third the previous year. He played in four Ryder Cup matches and led the US team in the 2006 Ryder Cup match at the K Club when the Americans lost 18½-9½ to the Europeans led by Ian Woosnam.

Leonard, Justin (USA)
Born Dallas, Texas, 15 June 1972
Turned professional 1994
Winner of the 1997 Open at Royal Troon when he beat Jesper Parnevik and Darren Clarke into second place with a closing 65 and nearly won the title again in 1999 when he lost a four-hole play-off with Jean Van de Velde and Paul Lawrie to the Scotsman at Carnoustie. In 1998 came from five back to beat Lee Janzen in the Players Championship and is remembered for his fight back against José Maria Olazábal on the final day of the

1999 Ryder Cup at Brookline. Four down after 11 holes he managed to share a half-point with the Spaniard to help America win the Cup. He was again a member of a winning Ryder Cup side when he played in the 2008 team captained by Paul Azinger at Valhalla.

Levet, Thomas (FRA)
Born Paris, 9 September 1968   Turned professional 1988
Although he was the first Frenchman to play full time on the US Tour, he lost his card and only regained his European Tour card when he was invited because of his French ranking to play in the 1998 Cannes Open – and won it. Sixth in the 1997 Open at Royal Troon he lost in a play-off to Ernie Els in the 2002 Open at Muirfield. Thomas made his Ryder Cup début at Oakland Hills in 2004, winning his singles game against Fred Funk. He is a gifted linguist speaking seven languages including Japanese. Has also turned his hand very successfully to commentating for French television.

Lima, José-Filipe (POR)
Born Versailles, 26 November 1981
Turned professional 2002
Although he played all his early golf in France and represented that country on the European Tour when he won the AA St Omer event in 2004, he has since changed nationalities. His mother is Portuguese and he represented that country in the 2005 WGC–World Cup of Golf.

Littler, Gene (USA)
Born San Diego, California, 21 July 1930
Turned professional 1954
Winner of the 1953 US Amateur Championship he had a distinguished professional career scoring 26 victories on the US Tour between 1955 and 1977. He scored his only major triumph at Pebble Beach in 1971 when he beat Bob Goalby and Doug Sanders at Oakland Hills. He had been runner-up in the US Open in 1954 and was runner-up in the 1977 US PGA Championship and the 1970 US Masters. A seven-time Ryder Cup player between 1961 and 1977 he is a former winner of the Ben Hogan, Bobby Jones and Byron Nelson awards. He won the Hogan award after successfully beating cancer.

Love III, Davis (USA)
Born Charlotte, North Carolina, 13 April 1964
Turned professional 1985
Son of one of America's most highly rated teachers who died in a plane crash in 1988, Love has won only one major – the 1997 US PGA Championship at Winged Foot where he beat Justin Leonard by five shots. He has been runner-up in the US Open (1996) and the US Masters (1999). In the World Cup of Golf he won the title in partnership with Fred Couples four years in a row (1992–1995). He has played in five Ryder Cups and enjoyed a superb 2003 winning four times between February and August. His victories were the AT&T Pebble Beach National Pro-Am, the Players Championship, The Heritage and The International. Just failed to make the 2006 Ryder Cup side but two weeks later he returned to the winner's circle when he won the Chrysler Greensboro event.

Lundberg, Mikael (SWE)
Born Helsingborg, 13 August 1973
Turned professional 1997
The former Challenge Tour player won his first main Tour event when he picked up the first prize in the Cadillac Russian Open at Le Meridien Moscow Country Club in 2005. He represented Sweden as an amateur in the Eisenhower Trophy.

Lyle MBE, Sandy (SCO)
Born Shrewsbury, 9 February 1958
Turned professional in 1977
With his win in the 1985 Open Championship at Royal St George's he became the first British player to take the title since Tony Jacklin in 1969. He was also the first British player to win a Green Jacket in the Masters at Augusta in 1988 helped by a majestic 7-iron second shot out of sand at the last for a rare winning birdie 3. Although he represented England as an amateur at boys', youths' and senior level he became Scottish when he turned professional, something he was entitled to do at the time because his late father, the professional at Hawkstone Park, was a Scot. This is no longer allowed. He made his international début at age 14 and, two years later, qualified for and played 54 holes in the 1974 Open at Royal Lytham and St Annes. A tremendously talented natural golfer he fell a victim later in his career to becoming over-technical. Now lives in Perthshire and is competing less and less frequently in the US and Europe. He was part of captain Ian Woosnam's team for the 2006 Ryder Cup at the K Club in 2006.

Lynn, David (ENG)
Born Billinge 20 October 1973
Turned professional 1995
Made his European Tour winning breakthrough when he won the 2004 KLM Dutch Open at Hilversum by three shots from Richard Green and Paul McGinley with a winning total of 264.

McDowell, Graeme (NIR)
Born Ballymoney, Northern Ireland, 30 July 1979
Turned professional 2002
A member of the winning Great Britain and Ireland Walker Cup team in 2001, he earned his European Tour card in just his fourth event as a professional. McDowell, who had been signed up to represent the Kungsangen Golf Club in Sweden just two weeks earlier, received a last minute sponsor's invitation to play there in the Volvo Scandinavian Masters ... and not only won the event but also broke the course record with an opening round of 64. He beat Trevor Immelman into second place with former USPGA champion Jeff Sluman third. McDowell's winning score of 270 – 14-under-par – earned him a first prize of over £200,000 and a place in the World Golf Championship NEC event at Sahalee in Washington. He was the European Tour's 12th first time winner of the season and at 23 the youngest winner of the title. In 2008 helped by victories in the Ballantine's Championship in Korea and the Barclays Scottish Open at Loch Lomond he qualified automatically for

the Ryder Cup at Valhalla and was one of the team's most successful performers. In his amateur days he attended the University of Alabama where he was rated No. 1 Collegiate golfer winning six of 12 starts with a stroke average of 69.6. In 2004, scored his second European success when he won the Telecom Italia Open. He found it difficult to compete on both sides of the Atlantic in 2006.

McEvoy OBE, Peter (ENG)
Born London, 22 March 1953
The most capped player for England who has had further success as a captain of Great Britain and Ireland's Eisenhower Trophy and Walker Cup sides. The Eisenhower win came in 1998 and the Walker Cup triumphs at Nairn in 1999 and at Ocean Forest, Sea Island, Georgia in 2001. On both occasions his team won 15–9. A regular winner of amateur events McEvoy was amateur champion in 1977 and 1978 and won the English stroke play title in 1980. He reached the final of the English Amateur the same year. In 1978 he played all four rounds in the Masters at Augusta and that year received the Association of Golf Writers' Trophy for his contribution to European golf. He was leading amateur in two Open Championships – 1978 and 1979. In 2003 he was awarded the OBE by Her Majesty the Queen for his services to golf.

McGimpsey, Garth (IRL)
Born Bangor, 17 July 1955
A long hitter who was Irish long-driving champion in 1977 and UK long-driving title holder two years later. He was amateur champion in 1985 and Irish champion the same year and again in 1988. He played in three Walker Cup matches and competed in the home internationals for Ireland in 1978 and from 1980 to 1998. He captained the winning Great Britain and Ireland Walker Cup side that beat American 12½–11½ at Ganton in 2003 and again two years later in Chicago when the Americans won by a point.

McGinley, Paul (IRL)
Born Dublin, 16 December 1966
Turned professional 1991
Popular Irish golfer who turned to the game after breaking his left kneecap playing Gaelic football. With Padraig Harrington won the 1977 World Cup at Kiawah and made his Ryder Cup début when the postponed 2001 match was played in 2002. In a tense finish to his match with Jim Furyk he holed from nine feet to get the half point the Europeans needed for victory. He made the side again in 2004 and was unbeaten as Europe beat the USA 18½–9½ and was one of three Irishmen who helped Europe win by the same margin in 2006. Europe might have won 19–9 had he not conceded a half to J. J. Henry at the last when a streaker ran over the line of the American's 20 foot downhill putt. In 2005 he finished third behind Colin Montgomerie and Michael Campbell in the European Tour Order of Merit making over £1.5 million. During the year he finished third behind Tiger Woods in the WGC–NEC Invitational at Firestone, lost the HSBC World MatchPlay at Wentworth to Michael Campbell but ended the season on a high note with victory in the Volvo Masters of Andalucia. In 2007 he was appointed

by Nick Faldo to be one of his vice-captains at the 2008 Ryder Cup but later declined in order to try and play himself into the side. He failed to do so. He had been a surprise omission from the Great Britain and Ireland side against the Continent of Europe for the Seve Trophy when it was played in Ireland the previous year. He remains one of the most popular and honest players on Tour.

Macgregor, George (SCO)
Born Edinburgh, 19 August 1944
After playing in five Walker Cup matches he captained the side in 1991 and later served as chairman of The R&A Selection committee. He won the Scottish Stroke Play title in 1982 after having been runner up three times.

McIlroy, Rory (NIR)
Born Holywood, May 4 1989
Turned professional 2007
Twice winner of the Irish and European Amateur titles – he was the youngest winner of the Irish event in 2005 – Rory won the silver medal as leading amateur in the 2007 Open at Carnoustie. After turning professional he won his European Tour card when finishing third in the Alfred Dunhill Links Championship – only his second event as a pro. In 2008 he missed a 15 in. putt to lose a play-off to Jean-François Lucquin at the Omega European Masters at Crans-sur-Sierre. This runner-up spot guaranteed him his Tour card for 2009.

McNulty, Mark (IRL)
Born Zimbabwe, 25 October 1953
Turned professional 1977
Recognised as one of the best putters in golf he was runner-up with the late Payne Stewart to Nick Faldo in the 1990 Open at St Andrews. Although hampered throughout his career by a series of injuries and illness he has scored 16 wins on the European Tour and 33 around the world including 23 on the South African Sunshine circuit. He won the South African Open in 1987 and again in 2001 holing an 18-foot putt on the last at East London to beat Justin Rose. Qualified in 2004 to join the US Champions Tour and although originally from Zimbabwe he now plays out of Ireland.

Maggert, Jeff (USA)
Born Columbia, Missouri, 20 February 1964
Turned professional 1986
A three times Ryder Cup player who competed in the 1995, 1997 and 1999 matches he won the World Golf Championship Match Play event in 1999 to land a $1 million cheque. A quiet achiever he came third in the US PGA Championship in 1995 and 1997.

Marks, Geoffrey (ENG)
Born Hanley, Stoke-on-Trent, November 1938
President of the English Golf Union in 1995 he captained the Walker Cup side in 1987 after having played on two previous occasions. He made eight appearances for England in the home internationals before captaining the team in a non-playing capacity at the start of the 1980s. He is a former England selector and was chairman of The R&A selection committee for four years from 1989.

Mamat, Mardan (SIN)
Born Singapore, 31 October 1967
Turned professional 1994
Became the first Singaporean to win an Asian/European joint venture in his home country when he took the Osim Singapore Masters in 2006.

Marsh, Dr David (ENG)
Born Southport, Lancashire, 29 April 1934
Twice winner of the English Amateur Championship in 1964 and 1970, he was captain of The R&A in 1990/1991. He played in the 1971 Walker Cup match at St Andrews and helped the home side win by scoring a vital one hole victory in the singles against Bill Hyndman. He captained the team in 1973 and 1975 and had a distinguished career as a player and then captain for England between 1956 and 1972. He was chairman of The R&A selection committee from 1979 to 1983 and in 1987 was president of the English Golf Union.

Marsh, Graham (AUS)
Born Kalgoorlie, Western Australia, 14 January 1944
Turned professional 1968
A notable Australian who followed up his international playing career by gaining a reputation for designing fine courses. Although he played in Europe, America and Australasia he spent most of his time on the Japanese circuit where he had 17 wins between 1971 and 1982. He won 11 times in Europe and scored victories also in the United States, India, Thailand and Malaysia. He now plays on the US Champions Tour and occasionally in Europe.

Martin, Pablo (ESP)
Born Malaga, 20 April 1986
Turned professional 2007
Became the first amateur to win on the PGA European Tour when he edged out Raphaël Jacquelin of France by a shot in the Estoril Open de Portugal in 2007. A former British Boys' champion (2001) and Carris Trophy winner in 2004, he played in two Eisenhower Trophy competitions and two Palmer Cups. Winner of the Jack Nicklaus award for top national amateur in 2006 when at Oklahoma State University he gave up his studies to join the professional ranks and hopes to play on both sides of the Atlantic. Curiously another Oklahoma "cowboy", Scott Verplank, has also won as an amateur in his case on the PGA Tour.

Mason, Carl (ENG)
Born Buxton, Derbyshire, 25 June 1953
Turned professional 1973
Carl won twice on the main European Tour in 1994 but has played his best golf on the European Seniors Tour. He finished second on the money list in his first two years and first for the next three years. In 2004 and again in 2007 he won five events in a season. By the end of 2008 he had won one tournament and moved to the top of the Senior Tour career money list with €1.7m.

Melnyk, Steve (USA)
Born Brunswick, Georgia, 26 February 1947
Turned professional 1971
US Amateur champion in 1969 and British champion in 1971. His professional career was cut short because of an ankle injury. For a time he commentated on American television.

Micheel, Shaun (USA)
Born Orlando, Florida, 5 January 1969
Turned professional 1962
Surprise winner of the US PGA Championship at Oak Hill in 2003. He fired rounds of 69, 68, 69 and 70 for a winning total of 276. He completed his victory with one of the most brilliant approach irons from the rough to just one foot of the hole at the last. In 2006 at Medinah, he finished second to Tiger Woods again in the US PGA Championship. Later he beat Woods en route to the final of the HSBC World Match Play at Wentworth but lost in the final to Paul Casey.

Mickelson, Phil (USA)
Born San Diego, California, 16 June 1970
Turned professional 1992
The world's leading left-hander who plays all sports right-handed except golf and claims to have started hitting golf balls at 18 months. One of only three players to win the NCAA Championship and US Amateur in the same year. The others were Jack Nicklaus and Tiger Woods. He has played in two Walker Cups, seven times in Presidents Cup and in seven Ryder Cup matches. Mickelson, who had won the Tour Championship in 2000, finally won his first major when he took the Green Jacket in the 2004 Masters at Augusta by a shot from Ernie Els. Mickelson birdied five of the last seven holes to do so He was pipped by Retief Goosen for the 2004 US Open at Shinnecock Hills and was third in The Open that year at Royal Troon. In 2005 he won four times on the US Tour including a second major – the USPGA Championship at Baltusrol. He started the 2006 season by winning The Masters for a second time and had the chance to win a third major in a row at the US Open at Winged Foot in June but double-bogeyed the last hole and finished joint second with Jim Furyk and Colin Montgomerie and behind Australian Geoff Ogilvy. In 2007 he won the AT&T pro-am for a third time, The Players Championship and the Deutsche Bank Open. At the end of 2007 he won the HSBC Champions event in Shanghai after a play-off with Lee Westwood and Ross Fisher. It was only his second victory outside America, the other having come at the Tournoi Perrier Paris in 1993. He remains one of America and the world's most consistent performers and was expected to compete in the Race to Dubai on the revamped European Tour.

Miller, Johnny (USA)
Born San Francisco, California, 29 April 1947
Turned professional 1969
Dreamed of winning The Open after Tony Lema, another member of the Olympic Club in San Francisco, did so in 1964. Realised his dream when he beat Jack Nicklaus and Seve Ballesteros into second place in the 1976 Open at Royal Birkdale. His US Open win in 1973 came with the help of a brilliant last round 63 which set the record, since equalled for the lowest round in the Championship. Was involved with Tom Weiskopf and Jack Nicklaus in one of the greatest finishes to a US Masters in 1975 which Nicklaus won. He scored 24 wins between 1971 and 1984 and in 1975 shot 49 under par when winning the Phoenix and Tucson Opens in successive weeks. Now is lead commentator for NBC.

Milligan, Jim (SCO)
Born Irvine, Ayrshire, 15 June 1963
The 1988 Scottish Amateur champion had his moment of international glory in the 1989 Walker Cup which was won by the Great Britain and Ireland side for only the third time in the history of the event and for the first time on American soil. With GB&I leading by a point at Peachtree in Atlanta only Milligan and his experienced opponent Jay Sigel were left on the course. The American looked favourite to gain the final point and force a draw when two up with three to play but Milligan hit his approach from 100 yards to a few inches to win the 16th with a birdie then chipped in after both had fluffed chips to square at the 17th. The last was halved leaving the Great Britain and Ireland side historic winners by a point.

Mize, Larry (USA)
Born Augusta, Georgia, 23 September 1958
Turned professional 1980
Only local player ever to win the Masters and he did it in dramatic style holing a 140-foot pitch and run at the second extra hole to edge out Greg Norman and Seve Ballesteros. He had made the play-off by holing a 10-foot birdie on the final green. In 1993 he beat an international field to take the Johnnie Walker World Championship title at Tryall in Jamaica. His middle name is Hogan.

Molinari, Eduardo (ITA)
Born Turin, 11 February 1981
Turned professional 2006
Became the first Italian to win the US Amateur Championship when he beat Dillon Dougherty 4 and 3 in the 2005 final at Merion, Pennsylvania. The 24-year-old, who has earned an engineering degree in his home country. joined his brother Francesco on the European Tour in 2006. He and his brother represented Italy in the 2007 World Cup of Golf at Mission Hills in Shenzhen, China.

Molinari, Francesco (ITA)
Born Turin, 8 November 1982
Turned professional 2004
Brother of Eduardo Molinari, winner of the US Amateur in 2005, he won his first European Tour title when he took the Italian Open at Castello di Tolcinasco in 2006.

Monasterio, Cesar (ARG)
Born Buenos Aires, 28 November 1963
Turned professional 1990
Became the latest Argentinian to win on the European Tour when he triumphed at the Aa St Omer Open.

Colin Montgomerie

Montgomerie OBE, Colin (SCO)
Born Glasgow, 23 June 1963   Turned professional 1987
Europe's most consistent golfer who topped the Volvo Order of Merit an unprecedented seven years in a row between 1993 and 1999 and again in 2004.. Although he has yet to win a major he has come close losing a play-off for the US Open to Ernie Els in 1994 and again being pipped by Els in the 1997 Championship. He was third behind Tom Kite in the 1992 US Open and was runner-up to Tiger Woods in the 2005 Open at St Andrews. In 1995 he was beaten in a play-off for the USPGA Championship by Australian Steve Elkington. He has had 31 victories around the world and has played with distinction in seven Ryder Cups. At Brookline in 1999, at The Belfry in 2002, Oakland Hills in 2004 where he holed the winning putt and at the K Club in 2006 when he was again a pillar of strength for the team in difficult on-course conditions. He did not play well enough to make the 2008 side and was passed over by Nick Faldo for a captain's pick. He has twice won the Association of Golf Writers' Golfer of the Year award and has been three times Johnnie Walker Golfer of the Year in Europe. His low round in Europe is 61 achieved at Crans-sur-Sierre in the Canon European Masters in 1996. He has been honoured by Her Majesty the Queen for his record-breaking golfing exploits with an MBE later upgraded to OBE. In 2004 he won in Singapore after being chosen as a captain's pick by Bernhard Langer for the European Ryder Cup side and played inspired golf, holing the winning putt. It was a remarkable performance considering a year of trauma off the course which culminated in divorce from wife Eimear. After a hesitant start to 2005, by which time he had slipped to 83rd in the world rankings, he staged a remarkable comeback in the latter half of the year. He produced his best ever finish in The Open when second behind Tiger Woods at St Andrews, won the Alfred Dunhill Links Championship – his first win since Singapore 2004 – and went on to finish

European No.1 for a remarkable eighth time. In Europe he earned almost £1.9 million and before the end of the year had clawed his way back into the top 15 in the world. In the 2006 European season, he won the Hong Kong Open and was the winner in 2007 of the Smurfit European Open to take his total victories on the European Tour to 31. Later in the year he teamed up with Marc Warren to win the World Cup of Golf at Mission Hills in China. It was Scotland's first win in the 54 year history of the event. In 2008 he struggled on the course to play his best golf but did well in the Open de France. Off the course he married for a second time to Gaynor and moved home to Perthshire in Scotland.

Nagle, Kel (AUS)
Born North Sydney, 21 December 1920
Turned professional 1946
In the dramatic Centenary Open at St Andrews in 1960 he edged out Arnold Palmer, winner already that year of the Masters and US Open, to become champion. It was the finest moment in the illustrious career of a golfer who has been a wonderful ambassador for his country. Along with Peter Thomson he competed nine times in the World Cup winning the event in 1954. He is an honorary member of the Royal and Ancient Golf Club of St Andrews and was inducted into the World Golf Hall of Fame in 2007.

Nelson, Larry (USA)
Born Fort Payne, Alabama, 10 September 1947
Turned professional 1971
Often underrated he learned to play by reading Ben Hogan's The Five Fundamentals of Golf and broke 100 first time out and 70 after just nine months. Active as well these days on course design he has won the Jack Nicklaus award. He has been successful in the US Open (1983 at Oakmont) and two US PGA Championships (in 1981 at the Atlanta Athletic Club and in 1987 after a play-off with Lanny Wadkins at PGA National). Three times a Ryder Cup player he has competed equally successfully as a Senior having won 15 titles. He did not play as a youngster but visited a driving range after completing his military service and was hooked. He was named Senior PGA Tour Player of the Year for finishing top earner and winning six times in 2000. At the end of his third full season on the Senior Tour and after 87 events he had won just short of $10 million.

Newton, Jack (AUS)
Born Sydney, 30 January 1950
Turned professional 1969
Runner-up to Tom Watson after a play-off in the 1975 Open at Carnoustie and runner-up to Seve Ballesteros in the 1980 Masters at Augusta, he was a popular personality on both sides of the Atlantic and in his native Australia only to have his playing career ended prematurely when he walked into the whirling propeller of a plane at Sydney airport. He lost an eye, an arm and had considerable internal injuries but the quick action of a surgeon who happened to be around saved his life. Learned to play one-handed and still competes in pro-ams successfully. Until his retirement in 2000 he was chairman of the Australasian Tour and for many years was Australia's most respected golf commentator.

Nicklaus, Jack (USA)

Born Columbus, Ohio, 21 January 1940
Turned professional 1961

The greatest golfer of the 20th century and possibly of all time depending on what Tiger Woods manages to achieve. After winning two US Amateurs he went on to win 18 professional major titles. His record is phenomenal. He won The Open in 1966, 1970 and 1978, the last two at St Andrews and was runner-up seven times and third on two further occasions. He won the US Open in 1962, 1967, 1972 and 1980 and came second four times. He won five US PGA titles in 1963, 1971, 1973, 1975 and 1980 and was runner-up four times and third on two further occasions and he won six Masters in 1963, 1965, 1966, 1972, 1975 and 1986 when at the age of 46 he became the oldest winner of a Green Jacket. In addition he was runner-up four times and twice third at Augusta. In 1966 he became the first player to successfully defend the Masters (a feat later matched by Nick Faldo in 1990). He won six Australian Opens (1964, 1968, 1971, 1975, 1976 and 1978) and played in six Ryder Cups, captaining two more in 1983 at Palm Beach Gardens when America won narrowly and in 1987 at Muirfield Village where his side were losers for the first time on home soil. Credited with saving the Cup match after suggesting that Continental golfers should be included in the side from 1979. Ten years earlier he conceded the 18-inch putt that Tony Jacklin had for a half at the last when the overall result of the match depended on the result of that game. The match was drawn. After winning 71 times between 1962 and 1984 on the main Tour he won a further ten times on the US Champions Tour. He has won almost every honour you can win in golf including the Byron Nelson, Ben Hogan and Walter Hagen awards. He was the US top money earner in 1964, 1965, 1967, 1971, 1972, 1973, 1975 and 1976 and is an honorary member of the Royal and Ancient Golf Club of St Andrews. Bobby Jones once said of Nicklaus that 'he played a game with which I am not familiar'. With the constant support of his wife Barbara, Nicklaus has been the personification of all that is good about the game. He has designed over 300 courses worldwide. He played in The Open Championship for the last time in 2005. It was his 44th appearance. He regularly captains the US Presidents Cup side against the Rest of the World and in 2007 he was named the most influential person in golf by an American golf magazine.

Nirat, Chapchai (THA)

Born Pitsanulok. Thailand, 5 June 1983
Turned professional 1998

Scored his first European Tour International circuit victory when he won the TCL Classic. He was the 13th Asian to win and was the ninth first-time winner of the 2007 season. He covered the first 36 holes in 127 (61, 66) and led from start to finish in that TCL Classic.

Nobilo, Frank (NZL)

Born Auckland, 14 May 1960   Turned professional 1979

Injury affected his playing career but he remains one of his country's most popular commentators with the

Greg Norman

Golf Channel. After winning regularly in Europe he moved to America where in 1997 he won the Greater Greensboro Classic. He has represented New Zealand in nine World Cup matches between 1982 and 1999, played in 11 Alfred Dunhill Cups and three Presidents Cup sides. In 2009 he will be deputy captain to Greg Norman for the Rest of the World team.

Norman, Greg (AUS)

Born Mount Isa, Queensland, 10 February 1955
Turned professional 1976

Australia's most prolific winner in recent years credited with 77 victories worldwide (as of July 2001) but has slowed down because of injury and trimmed his schedule in recent times. He won The Open in tough conditions at Turnberry in 1986 and again in glorious weather at Royal St George's in 1993 when he fired the lowest winning aggregate of 267 (66, 68, 69, 64). Decided to take up golf after caddying for his mother and abandoned plans to join the Australian Air Force. One of the few golfers to have topped the official money lists on both sides of the Atlantic he received his first winner's cheque in the Westlake Classic on the Australian Tour in 1976. Has the unhappy reputation of having lost Majors in three different types of play-off – the 1987 Masters to Larry Mize and the 1993 US PGA to Paul Azinger in sudden death, The Open to Mark Calcavecchia at Royal Troon in a four-hole play-off in 1989 and the US Open over 18 holes to Fuzzy Zoeller at Winged Foot in 1984. In 1986 he led going into the final round of all four Majors that year and won only The Open. During his career he has set all kinds of money records on the US Tour but is jinxed at the US Masters where he has finished second three times. He has also been runner-up on five other occasions in Majors. Today spends more time in the boardroom looking after his business interests than

Arnold Palmer

playing. Made the news pages in 2007 when he and his wife Laura divorced and in 2008 he married former tennis star Chris Evert who was with him when he played in the 2008 Open Championship at Royal Birkdale as a "warm-up" for the British Senior Open being played the following week at Royal Troon. In fact Norman turned the clock back to finish third behind Padraig Harrington in The Open after leading with nine to play. The following week he was fourth at Royal Troon behind Bruce Vaughan and the next week was fourth again to Eduardo Romero in the US Senior Open.

North, Andy (USA)
Born Thorp, Wisconsin, 9 March 1950
Turned professional 1972
Although this tall American found it difficult to win Tour events he did pick up two US Open titles. His first Championship success came at Cherry Hills in Denver in 1986 when he edged out Dave Stockton and J.C. Snead and the second at Oakland Hills in 1985 when he finished just a shot ahead of Dave Barr, T.C. Chen and Denis Watson who had been penalised a shot during the Championship for waiting longer than the regulation 10 seconds at one hole to see if his ball would drop into the cup. North is now a golf commentator.

O'Connor Sr, Christy (IRL)
Born Galway, 21 December 1924
Turned professional 1946
Never managed to win The Open but came close on three occasions finishing runner-up to Peter Thomson in 1965 and being third on two other occasions. Played in ten Ryder Cup matches between 1955 and 1973 and scored 24 wins in tournament play between 1955 and 1972. Known affectionately as 'Himself' by Irish golfing fans who have long admired his talent with his clubs.

He is a brilliant shot maker. He is an Honorary Member of the PGA European Tour. In 2006, a special dinner was staged in his honour in Dublin by the Irish Food Board on the eve of the Ryder Cup.

O'Connor Jr, Christy (IRL)
Born Galway, 19 August 1948
Turned professional 1965
Nephew of Christy Sr, he finished third in the 1985 Open Championship. A winner on the European and Safari circuits he won the 1999 and 2000 Senior British Open – only the second man to successfully defend. Played in two Ryder Cup matches hitting a career best 2-iron to the last green at The Belfry in 1989 to beat Fred Couples and ensure a drawn match enabling Europe to keep the trophy. His US Champions Tour career was interrupted when he broke a leg in a motorcycle accident.

Olazábal, José María (ESP)
Born Fuenterrabia, 5 February 1966
Turned professional 1985
Twice a winner of the Masters, his second triumph was particularly emotional. He had won in 1994 but had to withdraw from the 1995 Ryder Cup with a foot problem eventually diagnosed as rheumatoid polyarthritis in three joints of the right foot and two of the left. He was out of golf for 18 months but treatment from Munich doctor Hans-Wilhelm Muller-Wohlfahrt helped him back to full fitness after a period when he was house bound and unable to walk. At that point it seemed as if his career was over, but he came back in 1999 to beat Davis Love III by two shots at Augusta. With over 20 victories in Europe and a further seven abroad, the son of a Real Sebastian greenkeeper who took up the game at the age of four has been one of the most popular players in the game. He competed in seven Ryder Cups between 1987 and 2006 frequently forming the most successful Cup partnership with Severiano Ballesteros winning 11 and losing only two of their 15 games together. He was Nick Faldo's backroom assistant at Valhalla in 2008 and will captain the side at some time in the future. Although he was side-lined again through rheumatic injury in 2008 he still believes he can make the side in 2010. He is a former British Boys', Youths' and Amateur champion. His best performances in The Open have been third behind Nick Faldo in the 1992 Championship at Muirfield and behind Tiger Woods in the 2005 event at St Andrews. Olazábal, who played on both sides of the Atlantic in 2005, finished 10th on the European Money list finishing strongly with a 2nd place finish in the Linde German Masters, victory in the Open de Mallorca and a third place behind Paul McGinley in the Volvo Masters of Andalucia. In 2006 he regained his place in the Ryder Cup team and played well with Sergio García in the fourballs, winning twice. He beat Phil Mickelson in the singles.

O'Leary, John (IRL)
Born Dublin, 19 August 1949   Turned professional 1979
After a successful career as a player including victory in the Carrolls Irish Open in 1982 he retired because of injury and now is director of golf at the

Buckinghamshire Club. He is a member of the PGA European Tour Board of Directors.

O'Meara, Mark (USA)

Born Goldsboro, North Carolina, 13 January 1957
Turned professional 1980

A former US Amateur Champion in 1979 Mark was 41 when he won his first Major – the US Masters at Augusta. That week in 1998 he did not three putt once on Augusta's glassy greens. Three months later he won The Open at Royal Birkdale battling with, among others, Tiger Woods with whom he has had a particular friendship. He is the oldest player to win two Majors in the same year and was chosen as PGA Player of the Year that season. When he closed birdie, birdie to win the Masters he joined Arnold Palmer and Art Wall as the only players to do that and became only the fifth player in Masters history to win without leading in the first three rounds. He won his Open championship title in a four hole play-off against Brian Watts. O'Meara played in five Ryder Cups between 1985 and 1999.

Ogilvy, Geoff (AUS)

Born Adelaide, South Australia
Turned professional 1998

He became the first Australian to win a major since Steve Elkington's success in the USPGA Championship in 1992 when he won the US Open at Winged Foot beating Colin Montgomerie, Jim Furyk and Phil Mickelson into second place. In 2007 he was beaten by Henrik Stenson in the final of the Accenture Match Play Championship and finished 14th on the US money list.

Oosterhuis, Peter (ENG)

Born London, 3 May 1948   Turned professional 1968

Twice runner up in The Open Championship in 1974 and 1982, he was also the leading British player in 1975 and 1978. He finished third in the US Masters in 1973, had multiple wins on the European Tour and in Africa and won the Canadian Open on the US Tour in 1981. He played in six Ryder Cups partnering Nick Faldo at Royal Lytham and St Annes in 1977 when Faldo made his début. He was top earner in Europe four years in a row from 1971. Following his retirement from top-line golf he turned to commentary work for the Golf Channel CBS and SKY. His contribution to European professional golf is frequently underrated.

Ozaki, 'Jumbo' Masashi (JPN)

Born Kaiman Town, Tokushima, 24 January 1947
Turned professional 1980

Along with Isao Aoki is Japan's best known player, but unlike Aoki has maintained his base in Japan where he has scored over 80 victories. His only overseas win was the New Zealand Open early in his career. He is a golfing icon in his native country. His two brothers Joe (Naomichi) and Jet also play professionally. In 2005 he was declared bankrupt.

Palmer, Arnold (USA)

Born Latrobe, Pennsylvania, 10 September 1929
Turned professional 1954

Winner of 61 titles on the US Tour between 1956 and 1980, he remains one of the most charismatic players in golf. Although now retired from top line competition he has been credited with starting the golfing boom in the latter part of the 20th century. A former US Amateur champion in 1954, his performances were always exciting to watch and for years he was followed around by his own ever-loyal army of fans ... indeed still is when he tees up in charity or exhibition matches. He won eight Major titles – the 1960 US Open and the 1961 and 1962 Opens at Royal Birkdale in very stormy weather and at Royal Troon where he beat Kel Nagle by six shots and the rest of the field by 13. He won the US Masters in 1958, 1960, 1962 and 1964 but never managed to win the US PGA although he finished second three times. The first player to pass the $1 million mark in earnings he helped Keith Mackenzie, the then secretary of the Royal and Ancient Golf Club of St Andrews, revive The Open and is now a distinguished honorary member of the club. In 1960 having won The Masters and US Open he came to St Andrews for the Centenary Open hoping to match three majors in a season – a record held at the time by Ben Hogan but he was beaten by Australian Kel Nagle. Son of the greenkeeper at Ligonier in the Pennsylvanian mountains – he later bought the club – he has remained a respected golfing idol noted for his remarkable strength and his attacking golf. With Jack Nicklaus and Gary Player he became a member of the modern Big Three – a concept developed by his manager – the late Mark McCormack whose first client he was. Palmer, who had already played his last Open, US Open and USPGA Championships, bowed out of The Masters in 2004. He helped to launch the now hugely successful Golf Channel in the United States and presented the Palmer Cup for annual competition between the best young college golfers in America and Europe. Retired from competitive golf in October 2006 after hitting two balls into the water at the fourth on the first day of the Adminstaff Bureau Classic. Having recovered from prostate cancer he is now concentrating on his other passion – building golf courses.

Pampling, Rod (AUS)

Born Redcliffe, Queensland, 23 September 1969
Turned professional 1994

Made his breakthrough as a winner on the US Tour when he took The International in 2004. His wife Angela is a clinical psychologist. In 2006 he won the Bay Hill Invitational and later in the year partnered Jerry Kelly to success in the Merrill Lynch Shoot Out.

Panton MBE, John (SCO)

Born Pitlochry, Perthshire, 9 October 1916
Turned professional 1935

Former honorary professional at the Royal and Ancient Golf Club of St Andrews he is one of Scotland's best known, admired and loved professionals. He was leading British player in the 1956 Open and beat Sam Snead for the World Senior's title in 1967. He played in three Ryder Cup matches and was 12 times a contestant in the World Cup with the late Eric Brown as his regular partner. He won the Association of Golf Writers' Trophy for his contribution to the game in 1967 and has been honoured with an MBE. Although now in his 90's still manages to hit the odd shot or two. Now lives with his daughter Cathy, herself a former golf professional, and her husband in Sunningdale.

Parnevik, Jesper (SWE)

Born Danderyd, Stockholm, 7 March 1965
Turned professional 1986

Son of a well-known Swedish entertainer he is one of the most extrovert of golfers best known for his habit of wearing a baseball cap with the brim turned up and brightly coloured drain-pipe style trousers. Winner of events on both sides of the Atlantic he plays most of his golf these days in America. He made history in 1995 when he became the first Swede to win in Sweden when he took the Scandinavian Masters at Barsebäck in Malmo. Has twice finished runner-up in The Open. At Turnberry in 1994 he was two ahead but made a bogey at the last and was passed by Nick Price who finished with an eagle and a birdie in the last three holes. He led by two with a round to go in 1998 but shot 73 and finished tied second with Darren Clarke behind Justin Leonard. Played in the 1997 and 1999 Ryder Cup teaming up successfully with Sergio García to win three and a half points in 1999. Was also in the 2002 team and halved with Tiger Woods in the singles. Has had health problems suffering injuries and illness and has resorted at times to unusual remedies including, at one stage, eating volcanic dust to cleanse the system. He saved his PGA Tour card in 2007 when finishing second to Justin Leonard in the Valero Texas Open. Parnevik had fired an opening 61 and only lost at the third hole of a play-off.

Parry Craig (AUS)

Born Sunshine, Victoria, Australia 12 January 1966.
Turned professional 1985.

Australian Parry, winner of 18 titles internationally including the 2002 World Golf Championship NEC Invitational at Sahalee in Washington where he picked up his largest career cheque – $1 million. After 15 years of trying to win in America the chances of him being successful at Salahee seemed slim having missed the four previous cuts. However, the 300–1 long-shot played and putted beautifully covering the last 48 holes without making a bogey to win by four from another Australian Robert Allenby and American Fred Funk. Tiger Woods, trying to win the event for a record fourth-successive year was fourth. Only Gene Sarazen and Walter Hagen have ever won the same four titles in successive years. It was Parry's 236th tournament in the United States and moved him from 118th in the world to 45th. In 2004 he eagled the hardest hole on the US Tour in a play-off with Scott Verplank to win the Ford Championship in Florida.

Pate, Jerry (USA)

Born Macon, Georgia, 16 September 1953
Turned professional 1975

Winner of the 1976 US Open when he hit a 5-iron across water to three feet at the 72nd hole at the Atlanta Athletic Club. He was a member of what is regarded as the strongest ever Ryder Cup side that beat the Europeans at Walton Heath in 1981. Has now retired from golf and commentates occasionally on American television.

Pavin, Corey (USA)

Born Oxnard, California, 26 May 1961
Turned professional 1983

Although not one of golf's longer hitters he battled with powerful Greg Norman to take the 1995 US Open title at Shinnecock Hills. A runner-up in the 1994 US PGA Championship and third in the 1992 US Masters he won 14 times between 1984 and 2006. His only victory in Europe came when he took the German Open title in 1983 while on honeymoon. In 2006, he ended a ten-year winning drought by taking the US Bank Championship in Milwaukee and was one of Tom Lehman's vice-captains at the Ryder Cup at the K Club.

Perry, Kenny (USA)

Born Elizabethtown, Kentucky, 10 August 1960
Turned professional 1982

After winning for times between 1991 and 2001, he had a marvellous 2003 winning the Bank of America Colonial, the Memorial Tournament and the Greater Milwaukee Open between May 25 and July 13. He made his Ryder Cup début at Detroit in 2004 having played in the 1996, 2003 and 2005 Presidents Cups. In 2008 he deliberately by-passed two major Championships in order to ensure he had a place in Paul Azinger's Ryder Cup side for the match against Europe at Valhalla in his home state of Kentucky. He achieved his goal and played with considerable success.

Phadungsil, Chinarat (THA)

Born Bangkok, Thailand   Turned professional 2005

He became the youngest winner on the Asian Tour when he beat Shiv Kapur at the second hole of their play-off for the Double A International title at the St Andrews Hill (2000) GC in Rayong, Thailand. The reigning World Junior champion, he was only 17 years and 5 days when he won and immediately turned professional.

Player, Gary (RSA)

Born Johannesburg, 1 November 1935
Turned professional 1953

One of the modern Big Three with Arnold Palmer and Jack Nicklaus, he has won 176 titles worldwide including nine Majors between 1959 and 1978 and nine senior Majors between 1986 and 1997. His Major wins include three Open Championships in 1959 at Muirfield, 1968 at Carnoustie and 1974 at Royal Lytham and St Annes, three US Masters in 1961, 1974 and 1978, the US Open in 1965 when he completed a Grand Slam of major titles and the US PGA Championship in 1962 and 1972. A life-long fitness fanatic who has won titles in six decades he is one of only five players to have won all four Major titles. Gene Sarazen, Jack Nicklaus, Ben Hogan and Tiger Woods are the others. He considers the greatest thrill of his life was becoming the third man in history to do so. Having never based himself full-time in the US he has travelled more miles than any other golfer during his career – an estimated 13 million by the end of 2008 He entered his first Open in 1955 and failed to qualify but finished fourth in 1956 and played for the last time at Royal

Lytham and St Annes in 2001 when 66. One of his most dramatic major performances came when he went into the last round seven shots behind Hubert Green at the 1974 US Masters, came home in 30 and equalled the then record 64 to win. He scored a record seven wins in the Australian Open, took the South African Open a record 13 times and won the World Match Play title five times coming from seven down after 19 holes in one tie in 1965 to beat Tony Lema at the 37th. Credited as being one of the game's greatest bunker players he remains as enthusiastic about competing today as he did when he first took up the game. In 2006, he received the Payne Stewart award for his services to golf and to charity work, especially in Africa. He has been a regular captain of the Rest of the World team playing in the Presidents Cup but handed over the captaincy to Greg Norman for the 2009 match.

Poulter, Ian (ENG)
Born Hitchen, England, 10 January 1976
Turned professional 1994
Having failed narrowly to make the 2002 European Ryder Cup side, he made the 2004 team and beat Chris Riley in the singles at Oakland Hills and later that year beat Sergio García in a play-off for the Volvo Masters Andalucia at Valderrama. He had won twice in 2003 at Celtic Manor and Copenhagen but had no victories in 2005. A real character with no shortage of talent, he insists he wants to be noticed for the quality of his golf rather than his hair-styles and colourful clothing. Missed out on the 2006 Ryder Cup but returned to winning ways when he won a European Tour event in Madrid in September. This victory moved him into the top 50 in the world. He also kept his card in America. Before the end of the season, he finished joint second to Tiger Woods in the American Express Championship at The Grove. In 2007 he spent most of his time in America where he finished 56th on the money list. He challenged Lee Westwood in the Quinn Direct British Masters but lost out to Westwood's powerful finish. He was successful in 2007 when he won the Dunlop Phoenix Open at Miyazaki in Japan then partnered Justin Rose into fourth place in the Mission Hills World Cup of Golf in China. In 2008 he came second to Padraig Harrington in The Open at Royal Birkdale and was chosen as a captain's pick by Nick Faldo to play in the Ryder Cup match at `Valhalla where he lived up to his captain's faith in him by ending up the week's top scorer from either side.

Price, Phillip (WAL)
Born Pontypridd, 21 October 1966
Turned professional 1989
Winner of the 1994 Portuguese Open he made his Ryder Cup début in 2002 and produced a sterling last day performance when he beat the world No.2 Phil Mickelson 3 and 2 for a vital point. He was named Asprey Golfer of the Month after winning the Smurfit European Open at the K-Club and finishing in the top 10 at the Barclays Scottish Open and The Open at Royal St George's. Played in the United States through 2005 with limited success and, back in Europe in 2006, found it difficult to re-discover the old magic.

Price, Nick (ZIM)
Born Durban, South Africa, 28 January 1957
Turned professional 1977
One of the game's most popular players his greatest season was 1990 when he took six titles including The Open at Turnberry when he beat Jesper Parnevik and the US PGA at Southern Hills when Corey Pavin was second. He had scored his first Major triumph two years earlier when he edged out John Cook, Nick Faldo, Jim Gallagher Jr and Gene Sauers at the US PGA at Bellerive, St Louis. Along with Tiger Woods his record of 15 wins in the 90s was the most by any player. One of only eight players to win consecutive Majors, the others being Ben Hogan, Jack Nicklaus, Arnold Palmer, Lee Trevino, Tom Watson, Tiger Woods and Padraig Harrington. Four times a Presidents Cup player he jointly holds the Augusta National record of 63 with Greg Norman. One of only two players in the 90s to win two Majors in a year, the others being Nick Faldo in 1990 and Mark O'Meara in 1998. Born of English parents but brought up in Zimbabwe he played his early golf with Mark McNulty and Tony Johnstone. Winner of 42 titles, by the end of 2008 he was named recipient in 2002 of the Payne Stewart Award which goes to the player who respects the traditions of the game and works to uphold them. In 2003, ten years after being named PGA Tour Player of the Year, he was inducted into the World Golf Hall of Fame.

Quigley, Dana (USA)
Born Lynnfield Centre, Massachussetts, 14 April 1947
Turned professional 1971
Iron man of the US Champions Tour who played in 278 consecutive events for which he was qualified before missing the 2005 Senior British Open at Royal Aberdeen. He had passed the million dollars mark in prize-money by early June that year and with official money of $2,170,258 he topped the Champions Tour money list at the end of the season.

Quiros, Alvaro (ESP)
Born Cadiz, Spain, 21 January 1983
Turned professional 2004
The Spaniard became the first player in European Tour history to win on his first appearance when he won the 2007 dunhill championship at Leopard Creek in South Africa. In 2008 he won again this time capturing the Portugal masters at Vilamoura.

Rafferty, Ronan (NIR)
Born Newry, Northern Ireland, 13 January 1964
Turned professional 1981
Won the Irish Amateur Championship as a 16 year old in 1980 when he also won the English Amateur Open Stroke Play title, competed in the Eisenhower Trophy and played against Europe in the home internationals. Winner of the British Boys', Irish Youths' and Ulster Youths' titles in 1979, he also played in the senior Irish side against Wales that year. A regular winner on the European tour between 1988 and 1993 he was also victorious in tournaments played in South America, Australia and New Zealand. A wrist injury curtailed his career but he is active on

the corporate golf front and often commentates for Setanata Sports. He has an impressive wine collection.

Ramsay, Richie (SCO)
Born Aberdeen, 15 June 1983
Turned professional 2007
A student at Stirling University he became the first Scot since 1898 and the first British golfer since 1911 to win the US Amateur Championship when he beat John Kelly from St Louis 4 and 2 in the final at Hazeltine. His victory earned him automatic entry into the 2007 US Open and The Open and The Masters at Augusta. A member of the 2005 Great Britain and Ireland Walker Cup team, he has played in the Palmer Cup and was the winner of the 2004 Scottish Open Stroke-play title and the 2005 Irish Open Stroke-play. He has shot a 62 at Murcur in Aberdeenshire. Ramsay turned professional after the 2007 Open, missing the chance to play again in the Walker Cup. He failed to survive the first stage of the European Tour School and competed on the 2008 Challenge Tour winning twice and earning his card for the main Tour in 2009.

Randhawa, Jyoti (IND)
Born New Delhi, 4 May 1972
Turned professional 1994
First Indian winner on the Japanese Tour when he triumphed in the 2003 Suntory Open. Son of an Indian general, he was top earner on the Asian PGA Tour in 2002 despite missing several events after breaking his collarbone in a motorcycle accident. Practices yoga.

Remesy, Jean-François (FRA)
Born Nimes, 5 June 1964   Turned professional 1987
Became the first Frenchman since Jean Garaialde in 1969 to win the Open de France in 2004 then successfully defended the title at Golf National, Versailles when beating Jean Van de Velde in a play-off. Now lives in the Seychelles.

Rivero, José (ESP)
Born Madrid, 20 September 1955
Turned professional 1973
One of only eight Spaniards who have played in the Ryder Cup he was a member of the winning 1985 and 1987 sides. Worked as a caddie but received a grant from the Spanish Federation to pursue his golf career. With José Maria Canizares won the World Cup in 1984 at Olgiata in Italy. Now plays regularly on the Senior Tour.

Roberts, Loren (USA)
Born San Luis Obispo, California, 24 June 1955
Turned professional 1975
An eight times winner on the PGA Tour, he earned the nickname "Boss of the Moss" because of his exceptional putting. He played in two Presidents Cup matches and the 1995 Ryder Cup before joining the Champions Tour. He had chalked up seven wins by the end of 2007 and for the second year running had the low average score on that Tour – an impressive 69.31.

Rocca, Costantino (ITA)
Born Bergamo, 4 December 1956
Turned professional 1981
The first and to date only Italian to play in the Ryder Cup. In the 1999 match at Valderrama he beat Tiger Woods 4 and 2 in a vital singles. Left his job in a polystyrene box making factory to become a club professional and graduated to the tournament scene through Europe's Challenge Tour. In 1995 he fluffed a chip at the final hole in The Open at St Andrews only to hole from 60 feet out of the Valley of Sin to force a play-off against John Daly which he then lost. In recent years he has met with limited success in European Tour events but won several times on the European Senior Tour. In 2007 he finished second on the European Senior Tour money list to Carl Mason.

Rogers, Bill (USA)
Born Waco, Texas, 10 September 1951
Turned professional 1974
US PGA Player of the Year in 1981 when he won The Open at Royal St George's and was runner-up in the US Open. That year he also won the Australian Open but retired from top line competitive golf not long after because he did not enjoy all the travelling. A former Walker Cup player in 1973 he only entered The Open in 1981 at the insistence of Ben Crenshaw. Now a successful club professional and sometime television commentator.

Romero, Eduardo (ARG)
Born Cordoba, Argentina, 12 July 1954
Turned professional 1982
Son of the Cordoba club professional he learned much from former Open champion Roberto de Vicenzo and has inherited his grace and elegance as a competitor. A wonderful ambassador for Argentina he briefly held a US Tour card in 1994 but prefers to play his golf these days on the European Tour where he has won seven times including impressively at the 1999 Canon European Masters where he improved his concentration after studying Indian yoga techniques. Used his own money to sponsor Angel Cabrera with whom he finished second in the 2000 World Cup in Buenos Aries behind Tiger Woods and David Duval. Beat Frederick Andersson in a play-off in 2002 to win the Barclays Scottish Open at Loch Lomond but lost to Padraig Harrington in a play-off for the US$800,000 first prize in the dunhill Links Championship at St Andrews. Continued playing well in 2003 and insists practising yoga helps. Joined the Senior ranks in July 2004 but still plays from time to time on the main European Tour. In 2008 he won the US Senior Open on the Champions Tour.

Rose, Justin (ENG)
Born Johannesburg, South Africa, 30 July 1980
Turned professional 1998
Walker Cup player who shot to attention in the 1998 Open Championship at Royal Birkdale when he finished top amateur and third behind winner Mark O'Meara after holing his third shot at the last on the final day for a closing birdie. Immediately after that Open he turned professional and missed his first 21 half-way cuts before

finding his feet. In 2002 was a multiple winner in Europe and also won in Japan and South Africa. Delighted his father who watched him win the Victor Chandler British Masters just a few weeks before he died of leukemia. He has found winning more difficult in the last four years when he played most of his golf in the United States from his base in Lake Nona but in a strong finish to the 2006 season he shot a 60 in the Funai Classic at Walt Disney World. Overall he finished 47th on the American money list with over $1.6 million. He will continue to play in America but rejoined the European Tour in 2007 in the hope of making the 2008 Ryder Cup side. He jumped from 69th to 51st in the world rankings when he scored his first win in four years in Melbourne at the 2006 MasterCard Masters, which was part of the 2007 European season. Although he played only 12 events on the European Tour in 2007, he won the end of season Volvo Masters at Valderrama to finish No.1 on the European money list and became the highest ranked British golfer in the world ranking, moving into seventh place. Later in the year he partnered Iain Poulter into fourth place in the Mission Hills World Cup of Golf in China. He made his début in the Ryder Cup in the 2008 match at Valhalla.

Saltman, Lloyd (SCO)

Born Edinburgh, 10 September 1985
Turned professional 2007
Had a wonderful 2005 season winning the Brabazon Trophy, the St Andrews Links Championship, taking the silver medal in The Open at St Andrews, being top scorer for Great Britain and Ireland in the Walker Cup in Chicago and helping Scotland win the Home Internationals series for the first time since 2000. Elected to stay amateur throughout 2006 but turned professional after playing in the 2007 Walker Cup at Royal County Down. He now plays on the European Challenge Tour.

Sandelin, Jarmo (SWE)

Born Imatra, Finland, 10 May 1967
Turned professional 1987
Extrovert Swede who made his début in the Ryder Cup at Brookline in 1999 although he did not play until the singles. Has always been a snazzy dresser on course where he is one of the game's longest hitters often in the early days with a 54-inch shafted driver. Five time winner on Tour he met his partner Linda when she asked to caddie for him at a Stockholm pro-am. In 2008 he made sure of keeping his card for 2009 with a sterling performance in the Alfred Dunhill Links Championship.

Schwartzel, Charl (RSA)

Born Johannesburg, 31 August 1984
Turned professional 2002
He was playing off plus 4 when he turned professional after an amateur career that had seen him represent South Africa in the Eisenhower Trophy. In only his third event as a professional he finished joint third in the South African Airways Open and became a winner in his 56th event when he won the dunhill championship in a play-off at Leopard Creek. He was South African No.1 in season 2004–5 and was again No.1 in the 2005–6 season. In the 2007 European Tour season he won the Spanish Open and was winless in 2008 until he again played well in Spain to take the Madrid Masters title.

Scott, Adam (AUS)

Born Adelaide, 16 July 1980   Turned professional 2000
Highly regarded young Australian who was ranked World No. 2 amateur when he turned professional in 2000. Coached in the early days by his father Phil, himself a golf professional, Scott now uses Butch Harmon whom he met while attending the University of Las Vegas. Swings very much like another Harmon client Tiger Woods. He made headlines as an amateur when he fired a 10-under-par 63 at the Lakes in the Greg Norman Holden International in 2000 but has shot 62 in the US Junior Championship at Los Coyotes CC. Made his European Tour card in just eight starts and secured his first Tour win when beating Justin Rose in the 2001 Alfred Dunhill Championship at Houghton in Johannesburg. In 2002 he won at Qatar and at Gleneagles Hotel when he won the Diageo Scottish PGA Championship by ten shots with a 26 under par total. He was 22 under par that week for the par 5 holes. In 2003 he was an impressive winner of the Scandinavian Masters at Barsebäck in Sweden and the Deutsche Bank Championship on the US Tour. In 2005 when he again played in the Presidents Cup, his victories included the Johnnie Walker Classic on the European and Asian Tours, the Singapore Open on the Asian Tour and the Nissan Open on the US Tour. In 2006, he won the Players Championship and Tour Championship in America moving to third in the World rankings in mid November. He also won the Singapore Open again. He continued to play well throughout 2008.

Senden, John (AUS)

Born Brisbane, Queensland, 20 April 1971
Turned professional 1992
After finishing in the top 10 of Australia's three main events in 2005 he played in America in 2006 and was one of seven Australian winners. His success came in the John Deere Classic. He made over $1 million and finished inside the top 50 on the money list. Later won the Australian Open, finishing with two birdies to beat Geoff Ogilvy.

Senior, Peter (AUS)

Born Singapore, 31 July 1959
Turned professional 1978
One of Australia's most likeable and underrated performers who has been a regular winner over the years on the Australian, Japanese and European circuits. Converted to the broomstick putter by Sam Torrance – a move that saved his playing career. A former winner of the Australian Open, Australian PGA and Australian Masters titles he had considerable success off the course when he bought a share in a pawn-broking business. Senior now plays irregularly outside Australia where he is now chairman of the Australasian Tour.

Sheehan, Paul (AUS)

Born Woolagong, NSW, 26 January 1977
Turned professional 1999
A former Australian junior tennis champion who turned to golf and played the Australasian, Asian and Japanese circuits. In 2006 he won the Japanese Open.

Siderowf, Dick (USA)
Born New Britain Connecticut, 1938
Twice a winner of the British Amateur title in 1973 when he beat Peter Moody at Royal Porthcawl and again in 1976 when he had to go to the 37th hole to beat John Davies. He was leading amateur in the 1968 US Open and played in four Walker Cups (1969, 1973, 1975 and 1977) before captaining the winning side in 1979.

Siem, Marcel (GER)
Born Mettmann, 15 July 1980   Turned Professional 2000
Became the latest German to win on the European Tour when he beat Frenchmen Gregory Havret and Raphaël Jaquelin in a play-off at Houghton to win the Dunhill Championship. Represented Germany in the 2000 Eisenhower Trophy. He lost his card in 2007 and had to return to the qualifying school to get it back.

Sigel, Jay (USA)
Born Narbeth, Pennsylvania, 13 November 1943
Turned professional 1993
Winner of the Amateur Championship in 1979 when he beat Scott Hoch 3 and 2 at Hillside, he also won the US Amateur in 1982 and 1983. He was leading amateur in the US Open in 1984 and leading amateur in the US Masters in 1981, 1982 and 1988. He played in nine Walker Cup matches between 1977 and 1993 and has a record 18 points to his credit. Turned professional in order to join the US Senior Tour where he has had several successes.

Simpson, Scott (USA)
Born San Diego, California, 17 September 1955
Turned professional 1977
Winner of the US Open in 1987 at San Francisco's Olympic Club, he was beaten in a play-off for the title four years later at Hazeltine when the late Payne Stewart won the 18-hole play-off.

Singh, Jeev Milkha (IND)
Born Chandigarh, India, 15 December 1971
Turned professional 1993
Stylish swinger, he won his first European event when he took the Volvo China Open in Beijing in 2006 but he scored an even greater triumph when he picked up the first prize at the Volvo Masters at Valderrama later in the year. He is the son of the former Olympian Milkha Singh who won a medal in the 1980 games. In 2007 he played in 30 European Tour events and finished 46th on the money list. In 2008 he won in Austria and came second twice finishing 12th on the money list. His victory in the Barclays Singapore Open meant he became the first player to make US$1 million in one season on the Asian Tour. He topped the money list on that circuit for the second time. His Singapore win also moved him into the top 50 in the world rankings for the second time.

Singh, Vijay (FIJ)
Born Lautoka, 22 February 1963
Turned professional 1982
An international player who began his career in Australasia, he became the first Fijian to win a major when he won the 1998 US PGA Championship at Sahalee but may well be remembered more for his victory in the 2000 US Masters which effectively prevented Tiger Woods winning all four Majors in a year. Tiger went on to win the US Open, Open and US PGA Championship that year and won the Masters the following year to hold all four Major titles at the one time. Introduced to golf by his father, an aeroplane technician, Vijay modelled his swing on that of Tom Weiskopf. Before making the grade on the European Tour where he won the 1992 Volvo German Open by 11 shots he was a club professional in Borneo. He has won tournaments in South Africa, Malaysia, the Ivory Coast, Nigeria, France, Zimbabwe, Morocco, Spain, England, Germany, Sweden, Taiwan and the United States. He ended Ernie Els' run of victories in the World Match Play Championship when he beat him in the final by one hole in 1997 when the South African was going for a fourth successive title. One of the game's most dedicated practisers. In 2003 he won the Phoenix Open, the EDS Byron Nelson Championship, the John Deere Classic and the Funai Classic. With 10 top ten finishes in his last 11 starts, Singh ended Woods' run as top money earner when he finished with a grand total of $7,753,907 – the second largest total in Tour history but was not named Player of the Year. Woods was again the players' choice. In 2004 he had his best ever season and by mid-October was approaching $10 million in year-long winnings on the US Tour, having won eight times, matching Johnnie Miller's eight wins in 1974. Finally edged out Woods for the No.1 spot and earned his third major and second USPGA Championship title with a play-off victory at Whistling Straits. He won four times in 2005 – the Sony Open, the Shell Houston Open, the Buick Open, and the Wachovia Championship – played 30 events on the US Tour but had to be content with second place in the money list to Tiger Woods. In 2006 he made $4.6 million and finished fourth on the US money list and in 2007 he was third with $4.3 million earned. In 2008 he won two events In the Fedex Cup series and finished top of the money list on the PGA Tour for the second time. His late season schedule was disrupted by injury.

Smyth, Des (IRL)
Born Drogheda, Ireland, 12 February 1953
Turned professional 1973
Became the oldest winner on the PGA European Tour when he won the Madeira Island Open in 2001. Smyth was 48 years and 34 days – 20 days older than Neil Coles had been when he won the Sanyo Open in Barcelona in 1982. One of the Tour's most consistent performers – he played 592 events before switching to the European Seniors Tour and qualifying for the US Champions Tour where he has been a winner. Five times Irish National champion he was a member of the winning Irish side in the 1988 Alfred Dunhill Cup. Won twice on US Champions Tour in 2005 and In Abu Dhabi on the European Senior Tour. He was vice-captain for the European team in the 2006 Ryder Cup.

Stadler, Craig (USA)
Born San Diego, California, 2 June 1953
Turned professional 1975
Nicknamed 'The Walrus' because of his moustache and stocky build, he was the winner of the 1982

Masters at Augusta. Winner of 12 titles on the US Tour between 1980 and 1996 he played in two Ryder Cups (1983 and 1985). As an amateur he played in the 1975 Walker Cup two years after winning the US Amateur. He won his first senior major title when he took the Ford Senior Players' Championship just a few weeks after turning 50 then went back to the main tour the following week and won the BC Open against many players half his age. In 2004 he was top earner on the US Champions Tour with over $2 million. His son Kevin is also a professional golfer.

Stadler, Kevin (USA)

Born Reno, Nevada, 5 February 1980
Turned professional 2002
Son of Craig Stadler, the former Masters champion, Kevin won the Abierto Visa de la Republica in Argentina on the European Challenge Tour in 2005 before making his breakthrough on the main tour when taking the first prize in the Johnnie Walker Classic at The Vines in Perth in 2006.

Stenson, Henrik (SWE)

Born Gothenburg, 5 April 1976
Turned professional 1998
Ended a run without success following his initial Tour win in 2001 at the old Benson and Hedges Festival at The Belfry by winning the inaugural Heritage event at Woburn. In 2005 he failed to add to his success but had nine top 10 finishes including three second place finishes and four thirds. He ended the season eighth on the European money list making just over a £1 million in prize-money. He played for Sweden in the 1998 Eisenhower Trophy and made the 2006 Ryder Cup side helping Europe beat America 18½–9½ at the K Club. In the singles he beat Vaughn Taylor. He again played in the 2008 match at Valhalla. Stenson finished the 2006 season in seventh place with €1.7 million earned in prize-money. He played the first part of 2007 in America and was quickly a winner of the Accenture Match-Play Championship. Earlier, he had picked up first prize in the Dubai Desert Classic. Stenson rounded off 2008 in style by winning the World Cup at Mission Hils with Robert Karlsson.

Sterne, Richard (RSA)

Born Pretoria 27 August 1981
Turned professional 2001
Former world junior champion he made history as an amateur in South Africa when becoming the first player to win the junior and senior stroke and matchplay titles. He scored his first European Tour success when he won the Open de Madrid in 2004 and in 2007 won the Celtic Manor Resort event in Wales after having lost a play-off to Anton Haig in the Johnnie Walker Classic in Phuket. In 2008 he won the Jo'burg Open.

Stockton, Dave (USA)

Born San Bernardino, California, 2 November 1941
Turned professional 1964
Winner of two US PGA Championships in 1970 and 1976, he has won more Senior Tour titles (14 as of end July 2001) than he did on the main Tour (11). Captained the American Ryder Cup team

controversially in the infamous 'War on the Shore' match at Kiawah Island in 1991. Chosen by Paul Azinger to assist him at the 2008 Ryder Cup.

Storm, Graeme (ENG)

Born Hartlepool, Durham, 13 March 1978
Turned professional 2000
He won his first European Tour title when he landed the French Open at Golf National. Later played in Nick Faldo's Seve Trophy side which beat Continental Europe at the Heritage Club in Ireland. When he played in The Masters as an amateur his mother caddied for him.

Stranahan, Frank R (USA)

Born Toledo, Ohio, 5 August 1922
Turned professional 1954
One of America's most successful amateurs he won the Amateur championship at Royal St George's in 1948 and 1950. He also won the US Amateur in 1950, the Mexican Amateur in 1946, 1948 and 1951 and the Canadian title in 1947 and 1948. He was also leading amateur in The Open in 1947, 1949, 1950, 1951 and 1953. He played in three Walker Cups in 1947, 1949 and 1951.

Strange, Curtis (USA)

Born Norfolk, Virginia, 20 January 1955
Turned professional 1976
Winner of successive US Opens in 1988 and again in 1989 when he beat Nick Faldo in an 18-hole play-off at The Country Club Brookline after getting up and down from a bunker at the last to tie on 278. Winner of 17 US Tour titles he won at least one event for seven successive years from 1983. Having played in five Ryder Cup matches he captained the US side when the 2001 match was played at The Belfry in 2002. In 2007 Strange, who won 17 PGA Tour events, was inducted into the World Golf Hall of Fame.

Stricker, Steve (USA)

Born Egerton, Wisconsin, 23 February 1967
Turned professional 1990
Started 2001 by winning the $1 million first prize in the Accenture Match Play Championship, one of the World Golf Championship series. In the final he beat Pierre Fulke. Was a member of the winning American Alfred Dunhill Cup side in 1996. In 2007 he won the Barclays Championship … one of the four end of season Fedex Cup events. In 2008 he was a captain's pick in the US Ryder Cup side at Valhalla. When he started on Tour his wife Nikki caddied for him. Her father Dennis Tiziani was his coach.

Suneson, Carl (ESP)

Born Las Palmas, 22 July 1967
Turned professional 1990
He won his first European title when he took the St Omer Open in 2007.

Sutton, Hal (USA)

Born Shreveport, Louisiana, 28 April 1958
Turned professional 1981
Winner of the 1983 US PGA Championship at the Riviera CC in Los Angeles beating Jack Nicklaus into

second place. Played in the 1985 and 1987 Ryder Cup matches and returned to the side in 1999 at Brookline when he beat Darren Clarke 4 and 2 in the singles. He made the 2002 side as well and captained the American team which lost to the Europeans at Oakland Hills in 2004. In 2007 he was given the Payne Stewart award for respecting and upholding the traditions of the game.

Taylor, Vaughn (USA)
Born Roanoke, Virginia, 9 March 1976
Turned professional 1999
Made his Ryder Cup début in the 2006 match at the K Club. Won the Reno-Tahoe Open in 2004 and 2005.

Thomas, Dave (WAL)
Born Newcastle-upon-Tyne, 16 August 1934
Turned professional 1949
Twice runner-up in The Open Championship, Welshman Thomas lost a play-off to Peter Thomson in 1958. And was runner-up to Jack Nicklaus in 1966. He played 11 times in the World Cup for Wales and four times in the Ryder Cup. In all he won 10 tournaments between 1961 and 1969 before retiring to concentrate on golf course design. Along with Peter Alliss designed the Ryder Cup course at The Belfry. He was captain of the Professional Golfers' Association for 2001 – their Centenary year – and for 2002.

Thomson CBE, Peter (AUS)
Born Melbourne, 23 August 1929
Turned professional 1949
He is one of only four players who have won five Open Championships. At the start of the 20th century J.H. Taylor and James Braid won five, and Tom Watson five in eight years from 1975 while Thomson completed his five victories between 1954 and 1965. In one seven-year spell from 1952 Thomson never finished worse than second in the Championship. His run of finishes from 1952 was 2, 2, 1, 1, 1, 2, 1. His fifth victory, arguably his most impressive, came at Royal Birkdale in 1965 when more Americans were in the field. He played only three times in the US Open finishing fourth in 1956. He played in five US Masters with fifth his best finish in 1957. He won three Australian Opens and in Europe had 24 victories between 1954 and 1972. With one of the most fluent and reliable swings he made golf look easy. Instrumental in developing the game throughout Asia, Africa and the Middle East he was ready to retire from golf and pursue a career in Australian politics but he was not elected and turned instead to the US Senior Tour with great success. In 1985 he won nine Senior Tour titles. Has captained three Rest of the World Presidents Cup sides, was elected to the World Golf Hall of Fame in 1988 and is an honorary member of the Royal and Ancient Golf Club of St Andrews. After his retirement from top-line golf he concentrated on his hugely successful golf course design business based in Melbourne completing projects in many countries around the world.

Toms, David (USA)
Born Monroe, LA, 4 January 1967
Turned professional 1989
Most important of his six wins on the US Tour was his first Major success by beating Phil Mickelson into

second place in the 2001 USPGA Championship. Toms shot 66, 65, 65 and 69 for a 265 record winning aggregate at the Atlanta Athletic Club. This is the lowest aggregate in any Major. The previous year he had come joint fourth to Tiger Woods in The Open. Made his Ryder Cup début in 2002 and was the American side's top points scorer with 3½ points. In 2003 he had won twice in the Wachovia Championship and the Fedex St Jude Classic by the end of August. In an injury-hit 2004 he still made the US Ryder Cup side at Oakland Hills and again at the K Club in 2006. In 2005 Toms won the WGC Accenture Match-play title beating Chris DiMarco 6 and 5 in the final.

Torrance OBE, Sam (SCO)
Born Largs, Ayrshire, 24 August 1953
Turned professional 1970
Between 1976 and 1998 he won 21 times on the European Tour in which he has played over 700 events. Captain of the 2002 European Ryder Cup side having previously played in eight matches notably holing the winning putt in 1985 to end a 28-year run of American domination. He was an inspired captain when the 2001 match was played in September 2002. Tied 8 points each, Torrance's men won the singles for only the third time since 1979 to win 15½–12½. His father Bob, who has been his only coach, looks after the swings these days of several others on the European Tour including Paul McGinley who holed the nine foot putt that brought the Ryder Cup back to Europe. He was awarded the MBE in 1996. European Tour officials worked out that in his first 28 years Torrance walked an estimated 14,000 miles and played 15,000 shots earning at the rate of £22 per stroke. In 2003 he retired from full-time competition on the European Tour and made his début in the Charles Church Scottish Seniors at The Roxburghe in late August. In 2004 he qualified for the US Champions Tour but returned to Europe to win the Travis Perkins Senior Masters with a brilliant final round of 61 over the Wentworth Edinburgh course. He played throughout 2005 and 2006 on the European Senior Tour and finished top earner both years. He hit the 700 mark on the main Tour at the Barclays Scottish Open at Loch Lomond. He is often a member of the BBC commentary team working with Peter Alliss and Ken Brown.

Trevino, Lee (USA)
Born Dallas, Texas, 1 December 1939
Turned professional 1961
Twenty times a winner on the US Tour between 1968 and 1981 'Supermex', as he was nicknamed by his peers, hit the headlines in 1971 when he won the US Open beating Jack Nicklaus in a play-off at Merion, the Canadian Open at Montreal and The Open at Royal Birkdale in succession. One of the most extrovert of golfers who followed up his 27 victories on the main Tour with 29 on the US Senior Tour he was entirely self-taught. He won six Majors – The Open in 1971 and 1972 when he chipped in at the 71st hole to end Tony Jacklin's hopes of winning, the US Open in 1968 and 1971 and the US PGA Championship in 1974 and 1984 but he never finished

better than tenth twice in the Masters at Augusta – a course with so many right to left dog-legs that he felt it did not suit his game. In 1975 he was hit by lightning while playing in the Western Open in Chicago and had to undergo back surgery in order to keep competing. He was involved in one of the low scoring matches in the World Match Play Championship with Tony Jacklin in 1972 when he again came out on top. In 2003 he was made an honorary member of the Royal and Ancient Golf Club of St Andrews. He retired from professional competition in 2007.

Van de Velde, Jean (FRA)
Born Mont de Marsan, 29 May 1966
Turned professional 1987
Who ever remembers who came second? Everybody will remember Jean Van de Velde, however, for finishing runner-up after a play-off with eventual winner Paul Lawrie and American Justin Leonard when The Open returned to a somewhat tricked-up Carnoustie in 1999. Playing the last hole he led by three but refused to play safe and paid a severe penalty. He ran up a triple bogey 7 after seeing his approach ricochet off a stand into the rough and his next into the Barry Burn. He appeared to contemplate playing the half-submerged ball when taking off his shoes and socks and wading in but that was never a possibility. Sadly, he was an absentee at the 2007 Open played at the same venue. Took up the game as a youngster when holidaying with his parents in Biarritz. Has scored only one win in Europe (the Roma Masters in 1993) and has returned to the European Tour after a spell in America. Made his Ryder Cup début at Brookline in 1999. Injury prevented him competing regularly in 2003 and 2004 during which time he was part of the BBC Golf Commentary team with, among others, Peter Alliss, Sam Torrance, Mark James and Ken Brown. Came close to winning his national title but lost out in a play-off to fellow Frenchman Jean-François Remesy at Golf National. Created headlines later in the year when he said that if it was to be made easier for women to play in The Open he thought it only fair that he should be allowed to enter the British Women's Open but never followed through on his threat.

Vancsik, Daniel (ARG)
Born Pasadas, Argentina, 7 January 1977
Turned professional 1997
Won his first European Tour title in 2007 in Madeira by seven shots. He was the ninth Argentinian to win on Tour.

Verplank, Scott (USA)
Born Dallas, Texas, 9 July 1964
Turned professional 1986
When he won the Western Open as an amateur in 1985 he was the first to do so since Doug Sanders took the 1956 Canadian Open. Missed most of the 1991 and 1992 seasons because of an elbow injury and the injury also affected his 1996 season. He has diabetes and wears an insulin pump while playing to regulate his medication. Curtis Strange chose him as one of his two picks for the 2002 US Ryder Cup side. In the singles on the final day he beat Lee Westwood 2 and 1. He was again a captain's pick in Tom

Lehman's side in 2006 and again won his singles, this time against Padraig Harrington. Surprisingly he failed to make the 2008 US side.

Wadkins, Lanny (USA)
Born Richmond, Virginia, 5 December 1949
Turned professional 1971
His 21 victories on the US Tour between 1972 and 1992 include the 1977 US PGA Championship, his only Major. He won that after a play-off with Gene Littler at Pebble Beach but lost a play-off for the same title in 1987 to Larry Nelson at Palm Beach Gardens. He was second on two other occasions to Ray Floyd in 1982 and to Lee Trevino in 1984. In other Majors his best finish was third three times in the US Masters (1990, 1991 and 1993), tied second in the US Open (1986) and tied fourth in the 1984 Open at St Andrews. One of the fiercest of competitors he played eight Ryder Cups between 1977 and 1993 winning 20 of his 33 games, but was a losing captain at Oak Hill in 1995.

Walton, Philip (IRL)
Born Dublin, 28 March 1962
Turned professional 1983
Twice a Walker Cup player he is best remembered for two-putting the last to beat Jay Haas by one hole and clinch victory in the 1995 Ryder Cup at Oak Hill. He played in five Alfred Dunhill Cup competitions at St Andrews and was in the winning side in 1990.

Watson, Tom (USA)
Born Kansas City, Missouri, 4 September 1949
Turned professional 1971
Winner of 34 career titles, he won at least three a year on the main US Tour in a six-year spell between 1977 and 1982. He is best known for having won five Open championships in eight years between 1975 and 1983 to match the feat of J.H. Taylor, James Braid and Peter Thomson. When he had a chance to win a sixth Open and tie Harry Vardon's record at St Andrews in 1984 he hit his second close to the wall through the green at the 17th and lost out to Seve Ballesteros. Watson's wins came at Carnoustie in 1975 after a play-off with Jack Newton; a memorable 1977 triumph in which he edged out Jack Nicklaus at Turnberry shooting 65, 65 over the weekend to Nicklaus' 65, 66; 1980 at Muirfield where he beat Lee Trevino; 1982 at Royal Troon where Peter Oosterhuis and Nick Price came second and 1983 when Andy Bean and Hale Irwin were runners-up. Watson also won the 1982 US Open at Pebble Beach chipping in from the rough at the 17th on the final day to go on and beat Nicklaus and two US Masters in 1977 and 1981 but he never did better than tied second in the 1977 US PGA Championship to miss out joining Gene Sarazen, Ben Hogan, Gary Player, Jack Nicklaus and Tiger Woods as a winner of all four Majors. Became the oldest winner on the US Tour when he won the Mastercard Colonial in 1998 nearly 24 years after scoring his first win in the Western Open. He was 48, two years older than the previous oldest Ben Hogan, when he won the same event for the fifth time in 1959. Six times Player of the Year, Tom played in four Ryder Cups and captained the

side to victory in 1993 at The Belfry. Inducted into the World Golf Hall of Fame in 1988, he is an honorary member of the Royal and Ancient Golf Club of St Andrews. Now plays on the US Senior Tour and returned in triumph to Turnberry in 2003 to win the Senior British Open 26 years after his memorable shoot-out for The Open over the same course. Although Nicklaus was again in the field, Watson's main rival this time was rookie European Senior Tour player Carl Mason who let a two shot lead playing the last slip then lost the play-off to the American at the second extra hole. Tom retained the British title in 2005 at Royal Aberdeen and finished second behind Dana Quigley on the US Champions Tour money list. In 2006 he won once on the Champions Tour but had two victories in 2007 including The Senior Open for a third time at Muirfield where he had won The Open 27 years earlier. By the end of 2007 he had played 106 Champions Tour events and made $10,051,484 in prize-money which compares with the $10,004,299 he made from 591 events on the main US circuit. He continued to play throughout 2008 but failed in his bid to win the Senior British Open at Royal Troon where he had won The Open in 1984. He has won The Open and Senior Open titles at both Muirfield and Carnoustie. Late in 2008 he had a hip operation.

Warren, Marc (SCO)
Born Rutherglen, near Glasgow, 1 April 1981
Turned professional 2002
Marc, who holed the winning putt in Great Britain and Ireland's Walker Cup victory over America in 2001, had two play-off victories on the European Challenge Tour in 2005 – in the Ireland Ryder Cup Challenge and the Rolex Trophy. His joint second place finish behind Carl Sunesson in the end of season Apulia San Domenica Grand Final saw him finish leader of the Challenge Tour. In 2006 Warren, who is coached by Bob Torrance, scored his first victory on the main Tour when he beat Robert Karlsson in a play-off for the Eurocard Masters at Barsebäck. At the start of the 2007 season he finished fifth behind winner Yang Yong-eun, Tiger Woods, Michael Campbell and Retief Goosen in the HSBC Champions event. He scored his second win in the Johnnie Walker Championship at Gleneagles Hotel by beating Simon Wakefield in a play-off. He was a wild card pick for the GB&I team in the Seve Trophy match and partnered Colin Montgomerie to a first-ever success for Scotland in the World Cup of Golf at Mission Hills in China. He had a quiet 2008 and left his long-time coach Bob Torrance.

Webster, Steve (ENG)
Born Nuneaton, England, 17 January 1975
Turned professional 1995
After five second place finishes on Tour twice in Spain, twice in South Africa and in Germany he finally hit the jackpot in Italy in 2005 when he won the Telecom Italia Open at Castello di Tolcinaco in Milan. He scored a second emotional success in the Open de Portugal at Vilamoura in 2007. He won the silver medal as leading amateur in The Open Championship at St Andrews in 2005.

Weekley, Boo (USA)
Born Milton, Florida 23 July 1973
Turned professional 1997
One of six players who made their débuts in the 2008 Ryder Cup at Valhalla. He played well and enjoyed every minute of the American success. Nicknamed Boo after Yogi Bear's sidekick, he made $500,000 on the Nationwide Tour before joining the main Tour. Studied at the Abraham Baldwin Agricultural College and won the Verizon Open in 2007 and 2008.

Weir, Mike (CAN)
Born Sarnia, Ontario, 12 May 1970
Turned professional 1992
A left-hander, he was the first Canadian to play in the Presidents Cup when he made the side in 2000 and the first from his country to win a World Golf Championship event when he took the American Express Championship at Valderrama in 2000. Wrote to Jack Nicklaus as a 13-year-old to enquire whether or not he should switch from playing golf left-handed to right-handed and was told not to switch. In 1997 he led the averages on the Canadian Tour with a score of 69.29 but his greatest triumph came when he became only the second left-hander to win a major when he played beautifully and putted outstandingly to beat Len Mattiace for a Masters Green Jacket. Weir had to hole from 15 feet at the last to take the tournament into extra holes but won his first major title when Mattiace failed to par the tenth – the first extra hole. He has now assumed hero status in Canada.

Weiskopf, Tom (USA)
Born Massillon, Ohio, 9 November 1942
Turned professional 1964
Winner of only one Major – the 1973 Open Championship at Royal Troon, he lived in the shadow of Jack Nicklaus throughout his competitive career. He was runner-up in the 1976 US Open to Jerry Pate and was twice third in 1973 and 1977. His best finish in the US PGA Championship was third in 1975 – the year he had to be content for the fourth time with second place at the US Masters. He had been runner-up for a Green Jacket in 1969, 1972 and 1974 but played perhaps his best golf ever in 1975 only to be pipped at the post by Nicklaus. With 22 wins to his name he now plays the US Senior Tour with a curtailed schedule because of his course design work for which he and his original partner Jay Morrish have received much praise. One of their designs is Loch Lomond, venue of the revived Scottish Open. Played in just two Ryder Cup matches giving up a place in the team one year in order to go Bighorn sheep hunting in Alaska.

Westwood, Lee (ENG)
Born Worksop, Nottinghamshire, 24 April 1973
Turned professional 1993
A former British Youths' champion who missed out on Walker Cup honours, he quickly made the grade in the professional ranks. In 2000 he ended the seven-year reign of Colin Montgomerie by taking the top spot in the Volvo Order of Merit. He was six-time winner that year in Europe and beat Montgomerie at the second extra hole of the Cisco World Match Play final at Wentworth.

Among his overseas victories are three successful Taiheiyo Masters titles in Japan, the Australian Open in 1997 when he beat Greg Norman in a play-off and the Freeport McDermott Classic at New Orleans on the US Tour. He has won titles on every major circuit. He is married to Laurae Coltart, sister of fellow professional Andrew Coltart. Lee has been a member of the last five Ryder Cup teams and in the 2002 match won 3 points out of 4. In 2004 he again produced some of his best golf, picking up points as Europe swept to a record win at Oakland Hills and more than justified being chosen as a captain's pick for the 2006 match in which he teamed up successfully with close friend Darren Clarke and won his singles against Chris DiMarco. He again made the 2008 side at Valhalla where he equalled Arnold Palmer's record run of 12 unbeaten matches in the event. Although he admits he had thoughts of giving up tournament play he persevered and won again for the first time in three years when he was successful in the BMW International at Nord Eichenried, Munich. A month later he picked up first prize in the Dunhill Links Championship bringing his earnings in five weeks to over $1 million. He credits David Leadbetter for sorting out his game. He had five top 10 finishes in 2005 in Europe and finished 27th on the money list. In 2006 he finished 24th in Europe. In 2007 Westwood won the Andalucian Open and the Quinn Direct British Masters at the Belfry but lost a play-off to Phil Mickelson in the first event on the 2008 European Tour schedule in Shanghai. Westwood again proved his consistency in 2008 with 13 top ten finishes, including four as runner-up, in Europe. He was third in the US Open and third on the European Tour money list.

Wetterich, Brett (USA)
Born Cincinnati, Ohio, 9 August 1973
Turned professional 1994
Was one of the four rookies in Tom Lehman's side which lost 18½–9½ to the Europeans at the K Club in 2006. During the year, he had won the EDS Byron Nelson Classic at Cottonwood Valley.

Wi, Charlie (KOR)
Born 3 January 1972   Turned professional 1995
The popular Korean-American won his first European Tour title when he won the jointly-promoted Asian/European event at Kuala Lumpur in 2006. His success in the Maybank Malaysian Open was well deserved.

Wilson, Oliver (ENG)
Born Mansfield, 14 September 1980
Turned professional 2003
Although he did not win in 2008 he did finish second three times including in a play-off to Miguel Angel Jimenez in the BMW PGA Championship at Wentworth. He played his way into the 2008 Ryder Cup side at Valhalla and impressed as a rookie, Having attended Augusta College he now lives much of the time in America. He was a member of the winning Great Britain and Ireland Walker Cup side in 2003.

Wirachant, Thawarn (THA)
Born Bangkok, Thailand, 28 December 1966
Turned professional 1987
He earned a full year's exemption on the European Tour when he won the Enjoy Jakarta Standard Chartered Indonesian Open – a joint venture between the Asian and European Tours. It was his sixth win on the Asian Tour which he joined 10 years earlier. Wirachant is best known for his unorthodox swing which works effectively for him. He is a former Thai Amateur champion.

Wolstenholme, Gary (ENG)
Born Egham, Surrey, 21 August 1960
Turned professional 2008
The 1991 Amateur champion he has been one of the most regular title winners in the past 11 years and regained the Amateur title in 2003 when beating Raphael De Sousa, the first Swiss to reach the final, by 6 and 5. At 42 he was the oldest player in the field and not one of the longest hitters on a course measuring 7126 yards. In 1991 he had beaten Bob May 8 and 6 in the final. A week after his triumph at Troon he won the Scottish StrokePlay title. Son of former professional the late Guy Wolstenholme, he won the 1995 and 1996 British Mid-Amateur Championship, the Chinese Amateur title in 1993, the Emirates Amateur in 1995 and the Finnish Amateur in 1996. He also won the 2002 Australian Amateur Championship title and the 2002 and 2003 South African strokeplay title. He was England County champion of champions in 1994 and 1996 and he highlighted his appearances in Walker Cup golf by beating Tiger Woods by one hole in the first day singles of the 1995 match at Royal Porthcawl. Great Britain and Ireland won that year but Woods gained his revenge on Wolstenholme by beating him on the second day. He was named 2003 Ping English Golfer of the Year. He made his sixth appearance in the Walker Cup in Chicago in 2005 and became Great Britain and Ireland's record points scorer with 10 from 19 ties when he won his singles match. He failed to make the 2007 Walker Cup side but was at Royal County Down as a member of the BBC commentating team. At the age of 48 he turned professional but failed to earn his Tour card at the Tour School.

Woods, Eldrick 'Tiger' (USA)
Born Cypress, California, 30 December 1975
Turned professional 1996
Tiger Woods has now won 14 majors following his remarkable success in the 2008 US Open at Torrey Pines in which he beat Riocco Mediate after an extra 18 holes and two play-off holes despite being in pain from a badly damaged knee. He ignored doctor's advice to play despite having hardly recovered from an earlier knee operation and suffering from cruciate ligament problems because he wanted so much to play at Torrey Pines where he had first competed as a youngster. Following his win he required further surgery and did not play again in 2008 and was an absentee at the start of the 2009 season. Woods has had an unprecedented career since becoming a professional golfer in the late summer of 1996. He has won 82 tournaments, 62 of those on the PGA Tour, including the 1997, 2001, 2002, and 2005 Masters Tournaments, 1999, 2000, 2006, and 2007 PGA Championships, 2000, 2002 and 2008 U.S. Open Championships, and 2000 2005, and 2006 Open Championships. With his second Masters victory in 2001, he became the first ever to hold all four

Tiger Woods

professional major championships at the same time. He is the career victories leader among active players on the PGA Tour and is the career money list leader. Up until November 2007 Woods had played in 266 events as a pro, of which he had won 86 worldwide (64 on the PGA Tour), finished second 35 times and third on 24 occasions. In all he has had 192 top-10 finishes and has finished top money earner on the US Tour eight times between 1997 and 2007. As a professional he has missed only four half-way cuts – the 1997 Bell Canadian Open, the 2005 EDS Byron Nelson Classic, the 2005 Funai Classic and the 2006 US Open. He has had to withdraw from events on only two occasions. He holds the record for consecutive cuts made on the PGA Tour – 142 stretching from the 1998 Buick Invitational to the 2005 Wachovia Championship. In comparison with Jack Nicklaus he had more wins before his 25th birthday than Jack – 24 to 12 – and won 46 times between the age of 20 and 29 – 16 more times than Nicklaus. By the end of 2007 he had won tournaments in the USA, Thailand, Germany, Spain, Scotland, Canada, Ireland, Japan, the UAE, England, Argentina and Malaysia. Woods won 11 tournaments in 2000, nine on the PGA Tour, one on the PGA European Tour and the PGA Grand Slam. In addition, Woods and David Duval won the World Cup team title for the United States. In 1999 he had eight PGA Tour victories and 11 worldwide and his nine PGA Tour wins in 2000 equalled the fifth highest total and were the most since Sam Snead won 11 in 1950. His 68.17 scoring average that year beat Byron Nelson's previous record of 68.33 in 1945. That year he matched the record of Ben Hogan in 1953 in winning

three professional major championships in the same year. In winning The Open in 2000, Woods became the youngest to complete the career Grand Slam of professional major championships and only the fifth ever to do so, following Hogan, Gene Sarazen, Gary Player and Jack Nicklaus. Tiger also was the youngest Masters champion ever, at the age of 21 years, three months and 14 days, and was the first major championship winner of African or Asian heritage. Woods holds or shares the record for the low score in relation to par in each of the four major championships. His records are 270 (18 under par) in the Masters, 272 (12 under par) in the US Open, 269 (19 under par) in The Open, and he shares the record of 270 (18 under par) with Bob May in the 2000 PGA Championship, which Tiger won by one stroke in a three-hole play-off. The US Open and Masters victories came by record margins, 15 strokes and 12 strokes respectively, and the US Open triumph swept aside the 13-stroke major championship standard which had stood for 138 years, established by Old Tom Morris in the 1862 Open. The record margin for the US Open had been 11 strokes by Willie Smith in 1899. In the Masters, Woods broke the record margin of nine strokes set by Nicklaus in 1965. Tiger won The Open by eight strokes, the largest margin since J.H. Taylor in 1913. He has lost only six times when leading at the 54-hole stage and never when in that position in a major. As an amateur, Woods compiled one of the most impressive records in golf history, winning six USGA national cham-pionships, plus the NCAA title, before turning professional on August 27, 1996. He concluded his amateur career by winning an unprecedented third consecutive US Amateur title, finishing with a record 18 consecutive match-play victories. Prior to his Amateur Championship successes he had had three successive victories in the US Junior Amateur Championship. He was the first to win that title more than once, he was the youngest ever winner in 1991 when only 15. He was the youngest ever to win the US Amateur in 1994 when 18. With his US Open victory, Tiger became the first ever to hold that title along with the US Junior Amateur and US Amateur titles. The son of the late Earl Woods, a retired lieutenant-colonel in the US Army, and Kultida, a native of Thailand, Woods was nicknamed Tiger after a Vietnamese soldier and friend of his father, Vuong Dang Phong, to whom his father had also given that nickname. Born on December 30, 1975, Woods grew up in Cypress, California, 35 miles southeast of Los Angeles. He took an interest in golf, at age 6 months, watching as his father hit golf balls into a net and imitating his swing. He appeared on the Mike Douglas Show at age 2, putting with Bob Hope. He shot 48 for nine holes at age 3 and was featured in Golf Digest at age 5. Tiger played in his first professional tournament – the Nissan Los Angeles Open in 1992 at age 16. He entered Stanford University in 1994 and in two years he won 10 collegiate events including the NCAA title. Among his other amateur victories was the 1994 Western Amateur. He was in the winning United States side in the 1994 World Amateur Team Championships in France – and was a member of the 1995 Walker Cup side which lost to Great Britain and Ireland in Wales. He played his first major

© Phil Sheldon Golf Picture Library

championship in 1995, making the 36-hole cuts in the Masters and The Open. He played in three more major championships in 1996, making the cuts in two of them That year, Tiger posted a 281 total to tie the record for an amateur in The Open, and his 66 in the second round equalled the lowest ever by an amateur. He tied for 22nd place. The week after winning his third US Amateur title, Woods played his first tournament as a professional in the Greater Milwaukee Open. It was one of only seven events in 1996 for him to finish among the top 125 money winners but he did it. He achieved No.1 on the Official World Golf Ranking for the most rapid progression ever to that position. On June 15, 1997, in his 42nd week as a professional, Woods became the youngest-ever No.1 golfer at age 21 years, 24 weeks. The previous youngest was Bernhard Langer, age 29 years, 31 weeks in 1986. His dominance in 1999 was such that Woods won 52 per cent of all the prize money he could have won. He won 81.7 per cent more than the runner-up, the highest margin since Byron Nelson in 1945 (87.2 per cent) and Hogan in 1946 (85 per cent). He chose Dubai as the location to build his first course. Tiger is married to Elin and has a daughter Samantha. In 2007 he won the US Tour Golfer of the Year for the ninth time in 11 years. With his victory in the 2008 US Open he became only the second player to have won all four majors at least three times. The other player to have achieved this is, of course, Jack Nicklaus.

Woosnam MBE, Ian (WAL)
Born Oswestry, Shropshire, 2 March 1958
Turned professional 1976

Highlight of his career was winning the Green Jacket at the Masters in 1991 after a last day battle with Spaniard José Maria Olazábal who went on to win in 1994 and again in 1999. Teamed up very successfully with Nick Faldo in Ryder Cup golf and was in four winning teams in 1985, 1987, 1995 and 1997. Was vice-captain in 2001 to Sam Torrance. He has scored 28 European Tour victories and twice won the World Match Play Championship in 1987 when he beat Sandy Lyle, with whom he used to play boys' golf in Shropshire, in 1990 when his opponent was Zimbabwean Mark McNulty and in 2001 when he beat Retief Goosen, then US Open Champion, Colin Montgomerie, Lee Westwood and then Padraig Harrington in the final. In 1989 he lost a low-scoring final to Nick Faldo on the last green. His lowest round was a 60 he returned in the 1990 Monte Carlo Open at Mont Agel. Partnered by David Llewellyn he won the World Cup of Golf in 1987 beating Scotland's Sam Torrance and Sandy Lyle in a play-off. Honoured with an MBE from Her Majesty the Queen he now lives with his family in Jersey. Finished joint third in the 2001 Open at Lytham after having been penalised two shots for discovering on the

second tee he had 15 clubs (one over the limit) in his bag. He lost out for the captaincy of the Ryder Cup in 2004 to Bernhard Langer but captained the side to victory in the 2006 match at the K Club just outside Dublin. Illness and injury curtailed his competitive appearances in 2007. He now plays on the European Senior Tour and when he topped the money list in 2008 he became the first player to be No. 1 on the European Tour and the European Seniors Tour.

Yang, Y-e (KOR)
Born Seoul, Korea, 15 January 1972
Turned professional 1996

Winner of four events on the Japanese Tour between 2004 and 2006 and with wins on the Korean circuit and Asian Tour on which he played from 1998 to 2003, he shot to prominence when he beat World No. 1 Tiger Woods into second place in the $5m dollar HSBC Champions tournament at Sheshan in Shanghai in 2006. Yong-eun, who won a first prize cheque of $833,300, by far his largest, not only beat Woods but had former US Open champions Michael Campbell (NZL) and Retief Goosen (RSA) behind him in joint third spot. It was only his 17th European Tour event. The HSBC event is the richest in Asia.

Yeh, Wei-tze (TPE)
Born Taiwan, 20 February 1973
Turned professional 1994

Fisherman's son who became the third Asia golfer after "Mr Lu" and Isao Aoki to win on the European Tour when he won the 2000 Benson and Hedges Malaysian Open. In 2003 he won the ANA Open on the Japanese Tour.

Zhang, Lian-Wei (CHN)
Born Shenzhen, 2 May 1965
Turned professional 1994

Leading Chinese player whose victory in the 2003 Caltex Singapore Open when he edged out Ernie Els was the first by a Chinese golfer on Tour. Initially he trained as a javelin thrower before turning to golf. Self-taught he was also the first Asian golfer to win on the Canadian Tour but remains a stalwart on the Asian circuit.

Zoeller, Fuzzy (USA)
Born New Albany, Indiana, 11 November 1951
Turned professional 1973

Winner of the US Masters in 1979 after a play-off with Ed Sneed (who had dropped shots at the last three holes in regulation play) and Tom Watson and the US Open in 1984 at Winged Foot after an 18-hole play-off with Greg Norman. A regular winner on the US Tour between 1979 and 1980, he played on three Ryder Cups in 1979, 1983 and 1985.

Who's Who in Golf – Women

Alfredsson, H.	Garvey, P.	Laing, A.	Ochoa, L.	Shin, JY
Andrew, K.	Geddes, J.	Lawrence, J.	Olamoto, A.	Sörenstam, A.
Bailey, D.	Gustafson, S.	Lee-Smith, J.	Otto, J.	Steinhauer, S.
Bisgood, J.	Harris, M.	Lopez, N.	Pak, S.R.	Stephenson, J.
Bonallack, A.	Haynie, S.	De Lorenzi, M.-L.	Panton-Lewis, C.	Streit, M.S.
Bradley, P.	Higuchi, H.	Lunn, K.	Park, G.	Suggs, L.
Butler, I.	Hjörth, M.	McIntire, B.	Park, I.	Stupples, K.
Caponi, D.	Hudson, R.	McKay, M.	Pepper, D.	Thomas, V.
Carner, J.A.	Hurst, P.	McKenna, M.	Petterson, S.	Tinning, I.
Cavalleri, S.	Inkster, J.	Mallon, M.	Prado, C.	Tseng, Y.
Coughlan, C.	Irvin, A.	Mann, C.	Rawls, B.	Varangot, B.
Creamer, P.	Jackson, B.	Massey, D.	Reid, D.	Walker, M.
Daniel. B.	Jang, J.	Matthew, C.	Robertson, B.	Webb, K.
Davidson, A.	Johnson, T.	Meunier-Lebouc,	Sanchez, A.B.	Whitworth, K.
Davies, L.	Kerr, C.	P.	Sander, A.	Wie, M.
Dibnah, C.	Kim, B.	Miyazato, A	Saunders, V.	Wright, J.
Dowling, C.	King, B.	Moodie, J.	Segard, P.	Wright, M.
Duggleby, E.	Klein, E.	Neumann, L.	Semple Thompson,	Wright, P.
Fudoh, Y.	Koch, K.	Nicholas, A.	C.	
Garrett, M.	Kuehne, K.	Nilsmark, C.	Sheehan, P.	

Alfredsson, Helen (SWE)
Born Gothenburg, 9 April 1965
Turned professional 1989
After earning Rookie of the Year on the 1989 European Tour she won the 1992 Ladies' British Open. Two years later she was Gatorade Rookie of the Year on the American LPGA Tour. She has competed in seven Solheim Cup matches and has won titles in Europe, America, Japan and Australia and captained the 2007 European Solheim Cup side which lost to America. She won the Evian Masters in 2008.

Andrew, Kim (née Rostron) (ENG)
Born 12 February 1974
After taking the English and Scottish Ladies' stroke play titles in 1997 she won the Ladies' British Open Amateur a year later. She played in the 1998 and 2000 Curtis Cup matches.

Bailey MBE, Mrs Diane (Frearson née Robb) (ENG)
Born Wolverhampton, 31 August 1943
After playing in the 1962 and 1972 Curtis Cup matches she captained the side in 1984, 1986 and 1988. In 1984 at Muirfield the Great Britain and Ireland side lost narrowly to the Americans but she led the side to a first ever victory on American soil at Prairie Dunes in Kansas two years later. The result was a convincing 13–5. She was in charge again when the GB&I side held on to the Cup two years later this time by 11–7 at Royal St George's.

Bisgood CBE, Jeanne (ENG)
Born Richmond, Surrey, 11 August 1923
Three times English Ladies champion in 1951, 1953 and 1957. Having played in three Curtis Cups she captained the side in 1970. Between 1952 and 1955 she won the Swedish, Italian, German, Portuguese and Norwegian Ladies titles.

Bonallack, Lady (née Angela Ward) (ENG)
Born Birchington, Kent, 7 April 1937
Wife of Sir Michael Bonallack OBE she played in six Curtis Cup matches. She was leading amateur in the 1975 and 1976 Colgate European Opens, won two English Ladies' titles and had victories, too, in Swedish, German, Scandinavian and Portuguese Championships.

Bradley, Pat (USA)
Born Westford, Massachusetts, 24 March 1951
Turned professional 1974
Winner of four US LPGA majors – the Nabisco Championship, the US Women's Open, the LPGA Championship and the du Maurier Classic, she won 31 times on the American circuit. An outstanding skier and ski instructor as well, she started playing golf when she was 11. Every time she won her mother would ring a bell on the porch of the family home whatever the time of day. The bell is now in the World Golf Hall of Fame. She played in four Solheim Cup sides and captained the team in 2000 at Loch Lomond. Inducted into the LPGA Hall of Fame in 1991 she was Rolex Player of the Year in 1986 and 1991.

Butler, Ita (née Burke) (IRL)
Born Nenagh, County Tipperary
Having played in the Curtis Cup in 1966, she captained the side that beat the Americans by 5 points at Killarney thirty years later.

Caponi, Donna (USA)
Born Detroit, Michigan, 29 January 1945
Turned professional 1965
Twice winner of the US Women's Open in 1969 and 1970 she collected 24 titles between 1969 and 1981 on the LPGA Tour. Winner of the 1975 Colgate European Open at Sunningdale, she is now a respected commentator/analyst for The Golf Channel in Orlando.

Carner, Jo Anne (née Gunderson) (USA)
Born Kirkland, Washington, 4 April 1939
Turned professional 1970
Had five victories in the US Ladies' Amateur Championship (1957, 1960, 1962, 1966 and 1968) before turning professional and winning the 1971 and 1976 US Women's Open. She remains the last amateur to win on the LPGA Tour after having taken the 1969 Burdine's Invitational. Between 1970 and 1985 scored 42 victories on the LPGA Tour and was Rolex Player of the Year in 1974, 1981 and 1982. She was inducted into the LPGA Hall of Fame in 1982 and the World Golf Hall of Fame in 1985. She won the Bobby Jones award in 1981 and the Mickey Wright award in 1974 and 1982.

Cavalleri, Silvia (ITA)
Born Milan, 10 October 1972
Turned professional 1997
Became the first Italian to win the US Amateur when she beat Robin Burke 5 and 4 at Brae Burn in the final. She was five times Italian National Junior champion and won the British Girls' title in 1990 with a 5 and 4 success over E. Valera at Penrith. As a professional her best finish to date is tied second in the 2000 Ladies' Italian Open.

Creamer, Paula (USA)
Born Pleasanton, California, 5 August 1986
Turned professional 2005
The youngest and first amateur to win the LPGA qualifying school in 2004. As an amateur she was top ranked American junior in 2003 and 2004 winning 19 national titles. She became a winner on the LPGA Tour in her ninth start after turning professional when she won the Sybase Classic. Later in 2005 she won the Evian Masters and played in the winning Solheim Cup side. She began playing golf at the age of 10. In 2006 she had 13 top 10 finishes in 26 starts but did not win. She won twice in 2007 and continued to play well in 2008.

Coughlan, Claire (IRL)
Born Cork, 11 March 1980
Made her début in the 2004 Curtis Cup and won three points.

Daniel, Beth (USA)
Born Charleston, South Carolina, 14 October 1956
Turned professional 1978
A member of the LPGA Hall of Fame she won 32 times between 1979 and 1995 including the 1990 US LPGA Championship. She was Rolex Player of the Year in 1980, 1990 and 1994. Before turning professional she won the US Women's Amateur title in 1975 and 1977 and played in the 1976 and 1978

Laura Davies

Curtis Cup teams. She has played in eight Solheim Cup competitions since it began in 1990 and was named as vice-captain to Betsy King at the 2007 match in Sweden. She will be captain of the US side in 2009 at Rich Harvest Farm in Sugar Grove, Illinois. During her career she has won 33 LPGA events and has won $8.7m in prize money. She works as an analyst on the Golf Channel.

Davidson, Alison (née Rose) (SCO)
Born Stirling, Scotland, 18 June 1968
Twice a Curtis Cup player in 1996 and 1998. She won the Ladies' British Open Amateur in 1997.

Davies CBE, Laura (ENG)
Born 10 October 1963
Turned professional 1985
Record-breaking performer who has won over 60 events worldwide including the US and British Women's Opens. For six days in 1987 she held both titles having won the American event before joining the US Tour. Was a founder member of the Women's Tour in Europe where she has won a record 33 times. Still holds the record for the number of birdies in a round – 11 which she scored in the 1987 Open de France Feminin. Her 16-shot victory, by a margin of five shots, in the 1995 Guardian Irish Holidays Open at St Margaret's remains the biggest in European Tour history. Her 267 totals in the 1988 Biarritz Ladies' Open and the 1995 Guardian Irish Holidays Open are the lowest on Tour and have been matched only by Julie Inkster in

© Phil Sheldon Golf Picture Library

the 2002 Evian Masters. Other major victories include the LPGA Championship twice and the du Maurier Championship. In 1999 she became the first European Tour player to pass through the £1 million in prize-money earnings and finished European No. 1 that year for a record fifth time. She was No.1 again in 2004. The 1996 Rolex Player of the Year in America, she has won almost $5.5 million in US prize-money. Originally honoured with an MBE by Her Majesty the Queen in 1988, she became a CBE in 2000. Enjoys all sports including soccer (she supports Liverpool FC). Among other awards she has received during her career have been the Association of Golf Writers' Trophy for her contribution to European golf in 1994 and the American version in 1994 and 1996 for her performances on the US Tour. In 1994 she became the first golfer to score victories on five different Tours – European, American, Australasian, Japanese and Asian in one calendar year. As an amateur she played for Surrey and was a Curtis Cup player in 1984. She has competed in all ten Solheim Cup matches. In 2000 was recognised by the LPGA in their top 50 players' and teachers' honours list. Laura proved how strong a competitor she still is when she took the No.1 spot on the women's tour in Europe for a seventh time in 2006. Although she only won once she had six second-place finishes and ended the year with a total of €471,727 from the 11 events she played. By the end of 2006 she had stretched her winning record to 67 titles and in 2007 made it 68 with victory in the Austrian Open a week after missing the cut in the Scottish Open, the first time she had missed in 23 years competing in events organised solely by the Ladies European Tour. She has failed only once – in 2005 – to win an event. When she successfully defended the Uniqua Ladies' Golf Open in 2008 she took her victory tally to 69.

Dibnah, Corinne (AUS)
Born Brisbane, 29 July 1962
Turned professional 1984
A former Australian and New Zealand amateur champion, she joined the European Tour after turning professional and won 13 times between 1986 and 1994. A pupil of Greg Norman's first coach Charlie Earp, she was Europe's top earner in 1991.

Dowling, Clare (née Hourihane) (IRL)
Born 18 February 1958
Won three Irish Ladies' Championships in a row – 1983, 1984 and 1985 and won the title again in 1987 and 1991. She won the 1986 British Ladies' Stroke play amateur title. Two years earlier she had made the first of five playing appearances in the Curtis Cup before acting as non-playing captain in 2000.

Duggelby, Emma (ENG)
Born Fulford, York, 5 October 1971
Talented English golfer who won the British Ladies' Open Amateur Championship in 1994 and the English Ladies in 2000 when she made her Curtis Cup début. She also played in the 2002 and 2004 matches, winning three points out of four in 2004.

Fudoh, Yuri (JPN)
Born Kumamoto, 14 October 1976
Turned professional 1996
A multiple winner on the Japanese Tour who won her first Japanese event in 2003 when she won the Japan LPGA Championship. She has won 20 events on the Japanese Tour and her winnings in 2000 of ¥120,443,924 was a record.

Garrett, Maureen (née Ruttle) (ENG)
Born 22 August 1922
President of the Ladies' Golf Union from 1982 to 1985, she captained the Curtis Cup (1960) and Vagliano Trophy (1961) teams. In 1983 won the Bobby Jones award presented annually by the United States Golf Association to a person who emulates Jones' spirit, personal qualities and attitude to the game and its players.

Garvey, Philomena (IRL)
Born Drogheda, Co Louth, 27 April 1927
Turned professional 1964 but later reinstated
Winner of the Irish Ladies' title 15 times between 1946 and 1970 and six times a Curtis Cup player between 1948 and 1960 she remains one of Ireland's most successful players. In 1957 she won the British Ladies' Open Amateur title.

Geddes, Jane (USA)
Born Huntingdon, New York, 5 February 1960
Turned professional 1983
In 1986 she was the 13th player on the LPGA Tour to score her first victory at the US Women's Open. A year later she won the US LPGA title and took the British Women's title in 1989. She won 11 times on the US Tour between 1986 and 1994.

Gustafson, Sophie (SWe)
Born Saro, 27 December 1973
Turned professional 1992
Winner of the 2000 Weetabix Women's British Open she had studied marketing, economics and law before turning to professional golf. Credits Seve Ballesteros and Laura Davies as the two players most influencing her career. Her first European victory was the 1996 Swiss Open and her first on the USLPGA Tour was the Chick-fil-A Charity Cup in 2000. She played in all the Solheim Cup sides since 1998.

Harris, Marley (née Spearman) (ENG)
Born January 11 1988
Superb ambassador for golf in the 1950s and 1960s whose exuberance and joie de vivre is legendary. Three times a Curtis Cup player she won the British Ladies in 1961 and again in 1962. She was English champion in 1964. In 1962 was awarded the Association of Golf Writers' Trophy for her services to golf.

Haynie, Sandra (USA)
Born Fort Worth, Texas, 4 June 1943
Turned professional 1961
Twice a winner of the US Open (1965 and 1974) she won 42 times between 1962 and 1982 on the US LPGA Tour. She was elected to the LPGA Hall of Fame in 1977.

Higuchi, Hisako "Chako" (JPN)

Born Saitama Prefecture, Japan, 13 October 1945
Turned professional 1967

A charter member and star of the Japan LPGA Tour she won 72 victories worldwide during her career. In 2003 she was elected to the World Golf Hall of Fame.

Hjörth, Maria (SWE)

Born Falun, 10 October 1973
Turned professional 1996

After an excellent amateur career when she won titles in Finland, Norway and Spain (where she won the prestigious Sherry Cup), she attended Stirling University in Scotland on a golf bursary and graduated with a BA honours degree in English before turning professional. In 2002, 2003, 2005 and 2007 she played in the Solheim Cup. She was a winner again on the LPGA Tour in 2007 and in 2008 the Swede was beaten in a play-off for the McDonald's LPGA Championship by Tseng Yani. In Europe she successfully defended the KSPoker.com English Open.

Hudson, Rebecca (ENG)

Born Doncaster, Yorkshire, 13 June 1979
Turned professional 2002

A member of the 1998, 2000 and 2002 Curtis Cup teams Rebecca is one of the most gifted of younger players. In 2000 she won both the British Match Play and Stroke Play titles, the Scottish and English Stroke play Championships and the Spanish Women's Open. In addition she made the birdie that ensured Great Britain and Ireland won a medal in the World Team Championship for the Espirito Santo Trophy in Berlin in 2000.

Hurst, Pat (USA)

Born San Leandro, California, 23 May 1969
Turned professional 1995

Had eight top 10 finishes in 2006 and nearly won the US Women's Open. An 18-hole play-off was required and she lost out to Annika Sörenstam.

Inkster, Juli (USA)

Born Santa Cruz, California, 24 June 1960
Turned professional 1983

Winner of two majors in 1984 (the Nabisco Championship and the du Maurier) she also had a double Major year in 1999 when she won the US Women's Open and the LPGA Championship which she won for a second time in 2000. In 2002 she won the US Women's Open for a second time. In all she has won seven major titles. In her amateur career she became the first player since 1934 to win the US Women's amateur title three years in a row (1980, 81, 82). Only four other women and one man (Tiger Woods) have successfully defended their national titles twice in a row. Coached for a time by the late London-based Leslie King at Harrods Store. She is a regular in the Solheim Cup competition. The 46 year old won again (the Safeway Classic) in 2006 and had 12 top 10 finishes in 20 starts on the LPGA Tour. Her career earnings have now gone through $12 million.

Hisako Higuchi

© Phil Sheldon Golf Picture Library

Irvin, Ann (ENG)

Born 11 April 1943

Winner of the British Ladies' title in 1973, she played in four Curtis Cup matches between 1962 and 1976. She was Daks Woman Golfer of the Year in 1968 and 1969 and has been active in administration at junior and county level.

Jackson, Bridget (ENG)

Born Birmingham, 10 July 1936

A former President of the Ladies' Golf Union she played in three Curtis Cup matches and captained the Vagliano Trophy side twice after having played four times. Although the best she managed in the British Championship was runner-up in 1964 she did win the English, German and Canadian titles.

Jang, Jeong (KOR)

Born Daejeon, Korea, 11 June 1980
Turned professional 1999

She scored her breakthrough win on the LPGA Tour when winning the Weetabix Women's British Open at Royal Birkdale – a joint venture with the Ladies European Tour. She led from start to finish. As an amateur she won the Korean Women's Open in 1997 and the following year was Korean Women's Amateur champion. Just 5ft tall, she started playing golf at age 13 and has been influenced throughout her career by her father. She has made over $2.75 million in prize money since 2000.

Johnson, Trish (ENG)

Born Bristol, 17 January 1966
Turned professional 1987

Another stalwart of the Women's Tour in Europe who learned the game at windy Westward Ho. Regular

Nancy Lopez

King, Betsy (USA)
Born Reading, Pennsylvania, 13 August 1955
Turned professional 1977
Another stalwart of the LPGA Tour in America she has won 34 times between 1984 and 2001. Winner of the British Open in 1985 she has also won the US Open in 1989 and 1990, the Nabisco Championship three times in 1987, 1990 and 1997 and the LPGA Championship in 1990. She never managed to win the du Maurier event although finishing in the top six on nine occasions. Three times Rolex Player of the Year in 1984, 1989 and 1993 she was elected to the LPGA Hall of Fame in 1995.

Klein, Emilee (USA)
Born Santa Monica, California, 11 June 1974
Turned professional 1994
The former Curtis Cup player who played in the 1994 match scored her biggest triumph as a professional when winning the Weetabix British Women's Open at Woburn in 1996.

Koch, Carin (SWE)
Born Kungalv, Sweden, 2 February 1971
Turned professional 1992
She has been playing golf since she was nine and in the 2000 and 2002 Solheim Cup matches was unbeaten. In 2000 she won three points out of three and in 2002 she won 2½ points out of three. She also played in the 2003 and 2005 matches.

Kuehne, Kelli (USA)
Born Dallas, Texas, 11 May 1977
Turned professional 1998
Having won the US Women's Amateur Championship in 1995 she successfully defended the title the following year when she also won the British Women's title – the first player to win both in the same year. She was also the first player to follow up her win in the US Junior Girls' Championship in 1994 with victory in the US Women's event the following year. Her brother Hank is also a professional.

winner on Tour both in Europe and America, she scored two and a half points out of four in Europe's dramatic Solheim Cup win over the Americans at Loch Lomond in 2000. She has played in eight Solheim Cup matches. She was European No.1 earner in 1990. A loyal supporter of Arsenal FC she regularly attends games at The Emirates Stadium.

Kerr, Cristie (USA)
Born Florida, 1977
Turned professional 1997
She scored her first major title victory when she won the 2007 US Women's Open at Pine Needles, North Carolina, which was her favourite course. Her official career earnings in the LPGA Tour amount to over $7.8m. In 2006 she had 19 top 10 finishes on the LPGA Tour. In 1996 she played in the Curtis Cup and was low amateur in the US Women's Open. She launched the Birdies for Breast Cancer programme. In 2008 she won the Safeway Classic.

Kim, Birdie (KOR)
Born Ik-San, Korea, 26 August 1981
Turned professional 2000
She became the 14th player in the history of the LPGA Tour to score her first win at the US Women's Open and she did it dramatically holing a bunker shot at the last to beat amateurs Brittany Lang and Morgan Pressel by two shots at Cherry Hills, Colorado. A silver medallist at the 1998 Asian Games she won 19 events as an amateur before joining the US Futures Tour in 2001.

Laing, Anne (SCO)
Born Alexandria, Dunbartonshire, 14 March 1975
Winner of three Scottish Championships in 1996, 2003 and 2004. She made her début in the Curtis Cup in 2004 having played in the Vagliano Trophy in 2003.

Lawrence, Joan (SCO)
Born Kinghorn, Fife, 20 April 1930
After a competitive career in which she three times won the Scottish championship and played in the 1964 Curtis Cup, she has played her part in golf administration. She had two four-year spells as an LGU selector, is treasurer of the Scottish Ladies' Golf Association and has also served on the LGU executive.

Lee-Smith, Jennifer (ENG)
Born Newcastle-upon-Tyne, 2 December 1948
Turned professional 1977
After winning the Ladies' British Open as an amateur in 1976 was named Daks Woman Golfer of the Year. She

© Phil Sheldon Golf Picture Library

played twice in the Curtis Cup before turning professional and winning nine times in a six year run from 1979. For a time she ran her own driving range in southern England and is back living in Kent again after having spent time in Florida.

Lopez, Nancy (née Knight) (USA)
Born Torrance, California, 6 January 1957
Turned professional 1977

One of the game's bubbliest personalities and impressive performers who took her first title – the New Mexico Women's Amateur title at age 12. Between 1978 and 1995 she won 48 times on the LPGA Tour and was Rolex Player of the Year on four occasions (1978, 79, 85 and 88). In 1978, her rookie year, she won nine titles including a record five in a row. That year she also lost two play-offs and remains the only player to have won the Rookie of the Year, Player of the Year and Vare Trophy (scoring average) in the same season. A year later she won eight tournaments. Three times a winner of the LPGA Championship in 1978, 1985 and 1989 she has never managed to win the US Open although she was runner-up in 1975 as an amateur, in 1977, 1989 and most recently 1997 when she lost out to Britain's Alison Nicholas. She retired from competitive golf and in 2002 was awarded the PGA's First Lady in Golf award for the contribution she has made to the game. In 2005 she captained the winning American Solheim Cup side at Crooked Stick. She started playing competitively again on a limited basis in 2007.

De Lorenzi, Marie-Laure (FRA)
Born Biarritz, 21 January 1961
Turned professional 1986

The stylish French golfer won 20 titles in Europe between 1987 and 1997 setting a record in 1988 when she won eight times but for family reasons never spent time on the US Tour. Jointly holds the record for 54 holes on the European Tour with her 201 total in the 1995 Dutch Open.

Lunn, Karen (AUS)
Born Sydney, 21 March 1966
Turned professional 1985

A former top amateur she won the British Women's Open in 1993 at Woburn following the success in the European Ladies' Open earlier in the year by her younger sister Mardi. She is the chairperson of the Ladies' European Tour.

McKay, Mhairi (SCO)
Born Glasgow 18 April 1975
Turned professional 1997

Former British Girls' Champion (1992 and 1993) she has played in the Vagliano Trophy and Curtis Cup. She was an All-American when studying at Stanford University and made her first appearance in the Solheim Cup at Barsebäck, Sweden, in 2003.

McKenna, Mary (IRL)
Born Dublin, 29 April 1949

Winner of the British Ladies' Amateur Stroke play title in 1979 and eight times Irish champion between 1969

and 1989. One of Ireland's most successful golfers she played in nine Curtis Cup matches and nine Vagliano Trophy matches between 1969 and 1987. She captained the Vagliano team in 1995. Three times a member of the Great Britain and Ireland Espirito Santo Trophy side she went on to captain the team in 1986. She was Daks Woman Golfer of the Year in 1979.

McIntire, Barbara (USA)
Born Toledo, Ohio, 1935

One of America's best amateurs who finished runner-up in the 1956 US Women's Open to Kathy Cornelius at Northland Duluth. Winner of the US Women's Amateur title in 1959 and 1964 she also won the British Amateur title in 1960. She played in six Curtis Cups between 1958 and 1962.

Mallon, Meg (USA)
Born Natwick, Maryland, 14 April 1963
Turned professional 1986

Winner of the 1991 US Women's Open, 1991 Mazda LPGA Championship, the 2000 du Maurier Classic and 11 other events between 1991 and 2002. In 2004 she won the US Women's Open for the second time. She holed the winning putt in the 2005 Solheim Cup.

Mann, Carole (USA)
Born Buffalo, New York, 3 February 1940
Turned professional 1960

Winner of 38 events on the LPGA Tour in her 22 years on Tour. A former president of the LPGA she was a key figure in the founding of the Tour and received the prestigious Babe Zaharias award. In 1964 she won the Western Open, then a Major, and in 1965 the US Women's Open but in 1968 she had a then record 23 rounds in the 60s, won 11 times and won the scoring averages prize with a score of 72.04. Enjoys a hugely successful corporate career within golf. In 2008 she was awarded the prestigious First Lady of Golf award from the PGA of America.

Massey, Debbie (USA)
Born Grosse Pointe, Michigan, 5 November 1950
Turned professional 1977

Best known for winning the British Women's Open in 1980 and 1981.

Matthew, Catriona (SCO)
Born Edinburgh, 25 August 1969
Turned professional 1995

Former Scottish Girls Under-21 and Amateur champion, Catriona also won the British Amateur in 1993. She played in the 1990, 1992 and 1994 Curtis Cup matches and made her début in the Solheim Cup at Barsebäck in 2003 and had the honour of holing the winning putt. She performed impressively throughout, showing considerable coolness under pressure. She was also a member of the 2005 and 2007 European teams. Now plays on both sides of the Atlantic. With Janice Moodie came second to Sweden's Annika Sörenstam and Liselotte Neumann in the 2006 Women's World Cup of Golf. In 2007 made the cut in all four women's majors and finished tied second in the Kraft Nabisco Championship. Her best US finish in

2008 was a second place in the Sybase Classic. Towards the end of 2008 she had amassed $5.5 million in prize-money.

Meunier-Lebouc, Patricia (FRA)
Born Dijon, 16 November 1972
Turned professional 1993
French amateur champion in 1992, she has been a regular winner on Europe's Evian Tour. She played in the 2000 Solheim Cup and again last year at Barsebäck. In 2003 she won the Kraft-Nabisco Championship on the US Tour.

Miyazato, Ai (JPN)
Born Okinawa, Japan, 1985
Turned professional 2005
A multiple winner on the Japanese women's circuit in her rookie year as a pro, she is being talked off as Japanese women's golf's Tiger Woods. Among her victories last year – the Japan Open, the Elleair Ladies, the Vernal Ladies and the Hisako Higuchi IDC Otsukakagu Ladies.

Moodie, Janice (SCO)
Born Glasgow, 31 May 1973
Turned professional 1997
The 1992 Scottish Women's Stroke play champion played in two winning Curtis Cup teams and earned All American honours at San José State University where she graduated with a degree in psychology. She plays both the European and American Tours and in 2000 finished 17th in America and ninth in Europe. Started playing at age 11 and has been helped considerably by Cawder professional Ken Stevely. In the 2000 Solheim Cup she won three out of four points but was controversially left out of the 2002 team despite having won the Asahi Ryokuken International on the LPGA tour. She was reinstated by captain Catrin Nilsmark for the 2003 match at Barsebäck in Sweden. She teamed up well with Catriona Matthew and also won her singles. She played well in the USA in 2004 without managing to win. With Catriona Matthew, came second to Sweden's Annika Sörenstam and Liselotte Neumann in the 2006 Women's World Cup of Golf at Sun City in South Africa.

Neumann, Liselotte (SWE)
Born Finspang, 20 May 1966
Turned professional 1985
Having won the US Women's Open in 1988 she won the Weetabix British Women's title in 1990 to become one of six players to complete the Transatlantic double. The others are Laura Davies, Alison Nicholas, Jane Geddes, Betsy King and Patty Sheehan. The 1988 Rookie of the Year on the LPGA Tour she played in the first six Solheim Cup matches but was a surprising omission from the team in 2005 when she had one of her best years on the US Tour. With Annika Sörenstam won the 2006 World Cup of Golf in South Africa.

Nicholas MBE, Alison (ENG)
Born Gibraltar, 6 February 1978
In Solheim Cup golf had a successful partnership with Laura Davies. In addition they have both won the British and US Open Championship. Alison's first win

on the European Tour came in the 1987 Weetabix British Open and she added the US Open ten years later after battling with Nancy Lopez who was trying to win her national title for the first time. Alison is a former winner of the Association of Golf Writers' Golfer of the Year award and has been honoured with an MBE. She announced her retirement from top-line competition in 2004. She will captain the European Solheim Cup side in 2009 in America.

Nilsmark, Catrin (SWE)
Born Gothenburg, Sweden, 28 Aug 1967
Turned professional 1987
Holed the winning putt in Europe's Solheim Cup victory in 1992. Her early career was affected by whiplash injury after a car crash. Used to hold a private pilot's licence but now rides Harley Davidson motorcycles. She captained the European team to victory in the 2003 Solheim Cup matches at Barsebäck in Sweden and captained the team again at Crooked Stick when America regained the trophy.

Ochoa, Lorena (MEX)
Born Guadalajara, 15 November 1981
Turned professional 2003
She won her first major when she took the Ricoh British Women's Open played for the first time over the Old Course at St Andrews. She had become the fastest player to reach $3million in prize-money on the LPGA Tour in 2006. She did not win a major that season, losing the Kraft Nabisco to Karrie Webb in a play-off at Palm Springs, but she topped the money list for the first time and was Player of the Year. In 2006 she had six victories, five second place finishes, two thirds, two fourths and a fifth earning more than $2.5million and did even better in 2007 when she won eight times and pocketed $4.36 million in prize-money. In 2008 she won another major – the Kraft Nabisco. From the beginning of March to April 20 she won five times and had two more late season victories by the end of September.

Okamoto, Ayako (JPN)
Born Hiroshima, 12 April 1951
Turned professional 1976
Although she won the British Women's Open in 1984 she managed only a runner-up spot in the US Women's Open and US LPGA Championships despite finishing in the top 20 28 times and missing the cut only four times. In the LPGA Championships she finished second or third five times in six years from 1986. She scored 17 victories in the USA between 1982 and 1992, won the 1990 German Open and was Japanese Women's champion in 1993 and 1997. The LPGA Tour's Player of the Year in 1987, she was inducted into the World Golf Hall of Fame in 2005.

Otto, Julie (née Wade) (ENG)
Born Ipswich, Suffolk, 10 March 1967
Secretary of the Ladies' Golf Union from 1996 to 2000 she was one of the most successful competitors in both individual and team golf. Among the many titles she won were the English Stroke Play in 1987 and 1993, the British Ladies' Stroke Play in 1993 and the Scottish

Stroke Play in 1991 and 1993. She shared Britain's Golfer of the Year award in 1993 and won it again in 1995 on her own. She played in five Curtis Cup matches including the victories at Royal Liverpool in 1992 and Killarney in 1996 and the drawn match in 1994 at Chattanooga.

Pak, Se Ri (KOR)
Born Daejeon, 28 September 1977
Turned professional 1996
In 1998 she was awarded the Order of Merit by the South Korean government – the highest honour given to an athlete – for having won two Majors in her rookie year on the US Tour. She won the McDonald's LPGA Championship matching Liselotte Neumann in making a major her first tour success. When she won the US Women's Open later that year after an 18-hole play-off followed by two extra holes of sudden death against amateur Jenny Chuasiriporn, she became the youngest golfer to take that title. By the middle of 2001 she had won 12 events on the US tour including the Weetabix Women's British Open at Sunningdale – an event included on the US Tour as well as the European Circuit for the first time. In 2002 she was again a multiple winner on the US Tour adding to her majors by winning the McDonald's LPGA Championship. As an amateur in Korea she won 30 titles and became the first lady professional to make the cut in a men's professional event for 58 years when she played four rounds in a Korean Tour event. In 2006 she returned to the major winner's circle when she beat Karrie Webb in a play off for the McDonald's LPGA Championship. It was her fifth major victory but her first since 2002. In 2007 she was inducted into the World Golf Hall of Fame.

Panton-Lewis, Cathy (SCO)
Born Bridge of Allan, Stirlingshire, 14 June 1955
Turned professional 1978
A former Ladies' British Open Amateur Champion in 1976 when she was named Scottish Sportswoman of the year. She notched up 13 victories as a professional on the European tour between 1979 and 1988. Daughter of John Panton, MBE.

Park, Grace (KOR)
Born Seoul, Korea, 6 March 1979
Turned professional 1999
After having lost a sudden-death play-off to Annika Sörenstam at the McDonald's LPGA Championship in 2003 she did win her first major in 2004 when she was successful in the Nabisco Dinah Shore at Mission Hills in Palm Springs. She was a graduate of the Futures Tour where in 1999 she won five of the ten events . Before turning professional she attended Arizona State University and in 1998 became the first player since Patty Berg in 1931 to win the US Amateur, Western Amateur and Trans-Amateur titles in the same year. She won 55 national junior, college and amateur titles and tied eighth as an amateur in the 1999 US Women's Open.

Park, Inbee (KOR)
Born South Korea, 1988
Turned professional 2006
Started playing golf at the age of 10 and won nine events on the American Junior Golf Association circuit. She

Catherine Prado

© Phil Sheldon Golf Picture Library

earned her LPGA card in 2006 and won her first major – the 2008 US Women's Open at Interlachen by four shots from Sweden's Helen Alfredsson.

Pepper (Mochrie, Scarinzi), Dottie (USA)
Born Saratoga Springs, Florida, 17 August 1965
Turned professional 1987
Winner of 17 events (through to July 2001) on the US LPGA Tour including two majors. A fierce competitor she took the Nabisco Dinah Shore title in 1992 and again in 1999. She played in all Solheim Cup matches to 2000. In 2004 she announced her retirement from the US LPGA Tour.

Petterson, Suzann (NOR)
Born Oslo, April 7 1981
Turned professional 2000
Five times Norwegian Amateur champion, Suzann was World Amateur champion in 2000. She won the French Open in 2001 and made her Solheim Cup début in the 2003 match at Barsebäck. One of the best performers on the week and was unbeaten going into the singles. She also played in the 2005 and 2007 matches and scored her first major success when she won the McDonald's LPGA Championship in 2007 and finished second to Lorena Ochoa in the LPGA money list.

Prado, Catherine (née Lacoste) (FRA)

Born Paris 27 June 1945

The only amateur golfer ever to win the US Women's Open she won the title at Hot Springs, Virginia in 1967. She was also the first non-American to take the title and the youngest. Two years later she won both the US and British Amateur titles. She was a four times winner of her own French Championship in 1967, 1969, 1970 and 1972 and won the Spanish title in 1969, 1972 and 1976. She comes from a well-known French sporting family.

Rawls, Betsy (USA)

Born Spartanburg, South Carolina, 4 May 1928
Turned professional 1951

Winner of the 1951, 1953, 1957 and 1960 US Women's Open and the US LPGA Championship in 1959 and 1969 as well as two Western Opens when the Western Open was a Major, she scored 55 victories on the LPGA Tour between 1951 and 1972. One of the best shot makers in women's golf who was noted for her game around and on the greens.

Reid MBE, Dale (SCO)

Born Ladybank, Fife, 20 March 1959
Turned professional 1979

Scored 21 wins in her professional career between 1980 and 1991 and was so successful in leading Europe's Solheim Cup side to victory against the Americans at Loch Lomond in 2000 that she was again captain in 2002 when the Americans won. Following the team's success in the 2000 Solheim Cup she received an MBE.

Robertson MBE, Belle (SCO)

Born Southend, Argyll, 11 April 1936

One of Scotland's most talented amateur golfers who was Scottish Sportswoman of the Year in 1968, 1971, 1978 and 1981. She was Woman Golfer of the Year in 1971, 1981 and 1985. A former Ladies' British Open Amateur Champion and six times Scottish Ladies' Champion, she competed in nine Curtis Cups acting as non-playing captain in 1974 and 1976.

Sanchez, Ana Belen (ESP)

Born Malaga, 16 February 1976
Turned professional 1997

As an amateur she was a member of the winning Spanish side in the 1995 European Team Championship. Now plays on the Ladies European Tour and made her Solheim Cup début at Barsebäck in 2003.

Sander, Anne (Welts, Decker, née Quast) (USA)

Born Marysville, 1938

A three times winner of the US Ladies' title in 1958, 1961 and 1963, she also won the British Ladies' title in 1980. She made eight appearances in the Curtis Cup stretching from 1958 to 1990. Only Carole Semple Thompson has played more often, having played ten times.

Saunders, Vivien (ENG)

Born Sutton, Surrey, 24 November 1946
Turned professional 1969

Founder of the Women's Professional Golfers' Association (European Tour) in 1978 and chairman for the first two years. In 1969 she was the first European golfer to qualify for the LPGA Tour in America. No longer playing top-line professional golf, she is keen to be reinstated as an amateur but not finding that easy.

Segard, Mme Patrick (de St Saveur, née Lally Vagliano) (FRA)

Former chairperson of the Women's Committee of the World Amateur Golf Council holding the post from 1964 to 1972. A four times French champion (1948, 50, 51 and 52) she also won the British (1950), Swiss (1949 and 1965), Luxembourg (1949), Italian (1949 and 1951) and Spanish (1951) amateur titles. She represented France from 1937 to 1939, from 1947 to 1965 and again in 1970.

Semple Thompson, Carol (USA)

Born 1950

Winner of six USLPGA titles including the US Ladies' title in 1973 and the British Ladies in 1974. She has played in 12 Curtis Cups between 1974 and 2002 and holed the 27-foot winning putt in the 2002 match. At 53 she is the oldest US Curtis Cup Player. She captained the side in the 2008 match played over the Old Course at St Andrews for the first time. In 2003 she was named winner of the Bob Jones award for sportsmanship and in 2005 received the PGA of America Lady of the Year trophy.

Sheehan, Patty (USA)

Born Middlebury, Vermont, 27 October 1956
Turned professional 1980

Scored 35 victories between 1981 and 1996 including six Majors – the LPGA Championship in 1983, 1984 and 1994, the US Women's Open in 1993 and 1994 and the Nabisco Championship in 1996. As an amateur she won all her four games in the 1980 Curtis Cup. She is a member of the LPGA Hall of Fame. Captained the 2003 US Solheim Cup side.

Shin, Ji Yai (KOR)

Born Chonnam, Korea, 28 April 1988
Turned professional 2006

She played 18 events on the Korean LPGA Tour in 2007 and won nine times, winning twice as much as her nearest rival with a record total of $725,000. She was Korea's Player of the Year – a title she retained in 2008 when she became the first player to win all three events that comprise that circuit's Grand Slam. She had broken almost every record set on the Korean Tour by Se Ri Pak before the start of the 2008 season. Last year she won her first major – the Ricoh British Women's Open at Sunningdale – and went on to win two more times on the LPGA Tour taking the Mizuno Classic and the end-of-season ADT Championship in which she beat Karrie Webb by a shot to win US $1 million. She was the first non-member to win three times on that Tour. In addition she had three other top 10 finishes, made

US$1.77 million and was playing that Tour full time this year instead of in Japan as she had previously planned. In all in 2008 she won 11 times – the three on the LPGA Tour, seven times in Korea and once in Japan.

Sörenstam, Annika (SWE)
Born Stockholm, 9 October 1970
Turned professional 1992
Winner of the US Open in 1995 and 1996 she and Karrie Webb of Australia have battled for the headlines on the USLPGA Tour over the past few years. A prolific winner of titles in America. She won four in a row in early summer 2000 as she and Webb battled again for the No. 1 spot in 2001. Sörenstam was the No. 1 earner in 1995, 1997 and 1998, Webb in 1996, 1999 and 2000. At the Standard Register Ping event she became the first golfer to shoot 59 on the LPGA Tour. Her second round score 59 included 13 birdies, 11 of them in her first 12 holes. Her 36-hole total of 124 beat the record set by Webb the previous season by three. Her 54-hole score of 193 matched the record set by Karrie Webb and her 72-hole total of 261 which gave her victory by three shots from Se Ri Pak matched the low total on Tour set by Se Ri Pak in 1998. Sörenstam's 27-under-par winning score was a new record for the Tour beating the 26-under-par score Webb returned in the Australian Ladies' Masters in 1999. Her sister Charlotta also plays on the LPGA and Evian Tours. Before turning professional she finished runner-up in the 1992 US Women's Championship. Sörenstam continued on her winning way in 2002 when her victories included another major – the Kraft Nabisco Championship. By the end of August she had won six times in the US and once more in Europe. By the beginning of October she had won nine times on the 2002 LPGA Tour and collected her 40th LPGA title. Only four players have won more than 9 events in one LPGA season. By October she had won $2.5 million world wide. In 2003 she was awarded the Golf Writers award in Britain for the golfer who had done most for European golf. In 2004 she quickly passed through the 50 mark in titles won in America. Before the middle of October her tally was 54 she had passed the $2 million mark in American Tour earnings for the year. In 2004 she added another major to her list of achievements winning the McDonald's LPGA Championship. She remains the dominant force in women's professional golf. When Annika won the Mizuno Classic in Japan she became the first player for 34 years to win 10 titles in a season. In 2003 she took up the challenge of playing on the US Men's Tour teeing up in a blaze of publicity in the Colonial event in Texas but missed the half-way cut. She won her fifth Major when she took the McDonald's LPGA Championship in June and when she won the Weetabix British Women's Open at Royal Lytham and St Annes she completed a Grand Slam of major titles. Her tally is now six Majors. Her win at Lytham was her sixth major success. By the end of August 2003 she had won 46 LPGA tournaments and was inducted into the World Golf Hall of Fame. When she won the Mizuno Classic for the third successive year she was winning her 46th LPGA title and had wrapped up the Player of the Year and top money earner award. In 2004 she quickly passed through the 50 mark in titles won and before the middle of October had passed the $2 million mark in US

PGA Tour earnings for a fourth successive year. She added another major to her personal tally when she won the McDonald's LPGA Championship. 2005 was another stellar year for Annika who took her career wins on the LPGA Tour to 66 with 10 more victories from her 20 starts. She easily topped the money list with over $2 million and moved her career earnings on the US Tour to $18,332,764. During the year she also won her own event in Sweden. Her majors total at the end of 2005 after further Grand Slam victories in the Kraft Nabisco Championship and McDonald's LPGA Championship moved to nine. Although she did not win Player of the Year honours in 2006 – that went to Mexico's Lorena Ochoa – Annika again had an excellent season, winning three times and coming second on a further five occasions. She has now won 69 times and her earnings in America have gone through $20 million. She added a further major win to her list of Grand Slam successes and with Liselotte Neumann won the World Cup of Golf in South Africa early in the year. She also hosted and then won her own event in Sweden and beat Helen Alfredsson and Karrie Webb to the first prize at the Dubai Ladies Masters in November. In 2007 her appearances were curtailed because of injury and she announced her retirement from full-time professional golf in 2008 despite having won the SBS Open in Hawaii. The Stanford International and the Michelob Ultra Open in the United States. In her last season she earned $1,617,411 taking her total on Tour since 1994 to $22,454,692. Now runs her own event in Sweden.

Steinhauer, Sherri (USA)
Born Madison, Wisconsin, 27 December 1962
Turned professional 1985
Winner of the Weetabix Women's British Open at Woburn in 1999 and at Royal Lytham and St Annes in 1998 and again there in 2006. Her third victory was her first major success because the British Women's Open was only recently awarded major status. She has also played in four Solheim Cup matches.

Stephenson, Jan (AUS)
Born Sydney, 22 December 1951
Turned professional 1973
She won three majors on the LPGA Tour – the 1981 du Maurier Classic, the 1982 LPGA Championship and the 1983 US Women's Open. She was twice Australian Ladies champion in 1973 and 1977.

Streit, Marlene Stewart (CAN)
Born Cereal, Alberta, 9 March 1934
One of Canada's most successful amateurs she won her national title ten times between 1951 and 1973. She won the 1953 British Amateur, the US Amateur in 1956 and the Australian Ladies in 1963. She was Canadian Woman Athlete of the Year in 1951, 1953, 1956, 1960 and 1963.

Stupples, Karen (ENG)
Born Dover, England, 24 June 1973
English professional who lives in Orlando but hit the headlines at Sunningdale in the summer of 2004 when she won the Weetabix British Women's Open with a

19 under par total of 269. In the final round she began by making an eagle at the first and holing her second shot for an eagle 2 at the second. She finally clinched victory with the help of three birdies in a row on the back nine. Earlier in the year she had won on the LPGA Tour which she had joined in 1999. She has played golf since she was 11. She made her début in the Solheim Cup in 2005 and was again in the side in 2007.

Suggs, Louise (USA)
Born Atlanta, Georgia, 7 September 1923
Turned professional 1948
Winner of 58 titles on the LPGA Tour after a brilliant amateur career which included victories in the 1947 US Amateur and the 1948 British Amateur Championships. She won 11 Majors including the US Open in 1949 and 1952 and the LPGA Championship in 1957. A founder member of the US Tour she was an inaugural honoree when the LPGA Hall of Fame was instituted in 1967. In 2006 she was awarded the Bob Jones award for outstanding sportsmanship and for being a perfect ambassador for the game. She comes from Atlanta and knew Bobby Jones when she was younger.

Thomas, Vicki (née Rawlings) (WAL)
Born Northampton, 27 October 1954
One of Wales' most accomplished players who took part in six Curtis Cup matches between 1982 and 1992. She won the Welsh Championship eight times between 1979 and 1994 as well as the British Ladies' Stroke Play in 1990.

Tinning, Iben (DEN)
Born Copenhagen, 4 February 1974
Turned professional 1995
Cousin of the European Tour player Steen Tinning she is Denmark's leading lady professional and made her Solheim Cup début in 2003 at Barsebäck. She was also in the Cup line-up in 2005 when she finished No.1 money earner in Europe.

Tseng, Yani (TPE)
Born Taoyuan, near Teipei, Taiwan, 1989
Turned professional 2007
A top-ranked Taiwanese amateur who was the Asia-Pacific Junior champion in 2003 and 2005. In 2004 she won the USGA Women's Amateur Public Links Championship and, after turning professional, competed initially on the Asian Golf Tour and in Canada. She won her first major on the LPGA circuit when she beat Sweden's Maria Hjorth at the fourth extra hole of a play-off for the McDonald's LPGA Championship.

Varangot, Brigitte (FRA)
Born Biarritz, 1 May 1940
Winner of the French Amateur title five times in six years from 1961 and again in 1973. Her run in the French Championship was impressive from 1960 when her finishes were 2, 1, 1, 2, 1, 1, 1, 2. She was also a triple winner of the British Championship in 1963, 1965 and 1968. One of France's most successful players she also won the Italian title in 1970.

Walker OBE, Mickey (ENG)
Born Alwoodley, Yorkshire, 17 December 1952
Turned professional 1973
Always a popular and modest competitor she followed up an excellent amateur career by doing well as a professional. Twice a Curtis Cup player she won the Ladies' British Open Amateur in 1971 and 1972, the English Ladies' in 1973 and had victories, too, in Portugal, Spain and America where she won the 1972 Trans-Mississippi title. She won six times as a professional but is perhaps best known for her stirring captaincy of the first four European Solheim Cup sides leading them to a five point success at Dalmahoy. In 1992 she galvanised her side by playing them tapes of the men's Ryder Cup triumphs. Now a club professional she also works regularly as a television commentator for Sky.

Webb, Karrie (AUS)
Born Ayr, Queensland, 21 December 1974
Turned professional 1994
Blonde Australian who is rewriting the record books with her performances on the LPGA Tour. Peter Thomson, the five times Open champion considers she is the best golfer male or female there is and Greg Norman, who was her inspiration as a teenager, believes she can play at times better than Tiger Woods although Webb herself hates comparisons. She scored her first Major win in 1995 when she took the Weetabix Women's British Open – a title she won again in 1997. When she joined the LPGA Tour she won the 1999 du Maurier Classic, the 2000 Nabisco Championship and the 2000 and 2001 US Women's Open – five Majors out of eight (by the end of July 2001) – the most impressive run since Mickey Wright won five out of six in the early 1960s. In 2002 she became the first player to complete a career Grand Slam when she won her third Weetabix British Open which had become an official major on the US LPGA Tour. It was her sixth major title in four years. Her winning total at Turnberry was 15 under par 273. Enjoys a close rivalry with Annika Sörenstam. In 2005 she was inducted into the World Golf Hall of Fame. She added to her majors tally in 2006 when she beat Lorena Ochoa in a play-off for the Kraft Nabisco Championship. Later she lost a play-off to Se Ri Pak for another major – the McDonald's LPGA Championship. She is the only player to have victories in the current four majors and the du Maurier event, now discarded as a major.

Whitworth, Kathy (USA)
Born Monahans, Texas, 27 September 1939
Turned professional 1958
Won 88 titles on the LPGA Tour between 1959 and 1991 – more than any one else male or female. Her golden period was in the 1960s when she won eight events in 1965, nine in 1966, eight in 1967 and 10 in 1968. When she finished third in the 1981 US Women's Open she became the first player to top $1 million in prize money on the LPGA Tour. She was the seventh member of the LPGA Tour Hall of Fame when inducted in 1975. Began playing golf at the age of 15 and made

golfing history when she teamed up with Mickey Wright to play in the previously all male Legends of Golf event. Winner of six Majors – including three LPGA Championship wins in 1967, 1971 and 1975. In addition she won two Titleholders' Championships (1966 and 1967) and the 1967 Western Open when they were Majors. Enjoyed a winning streak of 17 successive years on the LPGA Tour.

Wie, Michelle

Born Hawaii, 11 October 1989
Turned professional 2005
As an amateur she finished third in the Weetabix British Women's Open in July 2005 and turned professional in October as a 16-year-old with multi-million contract guarantees. In her first event as a professional in the Samsung Championship she finished fourth behind Annika Sörenstam but then was disqualified for a dropped ball infringement incurred in the third round – and spotted by an American journalist who did not report it until the following day. In 2006 she continued to play in a few men's events including the Omega European Masters at Crans-sur-Sierre but failed to make the cut in any. She did make the cut in all four majors in 2006. She combines her professional career with her school work in Hawaii and it is reported she hopes to go eventually to Stanford University. In 2008 she earned a card on the LPGA Tour at the Qualifying School.

Wright, Janette (née Robertson) (SCO)

Born Glasgow, 7 January 1935
Another of Scotland's most accomplished amateur players she competed four times in the Curtis Cup and was four times Scottish champion between 1959 and 1973. Formerly married to the late golf professional Innes Wright, her daughter Pamela plays professionally on the LPGA Tour in America.

Wright, Mickey (USA)

Born San Diego, California, 14 February 1935
Turned professional 1954
Her 82 victories on the LPGA Tour between 1956 and 1973 was bettered only by Kathy Whitworth who has 88 official victories. One of the greatest golfers in the history of the Tour she had a winning streak of 14 successive seasons. Winner of 13 Major titles she is the only player to date to have won three in one season. In 1961 she took the US Women's Open, the LPGA Championship and the Titleholders' Championship. That year she became only the second player to win both the US Women's Open and LPGA Championship in the same year having done so previously in 1958. Scored 79 of her victories between 1956 and 1969 when averaging almost eight wins a season. During this time she enjoyed a tremendous rivalry with Miss Whitworth. Truly a golfing legend.

Wright, Pamela (SCO)

Born Aboyne, Scotland, 26 June 1964
Turned professional 1988
Daughter of former Scottish champion and Curtis Cup golfer Janette Wright and the late Aboyne professional Innes Wright. She played in the first three Solheim Cup matches being a member of the winning team at Dalmahoy in 1992 and was vice-captain in 2000. She was an All-American in 1987 and again in 1988 when she also won Collegiate Golfer of the Year honours. She was LPGA Tour rookie of the year in 1989.

Famous Personalities of the Past

In making the difficult choice of the names to be included, effort has been made to acknowledge the outstanding players and personalities of each successive era from the early pioneers to the stars of recent times.

Alliss, Percy	Cotton, Sir Henry	Jones, Bob	Norman, Moe	Tait, Freddie
Anderson, Jamie	Crawley, Leonard	King, Sam	Ouimet, Francis	Taylor, JH
Anderson, Willie	Curtis, The Sisters	Kirkaldy, Andrew	Park, Mungo	Tolley, Cyril
Archer, George	Daly, Fred	Laidlay, John	Park, Willie	Travis, Walter
Armour, Tommy	Darwin, Bernard	Leitch, Cecil	Park, Willie Jnr	Valentine, Jessie
Auchterlonie,	Demeret, Jimmy	Lema, Tony	Philp, Hugh	Vardon, Harry
Willie	Dobereiner, Peter	Little, Lawson	Picard, Henry	Von Nida, Norman
Balding, Al	Duncan, George	Locke, Bobby	Price-Fisher,	Vare, Glenna
Ball, John	Faulkner, Max	Longhurst, Henry	Elizabeth	Walker, George
Barton, Pamela	Ferguson, Bob	Lunt, Michael	Ray, Ted	Ward, Charlie
Berg, Patty	Fernie, Willie	McCormack, Mark	Rees, Dai	Ward, Harvie
Bolt, Tommy	Goldschmid, Isa	McDonald, CB	Robertson, Allan	Wethered, Joyce
Boros, Julis	Hagen, Walter	Mackenzie, Alister	Ryder, Samuel	Wethered, Roger
Bousfield, Ken	Harper, Chandler	Massy, Arnaud	Sarazen, Gene	Whitcombes, The
Bradshaw, Harry	Henning, Harold	Micklem, Gerald	Shade, Ronnie	White, Ronnie
Braid, James	Herd, Sandy	Middlecoff, Cary	Smith, Frances	Wilson, Enid
Brewer, Gay	Hilton, Harold	Mitchell, Abe	Smith, Horton	Wind, Herbert
Brown, Eric	Hogan, Ben	Moody, Orville	Smith, Macdonald	Warren
Bruen, Jimmy	Howard, Barclay	Morgan, Wanda	Snead, Sam	Wood, Craig
Campbell, Dorothy	Hutchinson,	Morris, Old Tom	Solheim, Karsten	Wooldridge, Ian
Carr, Joe	Horace	Morris, Young Tom	Souchak, Mike	Yates, Charlie
Compston, Archie	Jarman, Ted	Nelson, Byron	Stewart, Payne	"Babe"

Alliss, Percy (1897–1975)

Father of Peter Alliss he finished in the top six in The Open Championship seven times, including joint third at Carnoustie in 1931, two strokes behind winner Tommy Armour. Twice winner of the Match Play Championship, five times German Open champion and twice winner of the Italian Open. He was a Ryder Cup player in 1933–35–37, an international honour also gained by his son. Spent much of his career as professional at the Wansee Club in Berlin.

Anderson, Jamie (1842–1912)

Winner of three consecutive Open Championships – 1877–78–79. A native St Andrean, he once claimed to have played 90 consecutive holes on the Old Course without a bad or unintended shot. He was noted for his straight hitting and accurate putting.

Anderson, Willie (1878–1910)

Took his typically Scottish flat swing to America where he won the US Open four times in a five year period from 1901. Only Bobby Jones, Ben Hogan and Jack Nicklaus have also won the US Open four times.

Archer, George (1940–2005)

The 6ft 5in tall former cowboy won The Masters in 1969 – one of four golfers who won their first major that year. A superb putter Archer was dogged throughout his career by injury but he won 12 times on the PGA Tour and a further 19 times on the US Senior Tour now the Champions Tour. Elizabeth, one of his two daughters, made headlines when she caddied for her father and became the first woman to do so at Augusta.

Armour, Tommy (1896–1968)

Born in Edinburgh, he played for Britain against America as an amateur and, after emigrating, for America against Britain as a professional in the forerunners of the Walker and Ryder Cup matches. Won the US Open in 1927, the USPGA in 1930 and the 1931 Open at Carnoustie. Became an outstanding coach and wrote several bestselling instruction books. Known as 'The Silver Scot'.

Auchterlonie, Willie (1872–1963)

Won The Open at Prestwick in 1893 at the age of 21 with a set of seven clubs he had made himself. Founded the famous family club-making business in St Andrews. He believed that golfers should master half, three-quarter and full shots with each club. Appointed Honorary Professional to The R&A in 1935.

Balding, Al (1924–2006)
A lovely swinger of the club, he was the first Canadian to win on the US Tour when he took the Mayfair Inn Open in Florida in 1955. In 1968, in partnership with Stan Leonard, he won the World Cup in Rome and was himself low individual scorer that year.

Ball, John (1861–1940)
Finished fourth in The Open of 1878 at the age of 16 and became the first amateur to win the title in 1890. He won the Amateur Championship eight times and shares with Bobby Jones the distinction of being the winner of The Open and Amateur in the same year. He grew up on the edge of the links area which became the Royal Liverpool Golf Club and the birthplace of the Amateur. He was a master at keeping the ball low in the wind, but with the same straight-faced club could cut the ball up for accurate approach shots. His run of success could have been greater but for military service in the South African campaign and the First World War.

Barton, Pamela (1917–1943)
At the age of 19 she held both the British and American Ladies Championships in 1936. She was French champion at 17, runner-up in the British in both 1934 and '35 and won the title again in 1939. A Curtis Cup team member in 1934 and '36 she was a Flight Officer in the WAAF when she was killed in a plane crash at an RAF airfield in Kent.

Berg, Patty (1915–2006)
The golf pioneer who won an LPGA Tour record 15 major titles and was one of the 13 founding members of the tour in 1950. She was the LPGA Tour's first president from 1950–52 and was the tour's money leader in 1954, '55 and '57 ending her career with 60 victories. She was a member of the LPGA Tour and World Golf Halls of Fame. She was described as a pioneer, an athlete, a mentor, a friend and an entertainer and had a great sense of humour.

Bolt, Tommy (1916–2008)
The 1958 US Open champion and two-time Ryder Cup player who is remembered as much for his short temper as his short game. He had a penchant for throwing clubs insisting it was better to throw them ahead of you in order to avoid having to walk back for them! Known as "Terrible Tommy" he was a funding member of the US Champions Tour. In the 1957 Ryder Cup at Lindrick he lost a bad-tempered game to fiery Scot Eric Brown.

Boros, Julius (1920–1994)
Became the oldest winner of a major championship when he won the USPGA in 1968 at the age of 48. He twice won the US Open, in 1952 and again 11 years

Tommy Armour   Doug Benc/Getty Images

later at Brookline when he was 43. In a play-off he beat Jackie Cupit by three shots and Arnold Palmer by six. He played in four Ryder Cup matches between 1959–67, winning nine of his 16 matches and losing only three.

Bousfield, Ken (1919–2000)
Although a short hitter even by the standards of his era, he won five out of 10 matches in six Ryder Cup appearances from 1949–61. He captured the PGA Match Play Championship in 1955, one of eight tournament victories in Britain, and also won six European Opens. He represented England in the World Cup at Wentworth in 1956 and Tokyo in 1957.

Bradshaw, Harry (1913–1950)
One of Ireland's most loved golfers whose swing Bernard Darwin described as "rustic and rugged". With Christy O'Connor he won the Canadian Cup (World Cup) for Ireland in Mexico in 1958 but he is also remembered for losing the 1949 Open to Bobby Locke after having hit one shot out of a bottle at the fifth on the second day. That bit of bad luck, it was later considered, cost him £10,000.

Braid, James (1870–1950)
Together with Harry Vardon and J.H. Taylor he formed the Great Triumvirate and dominated the game for 20 years before the 1914–18 war. In a 10-year period from 1901 he became the first player in the history of the event to win The Open five times – and also finished second on three occasions. In that same period he won the Match Play Championship four times and the French Open. He was a tall, powerful player who hit the ball hard but always retained an appearance of outward calm. He was one of the

founder members of the Professional Golfers' Associ-ation and did much to elevate the status of the profes-sional golfer. He was responsible for the design of many golf courses and served as professional at Wal-ton Heath for 45 years. He was an honorary member of that club for 25 years and became one of its direc-tors. He was also an honorary member of The R&A.

Brewer, Gay   (1932–2007)

Winner of the 1967 Masters he was one of the most popular figures on the US Tour and later the Cham-pions Tour. His love of the game, his joviality and his story-telling were all part of the legacy of the man from Lexington, Kentucky, whose loopy swing was one of the most unorthodox.

Brown, Eric   (1925–1986)

Twice captained the Ryder Cup side and for many years partnered John Panton for Scotland in the World Cup. A larger-than-life personality, he was one of two Cup captains who came from the Bathgate club. The other was Bernard Gallacher, who played in the 1969 match which Brown captained.

Bruen, Jimmy   (1920–1972)

Won the Irish Amateur at the age of 17 and defended the title successfully the following year. At 18 he became the youngest ever Walker Cup player at that time and in practice for the match at St Andrews in 1938 equalled the then amateur course record of 68 set by Bobby Jones.

Campbell, Dorothy Iona   (1883–1946)

One of only two golfers to win the British, American and Canadian Ladies titles. In total she won these three major championships seven times.

Carr, Joe   (1922–2004)

The first Irishman to captain the Royal and Ancient Golf Club of St Andrews, he was winner of three British Amateur Championship titles in 1953, 1958 and 1960. He played or captained Walker Cup sides from 1947 to 1963 making a record 11 appearances. He was the first Irishman to play in The Masters at Augusta, made 23 consecutive appearances for Ireland in the Home Internationals and was a regular winner of the West of Ireland and East of Ireland Championships. At one point in an illustrious career he held 18 different course records. An ebullient, fast-talking personality with a somewhat eccentric swing, he was one of Ire-land's best known and best loved golfers. In 2007 he was inducted posthumously into the World Golf Hall of Fame in St Augustine, Florida.

Coe, Charlie   (1923–2007)

Another fine American amateur golfer who finished runner-up with Arnold Palmer to Gary Player in the 1961 Masters at Augusta. Twice US Amateur champi-on in 1949 and 1958, he played in six Walker Cup matches and was non-playing captain in 1959. He won seven and halved two of the 13 games he played. Win-ner of the Bobby Jones award in 1964. Born in Okla-homa City, he never considered turning professional.

Compston, Archie   (1893–1962)

Beat Walter Hagen 18 and 17 in a 72-hole challenge match at Moor Park in 1928 and tied for second place in the 1925 Open. Played in the Ryder Cup in 1927–29–31.

Cotton, Sir Henry   (1907–1987)

The first player to be knighted for services to golf, he died a few days before the announcement of the award was made. He won The Open Championship three times, which included a round of 65 at Royal St George's in 1934 after which the famous Dunlop golf ball was named. His final 71 at Carnoustie to win the 1937 Championship in torrential rain gave him great satisfaction and he set another record with a 66 at Muirfield on the way to his third triumph in 1948. He won the Match Play Championship three times and was runner-up on three occasions. He also won 11 Open titles in Europe, played three times in the Ryder Cup and was non-playing captain in 1953. Sir Henry worked hard to promote the status of professional golf and also championed the cause of young golfers, becoming a founder member of the Golf Foundation. He was a highly successful teacher, author and archi-tect, spending much time at Penina, a course he creat-ed in southern Portugal. He was an honorary member of The R&A.

Crawley, Leonard   (1903–1981)

Played four times in the Walker Cup in 1932–34–38–47 and won the English Amateur in 1931. He also played first-class cricket for Worcestershire and Essex and toured the West Indies with the MCC in 1936. After the Second World War he was golf cor-respondent for the Daily Telegraph for 30 years.

The Curtis sisters, Harriet   (1878–1944)
Margaret   (1880–1965)

Donors of the Curtis Cup still contested biennially between the USA and GB&I. Harriet won the US Women's Amateur in 1906 and lost in the following year's final to her sister Margaret, who went on to win the championship three times.

Daly, Fred   (1911–1990)

Daly won The Open at Royal Liverpool in 1947 and in four of the next five years was never out of the top four in the Championship. At Portrush, where he was born, he finished fourth to Max Faulkner in 1951, the only time The Open has been played in Northern Ire-land. He was Ulster champion 11 times and three times captured the prestigious PGA Match Play Cham-pionship. He was a member of the Ryder Cup team four times, finishing on a high note at Wentworth in 1953 when he won his foursomes match in partner-ship with Harry Bradshaw and then beat Ted Kroll 9 and 7 in the singles.

Darwin, Bernard   (1876–1961)

One of the most gifted and authoritative writers on golf, he was also an accomplished England internation-al player for more than 20 years. While in America to report the 1922 Walker Cup match for The Times, he was called in to play and captain the side when Robert Harris became ill. A grandson of Charles Darwin, he was captain of The R&A in 1934–35. In 1937 he was awarded the CBE for services to literature. He was inducted into the World Golf Hall of Fame in 2005.

Demaret, Jimmy (1910–1983)
Three times Masters champion, coming from five strokes behind over the final six holes to beat Jim Ferrier by two in 1950, he also won six consecutive tournaments in 1940 while still performing as a night club singer. He won all six Ryder Cup matches he played in the encounters of 1947–49–51.

Dobereiner, Peter (1925–1996)
A multi-talented journalist in various fields who wrote eloquently, knowledgeably and amusingly on golf in many books, Golf Digest, and Golf World magazines and in The Observer and Guardian newspapers for whom he was correspondent for many years. Born of English-Scottish-Danish-Red Indian and German parentage he claimed he stubbornly refused all efforts by King's College, Taunton and Lincoln College, Oxford to impart a rudimentary education so chose journalism as a profession.

Duncan, George (1884–1964)
Won The Open in 1920 by making up 13 shots on the leader over the last two rounds and came close to catching Walter Hagen for the title two years later. Renowned as one of the fastest players, his book was entitled Golf at the Gallop.

Faulkner, Max (1916–2005)
One of the game's most extrovert and colourful personalities, who won the 1951 Open Championship at Royal Portrush, the only time the event was played in Northern Ireland. He played in five Ryder Cups and was deservedly if belatedly recognised for his contribution to the game with an honour in 2001 when he was awarded the OBE. His son-in-law is Brian Barnes, another golfing extrovert.

Ferguson, Bob (1848–1915)
The Open Championship winner three times in succession between 1880–82. He then lost a 36-hole play-off for the title by one stroke to Willie Fernie in 1883. At 18 he had won the Leith Tournament against the game's leading professionals.

Fernie, Willie (1851–1924)
In 1882 he was second to Bob Ferguson in The Open over his home course at St Andrews. The following year he beat the same player in a 36-hole play-off for the championship over Ferguson's home links at Musselburgh.

Goldschmid Isa (née Bevione) (1925–2002
One of Italy's greatest amateurs, she won her national title 21 times between 1947 and 1974 and was ten times Italian Open champion between 1952 and 1969. Among her other triumphs were victories in the 1952 Spanish Ladies and the 1973 French Ladies.

Hagen, Walter (1892–1969)
A flamboyant character who used a hired Rolls Royce as a changing room because professionals were not allowed in many clubhouses, he once gave his £50 cheque for winning The Open to his caddie. He won four consecutive USPGA Championships from 1924 when it was still decided by matchplay. He was four times a winner of The Open, in 1922–24–28–29 and captured the US Open title in 1914 and 1919. He captained and played in five Ryder Cup encounters between 1927–35, winning seven of his nine matches and losing only once. He was non-playing captain in 1937.

Harper, Chandler (1914–2004)
Born in Portsmouth, VA, he was winner of the 1950 US PGA Championship. He won over ten tournaments and was elected to the US PGA Hall of Fame in 1969. Once shot 58 (29-29) round a 6100 yards course in Portsmouth.

Henning, Harold (1934–2005)
One of three brothers from a well-known South African golf family he was a regular winner of golf events in his home country and Europe and had two wins on the US Tour. Played ten times for South Africa in the World Cup winning the event with Gary Player in Madrid in 1965.

Herd, Alexander 'Sandy' (1868–1944)
When he first played in The Open at the age of 17 he possessed only four clubs. His only Championship success came in the 1902 Open at Hoylake, the first player to capture the title using the new rubber-cored ball. He won the Match Play Championship at the age of 58 and took part in his last Open at St Andrews in 1939 at the age of 71.

Hilton, Harold (1869–1942)
Winner of the Amateur Championship four times between 1900 and 1913, he also became the first player and the only Briton to hold both the British and US Amateur titles in the same year 1911. He won The Open in 1892 at Muirfield, the first time the Championship was extended to 72 holes. A small but powerful player he was the first editor of Golf Monthly.

Hogan, Ben (1912–1997)
One of only five players to have won all four major championships, his record of capturing three in the same season has been matched by Tiger Woods. He dominated the golfing scene in America after the Second World War and in 1953 won the Masters, US Open and The Open Championship. A clash of dates between The Open and USPGA prevented an attempt on the Grand Slam, but his poor state of health after a near fatal car crash four years earlier would have made the matchplay format of 10 rounds in six days in the USPGA an impossibility. After his car collided with a Greyhound bus in fog, it was feared that Hogan might never walk again. He had won three majors before the accident and he returned to capture six more. His

Bobby Jones   Popperfoto

other appearance in The Open was in his tremendous season of 1953 and he recorded rounds of 73-71-70-68 to win by four strokes at Carnoustie. His dramatic life story was made into a Hollywood film entitled Follow the Sun.

Howard, Barclay (1953 – 2008)
Leading amateur in the 1997 Open at Royal Troon he battled leukaemia after playing in the 1995 Walker Cup. When Dean Robertson won the 1999 Italian Open he dedicated his victory to Barclay as tribute to the courage and adversity he showed in attempting to beat the disease.

Hutchinson, Horace (1859–1932)
Runner-up in the first Amateur Championship in 1885, he won the title in the next two years and reached the final again in 1903. Represented England from 1902–07. He was a prolific writer on golf and country life and became the first English captain of The R&A in 1908.

Jarman, Ted (1907–2003)
He competed in the 1935 Ryder Cup at Ridgewood, New Jersey, and until his death in 2003 he had been the oldest living Cup golfer. When he was 76 years old and before he had to stop playing because of arthritis he shot a 75.

Jones, Bobby (1902–1971)
Always remembered for his incredible and unrepeatable achievement in 1930 of winning The Open and Amateur Championships of Britain and America in one outstanding season – the original and unchallenged Grand Slam. At the end of that year he retired from competitive golf at the age of 28. His victories included four US Opens, five US Amateur titles, three Opens in Britain and one Amateur Championship. Although his swing was stylish and fluent, he suffered badly from nerves and was often sick and unable to eat during championships. He was also an accomplished scholar, gaining first-class honours degrees in law, English literature and mechanical engineering at three different universities. He subsequently opened a law practice in Atlanta and developed the idea of creating the Augusta National course and staging an annual invitation event which was to become known as The Masters. He was made an honorary member of the Royal and Ancient Golf Club in 1956 and two years later was given the freedom of the Burgh of St Andrews at an emotional ceremony. He died after many years of suffering from a crippling spinal disease. The tenth hole on the Old Course bears his name.

King, Sam (1911–2003)
He played Ryder Cup golf immediately before and after World War II and came third in the 1939 Open behind Dick Burton at Royal St George's. In the 1947 Ryder Cup he prevented an American whitewash in the singles by beating Herman Kaiser. He was British Senior Champion in 1961 and 1962 and was often described as "the old master" – a golfer noted for his long, straight drives and superb putting.

Kirkaldy, Andrew (1860–1934)
First honorary professional appointed by The R&A, he lost a play-off for The Open Championship of 1889 to Willie Park at Musselburgh. He was second in the championship three times, a further three times finished third and twice fourth. A powerful player, he was renowned for speaking his mind.

Laidlay, John Ernest (1860–1940)
The man who first employed the overlapping grip which was later credited to Harry Vardon and universally known as the Vardon grip, Laidlay was a finalist in the Amateur Championship six times in seven years from 1888, winning the title twice at a time when John Ball, Horace Hutchinson and Harold Hilton were at their peak. He was runner-up in The Open to Willie Auchterlonie at Prestwick in 1893. Among the 130 medals he won, were the Gold Medal and Silver Cross in R&A competitions.

Leitch, Charlotte Cecilia 'Cecil' (1891–1977)
Christened Charlotte Cecilia, but universally known as Cecil, her list of international victories would

undoubtedly have been greater but for the blank golfing years of the first world war. She first won the British Ladies Championship in 1908 at the age of 17. In 1914 she took the English, French and British titles and successfully defended all three when competition was resumed after the war. In all she won the French Championship five times, the British four times, the English twice, the Canadian once. Her total of four victories in the British has never been beaten and has been equalled only by her great rival Joyce Wethered. The victory in Canada was by a margin of 17 and 15 in the 36-hole final.

Lema, Tony (1934–1966)

His first visit to Britain, leaving time for only 27 holes of practice around the Old Course at St Andrews, culminated in Open Championship victory in 1964 by five shots over Jack Nicklaus. He had won three tournaments in four starts in America before arriving in Scotland and gave great credit for his Open success to local caddie Tip Anderson. He played in the Ryder Cup in 1963 and 1965 with an outstanding record. He lost only once in 11 matches, halved twice and won eight. Lema and his wife were killed when a private plane in which they were travelling to a tournament crashed in Illinois.

Little, Lawson (1910–1968)

Won the Amateur Championships of Britain and America in 1934 and successfully defended both titles the following year. He then turned his amateur form into a successful professional career, starting in 1936 with victory in the Canadian Open. He won the US Open in 1940 after a play-off against Gene Sarazen.

Locke, Bobby (1917–1987)

The son of Northern Irish emigrants to South Africa, Arthur D'Arcy Locke was playing off plus four by the age of 18 and won the South African Boys, Amateur and Open Championships. On his first visit to Britain in 1936 he was leading amateur in The Open Championship. Realising that his normal fade was leaving him well short of the leading players, he deliberately developed the hook shot to get more run on the ball. It was to become his trade-mark throughout a long career. He was encouraged to try the American tour in 1947 and won five tournaments, one by the record margin of 16 shots. More successes followed and the USPGA framed a rule which banned him from playing in their events, an action described by Gene Sarazen as 'the most disgraceful action by any golf organisation'. Disillusioned by the American attitude, Locke then played most of his golf in Europe, winning The Open four times. He shared a period of domination with Peter Thomson between 1949–1958 when they won the championship four times each, only Max Faulkner and Ben Hogan breaking the sequence. In his final Open victory at St Andrews in 1957 he failed to replace his ball in the correct spot on the 18th green after moving it from fellow competitor Bruce Crampton's line. The mistake, which could have led to disqualification, was only spotted on television replays. The R&A Championship Committee rightly decided that Locke, who

Bobby Locke   Popperfoto

had won by three strokes, had gained no advantage, and allowed the result to stand. Following a career in which he won over 80 events around the world he was made an honorary member of The R&A in 1976.

Longhurst, Henry (1909–1978)

Captain of Cambridge University golf team, runner-up in the French and Swiss Amateur Championships and winner of the German title in 1936, he became the most perceptive and readable golf correspondent of his time and a television commentator who never wasted a single word. His relaxed, chatty style was based on the premise that he was explaining the scene to a friend in his favourite golf club bar. For 25 years his Sunday Times column ran without a break and became compulsory reading for golfers and non-golfers alike. He had a brief spell as a member of parliament and was awarded the CBE for services to golf.

Lunt, Michael (1935–2007)

The former Amateur and English Amateur champion who played most of his golf at Walton Heath died during his captaincy of the Royal and Ancient Golf Club of St Andrews – an honour which was well-deserved for a golfer who was liked and admired as much for his work as an administrator as his prowess on the links. Son of Stanley Lunt, the 1934 English amateur champion, Michael played on four Walker Cup teams including the one that shocked the Americans by drawing at Five Farms in 1965. He was also a member of the winning Great Britain and Ireland side captained by Joe Carr in the World Amateur Team Championship for the Eisenhower Trophy a year earlier at Olgiata in Rome. After working in the family business he moved to the Slazenger company and later was secretary manager at the Royal Mid-Surrey club before he retired. He is survived by his wife Vicki and son and daughter.

McCormack, Mark (1931–2003)

The Cleveland lawyer who created a golf management empire after approaching Arnold Palmer to look after his affairs. A keen golfer himself, he became one of the most influential and powerful men in sport, managing many golfing legends including Tiger Woods. He was responsible for the development of the modern game commercially and started the World Match Play Championship at Wentworth in 1964.

McDonald, C.B. (1855–1939)

Credited with building the first 18-hole golf course in the United States and instrumental in forming the United States Golf Association. He won the first US Amateur Championship in 1895. He was elected to the World Golf Hall of Fame in 2007.

Mackenzie, Alister (1870–1934)

A family doctor and surgeon, he became involved with Harry S. Colt in the design of the Alwoodley course in Leeds, where he was a founder member and honorary secretary and eventually abandoned his medical career and worked full time at golf course architecture. There are many outstanding examples of his work in Britain, Australia, New Zealand and America. His most famous creation, in partnership with Bobby Jones, is the Augusta National course in Georgia, home of The Masters.

Massy, Arnaud (1877–1958)

The first non-British player to win The Open Championship. Born in Biarritz, France, he defeated J.H. Taylor by two strokes at Hoylake in 1907. Four years later he tied for the title with Harry Vardon at Royal St George's, but in the play-off conceded at the 35th hole when he was five strokes behind. He won the French Open four times, the Spanish on three occasions and the Belgian title once.

Micklem, Gerald (1911–1988)

A pre-war Oxford Blue, he won the English Amateur Championship in 1947 and 1953 and played in the Walker Cup team four times between 1947 and 1955. He was non-playing captain in 1957 and 1959. In 1976 he set a record of 36 consecutive appearances in the President's Putter, an event that he won in 1953. In addition to his playing success he was a tireless administrator, serving as chairman of The R&A Rules, Selection and Championship Committees. He was president of the English Golf Union and the European Golf Association and captain of The R&A. In 1969 he received the Bobby Jones award for distinguished sportsmanship and services to the game. He was elected to the World Golf Hall of Fame in 2007.

Middlecoff, Cary (1921–1998)

Dentist turned golf professional, he became one of the most prolific winners on the US tour, with 37 victories that included two US Opens and a Masters victory. In the US Open of 1949 he beat Sam Snead and Clayton Heafner at Medinah, and seven years later recaptured the title by one shot ahead of Ben Hogan and Julius Boros at Oak Hill. His Masters success came in 1955 when he established a record seven-shot winning margin over Hogan.

Mitchell, Abe (1897–1947)

Said by J.H. Taylor to be the finest player never to win an Open, he finished in the top six five times. He was more successful in the Match Play Championship, with victories in 1919, 1920 and 1929. He taught the game to St Albans seed merchant Samuel Ryder and is the figure depicted on top of the famous trophy.

Moody, Orville (1933–2008)

His only victory on the PGA Tour came in the 1969 US Open for which he had had to qualify. A descendent of the native American Choctaw tribe, he is best remembered, however, for popularising the long-shafted (broom handle) putter which he had first seen used by Charlie Owens, another "yips" sufferer. If Owens invented the 50in shafted putter Moody brought it to everyone's attention when he won the 1989 US Senior Open using one. Sam Torrance, Peter Senior and Bernhard Langer all started using it after golf's ruling bodies declared the putter legal.

Morgan, Wanda (1910–1995)

Three-time English Amateur champion, in 1931–36–37, she also captured the British title in 1935 and played three times in the Curtis Cup from 1932–36.

Morris, Old Tom (1821–1908)

Apprenticed as a feathery ball maker to Allan Robertson in St Andrews at the age of 18 he was one of the finest golfers of his day when he took up the position of Keeper of the Green at Prestwick, where he laid out the original 12-hole course. He was 39 when he finished second in the first Open in 1860, but subsequently won the title four times. His success rate might have been much greater if he had been a better putter. His son once said: 'He would be a much better player if the hole was a yard closer.' A man of fierce conviction, he returned to St Andrews to take up the duties of looking after the Old Course at a salary of £50 per year, paid by The R&A. He came to regard the course as his own property and was once publicly reprimanded for closing it without authority because he considered it needed a rest. A testimonial in 1896 raised £1,240 pounds towards his old age from golfers around the world and when he retired in 1903 The R&A continued to pay his salary. He died after a fall on the stairs of the New Club in 1908, having outlived his wife, his daughter and his three sons.

Morris, Young Tom (1851–1875)

Born in St Andrews, but brought up in Prestwick, where his father had moved to become Keeper of the Green, he won a tournament against leading professionals at the age of 13. He was only 17 when he succeeded his father as Open champion in 1868 and then defended the title successfully in the following two years to claim the winner's belt outright. There was no championship in 1871, but when the present silver trophy became the prize in 1872, Young Tom's was the first name engraved on its base. His prodigious talent was best demonstrated in his third successive Open victory in 1870 when he played 36 holes at Prestwick in 149 strokes, 12 shots ahead of his nearest rival, superb scoring given the equipment and the condition of the course at that time. He married in November 1874 and was playing with his father in a money match at North Berwick the following year when a telegram from St Andrews sent them hurrying back across the Firth of Forth in a private yacht. Young Tom's wife and baby had both died in childbirth. He played golf only twice after that, in matches that had been arranged long in advance, and fell into moods of deep depression. He died on Christmas morning of that same year from a burst artery in the lung. He was 24 years old. A public subscription paid for a memorial which still stands above his grave in the cathedral cemetery.

Nelson, Byron (1912–2006)

John Byron Nelson left a legacy which many will aspire to emulate but which few will achieve. He joined the professional circuit in 1935 after a caddie shack apprenticeship which he shared with Ben Hogan and quickly established himself, winning the New Jersey Open in 1935 and going on to take The Masters title a mere two years later. Between 1935 and 1946 he had 54 wins but although he won The Masters in 1937 and 1942, the US Open in 1939 and the US PGA Championship in 1940 and 1945 he didn't manage to pull off a Grand Slam having never won The Open Championship. The 1939 US Open is probably best remembered as the tournament Sam Snead threw away, history tending to overlook the achievement of Byron Nelson, the man who eventually took the title. After a three-way play-off with Craig Wood and Densmore Shute, Nelson went on to win the decisive 18 holes by three shots from Wood. America's entry into the second world war called a temporary halt to competitive golf for many. Nelson, denied the opportunity to serve his country due to a blood disorder, continued to play throughout 1943 and 1944, re-establishing his prominent position when full competition resumed in 1945, winning 18 times including 11 events in a row between March and August – a record unlikely ever to be broken. He was twice a member of US Ryder Cup teams – in 1937 and 1947 and had been picked for the postponed matches in 1939 and 1941. He returned to that competition in 1965 when he captained the victorious US team. His only win in Europe was the 1955 French Open. He was a father figure in US golf and until he retired in 2001 was one of The Masters honorary starters along with the late Gene Sarazen and Sam Snead. In company with Snead and his old sparring partner Ben Hogan, Byron Nelson was one of the sport's most revered figures and had a particularly close friendship with five times Open champion Tom Watson.

Norman, Moe (1929–2004)

Eccentric Canadian golf star who was renowned for the accuracy of his unusual swing. Twice Canadian Amateur Champion and winner of 13 Canadian Tour titles, he was inducted into the Canadian Golf Hall of Fame in 1995. He played very quickly, seldom slowing to line up a putt. He never had a lesson. He was such a character that Wally Uihlein, president of Titleist and Footjoy, paid him $5,000 a month for the last 10 years of his life for just "being himself".

Ouimet, Francis (1893–1967)

Regarded as the player who started the American golf boom after beating Harry Vardon and Ted Ray in a play-off for the 1913 US Open as a young amateur. Twice a winner of the US Amateur, he was a member of every Walker Cup team from 1922 to 1934 and non-playing captain from then until 1949. In 1951 he became the first non-British national to be elected captain of The R&A and was a committee member of the USPGA for many years.

Park, Willie (1834–1903)

Winner of the first Open Championship in 1860. He won the title three more times, in 1863, 1866 and 1875, and was runner-up on four occasions. For 20 years he issued a standing challenge to play any man in the world for £100 a side. His reputation was built largely around a successful putting stroke and he always stressed the importance of never leaving putts short.

Park, Mungo (1839–1904)

Younger brother to Willie Park, he spent much of his early life at sea, but won The Open Championship in 1874 at the age of 35, beating Young Tom Morris into second place by two shots on his home course at Musselburgh.

Park Jr, Willie (1864–1925)

Son of the man who won the first Open Championship, Willie Park Jr captured the title twice – in 1887 and 1889 – and finished second to Harry Vardon in 1898. He was also an accomplished clubmaker who did much to popularise the bulger driver with its convex face and he patented the wry-neck putter in 1891. One of the first and most successful professionals to design golf courses, he was responsible for many layouts in Britain, Europe and America and also wrote two highly successful books on the game.

Philp, Hugh (1782–1856)

One of the master craftsmen in St Andrews in the early days of the 19th century, he was renowned for his skill in creating long-nosed putters. After his death his business was continued by Robert Forgan. Philp's clubs are much prized collector's items.

Picard, Henry (1907–1997)

Winner of The US Masters in 1938 and the 1939 USPGA Championship, where he birdied the final hole to tie with Byron Nelson and birdied the first extra

Dai Rees   Popperfoto

hole for the title. Ill health cut short a career in which he won 27 tournaments.

Price-Fisher, Elizabeth (1923–2008)

Born in London she played in six Curtis Cup matches and, in addition to winning the 1959 British Women's Championship. Took titles in Denmark and Portugal, She turned professional in 1968 but was later re-instated as an amateur in 1971. For many years she worked as the ladies golf correspondent for the *Daily Telegraph* in London.

Ray, Ted (1877–1943)

Born in Jersey, his early years in golf were in competition with Channel Islands compatriot Harry Vardon and his fellow members of the Great Triumvirate, J.H. Taylor and James Braid. His only victory in The Open came in 1912, but he was runner-up to Taylor the following year and second again, to Jim Barnes of America, in 1925 when he was 48 years of age He claimed the US Open title in 1920 and remains one of only three British players to win The Open and the US Open on both sides of the Atlantic. The others are Harry Vardon and Tony Jacklin.

Rees, Dai (1913–1983)

One of Britain's outstanding golfers for three decades, he played in nine Ryder Cup matches between 1937 and 1961 and was playing captain of the 1957 team which won the trophy for the first time since 1933. He was non-playing captain in 1967. He was runner-up in The Open three times and won the PGA Match Play

title four times. He was made an honorary member of the Royal and Ancient Golf Club in 1976.

Robertson, Allan (1815–1858)

So fearsome was Robertson's reputation as a player that when The R&A staged an annual competition for local professionals, he was not allowed to take part so as to give the others a chance. A famous maker of feather golf balls, he strongly resisted the advance of the more robust gutta percha. Tom Morris senior was his apprentice and they were reputed never to have lost a foursomes match in which they were partners.

Ryder, Samuel (1858–1936)

The prosperous seed merchant was so impressed with the friendly rivalry between British and American professionals at an unofficial match at Wentworth in 1926 that he donated the famous gold trophy for the first Ryder Cup match the following year. The trophy is still presented today for the contest between America and Europe.

Sarazen, Gene (1902–1999)

Advised to find an outdoor job to improve his health, Sarazen became a caddie and then an assistant professional. At the age of 20 he became the first player to win the US Open and PGA titles in the same year. In claiming seven major titles he added The Open at Prince's in 1932 and when he won the second Masters tournament in 1935 he became the first of only five players to date who have won all four Grand Slam trophies during their careers. He played 'the shot heard around the world' on his way to Masters victory, holing a four-wood across the lake at the 15th for an albatross two. At the age of 71 he played in The Open at Troon and holed-in-one at the Postage Stamp eighth. The next day he holed from a bunker for a two at the same hole. He acted as an honorary starter at the Masters, hitting his final shot only a month before his death at 97.

Sayers, Ben (1857–1924)

A twinkling, elphin figure, the diminutive Sayers played a leading part in the game for more than four decades. He represented Scotland against England from 1903 to 1913 and played in every Open from 1880 to 1923.

Shade, Ronnie D.B.M. (1938–1984)

One of Scotland's greatest golfers whom many considered the world's top amateur in the mid 60s. After losing the 1962 Scottish Amateur Golf Championship final to Stuart Murray, he won that title five years in a row winning 43 consecutive ties before losing in the fourth round to Willie Smeaton at Muirfield in 1968. Taught by his father John, professional at the Duddingston club in Edinburgh, he was often referred to as "Right Down the Bloody Middle" because of his initials and consistent play. Shade won the Scottish and Irish Open Championships as a professional but was reinstated as an amateur before his death from cancer at the age of 47.

Smith, Frances – née Bunty Stephens (1925–1978)

Dominated post-war women's golf, winning the British Ladies Championship in 1949 and 1954, was three times a winner of the English and once the victor in the French Championship. She represented Great Britain & Ireland in six consecutive encounters from 1950, losing only three of her 11 matches, and was non-playing captain of the team in 1962 and 1972. She was awarded the OBE for her services to golf.

Smith, Horton   (1908–1963)

In his first winter on the US professional circuit as a 20-year-old in 1928–29 he won eight out of nine tournaments. He was promoted to that year's Ryder Cup team and played in 1933 and 1935 and remained unbeaten He won the first Masters in 1934 and repeated that success two year's later. He received the Ben Hogan Award for overcoming illness or injury and the Bobby Jones Award for distinguished sportsmanship in golf.

Smith, Macdonald   (1890–1949)

Born into a talented Carnoustie golfing family, he was destined to become one of the finest golfers never to win The Open. He was second in 1930 and 1932, was twice third and twice fourth. His best chance came at Prestwick in 1925 when he led the field by five strokes with one round to play, but the enthusiastic hordes of Scottish supporters destroyed his concentration and he finished with an 82 for fourth place.

Snead, Sam   (1912–2002)

Few would argue that 'Slammin' Sam Snead' possessed the sweetest swing in the history of the game. 'He just walked up to the ball and poured honey all over it', it was said. Raised during the Depression in Hot Springs, Virginia, he also died there on May 23 2002, four days short of his 90th birthday. His seven major titles comprised three Masters, three USPGA Championships and the 1946 Open at St Andrews, while he was runner-up four times in the US Open. But for the Second World War he would surely have added several more. He achieved a record 82 PGA Tour victories in America, the last of them at age 52, and was just as prolific round the world across six decades. He played in seven Ryder Cup matches, captained the 1969 United States team which tied at Royal Birkdale and after his retirement acted as honorary starter at The Masters until his death. Perhaps his greatest achievement came in the 1979 Quad Cities Open when he scored 67 and 66. He was 67 years of age at the time.

Solheim, Karsten   (1912–2000)

A golfing revolutionary who discovered the game at the age of 42 and, working in his garage, invented the Ping putter with its unique heel-toe weighting design, later adopted in his irons. A keen supporter of women's golf, he presented the Solheim Cup for a biennial competition between the American and European Ladies' Tours.

Souchak, Mike (1927 – 2008)

He won 15 times on the PGA Tour in the 1950's and 1960's, competed in the 1959 and 1961 Ryder Cups and played for 11 years on the Champions Tour before retiring. Although he never won a major title he finished 11 times in the top 10 in majors coming third twice in the US Open.

Stewart, Payne   (1957–1999)

Four months after winning his second US Open title Payne Stewart was killed in a plane crash. Only a month earlier he had been on the winning United States Ryder Cup team. His first major victory was in the 1989 USPGA Championship and he claimed his first US Open title two years later after a play-off against Scott Simpson. In 1999 he holed an 18-foot winning putt to beat Phil Mickleson for the US title he was never able to defend. In 1985 he finished a stroke behind Sandy Lyle in The Open at Royal St George's and five years later he shared second place as Nick Faldo won the Championship at St Andrews.

Tait, Freddie   (1870–1900)

In 1890 Tait set a new record of 77 for the Old Course, lowering that to 72 only four years later. He was three times the leading amateur in The Open Championship and twice won the Amateur Championship, in 1896 and 1898. The following year he lost at the 37th hole of an historic final to John Ball at Prestwick. He was killed while leading a charge of the Black Watch at Koodoosberg Drift in the Boer War.

Taylor, J.H.   (1871–1963)

Winner of The Open Championship five times between 1894 and 1913, Taylor was part of the Great Triumvirate with James Braid and Harry Vardon. He tied for the title with Vardon in 1896, but lost in the play-off and was runner-up another five times. He also won the French and German Opens and finished second in the US Open. A self-educated man, he was a thoughtful and compelling speaker and became the founding father of the Professional Golfers' Association. He was made an honorary member of The R&A in 1949.

Tolley, Cyril   (1896–1978)

Won the first of his two Amateur Championships in 1920 while still a student at Oxford and played in the unofficial match which preceded the Walker Cup a year later. He played in six Walker Cup encounters and was team captain in 1924. Tolley is the only amateur to have won the French Open, a title he captured in 1924 and 1928. After winning the Amateur for the second time in 1929 he was favourite to retain the title at St Andrews the following summer but was beaten by a stymie at the 19th hole in the fourth round by Bobby Jones in the American's Grand Slam year.

Travis, Walter   (1862–1925)

Born in Australia, he won the US Amateur Championship in 1900 at the age of 38, having taken up the game only four years earlier. He won again the following year and in 1903. He became the first overseas player to win the Amateur title in Britain in 1904, using a centre-shafted Schenectady putter he had just acquired. The club was banned a short time later. He was 52 years old when he last reached the semi-finals of the US Amateur in 1914.

Valentine, Jessie   (1915–2006)

A winner of titles before and after World War II, she was an impressive competitor and was one of the first ladies to make a career out of professional golf. She won the British Ladies as an amateur in 1937 and again in 1955 and 1958 and was Scottish champion in 1938 and 1939 and four times between 1951 and 1956. But for the war years it is certain she would have had more titles and victories. She played in seven Curtis Cups between 1936 and 1958 and represented Scotland in the Home Internationals on 17 occasions between 1934 and 1958.

Vardon, Harry   (1870–1937)

Still the only player to have won The Open Championship six times, Vardon, who was born in Jersey, won his first title in 1896, in a 36-hole play-off against J.H. Taylor and his last in 1914, this time beating Taylor by three shots. He won the US Open in 1900 and was beaten in a play-off by Francis Ouimet in 1913. He was one of the most popular of the players at the turn of the century and did much to popularise the game in America with his whistle-stop exhibition tours. He popularised the overlapping grip which still bears his name, although it was first used by Johnny Laidlay. He was also the originator of the modern upright swing, moving away from the flat sweeping action of previous eras. After his Open victory of 1903, during which he was so ill he thought he would not be able to finish, he was diagnosed with tuberculosis. His legendary accuracy and low scoring are commemorated with the award of two Vardon Trophies – in America for the player each year with the lowest scoring average and in Europe for the golfer who wins the money list.

Von Nida, Norman   (1914–2007)

Generally considered the father of Australian golf, he won over 80 titles worldwide. The Australian development Tour is named after him. Played extensively in Britain in the 1940s and 1960s. In later life he was registered bind. Generally regarded as the first golfer to make his income on Tour rather than being based at a club.

Vare, Glenna – née Collett   (1903–1989)

Won the first of her six US Ladies Amateur titles at the age of 19 in 1922 and the last in 1935. A natural athlete, she attacked the ball with more power than was normal in the women's game. The British title eluded her, although at St Andrews in 1929 she was three-under par and five up on Joyce Wethered after 11 holes, but lost to a blistering counter-attack. She played in the first Curtis Cup match in 1932 and was a member of the team in 1936, 1938 and 1948 and was captain in 1934 and 1950.

Walker, George   (1874–1953)

The President of the United States Golf Association who donated the trophy for the first match in 1922, at Long Island, New York, and which is still presented to the winning team in the biennial matches between USA and Great Britain & Ireland. His grandson and great grandson, George Walker Bush and George Bush Jr have both become Presidents of the United States.

Ward, Charles Harold   (1911–2001)

Charlie Ward played in three Ryder Cup matches from 1947–1951 and was twice third in The Open, behind Henry Cotton at Muirfield in 1948 and Max Faulkner at Royal Portrush in 1951.

Ward, Harvie   (1926–2004)

Born in Tarboro, North Carolina, he was winner of the Amateur Championship in 1952 when he beat Frank Stranahan 6 and 5 at Prestwick, he went on to win the US title in 1955 and 1956 and the Canadian Amateur in 1964. He played in the 1953, 1955 and 1959 Walker Cup matches and won all of his six games.

Wethered, Joyce – Lady Heathcoat-Amory   (1901–1997)

Entered her first English Ladies Championship in 1920 at the age of 18 and beat holder Cecil Leitch in the final. She remained unbeaten for four years, winning 33 successive matches. After they had played together at St Andrews, Bobby Jones remarked: 'I had never played golf with anyone, man or woman, amateur or professional, who made me feel so utterly outclassed.'

Wethered, Roger   (1899–1983)

Amateur champion in 1923 and runner-up in 1928 and 1930, he played five times in the Walker Cup, acting as playing captain at Royal St George's in 1930, and represented England against Scotland every year from 1922 to 1930. In The Open Championship at St Andrews in 1921 he tied with Jock Hutchison despite incurring a penalty for treading on his own ball. Due to play in a cricket match in England the following day, he was persuaded to stay in St Andrews for the play-off, but lost by 150–159 over 36 holes.

Whitcombe, Ernest   (1890–1971)
Charles   (1895–1978)
Reginald   (1898–1957)

The remarkable golfing brothers from Burnham, Somerset, were all selected for the Ryder Cup team of 1935. Charlie and Eddie were paired together and won the only point in the foursomes in a heavy 9–3 defeat by the American team. Reg won the gale-lashed Open at Royal St George's in 1938, with a final round of 78 as the exhibition tent was blown into the sea. Ernest finished second to Walter Hagen in 1924 and Charlie was third at Muirfield in 1935.

White, Ronnie   (1921–2005)

A five times Walker Cup team member between 1947 and 1953 he was one of the most impressive players in post-war amateur golf. He won six and halved one of the 10 Walker Cup matches he played and won the English Amateur in 1949 and the English Open stroke play title the following two years.

Wilson, Enid   (1910–1996)

Completed a hat-trick of victories in the Ladies British Amateur Championship from 1931–33. She was twice a semi-finalist in the American Championship, won the British Girls' and English Ladies' titles and played in the inaugural Curtis Cup match, beating Helen Hicks 2 and 1 in the singles. Retiring early from competitive golf, she was never afraid to express strongly held views on the game in her role as women's golf correspondent of the Daily Telegraph.

Wind, Herbert Warren   (1917–2005)

One of if not the most distinguished writers on golf in America, he authored 14 books on the game he loved with a passion. A long-time contributor to the New Yorker magazine, he is still the only writer to have received the United States Golf Association's Bobby Jones award for distinguished sportsmanship – an honour bestowed on him in 1995, the year the Association celebrated its centenary. The award was appropriate because he was a life-long admirer of Jones and was a regular at The Masters each year where he has been given the credit for naming, in 1958, the difficult stretch of holes from the 11th to the 13th as Amen Corner, arguing you said "Amen" if you negotiated them without dropping a shot.

Wood, Craig   (1901–1968)

Both Masters and US Open champion in 1941, Wood finally made up for a career of near misses, having lost play-offs for all four major championships between 1933 and 1939. He was three times a member of the American Ryder Cup team.

Wooldridge, Ian   (1932–2007)

One of the most respected sports writers who enjoyed nothing more than covering golf. His Daily Mail column was required reading for 40 years.

Yates, Charlie   (1913–2005)

Great friend of the late Bobby Jones he was top amateur in the US Masters in 1934, 1939 and 1940. In 1938 came to Royal Troon and won the British Amateur title beating R. Ewing 3 and 2. For many years acted as chairman of the press committee at The Masters and staged annual parties for visiting golf writers in the Augusta Clubhouse. He was a long-time Vice President of the Association of Golf Writers.

Zaharias, Mildred "Babe" – née Didrickson   (1915–1956)

As a 17-year-old, Babe, as she was universally known, broke three records in the 1932 Los Angeles Olympics – the javelin, 80 metres hurdles and high jump, but her high jump medal was denied her when judges decided her technique was illegal. Turning her attention to golf, she rapidly established herself as the most powerful woman golfer of the time and in 1945 played and made the cut in the LA Open on the men's PGA Tour. She won the final of the US Amateur by 11 and 9 in 1946, became the first American to win the British title the following year, then helped launch the women's professional tour. She won the US Women's Open in 1948, 1950 and 1954 and in 1950 won six of the nine events on the tour. In 1952 she had a major operation for cancer, but when she won her third and final Open two years later it was by the margin of 12 shots. She was voted Woman Athlete of the Year five times between 1932 and 1950 and Greatest Female Athlete of the Half-Century in 1949.

British Isles International Players

Professional Men

Key

RC	Ryder Cup GBI till 1977; Europe thereafter.	**DC**	Dunhill Cup – by home country
		CC	Canada Cup
USA	1921, 1926: pre-Ryder Cup	**WbC**	Warburg Cup
RoW	Rest of World	**(S)Eur**	European Seniors v Ladies European Tour
FT	Four Tours World Championship, Players represented European Tour; also in Nissan Cup and Kirin Cup	*	indicates winning team
			'to' indicates inclusive dates: e.g.'1908 to 1911' means '1908-09-10-11'; otherwise individual years are shown.
Eur	GBI v Continent of Europe (Seve Trophy)		
WC	World Cup – by home country; was Canada (Cup) till 1966		Captaincy is indicated by the year printed in bold type; non-playing captaincy in brackets

ENGLAND

Alliss, Percy – **RC** 1929-31-33-35-37; Sco 1932 to 1937; Irl 1932-38; Wal 1938. GBI: Fra 1939

Alliss, Peter – **RC** 1953-57-59-61-63-65-67-69; CC 1954-55-57-58-59-61-62-64-66; WC 1967

Archer, Phillip – Eur 2007

Baker, Peter – **RC** 1993; DC 1993 (r/u)-98; WC 1999

Bamford, BJ – CC 1961

Barber, T – Irl 1932-33

Batley, JB – Sco 1912

Beck, AG – Wal, Irl 1938

Bembridge, Maurice – **RC** 1969-71-73-75; SA 1976; WC 1974-75; (S)Eur 1997

Bickerton, J – Eur 2000

Boomer, Aubrey – USA 1926; **RC** 1927-29

Bousfield, Ken – **RC** 1949-51-55-57-59-61; CC 1956-57

Boxall, R – WC 1990; DC 1990

Branch, WJ – Sco 1936

Brand, Gordon J – **RC** 1983; Nissan 1986; WC 1983; DC 1986-87*

Broadhurst, Paul – **RC** 1991; FT 1991-95; WC 1997; DC 1991

Burton, J – Irl 1933

Burton, R (Dick) – **RC** 1935-37-49; Sco 1935-36-37; Sco, Wal, Irl 1938

Busson, JH – Sco 1938

Busson, Jack J – **RC** 1935; Sco 1934-35-36-37

Butler, Peter J – **RC** 1965-69-71-73; Eur 1976; WC 1969-70-73

Carter, D – DC 1998; WC 1998*

Casey, Paul – **RC** 2004-06-08; WC 2004; Eur 2003-05-07

Cawsey, GH – Sco 1906-07

Caygill, G Alex – **RC** 1969

Chapman, R – DC 2000

Clark, Clive – **RC** 1973

Clark, Howard K – **RC** 1977-81-85-87-89-95; Aus 1988; Eur 1978-84; Nissan 1985; WC 1978-84-85-87; DC 1985-86-87*-89-90-94-95

Claydon, R – DC 1997

Coles, Neil C – **RC** 1961-63-65-67-69-71-73-77; Eur 1974-76-78-80; (S)Eur 1998-99; Can 1963; WC 1968

Collinge, T – Sco 1937

Collins, JF – Sco 1903-04

Compston, Archie – USA 1926; **RC** 1927-29-31; Fra 1929; Sco, Irl 1932; Sco 1935

Cotton, T Henry – **RC** 1929-37-47; Fra 1929

Cox, WJ (Bill) – **RC** 1935-37; Sco 1935-36-37

Curtis, D – Sco 1934; Sco, Wal, Irl 1938

Davis, Brian – DC 2000; Eur 2005

Davies, William H – **RC** 1931-33; Sco, Irl 1932-33

Dawson, Peter – **RC** 1977; WC 1977

Denny, Charles S – Sco 1936

Donald, Luke – **RC** 2004-06; WC 2004-06

Dougherty, Nick – Eur 2005-07

Durnian, Denis – WC 1989; DC 1989; WbC 2001-02

Dyson, Simon – Eur 2007

Easterbrook, Syd – **RC** 1931-33; Sco 1932 to 35, 38; Irl 1933

Faldo, Nick A – **RC** 1977-79-81-83-85-87-89-91-93-95-97-(08); Eur 1978-80-82-84; RoW 1982; Nissan 1986; Kirin 1987; FT 1990; WC 1977-91-98*; DC 1985-86-87*-88-91-93; WbC 2001-02

Faulkner, Max – **RC** 1947-49-51-53-57

Foster, M – Eur 1976; WC 1976

Gadd, B – Sco, Irl 1933; Sco 1935; Sco, Irl, Wal 1938

Gadd, George – USA 1926; **RC** 1927

Garner, John R – **RC** 1971-71

Gaudin, PJ – Sco 1905-06-07-09-12-13

Gilford, David – **RC** 1991-95; WC 1992-93; DC 1992*

Gray, E – Sco 1904-05-07

Green, Eric – **RC** 1947

Green, T – Sco 1935; also Wal v Sco, Irl 1937 and Sco, Eng 1938

Gregson, Malcolm – RC 1967; WC 1967; (S)Eur 1997

Hargreaves, Jack – RC 1951

Havers, AG – USA 1921-26; RC 1927-31-33; Fra 1929; Sco, Irl 1932-33; Sco 1934

Hitchcock, Jimmy – RC 1965

Horne, Reg – RC 1947

Horton, Tommy – RC 1975-77; Eur 1974-76; WC 1976; (S)Eur 1997-(98)-(99)

Howell, David – RC 2004-06; Eur 2000-03-05; DC 1999; WC 2005

Hunt, Bernard J – RC 1953-57-59-61-63-65-67-69; Can 1958-59-60-62-63-64; WC 1968

Hunt, Guy L – RC 1975; Eur 1974; WC 1972-75

Hunt, Geoffrey M – RC 1963

Jacklin, A (Tony) – RC 1967-69-71-73-75-77-79-(83)-(85)-(87)-(89); Eur 1976-82; RoW 1982; Can 1966; WC 1970-71-72

Jacobs, John RM – RC 1955

Jagger, D – Eur 1976

James, Mark H – RC 1977-79-81-89-91-93-95-(99); Eur 1978-80-82; RoW 1982; Aus 1988; Kirin 1988; FT 1989-90; WC 1978-79-82-84-87-88-93-97-99; DC 1988-89-90-93-95-97-99

Jarman, Edward W – RC 1935; Sco 1935

Job, Nick – Eur 1980

Jolly, Herbert C – USA 1926; RC 1927; Fra 1929

Jones, D – (S)Eur 1998-99

Jones, R – Sco 1903 to 07, 09-10-12-13

Kenyon, EWH – Sco, Irl 1932

King, Michael – RC 1979; WC 1979

King, Sam L – RC 1937-47-49; Sco 1934-36-37; Sco, Wal, Irl 1938

Lacey, Arthur J – RC 1933-37; Sco, Irl 1932-33; Sco 1934-36-37; Sco, Irl, Wal 1938

Lane, Barry – RC 1993; WC 1988-94; DC 1988-94-95-96; WbC 2002

Lees, Arthur – RC 1947-49-51-55; Sco, Wal, Irl 1938

Mason, SC – Eur 1980; WC 1980

Mayo, CH – Sco 1907-09-10-12-13

Mills, R Peter – RC 1957-59

Mitchell, Abe – USA 1921-26; RC 1929-31-33; Sco 1932-33-34

Mitchell, P – WC 1996

Moffitt, Ralph – RC 1961

Morgan, J – (S)Eur 1997-99

Ockenden, J – USA 1921

Oke, WG – Sco 1932

Oosterhuis, Peter A – RC 1971-73-75-77-79-81; Eur 1974; WC 1971

O'Sullivan, DF – (S)Eur 1998

Padgham, Alf H – RC 1933-35-37; Sco, Irl 1932-33; Sco 1934 to 37; Sco, Irl, Wal 1938

Payne, J – WC 1996

Perry, Alf – RC 1933-35-37; Irl 1932; Sco 1933-36-38

Platts, Lionel – RC 1965

Poulter, Ian – RC 2004-08; Eur 2005; WC 2007

Price, Phillip – Eur 2003

Rainford, P – Sco 1903-07

Ray, E (Ted) – USA 1921-26; RC 1927; Sco 1903 to 07, 09-10-12-13

Reid, W – Sco 1906-07

Renouf, TG – Sco 1903-04-05-10-13

Rhodes, J – (S)Eur 1998

Richardson, Steven – RC 1991; FT 1991; WC 1992; DC 1991-92*

Robson, F – USA1926; RC 1927-29-31; Sco 1909-10

Roe, Mark – WC 1989-94-95; DC 1994

Rose, Justin – RC 2008; Eur 2003-07; WC 2007

Rowe, AJ – Sco 1903-06-07

Scott, Syd S – RC 1955

Seymour, M – sco: Irl 1932. ENG: Sco, Irl 1932-33

Sherlock, JG – USA 1921; Sco 1903 to 07, 09-10-12-13

Snell, D – Canada 1965

Spence, J – DC 1992*-2000

Storm, Graeme – Eur 2007

Sutton, M – Can 1955

Taylor, JH – USA 1921; Sco 1903 to 07, 09-10-12-13

Taylor, JJ – Sco 1937

Taylor, Josh – USA 1921; Sco 1913

Tingey, A – Sco 1903-05

Townsend, Peter – RC 1969-71; Eur 1974; WC 1969-74

Twine, WT – Irl 1932

Vardon, Harry – USA 1921

Waites, Brian J – RC 1983; Eur 1980-82-84; RoW 1982; WC 1980-82-83; (S)Eur 1997-98

Ward, Charlie H – RC 1947-49-51; Irl 1932

Way, Paul – RC 1983-85; WC 1985; DC 1985-99

Weetman, Harry – RC 1951-53-55-55*-59-61-63; Can 1954-56-60

Westwood, Lee – RC 1997-99-2002-04-06-08; Eur 2000-03; DC 1996-97-98-99

Whitcombe, Charles A – RC 1927-29-31-33-35-37; Fra 1929; Sco 1932 to 38; Irl 1933

Whitcombe, EE – Sco, Wal, Irl 1938

Whitcombe, Ernest R – USA 1926; RC 1929-31-35; Fra 1929; Sco 1932; Irl 1933

Whitcombe, Reg A – RC 1935; Sco 1933 to 38

Wilcock, P – WC 1973

Williamson, T – Sco 1904 to 07, 09-10-12-13

Wilson, Oliver – RC 2008; Eur 2007

Wilson, RG – Sco 1913

Wolstenholme, Guy B – Can 1965

IRELAND

Boyle, Hugh F – RC 1967; WC 1967

Bradshaw, Harry – RC 1953-55-57; Can 1954 to 1959; Sco 1937-38; Wal 1937; Eng 1938

Carrol, LJ – Sco, Wal 1937; Sco, Eng 1938

Cassidy, D – Sco 1936; Sco, Wal 1937

Cassidy, J – Eng 1933; Sco 1934-35

Clarke, Darren – RC 1997-99-2002-04-06; Eur 2000; DC 1994 to 99; WC 1994-95-96

Daly, Fred – RC 1947-49-51-53; Sco 1936; Sco, Wal 1937; Sco, Eng 1938; Can 1954-55

Darcy, Eamonn – RC 1975-77-81-87; Eur 1976-84; SA 1976; WC 1976-77-83-84-85-87; DC 1987-88*-91

Drew, Norman V – RC 1959; Can 1960-61

Edgar, J – Sco 1938

Fairweather, S – Eng 1932; Sco 1933. sco: Eng 1933-35-36; Irl, Wal 1938

Feherty, David – RC 1991; FT 1990-91; DC 1985-86-90*-91-93; WC 1990

Greene, C – Can 1965

Hamill, J – Eng 1932; Eng, Sco 33; Sco 34-35

Harrington, Padraig – RC 1999-2002-04-06-08; Eur 2000-03-05; DC 1996 to 99; WC 1996-97*-98-99-2000-04-05-06

Hoey, M – WC 2007

Holley, W – Sco 1933-34-35-36-38; Eng 1932-33-38

Jackson, H – WC 1970-71

Jones, E – Can 1965

Kinsella, J – WC 1968-69-72-73

Kinsella, W – Sco 1937; Sco, Eng 1938

McCartney, J – Sco 1932 to 38; Eng 1932-33-38; Wal 1937

McDermott, M – Sco, Eng 1932

McDowell, Graeme – RC 2008; Eur 2005

McGinley, Paul – RC 2002-04-06; WC 1993-94-97*-98-99-2000-05-06; DC 1993-94-96-97-98-99-04; Eur 2005

McKenna, J – Sco 1936; Sco, Wal 1937; Sco, Wal, Eng 1938

McKenna, R – Sco, Eng 1933; Sco 1935

McNeill, H – Eng 1932

Mahon, PJ – Sco 1932 to 38; Eng 1932-33-38; Wal 1937-38

Martin, Jimmy – RC 1965; Can 1962-63-64-66; WC 1970

Maybin, G – WC 2007

O'Brien, W – Sco 1934-36; Sco, Wal 1937

O'Connor, Christy – RC 1955-57-59-61-63-65-67-69-71-73; Can 1956 to 64, 65, 66; WC 1967-68-69-71-73

O'Connor, Christy jr – RC 1975-89; Eur 1974-84; SA 1976; (S)Eur 1998; WC 1974-75-78-85-89-92; DC 1985-89-92

O'Connor, CJ – (S)Eur 1998

O'Connor, P – Sco, Eng 1932-33; Sco 1934-35-36

O'Leary, John E – RC 1975; Eur 1976-78-82; RoW 1982; WC 1972-80-82

O'Neill, J – Eng 1933

O'Neill, M – Sco, Eng 1933; Sco 1934

Patterson, E – Sco 1933 to 36; Eng 1933; Wal 1937

Polland, Eddie – RC 1973; Eur 1974-76-78-80; (S)Eur 1998-99; WC 1973-74-76-77-78-79

Pope, CW – Sco, Eng 1932

Rafferty, Ronan – RC 1989; Eur 1984; Kirin 1988; FT 1989-90-91; Aus 1988; WC 1983-84-87-88, 90 to 93; DC 1986-87-88*-89-90*-91-92-93-95

Smyth, Des – RC 1979-81; Eur 1980-82-84; RoW 1982; WC 1979-80-82-83-88-89; DC 1985-86-87-88*-2000; WbC 2001

Stevenson, P – Sco 1933 to 36, 38; Eng 1933-38

Wallace, L – Sco, Eng 1932

Walton, Philip – RC 1995; WC 1995; DC 1989-90*-92-94-95

SCOTLAND

Adams, J – RC 1947-49-51-53; Eng 1932 to 1938; Wal 1937-38; Irl 1937-38

Ainslie, T – Irl 1936

Anderson, Joe – Irl 1932

Anderson, W – Irl 1936; Eng, Wal 1937

Ayton, LB – Eng 1910-12-13-33-34

Ayton, Laurie B jr – RC 1949; Eng 1937

Ballantine, J – Eng 1932-36

Ballingall, J – Eng, Irl, Wal 1938

Bannerman, Harry – RC 1993; WC 1967-72

Barnes, Brian – RC 1969-71-73-75-77-79; Eur 1974-76-78-80; SA 1976; WC 1974-75-76-77

Braid, James – USA 1921; Eng 1903 to 07, 1910-12

Brand, Gordon jr – RC 1987-89; Aus 1988; Nissan 1985; Kirin 1988; FT 1989; WC 1984-85-88-89-90-92-94; DC 1985 to 89, 91 to 94, 97

Brown, Eric C – RC 1953-55-57-59; Can 1954 to 62, 65-66; WC 1967-68

Brown, Ken – RC 1977-79-83-85-87; Eur 1978; Kirin 1987; WC 1977-78-79-83

Burns, Stewart – RC 1929; Eng 1932

Callum, WS – Irl 1935

Campbell, J – Irl 1936

Coltart, Andrew – RC 1999; DC 1994-95*-96-98-2000; WC 1994-95-96-98

Coltart, F – Eng 1909

Dailey, Allan – RC 1933; Eng 1932 to 36; Eng, Irl, Wal 1938

Davis, W – Irl 1933 to 36; Irl, Eng, Wal 1937-38

Dobson, T – Eng, Irl 1932 to 1936; Eng, Irl, Wal 1937; Irl, Wal 1938

Don, W – Irl 1935-36

Donaldson, J – Eng 1932-35-38; Irl, Wal 1937

Dorman, R – Irl 1932

Drummond, Scott – WC 2005-06

Duncan, George – USA 1921-26; RC 1927-29-31; Eng 1906-07-09-10-12-13-32-34 to 37

Durward, JG – Irl 1934; Eng 1937

Fairweather, S – IRL: Eng 1932; Sco 1933. SCO: Eng 1933-35-36; Irl, Wal 1938

Fallon, John – RC 1955; Eng 1936; Eng, Irl, Wal 1937-38

Fenton, WB – Eng, Irl 1932; Irl 1933

Fernie, TR – Eng 1910-12-13-33

Gallacher, Bernard – RC 1969-71-73-75-77-79-81-83-(91)-(93)-(95); Eur 1974-78-82-84; SA 1976; RoW 1982; WC 1969-71-74-82-83

Gallacher, Stephen – WC 2005-06

Good, G – Eng 1934-36

Gow, A – Eng 1912

Grant, T – Eng 1913

Haliburton, Tom B – RC 1961-63; Can 1954; Irl 1935-36; Irl, Wal, Eng 1938

Hastings, W – Eng, Wal, Irl 1937-38

Hepburn, J – Eng 1903-05-06-07-09-10-12-13

Herd, A (Sandy) – Eng 1903-04-05-06-09-10-12-13-32

Houston, D – Irl 1934

Huish, D – WC 1973

Hunter, W – Eng 1906-07-09-10

Hutton, GC – Irl 1936; Irl, Eng, Wal 1937; Eng 1938

Ingram, D – WC 1973

Knight, G – Eng 1937

Laidlaw, W – Eng 1935-36-38; Irl, Wal 1937

Lawrie, Paul – RC 1999-06; WC 1996; DC 1999; Eur 2003

Lockhart, G – Irl 1934-35

Lyle, AWB (Sandy) – RC 1979-81-83-85-87; Eur 1980-82-84; RoW 1982; Aus 1988; Nissan 1985-86; Kirin 1987; WC 1979-80-87; DC 1985 to 90, 92

McCulloch, D – Eng, Irl 1932 to 35; Eng 1936-37

McDowall, J – Eng 1932; Eng, Irl 1933 to 36

McEwan, P – Eng 1907

McIntosh, G – Eng, Irl, Wal 1938

McMillan, J – Eng, Irl 1933-34; Eng 1935

McMinn, W – Eng 1932-33-34

Martin, S – WC 1980

Montgomerie, Colin – RC 1991-93-95-97-99-2002-04-06; Eur 2000-03-05-07; FT 1991; WC 1988-91-92-93-97 (individual winner)-98-99-2006-07*; DC 1988, 91 to 98 (winners 95), 2000

Orr, Gary – Eur 2000; DC 1998-99-2000

Panton, John – RC 1951-53-61; Can 1955 to 66; WC 1968

Park, J – Eng 1909

Ritchie, WL – Eng 1913

Robertson, F – Irl 1933; Eng 1938

Robertson, P – Eng, Irl 1932; Irl 1934

Russell, Raymond – WC 1997; DC 1996-97

Sayers, Ben jr – Eng 1906-07-09

Seymour, M – Irl 1932. ENG: Sco, Irl 1932-33

Shade, Ronnie DBM – WC 1970-71-72

Simpson, A – Eng 1904

Smith, CR – Eng 1903-04-07-09-13
Smith, GE – Irl 1932
Spark, W – Irl 1933; Irl, Eng 1935; Irl, Wal 1937
Thompson, R – Eng 1903 to 07, 09-10-12
Torrance, Sam – **RC** 1981-83-85-87-89-91-93-95-**(2002)**; Eur 1976-78-80-82-84; RoW 1982; Nissan 1985; FT 1991; WC 1976-78-82-84-85-87-89-90-93-95; DC 1985-86-87-89-90-91-93-95*; WbC 2001-02
Walker, RT – Can 1964
Warren, Marc – Eur 2007; WC 2006-07*
Watt, T – Eng 1907
Watt, W – Eng 1912-13
White, J – Eng 1903 to 07, 09, 12-13
Will, George – **RC** 1963-65-67; Can 1963; WC 1969-70
Wilson, T – Irl 1932; Irl, Eng 1933-34
Wood, Norman – **RC** 1975; WC 1975

WALES

Affleck, P – DC 1995-96
Cox, S – WC 1975
Davies, R – WC 1968

De Foy, Craig B – WC 1971, 73 to 78
Dobson, K – WC 1972
Dodd, Stephen – Eur 2005; WC 2005*-06-07
Dredge, Bradley – Eur 2005-07; WC 2005*-06-07
Gould, H – Can 1954-55
Grabham, C – Eng, Sco 1938
Healing, SF – Sco 1938
Hill, EF – Sco, Irl 1937; Sco, Eng 1938
Hodson, Bert – **RC** 1931; Sco, Irl 1937; Sco, Eng 1938; also Eng v Irl 1933
Huggett, Brian GC – **RC** 1963-67-69-71-73-75; Eur 1974-78; Can 1963-64-65; WC 1968-69-70-71-76-79; (S)Eur 1998
James, G – Sco, Irl 1937
Jones, DC – Sco, Irl 1937; Sco, Eng 1938
Jones, T – Sco 1936; Irl 1937; Eng 1938
Llewellyn, D – Eur 1984; WC 1974-85-87*-88; DC 1985-88
Lloyd, F – Sco, Irl 1937; Sco, Eng 1938
Mayo, Paul – DC 1993
Mouland, Mark – Kirin 1988; WC 1988-89-90-92-93-95-96; DC 1986-87-88-89-93-95-96

Mouland, S – Can 1965-66; WC 1967
Park, D – DC 2000
Parkin, P – Eur 1984; WC 1984-89; DC 1985-86-87-89-90-91
Pickett, C – Sco, Irl 1937; Sco, Eng 1938
Price, Phillip – **RC** 2002; Eur 2000; WC 1994-95-97-98-2000; DC 1991-96
Rees, Dai J – **RC** 1937-47-49-51-53-**(55)**-**(57)***-**(59)**-**(61)**-**(67)**
Smalldon, D – Can 1955-56
Thomas, Dave C – **RC** 1959-63-65-67; Can 1957 to 63, 66; WC 1967-69-70
Vaughan, DI – WC 1972-73-77-78-79-80
Williams, K – Sco, Irl 1937; Sco, Eng 1938
Williams, KL – WC 1982
Woosnam, Ian – **RC** 1983-85-87-89-91-93-95-97-**(2006)**; Eur 1982-84-2000; RoW 1982; Aus 1988; Nissan 1985-86; Kirin 1987; FT 1989-90; WC 1980, 82 to 85, 87*, 90 to 94, 96-97-98; DC 1985 to 91, 93-95-2000; WbC 2001-02

Professional Women   Non-playing captaincy in brackets

ENGLAND

Davies, Laura – SOLHEIM CUP 1990-92-94-96-98-2000-2002-03-05-07; World Cup 2006

Douglas, Kitrina – SOLHEIM CUP 1992

Fairclough, Lora – SOLHEIM CUP 1994

Hackney, Lisa – SOLHEIM CUP 1996-98

Johnson, Trish – SOLHEIM CUP 1990-92-94-96-98-2000-05-07

Masters, Danielle – World Cup 2008

Morley, Joanne – SOLHEIM CUP 1996

Nicholas, Alison – SOLHEIM CUP 1990-92-94-96-98-2000

Stupples, Karen – SOLHEIM CUP 2005

Taylor, Kirsty – World Cup 2006

Walker, Mickey – SOLHEIM CUP **(1990)-(92)-(94)-(96)**

SCOTLAND

McKay, Mhairi – SOLHEIM CUP 2002-03; World Cup 2008

Marshall, Kathryn – SOLHEIM CUP 1996

Matthew, Catriona – SOLHEIM CUP 1998-2003-05-07; World Cup 2006-08

Moodie, Janice – SOLHEIM CUP 2000-03; World Cup 2006

Reid, Dale – SOLHEIM CUP 1990-92-94-96-**(2000)-(2002)**

Wright, Pam – SOLHEIM CUP 1990-92-94

WALES

Brewerton, Becky – SOLHEIM CUP 2007; World Cup 2006-08

Morgan, Becky – World Cup 2006-08

Amateur Men

Key

WC	Walker Cup
AP	Europe v Asia-Pacific (Bonallack Trophy)
CT	Commonwealth Tournament
ET	Eisenhower Trophy
ETC	played in European Team Championship for home country
Eur	GBI v Cont of Europe (St Andrews Trophy)
HI	played in Home International matches

NNC	Nixdorf Nations Cup
Scan	Scandinavia
*	indicates winning team

'to' indicates inclusive dates: e.g.'1908 to 1911' means '1908-09-10-11'; otherwise individual years are shown.

Captaincy is indicated by the year printed in bold type; non-playing captaincy in brackets

ENGLAND

Adcock, Todd – HI 2008

Ashby, H – Dominican Int 1973; Eur 1974; HI 1972-73-74

Attenborough, MF – WC 1967; Eur 1966-68; HI 1964-66-67-68; ETC 1967

Aylmer, CC – USA 1921; **WC** 1922; Sco 1911-22-23-24

Baker, P – WC 1985; Eur 1986; HI 1985

Baldwin, Matt – HI 2007

Ball, J – Sco 1902 to 12

Banks, C – HI 1983

Banks, SE – HI 1934-38

Bardsley, R – HI 1987; Fra 1988

Barker, HH – Sco 1907

Barry, AG – Sco 1906-07

Bathgate, D – HI 1990

Bayliss, RP – Irl 1929; HI 1933-34

Beck, JB – WC 1928-**(38)***-**(47)**; Sco 1926-30; HI 1933

Beddard, JB – Wal/Irl 1925; Sco 1927-28; Sco, Irl 1929

Beharrell, JC – HI 1956

Bell, RK – HI 1947

Benka, PJ – WC 1969; Eur 1970; HI 1967-68-69-70; ETC 1969

Bennett, H – HI 1948-49-51

Bennett, S – Sco 1979

Bennett, S – ET 1994; Eur 1994; HI 1992-93-94; Fra 1994

Benson, Seve – Aus 2007

Bentley, AL – HI 1936-37; Fra 1937-39

Bentley, HG – WC 1934-36-38; Sco, Irl 1931; HI 1932 to 38, 47; Fra 1934 to 37, 39, 54

Berry, P – Eur 1972; HI 1972

Birtwell, SG – HI 1968-70-73

Blackey, M – HI 1995-96-97; ETC 1997; Fra 1994-96; Esp 1995

Bladon,W – Eur 1996; HI 1996

Blakeman, D – HI 1981; Fra 1982

Bland, R – HI 1994-95; Esp 1995

Bloxham, JA – HI 1966

Bonallack, Sir Michael F – WC 1957 to 73, **(69-71*)**; ET 1960 to 72; CT 1959-63-67-71; Eur 1958, 62 to 72; HI 1957 to 74; ETC 1969-71

Bottomley, S – HI 1986

Bourn, TA – Aus 1934; Irl 1928; Sco 1930; HI 1933-34; Fra 1934

Bowman, TH – HI 1932

Boyd, Gary – HI 2006-07; ETC 2007; Aus 2007

Boxall, R – HI 1980-81-82; Fra 1982

Bradshaw, AS – HI 1932

Bradshaw, EI – Sco 1979; ETC 1979

Bradshaw, Paul – HI 2003

Bramston, JAT – Sco 1902

Brand, GJ – Eur 1976; HI 1976

Bretherton, CF – Sco 1922 to 25; Wal/Irl 1925

Bristowe, OC – WC 1923-24

Broadhurst. P – Eur 1988; HI 1986-87; Fra 1988

Bromley-Davenport, E – HI 1938-51

Brough, S – Eur 1960; HI 1952-55-59-60; Fra 1952-60

Brownlow, Hon WGE – WC 1926

Burch, N – HI 1974

Burgess, MJ – HI 1963-64-67; ETC 1967

Butterworth, JR – Fra 1954

Cage, S – WC 1993; HI 1992

Caldwell, I – WC 1951-55; HI 1950 to 59, 61; Fra 1950

Cannon, JHS – Irl/Wal 1925

Carman, A – Sco 1979; HI 1980

Carr, FC – Sco 1911

Carrigill, PM – HI 1978

Carver, M – HI 1996; ETC 1997

Casey, P – WC 1999; ET 2000; Eur 2000; HI 1999

Cassells, C – HI 1989

Castle, H – Sco 1903-04

Chapman, BHG – WC 1961; Eur 1962; HI 1961-62

Chapman, R – WC 1981; Eur 1980; Sco 1979; HI 1980-81; ETC 1981

Christmas, MJ – WC 1961-63; Eur 1962-64; ET 1962; HI 1960 to 64

Clark, CA – WC 1965; Eur 1964; HI 1964

Clark, Graeme – HI 1995-2002-03; ETC 2001; Esp 2001-03 Fra 2002

Clark, GJ – WC 1965; Eur 1964-66

Clark, HK – WC 1973; HI 1973

Claydon, Russell – WC 1989; HI 1988; ETC 1989

Colt, HS – Sco 1908

Cook, J – HI 1989-90

Cook, JH – 1969

Corfield, Lee – Eur 2004; HI 2002-04; Esp 2005

Crampton, James – HI 2005

Crawley, Leonard G – WC 1932-34-38-47; Sco, Irl 1931; HI 1932-33-34-36-37-38-47-48-49-54-55; Fra 1936-37-38-49

Critchley, MJ – WC 1969; Eur 1970; HI 1962-69-70; ETC 1969

Cryer, Matthew – HI 2005-07; Fra 2006

Curry, DH – WC 1987; ET 1986; Eur 1986-88; HI 1984-86-87; Fra 1988

Darwin, Bernard – WC 1922; Sco 1902-04-05-08-09-10-23-24

Davies, JC – WC 1973-75-77-79; ET 1974-76*; Eur 1972-74-76-78; HI 1969-71-72-73-74-78; ETC 1973-75-77

Davies, M – HI 1984-85

Davison, C – HI 1989

Dawson, P – HI 1969

De Bendern, Count J (John de Forest) – WC 1932; Sco, Irl **1931**

Deeble, P – WC 1977-81; Eur 1978; Colombian Int 1978; HI 1975-76-77-78-80-81-83-84; Sco 1979; ETC 1979-81; Fra 1982

Dinwiddie, Robert – WC 2005; HI 2004-05-06; Eur 2006; Esp 2005; Fra 2006

Dixon, D – HI 2000; RSA Esp 2001

Dodd, Laurence – HI 2004

Donald, Luke – WC 1999-2001; ET 1998*-2000; Eur 2000; HI 1996-97-98; ETC 1999-2001; Fra 1996

Dougherty, Nick – WC 2001; Eur 2000; HI 2000; ETC 2001; Fra 2000; Esp 2001

Downes, P – Eur 1980; HI 1976-77-78-80-81-82; ETC 1977-79-81

Downie, JJ – HI 1974

Drummond, S – HI 1995

Duck, R – HI 1997

Dunn, NW – Irl 1928

Durrant, RA – HI 1967; ETC 1967

Dyson, S – WC 1999; HI 1998-99; ETC 1999; Esp 1999

Edwards, CS – AP 2002; HI 1991 to 95, 97-98, 2003; ETC 1995-99; Fra 1992-94-96-2000; Esp 1993-95-99-2001

Eggo, R – WC 1987; Eur 1988; HI 1986 to 90; Fra 1988

Ellis, HC – Sco 1902-12

Ellison, TF – Sco 1922-25-26-27

Elson, Jamie – WC 2001; HI 2000-01-02; Fra 2000-02; Esp 2001

Evans, Ben – HI 2007

Evans, G – HI 1961

Evans, G – WC 1991; ET 1990; HI 1990; ETC 1991

Eyles, GR – WC 1975; ET 1974; Eur 1974; HI 1974-75; ETC 1975

Fairbairn, KA – HI 1988

Faldo, N – CT 1975; HI 1975

Fenton, P – HI 1996

Ferrie, K – HI 1998

Fiddian, EW – WC 1932-34; Sco, Irl 1929-30-31; HI 1932 to 35; Fra 1934

Finch, Richard – HI 2000-02; ETC 2003; Fra 2000-02; Esp 2003

Fisher, D – Eur 1994; HI 1993-94; Fra 1994

Fisher, Oliver – WC 2005; ET 2006; ETC 2005; AP 2006; Eur 2006; HI 2005-06

Fisher, Ross – HI 2003; ETC 2003

Fogg, HN – HI 1933

Fleetwood, Tommy – HI 2008

Ford, Charles – HI 2007-08; ETC 2008

Foster, M – WC 1995; HI 1994-95; ETC 1995; Esp 1995

Foster, MF – HI 1973

Foster, R – WC 1965-67-69-71-73-(79)-(81); ET 1964-70-80; Eur 1964-66-68-70; CT 1967-71; HI 1963-64, 66 to 72; ETC 1967-69-71-73

Fowler, WH – Sco 1903-04-05

Fox, SJ – HI 1956-57-58

Frame, DW – WC 1961; HI 1958 to 63

Francis, F – HI 1936; Fra 1935-36

Frazier, K – HI 1938

Fry, SH – Sco 1902 to 09

Garbutt, I – Eur 1992; HI 1990-91-92; ETC 1991; Fra 1992

Garner, PF – HI 1977-78-80; Sco 1979

Garnet, LG – Aus 1934; Fra 1934

Gee, Adam – HI 2004-06; Esp 2005; Fra 2006

Gent, J – Irl 1930; HI 1938

Gilford, David – WC 1985; ET 1984; Eur 1986; HI 1983-84-85

Gillies, HD – Sco 1908-25-26-27

Goddard, Luke – WC 2008; HI 2008

Godfrey, S – HI 2001

Godwin, G – WC 1979-81; HI 1976-77-78-80-81; Sco 1979; ETC 1979-81; Fra 1982

Gray, CD – HI 1932

Green, HB – Sco 1979

Green, PO – CT 1963; HI 1961-62-63

Griffiths, D – HI 1999-2000-01; Fra 2000; RSA, Esp 2001

Haines, Matt – ETC 2008; Eur 2008; Fra 2008

Hambro, AV – Sco 1905-08-09-10-22

Hamer, S – HI 1983-84

Hardman, RH – WC 1928; Sco 1927-28

Hare, A – WC 1989; HI 1988; ETC 1989

Harris, G – HI 1994; ETC 1995; Esp 1995

Harris, M – Eur 2000; HI 1998-99

Hartley, RW – WC 1930-32; Sco 1926 to 31; Irl 1928 to 31; HI 1933-34-35

Hartley, WL – WC 1932; Irl/Wal 1925; Sco 1927-31; Irl 1928-31; HI 1932-33; Fra 1935

Hassall, JE – Sco 1923; Irl/Wal 1925

Hawksworth, J – WC 1985; HI 1984-85

Hayward, CH – Sco 1925; Irl 1928

Heath, James – ET 2004; Eur 2004; AP 2004; HI 2003-04

Hedges, PJ – WC 1973-75; ET 1976; Eur 1974-76; HI 1970, 73 to 78, 82-83; ETC 1973-75-77

Helm, AGB – HI 1948

Henriques, GLQ – Irl 1930

Henry, W – HI 1987; Fra 1988

Hill, GA – WC 1936-(1955); HI 1936-37

Hilton, HH – Sco 1902 to 07, 09 to 12

Hilton, M – Esp 1999

Hoad, PGJ – HI 1978; Sco 1979

Hodgson, C – Sco 1924

Hodgson, J – HI 1994

Holderness, Sir EWE – USA 1921; WC 1923-26-30; Sco 1922 to 26, 28

Holmes, AW – HI 1962

Homer, TWB – WC 1973; ET 1972; Eur 1972; HI 1972-73; ETC 1973

Homewood, G – HI 1985-91; ETC 1991

Hooman, CVL – WC 1922-23; Sco 1910-22

Horsey, David – Fra 2006; ETC 2007; Aus 2007

Howell, D – WC 1995; HI 1994-95; ETC 1995; Esp 1995

Huddy, G – WC 1961; HI 1960-61-62

Humphreys, W – WC 1971; Eur 1970; HI 1970-71; ETC 1971

Hutchings, C – Sco 1902

Hutchinson, HG – Sco 1902-03-04-06-07-09

Hutsby, Sam – WC 2008; ETC 2008; Eur 2008; HI 2007-08; Fra 2008

Hutt, R – HI 1991-92-93

Hyde, GE – HI 1967-68

Illingworth, G – Sco 1929; Fra 1937

Inglis, MJ – HI 1977

James, L – WC 1995; ET 1994; Eur 1994; HI 1993-94-95; ETC 1995; Fra 1994; Esp 1995

James, M – WC 1975; HI 1974-75; ETC 1975

James, RD – HI 1974-75

Jobson, RH – Irl 1928

Jones, JW – HI 1948 to 52, 54-55

Keenan, Farren – HI 2008

Kelley, MJ – WC 1977-79; ET 1976*; Eur 1976-78; Colombian Int 1978; HI 1974 to 78, 80-81-82-**(88)**; ETC 1977-79; Fra 1982

Kelley, PD – HI 1965-66-68

Kemp, John – HI 2003

Keppler, SD – WC 1983; HI 1982-83; Fra 1982

King, M – WC 1969-73; Eur 1970-72; CT 1971; HI 1969 to 73; ETC 1971-73

Kitchin, JE – Fra 1949

Knight, J – Fra 1996

Langley, JDA – WC 1936-51-53; HI 1950 to 53; Fra 1950

Langmead, J – HI 1986

Lassen, EA – Sco 1909 to 12

Laurence, C – HI 1983-84-85

Layton, EN – Sco 1922-23-26; Irl/Wal 1925

Lee, M – HI 1950

Lee, MG – HI 1965

Lewis, ME – WC 1983; HI 1980-81-82-**(99)-(2001)**; Fra 1982

Lewton, Stephen – HI 2006; Aus 2007

Lincoln, AC – Sco 1907

Lockerbie, Gary – WC 2005, HI 2003-04; ETC 2005; Esp 2005

Logan, GW – HI 1973

Lucas, D – HI 1996

Lucas, PB – WC 1936-47-**(49)**; HI 1936-48-49; Fra 1936

Ludwell, N – HI 1991; Fra 1992

Lunt, MSR – WC 1959-61-63-65; ET 1964; Eur 1964; CT 1963; HI 1956 to 60, 62-63-64-66

Lunt, S – HI 1932 to 35; Fra 1934-35-39

Lupton, Jonathan – HI 2001-02; ETC 2003; Fra 2002; Esp 2003

Lyle, AWB (Sandy) – WC 1977; Eur 1976; CT 1975; HI 1975-76-77; ETC 1977

Lynn, D – HI 1995

Lyon, JS – HI 1937-38

McCarthy, S – HI 1998

McEvoy, Peter – WC 1977-79-81-85-89**(1999)*-(2001)***; ET 1978-80-84-86-88*; Eur 1978-80-86-88; HI 1976-77-78, 80-81, 83 to 89, 91, **(94) to (97)**; Sco 1979; ETC 1977-79-81-89; Fra 1982-88-92-**(02)**

McEvoy, R – WC 2001; HI 2000-01; ETC 2001; Fra 2000; Esp 2001

McGowan, Ross – ET 2006; Eur 2006; HI 2006

McGuire, M – HI 1992

Marks, GC – WC 1969-71-**(87)-(89)***; ET 1970; Eur 1968-70; CT 1975; Colombian Int 1975; HI 1963, 67 to 71, 74-75-82; ETC 1967-69-71-75; Fra **(1982)**

Marsh, David M – WC 1959-71-**(73)-(75)**; Eur 1958; HI 1956 to 60, 64-66, 68 to 72; ETC 1971

Martin, DHR – HI 1938; Fra 1934-49

Mason, B – HI 1998-99; Esp 1999

Mason, SC – HI 1973

Mellin, GL – Sco 1922

Metcalfe, J – Eur 1990; HI 1989

Micklem, Gerald H – WC 1947-49-53-55-**(57)-(59)**; ET 1958; HI 1947 to 55

Millensted, Dudley J – WC 1967; CT 1967; HI 1966; ETC 1967

Millward, EB – WC 1949-55; HI 1950, 52 to 55

Mitchell, Abe – Sco 1910-11-12

Mitchell, CS – HI 1975-76-78

Mitchell, FH – Sco 1906-07-08

Moffat, DM – HI 1961-63-67; Fra 1959-60

Montmorency, RH de – USA 1921; Sco 1908; Wal/Irl 1925; SA 1927

Moody, PH – Eur 1972; HI 1971-72

Morgan, J – Fra 2000

Morrison, JSF – Irl 1930

Mosey, IJ – HI 1971

Moul, Jamie – ET 2006; ETC 2005-07; Eur 2006; HI 2005-06; Esp 2005; Fra 2006; Aus 2007

Muscroft, R – HI 1986

Nash, A – HI 1988-89

Neech, DG – HI 1961

Nelson, P – Fra 1996

Newey, AS – HI 1932

Oldcorn, Andrew – WC 1983; ET 1982; HI 1982-83

Oosterhuis, Peter A – WC 1967; ET 1968; Eur 1968; HI 1966-67-68

Oppenheimer, RH – WC **(1951)**; Irl 1928-29; Irl, Sco 1930

Osborne, Sam – Eur 2004

Page, P – WC 1993; HI 1993

Paisley, Chris – Eur 2008

Palmer, DJ – HI 1962-63

Parker, Ben – HI 2006-07; Aus 2007

Parry, John – Fra 2006; ETC 2007

Patey, IR – HI 1925; Fra 1948-49-50

Pattinson, R – HI 1949

Payne, J – HI 1950-51

Payne, J – WC 1991; Eur 1990; HI 1989-90; ETC 1991

Pearson, AG – SA 1927

Pearson, MJ – HI 1951-52

Pease, JWB (Lord Wardington) Sco 1903 to 06

Pennink, JJF – WC 1938; HI 1937-38-47; Fra 1937-38-39

Pepperell, Eddie – HI 2008

Perkins, TP – WC 1928; Sco 1927-28-29

Perowne, AH – WC 1949-53-59; ET 1958; HI 1947 to 51, 53-54-55-57

Philipson, S – HI 1997

Phillips, V – WC 1993

Plaxton, Jonathan – HI 1983-84-**(08)**; ETC **(2007)**

Pollock, VA – Sco 1908

Powell, WA – Sco 1923-24; Wal/Irl 1925

Poxon, Martin A – WC 1975; HI 1975-76; ETC 1975

Prosser, D – ETC 1989

Pullan, M – HI 1991-92

Pyman, I – WC 1993; HI 1993

Rawlinson, D – HI 1949-50-52-53

Ray, D – HI 1982; Fra 1982

Revell, RP – HI 1972-73; ETC 1973

Reynard, M – HI 1996-97; Fra 1996

Richardson, Edward – HI 2005-06; Fra 2006

Richardson, Matthew – WC 2005; ET 2004; Eur 2004; HI 2004; Esp 2003; ETC 2005; Esp 2005

Richardson, S – HI 1986-87-88

Risdon, PWL – HI 1935-36
Roberts, GP – HI 1951-53; Fra 1949
Roberts, HJ – HI 1947-48-53
Robertson, A – HI 1986-87; Fra 1988
Robinson, J – Irl 1928
Robinson, J – **WC** 1987; HI 1986
Robinson, S – Sco 1925; Irl 1928-29-30
Rodgers, C – HI 1999; Esp 1999
Rogers, A – HI 1991; Fra 1992
Roper, HS – Sco, Irl 1931
Roper, R – HI 1984 to 87
Rose, Justin – **WC** 1997; HI 1997; ETC 1997
Rothwell, J – HI 1947-48
Rowe, Philip – **WC** 1999; AP 2000; HI 1997-98-2000; ETC 1999; Esp 1999
Ruth, James – HI 2004-05; Esp 2005
Ryles, D – HI 2000
Sanders, M – HI 1998-99; Esp 1999
Sandywell, A – HI 1990; ETC 1991
Scotland, Zane – HI 2000-01-02; Fra 2000-02
Scott, KB – HI 1937-38; Fra 1938
Scott, Hon Michael – **WC** 1924-**(34)**; Aus 1934; Sco 1911-12, 23 to 26
Scott, Hon O – Sco 1902-05-06
Scrutton, EWHB – Sco 1912
Scrutton, PF – **WC** 1955-57; HI 1950-55
Sell, Martin – Esp 2003
Sewell, D – **WC** 1957-59; ET 1960; CT 1959; HI 1956 to 60
Shepperson, AE – **WC** 1957-59; HI 1956 to 60, 62
Sherborne, A – HI 1982-83-84
Sherreard, Tom – HI 2008
Shingler, TR – HI 1977
Shorrock, TJ – Fra 1952
Side, M – HI 1999
Skelton, Michael – **WC** 2003*; HI 2003-04
Skinns, David – HI 2001-02-03; Fra 2002
Slark, WA – HI 1957
Slater, A – HI 1955-62
Smith, Eric M – Sco, Irl 1931
Smith, Everard – Sco 1908-09-10-12
Smith, GF – Sco 1902-03
Smith, JR – HI 1932

Smith, LOM – HI 1963
Smith, W – Eur 1972; HI 1972
Snowdon, J – HI 1934
Stanford, M – **WC** 1993; ET 1992; Eur 1992; HI 1991-92-93; Fra 1992
Steel, Donald MA – HI 1970
Stevens, LB – Sco 1912
Storey, EF – **WC** 1924-26-28; Sco 1924 to 28, 30; HI 1936; Fra 1936
Storm, G – **WC** 1999; HI 1999; ETC 1999
Stott, HAN – HI 1976-77
Stout, JA – **WC** 1930-32; Sco 1928 to 31; Irl 1929-31
Stowe, C – **WC** 1938-47; HI 1935 to 38, 47-49-54; Fra 1938-39-49
Straker, R – HI 1932
Streeter, P – HI 1992; Fra 1994-96
Stubbs, AK – HI 1982
Suneson, C – HI 1988; ETC 1989
Sutherland, DMG – HI 1947
Sutton, W – Sco 1929-31; Irl 1929-30-31
Tate, JK – HI 1954-55-56
Taylor, HE – Sco 1911
Thirlwell, A – **WC** 1957; Eur 1956-58-64; CT 1953-64; HI 1951-52, 54 to 58, 63-64
Thirsk, TJ – Irl 1929; HI 1933 to 38; Fra 1935 to 39
Thom, KG – **WC** 1949; HI 1947-48-49-53
Thomas, I – HI 1933
Thompson, ASG – HI 1935-37
Thompson, MS – **WC** 1983; HI 1982
Tiley, Steven – HI 2004-05; ETC 2005; Esp 2005
Timmis, CT – Irl 1930; HI 1936-37
Tipping, EB – Irl 1930
Tipple, ER – Irl 1928-29; HI 1932
Tolley, Cyril JH – USA 1921; **WC** 1922-23-**24**-26-30-34; SA 1927; Sco 1922 to 30; Irl/Wal 1925; HI 1936-37-38; Fra 1938
Townsend, Peter M – **WC** 1965; ET 1966; Eur 1966; HI 1965-66
Tredinnick, SV – HI 1950
Tupling, LP – **WC** 1969; HI 1969; ETC 1969
Turner A – HI 1952
Tweddell, W – **WC** 1928-**(36)**; Sco 1928-29-30; HI 1935

Uzzell, Steve – HI 2008 ETC 2008 Fra 2008; Eur 2008
Wainwright, A – HI 1997-99
Walker, MS – Irl/Wal 1925
Walker, Richard – ET 2002; HI 2001-02-03; ETC 2003; Fra 2002; Esp 2003
Wallbank, K – HI 1996-97; Fra 1996
Walls, MPD – HI 1980-81-85
Walters, Justin – Esp 2003
Walton, AR – HI 1934-35
Wardrop, Daniel – Esp 2003
Waring, Paul – HI 2005-06; Fra 2006; ETC 2007
Warren, KT – HI 1962
Watts, C – HI 1991-92; Fra 1992
Way, Paul – **WC** 1981; HI 1981; ETC 1981
Webster, S – HI 1995-96; ETC 1997
Weeks, K – HI 1987-88; Fra 1988
Welch, M – HI 1993-94; Fra 1994
Wells, J – HI 1999
Westwood, Lee – HI 1993
Wethered, Roger H – USA 1921; **WC** 1922-23-26-**30**-34; Sco 1922 to 30
White, L – **WC** 1991; HI 1990; ETC 1991
White, RJ – **WC** 1947-49-51-53-55; HI 1947-48-49-53-54
Whitehouse, Tom – HI 2000
Whitnell, Dale – WC 2008; HI 2007-08; ETC 2008; Eur 2008; Fra 2008
Wiggett, M – HI 1990
Wiggins, R – Eur 1996; HI 1996; ETC 1997
Willett. Daniel – AP 2008; HI 2007; Fra 2008
Williams, DF – Sco 1979
Willison, R – **WC** 1991; ET 1990; Eur 1990; HI 1988-89-90; ETC 1989-91
Wilson, Oliver – WC 2003*; HI 2002; ETC 2003, Fra 2002
Winchester, R – HI 1985-87-89
Winter, G – HI 1991
Wise, WS – HI 1947
Wolstenholme, Gary P – **WC** 1995-97-99*-2001*-03*-05; ET 1996-98*-2002-**04**; Eur 1992-94-2004; AP 2000-04-06; HI 1988 to 2007; ETC 1995-97-99-2001-03-**05**-07; Fra 1988-92-94-2000-02-06; Esp 1989-91-95-99-2001-03-05; RSA 2001
Wolstenholme, Guy G – **WC** 1957-59; ET 1958-60; CT 1959; HI 1953, 55 to 60

Wood, Chris – AP 2008; HI 2007; ETC 2008; Fra 2008

Woollam, J – HI 1933-34-35; Fra 1935

Woolley, FA – Sco 1910-11-12

Worthington, JS – Sco 1905

Yasin Ali – HI 2002

Yeo, J – HI 1971

Zacharias, JP – HI 1935

Zoete, HW de – Sco 1903-04-06-07

IRELAND

Allison, A – Eng 1928; Sco 1929

Anderson, N – Eur 1988; HI 1985 to 90, 93; ETC 1989

Arthurs, Eoin – HI 2008

Babington, A – Wal 1913

Baker, RN – HI 1975

Bamford, JL – HI 1954-56

Beamish, CH – HI 1950-51-53-56

Bell, HE – Wal 1930; HI 1932

Bowden, Greg – HI 2004

Bowen, J – HI 1961

Boyd, HA – Wal 1913-23

Brady, E – HI 1995-98; ETC 1999

Branigan, D – HI 1975-76-77-80-81-82-86; ETC 1977-81; WGer, Fra, Swe 1976

Briscoe, A – Eng 1928 to 31; Sco, Wal 1929-30-31; HI 1932-33-38

Brown, JC – HI 1933 to 38, 48-52-53

Browne, S – HI 2001; ETC 2001

Bruen, J – WC 1938-49-51; HI 1937-38-49-50

Burke, J – WC 1932; Eng, Wal 1929; Eng, Wal, Sco 1930-31; HI 1932 to 38, 47-48-49

Burns, M – HI 1973-75-83; ETC **(2007)**

Burns, R – WC 1993; ET 1992; Eur 1992; HI 1991-92

Cairnes, HM – Sco, Eng 1904; Wal 1913-25; Sco 1927

Caldwell, Jonathan – WC 2008; HI 2006-08; ETC 2007-08; Eur 2008

Campbell, MK – HI 1999-2003-04

Carr, Joe B – WC 1947 to 63, **(65)-(67)**; ET 1958-60; Eur 1954-56-64-66-68; HI 1947 to 69; ETC 1965-67-69

Carr, JJ – HI 1981-82-83

Carr, JR – Wal 1930; Wal, Eng 1931; HI 1933

Carr, R – WC 1971; HI 1970-71; ETC 1971

Carroll, CA – Wal 1924

Carroll, JP – HI 1948-49-50-51-62

Carroll, W – Wal 1913-23-24-25; Eng 1925; Sco 1929; HI 1932

Carvill, J – Eur 1990; HI 1989; ETC 1989

Carvill, Jim – ETC 2005

Cashell, BG – HI 1978; Fra, WGer, Swe 1978

Caul, P – HI 1968-69, 1971 to 75

Clarke, D – Eur 1990; HI 1987-89

Cleary, T – HI 1976-77-78, 82 to 86; Wal 1979; Fra, WGer, Swe 1976

Corcoran, DK – HI 1972-73; ETC 1973

Corridan, T – HI 1983-84-91-92

Coughlan, R – WC 1997; HI 1991-94; ETC 1997

Crabbe, JL – Wal 1925; Sco 1927-28

Craddock, T – WC 1967-69; HI 1955 to 60, 67 to 70

Craigan, RM – HI 1963-64

Crosbie, GF – HI 1953-55-56-57-(88)

Crowe, Darren – ET 2004; HI 2002-03-04-05-06; ETC 2005

Crowley, M – Eng 1928 to 31; Wal 1929-31; Sco 1929-30-31; HI 1932

Cullen, G – AP 2000; HI 1999; ETC 1999

Curley, Cian – HI 2007-08

Cutler. Paul – WC 2008; HI 2007-08; ETC 2008

Davies, FE – Wal 1923

Dickson, JR – HI 1980; ETC 1977

Donellan, B – HI 1952

Dooley, Padraig – HI 2002

Doran, Connor – HI 2005-07

Drew, Norman V – WC 1953; HI 1952-53

Dunbar, Alan – HI 2008

Duncan, J – HI 1959-60-61

Dunne, D – HI 1997

Dunne, E – HI 1973-74-76-77-**(2001)**; Wal 1979; ETC 1975

Edwards, B – HI 1961-62, 64 to 69, 73

Edwards, M – HI 1956-57-58-60-61-62

Egan, TW – HI 1952-53-59-60-62-67-68; ETC 1967-69

Elliot, IA – HI 1975-77-78; ETC 1975; Fra, WGer, Swe 1978

Errity, D – HI 1990

Ewing, RC – WC 1936-38-47-49-51-55; HI 1934 to 38, 47 to 51, 53 to 58

Fanagan, J – WC 1995; Eur 1992-96; HI 1989 to 97; ETC 1995-97

Ferguson, M – HI 1952

Ferguson, WJ – HI 1952-54-55-58-59-61

French, WF – Sco 1929; HI 1932

Fitzgibbon, JF – HI 1955-56-57

Fitzsimmons, J – HI 1938-47-48

Flaherty, JA – HI 1934 to 37

Flaherty, PD – HI 1967; ETC 1967-69

Fleury, RA – HI 1974

Fogarty, GN – HI 1956-58-63-64-67

Foster, J – HI 1998-2000-01-03

Fox, Noel – WC 2003*; ET 2002; Eur 2000; AP 2004; HI 1996 to 99, 2001-02-03-04; ETC 1997-2001-03

Froggatt, P – HI 1957

Gannon, MA – Eur 1974-78; HI 1973-74-77-78-80-81-83-84, 87 to 90; ETC 1979-81-89-**(2005)**; Fra, WGer, Swe 1978-80

Gill, WJ – Wal 1931; HI 1932 to 37

Glover, J – HI 1951-52-53-55-59-60-70

Goulding, N – HI 1988 to 92; ETC 1991

Graham, JSS – HI 1938-50-51

Greene, R – HI 1933

Gribben, P – WC 1999; ET 1998*; HI 1997-98-99

Guerin, M – HI 1961-62-63

Hanway, M – HI 1971-74

Harrington, J – HI 1960-61-74-75-76; Wal 1979; ETC 1975

Harrington, Padraig – WC 1991-93-95; Eur 1992-94; HI 1990 to 95; ETC 1991-95

Hayes, JA – HI 1977

Healy, TM – Sco, Eng 1931

Heather, D – HI 1976; Fra, WGer, Swe 1976

Hegarty, J – HI 1975

Hegarty, TD – HI 1957

Henderson, J – Wal 1923

Herlihy, B – HI 1950

Heverin, AJ – HI 1978; Fra, WGer, Swe 1978

Hezlet, CO – WC 1924-26-28; SA 1927; Wal 1923-25-27-29-31; Sco 1927 to 31; Eng 1929-30-31

Higgins, D – HI 1993-94

Higgins, L – HI 1968-70-71

Hoey, M – WC 2001; HI 1999-2000-01; ETC 1999-2001

Hoey, TBC – HI 1970 to 73, 77-84; ETC 1971-77

Hogan, P – HI 1985 to 88; ETC 1991

Hulme, WJ – HI 1955-56-57

Humphreys, AR – Eng 1957

Hutton, R – HI 1991

Jameson, JF – Wal 1913-24

Johnson, TWG – Eng 1929

Jones, D – HI 1998

Kane, RM – Eur 1974; HI 1967-68-71-72-74-78; Wal 1979; ETC 1971-79

Kearney, Ken – HI 1988-89-90-92-94-95-97-98-2002; ETC 1999

Kearney, Niall – HI 2006-07-08; ETC 2008

Keenan, S – HI 1989

Kehoe, Justin – ET 2002; HI 2000-01-02-03; ETC 2003

Kelleher, WA – HI 1962

Kelly, NS – HI 1966

Kilduff, AJ – Sco 1928

Kilpatrick, Richard – HI 2003-04-05; ETC 2007

Kissock, B – HI 1961-62-74-76; Fra, WGer, Swe 1978

Lawrie, P – HI 1996; ETC 1997

Lehane, N – HI 1976; Fra, WGer, Swe 1976

Lernahan, Dara – HI 2008

Leyden, PJ – HI 1953-55-56-57-59

Long, D – HI 1973-74, 80 to 84; Wal 1979; ETC 1979

Lowe, A – Wal 1924; Eng 1925-28; Sco 1927-28

Lowry, Shane – WC 2008; AP 2008; HI 2006-07-98; ETC 2007-08; Eur 2008

Lyons, Joe – HI 2007

Lyons, P – HI 1986

McCarroll, F – HI 1968-69

McCarthy, L – HI 1953 to 56

McConnell, FP – Wal, Eng 1929; Wal, Eng, Sco 1930-31; HI 1934

McConnell, RM – Wal 1924-25-29-30-31; Eng 1925, 28 to 31; Sco 1927-28-29-31; HI 1934 to 37

McConnell, WG – Eng 1925

McCormack, JD – Wal 1913-24; Eng 1928; HI 1932 to 37

McCormick, Andrew – HI 1997 to 2002

McCrea, WE – HI 1965-66-67; ETC 1965

McCready, SM – WC 1949-51; HI 1947-49-50-52-54

McDaid, B – Wal 1979

McDermott, M – HI 2000-01; ETC 2001

McDowell, G – WC 2001; HI 2000; ETC 2001

McElhinney, Brian – WC 2005; ET 2004; AP 2004; HI 2003-04-05; ETC 2003-05

McGeady, Michael – HI 2003-04-05; ETC 2003-05

McGimpsey, G – WC 1985-89-91-(2003)*-(05); ET 1984-86-88*; Eur 1986-88-90-92-(2004); HI 1978, 80 to 99; Wal 1979; ETC 1981-89-91-95-97-99

McGinley, M – HI 1996

McGinley, P – WC 1991; HI 1989-90; ETC 1991

McGinn, John – HI 2002

McHenry, J – WC 1987; HI 1985-86

McIlroy, Rory – ET 2006; Eur 2006; AP 2006; HI 2005; ETC 2005-07

McInally, RH – HI 1949-51

Mackeown, HN – HI 1973; ETC 1973

McMenamin, E – HI 1981

McMonagle, C – HI 1999-2000; ETC 1999

McMullan, C – HI 1933-34-35

McNamara, Cian – HI 2004-05-07

MacNamara, L – HI 1977, 83 to 92; ETC 1977-91

McNeill, G – HI 1991-93-2001

McTernan, Sean – ET 2004; HI 2002-04-05; ETC 2005

Madeley, JFD – WC 1963; Eur 1962; HI 1959 to 64

Mahon, RJ – HI 1938-52-54-55

Malone, B – HI 1959-64-69-71-75; ETC 1971-75

Manley, N – Wal 1924; Sco 1927-28; Eng 1928

Marren, JM – Wal 1925

Martin, GNC – WC 1928; Wal 1923-29; Sco 1928-29-30; Eng 1929-30

Maybin, Gareth – HI 2002-04; ETC 2003

Meharg, W – HI 1957

Moore, GJ – Eng 1928; Wal 1929

Moriarty, Colm – WC 2003*; ET 2002; HI 2001-02; ETC 2003

Morris, JC – HI 1993 to 98; ETC 1995

Morris, MF – HI 1978-80-82-83-84; Wal 1979; ETC 1979; Fra, WGer, Swe 1980

Morrow, AJC – HI 1975-83-92-93-96-97-99-2000

Mulcare, P – WC 1975; Eur 1972; HI 1968 to 72, 74-78-80; ETC 1975-79; Fra, WGer, Swe 1978-80

Mulholland, D – HI 1988

Munn, E – Wal 1913-23-24; Sco 1927

Munn, L – Wal 1913-23-24; HI 1936-37

Murphy, G – HI 1992 to 95; ETC 1995

Murphy, M – HI 2000

Murphy, P – HI 1985-86

Murray, P – HI 1995-96

Murray, Pat – HI 1995-96-2005-06-07

Neill, JH – HI 1938-47-48-49

Nestor, JM – HI 1962-63-64

Nevin, V – HI 1960-63-65-67-69-72; ETC 1967-69-73

Nicholson, J – HI 1932

Nolan, K – WC 1997; ET 1996; Eur 1996; HI 1992 to 96; ETC 1995-97

O'Boyle, P – ETC 1977

O'Braian, Neil – HI 2007

O'Brien, MD – HI 1968 to 72, 75-76-77; ETC 1971; Fra, WGer, Swe 1976

O'Callaghan, Aaron – HI 2005-06

O'Connell, A – HI 1967-70-71

O'Connell, E – WC 1989; ET 1988*; Eur 1988; HI 1985; ETC 1989

O'Hanlon, Paul – HI 2007-08; ETC 2008

O'Leary, JE – HI 1969-70; ETC 1969

O'Malley, Cathal – HI 2008

O'Neill, JJ – HI 1968

O'Rourke, P – HI 1980-81-82-84-85

O'Sullivan, DF – HI 1976-85-86-87-91; ETC 1977

O'Sullivan, Mark – HI 2003

O'Sullivan, WM – HI 1934 to 38, 47 to 51, 53-54

Omelia, B – HI 1994 to 97

Owens, M – HI 2003

Ownes, GH – HI 1935-37-38-47

Patterson, AH – Wal 1913

Paul, Stuart – HI 2001-02

Pierse, AD – WC 1983; ET 1982; Eur 1980; HI 1976-77-78, 80 to 85, 87-88; Wal 1979; ETC 1981; Fra, WGer, Swe 1980

Pollin, RKM – HI 1971; ETC 1973

Power, E – HI 1987-88-93-94-95-97-98-99

Power, M – HI 1947 to 52, 54

Power, Seamus – HI 2006

Purcell, M – HI 1973

Rafferty, Ronan – **WC** 1981; ET 1980; Eur 1980; Wal 1979; HI 1980-81; ETC 1981; Fra, WGer, Swe 1980

Rainey, WHE – HI 1962

Rayfus, P – HI 1986-87-88

Reade, HE – Wal 1913

Reddan, B – HI 1987

Rice, JH – HI 1947-52

Rice, T – HI 2000-01; ETC 2001

Robertson, CT – Wal, Sco 1930

Scannel, BJ – HI 1947 to 51, 53-54

Shaw, Gareth – ET 2006; HI 2005-06; ETC 2007-08

Sheals, HS – Wal 1929; Eng 1929-30-31; Sco 1930; HI 1932-33

Sheahan, D – **WC** 1963; Eur 1962-64-67; HI 1961 to 67, 70

Simcox, R – Wal, Sco 1930; Wal, Sco, Eng 1931; HI 1932 to 36, 38

Sinclair, Michael – HI 1999-04

Slattery, B – HI 1947-48

Sludds, MF – HI 1982

Smyth, D – HI 1972-73; ETC 1973

Smyth, DW – Wal 1923-30; Eng 1930; Sco 1931; HI 1933

Smyth, V – HI 1981-82

Soulby, DEB – Sco, Wal, Eng 1929-30

Spiller, EF – Wal 1924; Eng 1928; Sco 1928-29

Spring, G – HI 1996

Staunton, R – HI 1964-65-72; ETC 1973

Stevenson, JF – Wal 1923-24; Eng 1925

Stevenson, K – HI 1972

Taggart, J – HI 1953

Timbey, JC – Sco 1928-31; Wal 1931

Waddell, G – Wal 1925

Walton, P – **WC** 1981-83; ET 1982; Wal 1979; HI 1980-81; ETC 1981; Fra, WGer, Swe 1980

Ward, Simon – ET 2006; HI 2006-07-08; ETC 2007

Webster, F – HI 1949

Welch, L – HI 1936

Werner, LE – Wal 1925

West, CH – Eng 1928; HI 1932

Young, D – HI 1969-70-77

SCOTLAND

Aitken, AR – Eng 1906-07-08

Alexander, DW – HI 1958; Scan 1958

Anderson, RB – HI 1962-63; Scan 1960-62

Andrew, R – Eng 1905 to 10

Armour, A – Eng 1922

Armour, TD – USA 1921

Bannerman, SJ – HI 1988; Swe 1990

Barrie, GC – HI 1981-83; Swe 1983

Beames, Roger – Eur 1996; HI 1995-96-99; Esp 1996; Fra, Swe 1997

Beveridge, HW – Eng 1908

Birnie, J – Irl 1927

Black, D – HI 1966-67

Black, FC – Eur 1966; HI 1962-64-65-66-68; ETC 1965-67; Scan 1962

Black, GT – HI 1952-53; SA 1954

Black, WC – HI 1964-65

Blackwell, EBH – Eng 1902, 1904 to 1907, 1909-10-12, 1923-24-25

Blair, DA – **WC** 1955-61; CT 1954; HI 1948-49-51-52-53-55-56-57; Scan 1956-58-62

Bloice, C – **WC** 1985; HI 1985-86; ETC 1985; Fra 1985; Ita, Swe 1986

Blyth, AD – Eng 1904

Bookless, JT – Eng, Irl 1930; Eng, Wal 1931

Booth, Wallace – **WC** 2008*; Eur 2008; AP 2008; Fra 2003; HI 2007-08

Braid, HM – Eng 1922-23

Brand, Gordon jr – **WC** 1979; ET 1978-80; Eur 1978-80; HI 1978-80

Brock, J – Irl 1929; HI 1932

Brodie, Allan – **WC** 1977-79; ET 1978; Eur 1974-76-78-80; HI 1970, 1972 to 1978, 1980; Eng 1979; ETC 1973-77; Bel, Esp 1977; Fra 1978; Ita 1979

Brodie, Andrew – HI 1968-69; Esp 1974

Brooks, A – **WC** 1969; HI 1968-69; ETC 1969

Brooks, CJ – Eur 1986; HI 1984-85; Swe 1984; Swe, Ita 1986

Brooks, M – **WC** 1997; ET 1996; Eur 1996; HI 1995-96; ETC 1997; Aut 1994; Esp 1996; Fra, Swe 1997

Brotherston, IR – HI 1984-85; ETC 1985; Fra 1985

Brown, Graeme – HI 2004

Bryson, WS – HI 1991-92-93; Swe, Ita 1992; Fra 1993; Esp 1994

Bucher, AMM – HI 1954-55-56; Scan 1956

Burnside, J – HI 1956-57

Burrell, TM – Eng 1924

Bussell, AF – **WC** 1957; Eur 1956-62; HI 1956-57-58-61; Scan 1956-60

Byrne, James – ETC 2007; HI 2007

Cairns, S – HI 1997

Cameron, D – HI 1938-51

Campbell, C – HI 1999

Campbell, Glenn – HI 2003-04-07-08; Esp 2006

Campbell, Sir Guy, Bt – Eng 1909-10-11

Campbell, HM – Eur 1964; HI 1962-64-68; ETC 1965-**(79)**; Scan 1962; Aus 1964

Campbell, JGS – HI 1947-48

Campbell, W – **WC** 1930; Irl 1927; Irl, Eng 1928-29-30; Irl, Eng, Wal 1931; HI 1933 to 36

Cannon, JM – HI 1969; Esp 1974

Carmichael, Steven – HI 1998-99-2001-02; Swe 1999; Esp, Ita 2002; Fra 2003

Carrick, DG – **WC** 1983-87; Eur 1986; HI 1981 to 89; ETC 1987-**(89)-(91)**; WGer 1987; Ita 1984-86-88; Fra 1987-89; Swe 1983-84-86

Carslaw, IA – **WC** 1979; Eur 1978; HI 1976-77-78-80-81; ETC 1977-79; Eng 1979; Esp 1977; Fra 1978-83; Bel 1978; Ita 1979

Cater, JR – **WC** 1955; HI 1952 to 56; SA 1954; Scan 1956

Caven, J – **WC** 1922; Eng 1926

Chillas, D – HI 1971

Cochran, JS – HI 1966

Collier, B – HI 1994; Aut 1994

Coltart, Andrew – **WC** 1991; ET 1990; Eur 1990; HI 1988-89-90; ETC 1989-91; NNC 1990; Ita, Swe 1990; Fra 1991

Cosh, GB – **WC** 1965; ET 1966-68; Eur 1966-68; CT 1967; HI 1964 to 69; ETC 1965-**(69)**

Coutts, FJ – HI 1980-81-82; ETC 1981-83; Fra 1981-82-83

Crawford, DR – HI 1990-91; ETC 1991; Fra 1991

Crawford, George – Esp 2002; ETC **(2005)-(2007)**; HI **(2008)**

Cuddihy, J – HI 1977-78

Dalgleish, CR – **WC** 1981; Eur 1982; HI 81-82-83-89-**(95)**; ETC

1981-83-**(93)-(95)**; Fra 1982; NNC 1989

Dawson, JE – Irl 1927-29; Irl, Eng 1930; Irl, Eng, Wal 1931; HI 1932-33-34-37

Dawson, M – HI 1963-65-66

Dear, Gavin – WC 2008*; HI 2007-08

Deboys, A – HI 1956-59-60; Scan 1960

Deighton, Frank WG – WC 1951-57; CT 1954-59; HI 1950-52-53-56-58-59-60; SA 1954; NZ 1954; Scan 1956

Denholm, RB – Irl 1927-29; Irl, Wal, Eng 1931; HI 1932-33-34

Dewar, FG – HI 1952-53-55; SA 1954; ETC **(1971)-(73)**

Dick, CE – Eng 1902-03-04-05-09-12

Dickson, HM – Irl 1929-31

Doherty, Jack – ET 2002; ETC 2003; HI 2001-02; Swe 2001; Esp, Ita 2002

Dowie, Andrew – HI 1949

Downie, D – HI 1993-94; Esp, Ita 1994; Fra, Swe 1995

Draper, JW – HI 1954

Dundas, S – HI 1992-93

Dykes, J Morton – WC 1936; HI 1934-35-36-48-49-51

Easingwood, SR – HI 1986-87-88-90; ETC 1989; Fra 1987-89; Ita 1988-90

Elliot, A – HI 1989; ETC 1989; Fra 1989

Elliot, C – HI 1982; Fra 1983

Everett, C – HI 1988-89-90; ETC 1989-91; NNC 1989-90; Ita 1988-90; Fra 1988-89-91; Swe 1990

Fairlie, WE – Eng 1912

Farmer, A – HI 1997; Swe 1999

Farmer, JC – HI 1970

Ferguson, S Mure – Eng 1902-03-04

Fleming, J – HI 1987

Flockhart, AS – HI 1948-49

Forbes, E – HI 1996-98-2000-01; Ita 1996-2000; Fra 1997; Swe 1997-99; Esp 2002

Forsyth, A – HI 1996; ETC 1997; Ita 1996; Fra, Swe 1997

Fotheringham, Bryan – HI 2005; Esp 2006

Fox, G – HI 1997-98-99; ETC 1999; Swe 1999

Gairdner, JR – Eng 1902

Gallacher, Bernard J – HI 1967

Gallacher, S – WC 1995; ET 1994; HI 1992 to 95; ETC 1993-95; Ita, Esp 1994; Fra, Swe 1995

Gallagher, John – HI 2007

Galloway, RF – HI 1957-58-59; Scan 1958

Garson, R – Irl 1927-28-29

Gibb, C – Eng 1927; Irl 1928

Gibson, WC – HI 1950-51

Girvan, P – WC 1987; HI 1986; ETC 1987; WGer 1987

Gordon, Graham – WC 2003*; ET 2002; ETC 2003; HI 2000-02

Graham, AJ – Eng 1925

Graham, J – Eng 1902 to 11

Green, CT – WC 1963-69-71-73-75-**(83)-(85)**; ET 1970-72-**(84)-(86)**; Eur 1962-66-68-70-72-74-76; CT 1971; HI 1961 to 78; Eng 1979; ETC 1965 to 83; Scan 1962; Aus 1964; Bel 1973-75-77-78; Esp 1977; Ita 1979

Greig, DG – CT 1975; HI 1972-73-75

Greig, K – HI 1933

Guild, WJ – Eng 1925; Eng, Irl 1927-28

Hall, AH – HI 1962-66-69

Hamilton, ED – HI 1936-37-38

Hare, WCD – HI 1953; NZ 1954

Harris, IR – HI 1955-56-58-59

Harris, R – WC **1922-23-26**; Eng 1905-08-10-11-12, 22 to 28

Hastings, JL – HI 1957-58; Scan 1958

Hay, G – WC 1991; Eur 1980; Eng 1979; HI 1980-88-90-91-92; ETC 1991-93; Bel 1980; Fra 1980-82-89-91-93; Ita 1988-92-94; Swe 1992; Esp 1994

Hay, J – HI 1972

Heap, Craig – HI 1999-2001; ETC 2001

Henderson, N – HI 1963-64

Henry, Scott – HI 2007-08

Hird, K – HI 1987-88-89; NNC 1989; Ita 1990

Hislop, Craig – HI 1994-96; Aut 1994; Ita 1996

Hope, WL – WC 1923-24-28; Eng 1923, 25 to 29

Horne, A – HI 1971

Horne, S – HI 1997-98

Hosie, JR – HI 1936

Howard, D Barclay – WC 1995-97; ET 1996; Eur 1980-94-96; Eng 1979; HI 1980 to 83, 93 to 96; ETC 1981-95-97; Bel 1980; Fra 1980-81-83-95-97; Ita 1984-94; Esp 1994-96; Swe 1995-97

Huggan, J – HI 1981 to 84; ETC 1981; Fra 1982-83; Swe 1983; Ita 1984

Hume, B – HI 1999-2000-01; ETC 2001; Ita 2000; Swe 2001

Hunter, NM – 1903-12

Hunter, R – HI 1966

Hunter, WI – Eng 1922

Hutcheon, I – WC 1975-77-79-81; ET 1974-76*-80; Eur 1974-76; CT 1975; Dominican Int 1973; Colombian Int 1975; HI 1971 to 78, 80; ETC 1973-75-77-79-81; Bel 1973-75-77-78-80; Esp 1977; Fra 1978-80-81; Ita 1979; Swe 1983

Hutchison, CK – Eng 1904 to 12

Inglis, David – WC 2003*; ETC 2003; HI 2001-02

Innes, Brian – HI 2003

Jack, R Reid – WC 1957-59; ET 1958; Eur 1956; CT 1959; HI 1950-51, 54 to 59, 61; NZ 1954; Scan 1956-58

Jack, WS (Billy) – HI 1955

James, D – HI 1985

Jamieson, A jr – WC 1926; Eng 1927; Eng, Irl 1928; Eng, Irl, Wal 1931; HI 1932-33-36-37

Jamieson, D – HI 1980

Jamieson, Scott – ET 2006; HI 2002-04-05; Esp 06

Jenkins, JLC – USA 1921; Eng 1908-12-22-24-26-28; Irl 1928

Johnston, JW – HI 1970-71

Kellett, Ross – HI 2008

Kelly, L – WC 1999; ET 1998*; HI 1997-98; ETC 1999; Swe 1999

Killey, GC – Irl 1928

King, Jonathan – HI 2001-02-03-04-07; Swe 2001; Esp 2002-06; Fra 2003 ETC 2005-07

Kirkpatrick, D – HI 1992; ETC 1993; Fra 1993

Knowles, ST – HI 1990-91-92; Fra 1991

Kyle, AT – WC 1938-47-51; SA 1952; HI 1938-47, 49 to 53

Kyle, DH – WC 1924; Eng 1924-30

Kyle, EP – Eng 1925

Laidlay, JE – Eng 1902 to 11

Laird, Martin – HI 2003

Lang, JA – WC 1930; Irl, Eng 1929; Irl 1930; Irl, Eng, Wal 1931

Lawrie, CD – WC **(1961)-(1963)**; ET **(1960)-(1962)**; Eur **(1960)-(1962)**; HI 1949-50, 55 to 58; Swe 1950; Scan 1956-58

Lee, IGF – HI 1958 to 62; Scan 1960

Lindsay, J – HI 1933 to 36

Little, E – Ita 1996

Lockhart, G – Eng 1911-12

Loftus, M – Eur 2000; HI 1999-2000; Ita 2000

Low, AJ – HI 1963-64; ETC 1965; Aus 1964

Low, JL – Eng 1904

Lowdon, CJ – Irl 1927

Lowson, AG – HI 1989-90-91-97; Swe 1990; Swe, Ita 1992

Lygate, M – HI 1970-75-**(88)**; ETC 1971-85-87

McAllister, SD – HI 1983; ETC 1983; Swe 1983

McAlpine, Kevin – ETC 2007; HI 2007

McArthur, Andrew – Eur 2004; ETC 2003-05; HI 2002-03-04-05

McArthur, W – HI 1952-54; SA 1954

Macaulay, Callum – WC 2008*; Eur 2008; AP 2008; HI 2007-08

McBeath, J – HI 1964

McBride, D – HI 1932

McCallum, AR – WC 1928; Eng 1929

McCart, DM – HI 1977-78; Bel, Fra 1978

MacDonald, GK – HI 1978-81-82; Eng 1979; Fra 1981-82-83

McDonald, H – HI 1970

Macdonald, J Scott – WC 1971; Eur 1970; HI 1969 to 72; ETC 1971; Bel 1973

McEwan, Steven – HI 2008; Esp 2006

Macfarlane, CB – Eng 1912

Macgregor, A – Scan 1956

Macgregor, G – WC 1971-75-83-85-87-**(91)-(93)**; ET 1982; Eur 1970-74-84; CT 1971-75; HI 1969 to 76, 80 to 87, **(99)**; Eng 1979; ETC 1971-73-75-81-83-85-87; Bel 1973-75-80; Fra 1981-82-85-87; Swe 1983-84-86; Ita 1984-86

MacGregor, RC – WC 1953; HI 1951 to 54; NZ 1954

McInally, H – HI 1937-47-48

McIntosh, EA – HI 1989

Macintosh, KW – Eur 1980; Eng 1979; HI 1980; Bel, Fra 1980

McKay, G – HI 1969

McKay, JR – HI 1950-51-52-54; NZ 1954

McKechnie, P – HI 1998

McKellar, PJ – WC 1977; Eur 1978; HI 1976-77-78; Eng 1979; Bel, Fra 1978

Mackenzie, F – Eng 1902-03

Mackenzie, S – ET 2002; HI 1990, 93 to 2001-03; ETC 1999-2001; Esp 1994-96-02; Ita 1994-2000; Fra 1997; Swe 1997-99

Mackenzie, WW – WC 1922-23; Eng 1923-26-27-29; Irl 1930

McKibbin, H – HI 1994-95; ETC 1995; Fra, Swe 1995; Esp 1996

Mackie, GW – HI 1948-50

McKinlay, SL – WC 1934; Eng 1929-30-31; Irl 1930; Wal 1931; HI 1932-33-35-37-47

McKinna, RA – HI 1938

McKinnon, A – HI 1947-52

McLean, J – WC 1934-36; Aus 1934; HI 1932 to 36

McLeary, Jamie – Eur 2004; HI 2002-03-04-05; ET 2004

McLeod, AE – HI 1937-38

McLeod, WS – HI 1935-37-38, 47 to 51; Swe 1950

McNair, AA – Irl 1929

McNicoll, Keir – ETC 2007; HI 2007-08

MacRae, Neil – HI 2003; Ita 2002

McRuvie, Eric A – WC 1932-34; Eng 1929; Eng, Irl 1930; Eng, Irl, Wal 1931; HI 1932 to 36

McTear, J – HI 1971

Manford, GC – Eng 1922-23

Mann, LS – WC 1983; HI 1982-83; ETC 1983; Swe 1983

Marchbank, Brian – WC 1979; ET 1978; Eur 1976-78; HI 1978; ETC 1979; Ita 1979

Martin, S – WC 1977; ET 1976; Eur 1976; HI 1975-76-77; ETC 1977; Bel, Esp 1977

Maxwell, R – Eng 1902 to 07, 09-10

Melville, LM Balfour – Eng 1902-03

Melville, TE – HI 1974

Menzies, A – Eng 1925

Mill, JW – HI 1953-54

Miller, AC – HI 1954-55

Miller, MJ – HI 1974-75-77-78; Bel, Fra 1978

Milligan, JW – WC 1989-91; ET 1988*-90; Eur 1988-92; HI 1986 to 92; ETC 1987-89-91; NNC 1989; Swe 1986-90-92; WGer 1987; Fra 1987-89-91; Ita 1988-90-92

Milne, WTG – WC 1973; HI 1972-73; ETC 1973; Bel 1973

Moir, A – Eur 1984; HI 1983-84; ETC 1985; Swe, Ita 1984; Fra 1985

Montgomerie, Colin S – WC 1985-87; ET 1984-86; Eur 1986; HI 1984-85-86; ETC 1985-87; Ita 1984; Swe 1984-86; Fra 1985; WGer 1987

Montgomerie, JS – HI 1957; ETC 1965; Scan 1958

Morris, FS – HI 1963

Morrison, JH – Scan 1960

Munro, RAG – HI 1960

Murdoch, D – HI 1964

Murphy, AR – HI 1961-67

Murray, George – ET 2004; HI 2004-05-06; ETC 2005; Esp 06

Murray, GH – WC 1977; Eur 1978; HI 1973 to 78, 83; ETC 1975-77; Esp 1974-77; Bel 1975-77

Murray, SWT – WC 1963; Eur 1958-62; HI 1959 to 63; Scan 1960

Murray, WA – WC 1923-24; Eng 1923 to 27

Murray, WB – HI 1967-68-69; ETC 1969

Neill, R – HI 1936

Noon, J – HI 1987

O'Hara, Paul – Esp 2006, HI 2007-08

O'Hara, Steven – WC 2001; ET 2000; Eur 2000; HI 1999-2000; ETC 2001; Ita 2000; Swe 2001

Osgood, TH – Eng 1925

Paton, DA – HI 1991

Patrick, D – WC 1999; AP 2000; HI 1997-98-99; ETC 1999; Swe 1999

Patrick, KG – HI 1937

Peters, GB – WC 1936-38; HI 1934 to 38

Pirie, AK – WC 1967; Eur 1970; HI 1966 to 75; ETC 1967-69; Bel 1973-75; Esp 1974

Pressley, J – HI 1947-48-49

Raeside, A – Irl 1929

Ramsay, Eric – HI 2002-03-04-05; Ita 2002; ETC 2005

Ramsay, Richie – WC 2005; ET 2006; AP 2006; Eur 2006; HI 2004-06; ETC 2005-07

Rankin, G – WC 1995-97-99; HI 1994-95-97-98; ETC 1995-97-99; Swe 1995-97-99; Fra 1995-97; Esp 1996

Reid, A – HI 1993-94-95; ETC 1993-95; Esp, Ita 1994; Fra 1995

Renfrew, RL – HI 1964

Robb, J jr – Eng 1902-03-05-06-07

Robb, WM – HI 1935

Roberts, AT – Irl 1931

Roberts, GW – HI 1937-38

Robertson, Dean – WC 1993; ET 1992; Eur 1992; HI 1991-92-93; ETC 1993; Swe, Ita 1992; Fra 1993

Robertson, DM – HI 1973-74; Esp 1974

Robertson-Durham, JA – Eng 1911

Russell, R – WC 1993; HI 1992-93; ETC 1993; Fra 1993

Rutherford, DS – Irl 1929

Rutherford, R – HI 1938-47

Saddler, AC – WC 1963-65-67-**(77)**; ET 1962-**(76)***; Eur 1960-62-64-66; CT 1959-63-67; HI 1959 to 64, 66; ETC 1965-67-**(75)-(77)**; Scan 1962

Saltman, Lloyd – WC 2005-07; Eur 2006; HI 2004-05-06; ETC 2005-07; Esp 06

Scott, R jr – WC 1924; Eng 1924-28

Scott, WGF – Irl 1927

Scroggie, FH – Eng 1910

Shade, Ronnie DBM – WC 1961-63-65-67; ET 1962-64-66-68; Eur 1960-62-64-66; CT 1963-67; Aus 1964; HI 1957, 60 to 68; ETC 1965-67; Scan 1960-62

Shaw, G – WC 1987; HI 1984-86-87-88-90; ETC 1987; Swe 1984; Fra, WGer 1987

Sherry, Gordon – WC 1995; ET 1994; Eur 1994; HI 1993-94-95; ETC 1995; Fra 1993-95; Esp 1994; Swe 1995

Shields, B – HI 1986

Simpson, AF – Eng 1927; Irl 1928

Simpson, JG – USA 1921; Eng 1907-08-09-11-12-22-24-26

Sinclair, A – HI 1950; ETC **(1967)**

Smith, JN – WC 1930; Irl 1928; Irl, Eng 1930; Irl, Eng, Wal 1931; HI 1932-33-34

Smith, S – Aut 1994

Smith, WD – WC 1959; Eur 1958; HI 1957 to 60, 63; Scan 1958-60

Stephen, AR (Sandy) – WC 1985; Eur 1972; HI 1971 to 77, 84-85; ETC 1975-85; Esp 1974; Bel 1975-77-78; Fra 1985

Stevenson, A – HI 1949

Stevenson, JB – Irl 1931; HI 1932-38-47-49-50-51

Stewart, Michael – HI 2008

Strachan, CJL – HI 1965-66-67; ETC 1967

Stuart, HB – WC 1971-73-75; ET 1972; Eur 1968-72-74; CT 1971; HI 1967 to 74, 76; ETC 1969-71-73-75; Bel 1973-75

Stuart, JE – HI 1959

Tait, AG – HI 1987-88-89; NNC 1989

Taylor, GN – HI 1948

Taylor, JS – Eng 1979; HI 1980; Bel, Fra 1980

Taylor, LG – HI 1955-56

Thomson, AP – HI 1970; ETC 1971

Thomson, G – HI 1996

Thomson, Hector – WC 1936-38; HI 1934 to 38

Thomson, JA – HI 1981 to 89, 91-92; ETC 1983; WGer 1987; Ita 1984-86-88-90; Swe 1990

Thomson, Mike – HI 1998

Thorburn, K – Irl 1927; Eng 1928

Torrance, TA – WC 1924-28-30-**32**-34; Eng 1922-23-25-26-28-29-30; HI 1933

Torrance, WB – WC 1922; Eng 1922-23-24-26-27-28-30; Irl 1928-29-30

Tulloch, W – Eng 1927-29; Eng, Irl 1930; Eng, Irl, Wal 1931; HI 1932

Turnbull, A – HI 1995-96-97; Fra 1995; Esp 1996

Twynholm, S – HI 1990; NNC 1990

Urquhart, M – HI 1993; Ita 1996

Vannet, Lee – HI 1984

Walker, J – WC 1961; Eur 1958-60; HI 1954-55-57-58, 60 to 63; Scan 1958-62

Walker, KH – HI 1985-86

Walker, RS – HI 1935-36

Warren, Marc – WC 2001; HI 2000-01; ETC 2001; Ita 2000; Swe 2001

Watson, Craig R – WC 1997; HI 1991-92, 94 to 2000, **2001**, 2003; ETC 1997-99-2001-03; Swe 1992-97-2001; Ita 1992; Aut 1994; Esp 1996-2002; Fra 1997

Watt, AW – HI 1987

Webster, AJ – HI 1978

Wemyss, DS – HI 1937

Whyte, AW – HI 1934

Wight, R – Swe 1950

Wilkie, DF – HI 1962-63-65-67-68

Wilkie, G – Eng 1911

Williamson, SB – HI 1947-48-49-51-52

Wilson, E – HI 1985

Wilson, J – WC 1923; Eng 1922-23-24-26; Irl 1932

Wilson, JC – WC 1947-53; CT 1954; SA 1954; HI 1947-48-49-51-52-53; Swe 1950; NZ 1954

Wilson, P – HI 1976; Bel 1977

Wilson, Stuart – WC 2003*; 2004; Eur 2004; AP 2002-04; ETC 2003; HI 2000-02-03-04; Esp, Ita 2002; Fra 2003

Wright, I – HI 1958 to 61; Scan 1960-62

Yates, Gordon – HI 2008

Young, ID – Eur 1982; HI 1981-82; Fra 1982

Young, JR – Eur 1960; HI 1960-61-65; Scan 1960

Young, S – WC 1997; HI 1996; ETC 1997; Ita 1996

WALES

Adams, MPD – HI 1969 to 72, 75-76-77

Atkinson, HN – Irl 1913

Barnett, A – HI 1989-90-91; ETC 1991

Bayne, PWGA – HI 1949

Bevan, RJ – HI 1964-65-66-67-73-74

Black, JL – HI 1932 to 1936

Bonnell, DJ – HI 1949-50-51

Broad, RD – Irl 1979; HI 1980-81-82-84; ETC 1981

Brookman, R – HI 1999-2000

Brown, CT – WC (1995)*-(97); Eur **(1996)**; HI 1970 to 75, 77-78-80-**(88)**; ETC 1973; Den 1977; Irl 1979; Den, Esp, Sui 1980

Brown, D – Irl 1923-30-31; Eng 1925; Sco 1931

Buckley, JA – WC 1979; HI 1967-68-69-76-77-78; ETC 1967-69; Den 1976-77

Calvert, M – HI 1983-84-86-87-89-91

Campbell, A – HI 1996-97-2000-01

Campbell, I – HI 1998-99-2001; ETC 1999-2001

Carr, JP – Irl 1913

Chapman, JA – Irl 1923-29-30-31; Eng 1925; Sco 1931

Chapman, R – Irl 1929; HI 1932-34-35-36

Charles, WB – Irl 1924

Clark, MD – Irl 1947

Clay, G – HI 1962

Clement, G – Irl 1979

Coulter, JG – HI 1951-52

Cousins, Chris – HI 2006

Cox, S – HI 1970 to 74; ETC 1971-73

Davies, EN – HI 1959 to 74; ETC 1969-71-73

Davies, G – HI 1981-82-83; Den 1977

Davies, HE – HI 1933-34-36

Davies, Rhys – WC 2005-07; ET 2006; Eur 2006; ET 2004; HI 2002-03-04-05-06; ETC 2005-07

Davies, TJ – HI 1954 to 60

Dinsdale, R – HI 1991-92-93

Disley, A – HI 1976-77-78-**(99)**; Irl 1979; Den 1977

Dodd, SC – WC 1989; HI 1985-87-88-89

Donaldson, J – ET 2000; Eur 2000; HI 1996 to 2000; ETC 1997-99

Dredge, Bradley – WC 1993; ET 1992; Eur 1994; HI 1992 to 95; ETC 1995

Duffy, I – HI 1975

Duncan, AA – WC **(1953)**; HI 1933-34-36-38, 47 to 59

Duncan, GT – HI 1952 to 58

Duncan, J jr – Irl 1913

Dykes, Tim – HI 2001-02-03-04-05-06; Fin 2004; ETC 2005

Eaves, CH – HI 1935-36-38-47-48-49

Edwards, Nigel – WC 2001*-03*-05-07-08; ET 2002-04-06; Eur 2004-06; AP 2002-04-06-08; HI 1995 to 2002, 2004-05-06-07-08; ETC 1997-99-2001-03-05-07-08

Edwards, S – HI 1992

Edwards, TH – HI 1947

Ellis, M – Eur 1996; HI 1992 to 96

Emerson, T – HI 1932

Emery, G – Irl 1925; HI 1933-36-38

Enoch, Ben – HI 2008; ETC 2008

Enoch, Rhys – WC 2008, ETC 2008; HI 2006-07-08

Evans, AD – Sco, Irl 1931; Sco 1935; HI 1932 to 35, 38, 47 to 56, 61

Evans, Craig – HI 2004-05-06-07-08; ETC 2007-08

Evans, C – 1990 to 95; ETC 1995

Evans, Craig – HI 2004-05

Evans, Duncan – WC 1981; Eur 1980; HI 1978-80-81; Irl 1979; ETC 1981

Evans, HJ – HI 1976-77-78-80-81-84-85-87-88; Irl 1979; ETC 1979-81;

Fra 1976; Den 1977-80; Esp, Sui 1980

Evans, M Gear – Irl 1930; Sco, Irl 1931

Fairchild, CEL – Irl 1923; Eng 1925

Fairchild, IJ – Irl 1924

Farr, Oliver – HI 2008

Frazer, James – HI 2008

Gilford, CF – HI 1963 to 67

Glossop, R – HI 1935-37-38-47

Gould, Zach – AP 2006; HI 2005-06; ETC 2005-08; HI 2007

Griffiths, HGB – Irl 1923-24-25

Griffiths, HS – Eng 1958

Griffiths, JA – HI 1933

Griffiths, M – HI 1999-2000-01; ETC 2001

Hales, JP – Sco 1963

Hall, A – HI 1994

Hall, D – HI 1932-37

Hall, K – HI 1955-59

Hamilton, CJ – Irl 1913

Harpin, Lee – ET 2002; HI 1996, 1998 to 2003; ETC 1999-2001

Harrhy, A – HI 1988-89-95

Harris, D – HI 1997

Harrison, JW – HI 1937-50

Hendriksen, Paul – Fin 2004

Herne, KTC – Irl 1913

Houston, G – HI 1990 to 95; ETC 1991-95

Howell, HR – Irl 1923-24-25-29-30-31; Eng 1925; Sco 1931; HI 1932, 34 to 38, 47

Howell H Logan – Irl 1925

Howie, James – HI 2007-08

Hughes, I – HI 1954-55-56

Humphrey, JG – Irl 1925

Humphreys, DI – HI 1972

Isitt, GH – Irl 1923

Jacob, NE – HI 1932 to 36

Jermine, JG – HI 1972 to 76, 82, 2000; ETC 1975-77; Fra 1975

Johnson, R – Eur 1994; HI 1990-92-93-94; ETC 1991

Jones, A – HI 1989-90; ETC 1991

Jones, DK – HI 1973

Jones, EO – HI 1983-85-86

Jones, JG Parry – HI 1959-60

Jones, JL – HI 1933-34-36

Jones, JR – HI 1970-72-73-77-78, 80 to 85; Irl 1979; ETC 1973-79-81; Den 1976; Den, Sui, Esp 1980

Jones, KG – HI 1988

Jones, MA – HI 1947 to 51, 53-54-57

Jones, Malcolm F – HI 1933

Jones, SP – HI 1981 to 86, 88-89-91-93

Knight, B – HI 1986

Knipe, RG – HI 1953 to 56

Knowles, WR – Eng 1948

Lake, AD – HI 1958

Laskey, Mark – HI 2004

Last, CN – HI 1975

Lee, JN – HI 1988-89; ETC 1991

Lewis, DH – HI 1935 to 38

Lewis, DR – Irl 1925-29-30-31; Sco 1931; HI 1932-34

Lewis, R Cofe – Irl 1925

Lloyd, HM – Irl 1913

Lloyd, RM de – Sco, Irl 1931; HI 1932 to 38, 47-48

Llyr, A – HI 1984-85

Lockley, AE – HI 1956-57-58-62

Macara, MA – HI 1983-84-85, 87, 89 to 93

McLean, D – HI 1968 to 78, 80 to 83, 85-86-88-90; Irl 1979; ETC 1975-77-79-81; Fra 1975; Fra, Den 1976; Den, Sui, Esp 1980

Maliphant, FR – HI 1932

Manley, Stuart – WC 2003*; HI 2001-02; ETC 2003

Marsden, G – HI 1994

Marshman, A – HI 1952

Marston, CC – Irl 1929-30; Irl, Sco 1931

Mathias-Thomas, FEL – Irl 1924-25

Matthews, Llewellyn – WC 2007; ET 2006; HI 2003-05-06-07; ETC 2007

Matthews, N – HI 1999; ETC 1999

Matthews, RL – HI 1935-37

Mayo, PM – WC 1985-87; HI 1982-88

Melia, TJ – HI 1976-77-78-80-81-82; Irl 1979; ETC 1977-79; Den 1976; Den, Sui, Esp 1980

Mills, Cennydd – HI 2003-05-06; Fin 2004

Mills, ES – HI 1957

Mitchell, JWH – HI 1964-65-66-67

Moody, JV – HI 1947-48-49-51-56, 58 to 61

Morgan, JL – WC 1951-53-55; HI 1948 to 62, 64-68

Morris, R – HI 1983-86-87

Morris, TS – Irl 1924-29-30

Morrow, JM – Irl 1979; HI 1980-81; ETC 1979-81; Den, Sui, Esp 1980

Moss, AV – HI 1965-66-68

Mouland, MG – HI 1978-81; Irl 1979; ETC 1979

Moxon, GA – Irl 1929-30

Newman, JE – HI 1932

Newton, H – Irl 1929

Noon, GS – HI 1935-36-37

Oakley, Neil – HI 2002

O'Carroll, C – HI 1989 to 93; ETC 1991

Owen, JB – HI 1971

Owens, GF – HI 1960-61

Palferman, H – HI 1950-53

Palmer, M – HI 1998

Pardoe, S – HI 1991

Parfitt, RWM – Irl 1924

Park, D – WC 1997; HI 1994 to 97; ETC 1995-97

Parkin, AP – WC 1983; HI 1980-81-82

Parry, JR – HI 1966-75-76-77; Fra 1976

Peet, M – HI 1995-96

Peters, JL – HI 1987-88-89

Phillips, LA – Irl 1913

Pilkington, M – HI 1997-98; ETC 1997

Pinch, AG – HI 1969

Povall, J – Eur 1962; HI 1960 to 63, 65 to 77; ETC 1967-69-71-73-75-77; Fra 1975; Fra, Den 1976

Pressdee, RNG – HI 1958 to 62

Price, David – ET 2002; HI 1999 to 2003; ETC 2003

Price, JP – HI 1986-87-88

Price, Rhodri – HI 1994-96-97

Pugh, RS – Irl 1923-24-29

Pughe, O – HI 1997-98

Rees, CN – HI 1986-88-89-91-92, 94 to 97

Rees, DA – HI 1961 to 64

Renwick, G jr – Irl 1923

Ricardo, W – Irl 1930; Irl, Sco 1931

Rice-Jones, L – Irl 1924

Richards, PM – HI 1960 to 63, 71

Roberts, H – HI 1992-93

Roberts, J – HI 1937

Roberts, S – HI 1998-99

Roberts, SB – HI 1932 to 35, 37-38, 47 to 54

Roberts, WJ – HI 1948 to 54

Roderick, RN – WC 1989; Eur 1988; HI 1983 to 88

Rolfe, B – HI 1963-65

Roobottom, EL – HI 1967

Roper, MS – Irl 1979

Runcie, Adam – HI 2007-08

Scott, Richard – HI 2003; Fin 2004

Sheppard, M – HI 1990

Shufflebotham, Jason – HI 2007

Smith, Alex – HI 1998-2000-02-03-04; ETC 2003; Fin 2004

Smith, Craig – HI 2002-03-04-05; ETC 2003

Smith, M – HI 1993 to 97; ETC 1995-97

Smith, VH – Irl 1924-25

Squirrel, HC – HI 1955 to 71, 73-74-75; ETC 1967-69-71-75; Fra 1975

Stevens, DI – HI 1968-69-70, 74 to 78, 80-82; ETC 1969-77; Fra 1976; Den 1977

Stoker, K – Irl 1923-24

Stokoe, GC – Eng 1925; Irl 1929-30

Sullivan, Kyron – HI 1998 to 2001; ETC 2001

Symonds, A – Irl 1925

Taylor, TPD – HI 1963

Taylor, Y – HI 1995-96-97; ETC 1995-97

Thomas, KR – HI 1951-52

Thomas, Luke – HI 2007

Thomas, Ryan – HI 2004-05-06-07; ETC 2007

Tooth, EA – Irl 1913

Toye, JL – HI 1963 to 67, 69 to 74, 76-78-**(2006)**; ETC 1971-73-75-77-**(2005)**; Fra 1975

Tucker, WI – HI 1949 to 72, 74-75; ETC 1967-69-75; Fra 1975

Turnbull, CH – Irl 1913-25

Turner, GB – HI 1947 to 52, 55-56

Vickery, Joe – HI 2008

Wakely, Carl – HI 2005

Wallis, G – HI 1934-36-37-38

Walters, EM – HI 1967-68-69; ETC 1969

Westgate, Ben – WC 2008; HI 2004-06-07-08; ETC 2008

Wilkie, GT – HI 1938

Wilkinson, S – HI 1990-91

Willcox, FS – Sco, Irl 1931

Williams, Craig – AP 2000; HI 1998 to 2001; ETC 1999-2001

Williams, James – HI 2001-02-03-04-05; Fin 2004; ETC 2005

Williams, KH – HI 1983 to 87

Williams, PG – Irl 1925

Wills, M – HI 1990

Winfield, HB – Irl 1913

Wood, DK – HI 1982 to 87

Woosnam, Ian – Fra 1976

Wright, Garwth – HI 2002-03-04; ETC 2003-05; ET 2004

Amateur Women

Key

Entries for the Curtis Cup, Commonwealth Tournament, World Amateur Team Championship and Vagliano Trophy, indicate that the player is representing Great Britain and Ireland. Other entries are for the home country.

CC	Curtis Cup
CT	Commonwealth Tournament
ES	World Amateur Team Championship (Espirito Santo)
VT	Vagliano Trophy
ELTC	played in European Ladies Team Championship for home country
HI	played in Home International matches
*	indicates winning team

'to' indicates inclusive dates: e.g.'1908 to 1911' means '1908-09-10-11'; otherwise individual years are shown.

Captaincy is indicated by the year printed in bold type; non-playing captaincy in brackets

[1998] indicates Espirito Santo Team selection which was subsequently advised not to travel to Chile

Maiden names are shown in brackets; other surnames and titles in square brackets

ENGLAND

Aitken, Claire – HI 2007

Allen, F – HI 1952

Andrew, Kim (Rostron) – CC 1998-2000; HI 1996-97-99-2001; ELTC 1997-2001; (GBI) VT 1997-99-2001; ES [1998]; CT 1999

Archer, A (Rampton) – HI **(1968)**

Bailey, D [Frearson] (Robb) – CC 1962-72-**(84)-(86)***-**(88)***; VT 1961-**(83)-(85)**; CT 1983; HI 1961-62-71; ELTC 1968-**(93)**

Ball, Lisa – HI 2004

Barber, S (Bonallack) – CC 1962; ES **(1996)**; VT 1961-63-69; CT **(1995)**; HI 1960-61-62-68-70-72-77-**(78)**; ELTC 1969-71

Bargh Etherington, B (Whitehead) – HI 1974

Barry, L – HI 1911 to 14

Barry, P – HI 1982

Barton, Pam – CC 1934-36; HI 1935 to 39

Barwood, Hannah – HI 2008

Bastin, G – HI 1920 to 25

Bayman, Linda (Denison Pender) – CC 1988; ES 1988; VT 1971-85-87; HI 1971-72-73-83-84-85-87-88-**(95)-(96)**; ELTC 1985-87-89-**(97)-(2001)**

Beharrell, Veronica (Anstey) – CC 1956; HI 1955-56-57-**(61)**

Bell, Rachel – HI 2006-07

Benka, Pam (Tredinnick) – CC 1966-68-**(2002)**; CT **(2003)**; VT 1967; HI 1967

Bennett, Elizabeth – CC 2008; ES 2008; HI 2006-07-08; ELTC 2008

Biggs, A (Whittaker) – VT 1959

Bisgood, Jeanne – CC 1950-52-54-**(70)**; HI 1949 to 54, 56-58

Blaymire, J – HI 1971-88-**(89)**

Boatman, Elizabeth A (Collis) – CC **(1992)***-**(94)**; CT **(1987)-(91)**; HI 1974-80-**(84)-(85)-(90)-(91)**; ELTC **(1985)-(87)**

Bolas, R – HI 1992

Bolton, Zara (Bonner Davis) – CC 1948-**(56)-(66)-(68)**; CT 1967; HI 1939, 48 to 51, **(55)-(56)**

Bonallack, Angela (Ward) [Lady Bonallack] – CC 1956-58-60-62-64-66; VT 1959-61-63; HI 1956 to 66, 72

Bostock, M – HI **(1954)**

Bourn, Mrs – HI 1909-12

Brown, Fiona – CC 1998-2000; VT 1999-2001; CT 1999; HI 1994, 96 to 2001; ELTC 1997-99-2001

Brown, J – HI 1984

Burnell, S – HI 1993; ELTC 1993

Burton, M – ELTC 1997

Cairns, Lady Katherine – CC **(1952)***; HI 1947-48, 50 to 54

Caldwell, Carole (Redford) – CC 1978-80; VT 1973; HI 1973-78-79-80

Cann, M (Nuttall) – HI 1966

Carrick, P (Bullard) – HI 1939-47

Cautley, B (Hawtrey) – HI 1912-13-14, 22 to 25, 27

Christison, D – HI 1981

Clark, G (Atkinson) – HI 1955

Clarke, Mrs ML – HI 1933-35

Clarke, Nickie – HI **(2002)**

Clarke, P – HI 1981

Clement, V – HI 1932-34-35

Close, M (Wenyon) – VT 1969; HI 1968-69; ELTC 1969

Collett, P – HI 1910

Collingham, J (Melville) – VT 1979-87; CT 1987; HI 1978-79-81-84-86-87-92; ELTC 1989

Comboy, Carol (Grott) – CC **(1978)-(80)**; ES **(1978)**; VT **(1977)-(79)**; CT **(1979)**; HI **(1975)-(76)**

Connor, Rachel – HI 2008

Corlett, Elsie – CC 1932-38-**(64)**; HI 1927, 29 to 33, 35 to 39

Cotton, S (German) – VT 1967; HI 1967-68; ELTC 1967

Court, C – HI 2000

Critchley, Diana (Fishwick) – CC 1932-34-**(50)**; HI 1930 to 33, 35-36-**(47)**

Croft, A – HI 1927

Crummack, Miss – HI 1909

Davies, Laura – CC 1984; HI 1983-84

Dobson, Helen – CC 1990; VT 1989; HI 1987-88-89; ELTC 1989

Dod, L – HI 1905

Douglas, K – CC 1982; VT 1983; HI 1981-82-83

Dowling, D – HI 1979

Duggleby, Emma – CC 2000-02-04; ES 2002-04; VT 1995-2001-03; HI 1994-95-96-99 to 2005; ELTC 1995-99-2001-03-05

Durrant, B [Green] (Lowe) – HI 1954

Eastwood, Laura – HI 2005

Edmond, F (Macdonald) – VT 1991; HI 1991; ELTC 1991

Marvin, Vanessa – CC 1978; VT 1977; HI 1977-78; ELTC 1977

Masters, Danielle – CC 2004; VT 2003; HI 2003; ELTC 2003

Matharu, Kiran – CC 2006; HI 2005

Merrill, Julia (Greenhalgh) – CC 1964-70-74-76-78; ES 1970-**74**-78; VT 1961-65-75-77; CT 1963; HI 1960-61-63-66-69-70-71, 75 to 78; ELTC 1971-77

Montgomery, Danielle – HI 2007

Moorcroft, S – HI 1985-86; ELTC 1985-87

Morant, E – HI 1906-10

More, Fame – CC 2002-04; VT 2001-03; HI 2000-01-02-03; ELTC 2001-03

Morgan, S – HI 1989; ELTC 1989

Morgan, Wanda – CC 1932-34-36; HI 1931 to 37

Morley, Joanne – CC 1992; ES 1992; VT 1991-93; HI 1990 to 93; ELTC 1991-93

Morris, L (Moore) – HI 1912-13

Morrison, G (Cheetham) – VT 1965; HI 1965-**(69)**

Morrison, G (Cradock-Hartopp) – HI 1936

Murray, Nicola (Buxton) – CC 1992; VT 1991-93; HI 1991-92-93; ELTC 1991-93

Murray, S (Jolly) – HI 1976

Nes, K (Garnham) – HI 1931-32-33, 36 to 39

Neville, E – HI 1905-06-08-10

New, Beverley – CC 1984; VT 1983; HI 1980 to 83

Newell, B – HI 1936

Newton, B (Brown) – HI 1930, 33 to 37

Oliver, J – HI 1995

Parker, Florentyna – CC 2008; HI 2006-08; ELTC 2008

Parker, S – HI 1973

Pearson, D – HI 1928 to 32, 34

Phillips, ME – HI 1905

Pickard, Margaret (Nichol) – CC 1968-70; VT 1959-61-67; HI 1958 to 61, 67-69, **(83)**

Pook, Elizabeth (Chadwick) – CC 1966; VT 1963-67; CT 1967; HI 1963-65-66-67

Porter, M (Lazenby) – HI 1931-32

Price, M (Greaves) – HI **(1956)**

Price Fisher, Elizabeth (Price) CC 1950-52-54-56-58-60;

VT 1959; CT 1959; HI 1948, 51 to 60

Prout, Rebecca – HI 2000

Rabbidge, R – HI 1931

Ratcliffe, Elaine – CC 1998; ES 1996; VT 1997; HI 1995-96-97; ELTC 1995-97

Read, P – HI 1922

Reddick, Sian – ELTC 2005

Reece, P (Millington) – HI 1966

Reid, Melissa – CC 2006; CT 2007; ES 2006; HI 2006

Remer, H – HI 1909

Richardson, Mrs – HI 1907-09

Robinson, S – HI 1989

Roskrow, M – HI 1948-50

Ross, Julie – HI 2004

Rudgard, G – HI 1931-32-50-51-52

Sabine, Diana (Plumpton) – CC 1934; HI 1934-35

Sanderson, Fay – HI 2004; ELTC 2005

Saunders, Vivien – CC 1968; VT 1967; CT 1967; HI 1967-68; ELTC 1967

Sheppard, E (Pears) – HI 1947

Simpson, Linda (Moore) – CC 1980; HI 1979-80

Slark, Ruth (Porter) – CC 1960-62-64; ES 1964-66; VT 1959-61-65; CT 1963; HI 1959 to 62, 64-65-66-68-78; ELTC 1965

Smillie, P – HI 1985-86

Smith, Anne [Stant] (Willard) – CC 1976; VT 1975; CT **1959-63**; HI 1974-75-76

Smith, E – HI 1991

Smith, Frances (Stephens) – CC 1950-52-54-56-58-60, **(62)-(72)**; VT 1959-71; CT 1959-63; HI 1947 to 55, 59, **(62)-(71)-(72)**

Smith, Kerry – CC 2002; CT 2007; ES 2006; VT 2001-05; HI 1997 to 2008; ELTC 1999-2003-05-08

Soulsby, Janet – CC 1982

Speak, Kirsty – CC 1994; ES 1994; VT 1993; HI 1993-94; ELTC 1993

Steel, E – HI 1905 to 08, 11

Stocker, J – HI 1922-23

Stupples, Karen – CC 1996-98; VT 1997; HI 1995 to 98; ELTC 1995-97

Sugden, J (Machin) – HI 1953-54-55

Sumpter, Mrs – HI 1907-08-12-14-24

Sutherland Pilch, R (Barton) – HI 1947-49-50-**(58)**

Swallow, C – HI 1985; ELTC 1985

Tamworth, Mrs – HI 1908

Tebbet, K – HI 1990-94

Temple, S – HI 1913-14

Temple Dobell, G (Ravenscroft) – HI 1911 to 14, 20-21-25-30

Thompson, M (Wallis) – HI 1948-49

Thornhill, J (Woodside) – CC 1984-86-88; VT 1965-83-85-87-**(89)**; CT 1983-87; HI 1965-74, 82 to 88; ELTC 1965-85-87

Thomlinson, J [Evans] – (Roberts) – CC 1962; VT 1963; HI 1962-64

Timmins, Nicola – CC 2004; HI 2003; ELTC 2003

Turner, B – HI 1908

Uzielli, Angela (Carrick) – CC 1978; VT 1977; HI 1976-77-78-90, **(92)-(93)**; ELTC 1977

Wade, Julie – CC 1988-90-92-94-96; ES 1988-90-94; VT 1989-91-93-95; CT 1991-95; HI 1987 to 95; ELTC 1987 to 95

Waite, Claire – CC 1984; ES 1984; VT 1983; CT 1983; HI 1981 to 84; ELTC 1985

Walker, B (Thompson) – HI 1905 to 09, 11

Walker, Mickey – CC 1972-74; VT 1971; CT 1971; HI 1970-72; ELTC 1971

Walker, Sophie – ES 2006; VT 2005; HI 2003-04-05-06; ELTC 2005

Walker-Leigh, F – HI 1907-08-09, 11 to 14

Walter, J – HI 1974-79-80-82-86

Walters, L – HI 1998

Watson, C (Nelson) – HI 1982

Westall, S (Maudsley) – HI 1973

Williamson, C (Barker) – HI 1979-80-81

Willock-Pollen, G – HI 1907

Wilson, Enid – CC 1932; HI 1928-29-30

Winn, J – HI 1920-21-23-25

Wragg, M – HI 1929

Wylie, Phyllis (Wade) – CC 1938; HI 1934 to 38, 47

IRELAND

Alexander, M – HI 1920-21-22-30

Arbuthnot, M – HI 1921

McNeile, CL – HI 1906

McQuillan, Y – HI 1985-86

McVeigh, Danielle – ES 2008; HI 2006-07-08; ELTC 2008

Madeley, M (Coburn) – HI 1964-69; ELTC 1969

Madill, Maureen – CC 1980; ES 1980; VT 1979-81-85; CT 1979; HI 1978 to 85

Madill, Mrs – HI 1920-24-25-27-28-29-33

Magill, J – HI 1907-11-13

Mahon, D – HI 1989-90

Mallam, Mrs S – HI 1922-23

Mangan, Tricia – CC 2006; ES 2006; VT 2003-05; HI 1998-2000-02-03-04-05-06; ELTC 2003-05

Marks, Mrs T – HI 1950

Marks, Mrs – HI 1930-31-33-35

Menton, D – HI 1949

Millar, D – HI 1928

Milligan, J (Mark) – HI 1971-72-73

Mitchell, J – HI 1930

Mooney, M – VT 1973; HI 1972-73; ELTC 1971

Moore, S – HI 1937-38-39-47-48-49-**(68)**

Moran, V (Singleton) – HI 1970-71-73-74-75; ELTC 1971-75

Moriarty, M (Irvine) – HI 1979

Morrin, Maura – HI 2003-04-05-06-07; ELTC 2003-08

Morris, Mrs de B – HI 1933

Murray, Rachel – HI 1952

Nolan, Heather – HI 2002-03-04-05; ELTC 2005

Nutting, P (Jameson) – HI 1927-28

O'Brien, A – HI 1969

O'Brien, Suzanne (Fanagan) – CC 2000; ES 2000; VT 1999; HI 1995 to 2000; ELTC 1997-99

O'Brien Kenney, S – HI 1977-78, 83 to 86

O'Donnell, Maire – CC **(1982)**; VT **(1981)**; HI 1974-77-**(78)-(79)**; ELTC **(1980)**

O'Donohue, A – HI 1948 to 51, 53, **(73)-(74)**

O'Hare, S – HI 1921-22

O'Leary, Gillian – HI 2007-08; ELTC 2008

O'Reilly, T (Moran) – HI 1977-78-86-88, **(95)**; ELTC 1987

O'Sullivan, Ada – CC **(2006)**; HI 1982-83-84-92-94-95-96; ELTC 1993-97

O'Sullivan, P – HI 1950 to 60, 63 to 67, **(69)-(70)-(71)**; ELTC **(1971)**

O'Sullivan, Sinead – HI 2004

Ormsby, Miss – HI 1909-10-11

Orr, P (Boyd) – HI 1971

Pim, Mrs – HI 1908

Power, Eileen Rose (McDaid) – CC 1994; VT 1995-97; HI 1987 to 97, 2001-02; ELTC 1987-93-97-99

Purcell, E – HI 1965-66-67-72-73

Purfield, O – HI 1998-99

Reddan, Clarrie (Tiernan) – CC 1938-48; HI 1935-36-38-39-47-48-49

Reddan, MV – HI 1955

Rice, J – HI 1924-27-29

Riordan, Marian – HI 2002-07

Roberts, E (Pentony) – HI 1932 to 36, 39

Roberts, E (Barnett) – HI 1961 to 65; ELTC 1964

Robinson, C (Nesbitt) – CC 1980; VT 1979; HI 1974 to 81

Robinson, R (Bayly) – HI 1947-56-57

Roche, Mrs – HI 1922

Rogers, A – HI 1992-93; ELTC 1993

Ross, M (Hezlet) – HI 1905 to 08, 11-12

Slade, Lady – HI 1906

Smith, Deirdre – HI 1999-2004-05-06; ELTC 2001-05

Smith, Mrs L – HI 1913-14-21-22-23-25

Smythe, M – HI 1947 to 56, 58-59, **(62)**

Starrett, L (Malone) – HI 1975 to 78, 80

Stuart, M – HI 1905-07-08

Stuart-French, Miss – HI 1922

Sweeney, L – HI 1991

Taylor, I – HI 1930

Thornhill, Miss – HI 1924-25

Thornton, Mrs – HI 1924

Todd, Mrs – HI 1931 to 36

Tynte, V – HI 1905-06-08-09, 11 to 14

Walker, Pat – CC 1934-36-38; HI 1928 to 39, 48

Walsh, R – HI 1987

Webb, L (Bolton) – HI 1981-82-88-89-91-92-94

Wickham, C – HI 1983-89

Wickham, P – HI 1976-83-87; ELTC 1987

Wilson, Mrs – HI 1931

SCOTLAND

Agnew, C – HI 1995

Aitken, E (Young) – HI 1954

Anderson, E – HI 1910-11-12-21-25

Anderson, F – VT 1987; HI 1977-79-80-81-83-84-87 to 92; ELTC 1979-83-87-91

Anderson, H – VT 1969; HI 1964-65-68-69-70-71; ELTC 1969

Anderson, Jean (Donald) – CC 1948-50-52; HI 1947 to 52

Anderson, L – HI 1986 to 89; ELTC 1987-89

Anderson, VH – HI 1907

Bald, J – HI 1968-69-71; ELTC 1969

Barclay, C (Brisbane) – HI 1953-61-68

Baynes, Mrs CE – HI 1921-22

Beddows, C [Watson] (Stevenson) – CC 1932; HI 1913-14-21-22-23-27, 29 to 37, 39, 47 to 51

Bennett, Lorna – HI 1977-80-81

Benton, MH – HI 1914

Bishop, Sara – HI 2006

Blair, N (Menzies) – HI 1955

Booth, Carly – CC 2008; HI 2007

Bowhill, M (Robertson-Durham) – HI 1936-37-38

Briggs, Megan – HI 2007-08

Broun, JG – HI 1905-06-07-21

Brown, Mrs FW (Gilroy) – HI 1905 to 11, 13-21

Brown, TWL – HI 1924-25

Burns, K – HI 1999

Burton, H (Mitchell) – VT 1961; HI 1931-55-56-**(59)**

Cadden, G – VT **(1997)**; HI 1974-75-**(95)-(96)**; ELTC **(1997)**

Caithness, Krystle – CC 2008; ES 2006-08; CT 2007; VT 2007; ES 2006; HI 2004-05-06; ELTC 2008

Campbell, J (Burnett) – HI 1960

Coats, Mrs G – HI 1931 to 34

Cochrane, K – HI 1924-25-28-29-30

Connachan, J – CC 1980-82; ES 1980-82; VT 1981-83; CT 1983; HI 1979 to 83

Copley, K (Lackie) – HI 1974-75

Couper, M – HI 1929, 34 to 37, 39-56

Craik, T – HI 1988

Crawford, I (Wylie) – HI 1970-71-72

Cresswell, K (Stuart) – HI 1909 to 12, 14

Cruickshank, DM – (Jenkins) – HI 1910-11-12

Davidson, Alison (Rose) – CC 1996-98; VT 1995-97; CT 1995; HI 1990 to 98, 2000; ELTC 1991-93-95-97-99

Davidson, B (Inglis) – HI 1928

Draper, Marjorie [Peel] (Thomas) – CC 1954; VT **(1963)**; HI 1929-34-38, 49 to 53, **(54)-(55)**, 56-57-58, **(61)**, 62

Duncan, MJ (Wood) – HI 1925-27-28-39

Falconer, V (Lamb) – HI 1932-36-37, 47 to 56

Farie-Anderson, J – HI 1924

Farquharson-Black, Elaine (Farquharson) – CC 1990-92; VT 1989-91; CT 1991; HI 1987 to 91, 97-98, **(2002)**; ELTC 1989-91

Feggans, Pamela – HI 2002-03; ELTC 2005

Ferguson, Marjory (Fowler) – CC 1966; VT 1965; HI 1959, 62 to 67, 69-70-85; ELTC 1965-67-71

Forbes, J – HI 1985 to 89; ELTC 1987-89

Ford, J – HI 1993-94-95

Gallagher, S – HI 1983-84

Gemmill, A – HI 1981-82, 84 to 89, 91-**(97)**

Glennie, H – HI 1959

Glover, A – HI 1905-06-08-09-12

Gow, J – HI 1923-24-27-28

Graham, MA – HI 1905-06

Granger Harrison, Mrs – HI 1922

Grant-Suttie, E – HI 1908-10-11-14-22-23

Grant-Suttie, R – HI 1914

Greenlees, E – HI 1924

Greenlees, Y – HI 1928-30-31-33-34-35-38

Hamilton, S (McKinven) – HI 1965

Hargan, Claire – ELTC 2001-03; HI 1999-2000-01

Hastings, Dorothea (Sommerville) – CC 1958; VT 1963; HI 1955 to 63

Hay, J (Pelham Burn) – HI 1959

Holm, Helen (Gray) – CC 1936-38-48; HI 1932 to 38, 47-48-50-51-55-57

Hope, LA – HI 1975-76-80, 84 to 87, **(88)-(89)-(90)**

Huggan, Shirley (Lawson) – CC 1988; VT 1989; HI 1985 to 89; ELTC 1985-87-89

Hurd [Howe] (Campbell) – HI 1905-06-08-09-11-28-30

Jack, E (Philip) – HI 1962-63-64-**(81)-(82)**

Jackson, D – HI 1990

Kelway Bamber, Mrs – HI 1923-27-33

Kenny, Louise – HI 2003-06-08; ELTC 2008

Kenny, Lynn – VT 2003; CT 2003; ELTC 2003; HI 2000-01-03-04

Kerr, J – HI 1947-48-49-54

Kinloch, Miss – HI 1913-14

Knight, Mrs – HI 1922

Kyle, E – HI 1909-10

Laing, A – VT 1967; HI 1966-67-70-71-**(73)-(74)**

Laing, Anne – CC 2004; VT 1999-2003-05; CT 1999-2003; HI 1995 to 99, 2001 to 05; ELTC 1997-99-2001-03-05

Laing, Susannah – HI 2002

Laing, Vicki – CC 2002; VT 2003; HI 1997-98; ELTC 2001-03

Lambie, S – HI 1976

Lawrence, Joan B – CC 1964; ES 1964; VT 1963-65; CT 1971; HI 1959 to 70, **(77)**; ELTC 1965-67-69-71

Leburn, Wilma (Aitken) – CC 1982; VT 1981-83; HI 1978 to 83, 85

Leete, Mrs IG – HI 1933

Little, S – HI 1993

Lockhart, Fiona – HI 2005; ELTC 2005

Lugton, C – HI 1968-72-73-**75-76**-77-78-80

MacAndrew, F – HI 1913-14

McCulloch, J – HI 1921 to 24, 27, 29 to 33, 35, **(60)**

MacDonald, Kelsey – HI 2007-08

Macdonald, K – HI 1928-29

MacIntosh, I – HI **(1991)-(92)-(93)**; ELTC **(1993)**

McKay, F – HI 1992-93-94; ELTC 1993

Mackay, Lesley – HI 1999 to 2003; ELTC 2001-03

McKay, Mhairi – CC 1994-96; ES 1996; VT 1993-95-97; CT 1995; HI 1991-93-94-96; ELTC 1993-95

Mackenzie, A – HI 1921

McKinlay, Myra – CC 1994; HI 1990-92-93; ELTC 1993

McLarty, E – HI **(1966)-(67)-(68)**

McMahon, Suzanne (Cadden) – CC 1976; VT 1975; HI 1974 to 77, 79

McMaster, S – HI 1994 to 97; ELTC 1995-97

McNeil, K – HI **(1969)-(70)**

MacRae, Heather – ES 2006; VT 2005; HI 2003-04-06; ELTC 2005

Main, M (Farquhar) – HI 1950-51

Maitland, M – HI 1905-06-08-12-13

Marr, H (Cameron) – HI 1927 to 31

Marshall, Kathryn (Imrie) – CC 1990; VT 1989; HI 1984-85-89; ELTC 1987-89

Mather, H – HI 1905-09-12-13-14

Matthew, Catriona (Lambert) – CC 1990-92-94; ES 1992; VT 1989-91-93; CT 1991; HI 1989 to 93; ELTC 1989-91-93

Mellis, Mrs – HI 1924-27

Melvin, V – HI 1994-96

Menzies, M – HI **(1962)**

Milton, Moira (Paterson) – CC 1952; HI 1948 to 52

Moffat, L – VT 1999; HI 1996-98-2001

Monaghan, Hilary – CC 1998; VT 1999; HI 1995 to 98, 2000; ELTC 1997-99

Moodie, Janice – CC 1994-96; ES 1996; VT 1993-95-97; CT 1995; HI 1990-91-92; ELTC 1991-93-95-97

Morton, Linzi – HI 2000-01-02; ELTC 2001

Murray, Laura – HI 2007-08; ELTC 2008

Myles, M – HI 1955-57-59-60-67

Neill-Fraser, M – HI 1905 to 14

Nicholson, J (Hutton) – CT 1971; HI 1969-70; ELTC 1971

Nicholson, Lesley – CC 2000; VT 1999; HI 1994 to 99-**(2008)**; ELTC 1995-97-99

Nicholson, Mrs WH – HI 1910-13

Nimmo, H – HI 1936-38-39

Niven, Roseanne – ES 2008; HI 2006

Norris, J (Smith) – VT 1977; HI 1966 to 72, 75 to 79, **(83)-(84)**; ELTC 1971

Patron of

THE OPEN
CHAMPIONSHIP

Uncompromising support

There are no shortcuts in business. Dedication and
perseverance are key to success. At RBS we are
on hand to offer you and your business support,
whenever and wherever you need it.   rbs.com

Make it happen™

RBS
The Royal Bank of Scotland

DRIVE LIKE THERE IS A TOMORROW

LS 600h There's a unique pleasure in taking an exceptional car out on a fast, open road. But what about your responsibility to the environment? Drive the Lexus LS 600h and you'll have the comfort of knowing that it is powered by unique Lexus Hybrid Drive technology that combines an advanced V8 petrol engine with an electric motor. Together they deliver extraordinary fuel efficiency, lower CO_2 emissions and 445 DIN hp of smooth, near silent power. **www.lexus.eu**

LEXUS HYBRID DRIVE

LS 600h fuel consumption figures: Extra-urban 8.0 L/100km (35.3 mpg), urban 11.3 L/100km (25.0 mpg), combined 9.3 L/100km (30.4 mpg). CO_2 emissions 219 g/km. Claims made when compared to other cars within the 'luxury' class.

Working for **Golf's**
development worldwide.

2008 China National Rules School.

Based in St Andrews, The R&A is golf's governing body and organiser of The Open Championship. The R&A is committed to working for golf and operates with the consent of 136 organisations, from the amateur and professional game, and on behalf of over thirty million golfers in 121 countries.

www.randa.org

R&A
WORKING FOR GOLF

THE OPEN CHAMPIONSHIP
Patron of The Open Championship

At the heart of the image

Nikon

With Nikon you get what you pay for.

Except with the new D300,
where you get more.

40 million NIKKOR   EXPEED

2008 AWARDS
TIPA
BEST
D-SLR PROFESSIONAL

What you get is pro camera features for a fraction of the cost. 12.3
Megapixel DX format image sensor. 6 fps frame advance. 51-point AF
system. ISO sensitivity up to 3200. EXPEED image processing engine.
Start up in 0.13 seconds. 3 inch LCD monitor with live view. Active
D-lighting. Self-cleaning sensor unit. Durable, magnesium alloy
body. The most advanced digital SLR in its class. Welcome to Nikon.

www.nikon.co.uk
0800 230 220

Rethink your approach

The 16th hole (Wee Burn) at Turnberry

Wee Burn, once a straightforward and relatively short par-4, has been extended and its fairway moved to create a more challenging approach shot to an elevated green. Often played into a prevailing wind, the green slopes backward toward a deep burn. Choosing the right club is critical.

Today's business environment can be just as challenging. In times like these professional advice is invaluable. At MMC, we understand the challenges brought on by changing conditions. Our companies excel at providing global advice and solutions in risk, strategy and human capital. We help clients act with certainty when changes demand a fresh approach. Visit mmc.com to see how we can help you.

THE OPEN CHAMPIONSHIP

MMC   MARSH   MERCER   KROLL
GUY CARPENTER   OLIVER WYMAN

Patron of The Open Championship

www.mmc.com

BREAK THE
INNOVATION BARRIER.
FREE IT.

No longer can IT be considered "the cost of doing business."
IT modernization can drive your organization forward with greater
strength, innovation and agility. Our approach leverages existing
investments with solutions and services to realize early savings that
are, in turn, reinvested in innovation projects until we achieve your
optimal IT model — at your pace. In short, modernization pays for
itself. From consulting to systems integration to outsourcing, Unisys
Secure Business Operations don't simply modernize IT, they unleash
your full potential.

Security unleashed.

© 2008 Unisys Corporation.
Unisys is a registered trademark of Unisys Corporation.

www.securityunleashed.com/FreeIT

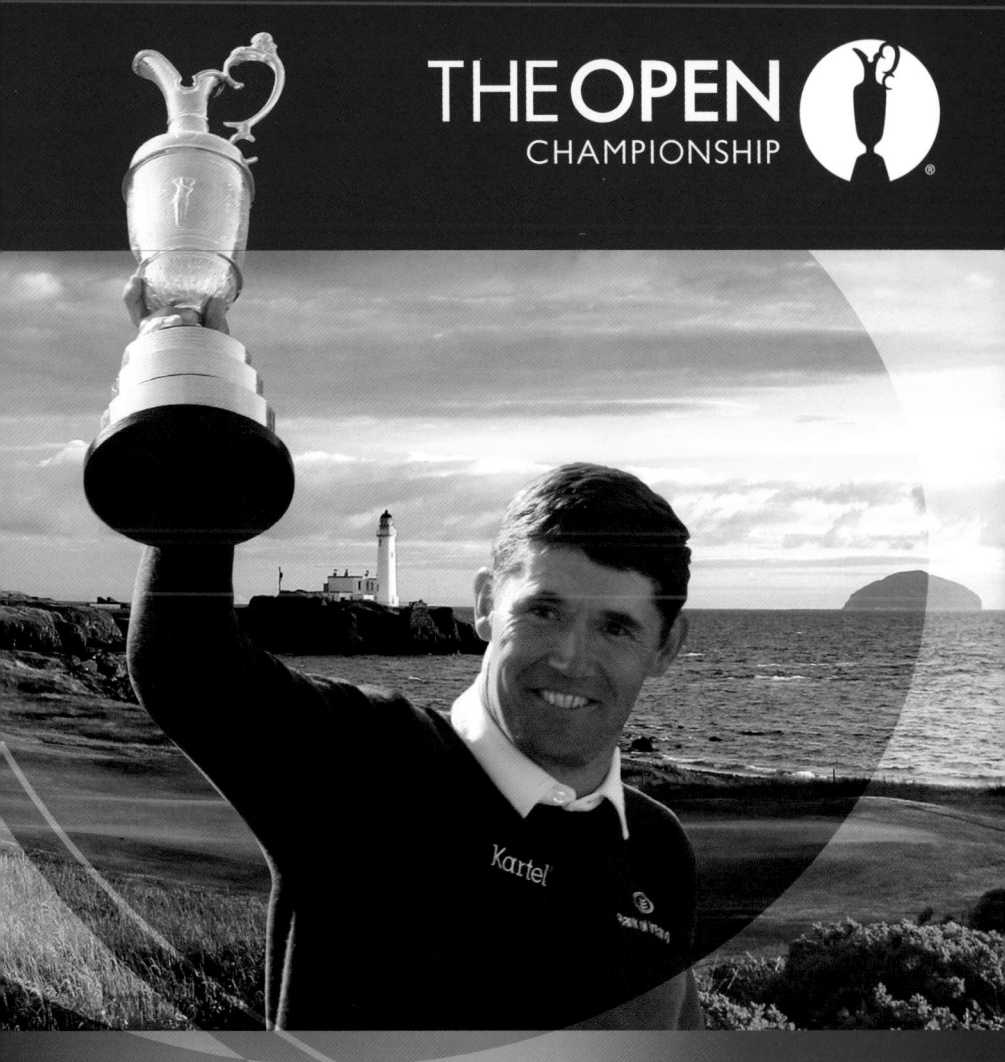

THE OPEN CHAMPIONSHIP

TURNBERRY, SCOTLAND, 12 – 19 JULY 2009

For Tickets and Open Championship News,
please visit the official website **www.opengolf.com**

FUTURE VENUES

St Andrews	Royal St George's	Royal Lytham & St Annes
15 – 18 July 2010	14 –17 July 2011	19 – 22 July 2012

RULES OF GOLF

R&A

Scotland. 1754. A group of men who understood the virtues of an exciting game called golf, and the conduct necessary to play it, established a set of rules. Little did they realise that the Rules of Golf would become a sacred and universal framework for playing the game fairly. For more than 250 years, The R&A has helped encourage and safeguard the rules of the game. Amended over time, the rules are in effect for every round – friendly or competitive. Sometimes challenged, but always adhered to. Respect the traditions of the game. Even if it means looking them up.

ROLEX. A CROWN FOR EVERY ACHIEVEMENT.

OYSTER PERPETUAL DAY-DATE II

ROLEX
ROLEX.COM

Norwell, I (Watt) – HI 1954

Ogilvy, Emily – HI 2007-08

Panton-Lewis, C (Panton) – ES 1976; VT 1977; HI 1972-73-76-77-78

Park, Mrs – HI 1952

Patey, Mrs – HI 1922-23

Percy, G (Mitchell) – HI 1927-28-30-31

Porter, Doris (Park) – CC 1932; HI 1922-25-27, 29 to 35, 37-38, 47-48

Pow, Martine – HI 2004-06

Pretswell, Pamela – HI 2007-08; ELTC 2008

Provis, I (Kyle) – HI 1910-11

Purvis-Russell-Montgomery, C – HI 1921-22-23-25, 28 to 39, 47 to 50, 52

Queen, Clare – VT 2003-05; ELTC 2003-05; HI 2002-03-04-05; ES 2004

Rawlinson, T (Walker) – VT 1973; HI 1970-71-73-76

Reid, A (Lurie) – VT 1961; HI 1960 to 64, 66

Reid, A (Kyle) – HI 1923-24-25

Reid, D – HI 1978-79

Rennie, J (Hastings) – CC 1966; VT 1961-67, 1961-65-66-67-71-72; ELTC 1967

Richmond, M (Walker) – CC 1974; VT 1975; HI 1972 to 75, 77-78

Rigby, F (Macbeth) – HI 1912-13

Ritchie, C (Park) – HI 1939-47-48-51-52-53-(64)

Roberts, M (Brown) – ES 1964; HI (1965)

Robertson, B (McCorkindale) – CC 1960-66-68-70-72-(74)-(76)-82-86; ES 1964-66-(68)-72-80-82; VT 1959-63-69-71-81-85; CT 1971-(75); HI 1958 to 66, 69-72-73-78-80-81-82-84-85-86; ELTC 1965-67-69-71

Robertson, D – HI 1907

Robertson, E – HI 1924

Robertson, G – HI 1907-08-09

Roxburgh, L – HI 1993-94-95

Roy, S (Needham) – VT 1973-75; HI 1969, 71 to 76, 83

Rusack, J – HI 1908

Singleton, B (Henderson) – HI 1939, 52 to 58, 60 to 65

Smith, J – HI 1999; ELTC 1999

Speir, Marigold – HI 1957-64-68-(71)-(72)

Stavert, M – HI 1979

Steel, Mrs DC – HI 1925

Stewart, Gillian – CC 1980-82; VT 1979-81-83; CT 1979-83; HI 1979 to 84; ELTC 1982-4

Stewart, L (Scraggie) – HI 1921-22-23

Stirling, Heather – CC 2002; HI 1999-2000-01-02

Summers, M (Mackie) – HI 1986

Teacher, F – HI 1908-09-11-12-13

Thompson, M – HI 1949

Thomson, D – HI 1982-83-85-87

Thomson, Michelle – CC 2008; HI 2007-08; ELTC 2008

Thomson, M – HI 1907

Thomson, Muriel – CC 1978; VT 1977; HI 1974 to 78; ELTC 1978

Valentine, Jessie (Anderson) – CC 1938-48-50-52-54-56-58; CT 1959; HI 1934 to 39, 47, 49 to 55, 56, 57-58

Veitch, F – HI 1912

Walker, Kylie – ES 2008; HI 2004-05-08; ELTC 2008

Wallace-Williamson, Verona – CC 1938; HI 1932

Walker, Kylie – HI 2004-05

Wardlaw, Nan (Baird) – CC 1938; HI 1932, 35 to 39, 47-48

Watson, Sally – CC 2008; HI 2005-06

Webster, Gemma – HI 2005

Wells, Laura – HI 2003

Wilson, A – HI 1973-74-(85)

Wilson, Jenna – ES 2006; HI 2004-05-06-07; ELTC 2005

Wood, S – HI 1999-2000

Wooldridge, W (Shaw) – HI 1982

Wright, Janette (Robertson) – CC 1954-56-58-60; VT 1959-61-63; CT 1959; HI 1952 to 61, 63-65-67-73, (78)-(79)-(80)-(86); ELTC 1965

Wright, M – HI 1990-91-92; ELTC 1991

Wright, P – VT 1981; HI 1981 to 84; ELTC 1987

WALES

Allington-Hughes, Miss – HI 1908-09-10-12-14-22-25

Archer, L – HI 1999

Ashcombe, Lady – HI 1950 to 54

Aubertin, Mrs – HI 1908-09-10

Baker, J – HI 1990

Barron, M – HI 1929-30-31, 34 to 39, 47 to 58, 60 to 63

Bayliss, Mrs – HI 1921

Bloodworth, D (Lewis) – HI 1954 to 57, 60

Boulden, Amy – HI 2008

Boulden, Kimberley – HI 2005

Boyes, S – HI 1992

Bradley, K (Rawlings) – HI 1975 to 79, 82-83

Brearley, M – HI 1937-38

Brewerton, R (Becky) – CC 2000; ES 2002; VT 2001-03; HI 1997 to 2003; ELTC 1999-2001-03

Bridges, Mrs – HI 1933-38-39

Briggs, A (Brown) – VT 1971-75; HI 1969 to 80, 81-82-83, 84, 93; ELTC 1971-75

Bromley-Davenport, I (Rieben) – HI 1932 to 36, 48, 50 to 56

Brook, D – HI 1913

Brown, E (Jones) – HI 1947 to 50, 52-53, 57 to 66, 68-69-70

Brown, J – HI 1960-61-62-64-65; ELTC 1965-69

Brown, Mrs – HI 1924-25-27

Bryan-Smith, S – HI 1947 to 52, 56

Burrell, Mrs – HI 1939

Caryl, M – HI 1929

Chugg, Pam (Light) – HI 1973 to 78, 86-87-88, 96, (2002); ELTC 1975-87-(2001)

Clarkson, H (Reynolds) – HI 1935-38-39

Clay, E – HI 1912

Cole, C – HI 1998

Cowley, Lady – HI 1907-09

Cox, Margaret – HI 1924-25

Cox, Nell – HI 1954

Cross, M – HI 1922

Cunninghame, S – HI 1922-25-29-31

Dampney, S – HI 1924-25, 27 to 30

David, Mrs – HI 1908

Davies, Karen – CC 1986-88; VT 1987; CT 1987; HI 1981-82-83; ELTC 1987

Davies, P (Griffiths) – HI 1965 to 68, 70-71-73; ELTC 1971

Davies, Tara – ES 2006; HI 2005-06-07-08

Davis, Louise – HI 1997-98-2000-01-02; ELTC 1997-99

Deacon, Mrs – HI 1912-14

Dermott, Lisa – **CC** 1996; HI 1987-88-89, 91 to 96; ELTC 1991-93

Donne, A – HI 1993-94; ELTC 1993

Duncan, B – HI 1907 to 10, 12

Duncan, M – HI 1922-23-28-34

Edwards, E – HI 1949-50

Edwards, J – HI 1932-33-34-36-37

Edwards, J (Morris) – HI 1962-63, 66 to 70, **(77)-(78)-(79)**; ELTC 1967-69-**(93)**

Ellis Griffiths, Mrs – HI 1907-08-09-12-13

Emery, MJ – HI 1928 to 38, 47

Evans, Kathryn – HI 1999-2000-01-02

Evans, N – HI 1908-09-10-13

Evans, Natalee – HI 1996 to 99, 2003-04; ELTC 1997-99-05

Evans, Stephanie – ES 2004; HI 2002-03-04-05-06-07-08; ELTC 2003-05-08

Franklin Thomas, E – HI 1909

Freeguard, C – HI 1927

Garfield Evans, PR (Whittaker) – HI 1948 to 54, **(55)-(56)-(57)-(58)**

Gear Evans, A – HI 1932-33-34

Gethin Griffith, S – HI 1914-22-23-24, 28 to 31, 35

Gibbs, S – HI 1933-34-39

Gould, Lucy – HI 2005-07-08

Griffith, W – HI 1981

Haig, J (Mathias Thomas) – HI 1938-39

Hall, Lydia – HI 2004-05-07; ELTC 2005

Harries, Rebecca Helen – HI 2006-07

Hartley, R – HI 1958-59-62

Hassan, Sahra – **VT** 2007; ES 2006-08; HI 2005-06-07-08; ELTC 2008

Hedley Hill, Miss – HI 1922

Highgate, Anna – **CC** 2004; CT 2003; HI 1999-2001-02-03-04; ELTC 2001-03

Hill, Mrs – HI 1924

Hort, K – HI 1929

Hughes, J – HI 1967-71-88-**(89)**; ELTC 1971

Hughes, Miss – HI 1907

Humphreys, A (Coulman) – HI 1969-70-71

Hurst, Mrs – HI 1921-22-23-25-27-28

Inghram, E (Lever) – HI 1947 to 58, 64-65

Irvine, Miss – HI 1930

Isaac, Mrs – HI 1924

Isherwood, L – HI 1972-76-77-78-80-86, 88 to 91

Jenkin, B – HI 1959

Jenkins, Hannah – HI 2008; ELTC 2008

Jenkins, J (Owen) – HI 1953-56

John, J – HI 1974

Johnson, A (Hughes) – HI 1964, 66 to 76, 78-79-85, **(95)**; ELTC 1965-67-69-71

Johnson, J (Roberts) – HI 1955

Johnson, R – HI 1955

Jones, A (Gwyther) – HI 1959

Jones, B – HI 1994-95-96-98; ELTC 1993

Jones, K – HI **(1959)-(60)-(61)**

Jones, M (De Lloyd) – HI 1951

Jones, Sarah – **CC** 2002; HI 2000-01-02-03-04-05; ELTC 2001-03-05

Jones, Mrs – HI 1932-35

Justice, M – HI 1931-32

Laming Evans, Mrs – HI 1922-23

Langford, Mrs – HI 1937

Lawson, H – HI 1989 to 92, 97-98; ELTC 1991-93-97

Leaver, B – HI 1912-14-21

Llewellyn, Miss – HI 1912-13-14-21-22-23

Lloyd, J – HI 1988

Lloyd, P – HI 1935-36

Lloyd Davies, VH – HI 1913

Lloyd Roberts, V – HI 1907-08-10

Lloyd Williams, Miss – HI 1909-10-12-14

Loucks, Breanne – **CC** 2006-08; VT 2007; CT 2007; ES 2006-08; HI 2004-05-06-08; ELTC 2005-08

Lovatt, S – HI 1994-95

MacKean, Mrs – HI 1938-39-47

MacTier, Mrs – HI 1927

Magee, A-M – HI 1991 to 94

Marley, MV – HI 1921-22-23-30-37

Martin, P [Whitworth Jones] (Low) – HI 1948-50-56-59-60-61

Mason, Mrs – HI 1923

Matthews, Tegwen [Thomas] (Perkins) – **CC** 1974-76-78-80; ES

1974; VT 1973-75-77-79; CT 1975-79; HI 1972 to 84

Mills, I – HI 1935-36-37-39-47-48

Morgan, R [Becky] – **CC** 1998-2000; ES [1998]; VT 1997-99; CT 1999; HI 1996 to 99; ELTC 2001

Morgan, Miss – HI 1912-13-14

Mountford, Sara – HI 1989 to 92; ELTC 1991-2001

Musgrove, Mrs – HI 1923-24

Newman, L – HI 1927-31

Nicholls, M – HI **(1962)**

Nicolson, Jo – HI 2003-04-06; ELTC 2005

O'Connor, Katherine – HI 2006; ELTC 2008

Oliver, M (Jones) – ES 1964; HI 1955, 60 to 66

Orr, Mrs – HI 1924

Owen, E – HI 1947

Perriam, A – HI 1988-90-91-92

Phelips, M – HI 1913-14-21

Phillips, Kate – CT 2003; HI 1999 to 2004; ELTC 2001-03

Phillips, Mrs – HI 1921

Pilgrim, Eleanor – HI 1995-97-2000-01; ELTC 1997-99-2001

Powell, M – HI 1908-09-10-12

Pritchard, Jo – HI 2002-03; ELTC 2003

Proctor, Mrs – HI 1907

Pyman, B – HI 1921-22-23-25, 28 to 39, 47 to 50, 52

Rawlings, M – VT 1981; HI 1979-80-81, 83 to 87

Rees, G – HI 1981

Rees, MB – HI 1927-31

Rhys, J – HI 1979

Richards, D – HI 1994-95-96

Richards, J – HI 1980-82-83-85

Richards, S – HI 1967

Rieben, Mrs – HI 1927 to 33

Roberts, B – HI **(1984)-(85)-(86)**

Roberts, G – HI 1949-52-53-54

Roberts, P – ES 1964; HI 1950-51-53, 55 to 63, **(64)-(65)-(66)-(67)**, 68-69-70; ELTC 1965-67-69

Roberts, S – HI 1983 to 90; ELTC 1983-87

Rogers, J – HI 1972

Scott Chard, Mrs – HI 1928-30

Seddon, N – HI 1962-63, **(74)-(75)-(76)**

Selkirk, H – HI 1925-28

Shaw, P – HI 1913

Sheldon, A – HI 1981

Slocombe, E (Davies) – HI 1974-75

Smalley, Mrs A – HI 1924-25, 31 to 34

Sowter, Mrs – HI 1923

Stark, K – HI 1995-96

Stockton, Mrs – HI 1949

Storry, Mrs – HI 1910-14

Stroud, N – HI 1989

Thomas, C (Phipps) – HI 1959, 63 to 73, 76-77-80

Thomas, I – HI 1910

Thomas, J (Foster) – HI 1984 to 87, 92-93-95; ELTC 1987-89-91-93

Thomas, O – HI 1921

Thomas, Rhian Wyn – ES 2008; HI 2007-08; ELTC 2008

Thomas, S (Rowlands) – HI 1977-82-84-85

Thomas, Vicki (Rawlings) – CC 1982-84-86-88-90; ES 1990; VT 1979-83-85-87-89-91; CT 1979-83-87-91; HI 1971 to 98; ELTC 1973 to 83, 87-91-97-99

Thompson, M – HI 1937-38-39

Treharne, A (Mills) – HI 1952-61

Turner, S (Jump) – HI 1982-84-85-86-91-93-(2008)

Valentine, P (Whitley) – HI 1973-74-75, 77 to 80, (90)

Wadsworth, Helen – CC 1984; HI 1987 to 90; ELTC 1987-90

Wakelin, H – HI 1955

Webster, S (Hales) – HI 1968-69-72, (91)

Wesley, N – HI 1986

Weston, R – HI 1927

Whieldon, Miss – HI 1908

Williams, M – HI 1936

Wilson Jones, D – HI 1952

Wright, N (Cook) – ES 1964; HI 1938-47-48-49, 51 to 54, 57 to 60, 62-63-64-66-67-68, (71)-(72)-(73); ELTC 1965, (71)

PART XIII

Governance of the Game

R&A Rules Limited

With effect from 1st January 2004, the responsibilities and authority of The Royal and Ancient Golf Club of St Andrews in making, interpreting and giving decisions on the Rules of Golf and on the Rules of Amateur Status were transferred to R&A Rules Limited.

Gender

In the Rules of Golf, the gender used in relation to any person is understood to include both genders.

Golfers with Disabilities

The R&A publication entitled "A Modification of the Rules of Golf for Golfers with Disabilities", that contains permissible modifications of the Rules of Golf to accommodate disabled golfers, is available through the R&A.

Handicaps

The Rules of Golf do not legislate for the allocation and adjustment of handicaps. Such matters are within the jurisdiction of the National Union concerned and queries should be directed accordingly.

RULES
OF GOLF

As Approved by
R&A Rules Limited
and the
United States Golf Association

31st EDITION
EFFECTIVE 1st JANUARY 2008

Copyright 2007©
Royal and Ancient Golf Club of St. Andrews
and the United States Golf Association.
All Rights Reserved.

How to use the rule book

It is understood that not everyone who has a copy of the Rules of Golf will read it from cover to cover. Most golfers only consult the Rule book when they have a Rules issue on the course that needs to be resolved. However, to ensure that you have a basic understanding of the Rules and that you play golf in a reasonable manner, it is recommended that you at least read the Quick Guide to the Rules of Golf and the Etiquette Section contained within this publication.

In terms of ascertaining the correct answer to Rules issues that arise on the course, use of the Rule book's Index should help you to identify the relevant Rule. For example, if a player accidentally moves his ball-marker in the process of lifting his ball on the putting green, identify the key words in the question, such as "ball-marker", "lifting ball" and "putting green" and look in the Index for these headings. The relevant Rule (Rule 20-1) is found under the headings "ball-marker" and "lifted ball" and a reading of this Rule will confirm the correct answer.

In addition to identifying key words and using the Index in the Rules of Golf, the following points will assist you in using the Rule book efficiently and accurately:

Understand the Words
The Rule book is written in a very precise and deliberate fashion. You should be aware of and understand the following differences in word use:

- "may" (e.g. the player may cancel the stroke) means the action is optional
- "should" (e.g. the marker should check the score) means the action is recommended but is not mandatory
- "must" (e.g. the player's clubs must conform) means it is an instruction and there is a penalty if it is not carried out
- "a ball" (e.g. drop a ball behind the point) means you may substitute another ball (e.g. Rules 26, 27 and 28)
- "the ball" (e.g. the player must lift the ball and drop it) means you must not substitute another ball (e.g. Rules 24-2 and 25-1)

Know the Definitions
There are over fifty defined terms (e.g. abnormal ground condition, through the green, etc) and these form the foundation around which the Rules of Play are written. A good knowledge of the defined terms (which are italicised throughout the book) is very important to the correct application of the Rules.

The Facts of the Case
To answer any question on the Rules you must consider the facts of the case in some detail. You should identify:

- The form of play (e.g. match play or stroke play, single, foursome or four-ball)
- Who is involved (e.g. the player, his partner or caddie, an outside agency)
- Where the incident occurred (e.g. on the teeing ground, in a bunker or water hazard, on the putting green)
- What actually happened
- The timing of the incident (e.g. has the player now returned his score card, has the competition closed)

Refer to the Book
As stated above, reference to the Rule book Index and the relevant Rule should provide the answer to the majority of questions that can arise on the course. If in doubt, play the course as you find it and play the ball as it lies. On returning to the Clubhouse, you can refer the matter to the Committee and it may be that reference to the "Decisions on the Rules of Golf" will assist in resolving any queries that are not entirely clear from the Rule book itself.

Contents

Section I —
Etiquette; Behaviour on the Course

Introduction

This section provides guidelines on the manner in which the game of golf should be played. If they are followed, all players will gain maximum enjoyment from the game. The overriding principle is that consideration should be shown to others on the course at all times.

The Spirit of the Game

Golf is played, for the most part, without the supervision of a referee or umpire. The game relies on the integrity of the individual to show consideration for other players and to abide by the Rules. All players should conduct themselves in a disciplined manner, demonstrating courtesy and sportsmanship at all times, irrespective of how competitive they may be. This is the spirit of the game of golf.

Safety

Players should ensure that no one is standing close by or in a position to be hit by the club, the ball or any stones, pebbles, twigs or the like when they make a stroke or practice swing.

Players should not play until the players in front are out of range.

Players should always alert greenstaff nearby or ahead when they are about to make a stroke that might endanger them.

If a player plays a ball in a direction where there is a danger of hitting someone, he should immediately shout a warning. The traditional word of warning in such situations is "fore".

Consideration for Other Players

No Disturbance or Distraction

Players should always show consideration for other players on the course and should not disturb their play by moving, talking or making unnecessary noise.

Players should ensure that any electronic device taken onto the course does not distract other players.

On the teeing ground, a player should not tee his ball until it is his turn to play.

Players should not stand close to or directly behind the ball, or directly behind the hole, when a player is about to play.

On the Putting Green

On the putting green, players should not stand on another player's line of putt or, when he is making a stroke, cast a shadow over his line of putt.

Players should remain on or close to the putting green until all other players in the group have holed out.

Scoring

In stroke play, a player who is acting as a marker should, if necessary, on the way to the next tee, check the score with the player concerned and record it.

Pace of Play

Play at Good Pace and Keep Up

Players should play at a good pace. The Committee may establish pace of play guidelines that all players should follow.

It is a group's responsibility to keep up with the group in front. If it loses a clear hole and it is delaying the group

behind, it should invite the group behind to play through, irrespective of the number of players in that group. Where a group has not lost a clear hole, but it is apparent that the group behind can play faster, it should invite the faster moving group to play through.

Be Ready to Play

Players should be ready to play as soon as it is their turn to play. When playing on or near the putting green, they should leave their bags or carts in such a position as will enable quick movement off the green and towards the next tee. When the play of a hole has been completed, players should immediately leave the putting green.

Lost Ball

If a player believes his ball may be lost outside a water hazard or is out of bounds, to save time, he should play a provisional ball.

Players searching for a ball should signal the players in the group behind them to play through as soon as it becomes apparent that the ball will not easily be found. They should not search for five minutes before doing so. Having allowed the group behind to play through, they should not continue play until that group has passed and is out of range.

Priority on the Course

Unless otherwise determined by the Committee, priority on the course is determined by a group's pace of play. Any group playing a whole round is entitled to pass a group playing a shorter round. The term "group" includes a single player.

Care of the Course

Bunkers

Before leaving a bunker, players should carefully fill up and smooth over all holes and footprints made by them and any nearby made by others. If a rake is within reasonable proximity of the bunker, the rake should be used for this purpose.

Repair of Divots, Ball-Marks and Damage by Shoes

Players should carefully repair any divot holes made by them and any damage to the putting green made by the impact of a ball (whether or not made by the player himself). On completion of the hole by all players in the group, damage to the putting green caused by golf shoes should be repaired.

Preventing Unnecessary Damage

Players should avoid causing damage to the course by removing divots when taking practice swings or by hitting the head of a club into the ground, whether in anger or for any other reason.

Players should ensure that no damage is done to the putting green when putting down bags or the flagstick.

In order to avoid damaging the hole, players and caddies should not stand too close to the hole and should take care during the handling of the flagstick and the removal of a ball from the hole. The head of a club should not be used to remove a ball from the hole.

Players should not lean on their clubs when on the putting green, particularly when removing the ball from the hole.

The flagstick should be properly replaced in the hole before the players leave the putting green.

Local notices regulating the movement of golf carts should be strictly observed.

Conclusion; Penalties for Breach

If players follow the guidelines in this section, it will make the game more enjoyable for everyone.

If a player consistently disregards these guidelines during a round or over a period of time to the detriment of others, it is recommended that the Committee considers taking appropriate disciplinary action against the offending player. Such action may, for example, include prohibiting play for a limited time on the course or in a certain number of competitions. This is considered to be justifiable in terms of protecting the interests of the majority of golfers who wish to play in accordance with these guidelines.

In the case of a serious breach of etiquette, the Committee may disqualify a player under Rule 33-7.

Section II — Definitions

The Definitions are listed alphabetically and, in the *Rules* themselves, defined terms are in *italics*.

Abnormal Ground Conditions

An "*abnormal ground condition*" is any *casual water, ground under repair* or hole, cast or runway on the *course* made by a *burrowing animal*, a reptile or a bird.

Addressing the Ball

A player has "*addressed the ball*" when he has taken his *stance* and has also grounded his club, except that in a *hazard* a player has *addressed the ball* when he has taken his *stance*.

Advice

"*Advice*" is any counsel or suggestion that could influence a player in determining his play, the choice of a club or the method of making a *stroke*.

Information on the *Rules*, distance or matters of public information, such as the position of *hazards* or the *flagstick* on the *putting green*, is not *advice*.

Ball Deemed to Move

See "*Move or Moved*".

Ball Holed

See "*Holed*".

Ball Lost

See "*Lost Ball*".

Ball in Play

A ball is "*in play*" as soon as the player has made a *stroke* on the *teeing ground*. It remains *in play* until it is *holed*, except when it is *lost, out of bounds* or *lifted*, or another ball has been *substituted*, whether or not the substitution is permitted; a ball so *substituted* becomes the *ball in play*.

If a ball is played from outside the *teeing ground* when the player is starting play of a hole, or when attempting to correct this mistake, the ball is not *in play* and Rule 11-4 or 11-5 applies. Otherwise, *ball in play* includes a ball played from outside the *teeing ground* when the player elects or is required to play his next *stroke* from the *teeing ground*.

Exception in match play: *Ball in play* includes a ball played by the player from outside the *teeing ground* when starting play of a hole if the opponent does not require the *stroke* to be cancelled in accordance with Rule 11-4a.

Best-Ball

See "*Forms of Match Play*".

Bunker

A "*bunker*" is a *hazard* consisting of a prepared area of ground, often a hollow, from which turf or soil has been removed and replaced with sand or the like.

Grass-covered ground bordering or within a *bunker*, including a stacked turf face (whether grass-covered or earthen), is not part of the *bunker*. A wall or lip of the *bunker* not covered with grass is part of the *bunker*. The margin of a *bunker* extends vertically downwards, but not upwards.

A ball is in a *bunker* when it lies in or any part of it touches the *bunker*.

Burrowing Animal

A "*burrowing animal*" is an animal (other than a worm, insect or the like) that makes a hole for habitation or shelter, such as a rabbit, mole, groundhog, gopher or salamander.

Note: A hole made by a non-burrowing animal, such as a dog, is not an *abnormal ground condition* unless marked or declared as *ground under repair*.

Caddie

A "*caddie*" is one who assists the player in accordance with the *Rules*, which may include carrying or handling the player's clubs during play.

When one *caddie* is employed by more than one player, he is always deemed to be the *caddie* of the player sharing the *caddie* whose ball (or whose *partner's* ball) is involved, and *equipment* carried by him is deemed to be that player's *equipment*, except when the *caddie* acts upon specific directions of another player (or the *partner* of another player) sharing the *caddie*, in which case he is considered to be that other player's *caddie*.

Casual Water

"*Casual water*" is any temporary accumulation of water on the *course* that is not in a *water hazard* and is visible before or after the player takes his *stance*. Snow and natural ice, other than frost, are either *casual water* or *loose impediments*, at the option of the player. Manufactured ice is an *obstruction*. Dew and frost are not *casual water*.

A ball is in *casual water* when it lies in or any part of it touches the *casual water*.

Committee

The "*Committee*" is the committee in charge of the competition or, if the matter does not arise in a competition, the committee in charge of the *course*.

Competitor

A "*competitor*" is a player in a stroke play competition. A "*fellow-competitor*" is any person with whom the *competitor* plays. Neither is *partner* of the other.

In stroke play *foursome* and *four-ball* competitions, where the context so admits, the word "*competitor*" or "*fellow-competitor*" includes his *partner*.

Course

The *"course"* is the whole area within any boundaries established by the *Committee* (see Rule 33-2).

Equipment

"Equipment" is anything used, worn or carried by the player or anything carried for the player by his *partner* or either of their *caddies,* except any ball he has played at the hole being played and any small object, such as a coin or a *tee,* when used to mark the position of a ball or the extent of an area in which a ball is to be dropped. *Equipment* includes a golf cart, whether or not motorised.

Note 1: A ball played at the hole being played is *equipment* when it has been lifted and not put back into play.

Note 2: When a golf cart is shared by two or more players, the cart and everything in it are deemed to be the *equipment* of one of the players sharing the cart.

If the cart is being moved by one of the players (or the *partner* of one of the players) sharing it, the cart and everything in it are deemed to be that player's *equipment.* Otherwise, the cart and everything in it are deemed to be the *equipment* of the player sharing the cart whose ball (or whose *partner's* ball) is involved.

Fellow-Competitor

See *"Competitor".*

Flagstick

The *"flagstick"* is a movable straight indicator, with or without bunting or other material attached, centred in the *hole* to show its position. It must be circular in cross-section. Padding or shock absorbent material that might unduly influence the movement of the ball is prohibited.

Forecaddie

A *"forecaddie"* is one who is employed by the *Committee* to indicate to players the position of balls during play. He is an *outside agency.*

Forms of Match Play

Single: A match in which one player plays against another player.

Threesome: A match in which one player plays against two other players, and each *side* plays one ball.

Foursome: A match in which two players play against two other players, and each *side* plays one ball.

Three-Ball: Three players play a match against one another, each playing his own ball. Each player is playing two distinct matches.

Best-Ball: A match in which one player plays against the better ball of two other players or the best ball of three other players.

Four-Ball: A match in which two players play their better ball against the better ball of two other players.

Forms of Stroke Play

Individual: A competition in which each *competitor* plays as an individual.

Foursome: A competition in which two *competitors* play as partners and play one ball.

Four-Ball: A competition in which two *competitors* play as partners, each playing his own ball. The lower score of the partners is the score for the hole. If one *partner* fails to complete the play of a hole, there is no penalty.

Note: For bogey, par and Stableford competitions, see Rule 32-1.

Four-Ball

See *"Forms of Match Play"* and *"Forms of Stroke Play".*

Foursome

See *"Forms of Match Play"* and *"Forms of Stroke Play".*

Ground Under Repair

"Ground under repair" is any part of the *course* so marked by order of the *Committee* or so declared by its authorised representative. All ground and any grass, bush, tree or other growing thing within the *ground under repair* are part of the *ground under repair. Ground under repair* includes material piled for removal and a hole made by a greenkeeper, even if not so marked. Grass cuttings and other material left on the *course* that have been abandoned and are not intended to be removed are not *ground under repair* unless so marked.

When the margin of *ground under repair* is defined by stakes, the stakes are inside the *ground under repair,* and the margin of the *ground under repair* is defined by the nearest outside points of the stakes at ground level. When both stakes and lines are used to indicate *ground under repair,* the stakes identify the *ground under repair* and the lines define the margin of the *ground under repair.* When the margin of *ground under repair* is defined by a line on the ground, the line itself is in the *ground under repair.* The margin of *ground under repair* extends vertically downwards but not upwards.

A ball is in *ground under repair* when it lies in or any part of it touches the *ground under repair.*

Stakes used to define the margin of or identify *ground under repair* are *obstructions.*

Note: The *Committee* may make a Local Rule prohibiting play from *ground under repair* or an environmentally-sensitive area defined as *ground under repair.*

Hazards

A *"hazard"* is any *bunker* or *water hazard.*

Hole

The *"hole"* must be 4¼ inches (108 mm) in diameter and at least 4 inches (101.6 mm) deep. If a lining is used, it must be sunk at least 1 inch (25.4 mm) below the *putting green* surface, unless the nature of the soil makes it impracticable to do so; its outer diameter must not exceed 4¼ inches (108 mm).

Holed

A ball is *"holed"* when it is at rest within the circumference of the *hole* and all of it is below the level of the lip of the *hole.*

Honour

The player who is to play first from the *teeing ground* is said to have the *"honour".*

Lateral Water Hazard

A *"lateral water hazard"* is a *water hazard* or that part of a *water hazard* so situated that it is not possible, or is deemed by the *Committee* to be impracticable, to drop a ball behind the *water hazard* in accordance with Rule 26-1b. All ground and water within the margin of a *lateral water hazard* are part of the *lateral water hazard.*

When the margin of a *lateral water hazard* is defined by stakes, the stakes are inside the *lateral water hazard,* and the margin of the *hazard* is defined by the nearest outside points of the stakes at ground level. When both stakes and lines are used to indicate a *lateral water hazard,* the stakes identify the *hazard* and the lines define the *hazard* margin. When the margin of a *lateral water hazard* is defined by a line on the ground, the line itself is in the *lateral water hazard.* The margin of a *lateral water hazard* extends vertically upwards and downwards.

A ball is in a *lateral water hazard* when it lies in or any part of it touches the *lateral water hazard.*

Stakes used to define the margin of or identify a *lateral water hazard* are *obstructions.*

Note 1: That part of a *water hazard* to be played as a *lateral water hazard* must be distinctively marked. Stakes or lines used to define the margin of or identify a *lateral water hazard* must be red.

Note 2: The *Committee* may make a Local Rule prohibiting play from an environmentally-sensitive area defined as a *lateral water hazard.*

Note 3: The *Committee* may define a *lateral water hazard* as a *water hazard.*

Line of Play

The "*line of play*" is the direction that the player wishes his ball to take after a *stroke*, plus a reasonable distance on either side of the intended direction. The *line of play* extends vertically upwards from the ground, but does not extend beyond the *hole*.

Line of Putt

The "*line of putt*" is the line that the player wishes his ball to take after a *stroke* on the *putting green*. Except with respect to Rule 16-1e, the *line of putt* includes a reasonable distance on either side of the intended line. The *line of putt* does not extend beyond the *hole*.

Loose Impediments

"*Loose impediments*" are natural objects, including:
* stones, leaves, twigs, branches and the like,
* dung, and
* worms, insects and the like, and the casts and heaps made by them,

provided they are not:
* fixed or growing,
* solidly embedded, or
* adhering to the ball.

Sand and loose soil are *loose impediments* on the *putting green*, but not elsewhere.

Snow and natural ice, other than frost, are either *casual water* or *loose impediments*, at the option of the player.

Dew and frost are not *loose impediments.*

Lost Ball

A ball is deemed "*lost*" if:

a. It is not found or identified as his by the player within five minutes after the player's *side* or his or their *caddies* have begun to search for it; or

b. The player has made a *stroke* at a *provisional ball* from the place where the original ball is likely to be or from a point nearer the *hole* than that place (see Rule 27-2b); or

c. The player has put another ball into play under penalty of stroke and distance (see Rule 27-la); or

d. The player has put another ball into play because it is known or virtually certain that the ball, which has not been found, has been moved by an *outside agency* (see Rule 18-1), is in an *obstruction* (see Rule 24-3), is in an *abnormal ground condition* (see Rule 25-1c) or is in a *water hazard* (see Rule 26-1); or

e. The player has made a *stroke* at a *substituted ball.*

Time spent in playing a *wrong ball* is not counted in the five-minute period allowed for search.

Marker

A "*marker*" is one who is appointed by the *Committee* to record a *competitor's* score in stroke play. He may be a *fellow-competitor*. He is not a *referee*.

Move or Moved

A ball is deemed to have "*moved*" if it leaves its position and comes to rest in any other place.

Nearest Point of Relief

The "*nearest point of relief*" is the reference point for taking relief without penalty from interference by an immovable *obstruction* (Rule 24-2), an *abnormal ground condition* (Rule 25-1) or a *wrong putting green* (Rule 25-3).

It is the point on the *course* nearest to where the ball lies:

(i) that is not nearer the *hole*, and

(ii) where, if the ball were so positioned, no interference by the condition from which relief is sought would exist for the *stroke* the player would have made from the original position if the condition were not there.

Note: In order to determine the *nearest point of relief* accurately, the player should use the club with which he would have made his next *stroke* if the condition were not there to simulate the *address* position, direction of play and swing for such a *stroke.*

Observer

An "*observer*" is one who is appointed by the *Committee* to assist a *referee* to decide questions of fact and to report to him any breach of a *Rule*. An *observer* should not attend the *flagstick*, stand at or mark the position of the *hole*, or lift the ball or mark its position.

Obstructions

An "*obstruction*" is anything artificial, including the artificial surfaces and sides of roads and paths and manufactured ice, except:

a. Objects defining *out of bounds*, such as walls, fences, stakes and railings;

b. Any part of an immovable artificial object that is *out of bounds*; and

c. Any construction declared by the *Committee* to be an integral part of the *course.*

An *obstruction* is a movable *obstruction* if it may be moved without unreasonable effort, without unduly delaying play and without causing damage. Otherwise, it is an immovable *obstruction.*

Note: The *Committee* may make a Local Rule declaring a movable *obstruction* to be an immovable *obstruction.*

Out of Bounds

"*Out of bounds*" is beyond the boundaries of the *course* or any part of the *course* so marked by the *Committee.*

When *out of bounds* is defined by reference to stakes or a fence or as being beyond stakes or a fence, the *out of bounds* line is determined by the nearest inside points at ground level of the stakes or fence posts (excluding angled supports). When both stakes and lines are used to indicate *out of bounds*, the stakes identify *out of bounds* and the lines define *out of bounds*. When *out of bounds* is defined by a line on the ground, the line itself is *out of bounds*. The *out of bounds* line extends vertically upwards and downwards.

A ball is *out of bounds* when all of it lies *out of bounds*. A player may stand *out of bounds* to play a ball lying within bounds.

Objects defining *out of bounds* such as walls, fences, stakes and railings are not *obstructions* and are deemed to be fixed. Stakes identifying *out of bounds* are not *obstructions* and are deemed to be fixed.

Note 1: Stakes or lines used to define *out of bounds* should be white.

Note 2: A *Committee* may make a Local Rule declaring stakes identifying but not defining *out of bounds* to be movable *obstructions.*

Outside Agency

In match play, an "*outside agency*" is any agency other than either the player's or opponent's *side*, any *caddie* of either *side*, any ball played by either *side* at the hole being played or any *equipment* of either *side.*

In stroke play, an *outside agency* is any agency other than the *competitor's side*, any *caddie* of the *side*, any ball played by the *side* at the hole being played or any *equipment* of the *side.*

An *outside agency* includes a *referee*, a *marker*, an *observer* and a *forecaddie*. Neither wind nor water is an *outside agency.*

Partner

A "*partner*" is a player associated with another player on the same *side.*

In *threesome, foursome, best-ball* or *four-ball* play, where the context so admits, the word "player" includes his *partner* or *partners*.

Penalty Stroke

A *"penalty stroke"* is one added to the score of a player or *side* under certain *Rules*. In a *threesome* or *foursome*, penalty strokes do not affect the order of play.

Provisional Ball

A *"provisional ball"* is a ball played under Rule 27-2 for a ball that may be *lost* outside a *water hazard* or may be *out of bounds*.

Putting Green

The *"putting green"* is all ground of the hole being played that is specially prepared for putting or otherwise defined as such by the *Committee*. A ball is on the *putting green* when any part of it touches the *putting green*.

R&A

The *"R&A"* means R&A Rules Limited.

Referee

A *"referee"* is one who is appointed by the *Committee* to accompany players to decide questions of fact and apply the *Rules*. He must act on any breach of a *Rule* that he observes or is reported to him.

A *referee* should not attend the *flagstick*, stand at or mark the position of the *hole*, or lift the ball or mark its position.

Rub of the Green

A *"rub of the green"* occurs when a ball in motion is accidentally deflected or stopped by any *outside agency* (see Rule 19-1).

Rule or Rules

The term *"Rule"* includes:

a.   The Rules of Golf and their interpretations as contained in "Decisions on the Rules of Golf";

b.   Any Conditions of Competition established by the *Committee* under Rule 33-1 and Appendix I;

c.   Any Local Rules established by the *Committee* under Rule 33-8a and Appendix I; and

d.   The specifications on clubs and the ball in Appendices II and III and their interpretations as contained in "A Guide to the Rules on Clubs and Balls".

Side

A *"side"* is a player, or two or more players who are *partners*.

Single

See *"Forms of Match Play"* and *"Forms of Stroke Play"*.

Stance

Taking the *"stance"* consists in a player placing his feet in position for and preparatory to making a *stroke*.

Stipulated Round

The *"stipulated round"* consists of playing the holes of the *course* in their correct sequence, unless otherwise authorised by the *Committee*. The number of holes in a *stipulated round* is 18 unless a smaller number is authorised by the *Committee*. As to extension of *stipulated round* in match play, see Rule 2-3.

Stroke

A *"stroke"* is the forward movement of the club made with the intention of striking at and moving the ball, but if a player checks his downswing voluntarily before the clubhead reaches the ball he has not made a *stroke*.

Substituted Ball

A *"substituted ball"* is a ball put into play for the original ball that was either *in play, lost, out of bounds* or lifted.

Tee

A *"tee"* is a device designed to raise the ball off the ground. It must not be longer than 4 inches (101.6 mm) and it must not be designed or manufactured in such a way that it could indicate the *line of play* or influence the movement of the ball.

Teeing Ground

The *"teeing ground"* is the starting place for the hole to be played. It is a rectangular area two club-lengths in depth, the front and the sides of which are defined by the outside limits of two tee-markers. A ball is outside the *teeing ground* when all of it lies outside the *teeing ground*.

Three-Ball

See *"Forms of Match Play"*.

Threesome

See *"Forms of Match Play"*.

Through the Green

"Through the green" is the whole area of the *course* except:

a.   The *teeing ground* and *putting green* of the hole being played; and

b.   All *hazards* on the *course*.

Water Hazard

A *"water hazard"* is any sea, lake, pond, river, ditch, surface drainage ditch or other open water course (whether or not containing water) and anything of a similar nature on the *course*. All ground and water within the margin of a *water hazard* are part of the *water hazard*.

When the margin of a *water hazard* is defined by stakes, the stakes are inside the *water hazard*, and the margin of the *hazard* is defined by the nearest outside points of the stakes at ground level. When both stakes and lines are used to indicate a *water hazard*, the stakes identify the *hazard* and the lines define the *hazard* margin. When the margin of a *water hazard* is defined by a line on the ground, the line itself is in the *water hazard*. The margin of a *water hazard* extends vertically upwards and downwards.

A ball is in a *water hazard* when it lies in or any part of it touches the *water hazard*.

Stakes used to define the margin of or identify a *water hazard* are *obstructions*.

Note 1: Stakes or lines used to define the margin of or identify a *water hazard* must be yellow.

Note 2: The *Committee* may make a Local Rule prohibiting play from an environmentally-sensitive area defined as a *water hazard*.

Wrong Ball

A *"wrong ball"* is any ball other than the player's:

•   *ball in play*;

•   *provisional ball*; or

•   second ball played under Rule 3-3 or Rule 20-7c in stroke play;

and includes:

•   another player's ball;

•   an abandoned ball; and

•   the player's original ball when it is no longer *in play*.

Note: *Ball in play* includes a ball *substituted* for the *ball in play*, whether or not the substitution is permitted.

Wrong Putting Green

A *"wrong putting green"* is any *putting green* other than that of the hole being played. Unless otherwise prescribed by the *Committee*, this term includes a practice *putting green* or pitching green on the *course*.

Section III — The Rules of Play

THE GAME

Rule 1 – The Game

Definitions
All defined terms are in *italics* and are listed alphabetically in the Definitions section – see pages 523–526.

1-1. General
The Game of Golf consists of playing a ball with a club from the *teeing ground* into the *hole* by a *stroke* or successive *strokes* in accordance with the *Rules*.

1-2. Exerting Influence on Ball
A player or *caddie* must not take any action to influence the position or the movement of a ball except in accordance with the *Rules*.
(Removal of loose impediment – see Rule 23-1)
(Removal of movable obstruction – see Rule 24-1)

 * PENALTY FOR BREACH OF RULE 1-2:
Match play – Loss of hole; Stroke play – Two strokes.

* In the case of a serious breach of Rule 1-2, the *Committee* may impose a penalty of disqualification.

Note: A player is deemed to have committed a serious breach of Rule 1-2 if the *Committee* considers that his act of influencing the position or movement of the ball has allowed him or another player to gain a significant advantage or has placed another player, other than his *partner*, at a significant disadvantage.

1-3. Agreement to Waive Rules
Players must not agree to exclude the operation of any *Rule* or to waive any penalty incurred.

 PENALTY FOR BREACH OF RULE 1-3:
  Match play – Disqualification of both *sides*;
Stroke play – Disqualification of *competitors* concerned.

(Agreeing to play out of turn in stroke play – see Rule 10-2c)

1-4. Points Not Covered by Rules
If any point in dispute is not covered by the *Rules*, the decision should be made in accordance with equity.

Rule 2 – Match Play

Definitions
All defined terms are in *italics* and are listed alphabetically in the Definitions section – see pages 523–526.

2-1. General
A match consists of one *side* playing against another over a *stipulated round* unless otherwise decreed by the *Committee*.

In match play the game is played by holes.

Except as otherwise provided in the *Rules*, a hole is won by the *side* that *holes* its ball in the fewer *strokes*. In a handicap match, the lower net score wins the hole.

The state of the match is expressed by the terms: so many "holes up" or "all square", and so many "to play".

A *side* is "dormie" when it is as many holes up as there are holes remaining to be played.

2-2. Halved Hole
A hole is halved if each *side holes* out in the same number of *strokes*.

When a player has *holed* out and his opponent has been left with a *stroke* for the half, if the player subsequently incurs a penalty, the hole is halved.

2-3. Winner of Match
A match is won when one *side* leads by a number of holes greater than the number remaining to be played.

If there is a tie, the *Committee* may extend the *stipulated round* by as many holes as are required for a match to be won.

2-4. Concession of Match, Hole or Next Stroke
A player may concede a match at any time prior to the start or conclusion of that match.

A player may concede a hole at any time prior to the start or conclusion of that hole.

A player may concede his opponent's next *stroke* at any time, provided the opponent's ball is at rest. The opponent is considered to have *holed* out with his next *stroke*, and the ball may be removed by either *side*.

A concession may not be declined or withdrawn.
(Ball overhanging hole – see Rule 16-2)

2-5. Doubt as to Procedure; Disputes and Claims
In match play, if a doubt or dispute arises between the players, a player may make a claim. If no duly authorised representative of the *Committee* is available within a reasonable time, the players must continue the match without delay. The *Committee* may consider a claim only if the player making the claim notifies his opponent (i) that he is making a claim, (ii) of the facts of the situation and (iii) that he wants a ruling. The claim must be made before any player in the match plays from the next *teeing ground* or, in the case of the last hole of the match, before all players in the match leave the *putting green*.

A later claim may not be considered by the *Committee*, unless it is based on facts previously unknown to the player making the claim and he had been given wrong information (Rules 6-2a and 9) by an opponent.

Once the result of the match has been officially announced, a later claim may not be considered by the *Committee*, unless it is satisfied that the opponent knew he was giving wrong information.

2-6. General Penalty
The penalty for a breach of a *Rule* in match play is loss of hole except when otherwise provided.

Rule 3 – Stroke Play

Definitions
All defined terms are in *italics* and are listed alphabetically in the Definitions section – see pages 523–526.

3-1. General; Winner
A stroke play competition consists of *competitors* completing each hole of a *stipulated round* or rounds and, for each round, returning a score card on which there is a gross score for each hole. Each *competitor* is playing against every other *competitor* in the competition.

The *competitor* who plays the *stipulated round* or rounds in the fewest *strokes* is the winner.

In a handicap competition, the *competitor* with the lowest net score for the *stipulated round* or rounds is the winner.

3-2. Failure to Hole Out
If a *competitor* fails to hole out at any hole and does not correct his mistake before he makes a *stroke* on the next *teeing ground* or, in the case of the last hole of the round, before he leaves the *putting green*, he is disqualified.

3-3. Doubt as to Procedure
a. Procedure
In stroke play, if a *competitor* is doubtful of his rights or the correct procedure during the play of a hole, he may, without penalty, complete the hole with two balls.

After the doubtful situation has arisen and before taking further action, the *competitor* must announce to his *marker* or *fellow-competitor* that he intends to play two balls and which ball he wishes to count if the *Rules* permit.

The *competitor* must report the facts of the situation to the *Committee* before returning his score card. If he fails to do so, he is disqualified.

Note: If the *competitor* takes further action before dealing with the doubtful situation, Rule 3-3 is not applicable. The score with the original ball counts or, if the original ball is not one of the balls being played, the score with the first ball put into play counts, even if the *Rules* do not allow the procedure adopted for that ball. However, the *competitor* incurs no penalty for having played a second ball, and any *penalty strokes* incurred solely by playing that ball do not count in his score.

b. Determination of Score for Hole
(i) If the ball that the *competitor* selected in advance to count has been played in accordance with the *Rules*, the score with that ball is the *competitor's* score for the hole. Otherwise, the score with the other ball counts if the *Rules* allow the procedure adopted for that ball.

(ii) If the *competitor* fails to announce in advance his decision to complete the hole with two balls, or which ball he wishes to count, the score with the original ball counts, provided it has been played in accordance with the *Rules*. If the original ball is not one of the balls being played, the first ball put into play counts, provided it has been played in accordance with the *Rules*. Otherwise, the score with the other ball counts if the *Rules* allow the procedure adopted for that ball.

Note 1: If a *competitor* plays a second ball under Rule 3-3, the *strokes* made after this Rule has been invoked with the ball ruled not to count and *penalty strokes* incurred solely by playing that ball are disregarded.

Note 2: A second ball played under Rule 3-3 is not a *provisional ball* under Rule 27-2.

3-4. Refusal to Comply with a Rule
If a *competitor* refuses to comply with a *Rule* affecting the rights of another *competitor*, he is disqualified.

3-5. General Penalty
The penalty for a breach of a *Rule* in stroke play is two strokes except when otherwise provided.

Clubs and the Ball

The *R&A* reserves the right, at any time, to change the Rules relating to clubs and balls (see Appendices II and III) and make or change the interpretations relating to these Rules.

Rule 4 – Clubs
A player in doubt as to the conformity of a club should consult the *R&A*.

A manufacturer should submit to the *R&A* a sample of a club to be manufactured for a ruling as to whether the club conforms with the *Rules*. The sample becomes the property of the *R&A* for reference purposes. If a manufacturer fails to submit a sample or, having submitted a sample, fails to await a ruling before manufacturing and/or marketing the club, the manufacturer assumes the risk of a ruling that the club does not conform with the *Rules*.

Definitions
All defined terms are in *italics* and are listed alphabetically in the Definitions section – see pages 523–526.

4-1. Form and Make of Clubs
a. General
The player's clubs must conform with this Rule and the provisions, specifications and interpretations set forth in Appendix II.

Note: The *Committee* may require, in the conditions of a competition (Rule 33-1), that any driver the player carries must have a clubhead, identified by model and loft, that is named on the current List of Conforming Driver Heads issued by the *R&A*.

b. Wear and Alteration
A club that conforms with the *Rules* when new is deemed to conform after wear through normal use. Any part of a club that has been purposely altered is regarded as new and must, in its altered state, conform with the *Rules*.

4-2. Playing Characteristics Changed and Foreign Material
a. Playing Characteristics Changed
During a *stipulated round*, the playing characteristics of a club must not be purposely changed by adjustment or by any other means.

b. Foreign Material
Foreign material must not be applied to the club face for the purpose of influencing the movement of the ball.

> ***PENALTY FOR CARRYING, BUT NOT MAKING STROKE WITH, CLUB OR CLUBS IN BREACH OF RULE 4-1 or 4-2:**
> Match play – At the conclusion of the hole at which the breach is discovered, the state of the match is adjusted by deducting one hole for each hole at which a breach occurred; maximum deduction per round – Two holes.
> Stroke play – Two strokes for each hole at which any breach occurred; maximum penalty per round – Four strokes.
> Match or stroke play – In the event of a breach between the play of two holes, the penalty applies to the next hole.
> Bogey and par competitions – See Note 1 to Rule 32-1a.
> Stableford competitions – See Note 1 to Rule 32-1b.

*Any club or clubs carried in breach of Rule 4-1 or 4-2 must be declared out of play by the player to his opponent in match play or his *marker* or a *fellow-competitor* in stroke play immediately upon discovery that a breach has occurred. If the player fails to do so, he is disqualified.

> **PENALTY FOR MAKING STROKE WITH CLUB IN BREACH OF RULE 4-1 or 4-2:**
> Disqualification.

4-3. Damaged Clubs: Repair and Replacement
a. Damage in Normal Course of Play
If, during a *stipulated round*, a player's club is damaged in the normal course of play, he may:
(i) use the club in its damaged state for the remainder of the *stipulated round*; or
(ii) without unduly delaying play, repair it or have it repaired; or
(iii) as an additional option available only if the club is unfit for play, replace the damaged club with any club. The replacement of a club must not unduly delay play and must not be made by borrowing any club selected for play by any other person playing on the *course*.

> **PENALTY FOR BREACH OF RULE 4-3a:**
> See Penalty Statements for Rule 4-4a or b, and Rule 4-4c.

Note: A club is unfit for play if it is substantially damaged, e.g. the shaft is dented, significantly bent or breaks into pieces; the clubhead becomes loose, detached or significantly deformed; or the grip becomes loose. A club is not unfit for play solely because the club's lie or loft has been altered, or the clubhead is scratched.

b. Damage Other Than in Normal Course of Play

If, during a *stipulated round*, a player's club is damaged other than in the normal course of play rendering it non-conforming or changing its playing characteristics, the club must not subsequently be used or replaced during the round.

c. Damage Prior to Round

A player may use a club damaged prior to a round, provided the club, in its damaged state, conforms with the *Rules*. Damage to a club that occurred prior to a round may be repaired during the round, provided the playing characteristics are not changed and play is not unduly delayed.

PENALTY FOR BREACH OF RULE 4-3b or c:
Disqualification.

(Undue delay – see Rule 6-7)

4-4. Maximum of Fourteen Clubs
a. Selection and Addition of Clubs

The player must not start a *stipulated round* with more than fourteen clubs. He is limited to the clubs thus selected for that round, except that if he started with fewer than fourteen clubs, he may add any number, provided his total number does not exceed fourteen.

The addition of a club or clubs must not unduly delay play (Rule 6-7) and the player must not add or borrow any club selected for play by any other person playing on the *course*.

b. Partners May Share Clubs

Partners may share clubs, provided that the total number of clubs carried by the *partners* so sharing does not exceed fourteen.

PENALTY FOR BREACH OF RULE 4-4a or b,
REGARDLESS OF NUMBER OF EXCESS CLUBS
CARRIED:

Match play – At the conclusion of the hole at which the breach is discovered, the state of the match is adjusted by deducting one hole for each hole at which a breach occurred; maximum deduction per round – Two holes.

Stroke play – Two strokes for each hole at which any breach occurred; maximum penalty per round – Four strokes.

Bogey and par competitions – See Note 1 to Rule 32-1a.
Stableford competitions – See Note 1 to Rule 32-1b.

c. Excess Club Declared Out of Play

Any club or clubs carried or used in breach of Rule 4-3a(iii) or Rule 4-4 must be declared out of play by the player to his opponent in match play or his *marker* or a *fellow-competitor* in stroke play immediately upon discovery that a breach has occurred. The player must not use the club or clubs for the remainder of the *stipulated round*.

PENALTY FOR BREACH OF RULE 4-4c:
Disqualification.

Rule 5 – The Ball

Definitions

All defined terms are in *italics* and are listed alphabetically in the Definitions section – see pages 523–526.

5-1. General

The ball the player plays must conform to the requirements specified in Appendix III.

Note: The *Committee* may require, in the conditions of a competition (Rule 33-1), that the ball the player plays must be named on the current List of Conforming Golf Balls issued by the *R&A*.

5-2. Foreign Material

Foreign material must not be applied to a ball for the purpose of changing its playing characteristics.

PENALTY FOR BREACH OF RULE 5-1 or 5-2:
Disqualification.

5-3. Ball Unfit for Play

A ball is unfit for play if it is visibly cut, cracked or out of shape. A ball is not unfit for play solely because mud or other materials adhere to it, its surface is scratched or scraped or its paint is damaged or discoloured.

If a player has reason to believe his ball has become unfit for play during play of the hole being played, he may lift the ball, without penalty, to determine whether it is unfit.

Before lifting the ball, the player must announce his intention to his opponent in match play or his *marker* or a *fellow-competitor* in stroke play and mark the position of the ball. He may then lift and examine it, provided that he gives his opponent, *marker* or *fellow-competitor* an opportunity to examine the ball and observe the lifting and replacement. The ball must not be cleaned when lifted under Rule 5-3.

If the player fails to comply with all or any part of this procedure, or if he lifts the ball without having reason to believe that it has become unfit for play during play of the hole being played, he incurs a penalty of one stroke.

If it is determined that the ball has become unfit for play during play of the hole being played, the player may *substitute* another ball, placing it on the spot where the original ball lay. Otherwise, the original ball must be replaced. If a player *substitutes* a ball when not permitted and makes a *stroke* at the wrongly *substituted* ball, he incurs the general penalty for a breach of Rule 5-3, but there is no additional penalty under this Rule or Rule 15-2.

If a ball breaks into pieces as a result of a *stroke*, the *stroke* is cancelled and the player must play a ball, without penalty, as nearly as possible at the spot from which the original ball was played (see Rule 20-5).

*PENALTY FOR BREACH OF RULE 5-3:
Match play – Loss of hole; Stroke play – Two strokes.

*If a player incurs the general penalty for a breach of Rule 5-3, there is no additional penalty under this Rule.

Note 1: If the opponent, *marker* or *fellow-competitor* wishes to dispute a claim of unfitness, he must do so before the player plays another ball.

Note 2: If the original lie of a ball to be placed or replaced has been altered, see Rule 20-3b.

(Cleaning ball lifted from putting green or under any other Rule –see Rule 21)

Player's Responsibilities

Rule 6 – The Player

Definitions

All defined terms are in *italics* and are listed alphabetically in the Definitions section – see pages 523–526.

6-1. Rules

The player and his *caddie* are responsible for knowing the *Rules*. During a *stipulated round*, for any breach of a *Rule* by his *caddie*, the player incurs the applicable penalty.

6-2. Handicap
a. Match Play

Before starting a match in a handicap competition, the players should determine from one another their respective handicaps. If a player begins a match having declared a handicap higher than that to which he is entitled and this affects the number of strokes given or received, he is disqualified; otherwise, the player must play off the declared handicap.

b. Stroke Play

In any round of a handicap competition, the *competitor* must ensure that his handicap is recorded on his score card before it is returned to the *Committee*. If no handicap is recorded on his score card before it is returned (Rule 6-6b), or if the recorded handicap is higher than that to which he is entitled and this affects the number of strokes received, he is disqualified from the handicap competition; otherwise, the score stands.

Note: It is the player's responsibility to know the holes at which handicap strokes are to be given or received.

6-3. Time of Starting and Groups
a. Time of Starting
The player must start at the time established by the *Committee*.

b. Groups
In stroke play, the *competitor* must remain throughout the round in the group arranged by the *Committee*, unless the *Committee* authorises or ratifies a change.

PENALTY FOR BREACH OF RULE 6-3:
Disqualification.

(Best-ball and four-ball play – see Rules 30-3a and 31-2)

Note: The *Committee* may provide, in the conditions of a competition (Rule 33-1), that if the player arrives at his starting point, ready to play, within five minutes after his starting time, in the absence of circumstances that warrant waiving the penalty of disqualification as provided in Rule 33-7, the penalty for failure to start on time is loss of the first hole in match play or two strokes at the first hole in stroke play instead of disqualification.

6-4. Caddie
The player may be assisted by a *caddie*, but he is limited to only one *caddie* at any one time.

PENALTY FOR BREACH OF RULE 6-4:
Match play – At the conclusion of the hole at which the breach is discovered, the state of the match is adjusted by deducting one hole for each hole at which a breach occurred; maximum deduction per round – Two holes.
Stroke play – Two strokes for each hole at which any breach occurred; maximum penalty per round – Four strokes.
Match or stroke play – In the event of a breach between the play of two holes, the penalty applies to the next hole.
A player having more than one *caddie* in breach of this Rule must immediately upon discovery that a breach has occurred ensure that he has no more than one *caddie* at any one time during the remainder of the *stipulated round*. Otherwise, the player is disqualified.
Bogey and par competitions – See Note 1 to Rule 32-1a.
Stableford competitions – See Note 1 to Rule 32-1b.

Note: The *Committee* may, in the conditions of a competition (Rule 33-1), prohibit the use of *caddies* or restrict a player in his choice of *caddie*.

6-5. Ball
The responsibility for playing the proper ball rests with the player. Each player should put an identification mark on his ball.

6-6. Scoring in Stroke Play
a. Recording Scores
After each hole the *marker* should check the score with the *competitor* and record it. On completion of the round the *marker* must sign the score card and hand it to the *competitor*. If more than one *marker* records the scores, each must sign for the part for which he is responsible.

b. Signing and Returning Score Card
After completion of the round, the *competitor* should check his score for each hole and settle any doubtful points with the *Committee*. He must ensure that the *marker* or *markers*

have signed the score card, sign the score card himself and return it to the *Committee* as soon as possible.

PENALTY FOR BREACH OF RULE 6-6b:
Disqualification.

c. Alteration of Score Card
No alteration may be made on a score card after the *competitor* has returned it to the *Committee*.

d. Wrong Score for Hole
The *competitor* is responsible for the correctness of the score recorded for each hole on his score card. If he returns a score for any hole lower than actually taken, he is disqualified. If he returns a score for any hole higher than actually taken, the score as returned stands.

Note 1: The *Committee* is responsible for the addition of scores and application of the handicap recorded on the score card – see Rule 33-5.

Note 2: In *four-ball* stroke play, see also Rule 31-3 and 31-7a.

6-7. Undue Delay; Slow Play
The player must play without undue delay and in accordance with any pace of play guidelines that the *Committee* may establish. Between completion of a hole and playing from the next *teeing ground*, the player must not unduly delay play.

PENALTY FOR BREACH OF RULE 6-7:
Match play – Loss of hole; Stroke play – Two strokes.
Bogey and par competitions – See Note 2 to Rule 32-1a.
Stableford competitions – See Note 2 to Rule 32-1b.
For subsequent offence – Disqualification.

Note 1: If the player unduly delays play between holes, he is delaying the play of the next hole and, except for bogey, par and Stableford competitions (see Rule 32), the penalty applies to that hole.

Note 2: For the purpose of preventing slow play, the *Committee* may, in the conditions of a competition (Rule 33-1), establish pace of play guidelines including maximum periods of time allowed to complete a *stipulated round*, a hole or a *stroke*.

In stroke play only, the *Committee* may, in such a condition, modify the penalty for a breach of this Rule as follows:

First offence – One stroke;
Second offence – Two strokes.
For subsequent offence – Disqualification.

6-8. Discontinuance of Play; Resumption of Play
a. When Permitted
The player must not discontinue play unless:
(i)   the *Committee* has suspended play;
(ii) he believes there is danger from lightning;
(iii) he is seeking a decision from the *Committee* on a doubtful or disputed point (see Rules 2-5 and 34-3); or
(iv) there is some other good reason such as sudden illness.
Bad weather is not of itself a good reason for discontinuing play.

If the player discontinues play without specific permission from the *Committee*, he must report to the *Committee* as soon as practicable. If he does so and the *Committee* considers his reason satisfactory, there is no penalty. Otherwise, the player is disqualified.

Exception in match play: Players discontinuing match play by agreement are not subject to disqualification, unless by so doing the competition is delayed.

Note: Leaving the *course* does not of itself constitute discontinuance of play.

b. Procedure When Play Suspended by Committee
When play is suspended by the *Committee*, if the players in a match or group are between the play of two holes, they

must not resume play until the *Committee* has ordered a resumption of play. If they have started play of a hole, they may discontinue play immediately or continue play of the hole, provided they do so without delay. If the players choose to continue play of the hole, they are permitted to discontinue play before completing it. In any case, play must be discontinued after the hole is completed.

The players must resume play when the *Committee* has ordered a resumption of play.

PENALTY FOR BREACH OF RULE 6-8b:
Disqualification.

Note: The *Committee* may provide, in the conditions of a competition (Rule 33-1), that in potentially dangerous situations play must be discontinued immediately following a suspension of play by the *Committee*. If a player fails to discontinue play immediately, he is disqualified, unless circumstances warrant waiving the penalty as provided in Rule 33-7.

c. Lifting Ball When Play Discontinued
When a player discontinues play of a hole under Rule 6-8a, he may lift his ball, without penalty, only if the *Committee* has suspended play or there is a good reason to lift it. Before lifting the ball the player must mark its position. If the player discontinues play and lifts his ball without specific permission from the *Committee*, he must, when reporting to the *Committee* (Rule 6-8a), report the lifting of the ball.

If the player lifts the ball without a good reason to do so, fails to mark the position of the ball before lifting it or fails to report the lifting of the ball, he incurs a penalty of one stroke.

d. Procedure When Play Resumed
Play must be resumed from where it was discontinued, even if resumption occurs on a subsequent day. The player must, either before or when play is resumed, proceed as follows:
(i) if the player has lifted the ball, he must, provided he was entitled to lift it under Rule 6-8c, place the original ball or a *substituted ball* on the spot from which the original ball was lifted. Otherwise, the original ball must be replaced;
(ii) if the player has not lifted his ball, he may, provided he was entitled to lift it under Rule 6-8c, lift, clean and replace the ball, or substitute a ball, on the spot from which the original ball was lifted. Before lifting the ball he must mark its position; or
(iii) if the player's ball or ball-marker is moved (including by wind or water) while play is discontinued, a ball or ball-marker must be placed on the spot from which the original ball or ball-marker was moved.
Note: If the spot where the ball is to be placed is impossible to determine, it must be estimated and the ball placed on the estimated spot. The provisions of Rule 20-3c do not apply.

*PENALTY FOR BREACH OF RULE 6-8d:
Match play – Loss of hole; Stroke play – Two strokes.

*If a player incurs the general penalty for a breach of Rule 6-8d, there is no additional penalty under Rule 6-8c.

Rule 7 – Practice

Definitions
All defined terms are in *italics* and are listed alphabetically in the Definitions section – see pages 30–43.

7-1. Before or Between Rounds
a. Match Play
On any day of a match play competition, a player may practise on the competition *course* before a round.

b. Stroke Play
Before a round or play-off on any day of a stroke play competition, a *competitor* must not practise on the competition

course or test the surface of any *putting green* on the *course* by rolling a ball or roughening or scraping the surface.

When two or more rounds of a stroke play competition are to be played over consecutive days, a *competitor* must not practise between those rounds on any competition *course* remaining to be played, or test the surface of any *putting green* on such *course* by rolling a ball or roughening or scraping the surface.

Exception: Practice putting or chipping on or near the first *teeing ground* before starting a round or play-off is permitted.

PENALTY FOR BREACH OF RULE 7-1b:
Disqualification.

Note: The *Committee* may, in the conditions of a competition(Rule 33-1), prohibit practice on the competition *course* on any day of a match play competition or permit practice on the competition *course* or part of the *course* (Rule 33-2c) on any day of or between rounds of a stroke play competition.

7-2. During Round
A player must not make a practice *stroke* during play of a hole.

Between the play of two holes a player must not make a practice *stroke*, except that he may practise putting or chipping on or near:
a. the *putting green* of the hole last played,
b. any practice *putting green*, or
c. the *teeing ground* of the next hole to be played in the round, provided a practice *stroke* is not made from a *hazard* and does not unduly delay play (Rule 6-7).

Strokes made in continuing the play of a hole, the result of which has been decided, are not practice *strokes*.

Exception: When play has been suspended by the *Committee*, a player may, prior to resumption of play, practise (a) as provided in this Rule, (b) anywhere other than on the competition *course* and (c) as otherwise permitted by the *Committee*.

PENALTY FOR BREACH OF RULE 7-2:
Match play – Loss of hole; Stroke play – Two strokes.
In the event of a breach between the play of two holes, the penalty applies to the next hole.

Note 1: A practice swing is not a practice *stroke* and may be taken at any place, provided the player does not breach the *Rules*.

Note 2: The *Committee* may, in the conditions of a competition (Rule 33-1), prohibit:
(a) practice on or near the *putting green* of the hole last played, and
(b) rolling a ball on the *putting green* of the hole last played.

Rule 8 – Advice; Indicating Line of Play

Definitions
All defined terms are in *italics* and are listed alphabetically in the Definitions section – see pages 523–526.

8-1. Advice
During a *stipulated round*, a player must not:
a. give *advice* to anyone in the competition playing on the *course* other than his *partner*, or
b. ask for *advice* from anyone other than his *partner* or either of their *caddies*.

8-2. Indicating Line of Play
a. Other Than on Putting Green
Except on the *putting green*, a player may have the *line* of *play* indicated to him by anyone, but no one may be positioned by the player on or close to the line or an extension of the line beyond the *hole* while the *stroke* is being made. Any mark

placed by the player or with his knowledge to indicate the line must be removed before the *stroke* is made.

Exception: Flagstick attended or held up – see Rule 17-1.

b. On the Putting Green

When the player's ball is on the *putting green*, the player, his *partner* or either of their *caddies* may, before but not during the *stroke*, point out a line for putting, but in so doing the *putting green* must not be touched. A mark must not be placed anywhere to indicate a line for putting.

PENALTY FOR BREACH OF RULE:

Match play – Loss of hole; Stroke play – Two strokes.

Note: The *Committee* may, in the conditions of a team competition (Rule 33-1), permit each team to appoint one person who may give *advice* (including pointing out a line for putting) to members of that team. The *Committee* may establish conditions relating to the appointment and permitted conduct of that person, who must be identified to the *Committee* before giving *advice*.

Rule 9 – Information as to Strokes Taken

Definitions

All defined terms are in *italics* and are listed alphabetically in the Definitions section – see pages 523–526.

9-1. General

The number of *strokes* a player has taken includes any *penalty strokes* incurred.

9-2. Match Play

a. Information as to Strokes Taken

An opponent is entitled to ascertain from the player, during the play of a hole, the number of *strokes* he has taken and, after play of a hole, the number of *strokes* taken on the hole just completed.

b. Wrong Information

A player must not give wrong information to his opponent. If a player gives wrong information, he loses the hole.

A player is deemed to have given wrong information if he:

(i) fails to inform his opponent as soon as practicable that he has incurred a penalty, unless (a) he was obviously proceeding under a *Rule* involving a penalty and this was observed by his opponent, or (b) he corrects the mistake before his opponent makes his next *stroke*; or

(ii) gives incorrect information during play of a hole regarding the number of *strokes* taken and does not correct the mistake before his opponent makes his next *stroke*; or

(iii) gives incorrect information regarding the number of *strokes* taken to complete a hole and this affects the opponent's understanding of the result of the hole, unless he corrects the mistake before any player makes a *stroke* from the next *teeing ground* or, in the case of the last hole of the match, before all players leave the *putting green*.

A player has given wrong information even if it is due to the failure to include a penalty that he did not know he had incurred. It is the player's responsibility to know the *Rules*.

9-3. Stroke Play

A *competitor* who has incurred a penalty should inform his *marker* as soon as practicable.

Order of Play

Rule 10 – Order of Play

Definitions

All defined terms are in *italics* and are listed alphabetically in the Definitions section – see pages 523–526.

10-1. Match Play

a. When Starting Play of Hole

The *side* that has the *honour* at the first *teeing ground* is determined by the order of the draw. In the absence of a draw, the *honour* should be decided by lot.

The *side* that wins a hole takes the *honour* at the next *teeing ground*. If a hole has been halved, the *side* that had the *honour* at the previous *teeing ground* retains it.

b. During Play of Hole

After both players have started play of the hole, the ball farther from the *hole* is played first. If the balls are equidistant from the *hole* or their positions relative to the *hole* are not determinable, the ball to be played first should be decided by lot.

Exception: Rule 30-3b (*best-ball* and *four-ball* match play).

Note: When it becomes known that the original ball is not to be played as it lies and the player is required to play a ball as nearly as possible at the spot from which the original ball was last played (see Rule 20-5), the order of play is determined by the spot from which the previous *stroke* was made. When a ball may be played from a spot other than where the previous *stroke* was made, the order of play is determined by the position where the original ball came to rest.

c. Playing Out of Turn

If a player plays when his opponent should have played, there is no penalty, but the opponent may immediately require the player to cancel the *stroke* so made and, in correct order, play a ball as nearly as possible at the spot from which the original ball was last played (see Rule 20-5).

10-2. Stroke Play

a. When Starting Play of Hole

The *competitor* who has the *honour* at the first *teeing ground* is determined by the order of the draw. In the absence of a draw, the *honour* should be decided by lot.

The *competitor* with the lowest score at a hole takes the *honour* at the next *teeing ground*. The *competitor* with the second lowest score plays next and so on. If two or more *competitors* have the same score at a hole, they play from the next *teeing ground* in the same order as at the previous *teeing ground*.

Exception: Rule 32-1 (handicap bogey, par and Stableford competitions).

b. During Play of Hole

After the *competitors* have started play of the hole, the ball farthest from the *hole* is played first. If two or more balls are equidistant from the *hole* or their positions relative to the *hole* are not determinable, the ball to be played first should be decided by lot.

Exceptions: Rules 22 (ball assisting or interfering with play) and 31-4 (*four-ball* stroke play).

Note: When it becomes known that the original ball is not to be played as it lies and the *competitor* is required to play a ball as nearly as possible at the spot from which the original ball was last played (see Rule 20-5), the order of play is determined by the spot from which the previous *stroke* was made. When a ball may be played from a spot other than where the previous *stroke* was made, the order of play is determined by the position where the original ball came to rest.

c. Playing Out of Turn

If a *competitor* plays out of turn, there is no penalty and the ball is played as it lies. If, however, the *Committee* determines that *competitors* have agreed to play out of turn to give one of them an advantage, they are disqualified.

(Making stroke while another ball in motion after stroke from putting green – see Rule 16-1f)

(Incorrect order of play in threesome and foursome stroke play – see Rule 29-3)

10-3. Provisional Ball or Another Ball from Teeing Ground

If a player plays a *provisional ball* or another ball from the *teeing ground*, he must do so after his opponent or *fellow-competitor* has made his first *stroke*. If more than one player elects to play a *provisional ball* or is required to play another ball from the *teeing ground*, the original order of play must be retained. If a player plays a *provisional ball* or another ball out of turn, Rule 10-1c or 10-2c applies.

Teeing Ground

Rule 11 – Teeing Ground

Definitions
All defined terms are in *italics* and are listed alphabetically in the Definitions section – see pages 523–526.

11-1. Teeing

When a player is putting a ball into play from the *teeing ground*, it must be played from within the *teeing ground* and from the surface of the ground or from a conforming *tee* in or on the surface of the ground.

For the purposes of this Rule, the surface of the ground includes an irregularity of surface (whether or not created by the player) and sand or other natural substance (whether or not placed by the player).

If a player makes a *stroke* at a ball on a non-conforming *tee*, or at a ball teed in a manner not permitted by this Rule, he is disqualified.

A player may stand outside the *teeing ground* to play a ball within it.

11-2. Tee-Markers

Before a player makes his first *stroke* with any ball on the *teeing ground* of the hole being played, the tee-markers are deemed to be fixed. In these circumstances, if the player moves or allows to be moved a tee-marker for the purpose of avoiding interference with his *stance*, the area of his intended swing or his *line of play*, he incurs the penalty for a breach of Rule 13-2.

11-3. Ball Falling off Tee

If a ball, when not *in play*, falls off a *tee* or is knocked off a *tee* by the player in *addressing* it, it may be re-teed, without penalty. However, if a *stroke* is made at the ball in these circumstances, whether the ball is moving or not, the *stroke* counts, but there is no penalty.

11-4. Playing from Outside Teeing Ground

a. Match Play
If a player, when starting a hole, plays a ball from outside the *teeing ground*, there is no penalty, but the opponent may immediately require the player to cancel the *stroke* and play a ball from within the *teeing ground*.

b. Stroke Play
If a *competitor*, when starting a hole, plays a ball from outside the *teeing ground*, he incurs a penalty of two strokes and must then play a ball from within the *teeing ground*.

If the *competitor* makes a *stroke* from the next *teeing ground* without first correcting his mistake or, in the case of the last hole of the round, leaves the *putting green* without first declaring his intention to correct his mistake, he is disqualified.

The *stroke* from outside the *teeing ground* and any subsequent *strokes* by the *competitor* on the hole prior to his correction of the mistake do not count in his score.

11-5. Playing from Wrong Teeing Ground

The provisions of Rule 11-4 apply.

Playing the Ball

Rule 12 – Searching for and Identifying Ball

Definitions
All defined terms are in *italics* and are listed alphabetically in the Definitions section – see pages 523–526.

12-1. Searching for Ball; Seeing Ball

In searching for his ball anywhere on the *course*, the player may touch or bend long grass, rushes, bushes, whins, heather or the like, but only to the extent necessary to find and identify it, provided that this does not improve the lie of the ball, the area of his intended *stance* or swing or his *line of play*.

A player is not necessarily entitled to see his ball when making a *stroke*.

In a *hazard*, if a ball is believed to be covered by *loose impediments* or sand, the player may remove by probing or raking with a club or otherwise, as many *loose impediments* or as much sand as will enable him to see a part of the ball. If an excess is removed, there is no penalty and the ball must be re-covered so that only a part of it is visible. If the ball is *moved* during the removal, there is no penalty; the ball must be replaced and, if necessary, re-covered. As to removal of *loose impediments* outside a *hazard*, see Rule 23-1.

If a ball lying in or on an *obstruction* or in an *abnormal ground condition* is accidentally *moved* during search, there is no penalty; the ball must be replaced, unless the player elects to proceed under Rule 24-1b, 24-2b or 25-1b as applicable. If the player replaces the ball, he may still proceed under Rule 24-1b, 24-2b or 25-1b if applicable.

If a ball is believed to be lying in water in a *water hazard*, the player may probe for it with a club or otherwise. If the ball is *moved*, it must be replaced, unless the player elects to proceed under Rule 26-1. There is no penalty for causing the ball to *move*, provided the movement of the ball was directly attributable to the specific act of probing. Otherwise, the player incurs a *penalty stroke* under Rule 18-2a.

PENALTY FOR BREACH OF RULE 12-1:
Match play – Loss of hole; Stroke play – Two strokes.

12-2. Identifying Ball

The responsibility for playing the proper ball rests with the player. Each player should put an identification mark on his ball.

If a player has reason to believe a ball at rest is his and it is necessary to lift the ball in order to identify it, he may lift the ball, without penalty, in order to do so.

Before lifting the ball, the player must announce his intention to his opponent in match play or his *marker* or a *fellow-competitor* in stroke play and mark the position of the ball. He may then lift the ball and identify it, provided that he gives his opponent, *marker* or *fellow-competitor* an opportunity to observe the lifting and replacement. The ball must not be cleaned beyond the extent necessary for identification when lifted under Rule 12-2.

If the ball is the player's ball and he fails to comply with all or any part of this procedure, or he lifts his ball in order to identify it when not necessary to do so, he incurs a penalty of one stroke. If the lifted ball is the player's ball, he must replace it. If he fails to do so, he incurs the general penalty for a breach of Rule 12-2, but there is no additional penalty under this Rule.

Note: If the original lie of a ball to be placed or replaced has been altered, see Rule 20-3b.

*PENALTY FOR BREACH OF RULE 12-2:
Match play – Loss of hole; Stroke play – Two strokes.

*If a player incurs the general penalty for a breach of Rule 12-2, there is no additional penalty under this Rule.

Rule 13 – Ball Played as It Lies

Definitions
All defined terms are in *italics* and are listed alphabetically in the Definitions section – see pages 523–526.

13-1. General
The ball must be played as it lies, except as otherwise provided in the *Rules*.

(Ball at rest moved – see Rule 18)

13-2. Improving Lie, Area of Intended Stance or Swing, or Line of Play
A player must not improve or allow to be improved:
- the position or lie of his ball,
- the area of his intended *stance* or swing,
- his *line of play* or a reasonable extension of that line beyond the *hole*, or
- the area in which he is to drop or place a ball, by any of the following actions:
- pressing a club on the ground,
- moving, bending or breaking anything growing or fixed (including immovable *obstructions* and objects defining *out of bounds*),
- creating or eliminating irregularities of surface,
- removing or pressing down sand, loose soil, replaced divots or other cut turf placed in position, or
- removing dew, frost or water.

However, the player incurs no penalty if the action occurs:
- in grounding the club lightly when *addressing the ball*,
- in fairly taking his *stance*,
- in making a *stroke* or the backward movement of his club for a *stroke* and the *stroke* is made,
- in creating or eliminating irregularities of surface within the *teeing ground* (Rule 11-1) or in removing dew, frost or water from the *teeing ground*, or
- on the *putting green* in removing sand and loose soil or in repairing damage (Rule 16-1).

Exception: Ball in *hazard* – see Rule 13-4.

13-3. Building Stance
A player is entitled to place his feet firmly in taking his *stance*, but he must not build a *stance*.

13-4. Ball in Hazard; Prohibited Actions
Except as provided in the *Rules*, before making a *stroke* at a ball that is in a *hazard* (whether a *bunker* or a *water hazard*) or that, having been lifted from a *hazard*, may be dropped or placed in the *hazard*, the player must not:
a. Test the condition of the *hazard* or any similar *hazard*;
b. Touch the ground in the *hazard* or water in the *water hazard* with his hand or a club; or
c. Touch or move a *loose impediment* lying in or touching the *hazard*.

Exceptions:
1. Provided nothing is done that constitutes testing the condition of the *hazard* or improves the lie of the ball, there is no penalty if the player (a) touches the ground or *loose impediments* in any *hazard* or water in a *water hazard* as a result of or to prevent falling, in removing an *obstruction*, in measuring or in marking the position of, retrieving, lifting, placing or replacing a ball under any *Rule* or (b) places his clubs in a *hazard*.
2. After making the *stroke*, if the ball is still in the *hazard* or has been lifted from the *hazard* and may be dropped or placed in the *hazard*, the player may smooth sand or soil in the *hazard*, provided nothing is done to breach Rule 13-2 with respect to his next *stroke*. If the ball is outside the *hazard* after the *stroke*, the player may smooth sand or soil in the *hazard* without restriction.

3. If the player makes a *stroke* from a *hazard* and the ball comes to rest in another *hazard*, Rule 13-4a does not apply to any subsequent actions taken in the *hazard* from which the *stroke* was made.
Note: At any time, including at *address* or in the backward movement for the *stroke*, the player may touch, with a club or otherwise, any *obstruction*, any construction declared by the *Committee* to be an integral part of the *course* or any grass, bush, tree or other growing thing.

PENALTY FOR BREACH OF RULE:
Match play – Loss of hole; Stroke play – Two strokes.

(Searching for ball – see Rule 12-1)
(Relief for ball in water hazard – see Rule 26)

Rule 14 – Striking the Ball

Definitions
All defined terms are in *italics* and are listed alphabetically in the Definitions section – see pages 523–526.

14-1. Ball to be Fairly Struck At
The ball must be fairly struck at with the head of the club and must not be pushed, scraped or spooned.

14-2. Assistance
In making a *stroke*, a player must not:
a. Accept physical assistance or protection from the elements; or
b. Allow his *caddie*, his *partner* or his *partner's caddie* to position himself on or close to an extension of the *line of play* or the *line of putt* behind the ball.

PENALTY FOR BREACH OF RULE 14-1 or 14-2:
Match play – Loss of hole; Stroke play – Two strokes.

14-3. Artificial Devices, Unusual Equipment and Unusual Use of Equipment
The *R&A* reserves the right, at any time, to change the Rules relating to artificial devices, unusual *equipment* and the unusual use of *equipment*, and to make or change the interpretations relating to these Rules.

A player in doubt as to whether use of an item would constitute a breach of Rule 14-3 should consult the *R&A*.

A manufacturer should submit to the *R&A* a sample of an item to be manufactured for a ruling as to whether its use during a *stipulated round* would cause a player to be in breach of Rule 14-3. The sample becomes the property of the *R&A* for reference purposes. If a manufacturer fails to submit a sample or, having submitted a sample, fails to await a ruling before manufacturing and/or marketing the item, the manufacturer assumes the risk of a ruling that use of the item would be contrary to the *Rules*.

Except as provided in the *Rules*, during a *stipulated round* the player must not use any artificial device or unusual *equipment*, or use any *equipment* in an unusual manner:
a. That might assist him in making a *stroke* or in his play; or
b. For the purpose of gauging or measuring distance or conditions that might affect his play; or
c. That might assist him in gripping the club, except that:
  (i) plain gloves may be worn;
  (ii) resin, powder and drying or moisturising agents may be used; and
  (iii) a towel or handkerchief may be wrapped around the grip.

Exceptions:
1. A player is not in breach of this Rule if (a) the *equipment* or device is designed for or has the effect of alleviating a medical condition, (b) the player has a legitimate medical reason to use the *equipment* or device, and (c) the *Committee* is satisfied that its use does not give the player any undue advantage over other players.

2. A player is not in breach of this Rule if he uses *equipment* in a traditionally accepted manner.

PENALTY FOR BREACH OF RULE 14-3:
Disqualification.

Note: The *Committee* may make a Local Rule allowing players to use devices that measure or gauge distance only.

14-4. Striking the Ball More Than Once

If a player's club strikes the ball more than once in the course of a *stroke*, the player must count the *stroke* and add a *penalty stroke*, making two *strokes* in all.

14-5. Playing Moving Ball

A player must not make a *stroke* at his ball while it is moving.

Exceptions:
- Ball falling off *tee* – Rule 11-3
- Striking the ball more than once – Rule 14-4
- Ball moving in water – Rule 14-6

When the ball begins to *move* only after the player has begun the *stroke* or the backward movement of his club for the *stroke*, he incurs no penalty under this Rule for playing a moving ball, but he is not exempt from any penalty under the following Rules:
- Ball at rest *moved* by player – Rule 18-2a
- Ball at rest moving after *address* – Rule 18-2b

(Ball purposely deflected or stopped by player, partner or caddie – see Rule 1-2)

14-6. Ball Moving in Water

When a ball is moving in water in a *water hazard*, the player may, without penalty, make a *stroke*, but he must not delay making his *stroke* in order to allow the wind or current to improve the position of the ball. A ball moving in water in a *water hazard* may be lifted if the player elects to invoke Rule 26.

PENALTY FOR BREACH OF RULE 14-5 or 14-6:
Match play – Loss of hole; Stroke play – Two strokes.

Rule 15 – Substituted Ball; Wrong Ball

Definitions

All defined terms are in *italics* and are listed alphabetically in the Definitions section – see pages 523–526.

15-1. General

A player must hole out with the ball played from the *teeing ground*, unless the ball is *lost* or *out of bounds* or the player *substitutes* another ball, whether or not substitution is permitted (see Rule 15-2). If a player plays a *wrong ball*, see Rule 15-3.

15-2. Substituted Ball

A player may *substitute* a ball when proceeding under a *Rule* that permits the player to play, drop or place another ball in completing the play of a hole. The *substituted ball* becomes the *ball in play*.

If a player *substitutes* a ball when not permitted to do so under the *Rules*, that *substituted ball* is not a *wrong ball*; it becomes the *ball in play*. If the mistake is not corrected as provided in Rule 20-6 and the player makes a *stroke* at a wrongly *substituted ball*, he loses the hole in match play or incurs a penalty of two strokes in stroke play under the applicable Rule and, in stroke play, must play out the hole with the *substituted ball*.

Exception: If a player incurs a penalty for making a *stroke* from a wrong place, there is no additional penalty for substituting a ball when not permitted.

(Playing from wrong place – see Rule 20-7)

15-3. Wrong Ball
a. Match Play

If a player makes a *stroke* at a *wrong ball*, he loses the hole.
If the *wrong ball* belongs to another player, its owner must place a ball on the spot from which the *wrong ball* was first played.

If the player and opponent exchange balls during the play of a hole, the first to make a *stroke* at a *wrong ball* loses the hole; when this cannot be determined, the hole must be played out with the balls exchanged.

Exception: There is no penalty if a player makes a *stroke* at a *wrong ball* that is moving in water in a *water hazard*. Any *strokes* made at a *wrong ball* moving in water in a *water hazard* do not count in the player's score. The player must correct his mistake by playing the correct ball or by proceeding under the *Rules*.

b. Stroke Play

If a *competitor* makes a *stroke* or *strokes* at a *wrong ball*, he incurs a penalty of two strokes.

The *competitor* must correct his mistake by playing the correct ball or by proceeding under the *Rules*. If he fails to correct his mistake before making a *stroke* on the next *teeing ground* or, in the case of the last hole of the round, fails to declare his intention to correct his mistake before leaving the *putting green*, he is disqualified.

Strokes made by a *competitor* with a *wrong ball* do not count in his score. If the *wrong ball* belongs to another *competitor*, its owner must place a ball on the spot from which the *wrong ball* was first played.

Exception: There is no penalty if a *competitor* makes a *stroke* at a *wrong ball* that is moving in water in a *water hazard*. Any *strokes* made at a *wrong ball* moving in water in a *water hazard* do not count in the *competitor's* score.

(Lie of ball to be placed or replaced altered – see Rule 20-3b)

(Spot not determinable – see Rule 20-3c)

The Putting Green

Rule 16 – The Putting Green

Definitions

All defined terms are in *italics* and are listed alphabetically in the Definitions section – see pages 523–526.

16-1. General
a. Touching Line of Putt

The *line of putt* must not be touched except:
(i) the player may remove *loose impediments*, provided he does not press anything down;
(ii) the player may place the club in front of the ball when *addressing* it, provided he does not press anything down;
(iii) in measuring – Rule 18-6;
(iv) in lifting or replacing the ball – Rule 16-1b;
(v) in pressing down a ball-marker;
(vi) in repairing old *hole* plugs or ball marks on the *putting green* – Rule 16-1c; and
(vii) in removing movable *obstructions* – Rule 24-1.

(Indicating line for putting on putting green – see Rule 8-2b)

b. Lifting and Cleaning Ball

A ball on the *putting green* may be lifted and, if desired, cleaned. The position of the ball must be marked before it is lifted and the ball must be replaced (see Rule 20-1).

c. Repair of Hole Plugs, Ball Marks and Other Damage

The player may repair an old *hole* plug or damage to the *putting green* caused by the impact of a ball, whether or not the player's ball lies on the *putting green*. If a ball or ball-marker is accidentally *moved* in the process of the repair, the ball or ball-marker must be replaced. There is no penalty, provided the movement of the ball or ball-marker is directly attributable to the specific act of repairing an old *hole* plug or damage to the *putting green* caused by the impact of a ball. Otherwise, Rule 18 applies.

Any other damage to the *putting green* must not be repaired if it might assist the player in his subsequent play of the hole.

d. Testing Surface

During the *stipulated round*, a player must not test the surface of any *putting green* by rolling a ball or roughening or scraping the surface.

Exception: Between the play of two holes, a player may test the surface of any practice *putting green* and the *putting green* of the hole last played, unless the *Committee* has prohibited such action (see Note 2 to Rule 7-2).

e. Standing Astride or on Line of Putt

The player must not make a *stroke* on the *putting green* from a *stance* astride, or with either foot touching, the *line of putt* or an extension of that line behind the ball.

Exception: There is no penalty if the *stance* is inadvertently taken on or astride the *line of putt* (or an extension of that line behind the ball) or is taken to avoid standing on another player's *line of putt* or prospective *line of putt*.

f. Making Stroke While Another Ball in Motion

The player must not make a *stroke* while another ball is in motion after a *stroke* from the *putting green*, except that if a player does so, there is no penalty if it was his turn to play.

(Lifting ball assisting or interfering with play while another ball in motion – see Rule 22)

PENALTY FOR BREACH OF RULE 16-1:
Match play – Loss of hole; Stroke play – Two strokes.

(Position of caddie or partner – see Rule 14-2)
(Wrong putting green – see Rule 25-3)

16-2. Ball Overhanging Hole

When any part of the ball overhangs the lip of the *hole*, the player is allowed enough time to reach the *hole* without unreasonable delay and an additional ten seconds to determine whether the ball is at rest. If by then the ball has not fallen into the *hole*, it is deemed to be at rest. If the ball subsequently falls into the *hole*, the player is deemed to have *holed* out with his last *stroke*, and must add a *penalty stroke* to his score for the hole; otherwise, there is no penalty under this Rule.

(Undue delay – see Rule 6-7)

Rule 17 – The Flagstick

Definitions

All defined terms are in *italics* and are listed alphabetically in the Definitions section – see pages 523–526.

17-1. Flagstick Attended, Removed or Held Up

Before making a *stroke* from anywhere on the *course*, the player may have the *flagstick* attended, removed or held up to indicate the position of the *hole*.

If the *flagstick* is not attended, removed or held up before the player makes a *stroke*, it must not be attended, removed or held up during the *stroke* or while the player's ball is in motion if doing so might influence the movement of the ball.

Note 1: If the *flagstick* is in the *hole* and anyone stands near it while a *stroke* is being made, he is deemed to be attending the *flagstick*.

Note 2: If, prior to the *stroke*, the *flagstick* is attended, removed or held up by anyone with the player's knowledge and he makes no objection, the player is deemed to have authorised it.

Note 3: If anyone attends or holds up the *flagstick* while a *stroke* is being made, he is deemed to be attending the *flagstick* until the ball comes to rest.

(Moving attended, removed or held-up flagstick while ball in motion – see Rule 24-1)

17-2. Unauthorised Attendance

If an opponent or his *caddie* in match play or a *fellow-competitor* or his *caddie* in stroke play, without the player's authority or prior knowledge, attends, removes or holds up the *flagstick* during the *stroke* or while the ball is in motion, and the act might influence the movement of ball, the opponent or *fellow-competitor* incurs the applicable penalty.

*PENALTY FOR BREACH OF RULE 17-1 or 17-2:
Match play – Loss of hole; Stroke play – Two strokes.

*In stroke play, if a breach of Rule 17-2 occurs and the *competitor's* ball subsequently strikes the *flagstick*, the person attending or holding it or anything carried by him, the *competitor* incurs no penalty. The ball is played as it lies, except that if the *stroke* was made on the *putting green*, the *stroke* is cancelled and the ball must be replaced and replayed.

17-3. Ball Striking Flagstick or Attendant

The player's ball must not strike:
a. The *flagstick* when it is attended, removed or held up;
b. The person attending or holding up the *flagstick* or anything carried by him; or
c. The *flagstick* in the *hole*, unattended, when the *stroke* has been made on the *putting green*.

Exception: When the *flagstick* is attended, removed or held up without the player's authority – see Rule 17-2.

PENALTY FOR BREACH OF RULE 17-3:
Match play – Loss of hole; Stroke play – Two strokes and the ball must be played as it lies.

17-4. Ball Resting Against Flagstick

When a player's ball rests against the *flagstick* in the *hole* and the ball is not *holed*, the player or another person authorised by him may move or remove the *flagstick*, and if the ball falls into the *hole*, the player is deemed to have *holed* out with his last *stroke*; otherwise, the ball, if *moved*, must be placed on the lip of the *hole*, without penalty.

Ball Moved, Deflected or Stopped

Rule 18 – Ball at Rest Moved

Definitions

All defined terms are in *italics* and are listed alphabetically in the Definitions section – see pages 523–526.

18-1. By Outside Agency

If a ball at rest is *moved* by an *outside agency*, there is no penalty and the ball must be replaced.

Note: It is a question of fact whether a ball has been *moved* by an *outside agency*. In order to apply this Rule, it must be known or virtually certain that an *outside agency* has *moved* the ball. In the absence of such knowledge or certainty, the player must play the ball as it lies or, if the ball is not found, proceed under Rule 27-1.

(Player's ball at rest moved by another ball – see Rule 18-5)

18-2. By Player, Partner, Caddie or Equipment
a. General

When a player's ball is *in play*, if:
(i) the player, his *partner* or either of their *caddies* lifts or moves it, touches it purposely (except with a club in the act of *addressing* it) or causes it to *move* except as permitted by a *Rule*, or
(ii) *equipment* of the player or his *partner* causes the ball to *move*, the player incurs a penalty of one stroke. If the ball is *moved*, it must be replaced, unless the movement of the ball occurs after the player has begun the *stroke* or the backward movement of the club for the *stroke* and the *stroke* is made.

Under the *Rules* there is no penalty if a player accidentally causes his ball to *move* in the following circumstances:

*   In searching for a ball in a *hazard* covered by *loose impediments* or sand, for a ball in an *obstruction* or *abnormal ground condition* or for a ball believed to be in water in a *water hazard* – Rule 12-1
*   In repairing a *hole* plug or ball mark – Rule 16-1c
*   In measuring – Rule 18-6
*   In lifting a ball under a *Rule* – Rule 20-1
*   In placing or replacing a ball under a *Rule* – Rule 20-3a
*   In removing a *loose impediment* on the *putting green* – Rule 23-1
*   In removing movable *obstructions* – Rule 24-1

b. Ball Moving After Address
If a player's *ball in play* moves after he has *addressed* it (other than as a result of a *stroke*), the player is deemed to have *moved* the ball and incurs a penalty of one stroke. The ball must be replaced, unless the movement of the ball occurs after the player has begun the *stroke* or the backward movement of the club for the *stroke* and the *stroke* is made.

18-3. By Opponent, Caddie or Equipment in Match Play
a. During Search
If, during search for a player's ball, an opponent, his *caddie* or his *equipment* moves the ball, touches it or causes it to *move*, there is no penalty. If the ball is *moved*, it must be replaced.

b. Other Than During Search
If, other than during search for a player's ball, an opponent, his *caddie* or his *equipment* moves the ball, touches it purposely or causes it to *move*, except as otherwise provided in the *Rules*, the opponent incurs a penalty of one stroke. If the ball is *moved*, it must be replaced.
(Playing a wrong ball – see Rule 15-3)
(Ball moved in measuring – see Rule 18-6)

18-4. By Fellow-Competitor, Caddie or Equipment in Stroke Play
If a *fellow-competitor*, his *caddie* or his *equipment* moves the player's ball, touches it or causes it to *move*, there is no penalty. If the ball is *moved*, it must be replaced.
(Playing a wrong ball – see Rule 15-3)

18-5. By Another Ball
If a *ball in play* and at rest is *moved* by another ball in motion after a *stroke*, the *moved* ball must be replaced.

18-6. Ball Moved in Measuring
If a ball or ball-marker is *moved* in measuring while proceeding under or in determining the application of a *Rule*, the ball or ball-marker must be replaced. There is no penalty, provided the movement of the ball or ball-marker is directly attributable to the specific act of measuring. Otherwise, the provisions of Rules 18-2a, 18-3b or 18-4 apply.

*PENALTY FOR BREACH OF RULE:
Match play – Loss of hole; Stroke play – Two strokes.

*If a player who is required to replace a ball fails to do so, or if he makes a *stroke* at a ball *substituted* under Rule 18 when such *substitution* is not permitted, he incurs the general penalty for breach of Rule 18, but there is no additional penalty under this Rule.

Note 1: If a ball to be replaced under this Rule is not immediately recoverable, another ball may be *substituted*.

Note 2: If the original lie of a ball to be placed or replaced has been altered, see Rule 20-3b.

Note 3: If it is impossible to determine the spot on which a ball is to be placed, see Rule 20-3c.

Rule 19 – Ball in Motion Deflected or Stopped

Definitions
All defined terms are in *italics* and are listed alphabetically in the Definitions section – see pages 523-526.

19-1. By Outside Agency
If a player's ball in motion is accidentally deflected or stopped by any *outside agency*, it is a *rub of the green*, there is no penalty and the ball must be played as it lies, except:
a. If a player's ball in motion after a *stroke* other than on the *putting green* comes to rest in or on any moving or animate *outside agency*, the ball must *through the green* or in a *hazard* be dropped, or on the *putting green* be placed, as near as possible to the spot directly under the place where the ball came to rest in or on the *outside agency*, but not nearer the *hole*, and
b. If a player's ball in motion after a *stroke* on the *putting green* is deflected or stopped by, or comes to rest in or on, any moving or animate *outside agency*, except a worm, insect or the like, the *stroke* is cancelled. The ball must be replaced and replayed.
If the ball is not immediately recoverable, another ball may be *substituted*.
Exception: Ball striking person attending or holding up *flagstick* or anything carried by him – see Rule 17-3b.
Note: If the *referee* or the *Committee* determines that a player's ball has been purposely deflected or stopped by an *outside agency*, Rule 1-4 applies to the player. If the *outside agency* is a *fellow-competitor* or his *caddie*, Rule 1-2 applies to the *fellow-competitor*.
(Player's ball deflected or stopped by another ball – see Rule 19-5)

19-2. By Player, Partner, Caddie or Equipment
If a player's ball is accidentally deflected or stopped by himself, his *partner* or either of their *caddies* or *equipment*, the player incurs a penalty of one stroke. The ball must be played as it lies, except when it comes to rest in or on the player's, his *partner's* or either of their *caddies'* clothes or *equipment*, in which case the ball must *through the green* or in a *hazard* be dropped, or on the *putting green* be placed, as near as possible to the spot directly under the place where the ball came to rest in or on the article, but not nearer the *hole*.
Exceptions:
1. Ball striking person attending or holding up *flagstick* or anything carried by him – see Rule 17-3b.
2. Dropped ball – see Rule 20-2a.
(Ball purposely deflected or stopped by player, partner or caddie – see Rule 1-2)

19-3. By Opponent, Caddie or Equipment in Match Play
If a player's ball is accidentally deflected or stopped by an opponent, his *caddie* or his *equipment*, there is no penalty. The player may, before another *stroke* is made by either side, cancel the *stroke* and play a ball, without penalty, as nearly as possible at the spot from which the original ball was last played (Rule 20-5) or he may play the ball as it lies. However, if the player elects not to cancel the *stroke* and the ball has come to rest in or on the opponent's or his *caddie's* clothes or *equipment*, the ball must *through the green* or in a *hazard* be dropped, or on the *putting green* be placed, as near as possible to the spot directly under the place where the ball came to rest in or on the article, but not nearer the *hole*.
Exception: Ball striking person attending or holding up *flagstick* or anything carried by him – see Rule 17-3b.
(Ball purposely deflected or stopped by opponent or caddie – see Rule 1-2)

19-4. By Fellow-Competitor, Caddie or Equipment in Stroke Play

See Rule 19-1 regarding ball deflected by *outside agency*.

Exception: Ball striking person attending or holding up *flagstick* or anything carried by him – see Rule 17-3b.

19-5. By Another Ball
a. At Rest

If a player's ball in motion after a *stroke* is deflected or stopped by a *ball in play* and at rest, the player must play his ball as it lies. In match play, there is no penalty. In stroke play, there is no penalty, unless both balls lay on the *putting green* prior to the *stroke*, in which case the player incurs a penalty of two strokes.

b. In Motion

If a player's ball in motion after a *stroke* is deflected or stopped by another ball in motion after a *stroke*, the player must play his ball as it lies. There is no penalty, unless the player was in breach of Rule 16-1f, in which case he incurs the penalty for breach of that Rule.

Exception: If the player's ball is in motion after a *stroke* on the *putting green* and the other ball in motion is an *outside agency* – see Rule 19-1b.

PENALTY FOR BREACH OF RULE:
Match play – Loss of hole; Stroke play – Two strokes.

Relief Situations and Procedure

Rule 20 – Lifting, Dropping and Placing; Playing from Wrong Place

Definitions

All defined terms are in *italics* and are listed alphabetically in the Definitions section – see pages 523–526.

20-1. Lifting and Marking

A ball to be lifted under the *Rules* may be lifted by the player, his *partner* or another person authorised by the player. In any such case, the player is responsible for any breach of the *Rules*.

The position of the ball must be marked before it is lifted under a *Rule* that requires it to be replaced. If it is not marked, the player incurs a penalty of one stroke and the ball must be replaced. If it is not replaced, the player incurs the general penalty for breach of this Rule but there is no additional penalty under Rule 20-1.

If a ball or ball-marker is accidentally *moved* in the process of lifting the ball under a *Rule* or marking its position, the ball or ball-marker must be replaced. There is no penalty, provided the movement of the ball or ball-marker is directly attributable to the specific act of marking the position of or lifting the ball. Otherwise, the player incurs a penalty of one stroke under this Rule or Rule 18-2a.

Exception: If a player incurs a penalty for failing to act in accordance with Rule 5-3 or 12-2, there is no additional penalty under Rule 20-1.

Note: The position of a ball to be lifted should be marked by placing a ball-marker, a small coin or other similar object immediately behind the ball. If the ball-marker interferes with the play, *stance* or *stroke* of another player, it should be placed one or more clubhead-lengths to one side.

20-2. Dropping and Re-Dropping
a. By Whom and How

A ball to be dropped under the *Rules* must be dropped by the player himself. He must stand erect, hold the ball at shoulder height and arm's length and drop it. If a ball is dropped by any other person or in any other manner and the error is not corrected as provided in Rule 20-6, the player incurs a penalty of one stroke.

If the ball, when dropped, touches any person or the *equipment* of any player before or after it strikes a part of the *course* and before it comes to rest, the ball must be re-dropped, without penalty. There is no limit to the number of times a ball must be re-dropped in these circumstances.

(Taking action to influence position or movement of ball – see Rule 1-2)

b. Where to Drop

When a ball is to be dropped as near as possible to a specific spot, it must be dropped not nearer the *hole* than the specific spot which, if it is not precisely known to the player, must be estimated.

A ball when dropped must first strike a part of the *course* where the applicable *Rule* requires it to be dropped. If it is not so dropped, Rules 20-6 and 20-7 apply.

c. When to Re-Drop

A dropped ball must be re-dropped, without penalty, if it:
(i) rolls into and comes to rest in a *hazard*;
(ii) rolls out of and comes to rest outside a *hazard*;
(iii) rolls onto and comes to rest on a *putting green*;
(iv) rolls and comes to rest *out of bounds*;
(v) rolls to and comes to rest in a position where there is interference from the condition from which relief was taken under Rule 24-2b (immovable obstruction), Rule 25-1 (abnormal ground conditions), Rule 25-3 (wrong putting green) or a Local Rule (Rule 33-8a), or rolls back into the pitch-mark from which it was lifted under Rule 25-2 (embedded ball);
(vi) rolls and comes to rest more than two club-lengths from where it first struck a part of the *course*; or
(vii) rolls and comes to rest nearer the *hole* than:
  (a) its original position or estimated position (see Rule 20-2b) unless otherwise permitted by the *Rules*; or
  (b) the *nearest point of relief* or maximum available relief (Rule 24-2, 25-1 or 25-3); or
  (c) the point where the original ball last crossed the margin of the *water hazard* or *lateral water hazard* (Rule 26-1).

If the ball when re-dropped rolls into any position listed above, it must be placed as near as possible to the spot where it first struck a part of the *course* when re-dropped.

Note 1: If a ball when dropped or re-dropped comes to rest and subsequently *moves*, the ball must be played as it lies, unless the provisions of any other *Rule* apply.

Note 2: If a ball to be re-dropped or placed under this Rule is not immediately recoverable, another ball may be *substituted*.

(Use of dropping zone – see Appendix I; Part B; section 8)

20-3. Placing and Replacing
a. By Whom and Where

A ball to be placed under the *Rules* must be placed by the player or his *partner*. If a ball is to be replaced, the player, his *partner* or the person who lifted or *moved* it must place it on the spot from which it was lifted or *moved*. If the ball is placed or replaced by any other person and the error is not corrected as provided in Rule 20-6, the player incurs a penalty of one stroke. In any such case, the player is responsible for any other breach of the *Rules* that occurs as a result of the placing or replacing of the ball.

If a ball or ball-marker is accidentally *moved* in the process of placing or replacing the ball, the ball or ball-marker must be replaced. There is no penalty, provided the movement of the ball or ball-marker is directly attributable to the specific act of placing or replacing the ball or removing the ball-marker. Otherwise, the player incurs a penalty of one stroke under Rule 18-2a or 20-1.

If a ball to be replaced is placed other than on the spot from which it was lifted or *moved* and the error is not corrected as provided in Rule 20-6, the player incurs the general penalty, loss of hole in match play or two strokes in stroke play, for a breach of the applicable *Rule*.

b. Lie of Ball to be Placed or Replaced Altered
If the original lie of a ball to be placed or replaced has been altered:
(i)   except in a *hazard*, the ball must be placed in the nearest lie most similar to the original lie that is not more than one club-length from the original lie, not nearer the *hole* and not in a *hazard*;
(ii) in a *water hazard*, the ball must be placed in accordance with Clause (i) above, except that the ball must be placed in the *water hazard*;
(iii) in a *bunker*, the original lie must be re-created as nearly as possible and the ball must be placed in that lie.

c. Spot Not Determinable
If it is impossible to determine the spot where the ball is to be placed or replaced:
(i)   *through the green*, the ball must be dropped as near as possible to the place where it lay but not in a *hazard* or on a *putting green*;
(ii) in a *hazard*, the ball must be dropped in the *hazard* as near as possible to the place where it lay;
(iii) on the *putting green*, the ball must be placed as near as possible to the place where it lay but not in a *hazard*.
Exception: When resuming play (Rule 6-8d), if the spot where the ball is to be placed is impossible to determine, it must be estimated and the ball placed on the estimated spot.

d. Ball Fails to Come to Rest on Spot
If a ball when placed fails to come to rest on the spot on which it was placed, there is no penalty and the ball must be replaced. If it still fails to come to rest on that spot:
(i)   except in a *hazard*, it must be placed at the nearest spot where it can be placed at rest that is not nearer the *hole* and not in a *hazard*;
(ii) in a *hazard*, it must be placed in the *hazard* at the nearest spot where it can be placed at rest that is not nearer the *hole*.
If a ball when placed comes to rest on the spot on which it is placed, and it subsequently *moves*, there is no penalty and the ball must be played as it lies, unless the provisions of any other *Rule* apply.

PENALTY FOR BREACH OF RULE 20-1, 20-2 or 20-3:
Match play – Loss of hole; Stroke play – Two strokes.

20-4. When Ball Dropped or Placed is in Play
If the player's *ball in play* has been lifted, it is again in play when dropped or placed.
A *substituted ball* becomes the *ball in play* when it has been dropped or placed.
(Ball incorrectly substituted – see Rule 15-2)
(Lifting ball incorrectly substituted, dropped or placed – see Rule 20-6)

20-5. Making Next Stroke from Where Previous Stroke Made
When a player elects or is required to make his next *stroke* from where a previous *stroke* was made, he must proceed as follows:
(a) On the Teeing Ground: The ball to be played must be played from within the *teeing ground*. It may be played from anywhere within the *teeing ground* and may be teed.
(b) Through the Green: The ball to be played must be dropped and when dropped must first strike a part of the *course through the green*.

(c) In a Hazard: The ball to be played must be dropped and when dropped must first strike a part of the *course* in the *hazard*.
(d) On the Putting Green: The ball to be played must be placed on the *putting green*.
PENALTY FOR BREACH OF RULE 20-5:
Match play – Loss of hole; Stroke play – Two strokes.

20-6. Lifting Ball Incorrectly Substituted, Dropped or Placed
A ball incorrectly *substituted*, dropped or placed in a wrong place or otherwise not in accordance with the *Rules* but not played may be lifted, without penalty, and the player must then proceed correctly.

20-7. Playing from Wrong Place
a. General
A player has played from a wrong place if he makes a *stroke* at his *ball in play*:
(i)   on a part of the *course* where the *Rules* do not permit a *stroke* to be played or a ball to be dropped or placed; or
(ii) when the *Rules* require a dropped ball to be re-dropped or a *moved* ball to be replaced.
Note: For a ball played from outside the *teeing ground* or from a wrong *teeing ground* – see Rule 11-4.

b. Match Play
If a player makes a *stroke* from a wrong place, he loses the hole.

c. Stroke Play
If a *competitor* makes a *stroke* from a wrong place, he incurs a penalty of two strokes under the applicable *Rule*. He must play out the hole with the ball played from the wrong place, without correcting his error, provided he has not committed a serious breach (see Note 1).
If a *competitor* becomes aware that he has played from a wrong place and believes that he may have committed a serious breach, he must, before making a *stroke* on the next *teeing ground*, play out the hole with a second ball played in accordance with the *Rules*. If the hole being played is the last hole of the round, he must declare, before leaving the *putting green*, that he will play out the hole with a second ball played in accordance with the *Rules*.
If the *competitor* has played a second ball, he must report the facts to the *Committee* before returning his score card; if he fails to do so, he is disqualified. The *Committee* must determine whether the *competitor* has committed a serious breach of the applicable *Rule*. If he has, the score with the second ball counts and the competitor must add two *penalty strokes* to his score with that ball. If the *competitor* has committed a serious breach and has failed to correct it as outlined above, he is disqualified.
Note 1: A *competitor* is deemed to have committed a serious breach of the applicable *Rule* if the *Committee* considers he has gained a significant advantage as a result of playing from a wrong place.
Note 2: If a *competitor* plays a second ball under Rule 20-7c and it is ruled not to count, *strokes* made with that ball and *penalty strokes* incurred solely by playing that ball are disregarded. If the second ball is ruled to count, the *stroke* made from the wrong place and any *strokes* subsequently taken with the original ball including *penalty strokes* incurred solely by playing that ball are disregarded.
Note 3: If a player incurs a penalty for making a *stroke* from a wrong place, there is no additional penalty for *substituting* a ball when not permitted.

Rule 21 – Cleaning Ball
Definitions
All defined terms are in *italics* and are listed alphabetically in the Definitions section – see pages 523–526.

A ball on the *putting green* may be cleaned when lifted under Rule 16-1b. Elsewhere, a ball may be cleaned when lifted, except when it has been lifted:

a.   To determine if it is unfit for play (Rule 5-3);
b.   For identification (Rule 12-2), in which case it may be cleaned only to the extent necessary for identification; or
c.   Because it is assisting or interfering with play (Rule 22).

If a player cleans his ball during play of a hole except as provided in this Rule, he incurs a penalty of one stroke and the ball, if lifted, must be replaced.

If a player who is required to replace a ball fails to do so, he incurs the general penalty under the applicable Rule, but there is no additional penalty under Rule 21.

Exception: If a player incurs a penalty for failing to act in accordance with Rule 5-3, 12-2 or 22, there is no additional penalty under Rule 21.

Rule 22 – Ball Assisting or Interfering with Play

Definitions
All defined terms are in *italics* and are listed alphabetically in the Definitions section – see pages 523–526.

22-1. Ball Assisting Play
Except when a ball is in motion, if a player considers that a ball might assist any other player, he may:

a.   Lift the ball if it is his ball; or
b.   Have any other ball lifted.

A ball lifted under this Rule must be replaced (see Rule 20-3). The ball must not be cleaned, unless it lies on the *putting green* (see Rule 21).

In stroke play, a player required to lift his ball may play first rather than lift the ball.

In stroke play, if the *Committee* determines that *competitors* have agreed not to lift a ball that might assist any *competitor*, they are disqualified.

22-2. Ball Interfering with Play
Except when a ball is in motion, if a player considers that another ball might interfere with his play, he may have it lifted.

A ball lifted under this Rule must be replaced (see Rule 20-3). The ball must not be cleaned, unless it lies on the *putting green* (see Rule 21).

In stroke play, a player required to lift his ball may play first rather than lift the ball.

Note: Except on the *putting green*, a player may not lift his ball solely because he considers that it might interfere with the play of another player. If a player lifts his ball without being asked to do so, he incurs a penalty of one stroke for a breach of Rule 18-2a, but there is no additional penalty under Rule 22.

PENALTY FOR BREACH OF RULE:
Match play – Loss of hole; Stroke play – Two strokes.

Rule 23 – Loose Impediments

Definitions
All defined terms are in *italics* and are listed alphabetically in the Definitions section – see pages 523–526.

23-1. Relief
Except when both the *loose impediment* and the ball lie in or touch the same *hazard*, any *loose impediment* may be removed without penalty.

If the ball lies anywhere other than on the *putting green* and the removal of a *loose impediment* by the player causes the ball to *move*, Rule 18-2a applies.

On the *putting green*, if the ball or ball-marker is accidentally *moved* in the process of the player removing a *loose impediment*, the ball or ball-marker must be replaced. There is no penalty, provided the movement of the ball or

ball-marker is directly attributable to the removal of the *loose impediment*. Otherwise, if the player causes the ball to *move*, he incurs a penalty of one stroke under Rule 18-2a.

When a ball is in motion, a *loose impediment* that might influence the movement of the ball must not be removed.

Note: If the ball lies in a *hazard*, the player must not touch or move any *loose impediment* lying in or touching the same *hazard* – see Rule 13-4c.

PENALTY FOR BREACH OF RULE:
Match play – Loss of hole; Stroke play – Two strokes.

(Searching for ball in hazard – see Rule 12-1)
(Touching line of putt – see Rule 16-1a)

Rule 24 – Obstructions

Definitions
All defined terms are in *italics* and are listed alphabetically in the Definitions section – see pages 523–526.

24-1. Movable Obstruction
A player may take relief, without penalty, from a movable *obstruction* as follows:

a.   If the ball does not lie in or on the *obstruction*, the *obstruction* may be removed. If the ball *moves*, it must be replaced, and there is no penalty, provided that the movement of the ball is directly attributable to the removal of the *obstruction*. Otherwise, Rule 18-2a applies.

b.   If the ball lies in or on the *obstruction*, the ball may be lifted and the *obstruction* removed. The ball must *through the green* or in a *hazard* be dropped, or on the *putting green* be placed, as near as possible to the spot directly under the place where the ball lay in or on the *obstruction*, but not nearer the *hole*.

The ball may be cleaned when lifted under this Rule.

When a ball is in motion, an *obstruction* that might influence the movement of the ball, other than *equipment* of any player or the *flagstick* when attended, removed or held up, must not be moved.

(Exerting influence on ball – see Rule 1-2)

Note: If a ball to be dropped or placed under this Rule is not immediately recoverable, another ball may be *substituted*.

24-2. Immovable Obstruction
a. Interference
Interference by an immovable *obstruction* occurs when a ball lies in or on the *obstruction*, or when the *obstruction* interferes with the player's *stance* or the area of his intended swing. If the player's ball lies on the *putting green*, interference also occurs if an immovable *obstruction* on the *putting green* intervenes on his *line of putt*. Otherwise, intervention on the *line of play* is not, of itself, interference under this Rule.

b. Relief
Except when the ball is in a *water hazard* or a *lateral water hazard*, a player may take relief from interference by an immovable *obstruction* as follows:

(i)   Through the Green: If the ball lies *through the green*, the player must lift the ball and drop it, without penalty, within one club-length of and not nearer the *hole* than the *nearest point of relief*. The *nearest point of relief* must not be in a *hazard* or on a *putting green*. When the ball is dropped within one club-length of the *nearest point of relief*, the ball must first strike a part of the *course* at a spot that avoids interference by the immovable *obstruction* and is not in a *hazard* and not on a *putting green*.

(ii) In a Bunker: If the ball is in a *bunker*, the player must lift the ball and drop it either:

(a)   Without penalty, in accordance with Clause (i) above, except that the *nearest point of relief* must be in the *bunker* and the ball must be dropped in the *bunker*; or

(b) Under penalty of one stroke, outside the *bunker* keeping the point where the ball lay directly between the *hole* and the spot on which the ball is dropped, with no limit to how far behind the *bunker* the ball may be dropped.

(iii) On the Putting Green: If the ball lies on the *putting green*, the player must lift the ball and place it, without penalty, at the *nearest point of relief* that is not in a *hazard*. The *nearest point of relief* may be off the *putting green*.

(iv) On the Teeing Ground: If the ball lies on the *teeing ground*, the player must lift the ball and drop it, without penalty, in accordance with Clause (i) above.

The ball may be cleaned when lifted under this Rule.

(Ball rolling to a position where there is interference by the condition from which relief was taken – see Rule 20-2c(v))

Exception: A player may not take relief under this Rule if (a) it is clearly unreasonable for him to make a *stroke* because of interference by anything other than an immovable *obstruction* or (b) interference by an immovable *obstruction* would occur only through use of an unnecessarily abnormal *stance*, swing or direction of play.

Note 1: If a ball is in a *water hazard* (including a *lateral water hazard*), the player may not take relief from interference by an immovable *obstruction*. The player must play the ball as it lies or proceed under Rule 26-1.

Note 2: If a ball to be dropped or placed under this Rule is not immediately recoverable, another ball may be *substituted*.

Note 3: The *Committee* may make a Local Rule stating that the player must determine the *nearest point of relief* without crossing over, through or under the *obstruction*.

24-3. Ball in Obstruction Not Found

It is a question of fact whether a ball that has not been found after having been struck toward an *obstruction* is in the *obstruction*. In order to apply this Rule, it must be known or virtually certain that the ball is in the *obstruction*. In the absence of such knowledge or certainty, the player must proceed under Rule 27-1.

a. Ball in Movable Obstruction Not Found

If it is known or virtually certain that a ball that has not been found is in a movable *obstruction*, the player may *substitute* another ball and take relief, without penalty, under this Rule. If he elects to do so, he must remove the *obstruction* and *through the green* or in a *hazard* drop a ball, or on the *putting green* place a ball, as near as possible to the spot directly under the place where the ball last crossed the outermost limits of the movable *obstruction*, but not nearer the hole.

b. Ball in Immovable Obstruction Not Found

If it is known or virtually certain that a ball that has not been found is in an immovable *obstruction*, the player may take relief under this Rule. If he elects to do so, the spot where the ball last crossed the outermost limits of the *obstruction* must be determined and, for the purpose of applying this Rule, the ball is deemed to lie at this spot and the player must proceed as follows:

(i) Through the Green: If the ball last crossed the outermost limits of the immovable *obstruction* at a spot *through the green*, the player may *substitute* another ball, without penalty, and take relief as prescribed in Rule 24-2b(i).

(ii) In a Bunker: If the ball last crossed the outermost limits of the immovable *obstruction* at a spot in a *bunker*, the player may *substitute* another ball, without penalty, and take relief as prescribed in Rule 24-2b(ii).

(iii) In a Water Hazard (including a Lateral Water Hazard): If the ball last crossed the outermost limits of the immovable *obstruction* at a spot in a *water hazard*, the player is not entitled to relief without penalty. The player must proceed under Rule 26-1.

(iv) On the Putting Green: If the ball last crossed the outermost limits of the immovable *obstruction* at a spot on the *putting green*, the player may *substitute* another ball, without penalty, and take relief as prescribed in Rule 24-2b(iii).

PENALTY FOR BREACH OF RULE:

Match play – Loss of hole; Stroke play – Two strokes.

Rule 25 – Abnormal Ground Conditions, Embedded Ball and Wrong Putting Green

Definitions

All defined terms are in *italics* and are listed alphabetically in the Definitions section – see pages 523–526.

25-1. Abnormal Ground Conditions

a. Interference

Interference by an *abnormal ground condition* occurs when a ball lies in or touches the condition or when the condition interferes with the player's *stance* or the area of his intended swing. If the player's ball lies on the *putting green*, interference also occurs if an *abnormal ground condition* on the *putting green* intervenes on his *line of putt*. Otherwise, intervention on the *line of play* is not, of itself, interference under this Rule.

Note: The *Committee* may make a Local Rule stating that interference by an *abnormal ground condition* with a player's *stance* is deemed not to be, of itself, interference under this Rule.

b. Relief

Except when the ball is in a *water hazard* or a *lateral water hazard*, a player may take relief from interference by an *abnormal ground condition* as follows:

(i) Through the Green: If the ball lies *through the green*, the player must lift the ball and drop it, without penalty, within one club-length of and not nearer the *hole* than the *nearest point of relief*. The *nearest point of relief* must not be in a *hazard* or on a *putting green*. When the ball is dropped within one club-length of the *nearest point of relief*, the ball must first strike a part of the *course* at a spot that avoids interference by the condition and is not in a *hazard* and not on a *putting green*.

(ii) In a Bunker: If the ball is in a *bunker*, the player must lift the ball and drop it either:

(a) Without penalty, in accordance with Clause (i) above, except that the *nearest point of relief* must be in the *bunker* and the ball must be dropped in the *bunker* or, if complete relief is impossible, as near as possible to the spot where the ball lay, but not nearer the *hole*, on a part of the *course* in the *bunker* that affords maximum available relief from the condition; or

(b) Under penalty of one stroke, outside the *bunker* keeping the point where the ball lay directly between the *hole* and the spot on which the ball is dropped, with no limit to how far behind the *bunker* the ball may be dropped.

(iii) On the Putting Green: If the ball lies on the *putting green*, the player must lift the ball and place it, without penalty, at the *nearest point of relief* that is not in a *hazard* or, if complete relief is impossible, at the nearest position to where it lay that affords maximum available relief from the condition, but not nearer the *hole* and not in a *hazard*. The *nearest point of relief* or maximum available relief may be off the *putting green*.

(iv) On the Teeing Ground: If the ball lies on the *teeing ground*, the player must lift the ball and drop it, without penalty, in accordance with Clause (i) above.

The ball may be cleaned when lifted under Rule 25-1b.

(Ball rolling to a position where there is interference by the condition from which relief was taken – see Rule 20-2c(v))

Exception: A player may not take relief under this Rule if (a) it is clearly unreasonable for him to make a *stroke* because of interference by anything other than an *abnormal ground condition* or (b) interference by an *abnormal ground condition* would occur only through use of an unnecessarily abnormal *stance*, swing or direction of play.

Note 1: If a ball is in a *water hazard* (including a *lateral water hazard*), the player is not entitled to relief, without penalty, from interference by an *abnormal ground condition*. The player must play the ball as it lies (unless prohibited by Local Rule) or proceed under Rule 26-1.

Note 2: If a ball to be dropped or placed under this Rule is not immediately recoverable, another ball may be *substituted*.

c. Ball in Abnormal Ground Condition Not Found
It is a question of fact whether a ball that has not been found after having been struck toward an *abnormal ground condition* is in such a condition. In order to apply this Rule, it must be known or virtually certain that the ball is in the *abnormal ground condition*. In the absence of such knowledge or certainty, the player must proceed under Rule 27-1.

If it is known or virtually certain that a ball that has not been found is in an *abnormal ground condition*, the player may take relief under this Rule. If he elects to do so, the spot where the ball last crossed the outermost limits of the *abnormal ground condition* must be determined and, for the purpose of applying this Rule, the ball is deemed to lie at this spot and the player must proceed as follows:

(i) Through the Green: If the ball last crossed the outermost limits of the *abnormal ground condition* at a spot *through the green*, the player may *substitute* another ball, without penalty, and take relief as prescribed in Rule 25-1b(i).

(ii) In a Bunker: If the ball last crossed the outermost limits of the *abnormal ground condition* at a spot in a *bunker*, the player may *substitute* another ball, without penalty, and take relief as prescribed in Rule 25-1b(ii).

(iii) In a Water Hazard (including a Lateral Water Hazard): If the ball last crossed the outermost limits of the *abnormal ground condition* at a spot in a *water hazard*, the player is not entitled to relief without penalty. The player must proceed under Rule 26-1.

(iv) On the Putting Green: If the ball last crossed the outermost limits of the *abnormal ground condition* at a spot on the *putting green*, the player may *substitute* another ball, without penalty, and take relief as prescribed in Rule 25-1b(iii).

25-2. Embedded Ball
A ball embedded in its own pitch-mark in the ground in any closely-mown area *through the green* may be lifted, cleaned and dropped, without penalty, as near as possible to the spot where it lay but not nearer the *hole*. The ball when dropped must first strike a part of the *course through the green*. "Closely-mown area" means any area of the *course*, including paths through the rough, cut to fairway height or less.

25-3. Wrong Putting Green
a. Interference
Interference by a *wrong putting green* occurs when a ball is on the *wrong putting green*.

Interference to a player's *stance* or the area of his intended swing is not, of itself, interference under this Rule.

b. Relief
If a player's ball lies on a *wrong putting green*, he must not play the ball as it lies. He must take relief, without penalty, as follows:

The player must lift the ball and drop it within one club-length of and not nearer the *hole* than the *nearest point of relief*. The *nearest point of relief* must not be in a *hazard* or on a *putting green*. When dropping the ball within one club-length of the *nearest point of relief*, the ball must first strike a part of the *course* at a spot that avoids interference by the *wrong putting green* and is not in a *hazard* and not on a *putting green*. The ball may be cleaned when lifted under this Rule.

PENALTY FOR BREACH OF RULE:
Match play – Loss of hole; Stroke play – Two strokes.

Rule 26 – Water Hazards (Including Lateral Water Hazards)

Definitions
All defined terms are in *italics* and are listed alphabetically in the Definitions section – see pages 523–526.

26-1. Relief for Ball in Water Hazard
It is a question of fact whether a ball that has not been found after having been struck toward a *water hazard* is in the *hazard*. In order to apply this Rule, it must be known or virtually certain that the ball is in the *hazard*. In the absence of such knowledge or certainty, the player must proceed under Rule 27-1.

If a ball is in a *water hazard* or if it is known or virtually certain that a ball that has not been found is in a *water hazard* (whether the ball lies in water or not), the player may under penalty of one stroke:

a. Play a ball as nearly as possible at the spot from which the original ball was last played (see Rule 20-5); or

b. Drop a ball behind the *water hazard*, keeping the point at which the original ball last crossed the margin of the *water hazard* directly between the *hole* and the spot on which the ball is dropped, with no limit to how far behind the *water hazard* the ball may be dropped; or

c. As additional options available only if the ball last crossed the margin of a *lateral water hazard*, drop a ball outside the *water hazard* within two club-lengths of and not nearer the *hole* than (i) the point where the original ball last crossed the margin of the *water hazard* or (ii) a point on the opposite margin of the *water hazard* equidistant from the *hole*.

When proceeding under this Rule, the player may lift and clean his ball or *substitute* a ball.

(Prohibited actions when ball is in a *hazard* – see Rule 13-4)

(Ball moving in water in a *water hazard* – see Rule 14-6)

26-2. Ball Played Within Water Hazard
a. Ball Comes to Rest in Same or Another Water Hazard
If a ball played from within a *water hazard* comes to rest in the same or another *water hazard* after the *stroke*, the player may:

(i) proceed under Rule 26-1a. If, after dropping in the *hazard*, the player elects not to play the dropped ball, he may:

(a) proceed under Rule 26-1b, or if applicable Rule 26-1c, adding the additional penalty of one stroke prescribed by the Rule and using as the reference point the point where the original ball last crossed the margin of this *hazard* before it came to rest in this *hazard*; or

(b) add an additional penalty of one stroke and play a ball as nearly as possible at the spot from which the last *stroke* from outside a *water hazard* was made (see Rule 20-5); or

(ii) proceed under Rule 26-1b, or if applicable Rule 26-1c; or

(iii) under penalty of one stroke, play a ball as nearly as possible at the spot from which the last stroke from outside a *water hazard* was made (see Rule 20-5).

b. Ball Lost or Unplayable Outside Hazard or Out of Bounds

If a ball played from within a *water hazard* is *lost* or deemed unplayable outside the *hazard* or is *out of bounds*, the player may, after taking a penalty of one stroke under Rule 27-1 or 28a:

(i) play a ball as nearly as possible at the spot in the *hazard* from which the original ball was last played (see Rule 20-5); or

(ii) proceed under Rule 26-1b, or if applicable Rule 26-1c, adding the additional penalty of one stroke prescribed by the Rule and using as the reference point the point where the original ball last crossed the margin of the *hazard* before it came to rest in the *hazard*; or

(iii) add an additional penalty of one stroke and play a ball as nearly as possible at the spot from which the last *stroke* from outside a *water hazard* was made (see Rule 20-5).

Note 1: When proceeding under Rule 26-2b, the player is not required to drop a ball under Rule 27-1 or 28a. If he does drop a ball, he is not required to play it. He may alternatively proceed under Rule 26-2b(ii) or (iii).

Note 2: If a ball played from within a *water hazard* is deemed unplayable outside the *hazard*, nothing in Rule 26-2b precludes the player from proceeding under Rule 28b or c.

PENALTY FOR BREACH OF RULE:
Match play – Loss of hole; Stroke play – Two strokes.

Rule 27 – Ball Lost or Out of Bounds; Provisional Ball

Definitions
All defined terms are in *italics* and are listed alphabetically in the Definitions section – see pages 523–526.

27-1. Stroke and Distance; Ball Out of Bounds; Ball Not Found Within Five Minutes

a. Proceeding Under Stroke and Distance

At any time, a player may, under penalty of one stroke, play a ball as nearly as possible at the spot from which the original ball was last played (see Rule 20-5), i.e. proceed under penalty of stroke and distance.

Except as otherwise provided in the *Rules*, if a player makes a *stroke* at a ball from the spot at which the original ball was last played, he is deemed to have proceeded under penalty of stroke and distance.

b. Ball Out of Bounds

If a ball is *out of bounds*, the player must play a ball, under penalty of one stroke, as nearly as possible at the spot from which the original ball was last played (see Rule 20-5).

c. Ball Not Found Within Five Minutes

If a ball is *lost* as a result of not being found or identified as his by the player within five minutes after the player's *side* or his or their *caddies* have begun to search for it, the player must play a ball, under penalty of one stroke, as nearly as possible at the spot from which the original ball was last played (see Rule 20-5).

Exceptions:

1. If it is known or virtually certain that the original ball that has not been found is in an *obstruction* (Rule 24-3) or is in an *abnormal ground condition* (Rule 25-1c), the player may proceed under the applicable Rule.

2. If it is known or virtually certain that the original ball that has not been found has been moved by an *outside agency* (Rule 18-1) or is in a *water hazard* (Rule 26-1), the player must proceed under the applicable Rule.

PENALTY FOR BREACH OF RULE 27-1:
Match play – Loss of hole; Stroke play – Two strokes.

27-2. Provisional Ball

a. Procedure

If a ball may be *lost* outside a *water hazard* or may be *out of bounds*, to save time the player may play another ball provisionally in accordance with Rule 27-1. The player must inform his opponent in match play or his *marker* or a *fellow-competitor* in stroke play that he intends to play a *provisional ball*, and he must play it before he or his *partner* goes forward to search for the original ball.

If he fails to do so and plays another ball, that ball is not a *provisional ball* and becomes the *ball in play* under penalty of stroke and distance (Rule 27-1); the original ball is *lost*.

(Order of play from teeing ground – see Rule 10-3)

Note: If a *provisional ball* played under Rule 27-2a might be *lost* outside a *water hazard* or *out of bounds*, the player may play another *provisional ball*. If another *provisional ball* is played, it bears the same relationship to the previous *provisional ball* as the first *provisional ball* bears to the original ball.

b. When Provisional Ball Becomes Ball in Play

The player may play a *provisional ball* until he reaches the place where the original ball is likely to be. If he makes a *stroke* with the *provisional ball* from the place where the original ball is likely to be or from a point nearer the *hole* than that place, the original ball is *lost* and the *provisional ball* becomes the *ball in play* under penalty of stroke and distance (Rule 27-1).

If the original ball is *lost* outside a *water hazard* or is *out of bounds*, the *provisional ball* becomes the *ball in play*, under penalty of stroke and distance (Rule 27-1).

If it is known or virtually certain that the original ball is in a *water hazard*, the player must proceed in accordance with Rule 26-1.

Exception: If it is known or virtually certain that the original ball is in an *obstruction* (Rule 24-3) or an *abnormal ground condition* (Rule 25-1c), the player may proceed under the applicable Rule.

c. When Provisional Ball to be Abandoned

If the original ball is neither *lost* nor *out of bounds*, the player must abandon the *provisional ball* and continue play with the original ball. If he makes any further *strokes* at the *provisional ball*, he is playing a *wrong ball* and the provisions of Rule 15-3 apply.

Note: If a player plays a *provisional ball* under Rule 27-2a, the *strokes* made after this Rule has been invoked with a *provisional ball* subsequently abandoned under Rule 27-2c and *penalty strokes* incurred solely by playing that ball are disregarded.

Rule 28 – Ball Unplayable

Definitions
All defined terms are in *italics* and are listed alphabetically in the Definitions section – see pages 523–526.

The player may deem his ball unplayable at any place on the *course*, except when the ball is in a *water hazard*. The player is the sole judge as to whether his ball is unplayable. If the player deems his ball to be unplayable, he must under penalty of one stroke:

a. Play a ball as nearly as possible at the spot from which the original ball was last played (see Rule 20-5); or

b. Drop a ball behind the point where the ball lay, keeping that point directly between the *hole* and the spot on which the ball is dropped, with no limit to how far behind that point the ball may be dropped; or

c. Drop a ball within two club-lengths of the spot where the ball lay, but not nearer the *hole*.

If the unplayable ball is in a *bunker*, the player may proceed under Clause a, b or c. If he elects to proceed under Clause b or c, a ball must be dropped in the *bunker*.

When proceeding under this Rule, the player may lift and clean his ball or *substitute* a ball.

PENALTY FOR BREACH OF RULE:
Match play – Loss of hole; Stroke play – Two strokes.

Other Forms of Play

Rule 29 – Threesomes and Foursomes

Definitions
All defined terms are in *italics* and are listed alphabetically in the Definitions section – see pages 523–526.

29-1. General
In a *threesome* or a *foursome*, during any *stipulated round* the *partners* must play alternately from the *teeing grounds* and alternately during the play of each hole. *Penalty strokes* do not affect the order of play.

29-2. Match Play
If a player plays when his *partner* should have played, his *side* loses the hole.

29-3. Stroke Play
If the *partners* make a *stroke* or *strokes* in incorrect order, such *stroke* or *strokes* are cancelled and the side incurs a penalty of two strokes. The *side* must correct the error by playing a ball in correct order as nearly as possible at the spot from which it first played in incorrect order (see Rule 20-5). If the *side* makes a *stroke* on the next *teeing ground* without first correcting the error or, in the case of the last hole of the round, leaves the *putting green* without declaring its intention to correct the error, the *side* is disqualified.

Rule 30 – Three-Ball, Best-Ball and Four-Ball Match Play

Definitions
All defined terms are in *italics* and are listed alphabetically in the Definitions section – see pages 523–526.

30-1. Rules of Golf Apply
The Rules of Golf, so far as they are not at variance with the following specific Rules, apply to *three-ball*, *best-ball* and *four-ball* matches.

30-2. Three-Ball Match Play
a. Ball at Rest Moved by an Opponent
Except as otherwise provided in the *Rules*, if the player's ball is touched or *moved* by an opponent, his *caddie* or *equipment* other than during search, Rule 18-3b applies. That opponent incurs a penalty of one stroke in his match with the player, but not in his match with the other opponent.

b. Ball Deflected or Stopped by an Opponent Accidentally
If a player's ball is accidentally deflected or stopped by an opponent, his *caddie* or *equipment*, there is no penalty. In his match with that opponent the player may, before another *stroke* is made by either *side*, cancel the *stroke* and play a ball, without penalty, as nearly as possible at the spot from which the original ball was last played (see Rule 20-5) or he may play the ball as it lies. In his match with the other opponent, the ball must be played as it lies.

Exception: Ball striking person attending or holding up *flagstick* or anything carried by him – see Rule 17-3b.

(Ball purposely deflected or stopped by opponent – see Rule 1-2)

30-3. Best-Ball and Four-Ball Match Play
a. Representation of Side
A *side* may be represented by one *partner* for all or any part of a match; all *partners* need not be present. An absent *partner* may join a match between holes, but not during play of a hole.

b. Order of Play
Balls belonging to the same *side* may be played in the order the *side* considers best.

c. Wrong Ball
If a player incurs the loss of hole penalty under Rule 15-3a for making a *stroke* at a *wrong ball*, he is disqualified for that hole, but his *partner* incurs no penalty even if the *wrong ball* belongs to him. If the *wrong ball* belongs to another player, its owner must place a ball on the spot from which the *wrong ball* was first played.

d. Penalty to Side
A *side* is penalised for a breach of any of the following by any *partner*:
*   Rule 4   Clubs
*   Rule 6-4   Caddie
*   Any Local Rule or Condition of Competition for which the penalty is an adjustment to the state of the match.

e. Disqualification of Side
(i) A *side* is disqualified if any *partner* incurs a penalty of disqualification under any of the following:
*   Rule 1-3   Agreement to Waive Rules
*   Rule 4   Clubs
*   Rule 5-1 or 5-2   The Ball
*   Rule 6-2a   Handicap
*   Rule 6-4   Caddie
*   Rule 6-7   Undue Delay; Slow Play
*   Rule 11-1   Teeing
*   Rule 14-3   Artificial Devices, Unusual Equipment and Unusual Use of Equipment
*   Rule 33-7   Disqualification Penalty Imposed by Committee

(ii) A *side* is disqualified if all *partners* incur a penalty of disqualification under any of the following:
*   Rule 6-3   Time of Starting and Groups
*   Rule 6-8   Discontinuance of Play

(iii) In all other cases where a breach of a *Rule* would result in disqualification, the player is disqualified for that hole only.

f. Effect of Other Penalties
If a player's breach of a *Rule* assists his *partner's* play or adversely affects an opponent's play, the *partner* incurs the applicable penalty in addition to any penalty incurred by the player.

In all other cases where a player incurs a penalty for breach of a *Rule*, the penalty does not apply to his *partner*. Where the penalty is stated to be loss of hole, the effect is to disqualify the player for that hole.

Rule 31 – Four-Ball Stroke Play

Definitions
All defined terms are in *italics* and are listed alphabetically in the Definitions section – see pages 523–526.

31-1. General
The Rules of Golf, so far as they are not at variance with the following specific Rules, apply to *four-ball* stroke play.

31-2. Representation of Side
A *side* may be represented by either *partner* for all or any part of a *stipulated round*; both *partners* need not be present. An absent *competitor* may join his *partner* between holes, but not during play of a hole.

31-3. Scoring

The *marker* is required to record for each hole only the gross score of whichever *partner's* score is to count. The gross scores to count must be individually identifiable; otherwise, the *side* is disqualified. Only one of the *partners* need be responsible for complying with Rule 6-6b.

(Wrong score – see Rule 31-7a)

31-4. Order of Play

Balls belonging to the same *side* may be played in the order the *side* considers best.

31-5. Wrong Ball

If a *competitor* is in breach of Rule 15-3b for making a *stroke* at a *wrong ball*, he incurs a penalty of two strokes and must correct his mistake by playing the correct ball or by proceeding under the *Rules*. His *partner* incurs no penalty, even if the *wrong ball* belongs to him.

If the *wrong ball* belongs to another *competitor*, its owner must place a ball on the spot from which the *wrong ball* was first played.

31-6 Penalty to Side

A *side* is penalised for a breach of any of the following by any *partner*:

- Rule 4   Clubs
- Rule 6-4   Caddie
- Any Local Rule or Condition of Competition for which there is a maximum penalty per round.

31-7. Disqualification Penalties
a. Breach by One Partner

A *side* is disqualified from the competition if either *partner* incurs a penalty of disqualification under any of the following:

• Rule 1-3	Agreement to Waive Rules
• Rule 3-4	Refusal to Comply with a Rule
• Rule 4	Clubs
• Rule 5-1 or 5-2	The Ball
• Rule 6-2b	Handicap
• Rule 6-4	Caddie
• Rule 6-6b	Signing and Returning Score Card
• Rule 6-6d	Wrong Score for Hole
• Rule 6-7	Undue Delay; Slow Play
• Rule 7-1	Practice Before or Between Rounds
• Rule 11-1	Teeing
• Rule 14-3	Artificial Devices, Unusual Equipment and Unusual Use of Equipment
• Rule 22-1	Ball Assisting Play
• Rule 31-3	Gross Scores to Count Not Individually Identifiable
• Rule 33-7	Disqualification Penalty Imposed by Committee

b. Breach by Both Partners

A *side* is disqualified from the competition:

(i) if each *partner* incurs a penalty of disqualification for a breach of Rule 6-3 (Time of Starting and Groups) or Rule 6-8 (Discontinuance of Play), or

(ii) if, at the same hole, each *partner* is in breach of a *Rule* the penalty for which is disqualification from the competition or for a hole.

c. For the Hole Only

In all other cases where a breach of a *Rule* would result in disqualification, the *competitor* is disqualified only for the hole at which the breach occurred.

31-8. Effect of Other Penalties

If a *competitor's* breach of a *Rule* assists his *partner's* play, the *partner* incurs the applicable penalty in addition to any penalty incurred by the *competitor*.

In all other cases where a *competitor* incurs a penalty for breach of a *Rule*, the penalty does not apply to his *partner*.

Rule 32 – Bogey, Par and Stableford Competitions

Definitions

All defined terms are in *italics* and are listed alphabetically in the Definitions section – see pages 523–526.

32-1. Conditions

Bogey, par and Stableford competitions are forms of stroke play in which play is against a fixed score at each hole. The *Rules* for stroke play, so far as they are not at variance with the following specific Rules, apply.

In handicap bogey, par and Stableford competitions, the *competitor* with the lowest net score at a hole takes the *honour* at the next *teeing ground*.

a. Bogey and Par Competitions

The scoring for bogey and par competitions is made as in match play. Any hole for which a *competitor* makes no return is regarded as a loss. The winner is the *competitor* who is most successful in the aggregate of holes.

The *marker* is responsible for marking only the gross number of *strokes* for each hole where the *competitor* makes a net score equal to or less than the fixed score.

Note 1: The *competitor's* score is adjusted by deducting a hole or holes under the applicable *Rule* when a penalty other than disqualification is incurred under any of the following:

- Rule 4   Clubs
- Rule 6-4   Caddie
- Any Local Rule or Condition of Competition for which there is a maximum penalty per round.

The *competitor* is responsible for reporting the facts regarding such a breach to the *Committee* before he returns his score card so that the *Committee* may apply the penalty. If the *competitor* fails to report his breach to the *Committee*, he is disqualified.

Note 2: If the *competitor* is in breach of Rule 6-7 (Undue Delay; Slow Play), the *Committee* will deduct one hole from the aggregate of holes. For a repeated offence, see Rule 32-2a.

b. Stableford Competitions

The scoring in Stableford competitions is made by points awarded in relation to a fixed score at each hole as follows:

Hole Played In	Points
More than one over fixed score or no score returned	0
One over fixed score	1
Fixed score	2
One under fixed score	3
Two under fixed score	4
Three under fixed score	5
Four under fixed score	6

The winner is the *competitor* who scores the highest number of points.

The *marker* is responsible for marking only the gross number of *strokes* at each hole where the *competitor's* net score earns one or more points.

Note 1: If a *competitor* is in breach of a *Rule* for which there is a maximum penalty per round, he must report the facts to the *Committee* before returning his score card; if he fails to do so, he is disqualified. The *Committee* will, from the total points scored for the round, deduct two points for each hole at which any breach occurred, with a maximum deduction per round of four points for each *Rule* breached.

Note 2: If the *competitor* is in breach of Rule 6-7 (Undue Delay; Slow Play), the *Committee* will deduct two points from the total points scored for the round. For a repeated offence, see Rule 32-2a.

32-2. Disqualification Penalties
a. From the Competition
A *competitor* is disqualified from the competition if he incurs a penalty of disqualification under any of the following:

• Rule 1-3	Agreement to Waive Rules
• Rule 3-4	Refusal to Comply with a Rule
• Rule 4	Clubs
• Rule 5-1 or 5-2	The Ball
• Rule 6-2b	Handicap
• Rule 6-3	Time of Starting and Groups
• Rule 6-4	Caddie
• Rule 6-6b	Signing and Returning Score Card
• Rule 6-6d	Wrong Score for Hole, i.e. when the recorded score is lower than actually taken, except that no penalty is incurred when a breach of this Rule does not affect the result of the hole
• Rule 6-7	Undue Delay; Slow Play
• Rule 6-8	Discontinuance of Play
• Rule 7-1	Practice Before or Between Rounds
• Rule 11-1	Teeing
• Rule 14-3	Artificial Devices, Unusual Equipment and Unusual Use of Equipment
• Rule 22-1	Ball Assisting Play
• Rule 33-7	Disqualification Penalty Imposed by Committee

b. For a Hole
In all other cases where a breach of a *Rule* would result in disqualification, the *competitor* is disqualified only for the hole at which the breach occurred.

Administration

Rule 33 – The Committee

Definitions
All defined terms are in *italics* and are listed alphabetically in the Definitions section – see pages 523–526.

33-1. Conditions; Waiving Rule
The *Committee* must establish the conditions under which a competition is to be played.

The *Committee* has no power to waive a Rule of Golf.

Certain specific *Rules* governing stroke play are so substantially different from those governing match play that combining the two forms of play is not practicable and is not permitted. The result of a match played in these circumstances is null and void and, in the stroke play competition, the *competitors* are disqualified.

In stroke play, the *Committee* may limit a *referee's* duties.

33-2. The Course
a. Defining Bounds and Margins
The *Committee* must define accurately:
(i) the *course* and *out of bounds*,
(ii) the margins of *water hazards* and *lateral water hazards*,
(iii) *ground under repair*, and
(iv) *obstructions* and integral parts of the *course*.

b. New Holes
New *holes* should be made on the day on which a stroke play competition begins and at such other times as the *Committee* considers necessary, provided all *competitors* in a single round play with each *hole* cut in the same position.

Exception: When it is impossible for a damaged *hole* to be repaired so that it conforms with the Definition, the *Committee* may make a new *hole* in a nearby similar position.

Note: Where a single round is to be played on more than one day, the *Committee* may provide, in the conditions of a competition (Rule 33-1), that the *holes* and *teeing grounds* may be differently situated on each day of the competition, provided that, on any one day, all *competitors* play with each *hole* and each *teeing ground* in the same position.

c. Practice Ground
Where there is no practice ground available outside the area of a competition *course*, the *Committee* should establish the area on which players may practise on any day of a competition, if it is practicable to do so. On any day of a stroke play competition, the *Committee* should not normally permit practice on or to a *putting green* or from a *hazard* of the competition *course*.

d. Course Unplayable
If the *Committee* or its authorised representative considers that for any reason the *course* is not in a playable condition or that there are circumstances that render the proper playing of the game impossible, it may, in match play or stroke play, order a temporary suspension of play or, in stroke play, declare play null and void and cancel all scores for the round in question. When a round is cancelled, all penalties incurred in that round are cancelled.

(Procedure in discontinuing and resuming play – see Rule 6-8)

33-3. Times of Starting and Groups
The *Committee* must establish the times of starting and, in stroke play, arrange the groups in which *competitors* must play.

When a match play competition is played over an extended period, the *Committee* establishes the limit of time within which each round must be completed. When players are allowed to arrange the date of their match within these limits, the *Committee* should announce that the match must be played at a stated time on the last day of the period, unless the players agree to a prior date.

33-4. Handicap Stroke Table
The *Committee* must publish a table indicating the order of holes at which handicap strokes are to be given or received.

33-5. Score Card
In stroke play, the *Committee* must provide each *competitor* with a score card containing the date and the *competitor's* name or, in *foursome* or *four-ball* stroke play, the *competitors'* names.

In stroke play, the *Committee* is responsible for the addition of scores and application of the handicap recorded on the score card.

In *four-ball* stroke play, the *Committee* is responsible for recording the better-ball score for each hole and in the process applying the handicaps recorded on the score card, and adding the better-ball scores.

In bogey, par and Stableford competitions, the *Committee* is responsible for applying the handicap recorded on the score card and determining the result of each hole and the overall result or points total.

Note: The *Committee* may request that each *competitor* records the date and his name on his score card.

33-6. Decision of Ties
The *Committee* must announce the manner, day and time for the decision of a halved match or of a tie, whether played on level terms or under handicap.

A halved match must not be decided by stroke play. A tie in stroke play must not be decided by a match.

33-7. Disqualification Penalty; Committee Discretion
A penalty of disqualification may in exceptional individual cases be waived, modified or imposed if the *Committee* considers such action warranted.

Any penalty less than disqualification must not be waived or modified.

If a *Committee* considers that a player is guilty of a serious breach of etiquette, it may impose a penalty of disqualification under this Rule.

33-8. Local Rules
a. Policy
The *Committee* may establish Local Rules for local abnormal conditions if they are consistent with the policy set forth in Appendix I.

b. Waiving or Modifying a Rule
A Rule of Golf must not be waived by a Local Rule. However, if a *Committee* considers that local abnormal conditions interfere with the proper playing of the game to the extent that it is necessary to make a Local Rule that modifies the Rules of Golf, the Local Rule must be authorised by the *R&A*.

Rule 34 – Disputes and Decisions
Definitions
All defined terms are in *italics* and are listed alphabetically in the Definitions section – see pages 523–526.

34-1. Claims and Penalties
a. Match Play
If a claim is lodged with the *Committee* under Rule 2-5, a decision should be given as soon as possible so that the state of the match may, if necessary, be adjusted. If a claim is not made in accordance with Rule 2-5, it must not be considered by the *Committee*.

There is no time limit on applying the disqualification penalty for a breach of Rule 1-3.

b. Stroke Play
In stroke play, a penalty must not be rescinded, modified or imposed after the competition has closed. A competition is closed when the result has been officially announced or, in stroke play qualifying followed by match play, when the player has teed off in his first match.

Exceptions: A penalty of disqualification must be imposed after the competition has closed if a *competitor:*
(i) was in breach of Rule 1-3 (Agreement to Waive Rules); or
(ii) returned a score card on which he had recorded a handicap that, before the competition closed, he knew was higher than that to which he was entitled, and this affected the number of strokes received (Rule 6-2b); or
(iii) returned a score for any hole lower than actually taken (Rule 6-6d) for any reason other than failure to include a penalty that, before the competition closed, he did not know he had incurred; or
(iv) knew, before the competition closed, that he had been in breach of any other *Rule* for which the penalty is disqualification.

34-2. Referee's Decision
If a *referee* has been appointed by the *Committee*, his decision is final.

34-3. Committee's Decision
In the absence of a *referee*, any dispute or doubtful point on the *Rules* must be referred to the *Committee*, whose decision is final.

If the *Committee* cannot come to a decision, it may refer the dispute or doubtful point to the Rules of Golf Committee of the R&A, whose decision is final.

If the dispute or doubtful point has not been referred to the Rules of Golf Committee, the player or players may request that an agreed statement be referred through a duly authorised representative of the *Committee* to the Rules of Golf Committee for an opinion as to the correctness of the decision given. The reply will be sent to this authorised representative.

If play is conducted other than in accordance with the Rules of Golf, the Rules of Golf Committee will not give a decision on any question.

Appendix I – Contents

Appendix I – Local Rules; Conditions of the Competition

Definitions

All defined terms are in *italics* and are listed alphabetically in the Definitions section – see pages 523–526.

Part A – Local Rules

As provided in Rule 33-8a, the *Committee* may make and publish Local Rules for local abnormal conditions if they are consistent with the policy established in this Appendix. In addition, detailed information regarding acceptable and prohibited Local Rules is provided in "Decisions on the Rules of Golf" under Rule 33-8 and in "Guidance on Running a Competition".

If local abnormal conditions interfere with the proper playing of the game and the *Committee* considers it necessary to modify a Rule of Golf, authorisation from the *R&A* must be obtained.

1. Defining Bounds and Margins

Specifying means used to define *out of bounds*, *water hazards*, *lateral water hazards*, *ground under repair*, *obstructions* and integral parts of the *course* (Rule 33-2a).

2. Water Hazards
a. Lateral Water Hazards

Clarifying the status of *water hazards* that may be *lateral water hazards* (Rule 26).

b. Ball Played Provisionally Under Rule 26-1

Permitting play of a ball provisionally under Rule 26-1 for a ball that may be in a *water hazard* (including a *lateral water hazard*) of such character that, if the original ball is not found, it is known or virtually certain that it is in the *water hazard* and it would be impracticable to determine whether the ball is in the *hazard* or to do so would unduly delay play.

3. Areas of the Course Requiring Preservation; Environmentally-Sensitive Areas

Assisting preservation of the *course* by defining areas, including turf nurseries, young plantations and other parts of the *course* under cultivation, as *ground under repair* from which play is prohibited.

When the *Committee* is required to prohibit play from environmentally-sensitive areas that are on or adjoin the *course*, it should make a Local Rule clarifying the relief procedure.

4. Course Conditions – Mud, Extreme Wetness, Poor Conditions and Protection of Course
a. Lifting an Embedded Ball, Cleaning

Temporary conditions that might interfere with proper playing of the game, including mud and extreme wetness, warranting relief for an embedded ball anywhere *through the green* or permitting lifting, cleaning and replacing a ball anywhere *through the green* or on a closely-mown area *through the green*.

b. "Preferred Lies" and "Winter Rules"

Adverse conditions, including the poor condition of the *course* or the existence of mud, are sometimes so general, particularly during winter months, that the *Committee* may decide to grant relief by temporary Local Rule either to protect the *course* or to promote fair and pleasant play. The Local Rule should be withdrawn as soon as the conditions warrant.

5. Obstructions
a. General

Clarifying status of objects that may be *obstructions* (Rule 24).

Declaring any construction to be an integral part of the *course* and, accordingly, not an *obstruction*, e.g. built-up sides of *teeing grounds*, *putting greens* and *bunkers* (Rules 24 and 33-2a).

b. Stones in Bunkers

Allowing the removal of stones in *bunkers* by declaring them to be movable *obstructions* (Rule 24-1).

c. Roads and Paths

(i) Declaring artificial surfaces and sides of roads and paths to be integral parts of the *course*, or
(ii) Providing relief of the type afforded under Rule 24-2b from roads and paths not having artificial surfaces and sides if they could unfairly affect play.

d. Immovable Obstructions Close to Putting Green

Providing relief from intervention by immovable *obstructions* on or within two club-lengths of the *putting green* when the ball lies within two club-lengths of the immovable *obstruction*.

e. Protection of Young Trees

Providing relief for the protection of young trees.

f. Temporary Obstructions

Providing relief from interference by temporary obstructions (e.g. grandstands, television cables and equipment, etc).

6. Dropping Zones

Establishing special areas on which balls may or must be dropped when it is not feasible or practicable to proceed exactly in conformity with Rule 24-2b or 24-3 (Immovable Obstruction), Rule 25-1b or 25-1c (Abnormal Ground Conditions), Rule 25-3 (Wrong Putting Green), Rule 26-1 (Water Hazards and Lateral Water Hazards) or Rule 28 (Ball Unplayable).

Part B – Specimen Local Rules

Within the policy established in Part A of this Appendix, the *Committee* may adopt a Specimen Local Rule by referring, on a score card or notice board, to the examples given below. However, Specimen Local Rules of a temporary nature should not be printed on a score card.

1. Water Hazards; Ball Played Provisionally Under Rule 26-1

If a *water hazard* (including a *lateral water hazard*) is of such size and shape and/or located in such a position that:
(i) it would be impracticable to determine whether the ball is in the *hazard* or to do so would unduly delay play, and
(ii) if the original ball is not found, it is known or virtually certain that it is in the *water hazard*,

the *Committee* may introduce a Local Rule permitting the play of a ball provisionally under Rule 26-1. The ball is played provisionally under any of the applicable options under Rule 26-1 or any applicable Local Rule. In such a case, if a ball is played provisionally and the original ball is in a *water hazard*, the player may play the original ball as it lies or continue with the ball played provisionally, but he may not proceed under Rule 26-1 with regard to the original ball.

In these circumstances, the following Local Rule is recommended:

"If there is doubt whether a ball is in or is *lost* in the *water hazard* (specify location), the player may play another ball provisionally under any of the applicable options in Rule 26-1.

If the original ball is found outside the *water hazard*, the player must continue play with it.

If the original ball is found in the *water hazard*, the player may either play the original ball as it lies or continue with the ball played provisionally under Rule 26-1.

If the original ball is not found or identified within the five-minute search period, the player must continue with the ball played provisionally.

PENALTY FOR BREACH OF LOCAL RULE:
Match play – Loss of hole; Stroke play – Two strokes."

2. Areas of the Course Requiring Preservation; Environmentally-Sensitive Areas
a. Ground Under Repair; Play Prohibited
If the *Committee* wishes to protect any area of the *course*, it should declare it to be *ground under repair* and prohibit play from within that area. The following Local Rule is recommended:

"The _____(defined by _____) is *ground under repair* from which play is prohibited. If a player's ball lies in the area, or if it interferes with the player's *stance* or the area of his intended swing, the player must take relief under Rule 25-1.

PENALTY FOR BREACH OF LOCAL RULE:
Match play – Loss of hole; Stroke play – Two strokes."

b. Environmentally-Sensitive Areas
If an appropriate authority (i.e. a Government Agency or the like) prohibits entry into and/or play from an area on or adjoining the *course* for environmental reasons, the *Committee* should make a Local Rule clarifying the relief procedure.

The *Committee* has some discretion in terms of whether the area is defined as *ground under repair*, a *water hazard* or *out of bounds*. However, it may not simply define the area to be a *water hazard* if it does not meet the Definition of a "*Water Hazard*" and it should attempt to preserve the character of the hole.

The following Local Rule is recommended:

"I. Definition
An environmentally-sensitive area (ESA) is an area so declared by an appropriate authority, entry into and/or play from which is prohibited for environmental reasons. These areas may be defined as *ground under repair*, a *water hazard*, a *lateral water hazard* or *out of bounds* at the discretion of the *Committee*, provided that in the case of an ESA that has been defined as a *water hazard* or a *lateral water hazard*, the area is, by definition, a *water hazard*.
Note: The *Committee* may not declare an area to be environmentally-sensitive.

II. Ball in Environmentally-Sensitive Area
a. Ground Under Repair
If a ball is in an ESA defined as *ground under repair*, a ball must be dropped in accordance with Rule 25-1b.

If it is known or virtually certain that a ball that has not been found is in an ESA defined as *ground under repair*, the player may take relief, without penalty, as prescribed in Rule 25-1c.

b. Water Hazards and Lateral Water Hazards
If it is known or virtually certain that a ball that has not been found is in an ESA defined as a *water hazard* or *lateral water hazard*, the player must, under penalty of one stroke, proceed under Rule 26-1.
Note: If a ball, dropped in accordance with Rule 26 rolls into a position where the ESA interferes with the player's *stance* or the area of his intended swing, the player must take relief as provided in Clause III of this Local Rule.

c. Out of Bounds
If a ball is in an ESA defined as *out of bounds*, the player must play a ball, under penalty of one stroke, as nearly as possi-

ble at the spot from which the original ball was last played (see Rule 20-5).

III. Interference with Stance or Area of Intended Swing
Interference by an ESA occurs when the ESA interferes with the player's *stance* or the area of his intended swing. If interference exists, the player must take relief as follows:
(a) Through the Green: If the ball lies *through the green*, the point on the *course* nearest to where the ball lies must be determined that (a) is not nearer the *hole*, (b) avoids interference by the ESA and (c) is not in a *hazard* or on a *putting green*. The player must lift the ball and drop it, without penalty, within one club-length of the point so determined on a part of the *course* that fulfils (a), (b) and (c) above.
(b) In a Hazard: If the ball is in a *hazard*, the player must lift the ball and drop it either:
(i) Without penalty, in the *hazard*, as near as possible to the spot where the ball lay, but not nearer the *hole*, on a part of the *course* that provides complete relief from the ESA; or
(ii) Under penalty of one stroke, outside the *hazard*, keeping the point where the ball lay directly between the *hole* and the spot on which the ball is dropped, with no limit to how far behind the *hazard* the ball may be dropped. Additionally, the player may proceed under Rule 26 or 28 if applicable.
(c) On the Putting Green: If the ball lies on the *putting green*, the player must lift the ball and place it, without penalty, in the nearest position to where it lay that affords complete relief from the ESA, but not nearer the *hole* or in a *hazard*.
The ball may be cleaned when lifted under Clause III of this Local Rule.
Exception: A player may not take relief under Clause III of this Local Rule if (a) it is clearly unreasonable for him to make a *stroke* because of interference by anything other than an ESA or (b) interference by an ESA would occur only through use of an unnecessarily abnormal *stance*, swing or direction of play.

PENALTY FOR BREACH OF LOCAL RULE:
Match play – Loss of hole; Stroke play – Two strokes.
Note: In the case of a serious breach of this Local Rule, the *Committee* may impose a penalty of disqualification."

3. Protection of Young Trees
When it is desired to prevent damage to young trees, the following Local Rule is recommended:
"Protection of young trees identified by _____. If such a tree interferes with a player's *stance* or the area of his intended swing, the ball must be lifted, without penalty, and dropped in accordance with the procedure prescribed in Rule 24-2b (Immovable Obstruction). If the ball lies in a *water hazard*, the player must lift and drop the ball in accordance with Rule 24-2b(i), except that the *nearest point of relief* must be in the *water hazard* and the ball must be dropped in the *water hazard* or the player may proceed under Rule 26. The ball may be cleaned when lifted under this Local Rule.
Exception: A player may not obtain relief under this Local Rule if (a) it is clearly unreasonable for him to make a *stroke* because of interference by anything other than the tree or (b) interference by the tree would occur only through use of an unnecessarily abnormal *stance*, swing or direction of play.

PENALTY FOR BREACH OF LOCAL RULE:
Match play – Loss of hole; Stroke play – Two strokes."

4. Course Conditions – Mud, Extreme Wetness, Poor Conditions and Protection of the Course

a. Relief for Embedded Ball

Rule 25-2 provides relief, without penalty, for a ball embedded in its own pitch-mark in any closely-mown area *through the green*. On the *putting green*, a ball may be lifted and damage caused by the impact of a ball may be repaired (Rules 16-1b and c). When permission to take relief for an embedded ball anywhere *through the green* would be warranted, the following Local Rule is recommended:

"*Through the green*, a ball that is embedded in its own pitch-mark in the ground may be lifted, without penalty, cleaned and dropped as near as possible to where it lay but not nearer the *hole*. The ball when dropped must first strike a part of the *course through the green*.

Exceptions:

1.   A player may not take relief under this Local Rule if the ball is embedded in sand in an area that is not closely mown.
2.   A player may not take relief under this Local Rule if it is clearly unreasonable for him to make a *stroke* because of interference by anything other than the condition covered by this Local Rule.

PENALTY FOR BREACH OF LOCAL RULE:
Match play – Loss of hole; Stroke play – Two strokes."

b. Cleaning Ball

Conditions, such as extreme wetness causing significant amounts of mud to adhere to the ball, may be such that permission to lift, clean and replace the ball would be appropriate. In these circumstances, the following Local Rule is recommended:

"(Specify area) a ball may be lifted, cleaned and replaced without penalty.

Note: The position of the ball must be marked before it is lifted under this Local Rule – see Rule 20-1.

PENALTY FOR BREACH OF LOCAL RULE:
Match play – Loss of hole; Stroke play – Two strokes."

c. "Preferred Lies" and "Winter Rules"

Ground under repair is provided for in Rule 25 and occasional local abnormal conditions that might interfere with fair play and are not widespread should be defined as *ground under repair*.

However, adverse conditions, such as heavy snows, spring thaws, prolonged rains or extreme heat can make fairways unsatisfactory and sometimes prevent use of heavy mowing equipment. When such conditions are so general throughout a *course* that the *Committee* believes "preferred lies" or "winter rules" would promote fair play or help protect the *course*, the following Local Rule is recommended:

"A ball lying on a closely-mown area *through the green* (or specify a more restricted area, e.g. at the 6th hole) may be lifted, without penalty, and cleaned. Before lifting the ball, the player must mark its position. Having lifted the ball, he must place it on a spot within (specify area, e.g. six inches, one club-length, etc.) of and not nearer the *hole* than where it originally lay, that is not in a *hazard* and not on a *putting green*.

A player may place his ball only once, and it is *in play* when it has been placed (Rule 20-4). If the ball fails to come to rest on the spot on which it is placed, Rule 20-3d applies. If the ball when placed comes to rest on the spot on which it is placed and it subsequently *moves*, there is no penalty and the ball must be played as it lies, unless the provisions of any other *Rule* apply.

If the player fails to mark the position of the ball before lifting it or *moves* the ball in any other manner, such as

rolling it with a club, he incurs a penalty of one stroke.

Note: "Closely-mown area" means any area of the *course*, including paths through the rough, cut to fairway height or less.

*PENALTY FOR BREACH OF LOCAL RULE:
Match play – Loss of hole; Stroke play – Two strokes.

*If a player incurs the general penalty for a breach of this Local Rule, no additional penalty under the Local Rule is applied."

d. Aeration Holes

When a *course* has been aerated, a Local Rule permitting relief, without penalty, from an aeration hole may be warranted. The following Local Rule is recommended:

"*Through the green*, a ball that comes to rest in or on an aeration hole may be lifted, without penalty, cleaned and dropped, as near as possible to the spot where it lay but not nearer the *hole*. The ball when dropped must first strike a part of the *course through the green*.

On the *putting green*, a ball that comes to rest in or on an aeration hole may be placed at the nearest spot not nearer the *hole* that avoids the situation.

PENALTY FOR BREACH OF LOCAL RULE:
Match play – Loss of hole; Stroke play – Two strokes."

e. Seams of Cut Turf

If a *Committee* wishes to allow relief from seams of cut turf, but not from the cut turf itself, the following Local Rule is recommended:

"*Through the green*, seams of cut turf (not the turf itself) are deemed to be *ground under repair*. However, interference by a seam with the player's *stance* is deemed not to be, of itself, interference under Rule 25-1. If the ball lies in or touches the seam or the seam interferes with the area of intended swing, relief is available under Rule 25-1. All seams within the cut turf area are considered the same seam.

PENALTY FOR BREACH OF LOCAL RULE:
Match play – Loss of hole; Stroke play – Two strokes."

5. Stones in Bunkers

Stones are, by definition, *loose impediments* and, when a player's ball is in a *hazard*, a stone lying in or touching the *hazard* may not be touched or moved (Rule 13-4). However, stones in *bunkers* may represent a danger to players (a player could be injured by a stone struck by the player's club in an attempt to play the ball) and they may interfere with the proper playing of the game.

When permission to lift a stone in a *bunker* is warranted, the following Local Rule is recommended:

"Stones in *bunkers* are movable *obstructions* (Rule 24-1 applies)."

6. Immovable Obstructions Close to Putting Green

Rule 24-2 provides relief, without penalty, from interference by an immovable *obstruction*, but it also provides that, except on the *putting green*, intervention on the *line of play* is not, of itself, interference under this Rule.

However, on some courses, the aprons of the *putting greens* are so closely mown that players may wish to putt from just off the green. In such conditions, immovable *obstructions* on the apron may interfere with the proper playing of the game and the introduction of the following Local Rule providing additional relief, without penalty, from intervention by an immovable *obstruction* would be warranted:

"Relief from interference by an immovable *obstruction* may be obtained under Rule 24-2. In addition, if a ball lies off the *putting green* but not in a *hazard* and an immovable *obstruction* on or within two club-lengths of the *putting green* and within two club-lengths of the ball intervenes on the *line of play* between the ball and the *hole*, the player may take relief as follows:

The ball must be lifted and dropped at the nearest point to where the ball lay that (a) is not nearer the *hole*, (b) avoids intervention and (c) is not in a *hazard* or on a *putting green*. The ball may be cleaned when lifted.

Relief under this Local Rule is also available if the player's ball lies on the *putting green* and an immovable *obstruction* within two club-lengths of the *putting green* intervenes on his *line of putt.* The player may take relief as follows:

The ball must be lifted and placed at the nearest point to where the ball lay that (a) is not nearer the *hole*, (b) avoids intervention and (c) is not in a *hazard*. The ball may be cleaned when lifted.

PENALTY FOR BREACH OF LOCAL RULE:
Match play – Loss of hole; Stroke play – Two strokes."

7. Temporary Obstructions

When temporary obstructions are installed on or adjoining the *course*, the *Committee* should define the status of such obstructions as movable, immovable or temporary immovable obstructions.

a. Temporary Immovable Obstructions

If the *Committee* defines such obstructions as temporary immovable obstructions, the following Local Rule is recommended:

"I. Definition

A temporary immovable obstruction (TIO) is a non-permanent artificial object that is often erected in conjunction with a competition and is fixed or not readily movable. Examples of TIOs include, but are not limited to, tents, scoreboards, grandstands, television towers and lavatories. Supporting guy wires are part of the TIO, unless the *Committee* declares that they are to be treated as elevated power lines or cables.

II. Interference

Interference by a TIO occurs when (a) the ball lies in front of and so close to the TIO that the TIO interferes with the player's *stance* or the area of his intended swing, or (b) the ball lies in, on, under or behind the TIO so that any part of the TIO intervenes directly between the player's ball and the *hole* and is on his *line of play*; interference also exists if the ball lies within one club-length of a spot equidistant from the *hole* where such intervention would exist.

Note: A ball is under a TIO when it is below the outer most edges of the TIO, even if these edges do not extend downwards to the ground.

III. Relief

A player may obtain relief from interference by a TIO, including a TIO that is *out of bounds*, as follows:

(a) Through the Green: If the ball lies *through the green*, the point on the *course* nearest to where the ball lies must be determined that (a) is not nearer the *hole*, (b) avoids interference as defined in Clause II and (c) is not in a *hazard* or on a *putting green*. The player must lift the ball and drop it, without penalty, within one club-length of the point so determined on a part of the *course* that fulfils (a), (b) and (c) above.

(b) In a Hazard: If the ball is in a *hazard*, the player must lift and drop the ball either:

(i) Without penalty, in accordance with Clause III(a) above, except that the nearest part of the *course* affording complete relief must be in the *hazard* and the ball must be dropped in the *hazard* or, if complete relief is impossible, on a part of the *course* within the *hazard* that affords maximum available relief; or

(ii) Under penalty of one stroke, outside the *hazard* as follows: the point on the *course* nearest to where the ball lies must be determined that (a) is not

nearer the *hole*, (b) avoids interference as defined in Clause II and (c) is not in a *hazard*. The player must drop the ball within one club-length of the point so determined on a part of the *course* that fulfils (a), (b) and (c) above.

The ball may be cleaned when lifted under Clause III.

Note 1: If the ball lies in a *hazard*, nothing in this Local Rule precludes the player from proceeding under Rule 26 or Rule 28, if applicable.

Note 2: If a ball to be dropped under this Local Rule is not immediately recoverable, another ball may be substituted.

Note 3: A *Committee* may make a Local Rule (a) permitting or requiring a player to use a dropping zone when taking relief from a TIO or (b) permitting a player, as an additional relief option, to drop the ball on the opposite side of the TIO from the point established under Clause III, but otherwise in accordance with Clause III.

Exceptions: If a player's ball lies in front of or behind the TIO (not in, on or under the TIO), he may not obtain relief under Clause III if:

1. It is clearly unreasonable for him to make a *stroke* or, in the case of intervention, to make a *stroke* such that the ball could finish on a direct line to the *hole*, because of interference by anything other than the TIO;

2. Interference by the TIO would occur only through use of an unnecessarily abnormal *stance*, swing or direction of play; or

3. In the case of intervention, it would be clearly unreasonable to expect the player to be able to strike the ball far enough towards the *hole* to reach the TIO.

A player not entitled to relief due to these exceptions may proceed under Rule 24-2, if applicable.

IV. Ball in TIO Not Found

If it is known or virtually certain that a ball that has not been found is in, on or under a TIO, a ball may be dropped under the provisions of Clause III or Clause V, if applicable. For the purpose of applying Clauses III and V, the ball is deemed to lie at the spot where it last crossed the outer-most limits of the TIO (Rule 24-3).

V. Dropping Zones

If the player has interference from a TIO, the *Committee* may permit or require the use of a dropping zone. If the player uses a dropping zone in taking relief, he must drop the ball in the dropping zone nearest to where his ball originally lay or is deemed to lie under Clause IV (even though the nearest dropping zone may be nearer the *hole*).

Note: A *Committee* may make a Local Rule prohibiting the use of a dropping zone that is nearer the *hole*.

PENALTY FOR BREACH OF LOCAL RULE:
Match play – Loss of hole; Stroke play – Two strokes."

b. Temporary Power Lines and Cables

When temporary power lines, cables, or telephone lines are installed on the *course*, the following Local Rule is recommended:

"Temporary power lines, cables, telephone lines and mats covering or stanchions supporting them are *obstructions*:

1. If they are readily movable, Rule 24-1 applies.

2. If they are fixed or not readily movable, the player may, if the ball lies *through the green* or in a *bunker*, obtain relief as provided in Rule 24-2b. If the ball lies in a *water hazard*, the player may lift and drop the ball in accordance with Rule 24-2b(i), except that the *nearest point of relief* must be in the *water hazard* and the ball must be dropped in the *water hazard* or the player may proceed under Rule 26.

3. If a ball strikes an elevated power line or cable, the *stroke* must be cancelled and replayed, without penalty (see

Rule 20-5). If the ball is not immediately recoverable another ball may be *substituted*.

Note: Guy wires supporting a temporary immovable *obstruction* are part of the temporary immovable *obstruction*, unless the *Committee*, by Local Rule, declares that they are to be treated as elevated power lines or cables.

Exception: A *stroke* that results in a ball striking an elevated junction section of cable rising from the ground must not be replayed.

4. Grass-covered cable trenches are *ground under repair*, even if not marked, and Rule 25-1b applies."

8. Dropping Zones

If the *Committee* considers that it is not feasible or practicable to proceed in accordance with a Rule providing relief, it may establish dropping zones in which balls may or must be dropped when taking relief. Generally, such dropping zones should be provided as an additional relief option to those available under the Rule itself, rather than being mandatory.

Using the example of a dropping zone for a *water hazard*, when such a dropping zone is established, the following Local Rule is recommended:

"If a ball is in or it is known or virtually certain that a ball that has not been found is in the *water hazard* (specify location), the player may:

(i) proceed under Rule 26; or

(ii) as an additional option, drop a ball, under penalty of one stroke, in the dropping zone.

PENALTY FOR BREACH OF LOCAL RULE:

Match play – Loss of hole; Stroke play – Two strokes."

Note: When using a dropping zone the following provisions apply regarding the dropping and re-dropping of the ball:

(a) The player does not have to stand within the dropping zone when dropping the ball.

(b) The dropped ball must first strike a part of the *course* within the dropping zone.

(c) If the dropping zone is defined by a line, the line is within the dropping zone.

(d) The dropped ball does not have to come to rest within the dropping zone.

(e) The dropped ball must be re-dropped if it rolls and comes to rest in a position covered by Rule 20-2c(i-vi).

(f) The dropped ball may roll nearer the *hole* than the spot where it first struck a part of the *course*, provided it comes to rest within two club-lengths of that spot and not into any of the positions covered by (e).

(g) Subject to the provisions of (e) and (f), the dropped ball may roll and come to rest nearer the *hole* than:

• its original position or estimated position (see Rule 20-2b);

• the *nearest point of relief* or maximum available relief (Rule 24-2, 24-3, 25-1 or 25-3); or

• the point where the original ball last crossed the margin of the *water hazard* or *lateral water hazard* (Rule 26-1).

9. Distance-Measuring Devices

If the *Committee* wishes to act in accordance with the Note under Rule 14-3, the following wording is recommended:

"(Specify as appropriate, e.g. In this competition, or For all play at this course, etc.), a player may obtain distance information by using a device that measures distance only. If, during a *stipulated round*, a player uses a distance-measuring device that is designed to gauge or measure other conditions that might affect his play (e.g. gradient, windspeed, temperature, etc.), the player is in breach of Rule 14-3, for which the penalty is disqualification, regardless of whether any such additional function is actually used."

Part C – Conditions of the Competition

Rule 33-1 provides, "The *Committee* must establish the conditions under which a competition is to be played." The conditions should include many matters such as method of entry, eligibility, number of rounds to be played, etc. which it is not appropriate to deal with in the Rules of Golf or this Appendix. Detailed information regarding these conditions is provided in "Decisions on the Rules of Golf" under Rule 33-1 and in "Guidance on Running a Competition".

However, there are a number of matters that might be covered in the Conditions of the Competition to which the *Committee's* attention is specifically drawn. These are:

1. Specification of Clubs and the Ball

The following conditions are recommended only for competitions involving expert players:

a. List of Conforming Driver Heads

On its web site (www.randa.org) the *R&A* periodically issues a List of Conforming Driver Heads that lists driving clubheads that have been evaluated and found to conform with the Rules of Golf. If the *Committee* wishes to limit players to drivers that have a clubhead, identified by model and loft, that is on the List, the List should be made available and the following condition of competition used:

"Any driver the player carries must have a clubhead, identified by model and loft, that is named on the current List of Conforming Driver Heads issued by the *R&A*.

Exception: A driver with a clubhead that was manufactured prior to 1999 is exempt from this condition.

*PENALTY FOR CARRYING, BUT NOT MAKING STROKE WITH, CLUB OR CLUBS IN BREACH OF CONDITION:

Match play – At the conclusion of the hole at which the breach is discovered, the state of the match is adjusted by deducting one hole for each hole at which a breach occurred; maximum deduction per round – Two holes.

Stroke play – Two strokes for each hole at which any breach occurred; maximum penalty per round – Four strokes.

Match or stroke play – In the event of a breach between the play of two holes, the penalty applies to the next hole.

Bogey and par competitions – See Note 1 to Rule 32-1a.

Stableford competitions – See Note 1 to Rule 32-1b.

*Any club or clubs carried in breach of this condition must be declared out of play by the player to his opponent in match play or his *marker* or a *fellow-competitor* in stroke play immediately upon discovery that a breach has occurred. If the player fails to do so, he is disqualified.

PENALTY FOR MAKING STROKE WITH CLUB IN BREACH OF CONDITION:
Disqualification."

b. List of Conforming Golf Balls

On its website (www.randa.org) the *R&A* periodically issues a List of Conforming Golf Balls that lists balls that have been tested and found to conform with the Rules of Golf. If the *Committee* wishes to require players to play a model of golf ball on the List, the List should be made available and the following condition of competition used:

"The ball the player plays must be named on the current List of Conforming Golf Balls issued by the *R&A*.

PENALTY FOR BREACH OF CONDITION:
Disqualification."

c. One Ball Condition

If it is desired to prohibit changing brands and models of golf balls during a *stipulated round*, the following condition is recommended:

"Limitation on Balls Used During Round: (Note to Rule 5-1)

(i) "One Ball" Condition

During a *stipulated round*, the balls a player plays must be of the same brand and model as detailed by a single entry on the current List of Conforming Golf Balls.

Note: If a ball of a different brand and/or model is dropped or placed it may be lifted, without penalty, and the player must then proceed by dropping or placing a proper ball (Rule 20-6).

PENALTY FOR BREACH OF CONDITION:

Match play – At the conclusion of the hole at which the breach is discovered, the state of the match must be adjusted by deducting one hole for each hole at which a breach occurred; maximum deduction per round – Two holes.

Stroke play – Two strokes for each hole at which any breach occurred; maximum penalty per round – Four strokes.

(ii) Procedure When Breach Discovered

When a player discovers that he has played a ball in breach of this condition, he must abandon that ball before playing from the next *teeing ground* and complete the round with a proper ball; otherwise, the player is disqualified. If discovery is made during play of a hole and the player elects to *substitute* a proper ball before completing that hole, the player must place a proper ball on the spot where the ball played in breach of the condition lay."

2. Time of Starting (Note to Rule 6-3a)

If the *Committee* wishes to act in accordance with the Note, the following wording is recommended:

"If the player arrives at his starting point, ready to play, within five minutes after his starting time, in the absence of circumstances that warrant waiving the penalty of disqualification as provided in Rule 33-7, the penalty for failure to start on time is loss of the first hole to be played in match play or two strokes in stroke play. Penalty for lateness beyond five minutes is disqualification."

3. Caddie (Note to Rule 6-4)

Rule 6-4 permits a player to use a *caddie*, provided he has only one *caddie* at any one time. However, there may be circumstances where a *Committee* may wish to prohibit caddies or restrict a player in his choice of *caddie*, e.g. professional golfer, sibling, parent, another player in the competition, etc. In such cases, the following wording is recommended:

Use of Caddie Prohibited

"A player is prohibited from using a *caddie* during the *stipulated round*."

Restriction on Who May Serve as Caddie

"A player is prohibited from having _____ serve as his *caddie* during the *stipulated round*.

PENALTY FOR BREACH OF CONDITION:

Match play – At the conclusion of the hole at which the breach is discovered, the state of the match is adjusted by deducting one hole for each hole at which a breach occurred; maximum deduction per round – Two holes.

Stroke play – Two strokes for each hole at which any breach occurred; maximum penalty per round – Four strokes.

Match or stroke play – In the event of a breach between the play of two holes, the penalty applies to the next hole. A player having a *caddie* in breach of this condition must immediately upon discovery that a breach has occurred ensure that he conforms with this condition for the remainder of the *stipulated round*. Otherwise, the player is disqualified."

4. Pace of Play (Note 2 to Rule 6-7)

The *Committee* may establish pace of play guidelines to help prevent slow play, in accordance with Note 2 to Rule 6-7.

5. Suspension of Play Due to a Dangerous Situation (Note to Rule 6-8b)

As there have been many deaths and injuries from lightning on golf courses, all clubs and sponsors of golf competitions are urged to take precautions for the protection of persons against lightning. Attention is called to Rules 6-8 and 33-2d. If the *Committee* desires to adopt the condition in the Note under Rule 6-8b, the following wording is recommended:

"When play is suspended by the *Committee* for a dangerous situation, if the players in a match or group are between the play of two holes, they must not resume play until the *Committee* has ordered a resumption of play. If they are in the process of playing a hole, they must discontinue play immediately and not resume play until the *Committee* has ordered a resumption of play. If a player fails to discontinue play immediately, he is disqualified, unless circumstances warrant waiving the penalty as provided in Rule 33-7.

The signal for suspending play due to a dangerous situation will be a prolonged note of the siren."

The following signals are generally used and it is recommended that all *Committees* do similarly:

Discontinue Play Immediately: One prolonged note of siren.

Discontinue Play: Three consecutive notes of siren, repeated.

Resume Play: Two short notes of siren, repeated.

6. Practice
a. General

The *Committee* may make regulations governing practice in accordance with the Note to Rule 7-1, Exception (c) to Rule 7-2, Note 2 to Rule 7 and Rule 33-2c.

b. Practice Between Holes (Note 2 to Rule 7)

If the *Committee* wishes to act in accordance with Note 2 to Rule 7-2, the following wording is recommended:

"Between the play of two holes, a player must not make any practice *stroke* on or near the *putting green* of the hole last played and must not test the surface of the *putting green* of the hole last played by rolling a ball.

PENALTY FOR BREACH OF CONDITION:

Match play – Loss of next hole.

Stroke play – Two strokes at the next hole.

Match or stroke play – In the case of a breach at the last hole of the *stipulated round*, the player incurs the penalty at that hole."

7. Advice in Team Competitions (Note to Rule 8)

If the *Committee* wishes to act in accordance with the Note under Rule 8, the following wording is recommended:

"In accordance with the Note to Rule 8 of the Rules of Golf, each team may appoint one person (in addition to the persons from whom *advice* may be asked under that Rule) who may give *advice* to members of that team. Such person (if it is desired to insert any restriction on who may be nominated insert such restriction here) must be identified to the *Committee* before giving *advice*."

8. New Holes (Note to Rule 33-2b)

The *Committee* may provide, in accordance with the Note to Rule 33-2b, that the *holes* and *teeing grounds* for a single round competition being held on more than one day may be differently situated on each day.

9. Transportation

If it is desired to require players to walk in a competition, the following condition is recommended:

"Players must not ride on any form of transportation during a *stipulated round* unless authorised by the *Committee*.

PENALTY FOR BREACH OF CONDITION:
Match play – At the conclusion of the hole at which the breach is discovered, the state of the match is adjusted by deducting one hole for each hole at which a breach occurred; maximum deduction per round – Two holes.
Stroke play – Two strokes for each hole at which any breach occurred; maximum penalty per round – Four strokes.
Match or stroke play – In the event of a breach between the play of two holes, the penalty applies to the next hole. Use of any unauthorised form of transportation must be discontinued immediately upon discovery that a breach has occurred. Otherwise, the player is disqualified."

10. Anti-Doping
The *Committee* may require, in the conditions of competition, that players comply with an anti-doping policy.

11. How to Decide Ties
In both match play and stroke play, a tie can be an acceptable result. However, when it is desired to have a sole winner, the *Committee* has the authority, under Rule 33-6, to determine how and when a tie is decided. The decision should be published in advance.

The *R&A* recommends:

Match Play
A match that ends all square should be played off hole by hole until one *side* wins a hole. The play-off should start on the hole where the match began. In a handicap match, handicap strokes should be allowed as in the *stipulated round*.

Stroke Play
(a) In the event of a tie in a scratch stroke play competition, a play-off is recommended. The play-off may be over 18 holes or a smaller number of holes as specified by the *Committee*. If that is not feasible or there is still a tie, a hole-by-hole play-off is recommended.
(b) In the event of a tie in a handicap stroke play competition, a play-off with handicaps is recommended. The play-off may be over 18 holes or a smaller number of holes as specified by the *Committee*. It is recommended that any such play-off consist of at least three holes.
In competitions where the handicap stroke allocation table is not relevant, if the play-off is less than 18 holes, the percentage of 18 holes played should be applied to the players' handicaps to determine their play-off handicaps. Handicap stroke fractions of one half stroke or more should count as a full stroke and any lesser fraction should be disregarded.

In competitions where the handicap stroke table is relevant, such as four-ball stroke play and bogey, par and Stableford competitions, handicap strokes should be taken as they were assigned for the competition using the players' respective stroke allocation table(s).
(c) If a play-off of any type is not feasible, matching score cards is recommended. The method of matching cards should be announced in advance and should also provide what will happen if this procedure does not produce a winner. An acceptable method of matching cards is to determine the winner on the basis of the best score for the last nine holes. If the tying players have the same score for the last nine, determine the winner on the basis of the last six holes, last three holes and finally the 18th hole. If this method is used in a competition with a multiple tee start, it is recommended that the "last nine holes, last six holes, etc." is considered to be holes 10-18, 13-18, etc.

For competitions where the handicap stroke table is not relevant, such as individual stroke play, if the last nine, last six, last three holes scenario is used, one-half, one-third, one-sixth, etc. of the handicaps should be deducted from the score for those holes. In terms of the use of fractions in such deductions, the *Committee*

should act in accordance with the recommendations of the relevant handicapping authority.

In competitions where the handicap stroke table is relevant, such as *four-ball* stroke play and bogey, par and Stableford competitions, handicap strokes should be taken as they were assigned for the competition, using the players' respective stroke allocation table(s).

12. Draw for Match Play
Although the draw for match play may be completely blind or certain players may be distributed through different quarters or eighths, the General Numerical Draw is recommended if matches are determined by a qualifying round.

General Numerical Draw
For purposes of determining places in the draw, ties in qualifying rounds other than those for the last qualifying place are decided by the order in which scores are returned, with the first score to be returned receiving the lowest available number, etc. If it is impossible to determine the order in which scores are returned, ties are determined by a blind draw.

UPPER HALF	LOWER HALF
64 QUALIFIERS	
1 vs. 64	2 vs. 63
32 vs. 33	31 vs. 34
16 vs. 49	15 vs. 50
17 vs. 48	18 vs. 47
8 vs. 57	7 vs. 58
25 vs. 40	26 vs. 39
9 vs. 56	10 vs. 55
24 vs. 41	23 vs. 42
4 vs. 61	3 vs. 62
29 vs. 36	30 vs. 35
13 vs. 52	14 vs. 51
20 vs. 45	19 vs. 46
5 vs. 60	6 vs. 59
28 vs. 37	27 vs. 38
12 vs. 53	11 vs. 54
21 vs. 44	22 vs. 43
32 QUALIFIERS	
1 vs. 32	2 vs. 31
16 vs. 17	15 vs. 18
8 vs. 25	7 vs. 26
9 vs. 24	10 vs. 23
4 vs. 29	3 vs. 30
13 vs. 20	14 vs. 19
5 vs. 28	6 vs. 27
12 vs. 21	11 vs. 22
16 QUALIFIERS	
8 vs. 9	7 vs. 10
4 vs. 13	3 vs. 14
8 QUALIFIERS	
1 vs. 8	2 vs. 7
4 vs. 5	3 vs. 6

Appendices II and III
The *R&A* reserves the right, at any time, to change the Rules relating to clubs and balls and make or change the interpretations relating to these Rules. For up to date information, please contact the *R&A* or refer to www.randa.org/equipmentrules.

Any design in a club or ball which is not covered by the *Rules*, which is contrary to the purpose and intent of the *Rules* or which might significantly change the nature of the game, will be ruled on by the *R&A*.

The dimensions and limits contained in Appendices II and III are given in the units by which conformance is determined. An equivalent imperial/metric conversion is also referenced for information, calculated using a conversion rate of 1 inch = 25.4 mm.

Appendix II – Design of Clubs

A player in doubt as to the conformity of a club should consult the *R&A*.

A manufacturer should submit to the *R&A* a sample of a club to be manufactured for a ruling as to whether the club conforms with the *Rules*. The sample becomes the property of the *R&A* for reference purposes. If a manufacturer fails to submit a sample or, having submitted a sample, fails to await a ruling before manufacturing and/or marketing the club, the manufacturer assumes the risk of a ruling that the club does not conform with the *Rules*.

The following paragraphs prescribe general regulations for the design of clubs, together with specifications and interpretations. Further information relating to these regulations and their proper interpretation is provided in "A Guide to the Rules on Clubs and Balls".

Where a club, or part of a club, is required to meet a specification within the *Rules*, it must be designed and manufactured with the intention of meeting that specification.

1. Clubs

a. General

A club is an implement designed to be used for striking the ball and generally comes in three forms: woods, irons and putters distinguished by shape and intended use. A putter is a club with a loft not exceeding ten degrees designed primarily for use on the *putting green*.

The club must not be substantially different from the traditional and customary form and make. The club must be composed of a shaft and a head and it may also have material added to the shaft to enable the player to obtain a firm hold (see 3 below). All parts of the club must be fixed so that the club is one unit, and it must have no external attachments. Exceptions may be made for attachments that do not affect the performance of the club.

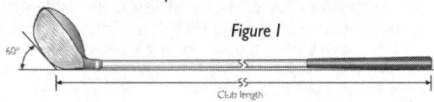

Figure I

b. Adjustability

All clubs may incorporate mechanisms for weight adjustment. Other forms of adjustability may also be permitted upon evaluation by the *R&A*. The following requirements apply to all permissible methods of adjustment:

(i) the adjustment cannot be readily made;

(ii) all adjustable parts are firmly fixed and there is no reasonable likelihood of them working loose during a round; and

(iii) all configurations of adjustment conform with the *Rules*.

During a *stipulated round*, the playing characteristics of a club must not be purposely changed by adjustment or by any other means (see Rule 4-2a).

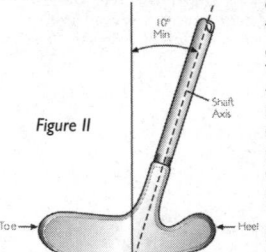

Figure II

c. Length

The overall length of the club must be at least 18 inches (0.457 m) and, except for putters, must not exceed 48 inches (1.219 m).

For woods and irons, the measurement of length is taken when the club is lying on a horizontal plane

and the sole is set against a 60 degree plane as shown in Fig. I. The length is defined as the distance from the point of the intersection between the two planes to the top of the grip. For putters, the measurement of length is taken from the top of the grip along the axis of the shaft or a straight line extension of it to the sole of the club.

d. Alignment

When the club is in its normal address position the shaft must be so aligned that:

(i) the projection of the straight part of the shaft on to the vertical plane through the toe and heel must diverge from the vertical by at least 10 degrees (see Fig. II). If the overall design of the club is such that the player can effectively use the club in a vertical or close-to-vertical position, the shaft may be required to diverge from the vertical in this plane by as much as 25 degrees;

(ii) the projection of the straight part of the shaft on to the vertical plane along the intended *line of play* must not diverge from the vertical by more than 20 degrees forwards or 10 degrees backwards (see Fig. III).

Except for putters, all of the heel portion of the club must lie within 0.625 inches (15.88 mm) of the plane containing the axis of the straight part of the shaft and the intended (horizontal) *line of play* (see Fig. IV).

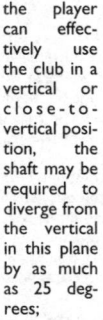

Figure III

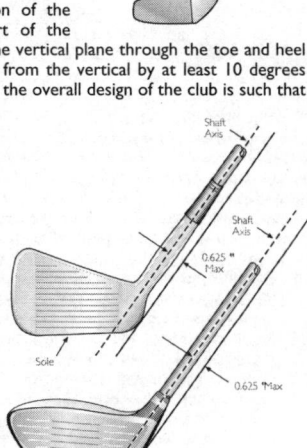

Figure IV

2. Shaft

a. Straightness

The shaft must be straight from the top of the grip to a point not more than 5 inches (127 mm) above the sole, measured from the point where the shaft ceases to be straight along the axis of the bent part of the shaft and the neck and/or socket (see Fig. V).

b. Bending and Twisting Properties

At any point along its length, the shaft must:

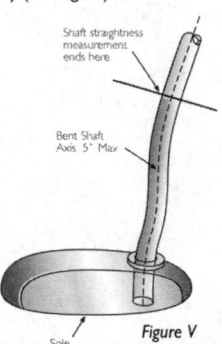

Figure V

(i) bend in such a way that the deflection is the same regardless of how the shaft is rotated about its longitudinal axis; and

(ii) twist the same amount in both directions.

c. Attachment to Clubhead

The shaft must be attached to the clubhead at the heel either directly or through a single plain neck and/or socket. The length from the top of the neck and/or socket to the sole of the club must not exceed 5 inches (127 mm), mea-

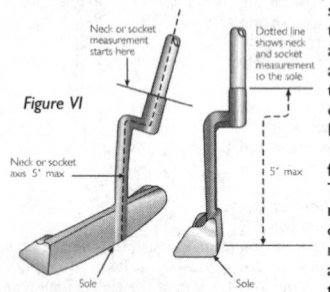

Figure VI

sured along the axis of, and following any bend in, the neck and/or socket (see Fig. VI).

Exception for Putters: The shaft or neck or socket of a putter may be fixed at any point in the head.

3. Grip (see Fig. VII)

The grip consists of material added to the shaft to enable the player to obtain a firm hold. The grip must be fixed to the shaft, must be straight and plain in form, must extend to the end of the shaft and must not be moulded for any part of the hands. If no material is added, that portion of the shaft designed to be held by the player must be considered the grip.

(i) For clubs other than putters the grip must be circular in cross-section, except that a continuous, straight, slightly raised rib may be incorporated along the full length of the grip, and a slightly indented spiral is permitted on a wrapped grip or a replica of one.

(ii) A putter grip may have a non-circular cross-section, provided the cross-section has no concavity, is symmetrical and remains generally similar throughout the length of the grip. (See Clause (v) overleaf).

(iii) The grip may be tapered but must not have any bulge or waist. Its cross-sectional dimensions measured in any direction must not exceed 1.75 inches (44.45 mm).

(iv) For clubs other than putters the axis of the grip must coincide with the axis of the shaft.

(v) A putter may have two grips provided each is circular in cross-section, the axis of each coincides with the axis of the shaft, and they are separated by at least 1.5 inches (38.1 mm).

4. Clubhead
a. Plain in Shape

The clubhead must be generally plain in shape. All parts must be rigid, structural in nature and functional. The clubhead or its

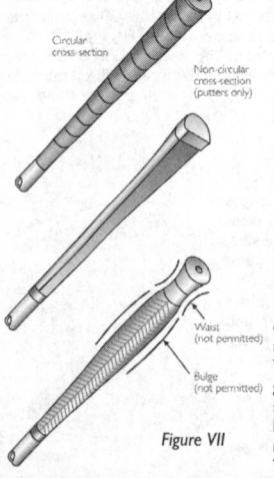

Figure VII

parts must not be designed to resemble any other object. It is not practicable to define plain in shape precisely and comprehensively. However, features that are deemed to be in breach of this requirement and are therefore not permitted include, but are not limited to:

(i) All Clubs
- holes through the face;
- holes through the head (some exceptions may be made for putters and cavity back irons);
- features that are for the purpose of meeting dimensional specifications;
- features that extend into or ahead of the face;
- features that extend significantly above the top line of the head;
- furrows in or runners on the head that extend into the face (some exceptions may be made for putters); and
- optical or electronic devices.

(ii) Woods and Irons
- all features listed in (i) above;
- cavities in the outline of the heel and/or the toe of the head that can be viewed from above;
- severe or multiple cavities in the outline of the back of the head that can be viewed from above;
- transparent material added to the head with the intention of rendering conforming a feature that is not otherwise permitted; and
- features that extend beyond the outline of the head when viewed from above.

b. Dimensions, Volume and Moment of Inertia
(i) Woods

When the club is in a 60 degree lie angle, the dimensions of the clubhead must be such that:
- the distance from the heel to the toe of the clubhead is greater than the distance from the face to the back;
- the distance from the heel to the toe of the clubhead is not greater than 5 inches (127 mm); and
- the distance from the sole to the crown of the clubhead, including any permitted features, is not greater than 2.8 inches (71.12 mm).

These dimensions are measured on horizontal lines between vertical projections of the outermost points of:
- the heel and the toe; and
- the face and the back (see Fig. VIII, dimension A);

and on vertical lines between the horizontal projections of the outermost points of the sole and the crown (see Fig. VIII, dimension B). If the outermost point of the heel is not clearly defined, it is deemed to be 0.875 inches (22.23 mm) above the horizontal plane on which the club is lying (see Fig. VIII, dimension C).

The volume of the clubhead must not exceed 460 cubic centimetres (28.06 cubic inches), plus a tolerance of 10 cubic centimetres (0.61 cubic inches).

When the club is in a 60 degree lie angle, the moment of inertia component around the vertical axis through the clubhead's centre of gravity must not exceed 5900 g cm^2 (32.259 oz in^2), plus a test tolerance of 100 g cm^2 (0.547 oz in^2).

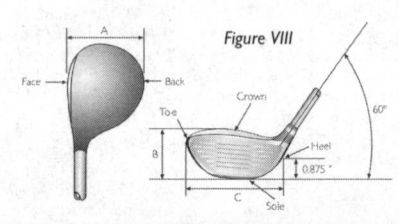

Figure VIII

(ii) Irons
When the clubhead is in its normal address position, the dimensions of the head must be such that the distance from the heel to the toe is greater than the distance from the face to the back.

(iii) Putters (see Fig. IX)
When the clubhead is in its normal address position, the dimensions of the head must be such that:
- the distance from the heel to the toe is greater than the distance from the face to the back;
- the distance from the heel to the toe of the head is less than or equal to 7 inches (177.8 mm);
- the distance from the heel to the toe of the face is greater than or equal to two thirds of the distance from the face to the back of the head;
- the distance from the heel to the toe of the face is greater than or equal to half of the distance from the heel to the toe of the head; and
- the distance from the sole to the top of the head, including any permitted features, is less than or equal to 2.5 inches (63.5 mm).

For traditionally shaped heads, these dimensions will be measured on horizontal lines between vertical projections of the outermost points of:
- the heel and the toe of the head;
- the heel and the toe of the face; and
- the face and the back;

and on vertical lines between the horizontal projections of the outermost points of the sole and the top of the head.

For unusually shaped heads, the toe to heel dimension may be made at the face.

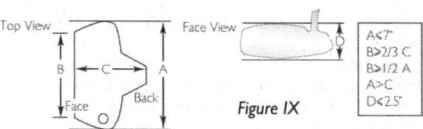

Figure IX

c. Spring Effect and Dynamic Properties
The design, material and/or construction of, or any treatment to, the clubhead (which includes the club face) must not:
(i) have the effect of a spring which exceeds the limit set forth in the Pendulum Test Protocol on file with the R&A; or
(ii) incorporate features or technology including, but not limited to, separate springs or spring features, that have the intent of, or the effect of, unduly influencing the clubhead's spring effect; or
(iii) unduly influence the movement of the ball.
Note: (i) above does not apply to putters.

d. Striking Faces
The clubhead must have only one striking face, except that a putter may have two such faces if their characteristics are the same, and they are opposite each other.

5. Club Face
a. General
The face of the club must be hard and rigid and must not impart significantly more or less spin to the ball than a standard steel face (some exceptions may be made for putters). Except for such markings listed below, the club face must be smooth and must not have any degree of concavity.

b. Impact Area Roughness and Material
Except for markings specified in the following paragraphs, the surface roughness within the area where impact is intended (the "impact area") must not exceed that of decorative sandblasting, or of fine milling (see Fig. X).

The whole of the impact area must be of the same material (exceptions may be made for clubheads made of wood).

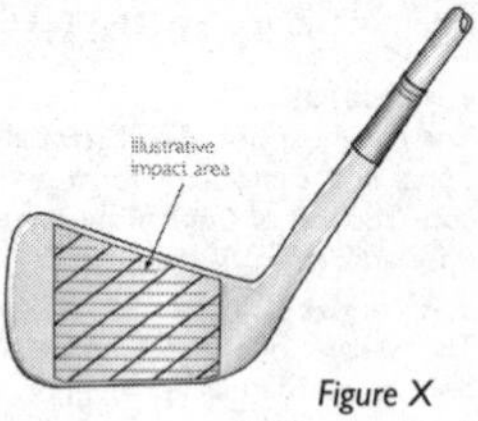

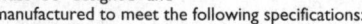

c. Impact Area Markings
If a club has grooves and/or punch marks in the impact area they must be designed and manufactured to meet the following specifications:

Figure X

(i) Grooves
- Grooves must not have sharp edges or raised lips (test on file).
- Grooves must be straight and parallel.
- Grooves must have a symmetrical cross-section and have sides which do not converge (see Fig. XI).
- The width, spacing and cross-section of the grooves must be consistent throughout the impact area.
- Any rounding of groove edges must be in the form of a radius which does not exceed 0.020 inches (0.508 mm).
- The width of each groove must not exceed 0.035 inches (0.9 mm), using the 30 degree method of measurement on file with the R&A.
- The distance between edges of adjacent grooves must not be less than three times the width of the grooves, and not less than 0.075 inches (1.905 mm).
- The depth of each groove must not exceed 0.020 inches (0.508 mm).

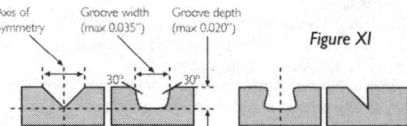

Figure XI

(ii) Punch Marks.
- The area of any punch mark must not exceed 0.0044 square inches (2.84 sq. mm).
- The distance between adjacent punch marks (or between punch marks and grooves) must not be less than 0.168 inches (4.27 mm), measured from centre to centre.
- The depth of any punch mark must not exceed 0.040 inches (1.02 mm).
- Punch marks must not have sharp edges or raised lips (test on file).

d. Decorative Markings
The centre of the impact area may be indicated by a design within the boundary of a square whose sides are 0.375 inches (9.53 mm) in length. Such a design must not unduly influence the movement of the ball. Decorative markings are permitted outside the impact area.

e. Non-Metallic Club Face Markings
The above specifications do not apply to clubheads made of wood on which the impact area of the face is of a material of hardness less than the hardness of metal and whose loft angle is 24 degrees or less, but markings which could unduly influence the movement of the ball are prohibited.

f. Putter Face Markings
Any markings on the face of a putter must not have sharp edges or raised lips. The specifications with regard to roughness, material and markings in the impact area do not apply.

Appendix III – The Ball

1. General
The ball must not be substantially different from the traditional and customary form and make. The material and construction of the ball must not be contrary to the purpose and intent of the *Rules*.

2. Weight
The weight of the ball must not be greater than 1.620 ounces avoirdupois (45.93 g).

3. Size
The diameter of the ball must not be less than 1.680 inches (42.67mm). This specification will be satisfied if, under its own weight, a ball falls through a 1.680 inches diameter ring gauge in fewer than 25 out of 100 randomly selected positions, the test being carried out at a temperature of 23 +/-1°C.

4. Spherical Symmetry
The ball must not be designed, manufactured or intentionally modified to have properties which differ from those of a spherically symmetrical ball.

5. Initial Velocity
The initial velocity of the ball must not exceed the limit specified (test on file) when measured on apparatus approved by the *R&A*.

6. Overall Distance Standard
The combined carry and roll of the ball, when tested on apparatus approved by the *R&A*, must not exceed the distance specified under the conditions set forth in the Overall Distance Standard for golf balls on file with the *R&A*.

RULES OF AMATEUR STATUS
As approved by R&A Rules Limited
Effective from 1st January 2008

Preamble
The *R&A* reserves the right to change the Rules of Amateur Status and to make and change the interpretations of the Rules of Amateur Status at any time.

In the Rules of Amateur Status, the gender used in relation to any person is understood to include both genders.

Definitions
The Definitions are listed alphabetically and, in the *Rules* themselves, defined terms are in *italics*.

Amateur Golfer
An "amateur golfer" is one who plays the game as a non-remunerative and non-profit making sport and who does not receive remuneration for teaching golf or for other activities because of *golf skill or reputation*, except as provided in the *Rules*.

Committee
The "Committee" is the appropriate *Committee* of the *Governing Body*.

Note: In Great Britain and Ireland, the *Committee* is the Amateur Status Committee of the *R&A*.

Golf Skill or Reputation
It is a matter for the *Governing Body* to decide whether a particular *amateur golfer* has *golf skill or reputation*.

Generally, an *amateur golfer* is only considered to have *golf skill* if he:
(a) has had competitive success at a local or national level or has been selected to represent his national, regional, state or county union or association; or
(b) competes at an elite level.

Golf reputation can only be gained through *golf skill* and does not include prominence for service to the game of golf as an administrator.

Governing Body
The "Governing Body" for the Rules of Amateur Status in any country is the national union of that country.

Note: In Great Britain and Ireland, the *R&A* is the *Governing Body*.

Instruction
"Instruction" covers teaching the physical aspects of playing golf, i.e. the actual mechanics of swinging a golf club and hitting a golf ball.

Note: *Instruction* does not cover teaching the psychological aspects of the game or the etiquette or Rules of Golf.

Junior Golfer
A "junior golfer" is an *amateur golfer* who has not reached a specified age as determined by the *Governing Body*.

Note: In Great Britain and Ireland, a *junior golfer* is an *amateur golfer* who has not reached his 18th birthday in the year prior to the event.

Prize Voucher
A "prize voucher" is a voucher or gift certificate issued by the Committee in charge of a competition for the purchase of goods from a professional's shop or other retail source.

R&A
The "R&A" means R&A Rules Limited.

Retail Value
The "retail value" of a prize is the price at which the prize is generally available from a retail source at the time of the award.

Rule or Rules
The term "Rule" or "Rules" refers to the Rules of Amateur Status as determined by the *Governing Body*.

Symbolic Prize
A "symbolic prize" is a trophy made of gold, silver, ceramic, glass or the like that is permanently and distinctively engraved.

Testimonial Award
A "testimonial award" is an award for notable performances or contributions to golf as distinguished from competition prizes. A testimonial award may not be a monetary award.

Rule 1 – Amateurism

1-1. General

An *amateur golfer* must play the game and conduct himself in accordance with the *Rules*.

1-2. Amateur Status

Amateur Status is a universal condition of eligibility for playing in golf competitions as an *amateur golfer*. A person who acts contrary to the *Rules* may forfeit his status as an *amateur golfer* and as a result will be ineligible to play in amateur competitions.

1-3. Purpose and Spirit of the Rules

The purpose and spirit of the *Rules* is to maintain the distinction between amateur golf and professional golf and to keep the amateur game as free as possible from the abuses that may follow from uncontrolled sponsorship and financial incentive. It is considered necessary to safeguard amateur golf, which is largely self-regulating with regard to the Rules of play and handicapping, so that it can be fully enjoyed by all *amateur golfers*.

1-4. Doubt as to Rules

A person who wishes to be an *amateur golfer* and who is in doubt as to whether taking a proposed course of action is permitted under the *Rules* should consult the *Governing Body*.

An organiser or sponsor of an amateur golf competition or a competition involving *amateur golfers* who is in doubt as to whether a proposal is in accordance with the *Rules* should consult the *Governing Body*.

Rule 2 – Professionalism

2-1. General

Except as provided in the *Rules*, an *amateur golfer* must not take any action for the purpose of becoming a professional golfer and must not identify himself as a professional golfer.

Note 1: Actions by an *amateur golfer* for the purpose of becoming a professional golfer include, but are not limited to:

(a) accepting the position of a professional golfer;
(b) receiving services or payment, directly or indirectly, from a professional agent;
(c) entering into a written or oral agreement, directly or indirectly, with a professional agent or sponsor; and
(d) agreeing to accept payment or compensation, directly or indirectly, for allowing his name or likeness as a player of *golf skill or reputation* to be used for any *commercial purpose*.

Note 2: An *amateur golfer* may enquire as to his likely prospects as a professional golfer, including applying unsuccessfully for the position of a professional golfer, and he may work in a professional's shop and receive payment or compensation, provided he does not infringe the *Rules* in any other way.

2-2. Membership of Professional Golfers' Organisations

a. Professional Golfers' Association

An *amateur golfer* must not hold or retain membership of **any Professional Golfers' Association.**

b. Professional Tours

An *amateur golfer* must not hold or retain membership of a Professional Tour limited exclusively to professional golfers.

Note: If an *amateur golfer* must compete in one or more qualifying competitions in order to be eligible for membership of a Professional Tour, he may enter and play in such qualifying competitions without forfeiting his Amateur Status, provided, in advance of play and in writing, he waives his right to any prize money in the competition.

Rule 3 – Prizes

3-1. Playing for Prize Money

An *amateur golfer* must not play golf for prize money or its equivalent in a match, competition or exhibition.

Note: An *amateur golfer* may participate in an event where prize money or its equivalent is offered, provided that prior to participation he waives his right to accept prize money in that event.

(Conduct contrary to the purpose and spirit of the Rules – see Rule 7-2)

(Policy on gambling – see Appendix)

Rule 3-2. Prize Limits

a. General

An *amateur golfer* must not accept a prize (other than a *symbolic prize*) or *prize voucher* of *retail value* in excess of £500 or the equivalent, or such a lesser figure as may be decided by the *Governing Body*. This limit applies to the total prizes or *prize vouchers* received by an *amateur golfer* in any one competition or series of competitions, excluding any hole-in-one prize (see Rule 3-2b).

b. Hole-in-One Prizes

The limits prescribed in Rule 3-2a apply to a prize for a hole-in-one. However, such a prize may be accepted in addition to any other prize won in the same competition.

c. Exchanging Prizes

An *amateur golfer* must not exchange a prize or *prize voucher* for cash.

Exception: An *amateur golfer* may submit a *prize voucher* to a national, regional, state or county union or association and thereafter be reimbursed from the value of that voucher for expenses incurred in participating in a golf competition, provided the reimbursement of such expenses is permitted under Rule 4-2.

Note 1: The responsibility to prove the *retail value* of a particular prize rests with the Committee in charge of the competition.

Note 2: It is recommended that the total value of prizes in a gross competition, or each division of a handicap competition, should not exceed twice the prescribed limit in an 18-hole competition, three times in a 36-hole competition, five times in a 54-hole competition and six times in a 72-hole competition.

3-3. Testimonial Awards

a. General

An *amateur golfer* must not accept a *testimonial award* of retail value in excess of the limits prescribed in Rule 3-2a.

b. Multiple Awards

An *amateur golfer* may accept more than one *testimonial award* from different donors, even though their total *retail value* exceeds the prescribed limit, provided they are not presented so as to evade the limit for a single award.

Rule 4 – Expenses

4-1. General

Except as provided in the *Rules*, an *amateur golfer* must not accept expenses, in money or otherwise, from any source to play in a golf competition or exhibition.

4-2. Receipt of Expenses

An *amateur golfer* may receive reasonable expenses, not exceeding the actual expenses incurred, to play in a golf competition or exhibition as follows:

a. Family Support

An *amateur golfer* may receive expenses from a member of his family or a legal guardian.

b. Junior Golfers

A *junior golfer* may receive expenses when competing in a competition limited exclusively to *junior golfers*.

c. Individual Events

An *amateur golfer* may receive expenses when competing in individual events provided he complies with the following provisions:

(i)　Where the competition is to take place in the player's own country the expenses must be approved by and paid through the player's national, regional, state or county union or association.

(ii)　Where the competition is to take place in another country the expenses must be approved by both the player's national union or association and the national union or association in the country in which the competition is to be staged. The expenses must be paid through the player's national, regional, state or county union or association or, subject to the approval of the player's national union or association, by the body controlling golf in the territory he is visiting.

The *Governing Body* may limit the receipt of expenses to a specific number of competitive days in any one calendar year and an *amateur golfer* must not exceed any such limit. In such a case, the expenses are deemed to include reasonable travel time and practice days in connection with the competitive days.

Exception: An *amateur golfer* must not receive expenses, directly or indirectly, from a professional agent (see Rule 2-1) or any other similar source as may be determined by the *Governing Body*.

Note: An *amateur golfer* of *golf skill or reputation* must not promote or advertise the source of any expenses received (see Rule 6-2).

d. Team Events

An *amateur golfer*, may receive expenses when he is representing:

• his country,
• his regional, state or county union or association,
• his golf club,
• his business or industry, or
• a similar body

in a team competition, practice session or training camp.

Note 1: A "similar body" includes a recognised educational institution or military service.

Note 2: Unless otherwise stated, the expenses must be paid by the body that the *amateur golfer* is representing or the body controlling golf in the country he is visiting.

e. Invitation Unrelated to Golf Skill

An *amateur golfer* who is invited for reasons unrelated to *golf skill* (e.g. a celebrity, a business associate or customer) to take part in a golf event may receive expenses.

f. Exhibitions

An *amateur golfer* who is participating in an exhibition in aid of a recognised charity may receive expenses, provided that the exhibition is not run in connection with another golfing event in which the player is competing.

g. Sponsored Handicap Competitions

An *amateur golfer* may receive expenses when competing in a sponsored handicap competition, provided the competition has been approved as follows:

(i)　Where the competition is to take place in the player's own country, the annual approval of the *Governing Body* must first be obtained in advance by the sponsor; and

(ii)　Where the competition is to take place in more than one country or involves golfers from another country, the approval of each *Governing Body* must first be obtained in advance by the sponsor. The application for this approval should be sent to the *Governing Body* in the country where the competition commences.

Rule 5 – Instruction

5-1. General

Except as provided in the *Rules*, an *amateur golfer* must not receive payment or compensation, directly or indirectly, for giving *instruction* in playing golf.

5-2. Where Payment Permitted
a. Schools, Colleges, Camps, etc.

An *amateur golfer* who is (i) an employee of an educational institution or system or (ii) a counsellor at a camp or other similar organised programme, may receive payment or compensation for golf *instruction* to students in the institution, system or camp, provided that the total time devoted to golf *instruction* comprises less than 50 percent of the time spent in the performance of all duties as such an employee or counsellor.

b. Approved Programmes

An *amateur golfer* may receive expenses, payment or compensation for giving golf *instruction* as part of a programme that has been approved in advance by the *Governing Body*.

5-3. Instruction in Writing

An *amateur golfer* may receive payment or compensation for golf *instruction* in writing, provided his ability or reputation as a golfer was not a major factor in his employment or in the commission or sale of his work.

Rule 6 – Use of Golf Skill or Reputation

6-1. General

Except as provided in the *Rules*, an *amateur golfer* of *golf skill or reputation* must not use that skill or reputation to promote, advertise or sell anything or for any financial gain.

6-2. Lending Name or Likeness

An *amateur golfer* of *golf skill or reputation* must not use that skill or reputation to obtain payment, compensation, personal benefit or any financial gain, directly or indirectly, for allowing his name or likeness to be used for the advertisement or sale of anything.

Exception: An amateur golfer of golf skill or reputation may allow his name or likeness to be used to promote:

(a)　his national, regional, state or county union or association; or

(b)　subject to the permission of his national union, (i) any golf competition or other event that is considered to be in the best interests of, or would contribute to the development of, the game or (ii) a recognised charity (or similar good cause).

The amateur golfer must not obtain any payment, compensation or financial gain, directly or indirectly, for doing so.

Note: An *amateur golfer* may accept golf equipment from anyone dealing in such equipment provided no advertising is involved.

6-3. Personal Appearance

An *amateur golfer* of *golf skill or reputation* must not use that skill or reputation to obtain payment, compensation, personal benefit or any financial gain, directly or indirectly, for a personal appearance.

Exception: An *amateur golfer* may receive actual expenses in connection with a personal appearance provided no golf competition or exhibition is involved.

6-4. Broadcasting and Writing

An *amateur golfer* of *golf skill or reputation* may receive payment, compensation, personal benefit or any financial gain from broadcasting or writing provided:

(a)　the broadcasting or writing is part of his primary occupation or career and golf *instruction* is not included (Rule 5); or

(b) the broadcasting or writing is on a part-time basis, the player is actually the author of the commentary, articles or books and *instruction* in playing golf is not included.

Note: An *amateur golfer* of *golf skill or reputation* must not promote or advertise anything within the commentary, article or books and must not lend his name or likeness to the promotion or sale of the commentary, article or books (see Rule 6-2).

6-5. Grants, Scholarships and Bursaries
An *amateur golfer* of *golf skill or reputation* must not accept the benefits of a grant, scholarship or bursary, except one whose terms and conditions have been approved by the *Governing Body*.

6-6. Membership
An *amateur golfer* of *golf skill or reputation* must not accept an offer of membership in a Golf Club or privileges at a golf course, without full payment for the class of membership or privilege, if such an offer is made as an inducement to play for that Club or course.

Rule 7 – Other Conduct Incompatible with Amateurism

7-1. Conduct Detrimental to Amateurism
An *amateur golfer* must not act in a manner that is detrimental to the best interests of the amateur game.

7-2. Conduct Contrary to the Purpose and Spirit of the Rules
An *amateur golfer* must not take any action, including actions relating to golf gambling, that is contrary to the purpose and spirit of the *Rules*.
(Policy on gambling – see Appendix)

Rule 8 – Procedure for Enforcement of the Rules

8-1. Decision on a Breach
If a possible breach of the *Rules* by a person claiming to be an *amateur golfer* comes to the attention of the *Committee*, it is a matter for the *Committee* to decide whether a breach has occurred. Each case will be investigated to the extent deemed appropriate by the *Committee* and considered on its merits. The decision of the *Committee* is final, subject to an appeal as provided in these *Rules*.

8-2. Enforcement
Upon a decision that a person has breached the *Rules*, the *Committee* may declare the Amateur Status of the person forfeited or require the person to refrain or desist from specified actions as a condition of retaining his Amateur Status.

The *Committee* should notify the person and may notify any interested golf union or association of any action taken under Rule 8-2.

8-3. Appeals Procedure
Each *Governing Body* should establish a process or procedure through which any decision concerning enforcement of these Rules may be appealed by the person affected.
Note: If a person, whose *Governing Body* is the R&A, is affected by a decision made by the Amateur Status Committee of the R&A in respect of the enforcement of these *Rules*, that person may raise an appeal of that decision with the R&A Appeals Committee.

Rule 9 – Reinstatement of Amateur Status

9-1. General
The *Committee* has the sole authority to reinstate a person to Amateur Status, prescribe a waiting period necessary for reinstatement or to deny reinstatement, subject to an appeal as provided in the *Rules*.

9-2. Applications for Reinstatement
Each application for reinstatement will be considered on its merits, with consideration normally being given to the following principles:

a. Awaiting Reinstatement
The professional golfer is considered to hold an advantage over the *amateur golfer* by reason of having devoted himself to the game as his profession; other persons infringing the *Rules* also obtain advantages not available to the *amateur golfer*. They do not necessarily lose such advantages merely by deciding to cease infringing the *Rules*. Therefore, an applicant for reinstatement to Amateur Status must undergo a period awaiting reinstatement as prescribed by the *Committee*.

The period awaiting reinstatement generally starts from the date of the person's last breach of the *Rules* unless the *Committee* decides that it starts from either (a) the date when the person's last breach became known to the *Committee*, or (b) such other date determined by the *Committee*.

b. Period Awaiting Reinstatement
(i) Professionalism
Generally, the period awaiting reinstatement is related to the period the person was in breach of the *Rules*. However, no applicant is normally eligible for reinstatement until he has conducted himself in accordance with the *Rules* for a period of at least one year.

It is recommended that the following guidelines on periods awaiting reinstatement be applied by the *Committee*:

Period of Breach	Period Awaiting Reinstatement:
under 5 years	1 year
5 years or more	2 years

However, the period may be extended if the applicant has played extensively for prize money, regardless of performance. In all cases, the *Committee* reserves the right to extend or to shorten the period awaiting reinstatement.

(ii) Other Breaches of the Rules
A period awaiting reinstatement of one year will normally be required. However, the period may be extended if the breach is considered serious.

c. Number of Reinstatements
A person is not normally eligible to be reinstated more than twice.

d. Players of National Prominence
A player of national prominence who has been in breach of the *Rules* for more than five years is not normally eligible for reinstatement.

e. Status While Awaiting Reinstatement
An applicant for reinstatement must comply with these *Rules*, as they apply to an *amateur golfer*, during his period awaiting reinstatement.

An applicant for reinstatement is not eligible to enter competitions as an *amateur golfer*. However, he may enter competitions and win a prize solely among members of a Club where he is a member, subject to the approval of the Club. He must not represent such a Club against other Clubs unless with the approval of the Clubs in the competition and/or the organising Committee.

An applicant for reinstatement may enter competitions that are not limited to *amateur golfers*, subject to the conditions of competition, without prejudicing his application, provided he does so as an applicant for reinstatement. He must waive his right to any prize money offered in the competition and must not accept any prize reserved for an *amateur golfer* (Rule 3-1).

9-3. Procedure for Applications
Each application for reinstatement must be submitted to the *Committee*, in accordance with such procedures as may

be laid down and including such information as the *Committee* may require.

9-4. Appeals Procedure

Each *Governing Body* should establish a process or procedure through which any decision concerning reinstatement of Amateur Status may be appealed by the person affected. Note: If a person, whose *Governing Body* is the *R&A*, is affected by a decision made by the Amateur Status Committee of the *R&A* in respect of reinstatement of Amateur Status, that person may raise an appeal of that decision with the *R&A* Appeals Committee.

Rule 10 – Committee Decision

10-1. Committee's Decision

The *Committee's* decision is final, subject to an appeal as provided in Rules 8-3 and 9-4.

10-2. Doubt as to Rules

If the *Committee* of a *Governing Body*, other than the *R&A*, considers the case to be doubtful or not covered by the *Rules*, it may, prior to making its decision, consult with the Amateur Status Committee of the *R&A*.

INDEX

The Rules of Golf are here indexed according to the pertinant rule number, definition or appendix that has gone before.

The R&A and the modern game

What is The R&A?

The R&A takes its name from The Royal and Ancient Golf Club of St Andrews, which traces its origins back 250 years. Although the golf club still exists to meet the needs of more than 2,000 international members, The R&A has grown apart to focus on its role as golf's world governance and development body and organiser of The Open Championship.

The R&A is golf's world rules and development body and organiser of The Open Championship. It operates with the consent of more than 130 national and international amateur and professional organisations from almost 120 countries and on behalf of an estimated 30 million golfers in Europe, Africa, Asia Pacific and the Americas.

The R&A and the United States Golf Association have jointly issued the Rules of Golf since 1952. The USGA is the governing body for the Rules of Golf in the United States and Mexico.

By making The Open Championship one of the world's great sporting events and an outstanding commercial success, The R&A is able to invest a substantial annual surplus for the development of the game through The R&A Foundation. The Foundation is the charitable body that channels money from The Open directly into grassroots development projects around the world.

Particular emphasis is placed on the encouragement of junior golf, on the development of the game in emerging golfing nations, on coaching and the provision of more accessible courses and improved practice facilities.

The R&A also provides best practice guidance on all aspects of golf course management, to help golf grow throughout the world in a commercially and environmentally sustainable way.

Useful links

www.randa.org
www.opengolf.com
www.bestcourseforgolf.org
www.theroyalandancientgolfclub.org
www.britishgolfmuseum.co.uk
wagr.randa.org

The future of the game

The R&A is committed to promoting and developing golf both nationally and internationally. Two factors make this possible. One is the annual surplus from The Open Championship and the other is The R&A's position of global influence. Combined, these give scope for the worldwide advancement of golf.

A major priority for The R&A is providing funding for training and the development of the game around the world. In recent years, a determined effort has been directed towards financing development in countries where golf is a relatively new sport. Major contributions are made to women's golf and the Golf Foundation receives substantial help to assist with its work of introducing young people to the game.

The R&A is highly conscious of the need and its obligation to serve the game worldwide. Since 1997 the R&A has provided financial support towards the African VI Tournament. The South American Men's and Women's Amateur Team Championship are also supported as are the equivalent events in the Asia-Pacific region.

The R&A Foundation supports University golf throughout Great Britain and Ireland with the aim of encouraging students to remain competitive while completing their formal education.

The R&A takes a lead in and offers advice on all aspects of golf course management worldwide, with developments in greenkeeping and environmental issues foremost among its concerns. Again, it is particularly concerned with offering assistance in countries where golf is still in its infancy.

Funding the future

Most of The R&A's funding comes from The Open Championship. Worldwide television rights are an important source of income, along with spectator ticket sales, catering, merchandising, corporate hospitality and sponsorship.

The Open Championship is broadcast throughout the world. Television coverage of The Open has a global household reach of 410 million and is delivered by 57 broadcasters in 162 territories. It is the world's largest annual televised sports event alongside Wimbledon.

In recent years The R&A has been at the forefront of modern technology, extending its range of activities to New Media rights, whereby income is generated through the internet, and mobile communication devices. These, combined with merchandising, licensing and publishing, increase the ways in which The R&A is able to provide financial assistance for the development of golf throughout the world.

In 2004, Rolex began to sponsor the publication and distribution of the Rules of Golf book, ensuring that golfers worldwide can have a copy of the current Rules of Golf free of charge. Over 4 million copies are distributed and the book is available in 21 different languages.

Marsh and McLennan, Nikon, Rolex, the Royal Bank of Scotland and Unisys are patrons of the Open Championship and they were joined in 2005 by luxury car-maker Lexus. Through their association with The Open, the Patrons provide additional income for the funding of golf development projects worldwide.

The rules of the game

In almost every country where the game is played, the rules followed are those set by The R&A. The exceptions are the USA and Mexico, where the code is set by the United States Golf Association, and Canada, which is self-governing but affiliated to The R&A. There are 130 associations and unions affiliated to The R&A.

The R&A is responsible for the Rules of Golf, the rules affecting equipment standards and the Rules of Amateur Status. The Rules of Golf Committee reviews the Rules of Golf and interprets and makes decisions on the playing Rules. The Equipment Standards Committee interprets and gives decisions on those rules that deal with the form and make of golf clubs and the specifications of the ball. The Amateur Status Committee reviews, interprets and amends the Rules of Amateur Status. All work closely with the equivalent committees of the USGA.

To meet the needs of golfers worldwide the Rules of Golf are published in over 20 languages and in audio CD format. Supplementing these are the biennial decisions on the Rules of Golf. Each volume contains over 1,100 decisions. Together, these help to ensure a consistent interpretation of the Rules throughout the world. The R&A also publish modifications of the Rules for golfers with disabilities.

The Rules Department answers thousands of queries from golf clubs, associations and professional tours on the playing Rules, the equipment Rules and on the Amateur Code.

Rules education is a priority for The R&A. Each year a Referees School is held in St Andrews, and overseas Rules Schools are held on a regular basis.

Since the beginning of 2001, countries visited include Argentina, Brazil, the Dominican Republic, Ecuador, Germany, Guatemala, Japan, Kenya, Luxembourg, New Zealand, Poland, Russia, Singapore, South Africa, South Korea, Thailand and the United Arab Emirates. In 2007, schools were also held in China, India and Malaysia.

R&A Championships

The R&A promotes, organises and controls a number of championships and matches at both national and international level. Of these events, the biggest and most prestigious is The Open Championship.

In 1920, the Royal and Ancient Golf Club took over the running of the Amateur and Open Championships. The Boys Amateur Championship followed in 1948 and the British Youths Open Championship in 1963. The British Mid-Amateur Championship replaced the Youths event in 1995 but was discontinued in 2007.

In 1969, the Club introduced the Seniors Open Amateur Championship for players aged 55 and over. In 1991, it became involved with and now organises the Senior British Open, in conjunction with the PGA European Seniors Tour. The Junior Open, first played in 1994, came under The R&A umbrella in 2000.

The Walker Cup, which is the largest of the international amateur matches, is played between teams from Great Britain & Ireland and the United States and is run jointly with the United States Golf Association.

The R&A also administers the St Andrews Trophy, inaugurated in 1956, and the Jacques Leglise Trophy, an event for boys. Both are played between teams from Great Britain & Ireland and the Continent of Europe. When these matches are played in Europe, they are organised by the European Golf Association.

The Great Britain and Ireland team selection for the Walker Cup and the St Andrews Trophy is undertaken by The R&A.

In 2004, The Royal and Ancient Golf Club transferred to The R&A the responsibilities and authority of the Club for all aspects of running championships and matches at national and international level.

Governing Organisations – Professional Golf

The Professional Golfers' Association (PGA)

The PGA was founded in 1901 and is the oldest PGA in the world. It has continued to develop steadily over the years; in the mid seventies major re-structuring of the Association took place with the development of two separate divisions. The administrative operation moved to The Belfry in 1977 to advance and develop the services available to club professionals, and shortly afterwards the Tournament Division established a new base at the Wentworth Club.

In 1984 it was decided that the interests of the members of each division would be best served by forming two separate organisations and on 1st January 1985 The Professional Golfers' Association and the European Tour became independent of each other.

The PGA's activities include training and further education of assistants and members and the organisation of tournaments at national level. National Headquarters is also the administrative base to accounts, marketing, media and the commercial activities of the Association.

There are seven regional headquarters located throughout Great Britain and Ireland and each region organises its own tournaments.

Classes of Membership

Class AA
Shall have passed the final examination of a PGA approved training programme, be actively engaged on a continuous basis in any field having a direct connection with or relevance to golf and has maintained the relevant requirements for the Professional Development Programme as defined by the Association.

Class A
Shall have passed the final examination of a PGA approved training programme and be actively engaged on a continuous basis in any field having a direct connection with or relevance to golf.

Class TP1
Must be a current full member of either the European Tour, Ladies' European Tour, European Seniors' Tour or any tour belonging to the International Federation of PGA Tours subject to the relevant categories as defined by the Association at the time.

Class TP2
Must be a current full member of either the European Tour, Ladies' European Tour or European Seniors' Tour subject to the relevant categories as defined by the Association at the time.

Class TP3
Must be a member of the PGA Europro Tour finishing 1–80 in the immediately preceding year's Order of Merit.

Life Member
Must be a member of the Association who has been recommended by the Board of Directors to Special General Meeting of the Association for appointment as a Life Member and whose recommendation has been approved.

Honorary Member
Must be a member who in the opinion of the Executive Committee through their past or continuing membership and contribution to the Association justifies retaining full privileges of membership as an Honorary Member.

Inactive Member
Shall have been a member for a continuous period of 10 years and no longer engaged in a direct or commercial capacity in the golf industry.

Retired Member
Shall be at least 60 years of age and been a member for a continuous period of 30 years.

Members may then proceed towards enhanced membership levels upon prior achievement and learning being recognised by the Association in the following categories:

Advanced Professional
Qualified members for a minimum of five years. Over a long period of time have demonstrated a strong desire to improve understanding and knowledge. Through attendance at courses, seminars and by taking qualifications related to golf, have shown commitment and willingness to develop self. Written articles and/or delivered seminars. Recognised by peers as having a high level of skill and knowledge, or qualified through the PGA Advanced Diploma programme.

Fellow Professional

Qualified members for a minimum of eight years. Consistently demonstrated an ability to work at a very high level with contribution to: development of players at different levels and/or a very strong reputation as an ethical business person who has established an extensive business that has benefited the golfing community and/or a strong reputation in equipment technology and/or repairs, which has enhanced the reputations of golf professionals and/or has written articles/books and presented at conferences, or has qualified through one of the PGA's Advanced Education programmes.

Advanced Fellow Professional

Qualified members for a minimum of ten years. Very strong national – possibly international reputation in one or more areas – coaching, course design, business, retail, equipment technology. Someone who has demonstrated strong leadership and has enhanced the world of golf and may have coached at the highest level or developed a programme method that has enabled ordinary players to play the game and/or designed a number of recognised golf courses and/or developed a strong golf business that has brought benefits to golf and golfers and/or innovative in the retail world with a strong sense of business ethics and/or designed/developed/improved some aspect of equipment (to include training aids or computer software) that has benefited a wide range of people in golf and/or a golf writer whose work has contributed strongly to the understanding and development of golf performance and/or a charity worker whose contribution has helped improve the lot of the disadvantaged through golf or in golf and/or written a number of books, articles and presented at prestigious conferences and seminars, or has qualified through one of the PGAís Advanced Education programmes.

Master Professional

Qualified member for a minimum of fifteen years. Held in high national or international esteem. Made a significant contribution to the development of golf as a player, coach, administrator or course designer. Someone who has left their mark at conferences and/or through books, articles or videos. Or an Advanced Fellow who has qualified as Master Professional through the submission of approved theses.

Tel 01675 470333   *Fax* 01675 477888

The Professional Golfers' Associations of Europe

The PGA of Europe was created in 1989 as an Association of national European PGAs to ensure uniformity of professional standards and objectives.

In its first ten years the PGAsE grew to a body comprising 33 member PGAs, five of them Associate Members from outside the continent of Europe. These 33 PGAs are made up of a total of 12,000 professionals comprising Directors of Golf, Club Professionals, Teaching Professionals, all of whom provide a comprehensive service to the entire golfing community.

The purpose of the PGAs of Europe is to:

(1) Unify and improve standards of education and qualification;

(2) Advise and assist golf professionals to achieve properly rewarded employment;

(3) Provide relevant playing opportunities;

(4) Be the central point of advice, information and support;

(5) Be a respected link with other golfing bodies throughout Europe and the rest of the world – all for the benefit of its members and the enhancement of the sport.

Tel 01675 477899

Fax 01675 4778980

European Tour

To be eligible to become a member of the European Tour a player must possess certain minimum standards which shall be determined by the Tournament Committee. In 1976 a Qualifying School for potential new members was introduced to be held annually. The leading players are awarded cards allowing them to compete in European Tour tournaments.

In 1985 the PGA European Tour became ALL EXEMPT with no more Monday pre-qualifying. Full details can be obtained from the Wentworth Headquarters.

Tel 01344 840400

Fax 01344 840444

Ladies' European Tour

The Ladies European Tour was founded in 1988 to further the development of women's professional golf throughout Europe and its membership is open to all nationalities. A qualifying school is held annually and an amateur wishing to participate must be 18 years of age and have a handicap of 1 or less. Full details can be obtained from the Tour Headquarters at Tytherington.

Tel 01625 611444

Fax 01625 610406

Governing Organisations – Amateur Golf

Home Unions

The English Golf Union

The English Golf Union was founded in 1924 and embraces 34 County Unions with 1895 affiliated clubs, 24 clubs overseas, and 500 Golfing Societies and Associations. Its objects are:

(1) To further the interests of Amateur Golf in England.

(2) To assist in maintaining a uniform system of handicapping.

(3) To arrange an English Championship; an English Strokeplay Championship; an English County Championship, International and other Matches and Competitions.

(4) To cooperate with The Royal and Ancient Golf Club of St Andrews and the Council of National Golf Unions.

(5) To cooperate with other National Golf Unions and Associations in such manner as may be decided.

Tel 01526 354500   *Fax* 01526 354020

The Scottish Golf Union

The Scottish Golf Union, the governing body for men's golf in Scotland, is dedicated to inspiring people to play golf and to developing and sustaining the game throughout the country. Its over-arching intention is to make golf available to everyone, in an environment that will actively encourage players to fulfil their potential.

Its aims are to:

- **Grow the game** – work with others to develop and grow golf in Scotland by increasing the number of people playing and enjoying golf

- **Develop talent** – ensure that the pathways to develop young talent are in place to produce excellent golfers at all levels

- **Support Clubs** – provide core services including handicapping, course rating, lobbying and training to improve the health and future success of member clubs.

The organisation is governed by a non executive board of directors who oversee the management of the organisation and an executive council, comprising representatives from 16 area associations, which provides the board with advice on policy matters.

Tel 01382 549500   *Fax* 01382 549510

Golfing Union of Ireland

The Golfing Union of Ireland, founded in 1891, embraces 398 Clubs. Its objects are:

(1) Securing the federation of the various Clubs.

(2) Arranging Amateur Championships, Inter-Provincial and Inter-Club Competitions, and International Matches.

(3) Securing a uniform standard of handicapping.

(4) Providing for advice and assistance, other than financial, to affiliated Clubs in all matters appertaining to Golf, and generally to promote the game in every way, in which this can be better done by the Union than by individual Clubs.

Its functions include the holding of the Close Championship for Amateur Golfers and Tournaments for Team Matches.

Its organisation consists of Provincial Councils in each of the four Provinces elected by the Clubs in the Province – each province electing a limited number of delegates to the Central Council which meets annually.

Tel 00 353 1 269411   *Fax* 00 353 1 693568

Welsh Golfing Union

The Welsh Golfing Union was founded in 1895 and is the second oldest of the four National Unions. Unlike the other Unions it is an association of Golf Clubs and Golfing Organisations. The present membership is 159. For the purpose of electing the Executive Council, Wales is divided into ten districts which between them return 22 members. The objects of the Union are:

(a) To take any steps which may be deemed necessary to further the interests of the amateur game in Wales.

(b) To hold a Championship Meeting or Meetings each year.

(c) To encourage, financially and/or otherwise, Inter-Club, Inter-County, and International Matches, and such other events as may be authorised by the Council.

(d) To assist in setting up and maintaining a uniform system of Handicapping.

(e) To assist in the establishment and maintenance of high standards of greenkeeping.

Note: The union recognises The Royal and Ancient Golf Club of St Andrews as the ruling authority.

Tel 01633 430830   *Fax* 01633 430843

The Council of National Golf Unions

At a meeting of Representatives of Golf Unions and Associations in Great Britain and Ireland, called at the special request of the Scottish Golf Union, and held in York, on 14th February, 1924, resolutions were adopted from which the Council of National Golf Unions was constituted.

The Council holds an Annual Meeting in March, and such other meetings as may be necessary. Two representatives are elected from each national Home Union – England, Scotland, Ireland and Wales and one from The Royal and Ancient Golf Club of St Andrews – and hold office until the next Annual meeting when they are eligible for re-election.

The principal function of the Council, as laid down by the York Conference, was to formulate a system of Standard Scratch Scores and Handicapping, and to co-operate with The Royal and Ancient Championship Committee in matters coming under their jurisdiction. The responsibilities undertaken by the Council at the instance of The Royal and Ancient Golf Club or the National Unions are as follows:

1 The Standard Scratch Score and Handicapping Scheme, formulated in March, 1926, approved by The Royal and Ancient, and last revised in 2001.
2 The nomination of one member on the Board of Management of The Sports Turf Research Institute, with an experimental station at St Ives, Bingley, Yorkshire.
3 The management of the Annual Amateur International Matches between the four countries – England, Scotland, Ireland and Wales.

Tel 00 353 416 861476

Government of the Amateur and Open Golf Championships

In December 1919, on the invitation of the clubs who had hitherto controlled the Amateur and Open Golf Championships, The Royal and Ancient Golf Club took over the government of those events. These two championships are now controlled by a committee appointed by The R&A.

Tel 01334 460000   *Fax* 01334 460001

European Golf Association
Association Européenne de Golf

Formed at a meeting held 20 November 1937 in Luxembourg, membership is restricted to European national amateur golf associations or unions. The Association concerns itself solely with matters of an international character. The association is presently composed of 30 member countries and is governed by the following committees:

• Executive Committee
• Championship Committee
• Professional Technical Committee
• EGA Handicapping & Course Rating Committee

Prime objectives are:

(a) To encourage international development of golf, to strengthen bonds of friendship existing between it members.
(b) To encourage the formation of new golf organisations representing the golf activities of European countries.
(c) To co-ordinate the dates of the Open and Amateur championships of its members and to arrange, in conjuction with host Federations, European championships and specific matches of international character.
(d) To ratify and publish the calendar dates of the major Amateur and Professional championships and international matches in Europe.
(e) To create and maintain international relationships in the field of golf and undertake any action useful to the cause of golf on an international level.

The headquarters are situated in Epalinges, Switzerland.

Ladies' Golf Union (LGU)

The Ladies' Golf Union was founded in 1893. Its objects are:

(1) To uphold the rules of golf, to advance and safeguard the interests of ladies' golf and to resolve any disputes related to the ladies' game;

(2) To employ the funds of the LGU in the best interests of ladies' golf, with power to borrow or raise money for the same purpose;

(3) To promote, maintain and regulate International Events, Championships and Competitions held under the LGU Regulations and to promote the interests of Great Britain and Ireland in ladies' international golf; and

(4) To maintain, enforce and publish such regulations as may be considered necessary for the above purposes.

Following a comprehensive review in 2007/08, the LGU has defined it strategic objectives as follows:

(1) To provide women and girls with opportunities to participate in the highest standard elite golf competitions;

(2) To achieve international success for Great Britain and Ireland women and girl golfers and teams;

(3) To increase awareness and raise the profile of women's and girls' golf through the Ricoh Women's British Open and other golf events;

(4) To provide a collective strong voice for, and represent the interests of, women's and girls' golf in partnership with the National Organisations for women's golf;

(5) To actively influence and drive equality in golf;

(6) To be operationally and financially sustainable.

Maureen Lockett, President of the Ladies' Golf Union

The constituents of the LGU are:

Home Countries. The English Women's Golf Association Ltd., the Irish Ladies' Golf Union Ltd., the Scottish Ladies' Golfing Association Ltd., the Golf Union of Wales Ltd., ladies' golf clubs and ladies' sections of recognised golf clubs affiliated to these organisations.

Overseas. Affiliated overseas ladies' golf unions, ladies' golf clubs and ladies' sections of recognised golf clubs affiliated to their respective Overseas Union and affiliated Overseas Clubs.

Annual playing lady members of clubs within the above categories are considered to be members of the LGU.

The Rules of Golf and of Amateur Status, which the LGU is bound to uphold, are those published by R&A Rules Limited.

In endeavouring to fulfil its responsibilities towards advancing and safeguarding women's golf, the LGU maintains contact with other golfing organisations – The R&A, the Council of National Golf Unions, the United States Golf Association, the European Golf Association, the Ladies' Professional Golf Association and the Ladies' European Tour. This contact enables the LGU to be informed of developments and projected developments and provides an opportunity to comment upon and to influence the future of the game for women.

Either directly or through its constituent national organisations, the LGU advises and is the ultimate authority on doubts or disputes which may arise in connection with the regulations governing competitions played under LGU conditions.

The funds of the LGU are administered on the authority of the Executive Council, and the accounts are submitted annually for adoption in General Meeting.

The Ricoh Women's British Open Championship, Ladies' British Open Amateur Championship, Ladies' British Open Amateur Stroke Play Championship, Girls' British Open Amateur Championship, Senior Ladies' British Open Amateur Championship and the three Home International matches are organised annually by the LGU. International events involving a Great Britain and Ireland team are organised and controlled by the LGU when held in this country and the LGU acts as the co-ordinating body for the 5 Nations Tournament in whichever of the five participating countries it is held, four-yearly, by rotation. The LGU selects and prepares the teams, provides the uniforms and pays the expenses of participation, whether held in this country or overseas. The LGU also maintains and regulates certain competitions played under handicap, such as the Peugeot Coronation Foursomes, the Challenge Bowls and the Australian Spoons, with the support of the National Organisations.

Membership subscriptions to the LGU are assessed on a per capita basis of a club's annual playing membership. They are collected by the National Organisations and forwarded to the LGU.

Policy is determined and control over the LGU's activities is exercised by an Executive Council of eight members – two each elected by the English, Irish, Scottish and Welsh national organisations. The Chairman is elected annually by the Councillors. During her chairmanship her place on the Council is taken by her Deputy and she has no vote other than a casting vote. The President and the Hon. Treasurer of the Union also attend and take part in Council meetings but with no vote. The Council meets five times a year.

The Annual General Meeting is held in January. The formal business includes presentation of the Financial & Executive Council's report for the previous year and the election or re-election of President, Vice-Presidents, Hon. Treasurer and Auditors, and a report of the election of Councillors and their Deputies for the ensuing year. Voting is on the following basis: Executive Council, one each (8); members in the four home countries, one per national organisation (4) and in addition one per 100 affiliated clubs or part thereof; one per overseas Commonwealth Union with a membership of 50 or more clubs, and one per 100 individually affiliated clubs.

The Rules of the Union and the regulations for British Championships, International Matches and other LGU competitions are published annually together with other useful information.

Tel 01334 475811   *Fax* 01334 472818

United States Golf Association

The USGA is the national governing body of golf in the United States, dedicated to promoting and conserving the best interests and true spirit of the game.

Founded on 22 December 1894 by representatives of five American golf clubs, the USGA was originally charged with conducting national championships, implementing a uniform code of rules, and maintaining a national system of handicapping.

Today, the principal functions of the association remain lagely unchanged. Each year, the USGA conducts thirteen national championships for amateur and professional golfers; biennial competitions include State Team Championships for men and women, the Walker Cup, Curtis Cup, and World Amateur Team Championships. In cooperation with the Royal & Ancient Golf Club of St. Andrews, Scotland, the USGA continues to write and interpret the Rules of Golf, and oversees the standards regulating the equipment used to play the game. The association also maintains a national handicapping system, providing handicap computation services to state and regional golf associations through the Golf Handicap and Information Network.

Additional responsibilities assumed by the association encompass turfgrass and environmental research conducted by the USGA Green Section; preservation and promotion of the game's rich history in the Museum and Archives; oversight of the Rules of Amateur Status; publication of *Golf Journal*, the USGA's official magazine; and direction of the USGA Members Program, with over 900,000 members globally. Since 1965, the USGA Foundation has functioned as the association's broad-based philanthropic arm, dedicated to maintaining and improving the opportunities for all individuals to participate fully in the game.

Tel 001 908 234 2300   *Fax* 001 908 234 9687

Major Championship and International Conditions

UK CHAMPIONSHIPS

Men

Amateur Championship

The Championship, until 1982, was decided entirely by match play over 18 holes except for the final which was over 36 holes. Since 1983 the Championship has comprised two stroke play rounds of 18 holes each from which the leading 64 players and ties over the 36 holes qualify for the match play stages. Matches are over 18 holes except for the final which is over 36 holes. Full particulars can be obtained from the Entries Department, R&A, St Andrews, Fife KY16 9JD. Tel: 01334 460000; Fax 01334 460005; e-mail entries@randa.org

Seniors Open Amateur Championship

The Championship consists of 18 holes on each of two days, the leading 60 players and ties over the 36 holes then playing a further 18 holes the following day. Entrants must have attained the age of 55 years prior to the first day of the Championship. Full particulars can be obtained from the Entries Department, R&A, St Andrews, Fife KY16 9JD. Tel 01344 460000; fax 01334 460005; e-mail entries@randa.org

National Championships

The English, Irish, Scottish and Welsh Amateur Championships are played by holes, each match consisting of one round of 18 holes except the final which is contested over 36 holes. Only the English Golf Union hold a 36-hole qualifier for their event. Full particulars of conditions of entry and method of play can be obtained from the secretaries of the respective national Unions.

English Open Amateur Stroke Play Championship (The Brabazon)

The Championship consists of one round of 18 holes on each of two days after which the leading 40 and those tying for 40th place play a further two rounds. The remainder are eliminated.

Conditions for entry include: entrants must have a handicap not exceeding one; where the entries exceed 130, an 18-hole qualifying round is held the day before the Championship. Certain players are exempt from qualifying.

Full particulars of conditions of entry and method of play can be obtained from the Secretary, English Golf Union, National Golf Centre, The Broadway, Woodhall Spa, Lincs LN10 6PU. Tel: 01526 354500; Fax: 01526 354020.

Scottish Open Amateur Stroke Play Championship

The Championship consists of one round of 18 holes on each of two days after which the leading 40 and those tying for 40th place play a further two rounds. The remainder are eliminated. Full particulars of conditions of entry and method of play can be obtained from the the from the Events Department of the Scottish Golf Union, The Duke's, St Andrews, Fife KY16 8NX. Tel: 01334 466477; Fax: 01334 466361.

Boys

Boys Amateur Championship

The Championship is played by match play, each match including the final 36 holes consisting of one round of 18 holes. Entrants must be under 18 years of age at 00.00 hours on 1st January in the year of the Championship. Full particulars can be obtained from the Entries Department, R&A, St Andrews, Fife KY16 9JD. Tel: 01334 460000; Fax: 01334 460005

Ladies

Ladies' British Open Amateur Championship

The Championship consists of one 18-hole qualifying round on each of two days. The players returning the 64 lowest scores over 36 holes shall qualify for match play. Ties for 64th place shall be decided by hole-by-hole play-off.

Ladies' British Open Amateur Stroke Play Championship

The Championship consists of 72 holes stroke play; 18 holes are played on each of two days after which the first 40 and all ties for 40th place qualify for a further 36 holes on the third day. Handicap limit is 6.4.

Ricoh Women's British Open Championship

The Ricoh Women's British Open is a designated major in ladies' professional golf and is the only such major played outside the USA. Owned by the Ladies' Golf Union, the championship consists of 72 holes stroke play. 18 holes are played on each of four days, the field being reduced after the first 36 holes. Certain categories of players gain automatic entry to the championship because of past performance in the Ricoh Women's British Open or from current performance in the Rolex Rankings and the LET, LPGA and JLPGA money lists. Those not automatically exempt can gain entry through pre-qualifying and final qualifying competitions.

Full particulars of the above three championships can be obtained from the Ladies' Golf Union, The Scores, St Andrews, Fife KY16 9AT.

Tel: 01334 475811; Fax: 01334 472818.

National Championships

Conditions of entry and method of play for the English, Scottish, Welsh and Irish Ladies' Close Championships can be obtained from the Registered Offices of the respective associations.

Other championships organised by the respective national associations, from whom full particulars can be obtained, include English Ladies', Intermediate, English Ladies' Stroke Play, Scottish Girls' Open Amateur Stroke Play (under 21) and Welsh Ladies' Open Amateur Stroke Play.

Girls

Girls' British Open Amateur Championship

The Championship consists of two 18-hole qualifying rounds, followed by match play in two flights, the first of 32 and the second of 16 players.

Conditions of entry include:

Entrants must be under 18 years of age on the 1st January in the year of the Championship.

Competitors are required to hold a certified LGU international handicap not exceeding 12.4.

Full particulars can be obtained from the Administrator, LGU, The Scores, St Andrews, Fife KY16 9AT. Tel: 01334 475811; Fax: 01334 472818.

National Championships

The English, Scottish, Irish and Welsh Girls' Close Championships are open to all girls of relevant nationality and appropriate age which may vary from country to country. A handicap limit may be set by some countries. Full particulars can be obtained via the secretaries of the respective associations.

EUROPEAN CHAMPIONSHIPS

Founded in 1986 by the European Golf Association, the International Amateur and Ladies Amateur Championships are held on an annual basis since 1990. These Championships consist of one round of 18 holes on each of three days after which the leading 70 and those tying for 70th place play one further round.

Full particulars of conditions of entry and method of play can be obtained from the European Golf Association.

Since 1991, the European Golf Association also holds an International Mid-Amateur Championship on an annual basis. The Championship consist of one round of 18 holes on each of two days after which the leading 90 and those tying for 90th place play one further round.

Full particulars of conditions of entry and method of play can be obtained from the European Golf Association.

Since 1996, the European Golf Association holds an International Seniors Championship for ladies and men on an annual basis.

The Championship consists of one round of 18 holes on each of two days after which there is a cut in both ladies and men categories. The competitors who pass the cut play one further round.

Additionally, a nation's cup is played within the tournament on the first two days. Teams are composed of three players. The two best gross scores out of three will count each day. The total aggregate of the four scores over two days will constitute the team's score.

Full particulars of conditions of entry and method of play can be obtained from the European Golf Association, Place de la Croix-Blanche 19, PO Box CH-1066 Epilanges, Switzerland. Tel: +41 21 784 32 32; Fax: +412 1 784 35 91.

TEAM CHAMPIONSHIPS

Men's Amateur

Walker Cup – Great Britain and Ireland v United States of America

Mr George Herbert Walker of the United States presented a Cup for international competition to be known as *The United States Golf Association International Challenge Trophy*, popularly described as *The Walker Cup.*

The Cup shall be played for by teams of amateur golfers selected from Clubs under the jurisdiction of the United States Golf Association on the one side and from England, Ireland, Scotland and Wales on the other.

The Walker Cup shall be held every two years in the United States of America and Great Britain and Ireland alternately.

The teams shall consist of not more than ten players and a captain.

The contest consists of four foursomes and eight singles matches over 18 holes on each of two days.

St Andrews Trophy – Great Britain and Ireland v Continent of Europe

First staged in 1956, the St Andrews Trophy is a biennial international match played between two selected teams of amateur golfers representing Great Britain and Ireland and the Continent of Europe. Each team consists of nine players and the match is played over two consecutive days with four morning foursomes followed each afternoon by eight singles. Selection of the Great Britain and Ireland team is carried out by the R&A Selection Committee. The European Golf Association select the Continent of Europe team.

Eisenhower Trophy – Men's World Team Championship

Founded in recognition of the need for an official world amateur team championship, the first event was played at St Andrews in 1958 and the Trophy has been played for every second year in different countries around the world.

Each country enters a team of four players who play strokeplay over 72 holes, the total of the three best individual scores to be counted for each round.

European Team Championship

Founded in 1959 by the European Golf Association for competition among member countries of the Association. The Championship has recently been changed to be played on an annual basis and played in rotation round the countries, which are grouped in four geographical zones.

Each team consists of six players who play two qualifying rounds of 18 holes, the five best scores of each round constituting the team aggregate. Flights for match play are then arranged according to qualifying rankings. The match play consists of two foursomes and five singles on each of three days.

A similar championship is held in alternate years for Youths teams, under 21 years of age and every year for Boys teams, under 18 years of age.

Raymond Trophy – Home Internationals

The first official International Match recorded was in 1902 at Hoylake between England and Scotland who won 32 to 25 on a holes up basis.

In 1932 International Week was inaugurated under the auspices of the British Golf Unions' Joint Advisory Council with the full approval of the four National Golf Unions who are now responsible for running the matches. Teams of 11 players from England, Ireland, Scotland and Wales engage in matches consisting of five foursomes and ten singles over 18 holes, the foursomes being in the morning and the singles in the afternoon. Each team plays every other team.

The eligibility of players to play for their country shall be their eligibility to play in the Amateur Championship of their country.

Sir Michael Bonallack Trophy – Europe v Asia /Pacific

First staged in 1998, the Sir Michael Bonallack Trophy is a biennial international match played between two selected teams of amateur golfers representing Europe and Asia/Pacific. Each team consists of 12 players and the match is played over three days with five four balls in the morning and five foursomes in the afternoon of the first two days, followed by 12 singles on the last day. Selection of the European team is carried out by the European Golf Association. The Asia/Pacific Golf Confederation selects the Asia/Pacific team.

Men's Professional

Ryder Cup – Europe v United States of America

This Cup was presented by Mr Samuel Ryder, St Albans, England (who died 2nd January, 1936), for competition between a team of British professionals and a team of American professionals. The trophy was first competed for in 1927. In 1929 the original conditions were varied to confine the British team to British-born professionals resident in Great Britain, and the American team to American-born professionals resident in the United States, in the year of the match. In 1979 the British team was extended to include European players. The matches are played biennially, in alternate continents, in accordance with the conditions as agreed between the respective PGAs.

World Cup

Founded in America by John Jay Hopkins in 1955 as a team event for professional golfers with the object of spreading international goodwill. Each country is represented by two players with the best team score over 72 holes producing the winners of the World Cup and the best individual score the winner of the International Trophy. Played for annually (but not in 1986) the event was run until 1999 by the International Golf Association. It then became part of the new World Championship series of events. Formerly known as the Canada Cup it is now run separately by the various world golf tours. The 2007 event was staged at Mission Hills, Shenzhen, China, where it will be staged for the next 11 years

Seve Ballesteros Trophy – Great Britain and Ireland v Continent of Europe

A match instituted in 2000 at Sunningdale and played along Ryder Cup lines in alternate years.

Llandudno Trophy (PGA Cup) – Great Britain and Ireland v United States of America

The Llandudno International Trophy was first awarded to England in 1939 after winning the first Home Tournament Series against Ireland, Scotland and Wales. With the outbreak of war the series was abolished and the Trophy formed part of Percy Alliss's personal collection. After Percy's death his son Peter donated the Llandudno Trophy to be awarded to the winner of the then annual PGA Cup Match. Now it is a biennial match played since 1973 in Ryder Cup format between Great Britain and Ireland and the United States of America involving top club professionals. No prize money is awarded to the competitors who compete solely for their country. Selection of the Great Britain and Ireland team is determined following completion of the Glenmuir PGA Club Professionals Championship.

Ladies Amateur

Curtis Cup – Great Britain and Ireland v United States

For a trophy presented by the late Misses Margaret and Harriot Curtis of Boston, USA, for biennial competition between amateur teams from the United States of America and Great Britain and Ireland. The match is sponsored jointly by the United States Golf Association and the Ladies' Golf Union who may select teams of not more than eight players.

The match, held over three days, consists of three foursomes and three four-ball matches on each of the first two days and eight singles of 18 holes on the final day.

Vagliano Trophy – Great Britain and Ireland v Continent of Europe

For a trophy presented to the Comité des Dames de la Fédération Française de Golf and the Ladies' Golf Union by Monsieur AA Vagliano, originally for annual competition between teams of women amateur golfers from France and Great Britain and Ireland but, since 1959, by mutual agreement, for competition between teams from the Continent of Europe and Great Britain and Ireland.

The match is played biennially, alternately in Great Britain and Ireland and on the Continent of Europe, with teams of not more than nine players plus a non-playing captain. The match consists of four foursomes and eight singles of 18 holes on each of two days. The foursomes are played each morning.

Espirito Santo Trophy – Women's World Team Championship

Presented by Mrs Ricardo Santo of Portugal for biennial competition between teams of not more than three women amateur golfers who represent a national association affiliated to the World Amateur Golf Council. First competed for in 1964. The Championship consists of 72 holes strokeplay, 18 holes on each of four days, the two best scores in each round constituting the team aggregate.

Lady Astor Trophy – Five Nations Tournament (formerly Commonwealth Tournament)

For a trophy presented by Nancy, Viscountess Astor CH, and the Ladies' Golf Union for competition once in every four years between teams of women amateur golfers from Commonwealth countries.

The inaugural Commonwealth Tournament was played at St Andrews in 1959 between teams from Australia, Canada, New Zealand, South Africa and Great Britain and was won by the British team. The tournament is played in rotation in the competing countries, Great Britain, Australia, Canada, New Zealand and South Africa, each country being entitled to nominate six players including a playing or non-playing captain. In 2011, a Great Britain and Ireland team will compete for the first time.

Each team plays every other team and each team match consists of two foursomes and four singles over 18 holes. The foursomes are played in the morning.

European Team Championships

Founded in 1959 by the European Golf Association for competition among member countries of the Association. The Championship is held annually and played in rotation round the countries, which are grouped in four geographical zones.

Each team consists of six players who play two qualifying rounds of 18 holes, the five best scores of each round constituting the team aggregate. Flights for matchplay are then arranged according to qualifying rankings. The matchplay consists of two foursomes and five singles on each of three days.

A similar championship is held in alternate years for Lady Juniors teams, under 21 years of age and every year for Girls teams, under 18 years of age.

Home Internationals

Teams from England, Scotland, Ireland and Wales compete annually for a trophy presented to the LGU by the late Mr TH Miller. The qualifications for a player being eligible to play for her country are the same as those laid down by each country for its Close Championship.

Each team, consisting of not more than eight players, plays each other team, a draw taking place to decide the order of play between the teams. The matches consist of three foursomes and six singles, each of 18 holes.

Ladies Professional

Solheim Cup – Europe v United States

The Solheim Cup, named after Karsten Solheim who founded the sponsoring Ping company, is the women's equivalent of the Ryder Cup. In 1990 the inaugural competition between the top women professional golfers from Europe and America took place in Florida.

The matches are played biennially in alternate continents. The format is foursomes and fourball matches on the first two days, followed by singles on the third in accordance with the conditions as agreed between the Ladies European Tour and the United States LPGA Tour.

World Cup

Started in 2000 by the LPGA and the International Management Group, the event is held along similar lines to the men's World Cup with each country represented by two players. There is also an individual competiton incorporated in the regulations. It had been planned as an annual fixture but after the inaugural event held in Malaysia the 2001 Championship scheduled for Adelaide was cancelled. The event was restarted in South Africa in 2004.

Boys

R & A Trophy – Home Internationals

Teams comprising 11 players from England, Scotland, Ireland and Wales compete against one another over three days in a single round robin format. Each fixture comprises five morning foursomes followed by ten afternoon singles.

To be eligible for selection, players must be under the age of 18 at 00.00 hours on 1st January in the year of the matches and have eligibility to play in their national championships

Jacques Léglise Trophy – Great Britain and Ireland v Continent of Europe

The Jacques Léglise Trophy is an annual international match played between two selected teams of amateur boy golfers representing Great Britain and Ireland and the Continent of Europe. Each team consists of nine players and the match is played over two consecutive days with four morning foursomes followed each afternoon by eight singles. Selection of the Great Britain and Ireland team is carried out by the R&A Selection Committee. The European Golf Association selects the Continent of Europe team

To be eligible for selection, players must be under the age of 18 at 00.00 hours on 1st January in the year of the matches.

Junior Ryder Cup

First staged in 1995, the Junior Ryder Cup is a biennial international match played between two selected teams of amateur golfers representing Europe and the USA, prior to the Ryder Cup. Each team consists of four girls and four boys under 16 as well as two girls and two boys under 18. The match is played over two consecutive days with six four balls on the first day and six mixed four balls on the second day.

Selection of the European team is carried out by the European Golf Association. Players and captains are then invited to watch the Ryder Cup.

Girls

Home Internationals

Teams from England, Ireland, Scotland and Wales compete annually for the Stroyan Cup. The qualifications for a player for the Girls' International Matches shall be the same as those laid down by each country for its Girls' Close Championship except that a player shall be under 18 years on the 1st January in the year of the Tournament.

Each team, consisting of not more than eight players, plays each other team, a draw taking place to decide the order of play between the teams. The matches consist of three foursomes and six singles, each of 18 holes.

PART XIV

Golf History

R&A Championships and Team Events

In 2004, The Royal and Ancient Golf Club of St Andrews devolved responsibility for the running of The Open Championship and other key golfing events to The R&A. The history of championships and team events organised by The R&A and by The R&A and other golfing bodies are outlined below. Current championship and match conditions are defined elsewhere in the volume.

Championships solely under the administration of The R&A:
The Open Championship
The Amateur Championship
The Seniors Open Amateur Championship
The Boys Amateur Championship
The Junior Open Championship

Team events organised by The R&A:
The Boys Home Internationals

Team events organised by The R&A and other golfing bodies:
The Walker Cup (R&A/USGA)
The World Amateur Team Championships (R&A as part of the International Golf Federation)
The St Andrews Trophy (R&A/EGA)
The Jacques Léglise Trophy (R&A/EGA)
The Senior Open Championship

The Open Championship

The Open Championship began in 1860 at the Prestwick Golf Club and the original trophy was an ornate Challenge Belt, which was subscribed for and presented by the members of Prestwick Golf Club. What is now recognised as the first Open Championship was played on October 17, 1860 at the end of the club's autumn meeting. A total of eight players competed in three rounds of the 12 hole course. No prize money for The Open was awarded until 1863, the winner simply received the Belt for a year. In 1863 it was decided to give money prizes to those finishing second, third and fourth but the winner still only received the Belt. It was not until 1864 that the winner received £6. The average field in the 1860s was only 12 players.

The original rules of the competition stated that the Belt "becomes the property of the winner by being won three years in succession". In 1870 Tom Morris Junior won for the third year in a row and took possession of the Belt. He won £6 for his efforts out of a total prize fund of £12. No Championship was held in 1871 whilst the Prestwick Club entered into discussions with The Royal and Ancient Golf

Club and the Honourable Company of Edinburgh Golfers over the future of the event.

One of the key turning points in the history of The Open took place at the Spring Meeting of the Prestwick Club in April 1871. At that meeting it was proposed that "in contemplation of St Andrews, Musselburgh and other clubs joining in the purchase of a Belt to be played for over four or more greens, it is not expedient for the Club to provide a Belt to be played solely for at Prestwick". From that date onwards, The Open ceased to be under the sole control of the Prestwick Golf Club.

The Championship was played again under this new agreement in 1872. A new trophy, the now famous Claret Jug, was purchased for presentation to the winner. Until 1891, the host club remained responsible for all arrangements regarding the Championship, which continued to be played over 36 holes in one day.

In 1892, the Honourable Company of Edinburgh Golfers took four radical steps to transform The Open Championship. It extended play to 72 holes over two days, imposed an entrance charge for all competitors, changed the venue to a new course at Muirfield and increased the total prize fund from £28 10s to £100. These actions were all taken unilaterally by the club. The increased purse to counter a rival tournament held at Musselburgh.

A meeting was held between the three host clubs on June 9, 1893, for the purpose of "placing the competition for The Open Championship on a basis more commensurate with its importance than had hitherto existed". Three resolutions were agreed. Two English clubs, St George's, Sandwich and Royal Liverpool, would be invited to stage the Championship and join the rota, now of five clubs. Four rounds of 18 holes would be played over two days. Each of the five clubs would contribute £15 annually to the cost and the balance would come from an entry fee for all competitors. The prize money would total £100, with £30 for the winner. The date of each year's championship would be set by the host club, which would also bear any additional necessary expenses. The representatives of the five clubs became known as the Delegates of the Associated Clubs.

The increasing number of entrants caused a cut to be introduced after two rounds in 1898 and between 1904 and 1906 the Championship was played over three days. It then reverted to two days in 1907 with the introduction of qualifying rounds. The entire field had to qualify and there were no exemptions.

On January 24, 1920, the Delegates of the Associated Clubs asked The Royal and Ancient Golf Club to take over "the management of the Championship and the custody of the Challenge Cup". The new Championship Committee was responsible for running both The Open and Amateur Championships and in 1922 it was decided that The Open should only be played over links courses. The venues included in today's circuit are: Carnoustie, Muirfield, Royal Birkdale, Royal Liverpool, Royal Lytham & St Annes, Royal St George's, Royal Troon, the Old Course, St Andrews and Turnberry.

Prestwick, birth place of The Open, played host to the Championship 24 times, the last in 1925. Other courses that have been used in the past are: Musselburgh (1874, 1877, 1880, 1883, 1886, 1889); Royal Cinque Ports, Deal (1909, 1920); Princes, Sandwich (1932) and Royal Portrush (1951).

The Open was played regularly over three days starting in 1926, with a round on each of the first two days and two rounds on the final day, which from 1927 onwards was a Friday. The total prize money had reached £500 by 1939. The prize money was increased to £1000 in 1946 and reached £5000 in 1959.

As The Open went into its second century in the 1960s, it grew tremendously both as a Championship and a spectator event. In 1963, exemptions from pre-qualifying were introduced for the leading players. Play was extended to four days in 1966, with the Championship finishing with a single round on the Saturday. In 1968, a second cut after 54 holes was introduced to further reduce the field on the final day and this remained in effect until 1985. To cope with the increasing spectator numbers, facilities were much improved. Grandstands were first introduced at The Open in 1960 and they became a standard feature from 1963 onwards.

Regional qualifying had been tried as an experiment for one year in 1926, but did not become a regular feature until 1977. Some players were exempt but had to take part in final qualifying, while others were exempt from both regional and final qualifying. In 2004, International Final Qualifying was introduced, enabling players around the world to qualify on five different Continents.

Since 1980, the Championship has been scheduled to end on a Sunday instead of a Saturday. In the event of a tie for first place, play-offs took place over 36 holes up until 1963, when they were reduced to 18 holes. In 1985 a four-hole play-off, followed by sudden death, was introduced.

The Open Championship was first televised live in 1955 and was shown on the BBC. In 1958, the television coverage lasted for a total of three hours, one and a half hours on each of the final two days. In 2008, the total coverage was 2,214 hours worldwide, of which 62% was live.

Admission charges to watch The Open were introduced in 1926. Paid admissions went over 50,000 for the first time in 1968 at Carnoustie and over 100,000 for the first time at St Andrews in 1978. The 200,000 attendance figure was reached for the

first time at St Andrews in 1990. A new record was set at the Home of Golf in 2000 when 238,787 watched the Millennium Open.

Growth of prize money

Year	Total Prize Money	First Prize
1860	£0	£0
1863	£10	£0
1868	£12	£6
1878	£20	£8
1888	£24	£8
1898	£90	£10
1908	£115	£50
1914	£125	£50
1920	£200	£75
1928	£250	£75
1938	£500	£100
1948	£1,000	£150
1958	£4,850	£1,000
1968	£20,000	£3,000
1978	£125,000	£12,500
1988	£700,000	£80,000
1998	£1,800,000	£300,000
2008	£4,200,000	£750,000

Harry Vardon has scored most victories in The Open Championship. He won it six times between 1896 and 1914. JH Taylor, James Braid, Peter Thomson and Tom Watson have each won The Open five times. Between 1860 and 1889, all of The Open winners were Scottish. John Ball Jr became the first Englishman and the first amateur to claim the title in 1890. Arnaud Massy from France was the first Continental winner in 1907.

Four players have completed a hat trick of Open wins: Tom Morris Jr 1868–1870; Jamie Anderson 1877–1879; Bob Ferguson 1880–1882; Peter Thomson 1954–1956.

The Open Championship has been won by an amateur player six times – John Ball in 1890, Harold Hilton in 1892 and 1897 and Bobby Jones in 1926, 1927 and 1930. Walter Hagen was the first native born American to win The Open when he triumphed in 1922. Jock Hutchison, who had won the previous year, was resident in America at the time of his victory although he was born in St Andrews.

The Amateur Championship

What became recognised as the first Amateur Championship was held at Hoylake in 1885, although earlier national amateur competitions had been played at St Andrews in 1857, 1858 and 1859. The Royal and Ancient Golf Club had considered holding a national amateur tournament in 1876 but decided not to proceed with the idea.

In December 1884, Thomas Owen Potter, the Secretary of Royal Liverpool Golf Club, proposed holding a championship for amateur players. The event was to be open to members of recognised clubs and it was hoped that it would make the game more popular and lead to improved standards of play.

A total of 44 players from 12 clubs entered the first championship. The format was matchplay, with the ruling that if two players tied they would both advance to the following round and play one another again. There were three semi-finalists: John Ball, Horace Hutchinson and Allan Macfie. After a bye to the final, Macfie beat Hutchinson 7 and 6.

Following the success of the first tournament, it was agreed that a championship open to all amateurs should be played at St Andrews, Hoylake and Prestwick in rotation.

Twenty-four golf clubs subscribed for the trophy, which was acquired in 1886. They were:

Alnmouth	Royal Aberdeen
Bruntsfield	Royal Albert (Montrose)
Dalhousie	Royal and Ancient
Formby	Royal Blackheath
Gullane	Royal Burgess
Honourable Company	Royal Liverpool
Innerleven	Royal North Devon
Kilspindie	Royal St George's
King James VI	Royal Wimbledon
North Berwick New	Tantallon
Panmure	Troon
Prestwick	West Lancashire

Representatives, known as Delegates of the Associated Clubs, were elected from these clubs to run the Championship and in 1919 they approached The Royal and Ancient Golf Club to accept future management. The Club agreed and in 1920 the Championship Committee was formed. This committee became responsible for organising the Amateur and Open and for making decisions on the conditions of play. It was not until 1922, however, that the 1885 tournament was officially recognised as the first Amateur Championship and Allan Macfie the first winner.

The venue circuit gradually increased. Sandwich was added in 1892, Muirfield in 1897 and Westward Ho! in 1912. The Championship was first played in Ireland in 1949 (Portmarnock) and Wales in 1951 (Porthcawl).

Prior to 1930, only two non-British players won the Amateur Championship title, Walter Travis, in 1904, and Jesse Sweetser, in 1926. Both hailed from the United States, the former via Australia.

The Americans began to make their presence felt more strongly in the 1930s, with four Americans winning five Amateur Championships. Bobby Jones took the title at St Andrews 1930, the year in which he achieved the Grand Slam. Lawson Little won in 1934 and 1935, Robert Sweeney in 1937 and Charles Yates in 1938.

Following a break during World War II, the Amateur Championship resumed in 1946 at Birkdale when the handicap limit was raised from one to two as an encouragement to those amateurs who had been on war service.

Attempts were made during the 1950s and 1960s to control large numbers of entries. In 1956 the field was limited to 200 so that the quarter-finals, semi-finals and the final could be played over 36 holes. This experiment lasted two years, when it was decided

that only the semi-finals and final should be played over two rounds.

Regional qualifying over 36 holes was introduced in 1958 when 14 courses throughout the UK were selected. Using this method, the original entry of 500 was reduced to 200. Any player with a handicap of 5 or better could enter.

In 1961 regional qualifying was scrapped and the quarter-finals and semi-finals were played over 18 holes. Then in 1983 at Turnberry, 36 holes of stroke-play qualifying were introduced during the first two days. This format continues, with the leading 64 players and ties qualifying for the matchplay stages.

The Senior Open Championship

The Senior Open Championship has been part of the European Seniors Tour since 1987, and in 2003 was added to the Champions Tour as one of the five major world events in senior golf. The European Seniors Tour jointly administers the event alongside The R&A. Previous winners include former Open champions Gary Player, Bob Charles and Tom Watson.

The Seniors Open Amateur Championship

The Seniors Open Amateur Championship was the first tournament to be initiated by The Royal and Ancient Golf Club. Prestwick Golf Club had been responsible for starting the Open Championship, while Royal Liverpool Golf Club had introduced the Amateur Championship. Other events, such as the Boys Amateur Championship and Boys Home Internationals were introduced by private individuals and then handed over, by agreement, to The R&A.

The Seniors Open Amateur Championship made its début in 1969. It started as a means to help choose a Great Britain and Ireland team for the World Senior Amateur Team Championship which had begun in 1967 at Pinehurst, North Carolina, under the auspices of the World Amateur Golf Council.

Initially, the World Senior team event was to be played every two years, alternating with the competition for the Eisenhower Trophy, but it did not survive beyond 1969. The success of the Seniors Open Amateur Championship, however, was evident from the start and it became a popular event in its own right.

It began as a 36-hole strokeplay event, held over two days for players over the age of 55. The handicap limit was 5 and the field was restricted to 100. The winner was Reg Pattinson, who duly played his way onto the World Amateur Senior team in which he was partnered by Alan Cave, AL Bentley and AT Kyle. The short-lived World Senior event was played in 1969 over the Old Course at St Andrews and was won for the second time by the United States. Great Britain and Ireland finished third out of an entry of only 13 teams.

Before the present format was introduced, various alternatives were tried, in order to satisfy increasing entry demands. Two courses were used in 1971, allowing an entry of 250 with the handicap limit being increased to 9. In 1974, a limit of 130 was imposed. Subsidiary competitions were introduced according to age group: 55–59, 60–64 and 65 and over. A fourth age group was added in 1975 for the over 70s and the entry limit was increased to 140. The special categories changed in 1999, to one only for the 65 and over age group.

Today, the Seniors Open Amateur Championship attracts a wide international field, the initial entry of 252 playing two rounds and the leading 50 and ties completing a further 18 holes. Scotland's Charlie Green is a multiple winner, having claimed the title six times between 1988 and 1994.

The Boys Amateur Championship

The Boys Amateur Championship was introduced in 1921 for the under-16 age group. For the first two years it was played at Royal Ascot under the guidance of DM Mathieson and Colonel Thomas South. In 1948, Colonel South announced his intention to retire from his duties in connection with the event, declaring that "nothing would give him greater pleasure than that The Royal and Ancient Golf Club should take over the conduct of the Championship".

The venue for the first Boys Amateur Championship to be played under the administration of The Royal and Ancient Golf Club was the Old Course, St Andrews. A sub-committee ran the event until 1952 when it was finally handed over to the Championship Committee.

Since that year a prize has been presented to the best performing 16-year-old. This, the Peter Garner Bowl, commemorates the death of a competitor who was killed in a road accident while returning from the 1951 Championship.

Sir Michael Bonallack enjoyed early success in the Boys Amateur Championship. He won in 1952, and went on to win the Amateur Championship in 1961, 1965, 1968, 1969 and 1970.

Professionals who won the title earlier in their careers include Ronan Rafferty (1979), José Maria Olazábal (1983) and more recently Sergio García (1997).

The Junior Open Championship

Inaugurated in 1994, the Junior Open Championship came under The R&A's administrative control in 2000. All national golf unions and federations are invited to send their leading boy and girl under the age of 16 to compete in the three-day event. In previous years, only one player from each union or federation could enter. The biennial event is run on a course close to The Open Championship and in the same week so that all participants can spend time watching the world's finest players in action.

To encourage entries worldwide, there are three categories of competition defined by varying handicap limits. Gold is for those with a handicap of 3 and under, silver 4–9 and bronze 10–21.

TEAM EVENTS

The Walker Cup

The United States Golf Association International Challenge Trophy was originally intended to be presented to the winners of a contest to which all golf playing nations would be invited to compete. However, as The R&A tactfully pointed out to their counterparts in the USGA in 1921, the only two countries capable of entering a team were Great Britain and America.

By this simple process of elimination the trophy presented by USGA President George Herbert Walker became the focal point of a biennial series between the finest amateur players of the two countries. The first unofficial match was played in 1921 on the eve of the Amateur Championship at Hoylake when 19-year-old Bobby Jones helped the American team to a 9–3 victory. For the next three years the event was played annually, but settled into its biennial pattern after 1924.

It was not until 1938 at St Andrews that Great Britain and Ireland recorded a first victory. In 1965 the score was 11–11. There were 2 halved matches.

Only after the first success in America, with a 12½–11½ victory at Peachtree in Georgia in 1989, did the GB&I team finally end American domination of matches. In the years that followed there were home wins at Porthcawl in 1995 and Nairn in 1999. The GB&I run of victories continued at Ocean Forest in 2001 and Ganton in 2003.

The man after whom the trophy and the matches are named has another claim to a place in world history. His grandson, George Herbert Walker Bush and his great-grandson have both held office as President of the United States of America.

The Eisenhower Trophy

The United States Golf Association approached The Royal and Ancient Golf Club in 1958 with the proposal that the two bodies should sponsor a worldwide amateur golf event. The new competition would take place biennially in non-Walker Cup years, with the first being played at St Andrews in 1958. All golfing bodies that observed the Rules of Golf and Amateur Status as approved by The R&A and the USGA were invited to send one representative to a meeting in Washington at which President Dwight D Eisenhower presented a trophy to be awarded to the winning country. The committee of the event was to be known as the World Amateur Golf Council, which is now the International Golf Federation.

The key objective of the new council was "to foster friendship and sportsmanship among the peoples of the world through the conduct of an Amateur Team Championship for The Eisenhower Trophy". In a meeting with the President in the Rose Garden of the White House, Eisenhower offered his advice to the delegates: "I suggest, aside from the four hotshot golfers you bring, that you take along some high-handicap fellows and let them play at their full handicaps ... This way golf doesn't become so important". This observation led to the creation of a "Delegates and Duffers Cup" for officials and non-playing captains.

The format decided for the Eisenhower Trophy was strokeplay. Each team consisted of four players who would play four rounds. The team score for each round was the three best individual scores. The first competition was held in St Andrews and attracted teams from 29 countries. After 72 holes of golf, the American and Australian teams were both tied on an aggregate score of 918. A play-off was held and the Australian team won by two strokes. So far this has been the only play-off in the history of the event.

Australia went on to win the trophy twice more, in 1966 and 1996. However, the USA have dominated the event, winning it 13 times in total. The Great Britain and Ireland team have won four times, in 1964, 1976, 1988 and 1998. In 2002 teams were reduced from four to three players with the best two scores counting in each round and for the first time England, Ireland, Scotland and Wales entered separate teams. In 2008, Scotland claimed its first victory in the Eisenhower Trophy at the Royal Adelaide Golf Club, Australia. Fifty years after the Australians won the first Championship at the Old Course in St Andrews, the Scots took the Trophy home from Australia. A parallel event for women, playing for the Espirito Santo Trophy, is held at the same venue prior to the Eisenhower.

The St Andrews Trophy

In November 1955 the Championship Committee of The Royal and Ancient Golf Club put forward a recommendation that "the European Golf Association should be approached with a view to arranging an international match between a Great Britain and Ireland and European side".

The GB&I team, captained by Gerald Micklem, duly triumphed by a score of 12½ to 2½ in the first match played over the West Course at Wentworth in 1956. A resounding success, it was immediately established as a biennial event in non-Walker Cup years and in 1964 the Club donated the St Andrews Trophy to be presented to the winning team.

Although Great Britain and Ireland have dominated the match, winning 23 of the 26 encounters, the Continent of Europe had a convincing victory at Villa d'Este in Italy in 1998 and suffered only a narrow 13–11 defeat at Turnberry in 2000. GB&I are the current holders of the trophy, winning in 2008 by a score of 13½ to 10½ at Kingsbarns in Fife, Scotland.

The Jacques Léglise Trophy

The annual boys international match involving GB&I against a team from the Continent of Europe was introduced in 1958. This event was dominated originally by the British and Irish side, which won every match through 1966 prompting the match to be discontinued because it was a one-sided affair.

The match was revived in 1977 when the Continental team won by 7 points to 6. A new trophy, donated by Jean-Louis Dupont on behalf of Golf de Chantilly in memory of Jacques Léglise, a leading French golf administrator, was presented for the first time in 1978 when the Continental team again won. Since then the Continental side has triumphed a further seven times, most recently in 2006. The 2008 match at Kingsbarns resulted in a 14–10 victory for GB&I. The match was played in conjunction with the Boys Amateur Championship and Home International events until 1995. Since 1996 it has been played concurrently with the St Andrews Trophy, although the Jacques Léglise Trophy remains an annual competition.

The Boys Home Internationals

Introduced at Dunbar in 1923, the Boys Home Internationals started off as a match played between England and Scotland. It was traditionally associated with the Boys Amateur Championship, being played the day before and acting as a prelude to the main event.

The Royal and Ancient Golf Club accepted responsibility for the Boys Amateur Championship in 1949 and with it the running of the England v Scotland match. The Championship Committee originally carried out team selection. Today, representatives from the four Home Unions select the teams.

In 1972, a team match between Ireland and Wales was added to the fixture and the current format was established in 1996. The four home countries compete against one another over three consecutive days in a round robin series. Each fixture comprises five morning foursomes, followed by ten afternoon singles.

In 1997, there was a significant break with the past when, for the first time, the venue chosen for the Boys Home Internationals differed to that for the Boys Amateur Championship. This practice has remained, helping to shape the individual identity of the inter-national matches. Since 1985, the R&A Trophy has been awarded to the winning team.

Important dates in the history of St Andrews, The Open Championship and The R&A

1123   King David I grants links to powerful bishops of St Andrews.

1413   Evidence of golf being a regular pastime on the links.

1457   Golf so popular King James II of Scotland bans it.

1552   Archbishop Hamilton grants citizens rights to play games including golf on the links.

1744   First set of 13 rules laid out by golfers at Leith.

1754   22 noblemen and gentlemen of Kingdom of Fife form Society of St Andrews golfers.

1764   Golfers at St Andrews play over 18 instead of 22 holes – and set the standard for a round of golf.

1834   King William IV confers his patronage and the Society of St Andrews Golfers becomes The Royal and Ancient Golf Club.

1854   Royal and Ancient Clubhouse completed and opened.

1860   First Open Championship held at Prestwick.

1870   Tom Morris jr wins Open Belt for third time and gets to keep it.

1872   The Royal and Ancient Golf Club, Prestwick and Honourable Company of Edinburgh Golfers take over running of The Open. Golfers play for Claret Jug.

1873   First Open at St Andrews.

1894   United States Golf Association responsible for rules in USA.

1897   Formation of Rules of Golf Committee. The R&A becomes accepted authority for golf.

1904   Lost ball search time reduced from 10 to five minutes.

1919   The R&A takes charge of Amateur Championship.

1920   The R&A takes charge of The Open Championship. First R&A–USGA rules conference.

1926   The Open Championship first played over three days.

1929   USGA legitimises larger ball (1.68in.). Smaller ball (1.62in.) still used elsewhere.

1929   Steel shafts legalised for the first time.

1951   The R&A and USGA meet to unify rules.

1952   The R&A and USGA standardise rules except for ball size. Stymie abolished.

1955   First live television coverage of The Open Championship.

1956   First four-yearly rules revision.

1960   First grandstands erected at The Open Championship.

1963   Last 36-hole play-off for The Open Championship.

1966   First live coverage of The Open Championship in America.

1966   Open played over four days for first time at Muirfield.

1974   Bigger American size ball (1.68in. compulsory in The Open Championship for first time).

1980   The Open Championship finished on a Sunday for the first time at Muirfield.

1985   The R&A change play-off arrangements for The Open Championship to four holes.

1984   New dropping procedure at arms length from the shoulder.

1990   The American size 1.68in. ball becomes the only legal ball.

2004   The Royal and Ancient Golf Club celebrates 250th anniversary.

2007   Old Course used for the first time for the Ricoh Women's British Open Championship.

2008   Old Course used for the first time for the Curtis Cup.

Interesting Facts and Unusual Incidents

Royal golf clubs

● The right to the designation *Royal* is bestowed by the favour of the Sovereign or a member of the Royal House. In most cases the title is granted along with the bestowal of royal patronage on the club. The Perth Golfing Society was the first to receive the designation *Royal*. That was accorded in June 1833. King William IV bestowed the honour on The Royal and Ancient Club in 1834. The most recent Club to be so designated is Royal Mayfair Golf & Country Club in Edmonton, Canada. The club was granted Royal status in October 2005. The next most recent was Royal Mariánské Lázně in the Czech Republic. In 2003, the club was given the Royal title as a result of its association in the early part of the 20th century with King Edward VII. A full list of Royal clubs can be found on pages 620–621.

Royal and Presidential golfers

● In the long history of the Royal and Ancient game no reigning British monarch has played in an open competition. In 1922 the Duke of Windsor, when Prince of Wales, competed in The Royal and Ancient Autumn Medal at St Andrews. He also took part in competitions at Mid-Surrey, Sunningdale, Royal St George's and in the Parliamentary Handicap. He occasionally competed in American events, sometimes partnered by a professional. On a private visit to London in 1952, he competed in the Autumn competition of Royal St George's at Sandwich, scoring 97. As Prince of Wales he played on courses all over the world and, after his abdication, as Duke of Windsor he continued to enjoy the game for many years.

● King George VI, when still Duke of York, in 1930, and the Duke of Kent, in 1937, also competed in the Autumn Meeting of The Royal and Ancient, when they had formally played themselves into the Captaincy of the Club and each returned his card in the medal round. So too did Prince Andrew, the Duke of York, when he became captain in 2003. He also played in the medal and won the mixed foursomes the following day playing with former British ladies champion Julie Otto.

● King Leopold of Belgium played in the Belgian Amateur Championship at Le Zoute, the only reigning monarch ever to have played in a national championship. The Belgian King played in many competitions subsequent to his abdication. In 1949 he reached the quarter-finals of the French Amateur Championship at St Cloud, playing as Count de Rethy.

● King Baudouin of Belgium in 1958 played in the triangular match Belgium–France–Holland and won his match against a Dutch player. He also took part in the Gleneagles Hotel tournament (playing as Mr B. de Rethy), partnered by Dai Rees in 1959.

● United States President George Bush accepted an invitation in 1990 to become an Honorary Member of The Royal and Ancient Golf Club of St Andrews. The honour recognised his long connection and that of his family with golf and The R&A. Both President Bush's father, Prescott Bush Sr, and his grandfather, George Herbert Walker – who donated the Walker Cup – were presidents of the United States Golf Association. Other Honorary Members of the R&A include Kel Nagle, Jack Nicklaus, Arnold Palmer, Gene Sarazen, Peter Thomson, Roberto de Vicenzo, Gary Player and five-times Open Championship winner Tom Watson, who was made an honorary member in 1999 on his 50th birthday.

● In September 1992, The Royal and Ancient Golf Club of St Andrews announced that His Royal Highness The Duke of York had accepted the Club's invitation of Honorary Membership. The Duke of York is the sixth member of the Royal Family to accept membership along with Their Royal Highnesses The Duke of Edinburgh and The Duke of Kent. He has since become a single handicapper, and has appeared in a number of pro-ams, partnering The Open and Masters champion Mark O'Meara to victory in the Alfred Dunhill Cup pro-am at St Andrews in 1998. His Royal Highness was Captain for 2003–2004, the year in which the Club celebrated its 250th anniversary.

First lady golfer

● Mary Queen of Scots, who was beheaded on 8th February, 1587, was probably the first lady golfer so mentioned by name. As evidence of her indifference to the fate of Darnley, her husband who was murdered at Kirk o' Field, Edinburgh, she was charged at her trial with having played at golf in the fields beside Seton a few days after his death.

Record championship victories

● In the Amateur Championship at Muirfield, 1920, Captain Carter, an Irish golfer, defeated an American entrant by 10 and 8. This is the only known instance where a player has won every hole in an Amateur Championship tie.

● In the final of the Canadian Ladies' Championship at Rivermead, Ottawa, in 1921, Cecil Leitch defeated Mollie McBride by 17 and 15. Miss Leitch lost only 1 hole in the match, the ninth. She was 14 up at the end of the first round, making only 3 holes necessary in the second. She won 18 holes out of 21 played, lost 1, and halved 2.
● In the final of the French Ladies' Open Championship at Le Touquet in 1927, Mlle de la Chaume (St Cloud) defeated Mrs Alex Johnston (Moor Park) by 15 and 14, the largest victory in a European golf championship.
● At Prestwick in 1934, W. Lawson Little of Presidio, San Francisco, defeated James Wallace, Troon Portland, by 14 and 13 in the final of the Amateur Championship, the record victory in the Championship. Wallace failed to win a single hole.

Players who have won two or more majors in the same year

(The first Masters Tournament was played in 1934.)
1922 Gene Sarazen – USPGA, US Open
1924 Walter Hagen – USPGA, The Open
1926 Bobby Jones – US Open, The Open
1930 Bobby Jones – US Open, The Open (Bobby Jones also won the US Amateur and British Amateur in this year.)
1932 Gene Sarazen – US Open, The Open
1941 Craig Wood – Masters, US Open
1948 Ben Hogan – USPGA, US Open
1949 Sam Snead – USPGA, Masters
1951 Ben Hogan – Masters, US Open
1953 Ben Hogan – Masters, US Open, The Open
1956 Jack Burke – USPGA, Masters
1960 Arnold Palmer – Masters, US Open
1962 Arnold Palmer – Masters, The Open
1963 Jack Nicklaus – USPGA, Masters
1966 Jack Nicklaus – Masters, The Open
1971 Lee Trevino – US Open, The Open
1972 Jack Nicklaus – Masters, The Open
1974 Gary Player – Masters, The Open
1975 Jack Nicklaus – USPGA, Masters
1977 Tom Watson – Masters, The Open
1980 Jack Nicklaus – USPGA, US Open
1982 Tom Watson – US Open, The Open
1990 Nick Faldo – Masters, The Open
1994 Nick Price – The Open, US PGA
1998 Mark O'Meara – Masters, The Open
2000 *Tiger Woods – US Open, The Open, USPGA

*Woods also won the 2001 Masters to become the first player to hold all four Majors at the same time. He was 65-under-par for the four events.

Outstanding records in championships, international matches and on the professional circuit

● The record number of victories in The Open Championship is six, held by Harry Vardon who won in 1896-98-99-1903-11-14.

● Five-time winners of the Championship are J.H. Taylor in 1894-95-1900-09-13; James Braid in 1901-05-06-08-10; Peter Thomson in 1954-55-56-58-65 and Tom Watson in 1975-77-80-82-83. Thomson's 1965 win was achieved when the Championship had become a truly international event. In 1957 he finished second behind Bobby Locke. By winning again in 1958 Thomson was prevented only by Bobby Locke from winning five consecutive Open Championships.
● Four successive victories in The Open by Young Tom Morris is a record so far never equalled. He won in 1868-69-70-72. (The Championship was not played in 1871.) Other four-time winners are Bobby Locke in 1949-50-52-57, Walter Hagen in 1922-24-28-29, Willie Park 1860-63-66-75, and Old Tom Morris 1861-62-64-67.
● Since the Championship began in 1860, players who have won three times in succession are Jamie Anderson, Bob Ferguson, and Peter Thomson.
● Robert Tyre Jones won The Open three times in 1926-27-30; the Amateur in 1930; the American Open in 1923-26-29-30; and the American Amateur in 1924-25-27-28-30. In winning the four major golf titles of the world in one year (1930) he achieved a feat unlikely ever to be equalled. Jones retired from competitive golf after winning the 1930 American Open, the last of these Championships, at the age of 28.
● Jack Nicklaus has had the most wins (six) in the US Masters Tournament, followed by Arnold Palmer with four.
● In modern times there are four championships generally regarded as standing above all others – The Open, US Open, US Masters, and USPGA. Five players have held all these titles, Gene Sarazen, Ben Hogan, Gary Player, Jack Nicklaus and Tiger Woods in that order. In 1978 Nicklaus became the first player to have held each of them at least three times. His record in these events is: The Open 1966-70-78; US Open 1962-67-72-80; US Masters 1963-65-66-72-75-86; USPGA 1963-71-73-75-80. His total of major championships is now 18. In 1998 at the age of 58, Nicklaus finished joint sixth in the Masters. By not playing in The Open Championship that year, he ended a run of 154 successive major championships for which he was eligible (stretching back to 1957).
In 1953 Ben Hogan won the Masters, US Open and The Open, but did not compete in the USPGA because of a dates clash with The Open.
In 2000 Tiger Woods won the US Open by 15 strokes (a major championship record), The Open by eight strokes, and the USPGA in the play-off. In 2001 he then added the Masters winning by two shots to become the first player to hold all four major titles at the same time. He was 65-under-par for the four events.
● In the 1996 English Amateur Championship at Hollinwell, Ian Richardson (50) and his son, Carl, of Burghley Park, Lincolnshire, both reached the semi-finals. Both lost.

● The record number of victories in the US Open is four, held by Willie Anderson, Bobby Jones, Ben Hogan and Jack Nicklaus.

● Bobby Jones (amateur), Gene Sarazen, Ben Hogan, Lee Trevino, Tom Watson and Tiger Woods are the only players to have won The Open and US Open Championships in the same year. Tony Jacklin won The Open in 1969 and the US Open in 1970 and for a few weeks was the holder of both.

● In winning the Amateur Championship in 1970 Michael Bonallack became the first player to win in three consecutive years.

● The English Amateur record number of victories is held by Michael Bonallack, who won the title five times.

● John Ball holds the record number of victories in the Amateur Championship, which he won eight times. Next comes Michael Bonallack (who was internationally known as The Duke) with five wins.

● Cecil Leitch and Joyce Wethered each won the British Ladies' title four times.

● The Scottish Amateur record was held by Ronnie Shade, who won five titles in successive years, 1963 to 1967. His long reign as Champion ended when he was beaten in the fourth round of the 1968 Championship after winning 44 consecutive matches.

● Joyce Wethered established an unbeaten record by winning the English Ladies' in five successive years from 1920 to 1924 inclusive.

● In winning the Amateur Championships of Britain and America in 1934 and 1935 Lawson Little won 31 consecutive matches. Other dual winners of these championships in the same year are R.T. Jones (1930) and Bob Dickson (1967).

● Peter Thomson's victory in the 1971 New Zealand Open Championship was his ninth in that event.

● In a four-week spell in 1971, Lee Trevino won in succession the US Open, the Canadian Open and The Open Championship.

● Michael Bonallack and Bill Hyndman were the Amateur Championship finalists in both 1969 and 1970. This was the first time the same two players reached the final in successive years.

● On the US professional circuit the greatest number of consecutive victories is 11, achieved by Byron Nelson in 1945. Nelson also holds the record for most victories in one calendar year, again in 1945 when he won a total of 18 tournaments.

● Raymond Floyd, by winning the Doral Classic in March 1992, joined Sam Snead as the only winners of US Tour events in four different decades.

● Sam Snead won tournaments in six decades. His first win was the 1936 West Virginia PGA. In 1980 he won the Golf Digest Commemorative and in 1982 the Legends of Golf with Don January.

● Neil Coles has won official Tour events in six decades. His first victory was in 1958 and he was a winner on the European Senior Tour in June 2000 when he took the Microlease Jersey Senior Open. Coles still plays well enough to beat his age. Now 67, he shot a closing 64 in the final round of the 2003

Travis Perkins Senior Open over the Edinburgh course he helped design.

● Jack Nicklaus and the late Walter Hagen have had five wins each in the USPGA Championship. All Hagen's wins were at match play; all Nicklaus's at stroke play.

● In 1953 Flory van Donck of Belgium had seven major victories in Europe, including The Open Championships of Switzerland, Italy, Holland, Germany and Belgium.

● Mrs Anne Sander won four major amateur titles each under a different name. She won the US Ladies' in 1958 as Miss Quast, in 1961 as Mrs Decker, in 1963 as Mrs Welts and the British Ladies' in 1980 as Mrs Sander.

● The highest number of appearances in the Ryder Cup matches is held by Nick Faldo who made his eleventh appearance in 1997.

● The greatest number of appearances in the Walker Cup matches is held by Irishman Joe Carr who made his tenth appearance in 1967.

● In the Curtis Cup Mary McKenna made her ninth consecutive appearance in 1986.

● Players who have represented their country in both Walker and Ryder Cup matches are: for the United States, Fred Haas, Ken Venturi, Gene Littler, Jack Nicklaus, Tommy Aaron, Mason Rudolph, Bob Murphy, Lanny Wadkins, Scott Simpson, Tom Kite, Jerry Pate, Craig Stadler, Jay Haas, Bill Rodgers, Hal Sutton, Curtis Strange, Davis Love III, Brad Faxon, Scott Hoch, Phil Mickelson, Corey Pavin, Justin Leonard, Tiger Woods and David Duval; and for Great Britain & Ireland, Norman Drew, Peter Townsend, Clive Clark, Peter Oosterhuis, Howard Clark, Mark James, Michael King, Gordon Brand Jr, Paul Way, Ronan Rafferty, Sandy Lyle, Philip Walton, David Gilford, Colin Montgomerie, Peter Baker, Padraig Harrington and Andrew Coltart.

Remarkable recoveries in matchplay

● There have been two remarkable recoveries in the Walker Cup Matches. In 1930 at Sandwich, J.A. Stout, Great Britain, round in 68, was 4 up at the end of the first round against Donald Moe. Stout started in the second round, 3, 3, 3, and was 7 up. He was still 7 up with 13 to play. Moe, who went round in 67, won back the 7 holes to draw level at the 17th green. At the 18th or 36th of the match, Moe, after a long drive placed his iron shot within three feet of the hole and won the match by 1 hole.

● In 1936 at Pine Valley, George Voigt and Harry Girvan for America were 7 up with 11 to play against Alec Hill and Cecil Ewing. The British pair drew level at the 17th hole, or the 35th of the match, and the last hole was halved.

● In the 1965 Piccadilly Match Play Championship Gary Player beat Tony Lema after being 7 down with 17 to play.

● Bobby Cruickshank, the old Edinburgh player, had an extraordinary recovery in a 36-hole match in a

USPGA Championship for he defeated Al Watrous after being 11 down with 12 to play.
● In a match at the Army GC, Aldershot, on 5th July, 1974, for the Gradoville Bowl, M.C. Smart was 8 down with 8 to play against Mike Cook. Smart succeeded in winning all the remaining holes and the 19th for victory.
● In the 1982 Suntory World Match Play Championship Sandy Lyle beat Nick Faldo after being 6 down with 18 to play.

Oldest champions

The Open Championship: Belt Tom Morris in 1867 – 46 years 99 days. *Cup* Roberto de Vicenzo, 44 years 93 days, in 1967; Harry Vardon, 44 years 42 days, in 1914; J.H. Taylor, 42 years 97 days, in 1913.
Amateur Championship Hon. Michael Scot, 54, at Hoylake in 1933.
British Ladies Amateur Mrs Jessie Valentine, 43, at Hunstanton in 1958.
Scottish Amateur J.M. Cannon, 53, at Troon in 1969.
English Amateur Terry Shingler, 41 years 11 months at Walton Heath 1977; Gerald Micklem, 41 years 8 months, at Royal Birkdale 1947.
Welsh Amateur John Jermine, 56, at St David's, in 2000
US Open Hale Irwin, 45, at Medinah, Illinois, in 1990.
US Amateur Jack Westland, 47, at Seattle in 1952 (He had been defeated in the 1931 final, 21 years previously, by Francis Ouimet).
US Masters Jack Nicklaus, 46, in 1986.
European Tour Des Smyth, 48 years, 14 days, Madeira Open 1982; Neil Coles, 48 years 14 days, Sanyo Open 1982
European Senior Tour Neil Coles, 65, in 2000
USPGA Julius Boros, 48, in 1968. Lee Trevino, 44, in 1984.
USPGA Tour Sam Snead, 52, at Greensborough Open in 1965. Sam Snead, 61, equal second in Glen Campbell Open 1974.

Youngest champions

The Open Championship: Belt Tom Morris, Jr, 17 years 5 months, in 1868. *Cup* Willie Auchterlonie, 21 years 24 days, in 1893; Tom Morris, Jr, 21 years 5 months, in 1872; Severiano Ballesteros, 22 years 103 days, in 1979.
Amateur Championship J.C. Beharrell, 18 years 1 month, at Troon in 1956; R. Cole (RSA) 18 years 1 month, at Carnoustie in 1966.
British Ladies Amateur May Hezlett, 17, at Newcastle, Co. Down, in 1899; Michelle Walker, 18, at Alwoodley in 1971.
English Amateur Nick Faldo, 18, at Lytham St Annes in 1975; Paul Downes, 18, at Birkdale in 1978; David Gilford, 18, at Woodhall Spa in 1984; Ian Garbutt, 18, at Woodhall Spa in 1990; Mark Foster, 18, at Moortown in 1994.
English Amateur Strokeplay Ronan Rafferty, 16, at Hunstanton in 1980.
British Ladies Open Strokeplay Helen Dobson, 18, at Southerness in 1989.

British Boys Championship Mark Mouland (WAL) 15 years 120 days at Sunningdale in 1976; Pablo Martin (ESP) 15 years 120 days at Ganton 2001.

More records can be found on pages 394–405

Disqualifications

Disqualifications are now numerous, usually for some irregularity over signing a scorecard or for late arrival at the first tee. We therefore show here only incidents in major events involving famous players or players who were in a winning position or incidents which were in themselves unusual.

● J.J. McDermott, the American Open Champion 1911–12, arrived for The Open Championship at Prestwick in 1914 to discover that he had made a mistake of a week in the date the championship began. The American could not play, as the qualifying rounds were completed on the day he arrived.
● In the Amateur Championship at Sandwich in 1937, Brigadier-General Critchley, arriving at Southampton from New York on the *Queen Mary*, which had been delayed by fog, flew by specially chartered aeroplane to Sandwich. He circled over the clubhouse, so the officials knew he was nearly there, but he arrived six minutes late, and his name had been struck out. At the same championship a player, entered from Burma, who had travelled across the Pacific and the American Continent, and was also on the *Queen Mary*, travelled from Southampton by motor car and arrived four hours after his starting time to find after journeying more than halfway round the world he was *struck out*.
● An unprecedented disqualification was that of A. Murray in the New Zealand Open Championship, 1937. Murray, who was New Zealand Champion in 1935, was playing with J.P. Hornabrook, New Zealand Amateur Champion, and at the 8th hole in the last round, while waiting for his partner to putt, Murray dropped a ball on the edge of the green and made a practice putt along the edge. Murray returned the lowest score in the championship, but he was disqualified for taking the practice putt.
● At The Open Championship at St Andrews in 1946, John Panton, Glenbervie, in the evening practised putting on a green on the New Course, which was one of the qualifying courses. He himself reported his inadvertence to The Royal and Ancient and he was disqualified.
● At The Open Championship, Sandwich, 1949, C. Rotar, an American, qualified by four strokes to compete in the championship but he was disqualified because he had used a putter which did not conform to the accepted form and make of a golf club, the socket being bent over the centre of the club head. This is the only case where a player has been disqualified in The Open Championship for using an illegal club.
● In the 1957 American Women's Open Championship, Mrs Jackie Pung had the lowest score, 298

over four rounds, but lost the championship. The card she signed for the final round read *five* at the 4th hole instead of the correct *six*. Her total of 72 was correct but the error, under rigid rules, resulted in her disqualification. Betty Jameson, who partnered Mrs Pung and also returned a wrong score, was also disqualified.

● Mark Roe and Jesper Parnevik were disqualified in bizarre circumstances in the 2003 Open at Royal St George's, Sandwich. Roe had shot 67 to move into contention but it was discovered after they left the recorder's hut that they had not exchanged cards. Roe's figures were returned on a card with Parnevik's name on it and vice versa. The R&A have since changed the rules to allow the official scorer to erase the wrong name and put the correct one on the card ensuring a Roe–Parnevik incident can never happen again.

● Teenager Michelle Wie will not be allowed to forget her début on the LPGA Tour as a professional in the Samsung World Championship. Although she completed four rounds and finished fourth behind Annika Sörenstam, she was disqualified for taking a drop nearer to the hole in the third round. A reporter, Michael Bamberger from *Sports Illustrated*, saw the incident but did not report it to officials until the next day after he had spoken with his editor. Officials only decided to disqualify the youngster after measuring out distances at the spot where she took the drop with a yard of string.

● Kevin Stadler, son of Ryder Cup and former Masters champion Craig Stadler, was disqualified in the 2005 Funai Classic in Orlando for disclosing he had a bent shaft in his wedge. Lying 163rd in the money list and needing a good finish to keep his card, he was lying joint fifth going into the final round. He discovered the shaft of his wedge was bent on the second hole on the final day and was disqualified for playing with an illegal club – ironically, one that could never have helped him play a decent shot.

Longest match

● W.R. Chamberlain, a retired farmer, and George New, a postmaster at Chilton Foliat, on 1st August, 1922, met at Littlecote, the 9-hole course of Sir Ernest Wills, and agreed to play every Thursday afternoon over the course. This continued until New's sudden death on 13th January, 1938. An accurate record of the match was kept, giving details of each round including wind direction and playing conditions. In the elaborate system nearly two million facts were recorded. They played 814 rounds, and aggregated 86,397 strokes, of which Chamberlain took 44,008 and New 42,371. New, therefore, was 1,637 strokes up. The last round of all was halved, a suitable end to such an unusual contest.

Longest ties

● The longest known ties in 18-hole match play rounds in major events were in an early round of the News of the World Match Play Championship at Turnberry in 1960, when W.S. Collins beat W.J.

Branch at the 31st hole, and in the third round of the same tournament at Walton Heath in 1961 when Harold Henning beat Peter Alliss also at the 31st hole.
● In the 1970 Scottish Amateur Championship at Balgownie, Aberdeen, E. Hammond beat J. McIvor at the 29th hole in their second round tie.
● C.A. Palmer beat Lionel Munn at the 28th hole at Sandwich in 1908. This is the record tie of the British Amateur Championship. Munn has also been engaged in two other extended ties in the Amateur Championship. At Muirfield, in 1932, in the semi-final, he was defeated by John de Forest, the ultimate winner, at the 26th hole, and at St Andrews, in 1936, in the second round he was defeated by J.L. Mitchell, again at the 26th hole.

The following examples of long ties are in a different category for they occurred in competitions, either stroke play or match play, where the conditions stipulated that in the event of a tie, a further stated number of holes had to be played – in some cases 36 holes, but mostly 18. With this method a vast number of extra holes was sometimes necessary to settle ties.

● The longest known was between two American women in a tournament at Peterson (New Jersey) when 88 extra holes were required before Mrs Edwin Labaugh emerged as winner.
● In a match on the Queensland course, Australia, in October, 1933, H.B. Bonney and Col H.C.H. Robertson versus B.J. Canniffe and Dr Wallis Hoare required to play a further four 18-hole matches after being level at the end of the original 18. In the fourth replay Hoare and Caniffe won by 3 and 2 which meant that 70 extra holes had been necessary to decide the tie.
● After finishing all square in the final of the Dudley GC's foursomes competition in 1950, F.W. Mannell and A.G. Walker played a further three 18-hole replays against T. Poole and E. Jones, each time finishing all square. A further 9 holes were arranged and Mannell and Walker won by 3 and 2 making a total of 61 extra holes to decide the tie.
● R.A. Whitcombe and Mark Seymour tied for first prize in the Penfold £750 Tournament at St Anneson-Sea, in 1934. They had to play off over 36 holes and tied again. They were then required to play another 9 holes when Whitcombe won with 34 against 36. The tournament was over 72 holes. The first tie added 36 holes and the extra 9 holes made an aggregate of 117 holes to decide the winner. This is a record in first-class British golf but in no way compares with other long ties as it involved only two replays – one of 36 holes and one of 9.
● In the American Open Championship at Toledo, Ohio, in 1931, G. Von Elm and Billy Burke tied for the title. Each returned aggregates of 292. On the first replay both finished in 149 for 36 holes but on the second replay Burke won with a score of 148 against 149. This is a record tie in a national open championship.
● Cary Middlecoff and Lloyd Mangrum were declared co-winners of the 1949 Motor City Open

on the USPGA Tour after halving 11 sudden death holes.

● Australian David Graham beat American Dave Stockton at the tenth extra hole in the 1998 Royal Caribbean Classic, a record on the US Senior Tour.

● Paul Downes was beaten by Robin Davenport at the 9th extra hole in the 4th round of the 1981 English Amateur Championship, a record marathon match for the Championship.

● Severiano Ballesteros was beaten by Johnny Miller at the 9th extra hole of a sudden-death play-off at the 1982 Million Dollar Sun City Challenge.

● José Maria Olazábal beat Ronan Rafferty at the 9th extra hole to win the 1989 Dutch Open on the Kennemer Golf and Country Club course. Roger Chapman had been eliminated at the first extra hole.

Long drives

It is impossible to state with any certainty what is the longest ever drive. Many long drives have never been measured and many others have most likely never been brought to our attention. Then there are several outside factors which can produce freakishly long drives, such as a strong following wind, downhill terrain or bonehard ground. Where all three of these favourable conditions prevail outstandingly long drives can be achieved. Another consideration is that a long drive made during a tournament is a different proposition from one made for length alone, either on the practice ground, a long driving competition or in a game of no consequence. All this should be borne in mind when considering the long drives shown here.

● When professional Carl Hooper hit a wayward drive on the 3rd hole (456 yards) at the Oak Hills Country Club, San Antonio, during the 1992 Texas Open, he wrote himself into the record books but out of the tournament. The ball kept bouncing and rolling on a tarmac cart path until it was stopped by a fence – 787 yards away. It took Hooper two recovery shots with a 4-iron and then an 8-iron to return to the fairway. He eventually holed out for a double bogey six and failed to survive the half-way qualifying cut.

● Tommie Campbell of Portmarnock hit a drive of 392 yards at Dun Laoghaire GC in July 1964.

● Playing in Australia, American George Bayer is reported to have driven to within chipping distance of a 589 yards hole. "It was certainly a drive of over 500 yards", said Bayer acknowledging the strong following wind, sharp downslope where his ball landed and the bone-hard ground.

● In September, 1934, over the East Devon course, T.H.V. Haydon, Wimbledon, drove to the edge of the 9th green which was a hole of 465 yards, giving a drive of not less than 450 yards.

● E.C. Bliss drove 445 yards at Herne Bay in August, 1913. The drive was measured by a government surveyor who also measured the drop in height from tee to resting place of the ball at 57 feet.

Long carries

● At Sitwell Park, Rotherham, in 1935 the home professional, W. Smithson, drove a ball which carried a dyke at 380 yards from the 2nd tee.

● George Bell, of Penrith GC, New South Wales, Australia, using a number 2 wood drove across the Nepean River, a certified carry of 309 yards in a driving contest in 1964.

● After the 1986 Irish Professional Championship at Waterville, Co. Kerry, four long-hitting professionals tried for the longest-carry record over water, across a lake in the Waterville Hotel grounds. Liam Higgins, the local professional, carried 310 yards and Paul Leonard 311, beating the previous record by 2 yards.

● In the 1972 Algarve Open at Penina, Henry Cotton vouched for a carry of 305 yards over a ditch at the 18th hole by long-hitting Spanish professional Francisco Abreu. There was virtually no wind assistance.

● At the Home International matches at Portmarnock in 1949 a driving competition was held in which all the players in all four teams competed. The actual carry was measured and the longest was 280 yards by Jimmy Bruen.

● On 6th April, 1976, Tony Jacklin hit a number of balls into Vancouver harbour, Canada, from the 495-foot high roof of a new building complex. The longest carry was measured at 389 yards.

Long hitting

There have been numerous long hits, not on golf courses, where an outside agency has assisted the length of the shot. Such an example was a "drive" by Liam Higgins in 1986, on the Airport runway at Baldonal, near Dublin, of 632 yards.

● How's this for a long shot? Odd Marthinussen was holidaying in Haparanda in Sweden when he holed in one at the 14th. So what! The curious thing about this ace is that while he teed up in Sweden the green is in Finland which is in a different time zone. Registered as an ace in both countries, the time it took for the ball to go from tee to cup was estimated at 1 hour and 4 seconds ... surely the longest hole ever reported by Simon Pia in his column in *The Scotsman* newspaper.

Longest albatrosses

● The longest-known albatrosses (three under par) recorded at par 5 holes are:

● 647 yards-2nd hole at Guam Navy Club by Chief Petty Officer Kevin Murray of Chicago on 3rd January, 1982.

● 609 yards-15th hole at Mahaka Inn West Course, Hawaii, by John Eakin of California on 12th November, 1972.

● 602 yards-16th hole at Whiting Field Golf Course, Milton, Florida, by 27-year-old Bill Graham with a drive and a 3-wood, aided by a 25 mph tail wind.

● The longest-known albatrosses in open championships are: 580 yards 14th hole at Crans-sur-Sierre, by American Billy Casper in the 1971 Swiss Open; 558 yards 5th hole at Muirfield by American Johnny Miller in the 1972 Open Championship.

● In the 1994 German Amateur Championship at Wittelsbacher GC, Rohrenfield, Graham Rankin, a member of the visiting Scottish national team, had a two at the 592 yard 18th.

Eagles (multiple and consecutive)

● Wilf Jones scored three consecutive eagles at the first three holes at Moor Hall GC when playing in a competition there on August Bank Holiday Monday 1968. He scored 3, 1, 2 at holes measuring 529 yards, 176 yards and 302 yards.

● In a round of the 1980 Jubilee Cup, a mixed foursomes match play event of Colchester GC, Mrs Nora Booth and her son Brendan scored three consecutive gross eagles of 1, 3, 2 at the eighth, ninth and tenth holes.

● Three players in a four-ball match at Kington GC, Herefordshire, on 22nd July, 1948, all had eagle 2s at the 18th hole (272 yards). They were R.N. Bird, R. Morgan and V. Timson.

● Four Americans from Wisconsin on holiday at Gleneagles in 1977 scored three eagles and a birdie at the 300-yard par-4 14th hole on the King's course. The birdie was by Dr Kim Lulloff and the eagles by Dr Gordon Meiklejohn, Richard Johnson and Jack Kubitz.

● In an open competition at Glen Innes GC, Australia on 13th November, 1977, three players in a four-ball scored eagle 3s at the 9th hole (442 metres). They were Terry Marshall, Roy McHarg and Jack Rohleder.

● David McCarthy, a member of Moortown Golf Club, Leeds, had three consecutive eagles (3, 3, 2) on the 4th, 5th and 6th holes during a Pro-Am competition at Lucerne, Switzerland, on 7th August, 1992.

Speed of golf ball and club head and effect of wind and temperature

● In *The Search for the Perfect Swing*, a scientific study of the golf swing, a first class golfer is said to have the club head travelling at 100 mph at impact. This will cause the ball to leave the club at 135 mph. An outstandingly long hitter might manage to have the club head travelling at 130 mph which would produce a ball send-off speed of 175 mph. The resultant shot would carry 280 yards.

● According to Thomas Hardman, Wilson's director of research and development, wind will reduce or increase the flight of a golf ball by approximately 1½ yards for every mile per hour of wind. Every two degrees of temperature will make a yard difference in a ball's flight.

Most northerly course

● Although the most northerly course used to be in Iceland, Björkliden Arctic Golf Club, Sweden, 250 km north of the Arctic Circle, has taken over that role. This may soon change, however, when a course opens in Narvic, Norway, which could be a few metres further north than Björkliden.

Most southerly course

● Golf's most southerly course is Scott Base Country Club, 13° north of the South Pole. The course is run by the New Zealand Antarctic Programme and players must be kitted in full survival gear. The most difficult aspect is finding the orange golf balls which tend to get buried in the snow. Other obstacles include penguins, seals and skuas. If the ball is stolen by a skua then a penalty of one shot is incurred; but if the ball hits a skua it counts as a birdie.

Highest golf courses

● The highest golf course in the world is thought to be the Tuctu GC in Peru which is 14,335 feet above sea-level. High courses are also found in Bolivia with the La Paz GC being about 13,500 feet. In the Himalayas, near the border with Tibet, a 9-hole course at 12,800 feet has been laid out by keen golfers in the Indian Army.

● The highest course in Europe is at Sestriere in the Italian Alps, 6,500 feet above sea-level.

● The highest courses in Great Britain are West Monmouthshire in Wales at 1,513 feet, Leadhills in Scotland at 1,500 feet and Kington in England at 1,284 feet.

Longest courses

● The longest course in the world is Dub's Dread GC, Piper, Kansas, USA measuring 8,101 yards (par 78).

● The longest course for The Open Championship was 7,361 yards at Carnoustie in 1999.

Longest holes

● The longest hole in the world, as far as is known, is the 6th hole measuring 782 metres (860 yards) at Koolan Island GC, Western Australia. The par of the hole is 7. There are several holes over 700 yards throughout the world.

● The longest hole for The Open Championship is the 577 yards 6th hole at Royal Troon.

Longest tournaments

● The longest tournament held was over 144 holes in the World Open at Pinehurst, N Carolina, USA, first held in 1973. Play was over two weeks with a cut imposed at the halfway mark.

● An annual tournament, played in Germany on the longest day of the year, comprises 100 holes' medal play. Best return, in 1995, was 399 strokes.

Largest entries

● The Open – 2,477, St Andrews, 2000.
● The Amateur – 537, Muirfield, 1998.
● US Open – 8,457, Pebble Beach, 2000.
● The largest entry for a PGA European Tour event was 398 for the 1978 Colgate PGA Championship. Since 1985, when the all-exempt ruling was introduced, all PGA tournaments have had 144 competitors, slightly more or less.

● In 1952, Bobby Locke, The Open Champion, played a round at Wentworth against any golfer in Britain. Cards costing 2s. 6d. each (12½p), were taken out by 24,000 golfers. The challenge was to beat the local par by more than Locke could beat the par at Wentworth. 1,641 competitors, including women, succeeded in *beating* the Champion and each received a certificate signed by him. As a result of this challenge the British Golf Foundation benefited to the extent of £3,026, the proceeds from the sale of cards. A similar tournament was held in the US and Canada when 87,094 golfers participated; 14,667 players bettered Ben Hogan's score under handicap. The fund benefited by $80,024.

Largest prize money

● The Machrie Tournament of 1901 was the first tournament with a first prize of £100. It was won by J.H. Taylor, then The Open Champion, who beat James Braid in the final.

● The richest event in the world (at time of writing) will be the American Express Championship scheduled for Mount Juliet in 2004. Total prize money will be $7 million. The richest first prize in Europe is the $1.3 million which goes to the winner of the Nedbank Golf Challenge at Sun City in South Africa.

Holing-in-one – odds against

● At the Wanderers Club, Johannesburg in January, 1951, forty-nine amateurs and professionals each played three balls at a hole 146 yards long. Of the 147 balls hit, the nearest was by Koos de Beer, professional at Reading Country Club, which finished 10½ inches from the hole. Harry Bradshaw, the Irish professional who was touring with the British team in South Africa, touched the pin with his second shot, but the ball rolled on and stopped 3 feet 2 inches from the cup.

● A competition on similar lines was held in 1951 in New York when 1,409 players who had done a hole-in-one held a competition over several days at short holes on three New York courses. Each player was allowed a total of five shots, giving an aggregate of 7,045 shots. No player holed-in-one, and the nearest ball finished 3½ inches from the hole.

● A further illustration of the element of luck in holing-in-one is derived from an effort by Harry Gonder, an American professional, who in 1940 stood for 16 hours 25 minutes and hit 1,817 balls trying to do a 160 yard hole-in-one. He had two official witnesses and caddies to tee and retrieve the balls and count the strokes. His 1,756th shot struck the hole but stopped an inch from the hole. This was his nearest effort.

● From this and other similar information an estimate of the odds against holing-in-one at any particular hole within the range of one shot was made at somewhere between 1,500 and 2,000 to 1 by a proficient player. Subsequently, however, statistical analysis in America has come up with the following odds: a male professional or top amateur 3,708 to 1; a female professional or top amateur 4,648 to 1; an average golfer 42,952 to 1.

Hole-in-one first recorded

● The earliest recorded hole-in-one was in 1869 at The Open Championship when Tom Morris Jr completed the 145-yard 8th hole at Prestwick in one.

This was the first ace in competition for The Open Championship Challenge Belt.

● The first hole-in-one recorded with the 1.66 in ball was in 1972 by John G. Salvesen, a member of the R&A Championship Committee. At the time this size of ball was only experimental. Salvesen used a 7-iron for his historical feat at the 11th hole on the Old Course, St Andrews.

Holing-in-one in important events

Since the day of the first known hole-in-one by Tom Morris Jr, at the 8th hole (145 yards) at Prestwick in the 1869 Open Championship, holes-in-one, even in championships, have become too numerous for each to be recorded. Only where other unusual or interesting circumstances prevailed are the instances shown here.

● All hole-in-one achievements are remarkable. Many are extraordinary. Among the more amazing was that of 2-handicap Leicestershire golfer Bob Taylor, a member of the Scraptoft Club. During the final practice day for the 1974 Eastern Counties Foursomes Championship on the Hunstanton Links, he holed his tee shot with a one-iron at the 188-yard 16th. The next day, in the first round of the competition, he repeated the feat, the only difference being that because of a change of wind he used a six-iron. When he stepped on to the 16th tee the following day his partner jokingly offered him odds of 1,000,000 to one against holing-in-one for a third successive time. Taylor again used his six-iron – and holed in one!

● 1878 – Jamie Anderson, competing in The Open Championship at Prestwick, holed in one at the 11th. In these days The Open was played over three rounds of 12 holes so his ace, the first hole-in-one in competition for the Claret Jug – came at his penultimate hole in his third round. Although it seemed then that he was winning easily, it turned out afterwards that if he had not taken this hole in one stroke he would very likely have lost. Anderson was just about to make his tee shot when Andy Stuart (winner of the first Irish Open Championship in 1892), who was acting as marker to Anderson, remarked he was standing outside the teeing ground, and that if he played the stroke from there he would be disqualified. Anderson picked up his ball and teed it in a proper place. Then he holed-in-one. He won the Championship by one stroke.

● On a Friday the 13th in 1990, Richard Allen holed-in-one at the 13th at the Barwon Heads Golf Club, Victoria, Australia, and then lost the hole. He was giving a handicap stroke to his opponent, brother-in-law Jason Ennels, who also holed-in-one.

● 1906 – R. Johnston, North Berwick, competing in The Open Championship, did the 14th hole at Muirfield in one. Johnston played with only one club throughout – an adjustable head club.

● 1959 – The first hole-in-one in the US Women's Open Championship was recorded. It was by Patty Berg on the 7th hole (170 yards) at Churchill Valley CC, Pittsburgh.

● 1962 – On 6th April, playing in the second round of the Schweppes Close Championship at Little Aston, H. Middleton of Shandon Park, Belfast, holed his tee shot at the 159-yard 5th hole, winning a prize of £1,000. Ten minutes later, playing two matches ahead of Middleton, R.A. Jowle, son of the professional, Frank Jowle, holed his tee shot at the 179-yard 9th hole. As an amateur he was rewarded by the sponsors with a £30 voucher.

● 1963 – By holing out in one stroke at the 18th hole (156 yards) at Moor Park on the first day of the Esso Golden round-robin tournament, H.R. Henning, South Africa, won the £10,000 prize offered for this feat.

● 1967 – Tony Jacklin in winning the Masters tournament at St George's, Sandwich, did the 16th hole in one. His ace has an exceptional place in the records for it was seen by millions on TV, the ball was in view in its flight till it went into the hole in his final round of 64.

● 1971 – John Hudson, 25-year-old professional at Hendon, achieved a near miracle when he holed two consecutive holes-in-one in the Martini Tournament at Norwich. They were at the 11th and 12th holes (195 yards and 311 yards respectively) in the second round.

● 1971 – In The Open Championship at Birkdale, Lionel Platts holed-in-one at the 212-yard 4th hole in the second round. This was the first instance of an Open Championship hole-in-one being recorded by television. It was incidentally Platts' seventh ace of his career.

● There have been four holes-in-one in the Ryder Cup: by Peter Butler at Muirfield in 1973, Nick Faldo at the Belfry in 1993, and by Costantino Rocca and Howard Clark at Oak Hill in 1995. No American has holed in one in the Cup competition.

● 1973 – In the 1973 Open Championship at Troon, two holes-in-one were recorded, both at the 8th hole, known as the Postage Stamp, in the first round. They were achieved by Gene Sarazen and amateur David Russell, who were by coincidence respectively the oldest and youngest competitors.

● Mrs Argea Tissies, whose husband Hermann took 15 at Royal Troon's Postage Stamp 8th hole in the 1950 Open, scored a hole-in-one at the 2nd hole at Punta Ala in the second round of the Italian Ladies' Senior Open of 1978. Exactly five years later on the same date, at the same time of day, in the same round of the same tournament at the same hole, she did it again with the same club.

● In less than two hours play in the second round of the 1989 US Open at Oak Hill Country Club, Rochester, New York, four competitors – Doug Weaver, Mark Wiebe, Jerry Pate and Nick Price – each holed the 167-yard 6th hole in one. The odds against four professionals achieving such a record in a field of 156 are reckoned at 332,000 to 1.

● On 20th May, 1998, British golf journalist Derek Lawrenson, an eight-handicapper, won a Lamborghini Diablo car, valued at over £180,000, by holing his three-iron tee shot to the 175-yard 15th hole at Mill Ride, Berkshire. He was taking part in a charity

day and was partnering England football stars Paul Ince and Steve McManaman.

● David Toms took the lead in the 2001 USPGA Championship at Atlanta Athletic Club with a hole-in-one at the 15th hole in the third round and went on to win. Nick Faldo (4th hole) and Scott Hoch (17th hole) also had holes-in-one during the event.

● In the 2006 Ryder Cup at the K Club, Ireland, Paul Casey holed his 4-iron shot at the 14th to score the fifth ace in the history of the competition. The following day, at the same hole, Scott Verplank became the first American to score a Ryder Cup hole-in-one.

Holing-in-one – longest holes

● Bob Mitera, as a 21-year-old American student, standing 5 feet 6 inches and weighing under 12 stones, claimed the world record for the longest hole-in-one. Playing over the appropriately named Miracle Hill course at Omaha, on 7th October, 1965, Bob holed his drive at the 10th hole, 447 yards long. The ground sloped sharply downhill.

● Two longer holes-in-one have been achieved, but because they were at dog-leg holes they are not generally accepted as being the longest holes-in-one. They were 496 yards (17th hole, Teign Valley) by Shaun Lynch in July 1995 and 480 yards (5th hole, Hope CC, Arkansas) by L. Bruce on 15th November, 1962.

● In March, 1961, Lou Kretlow holed his tee shot at the 427-yard 16th hole at Lake Hefner course, Oklahoma City, USA.

● The longest known hole-in-one in Great Britain was the 393-yard 7th hole at West Lancashire GC, where in 1972 the assistant professional Peter Parkinson holed his tee shot.

● Paul Neilson, a 34-year-old golfer at South Winchester, holed in one at the club's par 4 fifth hole – 391 yards.

● Other long holes-in-one recorded in Great Britain have been 380 yards (5th hole at Tankersley Park) by David Hulley in 1961; 380 yards (12th hole at White Webbs) by Danny Dunne on 30th July, 1976; 370 yards (17th hole at Chilwell Manor, distance from the forward tee) by Ray Newton in 1977; 365 yards (10th hole at Harewood Downs) by K. Saunders in 1965; 365 yards (7th hole at Catterick Garrison GC) by Leslie Bruckner on 18th July, 1980.

● The longest-recorded hole-in-one by a woman was that accomplished in September, 1949 by Marie Robie – the 393-yard hole at Furnace Brook course, Wollaston, Mass, USA.

Holing-in-one – greatest number by one person

59–Amateur Norman Manley of Long Beach, California.

50–Mancil Davis, professional at the Trophy Club, Fort Worth, Texas.

31–British professional C.T. le Chevalier who died in 1973.

22–British amateur, Jim Hay of Kirkintilloch GC.

At One Hole
13–Joe Lucius at 15th hole of Mohawk, Ohio.
5–Left-hander, the late Fred Francis at 7th (now 16th) hole of Cardigan GC.

Holing-in-one – greatest frequency

● The record for the greatest number of holes-in-one in a calendar year is 14, claimed in 2007 by Californian Jacqueline Gagne who hit her fourteenth ace at Mission Hills in front of a television crew who had been sent to check if her claims for the previous 13 were true

● J.O. Boydstone of California made 11 aces in 1962.

● John Putt of Frilford Heath GC had six holes-in-one in 1970, followed by three in 1971.

● Douglas Porteous, of Ruchill GC, Glasgow, achieved seven holes-in-one in the space of eight months. Four of them were scored in a five-day period from 26th to 30th September, 1974, in three consecutive rounds of golf. The first two were achieved at Ruchill GC in one round, the third there two days later, and the fourth at Clydebank and District GC after another two days. The following May, Porteous had three holes-in-one, the first at Linn Park GC incredibly followed by two more in the one round at Clober GC.

● Mrs Kathleen Hetherington of West Essex has holed-in-one five times, four being at the 15th hole at West Essex. Four of her five aces were within seven months in 1966.

● Mrs Dorothy Hill of Dumfries and Galloway GC holed-in-one three times in 11 days in 1977.

● James C. Reid of Brodick, aged 59 and 8 handicap in 1987, achieved 14 holes-in-one, all but one on Isle of Arran courses. His success was in spite of severe physical handicaps of a stiff left knee, a damaged right ankle, two discs removed from his back and a hip replacement.

● Jean Nield, a member at Chorlton-cum-Hardy and Bramall Park, has had eleven holes-in-one and her husband Brian, who plays at Bramall Park, has had five – a husband and wife total of 16.

● Peter Gibbins holed his tee shot at the 359 yards par 4 13th hole at Hazlemere on November 2 1984 using a 3-wood that was in his bag for the first time. That spectacular ace was his third but he has had nine more since then.

Holing successive holes-in-one

● Successive holes-in-one are rare; successive par 4 holes-in-one may be classed as near miracles. N.L. Manley performed the most incredible feat in September, 1964, at Del Valle Country Club, Saugus, California, USA. The par 4 7th (330 yards) and 8th (290 yards) are both slightly downhill, dog-leg holes. Manley had *aces* at both, en route to a course record of 61 (par 71).

● The first recorded example in Britain of a player holing-in-one stroke at each of two successive holes was achieved on 6th February, 1964, at the Walmer and Kingsdown course, Kent. The young assistant professional at that club, Roger Game (aged 17)

holed out with a 4-wood at the 244-yard 7th hole, and repeated the feat at the 256-yard 8th hole, using a 5-iron.

● The first occasion of holing-in-one at consecutive holes in a major professional event occurred when John Hudson, 25-year-old professional at Hendon, holed-in-one at the 11th and 12th holes at Norwich during the second round of the 1971 Martini tournament. Hudson used a 4-iron at the 195-yard 11th and a driver at the 311-yard downhill 12th hole.

● Assistant professional Tom Doty (23 years), playing in a friendly match on a course near Chicago in October, 1971, had a remarkable four-hole score which included two consecutive holes-in-one, sandwiched either side by an albatross and an eagle: 4th hole (500 yards)-2; 5th hole (360 yards dog-leg)-1; 6th hole (175 yards)-1; 7th hole (375 yards)-2. Thus he was 10 under par for four consecutive holes.

● At the Standard Life Loch Lomond tournament on the European Tour in July 2000 Jarmo Sandelin holed-in-one at the 17th with the final shot there in the third round and fellow Swede Mathias Gronberg holed-in-one with the first shot there in the last round. A prize of $100,000 was only on offer in the last round.

Holing-in-one twice (or more) in the same round by the same person

What might be thought to be a very rare feat indeed – that of holing-in-one twice in the same round – has in fact happened on many occasions as the following instances show. It is, nevertheless, compared to the number of golfers in the world, still something of an outstanding achievement. The first known occasion was in 1907 when J. Ireland playing in a three-ball match at Worlington holed the 5th and 18th holes in one stroke and two years later in 1909 H.C. Josecelyne holed the 3rd (175 yards) and the 14th (115 yards) at Acton on 24th November.

● The first mention of two holes-in-one in a round by a woman was followed later by a similar feat by another lady at the same club. On 19th May, 1942, Mrs W. Driver, of Balgowlah Golf Club, New South Wales, holed out in one at the 3rd and 8th holes in the same round, while on 29th July, 1948, Mrs F. Burke at the same club holed out in one at the second and eighth holes.

● The Rev Harold Snider, aged 75, scored his first hole-in-one on 9th June, 1976 at the 8th hole of the Ironwood course, near Phoenix. By the end of his round he had scored three holes-in-one, the other two being at the 13th (110 yards) and 14th (135 yards). Ironwood is a par-3 course, giving more opportunity for scoring holes-in-one, but, nevertheless, three holes-in-one in one round on any type of course is an outstanding achievement.

● When the Hawarden course in North Wales comprised only nine holes, Frank Mills in 1994 had two holes-in-one at the same hole in the same round. Each time, he hit a seven iron to the 134-yard 3rd and 12th.

● The youngest player to achieve two holes-in-one in the same round is thought to be Christopher Anthony Jones on 14 September, 1994. At the age of 14 years and 11 months he holed-in-one at the Sand Moor, Leeds, 137-yard 10th and then at the 156-yard 17th.

● The youngest woman to have performed the feat was a 17-year-old, Marjorie Merchant, playing at the Lomas Athletic GC, Argentina, at the 4th (170 yards) and 8th (130 yards) holes.

● Tony Hannam, left-handed, handicap 16 and age 71, followed a hole-in-one at the 142 yards 4th of the Bude and North Cornwall Golf Club course with another at the 143-yard 10th on Friday, 18th September, 1992.

● Brothers Eric and John Wilkinson were playing together at the Ravensworth Golf Club on Tyneside in 2001 and both holed-in-one at the 148 yards eighth. Eric (46) played first and then John to the hidden green but there is no doubting this unusual double ace. The club's vice-captain Dave Johnstone saw both balls go in! Postman Eric plays off 9. John, a county planner, has a handicap of 20. Next time they played the hole both missed the green.

● Chris Valerro, a 22-handicapper from the Liberty Lake Golf Club, Spokane, Washington, aced the 143 yards 3rd hole at his home club with a 7-iron and then the 140 yards 11th hole with his 8-iron.

● Edinburgh golfer, 25-year-old Chris Tugwell, was representing the Lothianburn club when he aced the 157-yard seventh with a nine iron and then went on to hole-in-one again at the 168-yard 12th with a five iron.

● Eugene O'Brien scored a hole-in-one double on one of Britain's most difficult courses when he aced the 13th and 16th holes at Carnoustie.

● Yusuka Miyazato, a multiple winner on the Japanese circuit, had two holes in one in the same round on the second day at the Montreux Golf Club in 2006.

● Milwaukee resident Sanjay Kuttemperoor scored two aces in 2006 at the Treetops Resort, Michigan, the first on the 150-yard fifth and the second on the 135-yard ninth.

Holes-in-one on the same day

● In July 1987, at the Skerries Club, Co Dublin, Rank Xerox sponsored two tournaments, a men's 18-hole four-ball with 134 pairs competing and a 9-hole mixed foursomes with 33 pairs. During the day each of the four par-3 holes on the course were holed-in-one: the 2nd by Noel Bollard, the 5th by Bart Reynolds, the 12th by Jackie Carr and the 15th by Gerry Ellis.

● Wendy Russell holed-in-one at the consecutive par threes in the first round of the British Senior Ladies' at Wrexham in 1989.

● Clifford Briggs, aged 65, holed-in-one at the 14th at Parkstone GC on the same day as his wife Gwen, 60, aced the 16th.

● In the final round of the 2000 Victor Chandler British Masters at Woburn Alastair Forsyth holed-in-one at the second. Playing partner Roger Chapman then holed-in-one at the eighth.

Two holes-in-one at the same hole in the same game

● First in World: George Stewart and Fred Spellmeyer at the 18th hole, Forest Hills, New Jersey, USA in October 1919.

● First in Great Britain: Miss G. Clutterbuck and Mrs H.M. Robinson at the 15th hole (120 yards), St Augustine GC, Ramsgate, on 8th May, 1925.

● First in Denmark: In a Club match in August 1987 at Himmerland, Steffan Jacobsen of Aalborg and Peter Forsberg of Himmerland halved the 15th hole in one shot, the first known occasion in Denmark.

● First in Australia: Dr & Mrs B. Rankine, playing in a mixed "Canadian foursome" event at the Osmond Club near Adelaide, South Australia in April 1987, holed-in-one in consecutive shots at the 2nd hole (162 metres), he from the men's tee with a 3-iron and his wife from the ladies' tee with a 1½ wood.

● Jack Ashton, aged 76, holed-in-one at the 8th hole of the West Kent Golf Club at Downe but only got a half. Opponent Ted Eagle, in receipt of shot, made a 2, net 1.

● Dr Martin Pucci and Trevor Ironside will never forget one round at the Macdonald Club in Ellon last year. Playing in an open competition the two golfers with Jamie Cowthorne making up the three-ball reached the tee at the 169yards short 11th. Dr Pucci, with the honour, hit a 5-iron, Mr Ironside a 6-iron at the hole where only the top of the flag is visible. Both hit good shots but when they reached the green they could spot only one ball   and that was Mr Cowthorne's. Then they realised that something amazing might have happened. When they reached the putting surface they discovered that both Dr Pucci's and Mr Ironside's balls were wedged into the

---

Brothers hole in one at same hole on same day

Brothers Hanks and Davis Massey were playing a late afternoon practice round at TPC Sawgrass in Florida when they came to the par 3 third. Eleven-year-old Hanks was up first and hit a 9-iron 108 yards into the hole. He and his father Scott ran up to the green in wild celebration forgetting that nine-year-old Davis had still to play. When he did he pulled out an 8-iron and also aced – a feat that experts considered was a 7 million to 1 chance!

hole. Both had made aces. It was Dr Pucci's sixth and Mr Ironside's second.

● Eric and John Wilkinson went out for their usual weekly game at the Ravensworth Golf Club in Wrekenton on Tyneside in 2001 and both holed in one at the 148 yards eighth. Neither Eric, a 46-year-old 9-handicapper who has been playing golf since he was 14, nor John, who has been playing golf for ten years and has a handicap of 20, saw the balls go in because the green is over a hill but club vice-captain Dave Johnston did and described the incident as "amazing". Next time the brothers played the hole both missed the green!

● Richard Evans and Mark Evans may not be related but they have one thing in common – they both holed in one at the same hole when playing in a club competition. The double ace occurred in 2003 at Glynhir Golf Club's third hole which measures 189 yards. Thirty-seven-year-old surveyor Richard, who plays off 7, hit first and made his first hole-in-one in the 15 years he has played the game. His opponent, car worker Mark whose handicap is 12, then followed him in.

● Richard Hall, who plays off 12, and high handicapper Peter McEvoy had never had a hole-in-one until one Saturday night in 2003 at Shandon Park Golf Club in Belfast. Friends since their schooldays they play a lot of golf together so there was much excitement when Hall holed his 5-iron shot for an ace at the 180 yards eighth. Then he challenged McEvoy to match it. And he did!

Three holes-in-one at the same hole in the same game

● During the October monthly medal at Southport & Ainsdale Golf Club on Saturday October 18, 2003, three holes-in-one were achieved at the 153-yard 8th by Stuart Fawcett (5 handicap), Brian Verinder (17 handicap) and junior member Andrew Kent (12 handicap). The players were not playing in the same group.

Holing-in-one – youngest and oldest players

● Elsie McLean, 102, from Chico, California, holed-in-one in April 2007.

● In January 1985 Otto Bucher of Switzerland holed-in-one at the age of 99 on La Manga's 130-yard 12th hole.

● In 2005, Bim Smith, a member of Rochester & Cobham Park Golf Club, Kent, hit a hole-in-one – his fourth – three days before his 91st birthday.

● Bob Hope had a hole-in-one at Palm Springs, California, at the age of 90.

● 76-year-old lady golfer Mrs Felicity Sieghart achieved two holes-in-one when playing in a club Stableford competition at the Aldeburgh club in 2003. Mrs Sieghart aced the 134 yards eighth and the 130 yards 17th – but sadly did not win the competition.

● The youngest player ever to achieve a hole in one is now believed to be Matthew Draper, who was only five when he aced the 122-yard fourth hole at Cherwell Edge, Oxfordshire, in June 1997. He used a wood.

● Six-year-old Tommy Moore aced the 145-yard fourth hole at Woodbrier, West Virginia, in 1968. He had another at the same hole before his seventh birthday.

● Keith Long was just five when he aced on a Mississippi golf course in 1998.

● Alex Evans, aged eight, holed-in-one with a 4-wood at the 136-yard 4th hole at Bromborough, Merseyside, in 1994.

● Nine-year-old Kate Langley from Scotter in Lincolnshire, is believed to have became the youngest girl to score an ace. It is reported that she holed in one at the 134 yards first hole at Forest Pines Beeches in Scunthorpe after having had a lesson from local professional David Edwards. Kate was nine years and 166 days when she hit the ace – 199 days younger than Australian Kathryn Webb who had held the record previously.

● In 2007, 13-year-old Lauren Taylor from Rugby scored two aces and made history at her club. Her first ace was scored on the 145 yard 12th, where she used a seven iron for her shot over the brook whilst playing in a junior medal competition. Her second came during the second round of the 36-hole Junior Championship This time it was achieved on the 100 yard 8th (which plays much harder due to it being all up-hill), using a pitching wedge. From the tee you cannot see what is happening on the green.

Holing-in-one – miscellaneous incidents

● Chemistry student Jason Bohn, aged 19, of State College, Pennsylvania, supported a charity golf event at Tuscaloosa, Alabama, in 1992 when twelve competitors were invited to try to hole-in-one at the 135-yard second hole for a special prize covered by insurance. One attempt only was allowed. Bohn succeeded and was offered US$1m (paid at the rate of $5,000 a month for the next 20 years) at the cost of losing his amateur status. He took the money.

● The late Harry Vardon, who scored the greatest number of victories in The Open Championship, only once did a hole-in-one. That was in 1903 at Mundesley, Norfolk, where Vardon was convalescing from a long illness.

● In a guest day at Rochford Hundred, Essex, in 1994, there were holes-in-one at all the par threes. First Paul Cairns, of Langdon Hills, holed a 4-iron at the 205-yard 15th, next Paul Francis, a member of the home club, sank a 7-iron at the 156-yard seventh and finally Jim Crabb, of Three Rivers, holed a 9-iron at the 136-yard 11th.

● In April 1988, Mary Anderson, a bio-chemistry student at Trinity College, Dublin, holed-in-one at the 290-yard 6th hole at Island GC, Co Dublin.

● In April 1984 Joseph McCaffrey and his son, Gordon, each holed-in-one in the Spring Medal at the 164-yard 12th hole at Vale of Leven Club, Dunbartonshire.

● In 1977, 14-year-old Gillian Field after a series of lessons holed-in-one at the 10th hole at Moor Place GC in her first round of golf.

● When he holed-in-one at the second hole in a match against D. Graham in the 1979 Suntory World Match Play at Wentworth, Japanese professional Isao Aoki won himself a Bovis home at Gleneagles worth, inclusive of furnishings, £55,000. Brian Barnes has aced the short 10th and Thomas Bjørn won a car when he aced the short 14th in 2003.

● On the morning after being elected captain for 1973 of the Norwich GC, J.S. Murray hit his first shot as captain straight into the hole at the 169-yard 1st hole.

● At Nuneaton GC in 1999 the men's captain and the ladies' captain both holed-in-one during their captaincies.

● Using the same club and ball, 11-handicap left-hander Christopher Smyth holed-in-one at the 2nd hole (170 yards) in two consecutive medal competitions at Headfort GC, Co. Meath, in January, 1976.

● Playing over Rickmansworth course at Easter, 1960, Mrs A.E. (Paddy) Martin achieved a remarkable sequence of aces. On Good Friday she sank her tee shot at the 3rd hole (125 yards). The next day, using the same ball and the same 8-iron, at the same hole, she scored another one. And on the Monday (same ball, same club, same hole) she again holed out from the tee.

● At Barton-on-Sea in February 1989 Mrs Dorothy Huntley-Flindt, aged 91, holed-in-one at the par-3 13th. The following day Mr John Chape, a fellow member in his 80s, holed the par- 3 5th in one.

● In 1995 Roy Marsland of Ratho Park, Edinburgh, had three holes-in-one in nine days: at Prestonfield's 5th, at Ratho Park's 3rd and at Sandilands' 2nd.

● Michael Monk, age 82, a member of Tandridge Golf Club, Surrey, waited until 1992 to record his first hole-in-one. It continued a run of rare successes for his family. In the previous 12 months, Mr Monk's daughter, Elizabeth, 52, daughter-in-law, Celia, 48, and grandson, Jeremy, 16, had all holed-in-one on the same course.

● Lou Holloway, a left-hander, recorded his second hole-in-one at the Mount Derby course in New Zealand 13 years after acing the same hole while playing right-handed.

● Ryan Procop, an American schoolboy, holed-in-one at a 168-yard par 3 at Glen Eagles GC, Ohio, with a putter. He confessed that he was so disgusted with himself after a 12 on the previous hole that he just grabbed his putter and hit from the tee.

● Ernie and Shirley Marsden, of Warwick Golf Club, are believed in 1993 to have equalled the record for holes-in-one by a married couple. Each has had three, as have another English couple, Mr and Mrs B.E. Simmonds.

● Russell Pughe, a 12-handicapper from Nottinghamshire, holed-in-one twice in three days at the 274-yard par-4 18th hole at Sidmouth in Devon in 1998. The hole has a blind tee shot.

● Robert Looney aced the 170 yards 13th at the Thorny Lea Golf Club in Brockton, Massachussetts, 30 years after his father made a hole-in-one at the same hole.

● The odds on the chances of two players having a hole in one when playing together are long but it happened to former club captain Robert Smallwood, a 58-year-old retired IBM manager, and current captain Mike Wheeler, a 57-year-old retired financial consultant, when they went out for a round at Irvine Golf Club in Ayrshire in 2005. Playing in the rain, Mr Smallwood, using a driver, had his ace at the 289 yards fourth before Mr Wheeler holed in one at the 279 yards fifth.

● Texan blind golfer Charles Adams, sank his tee shot on the 102-yard 14th hole at Stone Creek Golf Club, Oregon City, Oregon, on October 4, 2006, during the US Blind Golf Association National Championship, the first hole-in-one in the 61-year history of the tournament.

● Blind golfer Sheila Drummond, a member of the US Blind Golf Association (USBGA), is believe to be the only blind woman golfer to have holed-in-one. Sheila's feat was accomplished in August 2007 at the 144-yard par-3 at Mahoning Valley CC in Lehighton, PA.

Challenge matches

One of the first recorded professional challenge matches was in 1843 when Allan Robertson beat Willie Dunn in a 20-round match at St Andrews over 360 holes by 2 rounds and 1 to play. Thereafter until about 1905 many matches are recorded, some for up to £200 a side – a considerable sum for the time. The Morrises, the Dunns and the Parks were the main protagonists until Vardon, Braid and Taylor took over in the 1890s. Often matches were on a home-and-away basis over 72 holes or more, with many spectators; Vardon and Willie Park Jr attracted over 10,000 at North Berwick in 1899.

Between the wars Walter Hagen, Archie Compston, Henry Cotton and Bobby Locke all played several such matches. Compston surprisingly beat Hagen by 18 up and 17 to play at Moor Park in 1928; yet typically Hagen went on to win The Open the following week at Sandwich. Cotton played classic golf at Walton Heath in 1937 when he beat Densmore Shute for £500-a-side at Walton Heath by 6 and 5 over 72 holes.

Curious and large wagers

(See also bets recorded under Cross-Country Matches and in Challenge Matches)

● In The Royal and Ancient Golf Club minutes an entry on 3rd November, 1820 was made in the following terms:

> Sir David Moncrieffe, Bart, of Moncrieffe, backs his life against the life of John Whyte-Melville, Esq, of Strathkinnes, for a new silver club as a present to the St Andrews Golf Club, the price of the club to be paid by the survivor and the arms of the parties to be engraved on the club, and the present bet inscribed on it. No balls to be attached to it. In testimony of which this bet is subscribed by the parties thereto.

Thirteen years later, Mr Whyte-Melville, in a feeling and appropriate speech, expressed his deep regret at the lamented death of Sir David Moncrieffe, one of the most distinguished and zealous supporters of the club. Whyte-Melville, while lamenting the cause that led to it, had pleasure in fulfilling the duty imposed upon him by the bet, and accordingly delivered to the captain the silver putter. Whyte-Melville in 1883 was elected captain of the club a second time; he died in his eighty-sixth year in July, 1883, before he could take office and the captaincy remained vacant for a year. His portrait hangs in The Royal and Ancient clubhouse and is one of the finest and most distinguished pictures in the smoking room.

● In 1914 Francis Ouimet, who in the previous autumn had won the American Open Championship after a triangular tie with Harry Vardon and Ted Ray, came to Great Britain with Jerome D. Travers, the holder of the American amateur title, to compete in the British Amateur Championship at Sandwich. An American syndicate took a bet of £30,000 to £10,000 that one or other of the two United States champions would be the winner. It only took two rounds to decide the bet against the Americans. Ouimet was beaten by a then quite unknown player, H.S. Tubbs, while Travers was defeated by Charles Palmer, who was 56 years of age at the time.

● In 1907 John Ball for a wager undertook to go round Hoylake during a dense fog in under 90, in not more than two and a quarter hours and without losing a ball. Ball played with a black ball, went round in 81, and also beat the time.

● The late Ben Sayers, for a wager, played the 18 holes of the Burgess Society course scoring a four at every hole. Sayers was about to start against an American, when his opponent asked him what he could do the course in. *Fours* replied Sayers, meaning 72, or an average of 4s for the round. A bet was made, then the American added, *Remember a three or a five is not a four.* There were eight bogey 5s and two 3s on the Burgess course at the time Old Ben achieved his feat.

Feats of endurance

Although golf is not a game where endurance, in the ordinary sense in which the term is employed in sport, is required, there are several instances of feats on the links which demanded great physical exertion.

● Four British golfers, Simon Gard, Nick Harley, Patrick Maxwell and his brother Alastair Maxwell, completed 14 rounds in one day at Iceland's Akureyri Golf Club, the most northern 18-hole course in the world, during June 1991 when there was 24-hour daylight. It was claimed a record and £10,000 was raised for charity.

● In 1971 during a 24-hour period from 6 pm on 27th November until 5.15 pm on 28th November, Ian Colston completed 401 holes over the 6,061 yards Bendigo course, Victoria, Australia. Colston was a top marathon athlete but was not a golfer. However prior to his golfing marathon he took some lessons and became adept with a 6-iron, the only club

he used throughout the 401 holes. The only assistance Colston had was a team of harriers to carry his 6-iron and look for his ball, and a band of motorcyclists who provided light during the night. This is, as far as is known, the greatest number of holes played in 24 hours on foot on a full-size course.

● In 1934 Col Bill Farnham played 376 holes in 24 hours 10 minutes at the Guildford Lake Course, Guildford, Connecticut, using only a mashie and a putter.

● To raise funds for extending the Skipton GC course from 12 to 18 holes, the club professional, 24-year-old Graham Webster, played 277 holes in the hours of daylight on Monday 20th June, 1977. Playing with nothing longer than a 5-iron he averaged 81 per 18-hole round. Included in his marathon was a hole-in-one.

● Michael Moore, a 7 handicap 26-year-old member of Okehampton GC, completed on foot 15 rounds 6 holes (276 holes) there on Sunday, 25th June, 1972, in the hours of daylight. He started at 4.15 am and stopped at 9.15 pm. The distance covered was estimated at 56 miles.

● On 21st June, 1976, 5-handicapper Sandy Small played 15 rounds (270 holes) over his home course Cosby GC, length 6,128 yards, to raise money for the Society of Physically Handicapped Children. Using only a 5-iron, 9-iron and putter, Small started at 4.10 am and completed his 270th hole at 10.39 pm with the aid of car headlights. His fastest round was his first (40 minutes) and slowest his last (82 minutes). His best round of 76 was achieved in the second round.

● During the weekend of 20th–21st June, 1970, Peter Chambers of Yorkshire completed over 14 rounds of golf over the Scarborough South Cliff course. In a non-stop marathon lasting just under 24 hours, Chambers played 257 holes in 1,168 strokes, an average of 84.4 strokes per round.

● Bruce Sutherland, on the Craiglockhart Links, Edinburgh, started at 8.15 pm on 21st June, 1927, and played almost continuously until 7.30 pm on 22nd June, 1927. During the night four caddies with acetylene lamps lit the way, and lost balls were reduced to a minimum. He completed fourteen rounds. Mr Sutherland, who was a physical culture teacher, never recovered from the physical strain and died a few years later.

● Sidney Gleave, motorcycle racer, and Ernest Smith, golf professional at Davyhulme Club, Manchester, on 12th June, 1939, played five rounds of golf in five different countries – Scotland, Ireland, Isle of Man, England and Wales. Smith had to play the five rounds under 80 in one day to win the £100 wager. They travelled by plane, and the following was their programme:

Start 3.40a.m. at Prestwick St Nicholas (Scotland), finished 1 hour 35 minutes later on 70.

2nd Course – Bangor, Ireland. Started at 7.15 a.m. and took 1 hour 30 minutes to finish on 76.

3rd Course – Castletown, Isle of Man. Started 10.15 am, scored 76 in 1 hour 40 minutes.

4th Course – Blackpool, Stanley Park, England. Started at 1.30 pm and scored 72 in 1 hour 55 minutes.

5th Course – Hawarden, Wales, started at 6 pm and finished 2 hours 15 minutes later with a score of 72.

● On 19th June, 1995, Ian Botham, the former England cricketer, played four rounds of golf in Ireland, Wales, Scotland and England. His playing companions were Gary Price, the professional at Branston, and Tony Wright, owner of Craythorne, Burton-on-Trent, where the last 18 holes were completed. The other courses were St Margaret's, Anglesey and Dumfries & Galloway. The first round began at 4.30 am and the last was completed at 8.30 pm.

● On Wednesday, 3rd July, 1974, E.S. Wilson, Whitehead, Co. Antrim and Dr G.W. Donaldson, Newry, Co. Down, played a nine-hole match in each of seven countries in the one day. The first 9 holes was at La Moye (Channel Islands) followed by Hawarden (Wales), Chester (England), Turnberry (Scotland), Castletown (Isle of Man), Dundalk (Eire) and Warrenpoint (N Ireland). They started their first round at 4.25 am and their last round at 9.25 pm. Wilson piloted his own plane throughout.

● In June 1986 to raise money for the upkeep of his medieval church, the Rector of Mark with Allerton, Somerset, the Rev Michael Pavey, played a sponsored 18 holes on 18 different courses in the Bath & Wells Diocese. With his partner, the well-known broadcaster on music, Antony Hopkins, they played the 1st at Minehead at 5.55 am and finished playing the 18th at Burnham and Berrow at 6.05 pm. They covered 240 miles in the "round" including the distances to reach the correct tee for the "next" hole on each course. Par for the "round" was 70. Together the pair raised £10,500 for the church.

● To raise funds for the Marlborough Club's centenary year (1988), Laurence Ross, the Club professional, in June 1987, played eight rounds in 12 hours. Against a par of 72, he completed the 576 holes in 3 under par, playing from back tees and walking all the way.

● As part of the 1992 Centenary Celebrations of the Royal Cinque Ports Golf Club at Deal, Kent, and to support charity, a six-handicap member, John Brazell, played all 37 royal courses in Britain and Ireland in 17 days. He won 22 matches, halved three, lost 12; hit 2,834 shots for an average score of 76.6; lost 11 balls and made 62 birdies. The aim was to raise £30,000 for Leukaemia Research and the Spastics Society.

● To raise more than £500 for the Guide Dogs for the Blind charity in the summer of 1992, Mrs Cheryle Power, a member of the Langley Park Golf Club, Beckenham, Kent, played 100 holes in a day – starting at 5 am and finishing at 8.45 pm.

● David Steele, a former European Tour player, completed 17½ rounds, 315 holes, between 6 am and 9.45 pm in 1993 at the San Roque club near Gibraltar in a total of 1,291 shots. Steele was assisted by a caddie cart and raised £15,000 for charity.

● In 2005 Bernard Wood, a member of Rossendale Golf Club, played all the 18-hole courses in Scotland – 377 in all – to raise money for the Kirsty Appeal which supports the Frances House Children's Hospice in Manchester.

Fastest rounds

● Dick Kimbrough, 41, completed a round on foot on 8th August, 1972, at North Platte CC, Nebraska (6,068 yards) in 30 minutes 10 seconds. He carried only a 3-iron.

● At Mowbray Course, Cape Town, November 1931, Len Richardson, who had represented South Africa in the Olympic Games, played a round which measured 6,248 yards in 31 minutes 22 seconds.

● The women's all-time record for the fastest round played on a course of at least 5,600 yards is held by Sue Ledger, 20, who completed the East Berks course in 38 minutes 8 seconds, beating the previous record by 17 minutes.

● In April, 1934, after attending a wedding in Bournemouth, Hants, Captain Gerald Moxom hurried to his club, West Hill in Surrey, to play in the captain's prize competition. With daylight fading and still dressed in his morning suit, he went round in 65 minutes and won the competition with a net 71 into the bargain.

● On 14th June, 1922, Jock Hutchison and Joe Kirkwood (AUS) played round the Old Course at St Andrews in 1 hour 20 minutes. Hutchison, out in 37, led by three holes at the ninth and won by 4 and 3.

● Fastest rounds can also take another form – the time taken for a ball to be propelled round 18 holes. The fastest known round of this type is 8 minutes 53.8 seconds on 25th August, 1979 by 42 members at Ridgemount CC Rochester, New York, a course measuring 6,161 yards. The Rules of Golf were observed but a ball was available on each tee; to be driven off the instant the ball had been holed at the preceding hole.

● The fastest round with the same ball took place in January 1992 at the Paradise Golf Club, Arizona. It took only 11 minutes 24 seconds; 91 golfers being positioned around the course ready to hit the ball as soon as it came to rest and then throwing the ball from green to tee.

● In 1992 John Daly and Mark Calcavecchia were both fined by the USPGA Tour for playing the final round of the Players' Championship in Florida in 123 minutes. Daly scored 80, Calcavecchia 81.

Curious scoring

● C.W. Allen of Leek Golf Club chipped-in four times in a round in which he was partnered by K. Brint against G. Davies and R. Hollins. The shortest chip was a yard, the longest 20 yards.

● Tony Blackwell, playing off a handicap of four, broke the course record at Bull Bay, Anglesey, by four strokes when he had a gross 60 (net 56) in winning the club's town trophy in 1996. The course measured 6,217 yards.

● In the third round of the 1994 Volvo PGA Championship at Wentworth, Des Smyth, of Ireland, made birdie twos at each of the four short holes, the 2nd, 5th, 10th and 14th. He also had a two at the second hole in the fourth round.

● Also at Wentworth, in the 1994 World Match Play Championship, Seve Ballesteros had seven successive twos at the short holes – and still lost his quarter-final against Ernie Els.

● R.H. Corbett, playing in the semi-final of the Tangye Cup at Mullion in 1916, did a score of 27. The remarkable part of Corbett's score was that it was made up of nine successive 3s, bogey being 5, 3, 4, 4, 5, 3, 4, 4, 3.

● At Little Chalfont in June 1985 Adrian Donkersley played six successive holes in 6, 5, 4, 3, 2, 1 from the 9th to the 14th holes against a par of 4, 4, 3, 4, 3, 3.

● On 2nd September, 1920, playing over Torphin, near Edinburgh, William Ingle did the first five holes in 1, 2, 3, 4, 5.

● In the summer of 1970, Keith McMillan, on holiday at Cullen, had a remarkable series of 1, 2, 3, 4, 5 at the 11th to 15th holes.

● Marc Osborne was only 14 years of age when he equalled the Betchworth Park amateur course record with a 66 in July, 1993. He was playing in the Mortimer Cup, a 36-hole medal competition, and had at the time a handicap of 6.8.

● Playing at Addington Palace, July, 1934, Ronald Jones, a member of Hendon Club, holed five consecutive holes in 5, 4, 3, 2, 1.

● Harry Dunderdale of Lincoln GC scored 5, 4, 3, 2, 1 in five consecutive holes during the first round of his club championship in 1978. The hole-in-one was the 7th, measuring 294 yards.

● At the Open Amateur Tournament of the Royal Ashdown Forest in 1936 Bobby Locke in his morning round had a score of 72, accomplishing every hole in 4.

● George Stewart of Cupar had a four at every hole over the Queen's course at Gleneagles despite forgetting to change into his golf shoes and therefore still wearing his street shoes.

● Henry Cotton told of one of the most extraordinary scoring feats ever. With some other professionals he was at Sestrieres in the 30s for the Italian Open Championship and Joe Ezar, a colourful character in those days on both sides of the Atlantic, accepted a wager from a club official – 1,000 lira for a 66 to break the course record; 2,000 for a 65; and 4,000 for a 64. I'll do 64, said Ezar, and proceeded to jot down the hole-by-hole score figures he would do next day for that total. With the exception of the ninth and tenth holes where his predicted score was 3, 4 and the actual score was 4, 3, he accomplished this amazing feat exactly as nominated.

● Nick Faldo scored par figures at all 18 holes in the final round of the 1987 Open Championship at Muirfield to win the title.

● During the Colts Championship at Knowle Golf Club, Bristol, Chris Newman (Cotswold Hills) scored eight consecutive 3s with birdies at four of the holes.

● At the Toft Hotel Golf Club captain's day event L. Heffernan had an ace, D. Patrick a 2, R. Barnett a 3 and D. Heffernan a 4 at the 240 yard par-4 ninth.

● In the European Club Championship played at the Parco de Medici Club in Rome in 1998, Belgian Dimitri van Hauwaert from Royal Antwerp had an albatross 2, Norwegian Marius Bjornstad from Oslo an eagle 3 and Scotsman Andrew Hogg from Turriff a birdie 4 at the 486 metre par-5 eighth hole.

● Earle F. Wilson from Brewerton, Alabama, has had an ace, an albatross and has fired eight birdies in a row.

High scores

● In the qualifying competition at Formby for the 1976 Open Championship, Maurice Flitcroft, a 46-year-old crane driver from Barrow-in-Furness, took 121 strokes for the first round and then withdrew saying, I have no chance of qualifying. Flitcroft entered as a professional but had never before played 18 holes. He had taken the game up 18 months previously but, as he was not a member of a club, had been limited to practising on a local beach. His round was made up thus: 7, 5, 6, 6, 6, 6, 12, 6, 7-61; 11, 5, 6, 8, 4, 9, 5, 7, 5-60, total 121. After his round Flitcroft said, "I've made a lot of progress in the last few months and I'm sorry I did not do better. I was trying too hard at the beginning but began to put things together at the end of the round". R&A officials, who were not amused by the bogus professional's efforts, refunded the £30 entry money to Flitcroft's two fellow-competitors. Flitcroft has since tried to qualify for The Open under assumed names: Gerard Hoppy from Switzerland and Beau Jolley (as in the wine)!

● Playing in the qualifying rounds of the 1965 Open Championship at Southport, an American self-styled professional entrant from Milwaukee, Walter Danecki, achieved the inglorious feat of scoring a total of 221 strokes for 36 holes, 81 over par. His first round over the Hillside course was 108, followed by a second round of 113. Walter, who afterwards admitted he felt a little discouraged and sad, declared that he entered because he was after the money.

● The highest individual scoring ever known in the rounds connected with The Open Championship occurred at Muirfield, 1935, when a Scottish professional started 7, 10, 5, 10, and took 65 to reach the 9th hole. Another 10 came at the 11th and the player decided to retire at the 12th hole. There he was in a bunker, and after playing four shots he had not regained the fairway.

● In 1883 in The Open Championship at Musselburgh, Willie Fernie, the winner, had a 10, the only time double figures appeared on the card of The Open Champion of the year. Fernie won after a tie with Bob Ferguson, and his score for the last hole in the tie was 2. He holed from just off the green to win by one stroke.

● In the first Open Championship at Prestwick in 1860 a competitor took 21, the highest score for one hole ever recorded in this event. The record is preserved in the archives of the Prestwick Golf Club, where the championship was founded.

● In the first round of the 1980 US Masters, Tom Weiskopf hit his ball into the water hazard in front of the par-3 12th hole five times and scored 13 for the hole.

● In the French Open at St Cloud, in 1968, Brian Barnes took 15 for the short 8th hole in the second round. After missing putts at which he hurriedly snatched while the ball was moving he penalised himself further by standing astride the line of a putt. The amazing result was that he actually took 12 strokes from about three feet from the hole. The highest scores on the European Tour were also recorded in the French Open. Philippe Porquier had a 20 at La Baule in 1978 and Ian Woosnam a 16 at La Boulie in 1986.

● US professional Dave Hill 6-putted the fifth green at Oakmont in the 1962 US Open Championship.

● Many high scores have been made at the Road Hole at St Andrews. Davie Ayton, on one occasion, was coming in a certain winner of The Open Championship when he got on the road and took 11. In 1921, at The Open Championship, one professional took 13. In 1923, competing for the Autumn Medal of The Royal and Ancient, J.B. Anderson required a five and a four to win the second award, but he took 13 at the Road Hole. Anderson was close to the green in two, was twice in the bunkers in the face of the green, and once on the road. In 1935, R.H. Oppenheimer tied for the Royal Medal (the first award) in the Autumn Meeting of The Royal and Ancient. On the play-off he was one stroke behind Captain Aitken when they stood on the 17th tee. Oppenheimer drove three balls out of bounds and eventually took 11 to the Road Hole.

● British professional Mark James scored 111 in the second round of the 1978 Italian Open. He played the closing holes with only his right hand due to an injury to his left hand.

● In the 1927 Shawnee Open, Tommy Armour took 23 strokes to the 17th hole. Armour had won the American Open Championship a week earlier. In an effort to play the hole in a particular way, Armour hooked ball after ball out of bounds and finished with a 21 on the card. There was some doubt about the accuracy of this figure and on reaching the clubhouse Armour stated that it should be 23. This is the highest score by a professional in a tournament.

Freak matches

● In 1912, the late Harry Dearth, an eminent vocalist, attired in a complete suit of heavy armour, played a match at Bushey Hall. He was beaten 2 and 1.

● In 1914, at the start of the First World War, J.N. Farrar, a native of Hoylake, was stationed at Royston, Herts. A bet was made of 10-1 that he would not go round Royston under 100 strokes, equipped in full infantry marching order, water bottle, full field kit and haversack. Farrar went round in 94. At the camp were several golfers, including professionals, who tried the same feat but failed.

● Captain Pennington took part in a match *from the air* against A.J. Young, the professional at Sonning.

Captain Pennington, with 80 golf balls in the locker of his machine, had to find the Sonning greens by dropping the balls as he circled over the course. The balls were covered in white cloth to ensure that they did not bounce once they struck the ground. The airman completed the course in 40 minutes, taking 29 *strokes*, while Young occupied two hours for his round of 68. Captain Pennington was eventually killed in an air crash in 1933.

● In April 1924, at Littlehampton, Harry Rowntree, an amateur golfer, played the better ball of Edward Ray and George Duncan, receiving an allowance of 150 yards to use as he required during the round. Rowntree won by 6 and 5 and had used only 50 yards 2 feet of his handicap. At one hole Duncan had a two – Rowntree, who was 25 yards from the hole, took this distance from his handicap and won the hole in one. Ray (died 1945) afterwards declared that, conceding a handicap of one yard per round, he could win every championship in the world. And he might, when reckoning is taken of the number of times a putt just stops an inch or two or how much difference to a shot three inches will make for the lie of the ball, either in a bunker or on the fairway. Many single matches on the same system have been played. An 18 handicap player opposed to a scratch player should make a close match with an allowance of 50 yards.

● The first known instance of a golf match by telephone occurred in 1957, when the Cotswold Hills Golf Club, Cheltenham, England, won a golf tournament against the Cheltenham Golf Club, Melbourne, Australia, by six strokes. A large crowd assembled at the English club to wait for the 12,000 miles telephone call from Australia. The match had been played at the suggestion of a former member of the Cotswold Hills Club, Harry Davies, and was open to every member of the two clubs. The result of the match was decided on the aggregate of the eight best scores on each side and the English club won by 564 strokes to 570.

Golf matches against other sports

● H.H. Hilton and Percy Ashworth, many times racket champion, contested a driving match, the former driving a golf ball with a driver, and the latter a racket ball with a racket. Best distances: Against breeze – Golfer 182 yards; Racket player 125 yards. Down wind – Golfer 230 yards; Racket player 140 yards. Afterwards Ashworth hit a golf ball with the racket and got a greater distance than with the racket ball, but was still a long way behind the ball driven by Hilton.

● In 1913, at Wellington, Shropshire, a match between a golfer and a fisherman casting a 2½ oz weight was played. The golfer, Rupert May, took 87; the fisherman J.J.D. Mackinlay, in difficulty because of his short casts, 102. His longest cast, 105 yards, was within 12 yards of the world record at the time, held by French angler, Decautelle. When within a rod's length of a hole he ran the weight to the rod end and dropped into the hole. Five times he broke his line, and was allowed another shot without penalty.

● In December, 1913, F.M.A. Webster, of the London Athletic Club, and Dora Roberts, with javelins, played a match with the late Harry Vardon and Mrs Gordon Robertson, who used the regulation clubs and golf balls. The golfers conceded two-thirds in the matter of distance, and they won by 5 up and 4 to play in a contest of 18 holes. The javelin throwers had a mark of two feet square in which to hole out while the golfers had to get their ball into the ordinary golf hole. Mr Webster's best throw was one of 160 feet.

● Several matches have taken place between a golfer on the one side and an archer on the other. The wielder of the bow and arrow has nearly always proved the victor. In 1953 at Kirkhill Golf Course, Lanarkshire, five archers beat six golfers by two games to one. There were two special rules for the match; when an archer's arrow landed six feet from the hole or the golfer's ball three feet from the hole, they were counted as holed. When the arrows landed in bunkers or in the rough, archers lifted their arrow and added a stroke. The sixth archer in this match called off and one archer shot two arrows from each of the 18 tees.

● In 1954, at the Southbroom Club, South Africa, a match over 9 holes was played between an archer and a fisherman against two golfers. The participants were all champions of their own sphere and consisted of Vernon Adams (archer), Dennis Burd (fisherman), Jeanette Wahl (champion of Southbroom and Port Shepstone), and Ron Burd (professional at Southbroom). The conditions were that the archer had holed out when his arrows struck a small leather bag placed on the green beside the hole and in the event of his placing his approach shot within a bow's length of the pin he was deemed to have 1-putted. The fisherman, to achieve a 1-putt, had to land his sinker within a rod's length of the pin. The two golfers were ahead for brief spells, but it was the opposition who led at the deciding 9th hole where Robin Hood played a perfect approach for a birdie.

● An Across England combined match was begun on 11th October, 1965, by four golfers and two archers from Crowborough Beacon Golf Club, Sussex, accompanied by Penny, a white Alsatian dog, whose duty it was to find lost balls. They teed off from Carlisle Castle via Hadrian's Wall, the Pennine Way, finally holing out in the 18th hole at Newcastle United GC in 612 teed shots. Casualties included 110 lost golf balls and 19 lost or broken arrows. The match took 5½ days, and the distance travelled was about 60 miles. The golfers were Miss P. Ward, K. Meaney, K. Ashdown and C.A. Macey; the archers were W.H. Hulme and T. Scott. The first arrow was fired from the battlements of Carlisle Castle, a distance of nearly 300 yards, by Cumberland Champion R. Willis, who also fired the second arrow right across the River Eden. R. Clough, president of Newcastle United GC, holed the last two putts. The match was in aid of Guide Dogs for the Blind and Friends of Crowborough Hospital.

Cross-country matches

● Taking 1 year, 114 days, Floyd Rood golfed his way from coast to coast across the United States. He took 114,737 shots including 3,511 penalty shots for the 3,397 mile course.

● Two Californian teenagers, Bob Aube (17) and Phil Marrone (18) went on a golfing safari in 1974 from San Francisco to Los Angeles, a trip of over 500 miles lasting 16 days. The first six days they played alongside motorways. Over 1,000 balls were used.

● In 1830, the Gold Medal winner of The Royal and Ancient backed himself for 10 sovereigns to drive from the 1st hole at St Andrews to the toll bar at Cupar, distance nine miles, in 200 teed shots. He won easily.

● In 1848, two Edinburgh golfers played a match from Bruntsfield Links to the top of Arthur's Seat – an eminence overlooking the Scottish capital, 822 feet above sea level.

● On a winter's day in 1898, Freddie Tait backed himself to play a gutta ball in 40 teed shots from Royal St George's Clubhouse, Sandwich, to the Cinque Ports Club, Deal. He was to hole out by hitting any part of the Deal Clubhouse. The distance as the crow flies was three miles. The redoubtable Tait holed out with his 32nd shot, so effectively that the ball went through a window.

● In 1900 three members of the Hackensack (NJ) Club played a game of four-and-a-half hours over an extemporised course six miles long, which stretched from Hackensack to Paterson. Despite rain, cornfields, and wide streams, the three golfers – J.W. Hauleebeek, Dr E.R. Pfaare, and Eugene Crassons – completed the round, the first and the last named taking 305 strokes each, and Dr Pfaare 327 strokes. The players used only two clubs, the mashie and the cleek.

● On 3rd December, 1920, P. Rupert Phillips and W. Raymond Thomas teed up on the first tee of the Radyr Golf Club and played to the last hole at Southerndown. The distance as the crow flies was 15½ miles, but circumventing swamps, woods, and plough, they covered, approximately, 20 miles. The wager was that they would not do the hole in 1,000 strokes, but they holed out at their 608th stroke two days later. They carried large ordnance maps.

● On 12th March, 1921, A. Stanley Turner, Macclesfield, played from his house to the Cat and Fiddle Inn, five miles distance, in 64 strokes. The route was broken and hilly with a rise of nearly 1,000 feet. Turner was allowed to tee up within two club lengths after each shot and the wagering was 6-4 against his doing the distance in 170 strokes.

● In 1919, a golfer drove a ball from Piccadilly Circus and, proceeding via the Strand, Fleet Street and Ludgate Hill, holed out at the Royal Exchange, London. The player drove off at 8 am on a Sunday, a time when the usually thronged thoroughfares were deserted.

● On 23rd April, 1939, Richard Sutton, a London stockbroker, played from Tower Bridge, London, to

White's Club, St James's Street, in 142 strokes. The bet was he would not do *the course* in under 200 shots. Sutton used a putter, crossed the Thames at Southwark Bridge, and hit the ball short distances to keep out of trouble.

● Golfers produced the most original event in Ireland's three-week national festival of An Tostal, in 1953 – a cross-country competition with an advertised £1,000,000 for the man who could hole out in one. The 150 golfers drove off from the first tee at Kildare Club to hole out eventually on the 18th green, five miles away, on the nearby Curragh course, a distance of 8,800 yards. The unusual hazards to be negotiated included the main Dublin-Cork railway line and highway, the Curragh Racecourse, hoofprints left by Irish thoroughbred racehorses out exercising on the plains from nearby stables, army tank tracks and about 150 telephone lines. The Golden Ball Trophy, which is played for annually – a standard size golf ball in gold, mounted on a black marble pillar beside the silver figure of a golfer on a green marble base, designed by Captain Maurice Cogan, Army GHQ, Dublin – was for the best gross. And it went to one of the longest hitters in international golf – Amateur Champion, Irish internationalist and British Walker Cup player Joe Carr, with the remarkable score of 52.

● In 1961, as a University Charities Week stunt, four Aberdeen University students set out to golf their way up Ben Nevis (4,406 feet). About half-way up, after losing 63 balls and expending 659 strokes, the quartet conceded victory to Britain's highest mountain.

● Among several cross-country golfing exploits, one of the most arduous was faced by Iain Williamson and Tony Kent, who teed off from Cained Point on the summit of Fairfield in the Lake District. With the hole cut in the lawn of the Bishop of Carlisle's home at Rydal Park, it measured 7,200 yards and passed through the summits of Great Rigg Mann, Heron Pike and Nab Scar, descending altogether 1,900 feet. Eight balls were lost and the two golfers holed out in a combined total of 303 strokes.

Long-lived golfers

● James Priddy, aged 80, played in the Seniors' Open at his home club, Weston-super-Mare, Avon, on 27th June, 1990, and scored a gross 70 to beat his age by ten shots.

● The oldest golfer who ever lived is believed to have been Arthur Thompson of British Columbia, Canada. He equalled his age when 103 at Uplands GC, a course of over 6,000 yards. He died two years later.

● Nathaniel Vickers celebrated his 103rd birthday on Sunday, 9th October, 1949, and died the following day. He was the oldest member of the United States Senior Golf Association and until 1942 he competed regularly in their events and won many trophies in the various age divisions. When 100 years old, he apologised for being able to play only nine holes a day. Vickers predicted he would live until 103 and he died a few hours after he had celebrated his birthday.

● American George Miller, who died in 1979 aged 102, played regularly when 100 years old.

● In 1999 94-year-old Mr W. Seneviratne, a retired schoolmaster who lived and worked in Malaysia, was still practising every day and regularly competing in medal competitions at the Royal Colombo Golf Club which was founded in 1879.

● Bim Smith, a member of Rochester & Cobham Park Golf Club, Kent, achieved a hole-in-one three days before his 91st birthday.

● Phyllis Tidmarsh, aged 90, won a Stableford competition at Saltford Golf Club, near Bath, when she returned 42 points. Her handicap was cut from 28 to 27.

● George Swanwick, a member of Wallasey, celebrated his 90th birthday with a lunch at the club on 1st April, 1971. He played golf several times a week, carrying his own clubs, and had holed-in-one at the ages of 75 and 85. His ambition was to complete the sequence aged 95 … but he died in 1973 aged 92.

● The 10th Earl of Wemyss played a round on his 92nd birthday, in 1910, at Craigielaw. At the age of 87 the Earl was partnered by Harry Vardon in a match at Kilspindie, the golf course on his East Lothian estate at Gosford. After playing his ball the venerable earl mounted a pony and rode to the next shot. He died on 30th June, 1914.

● F.L. Callender, aged 78, in September 1932, played nine consecutive rounds in the Jubilee Vase, St Andrews. He was defeated in the ninth, the final round, by 4 and 2. Callender's handicap was 12. This is the best known achievement of a septuagenarian in golf.

● George Evans shot a remarkable one over par 71 at Brockenhurst Manor – remarkable because Mr Evans was 87 at the time. Playing with him that day was Hampshire, Isle of Wight and Channel Islands President John Nettell and former Ferndown pro Doug Sewell. "It's good to shoot a score under your age, but when its 16 shots better that must be a record", said Mr Nettell. Mr Evans qualified for four opens while professional at West Hill, Surrey.

● Bernard Matthews, aged 82, of Banstead Downs Club, handicap 6, holed the course in 72 gross in August 1988. A week later he holed it in 70, twelve shots below his age. He came back in 31, finishing 4, 3, 3, 2, 3, against a par of 5, 4, 3, 3, 4. Mr Matthews's eclectic score at his Club is 37, or one over 2's.

Playing in the dark

On numerous occasions it has been necessary to hold lamps, lighted candles, or torches at holes in order that players might finish a competition. Large entries, slow play, early darkness and an eclipse of the sun have all been causes of playing in darkness.

● Since 1972, the Whitburn Golf Club at South Shields, Tyne and Wear, has held an annual Summer Solstice Competition. All competitors, who draw lots for starting tees, must begin before 4.24 and 13 seconds am, the time the sun rises over the first hole on the longest day of the year.

● At The Open Championship in Musselburgh in November 1889 many players finished when the light had so far gone that the adjacent street lamps were lit. The cards were checked by candlelight. Several players who had no chance of the championship were paid small sums to withdraw in order to permit others who had a chance to finish in daylight. This was the last championship at Musselburgh.

● At the Southern Section of the PGA tournament on 25th September, 1907, at Burnham Beeches, several players concluded the round by the aid of torch lights placed near the holes.

● In the Irish Open Championship at Portmarnock in September, 1907, a tie in the third round between W.C. Pickeman and A. Jeffcott was postponed owing to darkness, at the 22nd hole. The next morning Pickeman won at the 24th.

● The qualifying round of the American Amateur Championship in 1910 could not be finished in one day, and several competitors had to stop their round on account of darkness, and complete it early in the morning of the following day.

● On 10th January, 1926, in the final of the President's Putter, at Rye, E.F. Storey and R.H. Wethered were all square at the 24th hole. It was 5 pm and so dark that, although a fair crowd was present, the balls could not be followed. The tie was abandoned and the Putter held jointly for the year. Each winner of the Putter affixes the ball he played; for 1926 there are two balls, respectively engraved with the names of the finalists.

● In the 1932 Walker Cup contest at Brooklyn, a total eclipse of the sun occurred.

● At Perth, on 14th September, 1932, a competition was in progress under good clear evening light, and a full bright moon. The moon rose at 7.10 and an hour later came under eclipse to the earth's surface. The light then became so bad that on the last three greens competitors holed out by the aid of the light from matches.

● At Carnoustie, 1932, in the competition for the *Craw's Nest Tassie* the large entry necessitated competitors being sent off in 3-ball matches. The late players had to be assisted by electric torches flashed on the greens.

● In February, 1950, Max Faulkner and his partner, R. Dolman, in a Guildford Alliance event finished their round in complete darkness. A photographer's flash bulbs were used at the last hole to direct Faulkner's approach. Several of the other competitors also finished in darkness. At the last hole they had only the light from the clubhouse to aim at and one played his approach so boldly that he put his ball through the hall doorway and almost into the dressing room.

● On the second day of the 1969 Ryder Cup contest, the last 4-ball match ended in near total darkness on the 18th green at Royal Birkdale. With the help of the clubhouse lights the two American players, Lee Trevino and Miller Barber, along with Tony Jacklin for

Britain each faced putts of around five feet to win their match. All missed and their game was halved.

The occasions mentioned above all occurred in competitions where it was not intended to play in the dark. There are, however, numerous instances where players set out to play in the dark either for bets or for novelty.

● On 29th November, 1878, R.W. Brown backed himself to go round the Hoylake links in 150 strokes, starting at 11 pm. The conditions of the match were that Mr Brown was only to be penalised *loss of distance* for a lost ball, and that no one was to help him to find it. He went round in 147 strokes, and won his bet by the narrow margin of three strokes.

● In 1876 David Strath backed himself to go round St Andrews under 100, in moonlight. He took 95, and did not lose a ball.

● In September 1928, at St Andrews, the first and last holes were illuminated by lanterns, and at 11 pm four members of The Royal and Ancient set out to play a foursome over the 2 holes. Electric lights, lanterns, and rockets were used to brighten the fairway, and the headlights of motor cars parked on Links Place formed a helpful battery. The 1st hole was won in four, and each side got a five at the 18th. About 1,000 spectators followed the freak match, which was played to celebrate the appointment of Angus Hambro to the captaincy of the club.

● In 1931, Rufus Stewart, professional, Kooyonga Club, South Australia, and former Australian Open Champion, played 18 holes of exhibition golf at night without losing a single ball over the Kooyonga course, and completed the round in 77.

● At Ashley Wood Golf Club, Blandford, Dorset, a night-time golf tournament was arranged annually with up to 180 golfers taking part over four nights. Over £6000 has been raised in four years for the Muscular Dystrophy Charity.

● At Pannal, 3rd July, 1937, R.H. Locke, playing in bright moonlight, holed his tee shot at the 15th hole, distance 220 yards, the only known case of holing-in-one under such conditions.

Fatal and other accidents on the links

The history of golf is, unfortunately, marred by a great number of fatal accidents on or near the course. In the vast majority of such cases they have been caused either by careless swinging of the club or by an uncontrolled shot when the ball has struck a spectator or bystander. In addition to the fatal accidents there is an even larger number on record which have resulted in serious injury or blindness. We do not propose to list these accidents except where they have some unusual feature. We would remind all golfers of the tragic consequences which have so often been caused by momentary carelessness. The fatal accidents which follow have an unusual cause and other accidents given may have their humorous aspect.

● English tournament professional Richard Boxall was three shots off the lead in the third round of the 1991 Open Championship when he fractured his left leg driving from the 9th tee at Royal Birkdale. He was taken from the course to hospital by ambulance and was listed in the official results as "retired" which entitled him to a consolation prize of £3000.

A month later, Russell Weir of Scotland, was competing in the European Teaching Professionals' Championship near Rotterdam when he also fractured his left leg driving from the 7th tee in the first round.

● In July, 1971, Rudolph Roy, aged 43, was killed at a Montreal course; in playing out of woods, the shaft of his club snapped, rebounded off a tree and the jagged edge plunged into his body.

● Harold Wallace, aged 75, playing at Lundin Links with two friends in 1950, was crossing the railway line which separates the fifth green and sixth tee, when a light engine knocked him down and he was killed instantly.

● In the summer of 1963, Harold Kalles, of Toronto, Canada, died six days after his throat had been cut by a golf club shaft, which broke against a tree as he was trying to play out of a bunker.

● At Jacksonville, Florida, on 18th March, 1952, two women golfers were instantly killed when hit simultaneously by the whirling propeller of a navy fighter plane. They were playing together when the plane with a dead engine coming in out of control, hit them from behind.

● In May, 1993, at Ponoka Community GC, Alberta, Canada, Richard McCulough hit a poor tee shot on the 13th hole and promptly smashed his driver angrily against a golf cart. The head of the driver and six inches of shaft flew through the air, piercing McCulough's throat and severing his carotid artery. He died in hospital.

● Britain's first national open event for competitors aged over 80, at Moortown, Leeds in September, 1992, was marred when 81-year-old Frank Hart collapsed on the fourth tee and died. Play continued and Charles Mitchell, aged 80, won the Stableford competition with a gross score of 81 for 39 points.

● Playing in the 1993 Carlesburg-Tetley Cornish Festival at Tehidy Park, Ian Cornwell was struck on the leg by a wayward shot from a player two groups behind. Later, as he was leaving the 16th green, he was hit again, this time below the ear, by the same player, knocking him unconscious. This may be the first time that a player has been hit twice in the same round by the same player.

Lightning on the links

There have been a considerable number of fatal and serious accidents through players and caddies having been struck by lightning on the course. The Royal and Ancient and the USGA have, since 1952, provided for discontinuance of play during lightning storms under the Rules of Golf (Rule 37, 6) and the United States Golf Association has given the following guide for personal safety during thunderstorms:

(a) Do not go out of doors or remain out during thunderstorms unless it is necessary. Stay inside of a building where it is dry, preferably away from fireplaces, stoves, and other metal objects.

(b) If there is any choice of shelter, choose in the following order:
1. Large metal or metal-frame buildings.
2. Dwellings or other buildings which are protected against lightning.
3. Large unprotected buildings.
4. Small unprotected buildings.

(c) If remaining out of doors is unavoidable, keep away from:
1. Small sheds and shelters if in an exposed location.
2. Isolated trees.
3. Wire fences.
4. Hilltops and wide open spaces.

(d) Seek shelter in:
1. A cave.
2. A depression in the ground.
3. A deep valley or canyon.
4. The foot of a steep or overhanging cliff.
5. Dense woods.
6. A grove of trees.

Note – Raising golf clubs or umbrellas above the head is dangerous.

● A serious incident with lightning involving well-known golfers was at the 1975 Western Open in Chicago when Lee Trevino, Jerry Heard and Bobby Nichols were all struck and had to be taken to hospital. At the same time Tony Jacklin had a club thrown 15 feet out of his hands.

● Two well-known competitors were struck by lightning in European events in 1977. They were Mark James of Britain in the Swiss Open and Severiano Ballesteros of Spain in the Scandinavian Open. Fortunately neither appeared to be badly injured.

● Two spectators were killed by lightning in 1991: one at the US Open and the other at US PGA Championship.

Spectators interfering with balls

● Deliberate interference by spectators with balls in play during important money matches was not unknown in the old days when there was intense rivalry between the *schools* of Musselburgh, St Andrews, and North Berwick, and disputes arose in stake matches caused by the action of spectators in kicking the ball into either a favourable or an unfavourable position.

● Tom Morris, in his last match with Willie Park at Musselburgh, refused to go on because of interference by the spectators, and in the match on the same course about 40 years later, in 1895, between Willie Park Jr and J.H. Taylor, the barracking of the crowd and interference with play was so bad that when the Park-Vardon match came to be arranged in 1899, Vardon refused to accept Musselburgh as a venue.

● Even in modern times spectators have been known to interfere deliberately with players' balls, though it is usually by children. In the 1972 Penfold Tournament at Queen's Park, Bournemouth, Christy O'Connor Jr had his ball stolen by a young boy, but not being told of this at the time had to take the penalty for a lost ball. O'Connor finished in a tie for first place, but lost the play-off.

● In 1912 in the last round of the final of the Amateur Championship at Westward Ho! between Abe Mitchell and John Ball, the drive of the former to the short 14th hit an open umbrella held by a lady protecting herself from the heavy rain, and instead of landing on the green the ball was diverted into a bunker. Mitchell, who was leading at the time by 2 holes, lost the hole and Ball won the Championship at the 38th hole.

● In the match between the professionals of Great Britain and America at Southport in 1937 a dense crowd collected round the 15th green waiting for the Sarazen-Alliss match. The American's ball landed in the lap of a woman, who picked it up and threw it so close to the hole that Sarazen got a two against Alliss' three.

● In a memorable tie between Bobby Jones and Cyril Tolley in the 1930 Amateur Championship at St Andrews, Jones' approach to the 17th green struck spectators massed at the left end of the green and led to controversy as to whether it would otherwise have gone on to the famous road. Jones himself had deliberately played for that part of the green and had requested stewards to get the crowd back. Had the ball gone on to the road, the historic Jones Quadrilateral of the year – The Open and Amateur Championships of Britain and the United States – might not have gone into the records.

● In the 1983 Suntory World Match Play Championship at Wentworth Nick Faldo hit his second shot over the green at the 16th hole into a group of spectators. To everyone's astonishment and discomfiture the ball reappeared on the green about 30ft from the hole, propelled there by a thoroughly misguided and anonymous spectator. The referee ruled that Faldo should play the ball where it lay on the green. Faldo's opponent, Graham Marsh, understandably upset by the incident, took three putts against Faldo's two, thus losing a hole he might well otherwise have won. Faldo won the match 2 and 1, but lost in the final to Marsh's fellow Australian Greg Norman by 3 and 2.

Golf balls killing animals and fish, and incidents with animals

● An astounding fatality to an animal through being hit by a golf ball occurred at St Margaret's-at-Cliffe Golf Club, Kent on 13th June, 1934, when W.J. Robinson, the professional, killed a cow with his tee shot to the 18th hole. The cow was standing in the fairway about 100 yards from the tee, and the ball struck her on the back of the head. She fell like a log, but staggered to her feet and walked about 50 yards before dropping again. When the players reached her she was dead.

● J.W. Perret, of Ystrad Mynach, playing with Chas R. Halliday, of Ralston, in the qualifying rounds of the Society of One Armed Golfers' Championship over the Darley course, Troon, on 27th August, 1935, killed two gulls at successive holes with his second shots. The *deadly* shots were at the 1st and 2nd holes.

● On the first day of grouse shooting of the 1975 season (12th August), 11-year-old schoolboy Willie Fraser, of Kingussie, beat all the guns when he killed a grouse with his tee shot on the local course.

● On 10th June, 1904, while playing in the Edinburgh High Constables' Competition at Kilspindie, Captain Ferguson sent a long ball into the rough at the Target hole, and on searching for it found that it had struck and killed a young hare.

● Playing in a mixed open tournament at the Waimairi Beach Golf Club in Christchurch, New Zealand, in the summer of 1961, Mrs R.T. Challis found her ball in fairly long spongy grass where a placing rule applied. She picked up, placed the ball and played her stroke. A young hare leaped into the air and fell dead at her feet. She had placed the ball on the leveret without seeing it and without disturbing it.

● In 1906 in the Border Championship at Hawick, a gull and a weasel were killed by balls during the afternoon's play.

● A golfer at Newark, in May, 1907, drove his ball into the river. The ball struck a trout 2lb in weight and killed it.

● On 24th April, 1975, at Scunthorpe GC, Jim Tollan's drive at the 14th hole, called The *Mallard*, struck and killed a female mallard duck in flight. The duck was stuffed and is displayed in the Scunthorpe Clubhouse.

● A. Samuel, Melbourne Club, at Sandringham, was driving with an iron club from the 17th tee, when a kitten, which had been playing in the long grass, sprang suddenly at the ball. Kitten and club arrived at the objective simultaneously, with the result that kitten took an unexpected flight through the air, landing some 20 yards away.

● As Susan Rowlands was lining up a vital putt in the closing stages of the final of the 1978 Welsh Girls' Championship at Abergele, a tiny mouse scampered up her trouser leg. After holing the putt, the mouse ran down again. Susan, who won the final, admitted that she fortunately had not known it was there.

Interference by birds and animals

● Crows, ravens, hawks and seagulls frequently carry off golf balls, sometimes dropping the ball actually on the green, and it is a common incident for a cow to swallow a golf ball. A plague of crows on the Liverpool course at Hoylake are addicted to golf balls – they stole 26 in one day – selecting only new balls. It was suggested that members should carry shotguns as a 15th club!

● A match was approaching a hole in a rather low-lying course, when one of the players made a crisp chip from about 30 yards from the hole. The ball trickled slowly across the green and eventually disappeared into the hole. After a momentary pause, the ball was suddenly ejected on to the green, and out jumped a large frog.

● A large black crow named Jasper which frequented the Lithgow GC in New South Wales, Australia, stole 30 golf balls in the club's 1972 Easter Tournament.

● As Mrs Molly Whitaker was playing from a bunker at Beachwood course, Natal, South Africa, a large monkey leaped from a bush and clutched her round the neck. A caddie drove it off by clipping it with an iron club.

● In Massachusetts a goose, having been hit rather hard by a golf ball which then came to rest by the side of a water hazard, took revenge by waddling over to the ball and kicking it into the water.

● In the summer of 1963, S.C. King had a good drive to the 10th hole at the Guernsey Club. His partner, R.W. Clark, was in the rough, and King helped him to search. Returning to his ball, he found a cow eating it. Next day, at the same hole, the positions were reversed, and King was in the rough. Clark placed his woollen hat over his ball, remarking, *I'll make sure the cow doesn't eat mine*. On his return he found the cow thoroughly enjoying his hat; nothing was left but the pom-pom.

● On 5 August 2000 in the first round of the Royal Westmoreland Club Championship in Barbados, Kevin Edwards, a five-handicapper, hit a tee shot at the short 15th to a few feet of the hole. A monkey then ran onto the green, picked up the ball, threw it into the air a few times, then placed it in the hole before running off. Mr Edwards had to replace his ball, but was obliged afterwards to buy everyone a drink at the bar by virtue of a newly written rule.

Armless, one-armed, legless and ambidextrous players

● In September, 1933, at Burgess Golfing Society of Edinburgh, the first championship for one-armed golfers was held. There were 43 entries and 37 of the competitors had lost an arm in the 1914–18 war. Play was over two rounds and the championship was won by W.E. Thomson, Eastwood, Glasgow, with a score of 169 (82 and 87) for two rounds. The Burgess course was 6,300 yards long. Thomson drove the last green, 260 yards. The championship and an international match are played annually.

● In the Boys' Amateur Championship 1923, at Dunbar and 1949 at St Andrews, there were competitors each with one arm. The competitor in 1949, R.P. Reid, Cupar, Fife, who lost his arm working a machine in a butcher's shop, got through to the third round.

● There have been cases of persons with no arms playing golf. One, Thomas McAuliffe, who held the club between his right shoulder and cheek, once went round Buffalo CC, USA, in 108.

● Group Captain Bader, who lost both legs in a flying accident prior to the World War 1939–45, took part in golf competitions and reached a single-figure handicap in spite of his disability.

● In 1909, Scott of Silloth, and John Haskins of Hoylake, both one-armed golfers, played a home and away match for £20-a-side. Scott finished five up at Silloth. He was seven up and 14 to play at Hoylake but Haskins played so well that Scott eventually only won by 3 and 1. This was the first match between one-armed golfers. Haskins in 1919 was challenged by Mr Mycock, of Buxton, another one-armed player. The match was 36 holes, home and away. The first half was played over the Buxton and High Peak Links, and the latter half over the Liverpool Links, and resulted in a win for Haskins by 11 and 10. Later in the same year Haskins received another challenge to play against Alexander Smart of Aberdeen. The match was 18 holes over the Balgownie Course, and ended in favour of Haskins.

● In a match, November, 1926, between the Geduld and Sub Nigel Clubs – two golf clubs connected with the South African gold mines of the same names – each club had two players minus an arm. The natural consequence was that the quartet were matched. The players were – A.W.P. Charteris and E. Mitchell, Sub Nigel; and E.P. Coles and J. Kirby, Geduld. This is the first record of four one-armed players in a foursome.

● At Joliet Country Club, USA, a one-armed golfer named D.R. Anderson drove a ball 300 yards.

● Left-handedness, but playing golf right-handed, is prevalent and for a man to throw with his left hand and play golf right-handed is considered an advantage, for Bobby Jones, Jesse Sweetser, Walter Hagen, Jim Barnes, Joe Kirkwood and more recently Johnny Miller were eminent golfers who were left-handed and ambidextrous.

● In a practice round for The Open Championship in July, 1927, at St Andrews, Len Nettlefold and Joe Kirkwood changed sets of clubs at the 9th hole. Nettlefold was a left-handed golfer and Kirkwood right-handed. They played the last nine, Kirkwood with the left-handed clubs and Nettlefold with the right-handed clubs.

● The late Harry Vardon, when he was at Ganton, got tired of giving impossible odds to his members and beating them, so he collected a set of left-handed clubs, and rating himself at scratch, conceded the handicap odds to them. He won with the same monotonous regularity.

● Ernest Jones, who was professional at the Chislehurst Club, was badly wounded in the war in France in 1916 and his right leg had to be amputated below the knee. He persevered with the game, and before the end of the year he went round the Clacton course balanced on his one leg in 72. Jones later settled in the United States where he built fame and fortune as a golf teacher.

● Major Alexander McDonald Fraser of Edinburgh had the distinction of holding two handicaps simultaneously in the same club – one when he played left-handed and the other for his right-handed play. In medal competitions he had to state before teeing up which method he would use.

● Former England test cricketer Brian Close once held a handicap of 2 playing right-handed, but after retiring from cricket in 1977 decided to apply himself as a left-handed player. His left-handed handicap at the time of his retirement was 7. Close had the distinction of once beating Ted Dexter, another distinguished test cricketer and noted golfer twice in the one day, playing right-handed in the morning and left-handed in the afternoon.

Blind and blindfolded golf

● Major Towse, VC, whose eyes were shot out during the South African War, 1899, was probably the first blind man to play golf. His only stipulations when playing the game were that he should be allowed to touch the ball with his hands to ascertain its position, and that his caddie could ring a small bell to indicate the position of the hole. Major Towse, who played with considerable skill, was also an expert oarsman and bridge player. He died in 1945, aged 81.

● The United States Blind Golfers' Association in 1946 promoted an Invitational Golf Tournament for the blind at Inglewood, California, to be held annually. In 1953 there were 24 competitors, of which 11 completed the two rounds of 36 holes. The winner was Charley Boswell who lost his eyesight leading a tank unit in Germany in 1944.

● In July, 1954, at Lambton Golf and Country Club, Toronto, the first international championship for the blind was held. It resulted in a win for Joe Lazaro, of Waltham, Mass., with a score of 220 for the two rounds. He drove the 215-yard 16th hole and just missed an ace, his ball stopping 18 inches from the hole. Charley Boswell, who won the United States Blind Golfers' Association Tournament in 1953, was second. The same Charles Boswell, of Birmingham, Alabama holed the 141-yard 14th hole at the Vestavia CC in one in October, 1970.

● Another blind person to have holed-in-one was American Ben Thomas while on holiday in South Carolina in 1978.

● Rick Sorenson undertook a bet in which, playing 18 holes blindfolded at Meadowbrook Course, Minneapolis, on 25th May, 1973, he was to pay $10 for every hole over par and receive $100 for every hole in par or better. He went round in 86 losing $70 on the deal.

● Alfred Toogood played blindfolded in a match against Tindal Atkinson at Sunningdale in 1912. Toogood was beaten 8 and 7. Previously, in 1908, I. Millar, Newcastle-upon-Tyne, played a match blindfolded against A.T. Broughton, Birkdale, at Newcastle, County Down.

● Wing-Commander *Laddie* Lucas, DSO, DFC, MP, played over Sandy Lodge golf course in Hertfordshire on 7th August, 1954, completely blindfolded and had a score of 87.

Trick shots

● Joe Kirkwood, Australia, specialised in public exhibitions of trick and fancy shots. He played all kinds of strokes after nominating them, and among his ordinary strokes nothing was more impressive than those hit for low flight. He played a full drive from the face of a wrist watch, and the toe of a spectator's shoe, full strokes at a suspended ball, and played for slice and pull at will, and exhibited his ambidexterity by playing left-handed strokes with right-handed clubs. Holing six balls, stymieing, a full shot at a ball catching it as it descended, and hitting 12 full shots in rapid succession, with his face turned away from the ball, were shots among his repertoire. In playing the last named Kirkwood placed the balls in a row, about six inches apart, and moved quickly along the line. Kirkwood, who was born in Australia lived for many years in America. He died in November, 1970 aged 73.

● On 2nd April, 1894, a 3-ball match was played over Musselburgh course between Messrs Grant, Bowden, and Waggot, the clubmaker, the latter teeing on the face of a watch at each tee. He finished the round in 41 the watch being undamaged in any way.

● In a match at Esher on 23rd November, 1931, George Ashdown, the professional, played his tee shot for each of the 18 holes from a rubber tee strapped to the forehead of Miss Ena Shaw.

● E.A. Forrest, a South African professional in a music hall turn of trick golf shots, played blindfolded shots, one being from the ball teed on the chin of his recumbent partner.

● The late Paul Hahn, an American trick specialist could hit four balls with two clubs. Holding a club in each hand he hit two balls, hooking one and slicing the other with the same swing. Hahn had a repertoire of 30 trick shots. In 1955 he flew round the world, exhibiting in 14 countries and on all five continents.

Balls colliding and touching

● Competing in the 1980 Corfu International Championship, Sharon Peachey drove from one tee and her ball collided in mid-air with one from a competitor playing another hole. Her ball ended in a pond.

● Playing in the Cornish team championship in 1973 at West Cornwall GC Tom Scott-Brown, of West Cornwall GC, and Paddy Bradley, of Tehidy GC, saw their drives from the fourth and eighth tees collide in mid-air.

● During a fourball match at Guernsey Club in June, 1966, near the 13th green from the tee, two of the players, D.G. Hare and S. Machin, chipped up simultaneously; the balls collided in mid-air and Machin's ball hit the green, then the flagstick, and dropped into the hole for a birdie 2.

● In May, 1926, during the meeting of the Army Golfing Society at St Andrews, Colonel Howard and Lieutenant-Colonel Buchanan Dunlop, while playing in the foursomes against J. Rodger and J. Mackie, hit full iron shots for the seconds to the 16th green. Each thought he had to play his ball first, and hidden by a bunker the players struck their balls simultaneously. The balls, going towards the hole about 20 yards from the pin and five feet in the air, met with great force and dropped either side of the hole five yards apart.

● In 1972, before a luncheon celebrating the centenary year of the Ladies' Section of Royal Wimbledon

GC, a 12-hole competition was held during which two competitors, Mrs L. Champion and Mrs A. McKendrick, driving from the eighth and ninth tees respectively, saw their balls collide in mid-air.

● In 1928, at Wentworth Falls, Australia, Dr Alcorn and E.A. Avery, of Leura Club, were playing with professional E. Barnes. The tee shots of Avery and Barnes at the 9th hole finished on opposite sides of the fairway. Both players unknowingly hit their seconds (chip shots) at the same time. Dr Alcorn, standing at the pin, suddenly saw two balls approaching the hole from different angles. They met in the air and dropped into the hole.

● At Rugby, 1931, playing in a 4-ball match, H. Fraser pulled his drive from the 10th tee in the direction of the ninth tee. Simultaneously a club member, driving from the ninth tee, pulled his drive. The tees were about 350 yards apart. The two balls collided in mid-air.

● Two golf balls, being played in opposite directions, collided in flight over Longniddry Golf Course on 27th June, 1953. Immediately after Stewart Elder, of Longniddry, had driven from the third tee, another ball, which had been pulled off line from the second fairway, which runs alongside the third, struck his ball about 20 feet above the ground. S.J. Fleming, of Tranent, who was playing with Elder, heard a loud crack and thought Elder's ball had exploded. The balls were found undamaged about 70 yards apart.

Three and two balls dislodged by one shot

● In 1934 on the short 3rd hole (now the 13th) of Olton Course, Warwickshire, J.R. Horden, a scratch golfer of the club, sent his tee shot into long wet grass a few feet over the back of the green. When he played an *explosion* shot three balls dropped on to the putting green, his own and two others.

● A.M. Chevalier, playing at Hale, Cheshire, March, 1935, drove his ball into a grass bunker, and when he reached it there was only part of it showing. He played the shot with a niblick and to his amazement not one but three balls shot into the air. They all dropped back into the bunker and came to rest within a foot of each other. Then came another surprise. One of the *finds* was of the same manufacture and bore the same number as the ball he was playing with.

● Playing to the 9th hole, at Osborne House Club, Isle of Wight, George A. Sherman lost his ball which had sunk out of sight on the sodden fairway. A few weeks later, playing from the same tee, his ball again was plugged, only the top showing. Under a local rule he lifted his ball to place it, and exactly under it lay the ball he had lost previously.

Balls in strange places

● Playing at the John O' Gaunt Club, Sutton, near Biggleswade (Beds), a member drove a ball which did not touch the ground until it reached London – over 40 miles away. The ball landed in a vegetable lorry

which was passing the golf course and later fell out of a package of cabbages when they were unloaded at Covent Garden, London.

● In the English Open Amateur Stroke Play at Moortown in 1974, Nigel Denham, a Yorkshire County player, in the first round saw his overhit second shot to the 18th green bounce up some steps into the clubhouse. His ball went through an open door, ricocheted off a wall and came to rest in the men's bar, 20 feet from the windows. As the clubhouse was not out of bounds Denham decided to play the shot back to the green and opened a window 4 feet by 2 feet through which he pitched his ball to 12 feet from the flag. (Several weeks later the R&A declared that Denham should have been penalised two shots for opening the window. The clubhouse was an immovable obstruction and no part of it should have been moved.)

● In The Open Championship at Sandwich, 1949, Harry Bradshaw, Kilcroney, Dublin, at the 5th hole in his second round, drove into the rough and found his ball inside a beer bottle with the neck and shoulder broken off and four sharp points sticking up. Bradshaw, if he had treated the ball as in an unplayable lie might have been involved in a disqualification, so he decided to play it where it lay. With his blaster he smashed the bottle and sent the ball about 30 yards. The hole, a par 4, cost him 6.

● Kevin Sharman of Woodbridge GC hit a low, very straight drive at the club's 8th hole in 1979. After some minutes' searching, his ball was found embedded in a plastic sphere on top of the direction post.

● On the Dublin Course, 16th July, 1936, in the Irish Open Championship, A.D. Locke, the South African, played his tee shot at the 100-yard 12th hole, but the ball could not be found on arrival on the green. The marker removed the pin and it was discovered that the ball had been entangled in the flag. It dropped near the edge of the hole and Locke holed the short putt for a birdie two.

● While playing a round on the Geelong Golf Club Course, Australia, Easter, 1923, Captain Charteris topped his tee shot to the short 2nd hole, which lies over a creek with deep and steep clay banks. His ball came to rest on the near slope of the creek bank. He elected to play the ball as it lay, and took his niblick. After the shot, the ball was nowhere to be seen. It was found later embedded in a mass of gluey clay stuck fast to the face of the niblick. It could not be shaken off. Charteris did what was afterwards approved by the R&A, cleaned the ball and dropped it behind without penalty.

● In October, 1929, at Blackmoor Golf Club, Bordon, Hants, a player driving from the first tee holed out his ball in the chimney of a house some 120 yards distant and some 40 yards out of bounds on the right. The owner and his wife were sitting in front of the fire when they heard a rattle in the chimney and were astonished to see a golf ball drop into the fire.

● A similar incident occurred in an inter-club match between Musselburgh and Lothianburn at Prestongrange in 1938 when a member of the former team hooked his ball at the 2nd hole and gave it up for lost.

To his amazement a woman emerged from one of the houses adjacent to this part of the course and handed back the ball which she said had come down the chimney and landed on a pot which was on the fire.

● In July, 1955, J. Lowrie, starter at the Eden Course, St Andrews, witnessed a freak shot. A visitor drove from the first tee just as a north-bound train was passing. He sliced the shot and the ball disappeared through an open window of a passenger compartment. Almost immediately the ball emerged again, having been thrown back on to the fairway by a man in the compartment, who waved a greeting which presumably indicated that no one was hurt.

● At Coombe Wood Golf Club, a player hit a ball towards the 16th green where it landed in the vertical exhaust of a tractor which was mowing the fairway. The greenkeeper was somewhat surprised to find a temporary loss of power in the tractor. When sufficient compression had built up in the exhaust system, the ball was forced out with tremendous velocity, hit the roof of a house nearby, bounced off and landed some three feet from the pin on the green.

● When carrying out an inspection of the air conditioning system at St John's Hospital, Chelmsford, in 1993, a golf ball was found in the ventilator immediately above the operating theatre. It was probably the result of a hooked drive from the first tee at Chelmsford Golf Club, which is close by, but the ball can only have entered the duct on a rebound through a three-inch gap under a ventilator hood and then descended through a series of sharp bends to its final resting place.

● There have been many occasions when misdirected shots have finished in strange places after an unusual line of flight and bounce. At Ashford, Middlesex, John Miller, aged 69, hit his tee shot out of bounds at the 12th hole (237 yards). It struck a parked car, passed through a copse, hit more cars, jumped a canopy, flew through the clubhouse kitchen window, finishing in a cooking stock-pot, without once touching the ground. Mr Miller had previously done the hole in one on four occasions.

Balls Hit To and From Great Heights

● In 1798 two Edinburgh golfers undertook to drive a ball over the spire of St Giles' Cathedral, Edinburgh, for a wager. Mr Sceales, of Leith, and Mr Smellie, a printer, were each allowed six shots and succeeded in sending the balls well over the weather-cock, a height of more than 160 feet from the ground.

● Some years later Donald McLean, an Edinburgh lawyer, won a substantial bet by driving a ball over the Melville Monument in St Andrew Square, Edinburgh – height, 154 feet.

● Tom Morris in 1860, at the famous bridge of Ballochmyle, stood in the quarry beneath and, from a stick elevated horizontally, attempted to send golf balls over the bridge. He could raise them only to the pathway, 400 feet high, which was in itself a great feat with the gutta ball.

● Captain Ernest Carter, on 28th September, 1922, drove a ball from the roadway at the 1st tee on Harlech Links against the wall of Harlech Castle. The embattlements are 200 feet over the level of the roadway, and the point where the ball struck the embattlements was 180 yards from the point where the ball was teed. Captain Carter, who was laid odds of £100 to £1, used a baffy.

● In 1896 Freddie Tait, then a subaltern in the Black Watch, drove a ball from the Rookery, the highest building on Edinburgh Castle, in a match against a brother officer to hole out in the fountain in Princes Street Gardens 350 feet below and about 300 yards distant.

● Prior to the 1977 Lancôme Tournament in Paris, Arnold Palmer hit three balls from the second stage of the Eiffel Tower, over 300 feet above ground. The longest was measured at 403 yards. One ball was hooked and hit a bus but no serious damage was done as all traffic had been stopped for safety reasons.

● Long drives have been made from mountain peaks, across the gorge at Victoria Falls, from the Pyramids, high buildings in New York, and from many other similar places. As an illustration of such freakish *drives* a member of the New York Rangers' Hockey Team from the top of Mount Edith Cavell, 11,033 feet high, drove a ball which struck the Ghost Glacier 5000 feet below and bounced off the rocky ledge another 1000 feet – a total drop of 2000 yards. Later, in June, 1968, from Pikes Peak, Colorado (14,110 feet), Arthur Lynskey hit a ball which travelled 200 yards horizontally but 2 miles vertically.

Remarkable Shots

● Remarkable shots are as numerous as the grains of sand; around every 19th hole, legends are recalled of astounding shots. One shot is commemorated by a memorial tablet at the 17th hole at the Lytham and St Annes Club. It was made by Bobby Jones in the final round of The Open Championship in 1926. He was partnered by Al Watrous, another American player. They had been running neck and neck and at the end of the third round, Watrous was just leading Jones with 215 against 217. At the 16th Jones drew level then on the 17th he drove into a sandy lie in broken ground. Watrous reached the green with his second. Jones took a mashie-iron (the equivalent to a 4-iron today) and hit a magnificent shot to the green to get his 4. This remarkable recovery unnerved Watrous, who 3-putted, and Jones, getting another 4 at the last hole against 5, won his first Open Championship with 291 against Watrous' 293. The tablet is near the spot where Jones played his second shot.

● Arnold Palmer (USA), playing in the second round of the Australian Wills Masters tournament at Melbourne, in October, 1964, hooked his second shot at the 9th hole high into the fork of a gum tree. Climbing 20 feet up the tree, Palmer, with the head of his 1-iron reversed, played a hammer stroke and knocked the ball some 30 yards forward, followed by a brilliant chip to the green and a putt.

● In the foursome during the Ryder Cup at Moortown in 1929, Joe Turnesa hooked the American side's second shot at the last hole behind the marquee adjoining the clubhouse, Johnny Farrel then pitched the ball over the marquee on to the green only feet away from the pin and Turnesa holed out for a 4.

Miscellaneous Incidents and Strange Golfing Facts

● Gary Player of South Africa was honoured by his country by having his portrait on new postage stamps which were issued on 12th December, 1976. It was the first time a specific golfer had ever been depicted on any country's postage stamps. In 1981 the US Postal Service introduced stamps featuring Bobby Jones and Babe Zaharias. They are the first golfers to be thus honoured by the United States.

● Gary Harris, aged 18, became the first player to make five consecutive appearances for England in the European Boys Team Championship at Vilamoura, Portugal, in 1994.

● In February, 1971, the first ever golf shots on the moon's surface were played by Captain Alan Shepard, commander of the Apollo 14 spacecraft. Captain Shepard hit two balls with an iron head attached to a makeshift shaft. With a one-handed swing he claimed he hit the first ball 200 yards aided by the reduced force of gravity on the moon. Subsequent findings put this distance in doubt. The second was a shank. Acknowledging the occasion the R&A sent Captain Shepard the following telegram: *Warmest congratulations to all of you on your great achievement and safe return. Please refer to Rules of Golf section on etiquette, paragraph 6, quote – before leaving a bunker a player should carefully fill up all holes made by him therein, unquote.* Shepard presented the club to the USGA Museum in 1974.

● Charles (Chick) Evans competed in every US Amateur Championship held between 1907 and 1962 by which time he was 72 years old. This amounted to 50 consecutive occasions discounting the six years of the two World Wars when the championship was not held.

● In winning the 1977 US Open at Southern Hills CC, Tulsa, Oklahoma, Hubert Green had to contend with a death threat. Coming off the 14th green in the final round, he was advised by USGA officials that a phone call had been received saying that he would be killed. Green decided that play should continue and happily he went on to win, unharmed.

● It was discovered at the 1977 USPGA Championship that the clubs with which Tom Watson had won The Open Championship and the US Masters earlier in the year were illegal, having grooves which exceeded the permitted specifications. The set he used in winning the 1975 Open Championship were then flown out to him and they too were found to be illegal. No retrospective action was taken.

● Mrs Fred Daly, wife of the former Open champion, saved the clubhouse of Balmoral GC, Belfast, from destruction when three men entered the professional's shop on 5th August, 1976, and left a bag containing a bomb outside the shop beside the clubhouse when refused money. Mrs Daly carried the bag over to a hedge some distance away where the bomb exploded 15 minutes later. The only damage was broken windows. On the same day several hours afterwards, Dungannon GC in Co. Tyrone suffered extensive damage to the clubhouse from terrorist bombs. Co. Down GC, proposed venue of the 1979 home international matches suffered bomb damage in May that year and through fear for the safety of team members the 1979 matches were cancelled.

● The Army Golfing Society and St Andrews on 21st April, 1934, played a match 200-a-side, the largest golf match ever played. Play was by foursomes. The Army won 58, St Andrews 31 and 11 were halved.

● Jamie Ortiz-Patino, owner of the Valderrama Golf Club at Sotogrande, Spain, paid a record £84,000 (increased to £92,400 with ten per cent buyers premium) for a late seventeenth- or early eighteenth-century rake iron offered at auction in Musselburgh in July, 1992. The iron, which had been kept in a garden shed, was bought to be exhibited in a museum being created in Valderrama.

● In 1986 Alistair Risk and three colleagues on the 17th green at Brora, Sutherland, watched a cow giving birth to twin calves between the markers on the 18th tee, causing them to play their next tee shots from in front of the tee. Their application for a ruling from the R&A brought a Rules Committee reply that while technically a rule had been broken, their action was considered within the spirit of the game and there should be no penalty. The Secretary added that the Rules Committee hoped that mother and twins were doing well.

● In view of the increasing number of people crossing the road (known as Granny Clark's Wynd) which runs across the first and 18th fairways of the Old Course, St Andrews, as a right of way, the St Andrews Links committee decided in 1969 to control the flow by erecting traffic lights, with appropriate green for go, yellow for caution and red for stop. The lights are controlled from the starter's box on the first tee. Golfers on the first tee must wait until the lights turn to green before driving off and a notice has been erected at the Wynd warning pedestrians not to cross at yellow or stop.

● A traffic light for golfers was also installed in 1971 on one of Japan's most congested courses. After putting on the uphill 9th hole of the Fukuoka course in Southern Japan, players have to switch on a go-ahead signal for following golfers waiting to play their shots to the green.

● A 22-year-old professional at Brett Essex GC, Brentwood, David Moore, who was playing in the Mufulira Open in Zambia in 1976, was shot dead it is alleged by the man with whom he was staying for the duration of the tournament. It appeared his host then shot himself.

● Peggy Carrick and her daughter, Angela Uzielli, won the Mothers and Daughters Tournament at Royal Mid-Surrey in 1994 for the 21st time.

● Patricia Shepherd has won the ladies' club championship at Turriff GC Aberdeenshire 30 consecutive times from 1959 to 1988.

● Mrs Jackie Mercer won the South African Ladies' Championship in 1979, 31 years after her first victory in the event as Miss Jacqueline Smith.

● During The Royal and Ancient Golf Club of St Andrews' medal meeting on 25th September, 1907, a member of The Royal and Ancient drove a ball which struck the sharp point of a hatpin in the hat of a lady who was crossing the course. The ball was so firmly impaled that it remained in position. The lady was not hurt.

● John Cook, former English Amateur Champion, narrowly escaped death during an attempted coup against King Hassan of Morocco in July 1971. Cook had been playing in a tournament arranged by King Hassan, a keen golfer, and was at the King's birthday party in Rabat when rebels broke into the party demanding that the King give up his throne. Cook and many others present were taken hostage.

● When playing from the 9th tee at Lossiemouth golf course in June, 1971, Martin Robertson struck a Royal Navy jet aircraft which was coming in to land at the nearby airfield. The plane was not damaged.

● At a court in Inglewood, California, in 1978, Jim Brown was convicted of beating and choking an opponent during a dispute over where a ball should have been placed on the green.

● During the Northern Ireland troubles a home-made hand grenade was found in a bunker at Dungannon GC, Co. Tyrone, on Sunday, 12th September, 1976.

● Tiger Woods, 18, became both the youngest and the first black golfer to win the United States Amateur Championship at Sawgrass in 1994. He went on to win the title three years in a row and then won the first major championship he played as a professional, the 1997 Masters, by a record 12 strokes and with a record low aggregate of 270, 18 under par.

● To mark the centenary of the Jersey Golf Club in 1978, the Jersey Post Office issued a set of four special stamps featuring Jersey's most famous golfer, Harry Vardon. The background of the 13p stamp was a brief biography of Vardon's career reproduced from the Golfer's Handbook.

● Forty-one-year-old John Mosley went for a round of golf at Delaware Park GC, Buffalo, New York, in July, 1972. He stepped on to the first tee and was challenged over a green fee by an official guard. A scuffle developed, a shot was fired and Mosley, a bullet in his chest, died on the way to hospital. His wife was awarded $131,250 in an action against the City of Buffalo and the guard. The guard was sentenced to 7½ years for second-degree manslaughter.

● When three competitors in a 1968 Pennsylvania pro-am event were about to drive from the 16th tee, two bandits (one with pistol) suddenly emerged from the bushes, struck one of the players and robbed them of wristwatches and $300.

● In the 1932 Walker Cup match at Brooklyn, Leonard Crawley succeeded in denting the cup. An errant iron shot to the 18th green hit the cup, which was on display outside the clubhouse.

● In Johannesburg, South Africa, three golf officials appeared in court accused of violating a 75-year-old Sunday Observance Law by staging the final round of the South African PGA championship on Sunday, 28th February, 1971. The Championship should have been completed on the Saturday but heavy rain prevented any play.

● In The Open Championship of 1876, at St Andrews, Bob Martin and David Strath tied at 176. A protest was lodged against Strath alleging he played his approach to the 17th green and struck a spectator. The Royal and Ancient ordered the replay, but Strath refused to play off the tie until a decision had been given on the protest. No decision was given and Bob Martin was declared the Champion.

● At Rose Bay, New South Wales, on 11th July, 1931, D.J. Bayly MacArthur, on stepping into a bunker, began to sink. MacArthur, who weighed 14 stone, shouted for help. He was rescued when up to the armpits. He had stepped on a patch of quicksand, aggravated by excess of moisture.

● The late Bobby Cruickshank was the victim of his own jubilation in the 1934 US Open at Merion. In the 4th round while in with a chance of winning he half-topped his second shot at the 11th hole. The ball was heading for a pond in front of the green but instead of ending up in the water it hit a rock and bounced on to the green. In his delight Cruickshank threw his club into the air only to receive a resounding blow on the head as it returned to earth.

● A dog with an infallible nose for finding lost golf balls was, in 1971, given honorary membership of the Waihi GC, Hamilton, New Zealand. The dog, called Chico, was trained to search for lost balls, to be sold back to the members, the money being put into the club funds.

● By 1980 Waddy, an 11-year-old beagle belonging to Bob Inglis, the secretary of Brokenhurst Manor GC, had found over 35,000 golf balls.

● Herbert M. Hepworth, Headingley, Leeds, Lord Mayor of Leeds in 1906, scored one thousand holes in 2, a feat which took him 30 years to accomplish. It was celebrated by a dinner in 1931 at the Leeds club. The first 2 of all was scored on 12th June, 1901, at Cobble Hall Course, Leeds, and the 1,000th in 1931 at Alwoodley, Leeds. Hepworth died in November, 1942.

● Fiona MacDonald was the first female to play in the Oxford and Cambridge University match at Ganton in 1986.

● Mrs Sara Gibbon won the Farnham (Surrey) Club's Grandmother's competition 48 hours after her first grand-child was born.

● At Carnoustie in the first qualifying round for the 1952 Scottish Amateur Championship a competitor drove three balls in succession out of bounds at the 1st hole and thereupon withdrew.

● In 1993, the Clark family from Hagley GC, Worcs, set a record for the county's three major professional events. The Worcestershire Stroke Play Championship was won by Finlay Clark, the eldest son, who beat his father Iain and younger brother Cameron, who tied second. In the Match Play Iain beat his son Finlay by 2 and 1 in the final; Cameron won the play-off for third place. Then in the Worcestershire Annual Pro-Am it was Cameron's turn to win, with his brother Finlay coming second and father Iain third. To add to the achievements of the family, Cameron also won the Midland Professional Match Play Championship.

● During a Captain–Pro foursomes challenge match at Chelmsford in 1993, Club Professional Dennis Bailey, put the ball into a hole only once in all 18 holes – when he holed-in-one at the fourth.

● In 1891, a new kind of matchplay – bogey – was introduced at Great Yarmouth Golf Club where the scratch score of the course was taken and each hole given a value known as the ground score. One of the club's members was described as a "regular bogeyman", a name suggested by a music hall song that was currently popular ... and the name stuck.

● Mrs C.C. Gray was Todmorden Golf Club's Ladies Champion 38 out of 42 times between 1951 and 1992, a fact recorded in the Guinness Book of Records.

● Llanymynech is a golf club situated in two countries with 15 holes in Wales and three in England. On the fourth tee, players drive from England and putt out in Wales.

Strange local rules

● The Duke of Windsor, who played on an extraordinary variety of the world's courses, once took advantage of a local rule at Jinja in Uganda and lifted his ball from a hippo's footprint without penalty.

● At the Glen Canyon course in Arizona a local rule provides that If your ball lands within a club length of a rattlesnake you are allowed to move the ball.

● Another local rule in Uganda read: If a ball comes to rest in dangerous proximity to a crocodile, another ball may be dropped.

● The 6th hole at Koolan Island GC, Western Australia, also serves as a local air strip and a local rule reads: Aircraft and vehicular traffic have right of way at all times.

● A local rule at the RAF Waddington GC reads: When teeing off from the 2nd, right of way must be given to taxiing aircraft.

Hannah's keen sense of smell was worth £10,000

Hannah was an English Springer Spaniel owned by Richard Williams, a member of the East Devon Golf Club. Her sense of smell was so acute that she could sniff out and retrieve golf balls with consummate ease.

So much so that in a period from 1993 to 2004 she found no fewer than 48,000 lost balls at East Devon which must indicate that the rough was reasonably thick or some of the members were somewhat erratic through the green – or both.

Her amazing exploits – an average of 4,000 balls retrieved a year – were reported in a French animal magazine, several golf magazines and a short documentary was even made about the incredible scenting ability of Hannah and shown on television around the world.

Julian Reynolds, managing secretary of the Club, reports that from the television fees and the sale of the recovered balls, Hannah's owner raised over £10,000 which he spent on a water fountain, a golf buggy, a weather station and numerous benches, tables and chairs for the club. Good girl Hannah!

Timeline for the Rules of Golf

The earliest known Rules of Golf were drawn up in 1744 by what was to become the Honourable Company of Edinburgh Golfers. For the next 100 years, each club could issue and revise its own code of Rules, and these were mainly based on the codes issued by The Royal and Ancient Golf Club, the Edinburgh Burgess Golfing Society or the Honourable Company. Some of the rules followed by individual clubs were identical to one of these codes, while others were worded with reference to the features of a particular course.

Starting in the second half of the 19th century, more and more clubs based their codes on those issued by The Royal and Ancient Golf Club. In 1897 its governance role was formalised with the creation of the Rules of Golf Committee.

1744 The Honourable company of Edinburgh Golfers produce a written code of rules. Known as the Thirteen Articles, Rule 1 states: "You must tee your ball within a club-length of the hole".

1754 Largely copying from the 1744 Rules, the Society of St Andrews Golfers (later to become The Royal and Ancient Golf Club) record their own Rules in the minutes.

1775 Methods of settling disputes first appear in the Honourable Company's Rules. "Any dispute arising between parties on the green shall be determined by the Captain for the time, if present, or by the latest Captain who may be on the ground".

1812 The R&A's 1754 code is revised and for the first time the Rules of Golf refer to bunkers and the putting green.

1842 The revised R&A code stipulates that "one round of the links, or 18 holes, is reckoned a match" for the first time.

1851 A revised R&A code is issued. In response to the advent of the gutta percha ball, a new rule allows that: "If a ball shall split into two or more pieces, a fresh ball shall be put down in playing for a medal".

1875 Attending the flagstick and dealing with balls resting against the flagstick appear in the Rules for the first time.

1882 The revised R&A code contains an index and a glossary of terms for the first time.

1882 The glossary of terms in the R&A code defines the size of the hole as being four inches in diameter and lined with iron.

1886 The Royal Isle of Wight Golf Club issues a version of the Rules of Golf, which defines the size of the hole as being four inches in diameter and six inches deep.

1888 Local Rules for Playing the Links at St Andrews are separated out from the main Rules of Golf for the first time by The R&A.

1891 The revised R&A code defines the hole as being four and a quarter inches in diameter and at least four inches deep. This remains the definition.

1897 The Royal and Ancient Golf Club is officially recognised as the game's governing body for the Rules of Golf.

1909 Limits on the form and make of clubs are applied for the first time.

1920 The R&A and the USGA agreed that from May 1st, 1921, "the weight of the ball should be no greater than 1.62 ounces and the size not less than 1.62 inches in diameter".

1929 Steel shafts are legalised.

1939 The maximum number of clubs that can be carried is 14.

1952 The R&A and the USGA establish a unified code of Rules.

1960 Distance measuring devices are banned.

1984 The ball is no longer dropped over the player's shoulder, but at arm's length and at shoulder height.

1988 First Joint Decisions on the Rules of Golf book published by The R&A and the USGA.

1990 The 1.68-inch ball becomes the only legal ball, marking the demise of the 1.62-inch British ball.

Royal Clubs

There are currently 62 clubs with royal titles granted by the British Royal family. In October 2005, the Mayfair Golf Club in Edmonton, Canada, was granted Royal status by Her Majesty Queen Elizabeth II. In 2004, Wellington Golf Club received the title from HRH The Duke of York. Mariánské Lázně Golf Club was honoured in 2003. The club had strong connections with British Royalty in the past; King Edward VII holidayed there, in what is now the Czech Republic. Apart from Mariánské Lázně, the Royal Clubs are in the United Kingdom or the Commonwealth. The oldest club with Royal connections is The Royal and Ancient Golf Club of St Andrews, founded in 1754 and given Royal patronage by King William IV in 1834. Royal Perth Golf Club, which was founded in 1824, received the patronage of King William IV a year earlier, in 1833.

Club	Year Founded	Year of Royal Patronage	Royal Patron
Royal Ancient Golf Club, St Andrews	1754	1834	William IV
Royal Aberdeen	1780	1903	Edward VII (Leopold patron in 1872)
Royal Adelaide	1892	1923	George V
Royal Ascot	1887	1887	Victoria 1887; Elizabeth II 1977
Royal Ashdown Forest	1888	1893	Victoria
Royal Belfast	1881	1885	Edward, Prince of Wales (later Edward VII)
Royal Birkdale	1889	1951	George VI
Royal Blackheath	1766	1857	Not known
Royal Burgess	1773	1929	George V
Royal Calcutta	1829	1912	George V
Royal Canberra	1926	1933	George V
Royal Cape	1885	1910	George V
Royal Cinque Ports	1892	1910	George V
Royal Colombo	1879	1928	George V
Royal Colwood	1913	1931	George V
Royal County Down	1889	1908	Edward VII
Royal Cromer	1888	1887	Edward, Prince of Wales (later Edward VII)
Royal Dornoch	1877	1906	Edward VII
Royal Dublin	1885	1891	Victoria
Duff House Royal	1909	1925	Princess Louise, Dowager Duchess of Fife
Royal Durban	1892	1932	George V
Royal Eastbourne	1887	1887	Victoria
Royal Epping Forest	1888	1888	Victoria
Royal Fremantle	1905	1930	George V
Royal Guernsey	1890	1891	Victoria

Club	Year Founded	Year of Royal Patronage	Royal Patron
Royal Harare	1898	1929	George V
Royal Hobart	1900	1925	George V
The Royal Household	1901	1901	Edward VII
Royal Jersey	1878	1879	Victoria
Royal Johannesburg	1890	1931	George V
Royal Liverpool	1869	1871	Prince Arthur, Duke of Connaught
Royal Lytham	1886	1926	George V
Royal Malta	1888	1888	Prince Alfred, Duke of Edinburgh
Royal Mariánské Lázně	1905	2003	Elizabeth II
Royal Mayfair	1922	2005	Elizabeth II
Royal Melbourne	1891	1895	Victoria
Royal Mid Surrey	1892	1926	George V
Royal Montreal	1873	1884	Victoria
Royal Montrose	1810	1845	Prince Albert
Royal Musselburgh	1774	1876	Prince Arthur, Duke of Connaught
Royal Nairobi	1906	1935	George V
Royal North Devon	1864	1866	Edward, Prince of Wales (later Edward VII)
Royal Norwich	1893	1893	George, Duke of York (later George V)
Royal Ottawa	1891	1912	George V
Royal Perth	1824	1833	William IV
Royal Perth (Australia)	1895	1937	George VI
Royal Port Alfred	1907	1924	George V
Royal Porthcawl	1891	1909	Edward VII
Royal Portrush	1888	1892	George, Duke of York (later George V)
Royal Quebec	1874	1934	George V
Royal Queensland	1920	1921	George V
Royal Regina	1899	1999	Elizabeth II
Royal St Davids	1894	1908	Edward, Prince of Wales (later Edward VII)
Royal St George's	1887	1902	Edward VII
Royal Sydney	1893	1897	Victoria
Royal Tarlair	1926	1926	Princess Louise, Dowager Duchess of Fife
Royal Troon	1878	1978	Elizabeth II
Royal Wellington	1895	2004	Prince Andrew, Duke of York
Royal West Norfolk	1892	1892	Edward, Prince of Wales (later Edward VII)
Royal Wimbledon	1865	1882	Victoria
Royal Winchester	1888	1913	George V
Royal Worlington and Newmarket	1893	1895	Victoria

Websites

The R&A	www.randa.org
United States Golf Association	www.usga.org
English Golf Union	www.englishgolfunion.org
Golf Union of Ireland	www.gui.ie
Scottish Golf Union	www.scottishgolfunion.org
Welsh Golf Union	www.welshgolf.org
European Golf Association	www.ega-golf.ch
Ladies Golf Union (LGU)	www.lgu.org
English Ladies (ELGA)	www.englishladiesgolf.org
Irish Ladies (ILGU)	www.ilgu.ie
European Tour	www.europeantour.com
US PGA Tour	www.pgatour.com
Australasian Tour	www.pgatour.com.au
Asian Tour	www.asiantour.com
Japanese Tour	www.jgto.org
South African Sunshine Tour	www.sunshinetour.com
LPGA Tour	www.lpga.com
Ladies European Tour (LET)	www.ladieseuropeantour.com
Japanese Ladies Tour	www.lpga.or.jp (Japanese only)
Asian Ladies Tour	www.lagt.org
Australian Ladies Tour	www.alpgtour.com
South African Ladies Tour	www.wpga.co.za
Futures Tour	www.duramedfuturestour.com
The Open	www.opengolf.com
US Open	www.usopen.com
The Masters	www.masters.org
US PGA Championship	www.pga.com/pgachampionship/2008
PGA (The Belfry)	www.pga.info
PGAs of Europe	www.pgae.com
PGA of America	www.pga.com

Severiano Ballesteros	www.seveballesteros.com
Angel Cabrera	www.angelcabrera.com
Michael Campbell	www.cambogolf.com
Paul Casey	www.paul-casey.com
Darren Clarke	www.darrenclarke.com
Ernie Els	www.ernieels.com
Nick Faldo	www.nickfaldo.com
Padraig Harrington	www.padraigharrington.com
David Howell	www.davidhowellgolf.com
Miguel Angel Jiménez	www.mmiworldwide.com
Bernhard Langer	www.bernhardlanger.de
Paul McGinley	www.paulmcginley.net
Phil Mickelson	www.phil-mickelson.com
Colin Montgomerie	www.colinmontgomerie.com
Jack Nicklaus	www.nicklaus.com
Ian Poulter	www.ianpoulter.co.uk
Eduardo Romero	www.eduardoromero.com
Justin Rose	www.justinrose.com
Adam Scott	www.adamscott.com.au
Henrik Stenson	www.henrikstenson.com
Lee Westwood	www.westyuk.com
Tiger Woods	www.tigerwoods.com
Ian Woosnam	www.woosie.com

PART XV

Directory of Golfing Organisations Worldwide

Directory of Golfing Organisations Worldwide

National Associations

The R&A
Ch Exec, Peter Dawson, St Andrews, Fife KY16 9JD
Tel (01334) 460000   Fax (01334) 460001
E-mail thechiefexecutive@randa.org
Website www.randa.org

Council of National Golf Unions
Sec, Kevin McIntyre, Dromin, Dunleer, Co. Louth,
Ireland
Tel +353 41 686 1476
E-mail golfinmcinere@hotmail.com
Website www.congu.com

Ladies European Tour
Exec Dir, A Armas, Buckinghamshire GC, Denham
Court Drive, Denham UB9 5PG
Tel (01895) 831028   Fax (01895) 832301
E-mail mail@ladieseuropeantour.com
Website www.ladieseuropeantour.com

Ladies' Golf Union
Ch Exec, S Malcolm, The Scores, St Andrews, Fife
KY16 9AT
Tel (01334) 475811   Fax (01334) 472818
E-mail info@lgu.org   Website www.lgu.org

The Professional Golfers' Association
Ch Exec, Sandy Jones, Centenary House,
The Belfry, Sutton Coldfield B76 9PT
Tel (01675) 470333   Fax (01675) 477888
Website www.pga.info

East Region: Sec, J Smith, Bishop's Stortford GC,
Dunmow Road, Bishop's Stortford, Herts
CM23 5HP
Tel (01279) 652070   Fax (01279) 652732
E-mail john.smith@pga.org.uk

Midland Region: Sec, J Sewell, Forest Hill GC,
Markfield Lane, Botcheston, Leicester LE9 9FS
Tel (01455) 824393   Fax (01455) 828751
E-mail jon.sewell@pga.org.uk

North Region: Sec, G Maly, No 2 Cottage, Bolton
GC, Lostock Park, Chorley New Rd, Bolton, Lancs
BL6 4AJ
Tel (01204) 496137   Fax (01204) 847959
E-mail graham.maly@pga.org.uk

South Region: Sec, L Greasley, Clandon Regis GC,
Epsom Rd, West Clandon, Guildford, Surrey
GU4 7TT
Tel (01483) 224200   Fax (01483) 223224
E-mail south.region@pga.org.uk

West Region: Sec, G Ross, Exeter G&CC,
Topsham Rd, Countess Wear, Exeter EX2 7AE
Tel (01392) 877657   Fax (01392) 876382
E-mail glenn.ross@pga.info

Irish Region: Sec, M McCumiskey, Dundalk GC,
Blackrock, Dundalk, Co Louth, Eire
Tel +353 42 932 1193   Fax +353 42 932 1899
E-mail michael.mccumiskey@pga.org.uk

Scottish Region: Sec, G Dewar, King's Lodge,
Gleneagles, Auchterarder PH3 1NE
Tel (01764) 661840   Fax (01764) 661841
E-mail gordon.dewar@pga.org.uk

PGA European Tour
Exec Dir, G O'Grady, PGA European Tour,
Wentworth Drive, Virginia Water, Surrey GU25 4LX
Tel (01344) 840400   Fax (01344) 840500
E-mail info@europeantour.com
Website www.europeantour.com

PGAs of Europe
Chief Exec, I Randell, Centenary House, The Belfry,
Sutton Coldfield, B76 9PT
Tel (01675) 477899   Fax (01675) 477890
E-mail info@pgae.com   Website www.pgae.com

Artisan Golfers' Association
Hon Sec, K Stevens, 48 The Avenue, Lightwater,
Surrey GU18 5RG
Tel (01276) 475103
E-mail kevin@stevens85.freeserve.co.uk
Website www.agagolf.co.uk

Association of Golf Writers
A group of 30 newspapermen attending the Walker
Cup match at St Andrews in 1938 founded the Association to protect the interests of golf writers. The
principal objective is to maintain a close liaison with
all the governing bodies and promoters to ensure
good working conditions.

Sec, Andrew Farrell, 1 Pilgrims Bungalow, Mulberry
Hill, Chilham, Kent CT4 8AH
Tel/Fax (01227) 732496
E-mail andyfarrell292@btinternet.com

**BAGCC – British Association of Golf Course
Constructors**
The BAGCC has a small but highly prestigious membership of constructors who have performed work to
the highest standard from initial consultation to survey
work and design through to the construction of a
course and then its regular maintenance. Membership

is granted only if the candidates satisfy the demanding criteria of experience, professionalism and workmanship set down by the Association.

Sec, Brian Pierson, 32 New Rd, Ringwood BH24 3AU
Tel (01424) 842380   *Fax* (01424) 843375
E-mail brian.pierson@btopenworld,com
Website www.bagcc.org.uk

BALASA – British Amputee & Les Autres Sports Association
Chair, Brian Cherrington, 16 Scott Ave, Crewe, Cheshire CW1 5JP
Tel /Fax (01270) 585508

British Golf Collectors' Society
Sec, A Thorpe, 22 Cherry Tree Close, Brinsley, Nottingham NG16 5BA
Tel/Fax (01773) 780420
E-mail anthonythorpe@ntlworld.com
Website www.britgolfcollectors.wyenet.co.uk

BGIA – British Golf Industry Association
Federation House, Stoneleigh Park, Warks CV8 2RF
Tel (024) 7641 7141
Fax (024) 7641 4990
E-mail bgia@sportsandplay.com
Website www.bgia.org.uk

British Golf Museum
Dir, PN Lewis, Bruce Embankment, St Andrews, Fife KY16 9AB
Tel (01334) 460046   *Fax* (01334) 460064
Website www.britishgolfmuseum.co.uk

BIGGA – British & International Golf Greenkeepers Association
BIGGA, which was formed in 1987, is an amalgamation of the English, Scottish and Northern Irish Associations and promotes and advances all aspects of greenkeeping and assists and encourages the proficiency of the members. In addition to its annual conference the Association organizes the annual Turf Management Exhibition, Europe's largest indoor turf show. Currently the Association has over 7,300 members.

Ch Exec, J Pemberton, BIGGA House, Aldwark, Alne, York YO61 1UF
Tel (01347) 833800   *Fax* (01347) 833801
E-mail reception@bigga.co.uk
Website www.bigga.org.uk

BRTMA – British Rootzone & Topdressing Manufacturers Association
Federation House, Stoneleigh Park, Warks CV8 2RF
Tel (024) 7641 4999
Fax (024) 7641 4990
E-mail brtma@sportsandplay.com
Website www.brtma.com

BTLIA – British Turf & Landscape Irrigation Association
Sec, M Jones, 41 Pennine Way, Great Eccleston, Preston PR3 0YS
Tel/Fax (01995) 670675
E-mail ntfoundation@btconnect.com
Website www.btlia.org.uk

EDGA – European Disabled Golf Association
Sec/Treas, Pieter van Duyn, Wederikof 8, 2215 GJ Voorhout, The Netherlands
Tel +31 6 429 201 98   *E-mail* p.vanduyn@tiscali.nl
Website www.edgagolf.com

EGIA – European Golf Industry Association
Federation House, Stoneleigh Park, Warks CV8 2RF
Tel (024) 7641 4999   *Fax* (024) 7641 4990
E-mail egia@sportsandplay.com

EIGCA – European Institute of Golf Course Architects
The EIGCA represents the vast majority of qualified and experienced golf course architects throughout Europe. Its goals are to enhance its professional status and to provide educational courses to train future architects.

Exec Off, Mrs Julia Green, Meadow View House, Tannery Lane, Bramley, Surrey GU5 0AJ
Tel/Fax (01483) 891831   *Fax* (01483) 891846
E-mail enquiries@eigca.org   *Website* www.eigca.org

Golf Club Managers Association
Membership of the Association is approximately 2500, consisting of managers/secretaries and owners of clubs and golfing associations situated mainly in the UK and Europe. The Association offers advice on all aspects of managing a golf club and has an extensive information library available to its members through its website.

Ch Exec, K Lloyd, 7a Beaconsfield Rd, Weston-super-Mare BS23 1YE
Tel (01934) 641166   *Fax* (01934) 644254
E-mail hq@gcma.org.uk   *Website* www.gcma.org.uk

Golf Club Stewards' Association
The Golf Club Stewards' Association was founded in 1912 to promote the interests of members and to serve as an employment agency for golf club stewards.

Sec, Peter Payne, 3 St George's Drive, Ickenham, Middx UB10 4HW
Tel (01895) 674325   *E-mail* golfclubstewards@aol.com
Website www.club_noticeboard.co.uk

Golf Consultants Association
Federation House, Stoneleigh Park, Warks CV8 2RF
Tel (024) 7641 4999
Fax (024) 7641 4990
E-mail gca@sportsandplay.com
Website www.golfconsultants.org.uk

Golf Foundation
Ch. Exec, Michael Round, The Spinning Wheel, High St, Hoddesdon, Herts EN11 8BP
Tel (01992) 449830   *Fax* (01992) 449840
E-mail info@golf-foundation.org
Website www.golf-foundation.org

Handigolf Foundation
Sec, Ray Lee, 404 Westthorne Ave, Eltham, London SE9 5TL
Tel (0208) 850 7407   *E-mail* rayndpam@hotmail.com
Website www.handigolf.org

National Association of Public Golf Courses

Affiliated to the English Golf Union, the Association was founded in 1927 by golf course architect FG Hawtree and five times Open champion JH Taylor to provide a relationship between public and proprietory golf clubs, and local councils and course owners.

Hon Sec, E Mitchell, 12 Newton Close, Redditch B98 7YR
Tel (01527) 542106   *Fax* (01527) 455320
E-mail eddiemitchell@blueyonder.co.uk
Website www.napgc.org.uk

National Golf Clubs' Advisory Association

Founded in 1922, the Association's aims are to protect the interests of golf clubs in general; to give legal advice and direction, under the opinion of Counsel, on the administrative and legal responsibilities of golf clubs;.and to provide a mediation service to members' clubs within the UK.

Ch Exec, Michael Shaw LLM
Nat Sec, J Howe, The Threshing Barn, Homme Castle Barns, Shelsley Walsh, Worcs WR6 6RR
Tel (01886) 812943   *Fax* (01886) 812935
E-mail jackie.ngaa@idealnet.co.uk
Website www.ngcaa.org.uk

One-Armed Golfers, Society of

Hon Sec, Peter Priscott, 25 Malsters Close, Mundford, Thetford, Norfolk IP26 5HJ
Tel (01842) 878554
E-mail PeterPriscott@aol.com

Public Schools Old Boys Golf Association

Hon Sec, P de Pinna, Bruins, Wythwood, Haywards Heath, West Sussex RH16 4RD
Tel/Fax (01444) 454883

Public Schools' Golfing Society

Hon Sec, N D Owen,1 Bruce Grove, Orpington, Kent BR6 0HF
Tel (01689) 810225
E-mail nick.owen@ndowen.com

STRI – Sports Turf Research Institute

STRI is an independent consultancy and research organisation specialising in golf courses. Recognised throughout the world for its expertise in both agronomic and environmental issues relating to golf, STRI is the official adviser to The R&A's Championship Committee for all 'Open' venues. STRI undertakes research into turfgrass and sports surface science, promoting innovative solutions. For golf courses, it provides advisory and architectural services and gives ecological advice. In addition, STRI organises training and produces publications.

Ch Exec, Dr IG McKillop; *Ext Affairs*, Anne Wilson, St Ives Estate, Bingley, West Yorks BD16 1AU
Tel (01274) 565131
Fax (01274) 561891
E-mail info@stri.co.uk
Website www.stri.co.uk

Home Unions and Regional Associations

England

English Golf Union

Ch Exec, John Petrie, National Golf Centre, The Broadway, Woodhall Spa, Lincs LN10 6PU
Tel (01526) 354500   *Fax* (01526) 354020
E-mail info@englishgolfunion.org
Website www.englishgolfunion.org

Midland Group: *Sec*, TG Arnold, 11 Duckworth Rd, Corby, Northants NN17 2RZ
Tel (01536) 743829   *Fax* (07005) 801 042
E-mail secretary@midlandgolfunion.co.uk
Website www.midlandgolfunion.co.uk

Northern Group: *Sec*, JD Trickett, 8 Derriman Grove, Sheffield S11 9LE
Tel/Fax (0114) 249 1625
E-mail dennistrickett@yahoo.co.uk
Website www.ncgu.co.uk

South Eastern Group: *Sec*, BJ Thompson, 5 Rookery Drive, Luton, Beds LU2 7FG
Tel (01582) 485638
E-mail secretary@southeastgolfunion.co.uk

South Western Group: *Sec*, TC Reynolds, The Haven, Velator, Nr Braunton, N Devon EX33 2DX
Tel/Fax (01271) 812228   *E-mail* swcga@talktalk.net

English Men's County Unions

Bedfordshire CGU

Sec, DA Parrett. 49 Manor Rd, Barton-le-Clay MK45 4NP
Tel (01582) 883089
E-mail secretary@bedsgolfunion.org
Website www.bedsgolfunion.org

Berks, Bucks & Oxon UGC

Sec, PMJ York, Bridge House, Station Approach, Great Missenden HP16 9AZ
Tel (01494) 867341   *Fax* (01494) 867342
E-mail secretary@bbogolf.com
Website www.bbogolf.com

Cambridgeshire Area GU

Sec, RAC Blows, 73 Pheasant Rise, Bar Hill, Cambridge CB23 8SB
Tel (01954) 780887
Website www.cagu.co.uk

Cheshire UGC

Sec, SJ Foster, County Office Chester GC, Curzon Park North, Chester CH4 8AR
Tel (01244) 678004
E-mail secretary@cheshiregolf.org.uk
Website www.cheshiregolf.org.uk

Cornwall GU

Hon Sec, P F Batty, 3 Clemens Close, Newquay, Cornwall TR7 2SG

Tel/Fax (01637) 873117
E-mail secretary@cornwallgolfunion.org.uk
Website www.cornwallgolfunion.org.uk

Cumbria UGC
Hon Sec, T F Stout, Kingston House, Moresby,
Whitehaven CA28 8UW
Tel/Fax (01946) 693036
E-mail cumbriaugcsec@yahoo.co.uk
Website www.cumbria-golf-union.org.uk

Derbyshire UGC
Hon Sec, P McGrath, 36 Ilkeston Rd, Stapleford, Notts
NG9 8JL
Tel (01159) 223603
E-mail secretary@dugc.co.uk
Website www.dugc.co.uk

Devon CGU
Sec, John Hirst, 20 Plymouth Rd, Tavistock PL19 8AY
Tel (01822) 610640   *Fax* (01822) 610540
E-mail info@devongolfunion.org.uk
Website www.devongolfunion.org.uk

Dorset CGU
Sec, Ian Hulse, 5 St James Rd, Ferndown, Dorset
BH22 9NY
Tel (01202) 861185
E-mail secretary@dcgu.org.uk
Website www.dcgu.org.uk

Durham CGU
Sec, GP Hope, 7 Merrion Close, Moorside,
Sunderland SR3 2QP
Tel/Fax (0191) 522 8605
E-mail secretary@durhamcountygolfunion.co.uk
Website www.durhamcountygolfunion.co.uk

Essex GU
Sec, AT Lockwood, 2d Maldon Rd, Witham, Essex
CM8 2AB
Tel (01376) 500998   *Fax* (01376) 500842
E-mail info@essexgolfunion.org
Website www.essexgolfunion.org

Gloucestershire GU
Sec, I Watkins, The Vyse, Olde Lane,
Toddington, Glos GL54 5DW
Tel/Fax (01242) 621476
E-mail secretary@gloucestershiregolfunion.co.uk
Website www.gloucestershiregolfunion.co.uk

Hampshire, Isle of Wight &
Channel Islands GU
Sec, Barry Morgan, c/o Liphook GC, Wheatsheaf
Enclosure, Liphook, Hants GU30 7EH
Tel/Fax (01428) 725580
E-mail hgu@hampshiregolf.co.uk
Website www.hampshiregolf.org.uk

Hertfordshire GU
Hon Sec, C Murray, Oak Tree House, 14 Main Rd,
Bramfield, SG14 2QJ
Tel (07801) 187317
E-mail secretary@hertsgolfunion.com
Website www.hertsgolfunion.com

Isle of Man GU
Hon Sec, Joe Boyd, Cheu-Ny-Hawiney,
Phildraw Rd, Ballasalla, Isle of Man IM9 3EG
Tel/Fax (01624) 823098
E-mail joeboyd@manx.net
Website www.isleofmangolf.com

Kent CGU
Sec, BL Sparkes, Littlestone GC, St Andrew's Rd,
Littlestone, New Romney, Kent TN28 8RB
Tel (01797) 367725   *Fax* (01797) 367726
E-mail kcgu@kentgolf.co.uk   *Website* www.kcgu.org

Lancashire UGC
Sec, AV Moss, 5 Dicconson Terrace, Lytham
St Annes FY8 5JY
Tel (01253) 733323   *Fax* (01253) 795721
E-mail secretary@lancashiregolf.org
Website www.lancashiregolf.org

Leicestershire & Rutland GU
Hon Sec, J Tolley, Fairbourne House, Spring Lane,
Shepshed, LE12 9JE
Tel (01509) 554664
E-mail lrgusecretary@gmail.com
Website www.lrgu.co.uk

Lincolnshire UGC
Hon Sec, H Harrison, 27 Orchard Close, Morton,
Gainsborough DN21 3BP
Tel (01427) 616904   *E-mail* secretary@lugc.co.uk
Website www.lugc.co.uk

Middlesex CGU
Sec, M Willcox, Northwick Park Golf Centre,
Watford Rd, Harrow HA1 3TZ
Tel (0208) 864 4744   *Fax* (0208) 864 4554
E-mail secretary@mcgu.co.uk
Website www.mcgu.co.uk

Norfolk CGU
Hon Sec, D Horsburgh, 5 Bishops Croft, Barningham,
Bury St Edmunds IP31 1BZ
Tel (01359) 221281
E-mail dandmhorsburgh@talktalk.net
Website www.norfolkcountygolfunion.co.uk

Northamptonshire GU
Hon Sec, J Pearson, 150 Church Green Rd, Bletchley,
Milton Keynes MK3 6DD
Tel (01908) 648657
E-mail secretary@northantsgolfunion.co.uk
Website www.northantsgolfunion.co.uk

Northumberland UGC
Hon Sec, WE Procter, Eastfield House, Moor Rd
South, Gosforth, Newcastle upon Tyne NE3 1NP
Tel (0191) 285 4981
E-mail secretary@nugc.org.uk
Website www.nugc.org.uk

Nottinghamshire UGC
Hon Sec, R Case, 68a Cropwell Rd, Radcliffe-on-Trent,
Nottingham NG12 2JG
Tel/Fax (0115) 933 4777
E-mail golfstuff@btinternet.com
Website www.nottsgolfunion.com

Shropshire & Herefordshire UGC
Hon Sec, JR Davies, 23 Poplar Crescent, Bayston Hill,
Shrewsbury SY3 0QB
Tel (01743) 872655
E-mail bdavies@blueyonder.co.uk
Website www.shugc.com

Somerset GU
Hon Sec, A King, Tweedside, Goosenford, Cheddon
Fitzpaine, Taunton TA2 8LJ

Tel/Fax (01823) 412510
E-mail secretary@somerset.golfunion.co.uk
Website www.somerset.golfunion.co.uk

Staffordshire UGC
Sec, MA Payne, 20 Kingsbrook Drive, Hillfield, Solihull
B91 3UU
Tel (0121) 704 4779   *Fax* (0121) 711 2841
E-mail martin@mpayne99.freeserve.co.uk
Website www.staffsgolf.com

Suffolk GU
Hon Sec, RA Kent, 77 Bennett Ave, Bury St Edmunds
IP33 3JJ
Tel (01284) 705765
E-mail golfsgu@btinternet.com
Website www.suffolkgolfunion.co.uk

Surrey CGU
Sec, JA Davies, Sutton Green GC, New Lane,
Sutton Green GU4 7QF
Tel (01483) 755788   *Fax* (01483) 751771
E-mail secretary@surreygolf.org
Website www.surreygolf.org

Sussex CGU
Sec, A Vasant, J.P., Eastbourne Down GC, East Dean
Rd, Eastbourne, East Sussex BN20 8ES
Tel (01323) 746677   *Fax* (01323) 746777
E-mail countyoffice@sussexgolf.org
Website www.sussexgolf.org

Warwickshire UGC
Sec, G G Hayes, 114 Stonebury Ave, Eastern Green,
Coventry CV5 7NX
Tel/Fax (02476) 422793
E-mail grahamhayes@warksgolf.co.uk
Website www.warksgolf.co.uk

Wiltshire CGU
Sec, EK Hodges, 13 Elm Close, Bowerhill,
Melksham, Wilts SN12 6SD
E-mail secretary@wcgu.org.uk
Website www.wcgu.org.uk

Worcestershire UGC
Hon Sec, A Boyd, The Bear's Den, Upper St,
Defford, Worcester WR8 9BG
Tel (01386) 750657   *Fax* (01386) 750472
E-mail menssecretary
                    @worcestershireamateurgolf.co.uk
Website www.worcestershireamateurgolf.co.uk

Yorkshire UGC
Hon Sec, KH Dowswell, 33 George St, Wakefield
WF1 1LX
Tel (01924) 383869   *Fax* (01924) 383634
E-mail yorkshiregolf@lineone.net
Website www.yorkshireunionofgolf.co.uk

English Women's Golf Association
Sec, Mrs P Perla, 11 Highfield Rd, Edgbaston,
Birmingham B15 3EB
Tel (0121) 456 2088   *Fax* (0121) 454 5542
E-mail office@englishwomensgolf.org
Website englishwomensgolf.org

Midlands Division: *Hon Sec*, Mrs S Ramsay, 35
Kooreman Ave, Wisbech PE13 3HY

Tel (01945) 467732
E-mail susan.ramsay@btinternet.com

Northern Division: *Hon Sec*, Mrs D V Wilson,
27 Wilton Ave, Hartlepool TS26 9PT
Tel (01429) 261473
E-mail diane.wilson@btinternet.com

South-Eastern Division: *Hon Sec*, Mrs A Green,
40a Woodside Ave, Beaconsfield HP9 1JH
Tel (01494) 674791
E-mail agreen.beaconsfield@virgin.net

South-Western Division: *Hon Sec*, Lady
Beauchamp, The Coach House, 4 Balfour Mews,
Sidmouth EX10 8XL
Tel (01395) 513141
E-mail margot.beauchamp@btinternet.com

English Senior Ladies Golf Association
(contact EWGA)

English Ladies' County Associations

Bedfordshire LCGA
Hon Sec, Miss K Harris, 14 Tanqueray Ave, Clophill
MK45 4AW
Tel (01525) 862180
E-mail Bkh.Home@btinternet.com
Website blcga.co.uk

Berkshire LCGA
Hon Sec, Mrs J Houghton, 5 Garden House, 41
St Peters Ave, Caversham RG4 7DH
Tel (01189) 483571
E-mail j.houghton161@btinternet.com

Buckinghamshire CLGA
Hon Sec, Mrs L Hilton, Peartree Cottage,
Hodgemoor View, Chalfont St Giles HP8 4LS
Tel (01404) 876303
E-mail lynda.hilton@btinternet.com
Website bclga.org.uk

Cambs & Hunts LCGA
Hon Sec, Mrs C Ratcliffe, 57 Alexander Chase, Ely
CB6 3SN
Tel (01353) 664136
E-mail christineratcliffe@sky.com *Website* chlgca.co.uk

Cheshire CLGA
Hon Sec, Mrs A McCormick, Frinton, 22 Buxton Rd
West, Disley, Stockport SK12 2LY
Tel (01663) 766807
E-mail ann.mccormick4@ntlworld.com

Cornwall LCGA
Hon Sec, Mrs C Ryder, 7 Choughs Close, Camborne
TR14 7XH
Tel (01209) 717 564
E-mail clcga@btinternet.com   *Website* clga.co.uk

Cumbria LCGA
Hon Sec, Mrs S Cotter, Park Rigg Bungalow, Easton,
nr Longtown CA6 5RS
Tel (01228) 577347
E-mail sue@cumbriakitchens.co.uk

Derbyshire LCGA
Hon Sec, Mrs V Kay, 60 Windsor Drive,
Wingerworth, Chesterfield S42 6TJ
Tel (01246) 237824
E-mail veda.kay@btinternet.com

Devon CLGA
Hon Sec, Mrs D Harris, Fairmile, 20 Church Rd,
Alphington, Exeter EX2 8SH
Tel (01392) 669504
E-mail deborah.harris@dwp.gsi.gov.uk

Dorset LCGA
Hon Sec, Mrs K Everett, 12 Holland Way, Blandford
Forum, DT11 7RU
Tel (01258) 454303
E-mail kaytel@logic-net.co.uk

Durham CLGA
Hon Sec, Mrs E Whittle, 9 Woodlands, Lanchester,
Co. Durham DH7 0NS
Tel (01207) 520581
E-mail alenawhittle@talktalk.net
Website durhamladiesgolf.org.uk

Essex LCGA
Hon Sec, W Wilcock, 24 Martingale, Thunderclay,
Benfleet SS7 3DP
Tel (01702) 554761   E-mail waw24m@talktalk.net
Website essexladiesgolf.org

Gloucestershire LCGA
Hon Sec, Mrs G Merry, Myles House, Ashmead, Cam,
Dursley GL11 5EN
Tel (01453) 542569   E-mail GillianMerry@talktalk.net

Hampshire LCGA
Hon Sec, Miss M Rook, 6 Adocet Way, Horndean,
Waterlooville PO8 9YE
Tel (02392) 593798
E-mail hlcgahonsec@freenet.co.uk
Website www.hampshireladiesgolf.co.uk

Hertfordshire CLGA
Hon Sec, Mrs L Hall, 1 Eaton Close, Weston Turville
HP22 5BQ
Tel (01296) 515557
E-mail lorna@nickhall.goladsl.co.uk
Website www.hclga.co.uk

Kent CLGA
Hon Sec, Mrs A Blackman, 17 Woodhayes, Willow
Grove, Chislehurst BR7 5EX
Tel (0208) 468 7398
E-mail alexdud@btinternet.com
Website kentladiesgolf.org.uk

Lancashire LCGA
Hon Sec, Mrs J Smart, Netherfield, Links Lane,
Pleasington, Blackburn BB2 5JH
Tel (01254) 208935
E-mail janettesmart@btinternet.com

Leicestershire & Rutland LCGA
Hon Sec, Mrs D Jones, 73 Cunningham Drive,
Lutterworth LE17 4YR
Tel (01455) 554310
E-mail k.t-djones_73@tiscali.co.uk

Lincolnshire LCGA
Hon Sec, Mrs K Craigs, 55 Main St, Scopwick, Lincs
LN4 3NW
Tel (01526) 321470   Fax (01526) 354403
E-mail kmcraigs@aol.com

Middlesex LCGA
Hon Sec, Mrs D Rowlands, 3 Meadowbank Close,
Bovingdon HP3 0FB
Tel (01442) 831414

Norfolk LCGA
Hon Sec, Mrs Y Douglas, 204 Norwich Rd, Fakenham
NR21 8LX
Tel (01328) 863296
E-mail douglas.yvette@btinternet.com

Northamptonshire LCGA
Hon Sec, Mrs S Butler, The Rookery, Hardwick, nr
Wellingborough NN9 5AL
Tel (01933) 679605
E-mail NLCGA@butler123.freeserve.co.uk

Northumberland LCGA
Hon Sec, Mrs S Gowens, 3 Lydbury Close,
Northburn Green, Cramlington NE23 3XY
Tel (01670) 735426
E-mail sue@gowens.org.uk
Website www.nlcga.co.uk

Nottinghamshire CLGA
Hon Sec, Mrs BA Patrick, 18 Delville Ave,
Keyworth, Nottingham NG12 5JA
Tel (0115) 937 3237
E-mail bapatrick@tiscali.co.uk

Oxfordshire LCGA
Hon Sec, Dr S Adams, Stable Barn, Milton Rd,
Stadhampton OX44 7UF
Tel (01865) 691827   Fax (01865) 691630
E-mail sallyeadams@btinternet.com
Website olcga.org.uk

Shropshire LCGA
Hon Sec, Mrs H Hampton, 17 Peregrine Way, Telford
TF1 6TH
Tel (01952) 248383   E-mail helenhampton@aol.com

Somerset LCGA
Hon Sec, Mrs R Gait, 12 Bathurst Close, Burnham-on-
Sea, TA8 2SZ
Tel (01278) 786507   E-mail rosgait@sky.com

Staffordshire LCGA
Hon Sec, Mrs P Siviter, 69 Ward St, Coseley,
W Midlands WV14 9LQ
Tel/Fax (01902) 689940
E-mail pam.siviter@blueyonder.co.uk

Suffolk LCGA
Hon Sec, Mrs T Pearson, 12 Rydal Ave, Felixstowe
IP11 9SE
Tel (01394) 270319
E-mail mojogolf@talktalknet
Website suffolkladiesgolf.org.uk

Surrey LCGA
Sec, Mrs P Hall, SLGCA, c/o Sutton Green GC, Sutton
Green, Guildford GU4 7QF
Tel (01483) 751622   Fax (01483) 751771
E-mail secretary@slcga.org
Website www.slcga.org

Sussex CLGA
Hon Sec, Mrs S Holman, The Wattles, Piltdown, East
Sussex TN22 3XL
Tel (01825) 723443
E-mail holman@wattles.force9.co.uk
Website sclga.com

Warwickshire LCGA
Hon Sec, Mrs E Murdoch, Plestowes House, Hareway
Lane, Warwick CV35 8DD

Tel (01926) 624503
E-mail e.murdoch@ukonline.co.uk
Website warksgolf.co.uk

Wiltshire LCGA
Hon Sec, Mrs P Telling, Swanborough Cottage, Mill Lane, Poulshot, Devizes SN10 1SA
Tel (01380) 828370
E-mail pennytelling@aol.com

Worcestershire and Herefordshire CLGA
Hon Sec, Miss J Freeman, Leacroft Rd, Crabbe Cross, Redditch B97 5LZ
Tel (01527) 401923
E-mail jayne.freeman@solihull-ct.nhs.uk

Yorkshire LCGA
Hon Sec, Mrs E Haw, Orchard Cross, Stonegate, Whixley, York YO26 8AS
Tel (01423) 339 503
E-mail johliz@btopenworld.com
Website www.ylcga.org

English County PGAs

Bedfordshire & Cambridgeshire PGA
Sec, B Wake, 6 Gazelle Close, Eaton Socon, St Neots PE19 8QF
Tel (01480) 219760
E-mail brian.wake@btopenworld.com

Berks, Bucks & Oxon PGA
Hon Sec, Mrs M Green, Wayside, Aylesbury Rd, Monks Risborough, Princes Risborough HP27 0JS
Tel (01844) 343012
E-mail monica@stbarbe-green.freeserve.co.uk

Cheshire and North Wales PGA
Sec, G Maly, No 2 Cottage, Bolton GC, Lostock Park, Chorley New Road, Bolton BL6 4AJ
Tel (01204) 496137   *Fax* (01204) 847959
E-mail graham.maly@pga.org.uk

Cornwall PGA
Sec, C Willis, Bowood Park GC, Camelford PL32 9RF
Tel (01840) 213017   *Fax* (01840) 212622

Derbyshire PGA
Sec, F McCabe, Hillside, Lower Hall Close, Holbrook, Derby DE56 0TN
Tel (01332) 880411
E-mail fcmccabe@hotmail.com

Devon PGA
Sec, R Goodey, 1 Brookside Cres., Exeter EX4 8NF
Tel (07967) 769485
E-mail robingoodey@blueyonder.co.uk
Website www.devonpga.co.uk

Dorset PGA
Sec, D Parsons, Bridport & West Dorset GC, Burton Rd, Bridport, Dorset DT6 4PS
Tel (01308) 421491
E-mail bridproshop@tesco.net

Essex PGA
Sec, S Garland-Collins, 27 Willowdene Court, Brentwood, Essex CM14 5ET
Tel/Fax (01277) 223510
E-mail entries@essexpga.co.uk
Website www.essexpga.co.uk

Gloucestershire & Somerset PGA
Sec, E Goodwin, Cotswold Hills GC, Ullenwood, Cheltenham GL53 9QT
Tel (01242) 515263

Hampshire PGA
Sec, DL Wheeler, South Winchester GC, Pitt, Winchester SO22 5QX
Tel (01962) 860928
E-mail hampshirepga@yahoo.co.uk
Website www.hampshire-pga.co.uk

Hertfordshire PGA
Sec, ME Plumbley, Stavonga Dell, Pasture Rd, Letchworth SG6 3LP
Tel/Fax (01462) 485268
E-mail meplumbley@hertspga.org
Website www.hertspga.org

Kent PGA
Contact South Region PGA

Lancashire PGA
Sec, G Maly, No 2 Cottage, Bolton GC, Lostock Park, Chorley New Road, Bolton BL6 4AJ
Tel (01204) 496137   *Fax* (01204) 847959
E-mail graham.maly@pga.org.uk

Leicestershire PGA
Sec, Jim Pochin, 28 Errington Close, Oadby, Leicester LE2 4RP
Tel (0116) 271 1381
E-mail jimpochin@btinternet.com

Lincolnshire PGA
Sec, D Drake, 23 Manor Rd, Saxilby, Lincoln LN1 2HX
Tel (01522) 703331

Middlesex PGA
Sec, B Eady, 8 Woodbank Drive, Chalfont St Giles HP8 4RP
Tel (01494) 874487
E-mail brian@eadyuk.plus.com

Norfolk PGA
Sec, John Paling, Squirrels Reach, Folgate Lane, Old Costessey, Norwich NR8 5EF
Tel (01603) 741301
E-mail jandjpaling@uwclub.net
Website www.club-noticeboard.co.uk

North East & North West PGA
Hon Sec, T Flowers, 10 Rosedale Rd, Belmont, Durham DH1 2AS
Tel (0191) 383 9385
E-mail tom.flowers@fsmail.net

Northamptonshire PGA
Sec, R Lobb, 15 Manor Rd, Pitsford, Northampton NN6 9AR
Tel (01604) 881367
E-mail richard.lobb@northamptonshiregolf.org.uk
Website www.northamptonshirepga.co.uk

Nottinghamshire PGA
Sec, D Revill, 132 Nuncargate Rd, Kirby-in-Ashfield, Nottingham NG17 9EQ
Tel (01623) 477934
E-mail dave.revill@ntlworld.com
Website www.nottspga.co.uk

Shropshire & Hereford PGA
Sec, P Hinton, 29 Stourbridge Rd, Bridgnorth,
WV15 5AZ
Tel (01746) 762045
E-mail paulhinton@enta.net
Website www.a1golf.biz

Staffordshire PGA
Sec, Richard Spragg, Great Barr GC, Chapel Lane,
Birmingham B43 7BA
Tel/Fax (0121) 358 4376
E-mail secrichspragg@aol.com

Suffolk PGA
Sec, AED Garnett, 9 Furness Close, Ipswich IP2 9YA
Tel (01473) 685529
E-mail tonygarnett@talktalk.net

Surrey PGA
Contact South Region PGA

Sussex PGU
Sec, C Pluck, 96 Cranston Ave, Bexhill,
East Sussex TN39 3NL
Tel/Fax (01424) 221298
E-mail sussexpgu@g.mail.com
Website www.spgu.co.uk

Warwickshire PGA
Sec, N Selwyn-Smith, 18 Cornfield Ave, Stoke Heath,
Bromsgrove B60 3QU
Tel (01527) 875 750   E-mail neilss@execgolf.co.uk

Wiltshire PGA
Sec, M Walters, Erlestoke Sands GC, Erlestoke,
Devizes SN10 5UB   Tel (01380) 831027

Worcestershire PGA
Sec, K Ball, 136 Alvechurch Rd, West Heath,
Birmingham B31 3PW   Tel (0121) 475 7400

Yorkshire PGA
Sec, J Pape, 22 The Locks, Pottery Lane, Woodlesford,
Leeds LS26 8PU   Tel (0113) 282 8984

English Blind Golf Association
Sec, B Richards, 1 Hampden Way, Bilton, Rugby
CV22 7NW   Tel/Fax (01788) 519835
E-mail bryan.richards@talktalk.net
Website www.blindgolf.co.uk

Ireland

Golfing Union of Ireland
Gen Sec, S Smith, National Headquarters, Carton
Demesne, Maynooth, Co. Kildare
Tel +353 1 505 4000   Fax +353 1 505 4001
E-mail information@gui.ie   Website www.gui.ie

Irish Men's Branches

Connacht Branch: Gen Sec, E Lonergan,
2 Springfield Terrace, Castlebar, Mayo
Tel +353 94 90 28141   Fax +353 94 90 28143
E-mail guicb@eircom.net

Leinster Branch: Hon Sec, K McIntyre, Carton
Demesne, Maynooth, Co.Kildare
Tel +353 1 601 6842   Fax +353 1 601685
E-mail info@leinster.gui.ie

Munster Branch: Hon Sec, J Moloughney,
6 Townview, Mallow, Co Cork
Tel +353 22 21026   Fax +353 22 42373
E-mail guimb@iol.ie

Ulster Branch: Sec, BG Edwards, MBE,
Unit 5, Forestgrove Business Park, Newtownbreda Rd,
Belfast BT8 6AW
Tel (028) 9049 1891   Fax (028) 9049 1615
E-mail ulster.gui@btconnect.com

Irish Ladies' Golf Union
Ch Exec, Mrs S Heraty, 103-105 Q House, 76 Furze
Rd, Sandyford Ind. Est., Dublin 18
Tel +353 1 293 4833   Fax +353 1 293 4832
E-mail info@ilgu.ie   Website www.ilgu.ie

Irish Ladies' Districts

Eastern District: Hon Sec, Mrs R Hayes, 51
College Grove, Castle Knock, Dublin 15
Tel +353 1 822 6380
E-mail easterndistrict@eircom.net

Midland District: Hon Sec, Ms R Tully, Kilmeany,
Carlow
Tel +353 59 913 7672
E-mail rosemarytully@eircom.net

Northern District: Hon Sec Mrs S Robinson, 41
Ballyreagh Rd, Portrush, Co.Antrim BT56 8LR
Tel 028 70 824253 E-mail dunlucevolvo@yahoo.co.uk

Southern District: Hon Sec, Ms E Smith, Prague,
30 Shamrock Hill, Clonmel, Co.Tipperary
Tel +353 52 89316   E-mail eilism1@eircom.net

Western District: Hon Sec, Mrs B Hughes,
Rampert Woods, Golf Cub Road, Westport, Co Mayo
Tel +353 98 25870   E-mail ilguwest@eircom.net

Scotland

Scottish Golf Union
Sec, H Grey, The Duke's, St Andrews KY16 8NX
Tel (01334) 466477   Fax (01334) 461361
E-mail sgu@scottishgolf.org
Website www.scottishgolf.org

Scottish Men's Area Golf Associations

Angus: Sec, D Speed, 7 Eastgate, Friockheim,
Arbroath DD11 4TG
Tel (01241) 828544   Fax (01241) 828455
E-mail david.speed2@btopenworld.com

Argyll & Bute: Sec, R Biggart, Rimrock, 4
Calderwood, Cluniter Rd, Innellan, Dunoon
PA23 9QA
Tel (07717) 434405   E-mail rwbiggart@aol.com
Website www.argyllandbutegolfunion.com

Ayrshire: Sec, R L Crawford, 81 Connel Crescent,
Mauchline, Ayrshire KA5 5AU
Tel/Fax (01290) 551078
E-mail ballochmylegolf@btconnect.com

Borders: Sec, RG Scott, 3 Whytbank Row,
Clovenfords, Nr Galashiels TD1 3NE
Tel/Fax (01896) 850570
E-mail rscott.bga@btinternet.com
Website www.bordergolf.co.uk

Clackmannanshire: Sec, T Johnson, 75 Dewar Ave, Kincardine on Forth FK10 4RR
Tel 01259) 731520   Fax (01259) 769445
E-mail thjohn01@aol.com

Dunbartonshire: Sec, AW Jones, 107 Larkfield Rd, Lenzie, Glasgow G66 3AS
Tel/Fax (0141) 776 4377
E-mail alanjones@larky14.fsnet.co.uk
Website www.dgu.org.uk

Fife: Sec, J Scott, Lauriston, East Links, Leven KY8 4JL
Tel (01333) 423798   Fax (01333) 439910
E-mail jscottfga@blueyonder.co.uk
Website www.fifegolf.org

Glasgow: Sec, RJG Jamieson, 32 Eglinton St, Beith KA15 1AH
Tel/Fax (01505) 503000
E-mail r.jamieson-accountants@fsmail.net
Website www.glasgowgolfunion.org

Lanarkshire: Sec, T Logan, 41 Woodlands Drive, Coatbridge ML5 1LB
Tel (01236) 428799   E-mail tlogan.lga@hotmail.co.uk

Lothians: Sec, AG Shaw, 34 Caroline Terrace, Edinburgh EH12 8QX
Tel 0131 334 7291   Fax 0131 334 9269
E-mail AllanGShaw@hotmail.com
Website www.lothiansgolfassociation.org.uk

North: Sec, PL Abbott, 21 Manse Rd, Nairn IV12 4RW
Tel (01667) 453625
E-mail p.l.a@btinternet.com
Website www.sgunorth.com

North-East: Sec, GM Young, 24 Shore St, Cairnbulg, Fraserburgh AB43 8YL
Tel (01346) 582324
E-mail georgemyoung24@btinternet.com
Website www.sgunortheast.com

Perth & Kinross: Sec, JJE Simpson, 11 Dunbarney Av, Bridgeof Earn, Perth PH2 9BP
Tel (01738) 812588
E-mail auntyeedie@hotmail.com
Website www.perthandkinrosscountygolf.net

Renfrewshire: Sec, IJ Walker, 12 Langcraigs Drive, Glenburn, Paisley PA2 8JW
Tel (0141) 569 3515   Fax (0141) 560 5649
E-mail walker.ian@ntlworld.com
Website www.renfrewshiregolfunion.co.uk

South: Sec, J Burns, Glanavon, 14 Millfield Ave, Stranraer DG9 0EG
Tel (01776) 704778   Fax (01776) 870445
E-mail stranraergolf@btclick.com

Stirlingshire: Sec, J Elliott, 65 Rosebank Ave, Falkirk FK1 5JR
Tel (01324) 634 118
E-mail johnelliott65@blueyonder.co.uk
Website www.stirlingshiregolfunion.co.uk

Scottish Blind Golf Society
Sec, R Clayden, 5 The Round, Dunfermline, Fife KY12 7YH   Tel (01383) 737717

Scottish Golfers Alliance
Sec, E Sherry, Lundin Tower, Pilmuir Rd, Lundin Links KY8 6BD

Scottish Ladies' Golfing Association
Sec, Dr S Hartley, The Den, 2 Dundee Rd, Perth PH2 7DW
Tel (01738) 442357   Fax (01738) 442380
E-mail secretary@slga.co.uk
Website www.slga.co.uk

Scottish Ladies County Golf Associations
Aberdeen LCGA
Hon Sec, Miss K Stalker, 2 Braemar Court, Fraserburgh AB43 9XE
Tel (01346) 513308
E-mail karen@fairways.eclipse.co.uk
Website www.alcga.co.uk

Angus LCGA
Hon Sec, Mrs M Raitt, 22 Briar Grove, Forfar DD8 1DG
Tel (01307) 464931
E-mail gordon.raitt@btinternet.com

Ayrshire LCGA
Hon Sec, Mrs S Young, Broomhill House, Riccarton, Kilmarnock KA1 5LP
Tel (01563) 540564   E-mail mops@aquatron.co.uk

Border Counties' LGA
Hon Sec, Mrs M Waddell, Nether Horsburgh, Innerleithen EH44 6RE
Tel (01896) 830188
E-mail marnywaddell@btinternet.com
Website www.borderladiesgolf.com

Dumfriesshire LCGA
Hon Sec, C Glen, 1A Annan Rd, Eastriggs, Annan DG12 6PZ
Tel (01461) 40266

Dunbartonshire & Argyll LCGA
Hon Sec, Mrs A Byiers, 43 Ballater Dr, Bearsden, Glasgow G61 1BZ
Tel (0141) 9430281
E-mail annebyiers@hotmail.com
Website www.dalcga.ik.com

East Lothian LCGA
Hon Sec, Mrs F Playfair, Dunaros, Ballencrieff Farm, Longniddry EH32 0PJ
Tel (01875) 870509   E-mail playfair@globalnet.co.uk

Fife CLGA
Hon Sec, Mrs M Muncey, 25 Lakeside Rd, Kirkcaldy KY2 5QJ
Tel (01592) 262980
E-mail david.muncey@zen.co.uk

Galloway LCGA
Hon Sec/Treas, Mrs A Furness, 57 South St, Port William, Newton Stewart DG8 9SH
Tel (01988) 700233

Lanarkshire LCGA
Hon Sec, Mrs J Macintyre, 4 Midcroft Place, Strathaven ML10 6EX
Tel (01357) 520648
E-mail jean.macintyre1@virgin.net
Website www.llcga.co.uk

Midlothian CLGA
Hon Sec, Mrs A Leslie, 18 Swanston Grove, Edinburgh EH10 7BW
Tel (0131) 445 2411
E-mail agnes.leslie@lbfire.org.uk
Website www.mclga.co.uk

Northern Counties' LGA
Hon Sec/Treas, Mrs M Alexander, 16 Grant St,
Whitehills AB45 2NU
Tel (01261) 861771
E-mail mayalexander@jenartie.wanadoo.com

Perth & Kinross LCGA
Hon Sec, Miss A Bushby, Braemore, Meigle PH12 8QX
Tel (01828) 640397   *E-mail* ahmb1@aol.com

Renfrewshire LCGA
Hon Sec, Mrs M Turner, 5 Westfield Dr, Kilmacolm
PA13 4JE
Tel (01505) 874429
E-mail moragturner@aol.com
Website rlgca.co.uk

Stirling & Clackmannan LGA
Hon Sec, Mrs A Hunter, 22 Muirhead Rd,
Stenhousemuir, FK5 4JA
Tel (01324) 554515
E-mail annahunter@btinternet.com

**Scottish Veteran Ladies' Golfing
Association**
Hon Sec, Mrs JC Lambert, Balcary, Barcloy Rd,
Rockcliffe, Dalbeattie DG5 4QJ
Tel (01556) 630419
E-mail jeanc.lambert@tesco.net
Website www.svlga.co.uk

Wales

Golf Union of Wales
Ch Exec, Richard Dixon, Catsash, Newport, Gwent
NP18 1JQ
Tel (01633) 436 040   *Fax* (01633) 430843
E-mail wgu@welshgolf.org
Website www.welshgolf.org.uk

Welsh Men's Golf Unions

Anglesey GU
Hon Sec, GP Jones, 20 Gwelfor Estate, Cemaes Bay,
Anglesey LL67 0NL
Tel (01407) 710755
E-mail garethgwelfor@aol.com

Brecon & Radnor GU
Hon Sec, DJ Davies, Garden House, Howey,
Llandrindod Wells, Powys LD1 5PU
Tel (01597) 824316

Caernarfonshire & District GU
Hon Sec, RE Jones, 23 Bryn Rhos, Rhosbodrual,
Caernarfon, Gwynedd LL55 2BT
Tel (01286) 673486

Denbighshire GU
Hon Sec, D Ethelston, Gwylfa, Garth Rd, Garth,
Llangollen LL20 7UR
Tel (01978) 820722   *E-mail* ethelgarth@aol.com

Dyfed GU
B Booth, Rhyd, Croes Y Llan, Llangoedmor, Cardigan
SA43 2LH
Tel (01239) 615334
E-mail wdjbooth@tiscali.co.uk
Website www.dyfedgolf.co.uk

Union of Flintshire Golf Clubs
Hon Sec, Mrs G Snead, 1 Cornist Cottages, Flint
CH6 5RH
Tel (01352) 732461
E-mail johnsnead@hotmail.co.uk

Glamorgan County GU
Hon Sec, P Austerberry, 10 Chestnut Tree Close,
Radyr, Cardiff CF15 8RY
Tel (02920) 419823

Gwent GU
Sec, G Harris, 4 Rolls Walk, Mount Pleasant,
Rogerstone, Gwent NP10 0AE
Tel (01633) 663750
E-mail w.graham.harris@ntlworld.com

North Wales PGA
See Cheshire & North Wales PGA, page 632

South Wales PGA
See West Region PGA, page 626

Welsh Ladies' Golf Union
See Golf Union of Wales

Welsh Ladies' County Golf Associations

Caernarvonshire & Anglesey LCGA
Hon Sec, Mrs J Harvey, 10 Craig y Don, Pensarn,
Abergele LL22 7RL
Tel (01745) 827239

Denbighshire & Flintshire LCGA
Hon Sec, Mrs K Harcombe, 6 Birch Drive, Gresford,
Wrexham LL12 8YZ
Tel (01978) 855933
E-mail kim.harcombe@btinternet.com

Glamorgan LCGA
Hon Sec, Mrs G J Phillips, 17 Martin Close, Heol
Gerrig, Merthyr Tydfil CF48 1TY
Tel (01685) 385245
E-mail gloheolg@aol.com

Mid Wales LCGA
Hon Sec, Mrs L Price, Coygen, Lower Chapel, Brecon,
Powys LD3 9RE
Tel (01874) 690 258
E-mail coygen@btclick.com

Monmouthshire LCGA
Hon Sec, Mrs EL Davidson, Jon-Len, Goldcliff,
Newport NP18 2AU
Tel (01633) 274477
E-mail lena_mlcga@hotmail.co.uk

Overseas Associations

Europe

European Golf Association
Gen Sec, Johnny Storjohann, Place de la Croix Blanche
19, Case Postale CH-1066 Epalinges, Switzerland
Tel +41 21 785 7060   Fax +41 21 785 7069
E-mail info@ega-golf.ch
Website www.ega-golf.ch

Austrian Golf Association
Gen Sec, Robert Fiegl, Marxergasse 25, AT-1030 Wien
Tel +43 1 505 3245   Fax +43 1 505 4962
E-mail oegv@golf.at   Website www.golf.at

Royal Belgian Golf Federation
Sec Gen, Christian Moyson, Chaussée de la Hulpe 110,
BE-1000 Brussels
Tel +32 2 672 2389   Fax +32 2 675 4619
E-mail info@golfbelgium.be
Website www.golfbelgium.be

Bulgarian Golf Association
Gen Sec, Seth Underwood, 19 Oborishte Street,
BG-1504 Sofia
Tel +359 2943 0610   Fax +359 2946 3740
E-mail seth@techno-link.com
Website www.golfbg.com

Croatian Golf Federation
Gen Sec, Dragutin Kasapović, Trg Krešimira Ćosića 11,
HR-10 000 Zagreb
Tel /Fax +385 1 309 2111
e-mail hgs@golf.hr   Website www.golf.hr

Cyprus Golf Federation
Gen Sec, Nick Rossides, Olympic House, Amfipoleos
21, Office B208, CY-2025 Nicosia
Tel +357 2244 9874   Fax +357 2244 9876
E-mail cgf@cgf.org.cy   Website www.cgf.org.cy

Czech Golf Federation
Gen Sec, Miroslav Holub, Erpet Golf Centre,
Strakonickà 2860, CZ-150 00 Prague 5-Smichov
Tel +420 2 5731 7865   Fax +420 2 5731 8618
E-mail cgf@cgf.cz   Website www.cgf.cz

Danish Golf Union
Gen Sec, Karsten Thuen, Idrættens Hus, Brøndby
Stadion 20, DK-2605 Brøndby
Tel +45 43 262 700   Fax +45 43 262 701
E-mail info@dgu.org   Website www.dgu.org

Estonian Golf Association
Sec Gen, Mrs Christine Marcus, Liivalaia 9, EE-10118
Tallinn
Fax +372 6 314 343
E-mail christine@golf.ee   Website www.golf.ee

Finnish Golf Union
Gen Sec, Risto Korpela, Radiokatu 20, FI-00093 SLU
Tel +358 9 3481 2520   Fax +358 9 147 145
E-mail office@golf.fi   Website www.golf.fi

French Golf Federation
Ch Exec, Christophe Muniesa, 68 rue Anatole France,
FR-92309 Levallois-Perret Cedex
Tel +33 1 41 497 700   Fax +33 1 41 497 701
E-mail ffg@ffgolf.org   Website www.ffgolf.org

German Golf Association
Pres, Dr Wolfgang Scheuer, Postfach 2106, DE-65011
Wiesbaden
Tel +49 611 990 2000   Fax +49 611 990 2040
E-mail info@dgv.golf.de   Website www.golf.de

Hellenic Golf Federation
Gen Sec, Michael Sideris, PO Box 70003, GR-166 10
Glyfada, Athens
Tel +30 210 894 1933   Fax +30 210 894 5162
E-mail info@hgf.gr   Website www.hgf.gr

Hungarian Golf Federation
Gen Sec, Mrs Tunde Fucskó, Istvanmezei út 1-3,
HU-1146 Budapest
Tel +36 1 460 6859   Fax +36 1 460 6860
E-mail hungolf@hungolf.hu
Website: www.hungolf.hu

Golf Union of Iceland
Gen Sec, Hordur Thorsteinsson, Sport Center,
Laugardal, IS-104 Reykjavik
Tel +354 514 4050   Fax +354 514 4051
E-mail gsi@golf.is   Website www.golf.is

Italian Golf Federation
Sec Gen, Stefano Manca, Viale Tiziano 74, IT-00196
Roma
Tel +39 06 323 1825   Fax +39 06 322 0250
E-mail fig@federgolf.it
Website www.federgolf.it

Kazakhstan Golf Federation
Gen Sec, Konstantin Lifanov, c/o Nurtau GC, Alatau
Sanatorium, Kamenka Village, KY-040918 Almat obl,
Kazakhstan
Tel +7 727 295 8823   Fax +7 727 295 8830
E-mail golfpro1@yandex.ru
Website www.nurtau.kz

Latvia Golf Federation
Gen Sec, Mrs Ineta Krodere-Imsa, Milgravja Iela 16,
LV-1034 Riga
Tel +371 739 4399   Fax +371 739 4034
E-mail info@golfaskola.lv
Website www.lgf.lv

Lithuanian Golf Federation
V-Pres, Darius Krasaitis, Veiveriu str 142b, LT-46353
Kaunas
Tel +370 686 00090
E-mail info@golfofederacija.lt

Luxembourg Golf Federation
Sec, Roger Weber, Domaine de Belenhaff, LU-6141
Junglinster
Tel +352 26 78 2383   Fax +352 26 78 2393
E-mail flgsecretariat@flgolf.lu
Website www.flgolf.lu

Malta Golf Association
Sec, Ian Restall, Aldo Moro St, MT-Marsa LQA 09,
Malta
Tel +356 2122 3704   Fax +356 2122 7020
E-mail association@maltagolf.org
Website www.maltagolf.org

Netherlands Golf Federation
Gen Sec, Henk L Heyster, PO Box 8585, NL-3503 RN
Utrecht
Tel +31 30 242 6370   Fax +31 30 242 6380
E-mail golf@ngf.nl   Website www.ngf.nl

Norwegian Golf Federation
Gen Sec, Geir Ove Berg, NO-0840 Oslo
Tel +47 21 029 150   Fax +47 21 029 151
E-mail post@golfforbundet.no
Website www.golfforbundet.no

Polish Golf Union
Sec, J A Gazecki, Lim Centre, Al.Jerozolimskie 65/79,
PL-00-697 Warszawa
Tel +48 22 630 5560   Fax +48 22 630 5561
E-mail pzg@pzgolf.pl
Website www.pzgolf.pl

Portuguese Golf Federation
Gen Sec, Pedro Vicente, Av das Túlipas Edifico
Miraflores17°, Miraflores, PT-1495-161 Algés
Tel +351 214 123 780   Fax +351 214 107 972
E-mail fpg@fpg.pt   Website www.fpg.pt

Romanian Golf Federation
Gen Sec, Ovidiu Brebene, 44 Carierei Str., Breaza,
RO-105400 Prahova
Tel +40 244 343 850   Fax +40 244 343 525
E-mail general.secretary@romaniangolffederation.com
Website www.romaniangolffederation.com

Russian Golf Association
Gen Sec, Denis Zherebko, 12 Khamovnitchesky Val,
RU-119871 Moskow
Tel +7 095 242 7464   Fax +7 095 242 7467
E-mail info@rusgolf.ru   Website www.rusgolf.ru

San Marino Golf Federation
Sec Gen, Dr E Casali, Via Rancagalia 30, SM-47899
Serravalle, San Marino
Tel +378 (0549) 885 600   Fax +378 (0549) 885 651
E-mail dzanotti@omniway.sm

Serbia Golf Association
Pres, Aleksander Andjelkovic, Ada Ciganlija 5,
YU-11000 Belgrade
Tel/Fax +381 11 305 6837
E-mail office@golfclub.co.yu
Website www.golfclub.co.yu

Slovak Golf Association
Gen Sec, Vladimir Balogh, Kukucínova 26, SK-831 02
Bratislava, Slovak Republic
Tel/Fax +421 2 4445 0727
E-mail skga@skga.sk   Website www.skga.sk

Slovenian Golf Association
Sec, Gorazd Kogoj, Dunajska 22, SI-1511 Ljubljana
Tel +386 1 430 3200   Fax +386 1 430 3201
E-mail golfzveza@golfzveza-slovenije.si
Website www.golfzveza-slovenije.si

Royal Spanish Golf Federation
Sec, Luiz Alvarez de Bohorques, c/o Provisional
Arroyo del Fresno Dos, 5, ES-280 35 Madrid
Tel +34 91 555 2682   Fax +34 91 556 3290
E-mail rfeg@golfspain.com
Website www.golfspainfederacion.com

Swedish Golf Federation
Gen Sec, Gunnar Hakansson, PO Box 84,
Kevingestrand, SE-182 11 Danderyd
Tel +46 8 622 1500   Fax +46 8 755 8439
E-mail info@sgf.golf.se   Website www.sgf.golf.se

Swiss Golf Association
Sec, John C Storjohann, Place de la Croix Blanche 19,
CH-1066 Epalinges
Tel +41 21 785 7000   Fax +41 21 785 7009
E-mail info@asg.ch   Website www.asg.ch

Turkish Golf Federation
Gen Sec, Ismet Aktekin, GSGM Ulus Is Hani A Blok 2,
Kat 205 Ulus 06050, TR-Ankara
Tel +90 312 309 3945   Fax +90 312 309 1840
E-mail info@tgf.org.tr   Website www.tgf.org.tr

Professional Associations

Austria PGA
Off, Monika Gross, 12/1, AT-8010 Graz
Tel +43 316 890 503   Fax +43 316 890 50315
E-mail office@apga.info   Website www.apga.info

Belgian PGA
Off, Bernard de Bruyckere, Jozef Mertenstraat 46,
BE-1702 Groot-Bijgaarden
Tel +32 2463 1963
E-mail info@pga.be   Website www.pga.be

Bulgarian PGA
Off, Pascal Simard, Oboriste Street 19. BG-1504 Sofia
Tel /Fax +359 2 943 0610
E-mail info@pga-bulgaria.com
Website www.pga-bulgaria.com

Croatia PGA
Off, Nikola Smoljenovic, Fancevljec Prilaz 16,
HR-10010 Zagreb
Tel +385 1 667 3308   Fax +385 1 660 6798
E-mail pga@pga.hr   Website www.pga.hr

Czech Republic PGA
Off, Petr Nitra, Villa Golfista, Amerika 782/1C,
CZ-353 01 Marianske Lazne
Tel +420 354 623071   Fax +420 354 621357
E-mail pga@pga.cz   Website www.pga.cz

Denmark PGA
Off, Joan Ejlertsen, Graensevej 1b, DK-9000, Aalborg
Tel +45 98 662 235   Fax +45 98 662 236
E-mail info@pga.dk   Website www.pga.dk

Finland PGA
Off, Teemu Laakso, Radiokatu 20, FI-00093 SLU
Tel +358 9 3481 2377   Fax +358 9 3481 2378
E-mail pgafinland@pga.fi   Website www.pga.fi

French PGA
Off, Yves Bechu, National Golf Club, 2 Avenue du
Golf, FR-78 280 Guyancourt
Tel +33 1 34 52 0846   Fax +33 1 34 52 0548
E-mail contact@pgafrance.net
Website www.pgafrance.net

PGA of Germany
Off, Felix Lechner, Arnulfstrasse 295, DE-80639
München
Tel +49 8917 95880   Fax +49 8917 958829
E-mail info@pga.de   Website www.pga.de

Greece PGA
Off, Vassilis Anastassiou, 9 Harilaou Trikoupi str,
GR-166 75 Glyfada Athens
Tel +30 22410 52798   *E-mail* info@greekpga.com
Website www.greekpga.com

Hungary PGA
Off, Áron Makszin, Diosd, Pacsirta u.3, Hungary
Tel +36 23 545 440   *Fax* +36 70 454 5663
E-mail makszin@yahoo.com
Website www.pgah.hu

Iceland PGA
Off, Arnar Már Ólafsson, Engjavegur 6, IS-104
Reykjavik
Tel +354 514 4050   *Fax* +354 514 4051
E-mail arnarmar@golf.is

Italy PGA
Off, Laura Rendina, Via Marangoni 3, IT-20124 Milano
Tel +39 02 670 5670   *Fax* +39 02 669 3600
E-mail pgaitaly@tin.it   *Website* www.pga.it

Luxembourg PGA
Off, Leslie Cain, GC Grand Ducal, 1 Route de Tréves,
LU-2633 Senningerberg
Tel/Fax +352 348394
E-mail info@pga.lu   *Website* www.pga.lu

Malta PGA
Off, William Beck, The Royal Malta GC, Aldo Moro
St, HMR-15 Marsa
Tel/Fax +356 239 320
E-mail association@maltagolf.org
Website www.maltagolf.org

Netherlands PGA
Off, Frank Kirsten, Huis Ter Heideweg 56, NL-3705
LZ Zeist
Tel +31 30 228 7018   *Fax* +31 30 225 0261
E-mail info@pgaholland.nl
Website www.pgaholland.nl

Norway PGA
Off, Peter Söder, PO Box 226, NO-2402 Elverum
Tel +47 993 44000
E-mail peter.sodor@pganorway.no
Website www.pganorway.no

Poland PGA
Off, Marek Podstolski, ul.Kwiatowa, PL-81638
Gdynia
Tel +48 58 624 7813   *Fax* +48 58 624 4309
E-mail m.podstolski@ndh.net
Website www.golf24.pl

Portugal PGA
Off, David Moura, Av Das Túlipas 6-Edif., Miraflores
17°, Miraflores, PT-1495-161 Algés
Tel +351 214 123 780
Fax +351 214 107 972
E-mail pgaportugal@gmail.com
Website www.pgaportugal.net

Russia PGA
Off, Denis Zherebko, Khamovnichesky val.12,
RU-119270 Moscow
Tel/Fax +7 095 977 7872
E-mail pga@russgolf.ru
Website www.rusga.ru

Slovakia PGA
Off, Martin Forro, Orenburska Str.66, SK-821 06
Bratislava
Tel +42 1903 256 316
E-mail forro@pga.sk   *Website* www.pga.sk

Slovenia PGA
Off, Metka Jamar, Dunajska, Cesta 22, SL-1000
Ljubljana
Tel +386 4 148 7280
E-mail info@pgaslo.si   *Website* www.pgaslo.si

Spain PGA
Off, Javier Roura, c/ Capitán Haya 22-5C, ES-28020
Madrid
Tel +34 91 555 1393   *Fax* +34 91 597 0170
E-mail apge@wanadoo.es
Website www.pgaspain.com

Swedish PGA
Off, A Strivall, Tylösand, SE-302 73 Halmstad
Tel +46 35 320 30   *Fax* +46 35 320 25
E-mail pga@pgasweden.com
Website www.pgasweden.com

Swiss PGA
Off, André Glauser, PO Box 107, CH-3177 Laupen
Tel +41 31 748 0312   *Fax* +41 31 748 0313
E-mail info@swisspga.ch
Website www.swisspga.ch

Turkey PGA
Off, Andrew McNabola, Doktorlar Sitesi A7 Blok
Daire 6, Nato Yolu, Bosna Bulvari, Cengelkoy,
Istanbul
Tel +90 533 773 3019   *E-mail* amc@igk.org.tr

North America: Canada and USA

Royal Canadian Golf Association
Exec Dir, Scott Simmons, Golf House, Suite 1 1333
Dorval Drive, Oakville, Ontario L6M 4X7
Tel 001 905 849 9700   *Fax* 001 905 845 7040
E-mail golfhouse@rcga.org
Website www.rcga.org

Canadian Ladies' Golf Association
See Royal Canadian Golf Association

National Golf Foundation
Ch Exec, Joseph Beditz, 1150 South US Highway One,
Jupiter, Florida 33477
Tel +1 561 744 6006
Website www.ngf.org

United States Golf Association
Pres, Walter W Driver jr, Golf House, PO Box 708,
Far Hills, NJ 07931-0708
Tel +1 908 234 2300   *Fax* +1 908 234 9687
E-mail usga@usga.org   *Website* www.usga.org

Professional Associations

Canadian PGA
Ch Exec, David J Colling, 13450 Dublin Line RR#1,
Acton, Ontario L7J 2W7
Tel +1 519 853 5450   *Fax* +1 519 853 5449
E-mail cpga@canadianpga.org
Website www.cpga.com

Canadian Tour
Comm, Ian Mansfield, 212 King Street West, Suite 203,
Toronto, Ontario M58 1K5
Tel +1 416 204 1564   Fax +1 416 204 1368
Website cantour.com

Ladies' Professional Golf Association
Comm, Carolyn Vesper Bivens, 100 International Golf
Drive, Daytona Beach, Florida 32124-1092
Tel +1 386 274 6200   Fax +1 386 274 1099
Website www.lpga.com

PGA of America
Ch Exec, Joe Steranka, 100 Avenue of the Champions,
Palm Beach Gardens, Florida 33418
Tel +1 561 624 8400   Fax +1 561 624 8448
Website www.pgaonline.com

PGA Tour
Comm, Tim Finchem, PGA Tour, 112 PGA Tour
Boulevard, Ponte Vedra Beach, Florida 32082
Tel +1 904 285 3700   Fax +1 904 285 7913
Website www.pgatour.com

The Caribbean and Central America

Caribbean Golf Association
Sec, David G Bird, PO Box 31329, Grand Cayman,
KY1-1206, Cayman Islands
Tel +345 947 1903   Fax +345 947 3439
E-mail bird@candw.ky
Website www.cgagolfnet.com

Bahamas Golf Federation
Sec, Dudley Martinborough, PO Box SS-19092,
Nassau, Grand Bahama
Tel +242 326 7415   Fax +242 326 7420
E-mail admin@bgfnet.com
Website www.bgfnet.com

Barbados Golf Association
Pres, Birchmore Griffith, PO Box 585, Bridgetown,
Barbados
Tel +246 430 0808   Fax +246 437 7792
E-mail carib@caribsurf.com
Website www.barbadosgolfassociation.com

Bermuda Golf Association
Sec, Richard Bartlett, PO Box HM 433, Hamilton
HM BX, Bermuda
Tel +1 441 295 9972   Fax +1 441 295 0304
Website www.bermudagolf.org

Cayman Islands Golf Association
Sec, David G Bird, PO Box 31329 SMB, Grand
Cayman, KY1-1206
Tel +345 947 1903   Fax +345 947 3439
E-mail bird@candw.ky
Website www.caymanislandsgolfassociation.com

Costa Rica Golf Federation
Sec, F T Deunas, PO Box 10969, San José 1000,
Costa Rica
Tel +506 296 5772   Fax +506 231 1914
E-mail info@anagolf.com
Website www.anagolf.com

Fedogolf (Dominican Republic)
Exec Dir, Carlos Lizarazo, Calle Macao No.7,
Urbanizacion Tennis Club, Arroyo Hondo, Santo
Domingo, Dominican Republic
Tel +809 338 1004   Fax +809 338 1008
E-mail administracion@fedogolf.org.do
Website www.golfdominicano.com

El Salvador Golf Federation
Pres, Jose Maria Duran Pacheco, VIP SAL 1256, PO
Box 2-5364, Miami FL 33102-5364
Tel +1 305 264 1583   Fax +1 305 298 3354
E-mail figueroa@telesal.net

National Golf Association of Guatemala
Pres, Gustavo Evertsz H., 23 Avenida 31-01 zona 5,
Edificio Espectrum oficina 210, Guatemala
Tel +502 2336 5079
E-mail asogolf@asogolfguatemala.org
Website www.asogolfguatemala.org

Hondureña Golf Association
Pres, Henry Kattan, Residential Piñares, Km 6.5
Paseo al Hatillo, PO Box 3555, Tegucigalpa, Honduras
Tel +504 211 9260   Fax +504 9992 3489
E-mail Hondurasgolf@gmail.com
Website www.hondurasgolf.org

Jamaica Golf Association
Hon Sec, William Brown, PO Box 743, Kingston 8
Tel +876 906 7636   Fax +876 906 7635
E-mail jamgolf@cwjamaica.com
Website www.jamaicagolfassociation.com

Mexican Golf Federation
Exec Dir, Fernando Erana, Av.Insurgentes Sur 1605
10° Piso Torre Mural, Col. San Jose Insurgentes,
C.P. 03900 México, D.F.
Tel +525 1084 2176   Fax +525 1084 2179
E-mail direccionfmg@mexgolf.org
Website www.mexgolf.org

Nicaraguan Golf Federation
Exec Sec, J A Narvaez, Nejapa GCC, Managua
Tel +505 822 5522
E-mail procalsa1@hotmail.com

OECS Golf Association
Sec, Ivan Browne, c/o PO Box 895, Basseterre,
St Kitts
Tel +869 465 3214   E-mail oecsgolf@gmail.com

Panama Golf Association
Exec Dir, Luiz Heley Bárcenas, PO Box 8613, Panama 5
Tel +507 266 7436   Fax +507 220 3994
E-mail apagolf@yahoo.es

Puerto Rico Golf Association
Pres, Sidney Wolf, 264 Matadero – Suite 11, San Juan,
Puerto Rico 00920
Tel +787 793 3444   Fax +787 723 3138
E-mail golfpuertorico@prga.org
Website www.prga.org

Trinidad & Tobago Golf Association
Pres, Asraph Ali, c/o St Andrews GC, PO Box 3403,
Moka, Maraval, Trinidad
Tel +868 629 7127   Fax +868 629 0411
E-mail ttga@tstt.net.tt
Website www.trinidadandtobagogolfassociation.com

Turks & Caicos Golf Association
Pres, Thomas Waite, PO Box 319, Providenciales,
Turks & Caicos Islands
Tel +649 946 4417   Fax +649 946 4437
E-mail thomasw@tciway.tc

Virgin Islands Golf Federation
Pres, Greg Manigault, PO Box 5187, Kingshill, St Croix,
US Virgin Islands 00851
Tel +340 779 2315   Fax +340 714 5393
E-mail gregmanigault@hotmail.com

Professional Association

Jamaica PGA
Chairman, O Marshall, 9 Park Ave., Kingston 5
Tel +876 881 4444   E-mail chairman@pgaj.com

Mexico PGA
Off, D Ross, Nadadores 30, Col.Country Club, Mexico
DF, CP 04210
Tel +52 55 5544 6644   Fax +52 55 5689 4254
E-mail info@pgamexico.org
Website www.pgamexico.org

South America

South American Golf Federation
Exec Sec, Rafael Enrique Otero D., Carrera 12
No 79-43 Of 704, Bogotá, Colombia
Tel +57 1 313 0624   Fax +57 1 313 0391
E-mail fedesud@cable.net.co
Website www.fedsudgolf.com

Argentine Golf Association
Exec Dir, Mark Lawrie, Av Corrientes 538-Pisos 11y12,
1043 CF, Buenos Aires
Tel +54 11 4325 1113   Fax +54 11 4325 8660
E-mail golf@aag.com.ar
Website www.aag.com.ar

Bolivian Golf Federation
Sec, Jaime Gonzalez, Ave. Mariscal Santa Cruz, Edif.
Camara de Comercio Of 604, Casilla Postal 10217,
La Paz
Tel/Fax +591 2 315853
E-mail fbgolf@ceibo.entelnet.bo
Website www.boliviagolf.com

Brasilian Golf Confederation
Exec Sec, M A Aguiar Giusti, Rua Paez de Araújo
29 conj 42, cep 04531 090 São Paulo-SP
Tel/Fax +55 11 3168 4366
E-mail golfe@cbg.com.br
Website www.cbg.com.br

Chilean Golf Federation
Sec Gen, Andrés Délano, Málaga 655, Las Condes,
Santiago
Tel +56 2 208 7080   Fax +56 2 208 6566
E-mail secretaria@chilegolf.cl
Website www.chilegolf.cl

Colombian Golf Federation
Sec, Jaime Rodríguez Posada, Carrera 7#72-64 Int 26,
Bogotá DC
Tel +57 1 310 7664   Fax +57 1 235 5091
E-mail fedegolf@federacioncolombianadegolf.com
Website www.federacioncolombianadegolf.com

Ecuador Golf Federation
Sec, Carlos Javier Vallarino, Av Amazonas N.28-17 y
Alemania, Edif.Skorpios Piso 8 of.812, Quito
Tel +593 2 2922 128
Fax +593 2 2442 986
E-mail fedecuat@feg.org.ec
Website www.feg.org.ec

Guyana Golf Union
Sec, c/o Demerara Bauxite Co Ltd, Mackenzie, Guyana

Paraguay Golf Association
Sec, Roberto Berino, Manduriva 709, Casilla de
Correo No 76, Asunción
Tel +595 21 494 8011   Fax +595 21 447 923
E-mail secretaria@apg.org.py
Website www.apg.com.py

Peru Golf Federation
Exec Dir, Eduardo Ibarra, Calle Conde de la Monclova
315 Of 308, San Isidro, Lima 27
Tel +51 1 441 1500
Fax +51 1 441 1992
E-mail fepegolf@terra.com,pe
Website www.fpg.org.pe

Uruguay Golf Association
Sec, Nelson Silva, Bulevar Artigas 379, Montevideo
Tel +598 2 7101 721   Fax +598 2 7115285
E-mail augolf@adinet.com.uy
Website www.aug.com.uy

Venezuela Golf Federation
Exec Dir, Julio L Torres, Av. Juan B Arismendi Unidad
Comercial La Florida, Nivel Mezzanina, local 8, La
Florida, Caracas 1050
Tel +582 12 731 7662
Fax +582 12 730 1660
E-mail fvg@fvg.org   Website www.fvg.or

Professional Association

Brazil PGA
Off, Claci Schneider, Rua Francisco de Paula Brito,
317-Planalto Paulista, cep 04071 050 São Paulo-SP
Tel +55 11 2276 0745
Fax +55 11 2276 0789
E-mail pgabrasil@aol.com.br
Website www.pgadobrasil.com.br/

Africa

African Golf Confederation
Pres, Gert Cloete, PO Box 2122, Windhoek, Namibia
Fax +264 64 403 165

Algerian Golf Federation
Sec, Ben Miloude Noureddine, rue Ahmed Ouaked,
Dely Ibrahim
Tel +213 213 75 362   Fax +213 213 75 790

Arab Golf Federation
Sec Gen, Dr Mohamed El Attar, 39 Abdel Moneim
Hafez St, Heliopolis, Cairo, Egypt
Tel +202 291 9101   Fax +202 291 9102
E-mail mohamedattar@eescoegypt.com
Website www.arabgolf.org

Botswana Golf Union
Exec Sec, Joseph Marudu, PO Box 1033, Gaborone
Tel +267 316 1116   Fax +267 391 2262
E-mail bgu@it.bw

Botswana Ladies Golf Union
Hon Sec, Mrs S Roberts, PO Box 1362, Gaborone

D R of Congo Golf Federation
Pres, Alain Nitu, c/o Rainbow Connections, Carrefour
des Jeunes, 5151 Avenue Kasa-Vuba, Q/Matonge,
Commune Kalamu, Kinshasa
E-mail alainnitu@hotmail.com

Egyptian Golf Federation
Sec Gen, Dr Mohamed El Attar, 39 Abdel Moneim
Hafez St, Heliopolis, Cairo
Tel +202 758 8433   Fax +202 757 5233
E-mail kat@katameyaheights.com
Website www.egf-eg.com

Gabon Golf Federation
Sec, BP 15159 Libreville
Tel +241 760 378   Fax +241 729 079
E-mail golfclublibreville@inet.ga

Ghana Golf Association
Sec, J Wartemberg, PO Box 8, Achimota
Tel/Fax +233 21 400221
E-mail ghanagolf@yahoo.co.uk
Website www.achimotagolf.com

Ghana Ladies Golf Union
Hon Sec, Mrs M Amu, PO Box 70, Accra

Ivory Coast (Côte d'Ivoire) Golf Federation
Sec, Bendey-Diby Valentin, O8 BP 01, Abidjan 08
Tel +225 2243 1076   Fax +225 2243 3772
E-mail f.golfci@aviso.ci   Website www.fgolfci.com

Kenya Golf Union
Hon Sec, Parshu Harini, PO Box 49609, 00100 Nairobi
Tel +254 2 76 3898   Fax +254 2 76 5118
E-mail kgu@iconnect.co.ke
Website www.kgu.org.ke

Kenya Ladies' Golf Union
Hon Sec, Mrs E Ilako, PO Box 7785, 00100 Nairobi
Tel +254 2 733 794

KwaZulu-Natal Golf Union
Sec, RT Runge, PO Box 1939, Durban 4000
Tel +27 (0)31 202 7636   Fax +27 (0)31 202 1022
E-mail kzngu@kzngolf.co.za

Libyan Golf Federation
Gen Sec, Mustafa Ewkaiat, PO Box 3674, Tripoli
Tel +218 21 478 0510
E-mail golf_libya@hotmail.com

Malawi Golf Union
Hon Sec, James Hinde, PO Box 1198, Blantyre 8
Tel +265 1 824 108   Fax +265 1 824 027
E-mail medlife@malawi.net

Malawi Ladies' Golf Union
Treas, Mrs A Matthews, PO Box 30328, Lilongwe 3

Mauritius Golf Federation
Pres, Raj Ramlackhan, 42 Sir William Newton Street,
Port Louis
Tel +230 208 4224   Fax +230 483 5163
E-mail mgolffed@intnet.mu

The Royal Moroccan Golf Federation
Sec Gen, Abdelal Latif Benali, Route des Zaers, Rabat,
Dar El Salam
Tel +212 3775 5636   Fax +212 3775 1026
E-mail abdellatif.benali@manara.ma

Namibia Golf Federation
Treas, Hugh Mortimer, PO Box 2122, Windhoek,
Namibia
Tel +264 61 205 5223   Fax +264 61 205 5220
E-mail gm@wccgolf.com.na
Website www.wccgolf.com.na

Nigeria Golf Federation
Sec, Patrick Uwagbale, National Stadium Surulere,
PO Box 145, Lagos
Tel +234 1 545 6209   Fax +234 1 545 0530
E-mail nigeriagolffederation@yahoo.com

Nigerian Ladies Golf Union
Sec, Mrs OR Ogunleye, c/o Ikoyi GC, PO Box 239,
Ikoyi, Lagos

Sierra Leone Golf Federation
Pres, Freetown GC, PO Box 237, Lumley Beach,
Freetown
E-mail fadi@sierratel.sl

South African Golf Association
Exec Dir, BA Younge, PO Box 65303, Benmore 2010
RSA
Tel +27 11 783 5474   Fax +27 11 783 5699
E-mail admin@saga.co.za
Website www.saga.co.za

Women's Golf South Africa
Hon Sec, Mrs V Horak, PO Box 209, Randfontein
1760, RSA
Tel/Fax +27 11 416 1263
E-mail salgu@global.co.za   Website www.salgu.co.za

Swaziland Golf Union
Sec, AP Dunn, PO Box 1739, Mbabane, H100
Swaziland
Tel +268 404 4735   Fax +268 404 5401
E-mail adunn2@fnb.co.za

Tanzania Golf Union
Hon Sec, Perfect A Lyimo, PO Box 15606, Arusha
Tel +255 22 250 4347
E-mail info@tgu.com   Website www.tgu.com

Tanzania Ladies Golf Union
Hon Sec, Mrs T Anthony, Gymkana Club, PO Box 286,
Dar es Salaam
E-mail magapye@netscape.net

Tunisian Golf Federation
Sec Gen, Mohamed Moncef Gaida, Maison de Fédéra-
cions Sportives, 1004 Cité Olympique, Tunis
Tel +216 71 237 087   Fax +216 71 237 299
E-mail ftg@ftg.org.tn
Website www.ftg.org.tn

Uganda Golf Union
Hon Sec, Gadi A Musasizi, Kitante Road, PO Box 2574,
Kampala
Tel +256 712 877 036   Fax +256 41 304 832
E-mail gmusasizi@yahoo.com

Uganda Ladies Golf Union
Hon Sec, Mrs R Tumusiime, PO Box 624, Kampala
E-mail ugagolf@africaonline.co.ug

Zaire Golf Federation
Pres, Tshilombo Mwin Tshitol, BP 1648, Lubumbashi

Zambia Golf Union
Hon Sec, A C Mwangata, 37A Twaliilubula Ave,
Parklands, PO Box 21602, Kitwe
Tel +260 96 780 095   Fax +260 2 226 884
E-mail anthony@coppernet.zm

Zambia Ladies Golf Union
Hon Sec, Mrs H Kapya, PO Box 22151, Kitwe

Zimbabwe Golf Association
Sec, John Nixon, PO Box 3327, Harare
Tel +263 4 746 141 Fax +263 4 746 228

Zimbabwe Ladies Golf Union
Hon Sec, Mrs JM Hall, PO Box HG 182, Highlands,
Harare

Professional Associations

South African PGA
Sec, Anne Du Toit, PO Box 949 Bedfordview 2008, RSA
Tel +27 11 485 1370   Fax +27 11 640 4372
E-mail admin@pgasa.com   Website www.pgasa.com

South African Women's PGA
Sec, Mrs V Harrington, PO Box 781547, Sandton 2146
Tel/Fax +27 11 477 8606

South Africa Sunshine Tour
Exec Dir, Louis Martin, 15 Postnet Suite #185,
Private Bag X15, Somerset West 7129
Tel +27 21 850 6500   Fax +27 21 852 8271

Middle East

Bahrain Golf Committee
Sec Gen, Daij Khalifa, PO Box 38938, Riffa,
Kingdom of Bahrain
Tel +973 1777 7179   Fax +973 1776 948
E-mail bgassoc@batelco.com.bh

Islamic Republic of Iran Golf Federation
Pres, E Eshaghi, Enghelab Club,Val-e-Asr Ave, PO Box
15815, 1881-Tehran
Tel/Fax +98 21 883 6040
E-mail info@golfir.com

Israel Golf Federation
Sec,Mrs Irit Peleg, PO Box 4858, Caesarea 38900
Tel +972 4 610 9600   Fax +972 4 636 1173
E-mail info@israelgolffed.org
Website www.israelgolffed.org

Jordan Golf Federation
Sec, Mr Jamal Bazzari, PO Box 850 888, Amman 11183
Tel +962 6593 4158   Fax +962 6593 4159
E-mail jamal@tedata.met.jo

Kuwait Golf Federation
Pres, Saud Al Hajeri, PO Box 1192, Fintas Z-code
51013
Tel +965 390 5287

Lebanese Golf Federation
Pres, Dr Faisal Alamuddin, c/o GC of Lebanon,
PO Box 11-3099, Beirut
Tel +961 1 822 470   Fax +961 1 822 474
E-mail info@golfclub.org.lb

Qatar Golf Association
Pres, Hassan Nasser Al Noaimi, PO Box 13530, Doha
Tel +974 483 7809   Fax +974 483 2610
E-mail info@qgagolf.com
Website www.qatargolfassociation.com

Saudi Golf Committee
Pres, Khaled Abunayyan, PO Box 325422, Riyadh
11371, Saudi Arabia
Tel +966 1 4090 009
Fax +966 1 4090 002
E-mail info@ksagolf.com
Website www.ksagolf.com

United Arab Emirates Golf Association
Gen Man, A Flaherty, PO Box 31410, Dubai, UAE
Tel +971 4 380 1777
Fax +971 4 380 1818
E-mail uaegolf@emirates.net.ae
Website www.ugagolf.com

Professional Associations

Israel PGA
Sec, R Cordoba-Core, Sokolov 10, Block B Floor 2,
Apartment 6, Hertzlya
Tel +972 4 6636 1172   Fax +972 4 6636 1173

United Arab Emirates PGA
Off, J Danby, Nad Al Sheba Golf, PO Box 52872,
Dubai
Tel +971 4 336 3666   Fax +971 4 336 1624
E-mail jdanby@dubaigolf.com

Asia

Asia-Pacific Golf Confederation
Hon Sec, Colin Phillips, Golf Australia, Level 3, 95
Coventry St, South Melbourne, Victoria-3205
Tel +613 9626 5050   Fax +613 9626 5095
E-mail apgc@agu.org.au

Bangladesh Golf Federation
Pres, General Moeen U Ahmed ndc, psc, c/o
Kurmitola GC, Dhaka Cantonment, Dhaka-1206
Tel +880 2 8752 000   Fax +880 2 8752 521
E-mail kgcdhaka@hotmail.com

Bhutan Golf Confederation
Sec Gen, D K Chhetri, PO Box 939, Thimphu, Bhutan
Tel 975 2 322 138   Fax 975 2 323 937
E-mail tsenchok@druknet.bt

Cambodian Golf Association
Sec, Pok Yuthea, No 202 Norodom Blvd, Senak
Building, Chamcar Morn, Phnom Penh

China Golf Association
Sec Gen, Zhang Xiao Ning, 5 Tiyuguan Rd, Beijing,
100763 China
Tel +86 10 6711 7897   Fax +86 10 6716 2993
E-mail chinagolf@263.net   Website www.golf.org.cn

Chinese Taipei Golf Association
Sec Gen, Bob Hsu, 12 F-1 125 Nanking East Rd,
Section 2, Taipei, Taiwan 104, Chinese Taipei
Tel +886 22 516 5611   Fax +886 22 516 3208
E-mail garoc.tw@msa.hinet.net
Website www.garoc.com.tw

National Golf Association of Fiji
Gen Sec, Mosese Waqavonovono, PO Box 5363,
Raiwaqa, Suva, Fiji
Tel/Fax +679 337 1191
E-mail ngaf@connect.com.fi

Guam National Golf Federation
Pres, Samuel Teker, Suite 2A 130 Aspinall Ave, Agana,
Guam 96910
Tel +1 671 653 3100   Fax +1 671 472 2601
E-mail st@tttguamlawyers.com

Hong Kong Golf Association Ltd
Ch Exec, F 1 Valentine, Rm 2003, Olympic House,
1 Stadium Path, So Kon Po, Causeway Bay,
Hong Kong
Tel +852 2504 8196   Fax +852 2845 1553
E-mail hkgolf@hkga.com   Website www.hkga.com

Indian Golf Union
Sec-Gen, W/Cdr Satish Aparajit (Retd), First Floor 24,
Adchina, New Delhi 110017
Tel +91 11 265 25772   Fax +91 11 265 25770
E-mail tigu@vsnl.net   Website www.tigu.in

Indonesian Golf Association
Sec Gen, Zaenel Soedjais, Gd Direksi Gelora Bung
Karno 2nd Floor, Jl.Pintu I, Senayan-Jakarta 10270
Tel +62 21 573 2811   Fax +62 21 573 1291
E-mail pgi@pgionline.org
Website www.pgionline.org

Japan Golf Association
Sec Gen, Ryo Shioda, Kyobashi YS Bldg 2nd Floor,
1-12-5 Kyobashi, Chuo-Ku, Tokyo 104-0031
Tel +81 3 3566 0003   Fax +81 3 3566 0101
E-mail info@jga.or.jp   Website www.jga.or.jp

Korean Golf Association
Exec Dir, Dong-Wook Kim, Rm 1318, Manhattan Bldg,
36-2 Yeo Eui Do-Dong, Yeong Deung Po-Ku, Seoul
150-749
Tel +82 2 783 4748   Fax +82 2 783 4747
E-mail kga@kgagolf.or.kr   Website www.kgagolf.or.kr

Lao National Golf Federation
Sec, Sangkhom Phomphakdy, PO Box 4300, 33 Wat
Xiengnhum St, Sethathirat Rd, Vientiane, Lao PDR
Tel/Fax +856 2121 7294
E-mail sangkhom52@hotmail.com

Golf Association of Macau
Sec, Michelle Leong, Rm 15, Estrada Vitoria S/N,
Centro Desportivo, Vitoria, Macau
Tel +853 831 555   Fax +853 832 555

Malaysian Golf Association
Hon Sec, Encik Zulkifli bin Dato 'Ismail, 14 Jalan 4/76C,
Desa Pandan, 55100 Kuala Lumpur
Tel +60 3 9283 7300
Fax +60 3 9282 9300
E-mail mga@mgaonline.com.my
Website www.mgaonline.com.my

Mongolian Golf Association
Sec Gen, Enkh-Amgalan.L., MCS Plaza, Seoul St – 4,
Ulaanbaatar – 210644, Mongolia
Tel +976 11 323 705   Fax +976 11 311 323
E-mail enkh_amgalan@mcs.mn

Golf Federation of the Union of Myanmar
Gen Sec, U Aung Hla Han, no.46 Pyay Rd, Building C 6
1 / 2 miles, Hlaing Township, Yangon
Tel +95 1 537 241   Fax +95 1 538 686
E-mail aunghhan@baganmail.net.mm

Nepal Golf Association
Sec, Prachanda Bdr Shrestha, GPO Box 1665 Naya,
Baneshwar, Kathmandu
Tel +977 1 449 4247   Fax +977 1 478 0141
E-mail pranec@mos.com.np

Pakistan Golf Federation
Pres, Lt Gen Ashfaq Kayani, Jhelum Road, PO Box
1295, Rawalpindi
Tel +92 51 556 8177   Fax +92 51 225 5440
E-mail pakgolffed@yahoo.com

National Golf Association of the Philippines
Exec Sec, S Facundo, 209 PSC Admin Bldg, Rizal
Memorial Sports Complex, Pablo Ocampo Sr. St,
Malate, Manila 1004
Tel +63 2 525 6987   Fax +63 2 521 1587
E-mail info@ngapgolf.com
Website www.ngapgolf.com

Singapore Golf Association
Hon Sec, Bob Tan, 249 Sembawang Rd, Singapore
758352
Tel +65 6 755 5976   Fax +65 6 755 1373
E-mail sga@pacific.net.sg
Website www.sga.org.sg

Sri Lanka Golf Union & Ladies Golf Union
Hon Sec, Lal Wikrematuuge, PO Box 309, 223 Model
Farm Rd, Colombo 8, Sri Lanka
Tel +94 11 266 7771
Fax +94 11 461 6056
E-mail golfsrilanka@rcgcsl.com

Thailand Golf Association
Sec Gen, Air Mrshl Bureerat Ratanavanich, PO Box
1190, Ramkamhaeng, Bangkok 10241
Tel +66 2 369 3777
Fax +66 2 369 3776
E-mail secretary@tga.or.th   Website www.tga.or.th

Vietnam Golf Association
Sec Gen, Dr Nguyen Ngoc Chu, Suite 114 National
Convention Centre, Me Tri, Tu Liem, Hanoi
Tel/Fax +844 7833 194
E-mail chunn@hn.vnn.vn

Professional Associations

Asian PGA
Sec, Ramlan Dato Harun, 415-417 Block A Kelana
Business Centre, 97 Jalan SS 7/2 Kelana Jaya,
Selangor, Malaysia
Tel +603 7492 0099   Fax +603 7492 0098
Website www.asianpgatour.com

Asia PGA Tour
Chief Exec, Justin Strachan, 15/F, One Harbourfront, 18 Tak Fung Street, Hunghom, Kowloon, Hong Kong
Tel +852 2330 8227   Fax +852 2801 5743
E-mail apgatour@asiaonline.net
Website www.asianpgatour.com

PGA Republic of China
2nd Floor 196 Cheng-Teh Road, Taipei, Taiwan
Tel +886 2 8220318   Fax +886 2 8229684
E-mail garoc.tw@msa.hinet.net
Website www.twgolf.org

Hong Kong PGA
Sec, Mr M Lai Wai Sing, Room 702 Landmark North, Sheung Shui, NT Hong Kong
Tel +852 523 3171

Indian PGA
Sec, P K Bhattacharyya, 109A, 1513 Guman Puri Complex (First Floor), Kotia, Mubarak Pur, New Delhi – 110 003
Tel +91 11 3250 5456   Fax +91 91 11 2461 6331
E-mail pgaofindia@gmail.com

Japan Ladies PGA
7-16-3 Ginza, Nitetsu Kobiki Bldg 8F, Chuo-ku, Tokyo 104-0061
Tel +81 3 3546 7801   Fax +81 3 3546 7805

Japan PGA
Int Com, Seien Kobayakawa, Top Hamamatsucho Bldg, 1-5-12 Shiba.Minato-Ku, 8FL, Tokyo 105-0014
Tel +81 3 5419 2614   Fax +81 3 5419 2622
E-mail bp@pga.or.jp

PGA of Malaysia
Sec, Brig-Gen Mahendran, 1B Jalan Mamanda 7, Ampang Point, 6800 Selangor Darul Ehsan, Malaysia

Australasia and the Pacific

Golf Australia
Ch Exec, Stephen Pitt, Level 3,95 Coventry St, South Melbourne, Victoria-3205
Tel +613 9626 5050   Fax +613 9626 5095
E-mail info@golfaustralia.org.au
Website www.golfaustralia.org.au

Womens Golf Australia
See Golf Australia

Cook Islands Golf Association
Sec, Mrs Tereapii Urlich, Rarotonga GC, PO Box 151, Rarotonga, Cook Islands
Tel +682 20621   Fax +682 20631
E-mail toots@oyster.net.ck

National Golf Association of Fiji
Pres, I Bainimara c/o Air Terminal Services (Fiji) Ltd, PO Box 18140, Suva, Fiji Islands
Tel +679 338 5089
Fax +679 992 2601
E-mail ibainimara@hotmail.com

New Zealand Golf Incorporated
Ch Exec, Bill MacGowan, PO Box 11-842, Wellington 6142, New Zealand
Tel +64 4 471 0990   Fax +64 4 471 0991
E-mail nzgolf@nzgolf.org.nz
Website www.nzgolf.org.nz

Womens' Golf New Zealand Inc
See New Zealand Golf Incorporated

Papua New Guinea Golf Association
Pres, S Walker, PO Box 4632, Boroko, NCD
Tel +675 323 1120   Fax +675 323 1300
E-mail swalker@brianbell.com.pg

Papua New Guinea Ladies Golf Association
Hon Sec, Mrs L Illidge, PO Box 348, Lae MP 411

Vanuatu Golf Association
Chairman, Bernie Cain, PO Box 358, Port Vila, Vanuatu, Pacific Ocean
Tel +678 22178   Fax +678 25037
E-mail vilare@vanuatu.com.vu

Professional Associations

Australian PGA
Ch Exec, Max Garske, PO Box 1314, Crows Nest, New South Wales
Tel +61 2 9439 8111   Fax +61 2 9439 7888
E-mail maxgpga@oze-mail.com.au
Website www.pga.org.au

Australian Ladies Professional Golf
Ch Exec, Warren Savil, PO Box 447, Mudgeeraba, Queensland 4213
Tel +61 7 5592 9343
Fax +61 7 5592 9344
E-mail warrens@alpg.com.au
Website www.alpg.com.au

PGA Tour Australasia
Exec Dir, Andrew Georgiou, Suite 302, 77 Berry St, North Sydney, NSW 2060
Tel +61 2 9956 0000
Fax +61 2 9956 0099
Website pgatour.com.au

New Zealand PGA
Exec Dir, PO Box 11-934, Wellington
Tel +64 4 4722 687   Fax +64 4 4722 925
E-mail postmaster@pga.org.nz
Website www.pga.org.nz

PART XVI

Clubs and Courses in the British Isles and Europe

Compiled by Paula Taylor

Club Centenaries

1909	1910	1911	1912
Arcot Hall	Abergele	Aberystwyth	Aberlady
Arkley	Bacup	Ardee	Aquarius
Bandon	Ballina	Beau Desert	Ashton-under-Lyne
Bexleyheath	Bishop's Stortford	Betchworth Park	Banbridge
Brampton (Talkin Tarn)	Blairbeth	Boyle	Bedford & County
Charleville	Carrick-on-Shannon	Breightmet	Boldon
Cowes	Castlebar	City of Derry	Branshaw
Craigie Hill	Dartmouth	Cliftonville	Camberley Heath
Denton	Delamere Forest	Clonmel	Childwall
Douglas	Denham	Consett and District	Clontarf
Filton	Dinsdale Spa	Coombe Hill	Cooden Beach
Glynhir	Dolgellau	Crewe	Dumfries & County
Greenway Hall	Duff House Royal	Croham Hurst	Essex Golf Centres,
Grim's Dyke	Dun Laoghaire	Davyhulme Park	Hainault Forest
Hickleton	Eaton	Gatley	Fishwick Hall
Hopeman	Edenderry	Hawarden	Heaton Park Golf Centre
Kidderminster	Elland	Heworth (N. Yorkshire)	Heworth (Tyne & Wear)
Laytown & Bettystown	Grange	Hillside	Holyhead
Lydney	Haggs Castle	Killin	Kinsale Ringenane
Merthyr Tydfil	Heysham	Kintore	Maesteg
Mold	Houldsworth	Luffenham Heath	Market Rasen & District
Moortown	Kirkhill	Renishaw Park	Muthill
Murcar Links	Knott End	Rothley Park	Northenden
Northamptonshire County	Langley Park	St Austell	Port Bannatyne
Parkstone	Longley Park	Silsden	Ravelston
Pike Fold	Malton & Norton	Sonning	Reddish Vale
Pitlochry	Milnathort	Warren	St George's Hill
Radcliffe-on-Trent	North Shore	Whickham	Saline
Ringway	Nottingham City	Whinhill	Southport Golf Links
Royal Town of Caernarfon	Old Fold Manor	Whitstable and Seasalter	Thetford
Runcorn	Omagh	Worksop	Waterford
Rushcliffe	Penmaenmawr		Werneth Low
Scarborough North Cliff	Reading		Whalley
Sheerness	Rhondda		Woodcote Park
Strathtay	Ryburn		
Swinley Forest	Sandy Lodge		
Tarbat	Tarbert		
Temple	West Hove		
Thurles	West Surrey		
Torquay	Western Park		
Troon St Meddans	Wetherby		
Walmer & Kingsdown			
West Hill			
Weymouth			
Withernsea			

Golf Clubs and Courses in the British Isles and Europe

How to use this section

Clubs in England, Ireland and Wales are listed in alphabetical order by country and county. Note that some clubs and courses are affiliated to a county different to that in which they are physically located. Clubs in Scotland are grouped under recognised administrative regions. The Great Britain and Ireland county index can be found on page 648.

European clubs are listed alphabetically by country and grouped under regional headings. The index for these can be found on page 845. In most European countries, only 18 hole courses are included.

All clubs and courses are listed in the the general index at the back of the book.

Contact details are shown for all clubs. Full course details are included where these have been made available.

Club details (see Key to Symbols below)
The date after the name of the club indicates the year it was founded. Courses are private unless otherwise stated. Many public courses play host to members' clubs. Information on these can be obtained from the course concerned.

The address is the postal address.

Telephone: club telephone number for general use.

Membership: total number of playing members. The number of lady members (L) and juniors (J) is sometimes shown separately.

Secretary/Professional: telephone numbers for secretaries and professionals are shown separately.

Holes: the length of the course refers in most cases to the yardage from the medal tees.

Visitors: indicates the playing opportunities and restrictions for unaccompanied visitors.

Fees: green fees, the most up-to-date supplied, are quoted for visitors playing without a member. The basic cost per round or per day (D) is shown first, with the weekend rate in brackets. The cost of a weekly (W) ticket is sometimes shown.

Location: general location of club/course.

Miscellaneous: other golf facilities.

Architect: course architect/designer.

Abbreviations

WD Weekdays.
WE Weekends.
BH Bank Holidays.
H Handicap certificate required.
M With a member, i.e. casual visitors are not allowed: only visitors playing with a member are permitted on the days stated.
NA No visitors allowed.
SOC Recognised Golfing Societies welcome if previous arrangements made with secretary.
U Unrestricted.
CR Course Rating (Europe)
SR Slope Rating (Europe)
We are indebted to club secretaries in the British Isles and continental Europe for the information supplied.

Key to Symbols		International Dialling Codes		
☎ Telephone	🏃 Visitors	Austria +43	Iceland +354	Poland +48
🖨 Fax	££ Fees	Belgium +32	Repubic of	Portugal +351
✉ E-mail	🚗 Location	Czech Republic	Ireland +353	Slovenia +386
📖 Membership	⊕ Miscellaneous	+420	Italy +39	Spain +34
🖋 Secretary	🏠 Architect	Denmark +45	Luxembourg	Sweden +46
✓ Professional	🖥 Website	Finland +358	+352	Switzerland
⛳ Holes		France +33	Malta +356	+41
		Germany +49	Netherlands	Turkey +90
		Greece +30	+31	
		Hungary +36	Norway +47	

Great Britain and Ireland County Index

England

Bedfordshire

Aspley Guise & Woburn Sands (1914)
West Hill, Aspley Guise, Milton Keynes, MK17 8DX
☎ (01908) 583596
🖵 (01908) 583596
✉ info@aspleyguisegolfclub.co.uk
🕮 590
🏌 Tony Hutchinson (01908) 583596
⛳ C Clingan (01908) 582974
▷ 18 L 6079 yds Par 71 SSS 70
⛳ WD–H WE/BH–MH SOC–Wed & Fri
££ £34 (£50)
⊕ 2 miles W of M1 Junction 13
⛫ Herd/Sandow
🖳 www.aspleyguisegolfclub.co.uk

Aylesbury Vale (1991)
Proprietary
Wing, Leighton Buzzard, LU7 0UJ
☎ (01525) 240196
🖵 (01525) 240848
✉ info@avgc.co.uk
🕮 550
🏌 C Wright (Sec/Mgr)
⛳ T Bunyan (01525) 240196
▷ 18 L 6612 yds Par 72 SSS 72
⛳ WD–U WE–phone first SOC–WD U, SOC–WE after 1pm
££ £23 D–£28 (£30) Twilight £14 plus optnl ½ pr Seniors Tues £11
⊕ 3 miles W of Leighton Buzzard on Wing-Stewkley road
⊕ Driving range
⛫ Sq Ldr Don Wright
🖳 www.avgc.co.uk

Beadlow Manor Hotel G&CC (1973)
Proprietary
Beadlow, Shefford, SG17 5PH
☎ (01525) 860800
🖵 (01525) 861345
✉ office@beadlowmanor.co.uk
🕮 700
🏌 Graham Wilson (Gen Mgr)
⛳ Paul Simpson (01525) 860666
▷ 18 L 6238 yds SSS 71
   18 L 6042 yds SSS 70
⛳ U SOC WD WE
££ Mon–Thur £17.50 (£20) Fri £20 WE+BH £25
⊕ 2 miles W of Shefford on A507
⊕ Driving range
🖳 www.beadlowmanor.co.uk

The Bedford (1999)
Proprietary
Carnoustie Drive, Great Denham Golf Village, Biddenham, MK40 4FF
☎ (01234) 320022
🖵 (01234) 320023
✉ thebedford@btopenworld.com
🕮 500

🏌 Simon Pepper (01234) 330559
⛳ Zac Thompson
▷ 18 L 6560 yds Par 72
⛳ WD–U WE–U SOC–WD
££ £40 (£60)
⊕ 2 miles W of Bedford (A428)
⊕ Driving range; chipping green; putting green
⛫ David Pottage
🖳 www.kolvengolf.com

Bedford & County (1912)
Green Lane, Clapham, Bedford, MK41 6ET
☎ (01234) 352617
🖵 (01234) 357195
✉ office@bedfordandcountygolfclub.co.uk
🕮 600
🏌 RP Walker (Mgr)
⛳ R Tattersall (01234) 359189
▷ 18 L 6420 yds SSS 70 Gents
   18 L 5641 yds SSS 73 Ladies
⛳ WD–U H SOC WE–M
££ £34 D–£42
⊕ 2 miles NW of Bedford on the old A6 in the village of Clapham
⛫ FG Howtee (1925)
🖳 www.bedfordandcountygolfclub.co.uk

Bedfordshire (1891)
Spring Lane, Stagsden, Bedford, MK43 8SR
☎ (01234) 822555
🖵 (01234) 825052
✉ office@bedfordshiregolf.com
🕮 700
🏌 Ross Ellens (Gen Mgr)
⛳ Geraint Dixon (01234) 826100
▷ 18 L 6565 yds Par 70 SSS 72
   9 L 1345 yds Par 28
⛳ WD–U (phone first) WE–M before noon SOC–WD
££ On application
⊕ 3 miles W of Bedford (A422). M1 Junction 14, 8 miles
⊕ 24-bay driving range
⛫ Cameron Sinclair
🖳 www.bedfordshiregolf.com

Caddington (1985)
Proprietary
Chaul End Road, Caddington, LU1 4AX
☎ (01582) 415573
🖵 (01582) 415314
✉ info@caddingtongolfclub.co.uk
🕮 400
🏌 D Isger
⛳ D Turner (07957) 309154
▷ 18 L 6226 yds Par 71 SSS 70
⛳ WD–U WE/BH–after 2pm
££ £19 (£30)
⊕ 3 miles W of Luton off A505 between Dunstable and Caddington. M1 Junction 10/11
⊕ Professional shop; Driving Range
🖳 www.caddingtongolfclub.co.uk

Chalgrave Manor (1994)
Proprietary
Dunstable Road, Chalgrave, Toddington, LU5 6JN
☎ (01525) 876556
🖵 (01525) 876556
✉ steve@chalgravegolf.co.uk
🕮 450
🏌 S Rumball
⛳ Martin Heanue
▷ 18 L 6382 yds Par 72 SSS 70
⛳ U SOC–WD WE–U after 1 pm
££ £22 (£34)
⊕ 2 miles W of M1 Jct 12 on A5120
⊕ Practice range
⛫ Mike Palmer
🖳 www.chalgravegolf.co.uk

Colmworth (1992)
Proprietary
New Road, Colmworth, MK44 2NN
☎ (01234) 378181
✉ julie@colmworthgc.fsnet.co.uk

Colworth (1985)
Colworth House, Sharnbrook, Bedford, MK44 1LQ
☎ (01933) 353269 (Sec)
✉ ewthompson@btinternet.com
🕮 350
🏌 E Thompson
▷ 9 L 5208 yds Par 68 SSS 66
⛳ M
££ D–£10
⊕ Sharnbrook, 10 miles N of Bedford, off A6

Dunstable Downs (1906)
Whipsnade Road, Dunstable, LU6 2NB
☎ (01582) 604472
🖵 (01582) 478700
✉ dunstabledownsgc@btconnect.com
🕮 640
🏌 Alan Sigee
⛳ D Charlton (01582) 662806
▷ 18 L 5923 yds SSS 69
⛳ WD–H WE–M SOC–WD exc Wed
££ On request
⊕ 2 miles SW of Dunstable on B4541. M1 Junction 11
⛫ James Braid
🖳 www.dunstable-golf.co.uk

Henlow (1985)
RAF Henlow, Henlow, SG16 6DN
☎ (01462) 851515 Ext 7083

John O'Gaunt (1948)
Sutton Park, Sandy, Biggleswade, SG19 2LY
☎ (01767) 260360
🖵 (01767) 262834
✉ admin@johnogauntgolfclub.co.uk
🕮 1450
🏌 TBA
⛳ L Scarbrow (01767) 260094

John O'Gaunt 18 L 6513 yds Par 71
SSS 71
Carthagena 18 L 5869 yds Par 69
SSS 69
H–phone first SOC–WD
££ £40 D–£50 (£60)
🚗 3 m NE of Biggleswade on B1040
🏠 Hawtree
🖳 www.johnogauntgolfclub.co.uk

Leighton Buzzard   (1925)
Plantation Road, Leighton Buzzard, LU7 3JF
☎ (01525) 244800
🖥 (01525) 244801
📧 secretary@leightonbuzzardgolf.net
📖 650
🏌 D Mutton (01525) 244800
🏌 M Campbell (01525) 244815
📏 18 L 6101 yds SSS 70
🏌 WD exc Tues–U H WE/BH–MH
££ £45 D–£45
🚗 Heath and Reach, 1 mile N of
Leighton Buzzard. M1 Junction 12
🖳 www.leightonbuzzardgolf.net

The Millbrook   (1980)
Ampthill, MK45 2JB
☎ (01525) 840252
🖥 (01525) 406249
📧 info@themillbrook.com
📖 500
🏌 DC Cooke (01525) 840252
🏌 R Brightman (01525) 402269
📏 18 L 6966 yds Par 73 SSS 73
🏌 WD–U WE after 12.00pm
SOC–after 1pm
££ £25 (£35)
🚗 4 miles from M1 Jcts 12/13 (A507)
⊕ Practice range; buggies–£15 per 18
holes
🏠 W Sutherland
🖳 www.themillbrook.com

Mount Pleasant   (1992)
Proprietary
Station Road, Lower Stondon, Henlow,
SG16 6JL
☎ (01462) 850999
🖥 (01462) 850257
📧 manager@mountpleasantgolfclub
.co.uk
📖 300
🏌 D Simkins (Prop) (01462) 850999
🏌 Glen Kemble (01462) 850999
📏 9 L 6185 yds Par 70 SSS 70
🏌 U SOC–WD
££ 9: £10 (£12.50); 18: £18 (£22)
🚗 4 miles N of Hitchin, off A600
⊕ Practice chipping green with
bunker; 9 hole putting green;
undercover nets
🏠 Derek Young
🖳 www.mountpleasantgolfclub.co.uk

Mowsbury   (1975)
Public
Kimbolton Road, Bedford, MK41 8BJ
☎ (01234) 772700
📖 350
🏌 TW Gardner (01234) 771041
🏌 M Summers (01234) 772700
📏 18 L 6451 yds Par 72 SSS 71
🏌 U

££ £14.90 (£19.50)
🚗 2 miles N of Bedford on B660
⊕ Driving range
🏠 Hawtree

Pavenham Park   (1994)
Proprietary
Pavenham, Bedford, MK43 7PE
☎ (01234) 822202
🖥 (01234) 826602
📧 kolvengolf@ukonline.co.uk
📖 850
🏌 S Pepper
🏌 ZL Thompson
📏 18 L 6351 yds Par 72 SSS 71
🏌 WD–U WE–M SOC–WD
££ £40 (£60)
🚗 4 miles NW of Bedford on A6
🏠 Zac Thompson
🖳 www.kolvengolf.com

South Beds   (1892)
Warden Hill Road, Luton, LU2 7AE
☎ (01582) 591500
🖥 (01582) 495381
📧 office@southbedsgolfclub.co.uk
📖 850
🏌 RJ Wright (01582) 591500
🏌 M Davis (01582) 591209
📏 Galley 18 L 6401 yds SSS 71
Warden 9 L 4784 yds SSS 63
🏌 Galley WD–H (Ladies Day–Tues)
WE/BH–H exc comp days–NA
Warden–U
££ Galley £23 D–£35 (£32 D–£45)
Warden £10 (£13)
🚗 3 miles N of Luton, E of A6
🖳 www.southbedsgolfclub.co.uk

Stockwood Park   (1973)
Public
Stockwood Park, London Rd, Luton,
LU1 4LX
☎ (01582) 413704
🖥 (01582) 481001
📧 spgc@hotmail.co.uk
📖 500
🏌 Brian E Clark (Club Admin
Officer) (01582) 431788
(answerphone)
🏌 Matt Green, Simon Wagstaffe
📏 18 L 6049 yds SSS 69
🏌 U SOC by prior arrangement
££ £12 D–£17 (£16)
🚗 Adjacent exit 10/10a M1 exit for
Luton Airport
⊕ Driving range; par 3 9-hole mini
course; buggies £15/rnd; practice
nets; putting green
🏠 Charles Lawrie

Tilsworth   (1972)
Pay and play
Dunstable Rd, Tilsworth, Dunstable,
LU7 9PU
☎ (01525) 210721/210722
🖥 (01525) 210465
📧 enquiries@tilsworthgolf.co.uk
📖 370
🏌 N Webb
🏌 N Webb (Mgr)
📏 18 L 5306 yds Par 69 SSS 67
🏌 U SOC

££ £17 (£19.50)
🚗 2 miles N of Dunstable (A5)
⊕ Driving range
🖳 www.tilsworthgolf.co.uk

Wyboston Lakes   (1978)
Public
Wyboston Lakes, Wyboston, MK44 3AL
☎ (01480) 223004
🖥 (01480) 407330
📖 300
🏌 DJ Little (Mgr)
🏌 P Ashwell (01480) 223004
📏 18 L 5995 yds Par 70 SSS 69
🏌 WD–U WE–booking SOC
££ Under revision
🚗 S of St Neots, off A1 and St Neots
by-pass
⊕ Driving range
🏠 Neil Ockden
🖳 www.wybostonlakes.co.uk

Berkshire

Bearwood   (1986)
Mole Road, Sindlesham, Wokingham,
RG41 5DB
☎ (0118) 976 0060

Bearwood Lakes   (1996)
Bearwood Road, Sindlesham, RG41 4SJ
☎ (0118) 979 7900
📧 info@bearwoodlakes.co.uk

The Berkshire   (1928)
Swinley Road, Ascot, SL5 8AY
☎ (01344) 621495
🖥 (01344) 623328
📧 golf@theberkshire.co.uk
📖 625
🏌 Lt Col JCF Hunt (01344) 621496
🏌 P Anderson (01344) 622351
📏 Red 18 L 6452 yds Par 72 SSS 71
Blue 18 L 6358 yds Par 71 SSS 71
🏌 WD–I WE/BH–M
££ On application
🚗 3 m from Ascot on A332. M3 Jct 3
⊕ Practice range and short course
academy
🏠 Herbert Fowler
🖳 www.theberkshire.co.uk

Billingbear Park   (1985)
Pay and play
The Straight Mile, Wokingham, RG40 5SJ
☎ (01344) 869259
🖥 (01344) 869259
📧 jacquie@billingbearpark.com
📖 100
🏌 Mrs JR Blainey
🏌 MW Blainey
📏 9 L 5700 yds Par 68
9 hole Par 3 course
🏌 U
££ £10 (£13)
🚗 2 miles E of Wokingham via B3034.
M4 Junction 10
⊕ Practice nets; putting green;
bunker; chipping green
🏠 Hawtree
🖳 www.billingbeargolf.co.uk

Bird Hills Golf Centre (1985)

Public
Drift Road, Hawthorn Hill, Maidenhead,
SL6 3ST
☎ **(01628) 771030**
📠 (01628) 631023
📧 info@birdhills.co.uk
📖 400
🏌 Hannah Edwards
✓ N Slimming
⏴ 18 L 6212 yds SSS 71
👥 U SOC–WD/WE
££ On application
⛳ 4 miles S of Maidenhead on A330
⊕ Floodlit driving range; putting green
🖥 www.birdhills.co.uk

Blue Mountain Golf Centre
(1993)

Pay and play
Wood Lane, Binfield, RG42 4EX
☎ **(01344) 300200**
📠 (01344) 360960
📧 bluemountain@crown-golf.co.uk
📖 350
🏌 Grant Convey (Gen Mgr)
✓ Matthew Grady
⏴ 18 L 6097 yds SSS 70
👥 U SOC
££ Mon–Thur £20, Fri £21 (£26)
⛳ 1 mile W of Bracknell on B3408.
M4 Junction 10
⊕ Driving range. Golf Academy
🖥 www.crown-golf.co.uk

Calcot Park (1930)

Bath Road, Calcot, Reading, RG31 7RN
☎ **(0118) 942 7124**
📠 (0118) 945 3373
📧 info@calcotpark.com
📖 550
🏌 Kim Brake
✓ M Grieve (0118) 942 7797
⏴ 18 L 6216 yds SSS 70
👥 WD–H WE/BH–M SOC–WD
££ £50. After 2pm–£35
⛳ 3 miles W of Reading on A4. 1¹/₂
miles E of M4 Junction 12
🏠 HS Colt
🖥 www.calcotpark.com

Castle Royle (1994)

Knowl Hill, Reading, RG10 9XA
☎ **(01628) 825442**

Caversham Heath (2000)

Proprietary
Chazey Heath, Mapledurham, Reading,
RG4 7UT
☎ **(0118) 947 8600**
📠 (0118) 947 8700
📧 info@cavershamgolf.co.uk
📖 600
🏌 Adam Harrison
✓ Adam Harrison (01189) 479400
⏴ 18 7151 yds Par 73 SSS 74
👥 U–restricted WD. WE–NA before
12.00pm SOC
££ £40 (£56)
⛳ 3 miles N of Reading
⊕ 310 yard Driving range; Buggies
available

🏠 David Williams
🖥 www.cavershamgolf.co.uk

Datchet (1890)

Buccleuch Road, Datchet, SL3 9BP
☎ **(01753) 543887 (Clubhouse)**
📠 (01753) 541872
📧 secretary@datchetgolfclub.co.uk
📖 435 60(L) 30(J)
✓ KR Smith (01753) 541872
✓ P Cook (01753) 545222
⏴ 9 L 6087 yds SSS 69
👥 WD–U SOC WE–U after 2pm
££ £25 D–£35 (£30)
⛳ Slough, Windsor 2 miles
🏠 JH Taylor
🖥 www.datchetgolfclub.co.uk

Deanwood Park (1995)

Pay and play
Stockcross, Newbury, RG20 8JP
☎ **(01635) 48772**
📠 (01635) 48772
📧 golf@deanwoodpark.co.uk
📖 400
🏌 John Bowness
✓ Claire Waite
⏴ 9 L 4230 yds Par 64 SSS 60
👥 U
££ 9: £10.00 (£12.00); 18: £18.00
(£22.00)
⛳ 2 miles W of Newbury (B4000).
M4 Junction 13, 2 miles
⊕ Driving range; putting green
🖥 www.deanwoodpark.co.uk

Donnington Valley
(1985)

Proprietary
Snelsmore House, Snelsmore Common,
Newbury, RG14 3BG
☎ **(01635) 568140**
📠 (01635) 568141
📧 golf@donningtonvalley.co.uk
📖 550
🏌 Peter Smith (01635) 568144
✓ M Balfour
⏴ 18 L 6353 yds SSS 71
👥 U
££ £27 (£36)
⛳ N of Newbury, off Old Oxford
road; 5 min M4 Jct 14
⊕ Putting green
🏠 Mike Smith
🖥 www.donningtonvalleygolfclub
.co.uk

Downshire (1973)

Public
Easthampstead Park, Wokingham,
RG40 3DH
☎ **(01344) 302030**
📠 (01344) 301020
📧 downshiregolf
@bracknell-forest.gov.uk
📖 500
🏌 P Stanwick (Golf Mgr)
(01344) 422708
✓ W Owers (01344) 302030
⏴ 18 L 6416 yds Par 73 SSS 69
👥 U SOC WD WE
££ £19.65 (£26.15)
⛳ Off Nine Mile Ride M4 J10 M3 J3

⊕ PowerTee driving range; 9-hole
pitch & putt
🖥 www.bracknell-forest.gov.uk
/downshiregolf

East Berkshire (1903)

Ravenswood Ave, Crowthorne, RG45 6BD
☎ **(01344) 772041**
📠 (01344) 777378
📧 thesecretary
@eastberkshiregolfclub.com
📖 700
🏌 C Day
✓ J Brant (01344) 774112
⏴ 18 L 6345 yds SSS 70
👥 WD–H SOC (only Thur/Fri)
WE/BH–M
££ £40
⛳ Nr Crowthorne Railway Station
🏠 P Paxton
🖥 www.eastberkshiregolfclub.com

Goring & Streatley (1895)

Rectory Road, Streatley-on-Thames,
RG8 9QA
☎ **(01491) 873229**
📠 (01491) 875224
📧 secretary@goringgc.org
📖 740 115(L) 50(J)
🏌 ABW James
✓ J Hadland (01491) 873715
⏴ 18 L 6355 yds SSS 71
👥 WD–U WE/BH–M SOC–WD
££ £34 D–£46 (£44)
⛳ 10 miles NW of Reading on A417
🏠 Tom Dunne
🖥 www.goringgc.org

Hennerton (1992)

Proprietary
Crazies Hill Road, Wargrave, RG10 8LT
☎ **(0118) 940 1000/4778**
📠 (0118) 940 1042
📧 info@hennertongolfclub.co.uk
📖 500
🏌 W Farrow (0118) 940 4778
✓ W Farrow (0118) 940 4778
⏴ 18 L 4391 yds Par 65 SSS 62
👥 WD+WE U after 10.30am SOC
WD only
££ 9: £14 (£18); 18: £20 (£30)
⛳ Half mile from Wargrave High
Street (A321); between
Maidenhead and Reading
⊕ Driving range, floodlit, covered;
practice putting green
🏠 Dion Beard; Gaunt & Marnoch
🖥 www.hennertongolfclub.co.uk

Hurst (1979)

Public
Sandford Lane, Hurst, Wokingham,
RG10 0SQ
☎ **(01734) 344355**

Lavender Park

Swinley Road, Ascot SL5 8BD
☎ **(01344) 893344**
✓ David Johnson, Master Pro
⏴ 9 holes
👥 U SOC WD WE
££ Prices on website
⛳ M3 jct 3

For list of abbreviations and key to symbols see page 647

⊕ Driving range, floodlit
🖳 www.lavenderparkgolf.co.uk

Maidenhead   (1896)
Shoppenhangers Road, Maidenhead,
SL6 2PZ
☎ (01628) 624693
🖳 (01628) 780758
📧 manager@maidenheadgolf.co.uk
🏛 600
♟ J Pugh
✓ S Geary (01628) 624067
ρ 18 L 6360 yds SSS 70
👥 WD–H Mon–Thur Fri M only H
SOC Tue am/Wed–Thur WD only
££ D–£37 W–£40
⛳ Off A308, nr Maidenhead Station
⊕ Conference facilities
🏠 A Simpson/JH Taylor
🖳 www.maidenheadgolf.co.uk

Mapledurham   (1992)
Mapledurham, Reading, RG4 7UD
☎ (0118) 946 3353
🖳 (0118) 946 3363
📧 d.reeves@clubhaus.com
🏛 750
♟ R Davies
✓ T Gilpin
ρ 18 L 5635 yds SSS 67
👥 WE–NA before 11am
££ On application
⛳ 4 miles NW of Reading, off A4074
🏠 MRM Sandow

Mill Ride   (1990)
Mill Ride, Ascot, SL5 8LT
☎ (01344) 886777
🖳 (01344) 886820
📧 info@mill-ride.com
🏛 300
♟ S Gillett
✓ T Wild
ρ 18 L 6752 yds SSS 72
👥 H SOC WD, WE–NA before noon
££ On application
⛳ 2 miles W of Ascot
🏠 Donald Steel
🖳 www.mill-ride.com

Newbury & Crookham
(1873)
Bury's Bank Road, Greenham Common,
Newbury, RG19 8BZ
☎ (01635) 40035
🖳 (01635) 40045
📧 steve.myers@newburygolf.co.uk
🏛 620
♟ S Myers MBE (01635) 40035
✓ DW Harris (01635) 31201
ρ 18 L 5961 yds SSS 69
👥 WD–U H WE–M (recognised club
members)
££ £40 D–£50
⛳ 4 miles SE of Newbury. M4 Jct 13
🖳 www.newburygolf.co.uk

Newbury Racecourse   (1994)
The Racecourse, Newbury, RG14 7NZ
☎ (01635) 551464

Parasampia G&CC
Donnington Grove, Grove Road, Donnington,
RG14 2LA
☎ (01635) 581000
📧 enquiries@parasampia.com

Reading   (1910)
17 Kidmore End Road, Emmer Green,
Reading, RG4 8SG
☎ (0118) 947 2909
🖳 (0118) 946 4468
📧 secretary@readinggolfclub.com
🏛 600
♟ A Chaundy (0118) 947 2909
✓ S Fotheringham (0118) 947 6115
ρ 18 L 6251 yds SSS 70
👥 Mon–Fri–UH WE/BH–M
SOC–Tues–Fri
££ £40 D–£50
⛳ 2 miles N of Reading, off Peppard
Road (B481)
🏠 James Braid
🖳 www.readinggolfclub.com

Royal Ascot   (1887)
Winkfield Road, Ascot, SL5 7LJ
☎ (01344) 625175
🖳 (01344) 872330
📧 secretaries@royalascotgolfclub
.co.uk
🏛 600
♟ Mrs S Thompson (01344) 625175
✓ A White (01344) 624656
ρ 18 L 6294 yds Par 70 SSS 70
👥 M SOC H
££ On application
⛳ Now on new course, formerly
Ascot Farm, off A330; Windsor 4
miles; M3
🏠 STRI
🖳 www.royalascotgolfclub.co.uk

The Royal Household
(1901)
Buckingham Palace, London SW1 1AA
☎ (0207) 930 4832
🖳 (0207) 839 5970
📧 rhgc@royal.gsx.gov.uk
🏛 250
♟ Peter Walter
ρ 9 (18 tees) L 4925 yds Par 66
SSS 64
👥 Strictly by invitation only
⛳ The Home Park, Windsor Castle;
M25 J13
🏠 Samuel Mure Fergusson

Sand Martins   (1993)
Proprietary
Finchampstead Road, Wokingham,
RG40 3RQ
☎ (0118) 979 2711
🖳 (0118) 977 0282
📧 info@sandmartins.com
🏛 750
♟ J McDonald (0118) 902 9965
✓ AJ Hall (0118) 977 0265
ρ 18 L 6235 yds Par 70 SSS 70
👥 WD–U WE–NA before 1pm SOC
££ £36 (£43)
⛳ 1 mile S of Wokingham. M4 Jct 10
⊕ Driving range

🏠 ET Fox
🖳 www.sandmartins.com

Sonning   (1911)
Duffield Road, Sonning, Reading, RG4 6GJ
☎ (0118) 969 3332
🖳 (0118) 944 8409
📧 secretary@sonning-golf-club.co.uk
🏛 750
♟ AJ Tanner
✓ RT McDougall (0118) 969 2910
ρ 18 L 6366 yds Par 70 SSS 70
👥 WD–H WE–M SOC–WD
££ £40 £25 with member
⛳ 1½ miles E of A329(M). S of A4, nr
Sonning
🏠 JH Taylor (1911)
🖳 www.sonning-golf-club.co.uk

Swinley Forest   (1909)
Coronation Road, Ascot, SL5 9LE
☎ (01344) 620197
🖳 (01344) 874733
📧 swinleyfgc@tiscali.co.uk
🏛 350
♟ Stewart Zuill (01344) 295283
✓ Stuart Hill (01344) 295282
ρ 18 L 6062 yds Par 69 SSS 70
👥 M
⛳ S of Ascot
🏠 HS Colt

Temple   (1909)
Henley Road, Hurley, Maidenhead,
SL6 5LH
☎ (01628) 824795
🖳 (01628) 828119
📧 templegolfclub@btconnect.com
🏛 465
♟ KGM Adderley (01628) 824795
✓ J Whiteley (01628) 824254
ρ 18 L 6266 yds SSS 70
👥 H SOC
££ £45 D–£55 (£50 D–£60)
⛳ Between Maidenhead and Henley
on A4130. M4 Jct 8/9. M40 Jct 4
🏠 Willie Park Jr
🖳 www.templegolfclub.co.uk

Theale
North Street, Theale, Reading, RG6 5EX
☎ (01189) 305331

West Berkshire   (1975)
Proprietary
Chaddleworth, Newbury, RG20 7DU
☎ (01488) 638574
🖳 (01488) 638781
📧 info@thewbgc.co.uk
🏛 450
♟ Mrs CM Clayton
✓ P Simpson (01488) 638851
ρ 18 L 7022 yds SSS 74
👥 WD–U WE–NA before noon
SOC–WD
££ £22 D–£30 (£28) Twilight rates
available
⛳ Off A338 to Wantage. M4 Junction
14
🖳 www.thewbgc.co.uk

Winter Hill (1976)
Proprietary
Grange Lane, Cookham, SL6 9RP
☎ **(01628) 527613**
🖳 (01628) 527479
✉ winterhilladministration
@johnlewis.co.uk
⌷ 750
♫ Hilary Spiers (01628) 536033
✐ Julian Goodman (PGA)
► 18 L 6408 yds SSS 71
♙ WD–U WE–M–H SOC
££ D–£36
⊙ Maidenhead 3 miles
⊕ Coaching; society days Wed & Fri,
Meeting Room Hire
⌂ Charles Lawrie
▤ www.winterhillgolfclub.net

Wokefield Park (1998)
Mortimer, Reading, RG7 3AE
☎ **(0118) 933 4013/4018/4017**
🖳 (0118) 933 4031
✉ wokefieldgolf@initialstyle.co.uk
✐ G Smith (0118) 933 4078
► 18 L 6961 yds Par 72 SSS 73
♙ WD–U WE–NA before 9.30am
SOC
££ £30 (£45)
⊙ 8 miles SW of Reading, off A33. M4
Junction 11
⊕ Driving range
⌂ Jonathan Gaunt
▤ www.golf-isc.co.uk

Buckinghamshire

Aylesbury Golf Centre
(1992)
Public
Hulcott Lane, Bierton, HP22 5GA
☎ **(01296) 393644**
♫ K Partington (Mgr)
✐ R Wooster
► 18 L 5965 yds SSS 69
♙ U
££ £12 (£17)
⊙ 1 mile N of Aylesbury on A418
⊕ Driving range
⌂ TS Benwell
▤ www.aylesburygolfclub.co.uk

Aylesbury Park (1996)
*Andrews Way, off Coldharbour Way,
Oxford Road, Aylesbury, HP17 8QQ*
☎ **(01296) 399196**
🖳 (01296) 336830
⌷ 360
♫ J Scheu
✐ G Legouix, J Scheu
► 18 L 6166 yds SSS 69
9-hole Par 3 short course
♙ U
££ 9: £5; 18: £20 (£25)
⊙ SW of Aylesbury (A418). M40
Junction 8, 12 miles
⊕ Practice nets & putting green
⌂ Martin Hawtree
▤ www.aylesburyparkgolf.com

Beaconsfield (1902)
Seer Green, Beaconsfield, HP9 2UR
☎ **(01494) 676545**
🖳 (01494) 681148
✉ secretary@beaconsfieldgolfclub
.co.uk
⌷ 850
♫ KR Wilcox
✐ M Brothers (01494) 676616
► 18 L 6508 yds Par 72 SSS 71
♙ WD–H WE–M SOC
££ £50 D–£60
⊙ 2 miles E of Beaconsfield. M40 Jct 2
⊕ Driving range
⌂ HS Colt
▤ www.beaconsfieldgolfclub.co.uk

Buckingham (1914)
Tingewick Road, Buckingham, MK18 4AE
☎ **(01280) 815566**
🖳 (01280) 821812
✉ admin@buckinghamgolfclub.co.uk
⌷ 700
♫ GL Pearce (Sec/Mgr)
✐ G Hannah (01280) 815210
► 18 L 6162 yds SSS 70
♙ WD–U WE–M SOC–Tues & Thurs
££ £40
⊙ 2 m SW of Buckingham on A421
⌂ Peter Jones
▤ www.buckinghamgolfclub.co.uk

Buckinghamshire (1992)
*Denham Court Mansion, Denham Court
Drive, Denham, UB9 5PG*
☎ **(01895) 835777**
🖳 (01895) 835210
✉ enquiries@buckinghamshiregc.co.uk
⌷ 550
♫ D Griffiths (01895) 836803
John O'Leary (Dir of Golf)
✐ Paul Schunter (01895) 836814
► 18 L 6880 yds Par 72 SSS 73
♙ 1 or M SOC–WD exc Fri
££ £90 Mon–Thur (£100 Fri–Sun)
⊙ Off A40(M). M25 Jct 16b/M40 Jct 1
⊕ Driving range; chipping green;
putting green
⌂ John Jacobs
▤ www.buckinghamshiregc.com

Burnham Beeches (1891)
Green Lane, Burnham, Slough, SL1 8EG
☎ **(01628) 661448**
🖳 (01628) 668968
✉ enquiries@bbgc.co.uk
⌷ 670
♫ TP Jackson (Mgr) (01628) 661448
✐ R Bolton (01628) 661661
► 18 L 6449 yds SSS 71
♙ WD–I WE/BH–M H
££ £45 D–£60
⊙ 4 miles W of Slough
⌂ J Taylor
▤ www.bbgc.co.uk

Chartridge Park (1989)
Chartridge, Chesham, HP5 2TF
☎ **(01494) 791772**
🖳 (01494) 786462
✉ info@cpgc.co.uk
⌷ 700

♫ E Roca
✐ J Reilly
► 18 L 5409 yds SSS 66
♙ U SOC
££ £20 (£30)
⊙ 2 miles NW of Chesham. 9 miles
W of M25 Junction 18
⌂ John Jacobs
▤ www.cpgc.co.uk

Chesham & Ley Hill (1900)
Ley Hill, Chesham, HP5 1UZ
☎ **(01494) 784541**
🖳 (01494) 785506
✉ secretary@cheshamgolf.co.uk
⌷ 300
♫ James Short
✐ James Short (07773) 367079
► 9 L 5240 yds Par 67 SSS 65
♙ WD–U exc Tues–NA before 3pm
WE/BH–M SOC–Thurs & Fri
££ £19
⊙ Chesham 2 miles
▤ www.cheshamgolf.co.uk

Chiltern Forest (1979)
Aston Hill, Halton, Aylesbury, HP22 5NQ
☎ **(01296) 631267**
🖳 (01296) 632709
✉ secretary@chilternforest.co.uk
⌷ 650
♫ R Clift (01296) 631267
✐ Simon Perks (01296) 631817
► 18 L 5765 yds Par 70 SSS 69
♙ WD–U WE–M SOC
££ £36
⊙ 5 miles SE of Aylesbury, off A4011
▤ www.chilternforest.co.uk

Denham (1910)
Tilehouse Lane, Denham, UB9 5DE
☎ **(01895) 832022**
🖳 (01895) 835340
⌷ 775
♫ JW Tucker
✐ S Campbell (01895) 832801
► 18 L 6470 yds SSS 71
♙ Mon–Fri–I H Sat–Sun/BH–M
££ £60
⊙ 2 miles NW of Uxbridge
⌂ HS Colt
▤ www.denhamgolfclub.co.uk

Ellesborough (1906)
Butlers Cross, Aylesbury, HP17 0TZ
☎ **(01296) 622114**
🖳 (01296) 622114
✉ admin@ellesboroughgolf.co.uk
⌷ 700
♫ PG Miles (Gen Mgr)
✐ M Squire (01296) 623126
► 18 L 6384 yds Par 71 SSS 72
♙ WD–U except Tues am WE/BH–M
H SOC–on application
££ On application
⊙ 1 mile W of Wendover
⊕ Practice areas; driving nets
▤ www.ellesboroughgolf.co.uk

Farnham Park (1974)
Public
Park Road, Stoke Poges, Slough, SL2 4PJ
☎ **(01753) 643332**

Flackwell Heath (1904)
Treadaway Road, Flackwell Heath, High Wycombe, HP10 9PE
☎ **(01628) 520929**
🖥 (01628) 530040
📖 700
♟ IR Hulley
✓ P Watson (01628) 523017
⟩ 18 L 6211 yds SSS 70
👫 WD–H WE–M SOC–Wed & Thurs
££ £36
⛳ Between High Wycombe and Beaconsfield, off A40. M40 Jct 3/4
⛪ J Turner
🖳 www.fhcb.co.uk

Gerrards Cross (1921)
Chalfont Park, Gerrards Cross, SL9 0QA
☎ **(01753) 883263**
🖥 (01753) 883593
✉ secretary@gxgolf.co.uk
📖 640
♟ Simon Maynard
✓ M Barr (01753) 885300
⟩ 18 L 6243 yds SSS 70
👫 WD–H WE/H–M SOC
££ £50
⛳ 1 mile from Station, off A413
⛪ B Pedlar
🖳 www.gxgolf.co.uk

Harewood Downs (1907)
Cokes Lane, Chalfont St Giles, HP8 4TA
☎ **(01494) 762184**
🖥 (01494) 766869
✉ secretary@hdgc.co.uk
📖 500
♟ SJ Thornton (01494) 762184
✓ GC Morris (01494) 764102
⟩ 18 L 6028 yds SSS 70
👫 H
££ £40 (£45)
⛳ 2 miles E of Amersham, off A413
⛪ JH Taylor
🖳 www.hdgc.co.uk

Harleyford (1996)
Harleyford Estate, Henley Road, Marlow, SL7 2SP
☎ **(01628) 816161**
🖥 (01628) 816160
✉ info@harleyfordgolf.co.uk
📖 750
♟ Ken McCrea
✓ Graham Finch (01628)816162
⟩ 18 L 6708 yds Par 72 SSS 72
👫 U SOC–WD after 10am SOC–WE after 1pm
££ £45 (£65)
⛳ 1 mile W of Marlow on A4155
⊕ Driving range
⛪ Donald Steel
🖳 www.harleyfordgolf.co.uk

Hazlemere (1982)
Penn Road, Hazlemere, High Wycombe, HP15 7LR
☎ **(01494) 719300**
🖥 (01494) 713914
✉ enquiries@hazlemeregolfclub.co.uk
📖 600
♟ PS Dawson

✓ G Cousins (01494) 719306
⟩ 18 L 5833 yds SSS 69
👫 WD–U WE–booking req SOC–WD
££ £36 (£45)
⛳ 3 m NE of High Wycombe (B474)
⛪ Terry Murray
🖳 www.hazlemeregolfclub.co.uk

Hedsor (2000)
Pay and play
Broad Lane, Wooburn Common, Bucks, HP10 0JW
☎ **(01628) 851285**
✉ info@hedsorgolfcourse.co.uk
📖 150
♟ S Morris (Gen Mgr) (01628) 851285
✓ S Cannon (01628) 851285
⟩ 9 L 5158 yds (18 holes) Par 68 SSS 64
👫 U
££ 9 holes £10 (£12); Seniors £7 WD
⛳ M40 Jct 2, take A355 to Slough and follow signs to Hedsor Golf Club
⊕ Practice area
⛪ Steve Morris
🖳 www.hedsorgolfcourse.co.uk

Huntswood (1996)
Taplow Common Road, Burnham, SL1 8LS
☎ **(01628) 667144**
🖥 (01628) 663145
✉ chrislewis.huntswood @btopenworld.com
📖 330
♟ R Balm (01628) 667144
✓ G Beynon (01628) 667144
⟩ 18 L 5613 yds Par 69 SSS 66
👫 U SOC WD WE
££ £16 (£20.50)
⛳ M4 Junction 7
⊕ Practice green; buggies; club hire
🖳 www.huntswoodgolf.com

Iver (1983)
Hollow Hill Lane, Iver, SL0 0JJ
☎ **(01753) 655615**
🖥 (01753) 654225
✉ ivergolf@fsmail.net
📖 500
♟ J Lynch (Golf Dir) – Fellow PGA
✓ J Lynch
⟩ 9 L 5146 yds SSS 66
👫 U SOC Book time WE
££ 9: £8 (£9.50); 18: £14 (£17) Short: Adults 9: £4 (£4.50) 18: £7 (£8) reductions for juniors
⛳ M4 Slough East Langley
⊕ Driving range on site
🖳 www.ivergolfcourse.co.uk

Ivinghoe (1967)
Wellcroft, Ivinghoe, Leighton Buzzard, LU7 9EF
☎ **(01296) 668696**
🖥 (01296) 662755
✉ ivinghoegolfclub@tesco.net
📖 150
♟ Mrs SE Garrad (01296) 668696
✓ M Flitney (01296) 668696
⟩ 9 L 4508 yds SSS 62

👫 WD–U WE–U after 8am SOC
££ 9: £6, 18: £10
⛳ 3 m N of Tring. M1 Jct 11, 5 miles
⛪ R Garrad
🖳 golfshopbuckinghamshire.co.uk

Kingfisher CC (1995)
Proprietary
Buckingham Road, Deanshanger, Milton Keynes, MK19 6JY
☎ **(01908) 560354**
🖥 (01908) 260857
✉ sales.kingfisher@btopenworld.com
📖 80
♟ Matthew Brand (01908) 562332
✓ Brian Mudge (01604) 643555
⟩ 9 L 5552 yds Par 70 SSS 67 (18 tees)
👫 U SOC
££ 9: £9.50 (£12.50); 18: £14 (£17)
⛳ 10 min W central Milton Keynes, Junction 15
⊕ Driving range – phone for availability
⛪ Donald Steele
🖳 www.kingfisher-uk.com

The Lambourne Club (1992)
Dropmore Road, Burnham, SL1 8NF
☎ **(01628) 666755**
🖥 (01628) 663301
✉ info@lambourneclub.co.uk
📖 600
♟ D Hart (Gen Mgr)
✓ D Hart (Golf Dir)/S Marshall (01628) 662936
⟩ 18 L 6798 yds SSS 73
👫 H SOC–Thur only
££ £60 (£90)
⛳ 1 mile N of Burnham. M40 Junction 2. M4 Junction 7
⊕ Driving range
⛪ Donald Steel
🖳 www.lambourneclub.co.uk

Little Chalfont (1981)
Lodge Lane, Chalfont St Giles, HP8 4AJ
☎ **(01494) 764877**
📖 200
♟ JM Dunne (01494) 762942
✓ A Dunne (01494) 762942
⟩ 9 L 5752 yds SSS 68
👫 U SOC
££ £14 D–£19 (£16)
⛳ Chalfont & Latimer Station ½ mile. M25 Junction 18, 1 mile
⛪ JM Dunne

Magnolia Park
Arncott Road, Boarstall, HP18 9XX
☎ **(01844) 239700**
🖥 (01844) 238991
✉ info@magnoliapark.co.uk
📖 400
♟ Debbie Ludlow
✓ Dusan Gavrilovic
⟩ 18 holes Par 73 SSS 73 9 hole course
👫 U SOC–WD
££ D–£40 (midweek), £50 WE after noon, No societies at WE
⛳ 10 miles NW of Thame (B4011); 10 miles West of Oxford

⊕ Practice ground; putting greens
⋔ Johnathan Gaunt
▤ www.magnoliapark.co.uk

Mentmore G&CC (1992)
Mentmore, Leighton Buzzard, LU7 0UA
☎ (01296) 662020
🖴 (01296) 662592
📧 rgriffiths@theclubcompany.co.uk
🕮 1100
⚐ R Griffiths
⌁ Alistair Halliday
⏦ Rothschild 18 L 6777 yds SSS 72
Rosebery 18 L 6850 yds SSS 73
👥 WD–U WE/BH–U after 11am SOC
££ £45 (£50)
⊷ 4 miles S of Leighton Buzzard
⊕ Driving range; swimming pool, gym, tennis courts
⋔ Bob Sandow
▤ www.theclubcompany.com

Oakland Park (1994)
Proprietary
Three Households, Chalfont St Giles, HP8 4LW
☎ (01494) 871277
🖴 (01494) 874692
📧 info@oaklandparkgolf.co.uk
🕮 600
⚐ I Donnelly (Gen Mgr)
⌁ A Thatcher (01494) 877333
⏦ 18 L 5246 yds Par 67 SSS 66
👥 U SOC–WD–WE
££ £28.50 (£30.50)
⊷ 3 miles N of M40 Junction 2
⊕ Driving range
⋔ Jonathan Gaunt
▤ www.oaklandparkgolf.co.uk

Princes Risborough (1990)
Proprietary with Pay & Play
Lee Road, Saunderton Lee, Princes Risborough, HP27 9NX
☎ (01844) 346989 (Clubhouse)
🖴 (01844) 274938
📧 mlgolfltd@uwclub.net
🕮 320
⚐ J Murray (Man Dir)
⌁ S Lowry (01844) 274567
⏦ 9 L 5440 yds Par 68 SSS 67
👥 U SOC Dress code applies
££ 9: £12 (£14); 18: £18 (£23)
⊷ 7 miles NW of High Wycombe on A4010; M40 Jct 4 or 5; follow signs for Aylesbury
⋔ Guy Hunt
▤ www.prgc.co.uk

Richings Park (1996)
Proprietary
North Park, Iver, SL0 9DL
☎ (01753) 655352
🖴 (01753) 655409
🕮 450
⚐ Steve Coles (01753) 655370
⌁ Ryan Kirby (01753) 655352
⏦ 18 L 6210 yds Par 70 SSS 70
👥 WD–U WE–U
££ £26 (£45)
⊷ Nr M4 Junction 5
⊕ Driving range
⋔ Alan Higgins
▤ www.richingspark.co.uk

Silverstone (1992)
Proprietary
Silverstone Road, Stowe, Buckingham, MK18 5LH
☎ (01280) 850005
🖴 (01280) 850156
📧 proshop@silverstonegolfclub.co.uk
🕮 500
⚐ S Barnes
⌁ R Holt
⏦ 18 L 6558 yds Par 72 SSS 71
👥 U–booking advisable SOC
££ £22 (£32.50)
⊷ Opposite Silverstone Race Circuit, N of Buckingham
⊕ Driving range
⋔ David Snell
▤ www.silverstonegolfclub.co.uk

Stoke Park (1908)
Park Road, Stoke Poges, SL2 4PG
☎ (01753) 717171
🖴 (01753) 717181
📧 info@stokeparkclub.com
🕮 850
⚐ Miss Kelly Ford (01753) 717116
⌁ S Collier
⏦ 18 L 6721 yds SSS 72
9 L 3074 yds
👥 M NA H SOC
⊷ 5 miles N of Windsor
⋔ HS Colt
▤ www.stokeparkclub.com

Stowe (1974)
Stowe, Buckingham, MK18 5EH

Tattenhoe (1972)
Pay and play
Tattenhoe Lane, Bletchley, MK3 7RB
☎ (01908) 631113 (Bookings)
🖴 (01908) 630034
📧 info@golfinmiltonkeynes.co.uk
🕮 90
⚐ Diana Allen (01908) 647615
⌁ C Clingan (01908) 378623
⏦ 18 L 6720 yds Par 73 SSS 72
👥 U SOC after 11am
££ £16.00 (£22 – £17.50 after 1pm)
⊷ W of Milton Keynes on A421. M1 Junctions 13 & 14
⊕ Driving range
⋔ Sir Henry Cotton
▤ www.golfinmiltonkeynes.co.uk

Thorney Park (1992)
Proprietary
Thorney Mill Lane, Iver, SL0 9AL
☎ (01895) 422095
📧 sales@thorneypark.co.uk

Three Locks (1992)
Great Brickhill, Milton Keynes, MK17 9BH
☎ (01525) 270050
🖴 (01525) 270470
📧 info@threelocksgolfclub.co.uk
🕮 300
⚐ P Critchley
⏦ 18 L 6025 yds Par 70 SSS 68
👥 U SOC exc Sun
££ £19.50 weekdays £26.50 weekends
⊷ N of Leighton Buzzard on A4146. M1 Junction 14

⋔ MRM Sandow
▤ www.threelocksgolfclub.co.uk

Wavendon Golf Centre (1990)
Pay and play
Lower End Road, Wavendon, Milton Keynes, MK17 8DA
☎ (01908) 281811
🖴 (01908) 281257
🕮 250
⚐ G Iron
⌁ G Iron
⏦ 18 L 5460 yds Par 67 SSS 66
9 hole par 3 pitch & putt course
👥 U SOC
££ Mon–Thur £16.50, Fri £17 (£22)
⊷ 2 miles W of M1 Junction 13
⊕ Floodlit driving range

Weston Turville (1973)
Proprietary
New Road, Weston Turville, Aylesbury, HP22 5QT
☎ (01296) 424084
🖴 (01296) 395376
📧 enquiries@westonturvillegolfclub.co.uk
🕮 500
⚐ D Allen
⌁ G George (01296) 425949
⏦ 18 L 6008 yds SSS 69
👥 U
££ £25 (£30)
⊷ 1½ miles SE of Aylesbury
▤ www.westonturvillegolfclub.co.uk

Wexham Park (1977)
Pay and play
Wexham Street, Wexham, Slough, SL3 6ND
☎ (01753) 663271
🖴 (01753) 663318
📧 info@wexhamparkgolfcourse.co.uk
🕮 900
⚐ J Dunne
⌁ J Kennedy (01753) 663425
⏦ 18 L 5251 yds SSS 66
Green 9 L 2219 yds SSS 32
Red 9 L 2727 yds SSS 34
👥 U SOC–WD/Sat pm
££ 9: £9 (£12.50) 18: £15.50 (£22.50)
⊷ 2 miles N of Slough. M4 Junction 4
⊕ Driving range (18 covered, 18 open); practice area; putting green
⋔ David Morgan
▤ www.wexhamparkgolfcourse.co.uk

Whiteleaf (1907)
Whiteleaf, Princes Risborough, HP27 0LY
☎ (01844) 343097/274058
🖴 (01844) 275551
📧 whiteleafgc@tiscali.co.uk
🕮 300
⚐ D Hill (01844) 274058
⌁ KS Ward (01844) 345472
⏦ 9 L 5391 yds SSS 66
👥 WD–U WE–M SOC
££ £20
⊷ Princes Risborough 2 miles
▤ www.whiteleafgolfclub.co.uk

Woburn   (1976)
Little Brickhill, Milton Keynes, MK17 9LJ
- ☎ (01908) 370756
- 🖳 (01908) 378436
- ✉ enquiries@woburngolf.com
- 🏛 1400
- ✎ Jason O'Malley (Gen Mgr)
  Glenna Beasley (Sec)
- ⌇ L Blacklock (01908) 626600
- ▷ Duke's 18 L 6976 yds SSS 74
  Duchess 18 L 6651 yds SSS 72
  Marquess 18 L 7214 yds SSS 74
- ⚇ WD–H (by arrangement) WE–M
- ££ By arrangement
- ⚘ ½ mile E of A5. 4 miles W of M1 ·
  Junction 13
- 🏛 Charles Lawrie (Duke's/Duchess),
  Peter Alliss and Clive Clark,
  European Golf Design (Ross
  McMurray), Alex Hay (Marquess)
- 🖳 www.discoverwoburn.co.uk

Wycombe Heights   (1991)
Pay and play
*Rayners Avenue, Loudwater, High
Wycombe, HP10 9SZ*
- ☎ (01494) 816686
- 🖳 (01494) 816728
- ✉ info@wycombeheightsgc.co.uk
- 🏛 625
- ✎ Steve West
- ⌇ Chris Reeve (Head Pro)
- ▷ 18 L 6300 yds Par 70 SSS 72
  18 hole Par 3 course
- ⚇ U SOC
- ££ £20 (£26)
- ⚘ ½ mile from M40 Junction 3, on
  A40 to Wycombe
- ⊕ 24-bay driving range; short game
  area; putting green
- 🏛 John Jacobs
- 🖳 www.wycombeheightsgc.co.uk

Cambridgeshire

Abbotsley   (1986)
Proprietary
Eynesbury Hardwicke, St Neots, PE19 6XN
- ☎ (01480) 474000
- 🖳 (01480) 403280
- ✉ abbotsley@crown-golf.co.uk
- 🏛 500
- ✎ Nicky Briggs (01480) 474000
- ⌇ S Connolly
- ▷ 18 L 6311 yds SSS 72
- ⚇ WD/BH–U WE–M before 1pm –U
  after 1pm SOC
- ££ £28 (£42.50)
- ⚘ 2 miles SE of St Neots on B1046.
  M11 Junction 13 (A428)
- 🏛 Vivien Saunders
- 🖳 www.abbotsleygolf.co.uk

Bourn   (1991)
Proprietary
Toft Road, Bourn, Cambridge, CB23 2TT
- ☎ (01954) 718057
- 🖳 (01954) 718908
- 🏛 600
- ✎ A.Lavers (01954) 718057
- ⌇ C Watson (01954) 718958

- ▷ 18 L 6528 yds SSS 71
- ⚇ WD–U WE–U after 12pm
  SOC–WD SOC–WE
- ££ On application
- ⚘ 8 miles W of Cambridge, off
  B1046. M11 Junction 12
- ⊕ Par 3 course; driving range; 2
  putting greens; practice bunker
- 🖳 www.bourngolfand leisure.co.uk

Brampton Park   (1991)
*Buckden Road, Brampton, Huntingdon,
PE28 4NF*
- ☎ (01480) 434700
- 🖳 (01480) 411145
- ✉ admin@bramptonparkgc.co.uk
- 🏛 720
- ✎ Mr Pete Holland
- ⌇ A Currie (01480) 434705
- ▷ 18 L 6300 yds SSS 71
- ⚇ U SOC
- ££ £27 D–£37 (£46)
- ⚘ 3 m W of Huntingdon, off A1/A14
- ⊕ Driving range; buggies
- 🏛 Simon Gidman
- 🖳 www.bramptonparkgc.co.uk

Cambridge
*Station Road, Longstanton, Cambridge,
CB4 5DS*
- ☎ (01954) 789388
- 🏛 300
- ✎ K Green
- ⌇ G Huggett, Phil Rains
- ▷ 18 L 6736 yds Par 72 SSS 74
- ⚇ U SOC
- ££ 9: £10 (£12) 18: £14 (£18)
- ⚘ 5 miles NW of Cambridge, off A14
  (B1050)
- ⊕ Floodlit driving range

Cambridge National   (1944)
Proprietary
*Comberton Road, Toft, Cambridge,
CB23 2RY*
- ☎ (01223) 264700
- 🖳 (01223) 264701
- ✉ meridian@golfsocieties.com
- 🏛 500
- ✎ Vivien Saunders
- ⌇ Craig Watson 01223 264702
- ▷ 18 L 6732 yds Par 73 SSS 72
- ⚇ U SOC
- ££ £28 (£35)
- ⚘ 3 miles SW of Cambridge on
  B1046. M11 Junction 12
- 🏛 Alliss/Clark
- 🖳 www.golfsocieties.com

Cromwell   (1986)
Proprietary
Eynesbury Hardwicke, St Neots, PE19 6XN
- ☎ (01480) 215153
- 🖳 (01480) 406463
- ✉ abbotsley@crown-golf.co.uk
- 🏛 300
- ✎ Nicky Briggs (01480) 474000
- ⌇ S Connolly
- ▷ 18 L 6087 yds SSS 69
  9 hole Par 3 course
- ⚇ U SOC
- ££ £17 (£23)

- ⚘ 2 miles SE of St Neots on B1046.
  M11 Junction 13 (A428)
- ⊕ 21-bay floodlit driving range; 9 hole
  par 3; grass driving range
- 🏛 Vivien Saunders
- 🖳 www.cromwellgolfclub.co.uk

Elton Furze   (1993)
Proprietary
*Bullock Road, Haddon, Peterborough,
PE7 3TT*
- ☎ (01832) 280189
- 🖳 (01832) 280299
- ✉ helen@efgc.co.uk
- 🏛 540
- ✎ Helen Barron (01832) 280189
- ⌇ G Krause (01832) 280614
- ▷ 18 L 6279 yds Par 70 SSS 71
- ⚇ WD–phone in advance SOC
- ££ £35 (£39)
- ⚘ 4 miles W of Peterborough on old
  A605
- ⊕ Driving range
- 🏛 Roger Fitton
- 🖳 www.efgc.co.uk

Ely City   (1961)
107 Cambridge Road, Ely, CB7 4HX
- ☎ (01353) 662751
- 🖳 (01353) 668636
- ✉ info@elygolf.co.uk
- 🏛 775
- ✎ MS Hoare (Mgr) (01353) 662751
- ⌇ A George (01353) 663317
- ▷ 18 L 6627 yds SSS 72
- ⚇ WD–H WE–H SOC–Mon–Fri
- ££ £34 (£40)
- ⚘ 12 miles N of Cambridge
- ⊕ Buggies available (Apr–Oct)
- 🏛 Henry Cotton
- 🖳 www.elygolf.co.uk

Girton   (1936)
Dodford Lane, Girton, CB3 0QE
- ☎ (01223) 276169
- 🖳 (01223) 277150
- ✉ info@girtongolf.co.uk
- 🏛 800
- ✎ Miss VM Webb
- ⌇ S Thomson (01223) 276991
- ▷ 18 L 6012 yds SSS 69
- ⚇ WD–U WE/BH–M SOC–WD
- ££ £25
- ⚘ 3 miles N of Cambridge (A14)
- 🖳 www.girtongolf.co.uk

The Gog Magog   (1901)
Shelford Bottom, Cambridge, CB22 3AB
- ☎ (01223) 247626
- 🖳 (01223) 414990
- ✉ secretary@gogmagog.co.uk
- 🏛 1300
- ✎ Mrs C Davison
- ⌇ I Bamborough (01223) 246058
- ▷ Old 18 L 6398 yds SSS 70
  Wandlebury 18 L 6735 yds SSS 72
- ⚇ WD–I or H WE/BH–M SOC on
  application, not Wed/Sat/Sun
- ££ £45 (£60) (fee reduction for
  winter)
- ⚘ 2 miles S of Cambridge on A1307
  (A604)
- ⊕ Driving range

Hemingford Abbots (1991)
Proprietary
New Farm Lodge, Cambridge Road,
Hemingford Abbots, PE28 9HQ
☎ (01480) 495000

Heydon Grange G&CC
(1994)
Heydon, Royston, SG8 7NS
☎ (01763) 208988
🖳 (01763) 208926
✉ enquiries@heydongrange.co.uk
📖 200
♞ S Akhtar
✓ Stuart Smith (07799) 088786
🏴 18 L 6512 yds SSS 72
9 L 3249 yds SSS 36
👥 U SOC WD U WE U
££ £20 (£25)
🚗 4 miles E of Royston on A505. M11
Junction 10
⊕ Driving range
🏠 Cameron Sinclair
🖳 www.heydongrange.co.uk

Lakeside Lodge (1992)
Fen Road, Pidley, Huntingdon, PE28 3DF
☎ (01487) 740540
🖳 (01487) 740852
✉ info@lakeside-lodge.co.uk
📖 800
♞ Mrs J Hopkins
✓ S Waterman (01487) 741541
🏴 18 L 6865 yds SSS 73
9 L 2601 yds SSS 33
👥 U SOC
££ £18 (£27)
🚗 4 miles N of St Ives on B1040
⊕ Driving range; 9 hole Manor
course; 12 hole Church course; Par
3 course
🏠 A Headley
🖳 www.lakeside-lodge.co.uk

Malton (1993)
Pay and play
Malton Lane, Meldreth, Royston, SG8 6PE
☎ (01763) 262200
🖳 (01763) 262209
✉ info@maltongolf.co.uk
📖 300
♞ P Bancroft
✓ K Evans
🏴 18 L 6708 yds Par 72 SSS 72
👥 U SOC inc WE
££ £13.50 D–£23 (£19.50)
🚗 8 miles SW of Cambridge, off A10.
5 miles SW of M11 Junction 11
⊕ Driving range; Chipping area;
Putting Green
🏠 Bruce Critchley/P Bancroft
🖳 www.maltongolf.co.uk

March (1922)
Frogs Abbey, Grange Rd, March, PE15 0YH
☎ (01354) 652364
✉ secretary@marchgolfclub.co.uk
📖 360
♞ M Simpson

✓ A Oldham (01354) 657255
🏴 9 L 6204 yds SSS 70
👥 H SOC–WD
££ £22 (£26)
🚗 18 m E of Peterborough on A141
🖳 www.marchgolfclub.co.uk

Menzies Cambridgeshire
(1974)
Proprietary
Bar Hill, Cambridge, CB23 8EU
☎ (01954) 780098
🖳 (01954) 780010
✉ cambridge.golfpro
@menzieshotels.co.uk
📖 500
♞ Tom Turner (Golf Ops Mgr)
✓ Michael Clemons
🏴 18 L 6750 yds Par 72 SSS 73
👥 U SOC–WD
££ £30 (£40)
🚗 5 miles NW of Cambridge on A14
🖳 www.menzieshotels.co.uk

Old Nene G&CC (1992)
Muchwood Lane, Bodsey, Ramsey,
PE26 2XQ
☎ (01487) 815622
(01487) 813610 (Golf Shop)
🖳 (01487) 813519
✉ george.stoneman@virgin.net
📖 200
♞ GHD Stoneman
✓ GHD Stoneman
🏴 9 L 5605 yds SSS 68
👥 U SOC
££ 9: £9 (£14) 18: £12 (£18)
🚗 1 mile N of Ramsey, towards
Ramsey Mereside; 10 miles A1(M)
⊕ Floodlit driving range

Orton Meadows (1987)
Public
Ham Lane, Peterborough, PE2 5UU
☎ (01733) 237478
📖 450
♞ WL Stocks (01733) 234769
✓ Stuart Brown
🏴 18 L 5664 yds SSS 68
👥 U–phone Pro
££ £14 (£19.50)
🚗 2 miles SW of Peterborough on old
A605
⊕ 12 hole pitch & putt
🏠 D & R Fitton
🖳 www.ortonmeadowsgolfcourse
.co.uk

Peterborough Milton (1937)
Milton Ferry, Peterborough, PE6 7AG
☎ (01733) 380489
🖳 (01733) 380489
✉ secretary
@peterboroughmiltongolfclub.co.uk
📖 730
♞ Andy Izod (01733) 380489
✓ Jasen Barker (01733) 380489
🏴 18 L 6505 yds SSS 72
👥 U SOC H WD
££ £40 D (£50 D)
🚗 4 miles W of Peterborough on A47
⊕ Driving Range; Short game practice
area.

James Braid
🖳 www.club-noticeboard.co.uk

Ramsey (1964)
4 Abbey Terrace, Ramsey, Huntingdon,
PE26 1DD
☎ (01487) 812600
🖳 (01487) 815746
✉ admin@ramseyclub.co.uk
📖 750
✓ S Scott (01487) 813022
🏴 18 L 6163 yds Par 71 SSS 70
👥 WD–H WE/BH–M SOC
££ £25
🚗 12 miles SE of Peterborough
🏠 J Hamilton Stutt
🖳 www.ramseyclub.co.uk

St Ives (1923)
Westwood Road, St Ives, PE27 6DH
☎ (01480) 468392 (Mgr)
🖳 (01480) 468392
✉ manager@stivesgolfclub.co.uk
📖 450
♞ Mike Kjenstad (01480) 468392
✓ M Pond (01480) 466067
🏴 9 L 6180 yds SSS 70
👥 WD–U H WE–M WD–SOC
££ D–£26
🚗 5 miles E of Huntingdon
⊕ Practice ground

St Neots (1890)
Crosshall Road, St Neots, PE19 7GE
☎ (01480) 472363
🖳 (01480) 472363
✉ office@stneots-golfclub.co.uk
📖 600
♞ M.V.Truswell
✓ P Toyer (01480) 476513
🏴 18 L 6087 yds SSS 70
👥 WD–H WE–M
££ On application
🚗 By A1/B1048 Junction
🏠 Harry Vardon
🖳 www.stneots-golfclub.co.uk

Stilton Oaks (1997)
Proprietary
High Street, Stilton, Peterborough, PE7 3RA
☎ (01733) 245233

Thorney Golf Centre (1991)
Public
English Drove, Thorney, Peterborough,
PE6 0TJ
☎ (01733) 270570
🖳 (01733) 270842
📖 400
♞ Jane Hind
✓ M Templeman
🏴 Fen 18 L 6104 yds SSS 69
Lakes 18 L 6402 yds SSS 71
9 hole Par 3 course
👥 Lakes WD–U SOC WE–M
££ Fen £10.00 (£12.00) Lakes £17.00
(£25.00)
🚗 8 miles E of Peterborough, off A47
⊕ Floodlit driving range
🏠 A Dow
🖳 www.thorneygolfcentre.com

Thorpe Wood (1975)
Pay and play
Nene Parkway, Peterborough, PE3 6SE
☎ **(01733) 267701**
🖥 (01733) 332774
✉ enquiries@thorpewoodgolfcourse
.co.uk
🏌 R Palmer
✓ R Fitton
🏳 18 L 7086 yds SSS 74
👥 U–booking required SOC–WD
££ £14.60 (£19.50)
🚗 3 miles W of Peterborough on A47
(Junction 15)
🏠 Alliss/Thomas
🖥 www.thorpewoodgolfcourse.co.uk

Waterbeach (1968)
Waterbeach Barracks, Waterbeach,
Cambridge, CB5 9PA
☎ **(01223) 441199 (Sec)**
🖥 (01223) 204636
✉ waterbeachgolfclub@gtnet.gov.uk
🏌 Maj (Retd) DA Hornby (Hon)
🏳 9 L 6237 yds Par 70 SSS 70
👥 M SOC–WD–WE
££ £10
🚗 6 miles NE of Cambridge, off A10
🖥 www.waterbeachgolfclub.co.uk

Channel Islands

Alderney
Route des Carrieres, Alderney, GY9 3YD
☎ **(01481) 822835**

La Grande Mare (1994)
Proprietary
Vazon Bay, Castel, Guernsey, GY5 7LL
☎ **(01481) 253544**
🖥 (01481) 255194
✉ golf@lagrandemare.com
📖 800
🏌 N Graham (01481) 253544
✓ M Groves (01481) 253432
🏳 18 L 4755 yds SSS 64
👥 U–booking necessary SOC
££ D–£39 (£45)
🚗 Vazon Bay, W coast of Guernsey
⊕ Driving range
🏠 Hawtree
🖥 www.lagrandemare.com

Les Mielles G&CC (1994)
St Ouens Bay, Jersey, JE3 7FQ
☎ **(01534) 482787**
🖥 (01534) 485414
✉ enquiries@lesmielles.co.je
📖 1500
🏌 J Le Brun (Golf Dir)
(01534) 482787
✓ Ms L Cummins (01534) 483699
W Osmand (01534) 483252
🏳 18 L 5770 yds Par 70 SSS 68
👥 U
££ £26.50 (£30)
🚗 Five Mile Road, St Ouens Bay
⊕ Driving range
🏠 Le Brun/Whitehead
🖥 www.lesmielles.com

La Moye (1902)
La Moye, St Brelade, Jersey, JE3 8GQ
☎ **(01534) 743401**
(01534) 747166 (Bookings)
🖥 (01534) 747289
✉ secretary@lamoyegolfclub.co.uk
📖 1350
🏌 IN Prentice
✓ M Deeley (01534) 743130
🏳 18 L 6664 yds SSS 73
👥 U H SOC–9.30–11am and
2.30–4pm WE–after 2.30pm
££ £62 (£67)
🚗 2 miles from Jersey Airport
⊕ Driving range
🏠 James Braid
🖥 www.lamoyegolfclub.co.uk

Les Ormes (1996)
Mont à la Brune, St Brelade, Jersey, JE3 8FL
☎ **(01534) 497000**
🖥 (01534) 499122
✉ reception@lesormes.je
📖 1000
🏌 M Harris (01534) 497015
✓ A Jones (07797) 747401
🏳 9 L 5018 yds Par 66 SSS 65
👥 U SOC
££ 9: £5–£15 18: £10–£32 depending
when playing
🚗 Mont à la Brune, nr Airport
⊕ Practice facilities
🖥 www.lesormes.je

Royal Guernsey (1890)
L'Ancresse, Guernsey, GY3 5BY
☎ **(01481) 246523**
🖥 (01481) 243960
✉ bob.rggc@cwgsy.net
📖 1000
🏌 R Bushby (01481) 246523 R Eggo
(Golf Mgr)
✓ C Douglas (01481) 245070
🏳 18 L 6215 yds SSS 70
👥 WD–H WE–M
££ £47
🚗 3 miles N of St Peter Port
⊕ Driving range
🖥 www.royalguernseygolfclub.com

Royal Jersey (1878)
Grouville, Jersey, JE3 9BD
☎ **(01534) 854416**
🖥 (01534) 854684
✉ thesecretary@royaljersey.com
📖 1300
🏌 DJ Attwood
✓ D Morgan (01534) 852234
🏳 18 L 6200 yds SSS 71
👥 WD 10–12 & 2–4 (H), WE/BH
after 2.30pm
££ £55 (£55)
🚗 4 miles E of St Helier
🖥 www.royaljersey.com

St Clements (1925)
Public
St Clements, Jersey, JE2 6QN
☎ **(01534) 721938**
🖥 (01534) 721938
✉ stclementsgolf@jerseymail.co.uk
📖 120

✓ L Elstone
🏳 9 L 3972 yds SSS 61
👥 U exc Sun am–NA
££ On application
🚗 1 mile E of St Helier
⊕ Driving range; junior golf academy

St Pierre Park
Rohais, St Peter Port, Guernsey, GY1 1FD
☎ **(01481) 727039**
📖 290
✓ G Roberts (Mgr)
🏳 9 hole Par 3 course
👥 U SOC
££ On application
🚗 1 mile W of St Peter Port
⊕ Driving range
🏠 Tony Jacklin

Cheshire

Alder Root (1993)
Alder Root Lane, Winwick, Warrington,
WA2 8RZ
☎ **(01925) 291919**
🖥 (01925) 291961
✉ admin@alderroot.wanadoo.co.uk
📖 450
🏌 E Lander
✓ C McKevitt (01925) 291932
🏳 11 L 6152 yds Par 71 SSS 70
👥 WD–U SOC
££ £15 (£20)
🚗 4 miles N of Warrington (A49). M6
Junction 22. M62 Junction 9
🏠 Millington/Lander
🖥 www.alderroot.com

Alderley Edge (1907)
Brook Lane, Alderley Edge, SK9 7RU
☎ **(01625) 586200**
📖 225 65(L) 60(J)
🏌 RC Harrison (01625) 583073
✓ P Bowring (01625) 584493
🏳 9 L 5823 yds SSS 68
👥 SOC U H
££ £30 (£35); 2 for 1 scheme
🚗 12 miles S of Manchester
🖥 www.aegc.co.uk

Aldersey Green (1993)
Proprietary
Aldersey, Chester, CH3 9EH
☎ **(01829) 782157**
✉ bradburygolf@aol.com
📖 300
🏌 S Bradbury
✓ S Bradbury (01829) 782157
🏳 18 L 6150 yds Par 70
👥 U SOC
££ £15 (£20)
🚗 8 miles S of Chester, off A41
🖥 alderseygreengolfclub.co.uk

Altrincham Municipal (1893)
Public
Stockport Road, Timperley, Altrincham,
WA15 7LP
☎ **(0161) 928 0761**
📖 130
🏌 C J Schofield 0161 861 0201

⌒ S Partington
▷ 18 L 6385 yds Par 71 SSS 70
⋈ U SOC
££ £11.50 (£16)
⊶ 1 mile W of Altrincham (A560)
⊕ Driving range
▤ www.altrinchamgolfclub.org

Alvaston Hall (1992)
Proprietary
Middlewich Road, Nantwich, CW5 6PD
☎ **(01270) 628473**
⌒ (01270) 623395
▥ 120
♨ N Walkington (01270) 628473
⌁ K Valentine
▷ 9 L 3710 yds Par 64 SSS 59
⋈ U
££ £11 (£10)
⊶ 11 miles W of M6 Jct 16 on A530
⊕ Driving range
♁ K Valentine

Antrobus (1993)
Proprietary
Foggs Lane, Antrobus, Northwich, CW9 6JQ
☎ **(01925) 730890**
▥ 400
⌁ P Farrance (01925) 730900
▷ 18 L 6220 yds Par 71 SSS 72
⋈ H SOC
££ £25 (£28)
⊶ Nr M56 Junction 10, on A559 to Northwich
⊕ Driving range
♁ Michael Slater
▤ www.antrobusgolfclub.co.uk

Ashton-on-Mersey (1897)
Church Lane, Sale, M33 5QQ
☎ **(0161) 976 4390 (Clubhouse)**
⌒ (0161) 976 4390
▥ golf.aomgc@dbnmail.co.uk
▥ 190 65(L) 40(J)
♨ R Coppock (0161) 976 4390
⌁ Kris Andrews (0161) 976 4390
▷ 9 L 3073 yds SSS 69
⋈ WD–U H exc Thurs–NA before 3pm WE–M
££ £25.50
⊶ 5 miles W of Manchester. M60 Junction 7, 1½ miles
▤ www.aomgc.co.uk

Astbury (1922)
Peel Lane, Astbury, Congleton, CW12 4RE
☎ **(01260) 272772**
⌒ (01260) 276420
▥ admin@astburygolfclub.com
▥ 700
♨ FM Reed (01260) 272772
⌁ N Dawson (01260) 272772
▷ 18 L 6296 yds SSS 70
⋈ WD–H or M WE–M SOC–Thurs only
££ £30 SOC–£27.50
⊶ 1 mile S of Congleton, off A34
▤ www.astburygolfclub.com

Birchwood (1979)
Kelvin Close, Birchwood, Warrington, WA3 7PB
☎ **(01925) 818819**

⌒ (01925) 822403
▥ enquiries@birchwoodgolfclub.co.uk
▥ 745
♨ A Harper (Facilities Mgr)
⌁ C Edwards (01925) 825216
▷ 18 L 6596 yds Par 71 SSS 72
⋈ U SOC–Mon/Wed/Thurs/Fri/Sat
££ £25 D–£30 (£30)
⊶ M62 Junction 11, 2 miles. Signs to 'Science Park North'
⊕ Trolley hire; electric trolley hire; practice greens; chipping area; putting green
♁ TJA Macauley
▤ www.birchwoodgolfclub.co.uk

Bramall Park (1894)
20 Manor Road, Bramhall, Stockport, SK7 3LY
☎ **(0161) 485 3119 (Clubhouse)**
⌒ (0161) 485 7101
▥ secretary@bramallparkgolfclub.co.uk
▥ 400 100(L) 95(J)
♨ DE Shardlow (Hon) (0161) 485 7101
⌁ M Proffitt (0161) 485 2205
▷ 18 L 6247 yds SSS 70
⋈ SOC–WD (enquire of Sec)
££ £34 D–£38 (£40 D–£45)
⊶ 8 miles S of Manchester (A5102)
▤ www.bramallparkgolfclub.co.uk

Bramhall (1905)
Ladythorn Road, Bramhall, Stockport, SK7 2EY
☎ **(0161) 439 6092**
⌒ (0161) 439 6092
▥ office@bramhallgolfclub.com
▥ 700
♨ R Attwater (Hon)(0161) 439 6092
⌁ R Green (0161) 439 1171
▷ 18 L 6340 yds SSS 70
⋈ U H exc Thurs SOC–Wed, Fri
££ £40 (£55)
⊶ S of Stockport, off A5102
▤ www.bramhallgolfclub.com

Carden Park
Chester, CH3 9DQ
☎ **(01829) 731534**
⌒ (01829) 731599
▥ golf.carden@devere-hotels.com
▥ 270
♨ TBC
⌁ A Taylor (01829) 731500
▷ Cheshire 18 L 6824 yds SSS 72
  Nicklaus 18 L 7096 yds Par 72
⋈ WD–U WE–U SOC–U
££ From £20 (from £25)
⊶ 10 miles S of Chester on A534
⊕ Golf Academy; driving range; short game area, CPS Buggies, Full Catering.
▤ www.devere.co.uk

Cheadle (1885)
Shiers Drive, Cheadle Road, Cheadle, SK8 1HW
☎ **(0161) 491 4452**
▥ cheadlegolfclub@msn.com
▥ 250

♨ J V Heyes
⌁ A Millar (0161) 428 9878
▷ 9 L 4993 yds SSS 65
⋈ H or I exc Tues & Sat–NA SOC
££ £22 (£30)
⊶ 1 mile S of Cheadle. M60 Jct 2
♁ Mr Renouf
▤ www.cheadlegolfclub.com

Chester (1901)
Curzon Park, Chester, CH4 8AR
☎ **(01244) 677760**
▥ secretary@chestergolfclub.co.uk
▥ 840
♨ DR Kevan (01244) 677760
⌁ Scott Booth (01244) 671185
▷ 18 L 6461 yds SSS 72
⋈ U H SOC
££ £30 (£35)
⊶ Chester 1 mile
▤ www.chestergolfclub.co.uk

Congleton (1898)
Biddulph Road, Congleton, CW12 3LZ
☎ **(01260) 273540**
⌒ (01260) 290902
▥ congletongolfclub@hotmail.com
▥ 440
♨ D Lancake
⌁ A Preston
▷ 12 L 5119 yds Par 68 SSS 65
⋈ U H SOC
££ £24 (£34)
⊶ 1½ miles E of Congleton on A527

Crewe (1911)
Fields Road, Haslington, Crewe, CW1 5TB
☎ **(01270) 584227 (Steward)**
⌒ (01270) 256482
▥ secretary@crewegolfclub.co.uk
▥ 628
♨ H Taylor (01270) 584099
⌁ D Wheeler (01270) 585032
▷ 18 L 6404 yds SSS 71
⋈ WD–U WE/BH–M SOC
££ £50 After 1pm–£40
⊶ Haslington, 2 miles NE of Crewe Station, off A534. 5 miles W of M6
▤ www.crewegolfclub.co.uk

Davenport (1913)
Worth Hall, Middlewood Road, Poynton, SK12 1TS
☎ **(01625) 876951**
⌒ (01625) 877489
▥ chris@davenportgolf.co.uk
▥ 650
♨ JC Souter (01625) 876951
⌁ T Stevens (01625) 877319
▷ 18 L 6034 yds SSS 69
⋈ U exc Wed & Sat–NA SOC–Tues & Thurs
££ £32 (£43)
⊶ 5 miles S of Stockport. 7 miles N of Macclesfield
⊕ Practice ground and indoor custom fit and training facilities
▤ www.davenportgolf.co.uk

Delamere Forest (1910)
Station Road, Delamere, Northwich, CW8 2JE
☎ **(01606) 883264**

For list of abbreviations and key to symbols see page 647

☎ (01606) 889444
⌨ delamere@btconnect.com
info@delameregolf.co.uk
📖 400
⛳ Michael Towers (01606) 883800
⟋ Martin Brown (01606) 883307
▷ 18 L 6348 yds Par 72 SSS 71
👤 WD–U WE–U (No societies)
££ £40 D–£60 (£55 D–£100)
⊙⊙ 10 miles E of Chester, off B5152
⊕ 9-bay warm-up area; practice bunker; nets
🏠 Herbert Fowler
▤ www.delameregolf.co.uk

Disley   (1889)
Stanley Hall Lane, Disley, Stockport, SK12 2JX
☎ (01663) 764001
⌨ (01663) 762678
⌨ secretary@disleygolfclub.co.uk
📖 500
⛳ P Smallwood
⟋ AG Esplin (01663) 764001
▷ 18 L 5942 yds Par 69
👤 WD–U exc Thurs WE/BH–M
££ £30 (£40)
⊙⊙ 6 miles S of Stockport on A6
🏠 James Braid
▤ www.disleygolfclub.co.uk

Dukinfield   (1913)
Yew Tree Lane, Dukinfield, SK16 5DB
☎ (0161) 338 2340
⌨ (0161) 303 0205
⌨ dgclub@tiscali.co.uk
📖 300 80(L) 65(J)
⛳ R Winterbottom (0161) 338 2340
⟋ D Green (0161) 338 2340
▷ 18 L 5338 yds SSS 66
👤 WD–U exc Wed pm WE–M SOC
££ £20
⊙⊙ 6 miles E of Manchester. M67 Jct 3
▤ www.dukinfieldgolfclub.co.uk

Dunham Forest G&CC   (1961)
Oldfield Lane, Altrincham, WA14 4TY
☎ (0161) 928 2605
⌨ (0161) 929 8975
⌨ enquiries@dunhamforest.com
📖 600
⛳ Mrs A Woolf
⟋ I Wrigley (0161) 928 2727
▷ 18 L 6636 yds SSS 72
👤 WD–U WE/BH SOC–U – phone for availability
££ £58 (£68)
⊙⊙ 1 mile SW of Altrincham. M56 Jct 7
⊕ Driving range, indoor facility
🏠 John Bealey/Dave Thomas
▤ www.dunhamforest.com

Eaton   (1965)
Guy Lane, Waverton, Chester, CH3 7PH
☎ (01244) 335885
⌨ (01244) 335782
⌨ office@eatongolfclub.co.uk
📖 550
⛳ K Brown
⟋ W Tye (01244) 335826
▷ 18 L 6580 yds SSS 72
👤 H SOC

££ On application
⊙⊙ 3 miles SE of Chester, off A41
⊕ Driving range; chipping area
🏠 Donald Steel
▤ www.eatongolfclub.co.uk

Ellesmere Port   (1971)
Public
Chester Road, Childer Thornton, South Wirral, CH66 1QF
☎ (0151) 339 7689

Frodsham   (1990)
Simons Lane, Frodsham, WA6 6HE
☎ (01928) 732159
⌨ (01928) 734070
⌨ office@frodshamgolf.co.uk
📖 600
⛳ El Roylance
⟋ G Tonge (01928) 739442
▷ 18 L 6328 yds SSS 70
👤 WD–U WE/BH–M SOC–WD
££ £40
⊙⊙ 9 miles NE of Chester (A56). M56 Junction 12, 3 miles
🏠 John Day
▤ www.frodshamgolf.co.uk

Gatley   (1911)
Waterfall Farm, Styal Road, Heald Green, Cheadle, SK8 3TW
☎ (0161) 437 2091
⌨ secretary@gatleygolfclub.com
📖 450
⛳ George Griffiths
⟋ J Cheetham (0161) 436 2830
▷ 9 L 5934 yds SSS 68
👤 WD exc Tues–arrange with Pro WE/Tues–NA
££ £25 (£28)
⊙⊙ 7 miles S of Manchester. Manchester Airport 2 miles
⊕ Practice ground and net
▤ www.gatleygolfclub.com

Hale   (1903)
Rappax Road, Hale, Altrincham WA15 0NU
☎ (0161) 980 4225
⌨ secretary@halegolfclub.com
📖 350
⛳ C M Wood
⟋ A Bickerdike (0161) 904 0835
▷ 9 L 5780 yds Par 70 SSS 68
👤 WD–U exc Thurs–NA before 5pm WE/BH–M SOC
££ D–£30
⊙⊙ 2 miles SE of Altrincham M56 J6
▤ www.halegolfclub.com

Hazel Grove   (1913)
Buxton Road, Hazel Grove, Stockport, SK7 6LU
☎ (0161) 483 3217 (Clubhouse)
⌨ secretary@hazelgrovegolfclub.com
📖 550
⛳ DJ Billington (0161) 483 3978
⟋ J Hopley (0161) 483 7272
▷ 18 L 6264 yds SSS 71
👤 U SOC–Mon, Thurs & Fri
££ £35.50 D–£40.50 (£40.50 D–£45.50)
⊙⊙ 3 miles S of Stockport (A6)
▤ www.hazelgrovegolfclub.com

Heaton Moor   (1892)
Mauldeth Road, Heaton Mersey, Stockport, SK4 3NX
☎ (0161) 432 2134
⌨ (0161) 432 2134
⌨ heatonmoorgolfclub@yahoo.co.uk
📖 550
⛳ J Whiston
⟋ SJ Marsh (0161) 432 0846
▷ 18 L 5970 yds Par 70 SSS 69
👤 U SOC WD WE
££ £32 (£40)
⊙⊙ 2 miles from M60 J1, Stockport Town Centre
⊕ Practice nets; practice ground; putting green
▤ www.heatonmoorgolfclub.co.uk

Helsby   (1901)
Tower's Lane, Helsby, WA6 0JB
☎ (01928) 722021
⌨ (01928) 725384
⌨ secathgc@aol.com
📖 640
⛳ LJ Norbury
⟋ M Jones (01928) 725457
▷ 18 L 6265 yds SSS 70
👤 H WE–NA SOC–Tues & Thurs
££ £27.50 (£37)
⊙⊙ 1 mile SE of M56 Junction 14, off Primrose Lane
⊕ Driving range
🏠 James Braid
▤ www.helsbygolfclub.org

Heyrose   (1989)
Proprietary
Budworth Road, Tabley, Knutsford, WA16 0HZ
☎ (01565) 733664
⌨ (01565) 734578
⌨ info@heyrosegolfclub.com
📖 600
⛳ Mrs H Marsh
⟋ P Bills (01565) 734267
▷ 18 L 6499 yds SSS 71
👤 U SOC
££ £26 (£31)
⊙⊙ 3 miles W of Knutsford, off Pickmere Lane, Tabley. M6 Junction 19, 1 mile
⊕ Driving range; practice bunker; practice net; pitching practice area
🏠 CN Bridge, B.Sc Hons
▤ www.heyrosegolfclub.com

Houldsworth   (1910)
Houldsworth Park, Houldsworth Street, Reddish, Stockport, SK5 6BN
☎ (0161) 442 1712
⌨ (0161) 947 9678
⌨ secretary@houldsworthgolfclub .co.uk
📖 625
⛳ G Foy (0161) 442 1712
⟋ D Marsh (0161) 442 1714
▷ 18 L 6209 yds Par 70 SSS 70
👤 U SOC
££ £30 (£36)
⊙⊙ 4 miles S of Manchester, M60 Jct 26
🏠 Redesigned 1992 by Dave Thomas
▤ www.houldsworthgolfclub.co.uk

Knights Grange (1983)
Public
Grange Lane, Winsford, CW7 2PT
☎ **(01606) 552780**
✉ p.littler@valeroyal.gov.uk
🏌 Mrs P Littler (Mgr)
🏁 18 L 6253 yds SSS 70
👥 U SOC
££ £10.10 (£12.40) Juniors playing
with adult half price
🚗 Knights Grange Sports Complex.
M6 Junctions 18 & 19

Knutsford (1891)
Mereheath Lane, Knutsford, WA16 6HS
☎ **(01565) 633355**
🖂 250
🏁 DM Burgess
🏁 9 L 6203 yds SSS 70
👥 H exc Wed–NA SOC
££ £28 (£35)
🚗 Knutsford ½ mile

Leigh (1906)
Kenyon Hall, Broseley Lane, Culcheth,
Warrington, WA3 4BG
☎ **(01925) 763130**
🖂 (01925) 765097
✉ golf@leighgolf.fsnet.co.uk
🖂 850
🏁 DA Taylor (01925) 762943
🏁 A Baguley (01925) 762013
🏁 18 L 5892 yds SSS 69
👥 U H SOC
££ D–£30 (£40)
🚗 5 m NE of Warrington on B5207
🏛 James Braid
🖥 www.leighgolf.co.uk

Lymm (1907)
Whitbarrow Road, Lymm, WA13 9AN
☎ **(01925) 755020**
🖂 (01925) 755020
✉ lymmgolfclub@btconnect.com
🖂 400 100(L) 75(J) 50(S)
🏁 TH Glover
🏁 S McCarthy (01925) 755054
🏁 18 L 6351 yds SSS 71
👥 WD–H WE–M SOC–Wed
££ £32 (£36)
🚗 5 m SE of Warrington. M6 Jct 20
🖥 www.lymm-golf-club.co.uk

Macclesfield (1889)
The Hollins, Macclesfield, SK11 7EA
☎ **(01625) 423227**
🖂 (01625) 260061
✉ secretary@maccgolfclub.co.uk
🖂 600
🏁 B Littlewood
🏁 T Taylor
🏁 18 L 5714 yds SSS 68
👥 WD/BH–H WE–M SOC–WD
££ £30 (£40)
🚗 SE edge of Macclesfield, off A523
🏛 Hawtree
🖥 www.maccgolfclub.co.uk

Malkins Bank Golf Course
(1980)
Public
Betchton Road, Malkins Bank, Sandbach,
CW11 4XN
☎ **(01270) 765931**

🖂 (01270) 764730
✉ phil.pleasance@congleton.gov.uk
🏁 P Pleasance (Mgr) (01270) 760233
🏁 D Hackney
🏁 18 L 6005 yds SSS 69
👥 U SOC
££ £12 (£14)
🚗 2 miles S of Sandbach via
A534/A533. M6 Junction 17
⊕ Practice area; net; putting green
🏛 Hawtree & Son
🖥 www.congleton.gov.uk

Marple (1892)
Barnsfold Road, Hawk Green, Marple,
Stockport, SK6 7EL
☎ **(0161) 427 2311 Ext 1**
(0161) 427 9525 Ext 1
🖂 (0161) 427 2311/ (0161) 427 95
✉ marple.golfclub@virgin.net
🖂 415 84(L) 90(J)
🏁 R Hough (0161) 427 2311/
427 9525
🏁 D Myers (0161) 4271195/4272311
Ext 6
🏁 18 L 5554 yds SSS 67
👥 WD–U exc Thurs–NA WE/BH–M
SOC
££ £30 (£40)
🚗 2 m from High Lane North, off A6
🖥 www.marplegolfclub.co.uk

Mellor & Townscliffe (1894)
Tarden, Gibb Lane, Mellor, Stockport,
SK6 5NA
☎ **(0161) 427 9700 (Clubhouse)**
🖂 (0161) 427 9700
🖂 600
🏁 JV Dixon (0161) 427 2208
🏁 G Broadley (0161) 427 5759
🏁 18 L 5925 yds SSS 69
👥 WD–U WE–M SOC
££ £24 (£32)
🚗 7 miles SE of Stockport, off A626
🖥 www.mellorgolf.co.uk

Mere G&CC (1934)
Chester Road, Mere, Knutsford, WA16 6LJ
☎ **(01565) 830155**
🖂 (01565) 830713
✉ enquiries@meregolf.co.uk
🖂 355 103(L) 62(J)
🏁 J Leeman
🏁 P Eyre (01565) 830219
🏁 18 L 6817 yds SSS 73
👥 WE/BH–M Wed & Fri–M
Mon/Tues/Thurs–H SOC
££ D–£75 summer D–£55 winter
🚗 1 mile E of M6 Junction 19. 2 miles
W of M56 Junction 7
⊕ Driving range-members and green
fees only; putting green; practice
area; buggies
🏛 James Braid
🖥 www.meregolf.co.uk

Mersey Valley (1995)
Proprietary
Warrington Road, Bold Heath, Widnes,
WA8 3XL
☎ **(0151) 424 6060**
🖂 (0151) 257 9097
✉ chrismgerrard@yahoo.co.uk

🖂 550
🏁 RM Bush (Man Dir)
Alan Robinson (Sec)
🏁 Advanced PGA Pro Andy
Stevenson
🏁 18 L 6511 yds SSS 71
👥 U SOC welcome
££ £20 (£25)
🚗 M62 Junction 7, 2 miles
🏛 RMR Bush
🖥 www.merseyvalleygolfclub.co.uk

Mobberley (1995)
Burleyhurst Lane, Mobberley, Knutsford,
WA16 7JZ
☎ **(01505) 880188**
🖂 (01505) 880178
✉ enquiries@mobgolfclub.co.uk
🏁 Mike Sheehan
🏁 Mr Gary Donnison (Tournament
Pro)
🏁 9 L 5542 yds Par 67
👥 U SOC
££ £16.50 (£20)
🚗 Mobberley. M56 Junction 6
🖥 www.mobgolfclub.co.uk

Mollington Grange (1999)
Townfield Lane, Mollington, Chester,
CH1 6NJ
☎ **(01244) 851185**
🖂 (01244) 851349
✉ info@mollingtongolfclub.co.uk
🖂 500
🏁 Ray Stringer
🏁 Alan Gibson
🏁 18 L 6696 yds Par 72 SSS 72
👥 WD–U WE–U before noon
SOC–WD/WE
££ £30 (£35)
🚗 2 miles N of Chester on A540. End
of M56, 2 miles
⊕ Driving range; putting green;
chipping area
🏛 Garry Chubb
🖥 www.mollingtongolfclub.co.uk

Mottram Hall Hotel (1991)
Wilmslow Road, Mottram St Andrew,
Prestbury, SK10 4QT
☎ **(01625) 820064**
🖂 (01625) 829284
✉ mhgolf@devere-hotels.com
🖂 300
🏁 Tim Hudspith (Head Golf &
Leisure)
🏁 M Turnock/T Maxwell
🏁 18 L 7006 yds SSS 74
👥 U H SOC
££ £60 (summer); £30 (winter)
🚗 4 miles SE of Wilmslow
⊕ Driving range; short game area; 2
putting greens
🏛 Dave Thomas
🖥 www.deveregolf.co.uk

Peover (1996)
Proprietary
Plumley Moor Road, Lower Peover,
WA16 9SE
☎ **(01565) 723337**
🖂 (01565) 723311
✉ mail@peovergolfclub.co.uk

☐ 350
🏌 PA Naylor (Man Dir), J Baker (Sec)
✓ Mike Grantham (07976) 894357
➤ 18 L 6702 yds Par 72
👥 U SOC–WD
££ £25 (£30)
🚗 3 miles SW of Knutsford, off A556. M6 Junction 19
🏠 Peter Naylor
🖥 www.peovergolfclub.co.uk

Portal G&CC   (1992)
Cobblers Cross Lane, Tarporley, CW6 0DJ
☎ (01829) 733933
✉ enquiries@portalgolf.co.uk

Portal Premier   (1990)
Forest Road, Tarporley, CW6 0JA
☎ (01829) 733884
✉ enquiries.premier@portalgolf.co.uk

Poulton Park   (1978)
Dig Lane, Cinnamon Brow, Warrington, WA2 0SH
☎ (01925) 812034/822802
🖥 (01925) 822802
✉ secretary@poultonparkgolfclub.co.uk
☐ 360
🏌 Jeff Perkin (01925) 822802
✓ Ian Orrell (01925) 825220
➤ 9 L 5048 m Par 68 SSS 67
👥 WD–NA 5–6pm WE–NA before 2pm
££ £20 (£22)
🚗 Off Crab Lane, Fearnhead (M6 Jct 21)
🖥 www.poultonparkgolfclub.co.uk

Prestbury   (1920)
Macclesfield Road, Prestbury, Macclesfield, SK10 4BJ
☎ (01625) 828241
🖥 (01625) 828241
✉ office@prestburygolfclub.com
☐ 650
🏌 N Young (01625) 828241
✓ N Summerfield (01625) 828242
➤ 18 L 6371 yds SSS 71
👥 WD–I WE–M SOC–Thurs
££ £50
🚗 2 miles NW of Macclesfield
⊕ Practice ground inc. driving range
🏠 HS Colt
🖥 www.prestburygolfclub.com

Pryors Hayes   (1993)
Proprietary
Willington Road, Oscroft, Tarvin, CH3 8NL
☎ (01829) 741250
🖥 (01829) 749077
✉ info@pryors-hayes.co.uk
☐ 600
🏌 JM Quinn
✓ M Redrup (01829) 740140
➤ 18 L 5915 yds Par 69 SSS 69
👥 U SOC
££ £30 (£40)
🚗 Tarvin, 5 miles E of Chester
🏠 John Day
🖥 www.pryorshayes.com

Queens Park   (1985)
Public
Queens Park Drive, Crewe, CW2 7SB
☎ (01270) 662378

Reaseheath   (1987)
Reaseheath College, Reaseheath, Nantwich, CW5 6DF
☎ (01270) 625131
🖥 (01270) 625665
✉ johnsoddy@aol.co.uk
☐ 450
🏌 John Soddy (01270) 629869
➤ 9 L 3668 yds SSS 58
👥 U SOC–WD/WE
££ Winter: D–£8 Summer: D–£10
🚗 2 miles NW of Nantwich on College campus
🏠 D Mortram
🖥 www.reaseheath.ac.uk/golf

Reddish Vale   (1912)
Southcliffe Road, Reddish, Stockport, SK5 7EE
☎ (0161) 480 2359
🖥 (0161) 480 2359
✉ admin@reddishvalegolfclub.co.uk
☐ 550
🏌 G Lee
✓ RE Freeman (0161) 480 2359
➤ 18 L 6086 yds SSS 69
👥 WD–U exc 12.30–1.30pm–M WE–M SOC–WD
££ £28 (£40)
🚗 1 mile NNE of Stockport
🏠 Dr A MacKenzie
🖥 www.reddishvalegolfclub.co.uk

Ringway   (1909)
Hale Mount, Hale Road, Hale Barns, Altrincham WA15 8SW
☎ (0161) 980 2630
🖥 (0161) 980 4414
✉ enquiries@ringwaygolfclub.co.uk
☐ 375 175(L) 90(J)
🏌 Mrs F Cornelius
✓ N Ryan
➤ 18 L 6482 yds SSS 72
👥 Tues–NA before 3pm, Fri–M, Sun–NA before 12.30pm, SOC–Thurs
££ £40 (£50)
🚗 8 miles S of Manchester, off M56 Junction 6 (A538)
⊕ 375
🏠 Harry Colt/James Braid
🖥 www.ringwaygolfclub.co.uk

Romiley   (1897)
Goosehouse Green, Romiley, Stockport, SK6 4LJ
☎ (0161) 430 2392
🖥 (0161) 430 7258
✉ office@romileygolfclub.org
☐ 625
🏌 DH Mason
✓ (0161) 430 7122
➤ 18 L 6412 yds Par 70 SSS 71
👥 U SOC
££ £30 (£40)
🚗 Station 3/4 mile (B6104)
🖥 www.romileygolfclub.org

Runcorn   (1909)
Clifton Road, Runcorn, WA7 4SU
☎ (01928) 572093 (Members)
🖥 (01928) 574214
✉ secretary@runcorngolfclub.co.uk
☐ 375 80(L) 60(J)
🏌 BR Griffiths (01928) 574214
✓ K Hartley (01928) 564791
➤ 18 L 6035 yds SSS 69
👥 WD–U H exc comp days WE–M SOC–Mon & Fri only
££ £30
🚗 Runcorn (A557). M56 Junction 12
🖥 www.runcorngolfclub.co.uk

Sale   (1913)
Sale Lodge, Golf Road, Sale, M33 2XU
☎ (0161) 973 1638
🖥 (0161) 962 4217
✉ mail@salegolfclub.com
☐ 675
🏌 CJ Boyes (Hon Sec)
✓ M Stewart (0161) 973 1730
➤ 18 L 6301 yds Par 70 SSS 70
👥 SOC–WD–WE
££ £40 (£40)
🚗 N of Sale. M60 Junction 6
🖥 www.salegolfclub.com

Sandbach   (1895)
Middlewich Road, Sandbach, CW11 1FH
☎ (01270) 762117

Sandiway   (1921)
Chester Road, Sandiway, CW8 2DJ
☎ (01606) 883247
🖥 (01606) 888548
✉ manager@sandiwaygolf.co.uk
☐ 730
🏌 K Melia (01606) 880811
✓ W Laird (01606) 883180
➤ 18 L 6435 yds SSS 71
👥 H SOC
££ £45 (£55)
🚗 15 miles E of Chester on A556, 10½ miles W of M6 J19 on A556
🏠 Ted Ray
🖥 www.sandiwaygolf.co.uk

Stamford   (1901)
Oakfield House, Huddersfield Road, Stalybridge, SK15 3PY
☎ (01457) 832126
✉ admin@stamford.golfclub.co.uk
☐ 600
🏌 J Kitchen
✓ M Smith (01457) 832126
➤ 18 L 5701 yds SSS 68
👥 WD–U WE comp days–after 2.30pm SOC–WD
££ £25 (£25)
🚗 NE boundary of Stalybridge on B6175
🖥 www.stamfordgolfclub.co.uk

Stockport   (1905)
Offerton Road, Offerton, Stockport, SK2 5HL
☎ (0161) 427 8369
🖥 (0161) 427 8369
✉ info@stockportgolf.co.uk
☐ 510

J S Howarth
M Peel
18 L 6326 yds SSS 71
SOC–WD
£€ £45 (£55)
4 miles SE of Stockport on A627
Herd/Hawtree
www.stockportgolf.co.uk

Styal (1994)
Proprietary
Station Road, Styal, SK9 4JN
☎ (01625) 531359 (Bookings)
(01625) 416373
gtraynor@styalgolf.co.uk
850
G Traynor (01625) 530063 ext 214
S Forrest (01625) 528910
18 L 6238 yds Par 70 SSS 70
9 9 L 1203 yds Par 27
U SOC
£€ 18 hole course £24 (£30) Par 3
course £8 for 9, £12 for 18
2 miles from M56 Junction 5.
Manchester Airport 5 mins
Floodlit driving range; tuition;
buggies for hire
T Holmes
www.styalgolf.co.uk

Sutton Hall
Proprietary
Aston Lane, Sutton Weaver, Runcorn,
WA7 3ED
☎ (01928) 790747
(01928) 759174
suttonhall@tiscali.co.uk
600 30(J)
M Faulkner
J Hope (01928) 714872
18 L 6618 yds Par 72
U SOC–WD
£€ £20 (£25)
2 miles E of M56 Junction 12
Steve Wundke

The Tytherington Club
(1986)
Macclesfield, SK10 2JP
☎ (01625) 506000
(01625) 506040
tytherington.events
@theclubcompany.com
750
Mark Law
Anthony Haste 07505 816755
18 L 6765 yds SSS 73 Par 72 143
acres
U H SOC–WD
£€ £39 D–£59 (£49 D–£69)
N of Macclesfield (A523)
Driving range, Putting Green, Short
game practice area, Golf Buggies.
Thomas/Dawson
www.theclubcompany.com

Upton-by-Chester (1934)
Upton Lane, Chester, CH2 1EE
☎ (01244) 381183
(01244) 376955
secretary@uptongc.com
750
F Hopley (01244) 381183

S Dewhurst (01244) 381183
18 L 5850 yds SSS 68
U SOC–WD
£€ £25 D–£35 (£25 D–£35)
Off Liverpool road, near 'Frog' PH
JW (Bill) Davies
www.uptonbychestergolfclub.co.uk

Vale Royal Abbey (1998)
Whitegate, Northwich, CW8 2BA
☎ (01606) 301291
(01606) 301414
golf@vra.co.uk
440
Steve Dunlop
D Ingman (01606) 301702
18 holes Par 72 SSS 71
M
2 miles W of Hartford, off A556
Simon Gidman
www.vra.co.uk

Vicars Cross (1939)
Tarvin Road, Great Barrow, Chester,
CH3 7HN
☎ (01244) 335174
(01244) 335686
manager@vicarscrossgolf.co.uk
800
Mrs K Hunt
G Beddon (01244) 335595
18 L 6446 yds SSS 71
U SOC–Tue, Thur, Fri
£€ £35 (£40)
3 miles E of Chester on A51
Driving range
E Parr
www.vicarscrossgolf.co.uk

Walton Hall (1972)
Public
Warrington Road, Higher Walton,
Warrington, WA4 5LU
☎ (01925) 266775
theclub@waltonhallgolfclub.co.uk
150
Dave Johnson (01925) 266775
J Jackson (01925) 263061
18 L 6647 yds Par 72 SSS 73
U SOC
£€ £13.75 (£18)
2 m S of Warrington. M56 J10/11
Dave Thomas/Peter Alliss
www.waltonhallgolfclub.co.uk

Warrington (1903)
Hill Warren, London Road, Appleton,
WA4 5HR
☎ (01925) 261775
(01925) 265933
secretary@warringtongolfclub
.co.uk
875
D S Macphee (01925) 261775
R Mackay (01925) 265431
18 L 6210 yds SSS 71
U SOC–Wed
£€ £35 (£40)
3 miles S of Warrington on A49.
M56 Junction 10
James Braid/Creative Golf Design
www.warringtongolfclub.co.uk

Werneth Low (1912)
Werneth Low Road, Gee Cross, Hyde,
SK14 3AF
☎ (0161) 368 2503

Widnes (1924)
Highfield Road, Widnes, WA8 7DT
☎ (0151) 424 2995
(0151) 495 2849
office@widnesgolfclub.co.uk
600
Miss Nicola Farrington
J O'Brien (0151) 420 7467
18 L 5729 yds SSS 68
WD–H WE–H NA on comp days
£€ D–£24 (£33)
Station 1/2 mile. M62 Junction 7

Wilmslow (1889)
Great Warford, Mobberley, Knutsford,
WA16 7AY
☎ (01565) 872148
(01565) 872172
info@wilmslowgolfclub.co.uk
760
Mrs MI Padfield
LJ Nowicki (01565) 873620
18 L 6635 yds SSS 72
U H exc Wed–NA before 3pm
£€ £45 (£55)
3 miles W of Alderley Edge
www.wilmslowgolfclub.co.uk

Woodside
Knutsford Road, Holmes Chapel, CW4 8HT
☎ (01477) 532388

Cornwall

Bowood Park (1992)
Valley Truckle, Lanteglos, Camelford,
PL32 9RF
☎ (01840) 213017
(01840) 212622
info@bowoodpark.org
300
Norman Street
Matt Stewart
18 L 6692 yds SSS 72
H (phone first) SOC WD WE
£€ From £20 (£22) to £28 (£30)
2 miles SW of Camelford, off A39,
on to B3266
Driving range; chipping green; 9
hole putting green
Bob Sandow
www.bowoodpark.org

Bude & North Cornwall
(1891)
Burn View, Bude, EX23 8DA
☎ (01288) 352006
(01288) 356855
secretary@budegolf.co.uk
682 106(L) 38(J)
Mrs PM Ralph
M Yeo (01288) 353635
18 L 6006 yds Par 71 SSS 70
WD–U after 9.30am
WE–restricted

For list of abbreviations and key to symbols see page 647

££   D–£30 (+BH £30)
⚘   Bude town centre
⊕   Buggies
🏠   Tom Dunn
▤   www.budegolf.co.uk

Budock Vean Hotel Golf & Country Club   (1932)
Mawnan Smith, Falmouth, TR11 5LG
☎   (01326) 252102
🖴   (01326) 250892
✉   relax@budockvean.co.uk
🕮   150
⚐   Keith Rashleigh (01326) 377091
     e-mail: keith.rashleigh@talktalk.net
✓   A Ramsden (Golf Mgr)
⮞   9 L 5286 yds Par 68 SSS 66
👤   H
££   D–£23 (D–£27)
⚘   Close to the village of Mawnan
     Smith and situated on Helford
     River about 5 miles from Falmouth
🏠   James Braid

Cape Cornwall G&CC   (1990)
St Just, Penzance, TR19 7NL
☎   (01736) 788611
✉   info@capecornwall.com

Carlyon Bay   (1926)
Proprietary
Carlyon Bay, St Austell, PL25 3RD
☎   (01726) 814250
🖴   (01726) 814250
✉   golf@carlyonbay.com
🕮   500
⚐   P Martin
✓   M Rowe (01726) 814228
⮞   18 L 6597 yds SSS 71
👤   U–book with Pro
££   £25–£42
⚘   2 miles E of St Austell
⊕   Large practice ground; golf tuition
     holidays, health spa
🏠   J Hamilton Stutt
▤   www.carlyongolf.com

China Fleet CC   (1991)
Saltash, PL12 6LJ
☎   (01752) 848668
🖴   (01752) 848456
✉   golf@china-fleet.co.uk
🕮   600
⚐   Mrs L Goddard
✓   Domonic Reehag (01752) 854665
⮞   18 L 6551 yds SSS 72
👤   H–by arrangement SOC
££   On application
⚘   1 mile from Tamar Bridge, off A38
⊕   Floodlit driving range
🏠   Martin Hawtree
▤   www.china-fleet.co.uk

Falmouth   (1894)
Proprietary
Swanpool Road, Falmouth, TR11 5BQ
☎   (01326) 311262/314296
🖴   (01326) 317783
✉   clubsec@falmouthgolfclub.com
🕮   500
⚐   (01326) 314296
✓   N Rogers

⮞   18 L 6037 yds Par 71 SSS 70
👤   U SOC
££   £32 D–£38
⚘   ¼ mile W of Swanpool Beach
⊕   Driving range
▤   www.falmouthgolfclub.com

Isles of Scilly   (1904)
Carn Morval, St Mary's, Isles of Scilly,
TR21 0NF
☎   (01720) 422692
🕮   170
⚐   Peter Leahy (Hon Sec)
⮞   9 L 5898 yds Par 73 SSS 69
👤   U
££   £22
⚘   Hughtown 1½ miles
🏠   Horace Hutchinson

Killiow   (1987)
Proprietary
Killiow, Kea, Truro, TR3 6AG
☎   (01872) 270246
🖴   (01872) 240915
✉   killiowsec@yahoo.co.uk
🕮   500
⚐   J Crowson (01872) 266876
⮞   18 L 6266 yds Par 72 SSS 71
👤   U
££   £15.50–£25 D–£30
⚘   2½ miles S of Truro, off A39
⊕   Driving range

Lanhydrock Hotel & Golf Club   (1991)
Proprietary
Lostwithiel Road, Bodmin, PL30 5AQ
☎   (01208) 262570
🖴   (01208) 262579
✉   info@lanhydrockhotel.com
🕮   300
⚐   G Bond (Dir)
✓   Richard O'Hanlon
⮞   18 L 6100 yds Par 70 SSS 70
👤   U SOC H
££   On application (see web page)
⚘   A30 exit for Bodmin; follow tourist
     signs for Lanhydrock then hotel; 1
     mile S of Bodmin on B3268
⊕   Driving range
🏠   J Hamilton Stutt
▤   www.lanhydrockhotel.com

Launceston   (1927)
St Stephen, Launceston, PL15 8HF
☎   (01566) 773442
🖴   (01566) 777506
✉   secretary@launcestongolfclub
     .co.uk
🕮   550
⚐   PM Jones
✓   J Tozer (01566) 775359
⮞   18 L 6385 yds Par 70 SSS 70
👤   WD–U H WE by prior
     arrangement SOC –WD
££   £28 D–£35
⚘   1 mile N of Launceston, off Bude
     road
🏠   J Hamilton Stutt
▤   www.launcestongolfclub.co.uk

Looe   (1933)
Bin Down, Looe, PL13 1PX
☎   (01503) 240239
🖴   (01503) 240864
✉   enquiries@looegolfclub.co.uk
🕮   450
⚐   T Day (Hon)
✓   J Bowen
⮞   18 L 5940 yds Par 70 SSS 69
👤   U SOC
££   On application
⚘   3 miles E of Looe
🏠   Harry Vardon
▤   www.looegolfclub.co.uk

Lostwithiel G&CC   (1990)
Lower Polscoe, Lostwithiel, PL22 0HQ
☎   (01208) 873550
🖴   (01208) 873479
✉   reception@golf-hotel.co.uk
🕮   350
⚐   D Higman
✓   A Hooper (01208) 873822
⮞   18 L 5907 yds Par 72
👤   U SOC
££   £25 (£30)
⚘   ½ mile E of Lostwithiel, off A390
⊕   Driving range
🏠   Stuart Wood
▤   www.golf-hotel.co.uk

Merlin   (1991)
Proprietary
Mawgan Porth, Newquay, TR8 4DN
☎   (01841) 540222
✉   rossoliver@merlingolfcourse
     .co.uk

Mullion   (1895)
Cury, Helston, TR12 7BP
☎   (01326) 240276
🖴   (01326) 241527
✉   secretary@mulliongolfclub.plus
     .com
🕮   700
⚐   G Fitter (01326) 240685
✓   I Harris (01326) 241176
⮞   18 L 6083 yds SSS 70
👤   H (restricted comp days and open
     days) SOC–WD
££   £30
⚘   6 miles S of Helston
⊕   Golf academy
🏠   W Sich
▤   www.mulliongolfclub.co.uk

Newquay   (1890)
Tower Road, Newquay, TR7 1LT
☎   (01637) 872091
🖴   (01637) 874066
✉   newquaygolf@btconnect.com
🕮   600
⚐   J Gilbert (01637) 874354
✓   Joel Cant (01637) 874830
⮞   18 L 6151 yds SSS 69
👤   WD/Sat–H Sun–H SOC
££   £30 (£35)
⚘   Newquay town centre
🏠   HS Colt
▤   www.newquaygolfclub.co.uk

Perranporth (1927)
Budnic Hill, Perranporth, TR6 0AB
- ☎ **(01872) 573701**
- ✉ secretary@perranporthgolfclub.co.uk
- 📖 600
- ♟ DC Mugford
- ✓ DC Michell (01872) 572317
- ► 18 L 6296 yds SSS 72
- ♟ WD–U WE–H SOC
- ££ £35 (£40)
- ♣ ¹/₂ mile NW of Perranporth
- ⊕ Golf Academy (computerised)
- ♮ James Braid
- 🖥 www.perranporthgolfclub.co.uk

Porthpean (1992)
Proprietary
Porthpean, St Austell, PL26 6AY
- ☎ **(01726) 64613**
- 📞 (01726) 64613
- ✉ info@porthpeangolfclub.co.uk
- 📖 430
- ♟ Roger French
- ► 18 L 5474 yds Par 68 SSS 67
- ♟ U SOC
- ££ £20
- ♣ 2 miles SE of St Austell on coast
- ⊕ Driving range
- 🖥 www.porthpeangolfclub.co.uk

Praa Sands Golf and Country Club (1971)
Public
Praa Sands, Penzance, TR20 9TQ
- ☎ **(01736) 763445**
- 📞 (01736) 763741
- ✉ praasands2@haulfryn.co.uk
- 📖 100
- ♟ Simon Spencer 01736 762201
- ► 9 L 4122 yds Par 62 SSS 60 (men)
  Par 64 SSS 65 (ladies)
- ♟ U exc Sun am
- ££ £18.50 D–£27
- ♣ 7 miles E of Penzance on A394
  Penzance-Helston road
- ⊕ Practice net; chipping green;
  putting green
- ♮ RA Hamilton
- 🖥 www.praa-sands.com

Roserrow (1996)
Proprietary
St Minver, Wadebridge, PL27 6QT
- ☎ **(01208) 863000**
- 📞 (01208) 863002
- ✉ mail@roserrow.co.uk
- 📖 300
- ♟ Sarah Sanderson
- ✓ John Witcomb
- ► 18 L 6494 yds Par 72 SSS 72
- ♟ U SOC
- ££ Winter £18; spring £22 D–£28,
  summer £28
- ♣ Polzeath, 15 min from A30
- ⊕ Driving range; Explanar tuition with
  Pro
- ♮ David Feherty
- 🖥 www.roserrow.co.uk

St Austell (1911)
Tregongeeves Lane, St Austell, PL26 7DS
- ☎ **(01726) 74756**

- 📞 (01726) 71978
- ✉ office@staustellgolf.co.uk
- 📖 550
- ♟ P Clemo
- ✓ T Pitts (01726) 68621
- ► 18 L 6091 yds SSS 69
- ♟ SOC U
- ££ On application
- ♣ 1¹/₂ miles W of St Austell
- ⊕ Covered floodlit driving range
- 🖥 www.staustellgolf.co.uk

St Enodoc (1890)
Rock, Wadebridge, PL27 6LD
- ☎ **(01208) 863216**
- 📞 (01208) 862976
- ✉ enquiries@st-enodoc.co.uk
- 📖 1360
- ♟ TD Clagett
- ✓ NJ Williams (01208) 862402
- ► Church 18 L 6547 yds SSS 70
  Holywell 18 L 4103 yds SSS 61
- ♟ Church H–max 24 SOC
  Holywell–U
- ££ Church £55 (£65) Holywell £19
  (£19)
- ♣ 6 miles NW of Wadebridge
- ⊕ Driving range
- ♮ James Braid
- 🖥 www.st-enodoc.co.uk

St Kew (1993)
Proprietary
St Kew Highway, Wadebridge, Bodmin,
PL30 3EF
- ☎ **(01208) 841500**
- 📞 (01208) 841500
- ✉ stkewgolf@btconnect.com
- 📖 350
- ♟ J Brown (Prop)
- ✓ Mike Derry
- ► 9 L 4543 yds SSS 62
- ♟ U SOC WE booking after midday
- ££ 9: £11; 18: £16
- ♣ 2¹/₂ miles N of Wadebridge on A39
- ⊕ Covered driving range; Shop;
  Showers; Food all day
- ♮ David Derry

Tehidy Park (1922)
Camborne, TR14 0HH
- ☎ **(01209) 842208**
- 📞 (01209) 842208
- ✉ secretary-manager@tehidyparkgolfclub.co.uk
- 📖 750
- ♟ I J Veale (Sec/Mgr)
- ✓ J Lamb (01209) 842914
- ► 18 L 6241 yds SSS 71
- ♟ H SOC
- ££ £30 (£40)
- ♣ 3 miles N of Camborne
- ⊕ Practice ground; putting green;
  buggies
- ♮ CK Cotton
- 🖥 www.tehidyparkgolfclub.co.uk

Tregenna Castle Hotel (1982)
St Ives, TR26 2DE
- ☎ **(01736) 795254**
- 📞 (01736) 796066
- ✉ hotel@tregenna-castle.co.uk

- 📖 297
- ♟ S Davey
- ► 14 L 1846 yds Par 42
- ♟ U SOC
- ££ On application
- ♣ St Ives 1 mile, off A3074
- 🖥 www.tregenna-castle.co.uk

Treloy (1991)
Treloy, Newquay, TR8 4JN
- ☎ **(01637) 878554**
- 📖 145
- ♟ J Paull
- ► 9 L 2143 yds SSS 32
- ♟ U SOC
- ££ 9: £9.50 18: £14.50
- ♣ 2 miles E of Newquay on A3059
- ⊕ Driving range
- ♮ MRM Sandow
- 🖥 www.treloygolfclub.co.uk

Trethorne (1991)
Kennards House, Launceston, PL15 8QE
- ☎ **(01566) 86903**
- ✉ gen@trethornegolfclub.com

Trevose (1924)
Constantine Bay, Padstow, PL28 8JB
- ☎ **(01841) 520208**
- 📞 (01841) 521057
- ✉ info@trevose-gc.co.uk
- 📖 1500
- ♟ P Gammon (Prop),
  N Gammon (Sec/Mgr)
- ✓ G Lenaghan (01841) 520261
- ► 18 L 6863 yds SSS 72
  9 L 3031 yds SSS 35
  9 L 1360 yds SSS 29
- ♟ H SOC
- ££ On application
- ♣ 4 miles W of Padstow
- ⊕ 3 & 4 ball times restricted until
  11am
- ♮ HS Colt
- 🖥 www.trevose-gc.co.uk

Truro (1937)
Treliske, Truro, TR1 3LG
- ☎ **(01872) 272640/278684**
- 📞 (01872) 225972
- ✉ trurogolfclub@tiscali.co.uk
- 📖 1000
- ♟ HWD Leicester
  (Sec/Mgr) (01872) 278684
- ✓ NK Bicknell (01872) 276595
- ► 18 L 5306 yds SSS 66
- ♟ U H SOC
- ££ £25 (£30)
- ♣ 1 mile W of Truro on A390
- ♮ Colt/Alison/Morrison
- 🖥 www.trurogolf.co.uk

West Cornwall (1889)
Lelant, St Ives, TR26 3DZ
- ☎ **(01736) 753401**
- 📞 (01736) 758468
- ✉ secretary@westcornwallgolfclub.co.uk
- 📖 825
- ♟ GM Evans
- ✓ J Broadway (01736) 753177
- ► 18 L 5902 yds SSS 69
- ♟ H SOC

££ £35 (£40)
🚗 2 miles E of St Ives
⊕ Practice ground
🏠 Rev RF Tyack
🖥 www.westcornwallgolfclub.co.uk

Whitsand Bay Hotel   (1906)
Portwrinkle, Torpoint, PL11 3BU
☎ **(01503) 230276 (Clubhouse)**

Cumbria

Alston Moor   (1906)
The Hermitage, Alston, CA9 3DB
☎ **(01434) 381675**
🖥 (01434) 381675
📖 106
🏌 Paul Parkin (01434) 381704
↟ 10 L 5380 yds SSS 66
👤 U SOC
££ D–£13 (D–£15)
🚗 2 miles S of Alston on B6277
🖥 www.cybermoor.org.guest.golf

Appleby   (1903)
Brackenber Moor, Appleby, CA16 6LP
☎ **(017683) 51432**
🖥 (017683) 52773
📧 enquiries@applebygolfclub.co.uk
📖 740
🏌 JMF Doig (Hon)
↗ Andrew Sowerby
↟ 18 L 5993 yds SSS 69
👤 U H
££ £23 (£29)
🚗 2 miles SE of Appleby. ¹/₂ mile N of A66
⊕ Practice area
🏠 Willie Fernie
🖥 www.applebygolfclub.co.uk

Barrow   (1922)
Rakesmoor Lane, Hawcoat, Barrow-in-Furness, LA14 4QB
☎ **(01229) 825444**
📧 barrowgolf@supanet.com
📖 505 91(L) 67(J)
🏌 S G Warbrick (Hon)
↗ Michael Newton 01229 832121
↟ 18 L 6184 yds Par 71 SSS 70
👤 U H Ladies Day–Fri SOC
££ D–£28 (£30 inc BH)
🚗 2 miles E of Barrow, off A590
🏠 AM Duncan
🖥 www.barrowgolfclub.co.uk

Brampton (Talkin Tarn)
(1909)
Tarn Road, Brampton, CA8 1HN
☎ **(0169) 772255**
🖥 (0169) 7741487
📧 secretary@bramptongolfclub.com
📖 750
🏌 IJ Meldrum (0169) 772255
↗ S Wilkinson (016977) 2000
↟ 18 L 6407 yds Par 72 SSS 71
👤 U
££ £30, D–£38 (+BH £36, D–£45)
🚗 B6413, 1 mile SE of Brampton
⊕ Driving range

🏠 James Braid
🖥 www.bramptongolfclub.com

Brayton Park   (1986)
Pay and play
The Garth, Home Farm, Brayton, Aspatria, CA7 3SX
☎ **(01697) 323539**
📖 60
🏌 J Gibson (01697) 322517
↗ Graham Batey (01697) 332072
↟ 9 L 2559 yds SSS 65
👤 U
££ 9: £7; 18: £12
🚗 1 mile N of Aspatria. 10 miles N of Cockermouth
🏠 JB Ward

Carlisle   (1908)
Aglionby, Carlisle, CA4 8AG
☎ **(01228) 513029**
🖥 (01228) 513303
📧 secretary@carlislegolfclub.org
📖 700
🏌 Roger Johnson
↗ Graeme Lisle (01228) 513241
↟ 18 L 6263 yds SSS 70
👤 WD–U exc Tues–NA Sat–M Sun–restricted SOC–Mon/Wed/Thur/Fri
££ £40 D–£60 (£50)
🚗 ¹/₂ mile E of M6 Jct 43, on A69
🏠 Mackenzie Ross
🖥 www.carlislegolfclub.org

Carus Green   (1996)
Proprietary
Burneside Road, Kendal, LA9 6EB
☎ **(01539) 721097**
🖥 (01539) 721097
📧 info@carusgreen.co.uk
📖 520
🏌 G Curtin
↗ D Turner
↟ 18 L 5642 yds Par 70 SSS 68
👤 U SOC
££ £20
🚗 1 mile N of Kendal on Burneside Road, 7 miles from M6 J36
⊕ 16 bay driving range
🖥 www.carusgreen.co.uk

Casterton   (1955)
Sedbergh Road, Casterton, Nr Kirkby Lonsdale, LA6 2LA
☎ **(015242) 71592**
🖥 (015242) 74387
📧 castertongc@hotmail.com
📖 300
🏌 J & E Makinson (Props)
↗ R Williamson
↟ 9 L 2900 yds Par 35 SSS 67
👤 U SOC
££ £15 (£18)
🚗 1 mile NE of Kirkby Lonsdale on A683. M6 Junction 36, 6 miles
🏠 Will Adamson
🖥 www.castertongolf.co.uk

Cockermouth   (1896)
Embleton, Cockermouth, CA13 9SG
☎ **(017687) 76223/76941**
🖥 (017687) 76941

📧 secretary@cockermouthgolf.co.uk
📖 405
🏌 RS Wimpress (01900) 825431
↗ None
↟ 18 L 5410 yds Par 69 SSS 66
👤 WD–U before 3.30pm exc Wed (also 10–11am) and Thur (also 9–10am) WE restricted – ring club
££ £22 (£27)
🚗 3 m E of Cockermouth, 2 m W of Bassenthwaite Lake
🏠 James Braid
🖥 www.cockermouthgolf.co.uk

Dalston Hall   (1990)
Dalston Hall, Dalston, Carlisle, CA5 7JX
☎ **(01228) 710165**
🖥 (01228) 710165
📖 290
🏌 PS Holder
↟ 9 L 2700 yds SSS 67
👤 U SOC WD WE
££ 9: £9 (£10); 18: £16 (£18)
🚗 3 miles SW of Carlisle on B5299. 6 miles W of M6 Junction 42
🖥 www.dalstonhall.co.uk

The Dunnerholme   (1905)
Duddon Road, Askam-in-Furness, LA16 7AW
☎ **(01229) 462675**
🖥 (01229) 462675
📧 dunnerholmegolfclub@btinternet.com
📖 400
🏌 LA Haines (01229) 826198
↟ 10 L 6138 yds SSS 70
👤 U
££ £15 any day
🚗 6 miles N of Barrow on A595

Eden   (1992)
Proprietary
Crosby-on-Eden, Carlisle, CA6 4RA
☎ **(01228) 573003**
🖥 (01228) 818435
📖 700
↗ S Harrison (01228) 573003
↟ Eden 18 L 6368 yds SSS 71 Hadrian 9 L Par 36 SSS 71
👤 U SOC
££ £30 (£35)
🚗 5 miles NE of Carlisle, off A689. M6 Junction 44
⊕ Driving range; golf academy; extensive practice facilities
🏠 G Wannop & Son
🖥 www.edengolf.co.uk

Furness   (1872)
Central Drive, Walney Island, Barrow-in-Furness, LA14 3LN
☎ **(01229) 471232**
🖥 (01229) 475100
📧 furnessgolfclub@chessbroadband.co.uk
📖 450
🏌 WT French
↗ None
↟ 18 L 6363 yds SSS 70
👤 H SOC
££ £25 D–£30 (£30)
🚗 Walney Island. M6 Junction 36
🖥 www.furnessgolfclub.co.uk

Grange Fell (1952)
Fell Road, Grange-over-Sands, LA11 6HB
- ☎ **(015395) 32536**
- 🕮 300
- ♟ JG Park (015395) 58513
- ⮞ 9 L 4840 metres SSS 66
- ⛹ U
- ££ £15 (£20)
- 🚗 W of Grange-over-Sands, towards Cartmel

Grange-over-Sands (1919)
Meathop Road, Grange-over-Sands, LA11 6QX
- ☎ **(015395) 33180**
- 🖶 (015395) 33754
- ✉ grangegolfclub@tiscali.co.uk
- 🕮 450 100(L) 50(J)
- ♟ D C Booth (015395) 33180
- ✓ N Lowe (015395) 35937
- ⮞ 18 L 6065 yds SSS 69
- ⛹ H SOC
- ££ £28 D–£35
- 🚗 E of Grange, off B5277
- 🏠 A Mackenzie
- 🖥 www.grangegolfclub.co.uk

Haltwhistle (1967)
Wallend Farm, Greenhead, Carlisle, CA8 7HN
- ☎ **(01697) 747367**
- 🕮 300
- ♟ KL Dickinson (Hon)
- ✓ None
- ⮞ 18 L 5532 yds Par 69 SSS 67
- ⛹ U SOC
- ££ D–£16 (£20)
- 🚗 3 miles W of Haltwhistle on A69
- 🏠 Andrew Mair
- 🖥 www.haltwhistlegolf.co.uk

Kendal (1891)
The Heights, Kendal, LA9 4PQ
- ☎ **(01539) 723499 (Bookings)**
- 🖶 (01539) 736466
- ✉ secretary@kendalgolfclub.co.uk
- 🕮 475
- ♟ I Clancy (01539) 733708
- ✓ P Scott (01539) 723499
- ⮞ 18 L 5785 yds Par 70 SSS 68
- ⛹ H SOC U–midweek WE–not Sat
- ££ £28 D–£36 (£34 D–£44)
- 🚗 I mile NW of Kendal
- ⊕ Buggy hire
- 🖥 www.kendalgolfclub.co.uk

Keswick (1978)
Threlkeld Hall, Threlkeld, Keswick, CA12 4SX
- ☎ **(017687) 79324**
- 🖶 (017687) 79861
- ✉ secretary@keswickgolfclub.com
- 🕮 500
- ♟ May Lloyd (017687) 79324 ext 1
- ✓ G Watson (017687) 79324 ext 2
- ⮞ 18 L 6225 yds Par 71 SSS 70
- ⛹ U SOC
- ££ £31 (£37)
- 🚗 4 miles E of Keswick (A66); 11 miles W of M6 Jct 40
- ⊕ Practice area; carts for hire; clubhouse and catering

- 🏠 E Brown
- 🖥 www.keswickgolfclub.com

Kirkby Lonsdale (1906)
Scaleber Lane, Barbon, Kirkby Lonsdale, LA6 2LJ
- ☎ **(015242) 76366**
- 🖶 (015242) 76503
- ✉ KLGolf@Dial.Pipex.com
- 🕮 550 50(J)
- ♟ D Towers (015242) 76365
- ✓ P Brunt (015242) 76366
- ⮞ 18 L 6542 yds Par 72 SSS 71
- ⛹ U SOC
- ££ D–£30 (D–£35)
- 🚗 3 miles N of Kirkby Lonsdale, off A683
- ⊕ Practice facilities
- 🏠 W Squires
- 🖥 www.klgolf.dial.pipex.com

Maryport (1905)
Bankend, Maryport, CA15 6PA
- ☎ **(01900) 812605**
- 🖶 (01900) 815626
- ✉ maryportgolfclub@tiscali.co.uk
- 🕮 475
- ♟ Mrs L Hayton (01900) 815626
- ⮞ 18 L 5982 yds SSS 70
- ⛹ U SOC
- ££ On application
- 🚗 I mile N of Maryport, off B5300

Penrith (1890)
Salkeld Road, Penrith, CA11 8SG
- ☎ **(01768) 891919/865429**
- 🖶 (01768) 891919
- ✉ secretary@penrithgolfclub.co.uk
- 🕮 750
- ♟ S D Wright (01768) 891919
- ✓ G Key (01768) 891919
- ⮞ 18 L 6026 yds SSS 69
- ⛹ WD–H WE/BH–H 10.06–11.30am & after 3pm SOC
- ££ £30 D–£35 (£35 D–£40)
- 🚗 ½ mile E of Penrith Jnc 41 M6
- 🖥 www.penrithgolfclub.com

Seascale (1893)
Seascale, CA20 1QL
- ☎ **(019467) 28202/28800**
- 🖶 (019467) 28042
- ✉ seascalegolfclub@googlemail.com
- 🕮 540
- ♟ JDH Stobart (019467) 28202
- ⮞ 18 L 6416 yds Par 71 SSS 71
- ⛹ U SOC
- ££ £35 D–£40 (£40 D–£45)
- 🚗 15 miles S of Whitehaven
- 🏠 Campbell/Lowe
- 🖥 www.seascalegolfclub.co.uk

Sedbergh (1896)
Dent Road, Sedbergh, LA10 5SS
- ☎ **(015396) 21551**
- 🖶 (015396) 21827
- ✉ sedberghgolfclub@tiscali.co.uk
- 🕮 170
- ♟ Craig or Steve Gardner
- ⮞ 9 L 5588 yds Par 70 SSS 67
- ⛹ U–phone in advance SOC
- ££ £20 D–£26 WD+WE
- 🚗 I mile S of Sedbergh on Dent road. M6 Junction 37, 5 miles

- 🏠 WG Squires
- 🖥 www.sedberghgolfclub.co.uk

Silecroft (1903)
Silecroft, Millom, LA18 4NX
- ☎ **(01229) 774250**
- 🖶 (01229) 774342
- ✉ silecroftgcsec@aol.com
- 🕮 206
- ♟ K Newton (01229) 770467
- ✓ None
- ⮞ 9 L 5877 yds Par 68 SSS 68
- ⛹ WD–U WE/BH–restricted
- ££ D–£15 (£20)
- 🚗 3 miles W of Millom
- 🖥 www.silecroftgolfclub.com

Silloth-on-Solway (1892)
Silloth, Wigton, CA7 4BL
- ☎ **(016973) 31304**
- 🖶 (016973) 31782
- ✉ office@sillothgolfclub.co.uk
- 🕮 700
- ♟ John Hill
- ✓ (016973) 32404
- ⮞ 18 L 6600 yds SSS 71
  Visitors normally play 6041 yds
  Par 72 SSS 69
- ⛹ U H–booking advisable SOC
- ££ D–£40 (£54)
- 🚗 22 miles W of Carlisle (B5302). M6 Junction 43
- 🏠 David Grant
- 🖥 www/sillothgolfclub.co.uk

Silverdale (1906)
Red Bridge Lane, Silverdale, Carnforth, LA5 0SP
- ☎ **(01524) 701300**
- 🖶 (01524) 702074
- ✉ info@silverdalegolfclub.co.uk
- 🕮 500
- ♟ B Hebdon (01524) 702074
- ✓ Ceri Cousins, PGA Pro
- ⮞ 18 Holes 5592 yds Par 70 SSS 67
- ⛹ U exc Sun (Summer)–M
- ££ £25 (£35) Discount tickets available
- 🚗 3 miles NW of Carnforth, by Silverdale Station, opp R.S.P.B. Leighton
- 🖥 www.silverdalegolfclub.co.uk

St Bees (1929)
Peckmill, Beach Road, St Bees, CA27 0EJ
- ☎ **(01946) 820319**
  (01946) 824300 (Clubhouse)
- 🕮 250
- ♟ L Hinde
- ⮞ 10 L 5307 yds SSS 66
- ⛹ WD–U exc Wed–NA after 4pm
  WE–NA before 3pm
- ££ £12 (£12)
- 🚗 4 miles S of Whitehaven
- 🖥 www.stbeesschoolgolfclub.net

Stony Holme (1974)
Public
St Aidan's Road, Carlisle, CA1 1LS
- ☎ **(01228) 625511**
- 🕮 275
- ♟ A McConnell (01228) 625511
- ✓ S Ling (01228) 625511

▶ 18 L 5775 yds Par 69 SSS 68
๗ U SOC
££ £10.50 (£13.50)
⊕ I mile E of Carlisle, off A69. M6 Junction 43
↑ Frank Pennink

Ulverston   (1895)
Bardsea Park, Ulverston, LA12 9QJ
☎ (01229) 582824
▤ (01229) 588910
✉ enquiries@ulverstongolf.co.uk
▥ 822
♬ R Rushforth
✓ PA Stoller (01229) 582806
▶ 18 L 6191 yds Par 71 SSS 70
๗ H or I SOC
££ £30 D–£35 (£35 D–£40) Summer
£15 D–£20 (£20 D–£25) Winter
⊕ 1¹/₂ m SW of Ulverston on A5087
⊕ Driving range/ball dispenser
↑ Herd/Colt
▤ www.ulverstongolf.co.uk

Windermere   (1891)
Cleabarrow, Windermere, LA23 3NB
☎ (015394) 43123
▤ (015394) 46370
✉ office@windermeregc.demon.co.uk
▥ 700
♬ B Grundy (Sec/Mgr)
✓ WSM Rooke (015394) 43550
▶ 18 L 5143 yds SSS 65
๗ H SOC
££ £34 D–£56 (£40 D–£60)
⊕ 1¹/₂ miles E of Bowness on B5264 M6 Jct 36
⊕ Short game practice area
↑ George Lowe
▤ www.windermeregolfclub.net

Workington   (1893)
Branthwaite Road, Workington, CA14 4SS
☎ (01900) 603460
✉ workingtongolf@aol.com

Derbyshire

Alfreton   (1892)
Oakerthorpe, Alfreton, DE55 7LH
☎ (01773) 832070
▥ 350
♬ S Bradley (07712) 136647
✓ (01773) 831901
▶ 11 L 5393 yds SSS 66
๗ WD–U H before 4.30pm –M after 4.30pm WE–M SOC H
££ £20 (£28)
⊕ W of Alfreton (A38). M1 Jct 28
▤ www.alfretongolfclub.co.uk

Allestree Park   (1949)
Public
Allestree Hall, Allestree, Derby, DE22 2EU
☎ (01332) 550616
▥ 200
♬ C Barker
✓ L Woodward
▶ 18 L 5714 yds SSS 68

---

๗ WD–U WE–booking req SOC
££ £12.40
⊕ 2 miles N of Derby on A6

Ashbourne   (1886)
Wyaston Road, Ashbourne, DE6 1NB
☎ (01335) 342078
▤ (01335) 347937
✉ ashbournegc@tiscali.co.uk
▥ 600
♬ John Hammond
✓ A Smith (01335) 347960
▶ 18 L 6365 yds SSS 71
๗ WD–U SOC
££ £28 D–£40 (£35)
⊕ 1¹/₂ m SW of Ashbourne, off A52
⊕ Telephone to confirm green fee and starting time. Practice area
↑ David Hemstock
▤ www.ashbournegolfclub.co.uk

Bakewell   (1899)
Station Road, Bakewell, DE4 1GB
☎ (01629) 812307
✉ steward@bakewellgolfclub.co.uk
▥ 305 67(L) 25(J)
♬ Mrs P Moody
✓ None
▶ 9 L 5244 yds SSS 65
๗ WD–U WE–NA before noon/BH–by arrangement SOC
££ D–£20 (D–£25)
⊕ ¹/₂ mile NE of Bakewell and A6
▤ www.bakewellgolfclub.co.uk

Birch Hall
Sheffield Road, Unstone, S18 5DH
☎ (01246) 291979
▥ 290
♬ E Gallagher (Hon Gen)
✓ P Ball
▶ 18 L 6505 yds Par 73 SSS 71
๗ U
££ On application
⊕ Jct 29 on M1 then 2 miles N of Chesterfield (B6057)
↑ David Tucker

Blue Circle   (1985)
Cement Works, Hope, S33 2RP
☎ (01433) 622315

Bondhay   (1991)
Bondhay Lane, Whitwell, Worksop, S80 3EH
☎ (01909) 723608
▤ (01909) 720226
✉ enquiries@bondhaygolfclub.com
▥ 520
♬ M J Hardisty (Mgr)
✓ M Ramsden
▶ 18 L 6871 yds Par 72
9 hole course Par 3
๗ U SOC
££ Mon/Tue £16; Wed–Fri £19 (£26)
⊕ 2 miles E of M1 Junction 30, off A619
⊕ Driving range plus Par 3 Academy Course; Putting Green; Practice Bunker.
↑ Donald Steel
▤ www.bondhaygolfclub.com

Brailsford   (1994)
Proprietary
Pools Head Lane, Brailsford, Ashbourne, DE6 3BU
☎ (01335) 360096
▤ (01335) 360077
✉ vivian.craig @clowes-developments.com
▥ 325
♬ K Wilson (01332) 553703
✓ D McCarthy (01335) 360096
▶ 12 L 5758 yds Par 68 SSS 68
๗ U SOC
££ 9: £13 (£18) 18: £15 (£23)
⊕ On A52 between Derby and Ashbourne
⊕ Driving range; PGA tuition
↑ RW Baldwin (EGU)

Breadsall Priory Hotel G&CC   (1976)
Moor Road, Morley, Derby, DE7 6DL
☎ (01332) 836106
▤ (01332) 833438
▥ 850
♬ I Knox (Dir of Golf)
✓ D Steels (01332) 836082
▶ 18 L 6201 yds SSS 70
18 L 6028 yds SSS 69
๗ U
££ £25–£50
⊕ Morley, 5 miles N of Derby (A61). M1 Junction 25, 9 miles
⊕ Driving range
↑ David Cox & Donald Steele
▤ www.marriottbreadsallpriory.co.uk

Broughton Heath   (1988)
Proprietary
Bent Lane, Church Broughton, DE65 5BA
☎ (01283) 521235
✉ info@broughtonheathgc.co.uk
▥ 520
♬ J Bentley (Mgr)
✓ A Hyland
▶ 18 L 3125 yds Par 54 SSS 53
๗ WD–U WE–booking necessary SOC
££ £10 (£15)
⊕ Church Broughton, I mile off A516 at Hatton
⊕ Driving range
↑ K Tunnicliffe
▤ www.broughtonheathgc.co.uk

Burton-on-Trent   (1894)
43 Ashby Road East, Burton-on-Trent, DE15 0PS
☎ (01283) 568708 (Clubhouse)
✉ thesecretary @burtonontrentgolfclub.co.uk
▥ 700
♬ G R Duckmanton (01283) 544551
✓ G Stafford (01283) 562240
▶ 18 L 6579 yds SSS 71
๗ H WD–NA before 9am or 12.30–14.00pm SOC WE–M
££ £38 D–£50 (£44 D–£57)
⊕ 3 miles E of Burton on A511
↑ HS Colt
▤ www.burtonontrentgolfclub.co.uk

For list of abbreviations and key to symbols see page 647

Buxton & High Peak (1887)
Townend, Buxton, SK17 7EN
☎ **(01298) 26263**
🖷 (01298) 26333
✉ sec@bhpgc.co.uk
▥ 450
♟ J Harris
✓ J Lines (01298) 23112
⟜ 18 L 5997 yds SSS 69
♙ U
££ £24 (£30)
⊕ NE boundary of Buxton (A6)
⊕ Driving range adj. to course
(separate business)
⌂ J Morris
▤ www.bhpgc.co.uk

Cavendish (1925)
Gadley Lane, Buxton, SK17 6XD
☎ **(01298) 79708**
🖷 (01298) 79708
✉ admin@cavendishgolfcourse.com
▥ 600
♟ S Davis
✓ S Townend
⟜ 18 L 5833 yds SSS 68
♙ U H SOC–by prior arrangement
with Sec
££ £30 (£33)
⊕ ¾ mile W of Buxton Station. St
John's Road (A53)
⊕ Practice area
⌂ Dr A Mackenzie
▤ www.cavendishgolfcourse.com

Chapel-en-le-Frith
(1905)
The Cockyard, Manchester Road, Chapel-
en-le-Frith, SK23 9UH
☎ **(01298) 812118**
🖷 (01298) 814990
✉ info@chapelgolf.co.uk
▥ 640
♟ Denise Goldfinch (01298) 813943
✓ DJ Cullen (01298) 812118
⟜ 18 L 6434 yds SSS 71
♙ U
££ £24 (£30)
⊕ 13 miles SE of Stockport, off A6
(B5470)
⊕ Practice nets & green;
▤ www.chapelgolf.co.uk

Chesterfield (1897)
Walton, Chesterfield, S42 7LA
☎ **(01246) 279256**
🖷 (01246) 276622
✉ secretary@chesterfieldgolfclub
.co.uk
▥ 600
♟ T Marshall
✓ M McLean (01246) 276297
⟜ 18 L 6281 yds Par 71 SSS 70
♙ WD–U H after 9.30am WE Sat M
Sun after 1.30pm (if not with
member) SOC–WD
££ £32–£40
⊕ 2 miles SW of Chesterfield on
A623 (Matlock Road)
⊕ Practice ground
▤ www.chesterfieldgolfclub.co.uk

Chevin (1894)
Duffield, Derby, DE56 4EE
☎ **(01332) 841864**
🖷 (01332) 844028
✉ secretary@chevingolf.fsnet.co.uk
▥ 500 100(L) 80(J) 70(5D)
♟ H E Riley
✓ W Bird (01332) 841112
⟜ 18 L 6057 yds SSS 69
♙ WD–U WE–M SOC–WD H
££ £30 D–£35
⊕ 5 miles N of Derby on A6
▤ www.chevingolf.co.uk

Derby (1923)
Public
off Wilmore Road, Sinfin, Derby, DE24 9HD
☎ **(01332) 766323**
✉ thesecretary@derbygolfclub.com
▥ 180
♟ DP Anderson
✓ Lee Woodward (01332) 766462
⟜ 18 L 6185 yds SSS 70
♙ U SOC
££ On application
⊕ 1 mile S of Derby, off A52
⊕ Practice area
▤ www.derbygolfclub.com

Erewash Valley (1905)
Stanton-by-Dale, DE7 4QR
☎ **(0115) 932 3258**
🖷 (0115) 944 0061
✉ secretary@erewashvalley.co.uk
▥ 850
♟ N Cockbill (0115) 932 2984
✓ D Bartlett (0115) 932 4667
⟜ 18 L 6547 yds SSS 71
♙ WE/BH–NA before noon
SOC–WD
££ £35 D–£45 (£45)
⊕ 10 miles E of Derby, off A52. M1
Junction 25, 3 miles
⊕ Practice ground; Putting and
Chipping Greens
⌂ Hawtree
▤ www.erewashvalley.co.uk

Glossop & District (1894)
Sheffield Road, Glossop, SK13 7PU
☎ **(01457) 865247 (Clubhouse)**
🖷 (01457) 864013
✉ glossopgolfclub@talktalk.net
▥ 300
♟ K Harrison
✓ M Williams (01457) 853117
⟜ 11 L 5800 yds SSS 68
♙ U SOC
££ £20 (£25)
⊕ 1 mile E of Glossop, off A57
▤ www.glossopgolfclub.co.uk

Grassmoor Golf Centre
(1990)
Proprietary
North Wingfield Road, Grassmoor,
Chesterfield, S42 5EA
☎ **(01246) 856044**
🖷 (01246) 853486
✉ enquiries@grassmoorgolf.co.uk
▥ 420
♟ H Hagues

✓ G Hagues
⟜ 18 L 5721 yds Par 69
♙ U–advance booking required SOC
££ £12 (£15)
⊕ 2 miles S of Chesterfield on B6038.
M1 Junction 29, 3 miles
⊕ Floodlit driving range, 26 bay with
electric tee system
⌂ Hawtree
▤ www.grassmoorgolf.co.uk

Horsley Lodge (1990)
Smalley Mill Road, Horsley, DE21 5BL
☎ **(01332) 780838**
🖷 (01332) 781118
✉ richard@horsleylodge.co.uk
▥ 650
♟ Dennis Wake
✓ Mark Whithorn (01332) 780838
⟜ 18 L 6418 yds SSS 71
♙ WD–U H WE–NA before noon
££ £30 (£30)
⊕ 4 miles NE of Derby. M1 Jct 28
⊕ Driving range
⌂ GM White/P McEvoy
▤ www.horsleylodge.co.uk

Kedleston Park (1947)
Kedleston, Quarndon, Derby, DE22 5JD
☎ **(01332) 840035**
🖷 (01332) 840035
✉ secretary
@kedleston-park-golf-club.co.uk
▥ 689
♟ S P Kay
✓ P Wesselingh (01332) 841685
⟜ 18 L 6731 yds SSS 72
♙ WD–H SOC
££ £38 (£38)
⊕ 3 miles NE of Derby. National
Trust signs to Kedleston Hall
⌂ James Braid
▤ www.kedlestonparkgolf.co.uk

Matlock (1906)
Chesterfield Road, Matlock Moor, Matlock,
DE4 5LZ
☎ **(01629) 582191**
🖷 (01629) 582135
✉ matlockcs@hotmail.co.uk
▥ 500 80(L) 65(J)
♟ M Wain (01629) 582191 option 4
✓ C Goodman (01629) 584934
⟜ 18 L 5804 yds SSS 68
♙ WD–U exc 12.30–1.30pm–NA
WE/BH–M SOC–WD
££ D–£28
⊕ 1½ miles NE of Matlock (A632)
⊕ Practice area
⌂ Tom Williamson
▤ www.matlockgolfclub.co.uk

Maywood (1990)
Proprietary
Rushy Lane, Risley, Derby, DE72 3SW
☎ **(0115) 939 2306**
✉ maywoodgolfclub@btinternet.com
▥ 350
♟ WJ Cockeram (0115) 932 6772
✓ S Jackson (0115) 949 0043
⟜ 18 L 6424 yds Par 72 SSS 71
♙ WD–U before 4pm WE–restricted
SOC

££ £18 weekday, D–£23 £22
    weekend, D–£27 + BH
⊷ Between Nottingham and Derby.
    M1 Junction 25
⌂ P Moon
▤ www.maywoodgolfclub.com

Mickleover   (1923)
Uttoxeter Road, Mickleover, DE3 9AD
☎ (01332) 516011 (Clubhouse)
☏ (01332) 516011
✉ secretary@mickleovergolfclub.com
▥ 600
♔ GW Finney (01332) 516011
✓ T Coxon (01332) 518662
⮡ 18 L 5708 yds SSS 68
♟ U SOC–Tues & Thurs
££ £30 (D–£40)
⊷ 3 miles W of Derby on
    A516/B5020
▤ www.mickleovergolfclub.com

New Mills   (1907)
Shaw Marsh, New Mills, High Peak,
SK22 4QE
☎ (01663) 743485
▥ 420
♔ John White (01457) 367466
✓ C Cross (01663) 746161
⮡ 18 L 5604 yds SSS 67
♟ WD–U WE–U SOC
££ £22 (£32)
⊷ 8 miles SE of Stockport
⌂ David Williams

Ormonde Fields   (1926)
Nottingham Road, Codnor, Ripley, DE5 9RG
☎ (01773) 742987
☏ (01773) 744848
▥ 660
♔ K Constable
✓ R White (01773) 570043
⮡ 18 L 6504 yds SSS 72
♟ U SOC
££ On application
⊷ A610 Ripley to Nottingham road.
    M1 Junction 26, 5 miles
⌂ John Fearn

Shirland   (1977)
Proprietary
Lower Delves, Shirland, DE55 6AU
☎ (01773) 834935
✉ geofftowle@hotmail.com
▥ 450
♔ G Towle (01773) 874224
⮡ 18 L 6072 yds SSS 70
♟ WD–U WE–U after 2pm SOC
££ £15 (£18)
⊷ 1 mile N of Alfreton, off A61 by
    Shirland Church

Sickleholme   (1898)
Bamford, Sheffield, S33 0BH
☎ (01433) 651306
☏ (01433) 659498
✉ sickleholme.gc@btconnect.com
▥ 300 125(L) 70(J)
♔ PH Taylor (Mgr)
✓ PH Taylor
⮡ 18 L 6064 yds SSS 69
♟ U exc Wed am
££ £29 (£34)

⊷ W of Sheffield, between
    Hathersage and Hope (A625)
▤ www.sickleholme.co.uk

Stanedge   (1934)
Walton Hay Farm, Chesterfield, S45 0LW
☎ (01246) 566156
✉ graemecooper@tiscali.co.uk
▥ 250
♔ Chris Shaw 01246 200846 (home)
⮡ 10 L 5786 yds SSS 68
♟ WD–U before 2pm –M after 2pm
    WE–M SOC
££ £15
⊷ 5 m SW of Chesterfield, off B5057
▤ www.stanedgegolfclub.co.uk

Devon

Ashbury   (1991)
Higher Maddaford, Okehampton,
EX20 4NL
☎ (01837) 55453
☏ (01837) 55468
▥ 100
♔ I Gill
⮡ 18 L 5460 yds SSS 67
    18 L 5628 yds SSS 67
    18 L 5400 yds SSS 66
    18 L 2018 yds Par 3
    18 L 6355 yds SSS 68
♟ Subject to availability
££ £25 (£30)
⊷ 4 m W of Okehampton, off A3079
⊕ Driving range on site
⌂ DJ Fensom
▤ www.ashburyhotel.co.uk

Axe Cliff   (1894)
Proprietary
Squires Lane, Axmouth, Seaton, EX12 4AB
☎ (01297) 21754
✉ D.Quinn@axecliff.co.uk

Bigbury   (1923)
Bigbury-on-Sea, South Devon, TQ7 4BB
☎ (01548) 810557
☏ (01548) 810207
✉ enquiries@bigburygolfclub.co.uk
▥ 750
♔ Nigel Blenkarne (Director of Golf)
✓ Tracey Loveys
⮡ 18 L 6049 yds Par 70 SSS 69
♟ U– see website for availability
    H–preferred SOC–by arr.
££ Please see Website
⊷ 15 miles SE of Plymouth on B3392
⌂ JH Taylor
▤ www.bigburygolfclub.com

Bovey Castle   (1929)
North Bovey, Devon TQ13 8RE
☎ (01647) 445009
☏ (01647) 440961
✉ richard.lewis@boveycastle.com
▥ 150
♔ R Lewis
✓ R Lewis
⮡ 18 L 6303 yds Par 70 SSS 70
♟ U H SOC
££ £100

⊷ 15 miles SW of Exeter on B3212;
    M5 Junction 31
⌂ JF Abercromby
▤ www.boveycastle.com

Chulmleigh   (1976)
Pay and play
Leigh Road, Chulmleigh, EX18 7BL
☎ (01769) 580519
☏ (01769) 580519
✉ chulmleighgolf@aol.com
▥ 100
♔ RW Dow
⮡ Summer 18 L 1407 yds SSS 54
    Winter 9 L 2430 yds SSS 54 (2 x 9)
♟ U
££ £9 £8 before 10 am D–£18
⊷ 1 mile N of A377 at Chulmleigh
⌂ John Goodban
▤ www.chulmleighgolf.co.uk

Churston   (1890)
Churston, Brixham, TQ5 0LA
☎ (01803) 842751
☏ (01803) 845738
✉ manager@churstongolf.com
▥ 983
♔ SR Bawden (01803) 842751
✓ R Butterworth (01803) 843442
⮡ 18 L 6208 yds SSS 70
♟ H exc Tues am–NA
    SOC–Mon/Thurs/Fri
££ £45 (£50)
⊷ 5 miles S of Torquay
⊕ Practice area
⌂ HS Colt
▤ www.churstongolf.com

Dainton Park   (1993)
Proprietary
Totnes Road, Ipplepen, Newton Abbot,
TQ12 5TN
☎ (01803) 815000
☏ (01803) 815001
✉ info@daintonparkgolf.co.uk
▥ 600
♔ Mrs M Selway
✓ M Cayless
⮡ 18 L 6400 yds SSS 71
♟ U SOC
££ £25 (£25)
⊷ 2 miles S of Newton Abbot on
    A381
⊕ Driving range
⌂ Adrian Stiff
▤ www.daintonparkgolf.co.uk

Dartmouth G&CC   (1992)
Blackawton, Nr Dartmouth, Devon
TQ9 7DE
☎ (01803) 712686
☏ (01803) 712628
✉ info@dgcc.co.uk
▥ 800
♔ J Waugh (Sec),
    A Chappell (Assist. Sec)
✓ R Glazier/S Barrett (01803) 712650
⮡ Ch'ship 18 L 7191 yds SSS 74
    Dartmouth 18 L 4791 yds SSS 64
♟ WD–U phone first WE SOC. No
    handicap required
££ Championship: £38 (£48).
    Dartmouth: £15 (£16)

4 miles NE of Dartmouth on A3122
⊕ Driving range; Hotel; Leisure Club; Stay & Play Golf Breaks.
⌂ Jeremy Pern
▤ www.dgcc.co.uk

Dinnaton – McCaulays Health Club (1989)

Ivybridge, PL21 9HU
☎ (01752) 892512
⌨ (01752) 698334
✉ info@mccaulays.com
▥ 300
🏌 P Hendriksen
✓ P Hendriksen
▷ 9 L 4089 yds Par 64
☖ U SOC WD–All WE–All
££ 9: £9.99; 18: £14.99 (all times)
⌖ 12 miles SE of Plymouth, off A38/B3213
⌂ Pink/Cotton
▤ www.mccaulays.com

Downes Crediton (1976)

Hookway, Crediton, EX17 3PT
☎ (01363) 773025
⌨ (01363) 775060
✉ secretary@downescreditongc.co.uk
▥ 700
🏌 PT Lee (01363) 773025
✓ B Austin (01363) 774464
▷ 18 L 5962 yds Par 70 SSS 69
☖ H SOC
££ £30 (£35)
⌖ 2 miles S of Crediton, off A377
▤ www.downescreditongc.co.uk

East Devon (1902)

Links Road, Budleigh Salterton, EX9 6DG
☎ (01395) 443370
⌨ (01395) 445547
✉ secretary@edgc.co.uk
▥ 850
🏌 J Reynolds (01395) 443370
✓ T Underwood (01395) 445195
▷ 18 L 6231 yds SSS 70
☖ H SOC–Thurs only
££ £40 D–£52
⌖ 12 miles SE of Exeter, M5 J30 A376
▤ www.edgc.co.uk

Elfordleigh Hotel G&CC (1932)

Proprietary
Colebrook, Plympton, Plymouth, PL7 5EB
☎ (01752) 348425
⌨ (01752) 344581
✉ enquiries@elfordleigh.co.uk
▥ 500
🏌 Derek Mills (01752) 556205
✓ Nick Cook (01752) 348425
▷ 18 L 5527 yds SSS 67
☖ U H–phone first SOC
££ £25 (£30)
⌖ 4 miles E of Plymouth, off Plympton road
⌂ JH Taylor
▤ www.elfordleigh.co.uk

Exeter G&CC (1895)

Countess Wear, Exeter, EX2 7AE
☎ (01392) 874139
⌨ (01392) 874914
✉ golf@exetergcc.co.uk
▥ 850
🏌 KJ Ham (Golf Sec)
✓ G Milne (01392) 875028
▷ 18 L 6023 yds SSS 69
☖ WD–U H WE–I H SOC–Thurs
££ On application
⌖ 4 miles SE of Exeter
⌂ James Braid
▤ www.exetergcc.com

Fingle Glen (1989)

Proprietary
Tedburn St Mary, Exeter, EX6 6AF
☎ (01647) 61817
⌨ (01647) 61135
✉ fingle.glen@btinternet.com
▥ 600
🏌 P Miliffe
✓ S Gould
▷ 18 L 5878 yds Par 70 SSS 68
☖ U SOC
££ £20 (£22)
⌖ 5 miles W of Exeter on A30
⊕ Covered driving range
▤ www.fingleglen.com

Hartland Forest (1980)

Hartland Forest Golf & Leisure Parc, Woolsery, Bideford, EX39 5RA
☎ (01237) 431777
✉ hfgolf@googlemail.com
▥ 150
▷ 18 L 6004 yds Par 71 SSS 70
Course being redesigned, please check before booking.
☖ U
££ £25 (£25)
⌖ 6 miles S of Clovelly, off A39
⊕ Buggies-£15/round
⌂ Alan Cartwright
▤ www.hartlandforestgolf.com

Hele Park Golf Centre (1993)

Proprietary
Ashburton Road, Newton Abbot, TQ12 6JN
☎ (01626) 336060
⌨ (01626) 332661
✉ info@heleparkgolf.co.uk
▥ 400
🏌 Wendy Stanbury
✓ Duncan Arnold (Dir of Golf)
▷ 9 L 2584 yds SSS 65
☖ U SOC
££ £20 (£22)
⌖ W of Newton Abbot on A383
⊕ Driving range with Power Tees
⌂ M Craig
▤ www.heleparkgolf.co.uk

Highbullen Hotel G&CC (1961)

Proprietary
Chittlehamholt, Umberleigh, EX37 9HD
☎ (01769) 540561
⌨ (01769) 540492
✉ info@highbullen.co.uk

▥ 205
🏌 John Aryes (01769) 540664
✓ P Weston (01769) 540530
▷ 18 L 5630 yds Par 68 SSS 67
☖ U SOC WE WD
££ £22 (£26)
⌖ Mid Devon, M5 Jct17, A361 to South Molton
⊕ Golf simulator and practice hole, Putting Green, and Chipping Hole
⌂ Martin Neil & Hamilton Stutt
▤ www.highbullen.co.uk

Holsworthy (1937)

Killatree, Holsworthy, EX22 6LP
☎ (01409) 253177
⌨ (01409) 253177
✉ info@holsworthygolfclub.co.uk
▥ 450
🏌 Mrs C F Harper
✓ AR Johnston (01409) 255390
▷ 18 L 6059 yds SSS 69
☖ WD–U Sun–U after 2.30pm
££ £26
⌖ 1 mile W of Holsworthy. 7 miles E of Bude (A3072)
▤ www.holsworthygolfclub.co.uk

Honiton (1896)

Middlehills, Honiton, EX14 9TR
☎ (01404) 44422
⌨ (01404) 46383
✉ secretary@honitongolfclub.fsnet.co.uk
▥ 750
🏌 BM Young
✓ A Cave (01404) 42943
▷ 18 L 5910 yds Par 69 SSS 68
☖ U (recognised club member) SOC
££ £28 (£32)
⌖ 2 miles S of Honiton towards Farway off A35
▤ www.honitongolf club.co.uk

Hurdwick (1990)

Tavistock Hamlets, Tavistock, PL19 0LL
☎ (01822) 612746
▥ 100
🏌 Maj RW Cullen (Mgr) R Hurle (Golf Sec)
▷ 18 L 5335 yds Par 67
☖ U SOC
££ £20
⌖ 1 mile N of Tavistock, on Brentor Church road
⌂ Hawtree/Bartlett

Ilfracombe (1892)

Hele Bay, Ilfracombe, EX34 9RT
☎ (01271) 862176
⌨ (01271) 867731
✉ ilfracombegolfclub@btinternet.com
▥ 500
🏌 A Williams
✓ M Davies (01271) 863328
▷ 18 L 5795 yds Par 69 SSS 68
☖ WD–H SOC WE/BH–U after 10am –NA 12–1pm
££ £25 D–£35 (£30 D–£40)
⌖ 2 miles E of Ilfracombe, towards Combe Martin
⊕ Driving range
⌂ TK Weir
▤ www.ilfracombegolfclub.com

Libbaton   (1988)
High Bickington, Umberleigh, EX37 9BS
☎ **(01769) 560269**
🖃 (01769) 560342
📠 gerald.herniman@tesco.net
🛄 475
👤 Gerald Herniman
🏌 David Jeffs (01769) 560167
⛳ 18 L 6481 yds SSS 71
👥 U SOC
££ £22 (£26)
🚗 1 mile S of High Bickington on B3217. M5 Junction 27
⊕ Floodlit driving range; buggy hire
🖳 www.libbaton-golf-club.com

Mortehoe & Woolacombe
(1992)
Easewell, Mortehoe, Ilfracombe, EX34 7EH
☎ **(01271) 870566**
🛄 225
👤 M Wilkinson (01271) 870745
⛳ 9 L 4729 yds Par 66 SSS 63
👥 U
££ 9: £10 18: £16 D–£20
🚗 E of Mortehoe village
🏛 David Hoare

Okehampton   (1913)
Okehampton, EX20 1EF
☎ **(01837) 52113**
🖃 (01837) 53541
📠 okehamptongc@btconnect.com
🛄 550
👤 C Yeo
🏌 A Moon (01837) 53541
⛳ 18 L 5294 yds SSS 66 Par 68
👥 H SOC
££ £25 D–£30 (£35)
🚗 S boundary of Okehampton
🏛 JH Taylor
🖳 www.okehamptongc.co.uk

Padbrook Park   (1992)
Pay and play
Cullompton, EX15 1RU
☎ **(01884) 836100**
🖃 (01884) 836101
📠 info@padbrookpark.co.uk
🛄 250
👤 Cary Rawlings (Mgr)
🏌 Mike Hawton/David Curle
⛳ 18 L 6500 yds SSS 71 April '09
👥 U SOC–WD
££ £25
🚗 10 m E of Exeter. M5 Jct 28, 1 mile
⊕ Driving range (10 bays); 40 bed Hotel; Gym; Indoor Bowls
🏛 M J Smith

Portmore Golf Park   (1993)
Proprietary
Landkey Road, Barnstaple, EX32 9LB
☎ **(01271) 378378**
📠 colin@portmoregolf.co.uk
🛄 600
👤 C Webber
🏌 D Everett
⛳ 27 holes
   Barum: 18 L 6500 yds Par 71 SSS 70
   Landkey: 9 hole Par 3
👥 U, SOC–U, WD–U, WE–U

££ Landkey: 9 holes £8 18 holes £13
   Barum: 9 holes £13, 18 holes £22
🚗 1 mile E of Barnstaple, off A361
⊕ 24-bay floodlit driving range & practice area. Golf Mark, High Achiever Club
🏛 Hawtree
🖳 www.portmoregolf.co.uk

Royal North Devon   (1864)
Golf Links Road, Westward Ho!, EX39 1HD
☎ **(01237) 473824 (Clubhouse)**
🖃 (01237) 423456
📠 info@royalnorthdevongolfclub.co.uk
🛄 650
👤 R Fowler (01237) 473817
🏌 I Parker (01237) 477598
⛳ 18 L 6665 yds Par 72 SSS 72
   9 hole short par 3 course
👥 U H
££ £42 D–£48 (£50 D–£60)
🚗 2 miles N of Bideford (A39)
⊕ Golf museum; indoor practice bays; practice ground, putting green, short game practice area
🏛 Old Tom Morris
🖳 www.royalnorthdevongolfclub.co.uk

Saunton   (1897)
Saunton, Braunton, EX33 1LG
☎ **(01271) 812436**
🖃 (01271) 814241
📠 gm4@sauntongolf.co.uk
🛄 1450
👤 D Cliffe
🏌 AT Mackenzie (01271) 812013
⛳ East 18 L 6779 yds Par 73 SSS 72
   West 18 L 6403 yds Par 71 SSS 71
👥 U H SOC
££ £65 D–£85 (£70 D–£100)
🚗 6 miles W of Barnstaple
⊕ Driving range
🏛 Fowler/Pennink
🖳 www.sauntongolf.co.uk

Sidmouth   (1889)
Cotmaton Road, Sidmouth, EX10 8SX
☎ **(01395) 513451**
🖃 (01395) 514661
📠 secretary@sidmouthgolfclub.co.uk
🛄 500
👤 JP Lee (Mgr) (01395) 513451
🏌 C Haigh (01395) 516407
⛳ 18 L 5088 yds SSS 65
👥 U SOC
££ £30 (£30)
🚗 ½ mile W of Sidmouth. 12 miles SE of M5 Junction 30
🏛 JH Taylor
🖳 www.sidmouthgolfclub.co.uk

Sparkwell   (1993)
Pay and play
Sparkwell, Plymouth, PL7 5DF
☎ **(01752) 837219**

Staddon Heights   (1904)
Plymstock, Plymouth, PL9 9SP
☎ **(01752) 402475**
🖃 (01752) 401998
📠 golf@shgc.uk.net
🛄 850

👤 TJH Aggett
🏌 (01752) 492630
⛳ 18 L 6164 yds SSS 70
👥 WE–H SOC–WD
££ D–£28 (D–£32)
🚗 SE Plymouth, via Plymstock
⊕ 2 practice putting greens; short game area; practice ground
🖳 www.staddon-heights.co.uk

Stover   (1930)
Bovey Road, Newton Abbot, TQ12 6QQ
☎ **(01626) 352460**
🖃 (01626) 330210
📠 info@stovergolfclub.co.uk
🛄 750
👤 W Hendry
🏌 J Langmead (01626) 362078
⛳ 18 L 5764 yds SSS 68
👥 U H SOC
££ £32 D–£40 (£40)
🚗 3 miles N of Newton Abbot on A382. A38 Drumbridges Junction
🏛 James Braid
🖳 www.stovergolfclub.co.uk

Tavistock   (1890)
Down Road, Tavistock, PL19 9AQ
☎ **(01822) 612344**
🖃 (01822) 612344
📠 tavygolf@hotmail.com
🛄 700
👤 J Coe
🏌 D Rehaag (01822) 612316
⛳ 18 L 6546 yds SSS 71
👥 H SOC–WD
££ £28 (£36)
🚗 Whitchurch Down
🖳 www.tavistockgolfclub.org.uk

Teign Valley   (1995)
Christow, Exeter, EX6 7PA
☎ **(01647) 253026**
🖃 (01647) 253026
📠 andy@teignvalleygolf.co.uk
🛄 400
👤 Andy Stubbs
🏌 S Amiet (01647) 253026
⛳ 18 L 5958 yds Par 70 SSS 69
👥 U SOC
££ £30 summer, £20 winter
🚗 SW of Exeter, via A38 (B3193)
🏛 Peter Nicholson
🖳 www.teignvalleygolf.co.uk

Teignmouth   (1924)
Haldon Moor, Exeter Road, Teignmouth TQ14 9NY
☎ **(01626) 777070**
🖃 (01626) 777304
📠 info@teignmouthgolfclub.co.uk
🛄 900
👤 Ian Evans
🏌 R Selley (01626) 7728984
⛳ 18 L 6073 yds SSS 69
👥 WD–H (recognised club member) WE–by appointment SOC–Tues & Thur only
££ £40
🚗 2 miles N of Teignmouth on B3192
🏛 Dr A Mackenzie
🖳 www.teignmouthgolfclub.co.uk

Thurlestone (1897)

Thurlestone, Kingsbridge, TQ7 3NZ
- ☎ **(01548) 560405**
- 🖳 (01548) 562149
- ✉ info@thurlestonegc.co.uk
- ☐ 820
- ♟ TE Gibbons (01548) 560405
- ✓ P Laugher (01548) 560715
- ⏵ 18 L 6340 yds Par 71 SSS 70
- ⚇ I or H
- ££ £40
- ⛳ 5 miles W of Kingsbridge, off A379
- ⌂ HS Colt
- 🖥 www.thurlestonegc.co.uk

Tiverton (1932)

Post Hill, Tiverton, EX16 4NE
- ☎ **(01884) 252114 (Clubhouse)**
- 🖳 (01884) 251607
- ✉ tivertongolfclub@lineone.net
- ☐ 600 150(L) 100(J)
- ♟ R Jessop (Gen Mgr) (01884) 252187
- ✓ M Hawton (01884) 254836
- ⏵ 18 L 6346 yds SSS 70
- ⚇ H
- ££ On application
- ⛳ 5 miles W of M5 Junction 27. 1½ miles E of Tiverton on B3391
- ⌂ James Braid
- 🖥 www.tivertongolfclub.co.uk

Torquay (1909)

Petitor Road, St Marychurch, Torquay, TQ1 4QF
- ☎ **(01803) 327471**
- 🖳 (01803) 316116
- ✉ info@torquaygolfclub.org.uk
- ☐ 800
- ♟ TJ Fensom (01803) 314591
- ✓ M Ruth (01803) 329113
- ⏵ 18 L 6164 yds Par 69 SSS 69
- ⚇ H SOC
- ££ £33.50 (£38.50)
- ⛳ 2 miles N of Torquay
- 🖥 www.torquaygolfclub.org.uk

Torrington (1895)

Weare Trees, Torrington, EX38 7EZ
- ☎ **(01805) 622229**
- 🖳 (01805) 623878
- ✉ theoffice@tottingtongolf.fsnet.co.uk
- ☐ 400
- ♟ Mrs JM Cudmore
- ✓ None
- ⏵ 9 L 4423 yds Par 64 SSS 62
- ⚇ U exc Sat/Sun am–NA SOC–Tues/Wed am
- ££ D–£18
- ⛳ 1 mile W of Torrington on Weare Giffard road
- 🖥 www.greattorringtongolfclub.co.uk

Warren (1892)

Dawlish Warren, EX7 0NF
- ☎ **(01626) 862255**
- 🖳 (01626) 888005
- ✉ golf@dwgc.co.uk
- ☐ 600
- ♟ R Goodey (Golf Co-ordinator)
- ✓ D Prowse (01626) 864002
- ⏵ 18 L 5954 yds Par 69 SSS 69

- ⚇ U SOC–WD–WE
- ££ £35 (£40)
- ⛳ 1½ miles E of Dawlish. M5 Jct 30
- ⌂ James Braid
- 🖥 www.dwgc.co.uk

Waterbridge (1992)

Pay and play
Down St Mary, Crediton, EX17 5LG
- ☎ **(01363) 85111**
- ☐ 100
- ♟ G & A Wren (Props)
- ✓ D Ridyard (01837) 83406
- ⏵ 9 L 1955 yds Par 32
- ⚇ U
- ££ 9: £8 (£9) 18: £13 (£15)
- ⛳ 1 mile N of Copplestone on A337
- ⌂ David Taylor
- 🖥 www.waterbridgegc.co.uk

Willingcott Valley (1996)

Willingcott, Woolacombe, EX34 7HN
- ☎ **(01271) 870173**
- 🖳 (01271) 870800
- ✉ secretary.willingcottgolfclub @virgin.net
- ☐ 239
- ♟ Andy Hodge
- ✓ David Elliott (01271) 8837801 Mobile: (07774) 211740
- ⏵ 18 L 6422 SSS 71 Par 72 (White tees)
  18 L 5865 SSS 68 Par 72 (Yellow tees)
  18 L 5195 SSS 70 Par 72 (Red tees)
- ⚇ U SOC
- ££ £22 (£28)
- ⛳ Near Barnstaple, 45 min from M5 J27
- ⊕ Practice facilities available
- ⌂ Hawtree (1st 9), Peter Lang (2nd 9)
- 🖥 www.willingcott.co.uk

Woodbury Park (1992)

Woodbury Castle, Woodbury, EX5 1JJ
- ☎ **(01395) 233500**

Wrangaton (1895)

Golf Links Road, Wrangaton, South Brent, TQ10 9HJ
- ☎ **(01364) 73229**
- 🖳 (01364) 73229
- ✉ wrangatongolf@btconnect.com
- ☐ 660
- ♟ M Daniels (01364) 73229
- ✓ G Richards (01364) 72161
- ⏵ 18 L 6065 yds Par 70 SSS 69
- ⚇ U SOC
- ££ £25 (£30)
- ⛳ Off A38 between South Brent and Ivybridge
- ⌂ Donald Steel
- 🖥 www.wrangatongolfclub.co.uk

Yelverton (1904)

Golf Links Road, Yelverton, PL20 6BN
- ☎ **(01822) 852824**
- 🖳 (01822) 854869
- ✉ secretary@yelvertongc.co.uk
- ☐ 600
- ♟ SM Barnes (01822) 852824
- ✓ T McSherry (01822) 853593
- ⏵ 18 L 6353 yds Par 71 SSS 71

- ⚇ H SOC
- ££ D–£38 (£40)
- ⛳ 6 miles N of Plymouth on A386
- ⊕ Practice ground; putting & chipping areas; Academy course
- ⌂ Herbert Fowler
- 🖥 www.yelvertongc.co.uk

Dorset

The Ashley Wood (1896)

Wimborne Road, Blandford Forum, DT11 9HN
- ☎ **(01258) 452253**
- 🖳 (01258) 450590
- ✉ generalmanager @ashleywoodgolfclub.com
- ☐ 600
- ♟ T Salmon
- ✓ J Shimmons (01258) 480379
- ⏵ 18 L 6308 yds Par 70 SSS 70
- ⚇ WD after 10am WE–H after 1pm SOC–WD SOC–WE after 1pm
- ££ Phone in advance
- ⛳ 1½ miles SE of Blandford on B3082
- ⊕ Practice area
- ⌂ Patrick Tallack
- 🖥 www.ashleywoodgolfclub.com

Bridport & West Dorset (1891)

The Clubhouse, Burton Road, Bridport DT6 4PS
- ☎ **(01308) 421095/422597 (Clubhouse)**
- 🖳 (01308) 421095
- ✉ secretary@bridportgolfclub.org.uk
- ☐ 600
- ♟ R Wilson (01308) 421095
- ✓ D Parsons (01308) 421491
- ⏵ 18 L 5875 yds Par 70 SSS 68
- ⚇ WD/Sat–U after 9.30am Sun–U after 1pm SOC
- ££ £28. Afternoon £22 Twilight £14
- ⛳ 1 mile E of A35 Bridport by-pass on B3157
- ⊕ Driving range. 9 hole pitch & putt course (Summer).
- ⌂ F Hawtree
- 🖥 www.bridportgolfclub.org.uk

Broadstone (Dorset) (1898)

Wentworth Drive, Broadstone, BH18 8DQ
- ☎ **(01202) 692595**
- 🖳 (01202) 642520
- ✉ admin@broadstonegolfclub.com
- ☐ 650
- ♟ Colin Robinson (01202) 642521
- ✓ Mathew Wilson (01202) 692835
- ⏵ 18 L 6349 yds SSS 70
- ⚇ WD–H from 9.30–11.30am and 2–4pm WE/BH–restricted SOC–WD
- ££ £52 (£75 D–£65)
- ⛳ 4 miles N of Poole, off A349
- ⊕ Incorporates The Dorset Golf Club. Practice ground; chipping and putting greens; teaching bay
- ⌂ Dunn (1898)/Colt (1920)/Sparks (2005)
- 🖥 www.broadstonegolfclub.com

Bulbury Woods (1989)
Bulbury Lane, Lytchett Minster, Poole,
BH16 6EP
☎ **(01929) 459574**
🖥 (01929) 459000
📧 enquiries@bulbury-woods.co.uk
📖 400
✓ D Adams
▷ 18 L 6002 yds Par 71 SSS 69
👥 U SOC–WD
££ £18 (£22)
⛳ 3 miles NW of Poole, off A35
🖳 www.bulbury-woods.co.uk

Came Down (1896)
Higher Came, Dorchester, DT2 8NR
☎ **(01305) 813494**
🖥 (01305) 815122
📧 manager@camedowngolfclub.co.uk
📖 700
♫ Julie Fry (Mgr) (01305) 813494
✓ N Rodgers (01305) 812670
▷ 18 L 6255 yds Par 70 SSS 70
👥 U Sun am–NA SOC H
££ £36 (£42)
⛳ 2 miles S of Dorchester on A354
🏠 Harry S Colt
🖳 www.camedowngolfclub.co.uk

Canford Magna (1994)
Proprietary
Knighton Lane, Wimborne, BH21 3AS
☎ **(01202) 592552**
🖥 (01202) 592550
📧 admin@canfordmagnagc.co.uk
📖 1000
♫ S Hudson (Dir) (01202) 592505
✓ M Cummins (01202) 591212
▷ Parkland 18 L 6515 yds Par 71
   SSS 71
   Riverside 18 L 6213 yds Par 70
   SSS 69
   Knighton 9 L 1377 yds Par 27
👥 U
££ £7–£23 (£8–£27)
⛳ 2 miles E of Wimborne on A341
⊕ Driving range. Golf Academy. 6
   hole pitch & putt course
🏠 Howard Swan
🖳 www.canfordmagnagc.co.uk

Canford School (1987)
Canford School, Wimborne, BH21 3AD
☎ **(01202) 841254**
🖥 (01202) 881009
📧 msb@canford.com
📖 360
♫ M Burley (Mgr) (01202) 847522
▷ 9 L 5787 yds SSS 68
👥 M SOC
££ £12
⛳ 1 mile SE of Wimborne, off A341
🏠 P Boult
🖳 www.canford.com

Charminster (1998)
Proprietary
Wolfedale Golf Course, Charminster,
Dorchester, DT2 7SG
☎ **(01305) 260186**
🖥 (01305) 257074
📖 140

♫ D Cox (Prop/Mgr) (01305) 260186
✓ T Lovegrove (01305) 260186
▷ 18 L 5467 yds Par 69 SSS 67
👥 U
££ £15.90 (£15.90)
⛳ 2 miles N of Dorchester
⊕ 6-hole beginners' course
🏠 D Cox

Chedington Court (1991)
South Perrott, Beaminster, DT8 3HU
☎ **(01935) 891413**
🖥 (01935) 891217
📧 admincgc@btconnect.com
📖 375
♫ B Ritchie
✓ S Ritchie
▷ 18 L 6047 yds SSS 70
   9 hole par 3
👥 U SOC
££ £21 (£27)
⛳ 4 miles SE of Crewkerne on A356
⊕ 15 acre practice field; driving range
   planned
🏠 Chapman/Hemstock/Steel
🖳 www.chedingtoncourtgolfclub.co.uk

Christchurch (1977)
Pay and play
Riverside Avenue, Bournemouth, BH7 7ES
☎ **(01202) 436436 (Bookings)**
🖥 (01202) 436400
📧 secretary@ifordgolfcentre.co.uk
📖 231
♫ Peter Gilbert
✓ Rod Davis (01202) 436436
▷ 18 L 6325 yds course
   9 hole short course
👥 U SOC
££ 9: £10 (£13); 18: £17 (£22)
⛳ Bournemouth/Christchurch
   boundary
⊕ Driving range
🖳 www.ifordgolfcentre.co.uk

Crane Valley (1992)
The Clubhouse, Verwood, BH31 7LE
☎ **(01202) 814088**
🖥 (01202) 813407
📧 general@crane-valley.co.uk
📖 700
♫ A Blackwell (Gen Mgr)
✓ D Ranson
▷ 18 L 6421 yds Par 72 SSS 71
   9 L 2060 yds Par 33 SSS 60
👥 U SOC (9 hole–U)
££ 9: £7 (£8) 18: £20 (£30)
⛳ Nr Ringwood, on B3081 Verwood-
   Cranborne road
⊕ Floodlit driving range
🏠 Donald Steel
🖳 www.crane-valley.co.uk

The Dorset G&CC (1978)
Bere Regis, Wareham, BH20 7NT
☎ **(01929) 472244**
🖥 (01929) 471294
📧 admin@dorsetgolfresort.com
📖 850
♫ G Packer (Gen Mgr)
✓ S Porter
▷ Lakeland 18 L 7027 yds Par 72
   SSS 72

   Woodland 18 L 4887 yds Par 66
   SSS 64
   Parkland 18 L 5901 yds Par 69
   SSS 68
👥 U SOC
££ £39 (£43)
⛳ 5 miles S of Bere Regis, off Wool
   road
⊕ Driving range; hotel; luxury log
   homes for rent
🏠 Martin Hawtree
🖳 www.dorsetgolfresort.com

Dudsbury (1992)
Proprietary
64 Christchurch Road, Ferndown,
BH22 8ST
☎ **(01202) 593499**
🖥 (01202) 594555
📧 golf@dudsbury.demon.co.uk
♫ Micella Chamberlain (Mgr)
✓ Steve Pocknell (01202) 584488
   Head Pro & Sec
▷ 18 L 6904 yds Par 71 SSS 73
👥 U
££ £35 (£40)
⛳ 3 miles N of Bournemouth (B3073)
⊕ Driving range. Academy course
🏠 Donald Steel
🖳 www.dudsburygolfclub.co.uk

Ferndown (1923)
119 Golf Links Road, Ferndown, BH22 8BU
☎ **(01202) 874602**
🖥 (01202) 873926
📧 ferndowngc@lineone.net
📖 700
♫ MC Davies (Mgr) (01202) 874602
✓ (01202) 873825
▷ 18 L 6509 yds Par 71 SSS 71
   9 L 5604 yds SSS 68
👥 WD–I H after 9.30am SOC–Tues
   & Fri
££ Old £60 (£70), President's £20
   (£25)
⛳ 6 miles N of Bournemouth
🏠 Harold Hilton
🖳 www.ferndown-golf-club.co.uk

Ferndown Forest (1993)
Forest Links Road, Ferndown, BH22 9PH
☎ **(01202) 876096**
🖥 (01202) 894095
📧 golf@ferndownforestgolf.co.uk
📖 300
♫ Chris Lawford
✓ G Howell (01202) 894990
▷ 18 L 5200 yds Par 68 SSS 65
👥 U SOC
££ £16 (£18)
⛳ 5 miles N of Bournemouth on
   Ferndown Bypass. Off A31
⊕ Floodlit driving range
🏠 Hunt/Grafham
🖳 www.ferndownforestgolf.co.uk

Halstock (1988)
Pay and play
Common Lane, Halstock, BA22 9SF
☎ **(01935) 891689**
🖥 (01935) 891839
📧 halstockgolf@yahoo.com
📖 200

🏌 John Page
🏳 18 L 4481 yds Par 66 SSS 63
👥 U SOC
££ £16 D–£30 (£18)
⛳ 6 miles S of Yeovil, off A37
⊕ Driving range

Highcliffe Castle (1913)

107 Lymington Road, Highcliffe-on-Sea, Christchurch, BH23 4LA
☎ (01425) 272210/272953
🖳 (01425) 272953
🏢 350 100(L) 50(J)
🏌 G Fisher (01425) 272210
🏳 18 L 4776 yds Par 64 SSS 63
👥 H SOC
££ £26 (£36)
⛳ 8 miles E of Bournemouth

Isle of Purbeck (1892)

Studland, BH19 3AB
☎ (01929) 450361
🖳 (01929) 450501
📧 iop@purbeckgolf.co.uk
🏢 400
🏌 Mrs C Robinson
✏ I Brake (01929) 450354
🏳 18 L 6295 yds SSS 70
9 L 2007 yds SSS 30
👥 U SOC
££ Mon–Thur £42 D–50 (Fri–Sun £48 D–£55) (2008)
⛳ 3 miles N of Swanage on B3351. Ferry from Sandbanks to Studland
🏠 HS Colt
🖳 www.purbeckgolf.co.uk

Knighton Heath (1976)

Francis Avenue, Bournemouth, BH11 8NX
☎ (01202) 572633
🖳 (01202) 590774
📧 khgc@btinternet.com
🏢 700
🏌 Mr G Davis
✏ D Miles (01202) 578275
🏳 18 L 6065 yds SSS 69
👥 WD–H after 9.30am WE–M WD–SOC
££ On application
⛳ 3 miles N of Poole, at junction of A348/A3049
🖳 www.knightonheathgolfclub.co.uk

Lyme Regis (1893)

Timber Hill, Lyme Regis, DT7 3HQ
☎ (01297) 442963
🖳 (01297) 442963
📧 secretary@lymeregisgolfclub.co.uk
🏢 750
🏌 Miss S Davidge (01297) 442963
✏ D Driver (01297) 443822
🏳 18 L 6283 yds SSS 70
👥 H WD–U after 9.30am (2.30pm Thurs) Sun–U after noon SOC
££ £34 Last 3 hours £16 inc drink
⛳ Between Lyme Regis and Charmouth, off A3502/A35
🖳 www.lymeregisgolfclub.co.uk

Meyrick Park (1890)

Pay and play
Central Drive, Meyrick Park, Bournemouth, BH2 6LH

☎ (01202) 786000
(01202) 786040 (Bookings)
📧 m.gracehaus.com

Moors Valley (1988)

Proprietary
Horton Road, Ringwood, BH24 2ET
☎ (01425) 479776
📧 golf@moorsvalleygolf.co.uk
🏢 300
🏌 Desmond Meharg (Mgr)
🏳 18 L 6337 yds Par 72 SSS 70
4-hole short course
👥 U
££ £17 Mon–Thur, £23 Fri–Sun Twilight £11
⛳ 4 miles SW of Ringwood, off A31
⊕ HSBC/Golf Monthly Regional Course Ranking Silver Medal
🏠 Martin Hawtree
🖳 www.moors-valley.co.uk/golf

Parkstone (1909)

Links Road, Parkstone, Poole, BH14 9QS
☎ (01202) 707138
🖳 (01202) 706027
📧 admin@parkstonegolfclub.co.uk
🏢 500 160(L) 75(J)
🏌 Christine Radford (Gen Mgr) (01202) 707138
✏ M Thompson (01202) 708092
🏳 18 L 6250 yds SSS 70
👥 H WD–NA before 9.30am and 12.30–2.10pm WE–NA before 9.45am and 12.30–2.30pm
££ Oct–Apr: £50 D–£75 (£60 D–£85) May–Sep: £55 D–£80 (£65 D–£90)
⛳ 3 miles W of Bournemouth, off A35
⊕ Practice range
🏠 W Park Jr/Braid
🖳 www.parkstonegolfclub.co.uk

Parley Court (1992)

Proprietary
Parley Green Lane, Hurn, Christchurch, BH23 6BB
☎ (01202) 591600
🖳 (01202) 579043
📧 info@parleygolf.co.uk
🏢 200
🏌 Mr Adrian Perry
✏ R Hill (07746) 850901/(01202) 591600
🏳 9 L 2469 yds Par 68 SSS 64
18 tee positions
👥 U SOC
££ 9: £10 (£11.50); 18: £14 (£15)
⛳ Opp Bournemouth Airport situated B3073
⊕ Driving Range 23 bays
🖳 www.parleygolf.co.uk

Queens Park (Bournemouth) (1905)

Public
Queens Park West Drive, Queens Park, Bournemouth, BH8 9BY
☎ (01202) 302611 Secretary
(01202) 437807 (Bookings)
Tee Times
🖳 (01202) 302611
📧 secretary@queensparkgolfclub.co.uk

🏢 350
🏌 P Greenwood (01202) 302611
🏳 18 L 6132 yds SSS 70
👥 U SOC
££ £17 (£23)
⛳ 2 miles NE of Bournemouth
🏠 James Braid
🖳 www.queensparkgolfclub.co.uk

Sherborne (1894)

Higher Clatcombe, Sherborne, DT9 4RN
☎ (01935) 812274
🖳 (01935) 814218
📧 secretary@sherbornegolfclub.co.uk
🏢 700
🏌 Geoff Scott
✏ A Tresidder (01935) 812274
🏳 18 L 6415 yds Par 72 SSS 71
👥 H SOC WD WE U
££ £25 (£36)
⛳ 1 mile N of Sherborne, off B3145
🏠 James Braid
🖳 www.sherbornegolfclub.co.uk

Solent Meads Golf Centre (1965)

Public
Rolls Drive, Southbourne, Bournemouth, BH6 4NA
☎ (01202) 420795
📧 solentmeads@yahoo.co.uk
🏌 Matt Steward (01202) 420795
✏ Roddy Watkins Warren Butcher
🏳 18 L 2159 yds Par 54
👥 U Groups welcome SOC
££ £5.90–£7.90
⛳ Hengistbury Head, 1 mile S of Christchurch, 4 miles E of Bournemouth
⊕ Driving range, 9 hole fun course
🖳 www.solentmeads.com

Sturminster Marshall (1992)

Pay and play
Moor Lane, Sturminster Marshall, BH21 4AH
☎ (01258) 858444
📧 mike@sturminstermarshallgolfclub.co.uk
🏢 160
🏌 Mike Dodd
✏ Mike Dodd, Colin Murray
🏳 9 L 3850 yds SSS 59
👥 U SOC
££ 9: £10; 18: £15
⛳ 8 miles N of Poole on A350
⊕ Coaching range/short game area; children's golf academy; ladies golf academy
🏠 John Sharkey
🖳 www.sturminstermarshallgolfclub.co.uk

Wareham (1908)

Sandford Road, Wareham, BH20 4DH
☎ (01929) 554147/557995
🖳 (01929) 557993
📧 warehamgolf@tiscali.co.uk
🏢 550
🏌 Richard Murgatroyd
🏳 18 L 5766 yds SSS 68

H SOC WD after 9.30 WE after 13.00
££ £25 D–£36 (£25)
⊕ N of Wareham on A351
↑ C Whitcombe
▤ www.warehamgolfclub.com

Weymouth   (1909)
Links Road, Weymouth, DT4 0PF
☎ (0844) 980 9909
⌂ (01305) 788029
✉ weymouthgolfclub@aol.com
▦ 700
♟ SB Elliott
✎ D Lochrie (01305) 773997
⏩ 18 L 5996 yds Par 70 SSS 69
♜ H SOC–WD
££ £32 D–£40 (£38)
⊕ 1 mile from town centre (A354), off Manor roundabout
⊕ Practice facility
↑ Braid/Hamilton Stutt
▤ www.weymouthgolfclub.co.uk

Durham

Barnard Castle   (1898)
Harmire Road, Barnard Castle, DL12 8QN
☎ (01833) 638355
⌂ (01833) 695551
▦ 700
♟ J Kilgarriff
✎ D Pearce (01833) 631980
⏩ 18 L 6406 yds SSS 71
♜ U SOC
££ £20 D–£26 (£27 D–£32)
⊕ N boundary of Barnard Castle on B6278
▤ www.barnardcastlegolfclub.org.uk

Beamish Park   (1906)
Beamish, Stanley, DH9 0RH
☎ (0191) 370 1382
⌂ (0191) 370 2937
✉ beamishgolf@btconnect.com
▦ 560
♟ G L Pickering (0191) 370 1382
✎ C Cole (0191) 370 1984
⏩ 18 L 6205 yds SSS 70
♜ WD/Sat–U before 4pm Sun–NA SOC
££ Ring Professional – variable fees
⊕ Beamish, nr Stanley. A1(M) Jct 63
⊕ Practice areas; Buggy Hire; Professional Shop
↑ Henry Cotton
▤ www.beamishgolfclub.co.uk

Billingham   (1967)
Sandy Lane, Billingham, TS22 5NA
☎ (01642) 554494/533816
⌂ (01642) 533816
✉ billingham@onetel.com
▦ 850
♟ Peter B Hodgson (Sec/Mgr) (01642) 533816
✎ M Ure (01642) 557060
⏩ 18 L 6346 yds Par 71 SSS 70
♜ WD–H after 9am WE/BH–H after 10am SOC
££ D–£28 Reduction for parties D–£40 weekends

⊕ W boundary of Billingham by A19, E of bypass
⊕ Practice ground
↑ Frank Pennink
▤ www.billinghamgolfclub.com

Bishop Auckland   (1894)
High Plains, Durham Road, Bishop Auckland, DL14 8DL
☎ (01388) 661618
⌂ (01388) 607005
✉ enquiries@bagc.co.uk
▦ 788
♟ MS Metcalf (01388) 661618
✎ D Skiffington (01388) 661618
⏩ 18 L 6504 yds SSS 71
♜ H (closed Good Friday and Christmas Day) SOC WD/WE
££ £30 D–£35 (£35 D–£40)
⊕ ½ mile NE of Bishop Auckland
↑ James Kay
▤ www.bagc.co.uk

Blackwell Grange   (1930)
Briar Close, Blackwell, Darlington, DL3 8QX
☎ (01325) 464458
⌂ (01325) 464458
✉ secretary@blackwellgrangegolf.com
▦ 700
♟ P Wraith (Hon) (01325) 464458
✎ J Furby (01325) 462088
⏩ 18 L 5621 yds Par 68 SSS 67
♜ U exc Wed 11am–2.30pm–NA Sat–booking req Sun–restricted SOC
££ £25 D–£35 (£35)
⊕ 1 mile S of Darlington on A66
⊕ Buggies for hire
↑ Frank Pennink
▤ www.blackwellgrangegolf.com

Brancepeth Castle   (1924)
The Clubhouse, Brancepeth Village, Durham, DH7 8EA
☎ (0191) 378 0075
⌂ (0191) 378 3835
✉ enquiries@brancepeth-castle-golf.co.uk
▦ 768 68(L) 100(J)
♟ D Young
✎ D Howdon (0191) 378 0183
⏩ 18 L 6400 yds Par 70 SSS 70
♜ SOC–WD WE–by arrangement
££ £40 (£50) Society discounts
⊕ 4 miles W of Durham on A690
⊕ Practice area
↑ HS Colt
▤ www.brancepeth-castle-golf.co.uk

Castle Eden   (1927)
Castle Eden, Hartlepool, TS27 4SS
☎ (01429) 836510
▦ 650
♟ S J Watkin
✎ P Jackson (01429) 836689
⏩ 18 L 6247 yds SSS 70
♜ U
££ £30 (£38)
⊕ 2 miles S of Peterlee
↑ Henry Cotton
▤ www.btinternet.com /~derek.livingston2

Chester-Le-Street   (1908)
Lumley Park, Chester-Le-Street, DH3 4NS
☎ (0191) 388 3218
⌂ none
✉ clsgcoffice@tiscali.co.uk
▦ 510 75(L) 78(J)
♟ Bill Routledge
✎ D Fletcher (0191) 389 0157
⏩ 18 L 6479 yds SSS 71 Par 71
♜ WD–H after 9.30am –NA 12–1pm WE–NA before 10.30am or 12–2pm
££ D £30 (£35)
⊕ E of Chester-Le-Street in grounds of Lumley Castle
⊕ Large practice area
↑ JH Taylor
▤ www.clsgolfclub.co.uk

Consett & District   (1911)
Elmfield Road, Consett, DH8 5NN
☎ (01207) 502186 (Clubhouse)
⌂ (01207) 505060
✉ consettgolfclub@btconnect.com
▦ 650
✎ S Cowell (01207) 580210
⏩ 18 L 6020 yds SSS 69
♜ WD–U SOC WE–limited to 20
££ £25 (£30)
⊕ 14 miles N of Durham on A691
↑ Harry Vardon
▤ www.consettgolfclub.com

Crook   (1919)
Low Job's Hill, Crook, DL15 9AA
☎ (01388) 762429
⌂ (01388) 762137
✉ secretary@crookgolfclub.co.uk
▦ 450
♟ L Shaw
✎ G Catrell (01388) 768145
⏩ 18 L 6102 yds SSS 69
♜ U SOC
££ From £18
⊕ ½ mile E of Crook (A689)
▤ www.crookgolfclub.co.uk

Darlington   (1908)
Haughton Grange, Darlington, DL1 3JD
☎ (01325) 355324
⌂ (01325) 366086
✉ office@darlington-gc.co.uk
▦ 725
♟ M Etherington
✎ C Dilley (01325) 484198
⏩ 18 L 6181 yds Par 70 SSS 69
♜ WD–U WE–M SOC
££ £28 D–£40
⊕ Off Salters Lane, NE of Darlington (A1150)
↑ Dr Alistair Mackenzie
▤ www.darlington-gc.co.uk

Dinsdale Spa   (1910)
Middleton St George, Darlington, DL2 1DW
☎ (01325) 332297
⌂ (01325) 332297
✉ dinsdalespagolf@btconnect.com
▦ 875
♟ A Patterson
✎ M Stubbings (01325) 332515
⏩ 18 L 6107 yds Par 71 SSS 69 Yellow

ꗥ WD–U exc Tues–NA WE–M SOC
£€ D–£28
⊕⊙ 5 miles SE of Darlington; A1(M)
J57/J58; Durham Tees Valley
Airport 2 miles
⊕ Large practice area; 2 bays
undercover
🖃 www.dinsdalespagolfclub.co.uk

Durham City (1887)
Littleburn, Langley Moor, Durham,
DH7 8HL
☎ (0191) 378 0069
📠 (0191) 378 4265
🖾 enquiries@durhamcitygolf.co.uk
🕮 750
🏌 LTI Wilson (0191) 386 4434
✓ S Corbally (0191) 378 0029
ⱶ 18 L 6326 yds SSS 70
ꗥ WD–U SOC
£€ £30 (£40)
⊕⊙ 1½ miles W of Durham, off A690
⌂ CC Stanton
🖃 www.durhamcitygolf.co.uk

Eaglescliffe (1914)
Yarm Road, Eaglescliffe, Stockton-on-Tees,
TS16 0DQ
☎ (01642) 780098 (Clubhouse)
(01642) 780238 (office)
📠 (01642) 780238
🖾 secretary@eaglescliffegolfclub.co.uk
🕮 835
🏌 Alan McNinch (01642) 780238
✓ Graeme Bell (01642) 790122
ⱶ 18 L 6289 yds SSS 70
ꗥ U SOC WD
£€ £32 D–£40 (£40 D–£55)
⊕⊙ 3 miles S of Stockton-on-Tees on
A135
⌂ Braid/Cotton
🖃 www.eaglescliffegolfclub.co.uk

Hartlepool (1906)
Hart Warren, Hartlepool, TS24 9QF
☎ (01429) 274398
📠 (01429) 274129
🖾 hartlepoolgolf@btconnect.com
🕮 700
🏌 G Laidlaw (Mgr) (01429) 261723
✓ G Laidlaw (01429) 267473
ⱶ 18 L 6267 yds SSS 70
ꗥ WD–U SOC
£€ £34 (£44)
⊕⊙ N boundary of Hartlepool
🖃 www.hartlepoolgolfclub.co.uk

High Throston (1997)
Hart Lane, Hartlepool, TS26 0UG
☎ (01429) 275325
🕮 100
🏌 Mrs J Sturrock
✓ None
ⱶ 18 L 6247 yds Par 71 SSS 70
ꗥ U SOC
£€ £16 (£20)
⊕⊙ 2 miles NW of Hartlepool (A179)
⌂ Jonathan Gaunt

Hobson (1978)
Hobson, Burnopfield, Newcastle-upon-Tyne,
NE16 6BZ
☎ (01207) 271605

Knotty Hill Golf Centre
(1992)
Pay and play
Sedgefield, Stockton-on-Tees, TS21 2BB
☎ (01740) 620320
📠 (01740) 622227
🖾 knottyhill@btconnect.com
🏌 D Craggs (Mgr)
ⱶ Princes 18 L 6433 yds Par 72
SSS 71
Bishops 18 L 5976 yds Par 70
Academy 9 L 2494 yds Par 32
ꗥ U SOC
£€ £13 (£15)
⊕⊙ 1 mile N of Sedgefield on A177.
A1(M) Junction 60, 2 miles
⊕ Floodlit driving range
⌂ Chris Stanton

Mount Oswald (1924)
South Road, Durham City, DH1 3TQ
☎ (0191) 386 7527
📠 (0191) 386 0975
🖾 info@mountoswald.co.uk
🕮 200
🏌 N Galvin
✓ C Calder (0191) 384 8941
ⱶ 18 L 5991 yds SSS 69
ꗥ U SOC
£€ £15.25 D–£27.50 (£17.50 D–£28)
⊕⊙ SW of Durham on A177
⊕ Driving range; putting green
🖃 www.mountoswald.co.uk

Norton (1989)
Pay and play
Junction Road, Norton, Stockton-on-Tees,
TS20 1SU
☎ (01642) 676385
📠 (01642) 608467
ⱶ 18 L 5870 yds SSS 71
ꗥ U SOC
£€ £11.50 (£13.50)
⊕⊙ 1 mile E of A177 on B1274
⌂ Tim Harper

Oakleaf Golf Complex
(1993)
Pay and play
School Aycliffe Lane, Newton Aycliffe,
DL5 6QZ
☎ (01325) 310820
📠 (01325) 300873
🖾 info@great-aycliffe.gov.uk
🏌 A Bailey (Mgr) (01325) 300700
✓ A Hartley (01325) 310820
ⱶ 18 L 5568 yds SSS 67
ꗥ WD–U WE–booking necessary
£€ £12.25 D–£15 (£14.50 D–£20)
⊕⊙ 1 mile W of Aycliffe on A6072,
from A68
⊕ Floodlit driving range; buggy hire
🖃 www.great-aycliffe.gov.uk

Ramside (1995)
Proprietary
Ramside Hall Hotel, Carrville, Durham,
DH1 1TD
☎ (0191) 386 9514
📠 (0191) 386 9519
🖾 golf@ramsidehallgolf.co.uk
🕮 400

🏌 Robin Smith 07721 722629
✓ K Jackson (0191) 386 9514
ⱶ 27 holes:
6217-6851 yds SSS 70-73
ꗥ U SOC Soft spikes only
£€ £37 (£45)
⊕⊙ 2 miles NE of Durham on A690.
A1(M) Junction 62
⊕ Driving range. Golf Academy,
Buggies
⌂ J Gaunt
🖃 www.ramsidehallgolf.co.uk

Roseberry Grange (1986)
Public
Grange Villa, Chester-Le-Street, DH2 3NF
☎ (0191) 370 0660
📠 (0191) 370 2047
🖾 chrisjones@chester-le-street.gov.uk
🕮 500
🏌 R McDermott (Hon)
✓ C Jones (0191) 370 0660
ⱶ 18 L 5892 yds SSS 68
ꗥ U SOC
£€ £16 (£22)
⊕⊙ 3 miles W of Chester-Le-Street on
A693
⊕ Driving range

Seaham (1911)
Shrewsbury Street, Dawdon, Seaham,
SR7 7RD
☎ (0191) 581 2354
🖾 seahamgolfclub@btconnect.com
🕮 550
🏌 T Johnson (0191) 581 1268
✓ A Blunt (0191) 513 0837
ⱶ 18 L 6009 yds SSS 69
ꗥ WE–NA before 3pm
£€ On application
⊕⊙ Seaham/Murton jct of A19 to A192
🖃 www.seahamgolfclub.co.uk

Seaton Carew (1874)
Tees Road, Hartlepool, TS25 1DE
☎ (01429) 266249
📠 (01429) 267952
🖾 seatoncarewgolfclub@btconnect
.com
🕮 700
🏌 C Jackson (01429) 296496
✓ M Rogers (01429) 890660
ⱶ Old 18 L 6603 yds SSS 71
Brabazon 18 L 6920 yds SSS 73
ꗥ U SOC WD and selective WE
£€ On application
⊕⊙ Hartlepool 2 m, A1(M) J60
⌂ Dr A Mackenzie
🖃 www.seatoncarewgolfclub.co.uk

South Moor (1923)
The Middles, Craghead, Stanley, DH9 6AG
☎ (01207) 232848/283525
📠 (01207) 284616
🖾 secretary@southmoorgc.co.uk
🕮 520
🏌 M Brennan (0191) 373 0391
✓ S Cowell (01207) 283525
ⱶ 18 L 6271 yds Par 72 SSS 70
ꗥ WD WE/BH SOC–WD/Sat
£€ £22 (£27)
⊕⊙ 6 miles W of Chester-le-Street

For list of abbreviations and key to symbols see page 647

🏠 Dr A Mackenzie
💻 www.southmoorgc.co.uk

Stressholme   (1976)
Public
Snipe Lane, Darlington, DL2 2SA
☎ **(01325) 461002**
🖂 (01325) 461002
✉ stressholme@btconnect.com
🏌 R Givens
⛳ R Givens
🏳 18 L 6511 yds SSS 71
👤 U
££ On application
🏌 2 miles S of Darlington on A66
⊕ Floodlit driving range
💻 www.darlington.gov.uk/golf

Woodham G&CC   (1983)
Proprietary
Burnhill Way, Newton Aycliffe, DL5 4PN
☎ **(01325) 320574**
🖂 (01325) 315254
✉ Ernie Wilson (01325) 315257
🏳 18 L 6688 yds Par 73 SSS 72
👤 WD–SOC–U WD/WE U call for
   details
££ £22 D–£30 (£35 D–£44)
🏌 1 mile N of Newton Aycliffe. 6
   miles from A1 (A689)
🏠 J Hamilton Stutt

The Wynyard Club   (1996)
Proprietary
Wellington Drive, Wynyard Park, Billingham,
TS22 5QJ
☎ **(01740) 644399**
🖂 (01740) 644599
✉ chris@wynardgolfclub.co.uk
🏛 350
🏌 C Mounter (Golf Dir)
✉ C Mounter
🏳 18 holes Par 72 SSS 73
👤 SOC–H WD WE
££ £60 (£60)
🏌 5 miles E of Sedgefield, between A1
   and A19
⊕ Floodlit driving range. David
   Leadbetter Golf Academy
🏠 Hawtree
💻 www.wynardgolfclub.co.uk

Essex

Abridge G&CC   (1964)
Epping Lane, Stapleford Tawney, RM4 1ST
☎ **(01708) 688396**
🖂 (01708) 688550
✉ info@abridgegolf.com
🏛 500
🏌 Scott Morley (Mgr)
✉ Steve Tyson
🏳 18 L 6704 yds SSS 72
👤 WD–H WE–NA before noon SOC
££ £42 (£52) after 12pm
🏌 Theydon Bois/Epping Stations 3
   miles; 7 miles from M25 Jct 26
⊕ Driving range & full practice
   facilities; British Open pre-
   qualifying course from 2009
🏠 Henry Cotton
💻 www.abridgegolf.com

Ballards Gore G&CC   (1980)
Proprietary
Gore Road, Canewdon, Rochford, SS4 2DA
☎ **(01702) 258917**
🖂 (01702) 258571
✉ secretary@ballardsgore.com
🏛 600
🏌 Iain Evans
✉ G McCarthy
🏳 18 L 6874 yds SSS 73
👤 WD–U WE–M after 12.30pm
   (summer) 11.30am (winter) SOC
££ £40
🏌 1½ miles NE of Rochford
⊕ Practice hole; practice field 250
   yards
🏠 Arthur Elvin
💻 www.ballardsgore.com

Basildon   (1967)
Public
Clayhill Lane, Kingswood, Basildon, SS16 5JP
☎ **(01268) 533297**
✉ basildongc@onetel.com

Belfairs   (1926)
Public
Eastwood Road North, Leigh-on-Sea,
SS9 4LR
☎ **(01702) 525345 (Starter)**

Belhus Park G&CC   (1972)
Pay and play
Belhus Park, South Ockendon, RM15 4QR
☎ **(01708) 854260**

Bentley   (1972)
Ongar Road, Brentwood, CM15 9SS
☎ **(01277) 373179**
🖂 (01277) 375097
✉ info@bentleygolfclub.com
🏛 650
🏌 Andy Hall
✉ N Garrett (01277) 372933
🏳 18 L 6709 yds SSS 72
👤 WD–UH WE–M after noon
   BH–after 11am SOC–WD
££ £27.50 D–£42
🏌 18 m E of London. M25 Jct 28, 3 m
🏠 Alec Swan
💻 www.bentleygolfclub.com

Benton Hall Golf & Country Club   (1993)
Proprietary
Wickham Hill, Witham, CM8 3LH
☎ **(01376) 502454**
🖂 (01376) 521050
✉ bentonhall.retail@theclubcompany
   .com
🏌 James Gathercole
✉ C Fairweather
🏳 18 L 6417 yds SSS 71
   9 hole Par 3 course
👤 U SOC–WD
££ £28 (£34)
🏌 Witham, 8 miles NE of
   Chelmsford, off A12
⊕ Refurbished Clubhouse; Indoor
   Swimming Pool; Sauna; Gym
🏠 Walker/Cox
💻 www.theclubcompany.com

Birch Grove   (1970)
Layer Road, Colchester, CO2 0HS
☎ **(01206) 734276**
🖂 (01206) 734276
🏛 280
🏌 Mrs M Marston
🏳 9 L 4532 yds SSS 63
👤 U exc Sun–U after 1pm SOC
££ D–£15 (£10 for nine holes)
🏌 3 miles S of Colchester on B1026
💻 www.birchgrovegolfclub.co.uk

Boyce Hill   (1921)
Vicarage Hill, Benfleet, SS7 1PD
☎ **(01268) 793625**
🖂 (01268) 750497
✉ secretary@boycehillgolfclub.co.uk
🏛 700
🏌 D Kelly
✉ G Burroughs (01268) 752565
🏳 18 L 6003 yds SSS 69
👤 WD–UH WE/BH–MH SOC–Thurs
   only
££ £35 D–£45
🏌 4 miles W of Southend
🏠 James Braid
💻 www.boycehillgolfclub.co.uk

Braintree   (1891)
Kings Lane, Stisted, Braintree, CM77 8DD
☎ **(01376) 346079**
🖂 (01376) 348677
✉ manager@braintreegolfclub.co.uk
🏛 700
🏌 Mrs N Wells
✉ T Parcell (01376) 343465
🏳 18 L 6228 yds SSS 70
👤 WD–U H SOC
££ £36.50 (£52)
🏌 1 mile E of Braintree, off A120
   towards Stisted
🏠 Hawtree
💻 www.braintreegolfclub.co.uk

Braxted Park   (1953)
Braxted Park, Witham, CM8 3EN
☎ **(01376) 572372**
🖂 (01376) 572372
✉ golf@braxtedpark.com
🏛 100
🏌 Mrs V Keeble
🏳 9 L 5704 yds Par 70 SSS 68
👤 WD–U SOC–WD
££ 9: £11; 18: £19
🏌 1½ miles off A12, nr Kelvedon
🏠 Sir Allen Clark
💻 www.braxtedpark.com

Bunsay Downs   (1982)
Public
Little Baddow Road, Woodham Walter,
Maldon, CM9 6RW
☎ **(01245) 412648/412369**

Burnham-on-Crouch   (1923)
Ferry Road, Creeksea, Burnham-on-Crouch,
CM0 8PQ
☎ **(01621) 782282/785508**
🖂 (01621) 784489
✉ burnhamgolf@hotmail.com
🏛 600

⌂ S K Golf
✓ S K Golf (01621) 782282
▷ 18 L 6056 yds SSS 69
☷ WD–H SOC WE–NA before 2pm
££ £42 (£48) 2–4–1 accepted
⊶ 1¹/₂ miles W of Burnham on
Crouch
⊕ Putting green; practice area,
buggies
⌂ D Swan
▤ www.burnhamgolfclub.co.uk

The Burstead (1993)
*Tye Common Road, Little Burstead,
Billericay, CM12 9SS*
☎ (01277) 631171

Canons Brook (1962)
Elizabeth Way, Harlow, CM19 5BE
☎ (01279) 421482
⌨ (01279) 626393
✉ manager@canonsbrook.com
▥ 700
⌂ Mrs SJ Langton
✓ A McGinn (01279) 418357
▷ 18 L 6763 yds SSS 73
☷ WD–U WE/BH–M
££ £30 D–£35
⊶ 25 miles N of London
⌂ Henry Cotton
▤ www.canonsbrook.com

Castle Point (1988)
Public
*Waterside Farm, Somnes Avenue, Canvey
Island, SS8 9FG*
☎ (01268) 510830

Channels (1974)
*Belsteads Farm Lane, Little Waltham,
Chelmsford, CM3 3PT*
☎ (01245) 440005
⌨ (01245) 442032
✉ info@channelsgolf.co.uk
▥ 650
⌂ Mrs SJ Larner
✓ IB Sinclair (01245) 441056
▷ Channels: 18 L 6413 yds Par 71
SSS 71
Belsteads: 18 L 4779 yds Par 67
SSS 63
☷ WD–U WE–M SOC
££ £40 D–£55
⊶ 3 miles NE of Chelmsford on A130
⊕ Pitch & putt course. Driving range
▤ www.channelsgolf.co.uk

Chelmsford (1893)
Widford Road, Chelmsford, CM2 9AP
☎ (01245) 256483
⌨ (01245) 256648
✉ office@chelmsfordgc.co.uk
▥ 650
⌂ G Winckless (01245) 256483
✓ M Welch (01245) 257079
▷ 18 L 5981 yds SSS 69
☷ WD–H WE/BH–M SOC
££ £40 D–£50
⊶ Off A414 at Widford roundabout
⌂ HS Colt
▤ www.chelmsfordgc.co.uk

Chigwell (1925)
High Road, Chigwell, IG7 5BH
☎ (020) 8500 2059
⌨ (020) 8501 3410
✉ info@chigwellgolfclub.co.uk
▥ 780
✓ J Fuller (020) 8500 2384
▷ 18 L 6296 yds SSS 70
☷ WD–H WE/BH–M
££ £35 D–£50
⊶ 13 miles NE of London (A113)
⌂ Hawtree/Taylor
▤ www.chigwellgolfclub.co.uk

Chingford (1923)
*158 Station Road, Chingford, London
E4 6AN*
☎ (0208) 529 2107
⌂ B Sinden
✓ A Trainor (0208) 529 5708
▷ 18 L 6342 yds Par 71 SSS 70
☷ U
££ £19 (£25)
⌂ James Braid

Clacton-on-Sea (1892)
West Road, Clacton-on-Sea, CO15 1AJ
☎ (01255) 421919
⌨ (01255) 424602
✉ secretary@clactongolfclub.com
▥ 650
⌂ Brian Telford
✓ SJ Levermore (01255) 426304
▷ 18 L 6448 yds SSS 71
☷ H WE/BH–H after 2pm SOC–WD
££ £30 (£35)
⊶ On Clacton sea front. 13 miles E of
Colchester (A120)
⊕ Practice field; driving nets; chip and
run; putting green; practice bunker
▤ www.clactongolfclub.com

Colchester GC (1907)
21 Braiswick, Colchester, CO4 5AU
☎ (01206) 853396
⌨ (01206) 852698
✉ secretary@colchestergolfclub.co.uk
▥ 790
⌂ JH Wiggam
✓ M Angel (01206) 853920
▷ 18 L 6347 yds SSS 70
☷ WD/WE–H BH–NA SOC
££ £38 D–£40 (£40)
⊶ ³/₄ mile NW of Colchester North
Station, towards West Berholt on
B1508
⊕ Driving range; practice area
⌂ James Braid
▤ www.colchestergolfclub.com

Colne Valley (1991)
Station Road, Earls Colne, CO6 2LT
☎ (01787) 224343
⌨ (01787) 224126
✉ info@colnevalleygolfclub.co.uk
▥ 500
⌂ T Smith (01787) 224343
✓ Warren Sargent (01787) 220770
▷ 18 L 6286 yds SSS 71
☷ WD–U WE/BH–after 10 (10.30am
SOC) BH–U
££ £30 (£35)
⊶ 12 miles W of Colchester (A1124)

⌂ Howard Swann
▤ www.colnevalleygolfclub.co.uk

Crondon Park (1994)
Proprietary
Stock Road, Stock, CM4 9DP
☎ (01277) 841115
⌨ (01277) 841356
▥ 875
⌂ P Cranwell
✓ F Sunderland (01277) 841887
▷ 18 L 6627 yds SSS 72
9 hole course
☷ WD–U WE–M SOC–WD
££ £25 (£40)
⊶ 5 miles S of Chelmsford on B1007.
Jct 16 off A12
⊕ Driving range. Function rooms
⌂ Martin Gillett
▤ www.crondon.com

Elsenham Golf Centre (1997)
*Hall Road, Elsenham, Bishop's Stortford,
CM22 6DH*
☎ (01279) 812865
⌂ Alan Mills (Gen Mgr)
✓ O McKenna
▷ 9 L 5854 yds Par 70
☷ U
££ 9: £13 (£15); 18: £18 (£20)
⊶ Off M11, by Stansted Airport
⊕ Driving range; gym; Cafe/Bar
▤ www.egcltd.co.uk

Essex G&CC (1990)
Earls Colne, Colchester, CO6 2NS
☎ (01787) 224466
✉ essex.golfops@theclubcompany.com

Essex Golf Centres, Hainault Forest (1912)
Public
Romford Road, Chigwell Row, IG7 4QW
☎ (020) 8500 2131
(Proshop/Reception)
✉ info@essexgolfcentre.com

Five Lakes Resort (1995)
*Colchester Road, Tolleshunt Knights,
Maldon, CM9 8HX*
☎ (01621) 868888 (Hotel)
(01621) 862307 (Bookings)
⌨ (01621) 869696
✉ office@fivelakes.co.uk
▥ 550
⌂ AD Bermingham (Dir)
(01621) 862326
✓ G Carter (01621) 862326
▷ Links 18 L 6250 yds SSS 70
Lakes 18 L 6765 yds SSS 72
☷ U BH–U after 1pm SOC
££ Links £25 (£32). Lakes £32 (£42)
⊶ 8 miles S of Colchester, on B1026
⊕ Driving range; chipping & putting
green
⌂ Neil Coles
▤ www.fivelakes.co.uk

Forrester Park (1975)
*Beckingham Road, Great Totham, Maldon,
CM9 8EA*

☎ (01621) 891406
🖥 (01621) 891406
📧 info@forresterparkltd.com
📖 900
🏌 T Forrester-Muir
🏐 G Pike (07801) 428174
🏴 18 L 6073 yds SSS 69
👫 WD–U WE–NA before noon
SOC–WD
££ £24 (£25)
🏐🏐 3 miles NE of Maldon on B1022
⊕ Practice ground; par 3 loop
🏠 Everett/Forrester-Muir
🖥 www.forresterparkltd.com

Frinton (1895)
1 The Esplanade, Frinton-on-Sea, CO13 9EP
☎ (01255) 674618
📧 frintongolf@lineone.net

Garon Park Golf Complex (1993)
Pay and play
Garon Park, Eastern Avenue, Southend-on-Sea, SS2 4PT
☎ (01702) 601701

Gosfield Lake (1986)
The Manor House, Gosfield, Halstead, CO9 1SE
☎ (01787) 474747
🖥 (01787) 476044
📧 gosfieldlakegc@btconnect.com
📖 800
🏌 JA O'Shea (Sec/Mgr)
(01787) 474747
🏐 R Wheeler (01787) 474488
🏴 Lakes 18 L 6756 yds Par 72 SSS 72
Meadows 9 L 4990 yds Par 66
👫 Lakes WD–H WE (pm)–H by
arrangement SOC. Meadows–U
££ Lakes £35 D–£45, Meadows £17
D–£22
🏐🏐 7 miles N of Braintree (A1017)
🏠 Sir H Cotton/Swann
🖥 www.gosfield-lake-golf-club.co.uk

Hanover G&CC (1991)
Proprietary
Hullbridge Road, Rayleigh, SS6 9QS
☎ (01702) 232377
📧 hanovergolf@aol.com

Hartswood (1967)
Pay and play
King George's Playing Fields, Brentwood, CM14 5AE
☎ (01277) 214830 (Bookings)
📖 270
🏌 JR Gander (01227) 218850
🏐 S Cole (01277) 218714
🏴 18 L 6192 yds SSS 70
👫 WD–U after 10am SOC
££ £13 (£18)
🏐🏐 E of Brentwood on A128

Harwich & Dovercourt (1906)
Station Road, Parkeston, Harwich, CO12 4NZ
☎ (01255) 503616
🖥 (01255) 503323

📧 harwichgolfclub@btinternet.com
📖 400
🏌 PJ Cole (Hon)
🏐 None
🏴 9 L 2950 yds SSS 69
👫 WD–H WE–U after 11 am SOC
££ £22
🏐🏐 A120 to roundabout to Parkeston
Village & Golf Club (first exit)
⊕ Practice ground

Ilford (1907)
291 Wanstead Park Road, Ilford, IG1 3TR
☎ (020) 8554 2930
🖥 (020) 8554 0822
📧 ilfordgolfclub@btconnect.com
📖 500
🏌 Janice Pinner (Mgr)
🏐 G Cant (020) 8554 0094
🏴 18 L 5299 yds SSS 66
👫 WD–U WE–phone Pro SOC
££ £19 (£24)
🏐🏐 S end of M11, off A406
🖥 www.ilfordgolfclub.com

Langdon Hills (1991)
Proprietary
Lower Dunton Road, Bulphan, RM14 3TY
☎ (01268) 548444/544300
🖥 (01268) 490084
📧 secretary@golflangdon.co.uk
📖 700
🏌 K Thompson (01268) 400064
🏐 T Moncur (01268) 544300
🏴 27 holes:
Langdon 9 L 3128 yds Par 35
Bulphan 9 L 3395 yds Par 37
Horndon 9 L 3028 yds Par 36
👫 U SOC WD WE–NA before noon
££ £20 (£30)
🏐🏐 SW of Basildon between A127 and
A13. M25 Junction 29, 8 miles
🏠 MRM Sandow
🖥 www.langdonhillsgolfclub.co.uk

Lexden Wood (1993)
Proprietary
Bakers Lane, Colchester, CO3 4AU
☎ (01206) 843333
🖥 (01206) 854775
📧 enquiries@lexdenwood.co.uk
📖 850
🏌 K Hanvey
🏐 P Grice
🏴 18 L 5895 yds Par 70 SSS 69
👫 U SOC
££ £22 (£30)
🏐🏐 SW of Colchester, off A12
⊕ Floodlit Driving range. Pitch & putt
course
🏠 Johnathan Gaunt
🖥 www.lexdenwood.co.uk

Lords Golf & CC Notley (1995)
The Green, Witham Road, White Notley, Witham, Essex, CM8 1RJ
☎ (01376) 329328
🖥 (01376) 569051
📧 julia@lordsgolf&countryclub.co.uk
📖 375
🏌 Julia Keenes
🏐 J Lowe

🏴 18 L 6022 yds Par 71
9 hole Par 3 course
9 further holes under construction
👫 U
££ £20 (£25 + BH)
🏐🏐 Black Notley, S of Braintree
⊕ Driving range; Dress Code to be
adhered to.
🏠 John Day
🖥 www.lordsgolf&countryclub.co.uk

Loughton (1981)
Pay and play
Clays Lane, Debden Green, Loughton, IG10 2RZ
☎ (020) 8502 2923
📖 60
🏌 A Day
🏴 9 L 4735 yds Par 66 SSS 63
👫 U–booking required SOC
££ 9: £9 (£10) 18: £14 (£16)
🏐🏐 M25 Junction 26

Maldon (1891)
Beeleigh Langford, Maldon, CM9 6LL
☎ (01621) 853212
🖥 (01621) 855232
📧 maldon.golf@virgin.net
📖 350
🏌 Viv Locke
🏴 9 L 6253 yds Par 71 SSS 70
👫 WD–U WE–M SOC
££ £18 D–£25
🏐🏐 3 miles NW of Maldon on B1019
🖥 www.maldon-golf.co.uk

Maylands (1936)
Proprietary
Colchester Road, Harold Park, Romford RM3 0AZ
☎ (01708) 341777
🖥 (01708) 343777
📧 maylands@maylandsgolf.com
📖 600
🏌 (01708) 341777
🏐 D Parker (017083) 46466
🏴 18 L 6361 yds SSS 70
👫 WD–U WE after 12 SOC
££ £30 (£18 after 12)
🏐🏐 2 miles E of Romford on A12. M25
Junction 28, half mile
⊕ Driving range; putting green
🏠 HS Colt
🖥 www.maylandsgolf.com

North Weald (1996)
Proprietary
Rayley Lane, North Weald, Epping, CM16 6AR
☎ (01992) 522118
🖥 (01992) 522881
📧 info@northwealdgolfclub.co.uk
📖 500
🏌 S Smith
🏴 18 L 6377 yds Par 71 SSS 71
👫 U SOC–WD/WE
££ £22.50 (£33)
🏐🏐 1½ miles E of M11 Jct 7 on A414
⊕ Chipping area; putting green;
driving range
🏠 David Williams
🖥 www.northwealdgolfclub.co.uk

Orsett (1899)

Brentwood Road, Orsett, RM16 3DS
- ☎ **(01375) 891352**
- 🖳 (01375) 892471
- 🖂 enquiries@orsettgolfclub.co.uk
- 📖 750
- ⚏ GH Smith (01375) 893409
- ✓ Richard Herring (01375) 891797
- ⌛ 18 L 6682 yds Par 72 SSS 73
- 🙋 WD–H WE–M SOC–WD
   Mon/Tue/Wed(Thurspm)Fri
- ££ £45 D–£60
- ⊕ 4 miles NE of Grays on A128. M25
   Junction 30/31
- ⌂ James Braid
- 🖳 www.orsettgolfclub.co.uk

Regiment Way Golf Centre
(1995)

Pay and play
Back Lane, Little Waltham, Chelmsford,
CM3 3PR
- ☎ **(01245) 361100**
- 🖳 (01245) 442032
- 🖂 info@regimentway.co.uk
- 📖 210
- ⚏ R Pamphilon
- ✓ D Marsh
- ⌛ 9 L 4887 yds Par 65 SSS 64
- 🙋 U
- ££ 9: £11 (£12) 18: £15 (£17)
- ⊕ 3 miles NE of Chelmsford (A130)
- ⊕ Floodlit driving range
- 🖳 www.channelgolf.co.uk

Risebridge (1972)

Pay and play
Risebridge Chase, Lower Bedfords Road,
Romford, RM1 4DG
- ☎ **(01708) 741429**
- 📖 175
- ⚏ P Jennings
- ✓ P Jennings (01708) 741429
- ⌛ 18 L 6394 yds SSS 71
   9 hole Par 3 course
- 🙋 U
- ££ £13.50 (£15.50)
- ⊕ 2 miles from M25 Jct 28, off A12
- ⊕ Driving range
- ⌂ F Hawtree

Rivenhall Oaks (1994)

Pay and play
Forest Road, Witham, Essex, CM8 2PS
- ☎ **(01376) 510222**
- 🖳 (01376) 500316
- 🖂 info@rivenhalloaksgolf.co.uk
- 📖 260
- ⚏ B Chapman
- ✓ B Chapman/J Hudson/O Williams
- ⌛ 9 L 3128 yds Par 36
   9 hole Par 3 course
- 🙋 U SOC
- ££ £10 (£14) D–£14.95
- ⊕ 4 miles E of Witham, off A12
- ⊕ Floodlit driving range
- ⌂ Alan Walker
- 🖳 www.rivenhalloaksgolf.co.uk

Rochford Hundred (1893)

Rochford Hall, Hall Road, Rochford,
SS4 1NW

- ☎ **(01702) 544302**
- 🖳 (01702) 541343
- 🖂 admin@rochfordhundredgolfclub
   .co.uk
- 📖 375 90(L) 60(J)
- ⚏ MA Boon
- ✓ GS Hill
- ⌛ 18 L 6256 yds SSS 70
- 🙋 WD–U H WE–NA before noon
- ££ £40 (£40)
- ⊕ 4 miles N of Southend-on-Sea
- ⌂ James Braid
- 🖳 www.rochfordhundredgolfclub
   .co.uk

Romford (1894)

Heath Drive, Gidea Park, Romford,
RM2 5QB
- ☎ **(01708) 740007 (Members)**
- 🖂 info@romfordgolfclub.co.uk

Royal Epping Forest (1888)

Forest Approach, Station Road, Chingford,
London E4 7AZ
- ☎ **(020) 8529 2195**
- 🖳 (020) 8559 4664
- 🖂 office@refgc.co.uk
- 📖 160 35(L) 35(J)
- ⚏ R Simmonds (0208) 529 2195
- ✓ A Traynor (0181) 529 5708
- ⌛ 18 L 6281 yds Par 71 SSS 70
- 🙋 U–booking necessary SOC
- ££ £20 (£25)
- ⊕ Nr Chingford station. M25 Jct 26
- ⊕ Red coats or trousers compulsory
- 🖳 www.refgc.co.uk

Saffron Walden (1919)

Windmill Hill, Saffron Walden, CB10 1BX
- ☎ **(01799) 522786**
- 🖳 (01799) 520313
- 🖂 office@swgc.com
- 📖 950
- ⚏ Stephanie Standen (Ms)
- ✓ Philip Davis (01799) 527728
- ⌛ 18 L 6632 yds SSS 72 (men),
   SSS 74 (ladies)
- 🙋 WD–U H SOC WE–M NA before
   1pm Sat
- ££ £44 D–£55 £33 18h or £44 for day
   for 3+ visitors playing together
- ⊕ Saffron Walden, on B184 towards
   Cambridge
- 🖳 www.swgc.com

South Essex G&CC

Herongate, Brentwood, CM13 3LW
- ☎ **(01277) 811289**
- 🖳 (01277) 811304
- 🖂 southessexgolf@crown-golf.co.uk
- 📖 300
- ⚏ P Lecras (Gen Mgr)
- ✓ M Herbert
- ⌛ 18 L 6851 yds Par 72 SSS 73
   9 L 3102 yds Par 35
- 🙋 U SOC
- ££ £21 (£27)
- ⊕ 2 miles E of M25 Junction 29
   (A127/A128)
- ⊕ Driving range. Golf Academy
- ⌂ Reg Plumbridge
- 🖳 www.crown-golf.co.uk

St Cleres

St Cleres Hall, Stanford-le-Hope, SS17 0LX
- ☎ **(01375) 361565**
- 🖳 (01375) 361565
- 🖂 david.wood@foremostgolf.com
- 📖 500
- ⚏ D Wood (01375) 361565
- ✓ D Wood (01375) 361565
- ⌛ 18 holes Par 72 SSS 71
   9 L Par 3
- 🙋 U H SOC
- ££ £17 (£23)
- ⊕ 5 miles E of M25 Jct 30/31 (A13)
- ⊕ Driving range; 9 hole par 3 course
   £5
- ⌂ Adrian Stiff

Stapleford Abbotts (1989)

Horseman's Side, Tysea Hill, Stapleford
Abbotts, RM4 1JU
- ☎ **(01708) 381108**
- **(01708) 381278 (bookings)**
- 🖂 staplefordabbotts
   @crown-golf.co.uk

Stock Brook Manor (1992)

Queen's Park Avenue, Stock, Billericay,
CM12 0SP
- ☎ **(01277) 658181**
- 🖳 (01277) 633063
- 🖂 events@stockbrook.com
- 📖 850
- ⚏ C Laurence (Golf Dir)
- ✓ C Laurence
- ⌛ 18 L 6905 yds SSS 73
   9 L 2952 yds SSS 69
- 🙋 After 12 noon WE+BH
- ££ £30 (£35 +BH))
- ⊕ 5 miles S of Chelmsford on B1007
- ⊕ Driving range; par 3 practice area
- ⌂ Martin Gillett
- 🖳 www.stockbrook.com

Theydon Bois (1897)

Theydon Road, Theydon Bois, Epping,
CM16 4EH
- ☎ **(01992) 813054**
- 🖳 (01992) 815602
- 🖂 theydonboisgolf@btconnect.com
- 📖 600
- ⚏ R Dale (01992) 813054
- ✓ RJ Hall (01992) 812460
- ⌛ 18 L 5490 yds SSS 67
- 🙋 U exc Thurs am–restricted SOC
- ££ £33/24 (£24)
- ⊕ 1 mile S of Epping. M25 Junction 26
- ⌂ James Braid
- 🖳 www.theydongolf.co.uk

Thorndon Park (1920)

Ingrave, Brentwood, CM13 3RH
- ☎ **(01277) 810345**
- 🖳 (01277) 810645
- 🖂 office@thorndonpark.com
- 📖 H26 L106 J50
- ⚏ Mr Giles Thomas (mgr)
- ✓ BV White (01277) 810736
- ⌛ 18 L 6511 yds SSS 71
- 🙋 WD–U WE/BH–M
- ££ £50 D–£65
- ⊕ 2 miles SE of Brentwood on A128
- ⌂ HS Colt
- 🖳 www.thorndonparkgolfclub.com

For list of abbreviations and key to symbols see page 647

Thorpe Hall   (1907)
Thorpe Hall Avenue, Thorpe Bay, SS1 3AT
- ☎ **(01702) 582205**
- 📠 (01702) 584498
- ✉ sec@thorpehallgc.co.uk
- 🏛 1000
- ♨ J Hetherington
- ✓ J Fryatt/G Scase (01702) 588195
- ▷ 18 L 6290 yds SSS 70
- ♔ WD–H SOC–Fri only
- ££ On application
- ♨ E of Southend-on-Sea
- 📧 www.thorpehallgc.co.uk

Three Rivers G&CC   (1973)
Stow Road, Purleigh, Chelmsford, CM3 6RR
- ☎ **(01621) 828631**

Toot Hill   (1991)
School Road, Toot Hill, Ongar, CM5 9PU
- ☎ **(01277) 365747**
- 📠 (01277) 364509
- ✉ office@toothillgolfclub.co.uk
- 🏛 350
- ♨ Mrs Cameron
- ✓ M Bishop
- ▷ 18 L 6053 yds Par 70 SSS 69
- ♔ WE after 1pm SOC–WD
- ££ £29 (£34)
- ♨ 2 miles W of Ongar
- ⊕ Practice range
- 🏛 Martin Gillett
- 📧 www.toothillgolfclub.co.uk

Top Meadow   (1986)
Fen Lane, North Ockendon, RM14 3PR
- ☎ **(01708) 852239 (Clubhouse)**
- ✉ info@topmeadow.co.uk
- ♨ D Stock
- ✓ J Sharp (01708) 859545
- ▷ 18 L 6227 yds Par 72
- ♔ WD–U WE–M SOC
- ££ £16
- ♨ N Ockendon, off B186
- ⊕ Driving range
- 📧 www.topmeadow.co.uk

Unex Towerlands   (1985)
Panfield Road, Braintree, CM7 5BJ
- ☎ **(01376) 326802**
- 📠 (01376) 552487
- ✉ info@unextowerlands.com
- 🏛 150
- ♨ Colin Cooper
- ▷ 9 L 5559 yds Par 68
- ♔ WD–U exc Wed–NA after 4.30pm
  WE–NA before 1pm SOC
- ££ 9: £10; 18: £15 (£17)
- ♨ 1 mile NW of Braintree (B1053)
- 📧 www.unextowerlands.com

Upminster   (1928)
114 Hall Lane, Upminster, RM14 1AU
- ☎ **(01708) 222788**
- 📠 (01708) 222484
- ✉ secretary@upminstergolfclub.co.uk
- 🏛 936
- ♨ RP Winmill
- ✓ Jodie Dartford (01708) 220000
- ▷ 18 L 6031 yds SSS 69
- ♔ WD–U H exc Tues am Ladies Day
  WE/BH–NA SOC

- ££ £30 D–£35
- ♨ Station 3/4 mile
- ⊕ Practice school; practice nets
- 📧 www.upminstergolfclub.co.uk

Wanstead   (1893)
Overton Drive, Wanstead, London
E11 2LW
- ☎ **(0208) 989 3938**
- 📠 (020) 8532 9138
- ✉ wgclub@aol.com
- 🏛 650
- ♨ K Jones (020) 8989 3938
- ✓ D Hawkins (020) 8989 9876
- ▷ 18 L 6015 yds SSS 69
- ♔ WD–H WE/BH–M
- ££ D–£40
- ♨ Off A12, nr Wanstead station
- 🏛 James Braid
- 📧 www.wansteadgolf.org.uk

Warley Park   (1975)
Magpie Lane, Little Warley, Brentwood,
CM13 3DX
- ☎ **(01277) 224891**
- ✉ enquiries@warleyparkgc.co.uk

Warren   (1932)
Woodham Walter, Maldon, CM9 6RW
- ☎ **(01245) 223258/223198**
- 📠 (01245) 223989
- ✉ enquiries@warrengolfclub.co.uk
- 🏛 800
- ♨ MFL Durham (01245) 223258
- ✓ D Brooks (01245) 224662
- ▷ 18 L 6263 yds SSS 70
- ♔ WD–H WE–M SOC
- ££ £30 D–£36
- ♨ 7 miles E of Chelmsford, off A414
- ⊕ Golf Academy (01245) 224662;
  large practice area
- 📧 www.warrengolf.co.uk

Weald Park   (1994)
Coxtie Green Road, South Weald,
Brentwood, CM14 5RJ
- ☎ **(01277) 375101**

West Essex   (1900)
Bury Road, Sewardstonebury, Chingford,
London E4 7QL
- ☎ **(020) 8529 7558**
- 📠 (020) 8524 7870
- ✉ sec@westessexgolfclub.co.uk
- 🏛 720
- ♨ Peter J Clarke
- ✓ R Joyce (020) 8529 4367
- ▷ 18 L 6289 yds SSS 70
- ♔ WD–U H WE/BH–M H
  SOC–Mon/Wed/Fri
- ££ £35 D–£40
- ♨ 2 miles N of Chingford BR station.
  M25 Junction 26
- ⊕ Driving range; short game area; dry
  bays; putting green; practice bunker
- 🏛 James Braid
- 📧 www.westessexgolfclub.co.uk

Woodford   (1890)
2, Sunset Avenue, Woodford Green,
IG8 0ST
- ☎ **(020) 8504 0553 (Clubhouse)**

- 📠 (020) 8559 0504
- ✉ office@woodfordgolf.co.uk
- 🏛 290
- ♨ PS Willett (020) 8504 3330
- ✓ A Baker (020) 8504 4254
- ▷ 9 L 5867 yds Par 70 SSS 69
- ♔ WD–U exc Tues am WE–NA Sat
  before 12.30pm U–Sun after
  9.45am SOC
- ££ £12–£18 (£14–£20)
- ♨ 11 miles NE of London
- ⊕ Major item of red clothing to be
  worn on course
- 🏛 Tom Dunn
- 📧 www.woodfordgolf.co.uk

Woolston Manor   (1994)
Woolston Manor, Abridge Road, Chigwell,
IG7 6BX
- ☎ **(020) 8500 2549**

Gloucestershire

Brickhampton Court Golf Complex   (1995)
Proprietary
Cheltenham Road East, Churchdown,
Gloucestershire GL2 9QF
- ☎ **(01452) 859444**
- 📠 (01452) 859333
- ✉ info@brickhampton.co.uk
- ♨ Nigel Broadhurst
- ✓ Bruce Wilson
- ▷ Spa 18 L 6449 yds Par 71 SSS 71
  Glevum 9 L 1859 yds Par 31
- ♔ U SOC–WD
- ££ Spa: Mon–Sun £23, Glevum: £8 (£10)
- ♨ Between Cheltenham and Glouc.
  on B4063. M5 Jct 11, 3 miles
- ⊕ 28-bay floodlit covered driving
  range
- 🏛 Simon Gidman
- 📧 www.brickhampton.co.uk

Bristol & Clifton   (1891)
Beggar Bush Lane, Failand, Clifton, Bristol
BS8 3TH
- ☎ **(01275) 393474/393117**
- 📠 (01275) 394611
- ✉ mansec@bristolgc.co.uk
- 🏛 850
- ♨ CR Vane Percy (01275) 393474
- ✓ P Mitchell (01275) 393031
- ▷ 18 L 6408 yds SSS 71
- ♔ WD–UH WE/BH–UH after 11am
  SOC
- ££ £42 (£55)
- ♨ 2 miles W of suspension bridge. 4
  miles S of M5 Junction 19
- ⊕ Driving range; chipping green;
  practice bunkers; pitching green
- 📧 www.bristolgolf.co.uk

Broadway   (1895)
Willersey Hill, Broadway, Worcs,
WR12 7LG
- ☎ **(01386) 853683**
- 📠 (01386) 858643
- ✉ secretary@broadwaygolfclub.co.uk
- 🏛 515 165(L) 75(J)
- ♨ Mr V Tofts (01386) 853683

✓ M Freeman (01386) 853275
ℙ 18 L 6228 yds Par 72 SSS 70
🏌 H exc Sat–M SOC
££ £32 (£40)
⛳ 1½ miles E of Broadway (A44)
⊕ Driving/practice range
🏠 James Braid
▣ www.broadwaygolfclub.co.uk

Canons Court (1982)
Bradley Green, Wotton-under-Edge, GL12 7PN
☎ (01453) 843128

Chipping Sodbury (1905)
Trinity Lane, Chipping Sodbury, Bristol BS37 6PU
☎ (01454) 319042 (Members)
☐ (01454) 320052
▣ info@chippingsodburygolfclub.co.uk
▦ 750
✍ Bob Williams
✓ M Watts (01454) 314087
ℙ 18 L 6786 yds SSS 73
🏌 WD–U WE–pm only
££ £32 (£45)
⛳ 12 miles NE of Bristol. M4 Jct 18, 5 miles. M5 Jct 14, 9 miles
⊕ Practice range
🏠 Fred Hawtree
▣ www.chippingsodburygolfclub.co.uk

Cirencester (1893)
Cheltenham Road, Bagendon, Cirencester, GL7 7BH
☎ (01285) 652465
☐ (01285) 650665
▣ info@cirencestergolfclub.co.uk
▦ 800
✍ R Caldecott (01285) 652465
✓ E Goodwin (01285) 656124
ℙ 18 L 6055 yds Par 70 SSS 69
🏌 H SOC–WD
££ £32 (£38)
⛳ 1½ miles N of Cirencester on A435
⊕ Driving range; 6 hole par 3 academy
🏠 James Braid
▣ www.cirencestergolfclub.co.uk

Cleeve Hill (1892)
Pay and play
Cleeve Hill, Cheltenham, GL52 3PW
☎ (01242) 672025
☐ (01242) 678444
▣ hugh.fitzsimons@btconnect.com
✍ Hugh Fitzsimons (Mgr)
✓ D Finch (01242) 672592
ℙ 18 L 6448 yds Par 72 SSS 71
🏌 U
££ £15 (£20+BH)
⛳ 3 miles N of Cheltenham on A46 to Winchcombe
⊕ Putting green
▣ www.cleevehillgolfcourse.co.uk

Cotswold Edge (1980)
Upper Rushmire, Wotton-under-Edge, GL12 7PT
☎ (01453) 844167
☐ (01453) 845120
▣ cotswoldedge@freenetname.com

▦ 800
✍ NJ Newman
✓ R Hibbitt (01453) 844398
ℙ 18 L 5816 yds SSS 69
🏌 WD–U WE–M
££ £20 (£25)
⛳ 2 miles NE of Wotton-under-Edge on B4058 Tetbury road. M5 Jct 14
▣ www.cotswoldedgegolfclub.org.uk

Cotswold Hills (1902)
Ullenwood, Cheltenham, GL53 9QT
☎ (01242) 515264
☐ (01242) 515317
▣ contact.us@cotswoldhills-golfclub.com
▦ 750
✍ Mrs A Hale (Mgr)
✓ J Latham (01242) 515263
ℙ 18 L 6849 yds Par 72 SSS 73 (blue)
🏌 U–recognised club members SOC After 9.30 until 12.30 then after 2pm H
££ £36 D–£46 (£42)
⛳ 3 miles S of Cheltenham. M5 Junction 11A
🏠 MD Little
▣ www.cotswoldhills-golfclub.com

Dymock Grange (1995)
The Old Grange, Leominster Road, Dymock, GL18 2AN
☎ (01531) 890840
☐ (01531) 890860
▦ 180
✍ B Crossman
✓ None
ℙ 9 L 2774 yds Par 36
   9 L 1695 yds Par 30
🏌 U
££ £12 (£15)
⛳ 14 m NW of Gloucester (B4215)

Filton (1909)
Golf Course Lane, Bristol, BS34 7QS
☎ (0117) 969 4169
☐ (0117) 931 4359
▣ thesecretary@filtongolfclub.co.uk
▦ 700
✍ T Atkinson (0117) 969 4169
✓ D Kelley (0117) 969 6968
ℙ 18 L 6174 yds SSS 70
🏌 WD–U WE/BH–M SOC–WD H
££ £32 D–£40
⛳ 4 miles N of Bristol, M5 J16
⊕ Three practice greens
🏠 Hawtree
▣ www.filtongolfclub.co.uk

Forest Hills (1992)
Proprietary
Mile End Road, Coleford, GL16 7BY
☎ (01594) 810620
☐ (01594) 810823
▦ 550
✍ D Bowen (01594) 837134
✓ R Ballard (01594) 810620
ℙ 18 L 6300 yds SSS 72
🏌 U SOC
££ £18 (£25)
⛳ 1 mile E of Coleford (B4028)
⊕ Driving range
🏠 Adrian Stiff
▣ www.fweb.org.uk/forestgolf

Forest of Dean (1973)
Lords Hill, Coleford, GL16 8BE
☎ (01594) 832583
☐ (01594) 832584
▣ enquiries@bellshotel.co.uk
▦ 500
✍ H Wheeler (Hon Sec)
   B Jackson (Mgr)
✓ Stewart Jenkins (01594) 833689
ℙ 18 L 5524 yds SSS 69
🏌 U SOC
££ £20 (£20)
⛳ ½ mile SE of Coleford on Parkend road. M50, 10 miles
🏠 John Day
▣ www.bellshotel.co.uk

The Gloucestershire (1976)
Tracy Park Estate, Bath Road, Wick, Bristol, BS30 5RN
☎ (0117) 937 2251
▣ golf@thegloucestershire.com

Gloucester Hotel (1976)
Matson Lane, Gloucester, GL4 9EA
☎ (01452) 525653

Henbury (1891)
Westbury-on-Trym, Bristol, BS10 7QB
☎ (0117) 950 0660

Hilton Puckrup Hall Hotel (1992)
Puckrup, Tewkesbury, GL20 6EL
☎ (01684) 296200/271591
☐ (01684) 850788
▦ 400
✍ J Stuart
✓ M Fenning
ℙ 18 L 6219 yds SSS 70
🏌 WD SOC WE–residents
££ £30 (£35)
⛳ 2 miles N of Tewkesbury on A38. M50 Junction 1. M5 Junction 8
🏠 Simon Gidman
▣ www.puckrupgolf.co.uk

The Kendleshire (1997)
Proprietary
Henfield Road, Coalpit Heath, Bristol, BS36 2TG
☎ (0117) 956 7007
☐ (0117) 957 3433
▣ info@kendleshire.com
▦ 750
✍ P Murphy
✓ T Mealing (0117) 956 7000
ℙ 27 L 6249-6544 yds Par 70-71
🏌 U SOC
££ Mon £25, Tue–Thur £35, Fri–Sun £40
⛳ 1 mile NE of Bristol. M32 Jct 1
⊕ Driving range. Golf Academy
🏠 Adrian Stiff/Peter McEvoy
▣ www.kendleshire.com

Knowle (1905)
Fairway, West Town Lane, Brislington, Bristol, BS4 5DF
☎ (0117) 977 0660
☐ (0117) 972 0615
▣ admin@knowlegolfclub.co.uk

🏳 600
🏴 (0117) 977 0660
✔ R Hayward (0117) 977 9193
🏴 18 L 6061 yds SSS 69
👥 WD exc Thurs–H WE/BH–H
   SOC–Thurs
££ £30 D–£40 (£40 D–£50)
🏴 Brislington Hill, 3 miles S of Bristol,
   off A4
🏠 JH Taylor
🖥 www.knowlegolfclub.co.uk

Lilley Brook   (1922)
Cirencester Road, Charlton Kings,
Cheltenham, GL53 8EG
☎ (01242) 526785
🖳 (01242) 256880
📧 secretary@lilleybrook.co.uk
🏛 750
🏴 Caroline Kirby (Office Mgr)
✔ K Hayler (01242) 525201
🏴 18 L 6226 yds SSS 70
👥 WD–H or I (recognised club
   members) WE–M SOC–WD
££ £35 D–£40 (£40)
🏴 3 miles SE of Cheltenham on A435.
   M5 Junction 11A
🏠 McKenzie
🖥 www.lilleybrook.co.uk

Long Ashton   (1893)
Clarken Coombe, Long Ashton, Bristol,
BS41 9DW
☎ (01275) 392229
🖳 (01275) 394395
📧 secretary@longashtongolfclub.co.uk
🏛 750
🏴 Mrs V Rose
✔ M Hart (01275) 392229
🏴 18 L 6077 yds SSS 70
👥 WD–U H WE/BH–I H SOC–Wed
   & Fri
££ £35 (£45)
🏴 3 miles S of Bristol on B3128
🏠 JH Taylor
🖥 www.longashtongolfclub.co.uk

Lydney   (1909)
The Links, Off Lakeside Avenue, Lydney,
GL15 5QA
☎ (01594) 842614
🏛 300
🏴 J Mills (01594) 841186
🏴 9 L 5430 yds SSS 66
👥 U SOC
££ £11
🏴 20 miles SW of Gloucester
🖥 www.members.tripod.co.uk/kenfar
   /lgc

Minchinhampton   (1889)
Minchinhampton, Stroud, GL6 9BE
☎ (01453) 832642 (Old)
   (01453) 833840 (New)
🖳 (01453) 837360
📧 secretary@mgcnew.co.uk
🏛 1860
🏴 R East (01453) 833866
✔ C Steele (01453) 837351
🏴 Old 18 L 6019 yds SSS 69
   Avening 18 L 6263 yds SSS 70
   Cherington 18 L 6430 yds SSS 71
👥 H SOC

££ Old–£16 (£19). New–£40 (£50)
   (2007 rates – subject to review)
🏴 Old-3 miles E of Stroud. New-5
   miles E of Stroud
⊕ Driving range for members and
   green fee visitors
🏠 Old: R Wilson. Avening: F Hawtree.
   Cherington: M Hawtree
🖥 www.mgcnew.co.uk

Naunton Downs   (1993)
Proprietary
Naunton, Cheltenham, GL54 3AE
☎ (01451) 850090
🖳 (01451) 850091
📧 admin@nauntondowns.co.uk
🏛 750
🏴 Jane Ayers
✔ N Ellis (01451) 850092
🏴 18 L 6186 yds Par 71 SSS 71
👥 WD–U–by arrangement WE–NA
   before 11am
££ £25 (£29)
🏴 5 miles SW of Stow-on-the-Wold,
   on B4068
🏠 Jacob Pott
🖥 www.nauntondowns.co.uk

Newent   (1994)
Pay and play
Coldharbour Lane, Newent, GL18 1DJ
☎ (01531) 820478

Painswick   (1891)
Golf Course Road, Painswick, Stroud,
GL6 6TL
☎ (01452) 812180
📧 hello@painswickgolf.com
🏛 300
🏴 Mrs Ann Smith
✔ None
🏴 18 L 4780 yds SSS 63
👥 WD/Sat–U SOC Sun–M
££ £19 (Sat £22). With member £14
   (Sat £14.50)
🏴 ¹/₂ mile N of Painswick on A46
⊕ Practice nets; putting green
🏠 David Brown
🖥 www.painswickgolf.com

Rodway Hill   (1991)
Pay and play
Newent Road, Highnam, GL2 8DN
☎ (01452) 384222
🖳 (01452) 313814
🏛 400
🏴 A Price
🏴 18 L 6040 yds Par 70 SSS 69
👥 U SOC
££ 9: £9 (£10); 18: £15 (£17)
🏴 2 miles W of Gloucester (B4215)
🏠 J Gabb
🖥 www.rodway-hill-golf-course.co.uk

Sherdons Golf Centre
(1993)
Pay and play
Tredington, Tewkesbury, GL20 7BP
☎ (01684) 274782
🖳 (01684) 275358
📧 info@sherdons.co.uk
🏛 300

🏴 R Chatham
✔ J. Lee/C. Gillick
🏴 9 L 2654 yds Par 34 SSS 65
👥 U
££ 9: £10 (£11); 18: £17 (£18)
🏴 2 miles S of Tewkesbury, off A38
⊕ Driving range
🖥 www.sherdons.co.uk

Shirehampton Park   (1904)
Park Hill, Shirehampton, Bristol, BS11 0UL
☎ (0117) 982 2083
🖳 (0117) 982 5280
📧 info@shirehamptonparkgolfclub
   .co.uk
🏛 400
🏴 Karen Rix (0117) 982 2083
✔ J Palmer (0117) 982 2488
🏴 18 L 5453 yds Par 67 SSS 66
👥 SOC WD–U WE–WA before noon
££ £24 (£20) Twilight rates after 6pm
   wdays 2 w/e in summer, after 2pm
   everyday in winter.
🏴 2 miles E of M5 Jct 18, on B4054
🖥 www.shirehamptonparkgolfclub
   .co.uk

Stinchcombe Hill   (1889)
Stinchcombe Hill, Dursley, GL11 6AQ
☎ (01453) 542015
🖳 (01453) 549545
📧 secretary@stinchcombehill.plus.com
🏛 550
🏴 Ian Crowther
✔ P Bushell (01453) 543878
🏴 18 L 5734 yds SSS 68
👥 U–phone Pro SOC
££ £28 D–£36 (£36 D–£42)
🏴 1 mile W of Dursley. M5 J14
   northbound, J13 southbound
🏠 A Hoare; James Braid redesign
🖥 www.stinchcombehillgolfclub.com

Tewkesbury Park Hotel
(1976)
Lincoln Green Lane, Tewkesbury,
GL20 7DN
☎ (01684) 295405 (Hotel)
🖳 (01684) 292386
📧 golfsec.tewkesburypark
   @foliohotels.com
🏛 600
🏴 Golf Sec (01684) 272322
✔ Marc Cottrell (01684) 272320
🏴 18 L 6533 yds Par 73 SSS 71
   6 hole Par 3 course
👥 WD–U H WE–restricted
   SOC–WD
££ £30 (£40) Twilight £18
🏴 ¹/₂ mile S of Tewkesbury on A38.
   M5 Junction 9, 2 miles
🏠 Pennick
🖥 www.tewkesburyparkgolfclub.co.uk

Thornbury Golf Centre
(1992)
Bristol Road, Thornbury, BS35 3XL
☎ (01454) 281144
🖳 (01454) 281177
📧 info@thornburygc.co.uk
🏛 500
🏴 K Pickett (Mgr)

✓ M Smedley
🏌 18 L 6308 yds SSS 70 Par 71
18 L 2195 yds Par 54
U SOC–WD
££ £19.50 (£23)
🚗 10 miles N of Bristol, off A38
⊕ Driving range
🏠 Hawtree
🖥 www.thornburygc.co.uk

Woodlands G&CC (1989)
Pay and play
Woodlands Lane, Almondsbury, Bristol,
BS32 4JZ
☎ (01454) 619319
🖂 (01454) 619397
✉ golf@woodlands-golf.com
✎ D Knipe
✓ L Riddiford
🏌 Masters Course
18 L 6111 yds SSS 70
Signature Course
18 L 5541 yds SSS 69
U SOC
££ £14 (£16)
🚗 Nr M5 Junction 16
⊕ Golf Design
🖥 www.woodlands-golf.com

Woodspring G&CC
(1994)
Yanley Lane, Long Ashton, Bristol, BS41 9LR
☎ (01275) 394378
🖂 (01275) 394473
✉ info@woodspring-golf.com
✎ D Knipe
✓ K Pitts
🏌 27 holes:
6209-6587 yds Par 71 SSS 70-71
WD WE SOC
££ £30 (£34). Fairway rate £15 (£17)
🚗 2 miles S of Bristol on A38.
⊕ Floodlit driving range
🏠 Allis/Clark/Steel
🖥 www.woodspring-golf.com

Hampshire

Alresford (1890)
Cheriton Road, Tichborne Down, Alresford,
SO24 0PN
☎ (01962) 733746
🖂 (01962) 736040
✉ secretary@alresfordgolf.co.uk
📖 625
✎ D Maskery
✓ M Scott (01962) 733998
🏌 18 L 5914 yds Par 69 SSS 69
U SOC–WD
££ £24–£32 (£30–£40)
🚗 1 m S of Alresford on B3046, 2 m
N of A272
⊕ Practice ground, covered bays;
putting and chipping green
🏠 Scott Webb Young
🖥 www.alresfordgolf.co.uk

Alton (1908)
Old Odiham Road, Alton, GU34 4BU
☎ (01420) 82042

Ampfield Par Three (1963)
Winchester Road, Ampfield, Romsey,
SO51 9BQ
☎ (01794) 368480

Andover (1907)
51 Winchester Road, Andover, SP10 2EF
☎ (01264) 323980
🖂 (01264) 358040
✉ secretary@andovergolfclub.co.uk
📖 433 42(L) 73(J)
✎ Jon Lecisie (01264) 358040
✓ W Acant (01264) 324151
🏌 9 L 6096 yds SSS 69
U SOC WD
££ £20 (£25)
🚗 ½ mile S of Andover on A3057
🏠 JH Taylor
🖥 www.andovergolfclub.co.uk

Army (1883)
Laffan's Road, Aldershot, GU11 2HF
☎ (01252) 337272
🖂 (01252) 337562
✉ secretary@armygolfclub.com
📖 750
✎ John Hiscock (01252) 337272
✓ G Cowley (01252) 336722
🏌 18 L 6579 yds SSS 71
WD–H–contact Sec/Mgr SOC
££ Special rates for military personnel
Twilight rates
🚗 Between Aldershot and
Farnborough; M3 Jct 4
⊕ Practice range; putting green
🖥 www.armygolfclub.com

Barton-on-Sea (1897)
Milford Road, New Milton, BH25 5PP
☎ (01425) 615308
🖂 (01425) 621457
✉ admin@barton-on-sea-golf.co.uk
📖 700
✎ G Prince
✓ P Rodgers (01425) 611210
🏌 27 holes:
L 6289-6505 yds Par 72
H NA before 9am SOC–WD exc
Tues
££ D–£44 (R–£55)
🚗 1 mile from New Milton, off B3058
🏠 J Hamilton Stutt/H Colt
🖥 www.barton-on-sea-golf.co.uk

Basingstoke (1907)
Kempshott Park, Basingstoke, RG23 7LL
☎ (01256) 465990
🖂 (01256) 331793
✉ enquiries@basingstokegolfclub.co.uk
📖 700
✎ S Lawrence
✓ R Woolley (01256) 351332
🏌 18 L 6350 yds SSS 70
WD–H WE–M SOC–WD
££ £40 D–£50
🚗 3 miles W of Basingstoke on A30;
1 mile from M3 Jct 7 on A30 to
Basingstoke
⊕ Practice area
🏠 James Braid
🖥 www.basingstokegolfclub.co.uk

Bishopswood (1978)
Proprietary
Bishopswood Lane, Tadley, Basingstoke,
RG26 4AT
☎ (0118) 981 2200/5213
🖂 (0118) 940 8606
📖 420
✎ Mrs J Jackson-Smith
(0118) 982 0312 (Sec)
Mrs B Goss (0118 981 2200 (Prop)
✓ S Ward
🏌 9 L 6474 yds Par 72 SSS 71
WD–U WE–M SOC
££ 9: £14; 18: £20
🚗 6 miles N of Basingstoke, off A340
⊕ 12- bay floodlit driving range
🏠 Blake/Phillips
🖥 www.bishopswoodgolfcourse.co.uk

Blackmoor (1913)
Whitehill, Bordon, GU35 9EH
☎ (01420) 472775
🖂 (01420) 487666
✉ admin@blackmoorgolf.co.uk
📖 680 100(L) 70(J)
✎ Mrs J Dean (Admin Mgr)
✓ S Clay (01420) 472345
🏌 18 L 6164 yds SSS 70
WD–H SOC–WD
££ £40 D–£55
🚗 ½ mile W of Whitehill on A325
🏠 HS Colt
🖥 www.blackmoorgolf.co.uk

Blacknest (1993)
Blacknest, GU34 4QL
☎ (01420) 22888
🖂 (01420) 22001
✉ blacknestgolfclub@yahoo.co.uk
📖 400
✎ A Corbett
✓ M Dowdell
🏌 18 L 5938 yds SSS 69
6 hole Par 3 course
U SOC
££ £20 (£25)
🚗 7 miles SW of Farnham, off A325
⊕ Driving range; Practice Bunker;
Putting Green

Blackwater Valley
Chandlers Lane, Yateley, Hampshire,
GU46 7SZ
☎ (01252) 874725

Botley Park Hotel G&CC
(1989)
Winchester Road, Boorley Green, Botley,
SO3 2UA
☎ (01489) 780888 Ext 451
🖂 (01489) 789242
✉ golf.botley@macdonald-
hotels.co.uk
📖 700
✎ Dean Rossilli (Gen Mgr)
✓ Mark Smith (01489) 789771
🏌 18 L 6389 yds SSS 70
SOC WD–U WE–NA before noon
££ £9 (£17.50)
🚗 6 miles E of Southampton on
B3354. M27 Junction 7. 8 miles SE
of M3 Junction 11
⊕ Driving range

🏠 Potterton/Murray
🖥 www.macdonald-hotels.co.uk

Bramshaw (1880)
Brook, Lyndhurst, SO43 7HE
☎ **(023) 8081 3433**
📠 (023) 8081 3460
📧 golf@bramshaw.co.uk
📖 1075
🏌 Ian Baker
🏌 Clive Bonner (023) 8081 3434
🏁 Forest 18 L 5774 yds SSS 68
Manor 18 L 6537 yds SSS 71
🏌 WD–U WE–by arrangement H
Soc–WD only
££ Forest: £30 D–£55 (£35) Manor:
£40 D–£55 (£50)
🚗 10 miles W of Southampton. M27
Junction 1, 1 mile
🖥 www.bramshaw.co.uk

Brokenhurst Manor (1915)
Sway Road, Brockenhurst, SO42 7SG
☎ **(01590) 623332**
📠 (01590) 624691
📧 secretary@brokenhurst-manor
.org.uk
📖 800
🏌 PE Clifford (Ext 5)
🏌 B Parker (01590) 623092
🏁 18 L 6222 yds SSS 70
🏌 WD–H after 9.30am exc
Tues–Ladies' Day SOC–Thurs only
££ £49 D–£67 (£60 D–£78)
🚗 1 mile SW of Brockenhurst on
B3055
🏠 HS Colt
🖥 www.brokenhurst-manor.org.uk

Burley (1905)
Cott Lane, Burley, Ringwood, BH24 4BB
☎ **(01425) 403737 (Clubhouse)**
📠 (01425) 404168
📧 secretary@burleygolfclub.co.uk
📖 520
🏌 DC Gough (01425) 402431
🏁 9 L 6151 yds Par 71 SSS 69
🏌 Bona fide club members only – H
preferred
££ £20 (£25) W–£90
🚗 4 miles SE of Ringwood
🖥 www.burleygolfclub.co.uk

Cams Hall Estate (1993)
Proprietary
Cams Hall Estate, Fareham, PO16 8UP
☎ **(01329) 827222**
📠 (01329) 827111
📧 camshall@crown-golf.co.uk
📖 950
🏌 R Climas (Sec/Mgr)
🏌 J Neve (01329) 837732
🏁 27 L 6244–6477 yds SSS 70-71
🏌 U SOC
££ £30 (£38)
🚗 8 miles W of Portsmouth. M27
Junction 11
🏠 Alliss/Clarke
🖥 www.camshallgolf.co.uk

Chilworth (1989)
Main Road, Chilworth, Southampton,
SO16 7JP
☎ **(023) 8074 0544**

Corhampton (1891)
Corhampton, Southampton, SO32 3LP
☎ **(01489) 877279**
📠 (01489) 877680
📧 secretary@corhamptongc.co.uk
📖 550
🏌 Margaret Middleton
🏌 I Roper (01489) 877638
🏁 18 L 6398 yds SSS 71
🏌 WD–U H WE/BH–M SOC–Mons
& Thurs
££ £35 D–£50
🚗 9 miles S of Winchester M3
S/bound Jct9 or M27 E/bound Jct 7
🖥 www.corhamptongc.co.uk

Dibden Golf Centre (1974)
Public
Main Road, Dibden, Southampton,
SO45 5TB
☎ **(023) 8020 7508 (Bookings)**

Dummer (1993)
Dummer, Basingstoke, RG25 2AD
☎ **(01256) 397950**
📠 (01256) 397889
📧 enquiries@dummergolfclub.com
📖 650
🏌 Steve Wright (Mgr)
(01256) 397888
🏌 A Fannon (01256) 397950
🏁 18 L 6500 yds SSS 71
🏌 U SOC WD WE
££ Mon–Thur £20 Fri £25 (£30)
Twilight rates available Monthly
Web offers
🚗 4 m SW of Basingstoke, by M3 Jct 7
⊕ 10 bay covered driving range, open
to public
🏠 Peter Alliss
🖥 www.dummergolfclub.com

Dunwood Manor (1969)
Danes Road, Awbridge, Romsey, SO51 0GF
☎ **(01794) 340549**
📠 (01794) 341215
📧 admin@dunwood-golf.co.uk
📖 537
🏌 Hazel Johnson/Kenny Bygate
🏌 Heath Teschner (01794) 340663
🏁 18 L 5655 yds SSS 68
🏌 WE/BH–restricted SOC–WD
££ £35 D–£45 (£45)
🚗 Romsey 4 miles, off A27
🖥 www.dunwoodgolf.co.uk

Fleetlands (1961)
Fareham Road, Gosport, PO13 0AW
☎ **(023) 9254 4492**

Four Marks (1994)
Headmore Lane, Four Marks, Alton,
GU34 3ES
☎ **(01420) 587214**
📠 (01420) 587324
📖 180
🏌 Steve Bassil (01420) 587214
🏁 9 L 2077 yds Par 62 SSS 61
🏌 U SOC
££ 9: £8.95 (£9.95)
🚗 4.4 miles SW of Alton, Hampshire
🏠 Wright/Falloon/Wrigglesworth
🖥 www.fourmarksgolf.co.uk

Furzeley (1993)
Pay and play
Furzeley Road, Denmead, PO7 6TX
☎ **(023) 9223 1180**
📠 (023) 9223 0921
📧 furzeleygc@btinternet.com
🏌 R Brown
🏌 D Brown
🏁 18 L 4488 yds Par 62 SSS 61
🏌 U SOC
££ £15 (£16.00) OAP Mon–Thur £12
🚗 2 miles NW of Waterlooville

Gosport & Stokes Bay (1885)
Fort Road, Haslar, Gosport, PO12 2AT
☎ **(023) 925 27941/587423**
📠 (023) 925 27941
📧 secretary
@gosportandstokesbaygolfclub.co.uk
📖 500
🏌 Mark Chivers (023) 925 27941
🏁 9 L 5995 yds SSS 69
🏌 U exc Sun am–NA
SOC–Mon/Tues/Wed/Fri/Sat
££ £20 (£25)
🚗 S boundary of Gosport
⊕ Putting green, chipping area, driving
nets
🖥 www.gosportandstokesbaygolfclub
.co.uk

The Hampshire (1993)
Winchester Road, Goodworth Clatford,
Andover, SP11 7TB
☎ **(01264) 357555**
📠 (01264) 356606
📧 enquiries@thehampshiregolfclub
.co.uk
📖 500
🏌 T Fiducia
🏌 R Spurrier
🏁 18 L 6145 yds Par 71
9 hole Par 3 course
🏌 U SOC WD WE after midday
££ £28 (£33)
🚗 1 mile SW of Andover (A3057)
⊕ Covered driving range
🏠 T Fiducia
🖥 www.thehampshiregolfclub.co.uk

Hartley Wintney (1891)
London Road, Hartley Wintney, Hook,
RG27 8PT
☎ **(01252) 844211**
📠 (01252) 844211
📧 office@hartleywintneygolfclub.com
📖 750
🏌 P J Gaylor
🏌 M Smith
🏁 18 L 6240 yds Par 71 SSS 71
🏌 Wed–Ladies Day
WE/BH–restricted SOC
££ £35 (£40)
🚗 A30 between Camberley and
Basingstoke
🖥 www.hartleywintneygolfclub.com

Hayling (1883)
Links Lane, Hayling Island, PO11 0BX
☎ **(023) 9246 4446**
📠 (023) 9246 1119

⊠ members@haylinggolf.co.uk
☐ 1020
🏌 Ian Walton (023) 9246 4446
✓ M Treleaven (023) 9246 4491
ⴉ 18 L 6531 yds SSS 71
👤 H WE/BH–after 10am SOC–Tues
& Wed
££ £49 (£62)
⛳ 5 miles S of Havant on A3023
🏠 Taylor (1905)/Simpson (1933)
🖥 www.haylinggolf.co.uk

Hockley   (1914)
Twyford, Winchester, SO21 1PL
☎ (01962) 713165
⊠ secretary@hockleygolfclub.com

Lee-on-the-Solent
(1905)
Brune Lane, Lee-on-the-Solent, PO13 9PB
☎ (023) 925 51170
☐ (023) 925 54233
⊠ enquiries@leeonthesolentgolfclub
.co.uk
☐ 700
🏌 Rob Henderson (Mgr) (023) 925
51170
✓ R Edwards (023) 925 51181
ⴉ 18 L 5926 yds SSS 69
👤 WD–U H WE H SOC–U
££ D–£36 (£40)
⛳ 3 miles S of Fareham. M27 Jct 11
⊕ Practice area; putting, chipping and
practice bunkers
🏠 John D Dunn & John H Stutt
🖥 www.leegolf.co.uk

Liphook   (1922)
Liphook, GU30 7EH
☎ (01428) 723271/723785
☐ (01428) 724853
⊠ secretary@liphookgolfclub.com
☐ 700
🏌 John Douglass
(01428) 723785/723271
✓ I Mowbray
ⴉ 18 L 6167 yds SSS 69
👤 I H (max 24) Sun–NA before 1pm
SOC welcome Wed–Fri
££ £53 D–£67
⛳ 1 mile S of Liphook on B2070 (old
A3)
🏠 ACG Croome
🖥 www.liphookgolfclub.com

Meon Valley   (1979)
Sandy Lane, Shedfield, Southampton,
SO32 2HQ
☎ (01329) 833455
☐ (01329) 834411
☐ 730
🏌 GF McMenemy (Golf Dir)
✓ N Grist
ⴉ 18 L 6520 yds SSS 71
9 L 2885 yds SSS 68
👤 H SOC
££ 9: £12; 18: £45 (£55)
⛳ 2 miles NW of Wickham. N off
A334
⊕ Driving range; full practice facilities
🏠 J Hamilton Stutt

New Forest   (1888)
Southampton Road, Lyndhurst, SO43 7BU
☎ (023) 8028 2752
⊠ secretarynfgc@aol.com
☐ 600
🏌 Golf Manager (023) 8028 2752
✓ K Caplehorn
ⴉ 18 L 5526 yds SSS 67
👤 U – subject to availability H – may
be required at peak times
££ £17 D–£27 (£23 D–£32) (£24/£30)
Peak Times Discounts available out
of peak times & groups of 4+
⛳ 8 miles W of Southampton on A35
🖥 www.newforestgolfclub.co.uk

North Hants   (1904)
Minley Road, Fleet, GU51 1RF
☎ (01252) 616443
☐ (01252) 811627
⊠ secretary@north-hants-fleetgc
.co.uk
☐ 650
🏌 C Donovan
✓ S Porter (01252) 616655
ⴉ 18 L 6472 yds Par 70 SSS 72
👤 WD–H by prior arrangement
WE/BH–MH SOC–Tues & Wed
££ On application
⛳ 3 miles W of Farnborough on
B3013. M3 Junction 4A
⊕ Practice Ground.
🏠 James Braid/H S Colt
🖥 www.northhantsgolf.co.uk

Old Thorns   (1982)
Longmoor Road, Griggs Green, Liphook,
GU30 7PE
☎ (01428) 724555
☐ (01428) 725036
⊠ proshop@oldthorns.com
🏌 S Meakin (Gen
Mgr) (01428) 725813
✓ P Chapman (01428) 725 880
ⴉ 18 L 6533 yds SSS 71 Par 72
👤 U SOC
££ £45 (£55)
⛳ Griggs Green exit off A3
⊕ Driving range; Hotel; Health Spa.
🏠 Cdr John Harris
🖥 www.oldthorns.com

Otterbourne Golf Centre
(1995)
Pay and play
Poles Lane, Otterbourne, Winchester,
SO21 2EL
☎ (01962) 775225
⊠ info@chilworthgolfclub.com
🏌 C Garner
ⴉ 9 L 1939 yds Par
👤 U
££ £4 (£6.00)
⛳ On A31 between Otterbourne and
Hursley
⊕ Driving range
🖥 www.chilworthgolfclub.com

Park   (1995)
Pay and play
Avington, Winchester, SO21 1DA
☎ (01962) 779945 (Clubhouse)
☐ (01962) 779530

⊠ office@avingtongolf.co.uk
☐ 350
🏌 R Stent (Prop) (01962) 779955
✓ None
ⴉ 9 L 1907 yds Par 61 SSS 58
👤 U SOC
££ 9: £9.80 (£12). 18: £14.70 (£18)
⛳ 4 miles E of Winchester. M3 Jct 9
🏠 R Stent
🖥 www.avingtongolf.co.uk

Paultons Golf Centre   (1922)
Pay and play
Old Salisbury Road, Ower, Romsey,
SO51 6AN
☎ (023) 8081 3992
☐ (023) 8081 3993
🏌 M Rollinson
✓ M Williamson
ⴉ 18 L 6238 yds SSS 71
9 hole Academy course Par 3
👤 U SOC
££ 9: £7.50 (£8) 18: £20 (£26)
⛳ Nr M27 Junction 2, at Ower
⊕ Driving range; practice area
🖥 www.crown-golf.co.uk

Petersfield   (1892)
Tankerdale Lane, Liss, GU33 7QY
☎ (01730) 895165
☐ (01730) 894713
⊠ manager@pgc1892.net
☐ 730
🏌 PD Badger
✓ G Hughes (01730) 895216
ⴉ 18 L 6450 yds Par 72 SSS 71
👤 WD–U WE/BH–NA before noon
SOC–Mon/Wed/Fri
££ £30 (£35)
⛳ Off A3, at Liss exit (B3006)
🏠 Hawtree
🖥 www.petersfieldgolfclub.co.uk

Petersfield Sussex Road
Pay and play
Sussex Road, Petersfield
☎ (01730) 267732
🏌 PD Badger
ⴉ 9 L 3005 yds
👤 U
££ 12 holes: £10 (£12)
⛳ Petersfield

Portsmouth   (1926)
Pay and play
Crookhorn Lane, Widley, Waterlooville,
PO7 5QL
☎ (023) 9237 2210
☐ 500
🏌 S Richard (023) 9220 1827
✓ (023) 9237 2210
ⴉ 18 L 6139 yds SSS 70
👤 U SOC–arrange with Pro
££ £17
⛳ 1 mile N of Portsmouth, on B2177
⊕ Practice area, putting green,
practice nets
🏠 Hawtree
🖥 www.portsmouthgc.co.uk

Quindell   (1997)
Skylark Meadows, Whiteley, Fareham,
PO15 6RS
☎ (01329) 844441

For list of abbreviations and key to symbols see page 647

Romsey   (1900)
Nursling, Southampton, SO16 0XW
- ☎ **(023) 8073 4637**
- 📠 (023) 8074 1036
- ✉ secretary@romseygolfclub.co.uk
- 🕮 655
- ♟ Mike Batty
- ⚲ James Pitcher (023) 8073 6673
- ⛳ 18 L 5856 yds SSS 68 Par 69
- ♟ WD–H WE/BH–M H
- ££ £32 D–£38
- 🚗 2 miles SE of Romsey on A3057. M27/M271 Junction 3
- 🖳 www.romseygolfclub.com

Rowlands Castle   (1902)
Links Lane, Rowlands Castle, PO9 6AE
- ☎ **(023) 9241 2784**
- 📠 (023) 9241 3649
- ✉ manager@rowlandscastlegolfclub .co.uk
- 🕮 800 150(L) 50(J)
- ♟ KD Fisher (023) 9241 2784
- ⚲ P Klepacz (023) 9241 2785
- ⛳ 18 L 6630 yds Par 72 SSS 72
- ♟ WD–U H exc Wed am–restricted WE–phone first Sat–M SOC–Tues & Thurs
- ££ D–£38 (D–£42)
- 🚗 9 miles S of Petersfield, off A3(M). 3 miles N of Havant
- ♟ HS Colt
- 🖳 www.rowlandscastlegolfclub.co.uk

Royal Winchester   (1888)
Sarum Road, Winchester, SO22 5QE
- ☎ **(01962) 852462**
- 📠 (01962) 865048
- ✉ manager@royalwinchestergolfclub .com
- 🕮 750
- ♟ A Buck
- ⚲ S Hunter (01962) 862473
- ⛳ 18 L 6387 yds SSS 72
- ♟ WD–U H WE/BH–M SOC–Mon/Tues/Wed/Fri
- ££ On application
- 🚗 W of Winchester. M3 Junction 11
- ♟ JH Taylor
- 🖳 www.royalwinchestergolfclub.com

Sandford Springs   (1988)
Wolverton, Tadley, RG26 5RT
- ☎ **(01635) 296800**
- 📠 (01635) 296801
- ✉ andreww@leaderboardgolf.co.uk
- 🕮 650
- ♟ Andrew Wild (01635) 296805
- ⛳ 27 L 6100 yds SSS 70
- ♟ WD–prior booking WE–M SOC–WD
- ££ Mon–Thur £35 4 ball £99, Fri £40 4 ball £120, Sat/Sun after 1pm £40 4 ball £120
- 🚗 8 miles N of Basingstoke on A339
- ♟ Hawtree
- 🖳 www.sandfordspringsgolf.co.uk

Somerley Park   (1995)
Somerley, Ringwood, BH24 3PL
- ☎ **(01425) 461496**
- 🕮 169

- ♟ C Trounce (01202) 820722
- ⚲ J Waring (01202) 821703
- ⛳ 9 L 2155 yds Par 33 SSS 62
- ♟ M SOC
- ££ £10 (£10)
- 🚗 5 miles W of Ringwood
- ♟ John Jacobs OBE

South Winchester
Romsey Road, Pitt, Winchester, SO22 5QX
- ☎ **(01962) 877800**
- ✉ winchester-sales@crown-golf.co.uk

Southampton Municipal   (1935)
Public
1 Golf Course Road, Bassett, Southampton, SO16 7AY
- ☎ **(023) 807 60546**
- ✉ mick.carter7@ntlworld.com
- ♟ E Hemsley (02380) 476582
- ⚲ Andy Gordon (02380) 760388
- ⛳ 18 L 6218 yds SSS 70 9 L 2391 yds SSS 33
- ♟ U
- ££ On application
- 🚗 2 miles N of Southampton
- ♟ JH Taylor
- 🖳 www.southamptongolfclub.co.uk

Southsea   (1914)
Public
The Clubhouse, Burrfields Road, Portsmouth, PO3 5JJ
- ☎ **(023) 9266 8667**
- 📠 (023) 9266 8667
- ✉ southseagolfclub@tiscali.co.uk
- 🕮 250
- ♟ R Collinson (02392) 699110
- ⚲ T Healy (02392) 664549
- ⛳ 18 Holes Par 69 Whites 5620 SSS 67; Yellow 5259 SSS 66; Red 5057 SSS 68
- ♟ U SOC
- ££ £16
- 🚗 1 mile off M27 on A2030
- ⊕ Driving range
- 🖳 www.southsea-golf.co.uk

Southwick Park   (1977)
Pinsley Drive, Southwick, PO17 6EL
- ☎ **(023) 9238 0131**
- 📠 (0871) 855 6809
- ✉ southwickpark@btconnect.com
- 🕮 650 80(L)
- ♟ SG Searle
- ⚲ E Rawlings (023) 9238 0442
- ⛳ 18 L 5884 yds Par 69 SSS 69
- ♟ WD–U booking necessary WE–NA before 10am SOC
- ££ Visitor £25 D–£32 (£28) Service personnel reduced rate
- 🚗 5 miles N of Portsmouth, off B2177
- ⊕ Practice ground; putting green; 9-hole pitch & putt
- ♟ Charles Lawrie
- 🖳 www.southwickparkgolfclub.co.uk

Southwood   (1977)
Public
Ively Road, Farnborough, GU14 0LJ
- ☎ **(01252) 548700**

- ♟ (01252) 549091
- ✉ ianattoe@ddesure.co.uk
- 🕮 350
- ♟ Chris Hudson (01252) 665452
- ⚲ C Hudson
- ⛳ 18 L 5669 yds Par 69 SSS 67
- ♟ U
- ££ £19 (£21.70)
- 🚗 1 mile W of Farnborough, off A325; 2 miles from M3 J4A
- ♟ M Hawtree
- 🖳 www.southwoodgolfclub.co.uk

Stoneham   (1908)
Monks Wood Close, Bassett, Southampton, SO16 3TT
- ☎ **(023) 8076 9272**
- 📠 (023) 8076 6320
- ✉ richard@stonehamgolfclub.org.uk
- 🕮 600
- ♟ R Penley-Martin (Mgr) (023) 8076 9272
- ⚲ I Young (023) 8076 8397
- ⛳ 18 L 6392 yds Par 72 SSS 71
- ♟ H SOC–Mon/Thurs/Fri
- ££ £46 D–£55 (£51 D–£61)
- 🚗 2 miles N of Southampton on A27; 2 miles from M27 J5 or M3 J14
- ♟ Willie Park jr
- 🖳 www.stonehamgolfclub.org.uk

Test Valley   (1992)
Micheldever Road, Overton, Basingstoke, RG25 3DS
- ☎ **(01256) 771737**
- 📠 (01256) 771285
- ✉ info@testvalleygolf.com
- 🕮 550
- ♟ A Briggs (Mgr) (01256) 771737
- ⚲ A Briggs
- ⛳ 18 L 6897 yds SSS 71
- ♟ U SOC WD–U WE–NA before noon SOC WD U WE NA before 2pm
- ££ £24 D–£36 (£30)
- 🚗 2 miles S of Overton on Micheldever road. M3 Jct 8 (A303)
- ⊕ 10-bay driving range; short game practice area; putting green
- ♟ Wright/Darcy
- 🖳 www.testvalleygolf.com

Tylney Park   (1973)
Proprietary
Rotherwick, Hook, RG27 9AY
- ☎ **(01256) 762079**
- 📠 (01256) 763079
- ✉ contact@tylneypark.co.uk
- 🕮 700
- ♟ MA Brain
- ⚲ A Hay (Mgr)
- ⛳ 18 L 7017 yds Par 72 SSS 74
- ♟ WD–U WE–H or WD SOC
- ££ D–£45 (D–£45)
- 🚗 2 miles NW of Hook. M3 J5, 8 miles S M4 J11
- ⊕ Driving range; practice ground
- ♟ Donald Steel/Tom MacKenzie
- 🖳 www.tylneypark.co.uk

Waterlooville   (1907)
Cherry Tree Ave, Cowplain, Waterlooville, PO8 8AP

For list of abbreviations and key to symbols see page 647

☎ (023) 9226 3388
📠 (023) 9224 2980
📧 secretary@waterloovillegolfclub
.co.uk
📖 800
🏌 D Nairne
/ J Hay (023) 9225 6911
➤ 18 L 6602 yds SSS 72
👥 WD/WE H SOC
££ £40
🚗 10 miles N of Portsmouth on A3
⊕ Practice area and putting green
🏠 Henry Cotton
🖥 www.waterloovillegolfclub.co.uk

Wellow   (1991)
Ryedown Lane, East Wellow, Romsey,
SO51 6BD
☎ (01794) 322872
📠 (01794) 323832
📖 600
🏌 Mrs C Gurd
/ N Bratley (01794) 323833
➤ 27 L 6000 yds SSS 69
👥 U SOC–WD
££ £22 (£27)
🚗 2 miles W of Romsey. M27
Junction 2, via A36
🏠 W Wiltshire
🖥 www.wellowgolfclub.co.uk

Weybrook Park   (1971)
Rooksdown Lane, Basingstoke, RG24 9NT
☎ (01256) 320347
📠 (01256) 812973
📧 info@weybrookpark.co.uk
📖 600
🏌 P Shearman
/ A Dillon (01256) 333232
➤ 18 L 6468 yds SSS 71
👥 WD–U WE–contact Mgr SOC
££ £24 (£28)
🚗 1½ miles N of Basingstoke
🖥 www.weybrookpark.co.uk

Wickham Park   (1991)
Proprietary
Titchfield Lane, Wickham, Fareham,
PO17 5PJ
☎ (01329) 833342
📠 (01329) 834798
📧 wickhampark@crown-golf.co.uk
🏌 Jonathan Tubb
/ Dean Elder
➤ 18 L 5868 yds Par 69 SSS 68
👥 U SOC–WD
££ £15 (£20)
🚗 2 miles N of Fareham. M27 Jct 10
⊕ Driving range
🏠 Jon Payn
🖥 www.crown-golf.co.uk

Worldham   (1993)
Proprietary
Cakers Lane, Worldham, Alton, GU34 3BF
☎ (01420) 543151/544606
📠 (01420) 544606
📧 manager@worldhamgolfclub.co.uk
📖 350
🏌 Ian Yates (01420) 544606
/ Anthony Cook (01420) 543151
➤ 18 L 6196 yds SSS 70
👥 WD–U WE–U SOC–WD/WE

££ £18 (£22)
🚗 ½ mile E of Alton on B3004 to
Bordon
⊕ Driving range
🏠 Troth/Whidborne
🖥 www.worldhamgolfclub.co.uk

Herefordshire

Belmont Lodge   (1983)
Ruckhall Lane, Belmont, Hereford, HR2 9SA
☎ (01432) 352666
📠 (01432) 358090
📧 info@belmont-hereford.co.uk
📖 500
🏌 Christopher T Smith (Gen Mgr)
/ Richard Hemming (01432) 352717
➤ 18 L 6369 yds SSS 71
👥 U SOC
££ On application
🚗 1½ miles S of Hereford on A465
🏠 B Sandow
🖥 www.belmont-hereford.co.uk

Burghill Valley   (1991)
Tillington Road, Burghill, Hereford,
HR4 7RW
☎ (01432) 760456
📠 (01432) 761654
📧 info@bvgc.co.uk
🏌 K Smith (Gen Mgr)
/ K Preece (01432) 760808
➤ 18 L 6204 yds SSS 70
👥 U SOC
££ £26 (£31)
🚗 3 miles N of Hereford, off A4110
🖥 www.bvgc.co.uk

Cadmore Lodge   (1990)
Pay and play
Berrington Green, Tenbury Wells,
Worcester, WR15 8TQ
☎ (01584) 810044
📠 (01584) 810044
📖 150
🏌 RV Farr
/ None
➤ 9 L 5129 yds Par 68 SSS 65
👥 U
££ D–£10 (D–£14)
🚗 2 miles S of Tenbury Wells on
A4112
🖥 www.cadmorelodge.demon.co.uk

Hereford Golf Club   (1983)
Public
Hereford Halo Leisure & Golf Club, Holmer
Road, Hereford, HR4 9UD
☎ (01432) 344376
📠 (01432) 266281
📖 200
🏌 G Morgan (Mgr)
/ G Morgan (01432) 344376
➤ 9 L 3060 yds Par 70 SSS 68
👥 U SOC
££ 9: £5.60; 18: £8.40
🚗 Hereford Halo Leisure Centre,
A49 Leominster road
⊕ Practice area and putting green;
leisure centre attached

Herefordshire   (1896)
Raven's Causeway, Wormsley, Hereford,
HR4 8LY
☎ (01432) 830219
📠 (01432) 830095
📧 herefordshire.golf@breathe.com
📖 770 150(L) 55(J)
🏌 D Gwynne
/ J Parry (01432) 830465
➤ 18 L 6031 yds Par 70 SSS 69
👥 U–phone first SOC
££ £25 D–£30 (£35 D–£40)
🚗 6 miles NW of Hereford
🏠 Maj SV Hotchkin, MC
🖥 www.herefordshiregolfclub.co.uk

Kington   (1926)
Bradnor Hill, Kington, HR5 3RE
☎ (01544) 230340
📠 (01544) 340270
📧 kington@ukonline.co.uk
📖 440
🏌 GR Wictome (01544) 340270
/ A Gealy (01544) 231320
➤ 18 L 5840 yds SSS 69
👥 WE–NA before 10.15am–
restricted 1.30–2.45pm SOC
££ £22 D–£28 (£28 D–£34)
🚗 1 mile N of Kington
⊕ Practice area
🏠 Major CK Hutchison
🖥 www.kingtongolf.co.uk

Leominster   (1967)
Ford Bridge, Leominster, HR6 0LE
☎ (01568) 612863 (Clubhouse)
📠 (01568) 610055
📧 contact@leominstergolfclub.co.uk
📖 450
🏌 L Green (01568) 610055
/ N Clarke (01568) 611402
➤ 18 L 6026 yds SSS 69
👥 U SOC
££ £20 D–£25 (£25 D–£30)
🚗 3 miles S of Leominster on A49
(Leominster Bypass)
🏠 R Sandow
🖥 leominstergolfclub.co.uk

Ross-on-Wye   (1903)
Two Park, Gorsley, Ross-on-Wye, HR9 7UT
☎ (01989) 720267
📠 (01989) 720212
📧 admin@therossonwyegolfclub.co.uk
📖 760
🏌 Sarah Creighton (Administrator)
/ Paul Middleton (01989) 720439
➤ 18 L 6500 yds Par 72 SSS 71
👥 U SOC–Wed–Fri (min 16 players)
££ £40–£50 SOC–£34–£44 (subject
to review)
🚗 5 miles N of Ross-on-Wye, by M50
Junction 3
⊕ Parkland driving range
🏠 CK Cotton
🖥 www.therossonwyegolfclub.co.uk

Sapey   (1991)
Proprietary
Upper Sapey, Worcester, WR6 6XT
☎ (01886) 853288
📠 (01886) 853485

✉ anybody@sapeygolf.co.uk
📖 380
🏌 Miss L Stevenson (01886) 853506
✓ C Knowles
▷ 18 L 5939 yds SSS 68
9 hole Par 3 course
⚭ WD–U WE–NA before 11am SOC
££ £27 D–£34 (£32 D–£39)
⛐ 6 miles N of Bromyard on B4203.
M5 Junction 5
🖥 www.sapeygolf.co.uk

South Herefordshire

(1992)

*Twin Lakes, Upton Bishop, Ross-on-Wye,
HR9 7UA*

☎ (01989) 780535
📠 (01989) 740611
✉ info@herefordshiregolf.co.uk
📖 350
🏌 James Leaver
✓ Lewis Hanney
▷ 18 L 6672 yds Par 71 SSS 72
9 hole Par 3 course
⚭ U SOC
££ £20 D–£30 (£25 D–£35)
⛐ 3 miles NE of Ross-on-Wye. M50
Junction 4
⊕ Floodlit driving range
🏠 John Day
🖥 www.herefordshiregolf.co.uk

Summerhill   (1994)

Proprietary
*Clifford, Nr. Hay-on-Wye, Hereford
HR3 5EW*

☎ (01497) 820451
✉ competitions
@summerhillgolfcourse.co.uk
📖 210
🏌 Michael Tom
✓ Travelling Pro Will Dowd
▷ 9 (18 tees) L 5675 yds Par 70
SSS 69
⚭ U
££ £15 (£20)
⛐ Near Hay-on-Wye
⊕ 3 x par 3s
🏠 Bob Sandow
🖥 www.summerhillgolfcourse.co.uk

Hertfordshire

Aldenham G&CC   (1975)

*Church Lane, Aldenham, Watford,
WD25 8NN*

☎ (01923) 853929
📠 (01923) 858472
✉ info@aldenhamgolfclub.co.uk
📖 350
🏌 Mrs J Phillips
✓ T Dunstan (01923) 857889
▷ 18 L 6456 yds SSS 71
9 L 2350 yds
⚭ WD–U WE–U after 12.30pm
££ 9: £12 (£15) 18: £30 (£40)
⛐ 3 miles E of Watford, off B462. M1
Junction 5
🖥 www.aldenhamgolfclub.co.uk

Aldwickbury Park   (1995)

Proprietary
*Piggottshill Lane, Wheathampstead Road,
Harpenden, AL5 1AB*

☎ (01582) 760112
📠 (01582) 760113
✉ info@aldwickburyparkgc.co.uk
📖 700
🏌 T Hall
✓ R Turley
▷ 18 L 6368 yds Par 71 SSS 71
9 hole Par 3 Academy course
⚭ WD–U booking necessary WE–U
after 12.00 SOC–WD–U,
SOC–WE after 12
££ £35 (£40)
⛐ E of Harpenden on
Wheathampstead road. M1
Junction 9. A1(M) Junction 4
⊕ Practice ground, chipping & bunker
zones, putting green & net
🏠 Martin Gillett/Ken Brown
🖥 www.aldwickburyparkgolfclub.com

Arkley   (1909)

Rowley Green Road, Barnet, EN5 3HL

☎ (020) 8449 0394
📠 (020) 8440 5214
✉ secretary@arkley.demon.co.uk
📖 350
🏌 DDR Campbell
✓ A Hurley (020) 8440 8473
▷ 9 L 6046 yds SSS 69 - 18 tees
⚭ WD–U WE–M
SOC–Mon–Wed–Fri
££ £25 D–£32 (£20)
⛐ NW of Barnet, off A1(M)
⊕ Practice area
🏠 James Braid
🖥 www.arkleygolfclub.co.uk

Ashridge   (1932)

Little Gaddesden, Berkhamsted, HP4 1LY

☎ (01442) 842244
📠 (01442) 843770
✉ info@ashridgegolfclub.ltd.uk
📖 740
🏌 MS Silver
✓ P Cherry (01442) 842307
▷ 18 L 6625 yds SSS 71
WD only–phone Sec
££ On application
⛐ 5 m N of Berkhamsted on B4506
🏠 Campbell/Hutchison/Hotchkin
🖥 www.ashridgegolfclub.ltd.uk

Barkway Park   (1992)

*Nuthampstead Road, Barkway, Royston,
SG8 8EN*

☎ (01763) 849070
📖 285
🏌 GS Cannon
✓ J Bates (01763) 848215
▷ 18 L 6997 yds SSS 74
⚭ U
££ £18 (£24)
⛐ 5 miles SE of Royston, on B1368
🏠 Vivien Saunders

Batchwood Hall   (1935)

Pay and play
Batchwood Drive, St Albans, AL3 5XA

☎ (01727) 833349

Batchworth Park   (1996)

London Road, Rickmansworth, WD3 1JS

☎ (01923) 711400
📠 (01923) 710200
✉ bpgc@crown-golf.co.uk
📖 750
🏌 AD Lawrence
✓ S Proudfoot (01923) 714922
▷ 18 L 6723 yds Par 72 SSS 72
⚭ M
££ N/A
⛐ 1 mile SE of Rickmansworth on
A404. M25 Junction 18
⊕ Indoor Academy. Practice range
🏠 Dave Thomas
🖥 www.crown-golf.co.uk

Berkhamsted   (1890)

The Common, Berkhamsted, HP4 2QB

☎ (01442) 865832
📠 (01442) 863730
✉ barryh@berkhamstedgc.co.uk
📖 450 120(L) 50(J)
🏌 BJ Hill
✓ J Clarke (01442) 865851
▷ 18 L 6605 yds Par 71 SSS 72
⚭ U H WD after 8.30am WE after
11.30am SOC Mon–Wed–Fri
££ On application
⛐ 1 mile N of Berkhamsted. M25
Junction 21 (A41). M1 Junction 8
🏠 HS Colt/James Braid
🖥 www.berkhamstedgolfclub.co.uk

Bishop's Stortford   (1910)

*Dunmow Road, Bishop's Stortford,
CM23 5HP*

☎ (01279) 654715
📠 (01279) 655215
✉ office@bsgc.co.uk
📖 900
🏌 Judy Barker
✓ S Sheppard (01279) 651324
▷ 18 L 6404 yds SSS 71
⚭ WD–U H WE–M SOC–WD exc
Tues
££ £40 D–£50
⛐ E of Bishop's Stortford on A1250;
M11 Jct 8
🏠 James Braid
🖥 www.bsgc.co.uk

Boxmoor   (1890)

18 Box Lane, Hemel Hempstead, HP3 0DJ

☎ (01442) 242434 (Clubhouse)
📖 290
🏌 B Swann
✓ None
▷ 9 L 4854 yds SSS 64
⚭ WE–Sun after 1pm WD–U
££ £10 (£12)
⛐ 1 mile W of Hemel Hempstead on
B4505 to Chesham
🖥 www.boxmoorgolfclub.co.uk

Brickendon Grange   (1964)

*Pembridge Lane, Brickendon, Hertford,
SG13 8PD*

☎ (01992) 511258
📠 (01992) 511411
✉ play@brickendongrangegc.co.uk
📖 700

🏌 Martin Bennet
✓ A Clapp (01992) 511218
🏳 18 L 6458 yds SSS 71
👥 WD–U H WE/BH–M SOC
££ £38 D–£47
⛳ Bayford, 3 miles S of Hertford
🏠 CK Cotton
🖥 www.brickendongrangegc.co.uk

Briggens Park (1988)
Briggens Park, Stanstead Road, Stanstead
Abbotts, SG12 8LD
☎ (01279) 793867
🖥 (01279) 793867
📧 briggensparkgolf@aol.com
📖 200
🏌 Trevor Mitchell
✓ Darren Hodgson (PGA)
🏳 9 L 5582 yds Par 72 SSS 69
👥 U SOC
££ 9: £10 (£12); 18: £15 (£18)
⛳ 4 miles E of Hertford, off A414;
M11 J4

Brocket Hall (1992)
Welwyn, AL8 7XG
☎ (01707) 368808
🖥 (01707) 390052
📧 johnwells@brocket-hall.co.uk
📖 950
🏌 John Wells (01707) 368890
✓ K Wood (01707) 390063
🏳 Melbourne 18 L 6616 yds SSS 72
Palmerston 18 L 7096 yds SSS 73
👥 WD (H) WE(H)
££ £85 (£85)
⛳ On B653 to Wheathampstead.
A1(M) Junction 4
⊕ Driving range. Faldo Golf Institute,
Melbourne Lodge
🏠 Melbourne-Alliss/Clark.
Palmerston-Steel
🖥 www.brocket-hall.co.uk

Brookmans Park (1930)
Brookmans Park, Hatfield, AL9 7AT
☎ (01707) 652487
📧 info@bpgc.co.uk

Bushey G&CC (1980)
High Street, Bushey, WD23 1TT
☎ (020) 8950 2283
🖥 (020) 8386 1181
📧 info@busheycountryclub.com
📖 446
🏌 B Worthington
✓ Martin Siggins (020) 8950 2215
🏳 9 L 3030 yds SSS 70
👥 WD–U except Wed/Thur before 6
pm WE–NA before 2 pm SOC
££ 9: £14 (£16) 18: £22 (£27)
⛳ 2 miles S of Watford on A4008
⊕ Driving range
🏠 Donald Steel
🖥 www.busheycountryclub.com

Bushey Hall (1890)
Bushey Hall Drive, Bushey, WD23 2EP
☎ (01923) 222253
📧 gordon@golfclubuk.co.uk

Chadwell Springs (1974)
Hertford Road, Ware, SG12 9LE
☎ (01920) 463647

Chesfield Downs (1991)
Pay and play
Jack's Hill, Graveley, Stevenage, SG4 7EQ
☎ (08707) 460020

Cheshunt (1976)
Public
Park Lane, Cheshunt, EN7 6QD
☎ (01992) 29777

Chorleywood (1890)
Common Road, Chorleywood, WD3 5LN
☎ (01923) 282009
🖥 (01923) 286739
📧 secretary@chorleywoodgolfclub
.co.uk
📖 320
🏌 RA Botham
✓ RM Mandeville
🏳 9 L 2843 yds SSS 67
👥 WD–U exc Tues am WE–U after
11.30am SOC
££ £20 (£25)
⛳ 3 miles N of Rickmansworth, off
A404. M25 Junction 18

Dyrham Park CC (1963)
Galley Lane, Barnet, EN5 4RA
☎ (020) 8440 3361
🖥 (020) 8441 9836
📧 enquiries@dyrhampark.com
📖 600
🏌 D Adams
✓ M Blake (020) 8440 3904
🏳 18 L 6422 yds SSS 71
👥 M SOC–Wed
⛳ 10 miles N of London. M25 Jct 23
🏠 CK Cotton
🖥 www.dyrhampark.com

East Herts (1899)
Hamels Park, Buntingford, SG9 9NA
☎ (01920) 821978
🖥 (01920) 823700
📧 secretary@easthertsgolfclub.co.uk
📖 735
🏌 Ms A McDonald
✓ D Field (01920) 821922
🏳 18 L 6408 yds SSS 71
👥 WD–H exc Wed–NA before 1pm
WE–M
££ £36 D–£50
⛳ ¼ mile N of Puckeridge on A10
🖥 www.easthertsgolfclub.co.uk

Elstree (1984)
Watling Street, Elstree, WD6 3AA
☎ (020) 8238 6947 (Clubhouse)
(020) 8953 6115 (General)
🖥 (020) 8207 6390
📧 admin@elstree-golf.co.uk
📖 400
🏌 K Roberts (020) 8238 6942
Director of Golf
✓ M Warwick (020) 8238 6941/9
🏳 18 L 6556 yds Par 73 SSS 72
👥 U SOC
££ £20 (£24)

⛳ A5183, 1 m N of Elstree. M1 Jct 4
⊕ Floodlit driving range
🏠 Donald Steel
🖥 www.elstree-golfclub.co.uk

Great Hadham (1993)
Great Hadham Road, Bishop's Stortford,
SG10 6JE
☎ (01279) 843558
🖥 (01279) 842122
📧 ian@ghgcc.co.uk
📖 700
🏌 I Bailey
✓ K Lunt (01279) 843888
🏳 18 L 6854 yds Par 72 SSS 73
👥 WD–U WE/BH–NA before 12
noon SOC
££ £21 Mon–Thur £24 Fri (£28) 9
holes £13; 18 holes £21
⛳ 3 miles SW of Bishops Stortford
(B1004). M11 Junction 8
⊕ Driving range
🖥 www.ghgcc.co.uk

The Grove (2003)
Chandler's Cross, Rickmansworth,
WD3 4TG
☎ (01923) 807807
🖥 (01923) 294268
📧 golf@thegrove.co.uk
🏌 Spencer Schaub (Dir. of Golf)
✓ Anna Darrell
🏳 18 L 7152 yds
👥 U
££ £105–£170 depending on time of
year
⛳ 2 miles S of M25 (J20) on the A411
⊕ Range; short game area
🏠 Kyle Phillips
🖥 www.thegrove.co.uk

Hadley Wood (1922)
Beech Hill, Hadley Wood, Barnet, EN4 0JJ
☎ (020) 8449 4328
🖥 (020) 8364 8633
📧 gm@hadleywoodgc.com
📖 660
🏌 WM Beckett (Gen Mgr)
✓ P Jones (020) 8449 3285
🏳 18 L 6514 yds SSS 71
👥 WD–H WE/BH–M SOC
Mon/Thur/Fri
££ £55 D–£75 (£60)
⛳ 10 miles N of London, off A111
between Potters Bar and
Cockfosters. 2 m S of M25 Jct 24
⊕ Practice range and nets; chipping
green
🏠 Dr A MacKenzie
🖥 www.hadleywoodgc.com

Hanbury Manor G&CC
(1990)
Ware, SG12 0SD
☎ (01920) 487722
🖥 (01920) 487692
📧 mhrs.stngs.golfevents
@marriotthotels.com
📖 350
🏌 Simon Clough (Dir of Golf)
✓ Tim Good (01920) 885000
🏳 18 L 7016 yds SSS 74
👥 M H + Hotel guests SOC

££   Peak Summer Hotel res. fee £90
🚗   13 miles N of M25 Junction 25 on
     A10 at Thundridge
🏠   Jack Nicklaus II
🖥   www.hanbury-manor.com

Harpenden   (1894)
Hammonds End, Harpenden, AL5 2AX
☎   (01582) 712580
📠   (01582) 712725
📧   office@harpendengolfclub.co.uk
🏢   800
🏌   FLK Clapp (Gen Mgr)
✓   Peter Lane (01582) 767124
🏁   18 L 6377 yds par 70 SSS 70
👥   WD–U exc Thurs WE/BH–H
     SOC–WD exc Thurs
££   £40 D–£50 (£45)
🚗   6 miles N of St Albans on B487
🏠   Hawtree/Taylor
🖥   www.harpendengolfclub.co.uk

Harpenden Common   (1931)
East Common, Harpenden, AL5 1BL
☎   (01582) 711320
📠   (01582) 711321
📧   admin@hcgc.co.uk
🏢   740
🏌   D Fitzsimmons (01582) 711325
✓   D Fitzsimmons (01582) 460655
🏁   18 L 6214 yds SSS 70
👥   WD–U H WE–M SOC
££   £35
🚗   4 miles N of St Albans, on A1081
     M1, J9
🏠   K Brown (1995) - new holes
🖥   www.hcgc.co.uk

Hartsbourne G&CC   (1946)
Hartsbourne Avenue, Bushey Heath,
WD23 1JW
☎   (020) 8421 7272
📠   (020) 8950 5357
🏢   750
🏌   I Thomas
✓   R Weedon (020) 8421 7266
🏁   18 L 6385 yds SSS 70
     9 L 5773 yds SSS 68
👥   NA SOC
🚗   5 miles SE of Watford, off A4008
🏠   Hawtree/Taylor

Hatfield London CC   (1976)
Bedwell Park, Essendon, Hatfield, AL9 6HN
☎   (01707) 260360
📠   (01707) 278475
📧   info@hatfieldlondon.co.uk
🏢   260
🏌   H Takeda
🏁   18 L 6808 yds SSS 72
     18 L 6938 yds SSS 73
     36 hole course
👥   U SOC
££   £25 (£35)
🚗   4 miles E of Hatfield on B158. M25
     Junction 24. A1(M) Junction 4
⊕   9 hole pitch & putt course
🏠   Fred Hawtree
🖥   www.hatfieldlondon.co.uk

The Hertfordshire   (1995)
Proprietary
Broxbournebury Mansion, White Stubbs
Lane, Broxbourne, EN10 7PY

☎   (01992) 466666
📧   hertfordshire@americangolf.co.uk

Kingsway Golf Centre
(1991)
Cambridge Road, Melbourn, Royston,
SG8 6EY
☎   (01763) 262943
📠   (01763) 263038
📧   kingswaygolf@btconnect.com
🏢   150
🏌   P Sarno
✓   Mark Sturgess
🏁   9 L 2500 yds Par 33
     9 hole Par 3 course
👥   U SOC
££   9: £7.50 (£9). 18: £11 (£13)
🚗   N of Royston on A10
⊕   Driving range; Par 3 course; golf
     shop
🖥   www.kingswaygolf.co.uk

Knebworth   (1908)
Deards End Lane, Knebworth, SG3 6NL
☎   (01438) 812752
     (Clubhouse)
📠   (01438) 815216
📧   knebworth1@btconnect.com
🏢   750
🏌   Mr Steve Barrett (Gen Mgr)
✓   G Parker (01438) 812757
🏁   18 L 6492 yds SSS 71
👥   WD–U H WE–M
     SOC–Mon/Tues/Thurs
££   £40
🚗   1 mile S of Stevenage on B197.
     A1(M) Junction 7
🏠   Willie Park
🖥   www.knebworthgolfclub.com

Lamerwood   (1996)
Codicote Road, Wheathampstead, AL4 8GB
☎   (01582) 833013
📧   lamerwood.cc@virgin.net

Letchworth   (1905)
Letchworth Lane, Letchworth Garden City,
SG6 3NQ
☎   (01462) 683203
📠   (01462) 484567
📧   secretary@letchworthgolfclub
     .com
🏢   900
🏌   Mrs Niki Hunter
✓   Karl Teschner (01462) 682713
🏁   18 L 6459 yds SSS 71
👥   WD–H WE–M SOC–Wed–Fri
££   £20 Mon Tue–Fri £37 D–£49
🚗   S of Letchworth, off A505. A1(M)
     Junction 9
⊕   Driving range; 9 hole course
🏠   Harry Vardon
🖥   www.letchworthgolfclub.com

Little Hay Golf Complex
(1977)
Pay and play
Box Lane, Bovingdon, Hemel Hempstead,
HP3 0DQ
☎   (01442) 833798

Manor of Groves G&CC
(1991)
Proprietary
High Wych, Sawbridgeworth, CM21 0JU
☎   (01279) 600777
📧   golfsecretary@manorofgroves.com

Mid Herts   (1892)
Gustard Wood, Wheathampstead, AL4 8RS
☎   (01582) 832242
📠   (01582) 834834
📧   secretary@mid-hertsgolfclub.co.uk
🏢   500(M) 125(L)
🏌   Mr M Bennet
✓   B Puttick (01582) 839294
🏁   18 L 6060 yds SSS 69
👥   WD–UH exc Tues & Wed pm
     WE/BH–M SOC
££   £35
🚗   6 miles N of St Albans on B651
🏠   James Braid
🖥   www.mid-hertsgolfclub.co.uk

Mill Green   (1994)
Gypsy Lane, Mill Green, Welwyn Garden
City, AL7 4TY
☎   (01707) 276900
📠   (01707) 276898
📧   millgreen@crown-golf.co.uk
🏌   Tim Hudson
✓   I Parker (01707) 270542
🏁   18 L 6615 yds Par 72 SSS 72
     Par 3 course
👥   SOC–WD Visitors–WD–U
     WE–NA before noon
££   £29.50 (£37.50)
🚗   S of Welwyn Garden City, off
     A414. A1 Junction 4
⊕   Driving range
🏠   Clark/Alliss
🖥   www.millgreengolf.co.uk

Moor Park   (1923)
Rickmansworth, WD3 1QN
☎   (01923) 773146
📠   (01923) 777109
📧   jon.moore@moorparkgc.co.uk
🏢   942
🏌   JM Moore (01923) 773146
✓   L Farmer (01923) 774113
🏁   High 18 L 6717 yds SSS 72
     West 18 L 5833 yds SSS 68
👥   WD–H SOC WE/BH–NA before
     2pm
££   High £80 D–£110 (£120). West
     £50 (£80)
🚗   1 mile SE of Rickmansworth, off
     Batchworth roundabout (A4145).
     M25 Junction 18, 2 miles
⊕   Practice ground and nets; chipping
     green
🏠   HS Colt
🖥   www.moorparkgc.co.uk

Old Fold Manor   (1910)
Old Fold Lane, Hadley Green, Barnet,
EN5 4QN
☎   (020) 8440 9185
📠   (020) 8441 4863
📧   manager@oldfoldmanor.co.uk
🏢   450
🏌   B Cullen (Mgr)

For list of abbreviations and key to symbols see page 647

✓ P McEvoy (020) 8440 7488
▷ 18 L 6466 yds SSS 71
🕯 WD–H WE–M after 3pm
SOC–Mon–Fri
££ £35 (Mon+Wed £25) D–£60
🏌 1 mile N of Barnet on A1000
🖳 www.oldfoldmanor.co.uk

Oxhey Park
Prestwick Road, South Oxhey, Watford,
WD19 7EX
☎ (01923) 248213/210118
✉ info@oxheyparkgolfclub.co.uk
🕮 110
🏌 AT Duggan (Prop)
✓ J Wright
▷ 9 L 1637 yds Par 58
🕯 U
££ 9 holes–£6 (£8). 18 holes–£8 (£10)
🏌 2 miles SW of Watford. M1 Jct 5
⊕ Driving range
🖳 www.oxheyparkgolfclub.co.uk

Panshanger Golf Complex
(1976)
Public
Old Herns Lane, Welwyn Garden City,
AL7 2ED
☎ (01707) 333312/333350
(Bookings)
🖳 (01707) 390010
✉ panshanger.golfclub@virgin.net
🕮 300
🏌 Trish Skinner (07982) 259475
▷ 18 L 6167 yds SSS 70
9 hole Par 3 course
🕯 U SOC
££ £15.50 (£19.60) Snr £8.30 (£19.60)
Jnr £6.70 (£9)
🏌 2 miles off A1, via B1000 to
Hertford
🖳 www.finesseleisure.co.uk

Porters Park
(1899)
Shenley Hill, Radlett, WD7 7AZ
☎ (01923) 854127
🖳 (01923) 855475
✉ enquiries@porterspark.com
🕮 850
🏌 P Marshall
✓ D Gleeson (01923) 854366
▷ 18 L 6313 yds Par 70 SSS 70
🕯 WD–H (phone first) WE/BH–M
SOC–Wed & Thurs
££ £50 (no WE) Twilight round
4–6pm £25
🏌 E of Radlett on Shenley road. M25
Junction 22
⊕ Two practice grounds

Potters Bar
(1923)
Darkes Lane, Potters Bar, EN6 1DE
☎ (01707) 652020
✉ info@pottersbargolfclub.com

Redbourn
(1970)
Proprietary
Kinsbourne Green Lane, Redbourn, St
Albans, AL3 7QA
☎ (01582) 793493
🖳 (01582) 794362
✉ info@redbourngc.co.uk

🕮 750
🏌 T Hall (01582) 793493
✓ S Hunter (01592) 793493
▷ 18 L 6506 yds SSS 71
9 hole Par 3 course
🕯 WD–U booking necessary
WE/BH–H SOC–WD WE
afternoon
££ 9: £7.25 (£8.25) 18: £30 (£35)
🏌 4 miles N of St Albans, off A5. 1
mile S of M1 Junction 9
⊕ Floodlit golf range
🖳 www.redbourngolfclub.com

Rickmansworth
(1937)
Public
Moor Lane, Rickmansworth, WD3 1QL
☎ (01923) 775278

Royston
(1892)
Baldock Road, Royston, SG8 5BG
☎ (01763) 242696
🖳 (01763) 246910
✉ roystongolf@btconnect.com
🕮 500
🏌 S Clark (Mgr)
✓ S Clark (01763) 243476
▷ 18 L 6042 yds SSS 70
🕯 WD–U WE–after 1pm SOC–WD
U WE after 1pm
££ £15–£35
🏌 SW of Royston on A505
🏵 H Vardon
🖳 www.roystongolfclub.co.uk

Sandy Lodge
(1910)
Sandy Lodge Lane, Northwood, Middx,
HA6 2JD
☎ (01923) 825429
🖳 (01923) 824319
✉ info@sandylodge.co.uk
🕮 700
🏌 C Bailey
✓ J Pinsent (01923) 825321
▷ 18 L 6328 yds SSS 71
🕯 H or M SOC
££ On application
🏌 Adjacent Moor Park Station
🏵 Harry Vardon
🖳 www.sandylodge.co.uk

Shendish Manor Hotel &
Golf Course
(1988)
Pay and play
Shendish Manor, London Road, Apsley,
HP3 0AA
☎ (01442) 251806
🖳 (01442) 230683
✉ golf@shendish-manor.com
🏌 Seema Patel (Mgr) (01442) 251806
▷ 18 L 5660 yds Par 70 SSS 68
🕯 U SOC
££ £18 (£28)
🏌 S of Hemel Hempstead, off A41.
M25 Junction 20
🏵 Cotton/Steel
🖳 www.shendish-manor.com

South Herts
(1899)
Links Drive, Totteridge, London, N20 8QU
☎ (020) 8445 0117
🖳 (020) 8445 7569

✉ secretary@southhertsgolfclub.co.uk
🕮 850
🏌 RJ Weeds (020) 8445 2035
✓ RY Mitchell (020) 8445 4633
▷ 18 L 6470 yds SSS 71
9 L 1581 yds
🕯 WD–IH WE/BH–M
££ On application
🏌 Totteridge Lane
🏵 Harry Vardon
🖳 www.southhertsgolfclub.co.uk

Stevenage
(1980)
Public
Aston Lane, Stevenage, SG2 7EL
☎ (01438) 880424
🕮 250
🏌 P Winston
✓ P Winston (01438) 880424
▷ 18 L 6451 yds SSS 71
9 hole Par 3 course
🕯 U
££ £19 (£23.50)
🏌 Off A602 to Hertford. A1(M) Jct 7
⊕ Driving range
🏵 John Jacobs

Verulam
(1905)
226 London Road, St Albans, AL1 1JG
☎ (01727) 853327
🖳 (01727) 812201
✉ gm@verulamgolf.co.uk
🕮 650
🏌 PK Watson
✓ N Burch (01727) 861401
▷ 18 L 6429 yds Par 72 SSS 71
🕯 WD–H WE/BH–M SOC
££ £35 D–£50 Mon–£25 (£50)
🏌 1 mile SE of St Albans on A1081.
M25 Junction 21A or 22. M1 Jct 6
⊕ Practice range
🏵 Braid/Steel
🖳 www.verulamgolf.co.uk

Welwyn Garden City
(1922)
Mannicotts, High Oaks Road, Welwyn
Garden City, AL8 7BP
☎ (01707) 325243
🖳 (01707) 393213
✉ secretary
@welwyngardencitygolfclub.co.uk
🕮 900
🏌 D Spring (Gen Mgr)
(01707) 325243
✓ R May (01707) 325525
▷ 18 L 6100 yds Par 70 SSS 69
🕯 WD–H WE/BH–NA
££ On application
🏌 1 mile N of Hatfield. A1(M)
Junction 4 – B197 to Valley Road
🏵 Hawtree
🖳 www.welwyngardencitygolfclub
.co.uk

West Herts
(1890)
Cassiobury Park, Watford, WD3 3GG
☎ (01923) 236484
🖳 (01923) 222300
🕮 700
🏌 TBA
✓ CS Gough (01923) 220352
▷ 18 L 6602 yds SSS 72
🕯 WD–U WE/BH–M SOC–Mon,
Wed & Fri

For list of abbreviations and key to symbols see page 647

££ £40 (£50)
⊛ Off A412, between Watford and Rickmansworth
🏠 Morris/Mackenzie
▣ www.westhertsgolfclub.co.uk

Wheathampstead   (2001)
Pay and play
Harpenden Road, Wheathampstead, St Albans, AL4 8EZ
☎ (01582) 833941
🖳 (01582) 833941
✉ wheathampsteadgolfcourse@hotmail.co.uk
♒ JD Edgar (mob - 07960 364212)
✓ JD Edgar
🏴 9 L 2100 yds Par 31 SSS 31
👤 U SOC
££ £13 (£14). 9 holes–£9 Seniors: 9: £7, 18: £10 Children under 14: 9: £6, 18: £10
⊛ 1 mile W of Wheathampstead (B653)
⊕ Driving range
🏠 JD Edgar
▣ www.wheathampstead.net /golf-course

Whipsnade Park   (1974)
Studham Lane, Dagnall, HP4 1RH
☎ (01442) 842330
🖳 (01442) 842090
✉ secretary@whipsnadeparkgolf.co.uk
📖 450
♒ R Whalley
✓ M Day (01442) 842310
🏴 18 L 6812 yds SSS 72
👤 WD–U WE–U after 1pm SOC–WD
££ £30 £40 (£35 D–£46)
⊛ 8 miles N of Hemel Hempstead, off A4147
⊕ Driving range; grass practice ground; putting green; chipping green
▣ www.whipsnadeparkgolf.co.uk

Whitehill   (1990)
Proprietary
Dane End, Ware, SG12 0JS
☎ (01920) 438495
🖳 (01920) 438891
✉ whitehillgolf@btconnect.com
📖 550
♒ Mr A Smith (Prop)
✓ M Belsham
🏴 18 L 6802 yds SSS 72
👤 U
££ £23 (£30)
⊛ 4 miles N of Ware (A10)
⊕ Floodlit driving range; practice putting green
▣ www.whitehillgolf.co.uk

Isle of Man

Castletown Golf Links
(1892)
Proprietary
Fort Island, Derbyhaven, IM9 1UA
☎ (01624) 822211

🖳 (01624) 829661
✉ Isttee@manx.net
📖 400
✓ (01624) 822211
🏴 18 L 6734 yds SSS 72
👤 U SOC
££ £47.50 (£52.50)
⊛ 1 mile E of Castletown. 3 miles from Airport
🏠 Old Tom Morris
▣ www.golfiom.com

Douglas   (1891)
Public
Pulrose Road, Douglas, IM2 1AE
☎ (01624) 675952 (Clubhouse)
🖳 (01624) 616865
✉ douglasgolfclub@manx.net
📖 280
♒ Mrs E Vincent (01624) 616865
✓ M Vipond/J Fletcher (01624) 661558
🏴 18 L 5922 yds Par 69 SSS 69
👤 U
££ £14 (£17) (2008)
⊛ Douglas Pier 2 miles
🏠 Dr A Mackenzie
▣ www.douglasgolfclub.com

King Edward Bay   (1893)
Groudle Road, Onchan, IM3 2JR
☎ (01624) 620430/673821

Mount Murray G&CC   (1994)
Santon, IM4 2HT
☎ (01624) 695308
🖳 (01624) 611116
✉ sales@mountmurray.com
📖 360
♒ A Laing
✓ A Laing
🏴 18 L 6361 yds SSS 71
👤 U H SOC
££ £20 (£25)
⊛ 3 miles SW of Douglas
⊕ Driving range, Chipping Green, Putting Green, Practice Area.
▣ www.mountmurray.com

Peel   (1895)
Rheast Lane, Peel, IM5 1BG
☎ (01624) 842227
🖳 (01624) 843456
✉ peelgc@manx.net
📖 600
♒ N Richmond (01624) 843456
✓ P O'Reilly
🏴 18 L 5874 yds SSS 69
👤 WD–U WE/BH–NA before 10.30am SOC
££ £22 (£30)
⊛ 10 miles W of Douglas via A1
🏠 James Braid
▣ www.peelgolfclub.com

Port St Mary   (1903)
Public
Kallow Road, Port St Mary, IM9 5EJ
☎ (01624) 834932
🖳 (01624) 837231
♒ N Swimmin (07624) 498848
🏴 9 L 2711 yds SSS 68
👤 WD–U WE–NA before 10.30am SOC

££ On application
⊛ 6 miles S of Castletown via A5
🏠 George Duncan

Ramsey   (1891)
Brookfield Avenue, Ramsey, IM8 2AH
☎ (01624) 813365/812244
🖳 (01624) 815833
✉ ramseygolfclub@manx.net
📖 700
♒ Jane Sayle (01624) 812244
✓ A Dyson (01624) 814736
🏴 18 L 5982 yds Par 71 SSS 70
👤 WD–U after 10am WE–M SOC
££ £28 (£38)
⊛ N of Douglas via A18. W boundary of Ramsey
🏠 James Braid
▣ www.ramseygolfclub.im

Rowany   (1895)
Rowany Drive, Port Erin, IM9 6LN
☎ (01624) 834108
🖳 (01624) 834072
✉ rowany@iommail.net
📖 500
♒ CA Corrin (Mgr) (01624) 834072
✓ A Patterson
🏴 18 L 5774 yds SSS 69
👤 U SOC
££ WD £24; WE £30
⊛ 6 miles W of Castletown via A5
▣ www.rowanygolfclub.com

Isle of Wight

Cowes   (1909)
Crossfield Avenue, Cowes, PO31 8HN
☎ (01983) 280135 (Steward)
🖳 (01983) 292303
✉ cowesgolfclub@tiscali.co.uk
📖 300
♒ C lacey (01983) 292303 Members (01983) 280135
🏴 9 L 5878 yds SSS 68
👤 H Thurs–NA before 3pm (Ladies Day) Sun am–NA
££ £25 (£25)
⊛ Nr Cowes High School
🏠 J Hamilton Stutt

Freshwater Bay   (1894)
Afton Down, Freshwater, PO40 9TZ
☎ (01983) 752955
🖳 (01983) 756704
✉ secretary@freshwaterbaygolfclub.co.uk
📖 550
♒ T Riddett (01983) 752955
✓ James Veal 07808 395320
🏴 18 L 5725 yds SSS 68
👤 NA before 9.30am SOC
££ £30 (£34)
⊛ 400 yds off Military Road (A3055)
▣ www.freshwaterbaygolfclub.co.uk

Newport   (1896)
St George's Down, Shide, Newport, PO30 3BA
☎ (01983) 525076
✉ info@newportgolfclub.co.uk

□ 350
✍ Dave Boon (01983) 525076
▷ 9 L 5674 yds SSS 68
(18 holes from Aug 2007)
♛ WD–U exc Wed–NA 12–2.30pm
Sat–NA before 3.30pm Sun–NA
before noon SOC
££ £20 (£25)
⊶ 1 mile SE of Newport
♙ Guy Hunt
▤ www.newportgolfclub.co.uk

Osborne   (1904)
Osborne House Estate, East Cowes,
PO32 6JX
☎ **(01983) 295421**
▯ (01983) 292781
✉ info@osbornegolfclub.wanadoo
.co.uk
□ 350
✍ AC Waite
◡ Mark Wright
▷ 9 L 6358 yds SSS 70
♛ WD–U exc Ladies Day (Tues)
9am–12.30pm–NA WE–NA before
noon SOC
££ £25 (£30) 5D–£85 (to Apr 1, 2008)
⊶ S of East Cowes in grounds of
Osborne House
▤ www.osbornegolfclub.co.uk

Ryde   (1895)
Binstead Road, Ryde, PO33 3NF
☎ **(01983) 614809**
▯ (01983) 567418
✉ ryde.golfclub@btconnect.com
□ 450
✍ RA Dean
◡ None
▷ 9 L 5772 yds Par 70 SSS 69
♛ WD–NA before 10am Wed–NA
before 2pm (Ladies Day) WE–NA
before 11am
££ £20 (£24) – 18 holes
⊶ On main Ryde/Newport road
♙ J Hamilton Stutt
▤ www.rydegolf.co.uk

Shanklin & Sandown   (1900)
The Fairway, Lake, Sandown, PO36 9PR
☎ **(01983) 403217**
▯ (01983) 403007
✉ club@ssgolfclub.com
□ 700
✍ AC Creed
◡ P Hammond (01983) 404424
▷ 18 L 6062 yds SSS 69
♛ WD–U WE–NA before 12 noon
££ £32 (£37.50) 3WD–£75
⊶ 1 mile off A3055 in Lake
♙ James Braid
▤ www.ssgolfclub.com

Ventnor   (1892)
Steephill Down Road, Ventnor, PO38 1BP
☎ **(01983) 853326/853388**
▯ (01983) 853326
✉ secretary@ventnorgolfclub.co.uk
□ 250
✍ S Blackmore
▷ 12 L 5767 yds Par 70 SSS 68 (18
tees)
♛ WD–U Sun–NA before 1pm SOC

££ £15 (£20 + BH)
⊶ NW boundary of Ventnor
⊕ Nets; putting green
▤ www.ventnorgolfclub.co.uk

Westridge   (1990)
Pay and play
Brading Road, Ryde, PO33 1QS
☎ **(01983) 613131**
▯ (01983) 567017
✉ westgc@aol.com
□ 220
✍ Simon Hayward
◡ Mark Wright
▷ 9 L 3960 yds Par 62
♛ U
££ D–£13.50 (£14.50)
⊶ 2 miles S of Ryde (A3054)
⊕ Driving range with power tees;
practice bunker, green, chipping
♙ Mark Wright
▤ www.westridgegc.co.uk

Kent

Aquarius   (1912)
Marmora Rd, Honor Oak, London,
SE22 0RY
☎ **(020) 8693 1626**
✉ aquariusgolfclub@btopenworld.com
□ 400
✍ J Halliday
◡ F Private
▷ 9 L 5246 yds SSS 66
♛ M
££ £10 with member

Ashford   (1903)
Sandyhurst Lane, Ashford, TN25 4NT
☎ **(01233) 622655**
▯ (01233) 627494
✉ info@ashfordgolfclub.co.uk
□ 650
✍ S Naylor (01233) 622655
◡ H Sherman (01233) 629644
▷ 18 L 6284 yds SSS 70
♛ WD WE/BH–H SOC
££ £37 (£47)
⊶ Ashford 1½ miles (A20)
♙ Cotton
▤ www.ashfordgolfclub.co.uk

Austin Lodge   (1991)
Upper Auston Lodge Road, Eynsford,
Swanley, DA4 0HU
☎ **(01322) 863000**

Barnehurst   (1903)
Public
Mayplace Road East, Bexley Heath,
DA7 6JU
☎ **(01322) 523746**
▯ (01322) 523860
□ 300
✍ Freda Sunley
◡ Bob Cameron
▷ 9 L 5448 yds SSS 69
♛ U SOC
££ £9 (£12.10)
⊶ Between Crayford and Bexleyheath
⊕ Practice area
♙ James Braid

Bearsted   (1895)
Ware Street, Bearsted, Maidstone,
ME14 4PQ
☎ **(01622) 738389**
▯ (01622) 735608
✉ info@bearstedgolfclub.co.uk
□ 780
✍ Stuart Turner (01622) 738198
◡ T Simpson (01622) 738024
▷ 18 L 6439 yds Par 71 SSS 71
♛ WD–H WE–H SOC
££ £32 D–£42 (£37)
⊶ 2½ m E of Maidstone; J7 off M20
▤ www.bearstedgolfclub.co.uk

Beckenham Place Park   (1907)
Public
Beckenham Hill Road, Beckenham,
BR3 2BP
☎ **(020) 8650 2292**
▯ (020) 8663 1201
✉ beckenhamgolf
@glendale-services.co.uk
◡ Jonathan Good
▷ 18 L 5722 yds SSS 68
♛ U SOC
££ £16 (£23)
⊶ Off A21 on A222
▤ www.glendale-services.co.uk

Bexleyheath   (1909)
Mount Road, Bexleyheath, DA6 8JS
☎ **(020) 8303 6951**
✉ bexleyheathgolf@aol.com
□ 350
✍ Mrs J Smith
▷ 9 L 5239 yds SSS 66
♛ WD–H before 4pm
££ £25
⊶ Station 1 mile

Birchwood Park   (1990)
Birchwood Road, Wilmington, Dartford,
DA2 7HJ
☎ **(01322) 662038**

Boughton   (1993)
Pay and play
Brickfield Lane, Boughton, Faversham,
ME13 9AJ
☎ **(01227) 752277**
▯ (01227) 752361
✉ greg@pentlandgolf.co.uk
□ 300
✍ G Haenen (Mgr)
◡ T Dungate, G Naenen
▷ 18 L 6452 yds SSS 71
9 hole par 3 course
♛ U SOC–WD/WE
££ £20 (£27.50)
⊶ NE of Boughton, nr M2/A2
interchange. 6 miles W of
Canterbury
⊕ Driving range; putting green; short
game area
♙ Philip Sparks
▤ www.pentlandgolf.co.uk

Broke Hill   (1993)
Sevenoaks Road, Halstead, TN14 7HR
☎ **(01959) 533225**
✉ broke-sales@crows-golf.co.uk

Bromley   (1948)
Public
Magpie Hall Lane, Bromley, BR2 8JF
☎ **(020) 8462 7014**
📠 (020) 8462 6916
📧 bromleygolfcourse@wanadoo.co.uk
📖 200
♠ Ian Smith
⚲ A Hodgson
🏌 9 L 5590 yds SSS 67
👤 U
££ £8.50 (£11)
♧ Off Bromley Common (A21)
⊕ Floodlit 20-bay driving range

Broome Park   (1981)
Broome Park Estate, Barham, Canterbury, CT4 6QX
☎ **(01227) 830728**
📠 (01227) 832591
📧 admin@broomepark.co.uk
📖 600
♠ G Robins
⚲ T Britz (01227) 831126
🏌 18 L 6580 yds SSS 71
👤 H WE–NA before noon SOC–WD
££ £40 (£50)
♧ M2/A2-A260 Folkestone road, 1½ miles on RH side
⊕ Driving range
🏠 Donald Steel
🖥 www.broomepark.co.uk

Canterbury   (1927)
Scotland Hills, Littlebourne Road, Canterbury, CT1 1TW
☎ **(01227) 453532**
📠 (01227) 784277
📧 general.manager @canterburygolfclub.co.uk
📖 750
♠ Michael Smith (Mgr)
⚲ P Everard (01227) 462865
🏌 18 L 6272 yds Par 71 SSS 70
👤 WD–U H WE–NA before 11.30am SOC–Tues/Thurs/Fri
££ £38 (£48)
♧ 1 mile E of Canterbury on A257
🏠 HS Colt
🖥 www.canterburygolfclub.org.uk

Chart Hills   (1993)
Weeks Lane, Biddenden, Ashford, TN27 8JX
☎ **(01580) 292222**
📠 (01580) 292233
📧 info@charthills.co.uk
📖 495
♠ David Colyer (Gen Mgr)
⚲ James Cornish, PGA (Dir of Golf) (01580) 292148
🏌 18 L 7135 yds SSS 74
👤 Mon–Fri restricted times, Sat–sun+BH pm only, SOC
££ £65 (£80) plus seasonal offers (see website)
♧ 12 miles W of Ashford (A262). M20 Jcts 8 or 9
⊕ The Peter Mitchell Golf Academy
🏠 Nick Faldo
🖥 www.charthills.co.uk

Chelsfield Lakes Golf Centre   (1992)
Pay and play
Court Road, Orpington, BR6 9BX
☎ **(01689) 896266**
📠 (01689) 824577
📧 chelsfieldlakes@crown-golf.co.uk
📖 650
♠ Alex Taylor (Mgr)
⚲ N Lee
🏌 18 L 6077 yds Par 71 SSS 69
   9 hole Par 3 course
👤 SOC
££ £20 (£28)
♧ 1 mile from M25 Junction 4 (A224)
⊕ Target golf range
🏠 MRM Sandow
🖥 www.chelsfieldlakesgolf.co.uk

Cherry Lodge   (1969)
Jail Lane, Biggin Hill, Westerham, TN16 3AX
☎ **(01959) 572250**
📠 (01959) 540672
📧 info@cherrylodgegc.co.uk
📖 650
♠ Trevor E Norman
⚲ Craig Sutherland (01959) 572989
🏌 18 L 6593 yds SSS 72
👤 WD–U WE–M SOC–WD before 3pm
££ £40 D–£55
♧ 3 miles N of Westerham, off A233
⊕ Practice facilities
🏠 John Day
🖥 www.cherrylodgegc.co.uk

Chestfield   (1925)
103 Chestfield Road, Whitstable, CT5 3LU
☎ **(01227) 794411**
📠 (01227) 794454
📧 secretary@chestfield-golfclub.co.uk
📖 700
♠ Nick Pout
⚲ J Brotherton (01227) 793563
🏌 18 L 6208 yds SSS 70
👤 WD–U WE–NA before noon SOC
££ £36 (£40)
♧ ½ mile S of A2990 and Chestfield Station
🏠 Donald Steel/James Braid
🖥 www.chestfield-golfclub.co.uk

Chislehurst   (1894)
Camden Place, Camden Park Road, Chislehurst, BR7 5HJ
☎ **(020) 8467 3055**
📠 (020) 8295 0874
📧 thesecretary@chislehurstgolfclub .co.uk
📖 740
♠ P Foord (020) 8467 2782
⚲ D Bicknell (020) 8467 6798
🏌 18 L 5128 yds SSS 66
👤 WD–H WE–M SOC
·££ £40
♧ M25 Junction 3/A20/A222
🖥 www.chislehurstgolfclub.co.uk

Cobtree Manor Park   (1984)
Public
Chatham Road, Boxley, Maidstone, ME14 3AZ
☎ **(01622) 753276**
📠 (01622) 620387
📧 paul@medwaygolf.co.uk
📖 300
♠ Steve Mattingly
⚲ Paul Foston (01622) 753276
🏌 18 L 5611 yds Par 69 SSS 69
👤 WD–U (booking advisable) WE/BH–(book 5 days in advance) SOC–WD WE–PM
££ From £20 (£25)
♧ 3 miles N of Maidstone on A229
🏠 F Hawtree
🖥 www.medwaygolf.co.uk

Darenth Valley   (1973)
Pay and play
Station Road, Shoreham, Sevenoaks, TN14 7SA
☎ **(01959) 522944 (Clubhouse)**
   (01959) 522922 (Bookings)
📠 (01959) 525089
📧 enquiries@dvgc.co.uk
♠ Mrs E Rolph
⚲ Bill Abbott and Pete Stopford (01959) 522922
🏌 18 L 6258 yds Par 72 SSS 71
👤 U–booking required SOC
££ £20 (£25) Daily special and twilight rates – phone for details
♧ 3 miles N of Sevenoaks, off A225. M25 Junctions 3 or 5
🖥 www.dvgc.co.uk

Dartford   (1897)
The Clubhouse, Heath Lane (Upper), Dartford DA1 2TN
☎ **(01322) 223616**
📠 (01322) 226455
📧 dartfordgolf@hotmail.com
📖 750
♠ Mrs Amanda Malas (01322) 226455
⚲ J Gregory (01322) 226409
🏌 18 L 5909 yds Par 69 SSS 69
👤 WD–I WE–M H
££ £25
♧ Dartford 2 miles. Dartford Heath turn off A2
🏠 James Braid
🖥 www.dartfordgolfclub.co.uk

Deangate Ridge   (1972)
Public
Duxcourt Road, Hoo, Rochester, ME3 8RZ
☎ **(01634) 254481 (Gen Mgr)**
   (01634) 254481 (Soc B/ings)
📧 leisure@medway.gov.uk
📖 460
♠ M Smith (Gen Mgr) (01634) 254481; Mrs CJ Williams (Sec) (01634) 251950
⚲ R Fox (01634) 251180
🏌 18 L 6300 yds SSS 70
👤 U SOC
££ On application
♧ 7 miles NE of Rochester on A228. M2, 5 miles
⊕ 11 bay driving range; pitch & putt (18 holes); 6 hole golf-cross course
🏠 Hawtree
🖥 www.medway.gov.uk/leisure

For list of abbreviations and key to symbols see page 647

Eastwell Manor (2008)
Boughton Lees, ASHFORD, Kent,
TN25 4HR
☎ **(01233) 213100**
🖷 (01233) 213105
🖂 enquiries@eastwellmanor.co.uk
🏌 Phil Redman (Mgr)
➢ 9 L 2132 yds Par 32
👥 WD WE SOC U
££ M £15, £99 Spa Day + Golf
🚗 M20 Jct9
⊕ Spa, Restaurant/Hotel
🏠 Lee Evans Partnership
🖃 www.eastwellmanor.co.uk

Eltham Warren (1890)
Bexley Road, Eltham, London, SE9 2PE
☎ **(0208) 331 2831**
🖷 (020) 8860 0522
🖂 secretary@elthamwarren.idps.co.uk
🖵 430
🏌 DJ Mabbott (020) 8850 4477
✓ G Brett (020) 8859 7909
➢ 9 L 5850 yds Par 69 SSS 68
👥 WD–H WE–M SOC welcome
££ D–£30
🚗 On A210 Bexley Road, ¼ mile
from Eltham town centre
🏠 James Braid
🖃 www.elthamwarrengolfclub.co.uk

Etchinghill (1995)
Pay and play
Canterbury Road, Etchinghill, Folkestone,
CT18 8FA
☎ **(01303) 863863**
🖷 (01303) 863210
🖵 550
🏌 D Francis (01303) 864576
✓ R Dowle (01303) 863966
➢ Valley: 18 L 6101 Par 70 SSS 69
Leas: 18 L 5824 Par 70 SSS 69
9 hole Par 3 course
👥 WD–U WE–NA 7am–11am
££ Leas: £22 (£29.50)
Valley: £19 (£22)
🚗 1 mile N of M20 Jct 12 on B2065
⊕ Driving range, floodlit and covered
🏠 John Sturdy

Faversham (1902)
Belmont Park, Faversham, ME13 0HB
☎ **(01795) 890561**
🖷 (01795) 890760
🖂 themanager@favershamgolf.co.uk
🖵 800
🏌 J Edgington
✓ S Rokes (01795) 890275
➢ 18 L 5978 yds Par 70 SSS 69
👥 WD–I or H WE–M
££ £35 D–£45
🚗 Faversham and M2, 2 miles
🖃 www.favershamgolf.co.uk

Fawkham Valley (1987)
Gay Dawn Farm, Fawkham, Dartford,
DA3 8LZ
☎ **(01474) 707144**
🖷 (01474) 707911
🖂 info@fawkhamvalleygolf.co.uk
🖵 300
🏌 J Marchant
✓ N Willis

➢ 9 L 6547 yds Par 72 SSS 72
👥 U SOC
££ £25 (£35)
🚗 4 miles S of Dartford Tunnel. E of
Brands Hatch along Fawkham
Valley road
⊕ Practice ground, nets & putting
green
🖃 www.fawkhamvalleygolf.co.uk

Gillingham (1905)
Woodlands Road, Gillingham, ME7 2AP
☎ **(01634) 853017/850999**
🖷 (01634) 574749
🖂 golf@gillinghamgolf.idps.co.uk
🖵 800
🏌 Miss K Snow (01634) 853017
✓ M Daniels (01634) 855862
➢ 18 L 5260 yds SSS 65
👥 WD–I H WE/BH–M
££ £25 D–£45
🚗 A2/M2, 2 miles
🏠 Braid/Steel
🖃 www.gillinghamgolfclub.co.uk

Hawkhurst (1968)
High Street, Hawkhurst, TN18 4JS
☎ **(01580) 752396**
🖷 (01580) 754074
🖂 hawkhurstgolfclub@tiscali.co.uk
🖵 250
🏌 John Roberts
✓ P Chandler (01580) 752396
➢ 9 L 5751 yds Par 70 SSS 68
👥 WD–U WE SOC
££ 9: £13.50 (£16.50) 18: £22 (£26)
🚗 14 miles S of Tunbridge Wells on
A268
🖃 HawkhurstGolfClub.org.uk

Hemsted Forest (1969)
Golford Road, Cranbrook, TN17 4AL
☎ **(01580) 712833**
🖷 (01580) 714274
🖂 golf@hemstedforest.co.uk
🏌 K Stevenson
✓ P Foston
➢ 18 L 6305 yds SSS 70
👥 WD–U WE/BH–restricted SOC
££ £30 (£40)
🚗 15 miles S of Maidstone. M25
Junction 5-A21/A262
🏠 Cdr J Harris
🖃 www.hemstedforest.co.uk

Herne Bay (1895)
Eddington, Herne Bay, CT6 7PG
☎ **(01227) 374097**
🖂 sue.brown@hernebaygolfclub.co.uk
🖵 500
🏌 SU Brown (01227) 373964
✓ D Ledingham (01227) 374727
➢ 18 L 5567 yds SSS 68
👥 WD–U WE/BH–H after noon
SOC–WD
££ £20 D–£27 (£27)
🚗 A2299 Thanet road
🖃 www.hernebaygolfclub.co.uk

Hever Castle (1993)
Proprietary
Hever Road, Hever, TN8 7NP
☎ **(01732) 700771**

🖷 (01732) 700775
🖂 mail@hevercastlegolfclub.co.uk
🖵 500
🏌 Jon Wittenberg
✓ Peter Parks
➢ 18 L 7002 yds SSS 75
9 L 2784 yds
👥 SOC WD–U after 11am WE–U
after 10.30am
££ £39.50 (£48) Championship course
£12.50 (£14.50) Princes 9 course
🚗 2 miles E of Edenbridge
⊕ Driving range; putting green;
chipping area; Bunker practice.
🏠 Peter Nicholson
🖃 www.hevercastlegolflcub.co.uk

High Elms (1969)
Public
High Elms Road, Downe, Orpington,
BR6 7SZ
☎ **(01689) 858175**
🖷 (01689) 856326
🖵 423
🏌 Mrs P O'Keeffe (Hon)
➢ 18 L 6221 yds Par 71 SSS 70
👥 U
££ On application
🚗 M25 J4, off A21 via Shire Lane
🏠 Hawtree
🖃 www.highelmsgolfclub.com

Hilden Golf Centre
Pay and play
Rings Hill, Hildenborough, Tonbridge,
TN11 8LX
☎ **(01732) 833607**
🖷 (01732) 834484
🖂 info@hildenpark.co.uk
🏌 Jan Parfett
✓ Rupert Hunter, Nick McNally,
Nicky Way, Jamie Knight
➢ 9 L 1554 yds Par 3 SSS 54 (men),
SSS 60 (ladies)
👥 U
££ 9: £7.50 (£10); 18: £11.25 (£15)
🚗 M25/A21
⊕ Driving range with power tees
🖃 www.hildenpark.co.uk

Hythe Imperial (1950)
Prince's Parade, Hythe, CT21 6AE
☎ **(01303) 233745**
🖷 (01303) 267554 (Professional)
🖵 445
🏌 B Duncan (01303) 267554
✓ (01303) 233745
➢ 9 L 5560 yds SSS 67
👥 H SOC
££ £18 (£20) Twilight £15
🚗 On coast, 4 miles W of Folkestone

The Kent & Surrey G&CC (1972)
Proprietary
Crouch House Road, Edenbridge, TN8 5LQ
☎ **(01732) 867381**
🖷 (01732) 867167
🖂 info@thekentandsurrey.com
🖵 350
🏌 Mark Hickson
➢ 18 L 6601 yds Par 72 SSS 72
9 hole course

For list of abbreviations and key to symbols see page 647

🏌 WD/WE–booking necessary
  SOC–WD/WE
££ £27 (£32)
🚗 2 miles W of Edenbridge. M25 Jct 6
⊕ Floodlit driving range
🏠 David Williams
🖥 www.thekentandsurrey.com

Kent National G&CC   (1993)
Watermans Lane, Brenchley, Tonbridge, TN12 6ND
☎ (01892) 724400
✉ info@kentnational.com

Kings Hill   (1996)
Kings Hill, West Malling, ME19 4AF
☎ (01732) 875040/842121
  (Bookings)

Knole Park   (1924)
Seal Hollow Road, Sevenoaks, TN15 0HJ
☎ (01732) 452150
🖥 (01732) 463159
✉ secretary@knoleparkgolfclub
  .co.uk
🏢 700
🏌 AP Mitchell (01732) 452150
✓ P Sykes (01732) 451740
▷ 18 L 6246 yds SSS 70
🏌 WD–restricted WE/BH–M H SOC
££ £39 D–£50
🚗 ½ mile from Sevenoaks centre
🏠 JF Abercromby
🖥 www.knoleparkgolfclub.co.uk

Lamberhurst   (1890)
Church Road, Lamberhurst, TN3 8DT
☎ (01892) 890241
🖥 (01892) 891140
✉ secretary@lamberhurstgolfclub
  .com
🏢 600
🏌 Mrs S Deadman (01892) 890591
✓ BM Impett (01892) 890552
▷ 18 L 6409 yds SSS 71
🏌 WD–U H WE–NA before noon
££ £31 D–£41 Oct–Mar £33 D–£43
  Apr–Sept
🚗 5 miles SE of Tunbridge Wells, off A21
⊕ Small limited club practice area
🖥 www.lamberhurstgolfclub.com

Langley Park   (1910)
Barnfield Wood Road, Beckenham, BR3 6SZ
☎ (020) 8658 6849
🖥 (020) 8658 6310
✉ manager@langleyparkgolf.co.uk
🏢 750
🏌 R Pollard (Gen Mgr)
  (020) 8658 6849
✓ C Staff (020) 8650 1663
▷ 18 L 6453 yds SSS 71
🏌 WD–H WE–M SOC–WD
££ £40
🚗 Bromley South Station 1 mile. M25 Junction 4
🏠 JH Taylor
🖥 www.langleyparkgolf.co.uk

Leeds Castle   (1928)
Pay and play
Leeds Castle, Hollingbourne, Maidstone, ME17 1PL
☎ (01622) 880467/767828
🖥 (01622) 735616
✉ stevepurves@leeds-castle.co.uk
✓ S Purves
▷ 9 L 2681 yds Par 33
🏌 U SOC–WD 6–day advance booking
££ 9: £12 (£15) 18: £19.50 (£26)
🚗 4 miles E of Maidstone (A20). M20 Junction 8, 1 mile
⊕ Practice ground and nets
🏠 Neil Coles
🖥 www.leeds-castle.com

Littlestone   (1888)
St Andrews Road, Littlestone, New Romney, TN28 8RB
☎ (01797) 362310
🖥 (01797) 362446
✉ secretary@littlestonegolfclub.org.uk
🏢 450
🏌 C Elgenia (01797) 363355
✓ A Jones (01797) 362231
▷ 18 L 6676 yds Par 71 SSS 73
🏌 WD–H WE–by arrangement SOC
££ £45 (£65)
🚗 2 miles E of New Romney. 15 miles SE of Ashford. M20 Junction 10
🏠 W Laidlaw Purves/Dr A Mackenzie
🖥 www.littlestonegolfclub.org.uk

London Beach   (1998)
Pay and play
Ashford Road, St Michaels, Tenterden, TN30 6SP
☎ (01580) 766279
✉ enquiries@londonbeach.net

The London Golf Club   (1993)
Stansted Lane, Ash, Nr Brands Hatch, Kent TN15 7EH
☎ (01474) 879899
🖥 (01474) 879912
✉ golf@londongolf.co.uk
🏢 1000
🏌 Heath Harvey
✓ P Stuart, A Robertson
▷ Heritage 18 L 7257 yds Par 72 SSS 74
  International 18 L 7005 yds Par 72 SSS 74
🏌 M WD WE NA H Heritage – WD WE SOC H International
££ On application
🚗 Jct 3 off M25 Off A20, nr Brands Hatch
⊕ Driving range. Academy; Practice Holes & Greens; Online time bookings
🏠 Jack Nicklaus/Ron Kirby
🖥 www.londongolf.co.uk

Lullingstone Park   (1967)
Public
Parkgate Road, Chelsfield, Orpington, BR6 7PX
☎ (01959) 533793

🏌 CJ Pocock (0208) 303 9535
✓ M Watt
▷ 18 L 6734 yds SSS 72
  9 L 2379 yds Par 33
🏌 U SOC WD/WE
££ On application
🚗 Off Orpington Bypass (A224) towards Well Hill. M25 Junction 4
⊕ Driving range; 9 hole pitch & putt

Lydd   (1994)
Proprietary
Romney Road, Lydd, Romney Marsh, TN29 9LS
☎ (01797) 320808
🖥 (01797) 321482
✉ info@lyddgolfclub.co.uk
🏢 350
🏌 Keith Osbourne
✓ Richard Perkins (01797) 321201
▷ 18 L 6529 yds Par 71 SSS 71
🏌 U SOC
££ £21 (£30)
🚗 15 miles SE of Ashford, by Lydd Airport (B2075). M20 Junction 10
⊕ Driving range; Academy course
🏠 M Smith
🖥 www.lyddgolfclub.com

Mid Kent   (1908)
Singlewell Road, Gravesend, DA11 7RB
☎ (01474) 568035
🖥 (01474) 564218
✉ secretary@mkgc.co.uk
🏢 870
🏌 P Gleeson (01474) 568035
✓ M Foreman (01474) 332810
▷ 18 L 6106 yds Par 70 SSS 69
🏌 WD–H WE–M
££ £35 D–£50
🚗 SE of Gravesend, nr A2
⊕ Practice range – irons only
🏠 Frank Pennink
🖥 www.mkgc.co.uk

Nizels   (1992)
Nizels Lane, Hildenborough, Tonbridge, TN11 8NU
☎ (01732) 833833
🖥 (01732) 835492
✉ nizels@theclubcompany.com
🏢 800
🏌 Vanessa Machen (Gen Mgr)
✓ A Weller (01732) 838926
▷ 18 L 6361 yds SSS 71
🏌 WD–U SOC
££ £30
🚗 4 miles from M25 on B245. A21 Tonbridge North Junction
🏠 Lennan/Purnell
🖥 www.theclubcompany.com

North Foreland   (1903)
Convent Road, Broadstairs, Kent, CT10 3PU
☎ (01843) 862140
🖥 (01843) 862663
✉ office@northforeland.co.uk
🏢 1100
🏌 AJ Adams (01843) 862140
✓ D Parris (01843) 604471
▷ 18 L 6430 yds SSS 71
  18 hole Par 3 course L 1752 yds
🏌 WD–H WE–NA am –H pm
££ £39 D–£51 (£51)

For list of abbreviations and key to symbols see page 647

⊕ B2052, 1¹/₂ miles N of Broadstairs
⊕ Practice ground and putting green
⋔ Fowler/Simpson
▤ www.northforeland.co.uk

Oastpark (1992)
Pay and play
Malling Road, Snodland, ME6 5LG
☎ (01634) 242661
▱ (01634) 240744
✉ oastparkgolfclub@btconnect.com
▦ 130
♙ Lesley Murrock (01634) 242818
✓ D Porthouse (01634) 242661
▷ 9 L 2850 yds Par 34 SSS 34
♔ U SOC
££ 9: £9 (£10); 18: £10 (£15)
⊕ 1 mile E of M20 Junction 4
⊕ Driving range

Park Wood (1994)
Proprietary
Chestnut Avenue, Tatsfield, Westerham, TN16 2EG
☎ (01959) 577744
▱ (01959) 572702
✉ mail@parkwoodgolf.co.uk
▦ 450
♙ Miss RL Goldsmith (Man Dir)
✓ N Terry (01959) 577177
▷ 18 L 6527 yds Par 72 SSS 72
♔ U SOC after 11am WE
££ On application
⊕ Tatsfield, nr Westerham. M25 J4/5
⊕ Large practice area with bunker and green; 18-hole putting green; practice nets
▤ www.parkwoodgolf.co.uk

Pedham Place Golf Centre
(1996)
Proprietary
London Road, Swanley, BR8 8PP
☎ (01322) 867000
▱ (01322) 861646
✉ golf@ppgc.co.uk
▦ 456
♙ Carole Harrodine
✓ Jon Woodroffe
▷ 18 L 6444 yds Par 72 SSS 71
9 hole Par 3 course
♔ WD–U WE–U SOC WD WE
££ £21 (£28)
⊕ Swanley 1 mile, M25 J3 300 m
⊕ Driving range; putting green
⋔ John Fortune
▤ www.carole@ppgc.co.uk

Poult Wood (1974)
Public
Higham Lane, Tonbridge, TN11 9QR
☎ (01732) 364039 (Bookings)
(01732) 366180 (Clubhouse)

Prince's (1906)
Proprietary
Sandwich Bay, Sandwich, CT13 9QB
☎ (01304) 611118
▱ (01304) 612000
✉ office@princesgolfclub.co.uk
▦ 330
♙ WM Howie (Dir) (01304) 626909

✓ R McGuirk (01304) 613797
▷ 27 hole course (3 x 9 holes): Dunes/Himalayas/Shore Length 6813-7275 yds Par 71-72 SSS 72-73
♔ U SOC
££ Winter: £40 (£50); Summer: £70 D–£80 (£80 D–£90)
⊕ Sandwich Bay (A256)
⊕ Driving range; extensive practice areas inc. bunkers, chipping area, practice hole
⋔ Morrison/Campbell
▤ www.princesgolfclub.co.uk

Redlibbets (1996)
Proprietary
West Yoke, Ash, Nr Sevenoaks, TN15 7HT
☎ (01474) 879190
▱ (01474) 879290
✉ redlibbets@golfandsport.co.uk
▦ 500
♙ J Potter
✓ R Taylor (01474) 872278
▷ 18 L 6651 yds Par 72
♔ WD SOC
££ £40
⊕ Off A20 between Fawkham and Ash. M20 Junction 2. M25 Jct 3
⊕ Practice ground; indoor net room
⋔ Jonathan Gaunt
▤ www.golfandsport.co.uk

The Ridge (1993)
Chartway Street, East Sutton, Maidstone, ME17 3JB
☎ (01622) 844382
▱ (01622) 844168
✉ info@theridgegolfclub.co.uk
♙ Jemma Stoner (Gen Mngr)
✓ Steve Mitchell
▷ 18 L 6214 yds SSS 72
♔ U SOC WD
££ £23 (£30)
⊕ 3 miles E of Maidstone, off A274. M20 Junction 8
⊕ Driving range
⋔ Patrick Dawson
▤ www.theridgegolfclub.co.uk

Rochester & Cobham Park
(1891)
Park Pale, by Rochester, ME2 3UL
☎ (01474) 823411
▱ (01474) 824446
✉ rcpgc@talk21.com
▦ 630
♙ JS Auchterloney (Mgr)
✓ W Wood (01474) 823658
▷ 18 L 6597 yds SSS 72
♔ WD–U H WE–M SOC–Tues & Thurs. Soft spikes only
££ £40
⊕ Cobham/Shorne turnoff A2
⊕ Full practice facilities
⋔ D Steel
▤ www.rochesterandcobhamgc.co.uk

Romney Warren (1993)
Pay and play
St Andrews Road, Littlestone, New Romney, TN28 8RB
☎ (01797) 362231

⊕ (01797) 362740
✉ secretary@romneywarrengolfclub.org.uk
▦ 300
♙ C Elgenia (Gen Mgr) 01797 363355
✓ A Jones
▷ 18 L 5126 yds SSS 65
♔ U SOC
££ £18 (£23)
⊕ 2 miles E of New Romney. 15 miles SE of Ashford
⊕ 9-bay driving range; video studio
⋔ Evans/Lewis
▤ www.romneywarrengolfclub.org.uk

Royal Blackheath (1608)
Court Road, Eltham, London, SE9 5AF
☎ (020) 8850 1795
▱ (020) 8859 0150
✉ info@rbgc.com
▦ 630
♙ MJ Miller
✓ M Johns (020) 8850 1763
▷ 18 L 6147 yds SSS 70
♔ WD–I or H WE/BH–M SOC
££ £55 D–£75
⊕ 5 miles W of M25 Junction 3
⊕ Golf Museum
⋔ James Braid
▤ www.royalblackheath.com

Royal Cinque Ports (1892)
Golf Road, Deal, CT14 6RF
☎ (01304) 374007 (Office)
▱ (01304) 379530
✉ ken.hannah@royalcinqueports.com
▦ 935
♙ Ken Hannah (01304) 374007
✓ A Reynolds (01304) 374170
▷ 18 L 6960 yds SSS 73
♔ WD–H after 9.30am SOC
££ On application
⊕ A258, N of Deal
⊕ Full practice facilities
⋔ H Hunter/J Braid
▤ www.royalcinqueports.com

Royal St George's (1887)
Sandwich, CT13 9PB
☎ (01304) 613090
▱ (01304) 611245
✉ secretary@royalstgeorges.com
▦ 725
♙ HCG Gabbey
✓ A Brooks (01304) 615236
▷ 18 L 7102 yds Par 70 SSS 74
♔ WD–I H WE–M SOC–WD
££ £120 D–£150
⊕ 1 mile E of Sandwich
⋔ Dr Laidlaw Purves
▤ www.royalstgeorges.com

Sene Valley (1888)
Sene, Folkestone, CT18 8BL
☎ (01303) 268513
✉ senevalleygolf@btconnect.com
▦ 650
♙ John Hemphrey (Mgr)
✓ N Watson (01303) 268514
▷ 18 L 6271 yds SSS 70 Par 71
♔ WD SOC Tue pm Wed, Fri & Thur all day; WE NA before noon; WD–U H

££ D–£30 (D–£45)
🚗 2 miles N of Hythe on B2065; M20 Jct 12
⊕ Undulating, good condition
🏠 Henry Cotton
🖥 www.senevalleygolfclub.co.uk

Sheerness　(1909)
Power Station Road, Sheerness, ME12 3AE
☎ (01795) 662585
🖶 (01795) 668100
📧 thesecretary @sheernessgc.freeserve.co.uk
📖 600
🏌 D Nehra
🏌 L Stanford (01795) 583060
🏳 18 L 6390 yds SSS 71
👥 WD–U SOC
££ £22
🚗 9 miles N of Sittingbourne. M20, M2 or A2 to A249
⊕ Practice facilities

Shooter's Hill　(1903)
Lowood, Eaglesfield Road, London, SE18 3DA
☎ (020) 8854 6368
🖶 (020) 8854 0469
📧 secretary@shgc.uk.com
📖 600 60(L) 60(J)
🏌 Trevor Norman (020) 8854 6368
🏌 D Brotherton (020) 8854 0073
🏳 18 L 5721 yds SSS 68
👥 WD–I WE/BH–M SOC–Tues & Thurs only H
££ £35 D–£45
🚗 Off A207 nr Blackheath off A102 Nr Blackwall Tunnel
🏠 Willie Park
🖥 www.shgc.uk.com

Shortlands　(1894)
Meadow Road, Shortlands, Bromley, BR2 0DX
☎ (020) 8460 2471
🖶 (020) 8460 8828
📧 shortlandsgolfclub.com
📖 525
🏌 PS May (020) 8460 8828
🏌 M Wood (020) 8464 6182
🏳 9 L 5222 yds SSS 65
👥 M
££ 9: £10, 18: £15
🚗 Ravensbourne Ave, Shortlands
🖥 www.shortlandsgolfclub.com

Sidcup　(1891)
Hurst Road, Sidcup, DA15 9AW
☎ (020) 8300 2150
🖶 (020) 8300 2150
📧 sidcupgolfclub@tiscali.co.uk
📖 400
🏌 S Armstrong (020) 8300 2150
🏳 9 L 5571 yds Par 68 SSS 68
👥 WD–H WE/BH–M SOC–WD
££ £25
🚗 On A222. A2/A20, 2 miles. Clubhouse located rear of Hurstmere School

Sittingbourne & Milton Regis　(1929)
Wormdale, Newington, Sittingbourne, ME9 7PX
☎ (01795) 842261
📧 sittingbournegc@btconnect.com
📖 725
🏌 Charles Maxted
🏌 John Hearn (01795) 842775
🏳 18 L 6291 yds SSS 70
👥 WD–U Sat–M Sun–M SOC–Tues & Thurs
££ £32 D–£40
🚗 N of M2 Junction 5, towards Danaway
🏠 Donald Steel
🖥 www.sittingbournegolfclub.com

Southern Valley　(1999)
Pay and play
Thong Lane, Shorne, Gravesend, DA12 4LF
☎ (01474) 740026 (01474) 568568 (Bookings)
📧 info@southernvalley.co.uk

St Augustines　(1907)
Cottington Road, Cliffsend, Ramsgate, CT12 5JN
☎ (01843) 590333
🖶 (01843) 590444
📧 sagc@ic24.net
📖 650 55(J)
🏌 RF Tranckle
🏌 DB Scott (01843) 590222
🏳 18 L 5254 yds SS 66
👥 H SOC–WD
££ £22 (£28)
🚗 2 miles SW of Ramsgate from A253 or A256. Signs to St Augustines Cross
🏠 Tom Vardon

Staplehurst Golf Centre
Cradducks Lane, Staplehurst, TN12 0DR
☎ (01580) 893362
🖶 (01580) 893372
🏌 C Jenkins
🏌 C Jenkins/R Stilman/S Stevens
🏳 9 L 6114 yds Par 72 SSS 70
👥 U
££ £11 (£14)
🚗 8 miles S of Maidstone on A229
⊕ Driving range
🏠 Sayner/Jenkins
🖥 www.staplehurstgolfcentre.co.uk

Sundridge Park　(1901)
Garden Road, Bromley, BR1 3NE
☎ (020) 8460 0278
🖶 (020) 8289 3050
📧 gm@spgc.co.uk
📖 1200
🏌 RJ Walden (020) 8460 0278
🏌 S Dowsett (020) 8460 5540
🏳 East 18 L 6538 yds SSS 71 West 18 L 6019 yds SSS 69
👥 H SOC–WD
££ D–£85 East £60, West £45
🚗 1 mile N of Bromley, by Sundridge Park Station. M25 Junctions 3/4
🖥 www.spgc.co.uk

Sweetwoods Park　(1994)
Cowden, Edenbridge, TN8 7JN
☎ (01342) 850729
🖶 (01342) 850866
📧 samhollingdale@sweetwoodspark .com
📖 750
🏌 Sam Hollingdale
🏌 J Reason (01342) 850729
🏳 18 L 5299-6610 yds Par 72 SSS 69-73
👥 U SOC
££ £30 (£36)
🚗 5 miles E of E Grinstead on A264
⊕ Driving range
🏠 P Strand
🖥 www.sweetwoodspark.com

Tenterden　(1905)
Woodchurch Road, Tenterden, TN30 7DR
☎ (01580) 763987
🖶 (01580) 763430
📧 enquiries@tenterdengolfclub.co.uk
📖 480
🏌 K Kelsall (01580) 762409
🏳 18 L 6001 yds Par 70 SSS 69
👥 WD–U WE/BH–M Sun–NA before noon SOC–WD
££ £22
🚗 1 mile E of Tenterden on B2067; M20 J10 10 miles
⊕ Practice area; short course
🖥 www.tenterdengolfclub.co.uk

Thameside Golf Centre　(1991)
Pay and play
Fairway Drive, Summerton Way, Thamesmead, London SE28 8PP
☎ (020) 8310 7975
🖶 (020) 8312 3441
🏌 S Morley
🏌 Mat Stables
🏳 9 L 5462 yds Par 70 SSS 66
👥 U SOC
££ 9: £6.50 (£8.50); 18: £10.50 (£12)
⊕ Floodlit driving range
🖥 www.tvgc.co.uk

Tudor Park　(1988)
Proprietary
Ashford Road, Bearsted, Maidstone, ME14 4NQ
☎ (01622) 734334
🖶 (01622) 735360
📖 750
🏌 J Ladbrook (01622) 737119
🏌 Jason Muller (01622) 739412
🏳 18 L 6085 yds SSS 69
👥 SOC WE–NA before 11am
££ £35 (£40)
🚗 3 miles E of Maidstone on A20. M20 Junction 8
⊕ Driving range (no woods allowed); putting and chipping area
🏠 Donald Steel

Tunbridge Wells　(1889)
Langton Road, Tunbridge Wells, TN4 8XH
☎ (01892) 523034
📧 tunbridgewellsgolf@btconnect.com

297 40(L) 18(J)
🏌 Peter Annington (01892) 536918
✓ Sharon Hinton (01892) 541386
🏴 18 L 4725 yds SSS 62
👥 U SOC
££ 9–holes £12, 18–holes £18
⛳ Tunbridge Wells, next to Spa Hotel
▣ www.tunbridgewellsgolf.com

Upchurch River Valley
(1991)
Pay and play
Oak Lane, Upchurch, Sittingbourne,
ME9 7AY
☎ **(01634) 360626**
📠 (01634) 387784
▦ 652
🏌 D Candy (01634) 260594
✓ R Cornwell (01634) 379592
🏴 18 L 6237 yds SSS 70; 9 hole course
👥 U SOC–WD
££ 9: £10.20 (£11.20) 18: £15.70
(£20.20) Long South 9 hole £12
(£14)
⛳ 3 miles NE of Rainham, off A2. M2
Jct 4
⊕ Floodlit driving range
🏠 David Smart
▣ www.rivervalleygolf.co.uk

Walmer & Kingsdown
(1909)
The Leas, Kingsdown, Deal, CT14 8EP
☎ **(01304) 373256**
📠 (01304) 382336
▦✉ info@kingsdowngolf.co.uk
▦ 627
🏌 R Harrison
✓ J Read (01304) 363017
🏴 18 L 6471 yds Par 72 SSS 71
👥 WD–H WE–after noon SOC
££ D–£32 (£40)
⛳ 2¹/₂ miles S of Deal on clifftop
🏠 James Braid
▣ www.kingsdowngolf.co.uk

Weald of Kent
(1992)
Proprietary
Maidstone Road, Headcorn, TN27 9PT
☎ **(01622) 890866**
📠 (01622) 890070
▦✉ proshop@weald-of-kent.co.uk
▦ 500
🏌 Rob Golding (Golf Dir)
✓ Jacques Gous (01622) 890866
🏴 18 L 6310 yds SSS 70
👥 U–booking 7 days in advance SOC
££ £20 (£27.50) 4 balls £22.50 at WE
⛳ 5 miles S of Maidstone on A274.
M20 J8
⊕ Practice green (USPGA spec)
🏠 John Millen
▣ www.weald-of-kent.co.uk

West Kent
(1916)
Milking Lane, Downe, Orpington, BR6 7LD
☎ **(01689) 851323**
📠 (01689) 858693
▦✉ golf@wkgc.co.uk
▦ 700
🏌 Sean Trussell
✓ CW Forsyth (01689) 856863

🏴 18 L 6426 yds Par 71 SSS 71
👥 WD–H or I–phone to arrange
££ £45
⛳ 5 miles S of Orpington
🏠 DHS Colt
▣ www.wkgc.co.uk

West Malling
(1974)
Addington, Maidstone, ME19 5AR
☎ **(01732) 844785**
📠 (01732) 844795
▦✉ mail@westmallinggolf.com
▦ 900
🏌 MR Ellis
✓ D Lambert
🏴 Spitfire 18 L 6142 yds Par 70
Hurricane 18 L 6240 yds Par 70
👥 WD–U WE–U H after 1pm
££ £30 D–£50 (£30 after 1pm)
⛳ 12 miles W of Maidstone (A20);
M20 Jct 4
⊕ Driving range
🏠 Max Faulkner
▣ www.westmallinggolf.com

Westerham
(1997)
Proprietary
Valence Park, Brasted Road, Westerham,
TN16 1LJ
☎ **(01959) 567100**
📠 (01959) 567101
▦✉ info@westerhamgc.co.uk
▦ 600
🏌 R Sturgeon (Gen Mgr)
✓ J Marshall
🏴 18 L 6270 yds Par 72
👥 WD–U WE–after 12.00pm
££ £35 (£45)
⛳ E of Westerham (A25), off M25
Junction 5
⊕ Driving range; short game practice
area
🏠 David Williams
▣ www.westerhamgc.co.uk

Westgate & Birchington
(1893)
176 Canterbury Road, Westgate-on-Sea,
CT8 8LT
☎ **(01843) 831115/833905**
▦✉ wandbgc@tiscali.co.uk
▦ 350
🏌 TJ Sharp
✓ M Young
🏴 18 L 4889 yds SSS 64
👥 WD–NA before 10am WE–NA
before 10am SOC
££ £21 (£18)
⛳ 1 mile W of Birchington (A28)

Whitstable & Seasalter
(1911)
Collingwood Road, Whitstable, CT5 1EB
☎ **(01227) 272020**

Wildernesse
(1890)
Seal, Sevenoaks, TN15 0JE
☎ **(01732) 761199**
📠 (01732) 763809
▦✉ secretary@wildernesse.co.uk
▦ 700
🏌 Maj (Ret.) KP Loosemore

✓ Craig Walker (01732) 761527
🏴 18 L 6532 yds Par 72 SSS 71
👥 WD–U H SOC–Mon/Thurs/Fri
££ £60 D–£90
⛳ 2 miles E of Sevenoaks (A25). M25
Junction 5
⊕ Large practice ground and short
game academy
▣ www.wildernesse.co.uk

Woodlands Manor
(1928)
Woodlands, Tinkerpot Lane, Sevenoaks,
TN15 6AB
☎ **(01959) 523806**
▦✉ info@woodlandsmanorgolf.co.uk
▦ 650
🏌 CG Robins (01959) 523806
✓ P Womack (01959) 523806
🏴 18 L 6100 yds SSS 69
👥 WD–U WE–H NA before noon
SOC–WD
££ On application
⛳ 4 miles S of M25 Junction 3. Off
A20 between West Kingsdown and
Otford
⊕ Driving range
🏠 Coles/Lyons
▣ www.woodlandsmanorgolf.co.uk

Wrotham Heath
(1906)
Seven Mile Lane, Comp, Sevenoaks
TN15 8QZ
☎ **(01732) 884800**
▦✉ wrothamheathgolf@btconnect.com
▦ 424 75(L) 50(J)
🏌 J Hodgson
✓ H Dearden (01732) 883854
🏴 18 L 5954 yds SSS 69
👥 WD–H SOC–Fri only
££ £35 D–£45
⛳ 8 miles W of Maidstone on B2016.
M26/A20 Junction, 1 mile
🏠 Donald Steel
▣ www.wrothamheathgolfclub.co.uk

Lancashire

Accrington & District
(1893)
West End, Oswaldtwistle, Accrington,
BB5 4LS
☎ **(01254) 381614**
📠 (01254) 350111
▦✉ info@accringtongolfclub.com
▦ 500
🏌 S Padbury (01254) 350112
✓ M Harling (01254) 231091
🏴 18 L 6031 yds SSS 69
👥 WD/WE–U H SOC–H
££ On application
⛳ 3 miles SW of Accrington. M65
Junctions 6/7
🏠 Original unknown – amendments
by James Braid
▣ www.accringtongolfclub.com

Ashton & Lea
(1913)
Tudor Ave, Off Blackpool Rd, Lea, Preston
PR4 0XA
☎ **(01772) 735282**
📠 (01772) 735762
▦✉ info@ashtonleagolfclub.com

655
M Caunce (01772) 735282
M Greenough (01772) 720374
18 L 6334 yds SSS 71
U SOC
£€ £30 (£35) Members times:
8.30–9.15am WD 12.15–1.30pm
WD
3 miles W of Preston, off A5085.
Nr M6, M55 and M65
J Steer
www.ashtonleagolfclub.co.uk

Ashton-in-Makerfield
(1902)
Garswood Park, Liverpool Road, Ashton-in-Makerfield, Wigan, WN4 0YT
(01942) 727267
(01942) 719330
secretary@ashton-in-makerfieldgolfclub.co.uk
675
HG Williams (01942) 719330
P Allan (01942) 724229
18 L 6205 yds SSS 70 Par 70
WD–U exc Wed WE/BH–M SOC
£€ £32
1 mile W of Ashton-in-Makerfield
on A58. M6 Junction 23/24
Fred Hawtree
www.ashton-in-makerfieldgolfclub.co.uk

Ashton-under-Lyne   (1912)
Gorsey Way, Hurst, Ashton-under-Lyne, OL6 9HT
(0161) 330 1537
(0161) 330 6673
info@ashtongolfclub.co.uk
600
A Jackson (0161) 330 1537
C Boyle (0161) 308 2095
18 L 6209 yds SSS 70
WD–U WE/BH–M SOC
£€ £27.50 (£13.75 with member)
8 miles E of Manchester; 3 miles
from M60 Jct 23
www.ashtongolfclub.co.uk

Bacup   (1910)
Maden Road, Bankside Lane, Bacup, OL13 8HN
(01706) 873170
(01706) 867726
secretary_bgc@btconnect.com
T Leyland (01706) 879644
9 L 6018 yds SSS 69
U
£€ On application
Bankside Lane

Baxenden & District   (1913)
Top o' th' Meadow, Baxenden, Accrington, BB5 2EA
(01254) 234555
baxgolf@hotmail.com
400
N Turner (01706) 225423
9 L 5702 yds SSS 68
WD–U WE/BH–M
£€ £15
2 miles SE of Accrington
Small practice area
www.baxendengolf.co.uk

Beacon Park G&CC   (1982)
Public
Beacon Lane, Dalton, Up Holland, WN8 7RU
(01695) 625551
(01695) 628362
info@beaconparkgolf.com
250
Mark Prosser
C Parkinson (01695) 622700
18 L 6155 yds SSS 70
U–book 6 days in advance SOC
£€ £12 (£17)
Nr Ashurst Beacon and M58/M6
Junction 26
Driving range; practice area
Donald Steel
www.beaconparkgolf.com

Blackburn   (1894)
Beardwood Brow, Blackburn, BB2 7AX
(01254) 51122
(01254) 665578
blackburngolfclub@tiscali.co.uk
476 65(L) 104(J)
(01254) 51122
A Rodwell (01254) 55942
18 L 6144 yds SSS 70
U SOC–WD WE/BH–restricted
£€ £32 (£38)
1 mile NW of Blackburn (A677).
M6 Junction 31

Blackpool North Shore
(1904)
Devonshire Road, Blackpool, FY2 0RD
(01253) 352054
(01253) 591240
office@bnsgc.com
750
JW Morris (01253) 352054 ext 1
A Richardson (01253) 354640
18 L 6443 yds SSS 71
WD–U WE–restricted SOC
£€ £29 D–£37 (£35 D–£44)
½ mile E of Queens Promenade
(B5124)
HS Colt
www.bnsgc.com

Blackpool Park   (1925)
Public
North Park Drive, Blackpool, FY3 8LS
(01253) 397916
(01253) 397916
secretary@blackpoolparkgc.co.uk
450
Charles Wright
B Purdie (01253) 391004
18 L 6048 yds SSS 70
U–no telephone booking SOC
(01253) 478478, Sat Members up
to 2.30pm
£€ £18 (£20.60)
2 miles E of Blackpool, signposted
off M55
Phone bookings for tee times –
(01253) 478176 (up to 1 week in
advance)
Dr A Mackenzie
www.blackpoolparkgc.co.uk

Bolton   (1891)
Lostock Park, Bolton, BL6 4AJ
(01204) 843278
(01204) 843067
secretary@boltongolfclub.co.uk
500
S Higham (01204) 843067
R Longworth (01204) 843073
18 L 6213 yds Par 70 SSS 70
U SOC
£€ Summer: £32, fourball £100
Winter: £22.50, fourball £80
3 miles W of Bolton. M61 Junction
6, 2 miles on A673

Bolton Old Links   (1891)
Chorley Old Road, Montserrat, Bolton, BL1 5SU
(01204) 840050
(01204) 842307
mail@boltonoldlinksgolfclub.co.uk
600
Mrs J Boardman (01204) 842307
P Horridge (01204) 843089
18 L 6419 yds SSS 71
U H exc comp Sats SOC
£€ £35 (£45)
3 miles NW of Bolton on B6226
Dr A Mackenzie
www.boltonoldlinksgolfclub.co.uk

Bolton Open Golf Course
Pay and play
Longsight Park, Longsight Lane, Harwood, BL2 4JX
(01204) 597659/309778
250
H Swindells (Sec/Mgr)
(01204) 597659
Grant Hammerton (01204) 597659
18 holes Par 70 SSS 68
WD–U WE–booking necessary
SOC
£€ £10 (£14)
2 miles NE of Bolton (A666)
Driving range

Brackley Municipal   (1977)
Public
Bullows Road, Little Hulton, Worsley, M38 9TR
(0161) 790 6076

Breightmet   (1911)
Red Bridge, Ainsworth, Bolton, BL2 5PA
(01204) 399275
400
ID Cooke
18 L 6405 yds Par 72 SSS 72
WD–H WE–NA SOC–WD
£€ £20
3 miles E of Bolton
David Griffiths

Brookdale   (1896)
Medlock Road, Woodhouses, Failsworth, M35 9WQ
(0161) 681 4534

Burnley   (1905)
Glen View, Burnley, BB11 3RW
(0870) 330 6655

☖ (01282) 451281
✉ burnleygolfclub@onthegreen.co.uk
☷ 600
♣ RDM Wills
⛳ M Baker
▷ 18 L 5939 yds SSS 69
♙ H SOC WD/WE–phone for
availability
££ £25 (£30)
⊶ Via Manchester Road to Glen View
Road
⊕ Two practice areas; putting green
⌂ James Braid
▤ www.burnleygolfclub.com

Bury (1890)
Unsworth Hall, Blackford Bridge, Bury,
BL9 9TJ
☎ (0161) 766 4897
☖ (0161) 796 3480
✉ secretary@burygolfclub.com
☷ 650
♣ R Adams
⛳ G Coope (0161) 766 2213
▷ 18 L 5927 yds Par 69 SSS 69
♙ SOC WD WE
££ £30 (£35)
⊶ A56, 5 miles N of Manchester. 3
miles N of M62 Junction 17
⌂ McKenzie
▤ www.burygolfclub.com

Castle Hawk (1975)
Chadwick Lane, Castleton, Rochdale,
OL11 3BY
☎ (01706) 640841
✉ teeoff@castlehawk.co.uk

Chorley (1897)
Hall o' th' Hill, Heath Charnock, Chorley,
PR6 9HX
☎ (01257) 480263
☖ (01257) 480722
✉ secretary@chorleygolfclub
.freeserve.co.uk
☷ 550
♣ Mrs A Green (01257) 480263
⛳ M Bradley (01257) 481245
▷ 18 L 6240 yds SSS 70
♙ WD–I or H WE–NA SOC
££ On application
⊶ I mile S of Chorley at junction
A6/A673
⌂ JA Steer
▤ www.chorleygolfclub.co.uk

Clitheroe (1891)
Whalley Road, Clitheroe, BB7 1PP
☎ (01200) 422618 (Clubhouse)
☖ (01200) 422292
✉ secretary@clitheroegolfclub.com
☷ 700
♣ Mr M P D Walls (01200) 422292
⛳ P McEvoy (01200) 424242
▷ 18 L 6530 yds SSS 71
♙ WD–U H SOC
££ £37 D–£49 (£49)
⊶ 2 miles S of Clitheroe
⊕ Range
⌂ James Braid
▤ www.clitheroegolfclub.com

Colne (1901)
Law Farm, Skipton Old Road, Colne,
BB8 7EB
☎ (01282) 863391
☖ (01282) 870547
✉ colnegolfclub@hotmail.co.uk
☷ 440
♣ A Turpin (Hon)
⛳ None
▷ 9 L 6053 yds SSS 69
♙ U exc comp days SOC–WD
££ £20 (£25)
⊶ 1½ miles N of Colne. From end of
M65, signs to Keighley and then
Lothersdale
⊕ Practice Ground, Putting Green

Crompton & Royton (1908)
High Barn, Royton, Oldham, OL2 6RW
☎ (0161) 624 2154
☖ (0161) 652 4711
✉ secretary
@cromptonandroytongolfclub.co.uk
☷ 620
♣ R Smith (0161) 624 0986
⛳ DA Melling (0161) 624 2154
▷ 18 L 6186 yds SSS 70
♙ U SOC–WD
££ £25 (£35)
⊶ 3 miles NW of Oldham
▤ www.cromptonandroytongolfclub
.co.uk

Darwen (1893)
Winter Hill, Duddon Avenue, Darwen,
BB3 0LB
☎ (01254) 701287
☖ (01254) 773833
✉ admin@darwengolfclub.com
☷ 350 42(L) 57(J)
♣ MJ Catterall (01254) 704367
⛳ W Lennon (01254) 776370
▷ 18 L6354 yds Par 71 SSS 71
♙ U exc Tues & Sat–NA
££ £25 (£30)
⊶ Darwen 1½ miles. M65 Junction 4
▤ www.darwengolfclub.com

Dean Wood (1922)
Lafford Lane, Up Holland, Skelmersdale,
WN8 0QZ
☎ (01695) 622219
☖ (01695) 622245
✉ ray.benton@deanwoodgolfclub.co.uk
☷ 750
♣ WR Benton
⛳ D Clarke (01695) 627480
▷ 18 L 6148 yds SSS 70
♙ WD–U WE/BH–M
SOC–Mon/Thur/Fri only
££ D–£30 (£35)
⊶ I mile W of M6 J26
⊕ Small driving range; chipping facility;
practice nets
⌂ James Braid
▤ www.deanwoodgolfclub.co.uk

Deane (1906)
Broadford Road, Deane, Bolton, BL3 4NS
☎ (01204) 61944
☖ (01204) 652047
✉ secretary@deanegolfclub.com
☷ 490

♣ P Parry (01204) 651808
⛳ D Martindale
▷ 18 L 5652 yds SSS 67
♙ WD–U WE–restricted
SOC–Tues/Thurs/Fri
££ £25 (£30)
⊶ 2 m W of Bolton. M61 Jct 5, I mile
▤ www.deanegolfclub.co.uk

Dunscar (1908)
Longworth Lane, Bromley Cross, Bolton,
BL7 9QY
☎ (01204) 303321
☖ (01204) 303321
✉ dunscargolfclub@uk2.net
☷ 660
♣ Mrs A E Jennings (01204) 303321
⛳ G Treadgold (01204) 592992
▷ 18 L 5995 yds Par 71 SSS 69
♙ WD–U WE–M H at all times
SOC–WD
££ £30 (£36)
⊶ 3 miles N of Bolton, off A666
⌂ G Lowe
▤ www.dunscargolfclub.co.uk

Duxbury Park (1975)
Public
Duxbury Hall Road, Duxbury Park, Chorley,
PR7 4AS
☎ (01257) 265380
(01257) 241634 (Clubhouse)
☖ (01257) 241378
♣ F Holding (01257) 262209
⛳ Pro shop (01257) 265380
▷ 18 L 6270 yds SSS 70
♙ U
££ £14 (£17)
⊶ 1½ miles S of Chorley, off Wigan
Lane

Fairhaven (1895)
Oakwood Avenue, Ansdell, Lytham St Annes,
FY8 4JU
☎ (01253) 736741
☖ (01253) 736741
✉ secretary@fairhavengolfclub.co.uk
☷ 650
♣ R Thompson
⛳ B Plunkett (01253) 736976
▷ 18 L 6883 yds SSS 73
♙ WD–H–SOC between 9.30–12 and
1.30–4 WE–H–M
££ £55 D–£75 (£65 D–£85)
⊶ Lytham 2 miles. St Annes 2 miles.
M55 Junction 4
⊕ Practice ground; chipping green;
putting green
⌂ James Braid & JA steer; upgraded
by Donald Steel
▤ www.fairhavengolfclub.co.uk

Fishwick Hall (1912)
Glenluce Drive, Farringdon Park, Preston,
PR1 5TD
☎ (01772) 798300
☖ (01772) 704600
✉ fishwickhallgolfclub@supanet.com
☷ 530
♣ RE Stamp
⛳ M Watson (01772) 795870
▷ 18 L 6045 yds Par 70 SSS 69
♙ Apply to Sec SOC U

££   £20 D–£28 (£32)
🚗 1 mile E of Preston, nr junction of
A59 and M6 Junction 31
🖳 www.fishwickhallgolfclub.co.uk

Fleetwood   (1932)
Golf House, Princes Way, Fleetwood,
FY7 8AF
☎ (01253) 773573
📧 secretary@fleetwoodgolf.co.uk
🏠 548
🏌 Ernie Langford
⚐ Ian Taylor (01253) 873661
🏳 L 18 L 6308 yds SSS 71
👤 U H exc Tues SOC
££   £35 D–£45 (£45 D–£50)
🚗 1 mile W of Fleetwood centre
🏠 A Steer
🖳 www.fleetwoodgolf.co.uk

Gathurst   (1913)
Miles Lane, Shevington, Wigan, WN6 8EW
☎ (01257) 252861 (Clubhouse)
🖳 (01257) 255953
📧 mail@gathurstgolfclub.ltd.uk
🏠 675
🏌 Mrs I Fyffe (01257) 255235
⚐ D Clarke (01257) 255882
🏳 18 L 6089 yds Par 70 SSS 69
👤 WD–U before 5pm
WE/BH/Wed–M SOC–WD
££   £30
🚗 4 miles W of Wigan. 1 mile S of M6
Junction 27
🏠 N Pearson-ADAS
🖳 www.gathurstgolfclub.co.uk

Ghyll   (1907)
Ghyll Brow, Barnoldswick, Colne,
BB18 6JH
☎ (01282) 842466
📧 secretary@ghyllgolfclub.co.uk
🏠 310
🏌 K J Wilkinson (01282) 865582
🏳 11 Holes Tudor Course 9 L 6259
SSS 70
York Course 9 L 5770 SSS 68
👤 U exc Sun–NA; Tues NA before
3pm
££   D–£15 (D–£20)
🚗 7 miles N of Colne, off A56
(B6252)
🖳 www.ghyllgolfclub.co.uk

Great Harwood   (1896)
Harwood Bar, Whalley Road, Great
Harwood, BB6 7TE
☎ (01254) 884391
🏠 295 65(L) 45(J)
🏌 J Spibey (01254) 879494
🏳 9 L 6404 yds Par 73 SSS 71
👤 U SOC
££   £20 (£26)
🚗 5 miles NE of Blackburn. M65 Jct 7
🖳 www.greatharwoodgolfclub.co.uk

Green Haworth   (1914)
Green Haworth, Accrington, BB5 3SL
☎ (01254) 237580
📧 enquiries@greenhaworth.co.uk

Greenmount   (1920)
Greenmount, Bury, BL8 4LH
☎ (01204) 883712
📧 secretary@greenmountgolfclub
.co.uk
🏠 220
🏌 D Beesley (Hon)
🏳 9 L 5874 yds SSS 69
👤 WD–U exc Tues WE–M
££   £20 (WE only with member £10)
🚗 3 miles N of Bury
⊕ Visiting Professional by
arrangement
🏠 M Renouf (1936)
🖳 www.greenmountgolfclub.com

Haigh Hall   (1972)
Public
Haigh Hall Country Park, Haigh, Wigan,
WN2 1PE
☎ (01942) 833337 (Clubhouse)
🖳 (01942) 831417
📧 secretary@haighhall-golfclub.co.uk
🏠 180
🏌 SG Eyres
⚐ I Lee (01942) 831107
🏳 9 L 1446 yds
18 L 6358 yds
👤 U WD/WE–NA SOC–WD/WE
££   9: £4.50 (£5.50); 18: £13 – £10
after 1pm (£17 – £12 after 3pm)
Summer prices
🚗 2 miles NW of Wigan. M6 Junction
27. M61 Junction 6
⊕ Driving range; short game practice
area
🏠 Gaunt/Marnoch
🖳 www.haighhall-golfclub.co.uk

Hart Common   (1995)
Proprietary
Westhoughton Golf Centre, Wigan Road,
Westhoughton, BL5 2BX
☎ (01942) 813195
🏌 B Hill (01942) 813195
⚐ S Reeves (01942) 813195
🏳 18 L 6243 yds (white) Par 72
SSS 70
L 5719 yds (yellow) Par 71 SSS 68
9 L 694 yds Par 27
👤 U SOC
££   18: £12 (£14)
🚗 In-between Bolton and Wigan on
A58, M61 J5
⊕ 27 bay driving range; Par 3
Academy Course (9 holes)

Harwood   (1926)
Roading Brook Road, Bolton, BL2 4JD
☎ (01204) 522878
🖳 (01204) 524233
📧 secretary@harwoodgolfclub
.co.uk
🏠 511
🏌 IW Lund (01204) 522878
⚐ Clive Loydall (01204) 522878
🏳 18 L 5915 yds Par 70 SSS 69
👤 WD WE–M SOC–WD
££   £25 (£12)
🚗 4 miles NE of Bolton off B6196
🏠 J Shuttleworth
🖳 www.harwoodgolfclub.co.uk

De Vere Herons Reach
(1993)
Proprietary
East Park Drive, Blackpool, FY3 8LL
☎ (01253) 766156
🖳 (01253) 798800
📧 richard.bowman
@devere-hotels.com
🏠 400
🏌 P Heaton
⚐ R Bowman (01253) 766156
🏳 18 L 6461 yds SSS 72
👤 U H SOC
££   £35 (£45)
🚗 M55 Junction 4. Follow signs to
Blackpool Zoo
⊕ Floodlit driving range; buggies
🏠 Peter Alliss & Clive Clark
🖳 www.deveregolf.co.uk

Heysham   (1910)
Trumacar Park, Middleton Road, Heysham,
Morecambe, LA3 3JH
☎ (01524) 851011
🖳 (01524) 853030
📧 secretary@heyshamgolfclub.co.uk
🏠 650
🏌 Mrs G E Gardner
⚐ R Dône (01524) 852000
🏳 18 L 6258 yds SSS 70
👤 U H SOC
££   £30 (£40)
🚗 2 miles S of Morecambe. M6
Junction 34, 5 miles
⊕ Floodlit driving range; buggy hire
🏠 A Herd
🖳 www.heyshamgolfclub.co.uk

Hindley Hall   (1905)
Hall Lane, Hindley, Wigan, WN2 2SQ
☎ (01942) 255131
🖳 (01942) 253871
📧 sechindley@aol.com
🏠 430
🏌 Simon Tyrer (01942) 255131
⚐ D Clarke (01942) 255991
🏳 18 L 5913 yds SSS 68
👤 U SOC WD/WE after 3pm
££   £25 (£30)
🚗 2 miles E of Wigan. M61 Junction 6
🖳 www.hindleyhallgolfclub.co.uk

Horwich   (1895)
Victoria Road, Horwich, BL6 5PH
☎ (01204) 696980

Hurlston Hall   (1994)
Proprietary
Hurlston Lane, Southport Road, Scarisbrick,
L40 8HB
☎ (01704) 840400
🖳 (01704) 841404
📧 info@hurlstonhall.co.uk
🏠 650
🏌 Aoife O'Brien (MD)
⚐ Golf Centre (01704) 842829
🏳 18 L 6601 yds SSS 72
👤 SOC
££   £40 (£45)
🚗 2 miles NW of Ormskirk (A570).
M58 Junction 3
⊕ Floodlit driving range with power
tee

Donald Steel
🖳 www.hurlstonhall.co.uk

Ingol (1981)
Proprietary
*Tanterton Hall Road, Ingol, Preston,
PR2 7BY*
☎ **(01772) 734556**
🖂 ingol@golfers.net

Knott End (1910)
*Wyreside, Knott End-on-Sea, Poulton-le-
Fylde, FY6 0AA*
☎ **(01253) 810576**
📠 (01253) 813446
🖂 louise@knottendgolfclub.com
🛏 660
🏌 Louise Freeman (01253) 810576
✒ P Walker (01253) 811365
➥ 18 L 5849 yds SSS 68
👥 WD–U WE/BH–by arrangement
  SOC–WD
££ £32 (£40)
🚗 Over Wyre, 12 miles NE of
  Blackpool (A588). M55 J3 off M6
⊕ Practice ground; driving net;
  lessons; buggies
🏠 James Braid
🖳 www.knottendgolfclub.com

Lancaster (1882)
*Ashton Hall, Ashton-with-Stodday,
Lancaster, LA2 0AJ*
☎ **(01524) 752090 (Clubhouse)**
📠 (01524) 752742
🖂 office@lancastergc.co.uk
🛏 530 170(L) 62(J)
🏌 E Burrow (01524) 751247
✒ DE Sutcliffe (01524) 751802
➥ 18 L 6500 yds SSS 71
👥 WD–H SOC–WD
££ £45 D–£50
🚗 2 miles S of Lancaster (A588)
⊕ Dormy House
🏠 James Braid
🖳 www.lancastergc.co.uk

Lansil (1947)
Caton Road, Lancaster, LA4 3PE
☎ **(01524) 39269**
🛏 450
🏌 D Burns (07751) 089702
➥ 9 L 5608 yds Par 70 SSS 67
👥 WD–U Sun–U after 1pm
££ £12 (£12)
🚗 A683, 2 miles E of Lancaster

Leyland (1924)
Wigan Road, Leyland, PR25 5UD
☎ **(01772) 436457**
📠 (01772) 435605
🖂 manager@leylandgolfclub.co.uk
🛏 750
🏌 S Drinkall
✒ C Burgess (01772) 423425
➥ 18 L 6276 yds SSS 70
👥 WD–U WE–M SOC–WD
££ Phone for details
🚗 M6 Junction 28, ¹/₂ mile
🖳 www.leylandgolfclub.co.uk

Lobden (1888)
Whitworth, Rochdale, OL12 8XJ
☎ **(01706) 343228**
📠 (01706) 343228
🖂 lobdengc@hotmail.com
🛏 230
🏌 B Harrison (01706) 852752
➥ 9 L 5697 yds Par 70 SSS 68
👥 U
££ £12 (£15)
🚗 4 miles N of Rochdale

Longridge (1877)
*Fell Barn, Jeffrey Hill, Longridge, Preston,
PR3 2TU*
☎ **(01772) 783291**
📠 (01772) 783022
🖂 secretary@longridgegolfclub.fsnet
  .co.uk
🛏 600
🏌 D Simpson
✒ S Taylor (01772) 783291
➥ 18 L 5969 yds SSS 69
👥 U
££ £17–£25
🚗 8 miles NE of Preston, off B6243
⊕ Large practice area
🖳 www.longridgegolfclub.com

Lowes Park (1915)
Hilltop, Lowes Road, Bury, BL9 6SU
☎ **(0161) 764 1231**
📠 (0161) 763 9503
🖂 lowesparkgc@btconnect.com
🛏 300
🏌 Alan Taylor
➥ 9 L 6006 yds Par 70 SSS 69
👥 WD–U exc Wed–NA WE/BH–by
  arrangement
££ Summer £20 (£20); Winter £15
  (£15)
🚗 1 mile NE of Bury, off A56
🖳 www.lowesparkgc.co.uk

Lytham Green Drive (1913)
Ballam Road, Lytham St Annes, FY8 4LE
☎ **(01253) 737390**
📠 (01253) 731350
🖂 secretary@lythamgreendrive.co.uk
🛏 700
🏌 I Stewart (01253) 737390
✒ A Lancaster (01253) 737379
➥ 18 L 6305 yds SSS 70
👥 WD–U H WE–NA SOC–WD
££ £38 (£45) to be confirmed
🚗 Lytham St Annes. M55 Junction 4
🏠 JA Steer
🖳 www.lythamgreendrive.co.uk

Marland (1928)
Public
*Springfield Park, Bolton Road, Rochdale,
OL11 4RE*
☎ **(01706) 649801**

Marsden Park (1969)
Public
Townhouse Road, Nelson, BB9 8DG
☎ **(01282) 661912**
📠 (01282) 661384
🖂 martin.robinson
  @pendleleisuretrust.co.uk

🛏 300
🏌 D Walton (01282) 835833
✒ Martin Robinson (Mgr)
➥ 18 L 5989 yds Par 70 SSS 69
👥 U SOC
££ On application
🚗 M65 Junction 13, signposted
  Walton Lane
🖳 www.pendleleisuretrust.co.uk

Morecambe (1905)
Bare, Morecambe, LA4 6AJ
☎ **(01524) 418050**
🖂 secretary@morecambegolfclub
  .com

Mossock Hall (1996)
Liverpool Road, Bickerstaffe, L39 0EE
☎ **(01695) 421717**
📠 (01695) 424961
🖂 jackie@mossockhallgolfclub.co.uk
🛏 600
🏌 Jacqueline Fray
✒ B Millar (01695) 424969
➥ 18 L 6375 yds Par 71 SSS 71
👥 WD–U WE–after 12.30 SOC
££ £27 (£34)
🚗 4 miles S of Ormskirk
🏠 Steve Marnoch
🖳 www.mossockhallgolfclub.co.uk

Mytton Fold Hotel & Golf
Complex (1994)
Proprietary
Whalley Road, Langho, BB6 8AB
☎ **(01254) 240662 (Hotel)**
📠 (01254) 248119
🖂 golfshop@myttonfold.co.uk
🛏 350
🏌 D Hargreaves
✒ M Bardi (01254) 245392
➥ 18 L 6164 yds SSS 70
👥 U SOC
££ £22.50 (£25)
🚗 6 miles N of Blackburn, off A59.
  M6 Junction 31
⊕ Buggies available all year round
🏠 F Hargreaves
🖳 www.myttonfold.co.uk

Nelson (1902)
*Kings Causeway, Brierfield, Nelson,
BB9 0EU*
☎ **(01282) 611834**
📠 (01282) 611834
🖂 secretary@nelsongolfclub.com
🛏 550
🏌 Richard M Lees
✒ S Eaton (01282) 617000
➥ 18 L 6006 yds Par 70 SSS 69
👥 WD–U H exc Thurs–NA WE–U
  exc Sat before 4pm SOC
££ £30 WDU–£35
🚗 2 miles N of Burnley. M65 Jct 12
⊕ Large practice field
🏠 Dr A MacKenzie
🖳 www.nelsongolfclub.com

Oldham (1892)
Lees New Road, Oldham, OL4 5PN
☎ **(0161) 624 4986**
🛏 230 45(L) 20(J)

🖉 J Brooks
✓ J R Rowlands (0161) 626 8346
ᑉ 18 L 5045 yds SSS 65
⛹ U SOC
££ On application
🚗 Off Oldham-Stalybridge road

Ormskirk   (1899)
Cranes Lane, Lathom, Ormskirk, L40 5UJ
☎ **(01695) 572112**

Pennington
Pennington Country Park, Leigh, WN7 3PA
☎ **(01942) 741873**
🕮 122
🖉 Mrs A Lythgoe
✓ (01942) 682852 – for bookings
ᑉ 9 L 5521 yds Par 70 SSS 67
⛹ U SOC
££ £4.90 (£6.20)
🚗 ¹/2 mile off A580, on Leigh By-Pass.
    Follow signs for Pennington Flash

Penwortham   (1908)
Blundell Lane, Penwortham, Preston,
PR1 0AX
☎ **(01772) 744630**
🖳 (01772) 740172
📧 admin@penworthamgc.co.uk
🕮 820
🖉 N Annandale
✓ D Hopwood (01772) 742345
ᑉ 18 L 5865 yds SSS 69
⛹ WD–U (except Tues) WE–no
    parties
££ £27 (£35)
🚗 1¹/2 miles W of Preston (A59)
🏛 Ken Moodie
🖥 www.penworthamgc.co.uk

Pleasington   (1891)
Pleasington, Blackburn, BB2 5JF
☎ **(01254) 202177**
🖳 (01254) 201028
📧 secretary-manager
    @pleasington-golf.co.uk
🕮 545
🖉 T Ashton
✓ GJ Furey (01254) 201630
ᑉ 18 L 6402 yds SSS 71
⛹ SOC WD WE–limited availability
££ £45 (£50)
🚗 3 miles SW of Blackburn; M65
    Junction 3
⊕ Practice range available
🏛 George Lowe/Sandy Herd
🖥 www.pleasington-golf.co.uk

Poulton-le-Fylde   (1982)
Public
Myrtle Farm, Breck Road, Poulton-le-Fylde,
FY6 7HJ
☎ **(01253) 892444**
📧 greenwood-golf@hotmail.co.uk
🕮 320
🖉 S Wilkinson
✓ J Greenwood
ᑉ 9 L 2979 yds SSS 69
⛹ U
££ 9: £8.75 (£10); 18: £15 (£17)
🚗 3 miles NE of Blackpool
⊕ Putting green; practice ground
🖥 www.poultonlefyldegolfclub.co.uk

Preston   (1892)
Fulwood Hall Lane, Fulwood, Preston,
PR2 8DD
☎ **(01772) 700011**
🖳 (01772) 794234
📧 secretary@prestongolfclub.com
🕮 800
🖉 Mark Caunce
✓ A Greenbank (01772) 700022
ᑉ 18 L 6312 yds SSS 71
⛹ WD–U H WE–M SOC–WD
££ £40 (£45)
🚗 1¹/2 miles W of M6 Junction 32
⊕ Driving range. Golf academy
🏛 James Braid
🖥 www.prestongolfclub.com

Regent Park (Bolton)   (1931)
Pay and play
Links Road, Chorley New Road, Bolton,
BL6 4AF
☎ **(01204) 495421**
🕮 260
🖉 K Taylor
✓ N Brazell
ᑉ 18 L 6221yds Par 71 SSS 70
⛹ U SOC–WD
££ £12 (£15)
🚗 A673, 3 m W of Bolton. M61 Jct 6
⊕ 20-bay automated driving range
🏛 James Braid

Rishton   (1927)
Eachill Links, Hawthorn Drive, Rishton,
BB1 4HG
☎ **(01254) 884442**
📧 rishtongc@onetel.net

Rochdale   (1888)
Edenfield Road, Bagslate, Rochdale,
OL11 5YR
☎ **(01706) 643818 (Clubhouse)**
🖳 (01706) 861113
📧 rochdale.golfclub@zen.co.uk
🕮 750
🖉 P Kershaw (01706) 643818 (opt 2)
✓ A Laverty (01706) 522104
ᑉ 18 L 6031 yds SSS 69
⛹ U
££ £22 (£29)
🚗 3 miles from M62 Jct 20 on A680
🏛 George Lowe

Rossendale   (1903)
Ewood Lane Head, Haslingden, Rossendale,
BB4 6LH
☎ **(01706) 831339**
🖳 (01706) 228669
📧 admin@rossendalegolfclub.net
🕮 600
🖉 K Wilson
✓ SJ Nicholls (01706) 213616
ᑉ 18 L 6293 yds SSS 71
⛹ WD/Sun–U Sat–M
££ £30 D–£40 (£35) £45 Sun/BH
🚗 7 miles N of Bury, nr end of M66
🖥 www.rossendalegolfclub.net

Royal Lytham & St Annes
    (1886)
Links Gate, Lytham St Annes, FY8 3LQ
☎ **(01253) 724206**

🖳 (01253) 780946
📧 bookings@royallytham.org
🕮 500
🖉 RJG Cochrane
✓ E Birchenough (01253) 720094
ᑉ 18 L 6685 yds SSS 73
⛹ WD–I H
££ £140 (£212 – inc. £13 lunch)
    D–£212 – inc. £13 lunch
🚗 St Annes 1 mile (A584)
⊕ Dormy House
🏛 George Lowe
🖥 www.royallytham.org

Saddleworth   (1904)
Mountain Ash, Uppermill, Oldham, OL3 6LT
☎ **(01457) 873653**
🖳 (01457) 820647
📧 secretary@saddleworthgolfclub
    .org.uk
🕮 700
🖉 Paul Green
✓ RI Johnson
ᑉ 18 L 6196 yds SSS 69
⛹ U SOC WD
££ £28 (£41)
🚗 Uppermill, 5 miles E of Oldham
🏛 Mackenzie/Leaver

Shaw Hill Hotel G&CC
    (1925)
Preston Road, Whittle-le-Woods, Chorley,
PR6 7PP
☎ **(01257) 269221**
🖳 (01257) 261223
📧 info@shaw-hill.co.uk
🕮 500
🖉 B Brodrick (Manager)
✓ D Clarke (01257) 279222
ᑉ 18 L 6246 yds Par 73 SSS 70
⛹ WD–U H SOC WE
££ £40 (£50)
🚗 A6, 1¹/2 miles N of Chorley. M61
    Junction 8. M6 Junction 28
⊕ Leisure Centre, Gym and Pool
🏛 Tom McCauley
🖥 www.shaw-hill.co.uk

St Annes Old Links   (1901)
Highbury Road East, Lytham St Annes,
FY8 2LD
☎ **(01253) 723597**
🖳 (01253) 781506
📧 secretary@stannesoldlinks.com
🕮 945
🖉 Mrs Jane Donohoe
✓ D Webster (01253) 722432
ᑉ 18 L 6684 yds SSS 72
⛹ WD–NA before 9.30am and
    12–1.30pm WE/BH–arrange with
    Sec SOC
££ Mon–Thur am £55, Fri am £65;
    £40 pm (£50)
🚗 Between St Annes and Blackpool,
    off A584
🏛 Herd
🖥 www.stannesoldlinks.com

Standish Court   (1995)
Pay and play
Rectory Lane, Standish, Wigan, WN6 0XD
☎ **(01257) 425777**
🖳 (01257) 425777

For list of abbreviations and key to symbols see page 647

✉ info@standishgolf.co.uk
▥ 300
♬ S McGrath
✓ S McGrath
► 18 L 4860 yds Par 68 SSS 64
♟ U SOC
££ £12.50–£15 (£20)
↝ M6 Junction 27, 2 miles
⌂ Patrick Dawson
▤ www.standishgolf.co.uk

Stonyhurst Park   (1979)
Stonyhurst, Hurst Green, Clitheroe,
BB7 9QB
☎ (01254) 826478 (not manned)
⌨ jandbaus@btinternet.com
▥ 436
♬ JR Austin (01254) 240314
► 9 L 5715 yds SSS 69
♟ WD–U WE–NA
££ £20
↝ 5 miles SW of Clitheroe (B6243)
⊕ Green fees payable at Bayley Arms
   or Shireburn Arms, Hurst Green

Towneley   (1932)
Public
Towneley Park, Todmorden Road, Burnley,
BB11 3ED
☎ (01282) 451636
✉ secretary@towneleygolfclub.co.uk
▥ 220
♬ B Walsh
✓ James Major (01282)438473
► 18 L 5811 yds Par 70 SSS 68
   9 hole course
♟ U, SOC
££ £14 (£16)
↝ 1½ miles E of Burnley
▤ www.towneleygolfclub.co.uk

Tunshill   (1901)
Kiln Lane, Milnrow, Rochdale, OL16 3TS
☎ (01706) 342095
▥ 300
♬ P Lowthian (01706) 342095
► 9 L 5745 yds SSS 68
♟ WD–U WE–M SOC
££ £16
↝ 2 miles E of Rochdale. M62
   Junction 21
▤ www.tunshillgolfclub.co.uk

Turton   (1908)
Wood End Farm, Hospital Road, Bromley
Cross, Bolton, BL7 9QD
☎ (01204) 852235
⌨ (01204) 856921
✉ info@turtongolfclub.com
▥ 500 56(L) 65(J)
♬ Andrew Scully (01204) 852235
✓ Andrew Green
► 18 L 6124 yds Par 70 SSS 69
♟ WD–U exc Wed–NA
   10.00–2.30pm WE Sat–NA before
   4 pm SOC
££ £30 D–£39 (£36 D–£49)
↝ 3½ miles N of Bolton, nr Last
   Drop Village
⌂ Alexander Herd
▤ www.turtongolfclub.com

Walmersley   (1906)
Garrett's Close, Walmersley, Bury, BL9 6TE
☎ (0161) 764 1429
⌨ (0161) 764 7770
▥ 450
♬ DL Thomas (0161) 764 7770
✓ SL Halsall (0161) 763 9050
► 18 L 5385 yds Par 69 SSS 67
♟ WD–U exc Tues–NA Sat–after
   1pm SOC Wed–Fri & Sun pm
££ D–£30 (£30)
↝ 2 m N of Bury (A56). S of M66 Jct 1
⌂ SG Marnoch

Werneth   (1908)
Green Lane, Garden Suburb, Oldham,
OL8 3AZ
☎ (0161) 624 1190
✉ secretary@wernethgolfclub.co.uk
▥ 400
♬ JH Barlow
✓ James Matterson (0161) 628 7136
► 18 L 5363 yds SSS 66
♟ WD–U WE–M SOC
££ D–£18
↝ 2 miles S of Oldham centre
⌂ Sandy Herd
▤ www.wernethgolfclub.co.uk

Westhoughton   (1929)
Long Island, Westhoughton, Bolton,
BL5 2BR
☎ (01942) 811085
⌨ (01942) 811085
✉ honsec.wgc@btconnect.com
▥ 364
♬ Dave Moores
► 18 L 5918 yds SSS 69
♟ WD–U WE/BH–M
££ D–£20
↝ 4 miles SW of Bolton on A58

Whalley   (1912)
Long Leese Barn, Clerkhill Road, Whalley,
BB7 9DR
☎ (01254) 822236

Whittaker   (1906)
Littleborough, OL15 0LH
☎ (01706) 378310
▥ 176
♬ S Noblett (01706) 842541
► 9 L 5666 yds SSS 67
♟ WD/Sat–U Sun–NA
££ £15 (£20)
↝ 1½ miles N of Littleborough, off
   A58. M62 Junction 21
⌂ NP Stott
▤ www.whittakergolfclub.co.uk

Wigan   (1898)
Arley Hall, Haigh, Wigan, WN1 2UH
☎ (01257) 421360
✉ info@wigangolfclub.co.uk
▥ 300
♬ E Walmsley
► 18 L 6008 yds SSS 70
♟ U exc Tues & Sat
££ £30 (£30)
↝ 4 miles N of Wigan, off
   A5106/B5239. M6 Junction 27
⌂ Gaunt/Marnoch
▤ www.wigangolfclub.co.uk

Wilpshire   (1890)
72 Whalley Road, Wilpshire, Blackburn,
BB1 9LF
☎ (01254) 248260
⌨ (01254) 246745
✉ admin@wilpshiregolfclub.co.uk
▥ 650
♬ SH Tart
✓ W Slaven (01254) 249558
► 18 L 5843 yds SSS 69
♟ WD–U WE/BH–on request
££ £25 (£30)
↝ 3 miles NE of Blackburn, off A666
⌂ James Braid
▤ www.wilpshiregolfclub.co.uk

Leicestershire

Beedles Lake   (1993)
170 Broome Lane, East Goscote, LE7 3WQ
☎ (0116) 260 6759/7086
⌨ (0116) 260 4414
✉ ian@jelson.co.uk
▥ 480
♬ Jon Coleman (0116) 260 4414
✓ S Byrne
► 18 L 6641 yds Par 72 SSS 72
♟ U SOC WD (WE restricted)
££ £15 D–£26 (£22)
↝ 4 miles N of Leicester on B5328,
   off A46. M1, 8 miles
⊕ Driving range; putting green;
   practice bunker Bar; Restaurant
⌂ D Tucker
▤ www.beedleslake.co.uk

Birstall   (1900)
Station Road, Birstall, Leicester, LE4 3BB
☎ (0116) 267 4450
⌨ (0116) 267 4322
✉ sue@birstallgolfclub.co.uk
▥ 400 80(L) 50(J)
♬ Mrs SE Chilton (0116) 267 4322
✓ D Clark (0116) 267 5245
► 18 L 6239 yds SSS 71
♟ WD–I WE–M SOC
££ £30 (£40)
↝ 3 miles N of Leicester (A6)
▤ www.birstallgolfclub.co.uk

Breedon Priory   (1990)
Green Lane, Wilson, Derby, DE73 1LG
☎ (01332) 863081
✉ bpgc@barbox.net

Charnwood Forest   (1890)
Breakback Road, Woodhouse Eaves,
Loughborough, LE12 8TA
☎ (01509) 890259
   (01509) 890925 (Steward)
✉ secretary
   @charnwoodforestgolfclub.com
▥ 360
♬ PK Field
► 9 L 5972 yds SSS 69
♟ UH SOC–Wed–Fri (not Tue)
££ £25 D–£30 (£30)
↝ M1 Junction 22/23, 3 miles
⌂ James Braid
▤ www.charnwoodforestgolfclub.com

Cosby   (1895)

Chapel Lane, Broughton Road, Cosby, Leicester, LE9 1RG
- ☎ **(0116) 286 4759**
- 🖷 (0116) 286 4484
- ✉ secretary@cosbygolfclub.co.uk
- 🛏 750
- ✍ Peggy Remington (0116) 286 4759
- 🏌 G Coysh (0116) 2864759
- ⛳ 18 L 6438 yds Par 71 SSS 71
- 👥 WD–U H before 4pm WE/BH–M H SOC–WD–H
- ££ £30 D–£40
- ⛴ The village of Cosby, 7 miles S of Leicester
- ⊕ Practice facilities; buggies for hire
- ⌂ Cameron Sinclair
- 🖳 www.cosbygolfclub.co.uk

Enderby   (1986)

Public
Mill Lane, Enderby, Leicester, LE19 4LX
- ☎ **(0116) 284 9388**
- 🖷 (0116) 284 9388
- 🏌 C D'Araujo
- ⛳ 9 L 5800 yds Par 72 SSS 71
- 👥 U SOC
- ££ 18 holes: £8.95 (£11.25)
- ⛴ Enderby 2 miles. M1 Junction 21
- ⊕ On-site leisure centre

Forest Hill   (1991)

Proprietary
Markfield Lane, Botcheston, LE9 9FJ
- ☎ **(01455) 824800**
- 🖷 (01455) 828522
- ✉ gerry@hyde14.fsnet.co.uk
- 🛏 650
- ✍ GD Hyde
- 🏌 G Quilter
- ⛳ 18 L 6450 yds Par 72 SSS 71
- 👥 WD–U WE–M
- ££ On application
- ⛴ 6 miles W of Leicester. M1 Junction 22, 4 miles
- ⊕ Driving range; putting green; 9 hole par 3
- ⌂ Redevelopment Gaunt & Marnock

Glen Gorse   (1933)

Glen Road, Oadby, Leicester, LE2 4RF
- ☎ **(0116) 271 4159**
- 🖷 (0116) 271 4159
- ✉ secretary@gggc.org
- 🛏 557 73(L) 97(J)
- ✍ Mrs J James (0116) 271 4159
- 🏌 D Fitzpatrick (0116) 271 3748
- ⛳ 18 L 6648 yds SSS 72
- 👥 WD–U WE/BH–M SOC–WD
- ££ £30 D–£35
- ⛴ 3 miles S of Leicester on A6
- 🖳 www.gggc.org

Hinckley   (1894)

Leicester Road, Hinckley, LE10 3DR
- ☎ **(01455) 615124**
- 🖷 (01455) 890841
- ✉ proshop@hinckleygolfclub.com
- 🛏 650
- ✍ D Gray (Sec), Y Watts (Finance & Admin)
- 🏌 R Jones (01455) 615014
- ⛳ 18 L 6527 yds SSS 71

- 👥 WD–U exc Tues before 2pm M after 11am SOC
- ££ £30 D–£40
- ⛴ NE of Hinckley on B4668, nr M69
- ⌂ Southern Golf
- 🖳 www.hinckleygolfclub.com

Humberstone Heights   (1978)

Public
Gipsy Lane, Leicester, LE5 0TB
- ☎ **(0116) 299 5570/1**
- 🖷 (0116) 299 5569
- ✉ admin@hhmgolfclub.freeserve.co.uk
- 🛏 350
- ✍ Mrs M Weston
- 🏌 D Butler (0116) 299 5570
- ⛳ 18 L 6343 yds SSS 70
- 👥 U SOC
- ££ On application
- ⛴ 3 miles E of Leicester, off A47
- ⊕ Driving range. Pitch & putt course
- ⌂ Hawtree
- 🖳 www.humberstoneheightsgc.co.uk

Kibworth   (1904)

Weir Road, Kibworth Beauchamp, Leicestershire, LE8 0LP
- ☎ **(0116) 279 2301**
- 🖷 (0116) 279 6434
- ✉ secretary@kibworthgolfclub.freeserve.co.uk
- 🛏 700
- ✍ Ella Corbett
- 🏌 Bryn Morris (0116) 279 2283
- ⛳ 18 L 6354 yds Par 71 SSS 71
- 👥 WD–U WE–M SOC–WD
- ££ £30 D–£40
- ⛴ 9 miles SE of Leicester, off A6
- ⊕ Driving range & practice area for members only.
- 🖳 www.kibworthgolfclub.co.uk

Kilworth Springs   (1993)

South Kilworth Road, North Kilworth, Lutterworth, LE17 6HJ
- ☎ **(01858) 575082** **(01858) 575974 (Pro Shop)**
- 🖷 (01858) 575078
- ✉ admin@kilworthsprings.co.uk
- 🛏 850
- ✍ Ann Vicary (Sec) Jeremy Wilkinson (Mgr)
- 🏌 A Mankert (01858) 575974
- ⛳ 18 L 6718 yds SSS 72
- 👥 U SOC
- ££ £25 (£27)
- ⛴ 4 miles E of M1 Junction 20
- ⊕ Floodlit driving range; additional practice facilities; computerised teaching studio
- ⌂ Ray Baldwin
- 🖳 www.kilworthsprings.co.uk

Kirby Muxloe   (1893)

Station Road, Kirby Muxloe, Leicester, LE9 2EP
- ☎ **(0116) 239 3457**
- 🖷 (0116) 238 8891
- ✉ kirbymuxloegolf@btconnect.com
- 🛏 630
- ✍ PD Jelly (0116) 239 3457
- 🏌 B Whipham (0116) 239 2813

- ⛳ 18 L 6428 yds Par 71 SSS 70
- 👥 WD–U before 4pm exc Tues–NA WE–by arrangement SOC–H
- ££ £35 D–£45
- ⛴ 3 miles W of Leicester. M1 Junctions 21 or 21A
- ⊕ Driving range for members and green fees only
- 🖳 www.kirbymuxloe-golf.co.uk

Lingdale   (1967)

Joe Moore's Lane, Woodhouse Eaves, Loughborough, LE12 8TF
- ☎ **(01509) 890703**
- 🖷 (01509) 890703
- ✉ secretary@lingdale-golf-club.com
- 🛏 718
- ✍ T Stephens
- 🏌 P Sellears
- ⛳ 18 L 6545 yds SSS 71
- 👥 SOC WD–U phone for availability WE–NA before 2pm
- ££ £30 D–£35 (£37.50 D–£48)
- ⛴ 6 miles S of Loughborough. M1 Junction 23, 4 miles
- ⊕ Practice ground
- ⌂ D Tucker/G Austin
- 🖳 www.lingdale-golf-club.com

Longcliffe   (1906)

Snells Nook Lane, Nanpantan, Loughborough, LE11 3YA
- ☎ **(01509) 239129**
- 🖷 (01509) 231286
- ✉ longcliffegolf@btconnect.com
- 🛏 650
- ✍ Mr B Jones
- 🏌 DC Mee (01509) 231450
- ⛳ 18 L 6625 yds SSS 72, 73
- 👥 WD–U WE–M SOC–WD
- ££ £35 (£45)
- ⛴ 3 miles SW of Loughborough. M1 Junction 23
- 🖳 www.longcliffegolf.co.uk

Lutterworth   (1904)

Rugby Road, Lutterworth, LE17 4HN
- ☎ **(01455) 552532**
- 🖷 (01455) 553586
- ✉ sec@lutterworthgc.co.uk
- 🛏 725
- ✍ J Faulks (01455) 552532
- 🏌 L Challinor (01455) 557199
- ⛳ 18 L 6226 yds SSS 70
- 👥 WD–U WE–M SOC–WD
- ££ D–£30
- ⛴ By M1 Jct 20 and M6 Jct 1
- 🖳 www.lutterworthgc.co.uk

Market Harborough   (1898)

Great Oxendon Road, Market Harborough, LE16 8NF
- ☎ **(01858) 463684**
- 🖷 (01858) 432906
- ✉ mhgc@premier-opt.co.uk
- 🛏 650
- ✍ F J Baxter
- 🏌 FJ Baxter (01858) 463684
- ⛳ 18 L 6095 yds Par 70 SSS 69
- 👥 WD–U WE–M SOC–WD
- ££ £30 D–£40
- ⛴ 1 mile S of Market Harborough on A508

⚘ Howard Swan/Cameron Sinclair
▤ www.mhgolf.co.uk

Melton Mowbray (1925)
Waltham Rd, Thorpe Arnold, Melton Mowbray, LE14 4SD
☎ (01664) 562118
⌨ (01664) 562118
✉ meltonmowbraygc@btconnect.com
▦ 600
⚘ Sue Millward/Marilyn Connelly
✓ N Curtis (01664) 569629
⛳ 18 L 6222 yds SSS 70
⛳ U Full green fee WD–U WE–U; 2–for–1 WD–U WE–Sat after 2pm, Sun after 12.30pm SOC
££ £25 D–£35 (£30)
⛳ 2 miles NE of Melton Mowbray on A607
⊕ Driving range; short game area; Putting Green; 2 buggies for hire.
▤ www.mmgc.org

Oadby (1974)
Public
Leicester Road, Oadby, Leicester, LE2 4AJ
☎ (0116) 270 9052/270 0215
▦ 350
⚘ RA Primrose (0116) 270 3828
✓ A Wells (0116) 270 9052
⛳ 18 L 6311 yds Par 72 SSS 70
⛳ WD–U WE/BH–book with Pro SOC–WD
££ D–£14 (£17)
⛳ Leicester Racecourse, 2 miles SE of Leicester (A6)
⊕ 4-bay driving range
⚘ C O'Connor

Park Hill (1994)
Park Hill, Seagrave, LE12 7NG
☎ (01509) 815454
⌨ (01509) 816062
✉ mail@parkhillgolf.co.uk
▦ 500
⚘ JP Hutson
✓ M Ulyett (01509) 815775
⛳ 18 L 7219 yds Par 73 SSS 74
⛳ U SOC
££ £27 D–£38 (£33 D–£48)
⛳ 6 miles N of Leicester on A46. 10 min from M1 Junction 21A
⊕ Driving range (20 bay), grass tees; practice bunker; Par 3 academy course
▤ www.parkhillgolf.co.uk

Rothley Park (1911)
Westfield Lane, Rothley, Leicester, LE7 7LH
⌨ (0116) 230 2809
✉ secretary@rothleypark.co.uk
▦ 600
⚘ Kaye Watts (Gen Mgr) (0116) 230 2809
✓ D Spillane (0116) 230 2809
⛳ 18 L 6487 yds SSS 71
⛳ WD–H exc Tues–NA WE/BH–NA SOC
££ D–£45
⛳ 6 miles N of Leicester, W of A6
▤ www.rothleypark.com

Scraptoft (1928)
Beeby Road, Scraptoft, Leicester, LE7 9SJ
☎ (0116) 241 9000
⌨ (0116) 241 9000
✉ secretary@scraptoft-golf.co.uk
▦ 600
⚘ Paul Henry (0116) 241 9000
✓ Simon Wood (0116) 241 9138
⛳ 18 L 6151 yds Par 70 SSS 70
⛳ WD–U WE–M SOC–WD
££ £24 D–£29 (£29 after noon)
⛳ 3 miles E of Leicester
▤ www.scraptoft-golf.co.uk

Six Hills (1986)
Pay and play
Six Hills, Melton Mowbray, LE14 3PR
☎ (01509) 881225
⌨ (01509) 881846
▦ 120
⚘ Mrs J Showler
✓ J Hawley
⛳ 18 L 5824 yds Par 71 SSS 68
⛳ U
££ £16 (£20)
⛳ 10 miles N of Leicester, off A46
⊕ Driving range

Stapleford Park (2000)
Stapleford park, Melton Mowbray, LE14 2EF
☎ (01572) 787044
⌨ (01572) 787001
✉ club@stapleford.co.uk
▦ 100
⚘ Richard Alderson
✓ Richard Alderson
⛳ 18 L 6944 yds Par 73 SSS 73
⛳ H WD–U WE–NA before 11am SOC–NA WE before 11am SOC–WD–U
££ 9: £25; 18: £50 D–£75 Same rates apply at WE
⛳ 4 miles E of Melton Mowbray off B676
⊕ Driving range; putting green; pro shop
⚘ Donald Steel
▤ www.staplefordpark.com

The Leicestershire (1890)
Evington Lane, Leicester, LE5 6DJ
☎ (0116) 273 8825
✉ secretary@leicestershiregolfclub.co.uk
▦ 750
⚘ CR Chapman (0116) 273 8825
✓ DT Jones (0116) 273 8825
⛳ 18 L 6329 yds SSS 71
⛳ U H SOC–arrange with Manager
££ £35 (£40)
⛳ 2 miles E of Leicester
⊕ Practice area
▤ www.leicestershiregolfclub.co.uk

Ullesthorpe Court Hotel (1976)
Frolesworth Road, Ullesthorpe, Lutterworth, LE17 5BZ
☎ (01455) 209023
⌨ (01455) 202537
▦ 600

⚘ AP Parr (ext 2446)
✓ J Salter (01455) 209150
⛳ 18 L 6650 yds SSS 72
⛳ U SOC–WD
££ £25 D–£35
⛳ 3 miles NW of Lutterworth, off B577. M1 Junction 20, 5 miles
▤ www.bw-ullesthorpecourt.co.uk

Western Park (1910)
Public
Scudamore Road, Leicester, LE3 1UQ
☎ (0116) 287 5211

Whetstone (1965)
Proprietary
Cambridge Road, Cosby, Leicester, LE9 5SH
☎ (0116) 286 1424
⌨ (0116) 286 1424
✉ daviddalbywgc@aol.com
▦ 550
⚘ D Dalby
✓ D Raitt
⛳ 18 L 6182 yds Par 70 SSS 70
⛳ U SOC
££ £18 (£20)
⛳ S boundary of Leicester
⊕ Driving range
⚘ E Callaway
▤ www.whetstonegolf.co.uk

Willesley Park (1921)
Measham Road, Ashby-de-la-Zouch, LE65 2PF
☎ (01530) 414596
⌨ (01530) 564169
✉ info@willesleypark.com
▦ 676 90(L) 70(J)
⚘ Tina Harlow (01530) 414596
✓ BJ Hill (01530) 414820
⛳ 18 L 6290 yds SSS 71
⛳ WD–H WE/BH–H after 9.30am SOC
££ £35 (£40)
⛳ 2 miles S of Ashby on B5006. M1 Jcts 22/23/24. A42(M) Jct 12
▤ www.willesleypark.com

Lincolnshire

Ashby Decoy (1936)
Ashby Decoy, Burringham Road, Scunthorpe, DN17 2AB
☎ (01724) 866561
⌨ (01724) 271708
✉ info@ashbydecoygolfclub.co.uk
▦ 640
⚘ Mrs J Harrison (01724) 866561
✓ A Miller (01724) 868972
⛳ 18 L 6281 yds SSS 71
⛳ WD–Mon/Wed/Thur/Fri, Tue after 2pm WE–NA
££ £25 D–£30
⛳ 2 miles SW of Scunthorpe
▤ www.ashbydecoy.co.uk

Belton Park (1890)
Belton Lane, Londonthorpe Road, Grantham, NG31 9SH
☎ (01476) 567399
⌨ (01476) 592078

☒ greatgolf@beltonpark.co.uk
▥ 900
🏌 S Rowley (01476) 542900
✓ S Williams (01476) 542903
▷ 27 holes:
Brownlow L 6427 yds SSS 71
Ancaster L 6227 yds SSS 70
Belmont L 6016 yds SSS 69
☷ U H SOC–WD exc Tues
££ £35 (£45)
⊛ 2 miles N of Grantham
⊕ Long & short game practice area
🏠 T Williamson
▣ www.beltonpark.co.uk

De Vere Belton Woods Hotel   (1991)
Belton, Grantham, NG32 2LN
☎ (01476) 593200
▭ (01476) 574547
☒ belton.woods
@devere-hotels.co.uk
▥ 350
🏌 A Cameron (01476) 514364
✓ S Sayers (01476) 514634
▷ Lakes 18 L 6831 yds SSS 73
Woodside 18 L 6623 yds SSS 72
9 hole Par 3 course
☷ U SOC
££ £35 D–£45 (£45 D–£60)
⊛ 2 miles N of Grantham on A607
towards Lincoln; 5 min from A1
⊕ Driving range
🏠 Cayford
▣ www.devere.co.uk

Blankney   (1904)
Proprietary
Blankney, Lincoln, LN4 3AZ
☎ (01526) 320263
▭ (01526) 322521
☒ grahambradley5@btconnect.com
▥ 664 138(L) 50(J)
🏌 G Bradley (01526) 320202
✓ G Bradley (01526) 320202
▷ 18 L 6638 yds SSS 73
☷ U SOC WD WE U
££ £28 D–£36 (£34)
⊛ 10 miles SE of Lincoln on B1188
⊕ Good practice facilities
🏠 Cameron Sinclair
▣ www.blankneygolf.co.uk

Boston   (1902)
Cowbridge, Horncastle Road, Boston,
PE22 7EL
☎ (01205) 350589
▭ (01205) 367526
☒ steveshaw@bostongc.co.uk
▥ 650 115(L) 60(J)
🏌 SP Shaw (01205) 350589
✓ N Hiom (01205) 362306
▷ 18 L 6415 yds Par 72 SSS 71
☷ WD–U WE/BH–U H
££ £24 D–£32 (£30)
⊛ 2 miles N of Boston on B1183
⊕ Driving range; putting green;
practice ground
▣ www.bostongc.co.uk

Boston West   (1995)
Proprietary
Hubbert's Bridge, Boston, PE20 3QX
☎ (01205) 290670

▭ (01205) 290725
☒ info@bostonwestgolfclub.co.uk
▥ 650
🏌 MJ Couture (01205) 290670
▷ 18 L 6354 yds Par 72 SSS 70
6 hole Par 3 course
☷ U SOC WD WE
££ £20 (£25)
⊛ 2 miles W of Boston on B1192
⊕ Floodlit driving range
🏠 Michael Zara
▣ www.bostonwestgolfclub.co.uk

Burghley Park   (1890)
St Martin's, Stamford, PE9 3JX
☎ (01780) 753789
▭ (01780) 753789
☒ secretary@burghleyparkgolfclub
.co.uk
▥ 750 140(L) 100(J)
🏌 S Last (Sec/Mgr)
✓ Glenn Davies (01780) 762100
▷ 18 L 6236 yds SSS 70
☷ WD–I or H WE/BH–M SOC–WD
££ £27 D–£35 (N/A)
⊛ 1 mile S of Stamford, off A1 to
B1081
🏠 Rev JD Day
▣ www.burghleyparkgolfclub.co.uk

Canwick Park   (1893)
Canwick Park, Washingborough Road,
Lincoln, LN4 1EF
☎ (01522) 542912/522166
▭ (01522) 526997
☒ manager@canwickpark.org
▥ 650
🏌 N Porteus (01522) 542912
✓ S Williamson (01522) 537862
▷ 18 L 6148 yds SSS 69
☷ WD–U WE–M before 2.30pm
SOC–WD
££ £18 D–£32 (£25)
⊛ 1 mile SE of Lincoln
⊕ Adjacent driving range
🏠 Hawtree and Sons
▣ www.canwickpark.org

Carholme   (1906)
Carholme Road, Lincoln, LN1 1SE
☎ (01522) 523725
▭ (01522) 533733
☒ info@carholme-golf-club.co.uk
▥ 500
🏌 J Lammin
▷ 18 L 6215 yds Par 71 SSS 70
☷ WD–U WE–U after 2pm BH–SOC
££ £20 (£24)
⊛ Lincoln 1 mile (A57)
🏠 William Park jr
▣ www.carholme-golf-club.co.uk

Cleethorpes   (1894)
Kings Road, Cleethorpes, DN35 0PN
☎ (01472) 814060 (Pro)
☒ secretary@cleethorpesgolfclub
.co.uk
▥ 650
🏌 AJ Thompson (01472) 816110
✓ P Davies (01472) 814060
▷ 18 L 6272 yds SSS 71
☷ WD–U exc Tues am Wed pm
SOC–exc Wed/Sat

££ £25 D–£35 (£30 D–£40)
⊛ 1 mile S of Cleethorpes
🏠 Harry Vardon/Dr Alister
Mackenzie
▣ www.cleethorpesgolfclub.co.uk

Elsham   (1900)
Barton Road, Elsham, Brigg, DN20 0LS
☎ (01652) 680291
▭ (01652) 680308
☒ office@elshamgolfclub.co.uk
▥ 650
🏌 T Hartley (Mgr) (01652) 680291
✓ S Brewer (01652) 680432
▷ 18 L 6426 yds SSS 71
☷ H SOC–WD
££ £30 D–£40
⊛ 3 miles N of Brigg. M180 Junction 5
🏠 Various
▣ www.elshamgolfclub.co.uk

Forest Pines G&CC Hotel   (1996)
Ermine Street, Brigg, DN20 0AQ
☎ (01652) 650756
☒ forestpines@qhotels.co.uk

Gainsborough   (1894)
Thonock, Gainsborough, DN21 1PZ
☎ (01427) 613088
▭ (01427) 810172
☒ vicki@gainsboroughgc.co.uk
▥ 700
🏌 D Bowers
✓ S Cooper
▷ 18 L 6266 yds Par 70 SSS 70
18 L 6724 yds Par 72 SSS 72
☷ U
££ £30 D–£40
⊛ N of Gainsborough
⊕ Floodlit driving range
🏠 Neil Coles
▣ www.gainsboroughgc.co.uk

Gedney Hill   (1991)
Public
West Drove, Gedney End Hill, PE12 0NT
☎ (01406) 330922
▭ (01945) 581903
▥ 115
🏌 R Newns (01945) 581903
▷ 18 L 5450 yds SSS 66
☷ U SOC–WD/WE
££ £9.50 (£13.50) D–£15 Seniors £7
(£13.50)
⊛ 4 miles from A47 on B1166
🏠 C Britton

Grange Park   (1992)
Pay and play
Butterwick Road, Messingham, Scunthorpe,
DN17 3PP
☎ (01724) 762945
☒ info@grangepark.com
🏌 I Cannon (Mgr)
✓ J Drury
▷ 18 L 6180 yds Par 70
9 hole Par 3 course
☷ U SOC–WD/WE
££ £16 (£18)
⊛ 5 m from Scunthorpe. M180 Jct 3
⊕ Floodlit driving range

⋔ RW Price
▤ www.grangepark.com

Grimsby (1922)
Littlecoates Road, Grimsby, DN34 4LU
☎ (01472) 342823 (Clubhouse) (01472)267727
✉ secretary@grimsbygc.fsnet.co.uk
🏛 650 150(L) 70(J)
♠ D McCully (01472) 342630
✓ R Smith (01472) 356981
▷ 18 L 6057 yds Par 70 SSS 69
♟ WD–U Sat pm/Sun am–XL SOC–Mon & Fri H
££ £25 (£30)
⊕ I mile W of Grimsby, off A46. I mile from M180
⋔ HS Colt
▤ www.grimsbygolfclub.com

Holme Hall (1908)
Holme Lane, Bottesford, Scunthorpe, DN16 3RF
☎ (01724) 862078
📠 (01724) 862081
✉ secretary@holmehallgolf.co.uk
🏛 470 90(L) 30(J)
♠ Roger B. Bickley
✓ R McKiernan (01724) 851816
▷ 18 L 6404 yds SSS 71
♟ WD–U WE–M H SOC–WD
££ £30 £35–27 holes D–£40
⊕ 4 m SE of Scunthorpe. M180 Jct 4

Horncastle (1990)
West Ashby, Horncastle, LN9 5PP
☎ (01507) 526800
✉ info@twinlakescentre.com

Humberston Park
Humberston Avenue, Humberston, DN36 4SJ
☎ (01472) 210404
🏛 230
♠ RTrish Neal (01472) 825822
▷ 9 L 3670 yds Par 60 SSS 57
♟ U exc Wed pm/Thurs am/Sun am SOC
££ 9: £7.50 (£8.50); 18: £11 (£13) Daily £16
⊕ Humberston, 3 miles S of Grimsby (A1031)
⋔ T Barraclough

Immingham (1975)
St Andrews Lane, Off Church Lane, Immingham, DN40 2EU
☎ (01469) 575298
📠 (01469) 577636
🏛 650
♠ C Todd (Mgr)
✓ N Harding (01469) 575493
▷ 18 L 6215 yds SSS 70
♟ WD–U WE–restricted (ring for details) SOC–WD
££ £24
⊕ N of St Andrew's Church, Immingham
⋔ Hawtree/Pennink
▤ www.immgc.com

Kenwick Park (1992)
Kenwick, Louth, LN11 8NY
☎ (01507) 605134
📠 (01507) 606556
✉ secretary@kenwickparkgolf.co.uk
🏛 450
♠ E Sharp (Dir of Golf)
✓ Paul Spencer/ Michael Langford (01507) 607161
▷ 18 L 6782 yds Par 72 SSS 73
White Tees L 6715 yds Par 71 SSS 73
Yellow Tees L 6257 yds Par 70 SSS 71
♟ U H SOC
££ £35 (£45)
⊕ 2 miles SE of Louth
⊕ Teaching Academy. Driving range
⋔ Patrick Tallack
▤ www.kenwickparkgolf.co.uk

Kirton Holme (1992)
Proprietary
Holme Road, Kirton Holme, Boston, PE20 1SY
☎ (01205) 290669
🏛 320
♠ Mrs T Welberry
✓ Alison Johns
▷ 9 L 2884 yds Par 70 SSS 68
♟ U SOC
££ £7.50 D–£11.50 (£8.50 D–£12.50
⊕ 3 miles W of Boston, off A52
⋔ DW Welberry
▤ www.kirtonholmegolfcourse.co.uk

Lincoln (1891)
Torksey, Lincoln, LN1 2EG
☎ (01427) 718721
📠 (01427) 718721
✉ info@lincolngc.co.uk
🏛 625
♠ DB Linton
✓ A Carter (01427) 718273
▷ 18 L 6438 yds SSS 71
♟ WD–H SOC
££ £40 D–£50 (£50 D–£60)
⊕ 12 miles NW of Lincoln, off A156
⊕ 3-hole pitch & putt practice course; large practice area; driving net
⋔ JH Taylor
▤ www.lincolngc.co.uk

Louth (1965)
Crowtree Lane, Louth, LN11 9LJ
☎ (01507) 603681
📠 (01507) 608501
✉ enquiries@louthgolfclub.com
🏛 700
♠ Simon Moody (Gen Mgr) T Moody (Golf Dev Mgr)
✓ AJ Blundell (01507) 604648
▷ 18 L 6436 yds SSS 71
♟ WD U SOC WE – not Sat/Sun after 11
££ £24 D–£30 (£30 D–£35)
⊕ W side of Louth
▤ www.louthgolfclub.com

Manor (Laceby) (1992)
Laceby Manor, Laceby, Grimsby, DN37 7LD
☎ (01472) 873468

✉ mackayj@grimsby.ac.co.uk
🏛 500
♠ Mrs J Mackay
✓ Stuart Warren
▷ 18 L 6354 yds SSS 70
♟ U SOC
££ D–£22 (£25)
⊕ 5 miles W of Grimsby at Barton Street (A18)
⋔ Nicholson/Rushton

Market Rasen & District (1912)
Legsby Road, Market Rasen, LN8 3DZ
☎ (01673) 842319
📠 (01673) 849245
✉ marketrasengolf@onetel.net
🏛 600
♠ JP Smith
✓ AM Chester (01673) 842416
▷ 18 L 6239 yds SSS 70
♟ WD–I WE/BH–M SOC
££ £28 D–£39
⊕ I mile E of Market Rasen
▤ www.marketrasengolfclub.co.uk

Market Rasen Racecourse (1990)
Pay and play
Legsby Road, Market Rasen, LN8 3EA
☎ (01673) 843434
📠 (01673) 844532
✉ marketrasen @jockeyclubracecourses.com
▷ 9 L 2350 yds Par
♟ U
££ On application
⊕ Market Rasen Racecourse
⊕ Putting Green
▤ www.marketrasenraces.co.uk

Martin Moor
Martin Road, Blankney, LN4 3BE
☎ (01526) 378243

Millfield (1984)
Laughterton, Lincoln, LN1 2LB
☎ (01427) 718473
📠 (01427) 718473
🏛 500
♠ Paul Grey-Guthrie
✓ Brian Cummings
▷ 18 L 6098 yds SSS 69
18 L 4585 yds
9 hole Par 3 course
♟ U
££ £10
⊕ 9 miles W of Lincoln, nr Torksey (B1133)
⊕ Driving range
⋔ C Watson

North Shore (1910)
Proprietary
North Shore Road, Skegness, PE25 1DN
☎ (01754) 763298
📠 (01754) 761902
✉ golf@northshorehotel.com
🏛 375
♠ B Howard (01754) 899030
✓ J Cornelius (01754) 764822
▷ 18 L 6214 yds Par 71 SSS 70

⑩ H–soft spikes only Apr–Oct
SOC–WD WE
££ £31 D–£41 (£39 D–£51)
⊶ I mile N of Skegness
⊕ 36 en-suite bedroom hotel on site
⌂ James Braid
▤ www.northshorehotel.com

Pottergate (1992)

Moor Lane, Branston, Lincoln
☎ (01522) 794867
▥ 450
♨ K Lovering
✓ L Tasker
▷ 9 L 5164 yds Par 68 SSS 65
⑩ U
££ £8.50 (£10)
⊶ 3 miles SE of Lincoln (B1188)
⊕ Indoor golf simulator
⌂ WT Bailey

RAF Coningsby (1972)

RAF Coningsby, Lincoln, LN4 4SY
☎ (01526) 342581 Ext 6828
▥ 220
♨ N Parsons (01526) 347946
▷ 9 L 5354 yds Par 68 SSS 66
⑩ WD–U before 5pm SOC–WD
££ £8
⊶ Between Woodhall Spa and
Coningsby on B1192

Sandilands (1901)

Proprietary
Sandilands, Sutton-on-Sea, LN12 2RJ
☎ (01507) 441432
▯ (01507) 441617
✉ grangeandlinkshotel@btconnect.com
▥ 300
♨ Philip Ross
✓ Simon Sherratt
▷ 18 L 6068 yds Par 70 SSS 69
⑩ U SOC WD WE
££ £22 D–£30 (£25 D–£38)
⊶ I mile S of Sutton-on-Sea, off A52
⊕ Owned and managed by The
Grange Links Hotel Ltd. Golf break
details – 01507 441334
▤ www.sandilandsgolfclub.co.uk

Seacroft (1895)

Drummond Road, Seacroft, Skegness,
PE25 3AU
☎ (01754) 763020
▯ (01754) 763020
✉ enquiries@seacroft-golfclub.co.uk
▥ 328 107(L) 87(J)
♨ R England (Sec/Mgr)
✓ R Lawie (01754) 769624
▷ 18 L 6492 yds SSS 71
⑩ U H SOC
££ £45 – D£55 (Sat £55, Sun £50)
⊶ S boundary of Skegness, nr Nature
Reserve
⌂ Willie Fernie/Tom Dunn
▤ www.seacroft-golfclub.co.uk

Sleaford (1905)

Greylees, Sleaford, Lincs, NG34 8PL
☎ (01529) 488273
▯ (01529) 488644
✉ sleafordgolfclub@btinternet.com
▥ 630
♨ Mr D R Carlisle

✓ N Pearce (01529) 488644
▷ 18 L 6503 yds SSS 71
⑩ U H exc Sun–NA (Winter)
SOC–WD
££ £28 D–£35 (£36)
⊶ I mile W of Sleaford on A153
⌂ Tom Williamson
▤ www.sleafordgolfclub.co.uk

South Kyme (1990)

Skinners Lane, South Kyme, Lincoln,
LN4 4AT
☎ (01526) 861113
▯ (01526) 861080
✉ southkymegc@hotmail.com
♨ P Chamberlain (Golf Dir)
✓ P Chamberlain
▷ 18 L 6482 yds Par 72 SSS 71
⑩ U SOC
££ £20 (£24)
⊶ 2 miles from A17 on B1395
⊕ 6 hole practice course
▤ www.skgc.co.uk

Spalding (1907)

Surfleet, Spalding, PE11 4EA
☎ (01775) 680386
▯ (01775) 680988
✉ secretary@spaldinggolfclub.co.uk
▥ 825
♨ BW Walker (01775) 680386
✓ J Spencer (01775) 680474
▷ 18 L 6483 yds SSS 71
⑩ U H SOC–Tues after 2pm & Thurs
all day
££ £30 D–£35 (£40)
⊶ 4 miles N of Spalding, off A16
⊕ Driving range; Large Practice area.
⌂ Spencer/Ward/Price
▤ www.spaldinggolfclub.co.uk

Stoke Rochford (1924)

Great North Rd, Grantham, NG33 5EW
☎ (01476) 530275
▯ (01476) 530237
✉ srgc@ntlworl.com
▥ 580
♨ J Martindale (01572) 756305 e-mail
jmartindale@66max.co.uk
✓ A Dow (01476) 530218
▷ 18 L 6252 yds SSS 70
⑩ WD–U WE/BH–U after 10.30am
££ On application
⊶ 6 miles S of Grantham (A1)
⌂ Maj Hotchkin (1935)
▤ www.stokerochfordgolfclub.co.uk

Sudbrook Moor (1991)

Charity Street, Carlton Scroop, Grantham,
NG32 3AT
☎ (01400) 250796 all enquiries
♨ Judith Hutton
✓ Tim Hutton (01400) 250796
▷ 9 L 4827 yds Par 66 SSS 64
⑩ U–phone first
££ £9 (£12)
⊶ Carlton Scroop, 6 miles NE of
Grantham (A607)
⊕ 12 bay Driving range; 2 coaching
bays; putting and practice facilities;
Golf Shop
⌂ Tim Hutton
▤ www.sudbrookmoor.co.uk

Sutton Bridge (1914)

New Road, Sutton Bridge, Spalding,
PE12 9RQ
☎ (01406) 350323 (Clubhouse)
✉ suttonbridgegc@yahoo.co.uk
▥ 280
♨ PL Land (01945) 582447
✓ Antony Lowther (01406) 351422
▷ 9 L 5820 yds SSS 68
⑩ WD–H WE–M SOC
££ £25 (£30)
⊶ 8 miles N of Wisbech (A17)
⊕ Driving range
▤ www.club-noticeboard.co.uk
/suttonbridge

Tetney (1993)

Station Road, Tetney, Grimsby, DN36 5HY
☎ (01472) 211644
▯ (01472) 211644
▥ 350
♨ J Abrams
✓ J Abrams
▷ 18 L 6100 yds Par 71 SSS 69
⑩ U SOC
££ £12
⊶ 5 miles S of Grimsby, off A16
⊕ Driving range

Toft Hotel (1988)

Proprietary
Toft, Bourne, PE10 0JT
☎ (01778) 590616

Waltham Windmill (1997)

Proprietary
Cheapside, Waltham, Grimsby, DN37 0HT
☎ (01472) 824109
▯ (01472) 828391
▥ 600
♨ S Bennett (01472) 821883
✓ N Burkitt (01472) 823963
▷ 18 L 6400 yds Par 71 SSS 71
⑩ WD–U SOC
££ £26 (£32)
⊶ 2 miles S of Grimsby, off A16
⌂ Fox/Payne
▤ www.walthamgolf.co.uk

Welton Manor (1995)

Proprietary
Hackthorn Road, Welton, LN2 3PD
☎ (01673) 862827
▯ (01673) 860917
✉ golf@weltonmanorgolfcentre
.co.uk
▥ 475
♨ TM Coates MBE (01522) 851696
✓ G Leslie (01673) 862827
▷ 18 L 5703 yds Par 70 SSS 67
⑩ U SOC
££ £15 (£20)
⊶ Off A46 Lincoln to Grimsby road
⊕ Driving range
▤ www.weltonmanorgolfcentre
.co.uk

Woodhall Spa (1891)

Proprietary
Woodhall Spa, LN10 6PU
☎ (01526) 351835
(01526) 352511 (Bookings)

☖ (01526) 352778
✉ secretary@woodhallspagolfclub
.co.uk
▦ 600
♬ Mike Underwood
✓ Alison Johns
⌖ Hotchkin 18 L 7080 yds SSS 75
Bracken 18 L 6735 yds SSS 74
♙ Booking essential SOC
£€ Hotchkin–£80 D–£120 (non–EGU
rate – 2008) Bracken–£50 D–£75
(non–EGU rate – 2008)
⌘ 19 miles SE of Lincoln (B1191)
⊕ Driving range. Teaching Academy
⌂ Hotchkin/Steel
▤ www.woodhallspagolfclub.co.uk

Woodthorpe Hall (1986)
Woodthorpe, Alford, LN13 0DD
☎ (01507) 450000
☖ (01507) 450000
✉ secretary@woodthorpehallgolfclub
.fsnet.co.uk
▦ 200
♬ Joan Smith (01507) 450000
⌖ 18 L 5140 yds Par 67 SSS 65
♙ U SOC
£€ £12 (£15 inc. BH)
⌘ 3 miles N of Alford, off B1373. 8
miles SE of Louth
▤ www.woodthorpehall.co.uk

London Clubs

Aquarius Kent
Bent Valley Middlesex
Bush Hill Park Middlesex
Central London Golf Centre Surrey
Chingford Essex
Dulwich & Sydenham Hill Surrey
Eltham Warren Kent
Finchley Middlesex
Hampstead Middlesex
Hendon Middlesex
Highgate Middlesex
Leaside Middlesex
London Scottish Surrey
Mill Hill Middlesex
Muswell Hill Middlesex
North Middlesex Middlesex
Richmond Park Surrey
Roehampton Club Surrey
Royal Blackheath Kent
Royal Epping Forest Essex
Royal Mid-Surrey Surrey
Royal Wimbledon Surrey
Shooter's Hill Kent
South Herts Hertfordshire
Thameside Golf Centre Kent
Trent Park Middlesex
Wanstead Essex
West Essex Essex
Wimbledon Common Surrey
Wimbledon Park Surrey

Manchester

Blackley (1907)
Victoria Avenue East, Manchester,
M9 7HW
☎ (0161) 643 2980
☖ (0161) 653 8300
✉ office@blackleygolfclub.com
▦ 800
♬ B Beddoes (0161) 654 7770
✓ C Gould (0161) 643 3912
⌖ 18 L 6235 yds SSS 70
♙ WD–U WE–M SOC–WD exc
Thurs
£€ £35
⌘ North Manchester – M60 J20
⊕ Practice area; Two putting greens
⌂ Gaunt and Marnoch
▤ www.blackleygolfclub.com

Boysnope Park (1998)
Proprietary
Liverpool Road, Barton Moss, Eccles,
M30 7RF
☎ (0161) 707 6125

Chorlton-cum-Hardy (1902)
Barlow Hall, Barlow Hall Road, Manchester,
M21 7JJ
☎ (0161) 881 3139
☖ (0161) 881 4532
✉ chorltongolf@hotmail.com
▦ 600
♬ IR Booth (0161) 881 5830
✓ DR Valentine (0161) 881 9911
⌖ 18 L 5994 yds SSS 69
♙ U H SOC–Thurs & Fri
£€ £30 (£35)
⌘ 4 miles S of Manchester
(A5103/A5145)
▤ www.chorltoncumhardygolfclub
.co.uk

Davyhulme Park (1911)
Gleneagles Road, Davyhulme, Manchester,
M41 8SA
☎ (0161) 748 2260
☖ (0161) 747 4067
✉ davyhulmeparkgolfclub@email.com
▦ 700
♬ GR Swarbrick
✓ D Butler (0161) 748 3931
⌖ 18 L 6237 yds SSS 70
♙ WD–H exc Wed–NA Sat––M
SOC–Mon/Tue/Thur/Fri
£€ £24. 27 holes–£30
⌘ 7 miles SW of Manchester; M60 Jct
9/10 – 2 miles
▤ www.davyhulmeparkgc.info

Denton (1909)
Manchester Road, Denton, Manchester,
M34 2GG
☎ (0161) 336 3218
☖ (0161) 336 4751
✉ info@dentongolfclub.com
▦ 674
♬ ID McIlvanney
✓ M Hollingworth (0161) 336 2070
⌖ 18 L 6461 yds SSS 71
♙ WD–U WE/BH–NA before
3.30pm SOC
£€ £28 (£35)

⌘ M60 Junction 24, A57 to
Manchester
⊕ Indoor Teaching Academy
▤ www.dentongolfclub.co.uk

Didsbury (1891)
Ford Lane, Northenden, Manchester,
M22 4NQ
☎ (0161) 998 9278
☖ (0161) 902 3060
✉ golf@didsburygolfclub.com
▦ 760
♬ John K Mort (Mgr)
✓ P Barber (0161) 998 2811
⌖ 18 L 6210 yds Par 70 SSS 70
♙ WD–H exc 9–10am &
12–1.30pm–NA WE–U H SOC
Thur/Fri & Sun 10–12pm & after
1.30pm
£€ £29 (£33) – includes insurance
⌘ 6 miles S of Manchester. M60 Jct 5
⌂ D Thomas & P Alliss
▤ www.didsburygolfclub.com

Ellesmere (1913)
Old Clough Lane, Worsley, Manchester,
M28 7HZ
☎ (0161) 790 2122
☖ (0161) 790 2122 option 4
✉ honsec@ellesmeregolfclub.co.uk
▦ 380 80(L) 75(J)
♬ MJ Farrington (0161) 799 0554
✓ S Wakefield (0161) 790 8591
⌖ 18 L 6238 yds SSS 70
♙ U exc comp days (check with Pro)
SOC–WD
£€ £30 D–£40 (£35)
⌘ 6 miles W of Manchester, nr
junction of M60/A580
▤ www.ellesmeregolfclub.co.uk

Fairfield Golf & Sailing Club
(1892)
Booth Road, Audenshaw, Manchester,
M34 5GA
☎ (0161) 301 4528
☖ (0161) 301 4524
✉ fairfieldgolf@btconnect.com
▦ 550
♬ M Jones (Sec/Mgr)
✓ SA Pownell (0161) 370 2292
⌖ 18 L 5664 yds SSS 68
♙ WD–U WE–NA before noon
SOC–WD
£€ £25 (£25)
⌘ 5 miles E of Manchester on A635

Flixton (1893)
Church Road, Flixton, Urmston, Manchester
M41 6EP
☎ (0161) 748 2116
☖ (0161) 748 2116
✉ flixtongolfclub@mail.com
▦ 367
♬ B Clifford
✓ A Bridgewood (0161) 746 7160
⌖ 9 L 6492 yds SSS 71
♙ WD–U exc Wed SOC
£€ £15 (£25)
⌘ 6 miles SW of Manchester on
B5213. M60 Junction 10
▤ www.flixtongolfclub.co.uk

For list of abbreviations and key to symbols see page 647

Great Lever & Farnworth
(1901)
Plodder Lane, Farnworth, Bolton, BL4 0LQ
☎ **(01204) 656493**
🖷 (01204) 656137
✉ greatlever@btconnect.com
📖 421
♋ MJ Ivill (01204) 656137
➤ 18 L 5791 yds SSS 69
👥 H SOC–WD
££ £25 (£30)
♨ 2 miles S of Bolton. M61 Junction 4

Heaton Park Golf Centre
(1912)
Pay and play
Heaton Park, Middleton Road, Prestwich, M25 2SW
☎ **(0161) 654 9899**
🖷 (0161) 653 2003
♋ Brian Dique (Gen Mgr)
✓ Gary Dermott
➤ 18 L 5755 yds Par 70 SSS 68
18 hole Par 3 course
👥 U SOC
££ £10.50 (£14) Concessions available
♨ North Manchester, via M60 Junction 19 to Middleton Road
⊕ Pitch & putt course; teaching academy
🏠 JH Taylor

Manchester   (1882)
Hopwood Cottage, Rochdale Road, Middleton, Manchester M24 6QP
☎ **(0161) 643 3202**
🖷 (0161) 643 9174
✉ secretary@mangc.co.uk
📖 650
♋ Stephen Armstead
✓ B Connor (0161) 643 2638
➤ 18 L 6450 yds SSS 72
👥 WD–H WE–NA SOC
££ £37.50 D–£45
♨ 7 m N of Manchester. M62 Jct 20
⊕ Driving range-members and green fees only
🏠 HS Colt
🖳 www.mangc.co.uk

New North Manchester
(1923)
Rhodes House, Manchester Old Road, Middleton, M24 4PE
☎ **(0161) 643 9033**
🖷 (0161) 643 7775
✉ tee@nmgc.co.uk
📖 540
♋ G Heaslip
✓ J Peel (0161) 643 7094
➤ 18 L 6598 yds SSS 71
👥 H WD
££ £32 (£37)
♨ 5 miles N of Manchester. M60 Junction 19
⊕ Putting Green; Driving Nets; Bunker & Chipping area; Practice Ground; Bar & Catering 7 days a week.
🏠 A Compston
🖳 www.northmanchestergolfclub .co.uk

Northenden   (1912)
Palatine Road, Manchester, M22 4FR
☎ **(0161) 998 4738**
🖷 (0161) 945 5592
✉ manager@northendengolfclub.com
📖 700
♋ Alison Davidson (Mgr) (0161) 998 4738
✓ J Curtis (0161) 945 3386
➤ 18 L 6432 yds SSS 72
👥 U SOC H
££ £32 (£36)
♨ 5 miles S of Manchester. M56 Jct 2
🖳 www.northendengolfclub.com

Old Manchester   (1818)
Club
☎ **(0161) 766 4157**
♋ PT Goodall
➤ Club without a course

Pike Fold   (1909)
Hills Lane, Pole Lane, Unsworth, Bury BL9 8QP
☎ **(0161) 766 3561**
✉ john@pikefold.co.uk

Prestwich   (1908)
Hilton Lane, Prestwich, M25 9XB
☎ **(0161) 772 0700**
🖷 (0161) 772 0700
✉ prestwichgolf@btconnect.com
📖 420
♋ R Mason
✓ M Pearson (0161) 773 1404
➤ 18 L 5103 yds SSS 65
👥 WD WE–NA before 2pm SOC
££ £15 (£20)
♨ 2¹/2 miles N of Manchester, off A56. M60 Junction 17
🖳 www.prestwichgolf.co.uk

Stand   (1904)
The Dales, Ashbourne Grove, Whitefield, Manchester M45 7NL
☎ **(0161) 766 2388**
🖷 (0161) 796 3234
✉ secretary@standgolfclub.co.uk
📖 600
♋ TE Thacker (0161) 766 3197
✓ M Dance (0161) 766 2214
➤ 18 L 6411 yds SSS 71
👥 U SOC–WD
££ £30 (£35)
♨ 5 miles N of Manchester. M60 Junction 17
🏠 Alex Herd
🖳 www.standgolfclub.co.uk

Swinton Park   (1926)
East Lancashire Road, Swinton, Manchester, M27 5LX
☎ **(0161) 794 0861**
🖷 (0161) 281 0698
✉ info@spgolf.co.uk
📖 600
♋ Barbara Wood (0161) 794 0861
✓ J Wilson (0161) 793 8077
➤ 18 L 6726 yds SSS 70
👥 WD–U WE–M SOC–not Thur/Sat/Bank Hols
££ On application + 2 for 1 vouchers accepted; on–line tee times

♨ On A580, 5 miles NW of Manchester
⊕ Corporate membership; 2 putting greens; practice area; membership now open (no entrance fee)
🏠 James Braid
🖳 www.spgolf.co.uk

Whitefield   (1932)
Higher Lane, Whitefield, Manchester, M45 7EZ
☎ **(0161) 351 2700**
🖷 (0161) 351 2712
✉ enquiries@whitefieldgolfclub.com
📖 538
♋ Mrs M Rothwell
✓ R Penney (0161) 351 2709
➤ 18 L 6047 yds SSS 69
18 L 5752 yds SSS 68
👥 U SOC–WD
££ £25 (£35)
♨ 4 m N of Manchester. M60 Jct 17
🖳 www.whitefieldgolfclub.co.uk

Withington   (1892)
243 Palatine Road, West Didsbury, Manchester, M20 2UE
☎ **(0161) 445 9544**
🖷 (0161) 445 5210
✉ secretary@withingtongolfclub.co.uk
📖 600
♋ PJ Keane
✓ S Marr (0161) 445 4861
➤ 18 L 6410 yds SSS 70
👥 WD–H exc Thurs SOC
££ On application
♨ 6 miles S of Manchester on B5166
🖳 www.withingtongolfclub.co.uk

Worsley   (1894)
Stableford Avenue, Monton Green, Eccles, Manchester M30 8AP
☎ **(0161) 789 4202**
🖷 (0161) 789 3200
✉ office@worsleygolfclub.co.uk
📖 625
♋ J Clarke (Hon)
✓ Andrew Cory
➤ 18 L 6217 yds SSS 70
👥 H SOC
££ £30 (£35)
♨ 5 miles W of Manchester M60 Jct 13
🖳 www.worsleygolfclub.co.uk

Merseyside

Allerton Municipal   (1934)
Public
Allerton Road, Liverpool, L18 3JT
☎ **(0151) 428 1046**
✓ B Large
➤ 18 L 5494 yds SSS 65
9 hole course
👥 U SOC
££ On application
♨ 5 miles S of Liverpool

Arrowe Park   (1931)
Public
Arrowe Park, Woodchurch, Birkenhead, CH49 5LW
☎ **(0151) 677 1527**

Bidston (1913)
Bidston Link Road, Wallasey, Wirral,
CH44 2HR
☎ (0151) 638 3412
▥ 550
⚲ W Effingham
✓ Alan Norwood (0151) 638 3412
▷ 18 L 6153 yds SSS 70
⚇ WD–U WE–U after 3pm SOC
££ On request
⛳ Off Bidston Link Road. M53 Jct 1
▤ www.bidstongolf.co.uk

Bootle (1934)
Pay and play
Dunnings Bridge Road, Litherland, L30 2PP
☎ (0151) 928 1371
▱ (0151) 949 1815
✉ bootlegolfcourse@btconnect.com
▥ 400
⚲ G Howarth
✓ A Bradshaw (0151) 928 1371
▷ 18 L 6362 yds SSS 70
⚇ U–book by phone SOC
££ £9.80 (£12.00)
⛳ 5 miles N of Liverpool (A565)
⌂ Fred Stevens

Bowring (1913)
Public
Bowring Park, Roby Road, Huyton,
L36 4HD
☎ (0151) 489 1901
✉ dgwalker36@tiscali.co.uk

Brackenwood (1933)
Public
Bracken Lane, Bebington, Wirral, L63 2LY
☎ (0151) 608 3093
✉ secretary@brackenwoodgolf.co.uk
▥ 220
⚲ GW Brogan (0151) 339 9817
✓ K Lamb (0151) 608 3093
▷ 18 L 6232 yds SSS 70
⚇ U SOC
££ £11.70 Jnr/Snr £6.50
⛳ Nr M53 Junction 4
▤ www.brackenwoodgolf.co.uk

Bromborough (1903)
Raby Hall Road, Bromborough, CH63 0NW
☎ (0151) 334 2155
▱ (0151) 334 7300
✉ enquiries@bromboroughgolfclub
.org.uk
▥ 800
⚲ Peter McMullen (0151) 334 2155
✓ G Berry (0151) 334 4499
▷ 18 L 6885 yds SSS 72
⚇ U–contact Pro in advance
££ £35
⛳ Mid Wirral, M53 Junction 4
⌂ JE Hassall (redesign 1972, Hawtree
& Son)
▤ www.bromboroughgolfclub.org.uk

Caldy (1907)
Links Hey Road, Caldy, Wirral, CH48 1NB
☎ (0151) 625 5660
▱ (0151) 625 7394
✉ secretarycaldygc@btconnect.com
▥ 900

⚲ Gail M Copple
✓ AG Gibbons (0151) 625 1818
▷ 18 L 6707 yds Par 72 SSS 72
⚇ WD–U exc before 9.30am and
from 1–2pm (booking necessary)
SOC
££ On application
⛳ 1½ miles S of West Kirby
⊕ Practice ground with ball collection
⌂ James Braid/Cameron Sinclair
▤ www.caldygolfclub.co.uk

Childwall (1912)
Naylors Road, Gateacre, Liverpool, L27 2YB
☎ (0151) 487 0654
▱ (0151) 487 0654
✉ office@childwallgolfclub.co.uk
▥ 650
⚲ Peter Bowen
✓ N Parr (0151) 487 9871
▷ 18 L 6470 yds SSS 71
⚇ WD–Tues–restricted.
WE/BH–restricted SOC
££ £40 (£45)
⛳ 7 miles E of Liverpool. M62
Junction 6, 2 miles
⌂ James Braid
▤ www.childwallgolfclub.co.uk

Eastham Lodge (1973)
117 Ferry Road, Eastham, Wirral,
CH62 0AP
☎ (0151) 327 1483 (Clubhouse)
▱ (0151) 327 7574
✉ easthamlodge.g.c@btinternet.com
▥ 800
⚲ Mrs JL Lyon (0151) 327 3003
✓ N Sargent (0151) 327 3008
▷ 18 L 5706 yds SSS 68
⚇ WD–U WE/BH–M SOC
££ £24.50
⛳ 6 miles S of Birkenhead, off A41.
M53 Junction 5. Signs to Eastham
Country Park
⌂ Hawtree/Hemstock
▤ www.easthamlodgegolfclub.co.uk

Formby (1884)
Golf Road, Formby, Liverpool, L37 1LQ
☎ (01704) 872164
▱ (01704) 833028
✉ info@formbygolfclub.co.uk
▥ 690
⚲ CCH Barker (01704) 872164
✓ A Witherup (01704) 835396
▷ 18 L 7024 yds SSS 74 Par 72
⚇ WD–H SOC WE–NA before
3.30pm WD–NA before 9.30am
££ £100 (£120)
⛳ By Freshfield Station, Formby. 8
miles S of Southport
⊕ Driving range and short practice
area
⌂ Willie Park
▤ www.formbygolfclub.co.uk

Formby Hall
Southport Old Road, Formby, L37 0AB
☎ (01704) 875699
▱ (01704) 832134
✉ proshop@formby-hall.co.uk
⚲ Joe Fleetwood (Dir of Golf)
✓ D Lloyd

▷ 18 L 6875 yds Par 73
⚇ WD–U SOC
££ On application
⛳ Off Formby by-pass
⊕ Floodlit driving range
▤ www.formbyhallgolfclub.co.uk

Formby Ladies' (1896)
Golf Road, Formby, Liverpool, L37 1YH
☎ (01704) 873493
▱ (01704) 834654
✉ secretary@formbyladiesgolfclub
co.uk
▥ 419
⚲ Mrs CA Bromley (01704) 873493
✓ A Witherup (01704) 873090
▷ 18 L 5374 yds SSS 72
⚇ U–phone first SOC
££ £48 (£55)
⛳ Formby, off A565
⊕ Practice ground
▤ www.formbyladiesgolfclub.co.uk

Grange Park (1891)
Prescot Road, St Helens, WA10 3AD
☎ (01744) 22980 (Members)
▱ (01744) 26318
✉ secretary@grangeparkgolfclub
.co.uk
▥ 730
⚲ G Brown (01744) 26318
✓ P Roberts (01744) 28785
▷ 18 L 6446 yds SSS 71
⚇ I SOC–WD exc Tues
££ £30 (£35)
⛳ 1½ miles W of St Helens on A58
⊕ Practice ground
▤ www.grangeparkgolfclub.co.uk

Haydock Park (1877)
Golborne Park, Newton Lane, Newton-le-
Willows, WA12 0HX
☎ (01925) 228525
▱ (01925) 224984
✉ secretary@haydockparkgc.co.uk
▥ 610 120(L)
⚲ David Hughes
✓ PE Kenwright (01925) 226944
▷ 18 L 6058 yds SSS 69
⚇ H SOC–WD exc Tues
££ £30
⛳ 1 mile E of M6 Junction 23
⊕ Large practice area
⌂ James Braid
▤ www.haydockparkgc.co.uk

Hesketh (1885)
Cockle Dick's Lane, Cambridge Road,
Southport, PR9 9QQ
☎ (01704) 536897
▱ (01704) 539250
✉ secretary@heskethgolfclub.co.uk
▥ 650
⚲ MG Senior (01704) 536897 ext 1
✓ S Astin (01704) 530050
▷ 18 L 6693 yds SSS 73
⚇ WD–U WE/BH–restricted SOC
££ £60 D–£75 (£75)
⛳ 1 mile N of Southport (A565)
⊕ Indoor golf academy; online Tee
booking
⌂ JOF Morris/Hawtree
▤ www.heskethgolfclub.co.uk

For list of abbreviations and key to symbols see page 647

Heswall   (1902)
Cottage Lane, Gayton, Heswall, CH60 8PB
- ☎ (0151) 342 1237
- 🖴 (0151) 342 6140
- ✉ dawn@heswallgolfclub.com
- 📖 902
- 🏌 A Brooker
- 🏌 AE Thompson (0151) 342 7431
- ⊳ 18 L 6882 yds SSS 74
- 🏌 U H BH–NA SOC–Wed & Fri
- ££ £40 (£40)
- 🚗 8 miles NW of Chester off A540.
  M53 Junction 4
- 🖥 www.heswallgolfclub.com

Hillside   (1911)
Hastings Road, Hillside, Southport, PR8 2LU
- ☎ (01704) 567169
- 🖴 (01704) 563192
- ✉ secretary@hillside-golfclub.co.uk
- 📖 800
- 🏌 SH Newland (01704) 567169
- 🏌 B Seddon (01704) 567169
- ⊳ 18 L 7029 yds SSS 75
- 🏌 By arrangement with Sec
- ££ £75 D–£95
- 🚗 Southport
- ⊕ Buggies for hire
- 🏔 Hawtree
- 🖥 www.hillside-golfclub.co.uk

Houghwood   (1996)
Proprietary
Billinge Hill, Crank Road, Crank, St Helens,
WA11 8RL
- ☎ (01744) 894754
- 🖴 (01744) 894754
- ✉ houghwoodgolf@btinternet.com
- 📖 600
- 🏌 P Turner (Man Dir)
- 🏌 P Dickenson (01744) 894444
- ⊳ 18 L 6283 yds SSS 70
- 🏌 WD–U SOC–WD
- ££ £30 (£40)
- 🚗 3 miles N of St Helens, off A580
  (B5201). M6 Junctions 23 or 26
- 🏔 N Pearson
- 🖥 www.houghwoodgolfclub.co.uk

Hoylake Municipal   (1933)
Public
Carr Lane, Hoylake, Wirral, CH47 4BG
- ☎ (0151) 632 2956/4883
  (Bookings)
- 🏌 P Davies (0151) 632 0523
- 🏌 S Hooton
- ⊳ 18 L 6330 yds SSS 70
- 🏌 WD–U WE–phone booking one
  week in advance SOC
- ££ £11
- 🚗 4 miles W of Birkenhead
- 🏔 James Braid
- 🖥 www.hoylakegolfclub.com

Huyton & Prescot   (1905)
Hurst Park, Huyton Lane, Huyton, L36 1UA
- ☎ (0151) 489 3948
- 🖴 (0151) 489 0797
- 📖 700
- 🏌 L Griffin(0151) 489 3948
- 🏌 J Fisher (0151) 489 2022
- ⊳ 18 L 5874 yds SSS 68

- 🏌 WD–U WE–H SOC–WD
- ££ On application
- 🚗 7 miles E of Liverpool. I mile S of
  Prescot on B5199. M57 Junction 2
- 🏔 James Braid

Leasowe   (1891)
Leasowe Road, Moreton, Wirral,
CH46 3RD
- ☎ (0151) 677 5852
- 🖴 (0151) 641 8519
- ✉ secretary@leasowegolfclub.co.uk
- 📖 610
- 🏌 L Jukes (0151) 677 5852
- 🏌 AJ Ayre (0151) 678 5460
- ⊳ 18 L 6276 yds SSS 70 Par 71
- 🏌 U SOC–H
- ££ D–£32.50 (D–£37.50)
- 🚗 I mile N of Queensway Tunnel.
  M53 Junction I
- 🏔 John Ball Jr
- 🖥 www.leasowegolfclub.co.uk

Lee Park   (1954)
Childwall Valley Road, Gateacre, Liverpool,
L27 3YA
- ☎ (0151) 487 3882 (Clubhouse)
- 🖴 (0151) 498 4666
- ✉ lee.park@virgin.net
- 📖 580
- 🏌 Steve Settle (0151) 487 3882
- 🏌 Paul Grannell (07866) 616369
- ⊳ 18 L 5959 yds Par 70 SSS 69
- 🏌 WD SOC (Mon/Thur/Fri)
- ££ £32 (£40)
- 🚗 7 miles SE of Liverpool (B5171); 10
  min from Liverpool Airport; M62
  Jct 6
- ⊕ Practice nets; practice area;
  chipping area; all weather practice
  bays.
- 🏔 Frank Pennick (CK Cotton)
- 🖥 www.leepark.co.uk

Prenton   (1905)
Golf Links Road, Prenton, Birkenhead,
CH42 8LW
- ☎ (0151) 609 3426
- ✉ nigel.brown@prentongolfclub
  .co.uk
- 📖 470 100(L) 80(J)
- 🏌 N Brown
- 🏌 R Thompson (0151) 608 1636
- ⊳ 18 L 6429 yds SSS 71
- 🏌 U SOC–Mon/Wed/Fri
- ££ £35 (£40)
- 🚗 Outskirts of Birkenhead. M53
  Junction 3
- 🖥 www.prentongolfclub.co.uk

RLGC Village Play   (1895)
Club
c/o 18 Waverley Road, Hoylake, Wirral,
CH47 3DD
- ☎ (07885) 507263
- 🖴 (0151) 632 5156
- ✉ pdwbritesparks@tiscali.co.uk
- 📖 40
- 🏌 PD Williams (0151) 632 5156
- ⊳ Play over Royal Liverpool, Hoylake
- 🚗 M53 Jct 2

Royal Birkdale   (1889)
Waterloo Road, Birkdale, Southport,
PR8 2LX
- ☎ (01704) 552020
- 🖴 (01704) 552021
- ✉ secretary@royalbirkdale.com
- 🏌 MC Gilyeat
- 🏌 B Hodgkinson (01704) 568857
- ⊳ 18 L 6817 yds Par 72 SSS 73
- 🏌 I H SOC
- ££ £165 (£195)
- 🚗 1½ miles S of Southport (A565)
- 🏔 George Lowe
- 🖥 www.royalbirkdale.com

Royal Liverpool   (1869)
Meols Drive, Hoylake, CH47 4AL
- ☎ (0151) 632 3101/3102
- 🖴 (0151) 632 6737
- ✉ secretary@royal-liverpool-golf.com
- 📖 810
- 🏌 D Gromie
- 🏌 J Heggarty (0151) 632 5868
- ⊳ 18 L 7222 yds SSS 74
- 🏌 H SOC
- ££ On application
- 🚗 On A553 from M53 Junction 2
- ⊕ Golf bookings: bookings
  @royal-liverpool-golf.com
- 🏔 Robert Chambers & George
  Morris/Donald Steel
- 🖥 www.royal-liverpool-golf.com

Sherdley Park Municipal
(1974)
Public
Eltonhead Road, Sutton, St Helens,
Merseyside WA9 5DE
- ☎ (01744) 813149
- 🖴 (01744) 817967
- ✉ sherdleyparkgolfcourse@sthelens
  .gov.uk
- 🏌 J Barston (Mgr)
- ⊳ 18 L 5974 yds SSS 69
- 🏌 U SOC weekday anytime; weekend
  after 12 noon
- ££ £13.75 (£15.75) £7.90 after 2pm
  Mon & Tues £7.90 after 5pm every
  other day
- 🚗 2 miles E of St Helens (A570). M62
  Junction 7, 2 miles
- ⊕ Driving range
- 🖥 www.sthelens.gov.uk

Southport & Ainsdale
(1906)
Bradshaws Lane, Ainsdale, Southport,
PR8 3LG
- ☎ (01704) 578000
- 🖴 (01704) 570896
- ✉ secretary@sandagolfclub.co.uk
- 📖 452 94(L) 51(J)
- 🏌 MJ Vanner
- 🏌 J Payne (01704) 577316
- ⊳ 18 L 6768 yds Par 72 SSS 74
- 🏌 WD–H WE–NA morning
- ££ £75 D–£100 (£90)
- 🚗 3 miles S of Southport on A565
- 🏔 James Braid
- 🖥 www.sandagolfclub.co.uk

Southport Golf Links (1912)

Public
Park Road West, Southport, PR9 0JS
☎ (01704) 535286
✓ C Easter
↱ 18 L 6253 yds SSS 69
👥 U SOC
££ £12 (£14)
🏌 N end of Southport promenade

Southport Old Links (1926)

Moss Lane, Southport, PR9 7QS
☎ (01704) 228207
🖥 (01704) 505353
📧 secretary@solgc.freeserve.co.uk
📖 450
🏌 BE Kenyon
✓ Gary Copeman (07802) 653909
↱ 9 L 6450 yds Par 72 SSS 71
👥 U exc Wed & Sun & B Hols NA/H
££ £25 (£30)
🏌 Churchtown, 3 miles NE of
Southport
🖥 www.solgc.freeserve.co.uk

Wallasey (1891)

Bayswater Road, Wallasey, CH45 8LA
☎ (0151) 691 1024
🖥 (0151) 638 8988
📧 wallaseygc@aol.com
📖 515 82(L) 61(J)
🏌 JT Barraclough (0151) 691 1024
✓ M Adams (0151) 638 3888
↱ 18 L 6572 yds SSS 73
👥 H SOC
££ £75 (£85)
🏌 M53- Junction 1 signs to New
Brighton
🏠 Tom Morris
🖥 www.wallaseygolfclub.com

Warren (1911)

Public
Grove Road, Wallasey, Wirral, CH45 0JA
☎ (0151) 639 8323 (Clubhouse)

West Derby (1896)

Yew Tree Lane, Liverpool, L12 9HQ
☎ (0151) 254 1034
🖥 (0151) 259 0505
📧 pmilne@westderbygc.freeserve
.co.uk
📖 550
🏌 AP Milne (0151) 254 1034
✓ S Danchin (0151) 254 1034
↱ 18 L 6275 yds SSS 70
👥 SOC–WD after 9.30am
££ £36 (£40)
🏌 2 miles E of Liverpool, off
A580–West Derby Junction

West Lancashire (1873)

Hall Road West, Blundellsands, Liverpool,
L23 8SZ
☎ (0151) 924 1076
🖥 (0151) 931 4448
📧 sec@westlancashiregolf.co.uk
📖 700
🏌 S King (0151) 924 1076
✓ G Edge (0151) 924 5662
↱ 18 L 6767 yds SSS 73
👥 H SOC–WD exc Tues

££ £68 D–£80 (£85)
🏌 Between Liverpool and Southport,
off A565
🏠 CK Cotton
🖥 www.westlancashiregolf.co.uk

Wirral Ladies (1894)

93 Bidston Road, Birkenhead, Wirral,
CH43 6TS
☎ (0151) 652 1255
🖥 (0151) 651 3775
📧 sue.headford@virgin.co.uk
📖 480
🏌 Mrs SA Headford
✓ A Law (0151) 652 2468
↱ 18 L 4948 yds SSS 69 (Ladies)
18 L 5185 yds SSS 65 (Men)
👥 U H SOC–WD
££ £30
🏌 Birkenhead ½ mile. M53, 2 miles

Woolton (1901)

Doe Park, Speke Road, Woolton, Liverpool,
L25 7TZ
☎ (0151) 486 2298
🖥 (0151) 486 1664
📧 golf@wooltongolf.co.uk
📖 450
🏌 Manager (0151) 486 2298 opt 4
✓ D Thompson (0151) 486 2298
opt 1
↱ 18 L 5747 yds SSS 68
👥 U exc comp days SOC WD/WE
after 2pm
££ £30 (£40)
🏌 SE Liverpool. End of M62/M57. 2
miles Liverpool airport
⊕ Teaching facilities
🖥 www.thewooltongolfclub.com

Middlesex

Airlinks (1984)

Public
Southall Lane, Hounslow, TW5 9PE
☎ (020) 8561 1418

Amida Golf (1977)

Pay and play
Staines Road, Twickenham, TW2 5JD
☎ (0208) 783 1698
🖥 (0208) 783 9475
📧 golfpro.hampton@amidaclubs.com
✓ Jamie Skinner (020) 8783 1698
↱ 9 L 2700/5420 yds SSS 69
👥 U
££ £11 (£13)
🏌 2 miles NW of Hampton Court, nr
end of M3
⊕ Floodlit driving range; junior golf;
short game academy
🖥 www.amidaclubs.com

Ashford Manor (1898)

Fordbridge Road, Ashford, TW15 3RT
☎ (01784) 424644
🖥 (01784) 424649
📧 secretary@amgc.co.uk
📖 700
🏌 Peter Dawson (Business Mgr)
✓ Robert Walton (01784) 424654

↱ 18 L 6351 yds SSS 71
👥 WD–U WE–M H SOC–WD
££ £40 WD
🏌 A308 Ashford. M25 Junction 13
🏠 T Hogg
🖥 www.amgc.co.uk

Brent Valley (1938)

Public
Church Road, Hanwell, London, W7 3BE
☎ (020) 8567 4230
(Clubhouse)
(020) 8567 1287 (Bookings)
📖 195
🏌 Ms M Griffin
✓ V Santos (020) 8567 1287
↱ 18 L 5426 yds SSS 66
👥 U SOC
££ On application

Bush Hill Park (1895)

Bush Hill, Winchmore Hill, London,
N21 2BU
☎ (020) 8360 5738
🖥 (020) 8360 5583
📧 info@bushhillparkgolfclub.co.uk
📖 630
🏌 Martin Berry
✓ L Fickling (020) 8360 4103
↱ 18 L 5825 yds SSS 68
👥 WD–H WE–M SOC. Members
only WE
££ £29.50
🏌 S of Enfield M25 Jct 24 or 25
🖥 www.bushhillparkgolfclub.co.uk

Crews Hill (1916)

Cattlegate Road, Crews Hill, Enfield,
EN2 8AZ
☎ (020) 8363 6674
🖥 (020) 8363 2343
📧 info@crewshillgolfclub.com
📖 600
🏌 Pauline Cullen
✓ N Wichelow (020) 8366 7422
↱ 18 L 6281 yds SSS 70
👥 WDU WE/BH–H SOC
££ £27.50 (£40)
🏌 2½ miles N of Enfield. M25
Junction 24
🏠 HS Colt
🖥 www.crewshillgolfclub.com

Ealing (1898)

Perivale Lane, Greenford, UB6 8TS
☎ (020) 8997 0937
🖥 (020) 8998 0756
📧 info@ealinggolfclub.co.uk
📖 600
🏌 Guy Stacey
✓ R Willison (020) 8997 3959
↱ 18 L 6191 yds SSS 70
👥 WD–U H WE/BH–M SOC
££ £40 (£50)
🏌 Marble Arch 6 miles on A40-
Perivale junction
🏠 HS Colt
🖥 www.ealinggolfclub.co.uk

Enfield (1893)

Old Park Road South, Enfield, EN2 7DA
☎ (020) 8363 3970
🖥 (020) 8342 0381

✉ secretary@enfieldgolfclub.co.uk
⌨ 450
♠ Peter Monument
✓ Martin Porter (020) 8366 4492
⊳ 18 L 6154 yds Par 72 SSS 70
♦ WD–H WE/BH–M SOC–WD
££ £28 D–£37 (£36)
⊶ 1 mile NE of Enfield. M25 Junction 24-A1005
⌂ James Braid
▤ www.enfieldgolfclub.co.uk

Finchley   (1929)
Nether Court, Frith Lane, London, NW7 1PU
☎ (020) 8346 2436
⌨ (020) 8343 4205
✉ secretary@finchleygolfclub.co.uk
⌨ 550
♠ MD Gottlieb
✓ DM Brown (020) 8346 5086
⊳ 18 L 6356 yds SSS 71
♦ WD–U WE–pm only SOC
££ On application
⊶ M1 Junction 2
⌂ James Braid
▤ www.finchleygolfclub.com

Fulwell   (1904)
Wellington Road, Hampton Hill, TW12 1JY
☎ (020) 8977 2733
⌨ (020) 8977 7732
✉ secretary@fulwellgolfclub.co.uk
⌨ 750
♠ Mark Walden
✓ N Turner (020) 8977 3844
⊳ 18 L 6529 yds SSS 71
♦ WD–U WE–NA before noon SOC
££ £40 (£55)
⊶ Opposite Fulwell Station, close to A316, M25, M3
⌂ John Morrison
▤ www.fulwellgolfclub.co.uk

Grim's Dyke   (1910)
Oxhey Lane, Hatch End, Pinner, HA5 4AL
☎ (020) 8428 4539
⌨ (020) 8421 5494
✉ secretary@grimsdyke.co.uk
⌨ 400
♠ R Jones (020) 8428 4539
✓ L Curling (020) 8428 4539
⊳ 18 L 5600 yds Par 69 SSS 67
♦ WD–U H WE–M SOC exc BH–NA
££ £36 D–£35 (£18 with member)
⊶ 2 miles NW of Harrow (A4008). M1 Junctions 4/5
⌂ James Braid
▤ www.club-noticeboard.co.uk /grimsdyke

Hampstead   (1893)
Winnington Road, London, N2 0TU
☎ (020) 8455 0203
⌨ (020) 8731 6194
✉ hampsteadgolf@btconnect.com
⌨ 450
♠ Bob Blower
✓ PJ Brown (020) 8455 7089
⊳ 9 L 5812 yds SSS 68
♦ H–phone Pro first

££ £30 (£35)
⊶ 1 mile from Hampstead, nr Spaniards Inn
⌂ Tom Dunn

Harrow Hill Golf Course   (1982)
Public
Kenton Road, Harrow, Middx HA1 2BW
☎ (0208) 8643754
✉ info@harrowgolf.co.uk
♠ S Bishop
✓ S Bishop
⊳ 9 holes Par 3
♦ U
££ £4.90 (£5.90)
⊶ A404 Kenton Road
▤ www.harrowgolf.co.uk

Harrow School   (1978)
High Street, Harrow-on-the-Hill, HA1 3HW
☎ (0208) 872 8000
⌨ 440 100(L) 10(J)
♠ CV Davies (020) 8872 8232
⊳ 9 L 3690 yds SSS 57
♦ M H NA
££ £10 with member only
⊶ Harrow School, NW London
⌂ Donald Steel
▤ www.harrowschool.org.uk

Haste Hill   (1930)
Public
The Drive, Northwood, HA6 1HN
☎ (01923) 825224
⌨ (01923) 826485
⌨ 250
♠ P Clasby
✓ C Smilie
⊳ 18 L 5736 yds SSS 68
♦ U SOC
££ £16 (£22)
⊶ Northwood-Hillingdon

Heath Park   (1975)
Stockley Road, West Drayton
☎ (01895) 444232
⌨ (01895) 444232
✉ heathparkgolf@yahoo.co.uk
⌨ 160
♠ B Sharma (Prop)
⊳ 9 L 3236 yds SSS 60
♦ WD–U Sun–NA before 11am SOC
££ £11 (£12.50)
⊶ Crowne Plaza Hotel, Heathrow
⌂ Neil Coles

Hendon   (1903)
Ashley Walk, Devonshire Road, London, NW7 1DG
☎ (020) 8346 6023
⌨ (020) 8343 1974
✉ info@hendongolfclub.co.uk
⌨ 560
♠ CH Bailey
✓ M Deal (020) 8346 8990
⊳ 18 L 6289 yds Par 70 SSS 70
♦ WD–U WE/BH–bookings SOC
££ £35 D–£45 (£45)
⊶ M1 Jct 2, on to Holders Hill Road
⊕ Practice ground; nets

⌂ HS Colt
▤ www.hendongolfclub.co.uk

Highgate   (1904)
Denewood Road, Highgate, London, N6 4AH
☎ (020) 8340 1906 (Clubhouse)
⌨ (020) 8348 9152
✉ admin@highgategc.co.uk
⌨ 700
♠ N Higginson (020) 8340 3745
✓ R Turner (020) 8340 5467
⊳ 18 L 5964 yds SSS 69
♦ WD–U exc Wed–NA before noon WE/BH–M SOC
££ £35
⊶ Off Sheldon Avenue/Hampstead Lane
⌂ Cuthbert Butchart
▤ www.highgategc.co.uk

Horsenden Hill   (1935)
Public
Woodland Rise, Greenford, UB6 0RD
☎ (020) 8902 4555
⌨ 84
♠ AK Witte (020) 8458 5433
✓ J Quarshie
⊳ 9 L 3264 yds SSS 56
♦ U
££ 9 holes–£5 (£8)
⊶ Greenford, near Sudbury Town tube station
▤ www.horsendenhillgolfclub.co.uk

Hounslow Heath   (1979)
Public
Staines Road, Hounslow, TW4 5DS
☎ (020) 8570 5271
✉ golf@hhgc.uk.com
⌨ 120
♠ J Swanson
⊳ 18 L 5901 yds Par 69 SSS 68
♦ WD–U WE SOC
££ £11 (£15)
⊶ Opposite Green Lane, Staines Road (A315)
⌂ Fraser
▤ www.hhgc.uk.com

Leaside GC   (1974)
Pay and play
Lee Valley Leisure, Picketts Lock Lane, Edmonton, London N9 0AS
☎ (020) 8803 3611

Mill Hill   (1925)
100 Barnet Way, Mill Hill, London, NW7 3AL
☎ (020) 8959 2339
⌨ (020) 8906 0731
✉ cluboffice@millhillgc.co.uk
⌨ 570
♠ R Bauser
✓ D Beal (020) 8959 7261
⊳ 18 L 6247 yds SSS 70
♦ WD–U SOC–WD. WE/BH: Prior booking in Pro Shop (WE pm only)
££ £30 (£37)
⊶ ½ mile N of Apex Corner, nr A1/A41 junction
⊕ Driving range; chipping area; putting green

♔ Abercrombie/Colt
🖥 www.millhillgc.co.uk

Muswell Hill (1893)
Rhodes Avenue, London, N22 7UT
☎ (020) 8888 1764
📠 (020) 8889 9380
📧 mhgcclubsecretary@btconnect .com
🏛 600
🏌 A Hobbs (020) 8888 1764
🏌 D Wilton (020) 8888 8046
🏳 18 L 6474 yds SSS 71
👥 WD–U WE–book with Pro SOC
££ £35 D–£45 (£40)
🚗 1 mile from Bounds Green Station. Central London 7 miles
♔ Braid/Wilson
🖥 www.muswellhillgolfclub.co.uk

North Middlesex (1905)
The Manor House, Friern Barnet Lane, Whetstone, London, N20 0NL
☎ (020) 8445 1604
📠 (020) 8445 5023
📧 manager@northmiddlesexgc.co.uk
🏛 500
🏌 Howard Till (020) 8445 1604
🏌 Freddy George (020) 8445 3060
🏳 18 L 5594 yds SSS 67
👥 WE/BH–restricted SOC–WD
££ £25 (£30)
🚗 5 miles S of M25 Junction 23, between Barnet and Finchley
♔ Willie Park Jr
🖥 www.northmiddlesexgc.co.uk

Northwood (1891)
Rickmansworth Road, Northwood, HA6 2QW
☎ (01923) 821384
📠 (01923) 840150
📧 secretary@northwoodgolf.co.uk
🏛 560
🏌 T Collingwood (01923) 821384
🏌 CJ Holdsworth (01923) 820112
🏳 18 L 6553 yds Par 71 SSS 71
👥 WD–H WE/BH–NA SOC
££ £40
🚗 3 miles SE of Rickmansworth (A404)
♔ James Braid
🖥 www.northwoodgolf.co.uk

Perivale Park (1932)
Public
Stockdove Way, Argyle Road, Greenford, UB6 8JT
☎ (020) 8575 7116
🏛 140
🏌 J Mealyer
🏌 P Bryant (020) 8575 7116
🏳 9 L 5296 yds SSS 67
👥 U
££ 9: £8 (£9) 18: £14.50 (£17)
🚗 1 mile E of Greenford, off A40

Pinner Hill (1927)
Southview Road, Pinner Hill, HA5 3YA
☎ (020) 8866 0963
📠 (020) 8868 4817
📧 phgc@pinnerhillgc.com
🏛 770
🏌 Michael Gottlieb (Gen Mgr)

🏌 C Duck (020) 8866 2109
🏳 18 L 6393 yds Par 71 SSS 71
👥 WD–H exc Wed & Thurs–U Sun/BH–M SOC
££ £35 (£35) exc Wed & Thurs–£18.50
🚗 1 mile W from Pinner Green
♔ JH Taylor
🖥 www.pinnerhillgc.com

Ruislip (1936)
Public
Ickenham Road, Ruislip, HA4 7DQ
☎ (01895) 638835/623980
📠 (01895) 635780
📧 ruislipgolf@btconnect.com
🏛 201
🏌 N Jennings
🏌 P Glozier
🏳 18 L 5571 yds Par 69 SSS 67
👥 U SOC
££ £16 (£22)
🚗 W Ruislip BR/LTE Station
⊕ Driving range
♔ A Herd

Stanmore (1893)
29 Gordon Avenue, Stanmore, HA7 2RL
☎ (020) 8954 2599
📠 (020) 8954 2599
📧 secretary@stanmoregolfclub.co.uk
🏛 500
🏌 Allan Knott (020) 8954 2599
🏌 J Reynolds (020) 8954 2599
🏳 18 L 5885 yds SSS 68
👥 WD–H WE/BH–M SOC
££ Mon & Fri £17, Tues, Wed, Thur £25, WE £35
🚗 Between Stanmore and Belmont, off Old Church Lane; 5 min from M1 Jct 4
🖥 www.stanmoregolfclub.co.uk

Stockley Park (1993)
Pay and play
The Clubhouse, Stockley Park, Uxbridge, UB11 1AQ
☎ (020) 8813 5700/561 6339 (Bookings)
📧 k.soper@stockleyparkgolf.com

Strawberry Hill (1900)
Wellesley Road, Strawberry Hill, Twickenham, TW2 5SD
☎ (020) 8894 0165 .
📧 secretary@shgc.net
🏛 350
🏌 Paul Astbury (020) 8894 0165
🏌 P Buchan (020) 8898 2082
🏳 9 L 2381 yds Par 64 SSS 62
👥 WD–U WE–M
££ £20 D–£30
🚗 Strawberry Hill Station
♔ JH Taylor
🖥 www.shgc.net

Sudbury (1920)
Bridgewater Road, Wembley, HA0 1AL
☎ (020) 8902 3713 (office)
(020) 8902 7910 (bookings)
📧 enquiries@sudburygolfclubltd.co.uk

Sunbury (1993)
Proprietary
Charlton Lane, Shepperton, TW17 8QA
☎ (01932) 771414
📠 (01932) 789300
📧 sunbury@crown-golf.co.uk
🏛 350
🏌 P Dawson (Gen Mgr)
🏌 A McColgan
🏳 18 L 5103 yds Par 68 SSS 65 9 L 2444 yds Par 33
👥 U–phone Pro SOC
££ £19.50 (£24)
🚗 SE of Queen Mary Reservoir, nr Chalton. M3 Junction 1, 2 miles
⊕ Floodlit driving range
♔ Peter Alliss
🖥 www.crown-golf.co.uk

Trent Park (1973)
Public
Bramley Road, Southgate, London, N14 4UW
☎ (020) 8367 4653
📠 (020) 8366 4581
📧 trentpark@crown-golf.co.uk
🏌 D Peck
🏳 18 L 6008 yds SSS 69
👥 WD/WE–U SOC WE–NA before 11am
££ £17 (£20)
🚗 Nr Oakwood Tube station
⊕ Driving range
🖥 www.trentparkgolf.co.uk

Uxbridge (1947)
Public
The Drive, Harefield Place, Uxbridge, UB10 8AQ
☎ (01895) 231169
📠 (01895) 810262
📧 uxbridgegolf@btconnect.com
🏌 Mrs A James (01895) 272457
🏌 Phil Howard (01895) 237287
🏳 18 L 5711 yds SSS 68
👥 U SOC
££ £16 (£22)
🚗 2 miles N of Uxbridge. B467 off A40 towards Ruislip. M25 Junction 16, 3 miles
🖥 www.uxbridgegolfclub.co.uk

West Middlesex (1891)
Greenford Road, Southall, UB1 3EE
☎ (020) 8574 3450
📠 (020) 8574 2383
📧 westmid.gc@virgin.net
🏛 377
🏌 Miss R Khanna
🏌 T Talbot (020) 8574 1800
🏳 18 L 6127 yds SSS 69
👥 WD–U WE–NA before 2pm (phone Pro) SOC–Tues/Thurs/Fri
££ Mon–£18 Tues/Thurs/Fri–£22 Wed–£20 WE–£30
🚗 Junction of Uxbridge Road and Greenford Road
♔ James Braid
🖥 www.westmiddxgolfclub.co.uk

Wyke Green (1928)
Syon Lane, Isleworth, Osterley, TW7 5PT
☎ (020) 8560 8777

For list of abbreviations and key to symbols see page 647

📞 (020) 8569 8392
📧 office@wykegreengolfclub.co.uk
🏛 550
🖉 D Pearson
⛳ N Smith (020) 8847 0685
🏴 18 L 6182 yds SSS 70
👥 WD–U WE/BH–H after 4pm
££ £35 D–£40, after 5pm–£20
   (Mon/Tues only) WE £40 after
   4pm
⛳ ¹/₂ mile from Gillette Corner (A4)
⊕ Practice range
🏠 Hawtree/Taylor
🖥 www.wykegreengolfclub.co.uk

Norfolk

Barnham Broom Hotel
(1977)
Honingham Road, Barnham Broom,
Norwich, NR9 4DD
📞 (01603) 759393 (Hotel)
   (01603) 757505 (Golf Shop)
📠 (01603) 758224
📧 golf@barnham-broom.co.uk
🏛 500
🖉 R Brooks (01603) 757504
⛳ I Rollett
🏴 Valley 18 L 6483 yds Par 72 SSS 71
   Hill 18 L 6495 yds Par 71 SSS 71
👥 U SOC
££ £40 (£50)
⛳ 10 miles SW of Norwich, off A47.
   5 miles NW of Wymondham, off
   A11
⊕ 3 Academy holes; driving range
🏠 Pennink/Steel
🖥 www.barnham-broom.co.uk

Bawburgh   (1978)
Glen Lodge, Marlingford Road, Bawburgh,
Norwich NR9 3LU
📞 (01603) 740404
📠 (01603) 740403
📧 info@bawburgh.com
🏛 600
🖉 I Ladbrooke (Gen Mgr)
⛳ C Potter (01603) 742323
🏴 18 L 6720 yds SSS 72 Par 72 from
   May 2009
👥 U–phone first SOC
££ £25 (£25)
⛳ 2 miles W of Norwich, off A47
   Norwich Southern Bypass
⊕ Floodlit driving range. Golf
   Academy
🏠 Barnard Family
🖥 www.bawburgh.com

Caldecott Hall   (1993)
Caldecott Hall, Beccles Road, Fritton, Great
Yarmouth, NR31 9EY
📞 (01493) 488488
📠 (01493) 488561
🏛 600
🖉 G Braybrooke
⛳ M Tungate
🏴 18 L 6685 yds Par 73 SSS 72
   18 L 2658 yds Par 3
👥 H SOC WD WE
££ £25 (£30)

⛳ 5 miles SW of Gt Yarmouth on
   A143
⊕ Floodlit driving range
🖥 www.caldecotthall.co.uk

Costessey Park   (1983)
Costessey Park, Costessey, Norwich,
NR8 5AL
📞 (01603) 746333
📧 cpgc@ljgroup.com

Dereham   (1934)
Quebec Road, Dereham, NR19 2DS
📞 (01362) 695900
📠 (01362) 695904
📧 derehamgolfclub@dgolfclub
   .freeserve.co.uk
🏛 400
🖉 D Mayers
⛳ N Allsebrook (01362) 695631
🏴 9 L 6267 yds SSS 70
👥 H
££ £20 D–£30
⛳ Dereham ¹/₂ mile
🖥 www.club-noticeboard.co.uk

Dunham   (1979)
Proprietary
Little Dunham, Swaffham, PE32 2DF
📞 (01328) 701906
📧 info@dunhamgolfclub.com

De Vere Dunston Hall
(1994)
Pay and play
Ipswich Road, Dunston, Norwich,
NR14 8PQ
📞 (01508) 470178

Eagles   (1990)
39 School Road, Tilney All Saints, Kings
Lynn, PE34 4RS
📞 (01553) 827147
📠 (01553) 829777
🏛 200
🖉 RK Shipman
⛳ N Pickerell/S Cubitt
🏴 9 L 2142 yds SSS 61
   9 hole Par 3 course
👥 U
££ 9: £12 (+BH £13) 18: £16.50 (+BH
   £18.50)
⛳ 5 miles W of Kings Lynn on A47
⊕ Driving range
🏠 David Horn
🖥 www.eagles-golf-tennis.co.uk

Eaton   (1910)
Newmarket Road, Norwich, NR4 6SF
📞 (01603) 451686
📠 (01603) 457539
📧 admin@eatongc.co.uk
🏛 906 160(L) 62(J)
🖉 K Tuck
⛳ M Allen (01603) 251394
🏴 18 L 6118 yds SSS 70
👥 H WE–NA before noon SOC–WD
££ D–£39 (£49)
⛳ S Norwich, off A11
⊕ Driving bays
🏠 Ernest Riseborough
🖥 www.eatongc.co.uk

Fakenham   (1973)
The Race Course, Fakenham, NR21 7NY
📞 (01328) 862867
📧 grahamc21@tiscali.com

Feltwell   (1976)
Thor Ave, Wilton Road, Feltwell, Thetford,
IP26 4AY
📞 (01842) 827644
📠 (01842) 829065
📧 sec.feltwellgc@virgin.net
🏛 400
🖉 Jonathan Moore
⛳ Jonathan Moore
🏴 9 L 6488 yds Par 72 SSS 71
👥 U SOC–WD
££ £20 (£30)
⛳ I mile S of Feltwell on B1112
⊕ Former Feltwell aerodrome
🖥 www.club-noticeboard.co.uk

Gorleston   (1906)
Warren Road, Gorleston, Gt Yarmouth,
NR31 6JT
📞 (01493) 661911
📠 (01493) 661911
📧 manager@gorlestongolfclub.co.uk
🏛 900
🖉 JE Woodhouse (01493) 661911
⛳ N Brown (01493) 662103
🏴 18 L 6391 yds SSS 71
👥 U H SOC
££ £25 (£30) W–£85
⛳ S of Gorleston, off A12
🏠 JH Taylor

Great Yarmouth & Caister
(1882)
Beach House, Caister-on-Sea, Gt Yarmouth,
NR30 5TD
📞 (01493) 728699
📠 (01493) 728831
📧 office@caistergolf.co.uk
🏛 570
🖉 RA Peck
⛳ M Clarke (01493) 720421
🏴 18 L 6330 yds SSS 70
👥 WE–NA before noon WD SOC
   after 9 am
££ £35 (£45) WD £25 after noon
⛳ Caister-on-Sea
⊕ Practice field
🏠 HS Colt
🖥 www.caistergolf.co.uk

Hunstanton   (1891)
Golf Course Road, Old Hunstanton,
PE36 6JQ
📞 (01485) 532811
📠 (01485) 532319
📧 secretary@hunstantongolfclub
   .com
🏛 662 136(L) 83(J)
🖉 BRB Carrick
⛳ J Dodds (01485) 532751
🏴 18 L 6759 yds SSS 73
👥 WD–H after 9.30am WE–H after
   10.30am SOC
££ D–£75 £60 after 12, £45 after 3
   (£85, £65 after 12, £55 after 3)
⛳ 1¹/₂ miles NE of Hunstanton
⊕ 2 ball play (4 ball on Tues) after
   10.30

George Fernie
www.hunstantongolfclub.com

King's Lynn (1923)
Castle Rising, King's Lynn, PE31 6BD
☎ (01553) 631654
🖷 (01553) 631036
✉ secretary@kingslynngc.co.uk
🕮 700
🏌 M Bowman (01553) 633000
✓ J Reynolds (01553) 631655
ℙ 18 L 6609 yds SSS 73
🕴 U H SOC
££ £45 (£55) £30 twilight after 3pm
(Mon–Thur) Winter deal available
(Nov–Mar)
⊷ 4 miles NE of King's Lynn, off A149
⊕ Practice ground
⌂ Alliss/Thomas
▤ www.club-noticeboard.co.uk

Links Country Park Hotel & Golf Club (1903)
West Runton, Cromer, NR27 9QH
☎ (01263) 838383
✉ sales@links-hotel.co.uk

Marriott Sprowston Manor Hotel (1980)
Wroxham Road, Sprowston, Norwich, NR7 8RP
☎ (0870) 400 7229
🖷 (0870) 400 7329
✉ keith.grant@marriotthotels.com
🕮 620
🏌 Keith Grant (0870) 400 7229
✓ G Ireson (0870) 400 7229
ℙ 18 L 6547 yds Par 71 SSS 71
🕴 U SOC
££ £35 Mon–Thurs £40 Fri–Sun
Varying rates on application
⊷ 4 miles NE of Norwich on A1151
⊕ Floodlit driving range
⌂ Ross McMurray
▤ www.marriott.co.uk/nwigs

Mattishall (1990)
South Green, Mattishall, Dereham
☎ (01362) 850464
🕮 180
🏌 B Hall
ℙ 9 L 6170 yds Par 70 SSS 69
🕴 WD–U WE–U before noon SOC
££ 9: £10 18: £14
⊷ 6 miles E of Dereham (B1063)
⊕ 9 hole pitch & putt
⌂ BC Todd

Middleton Hall (1989)
Proprietary
Middleton, King's Lynn, PE32 1RH
☎ (01553) 841800
🖷 (01553) 841800
✉ middleton-hall@btclick.com
🕮 600
🏌 J Holland
✓ S White (01553) 841801
ℙ 18 L 5756 yds Par 71 SSS 68
🕴 U SOC
££ £25 D–£40 (£30)
⊷ 2 miles SE of King's Lynn on A47
⊕ Driving range

D Scott
www.middletonhall.co.uk

Mundesley (1901)
Links Road, Mundesley, NR11 8ES
☎ (01263) 720095
🖷 (01263) 722849
✉ manager@mundesleygolfclub.co.uk
🕮 500
🏌 TE Duke (Gen Mgr) (01263) 720095
✓ TG Symmons (01263) 720279
ℙ 9 L 5377 yds SSS 66
🕴 WD–U H exc Wed 10.00–2.30pm
WE–NA before 11.30am
££ £28 (£30) D–£30
⊷ 5 miles SE of Cromer
⊕ Driving range and practice area
⌂ Harry Vardon
▤ www.mundesleygolfclub.co.uk

The Norfolk G&CC (1993)
Proprietary
Hingham Road, Reymerston, Norwich, NR9 4QQ
☎ (01362) 850297
🖷 (01362) 850614
✉ norfolkgolfse@ukonline.co.uk
🕮 530
🏌 M de Boltz
✓ T Varney (01362) 850297
ℙ 18 L 6609 yds SSS 72
🕴 WD–U before 4pm –M after 4pm
WE/BH–NA before noon SOC
££ £30 (£30)
⊷ 14 miles W of Norwich, off B1135
Dereham to Wymondham road
⊕ Driving range. 9 hole pitch & putt course
▤ www.thenorfolk.co.uk

RAF Marham (1974)
RAF Marham, Kings Lynn, PE33 9NP
☎ (01760) 337261 ext 7262
🕮 290
🏌 PG Williams (ext 7387)
ℙ 9 L 5976 yds Par 71 SSS 69
🕴 SOC by prior arrangement
WD/WE subject to security clearance and state
££ £10 non–member, £7 with member,
⊷ 11 miles SE of King's Lynn, nr Narborough
⊕ Course situated on MOD land, and may be closed without prior notice
▤ www.marhamgolf.co.uk

Richmond Park (1990)
Saham Road, Watton, IP25 6EA
☎ (01953) 881803
🖷 (01953) 881817
✉ info@richmondpark.co.uk
🕮 500
🏌 S Jessop
✓ A Hemsley
ℙ 18 L 6300 yds SSS 71
🕴 WD–U WE–H before noon SOC
££ £30 (£45)
⊷ 1/2 mile NW of Watton
⊕ Driving range

Scott/Jessup
www.richmondpark.co.uk

Royal Cromer (1888)
Overstrand Road, Cromer, NR27 0JH
☎ (01263) 512884
🖷 (01263) 512430
✉ general.manager@royal-cromer.com
🕮 700
🏌 Gary Richardson
✓ Lee D Patterson (01263) 512267
ℙ 18 L 6508 yds SSS 72
🕴 H SOC–WD after 9.30 pm; WE after 10.30 pm
££ D–£50 (D–£60)
⊷ 1 mile E of Cromer on B1159
⌂ Morris/Taylor/Braid/Pennink
▤ www.royalcromergolfclub.com

Royal Norwich (1893)
Drayton High Road, Hellesdon, Norwich, NR6 5AH
☎ (01603) 425712
🖷 (01603) 417945
✉ mail@royalnorwichgolf.co.uk
🕮 650
🏌 Ryan O'Connor (Gen Mgr) (01603) 429928
✓ S Youd (01603) 408459
ℙ 18 L 6506 yds Par 72 SSS 72
🕴 WE/BH–restricted SOC
££ £30 D–£48 (£35 D–£48) Discount rates available for groups of 12 or more on request
⊷ 1/2 mile W of Norwich ring road, on Fakenham road (A1067)
⌂ James Braid
▤ www.royalnorwichgolf.co.uk

Royal West Norfolk (1892)
Brancaster, King's Lynn, PE31 8AX
☎ (01485) 210087
🖷 (01485) 210087
✉ secretary@rwngc.org
🕮 890
🏌 Ian Symington (01485) 210087
✓ S Rayner (01485) 210616
ℙ 18 L 6457 yds SSS 71
🕴 M mid July–mid Sept WE–NA before 10am SOC No three or four balls
££ £75 (£85)
⊷ 7 miles E of Hunstanton on A419
⊕ Practice ground
⌂ Holcombe Ingleby

Ryston Park (1932)
Ely Road, Denver, Downham Market, PE38 0HH
☎ (01366) 382133
🖷 (01366) 383834
✉ rystonparkgc@tiscali.co.uk
🕮 320
🏌 WJ Flogdell
✓ None
ℙ 9 L 6310 yds SSS 70
🕴 WD–H WE/BH–M SOC
££ £25 D–£35 playing with member £15 juniors £7.50
⊷ 1 m S of Downham Market on A10
⌂ James Braid
▤ www.club-noticeboard.co.uk

Sheringham   (1891)
Sheringham, NR26 8HG
☎ **(01263) 822038**
(Bar & Catering)
📠 (01263) 826129
📧 info@sheringhamgolfclub.co.uk
📖 800
♉ PJ Mounfield (01263) 823488
✒ MW Jubb (01263) 822980
🏌 18 L 6456 yds SSS 71
👥 WD & WE NA before 9–30am H
SOC
£€ £55 (£60)
🚗 ¹/₂ mile W of Sheringham (A149)
🏠 Tom Dunn
💻 www.sheringhamgolfclub.co.uk

Swaffham   (1922)
Cley Road, Swaffham, PE37 8AE
☎ **(01760) 721621**
📠 (01760) 336998
📧 manager@swaffhamgc.co.uk
📖 600
♉ Mr C T Wellstead
✒ Peter Field (01760) 721611
🏌 18 L 6525 yds SSS 71 Par 71
👥 WD–U from 10.00am WD–U SOC
from 10.00am WE – Pre book only
£€ £50 day, £30 half day £30 18 holes,
£25 county cards £10 juniors
🚗 1¹/₂ miles SW of Swaffham
⊕ 4 acre practice area with bunkers;
Putting Green and Short game
practice area.
🏠 Gaunt & Marnoch Ltd
💻 www.club-noticeboard.co.uk

Thetford   (1912)
Brandon Road, Thetford, IP24 3NE
☎ **(01842) 752258 (Clubhouse)**
📠 (01842) 766212
📧 thetfordgolfclub@btconnect.com
📖 700
♉ Mrs Diane Hopkins
(01842) 752169
✒ G Kitley (01842) 752662
🏌 18 L 6879 yds SSS 73
👥 H SOC–Mon/Wed/Thur/Fri WE
after 2pm
£€ £38 D–£50. Soc from £35
🚗 2 miles W of Thetford (B1107), off
A11 By-pass
⊕ Long and short game practice
grounds
🏠 CH Mayo
💻 www.thetfordgolfclub.co.uk

Wensum Valley   (1990)
Beech Avenue, Taverham, Norwich,
NR8 6HP
☎ **(01603) 261012**
📠 (01603) 261664
📧 enqs@wensumvalleyhotel.co.uk
📖 600
♉ Mrs B Hall
🏌 18 L 6223 yds SSS 70
18 L 6942 yds SSS 73
👥 U SOC
£€ £30
🚗 4 miles NW of Norwich on A1067
⊕ Floodlit driving range
🏠 BC Todd
💻 www.wensumvalleyhotel.co.uk

Weston Park   (1993)
Weston Longville, Norwich, NR9 5JW
☎ **(01603) 872363**
📠 (01603) 873040
📧 golf@weston-park.co.uk
📖 550
♉ Gary Stanger (Gen
Mgr) (01603) 876300
✒ MR Few (01603) 872998
🏌 18 L 6603 yds SSS 72
👥 WD–U H
£€ £37 (£47)
🚗 9 miles NW of Norwich, off A1067
⊕ Practice ground
🏠 John Glasgow
💻 www.weston-park.co.uk

Northamptonshire

Brampton Heath   (1995)
Sandy Lane, Church Brampton, NN6 8AX
☎ **(01604) 843939**
📠 (01604) 843885
📧 info@bhgc.co.uk
📖 500
♉ Sally Carter-Jones
✒ A Wright
🏌 18 L 6566 yds Par 72 SSS 71
9 hole short course
👥 U SOC
£€ £20 (£25)
🚗 4 miles N of Northampton
between A508 and A428
⊕ 18-bay floodlit driving range
🏠 David Snell
💻 www.bhgc.co.uk

Cold Ashby   (1974)
Proprietary
Stanford Road, Cold Ashby, Northampton,
NN6 6EP
☎ **(01604) 740548**
📠 (01604) 740548
📧 info@coldashbygolfclub.co.uk
📖 600 40(L) 40(J)
♉ DA Croxton
(Prop) (01604) 740548
✒ S Rose (01604) 740099
🏌 27 L 6308 yds Par 72 SSS 71
👥 U–WD/WE SOC–WD/WE
£€ £19 D–£24 (£27)
🚗 11 miles N of Northampton, nr
A5199/A14 Junction 1. 7 miles E of
M1 Junction 18
⊕ Driving range
🏠 David Croxton
💻 www.coldashbygolfclub.com

Collingtree Park Golf
Course   (1990)
Proprietary
Windingbrook Lane, Northampton,
NN4 0XN
☎ **(01604) 700000**
📠 (01604) 702600
📧 enquiries@collingtreeparkgolf.com
📖 900
♉ Kevin Whitehouse (Dir of
Golf) Les Pullan (Sec)
✒ Geoff Pook, Brian Mudge
🏌 18 L 6776 yds SSS 72

👥 H SOC WD WE (after 12.30)
£€ £40
🚗 ¹/₂ mile E of M1 Junction 15
⊕ Floodlit driving range
🏠 Johnny Miller
💻 www.collingtreeparkgolf.com

Daventry & District   (1907)
Norton Road, Daventry, NN11 2LS
☎ **(01327) 702829**
📧 ddgc@hotmail.co.uk
📖 350
♉ Colin Long
✒ None
🏌 9 L 5812 yds Par 69 SSS 68
👥 WD–U Sun–NA before 11am
SOC–phone Sec
£€ £15 (£20)
🚗 ¹/₂ mile E of Daventry
⊕ Practice area; putting green

Delapre   (1976)
Pay and play
Eagle Drive, Nene Valley Way,
Northampton, NN4 7DU
☎ **(01604) 764036**
📠 (01604) 706378
📧 delapre@jbgolf.co.uk
📖 350
♉ Andrew Coleman (Mgr)
(01604) 764036
✒ J Cuddihy/M Chapman (Teaching
Pro), A Coleman (Head Pro)
🏌 Oaks 18 L 6299 yds SSS 70
Hardingstone 9 L 2109 yds SSS 32
2 x 9 holes Par 3 courses
👥 U SOC
£€ £14.50, £16 Fri (£18.50) Online
booking available
🚗 3 miles from M1 Junction 15, on
A508/A45
⊕ Pitch & putt. Driving range; Srixon
range balls
🏠 Jacobs/Corby
💻 www.jackbarker.com

Farthingstone Hotel   (1974)
Farthingstone, Towcester, NN12 8HA
☎ **(01327) 361291**
📠 (01327) 361645
📧 interest@farthingstone.co.uk
📖 350
♉ DC Donaldson (Prop/Mgr)
✒ M Gallagher (01327) 361533
🏌 18 L 6299 yds SSS 70
👥 U SOC
£€ £20 D–£32 (£28 D–£40) SOC–£20
🚗 4 miles W of A5 on Farthingstone-
Everdon road. M1 Junction 16, 6
miles
💻 www.farthingstone.co.uk

Hellidon Lakes Hotel G&CC
(1991)
Hellidon, Daventry, NN11 6GG
☎ **(01327) 262550**

Kettering   (1891)
Headlands, Kettering, NN15 6XA
☎ **(01536) 511104**
📠 (01536) 523788
📧 secretary@kettering-golf.co.uk

630 95(L) 50(J)
🏊 JM Gilding (01536) 511104
✓ K Theobald (01536) 481014
⊳ 18 L 6057 yds SSS 69
👤 WD–U WE/BH–M SOC
££ £36 D–£45 2–fore–I accepted
⊛ Jct 8 of A14, follow signs
⊕ Two large practice areas
🏠 Tom Morris
▤ www.kettering-golf.co.uk

Kingfisher Hotel   (1995)
Proprietary
Buckingham Road, Deanshanger, Milton Keynes, MK19 6JY
☎ **(01908) 560354/562332**
🖥 (01908) 260857
✉ sales.kingfisher@btopenworld.com
🛏 98
🏊 Roland Carlish
✓ B Mudge
⊳ 9 L 5552 yds Par 70 SSS 67 (18 tees)
👤 U SOC
££ 9: £9.50 (£12.50) 18: £14 (£17)
⊛ NW of Milton Keynes on A422 to Buckingham. M1 Junction 15
⊕ Driving range
🏠 Donald Steel
▤ www.kingfisher-hotelandgolf.co.uk

Kingsthorpe   (1908)
Kingsley Road, Northampton, NN2 7BU
☎ **(01604) 711173**
🖥 (01604) 710610
✉ secretary@kingsthorpe-golf.co.uk
🛏 600
🏊 S Wade (01604) 710610
✓ P Armstrong (01604) 719602
⊳ 18 L 5903 yds SSS 69
👤 WD–U WE/BH–M H SOC–WD
££~ £30 D–£40
⊛ 2 miles N of Northampton centre, off A508
⊕ Putting green
🏠 Alison /Colt
▤ www.kingsthorpe-golf.co.uk

Northampton   (1893)
Harlestone, Northampton, NN7 4EF
☎ **(01604) 845155**
🖥 (01604) 820262
✉ golf@northamptongolfclub.co.uk
🛏 700
🏊 Gavin Reed
✓ B Randall (01604) 845167
⊳ 18 L 6615 yds Par 72 SSS 72
👤 H WD–U (except Weds) WE–M SOC–WD (except Weds)
££ D–£40
⊛ 4 miles NW of Northampton, on A428 beyond Harlestone
🏠 Donald Steel
▤ www.northamptongolfclub.co.uk

Northamptonshire County   (1909)
Church Brampton, Northampton, NN6 8AZ
☎ **(01604) 843025**
🖥 (01604) 843463
✉ secretary@countygolfclub.org.uk
🛏 650
🏊 Peter Walsh (01604) 843025

✓ T Rouse (01604) 842226
⊳ 18 L 6721 yds Par 70 SSS 73
+3 holes +6 holes Par 3 course
👤 H SOC
££ Summer: 18 £45, 27/36 £55
Winter: £35
⊛ 5 miles NW of Northampton, between A428 and A50
⊕ Driving range; Par 3 Course
🏠 HS Colt
▤ www.countygolfclub.org.uk

Oundle   (1893)
Benefield Road, Oundle, PE8 4EZ
☎ **(01832) 273267**
🖥 (01832) 273008
✉ office@oundlegolfclub.com
🛏 630
🏊 L Quantrill (01832) 272267
✓ R Keys (01832) 272267
⊳ 18 L 6265 yds Par 72 SSS 70
👤 WD–U H WE–M before 10.30am –U H after 10.30am SOC
££ £26.50 D–£35.50 (£30.50)
⊛ 1½ miles W of Oundle on A427
▤ www.oundlegolfclub.com

Overstone Park   (1994)
Proprietary
Overstone Park Ltd, Billing Lane, Northampton, NN6 0A5
☎ **(01604) 647666**
🖥 (01604) 642635
✉ enquiries@overstonepark.com
🛏 450
🏊 Allan McLundie (Gen Mgr)
✓ S Kier (01604) 643555
⊳ 18 L 6462 yds SSS 72
👤 WD–U SOC
££ £30 (£40)
⊛ 4 miles E of Northampton, off A45. M1 Junction 15
⊕ Practice area
🏠 Donald Steel
▤ www.overstonepark.com

Priors Hall   (1965)
Public
Stamford Road, Weldon, Corby, NN17 3JH
☎ **(01536) 260756**
🖥 (01536) 260756
✉ p.ackroyd1@btinternet.com
🛏 300
🏊 P Ackroyd
✓ G Bradbrook
⊳ 18 L 6631 yds SSS 72
👤 U SOC–WD+WE
££ On application
⊛ 4 miles E of Corby (A43)
⊕ Practice nets; buggies
🏠 Hawtree

Rushden   (1919)
Kimbolton Road, Chelveston, Wellingborough, Northamptonshire NN9 6AN
☎ **(01933) 418511**
🖥 (01933) 418511
✉ secretary@rushdengolfclub.org
🛏 400
🏊 EJ Williams
✓ Adrian Clifford (07710) 759265
⊳ 10 L 6249 yds Par 71 SSS 70

👤 WD–U exc Wed pm WE/BH–M SOC
££ £25
⊛ On B645, 2 miles E of Higham Ferrers
▤ www.rushdengolfclub.org

Staverton Park   (1977)
Staverton Park, Staverton, Daventry, NN11 6JT
☎ **(01327) 302000/302118**

Stoke Albany   (1995)
Proprietary
Ashley Road, Stoke Albany, Market Harborough, LE16 8PL
☎ **(01858) 535208**
🖥 (01858) 535505
✉ info@stokealbanygolfclub.co.uk
🛏 450
🏊 R Want
✓ A Clifford (07710) 759265
⊳ 18 L 6175 yds Par 71 SSS 70
👤 U SOC
££ D–£20 (£25 before 11, £23 after 11)
⊛ Between Market Harborough and Corby (A427)
⊕ Large practice area and putting green
🏠 Hawtree
▤ www.stokealbanygolfclub.com

Wellingborough   (1893)
Harrowden Hall, Great Harrowden, Wellingborough, NN9 5AD
☎ **(01933) 677234/673022**
🖥 (01933) 679379
✉ david.waite @wellingboroughgolfclub.com
🛏 850
🏊 David Waite (01933) 677234
✓ D Clifford (01933) 678752
⊳ 18 L 6721 yds SSS 72
👤 WD–U H exc Tues WE–M SOC–WD exc Tues
££ £36 D–£48
⊛ 2 miles N of Wellingborough on A509
⊕ No metal spikes May 1-Oct 31
🏠 Hawtree
▤ www.wellingboroughgolfclub.org

Whittlebury Park G&CC   (1992)
Whittlebury, Towcester, NN12 8WP
☎ **(01327) 850000**
✉ enquiries@whittlebury.com

Northumberland

Allendale   (1906)
High Studdon, Allenheads Road, Allendale, Hexham NE47 9DH
☎ **(0700) 580 8246**
🛏 96
🏊 N Harris (Hon)
⊳ 9 L 4541 yds Par 66 SSS 64
👤 U
££ D–£12 (D–£15) 2008

⊶ 1½ miles S of Allendale on B6295
🖰 www.allendale-golf.co.uk

Alnmouth   (1869)
Foxton Hall, Alnmouth, NE66 3BE
☎ **(01665) 830231**
🖳 (01665) 830922
✉ secretary@alnmouthgolfclub.com
🕮 750
♘ H Sutherland
✎ Shop (01665) 830043
🏌 18 L 6484 yds SSS 71
👥 Mon/Tues/Wed/Thurs/Sun–H SOC
££ £30 D–£40 (£35)
⊶ 5 miles SE of Alnwick
⊕ Dormy House
♙ HS Colt
🖰 www.alnmouthgolfclub.com

Alnmouth Village   (1869)
Marine Road, Alnmouth, NE66 2RZ
☎ **(01665) 830370**
✉ bobhill53@live.co.uk
🕮 340
♘ R A Hill (01665) 833189
🏌 9 L 6020 yds SSS 70
👥 U
££ £20 (£20)
⊶ Alnmouth
♙ Mungo Park
🖰 www.alnmouthvillagegolfclub.co.uk

Alnwick   (1907)
Swansfield Park, Alnwick, NE66 1AB
☎ **(01665) 602632**
✉ neil@neil448.orangehome.co.uk
🕮 400
♘ The Secretary (01665) 605725
🏌 18 L 6250 yds SSS 70
👥 U
££ D–£20 (D–£25)
⊶ Alnwick, off A1
♙ Rochester/Rae
🖰 www.alnwick-golfclub.co.uk

Arcot Hall   (1909)
Dudley, Cramlington, NE23 7QP
☎ **(0191) 236 2794**
🖳 (0191) 217 0370
✉ arcothall@tiscali.co.uk
🕮 700
♘ F Elliott (0191) 236 2794
✎ G Nicholls (0191) 236 2794
🏌 18 L 6389 yds SSS 70
👥 WD–H WE SOC
££ D–£28 (£32) After 3pm–£23
⊶ 7 miles N of Newcastle, off A1
♙ James Braid
🖰 www.arcothallgolfclub.com

Bamburgh Castle   (1904)
The Club House, 40 The Wynding,
Bamburgh, NE69 7DE
☎ **(01668) 214378**
🖳 (01668) 214607
✉ sec@bamburghcastlegolfclub.co.uk
🕮 730
♘ MND Robinson (01668) 214321
🏌 18 L 5621 yds Par 68 SSS 67
👥 WD–U H WE/BH– NA before
noon SOC
££ £35 (£40)
⊶ 5 miles E of A1, via B1341 or
B1342

♘ George Rochester
🖰 www.bamburghcastlegolfclub.co.uk

Bedlingtonshire   (1972)
Acorn Bank, Hartford Road, Bedlington,
NE22 6AA
☎ **(01670) 822457**
🖳 (01670) 823048
✉ secretary@bedlingtongolfclub.com
🕮 820
♘ J Laverick (01670) 822457
✎ M Webb (01670) 822457
🏌 18 L 6224 metres SSS 73
👥 U SOC
££ £25 (£35)
⊶ 12 miles N of Newcastle (A1068)
♙ Frank Pennink
🖰 www.bedlingtongolfclub.com

The Belford   (1993)
South Road, Belford, NE70 7DP
☎ **(01668) 213323**
🖳 (01668) 213282
🕮 250
♙ HS Adair
🏌 9 L 6412 yds SSS 71 (18 tee boxes)
👥 U SOC
££ 9: £14 (£16); 18: £20 (£22)
⊶ 15 miles N of Alnwick, off A1
⊕ Driving range
♙ Nigel Williams
🖰 www.thebelford.com

Bellingham   (1893)
Boggle Hole, Bellingham, NE48 2DT
☎ **(01434) 220530/220152**
✉ admin@bellinghamgolfclub.com
🕮 400
♘ Jaimie Self
🏌 18 L 6093 yds Par 70 SSS 70
👥 U SOC
££ £25 (£30)
⊶ 15 miles N of Hexham, off B6320
⊕ Driving range
♙ I Wilson
🖰 www.bellinghamgolfclub.com

Berwick-upon-Tweed (Goswick)   (1890)
Goswick, Berwick-upon-Tweed, TD15 2RW
☎ **(01289) 387256**
🖳 (01289) 387392
✉ goswickgc@btconnect.com
🕮 700
♘ IAM Alsop
✎ P Terras (01289) 387380
🏌 18 L 6803 yds SSS 72
👥 WD–U 9.30–11.30am & after 2pm
WE–U 10–11.30am & after 2.30pm
SOC
££ £33 D–£42 (£38 D–£48)
⊶ 5 miles S of Berwick, off A1
⊕ Driving range and large practice
area
♙ James Braid
🖰 www.goswicklinksgc.co.uk

Blyth   (1905)
New Delaval, Blyth, NE24 4DB
☎ **(01670) 540110**
🖳 (01670) 540134
✉ clubmanager@blythgolf.co.uk

🕮 800
♘ J Ritson
✎ A Brown (01670) 356514
🏌 18 L 6424 yds SSS 71
👥 WD–U before 4pm WE/BH–U
after 11.30am SOC
££ £23.50 D–£30 (£26)
⊶ 10 miles NE of Newcastle. Close
to Northumberland Spine Road
A189
♙ J Hamilton Stutt
🖰 www.blythgolf.co.uk

Burgham Park Golf and Leisure Club   (1994)
Felton, Morpeth, NE65 9QP
☎ **(01670) 787898**
🖳 (01670) 787164
✉ info@burghampark.co.uk
🕮 570
♘ William Kiely
✎ D Mather (01670) 787898
🏌 18 L 6804 yds SSS 72 Par 72
Championship Tee 7065 Par 71
SSS 74
👥 U SOC
££ £26 (£32)
⊶ 7 miles N of Morpeth on A1
⊕ Pitch & putt course; driving range.
Home to the North Region PGA
Championship, Putting Green
♙ Andrew Mair/Mark James
🖰 www.burghampark.co.uk

Close House Country Club   (1968)
Proprietary
Close House, Heddon-on-the-Wall,
Newcastle-upon-Tyne, NE15 0HT
☎ **(01661) 852953**
🖳 (01661) 853322
✉ events@closehouse.co.uk
🕮 900
♘ John Glendinning
✎ Jonathan Greenwood
🏌 18 L 5956 yds Par 70 SSS 70
👥 U–SOC
££ £25 (£35)
⊶ 9 miles W of Newcastle on A69
⊕ Driving range; buggies
♙ Hawtree
🖰 www.closehouse.co.uk

Dunstanburgh Castle   (1900)
Embleton, NE66 3XQ
☎ **(01665) 576562**
✉ enquiries@dunstanburgh.com

Hexham   (1892)
Spital Park, Hexham, NE46 3RZ
☎ **(01434) 603072**
🖳 (01434) 601865
✉ info@hexhamgolf.co.uk
🕮 750
♘ Dawn Wylie (01434) 603072
✎ Ben West
🏌 18 L 6272 yds SSS 70
👥 U
££ £35 (£45)
⊶ 21 miles W of Newcastle (A69)
♙ Vardon/Caird
🖰 www.hexhamgolf.co.uk

For list of abbreviations and key to symbols see page 647

Linden Hall   (1997)

Proprietary
Longhorsley, Morpeth, NE65 8XF
☎ **(01670) 500011**
🖀 (01670) 500001
✉ golf@lindenhall.co.uk
📖 303
🏌 G Dixon (Director of
    Golf) (01670) 500000
⛳ G Morrison (01670) 500011
▷ 18 L 6846 yds Par 72 SSS 73
👥 U SOC WD WE
££ £36 (£48)
⊕ 8 miles NW of Morpeth, off A697
⊕ Driving range
🏠 Jonathan Gaunt
🖥 www.macdonaldhotels.co.uk
    /lindenhall

Longhirst Hall Golf Course
(1997)

Longhirst Hall, Longhirst, NE61 3LL
☎ **(01670) 791562 (Clubhouse)**
    (01670) 791562 (Admin)
🖀 (01670) 791768
✉ enquiries@longhirstgolf.co.uk
📖 1400
🏌 Graham Chambers (01670) 791562
⛳ G Cant (07946) 474370 Wayne
    Tyrie (07804) 972985
▷ The Lakes 18 L 6101 yds
    White tees Par 70
    Dawson 18 L 6713 yds
    White tees Par 72
    Old Course (Nov-Mar) 18 L
    6572 yds
👥 U SOC
££ £30, £20, £15 (depending on tee
    time) subject to review
⊕ 4 miles NE of Morpeth, via
    A197/B1337
⊕ Driving range; Chipping Green;
    Two practice Putting Greens
🏠 B Poole
🖥 www.longhirstgolf.co.uk

Magdalene Fields   (1903)

Pay and play
*Magdalene Fields, Berwick-upon-Tweed,
TD15 1NE*
☎ **(01289) 306130**
🖀 (01289) 306384
✉ mail@magdalene-fields.co.uk
📖 330
🏌 MJ Lynch
▷ 18 L 6407 yds SSS 71
👥 U SOC
££ £22 (£26) D–£30 (£32)
⊕ Berwick-upon-Tweed 1 mile
🏠 Park/Jefferson/Thompson
🖥 www.magdalene-fields.co.uk

Matfen Hall Hotel   (1994)

Matfen, Hexham, NE20 0RH
☎ **(01661) 886500 (Hotel)**
    (01661) 886400 (Bookings)
🖀 (01661) 886055
✉ golf@matfenhall.com
📖 500
🏌 D Burton
⛳ J Harrison (01661) 886146
▷ 18 L 6700 yds Par 72
    9 hole Par 3 course

👥 WD–U WE–U after 11am
££ £35 (£40)
⊕ 12 miles W of Newcastle, off
    B6318
⊕ Driving range; new 9 holes opening
    May 2007
🏠 Mair/James/Gaunt
🖥 www.matfenhall.com

Morpeth   (1906)

The Clubhouse, Morpeth, NE61 2BT
☎ **(01670) 504942**
🖀 (01670) 504918
✉ morpethgolfclub@btconnect.com
📖 800
🏌 Terry Minett
⛳ MR Jackson (01670) 515675
▷ 18 L 5834 metres SSS 70
👥 SOC
££ £27 (£37)
⊕ 1 mile S of Morpeth on A197
🏠 Harry Vardon
🖥 www.morpethgolf.co.uk

Newbiggin   (1884)

Newbiggin-by-the-Sea, NE64 6DW
☎ **(01670) 817344 (Clubhouse)**
✉ info@newbiggingolfclub.co.uk
📖 500
🏌 J Storey
⛳ James Kerr
▷ 18 L 6516 yds SSS 71
👥 U after 10am exc comp days SOC
    by arrangement with Sec
££ D–£20 (D–£27)
⊕ Newbiggin, nr Church Point
🏠 Willie Park
🖥 www.newbiggingolfclub.co.uk

Percy Wood Golf &
Country Retreat   (1993)

Coast View, Swarland, Morpeth, NE65 9JG
☎ **(01670) 787940 (Clubhouse)**
✉ enquiries@percywood.com
📖 400
🏌 (01670) 787010
⛳ Peter Ritchie Shop (01670) 787010
▷ 18 L 6628 yds SSS 72
👥 U
££ £20 (£25)
⊕ 8 miles S of Alnwick, 1 mile W of A1
⊕ Log Cabin Accommodation,
    Floodlit Driving Range
🖥 www.percywood.co.uk

Ponteland   (1927)

*53 Bell Villas, Ponteland, Newcastle-upon-
Tyne, NE20 9BD*
☎ **(01661) 822689**
🖀 (01661) 860077
✉ secretary@thepontelandgolfclub
    .co.uk
📖 480 170(L) 115(J)
🏌 C Espiner
⛳ A Robson-Crosby
▷ 18 L 6587 yds SSS 72
👥 WD–U SOC–Tues & Thurs
££ £30
⊕ 6 miles NW of Newcastle on
    A696, nr Airport
🖥 www.thepontelandgolfclub.co.uk

Prudhoe   (1930)

*Eastwood Park, Prudhoe-on-Tyne,
NE42 5DX*
☎ **(01661) 832466 ext 20**
🖀 (01661) 830710
✉ secretary@prudhoegolfclub.co.uk
📖 500
🏌 ID Pauw
⛳ J Crawford (01661) 832466 ext 23
▷ 18 L 5839 yds SSS 69
👥 WD–U WE–NA before 3pm SOC
££ £24 (£32)
⊕ 12 miles W of Newcastle (A1/A695
    junction)
🖥 www.prudhoegolfclub.co.uk

Rothbury   (1891)

*Whitton Bank Road, Rothbury, Morpeth,
NE65 7RX*
☎ **(01669) 621271**
✉ secretary@rothburygolfclub.com
📖 300
🏌 LF Brown (0191) 215 0268
⛳ None
▷ 18 L 6160 yds Par 71
👥 Members only until 9.30pm and Fri
    after 4.30 otherwise H, SOC
££ £25 (£30)
⊕ 15 miles N of Morpeth on A697. S
    side of Rothbury
⊕ Practice field and bunker
🏠 JB Radcliffe
🖥 www.rothburygolfclub.com

Seahouses   (1913)

Beadnell Road, Seahouses, NE68 7XT
☎ **(01665) 720794**
🖀 (01665) 721799
✉ secretary@seahousesgolf.co.uk
📖 500
🏌 Angela Clough
▷ 18 L 5542 yds SSS 66
👥 U SOC
££ £24 (£32 +Bank Hols)
⊕ 14 miles N of Alnwick. 9 miles E of
    A1 on B1340
⊕ Practice area; Trolley and Club
    hire.
🖥 www.seahousesgolf.co.uk

De Vere Slaley Hall   (1988)

Slaley, Hexham, NE47 0BX
☎ **(01434) 673154**
🖀 (01434) 673350
✉ slaley.hall@devere-hotels.com
📖 350
🏌 M Stancer (Golf Mgr)
⛳ M Stancer (01434) 673350
▷ Hunting 18 L 7073 yds Par 72
    SSS 71-74
    Priestman 18 L 6951 Par 72 SSS 71-
    74
👥 U SOC
££ Hunting: Low season £40, High
    season £80; Priestman: Low season
    £32, High season £45
⊕ 20 miles W of Newcastle. 7 miles S
    of Corbridge, off A68
⊕ Driving range. Golf Academy
🏠 Hunting-Dave Thomas. Priestman-
    Neil Coles
🖥 www.devere.co.uk

Stocksfield (1913)

New Ridley, Stocksfield, NE43 7RE
- ☎ **(01661) 843041**
- ☖ (01661) 843046
- ✉ info@sgcgolf.co.uk
- ☷ 570 70(L) 160(J)
- ✎ S Harrison
- ⏵ 18 L 5991 yds SSS 70
- ☷ U SOC–exc Wed am
- ££ £20 D–£25 (£25)
- ⬡ Off A695 at Branch End, 3 miles E of A68
- ⌂ F Pennink
- ▤ www.sgcgolf.co.uk

Warkworth (1891)

The Links, Warkworth, Morpeth, NE65 0SW
- ☎ **(01665) 711596**
- ☷ 400
- ✎ J A Gray
- ⏵ 9 L 5986 yds Par 70 SSS 69
- ☷ U exc Tues & Sat SOC
- ££ D–£15 (D–£20)
- ⬡ 9 miles SE of Alnwick (A1068)
- ⌂ Old Tom Morris

Wooler (1975)

Dod Law, Doddington, Wooler, NE71 6AL
- ☎ **(01668) 282135**

Nottinghamshire

Beeston Fields (1923)

Beeston, Nottingham, NG9 3DD
- ☎ **(0115) 925 7062**
- ☖ (0115) 925 4280
- ✉ beestonfields@btconnect.com
- ☷ 470 100(L) 60(J)
- ✎ J Lewis
- ✎ A Wardle (0115) 925 7062
- ⏵ 18 L 6404 yds SSS 71
- ☷ U H SOC
- ££ £34 D–£43 (£39)
- ⬡ 4 m W of Nottingham. M1 Jct 25
- ⌂ Tom Williamson
- ▤ www.beestonfields.co.uk

Brierley Forest (1993)

Main Street, Huthwaite, Sutton-in-Ashfield, NG17 2LG
- ☎ **(01623) 550761**
- ☖ (01623) 550761
- ☷ 400
- ✎ D Crafts (01623) 514234
- ✎ T Liegh
- ⏵ 18 L 6008 yds Par 72 SSS 69
- ☷ WD–U bookings only WE–U before noon
- ££ £10 (£15)
- ⬡ W of Sutton-in-Ashfield. M1 Junction 28, 2 miles
- ⌂ Dave Hibbert, Malc Walsh, P Roberts

Bulwell Forest (1902)

Hucknall Road, Bulwell, Nottingham, NG6 9LQ
- ☎ **(0115) 977 0576 (Professional & Sec)**

- ☖ (0115) 976 3172 (Clubhouse & F
- ✉ secretarybfgc@hotmail.co.uk
- ☷ 350
- ✎ J Bush
- ✎ B Hurt
- ⏵ 18 L 5746 yds Par 68 SSS 68
- ☷ U SOC
- ££ £14 (£17)
- ⬡ 4 miles N of Nottingham. M1 Junction 26, 3 miles
- ▤ www.bulwellforestgolfclub.co.uk

Chilwell Manor (1906)

Meadow Lane, Chilwell, Nottingham, NG9 5AE
- ☎ **(0115) 925 8958**
- ☖ (0115) 922 0575
- ✉ info@chilwellmanorgolfclub.co.uk
- ☷ 700
- ✎ C Lawrence
- ✎ P Wilson (0115) 925 8993
- ⏵ 18 L 6028 yds Par 70 SSS 71
- ☷ U SOC
- ££ £25 D–£30 (£30)
- ⬡ 4 miles W of Nottingham on A6005
- ⌂ Tom Williamson
- ▤ www.chilwellmanorgolfclub.co.uk

College Pines (1994)

Proprietary
Worksop College Drive, Sparken Hill, Worksop, S80 3AL
- ☎ **(01909) 501431**
- ☖ (01909) 481227
- ✉ snelljunior@btinternet.com
- ☷ 550
- ✎ C Snell (Golf Dir)
- ✎ C Snell (01909) 501431
- ⏵ 18 L 6801 yds SSS 73
- ☷ U–phone first SOC
- ££ £16 round, £22 w/e (£24day/ £3
- ⬡ 1 mile SE of Worksop on B6034, off Worksop Bypass
- ⊕ Driving range; buggies for hire
- ⌂ David Snell
- ▤ www.collegepinesgolfclub.co.uk

Cotgrave Place G&CC (1991)

Stragglethorpe, Nr Cotgrave Village, Cotgrave, NG12 3HB
- ☎ **(0115) 933 3344**
- ✉ cotgrave@crown-golf.co.uk

Coxmoor (1913)

Coxmoor Road, Sutton-in-Ashfield, NG17 5LF
- ☎ **(01623) 557359**
- ☖ (01623) 557435
- ✉ secretary@coxmoorgolfclub.co.uk
- ☷ 650
- ✎ P Snow
- ✎ C Wright (01623) 557359/559906
- ⏵ 18 L 6577 yds SSS 72
- ☷ H WE–NA SOC–WD
- ££ £45 D–£58
- ⬡ 1½ miles S of Mansfield. 4 miles NE of M1 Junction 27 on A611
- ⊕ Practice nets/area
- ⌂ Tom Williamson
- ▤ www.coxmoorgolfclub.co.uk

Edwalton (1982)

Wellin Lane, Edwalton, Nottingham NG12 4AS
- ☎ **(0115) 923 4775**
- ☖ (0115) 923 1647
- ✉ edwalton@glendale-services.co.uk
- ☷ 700
- ✎ Mrs DJ Parkes (Hon) (0115) 914 8978
- ✎ L Rawlings
- ⏵ 9 L 3336 yds SSS 36 9 hole Par 3 course
- ☷ U SOC
- ££ £7.95 (£8.95)
- ⬡ 2 miles S of Nottingham (A606)
- ⊕ Driving range/practice facilities; putting green; buggy and club hire
- ▤ www.glendale-golf.com

Hucknall Golf Centre (1994)

Pay and play
Wigwam Lane, Hucknall, NG15 7TA
- ☎ **(0115) 964 2037**
- ☖ (0115) 964 2724
- ✉ leen@jbgolf.co.uk
- ☷ 200
- ✎ Maureen Foodman
- ✎ Cyril Jepson (07919) 853375
- ⏵ 18 L 6102 yds Par 70 SSS 69
- ☷ U SOC, WD, WE
- ££ £12.50 (£15 +BH)
- ⬡ ½ mile from Hucknall town centre
- ⊕ Driving Range on site.
- ⌂ Tom Hodgetts
- ▤ www.jackbarker.com

Kilton Forest (1978)

Public
Blyth Road, Worksop, S81 0TL
- ☎ **(01909) 486563**
- ☷ 300
- ✎ JA Eyre (Hon)
- ✎ S Betteridge (01909) 486563
- ⏵ 18 L 6424 yds Par 72 SSS 71
- ☷ WD–U WE–booking necessary SOC
- ££ £12 (£15.50)
- ⬡ 1 mile NE of Worksop on B6045

Mapperley (1907)

Central Avenue, Plains Road, Mapperley, Nottingham, NG3 6RH
- ☎ **(0115) 955 6672**
- ☖ (0115) 955 6670
- ✉ secretary@mapperleygolfclub.org
- ☷ 735
- ✎ Michael Mulhern
- ✎ Jon Newham (0115) 955 6672
- ⏵ 18 L 6307 yds SSS 70
- ☷ U H SOC WD + Sundays
- ££ £27 (£30)
- ⬡ 3 miles NE of Nottingham, off B684
- ⌂ J Mason
- ▤ www.mapperleygolfclub.org

Newark (1901)

Coddington, Newark, NG24 2QX
- ☎ **(01636) 626282**
- ☖ (01636) 626497
- ✉ manager@newarkgolfclub.co.uk
- ☷ 650
- ✎ DA Collingwood (01636) 626282

For list of abbreviations and key to symbols see page 647

✓ PA Lockley (01636) 626492
Teaching Professional
⊵ 18 L 6458 yds SSS 71
👥 H SOC
££ £36 (£42)
⊕ 4 miles E of Newark on A17
⊕ Driving range on site
🏠 Tom Williamson
🖥 www.newarkgolfclub.co.uk

Norwood Park (1999)

Norwood Park, Southwell, NG25 0PF
☎ (01636) 816626
🖂 golf@norwoodpark.co.uk
🛄 600
🏌 Ron Beckett
✓ P Thornton (01636) 816626
⊵ 18 L 6805 yds Par 72 SSS 72
9 L 1364 yds Par 27
👥 U SOC
££ Mon–Thur £20 D–£32 Fri £24
D–£38 Sat–Sun £28 D–£44
⊕ ½ mile W of Southwell, off
Kirklington road. Nearest road
A617/612
⊕ Driving range; buggies; par 3
academy course
🏠 Clyde Johnston
🖥 www.norwoodpark.org.uk

Nottingham City (1910)

Public
Norwich Gardens, Bulwell, Nottingham,
NG6 8LF
☎ (0115) 927 2767 (Pro Shop)
🛄 460
🏌 GJ Chappell (0115) 927 2606
⊵ 18 L 6218 yds SSS 70
👥 WD–U WE–U SOC
££ £12.50 (£16)
⊕ 5 miles N of Nottingham. M1 Jct 26

Notts (1887)

Hollinwell, Kirkby-in-Ashfield, NG17 7QR
☎ (01623) 753225
🖳 (01623) 753655
🖂 office@nottsgolfclub.co.uk
🛄 330
🏌 JB Noble (Mgr)
✓ M Bradley (01623) 753087
⊵ 18 L 7250 yds Par 72 SSS 76
👥 WD–H WE/BH–M
££ £70 D–£100
⊕ 4 miles S of Mansfield on A611. M1
Junction 27
⊕ Driving range-green fees only
🏠 Willie Park Jr
🖥 www.nottsgolfclub.co.uk

Oakmere Park (1974)

Oaks Lane, Oxton, NG25 0RH
☎ (0115) 965 3545
🖳 (0115) 965 5628
🖂 enquiries@oakmerepark.co.uk
🛄 450
🏌 D St-John Jones
✓ D St-John Jones (0115) 965 3545
⊵ 18 L 6617 yds SSS 72
9 L 3495 yds SSS 37
👥 WD–U WE/BH–arrange times with
Mgr SOC
££ 9: £8 (£12); 18: £22 (£32)
⊕ 8 miles NE of Nottingham on A614

⊕ Floodlit driving range
🏠 F Pennink
🖥 www.oakmerepark.co.uk

Radcliffe-on-Trent (1909)

Dewberry Lane, Cropwell Road, Radcliffe-
on-Trent, NG12 2JH
☎ (0115) 933 3000
🖳 (0115) 911 6991
🖂 les.wake@radcliffeontrentgc.co.uk
🛄 700
🏌 L Wake
✓ C George
⊵ 18 L 6374 yds Par 70 SSS 71
👥 H SOC–Wed only
££ 18: £22 (£34); 18+: £37 (£42)
⊕ 6 miles E of Nottingham, off A52
🏠 Tom Williamson
🖥 www.radcliffeontrentgc.co.uk

Ramsdale Park Golf Centre (1992)

Pay and play
Oxton Road, Calverton, NG14 6NU
☎ (0115) 965 5600
🖳 (0115) 965 4105
🖂 info@ramsdaleparkgc.co.uk
🛄 400
🏌 N Birch (Mgr)
✓ R Macey
⊵ Seely: 18 L 6546 yds SSS 71
Lee: 18 hole Par 3 course
👥 U SOC–WD WE restricted
££ £20.50 D–£32 (£26)
⊕ 5 miles NE of Nottingham on
B6386. M1 Junction 27
⊕ 26 bay floodlit driving range
🏠 Hawtree
🖥 www.ramsdaleparkgc.co.uk

Retford (1921)

Brecks Road, Ordsall, Retford, DN22 7UA
☎ (01777) 703733
🖳 (01777) 710412
🖂 retfordgolfclub@lineone.net
🛄 500
🏌 Lesley Redfearn & Diane Moore
(01777) 711188
✓ C Morris
⊵ 18 L 6370 yds SSS 70
👥 WD–U WE–after 2pm SOC–WD
££ £30 D–£30 (£30)
⊕ 2 miles SW of Retford, off A638 or
A620. M1 Junction 30
🖥 www.retfordgolfclub.co.uk

Ruddington Grange (1988)

Wilford Road, Ruddington, Nottingham,
NG11 6NB
☎ (0115) 984 6141
🖳 (0115) 940 5165
🖂 info@ruddingtongrange.co.uk
🛄 700
🏌 P Deacon
✓ R Simpson (0115) 921 1951
⊵ 18 L 6515 yds SSS 72
👥 WD–U SOC
££ D–£25 (£30) D–£40
⊕ 3 miles S of Nottingham
🏠 J Small
🖥 www.ruddingtongrange.co.uk

Rufford Park G&CC

Rufford Lane, Rufford, Newark, NG22 9DG
☎ (01623) 825253
🖳 (01623) 825254
🖂 enquiries@ruffordpark.co.uk
🛄 500
🏌 Mrs K Whitehead (01623) 825253
✓ J Vaughan, J Thompson
⊵ 18 L 6368 yds Par 70 SSS 71
👥 U–booking necessary
SOC–WD/WEpm
££ £22 (£28)
⊕ Nr Rufford Abbey on A614. 8 miles
S of A1/A614 junction
⊕ Floodlit driving range
🏠 Ken Moodie/Ken Brown
🖥 www.ruffordpark.co.uk

Rushcliffe (1909)

Stocking Lane, East Leake, Loughborough,
LE12 5RL
☎ (01509) 852959
🖳 (01509) 852688
🖂 secretary@rushcliffegolfclub.com
🛄 720
🏌 C Bee
✓ C Hall (01509) 852701
⊵ 18 L 6193 yds SSS 71
👥 SOC–WD
££ £31 (£40)
⊕ 9 miles S of Nottingham. M1 Jct 24
🖥 www.rushcliffegolfclub.com

Serlby Park (1906)

Serlby, Doncaster, DN10 6BA
☎ (01777) 818268

Sherwood Forest (1895)

Eakring Road, Mansfield, NG18 3EW
☎ (01623) 626689/627403
🖳 (01623) 420412
🖂 info@sherwoodforestgolfclub
.co.uk
🛄 648
🏌 Maj Gary J Mason BEM
(01623) 626689
✓ K Hall (01623) 627403
⊵ 18 L 6860 yds SSS 74
👥 H SOC–WD
££ 18: £50; 32: £70
⊕ 2 miles E of Mansfield (A617)
⊕ Large practice areas
🏠 Harry S Colt/James Braid
🖥 www.sherwoodforestgolfclub.co.uk

Southwell (1993)

Proprietary
Southwell Racecourse, Rolleston, Newark,
NG25 0TS
☎ (01636) 813706/816501
🖳 (01636) 812271
🖂 info@southwellgolfclub.com
🛄 450
🏌 M Harness (01636) 821651
✓ Chris White (01636) 813706
⊵ 18 L 5767 yds Par 69 SSS 68
👥 U SOC
££ £18 (£21)
⊕ 6 miles W of Newark on A617.
Course adjacent to racetrack
🏠 RA Muddle
🖥 www.southwellgolfclub.com

Springwater   (1991)
Proprietary
Moor Lane, Calverton, Nottingham,
NG14 6FZ
☎ (0115) 965 4946
🖬 (0115) 965 2344
✉ dave.putlan@springwatergolfclub
  .com
🏛 450
♟ E Brady (0115) 952 3956
✓ P Drew (0115) 965 2129
⊳ 18 L 6262 yds Par 71
👤 H U SOC WD WE after 1.30pm
££ £22 (£27)
♠ Off A6097 between Lowdham and
  Oxton
⊕ Driving range
🏠 N Footit/P Wharmsby
🖥 www.springwatergolfclub.com

Stanton-on-the-Wolds
(1906)
Golf Course Road, Stanton-on-the-Wolds,
Nottingham, NG12 5BH
☎ (0115) 937 4885
🖬 (0115) 937 4885
✉ info@stantongc.co.uk
🏛 500 167(L) 100(J)
♟ MJ Price (0115) 937 1650
✓ N Hernon ((0115) 937 2390
⊳ 18 L 6421 yds SSS 71
👤 WD–U SOC exc comp days
  WE–M
££ On application
♠ 9 miles S of Nottingham
⊕ Practice field and putting green;
  Restaurant
🏠 T Williamson
🖥 www.stantongolfclub.co.uk

Trent Lock Golf Centre
(1991)
Lock Lane, Sawley, Long Eaton, NG10 2FY
☎ (0115) 946 4398
🖬 (0115) 946 1183
✉ trentlockgolf@aol.com
🏛 550
♟ R Prior (F & B Mgr)
✓ M Taylor
⊳ 18 L 5883 yds Par 69 SSS 68
  9 L 2911 yds Par 36
👤 U SOC
££ 9: £6 (£7.50) 18: £17.50 (£22.50)
  Summer rates
♠ S of Long Eaton. M1 Junction 25
⊕ Driving range, 22 bays; power tees
  (floodlit); custom fitting centre;
  short game area
🏠 E McCausland
🖥 www.trenlock.co.uk

Wollaton Park   (1927)
Wollaton Park, Nottingham, NG8 1BT
☎ (0115) 978 7574
🖬 (0115) 970 0736
✉ wollatonparkgc@aol.com
🏛 700
♟ Avril J Jamieson
✓ J Lower (0115) 978 4834
⊳ 18 L 6445 yds SSS 71
👤 U SOC
££ £37 (£42) D–£51 (D–£58)

♠ 2 miles SW of Nottingham. M1
  Junction 25, 5 miles
🏠 T Williamson
🖥 www.wollatonparkgolfclub.com

Worksop   (1911)
Windmill Lane, Worksop, S80 2SQ
☎ (01909) 477731
🖬 (01909) 530917
✉ thesecretary@worksopgolfclub.com
🏛 500
♟ DA Dufall (01909) 477731
✓ K Crossland
⊳ 18 L 6628 yds Par 72 SSS 72
👤 WD–H (phone first) WE/BH–M
  SOC
££ On application
♠ 1 mile SE of Worksop, off A6034
  via by-pass (A57). M1 Junction 30,
  9 miles
🖥 www.worksopgolfclub.com

Oxfordshire

Aspect Park   (1988)
Remenham Hill, Henley-on-Thames,
RG9 3EH
☎ (01491) 578306

Badgemore Park   (1972)
Proprietary
Henley-on-Thames, RG9 4NR
☎ (01491) 637300
🖬 (01491) 576899
✉ info@badgemorepark.com
🏛 600
♟ J Connell (Mgr) (01491) 637300
✓ J Dunn (01491) 574175
⊳ 18 L 6129 yds SSS 69
👤 WD–U exc Tue am–NA WE–U
  after noon SOC–Wed to Sun
££ £30 (£39) Twilight £25
♠ 1 mile NW of Henley on
  Rotherfield Greys road
⊕ Nets; Pitch + Putt areas.
🏠 B Sandow
🖥 www.badgemorepark.com

Banbury Golf Centre   (1993)
Aynho Road, Adderbury, Banbury,
OX17 3NT
☎ (01295) 810419
🖬 (01295) 810056
✉ office@banburygolfcentre.co.uk
🏛 350
♟ Mrs A Prestidge
✓ (01295) 812880
⊳ 27 holes:
  L 5766–6706 yds Par 72 SSS 72
👤 U SOC
££ £23 (£29)
♠ 6 miles S of Banbury on B4100.
  M40 Junction 10/11
🏠 Reed/Payn
🖥 www.banburygolfcentre.co.uk

Bicester G&CC   (1973)
Chesterton, Bicester, OX26 1TE
☎ (01869) 241204
✉ bicestergolf@ukonline.co.uk

Brailes   (1992)
Proprietary
Sutton Lane, Lower Brailes, Banbury,
OX15 5BB
☎ (01608) 685633
🖬 (01608) 685205
✉ office@brailesgolfclub.co.uk
🏛 580
♟ P Gibbs (Gen Mgr) (01608) 685336
✓ Mark McGeehan (07787) 937672
⊳ 18 L 6304 yds Par 71 SSS 70
👤 U SOC–WD anytime WE after
  noon
££ £25 (£35)
♠ 4 miles E of Shipston-on-Stour on
  B4035. M40 Junction 11, 10 miles
⊕ Golf Academy & driving range
🏠 R Baldwin
🖥 www.brailesgolfclub.co.uk

Burford   (1936)
Burford, OX18 4JG
☎ (01993) 822583
🖬 (01993) 822801
✉ secretary@burfordgolfclub.co.uk
🏛 785
♟ RP Thompson
✓ M Ridge (01993) 822344
⊳ 18 L 6401 yds SSS 71
👤 WD–H SOC
££ On application
♠ 19 miles W of Oxford on A40
🏠 JH Turner
🖥 www.burfordgolfclub.co.uk

Carswell CC   (1993)
Carswell, Faringdon, SN7 8PU
☎ (01367) 870422
🖬 (01367) 870592
✉ info@carswellgolfandcountryclub
  .co.uk
🏛 500
♟ G Lisi (Prop)
✓ John Strode
⊳ 18 L 6133 yds Par 72
👤 U SOC–WD
££ £20 (£28)
♠ 12 miles W of Oxford on A420
⊕ Floodlit driving range
🏠 J & E Ely
🖥 www.carswellgolfandcountryclub
  .co.uk

Cherwell Edge   (1980)
Chacombe, Banbury, OX17 2EN
☎ (01295) 711591
🖬 (01295) 713674
✉ enquiries@cherwelledgegolfclub
  .co.uk
🏛 530
♟ RA Beare (Sec)
  David Newman (Gen Mgr)
✓ Jason Roberts-Newman
⊳ 18 L 6085 yds SSS 69
👤 U SOC–WD WE after 11am
££ From £20 (from £25)
♠ 2 miles N M40 Jct 11 (see website)
⊕ Driving range
🖥 www.cherwelledgegolfclub.co.uk

Chipping Norton   (1890)
Southcombe, Chipping Norton, OX7 5QH

☎ **(01608) 642383**
🖳 (01608) 645422
📧 chipping.nortongc@virgin.net
📖 900
🏌 N Clayton
✓ N Rowlands (01608) 643356
🏁 18 L 6316 yds Par 71 SSS 70
🕴 WD–U WE–M
££ £32
⛳ 1 mile E of Chipping Norton on A44

Drayton Park (1992)
Pay and play
Steventon Road, Drayton, Abingdon, OX14 4la
☎ **(01235) 550607/528989**
🖳 (01235) 525731
📧 draytonpark@btclick.com
📖 400
🏌 Jon Northover (Gen Mgr)
✓ M Morbey (01235) 550607
🏁 18 L 6214 yds SSS 70
9 hole Par 3 course
🕴 U SOC
££ £20 (£26)
⛳ 10 miles S of Oxford on A34. M4 J13
⊕ Floodlit driving range; chipping green; putting green
🏠 Hawtree
🖳 www.draytonparkgolfclubabingdon .co.uk

Frilford Heath (1908)
Frilford Heath, Abingdon, OX13 5NW
☎ **(01865) 390864**
🖳 (01865) 390823
📧 secretary@frilfordheath.co.uk
📖 1350 210(L)
🏌 S Styles
✓ DC Craik (01865) 390887
🏁 Red 18 L 6961 yds SSS 73
Green 18 L 6006 yds SSS 69
Blue 18 L 6761 yds SSS 72
🕴 H SOC
££ £65 (£80)
⛳ 3 miles W of Abingdon on A338
🏠 Blue-Simon Gidman
🖳 www.frilfordheath.co.uk

Hadden Hill (1990)
Proprietary
Wallingford Road, Didcot, OX11 9BJ
☎ **(01235) 510410**
🖳 (01235) 511260
📧 info@haddenhillgolf.co.uk
📖 400 50(L)
🏌 A.C.Smith
✓ I Mitchell
🏁 18 L 6563 yds SSS 71
🕴 WD–U SOC–WD & WE WE–U
££ £20 (£25) D32
⛳ E of Didcot on A4130
⊕ Floodlit driving range, 6 hole par 3 course
🏠 MV Morley
🖳 www.haddenhillgolf.co.uk

Henley (1907)
Harpsden, Henley-on-Thames, RG9 4HG
☎ **(01491) 575742**
🖳 (01491) 412179
📧 info@henleygc.com
📖 750
🏌 Gary Oatham (01491) 635305
✓ Mark Howell (01491) 575710
🏁 18 L 6264 yds SSS 70
🕴 WD–H WE–M SOC
££ £48
⛳ 1 mile S of Henley (A4155)
⊕ 160 yd short game area by club. 350 yd driving range opening Spring 2009
🏠 James Braid
🖳 www.henleygc.com

Hinksey Heights (1995)
Public
South Hinksey, Oxford, OX1 5AB
☎ **(01865) 327775**
🖳 (01865) 736930
📧 play@oxford-golf.co.uk
📖 575
🏌 K McCallum (01865) 327775 ext 2
✓ D Davis (01865) 327775 ext 1
🏁 18 L 6936 yds Par 72 SSS 73
9 hole Par 3 course
9/18 L 5212 yds Par 70 SSS 65
🕴 U SOC
££ £20 (£26)
⛳ W of Oxford, off A34 at South Hinksey, between Oxford and Abingdon
⊕ Practice rang; golf academy
🏠 D Heads
🖳 www.oxford-golf.co.uk

Huntercombe (1901)
Nuffield, Henley-on-Thames, RG9 5SL
☎ **(01491) 641207**
🖳 (01491) 642060
📧 office@huntercombegolfclub.co.uk
📖 650
🏌 GNV Jenkins
✓ IM Roberts (01491) 641241
🏁 18 L 6271 yds SSS 70
🕴 H–by appointment only SOC– WD
££ £45 D–£60 (£60 D–£75)
⛳ 6 miles W of Henley on A4130
⊕ Practice ground
🏠 Willie Park Jr
🖳 www.huntercombegolfclub.co.uk

Kirtlington (1995)
Proprietary
Kirtlington, Oxon OX5 3JY
☎ **(01869) 351133**
🖳 (01869) 331143
📧 info@kirtlingtongolfclub.com
📖 450
🏌 P Smith (Sec/Mgr)
✓ Andy Taylor (0800) 587 2489
🏁 18 holes Par 70 SSS 69
9 hole Par 30
🕴 U SOC
££ £25 (£30)
⛳ 1 mile from Kirtlington on A4095. M40 Junction 9
⊕ Driving range; putting green; short game practice area
🏠 G Webster
🖳 www.kirtlingtongolfclub.com

North Oxford (1907)
Banbury Road, Oxford, OX2 8EZ
☎ **(01865) 554415**
🖳 (01865) 515921
📧 adminmanager@nogc.co.uk
📖 565
🏌 SC Smith (01865) 554924
✓ R Harris (01865) 553977
🏁 18 L 5689 yds SSS 67
🕴 WD–U SOC–WD exc Thurs
££ £28 D–£33 (£33 D–£42)
⛳ 4 miles N of Oxford, off A4260 to Kidlington
⊕ Practice nets, bunker and putting green
🏠 JH Turner
🖳 www.nogc.co.uk

The Oxfordshire (1993)
Proprietary
Rycote Lane, Milton Common, Thame, OX9 2PU
☎ **(01844) 278300**
🖳 (01844) 278003
📧 info@theoxfordshiregolfclub.com
📖 470
🏌 Mr M Harris
✓ Justin Barnes (01844) 278505
🏁 18 L 7187 yds Par 72 SSS 75
🕴 1 H before noon SOC WD WE–NA before noon
££ On application
⛳ 1½ miles W of Thame on A329. M40 Junction 7, 1½ miles. M40 Junction 8, 4 miles
⊕ Driving range
🏠 Rees Jones
🖳 www.theoxfordshiregolfclub.com

RAF Benson (1975)
Royal Air Force, Benson, Wallingford, OX10 6AA
☎ **(01491) 837766 Ext 7322**
📖 200
🏌 M Vincent (01491) 824342
🏁 9 L 4412 yds Par 63 SSS 61
🕴 M
££ £7 Daily
⛳ 3½ miles NE of Wallingford

Rye Hill (1992)
Proprietary
Milcombe, Banbury, OX15 4RU
☎ **(01295) 721818**
🖳 (01295) 720089
📧 info@ryehill.co.uk
📖 900
🏌 Tony Pennock
✓ T Pennock (01295) 721818
🏁 18 L 6919 yds Par 72 SSS 73 White Tees
🕴 U–booking necessary SOC
££ £28 D–£36 (£32 D–£55) Ask for special deals
⛳ 5 miles SW of Banbury, off A361. M40 Junction 11
⊕ Golf Parc, purpose-built junior golf facility inc. driving school
🖳 www.ryehill.co.uk

Southfield (1875)

Hill Top Road, Oxford, OX4 1PF
☎ **(01865) 242158**
📠 (01865) 250023
✉ sgcltd@btopenworld.com
📖 550
🏌 Colin Whittle (01865) 242158
🏌 A Rees (01865) 244258
▷ 18 L 6230 yds SSS 70
⚭ WD–U WE/BH–M H SOC
££ £40
⚙ 2 miles E of Oxford City Centre
⊕ Members practice area
🏠 HS Colt
🖥 www.southfieldgolf.com

The Springs Hotel & Golf Club (1998)

Proprietary
Wallingford Road, North Stoke, Wallingford, OX10 6BE
☎ **(01491) 827310**
📠 (01491) 827312
✉ proshop@thespringshotel.com
📖 600
🏌 D Allen (01491) 827315
🏌 D Boyce (01491) 827310
▷ 18 L 6470 yds Par 72 SSS 71
  18 L 5651 yds Par 72 SSS 72 (ladies)
⚭ By arrangement SOC; U of handicap standard
££ £29 D–£37 (£35 D–£45)
⚙ 2 miles SW of Wallingford on B4009. M40 Junction 6
⊕ Short game practice area; buggies, trollies, clubs for hire; tuition
🏠 Brian Huggett
🖥 www.thespringshotel.com

Studley Wood (1996)

Proprietary
The Straight Mile, Horton-cum-Studley, Oxford, OX33 1BF
☎ **(01865) 351144**
📠 (01865) 351166
✉ admin@swgc.co.uk
📖 600
🏌 Ken Heathcote (01865) 351144
🏌 Matt Avaun (01865) 351122
▷ 18 L 6722 yds Par 73 SSS 72
⚭ WD–U WE–NA before noon SOC
££ £37.50
⚙ 4 miles NE of Oxford. M40 J8 from London, J9 from Birmingham
⊕ Driving range. Golf academy
🏠 Simon Gidman
🖥 www.studleywoodgolfclub.co.uk

Tadmarton Heath (1922)

Wigginton, Banbury, OX15 5HL
☎ **(01608) 737278**
📠 (01608) 730548
✉ secretary@tadmartongolf.com
📖 520
🏌 JR Cox (01608) 737278
🏌 T Stubbs (01608) 730047
▷ 18 L 5936 yds Par 69 SSS 69
⚭ WD–H by appointment WE–M SOC–WD (Tue/Wed/Fri)
££ £45 (£50). After 10am–£40 (12 noon £40)

⚙ 5 miles SW of Banbury, off B4035
🏠 Maj CJ Hutchison
🖥 www.tadmartongolf.com

Waterstock (1994)

Pay and play
Thame Road, Waterstock, Oxford, OX33 1HT
☎ **(01844) 338093**
📠 (01844) 338036
✉ wgc_oxford@btinternet.com
📖 500
🏌 AJ Wyatt
🏌 P Bryant
▷ 18 L 6535 yds Par 72
⚭ U SOC
££ £23 D–£36 (£28 D–£43); 9–hole, day fees available and twilight fees available
⚙ E of Oxford on A418. M40 Jct 8 and Jct 8A
⊕ 22-bay floodlit driving range; practice putting green; grass practice area
🏠 Donald Steel
🖥 www.waterstockgolf.co.uk

Witney Lakes (1994)

Downs Road, Witney, OX29 0SY
☎ **(01993) 893011**
📠 (01993) 778866
✉ golf@witney-lakes.co.uk
📖 450
🏌 G Brown
🏌 John Cook
▷ 18 L 6460 yds SSS 71
⚭ U SOC WD/WE
££ £23 (£32)
⚙ 2 miles W of Witney on B4047
⊕ Floodlit driving range; John Cook School of Golf
🏠 Simon Gidman
🖥 www.witney-lakes.co.uk

The Wychwood (1992)

Proprietary
Lyneham, Chipping Norton, OX7 6QQ
☎ **(01993) 831841**
📠 (01993) 831775
✉ info@thewychwood.com
📖 650
🏌 Susan Lakin (administrator)
🏌 A Souter
▷ 18 L 6844 yds SSS 72
⚭ WD–U WE–U after 11am SOC
££ £27 (£32)
⚙ 4 miles W of Chipping Norton, off A361
⊕ Driving range; Catering facilities open to general public.
🏠 D Carpenter
🖥 www.thewychwood.com

Rutland

Greetham Valley (1992)

Greetham, Oakham, LE15 7NP
☎ **(01780) 460444**
📠 (01780) 460623
✉ info@greethamvalley.co.uk
📖 1000

🏌 RE Hinch
🏌 Neil Evans (01780) 460666
▷ 18 holes SSS 71
  18 holes SSS 68
  9 hole Par 3 course
⚭ U SOC–WD
££ £26 (£32)
⚙ 5 miles NE of Oakham (B668), nr A1
⊕ Floodlit driving range; 35 room hotel
🏠 B Stephens & FE Hinch
🖥 www.greethamvalley.co.uk

Luffenham Heath (1911)

Ketton, Stamford, PE9 3UU
☎ **(01780) 720205**
📠 (01780) 722146
✉ jringleby@theluffenhamheathgc.co.uk
📖 555
🏌 JR Ingleby
🏌 I Burnett (01780) 720298
▷ 18 L 6563 yds Par 70 SSS 72
⚭ U H SOC–WD WE between 10.30–12.00 and after 2.30pm
££ £45 D–£55 (£45 D–£55) (under review)
⚙ 5 miles W of Stamford on A6121
🏠 James Braid
🖥 www.luffenhamheath.co.uk

RAF Cottesmore (1982)

Oakham, Leicester, LE15 7BL
☎ **(01572) 812241 Ext 8112**
📠 (01572) 812241 ext 7834
✉ ctsdepth-aesffs@cottesmore.raf.mod.uk
📖 150
🏌 S Hopkins
▷ 9 L 5767 yds SSS 69 (18 tees)
⚭ By arrangement
££ £5
⚙ RAF Cottesmore

Rutland County (1991)

Great Casterton, Stamford, PE9 4AQ
☎ **(01780) 460239/460330**
📠 (01780) 460437
✉ info@rutlandcountygolf.co.uk
🏌 G Lowe (Golf Dir)
🏌 Ian Melville (01780 460330 ext 2)
▷ 18 L 6422 yds SSS 71
  9 hole Par 3 course
⚭ U H SOC
££ Mon–Fri £25; £20 12–3pm Twilight £12.50 after 3pm W/E £30 am–12noon £30 – D £15 after 3pm
⚙ 3 miles N of Stamford on A1
⊕ Driving range; par 3 course
🏠 Cameron Sinclair
🖥 www.rutlandcountygolf.co.uk

Shropshire

Aqualate (1995)

Pay and play
Stafford Road, Newport, TF10 9JT
☎ **(01952) 811699**

Arscott (1992)

Arscott, Pontesbury, Shrewsbury, SY5 0XP
☎ (01743) 860114
📠 (01743) 860114
✉ golf@arscott.dydirect.net
🏛 650
⛳ Sian Cadwallader-Hinkins
✔ Glynn Sadd (01743) 860881
▶ 18 L 6112 yds SSS 69
👥 WD–U WE/BH–M before 2pm SOC
££ £24 (£29)
🚗 5 miles SW of Shrewsbury, off A488
🏠 Martin Hamer
🖥 www.arscottgolfclub.co.uk

Bridgnorth (1889)

Stanley Lane, Bridgnorth, WV16 4SF
☎ (01746) 763315
📠 (01746) 763315
✉ bridgnorthgolfclub@tiscali.co.uk
🏛 690
⛳ GC Kelsall
✔ S Russell (01746) 762045
▶ 18 L 6582 yds Par 73 SSS 72
👥 H SOC WD
££ £25 (£35)
🚗 1 mile N of Bridgnorth
🖥 www.bridgnorthgolfclub.co.uk

Brow

Proprietary
Welsh Frankton, Ellesmere, SY12 9HW
☎ (01691) 622628
✉ browgolf@btinternet.com

Chesterton Valley (1993)

Chesterton, Worfield, Bridgnorth, WV15 5NX
☎ (01746) 783682
🏛 450
⛳ P Hinton
✔ P Hinton
▶ 18 L 6000 yds Par 71 SSS 69
👥 U–phone first SOC
££ £15.50 (£18)
🚗 10 miles W of Wolverhampton on B4176
🏠 Mike Davis

Church Stretton (1898)

Trevor Hill, Church Stretton, SY6 6JH
☎ (01694) 722281
✉ secretary@churchstrettongolfclub.co.uk
🏛 410
⛳ J Townsend (Mgr) (01743) 860679
✔ J Townsend (01694) 722281
▶ 18 L 5020 yds SSS 65
👥 U WE–NA before 10.30am SOC
££ £20 (£25)
🚗 ½ mile W of Church Stretton, off A49 above Carding Mill Valley
🏠 Jack Morris, James Hepburn, Harry Vardon, James Braid
🖥 www.churchstrettongolfclub.co.uk

Cleobury Mortimer (1993)

Proprietary
Wyre Common, Cleobury Mortimer, DY14 8HQ

☎ (01299) 271112 (Clubhouse)
📠 (01299) 271468
✉ enquiries@cleoburygolfclub.com
🏛 600
⛳ G Pain (Gen Mgr)
✔ M Payne/T Hall
▶ 27 holes:
   L 6147-6438 yds SSS 69-71
👥 WD–U H WE–M H SOC
££ £24 (£32)
🚗 10 miles SW of Kidderminster on A4117
⊕ Practice area, Four Self Catering Cottages on site.
🏠 Ray Baldwin E.G.U.
🖥 www.cleoburygolfclub.com

Hawkstone Park (1920)

Weston-under-Redcastle, Shrewsbury, SY4 5UY
☎ (01939) 200611
📠 (01939) 200311
✉ secretary@hawkstone.co.uk
🏛 700
⛳ T Harrop
✔ S Leech
▶ Hawkstone 18 L 6491 yds SSS 72
   Championship 18 L 6764 yds SSS 72
   Academy 6 holes Par 3 course
👥 U SOC
££ £35 D–£50 (£45 D–£65)
🚗 10 miles S of Whitchurch. 14 miles N of Shrewsbury on A49
⊕ Driving range
🏠 Braid/Huggett
🖥 www.hpgcgolf.com

Hill Valley G&CC (1975)

Proprietary
Terrick Road, Whitchurch, SY13 4JZ
☎ (01948) 667788
✉ general.hillvalley@mcdonald-hotels.co.uk

Horsehay Village Golf Centre (1999)

Pay and play
Wellington Road, Horsehay, Telford, TF4 3BT
☎ (01952) 632070
📠 (01952) 632074
✉ horsehayvillagegolfcentre@telford.gov.uk
🏛 350
⛳ S Whitmore (Mgr)
✔ D Thorp & M Lea (01952) 382639
▶ 18 L 5929 yds Par 70 SSS 69
👥 U SOC
££ £12 (£14)
🚗 Nr M54 Junction 6
⊕ Driving range. Pitch & putt course
🏠 Howard Swan

Lilleshall Hall (1937)

Abbey Road, Lilleshall, Newport, TF10 9AS
☎ (01952) 604776
📠 (01952) 604272
✉ honsec@lhgc.entdsl.com
🏛 700
⛳ A Marklew (01952) 604776
✔ R Bluck (01952) 604104
▶ 18 L 5813 yds SSS 68

👥 WD–U WE SOC
££ £30 (£40)
🚗 3 miles S of Newport between Lilleshall and Sheriffhales. M54 Jct 4
⊕ Indoor teaching academy
🏠 HS Colt
🖥 www.lilleshallhallgolfclub.co.uk

Llanymynech (1933)

Pant, Oswestry, SY10 8LB
☎ (01691) 830983
📠 (01691) 183 9184
✉ secretary.llanygc@btinternet.com
🏛 700
⛳ Howard Jones
✔ A Griffiths (01691) 830879
▶ 18 L 6114 yds Par 70 SSS 69
👥 U between 9.30–4pm U SOC–WD
££ £32 D–£42 (£42 per round)
🚗 5 miles S of Oswestry on A483
⊕ Practice area
🖥 www.llanymynechgolfclub.co.uk

Ludlow (1889)

Bromfield, Ludlow, SY8 2BT
☎ (01584) 856285
📠 (01584) 856366
✉ secretary@ludlowgolfclub.com
🏛 650
⛳ E Wilks (01584) 856285
✔ R Price (01584) 856366
▶ 18 L 6277 yds SSS 70
👥 H SOC–WD
££ £28 D–£35 (£35)
🚗 2 miles N of Ludlow (A49)
⊕ Buggies available
🖥 www.ludlowgolfclub.com

Market Drayton (1906)

Sutton, Market Drayton, TF9 2HX
☎ (01630) 652266
📠 (01630) 656564
✉ market.draytongc@btconnect.com
🏛 650
⛳ CK Stubbs
✔ R Clewes (01630) 656237
▶ 18 L 6290 yds SSS 71
👥 WD–U WE–by arrangement with professional
££ £30 (£40)
🚗 1 mile S of Market Drayton off A41
⊕ On course bungalow for rental, sleeps 6, Price includes golf.
🖥 www.marketdraytongolfclub.co.uk

Mile End (1992)

Proprietary
Mile End, Oswestry, SY11 4JF
☎ (01691) 671246
📠 (01691) 670580
✉ info@mileendgolfclub.co.uk
⛳ R Thompson
✔ S Carpenter (01691) 671246
▶ 18 L 6233 yds SSS 70
👥 U SOC
££ Mon–Thur £17 D–£25 Fri £19 D–£28 Sat–Sun £26 D–£38
🚗 1 mile SE of Oswestry, off A5/A483
⊕ Driving range, PGA tuition, Practice Ground, Putting Green, Custom Fit Centre.
🏠 Price/Gough
🖥 www.mileendgolfclub.co.uk

Oswestry (1903)

Aston Park, Queens Head, Oswestry,
SY11 4JJ
- ☎ **(01691) 610535**
- 🖷 (01691) 610535
- 🖂 secretary@oswestrygolfclub.co.uk
- 🕮 880
- ✍ Peter Turner (01691) 610535
- ✓ Jason Davies (01691) 610448
- ⊩ 18 L 6051 yds Par 70 SSS 69
- 👯 M or H SOC–WD + some WE
- ££ £30 (£35 Sat)
- ⚙ 3 miles SE of Oswestry on A5
- ⊕ Practice area.
- ⌂ James Braid
- 🖳 www.oswestrygolfclub.co.uk

Patshull Park Hotel G&CC

(1980)
Pattingham, WV6 7HR
- ☎ **(01902) 700100**
- 🖷 (01902) 700874
- 🕮 395
- ✍ I Stevens
- ✓ R Bissell (01902) 700342
- ⊩ 18 L 6345 yds SSS 71
- 👯 U H SOC
- ££ £40
- ⚙ 7 miles W of Wolverhampton, off A41. M54 Junction 3, 5 miles
- ⊕ Practice facilities, putting green, on-site hotel
- ⌂ John Jacobs
- 🖳 www.patshull-park.co.uk

Severn Meadows

(1990)
Pay and play
Highley, Bridgnorth, WV16 6HZ
- ☎ **(01746) 862212**

Shifnal (1929)

Decker Hill, Shifnal, TF11 8QL
- ☎ **(01952) 460330**
- 🖷 (01952) 460330
- 🖂 secretary@shifnalgolfclub.co.uk
- 🕮 700
- ✍ NR Milton (01952) 460330
- ✓ D Ashton (01952) 460330 ext 3
- ⊩ 18 L 6422 yds SSS 71
- 👯 WD–phone first WE/BH–M
- ££ £32
- ⚙ 1 mile NE of Shifnal. M54 Junction 4, 2 miles
- ⌂ Pennink
- 🖳 www.shifnalgolfclub.com

Shrewsbury (1891)

Condover, Shrewsbury, SY5 7BL
- ☎ **(01743) 872977**
- 🖷 (01743) 872977
- 🖂 info@shrewsbury-golf-club.co.uk
- 🕮 525 184(L) 70(J)
- ✍ David Knight (01743) 872977
- ✓ John Richards (01743) 872977
- ⊩ 18 L 6178 yds Par 70 SSS 69
- 👯 H SOC
- ££ £28 (£34)
- ⚙ 4 miles S of Shrewsbury
- 🖳 www.shrewsburygolfclub.co.uk

The Shropshire (1992)

Muxton, Telford, TF2 8PQ
- ☎ **(01952) 677800**
- 🖷 (01952) 677622
- 🖂 sales@theshropshire.co.uk
- 🕮 300
- ✍ James Lever
- ✓ Mark Sutcliffe
- ⊩ 27 L 6589-6637 yds SSS 70-72
- 👯 U SOC WD WE
- ££ £18 (£22)
- ⚙ 3 miles NW of Telford (B5060). M54 Junction 4
- ⊕ Floodlit driving range; pitch & putt course
- ⌂ Martin Hawtree
- 🖳 www.theshropshire.co.uk

Telford (1976)

Proprietary
Great Hay Drive, Sutton Heights, Telford,
TF7 4DT
- ☎ **(01952) 429977**
- 🖷 (01952) 586602
- 🖂 ibarklem@aol.com
- 🕮 340
- ✍ I Lucas
- ✓ George Boden (01952) 586052
- ⊩ 18 L 6741 yds Par 72 SSS 72
- 👯 H SOC
- ££ On application
- ⚙ 4 miles SE of Telford, M54 J4, off A442
- ⊕ Driving range
- ⌂ John Harris
- 🖳 www.telford-golfclub.co.uk

Worfield (1991)

Proprietary
Worfield, Bridgnorth, WV15 5HE
- ☎ **(01746) 716541**
- 🖷 (01746) 716302
- 🖂 enquiries@worfieldgolf.co.uk
- 🕮 500
- ✍ W Weaver (Gen Mgr) (01746) 716372
- ✓ N Doody (01746) 716541
- ⊩ 18 L 6660 yds SSS 72
- 👯 U SOC
- ££ £22 (£25)
- ⚙ 7 miles W of Wolverhampton on A454
- ⌂ Williams
- 🖳 www.worfieldgolf.co.uk

Wrekin (1905)

Wellington, Telford, TF6 5BX
- ☎ **(01952) 244032**
- 🖷 (01952) 252906
- 🖂 wrekingolfclub@lineone.net
- 🕮 500 100(L) 90(J)
- ✍ D Briscoe
- ✓ O Evans 01952 244032
- ⊩ 18 L 5570 yds SSS 67
- 👯 WD–U before 5pm –M after 5pm SOC
- ££ £27 (£35)
- ⚙ Wellington, off B5061

Somerset

Bath (1880)

Sham Castle, North Road, Bath, BA2 6JG
- ☎ **(01225) 463834**
- 🖷 (01225) 331027
- 🖂 enquiries@bathgolfclub.org.uk
- 🕮 730
- ✍ (01225) 463834
- ✓ R Covey (01225) 466953
- ⊩ 18 L 6505 yds Par 71 SSS 71
- 👯 H SOC WD–NA before 9.30 am WE
- ££ £36 (£40)
- ⚙ 1½ miles SE of Bath, off A36. M4 Jct 18 (A46)
- ⊕ Warm-up range
- ⌂ HS Colt
- 🖳 www.bathgolfclub.org.uk

Brean (1973)

Coast Road, Brean, Burnham-on-Sea,
TA8 2QY
- ☎ **(01278) 752111**
- 🖷 (01278) 752111
- 🖂 proshop@brean.com
- 🕮 400
- ✍ A.P.Roper (Hon)
- ✓ D Haines (01278) 752111
- ⊩ 18 L 5565 yds SSS 67
- 👯 WD–U WE–pm only SOC
- ££ £25 (£30) D–£30 (£35)
- ⚙ 4 miles N of Burnham-on-Sea. M5 Junction 22, 6 miles
- 🖳 www.brean.com

Burnham & Berrow (1890)

St Christopher's Way, Burnham-on-Sea,
TA8 2PE
- ☎ **(01278) 785760**
- 🖷 (01278) 795440
- 🖂 secretary.bbgc@btconnect.com
- 🕮 800
- ✍ MA Blight (01278) 785760
- ✓ M Crowther-Smith (01278) 785760
- ⊩ 18 L 6616 yds Par 71 SSS 73
- 9 L 5819 yds Par 70 SSS 69
- 👯 I H SOC
- ££ 9: £17 (£20) 18: £60 (£80)
- ⚙ 1 mile N of Burnham-on-Sea on B3140. M5 Junction 22
- ⊕ Dormy House; driving range
- ⌂ HS Colt
- 🖳 www.burnhamandberrowgolfclub .co.uk

Cannington (1993)

Pay and play
Cannington Centre for Land Based Studies,
Bridgwater, TA5 2LS
- ☎ **(01278) 655050**
- 🖷 (01278) 655055
- 🕮 280
- ✍ R Macrow (Mgr)
- ✓ R Macrow
- ⊩ 9 L 6077 yds Par 68 SSS 70
- 👯 U exc Wed eve–restricted
- ££ 9: £10 (£13); 18: £14 (£18.50)
- ⚙ 4 miles NW of Bridgwater on A39. M5 Junction 24
- ⊕ Driving range
- ⌂ Hawtree
- 🖳 www.bridgwater.ac.uk

Clevedon (1891)
Castle Road, Clevedon, BS21 7AA
☎ (01275) 874057
✆ (01275) 341228
✉ secretary@clevedongolfclub.co.uk
📖 800
♟ J Cunning (01275) 874057
✓ R Scanlan (01275) 874704
▷ 18 L 6557 yds Par 72 SSS 72
♟ WD–U H exc Wed am WE/BH–U H (phone first) SOC–WD
££ £35 (£45)
♠ Off Holly Lane, Walton, Clevedon. M5 Junction 20
⚑ JH Taylor
🖥 www.clevedongolfclub.co.uk

Enmore Park (1906)
Enmore, Bridgwater, TA5 2AN
☎ (01278) 672100
✆ (01278) 672101
✉ manager@enmorepark.co.uk
📖 780
♟ S.Varcoe (01278) 672100
✓ N Wixon (01278) 672102
▷ 18 L 6411 yds SSS 71
♟ SOC–WD–WE–H
££ £36 D–£48 (£46)
♠ 3 miles W of Bridgwater, off Durleigh road. M5 Junctions 23/24
⊕ Full practice range 300 yds
⚑ Hawtree
🖥 www.enmorepark.co.uk

Entry Hill (1985)
Public
Entry Hill, Bath, BA2 5NA
☎ (01225) 834248

Farrington (1992)
Proprietary
Marsh Lane, Farrington Gurney, Bristol, BS39 6TS
☎ (01761) 451596
✆ (01761) 451021
✉ info@farringtongolfclub.net
📖 750
♟ J Cowgill
✓ J Lawrence (01761) 451046
▷ 18 L 6716 yds Par 72 SSS 72 9 L 3002 yds Par 54 SSS 53
♟ WD–U H SOC–WD WD–U WE–U after 12pm sat SOC–U
££ 9: £6.50 (£7.50); 18: £18–£20 (£27)
♠ 12 miles S of Bristol (A37). 10 miles S of Bath (A39)
⊕ Floodlit driving range; practice ground; chipping/putting greens
⚑ Peter Thompson
🖥 www.farringtongolfclub.net

Fosseway CC (1970)
Charlton Lane, Midsomer Norton, Radstock, BA3 4BD
☎ (01761) 412214
✆ (01761) 418357
✉ club@centurionhotel.co.uk
📖 240
♟ Gavin Jones (Mgr)
✓ Terry Williams
▷ 9 L 4565 yds SSS 63
♟ WD–U exc Wed–M after 5pm NA–Sundays before 12 noon

££ From £5 Juniors and £8 Adults
♠ 10 miles SW of Bath on A367
⊕ Practice ground; Putting Green; six hole Pitch + Putt
⚑ K C Cotton, F Penncik & I Horler
🖥 www.centurionhotel.co.uk

Frome (1994)
Proprietary
Critchill Manor, Frome, BA11 4LJ
☎ (01373) 453410
✉ fromegolfclub@yahoo.co.uk
📖 460
♟ Mrs S Austin
✓ Lawrence Wilkin
▷ 18 L 5527 yds Par 69 SSS 67
♟ U
££ £22 D–£26.50 (£25.50 D–£28)
♠ 1 mile from centre of Frome (easiest access from A361 Nunney jct following signs back to Frome)
⊕ Covered floodlit driving range; putting green; practice bunker & pitching area. Course can be played as 2 x 9 if time limited
🖥 www.fromegolfclub.fsnet.co.uk

Isle of Wedmore (1992)
Lineage, Lascots Hill, Wedmore, BS28 4QT
☎ (01934) 712452
✆ (01934) 713696
✉ info@wedmoregolfclub.com
📖 670
♟ AC Edwards (01934) 712222
✓ N Pope (01934) 712452
▷ 18 L 6006 yds Par 70 SSS 69
♟ U SOC–WD
££ £26 (£26)
♠ ³⁄₄ mile N of Wedmore. M5 Junction 22
⚑ Terry Murray
🖥 www.wedmoregolfclub.com

Kingweston (1983)
(Sec) 12 Lowerside Road, Glastonbury, Somerset BA6 9BH
☎ (01458) 834086
📖 200
♟ I Price
▷ 9 L 4809 yds SSS 65
♟ M exc Wed & Sat 2–5pm–NA
££ NA
♠ 1 mile SE of Butleigh. 2 miles SE of Glastonbury

Lansdown (1894)
Lansdown, Bath, BA1 9BT
☎ (01225) 422138
✆ (01225) 339252
✉ admin@lansdowngolfclub.co.uk
📖 750
♟ Mrs E Bacon
✓ S Readman (01225) 420242
▷ 18 L 6428 yds SSS 71
♟ H SOC
££ £30 (£35)
♠ 2 miles NW of Bath, by racecourse. M4 Junction 18, 6 miles
⚑ HS Colt
🖥 www.lansdowngolfclub.co.uk

Long Sutton (1991)
Pay and play
Long Load, Langport, TA10 9JU
☎ (01458) 241017
✆ (01458) 241022
✉ reservations@longsuttongolf.com
📖 700
♟ Gareth Harding
✓ A Hayes & Gareth Harding
▷ 18 L 6367 yds SSS 71
♟ WD–U WE–booking required SOC
££ £20 (£25)
♠ 3 miles E of Langport
⊕ Floodlit driving range
⚑ Patrick Dawson
🖥 www.longsuttongolf.com

The Mendip (1908)
Gurney Slade, Radstock, BA3 4UT
☎ (01749) 840570
✆ (01749) 841439
✉ secretary@mendipgolfclub.com
📖 800
♟ J Scott
✓ A Marsh (01749) 840793
▷ 18 L 6383 yds SSS 71
♟ WD–U WE–H SOC–WD
££ £27 (£38)
♠ 3 miles N of Shepton Mallet (A37)
⚑ CK Cotton
🖥 www.mendipgolfclub.com

Mendip Spring (1992)
Honeyhall Lane, Congresbury, BS49 5JT
☎ (01934) 853337/852322
✆ (01934) 853021
✉ info@mendipspringgolfclub.com
📖 500
♟ A Melhuish
✓ J Blackburn, R Moss
▷ 18 L 6412 yds SSS 70 9 L 4658 yds SSS 66
♟ U
££ 9: £9.50 (£10); 18: £30 (£38)
♠ Congresbury. M5 Junction 21
⊕ Driving range
⚑ Langholt
🖥 www.mendipspringgolfclub.com

Minehead & West Somerset (1882)
The Warren, Minehead, TA24 5SJ
☎ (01643) 702057
✆ (01643) 705095
✉ secretary.mwsgc@btconnect.com
📖 500
♟ G Mason
✓ I Read (01643) 704378
▷ 18 L 6153 yds SSS 69
♟ U after 9.30am SOC
££ £40 (£47) W–£150
♠ E end of sea front
🖥 www.minehead-golf-club.co.uk

Oake Manor (1993)
Oake, Taunton, TA4 1BA
☎ (01823) 461993
✆ (01823) 461995
✉ golf@oakemanor.com
📖 600
♟ R Gardner (Golf Mgr)

✓ R Gardner/J Smallacombe
▷ 18 L 6109 yds Par 70 SSS 69
⚇ U–phone first SOC
££ Mon–Thur £26 Fri £29 (£30)
⊕⊕ 4 miles W of Taunton, off B3227.
   M5 Junctions 25/26 onto A38 only
   6 minutes
⊕ Driving range; academy course;
   practice ground; short game area
⌂ Adrian Stiff
▤ www.oakemanor.com

Orchardleigh   (1996)
Frome, BA11 2PH
☎ (01373) 454200
⌨ (01373) 454202
✉ info@orchardleighgolf.co.uk
▥ 500
♪ David Nelson (Gen Mgr)
✓ I Ridsdale/S Clark
▷ 18 L 6824 yds Par 72 SSS 73
⚇ WD/BH–U WE–U after 11am SOC
££ £40 (£50)
⊕⊕ 2 miles NW of Frome on A362. 12
   miles S of Bath
⊕ Covered Driving range and
   practice facilities
⌂ Brian Huggett
▤ www.orchardleighgolf.co.uk

Saltford   (1904)
Golf Club Lane, Saltford, Bristol, BS31 3AA
☎ (01225) 873513
⌨ (01225) 873525
✉ secretary@saltfordgolfclub.co.uk
▥ 650
♪ M Penn (01225) 873513
✓ D Read (01225) 872043
▷ 18 L 6225 yds SSS 70
⚇ WD–U SOC–Mon & Thurs
££ £30 (£35)
⊕⊕ 7 miles SE of Bristol
⊕ Practice tees; chipping green;
   buggies for hire
▤ www.saltfordgolfclub.co.uk

Stockwood Vale
(1991)
Public
Stockwood Lane, Keynsham, Bristol,
BS31 2ER
☎ (0117) 986 6505
✉ stockwoodvale@aol.com

Tall Pines   (1990)
Proprietary
Cooks Bridle Path, Downside, Backwell,
Bristol, BS48 3DJ
☎ (01275) 472076
⌨ (01275) 474869
▥ 500
♪ T Murray
✓ A Murray
▷ 18 L 6067 yds Par 70 SSS 70
⚇ U SOC
££ £20 (£20)
⊕⊕ 8 miles SW of Bristol
   (A470/A38)
⊕ Practice area; Motel
   accommodation
⌂ Terry Murray
▤ www.tallpinesgolf.co.uk

Taunton & Pickeridge
(1892)
Corfe, Taunton, TA3 7BY
☎ (01823) 421537
⌨ (01823) 421742
✉ mail@tauntongolf.co.uk
▥ 660
♪ S Stevenson (01823) 421537
✓ S Stevenson (01823) 421790
▷ 18 L 6106 yds Par 69 SSS 69
⚇ H SOC
££ £30 (£45)
⊕⊕ 5 miles S of Taunton on B3170
⌂ H Fowler
▤ www.tauntongolf.co.uk

Taunton Vale   (1991)
Proprietary
Creech Heathfield, Taunton, TA3 5EY
☎ (01823) 412220
⌨ (01823) 413583
✉ admin@tauntonvalegolf.co.uk
▥ 700
♪ Mrs J Wyatt
✓ M Keitch (01823) 412880
▷ 18 L 6237 yds Par 70 SSS 70
   9 L 2004 yds Par 64 SSS 60
⚇ U SOC
££ 9: £10 (£12); 18: £23 (£28)
⊕⊕ 3 miles N of Taunton, off A361. M5
   Junctions 24/25
⊕ Floodlit driving range; practice
   putting green
⌂ John Pyne
▤ www.tauntonvalegolf.co.uk

Tickenham   (1994)
Clevedon Road, Tickenham, Bristol,
BS21 6RY
☎ (01275) 856626
✉ info@tickenhamgolf.co.uk
✓ A Sutcliffe, S Jarrett, A Smith, F
   Amey
▷ 9 L 2000 yds Par 60 SSS 58
⚇ U–phone first SOC
££ 18 holes–£12 (£15)
⊕⊕ 2 miles E of M5 Junction 20 on
   B3130, nr Nailsea
⊕ Floodlit driving range; Golfmark
   awarded; PGA Teaching Centre
⌂ Andrew Sutcliffe
▤ www.tickenhamgolf.co.uk

Vivary   (1928)
Public
Vivary Park, Taunton, TA1 3JW
☎ (01823) 289274 (Clubhouse)
⌨ 01823 353757
▥ 300
♪ Bob Stout
✓ R Coffin (01823) 333875
▷ 18 L 4533 yds SSS 63 Par 65
⚇ U SOC–WD
££ £13.50 (£15.00)
⊕⊕ Centre of Taunton
⊕ Practice Area
⌂ Herbert Fowler

Wells   (1893)
East Horrington Blackheath Lane, Wells,
BA5 3DS
☎ (01749) 675005

☎ (01749) 683170
✉ secretary@wellsgolfclub.co.uk
▥ 600
♪ Beverley New (01749) 683171
✓ A Bishop (01749) 679059
▷ 18 L 6004 yds SSS 69
⚇ WD–U WE–H SOC–WD
££ £30 (£35)
⊕⊕ 1½ miles E of Wells, off Bath road
   (B3139)
⊕ Floodlit driving range
▤ www.wellsgolfclub.co.uk

Weston-super-Mare   (1892)
Uphill Road North, Weston-super-Mare,
BS23 4NQ
☎ (01934) 626968
⌨ (01934) 621360
✉ wsmgolfclub@eurotelbroadband
   .com
▥ 752
♪ Mrs K Drake (01934) 626968
✓ M La Band (01934) 633360
▷ 18 L 6251 yds SSS 70
⚇ H SOC
££ £36 D–£48
⊕⊕ Weston-super-Mare, M5 J21
⌂ T Dunn – redesigned A Mackenzie
▤ www.westonsupermaregolfclub
   .com

Wheathill   (1993)
Wheathill, Somerton, TA11 7HG
☎ (01963) 240667
⌨ (01963) 240230
✉ wheathill@wheathill.fsnet.co.uk
▥ 600
♪ A England
✓ A England
▷ 18 L 5362 yds SSS 66
   8 hole Par 3 course
⚇ U
££ £20 D–£30 (£20 D–£30) Twilight
   e/day after 4pm £15 Twilight e/day
   after 6pm £10
⊕⊕ 3 miles W of Castle Cary on B3153
⊕ 10 acre practice ground; 8 hole
   academy course
⌂ John Baine

Wincanton Golf Course
(1994)
Proprietary
The Racecourse, Wincanton, BA9 8BJ
☎ (01963) 435850
✉ wincanton@rht.net
▥ 200
♪ Andrew England
✓ Andrew England
▷ 9/18 L 6182 yds Par 70 SSS 69
⚇ U SOC
££ 9: £10 (£12) 18: £15 (£17)
⊕⊕ A303 Wincanton
⊕ Practice ground; putting green;
   practice net; Coaching; Buggies;
   Golf shop
⌂ Eagle Golf
▤ wincantonracecourse.co.uk

Windwhistle   (1932)
Cricket St Thomas, Chard, TA20 4DG
☎ (01460) 30231
⌨ (01460) 30055

⊠ info@windwhistlegolfclub.co.uk
⌂ 550
♠ IN Dodd
✓ P Deeprose
▷ 18 L 6510 yds SSS 71
⚑ U–phone first SOC
££ £25 (£30)
♣ Windwhistle, 3 miles E of Chard on A30. M5 Junction 25, 12 miles
⊕ Driving range
⌂ JH Taylor/L Fisher
▤ www.windwhistlegolfclub.co.uk

Worlebury (1908)

Monks Hill, Worlebury, Weston-super-Mare, BS22 9SX

☎ (01934) 625789
⌨ (01934) 621935
⊠ secretary@worleburygc.co.uk
⌂ 530
♠ MW Wake
✓ G Marks (01934) 623932
▷ 18 L 5963 yds SSS 68
⚑ H SOC–WD
££ £30 (£35)
♣ 2 miles NE of Weston, off A370
⌂ H Vardon
▤ www.worleburygc.co.uk

Yeovil (1907)

Sherborne Road, Yeovil, BA21 5BW

☎ (01935) 422965
⌨ (01935) 411283
⊠ office@yeovilgolfclub.com
⌂ 710 122(L) 101(J)
♠ M Betteridge (01935) 422965
✓ G Kite (01935) 473763
▷ 18 L 6150 yds SSS 70 Par 71
   9 L 4905 yds SSS 65 Par 68
⚑ WD–U H WE/BH–H
   (WD/WE–phone Pro) SOC
££ 18: £40 (£40) 9: £25 (£25)
♣ 1 mile from Yeovil on A30 to Sherborne
⊕ 20-bay floodlit driving range open 7am-9pm WD, 7am-6pm WE
⌂ Alison
▤ www.yeovilgolfclub.com

Staffordshire

3 Hammers Golf Complex

Pay and play

Old Stafford Road, Cross Green, Wolverhampton WV10 7PP

☎ (01902) 790428
⌨ (01902) 791777
⊠ Info@3hammers.co.uk
✓ Piers Ward/Andrew Proudman
▷ 18 hole par 3 short course
⚑ U
££ £7.95 C (£8.95) D
♣ M54 Junction 2
⊕ Driving range
⌂ Henry Cotton
▤ www.3hammers.co.uk

Alsager G&CC (1992)

Audley Road, Alsager, Stoke-on-Trent, ST7 2UR

☎ (01270) 875700

Aston Wood (1994)

Blake Street, Sutton Coldfield, B74 4EU

☎ (0121) 580 7803
⌨ (0121) 353 0354
⊠ enquiries@astonwoodgolfclub.co.uk
⌂ 850
♠ George Briffa (0121) 580 7807
✓ Simon Smith (0121) 580 7801
▷ 18 holes Par 71 SSS 71
⚑ WD–SOC before 5pm WE–M after 1pm
££ £30 D–£35 (£35)
♣ 3 miles NE of Sutton Coldfield on A4026. M6 Jct 7; M42 Jct 9; M6 Toll T3
⊕ Driving range; practice chipping area
⌂ Peter Alliss
▤ www.astonwoodgolfclub.co.uk

Barlaston (1987)

Meaford Road, Stone, ST15 8UX

☎ (01782) 372867
⌨ (01782) 373648
⊠ barlaston.gc@virgin.net
⌂ 650
♠ M Emberton (01782 372867)
✓ I Rogers (01782) 372795
▷ 18 L 5800 yds SSS 68
⚑ WD–U WE–NA before 10am
££ £23 D–£35 (£35)
♣ 1/2 mile S of Barlaston. M6 Jct 14/15
⌂ P Aliss
▤ www.barlastongc.com

Beau Desert (1911)

Hazel Slade, Cannock, WS1 0PJ

☎ (01543) 422626/422773
⌨ (01543) 451137
⊠ enquiries@bdgc.co.uk
⌂ 650
♠ 01543) 422626
✓ Barrie Stevens (01543) 422492
▷ 18 L 6247 yds Par 70 SSS 71
⚑ WD–U WE–phone in advance BH–NA SOC
££ £50 (£60)
♣ 4 miles NE of Cannock, off A460
⊕ Driving range
⌂ WH Fowler
▤ www.bdgc.co.uk

Bloxwich (1924)

136 Stafford Road, Bloxwich, WS3 3PQ

☎ (01922) 476593
⌨ (01922) 493449
⊠ secretary@bloxwichgolfclub.com
⌂ 700
♠ RJ Wormstone
✓ RJ Dance (01922) 476889
▷ 18 L 6257 yds SSS 71
⚑ WD–U WE–M SOC
££ Mon £30, Tue–Thu £33, Fri £35 all per round
♣ N of Walsall on A34; 4m M6 J11
▤ www.bloxwichgolfclub.com

Branston G&CC (1975)

Burton Road, Branston, Burton-on-Trent, DE14 3DP

☎ (01283) 528320
⌨ (01283) 566984

⊠ sales@branston-golf-club.co.uk
⌂ 800
♠ G Pyle (Golf Mgr)
✓ J Sture
▷ 18 L 6697 yds Par 72 SSS 72
   9 L 1856 yds Par 30
⚑ WD–U WE–M before noon SOC
££ £36 (£44)
♣ 1/2 mile S of Burton (A38)
⊕ Driving range
⌂ G Hamshall
▤ www.branston-golf-club.co.uk

Brocton Hall (1894)

Brocton, Stafford, ST17 0TH

☎ (01785) 661901
⌨ (01785) 661591
⊠ secretary@broctonhall.com
⌂ 500
♠ JDS Duffy (01785) 661901
✓ N Bland (01785) 661485
▷ 18 L 6095 yds SSS 69
⚑ I H SOC
££ £45 (£50)
♣ 4 miles SE of Stafford, off A34
⌂ Harry Vardon
▤ www.broctonhall.com

Burslem (1907)

Wood Farm, High Lane, Stoke-on-Trent, ST6 7JT

☎ (01782) 837006
⌂ 300
♠ A Porter (01782) 839645
▷ 9 L 5274 yds SSS 66
⚑ WD–U WE–NA
££ £10 D–£16
♣ Burslem 2 miles

Calderfields (1983)

Proprietary

Aldridge Road, Walsall, WS4 2JS

☎ (01922) 646888 (Clubhouse)
   (01922) 632243 (Bookings)
⌨ (01922) 640540
⊠ calderfields@bigfoot.com
⌂ 750
♠ MR Andrews
✓ Cranfield Academy (01922) 613675
▷ 18 L 6509 yds Par 73 SSS 71
⚑ U SOC
££ £18 (£20) – under review
♣ 1 m N of Walsall (A454). M6 Jct 10
⊕ 27 bay floodlit driving range with Auto Tech golf tees; 18 hole putting green
▤ www.calderfieldsgolf.com

Cannock Park (1993)

Public

Stafford Road, Cannock, WS11 2AL

☎ (01543) 578850
⌨ (01543) 578850
⊠ seccpgc@yahoo.co.uk
⌂ 125
♠ CB Milne (01543) 571091
▷ 18 L 5149 yds SSS 65
⚑ U SOC–WD
££ £11.50 (£15.00)
♣ 1/2 mile N of Cannock on A34. M6 Junction 11, 2 miles
⌂ John Mainland
▤ www.cpgc.freeserve.co.uk

For list of abbreviations and key to symbols see page 647

The Chase (1999)
Pottal Pool Road, Penkridge, ST19 5RN
- ☎ **(01785) 712888**
- 🖷 (01785) 712692
- ✉ chase-sales@crown-golf.co.uk
- ☷ 800
- ⚐ 18 L 6354 yds Par 72 SSS 72
- 👥 U H SOC
- ££ £25
- ⛳ 10 miles S of Stafford, off A449. M6 Junctions 12 & 13
- ⊕ Driving range (20 bays)
- 🖳 www.crown-golf.co.uk

The Craythorne (1974)
Craythorne Road, Rolleston on Dove, Burton upon Trent, DE13 0AZ
- ☎ **(01283) 564329**
- 🖷 (01283) 511908
- ✉ admin@craythorne.co.uk
- ☷ 450
- ♟ AA Wright (Man Dir/Owner)
- ✓ S Hadfield (01283) 533745
- ⚐ 18 L 5641 yds Par 68 SSS 68
- 👥 WD–U SOC
- ££ £25 (£30) £15 Twilight during summer
- ⛳ Stretton, 1½ miles N of Burton. A38/A5121 Junction – follow brown tour
- ⊕ Floodlit driving range; buggies for hire, conference and pub
- ♟ A.A. Wright
- 🖳 www.craythorne.co.uk

Dartmouth (1910)
Vale Street, West Bromwich, B71 4DW
- ☎ **(0121) 588 2131**
- 🖷 (0121) 588 5746
- ☷ 350
- ♟ CF Wade (0121) 532 4070
- ⚐ 9 L 6036 yds SSS 71
- 👥 WD–U WE–M after 12 SOC–Tues & Thurs
- ££ D–£25 (£17)
- ⛳ 1 mile from W Bromwich, behind site of new estate. M5 J1, M6 J7
- 🖳 www.dartmouth-golf-club.co.uk

Denstone College (1991)
Denstone, Uttoxeter, ST14 5HN
- ☎ **(01889) 590484**
- 🖷 (01889) 590744
- ✉ moor.house.farm@btinternet.com
- ☷ 170(M) 24(J) 41(L)
- ♟ Ann Tweddle
- ✓ None
- ⚐ 9 L 4404 yds Par 64 SSS 62
- 👥 M SOC
- ££ £7.50
- ⛳ Grounds of Denstone College. 6 miles N of Uttoxeter
- ♟ MP Raisbeck
- 🖳 www.denstonecollege.org

Drayton Park (1897)
Drayton Park, Tamworth, B78 3TN
- ☎ **(01827) 251139**
- 🖷 (01827) 284035
- ✉ admin@draytonparkgc.com
- ☷ 650
- ♟ DO Winter

- ✓ MW Passmore (01827) 251478
- ⚐ 18 L 6473 yds SSS 71
- 👥 WD–H WE/BH–NA SOC–Tues & Thurs
- ££ £44 D–£44
- ⛳ 2 miles S of Tamworth (A4091); M42 J9 or 10
- ♟ James Braid
- 🖳 www.draytonparkgc.com

Druids Heath (1974)
Stonnall Road, Aldridge, WS9 8JZ
- ☎ **(01922) 455595**
- 🖷 (01922) 452887
- ✉ admin@druidsheathgc.co.uk
- ☷ 539 80(L) 50(J)
- ♟ KI Taylor
- ✓ G Williams (01922) 459523
- ⚐ 18 L 6661 yds Par 72 SSS 73
- 👥 WD–U WE–NA before 2pm SOC–WD
- ££ £40 (£43)
- ⛳ 6 miles NW of Sutton Coldfield, off A452
- 🖳 www.druidsheathgc.co.uk

Enville (1935)
Highgate Common, Enville, Stourbridge, DY7 5BN
- ☎ **(01384) 872074**
- 🖷 (01384) 873396
- ✉ secretary@envillegolfclub.com
- ☷ 900
- ♟ JJ Bishop (Sec/Mgr) (01384) 872074
- ✓ S Power (01384) 872585
- ⚐ Highgate 18 L 6592 yds SSS 73 Lodge 18 L 6417 yds SSS 71
- 👥 WD–U WE/BH–M H SOC
- ££ £45–£50
- ⛳ 6 miles W of Stourbridge
- 🖳 www.envillegolfclub.com

Great Barr (1961)
Chapel Lane, Birmingham, B43 7BA
- ☎ **(0121) 358 4376**
- 🖷 (0121) 358 4376
- ✉ info@greatbarrgolfclub.co.uk
- ☷ 600
- ♟ Mrs D Smith (0121) 358 4376
- ✓ R Spragg (0121) 357 5270
- ⚐ 18 L 6459 yds SSS 72
- 👥 WD–U WE–I (h'cap max 18) SOC
- ££ £32
- ⛳ 6 miles NW of Birmingham. M6 Junction 7
- 🖳 www.greatbarrgolfclub.co.uk

Greenway Hall (1909)
Pay and play
Stockton Brook, Stoke-on-Trent, ST9 9LJ
- ☎ **(01782) 503158**
- 🖷 (01782) 504691
- ✉ jackbarker_greenwayhallgolfclub @hotmail.com
- ☷ 250
- ♟ J Latham (Mgr)
- ⚐ 18 L 5676 yds SSS 67
- 👥 U SOC + Pay & Play WD WE
- ££ Mon–Thur £10 Fri £12 Sat–Sun £15
- ⛳ 5 miles N of Stoke, off A53
- 🖳 www.jackbarker.com

Handsworth (1895)
11 Sunningdale Close, Handsworth Wood, Birmingham, B20 1NP
- ☎ **(0121) 554 3387**
- 🖷 (0121) 554 6144
- ✉ info@handsworthgolfclub.net
- ☷ 850
- ♟ PS Hodnett (Hon)
- ✓ L Bashford (0121) 523 3594
- ⚐ 18 L 6325 yds SSS 71
- 👥 WD–U WE/BH–M SOC
- ££ £40
- ⛳ 3 miles NW of Birmingham. M5 Junction 1. M6 Junction 7
- ♟ HS Colt
- 🖳 www.handsworthgolfclub.com

Himley Hall (1980)
Pay and play
Himley Hall Park, Dudley, DY3 4DF
- ☎ **(01902) 895207**
- 🖷 (01902) 895207
- ✉ msgplt@aol.com
- ☷ 63
- ♟ B Sparrow (01902) 894973 Mobile: 07515 284196
- ✓ Mark Sparrow (07951) 440777
- ⚐ 9 L 3145 yds SSS 36 9 hole short course
- 👥 WD–U WE/BH–restricted
- ££ 9: £8.80, 18: £13 all week
- ⛳ Grounds of Himley Hall Park. B4176, off A449
- ⊕ Practice area
- ♟ A & K Baker
- 🖳 www.himleygolf.co.uk

Ingestre Park (1977)
Ingestre, Stafford, ST18 0RE
- ☎ **(01889) 270845**
- 🖷 (01889) 271434
- ✉ manager@ingestregolf.co.uk
- ☷ 740
- ♟ D Warrilow (Mgr) (01889) 270845
- ✓ D Scullion (01889) 270304
- ⚐ 18 L 6352 yds SSS 71
- 👥 WD–H before 3.30pm WE/BH–M SOC–WD exc Wed
- ££ £40 D–£50
- ⛳ 6 miles E of Stafford, off Tixall Road. M6 Junctions 13/14
- ♟ Hawtree
- 🖳 www.ingestregolf.com

Izaak Walton (1993)
Cold Norton, Stone, ST15 0NS
- ☎ **(01785) 760900**
- ✉ secretary@izaakwaltongolfclub .co.uk
- ☷ 500
- ♟ Charlie Lightbown
- ✓ Rob Grier (01785) 760900
- ⚐ 18 L 6398 yds SSS 72
- 👥 U SOC
- ££ £20 (£25 D–£30)
- ⛳ 7 miles NW of Stafford on B5026. M6 Junction 14
- ⊕ Driving range
- 🖳 www.izaakwaltongolfclub.co.uk

Keele Golf Centre (1973)
Pay and play
Keele Road, Newcastle-under-Lyme,
ST5 5AB
☎ (01782) 627596

Lakeside (1969)
Rugeley Power Station, Rugeley, WS15 1PR
☎ (01889) 575667
🖥 (01889) 572146
📧 lakeside-golfclub
@unicombox.co.uk
🏠 500
♟ TA Yates
✓ Phil Cary 07906 526061
🏳 18 L 5686 yds Par 69 SSS 68
👤 M SOC
££ £10 D (£15)
🞉 2 miles SE of Rugeley on A513
🖥 www.lakesidegolf.20m.com

Leek (1892)
Birchall, Leek, ST13 5RE
☎ (01538) 384779
🖥 (01538) 384779
📧 enquiries@leekgolfclub.co.uk
🏠 520 135(L) 65(J)
♟ DT Brookhouse
✓ Fred Fearn
🏳 18 L 6218 yds SSS 70
👤 U H before 3pm –M after 3pm
SOC–Wed
££ £26 (£32)
🞉 1 mile S of Leek on A520
🖥 www.leekgolfclub.co.uk

Little Aston (1908)
Roman Road, Streetly, Sutton Coldfield,
B74 3AN
☎ (0121) 353 2066
🖥 (0121) 580 8387
📧 manager@littleastongolf.co.uk
🏠 250
♟ Glyn Ridley (Mgr) (0121) 353 2942
✓ Brian Rimmer (0121) 353 0330
🏳 18 L 6813 yds SSS 74
👤 H WE–by prior arrangement
SOC–WD
££ £80 D–£110
🞉 4 miles NW of Sutton Coldfield, off
A454
⊕ Professional all-weather teaching
academy
🏠 Harry Vardon
🖥 www.littleastongolf.co.uk

Lichfield Golf and Country
Club (1991)
Proprietary
Elmhurst, Lichfield, WS13 8HE
☎ (01543) 417333
🖥 (01543) 418098
📧 r.gee@theclubcompany.com
🏠 1000
♟ Richard Gee
✓ Simon Joyce
🏳 18 L 6305 yds SSS 70
9 hole Par 3 course
👤 WD–U WE after 2 pm SOC
££ £35 (£40)
🞉 2 miles N of Lichfield on A515
⊕ Floodlit driving range

🏠 Hawtree
🖥 www.theclubcompany.com

Manor (Kingstone) (1991)
Proprietary
Leese Hill, Kingstone, Uttoxeter, ST14 8QT
☎ (01889) 563234
🖥 (01889) 563234
📧 manorgc@btinternet.com
🏠 300
♟ A Foulds
✓ Chris Miller
🏳 18 L 6206 yds Par 71 SSS 70
👤 U–SOC (SOC WD)
££ £20 (£30)
🞉 4 miles W of Uttoxeter on A518
🏠 A Foulds

Newcastle-under-Lyme
(1908)
Whitmore Road, Newcastle-under-Lyme,
ST5 2QB
☎ (01782) 616583
🖥 (01782) 617531
📧 info@newcastlegolfclub.co.uk
🏠 575
♟ Vicki Wiseman
(Sec/Mgr) (01782) 617006
✓ A Salt (01782) 618526
🏳 18 L 6395 yds SSS 71
👤 WD–U H WE/BH–M SOC
££ 18 holes £30; 36 holes £40
🞉 2 miles SW of Newcastle-under-
Lyme on A53
🖥 www.newcastlegolfclub.co.uk

Onneley (1968)
Onneley, Crewe, Cheshire, CW3 9QF
☎ (01782) 750577
📧 all@onneleygolf.co.uk
🏠 410
♟ P Ball (01782) 846759
🏳 18 L 5728 yds Par 70 SSS 68
👤 WD–U Sat/BH–M Sun–NA
SOC–by appointment
££ D–£20
🞉 8 miles W of Newcastle, off A525
🏠 A Benson
🖥 www.onneleygolf.co.uk

Oxley Park (1913)
Stafford Road, Bushbury, Wolverhampton,
WV10 6DE
☎ (01902) 425892
📧 secretary@oxleyparkgolfclub
.fsnet.co.uk

Parkhall (1989)
Public
Hulme Road, Weston Coyney, Stoke-on-
Trent, ST3 5BH
☎ (01782) 599584
🖥 (01782) 599584
♟ M Robson
✓ T Earl
🏳 18 L 2335 yds Par 54
👤 WE–booking necessary SOC
££ On application
🞉 3 miles E of Stoke. Longton 1 mile

Penn (1908)
Penn Common, Wolverhampton, WV4 5JN
☎ (01902) 341142
🖥 (01902) 620504
📧 secretary@penngolfclub.co.uk
🏠 650
♟ MH Jones
✓ (01902) 330472 Mr G Dean
🏳 18 L 6492 yds SSS 72
👤 WD–U WE–M SOC
££ £33. Nov–Feb £20
🞉 2 miles SW of Wolverhampton, off
A449
🖥 www.penngolfclub.co.uk

Perton Park (1990)
Proprietary
Wrottesley Park Road, Perton,
Wolverhampton, WV6 7HL
☎ (01902) 380073
🖥 (01902) 326219
📧 admin@pertongolfclub.co.uk
🏠 500
♟ Simon Edwin (Gen Mgr)
🏳 18 L 6520 yds SSS 72
👤 U SOC
££ £20 (£25)
🞉 6 miles W of Wolverhampton, off
A454
⊕ Driving range, Bowling Greens,
Tennis Courts.
🖥 www.pertongolfclub.co.uk

Sandwell Park (1895)
Birmingham Road, West Bromwich, B71 4JJ
☎ (0121) 553 4637
🖥 (0121) 525 1651
📧 secretary@sandwellparkgolfclub
.co.uk
🏠 600
♟ Andy Turner (0121) 553 4637
✓ N Wylie (0121) 553 4384
🏳 18 L 6468 yds Par 71 SSS 73
👤 WD–U WE–MH SOC–WD
££ £40 D–£50
🞉 West Bromwich/Birmingham
boundary. By M5 Junction 1
🏠 HS Colt
🖥 www.sandwellparkgolfclub.co.uk

Sedgley (1992)
Pay and play
Sandyfields Road, Sedgley, Dudley,
DY3 3DL
☎ (01902) 880503
📧 sedgleygolfcentre@yahoo.co.uk
🏠 150
♟ David Cox
✓ G Mercer
🏳 9 L 3150 yds SSS 71
👤 U
££ 9: £7.50 18: £10
🞉 ½ mile from Sedgley, off A463
between Dudley and
Wolverhampton
⊕ Driving range
🏠 WG Cox

South Staffordshire (1892)
Danescourt Road, Tettenhall,
Wolverhampton, WV6 9BQ
☎ (01902) 751065

📞 (01902) 751159
📠 suelebeau@southstaffsgc.co.uk
🏤 550
🗝 P Baker (Dir of Golf)
✓ Shaun Ball
🏌 18 L 6500 yds SSS 71
🏑 WD–U WE/BH–M or by
   arrangement SOC
💶 £36
🚗 3 miles W of Wolverhampton, off
   A41; 7 miles off M54 J3
⊕ Driving range (under construction)
🏠 Harry Vardon
🖥 www.southstaffordshiregolfclub
   .co.uk

St Thomas's Priory   (1995)

Armitage Lane, Armitage, Rugeley,
WS15 1ED
📞 (01543) 492096
📠 (01543) 492096
📧 rohanlonpro@acl.com
🏤 450
🗝 RMR O'Hanlon
✓ RMR O'Hanlon (01543) 492096
🏌 18 L 5969 yds SSS 70
🏑 SOC–WD/WE
💶 £30 (£40) 2 for 1 except WE
🚗 1 mile SE of Rugeley on A513, opp
   Ash Tree Inn
🏠 Paul Mulholland
🖥 www.st-thomass-golfclub.com

Stafford Castle   (1906)

Newport Road, Stafford, ST16 1BP
📞 (01785) 223821
📠 (01785) 223821
📧 staffordcastle.golfclub@globaluk
   .net
🏤 440
🗝 Mrs S Calvert
🏌 9 L 6383 yds Par 71 SSS 70
🏑 WD–U (phone prior to visit)
   WE–after 1pm
💶 D–£18 (D–£22)
🚗 ½ mile W of Stafford

Stone   (1896)

The Fillybrooks, Stone, ST15 0NB
📞 (01785) 813103
🏤 314
🗝 PR Farley (01785) 284875
🏌 9 L 6307 yds Par 71 SSS 70
🏑 WD–U WE/BH–M SOC–WD
💶 £20
🚗 ½ mile W of Stone on A34
🖥 www.stonegolfclub.co.uk

Swindon   (1976)

Proprietary
Bridgnorth Road, Swindon, Dudley,
DY3 4PU
📞 (01902) 897031
📠 (01902) 326219
📧 admin@swindongolfclub.co.uk
🏤 500
🗝 Simon Edwin (Gen Mgr)
🏌 18 L 6121 yds Par 71 SSS 70
🏑 U SOC–WD/WE
💶 £25 (£28)
🚗 5 miles SW of Wolverhampton on
   B4176, Dudley to Bridgnorth road
⊕ Driving range
🖥 www.swindongolfclub.co.uk

Tamworth   (1976)

Public
Eagle Drive, Amington, Tamworth, B77 4EG
📞 (01827) 709303
📠 (01827) 709304
🏤 395
🗝 Elaine Pugh
✓ W Alcock
🏌 18 L 6488 yds SSS 72
🏑 U SOC–WD WE
💶 £16.80 (£18.90)
🚗 2½ miles E of Tamworth on
   B5000. M42 Jct 10, 3 miles
⊕ Practice range
🏠 Hawtree

Trentham   (1894)

14 Barlaston Old Road, Trentham, Stoke-
on-Trent, ST4 8HB
📞 (01782) 658109
📠 (01782) 644024
📧 secretary@trenthamgolf.org
🏤 420
🗝 S K Owen
✓ S Wilson (01782) 657309
🏌 18 L 6644 yds SSS 72
🏑 WD–H WE/BH–M (or enquire
   Sec) SOC–WD
💶 £50 (£50)
🚗 3 miles S of Newcastle-under-Lyme
   on A5305, off A34. M6 Junction 15
🖥 www.trenthamgolf.org

Trentham Park   (1936)

Trentham Park, Stoke-on-Trent, ST4 8AE
📞 (01782) 642245
📠 (01782) 658800
📧 manager@trenthamparkgolfclub
   .com
🏤 500 100(L) 50(J)
🗝 John Adams (01782) 658800
✓ S Lynn (01782) 642125
🏌 18 L 6425 yds SSS 71
🏑 H SOC–Wed & Fri
💶 £38 (£43)
🚗 4 miles S of Newcastle on A34. M6
   Junction 15, 1 mile
🖥 www.trenthamparkgolfclub.com

Uttoxeter   (1970)

Wood Lane, Uttoxeter, ST14 8JR
📞 (01889) 566552
📠 (01889) 566552
📧 admin@uttoxetergolfclub.com
🏤 700
🗝 RW Harvey
✓ AD McCandless (01889) 564884
🏌 18 L 5801 yds Par 70 SSS 69
🏑 WD–U WE–by arrangement SOC
💶 D–£28 (£30)
🚗 Close to A50, ½ mile past
   entrance to Uttoxeter racecourse
🖥 www.uttoxetergolfclub.com

Walsall   (1907)

Broadway, Walsall, WS1 3EY
📞 (01922) 613512
📠 (01922) 616460
📧 secretary@walsallgolfclub.com
🏤 600
🗝 HJ Durkin (01922) 613512
✓ R Lambert (01922) 626766

🏌 18 L 6259 yds SSS 70
🏑 WD–U WE–M SOC
💶 £33
🚗 1 mile S of Walsall, off A34. M6
   Junction 7
🏠 McKenzie
🖥 www.walsallgolfclub.co.uk

Wergs   (1990)

Pay and play
Keepers Lane, Tettenhall, WV6 8UA
📞 (01902) 742225
📠 (01902) 844553
📧 wergs.golfclub@btinternet.com
🏤 100
🗝 Mrs G Parsons
✓ S Weir (07973) 899607
🏌 18 L 6949 yds Par 72 SSS 73
🏑 U
💶 D–£17 (£22)
🚗 3 miles W of Wolverhampton on
   A41
⊕ 20 acre practice area
🏠 CW Moseley
🖥 www.wergs.com

Westwood   (1923)

Newcastle Road, Wallbridge, Leek,
ST13 7AA
📞 (01538) 398385
📠 (01538) 382485
📧 westwoodgolfclub-leek@zen.co.uk
🏤 484
🗝 Tony Horton
✓ Greg Rogula 01538 398897
🏌 18 L 6105 yds SSS 70
🏑 U SOC–WD–WE
💶 £25 (£30) D £35 (£40)
🚗 W boundary of Leek on A53
🖥 www.leekwestwoodgolfclub.co.uk

Whiston Hall   (1971)

Whiston, Cheadle, ST10 2HZ
📞 (01538) 266260
📠 (01538) 266820
📧 enq@whistonhall.com
🏤 500
🗝 LC & RM Cliff (Mgr)
🏌 18 L 5742 yds SSS 69
🏑 U SOC
💶 £10
🚗 8 miles NE of Stoke-on-Trent on
   A52, nr Alton Towers (3 miles)
⊕ Hotel available for golfing breaks
🏠 T Cooper
🖥 www.whistonhall.com

Whittington Heath   (1886)

Tamworth Road, Lichfield, WS14 9PW
📞 (01543) 432317 (Admin)
   (01543) 432212 (Steward)
📠 (01543) 433962
📧 info@whittingtonheathgc.co.uk
🏤 670
🗝 Mrs JA Burton
✓ AR Sadler (01543) 432261
🏌 18 L 6490 yds SSS 71
🏑 WD–H or I WE/BH–M SOC–Wed
   & Thurs, Mon/Tue/Fri pm
💶 £40 D–£55
🚗 2½ miles E of Lichfield on
   Tamworth road (A51)
🖥 www.whittingtonheathgc.co.uk

Wolstanton (1904)
Dimsdale Old Hall, Hassam Parade,
Wolstanton, Newcastle, ST5 9DR
- ☎ (01782) 616995
- 📠 (01782) 622413
- 🏛 625
- 🖎 Mrs VJ Keenan (01782) 622413
- 🏌 S Arnold (01782) 622718
- ⛳ 18 L 5533 yds SSS 68
- 👥 WD–H WE–M SOC–WD
- ££ £27.50
- 🚗 1½ miles NW of Newcastle (A34)
- 💻 www.wolstantongolfclub.com

Suffolk

Aldeburgh (1884)
Aldeburgh, IP15 5PE
- ☎ (01728) 452890
- 📠 (01728) 452937
- 🖎 info@aldeburghgolfclub.co.uk
- 🏛 847
- 🏌 G Hogg
- 🏌 K Preston (01728) 453309
- ⛳ 18 L 6603 yds Par 68 SSS 71
  9 L 2114 yds SSS 64
- 👥 H–2 ball play only SOC
- ££ On application
- 🚗 6 miles E of A12 (A1094)
- ⊕ Practice ground; chipping and
  putting greens.
- 🏠 W Fernie/J Thompson
- 💻 www.aldeburghgolfclub.co.uk

Beccles (1899)
The Common, Beccles, NR34 9BX
- ☎ (01502) 712244
- 🖎 alan@ereira.wanadoo.co.uk
- 🏛 145
- 🏌 A Ereira (01502) 715222
  (07896) 087297
- ⛳ 9 L 2696 yds SSS 68
- 👥 WD–U Sun–M SOC
- ££ £5 (£10)
- 🚗 10 miles W of Lowestoft (A146)
- 💻 www.becclesgolfclub.co.uk

Brett Vale (1992)
Proprietary
Noakes Road, Raydon, Ipswich, IP7 5LR
- ☎ (01473) 310718
- 🖎 info@brettvalegolf.com
- 🏛 500
- 🏌 S Williams
- 🏌 Paul Bate
- ⛳ 18 L 5813 yds Par 70 SSS 67
- 👥 U–booking advisable. Soft spikes
  only. SOC–WD
- ££ £25 (£30)
- 🚗 5 miles N of Colchester, off A12
  (B1070), towards Hadleigh
- ⊕ Driving range. 3 x 3 Par 3 holes
- 🏠 Howard Swan
- 💻 www.brettvale.com

Bungay & Waveney Valley
(1889)
Outney Common, Bungay, NR35 1DS
- ☎ (01986) 892337

Bury St Edmunds (1922)
Tut Hill, Fornham All Saints, Bury St
Edmunds, IP28 6LG
- ☎ (01284) 755979
- 📠 (01284) 763288
- 🖎 info@burygolf.co.uk
- 🏛 632(M) 145(L)
- 🏌 JF Taylor
- 🏌 M Jillings (01284) 755978
- ⛳ 18 L 6675 yds Par 72 SSS 72
  9 L 2184 yds Par 31 SSS 31 (Pay &
  Play)
- 👥 18 WD–U SOC–WD 9 U
- ££ 9: £16 (£18); 18: £38 D–£50
- 🚗 2 miles W of Bury St Edmunds on
  B1106, off A14 Jct 42
- 🏠 Ted Ray
- 💻 www.club-noticeboard.co.uk
  /burystedmunds

Cretingham (1984)
Grove Farm, Cretingham, Woodbridge,
IP13 7BA
- ☎ (01728) 685275
- 📠 (01728) 685488
- 🏛 400
- 🏌 Mrs K Jackson
- 🏌 N Jackson
- ⛳ 18 L 5278 yds
  9 L 4969 yds Par 34
- 👥 U SOC
- ££ 18: £20 D–£26 (+BH £22 D–£28)
- 🚗 2 miles SE of Earl Soham. 11 miles
  N of Ipswich
- ⊕ Practice range; putting green
- 🏠 J Austin

Diss (1903)
Stuston Common, Diss, IP21 4AA
- ☎ (01379) 641025
- 📠 (01379) 644586
- 🖎 sec.dissgolf@virgin.net
- 🏛 650
- 🏌 Tom Bailey (01379) 641025
- 🏌 Nigel Taylor (01379) 644399
- ⛳ 18 L 6206 yds Par 70 SSS 70
- 👥 WD–U WE–phone first (SOC)
- ££ £28 D–£36
- 🚗 1 mile SE of Diss, off A140, on
  B1077
- ⊕ Driving range 1 mile E of clubhouse
  on A143/A140 junction
- 🏠 Michael Pinner (extension to 18
  holes)
- 💻 www.club-noticeboard.co.uk

Felixstowe Ferry (1880)
Ferry Road, Felixstowe, IP11 9RY
- ☎ (01394) 286834
- 📠 (01394) 273679
- 🖎 secretary@felixstowegolf.co.uk
- 🏛 900
- 🏌 M Tinge (01394) 286834
- 🏌 I Macpherson (01394) 283975
- ⛳ 18 L 6379 yds SSS 71
  9 L 2986 yds Par 35
- 👥 WD–H after 9am WE–H after
  2.30pm SOC. 9 hole course–U
- ££ 9: £13 D–£16; 18: £27.50
  D–£37.50 (£40)
- 🚗 2 miles NE of Felixstowe, towards
  Ferry
- 🏠 Henry Cotton (1947)
- 💻 www.felixstowegolf.co.uk

Flempton (1895)
Bury St Edmunds, IP28 6EQ
- ☎ (01284) 728291
- 🖎 flemptongolfclub@freebie.net
- 🏛 260
- 🏌 MS Clark
- 🏌 K Canham
- ⛳ 9 L 6184 yds Par 70 SSS 70
- 👥 WD–H WE/BH–H by prior
  arrangement
- ££ £35 D–£40 (£35 (D–£40)
- 🚗 4 miles NW of Bury St Edmunds
  on A1101
- 🏠 JH Taylor

Fynn Valley (1991)
Proprietary
Witnesham, Ipswich, IP6 9JA
- ☎ (01473) 785267
- 📠 (01473) 785632
- 🖎 enquiries@fynn-valley.co.uk
- 🏛 650
- 🏌 AR Tyrrell (01473) 785267
- 🏌 P Wilby (01473) 785463
- ⛳ 18 L 6391 yds Par 70 SSS 71
  9 hole Par 3 course
- 👥 U exc Sun am SOC
- ££ £26 (£32)
- 🚗 2 miles N of Ipswich on B1077
- ⊕ Driving range; restaurant;
  conference facilities
- 🏠 Antonio Primavera
- 💻 www.fynn-valley.co.uk

Halesworth (1990)
Proprietary
Bramfield Road, Halesworth, IP19 9XA
- ☎ (01986) 875567
- 📠 (01986) 874565
- 🖎 info@halesworthgc.co.uk
- 🏛 400
- 🏌 Chris Aldred (Mgr)
- 🏌 Richard Davies
- ⛳ 18 L 6506 yds SSS 72
  9 L 2280 yds SSS 33
- 👥 U
- ££ 9: £7 (£8); 18: £20 D–£25 (£25)
- 🚗 1 mile S of Halesworth, off A144
- ⊕ Floodlit driving range
- 🏠 JW Johnson
- 💻 www.halesworthgc.co.uk

Haverhill (1974)
Coupals Road, Haverhill, CB9 7UW
- ☎ (01440) 761951
- 📠 (01440) 761951
- 🖎 HAVERHILLGOLF
  @coupalsroad.eclipse.co.uk
- 🏛 700
- 🏌 Mrs L Farrant, D Renyard (Mgr)
- 🏌 Paul Wilby (01440) 712628
- ⛳ 18 L 5986 yds SSS 69
- 👥 U–phone Pro SOC–WD
- ££ £25 (£35)
- 🚗 1 mile E of Haverhill, off A1107
- 🏠 Lawrie/Pilgrem
- 💻 www.club-noticeboard.co.uk

Hintlesham (1991)
Hintlesham, Ipswich, IP8 3JG
- ☎ (01473) 652761
- 📠 (01473) 652750
- 🖎 sales@hintleshamgolfclub.com

🕮 425
🏌 D Roblin
✓ H Roblin
ℙ 18 L 6580 yds SSS 72
👥 WD–U WE SOC
££ £36 (£46)
🚗 4 miles W of Ipswich on A1071
🏠 Hawtree
🖳 www.hintleshamgolfclub.com

Ipswich (Purdis Heath) (1895)

Purdis Heath, Bucklesham Road, Ipswich, IP3 8UQ
☎ (01473) 728941
🖵 (01473) 715236
📧 neill@ipswichgolfclub.com
🕮 740
🏌 NM Ellice (01473) 728941
✓ K Lovelock (01473) 724017
ℙ 18 L 6439 yds Par 71 SSS 71
   9 L 1930 yds Par 31
👥 18 hole: H SOC; 9 hole: U
££ 9: D–£10 (£15); 18: £40 (£45)
   (D–£50 D–£55)
🚗 3 miles E of Ipswich
🏠 James Braid
🖳 www.ipswichgolfclub.com

Links (Newmarket) (1902)

Cambridge Road, Newmarket, CB8 0TG
☎ (01638) 663000
🖵 (01638) 661476
📧 secretary@linksgc.fsbusiness.co.uk
🕮 750
🏌 ML Hartley
✓ J Sharkey (01638) 662395
ℙ 18 L 6558 yds SSS 72
👥 H exc Sun–M before 11.30am SOC
££ £30 D–£38 (£34 D–£42) (2008)
🚗 1 mile SW of Newmarket
🖳 www.club-noticeboard.co.uk
   /newmarket

Newton Green (1907)

Newton Green, Sudbury, CO10 0QN
☎ (01787) 377217
🖵 (01787) 377549
📧 info@newtongreengolfclub.co.uk
🕮 550
🏌 Mrs C List
✓ T Cooper (01787) 313215
ℙ 18 L 5961 yds SSS 69
👥 WD WE SOC WE&BH after
   12.30pm
££ £23 (£27)
🚗 4 miles S of Sudbury on A134
🖳 www.newtongreengolfclub.co.uk

Rookery Park (1891)

Beccles Road, Carlton Colville, Lowestoft, NR33 8HJ
☎ (01502) 509190
🖵 (01502) 509191
📧 office@rookeryparkgolfclub.co.uk
🕮 860
🏌 RF Jones
✓ M Elsworthy (01502) 515103
ℙ 18 L 6714 yds Par 72 SSS 72
   9 hole Par 3 course
👥 WD–U SBH–after 11am
   Sun–NA SOC H
££ £35 D–£42 (£42 D–£48 – inc BH)

🚗 3 miles W of Lowestoft (A146)
⊕ Par 3 9-hole course; driving range
   with teaching facilities
🏠 CD Lawrie
🖳 www.club-noticeboard.co.uk

Royal Worlington & Newmarket (1893)

Golf Links Road, Worlington, Bury St Edmunds, IP28 8SD
☎ (01638) 712216 (Clubhouse)
🖵 (01638) 717787
📧 secretary@royalworlington.co.uk
🕮 330
🏌 S Ballentine (01638) 717787
✓ R Beadles (01638) 715224
ℙ 9 L 6246 yds SSS 70
👥 Phone for availability
££ 18 holes £45 D–£60
🚗 6 miles NE of Newmarket, off A11
🏠 Tom Dunn
🖳 www.royalworlington.co.uk

Rushmere (1927)

Rushmere Heath, Ipswich, IP4 5QQ
☎ (01473) 725648
🖵 (01473) 273852
📧 rushmeregolfclub@btconnect.com
🕮 770
🏌 RWG Tawell (01473) 725648
✓ K Vince (01473) 728076
ℙ 18 L 6262 yds SSS 70
👥 WD–H WE/BH–H after 2.30pm
££ £38
🚗 3 miles E of Ipswich, off
   Woodbridge road (A1214)
🏠 David Williams (bunkers 1999)
🖳 www.club-
   noticeboard.co.uk/rushmere

Seckford (1991)

Seckford Hall Road, Great Bealings, Woodbridge, IP13 6NT
☎ (01394) 388000
🖵 (01394) 382818
📧 secretary@seckfordgolf.co.uk
🕮 400
🏌 G Cook
✓ S Jay
ℙ 18 L 4881 yds Par 67 SSS 64
👥 U–booking necessary SOC WD
   WE after 12 online booking
   available
££ Summer: £25 (£30) Winter: Please
   apply
🚗 SW of Woodbridge, off A12, 7
   miles Ipswich
⊕ Driving range, practice green,
   practice bunker
🏠 J Johnson
🖳 www.seckfordgolf.co.uk

Southwold (1884)

The Common, Southwold, IP18 6TB
☎ (01502) 723234
📧 mail@southwoldgolfclub.co.uk
🕮 380
🏌 R Wilshaw (01502) 723248
✓ B Allen (01502) 723790
ℙ 9 L 6052 yds Par 70 SSS 69
👥 U (subject to fixtures) SOC
££ £26 (£28) £15 after 2.30 summer/
   12.30 winter

🚗 35 miles NE of Ipswich
🏠 J Braid

Stoke-by-Nayland (1972)

Keepers Lane, Leavenheath, Colchester, CO6 4PZ
☎ (01206) 262836
🖵 (01206) 263356
📧 golfsecretary@stokebynayland.com
🕮 1400
🏌 M Verhelst (01206) 265815
✓ R Hitchcock (01206) 265812
ℙ Gainsborough 18 L 6498 yds
   SSS 71
   Constable 18 L 6544 yds SSS 71
👥 WD–U WE/BH–H after 12 noon
   SOC
££ £35 (£45)
🚗 Off A134 Colchester-Sudbury road
   on B1068
⊕ Driving range – 20 bays covered
🖳 www.stokebynayland.com

Stowmarket (1962)

Lower Road, Onehouse, Stowmarket, IP14 3DA
☎ (01449) 736473
🖵 (01449) 736826
📧 mail@stowmarketgolfclub.co.uk
🕮 600
🏌 GR West (01449) 736473
✓ D Burl
ℙ 18 L 6119 yds SSS 69
   9-hole short course
👥 H SOC–Thurs & Fri
££ £34 (£44)
🚗 2½ miles SW of Stowmarket
⊕ Driving range;
🖳 www.club-noticeboard.co.uk
   /stowmarket

The Suffolk Golf & Spa Hotel (1974)

Fornham St Genevieve, Bury St Edmunds, IP28 6JQ
☎ (01284) 706777
🖵 (01284) 706721
📧 sales.suffolkgolf@ohiml.com
🕮 652
🏌 P Thorpe
✓ S Hall
ℙ 18 L 6376 yds SSS 71
👥 U SOC WD WE
££ £32 (£37)
🚗 2 miles NW of Bury St Edmunds
   (A14), off B1106
🖳 www.oxfordhotelsandinns.com

Thorpeness Hotel & Golf Course (1923)

Thorpeness, Leiston, IP16 4NH
☎ (01728) 452176
🖵 (01728) 453868
📧 charlie@thorpeness.co.uk
🕮 700
🏌 Charlie Damonsing (01728) 452176
✓ F Hill (01728) 454926
ℙ 18 L 6281 yds SSS 71
👥 H
££ £37 (£42)
🚗 2 miles N of Aldeburgh
⊕ Buggies available for hire

♟ James Braid
🖥 www.thorpeness.co.uk

Ufford Park (1992)
Yarmouth Road, Ufford, Woodbridge, IP12 1QW
☎ (01394) 382836
🖥 (01394) 383582
✉ golf@uffordparkco.uk
🏠 400
♟ Ray Baines (Sec) (part time) Alan Knight (Mgr) (full time)
🏌 S Robertson (01394) 383480
🏴 18 L 6312 yds SSS 71
♟ U H SOC
£€ £30 (£40)
🚗 2 miles N of Woodbridge, off A12
⊕ Golf Academy; 32 bay 2-storey driving range
♟ P Pilgrim
🖥 www.uffordpark.co.uk

Waldringfield (1983)
Newbourne Road, Waldringfield, Woodbridge, IP12 4PT
☎ (01473) 736768
🖥 (01473) 736793
✉ patgolf1@aol.com
🏠 550
♟ Pat Whitham
🏌 A Lucas (01473) 736417
🏴 18 L 6141 yds SSS 69
♟ WD–U WE/BH–M before noon SOC–WD
£€ £25 (30)
🚗 3 miles E of Ipswich, off A12
♟ P Pilgrem
🖥 www.club-noticeboard.co.uk

Woodbridge (1893)
Bromeswell Heath, Woodbridge, IP12 2PF
☎ (01394) 382038
🖥 (01394) 382392
✉ info@woodbridgegolfclub.co.uk
🏠 700
♟ AJ Bull
🏌 T Johnson (01394) 383213
🏴 18 L 6299 yds Par 70 SSS 71
9 L 6382 yds SSS 70
♟ 9:U 18:H WE/BH–M SOC
£€ 9: £15 (£15); 18: £42 (£42) Call office for special deals
🚗 2 miles E of Woodbridge on A1152 towards Orford
♟ F Hawtree
🖥 www.woodbridgegolfclub.co.uk

Surrey

Abbey Moor (1991)
Pay and play
Green Lane, Addlestone, KT15 2XU
☎ (01932) 570741/570765

The Addington (1913)
Proprietary
205 Shirley Church Road, Croydon, CRO 5AB
☎ (020) 8777 1055
🖥 (020) 8777 6661
✉ info@addingtongolf.com

✎ Oliver Peel
🏌 Malcolm Churchill
🏴 18 L 6338 yds SSS 71
♟ SOC–WD WE–after 12pm
£€ Mon–Thur £60 Fri £65 (£100)
🚗 E Croydon 2½ miles
⊕ Practice hole, par 4
♟ JF Abercromby
🖥 www.addingtongolf.com

Addington Court (1932)
Pay and play
Featherbed Lane, Addington, Croydon, CRO 9AA
☎ (020) 8657 0281 (Bookings)
🖥 (020) 8651 0282
✉ addington@crown-golf.co.uk
🏠 600
✎ Bradley Chard (020) 657 0281
🏌 David Bailey 07951 025252
🏴 Championship 18 L 5599 yds SSS 67
Falconwood 18 L 5472 yds SSS 67
Academy 9 L 1804 yds SSS 62
Pitch & putt 18 holes
♟ U SOC
£€ Championship £19 (£25); Falconwood £17 (£22); Academy £10 (£11); Pitch & Putt £2 (£2)
🚗 3 miles SE of Croydon
⊕ Driving range
♟ F Hawtree Sr
🖥 www.addingtoncourt-golfclub.co.uk

Addington Palace (1930)
Addington Park, Gravel Hill, Addington, CRO 5BB
☎ (020) 8654 3061
🖥 (020) 8655 3632
✉ info@addingtonpalacegolf.co.uk
🏠 600
🏌 R Williams (020) 8654 1786
🏴 18 L 6373 yds Par 71 SSS 70
♟ WD–M WD–U SOC
£€ £45 D–£50
🚗 2 miles E of Croydon Station
♟ JH Taylor
🖥 www.addingtonpalacegolf.co.uk

Banstead Downs (1890)
Burdon Lane, Belmont, Sutton, SM2 7DD
☎ (020) 8642 2284
🖥 (020) 8642 5252
✉ secretary@bansteaddowns.com
🏠 708
✎ Mrs KS Cote
🏌 I Golding (020) 8642 6884
🏴 18 L 6192 yds SSS 69
♟ WD–H M,T,W,T/BH–M SOC–Thurs Fri,Sat,Sun with members only BH with members only
£€ £45 am, £35 pm
🚗 6 miles north of M25 J8
♟ JH Braid
🖥 www.bansteaddowns.com

Barrow Hills (1970)
Longcross, Chertsey, KT16 0DS
☎ (01344) 635770
🏠 300
✎ R Hammond (01483) 234807
🏴 18 L 3090 yds SSS 53

♟ M
£€ On application
🚗 4 miles W of Chertsey

Betchworth Park (1911)
Reigate Road, Dorking, RH4 1NZ
☎ (01306) 882052
🖥 (01306) 877462
✉ manager@betchworthparkgc.co.uk
🏠 560
♟ Richard Hall (Sec/Mgr)
🏌 Andy Tocher (01306) 884334
🏴 18 L 6325 yds Par 69 SSS 70
♟ WD exc Tues am WE–NA exc Sun pm SOC–Mon & Thurs
£€ £40 (£50); after 4pm £20 (£30)
🚗 1 mile E of Dorking on A25; Jcts 8 & 9 M25
⊕ Large practice area; buggies for hire
♟ HS Colt
🖥 www.betchworthparkgc.co.uk

Bletchingley (1993)
Proprietary
Church Lane, Bletchingley, RH1 4LP
☎ (01883) 744666
🖥 (01883) 744284
✉ info@bletchingleygolf.co.uk
🏠 500
✎ Steven Cockson (Golf Operations Mgr)
🏌 Steven Cockson (01883) 744848
🏴 18 L 6585 yds Par 72 SSS 72
♟ WD–U WE after 12 noon
£€ £28 (£40)
🚗 1 mile S of M25 Junction 6 on A25
🖥 www.bletchingleygolf.co.uk

Bowenhurst Golf Centre
Mill Lane, Crondall, Farnham, GU10 5RP
☎ (01252) 851695
🖥 (01252) 852225
✎ GL Corbey (01252) 851695
🏌 Alastair Hardaway (01252) 851344
🏴 9 L 2023/4046 yds Par 62 SSS 63
♟ U SOC WD
£€ 9: £10 (£12) 18: £14 (£16.50). WD reduced fees for Snr/Jnr
🚗 2 miles SW of Farnham on A287. M3 Jct 5 (4 miles)
⊕ 20 bay floodlit driving range open 8–10pm
♟ G Finn, N Finn

Bramley (1913)
Bramley, Guildford, GU5 0AL
☎ (01483) 892696
🖥 (01483) 894673
✉ secretary@bramleygolfclub.co.uk
🏠 775
✎ Gary Peddie (Gen Mgr) (01483) 892696
🏌 G Peddie (01483) 893685
🏴 18 L 5930 yds SSS 69
♟ WD–U WE–M SOC–WD
£€ £40
🚗 3 miles S of Guildford on A281
⊕ Driving range – members and green fees only
♟ Mayo/Braid
🖥 www.bramleygolfclub.co.uk

For list of abbreviations and key to symbols see page 647

Broadwater Park
Guildford Road, Farncombe, Godalming,
GU7 3BU
- ☎ **(01483) 429955**
- ⌨ 126
- ✍ MJ Winwright (Dir)
- ✓ KD Milton
- ↦ 9 L 1301 yds Par 27
- ※ U
- ££ £5.25 (£6)
- ⇔ 1 mile SE of Godalming (A3100)
- ⊕ 16-bay floodlit driving range
- ⌂ KD Milton

Burhill   (1907)
Burwood Road, Walton-on-Thames,
KT12 4BL
- ☎ **(01932) 227345**
- ⌨ (01932) 267159
- ✉ info@burhillgolf-club.co.uk
- ⌨ 1100
- ✍ D Cook (Gen Mgr)
- ✓ Pip Elson (01932) 221729
- ↦ Old 18 L 6479 yds Par 70 SSS 71
     New 18 L 6597 yds Par 72 SSS 71
- ※ WD–H WE/BH–M
- ££ On application
- ⇔ Between Walton-on-Thames and
     Cobham, off Burwood Road; M25
     Jct 10
- ⊕ Driving range
- ⌂ Willie Park/Gidman
- ✉ www.burhillgolf-club.co.uk

Camberley Heath   (1912)
Golf Drive, Camberley, GU15 1JG
- ☎ **(01276) 23258**
- ⌨ (01276) 692505
- ✉ info@camberleyheathgolfclub
     .co.uk
- ⌨ 765
- ✍ J Hiscock
- ✓ G Ralph (01276) 27905
- ↦ 18 L 6426 yds SSS 71
- ※ WD–H WE–M SOC H
- ££ £60 (£80)
- ⇔ 1½ miles S of Camberley on
     A325
- ⊕ Practice Area; Putting Green
- ⌂ HS Colt
- ✉ www.camberleyheathgolfclub
     .co.uk

Central London Golf Centre
(1992)
Public
Burntwood Lane, Wandsworth, London,
SW17 0AT
- ☎ **(020) 8871 2468**
- ⌨ (020) 8874 7447
- ✉ info@clgc.co.uk
- ⌨ 200
- ✍ Bjoern Lueschen (Mgr)
- ✓ Gary Clements
- ↦ 9 L 4658 yds SSS 62
- ※ U SOC
- ££ £11 (£13.50)
- ⇔ Off Burntwood Lane SW17
- ⊕ Driving range; cart hire £7.50
- ⌂ Patrick Tallack
- ✉ www.clgc.co.uk

Chessington Golf Centre
(1983)
Pay and play
Garrison Lane, Chessington, KT9 2LW
- ☎ **(020) 8391 0948**
- ⌨ (020) 8397 2068
- ✉ info@chessingtongolf.co.uk
- ⌨ 85
- ✍ M Bedford
- ✓ M Janes
- ↦ 9 L 1679 yds Par 60 SSS 55
- ※ U
- ££ £9 (£11)
- ⇔ Off A243, opp Chessington South
     Station. M25 Junction 9
- ⊕ Driving range (floodlit)
- ⌂ Patrick Tullach
- ✉ www.chessingtongolf.co.uk

Chiddingfold   (1994)
Petworth Road, Chiddingfold, GU8 4SL
- ☎ **(01428) 685888**
- ⌨ (01428) 685939
- ✉ chiddingfoldgolf@btconnect.com
- ↦ 18 L 5482 yds Par 70 SSS 67
- ※ U SOC
- ££ £18 (£23)
- ⇔ On A283 between Petworth and
     Guildford
- ⌂ Johnathan Gaunt

Chipstead   (1906)
How Lane, Chipstead, Coulsdon, CR5 3LN
- ☎ **(01737) 555781**
- ⌨ (01737) 555404
- ✉ office@chipsteadgolf.co.uk
- ⌨ 600
- ✍ Mrs SA Wallace (Admin)
     (01737) 555781
- ✓ G Torbett (Golf Dir)
     (01737) 554939
- ↦ 18 L 5450 yds SSS 67
- ※ WD–U WE/BH–M
- ££ £30. After 4pm–£20
- ⇔ M25 Junction 8 (A217)
- ✉ www.chipsteadgolf.co.uk

Chobham   (1994)
Chobham Road, Knaphill, Woking,
GU21 2TZ
- ☎ **(01276) 855584**
- ⌨ (01276) 855663
- ✉ info@chobhamgolfclub.co.uk
- ⌨ 750
- ✍ Pam Reade-Hill
- ✓ T Coombes (01276) 855748
- ↦ 18 L 5959 yds Par 69 SSS 69
- ※ WD–H WD–SOC
- ££ £44
- ⇔ 3 miles E of M3 Junction 3 between
     Chobham and Knaphill
- ⌂ Alliss/Clark
- ✉ www.chobhamgolfclub.co.uk

Clandon Regis   (1994)
Epsom Road, West Clandon, GU4 7TT
- ☎ **(01483) 224888**
- ⌨ (01483) 211781
- ✉ office@clandonregis-golfclub.co.uk
- ⌨ 650
- ✍ Paul Napier (Gen Mgr)
- ✓ S Lloyd (01483) 223922

- ↦ 18 L 6485 yds Par 72 SSS 71
- ※ WD–U WE–NA before 10.30am
     SOC–WD
- ££ £40 (£50)
- ⇔ 3 miles E of Guildford on A246
- ⊕ Practice area; chipping area; indoor
     nets
- ⌂ David Williams
- ✉ www.clandonregis-golfclub.co.uk

Coombe Hill   (1911)
Golf Club Drive, Coombe Lane West,
Kingston, KT2 7DF
- ☎ **(0208) 336 7600**
- ⌨ (0208) 336 7601
- ✉ thesecretary@chgc.net
- ⌨ 527
- ✍ DR Cromie
- ✓ A Dunn (0208) 336 7615
- ↦ 18 L 6403 yds SSS 71
- ※ WD–I or H WE–NA SOC
- ££ £80 D–£100
- ⇔ 1 mile W of New Malden on A238
- ⌂ JF Abercromby
- ✉ www.coombehillgolfclub.com

Coombe Wood   (1904)
George Road, Kingston Hill, Kingston-upon-
Thames, KT2 7NS
- ☎ **(0208) 942 0388 (Clubhouse)**
- ⌨ (0208) 942 5665
- ✉ geoff.seed@coombewoodgolf.com
- ⌨ 600
- ✍ G Seed (0208) 942 0388
- ✓ P Wright (020) 8942 6764
- ↦ 18 L 5312 yds SSS 65
- ※ WD–U WE–NA before 2.30pm
     SOC–WD
- ££ £35 (£45)
- ⇔ 1 mile E of Kingston-upon-Thames,
     off A3 at Robin Hood roundabout
     or Coombe junction
- ⌂ Williamson
- ✉ www.coombewoodgolf.com

Coulsdon Manor   (1937)
Pay and play
Coulsdon Court Road, Old Coulsdon,
Croydon, CR5 2LL
- ☎ **(020) 8660 6083**
- ⌨ (020) 8668 3118
- ✉ sales.coulsdon@ohiml.com
- ⌨ 350
- ✍ A Oxby (020) 8668 0414
- ✓ Matt Asbury (020) 8660 6083
- ↦ 18 L 6037 yds SSS 70
- ※ U
- ££ £23 (£29.50)
- ⇔ 5 miles S of Croydon on B2030.
     M25 Junction 7
- ⊕ Practice ground; Practice nets;
     Putting green
- ⌂ HS Colt
- ✉ www.oxfordhotelsandinns.com

Cranfield Golf at Sandown
(1970)
Public
More Lane, Esher, KT10 8AN
- ☎ **(01372) 468093**

The Cranleigh (1985)
Barhatch Lane, Cranleigh, GU6 7NG
- ☎ (01483) 268855
- ✉ clubshop@cranleighgolfandleisure.co.uk

Croham Hurst (1911)
Croham Road, South Croydon, CR2 7HJ
- ☎ (020) 8657 5581
- ☎ (020) 8657 3229
- ✉ secretary@chgc.co.uk
- ☐ 515 110(L) 50(J)
- ♙ S Mackinson
- ✎ D Green (020) 8657 7705
- ⊳ 18 L 6373 yds SSS 70
- ☵ WD–I WE/BH–M
- ££ £40 (£50)
- ❀ I mile from S Croydon. M25 Junction 6–A22–B270–B269
- ⌂ Braid/Hawtree
- ▤ www.chgc.co.uk

Cuddington (1929)
Banstead Road, Banstead, SM7 1RD
- ☎ (020) 8393 0952
- ☎ (020) 8786 7025
- ✉ secretary@cuddingtongc.co/uk
- ☐ 760
- ✎ S Davis (020) 8393 0952
- ✎ M Warner (020) 8393 5850
- ⊳ 18 L 6614 yds SSS 71
- ☵ WD–I WE–M H
- ££ £45 (£55)
- ❀ M25 Jct 8 Nr Banstead Station
- ⊕ Driving range; nets; practice putting green.
- ⌂ HS Colt
- ▤ www.cuddingtongc.co.uk

Dorking (1897)
Deepdene Avenue, Chart Park, Dorking, RH5 4BX
- ☎ (01306) 886917
- ✉ info@dorkinggolfclub.co.uk

Drift (1975)
Proprietary
The Drift, East Horsley, KT24 5HD
- ☎ (01483) 284641
- ☎ (01483) 284642
- ✉ info@driftgolfclub.com
- ☐ 700
- ✎ R Gumbrell (GM)
- ✎ (01483) 284772 Sam Quirke
- ⊳ 18 L 6425 yds SSS 72
- ☵ WD–U WE–U after 12.00 SOC
- ££ £40 (£45)
- ❀ 2 miles off A3 (B2039). M25 Jct 10
- ⊕ Grass driving range in season
- ⌂ Sir Henry Cotton & Robert Sandow
- ▤ www.driftgolfclub.com

Dulwich & Sydenham Hill (1894)
Grange Lane, College Road, London, SE21 7LH
- ☎ (020) 8693 3961
- ☎ (020) 8693 2481
- ✉ secretary@dulwichgolf.co.uk
- ☐ 850
- ✎ MP Hickson

- ✎ D Baillie (020) 8693 8491
- ⊳ 18 L 6079 yds SSS 69
- ☵ WD–UH SOC by arrangements WE/BH–M before 2pm U after 2pm
- ££ £40
- ❀ Half mile from Dulwich College off A205
- ⌂ HS Colt
- ▤ www.dulwichgolf.co.uk

Effingham (1927)
Guildford Road, Effingham, KT24 5PZ
- ☎ (01372) 452203
- ☎ (01372) 459959
- ✉ secretary@effinghamgolfclub.com
- ☐ 710
- ✎ Robin Easton
- ✎ Steve Hoatson (01372) 452606
- ⊳ 18 L 6524 yds Par 72 SSS 71
- ☵ WD–H WE/BH–M
- ££ On application
- ❀ 8 miles E of Guildford on A246. M25 J9 (clockwise) or J10 (anti-clockwise)
- ⊕ Practice facilities available
- ⌂ HS Colt
- ▤ www.effinghamgolfclub.com

Epsom (1889)
Longdown Lane South, Epsom Downs, Epsom, KT17 4JR
- ☎ (01372) 721666
- ✉ secretary@epsomgolfclub.co.uk

Farnham (1896)
The Sands, Farnham, GU10 1PX
- ☎ (01252) 782109
- ☎ (01252) 781185
- ✉ enquiries@farnhamgolfclub.co.uk
- ☐ 750
- ✎ G Cowlishaw (01252) 782109
- ✎ R Colborne (01252) 782198
- ⊳ 18 L 6571 yds SSS 71
- ☵ WD–H WE–M SOC–Wed/Thurs/Fri
- ££ £45 D–£50
- ❀ I mile E of Farnham, off A31
- ▤ www.farnhamgolfclub.co.uk

Farnham Park (1966)
Pay and play
Farnham Park, Farnham, GU9 0AU
- ☎ (01252) 715216
- ☎ (01252) 718246
- ✉ admin@farnhamparkgolf.com
- ☐ 75
- ✎ G Hutton
- ✎ G Hutton
- ⊳ 9 L 1163 yds Par 54
- ☵ U
- ££ £6 (£7)
- ❀ Behind Farnham Castle
- ⊕ Putting green; golf lessons; club hire; no bookings required
- ⌂ Sir Henry Cotton
- ▤ www.farnhamparkgolf.com

Foxhills (1975)
Stonehill Road, Ottershaw, KT16 0EL
- ☎ (01932) 872050
- ☎ (01932) 874762
- ✉ golf@foxhills.co.uk

- ☐ 1200
- ♙ R Hyder
- ✎ R Summerscales (01932) 704465
- ⊳ 18 L 6680 yds SSS 73
- 18 L 6547 yds SSS 72
- 9 hole course
- ☵ WD–U WE–NA before noon SOC–WD am
- ££ £75 D–£95 (£95)
- ❀ 2 miles off M25 Jct 11
- ⊕ Driving range, conference centre, spa, 70 bedrooms, 3 restaurants
- ⌂ FW Hawtree
- ▤ www.foxhills.co.uk

Gatton Manor Hotel & Golf Club (1969)
Proprietary
Standon Lane, Ockley, Dorking, Surrey RH5 5PQ
- ☎ (01306) 627555
- ☎ (01306) 627713
- ✉ info@gattonmanor.co.uk
- ☐ 350
- ♙ Patrick Kiely (owner)
- ⊳ 18 L 6563 yds Par 72 SSS 72
- ☵ U exc Sun before 12 noon SOC–WD
- ££ £30 D–£47 (£40)
- ❀ 1½ miles SW of Ockley, off A29. M25 Junction 9, S on A24
- ⊕ Driving range; chipping green; bookings via website; putting green; 18 bed hotel
- ⌂ Cmdr John D Harris
- ▤ www.gattonmanor.co.uk

Goal Farm Par Three (1978)
Proprietary
Gole Road, Pirbright, GU24 0PZ
- ☎ (01483) 473183
- ☎ (01483) 473205
- ✉ secretary@goalfarmgolfclub.co.uk
- ☐ 320
- ♙ R Little
- ⊳ 9 hole Par 3 course
- ☵ Sat/Thurs am–restricted SOC–WD
- ££ £5.95 (£6.40)
- ❀ 7 miles NW of Guildford
- ▤ www.goalfarmgolfclub.co.uk

Guildford (1886)
High Path Road, Merrow, Guildford, GU1 2HL
- ☎ (01483) 563941
- ☎ (01483) 453228
- ✉ admin@guildfordgolfclub.co.uk
- ☐ 600
- ♙ BJ Green
- ✎ Andy Kirk (01483) 566765
- ⊳ 18 L 6160 yds SSS 70
- ☵ WD–U WE–M SOC–WD
- ££ £44
- ❀ 2 miles E of Guildford on A246
- ⌂ Taylor/Hawtree
- ▤ www.guildfordgolfclub.co.uk

Hampton Court Palace (1895)
Hampton Wick, Kingston-upon-Thames, KT1 4AD
- ☎ (020) 8977 2423

For list of abbreviations and key to symbols see page 647

📞 (020) 8614 4747
📧 hamptoncourtpalace@crown-golf.co.uk
🏫 650
🏌 Matthew Hazelden
✓ Karl Wesson (020) 8977 2658
🏳 18 L 6514 yds SSS 71
🏌 WD–U WE–U after 12pm
£€ Mon–Thur £40 Fri £45 (£50) WE after 12pm £45, £65 before 12pm
🏌 1 mile W of Kingston
🏠 Willie Park

Hankley Common   (1896)
Tilford, Farnham, GU10 2DD
📞 (01252) 792493
🏫 (01252) 795699
📧 jhay@hankley-commongc.co.uk
🏫 700
🏌 IM McColl
✓ P Stow (01252) 793761
🏳 18 L 6702 yds SSS 72
🏌 WD–U WE–H at discretion of Sec SOC (T+W only)
£€ £75 D–£85 (£85)
🏌 3 miles SE of Farnham on Tilford road
🏠 James Braid/Harry Colt
🖥 www.hankley.co.uk

Hazelwood Golf Centre
(1992)
Pay and play
Croysdale Avenue, Green Street, Sunbury-on-Thames, TW16 6QU
📞 (01932) 770932
🏫 (01932) 770933
🏫 200
🏌 AP Oades
✓ R Catley-Smith (01932) 770932
🏳 9 L 5660 yds Par 35 SSS 67
🏌 U SOC
£€ 9: £9.50 (£12.50); 18: £15 (£19)
🏌 M3 Junction 1, 1 mile
⊕ Driving range (36 bays, floodlit). Golf academy
🏠 Jonathan Gaunt

Hersham Village (Surrey)
(1997)
Assher Road, Hersham, Surrey, KT12 4RA
📞 (01932) 267666
🏫 (01932) 240975
📧 hvgolf@tiscali.co.uk
🏌 R Hutton (Golf Dir)
✓ R Hutton
🏳 18 hole Par 67
🏌 U SOC WD WE
£€ £20 (£25)
🏌 3 miles N of M25 Jct 10 (B365)
⊕ 22 bay floodlit driving range; golf academy

The Hindhead   (1904)
Churt Road, Hindhead, GU26 6HX
📞 (01428) 604614
🏫 (01428) 608508
📧 secretary@the-hindhead-golf-club.co.uk
🏫 500 76(L) 81(J)
🏌 N Hallam Jones
✓ I Benson (01428) 604458

🏳 18 L 6356 yds SSS 70
🏌 WD–U WE–by arrangement H SOC–Wed & Thurs
£€ £60 D–£70 (£70 D–£80)
🏌 1½ miles N of A3 on A287. M25 Junction 10, 25 miles
🏠 J H Taylor
🖥 www.the-hindhead-golf-club.co.uk

Hoebridge Golf Centre
(1982)
Public
Old Woking Road, Old Woking, GU22 8JH
📞 (01483) 722611
🏫 (01483) 740369
🏫 700
🏌 M O'Connell (Mgr)
✓ D Brewer
🏳 18 L 6549 yds SSS 72
Inter 9 L 2294 yds Par 33
18 hole Par 3 course
🏌 U SOC–WD
£€ 18 hole: £23 (£31) Inter: £12.50. Par 3: £10
🏌 Between Old Woking and West Byfleet on B382
⊕ Floodlit driving range; Book online (see below); SOC bookings taken 7 days a week
🏠 Jacobs/Hawtree
🖥 www.hoebridgegc.co.uk

Horne Park
Proprietary
Croydon Barn Lane, Horne, South Godstone, RH9 8JP
📞 (01342) 844443
🏫 (01342) 841828
📧 info@hornepark.co.uk
🏫 360
🏌 Neil Burke
✓ Neil Burke (01342) 844443
🏳 9 L 2718 yds Par 34
🏌 U
£€ 9 holes–£11.50 (£12.50)
🏌 Off A22. M25 Junction 6
⊕ Driving range; chipping green
🏠 Howard Swann
🖥 www.hornepark.co.uk

Horton Park G&CC   (1987)
Pay and play
Hook Road, Epsom, KT19 8QG
📞 (020) 8393 8400 (Enquiries)
(020) 8394 2626 (Bookings)
📧 hortonparkgc@aol.com

Hurtmore   (1992)
Pay and play
Hurtmore Road, Hurtmore, Surrey, GU7 2RN
📞 (01483) 426492
🏫 (01483) 426121
📧 general@hurtmore-golf.co.uk
🏫 200
🏌 Maxine Burton (01483) 426492
✓ Maxine Burton (01483) 424440
🏳 18 L 5530 yds Par 70 SSS 67
🏌 U SOC
£€ £15 (£21)
🏌 6 miles S of Guildford on A3. M25 Junction 10
⊕ Practice nets and putting green

🏠 Alliss/Clark
🖥 www.hurtmore-golf.co.uk

Kingswood   (1928)
Proprietary
Sandy Lane, Kingswood, Tadworth, KT20 6NE
📞 (01737) 832188
🏫 (01737) 833920
📧 sales@kingswood-golf.co.uk
🏫 650
🏌 Elaine Labbett (Corporate Golf Admin) Jackie Dunne (Membership Admin)
✓ T Sims (01737) 832334
🏳 18 L 6904 yds SSS 73
🏌 U SOC
£€ £30 (£60 Sat, £45 Sun)
🏌 5 miles S of Sutton on A217. M25 Junction 8, 2 miles
⊕ Driving range
🏠 James Braid
🖥 www.kingswood-golf.co.uk

Laleham   (1903)
Laleham Reach, Chertsey KT16 8RP
📞 (01932) 564211
🏫 (01932) 564448
📧 sec@laleham-golf.co.uk
🏫 400
🏌 B Lonsdale
✓ Paul Smith (01932) 562877
🏳 18 L 6291 yds SSS 70
🏌 NA–WE SOC exc we before 12 noon peak season and 11am off season WD–U WE after 12 noon peak 11am off peak
£€ £30 – £36
🏌 2 miles S of Staines, opp Thorpe Park
🏠 Jack White open champion 1904
🖥 www.laleham-golf.co.uk

Leatherhead   (1903)
Proprietary
Kingston Road, Leatherhead, KT22 0EE
📞 (01372) 843966
🏫 (01372) 842241
📧 sales@lgc-golf.co.uk
🏫 600
🏌 Timothy Lowe
✓ Timothy Lowe (01372) 849413
🏳 18 L 6203 yds Par 71 SSS 70
🏌 WD–U WE–NA before 2pm SOC
£€ £38 Twilight £21 (£40 Twilight £25)
🏌 On A243 to Chessington. M25 Junction 9
⊕ Practice area (own balls); putting green; practice nets
🖥 www.lgc-golf.co.uk

Limpsfield Chart   (1889)
Westerham Road, Limpsfield, RH8 0SL
📞 (01883) 723405/722106
📧 secretary@limpsfieldchartgolf.co.uk
🏫 300
🏌 RJ Smitherman
✓ M McLean
🏳 9 L 5718 yds SSS 68
🏌 WD–U exc Thurs (Ladies Day) WE–M or by appointment SOC
£€ £20 (£22)

For list of abbreviations and key to symbols see page 647

🚗 1 mile E of Oxted on A25
🖥 www.limpsfieldchartgolf.co.uk

Lingfield Park (1987)
Racecourse Road, Lingfield, RH7 6PQ
☎ (01342) 834602
🖂 cmorley@lingfieldpark.co.uk

London Scottish (1865)
Windmill Enclosure, Wimbledon Common, London, SW19 5NQ
☎ (020) 8788 0135
🖷 (020) 8789 7517
🖂 secretary.lsgc@virgin.net
🏛 250
🏌 S Barr (020) 8789 7517
⛳ S Barr (020) 8789 1207
⛳ 18 L 5458 yds Par 68 SSS 66
👥 WD–U WE/BH–NA SOC
££ £20 Mon–£15
🚗 Wimbledon Common
⊕ Red upper garment must be worn
🏠 Willie Dunn/Tom Dunn
🖥 www.londonscottishgolfclub.co.uk

Malden (1893)
Traps Lane, New Malden, KT3 4RS
☎ (020) 8942 0654
🖂 manager@maldengolfclub.com

Merrist Wood (1997)
Coombe Lane, Worplesdon, Guildford, GU3 3PE
☎ (01483) 238890
🖷 (01483) 238896
🏛 700
🏌 Nicholas Hughes
⛳ Simon Fowler (01483) 238897
⛳ 18 L 6575 yds Par 72 SSS 71
👥 Soft spikes only SOC
££ £30 (£35)
🚗 2 miles W of Guildford, off A323
⊕ Driving range
🏠 David Williams
🖥 www.merristwood-golfclub.co.uk

Milford
Proprietary
Station Lane, Milford, GU8 5HS
☎ (01483) 419200
🖷 (01483) 419199
🖂 milford@crown-golf.co.uk
🏛 750
🏌 N Hughes
⛳ P Creamer (01483) 416291
⛳ 18 L 5960 yds Par 69 SSS 68
👥 WD–U WE–after 12 noon SOC
££ £25 £42
🚗 3 miles SW of Guildford, off A3
⊕ Practice range
🏠 Alliss/Clark
🖥 www.milfordgolf.co.uk

Mitcham (1924)
Carshalton Road, Mitcham Junction, CR4 4HN
☎ (020) 8640 4280 (Bookings)
🖷 (020) 8648 4197
🖂 mitchamgc@hotmail.co.uk
🏛 500
🏌 DJ Tilley (020) 8648 4197
⛳ P Burton (020) 8640 4280

⛳ 18 L 6022 yds SSS 69
👥 WD–U WE–NA before 1.30pm SOC
££ £18, £13 after 3pm (£25, £16 after 6pm) BH £27
🚗 Mitcham Junction Station
🏠 Old Tom Morris
🖥 www.mitchamgolfclub.co.uk

Moore Place (1926)
Public
Portsmouth Road, Esher, KT10 9LN
☎ (01372) 463533
🖷 (01372) 463533
🏛 80
🏌 R Egan (020) 8715 8851
⛳ N Gadd
⛳ 9 L 2078 yds SSS 61
👥 U
££ £10 (£12.50)
🚗 Centre of Esher
🏠 D Allen
🖥 www.moore-place.co.uk

New Zealand (1895)
Woodham Lane, Addlestone, KT15 3QD
☎ (01932) 345049
🖷 (01932) 342891
🖂 roger.marrett@nzgc.org
🏛 300
🏌 RA Marrett (01932) 342891
⛳ VR Elvidge (01932) 349619
⛳ 18 L 5947 yds SSS 69
👥 By request
££ On application
🚗 Woking 3 miles. West Byfleet 1 mile. Weybridge 5 miles
🏠 Simpson/Fergusson

North Downs (1899)
Northdown Road, Woldingham, Caterham, CR3 7AA
☎ (01883) 652057
🖷 (01883) 652832
🖂 info@northdownsgolfclub.co.uk
🏛 500
🏌 DM Sinden (Sec/Mgr) (01883) 652057
⛳ MJ Homewood (01883) 653004
⛳ 18 L 5857 yds Par 69 SSS 68
👥 WD–U WE–NA before 2pm (summer), 12 noon (winter) SOC–WD
££ £25 (£25)
🚗 3 miles E of Caterham. M25 Jct 6
⊕ Practice ground; putting green
🏠 JF Pennink
🖥 www.northdownsgolfclub.co.uk

Oak Park (1984)
Proprietary
Heath Lane, Crondall, Farnham, GU10 5PB
☎ (01252) 850850
🖷 (01252) 850851
🖂 oakpark@crown-golf.co.uk
🏛 800+
🏌 R Pilbury
⛳ Paul Archer (01252) 850850 ext 1
⛳ Woodland 18 L 6352 yds Par 70 SSS 70
⛳ Village 9 L 3279 yds Par 36
££ Woodland Mon–Thur £30, Fri £32
Village Mon–Thur £15, Fri £14 (£16)

🚗 Off A287 Farnham-Odiham road. M3 Junction 5, 4 miles
⊕ Driving range; Teaching Academy; Buggies
🏠 Patrick Dawson
🖥 www.oakparkgolf.co.uk

Oaks Sports Centre (1973)
Public
Woodmansterne Road, Carshalton, SM5 4AN
☎ (020) 8643 8363
🖷 (020) 8661 7880
🖂 info@theoaksgolf.co.uk
🏛 1000
🏌 M Burridge
⛳ M Pilkington
⛳ 18 L 6026 yds SSS 69
9 hole course 1497
👥 U SOC WD–U WE–U
££ 9: £9.50 (£11.50); 18: £18 (£22)
🚗 2 miles from Sutton on B278
⊕ Floodlit driving range
🖥 www.theoaksgolf.co.uk

Pachesham Park Golf Centre (1990)
Pay and play
Oaklawn Road, Leatherhead, KT22 0BT
☎ (01372) 843453
🖂 enquiries@pacheshamgolf.co.uk
🏛 120
🏌 P Taylor
⛳ P Taylor
⛳ 9 L 2804 yds Par 35
👥 U SOC WD/WE
££ 9: £10 (£14); for offers see website; reduced rates for juniors u–18
🚗 NW of Leatherhead, off A244. M25 Junction 9
⊕ Driving range
🏠 P Taylor
🖥 www.pacheshamgolf.co.uk

Pine Ridge (1992)
Pay and play
Old Bisley Road, Frimley, Camberley, GU16 9NX
☎ (01276) 20770
🖷 (01276) 678837
🖂 enquiry@pineridgegolf.co.uk
🏌 Patrick Dawson (Sec/Mgr)
⛳ P Sefton
⛳ 18 L 6458 yds SSS 71
👥 U SOC
££ TBA
🚗 Off Maultway, between Lightwater and Frimley. M3 Junction 3, 2 miles
⊕ Floodlit driving range
🏠 Clive D Smith
🖥 www.pineridgegolf.co.uk

Purley Downs (1894)
106 Purley Downs Road, South Croydon, CR2 0RB
☎ (020) 8657 8347
🖷 (020) 8651 5044
🖂 info@purleydowns.co.uk
🏛 660
🏌 Mrs SJ Burr
⛳ S Iliffe (020) 8651 0819
⛳ 18 L 6308 yds SSS 70

⑭ WD–I WE–M SOC–WD exc Tues
am
£€ £40
⊕ 3 miles S of Croydon (A235)
▣ www.purleydowns.co.uk

Puttenham (1894)
Puttenham, Guildford, GU3 1AL
☎ (01483) 810498
🖳 (01483) 810988
✉ enquiries@puttenhamgolfclub
.co.uk
▥ 600
♟ G Simmons
✓ D Lintott (01483) 810277
➤ 18 L 6220 yds SSS 70
⑭ WE–by prior appointment pm only.
SOC–Wed, Thurs & Fri
£€ On application
⊕ Between Guildford and Farnham
on B3000, just off Hog's Back
⊕ Driving range for green fee/society
visitors & members
♙ Donald Steel
▣ www.puttenhamgolfclub.co.uk

Pyrford (1993)
Warren Lane, Pyrford, GU22 8XR
☎ (01483) 723555
🖳 (01483) 729777
✉ pyrford@crown-golf.co.uk
▥ 650
♟ Andrew Lawrence
✓ A Blackman (01483) 751070
➤ 18 L 6256 yds SSS 70
⑭ WD–U WE–M before noon
SOC–WD and WE after 1pm
£€ £40 (£45)
⊕ 2 miles from A3 at Ripley
⊕ Driving Range
♙ Alliss/Clark
▣ www.pyrfordgolf.co.uk

Redhill (1993)
Pay and play
Canada Avenue, Redhill, RH1 5BF
☎ (01737) 770204
✉ info@redhillgolfcentre.co.uk
▥ 50
♟ S Furlonger
✓ N A Golf
➤ 9 L 1903 yds Par 31 SSS 59
⑭ U SOC
£€ £5 (£6)
⊕ 1½ miles S of Redhill on A23, off
Three Arch Road
⊕ Floodlit driving range
▣ www.redhillgolfcentre.co.uk

Redhill & Reigate (1887)
Clarence Lodge, Pendleton Road, Redhill,
RH1 6LB
☎ (01737) 244626/244433
🖳 (01737) 242117
✉ mail@rrgc.net
▥ 500
♟ D Simpson (01737) 240777
✓ W Pike (01737) 244433
➤ 18 L 5272 yds SSS 68
⑭ WD–U WE–phone first SOC
£€ £25 (£28)
⊕ 1 mile S of Redhill on A23
⊕ Practice ground
▣ www.rrgc.net

Reigate Heath (1895)
The Club House, Reigate Heath, RH2 8QR
☎ (01737) 242610
✉ manager@reigateheathgolfclub
.co.uk
▥ 330 80(L) 60(J)
♟ Richard Arnold (01737) 226793
✓ Adam Aram
➤ 9 L 5658 yds SSS 68
⑭ WD–U, WE–M before 12, WE–U
after 12
£€ £35 before 2pm, £25 between 2
and 4pm, £20 after 4pm
⊕ W boundary of Reigate Heath on
Flanchford Road (off A25)
⊕ 2 balls only before 12 (except
Mondays)
▣ www.reigateheathgolfclub.co.uk

Reigate Hill
Gatton Bottom, Reigate, RH2 0TU
☎ (01737) 645577

The Richmond (1891)
Sudbrook Park, Richmond, TW10 7AS
☎ (020) 8940 4351
🖳 (020) 8332 7914
✉ admin@therichmondgolfclub.co.uk
▥ 600
♟ J Maguire (020) 8940 4351
✓ S Burridge (020) 8940 7792
➤ 18 L 6100 yds SSS 70
⑭ WD–H
£€ £50
⊕ Between Richmond and Kingston-
upon-Thames
⊕ Driving range
♙ T Dunn
▣ www.therichmondgolfclub.co.uk

Richmond Park (1923)
Public
Roehampton Gate, Richmond Park, London,
SW15 5JR
☎ (020) 8876 3205/1795
🖳 (020) 8878 1354
✉ richmondpark@glendale-services
.co.uk
♟ AJ Gourvish
✓ D Bown, A Ocana, Stuart Hill, J
Gillespie
➤ Dukes 18 L 6036 yds SSS 68
Princes 18 L 5868 yds SSS 67
⑭ WD–U WE–booking necessary
SOC–WD
£€ On application
⊕ In Richmond Park
⊕ Driving range
♙ Hawtree
▣ www.richmondparkgolf.co.uk

Roehampton Club (1901)
Roehampton Lane, London, SW15 5LR
☎ (020) 8480 4200
🖳 (020) 8480 4265
✉ alistair.cook@roehampton club
.co.uk
▥ 400
♟ M Bouaird (Chief Exec)
(020) 8480 4200; A Cook (Sports
Mgr) (020) 8480 4200
✓ AL Scott (020) 8876 3858
➤ 18 L 6065 yds Par 71

⑭ WD/WE–Introduced by member
£€ On application
⊕ 1 mile W of Putney, off South
Circular
▣ www.roehamptonclub.co.uk

Roker Park (1993)
Pay and play
Holly Lane, Aldershot Road, Guildford,
GU3 3PB
☎ (01483) 236677
▥ 200
♟ C Tegg
✓ A Carter (01483) 236677
➤ 9 L 3037 yds SSS 72
⑭ U SOC
£€ £9.50 D–£12.50 (£12.50)
⊕ 2 miles W of Guildford on A323
⊕ Driving range
♙ Alan Helling

Royal Automobile Club
(1913)
Woodcote Park, Epsom, KT18 7EW
☎ (01372) 276311
🖳 (01372) 276117
♟ D Adams (01372) 273091
✓ I Howieson (01372) 279514
➤ Old 18 L 6709 yds SSS 72
Coronation 18 L 6223 yds SSS 70
⑭ M SOC
⊕ Epsom Station 2 miles
♙ Fowler/Myddleton

Royal Mid-Surrey (1892)
Old Deer Park, Richmond, TW9 2SB
☎ (020) 8940 1894
🖳 (020) 8939 0150
✉ secretary@rmsgc.co.uk
▥ 1270
♟ Marc Newey
✓ (020) 8939 0148
➤ Outer 18 L 6402 yds Par 69 SSS 71
Inner 18 L 5544 yds Par 68 SSS 67
⑭ WD–H or M WE/BH–M SOC
£€ Outer £75 D–£90 WD only Inner
£65 D–£90 WD only
⊕ Nr Richmond roundabout, off
A316
⊕ Practice ground; short game
practice area; indoor nets
♙ Outer: JH Taylor; Inner: JH
Taylor/Hawtree
▣ www.rmsgc.co.uk

Royal Wimbledon (1865)
29 Camp Road, Wimbledon, London,
SW19 4UW
☎ (020) 8946 2125
🖳 (020) 8944 8652
✉ secretary@rwgc.co.uk
▥ 800
♟ NI Smith
✓ DR Jones (020) 8946 2125
➤ 18 L 6348 yds SSS 71
⑭ WD–H except Fri by prior
arrangement SOC–Wed & Thur
only
£€ £75 D–£100
⊕ Wimbledon Common, 2 miles S of
A23 Tibbets Corner
⊕ Driving range, Practice Bunker and
Chipping area.

� HS Colt
🖥 www.rwgc.co.uk

Rusper (1992)
Proprietary
Rusper Road, Newdigate, RH5 5BX
☎ **(01293) 871456**
(01293) 871871 (Bookings)
🖂 (01293) 871456
🖾 jill@ruspergolfclub.co.uk
🛏 350
🏌 Mrs J Thornhill
🏌 Janice Arnold (01293) 871871
🏴 18 L 6724 yds SSS 72 Yellow Tees
🚺 U SOC WD WE
££ Fees available from Golf Shop
🚗 5 miles S of Dorking, off A24
⊕ Driving range
� AW Blunden
🖥 www.ruspergolfclub.co.uk

Selsdon Park Hotel (1929)
Proprietary
Addington Road, Sanderstead, South
Croydon, CR2 8YA
☎ **(020) 768 3116**
🖂 (020) 8657 3401
🖾 chris.baron@principal-hayley.com
🛏 200
🏌 Mr C Baron
🏌 Mr C Baron (020) 768 3116
🏴 18 L 6473 yds SSS 71
🚺 U SOC (min 12 golfers)
££ £35 (£50)
🚗 3 miles S of Croydon on A2022
Purley-Addington road
⊕ Driving range; putting green
� JH Taylor
🖥 www.principal-hayley.com

Shirley Park (1913)
194 Addiscombe Road, Croydon, CR0 7LB
☎ **(020) 8654 1143**
🖂 (020) 8654 6733
🖾 secretary@shirleyparkgolfclub
.co.uk
🛏 600
🏌 Steve Murphy
🏌 Michael Taylor (020) 8654 8767
🏴 18 L 6170 yds Par 71 SSS 69
🚺 WD–U WE after 3pm SOC
££ £40 (£48)
🚗 On A232, 1 mile E of East Croydon
Station
⊕ Large practice area
🏕 Simpson/Fowler
🖥 www.shirleyparkgolfclub.co.uk

Silvermere (1976)
Pay and play
Redhill Road, Cobham, KT11 1EF
☎ **(01932) 584300**
🖂 (01932) 584301
🖾 sales@silvermere-golf.co.uk
🛏 500
🏌 Mrs P Devereux (01932) 584306
🏌 D McClelland (01932) 584348
🏴 18 L 6027 yds SSS 71
🚺 WD–U WE–NA before 11am SOC
££ £25 (£35)
🚗 ½ mile from M25 Junction 10 on
B366 to Byfleet
⊕ Floodlit driving range
🖥 www.silvermere-golf.co.uk

St George's Hill (1912)
Golf Club Road, St George's Hill, Weybridge,
KT13 0NL
☎ **(01932) 847758**
🖂 (01932) 821564
🖾 admin@stgeorgeshillgolfclub.co.uk
🛏 600
🏌 J Robinson
🏌 AC Rattue (01932) 843523
🏴 27 L 6163-6526 yds SSS 69-71
🚺 WD–I H WE/BH–M
SOC–Wed–Fri
££ £80–£115 D–£80–£115
🚗 2 miles N of M25/A3 Jct, on B374
🏕 HS Colt
🖥 www.stgeorgeshillgolfclub.co.uk

Sunningdale (1900)
Ridgemount Road, Sunningdale, Berks,
SL5 9RR
☎ **(01344) 621681**
🖂 (01344) 624154
🖾 info@sunningdalegolfclub.co.uk
🛏 900
🏌 S Toon
🏌 K Maxwell (01344) 620128
🏴 Old 18 L 6581 yds SSS 72
New 18 L 6617 yds SSS 73
🚺 Mon–Thurs–I Fri/WE–M H
££ Old–£190 New–£155
🚗 Sunningdale Station ¼ mile, off A30
🏕 Willie Park/HS Colt
🖥 www.sunningdale-golfclub.co.uk

Sunningdale Ladies (1902)
Cross Road, Sunningdale, SL5 9RX
☎ **(01344) 620507**
🖂 (01344) 620507
🖾 slgolfclub@tiscali.co.uk
🛏 400
🏌 A Cook (Mgr); Mrs Cathy Panton-
Lewis (Sec)
🏴 18 L 3616 yds SSS 60
🚺 H WD/WE–by appointment. No 3
or 4 balls before 10.30am
££ £27 (£32)
🚗 Sunningdale Station ¼ mile. M3 J3
🏕 HS Colt
🖥 www.sunningdaleladies.co.uk

Surbiton (1895)
Woodstock Lane, Chessington, KT9 1UG
☎ **(020) 8398 3101**
🖂 (020) 8339 0992
🖾 surbitongolfclub@btconnect.com
🛏 717
🏌 CJ Cornish
🏌 P Milton (020) 8398 6619
🏴 18 L 6056 yds SSS 69
🚺 WD–H WE/BH–M
££ £35 D–£45
🚗 2 miles E of Esher
🖥 www.surbitongolfclub.com

Surrey Downs (2001)
Proprietary
Outwood Lane, Kingswood, KT20 6JS
☎ **(01737) 839090**
🖂 (01737) 839080
🖾 booking@surreydownsgc.co.uk
🏌 S Blacklee
🏌 S Blacklee (01737) 832726

🏴 18 L 6356 yds Par 71 SSS 70
🚺 U SOC
££ £25 (£35)
🚗 N of Kingswood, off A217/B2032.
M25 Junction 8
⊕ Golf academy and range
🏕 Peter Alliss
🖥 www.surreydownsgc.co.uk

Surrey National (1999)
Rook Lane, Chaldon, Caterham, CR3 5AA
☎ **(01883) 344555**
🖂 (01883) 344422
🖾 caroline@surreynational.co.uk
🛏 550
🏌 S Hodsdon (Gen Mgr)
🏌 D Kent
🏴 18 L 6858 yds Par 72 SSS 73
🚺 WD–U WE–NA before 11.00am
SOC
££ £30 (£32)
🚗 5 miles S of Croydon. M25 Jct 7
⊕ Driving range, function room,
conference facilities
🏕 David Williams
🖥 www.surreynational.co.uk

Sutton Green (1994)
New Lane, Sutton Green, Guildford,
GU4 7QF
☎ **(01483) 747898**
🖂 (01483) 750289
🖾 admin@suttongreengc.co.uk
🛏 600
🏌 J Buchanan
🏌 P Tedder (01483) 766849
🏴 18 L 6300 yds Par 71 SSS 70
🚺 WD–U WE–U after 2pm
££ £50 (£60) Reduced fees available
online via club's website
🚗 2 miles S of Woking, just off A3,
M25 J10
🏕 Walker/Davies
🖥 www.suttongreengc.co.uk

The Swallow Farleigh Court (1997)
Proprietary
Old Farleigh Road, Farleigh, CR6 9PX
☎ **(01883) 627711**
🖂 (01883) 627722
🖾 swallow.farleigh@swallowhotels
.com
🛏 550
🏌 Scott Graham (Mgr)
🏌 Scott Graham (01883) 627733
🏴 18 black tees L 7616 yds SSS 72
18 white tees L 6409 yds SSS 70
9 white tees L 3255 yds
🚺 SOC WD/WE
££ 9: £9 (£12) 18 (Members): £30
(£40) 18: (Combination): £18 (£25)
🚗 5 miles SE of Croydon. M25
Junction 6
⊕ Driving range; chipping area and
putting green
🏕 John Jacobs
🖥 www.swallowhotels.com

Tandridge (1924)
Oxted, RH8 9NQ
☎ **(01883) 712273 (Clubhouse)**
🖂 (01883) 730537

✉ secretary@tandridgegolfclub.com
☎ 750
🏌 Lt Cdr SE Kennard RN
(01883) 712274
✓ C Evans (01883) 713701
⟩ 18 L 6277 yds SSS 70
👤 Mon/Wed/Thurs only–H
SOC–Mon/Wed/Thurs
££ On application
🚗 8 miles E of Redhill, off A25. M25
Junction 6
🏠 HS Colt
▤ www.tandridgegolfclub.com

Thames Ditton & Esher
(1892)
Portsmouth Road, Esher, KT10 9AL
☎ (020) 8398 1551

Tyrrells Wood   (1924)
The Drive, Tyrrells Wood, Leatherhead,
KT22 8QP
☎ (01372) 376025 (2 lines)
🖥 (01372) 360836
☎ 744
🏌 L Edgcumbe
✓ S DeFoy (01372) 375200
⟩ 18 L 6282 yds SSS 70
👤 WD–I BH/Sat+Sun NA before
noon SOC
££ £40 (£55)
🚗 2 miles SE of Leatherhead, off A24
nr Headley. M25 Junction 9, 1 mile
🏠 James Braid
▤ www.tyrrellswoodgolfclub.com

Walton Heath   (1903)
Deans Lane, Walton-on-the-Hill, Tadworth,
KT20 7TP
☎ (01737) 812060
🖥 (01737) 814225
✉ secretary@whgc.co.uk
☎ 900
🏌 MW Bawden (01737) 812380
✓ K Macpherson (01737) 812152
⟩ Old 18 L 6836 yds SSS 73
New 18 L 6613 yds SSS 72
👤 WD/WE/BH booking necessary
SOC–WD
££ On application
🚗 18 miles S of London on
A217/B2032. 2 miles N of M25
Junction 8
🏠 WH Fowler
▤ www.whgc.co.uk

Wentworth Club   (1924)
Wentworth Drive, Virginia Water,
GU25 4LS
☎ (01344) 842201
🖥 (01344) 842804
🏌 Stuart Christie (Admin)
✓ Stephen Gibson (Dir of
Golf) (01344) 846306
⟩ West 18 L 7308 yds SSS 74
East 18 L 6201 yds SSS 70
Edinburgh 18 L 7004 yds SSS 74
Executive 9 L 1902 yds Par 27
👤 WD–H by prior arrangement
WE–M SOC–WD
££ On application
🚗 21 miles SW of London at
A30/A329 jct. M25 Jct 13, 3 miles

⊕ Driving range; tennis and health
club
🏠 HS Colt (East/West). Jacobs/Player
(Edinburgh)
▤ www.wentworthclub.com

West Byfleet   (1906)
Sheerwater Road, West Byfleet, KT14 6AA
☎ (01932) 345230
🖥 (01932) 343433
✉ admin@wbgc.co.uk
☎ 600
🏌 DG Lee (Gen Mgr) (01932) 343433
✓ D Regan
⟩ 18 L 6211 yds SSS 70
👤 WD–U WE/BH–M SOC
££ £50 D–£75
🚗 West Byfleet 1/2 mile on A245. M25
Junction 10 or 11
⊕ Practice area (balls provided);
buggy hire
🏠 CS Butchart
▤ www.wbgc.co.uk

West Hill   (1909)
Bagshot Road, Brookwood, GU24 0BH
☎ (01483) 474365
🖥 (01483) 474252
✉ secretary@westhill-golfclub.co.uk
☎ 550
🏌 Lt Col RM Estcort (01483) 485760
✓ G Shoesmith (01483) 473172
⟩ 18 L 6350 yds Par 69 SSS 71
👤 WD–H WE–M SOC
££ £65 D–£85
🚗 5 miles S M3 J3 on A322
⊕ Winter packages available from £40
🏠 CS Butchart
▤ www.westhill-golfclub.co.uk

West Surrey   (1910)
Enton Green, Godalming, GU8 5AF
☎ (01483) 421275
🖥 (01483) 415419
✉ office@wsgc.co.uk
☎ 620
🏌 Adrian Jackson
✓ A Tawse (01483) 417278
⟩ 18 L 6482 yds SSS 71
👤 H SOC–Wed/Thurs/Fri
££ £50 (£60)
🚗 1/2 mile SE of Milford Station
⊕ Driving range; buggy hire
🏠 Herbert Fowler
▤ www.wsgc.co.uk

Wildwood Golf & CC   (1992)
Proprietary
Horsham Road, Alfold, GU6 8JE
☎ (01403) 753255
🖥 (01403) 752005
✉ info@wildwoodgolf.co.uk
☎ 640
🏌 J Hansen
✓ Phil Harrison
⟩ 27 L 6655 yds SSS 73
Par 3 course
👤 U SOC
££ £40 (£50) Tee Time £80 midweek,
£100 WE pm, £120 WE am
🚗 10 miles S of Guildford on A281
⊕ Driving range; golf academy; junior
academy; practice room

🏠 Hawtree
▤ www.wildwoodgolf.co.uk

Wimbledon Common   (1908)
19 Camp Road, Wimbledon Common,
London, SW19 4UW
☎ (020) 8946 0294
🖥 (020) 8947 8697
✉ secretary@wcgc.co.uk
☎ 300
🏌 B James (020) 8946 7571
✓ JS Jukes
⟩ 18 L 5438 yds SSS 66 Par 68
👤 WD–U WE–M SOC
££ WD–£20 D–£35 exc Mon–£15
D–£25
🚗 Wimbledon Common
⊕ Pillarbox red outer garment must
be worn. London Scottish play
here
🏠 Willie Dunn/Tom Dunn
▤ www.wcgc.co.uk

Wimbledon Park   (1898)
Home Park Road, London, SW19 7HR
☎ (020) 8946 1250
🖥 (020) 8944 8688
✉ secretary@wpgc.co.uk
☎ 881
🏌 P Shanahan
✓ D Wingrove (020) 8946 4053
⟩ 18 L 5483 yds SSS 66
👤 WD–H I WE/BH–after 3pm SOC
££ D–£60 (£60)
🚗 2 miles from A3 at Tibbetts
Corner
🏠 Willie Park Jnr
▤ www.wpgc.co.uk

Windlemere   (1978)
Pay and play
Windlesham Road, West End, Woking,
GU24 9QL
☎ (01276) 858727 or
(01276) 858271
🖥 (01276) 858271
✉ mikew@windlemeregolf.co.uk
☎ Public course
🏌 Clive D Smith
✓ D Thomas
⟩ 9 L 5346 yds SSS 66
👤 U
££ £11 (£12.50)
🚗 A319 at Lightwater/West End
⊕ Floodlit driving range ; 12 bays
🏠 Clive D Smith

Windlesham   (1994)
Proprietary
Grove End, Bagshot, GU19 5HY
☎ (01276) 452220
🖥 (01276) 452290
✉ admin@windleshamgolf.com
☎ 800
🏌 R Griffiths
✓ L Mucklow (01276) 472323
⟩ 18 L 6650 yds SSS 72
👤 H–phone first WE–pm only
SOC–WD
££ £35 (£40) – after 12
🚗 1/2 mile N of M3 Junction 3, off
A30/A322
⊕ Driving range; teaching school

🏠 Tommy Horton
🖳 www.windleshamgolf.com

The Wisley (1991)
Ripley, Woking, GU23 6QU
☎ (01483) 211022
🖳 (01483) 211662
📧 reception@thewisley.com
🕮 700
♫ Wayne Sheffield
✓ J Hall (01483) 211213
🏴 27 holes SSS 73:
Church 9 L 3356 yds; Garden 9 L 3385 yds; Mill 9 L 3473 yds
👥 M
££ £50 midweek £80 weekend
🚗 1 mile S of M25 Jct 10 (A3)
⊕ Driving range; short game practice area; complete learning centre
🏠 Robert Trent Jones Jr
🖳 www.thewisley.com

Woking (1893)
Pond Road, Hook Heath, Woking, GU22 0JZ
☎ (01483) 760053
🖳 (01483) 772441
📧 woking.golf@btconnect.com
🕮 500
♫ G Ritchie
✓ C Bianco (01483) 769582
🏴 18 L 6561 yds SSS 72
👥 WD–H WE/BH–M SOC–WD
££ £55 D–£75
🚗 W of Woking in St John's / Hook Heath area
🏠 Tom Dunn
🖳 www.wokinggolfclub.co.uk

Woldingham (1996)
Halliloo Valley Road, Woldingham, CR3 7HA
☎ (01883) 653501
🖳 (01883) 653502
📧 enquiries@woldingham-golfclub.co.uk
🕮 300
♫ Simon Hodsdon
✓ James Hillen (01883) 653541
🏴 18 L 6393 yds Par 71 SSS 70
👥 WD–U WE–NA before 10.30 SOC
££ £26 (£30)
🚗 2½ miles N of M25 Jct 6, off A22
⊕ Driving range; putting green; GPS buggies; Pro Shop
🏠 Bradford Benz
🖳 www.woldingham-golfclub.co.uk

Woodcote Park (1912)
Meadow Hill, Bridle Way, Coulsdon, CR5 2QQ
☎ (0208) 668 2788
🖳 (0208) 660 0918
📧 info@woodcotepgc.com
🕮 630
♫ AP Dawson
✓ W Grant (0208) 668 2788
🏴 18 L 6720 yds Par 71 SSS 72
👥 WD WE–M SOC
££ £50 round or all day
🚗 Purley 2 miles. M25 Junction 7
⊕ Full practice area
🏠 HS Colt
🖳 www.woodcotepgc.com

Worplesdon (1908)
Heath House Road, Woking, GU22 0RA
☎ (01483) 472277
🖳 (01483) 473303
📧 office@worplesdongc.co.uk
🕮 600
♫ CK Symington
✓ JT Christine (01483) 473287
🏴 18 L 6431 yds SSS 71
👥 WD–H WE–M
££ On application
🚗 E of Woking, off A322. 6 miles N of Guildford (A3). 6 miles S of M3 Junction 3
🖳 www.worplesdongc.co.uk

Sussex (East)

Beauport Park Golf Course (1973)
Battle Road, St Leonards-on-Sea, East Sussex, TN37 7BP
☎ (01424) 854245
🖳 (01424) 854245
🕮 200
♫ C Giddins
✓ C Giddins (01424) 854245
🏴 18 L 6180 yds SSS 71
👥 U–booking necessary SOC
££ £18 (£23)
🚗 3 miles N of Hastings, off A2100 Battle road
⊕ Driving range, Pitch + Putt
🖳 www.beauportparkgolf.co.uk

Brighton & Hove (1887)
Devils Dyke Road, Brighton, BN1 8YJ
☎ (01273) 556482
🖳 (01273) 554247
📧 phil@brightongolf.co.uk
🕮 380
♫ P Bonsall (Golf Dir)
✓ P Bonsall (01273) 556686
🏴 9 L 5704 yds SSS 68
👥 U SOC Sun–NA before noon
££ £22 (£27.50)
🚗 4 miles N of Brighton
🏠 James Braid
🖳 www.brightonandhovegolfclub.co.uk

Cooden Beach (1912)
Cooden Sea Road, Bexhill-on-Sea, TN39 4TR
☎ (01424) 842040
🖳 (01424) 842040
📧 enquiries@coodenbeachgc.com
🕮 630
♫ KP Wiley (01424) 842040
✓ J Sim (01424) 843938
🏴 18 L 6504 yds Par 72 SSS 71
👥 H SOC
££ £40 (£46)
🚗 W boundary of Bexhill
⊕ Full practice facility (inc driving range)
🏠 Herbert Fowler
🖳 www.coodenbeachgc.com

Crowborough Beacon (1895)
Beacon Road, Crowborough, TN6 1UJ
☎ (01892) 661511
🖳 (01892) 611988
📧 secretary@cbgc.co.uk
🕮 700
♫ Mrs V Harwood (01892) 661511
✓ D Newnham (01892) 661511/653877
🏴 18 L 6319 yds SSS 70
👥 WD–H WE/BH–H after 2.30pm SOC
££ 2008: £56 D–£66 (£66)
🚗 9 miles S of Tunbridge Wells on A26
🖳 www.crowboroughbeacongolfclub.co.uk

Dale Hill Hotel & GC (1973)
Ticehurst, Wadhurst, TN5 7DQ
☎ (01580) 200112
🖳 (01580) 201249
📧 golf@dalehill.co.uk
🕮 1000
♫ John Tolliday (Dir of Golf)
✓ M Woods (01580) 201090
🏴 18 L 5856 yds SSS 69
Woosnam 18 L 6512 yds SSS 72
👥 U SOC
££ £25 (£35) Woosnam–£60 (£70)
🚗 B2087, off A21 at Flimwell from M25 Jct 5
⊕ Driving range; 65 buggy fleet
🖳 www.dalehill.co.uk

Dewlands Manor (1992)
Cottage Hill, Rotherfield, TN6 3JN
☎ (01892) 852266
🖳 (01892) 853015
♫ T Robins
✓ N Godin
🏴 9 L 3186 yds Par 36
👥 U–phone first
££ 9: £17 (£19); 18: £27 (£32) 15 minute tee times Senior (midweek only): 9: £15; 18: £23
🚗 ½ mile S of Rotherfield, off A267/B2101. 10 miles S of Tunbridge Wells. M25 Junction 5
🏠 Reg Godin

The Dyke (1906)
Devil's Dyke, Devil's Dyke Road, Brighton, BN1 8YJ
☎ (01273) 857296
🖳 (01273) 857078
📧 office@dykegolfclub.co.uk
🕮 750
♫ SL Wise (Sec/Mgr)
✓ M Stuart-William (01273) 857260
🏴 18 L 6627 yds Par 72 SSS 72
👥 WD–U WE–U after noon SOC–WD
££ £36.50 D–£45 (£45)
🚗 4 miles N of Brighton
⊕ Practice area
🏠 Fred Hawtree
🖳 www.dykegolf.com

East Brighton   (1893)
Roedean Road, Brighton, BN2 5RA
- ☎ **(01273) 604838**
- 🖥 (01273) 680277
- ✉ office@ebgc.co.uk
- ☷ 650
- ♣ G McKay
- ⚲ Adrian Milligan (01273) 603989
- ⛳ 18 L 6426 yds SSS 71
- 👤 WD–U after 9am WE–NA before 11am SOC–WD
- ££ £25 (£30) 2 for 1 after 9am WD
- 🚗 1¹/₂ miles E of Town Centre, overlooking Marina
- 🏠 James Braid
- 🖥 www.ebgc.co.uk

East Sussex National Golf Resort and Spa   (1989)
Little Horsted, Uckfield, TN22 5ES
- ☎ **(01825) 880088**
- 🖥 (01825) 880066
- ✉ events@eastsussexnational.co.uk
- ☷ 770
- ♣ DT Howe (Gen Mgr)
- ⚲ S MacLennan (01825) 880088
- ⛳ East 18 L 7138 yds SSS 74
  West 18 L 7154 yds SSS 74
- ££ Summer–£55 (£60). Winter–£35 (£40)
- 🚗 2 miles S of Uckfield, on A22
- ⊕ Driving range; golf academy; hotel
- 🏠 Robert E Cupp
- 🖥 www.eastsussexnational.co.uk

Eastbourne Downs   (1908)
East Dean Road, Eastbourne, BN20 8ES
- ☎ **(01323) 720827**
- 🖥 (01323) 412506
- ✉ tony.reeves@btconnect.com
- ☷ 550
- ♣ AJ Reeves
- ⚲ T Marshall (01323) 732264
- ⛳ 18 L 6601 yds SSS 71
- 👤 WD–U WE–NA after 11am
- ££ £24–£30 (£35–£40))
- 🚗 ¹/₂ mile W of Eastbourne on A259
- ⊕ Driving range
- 🏠 JH Taylor
- 🖥 www.eastbournedownsgolfclub.co.uk

Eastbourne Golfing Park   (1992)
Pay and play
Lottbridge Drove, Eastbourne, BN23 6QJ
- ☎ **(01323) 520400**
- 🖥 (01323) 520400
- ✉ egpltd@uk2.net
- ☷ 250
- ♣ Maggie Garbutt
- ⚲ Matthew Tucknett (01323) 503500
- ⛳ 9 L 5046 yds SSS 65
- 👤 U
- ££ £11 D–£23 (£12)
- 🚗 ¹/₂ mile S of Hampden Park
- ⊕ All weather floodlit driving range
- 🏠 David Ashton

Highwoods   (1925)
Ellerslie Lane, Bexhill-on-Sea, TN39 4LJ
- ☎ **(01424) 212625**
- 🖥 (01424) 216866
- ✉ highwoods@btconnect.com
- ☷ 800
- ♣ AP Moran
- ⚲ MJ Andrews (01424) 212770
- ⛳ 18 L 6218 yds SSS 70
- 👤 WD/Sat–H M Sun pm–H
- ££ £35
- 🚗 2 miles N of Bexhill
- 🏠 JH Taylor
- 🖥 www.highwoodsgolfclub.co.uk

Hollingbury Park   (1908)
Public
Ditchling Road, Brighton, BN1 7HS
- ☎ **(01273) 552010**
- 🖥 (01273) 552010
- ☷ 200
- ♣ Mrs M Bailey
- ⚲ G Crompton (01273) 500086
- ⛳ 18 L 6482 yds SSS 71
- 👤 U SOC
- ££ £17 (£24)
- 🚗 1 mile NE of Brighton
- 🖥 www.hollingburygolfclub.co.uk

Holtye   (1893)
Holtye, Cowden, Nr Edenbridge, TN8 7ED
- ☎ **(01342) 850635**
- 🖥 (01342) 851139
- ✉ secretary@holtye.com
- ☷ 300
- ♣ Mrs DM Botham (01342) 850635
- ⚲ K Hinton (01342) 850957
- ⛳ 9 L 5325 yds SSS 66
- 👤 WD–U exc Wed/Thurs am–NA WE–NA before 9.30 SOC–Tues & Fri
- ££ D–£18 (£22)
- 🚗 4 miles S of E Grinstead on A264
- ⊕ 3-bay driving range
- 🖥 www.holtye.com

Horam Park   (1985)
Pay and play
Chiddingly Road, Horam, TN21 0JJ
- ☎ **(01435) 813477**
- 🖥 (01435) 813677
- ✉ angie@horampark.com
- ☷ 400
- ♣ Mrs A Briggs
- ⚲ G Velvick
- ⛳ 9 L 6128 yds SSS 70
- 👤 U SOC
- ££ 9: £12 (£13); 18: £18 (£20)
- 🚗 ¹/₂ mile S of Horam towards Chiddingley. 12 miles N of Eastbourne on A267
- ⊕ Floodlit driving range; pitch & putt course; putting green
- 🏠 Glen Johnson
- 🖥 www.horampark.com

Lewes   (1896)
Chapel Hill, Lewes, BN7 2BB
- ☎ **(01273) 473245**
- 🖥 (01273) 483474
- ✉ secretary@lewesgolfclub.co.uk
- ☷ 500
- ♣ Miss J Raffety (01273) 483474
- ⚲ T Hilton (01273) 483823
- ⛳ 18 L 6224 yds Par 71 SSS 70
- 👤 WD–U WE–NA before 11am SOC

££ £36 (£36)
- 🚗 ¹/₂ mile from Lewes at E end of Cliffe High Street
- 🖥 www.lewesgolfclub.co.uk

Mid Sussex   (1995)
Proprietary
Spatham Lane, Ditchling, BN6 8XJ
- ☎ **(01273) 846567**
- 🖥 (01273) 847815
- ✉ admin@midsussexgolfclub.co.uk
- ☷ 675
- ♣ A McNiven (Golf Dir)
- ⚲ N Plimmer
- ⛳ 18 L 6450 yds Par 71 SSS 71
- 👤 WD–U WE–pm only SOC–WD
- ££ £28 (£30)
- 🚗 1 mile E of Ditchling
- ⊕ Driving range
- 🏠 David Williams
- 🖥 www.midsussexgolfclub.co.uk

Nevill   (1914)
Benhall Mill Road, Tunbridge Wells, TN2 5JW
- ☎ **(01892) 525818**
- 🖥 (01892) 517861
- ✉ manager@nevillgolfclub.co.uk
- ☷ 800
- ♣ FW Prescott
- ⚲ P Huggett (01892) 532941
- ⛳ 18 L 6349 yds SSS 70
- 👤 WD–H WE/BH–M
- ££ £33 D–£50
- 🚗 Tunbridge Wells 1 mile
- 🖥 www.nevillgolfclub.co.uk

Peacehaven   (1895)
Proprietary
Brighton Road, Newhaven, BN9 9UH
- ☎ **(01273) 514049**
- ☷ 400
- ♣ Henry Hilton (01273) 514049 (Mgr)
- ⚲ James Morrall (01273) 514049 (PGA)
- ⛳ 9 L 5488 yds Par 70 SSS 66
- 👤 WD–U WE–U SOC–U
- ££ £10 (£15)
- 🚗 8 miles E of Brighton on A259 between Peacehaven and Newhaven
- 🏠 James Braid
- 🖥 www.golfatpeacehaven.co.uk

Piltdown   (1904)
Piltdown, Uckfield, TN22 3XB
- ☎ **(01825) 722033**
- 🖥 (01825) 724192
- ✉ secretary@piltdowngolfclub.co.uk
- ☷ 400
- ♣ Iain Wallace
- ⚲ J Partridge (01825) 722389
- ⛳ 18 L 6076 yds Par 68 SSS 69
- 👤 I or H exc BH/Tues am/Thurs am/Sun am SOC
- ££ £35
- 🚗 1 mile W of Maresfield, off A272 towards Isfield
- ⊕ Driving range; pitching area
- 🖥 www.piltdowngolfclub.co.uk

Royal Ashdown Forest

(1888)

*Chapel Lane, Forest Row, East Sussex,
RH18 5LR*

- ☎ **(01342) 822018 (Old)**
  (01342) 824866 (West)
- 🖳 (01342) 825211
- 🖂 office@royalashdown.co.uk
- 📖 450
- 🏌 DED Neave
- ✎ MA Landsborough (01342) 822247
- ⮑ Old 18 L 6518 yds SSS 71
  West 18 L 5606 yds SSS 67
- 🚶 West: U SOC welcome; Old:
  please phone – SOC welcome
- ££ Old: £55 D–£75 (£75 R) West:
  £29 D–£39 (£34 R)
- ⚲ 4 miles S of E Grinstead on B2110
  Hartfield road. M25 Junction 6
- ⊕ Computer-enhanced video swing
  analysis
- ⌂ Rev AT Scott
- 🖳 www.royalashdown.co.uk

Royal Eastbourne   (1887)

Paradise Drive, Eastbourne, BN20 8BP

- ☎ **(01323) 744045**
- 🖳 (01323) 744048
- 🖂 sec@regc.co.uk
- 📖 850
- ✎ David Lockyer (01323) 744045
- ✎ A Harrison (01323) 744041
- ⮑ Devonshire 18 L 6076 yds SSS 69
  Hartington 9 L 2147 yds SSS 61
- 🚶 U H SOC–WD
- ££ Devonshire: £37 (£45) Hartington:
  £21 (£21)
- ⚲ ½ mile from Town Hall
- 🖳 www.regc.co.uk

Rye   (1894)

New Lydd Road, Camber, Rye, TN31 7QS

- ☎ **(01797) 225241**
- 🖳 (01797) 225460
- 🖂 links@ryegolfclub.co.uk
- 📖 1000 125(L) 100(J)
- ✎ JAL Smith
- ✎ MP Lee (01797) 225218
- ⮑ 18 L 6278 yds SSS 71
  9 L 5848 yds SSS 68
- 🚶 M
- ££ Enquiry necessary – see website
- ⚲ 3 miles E of Rye on B2075
- ⌂ HS Colt
- 🖳 www.ryegolfclub.co.uk

Seaford   (1887)

Firle Road, Seaford, BN25 2JD

- ☎ **(01323) 892442**
- 🖳 (01323) 894113
- 🖂 secretary@seafordgolfclub.co.uk
- 📖 420 110(L) 37(J)
- ✎ LM Dennis-Smither (Gen Sec)
- ✎ David Mills (01323) 894160
- ⮑ 18 L 6546 yds SSS 71
- 🚶 WD–H after 10am exc Tues
  WE–M SOC
- ££ D–£40 (£50)
- ⚲ 1 mile N of Seaford (A259)
- ⊕ Driving range
- ⌂ JH Taylor
- 🖳 www.seafordgolfclub.co.uk

Seaford Head   (1887)

Public

Southdown Road, Seaford, BN25 4JS

- ☎ **(01323) 890139**
- ✎ RW Andrews (01323) 894843
- ✎ F Morley (01323) 890139
- ⮑ 18 L 5812 yds SSS 68
- 🚶 U
- ££ £19 (£22)
- ⚲ 8 miles W of Eastbourne. ¾ mile S
  of A259

Sedlescombe   (1990)

Kent Street, Sedlescombe, TN33 0SD

- ☎ **(01424) 871700**
- 🖂 golf@golfschool.co.uk

Wellshurst G&CC   (1992)

North Street, Hellingly, BN27 4EE

- ☎ **(01435) 813636**
- 🖳 (01435) 812444
- 🖂 info@wellshurst.com
- 📖 400
- ✎ M Adams (Man Dir)
- ✎ R Hollands (01435) 813456
- ⮑ 18 L 6084 yds SSS 70
- 🚶 U SOC
- ££ £20 (£24)
- ⚲ 2 miles N of Hailsham on A267
- ⊕ Driving range
- 🖳 www.wellshurst.com

West Hove   (1910)

Badgers Way, Hangleton, Hove, BN3 8EX

- ☎ **(01273) 413411 (Clubhouse)**
- 🖳 (01273) 439988
- 🖂 info@westhovegolfclub.co.uk
- 📖 600
- ✎ Megan Bibby (Mgr) (01273) 419738
- ✎ D Cook (01273) 413494
- ⮑ 18 L 6238 yds Par 70 SSS 70
- 🚶 U–phone first SOC
- ££ £25 (£30); after 3pm: £16 (£21)
- ⚲ N of Brighton By-pass. 2nd junction
  W from A23 flyover
- ⊕ Practice driving range (18 bays)
- ⌂ Hawtree
- 🖳 www.westhovegolfclub.info

Willingdon   (1898)

Southdown Road, Eastbourne, BN20 9AA

- ☎ **(01323) 410981**
- 🖳 (01323) 411510
- 🖂 secretary@willingdongolfclub.co.uk
- 📖 630
- ✎ Mrs J Packham (01323) 410981
- ✎ T Moore (01323) 410984
- ⮑ 18 L 6158 yds SSS 69
- 🚶 WD–U WE–MH exc Sun am–NA
  SOC
- ££ D–£24 (£35)
- ⚲ ½ mile N of Eastbourne, off A2200
- ⌂ JH Taylor/Dr A Mackenzie
- 🖳 www.willingdongolfclub.co.uk

Sussex (West)

Avisford Park   (1990)

Pay and play

*Yapton Lane, Walberton, Arundel,
BN18 0LS*

- ☎ **(01243) 554611**
- 🖳 (01243) 554958
- 🖂 avisfordparkgolf@aol.com
- 📖 240
- ✎ Sarah Chitty
- ✎ Guy McQuitty
- ⮑ 18 L 5602 yds Par 70 SSS 66
- 🚶 U SOC
- ££ £20 (£25) Twilight after 1pm £14
  Mon–Fri
- ⚲ 4 miles W of Arundel on A27
- ⊕ In grounds of Hilton Hotel

Bognor Regis   (1892)

*Downview Road, Felpham, Bognor Regis,
PO22 8JD*

- ☎ **(01243) 865867**
- 🖳 (01243) 860719
- 🖂 sec@bognorgolfclub.co.uk
- 📖 750
- ✎ Pl Bodle (01243) 821929
- ✎ M Kirby (01243) 865209
- ⮑ 18 L 6121 yds Par 70 SSS 69
- 🚶 WD–I or H after 9.30am
  WE/BH–M (Apr–Sept) –I H
  (Oct–Mar) SOC–WD
- ££ £30 (£35)
- ⚲ 2 miles E of Bognor Regis, off A259
- ⌂ James Braid
- 🖳 www.bognorgolfclub.co.uk

Burgess Hill Golf Centre

(1995)

Pay and play

Cuckfield Road, Burgess Hill

- ☎ **(01444) 242993 (office)**
  (01444) 258585 (shop)
- 🖳 (01444) 247318
- 🖂 enquiries@burgesshillgolfcentre
  .co.uk
- ✎ CJ Collins (Mgr)
- ✎ M Groombridge
- ⮑ 9 hole Par 3 course
- 🚶 U
- ££ On application
- ⚲ N of Burgess Hill
- ⊕ Floodlit driving range; PGA Short
  Course Championship (annually)
- ⌂ Steel/Collins
- 🖳 www.burgesshillgolfcentre.co.uk

Chartham Park   (1993)

Proprietary

Felcourt, East Grinstead, RH19 2JT

- ☎ **(01342) 870340**
- 🖳 (01342) 870719
- 🖂 d.hobbs@clubhaus.com
- ✎ V Machin
- ✎ D Hobbs (01342) 870008
- ⮑ 18 L 6688 yds Par 72 SSS 72
- 🚶 WD–U WE–U after 2pm
- ££ £50 (£60)
- ⚲ 2 miles N of East Grinstead, off
  A22. M25 Junction 6
- ⊕ Driving range
- ⌂ Neil Coles
- 🖳 www.clubhaus.com

Chichester   (1990)

Hunston Village, Chichester, PO20 1AX

- ☎ **(01243) 533833**
- 🖳 (01243) 528989
- 🖂 enquiries@chichestergolf.com

For list of abbreviations and key to symbols see page 647

☐ 750
🏌 Sally Haygarth (01243) 536666
🏌 James Willmott (01243) 528999
🏌 Tower: 18 L 5906 yds Par 71
    SSS 68
    Cathedral: 18 L 6158 yds Par 71
    SSS 69
👥 Tower: WD+WE–U+Sov;
    Cathedral: WE M before 11am
££ Tower: £17.50 D–£28.50 (£21.50
    D–£36) Cathedral: £22 D–£35
    (£30) (prices may change April 08)
🚗 2 miles S of A27 at Chichester on
    B2145 towards Selsey
⊕ 27-bay floodlit driving range; par 3
    9-hole course; teaching academy
🏠 Phillip Sanders
🖥 www.chichestergolf.com

Copthorne   (1892)
Borers Arms Road, Copthorne, RH10 3LL
☎ **(01342) 712508**
🖷 (01342) 717682
✉ info@copthornegolfclub.co.uk
☐ 565
🏌 JP Pyne (01342) 712033
🏌 J Burrell (01342) 712405
🏌 18 L 6435 yds SSS 71
👥 WD–U SOC
££ £40
🚗 1 mile E of M23 Jct 10, on A264
🏠 James Braid
🖥 www.copthornegolfclub.co.uk

Cottesmore   (1975)
Proprietary
Buchan Hill, Pease Pottage, Crawley,
RH11 9AT
☎ **(01293) 528256**
🖷 (01293) 522819
✉ cottesmore@crowngolf.co.uk
☐ 800
🏌 N Miller
🏌 C Callan (01293) 861777
🏌 Griffin 18 L 6248 yds Par 71
    SSS 70
    Phoenix 18 L 5514 yds Par 69
    SSS 66
👥 U SOC
££ Griffin–£29 (£33); Phoenix–£16
    (£20)
🚗 Pease Pottage S of Crawley, 1.5m
    from M23 J11
🏠 MD Rogerson
🖥 www.cottesmoregolf.co.uk

Cowdray Park   (1920)
Petworth Road, Midhurst, GU29 0BB
☎ **(01730) 813599**
🖷 (01730) 815900
✉ enquiries@cowdraygolf.co.uk
☐ 700
🏌 M Upfield
🏌 S Brown (01730) 813599
🏌 18 L 6265 yds SSS 70
👥 H U SOC Mon–Fri
££ £50
🚗 1 mile E of Midhurst on A272
⊕ Driving range on site
🏠 T Simpson
🖥 www.cowdraygolf.co.uk

Effingham Park   (1980)
Proprietary
West Park Road, Copthorne, RH10 3EU
☎ **(01342) 716528**
✉ mark.root@mill-cop/com

Foxbridge   (1993)
Foxbridge Lane, Plaistow, RH14 0LB
☎ **(01403) 753303 (Bookings)**

Golf At Goodwood   (1892)
Kennel Hill, Goodwood, Chichester,
PO18 0PN
☎ **(01243) 755133**
🖷 (01243) 755135
✉ golf@goodwood.co.uk
☐ 1200
🏌 Rob Greig (01243) 755130
🏌 Damon Allard (01243) 755133
🏌 36 L 7104 yds Par 71 SSS 74
    Downs Course
    36 L 6650 yds Par 72 SSS 72 Park
    Course
👥 Downs – M – Park – M and SOC
££ £30 (£40)
🚗 3 miles NE of Chichester, on road
    to racecourse
⊕ Driving range and short game
    practice area
🏠 James Braid/Howard Swan
    (Downs), Donald Steel (Park)
🖥 www.goodwood.co.uk

Ham Manor   (1936)
West Drive, Angmering, Littlehampton,
BN16 4JE
☎ **(01903) 783288**
🖷 (01903) 850886
✉ secretary@hammanor.co.uk
☐ 860
🏌 TBA
🏌 S Buckley (01903) 783732
🏌 18 L 6301 yds SSS 70
👥 WD/WE–H
££ £35 (£50)
🚗 Between Worthing and
    Littlehampton
🏠 HS Colt
🖥 www.hammanor.co.uk

Hassocks   (1995)
Pay and play
London Road, Hassocks, BN6 9NA
☎ **(01273) 846990**
🖷 (01273) 846070
✉ hassocksgolfclub@btconnect.com
☐ 350
🏌 Mrs J Brown (Gen Mgr)
    (01273) 846630
🏌 C Ledger (01273) 846990
🏌 18 L 5703 yds Par 70 SSS 67
👥 U
££ £20 (£25)
🚗 1 mile S of Burgess Hill on A273. 7
    miles N of Brighton
⊕ Driving range, irons only
🏠 Paul Wright
🖥 www.hassocksgolfclub.co.uk

Haywards Heath   (1922)
High Beech Lane, Haywards Heath,
RH16 1SL

☎ **(01444) 414457**
🖷 (01444) 458319
✉ info@haywardsheathgolfclub.co.uk
☐ 752
🏌 J E Cann
🏌 M Henning (01444) 414866
🏌 18 L 6216 yds Par 71 SSS 70
👥 WD/WE–H–restricted
    SOC–Wed/Thurs WD/WE–M
    before 12 noon–H
££ £32 (£42)
🚗 1.5 miles N of Haywards Heath, off
    B2028
⊕ Driving range; short game practice
    area; putting green
🏠 James Braid
🖥 www.haywardsheathgolfclub.co.uk

Hill Barn   (1935)
Public
Hill Barn Lane, Worthing, BN14 9QE
☎ **(01903) 237301**
🖷 (01903) 217613
✉ info@hillbarn.com
☐ 300
🏌 R Haygarth (01903) 237301
🏌 18 L 6229 yds SSS 70
👥 U
££ £18.50 (£24.50) Twilight after
    1.00pm £14.00 (£19.50)
🚗 NE of A27 at Warren Road
    roundabout
🏠 Hawtree
🖥 www.hillbarngolf.com

Horsham   (1993)
Pay and play
Worthing Road, Horsham, RH13 0AX
☎ **(01403) 271525**
🖷 (01403) 274528
✉ secretary@horshamgolfandfitness
    .co.uk
☐ 300
🏌 Warren Pritchard
🏌 Warren Pritchard
🏌 9 L 2061 yds Par 33 SSS 30
👥 U SOC
££ 9: £9 (£12); 18: £13.50 (£18) WE
    after 1pm – 9:£10, 18: £15
🚗 1 mile S of Horsham, off A24
🖥 www.horshamgolfandfitness.co.uk

Ifield   (1927)
Rusper Road, Ifield, Crawley, RH11 0LN
☎ **(01293) 520222**

Lindfield   (1990)
Proprietary
East Mascalls Lane, Lindfield, RH16 2QN
☎ **(01444) 484467**
🖷 (01444) 482709
✉ info@thegolfcollege.com
☐ 300
🏌 Louise Marks
🏌 Paul Lyons
🏌 18 L 5957 yds SSS 68 Par 70
👥 WD–U WE–U SOC
££ £20 (£25)
🚗 1 mile N of Lindfield, off B2028. 4
    miles NE of Haywards Heath
⊕ Driving range
🏠 Patrick Tallack
🖥 www.thegolfcollege.com

Littlehampton (1889)
170 Rope Walk, Littlehampton, BN17 5DL
- ☎ (01903) 717170
- 📠 (01903) 726629
- ✉ lgc@talk21.com
- 🔢 650
- ♠ S Graham
- ✓ S Fallow (ext 225)
- ⊳ 18 L 6244 yds SSS 70
- ☗ WD–U after 9am WE/BH–NA before 1pm
- ££ £33 (£45)
- ⊕ W bank of River Arun, Littlehampton
- ♖ Hawtree
- 🖥 www.littlehamptongolf.co.uk

Mannings Heath (1905)
Proprietary
Fullers, Hammerpond Road, Mannings Heath, Horsham, RH13 6PG
- ☎ (01403) 210228
- 📠 (01403) 270974
- ✉ enquiries@manningsheath.com
- 🔢 730
- ♠ S Slinger (01403) 220340
- ✓ C Tucker and Neil Darnell (01403) 210228
- ⊳ Waterfall 18 L 6683 yds Par 72 SSS 70
  Kingfisher 18 L 6217 yds Par 70 SSS 70
- ☗ Kingfisher: U SOC WD WE; Waterfall: M WD WE
- ££ From £30
- ⊕ 3 miles SE of Horsham (A281). M23 Junction 11
- ⊕ Driving range; steam room; 2 putting greens; buggies
- ♖ Kingfisher–David Williams, Waterfall–unknown
- 🖥 www.exclusivehotels.co.uk

Pease Pottage (1986)
Horsham Road, Pease Pottage, Crawley, RH11 9AP
- ☎ (01293) 521706

Petworth (1989)
Pay and play
Osiers Farm, London Road, Petworth GU28 9LX
- ☎ (01798) 344097/ (07932) 163941 (01798) 344097 (Mgr)
- ✉ info@petworthgolfcourse.co.uk
- 🔢 150
- ♠ John Davis (01903) 610859
- ✓ S Hall (01798) 873487
- ⊳ 18 L 6191 yds Par 71 SSS 69
- ☗ U SOC
- ££ £15 D–£25
- ⊕ 2½ miles N of Petworth on A283
- ⊕ Practice net/green
- ♖ C & T Duncton
- 🖥 www.petworthgolfcourse.co.uk

Pyecombe (1894)
Clayton Hill, Pyecombe, Brighton, BN45 7FF
- ☎ (01273) 845372
- 📠 (01273) 843338
- ✉ info@pyecombegolfclub.com
- 🔢 550

- ♠ JM Wilkinson
- ✓ CR White (01273) 845398
- ⊳ 18 L 6221 yds SSS 70
- ☗ WD–U exc Tues after 9.15am WE–U after 2pm SOC–Mon/Wed/Thurs
- ££ £25 (£30); D–£30 (D–£30)
- ⊕ 6 miles N of Brighton on A273
- 🖥 www.pyecombegolfclub.com

Rustington (1992)
Public
Golfers Lane, Angmering, BN16 4NB
- ☎ (01903) 850790
- 📠 (01903) 850982
- ✉ info@rgcgolf.com
- ♠ Mr G Salt
- ✓ (01903) 850790
- ⊳ 18 L 5735 yds Par 70 SSS 68 9 hole Par 3 course
- ☗ U SOC
- ££ On application
- ⊕ On A259 between Worthing and Littlehampton
- ⊕ Floodlit driving range
- ♖ David Williams
- 🖥 www.rgcgolf.com

Selsey (1908)
Golf Links Lane, Selsey, PO20 9DR
- ☎ (01243) 605176 (Members)
- 📠 (01243) 607101
- ✉ secretary@selseygolfclub.co.uk
- 🔢 300
- ♠ BE Rogers (01243) 608935
- ✓ P Grindley (01243) 608936
- ⊳ 9 L 5834 yds SSS 68
- ☗ U SOC
- ££ 9: £11 (£12); 18: £16 (£20)
- ⊕ 7 miles S of Chichester
- ♖ JH Taylor
- 🖥 www.selseygolfclub.co.uk

Shillinglee Park (1980)
Pay and play
Chiddingfold, Godalming, GU8 4TA
- ☎ (01428) 653237

Singing Hills (1992)
Proprietary
Albourne, Brighton, BN6 9EB
- ☎ (01273) 835353
- 📠 (01273) 835444
- ✉ info@singinghills.co.uk
- 🔢 485
- ♠ Kevin Parker
- ✓ W Street
- ⊳ 27 holes SSS 69-72: River 9 L 2826 yds Valley 9 L 3348 yds Lakes 9 L 3253 yds
- ☗ U SOC
- ££ £25 (£33.50)
- ⊕ 6 miles N of Brighton, off B2117
- ⊕ Driving range
- ♖ MRM Sandow
- 🖥 www.singinghills.co.uk

Slinfold Park (1993)
Stane Street, Slinfold, Horsham, RH13 7RE
- ☎ (01403) 791154 (Clubhouse)

Tilgate Forest (1982)
Public
Titmus Drive, Tilgate, Crawley, RH10 5EU
- ☎ (01293) 530103

West Chiltington (1988)
Proprietary
Broadford Bridge Road, West Chiltington, RH20 2YA
- ☎ (01798) 813574
- 📠 (01798) 812631
- ✉ richard@westchiltgolf.co.uk
- 🔢 500
- ♠ R Gough
- ✓ James Crawford (01798) 812115
- ⊳ 18 L 5969 yds Par 70 SSS 68 9 hole Par 3 course
- ☗ U SOC
- ££ £27 (£32)
- ⊕ 2 miles E of Pulborough
- ⊕ Driving range
- ♖ Faulkner/Barnes
- 🖥 www.westchiltgolf.co.uk

West Sussex (1931)
Golf Club Lane, Wiggonholt, Pulborough, RH20 2EN
- ☎ (01798) 872563
- 📠 (01798) 872033
- ✉ secretary@westsussexgolf.co.uk
- 🔢 800
- ♠ CP Simpson
- ✓ T Packham (01798) 872426
- ⊳ 18 L 6264 yds SSS 70
- ☗ WD–I H after 9.30am exc Fri–M SOC–Wed & Thurs
- ££ On application
- ⊕ 1½ miles E of Pulborough on A283
- ⊕ Driving range
- ♖ Campbell/Hutcheson/Hotchkin
- 🖥 www.westsussexgolf.co.uk

Worthing (1905)
Links Road, Worthing, BN14 9QZ
- ☎ (01903) 260801
- 📠 (01903) 694664
- ✉ enquiries@worthinggolf.com
- 🔢 1000
- ♠ John Holton (01903) 260801
- ✓ S Rolley (01903) 260718
- ⊳ Lower 18 L 6505 yds Par 71 SSS 71 Upper 18 L 5211 yds Par 66 SSS 65
- ☗ WD–U H WE–confirm in advance with Pro
- ££ On application
- ⊕ Central Station 1½ miles (A27), nr A24 Junction
- ♖ HS Colt
- 🖥 www.worthinggolf.co.uk

Tyne & Wear

Backworth (1937)
The Hall, Backworth, Shiremoor, Newcastle-upon-Tyne, NE27 0AH
- ☎ (0191) 268 1048

Birtley (1922)
Birtley Lane, Birtley, DH3 2LR
- ☎ (0191) 410 2207

☎ (0191) 410 2207
✉ birtleygolfclub@aol.com
▥ 360
▷ 9 L 5729 yds SSS 67 (men)
    9 L 5098 yds SSS 69 (ladies)
▨ WD–U before 4.30 pm WE/BH–M
    SOC
££ £15
⟡ 3 miles from Birtley service area on
    A1(M)
▤ www.birtleyportobellogolfclub
    .co.uk

Boldon   (1912)
Dipe Lane, East Boldon, Tyne & Wear,
NE36 0PQ
☎ **(0191) 536 5360 (Clubhouse)**
▯ (0191) 537 2270
✉ info@boldongolfclub.co.uk
▥ 700
⚲ Alastair Greenfield (0191) 536
    5360
✓ Phipps Golf (0191) 536 5835
▷ 18 L 6414 yds SSS 71
▨ WD–U WE/BH–NA before 2pm
    Sun – 12 noon Sat
££ £22.50 (£25.50)
⟡ 8 miles SE of Newcastle
⊕ Practice ground
⌂ H Vardon
▤ www.boldongolfclub.co.uk

City of Newcastle   (1891)
Three Mile Bridge, Gosforth, Newcastle-
upon-Tyne, NE3 2DR
☎ **(0191) 285 1775**
▯ (0191) 284 0700
✉ info@cityofnewcastlegolfclub.co.uk
▥ 400 110(L) 60(J)
⚲ AJ Matthew (Mgr)
✓ S McKenna (0191) 285 5481
▷ 18 L 6523 yds SSS 71
▨ U SOC
££ £28 D–£34 (£25)
⟡ B1318, 3 miles N of Newcastle
⌂ Harry Vardon
▤ www.cityofnewcastlegolfclub.co.uk

Garesfield   (1922)
Chopwell, NE17 7AP
☎ **(01207) 561309**
▯ (01207) 561309
✉ garesfieldgc@btconnect.com
▥ 700
⚲ WG Dunn, BEM
✓ S Cowell (01207) 563082
▷ 18 L 6458 yds SSS 71
▨ U (NA Sat)
££ On application
⟡ On B6315 to High Spen off A694
    from A1 to Rowlands Gill
⌂ William Woodend
▤ www.garesfieldgolf.com

Gosforth   (1906)
Broadway East, Gosforth, Newcastle upon
Tyne, NE3 5ER
☎ **(0191) 285 0553**
▯ (0191) 284 6274
✉ gosforth.golf@virgin.net
▥ 380 100(L) 60(J)
⚲ G Waugh (0191) 285 3495
✓ G Garland (0191) 285 0553

▷ 18 L 6024 yds SSS 69
▨ U SOC
££ £25 (£28)
⟡ 3 miles N of Newcastle, off A6125
▤ www.gosforthgolfclub.com

Hetton-le-Hill
Pay and play
Elemore Golf Course, Elemore Lane,
DH5 0QB
☎ **(0191) 517 3057**
▯ (0191) 517 3054
▥ 200
⚲ William Allen
▷ 18 L 5963 yds Par 69 SSS 68
▨ U SOC
££ £12 (£15)
⟡ 4 miles E of A1(M)/A690 junction

Heworth   (1912)
Gingling Gate, Heworth, Gateshead,
NE10 8XY
☎ **(0191) 469 9832**
▯ (0191) 469 9898
✉ secretary@theheworthgolfclub
    .co.uk
▥ 800
⚲ CJ Watson
✓ A Marshall (0191 483 4223)
▷ 18 L 6404 yds SSS 71
▨ WD–U WE–M before 10am, U
    after 10am
££ Without member £25 (Sun–Sat),
    with member £15 (Sun–Sat)
⟡ Off A194(M); A195
▤ www.theheworthgolfclub.co.uk

Houghton-le-Spring
    (1908)
Copt Hill, Houghton-le-Spring, Tyne &
Wear, DH5 8LU
☎ **(0191) 584 1198 (Clubhouse)**
    (0191) 584 0048 (Office)
▯ (0191) 584 0048
✉ houghton.golf@ntlworld.com
▥ 600
⚲ Kevin Gow (Club
    Administrator) (0191) 584 0048
✓ K Gow (0191) 584 7421
▷ 18 L 6381 yds Par 72 SSS 71
▨ U SOC
££ £25 D–£30 (£30 D–£35)
⟡ 3 miles SW of Sunderland
▤ www.houghtongolfclub.co.uk

Newcastle United   (1892)
Ponteland Road, Cowgate, Newcastle-upon-
Tyne, NE5 3JW
☎ **(0191) 286 9998 (Clubhouse)**
▯ (0191) 286 4323
✉ info@nugc.co.uk
▥ 650
⚲ S Darbyshire (Hon)
✓ (0191) 286 9998
▷ 18 L 6617 yds SSS 72
▨ WD–U WE/BH–M
££ On application
⟡ Nuns Moor, 2 miles W of city
    centre
⌂ Tom Morris
▤ www.nugc.co.uk

Northumberland   (1898)
High Gosforth Park, Newcastle-upon-Tyne,
NE3 5HT
☎ **(0191) 236 2498/2009**
▯ (0191) 236 2036
✉ sec@thengc.co.uk
▥ 500
⚲ Jamie Forteath
✓ None
▷ 18 L 6680 yds SSS 72
▨ WD/WE/BH–U H
££ £40 D–£50 (£50)
⟡ 5 miles N of Newcastle
⌂ HS Colt/James Braid
▤ www.thengc.co.uk

Parklands   (1971)
Proprietary
High Gosforth Park, Newcastle-upon-Tyne,
NE3 5HQ
☎ **(0191) 236 3322**
✉ parklands@newcastle-racecourse
    .co.uk
▥ 700
⚲ G Brown
✓ Mark Watkins
▷ 18 L 6013 yds Par 71 SSS 69
▨ U
££ £20 (£27)
⟡ 5 miles N of Newcastle
⊕ 18 hole mini golf course; 28-bay
    floodlit driving range
▤ www.parklandsgolf.co.uk

Ravensworth   (1906)
Angel View, Long Bank, Gateshead,
NE9 7NE
☎ **(0191) 487 6014**
✉ ravensworth.golfclub@virgin.net
▥ 550
⚲ John Jackson
✓ S Cowell (0191) 491 3475
▷ 18 L 5872 yds SSS 69
▨ U H SOC–contact Pro
££ £20 (£25)
⟡ J65 A1(M), take A1 northbound; at
    next junction take B1296
    Wrekenton
▤ www.ravensworthgolfclub.co.uk

Ryton   (1891)
Doctor Stanners, Clara Vale, Ryton,
NE40 3TD
☎ **(0191) 413 3253**
▯ (0191) 413 1642
✉ secretary@rytongolfclub.co.uk
▥ 600
⚲ Mrs H Oliver
▷ 18 L 5499 metres SSS 69
▨ WD–U WE–M SOC
££ £20 (£24)
⟡ 7 miles W of Newcastle, off A695
⊕ Practice area; putting green
▤ www.rytongolfclub.co.uk

South Shields   (1893)
Cleadon Hills, South Shields, NE34 8EG
☎ **(0191) 456 0475**
✉ thesecretary@south-shields-
    golf.freeserve.co.uk

Tynemouth (1913)
Spital Dene, Tynemouth, North Shields,
NE30 2ER
☎ **(0191) 257 4578**
🖳 (0191) 259 5193
📧 secretary@tynemouthgolfclub.com
📖 855
🏌 TJ Scott (0191) 257 3381
⛳ J McKenna (0191) 258 0728
🏳 18 L 6359 yds SSS 70
👥 WD–U (except Tue am)
9.30am–5pm –NA before 9.30am
and after 5pm WE/BH–M
££ £25 D–£30
🚗 8 miles E of Newcastle
🏠 Willie Park
🖥 www.tynemouthgolfclub.com

Tyneside (1879)
Westfield Lane, Ryton, NE40 3QE
☎ **(0191) 413 2742**
🖳 (0191) 413 0199
📧 shanabeattie@tynesidegolfclub
.fsbusiness.co.uk
📖 660
🏌 S Beattie (0191) 413 2742
⛳ G Vickers (0191) 413 1600
🏳 18 L 6103 yds SSS 70
👥 WD–U exc 11.30–1.30pm Sat–NA
Sun–NA before 3pm SOC
££ £25 (£25)
🚗 7 miles W of Newcastle. S of river,
off A695
🏠 HS Colt
🖥 www.tynesidegolfclub.co.uk

Wallsend (1973)
Rheydt Avenue, Bigges Main, Wallsend,
NE28 8SU
☎ **(0191) 262 1973**
🏌 D Souter
⛳ S Richardson (0191) 262 4231
🏳 18 L 6031 yds Par 70 SSS 69
👥 U
££ £20 (£24)
🚗 Between Newcastle and Wallsend
on coast road
⊕ Driving range
🏠 G Showball

Washington (1979)
Stone Cellar Road, High Usworth,
Washington, NE37 1PH
☎ **(0191) 417 8346**
🖳 (0191) 415 1166
📧 graeme.amanda@btopenworld.com
📖 600
🏌 G Robinson
⛳ G Robinson
🏳 18 L 6604 yds SSS 71
7 hole Par 3 course
👥 WD–U WE–after 10.30am SOC
££ £25 (£30)
🚗 Off A194 on A195
⊕ Driving range; 100 room hotel
🖥 www.georgewashington.co.uk

Wearside (1892)
Coxgreen, Sunderland, SR4 9JT
☎ **(0191) 534 2518**
📧 secretary@wearsidegolf.com

Westerhope (1941)
Whorlton Grange, Westerhope, Newcastle-upon-Tyne, NE5 1PP
☎ **(0191) 286 9125**
🖳 (0191) 214 6287
📧 wgc@btconnect.com
📖 778
🏌 D Souter (0191) 286 7636
⛳ M Nesbit (0191) 286 0594
🏳 18 L 6392 yds SSS 71 Par 72
👥 WD–U
££ £26 (£30)
🚗 5 miles W of Newcastle

Whickham (1911)
Hollinside Park, Fellside Road, Whickham,
Newcastle-upon-Tyne NE16 5BA
☎ **(0191) 488 1576 (Clubhouse)**
🖳 (0191) 488 1577
📧 enquiries@whickhamgolfclub.co.uk
📖 650
🏌 AJ Davidson (0191) 488 1576
⛳ S Williamson (0191) 488 8591
🏳 18 L 6252 yds SSS 72
👥 U SOC–WD WE–NA Sat
££ £25 D–£30 (£30 D–£35))
🚗 5 miles SW of Newcastle
🖥 www.whickhamgolfclub.co.uk

Whitburn (1931)
Lizard Lane, South Shields, NE34 7AF
☎ **(0191) 529 2144**
🖳 (0191) 529 4944
📧 wgsec@ukonline.co.uk
📖 580 73(L) 85(J)
🏌 Mr A Atkinson (0191) 529 4944
⛳ N Whinham (0191) 529 4210
🏳 18 L 5899 yds Par 70 SSS 68
👥 U SOC–WD exc Tues
££ £22 (£27)
🚗 2 miles N of Sunderland on coast
road overlooking mouth of River
Tyne
🏠 Colt/Alison/Morrison
🖥 www.golf-whitburn.co.uk

Whitley Bay (1890)
Claremont Road, Whitley Bay, NE26 3UF
☎ **(0191) 252 0180**
🖳 (0191) 297 0030
📧 whtglfclb@aol.com
📖 700
🏌 P Simpson (0191) 252 0180
⛳ P Crosby (0191) 252 5688
🏳 18 L 6579 yds SSS 71
👥 WD–U WE–Sun only after noon
££ £30 D–£40 (£35)
🚗 10 miles E of Newcastle
🖥 www.whitleybaygolfclub.co.uk

Warwickshire

Ansty (1990)
Pay and play
Brinklow Road, Ansty, Coventry, CV7 9JL
☎ **(024) 7662 1341/7660 2568**
🖳 (024) 7660 2568
📖 309
🏌 K Smith
⛳ M Goodwin (02476) 621341
🏳 18 L 6079 yds Par 71 SSS 69

Par 3 course
👥 U SOC WD–WE
££ £15 (£18)
🚗 Between Ansty and Brinklow
(B4029). M6 Junction 2, 1 mile.
⊕ Driving range; putting green;
practice area
🏠 D Morgan
🖥 www.anstygolfcentre.co.uk

Atherstone (1894)
The Outwoods, Coleshill Road, Atherstone,
CV9 2RL
☎ **(01827) 713110**
🖳 (01827) 715686
📖 400 40(L) 40(J)
🏌 VA Walton (01827) 892568
🏳 18 L 6012 yds Par 72 SSS 70
👥 WD–U BH/Sat–M Sun–M after
5pm SOC–WD
££ D–£25
🚗 ¼ mile from Atherstone on
Coleshill road. M42 Jct 10
⊕ Buggies for hire – phone for details

The Belfry (1977)
Public
Wishaw, Sutton Coldfield, B76 9PR
☎ **(01675) 470301**
🖳 (01675) 470174
📖 515
🏌 Gary Silcock (Dir. of Golf)
⛳ M Reed
🏳 Brabazon 18 L 7153 yds SSS 74
Derby 18 L 6057 yds SSS 69
PGA National 18 L 7053 yds
SSS 74
👥 H SOC U WD WE
££ Brabazon £50–£165. PGA National
£25–£90. Derby £15–£50
🚗 1 mile N of M42 Jct 9, off A446
⊕ PGA National Golf Academy;
National Custom Fit Centre
🏠 Brabazon & Derby-Alliss/Thomas;
PGA National-Thomas
🖥 www.thebelfry.co,m

Boldmere (1936)
Public
Monmouth Drive, Sutton Coldfield,
Birmingham, BJ3 6JR
☎ **(0121) 354 3379**
🖳 (0121) 353 5576
📧 boldmeregolfclub@hotmail.com
📖 250
🏌 R Leeson
⛳ T Short
🏳 18 L 4463 yds SSS 62
👥 U
££ £14 (£16)
🚗 By Sutton Park, 1 mile W of Sutton
Coldfield
🏠 Carl Bretherton designed 9 extra
holes in 1972
🖥 www.boldmeregolfclub.co.uk

Bramcote Waters
Pay and play
Bazzard Road, Bramcote, Nuneaton,
CV11 6QJ
☎ **(01455) 220807**
🖳 (02476) 388775
📖 137

🏷 Sara Britain (01455) 220807
✓ N Gilks
🏳 9 L 4995 yds Par 66 SSS 64
👤 U
££ 9: £9 (£10) 18: £16 (£17)
🚗 4 miles SE of Nuneaton, off B4114
🏠 David Snell

City of Coventry (Brandon Wood)   (1977)

Public
Brandon Lane, Coventry, CV8 3GQ
☎ (024) 7654 3141
🖷 (024) 7654 5108
🖂 brandongolf@coventrysports.uk
🎫 300
🏷 C Gledhill
✓ C Gledhill
🏳 18 L 6521 yds SSS 71
👤 U SOC
££ On application
🚗 6 miles SE of Coventry, off A45(S)
⊕ Floodlit driving range
🖳 www.brandonwood.co.uk

Copsewood Grange   (1924)

The Pavilion, Allard Way, Copsewood, Coventry   CV3 1JP
☎ (024) 76448355
🎫 300
🏷 REC Jones (024) 7645 2973
🏳 9 L 6048 yds SSS 71
👤 WD—U exc Wed—NA before 1.00pm, Sat—NA Sun—NA before noon
££ £15 (£20)
🚗 2¹/₂ miles E of Coventry on A428
🏠 TJ McAuley

Copt Heath   (1907)

1220 Warwick Road, Knowle, Solihull, B93 9LN
☎ (01564) 731620
🖷 (01564) 731621
🖂 golf@copt-heath.co.uk
🎫 700
🏷 CV Hadley
✓ BJ Barton (01564) 776155
🏳 18 L 6528 yds SSS 71
👤 WD/WE—H BH—M SOC
££ £45 – £55
🚗 2 miles S of Solihull on A4141. M42 Jct 5, half a mile
🖳 www.coptheathgolf.co.uk

Coventry   (1887)

St Martins Road, Finham Park, Coventry, CV3 6RJ
☎ (024) 7641 4152
🖷 (024) 7669 0131
🖂 secretary@coventrygolfclub.net
🎫 750
🏷 A Smith (024) 7641 4152
✓ P Weaver (024) 7641 1298
🏳 18 L 6601 yds SSS 73
👤 WD—H
££ D—£50
🚗 2 miles S of Coventry on A444/B4113
🏠 Vardon/Hawtree
🖳 www.coventrygolfclub.net

Coventry Hearsall   (1894)

Beechwood Avenue, Coventry, CV5 6DF
☎ (024) 7671 3470
🖷 (024) 7669 1534
🖂 secretary@hearsallgolfclub.co.uk
🎫 600
🏷 R Meade
✓ M Tarn (024) 7671 3156
🏳 18 L 6005 yds SSS 69
👤 WD—U WE—M
££ D—£35
🚗 1¹/₂ miles S of Coventry, off A45
🖳 www.hearsallgolfclub.co.uk

Edgbaston   (1896)

Church Road, Edgbaston, Birmingham, B15 3TB
☎ (0121) 454 1736
🖷 (0121) 454 2395
🖂 secretary@edgbastongc.co.uk
🎫 950
🏷 AD Grint
✓ J Cundy (0121) 454 3226
🏳 18 L 6132 yds SSS 69
👤 H SOC
££ £47 (£57)
🚗 1¹/₂ miles S of Birmingham, off A38
🏠 HS Colt
🖳 www.edgbastongc.co.uk

Harborne   (1893)

40 Tennal Road, Harborne, Birmingham, B32 2JE
☎ (0121) 427 3058
🖷 (0121) 427 4039
🖂 adrian@harbornegolfclub.org.uk
🎫 600
🏷 Adrian Cooper (0121) 427 3058
✓ S Mathews (0121) 427 3512
🏳 18 L 6210 yds SSS 70
👤 WD—U WE/BH—M SOC
££ £30 D—£35
🚗 3 miles SW of Birmingham. M5 Junction 3
🏠 HS Colt
🖳 www.harbornegolfclub.com

Harborne Church Farm   (1926)

Public
Vicarage Road, Harborne, Birmingham, B17 0SN
☎ (0121) 427 1204
🖷 (0121) 428 3126
🎫 120
✓ P Johnson
🏳 9 L 4882 yds Par 66 SSS 64
👤 U
££ 9: £8 (£8.50); 18: £11.50 (£14.50)
🚗 3 miles SW of Birmingham
⊕ Practice net ; Putting Green
🖳 www.golfbirmingham.co.uk

Hatchford Brook   (1969)

Public
Coventry Road, Sheldon, Birmingham, B26 3PY
☎ (0121) 743 9821
🖷 (0121) 743 3420
🖂 idt@hbgc.freeserve.co.uk
🎫 300
🏷 ID Thomson (0121) 742 6643

✓ M Hampton
🏳 18 L 6137 yds Par 70 SSS 69
👤 U SOC
££ £14 (£16) concessions
🚗 City boundary close to airport. A45/M42 Junction
🖳 www.golfpro-direct.co.uk/hbgc

Henley G&CC   (1994)

Proprietary
Birmingham Road, Henley-in-Arden, B95 5QA
☎ (01564) 793715
🖷 (01564) 795754
🖂 enquiries@henleygcc.co.uk
🎫 500
🏷 G Wright (Ch Exec)
✓ N Hyde
🏳 18 L 6933 yds SSS 73
9 hole Par 3 course
👤 U—booking required SOC
££ £30 (£38)
🚗 Henley-in-Arden
⊕ Driving range; buggies available
🏠 N Selwyn-Smith
🖳 www.henleygcc.co.uk

Hilltop   (1979)

Public
Park Lane, Handsworth, Birmingham, B21 8LJ
☎ (0121) 554 4463
🏷 K Highfield (Mgr & Sec)
✓ K Highfield
🏳 18 L 6114 yds SSS 69
👤 U but phone to book start time
££ £14 (£16)
🚗 Sandwell Valley. M5 Jct 1 or M6 Jct
🏠 Hawtree

Ingon Manor   (1993)

Proprietary
Ingon Lane, Snitterfield, Stratford-on-Avon, CV37 0QE
☎ (01789) 731857
🖷 (01789) 731657
🖂 info@ingonmanor.co.uk
🎫 350
🏷 Richard James Hampton
✓ N Evans (01789) 731938
🏳 18 L 6469 yds Par 72 SSS 71
👤 U H SOC
££ £30 (£40)
🚗 3 miles N of Stratford-on-Avon, off A461. M40 Junction 15
⊕ Driving range
🏠 David Hemstock
🖳 www.ingonmanor.co.uk

Kenilworth   (1889)

Crewe Lane, Kenilworth, CV8 2EA
☎ (01926) 854296
🖷 (01926) 864453
🖂 secretary@kenilworthgolfclub.co.uk
🎫 750
🏷 John McTavish (01926) 858517
✓ Steve Yates (01926) 512732
🏳 18 L 6261 yds SSS 70
👤 U H BH—M SOC—WD
££ £36 (£36) per round/day
🚗 1¹/₂ miles E of Kenilworth. 5 miles S of Coventry
🏠 Hawtree
🖳 www.kenilworthgolfclub.co.uk

Ladbrook Park (1908)

Poolhead Lane, Tanworth-in-Arden, Solihull, B94 5ED
- ☎ **(01564) 742264**
- 📠 (01564) 742909
- ✉ secretary@ladbrookparkgolf.co.uk
- 🔢 700
- ✍ MR Newman
- ⛳ R Mountford (01564) 742581
- ▷ 18 L 6500 yds SSS 71
- ⛳ WD–U H WE/BH–M H WD–SOC
- ££ £40
- ⚲ 12 miles S of Birmingham. M42 Jct 3
- ⌂ HS Colt
- ▤ www.ladbrookparkgolf.co.uk

Lea Marston Hotel & Leisure Complex

Haunch Lane, Lea Marston, Warwicks B76 0BY
- ☎ **(01675) 470707**
- 📠 (01675) 470871
- ✉ golf@shopleamarston.co.uk
- 🔢 284
- ✍ Darren Lewis (Mgr)
- ⛳ Darren Lewis
- ▷ 9 holes Par 62
- ⛳ M SOC WD WE
- ££ £8.50 (£13.95)
- ⚲ M42 Junction 9
- ⊕ Driving range; golf simulator
- ▤ www.leamarstonhotel.co.uk

Leamington & County
(1907)

Golf Lane, Whitnash, Leamington Spa, CV31 2QA
- ☎ **(01926) 425961**
- 📠 (01926) 425961
- ✉ secretary@leamingtongolf.co.uk
- 🔢 650
- ✍ David M Beck
- ⛳ J Mellor (01926) 428014
- ▷ 18 L 6418 yds SSS 72
- ⛳ U SOC H
- ££ £35 (£40)
- ⚲ 1½ miles S of Leamington Spa
- ⌂ HS Colt
- ▤ www.leamingtongolf.co.uk

Marriott Forest of Arden Hotel (1970)

Maxstoke Lane, Meriden, Coventry, CV7 7HR
- ☎ **(01676) 526113**
- 📠 (01676) 523711
- ✉ mhrs/cvtgs.golf@marriotthotels.com
- 🔢 650
- ✍ I Burns (Golf Dir)
- ⛳ P Hoye
- ▷ Arden 18 L 6707 yds Par 72 SSS 73
  Aylesford 18 L 5801 yds Par 69 SSS 68
- ⛳ WD–U SOC–WE
- ££ Arden–£100 (£110 Fri–Sun)
  Aylesford–£45 (£55 Fri–Sun)
- ⚲ 9 miles W of Coventry, off A45. M6 Jct 4 and M42 Jct 6
- ⊕ Driving range; practice area; buggies with gps; putting green
- ⌂ Donald Steel
- ▤ www.marriott.com/cvtgs

Maxstoke Park (1898)

Castle Lane, Coleshill, Birmingham, B46 2RD
- ☎ **(01675) 466743**
- 📠 (01675) 466185
- ✉ info@maxstokeparkgolfclub.com
- 🔢 700
- ✍ AJ Brown
- ⛳ N McEwan (01675) 464915
- ▷ 18 L 6442 yds SSS 71
- ⛳ WD–U H WE–M
- ££ £30
- ⚲ 3 miles SE of Coleshill. M6 Jct 6
- ▤ www.maxstokeparkgolfclub.com

Menzies Welcombe Hotel & Golf Course

Warwick Road, Stratford-on-Avon, CV37 0NR
- ☎ **(01789) 413800**

Moor Hall (1932)

Moor Hall Drive, Four Oaks, Sutton Coldfield, B75 6LN
- ☎ **(0121) 308 6130**
- 📠 (0121) 308 9560
- ✉ secretary@moorhallgolfclub.co.uk
- 🔢 730
- ✍ DJ Etheridge
- ⛳ Cameron Clark (0121) 308 5106
- ▷ 18 L 6293 yds SSS 70
- ⛳ WD–U H exc Thurs–U after 1pm WE/BH–M
- ££ £45 D–£60
- ⚲ 1 mile E of Sutton Coldfield
- ⌂ Hawtree & Taylor
- ▤ www.moorhallgolfclub.co.uk

Newbold Comyn (1973)
Public

Newbold Terrace East, Leamington Spa, CV32 4EW
- ☎ **(01926) 421157**
- ✉ ian@viscount5.freeserve.co.uk
- 🔢 191
- ✍ L Ryan and I Shepherd
- ⛳ David Playdon
- ▷ 18 L 6315 yds SSS 70
- ⛳ U WE–booking 1 week in advance SOC WD–booking 1 week in advance
- ££ £11.50 (£14.50)
- ⚲ Off Willes Road (B4099)
- ⊕ 9-hole pitch and putt

North Warwickshire (1894)

Hampton Lane, Meriden, Coventry, CV7 7LL
- ☎ **(01676) 522464 (Clubhouse)**
- 📠 (01676) 523004
- ✉ nwgcltd@btconnect.com
- 🔢 450
- ✍ IW Ford (Hon) (01676) 522915
- ⛳ A Bownes (01676) 522259
- ▷ 9 L 6374 yds SSS 71
- ⛳ WD–U WE/BH–M SOC
- ££ £25 (£27)
- ⚲ 6 miles W of Coventry, off A45
- ▤ www.northwarwickshiregolfclubltd.co.uk

Nuneaton (1905)

Golf Drive, Whitestone, Nuneaton, CV11 6QF
- ☎ **(024) 7634 7810**
- 📠 (024) 7632 7563
- ✉ nuneatongolfclub@btconnect.com
- 🔢 650
- ✍ P Smith
- ⛳ C Phillips (024) 7634 0201
- ▷ 18 L 6412 yds SSS 71
- ⛳ WD–U H WE–M SOC
- ££ £29 D–£35
- ⚲ 2 miles S of Nuneaton, off Lutterworth road
- ▤ www.nuneatongolf.com

Oakridge (1993)

Arley Lane, Ansley Village, Nuneaton, CV10 9PH
- ☎ **(01676) 541389**
- 📠 (01676) 542709
- ✉ shane-lovric@golfatoakridge.com
- 🔢 500
- ✍ Mrs S Lovric (Admin)
- ▷ 18 L 6242 yds Par 72 SSS 70
- ⛳ U SOC–WD
- ££ £18
- ⚲ B4112 from Nuneaton. M6 Jct 3
- ⌂ Algie Jayes

Olton (1893)

Mirfield Road, Solihull, B91 1JH
- ☎ **(0121) 704 1936**
- 📠 (0121) 711 2010
- ✉ oltongolfclub@tiscali.co.uk
- 🔢 700
- ✍ R Gay (0121) 704 1936
- ⛳ C Haynes (0121) 705 7296
- ▷ 18 L 6230 yds SSS 70
- ⛳ WD–U exc Wed am WE–M SOC–WD
- ££ £40
- ⚲ 7 m SE of Birmingham (A41); 2 m N of M42 Jct 5 (A41)
- ⊕ Driving range
- ▤ www.oltongolf.co.uk

Purley Chase (1980)

Pipers Lane, Ridge Lane, Nuneaton, CV10 0RB
- ☎ **(024) 7639 3118**
- ✉ enquiries@purley-chase.co.uk

Pype Hayes (1932)
Public

Eachelhurst Road, Walmley, Sutton Coldfield, B76 8EP
- ☎ **(0121) 351 1014**

Robin Hood (1893)

St Bernards Road, Solihull, B92 7DJ
- ☎ **(0121) 706 0061**
- 📠 (0121) 700 7502
- ✉ manager@robinhoodgolfclub.co.uk
- 🔢 650
- ✍ Martin J Ward
- ⛳ A Harvey (0121) 706 0806
- ▷ 18 L 6506 yds SSS 72
- ⛳ WD–U WE/BH–M SOC–WD H
- ££ £35 D–£48
- ⚲ 7 miles S of Birmingham
- ⌂ HS Colt
- ▤ www.robinhoodgolfclub.co.uk

Rugby   (1891)
Clifton Road, Rugby, CV21 3RD
- ☎ **(01788) 544637 (Clubhouse)**
- 🖳 (01788) 542306
- ✉ rugbygolfclub@tiscali.co.uk
- 🏠 750
- ♟ John Drake (01788) 542306
- ✓ D Quinn (01788) 575134
- ⚐ 18 L 5614 yds SSS 67
- ⚐ WD–U WE–M SOC–WD
- ££ £20 (£10 with member) D–£30
- ⊶ 1 mile N of Rugby on B5414. M6 Jct 1, M1 Jct 18 or 19
- 🖳 www.rugbygc.co.uk

Shirley   (1956)
Stratford Road, Monkspath, Shirley, Solihull, B90 4EW
- ☎ **(0121) 744 6001**
- 🖳 (0121) 746 5645
- ✉ shirleygolfclub@btclick.com
- 🏠 550
- ♟ Steve Wilkins (Gen Mgr)
- ✓ S Bottrill (0121) 746 5646
- ⚐ 18 L 6524 yds Par 72 SSS 71
- ⚐ WD–U WE–M SOC (Mon–Thur)
- ££ D–£35
- ⊶ 8 miles S of Birmingham, nr M42 J4
- ⊕ 4 practice areas inc. covered range (mid-iron play); caddy cars for hire
- 🏠 John Morrison
- 🖳 www.shirleygolfclub.co.uk

Stonebridge   (1996)
Proprietary
Somers Road, Meriden, CV7 7PL
- ☎ **(01676) 522442**
- 🖳 (01676) 522447
- ✉ sales@stonebridge.co.uk
- 🏠 400
- ♟ Mark Clarke
- ✓ Darren Murphy
- ⚐ 27 L 3316 yds Par 37, L 2786 yds Par 33, L 2757 yds Par 33
- ⚐ U
- ££ £20 (£30)
- ⊶ 2 miles E of M42 Junction 6
- ⊕ Driving range; chipping green; putting green
- 🏠 Simon Gidman/Mark Jones/ Julian Covey
- 🖳 www.stonebridgegolf.co.uk

Stoneleigh Deer Park (1992)
The Clubhouse, Coventry Road, Stoneleigh, CV8 3DR
- ☎ **(024) 7663 9991**
- 🖳 (024) 7651 1533
- ✉ stoneleighdeerpark@ukgateway.net
- 🏠 800
- ♟ C Reay
- ✓ Matt McGuire
- ⚐ 18 L 6023 yds SSS 71 9 hole Par 3 course
- ⚐ WD–U WE–NA before 2pm SOC
- ££ On application
- ⊶ ½ mile E of Stoneleigh
- ⊕ 9 hole par 3 course; practice area; putting green

Stratford Oaks   (1991)
Bearley Road, Snitterfield, Stratford-on-Avon, CV37 0EZ
- ☎ **(01789) 731980**
- ✉ admin@stratfordoaks.co.uk

Stratford-on-Avon   (1894)
Tiddington Road, Stratford-on-Avon, CV37 7BA
- ☎ **(01789) 205749**
- ✉ sec@stratford.co.uk

Sutton Coldfield   (1889)
110 Thornhill Road, Sutton Coldfield, B74 3ER
- ☎ **(0121) 580 7878**
- 🖳 (0121) 353 5503
- ✉ admin@suttoncoldfieldgc.com
- 🏠 600
- ♟ RG Mitchell, KM Tempest (0121) 353 9633
- ✓ JK Hayes (0121) 580 7878
- ⚐ 18 L 6541 yds SSS 71
- ⚐ U H SOC
- ££ £33 D–£44 (£44)
- ⊶ 9 miles N of Birmingham, off B4138
- 🏠 Dr Mackenzie
- 🖳 www.suttoncoldfieldgc.com

Walmley   (1902)
Brooks Road, Wylde Green, Sutton Coldfield, B72 1HR
- ☎ **(0121) 373 0029**
- 🖳 (0121) 377 7272
- ✉ walmleygolfclub@aol.com
- 🏠 650
- ♟ E Barnsley Hon Sec
- ✓ CJ Wicketts (0121) 373 0029 ext 5
- ⚐ 18 L 6603yds SSS 72
- ⚐ WD–U WE–M SOC H
- ££ £30 D–£40
- ⊶ Off A5127 (Birmingham Road), half mile N of junction with A452. M6 Jct
- ⊕ Practice ground – covered bays
- 🖳 www.walmleygolfclub.co.uk

Warwick   (1971)
Public
Warwick Racecourse, Warwick, CV34 6HW
- ☎ **(01926) 494316**
- ♟ Mrs R Dunkley
- ✓ P Sharp
- ⚐ 9 L 2682 yds SSS 66
- ⚐ U exc while racing in progress & Sun am
- ££ £15 (£16)
- ⊶ Centre of Warwick Racecourse
- ⊕ Driving range
- 🏠 DG Dunkley

The Warwickshire   (1993)
Proprietary
Leek Wootton, Warwick, CV35 7QT
- ☎ **(01926) 409409**

West Midlands   (2003)
Marsh House Farm Lane, Barston, Solihull, B92 0LB
- ☎ **(01675) 444890**
- 🖳 (01675) 444891

- ✉ mark@wmgc.co.uk
- 🏠 460
- ♟ Ron Guthrie (01675) 444894
- ⚐ 18 L 6624 yds Par 72 SSS 72
- ⚐ WD–U WE–M before 10am
- ££ £19.95 (£29.95am, £19.95pm)
- ⊶ 10 min from Birmingham and Coventry, 5 min from NEC
- 🏠 Nigel Harrhy, Mark Harrhy, David Griffith
- 🖳 www.wmgc.co.uk

Whitefields   (1992)
Proprietary
London Road, Thurlaston, Rugby, CV23 9LF
- ☎ **(01788) 815555**
- 🖳 (01788) 521695
- ✉ mail@draycote-hotel.co.uk
- 🏠 550
- ♟ B Coleman (01788) 815555
- ⚐ 18 L 6289 yds Par 71 SSS 70
- ⚐ U SOC WE
- ££ £20 (£30)
- ⊶ 3 miles SW of Rugby at A45/M45 Junction
- ⊕ Driving range (floodlit); Draycote Hotel - 50 beds (adjoining); buggies
- 🖳 www.draycote-hotel.co.uk

Widney Manor   (1993)
Pay and play
Saintbury Drive, Widney Manor, Solihull, B91 3SZ
- ☎ **(0121) 704 0704**

Windmill Village   (1990)
Birmingham Road, Allesley, Coventry, CV5 9AL
- ☎ **(024) 7640 4041**
- 🖳 (024) 7640 4042
- ✉ leisure@windmillvillagehotel.co.uk
- 🏠 450
- ♟ M Hartland (Mgr)
- ✓ R Hunter (024) 7640 4041
- ⚐ 18 L 5213 yds Par 70
- ⚐ U SOC
- ££ £18 (£20)
- ⊶ 10 min from NEC and M42 link
- ⊕ Putting green; driving nets
- 🏠 Hunter/Harrhy
- 🖳 www.windmillvillagehotel.co.uk

Wishaw   (1995)
Proprietary
Bulls Lane, Wishaw, Sutton Coldfield, B76 9QW
- ☎ **(0121) 313 2110**
- ✉ wishawgolfclub@blueyonder.co.uk
- 🏠 375
- ♟ PH Burwell
- ✓ A Partridge (Wishaw Academy)
- ⚐ 18 L 5745 yds Par 70 SSS 68
- ⚐ U SOC
- ££ £15 (£22)
- ⊶ 2 miles NW of M42 Junction 9
- ⊕ Chipping/putting area; practice nets
- 🏠 RS Wallis
- 🖳 www.wishaw-golfclub.co.uk

Wiltshire

Bowood G&CC (1992)
Proprietary
Derry Hill, Calne, SN11 9PQ
☎ (01249) 822228
🖷 (01249) 822218
✉ j.hansel@bowood.org
🕮 500
♟ John Hansel
✓ John Hansel
🏌 18 L 7317 yds Par 72 SSS 73
👤 U–booking required WE–M before noon SOC
££ £48 (£60)
🚗 3 miles SE of Chippenham on A342. M4 Junction 14 (A4)
⊕ Driving range; 3 Academy holes, PGA Tuition
🏛 David Thomas
🖥 www.bowood.org

Broome Manor (1976)
Public
Pipers Way, Swindon, SN3 1RG
☎ (01793) 532403
✉ bmgc.sec@eclipse.co.uk
🕮 800
♟ C Beresford 01793 526544
✓ B Sandry (01793) 532403
🏌 18 L 6283 yds SSS 70
9 L 2690 yds SSS 67
👤 U
££ 18 hole: £19.10 9 hole: £11.60
🚗 Swindon 2 miles. M4 Junction 15
⊕ Floodlit driving range
🏛 F Hawtree
🖥 www.bmgc.co.uk

Chippenham (1896)
Malmesbury Road, Chippenham, SN15 5LT
☎ (01249) 652040
🖷 (01249) 446681
✉ chippenhamgolf@btconnect.com
🕮 650
♟ B Cook
✓ W Creamer (01249) 655519
🏌 18 L 5783 yds SSS 68
👤 U WE–M SOC
££ £28 D–£32 (£35)
🚗 1 mile N of Chippenham, off A350. 2 m S of M4 Junction 17
🖥 www.chippenhamgolfclub.com

Cricklade Hotel (1992)
Common Hill, Cricklade, SN6 6HA
☎ (01793) 750751
🖷 (01793) 751767
✉ reception@crickladehotel.co.uk
🕮 70
♟ C Withers/P Butler
✓ I Bolt
🏌 9 L 1830 yds Par 62
Men: SSS 58; Women: SSS 62
👤 WD–U SOC–WD
££ £16 D–£25
🚗 ½ mile W of Cricklade on B4040. M4 Junctions 15/16
🏛 Bolt/Smith
🖥 www.crickladehotel.co.uk

Cumberwell Park (1994)
Bradford-on-Avon, BA15 2PQ
☎ (01225) 863322
🖷 (01225) 868160
✉ enquiries@cumberwellpark.com
🕮 1250
✓ J Jacobs (Golf Dir)
🏌 27 hole course
👤 U SOC
££ £27 (£33)
🚗 Between Bradford-on-Avon and Bath on A363. M4 Junction 18
⊕ Driving range
🏛 Adrian Stiff
🖥 www.cumberwellpark.com

Defence Academy (1953)
Shrivenham, Swindon, SN6 8LA
☎ (01793) 785725
✉ golfclub.hq@da.mod.uk
🕮 500
♟ A Willmett (Mgr)
🏌 18 L 5671 yds SSS 68
👤 M SOC
££ £12
🚗 Grounds of Defence Academy. Entry must be arranged with Mgr

Erlestoke (1992)
Erlestoke, Devizes, SN10 5UB
☎ (01380) 831069
✉ info@erlestokegolfclub.co.uk
🕮 620
♟ R Gobardansingh
✓ S Blazey (01380) 830300
🏌 18 L 6759-6102 yds Par 72 SSS 72-69
👤 U–book with Pro SOC
££ £27 (£32)
🚗 6 miles E of Westbury on B3098
⊕ Driving range; 3 Academy holes
🏛 Adrian Stiff
🖥 www.erlestokegolfclub.co.uk

Hamptworth G&CC (1994)
Elmtree Farmhouse, Hamptworth Road, Landford, SP5 2DU
☎ (01794) 390155
🖷 (01794) 390022
✉ info@hamptworthgolf.co.uk
♟ Janet Facer
✓ A Beal
🏌 18 L 6516 yds SSS 71
👤 H
££ £30 (£40)
🚗 10 miles SE of Salisbury, off A36/B3079. M27 Junction 2, 6 miles
⊕ Driving range, croquet lawns & fitness centre & tennis courts
🖥 www.hamptworthgolf.co.uk

High Post (1922)
Great Durnford, Salisbury, SP4 6AT
☎ (01722) 782356
🖷 (01722) 782674
✉ manager@highpostgolfclub.co.uk
🕮 625
♟ P Hickling (01722) 782356
✓ T Isaacs
🏌 18 L 6305 yds Par 70 SSS 70
👤 WD–U WE/BH–H SOC
££ £34 D–£50 (£42 D–£50) SOC £35 (£45)

[High Post continued]
🚗 4 miles N of Salisbury on A345
⊕ Driving range (members, fee payers & societies only)
🏛 Hawtree
🖥 www.highpostgolfclub.co.uk

Highworth (1990)
Swindon Road, Highworth, SN6 7SJ
☎ (01793) 766014

Kingsdown (1880)
Kingsdown, Corsham, SN13 8BS
☎ (01225) 742530
🖷 (01225) 743472
✉ kingsdowngolfclub@btconnect.com
🕮 640 105(L) 55(J)
♟ N Newman (01225) 743472
✓ A Butler (01225) 742634
🏌 18 L 6445 yds SSS 71
👤 WD–H WE–M
££ £36
🚗 5 miles E of Bath
⊕ Practice area; chipping green; putting green
🖥 www.kingsdowngolfclub.co.uk

Manor House (1992)
Proprietary
Castle Combe, SN14 7JW
☎ (01249) 782982
🖷 (01249) 782992
✉ enquiries@manorhousegolfclub.com
🕮 400
♟ Paul Thompson (Gen Mgr)
✓ S Slinger (Dir of Golf)
🏌 18 L 6500 yds SSS 72
👤 U H–booking necessary SOC
££ £75 Mon–Thur (£90 Fri–Sun)
🚗 N of Castle Combe, off B4039. M4 Junction 17, 4 miles
⊕ Driving range
🏛 Alliss/Clarke
🖥 www.manorhousegolfclub.com

Marlborough (1888)
The Common, Marlborough, SN8 1DU
☎ (01672) 512147
🖷 (01672) 513164
✉ gm@marlboroughgolfclub.co.uk
🕮 750
♟ Les Trute
✓ S Amor (01672) 512493
🏌 18 L 6409yds SSS 71
👤 WD/WE–H SOC
££ £30 D–£42 (£40 D–£55)
🚗 ½ mile N of Marlborough (A346). 7 miles S of M4 Junction 15
🖥 www.marlboroughgolfclub.co.uk

Monkton Park Par Three (1965)
Pay and play
Chippenham, SN15 3PP
☎ (01249) 653928

North Wilts (1890)
Bishops' Cannings, Devizes, SN10 2LP
☎ (01380) 860257
🖷 (01380) 860877
✉ secretary@northwiltsgolf.com
🕮 625 105(L) 90(J)
♟ Mrs P Stephenson (01380) 860627

GJ Laing (Golf Mgr)
(01380) 860330
18 L 6414 yds SSS 71
U exc Xmas Day–Jan 31–M SOC
D–£32 (£37/round)
1 mile from A4, E of Calne
H Colt
www.northwiltsgolf.com

Oaksey Park   (1991)
Pay and play
Oaksey, Malmesbury, SN16 9SB
☎ (01666) 577995
(01666) 577174
info@oakseypark.co.uk
John Cooper
Andy Leith
9 L 2900 yds SSS 68
U SOC
£10 (£15)
8 miles NE of Malmesbury, off A429
Driving range
Chapman/Warren
www.oakseyparkgolf.co.uk

Ogbourne Downs   (1907)
Ogbourne St George, Marlborough, SN8 1TB
☎ (01672) 841327
kevinpickett1@googlemail.com
600
Kevin Pickett (01672) 841327
Rob Ralph (01672) 841287
18 L 6422 yds Par 71 SSS 71
WD–H WE–M SOC–WD
£30 D–£40
5 miles S of M4 Jct 15, on A346
Driving range; buggy hire
JH Taylor
www.ogdgc.co.uk

Rushmore
Tollard Royal, Salisbury, SP5 5QB
☎ (01725) 516326
(01725) 516437
andrea@rushmoregolf.co.uk
Andrea Cooper (01725) 516391
P Jenkins (01725) 516326
18 L 6131 yds Par 71 SSS 70
U SOC
£25 (£30)
8 miles SE of Shaftesbury (B3081)
Driving range
www.rushmoregolfclub.co.uk

Salisbury & South Wilts
(1888)
Netherhampton, Salisbury, SP2 8PR
☎ (01722) 742645 ext.1
(01722) 742676
mail@salisburygolf.co.uk
900
Pat Clash (Gen Mgr)
Jon Waring (01722) 742645 ext 4
18 L 6485 yds SSS 71
9 hole course Par 34
WD–U SOC–WD
£36 (£55, £40 after 2.30)
Wilton, 3 miles SW of Salisbury on A3094
Practice ground; putting green
Taylor/Gidman
www.salisburygolf.co.uk

Shrivenham Park   (1967)
Pay and play
Pennyhooks Lane, Shrivenham, Swindon, SN6 8EX
☎ (01793) 783853

Tidworth Garrison   (1908)
Bulford Road, Tidworth, SP9 7AF
☎ (01980) 842301 (Clubhouse)
(01980) 842301
tidworthgolfclub@btconnect.com
750
RG Moan (01980) 842301
T Gosden (01980) 842301
18 L 6320 yds Par 70 SSS 70
WD–U H SOC–Tues & Thurs
£35 County Cards welcome
1 mile SW of Tidworth on Bulford road (A338)
Donald Steel
www.tidworthgolfclub.co.uk

Upavon   (1913)
Douglas Avenue, Upavon, SN9 6BQ
☎ (01980) 630787
(08712) 300800 daily course info line
(01980) 635103
play@upavongolfclub.co.uk
550
L Mitchell
R Blake (01980) 630281
18 L 6415 yds Par 71 SSS 71
WD–U WE–M before noon –U after noon SOC–WD/WE after noon
D–£30 (£40) 2 for 1 accepted
1½ miles SE of Upavon on A342, Andover Road
R Blake
www.upavongolfclub.co.uk

West Wilts   (1891)
Elm Hill, Warminster, BA12 0AU
☎ (01985) 213133
(01985) 219809
sec@westwiltsgolfclub.co.uk
570 70(L) 50(J)
GN Morgan
R Morris (01985) 212110
18 L 5754 yds SSS 68
WD–U H WE–M H NA Sat
£35 D–£35 (£40)
1 mile off A350, on Westbury to Warminster road
Indoor and outdoor practice facilities
JH Taylor
www.westwiltsgolfclub.co.uk

Whitley   (1993)
Pay and play
Corsham Road, Whitley, Melksham, SN12 8QE
☎ (01225) 790099
whitleygolfclub@onetel.com
250
C Tomkins (01225) 790099
None
9 L 2200 yds Par 33 SSS 61
U
9: £8; 18: £14
1 mile N of Melksham on B3553

Shrivenham Park   (duplicate entry)

Driving range
Laurence Ross
www.whitleygolfclub.com

The Wiltshire Golf & Country Club   (1991)
Proprietary
Vastern, Wootton Bassett, Swindon, SN4 7PB
☎ (01793) 849999
(01793) 849988
reception@the-wiltshire.co.uk
450
Jennifer Shah (Gen Mgr)
Richard Lawless
Lakes: 18 L 6628 yds Par 72 SSS 72
Garden: 9 L 3027 yds SSS 71
U SOC
£30 (46)
1 mile S of Wootton Bassett on A3102. M4 Junction 16
Driving range; Halfway House; Putting Green; Practice bunker
Alliss/Swan
www.the-wiltshire.co.uk

Wrag Barn G&CC   (1990)
Shrivenham Road, Highworth, Swindon, SN6 7QQ
☎ (01793) 861327
(01793) 861325
manager@wragbarn.com
600
T Lee
C Game (01793) 766027
18 L 6622 yds SSS 72
WD–U WE–NA before noon SOC–WD
£40 (£45)
6 miles NE of Swindon on B4000. M4 Junction 15, 8 miles
Driving range; 6-hole Academy course
Hawtree (Simon Gidman)
www.wragbarn.com

Worcestershire

Abbey Hotel G&CC   (1985)
Dagnell End Road, Redditch, B98 9BE
☎ (01527) 406600
(01527) 406514
info@theabbeyhotel.co.uk
400
R Davies (01527) 406500
18 L 6691 yds SSS 72
WD–U SOC
£30 (£30)
B4101, off A441 Birmingham road. M42 Junction 2
Driving range
Donald Steel

Bank House Hotel G&CC   (1992)
Bransford, Worcester, WR6 5JD
☎ (01886) 833545
(01886) 833545
350
Matt Nixon

For list of abbreviations and key to symbols see page 647

✓ Matt Nixon
⊬ 18 L 6204 yds SSS 71
ඔ U SOC Restrictions after 10.00 am
££ £22 (£30)
⊕ 3 miles SW of Worcester on A4103 Hereford road. M5 Jct 7
⊕ Driving range
🏠 Bob Sandow
✉ www.bankhouse@brook-hotels.co.uk

Blackwell (1893)
Blackwell, Bromsgrove, Worcestershire, B60 1PY
☎ (0121) 445 1994
📠 (0121) 445 4911
✉ info@blackwellgolfclub.com
📖 269 81(L) 11(J)
♟ JT Mead
✓ F Clark (0121) 445 3113
⊬ 18 L 6260 yds Par 70 SSS 71
ඔ WD–U H WE/BH–M
££ £70 D–£80, reductions for soc over 25 players, and winter season
⊕ 3 miles E of Bromsgrove. M42 Junction 1 (South)
⊕ Practice area
🏠 Herbert Fowler/Tom Simpson
✉ www.blackwellgolfclub.com

Brandhall (1906)
Public
Heron Road, Oldbury, Warley, B68 8AQ
☎ (0121) 552 2195
📠 (0121) 552 1758
✉ john_robinson@sandwell.gov.uk
📖 300
♟ J Robinson (Sandwell Leisure Trust)
✓ C Yates (0121) 552 2195
⊬ 18 L 5813 yds Par 71 SSS 68
ඔ U exc first 1½ hrs Sat/Sun
££ £12
⊕ 6 miles NW of Birmingham. M5 Junction 2, 1½ miles
✉ www.slt@sandwell.gov.uk

Bromsgrove Golf Centre
(1992)
Proprietary
Stratford Road, Bromsgrove, B60 1LD
☎ (01527) 575886
📠 (01527) 570964
✉ enquiries@bromsgrovegolfcentre.com
📖 900
♟ P Morris
✓ G Long (01527) 575886
⊬ 18 L 5969 yds SSS 69
ඔ U SOC
££ £20.90 (£27.80) check prices are current at time of booking.
⊕ Junction of A38/A448. M42 Junction 1. M5 Junction 4/5
⊕ Driving range
🏠 Hawtree
✉ www.bromsgrovegolfcentre.com

Churchill & Blakedown
(1926)
Churchill Lane, Blakedown, Kidderminster, DY10 3NB

☎ (01562) 700018
📠 (08712) 422049
✉ cbgolfclub@tiscali.co.uk
📖 380
♟ Peter Bailey (01562) 700018
✓ Debbie Garbett (07809) 769047/(01562) 700454
⊬ 9 L 6472 yds Par 72 SSS 71
ඔ WD–U WE–M M–H–SOC–WD (WEM)
££ £25
⊕ 3 miles N of Kidderminster on A456
✉ www.churchillblakedowngolfclub.co.uk

Cocks Moor Woods (1926)
Public
Alcester Road, South King's Heath, Birmingham, B14 4ER
☎ (0121) 464 3584

Droitwich G&CC (1897)
Ford Lane, Droitwich, WR9 0BQ
☎ (01905) 774344
📠 (01905) 796503
📖 782
♟ CS Thompson
✓ Phil Cundy (01905) 770207
⊬ 18 L 6058 yds SSS 69
ඔ WD–U WE/BH–M SOC–Wed & Fri
££ £30 – £35 £15 with member
⊕ 1 mile N of Droitwich, off A38. M5 Junction 5
⊕ Practice ground
🏠 George Cawsey, James Braid
✉ www.droitwichgolfclub.co.uk

Dudley (1893)
Turners Hill, Rowley Regis, B65 9DP
☎ (01384) 233877
📠 (01384) 233877
✉ secretary@dudleygolfclub.com
📖 320
♟ BM Clee
✓ G Kilmister (01384) 254020
⊬ 18 L 5730 yds Par 69 SSS 68
ඔ WD–U WE–SOC
££ See Website
⊕ 2 miles S of Dudley
⊕ Buggies available
✉ www.dudleygolfclub.com

Evesham (1894)
Craycombe Links, Fladbury, Pershore, WR10 2QS
☎ (01386) 860395
📠 (01386) 861356
✉ eveshamgolf@btopenworld.com
📖 360
♟ Mr J Dale (01386) 860395
✓ Daniel Clee (01386) 861011
⊬ 9 L 6415 yds SSS 71
ඔ WD–H WE–M NA on comp/match days SOC
££ D–£25 (D–£25)
⊕ Fladbury, 4 miles W of Evesham (A44)
✉ www.eveshamgolfclub.co.uk

Fulford Heath (1933)
Tanners Green Lane, Wythall, Birmingham, B47 6BH

☎ (01564) 822806 (Clubhouse)
📠 (01564) 822629
✉ secretary@fulfordheathgolfclub.co.uk
📖 660
♟ Mrs J Morris (01564) 824758
✓ R Dunbar (01564) 822930
⊬ 18 L 6179 yds SSS 70
ඔ WD–H WE/BH–M SOC by arrangement WD
££ On application
⊕ 3 miles S of Birmingham. M42 Jct 3
🏠 Braid/Hawtree
✉ www.fulfordheathgolfclub.co.uk

Gay Hill (1913)
Hollywood Lane, Birmingham, B47 5PP
☎ (0121) 430 6523/8544
📠 (0121) 436 7796
✉ secretary@ghgc.org.uk
📖 660
♟ Mrs D O'Reilly (0121) 430 8544
✓ C Harrison (0121) 474 6001
⊬ 18 L 6406 yds SSS 72
ඔ WD–U H WE–U SOC
££ £35.50 (18 holes)
⊕ 7 miles S of Birmingham on A435. M42 Junction 3, 3 miles
✉ www.ghgc.org.uk

Habberley (1924)
Low Habberley, Kidderminster, DY11 5RF
☎ (01562) 745756
📖 120
♟ DS McDermott
⊬ 9 L 5401 yds Par 69 SSS 67
ඔ WD–U WE–M SOC
££ £15 (£15)
⊕ 3 miles NW of Kidderminster
✉ www.habberleygolfclub.co.uk

Hagley (1980)
Proprietary
Wassell Grove, Hagley, Stourbridge, DY9 9JW
☎ (01562) 883701
📠 (01562) 887518
✉ manager@hagleygc.freeserve.co.uk
📖 700
♟ GF Yardley (01562) 883701
✓ I Clark (01562) 883852
⊬ 18 L 6376 yds SSS 72
ඔ WD–U WE–M after 10am SOC–WD
££ £31 D–£36
⊕ 5 miles SW of Birmingham on A456. M5 Junction 3
⊕ 20 bay floodlit Driving Range incorporating Golf Academy
✉ www.hagleygolfandcountryclub.co.uk

Halesowen (1906)
The Leasowes, Halesowen, B62 8QF
☎ (0121) 501 3606
📠 (0121) 501 3606
✉ halesowengolfclub@btconnect.com
📖 680
♟ P Crumpton
✓ J Nicholas (0121) 503 0593
⊬ 18 L 5754 yds SSS 69
ඔ WD–U WE–M SOC–WD
££ £28 D–£31
⊕ M5 Junction 3, 2 miles

For list of abbreviations and key to symbols see page 647

⊕ Practice area; putting green
🖳 www.halesowengc.co.uk

Kidderminster   (1909)
Russell Road, Kidderminster, DY10 3HT
☎ (01562) 822303
🖳 (01562) 827866
✉ info@kidderminstergolfclub.com
📖 900
✏ P Smith (01562) 740090
🏌 18 L 6422 yds Par 72 SSS 71
👥 WD–H WE–M SOC–Thurs
££ £35 D–£35 WE with member only
🚗 Signposted off A449
Wolverhampton-Worcester road;
in Kidderminster
🖳 www.kidderminstergolfclub.com

Kings Norton   (1892)
Brockhill Lane, Weatheroak, Alvechurch,
Birmingham B48 7ED
☎ (01564) 826789
🖳 (01564) 826955
✉ info@kingsnortongolfclub.co.uk
📖 1000
✏ T Webb (Mgr)
✏ K Hayward (01564) 822635
🏌 18 L 6748 yds SSS 72
9 L 3290 yds SSS 36
👥 WD–U WE–NA SOC
££ £35 D–£40
🚗 7 miles S of Birmingham. 1 mile N
of M42 Junction 3
⊕ 12 hole short course
🏛 Fred Hawtree
🖳 www.kingsnortongolfclub.co.uk

Little Lakes   (1975)
Lye Head, Bewdley, Worcester,
DY12 2UZ
☎ (01299) 266385
🖳 (01299) 266398
✉ info@littlelakes.co.uk
📖 400 50(L)
✏ J Dean (01562) 741704
✏ M Laing
🏌 18 L 6278 yds SSS 71
👥 U SOC
££ £20 (£25)
🚗 3 miles W of Bewdley, off A456
🏛 MA Laing
🖳 www.littlelakes.co.uk

Moseley   (1892)
Springfield Road, Kings Heath, Birmingham,
B14 7DX
☎ (0121) 444 4957
🖳 (0121) 441 4662
✉ secretary@moseleygolfclub.co.uk
📖 600
✏ Mr M J Knowle
✏ M Griffin (0121) 444 2063
🏌 18 L 6315 yds SSS 71 Par 70
👥 WD–H or M
££ £40
🚗 2 miles S of Birmingham off A435;
5 miles N of M42 Jct 3
⊕ Practice ground.
🏛 HS Colt
🖳 www.moseleygolf.co.uk

North Worcestershire   (1907)
Frankley Beeches Road, Northfield,
Birmingham, B31 5LP
☎ (0121) 475 1047
🖳 (0121) 476 8681
📖 550
✏ D Wilson
✏ D Cummins (0121) 475 5721
🏌 18 L 5907 yds SSS 69
👥 WD–U WE/BH–M
££ £25 D–£35
🚗 7 miles SW of Birmingham, off A38
🏛 James Braid

Ombersley   (1991)
Bishopswood Road, Ombersley, Droitwich,
WR9 0LE
☎ (01905) 620747
🖳 (01905) 620047
✉ enquiries@ombersleygolfclub.co.uk
📖 750
✏ G Glenister (Gen Mgr)
✏ G Glenister
🏌 18 L 6139 yds SSS 69
👥 U
££ £20.50 (£29.10) Variable extra
discounts
🚗 6 miles N of Worcester, off A449
⊕ Driving range; putting green;
chipping green; practice bunker
🏛 David Morgan
🖳 www.ombersleygolfclub.co.uk

Perdiswell Park   (1978)
Pay and play
Bilford Road, Worcester, WR3 8DX
☎ (01905) 754668
🖳 (01905) 756608
📖 286
✏ B F Hodgetts (01905) 640456
✏ M Woodward (01905) 754668
🏌 18 L 5297 yds Par 68 SSS 66
👥 U
££ 9: £7.75 (£9.75); 18: £11.50
(£15.50)
🚗 Worcester. M5 Junction 6

Pitcheroak   (1973)
Public
Plymouth Road, Redditch, B97 4PB
☎ (01527) 541054
📖 148
✏ R Barnett
✏ D Stewart
🏌 9 L 4561 yds Par 65 SSS 62
👥 U
££ 9: £10; 18: £14
🚗 Redditch Nr. Town Centre

Ravenmeadow   (1995)
Hindlip Lane, Clanes, Worcester, WR3 8SA
☎ (01905) 757525
🖳 (01905) 458876
📖 300
✏ T Senter (Mgr) (01905) 458876
✏ M Slater (01905) 756665
🏌 9 L 5440 yds 18 tees Par 68 SSS 68
👥 U–SOC WD WE
££ D–£10–£14 (D–£12–£17)
🚗 3 miles N of Worcester, off A38.
M5 Junction 6

⊕ Driving range; chipping greens;
putting greens; 9 hole par 3 pitch &
putt course
🏛 R Baldwyn

Redditch   (1913)
Lower Grinsty, Green Lane, Callow Hill,
Redditch B97 5PJ
☎ (01527) 543079
🖳 (01527) 547413
✉ lee@redditchgolfclub.com
📖 883
✏ W Kerr
✏ D Down (01527) 546372
🏌 18 L 6494 yds SSS 72
👥 WD–U SOC
££ £35
🚗 3 miles SW of Redditch, off A441
🏛 F Pennink
🖳 www.redditchgolfclub.com

Rose Hill   (1921)
Public
Lickey Hills, Rednal, Birmingham, B45 8RR
☎ (0121) 453 3159
🖳 (0121) 457 8779
✉ mark.toombs@birmingham.gov.uk
📖 200
✏ D C Walker
✏ Mark Toombs (Mgr)
🏌 18 L 6010 yds SSS 69
👥 U Pre–book tee times
££ £14 (£16)
🚗 10 miles SW of Birmingham. M5 Jct
4. M42 Jct 2

Stourbridge   (1892)
Worcester Lane, Pedmore, Stourbridge,
DY8 2RB
☎ (01384) 395566
🖳 (01384) 444660
✉ secretary@stourbridge-golf-club
.co.uk
📖 600
✏ Ms M Kite
✏ M Male (01384) 393129
🏌 18 L 6231 yds SSS 70
👥 WD–U exc Wed before 1.30pm–M
WE/BH–M
££ £30
🚗 1 mile S of Stourbridge on
Worcester Lane. M5 Junctions 3/4
🖳 www.stourbridge-golf-club.co.uk

Tolladine   (1898)
The Fairway, Tolladine Road, Worcester,
WR4 9BA
☎ (01905) 21074
(Clubhouse)

The Vale   (1991)
Bishampton, Pershore, WR10 2LZ
☎ (01386) 462781 ext 229
🖳 (01386) 462597
✉ vale-sales@crown-golf.co.uk
📖 1000
✏ Melanie Drake (Gen Mgr)
✏ Richard Jenkins (01386) 462520
🏌 18 L 6644 yds SSS 72
9 L 2628 yds SSS 65
👥 WD–U WE–U after 1pm
SOC–WD
££ £25 (£35)

℮ 6 miles NW of Evesham, off A44.
M5 Junction 6, 12 miles
⊕ Driving range; putting green;
chipping area
⌂ M Sandow
≡ www.crown-golf.co.uk

Warley   (1921)
Pay and play
Lightwoods Hill, Warley, B67 5ED
☏ **(0121) 429 2440**
🖪 (0121) 420 4430
🗩 golfshop@warleywoods.org.uk
👁 150
ℝ 9 L 2646 yds SSS 68
👥 U SOC
££ 9 L: £7 (£8) 18 L: £11 (£13)
concessions available
℮ 5 miles W of Birmingham, off
A456; 2 miles from M25 Jct 2
⊕ Practice nets; putting greens; cafe;
changing rooms.
≡ www.warleywoods.org.uk

Wharton Park   (1992)
Proprietary
Longbank, Bewdley, DY12 2QW
☏ **(01299) 405222 (restaurant)**
(01299) 405163 (pro shop)
🖪 (01299) 405121
🗩 enquiries@whartonpark.co.uk
👁 500
⛪ Kevin Fincher
Ⓩ A Hoare (01299) 405163
ℝ 18 L 6435 yds Par 72 SSS 71
👥 U SOC–WD WE–NA before noon
££ £40 (£50)
℮ Bewdley Bypass on A456/ M5
Junctions 3 or 6
⊕ Practice ground; practice putting
green; driving range
⌂ Howard Swann
≡ www.whartonpark.co.uk

Worcester G&CC   (1898)
Boughton Park, Worcester, WR2 4EZ
☏ **(01905) 422555**
🖪 (01905) 749090
🖪 worcestergcc@btconnect.com
👁 750
⛪ PA Tredwell (01905) 422555
Ⓩ G Farr (01905) 422044
ℝ 18 L 6251 yds SSS 70
👥 WD–H WE–M SOC
££ £35
℮ 1 mile W of Worcester on B4485
(formerly A4103); M5 Jct 7
⌂ Dr A Mackenzie (1926)/C Colenso
(1991)
≡ www.worcestergcc.co.uk

Worcestershire   (1879)
Wood Farm, Malvern Wells, WR14 4PP
☏ **(01684) 575992**
🖪 (01684) 893334
🖪 secretary@worcsgolfclub.co.uk
👁 770
⛪ David Wilson (Sec/Mgr)
(01684) 575992
Ⓩ RAF Lewis (01684) 564428
ℝ 18 L 6449 yds SSS 71
👥 WD–H
££ £36 D–£42 (£40 D–£46)

℮ 2 miles S of Gt Malvern, off
A449/B4209
⌂ Dr Alistair MacKenzie
≡ www.worcsgolfclub.co.uk

Wyre Forest Golf Centre
Pay and play
Zortech Avenue, Kidderminster, DY11 7EX
☏ **(01299) 822682**
🖪 chris@wyreforestgolf.com

Yorkshire (East)

Allerthorpe Park   (1994)
Proprietary
Allerthorpe, York, YO42 4RL
☏ **(01759) 306686**
🖪 (01759) 305106
🖪 enquiries@allerthorpeparkgolfclub
.co.uk
👁 500
⛪ Mrs A Drinkall (01759) 306686
Ⓩ J Drinkall (01759) 306686
proshop@allerthorpeparkgolfclub
.com
ℝ 18 L 6430 yds Par 70 SSS 70
👥 U SOC
££ £25 D–£35
℮ 2 miles W of Pocklington, off
A1079
⊕ Teaching academy
⌂ JG Hatcliffe & Partners
≡ www.allerthorpeparkgolfclub.com

Beverley & East Riding
    (1889)
The Westwood, Beverley, HU17 8RG
☏ **(01482) 868757**
🖪 (01482) 868757
🖪 golf@beverleygolfclub.karoo.co.uk
👁 550
⛪ M Drew (01482) 868757
Ⓩ A Ashby (01482) 869519
ℝ 18 L 6017 yds SSS 69
👥 U SOC
££ £17 (£24)
℮ Beverley-Walkington road (B1230)
≡ www.beverleygolfclub.co.uk

Boothferry   (1982)
Proprietary
Spaldington Lane, Spaldington, Nr Howden,
DN14 7NG
☏ **(01430) 430364**
🖪 (01430) 430567
🖪 info@boothferrygolfclub.co.uk
👁 300
⛪ Matthew Rumble
Ⓩ Matthew Rumble (Dir of Golf)
ℝ 18 L 6651 yds SSS 72 Par 73
👥 U SOC
££ £17 (£20)
℮ 3 miles N of Howden on B1288.
M62 Junction 37, 2 miles
⊕ Driving range; 9 hole pay & play
course; large practice ground;
short game area
⌂ Donald Steel
≡ www.boothferrygolfclub.co.uk

Bridlington   (1905)
Belvedere Road, Bridlington, YO15 3NA
☏ **(01262) 672092/606367**
🖪 enquiries@bridlingtongolfclub.co.uk
👁 500
⛪ ARA Howarth (01262) 606367
Ⓩ ARA Howarth (01262) 674721
ℝ 18 L 6638 yds Par 72 SSS 72
👥 U
££ £25 D–£32 (£32 D–£40)
℮ 1½ miles S of Bridlington, off A165
⌂ James Braid
≡ www.bridlingtongolfclub.co.uk

The Bridlington Links   (1993)
Pay and play
Flamborough Road, Marton, Bridlington,
YO15 1DW
☏ **(01262) 401584**

Brough   (1893)
Cave Road, Brough, HU15 1HB
☏ **(01482) 667374**
🖪 (01482) 669873
🖪 gt@brough-golfclub.co.uk
👁 700
⛪ GW Townhill (Golf
Dir) (01482) 667291
Ⓩ GW Townhill (01482) 667483
ℝ 18 L 6067 yds Par 68 SSS 69
👥 WD–U exc Wed–NA
££ £35 (£50)
℮ 10 miles W of Hull on A63
≡ www.brough-golfclub.co.uk

Cave Castle   (1989)
South Cave, Nr Brough, HU15 2EU
☏ **(01430) 421286**
🖪 admin@cavecastlegc.co.uk
≡ www.cavecastlegolf.co.uk

Cherry Burton   (1993)
Proprietary
Leconfield Road, Cherry Burton, Beverley,
HU17 7RB
☏ **(01964) 550924**
🖪 info@cherryburtongolf.co.uk
👁 220
⛪ John Gray 01964 550924
Ⓩ John Gray (01964) 550924
ℝ 9 L 3290 yds Par 36 SSS 71
👥 U SOC
££ 9: £10 (12); 18: £16
℮ 2 miles N of Beverley, off Malton
road
⊕ Floodlit driving range
⌂ Will Adamson
≡ cherryburtongolf.co.uk

Cottingham   (1994)
Woodhill Way, Cottingham, Hull,
HU16 5SW
☏ **(01482) 846030**
🖪 (01482) 845932
👁 600
⛪ RJ Wiles (01482) 846030
Ⓩ CW Gray (01482) 842394
ℝ 18 L 6453 yds Par 72 SSS 71
👥 WD–U WE/BH–restricted SOC
after 2pm
££ £20 D–£30 (£30 D–£45)
℮ 3 miles N of Hull, off A164

⊕ Driving range
🏠 Wiles/Litten
🖥 www.cottinghamparks.co.uk

Driffield   (1923)
Sunderlandwick, Driffield, YO25 9AD
☎ **(01377) 240448 (Clubhouse)**
   (01377) 253116 (Office)
📞 (01377) 240599
🖂 info@driffieldgolfclub.co.uk
📖 670
🔑 SD Collingwood
⚲ K Wright (01377) 241224
▷ 18 L 6212 yds SSS 70
🕴 H I SOC
££ £30 D–£40 (£40 D–£45)
🚗 S of Driffield on A164
🖥 www.driffieldgolfclub.co.uk

Flamborough Head   (1931)
Lighthouse Road, Flamborough, Bridlington, YO15 1AR
☎ **(01262) 850333/850279**
📞 (01262) 850333
🖂 enquiries@flamboroughheadgolfclub.co.uk
📖 400
🔑 GS Thornton
⚲ TM Dixon – Co-ordinator/C J Feast (01262) 850333 ext 21
▷ 18 L 6185 yds Par 71 SSS 69
🕴 U
££ £20 D–£30 (£29 D–£36)
🚗 5 miles NE of Bridlington
⊕ Buggies; free junior coaching
🖥 www.flamboroughheadgolfclub.co.uk

Ganstead Park   (1976)
Longdales Lane, Coniston, Hull, HU11 4LB
☎ **(01482) 811280 (Steward)**
📞 (01482) 817754
🖂 secretary@gansteadpark.co.uk
📖 700
🔑 M Milner (01482) 817754
⚲ M Smee (01482) 811121
▷ 18 L 6801 yds SSS 73
🕴 U H WE–NA before noon SOC
££ On application
🚗 5 miles E of Hull on A165
🏠 Peter Green
🖥 www.gansteadpark.co.uk

Hainsworth Park   (1983)
Brandesburton, Driffield, YO25 8RT
☎ **(01964) 542362**
📞 (01964) 542362
🖂 sec@hainsworthparkgolfclub.co.uk
📖 550
🔑 R Hounsfield, BW Atkin (Prop) Sec (01377) 253751
⚲ P Myers (01964) 542362
▷ 18 L 6362 yds SSS 71
🕴 SOC
££ £20–£24 (£24–£29)
🚗 6 miles NW of Beverley, off A165 at Brandesburton roundabout
🖥 www.hainsworthparkgolfclub.co.uk

Hessle   (1898)
Westfield Road, Raywell, Cottingham, HU16 5ZA
☎ **(01482) 306840**
📞 (01482) 652679

🖂 secretary@hesslegolfclub.co.uk
📖 680
🔑 D Pettit
⚲ G Fieldsend (01482) 306842
▷ 18 L 6608 yds SSS 72
🕴 WD–U exc Tues 9am–1pm WE–NA before 12 noon
££ £30 D–£40 (£40)
🚗 3 miles SW of Cottingham
🏠 Thomas/Alliss
🖥 www.hesslegolfclub.co.uk

Hornsea   (1898)
Rolston Road, Hornsea, HU18 1XG
☎ **(01964) 532020**
📞 (01964) 532080
🖂 hornseagolfclub@aol.com
📖 600
🔑 Matthew Staveley (01964) 532020
⚲ S Wright (01964) 534989
▷ 18 L 6647 yds SSS 72
🕴 WD–U WE–restricted SOC
££ £30 D–£40
🚗 300 yds past Hornsea Free Port
🏠 Mackenzie/Braid
🖥 www.hornseagolfclub.co.uk

Hull   (1904)
The Hall, 27 Packman Lane, Kirk Ella, Hull HU10 7TJ
☎ **(01482) 653026/658919**
📞 (01482) 658919
🖂 info@hullgolfclub@virgin.net
📖 600
🔑 DJ Crossley (01482) 658919
⚲ D Jagger (01482) 653074/658919
▷ 18 L 6246 yds SSS 70
🕴 WD–U WE–by arrangement
££ £36 D–£45 (£45)
🚗 5 miles W of Hull
⊕ New teaching studio with GASP equipment
🏠 James Braid
🖥 www.hullgolfclub.co.uk

Kilnwick Percy   (1995)
Proprietary
Pocklington, York, East Yorkshire, YO42 1UF
☎ **(01759) 303090**
🖂 info@kilnwickpercygolfclub.co.uk
📖 450
🔑 Aaron Pheasant
⚲ Aaron Pheasant
▷ 18 L 6218 yds Par 70 SSS 70
🕴 U SOC
££ £20 (£25)
🚗 1 mile E of Pocklington, off B1246
🏠 John Day
🖥 www.kilnwickpercygolfclub.co.uk

Springhead Park   (1930)
Public
Willerby Road, Hull, HU5 5JE
☎ **(01482) 656309**
🔑 P Smith (01482) 654875
▷ 18 L 6402 yds SSS 71
🕴 U SOC–WD
££ £13.50 7 days
🚗 4 miles W of Hull

Sutton Park   (1935)
Public
Salthouse Road, Hull, HU8 9HF
☎ **(01482) 374242**

Withernsea   (1909)
Chestnut Avenue, Withernsea, HU19 2PG
☎ **(01964) 612258 (Clubhouse)**
📞 (01964) 612078
🖂 info@withernseagolfclub.co.uk
📖 210 12(L) 40(J)
🔑 J Boasman (Admin) (01964) 612078
▷ 9 L 6207 yds Par 72 SSS 70
🕴 WD–U WE/BH–M before 1pm SOC
££ £15
🚗 17 miles E of Hull on A1033. S side of Withernsea
🖥 www.withernseagolfclub.co.uk

Yorkshire (North)

Aldwark Manor   (1978)
Aldwark, Alne, York, YO61 1UF
☎ **(01347) 838353**
📞 (01347) 833991
📖 400
🔑 A Grindlay (01347) 838353
⚲ Alastair J Grindlay (PGA)
▷ 18 L 6187 yds Par 72 SSS 70
🕴 U SOC
££ £35 D–£45 (£40 D–£50)
🚗 5 miles SE of Boroughbridge, off A1. 13 miles NW of York, off A19
⊕ Practice ground; short game area; putting green
🖥 www.Qhotels.co.uk

Ampleforth College   (1972)
Castle Drive, Gilling East, York, YO62 4HP
☎ **(01439) 788212**
📞 (01904) 762012
🖂 sec@ampleforthgolf.co.uk
📖 240
🔑 Dr M Wilson (01904) 768861
⚲ Ken Howarth (07952) 476729
▷ 9 L 5600 yds Par 69 SSS 69
🕴 U exc 2–4pm during term time when college pupils have precedence on course.
££ D–£15 (D–£15)
🚗 Gilling East, 18 miles N of York (B1363)
⊕ Short game practice area
🏠 Rev Jerome Lambert OSB
🖥 www.ampleforthgolf.co.uk

Bedale   (1894)
Leyburn Road, Bedale, DL8 1EZ
☎ **(01677) 422451**
📞 (01677) 427143
🖂 bedalegolfclub@aol.com
📖 600 100(J)
🔑 Jackie Wanless (01677) 422451
⚲ AD Johnson (01677) 422443
▷ 18 L 6610 yds SSS 72
🕴 U SOC
🚗 N boundary of Bedale
⊕ Practice ground
🏠 Hawtree
🖥 www.bedalegolfclub.com

For list of abbreviations and key to symbols see page 647

Bentham (1922)

Robin Lane, Bentham, Lancaster, LA2 7AG
- ☎ (015242) 62470
- ✉ secretary@benthamgolfclub.co.uk
- ⌂ 450
- ♙ J Mann (015242) 62470
- ✓ A Watson (01524) 262455
- ⏥ 18 L 6000 yds SSS 69
- ♟ U SOC
- ££ D–£30 (£35)
- ⛳ NE of Lancaster on B6480 towards Settle. 13 miles E of M6 Junction 34
- 🖅 www.benthamgolfclub.co.uk

Catterick (1930)

Leyburn Road, Catterick Garrison, DL9 3QE
- ☎ (01748) 833268
- 🖷 (01748) 833268
- ✉ secretary@catterickgolfclub.co.uk
- ⌂ 440
- ♙ M Young
- ✓ A Marshall (01748) 833671
- ⏥ 18 L 6378 yds SSS 70
- ♟ U – check with Sec first
- ££ £25 (£30)
- ⛳ 6 miles SW of Scotch Corner, via A1
- ⊕ Large practice ground
- ⏡ Arthur Day
- 🖅 www.catterickgolfclub.co.uk

Cleveland (1887)

Majuba Road, Redcar, TS10 5BJ
- ☎ (01642) 471798
- 🖷 (01642) 487619
- ✉ majuba@btconnect.com
- ⌂ 800
- ♙ W E Pattison (01642) 471798
- ✓ A Scott (01642) 483462
- ⏥ 18 L 6696 yds SSS 72
- ♟ WD–U WE/BH–by arrangement SOC
- ££ £10 to £20 Daily varying scale – ring for details
- ⛳ S bank of River Tees
- 🖅 www.clevelandgolfclub.co.uk

Cocksford (1992)

Stutton, Tadcaster, LS24 9NG
- ☎ (01937) 834253

Crimple Valley (1976)

Pay and play
Hookstone Wood Road, Harrogate, HG2 8PN
- ☎ (01423) 883485
- 🖷 (01423) 881018
- ⌂ 200
- ♙ Paul Johnson
- ✓ Paul Johnson
- ⏥ 9 L 2500 yds SSS 33
- ♟ U
- ££ 9: £9 (£13); 18: £10 D–£15
- ⛳ 1 mile S of Harrogate, off A61, by Yorkshire Showground
- ⏡ R Lumb

Drax (1989)

Drax, Selby, YO8 8PQ
- ☎ (01757) 617228
- 🖷 (01757) 617228
- ✉ draxgolfclub@btinternet.com

- ⌂ 350
- ♙ Mrs D A Smith
- ✓ Professional teaching available
- ⏥ 9 (12 tees) Par 69 SS 67
- ♟ M SOC WD WE Small groups contact Sec
- ££ £12; Juniors £6
- ⛳ 5 miles S of Selby, off A1041
- ⊕ Following a sport England Grant a further 3 holes are being developed and a short Par 3 has also been constructed, both will be open sometime in 2009
- ⏡ J Scott
- 🖅 www.draxgolfclub.co.uk

Easingwold (1930)

Stillington Road, Easingwold, York, YO61 3ET
- ☎ (01347) 822474
- 🖷 (01347) 822474
- ✉ enquiries@easingwoldgolfclub.co.uk
- ⌂ 688
- ♙ T Jenkinson (01347) 822474
- ✓ J Hughes (01347) 821964
- ⏥ 18 L 6699 yds Par 73 SSS 72
- ♟ U SOC WD after 9.30, WE by arrangement
- ££ £28 D–£35 (£35) – £12 junior
- ⛳ 12 miles N of York on A19. E end of Easingwold
- ⊕ Full practice facilities
- ⏡ Hawtree/OCM
- 🖅 www.easingwoldgolfclub.co.uk

Filey (1897)

West Ave, Filey, YO14 9BQ
- ☎ (01723) 513293
- 🖷 (01723) 514952
- ✉ secretary@fileygolfclub.com
- ⌂ 641
- ✓ Darren Squire (01723) 513134
- ⏥ 18 L 6112 yds SSS 69
- 9 L 1513 yds Par 30
- ♟ U H SOC
- ££ £30 (£35) Summer. £25 (£30) Winter
- ⛳ 1 mile S of Filey centre
- ⏡ James Braid
- 🖅 www.fileygolfclub.com

Forest of Galtres (1993)

Proprietary
Moorlands Road, Skelton, York, YO32 2RF
- ☎ (01904) 766198
- 🖷 (01904) 769400
- ✉ secretary@forestofgaltres.co.uk
- ⌂ 450
- ♙ Mrs SJ Procter
- ✓ P Bradley
- ⏥ 18 L 6534 yds Par 72 SSS 71
- ♟ U SOC–WD/Sun
- ££ £25 (£30)
- ⛳ Skelton, 4 miles N of York. 1½ miles off A19 Thursk Rd
- ⊕ Driving range
- ⏡ Simon Gidman
- 🖅 www.forestofgaltres.co.uk

Forest Park (1991)

Stockton-on Forest, York, YO32 9UW
- ☎ (01904) 400425
- ✉ admin@forestparkgolfclub.co.uk

- ⌂ 650
- ♙ S Crossley (01904) 400688
- ✓ M Winterburn (01904) 400425
- ⏥ 18 L 6673 yds Par 71 SSS 72
- 9 L 3186 yds Par 70 SSS 70
- ♟ U SOC
- ££ 9: £10 (£12) 18: £25 D–£32 (£30 D–£40)
- ⛳ 1½ miles from E end of A64 York By-pass
- ⊕ Driving range + undercover driving range
- 🖅 www.forestparkgolfclub.co.uk

Fulford (York) Golf Club (1906)

Heslington Lane, York, YO10 5DY
- ☎ (01904) 413579
- 🖷 (01904) 416918
- ✉ info@fulfordgolfclub.co.uk
- ⌂ 750
- ♙ GS Pearce
- ✓ G Wills (01904) 412882
- ⏥ 18 L 6775 yds SSS 72
- ♟ By arrangement with Mgr SOC WD H
- ££ From £42.50 D–£65
- ⛳ 2 miles S of York (A64)
- ⏡ Major C McKenzie
- 🖅 www.fulfordgolfclub.co.uk

Ganton (1891)

Station Road, Ganton, Scarborough, YO12 4PA
- ☎ (01944) 710329
- 🖷 (01944) 710922
- ✉ secretary@gantongolfclub.com
- ⌂ 550
- ♙ PE Ware
- ✓ G Brown (01944) 710260
- ⏥ 18 L 6724 yds SSS 73
- ♟ By prior arrangement
- ££ £75 (£85)
- ⛳ 11 miles SW of Scarborough on A64
- ⏡ Dunn/Vardon/Braid/Colt
- 🖅 www.gantongolfclub.com

Harrogate (1892)

Forest Lane Head, Harrogate, HG2 7TF
- ☎ (01423) 863158 (Clubhouse)
- 🖷 (01423) 860073
- ✉ secretary@harrogate-gc.co.uk
- ⌂ 700
- ♙ Peter Banks (01423) 862999
- ✓ S Everson/G Stothard
- ⏥ 18 L 6241 yds SSS 70
- ♟ WD–U WE/BH–enquire first SOC–WD exc Tues
- ££ £40 D–£45 (£50)
- ⛳ 2 miles E of Harrogate on Knaresborough road (A59)
- ⏡ Sandy Herd
- 🖅 www.harrogate-gc.co.uk

Heworth (1911)

Muncaster House, Muncastergate, York, YO31 9JY
- ☎ (01904) 424618
- 🖷 (01904) 426156
- ✉ golf@heworth-gc.fsnet.co.uk
- ⌂ 345 80(L) 50(J)
- ♙ RJ Hunt (01904) 426156

For list of abbreviations and key to symbols see page 647

✓ S Burdett (01904) 422389
⊵ 12 L 6105 yds Par 69 SSS 69
⋔ U
££ £15 (£20)
⊕ NE boundary of York (A1036)
⋔ C Heal
✉ www.heworthgolfclub.co.uk

Hunley Hall   (1993)
Brotton, Saltburn, TS12 2QQ
☎ (01287) 676216
⌂ (01287) 678250
⊠ enquiries@hunleyhall.co.uk
▥ 500
✍ E Lillie (01287) 676216
✓ A Brook (01287) 677444
⊵ 27 holes:
5948-6918 yds Par/SSS 68-73
⋔ U SOC–exc Sun
££ £25 (£35)
⊕ 15 miles N of Whitby on A174
⊕ Buggies; floodlit driving range
⋔ John Morgan
✉ www.hunleyhall.co.uk

Kirkbymoorside   (1951)
Manor Vale, Kirkbymoorside, York,
YO62 6EG
☎ (01751) 431525
⌂ (01751) 433190
⊠ enqs@kirkbymoorsidegolf.co.uk
▥ 550
✍ Mrs R Rivis
✓ J Hinchliffe (01751) 430402
⊵ 18 L 6207 yds SSS 69
⋔ U after 9.30am
££ £22 (£32)
⊕ A170 between Helmsley and
Pickering
✉ www.kirkbymoorsidegolf.co.uk

Knaresborough   (1920)
Boroughbridge Road, Knaresborough,
HG5 0QQ
☎ (01423) 862690
⌂ (01423) 869345
⊠ secretary@kgc.uk.com
▥ 700
✍ C Hill
✓ A Turner (01423) 864865
⊵ 18 L 6780 yds Par 72 SSS 72
⋔ U SOC WD WE
££ £34 (£39)
⊕ 1½ miles N of Knaresborough on
A6055
⊕ Practice facilities
⋔ Hawtree
✉ www.knaresboroughgolfclub.co.uk

Malton & Norton   (1910)
Welham Park, Welham Road, Norton,
Malton YO17 9QE
☎ (01653) 697912
⌂ (01653) 697844
⊠ maltonandnorton@btconnect
.com
▥ 820
✍ Mrs L Gurnell (01653) 697912
✓ M Brooks (01653) 693882
⊵ 27 holes:
Welham L 6456 yds SSS 71
Park L 6242 yds SSS 70
Derwent L 6286 yds SSS 70

⋔ WD–U WE–restricted on match
days H SOC
££ £29 (£35)
⊕ 18 miles NE of York (A64)
⊕ Driving range; short game practice
area
✉ www.maltonandnortongolfclub
.co.uk

Masham   (1895)
Burnholme, Swinton Road, Masham, Ripon,
HG4 4HT
☎ (01765) 688054
⌂ (01765) 688054
⊠ info@mashamgolfclub.co.uk
▥ 280
✍ H Macdonald
⊵ 9 L 6204 yds Par 70 SSS 70
⋔ WD–U WE–M BH–NA
££ £20 (18 holes) D–£25
⊕ 10 miles N of Ripon, off A6108
✉ www.mashamgolfclub.co.uk

Middlesbrough   (1908)
Brass Castle Lane, Marton, Middlesbrough,
TS8 9EE
☎ (01642) 311515
⌂ (01642) 319607
⊠ enquiries@middlesbroughgolfclub
.co.uk
▥ 975
✍ PM Jackson
✓ (01642) 311766
⊵ 18 L 6302 yds SSS 70
⋔ WD–U exc Tues–H Sat–NA SOC
££ D–£37 (£42)
⊕ 5 miles S of Middlesbrough
⋔ James Braid
✉ www.middlesbroughgolfclub.co.uk

Middlesbrough Municipal
(1977)
Public
Ladgate Lane, Middlesbrough, TS5 7YZ
☎ (01642) 315533
⌂ (01642) 300726
⊠ maurice_gormley@middlesbrough
.gov.uk
▥ 480
✍ M Gormley (Mgr)
✓ A Hope (01642) 300720
⊵ 18 L 6333 yds SSS 70
⋔ U
££ £14 (£17)
⊕ 2 miles S of Middlesbrough on
A174
⊕ Floodlit driving range
⋔ Shuttleworth
✉ www.middlesbroughcouncil.gov.uk

Oakdale   (1914)
Oakdale, Harrogate, HG1 2LN
☎ (01423) 567162
⌂ (01423) 536030
⊠ sec@oakdale-golfclub.com
▥ 775
✍ MJ Cross
✓ C Dell (01423) 560510
⊵ 18 L 6456 yds SSS 71
⋔ WD–U 9.30–12.30 and after 2pm
SOC–WD
££ £44 (£61)
⊕ ½ mile NE of Royal Hall,
Harrogate

⋔ Dr A Mackenzie
✉ www.oakdale-golfclub.com

The Oaks   (1996)
Proprietary
Aughton Common, Aughton, York,
YO42 4PW
☎ (01757) 288001 (Clubhouse)
(01757) 288007 (Bookings)
⌂ (01757) 288232
⊠ sheila@theoaksgolfclub.co.uk
▥ 700
✍ Mrs S Nutt (01757) 288577
✓ Graham Walker & Lysa Jones
(01757) 288007
⊵ 18 L 6792 yds Par 72 SSS 72
⋔ WD–U WE–M SOC–WD
££ D–£28 (D–£40)
⊕ 1 mile N of Bubwith on B1228. 14
miles SE of York. M62 Junction 37
⊕ Driving range; full practice facilities;
Graham Walker Golf Academy
⋔ Julian Covey
✉ www.theoaksgolfclub.co.uk

Pannal   (1906)
Follifoot Road, Pannal, Harrogate, HG3 1ES
☎ (01423) 872628
⌂ (01423) 870043
⊠ secretary@pannalgc.co.uk
▥ 780
✍ NG Douglas
✓ D Padgett
⊵ 18 L 6622 yds SSS 72
⋔ WD–H 9.30–12 and after 1.30pm
WE–H 11–12 and after 2.30pm
SOC
££ £55 D–£65 (£70)
⊕ 2½ miles S of Harrogate, on A61
⊕ Driving range
⋔ Herd/Mackenzie
✉ www.pannalgc.co.uk

Pike Hills   (1904)
Tadcaster Road, Askham Bryan, York,
YO23 3UW
☎ (01904) 700797
⌂ (01904) 700797
⊠ secretary@pikehillsgolfclub.co.uk
▥ 750
✍ Garry Dunn (01904) 700765
✓ I Gradwell (01904) 708756
⊵ 18 L 6146 yds SSS 70
⋔ WD–U H before 4.30pm –M after
4.30pm SOC–WD
££ £26 D–£32
⊕ 3 miles SW of York on A64
(eastbound)
⊕ Driving range
✉ www.pikehillsgolfclub.co.uk

Richmond   (1892)
Bend Hagg, Richmond, DL10 5EX
☎ (01748) 825319
⌂ (01748) 821709
⊠ secretary@richmondyorksgolfclub
.co.uk
▥ 600
✍ AE Lancaster (01748) 823231
✓ J Cousins (01748) 822457
⊵ 18 L 6073 yds SSS 69
⋔ U
££ £23 D–£25 (£25 D–£30)

⇔ 3 miles SW of Scotch Corner
⌂ Frank Pennink
▤ www.richmondyorksgolfclub.co.uk

Ripon City Golf Club
(1907)
Palace Road, Ripon, HG4 3HH
☎ **(01765) 603640**
⌨ (01765) 692880
✉ secretary@riponcitygolfclub.com
▦ 671 86(L) 59(J)
⚴ MJ Doig MBE
✓ T Davis (01765) 600411
⊳ 18 L 6084 yds SSS 69
⚙ U SOC
££ £30 (£40)
⇔ 1 mile N of Ripon on A6108
⊕ Driving range
⌂ ADAS
▤ www.riponcitygolfclub.com

Romanby Golf and Country Club
(1993)
Pay and play
Yafforth Road, Northallerton, DL7 0PE
☎ **(01609) 778855**
⌨ (01609) 779084
✉ info@romanby.com
▦ 550
⚴ R Boucher (Gen Mgr)
✓ R Wood (01609) 760777
   richard@romanby.com
⊳ 18 L 6663 yds SSS 72
   6 hole par 3 academy course
⚙ U SOC
££ To be decided
⇔ 1 mile W of Northallerton on B6271
⊕ Floodlit driving range; practice facilities; putting green
⌂ Will Adamson
▤ www.romanby.com

Rudding Park
(1995)
Pay and play
Rudding Park, Harrogate, HG3 1JH
☎ **(01423) 872100**
⌨ (01423) 873011
✉ sales@ruddingpark.com
▦ 700
⚴ J King
✓ M Moore (01423) 873400
⊳ 18 L 6883 yds SSS 73
⚙ U H SOC
££ £35, Fri/WE–£39.50
⇔ 2 miles S of Harrogate (A658)
⊕ Driving range; Golf Academy; 6-hole short course opening April 2008
⌂ Hawtree
▤ www.ruddingpark.com

Saltburn
(1894)
Hob Hill, Saltburn-by-the-Sea, TS12 1NJ
☎ **(01287) 622812**
⌨ (01287) 625988
✉ info@saltburngolf.co.uk
▦ 900
⚴ M Murtha
✓ P Bolton (01287) 624653
⊳ 18 L 5974 yds Par 70 SSS 70
⚙ U H SOC

££ £32 (£36)
⇔ East on A174, right at Quarry Lane roundabout, left at lights, 1 mile
⌂ James Braid
▤ www.saltburngolf.co.uk

Sandburn Hall
(2005)
Proprietary
Scotchman Lane, Flaxton, York YO60 7RB
☎ **(01904) 469929 Shop**
⌨ (01904) 469923
✉ alistair@sandburnhall.co.uk
▦ 420
⚴ Alistair Nicol (Golf Mgr)
✓ Steve Robinson (01904) 469926
⊳ 18 L 6723 yds par 72 SSS 72
   SOC, WD–U WE–NA before noon
££ £25 WD, £30 WE, £45 D Twilight £15
⇔ 8 miles NE of York. Turn left at Flaxton off A64
⊕ 18-bay driving range; short game area; sports bar
⌂ Bryan Moor
▤ www.sandburnhall.co.uk

Scarborough North Cliff
(1909)
North Cliff Avenue, Burniston Road, Scarborough, YO12 6PP
☎ **(01723) 355397**
⌨ (01723) 362134
✉ info@northcliffgolfclub.co.uk
▦ 600
⚴ Mrs JH Lloyd
✓ SN Deller (01723) 365920
⊳ 18 L 6493 yds Par 72 SSS 71
⚙ U H exc Sat am/Sun before 10am and comp days SOC
££ £35 D–£40 (£40 D–£45)
⇔ 2 miles N of Scarborough on coast road
⌂ James Braid
▤ www.northcliffgolfclub.co.uk

Scarborough South Cliff
(1902)
Deepdale Avenue, Scarborough, YO11 2UE
☎ **(01723) 374737**
⌨ (01723) 374737
✉ clubsecretary@southcliffgolfclub.com
▦ 600
⚴ D Roberts
✓ T Skingle (01723) 365150
⊳ 18 L 6432 yds Par 72 SSS 71
⚙ U H SOC WE NA before 1.30 (Sat only)
££ RD–£30 D–£35 Mon–Thurs
   RD–£35 D–£40 Fri–Sun, and BH
⇔ 1 mile S of Scarborough, off A165
⊕ Practice area, 5 Hole Pitch + Putt
⌂ Dr A Mackenzie
▤ www.southcliffgolfclub.com

Scarthingwell
(1993)
Scarthingwell, Tadcaster, LS24 9DG
☎ **(01937) 557878**
⌨ (01937) 557909
▦ 400
✓ S Danby (01937) 557864
⊳ 18 L 6642 yds Par 72 SSS 72

⚙ U SOC
££ £20 (£25)
⇔ 4 miles S of Tadcaster on A162
▤ www.scarthingwellgolfcourse.co.uk

Selby
(1907)
Mill Lane, Brayton, Selby, YO8 9LD
☎ **(01757) 228622**
⌨ (01757) 228785
✉ selbygolfclub@aol.com
▦ 749
⚴ JN Proctor
✓ N Ludwell (01757) 228785
⊳ 18 L 6374 yds SSS 71
⚙ WD–H WE–NA SOC–WD
££ £33 D–£37
⇔ 3 miles SW of Selby, off A63 Selby bypass; 5 miles N of M62 Jct 34
⌂ JH Taylor/Hawtree
▤ www.selbygolfclub.co.uk

Settle
(1895)
Giggleswick, Settle, BD24 0DH
☎ **(01729) 825288**
✉ info@settlegolfclub.co.uk
▦ 250
⚴ J Ketchell (01729) 841140
⊳ 9 L 6089 yds SSS 72
⚙ U exc Sun–restricted SOC
££ D–£20
⇔ 1 mile N of Settle on A65
⌂ Tom Vardon
▤ www.settlegolfclub.co.uk

Skipton
(1893)
Short Lee Lane, Skipton, BD23 3LF
☎ **(01756) 793922 (bar)**
⌨ (01756) 796665
✉ enquiries@skiptongolfclub.co.uk
▦ 720
⚴ Karen Chapman (01756) 795657
✓ P Robinson (01756) 793257
⊳ 18 L 6090 yds SSS 70
⚙ U SOC
££ £30 (£32)
⇔ 1 mile N of Skipton on A59
▤ www.skiptongolfclub.co.uk

Teesside
(1901)
Acklam Road, Thornaby, TS17 7JS
☎ **(01642) 676249**
⌨ (01642) 676252
✉ teessidegolfclub@btconnect.com
▦ 715
⚴ M Fleming (01642) 616516
✓ S Pilgrim (01642) 673822
⊳ 18 L 6535 yds Par 72 SSS 71
⚙ WD–U before 4.30pm WE–U after 11am BH–M before 11am SOC
££ D–£26 (£30)
⇔ 2 miles S of Stockton on A1130. ½ mile from A19 on A1130
⊕ Function & conference facilities
⌂ Makepeace/Summerville
▤ www.teessidegolfclub.com

Thirsk & Northallerton
(1914)
Thornton-le-Street, Thirsk, YO7 4AB
☎ **(01845) 525115**
⌨ (01845) 525115
✉ secretary@tngc.co.uk

📖 600
🏌 J Brown (01845) 525115
⛳ R Garner (01845) 526216
🏳 18 L 6495 yds SSS 71
👤 WD/Sat–U H Sun–M SOC
££ £30 D–£36 Sat/BH–£36 D–£46
🚗 2 miles N of Thirsk, nr A19 and
A168 roundabout
🏠 ADAS
🖥 www.tngc.co.uk

Whitby   (1892)
Sandsend Road, Low Straggleton, Whitby,
YO21 3SR
☎ **(01947) 600660**
🖥 (01947) 600660
📧 office@whitbygolfclub.co.uk
📖 450
🏌 T Mason
⛳ T Mason (01947) 602719
🏳 18 L 6259 yds SSS 70
👤 U SOC WD WE
££ £26 (£32)
🚗 2 miles N of Whitby on A174
🏠 Simon Gidman (new holes only)
🖥 www.whitbygolfclub.co.uk

Wilton   (1952)
Wilton, Redcar, Cleveland, TS10 4QY
☎ **(01642) 465265**
🖥 (01642) 465463
📧 secretary@wiltongolfclub.co.uk
📖 650
🏌 R Douglas (01642) 465265
⛳ Pat Smillie (01642) 465265
🏳 18 L 6276 yds Par 70 SSS 70
👤 Mon–Fri after 10 am U; Sat NA;
Sun after 10.30 am U
££ D–£26 (D–£32)
🚗 3 miles W of Redcar on A174-signs
to Wilton Castle
🏠 JFS Morrison
🖥 www.wiltongolfclub.co.uk

York   (1890)
Lords Moor Lane, Strensall, York,
YO32 5XF
☎ **(01904) 491840**
🖥 (01904) 491852
📧 secretary@yorkgolfclub.co.uk
📖 468(M) 160(L) 80(J)
🏌 MJ Wells
⛳ AP Hoyles (01904) 490304
🏳 18 L 6301 yds SSS 70
👤 U–phone Sec SOC
££ £36–£50 (£45–£50)
🚗 4 miles N of York ring road
(A1237)
🏠 JH Taylor
🖥 www.yorkgolfclub.co.uk

Yorkshire (South)

Abbeydale   (1895)
Twentywell Rise, Twentywell Lane, Dore,
Sheffield, S17 4QA
☎ **(0114) 236 0763**
🖥 (0114) 236 0762
📧 abbeygolf@btconnect.com
📖 500
🏌 Mrs JL Wing (Office Mgr)

⛳ N Perry (Golf Mgr/Pro)
(0114) 236 0763/5633
🏳 18 L 6241 yds SSS 70
👤 U SOC–H by arrangement
££ £35 (£45)
🚗 5 miles S of Sheffield, off A621
🏠 Herbert Fowler
🖥 www.abbeydalegolfclub.co.uk

Barnsley   (1925)
Public
Wakefield Road, Staincross, Barnsley,
S75 6JZ
☎ **(01226) 382856**
📧 barnsleygolfclub@hotmail.com
📖 363
🏌 Trevor Jones
⛳ S Wyke (01226) 380358
🏳 18 L 5951 yds Par 69 SSS 69
👤 U
££ £15 (£17)
🚗 4 miles N of Barnsley on A61
⊕ Buggies

Bawtry   (1974)
Cross Lane, Austerfield, Doncaster,
DN10 6RF
☎ **(01302) 711409**
🖥 (01302) 711445
📧 enquiries@bawtrygolfclub.co.uk
📖 460 34(L) 40(J)
🏌 D Gregory and M Beck
(01302) 710841
🏳 18 L 6994 yds Par 73 SSS 73
👤 U SOC WE–after noon
££ £20 (£28)
🚗 2 miles NE of Bawtry, on A614
⊕ Driving range
🏠 E & M Baker
🖥 www.bawtrygolfclub.co.uk

Beauchief   (1925)
Public
Abbey Lane, Beauchief, Sheffield,
S8 0DB
☎ **(0114) 236 7274**
📧 e-mail@beauchiefgolfclub.co.uk
📖 450
🏌 Mrs B Fryer
⛳ Mark Trippett
🏳 18 L 5452 yds SSS 66
👤 U
££ £12 (£14)
🚗 A621 Sheffield. M1 jct 33
🖥 www.beauchiefgolfclub.co.uk

Birley Wood   (1974)
Public
Birley Lane, Sheffield, S12 3BP
☎ **(0114) 264 7262**
📧 birleysec@hotmail.com

Concord Park   (1952)
Pay and play
Shiregreen Lane, Sheffield, S5 6AE
☎ **(0114) 257 7378**
📧 concordparkgc@tiscali.co.uk

Crookhill Park   (1974)
Public
Conisborough, Doncaster, DN12 2AH
☎ **(01709) 862979**

Doncaster   (1894)
Bawtry Road, Bessacarr, Doncaster,
DN4 7PD
☎ **(01302) 865632**
📧 doncastergolf@aol.com

Doncaster Town Moor
(1895)
Bawtry Road, Belle Vue, Doncaster,
DN4 5HU
☎ **(01302) 533778**
🖥 (01302) 533778
📧 dtmgc@btconnect.com
📖 540
🏌 Mr R Smith
⛳ S Shaw (01302) 535286
🏳 18 L 6141 yds SSS 69
👤 U exc Sun–NA before 3.30pm
SOC
££ £19 (£24)
🚗 Inside racecourse, clubhouse on
A638
⊕ Practice facility; junior coaching; full
catering facility
🖥 www.doncastertownmoorgolfclub
.co.uk

Dore & Totley   (1913)
Bradway Road, Bradway, Sheffield,
S17 4QR
☎ **(0114) 236 0492**
🖥 (0114) 235 3436
📧 dore.totley@btconnect.com
📖 580
🏌 Mrs SD Haslehurst (0114) 236
9872
⛳ G Roberts (0114) 236 6844
🏳 18 L 6763 yds Par 72 SSS 72
👤 WD–restricted Sat–NA
Sun–restricted before 1pm
SOC–by arrangement
££ £32 (£36) Sun–£24 after 4pm
🚗 5 miles SW of Sheffield, off A61
⊕ Practice area, Restaurant, Bar,
Snooker Table, 2-4-1's available –
must book in advance.
🖥 www.doreandtotleygolf.co.uk

Grange Park   (1972)
Pay and play
Upper Wortley Road, Kimberworth,
Rotherham, S61 2SJ
☎ **(01709) 558884**

Hallamshire   (1897)
Sandygate, Sheffield, S10 4LA
☎ **(0114) 230 1007**
🖥 (0114) 230 5413
📧 secretary@hallamshiregolfclub.com
📖 600
🏌 R Hill (0114) 230 2153
⛳ G Tickell (0114) 230 5222
🏳 18 L 6346 yds SSS 71
👤 H SOC–WD
££ £45 (£60)
🚗 W boundary of Sheffield

Hallowes   (1892)
Dronfield, Sheffield, S18 1UR
☎ **(01246) 413734**
🖥 (01246) 413753
📧 secretary@hallowesgolfclub.org

☐ 665
🖉 N Ogden
✍ J Oates (01246) 411196
🏌 18 L 6342 yds SSS 71
💂 WD–U WE–M SOC
££ £38 D–£42 (£25)
🚗 6 miles S of Sheffield on B6057
⊕ Practice ground
✉ www.hallowesgolfclub.org

Hickleton (1909)
Hickleton, Doncaster, DN5 7BE
☎ (01709) 896081
🖥 (01709) 896083
✉ john@hickletongolfclub.co.uk
☐ 600
🖉 JM Little (Mgr)
✍ PJ Audsley (01709) 888436
🏌 18 L 6446 yds SSS 71
💂 WD–U WE–NA before noon SOC
££ £32 (£40)
🚗 On A635 3 miles A1(M) J37
🏠 Huggett/Coles
✉ www.hickletongolfclub.co.uk

Hillsborough (1920)
Worrall Road, Sheffield, S6 4BE
☎ (0114) 234 9151 (Secretary)
🖥 (0114) 229 4105
✉ admin@hillsboroughgolfclub.co.uk
☐ 530
🖉 G Smalley (0114) 234 9151
✍ L Horsman (0114) 229 4100
🏌 18 L 6035 yds SSS 70
💂 H SOC
££ £30 (£35)
🚗 Wadsley, Sheffield

Lees Hall (1907)
Hemsworth Road, Norton, Sheffield, S8 8LL
☎ (0114) 255 4402
✉ secretary@leeshallgolfclub.co.uk

Lindrick (1891)
Lindrick Common, Worksop, Notts,
S81 8BH
☎ (01909) 485802
🖥 (01909) 488685
✉ lgc@ansbronze.com
☐ 500
🖉 (01909) 475282
✍ JR King (01909) 475820
🏌 18 L 6486 yds Par 71 SSS 71
💂 U H–by prior arrangement exc
Tues SOC–WD WE (limited Sun)
££ £60 D–£80 (£80)
🚗 4 miles W of Worksop on A57. M1
Junction 31
⊕ Practice grounds; teaching bays
🏠 Various
✉ www.lindrickgolfclub.co.uk

Owston Hall (the Robin Hood golf course) (1996)
Owston Hall, Owston, Doncaster, DN6 9JF
☎ (01302) 722800
🖥 (01302) 728885
✉ proshop@owstonhall.com
☐ 250
🖉 Gerry Briggs
✍ J Laszkowicz (01302) 722231
🏌 18 L 6937 yds Par 72 SSS 73
💂 U SOC

££ £22 (£30)
🚗 7 miles N of Doncaster on A19
(B1220)
🏠 Will Adamson
✉ www.owstonhall.com

Owston Park (1988)
Public
Owston Lane, Owston, Carcroft, DN6 8EF
☎ (01302) 330821
🖥 michael.parker@foremostgolf.com
🖉 MT Parker
✍ M Parker
🏌 9 L 6148 yds SSS 71
💂 U
££ On application
🚗 5 miles N of Doncaster on A19
🏠 Michael Parker
✉ www.owstonparkgolfcourse.co.uk

Phoenix (1932)
Pavilion Lane, Brinsworth, Rotherham,
S60 5PA
☎ (01709) 363788
🖥 (01709) 363788
✉ secretary@phoenixgolfclub.co.uk
☐ 700
🖉 I Gregory (01709) 363788
✍ M Roberts (01709) 382624
🏌 18 L 6181 yds SSS 70
💂 U
££ £19 D–£25 (£25 D–£35)
🚗 2 miles S of Rotherham. M1 Jct 34
⊕ Driving range
🏠 H Cotton
✉ www.phoenixgolfclub.co.uk

Renishaw Park (1911)
Golf House, Mill Lane, Renishaw, Sheffield
S21 3UZ
☎ (01246) 432044
🖥 (01246) 432116
☐ 550
🖉 TJ Childs
✍ N Parkinson (01246) 435484
🏌 18 L 6262 yds SSS 70
💂 H SOC
££ £28 D–£38.00 (£42)
🚗 7 miles SE of Sheffield. 2 miles W
of M1 Junction 30
✉ www.renishawparkgolf.co.uk

Rother Valley Golf Centre (1997)
Mansfield Road, Wales Bar, Sheffield,
S26 5PQ
☎ (0114) 247 3000
🖥 (0114) 247 6000
✉ rother-jackbarker@btinternet.com
☐ 300
🖉 Mrs M Goodman
✍ JK Ripley
🏌 18 L 6602 yds Par 72 SSS 72
9 hole Par 3 course
💂 U SOC
££ Mon–Thur £15, Fri £17, Sat–Sun
£19.50
🚗 Rother Valley Country Park, 2
miles S of M1 Junction 31
⊕ Floodlit driving range
🏠 Shattock/Roe
✉ www.jackbarker.com

Rotherham (1903)
Thrybergh Park, Rotherham, S65 4NU
☎ (01709) 850466
✉ manager@rotherhamgolfclub
.com

Roundwood (1976)
Green Lane, Rawmarsh, Rotherham,
S62 6LA
☎ (01709) 523471

Sandhill (1993)
Proprietary
Little Houghton, Barnsley, S72 0HW
☎ (01226) 753444
🖥 (01226) 753444
✉ ken9sqnre@talktalk.co.uk
☐ 420
🖉 K Walls (01226) 758903
🏌 18 L 6309 yds SSS 71 white
6037 yds yellow
5620 yds Ladies Par 73
💂 U SOC
££ £17.50 (£22.50) after 3pm Sun
£17.00
🚗 6 miles E of Barnsley, off A635
⊕ Driving range next door – not
owned by Sandhill
🏠 John Royston
✉ www.sandhillgolfclub.co.uk

Sheffield Transport (1923)
Meadow Head, Sheffield, S8 7RE
☎ (0114) 237 3216

Silkstone (1893)
Field Head, Elmhirst Lane, Silkstone,
Barnsley, S75 4LD
☎ (01226) 790328
🖥 (01226) 794902
✉ silkstonegolf@hotmail.co.uk
☐ 600
🖉 Alan Butcher
✍ K Guy (01226) 790128
🏌 18 L 6648 yds SSS 72
💂 WD–U SOC–WD
££ £28 D–£36
🚗 1 mile W of M1 Jct 37 on A628
✉ www.silkstone-golf-club.co.uk

Sitwell Park (1913)
Shrogs Wood Road, Rotherham,
S60 4BY
☎ (01709) 541046
🖥 (01709) 703637
✉ secretary@sitwellgolf.co.uk
☐ 500
🖉 S G Bell
✍ N Taylor (01709) 540961
🏌 18 L 6250 yds SSS 70
💂 WD–U Sat–M Sun–NA before
11.30am SOC
££ £26 (£32); D–£34 (£40)
🚗 2½ miles E of Rotherham on A631.
M18 Junction 1
⊕ Buggie Hire; Catering facilities;
Lessons from PGA Professionals.
🏠 Dr A Mackenzie
✉ www.sitwellgolf.co.uk

Stocksbridge & District

(1924)
Royd Lane, Deepcar, Sheffield, S36 2RZ
- ☎ (0114) 288 7479/288 2003
- 📠 (0114) 283 1460
- ✉ secretary
  @stocksbridgeanddistrictgolfclub
  .com
- 🏠 400
- ♣ D Haley (0114) 288 2003
- ✓ R Broad (0114) 288 2779
- ▷ 18 L 5200 yds Par 65 SSS 65
- ♛ U SOC
- ££ £25 (£37)
- ⊕ 9 miles W of Sheffield (A616)
- 🖥 www.stocksbridgeanddistrictgolfclub
  .com

Styrrup Hall   (2000)

Proprietary
Main Street, Styrrup, Doncaster DN11 8NB
- ☎ (01302) 751112 (Golf)
  (01302) 759933
  (Clubhouse)
- 📠 (01302) 750622
- ✉ office@styrrupgolf.co.uk
- 🏠 400
- ♣ Dianne Stokoe (Sec/Mgr)
- ✓ Richard Allen
- ▷ 18 L 6745 yds SSS 72
- ♛ SOC WD–U WE–afternoons
- ££ £18 (£25 + Bank Hols)
- ⊕ 2 miles from Blyth Services on
  A1M
- ⊕ Driving range; function room
- 🖥 www.styrrupgolf.co.uk

Tankersley Park   (1907)

Park Lane, High Green, Sheffield,
S35 4LG
- ☎ (0114) 246 8247
- 📠 (0114) 245 7818
- ✉ secretary@tpgc.freeserve.co.uk
- 🏠 574
- ♣ A Brownhill (0114) 246 8247
- ✓ I Kirk (0114) 245 5583
- ▷ 18 L 6212 yds Par 69 SSS 70
- ♛ WD–U WE–M SOC–WD
- ££ £27 D–£36 (£36)
- ⊕ Chapeltown, 7 miles N of Sheffield.
  M1 Junctions 35A/36
- 🏠 Hawtree
- 🖥 www.tankersleyparkgolfclub.org.uk

Thorne   (1980)

Pay and play
Kirton Lane, Thorne, Doncaster,
DN8 5RJ
- ☎ (01405) 815173
- 📠 (01405) 741899
- 🏠 120
- ♣ R Highfield
- ✓ ED Highfield (01405) 812084
- ▷ 18 L 5294 yds SSS 66 Par 68
- ♛ U SOC WD+WE
- ££ £12 (£13) Jun/Twilight £8 (£9)
- ⊕ 10 miles NE of Doncaster. M18
  Junction 5/6
- 🏠 RD Highfield
- 🖥 www.thornegolf.co.uk

Tinsley Park   (1920)

Public
High Hazels Park, Darnall, Sheffield,
S9 4PE
- ☎ (0114) 203 7435

Wath   (1904)

Abdy Rawmarsh, Rotherham, S62 7SJ
- ☎ (01709) 878609
- 📠 (01709) 877097
- ✉ golf@wathgolfclub.co.uk
- 🏠 630
- ♣ M Godfrey (01709) 583174
- ✓ C Bassett (01709) 878609
- ▷ 18 L 6086 yds SSS 70
- ♛ WD–U WE/BH–M SOC
- ££ £18–£36 (£36)
- ⊕ Abdy Farm, 1½ miles S of Wath-
  upon-Dearne. M1 junction 36. A1M
  junction if appropriate
- ⊕ Practice area; buggie & trolly hire
- 🖥 www.wathgolfclub.co.uk

Wheatley   (1913)

Armthorpe Road, Doncaster, DN2 5QB
- ☎ (01302) 831655
- 📠 (01302) 812736
- ✉ secretary@wheatleygolfclub.co.uk
- 🏠 430 100(L) 50(J)
- ♣ Trevor Roberts
- ✓ S Fox (01302) 834085
- ▷ 18 L 6405 yds SSS 71
- ♛ U SOC
- ££ £30 (£40)
- ⊕ 3 miles NE of Doncaster
- 🏠 George Duncan
- 🖥 www.wheatleygolfclub.co.uk

Wortley   (1894)

Hermit Hill Lane, Wortley, Sheffield,
S35 7DF
- ☎ (0114) 288 8469
- 📠 (0114) 288 8488
- ✉ wortley.golfclub@btconnect.com
- 🏠 500
- ♣ Tony Potter
- ✓ I Kirk (0114) 288 6490
- ▷ 18 L 6035 yds SSS 69
- ♛ WD–U WE–NA before 10.30am
  SOC
- ££ £30 (£35)
- ⊕ 2 miles W of M1 Jct 36, off A629
- ⊕ Large practice area
- 🖥 www.wortleygolfclub.co.uk

Yorkshire (West)

The Alwoodley   (1907)

Wigton Lane, Alwoodley, Leeds, LS17 8SA
- ☎ (0113) 268 1680
- ✉ alwoodley@btconnect.com
- 🏠 450
- ♣ Mrs J Slater
- ✓ JR Green (0113) 268 9603
- ▷ 18 L 6338 yds SSS 71 Yellow
- ♛ U SOC–WD SOC–WE after 3pm
  Sat/2pm Sun
- ££ £75 (£90) summer £55 winter WD
  £40 Twilight WD 4pm+4.10pm
- ⊕ 5 miles N of Leeds on A61
- ⊕ Practice ground; putting area

Dr A MacKenzie
- 🏠 Dr A MacKenzie
- 🖥 www.alwoodley.co.uk

Bagden Hall Hotel   (1993)

Wakefield Road, Scissett, HD8 9LE
- ☎ (01484) 865330

Baildon   (1896)

Moorgate, Baildon, Shipley, BD17 5PP
- ☎ (01274) 584266
- ✉ secretary@baildongolfclub.com
- 🏠 750
- ♣ N J Redman (01274) 584266
- ✓ R Masters (01274) 595162
- ▷ 18 L 6231 yds par 70 SSS 70
- ♛ WD–U before 5pm (restricted
  Tues) WE/BH–restricted
- ££ £15 (£15)
- ⊕ 5 miles N of Bradford, off A6038
- 🏠 Tom Morris/James Braid
- 🖥 www.baildongolfclub.com

Ben Rhydding   (1947)

High Wood, Ben Rhydding, Ilkley, LS9 8SB
- ☎ (01943) 608759
- ✉ secretary@benrhyddinggc
  .freeserve.co.uk
- 🏠 180 45(L) 40(J)
- ♣ J D B Watts
- ▷ 9 L 4611 yds SSS 63
- ♛ WD–U exc Wed pm & Thurs am
  WE–after 4pm
- ££ £15 (£20)
- ⊕ 2 miles SE of Ilkley

Bingley St Ives   (1931)

St Ives Estate, Bingley, BD16 1AT
- ☎ (01274) 562436
- 📠 (01274) 511788
- ✉ secretary@bingleystivesgc.co.uk
- 🏠 350 L80 J100
- ♣ RA Adams
- ✓ N Barber (01274) 562436
- ▷ 18 L 6480 yds SSS 71
- ♛ WD–U before 4pm
- ££ £30 D–£35 (£40)
- ⊕ 6 miles NW of Bradford, off A650
- ⊕ Driving range
- 🏠 Alistair Mackenzie, Bobby Jones
  involved
- 🖥 www.bingleystivesgc.co.uk

Bracken Ghyll   (1993)

Skipton Road, Addingham, Ilkley, LS29 0SL
- ☎ (01943) 831207
- 📠 (01943) 839453
- ✉ office@brackenghyll.co.uk
- 🏠 350
- ♣ Patrick J Lee
- ✓ None
- ▷ 18 L 5600 yds Par 69 SSS 67
- ♛ WD/BH–U WE–NA before 11am
  SOC
- ££ £20 D–£30 (£24 D–£36)
- ⊕ 3 miles W of Ilkley on old Skipton
  Road
- ⊕ Indoor practice area; practice
  putting green; chipping practice
  area
- 🏠 STRI
- 🖥 www.brackenghyll.co.uk

Bradford   (1891)
Hawksworth Lane, Guiseley, Leeds,
LS20 8NP
☎ (01943) 875570
🖃 (01943) 875570
✉ bradford-golfclub@tiscali.co.uk
📖 700
🏌 T Eagle
⌁ A Hall (01943) 873719
🏴 18 L 6303 yds SSS 71
👤 WD–U WE–NA before noon
SOC–WD
££ On application
🚗 8 miles N of Bradford, off A6038.
10 miles N of Leeds on A650
⊕ Range available for members and
green fee paying visitors
🏠 WH Fowler
🖥 www.bradfordgolfclub.co.uk

Bradford Moor   (1906)
Scarr Hall, Pollard Lane, Bradford,
BD2 4RW
☎ (01274) 640202
✉ bfdmoorgc@hotmail.co.uk
📖 300
🏌 GW Lee (01274) 771693
🏴 9 L 5854 yds SSS 68
👤 WD–U WE–M SOC
££ £12
🚗 2 miles N of Bradford
⊕ clubhouse open weekdays 4pm
weekends 12 noon

Bradley Park   (1978)
Public
Bradley Road, Huddersfield, HD2 1PZ
☎ (01484) 223772

Branshaw   (1912)
Branshaw Moor, Oakworth, Keighley,
BD22 7ES
☎ (01535) 643235
🖃 (01535) 643235
✉ simonjowitt@tiscali.co.uk
📖 525
🏌 Simon Jowitt
⌁ S Jowitt (01535) 647441
🏴 18 L 5858 yds SSS 68
👤 WD–U SOC–WD
££ D–£20 (D–£30)
🚗 2 miles SW of Keighley on B6143
🏠 James Braid/Dr A Mackenzie
🖥 www.branshawgolfclub.co.uk

Calverley   (1980)
Woodhall Lane, Pudsey, LS28 5QY
☎ (0113) 256 9244
🖃 (0113) 256 4362
✉ calverleygolf@btconnect.com
📖 480
🏌 N Wendel-Jones (Mgr)
⌁ N Wendel-Jones
🏴 18 L 5527 yds SSS 67
9 L 3100 yds Par 36
👤 WD–U WE–pm only H SOC
££ £16 (£20)
🚗 4 miles NE of Bradford

Castlefields   (1903)
Rastrick Common, Brighouse, HD6 3HL
☎ (01484) 402429

📖 180
🏌 DJ Bartliff
🏴 6 L 2406 yds Par 54 SSS 50
👤 M
££ £6 (£10)
🚗 I mile S of Brighouse

City Golf Course   (1997)
Pay and play
Red Cote Lane, Kirkstall Road, Leeds
LS4 2AW
☎ (0113) 263 3030
🖃 (0113) 263 3044
🏌 P Cole (Mgr)
🏴 9 L 1734 yds, pay and play
👤 U
££ £5 9–18 holes
🚗 2 miles from Leeds centre, M62 –
M1
⊕ Putting green

City of Wakefield   (1936)
Public
Lupset Park, Horbury Road, Wakefield,
WF2 8QS
☎ (01924) 367442
⌁ D Bagg (01924) 360282
🏴 18 L 6319 yds SSS 70
👤 U SOC–WD
££ On application
🚗 A642, 2 miles W of Wakefield. 2
miles E of M1 Junction 39/40
🏠 JSF Morrison

Clayton   (1906)
Thornton View Road, Clayton, Bradford,
BD14 6JX
☎ (01274) 880047
✉ tking@otto-uk.com
📖 168 17(L) 56(J)
🏌 DA Smith (01274) 572311
🏴 9 L 6237 yds SSS 70
👤 WD–U Sat–U Sun–after 4pm
££ D–£17 (£18)
🚗 3 miles W of Bradford, off A647
🖥 www.claytongolfclub.co.uk

Cleckheaton & District
   (1900)
483 Bradford Road, Cleckheaton,
BD19 6BU
☎ (01274) 851266 (Manager)
🖃 (01274) 871382
✉ info@cleckheatongolfclub.co.uk
📖 610
🏌 Andrew Callaway
⌁ Warren Lockett (01274) 851267
🏴 18 L 5860 yds SSS 69
👤 U SOC
££ £30 (£35)
🚗 Nr M62 Junction 26-A638
🏠 Alister Mackenzie
🖥 www.cleckheatongolfclub.fsnet
.co.uk

Cookridge Hall   (1997)
Proprietary
Cookridge Lane, Cookridge, Leeds,
LS16 7NL
☎ (0113) 230 0641
🖃 (0113) 203 0198
✉ info@cookridgehall.co.uk

📖 570
🏌 Gary Day (0113) 230 0641
⌁ M Pinkett
🏴 18 L 6788 yds Par 72 SSS 72
👤 WD–U Sat–U after 2pm Sun–U
after 12 noon SOC
££ £25 (£30)
🚗 5 miles NW of Leeds, via A660
⊕ 22 bay floodlit driving range
🏠 Karl Litten
🖥 www.cookridgehall.co.uk

Crosland Heath   (1914)
Felks Stile Road, Crosland Heath,
Huddersfield, HD4 7AF
☎ (01484) 653216
🖃 (01484) 461079
✉ golf@croslandheath.co.uk
📖 600
🏌 S Robinson (01484) 653216
⌁ Richard Lambert (01484) 653877
🏴 18 L 6087 yds Par 71 SSS 70
👤 U SOC H WD
££ On application
🚗 3 miles W of Huddersfield, off A62
🏠 Dr A Mackenzie
🖥 www.croslandheath.co.uk

Crow Nest Park   (1994)
Coach Road, Hove Edge, Brighouse,
HD6 2LN
☎ (01484) 401121
🖃 (01484) 720975
✉ info@crownestgolf.co.uk
📖 300
🏌 A Naylor
⌁ P Everitt (01484) 401121
🏴 9 L 6020 yds Par 70 SSS 69
👤 WD–U WE–U before noon
££ 9: £15 (£16); 18: £25 (£26)
🚗 5 miles E of Halifax. M62 Jct 25
⊕ Driving range with Power Tees and
Swingcam
🏠 Will Adamson
🖥 www.crownestgolf.co.uk

Dewsbury District   (1891)
The Pinnacle, Sands Lane, Mirfield,
WF14 8HJ
☎ (01924) 492399
🖃 (01924) 492399
✉ dewsbury.golf@btconnect.com
📖 650
🏌 B Foster
⌁ N Hirst (01924) 496030
🏴 18 L 6360 yds SSS 71
👤 WD–U WE–U after 3pm SOC
££ D £24 (£20 after 2pm)
🚗 2 miles W of Dewsbury, off A644
🏠 Tom Morris/Alliss/Thomas
🖥 www.dewsburygolf.co.uk

East Bierley   (1928)
South View Road, Bierley, Bradford,
BD4 6PP
☎ (01274) 681023
✉ rjwelch@ebgc.fsnet.co.uk
📖 156 47(L) 30(J)
🏌 RJ Welch (01274) 683666
⌁ J Whittam (07904) 141248
🏴 9 L 4692 yds SSS 63
👤 U exc Mon–NA after 4pm Sun–by
prior arrangement

££   £14 (£16)
⊕⊖   4 miles SE of Bradford. M62-M606

Elland   (1910)
Hammerstone Leach Lane, Hullen Edge,
Elland, HX5 0TA
☎   (01422) 372505
✉   ellandgolfclub@ellandgolfclub.plus
      .com
☐   280
✍   PA Green (01422) 251431
✓   N Krzywicki (01422) 374886
☞   9 L 5498 yds Par 66 SSS 67
✿   U
££   £18 (£30)
⊕⊖   Elland 1 mile. M62 Junction 24,
      signpost Blackley
▤   www.ellandgolfclub.plus.com

Fardew   (1993)
Pay and play
Nursery Farm, Carr Lane, East Morton,
Keighley, BD20 5RY
☎   (01274) 561229
✉   davidheaton@btconnect.com
☐   100
✍   A Stevens
✓   M Tyler (07986) 969853
☞   9 L 3104 yds Par 72 SSS 70
✿   U SOC
££   9: £9 (£10); 18: £12 (£16)
⊕⊖   2 miles W of Bingley on B6265
⊕   Grass Tee Driving Range
⌂   Will Adamson
▤   www.fardewgolfclub.co.uk

Ferrybridge   (2002)
PO Box 39, Stranglands Lane, Knottingley,
WF11 8SQ
☎   (01977) 884165
☐   (01977) 884001
✉   Trevor.Ellis@Scottish-southern
☐   250
✍   TD Ellis
✓   Alistair Cobbett (01977) 884204
☞   9 L 6047 yds SSS 69 Par 71
✿   U
££   D–£15 (D–£17)
⊕⊖   ¹/₂ mile off A1, on B6136
⊕   Practice area; buggies available
⌂   G Barton

Fulneck   (1892)
Fulneck, Pudsey, LS28 8NT
☎   (0113) 256 5191

Garforth   (1913)
Long Lane, Garforth, Leeds, LS25 2DS
☎   (0113) 286 3308
☐   (0113) 286 3308
✉   garforthgcltd@lineone.net
☐   629
✍   Richard H Green
      (0113) 286 3308
✓   K Findlater (0113) 286 2063
☞   18 L 6378 yds SSS 70
✿   WD–U WE/BH–M SOC
££   £36 D–£42
⊕⊖   9 miles E of Leeds, between
      Garforth and Barwick-in-Elmet
⊕   Practice grounds
⌂   Dr A Mackenzie
▤   www.garforthgolfclub.co.uk

Gotts Park   (1933)
Public
Armley Ridge Road, Armley, Leeds,
LS12 2QX
☎   (0113) 234 2019
☐   300
✍   M Gill (0113) 256 2994
✓   J Marlor
☞   18 L 4960 yds SSS 64
✿   U
££   On application
⊕⊖   2 miles W of Leeds

Halifax   (1895)
Union Lane, Ogden, Halifax, HX2 8XR
☎   (01422) 244171
☐   (01422) 241459
✉   halifax.golfclub@virgin.net
☐   450
✍   John Abson
✓   M Delaney (01422) 240047
☞   18 L 6037 yds SSS 69
✿   U WD–parties welcome SOC WE
      by arrangement; special offers
      Tues/Wed
££   £30 (£36)
⊕⊖   4 miles N of Halifax on A629
⌂   Alex Herd/James Braid
▤   www.halifaxgolfclub.co.uk

Halifax Bradley Hall   (1907)
Holywell Green, Halifax, HX4 9AN
☎   (01422) 374108
✉   bhgc@gotadsl.co.uk
☐   608
✍   M Dredge
✓   P Wood (01422) 370231
☞   18 L 6138 yds SSS 70
✿   U SOC
££   £27 (£34)
⊕⊖   S of Halifax on A6112 M62 Jct 24
⊕   Practice Ground
▤   www.bradleyhallgolf.co.uk

Halifax West End   (1906)
Paddock Lane, Highroad Well, Halifax,
HX2 0NT
☎   (01422) 341878
☐   (01442) 341878
✉   westendgc@btinternet.com
☐   580 100(L) 60(J)
✍   G Gower (01422) 341878
✓   D Rishworth (01422) 341878
☞   18 L 5951 yds SSS 69
✿   U SOC
££   £30 (£35) plus special offers
⊕⊖   2 miles NW of Halifax
▤   www.westendgc.co.uk

Hanging Heaton   (1922)
Whitecross Road, Bennett Lane, Dewsbury,
WF12 7DT
☎   (01924) 461606
☐   (01924) 430100
✉   derek.atkinson@hhgc.org
☐   400
✍   Derek Atkinson (01924) 430100
✓   Gareth Moore (01924) 467077
☞   9 L 2923 yds SSS 68
✿   WD–U WE–M
££   £16
⊕⊖   Dewsbury ³/₄ mile (A653)

Headingley   (1892)
Back Church Lane, Adel, Leeds, LS16 8DW
☎   (0113) 267 9573 (Clubhouse)
☐   (0113) 281 7334
✉   manager@headingleygolfclub.co.uk
☐   675
✍   TBA
✓   NM Harvey (0113) 267 5100
☞   18 L 6608 yds Par 71 SSS 72
✿   WD–U before 3.30pm SOC
££   £40 D–£45 (£45)
⊕⊖   5 miles NW of Leeds, off A660
      (Church Lane lights)
⌂   Dr A MacKenzie
▤   www.headingleygolfclub.co.uk

Headley   (1907)
Headley Lane, Thornton, Bradford,
BD13 3LX
☎   (01274) 833481
☐   (01274) 833481
☐   220 15(L) 35(J)
✍   D Britton
☞   9 L 4914 yds SSS 65
✿   WD–U WE–M SOC
££   On application
⊕⊖   5 miles W of Bradford (B6145)
▤   www.headleygolfclub.co.uk

Hebden Bridge   (1930)
Great Mount, Wadsworth, Hebden Bridge,
HX7 8PH
☎   (01422) 842896
✉   hbgc@btconnect.com
☐   300
✍   A Platten (01422) 842896
☞   9 L 5242 yds Par 68 SSS 67
✿   WD–U WE–Sun by appointment
££   £10–£12 (£15)
⊕⊖   1 mile N of Hebden Bridge past
      Birchcliffe Centre

Horsforth   (1906)
Layton Rise, Layton Road, Horsforth, Leeds,
LS18 5EX
☎   (0113) 258 6819
☐   (0113) 258 9336
✉   secretary@horsforthgolfclubltd
      .co.uk
☐   365 90(L) 85(J)
✍   Mrs LA Harrison
✓   Simon Booth & Dean Stokes
      (0113) 258 5200
☞   18 L 6258 yds SSS 70
✿   WD–U WD–SOC WE–after 3pm
      (contact Pro)
££   D–£36 (£40)
⊕⊖   M62 – follow signs for Leeds
      Bradford Airport
⊕   Practice field; buggies available
⌂   Dr Alistair Mackenzie
▤   www.horsforthgolfclubltd.co.uk

Howley Hall   (1900)
Scotchman Lane, Morley, Leeds, LS27 0NX
☎   (01924) 350100
☐   (01924) 350104
✉   office@howleyhall.co.uk
☐   492
✍   D Jones (01924) 350100
✓   G Watkinson (01924) 350102
☞   18 L 6454 yds Par 71 SSS 71
✿   U SOC–WD/Sun

For list of abbreviations and key to symbols see page 647

££ £30 D–£36 (£40)
⊛ 4 miles SW of Leeds on B6123
🖥 www.howleyhall.co.uk

Huddersfield (1891)

Fixby Hall, Lightridge Road, Huddersfield,
HD2 2EP
☎ (01484) 426203
📠 (01484) 424623
✉ secretary@huddersfield-golf.co.uk
🏢 686
♙ Mrs D Lockett
🏌 P Carman (01484) 426463
🏳 18 L 6458 yds SSS 72
👥 U SOC–WD–H
££ £45 D–£55 (£55 D–£65)
⊛ 2 miles N of Huddersfield, off
A6107. M62 Junction 24
🏠 Tom Dunn
🖥 www.huddersfield-golf.co.uk

Ilkley (1890)

Myddleton, Ilkley, LS29 0BE
☎ (01943) 607277
📠 (01943) 816130
✉ honsec@ilkleygolfclub.co.uk
🏢 530
♙ N Hudson (01943) 600214
🏌 JL Hammond (01943) 607463
🏳 18 L 6260 yds SSS 70
👥 U–H
££ £50 (£55). Winter rate 01/11 to
31/03 £35
⊛ NW of Ilkley, off A65
⊕ Practice ground
🖥 www.ilkleygolfclub.co.uk

Keighley (1904)

Howden Park, Utley, Keighley, BD20 6DH
☎ (01535) 604778
📠 (01535) 604778
✉ manager@keighleygolfclub.com
🏢 600
♙ G Cameron Dawson
🏌 A Rhodes (01535) 604778 option 2
🏳 18 L 6141 yds Par 69 SSS 70
👥 WD–NA before 9.30am &
12–1.30pm Sat–NA Sun/BH–NA
before 2pm
££ £35 D–£43 (£39 D–£47)
⊛ 1 mile W of Keighley on B6265
🖥 www.keighleygolfclub.com

Leeds (1896)

Elmete Road, Roundhay, Leeds, LS8 2LJ
☎ (0113) 265 8775
📠 (0113) 232 3369
✉ secretary@leedsgolfclub.com
🏢 545
♙ SJ Clarkson (0113) 265 9203
🏌 S Longster (0113) 265 8786
🏳 18 L 6092 yds SSS 69
👥 WD–U WE–M SOC
££ £32 D–£40
⊛ 4 miles NE of Leeds, off A58
🏠 Part design by Dr A McKenzie
🖥 www.leedsgolfclub.com

Leeds Golf Centre (1994)

Pay and play
Wike Ridge Lane, Shadwell, Leeds,
LS17 9JW
☎ (0113) 288 6000

📠 (0113) 288 6185
✉ info@leedsgolfcentre.com
🏢 500
♙ A Levine (Mgr)
🏌 T Tomlinson
🏳 18 L 6332 yds SSS 72
12 hole Par 3 course
👥 U SOC WD WE
££ £17.50 (£25)
⊛ NE of Leeds, between A58 and
A61
⊕ Driving range; Golf Academy;
practice areas
🏠 Donald Steel
🖥 www.leedsgolfcentre.com

Lightcliffe (1907)

Knowle Top Road, Lightcliffe,
HX3 8SW
☎ (01422) 202459
🏢 180 95(L) 84(J)
♙ RP Crampton (01484) 384672
🏌 R Tickle
🏳 9 L 5368 metres SSS 68
👥 U H–exc Wed Sun am–M SOC
££ £18 (£20)
⊛ 3 miles E of Halifax (A58)
⊕ Practice field adjacent

Lofthouse Hill

Leeds Road, Lofthouse Hill, Wakefield,
WF3 3LR
☎ (01924) 823703
📠 (01924) 823703
♙ P Moon
🏌 D Johnson (01924) 823703
🏳 18 L 5988 yds Par 70
👥 U
££ 9: £7; 18: £14
⊛ Between Leeds and Wakefield on
A61
🖥 www.lofthousehillgolfclub.co.uk

Longley Park (1910)

Maple Street, Huddersfield, HD5 9AX
☎ (01484) 426932
📠 (01484) 515280
✉ longleyparkgolfclub@12freeukisp
.co.uk
🏢 400
♙ D Palliser (01484) 422304
🏌 J Ambler (01484) 422304
🏳 9 L 5212 yds Par 66 SSS 66
👥 WD–U exc Thurs WE–restricted
££ £20 (£25)
⊛ Huddersfield ½ mile

Low Laithes (1925)

Park Mill Lane, Flushdyke, Ossett, WF5 9AP
☎ (01924) 273275
📠 (01924) 266266
✉ info@low-laithes-golf-club.co.uk
🏢 610
♙ P Browning
(Sec/Mgr) (01924) 266067
🏌 P Browning (01924) 274667
🏳 18 L 6468 yds SSS 71
👥 U WE–no parties SOC–WD
££ £25 D–£30 (£36)
⊛ 2 miles W of Wakefield. M1 Jct 40
🏠 Dr A Mackenzie

The Manor

Proprietary
Bradford Road, Drighlington, Bradford,
BD11 1AB
☎ (01132) 852644
📠 (01332) 879961
✉ themanorgolfclub@hotmail.co.uk
🏢 300
♙ G Thompson (Sec/Mgr)
🏌 G Thompson
🏳 18 L 6508 yds Par 72 SSS 71
👥 U SOC–exc Sat
££ £17 (£21) WE after 3.30pm
£12.50)
⊛ 3 miles from M62 J27, off A650
⊕ Floodlit driving range; 6 holes pitch
& putt course
🏠 David Hemstock

Marriott Hollins Hall Hotel (1999)

Hollins Hill, Baildon, Shipley, BD17 7QW
☎ (01274) 534212
📠 (01274) 534220
✉ mhrs.lbags@marriotthotels.com
🏢 300
♙ Peter Rishworth
(01274) 534250
🏌 Gordon Brand Jr, Mark Wood
🏳 18 L 6700 yds Par 71 SSS 72
👥 H WD–U WE–NA before 1pm
££ £40 (£50)
⊛ 6 miles N of Bradford on A6038
⊕ Driving range, leisure facilities, 4-
star hotel; short game practice area
🏠 Ross McMurray
🖥 www.marriotthollinshall.com

Marsden (1921)

Hemplow, Marsden, Huddersfield,
HD7 6NN
☎ (01484) 844253
✉ secretary@marsdengolf.co.uk
🏢 250 50(L) 50(J)
♙ SJ Boustead (01457) 874158
🏌 J Crompton
🏳 9 L 5702 yds SSS 68
👥 WD–U Sat–NA before 4pm Sun–M
SOC
££ £15 (£20)
⊛ 8 miles W of Huddersfield, off A62
🏠 Dr A Mackenzie
🖥 www.marsdengolf.co.uk

Meltham (1908)

Thick Hollins Hall, Meltham, Huddersfield,
HD9 4DQ
☎ (01484) 850227
📠 (01484) 850227
✉ admin@meltham-golf.co.uk
🏢 700
♙ J R Dixon (Hon)
🏌 PF Davies (01484) 851521
🏳 18 L 6407 yds Par 71 SSS 70
👥 SOC WD–WE
££ £28 (£33)
⊛ 5 miles SW of Huddersfield
(B6107)
🏠 W H Fowler
🖥 www.meltham-golf.co.uk

Mid Yorkshire (1993)
Proprietary
Havercroft Lane, Darrington, Pontefract,
WF8 3BP
- ☎ (01977) 704522
- ✉ (01977) 600823
- 🖂 admin@midyorkshiregolfclub.com
- 🕮 450
- ♠ Tony Harris MInstGCM
- ✏ Michael Hessay (01977) 600844
- ⊳ 18 L 6308 yds Par 70 SSS 70
- ♙ U SOC WD WE
- ££ £25 (£35)
- ⊸ Nr A1/M62 junction
- ⊕ Floodlit driving range
- ⌂ Steve Marnoch
- 🖳 www.midyorkshiregolfclub.com

Middleton Park (1933)
Public
Ring Road, Beeston Park, Middleton,
LS10 3TN
- ☎ (0113) 270 0449
- 🖂 secretary@middletonparkgolfclub
  .co.uk

Moor Allerton (1923)
Coal Road, Wike, Leeds, LS17 9NH
- ☎ (0113) 266 1154
- ✉ (0113) 268 0059
- 🕮 750
- ♠ RM Crann (Mgr)
- ✏ R Lane (0113) 266 5209
- ⊳ 27 L 6470-6843 yds SSS 73-74
- ♙ WD/Sat–U Sun–NA SOC
- ££ £55 D–£75 (£65 D–£85)
- ⊸ 5½ miles N of Leeds, off A61
- ⊕ Driving range
- ⌂ Robert Trent Jones Sr

Moortown (1909)
Harrogate Road, Leeds, LS17 7DB
- ☎ (0113) 268 6521
- ✉ (0113) 268 0986
- 🖂 secretary@moortown-gc.co.uk
- 🕮 600
- ♠ RSG Limbert
- ✏ Martin Heggie (0113) 268 3636
- ⊳ 18 L 7002 yds SSS 74
- ♙ U
- ££ £65 D–£75
- ⊸ 5½ miles N of Leeds on A61
- ⊕ Complimentary warm-up facilities
  for visitors
- ⌂ Dr A Mackenzie
- 🖳 www.moortown-gc.co.uk

Normanton (1903)
Hatfeild Hall, Aberford Road, Stanley,
Wakefield, WF3 4JP
- ☎ (01924) 377943
- ✉ (01924) 200777
- 🖂 office@normantongolf.co.uk
- 🕮 800
- ♠ D Holt/J Fox
- ✏ G Pritchard (01924) 200900
- ⊳ 18 L 6191 yds Par 72 SSS 69
- ♙ WD SOC
- ££ £28
- ⊸ 3 miles N of Wakefield (A642).
  M62 Junction 30
- ⌂ Patrick Dawson
- 🖳 www.normantongolf.co.uk

Northcliffe (1921)
High Bank Lane, Shipley, Bradford,
BD18 4LJ
- ☎ (01274) 584085
- ✉ (01274) 584148
- 🖂 northcliffegc@hotmail.com
- 🕮 500
- ♠ I Collins (01274) 596731
- ✏ M Hillas (01274) 587193
- ⊳ 18 L 6113 yds SSS 71
- ♙ U SOC
- ££ £25 (£30)
- ⊸ 3 miles NW of Bradford, off A650
  Keighley road
- ⌂ James Braid
- 🖳 www.northcliffegolfclubshipley.co.uk

Otley (1906)
West Busk Lane, Otley, LS21 3NG
- ☎ (01943) 465329
- ✉ (01943) 850387
- 🖂 office@otley-golfclub.co.uk
- 🕮 700
- ♠ PJ Clarke Ext 202
- ✏ S Tomkinson Ext 203
- ⊳ 18 L 6211 yds SSS 70
- ♙ U exc Sat–NA SOC
- ££ £36 D–£43 (£43)
- ⊸ 1 mile W of Otley, off A6038
- ⊕ Extensive practice facilities
- 🖳 www.otley-golfclub.co.uk

Oulton Park (1990)
Public
Oulton, Rothwell, Leeds, LS26 8EX
- ☎ (0113) 282 3152

Outlane (1906)
Slack Lane, off New Hey Road, Outlane,
Huddersfield HD3 3FQ
- ☎ (01422) 374762
- ✉ (01422) 311789
- 🖂 secretary@outlanegolfclub.ltd.uk
- 🕮 500
- ♠ P Jackson
- ✏ D Chapman
- ⊳ 18 L 6010 yds SSS 69
- ♙ U SOC
- ££ £20 (£28)
- ⊸ 4 miles W of Huddersfield, off
  A640. M62 Junction 23
- ⊕ Practice ground and nets; putting
  green
- ⌂ Dr Alistair Mackenzie
- 🖳 www.outlanegolfclub.ltd.uk

Phoenix Park (1922)
Dick Lane, Thornbury, Bradford, BD3 7AT
- ☎ (01274) 667573

Pontefract & District (1904)
Park Lane, Pontefract, WF8 4QS
- ☎ (01977) 792241
- ✉ (01977) 792241
- 🖂 manager@pdgc.co.uk
- 🕮 620
- ♠ J Heald (Mgr) (01977) 792241
- ✏ I Marshall (01977) 706806
- ⊳ 18 L 6519 yds SSS 72
- ♙ WD–U 9.30–12 noon and after 2
  pm WE–after 3pm SOC–WD exc
  Wed & WE

- ££ £30 (£35)
- ⊸ Pontefract 1 mile on B6134. M62
  Junction 32
- ⌂ Alistair Mackenzie
- 🖳 www.pdgc.co.uk

Queensbury (1923)
Brighouse Road, Queensbury, Bradford,
BD13 1QF
- ☎ (01274) 882155
- ✉ (01274) 882155
- 🖂 queensburygolf@supanet.com
- 🕮 400 48(L) 47(J)
- ♠ MH Heptinstall
- ✏ N Stead (01274) 816864
- ⊳ 9 L 5008 yds SSS 65
- ♙ U
- ££ £15 (£30)
- ⊸ 4 miles SW of Bradford (A647)
- 🖳 www.queensburygc.co.uk

Rawdon (1896)
Buckstone Drive, Micklefield Lane, Rawdon,
LS19 6BD
- ☎ (0113) 250 6040
- 🖂 info@rgltc.co.uk
- 🕮 220 55(L) 50(J)
- ♠ Ian Scuffins
- ✏ (0113) 250 5017
- ⊳ 9 L 5982 yds Par 72 SSS 69
- ♙ WD–H WE/BH–M SOC
- ££ £15 (£18)
- ⊸ 6 miles NW of Leeds nr A65/A658
  junction
- 🖳 www.rgltc.co.uk

Riddlesden (1927)
Howden Rough, Riddlesden, Keighley,
BD20 5QN
- ☎ (01535) 602148
- 🕮 400
- ♠ S Morton (01535) 602148
- ⊳ 18 L 4295 yds Par 63 SSS 61
- ♙ U exc Sun–NA before 2pm WD–U
  before 5pm SOC WE after 2pm
- ££ £10
- ⊸ 1 mile from Riddlesden, off Scott
  Lane West. 3 miles N of Keighley,
  off A650

Roundhay (1923)
Public
Park Lane, Leeds, LS8 2EJ
- ☎ (0113) 266 2695
- 🕮 230
- ♠ RH McLauchlan (0113) 266 4225
- ✏ A Newboult (0113) 266 1686
- ⊳ 9 L 5322 yds SSS 65
- ♙ U
- ££ On application
- ⊸ N of Leeds, off Moortown Ring
  Road

Ryburn (1910)
Norland, Sowerby Bridge, Halifax,
HX6 3QP
- ☎ (01422) 831355
- 🖂 secretary@ryburngolfclub.co.uk
- 🕮 300
- ♠ James Washington (07974) 359825
- ⊳ 9 L 5127 yds SSS 65
- ♙ U
- ££ £15 (£20)

⛳ 3 miles S of Halifax
🖥 www.ryburngolfclub.co.uk

Sand Moor   (1926)
Alwoodley Lane, Leeds, LS17 7DJ
☎ (0113) 268 5180
🖷 (0113) 266 1105
✉ info@sandmoorgolf.co.uk
🕮 540
♣ I Kerr (0113) 268 5180
♦ F Houlgate (0113) 268 3925
▷ 18 L 6446 yds SSS 71
♟ WD–H by arrangement SOC
££ £45 (£55)
⛳ 5 miles N of Leeds, off A61
⊕ Practice ground
🏠 Dr A Mackenzie
🖥 www.sandmoorgolf.co.uk

Scarcroft   (1937)
Syke Lane, Leeds, LS14 3BQ
☎ (0113) 289 2311
🖷 (0113) 289 3835
✉ secretary@scarcroftgolfclub.com
🕮 660
♣ M Gallagher (Sec/Mgr) (0113) 289 2311
♦ D Hughes (0113) 289 2780
▷ 18 L 6456 yds SSS 71
♟ WD–U WE/BH by arrangement SOC
££ £41 D–£52 (£52)
⛳ 7 miles N of Leeds, off A58
⊕ Driving range
🏠 A Mackenzie
🖥 www.scarcroftgolfclub.com

Shipley   (1896)
Beckfoot Lane, Cottingley Bridge, Bingley, BD16 1LX
☎ (01274) 568652
🖷 (01274) 567739
✉ office@shipleygc.co.uk
🕮 500
♣ Mrs MJ Simpson (01274) 568652
♦ JR Parry (01274) 563674
▷ 18 L 6209 yds SSS 70
♟ WD–U exc Tues–NA before 2pm Sat–NA before 4pm
££ D–£35 (D–£40)
⛳ 6 miles N of Bradford on A650
🏠 Colt/Alison/Mackenzie/Braid
🖥 www.shipleygolfclub.com

Silsden   (1911)
Brunthwaite Lane, Brunthwaite, Silsden, BD20 0ND
☎ (01535) 652998
✉ info@silsdengolfclub.co.uk
🕮 300
♣ T Starkie
▷ 18 L 5113 yds Par 67 SSS 65
♟ Sat–restricted
££ £15 (£25 Sat only)
⛳ 5 miles N of Keighley, off A6034
🖥 www.silsdengolfclub.co.uk

South Bradford   (1906)
Pearson Road, Odsal, Bradford, BD6 1BH
☎ (01274) 679195
🕮 200
♣ B Broadbent (01274) 690643
♦ P Cooke (01274) 673346

▷ 9 L 6076 yds SSS 69
♟ WD–U WE–M
££ On application
⛳ Bradford 2 miles, nr Odsal Stadium

South Leeds   (1906)
Gipsy Lane, Ring Road, Beeston, Leeds LS11 5TU
☎ (0113) 277 1676
🖷 (0113) 277 1676
✉ sec@slgc.freeserve.co.uk
🕮 450
♣ B Clayton (0113) 277 1676
♦ N Sheard (0113) 272 3757
▷ 18 L 5865 yds SSS 68
♟ WD–U WE–U SOC – time restriction WE
££ £22 D–27 (£30 D–£35) After 1.30 £12 (£15)
⛳ 4 miles S of Leeds. 2 miles from M62 and M1
🏠 Dr Alister Mackenzie
🖥 www.southleedsgolfclub.co.uk

Temple Newsam   (1923)
Public
Temple Newsam Road, Halton, Leeds, LS15 0LN
☎ (0113) 264 5624
✉ secretary@tngc.co.uk
🕮 300
♣ Mrs Christine P Wood
♦ A Newboult (0113) 264 7362
▷ Lord Irwin 18 L 6448 yds SSS 71 Lady Dorothy Wood 18 L 6229 yds SSS 70
♟ U SOC
££ £10 (£13)
⛳ 5 miles E of Leeds, off A63
⊕ Practice green; bunker area; putting green
🖥 www.tngolfclub.co.uk

Todmorden   (1894)
Rive Rocks, Cross Stone, Todmorden, OL14 8RD
☎ (01706) 812986
✉ secretarytodgolfclub@msn.com
🕮 165 43(L) 24(J)
♣ Peter H Eastwood
▷ 9 L 5874 yds SSS 68
♟ WD/BH–U WE–M SOC–WD
££ £20 (£25)
⛳ 1 mile N of Todmorden, off A646
🖥 www.todmordengolfclub.co.uk

Wakefield   (1891)
28 Woodthorpe Lane, Sandal, Wakefield, WF2 6JH
☎ (01924) 258778
🖷 (01924) 242752
✉ wakefieldgolfclub @woodthorpelane.freeserve.co.uk
🕮 500
♣ Elizabeth Newton (01924) 258778
♦ IM Wright (01924) 258778
▷ 18 L 6663 yds SSS 72
♟ U H SOC
££ £32 D–£37 (£40)
⛳ 3 miles S of Wakefield on A61. M1 Junction 39
🏠 Alex Herd
🖥 www.wakefieldgolfclub.co.uk

Waterton Park   (1995)
The Balk, Walton, Wakefield, WF2 6QL
☎ (01924) 259525
🖷 (01924) 256969
✉ watertonparkgolfclub@tiscali.co.uk
🕮 600
♣ M Pearson (01924) 255557
♦ M Pearson (01924) 255557
▷ 18 L 6843 yds Par 72 SSS 73
♟ WD–H SOC
££ D–£50 (£60)
⛳ 4 miles SE of Wakefield centre
⊕ Driving range
🏠 Simon Gidman

West Bradford   (1900)
Chellow Grange Road, Haworth Road, Bradford, BD9 6NP
☎ (01274) 542767
🖷 (01274) 482079
✉ secretary@westbradfordgolfclub .co.uk
🕮 450
♣ NS Bey (Hon) (01274) 542767
♦ W Kemp (01274) 542102
▷ 18 L 5738 yds SSS 68 Par 69
♟ WD–U WE–U after 3.00 pm
££ £32 (£32) – offers available
⛳ 3 miles NW of Bradford (B6144)
🖥 www.westbradfordgolfclub.co.uk

Wetherby   (1910)
Linton Lane, Linton, Wetherby, LS22 4JF
☎ (01937) 580089
✉ manager@wetherbygolfclub.co.uk
🕮 760
♦ M Daubney
▷ 18 L 6670 yds SSS 72
♟ WE–U after 10am SOC–WD H
££ £30 (£44)
⛳ 3/4 mile W of Wetherby. A1 Wetherby roundabout
⊕ Driving range
🖥 www.wetherbygolfclub.co.uk

Whitwood   (1987)
Public
Altofts Lane, Whitwood, Castleford, WF10 5PZ
☎ (01977) 512835
♣ J Deakin
♦ D Bagg
▷ 9 L 6176 yds SSS 69
♟ WD–U WE–booking necessary
££ On application
⛳ 2 miles SW of Castleford (A655). M62 Junction 31

Willow Valley   (1993)
Pay and play
Clifton, Brighouse, HD6 4JB
☎ (01274) 878624
✉ sales@wvgc.co.uk
🕮 260
♣ H Newton
♦ J Haworth
▷ Willow Valley 18 L 7030 Par 72 SSS 74
Pine Valley 18 L 5032 Par 66 SSS 62
Fountain Ridge 9 L 2039 Par 60 SSS 60
♟ U

££ Willow Valley £26 (£38), Pine
    Valley £15 (£17), Fountain Ridge
    £7.50 (£9)
⊷ SW of Leeds, M62 Junction 25
⊕ Driving range (floodlit); academy
    course
⌂ Jonathan Gaunt
🖳 www.wvgc.co.uk

Woodhall Hills   (1905)
Woodhall Road, Calverley, Pudsey,
LS28 5UN
☎ (0113) 256 4771 (Clubhouse)
🖵 (0113) 295 4594
✉ whhgc@tiscali.co.uk
🕮 550
♤ BM Court (0113) 255 4594
✓ W Lockett (0113) 256 2857
↦ 18 L 6184 yds SSS 70
👥 WD–U Sat–U after 4.30pm Sun–U
    after 9.30am

££ £24 (£29)
⊷ 4 miles E of Bradford, off A647,
    past Calverley GC

Woodsome Hall   (1922)
Woodsome Hall, Fenay Bridge,
Huddersfield, HD8 0LQ
☎ (01484) 602971
🖵 (01484) 608260
🕮 360 130(L) 90(J)
♤ TJ Mee (01484) 602739 (Gen Mgr)
✓ J Eyre (01484) 602034
↦ 18 L 6080 yds SSS 69
👥 U H exc Tues–NA before 4pm
    SOC
££ £32 D–£43 (£43 D–£53)
⊷ 6 miles SE of Huddersfield on A629
    Penistone road
🖳 www.woodsomehall.co.uk

Woolley Park   (1995)
Proprietary
New Road, Woolley, Wakefield, WF4 2JS
☎ (01226) 380144 (Bookings)
🖵 (01226) 390295
✉ woolleyparkgolf@yahoo.co.uk
🕮 500
♤ RP Stoffel (01226) 382209
✓ J Baldwin
↦ 18 L 6636 yds Par 71 SSS 72
👥 WD–U WE–restricted SOC
££ £20 (£27.50)
⊷ 5 miles S of Wakefield on A61. M1
    Junction 38, 2 miles
⊕ Driving range; putting green
⌂ M Shattock
🖳 www.woolleyparkgolfclub.co.uk

Ireland

Co Antrim

Antrim (1997)
Allen Park Golf Centre, 45 Castle Road, Antrim, BT41 4NA
☎ (028) 9442 9001
✉ allenpark@antrim.gov.uk
🏨 500
✍ Marie Agnew (Mgr)
✓ Maurice Kelly
▷ 18 L 6110 m Par 72 SSS 72
⚭ U
££ £17 (£19)
⊕ Antrim
⊕ Driving range
🏠 Tom Macauley
🖥 www.antrim.gov.uk

Ballycastle (1890)
Cushendall Road, Ballycastle, BT64 6QP
☎ (028) 2076 2536
📠 (028) 2076 9909
✉ info@ballycastlegolfclub.com
🏨 820
✍ BJ Dillon (Hon)
✓ I McLaughlin (028) 2076 2506
▷ 18 L 5927 yds SSS 70
⚭ U H SOC
££ £25 (£35)
⊕ Between Portrush and Cushendall (A2)
🖥 www.ballycastlegolfclub.com

Ballyclare (1923)
25 Springvale Road, Ballyclare, BT39 9JW
☎ (028) 9334 2352 (Clubhouse)
(028) 9332 2696 (Office)
📠 (028) 9332 2696
✉ info@ballyclaregolfclub.net
🏨 460
✍ Michael Stone (028) 9332 2696
✓ Colin Lyttle (028) 9332 4541
▷ 18 L 5840 yds SSS 71
⚭ WD–U WE–NA before 4pm
££ £22 (£28)
⊕ 1½ miles N of Ballyclare. 14 miles N of Belfast
⊕ Practice range; buggy hire
🏠 T McAuley
🖥 www.ballyclaregolfclub.net

Ballymena (1903)
128 Raceview Road, Ballymena, BT42 4HY
☎ (028) 2586 1207/1487

Bentra
Public
Slaughterford Road, Whitehead, BT38 9TG
☎ (028) 9335 8000
📠 (028) 9336 6676
✉ greenspace@carrickfergus.org
✍ S Daye (028) 9335 8039
▷ 9 L 3042 yds Par 36 SSS 35
⚭ U
££ 18 holes, adult: £10 (£14) 18 holes, U16/OAP: £5 (£7) Membership £260 (£200)

4 miles N of Carrickfergus on A2
Larne road
🏠 James Braid
🖥 www.bentragolf.co.uk

Burnfield House
10 Cullyburn Road, Newtownabbey, BT36 5BN
☎ (028) 9083 8737
✉ michaelhj@ntlworld.com

Bushfoot (1890)
50 Bushfoot Road, Portballintrae, BT57 8RR
☎ (028) 2073 1317
📠 (028) 2073 1852
✉ bushfootgolfclub@btconnect.com
🏨 684
✍ J Knox Thompson (Sec/Mgr)
▷ 9 L 6001 yds SSS 68
⚭ U Sat–NA after noon SOC
££ £9 D–£16 (£9) – 9 hole rate
⊕ 1 mile N of Bushmills. 4 miles E of Portrush
⊕ Pitch & putt 9 hole course

Cairndhu (1928)
192 Coast Road, Ballygally, Larne, BT40 2QG
☎ (028) 285 83954
📠 (028) 285 83324
✉ cairndhugc@btconnect.com
🏨 875
✍ M Keown (028) 285 83324
✓ S Hood (028) 285 83954
▷ 18 L 6112 yds SSS 69
⚭ U exc Sat–NA
££ £20 (£25)
⊕ 4 miles N of Larne
⊕ Driving range
🏠 JSF Morrison
🖥 www.cairndhugolfclub.co.uk

Carrickfergus (1926)
35 North Road, Carrickfergus, BT38 8LP
☎ (028) 9336 3713
📠 (028) 9336 3023
✉ carrickfergusgc@btconnect.com
🏨 967
✍ I McLean (Hon Sec)
✓ Gary Mercer
▷ 18 L 5713 yds SSS 68
⚭ U SOC
££ £19 (£25)
⊕ 7 miles E of Belfast via M5

Cushendall (1937)
21 Shore Road, Cushendall, BT44 0NG
☎ (028) 2177 1318
📠 (028) 2177 1318
✉ cushendallgc@btconnect.com
🏨 834
✍ S McLaughlin (028) 2175 8366
▷ 9 L 4834 m SSS 63
⚭ WE–restricted SOC
££ £13 (£18)
⊕ Cushendall, 25 miles N of Larne
⊕ Practice green/area/bunker
🏠 Denis Delargy

Down Royal (1990)
Dungarton Road, Maze, Lisburn, BT27 5RT
☎ (028) 9262 1339

Galgorm Castle (1997)
200 Galgorm Road, Ballymena, BT42 1HL
☎ (028) 256 46161
✉ golf@galgormcastle.com

Gracehill (1995)
Proprietary
141 Ballinlea Road, Stranocum, Ballymoney, BT53 8PX
☎ (028) 2075 1209
📠 (028) 2075 1074
✉ info@gracehillgolfclub.co.uk
🏨 425
✍ M McClure (Mgr)
▷ 18 L 6600 yds Par 72
⚭ U SOC
££ £25 (£30 +BH)
⊕ 6 miles N of Ballymoney (B66)
⊕ Driving range
🏠 Frank Ainsworth
🖥 www.gracehillgolfclub.co.uk

Greenacres (1996)
153 Ballyrobert Road, Ballyclare, BT39 9RT
☎ (028) 933 54111
📠 (028) 933 44509
🏨 511
✍ Colin Crawford
▷ 18 L 6031 yds Par 70 SSS 68
⚭ U
££ £16 (£22)
⊕ 3 miles from Corrs Corner on B56
⊕ Floodlit driving range; Par 3 course; 18-hole minigolf
🖥 www.greenacresgolfclub.co.uk

Greenisland (1894)
156 Upper Road, Greenisland, Carrickfergus, BT38 8RW
☎ (028) 9086 2236
✉ greenisland.golf@btconnect.com
🏨 469
✍ FF Trotter (Hon) (028) 9086 3518
▷ 9 L 6090 yds Par 71 SSS 69
⚭ WD–U Sat–NA before 5pm SOC–exc Sat
££ £12 (£18)
⊕ 9 miles NE of Belfast
🏠 F Middleton

Hilton Templepatrick (1999)
Proprietary
Castle Upton Estate, Paradise Walk, Templepatrick, BT39 0DD
☎ (028) 9443 5542
📠 (028) 9443 5511
✉ eamonn.logue@hilton.com
🏨 250
✍ Eamonn Logue (Golf Ops Mgr)
✓ E Logue and M Twitchett
▷ 18 L 7077 yds Par 71 SSS 71
⚭ U SOC WD WE
££ £45 (£45)

🚗 12 miles N of Belfast. M2 Junction
5. Belfast Airport 6 miles
⊕ Driving range
🏠 Jones/Feherty
🖳 www.hilton.com

Larne   (1894)
54 Ferris Bay Road, Islandmagee, Larne,
BT40 3RJ
☎ (028) 9338 2228
🖂 info@larnegolfclub.co.uk

Lisburn   (1891)
68 Eglantine Road, Lisburn, BT27 5RQ
☎ (028) 9267 7216
🖵 (028) 9260 3608
🖂 info@lisburngolfclub.com
🕮 1250
🏌 Andrew Crawford (Hon Sec)
⚲ Stephen Hamill (028) 9267 7217
🏴 18 L 6647 yds Par 72 SSS 72
👤 WD–U WE–M SOC–Mon & Thurs
££ £35 (£40)
🚗 3 miles S of Lisburn on A1
🏠 Hawtree
🖳 www.lisburngolfclub.com

Mallusk   (1992)
Antrim Road, Glengormley, Newtownabbey,
BT36 4RF
☎ (028) 9084 3799

Massereene   (1895)
51 Lough Road, Antrim, BT41 4DQ
☎ (028) 9442 8096 (office)
(028) 9442 9293 (bar)
🖵 (028) 9448 7661
🖂 info@massereene.com
🕮 850
🏌 G Henry (028) 9442 8096
⚲ J Smyth (028) 9446 4074
🏴 18 L 6603 yds SSS 72
👤 U SOC
££ £22 (£30)
🚗 1 mile S of Antrim
🏠 Fred Hawtree
🖳 www.massereene.com

Rathmore
Bushmills Road, Portrush, BT56 8JG
☎ (028) 7082 2996
🖂 rathmoregolfclubvalley@msn.com
🕮 155
🏌 W McIntyre (Club Admin.)
🏴 18 L 6304 yds Par 69
👤 U
££ £30 (£35)
🚗 Portrush
⊕ Tee reservations via Royal
Portrush GC – 028 708 23111

Royal Portrush   (1888)
Dunluce Road, Portrush, BT56 8JQ
☎ (028) 7082 2311
🖵 (028) 7082 3139
🖂 info@royalportrushgolfclub.com
🕮 997 297(L)
🏌 Miss W Erskine
⚲ G McNeill (028) 7082 3335
🏴 Dunluce 18 L 6867 yds SSS 73
Valley 18 L 6273 yds SSS 70
Skerries-9 hole course

👤 WD–I H exc Mon, Wed & Fri
pm–NA Sat–NA before 3pm
Sun–NA before 10.30am SOC
££ Dunluce £120 (£135) Valley £35
(£40)
🚗 Portrush Coastal Rd ½ mile
⊕ Driving range
🏠 HS Colt
🖳 www.royalportrushgolfclub.com

Whitehead   (1904)
McCrae's Brae, Whitehead, Carrickfergus,
BT38 9NZ
☎ (028) 9337 0820
🖂 robin@whiteheadgc.fsnet.co.uk

Co Armagh

Ashfield   (1990)
Freeduff, Cullyhanna, Newry, BT35 0JJ
☎ (028) 3086 8180

Cloverhill
Lough Road, Mullaghbawn, BT35 9XP
☎ (028) 3088 9374

County Armagh   (1893)
7 Newry Road, Armagh, BT60 1EN
☎ (028) 3752 2501
🖵 (028) 3752 2868
🖂 lynne@golfarmagh.co.uk
🕮 1350
🏌 Mrs Lynne Fleming
(028) 3752 5861
⚲ A Rankin (028) 3752 5864
🏴 18 L 6184 yds SSS 69
👤 SOC
££ £17 (£22)
🚗 40 miles SW of Belfast by M1
🖳 www.golfarmagh.co.uk

Edenmore G&CC   (1992)
Edenmore House, 70 Drumnabreeze Road,
Magheralin, Craigavon BT67 0RH
☎ (028) 9261 1310
🖵 (028) 9261 3310
🖂 info@edenmore.com
🕮 620
🏌 K Logan (Sec/Mgr)
⚲ Andrew Manson (028) 9261 9241
🏴 18 L 6278 yds Par 71 SSS 69
👤 WD–U WE–Sat after 3pm, Sun
booking required
££ £18 (£24)
🚗 Central location 4 miles E of
Lurgan on A3
⊕ Five practice greens
🏠 F Ainsworth
🖳 www.edenmore.com

Loughgall Country Park & Golf Course
11-14 Main Street, Loughgall
☎ (028) 3889 2900
🖵 (028) 3889 2902
🖂 g.ferson@btinternet.com
🏌 G Ferson (Mgr)
🏴 18 L 6229 yds Par 72
👤 U SOC
££ £15 (£17.50)

🚗 8 miles W of Portadown (B77)
⊕ Practice area; putting green
🏠 Don Patterson
🖳 www.armagh.gov.uk

Lurgan   (1893)
The Demesne, Lurgan, BT67 9BN
☎ (028) 3832 2087 (Clubhouse)
🖵 (028) 3831 6166
🖂 lurgangolfclub@btconnect.com
🕮 918
🏌 Mrs M Sharpe
⚲ D Paul (028) 3832 1068
🏴 18 L 6257 yds SSS 70
👤 U SOC–Mon/Thurs/Fri am/Sun am
££ £17 (£22)
🚗 Nr Brownlow Castle, Lurgan
🏠 Frank Pennink
🖳 www.lurgangolfclub.com

Portadown   (1902)
192 Gilford Road, Portadown, BT63 5LF
☎ (028) 383 55356
🖵 (028) 383 91394
🖂 portadown.gc@btconnect.com
🕮 700
🏌 Barbara Currie (Sec/Mgr)
⚲ P Stevenson (028) 383 34655
🏴 18 L 5786 yds SSS 70
👤 WD–U exc Tues SOC WE after
3pm Sat
££ £18 (£22)
🚗 3 miles from centre of Portadown,
towards Gilford and Banbridge
⊕ Practice area; indoor teaching area
🖳 www.portadowngolfclub.co.uk

Silverwood   (1983)
Turmoyra Lane, Silverwood, Lurgan,
BT66 6NG
☎ (028) 3832 6606

Tandragee   (1922)
Markethill Road, Tandragee, BT62 2ER
☎ (028) 3884 0727 (Clubhouse)
🖵 (028) 3884 0664
🖂 office@tandragee.co.uk
🕮 1205
🏌 A Hewitt (028) 3884 1272
⚲ D Keenan (028) 3884 1761
🏴 18 L 5754 m Par 71 SSS 70
👤 U SOC
££ £16 (£21)
🚗 5 miles S of Portadown on A27
🏠 F Hawtree
🖳 www.tandragee.co.uk

Belfast

Ballyearl Golf Centre
Public
585 Doagh Road, Newtownabbey,
BT36 5RZ
☎ (028) 9084 8287
🖂 sbartley@newtownabbey.gov.uk

Balmoral   (1914)
518 Lisburn Road, Belfast, BT9 6GX
☎ (028) 9038 1514
🖂 admin@balmoralgolf.com

Belvoir Park (1927)
73 Church Road, Newtownbreda, Belfast, BT8 7AN
- ☎ (028) 9049 1693
- 🖂 info@belvoirparkgolfclub.com

Dunmurry (1905)
91 Dunmurry Lane, Dunmurry, Belfast, BT17 9JS
- ☎ (028) 9061 0834
- 🖂 dunmurrygc@hotmail.com

Fortwilliam (1891)
Downview Avenue, Belfast, B15 4EZ
- ☎ (028) 9037 0770
- 🖵 (028) 9078 1891
- 🖂 michael@fortwilliam.co.uk
- 📖 1100
- 🏌 M Purdy
- ✓ P Hanna (028) 9077 0980
- ↦ 18 L 6030 yds SSS 69
- 👥 U SOC
- ££ £22 (£29)
- 🚗 2 miles N of Belfast on M2
- ⊕ Driving range; 2-seater buggies
- 🏠 Mr Butchart
- 🖥 www.fortwilliam.co.uk

Gilnahirk (1983)
Manns Corner, Upper Braniel Road, Belfast, BT5 7TX
- ☎ (028) 9044 8477

The Knock Club (1895)
Summerfield, Dundonald, Belfast, BT16 2QX
- ☎ (028) 9048 2249
- 🖵 (028) 9048 7277
- 🖂 knockgolfclub@btconnect.com
- 📖 900
- 🏌 Anne Armstrong (028) 9048 3251
- ✓ R Whitford (028) 9048 3825
- ↦ 18 L 6407 yds SSS 71
- 👥 U SOC–Mon & Thurs
- ££ D–£25 (£40)
- 🚗 4 miles E of Belfast on the Upper Newtownards Road
- 🏠 Colt/Mackenzie/Alison

Malone (1895)
240 Upper Malone Road, Dunmurry, Belfast, BT17 9LB
- ☎ (028) 9061 2758
- 🖂 manager@malonegolfclub.co.uk

Ormeau (1893)
50 Park Road, Belfast, BT7 2FX
- ☎ (028) 9064 1069 (Members)

Shandon Park (1926)
73 Shandon Park, Belfast, BT5 6NY
- ☎ (028) 9080 5030
- 🖵 (028) 9080 5999
- 🖂 shandonpark@btconnect.com
- 📖 1100
- 🏌 GA Bailie (Gen Mgr)
- ✓ B Wilson (028) 9080 5031
- ↦ 18 L 6261 yds SSS 70
- 👥 WD–U Sat–NA Sun NA
- ££ £25 (£27.50)
- 🚗 3 miles E of Belfast on the Knock road
- 🖥 www.shandonpark.com

Co Carlow

Borris (1907)
Deerpark, Borris
- ☎ (059) 977 3310 (office)
- (059) 977 3143 (bar)
- 🖵 (059) 73750
- 🖂 borrisgolfclub@eircom.net
- 📖 675
- 🏌 Nollaig Lucas (Sec/Mgr) (0503) 73310
- ↦ 9 L 5680 m Par 70 SSS 69
- 👥 WD–U Sun–M SOC–WD/Sat
- ££ €25 (18 holes)
- 🚗 Borris

Carlow (1899)
Deer Park, Dublin Road, Carlow
- ☎ (059) 913 1695
- 🖂 carlowgolfclub@eircom.net

Mount Wolseley (1996)
Tullow
- ☎ (059) 915 1674
- 🖵 (059) 915 2123
- 🖂 golf@mountwolseley.ie
- 📖 250
- 🏌 John Lawler (Director of Golf)
- ↦ 18 L 7172 yds Par 72 SSS 74
- 👥 U SOC
- ££ €60 (€80)
- 🚗 1 Hr from Dublin, Wexford
- ⊕ Buggie and club hire available
- 🏠 Christy O'Connor Jr
- 🖥 www.mountwolseley.ie

Co Cavan

Belturbet (1950)
Erne Hill, Belturbet
- ☎ (049) 952 2287

Blacklion (1962)
Toam, Blacklion, via Sligo
- ☎ (071) 985 3024
- 🖵 (071) 985 3024
- 📖 250
- 🏌 P Gallery (Hon)
- ↦ 9 L 5785 m SSS 69
- 👥 U SOC
- ££ €20 (€25)
- 🚗 12 miles SW of Enniskillen on A4 to N16
- 🏠 Eddie Hackett
- 🖥 www.blackliongolf.eu

Cabra Castle (1978)
Kingscourt
- ☎ (042) 966 7030
- 🖵 (042) 966 7039
- 🖂 gkellett@gilmores.ie
- 📖 160
- 🏌 George Kellett (085) 843 9121
- ↦ 9 L 5261 m Par 70
- 👥 U exc Sun–NA SOC
- ££ €15
- 🚗 2 miles E of Kingscourt

County Cavan (1894)
Arnmore House, Drumelis, Cavan
- ☎ (049) 433 1541
- 🖵 (049) 433 1541
- 🖂 info@cavangolf.ie
- 📖 800
- 🏌 James Fraker
- ✓ B Noble (049) 433 1388
- ↦ 18 L 5534 m SSS 69
- 👥 U
- ££ €30 (€35)
- 🚗 1 mile W of Cavan on Killeshandra road
- ⊕ Driving range
- 🏠 Eddie Hackett/Arthur Spring
- 🖥 www.cavangolf.ie

Slieve Russell G&CC (1994)
Ballyconnell
- ☎ (049) 952 6458
- 🖵 (049) 952 6640
- 🖂 slieve-russell@quinn-hotels.com
- 📖 500
- 🏌 L McCool (049) 952 5091
- ✓ L McCool (049) 952 5090
- ↦ 18 L 7053 yds Par 72 SSS 74 9 hole Par 3 course
- 👥 U SOC
- ££ €75 Sat–€90 Discounts apply for groups
- 🚗 15 miles N of Cavan Town
- ⊕ Driving range
- 🏠 Paddy Merrigan

Virginia (1945)
Park Hotel, Virginia
- ☎ (049) 854 8066

Co Clare

Clonlara (1993)
Clonlara
- ☎ (061) 354141
- 🖂 clonlaragolfclub@eircom.net
- 📖 142
- 🏌 Tom Carroll
- ↦ 12 L 5289 m Par 71 SSS 69
- 👥 U
- ££ €15 (€20)
- 🚗 8 miles NE of Limerick

Doonbeg (2002)
Doonbeg, Co Clare
- ☎ (065) 905 5600
- 🖵 (065) 905 5247
- 🖂 reservations@doonbeggolfclub.com
- 📖 400
- 🏌 Joe Russell (Gen Mgr)
- ✓ Brian Shaw (Head Pro)
- ↦ 18 L 6870 yds Par 72 SSS 74
- 👥 U
- ££ On application
- 🚗 10 miles N of Kilkee
- ⊕ Driving range; caddies
- 🏠 Greg Norman
- 🖥 www.doonbeggolfclub.com

Dromoland Castle (1964)
Newmarket-on-Fergus
- ☎ 353 (61) 368444

353 (61) 368498
🖂 golf@dromoland.ie
🏛 500
🏌 J O'Halloran
✒ D Foley
⛳ 18 L 6824 yds Par 72 SSS 72
👥 U H SOC WD WE
££ €60–€110
🚗 N18 to Dromoland Interchange, 18 miles NW of Limerick. Shannon Airport 8 miles
⊕ Buggies and trolley available. Caddies must be booked in advance
🏚 R Kirby and JB Carr (2004)
🖥 www.dromoland.ie

East Clare   (1992)
Bodyke
☎ (061) 921322

Ennis   (1907)
Drumbiggle, Ennis
☎ (065) 682 4074
🖷 (065) 684 1848
🖂 info@ennisgolfclub.com
🏛 1383
🏌 Pat McCarthy
⛳ 18 L 5706 m Par 70 SSS 69
👥 U SOC
££ €35
🚗 ¹/₂ mile NW of Ennis, off N18
🖥 www.ennisgolfclub.com

Kilkee   (1896)
East End, Kilkee
☎ (065) 905 6048
🖷 (065) 905 6977
🖂 kilkeegolfclub@eircom.net
🏛 750
🏌 M Culligan (Sec/Mgr)
⛳ 18 L 5555 m Par 70 SSS 69
👥 U SOC
££ €24 (€30)
🚗 End of Kilkee Promenade. 50 miles west of Shannon Airport
🏚 Eddie Hackett
🖥 www.kilkeegolfclub.ie

Kilrush   (1934)
Parknamoney, Kilrush
☎ (065) 905 1138
🖂 info@kilrushgolfclub.com

Lahinch   (1892)
Lahinch
☎ (065) 708 1003
🖷 (065) 708 1592
🖂 info@lahinchgolf.com
🏛 1250
🏌 A Reardon (Sec/Mgr)
✒ R McCavery (065) 708 1408
⛳ Old 18 L 6950 yds SSS 74
   Castle 18 L 5556 yds SSS 67
👥 WD–U WE–NA 8–10.30am and 1–2pm SOC
££ Old–€165. Castle–€55 (2008)
🚗 20 miles NW of Ennis on T69
⊕ Practice net and practice ground; Chipping green with practice bunker
🏚 Old: Morris/Gibson/Mackenzie/ Hawtre; Castle: Harris
🖥 www.lahinchgolf.com

Shannon   (1966)
Shannon
☎ (061) 471849
🖷 (061) 471507
🖂 info@shannongolfclub.ie
🏛 1050
🏌 M Corry (061) 471849
✒ Artle Pyke (061) 471551
⛳ 18 L 6515 yds Par 72 SSS 72
👥 WD–U SOC WE
££ €55 (€65)
🚗 Shannon Airport
⊕ Driving range; chipping facility
🏚 John D Harris
🖥 www.shannongolfclub.ie

Spanish Point   (1915)
Spanish Point, Miltown Malbay
☎ (065) 708 4219

Woodstock   (1993)
Shanaway Road, Ennis
☎ (065) 682 9463
🖷 (065) 682 0304
🖂 proshopwoodstock@eircom.net
🏛 400
🏌 Avril Guerin (Sec/Mgr)
⛳ 18 L 5879 m SSS 71
👥 U
££ €45 (€48 + BH)
🚗 Ennis, 18 miles from Shannon Airport N 85
🏚 Arthur Spring
🖥 www.woodstockgolfclub.com

Co Cork

Bandon   (1909)
Castlebernard, Bandon
☎ (023) 41111
🖷 (023) 44690
🖂 enquiries@bandongolfclub.com
🏛 1200
🏌 Kay Walsh
✒ P O'Boyle (023) 42224
⛳ 18 L 6334 m Par 71 SSS 72
👥 U SOC
££ On application
🚗 Bandon 1¹/₂ miles. 18 miles SW of Cork
🖥 www.bandongolfclub.com

Bantry Bay   (1975)
Donemark, Bantry, West Cork
☎ (027) 50579/53773
🖷 (027) 53790
🖂 info@bantrygolf.com
🏛 750
🏌 J O'Sullivan (Mgr) (027) 50579
⛳ 18 L 6117 m Par 71 SSS 72
👥 WE/BH–booking necessary SOC
££ €40 (€50)
🚗 1 mile N of Bantry on Glengarriff road (N71)
🏚 E Hackett/C O'Connor, Jnr
🖥 www.bantrygolf.com

Berehaven   (1902)
Millcove, Castletownbere
☎ (027) 70700

(027) 71957
🖂 info@berehavengolf.com
🏛 208
🏌 B Twomey (Hon)
⛳ 9 L 5121 m SSS 70 (ladies), SSS 67 (men)
👥 U SOC
££ €20 (€25)
🚗 2 miles E of Castletownbere on Glengarriff road
⊕ Practice putting green
🏚 James Healy
🖥 www.berehavengolf.com

Charleville   (1909)
Charleville
☎ (063) 81257
🖂 charlevillegolf@eircom.net

Cobh   (1987)
Ballywilliam, Cobh
☎ (021) 812399

Coosheen   (1989)
Coosheen, Schull
☎ (028) 28182

Cork   (1888)
Little Island, Cork
☎ (021) 435 3451/3037
🖷 (021) 435 3410
🖂 corkgolfclub@eircom.net
🏛 366 176 (L)
🏌 M Sands (021) 435 3451
✒ P Hickey (021) 435 3421
⛳ 18 L 6065 m SSS 72
👥 WD–U H exc 12–2pm –M after 4pm Thurs–(Ladies Day)–phone in advance WE–NA before 2.30pm H
££ €85 (€95)
🚗 5 miles E of Cork, off N25
⊕ Range balls for hire; buggy hire
🏚 Dr A Mackenzie
🖥 www.corkgolfclub.ie

Doneraile   (1927)
Doneraile
☎ (022) 24137
🖂 info@donerailegolfclub.com
🏛 750
🏌 J O'Leary (022) 24379
⛳ 9 L 5528 yds SSS 67
👥 WD/Sat–U
££ €25
🚗 8 miles NW of Mallow
🖥 www.donerailegolfclub.com

Douglas   (1909)
Douglas, Cork
☎ (021) 489 1086
🖷 (021) 436 7200
🖂 admin@douglasgolfclub.ie
🏛 839
🏌 Ronan Burke (Mgr)
✒ GS Nicholson (021) 436 2055
⛳ 18 L 5972 m SSS 71
👥 WD–U exc Tues WE–NA before 2pm
££ €45 (€50)
🚗 Cork 3 miles
⊕ Driving range; practice chipping & putting greens

🏠 Jeff Howes
🖳 www.douglasgolfclub.ie

Dunmore (1967)
Muckross, Clonakilty
☎ (023) 34644
📧 info@dunmoregolfclub.com
📖 430
✍ Liam Santry
🏴 9 L 4464 yds SSS 61
👥 WD–U exc Wed WE–M SOC–Sat
££ €25
🚗 3 miles S of Clonakilty
🏠 Eddie Hackett
🖳 www.dunmoregolfclub.com

East Cork (1971)
Gortacrue, Midleton
☎ (021) 463 1687
🖳 (021) 461 3695
📧 eastcorkgolfclub@eircom.net
📖 900
✍ M Moloney (Sec/Mgr)
✍ D MacFarlane
🏴 18 L 5207 m SSS 67
👥 WD–U WE–NA before noon
BH–U
££ €30
🚗 2 miles N of Midleton on L35
⊕ Driving range
🏠 Eddie Hackett
🖳 www.eastcorkgolfclub.com

Fermoy (1892)
Corrin, Fermoy
☎ (025) 32694
🖳 (025) 33072
📧 fermoygolfclub@eircom.net
📖 1000
✍ K Murphy
✍ B Moriarty (025) 31472
🏴 18 L 5847 m SSS 70
👥 U SOC
££ €20 (€30)
🚗 2 miles S of Fermoy, off N8
🏠 Cdr John Harris
🖳 www.fermoygolfclub.ie

Fernhill (1994)
Carrigaline
☎ (021) 437 2226
🖳 (021) 437 1011
📧 fernhill@iol.ie
📖 120
✍ A Bowes (Mgr)
✍ W Callaghan (087) 284 1365
🏴 18 L 5766 m Par 70 SSS 67
👥 U
££ €20 Mon–Thur (€30 Fri–Sun)
🚗 7 miles SE of Cork (R609), nr
Ringskiddy
🏠 ML Bowes
🖳 www.fernhillgolfhotel.com

Fota Island Resort (1993)
Proprietary
Fota Island, Cork
☎ (021) 488 3700
🖳 (021) 488 3713
📧 reservations@fotaisland.ie
📖 650
✍ Jonathon Woods
✍ K Morris (021) 488 3700

🏴 27 Holes
Deerpark 6327 yds Par 71 SSS 73
Belvelly 7121 yds Par 72 SSS 74
Barryscourt 7362 yds Par 73
SSS 75
👥 U
££ €75–€120
🚗 8 miles East of Cork on N25 Take
R625 to Cobh
⊕ Full State of art Golf Academy
🏠 O'Connor Jr/McEvoy/Howes
🖳 www.fotaisland.ie

Frankfield (1984)
Frankfield, Douglas
☎ (0214) 363124/3611299

Glengarriff (1935)
Glengarriff
☎ (027) 63150

Harbour Point (1991)
Proprietary
Clash Road, Little Island
☎ (021) 435 3094
🖳 (021) 435 4408
📧 hpoint@iol.ie
📖 300 176(L)
✍ Aylmer Barrett
✍ Morgan O'Donovan (086 603
0318)
🏴 18 L 6102 m SSS 72 (M)
SSS 73 (L)
👥 U SOC
££ €35 (€45)
🚗 5 miles E of Cork
⊕ Floodlit driving range
🏠 Paddy Merrigan
🖳 www.harbourpointgolfclub.com

Kanturk (1971)
Fairyhill, Kanturk
☎ (029) 50534

Kinsale Farrangalway (1993)
Farrangalway, Kinsale
☎ (021) 477 4722
🖳 (021) 477 3114
📧 office@kinsalegolf.com
📖 830
✍ Michael Power
✍ G Broderick (021) 477 3258
🏴 18 L 6609 yds SSS 72
👥 WD–U WE–NA SOC
££ €35 (€40)
🚗 3 miles NW of Kinsale. 18 miles S
of Cork
🏠 Jack Kenneally
🖳 www.kinsalegolf.com

Kinsale Ringenane (1912)
Ringenane, Belgooly, Kinsale
☎ (021) 477 2197
📖 740
✍ Michael Power
🏴 9 L 5332 yds SSS 68
👥 U SOC
££ €25
🚗 2 miles E of Kinsale (R600). 16
miles S of Cork

Lee Valley G&CC (1993)
Clashanure, Ovens, Cork
☎ (021) 733 1721
🖳 (021) 733 1695
📧 reservations@leevalleygcc.ie
📖 450
✍ D Keohane
✍ J Savage (021) 733 1758
🏴 18 L 6800 yds SSS 72
👥 U SOC WD WE
££ €50 (€60)
🚗 8 miles W of Cork (N22)
⊕ 4* accom; comp/tary bus service
🏠 C O'Connor Jr
🖳 www.leevalleygcc.ie

Macroom (1924)
Lackaduve, Macroom
☎ (026) 41072
🖳 (026) 41391
📧 mcroomgc@iol.net
📖 750
✍ C O'Sullivan (Mgr)
🏴 18 L 5605 m Par 71 SSS 69
👥 U SOC
££ €35 (€40)
🚗 Macroom Town, through Castle
Arch. 25 miles W of Cork
⊕ Putting Green
🏠 Eddie Hackett
🖳 www.macroomgolfclub.com

Mahon (1980)
Clover Hill, Blackrock, Cork
☎ (021) 429 2543
📧 mahon@golfnet.ie

Mallow (1948)
Ballyellis, Mallow
☎ (022) 21145
🖳 (022) 42501
📧 mallowgolfclubmanager@eircom.net
📖 1500
✍ D Curtin (Sec/Mgr)
✍ S Conway (022) 43424
🏴 18 L 6559 yds SSS 72
👥 WD–U before 5pm SOC
££ €45 (€50)
🚗 1 mile SE of Mallow Bridge on
Killavullen road
⊕ Practice facility
🏠 J Harris
🖳 www.mallowgolfclub.net

Mitchelstown (1908)
Gurrane, Mitchelstown
☎ (025) 24072
🖳 (025) 86631
📧 info@mitchelstown-golf.com
📖 750
✍ Sean Buckley
✍ Denis Doyle (086) 395 1182
🏴 18 L 5773 m Par 71
👥 U SOC
££ €25 (€30)
🚗 30 miles NE of Cork off N8
🏠 David Jones
🖳 www.mitchelstown-golf.com

Monkstown (1908)
Parkgarriffe, Monkstown
☎ (021) 484 1376

📖 (021) 484 1722
📧 office@monkstowngolfclub.com
📖 900
🏌 H Madden (Sec/Mgr)
(021) 486 3910
✓ B Murphy (021) 486 3912
🏌 18 L 5669 m Par 70 SSS 69
👤 U SOC
££ €43 (€50)
🚗 7 miles SE of Cork
🏠 Tom Carey and Peter O'Hare
🖳 www.monkstowngolfclub.com

Muskerry   (1907)
Carrigrohane, Co. Cork
☎ (021) 438 5297
📖 (021) 451 6860
📧 muskgc@eircom.net
📖 803
🏌 H Gallagher
✓ WM Lehane (021) 438 1445
🏌 18 L 5786 m SSS 70
👤 Restricted at certain times–phone first SOC
££ €35
🚗 7 miles NW of Cork. 2 miles W of Blarney
🏠 Dr A McKenzie contribution

Old Head Golf Links
(1997)
Kinsale
☎ (021) 477 8444
📖 (021) 477 8022
📧 info@oldhead.com
📖 400
🏌 Danny Brassil (Dir of Golf)
🏌 18 L 7200 yds SSS 72
👤 U H
££ €295
🚗 7 miles S of Kinsale
⊕ Driving range; putting green; chipping green
🏠 Carr/Merrigan/Kirby/Hackett
🖳 www.oldhead.com

Raffeen Creek   (1989)
Ringaskiddy
☎ (021) 437 8430

Skibbereen   (1904)
Licknavar, Skibbereen
☎ (028) 21227
📖 (028) 22994
📧 info@skibbgolf.com
📖 650
🏌 S Brett (Mgr)
🏌 18 L 5474 m Par 71 SSS 69
👤 U SOC–Sat
££ €40
🚗 1 mile W of Skibbereen. 52 miles SW of Cork
🏠 Eddie Hackett
🖳 www.skibbgolf.com

Youghal   (1898)
Knockaverry, Youghal
☎ (024) 92787/92861
📧 youghalgolfclub@eircom.net

Co Donegal

Ballybofey & Stranorlar
(1957)
The Glebe, Stranorlar
☎ (074) 31093
📖 (074) 31058
📖 655
🏌 Patsy O'Donnell (074) 914 1613
✓ (074) 31093 (shop)
🏌 18 L 5922 yds Par 68 SSS 68
👤 U SOC
££ €25 (€35)
🚗 Stranorlar 1 mile
🏠 PC Carr

Ballyliffin   (1947)
Ballyliffin, Inishowen
☎ (07493) 76119
📖 (07493) 76672
📧 info@ballyliffingolfclub.com
📖 1200
🏌 John Farren (Gen Mgr)
✓ John Dolan
🏌 Old 18 L 6910 yds Par 71 SSS 72
Glashedy 18 L 7217 yds Par 72 SSS 74
👤 U SOC–WD/WE
££ Old: €60/€65 Glashedy: €70/€80
🚗 8 miles N of Buncrana. 15 miles N of Londonderry
⊕ Driving range; practice bay; practice holes
🏠 Glashedy-Craddock/Ruddy/Faldo
🖳 www.ballyliffingolfclub.com

Buncrana   (1951)
Public
Buncrana
☎ (07493) 62279/20749
📧 buncranagc@eircom.net
📖 300
🏌 F McGrory (Hon) (07493) 20749
✓ J Doherty
🏌 9 L 4310 m SSS 62
👤 U
££ Men: €15; Women: €10; Juv. €8
🚗 In Buncrana, nr Inishowen (Gateway Hotel)

Bundoran   (1894)
Bundoran
☎ (072) 41302
📖 (072) 42014
📧 bundorangolfclub@eircom.net
📖 620
🏌 Paul Norman (Sec/Mgr)
✓ D Robinson
🏌 18 L 5688 m Par 70 SSS 70
👤 WD–U WE–restricted SOC
££ €45 (€55)
🚗 E boundary of Bundoran. 20 miles S of Donegal
🏠 H Vardon
🖳 www.bundorangolfclub.com

Cruit Island   (1985)
Kincasslagh, Dunglow
☎ (074) 954 3296

Donegal   (1960)
Murvagh, Laghey
☎ (074) 973 4054
📖 (074) 973 4377
📧 info@donegalgolfclub.ie
📖 720
🏌 Grainne Dorrian
✓ Leslie Robinson
🏌 18 L 7271 yds SSS 73
👤 H SOC
££ €55 (€70)
🚗 7 miles S of Donegal, off N15
⊕ Driving Range; Putting Green; Pitching Area;
🏠 Eddie Hackett
🖳 www.donegalgolfclub.ie

Dunfanaghy   (1906)
Kill, Dunfanaghy, Letterkenny
☎ (074) 913 6335
📖 (074) 913 6684
📧 dunfanaghygolf@eircom.net
📖 390
🏌 Mary Lafferty
🏌 18 L 5350 m Par 68 SSS 66
👤 Timesheets in operation – please phone
££ €30 (€40)
🚗 25 m NW of Letterkenny on N56
⊕ Practice area
🏠 Harry Vardon
🖳 www.dunfanaghygolfclub.com

Greencastle   (1892)
Greencastle
☎ (074) 93 81013
📖 (074) 93 81015
📧 b_mc_caul@yahoo.com
📖 750
🏌 Billy McCaul
🏌 18 L 5269 m SSS 67
👤 WD–U WE–restricted SOC
££ €30 (€40)
🚗 21 miles NE of Londonderry, nr Moville
🏠 Eddie Hackett/David Jones
🖳 www.greencastlegolfclub.com

Gweedore   (1926)
Pay and play
Magheragallon, Derrybeg, Letterkenny
☎ (07495) 31140
📧 eugenemccafferty@hotmail.com
📖 250
🏌 Eugene McCafferty
🏌 9 L 6201 yds SSS 69
👤 U
££ €20 (€20)
🚗 3 miles N of Gweedore, off R257
⊕ Practice Area; Putting Green
🖳 www.gweedoregolfclub.com

Letterkenny   (1913)
Barnhill, Letterkenny
☎ (+353) 7491 21150
📖 (+353) 7491 21175
📧 letterkennygc@eircom.net
📖 800
🏌 D Rainey(+353) 7491 21150
✓ S Duffy
🏌 18 L 6353 yds SSS 72
👤 U–booking necessary SOC

££ €25 (€35 + BH)
⊶ I mile E of Letterkenny
⊕ Buggy Hire; Trolley Hire, Pre-booking available
⌂ Declan Brannigan
▣ www.letterkennygolfclub.com

Narin & Portnoo   (1930)
Narin, Portnoo
☎ **(074) 954 5107**
🖳 (074) 945 5994
📧 narinportnoo@eircom.net
⌼ 750
♣ Willie Quinn (Hon)
�🏴 18 L 6269 m Par 73
👤 WD WE SOC–WE after 11.30am
££ €40 (€45) SOC–€30 (€35)
⊶ 6 miles N of Ardara. West Donegal. 30 min from Donegal Airport
⊕ Practice net
⌂ Leo Wallace, Hughie McNeill
▣ www.narinportnoogolfclub.ie

North West   (1891)
Lisfannon, Buncrana
☎ **(074) 936 0127**
   New Golf Shop
   (074) 936 1715
🖳 (074) 936 3284
📧 secretary@northwestgolfclub.com
⌼ 555
♣ Eugene O'Connell (086) 604 7299
⚐ S McBriarty (074) 936 1715
🏴 18 L 6239 yds SSS 70
👤 U SOC
££ €30 (€35)
⊶ 2 km S of Buncrana. 15 km N of Derry
⊕ Buggies for Hire.
▣ www.northwestgolfclub.com

Otway   (1893)
Saltpans, Rathmullan, Letterkenny
☎ **(074) 915 1665**
   (074) 915 8319 (Club House)
📧 tolandkevin@eircom.net
⌼ 97
♣ Kevin Toland
🏴 9 L 4234 yds SSS 60
👤 U
££ €15
⊶ 15 miles NE of Letterkenny, by Lough Swilly

Portsalon   (1891)
Portsalon, Fanad
☎ **(074) 915 9459**
🖳 (074) 915 9919
📧 portsalongolfclub@eircom.net
⌼ 550
♣ P Doherty
⚐ Seamus Clinton (086) 867 4201
🏴 18 L 6185m Par 72 SSS 72
👤 U–phone in advance
££ €50 (€60 +BH) €20 with member
⊶ 20 miles N of Letterkenny (R246)
⌂ Pat Ruddy
▣ www.portsalongolfclub.ie

Redcastle   (1983)
Redcastle, Moville
☎ **(074) 938 5555**

🖳 (074) 938 2214
⌼ 190
♣ M Wilson
🏴 9 L 6128 yds Par 72 SSS 69
👤 U
££ €20 (€25)
⊶ 15 miles N of Londonderry, by Lough Foyle (R238)

Rosapenna   (1894)
Downings, Rosapenna
☎ **(074) 55301**
🖳 (074) 55128
📧 rosapenna@eircom.net
⌼ 250
♣ J Sweeney
⚐ B Patterson
🏴 Old: 18 L 7155 yds Par 71 SSS 73
   Sandy Hill Links: 18 L 6254 yds Par 70 SSS 71
👤 U
££ Old: €50; Sandy Hills: €75
⊶ 20 miles N of Letterkenny
⊕ Golf academy; driving range
⌂ Morris/Vardon/Braid/Ruddy; Sandy Hills designed by Pat Ruddy
▣ www.rosapenna.ie

St Patricks Courses   (1994)
Carrigart
☎ **(074) 55114**

Co Down

Ardglass   (1896)
Castle Place, Ardglass, BT30 7PP
☎ **(028) 4484 1219**
🖳 (028) 4484 1841
📧 info@ardglassgolfclub.com
⌼ 840
♣ Mrs D Purley
⚐ P Farrell (028) 4484 1022
🏴 18 L 6268 yds Par 70 SSS 70
👤 U SOC
££ €40 (€55)
⊶ 7 miles SE of Downpatrick on B1
▣ www.ardglassgolfclub.com

Ardminnan   (1995)
15 Ardminnan Road, Portaferry, BT22 1QJ
☎ **(028) 4277 1321**
🖳 (028) 4277 1321
📧 lesliejardine104@yahoo.co.uk
⌼ 100
♣ L Jardine
🏴 9 L 2766 m Par 70
👤 U
££ £10 (£15)
⊶ 10 m E of Downpatrick via ferry. 18 m SE of Newtownards (A20)
⌂ Frank Ainsworth

Banbridge   (1912)
116 Huntly Road, Banbridge, BT32 3UR
☎ **(028) 4066 2342 (restaurant)**
🖳 (028) 4066 9400
⌼ 850
♣ J McKeown (028) 4066 2211
⚐ Jason Greenaway
🏴 18 L 5590 m SSS 69
👤 U SOC

££ £17 (£22)
⊶ I mile W of Banbridge
⌂ F Ainsworth
▣ www.banbridge-golf
   @btconnect.com

Bangor   (1903)
Broadway, Bangor, BT20 4RH
☎ **(028) 9127 0922**
🖳 (028) 9145 3394
📧 office@bangorgolfclubni.co.uk
⌼ 900
♣ Mrs EP Roberts
⚐ M Bannon
🏴 18 L 6424 yds SSS 71
👤 WD–U exc –M 1–2pm Wed–U before 4pm Sat–NA SOC
££ £26 (£34) SOC £21 (£26)
⊶ I mile S of Bangor, off Donaghadee road
⌂ James Braid
▣ www.bangorgolfclubni.co.uk

Blackwood   (1995)
150 Crawfordsburn Road, Bangor, BT19 1GB
☎ **(028) 9185 2706**
📧 blackwoodgc@btopenworld.com

Bright Castle   (1970)
14 Coniamstown Road, Bright, Downpatrick, BT30 8LU
☎ **(028) 4484 1319**

Carnalea   (1927)
Station Road, Bangor, BT19 1EZ
☎ **(028) 9146 5004**
🖳 (028) 9127 3989
⌼ 800
♣ GY Steele (028) 9127 0368
⚐ T Loughran (028) 9127 0122
🏴 18 L 5647 yds SSS 68
👤 U SOC–WD
££ £17.50 (£22)
⊶ By Carnalea Station, Bangor

Clandeboye   (1933)
Conlig, Newtownards, BT23 7PN
☎ **(028) 9127 1767 (office)**
   (028) 9147 3706 (bar)
🖳 (028) 9147 3711
📧 cgc-ni.@btconnect.com
⌼ 1456
♣ B Mills (Hon Sec) (028) 9127 1767
⚐ P Gregory (028) 9127 1750
🏴 Dufferin 18 L 6550 yds SSS 71
   Ava 18 L 5755 yds SSS 68
👤 WD–U WE–M SOC
££ Dufferin–£32 (£36); Ava £26 (£30)
⊶ Conlig, off A21 Bangor-Newtownards road
⌂ Von Limburger/Alliss/Thomas
▣ www.cgc-ni.com

Crossgar   (1993)
231 Derryboye Road, Crossgar, BT30 9DL
☎ **(028) 4483 1523**

Donaghadee   (1899)
84 Warren Road, Donaghadee, BT21 0PQ
☎ **(028) 9188 3624**
🖳 (028) 9188 8891

deegolf@freenet.co.uk
🛒 1135
🏌 Gareth Boyd
✓ G Drew (028) 9188 2392
🏴 18 L 5614 m Par 71
👥 U exc Sat–NA SOC–exc Sat
££ £23 (£26)
🚗 6 miles S of Bangor on coast road. 18 miles E of Belfast

Downpatrick   (1930)
Saul Road, Downpatrick, BT30 6PA
☎ (028) 4461 5947
🖨 (028) 4461 7502
🖂 office@downpatrickgolf.org.uk
🛒 960
🏌 Elaine Carson (028) 4461 5947
✓ Robert Hutton (028) 4461 5167
🏴 18 L 5702 m SSS 69
👥 U SOC
££ £23 (£28)
🚗 25 miles SE of Belfast (A1). Downpatrick 1½ miles
🏠 Hawtree
🖥 www.downpatrickgolfclub.org.uk

Helen's Bay   (1896)
Golf Road, Helen's Bay, Bangor, BT19 1TL
☎ (028) 9185 2815 (office)
🖨 (028) 9185 2660
🖂 mail@helensbaygc.com
🛒 700
🏌 Robin Longmore
🏴 9 L 5644 yds Par 68 SSS 67
👥 WD/Sun–U
Tues/Thurs/Sat–restricted
SOC–WD
££ £20 (£25)
🚗 9 miles E of Belfast, off A2
⊕ Excellent Catering
🖥 www.helensbaygc.com

Holywood   (1904)
Nuns Walk, Demesne Road, Holywood, BT18 9LE
☎ (028) 9042 2138
🖨 (028) 9042 5040
🖂 mail@holywoodgolfclub.co.uk
🛒 1000
🏌 Paul Gray (Gen Mgr) (028) 9042 3135
✓ Stephen Crooks (028) 9042 5503
🏴 18 L 5885 yds SSS 68
👥 WD–U Sat after 3pm
££ £25 (£29)
🚗 5 miles E of Belfast on Bangor road
🖥 www.holywoodgolfclub.co.uk

Kilkeel   (1948)
Mourne Park, Kilkeel, BT34 4LB
☎ (028) 4176 2296/5095
🖨 (028) 4176 5579
🖂 info@kilkeelgolfclub.org
🛒 720
🏌 SC McBride (Hon) (028) 4176 5095
🏴 18 L 6579 yds SSS 72
👥 U SOC–exc Sat
££ TBA
🚗 3 miles W of Kilkeel on Newry road
🏠 Badington/Hackett
🖥 www.kilkeelgolfclub.org

Kirkistown Castle   (1902)
142 Main Road, Cloughey, Newtownards, BT22 1JA
☎ (028) 4277 1233
🖨 (028) 4277 1699
🖂 kirkistown@supanet.com
🛒 948
🏌 R Coulter (028) 4277 1233
✓ N Graham (028) 4277 1004
🏴 18 L 5616 m Par 69 SSS 70
👥 WD/Sun–U Sat–NA before 2.30pm
££ £25 (£30)
🚗 25 miles SE of Belfast
🏠 James Braid
🖥 www.linksgolfkirkistown.com

Mahee Island   (1929)
Comber, 14 Mahee Island, Newtownlands BT23 6ET
☎ (028) 9754 1234
🖨 (028) 9754 1234
🖂 adrian.ross@ntlworld.com
🛒 500
🏌 M Marshall (Hon)
✓ C Macaw (shop)
🏴 9 L 5822 yds Par 71 SSS 70
👥 U exc Sat–NA before 5pm
SOC–WD exc Mon
££ £13 (£18)
🚗 Strangford Lough, 14 miles SE of Belfast
🏠 Mr Robinson
🖥 www.maheeislandgolfclub.com

Mount Ober G&CC   (1985)
Ballymaconaghy Road, Knockbracken, Belfast, BT8 6SB
☎ (028) 9079 2108 (Bookings)
🖨 (028) 9070 5862
🖂 mt.ober@ukonline.co.uk
🛒 500
🏌 E Williams (Sec/Mgr)
✓ W Ramsay (028) 9070 1648
🏴 18 L 5281 yds SSS 66
👥 WD–U Sat–NA before 3pm
Sun–NA before 10.30am SOC
££ £19 (£21)
🚗 2 m SW of Belfast, nr Four Winds
⊕ Floodlit driving range
🖥 www.mountober.com

Mourne   (1946)
Club
36 Golf Links Road, Newcastle, BT33 0AN
☎ (028) 4372 3218
🖨 (028) 4372 2575
🖂 secretary@mournegolfclub.co.uk
🛒 385
🏌 P Keown (Hon)
✓ See Royal Co Down
🏴 Play over Royal Co Down
👥 See Royal Co Down
££ See Royal Co Down
🚗 See Royal Co Down
🏠 See Royal Co Down
🖥 www.mournegolfclub.co.uk

Ringdufferin G&CC   (1993)
Ringdufferin Road, Toye, Downpatrick, BT30 9PH
☎ (028) 4482 8812
🖂 willismarshall@utvinternet.com

🛒 165
🏌 Willis Marshall (Hon)
✓ Mervyn Stewart
🏴 18 L 4652 m Par 68 SSS 66
👥 WE–NA
££ £12 (£15)
🚗 2 miles N of Killyleagh, off A22

Rockmount   (1995)
28 Drumalig Road, Carryduff, Belfast, BT8 8EQ
☎ (028) 9081 2279
🖨 (028) 9081 5851
🖂 d.patterson@btconnect.com
🛒 800
🏌 D Patterson (Mgr)
🏴 18 L 6373 yds Par 72 SSS 71
👥 U
££ £25 (£30)
🚗 8 miles S of Belfast (A24)
🖥 www.rockmountgolfclub.co.uk

Royal Belfast   (1881)
Holywood, Craigavad, BT18 0BP
☎ (028) 9042 8165
🖨 (028) 9042 1404
🖂 royalbelfast@btconnect.com
🛒 1200
🏌 Mrs SH Morrison
✓ A Ferguson (028) 9042 8586
🏴 18 L 6184 yds SSS 70
👥 1 Sat–NA before 4.30pm
££ £60 (£70)
🚗 E of Belfast on A2
🏠 HC Colt
🖥 www.royalbelfast.com

Royal County Down   (1889)
Newcastle, BT33 0AN
☎ (028) 4372 3314
🖨 (028) 4372 6281
🖂 golf@royalcountydown.org
🛒 450
🏌 JH Laidler
✓ KJ Whitson (028) 4372 2419
🏴 Ch'ship 18 L 7181 yds SSS 74
Annesley 18 L 4708 yds SSS 65
👥 See Web site
££ Ch'ship–£155 (£175) Annesley–£35 (£40)
🚗 30 miles S of Belfast
🏠 Tom Morris and others
🖥 www.royalcountydown.org

Scrabo   (1907)
233 Scrabo Road, Newtownards, BT23 4SL
☎ (028) 9181 2355
🖨 (028) 9182 2919
🖂 admin.scrabogc@btconnect.com
🛒 600
🏴 18 L 5699 m SSS 71
👥 WD–U WE–11am Sun SOC
££ £19 (£24)
🚗 2 miles W of Newtownards, by Scrabo Tower
⊕ 6-hole pitch & putt course
🖥 www.scrabo-golf-club.org

The Spa   (1907)
Grove Road, Ballynahinch, BT24 8BR
☎ (028) 9756 2365
🖨 (028) 9756 4158
🖂 spagolfclub@btconnect.com

☐ 920
✍ TG Magee
▷ 18 L 6003 m SSS 72
👥 U exc Wed–NA after 3pm Sat–NA
££ £18 (£23)
🚗 1 mile S of Ballynahinch. 15 miles S of Belfast

Temple   (1994)
60 Church Road, Boardmills, Lisburn, BT27 6UP
☎ **(028) 9263 9213**
☐ (028) 9263 8637
✉ info@templegolf.com
☐ 210
✍ B McConnell (Mgr)
▷ 9 L 5495 yds Par 68 SSS 68 (18 different Tees)
👥 WE after 4 pm SOC (sat) Sun – ring for bookings
££ £13 (£20) 9 hole £11 (£15)
🚗 5 miles S of Belfast on A24 Newcastle road
⊕ Award winning Restaurant
🏠 Frank Ainsworth
🖥 www.templegolf.com

Warrenpoint   (1893)
Lower Dromore Rd, Warrenpoint, BT34 3LN
☎ **(028) 4175 2219 (Clubhouse)**
☐ (028) 4175 2918
✉ office@warrenpointgolf.com
☐ 1575
✍ M Trainor (028) 4175 3695
✓ N Shaw (028) 4175 2371
▷ 18 L 5628 m SSS 70
👥 U SOC
££ £34 (£40)
🚗 5 miles S of Newry
🏠 Tom Craddock
🖥 www.warrenpointgolf.com

Co Dublin

Balbriggan   (1945)
Blackhall, Balbriggan
☎ **(01) 841 2229**
☐ (01) 841 3927
✉ balbriggangolfclub@eircom.net
☐ 600
✍ Peter Slevin (Hon Sec)
✓ Nigel Howley
▷ 18 L 5881 m SSS 71
👥 WD–U WE–M SOC
££ Mon–Tue €35, Wed–Fri €40 (€50) Earlybirds before 9 Mon–Wed & Thur–Fri €20
🚗 1 mile S of Balbriggan on N1. 18 miles N of Dublin
🏠 Eddie Connaughton
🖥 www.balbriggangolfclub.com

Balcarrick   (1972)
Corballis, Donabate
☎ **(01) 843 6957**

Beaverstown   (1985)
Beaverstown, Donabate
☎ **(01) 843 6439/6721**
☐ (01) 843 5059

✉ manager@beaverstown.com
☐ 921
✍ Stephen Ennis (Sec Mgr)
✓ Ed Martin PGA (01) 843 4655
▷ 18 L 5972 m Par 72 SSS 72
👥 WD–U WE–phone first SOC
££ €50 (€60)
🚗 4 miles N of Dublin Airport
⊕ Chipping and putting practice area; pro shop
🏠 Hackett/McEvoy
🖥 www.beaverstown.com

Beech Park   (1983)
Johnstown, Rathcoole
☎ **(01) 458 0522**
☐ (01) 458 8365
✉ info@beechpark.ie
☐ 1040
✍ E Burke (Hon), K M Young (Mgr)
✓ Zak Rouiller
▷ 18 L 5762 m SSS 72
👥 WD–U exc Tues/Wed–M WE–M BH–NA
££ €45
🚗 Rathcoole is on N7; club is 2 miles on Kilteel road from Rathcoole Vil
🏠 Eddie Hackett
🖥 www.beechpark.ie

Coldwinters   (1994)
Newtown House, St Margaret's
☎ **(01) 864 0324**

Corrstown   (1993)
Corrstown, Killsallaghan
☎ **(01) 864 0533**
☐ (01) 864 0537
✉ info@corrstowngolfclub.com
☐ 1050
✍ M Jeanes
✓ P Gittens (01) 864 3322
▷ River 18 L 6077 m Par 72 SSS 71 Orchard 9 L 2792 m Par 35 SSS 69
👥 Booking necessary
££ €50 (€60)
⊕ Dublin Airport 6 miles
⊕ Driving range
🏠 E Connaughton
🖥 www.corrstowngolfclub.com

Donabate   (1925)
Balcarrick, Donabate
☎ **(01) 843 6346**
☐ (01) 843 4488
✉ info@donabategolfclub.com
☐ 913
✍ Betty O'Connor (01) 843 6346 Brian May (01) 843 6346 (Golf Administrator)
✓ H Jackson
▷ 18 L 6670 yds SSS 73 9 L 3200 yds Par 36
👥 U (booking system)
££ €50 (€65); €30 (€40) before 10
🚗 6 miles N of Dublin Airport on N1
⊕ Practice range, putting green, buggy hire
🖥 www.donabategolfclub.com

Dublin Mountain   (1993)
Gortlum, Brittas
☎ **(01) 458 2622**

☐ (01) 458 2048
✉ dmgc.ie
☐ 430
✍ F Carolan
▷ 18 L 5433 m Par 71
👥 U
££ €18 (€25)
🚗 SW of Dublin
🖥 www.dublinmountaingolf.com

Dun Laoghaire   (1910)
Eglinton Park, Tivoli Road, Dun Laoghaire
☎ **(01) 280 3916**

Forrest Little   (1940)
Forrest Little, Cloghran, Swords
☎ **(01) 840 1763**
☐ (01) 840 1000
✉ margaret@forrestlittle.ie
☐ 1000
✍ Margaret Moynihan
✓ T Judd (01) 840 7670
▷ 18 L 5900 m Par 71 SSS 72
👥 WD–U WE–NA SOC
££ €50
🚗 Approx. ½ mile from Dublin Airport
⊕ Practice ground; chipping green; putting greens
🏠 F Hawtree/E Connaughton
🖥 www.forrestlittle.ie

Glencullen
Glencullen, Co Dublin
☎ **(01) 295 2895**

Hermitage   (1905)
Lucan
☎ **(01) 626 5396**
☐ (01) 623 8881
✉ hermitagegolf@eircom.net
☐ 1153
✍ Eddie Farrell
✓ S Byrne (01) 626 8072
▷ 18 L 6060 m SSS 72
👥 U SOC–WD
££ €75 (€85)
🚗 Lucan 2 miles. 8 miles W of Dublin
🏠 James McKenna
🖥 www.hermitagegolf.ie

Hibernian   (1994)
City West Hotel, Saggert
☎ **(01) 851 0565**

Hollywood Lakes   (1992)
Ballyboughal, Co Dublin
☎ **(01) 843 3406/7**
✉ hollywoodlakesgc@eircom.net

The Island   (1890)
Corballis, Donabate, Co Dublin
☎ **+353 1843 6205**
☐ +353 1843 6860
✉ reservations@theislandgolfclub.com
☐ 1000
✍ P McDunphy (01) 843 6205
✓ K Kelliher (01) 843 5005
▷ 18 L 6236 m SSS 73
👥 WD/WE–some restrictions, please enquire
££ €125

⊷ 14 miles N of Dublin. 15 min from
airport off M1 motorway
⊕ Practice ground
⌂ Hawtree
▤ www.theislandgolfclub.com

Killiney   (1903)
Ballinclea Road, Killiney
☎ **(01) 285 2823**
🖳 (01) 285 2861
✉ killineygolfclub@eircom.net
▦ 520
🏌 MF Walsh
✓ Lee Owens (01) 285 6294
➴ 9 L 6220 yds SSS 70
👥 WD
££ €50
⊷ 8 miles S of Dublin
⌂ E Connaughton
▤ www.killineygolfclub@eircom.net

Kilternan   (1987)
Kilternan
☎ **(01) 295 5559**
🖳 (01) 295 5670
✉ kgc@kilternan-hotel.ie
⊕ Closed until further notice due to
redevelopment

Lucan   (1897)
Celbridge Road, Lucan
☎ **(01) 628 2106**
🖳 (01) 628 2929
✉ lucangolf@eircom.net
▦ 840
🏌 Eddie Meehan (Sec/Mgr) (01) 628
2106
➴ 18 L 5979 m Par 71 SSS 71
👥 WD–U WE/BH–M SOC–WD exc
Wed/Thurs
££ €45
⊷ 14 miles W of Dublin, nr Lucan on
N4
⌂ Eddie Hackett
▤ www.lucangolfclub.ie

Luttrellstown Castle G&CC
(1993)
Castleknock, Dublin 15
☎ **(353) 1 808 9988**
✉ golf@luttrellstown.ie

Malahide   (1892)
Beechwood, The Grange, Malahide
☎ **(01) 846 1611**
✉ malgc@clubi.ie

Milltown   (1907)
Lower Churchtown Road, Milltown,
Dublin 14
☎ **(01) 497 6090**
🖳 (01) 497 6008
✉ info@milltowngolfclub.ie
▦ 1432
🏌 E Lawless (Gen Mgr)
✓ J Harnett (01) 497 7072
➴ 18 L 5638 m Par 71 SSS 70
👥 WD–U exc Tues & Wed pm
Fri/WE–M BH–NA SOC–Mon &
Thurs before 3.45pm
££ €85
⊷ 4 miles S of Dublin centre

⌂ Freddie Davis
▤ www.milltowngolfclub.ie

Portmarnock   (1894)
Portmarnock
☎ **(01) 846 2968 (Clubhouse)**
🖳 (01) 846 2601
▦ 971
🏌 JJ Quigley (01) 846 2968
(Gen Mgr)
✓ J Purcell (01) 846 2634
➴ 27 holes: 6997-7400 yds SSS 72-74
👥 I WE–XL
££ €180 (€215)
⊷ 8 miles NE of Dublin Off M50
North
▤ www.portmarnockgolfclub.ie

Portmarnock Hotel & Golf Links   (1995)
Proprietary
Strand Road, Portmarnock
☎ **(01) 846 1800**
🖳 (01) 846 1077
✉ golfres@portmarnock.com
🏌 Moira Cassidy (Golf Dir) (01) 846
1800
➴ 18 L 6342 m Par 71 SSS 73
👥 U H
££ €140
⊷ 8 miles NE of Dublin. Airport 15
mins
⌂ Bernhard Langer
▤ www.portmarnock.com

Rush   (1943)
Rush
☎ **(01) 843 8177**
🖳 (01) 843 8177
✉ info@rushgolfclub.com
▦ 450
🏌 Noeline Quirke (Sec/Mgr)
➴ 9 L 5639 m Par 69 SSS 68
👥 WD–U WE–M
££ €35
⊷ 16 miles N of Dublin, off N1
▤ www.rushgolfclub.com

Silloge Park   (1994)
Ballymun Road, Swords, Co Dublin
☎ **(01) 862 0464**
🖳 (01) 842 9956
✉ peteroconnorgolf@gmail.com
▦ 400
🏌 Leo Lennon Maher
✓ P O'Connor
➴ 18 L 5924 m Par 71
👥 U
££ €18 (€25)
⊷ Swords, N of Dublin
⊕ Practice ground
⌂ Gerry Barry & Eoin Ward
▤ www.christyoconnor.com

Skerries   (1905)
Hacketstown, Skerries
☎ **(01) 849 1567 (Clubhouse)**
🖳 (01) 849 1591
✉ skerriesgolfclub@eircom.net
▦ 1060
🏌 B Meehan (01) 849 1567
✓ J Kinsella (01) 849 0925

➴ 18 L 6107 m Par 73 SSS 72
👥 U SOC
££ €50 (€60)
⊷ 20 miles N of Dublin
▤ www.skerriesgolfclub.ie

Slade Valley   (1970)
Lynch Park, Brittas
☎ **(01) 458 2183**
🖳 (01) 458 2784
✉ info@sladevalleygolfclub.ie
▦ 900
🏌 D Clancy
✓ J Dignam
➴ 18 L 5468 m SSS 68
👥 WD–U am WE–M
££ €30 (€40)
⊷ 8 miles W of Dublin, off N4
⌂ Sullivan/O'Brien
▤ www.sladevalleygolfclub.ie

The South County   (1998)
Lisheen Road, Brittas, Co Dublin
☎ **(01) 458 2965**
🖳 (01) 458 2842
✉ info@southcountygolf.ie
▦ 500
🏌 Marie Branagan
✓ Raymond Burns (01) 458 3300
➴ 18 L 7013 yds Par 72
👥 U SOC
££ €50 (€60)
⊷ SW of Dublin (N81) 20 km from
City Centre
⊕ Practice area; covered bays;
pitching area; practice putting
green; Bar, Restaurant.
⌂ Dr N Bielenberg
▤ www.southcountygolf.com

St Margaret's G&CC   (1992)
St Margaret's, Dublin
☎ **(01) 864 0400**
🖳 (01) 864 0289
✉ reservations@stmargaretsgolf.com
▦ 260
🏌 Ronan Walsh (Gen Mgr)
✓ Gary Kearney
➴ 18 L 6900 yds Par 73 SSS 74
👥 U SOC
££ €50–€60 (€80)
⊷ 3 miles NW of Dublin Airport,
between N1/N2
⊕ Driving range; Putting Green;
Shortgame practice; Golf Academy,
Lessons
⌂ Craddock/Ruddy
▤ www.stmargaretsgolf.com

Swords   (1996)
Balheary Avenue, Swords
☎ **(01) 840 9819/890 1030**
🖳 (01) 840 9819
✉ info@swordsopengolfcourse.com
▦ 505
🏌 O McGuinness (Mgr)
➴ 18 L 5631 m Par 71 SSS 69
👥 U
££ €20 (€25)
⊷ 10 miles N of Dublin, nr Airport
⊕ Putting green
⌂ T Halpin
▤ www.swordsopengolfcourse.com

Turvey (1994)
Turvey Avenue, Donabate
- ☎ **(01) 843 5169**
- 📠 (01) 843 5179
- ✉ turveygc@eircom.net
- 🏠 335
- ♟ Sean McNelis
- ✓ Domnic Carty
- ⏐ 18 L 5825 m Par 71 SSS 71
- ♟ U WE–NA before noon
- ££ €35 (€40)
- ⛳ Donabate off M1 near airport
- ⊕ Practice area; putting green
- 🏠 Paddy McGuirk
- 🖥 www.turveygolfclub.com

Westmanstown (1988)
Clonsilla, Dublin 15
- ☎ **(01) 820 5817**
- ✉ info@westmanstowngolfclub.ie

Woodbrook (1926)
Dublin Road, Bray
- ☎ **(01) 282 4799**
- 📠 (01) 282 1950
- ✉ golf@woodbrook.ie
- 🏠 1100
- ♟ PF Byrne (Gen Mgr) (01) 282 4799
- ⏐ 18 L 6221 m SSS 72
- ♟ WD–U WE–phone Sec SOC
- ££ €95 (€100)
- ⛳ 11 miles SE of Dublin on N11
- 🏠 P McEvoy
- 🖥 www.woodbrook.ie

Dublin City

Carrickmines (1900)
Golf Lane, Carrickmines, Dublin 18
- ☎ **(01) 295 5972**
- 📠 (01) 214 9674
- 🏠 650
- ♟ CR Bailey (Hon)
- ⏐ 9 L 6063 yds Par 71 SSS 69
  Alternate tees make 18 holes
- ♟ U exc Wed/Sat–NA
- ££ 9: €20 Mon–Sat (€25 Sun) 18: €35 Mon–Sat (€40 Sun)
- ⛳ 6 miles S of Dublin

Castle (1913)
Woodside Drive, Rathfarnham, Dublin 14
- ☎ **(01) 490 4207**
- 📠 (01) 492 0264
- ✉ info@castlegc.ie
- 🏠 1400
- ♟ John McCormack (Gen Mgr)
- ✓ D Kinsella (01) 492 0272
- ⏐ 18 L 6270 yds SSS 71
- ♟ Mon/Thurs/Fri–U Wed–U before 12.30pm WE/BH–M SOC
- ££ €85
- ⛳ 5 miles S of Dublin
- 🏠 Harry Colt
- 🖥 www.castlegc.ie

Clontarf (1912)
Donnycarney House, Malahide Road, Dublin 3
- ☎ **(01) 833 1892**

- 📠 (01) 833 1933
- ✉ info.cgc@indigo.ie
- 🏠 1066
- ♟ A Cahill (Mgr)
- ✓ E Brady (01) 833 1877
- ⏐ 18 L 5317 m SSS 68
- ♟ U SOC
- ££ €50 (€60)
- ⛳ 2 miles NE of Dublin city centre
- 🏠 HS Colt
- 🖥 www.clontarfgolfclub.ie

Deer Park (1974)
Deer Park Hotel, Howth
- ☎ **(01) 832 6039**

Edmondstown (1944)
Rathfarnham, Dublin 16
- ☎ **(01) 493 2461**
- 📠 (01) 493 3152
- ✉ info@edmondstowngolfclub.ie
- 🏠 700
- ♟ SS Davies (01) 493 1082
- ✓ G McShea (01) 494 1049
- ⏐ 18 L 6011 m Par 71 SSS 73
- ♟ WD/BH–U SOC
- ££ €55 (€65)
- ⛳ 5 miles S of Dublin. M50 Jct 12
- 🏠 McEvoy/Cooke
- 🖥 www.edmondstowngolfclub.ie

Elm Park (1927)
Nutley House, Donnybrook, Dublin 4
- ☎ **(01) 269 3438/269 3014**
- 📠 (01) 269 4505
- ✉ office@elmparkgolfclub.ie
- 🏠 1750
- ♟ A McCormack (01) 269 3438
- ✓ S Green (01) 269 2650
- ⏐ 18 L 5374 m SSS 69
- ♟ U–phone Pro
- ££ €70 (€90)
- ⛳ 3 miles S of Dublin
- 🖥 www.elmparkgolfclub.ie

Grange (1910)
Whitechurch Road, Rathfarnham, Dublin 14
- ☎ **(01) 493 2889**
- 📠 (01) 493 9490
- 🏠 1200
- ♟ Angus Murray (Sec/Mgr)
- ✓ Declan Leigh
- ⏐ 18 L 5396 m Par 68 SSS 69
- ♟ WD–U exc Tues/Wed pm–NA WE–M SOC
- ££ €80
- ⛳ Rathfarnham, 5 miles from centre of Dublin
- 🏠 James Braid

Hazel Grove (1988)
Mount Seskin Road, Jobstown, Dublin 24
- ☎ **(01) 452 0911**

Howth (1916)
Carrickbrack Road, Sutton, Dublin 13
- ☎ **(01) 832 3055**
- 📠 (01) 832 1793
- ✉ gm@howthgolf.ie
- 🏠 1200
- ♟ Darragh Tighe MPGA (01) 832 3055

- ✓ John McGuirk (01) 839 3895
- ⏐ 18 L 5672 m SSS 69
- ♟ WD–U exc Wed & Thur WE after 4pm SOC Mon, Tue, Fri SOC by prior arrangement WE–booking essential
- ££ €50 (+BH €65) Soc rates beg; corporate days
- ⛳ 9 miles NE of Dublin, nr Sutton Cross; 20 min from Dublin Airport
- ⊕ Practice putting green; driving range; chipping green; buggy and club hire
- 🏠 James Braid
- 🖥 www.howthgolfclub.ie

Kilmashogue (1994)
St Columba's College, Whitechurch, Dublin 16
- ☎ **(087) 274 9844**

Newlands (1926)
Newlands Cross, Dublin 22
- ☎ **(01) 459 3157**
- 📠 (01) 459 3498
- ✉ info@newlandsgolf.com
- 🏠 1086
- ♟ Amber Dungan (Golf Operations) (01) 459 3157
- ✓ K O'Donnell (01) 459 3538
- ⏐ 18 L 5947 m SSS 71
- ♟ WD–U am WE/BH–NA SOC
- ££ €75 – discounts may apply
- ⛳ 6 miles SW of Dublin at Newlands Cross (N7)
- 🏠 James Braid
- 🖥 www.newlandsgolf.com

Rathfarnham (1899)
Newtown, Dublin 16
- ☎ **(01) 493 1201/493 1561**
- 📠 (01) 493 1561
- ✉ rgc@oceanfree.net
- 🏠 570
- ♟ C McInerney (01) 493 1201
- ✓ B O'Hara
- ⏐ 14 L 5529 m SSS 70
- ♟ U exc Tues & Sat–NA SOC–WD exc Tue/Wed
- ££ €40
- ⛳ 6 miles S of Dublin off M50 (Firhouse exit)
- 🏠 John Jacobs and Jeff Howes
- 🖥 www.rathfarnhamgolfclub.ie

Royal Dublin (1885)
North Bull Island Nature Reserve, Dollymount, Dublin 3
- ☎ **(01) 833 6346/1262**
- 📠 (01) 833 6504
- ✉ info@theroyaldublingolfclub.com
- 🏠 1250
- ♟ Paul Muldowney (01) 833 6346
- ✓ Leonard Owens (01) 833 6477 (Senior Pro Christy O'Connor Snr)
- ⏐ 18 L 7269 yds Par 72 SSS 76
- ♟ U H exc Wed Sat. Sun 10–12 and after 2pm SOC M, Tu, Th & Fri.
- ££ €170
- ⛳ 3 miles NE of Dublin, on coast road to Howth on Bull Island
- ⊕ Practice range
- 🏠 HS Colt and Martin Hawtree
- 🖥 www.theroyaldublingolfclub.com

St Anne's (1921)
North Bull Nature Reserve, Dollymount, Dublin 5
☎ **(01) 833 6471**
📠 (01) 833 4618
✉ info@stanneslinksgolf.com
📖 850
🏌 Ted Power
🏳 18 L 6443 m Par 71 SSS 72
👥 WE/BH–NA SOC WD available, Sat am
££ €80 (€95)
⛳ Dublin 5 miles. M50, 5 miles
🏠 Eddie Hackett
📧 www.stanneslinksgolf.com

Stackstown (1975)
Kellystown Road, Rathfarnham, Dublin 16
☎ **(01) 494 1993**
📠 (01) 493 3934
✉ stackstowngc@eircom.net
📖 1300
🏌 Larry Clarke (Gen Mgr) (01) 494 1993
✓ M Kavanagh (01) 494 4561
🏳 18 L 6494 m SSS 70
👥 WD Mon/Thur/Fri; WE Sun 12–2.00
££ €30 (€40)
⛳ 7 miles SE of Dublin. M50 junction 13, 2 miles
📧 www.stackstowngolfclub.com

Sutton (1890)
Cush Point, Sutton, Dublin 13
☎ **(01) 832 3013**
📠 (01) 832 1603
✉ info@suttongolfclub.org
📖 625
🏌 E O'Brien (Hon Sec)
✓ C Russell (01) 832 1703
🏳 9 L 5624 m Par 70 SSS 67
👥 Tues–NA Sat–NA before 5.30pm
££ €50
⛳ 7 miles E of Dublin, 15 min Dublin Airport
📧 www.suttongolfclub.org

Co Fermanagh

Castle Hume (1991)
Belleek Road, Enniskillen, BT93 7ED
☎ **(028) 6632 7077**
📠 (028) 6632 7076
✉ info@castlehumegolf.com
📖 270
🏌 Gloria Rogers (Admin)
✓ S Donnelly (028) 6632 7077
🏳 18 L 5932 m Par 72 SSS 71
Additional 18-hole championship course under construction
👥 U
££ £25 (+BH £35) Special rates for groups and societies
⛳ A46 Belleek/Donegal road
⊕ 5-bay driving range, covered and floodlit; putting/pitching green
🏠 Tony Carroll
📧 www.castlehumegolf.com

Enniskillen (1896)
Castlecoole, Enniskillen, BT74 6HZ
☎ **(028) 6632 5250**
✉ enquiries@enniskillengolfclub.com

Co Galway

Ardacong
Milltown Road, Tuam, Co Galway
☎ **(093) 25525**

Athenry (1902)
Palmerstown, Oranmore
☎ **(091) 794466**
📠 (091) 794971
✉ athenrygc@eircom.net
📖 1200
🏌 P Flattery (Gen Mgr) (086) 825 4454
✓ R Ryan (091) 790599
🏳 18 L 6300 yds Par 70 SSS 70
👥 WD/Sat–U Sun–NA SOC
££ D–€40 (D–€50)
⛳ 10 miles E of Galway on Athenry road (R348), off N6
⊕ Driving range; tuition
🏠 Eddie Hackett
📧 www.athenrygolfclub.net

Ballinasloe (1894)
Rosgloss, Ballinasloe
☎ **(0905) 42126**

Bearna (1996)
Corboley, Bearna
☎ **(091) 592677**
📠 (091) 592674
✉ info@bearnagolfclub.com
📖 500
🏌 Pat Donnellan
✓ Declan Cunningham
🏳 18 L 5746 m Par 72 SSS 72
👥 U
££ Mon–Fri + Sun €40 (€40) Sat €50
⛳ Approx 5 miles W of Galway City
⊕ Practice putting green; driving range under construction
🏠 RJ Browne
📧 www.bearnagolfclub.com

Connemara (1973)
Public
Ballyconneely, Clifden
☎ **(095) 23502/23602**
📠 (095) 23662
✉ info@connemaragolflinks.net
📖 900
🏌 R Flaherty (Sec/Mgr)
✓ H O'Neill (095) 23502
🏳 27 L 6560 m SSS 72
👥 U H SOC
££ €75
⛳ 8 miles SW of Clifden
⊕ Practice area; buggy hire; club rental
🏠 Eddie Hackett
📧 www.connemaragolflinks.com

Connemara Isles
Annaghvane, Lettermore, Connemara
☎ **(091) 572498**

Curra West (1996)
Curra, Kylebrack, Loughrea
☎ **(091) 45121**

Galway (1895)
Blackrock, Salthill, Galway
☎ **(091) 522033**
📠 (091) 529783
✉ galwaygolf@eircom.net
📖 1350
🏌 P Fahy
✓ D Wallace (091) 523038
🏳 18 L 5828 m SSS 70
👥 Restricted Tues & Sun
££ €50 (€60)
⛳ 3 miles W of Galway City
🏠 Dr Alister MacKenzie
📧 www.galwaygolf.com

Galway Bay Golf Resort (1993)
Renville, Oranmore
☎ **+353 (91) 790711/2**

Glenlo Abbey
Glenlo Abbey Hotel, Bushy Park, Galway
☎ **(091) 519698**

Gort (1924)
Castlequarter, Gort
☎ **(091) 632244**
📠 (091) 632387
✉ info@gortgolf.com
📖 997
🏌 J Skehill (Hon) (091) 631789
🏳 18 L 5974 m Par 71
👥 U exc Sun am SOC Saturday
££ €30 (€35)
⛳ 20 miles S of Galway
🏠 C O'Connor Jr
📧 www.gortgolf.com

Loughrea (1924)
Graigue, Loughrea
☎ **(091) 841049**
✉ loughreagolfclub@eircom.net

Mountbellew (1929)
Shankill, Mountbellew, Ballinasloe
☎ **(090) 967 9259**
📠 (090) 967 9973
📖 380
🏌 John Gilmore (090) 967 9202
🏳 9 L 5214 m Par 69
👥 U SOC
££ D–€20
⛳ 50km NE of Galway on N63

Oughterard (1973)
Gortreevagh, Oughterard
☎ **(091) 552131**
📠 (091) 552733
✉ oughterardgc@eircom.net
📖 1000
🏌 Michael Heaney
✓ M Ryan (Ext 201)
🏳 18 L 6752 yds SSS 69

U SOC
£€ €35
ᗏ 15 miles NW of Galway on N59
ᐱ Harris/Merrigan
▤ www.oughterardgolf.com

Portumna   (1913)
Ennis Road, Portumna
☎ **(090) 97 41059**
▯ (090) 97 41798
✉ portumnagc@eircom.net
▦ 1100
⚐ J Harte (Hon)
✓ R Clarke
▷ 18 L 6100 m Par 72 SSS 72
👥 U WD WE except Sat/Sun pm
SOC
£€ €30 (€35 subject to availability)
ᗏ 40 miles SE of Galway on Lough
Derg
⊕ Practice area
ᐱ E Connaughton
▤ www.portumnagolfclub.ie

Tuam   (1904)
Barnacurragh, Tuam
☎ **(093) 28993**
✉ tuamgolfclub@eircom.net

Co Kerry

Ardfert   (1993)
Sackville, Ardfert, Tralee
☎ **(066) 713 4744**

Ballybeggan Park
Ballybeggan, Tralee, Co Kerry
☎ **(066) 712 6188**

Ballybunion   (1893)
Sandhill Road, Ballybunion
☎ **(068) 27146**
▯ (068) 27387
▦ 648
⚐ J McKenna (Sec/Mgr)
✓ B O'Callaghan
▷ Old 18 L 6542 yds SSS 72
Cashen 18 L 6477 yds SSS 70
👥 U am SOC WE–NA H
£€ Old: €165 Ashen: €110 Both same
day: €240
ᗏ 2 miles S of Ballybunion. 50 miles
W of Limerick, via Tarbert
⊕ Driving range; practice facility
ᐱ Simpson

Ballyheigue Castle   (1995)
Ballyheigue, Tralee
☎ **(066) 713 3555**

Beaufort   (1994)
Churchtown, Beaufort, Killarney
☎ **(064) 44440**
▯ (064) 44752
✉ beaufortgc@eircom.net
▦ 350
⚐ C Kelly
✓ Keith Coveney
▷ 18 L 6605 yds Par 71 SSS 72
👥 WD–H SOC WE

£€ €50 (€60)
ᗏ 7 miles W of Killarney, off N72
ᐱ Dr Arthur Spring
▤ www.beaufortgolfclub.com

Castlegregory   (1989)
Stradbally, Castlegregory
☎ **(066) 713 9444**
▯ (066) 713 9958
▦ 400
⚐ M Lynch (Hon Sec)
▷ 9 L 5340 m SSS 68
👥 U SOC
£€ €30
ᗏ 18 miles W of Tralee
ᐱ Arthur Spring

Ceann Sibeal   (1924)
Ballyferriter
☎ **(066) 915 6255/6408**
▯ (066) 915 6409
✉ dinglegc@iol.ie
▦ 460
⚐ S Fahy (Mgr)
▷ 18 L 6690 yds SSS 71
👥 U SOC
£€ €60 – €80
ᗏ Dingle Peninsula, W of Tralee
ᐱ Hackett/O'Connor Jr
▤ www.dinglelinks.com

Dooks   (1889)
Glenbeigh
☎ **(066) 976 8205**
▯ (066) 976 8476
✉ office@dooks.com
▦ 1300
⚐ Brian Hurley
▷ 18 L 6000 m Par 71 SSS 71
👥 WD–U H before 5pm
WE/BH–phone first SOC
£€ €85
ᗏ 3 miles N of Glenbeigh, on Ring of
Kerry (N70)
ᐱ M Hawtree
▤ www.dooks.com

Kenmare   (1903)
Kenmare
☎ **(064) 41291**
▯ (064) 42061
✉ info@kenmaregolfclub.com
▦ 600
⚐ John Richardson
▷ 18 L 5441 m SSS 69
👥 U SOC
£€ €50 (€55)
ᗏ 20 miles S of Killarney on Cork
road
ᐱ Eddie Hackett
▤ www.kenmaregolfclub.com

Kerries   (1995)
Tralee
☎ **(066) 712 2112**

Killarney   (1893)
Mahoney's Point, Killarney
☎ **(064) 31034**
▯ (064) 33065
✉ reservations@killarney-golf.com
▦ 1500

⚐ Maurice O'Meara (Gen Mgr)
✓ David Keating (064) 31615
▷ Mahoney's Point 18 L 6164 m
SSS 72
Killeen 18 L 6475 m SSS 73
Lackabane 18 L 6410 m SSS 73
👥 H SOC
£€ On application
ᗏ 3 miles W of Killarney (N72)
⊕ Driving range
ᐱ Mahoney's Point-Longhurst/
Campbell; Killeen-Hackett/
O'Sullivan; Lackabane-Donald Steel
▤ www.killarney-golf.com

Killorglin   (1992)
Stealroe, Killorglin
☎ **(669) 761 979**
▯ (669) 761 437
✉ kilgolf@iol.ie
▦ 450
⚐ B Dodd
▷ 18 L 6464 yds SSS 72
👥 U SOC
£€ €35
ᗏ 1 mile from Killorglin on Tralee
road (N70). 12 miles W of
Killarney;
ᐱ Eddie Hackett
▤ www.killorglingolf.ie

Parknasilla   (1974)
Parknasilla, Sneem
☎ **(064) 45195**
✉ parknasillagolfclub@eircom.net

Ring of Kerry G&CC   (1998)
Proprietary
Templenoe, Kenmare
☎ **(064) 42000**
▯ (064) 42533
✉ james@ringofkerrygolf.com
▦ 300
⚐ James Mitchell (Gen Mgr)
✓ Adrian Whitehead
▷ 18 L 6820 yds Par 72 SSS 73
👥 U H SOC
£€ €60 (€40 after 2pm)
ᗏ 4 miles W of Kenmare on N70
⊕ Driving range; putting green;
buggies; club rental; teaching pro
ᐱ Eddie Hackett
▤ www.ringofkerrygolf.com

Tralee   (1896)
West Barrow, Ardfert
☎ **(066) 713 6379**
✉ info@traleegolfclub.com

Waterville   (1889)
Waterville Golf Links, Ring of
Kerry, Waterville
☎ **+353-66-947 4102**
▯ +353-66-947 4482
✉ wvgolf@iol.ie
▦ 466
⚐ Noel Cronin (Sec/Mgr)
✓ Liam Higgins
▷ 18 L 7341 yds Par 72 SSS 74
👥 U H SOC
£€ €180 (€190) Mon–Thur before
8am and after 4pm €115 (exl BH)
ᗏ 55 miles from Kilarney and Tralee,
half-way around the Ring of Kerry

⊕ Practice range
⋔ Hackett/Mulcahy/Fazio
▤ www.watervillegolflinks.ie

Co Kildare

Athy   (1906)
Geraldine, Athy
☎ (059) 863 1729
🖷 (059) 863 4710
▧ info@athygolfclub.com
▥ 848
🏌 Ger Ennis (Hon)
↳ 18 L 6475 yds Par 72 SSS 71
👥 W–U (Mon, Tue, Wed, Fri), Thur
    (Ladies Day) 11.30–1pm only)
    Sat–M SOC
££ €30 (€40)
🚗 1 mile N of Athy on Kildare road
⋔ Geoff Howes
▤ www.athygolfclub.com

Bodenstown   (1972)
Bodenstown, Sallins
☎ (045) 897096
🖷 (045) 898126
▧ bodenstown@eircom.net
▥ 650
🏌 Tom Keightley (0872 264133)
↳ Bodenstown 18 L 6134 m SSS 72
    Ladyhill 18 L 5618 m SSS 71
👥 U exc WE–NA (Old course)
££ Bodenstown €20 (7 days) Ladyhill
    €18 (7 days)
🚗 4 miles N of Naas on Clane road.
    18 miles W of Dublin, off N7
⋔ Eddie Hackett
▤ www.bodenstown.com

Carton House   (2002)
Carton House, Maynooth, Co Kildare
☎ +353 (0)1 505 2000
🖷 +353 (0)1 628 6555
▧ reservations@cartonhouse.com
▥ 730
🏌 John Lawler (Ops Mgr)
✎ Francis Howley
↳ O'Meara: 18 L 7006 yds Par 72
    Montgomerie: 18 L 7300 yds par 72
👥 SOC/U
££ €75–€115 (€135)
🚗 14 miles W of Dublin (N4)
⊕ Driving range; putting green; tuition
    with Pro
⋔ Mark O'Meara/Colin Montgomerie
▤ www.cartonhouse.com

Castlewarden G&CC   (1989)
Straffan
☎ (01) 458 9254
🖷 (01) 458 8972
▧ info@castlewardengolfclub.com
▥ 565 225(L)
🏌 Emer OBradford Flynn (Hon)
✎ B O'Brien
↳ 18 L 6731 yds Par 72 SSS 71
👥 WD–U WE–M SOC
££ €35–€45
🚗 13 miles W of Dublin, off N7, exit 6
⋔ Halpin/Browne
▤ www.castlewardengolfclub.com

Celbridge Elm Hall
Elmhall, Celbridge, Co Kildare
☎ (01) 628 8208

Cill Dara   (1920)
Little Curragh, Kildare Town
☎ (045) 521295

Craddockstown   (1991)
Blessington Road, Naas
☎ (045) 897610
🖷 (045) 896968
▧ enquiries@craddockstown.com
▥ 750
🏌 Pat Meagher
↳ 18 L 6134 m Par 71 SSS 70
👥 U
££ €43 (€53)
🚗 Naas
⋔ Arthur Spring
▤ www.craddockstown.com

The Curragh   (1883)
Curragh
☎ (045) 441238/441714
🖷 (045) 442476
▧ curraghgolf@eircom.net
▥ 500 176(L)
🏌 P Young (045) 441714
✎ G Burke (045) 441896
↳ 18 L 6586 yds Par 72 SSS 71
👥 WD–U exc Tues–phone Sec SOC
    (ex Sun)
££ €35 (€45)
🚗 3 m S of Newbridge via M7 Jct 12
▤ www.curraghgolf-club.com

Highfield   (1992)
Proprietary
Carbury
☎ (046) 973 1021
🖷 (046) 973 1021
▧ highfieldgolf@eircom.net
▥ 550
🏌 Philomena Duggan (Sec/Mgr)
↳ 18 L 5707 m SSS 69
👥 WD–U WE–U after 12 noon
££ €30 (€40)
🚗 32 miles W of Dublin off N4
⊕ Driving range
⋔ Alan Duggan
▤ www.highfield-golf.ie

The K Club   (1991)
Straffan
☎ (01) 601 7300
🖷 (01) 601 7399
▧ golf@kclub.ie
▥ 700
🏌 B Donald (Golf Dir) 01601 7302
✎ Lynn McCool
↳ Palmer: 18 L 7377 yds SSS 74
    Smurfit: 18 L 7277 yds SSS 74
👥 U H SOC–WD–WE
££ Prices on request Peak season
    prices – reduced in off season
🚗 18 miles SW of Dublin (N7)
⊕ Driving range; chipping green;
    putting green
⋔ Arnold Palmer (Palmer & Smurfit)
▤ www.kclub.ie

Kilkea Castle   (1995)
Castledermot
☎ (059) 914 5555
🖷 (059) 914 5505
▧ kilkeagolfclub@eircom.net
▥ 300
🏌 J Kissane (Gen Mgr)
↳ 18 L 6200 m Par 71 SSS 71
👥 U SOC WD+WE
££ €40 Mon–Thur (€50 Fri–Sun)
🚗 7 miles N of Castledermot
    (R418)
⊕ Driving range; putting area
⋔ David Conway
▤ www.kilkeacastlehotelgolf.com

Killeen   (1986)
Killeenbeg, Kill
☎ (045) 866003
🖷 (045) 875881
▧ admin@killeengc.ie
▥ 170
🏌 M Kelly
↳ 18 L 6732 yds Par 72 SSS 72
👥 WD–U WE–NA before 10am
££ €35 (€50)
🚗 2 miles off N7 on Sallins road
⋔ Ruddy/Craddock
▤ www.killeengolf.com

Knockanally   (1985)
Donadea, Naas, North Kildare
☎ (045) 869322
▧ golf@knockanally.com
▥ 500
🏌 Helen Melady
✎ M Darcy (045) 869 671
↳ 18 L 6424 yds SSS 72
👥 U
££ €35 (€50)
🚗 20 miles W of Dublin on Galway
    road (M4), Jct 8
⋔ N Lyons
▤ www.knockanally.com

Naas   (1896)
Kerdiffstown, Naas
☎ (045) 874644
🖷 (045) 896109
▧ info@naasgolfclub.com
▥ 1400
🏌 Denis Mahon (Mgr)
✎ Gavin Lunny
↳ 18 L 6278 yds Par 71 SSS 71
👥 U SOC
££ €40 (€45)
🚗 Exit 8 off N 7 Motorway, 2 miles N
    of Naas
⊕ Privately-owned driving range
    beside course
⋔ Jeff Howes Design
▤ www.naasgolfclub.com

Newbridge   (1997)
Tankardsgarden, Newbridge
☎ (045) 486110
🖷 (045) 446840
▥ 220
🏌 Jamie Stafford (Mgr)
↳ 18 L 5960 m Par 72 SSS 72
👥 U
££ €25 (€30)

🚗 30 mins from Dublin on M7; 20 min Red Cow roundabout
🏠 Pat Suttle

Co Kilkenny

Callan   (1929)
Geraldine, Callan
☎ (056) 7725136/7725949
🖥 (056) 7755155
📧 info@callangolfclub.com
📖 750
🏌 L Duggan (Sec/Mgr) (056) 7755875
⚐ M O'Shea (087) 6240599
🏁 18 L 6422 yds Par 71 SSS 69
👤 U SOC
££ €30 (€35)
🚗 1 mile SE of Callan. 10 miles SW of Kilkenny
🏠 Bryan Moor
🖥 www.callangolfclub.com

Castlecomer   (1935)
Dromgoole, Castlecomer
☎ (056) 4441139
🖥 (056) 4441139
📧 castlecomergolf@eircom.net
📖 700
🏌 M Dooley (Hon)
🏁 18 L 6175 m Par 72 SSS 72
👤 U SOC–WD WE
££ €35 (€40)
🚗 11 miles N of Kilkenny on N7
🏠 Pat Ruddy
🖥 www.castlecomergolfclub.com

Kilkenny   (1896)
Glendine, Kilkenny
☎ (056) 776 5400
🖥 (056) 772 3593
📧 enquiries@kilkennygolfclub.com
📖 1100
🏌 Sean Boland (056) 776 5400
⚐ J Bolger (056) 776 1730
🏁 18 L 6500 yds Par 71 SSS 70
👤 U
££ €35 (€45); special rates available for groups and early birds
🚗 1 mile N of Kilkenny, off N77 Close to Castlecomer Road Roundabout
⊕ Driving range within 1 mile
🖥 www.kilkennygolfclub.com

Mount Juliet   (1991)
Thomastown
☎ (056) 777 3071
🖥 (056) 777 3078
📧 golfinfo@mountjuliet.ie
📖 500
🏌 S O'Neill (Golf Mgr) (056) 777 3063
⚐ S Cotter
🏁 18 L 7264 yds SSS 75
👤 U
££ €125–€185 May/June/July/Sept €100–€150 Apr/Aug/Oct €85–€105 Nov–Mar
🚗 10 miles S of Kilkenny, off Dublin-Waterford road (N9)
⊕ Driving range-residents and green fees; Golf Academy

Co Laois

Abbeyleix   (1895)
Rathmoyle, Abbeyleix
☎ (0502) 31450
🖥 (0502) 130108
📧 info@abbeyleixgolfclub.ie
📖 601
🏌 M Fogarty (Hon Sec)
🏁 18 L 6031 yds Par 72 SSS 70
👤 WD–U WE–NA SOC–WD/WE
££ €20 (€30)
🚗 10 miles S of Portlaoise. 60 miles SW of Dublin on Cork road
⊕ Open singles every Fri during summer
🏠 Mel Flanagan
🖥 www.abbeyleixgolfclub.ie

The Heath   (1930)
The Heath, Portlaoise
☎ (057) 864 6533
🖥 (057) 864 6735
📧 info@theheathgc.ie
📖 830
🏌 Christy Crawford (Hon)
⚐ Mark O'Boyle (057) 864 6622
🏁 18 L 5873 m Par 71 SSS 70
👤 U
££ €20 (€30)
🚗 4 miles E of Portlaoise, M7 Motorway Jct 16, then 1st exit at roundabout
⊕ Floodlit driving range; Putting Green
🖥 www.theheathgc.ie

The Heritage Golf & Spa Resort   (2004)
Proprietary
The Heritage Golf & Spa Resort, Killenard
☎ (057) 864 2321
🖥 (057) 864 2392
📧 info@theheritage.com
📖 200
🏌 Niall Carroll (Golf Ops Mgr)
⚐ Eddie Doyle, head pro (057) 864 5500 Eamonn O'Flanagan - teaching pro (057) 864 5500
🏁 18 L 7319 yds Par 72
👤 H SOC WD WE
££ €135 (€140)
🚗 2 miles off M7, 40 miles S of Dublin
⊕ Driving range; Seve Ballesteros Natural Golf School
🏠 Seve Ballesteros/Jeff Howes
🖥 www.theheritage.com

Mountrath   (1929)
Knockanina, Mountrath
☎ (0502) 32558/32643
🖥 (0502) 56735
📧 mountrathgc@eircom.net
📖 800
🏌 Lar Sculls (057) 862 0375
🏁 18 L 5643 m Par 71 SSS 69
👤 U WD WE after 4pm SOC
££ €20 (€30)

🏠 Jack Nicklaus
🖥 www.mountjuliet.com

🚗 10 miles W of Portlaoise. Mountrath 2 miles; N7/M7
🖥 www.mountrathgolfclub.ie

Portarlington   (1908)
Garryhinch, Portarlington
☎ (057) 862 23115
   Golf (057) 864 2916
🖥 (057) 862 23044
📧 portarlingtongc@eircom.net
📖 646
🏌 Jerry Savage
🏁 18 L 5906 m Par 71 SSS 71
👤 WD–U WE–restricted SOC WD+WE Sat before 1pm
££ €35 (€40)
🚗 Between Portarlington and Mountmellick on L116
⊕ Practice ground; buggy hire
🏠 Eddie Hackett
🖥 www.portarlingtongolf.com

Rathdowney   (1930)
Coulnaboul West, Rathdowney
☎ (0505) 46170
🖥 (0505) 46065
📧 rathdowneygolf@eircom.net
📖 700
🏌 Martin O'Brian (Hon) (0505) 46338
🏁 18 L 5864 m Par 71 SSS 70
👤 U exc Sun–NA Sat–SOC
££ €25
🚗 Half mile S of Rathdowney. 20 miles SW of Portlaoise
🏠 Hackett/Suttle
🖥 www.rathdowneygolfclub.com

Co Leitrim

Ballinamore   (1941)
Creevy, Ballinamore
☎ (078) 964 4346
📖 250
🏌 G Mahon (078) 964 4031, (087) 767 8392
🏁 9 L 5514 m Par 70 SSS 68
👤 U SOC
££ D–€20 (D–€20)
🚗 11 miles N of Ballinamore. 17 miles NE of Carrick-on-Shannon
🏠 Arthur Spring

Co Limerick

Abbeyfeale   (1993)
Dromtrasna, Collins Abbeyfeale
☎ (068) 32033
📧 abbeyfealegolf@eircim.net

Adare Manor   (1900)
Adare
☎ (061) 396204
🖥 (061) 396800
📧 info@adaremanorgolfclub.com
📖 750
🏌 TP Healy
🏁 18 L 5764 yds SSS 69
👤 WD–U (advance booking advised) WE/SOC & Sat if tee times free (check with club)

£€ €40
🚗 10 miles SW of Limerick (N21)
⊕ Club hire
🏠 Sayers/Hackett
🖥 www.adaremanorgolfclub.com

Castletroy   (1937)
Golf Links Road, Castleroy, Co. Limerick
☎ (061) 335753 (club)
🖂 (061) 335373
🖂 golf@castletroygolfclub.ie
🕮 1033
🚺 Patrick Keane (Gen Mgr)
🏴 18: Blue L 6284 m Par 72 SSS 73;
White L 6046 m Par 72 SSS 72;
Red L 5453 Par 74 SSS 75
🚹 WD–U Sat am–U Sat pm/Sun–M
SOC–Mon/Wed/Fri/Sat
£€ €50 (€60)
🚗 Less than 3 miles from Limerick
City off N7 to Dublin
🏠 Eddie Connaughton
🖥 www.castletroygolfclub.ie

Limerick   (1891)
Ballyclough, Limerick
☎ (061) 414083
🖂 (061) 319219
🖂 information@limerickgolfclub.ie
🕮 1325
🚺 P Murray (Gen Mgr) (061) 415146
✓ L Harrington (061) 431344
🏴 18 L 6601 yds SSS 72
🚹 WD–U before 5pm exc Tues
WE–M SOC–WD prior booking
essential
£€ €50 (€70)
🚗 3 miles S of Limerick
🖥 www.limerickgolfclub.ie

Limerick County G&CC
(1994)
Ballyneety
☎ (061) 351881
🖂 (061) 351384
🖂 lcgolf@iol.ie
🕮 800
🚺 Gerry McKeon (Mgr)
✓ Donal McSweeney
🏴 18 L 5686 m Par 71 SSS 70
🚹 U SOC
£€ €40 (€50)
🚗 5 miles S of Limerick (R512)
⊕ Driving range
🏠 Des Smyth
🖥 www.limerickcounty.com

Newcastle West   (1938)
Rathgonan, Ardagh, Co. Limerick
☎ (069) 76500
🖂 (069) 76511
🖂 info@newcastlewestgolf.com
🕮 950
🚺 Kevin Mulcany (Mgr)
✓ Conor McCormick (069) 76500
ext 21
🏴 18 L 6141 m Medal 6446 m
Championship SSS 72
🚹 U exc Sun–U after 4pm SOC
£€ €45 (€55)
🚗 6 miles N of Newcastle West, off
N21
⊕ Floodlit driving range; putting
green; buggy hire

🏠 Arthur Spring
🖥 www.newcastlewestgolf.com

Rathbane   (1998)
Public
Rathbane, Crossagalla, Limerick
☎ (061) 313655
🖂 (061) 313655
🕮 800 approx
🚺 John O'Sullivan
✓ Barbara Hackett (086) 811 6255
🏴 18 L 5671 m Par 70
🚹 U
£€ Mon–Thur €15–€20 Fri–Sat + BH
€20–€27 Sun €17 Juniors Mon–Fri
€10
🚗 Limerick
⊕ Buggies & clubs for hire

Co Londonderry

Benone Par Three
53 Benone Avenue, Benone, Limavady,
BT49 0LQ
☎ (028) 7775 0555
🚺 MI Clark
🏴 9 L 1427 yds Par 3 course
🚹 U
£€ On request
🚗 12 miles N of Limavady on A2
coast road
⊕ Driving range (seasonal)

Brown Trout   (1984)
209 Agivey Road, Aghadowey, Coleraine,
BT51 4AD
☎ (028) 7086 8209
🖂 (028) 7086 8878
🖂 bill@browntroutinn.com
🕮 150
🚺 B O'Hara (Sec/Mgr)
✓ K Revie
🏴 9 L 2800 yds SSS 68
🚹 U SOC
£€ £10 (£15)
🚗 8 miles S of Coleraine at junction
of A54/B66
🏠 W O'Hara Sr
🖥 www.browntroutinn.com

Castlerock   (1901)
65 Circular Road, Castlerock, BT51 4TJ
☎ (028) 7084 8314
🖂 (028) 7084 9440
🖂 info@castlerockgc.co.uk
🕮 1260
🚺 M Steen (Sec/Mgr)
✓ Thomas Johnston (028) 7084 9424
🏴 18 L 6121 m SSS 72
9 L 2457 m SSS 34
🚹 WD–U exc Fri SOC
£€ 9 (Bann): £12 (£15); 18 (Mussenden
Links): £65 Mon–Fri, £80 weekends
& BH
🚗 5 miles W of Coleraine on A2
🏠 Ben Sayers
🖥 www.castlerockgc.co.uk

City of Derry   (1912)
49 Victoria Road, Londonderry, BT47 2PU
☎ (028) 7134 6369
🖂 info@cityofderrygolfclub.com

Foyle   (1994)
Proprietary
12 Alder Road, Londonderry, BT48 8DB
☎ (028) 7135 2222
🖂 (028) 7135 3967
🖂 mail@foylegolf.club24.co.uk
🕮 265
🚺 M Lapsley (028) 7135 2222
✓ D Morrison and S Young
🏴 18 L 6643 m Par 71 SSS 71
9 hole course
🚹 U
£€ £17 (£20)
🚗 Londonderry
⊕ Driving range; 2 putting greens
🏠 Frank Ainsworth
🖥 www.foylegolfcentre.co.uk

Kilrea   (1920)
47a Lisnagrot Road, Kilrea
☎ (028) 295 40044
🖂 kilreagc@hotmail.co.uk
🕮 310
🚺 B McGill (028) 295 40044
🏴 9 L 5615 yds Par 69 SSS 67
🚹 U SOC Tues & Wed–NA after
5pm Sat–NA before 4pm
£€ £15 (£20) Week £10 with member
🚗 Kilrea, 15 miles S of Coleraine
🖥 www.kilreagolfclub.co.uk

Moyola Park   (1976)
15 Curran Road, Castledawson,
Magherafelt, BT45 8DG
☎ (028) 7946 8468
🖂 (028) 7946 8626
🖂 moyolapark@btconnect.com
🕮 940
🚺 S McKenna (Hon)
✓ Bob Cockcroft (028) 7946 8830
🏴 18 L 6519 yds Par 71
🚹 U SOC exc Sat
£€ £24 (£30)
🚗 40 miles NW of Belfast by M2. 35
miles S of Coleraine
🏠 Don Patterson
🖥 www.moyolapark.com

Portstewart   (1894)
117 Strand Road, Portstewart, BT55 7PG
☎ (028) 7083 2015
🖂 (028) 7083 4097
🖂 info@portstewartgc.co.uk
🕮 1718
🚺 M Moss BA (028) 7083 3839
✓ A Hunter (028) 7083 2601
🏴 Strand: 18 L 6895 yds SSS 73
Riverside: 18 L 5725 yds SSS 68
Old: 18 L 4733 yds SSS 62
🚹 SOC–by arrangement
£€ Strand: £80 (£95) Riverside: £20
(£25) Old £12.50 (£17.50)
🚗 W boundary of Portstewart
🏠 Des Giffin
🖥 www.portstewartgc.co.uk

Roe Park   (1993)
Roe Park Golf Club, Radisson SAS Roe Park
Resort, Roe Park, Limavady, BT49 9LB
☎ (028) 7776 0105
🖂 (028) 777 22313
🖂 info@roegolf.com

For list of abbreviations, key to symbols and international dialling codes see page 647

☐ 550
🏌 Terry Kelly (028) 777 60105
✓ Shaun Devenney
⛳ 18 L 6318 yds Par 70 SSS 71
👫 U
££ £25 (£30)
🚌 Limavady
⊕ Covered driving range; golf
academy; Outdoor Bays
▤ www.radissonroepark.com

Traad Ponds
Shore Road, Magherafelt, BT45 6LR
☎ (028) 7941 8865

Co Longford

County Longford
(1900)
Glack, Dublin Road, Longford
☎ (043) 46310
☐ (043) 47082
📧 colongolf@eircom.net
☐ 800
🏌 M Glancy
✓ David Byrne
⛳ 18 L 6008 yds SSS 69
👫 U SOC
££ On application
🚌 Longford ¹/₂ mile on Dublin road
🏠 Mel Flanagan
▤ www.countylongfordgolfclub.com

Co Louth

Ardee   (1911)
Townparks, Ardee
☎ (041) 685 3227
☐ (041) 685 6137
📧 ardeegolfclub@eircom.net
☐ 700
🏌 Seamus Rooney (Sec/Mgr)
✓ Scott Kirkpatrick
⛳ 18 L 6490 yds Par 71 SSS 72
👫 U SOC
££ £35 (€50)
🚌 1km N of Ardee, 7km to M1
⊕ Driving range
🏠 Eddie Hackett
▤ www.ardeegolfclub.com

Carnbeg   (1996)
Carnbeg, Dundalk, Co Louth
☎ (042) 933 2518
☐ (042) 939 5731
📧 carnbeggolfcourse@eircom.net
🏌 P Kirk
✓ J Frawley
⛳ Championship: 18 L 5645 m Par 72
Ladies: 18 L 4656 m Par 72
👫 U
££ €25 (€33)
🚌 1 mile from Dundalk Road on R177
Armagh Road
⊕ Practice green and net
🏠 Eddie Hackett and Tom Croddock
▤ www.dundalk.parkinn.ie

County Louth   (1892)
Baltray, Drogheda
☎ (041) 988 1530
☐ (041) 988 1531
📧 reservations@countylouthgolfclub
.com
☐ 1400
🏌 M Delany
✓ P McGuirk (041) 988 1536
⛳ 18 L 7035 yds SSS 73
👫 By prior arrangement
££ €125
🚌 3 miles NE of Drogheda
🏠 Tom Simpson
▤ www.countylouthgolfclub.com

Dundalk   (1905)
Blackrock, Dundalk
☎ (042) 932 1731
☐ (042) 932 2022
📧 manager@dundalkgolfclub.ie
☐ 1250
🏌 T Sloane (Sec/Mgr)
✓ Leslie Walker (042) 932 2102
⛳ 18 holes
Championship tees: L 6206 m Par
72 SSS 72
Medal tees: L 6024 m Par 72 SSS 71
Forward tees: L 5713 Par 72
SSS 70
Ladies tees: L 5222 m Par 73
SSS 72
👫 U SOC
££ €60 (€25 with member)
🚌 3 miles S of Dundalk; m/way
junction is Dundalk South
⊕ Large practice area; pitching green;
putting green; driving range
🏠 Dave Thomas, Peter Alliss
▤ www.dundalkgolfclub.ie

Greenore   (1896)
Greenore
☎ (042) 937 3212/3678
☐ (042) 937 3678
📧 greenoregolfclub@eircom.net
☐ 1100
🏌 Linda Clarke
✓ Robert Giles (042) 937 3951
⛳ 18 L 6514 yds Par 71 SSS 71
👫 WD–U before 5pm WE/BH–by
arrangement SOC
££ €40 (€50)
🚌 15 miles E of Dundalk on
Carlingford Lough. M1
Dublin/Belfast
⊕ Driving range
🏠 Eddie Hackett
▤ www.greenoregolfclub.com

Killinbeg   (1991)
Killin Park, Dundalk
☎ (042) 933 9303
☐ (042) 932 0848
☐ 400
🏌 Pat Reynolds (Sec/Mgr)
⛳ 18 L 4717 m Par 69 SSS 66
👫 U SOC
££ €25 (€30)
🚌 2 miles NW of Dundalk on
Castletown road; M1 Castlebury
Road junction
🏠 Eddie Hackett

Seapoint   (1993)
Termonfeckin, Drogheda
☎ (041) 982 2333
☐ (041) 982 2331
📧 golflinks@seapoint.ie
☐ 630
✓ D Carroll (041) 988 1066
⛳ 18 L 6473 m Par 72 SSS 75 –
links course
👫 WD WE (limited availability) SOC
££ €60 (Sat €75, Sun €100)
🚌 M1
⊕ Driving range; large short game
practice academy; bunker play
practice
🏠 Des Smyth & Declan Branigan
▤ www.seapointgolflinks.ie

Townley Hall   (1994)
Tullyallen, Drogheda
☎ (041) 984 2229
☐ (041) 984 2229
📧 townleyhall@oceanfree.net
☐ 200
🏌 M Foley (Hon)
⛳ 9 L 5221 m Par 71 SSS 69
👫 U Sun–NA before 2pm
££ €15 (€18)
🚌 5 miles NW of Drogheda, off M1
Take Collon exit on roundabout
and next left turn for Tullyallen
⊕ Driving range

Co Mayo

Achill   (1951)
Keel, Achill
☎ (098) 43456
☐ (098) 43456
📧 achillgolfclub@aircom.net
☐ 100
🏌 Michael McGinty
⛳ 9 L 2689 m Par 70 SSS 67
👫 U H SOC
££ €15 (€20)
🚌 50 miles NW of Westport, on
Achill Island
⊕ Clubs & trollies for hire €12 & €3
🏠 P Skerritt
▤ www.achillgolfclub.com

Ashford Castle
Cong
☎ (092) 46003

Ballina   (1910)
Mossgrove, Shanaghy, Ballina
☎ (096) 21050
☐ (096) 21718
📧 ballinagc@eircom.net
☐ 460
🏌 Dick Melrose
✓ Eddie Tracey (096 76566)
⛳ 18 L 6103 yds SSS 69
👫 WD–U Sun–NA before noon
SOC–WD/WE
££ €30 (€40) Wed ££20 open day
🚌 1 mile E of Ballina
🏠 Eddie Hackett
▤ www.ballina-golf.com

Ballinrobe   (1895)
Clooncastle, Ballinrobe
☎ **(04) 954 1118**
📠 (094) 954 1889
🖂 info@ballinrobegolfclub.com
▦ 1150
♨ J McMahon (Sec/Mgr)
↟ 18 L 6354 m Par 73 SSS 72
🙆 U exc Sun–NA SOC
££ €30–€38
⛳ 2 miles NW of Ballinrobe on R331
⊕ Foodlit driving range
🏠 Eddie Hackett
🖥 www.ballinrobegolfclub.com

Ballyhaunis   (1929)
Coolnaha, Ballyhaunis
☎ **(0907) 30014**

Belmullet   (1925)
Carne, Belmullet
☎ **(00353) 97 82292**
🖂 terryswinson@esatclear.ie
▦ 386
♨ T Swinson (Hon Sec)
   (00353) 97 85786
↟ Blue: 18 L 6119 m SSS 72
   Medal: 18 L 5819 m Par 72 SSS 71
🙆 U
££ €65 (€65, 27h €72, 35h €90)
⛳ 1 mile from Belmullet
⊕ Belmullet is the permanent resident
   club of Carne Golf Links
🏠 Eddie Hackett
🖥 www.belmulletgolfclub.ie

Castlebar   (1910)
Hawthorn Avenue, Rocklands, Castlebar
☎ **(094) 21649**
📠 (094) 26088
▦ 950
♨ Bernie Murray (087) 657 7640
✓ David McQuillan
↟ 18 L 6500 yds Par 71 SSS 72
🙆 WD/Sat–U Sun–NA Pre-booking
   for time sheets advisable
££ €24 (€30)
⛳ 1 mile S of Castlebar, on Galway
   road
🏠 P McEvoy (1999)
🖥 www.castlebar.ie/golf

Claremorris   (1917)
Castlemacgarrett, Claremorris
☎ **(094) 937 1527**
📠 (094) 937 2919
🖂 info@claremorrisgolfclub.com
▦ 700
♨ W Feeley (Hon)
✓ Jimmy Heggarty
↟ 18 L 5827 yds Par 73 SSS 71
🙆 WD–U before noon Sat–U before
   noon SOC
££ €30 (€33)
⛳ 2 miles S of Claremorris (N17)
🏠 Tom Craddock
🖥 www.claremorrisgolfclub.com

Mulranny   (1968)
Mulranny, Westport
☎ **(098) 36262**

Swinford   (1922)
Brabazon Park, Swinford
☎ **(+353) 94 925 1378**

Westport   (1908)
Carrowholly, Westport
☎ **(098) 28262**
📠 (098) 24648
🖂 info@westportgolfclub.com
▦ 850
♨ Sean Durkan
✓ Alex Mealia
↟ 18 L 6724 yds SSS 72
🙆 U SOC
££ €45 (€60)
⛳ 2 miles W of Westport
⊕ Driving range
🏠 F Hawtree
🖥 www.westportgolfclub.com

Co Meath

Ashbourne   (1991)
Archerstown, Ashbourne
☎ **(01) 835 2005**
📠 (01) 835 9261
🖂 info@ashbournegolfclub.ie
▦ 700
♨ Paul Wisniewski
✓ J Dwyer
↟ 18 L 5778 m Par 71 SSS 70
🙆 WD–U WE–NA
££ €40 (€50)
⛳ 12 miles N of Dublin, off N2
⊕ Small practice fairway; putting
   green; chipping green
🏠 Des Smyth
🖥 www.ashbournegolfclub.ie

Black Bush   (1987)
Thomastown, Dunshaughlin
☎ **(01) 825 0021**
📠 (01) 825 0400
🖂 info@blackbushgolfclub.ie
▦ 1050
♨ Kate O'Rourke (Admin)
   (01) 825 0021
✓ S O'Grady (01) 825 0793
↟ 18 L 6930 yds SSS 73
   9 L 2800 yds SSS 35
🙆 WD–to 4pm WE–2 hrs Sat
   Sun–NA SOC to 4pm
££ €30 (€45)
⛳ 1 mile E of Dunshaughlin, off N3.
   20 miles NW of Dublin
⊕ Driving range for members and
   green fees
🏠 Robert J Browne
🖥 www.blackbushgolfclub.ie

County Meath   (1898)
Newtownmoynagh, Trim
☎ **(046) 9431463**
📠 (046) 9437554
▦ 800
♨ J Higgins (086) 274 9859
✓ R Machin
↟ 18 L 6720 yds SSS 72
🙆 WD–U WE–restricted SOC–exc
   Sun
££ €30 (€35)

⛳ 2 miles SW of Trim. 25 miles NW
   of Dublin
⊕ 15-bay (indoor & outdoor) driving
   range
🏠 Hackett/Craddock
🖥 www.trimgolf.net

Glebe
Kildalkey Road, Trim, Meath
☎ **(00353) 4694 31926**
📠 (00353) 4694 31926
🖂 glebegc@eircom.net
▦ 150
♨ Chris Bligh
↟ 18 L 6466 yds Par 73 SSS 71
🙆 WD–U all day WE–U Sat, after
   10am Sun SOC–U
££ €20 (€25)
⛳ Trim, Co Meath
⊕ Large practice facility
🏠 Eddie Hackett
🖥 www.glebegolfclub.com

Gormanston College
   (1961)
Franciscan College, Gormanston
☎ **(01) 841 2203**
📠 (01) 841 2685
▦ 200
♨ Br Laurence Brady
✓ B Browne
↟ 9 L 1973 m Par 32
🙆 NA
⛳ 22 miles N of Dublin
🖥 www.gormanstoncollege.ie

Headfort   (1928)
Kells
☎ **(046) 924 0146**
📠 (046) 924 9282
🖂 hgcadmin@eircom.net
▦ 1100
♨ Nora Murphy (Admin)
   (046) 924 0146
✓ B McGovern (046) 924 0639
↟ New 18 L 6164 m SSS 74
   Old 18 L 5973 m SSS 71
🙆 U exc NA 12.30–2pm SOC
££ New: €55 Mon–Thur (€65
   Fri–Sun) over 16 €50 Old: €45
   Mon–Thur (€55 Fri–Sun) over 16
   €40
⛳ 65km NW of Dublin on N3
⊕ Putting/chipping greens; practice
   nets
🏠 Christy O'Connor Jr
🖥 www.headfortgolfclub.ie

Kilcock   (1985)
Gallow, Kilcock
☎ **(01) 628 7592**
📠 (01) 628 7283
🖂 info@kilcockgolfclub.ie
▦ 650
♨ Martha Dalton (Sec)
↟ 18 L 5794 m SSS 71
🙆 U SOC
££ Mon–Thur €25, Fri €32
   (+BH €35)
⛳ 20 miles W of Dublin (N4)
🏠 E Hackett
🖥 www.kilcockgolfclub.ie

Laytown & Bettystown
(1909)
Bettystown, Co. Meath
☎ **(041) 982 7170**
📠 (041) 982 8506
✉ links@landb.ie
🔲 850
♟ Helen Finnegan (041) 982 7170 ext 1
✓ RJ Browne (041) 982 8793
↪ 18 L 6454 yds SSS 72
👥 U SOC–WD
££ €60 (€75) – 2009 prices
🚗 25 miles N of Dublin; junction Laytown and Drogheda South
⊕ Centenary Year 2009
🖥 www.landb.ie

Moor Park   (1993)
Moortown, Navan
☎ **(046) 27661**

Navan   (1996)
Public
Proudstown, Navan, Co Meath
☎ **(046) 907 2888**
📠 (046) 907 6722
✉ info@navangolfclub.ie
🔲 530
↪ 18 L 6114 m Par 72
👥 U
££ €23
🚗 2 miles N of Navan
🏠 RJ Browne
🖥 www.navangolfclub.ie

Royal Tara   (1906)
Bellinter, Navan
☎ **(046) 902 5244/902 5508/902 5584**
📠 (046) 9026684
✉ info@royaltaragolfclub.ie
🔲 1000
♟ John McGarth (Hon), F Duffy (Gen Mgr)
✓ J Byrne (046) 902 6009
↪ 18 L 5757 yds Par 71
9 L 3184 yds Par 35
👥 U
££ €35 (€45)
🚗 25 miles N of Dublin, off N3
🏠 Des Smyth
🖥 www.royaltaragolfclub.com

Summerhill
Agher, Rathmoylan, Co Meath
☎ **(046) 955 7857**

Co Monaghan

Castleblayney   (1985)
Onomy, Castleblayney
☎ **(042) 974 9485**
✉ castleblayney@golfnet.ie
🔲 275
♟ Frank McDonnell (042) 974 6098
↪ 9 L 2678 yds SSS 66
👥 U SOC
££ €12 (€15)
🚗 Castleblayney town centre. 18 miles SE of Monaghan

📠 R Browne
🖥 www.castleblayneygolfclub.com

Clones   (1913)
Hilton Demesne, Clones
☎ **(047) 56017**
📠 (047) 56017
✉ clonesgolfclub@eircom.net
🔲 400
♟ M Taylor (049) 555 2354
↪ 18 L 6600 yds Par 71 SSS 70
👥 WD–U WE–book in advance
££ €30 (€35)
🚗 Hilton Park, 3km from Clones on Scotshouse Road
⊕ Practice putting area; practice ground
🏠 Dr Arthur Spring
🖥 www.clonesgolfclub.com

Nuremore Hotel & CC
(1964)
Nuremore Hotel, Carrickmacross
☎ **(042) 966 1438**
📠 (042) 966 1853
✉ info@nuremore.com
🔲 300
♟ N Power
✓ M Cassidy
↪ 18 L 5870 m Par 71 SSS 69
👥 U
££ €40 (€45)
🚗 1 mile S of Carrickmacross off M1, take Derry exit
🏠 Eddie Hackett
🖥 www.nuremore.com

Rossmore   (1916)
Rossmore Park, Cootehill Road, Monaghan
☎ **(047) 81316**
📠 (047) 71227
✉ rossmoregolfclub@eircom.net
🔲 750
♟ J McKenna (Hon)
✓ Ciaran Smyth (047) 71222
↪ 18 L 6082 yds Par 70 SSS 69
👥 WD–U SOC WE/BH–U SOC
££ €30 (€40)
🚗 2 miles S of Monaghan on Cootehill road
⊕ Double driving/practice nets; Golf carts, Pull Trolleys, and electric trolleys for hire; Pro shop (fully stocked)
🏠 Des Smyth
🖥 www.rossmoregolfclub.com

Co Offaly

Birr   (1893)
The Glenns, Birr
☎ **(057) 91 20082**
📠 (057) 91 22155
✉ birrgolfclub@eircom.net
🔲 750
♟ Tony Hogan (Hon)
✓ Kevin McGrath (057) 91 21606
↪ 18 L 5824 m SSS 71
Men: Par 70; Ladies: Par 72
👥 U SOC–exc Sun–NA (except 11–12 on certain Sundays)

££ €30
🚗 2 miles W of Birr
⊕ Driving range
🖥 www.birrgolfclub.ie

Castle Barna   (1992)
Castlebarnagh, Daingean
☎ **(057) 935 3384**
📠 (057) 935 3077
✉ info@castlebarna.ie
🔲 600
♟ E Mangan
↪ 18 L 5595 m Par 72 SSS 69
👥 U
££ €25 (€35)
🚗 10 miles E of Tullamore (R402); or Jct 3 from N6 Dublin-Galway road, follow signs for Rhode then Daingean
🏠 Alan Duggan
🖥 www.castlebarna.ie

Edenderry   (1910)
Kishawanny, Edenderry
☎ **(046) 973 1072**
📠 (046) 973 3911
✉ enquiries@edenderrygolfclub.com
🔲 1000
♟ Noel Usher
↪ 18 L 6121 m Par 72 SSS 72
👥 WD–U exc Thurs (Ladies Day) WE–restricted SOC
££ €30 (€35) Reduction for groups on request
🚗 1 mile E of Edenderry town
🏠 Havers/Hackett
🖥 www.edenderrygolfclub.com

Esker Hills G&CC
(1996)
Proprietary
Tullamore, Co Offaly
☎ **(057) 93 55999**
📠 (057) 93 55021
✉ info@eskerhillsgolf.com
🔲 260
♟ C Guinan
↪ 18 L 6669 yds Par 71
👥 U
££ €35 (€45)
🚗 Tullamore
⊕ Putting green; practice area
🏠 Christy O'Connor Jr
🖥 www.eskerhillsgolf.com

Tullamore   (1896)
Brookfield, Tullamore
☎ **(057) 93 21439**
📠 (057) 83 41806
✉ tullamoregolfclub@eircom.net
🔲 1000
♟ H Egan (057) 93 21439
✓ D McArdle (057) 93 51757
↪ 18 L 6472 yds Par 70 SSS 70
👥 WD exc Tues–U Sat–restricted Sun–NA SOC
££ €37 (€48)
🚗 2½ miles S of Tullamore, off N52 on the R421
🏠 Braid/Merrigan
🖥 www.tullamoregolfclub.com

For list of abbreviations, key to symbols and international dialling codes see page 647

Co Roscommon

Athlone   (1892)
Hodson Bay, Athlone
☎ **(090) 649 2073/649 2235**
📠 (090) 649 4080
📧 athlonegolfclub@eircom.net
🕮 1000
🏌 I Dockery
✓ Kevin Grealy (090) 644 6008
▷ 18 L 5983 m SSS 71 white, 73 blue
👥 U SOC (H for open competitions)
££ D–€35 (€40)
🏴 3 miles from Athlone on
   Roscommon road, N61
⊕ Practice ground; putting green;
   buggy hire; Clubs for Hire
🏠 F Hawtree
🖥 www.athlonegolfclub.ie

Ballaghaderreen   (1937)
Aughalustia, Ballaghaderreen
☎ **(094) 986 0295**

Boyle   (1911)
Knockadoo, Brusna, Boyle
☎ **(071) 966 2594**
🕮 145
🏌 J Mooney (Hon) (087) 776 0161
▷ 9 L 5105 m Par 68 SSS 66
👥 U SOC
££ D–€15
🏴 1½ miles S of Boyle
🏠 Eddie Hackett

Castlerea   (1905)
Clonallis, Castlerea
☎ **(0907) 21214**

Roscommon   (1904)
Mote Park, Roscommon
☎ **(09066) 26382**
📠 (09066) 26043
📧 rosgolf@eircom.net
🕮 720
🏌 M Dolan (087) 225 4695
▷ 18 L 6059 m Par 72 SSS 71
👥 WD–U WE/BH–restricted SOC
££ €30 (€35)
🏴 I mile S of Roscommon
⊕ Practice area; putting green
🏠 Eddie Connaughton/Ken Kearney

Strokestown   (1995)
Strokestown
🕮 350
🏌 L Glover (Hon) (07196) 33528
▷ 9 L 5230 m Par 68 SSS 67
👥 U
££ €15
🏴 15 miles N of Roscommon (R368).
   N5 to Longford/Westport

Co Sligo

Ballymote   (1943)
Ballinascarrow, Ballymote
☎ **(071) 83504**

County Sligo   (1894)
Rosses Point
☎ **(071) 9177134/9177186**
📠 (071) 9177460
📧 teresa@countysligogolfclub.ie
🕮 1200
🏌 H O'Neill (Mgr) (071) 9177134
✓ J Robinson (071) 9177171
▷ 18 L 6162 m SSS 72
   9 L 2795 m SSS 35
👥 U H–booking required SOC
££ Mon–Thur €75 Fri/WE–€90
🏴 5 miles NW of Sligo
🏠 Colt/Allison
🖥 www.countysligogolfclub.ie

Enniscrone   (1931)
Ballina Road, Enniscrone
☎ **(096) 36297**

Strandhill   (1932)
Strandhill
☎ **(00353) 71 91 68188**
📧 strandhillgc@eircom.net

Tubbercurry   (1990)
Ballymote Road, Tubbercurry
☎ **(071) 918 5849**
📧 contact@tubbercurrygolfclub.com
🕮 300
🏌 Billy Kilgannon (071) 918 6124
▷ 9 L 5478 m SSS 69
👥 U SOC
££ €20
🏴 On N17 20 miles S of Sligo/15
   miles off motorway
🏠 Eddie Hackett
🖥 www.tubbercurrygolfclub.com

Co Tipperary

Ballykisteen Hotel & Golf
Resort   (1994)
Proprietary
Ballykisteen, Limerick Junction
☎ **(+353) 062 33333 (hotel)**
   (+353) 062 32117 (golf)
📠 (+353) 062 31555
📧 golf.ballykisteen@ballykisteenhotel
   .com
🕮 420
🏌 Mike Keegan (+353 087 667 9495)
✓ James Harris, PGA
▷ 18 L 6809 yds Par 72
   White tees SSS 72
   Blue tees SSS 74
👥 U SOC WD WE
££ €40 (€50), Wed singles €25, Mon
   Seniors singles €15
🏴 3 miles NW of Tipperary town; 25
   min from Limerick City
⊕ Driving range; practice facilities;
   Putting Green; Chipping Green;
   Practice Bunker
🏠 Des Smyth
🖥 www.ballykisteenhotel.com

Cahir Park   (1967)
Kilcommon, Cahir, Co Tipperary
☎ **(052) 41474**

📠 (052) 42717
📧 management@cahirparkgolfclub.com
🕮 700
🏌 J Costigan (052) 41146
✓ D Ryan (052) 43944
▷ 18 L 6351 yds Par 71 SSS 71
👥 U SOC–WD/Sat
££ €30 (€35)
🏴 I mile S of Cahir
⊕ Driving range
🏠 Eddie Hackett
🖥 www.cahirgolfclub.com

Carrick-on-Suir   (1939)
Garravoone, Carrick-on-Suir
☎ **(051) 640047**

Clonmel   (1911)
Lyreanearla, Mountain Road, Clonmel
☎ **(052) 24050**
📠 (052) 83349
📧 cgc@indigo.ie
🕮 820
🏌 A Myles-Keating (052) 24050
✓ R Hayes (052) 24050
▷ 18 L 6347 yds SSS 71
👥 WD–U WE–SOC before noon
££ €30 (€35) €20 with member WD:
   3 courses for €60 (Carrick,
   Clonmel, Cahir Park)
🏴 3 miles SW of Clonmel
⊕ Putting green
🏠 Eddie Hackett
🖥 www.clonmelgolfclub.com

County Tipperary
   (1993)
Dundrum, Cashel
☎ **(062) 71717**
📠 (062) 71718
📧 golfshop@dundrumhouse.ie
🕮 400
🏌 W Crowe (Mgr) (062) 71717
▷ 18 L 7160 yds SSS 74
👥 U SOC
££ €60 (€70)
🏴 6 miles W of Cashel
🏠 Philip Walton
🖥 www.dundrumhousehotel.com

Nenagh   (1929)
Beechwood, Nenagh
☎ **(067) 31476**
📠 (067) 34808
📧 nenaghgolfclub@eircom.net
🕮 1200
🏌 Sean Minogue
✓ Ryan McCann (067) 33242
▷ 18 L 6009 m Par 72 SSS 72
👥 U SOC
££ €30 reduced fees for groups
🏴 3 miles NE of Nenagh on old Birr
   road
🏠 Patrick Merrigan
🖥 www.nenaghgolfclub.com

Roscrea   (1892)
Derryvale, Roscrea
☎ **00353 (0) 505 21130**
📠 00353 (0) 505 23410
📧 info@roscreagolfclub.ie
🕮 500

✍ J Ryan
➤ 18 L 5862 Par 71 SSS 72 (men)
   L 4985 Par 72 SSS 72 (ladies)
⛳ U
££ €30 (€35)
⊕ 2 miles E of Roscrea on Dublin
   road (N7)
⌂ Arthur Spring
▤ www.roscreagolfclub.ie

Slievenamon   (1999)
Proprietary
Clonacody, Lisronagh, Co Tipperary
☎ (052) 32213
⌨ (052) 30875
✉ info@slievnamongolfclub.com
⌑ 1200
✍ B Kenny (052) 32213
✓ S O'Brien (087) 677 6474
➤ 18 L 5000 m Par 67
⛳ U
££ €15 (€20)
⊕ 4 miles N of Clonmel off Fethard
   Road
⊕ Practice area
▤ www.slievnamongolfclub.com

Templemore   (1970)
Manna South, Templemore
☎ (0504) 32923/31400
✉ johnkm@tinet.ie

Thurles   (1909)
Turtulla, Thurles
☎ (0504) 21983
⌨ (0504) 90806
✉ thurlesgolf@eircom.net
⌑ 1200
✍ Mark Taylor
✓ S Hunt
➤ 18 L 5904 m Par 72 SSS 71
⛳ U
££ €40 (€50)
⊕ 1 mile S of Thurles
⊕ Driving range
⌂ Lionel Hewson
▤ www.thurlesgolfclub.com

Tipperary   (1896)
Rathanny, Tipperary
☎ (062) 51119
✉ tipperarygolfclub@eircom.net

Co Tyrone

Auchnacloy   (1995)
99 Tullyvar Road, Auchnacloy
☎ (028) 8255 7050
✉ sidney.houston@yahoo.co.uk
⌑ 180
✍ S Houston
➤ 9 L 5017 m Par 70 SSS 68
⛳ U
££ (£15)
⊕ 12 miles SW of Dungannon (B35)
⊕ Driving range. Bar, Restaurant.

Benburb Valley
Maydown Road, Benburb, BT71 7LJ
☎ (028) 3754 9868

Dungannon   (1890)
34 Springfield Lane, Mullaghmore,
Dungannon, BT70 1QX
☎ (028) 8772 2098
⌨ (028) 8772 7338
✉ info@dungannongolfclub.com
⌑ 840
✍ ST Hughes
✓ Vivian Teague
➤ 18 L 6046 yds SSS 72
⛳ U
££ £20, £14 with member (£25, £16
   with member)
⊕ ½ mile NW of Dungannon on
   Donaghmore road
▤ www.dungannongolfclub.com

Fintona   (1904)
Eccleville Desmesne, 1 Kiln Street, Fintona,
BT78 2BJ
☎ (028) 8284 1480
⌨ (028) 8284 1480
✉ fintonagolfclub@btconnect.com
⌑ 400
✍ Raymond D Scott
✓ P Leonard (028) 8284 1480
➤ 9 L 5765 m Par 72 SSS 70
⛳ U exc comp days SOC
££ £10 (£15)
⊕ 8 miles S of Omagh

Killymoon   (1889)
200 Killymoon Road, Cookstown,
BT80 8TW
☎ (028) 8676 3762
⌨ (028) 8676 3762
✉ killymoongolf@btconnect.com
⌑ 950
✍ N Weir
✓ G Chambers
➤ 18 L 6202 yds SSS 70
⛳ U H SOC
££ £22 (£27)
⊕ 1 mile S of Cookstown, off A29
▤ www.killymoongolfclub.com

Newtownstewart   (1914)
38 Golf Course Road, Newtownstewart,
BT78 4HU
☎ (028) 8166 1466
   (028) 8166 2242 Shop
⌨ (028) 8166 2506
✉ newtown.stewart@lineone.net
⌑ 700
✍ H Friar (028) 8165 8237
➤ 18 L 5320 m Par 70 SSS 69
⛳ WD–U WE–NA after noon SOC
££ £17 (£25)
⊕ 2 miles SW of Newtownstewart on
   B84
⌂ Frank Pennink
▤ www.globalgolf.com
   /newtownstewart

Omagh   (1910)
83A Dublin Road, Omagh, BT78 1HQ
☎ (028) 8224 3160/1442
⌨ (028) 8224 3160
⌑ 817
✍ Mrs F Caldwell
➤ 18 L 5364 m SSS 68
⛳ U SOC
££ £15 (£20)

⊕ 1 mile from Omagh on Belfast-
   Dublin road

Strabane   (1908)
Ballycolman, Strabane, BT82 9PH
☎ (028) 7138 2271/2007
⌨ (028) 7188 6514
✉ strabanegc@btconnect.com
⌑ 600
✍ Claire Keys (028) 7138 2007
➤ 18 L 5552 m SSS 69
⛳ WD–U WE–by arrangement
   SOC
££ £12 (£15)
⊕ ½ mile from Strabane, nr Fir Trees
   Hotel

Co Waterford

Dungarvan   (1924)
Knocknagranagh, Dungarvan
☎ (058) 43310/41605
⌨ (058) 44113
✉ dungarvangc@eircom.net
⌑ 900
✍ Irene Lynch (Mgr) (058) 43310
✓ D Hayes (058) 44707
➤ 18 L 6134 m Par 72 SSS 72
⛳ U SOC
££ €35 (€45)
⊕ 2 miles E of Dungarvan on N25. 25
   miles W of Waterford
⌂ Maurice Fives
▤ www.dungarvangolfclub.com

Dunmore East   (1993)
Dunmore East
☎ (051) 383151
⌨ (051) 383151
✉ info@dunmoreeastgolfclub.ie
⌑ 450
✍ Paul O'Neill
✓ On request
➤ 18 L 6070 m Par 72 SSS 70
⛳ U
££ €30 (€35)
⊕ 10 miles S of Waterford (R684)
⊕ Accom. on site
⌂ J O'Riordan
▤ www.dunmoreeastgolfclub.ie

Faithlegg   (1993)
Faithlegg House, Faithlegg
☎ (051) 382000
⌨ (051) 382010
✉ golf@fhh.ie
✍ Ryan Hunt (051) 380588
✓ Ryan Hunt
➤ 18 L 6690 yds SSS 72
⛳ U SOC (corporate specialists)
   WD–U WE–Sun U after 12
££ €50 (€65) Soc negotiated
⊕ 6 miles E of Waterford City on
   Dunmore East road
⊕ Short game practice area; putting
   green; driving nets; practice
   bunkers
⌂ Patrick Merrigan
▤ www.faithlegg.com

Gold Coast   (1993)
Ballinacourty, Dungarvan
☎ **(058) 42249/44055**
☐ (058) 43378
✉ info@goldcoastgolfclub.com
▥ 600
♟ T Considine (058) 44055
⊩ 18 L 6171 m Par 72 SSS 72
⚇ U SOC
££ €35 (€45)
⚌ E of Dungarvan, off R675
⌂ M Fives
▤ www.goldcoastgolfclub.com

Lismore   (1965)
Ballyin, Lismore
☎ **(058) 54026**
☐ (058) 53338
✉ lismoregolfclub@eircom.net
▥ 550
♟ K Moynihan
✒ TW Murphy (058) 54558/
(086) 352 1070
⊩ 9 L 5871 yds Par 69 SSS 68
⚇ WD–U before 5pm –M after 5pm
WE–phone first SOC–exc Sun
££ €20 (€20)
⚌ 1 mile N of Lismore, off N72
▤ www.lismoregolf.org

Tramore   (1894)
Newtown, Tramore
☎ **(051) 386170/381247**
☐ (051) 390961
✉ info@tramoregolfclub.com
▥ 1396
♟ Alan Briggs (Gen Mgr)
✒ D Brennan
⊩ 18 L 6055 m SSS 73
⚇ U
££ €45 (€60)
⚌ 7 miles S of Waterford
⌂ Capt Tippett/Jeff Howes (new nine holes)
▤ www.tramoregolfclub.com

Waterford   (1912)
Newrath, Waterford
☎ **+353 (0) 51 876748**
☐ +353 (0) 51 853405
✉ info@waterfordgolfclub.com
▥ 961
♟ Damien Maquire (Sec/Mgr) (051) 876748
✒ Harry Ewing +353 (0) 51 830628
⊩ 18 L 5722 m Par 71 SSS 70
⚇ U
££ €40 (€50)
⚌ 1 mile N of Waterford
⊕ Practice ground; driving range; buggy hire
⌂ Willie Park/James Braid
▤ www.waterfordgolfclub.com

Waterford Castle   (1991)
Proprietary
The Island, Ballinakill, Waterford
☎ **(051) 871633**
☐ (051) 871634
✉ golf@waterfordcastle.com
▥ 750
♟ M Garland (Dir of Golf)
⊩ 18 L 6231 m Par 72 SSS 71

⚇ U H SOC
££ €52 (€62+BH)
⚌ 2 miles E of Waterford, off R683. Island in River Suir. Access by private ferry
⊕ Driving range; putting green; chipping area
⌂ Des Smyth
▤ www.waterfordcastle.com

West Waterford G&CC   (1993)
Dungarvan
☎ **(058) 43216/41475**
☐ (058) 44343
✉ info@westwaterfordgolf.com
▥ 485
♟ T Whelan (Sec/Mgr)
✒ TW Murphy (00353 86 352 1070)
⊩ 18 L 6719 yds Par 72
⚇ U SOC
££ €35 (€45)
⚌ 4km W of Dungarvan, off N25
⊕ Practice range
⌂ Eddie Hackett
▤ www.westwaterfordgolf.com

Co Westmeath

Ballinlough Castle
Clonmellon, Co Westmeath
☎ **(044) 64544**

Delvin Castle   (1992)
Clonyn, Delvin
☎ **(044) 96 64315**
✉ info@delvincastlegolf.com
▥ 450
♟ F Dillon
✒ D Keenaghan
⊩ 18 L 5818 m Par 70 SSS 68
⚇ U SOC
££ €28 (€38)
⚌ 15 miles NE of Mullingar (N52)
⌂ John Day
▤ www.delvincastlegolf.com

Glasson Golf Hotel   (1993)
Glasson, Athlone
☎ **(090) 648 5120**
☐ (090) 648 5444
✉ info@glassongolf.ie
▥ 230
♟ Gareth Jones
✒ Touring Pro – Colm Moriarty
⊩ 18 L 7215 yds Par 73 SSS 74
⚇ U
££ €60 (€75)
⚌ 6 miles NE of Athlone (N55)
⊕ Golf Academy
⌂ C O'Connor Jr
▤ www.glassongolf.ie

Moate   (1900)
Aghanargit, Moate
☎ **(090) 648 1271**
☐ (090) 648 2645
✉ moategolfclub@eircom.net
▥ 600
♟ A O'Brien

✒ Paul Power
⊩ 18 L 6294 yds SSS 70
⚇ U SOC–WD Sun after 3pm
££ €30 – €10 with member (€35 – €15 with member)
⚌ Moate town centre
⊕ Caddy Cars and Motorised Buggies; Full Catering facilities.
⌂ Bobby Browne
▤ www.moategolfclub.ie

Mount Temple G&CC   (1991)
Proprietary
Mount Temple, Moate
☎ **(090) 648 1841**
☐ (090) 648 1957
✉ mttemple@iol.ie
▥ 150
♟ M Dolan
✒ David Byrne
⊩ 18 L 6670 yds Par 72 SSS 72
⚇ U SOC WD+WE
££ €30 (€40)
⚌ 3 miles N of N6, between Athlone and Moate
⊕ Golf academy with driving range
⌂ Michael Dolan
▤ www.mounttemplegolfclub.com

Mullingar   (1894)
Belvedere, Mullingar
☎ **(0 0353 44) 934 8366**
☐ (0 0353 44) 934 1499
✉ mullingargolfclub@hotmail.com
▥ 1,000
♟ Ann McLoughlin (Sec/Mgr)
✒ John Burns
⊩ 18 L 6685 yds SSS 73
⚇ U SOC
££ €45 (€50)
⚌ 3 miles S of Mullingar on N52 at Belvedere
⊕ Practice chipping and putting areas
⌂ James Braid/David Jones
▤ www.mullingargolfclub.com

Co Wexford

Courtown   (1936)
Kiltennel, Gorey
☎ **(055) 25166**
✉ courtown@aol.ie

Enniscorthy   (1907)
Knockmarshall, Enniscorthy
☎ **(053) 92 33191**
☐ (053) 92 37637
✉ info@enniscorthygc.ie
▥ 1200
♟ AP Colley
✒ M Sludds (053) 923 7600
⊩ 18 L 6115 m Par 72 SSS 72
⚇ U–phone first SOC
££ Mon–Thur €30 (Fri–Sun + PH €40)
⚌ 1½ miles SW of Enniscorthy on New Ross road, N30
⊕ Driving range; trolleys; golf carts; on-line booking system
⌂ Eddie Hackett
▤ www.enniscorthygc.ie

New Ross (1905)

Tinneranny, New Ross
☎ **(051) 421433**
🖳 (051) 420098
📧 newrossgolf@eircom.net
⌨ 880
🏌 Kathleen Daly (Sec/Mgr)
  (051) 421433
➤ 18 L 5795 m
  Men: White Par 70 SSS 70, Yellow
  Par 70 SSS 69
  Ladies: Red Par 72 SSS 72
👥 U exc Sun SOC
££ €30 (€40)
🚗 1 mile W of New Ross
🖥 www.newrossgolfclub.net

Rosslare (1905)

Rosslare Strand, Rosslare
☎ **(053) 913 2113 (Clubhouse)**
  (053) 913 2203 (Bookings)
🖳 (053) 913 2263
📧 office@rosslaregolf.com
⌨ 1000
🏌 JP Hanrick (Gen Mgr)
✓ J Young (053) 913 2032
➤ 18 L 6782 yds Par 72 SSS 72
  12 L 3887 yds Par 46
👥 U SOC
££ 12: €20 (€25) 18: €50 (€70)
🚗 10 miles S of Wexford. Rosslare
  Ferry 6 miles
⊕ Iron range; chipping green
🏠 Hawtree/Taylor/O'Connor Jr
🖥 www.rosslaregolf.com

St Helen's Bay (1993)

Proprietary
St Helen's, Kilrane, Rosslare Harbour
☎ **(053) 91 33234**
🖳 (053) 91 33803
📧 info@sthelensbay.com
⌨ 650
🏌 A Howard
➤ 18 L 6091 m SSS 72
👥 U SOC
££ €25 (€30) Nov–Mar €40 (€50)
  Apr–Oct
🚗 Nr Rosslare Ferry terminal
⊕ Golf academy; driving range
  adjacent to course
🏠 Philip Walton
🖥 www.sthelensbay.com

Tara Glen (1993)

Ballymoney, Gorey, Co Wexford
☎ **(053) 942 5413**
🖳 (053) 942 5612
📧 taraglen@eircom.net
🏌 Marion Siggins
➤ 9 L 5826 m Par 72 SSS 70
👥 U H SOC WD WE (not during
  June, July Aug)
££ €22
🚗 4 miles E of Gorey. 12 miles S of
  Arklow

Wexford (1960)

Mulgannon, Wexford
☎ **(053) 42238**
🖳 (053) 42243
📧 info@wexfordgolfclub.ie
⌨ 805

🏌 Roy Doyle (Hon)
✓ Liam Bowler (053) 46300
➤ 18 L 5950 m Par 71 SSS 73
👥 U SOC
££ €40 (€45)
🚗 Wexford ¹/₂ mile
🏠 Jeff Howes
🖥 www.wexfordgolfclub.ie

Co Wicklow

Arklow (1927)

Abbeylands, Arklow
☎ **(0402) 32492**
🖳 (0402) 91604
📧 arklowgolflinks@eircom.net
⌨ 750
🏌 R Kavanagh (Hon)
➤ 18 L 6475 yds Par 69 SSS 67
👥 WD–U Sat–U after 5pm Sun–NA
  SOC
££ €40
🚗 1 mile from Arklow
🏠 Hawtree/Taylor/Hackett/
  Connaughton
🖥 www.arklowgolfclublinks.com

Baltinglass (1928)

Baltinglass
☎ **(059) 648 1350**
🖳 (059) 648 2842
📧 baltinglassgolfclub@eircom.net
⌨ 550
➤ Men: 18 L 5912 Par 71
  Ladies: L 4707 Par 72
👥 U SOC
££ €25 (+BH €35)
🚗 38 miles S of Dublin (N81)
⊕ Driving range; putting green; buggy
  hire
🏠 Eddie Connaughton
🖥 www.baltinglassgolfclub.ie

Blainroe (1978)

Blainroe
☎ **(0404) 68168**
🖳 (0404) 69369
📧 info@blainroe.com
⌨ 1150
🏌 Patrick Bradshaw
✓ J McDonald (0404) 66470
➤ 18 L 6175 m SSS 72
👥 U
££ €55 (€75)
🚗 3 miles S of Wicklow on coast
⊕ Putting green; practice area
🏠 FW Hawtree
🖥 www.blainroe.com

Boystown

Baltyboys, Blessington, Co Wicklow
☎ **(045) 867146**

Bray (1897)

Greystones Road, Bray
☎ **(01) 276 3200**
🖳 (01) 276 3262
📧 info@braygolfclub.com
⌨ 816
🏌 Alan Threadgold (Gen Mgr)
✓ Ciaran Carroll

➤ Men: Blue tees 18 L 5990 m Par 71
  SSS 72
  White tees 18 L 5545 m Par 71
  SSS 71
  Yellow tees 18 L 5198 m Par 71
  SSS 69
  Ladies: Red tees 18 L 5077 m Par
  72 SSS 72
👥 U before 4.30pm SOC–WD
££ €25 winter, €25.50 (€70 Sat/Bank
  Hol) summer
🚗 12 miles S of Dublin
⊕ Driving range; chipping green;
  putting green
🏠 Des Smyth/Declan Brannigan
🖥 www.braygolfclub.com

Charlesland (1992)

Greystones
☎ **(01) 287 4350**
🖳 (01) 287 0078
📧 teetimes@charlesland.com
⌨ 830
🏌 Gerry O'Brien (Mgr) (01) 287 8200
✓ P Duignan
➤ 18 L 6739 yds Par 72 SSS 71
👥 U SOC
££ €50 (€60) Early Bird €35
🚗 18 miles SE of Dublin, take
  Greystones exit on N11
⊕ Full practice ground/range
  facilities
🏠 Eddie Hackett
🖥 www.charlesland.com

Delgany (1908)

Delgany
☎ **(01) 287 4536**
🖳 (01) 287 3977
📧 delganygolf@eircom.net
⌨ 1209
🏌 Peter Ribeiro (Gen Mgr)
✓ G Kavanagh (01) 287 4697
➤ 18 L 5473 yds SSS 69
👥 U exc comp days
  SOC–Mon/Thurs/Fri
££ €45 (€55)
🚗 30 min from Dublin City Centre
  just off N11 to Wexford
🏠 H Vardon/P Merrigan
🖥 www.delganygolfclub.com

Djouce (1995)

Roundwood
☎ **(01) 281 8585**

Druid's Glen (1995)

Newtownmountkennedy
☎ **(01) 287 3600**
🖳 (01) 287 3699
📧 info@druidsglen.ie
⌨ 250
🏌 D Flinn (Gen Mgr)
✓ G Henry
➤ 18 L 7026 yds Par 71 SSS 74
👥 U SOC
££ €190
🚗 20 miles S of Dublin (N11)
⊕ Golf Academy
🏠 Craddock/Ruddy
🖥 www.druidsglen.ie

Druid's Heath   (2003)
Newtownmountkennedy
- ☎ **(01) 287 3600**
- 🖳 (01) 287 3699
- ✉ info@druidsglen.ie
- 🏛 250
- ♟ D Flinn (Gen Mgr)
- ⚲ G Henry
- ⛳ 18 L 7434 yds Par 71 SSS 75
- 👥 U SOC
- ££ €140
- ⛱ 20 miles S of Dublin (N11)
- ⊕ Golf academy
- 🏠 Pat Ruddy
- 🖥 www.druidsglen.ie

The European Club   (1989)
Brittas Bay, Wicklow
- ☎ **(0404) 47415**
- 🖳 (0404) 47449
- ✉ info@theeuropeanclub.com
- 🏛 100
- ♟ P Ruddy
- ⛳ 18 L 7323 yds SSS 71
- 👥 H SOC
- ££ €100 – €180
- ⛱ 30 miles S of Dublin, off N11
- ⊕ Large practice area; pitching green; 3 putting greens
- 🏠 Pat Ruddy
- 🖥 www.theeuropeanclub.com

Glen of the Downs   (1998)
Coolnaskeagh, Delgany, Co Wicklow
- ☎ **(01) 287 6240**
- 🖳 (01) 287 0063
- ✉ info@glenofthedowns.com
- 🏛 650
- ♟ Derek Murphy
- ⛳ 18 L 5891 m Par 71
- 👥 U
- ££ Summer €65 (€80) – early bird rates also available Winter €65 (€50)
- ⛱ Off N11, nr Delgany
- 🏠 Peter McEvoy
- 🖥 www.glenofthedowns.com

Glenmalure   (1993)
Greenane, Rathdrum
- ☎ **(0404) 46679**
- ✉ glenmal@glenmalure-golf.ie

Greystones   (1895)
Greystones
- ☎ **(01) 287 4136**
- 🖳 (01) 287 3749
- ✉ secretary@greystonesgc.com
- 🏛 850
- ♟ Angus Murray (Mgr)
- ⚲ K Holmes
- ⛳ 18 L 5350 m SSS 69
- 👥 U Mon & Fri (Tues & Sun pm), M Wed & Sat (Thur pm) on request, SOC
- ££ see website for details
- ⛱ Greystones, 18 miles S of Dublin
- 🏠 Ron Kirby
- 🖥 www.greystonesgc.com

Kilcoole   (1992)
Kilcoole
- ☎ **(01) 287 2066**
- ✉ adminkg@eircom.net

Old Conna   (1987)
Ferndale Road, Bray
- ☎ **(01) 282 6055**
- 🖳 (01) 282 5611
- ✉ info@oldconna.com
- 🏛 1000
- ♟ Tom Sheridan (Gen Mgr)
- ⚲ M Langford (01) 272 0022
- ⛳ 18 L 6551 yds SSS 72
- 👥 WD–U before 4pm WE/BH–NA SOC
- ££ €50 WD before 4pm
- ⛱ 2 miles N of Bray. 12 miles S of Dublin
- 🏠 Eddie Hackett
- 🖥 www.oldconna.com

Powerscourt (East)   (1996)
Powerscourt Estate, Enniskerry
- ☎ **(01) 204 6033**
- 🖳 (01) 276 1303
- 🏛 627
- ♟ B Gibbons (Mgr)
- ⚲ P Thompson
- ⛳ East: 18 L 5858 m Par 72 SSS 72 West: 18 L 6345 m
- 👥 U
- ££ East: €130 West: €130
- ⛱ Half hour outside Dublin city centre
- ⊕ Driving range; putting green; chipping area
- 🏠 Peter McEvoy/ David McLay Kidd
- 🖥 www.powerscourt.ie

Powerscourt (West)   (2003)
Powerscourt Estate, Enniskerry
- ☎ **(01) 204 6033**
- 🖳 (01) 276 1303
- ♟ B Gibbons (Mgr)
- ⚲ P Thompson
- ⛳ 18 L 5906 m Par 72 SSS 72
- 👥 U
- ££ €130
- ⛱ Half an hour outside Dublin City Centre
- ⊕ Driving range; putting green; chipping area; apartments; conference facilities
- 🏠 David McLay Kidd
- 🖥 www.powerscourt.ie

Rathsallagh   (1993)
Proprietary
Dunlavin
- ☎ **(045) 403316**
- 🖳 (045) 403295
- ✉ info@rathsallagh.com/golf @rathsallagh.com
- 🏛 406
- ♟ J O'Flynn (045) 403316
- ⚲ B McDaid (045) 403316
- ⛳ 18 L 6885 yds Par 72 SSS 72
- 👥 U
- ££ Mon–Fri €60 (€80)

- ⛱ 14 miles S of Naas (R412). Just off N9 and N81
- ⊕ Driving range; pitching and putting greens; Golfing Academy
- 🏠 McEvoy/O'Connor Jr
- 🖥 www.rathsallagh.com

Roundwood   (1995)
Ballinahinch, Newtownmountkennedy
- ☎ **(01) 281 8488**
- 🖳 (01) 284 3642
- ✉ rwood@indigo.ie
- ♟ M McGuirk
- ⛳ 18 L 6685 yds Par 72 SSS 72
- 👥 U
- ££ €38 (€55)
- ⛱ 2.5 miles from N11 at Druids Glen exit on R765
- 🖥 www.roundwoodgolf.com

Tulfarris   (1987)
Blessington Lakes, Blessington
- ☎ **(045) 867644**
- 🖳 (045) 867601
- ✉ golf@tulfarris.com
- 🏛 300
- ♟ A Williams (Mgr)
- ⛳ 18 L 7172 m SSS 74
- 👥 U SOC
- ££ €80 (€100)
- ⛱ 30 miles S of Dublin, off N81
- ⊕ Driving range
- 🏠 Patrick Merrigan

Vartry Lakes   (1997)
Proprietary
Roundwood
- ☎ **(01) 281 7006**

Wicklow   (1904)
Dunbur Road, Wicklow
- ☎ **(0404) 67379**
- 🖳 (0404(64756
- ✉ info@wicklowgolfclub.ie
- 🏛 550
- ♟ J Kelly
- ⚲ E McLoughlin (0404) 66122
- ⛳ 18 L 5695 m SSS 70
- 👥 SOC–WD/Sat U–WD/Sat
- ££ €40 (€45)
- ⛱ 30 miles S of Dublin, in Wicklow town off main N11 route
- 🏠 Craddock/Ruddy
- 🖥 www.wicklowgolfclub.ie

Woodenbridge   (1884)
Vale of Avoca, Arklow
- ☎ **(0402) 35202**
- 🖳 (0402) 35754
- ✉ info@woodenbridge.ie
- 🏛 750
- ♟ Kevin Mulcahy
- ⛳ 18 L 6400 yds Par 71 SSS 70
- 👥 U exc Sat & Thurs
- ££ €55 (€65)
- ⛱ 4 miles W of Arklow. 45 miles S of Dublin
- ⊕ Practice ground
- 🏠 Patrick Merrigan
- 🖥 www.woodenbridgegolfclub.com

Scotland

Aberdeenshire

Aboyne (1883)
Formaston Park, Aboyne, AB34 5HP
- ☎ (013398) 86328
- 📠 (013398) 87078
- ✉ aboynegolfclub@btconnect.com
- 🏠 725 180(J)
- 🏌 Mrs M Ferries (013398) 87078
- 🏌 S Moir (013398) 86328
- ⛳ 18 L 6009 yds SSS 69
- 👥 U
- ££ On application
- ⚐ E end of Aboyne. 30 miles W of Aberdeen (A93)
- 🖥 www.aboynegolfclub.co.uk

Aboyne Loch Golf Centre (2000)
Pay and play
Aboyne Loch, Aboyne, AB34 5BR
- ☎ (013398) 86444
- 📠 (013398) 86488
- ✉ info@thelodgeontheloch.com
- 🏠 50
- 🏌 Derek McCulloch
- ⛳ 9 L 2610 yds Par 34(68) SSS 65
- 👥 U
- ££ £10 D–£14 (£12 D–£16)
- ⚐ 1 mile east of Aboyne on A93
- 🏠 Derek McCulloch
- 🖥 www.thelodgeontheloch.com

Alford (1982)
Montgarrie Road, Alford, AB33 8AE
- ☎ (019755) 62178
- 📠 (019755) 64910
- ✉ info@alford-golf-club.co.uk
- 🏠 580
- 🏌 Mr Victor Harker
- ⛳ 18 L 5483 yds Par 69 SSS 66
- 👥 WD–U WE–restricted on comp days SOC
- ££ £20 D–£25 (£25 D–£30)
- ⚐ 25 miles W of Aberdeen on A944
- 🏠 David Hird
- 🖥 www.alford-golf-club.co.uk

Auchenblae (1894)
Pay and play
Auchenblae, Laurencekirk, AB30 1TX
- ☎ (01561) 320002 (Bookings)
- 🏠 480
- 🏌 J Thomson (01561) 320245
- ⛳ 9 L 2217 yds Par 64 SSS 61
- 👥 U–WD/WE WED–U till 5.30pm
- ££ D–£13 (D–£16)
- ⚐ 11 miles SW of Stonehaven. 3 miles W of A90
- 🏠 Latest addition: Robin Hiseman
- 🖥 www.auchenblae.org.uk

Ballater (1892)
Victoria Road, Ballater, AB35 5LX
- ☎ (013397) 55567
- ✉ sec@ballatergolfclub.co.uk
- 🏠 700

Colin Smith
- 🏌 W Yule (013397) 55658
- ⛳ 18 L 6094 yds SSS 69
- 👥 U
- ££ On application
- ⚐ 42 miles W of Aberdeen on A93
- ⊕ Putting Green
- 🖥 www.ballatergolfclub.co.uk

Ballindalloch Castle (2003)
Pay and play
Lagmore, Ballindalloch, Banffshire, AB37 9AA
- ☎ (01807) 500305
- 📠 (01807) 500226
- ✉ golf@ballindallochcastle.co.uk
- 🏌 Alan Rodger
- ⛳ 9 greens 18 tees L 6495 yds Par 72 SSS 71
- 👥 WD & WE U & SOC
- ££ 9: £15 18: £20
- ⚐ Just off A95 between Grantown-on-Spey and Aberlour
- ⊕ Practice area (230 yds); putting green
- 🏠 Donald Steel and Tom Mackenzie
- 🖥 www.ballindallochcastle.co.uk

Banchory (1905)
Kinneskie Road, Banchory, AB31 5TA
- ☎ (01330) 822365
- 📠 (01330) 822491
- ✉ info@banchorygolfclub.co.uk
- 🏠 1000
- 🏌 W Crighton
- 🏌 D Naylor (01330) 822447
- ⛳ 18 L 5801 yds Par 69 SSS 68
- 👥 WD–U WE–restricted H
- ££ £26 D–£35 (£35 D–£45)
- ⚐ W of Banchory, off A93
- 🖥 www.banchorygolfclub.co.uk

Braemar (1902)
Cluniebank Road, Braemar, AB35 5XX
- ☎ (013397) 41618
- ✉ info@braemargolfclub.co.uk
- 🏠 450
- 🏌 C McIntosh (01339) 741595
- ⛳ 18 L 4916 yds SSS 64
- 👥 U SOC WD WE
- ££ £25 D–£30 (£25 D–£30) W–£100
- ⚐ Braemar ½ mile. 17 miles W of Ballater
- 🏠 J Anderson
- 🖥 www.braemargolfclub.co.uk

Craibstone (1999)
Public
Craibstone Estate, Bucksburn, Aberdeen, AB29 9YA
- ☎ (01224) 716777
- ✉ craibstonegolf@sac.co.uk

Cruden Bay (1899)
Cruden Bay, Peterhead, AB42 0NN
- ☎ (01779) 812285
- **bookings@crudenbaygolfclub.co.uk**

- 📠 (01779) 812945
- ✉ secretary@crudenbaygolfclub.co.uk
- 🏠 1070
- 🏌 Mrs R Pittendrigh (Sec/Mgr)
- 🏌 RG Stewart (01779) 812414
- ⛳ 18 L 6287 yds SSS 71
- ⛳ 9 L 4905 yds SSS 64
- 👥 WD–U WE–H exc comp days
- ££ £65 D–£85 (£75)
- ⚐ 22 miles NE of Aberdeen (A90)
- ⊕ Driving range
- 🏠 Thomas Simpson
- 🖥 www.crudenbaygolfclub.co.uk

Cullen (1879)
The Links, Cullen, Buckie, AB56 4WB
- ☎ (01542) 840685
- ✉ cullengolfclub@btinternet.com
- 🏠 625
- 🏌 Mrs H Bavidge
- ⛳ 18 L 4610 yds Par 63 SSS 62
- 👥 U SOC
- ££ £22 D–£30 (£25 D–30) 2008
- ⚐ 5 miles E of Buckie, off A98 between Aberdeen and Inverness
- ⊕ Practice nets; putting green
- 🏠 Tom Morris
- 🖥 www.cullengolfclub.co.uk

Duff House Royal (1910)
The Barnyards, Banff, AB45 3SX
- ☎ (01261) 812062
- 📠 (01261) 812224
- ✉ duff_house_royal@btinternet.com
- 🏠 547 167(L) 132(J)
- 🏌 Graham MacKenzie
- 🏌 Gary Holland (01261) 812075
- ⛳ 18 L 6161 yds SSS 70
- 👥 WD–U H WE–H 8.30–11am and 12.30–3pm
- ££ £30–£40 (£36–£50) – 2008 rates
- ⚐ Moray Firth coast, between Buckie and Fraserburgh
- 🏠 Dr A & Maj CA Mackenzie
- 🖥 www.theduffhouseroyalgolfclub.co.uk

Fraserburgh (1777)
Philorth Links, Fraserburgh, AB43 8TL
- ☎ (01346) 516616
- 📠 (01346) 510611
- ✉ secretary@fraserburghgolfclub.org
- 🏠 642 56(L) 119(J)
- 🏌 Nicola Carono
- ⛳ 18 L 6308 yds Par 70 SSS 71
- ⛳ 9 L 2400 yds Par 64
- 👥 U SOC WD WE
- ££ £30 D–£40 (£35 D–£45)
- ⚐ 1 mile SE of Fraserburgh
- ⊕ Practice area and practice putting green
- 🏠 James Braid
- 🖥 www.fraserburghgolfclub.org

Huntly (1892)
Cooper Park, Huntly, AB54 4SH
- ☎ (01466) 792643
- 📠 (01466) 792643

✉ huntlygc@btconnect.com
🚪 500
🏌 A Donald (01466) 792643
➤ 18 L 5399 yds Par 67 SSS 66
👥 U SOC
£€ £17 D–£22.50 (£24 D–£30)
   W–£10
🚗 N side of Huntly. 38 miles NW of
   Aberdeen, off A96
🏠 Tom Morris
🖥 www.huntlygolf.com

Inchmarlo   (1995)
Proprietary
Glassel Road, Banchory, AB31 4BQ
☎ **(01330) 826424**
🖨 (01330) 826425
✉ secretary@inchmarlo.com
🚪 750
🏌 Andrew Shinie (01330) 826427
✓ P Lovie (01330) 826422
➤ 18 L 6218 yds Par 71 SSS 71
   9 L 4300 yds Par 64 SSS 62
👥 U SOC–WD
£€ 9: £16 (£18) 18: £32 (£37)
🚗 ¹/₂ mile W of Banchory on A93
⊕ 30 bay floodlit driving range;
   practice putting green
🏠 Graeme Webster
🖥 www.inchmarlogolf.com

Insch   (1906)
Golf Terrace, Insch, AB52 6JY
☎ **(01464) 820363**
🖨 (01464) 820363
✉ administrator@inschgolfclub.co.uk
🚪 400
🏌 Jill Townsend (Administrator)
➤ 18 L 5350 yds SSS 67
👥 U
£€ £16 (£22) special offers on app.
🚗 28 miles NW of Aberdeen, off A96
⊕ Practice area
🏠 Greens of Scotland
🖥 www.inschgolfclub.co.uk

Inverallochy
Public
*Whitelink, Inverallochy, Fraserburgh,
AB43 8XY*
☎ **(01346) 582000**

Inverurie   (1923)
Davah Wood, Inverurie, AB51 5JB
☎ **(01467) 624080**
🖨 (01467) 672869
✉ administrator@inveruriegc.co.uk
🚪 780
🏌 Alan Donald (01467) 624080
✓ Steven McLean (01467) 672863
➤ 18 L 5711 yds SSS 68
👥 U SOC
£€ £22 D–£25 (£25 D–£32)
🚗 Off the A96 at the Blackhall
   roundabout
🖥 www.inveruriegc.co.uk

Keith   (1963)
Mar Court, Fife Keith, Keith, AB55 5GF
☎ **(01542) 882469**
✉ secretary@keithgolfclub.org.uk
🚪 250
🏌 Graeme Cruickshank

➤ 18 L 5802 yds SSS 69
👥 U
£€ £15 D–£15 (£20 D–£20)
🚗 Fife Park, W side of Keith
🖥 www.keithgolfclub.org.uk

Kemnay   (1908)
Monymusk Road, Kemnay, AB51 5RA
☎ **(01467) 642060
   (Bar/Restaurant)
   (01467) 643746 (Office)**
🖨 (01467) 643746
✉ administrator@kemnaygolfclub
   .co.uk
🚪 820
🏌 S Booth
✓ D J Brown (01647) 642225
➤ 18 L 6362 yds Par 71 SSS 71
👥 U
£€ £24 D–£30 (£30 D–£36)
🚗 15 miles W of Aberdeen (B994, off
   A96)
🖥 www.kemnaygolfclub.co.uk

Kintore   (1911)
Balbithan Road, Kintore, AB51 0UR
☎ **(01467) 632631**
🖨 (01467) 632995
✉ kintoregolfclub@lineone.net
🚪 700
🏌 C Lindsay
➤ 18 L 6019 yds SSS 69
👥 U
£€ £20 (£25)
🚗 12 miles NW of Aberdeen on A96
🖥 www.kintoregolfclub.net

Longside   (1973)
West End, Longside, Peterhead, AB42 7XJ
☎ **(01779) 821558**
🖨 (01779) 821564
✉ info@longsidegolf.wanadoo.co.uk
🚪 700
🏌 K Allan (01771) 622424
➤ 18 L 5225 yds Par 66 SSS 66
👥 U exc Sun–NA before 10.30am
   SOC
£€ £13 D–£18 Sun–£19 D–£24
🚗 5 miles W of Peterhead on A590
🖥 www.longsidegolfclub.co.uk

Lumphanan   (1924)
*10 Main Road, Lumphanan, Banchory,
AB31 4PY*
☎ **(01339) 883480**
✉ lumphanan.golf.club@lineone.net
🏌 DJ Shaw (01339) 883440
➤ 9 L 3718 yds Par 62 SSS 62
👥 U
£€ £8 D–£12 (£10 D–£15)
🚗 25 miles W of Aberdeen on A980
🖥 www.lineone.net/~lumphanan
   .golf.club

McDonald   (1927)
Hospital Road, Ellon, AB41 9AW
☎ **(01358) 720576**
🖨 (01358) 720001
✉ mcdonald.golf@virgin.net
🚪 750
🏌 G Ironside
✓ R Urquhart (01358) 722891
➤ 18 L 5991 yds Par 70 SSS 70

👥 WD/WE–U after 10am
£€ On application
🚗 15 miles N of Aberdeen, off A90
🖥 www.ellongolfclub.co.uk

Meldrum House   (1998)
*Meldrum House Estate, Oldmeldrum,
AB51 0AE*
☎ **(01651) 873553**
🖨 (01651) 873635
✉ info@meldrumhousegolfclub.co.uk
🚪 400
🏌 B Smith (Operations Mgr)
✓ N Marr
➤ 18 L 6379 yds Par 70 SSS 72
👥 M
£€ N/A
🚗 11 miles N of Aberdeen on A947
🏠 Graeme Webster
🖥 www.meldrumhousegolfclub.com

Newburgh-on-Ythan
   (1888)
*Beach Road, Newburgh, Aberdeenshire,
AB41 6BY*
☎ **(01358) 789058**
🖨 (01358) 788104
✉ secretary@newburghgolfclub.co.uk
🚪 400 40(L) 120(J)
🏌 Administrator: (01358) 789084
✓ Ian Bratton
   pro@newburghgolfclub.co.uk
➤ 18 L 6423 yds Par 72 SSS 72
👥 WD–U WE–Sat before noon NA
£€ £35 D–£40 (£45 D–£55)
🚗 12 miles N of Aberdeen (A975); 14
   miles from Dyce Airport
⊕ 6 hole practice course; putting
   green; nets; indoor swing studio;
   driving range, buggies
🏠 Taylor
🖥 www.newburghgolfclub.co.uk

Newmachar   (1989)
*Swailend, Newmachar, Aberdeen,
AB21 7UU*
☎ **(01651) 863002**
🖨 (01651) 863055
✉ info@newmachargolfclub.co.uk
🚪 1040
🏌 Carol O'Neill
✓ A Cooper (01651) 863222
➤ 18 L 6700 yds Par 72 SSS 74
   18 L 6388 yds Par 72 SSS 71
👥 H SOC
£€ Hawkshill £40 (£60); Swailend £25
   (£35)
🚗 12 miles N of Aberdeen on A947
⊕ Driving range
🏠 Dave Thomas
🖥 www.newmachargolfclub.co.uk

Oldmeldrum   (1885)
Kirk Brae, Oldmeldrum, AB51 0DJ
☎ **(01651) 872648/873555**
🖨 (01651) 872896
✉ admin@oldmeldrumgolf.co.uk
🚪 800
🏌 S.Jones (Sec),
   Eva Beech-Campbell (Mgr)
✓ H Love (01651) 873555
➤ 18 L 5683 yds Par 70 SSS 70
👥 WD–U before 5pm WE–phone
   first

££ £24 (D–£30)
⊕ᴏ̃ 17 miles N of Aberdeen on A947
⊕ Driving Range
▤ www.oldmeldrumgolf.co.uk

Peterhead (1841)
Craigewan Links, Peterhead, AB42 1LT
☎ (01779) 472149/480725
📠 (01779) 480725
✉ phdgc@freenetname.co.uk
📖 500 45(L)
♫ᴏ D.G.Wood
✓ H Dougal
⊱ 18 L 6147 yds SSS 71
9 L 2237 yds SSS 62
👯 U exc Sat–restricted
££ On application
⊕ᴏ̃ 1 mile N of Peterhead
⊕ Practice nets; practice area
🏠 Willie Park Jr/James Braid
▤ www.peterheadgolfclub.co.uk

Rosehearty (1874)
c/o Mason's Arms Hotel, Rosehearty,
Fraserburgh, AB43 7JJ
☎ (01346) 571250 (Capt)
📠 (01346) 571306
✉ scotthornal@cbtinternet.com
📖 220
♫ᴏ S Hornal
✓ S Hornal (01346) 571250
⊱ 9 L 2197 yds SSS 62
👯 U
££ D–£10 (D–£15)
⊕ᴏ̃ 4 miles W of Fraserburgh (B9031)
⊕ Driving range; tuition bays

Rothes (1990)
Blackhall, Rothes, Aberlour, AB38 7AN
☎ (01340) 831443
📠 (01340) 831443
✉ rothesgolfclub.co.uk
📖 340
♫ᴏ Kenneth MacPhee (01340) 831676
⊱ 9 L 4972 yds Par 68 SSS 64
👯 U SOC
££ 9: £19 (£12) 18: £15 (£20)
⊕ᴏ̃ ¹/₂ mile SW of Rothes. 10 miles S
of Elgin on A941
🏠 John Souter
▤ www.rothesgolfclub.co.uk

Royal Tarlair (1926)
Buchan Street, Macduff, AB44 1TA
☎ (01261) 832897
📠 (01261) 833455
✉ info@royaltarlair.co.uk
📖 520
♫ᴏ Mrs Muriel McMurray
⊱ 18 L 5866 yds SSS 68
👯 U
££ £20 D–£25 (£25 D–£30)
⊕ᴏ̃ Macduff, 4 miles E of Banff. 45 miles
N of Aberdeen A98, Bariff to
Fraserburgh Road
▤ www.royaltarlair.co.uk

Stonehaven (1888)
Cowie, Stonehaven, AB39 3RH
☎ (01569) 762124
📠 (01569) 765973
✉ stonehavengc@btconnect.com
📖 500

♫ᴏ WA Donald
⊱ 18 L 5128 yds Par 66 SSS 65
👯 Sat–NA before 3.45pm Sun–NA
before 10.45am
££ £18 (£20)
⊕ᴏ̃ 1 mile N of Stonehaven
🏠 A Simpson
▤ www.stonehavengolfclub.com

Strathlene (1877)
Portessie, Buckie, AB56 2DJ
☎ (01542) 831798
📠 (01542) 831798
✉ strathgolf@ukonline.co.uk
📖 375
♫ᴏ G Jappy
⊱ 18 L 5977 yds SSS 69
👯 U SOC
££ £20 D–£24 (£23 D–£32)
⊕ᴏ̃ ¹/₂ mile E of Buckie
⊕ Driving range on site; pitch & putt
and putting facilities
🏠 G Smith
▤ www.strathlenegolfclub.co.uk

Tarland (1908)
Aberdeen Road, Tarland, AB34 4TB
☎ (013398) 81000
📠 (013398) 81000
📖 350
♫ᴏ Mrs J Joseph
⊱ 9 L 5875 yds SSS 68
👯 WD–U WE–enquiry advisable
SOC–WD only
££ D–£18 (£24)
⊕ᴏ̃ 5 miles NW of Aboyne. 30 miles
W of Aberdeen
🏠 Tom Morris

Torphins (1896)
Bog Road, Torphins, AB31 4JU
☎ (013398) 82115
✉ stuartmacgregor5@btinternet.com
📖 310
♫ᴏ S MacGregor (013398) 82402
⊱ 9 L 4777 yds SSS 64
👯 U SOC
££ £14 (£16); £9 for 9 holes
⊕ᴏ̃ 1¹/₂ miles W of Torphins towards
Lumphanan
▤ www.torphinsgolfclub.com

Turriff (1896)
Rosehall, Turriff, AB53 4HD
☎ (01888) 562982
📠 (01888) 568050
✉ secretary@turriffgolf.sol.co.uk
📖 700
♫ᴏ M Smart
✓ J Mooney (01888) 563025
⊱ 18 L 6145 yds SSS 70
👯 WD–U before 5pm WE after 10am
££ £23 D–£27 (£27 D–£33)
⊕ᴏ̃ 35 miles N of Aberdeen (A947)
⊕ Putting green; practice areas; buggy
hire
🏠 GM Fraser
▤ www.turriffgolfclub.com

Aberdeen Clubs

Bon Accord (1872)
Club
19 Golf Road, Aberdeen, AB24 5QB
☎ (01224) 633464

Caledonian (1899)
Club
20 Golf Road, Aberdeen, AB2 1QB
☎ (01224) 632443

Northern (1897)
Public
22 Golf Road, Aberdeen, AB24 5QB
☎ (01224) 636440
📠 (01224) 622679
📖 561
♫ᴏ D Sangster
⊱ Play over King's Links Municipal
18 L Medal 71 6270 yds, Yellow 67
5762 yds
££ £11.25
⊕ᴏ̃ Alongside Pittodrie Stadium
⊕ Driving range 100 yds from tee

Aberdeen Courses

Auchmill (1975)
Bonnyview Road, West Heatheryfold,
Aberdeen, AB2 7FQ
☎ (01224) 715214
✉ auchmill.golfclub@virgin.net

Balnagask (1955)
Public
St Fitticks Road, Aberdeen
☎ (01224) 871286

Deeside (1903)
Golf Road, Bieldside, Aberdeen, AB15 9DL
☎ (01224) 869457
📠 (01224) 861800
✉ admin@deesidegolfclub.com
📖 1100
♫ᴏ Ms D Pern (01224) 869457
✓ FJ Coutts (01224) 861041
⊱ 18 L 6407 yds SSS 72
9 L 5042 yds SSS 68
👯 H
££ £50 (£65)
⊕ᴏ̃ 3 miles SW of Aberdeen on A93
▤ www.deesidegolfclub.com

Fyvie (2003)
Pay and play
Fyvie, Turriff, Aberdeenshire AB53 8QR
☎ (01651) 891166
📠 (01651) 891166
✉ info@fyviegolfcourse.co.uk
📖 44
♫ᴏ Alexander Rankin
⊱ 9 L 5476 yds Par 35 SSS 67
👯 U SOC
££ 9: £10 D–£20 (£12) 18: £15 D–£25
(£18)
⊕ᴏ̃ 8 m south of Turriff off A947
🏠 Alexander Rankin & George McRae
▤ www.fyviegolfcourse.co.uk

Murcar Links   (1909)
Bridge of Don, Aberdeen, AB23 8BD
- ☎ **(01224) 704354**
- 📞 (01224) 704354
- ✉ golf@murcarlinks.com
- 🏠 850
- 🖊 Joanne Mitchell
- ⚑ Gary Forbes (01224) 704370
- ▷ 18 L 6325 yds SSS 71
  9 L 5369 yds SSS 67
- 🏌 H
- ££ £70 (£90) D–£95
- ⛳ 5 miles N of Aberdeen, off A90
- ⊕ Driving range; practice facilities
- 🏠 Archie Simpson/James Braid
- 💻 www.murcarlinks.com

Peterculter   (1989)
Oldtown, Burnside Road, Peterculter, AB14 0LN
- ☎ **(01224) 735245**
- 📞 (01224) 735580
- ✉ info@petercultergolfclub.co.uk
- 🏠 925
- 🖊 D Vannet
- ⚑ D Vannet (01224) 734994
- ▷ 18 L 6219 yds SSS 70
- 🏌 WD–U before 3pm WE–U SOC
- ££ £25–£30 (£30–£35)
- ⛳ 8 miles W of Aberdeen on A93
- 💻 www.petercultergolfclub.co.uk

Portlethen   (1983)
Badentoy Road, Portlethen, Aberdeen, AB12 4YA
- ☎ **(01224) 781090**
- 📞 (01224) 783383
- ✉ info@portlethengc.fsnet.co.uk
- 🏠 1100
- ⚑ Muriel Thomson (01224) 782571
- ▷ 18 L 6670 yds SSS 72
- 🏌 WD–U exc Wed after 2pm
  Sat–NA before 4pm
- ££ £24 D–£36 (£36)
- ⛳ 6 miles S of Aberdeen on A90
- ⊕ Driving range; putting green
- 🏠 Donald Steel
- 💻 www.portlethengolfclub.com

Royal Aberdeen   (1780)
Links Road, Bridge of Don, Aberdeen, AB23 8AT
- ☎ **(01224) 702571**
- 📞 (01224) 826591
- ✉ admin@royalaberdeengolf.com
- 🏠 350 100(J)
- 🖊 GF Webster
- ⚑ R MacAskill (Golf Dir) (01224) 702221
- ▷ 18 L 6900 yds SSS 74
  18 L 4066 yds SSS 60
- 🏌 I H SOC
- ££ £100 D–£150 (£120)
- ⛳ 2 miles N of Aberdeen on A90
- ⊕ Short game practice area
- 🏠 Simpson/Braid
- 💻 www.royalaberdeengolf.com

Westhill   (1977)
Westhill Heights, Westhill, AB32 6RY
- ☎ **(01224) 742567**
- 📞 (01224) 749124
- ✉ westhillgolf@btconnect.com
- 🏠 900
- 🖊 George Bruce (Admin)
- ⚑ G Bruce (01224) 740159
- ▷ 18 L 5849 yds SSS 69
- 🏌 WD–U WE–U SOC–U
- ££ £20 D–£25 (£25 D–£30)
- ⛳ 8 miles W of Aberdeen, off A944
- ⊕ Putting green, practice area; buggy hire
- 🏠 Charles Lawrie
- 💻 www.westhillgolfclub.co.uk

Angus

Arbroath Artisan   (1903)
Public
Elliot, Arbroath, DD11 2PE
- ☎ **(01241) 872069**
  (01241) 875837 (Bookings)
- 📞 (01241) 875837
- ✉ captain@arbroathartisangolfclub.co.uk
- 🏠 650
- 🖊 J R Tollerton
- ⚑ L Ewart (01241) 875837
- ▷ 18 L 6185 yds Par 70 SSS 69
- 🏌 WD–U SOC WE–NA before 10am
- ££ £26 D–£32 (£32 D–£40)
- ⛳ 1 mile SW of Arbroath on A92
- 🏠 James Braid
- 💻 www.arbroathartisangolfclub.co.uk

Ballumbie Castle   (2000)
3 Old Quarry Road, Dundee, DD4 0SY
- ☎ **(01382) 770028**
- 📞 (01382) 730008
- ✉ ballumbie2000@yahoo.com
- 🏠 620
- 🖊 Stephen Harrod
- ⚑ Lee Sutherland
- ▷ 18 L 6157 yds Par 69 SSS 70
- 🏌 U SOC
- ££ £30 7 days a week
- ⛳ NE outskirts of Dundee, off A90 to Arbroath
- ⊕ 20-bay driving range with power tees; putting green; chipping green; state of the art clubhouse.
- 🏠 Duncan Gray
- 💻 www.ballumbiecastlegolfclub.com

Brechin   (1893)
Trinity, Brechin, DD9 7PD
- ☎ **(01356) 622383/625270**
- 📞 (01356) 625270
- ✉ brechingolfclub@tiscali.co.uk
- 🏠 750
- 🖊 IA Jardine
- ⚑ S Rennie (01356) 625270
- ▷ 18 L 6162 yds SSS 70
- 🏌 U SOC welcome 7 days
- ££ £30 D–£37 (£32 sat/sun D–£40)
- ⛳ 1 mile N of Brechin on M90
- ⊕ Putting green/practice area; Full catering facilities
- 🏠 James Braid
- 💻 www.brechingolfclub.co.uk

Caird Park   (1926)
Public
Mains Loan, Caird Park, Dundee, DD4 9BX
- ☎ **(01382) 453606/461460**
  (01382) 438871 (Starter)
- ✉ cairdparkgolfclub@tiscali.co.uk

Camperdown   (1960)
Public
Camperdown Park, Dundee, DD2 4TF
- ☎ **(01382) 623398**

Downfield   (1932)
Turnberry Ave, Dundee, DD2 3QP
- ☎ **(01382) 825595**
- 📞 (01382) 813111
- ✉ downfieldgc@aol.com
- 🏠 750
- 🖊 Mrs M Campbell
- ⚑ KS Hutton (01382) 889246
- ▷ 18 L 6822 yds SSS 73
- 🏌 WD–U 9.30–11.16 and 2.18–3.42pm WE–limited access after 2pm (Sun only)
- ££ 18 holes: £50 D–£60 36 hole package £72 – 2008 prices
- ⛳ N of Dundee, off A923
- 🏠 James Braid, CK Cotton
- 💻 www.downfieldgolf.co.uk

Edzell   (1895)
High St, Edzell, DD9 7TF
- ☎ **(01356) 647283**
- 📞 (01356) 648094
- ✉ secretary@edzellgolfclub.net
- 🏠 885
- 🖊 IG Farquhar (01356) 647283
- ⚑ AJ Webster (01356) 648462
- ▷ 18 L 6427 yds SSS 71
  9 L 2057 yds Par 32
  West Water 9 hole course
  9 holes £12, 18 holes £16
- 🏌 WD–NA 4.45–6.15pm WE–NA 7.30–3pm SOC
- ££ £36 D–£48 (£42 D–£60)
- ⛳ 6 miles N of Brechin on B966
- ⊕ Driving range
- 🏠 Bob Simpson/James Braid
- 💻 www.edzellgolfclub.net

Forfar   (1871)
Cunninghill, Arbroath Road, Forfar, DD8 2RL
- ☎ **(01307) 463773/462120**
- 📞 (01307) 468495
- ✉ info@forfargolfclub.com
- 🏠 730
- 🖊 S Wilson
- ⚑ P McNiven (01307) 465683
- ▷ 18 L 6066 yds Par 69 SSS 69
- 🏌 U (SOC: WD & Sun 10–11.30am and 2.30–4pm, Sat 2.30–4pm)
- ££ £32 D–£40 (£35 D–£45)
- ⛳ 1½ miles E of Forfar on A932
- 🏠 Tom Morris/James Braid
- 💻 www.forfargolfclub.com

Kirriemuir   (1884)
Northmuir, Kirriemuir, DD8 4LN
- ☎ **(01575) 573317**
- 📞 (01575) 574608
- 🏠 850

⚗ C Gowrie
✓ Mrs K Dallas (01575) 573317
► 18 L 5510 yds SSS 67
👥 WD–U WE–by arrangement SOC
££ £25 D–£32 (£33 D–£43.50)
🚗 NE outskirts of Kirriemuir. 17 miles N of Dundee
🏠 James Braid

Monifieth Golf Links
Medal Starter's Box, Princes Street, Monifieth, DD5 4AW
☎ **(01382) 532767 (Medal)**
  (01382) 532967 (Ashludie)
🖥 (01382) 535816
✉ monifiethgolf@freeuk.com
📖 1450
⚗ J Brodie (Managing Sec), S McFarlane (GolfMgr) (01382) 535553
✓ I McLeod (01382) 532945
► Medal 18 L 6650 yds SSS 72 Ashludie 18 L 5123 SSS 66
👥 WD–U Sat–NA before 2pm Sun–NA before 10am SOC
££ Medal £49 (£59); Ashludie £24 (£26) Medal + Ashludie £69 (incl catering)
🚗 6 miles E of Dundee
⊕ Broughty, Grange and Monifieth clubs play here; buggies available
🖥 www.monifiethgolf.co.uk

Montrose (1562)
Public
Traill Drive, Montrose, DD10 8SW
☎ **(01674) 672932**
🖥 (01674) 671800
✉ secretary@montroselinks.co.uk
📖 1300
⚗ Mrs M Stewart
✓ J Boyd (01674) 672634
► Medal 18 L 6544 yds SSS 72 Broomfield 18 L 4830 yds SSS 63
👥 Medal–WD–U Sat–NA before 2.30pm Sun–NA before 10am Broomfield–U
££ Medal £47 (£52) Broomfield £20 (£22)
🚗 1 mile from Montrose centre, off A92
⊕ Royal Montrose, Caledonia and Mercantile clubs play here
🏠 Willie Park (1903)
🖥 www.montroselinks.co.uk

Montrose Caledonia (1896)
Club
Dorward Road, Montrose, DD10 8SW
☎ **(01674) 672313**
⚗ Mrs S Burness (01674 672416)
► Play over Montrose courses

Panmure (1845)
Barry, Carnoustie, DD7 7RT
☎ **(01241) 855120**
🖥 (01241) 859737
✉ secretary@panmuregolfclub.co.uk
📖 500
⚗ Charles JR Philip (01241) 855120
✓ Andrew Crerar (01241) 852460
► 18 L 6501 yds Par 70 SSS 72
👥 WD/Sun–U Sat–NA before 4 pm

££ On application
🚗 2 miles W of Carnoustie, off A930
⊕ Practice range
🏠 Morris/Braid
🖥 www.panmuregolfclub.co.uk

Royal Montrose (1810)
Club
Dorward Road, Montrose, DD10 8SW
☎ **(01674) 672376**
🖥 (01674) 678125
✉ secretary@royalmontrosegolf.com
📖 650
⚗ Michael J Cummins (01674) 662045
✓ Jason Boyd (01674) 672643
► Play over Montrose courses
👥 See Montrose Golf Links
££ See Montrose Golf Links
🚗 Adjacent to Montrose Medal 1st and 18th
🏠 Willie Park Jr, Old Tom Morris *et al*
🖥 www.royalmontrosegolf.com

Carnoustie Clubs

Carnoustie (1842)
Club
3 Links Parade, Carnoustie, DD7 7JF
☎ **(01241) 852480**
🖥 (01241) 856459
✉ admin@carnoustiegolfclub.com
📖 900
⚗ AJR Mackenzie
► Play over Carnoustie courses
🚗 Adjacent to 1st tee of Championship Course
⊕ Catering/bar facilities available for visitors/parties playing over Carnoustie courses
🖥 www.carnoustiegolfclub.com

Carnoustie Caledonia (1887)
Club
Links Parade, Carnoustie, DD7 7JF
☎ **(01241) 852115**
📖 413
⚗ R Reyner
► Play over Carnoustie courses
🖥 www.carnoustiecaledonia.co.uk

Carnoustie Ladies (1873)
Club
12 Links Parade, Carnoustie, DD7 7JF
☎ **(01241) 855252**

Carnoustie Mercantile (1896)
Club
Links Parade, Carnoustie, DD7 7JE
📖 40
⚗ GJA Murray (01241) 854420
► Play over Carnoustie courses

Carnoustie Courses

Buddon Links (1981)
Public
20 Links Parade, Carnoustie, DD7 7JF
☎ **(01241) 802280 (Starter)**
  (01241) 802270 (Bookings)
🖥 (01241) 802271

✉ golf@carnoustiegolflinks.co.uk
⚗ G Duncan
► 18 L 5420 yds SSS 66
👥 WD–U WE–U after 11.30am
££ £30
🚗 12 miles E of Dundee, by A92 or A930
⊕ Practice facilities
🏠 Peter Alliss/David Thomas
🖥 www.carnoustiegolflinks.co.uk

Burnside (1914)
Public
20 Links Parade, Carnoustie, DD7 7JF
☎ **(01241) 802290 (Starter)**
  (01241) 802270 (Bookings)
🖥 (01241) 802271
✉ golf@carnoustiegolflinks.co.uk
⚗ G Duncan
► 18 L 6028 yds SSS 70
👥 WD–U Sat–U after 2pm Sun–U after 11.30am
££ £35
🚗 12 miles E of Dundee, by A92 or A930
⊕ Practice facilities
🖥 www.carnoustiegolflinks.co.uk

Carnoustie Championship (16th Century)
Public
20 Links Parade, Carnoustie, DD7 7JF
☎ **(01241) 802280 (Starter)**
  (01241) 802270 (Bookings)
🖥 (01241) 802271
✉ golf@carnoustiegolflinks.co.uk
⚗ G Duncan
► 18 L 6941 yds SSS 75
👥 WD–H Sat–H after 2pm Sun–H after 11.30am
££ £130
🚗 12 miles E of Dundee, by A92 or A930
⊕ Practice facilities
🏠 Allan Robertson
🖥 www.carnoustiegolflinks.co.uk

Argyll & Bute

Blairmore & Strone (1896)
High Road, Strone, Dunoon, PA23 8JJ
☎ **(01369) 840676**
📖 120
⚗ JC Fleming (01369) 860307
► 9 L 2122 yds SSS 62
👥 Mon–NA after 6pm Sat–NA 12–4pm Wed–NA 6–7pm
££ D–£12
🚗 Strone, 8 miles N of Dunoon
🏠 James Braid

Bute (1888)
32 Marine Place, Ardbeg, Rothesay, Isle of Bute PA20 0LF
☎ **(01700) 503091**
✉ administrator@butegolfclub.com
📖 200
⚗ F Robinson (01700) 503091
► 9 L 2497 yds SSS 64
👥 U Sat–U after 11.30am
££ D–£10; Juniors £5

For list of abbreviations and key to symbols see page 647

🏌 Stravanan Bay, 6 miles S of
Rothesay, off A845
🖥 www.butegolfclub.com

Carradale   (1906)

Carradale, Campbeltown, PA28 6QT
☎ (01583) 431321
📧 archbiscuits@aol.com
🖽 260
🏌 Dr RJ Abernethy
🏳 9 L 2370 yds SSS 62
👤 U
££ £15 D–£20
🏌 Carradale, 15 miles N of
Campbeltown (B842)
🖥 www.carradalegolfclub.co.uk

Colonsay

Owned privately
Isle of Colonsay, PA61 7YR
☎ (01951) 200290
📠 (01951) 200290
🖽 200
🏌 Eleanor McNeill (01951) 200210
🏳 18 L 4775 yds Par 72
👤 U
££ On application
🏌 W coast of Colonsay, at Machrins

Cowal   (1891)

Ardenslate Road, Dunoon, PA23 8LT
☎ (01369) 705673
📠 (01369) 705673
📧 secretary@cowalgolfclub.com
🖽 900
🏌 A Douglas (01369) 705673
🏌 RD Weir (01369) 702395
🏳 18 L 6063 yds SSS 70
👤 U
££ £18 (£22)
🏌 NE boundary of Dunoon
🏟 James Braid (1928)

Craignure   (1895)

Scallastle, Craignure, Isle of Mull, PA65 6BA
☎ (01688) 302517
📧 pvnbook2@aol.com

Dalmally   (1986)

Old Saw Mill, Dalmally, PA33 1AS
☎ (01838) 200370
📧 dalmallygolfclub@btinternet.com
🖽 150
🏌 R Johnston (01838) 200487
🏳 9 L 2277 yds Par 64 SSS 63
👤 U SOC
££ D–£12
🏌 1 mile W of Dalmally on A85
⊕ Phone for special outings
🖥 www.loch-awe.com/golfclub

Dunaverty   (1889)

Southend, Campbeltown, PA28 6RW
☎ (01586) 830677
📠 (01586) 830677
📧 dunavertygc@aol.com
🖽 430
🏌 James Robertson
🏳 18 L 4799 yds SSS 63
👤 U
££ £19 (£23)
🏌 10 miles S of Campbeltown

Gigha   (1992)

Isle of Gigha, Kintyre, PA41 7AA
☎ (01583) 505242
📧 johngigha@hotmail.co.uk
🖽 30
🏌 J Bannatyne
🏳 9 L 5042 yds SSS 65
👤 U
££ D–£10
🏌 Off W coast of Kintyre A83 to
Tayinloan Ferry Terminal
🏟 Founder members in 1989
🖥 www.gigha.org

Glencruitten   (1908)

Glencruitten Road, Oban, PA34 4PU
☎ (01631) 562868
📧 enquiries@obangolf.com
🖽 450
🏌 AG Brown (01631) 564604
🏌 Shop (01631) 564115
🏳 18 L 4452 yds SSS 63
👤 U
££ £25 D or R (£30 D or R)
🏌 Oban 1 mile
⊕ Practice area; putting green
🏟 James Braid
🖥 www.obangolf.com

Helensburgh   (1893)

25 East Abercromby Street, Helensburgh,
G84 9HZ
☎ (01436) 674173
📠 (01436) 671170
📧 thesecretary@helensburghgolfclub
.co.uk
🖽 850
🏌 DW Deas (01436) 674173
🏌 F Hall (01436) 675505
🏳 18 L 5942 yds Par 69 SSS 69
👤 WD–U WE–NA
££ £35 D–£45
🏌 N of Helensburgh and A814. 8
miles W of Dumbarton
🏟 Tom Morris
🖥 www.helensburghgolfclub.co.uk

Innellan   (1891)

Knockamillie Road, Innellan, Dunoon
☎ (01369) 830242
🖽 200
🏌 A Wilson (01369) 702573
🏳 9 L 4878 yds SSS 64
👤 U SOC
££ 18: £15
🏌 4 miles S of Dunoon (A815)

Inveraray   (1893)

North Cromalt, Inveraray, Argyll
☎ (01499) 302079
🖽 140
🏌 D MacNeill
🏳 9 L 5600 yds SSS 69
👤 U SOC
££ D–£15
🏌 1 mile S of Inveraray on A83

Islay   (1891)

25 Charlotte St, Port Ellen, Isle of Islay,
PA42 7DF
☎ (01496) 300094

Isle of Seil   (1996)

Pay and play
Balvicar, Isle of Seil, PA34 4TL
☎ (01852) 300347
📧 jbseas@hotmail.com
🖽 100
🏌 J Blackstock
🏳 9 L 2141 yds Par 31
👤 U
££ D–£12
🏌 13 miles S of Oban, Argyll. Take
A816 to Kilniver then B844 to
Balvica
🏟 Donald Campbell

Kyles of Bute   (1906)

The Moss, Kames, Tighnabruaich,
PA21 2AB
🖽 160
🏌 Dr J Thomson (01700) 811 603
🏳 9 L 2389 yds SSS 32
👤 U
££ D–£10 (£10) Honesty box
🏌 26 miles W of Dunoon

Lochgilphead   (1963)

Blarbuie Road, Lochgilphead, PA31 8LE
☎ (01546) 602340
🖽 250
🏌 E Hunter
🏳 9 L 4484 yds SSS 63
👤 U SOC
££ D–£15 (D–£20)
🏌 1/2 mile N of Lochgilphead by
Hospital
🖥 www.lochgilphead-golf.com

Lochgoilhead   (1994)

Public
Drymsynie Estates, Lochgoilhead, PA24 8AD
☎ (01301) 703247
📠 (01301) 703538
📧 info@drimsynie.co.uk
🏳 9 L 3970 yds Par 62 SSS 61
👤 N of Lochgoilhead, off Rest & Be
Thankful Road
££ £11 (£11)
🖥 www.argyllholidays.com

Machrihanish   (1876)

Machrihanish, Campbeltown, PA28 6PT
☎ (01586) 810213
📠 (01586) 810221
📧 secretary@machgolf.com
🖽 890 152(L) 150(J)
🏌 Mrs A Anderson
🏌 K Campbell (01586) 810277
🏳 18 L 6225 yds SSS 71
9 hole course
👤 U
££ £50 D–£80 exc Sat £60 D–£90
🏌 5 miles W of Campbeltown
🏟 Tom Morris
🖥 www.machgolf.com

Millport   (1888)

Millport, Isle of Cumbrae, KA28 0HB
☎ (01475) 530311
📠 (01475) 530306
📧 secretary@millportgolfclub.co.uk
🖽 288 120(L) 78(J)
🏌 William Reid (01475) 530306

✓ (01475) 530305
℣ 18 L 5828 yds SSS 69
🖳 U SOC
££ £22 D–£28 (£30 D–£35) W–£90
🏌 W of Millport (Largs car ferry)
⊕ Driving range
🏠 James Braid
🖵 www.millportgolfclub.co.uk

Port Bannatyne   (1912)
Bannatyne Mains Road, Port Bannatyne, Isle
of Bute, PA20 0PH
☎ **(01700) 504544**
▥ 170
🏌 J Bicker (01700) 504270
℣ 13 L 5085 yds Par 68 SSS 65
🖳 U
££ £15 (£18) – special packages
   available on website
🏌 2 miles N of Rothesay
🏠 Peter Morrison
🖵 www.portbannatynegolf.co.uk

Rothesay   (1892)
Canada Hill, Rothesay, Isle of Bute,
PA20 9HN
☎ **(01700) 503554**
▤ (01700) 503554
▨ info@rothesaygolfclub.com
▥ 500
✓ J Dougal (01700) 503554
℣ 18 L 5419 yds SSS 67
🖳 WD–U WE–book with Pro SOC
££ On application
🏌 1 mile E of Rothesay
⊕ Practice range
🏠 Braid/Sayers
🖵 www.rothesaygolfclub.com

Tarbert   (1910)
Kilberry Road, Tarbert, PA29 6XX
☎ **(01880) 820565**
▥ 101
🏌 P Cupples (01546) 606896
℣ 9 L 4460 yds SSS 63
🖳 U SOC
££ D–£15
🏌 1 mile W of Tarbert on B8024, off
   A83

Taynuilt   (1987)
Taynuilt, PA35 1JE
☎ **(01866) 822429**
▤ (01866) 822255 (phone first)
▨ michaelurwin152@btinternet.com
▥ 180
🏌 MJP Urwin (Hon) (01866) 833341
℣ 9 L 4510 yds Par 64 SSS 63
🖳 U SOC
££ £12 per day
🏌 12 miles E of Oban on A85
🖵 www.taynuiltgolfclub.co.uk

Tobermory   (1896)
Erray Road, Tobermory, Isle of Mull,
PA75 6PS
☎ **(01688) 302387**
▤ (01688) 302140
▨ secretary@tobermorygolfclub.com
▥ 180
🏌 M Campbell (01688) 302743
℣ 9 L 2492 yds SSS 64
🖳 U

££ D–£186 W–£72
🏌 Tobermory, Isle of Mull
⊕ Tickets from Western Isles Hotel,
   Brown's shop and Ptarmigan
   clubhouse (Apr-Sep); practice
   ground and net
🏠 David Adams
🖵 www.tobermorygolfclub.com

Vaul   (1920)
Scarinish, Isle of Tiree, PA77 6TP

Ayrshire

Annanhill   (1957)
Public
Irvine Road, Kilmarnock, KA1 2RT
☎ **(01563) 521512 (Starter)**
▥ 235
🏌 T Denham (01563) 521644/525557
℣ 18 L 6270 yds SSS 70
🖳 WD/Sat/Sun–U SOC–exc Sat
££ On application
🏌 1 mile N of Kilmarnock
🏠 J McLean

Ardeer   (1880)
Greenhead Avenue, Stevenston, KA20 4LB
☎ **(01294) 464542**
▤ (01294) 464542
▨ info@ardeergolfclub.co.uk
▥ 700
🏌 P Watson (01294) 465316
℣ 18 L 6409 yds SSS 71
🖳 U exc Sat–NA SOC–WD
££ £25 D–£40 Sun–£35 D–£50
🏌 ½ mile N of Stevenston, off A78
🏠 H Stutt
🖵 www.ardeergolfclub.co.uk

Ballochmyle   (1937)
Ballochmyle, Mauchline, KA5 6LE
☎ **(01290) 550469**
▤ (01290) 553657
▨ ballochmylegolf@btconnect.com
▥ 750
🏌 J Davidson
℣ 18 L 5952 yds SSS 69
🖳 WD/WE–U BH–M SOC exc Sat
££ £22.50 D–£32.50 (£27.50
   D–£37.50)
🏌 1 mile S of Mauchline on B705, off
   A76

Beith   (1896)
Threepwood Road, Beith, KA15 2JR
☎ **(01505) 503166 (Clubhouse)**
   (01505) 506814 (Secretary)
▨ beith_secretary@btconnect.com
▥ 550
🏌 M Murphy (01505) 506814
℣ 18 L 5625 yds SSS 68
🖳 WD–U exc Tues
   9–10.30am/4.30–6.30pm; Thur
   9–10.30am; Sat–NA before 2pm;
   Sun–NA
££ £20 (£25)
🏌 Off Beith By-pass on A737
🖵 www.beithgolfclub.co.uk

Brodick   (1897)
Brodick, Isle of Arran, KA27 8DL
☎ **(01770) 302349**
▨ secretary@brodickgolfclub.org

Brunston Castle   (1992)
Golf Course Road, Dailly, Girvan, KA26 9GD
☎ **(01465) 811471**
▤ (01465) 811545
▨ golf@brunstoncastle.co.uk
▥ 450
🏌 M Edens
✓ S Smith (01465) 811825
℣ 18 L 6792 yds SSS 72
🖳 U–booking necessary SOC
££ £28 D–£45
🏌 4 miles E of Girvan
⊕ Floodlite Driving range; Putting
   green; Chipping green;
   Bar/Restaurant; Showers/Changing
   rooms; Lockers
🏠 Donald Steel
🖵 www.brunstoncastle.co.uk

Caprington   (1958)
Public
Ayr Road, Kilmarnock, KA1 4UW
☎ **(01563) 53702 (Club)**
   (01563) 521915 (Starter)
▨ caprington.golf@btconnect.com
▥ 400
🏌 Jim Pearson (Club Sec) 07912
   377124 Billy Richmond (Match
   Sec) 07803 592970
℣ 18 L 5810 yds SSS 68
   9 L 1731 yds SSS 30
🖳 U
££ On application
🏌 1 mile S of Kilmarnock (B7038)

Corrie   (1892)
Corrie, Sannox, Isle of Arran, KA27 8JD
☎ **(01770) 810223/810606**
▥ 270
🏌 J Miles (01770) 850247
℣ 9 L 1948 yds SSS 61
🖳 U exc Thurs 12–2.30pm & Sat–NA
££ D–£15 W–£60
🏌 6 miles N of Brodick

Dalmilling   (1961)
Public
Westwood Avenue, Ayr, KA8 0QY
☎ **(01292) 263893**
▤ (01292) 610543
▥ 110
🏌 G Campbell (01292) 521351
✓ P Cheyney (Golf Mgr)
℣ 18 L 5724 yds SSS 68
🖳 U – phone to book tee times
££ £14 D–£20 (£17.50 D–£27)
🏌 NE boundary of Ayr, nr Ayr
   racecourse

Doon Valley   (1927)
1 Hillside, Patna, Ayr, KA6 7JT
☎ **(01292) 531607**
▤ (01292) 532489
▥ 90
🏌 H Johnstone
℣ 9 L 5858 yds SSS 70
🖳 U

££ £14
⊸⊸ 8 miles SE of Ayr (A713)

Dundonald Links
Ayr Road, Irvine KA11 5BF
☎ **(01294) 314000**
▭ (01294) 314001
▣ dundonaldlinks@lochlomond.com
✔ Guy Redford (01294) 314006
▷ 18 L 7100 ydsPar 72 SSS 76
⚭ U
££ High season from £95, low season from £50
⊸⊸ 4 miles N of Troon A78, Gailes
⊕ Driving range; short game area; trolley & club hire
⌂ Kyle Phillips
▤ www.dundonaldlinks.com

Girvan   (1860)
Public
Golf Course Road, Girvan, KA26 9HW
☎ **(01465) 714272/714346 (Starter)**
▭ (01465) 714346
▥ 170
⚤ WB Tait
▷ 18 L 5095 yds SSS 64
⚭ U
££ £13–£25
⊸⊸ N side of Girvan (A77). 22 miles S of Ayr
⌂ James Braid

Glasgow GC Gailes Links
(1892)
Gailes, Irvine, KA11 5AE
☎ **(01294) 311258**
▭ (01294) 279366
▣ secretary@glasgow-golf.com
▥ 1200
⚤ AG McMillan (0141) 942 2011 Fax (0141) 942 0770
✔ J Greaves (01294) 311561
▷ 18 L 6535 yds Par 71 SSS 72
⚭ WD WE/BH–NA before 2.30pm SOC
££ £60 D–£75 (£70)
⊸⊸ 1 mile S of Irvine, off A78
⊕ Practice area
⌂ Willie Park Jr
▤ www.glasgowgolfclub.com

Irvine   (1887)
Bogside, Irvine, KA8 8SN
☎ **(01294) 275979**
▭ (01294) 278209
▣ secretary@theirvinegolfclub.co.uk
▥ 450
⚤ W McMahon
✔ J McKinnon (01294) 275626
▷ 18 L 6408 yds SSS 71
⚭ U SOC–WD
££ On application
⊸⊸ 1 mile N of Irvine towards Kilwinning
⌂ James Braid

Irvine Ravenspark   (1907)
Public
Kidsneuk Lane, Irvine, KA12 8SR
☎ **(01294) 271293**

▣ secretary@irgc.co.uk
▭ 400
⚤ M Murray (Sec) (01294) 213537 A Campbell (Steward) (01294) 271293
✔ P Bond (01294) 276467
▷ 18 L 6429 yds SSS 71
⚭ U exc Sat–U after 2.30pm Apr–Sep only SOC
££ £16 D–£29
⊸⊸ N side of Irvine, off A737. 7 miles N of Troon
▤ www.irgc.co.uk

Kilbirnie Place   (1922)
Largs Road, Kilbirnie, KA25 7AT
☎ **(01505) 683398**
▭ 01505 684444
▣ kilbirnie.golfclub@tiscali.co.uk
▭ 450
⚤ Mrs C McGurk
▷ 18 L 5411 yds SSS 67
⚭ WD/Sun–U
££ On application
⊸⊸ ¹/₂ mile W of Kilbirnie, S of A760. 15 miles SW of Paisley
▤ www.kilbirnieplacegolfclub.co.uk

Kilmarnock (Barassie)
(1887)
29 Hillhouse Road, Barassie, Troon, KA10 6SY
☎ **(01292) 313920/311077**
▭ (01292) 318300
▣ golf@kbgc.co.uk
▭ 600
⚤ D Wilson (01292) 313920
✔ G Howie (01292) 311322
▷ 18 L 6484 yds SSS 72 9 L 2888 yds SSS 34
⚭ WD–U WE–NA before 2pm Sat + Sun SOC–Mon/Tues & Thurs
££ D–£50 (£60) Sun pm Apr–Sep £75
⊸⊸ Opp Barassie Railway Station
⌂ Theodore Moone
▤ www.kbgc.co.uk

Lamlash   (1889)
Lamlash, Isle of Arran, KA27 8JU
☎ **(01770) 600296 (Clubhouse) (01770) 600196 (Starter)**
▭ (01770) 600296
▣ lamlashgolfclub@btconnect.com
▭ 450
⚤ J Henderson
▷ 18 L 4510 yds SSS 64
⚭ U SOC
££ On application
⊸⊸ 3 miles S of Brodick on A841
⌂ Auchterlonie/Fernie
▤ www.lamlashgolfclub.co.uk

Largs   (1891)
Irvine Road, Largs, KA30 8EU
☎ **(01475) 673594 (Secretary's office)**
▭ (01475) 673594
▣ secretary@largsgolfclub.co.uk
▭ 800
✔ Andrew Fullen (01475) 686192
▷ 18 L 6140 yds Par 70 SSS 71
⚭ U SOC–WD
££ £36 D–£48 (£40)

⊸⊸ 1 mile S of Largs on A78
⌂ JH Stutt
▤ www.largsgolfclub.co.uk

Lochranza   (1991)
Pay and play
Lochranza, Isle of Arran, KA27 8HJ
☎ **(0177083) 0273**
▣ office@lochgolf.demon.co.uk
⚤ IM Robertson
▷ 18 L 5470 yds SSS 70
⚭ U SOC–Apr–Oct
££ £18 (£18)
⊸⊸ 14 miles N of Brodick
⊕ PowerPlay Golf
⌂ IM Robertson
▤ www.lochranzagolf.com

Loudoun Gowf   (1909)
Galston, KA4 8PA
☎ **(01563) 821993**
▭ (01563) 820011
▣ secy@loudoungowfclub.co.uk
▭ 900
⚤ WB Buchanan (01563) 821993
▷ 18 L 6005 yds SSS 69 WE–NA WD–R 9–12 and 2–3 only
££ £25 D–£35
⊸⊸ 5 miles E of Kilmarnock on A71
▤ www.loudoungowfclub.co.uk

Machrie Bay   (1900)
Machrie Bay, Brodick, Isle of Arran, KA27 8DZ
☎ **(01770) 850232**

Muirkirk   (1991)
Pay and play
c/o 65 Main Street, Muirkirk, KA18 3QR
☎ **(01290) 660184 (night) (01290) 570728 (day)**
▭ 100
⚤ R Bradford
▷ 9 L 5366 yds SSS 66
⚭ U SOC
££ £10
⊸⊸ 12 miles W of M74 Jct 12 on A70

New Cumnock   (1902)
Lochill, Cumnock Road, New Cumnock, KA18 4BQ
☎ **(01290) 338000**

Prestwick   (1851)
2 Links Road, Prestwick, KA9 1QG
☎ **(01292) 477404**
▭ (01292) 477255
▣ bookings@prestwickgc.co.uk
▭ 580
⚤ IT Bunch
✔ DA Fleming (01292) 479483
▷ 18 L 6544 yds SSS 73 Medal Course 18 L 6808 yds SSS 74 Championship Course
⚭ WD/WE
££ £120 D–£175 (2009) WE £145
⊸⊸ Prestwick Airport 1 mile, nr Railway Station
⌂ Tom Morris
▤ www.prestwickgc.co.uk

Prestwick St Cuthbert
(1899)
East Road, Prestwick, KA9 2SX
- ☎ **(01292) 477101**
- 📠 (01292) 671730
- ✉ secretary@stcuthbert.co.uk
- 📖 803
- ♟ Jim Jess
- ↦ 18 L 6470 yds SSS 71
- 👥 WD–U WE/BH–M SOC–WD
- ££ £30 D–£45 Winter half price
- 🚗 ½ mile E of Prestwick
- ⊕ Practice facilities; putting greens
- 🏠 JR Stutt
- 🖥 www.stcuthbert.co.uk

Prestwick St Nicholas
(1851)
Grangemuir Road, Prestwick,
KA9 1SN
- ☎ **(01292) 477608**
- 📠 (01292) 473900
- ✉ secretary@prestwickstnicholas
  .com
- 📖 600 155(L) 68(J)
- ♟ Tom Hepburn
- ✓ Starter (01292) 473904
- ↦ 18 L 6044 yds SSS 69
- 👥 WD–U WE–NA exc Sun pm
- ££ £55 D–£75 Sun pm–£60
- 🚗 Prestwick
- 🏠 C Hunter
- 🖥 www.prestwickstnicholas.com

Routenburn
(1914)
Greenock Road, Largs, KA30 9AH
- ☎ **(01475) 673230 – public**
  (01475) 686475 – steward
- 📖 350
- ♟ RB Connal (Mgr) (01475) 672757
- ✓ G McQueen (01475) 687240
- ↦ 18 L 5650 yds SSS 68
- 👥 U–phone Pro SOC–WD/WE
- ££ £16.50
- 🚗 N of Largs, off A78
- ⊕ Routenburn GC is a private club
  attached to a public course
- 🏠 James Braid

Royal Troon
(1878)
Craigend Road, Troon, KA10 6EP
- ☎ **(01292) 311555**
- 📠 (01292) 318204
- ✉ admin@royaltroon.com
- 📖 800
- ♟ JW Chandler
- ✓ K Stevenson (01292) 310063
- ↦ Old 18 L 7150 yds SSS 74
  Portland 18 L 6289 yds SSS 75
- 👥 Booking required – h/cap limit:
  men 20, ladies 30. Mon/Tues/Thurs
  only–H
- ££ Old + Portland D–£220 (incl
  Lunch). Portland D–£125 (inc
  Lunch)
- 🚗 SE of Troon (B749). Prestwick
  Airport 3 miles
- ⊕ Practice range
- 🏠 W Fernie
- 🖥 www.royaltroon.com

Seafield
(1930)
Public
Belleisle Park, Doonfoot Road, Ayr,
KA7 4DU
- ☎ **(01292) 441258**
- 📠 (01292) 442632
- ✉ info@ayrseafieldgolfclub.co.uk
- 📖 105
- ♟ Brian Milligan (01292) 445144
- ✓ Richard Gordon
  (01292) 441314
- ↦ 18 L 5481 yds SSS 67
- 👥 U
- ££ £17.50 (£20)
- 🚗 S of Ayr in Belleisle Park
- 🏠 James Braid
- 🖥 www.ayrseafieldgolfclub.co.uk

Shiskine
(1896)
Shiskine, Blackwaterfoot, Isle of Arran,
KA27 8HA
- ☎ **(01770) 860226**
- 📠 (01770) 860205
- ✉ info@shiskinegolf.com
- 📖 550 154(L) 42(J)
- ♟ Douglas Bell (01770) 860548
- ✓ Douglas Bell
- ↦ 12 L 2990 yds SSS 42
- 👥 U SOC
- ££ £19 D–£32 (£24 D–£37)
- 🚗 11 miles SW of Brodick
- ⊕ Putting green; pro shop all year
- 🏠 Willie Fernie
- 🖥 www.shiskinegolf.com

Skelmorlie
(1891)
Skelmorlie, PA17 5ES
- ☎ **(01475) 520152**
- ✉ sgcsec@yahoo.co.uk
- 📖 387
- ♟ Mrs Ellen Linton
  (Hon) (01475) 522626
- ↦ 18 L 5030 yds SSS 65
- 👥 U exc Sat (Apr–Oct)
- ££ D–£22 Sun–£27
- 🚗 Wemyss Bay Station 1½ miles
- 🏠 James Braid
- 🖥 www.skelmorliegolf.co.uk

Troon Municipal
Public
Harling Drive, Troon, KA10 6NF
- ☎ **(01292) 312464**
- 📠 (01292) 312578
- ✓ G McKinlay
- ↦ Lochgreen 18 L 6785 yds SSS 73
  Darley 18 L 6501 yds SSS 72
  Fullarton 18 L 4822 yds SSS 63
- 👥 U SOC
- ££ Lochgreen £19–£31. Darley
  £15–£29. Fullarton £13–£25
- 🚗 4 miles N of Prestwick at Station
  Brae

Troon Portland
(1894)
Club
1 Crosbie Road, Troon KA10
- ☎ **(01292) 313488**
- 📖 120
- ♟ R McEwan (01292) 313602
- ↦ Play over Portland at Royal Troon

Troon St Meddans
(1909)
Club
Harling Drive, Troon, KA10 6NF
- ✉ troonstmeddans@btinternet.com
- 📖 264
- ♟ John Dedholm (01560) 482748
- ↦ Play over Troon Municipal courses
  Lochgreen and Darley

Turnberry Hotel
(1906)
Turnberry, KA26 9LT
- ☎ **(01655) 331000**
- 📠 (01655) 331069
- ✉ turnberry.reservations@westin
  .com
- 📖 440
- ♟ Richard Hall (Head golf
  Proff) (01655) 334062
- ✓ Richard Hall (01655) 334062
- ↦ Ailsa 18 L 7224 yds SSS 73
  Kintyre 18 L 6861 yds SSS 72
  Arran 9 L 1996 yds Par 31
- 👥 On application
- ££ On application
- 🚗 18 miles S of Ayr on A77
- ⊕ Colin Montgomerie Links Golf
  Academy
- 🏠 Ailsa-Mackenzie Ross. Kintyre-
  Donald Steel
- 🖥 www.westin.com/turnberry

West Kilbride
(1893)
Fullerton Drive, Seamill, West Kilbride,
KA23 9HT
- ☎ **(01294) 823911**
- 📠 (01294) 829573
- ✉ golf@westkilbridegolfclub.com
- 📖 900
- ♟ H Armour
- ✓ I Darroch (01294) 823042
- ↦ 18 L 6548 yds SSS 71
- 👥 WD–U WE–M BH–NA SOC
- ££ On application
- 🚗 West Kilbride
- 🏠 Old Tom Morris/James Braid
- 🖥 www.westkilbridegolfclub.com

Western Gailes
(1897)
Gailes, Irvine, KA11 5AE
- ☎ **(01294) 311649**
- 📠 (01294) 312312
- ✉ enquiries@westerngailes.com
- 📖 450
- ♟ BJ Knowles
- ↦ 18 L 6639 yds SSS 74
- 👥 WD–H Mon/Wed/Fri only
  (booking necessary) Sun pm
- ££ £115 D–£165 Sun pm–£125
- 🚗 3 miles N of Troon (A78), Marine
  Drive
- ⊕ Practice, chipping and bunker area;
  putting green
- 🖥 www.westerngailes.com

Whiting Bay
(1895)
Golf Course Road, Whiting Bay, Isle of
Arran, KA27 8PR
- ☎ **(01770) 700487**
- ✉ m.auld@connectfree.co.uk
- 📖 290
- ♟ Mrs M Auld (01770) 820208
- ↦ 18 L 4405 yds SSS 63
- 👥 U

££ £20 (£22)
⋀ 8 miles S of Brodick

Borders

Duns   (1894)
Hardens Road, Duns, TD11 3NR
☎ (01361) 882194
⌨ (01361) 883599
✉ secretary@dunsgolfclub.com
𝄢 400
♠ G Clark (01361) 882194
ᐁ 18 L 6298 yds Par 71 SSS 70
♟ U SOC WD WE
££ £26 D–£33 (£31 D–£39)
⋀ 1 mile W of Duns, off A6105
⊕ Driving range 2 miles S of course
⌂ EH Scott
🖥 www.dunsgolfclub.com

Eyemouth   (1894)
Gunsgreen House, Eyemouth, TD14 5DX
☎ (018907) 50551 (Clubhouse)

Galashiels   (1884)
Ladhope Recreation Ground, Galashiels,
TD1 2NJ
☎ (01896) 753724
✉ secretary@galashiels-golfclub.co.uk
𝄢 185
♠ R Gass (01896) 755307
ᐁ 9 Holes L 5483 yds SSS 68
♟ U SOC
££ 9=£10; 18=£20; 27=£25; 36=£30
⋀ ¼ mile NE of Galashiels, off A7
⌂ James Braid
🖥 www.galashiels-golfclub.co.uk

Hawick   (1877)
Vertish Hill, Hawick, TD9 0NY
☎ (01450) 372293
⌨ (01450) 375594
✉ thesecretary@hawickgolfclub
.fsnet.com
𝄢 600
♠ J Reilly
ᐁ 18 L 5929 yds SSS 69
♟ U
££ £30
⋀ 46 miles from M6 at Carlisle. 50
miles S of Edinburgh
⊕ Practice Area, Practice Green.
🖥 www.hawickgolfclub.com

The Hirsel   (1948)
Kelso Road, Coldstream, TD12 4NJ
☎ (01890) 882678
⌨ (01890) 882233
✉ bookings@hirselgc.co.uk
𝄢 500
♠ Mrs Diane Nichol
ᐁ 18 L 6024 yds SSS 70
♟ U SOC
££ £33 (£39)
⋀ ½ mile W of Coldstream (A697)
⊕ Practice area; Buggies for hire.
🖥 www.hirsel.co.uk

Jedburgh   (1892)
Dunion Road, Jedburgh, TD8 6TA
☎ (01835) 863587

⌨ (01835) 862360
✉ info@jedburghgolfclub.co.uk
𝄢 300
♠ H Hogg (01835) 862851
ᐁ 18 Holes, 5950 yds, Par 69, SSS 68
♟ U
££ Weekday – £25 per round £30 per
day Weekend – £28 per round £35
per day
⋀ Jedburgh 1 mile (signposted from
centre)
⊕ Discounts available for parties of
12 or more.
⌂ Willie Park
🖥 www.jedburghgolfclub.co.uk

Kelso   (1887)
Golf Course Road, Kelso, TD5 7SL
☎ (01573) 223009
✉ golf@kelsogc.fsnet.co.uk

Langholm   (1892)
Langholm, DG13 0JR
☎ (07724) 875151
✉ golf@langholmgolfclub.co.uk
𝄢 150
♠ WT Goodfellow
ᐁ 9 L 3090 yds SSS 69
♟ U
££ £20 (£20)
⋀ 21 miles N of Carlisle on A7
⊕ Practice Range
🖥 www.langholmgolfclub.co.uk

Lauder   (1896)
Pay and play
Galashiels Road, Lauder, TD2 6RS
☎ (01578) 722526
⌨ (01578) 722526
✉ secretary@laudergolfclub.co.uk
𝄢 250
♠ D Dickson (01578) 722526
♪ Craig Lumsden (07759) 591252
ᐁ 9 L 6050 yds Par 72 SSS 69
♟ U SOC WD Tues before 5pm
££ £15 (£15)
⋀ ½ mile W of Lauder
⊕ Practice fairway
⌂ W Park Jr
🖥 www.laudergolfclub.co.uk

Melrose   (1880)
Dingleton Road, Melrose, TD6 9HS
☎ (01896) 822855
⌨ (01896) 822855
✉ melrosegolfclub@tiscali.co.uk
𝄢 360
♠ LM Wallace (01835) 823553
ᐁ 9 L 5562 yds Par 70 SSS 68
♟ U exc during competitions
££ D–£25 £15 for 9 Holes
⋀ S boundary of Melrose, off A68
⌂ James Braid

Minto   (1928)
Denholm, Hawick, TD9 8SH
☎ (01450) 870220
⌨ (01450) 870126
✉ mintogolfclub@btconnect.com
𝄢 500
♠ J Simpson
ᐁ 18 L 5542 yds SSS 68
♟ H SOC WD–U WE–certain times

££ £30 (£40)
⋀ Minto near Denholm. 6 miles E of
Hawick along A698
🖥 www.mintogolf.co.uk

Newcastleton   (1894)
Holm Hill, Newcastleton, TD9 0QD
☎ (013873) 75608
♠ GA Wilson
ᐁ 9 L 5491 yds Par 69 SSS 70
♟ U SOC
££ £12 D–£12 (£12) 9 holes half price
⋀ W of Newcastleton, off B6357 (via
A7). M6 Junction 44
⌂ John Shade

Peebles   (1892)
Kirkland Street, Peebles, EH45 8EU
☎ (01721) 720197
✉ secretary@peeblesgolfclub.co.uk
𝄢 770
♠ H Gilmore
♪ C Imlah
ᐁ 18 L 6160 yds SSS 70
♟ SOC WD–U WE–Sun only
££ From £25 (£30) Group discounts
apply
⋀ 23 miles S of Edinburgh, via A703
⊕ Buggy hire
⌂ James Braid/HS Colt
🖥 www.peeblesgolfclub.co.uk

The Roxburghe Hotel   (1997)
Heiton, Kelso, TD5 8JZ
☎ (01573) 450333
⌨ (01573) 450611
✉ golf@roxburghe.net
𝄢 300
♪ C Montgomerie (01573) 450333
ᐁ 18 L 6925 yds Par 72 SSS 73
♟ By arrangement SOC
££ £50 (£70)
⋀ On A698 between Jedburgh and
Kelso
⊕ Driving range
⌂ Dave Thomas
🖥 www.roxburghe.net

Selkirk   (1883)
The Hill, Selkirk, TD7 4NW
☎ (01750) 20621
  (01750) 20857 (Bookings)
✉ secretary@selkirkgolfclub.co.uk
𝄢 300
♠ JM Hay (01750 20857 pm)
ᐁ 9 L 5560 yds SSS 68
♟ WD–U exc Thurs pm WE–phone
first SOC
££ D–£20 (£20) 9 holes £12 (£12)
⋀ 1 mile S of Selkirk on A7
⌂ Willie Park
🖥 www.selkirkgolfclub.co.uk

St Boswells   (1899)
St Boswells, Melrose, TD6 0DE
☎ (01835) 823527
⌨ (01835) 823527
✉ secretary@stboswellsgolfclub.co.uk
𝄢 330
♠ Linda Cessford
ᐁ 9 L 5274 yds SSS 66
♟ U SOC
££ 9: £12, 18: £20, D–£24

⛳ Off A68 at St Boswells Green, by River Tweed
🏠 Willie Park/Shade

Torwoodlee   (1895)
Edinburgh Road, Galashiels, Torwoodlee, TD1 2NE
☎ **(01896) 752260**
📧 thesecretary@torwoodleegolfclub .org.uk

Woll Golf Course   (1993)
Proprietary
New Woll Estate, Ashkirk, Selkirkshire, TD7 4PE
☎ **(01750) 32711**
📧 wollgolf@tiscali.co.uk
📖 475
🏌 Nicholas Brown (01750) 32711
🏳 18 L 6051 yds Par 70 SSS 70
👫 U SOC
££ £28 D–£40 (£32 D–£40)
⛳ Ashkirk, just off A7 between Selkirk and Hawick
⊕ Driving range nearby
🖥 www.wollgolf.co.uk

Clackmannanshire

Alloa   (1891)
Schawpark, Sauchie, Alloa, FK10 3AX
☎ **(01259) 722745**
📠 (01259) 218796
📧 alloagolf2@tiscali.co.uk
📖 550 80(L) 130(J)
🏌 W Wallace (Admin)
✎ D Herd (01259) 724476
🏳 18 L 6266 yds Par 71 SSS 71
👫 WD–U WE–parties restricted
££ £28 D–£38 (£34)
⛳ Sauchie, N of Alloa on A908
🏠 James Braid
🖥 www.alloagolfclub.co.uk

Alva
Beauclerc Street, Alva, FK12 5LH
☎ **(01259) 760431**

Braehead   (1891)
Cambus, Alloa, FK10 2NT
☎ **(01259) 725766**
📠 (01259) 214070
📧 braehead.gc@btinternet.com
📖 800
🏌 Ronald Murray
✎ Jamie Stevenson (01259) 722078
🏳 18 L 6053 yds SSS 69
👫 U–booking necessary SOC
££ £24 D–£32 (£32 D–£40)
⛳ 2 miles W of Alloa (A907)
⊕ Small practice area
🏠 Robert Tait
🖥 www.braeheadgolfclub.com

Dollar   (1890)
Brewlands House, Dollar, FK14 7EA
☎ **(01259) 742400**
📠 (01259) 743497
📧 info@dollargolfclub.com
📖 375
🏌 J McMillan/J Crossan

🏳 18 L 5242 yds SSS 66
👫 U SOC
££ £13.50 D–£17.50 (£22)
⛳ Dollar, off A91
🏠 Ben Sayers
🖥 www.dollargolfclub.com

Tillicoultry   (1899)
Alva Road, Tillicoultry, FK13 6BL
☎ **(01259) 750124**
📠 (01259) 750124
📧 golf@tillygc.freeserve.co.uk
📖 400
🏌 M Todd
🏳 9 L 2761 yds SSS 67
👫 WD/WE–U SOC
££ £12 (£17)
⛳ 9 miles E of Stirling on A91

Tulliallan   (1902)
Kincardine, Alloa, FK10 4BB
☎ **(01259) 730396**
📠 (01259) 733950
📧 tulliallangolf@btconnect.com
📖 600 50(L) 50(J)
🏌 Amanda Maley
✎ S Kelly (01259) 730798
🏳 18 L 5982 yds SSS 69
👫 U exc comp days
££ £22 D–£36 (£26 D–£43)
⛳ 5 miles SE of Alloa; 2 miles from M876–Glasgow
⊕ Putting green; practice area
🖥 www.tulliallangolf.co.uk

Dumfries & Galloway

Brighouse Bay   (1999)
Pay and play
Borgue, Kirkcudbright, DG6 4TS
☎ **(01557) 870509**
📧 admin@brighousebaygolfclub.co.uk

Castle Douglas   (1905)
Abercromby Road, Castle Douglas, DG7 1BA
☎ **(01556) 502801**
📧 cdgolfclub@aol.com
📖 300
🏌 J Dugold (01556) 503527
🏳 9 L 5390 yds SSS 66
👫 WD–U before 4pm Tue+Thur WE–U SOC
££ D–£18 (2008 price) 9–hole ticket £12
⛳ Off A75/A713, NE of Castle Douglas
⊕ Buggy hire
🖥 www.cdgolf.co.uk

Colvend   (1905)
Sandyhills, Dalbeattie, DG5 4PY
☎ **(01556) 630398**
📠 (01556) 630495
📧 sec.@colvendgolfclub.co.uk
📖 500
🏌 JB Henderson
🏳 18 L 5341 yds SSS 67
👫 U
££ D–£25
⛳ 6 miles S of Dalbeattie on A710

🏠 Fernie/Soutar
🖥 www.colvendgolfclub.co.uk

Crichton   (1884)
Bankend Road, Dumfries, DG1 4TH
☎ **(01387) 247894**
📠 (01387) 257616
📧 admin@crichton.co.uk
📖 400
🏌 Lee Sterritt (Match Sec) 0777 055 3320
🏳 9 L 2976 yds SSS 69
👫 WD–U before 3pm SOC WE–Sun by arrangement with Sec
££ £18.50 (£18.50)
⛳ 1 mile from Dumfries, nr Hospital
⊕ Practice area; putting green

Dalbeattie   (1894)
Maxwell Park, Dalbeattie, DG5 4JR
☎ **(01556) 611421**
📧 ocm@associates.ltd.fsnet.co.uk
📖 300
🏌 T Moffat
🏳 9 L 5710 yds SSS 68
👫 U SOC
££ 18: £16; 9: £10; D–£20
⛳ 14 miles SW of Dumfries on A711/B794
⊕ Practice ground; putting green
🏠 OCM Golf Design
🖥 www.dalbeattiegc.co.uk

Dumfries & County   (1912)
Nunfield, Edinburgh Road, Dumfries, DG1 1JX
☎ **(01387) 253585**
📠 (01387) 253585
📧 admin@thecounty.co.uk
📖 630 120(J)
🏌 BRM Duguid (01387) 253585
✎ S Syme (01387) 268918
🏳 18 L 5918 yds Par 69 SSS 69
👫 WD–U ex 11.30–2pm–NA Sat–NA Sun–NA before 10am
££ £33 D–£45 (Sun £38 D–£52)
⛳ 1 mile N of Dumfries, on A701
🏠 W Fernie with alterations by James Braid in 1929
🖥 www.thecounty.org.uk

Dumfries & Galloway   (1880)
2 Laurieston Avenue, Maxwelltown, Dumfries, DG2 7NY
☎ **(01387) 253582**
📠 (01387) 263848
📧 info@dandggolfclub.co.uk
📖 750
🏌 AT Miller (01387) 263848
✎ J Fergusson (01387) 256902
🏳 18 L 6222 yds Par 70 SSS 71
👫 U
££ £30 (£38)
⛳ Dumfries
🏠 Willie Fernie
🖥 www.dandggolfclub.co.uk

Gatehouse   (1921)
Lauriston Road, Gatehouse of Fleet, Castle Douglas, DG7 2BE
☎ **(01557) 814766 (Clubhouse – unmanned)**
📖 300

🖉 P Benney (01557) 814428
🏳 9 L 2521 yds SSS 66
👥 WD–U WE–not before noon Sun
££ D–£15 (D–£15)
🚗 ¾ mile N of Gatehouse, off A75. 9
miles NW of Kirkcudbright

Hoddom Castle   (1973)
Pay and play
Hoddom Bridge, Ecclefechan, DG11 1AS
☎ (01576) 300251
📠 (01576) 300757
📧 hoddomcastle@aol.com
🖉 G Condron
🏳 9 L 2274 yds SSS 33
👥 U
££ £8.10 (£12)
🚗 2 miles SW of Ecclefechan on
B725. M74 J19
🏠 David Rothwell
🖥 www.hoddomcastle.co.uk

Kirkcudbright   (1893)
Stirling Crescent, Kirkcudbright, DG6 4EZ
☎ (01557) 330314
📠 (01557) 330314
📧 kirkcudbrightgolf@lineone.net
📖 500
🖉 N Little (Manager)
🏳 18 L 5739 yds SSS 69
👥 U after 10 am H–phone first SOC
££ £25 D–£30
🚗 ½ mile from Kirkcudbright town
centre
🖥 www.kirkcudbrightgolf.co.uk

Lochmaben   (1926)
Castlehill Gate, Lochmaben, DG11 1NT
☎ (01387) 810552
📧 lgc@naims.co.uk
📖 660
🖉 JM Dickie
🏳 18 L 5933 yds SSS 70
👥 WD–U before 5pm WE–U exc
comp days SOC
££ £28 D–£38 (£30 D–£40)
🚗 4 miles W of Lockerbie on A709. 8
miles NE of Dumfries
🏠 James Braid
🖥 www.lochmabengolf.co.uk

Lockerbie   (1889)
Corrie Road, Lockerbie, DG11 2ND
☎ (01576) 203363
📠 (01576) 203363
📧 enquiries@lockerbiegolf
📖 430
🖉 J Thomson
🏳 18 L 5418 yds SSS 67
👥 U exc Sun–NA before 11.30am
££ £22 (£25)
🚗 ½ mile NE of Lockerbie, on Corrie
road
🏠 James Braid

Moffat   (1884)
Coatshill, Moffat, DG10 9SB
☎ (01683) 220020
📧 bookings@moffatgolfclub.co.uk
📖 380
🖉 J Rogers (01683) 220020
🏳 18 L 5259 yds Par 69 SSS 67
👥 U exc Wed–NA after 3pm SOC

££ £24 D–£30 (£30 D–£36)
🚗 A74(M) Junction 15. Follow signs
to Moffat
⊕ Electric buggies available
🏠 Ben Sayers
🖥 www.moffatgolfclub.co.uk

New Galloway   (1902)
New Galloway, Dumfries, DG7 3RN
☎ (01644) 420737
📖 280
🖉 NE White
🏳 9 L 5006 yds Par 68 SSS 67
👥 U
££ D–£18
🚗 S of New Galloway on A762. 20
miles N of Kirkcudbright
⊕ Buggies now available
🏠 Baillie

Newton Stewart   (1981)
Kirroughtree Avenue, Minnigaff, Newton
Stewart, DG8 6PF
☎ (01671) 402172
📧 enquiries@newtonstewartgolfclub
.com
📖 380
🖉 Mrs L Hamilton
🏳 18 L 5840 yds Par 69 SSS 70
👥 U
££ £27 D–£36 (£31 D–£42)
🚗 E of Newton Stewart, off A75
⊕ Nets & practice area
🖥 www.newtonstewartgolfclub.com

Pines Golf Centre   (1998)
Pay and play
Lockerbie Road, Dumfries, DG1 3PF
☎ (01387) 247444
📠 (01387) 249600
📧 admin@pinesgolf.com
📖 160
🖉 Bruce Gray
⚲ Richard Smith (01387) 247444
🏳 18 L 5870 yds Par 68 SSS 68
👥 U SOC
££ £22 (£26)
🚗 On Lockerbie Road (A701) By A75
Dumfries by-pass. M74 Junctions 15
or 17
⊕ Driving range; short game area;
public putting green
🏠 Duncan Gray
🖥 www.pinesgolf.com

Portpatrick   (1903)
Golf Course Road, Portpatrick, DG9 8TB
☎ (01776) 810273
📠 (01776) 810811
📧 enquiries@portpatrickgolfclub.com
📖 550
🖉 AN Russ
⚲ H Lee (01776) 810880
🏳 Dunskey 18 L 5913 yds SSS 69
Dinvin 9 L 1504 yds Par 27
👥 U H SOC
££ £32 D–£42.50 (£42.50 D–£48)
W–£135; Dinvin £12 D–£18
🚗 8 miles SW of Stranraer
🏠 CW Hunter
🖥 www.portpatrickgolfclub.com

Powfoot   (1903)
Cummertrees, Annan, DG12 5QE
☎ (01461) 204100
📠 (01461) 204111
📧 info@powfootgolfclub.com
📖 660
🖉 SR Gardner (Mgr)
🏳 18 L 6266 yds SSS 71
👥 WD 9.00–11.00, 13.00–15.30 Sat
14.30–15.30 Sun 10.30–11.15,
13.00–15.30
££ Winter £20 D–£21 Summer £37
D–£48 Weekday (£43 D–£60)
Weekend
🚗 4 miles W of Annan. 15 miles SE of
Dumfries, off B724
🏠 James Braid
🖥 www.powfootgolfclub.com

Sanquhar   (1894)
Blackaddie Road, Sanquhar, Dumfries,
DG4 6JZ
☎ (01659) 50577
📧 tich@rossirene.fsnet.co.uk
📖 180
🖉 Ian Macfarlane
🏳 9 L 5630 yds SSS 68
👥 U–parties welcome
££ D–£12 (D–£15); parties of 12 and
over £28 per person, Senior and
Junior £8
🚗 ½ mile W of Sanquhar (A76). 30
miles N of Dumfries
🏠 W Fernie
🖥 www.scottishgolf.com

Southerness   (1947)
Southerness, Dumfries, DG2 8AZ
☎ (01387) 880677
📠 (01387) 880471
📧 admin@southernessgc.sol.co.uk
📖 800
🖉 J R Handley
🏳 18 L 6566 yds SSS 73
👥 H–phone first SOC
££ £50 D–£65 (D–£75)
🚗 16 miles S of Dumfries, off A710
🏠 Mackenzie Ross
🖥 www.southernessgolfclub.com

St Medan   (1904)
Monreith, Newton Stewart, DG8 8NJ
☎ (01988) 700358
📧 mail@stmedangolfclub.co.uk
📖 150
🏳 9 L 4520 yds Par 64 SSS 64
👥 U SOC
££ 9: £15; 18: £20 Day ticket £25
🚗 3 miles S of Port William, off A747
🏠 James Braid
🖥 www.stmedangolfclub.co.uk

Stranraer   (1905)
Creachmore, Leswalt, Stranraer, DG9 0LF
☎ (01776) 870245
📠 (01776) 870445
📧 stranraergolf@btclick.com
📖 700
🖉 J Burns
🏳 18 L 6308 yds SSS 72
👥 WE–NA before 9.30am and
11.45am–1.45pm

££ £28 (£33)
⊕⊕ 2 miles NW of Stranraer on A718
⌂ James Braid
▤ www.stranraergolfclub.net

Thornhill (1893)
Blacknest, Thornhill, DG3 5DW
☎ **(01848) 330546 (clubhouse)**
(01848) 331779 (office)
✉ info@thornhillgolfclub.co.uk
⌑ 529
🖊 T Croager
▷ 18 L 6085 yds SSS 70
👥 U
££ On application
⊕⊕ 14 miles N of Dumfries (A76)
⊕ Two practice area; practice putting
green
⌂ W Ferne
▤ www.thornhillgolfclub.co.uk

Wigtown & Bladnoch (1960)
Lightlands Terrace, Wigtown, DG8 9EF
☎ **(01988) 403354**
⌑ 170
🖊 IM Thin
▷ 9 L 2731 yds SSS 67
👥 U SOC
££ £20 D–£25 (£20)
⊕⊕ Between Wigtown and Bladnoch,
off A714
⌂ J Muir

Wigtownshire County (1894)
Mains of Park, Glenluce, Newton Stewart,
DG8 0NN
☎ **(01581) 300420**
⌑ (01581) 300420
✉ enquiries
@wigtownshirecountygolfclub.com
⌑ 420
🖊 R McKnight
▷ 18 L 6104 yds SSS 69
👥 U exc Wed–NA after 6pm
££ £26 D–£33 (£28 D–£35)
⊕⊕ 8 miles E of Stranraer on A75
⊕ Practice area
⌂ W Gordon Cunningham
▤ www.wigtownshirecountygolfclub
.com

Dunbartonshire

Balmore (1894)
Balmore, Torrance, G64 4AW
☎ **(01360) 620284**
✉ secretary@balmoregolfclub.co.uk

Bearsden (1891)
Thorn Road, Bearsden, Glasgow, G61 4BP
☎ **(0141) 586 5300**
⌑ (0141) 586 5300
✉ secretary@bearsdengolfclub.com
⌑ 500
🖊 Alan Harris
▷ 9 L 6014 yds SSS 69
👥 By arrangement
££ £20 D–£30
⊕⊕ 6 miles NW of Glasgow
▤ www.bearsdengolfclub.com

Cardross (1895)
Main Road, Cardross, Dumbarton, G82 5LB
☎ **(01389) 841213 (Clubhouse)**
⌑ (01389) 842162
✉ golf@cardross.com
⌑ 810
🖊 IT Waugh (01389) 841754
✎ R Farrell (01389) 841350
▷ 18 L 6469 yds SSS 72
👥 WD–U WE–M
££ £35 D–£50 (party discount–see
website)
⊕⊕ 4 miles W of Dumbarton on A814
⌂ Fernie (1904)/Braid (1921)
▤ www.cardross.com

Clober (1951)
Craigton Road, Milngavie, Glasgow,
G62 7HP
☎ **(0141) 956 1685**
✉ clobergolfclub@btopenworld.com
⌑ 700
🖊 B Davidson
✎ Gary McFarlane (0141) 956 6963
(Golf Shop)
▷ 18 L 4963 yds SSS 65
👥 WD–U before 4pm WE–M
BH–NA SOC–WD
££ £18
⊕⊕ 7 miles NW of Glasgow
▤ www.clober.com

Clydebank & District (1905)
Hardgate, Clydebank, G81 5QY
☎ **(01389) 383833**
⌑ (01389) 383831
✉ clydebankanddgc@yahoo.com
⌑ 780
🖊 Mrs M Higgins (01389) 383831
✎ A Waugh (01389) 383835
▷ 18 L 5823 yds SSS 69
👥 WD–H
££ On application
⊕⊕ 2 miles N of Clydebank
▤ www.clydebankanddistrictgolfclub
.co.uk

Clydebank Overtoun (1927)
Public
Overtoun Road, Dalmuir, Clydebank,
G81 3RE
☎ **(0141) 952 2070 (Clubhouse)**
(0141) 952 6372
(Pro Shop/Starter)

Dougalston (1977)
Strathblane Road, Milngavie, Glasgow,
G62 8HJ
☎ **(0141) 955 2404**
⌑ (0141) 955 2406
⌑ 700
🖊 Mrs H Everett
✎ C Everett
▷ 18 L 6120 yds Par 70 SSS 71
👥 WD–U SOC WE afternoon subject
to availability
££ £25 (£32)
⊕⊕ 7 miles N of Glasgow on A81
⊕ Putting green & practice area
⌂ J Harris
▤ www.esporta.com

Douglas Park (1897)
Hillfoot, Bearsden, Glasgow, G61 2TJ
☎ **(0141) 942 2220 (Clubhouse)**
⌑ (0141) 942 0985
✉ secretary@douglasparkgolfclub
.co.uk
⌑ 585 180(L) 140(J)
🖊 Colin A Melville (0141) 942 0985
✎ D Scott (0141) 942 1482
▷ 18 L 5962 yds SSS 69
👥 M SOC
££ WD–£25 D–£35
⊕⊕ 6 miles NW of Glasgow, nr
Hillfoot Station
⌂ Willie Fernie
▤ www.douglasparkgolfclub.co.uk

Dullatur (1896)
1a Glendouglas Drive, Craigmarloch,
Cumbernauld, G68 0DW
☎ **(01236) 723230**
⌑ (01236) 727271
✉ secretary@dullaturgolf.com
⌑ 580 64(L)
🖊 William Crombie (01236) 723230
✎ D Sinclair (01236) 794721
▷ 18 L 6312 yds SSS 70
18 L 5875 yds SSS 68
👥 WD–U WE SOC
££ £21 D–£31 (£26 D–£36) £13.50
(£18.50)
⊕⊕ 3 miles N of Cumbernauld
▤ www.dullaturgolf.com

Dumbarton (1888)
Broadmeadow, Dumbarton, G82 2BQ
☎ **(01389) 765995**
✉ info@dumbartongolfclub.co.uk
⌑ 700
🖊 M Buchanan
✎ David Muir (01389) 600537
▷ 18 L 6018 yds SSS 69
👥 WD–U WE–NA
££ £22 D–£32
⊕⊕ 1 mile off A82
▤ www.dumbartongolfclub.co.uk

Hayston (1926)
Campsie Road, Kirkintilloch, Glasgow,
G66 1RN
☎ **(0141) 775 0723**
⌑ (0141) 776 9030
✉ secretary@haystongolf.com
⌑ 440 59(L) 80(J)
🖊 Tom Cowan
✎ S Barnett (0141) 775 0882
▷ 18 L 6080 yds Par 70 SSS 69
👥 WD–I before 4.30pm –M after
4.30pm WE–M
££ £35 D–£45
⊕⊕ 1 mile N of Kirkintilloch
⌂ James Braid
▤ www.haystongolf.com

Hilton Park (1927)
Auldmarroch Estate, Stockiemuir Road,
Milngavie, G62 7HB
☎ **(0141) 956 4657/5124**
✉ info@hiltonparkgolfclub.fsnet.co.uk

Kirkintilloch (1895)
Todhill, Campsie Road, Kirkintilloch,
G66 1RN

☎ **(0141) 776 1256**
📠 (0141) 775 2424
✉ secretary@kirkintillochgolfclub
.co.uk
🏢 450 100(L) 100(J)
♙ T Cummings (0141) 775 2387
✓ Jamie Good (07789) 207101
👉 18 L 5860 yds SSS 69
👤 M SOC
££ £10 D–£20 (WE on application)
⚙ 7 miles NE of Glasgow
⊕ Large practice ground; practice net
🏢 James Braid
🖥 www.kirkintillochgolfclub.co.uk

Lenzie   (1889)
19 Crosshill Road, Lenzie, G66 5DA
☎ **(0141) 776 1535**
📠 (0141) 777 7748
🏢 501 125(L) 125(J)
♙ SM Davidson (0141) 812 3018
✓ J McCallum (0141) 777 7748
👉 18 L 5984 yds SSS 69
👤 M SOC
££ £25 D–£30
⚙ 6 miles NE of Glasgow
🖥 www.lenziegolfclub.co.uk

Loch Lomond   (1994)
Rossdhu House, Luss, G83 8NT
☎ **(01436) 655555**
📠 (01436) 655500
✉ info@lochlomond.com
♙ N Flanagan
✓ J Caven
👉 18 L 7140 yds Par 72
👤 M
⚙ 20 miles NW of Glasgow on A82
🏢 Weiskopf/Morrish
🖥 www.lochlomond.com

Milngavie   (1895)
Laighpark, Milngavie, Glasgow, G62 8EP
☎ **(0141) 956 1619**
📠 (0141) 956 4252
✉ secretary@milngaviegc.fsnet.co.uk
🏢 700
♙ S Woods
👉 18 L 5818 yds SSS 68
👤 M SOC
££ £30 D–£55 (£40 D–£60)
⚙ 7 miles NW of Glasgow
🖥 www.milngaviegc.com

Palacerigg   (1975)
Public
Palacerigg Country Park, Cumbernauld, G67 3HU
☎ **(01236) 734969**
📠 (01236) 721461
✉ palacerigg-golfclub@lineone.net
🏢 300
♙ DSA Cooper
✓ J Murphy (Starter) (01236) 721461
👉 18 L 6444 yds Par 72 SSS 72
👤 U SOC
££ £8 (£10.50)
⚙ 3 miles SE of Cumbernauld, off A80. Within Palacerigg Country Park
🏢 Henry Cotton
🖥 www.palacerigggolfclub.co.uk

Ross Priory   (1978)
Proprietary
Ross Loan, Gartocharn, Alexandria, G83 8NL
☎ **(01389) 830398**
📠 (01389) 830357
✉ ross.priory@strath.ac.uk
🏢 800
♙ R Cook 0141 548 2960
👉 18 L 5758 yds Par 70 SSS 68
👤 M SOC WD–U
££ D–£17
⚙ Off A881 at Gartocharn
🏢 George Campbell
🖥 www.strath.ac.uk/rosspriory/golf

Vale of Leven   (1907)
Northfield Road, Bonhill, Alexandria, G83 9ET
☎ **(01389) 752351**
📠 (08707) 498950
✉ rbarclay@volgc.org
🏢 750
♙ R Barclay
✓ B Campbell (01389) 757880
👉 18 L 5277 yds Par 67 SSS 67
👤 U H exc Sat (Apr–Sept) SOC
££ £20 D–£30 (£25 D–£37.50)
⚙ Bonhill, 3 miles N of Dumbarton, off A82
🖥 www.volgc.org

Westerwood Hotel G&CC
(1989)
St Andrews Drive, Cumbernauld, G68 0EW
☎ **(01236) 725281**
📠 (01236) 738478
✉ westerwoodgolf@qhotels.co.uk
🏢 400
♙ Vincent Brown
✓ Vincent Brown
👉 18 L 6616 yds SSS 72
👤 U SOC WD WE
££ £35 (£40)
⚙ 13 miles NE of Glasgow, off A80
🏢 Thomas/Ballesteros
🖥 www.qhotels.co.uk

Windyhill   (1908)
Windyhill, Bearsden, G61 4QQ
☎ **(0141) 942 2349**
📠 (0141) 942 5874
✉ secretary@windyhillgolfclub.co.uk
🏢 650
♙ JM Young
✓ C Duffy (0141) 942 7157
👉 18 L 6254 yds SSS 70
👤 WD–U Sun–M SOC–WD
££ £25
⚙ 8 miles NW of Glasgow
🏢 James Braid
🖥 www.windyhillgolfclub.co.uk

Fife

Aberdour   (1896)
Seaside Place, Aberdour, KY3 0TX
☎ **(01383) 860080**
📠 (01383) 860050
✉ manager@aberdourgolfclub.co.uk
🏢 670

♙ Jane Cuthill
✓ D Gemmell (01383) 860256
👉 18 L 5460 yds Par 67 SSS 66
👤 WD–book with Pro Sat–NA SOC
££ £25 D–£35 (£40 Sun)
⚙ 8 miles SE of Dunfermline, on coast
🏢 Robertson/Anderson
🖥 www.aberdourgolfclub.co.uk

Anstruther   (1890)
Marsfield Shore Road, Anstruther, KY10 3DZ
☎ **(01333) 310956**
📠 (01333) 310956
✉ captain@anstruther.co.uk
🏢 500
♙ M MacDonald
👉 9 L 4504 yds Par 62 SSS 63
👤 U SOC
££ 9 = £15 18 = £20 all week
⚙ 9 miles S of St Andrews, Turn down at Symphany Craws Nest Hotel
⊕ Hardest Par 3 (5th hole) in UK, Todays Golfer Magazine 2007
🏢 T Morris Snr
🖥 www.anstruther.co.uk

Auchterderran   (1904)
Public
Woodend Road, Cardenden, KY5 0NH
☎ **(01592) 721579**

Balbirnie Park   (1983)
Balbirnie Park, Markinch, Fife, KY7 6NR
☎ **(01592) 612095**
📠 (01592) 612383
✉ bp-gc@tiscali.co.uk
🏢 800
♙ S Oliver (Club Administrator)
✓ C Donnelly (01592) 752006
👉 18 L 6313 yds SSS 71
👤 WE–booking essential
££ £40 D–£50 (£45 D–£60)
⚙ 2 miles E of Glenrothes
🏢 Fraser Middleton
🖥 www.balbirniegolf.com

Ballingry
Pay and play
Lochore Meadows Country Park, Crosshill, Lochgelly, KY5 8BA
☎ **(01592) 860086**

Burntisland   (1797)
Club
51 Craigkennochie Terrace, Burntisland, KY3 9EN
☎ **(01592) 872728**
✉ bigmac@waitrose.com
🏢 70
♙ AD McPherson
👉 Play over Dodhead Course, Burntisland
🏢 Willie Park
🖥 www.burntislandgolfclub.co.uk

Burntisland Golf House Club   (1898)
Dodhead, Kircaldy Road, Burntisland, KY3 9LQ
☎ **(01592) 874093**

✉ infobghc@aol.com
☎ 600
✍ Administration (01592) 874093 Ext 4
✓ Paul Wytrazek (01592) 872116
☞ 18 L 5965 yds SSS 70
⚭ U SOC WE NA Sat before 2.30pm
££ £25 D–£35 (£30 D–£42)
⚘ 1 mile E of Burntisland on B923; 9 miles E of M90 J1
⊕ Practice ground; putting green; buggies, power trollies
⌂ Willie Park Jr/James Braid
✉ www.burntislandgolfhouseclub.co.uk

Canmore (1897)
Venturefair Avenue, Dunfermline, KY12 0PE
☎ (01383) 724969
☎ (01383) 731649
✉ canmoregolfclub@aol.com
☎ 547 70(L) 85(J)
✍ A Watson (01383) 513604
✓ D Gemmell (01383) 728416
☞ 18 L 5437 yds SSS 66
⚭ WD–U WE–restricted
££ £24 D–£30 (£29 D–£35)
⚘ 1 mile N of Dunfermline on A823
⌂ Ben Sayers
✉ www.canmoregolf.co.uk

Charleton (1994)
Proprietary
Charleton, Colinsburgh, KY9 1HG
☎ (01333) 340505
☎ (01333) 340583
✉ clubhouse@charleton.co.uk
✍ David McOwat
✓ George Finlayson (01334) 460762
☞ 18 L 6464 yds Par 72 SSS 72
⚭ U SOC
££ £27 (£32)
⚘ 1 mile W of Colinsburgh, off B492
⊕ Driving range; 9 holes pitch & putt course; drive-on buggies
⌂ John Salvesen
✉ www.charleton.co.uk

Cowdenbeath (1991)
Public
Seco Place, Cowdenbeath, KY4 8PD
☎ (01383) 511918
☎ 200
✍ LH Connelly
☞ 18 L 6207 yds Par 71 SSS 70
⚭ U SOC
££ On application
⚘ In Cowdenbeath, signposted from A909/A92
⊕ Practice ground & putting green; separate chipping area

Crail Golfing Society (1786)
Balcomie Clubhouse, Fifeness, Crail, KY10 3XN
☎ (01333) 450686
☎ (01333) 450416
✉ info@crailgolfingsociety.co.uk
☎ 1600
✍ D Roy (01333) 450686
✓ G Lennie (01333) 450960/450967
☞ Balcomie 18 L 5922 yds SSS 69
Craighead 18 L 6728 yds Par 72 SSS 74

⚭ U
££ £51 (£63)
⚘ 11 miles SE of St Andrews
⊕ Driving range
⌂ Balcomie: Tom Morris
Craighead: Gil Hanse
✉ www.crailgolfingsociety.co.uk

Cupar (1855)
Hilltarvit, Cupar, KY15 5JT
☎ (01334) 653549
☎ (01334) 653549
✉ cupargc@fsmail.net
☎ 350
✍ James Elder 01334 650325
☞ 2 x 9 L 5153 yds SSS 66
⚭ WD–U SOC–WD/WE, WE after 2pm
££ D–£15
⚘ 10 miles W of St Andrews
⊕ Putting green
✉ www.cupargolfclub.co.uk

Drumoig (1996)
Drumoig Hotel, Drumoig, Leuchars, St Andrews, Fife KY16 0BE
☎ (01382) 541898
☎ (01382) 541898
✉ drumoiggolf@btconnect.com
☎ 350
✍ Margaret Sumner
Gordon Taylor (Mgr)
☞ 18 L 6835 yds par 72
⚭ U
££ £22 D–£30 (£30 D–£40) Special deals for visiting parties
⚘ 7 miles NW of St Andrews on A919; 4 miles S of Dundee
⊕ Driving range (01382 541529) with covered bays; buggies; online Booking
⌂ Dave Thomas
✉ www.drumoigleisure.com

Dunfermline (1887)
Pitfirrane, Crossford, Dunfermline, KY12 8QW
☎ (01383) 723534
☎ (01383) 723547
✉ secretary@dunfermlinegolfclub.com
☎ 720
✍ R De Rose
✓ C Nugent (01383) 729061
☞ 18 L 6121 yds SSS 70
⚭ WD–U 9.30am–4pm Sat–NA SOC–WD 9.30am–3.30pm
££ £32 D–£48 (£40)
⚘ 2 miles W of Dunfermline on A994
⌂ JR Stutt
✉ www.dunfermlinegolfclub.com

Dunnikier Park (1963)
Public
Dunnikier Way, Kirkcaldy, KY1 3LP
☎ (01592) 261599
☎ (01592) 642541
✉ dunnikierparkgolfclub@btinternet.com
☎ 600 35(L) 75(J)
✍ R Johnston
✓ G Whyte (01592) 642121
☞ 18 L 6601 yds SSS 72
⚭ U SOC

££ £15 (£20)
⚘ N boundary of Kirkcaldy
⌂ R Stutt
✉ www.dunnikierparkgolfclub.com

Earlsferry Thistle (1875)
Club
Melon Park, Elie, KY9 1AS
☎ 60
✍ J Peters (01333) 424315
☞ Play over Elie Golf House Club Course
See Elie Golf House Club for other info

Elmwood Golf Course
Pay and play
Stratheden, Nr Cupar, KY15 5RS
☎ (01334) 658780
☎ (01334) 658781
✉ clubhouse@elmwood.co.uk
✍ Sharif Sulaiman (Golf Admin) (01334) 658780
✓ Graeme McDowall (01334) 658780
☞ 18 L 5653 yds SSS 67
⚭ U SOC
££ £22 (£25 +BH)
⚘ M90 J7 (southbound)/J8 (northbound). A91 to St Andrews
⊕ Practice area; indoor video analysis studio
✉ www.elmwoodgc.co.uk

Falkland (1976)
The Myre, Falkland, KY15 7AA
☎ (01337) 857404
☎ 350
✍ Mrs H Brough
☞ 9 SSS 65
Yellow tees: L 2281 m
Medal tees: L 2343 m
⚭ WD WE restricted on comp. days SOC
££ On application
⚘ 5 miles N of Glenrothes on A912
✉ www.falklandgolfclub.com

Glenrothes (1958)
Public
Golf Course Road, Glenrothes, KY6 2LA
☎ (01592) 754561/758686
☎ (01592) 754561
✉ secretary@glenrothesgolf.org.uk
☎ 600 35(L) 50(J)
✍ Miss C Dawson
☞ 18 L 6444 yds SSS 71
⚭ U
££ £19 (£30)
⚘ Glenrothes West, off A92. M90 Junction 29
⌂ JR Stutt
✉ www.glenrothesgolf.org.uk

Golf House Club (1875)
Elie, Leven, KY9 1AS
☎ (01333) 330301
☎ (01333) 330895
✉ secretary@golfhouseclub.org
☎ 500
✍ G Scott (01333) 330301
✓ I Muir (01333) 330955
☞ 18 L 6273 yds SSS 70
9 L 2277 yds SSS 32

⚇ July–Aug ballot. WD–NA before
    10am. WE–NA before 10am
££ £65 D–£85 (£75 D–£95)
⊶ 12 miles S of St Andrews
⊕ Driving range; putting green
▤ www.golfhouseclub.org

Kinghorn   (1887)
Public
McDuff Crescent, Kinghorn, KY3 9RE
☎ **(01592) 890345**
▢ (01592) 891008
▥ 160
✍ Gordon Tulloch (01592) 891008
▷ 18 L 5629 yds Par 65 SSS 66
⚇ U SOC
££ £19 (£24)
⊶ 3 miles S of Kirkcaldy (A921)
⊕ Kinghorn and Kinghorn Thistle
    Clubs play here
⌂ Tom Morris
▤ www.kinghorngolfclub.co.uk

Kinghorn Ladies   (1894)
Club
Golf Clubhouse, McDuff Crescent, Kinghorn,
KY3 9RE
☎ **(01592) 890345**

Kingsbarns Golf Links
(2000)
Pay and play
Kingsbarns, Fife, KY16 8QD
☎ **(01334) 460860**
▢ (01334) 460877
▨ info@kingsbarns.com
✍ S McEwen (Gen Mgr)
✓ D Scott
▷ 18 hole course
⚇ U
££ Apr–May £130 D–£190, Jun–Nov
    £160 D–£240
⊶ Between St Andrews and Crail on
    coast road (A917)
⊕ Driving range
⌂ Phillips/Parsinen
▤ www.kingsbarns.com

Kirkcaldy   (1904)
Balwearie Road, Kirkcaldy, KY2 5LT
☎ **(01592) 205240**
▢ (01592) 205240
▨ enquiries@kirkcaldygolfclub.sol
    .co.uk
▥ 600
✍ A Wood
✓ A Caira (01592) 203258
▷ 18 L 6086 yds SSS 69
⚇ U exc Sat–NA
££ £28 D–£34 (£34 D–£42)
⊶ W side of Kirkcaldy; A92 exit
    Kirkcaldy West
⌂ Old Tom Morris
▤ www.kirkcaldygolfclub.co.uk

Ladybank   (1879)
Annsmuir, Ladybank, Fife KY15 7RA
☎ **(01337) 830814**
▢ (01337) 831505
▨ info@ladybankgolf.co.uk
▥ 1000
✍ FH McCluskey

✓ S Smith (01337) 830725
▷ 18 L 6601 yds SSS 72
⚇ WD–U 9.30am–4pm M–after 4pm
    WE–NA Sat
££ £50 (£60)
⊶ 6 miles SW of Cupar, off A92 from
    Melville Lodges roundabout
⌂ Old Tom Morris
▤ www.ladybankgolf.co.uk

Leslie   (1898)
Balsillie Laws, Leslie, Glenrothes, KY6 3EZ
☎ **(01592) 620040**
▨ g.lewis@blueyonder.co.uk
▥ 120
✍ G Lewis
▷ 9 L 4940 yds Par 62 SSS 65
⚇ U
££ £10 (£12)
⊶ 3 miles W of Glenrothes. M90
    Junction 5/7, 11 miles

Leven Golfing Society
(1820)
Club
Links Road, Leven, KY8 4HS
☎ **(01333) 426096/424229**
▢ (01333) 424229
▨ secretary@levengolfingsociety.co.uk
▥ 500
✍ Verne Greger
▷ Play over Leven Links:
    18 L 6506 yds Par 71 SSS 72
⚇ U Fri–NA after 12
££ £40 D–£50 (£50 D–£60)
⊶ See website
⌂ Tom Morris
▤ www.levengolfingsociety.co.uk

Leven Links   (1846)
The Promenade, Leven, KY8 4HS
☎ **(01333) 421390 (Starter)**
▢ (01333) 428859
▨ secretary@leven-links.com
▥ 1200
✍ (01333) 428859 (Links
    Committee)
▷ 18 L 6506 yds Par 71 SSS 72
⚇ WD–U before 5pm Sat–no parties
    Sun–NA before 10.30am SOC
££ £40 (£50)
⊶ E of Leven, on promenade. 12
    miles SW of St Andrews
▤ www.leven-links.com

Leven Thistle   (1867)
Club
Balfour Street, Leven, KY8 4JF
☎ **(01333) 426333**
▢ (01333) 439910
▨ leventhistlegolf@madasafish.com
▥ 500
✍ J Scott (01333) 426333
▷ Play over Leven Links

Lundin   (1868)
Golf Road, Lundin Links, KY8 6BA
☎ **(01333) 320202**
▢ (01333) 329743
▨ secretary@lundingolfclub.co.uk
▥ 950
✍ AJ McDonald

✓ DK Webster (01333) 320051
▷ 18 L 6371 yds SSS 71
⚇ WD–U between 9am–3pm Sat–NA
    before 2.30pm Sun–restricted 12
    noon–3pm
££ £52 D–£75 (£60)
⊶ 3 miles E of Leven
⌂ James Braid
▤ www.lundingolfclub.co.uk

Lundin Ladies   (1891)
Woodielea Road, Lundin Links, KY8 6AR
☎ **(01333) 320022 (Starter)**
    (01333) 320832 (Sec)
▨ llgolfclub@tiscali.co.uk
▥ 275
▷ 9 L 2365 yds SSS 68 Par 68
⚇ U Tue, Thur, Fri, Sat, Sun.
    Restricted Wed April–Sept
££ On application
⊶ 3 miles E of Leven
⌂ James Braid

Methil   (1892)
Club
Links House, Links Road, Leven, KY8 4HS
☎ **(01333) 425535**
▢ (01333) 425187
▥ 50
✍ ATJ Traill
▷ Play over Leven Links

Pitreavie   (1922)
Queensferry Road, Dunfermline, KY11 8PR
☎ **(01383) 722591**
▢ (01383) 722591
▥ 800
✍ E Comerford
✓ P Brookes (01383) 723151
▷ 18 L 6031 yds SSS 69
⚇ U–phone Pro SOC (Parties–max
    36–must be booked in advance)
££ £25 D–£35 (£30 D–£40)
⊶ 2 miles off M90 Junction 2,
    between Rosyth and Dunfermline
⌂ Dr A Mackenzie

Saline   (1912)
Kinneddar Hill, Saline, KY12 9LT
☎ **(01383) 852591/**
    (05601) 159055
▢ (01383) 852591
▨ salinegolfclub@btconnect.com
▥ 300
✍ A Lyon (01383) 852218
▷ 9 L 5384 yds SSS 66
⚇ U exc medal Sat
££ £11.50 (£14) Reduction for Jun &
    OAP
⊶ 5 miles NW of Dunfermline; M90
    Jct 4
⊕ Nets and putting green
▤ www.saline-golf-club.co.uk

Scoonie   (1951)
Public
North Links, Leven, KY8 4SP
☎ **(01333) 307007**
▢ (01333) 307008
▨ manager@scooniegolfclub.com
✍ S Kuczerepa
▷ 18 L 4979 metres Par 67 SSS 66
⚇ U SOC contact manager

For list of abbreviations and key to symbols see page 647

££   On application
⌒o   Adjoins Leven Links
☰   www.scooniegolfclub.com

Scotscraig   (1817)
Golf Road, Tayport, DD6 9DZ
☎   (01382) 552515
🖳   (01382) 553130
📧   scotscraig@scotscraiggolfclub.com
📖   850
🏌   BD Liddle
✓   C Mackie (0138) 552855
🏳   18 L 6550 yds SSS 72
👥   WD–U WE–by prior arrangement
    SOC
££   On application
⌒o   10 miles N of St Andrews
⊕   Practice area
🏠   James Braid
☰   www.scotscraiggolfclub.com

St Michaels   (1903)
Gallow Hill, Leuchars, KY16 0DX
☎   (01334) 839365 (Clubhouse)
🖳   (01334) 838789
📧   stmichaelsgc@btclick.com
📖   400
🏌   GD Dignan (01334) 838666
🏳   18 L 5802 yds SSS 68
👥   Sun am–NA (Mar–Oct) SOC
££   £29 (£37)
⌒o   5 miles N of St Andrews on
    Dundee road (A919)
⊕   Driving net; putting green; electric
    buggies
☰   www.stmichaelsgc.co.uk

Thornton   (1921)
Station Road, Thornton, KY1 4DW
☎   (01592) 771173 (Starter)
🖳   (01592) 774955
📧   thorntongolf@btconnect.com
📖   700
🏌   WD Rae (01592) 771111
🏳   18 L 6210 yds Par 70 SSS 70
👥   U
££   £25 D–£35 (£35 D–£50)
⌒o   5 miles N of Kirkcaldy, off A92
☰   www.thorntongolfclub.co.uk

St Andrews Clubs

New   (1902)
Club
3-5 Gibson Place, St Andrews, KY16 9JE
☎   (01334) 473426
🖳   (01334) 477570
📧   admin@newgolfclubstandrews.co.uk
📖   1750
🏌   The Secretary
🏳   Play over St Andrews Links courses
⌒o   18th fairway, Old Course
☰   www.newgolfclubstandrews.co.uk

The Royal and Ancient Golf
Club of St Andrews   (1754)
Club
St Andrews, KY16 9JD
☎   (01334) 460000
🖳   (01334) 460001
📧   thesecretary@randagc.org

📖   1900
🏌   P Dawson
🏳   Play over St Andrews Links
☰   www.theroyalandancientgolfclub.org

St Andrews Thistle Golf
Club   (1817)
Club
Lade Braes Hollow, 34 Lade Braes, St.
Andrews, Fife   KY16 9DA
☎   (01334) 477377
📧   thistle-secretary@tiscali.co.uk
📖   200
🏌   Randall Morrison
🏳   Play over St Andrews Links
⊕   Non-Course owning

St Regulus Ladies'   (1913)
Club
9 Pilmour Links, St Andrews, KY16 9JG
☎   (01334) 477797
🖳   (01334) 477887
📧   admin@st-regulus-lgc.co.uk
📖   293
🏌   Mrs L Graham
🏳   Play over St Andrews Links (7
    courses)
👥   WD–U
££   Varies depending on course
⊕   Practice facilities are available at
    the Links Trust Driving Range
☰   www.st-regulus-lgc.co.uk

The St Rule Club   (1898)
Club
12 The Links, St Andrews, KY16 9JB
☎   (01334) 472988
🖳   (01334) 472988
📧   struleclub@fsmail.net
📖   300
🏌   Mr Neil Doctor
🏳   Play over St Andrews Links
⌒o   St Andrews

The St Andrews   (1843)
Club
Links House, 13 The Links, St Andrews,
KY16 9JB
☎   (01334) 479799
🖳   (01334) 479577
📧   sec@thestandrewsgolfclub.co.uk
📖   2000
🏌   T Gallacher (01334) 479799
🏳   Play over St Andrews Links
☰   www.thestandrewsgolfclub.co.uk

St Andrews Courses

Balgove Course   (1993)
Public
St Andrews Links Trust, Pilmour House, St
Andrews, KY16 9SF
☎   (01334) 466666
🖳   (01334) 479555
📧   reservations@standrews.org.uk
🏌   AJR McGregor (Gen Mgr)
🏳   9 L 1520 yds Par 30
👥   U
££   £8–£12, 3–D £15–£21
    W £30–£42
⌒o   St Andrews Links, on A91

⊕   Driving range: St Andrews Links
    Golf Academy; Clubhouse;   Eden
    Clubhouse
🏠   Donald Steel
☰   www.standrews.org.uk

The Castle Course   (2008)
Public
St. Andrews Links Trust, Pilmour House, St.
Andrews, KY16 9SF
☎   (01334) 466666
🖳   (01334) 479555
📧   reservations@standrews.org.uk
🏌   AJR McGregor (Gen Mgr)
🏳   18 L 5460-7188 yds Par 71
👥   U SOC open 1 April – 31 October
££   £84 – £120
⌒o   The Castle Course, by Kinkell, Fife,
    Follow the A917 through St
    Andrew (North Street) heading
    towards Crail.
⊕   Warm-up area, Putting Green,
    Clubhouse
🏠   David McLay Kidd
☰   www.standrews.org.uk

Duke's   (1995)
Craigtoun, St Andrews, KY16 8NS
☎   (01334) 474371
🖳   (01334) 477668
📧   reservations@oldcoursehotel.co.uk
📖   350
🏌   David Scott (Mgr) (01334) 470214
✓   R Walker (01334) 470214
🏳   18 L 7512 yds Par 72 SSS 75
👥   U H SOC
££   £65 (£75) Low Season £70 High
    Season £110
⌒o   3 miles S of St Andrews on
    Pitscottie road
⊕   Golf academy
🏠   Peter Thomson CBE
☰   www.oldcoursehotel.co.uk

Eden Course   (1914)
Public
St Andrews Links Trust, Pilmour House, St
Andrews, KY16 9SF
☎   (01334) 466666
🖳   (01334) 479555
📧   reservations@standrews.org.uk
🏌   AJR McGregor (Gen Mgr)
🏳   18 L 6250 yds Par 70 SSS 70
👥   U SOC
££   £20–£40 3D–£70–£145
    W–£140–£290 (unlimited
    play–Jubilee, New, Eden &
    Strathtyrum courses)
⌒o   St Andrews Links, on A91
⊕   Driving range; St Andrews Links
    Golf Academy; St Andrews Links
    Clubhouse; Eden Clubhouse
🏠   HS Colt
☰   www.standrews.org.uk

Jubilee Course   (1897)
Public
St Andrews Links Trust, Pilmour House, St
Andrews, KY16 9SF
☎   (01334) 466666
🖳   (01334) 479555
📧   reservations@standrews.org.uk
🏌   AJR McGregor (Gen Mgr)

🏳 18 L 6742 yds Par 72 SSS 73
🏌 U SOC
££ £32–£65 3D–£70–£145
W–£140–£290 (unlimited play–Jubilee, New, Eden & Strathtyrum courses)
⛳ St Andrews Links, on A91. Signs to West Sands
⊕ Driving range; St Andrews Links Golf Academy; St Andrews Links Clubhouse; Eden Clubhouse
🏠 Angus/Auchterlonie/Steel
🖥 www.standrews.org.uk

New Course   (1895)
Public
St Andrews Links Trust, Pilmour House, St Andrews, KY16 9SF
☎ (01334) 466666
🖬 (01334) 479555
📧 reservations@standrews.org.uk
🖊 AJR McGregor (Gen Mgr)
🏳 18 L 6625 yds Par 71 SSS 73
🏌 U SOC
££ £32–£65 3D–£70–£145
W–£140–£290 (unlimited play–Jubilee, New, Eden & Strathtyrum courses)
⛳ St Andrews Links, on A91. Signs to West Sands
⊕ Driving range; St Andrews Links Golf Academy; St Andrews Links Clubhouse; Eden Clubhouse
🏠 Old Tom Morris
🖥 www.standrews.org.uk

Old Course   (15th Century)
Public
St Andrews Links Trust, Pilmour House, St Andrews, KY16 9SF
☎ (01334) 466666
🖬 (01334) 479555
📧 reservations@standrews.org.uk
🖊 AJR McGregor (Gen Mgr)
🏳 18 L 6721 yds Par 72 SSS 73
🏌 H No Sun play
££ £64–£130
⛳ St Andrews Links, on A91. Signs to West Sands
⊕ Driving range; St Andrews Links Golf Academy; St Andrews Links Clubhouse; Eden Clubhouse
🖥 www.standrews.org.uk

Strathtyrum Course   (1993)
Public
St Andrews Links Trust, Pilmour House, St Andrews, KY16 9SF
☎ (01334) 466666
🖬 (01334) 479555
📧 reservations@standrews.org.uk
🖊 AJR McGregor (Gen Mgr)
🏳 18 L 5620 yds Par 69 SSS 67
🏌 U SOC
££ £12–£25 3D–£70–£145
W–£140–£290 (unlimited play–Jubilee, New, Eden & Strathtyrum courses)
⛳ St Andrews Links, on A91
⊕ Driving range; St Andrews Links Golf Academy; St Andrews Links Clubhouse; Eden Clubhouse
🏠 Donald Steel
🖥 www.standrews.org.uk

Glasgow

Alexandra Park   (1880)
Public
Alexandra Park, Dennistoun, Glasgow, G31 8SE
☎ (0141) 276 0600
🖬 250
🖊 F Derwin
🏳 9 L 4562 yds Par 62
🏌 U
££ On application
⛳ ½ mile E of Glasgow, nr M8
🏠 Graham McArthur

Bishopbriggs   (1906)
Brackenbrae Road, Bishopbriggs, Glasgow, G64 2DX
☎ (0141) 772 1810
🖬 (0141) 762 2532
📧 thesecretarybgc@yahoo.co.uk
🖬 400 150(A) 120(J)
🖊 A Smith (0141) 772 8938
🏳 18 L 6262 yds SSS 71
🏌 H SOC–WD
££ £30 D–£40
⛳ 6 miles N of Glasgow on A803
⊕ 9 hole & Golf Academy area with driving bays
🏠 James Braid
🖥 www.thebishopbriggsgolfclub.com

Cathcart Castle   (1895)
Mearns Road, Clarkston, G76 7YL
☎ (0141) 638 9449
🖬 (0141) 638 1201
📧 secretary@cathcartcastle.com
🖬 950
🖊 IG Sutherland (0141) 638 9449
∕ S Duncan (0141) 638 3436
🏳 18 L 5865 yds SSS 69
🏌 M SOC
££ £30 D–£45
⛳ 1 mile from Clarkston on B767
🖥 www.cathcartcastle.com

Cawder   (1933)
Cadder Road, Bishopbriggs, Glasgow, G64 3QD
☎ (0141) 761 1281
🖬 (0141) 761 1285
📧 secretary@cawdergolfclub.cu.uk
🖬 1400
🖊 Fraser Gemmell (0141) 761 1283
∕ Gordon Stewart (0141) 772 7102
🏳 Cawder 18 L 6279 yds SSS 71
Keir 18 L 5880 yds SSS 68
🏌 WD–H SOC–WD
££ 1 round £35, 2 rounds £45
⛳ N of Glasgow, off A803 Kirkintilloch Road
🏠 Braid/Steel
🖥 www.cawdergolfclub.co.uk

Cowglen   (1906)
301 Barrhead Road, Glasgow, G43 1EU
☎ (0141) 632 0556
🖬 (01505) 503000
📧 r.jamieson-accountants@fsmail.net
🖬 625
🖊 RJG Jamieson (01505) 503000
∕ S Payne (0141) 649 9401

🏳 18 L 6079 yds SSS 69
🏌 WD–by arrangement with Sec WE–M
££ £35 D–£45
⛳ Take Pollok junction from M77 and course is half mile towards Pollok
⊕ Driving/long iron facilities; pitching green and putting green
🏠 James Braid
🖥 www.cowglengolfclub.co.uk

Glasgow   (1787)
Killermont, Bearsden, Glasgow, G61 2TW
☎ (0141) 942 1713
🖬 (0141) 942 0770
📧 secretary@glasgowgolfclub.com
🖬 800
🖊 AG McMillan (0141) 942 2011
∕ J Greaves (0141) 942 8507
🏳 18 L 5957 yds Par 70 SSS 69
🏌 M SOC WD
⛳ 4 miles NW of Glasgow
🏠 Tom Morris Sr
🖥 www.glasgowgolfclub.com

Haggs Castle   (1910)
70 Dumbreck Road, Dumbreck, Glasgow, G41 4SN
☎ (0141) 427 0480
🖬 (0141) 427 1157
📧 secretary@haggscastlegolfclub.com
🖬 900
🖊 A Williams (0141) 427 1157
∕ C Elliott (0141) 427 3355
🏳 18 L 6426 yds SSS 71
🏌 WD–H SOC–Weds only
££ SOC–£40
⛳ SW Glasgow (B768). M77 Jct 1
🏠 Dave Thomas (1998)
🖥 www.haggscastlegolfclub.com

Knightswood   (1929)
Public
Knightswood Park, Lincoln Avenue, Glasgow, G13 3DN
☎ (0141) 959 6358

Lethamhill   (1933)
Public
Cumbernauld Road, Glasgow, G33 1AH
☎ (0141) 770 6220

Linn Park   (1924)
Public
Simshill Road, Glasgow, G44 5TA
☎ (0141) 633 0377
🏳 18 L 5295 yds SSS 65
🏌 U–phone 1 day in advance
££ £10
⛳ 4 miles S of Glasgow, W of B766

Pollok   (1892)
90 Barrhead Road, Glasgow, G43 1BG
☎ (0141) 632 1080
🖬 (0141) 649 1398
📧 secretary@pollokgolf.com
🖬 650
🖊 D Morgan (0141) 632 4351
🏳 18 L 6358 yds SSS 70
🏌 WD/WE by arrangement SOC–WD
££ £50

⊕ 3 miles SW of Glasgow (B762).
M77 Junction 2
⌂ James Douglas, altered by Dr
Alastair McKenzie
▤ www.pollokgolf.com

Ralston (1904)
Strathmore Avenue, Ralston, Paisley,
PA1 3DT
☎ (0141) 882 1349
⌕ (0141) 883 9837
✉ thesecretary@ralstongolf.co.uk
▥ 440 165(L) 100(J)
♞ B W Hanson
⚐ C Munro (0141) 882 1349
ⴑ 18 L 6100 yds SSS 69
♔ M SOC
££ £27 D–£42 (£27 D–£42)
⊕ 2 m E of Paisley (A761); M8 Jct 26
⌂ Braid
▤ www.ralstongolfclub.co.uk

Rouken Glen (1922)
Pay and play
Stewarton Road, Thornliebank, Glasgow,
G46 7UZ
☎ (0141) 638 7044
⌕ (0141) 638 6115
✉ deaconsbank@ngclubs.co.uk
♞ S Armstrong
ⴑ 18 L 4800 yds SSS 63
♔ U SOC
££ £11 D–£19 (£14 D–£25)
⊕ 5 miles S of Glasgow, W of A77
⊕ Driving range
⌂ James Braid

Sandyhills (1905)
223 Sandyhills Road, Glasgow, G32 9NA
☎ (0141) 778 1179
▥ 700
♞ D Berry
ⴑ 18 L 6253 yds SSS 71
♔ M SOC
££ £30 D–£40
⊕ 4 miles SE of Glasgow, N of A74

Williamwood (1906)
Clarkston Road, Netherlee, Glasgow,
G44 3YR
☎ (0141) 637 1783
⌕ (0141) 571 0166
✉ secretary@williamwoodgc.co.uk
▥ 911
♞ LW Conn (0141) 629 1981
⚐ S Marshall (0141) 637 2715
ⴑ 18 L 5878 yds SSS 69
♔ WD–H
££ £30 D–£40
⊕ 5 miles S of Glasgow
⌂ James Braid
▤ www.williamwoodgc.co.uk

Highland

Caithness & Sutherland

Bonar Bridge/Ardgay (1904)
Bonar-Bridge, Ardgay, IV24 3EJ
☎ (01863) 766199 (Clubhouse)
✉ bonarardgaygolf@aol.com

▥ 250
♞ R Thomson (01862) 892443
ⴑ 9 L 5162 yds SSS 65 Par 68
♔ U
££ D–£15 (£15)
⊕ ½ mile N of Bonar-Bridge on
A836. 12 miles W of Dornoch

Brora (1891)
Golf Road, Brora, KW9 6QS
☎ (01408) 621417
⌕ (01408) 622157
✉ secretary@broragolf.co.uk
♞ AJA Gill
⚐ B Anderson (01408) 621473
ⴑ 18 L 6110 yds SSS 70
♔ U exc comp days –H for open
comps SOC
££ £37 D–£47 (£42 D–£52)
⊕ 18 miles N of Dornoch (A9)
⌂ James Braid
▤ www.broragolf.co.uk

The Carnegie Club (1995)
Skibo Castle, Dornoch, Sutherland,
IV25 3RQ
☎ (01862) 881 260
⌕ (01862) 881 260
✉ sharon.stewart@carnegieclubs.com
▥ 500
♞ Sharon Stewart
⚐ D Thomson (Dir of Golf)
ⴑ 18 L 6671 yds Par 71 SSS 72
⊕ 3 miles SW of Dornoch
⌂ Donald Steel
▤ www.carnegieclubs.com

Durness (1988)
Pay and play
Balnakeil, Durness, IV27 4PN
☎ (01971) 511364
⌕ (01971) 511321
✉ lucy@durnessgolfclub.org
▥ 150
♞ Mrs L Mackay (01971) 511364
ⴑ 9 L 5555 yds SSS 67
♔ U WE–Sun before 2pm
££ 9 Holes £15 18 Holes £18 D–£20
(£50)
⊕ 57 miles NW of Lairg on A838
⊕ Putting green; practice net
⌂ I Morrison, LJ Ross, F Keith
▤ www.durnessgolfclub.org

Golspie (1889)
Ferry Road, Golspie, KW10 6ST
☎ (01408) 633266
✉ info@golspie-golf-club.co.uk
▥ 260
♞ RI Beaton (Hon) (01408 633927)
ⴑ 18 L 5990 yds SSS 68
♔ U after 9.30 am daily SOC
WD/WE
££ £35 D–£45
⊕ Golspie on A9, 11 miles N of
Dornoch
⌂ Archibald Sumpson (1908),
James Braid (1925)
▤ www.golspie-golf-club.co.uk

Helmsdale (1895)
Strath Road, Helmsdale, KW8 6JL
☎ (01431) 821063

▥ 50
♞ R Sutherland
ⴑ 9 L 3360 yds SSS 60
♔ U
££ D–£15 (£15)
⊕ 30 miles N of Dornoch (A9)
▤ www.helmsdale.org

Lybster (1926)
Main Street, Lybster, KW1 6BL
▥ 100
♞ AG Calder (01595) 721316
ⴑ 9 L 2002 yds SSS 61
♔ U
££ D–£10
⊕ 13 miles S of Wick on A99
▤ www.lybstergolfclub.co.uk

Reay (1893)
Reay, Thurso, Caithness, KW14 7RE
☎ (01847) 811288
✉ info@reaygolfclub.co.uk
▥ 240
♞ W McIntosh
ⴑ 18 L 5854 yds Par 69 SSS 69
♔ U SOC
££ £25 D–£35 W–£90
⊕ 11 miles W of Thurso
⌂ James Braid
▤ www.reaygolfclub.co.uk

Royal Dornoch (1877)
Golf Road, Dornoch, IV25 3LW
☎ (01862) 810219
⌕ (01862) 810792
✉ bookings@royaldornoch.com
▥ 1115 217(L) 62(J) 346(Struie)
♞ JS Duncan
(Sec/Mgr) (01862) 811220
ext 22
⚐ A Skinner (01862) 810902
ⴑ C'ship 18 L 6562 yds SSS 73
Struie 18 L 6276 yds SSS 70
♔ C'ship–H Struie–U
££ £78 (£88) Championship £35
Struie
⊕ 45 miles N of Inverness, off A9, N
of Dornoch
⊕ Helipad by clubhouse; airstrip
nearby; practice ground nearby
⌂ Morris/Sutherland/Duncan
▤ www.royaldornoch.com

Thurso (1893)
Pay and play
Newlands of Geise, Thurso, KW14 7XD
☎ (01847) 893807
⌕ (01847) 892575
✉ info@thursogolfclub.co.uk
▥ 300
♞ RM Black (01847) 892575
ⴑ 18 L 5828 yds SSS 69
♔ U
££ £20 (£20)
⊕ 2 miles SW of Thurso
⊕ Two-bay driving range
⌂ WS Stewart
▤ www.thursogolfclub.co.uk

Ullapool (1998)
Pay and play
North Road, Ullapool, IV26 2TH
☎ (01854) 613323

☎ (01854) 612911
🏠 180
♣ A Paterson
🏌 9 L 5281 yds Par 70 SSS 67 (18 tees)
👥 U (outwith competitions)
££ Mon–Sun: D–£20 (9 holes £15) Mon–Fri £55
♨ Ullapool
⊕ Practice area; Putting Green
🏠 Souters

Wick   (1870)
Reiss, Wick, KW1 5LJ
☎ (01955) 602726
✉ wickgolfclub@hotmail.com

Inverness

Abernethy   (1893)
Nethy Bridge, PH25 3EB
☎ (01479) 821305
✉ info@abernethygolfclub.com
🏠 400
♣ Mrs J McCool
🏌 9 L 2526 yds SSS 66
👥 U SOC
££ £18 (£20)
♨ 5 miles S of Grantown (B970)
💻 www.abernethygolfclub.com

Aigas   (1993)
Proprietary
mains of Aigas, Beauly, Inverness, IV4 7AD
☎ (01463) 782942
✉ info@aigas-holidays.co.uk
🏠 120
🏌 9 L 2339 yds Par 66 SSS 63
👥 U SOC WD WE
££ £17 (£19)
♨ 6 miles west of Beauly on A831
⊕ Practice net; putting green
💻 www.aigas-holidays.co.uk

Alness   (1904)
Ardross Rd, Alness, Ross-shire, IV17 0QA
☎ (01349) 883877
✉ info@alnessgolfclub.co.uk
🏠 300
♣ Mrs A Black
✓ Gary Lister
🏌 18 L 4976 yds Par 67 SSS 64
👥 U SOC
££ £23 D–£28 (£25 D–£30)
♨ ¼ mile N of Alness. 20 miles N of Inverness
🏠 I Scott Taylor
💻 www.alness-golf.com

Boat-of-Garten   (1898)
Boat-of-Garten, PH24 3BQ
☎ (01479) 831282
🖂 (01479) 831523
✉ office@boatgolf.com
🏠 650
♣ W.N McConachie (clubsec@boatgolf.com)
✓ Ross Harrower (proshop@boatgolf.com)
🏌 18 L 5876 yds SSS 69
👥 WD–U after 9am WE–U after 9.30am Booking advisable

££ £35 D–£45 (£40 D–£50)
♨ 27 miles SE of Inverness (A95)
⊕ Driving range, net & putting green
🏠 James Braid
💻 www.boatgolf.com

Carrbridge   (1980)
Inverness Road, Carrbridge, PH23 3AU
☎ (08444) 141415 (Clubhouse) (01479) 811109 (Office)
🖂 (0871) 288 1014
✉ katie@carrbridgegolf.co.uk
🏠 450
♣ Mrs Katie Fenton
🏌 9 L 2623 yds Par 71 SSS 68
👥 U exc comp days; please phone to book and check availability; visitors/party books welcome
££ 9: £15 D–£21 18: £16 D–£21 (£23)
♨ 20 miles SE of Inverness, off A9
⊕ Putting green & practice area
💻 www.carrbridgegolf.com

Fort Augustus   (1926)
Pay and play
Markethill, Fort Augustus, PH32 4AU
☎ (01320) 366660
✉ fortaugustusgc@aol.com
🏠 110
♣ K Cheeseman
🏌 9 L 5454 yds SSS 67
👥 U
££ £15 D–£20
♨ W end of Fort Augustus on A82
🏠 Harry S Colt
💻 www.fortaugustusgc.webeden.co.uk

Fort William   (1974)
North Road, Fort William, PH33 6SN
☎ (01397) 704464
🏠 430
♣ R Macintyre
🏌 18 L 5686 metres SSS 70
👥 U
££ £25 (£28)
♨ 3 miles N of Fort William (A82)
🏠 JR Stutt
💻 www.fortwilliamgolf.co.uk

Fortrose & Rosemarkie   (1888)
Ness Road East, Fortrose, IV10 8SE
☎ (01381) 620529
🖂 (01381) 621328
✉ secretary@fortrosegolfclub.co.uk
🏠 800
♣ M MacDonald
🏌 18 L 5890 yds Par 71 SSS 69
👥 U SOC
££ £34 (£40)
♨ Black Isle, 12 miles N of Inverness
⊕ Driving range; 2 putting greens; practice net; golf shop
🏠 James Braid
💻 www.fortrosegolfclub.co.uk

Grantown-on-Spey   (1890)
Golf Course Road, Grantown-on-Spey, PH26 3HY
☎ (01479) 872079
🖂 (01479) 873725

✉ secretary@grantownonspeygolfclub.co.uk
🏠 800
♣ PR Mackay
🏌 18 L 5710 yds Par 70 SSS 68
👥 WD–U WE–U after 10am SOC
££ £28 D–£35 (£33 D–£40)
♨ E side of Grantown (A95)
🏠 Park/Braid/Brown
💻 www.grantownonspeygolfclub.co.uk

Invergordon   (1893)
King George Street, Invergordon, IV18 0BD
☎ (01349) 852715
✉ invergordongolf@tiscali.co.uk
🏠 170 30(L) 50(J)
🏌 18 L 6030 yds Par 69 SSS 69
👥 U SOC
££ £25
♨ 15 miles NE of Dingwall (A9/B817)
🏠 A Rae (1994)
💻 www.invergordongolf.co.uk

Inverness   (1883)
Culcabock Road, Inverness, IV2 3XQ
☎ (01463) 239882
🖂 (01463) 240616
✉ igc@freeuk.com
🏠 1100
♣ E Forbes
✓ AP Thomson (01463) 231989
🏌 18 L 6256 yds Par 69 SSS 70
👥 WE–restricted H SOC WD–after 10am, before 4pm
££ £38 D–£52 (£38 D–£52)
♨ 1 mile S of Inverness
🏠 George Smith/JJ Fraser; alterations by James Braid
💻 www.invernessgolfclub.co.uk

Kingussie   (1891)
Gynack Road, Kingussie, PH21 1LR
☎ (01540) 661600 (Office)
🖂 (01540) 662066
✉ sec@kingussie-golf.co.uk
🏠 600
♣ Ian Chadburn
🏌 18 L 5501 yds SSS 67
👥 U
££ Midweek £28 round/£36 day tkt Weekends £32 round/£38 day tkt
♨ Kingussie (A9)
🏠 H Vardon
💻 www.kingussie-golf.co.uk

Loch Ness   (1996)
Castle Heather, Inverness, IV2 6AA
☎ (01463) 713335
🖂 (01463) 712695
✉ info@golflochness.com
🏠 550
♣ ND Hampton (01463) 713335
✓ M Piggot (01463) 713334
🏌 18 L 5907 yds Par 70 SSS 69 9 L 1442 yds Par 29
👥 U SOC
££ £30 D–£45 (£35 D–£55)
♨ Culduthel, SW Inverness (A9)
⊕ Floodlit driving range; putting green; pitching/bunker area
🏠 Caddies Golf Course Design
💻 www.golflochness.com

Muir of Ord (1875)
Great North Road, Muir of Ord, IV6 7SX
☎ **(01463) 870825**
🖥 (01463) 871867
📧 muirgolf@supanet.com
📖 700
🏌 Mr A Pollock
✓ Shop (01463) 871311
🏴 18 L 5557 yds SSS 68
👥 U SOC
££ £23 D–£27 (£33 D–£38) week £50
🚗 15 miles N of Inverness (A862)
🏛 James Braid

Nairn (1887)
Seabank Road, Nairn, IV12 4HB
☎ **(01667) 453208**
🖥 (01667) 456328
📧 bookings@nairngolfclub.co.uk
📖 1330
🏌 D Corstorphine (01667) 453208
✓ R Fyfe (01667) 452787
🏴 18 L 6721 yds Par 72 SSS 73
9 hole course
👥 U SOC
££ On application
🚗 Nairn West Shore (A96). 15 miles
E of Inverness
🏛 Old Tom Morris/Braid/Simpson
🖥 www.nairngolfclub.co.uk

Nairn Dunbar (1899)
Lochloy Road, Nairn, IV12 5AE
☎ **(01667) 452741**
🖥 (01667) 456897
📧 secretary@nairndunbar.com
📖 1200
🏌 JS Falconer
✓ DH Torrance (01667) 453964
🏴 18 L 6765 yds SSS 74 SR 139
👥 U
££ £42 D–£60 (£50 D–£70)
🚗 In Nairn
⊕ Practice area
🖥 www.nairndunbar.com

Newtonmore (1893)
Golf Course Road, Newtonmore, PH20 1AT
☎ **(01540) 673878**
📧 secretary@newtonmoregolf.com

Strathpeffer Spa (1888)
Golf Course Road, Strathpeffer, IV14 9AS
☎ **(01997) 421219**
🖥 (01997) 421011
📧 mail@strathpeffergolfclub.co.uk
📖 360 50(L) 85(J)
🏌 Mrs Margaret Spark
🏴 18 L 5001 yds SSS 65
👥 U SOC
££ D–£24 (£28)
🚗 ¹/₄ mile N of Strathpeffer. 5 miles
W of Dingwall
⊕ Putting green + small practice area
🏛 Willie Park/Tom Morris
🖥 www.strathpeffergolf.co.uk

Tain (1890)
Chapel Road, Tain, IV19 1JE
☎ **(01862) 892314**
🖥 (01862) 892099
📧 info@tain-golfclub.co.uk

📖 560
🏌 Mrs J Bell
✓ Stuart Morrison
🏴 18 L 6404 yds SSS 72
👥 U
££ £40 D–£55 (£45 D–£60)
🚗 35 miles N of Inverness (A9). 8
miles S of Dornoch
⊕ Practice area; 3 nets; 2 putting
greens; designated short game area;
3 bay covered practice facility.
🏛 Old Tom Morris
🖥 www.tain-golfclub.co.uk

Tarbat (1909)
Pay and play
Portmahomack, Tain, IV20 1YB
☎ **(01862) 871278**
🖥 (01862) 871598
📖 240
🏴 9 L 2568 yds SSS 65
👥 U SOC
££ D–£17
🚗 10 miles E of Tain

Torvean (1962)
Public
Glenurquhart Road, Inverness, IV3 8JN
☎ **(01463) 225651**
x21 Starter x23 Office
🖥 (01463) 711417
📧 sarah@torveangolfclub.co.uk
📖 700
🏌 Sarah Downer (Mgr)
(01463) 225651
🏴 18 L 5799 yds SSS 68
👥 U
££ £24 (£26.50)
🚗 SW of Inverness on A82 1 mile
from city centre
⊕ Practice nets; putting green
🖥 www.torveangolfclub.co.uk

Orkney & Shetland

Orkney (1889)
Grainbank, Kirkwall, Orkney, KW15 1RD
☎ **(01856) 872457**

Sanday (1977)
Sanday, Orkney, KW17 2BW
☎ **(01857) 600341**
🖥 (01857) 600341
📖 20
🏌 R Thorne
🏴 9 L 2600 yds Par 35 SSS 36
👥 U
££ D–£5, £10 per annum, no further
green fees
🚗 2 miles N of Lady on B9069

Shetland (1891)
Dale, Gott, Shetland, ZE2 9SB
☎ **(01595) 840369**
🖥 (01595) 840369
📧 info@shetlandgolfclub.co.uk
📖 400
🏌 C J Wishart
🏴 18 L 5562 yds SSS 68
👥 U SOC
££ D–£20
🚗 4 miles N of Lerwick (A907)

⊕ Putting green; chipping green;
driving nets
🏛 Fraser Middleton
🖥 www.shetlandgolfclub.co.uk

Stromness (1890)
Stromness, Orkney, KW16 3DU
☎ **(01856) 850772**
📖 250
🏌 Colin McLeod
🏴 18 L 4762 yds SSS 63
👥 U
££ D–£20
🚗 Stromness, 16 miles W of Kirkwall
on Hoy Sound
🖥 www.stromnessgc.co.uk

Whalsay (1976)
Skaw Taing, Whalsay, Shetland, ZE2 9AL
☎ **(01806) 566450/566481**
📧 alan.solvei@lineone.net
📖 200
🏌 HA Sandison, C Hutchison
🏴 18 L 6140 yds Par 71 SSS 69
👥 U SOC
££ £20 round or day
🚗 5 miles N of Symbister Ferry
🖥 www.whalsaygolfclub.com

West Coast

Askernish (1891)
Lochboisdale, Askernish, South Uist,
HS81 5ST
☎ **(01878) 710312**

Gairloch (1898)
Gairloch, IV21 2BE
☎ **(01445) 712407**
🖥 (01445) 712865
📧 gairlochgolfclub@hotmail.co.uk
📖 240
🏌 B Jeffrey
🏴 9 L 2036-2072 yds SSS 62
👥 U–phone first
££ D–£16 W–£60 D–£10 W–£35
(Junior)
🚗 60 miles W of Dingwall in Wester
Ross
🏛 Capt AW Burgess
🖥 www.gairlochgolfclub.com

Isle of Harris (1891)
Scarista, Isle of Harris, HS5 3HX
☎ **(01859) 550226**
📧 harrisgolf@ic24.net
📖 72
🏌 J MacLean
🏴 9 L 2442 yds Par 68 SSS 64
👥 U
££ £15 (£15)
🚗 13 miles S of Tarbert on W coast
🖥 www.harrisgolf.com

Isle of Skye (1964)
Sconser, Isle of Skye, IV48 8TD
☎ **(01478) 650414**

Lochcarron (1908)
Lochcarron, Strathcarron, IV54 8YS
📧 secretary@lochcarrongolf.co.uk

Skeabost　(1982)
Skeabost Bridge, Isle of Skye, IV51 9NP
☎ **(01470) 532202**

Stornoway　(1890)
Lady Lever Park, Stornoway, Isle of Lewis, HS2 0XP
☎ **(01851) 702240**
✉ admin@stornowaygolfclub.co.uk
📖 400
🏌 KW Galloway (01851) 702533
🏳 18 L 5252 yds Par 68 SSS 67
👥 U exc Sun–NA SOC
££ D–£20 W–£60
⛳ Off A857 in Lews Castle grounds, Isle of Lewis
🏠 J & R Stutt (most recent alterations)
🖥 www.stornowaygolfclub.co.uk

Traigh　(1947)
Arisaig, Inverness-shire, PH39 4NT
☎ **(01687) 450337**

Lanarkshire

Airdrie　(1877)
Rochsoles, Airdrie, ML6 0PQ
☎ **(01236) 762195**
📟 (01236) 760584
✉ airdrie.golfclub@virgin.net
📖 450
🏌 R M Marshall
✍ S McLean (01236) 754360
🏳 18 L 5772 yds SSS 68
👥 U SOC WD WE H
££ £25 D–£30
⛳ Airdrie 1 mile
⊕ Putting green; practice net
🏠 James Braid

Bellshill　(1905)
Community Road, Orbiston, Bellshill, ML4 2RZ
☎ **(01698) 745124**
📟 (01698) 292576
✉ info@bellshillgolfclub.com
📖 680
🏌 T McLaughlin
🏳 18 L 5900 yds Par 69 SSS 69
👥 WD–U Sun–NA before 1.30pm SOC. No visiting parties
££ £20 D–£25 (+ BH £25 D–£30) Juniors £5 (£10) – must be accompanied by adult
⛳ 30 miles W (A725) M74 Junction 5
🖥 www.bellshillgolfclub.com

Biggar　(1895)
Public
The Park, Broughton Road, Biggar, ML12 6AH
☎ **(01899) 220618 (Clubhouse)**
　(01899) 220319 (Bookings)

Blairbeth　(1910)
Burnside, Rutherglen, Glasgow, G73 4SF
☎ **(0141) 634 3355 (Clubhouse)**
✉ secretary@blairbethgolfclub.co.uk
📖 205

📟 (0141) 634 3325
🏳 18 L 5537 yds Par 70 SSS 68
👥 SOC–WD WE–NA after 2pm
££ £15 D–£22 (£20)
⛳ 1 mile S of Rutherglen
🖥 www.blairbethgolfclub.co.uk

Bothwell Castle　(1922)
Uddington Road, Bothwell, Glasgow, G71 8TD
☎ **(01698) 801971**
📟 (01698) 801971
✉ secretary@bcgolf.co.uk
📖 1000
🏌 J Callaghan (01698) 801971
✍ A McCloskey (01698) 801969
🏳 18 L 6220 yds SSS 70
👥 WD–U 9.30–10.30am & 2.30–3.30pm SOC by arrangement (tel 01698 801972 Handicap Certificate required.
££ £35 D–£45
⛳ 2 miles N of Hamilton. M74 Jct 5
🖥 www.bcgolf.co.uk

Calderbraes　(1891)
57 Roundknowe Road, Uddington, G71 7TS
☎ **(01698) 813425**
📖 300
🏌 S McGuigan (0141) 573 2497
🏳 9 L 5046 yds Par 66 SSS 67
👥 WD–U WE–M
££ D–£13
⛳ Start of M74

Cambuslang　(1892)
30 Westburn Drive, Cambuslang, G72 7NA
☎ **(0141) 641 3130**
📟 (0141) 641 3130
✉ cambuslanggolfclub@tiscali.co.uk
📖 200 100(L) 40(J)
🏌 RM Dunlop
🏳 9 L 5942 yds SSS 69
👥 M
££ On application
⛳ Cambuslang Station ³/₄ mile

Carluke　(1894)
Hallcraig, Mauldslie Road, Carluke, ML8 5HG
☎ **(01555) 770574/771070**
📟 (01555) 770574
✉ carlukegolfsecy@tiscali.com
📖 505 100(L)
🏌 DT Stewart (01555) 770574
✍ C Ronald (01555) 751053
🏳 18 L 5919 yds SSS 69
👥 WD–U before 4pm WE–NA SOC
££ £25 D–£35
⛳ 20 miles SE of Glasgow
🖥 www.carlukegolfclub.com

Carnwath　(1907)
1 Main Street, Carnwath, ML11 8JX
☎ **(01555) 840251**
📟 (01555) 841070
✉ carnwathgc@hotmail.co.uk
📖 582
🏌 Mrs L McPate
🏳 18 L 5955 yds SSS 69
👥 WD–U before 4pm Sat–NA Sun–restricted

££ £22 D–£32 (Sun–£28 D–£38)
⛳ 7 miles E of Lanark
🖥 www.carnwathgc.co.uk

Cathkin Braes　(1888)
Cathkin Road, Rutherglen, Glasgow, G73 4SE
☎ **(0141) 634 6605**
✉ secretary@cathkinbraesgolfclub.co.uk
📖 1000
🏌 DE Moir
✍ S Bree (0141) 634 0650
🏳 18 L 6208 yds SSS 71
👥 WD–U
££ £35
⛳ 5 miles S of Glasgow (B759)
🏠 James Braid
🖥 www.cathkinbraesgolfclub.co.uk

Coatbridge Municipal　(1971)
Public
Townhead Road, Coatbridge, ML52 2HX
☎ **(01236) 28975**

Colville Park　(1923)
Jerviston Estate, Motherwell, ML1 4UG
☎ **(01698) 263017**
📟 (01698) 230418
📖 900 64(L) 140(J)
🏌 L Innes (01698) 262808
✍ J Stark (01698) 265779
🏳 18 L 6301 yds Par 71 SSS 70
👥 WD–U 11am–3pm (exc Fri–NA) WE–NA SOC–WD
££ £18 D–£27
⛳ 1 mile NE of Motherwell on A723
🏠 James Braid
🖥 www.colvillepark.co.uk

Crow Wood　(1925)
Cumbernauld Road, Muirhead, Glasgow, G69 9JF
☎ **(0141) 799 2011**
📟 (0141) 779 4873
✉ secretary@crowwood-golfclub.co.uk
📖 700
🏌 G Blyth (0141) 779 4954
✍ B Moffat (0141) 779 1943
🏳 18 L 6168 yds Par 71 SSS 70
👥 WD–H (prior notice required) SOC
££ £30 D–£40
⛳ 5 miles NE of Glasgow, off A80
🏠 James Braid
🖥 www.crowwood-golfclub.co.uk

Dalziel Park　(1997)
100 Hagen Drive, Motherwell, ML1 5RZ
☎ **(01698) 862862**

Douglas Water　(1922)
Rigside, Lanark, ML11 9NB
☎ **(01555) 880361**
📟 (01555) 880361
📖 190
🏌 D Hogg
🏳 9 L 2916 yds SSS 69
👥 U exc Sat–restricted
££ £10 (£12)
⛳ 7 miles S of Lanark. M74 Jcts 11/12

Drumpellier (1894)

Drumpellier Ave, Coatbridge, ML5 1RX
- ☎ (01236) 424139
- 🖬 (01236) 428723
- 📠 administrator@drumpelliergolfclub.com
- 🔲 460
- ♟ JM Craig
- ✓ Ian Taylor (01236) 432971
- ⛳ 18 L 6227 yds Par 71 SSS 70
- 👥 I H SOC WD
- ££ £35 D–£50 (no WE visitors)
- ⛀ 8 miles E of Glasgow
- ⌂ James Braid

East Kilbride (1900)

Chapelside Road, Nerston, East Kilbride, G74 4PH
- ☎ (01355) 220913 (Clubhouse)
- 🖬 (01355) 247728
- 📠 secretary@ekgolfclub.co.uk
- 🔲 850
- ♟ WG Gray (01355) 247728
- ✓ P McKay (01355) 222192
- ⛳ 18 L 6402 yds SSS 71
- 👥 M SOC–WD
- ££ £25 D–£35
- ⛀ 8 miles SE of Glasgow
- ⊕ Practice ground, practice putting green and chipping area; pro shop

Easter Moffat (1922)

Mansion House, Plains, Airdrie, ML6 8NP
- ☎ (01236) 842878
- 🖬 (01236) 842904
- 📠 secretary@emgc.co.uk
- 🔲 600
- ♟ G Miller (01236) 620972
- ✓ G King (01236) 843015
- ⛳ 18 L 6221 yds SSS 70
- 👥 WD only
- ££ £22 D–£33
- ⛀ 3 miles E of Airdrie

Hamilton (1892)

Riccarton, Ferniegair, Hamilton, ML3 7UE
- ☎ (01698) 282872
- 🖬 (01698) 204650
- 📠 secretary@hamiltongolfclub.co.uk
- 🔲 500
- ♟ GM Chapman
- ✓ D Wright
- ⛳ 18 L 6463 yds SSS 71
- 👥 M or by arrangement with Sec SOC
- ££ On application
- ⛀ 1½ miles S of Hamilton
- ⌂ James Braid
- 🖥 www.hamiltongolfclub.co.uk

Hollandbush (1954)

Public
Acre Tophead, Lesmahagow, Coalburn, ML11 0JS
- ☎ (01555) 893484
- 📠 mail@hollandbushgolfclub.co.uk
- 🔲 420
- ♟ J Hamilton
- ⛳ 18 L 6246 yds SSS 70
- 👥 U
- ££ £9.70 (£11.20)
- ⛀ 10 miles SW of Lanark, off A74, between Lesmahagow and Coalburn

- ⊕ 3 full hole practice area
- 🖥 www.hollandbushgolfclub.co.uk

Kirkhill (1910)

Greenlees Road, Cambuslang, Glasgow, G72 8YN
- ☎ (0141) 641 3083 (Clubhouse)
- 🖬 (0141) 641 8499
- 📠 secretary@kirkhillgolfclub.org.uk
- 🔲 570
- ♟ C Downes (0141) 641 8499
- ✓ D Williamson (0141) 641 7972
- ⛳ 18 L 6030 yds SSS 70
- 👥 WD–by prior arrangement WE/BH–NA SOC
- ££ On application
- ⛀ Cambuslang, SE Glasgow
- ⌂ James Braid
- 🖥 www.kirkhillgolfclub.org.uk

Lanark (1851)

The Moor, Lanark, ML11 7RX
- ☎ (01555) 663219
- 🖬 (01555) 663219
- 📠 lanarkgolfclub@supanet.com
- 🔲 550 130(L) 150(J)
- ♟ GH Cuthill
- ✓ A White (01555) 661456
- ⛳ 18 L 6306 yds SSS 71
  9 hole course
- 👥 WD–U until 4pm WE–M
- ££ 9: £8 adult, £4 under 18, 18: £40 D–£50
- ⛀ 30 miles S of Glasgow, off A74
- ⌂ Tom Morris
- 🖥 www.lanarkgolfclub.co.uk

Langlands (1985)

Public
Langlands Road, East Kilbride, G75 0QQ
- ☎ (01355) 248173
  (01355) 224685 (Starter)

Larkhall

Public
Burnhead Road, Larkhall, Glasgow
- ☎ (01698) 881113

Leadhills (1895)

The Lowthers, Horners Place, Leadhills, Nr Biggar ML12 6YQ
- ☎ (01659) 74272
- 📠 jack@gsx-r750cc.fsnrt.co.uk
- 🔲 80
- ♟ Jack Arrigoni
- ⛳ 9 L 4404 yds Par 66 SSS 64
- 👥 U
- ££ Over 18 years: £10 round or day
  Under 18 years: £7 round or day
- ⛀ 6 miles S of Abington, off M74
- ⊕ Trolley and club hire
- 🖥 See Golf Central

Mount Ellen (1904)

Lochend Road, Gartcosh, Glasgow, G69 9EY
- ☎ (01236) 872277
- 🖬 (01236) 872249
- 📠 archiewylie@hotmail.com
- 🔲 480
- ♟ Archie Wylie
- ✓ I Bilsborough (01236) 872632
- ⛳ 18 L 5525 yds SSS 68
- 👥 WD–U from 9am–4pm WE–NA

- ££ £25 D–£32 (NA)
- ⛀ 8 miles NE of Glasgow, W of M73
- 🖥 www.ourgolfclub.co.uk/megc.php

Mouse Valley (1993)

East End, Cleghorn, Lanark, ML11 8NR
- ☎ (01555) 870015
- 🖬 (01555) 870022
- 📠 info@kames-golf-club.com
- 🔲 300
- ♟ Mr John Kelly
- ⛳ 18 L 6300 yds SSS 72
  9 L 2200 yds SSS 65
- 👥 U
- ££ 18 hole: £19 (£25) 9 hole: £15
- ⛀ 2 miles W of Carnwath on A721
- ⊕ Coaching Centre - includes Driving Range; Indoor Green
- ⌂ Graham Taylor
- 🖥 www.kames-golf-club.com

Shotts (1895)

Blairhead, Benhar Road, Shotts, ML7 5BJ
- ☎ (01501) 820431
- 🖬 (01501) 825868
- 📠 info@shottsgolfclub.co.uk
- 🔲 700
- ♟ GT Stoddart (01501) 825868
- ✓ J Strachan (01501) 822658
- ⛳ 18 L 6205 yds SSS 70
- 👥 WD–U Sat–NA before 4.30pm
- ££ £22 (£30)
- ⛀ 18 miles E of Glasgow on B7057. M8 Junction 5, 1½ miles
- ⌂ James Braid
- 🖥 www.shottsgolfclub.co.uk

Strathaven (1908)

Glasgow Road, Strathaven, ML10 6NL
- ☎ (01357) 520421
- 🖬 (01357) 520539
- 📠 info@strathavengc.com
- 🔲 1000
- ♟ IF Neil
- ✓ S Kerr (01357) 521812
- ⛳ 18 L 6250 yds SSS 71
- 👥 WD–I before 4pm WE–NA
- ££ £31 D–£41
- ⛀ N of Strathaven, off Glasgow road (A726)
- ⌂ Willie Fernie
- 🖥 www.strathavengc.com

Strathclyde Park

Public
Mote Hill, Hamilton, ML3 6BY
- ☎ (01698) 429350
- 🔲 120
- ♟ K Will
- ✓ W Walker (01698) 285511
- ⛳ 9 L 6350 yds SSS 70
- 👥 U exc medal days (phone booking)
- ££ 18: jun/sen £4.50, adult £9; 9: £1.80 (£2.10) – Jnr, unwaged & senior
- ⛀ Hamilton. M74 Junction 5
- ⊕ Driving range; putting green; practice area

Torrance House (1969)

Public
Strathaven Road, East Kilbride, Glasgow, G75 0QZ
- ☎ (01355) 248638

Wishaw　(1897)

55 Cleland Road, Wishaw, ML2 7PH
- ☎ **(01698) 372869 (Clubhouse)**
- 🖳 (01698) 356930
- 🖂 jwdouglas@btconnect.com
- 🕮 475 80(L)
- ✍ JW Douglas (01698) 357480
- ⌁ S Adair (01698) 358247
- �📏 18 L 5999 yds SSS 69
- 🕴 WD–U until 4pm NA–Sat Sun–U
- ££ £26 D–£36 Sun–£30 D–£40
- ⬡ N of Wishaw town centre
- ⌂ James Braid

Lothians

East Lothian

Aberlady　(1912)

Club
Aberlady, EH32 0RB
- 🖂 ithomps3@aol.com

Archerfield Links　(2004)

Dirleton, East Lothian, EH39 5HU
- ☎ **(01620) 897050**
- 🖳 (08700) 515487
- 🖂 mail@archerfieldgolfclub.com
- ✍ Stuart Bayne (Dir of Golf) (01620) 850552
- ⌁ Stuart Bayne (Dir of Golf)
- 📏 36
- 🕴 M
- ⊕ Double-ended driving range, 2 short game areas; putting green
- ⌂ DJ Russell
- 🖳 www.archerfieldgolfclub.com

Bass Rock　(1873)

Club
43a High Street, North Berwick, EH39 4HH
- ☎ **(01620) 894071**
- 🖂 bassrockgolfclub@hotmail.com
- 🕮 110
- ✍ J Bullough (01620) 894071
- 📏 Play over North Berwick
- 🕴 All enquiries should be directed to North Berwick GC

Castle Park　(1994)

Pay and play
Gifford, Haddington, EH41 4PL
- ☎ **(01620) 810733**
- 🖳 (01620) 810691
- 🖂 castleparkgolf@hotmail.com
- 🕮 450
- ✍ JT Wilson (01620) 810733
- ⌁ D Small (01368) 862872
- 📏 18 L 6443 yds Par 72 SSS 71
- 🕴 U SOC
- ££ £24 D–£35 (£32 D–£45)
- ⬡ 2 miles S of Gifford on Longyester road
- ⊕ Driving range
- ⌂ A Baird
- 🖳 www.castleparkgolfclub.co.uk

Dirleton Castle　(1854)

Club
15 The Pines, Gullane, EH31 2DT

- ☎ **(01620) 843591**
- 🕮 100
- ✍ J Taylor
- 📏 Play over Gullane courses
- 🖳 www.dirletoncastlegolfclub.org.uk

Dunbar　(1856)

East Links, Dunbar, EH42 1LL
- ☎ **(01368) 862317**
- 🖳 (01368) 865202
- 🖂 secretary@dunbargolfclub.com
- 🕮 998
- ✍ John I Archibald (Club Mgr)
- ⌁ J Montgomery (01368) 862086
- 📏 18 L 6597 yds Par 71 SSS 72
- 🕴 U SOC–exc Thurs
- ££ £50 D–£65 (£60 D–£85) 2007 rates – subject to change
- ⬡ ¹/₂ mile E of Dunbar. 30 miles E of Edinburgh, off A1
- ⊕ Practice pitching area; practice ground; practice nets (indoor & outdoor)
- ⌂ Tom Morris
- 🖳 www.dunbargolfclub.com

Gifford　(1904)

Edinburgh Road, Gifford, EH41 4JE
- ☎ **(01620) 810591 (Starter)**
- 🖳 (01620) 810267
- 🖂 secretary@giffordgolfclub.com
- 🕮 570
- ✍ Robert Stewart (01620) 810267
- 📏 9 L 6050 yds SSS 69
- 🕴 U–booking required
- ££ 9: £14 18: £20 D–£30
- ⬡ 4 miles S of Haddington. 20 miles SE of Edinburgh (B6355)
- 🖳 www.giffordgolfclub.com

Glen (North Berwick)　(1906)

East Links, Tantallon Terrace, North Berwick, EH39 4LE
- ☎ **(01620) 892726**
- 🖳 (01620) 895447
- 🖂 secretary@glengolfclub.co.uk
- 🕮 650
- ✍ Rita Wilson (Office Mgr)
- ⌁ Shop (01620) 892726
- 📏 18 L 6243 yds SSS 70
- 🕴 U–booking recommended
- ££ £37 D–£47 (£49 D–£59)
- ⬡ 20 miles E of Edinburgh, take A198 off A1
- ⌂ Braid/Sayers/Mackenzie Ross
- 🖳 www.glengolfclub.co.uk

Gullane　(1882)

Gullane, EH31 2BB
- ☎ **(01620) 842255**
- **(01620) 843115 (Starter)**
- 🖳 (01620) 842327
- 🖂 secretary@gullanegolfclub.com
- 🕮 1100 450(L) 100(J)
- ✍ S Anthony (01620) 843760
- ⌁ AL Good (01620) 843111
- 📏 No 1 18 L 6466 yds SSS 72
- No 2 18 L 6244 yds SSS 71
- No 3 18 L 5252 yds SSS 66
- 6 hole children's course
- 🕴 No 1–H Nos 2/3–U
- ££ No 1 £85 D–£120 (£100) No 2 £40 D–£50 (£45) No 3 £24 D–£30 (£30) Children's course free

---

- ⬡ 18 miles E of Edinburgh on A198
- ⊕ Advance booking advisable; Visitors and Society bookings welcome
- 🖳 www.gullanegolfclub.com

Haddington　(1865)

Amisfield Park, Haddington, EH41 4PT
- ☎ **(01620) 823627**
- 🖳 (01620) 826580
- 🖂 info@haddingtongolf.co.uk
- 🕮 850
- ✍ N Edmonds (office Mgr)
- ⌁ J Sandilands (01620) 822727
- 📏 18 L 6335 yds Par 71 SSS 71
- 🕴 WD–U WE–U 10am–12 & 2–4pm SOC
- ££ £28 (£38)
- ⬡ 17 miles E of Edinburgh on A1. ³/₄ mile E of Haddington
- 🖳 www.haddingtongolf.co.uk

The Honourable Company of Edinburgh Golfers　(1744)

Muirfield, Gullane, EH31 2EG
- ☎ **(01620) 842123**
- 🖳 (01620) 842977
- 🖂 hceg@muirfield.org.uk
- ✍ ANG Brown
- 📏 18 L 6673 yds SSS 73 (Championship L 7034 yds)
- 🕴 WD–Tues & Thurs only except public hols H
- ££ 1 round £175, 2 rounds £220
- ⬡ NE outskirts of Gullane, opposite sign for Greywalls on A198
- ⊕ Practice range
- ⌂ Harry Colt
- 🖳 www.muirfield.org.uk

Kilspindie　(1867)

Aberlady, EH32 0QD
- ☎ **(01875) 870358**
- 🖂 kilspindie@btconnect.com
- 🕮 440 160(L) 70(J)
- ✍ PB Casely
- ⌁ GJ Sked (01875) 870695
- 📏 18 L 5030 m SSS 66
- 🕴 Phone Sec in advance WD–U after 9.45am WE–U after 11am SOC
- ££ £37 D–£57.50 (£47.50 D–£67.50)
- ⬡ Aberlady, 17 miles E of Edinburgh on A198 (off A1)
- ⊕ Putting green; practice nets; practice green with bunker
- ⌂ Ross/Sayers
- 🖳 www.golfeastlothian.com

Longniddry　(1921)

Links Road, Longniddry, EH32 0NL
- ☎ **(01875) 852141**
- 🖳 (01875) 853371
- 🖂 secretary@longniddrygolfclub.co.uk
- 🕮 1100
- ✍ RMS Gunning
- ⌁ WJ Gray (01875) 852228
- 📏 18 L 6260 yds SSS 70
- 🕴 WD–U H SOC–WD after 9.18am
- ££ £45 D–£70 (£65)
- ⬡ 13 miles E of Edinburgh, off A1
- ⌂ HS Colt
- 🖳 www.longniddrygolfclub.co.uk

For list of abbreviations and key to symbols see page 647

Luffness New (1894)

Aberlady, EH32 0QA

☎ **(01620) 843114**
📠 (01620) 842933
✉ secretary@luffnessnew.com
📖 700
🏌 Gp Capt AG Yeates
(01620) 843336
🏷 18 L 6328 yds SSS 71
👤 H or I WE/BH–NA SOC
££ £70 D–£95
🚗 1 mile W of Gullane (A198)
⊕ Practice area
🏠 Morris/Braid
🖳 www.luffnessgolf.com

Musselburgh (1938)

Monktonhall, Musselburgh, EH21 6SA

☎ **(0131) 665 2005**
📠 (0131) 665 4435
✉ secretary@themusselburghgolfclub
.com
📖 1000
🏌 P Millar
/ F Mann (0131) 665 7055
🏷 18 L 6725 yds SSS 72
👤 WD–U before 4.30pm WE–NA Sat
££ £35 D–£50 (£45 D–£50)
🚗 1 mile S of Musselburgh on B6415
🏠 James Braid
🖳 www.themusselburghgolfclub.com

Musselburgh Old Course

(1982)
Public
10 Balcarres Road, Musselburgh,
EH21 7SD

☎ **(0131) 665 6981**
(0131) 665 5438 (Starter)
📠 (0131) 653 1770
✉ secretary@mocgc.com
📖 270
🏌 R McGregor (0771) 461 0549
/ Jane Caunaghan
🏷 9 L 5748 yds SSS 68
👤 WD/BH–U WE–U after 1pm
££ 9: £11
🚗 7 miles E of Edinburgh on A1
🖳 www.mocgc.com

North Berwick (1832)

West Links, Beach Road, North Berwick,
EH39 4BB

☎ **(01620) 890312**
📠 (01620) 893274
✉ secretary@northberwickgolfclub
.com
📖 550
🏌 Christopher Spencer
(01620) 895040
/ D Huish (01620) 893233
🏷 18 L 6456 yds SSS 71
👤 U H
££ £75 D–£115 (£95) Winter–£35
D–£55 (£55) (2009 fees)
🚗 Centre of North Berwick. 24 miles
E of Edinburgh (A198)
🖳 www.northberwickgolfclub.com

Royal Musselburgh (1774)

Prestongrange House, Prestonpans,
EH32 9RP

☎ **(01875) 810276**
(advance bookings)
📠 (01875) 810276
✉ enquiries@royalmusselburgh.co.uk
📖 800
🏌 TH Hardie (Sec/Mgr); D Thomson
(Golf Sec) (01875) 819000
/ J Henderson (01875) 810139
🏷 18 L 6254 yds SSS 70
👤 U SOC
££ £30 D–£40 (£35)
🚗 8 miles E of Edinburgh on B1361
North Berwick road
⊕ Driving range
🏠 James Braid
🖳 www.royalmusselburgh.co.uk

Tantallon (1853)

Club
32 Westgate, North Berwick, EH39 4AH

☎ **(01620) 892114**
📠 (01620) 894399
✉ secretary@tantallongolfclub.co.uk
📖 441
🏌 I F Doig
/ D Huish (01620) 893233
🏷 Play over North Berwick West
Links
👤 See North Berwick Golf Club
££ See North Berwick Golf Club
🖳 www.north-berwick.co.uk/tantallon

Thorntree Golf Club

(1856)
Club
Prestongrange House, Prestonpans,
EH32 9RP

☎ **(0131) 552 3559**
📖 100
🏌 Arthur Reid
🏷 Play over Royal
Musselburgh course

Whitekirk (1995)

Whitekirk, North Berwick, EH39 5PR

☎ **(01620) 870300**
📠 (01620) 870330
✉ countryclub@whitekirk.com
📖 400
🏌 D Brodie
/ P Wardell
🏷 18 L 6526 yds Par 72 SSS 72
👤 U SOC
££ £30 (£40) Apr–Sep 2008
🚗 3 miles SE of North Berwick
(A198)
⊕ Practice range
🏠 Cameron Sinclair
🖳 www.whitekirk.com

Winterfield (1935)

Public
St Margarets, North Road, Dunbar,
EH42 1AU

☎ **(01368) 862280**
✉ kevinphillips@tiscali.co.uk
📖 350
/ K Phillips (01368) 863562
🏷 18 L 5053 yds SSS 65
👤 U
££ On application–phone Pro
🚗 W side of Dunbar. 28 miles E of
Edinburgh (A1)

Midlothian

Baberton (1893)

50 Baberton Avenue, Juniper Green,
Edinburgh, EH14 5DU

☎ **(0131) 453 4911**
📠 (0131) 453 4678
✉ manager@baberton.co.uk
📖 900
🏌 BM Flockhart (0131) 453 4911
/ K Kelly (0131) 453 3555
🏷 18 L 6119 yds SSS 70
👤 WD–U before 5pm; Sat–after 3pm;
Sun–after 1pm
££ £30 D–£40 (£32 D–£45)
🚗 5 miles SW of Edinburgh (A70)
🏠 Willie Park Jr
🖳 www.baberton.co.uk

Braid Hills (1893)

Public
Braid Hills Road, Edinburgh, EH10 6JY

☎ **(0131) 447 6666 (Starter)**

Braids United (1897)

Club
22 Braid Hills Approach, Edinburgh,
EH10 6JY

☎ **(0131) 452 9408**

Broomieknowe (1905)

36 Golf Course Road, Bonnyrigg,
EH19 2HZ

☎ **(0131) 663 9317**
📠 (0131) 663 2152
✉ administrator@broomieknowe.com
📖 500
🏌 R H Beattie
/ M Patchett (0131) 660 2035
🏷 18 L 6150 yds Par 70 SSS 70
👤 WD–U WE/BH–U
££ £30 D–£45 (£34)
🚗 7 miles SE of Edinburgh
⊕ Buggies for hire
🏠 Braid/Hawtree
🖳 www.broomieknowe.com

Bruntsfield Links Golfing

Society (1761)

The Clubhouse, 32 Barnton Avenue,
Edinburgh, EH4 6JH

☎ **(0131) 336 2006**
📠 (0131) 336 5538
✉ secretary@bruntsfield.sol.co.uk
📖 1185
🏌 Cdr DM Sandford (0131) 336 1479
/ R Brian (0131) 336 4050
🏷 18 L 6446 yds SSS 71
👤 WD–U WE–apply to Sec SOC–H
££ £60 D–£85 (£65 D–£90)
🚗 3 miles NW of Edinburgh, off A90
at Davidson Mains
🏠 Willie Park/Mackenzie/Hawtree
🖳 www.bruntsfieldlinks.co.uk

Carrick Knowe (1930)

Public
Glendevon Park, Edinburgh, EH12 5VZ

☎ **(0131) 337 1096 (Starter)**

Cogarburn   (1975)
Newbridge, Midlothian EH28 8NN
- ☎ **(0131) 333 4718**
- 🛄 460
- 🏌 Sandra Raine (0131) 333 4110
- ▶ 12 Parkland Par 66
- 👥 U WD/WE except for competitions
- ££ £15 (£20)
- 🏌️ 1 mile from Cogarburn roundabout

Craigmillar Park   (1895)
1 Observatory Road, Edinburgh, EH9 3HG
- ☎ **(0131) 667 2837**
- 🛄 (0131) 662 8091
- 🖂 secretary@craigmillarpark.co.uk
- 🛄 592 103L 18Y 69J
- 🏌 G Gillespie (0131) 667 0047
- ⚲ S Gourlay (0131) 667 2850
- ▶ 18 L 5825 yds SSS 68
- 👥 SOC WD–U WE–U after 3.30pm
- ££ On application
- 🏌️ Blackford, S of Edinburgh
- ⊕ Putting Green, Practice Ground, Bar and Catering Facilities, Golf club hire, showers.
- 🏠 James Braid
- 🖥 www.craigmillarpark.co.uk

Duddingston   (1895)
Duddingston Road West, Edinburgh, EH15 3QD
- ☎ **(0131) 661 7688**
- 🛄 (0131) 652 6057
- 🖂 admin@duddingstongolf.co.uk
- 🛄 800
- 🏌 Terry Christie
- ⚲ Alistair McLean (0131) 661 4301 Fax (0131) 661 4301
- ▶ 18 L 4525 yds SSS 72
- 👥 WD–U WE–phone Pro SOC–Tues & Thurs
- ££ £38 D–£48 SOC–£30 D–£40
- 🏌️ SE Edinburgh
- ⊕ Two practice areas; putting green; buggies
- 🏠 Willie Park
- 🖥 www.duddingstongolfclub.co.uk

Glencorse   (1890)
Milton Bridge, Penicuik, EH26 0RD
- ☎ **(01968) 677177**
- 🛄 (01968) 674399
- 🖂 secretary@glencorsegolfclub.com
- 🛄 700
- 🏌 W Oliver (01968) 677189
- ⚲ C Jones (01968) 676481
- ▶ 18 L 5217 yds Par 64 SSS 66
- 👥 WD–U SOC–WD/Sun pm
- ££ £25 (£32)
- 🏌️ 8 miles S of Edinburgh (A701)
- 🏠 Willie Park
- 🖥 www.glencorsegolfclub.com

Kings Acre   (1997)
Lasswade, EH18 1AU
- ☎ **(0131) 663 3456**
- 🛄 (0131) 663 7076
- 🖂 info@kings-acregolf.com
- 🏌 Alan Murdoch (Dir of Golf)
- ⚲ A Murdoch (0131) 663 3456
- ▶ 18 L 6031 yds Par 70 Junior Par 3 course

- 👥 U SOC
- ££ £26 (£35)
- 🏌️ 3 miles S of Edinburgh, off A720
- ⊕ Floodlit driving range
- 🏠 Graeme Webster
- 🖥 www.kings-acregolf.com

Kingsknowe   (1908)
326 Lanark Road, Edinburgh, EH14 2JD
- ☎ **(0131) 441 1144**
- 🛄 (0131) 441 2079
- 🖂 louise@kingsknowe.com
- 🛄 871
- 🏌 LI Fairlie (0131) 441 1145
- ⚲ C Morris (0131) 441 4030
- ▶ 18 L 5981 yds SSS 69
- 👥 WD–U before 4pm WE–phone Pro SOC–WD before 4pm
- ££ £25 (£32)
- 🏌️ SW Edinburgh
- 🏠 Herd/Braid
- 🖥 www.kingsknowe.com

Liberton   (1920)
Kingston Grange, 297 Gilmerton Road, Edinburgh, EH16 5UJ
- ☎ **(0131) 664 3009**
- 🖂 info@libertongc.co.uk
- 🛄 797
- 🏌 Duncan Ireland
- ⚲ Iain Seath (0131) 664 1056
- ▶ 18 L 5344 yds SSS 66
- 👥 WD–U before 5pm WE–NA before 2pm
- ££ £28 D–£33 (£33)
- 🏌️ 3 miles S of Edinburgh
- 🖥 www.libertongc.co.uk

Lothianburn   (1893)
106a Biggar Road, Edinburgh, EH10 7DU
- ☎ **(0131) 445 2206**
- 🛄 (0131) 445 5067
- 🖂 info@lothianburngc.co.uk
- 🛄 600 75(L) 100(J)
- 🏌 DP MacLaren (0131) 445 5067
- ⚲ K Mungall (0131) 445 2288
- ▶ 18 L 5662 yds SSS 69 Par 71
- 👥 WD–U before 4.30pm –M after 4.30pm WE–NA SOC–H
- ££ £21 D–£27 (£26 D–£32)
- 🏌️ S of Edinburgh, on A702. Lothianburn exit from Edinburgh Bypass
- ⊕ Motorised buggies for hire
- 🏠 James Braid (1928)
- 🖥 www.lothianburngc.co.uk

Marriott Dalmahoy Hotel & CC
Dalmahoy, Kirknewton, EH27 8EB
- ☎ **(0131) 335 8010**
- 🛄 (0131) 335 3577
- 🏌 Neal Graham (Golf Dir), Gordon Watt
- ⚲ Scott Dixon
- ▶ East 18 L 7055 yds SSS 74 West 18 L 5168 yds SSS 65
- 👥 WD–U H SOC–WD
- ££ East–£65 (£80) West–£40 (£45)
- 🏌️ 7 miles W of Edinburgh on A71
- ⊕ Floodlit driving range
- 🏠 James Braid

Melville Golf Centre   (1995)
Proprietary
Lasswade, Edinburgh, EH18 1AN
- ☎ **(0131) 663 8038 (range, shop, tuition)**
  (0131) 654 0224 (course)
- 🛄 (0131) 654 0814
- 🖂 golf@melvillegolf.co.uk
- 🛄 60
- 🏌 Mr & Mrs MacFarlane (Props)
- ⚲ Ryan Scott (0131) 663 8038
- ▶ 9 L 4604 yds Par 66 SSS 62
- 👥 U SOC
- ££ £12–£20 (£14–£25)
- 🏌️ 7 miles S of Edinburgh, signposted, 3 mins off city bypass on A7 (South)
- ⊕ Floodlit range; practice bunker; Pay & Play 9-hole course; 4-hole practice area; putting green; golf shop & tuition; junior golf academy
- 🏠 G Webster
- 🖥 www.melvillegolf.co.uk

Merchants of Edinburgh   (1907)
10 Craighill Gardens, Morningside, Edinburgh, EH10 5PY
- ☎ **(0131) 447 1219**
- 🛄 (0131) 446 9833
- 🖂 admin@merchantsgolf.com
- 🛄 1011
- 🏌 J Leslie
- ⚲ NEM Colquhoun (0131) 447 8709
- ▶ 18 L 4924 yds SSS 64
- 👥 WD–U before 4pm SOC–WD
- ££ £20 (£27)
- 🏌️ SW of Edinburgh, off A701
- 🏠 Braid/Letters
- 🖥 www.merchantsgolf.com

Mortonhall   (1892)
231 Braid Road, Edinburgh, EH10 6PB
- ☎ **(0131) 447 6974**
- 🛄 (0131) 447 8712
- 🖂 clubhouse@mortonhallgc.co.uk
- 🛄 1000
- 🏌 Ms BM Giefer
- ⚲ MT Leighton (0131) 447 5185
- ▶ 18 L 6530 yds SSS 72
- 👥 SOC WE–NA before 10.30
- ££ £40 D–£60
- 🏌️ 2 miles S of Edinburgh on A702
- 🏠 James Braid/FW Hawtree
- 🖥 www.mortonhallgc.co.uk

Murrayfield   (1896)
43 Murrayfield Road, Edinburgh, EH12 6EU
- ☎ **(0131) 337 3478**
- 🛄 (0131) 313 0721
- 🖂 manager@murrayfieldgolfclub.co.uk
- 🛄 815
- 🏌 Mrs MK Thomson (0131) 337 3478
- ⚲ Jonnie Cliffe
- ▶ 18 L 5799 yds Par 70 SSS 69
- 👥 WD–I WE–M
- ££ £37 (£47)
- 🏌️ 2 miles W of Edinburgh centre, 2 miles E of airport
- 🖥 www.murrayfieldgolfclub.co.uk

Newbattle (1896)

Abbey Road, Eskbank, Dalkeith,
EH22 3AD
- ☎ **(0131) 663 2123**
- 📠 (0131) 654 1810
- ✉ mail@newbattlegolfclub.com
- 🏠 600
- ✍ HG Stanners (0131) 663 1819
- ✓ S McDonald (0131) 660 1631
- ⌕ 18 L 6025 yds SSS 69
- ⚘ WD–U before 4pm WE–after 2pm
- ££ £25 D–£35
- ⚙ 6 miles S of Edinburgh on A7 and A68
- ⌂ HS Colt
- 🖥 www.newbattlegolfclub.com

Prestonfield (1920)

6 Priestfield Road North, Edinburgh,
EH16 5HS
- ☎ **(0131) 667 9665**
- 📠 (0131) 777 2727
- ✉ generalmanager@prestonfieldgolf .com
- 🏠 900
- ✍ Jl Archibald (Gen Mgr) (0131) 667 9665
- ✓ G Cook (0131) 667 8597
- ⌕ 18 L 6207 yds SSS 70 Par 70
- ⚘ WD–U WE–Sat/Sun after 3.00pm SOC–WD & Sat/Sun after 3pm
- ££ £29 D–£39 (£35)
- ⚙ 2 miles NE of Edinburgh City Centre, off A7 Dalkeith Road
- ⊕ Two practice areas with full facilities
- ⌂ Peter Robertson, modified by James Braid
- 🖥 www.prestonfieldgolf.com

Ratho Park (1928)

Ratho, Edinburgh, EH28 8NX
- ☎ **(0131) 335 0068**
- 📠 (0131) 333 1752
- ✉ secretary@rathoparkgolfclub .co.uk
- 🏠 550 106(L) 72(J)
- ✍ CR Innes (0131) 335 0068
- ✓ A Pate (0131) 333 1406
- ⌕ 18 L 5960 yds SSS 68
- ⚘ U SOC – Mon–Fri
- ££ £32 D–£45 (£45)
- ⚙ 8 miles W of Edinburgh centre (A71)
- ⌂ James Braid
- 🖥 www.rathoparkgolfclub.co.uk

Ravelston (1912)

24 Ravelston Dykes Road, Edinburgh,
EH4 3NZ
- ☎ **(0131) 315 2486**
- 📠 (0131) 315 2486
- ✉ ravelstongc@hotmail.com
- 🏠 675
- ✍ Jim Lowrie
- ⌕ 9 L 5170 yds SSS 66
- ⚘ WD–H
- ££ WD–£25
- ⚙ Off Queensferry Road (A90). Turn S at Blackhall
- ⌂ James Braid

Royal Burgess Golfing Society of Edinburgh (1735)

181 Whitehouse Road, Barnton, Edinburgh,
EH4 6BU
- ☎ **(0131) 339 2075**
- 📠 (0131) 339 3712
- ✉ secretary@royalburgess.co.uk
- 🏠 635 70(J)
- ✍ G Seeley (0131) 339 2075
- ✓ S Brian (0131) 339 6474
- ⌕ 18 L 6511 yds Par 71 SSS 71
- ⚘ SOC WD WE
- ££ £55 D–£55 (£75)
- ⚙ Queensferry Road (A90)
- ⊕ Putting green
- ⌂ Tom Morris
- 🖥 www.royalburgess.co.uk

Silverknowes (1947)

Public
Silverknowes Parkway, Edinburgh, EH4 5ET
- ☎ **(0131) 336 3843 (Starter)**

Swanston (1927)

111 Swanston Road, Fairmilehead,
Edinburgh, EH10 7DS
- ☎ **(0131) 445 5744**
- 🏠 350
- ✍ Capt Stewart Snedden
- ⌕ 18 L 5004 yds SSS 65
- ⚘ U SOC
- ££ £15 D–£20 (£20 D–£25)
- ⚙ S of Edinburgh, off Biggar road (A702) Edinburgh Bypass
- ⊕ Driving range
- 🖥 www.swanstongolf.co.uk

Torphin Hill (1895)

37-39 Torphin Road, Edinburgh, EH13 0PG
- ☎ **(0131) 441 1100**
- ✉ torphinhillgc@btconnect.com

Turnhouse (1897)

154 Turnhouse Road, Corstorphine,
Edinburgh, EH12 0AD
- ☎ **(0131) 339 1014**
- 📠 (0131) 339 1844
- ✉ secretary@turnhousegc.com
- 🏠 720
- ✍ DA Cleeton
- ✓ J Murray (0131) 339 7701
- ⌕ 18 L 6153 yds SSS 70
- ⚘ WD WE SOC
- ££ On application
- ⚙ W of Edinburgh (A9080) at end of city bypass
- ⊕ Large practice and pitching area
- ⌂ James Braid
- 🖥 www.turnhousegc.com

West Lothian

Bathgate (1892)

Edinburgh Road, Bathgate, EH48 1BA
- ☎ **(01506) 652232**
- 📠 (01506) 636775
- ✉ bathgate.golfclub@lineone.net
- 🏠 760
- ✍ WA Osborne (01506) 630505
- ✓ S Callan (01506) 630553
- ⌕ 18 L 6328 yds SSS 71

- 👥 U
- ££ £25 (£30)
- ⚙ 15 miles W of Edinburgh. M8 Jct 4
- ⌂ Wm Park Sr
- 🖥 www.bathgategolfclub.co.uk

Bridgend & District (1994)

Willowdean, Bridgend, Linlithgow,
EH49 6NW
- ☎ **(01506) 834140**
- 📠 (01506) 834706
- ✍ George Green
- ⌕ 9 L 5451 yds Par 67 SSS 66
- 👥 U
- ££ £13 (£15)
- ⚙ Nr Linlithgow M9
- 🖥 www.bridgendgolfclub.com

Deer Park G&CC (1978)

Golf Course Road, Knightsridge, Livingston,
EH54 8AB
- ☎ **(01506) 446699**
- 📠 (01506) 435608
- ✉ cmoir@muir-group.co.uk
- 🏠 850
- ✍ Joe Gallacher (Gen Mgr)
- ✓ Sandy Strachan
- ⌕ 18 L 6688 yds SSS 72
- 👥 U SOC
- ££ £28 (£38)
- ⚙ N of Livingston. M8 Junction 3
- 🖥 www.deer-park.co.uk

Dundas Parks (1957)

South Queensferry, EH30 9SS
- ☎ **(0131)331 4252**
- 🏠 550
- ✍ Mrs C Wood (07747) 854802
- ⌕ 9 L 6056 yds SSS 69
- 👥 M1 SOC
- ££ D–£15
- ⚙ Dundas Estate (Private). 1 mile S of Queensferry (A8000)
- 🖥 www.dundasparks.co.uk

Greenburn (1953)

6 Greenburn Road, Fauldhouse, EH47 9HJ
- ☎ **(01501) 770292**
- 📠 (01501) 772615
- ✉ administrator@greenburngolfclub .co.uk
- 🏠 730
- ✍ Adrian McGowan
- ✓ Scott Catlin (01501) 771187
- ⌕ 18 L 6067 yds SSS 70
- 👥 U
- ££ £23 D–£31 (£30 D–£38)
- ⚙ 4 miles S of M8 Junction 4 (East)/Junction 5 (West)
- ⊕ Practice area; putting green; pitching area
- 🖥 www.greenburngolfclub.co.uk

Harburn (1933)

West Calder, EH55 8RS
- ☎ **(01506) 871256**
- 📠 (01506) 870286
- ✉ info@harburngolf.co.uk
- 🏠 600 80(L) 120(J)
- ✍ J McLinden (01506) 871131
- ✓ S Mills (01506) 871582
- ⌕ 18 L 6125 yds Par 71 SSS 70
- 👥 U

££ £20 (£30)
⊕⊕ 2 miles S of W Calder on B7008, via A70 or A71
⊕ Buggies for hire
🖻 www.harburngolfclub.co.uk

Linlithgow (1913)
Braehead, Linlithgow, EH49 6QF
☎ (01506) 842585
📠 (01506) 842764
🖂 linlithgowgolf@talk21.com
🏛 900
♟ TI Adams
✏ G Bell (01506) 844356
🏌 18 L 5813 yds SSS 68
👥 U exc Sat–NA SOC
££ £20 D–£25 Sun–£25 D–£30
⊕⊕ SW of Linlithgow, off M9
⌂ Robert Simpson

Niddry Castle (1983)
Castle Road, Winchburgh, EH52 2RQ
☎ (01506) 891097
🖂 secretary@niddrycastlegc.co.uk
🏛 500
♟ G McLeod
🏌 18 L 5914 yds SSS 69
👥 U
££ £17 (£24)
⊕⊕ 12 miles W of Edinburgh (B9080)
🖻 www.niddrycastlegc.co.uk

Oatridge (2000)
Pay and play
Ecclesmachen, Broxburn, West Lothian, EH52 6NH
☎ (01506) 859636
🖂 oatridge@btconnect.com
🏛 250
♟ Brian Inglis
🏌 9 L 2770 yds Par 69 SSS 67 for 18 holes
👥 U
££ 9: £10 (£13); 18: £16 (£20)
⊕⊕ 1 mile W of Broxham off M8 J3
🖻 www.oatridge.ac.uk

Polkemmet (1981)
Public
Whitburn, Bathgate, EH47 0AD
☎ (01501) 743905
📠 (01501) 744780
🖂 mail@beecraigs.com
🏌 9 L 2946 metres SSS 37
👥 U
££ £5.50 (£6.50)
⊕⊕ Between Whitburn and Harthill on B7066. M8 Junctions 4/5
⊕ Driving range

Pumpherston (1895)
Drumshoreland Road, Pumpherston, EH53 0LH
☎ (01506) 432869/433336
📠 (01506) 438250
🖂 sheena.corner@tiscali.co.uk
🏛 537 33(L) 126(J)
♟ James Taylor (01506) 433336
✏ R Fyvie (01506) 433337
🏌 18 L 6006 yds Par 70 SSS 69
👥 WD–U SOC–WD
££ £25 D–£35 (£30 D–£42)
⊕⊕ 14 miles W of Edinburgh. M8 Jct 3

⊕ Practice putting, bunkers & pitching area; driving range
⌂ Graeme Webster
🖻 www.pumpherstongolfclub.co.uk

Rutherford Castle (1998)
West Linton, EH46 7AS
☎ (01968) 661233
📠 (01968) 661233
🖂 clubhouse@rutherfordcastle.org.uk
🏛 150
♟ Derek Mitchell (Mgr)
🏌 18 L 6466 yds Par 72 SSS 71
👥 U SOC
££ £15 (£25)
⊕⊕ 10 miles S of Edinburgh on A702
⌂ Bryan Moor
🖻 www.rutherfordcastlegc.org.uk

Uphall (1895)
Houston Mains, Uphall, EH52 6JT
☎ (01506) 856404
📠 (01506) 855358
🖂 uphallgolfclub@btconnect.com
🏛 650
♟ Miss M O'Connor (Club Administrator Mgr)
✏ G Law (01506) 855553
🏌 18 L 5588 yds Par 69 SSS 67
👥 U SOC
££ £23 D–£30 (£30 D–£40)
⊕⊕ 7 miles W of Edinburgh Airport (A8). M8 Junction 3
🖻 www.uphallgolfclub.com

West Linton (1890)
Medwyn Road, West Linton, EH46 7HN
☎ (01968) 660970
📠 (01968) 660622
🖂 secretarywlgc@btinternet.com
🏛 750 100 (J)
♟ John Johnson (01968) 661121
✏ I Wright (01968) 660256
🏌 18 L 6161 yds SSS 70
👥 WD–U WE–phone Pro
££ £30 D–£40 (£40)
⊕⊕ 18 miles S of Edinburgh on A702
🖻 www.wlgc.co.uk

West Lothian (1892)
Airngath Hill, Bo'ness, EH49 7RH
☎ (01506) 826030
📠 (01506) 826030
🖂 secretary@thewestlothiangolfclub.co.uk
🏛 850
♟ I Osborough (01506) 826030
✏ Alan Reid (01506) 825060
🏌 18 L 6249 yds SSS 71
👥 WD–NA after 4pm WE–by arrangement
££ On application
⊕⊕ 1 mile N of Linlithgow, towards Bo'ness
⊕ Buggies for hire
⌂ W Park Jr/Adams/Middleton
🖻 www.thewestlothiangolfclub.co.uk

Moray

Buckpool (1933)
Barhill Road, Buckie, AB56 1DU

☎ (01542) 832236
🖂 golf@buckpoolgolf.com

Dufftown (1896)
Tomintoul Road, Dufftown, AB55 4BS
☎ (01340) 820325
📠 (01340) 820325
🖂 admin@dufftowngolfclub.com
🏛 310
♟ IR Montgomery
🏌 18 L 5308 yds SSS 67
👥 U
££ £20 D–£20 (£20)
⊕⊕ 1 mile SW of Dufftown on B9009
⊕ Practise net. Putting area.
⌂ A Simpson
🖻 www.dufftowngolfclub.com

Elgin (1906)
Hardhillock, Birnie Road, Elgin, IV30 8SX
☎ (01343) 542338
📠 (01343) 542341
🖂 secretary@elgingolfclub.com
🏛 732 150(L) 144(J)
♟ JS Macpherson
✏ K Stables (01343) 542884
🏌 18 L 6449 yds SSS 71
👥 WD–U after 9.30am WE–U after 10am SOC–WD SOC–WE by arrangement
££ £35 D–£45 (£37 D–£47)
⊕⊕ 1 mile S of Elgin on A941
⊕ Driving range
⌂ John MacPherson
🖻 www.elgingolfclub.com

Forres (1889)
Muiryshade, Forres, IV36 2RD
☎ (01309) 672949
📠 (01309) 672261
🖂 forresgolfclub@tiscali.co.uk
🏛 950 150(J)
♟ David Mackintosh
✏ S Aird (01309) 672250
🏌 18 L 6141 yds SSS 70
👥 U SOC
££ £24 (£22)
⊕⊕ 1 mile SE of Forres, off B9010
⊕ Practice range
🖻 www.forresgolf.org.uk

Garmouth & Kingston (1932)
Spey Street, Garmouth, Fochabers, IV32 7NJ
☎ (01343) 870388
📠 (01343) 870388
🖂 garmouthgolfclub@aol.com
🏛 600
♟ Mrs I Fraser
🏌 18 L 5903 yds SSS 69
👥 U SOC
££ £20 D–£25 (£25 D–£28)
⊕⊕ 8 miles NE of Elgin
🖻 www.garmouthkingstongolfclub.com

Hopeman (1909)
Hopeman, Moray, IV30 5YA
☎ (01343) 830578
📠 (01343) 830152
🖂 hopemangc@aol.com
🏛 700

🛏 J Fraser (01343) 835068
⛳ 18 L 5624 yds SSS 68
👤 WD–NA between 12.45–1.15
Sat–NA before 10am and
12.30–2pm Sun–NA before 9am
SOC
££ £22 (£28)
🚗 7 miles NW of Elgin on B9012
🏠 J McKenzie
🖥 www.hopemangc.co.uk

Moray (1889)
Stotfield Road, Lossiemouth, IV31 6QS
☎ (01343) 812018
🖶 (01343) 815102
✉ secretary@moraygolf.co.uk
📖 1500
🛏 SM Crane
✓ A Thomson (01343) 813330
⛳ Old 18 L 6687yds SSS 73
New 18 L 6008 yds SSS 69
👤 U H SOC WD/WE after 10am
££ On application
🚗 6 miles N of Elgin
⊕ Practice range; golf buggies
🏠 Old Tom Morris
🖥 www.moraygolf.co.uk

Spey Bay (1904)
The Links, Spey Bay, Fochabers, IV32 7PJ
☎ (07826) 748071
✉ speybaygolf@freeuk.com
📖 200
🛏 Mrs H Barron
⛳ 18 L 6220 yds Par 70 SSS 70
👤 U
££ £20 D–£30
🚗 5 miles N of Fochabers off A96 on
B9210
⊕ Currently no catering facilities.
🏠 Ben Sayers

Perth & Kinross

Aberfeldy (1895)
Taybridge Road, Aberfeldy, PH15 2BH
☎ (01887) 820535
🖶 (01887) 820535
✉ feldyde@tiscali.co.uk
📖 130
🛏 Tomy Walsh
⛳ 18 L 5600 yds Par 68 SSS 66
👤 U
££ £22 (£27)
🚗 10 miles W of Ballinluig, off A9
🏠 Souters
🖥 www.aberfeldygolfclub.co.uk

Alyth (1894)
Pitcrocknie, Alyth, PH11 8HF
☎ (01828) 632268
🖶 (01828) 633491
✉ enquiries@alythgolfclub.co.uk
📖 850
🛏 J Docherty
✓ T Melville (01828) 632411
⛳ 18 L 6205 yds SSS 70
👤 U SOC
££ On application
🚗 16 miles NW of Dundee (A91)
🏠 Tom Morris/James Braid
🖥 www.alythgolfclub.co.uk

Auchterarder (1892)
Orchil Road, Auchterarder, PH3 1LS
☎ (01764) 662804
🖶 (01764) 664423
✉ secretary@auchterardergolf
.co.uk
📖 820
🛏 B G Johnston
✓ G Baxter
⛳ 18 L 5757 yds SSS 68
👤 U SOC
££ £27.50 D–£39 (£33 D–£50)
🚗 1 mile SW of Auchterarder
🖥 www.auchterardergolf.co.uk

Bishopshire (1903)
Pay and play
Kinnesswood, Woodmarch, Kinross,
KY13 9HX
✉ ian-davidson@tiscali.co.uk
📖 100
🛏 Ian Davidson (01592) 773224
⛳ 10 L 4707 yds SSS 63
👤 U
££ £8 (£12)
🚗 3 miles E of Kinross (A911). M90
Junction 6
🏠 W Park

Blair Atholl (1896)
Invertilt Road, Blair Atholl, PH18 5TG
☎ (01796) 481407
📖 385
🛏 T Boon 01796 481611
⛳ 9 L 5816 yds SSS 68
👤 U
££ £23 (£25)
🚗 35 miles N of Perth, off A9

Blairgowrie (1889)
Rosemount, Blairgowrie, PH10 6LG
☎ (01250) 872622
🖶 (01250) 875451
✉ office@theblairgowriegolfclub
.co.uk
📖 1700
✓ C Dernie (01250) 873116
⛳ Rosemount 18 L 6689 yds SSS 72
Lansdowne 18 L 7007 yds SSS 72
Wee 9 L 4704 yds SSS 64
👤 Mon–Fri 10–12 & 1.30–3.30 U–H
WE–restricted
££ On application
🚗 1 mile S of Blairgowrie, off A93. 15
miles N of Perth
🏠 Rosemount-Braid; Lansdowne-
Alliss/Thomas; Wee-Old Tom
Morris
🖥 www.theblairgowriegolfclub.co.uk

Callander (1890)
Aveland Road, Callander, FK17 8EN
☎ (01877) 330090
🖶 (01877) 330062
✉ callandergolf@btconnect.com
📖 500
🛏 Miss E Macdonald
✓ A Martin (01877) 330975
⛳ 18 L 5185 yds SSS 65
👤 U SOC
££ £22 (£30)
🚗 Off A84, E end of Callander

⊕ Putting green; practice area
(covered bays); swing analysis
(indoor); indoor training room
🏠 Old Tom Morris
🖥 www.callandergolfclub.co.uk

Comrie (1891)
Laggan Braes, Comrie, PH6 2LR
☎ (01764) 670055
✉ enquiries@comriegolf.co.uk

Craigie Hill (1909)
Cherrybank, Perth, PH2 0NE
☎ (01738) 620829
🖶 (01738) 624250
✉ golf@craigiehill.com
📖 625
🛏 Administration (01738) 620829
✓ Niall McGill (01738) 622644
⛳ 18 L 5386 yds SSS 67
👤 U exc Sat
££ £20 (£25)
🚗 W boundary of Perth
⊕ Practice area; putting green
🏠 Fernie/Anderson
🖥 www.craigiehill.scottishgolf.co.uk

Crieff (1891)
Perth Road, Crieff, PH7 3LR
☎ (01764) 652909 (Bookings)
🖶 (01764) 655096
✉ secretary@crieffgolf.co.uk
📖 803
🛏 JS Miller (01764) 652397
✓ DJW Murchie
⛳ Ferntower 18 L 6493 yds SSS 72
Dornock 9 L 4772 yds SSS 63
👤 U H NA–12–2pm or after 5pm
SOC
££ Ferntower £35 (£43) Dornock £16
🚗 1 mile NE of Crieff (A85). 17 miles
W of Perth
🏠 James Braid
🖥 www.crieffgolf.co.uk

Dalmunzie (1948)
Glenshee, Blairgowrie, PH10 7QE
☎ (01250) 885226
✉ enquiries@dalmunziecottages.com
📖 80
🛏 S Winton (Mgr)
⛳ 9 L 2099 yds SSS 61
👤 U
££ D–£14
🚗 20 miles N of Blairgowrie on A93.
(Dalmunzie Hotel sign)
🏠 James Braid
🖥 www.dalmunziecottages.com

Dunkeld & Birnam (1892)
Fungarth, Dunkeld, PH8 0ES
☎ (01350) 727524
🖶 (01350) 728660
✉ secretary-dunkeld@tiscali.co.uk
📖 590
🛏 RW Baldie
⛳ 18 L 5511 yds SSS 67
👤 WD–U WE–phone first
££ On application
🚗 Dunkeld 1 mile, off A923. 15 miles
N of Perth
⊕ Buggies for hire
🖥 www.dunkeldandbirnamgolfclub
.co.uk

Dunning (1953)
Rollo Park, Dunning, PH2 0QX
- ☎ (01764) 684747

Foulford Inn (1995)
Pay and play
Crieff, PH7 3LN
- ☎ (01764) 652407
- 🖳 (01764) 652407
- ✉ foulford@btconnect.com
- ✍ M Beaumont
- ⊳ 9 hole Par 3 course
- 👥 U
- ££ £6 D–£9
- ⊕ 5 Miles North of Crieff
- 🖥 www.foulfordinn.co.uk

The Gleneagles Hotel (1924)
Auchterarder, PH3 1NF
- ☎ (01764) 662231
- (01764) 662231 (Hotel)
- 🖳 (01764) 662134
- ✉ resort.sales@gleneagles.com
- ✍ Bernard Murphy (Hotel)
- ✓ Russell Smith (01764) 694343
- ⊳ King's 18 L 6471 yds SSS 71
  Queen's 18 L 5965 yds SSS 69
  PGA Centenary 18 L 7320 SSS 74
  9 hole Par 3 course
- 👥 U
- ££ May–Sept £155
- ⊕ 16 miles SW of Perth on A9
- ⊕ Driving range; golf academy; pitch 'n' putt
- 🏠 Braid/Nicklaus
- 🖥 www.gleneagles.com

Glenisla (1998)
Proprietary
Pitcrocknie Farm, Alyth, PH11 8JJ
- ☎ (01828) 632445

Kenmore (1992)
Pay and play
Mains of Taymouth, Kenmore, Aberfeldy, PH15 2HN
- ☎ (01887) 830226
- 🖳 (01887) 830775
- ✉ info@taymouth.co.uk
- 🕮 200
- ✍ R Menzies (Mgr)
- ⊳ 9 L 6052 yds SSS 69
- 👥 U SOC
- ££ 9: £15 (£17) 18: £20 (£25)
- ⊕ Kenmore, 6 miles W of Aberfeldy on A827
- 🏠 D Menzies & Partners
- 🖥 www.kenmoregolfcourse.co.uk

Killin (1911)
Killin, FK21 8TX
- ☎ (01567) 820312
- 🖳 (01567) 820312
- ✉ info@killingolfclub.co.uk
- 🕮 253
- ⊳ 9 L 5036 yds Par 66 SSS 65
- 👥 U SOC–Apr–Oct
- ££ £20 weekday, £24 weekends
- ⊕ Killin, W end of Loch Tay
- 🏠 John Duncan
- 🖥 www.killingolfclub.co.uk

King James VI (1858)
Moncreiffe Island, Perth, PH2 8NR
- ☎ (01738) 625170
  (01738) 632460 (Starter)
- 🖳 (01738) 445132
- ✉ mansec@kingjamesvi.com
- 🕮 675
- ✍ M Butler (01738) 445132
- ✓ A Crerar (01738) 632460
- ⊳ 18 L 6038 yds SSS 69
- 👥 U exc Sat Sun–by reservation
- ££ £24 D–£32 Sun D–£32
- ⊕ Island in River Tay, Perth
- 🏠 Tom Morris
- 🖥 www.kingjamesvi.com

Kinross Golf Courses (1900)
c/o The Green Hotel, 2 The Muirs, Kinross, KY13 8AS
- ☎ (01577) 863407
- 🖳 (01577) 863180
- ✉ bookings@golfkinross.com
- 🕮 450
- ✍ Eileen Gray
- ✓ Greg McSporran (01577) 865125
- ⊳ The Bruce: 18 L 6231 yds SSS 71
  The Montgomery: 18 L 6452 yds SSS 72
- 👥 U
- ££ Bruce: £27 D–£38 (£37 D–£48
  Montgomerey: £32 D–£48 (£42
  D–£58); 1 round on each course:
  D–£43 (D–£53)
- ⊕ Mile from M90 Jct 6
- ⊕ 50% discount for guests at Green Hotel and The Windlestrae
- 🏠 Sir David Montgomery
- 🖥 www.golfkinross.com

Milnathort (1910)
South Street, Milnathort, Kinross, KY13 9XA
- ☎ (01577) 864069
- ✉ milnathort.gc@btconnect.com
- 🕮 575
- ✍ K Dziennik (Admin. Mgr)
- ⊳ 9 L 5985 yds SSS 69
- 👥 U SOC
- ££ £15 D–£22 (£17 D–£25)
- ⊕ 1 mile N of Kinross. M90 Jct 6/7

Muckhart (1908)
Drumburn Road, Muckhart, Dollar, FK14 7JH
- ☎ (01259) 781423
- ✉ enquiries@muckhartgolf.com
- 🕮 593(G) 131(L) 120(J)
- ✍ A Houston
- ✓ K Salmoni (01259) 781493
- ⊳ 27 L 6174-6069 yds SSS 70-71
- 👥 U SOC
- ££ £30 D–£40 (£35 D–£45)
- ⊕ A91, 3 miles E of Dollar, towards Rumbling Bridge
- ⊕ 593(G)Practice area; pro shop
- 🖥 www.muckhartgolf.com

Murrayshall (1981)
Murrayshall, New Scone, Perth, PH2 7PH
- ☎ (01738) 554804
- ✉ info@murrayshall.co.uk

Muthill (1912)
Peat Road, Muthill, PH5 2DA
- ☎ (01764) 681523
- 🖳 (01764) 681557
- ✉ muthillgolfclub@btconnect.com
- 🕮 350
- ⊳ 9 L 2371 yds SSS 63
  Different tees for back 9
- 👥 U SOC
- ££ £15 (£18)
- ⊕ 3 miles S of Crieff on A822
- 🖥 www.muthillgolfclub.co.uk

North Inch
Public
c/o Perth & Kinross Council, The Environment Services, Pullar House, 35 Kinncoll St, Perth PH1 5GD
- ☎ (01738) 636481 (Starter)
- ✍ M Richmond
- ⊳ 18 L 5154 metres Par 68 SSS 66
- 👥 U SOC WD WE
- ££ On application
- ⊕ Nr Perth and A9, by River Tay. Signs to Bell's Sports Centre
- ⊕ Practice nets; putting green; trolley hire
- 🏠 Based on Old Tom Morris design
- 🖥 www.perthshire.com

Pitlochry (1909)
Pitlochry Estate Office, Golf Course Road, Pitlochry, PH16 5QY
- ☎ (01796) 472792 (Bookings)
- 🖳 (01796) 473947 (bookings)
- ✉ pro@pitlochrygolf.co.uk
- 🕮 400 approx.
- ✍ Bidwell Perth (01738) 630666
- ✓ M Pirie (01796) 472792 (PGA Pro)
- ⊳ 18 L 5670 yds SSS 69
- 👥 U SOC
- ££ On application
- ⊕ N side of Pitlochry (A9). 28 miles NW of Perth
- ⊕ Putting green; practice area with bunker and golf net
- 🏠 Fernie/Hutchison
- 🖥 www.pitlochrygolf.co.uk

Royal Perth Golfing Society (1824)
Club
1/2 Atholl Crescent, Perth, PH1 5NG
- ☎ (01738) 622265
- ✉ royal.perth@virgin.net
- 🕮 100
- ✍ DP McDonald (Gen Sec) (01738) 622265, Andrew Christie (Golf Sec) (01250) 873229
- ✓ Charles Dernie (01250) 873116
- ⊳ Play over North Inch, Perth & Strathmore courses
- 🖥 www.royal-perth-golfing-society.org.uk

St Fillans (1903)
South Lochearn Rd, St Fillans, PH26 2NJ
- ☎ (01764) 685312
- 🖳 01764 685312
- ✉ stfillansgolf@aol.com
- 🕮 400
- ✍ G Hilbert 19764 685312

▶ 9 L 6054 yds SSS 69
👥 U SOC
££ £16 (£20)
🚗 12 miles W of Crieff, on A85
⊕ Golf trolleys and buggies for hire.
🏠 W Auchterlonie
🖥 www.st-fillans-golf.com

Strathmore Golf Centre
(1995)
Pay and play
Leroch, Alyth, Blairgowrie, PH11 8NZ
☎ (01828) 633322
📠 (01828) 633533
✉ enquiries@strathmoregolf.com
📖 500
🏌 David Norman
⌐ Margot Smith
▶ 18 L 6454 yds Par 72 SSS 72
   9 L 1666 yds Par 29 SSS 58
👥 U SOC
££ £26 D–£34 (£32 D–£40)
🚗 5 miles E of Blairgowrie, off A926
⊕ Floodlit driving range; large short-game practice area with bunkers; putting green; practice nets
🏠 John Salvesen
🖥 www.strathmoregolf.com

Strathtay (1909)
Upper Derculich, Strathtay, Pitlochry, PH9 0LR
☎ (01887) 840373
📠 (01887) 840777
✉ aivr@aol.com
📖 210
🏌 AIV Robinson
▶ 9 L 4082 yds Par 62 SSS 61
👥 U SOC Tee reserved Sun 12–2
££ D–£12 (£15)
🚗 4 miles W of Ballinluig (A827), towards Aberfeldy

Taymouth Castle (1923)
Kenmore, Aberfeldy, PH15 2NT
☎ (01887) 830228

Whitemoss (1994)
Whitemoss Road, Dunning, Perth, PH2 0QX
☎ (01738) 730300
📠 (01738) 730490
✉ info@whitemossgolf.com
📖 300
🏌 A Nicolson
▶ 18 L 6200 yds Par 69 SSS 69
👥 U SOC
££ £15 D–£25 (£20 D–£30)
🚗 Aberuthven, 10 miles SW of Perth, off A9
⊕ Driving/practice range; driving nets; practice putting green
🖥 www.whitemossgolf.com

Renfrewshire

Barshaw (1927)
Public
Barshaw Park, Glasgow Road, Paisley, PA2
☎ (0141) 889 2908

Bonnyton (1957)
Eaglesham, Glasgow, G76 0QA
☎ (01355) 303030
📠 (01355) 303151
✉ secretarybgc@btconnect.com
📖 950
🏌 M Crichton
⌐ D Andrews (01355) 303030
▶ 18 L 6255 yds SSS 71
👥 I SOC–WD
££ £45
🚗 2 miles W of Eaglesham. 6 miles S of Glasgow
🖥 www.bonnytongolfclub.com

Caldwell (1903)
Caldwell, Uplawmoor, G78 4AU
☎ (01505) 850329
📠 (01505) 850604
✉ Secretary@caldwellgolfclub.co.uk
📖 450
🏌 K Morrison (01505) 850366
⌐ C Everett (01505) 850616
▶ 18 L 6335 yds SSS 71
👥 WD–booking before 4pm–M after 4pm WE–M
££ On application
🚗 5 miles SW of Barrhead on A736 Glasgow-Irvine road
🖥 www.caldwellgolfclub.i8.com

Cochrane Castle (1895)
Scott Avenue, Craigston, Johnstone, PA5 0HF
☎ (01505) 320146
📠 (01505) 325338
✉ secretary@cochranecastle.com
📖 425
🏌 Mrs PIJ Quin
⌐ A Logan (01505) 328465
▶ 18 L 6194 yds Par 71 SSS 71
👥 WD–U WE–M
££ £25 (£35)
🚗 ½ mile S of Beith Road, Johnstone
🏠 Charles Hunter
🖥 www.cochranecastle.com

East Renfrewshire (1922)
Pilmuir, Newton Mearns, G77 6RT
☎ (01355) 500256
📠 (01355) 500323
✉ secretary@eastrengolf.co.uk
📖 850 inc Ladies and Juniors
🏌 G J Tennant (01355) 500256
⌐ S Russell (01355) 500206
▶ 18 L 6107 yds Par 70 SSS 70
👥 WD–H SOC on application
££ £45 D–£60
🚗 2 miles SW of Newton Mearns - M77 J5
🏠 James Braid
🖥 www.eastrengolf.co.uk

Eastwood (1893)
Muirshield, Loganswell, Newton Mearns, Glasgow G77 6RX
☎ (01355) 500261
📠 (01355) 500333
✉ eastwoodgolfclub@btconnect.com
📖 900
🏌 S Wilson (01355) 500280
⌐ I Darroch (01355) 500285

▶ 18 L 6071 yds SSS 70
👥 WD SOC
££ £30 D–£40
🚗 9 miles SW of Glasgow off M77. Take A726/A77 turnoff then A77 S 1m then left to Mearnskirk, Eastwood is on right.
🏠 Theodore Moone/Graeme Webster
🖥 www.eastwoodgolfclub.co.uk

Elderslie (1908)
63 Main Road, Elderslie, PA5 9AZ
☎ (01505) 323956
📠 (01505) 340346
✉ eldersliegolfclub@btconnect.com
📖 450
🏌 Mrs A Anderson
⌐ R Bowman (01505) 320032
▶ 18 L 6165 yds SSS 70
👥 M–WE SOC–WD
££ £30 D–£45
🚗 2 miles SW of Paisley
⊕ Practice area; putting green
🖥 www.eldersliegolfclub.com

Erskine (1904)
Golf Road, Bishopton, PA7 5PH
☎ (01505) 862302
📠 (01505) 862898
✉ secretary@erskinegolfclub.wanadoo.co.uk
📖 850
🏌 DF McKellar
⌐ P Thomson (01505) 862108
▶ 18 L 6372 yds SSS 71
👥 WD SOC
££ £31 D–£42
🚗 5 miles NW of Paisley; M8
🏠 James Braid, Willie Fernie, Dr Alister Mackenzie
🖥 www.erskinegolfclublimited.co.uk

Fereneze (1904)
Fereneze Avenue, Barrhead, G78 1HJ
☎ (0141) 881 1519
📠 (0141) 881 1519
✉ ferenezegc@lineone.net
📖 700
🏌 G McCreadie (0141) 881 7149
⌐ J Smallwood (0141) 880 7058
▶ 18 L 5962 yds SSS 70
👥 SOC–WD
££ £30 D–£35
🚗 9 miles SW of Glasgow
🖥 www.ferenezegolfclub.co.uk

Gleddoch (1974)
Langbank, PA14 6YE
☎ (01475) 540711

Gourock (1896)
Cowal View, Gourock, PA19 1HD
☎ (01475) 631001
📠 (01475) 631001
✉ secretary@gourockgolfclub.com
📖 497 79(L) 198(J)
🏌 Margaret Paterson
⌐ D Watters (01475) 636834
▶ 18 L 6408 yds Par 73 SSS 72
👥 WD–I before 4.30pm SOC
££ £25 (D–£32) (to be reviewed for 2009)

⌆ 3 miles SW of Greenock, off A770.
7 miles W of Port Glasgow
€© Robert Braid/Henry Cotton
📠 www.gourockgolfclub.com

Greenock (1890)

Forsyth Street, Greenock, PA16 8RE
☎ **(01475) 720793**
🖨 (01475) 791912
🖨 secretary@greenockgolfclub.co.uk
📚 500 111(L) 110(J)
🖥 Mrs Heather Sinclair
(01475) 791912
✓ JH Duncan
(Starter) (01475) 787236
› 18 L 5888 yds SSS 69
9 L 2149 yds SSS 32
💀 WD–U WE/BH–M
££ D–£25 (£30)
⌆ 1 mile SW of Greenock on A8
€© James Braid
📠 www.greenockgolfclub.co.uk

Kilmacolm (1891)

Porterfield Road, Kilmacolm, PA13 4PD
☎ **(01505) 872139**

Lochwinnoch (1897)

Burnfoot Road, Lochwinnoch, PA12 4AN
☎ **(01505) 842153**
🖨 (01505) 843668
📚 600
🖥 RJG Jamieson
✓ G Reilly (01505) 843029
› 18 L 6243 yds SSS 71
💀 WD–U before 4.30pm SOC–WD
££ £25
⌆ 9 miles SW of Paisley
📠 www.lochwinnochgolf.co.uk

Old Ranfurly – Old Course
Ranfurly (1905)

Ranfurly Place, Bridge of Weir, PA11 3DE
☎ **(01505) 613612**
(Clubhouse)
🖨 (01505) 613214
🖨 secretary@oldranfurly.com
📚 817
🖥 J W Campbell (01505) 613214
✓ Grant Miller
› 18 L 6089 yds SSS 70
💀 WD–I M SOC
££ £25–£35 round/day. No WE
visitors
⌆ 7 miles W of Paisley, off A761
€© W Campbell
📠 www.oldranfurly.com

Paisley (1895)

Braehead Road, Paisley, PA2 8TZ
☎ **(0141) 884 2292**
(Clubhouse)
🖨 (0141) 884 3903
🖨 paisleygolfclub@btconnect.com
📚 820
🖥 J Hillis (0141) 884 3903
✓ D Gordon (0141) 884 4114
› 18 L 6466 yds Par 71 SSS 72
💀 WD–H SOC
££ £40 D–£50
⌆ Glenburn, S of Paisley, M8 Jct 27
⊕ Practise area

€© John H Stutt
📠 www.paisleygolfclub.com

Port Glasgow (1895)

Devol Road, Port Glasgow, PA14 5XE
☎ **(01475) 704181**
🖨 01475 700334
🖨 secretary@portglasgowgolfclub.com
📚 265
🖥 Chris McEwan
› 18 L 5712 yds SSS 68
💀 WD–U before 5pm –M after 5pm
WE–NA SOC
££ £20–£28 (sat after 2pm £22) (sun
18 hoes £22) round with buggy £32
pay with buggy £43
⌆ 1 mile S of Port Glasgow at end of
M8 west
⊕ Buggies, Practice area, Putting
Green.
€© James Braid
📠 www.portglasgowgolfclub.com

Ranfurly Castle (1889)

Golf Road, Bridge of Weir, PA11 3HN
☎ **(01505) 612609**
🖨 (01505) 610406
🖨 secranfur@aol.com
📚 400 160(A) 120(J)
🖥 J King
✓ T Eckford (01505) 614795
› 18 L 6284 yds SSS 71
💀 WD–H WE–NA before noon
SOC–WD
££ £30 D–£40
⌆ 7 miles W of Paisley (A761)
€© Kirkcaldy/Auchterlonie
📠 www.ranfurlycastle.co.uk

Renfrew (1894)

Blythswood Estate, Inchinnan Road,
Renfrew, PA4 9EG
☎ **(0141) 886 6692**
🖨 (0141) 886 1808
🖨 secretary@renfrew.scottishgolf.com
📚 465 110(L) 80(J)
🖥 David Cameron
✓ D Grant (0141) 885 1754
› 18 L 6818 yds SSS 73
💀 WD–H WE–M SOC–WD
££ £35 (£45)
⌆ 3 miles N of Paisley, nr Airport. M8
Junctions 26 or 27
€© Cdr JD Harris
📠 www.renfrewgolfclub.co.uk

Whitecraigs (1905)

72 Ayr Road, Giffnock, Glasgow, G46 6SW
☎ **(0141) 639 4530**
🖨 (0141) 616 3648
🖨 whitecraigsgc@btconnect.com
📚 1150
🖥 AG Keith CA
✓ A Forrow (0141) 639 2140
› 18 L 6013 yds SSS 70
💀 WD–U before 5pm WE–M
SOC–WD
££ £40 D–£50 (£40 D–£50)
⌆ 6 miles S of Glasgow (A77), nr
Whitecraigs Station
⊕ Practice ground
€© Fernie
📠 www.whitecraigsgolfclub.co.uk

Stirlingshire

Aberfoyle (1890)

Braeval, Aberfoyle, FK8 3UY
☎ **(01877) 382493**
🖨 secretary@aberfoylegolf.co.uk
📚 530
🖥 EJ Barnard (01360) 550847
› 18 L 5158 yds SSS 66
💀 WD–U WE–NA before 11 am
££ £18 D–£24 (£24 D–£30)
⌆ Aberfoyle, 18 miles W of Stirling
(A81)
⊕ Buggies available £18/round; club
hire available
📠 www.aberfoylegolf.com

Balfron (1992)

Kepculloch Road, Balfron, G63 0QP
☎ **(0781) 482 7620**
🖨 brian.a.davidson23@btinternet.com
📚 600
🖥 Brian Davidson (01360) 550613
› 18 L 5903 yds Par 72 SSS 70
💀 WD–U before 4pm WE–restricted
SOC
££ £15 (£20)
⌆ 18 miles NW of Glasgow, off A81
📠 www.balfrongolfsociety.org.uk

Bonnybridge (1925)

Larbert Road, Bonnybridge, Falkirk,
FK4 1NY
☎ **(01324) 812822/812323**
🖨 (01324) 812323
🖨 bgcl@hotmail.co.uk
📚 425
🖥 C McAteer (01324) 812323
› 9 L 6058 yds SSS 70
💀 WD–I SOC
££ £16 D–£20
⌆ 3 miles W of Falkirk. M876 Jct 1
⊕ Practice area

Bridge of Allan (1895)

Sunnylaw, Bridge of Allan, Stirling
☎ **(01786) 832332**
🖨 secretary@bofagc.com
📚 513
🖥 Scot Benson
✓ Gordon Niven
› 9 L 4932 yds SSS 66
💀 SOC WD WE after 4pm
££ £15 (£20)
⌆ 4 miles N of Stirling, off A9
⊕ Putting green; trolly hire
€© Tom Morris Sr
📠 www.bofagc.com

Buchanan Castle (1936)

Proprietary
Drymen, G63 0HY
☎ **(01360) 660307**
🖨 (01360) 660993
🖨 info@buchanancastlegolfclub.co.uk
📚 730
🖥 Ms JA Dawson
✓ K Baxter (01360) 660330
› 18 L 6047 yds SSS 69
💀 By prior arrangement with Pro
££ £38 D–£48 (D–£48)
⌆ 18 miles NW of Glasgow. 25 miles
W of Stirling, off A811

🏠 James Braid
🖥 www.buchanancastlegolfclub.com

Campsie (1897)
Crow Road, Lennoxtown, Glasgow, G66 7HX
☎ **(01360) 310244**
📧 campsiegolfclub@aol.com
🛏 650
🏌 K Stoddart (Mgr)
⛳ M Brennan (01360) 310920
🏴 18 L 5517 yds SSS 68
👥 WD–U before 4.30pm SOC; Visitors WE by arrangement
££ £15 D–£25 (£20)
🚗 N of Lennoxtown on B822 Fintry road
🏠 Auchterlonie/Stark
🖥 www.campsiegolfclub.org.uk

Dunblane New (1923)
Perth Road, Dunblane, FK15 0LJ
☎ **(01786) 821521**
📠 (01786) 821522
📧 secretary@dngc.co.uk
🛏 700
🏌 RD Morrison
⛳ RM Jamieson
🏴 18 L 5930 yds SSS 69
👥 WD–U WE–M SOC
££ £30 (£40)
🚗 E side of Dunblane. 6 miles N of Stirling
🏠 James Braid
🖥 www.dngc.co.uk

Falkirk (1922)
Stirling Road, Camelon, Falkirk, FK2 7YP
☎ **(01324) 611061/612219**
📠 (01324) 639573
📧 falkirkgolfclub@btconnect.com
🛏 700
🏌 J Elliott
⛳ Stewart Craig
🏴 18 L 6282 yds SSS 70
👥 WD–U until 4pm Sat–NA SOC–exc Sat

££ £30 D–£40 Sun–£45
🚗 1½ miles W of Falkirk on A9
⊕ Practice facilities, 3 Hole Par 3 Course
🏠 James Braid
🖥 www.falkirkgolfclub.co.uk

Falkirk Tryst (1885)
86 Burnhead Road, Larbert, FK5 4BD
☎ **(01324) 562415**
📠 (01324) 562054
📧 secretary@falkirktrystgolfclub.com
🛏 800
🏌 RC Chalmers (01324) 562054
⛳ S Dunsmore (01324) 562091
🏴 18 L 6053 yds SSS 69
👥 WD–U WE–M SOC–WD
££ £26 D–£35 (£35)
🚗 3 miles NW of Falkirk on A88
🖥 www.falkirktrystgolfclub.com

Glenbervie (1932)
Stirling Road, Larbert, FK5 4SJ
☎ **(01324) 562605**
📠 (01324) 551054
📧 secretary@glenbervegolfclub.com
🛏 800
🏌 A Turner CA
⛳ Steven Rosie (01324) 562725
🏴 18 L 6438 yds Par 71 SSS 71
👥 WD–U before 4pm WE–M SOC–Tues & Thurs
££ £35 D–£50
🚗 1 mile N of Larbert on A9. M876 Junction 2 (from Cumbernauld)
🏠 James Braid
🖥 www.glenbervegolfclub.com

Grangemouth (1973)
Public
Polmonthill, Polmont, FK2 0YA
☎ **(01324) 711500**
🛏 700
🏌 Jim McNairney
⛳ G McFarlane (01324) 503840
🏴 18 L 6527 yds SSS 70
👥 U–book with Pro SOC

££ £19 D–£27 (£23 D–£33)
🚗 3 miles NE of Falkirk. M9 Jct 4

Kilsyth Lennox (1905)
Tak-Ma-Doon Road, Kilsyth, G65 0RS
☎ **(01236) 824115 (Bookings)**
📧 info@klgs.co.uk

Polmont (1901)
Manuel Rigg, Maddiston, Falkirk, FK2 0LS
☎ **(01324) 711277 (Clubhouse)**
📠 (01324) 712504
📧 polmontgolfclub@btconnect.com
🛏 300
🏌 Mrs M Fellows (01324) 711277
🏴 9 L 3044 yds SSS 70
👥 WE–NA Saturday; Sunday by arrangement.
££ £10, Sun–£15
🚗 4 miles SE of Falkirk on B805

Stirling (1869)
Queen's Road, Stirling, FK8 3AA
☎ **(01786) 464098**
📠 (01786) 460090
📧 enquiries@stirlinggolfclub.tv
🛏 1000
🏌 AMS Rankin (01786) 464098
⛳ I Collins (01786) 471490
🏴 18 L 6409 yds SSS 71
👥 WD–U SOC WE–NA
££ £30 D–£45
🚗 ½ m from Stirling centre. M9 Jct 10
🏠 Braid/Cotton
🖥 www.stirlinggolfclub.com

Strathendrick (1901)
Glasgow Road, Drymen, G63 0AA
☎ **(01360) 660695**
🛏 480
🏌 M Quyn (01360) 660733
🏴 9 L 4982 yds SSS 64
👥 WD–U SOC–WD before 5pm
££ £15 All Day No weekends
🚗 25 miles W of Stirling, off A811
🏠 W Fernie

Wales

Cardiganshire

Aberystwyth (1911)
Bryn-y-Mor, Aberystwyth, SY23 2HY
- ☎ **(01970) 615104**
- 🖷 (01970) 626622
- 📧 aberystwythgolf@talk21.com
- 📖 390
- ♨ 01970 615104
- ✓ (01970) 625301
- ▷ 18 L 6119 yds Par 70 SSS 71
- ♙ U SOC
- ££ £25 (£30)
- ♨ Aberystwyth ¹/₂ mile
- ⊕ Par 3 Pay & Play; driving range
- ⌂ H Varden
- 🖥 www.aberystwythgolfclub.com

Borth & Ynyslas (1885)
Borth, Ceredigion, SY24 5JS
- ☎ **(01970) 871202**
- 🖷 (01970) 871202
- 📧 secretary@borthgolf.co.uk
- 📖 550
- ♨ GJ Pritchard
- ✓ JG Lewis (01970) 871557
- ▷ 18 L 6100 yds SSS 70
- ♙ WD–U WE/BH–by prior arrangement SOC
- ££ £28
- ♨ 8 miles N of Aberystwyth (B4353), off A487
- ⊕ Practice ground
- 🖥 www.borthgolf.co.uk

Cardigan (1895)
Gwbert-on-Sea, Cardigan, SA43 1PR
- ☎ **(01239) 612035/621775**
- 🖷 (01239) 621775
- 📧 golf@cardigan.fsnet.co.uk
- 📖 600
- ♨ JJ Jones (01239) 621775
- ✓ S Parsons (01239) 615359
- ▷ 18 L 6687 yds SSS 73
- ♙ H SOC
- ££ D–£27.50 (£35) W–£110
- ♨ 3 miles N of Cardigan
- ⊕ Practice area; junior golf academy
- ⌂ Grant/Hawtree
- 🖥 www.cardigangolf.co.uk

Cilgwyn (1905)
Llangybi, Lampeter, SA48 8NN
- ☎ **(01570) 493286**
- 📖 160
- ♨ JD Morgan
- ▷ 9 L 5327 yds SSS 67
- ♙ U SOC
- ££ £15 (£20)
- ♨ 5 miles NE of Lampeter, off A485 at Llangybi
- ⊕ Practice area
- 🖥 www.cilgwyngolf.co.uk

Penrhos G&CC (1991)
Llanrhystud, Ceredigion, SY23 5AY
- ☎ **(01974) 202999**
- 🖷 (01974) 202100
- 📧 info@penrhosgolf.co.uk
- 📖 300
- ♨ R Rees-Evans
- ✓ P Diamond
- ▷ 18 L 6660 yds SSS 73
  9 hole Par 3 course/Par 4
- ♙ U SOC
- ££ 9: £6 (£6); 18: £25 (£35)
- ♨ 9 miles S of Aberystwyth, signposted off A487
- ⊕ Floodlit driving range; buggy hire; Pro Shop;
- ⌂ Jim Walters
- 🖥 www.penrhosgolf.co.uk

Carmarthenshire

Ashburnham (1894)
Cliffe Terrace, Burry Port, SA16 0HN
- ☎ **(01554) 832269**
- 🖷 (01554) 836974
- 📧 golf@ashburnhamgolfclub.co.uk
- 📖 500
- ♨ Ian K Church
- ✓ Martin Stimson (01554) 833846
- ▷ 18 L 6916 yds SSS 73
- ♙ WD–H WE–H after 3pm only
- ££ £50 D–£60 (£39 after 3pm)
- ♨ 5 miles W of Llanelli (A484)
- ⌂ JH Taylor
- 🖥 www.ashburnhamgolfclub.co.uk

Carmarthen (1907)
Blaenycoed Road, Carmarthen, SA33 6EH
- ☎ **(01267) 281588**
- 🖷 (01267) 281493
- 📧 carmarthengolfclub@btinternet.com
- 📖 400
- ♨ Peter Ward
- ✓ John Hartley (01267) 281493
- ▷ 18 L 6242 yds SSS 71
- ♙ U
- ££ £25 (£30)
- ♨ 4 miles NW of Carmarthen
- ⊕ Driving range
- ⌂ JH Taylor
- 🖥 www.carmarthengolfclub.com

Derllys Court (1993)
Proprietary
Derllys Court, Llysonnen Road, Carmarthen, SA33 5DT
- ☎ **(01267) 211575**
- 🖷 (01267) 211575
- 📧 derllys@hotmail.com
- 📖 300+
- ♨ R Walters
- ✓ Robert Ryder (07771) 902604
- ▷ 18 L 5847 yds Par 70 SSS 68
- ♙ U SOC
- ♨ 4 miles W of Carmarthen, off A40
- ⊕ Practice area
- ⌂ P Johnson/S Finney
- 🖥 www.derllyscourtgolfclub.com

Garnant Park (1997)
Garnant, Ammanford, SA18 1NP
- ☎ **(01269) 823365**
- 🖷 (01269) 823365
- 📧 garnantgolf@carmarthenshire.gov.uk
- 📖 400
- ♨ Vince Mosson
- ✓ Gethin Collins (01269) 820865
- ▷ 18 L 6575 yds Par 72 SSS 72
- ♙ U SOC
- ££ £17.50 (£22.50)
- ♨ On A474, between Ammanford and Pontardawe. M4 Junction 45
- ⊕ Driving range; starter course; practice nets
- ⌂ Roger Jones
- 🖥 www.parcgarnantgolf.co.uk

Glyn Abbey (1992)
Proprietary
Trimsaran, SA17 4LB
- ☎ **(01554) 810278**
- 🖷 (01554) 810889
- 📧 course-enquiries@glynabbey.co.uk
- 📖 450
- ♨ Martin Lane (Mgr) (01554) 810278
- ✓ Darren Griffiths (01554) 810278
- ▷ 18 L 6202 yds Par 70 SSS 70
- ♙ U SOC
- ££ £20 (£25)
- ♨ 4 miles NW of Llanelli, between Trimsaran and Carway
- ⊕ Driving range; gym; 9-hole course
- ⌂ Hawtree
- 🖥 www.glynabbey.co.uk

Glynhir (1909)
Glynhir Road, Llandybie, Ammanford, SA18 2TF
- ☎ **(01269) 850472**
- 🖷 (01269) 851365
- 📧 glynhir.golfclub@virgin.net
- 📖 415
- ♨ D Davies, M Smith (01269) 851365
- ✓ Richard Herbert (01269) 851010
- ▷ 18 L 6006 yds SSS 70
- ♙ WD/Sat–H Sun–NA SOC–WD
- ££ Winter £13 (£16) 5D–£45 Summer £20 (£25) 5D–£70
- ♨ 3¹/₂ miles N of Ammanford; 6¹/₂ m from J49 of M4
- ⌂ Hawtree
- 🖥 www.glynhirgolfclub.co.uk

Saron Golf Course (1990)
Pay and play
Penwern, Saron, Llandysul, SA44 4EL
- ☎ **(01559) 370705**
- 📧 c9mbl@sarongolf.freeserve.co.uk
- ♨ Mr C Searle
- ▷ 9 L 2091 yds Par 32 (18 tees) 18 L 4412 yds par 66
- ♙ U
- ££ 9: £10 (Jnr £5) 18: £13 (Jnr £8) As Jan 1st 2009

⛳ On A484 Newcastle Emlyn to Carmarthen road
⊕ Putting green

Conwy

Abergele (1910)
Tan-y-Gopa Road, Abergele, LL22 8DS
☎ (01745) 824034
🖥 (01745) 824772
✉ secretary@abergelegolfclub.co.uk
🏠 1250
🖊 CP Langdon
🏌 I Runcie (01745) 823813
🏳 18 L 6520 yds SSS 71
👥 U SOC
£€ On application
⛳ Abergele Castle Grounds
🏠 David Williams
🖥 www.abergelegolfclub.co.uk

Betws-y-Coed (1977)
Clubhouse, Betws-y-Coed, LL24 0AL
☎ (01690) 710556
✉ info@golf-betws-y-coed.co.uk
🏠 280
🖊 D Hughes
🏳 9 L 4996 yds SSS 64
9 greens 18 tees
👥 U SOC
£€ £20 (£25) Half price golf every Thurs
⛳ 1/4 mile off A5, in Betws-y-Coed
🖥 www.golf-betws-y-coed.co.uk

Conwy (Caernarvonshire) (1890)
Beacons Way, Morfa, Conwy, LL32 8ER
☎ (01492) 592423
🖥 (01492) 593363
✉ secretary@conwygolfclub.com
🏠 1000
🖊 A Jones (01492) 592423
🏌 JP Lees (01492) 593225
🏳 18 L 6936 yds SSS 74
👥 H WE–restricted SOC
£€ £45 D–£50
⛳ 1/2 mile W of Conway, off A55 Jct 17
🖥 www.conwygolfclub.com

Llandudno (Maesdu) (1915)
Hospital Road, Llandudno, LL30 1HU
☎ (01492) 876450
🖥 (01492) 876450
✉ secretary@maesdugolfclub.co.uk
🏠 1109
🖊 G Dean
🏌 S Boulden (01492) 875195
🏳 18 L 6513 yds SSS 72
👥 U H–recognised GC members SOC
£€ £28 (£33)
⛳ 1 mile S of Llandudno Station, nr Hospital
🖥 www.maesdugolfclub.co.uk

Llandudno (North Wales) (1894)
72 Bryniau Road, West Shore, Llandudno, LL30 2DZ

☎ (01492) 875325
🖥 (01492) 873355
✉ enquiries@northwalesgolfclub.co.uk
🏠 691
🖊 Nick Kitchen (01492) 875325
🏌 RA Bradbury (01492) 876878
🏳 18 L 6247 yds Par 71 SSS 71
👥 U SOC–phone Sec WE–NA before 10.30 am
£€ £22 D–£22 (£40 D–£50)
⛳ 3/4 mile from Llandudno on West Shore. Jct 18 A55 Expressway
⊕ Practice ground; putting green; pitch and putt area
🖥 www.northwalesgolfclub.co.uk

Llanfairfechan (1971)
Llannerch Road, Llanfairfechan, LL33 0EB
☎ (07737) 385070 - Daytime
(01248) 680144 Eve & WE
🏠 16
🖊 R Ingham
🏳 9 L 3119 yds SSS 57
👥 U
£€ £10 (£10)
⛳ 7 miles E of Bangor on A55

Old Colwyn (1907)
Woodland Avenue, Old Colwyn, LL29 9NL
☎ (01492) 515581

Penmaenmawr (1910)
Conway Old Road, Penmaenmawr, LL34 6RD
☎ (01492) 623330
🖥 (01492) 622105
✉ clubhouse@pengolfclub.co.uk
🏠 600
🖊 Mrs AH greenwood
🏳 9 L 5143 yds SSS 66
👥 U SOC
£€ £15 (£20)
⛳ 4 miles W of Conway
🖥 www.pengolf.co.uk

Rhos-on-Sea (1899)
Penrhyn Bay, Llandudno, LL30 3PU
☎ (01492) 549641
🖥 (01492) 549100
✉ rhosonseagolfclub@btinternet.com
🏠 600
🖊 Ken Breeze
🏌 Jon Kelly
🏳 18 L 6064 yds SSS 69
👥 U
£€ £15 (£22)
⛳ On coast at Rhos-on-Sea. 4 miles E of Llandudno
⊕ 12 en-suite rooms (01492) 549641
🏠 Simpson
🖥 www.rhosgolf.co.uk

Denbighshire

Bryn Morfydd Hotel (1982)
Llanrhaeadr, Denbigh, LL16 4NP
☎ (01745) 890280
🖥 (01745) 890488
✉ brynmorfydd@live.co.uk
🏠 250
🖊 BW Astle (07752) 527257

🏌 David Frith
🏳 18 L 5800 yds Par 70 SSS 67
9 hole Par 3 course
And 18 Hole Course
👥 U SOC
£€ £15 (£20) £5 9 Hole Course
⛳ 2 1/2 miles SE of Denbigh on A525
⊕ 3 Star Hotel on Site; Function Room 200+ covers
🏠 Duchess-Alliss/Thomas. Dukes-Frith/Henderson
🖥 www.bryn-morfydd.co.uk

Denbigh (1908)
Henllan Road, Denbigh, LL16 5AA
☎ (01745) 816669
🖥 (01745) 814888
✉ denbighgolfclub@aol.com
🏠 585
🖊 JR Williams (01745) 816669
🏌 M Jones (01745) 814159
🏳 18 L 5826 yds SSS 68
👥 U SOC
£€ On application
⛳ 1 mile NW of Denbigh (B5382)
🖥 www.denbighgolfclub.co.uk

Kinmel Park (1989)
Pay and play
Bodelwyddan, LL18 5SR
☎ (01745) 833548
✉ info@kinmelgolf.co.uk
🖊 Mrs Fetherstonhaugh
🏌 Rhodri Lloyd Jones (07916) 346602
🏳 9 L 1550 yds Par 29
👥 U
£€ £5 (£6)
⛳ Off A55, Jct 25
⊕ Driving range
🏠 Peter Stebbings
🖥 www.kinmelgolf.co.uk

Prestatyn (1905)
Marine Road East, Prestatyn, LL19 7HS
☎ (01745) 854320
🖥 (01745) 834320
✉ prestatyngcmanager@freenet.co.uk
🏠 480
🖊 D Ames
🏳 18 L 6825 yds SSS 73
👥 H SOC WD WE
£€ £25 (£30)
⛳ 1 mile E of Prestatyn
🏠 S Collins
🖥 www.prestatyngolfclub.co.uk

Rhuddlan (1930)
Meliden Road, Rhuddlan, LL18 6LB
☎ (01745) 590217
🖥 (01745) 590472
✉ secretary@rhuddlangolfclub.co.uk
🏠 560(M) 109(L) 122(J)
🖊 Mrs J Roberts
🏌 A Carr (01745) 590898
🏳 18 L 6473 yds SSS 70
👥 H SOC–WD
£€ £30 (£35)
⛳ 2 miles N of St Asaph, J27 off A55
⊕ Pro shop
🏠 F Hawtree
🖥 www.rhuddlangolfclub.co.uk

Rhyl (1890)
Coast Road, Rhyl, LL18 3RE
- ☎ **(01745) 353171**
- 📠 (01745) 353171
- ✉ rhylgolfclub@il2.com
- 📖 450
- 🏌 Gill Davies
- 🏌 John Stubbs
- ⛳ 9 L 6220 yds SSS 70
- 🏌 U SOC
- ££ £20 (£25)
- ⛳ On A548 between Rhyl and Prestatyn
- 🏗 James Braid
- 💻 www.rhylgolfclub.com

Ruthin-Pwllglas (1920)
Pwllglas, Ruthin, LL15 2PE
- ☎ **(01824) 702296**
- 📖 360
- 🏌 Eric Owen (01824) 702383
- 🏌 Richard Heginbotham
- ⛳ 10 L 5362 yds SSS 66
- 🏌 U SOC
- ££ £16 (£22)
- ⛳ 2¹/₂ miles S of Ruthin in village of Pwllglas on Ruthin to Corwen road (A494)

St Melyd (1922)
The Paddock, Meliden Road, Prestatyn, LL19 8NB
- ☎ **(01745) 854405**
- 📠 (01745) 856908
- ✉ info@stmelydgolf.co.uk
- 📖 400
- ⛳ 9 L 5857 yds SSS 68
- 🏌 U SOC
- ££ £18 (£22)
- ⛳ S of Prestatyn on A547
- 💻 www.stmelydgolf.co.uk

Vale of Llangollen (1908)
Holyhead Road, Llangollen, LL20 7PR
- ☎ **(01978) 860906**
- 📠 (01978) 869165
- ✉ secretary@vlgc.co.uk
- 📖 850
- 🏌 Bob Hardy
- 🏌 Dl Vaughan (01978) 860040
- ⛳ 18 L 6656 yds Par 72 SSS 73
- 🏌 U–check first SOC–WD only
- ££ £35 D–£55 (£40 D–£60)
- ⛳ 1¹/₂ miles E of Llangollen on A5; 20 miles S of Chester
- ⊕ Practice ground; chipping area; buggies for hire
- 💻 www.vlgc.co.uk

Flintshire

Caerwys (1989)
Pay and play
Caerwys, Mold, CH7 5AQ
- ☎ **(01352) 721222**

Hawarden (1911)
Groomsdale Lane, Hawarden, Deeside, CH5 3EH
- ☎ **(01244) 531447**
- 📠 (01244) 536901
- ✉ secretary@hawardengolfclub.co.uk
- 📖 750
- 🏌 A Rowland
- 🏌 A Rowland (01244) 520809
- ⛳ 18 L 5809 yds SSS 69
- 🏌 H SOC–WD
- ££ Mon/Tue £14 or £50 for a 4ball Wed–Fri £30 Sat/Sun + BH £25
- ⛳ 6 miles W of Chester, off A55
- 💻 www.hawardengolfclub.co.uk

Holywell (1906)
Brynford, Holywell, CH8 8LQ
- ☎ **(01352) 710040/713937**
- 📠 (01352) 713937
- ✉ holywell_golf_club@lineone.net
- 📖 400 50(L)
- 🏌 RF Fiddaman (01352) 713937
- 🏌 M Parsley (01352) 710040
- ⛳ 18 L 6100 yds Par 70 SSS 70
- 🏌 WD–U WE–SOC
- ££ £22 (£25)
- ⛳ 2 miles S of Holywell, off A5026
- 💻 www.holywellgc.co.uk

Kinsale (1996)
Pay and play
Llanerchymor, Holywell, CH8 9DX
- ☎ **(01745) 561080**
- 📖 85
- 🏌 S Leverett
- ⛳ 9 holes Par 71 SSS 70
- 🏌 U
- ££ 9: £10. 18: £15
- ⛳ 4 miles N of Holywell on A548
- ⊕ Floodlit driving range
- 🏗 K Smith

Mold (1909)
Cilcain Road, Pantymwyn, Mold, CH7 5EH
- ☎ **(01352) 740318/741513**
- 📠 (01352) 741517
- ✉ info@moldgolfclub.co.uk
- 📖 450 90(L) 95(J)
- 🏌 C Mills (01352) 741513
- 🏌 M Jordan (01352) 740318
- ⛳ 18 L 5512 yds Par 68 SSS 67
- 🏌 U SOC
- ££ £25 (£30)
- ⛳ 3 miles W of Mold
- 🏗 Hawtree
- 💻 www.moldgolfclub.co.uk

Northop Country Park (1994)
Northop, Chester, CH7 6WA
- ☎ **(01352) 840440**
- 📠 (01352) 840445
- ✉ john@northoppark.co.uk
- 🏌 John Nolan (01352) 840440 press 1
- 🏌 John Nolan
- ⛳ 18 L 6802 yds Par 72
- 🏌 U–phone first SOC
- ££ £40 (£45)
- ⛳ 3 miles S of Flint, off A55
- ⊕ Driving range, leisure club, gym.
- 🏗 John Jacobs
- 💻 www.northoppark.co.uk

Old Padeswood (1978)
Station Road, Padeswood, Mold, CH7 4JL
- ☎ **(01244) 547701 (Clubhouse)**

Padeswood & Buckley (1933)
The Caia, Station Lane, Padeswood, Mold, CH7 4JD
- ☎ **(01244) 550537**
- 📠 (01244) 541600
- ✉ admin@padeswoodgolf.plus.com
- 📖 592
- 🏌 Mrs S A Davies
- 🏌 D Ashton (01244) 543636
- ⛳ 18 L 6042 yds Par 70 SSS 69
- 🏌 WD–U 9am–4pm –M after 4pm Sat–U Sun–NA SOC–WD Ladies Day–Wed
- ££ £28 (£32)
- ⛳ 8 miles W of Chester, off A5118. 2nd golf club on right
- ⊕ Practice area; nets
- 🏗 D Williams Partnership
- 💻 www.padeswoodgolfclub.com

Pennant Park (1998)
Proprietary
Whitford, Holywell, CH8 9AE
- ☎ **(01745) 563000**
- 📖 300
- 🏌 M Foster
- 🏌 Matthew Pritchard
- ⛳ 18 L 6059 yds Par 70 whites
- 🏌 U SOC WD WE
- ££ £20 (£25)
- ⛳ Nr North Wales Expressway (A55); take Jct 32 to Holywell and follow signs
- ⊕ Practice range. Academy course
- 🏗 Roger Jones
- 💻 www.pennant-park.co.uk

oldpad@par72.fsbusiness.co.uk
- ✉ oldpad@par72.fsbusiness.co.uk
- 📖 500
- 🏌 Gail Jones (01244) 550414
- 🏌 A Davies (01244) 547401
- ⛳ 18 L 6728 yds SSS 72
- 🏌 U exc comp days SOC–WD–WE
- ££ £13 (£15) with member
- ⛳ 2 miles from Mold on A5118
- ⊕ Driving range nearby
- 💻 www.oldpadeswoodgolfclub.co.uk

Gwynedd

Aberdovey (1892)
Aberdovey, LL35 0RT
- ☎ **(01654) 767493**
- 📠 (01654) 767027
- ✉ sec@aberdoveygolf.co.uk
- 📖 664
- 🏌 Ian Hamilton (Mgr) (01654) 767493
- 🏌 J Davies (01654) 767602
- ⛳ 18 L 6615 yds Par 71
- 🏌 NA–8.00–9.00am & 12.00–13.30pm
- ££ On application (guide: £40 per round)
- ⛳ ¹/₂ mile W of Aberdovey (A493)
- 🏗 Braid/Fowler/Colt
- 💻 www.aberdoveygolf.co.uk

Abersoch (1907)
Golf Road, Abersoch, LL53 7EY
- ☎ **(01758) 712636**
- 📠 (01758) 712777

✉ admin@abersochgolf.co.uk
▥ 700
♟ A Drosinos Jones (01758) 712622
✓ A Drosinos Jones
▷ 18 L 5819 yds SSS 69
👥 U H SOC
££ £25
⛳ ¹/₂ mile S of Abersoch (A55). 7 miles S of Pwllheli
🏠 Harry Vardon
🖥 www.abersochgolf.co.uk

Bala (1973)
Penlan, Bala, LL23 7YD
☎ (01678) 520359
📠 (01678) 521361
✉ balagolfclub@onetel.com
▥ 340
♟ G Rhys Jones
✓ T Davies (visiting)
▷ 10 L 4962 yds SSS 64
👥 WD–U WE–NA pm SOC
££ £20 (£25) W–£50
⛳ ¹/₂ mile SW of Bala, off A494 to Dolgellau
⊕ Practice net; putting green
🏠 Sid Collins
🖥 www.golffbala.co.uk

Dolgellau (1910)
Proprietary
Hengwrt Estate, Pencefn Road, Dolgellau, LL40 2ES
☎ (01341) 422603
✉ richard@dolgellaugolfclub.com
▥ 300
♟ R Stockdale
✓ R Stockdale
▷ 9 L 4671 yds Par 66 SSS 63
👥 U
££ £18 (£22.50)
⛳ ¹/₂ mile N of Dolgellau
⊕ Practice area; chipping green
🏠 J Medway
🖥 www.dolgellaugolfclub.com

Ffestiniog (1893)
Y Cefn, Ffestiniog
☎ (01766) 762637 (Clubhouse)
✉ info@ffestinioggolf.org
▥ 138
♟ A Roberts (01766) 831829
▷ 9 L 4570 metres Par 68 SSS 66
👥 U
££ £10 (£10)
⛳ 1 mile E of Ffestiniog on Bala road (B4391)
🖥 www.ffestinioggolf.org

Nefyn & District (1907)
Morfa Nefyn, Pwllheli, LL53 6DA
☎ (01758) 720966 (Clubhouse)
📠 (01758) 720476
✉ secretary@nefyn-golf-club.com
▥ 880
♟ S Dennis (01758) 720966
✓ J Froom (01758) 720102
▷ 26 holes in total
New Course: 18 holes 6718 yds SSS 71
Old Course: 18 holes 6267 yds SSS 71
👥 U SOC–U WD–U WE–U

££ Mon–Thurs Round £37 D–£50
Fri–Sun + Bank Hols Round £44 D–£60
⛳ 1¹/₂ miles W of Nefyn. 50 miles W of Colwyn Bay. 2 hours Manchester and 20 miles W of Caernarfon
⊕ Buggy & Trolley hire, Club Hire, Practice ground & net
🏠 James Braid, J H Taylor
🖥 www.nefyn-golf-club.com

Porthmadog (1905)
Morfa Bychan, Porthmadog, LL49 9UU
☎ (01766) 514124
📠 (01766) 514124
✉ secretary@porthmadog-golf-club .co.uk
▥ 860
♟ GT Jones (Mgr)
✓ P Bright (01766) 513828
▷ 18 L 6322 yds Par 71 SSS 71
👥 U H SOC
££ £30 D–£40 (£35 D–£45)
⛳ 2 miles S of Porthmadog, towards Black Rock Sands
🏠 James Braid
🖥 www.porthmadog-golf-club.co.uk

Pwllheli (1900)
Golf Road, Pwllheli, LL53 5PS
☎ (01758) 701644
📠 (01758) 701644
✉ admin@pwllheligolfclub.co.uk
▥ 920
♟ Dennis Moore (Gen Mgr)
✓ S Pilkington (01758) 701644
▷ 18 L 6108 yds SSS 70
👥 U
££ £33 D–£44 (£36 D–£44)
⛳ ¹/₂ mile SW of Pwllheli
🏠 James Braid/Tom Morris
🖥 www.pwllheligolfclub.co.uk

Royal St David's (1894)
Harlech, LL46 2UB
☎ (01766) 780203
📠 (01766) 781110
✉ secretary@royalstdavids.co.uk
▥ 880
♟ T Davies (01766) 780361
✓ J Barnett (01766) 780857
▷ 18 L 6629 yds Par 69 SSS 73
👥 U H–booking necessary SOC
££ £50 D–£65 (£60 D–£75)
⛳ W of Harlech on A496
⊕ Driving range, baskets of balls available, Buggies and trolleys for hire at Pro-shop
🏠 H Finch-Hatton
🖥 www.royalstdavids.co.uk

Royal Town of Caernarfon (1909)
Aberforeshore, LLanfaglan, Caernarfon, LL54 5RP
☎ (01286) 673783
📠 (01286) 673783
✉ secretary@caernarfongolfclub.co.uk
▥ 625
♟ EG Angel
✓ A Owen (01286) 678359
▷ 18 L 5941 yds Par 69 SSS 69

👥 U SOC
££ Apr–May £25 (£30) Jun–Sep £30 (£35) Oct–Mar £25 (£30) + special offers
⛳ 2¹/₂ miles SW of Caernarfon
⊕ Practice ground
🖥 www.caernarfongolfclub.co.uk

St Deiniol (1906)
Penybryn, Bangor, LL57 1PX
☎ (01248) 353098
📠 (01248) 370792
✉ secretary@st-deiniol.co.uk
▥ 300
♟ RD Thomas MBE (01248) 353098
✓ No pro - golf shop proprietor
▷ 18 L 5656 yds SSS 67
👥 U SOC
££ £20 (£25)
⛳ Off A5/A55 Junction 11, 1 mile E of Bangor on A5122
⊕ Buggies available; practice nets
🏠 James Braid
🖥 www.st-deiniol.co.uk

Isle of Anglesey

Anglesey (1914)
Station Road, Rhosneigr, LL64 5QX
☎ (01407) 810219
📠 (01407) 811127
✉ info@theangleseygolfclub.com
▥ 450
♟ MI Parry (01407) 811127
✓ M Parry (01407) 811202
▷ 18 L 6330 yds SSS 71
👥 U H SOC
££ £30 (£35)
⛳ 8 miles SE of Holyhead, off A55 J5
⊕ Practice facilities
🏠 H Hilton
🖥 www.angleseygolfclub.co.uk

Baron Hill (1895)
Beaumaris, LL58 8YW
☎ (01248) 810231
📠 (01248) 810231
✉ golf@baronhill.co.uk
▥ 360
♟ A Pleming
▷ 9 L 5062 metres SSS 68
👥 U exc comp days SOC–WD & Sat (apply Sec)
££ £20 D (£60)
⛳ Off A545 on approach to Beaumaris
🏠 Evolved over 110 years, with adjustments by Frank Pennink
🖥 www.baronhill.co.uk

Bull Bay (1913)
Bull Bay Road, Amlwch, LL68 9RY
☎ (01407) 830960
📠 (01407) 832612
✉ info@bullbaygc.co.uk
▥ 550
♟ John Burns (01407) 830960
✓ J Burns (01407) 831188
▷ 18 L 6276 yds SSS 72
👥 U SOC WD WE
££ £33 (£38) D–£45 (£50)

For list of abbreviations and key to symbols see page 647

∞ ½ mile W of Amlwch on A5025
⌂ WH Fowler
▤ www.bullbaygc.co.uk

Henllys Hall
Llanfaes, Beaumaris, LL58 8HU
☎ **(01248) 811717**
⌨ (01248) 811511
✉ hg@hpb.co.uk
✓ P Maton
⊳ 18 L 6062 yds Par 71
♟ U SOC
££ £30 Mon–Sun
∞ 2 miles N of Beaumaris (B5109)
⌂ Roger Jones
▤ www.henllysgolfclub.co.uk

Holyhead   (1912)
Trearddur Bay, Anglesey, LL65 2YL
☎ **(01407) 763279/762119**
⌨ (01407) 763279
✉ holyheadgolfclub@tiscali.co.uk
⌑ 534 147(L)
⚐ S Elliott (01407) 763279
✓ S Elliott (01407) 762022
⊳ 18 L 6090 yds SSS 70
♟ H SOC
££ £30 (£35)
∞ 2 miles S of Holyhead off A55
⊕ On site Dormy House sleeping upto 14 golfers.
⌂ James Braid
▤ www.holyheadgolfclub.co.uk

Llangefni   (1983)
Public
Llangefni, LL77 8YQ
☎ **(01248) 722193**

RAF Valley
Anglesey, LL65 3NY
☎ **(01407) 762241**
✉ constables@constables.wanadoo.com

Storws Wen   (1996)
Proprietary
Brynteg, Benllech, LL78 8JY
☎ **(01248) 852673**
⌨ (01248) 852673
✉ storws.wen.golf@hotmail.co.uk
⌑ 100
⚐ E Rowlands (Gen Mgr)
⊳ 9 L 5589 yds Par 70 SSS 68
♟ U SOC
££ £9 (for 9); £12 (for 18) W/E £9 (for 9); £15 (for 18)
∞ 2 miles from Benllech on B5108
⊕ Restaurant and accommodation on site.
⌂ K Jones

Mid Glamorgan

Aberdare   (1921)
Abernant, Aberdare, CF44 0RY
☎ **(01685) 871188 (Clubhouse)**
⌨ (01685) 872797
✉ sec-agc@tiscali.co.uk
⌑ 500
⚐ T Mears (01685) 872797

✓ Mrs K Price (01685) 878735
⊳ 18 L 5875 yds SSS 69
♟ H SOC
££ £17 (£21)
∞ ½ mile E of Aberdare. 12 miles NW of Pontypridd
⊕ 3 practice nets; putting green
▤ www.aberdaregolfclub.com

Bargoed   (1913)
Heolddu, Bargoed, CF81 9GF
☎ **(01443) 830143**
⌨ (01443) 830608
⌑ 548
⚐ Mrs Denise Richards (01443) 830608
✓ Craig Easton (01443) 836179
⊳ 18 L 6086 yds SSS 70
♟ WD–U WE–M SOC–WD
££ £18
∞ NW boundary of Bargoed. 8 miles N of Caerphilly (A469)

Bryn Meadows Golf Hotel   (1973)
Maes-y-Cwmmer, Ystrad Mynach, Nr Caerphilly, CF82 7SN
☎ **(01495) 225590/224103**
⌨ (01495) 228272
✉ reception@brynmeadows.co.uk
⌑ 550
⚐ S Mayo
⊳ 18 L 6156 yds SSS 69
♟ U
££ £20 (£35)
∞ 6 miles N of Caerphilly (A469)
⌂ Mayo/Jefferies
▤ www.brynmeadows.co.uk

Caerphilly   (1905)
Pencapel, Mountain Road, Caerphilly, CF83 1HJ
☎ **(029) 2086 3441**
⌨ (029) 2086 3441
✉ secretary&caerphillygolfclub.com
⌑ 540
⚐ Roger Chaffey (029) 2086 3441
✓ J Lee (029) 2086 9104
⊳ 18 L 5728 yds SSS 69 Par 71
♟ WD–U H WE–M
££ £12.50 with member (£30 without member/ £10 with member)
∞ 7 miles N of Cardiff, off A469
▤ www.caerphillygolfclub.com

Coed-y-Mwstwr   (1994)
Coychurch, Bridgend, CF35 6AF
☎ **(01656) 864934**
⌨ (01656) 864934
✉ secretary@coed-y-mwstwr.co.uk
⌑ 490
⚐ Gareth Summerton
✓ Paul Thomas
⊳ 18 L 5703 yds par 69 SSS 68
♟ WE–U Sun WE–M Sat WD–U SOC–WD only
££ £20 (£25)
∞ 2 miles W of M4 Junction 35
⊕ Putting green; chipping green; bunker; nets
▤ www.coed-y-mwstwr.co.uk

Creigiau   (1921)
Creigiau, Cardiff, CF15 9NN
☎ **(029) 2089 0263**
⌨ (029) 2089 0706
✉ creigiaugolfclub@btconnect.com
⌑ 810
⚐ Philip Gershon
✓ I Luntz (029) 2089 0263
⊳ 18 L 6063 yds SSS 70 Par 71
♟ WD–U WE/BH–M SOC–WD
££ £35 (£15)
∞ 7 miles NW of Cardiff. M4 Jct 34
▤ www.creigiaugolf.co.uk

Grove
South Cornelly, Bridgend, CF33 4RP
☎ **(01656 788771**
⌨ (01656) 788414
✉ enquiries@grovegolf.com
⌑ 540
⚐ M Thomas
✓ L Warne (01656) 788300
⊳ 18 L 5884 yds Par 70 SSS 69
♟ WD–U WE–NA before 3pm WD/WE–SOC contact Sec`
££ £20 (£25)
∞ 1.5 miles from Porthcawl, M4 J37
▤ www.grovegolf.com

Llantrisant & Pontyclun   (1927)
Ely Valley Road, Talbot Green, Llantrisant, CF72 8AL
☎ **(01443) 224601**
✉ llantrisantgolf@btconnect.com
⌑ 600
⚐ Theresa Morgan (Admin) (01443) 224601
✓ Andrew Bowen (01443) 228169
⊳ 18 L 5328 yds SSS 68
♟ WD–H WE/BH–M SOC–WD
££ On application
∞ 10 miles NW of Cardiff. 2 miles N of M4 Junction 34
▤ www.llantristantandpontyclungc.co.uk

Maesteg   (1912)
Mount Pleasant, Neath Road, Maesteg, CF34 9PR
☎ **(01656) 734106**
⌨ (01656) 731822
✉ ijm@fsmail.net info@maesteg-golf.co.uk
⌑ 485
⚐ Ralph Evans (01656) 734106
⊳ 18 L 5989 yds SSS 69
♟ WD–H SOC WE
££ £20 (£25)
∞ 1 mile W of Maesteg on B4282. M4 Junctions 36 or 40
⌂ James Braid
▤ www.maesteg-golf.co.uk

Merthyr Tydfil   (1909)
Cilsanws Mountain, Cefn Coed, Merthyr Tydfil, CF48 2NT
☎ **(01685) 723308**
⌑ 200
⚐ V Price
✓ None
⊳ 18 L 5622 yds SSS 68

👤 U SOC–WD
££ £10 (£15)
🚗 2 miles N of Merthyr Tydfil, off A470 at Cefn Coed
🏠 Viv Price/Richard Mathias (new holes); original architect unknown

Mountain Ash   (1907)
Cefnpennar, Mountain Ash, CF45 4DT
☎ **(01443) 472265 (Clubhouse)**
🖥 (01443) 479628
📧 sec@magc.fsnet.co.uk
🏛 530
🏌 Sharon Rees (01443) 479459
⛳ No Pro at present
🏳 18 L 5535 yds SSS 67
👤 WD–U H WE–M
££ £20 (£30)
🚗 9 miles NW of Pontypridd
🖥 www.mountainashgc.co.uk

Mountain Lakes   (1988)
Heol Penbryn, Blaengwynlais, Caerphilly, CF83 ING
☎ **(029) 2086 1128**
🖥 (029) 2086 3243
🏛 480
🏌 GM Richards (Hon)
🏳 18 L 6300 yds SSS 72
👤 U SOC
££ £18 (£18)
🚗 4 miles from M4 Junction 32
🏠 R Sandow

Pontypridd   (1905)
Ty Gwyn Road, Pontypridd, CF37 4DJ
☎ **(01443) 409904**
📧 secretary.pontypriddgc@virgin.net
🏛 850
🏌 Sonja McFadden (01443) 409904
⛳ W Walters (01443) 409904
🏳 18 L 5725 yds SSS 68
👤 WD–U H WE/BH–M H SOC–WD H
££ On application
🚗 E of Pontypridd, off A470. 12 miles NW of Cardiff
🖥 www.pontypriddgolfclub.co.uk

Pyle & Kenfig   (1922)
Waun-y-Mer, Kenfig, Bridgend, CF33 4PU
☎ **(01656) 783093**
🖥 (01656) 772822
📧 secretary@pandkgolfclub.co.uk
🏛 875
🏌 Mrs Bev Cronin (01656) 771613
⛳ R Evans (01656) 772446
🏳 18 L 6580 yds white boxed 6824 slates/blue Par 71 SSS 73
👤 WD–U WE (Sun) H SOC
££ D–£50 (£70) w/ends Groups on application.
🚗 2 miles NW of Porthcawl. M4 J37
⊕ Practice facilities
🏠 HS Colt
🖥 www.pandkgolfclub.co.uk

Rhondda   (1910)
Penrhys, Ferndale, Rhondda, CF43 3PW
☎ **(01443) 441384**
🖥 (01443) 441384
📧 rhonddagolf@aol.com
🏛 500

🏌 Ian Ellis (01443) 441384
🏳 18 L 6428 yds SSS 71
👤 U H SOC
££ May–Oct: £20 (£25) Winter: £15 (£20)
🚗 6 miles W of Pontypridd

Ridgeway   (1997)
Caerphilly Mountain, Caerphilly, CF83 ILY
☎ **(029) 2088 2255**
📧 petethepro@tiscali.co.uk
🏛 300
🏌 Tim James
⛳ Peter Johnson
🏳 9 L 4800 yds SSS 65 (18 tees)
👤 U
££ D–£10
🚗 3 miles from M4 J32 at top of Caerphilly Mountain on A469
⊕ 22 bay driving range
🖥 www.ridgeway-golf.co.uk

Royal Porthcawl   (1891)
Rest Bay, Porthcawl, CF36 3UW
☎ **(01656) 782251**
🖥 (01656) 771687
📧 office@royalporthcawl.com
🏛 800
🏌 MK Bond
⛳ P Evans (01656) 773702
🏳 18 L 7065 yds Par 72 SSS 74 (Black Tees)
👤 WD–I or H WE/BH–M SOC–H
££ Midweek 18 holes £95 inc green Midweek 36 holes £140 Weekend 18 holes £120 Weekend 36 holes £175
🚗 22 miles W of Cardiff. M4 Jct 37
⊕ Driving range; Dormy House (12 people per night) B+B
🏠 Charles Gibson
🖥 www.royalporthcawl.com

Southerndown   (1905)
Ogmore-by-Sea, Bridgend, CF32 0QP
☎ **(01656) 880476**
🖥 (01656) 880317
📧 southerndowngolf@btconnect.com
🏛 600
🏌 AJ Hughes (01656) 881111
⛳ DG McMonagle
🏳 18 L 6449 yds SSS 72
👤 U H
££ £45 D–£55 (£65 £75)
🚗 3 miles S of Bridgend, nr Ogmore Castle ruins
🏠 W Fernie
🖥 www.southerndowngolfclub.co.uk

Whitehall   (1922)
The Pavilion, Nelson, Treharris, CF46 6ST
☎ **(01443) 740245**
📧 m.wilde001@tiscali.co.uk
🏛 300
🏌 PM Wilde
🏳 9 L 5666 yds SSS 68
👤 WD–U WE–M SOC
££ £10
🚗 15 miles NW of Cardiff
🖥 www.whitehallgolfclub1922.co.uk

Monmouthshire

Alice Springs   (1989)
Kemeys Commander, Usk, NP15 IPP
☎ **(01873) 880708**
🖥 (01873) 881381
📧 alice_springs@btconnect.com
🏛 520
🏌 David J Rowlands
⛳ Stuart Steel (01873) 880914
🏳 Red 18 L 5870 yds SSS 69
Green 18 L 6438 yds SSS 72
👤 U SOC
££ £22 (£25)
🚗 3 miles N of Usk on B4598
⊕ Driving range; buggies with gps; all year round course
🏠 Keith Morgan
🖥 www.alicespringsgolfclub.com

Blackwood   (1914)
Cwmgelli, Blackwood, NP12 IBR
☎ **(01495) 223152**
🏛 300
🏌 GA Batty
⛳ None
🏳 9 L 5304 yds SSS 66
👤 WD–I SOC WE/BH–M
££ £14
🚗 ¼ mile N of Blackwood

The Celtic Manor Resort   (1995)
Coldra Woods, The Usk Valley, NP18 IHQ
☎ **(01633) 413000**
🖥 (01633) 410309
📧 postbox@celtic-manor.com
🏌 Matthew Lewis (Clubhouse Mgr) (01633) 410449
⛳ Golf Academy (01633) 410312
🏳 2010: 18 L 7439yds Par 71 SSS 77
Roman Road: 18 L 6515 yds Par 70 SSS 72
Montgomerie: 18 L 6294 yds Par 69 SSS 71
👤 H SOC WD WE
££ On application
🚗 E of Newport on A48. M4 Jct 24
⊕ Golf Academy; driving range; short game area. Venue for 2010 Ryder Cup
🏠 European Golf Design, Robert Trent Jones Sr, Colin Montgomerie
🖥 www.celtic-manor.com

Dewstow   (1988)
Proprietary
Caerwent, Monmouthshire, NP26 5AH
☎ **(01291) 430444**
🖥 (01291) 425816
📧 info@dewstow.com
🏛 850
🏌 D Bradbury
⛳ Steve Truman
🏳 Valley 18 L 6091 yds Par 72 SSS 70
Park 18 L 6226 yds Par 69 SSS 69
👤 U SOC
££ £22 (£25)
🚗 Caerwent, 5 miles W of old Severn Bridge, off A48
⊕ Driving range
🖥 www.dewstow.com

Greenmeadow G&CC
(1979)
Treherbert Road, Croesyceiliog, Cwmbran,
NP44 2BZ
- ☎ **(01633) 869321**
- 🖥 (01633) 868430
- ✉ info@greenmeadowgolf.com
- 📖 400
- ♠ PJ Richardson (01633) 869321
- ✓ D Woodman (01633) 862626
- ⏱ 18 L 6078 yds Par 70 SSS 70
- ♟ WD–U WE–NA before 11am SOC
- ££ On application
- ⛳ 4 miles N of Newport on A4042.
  M4 Junction 26
- ⊕ Floodlit driving range
- 🖳 www.greenmeadowgolf.com

Llanwern
(1928)
Tennyson Avenue, Llanwern, Newport,
NP18 2DY
- ☎ **(01633) 412029**
- 🖥 (01633) 412029
- ✉ llanwerngolfclub@btconnect.com
- 📖 550
- ♠ Peter Probert
- ✓ S Price (01633) 413233
- ⏱ 18 L 6177 yds SSS 70
- ♟ WD–U WE–restricted I H SOC
- ££ £25 (£30)
- ⛳ 1 mile S of M4 Junction 24
- ⊕ 2 practice grounds; putting green
- 🖳 www.llanwerngolfclub.co.uk

Marriott St Pierre Hotel & CC
(1962)
St Pierre Park, Chepstow, NP16 6YA
- ☎ **(01291) 625261**
- 🖥 (01291) 629975
- ✉ chepstow.golf@btconnect.com
- 📖 840
- ♠ Mr Arnie Pidgeon (01291) 635218
- ✓ Craig Dun (01291) 635205
- ⏱ Old 18 L 6818 yds SSS 74;
  Mathern 18 L 5732 yds SSS 68
- ♟ H SOC–WD
- ££ On application
- ⛳ 2 miles W of Chepstow (A48)
- ⊕ Driving range
- 🏠 CK Cotton

Monmouth
(1896)
Leasbrook Lane, Monmouth, NP25 3SN
- ☎ **(01600) 712212**
- 🖥 (01600) 772399
- ✉ sec@monmouthgolfclub.co.uk
- 📖 450
- ♠ P Tully (01600) 712212
- ✓ Mike Waldron and Tim Morgan
  (01600) 712212
- ⏱ 18 L 5582 yds Par 69 SSS 68
- ♟ U SOC WD WE (Sun only after
  11.30am)
- ££ £20 (£24) D–£34 (£28)
- ⛳ Signposted ¼ mile along A40
  Monmouth-Ross road
- ⊕ Putting green; practice area; driving
  net
- 🏠 George Walden
- 🖳 www.monmouthgolfclub.co.uk

Monmouthshire
(1892)
Llanfoist, Abergavenny, NP7 9HE
- ☎ **(01873) 852606**
- 🖥 (01873) 850470
- ✉ monmouthshiregc@btconnect.com
- 📖 518 99(L) 45(J)
- ♠ R Bradley
- ✓ B Edwards (01873) 852532
- ⏱ 18 L 5978 yds SSS 70
- ♟ WD–H SOC
- ££ D–£35 (D–£40)
- ⛳ 2 miles SW of Abergavenny on
  B4269
- 🏠 James Braid
- 🖳 www.monmouthshiregolfclub.co.uk

Newport
(1903)
Great Oak, Rogerstone, Newport,
NP10 9FX
- ☎ **(01633) 892643/894496**
- 🖥 (01633) 896676
- ✉ newportgolfclub@btconnect.com
- 📖 800
- ♠ R Thomas (01633) 892643
- ✓ PM Mayo (01633) 893271
- ⏱ 18 L 6500 yds SSS 71
- ♟ WD–H
- ££ £40 (£45)
- ⛳ 3 miles W of Newport on B4591.
  M4 Junction 27, 1 mile
- 🏠 Ross/Fernie
- 🖳 www.newportgolfclub.org.uk

Oakdale
(1990)
Pay and play
Llwynon Lane, Oakdale, NP12 0NF
- ☎ **(01495) 220044**
- ♠ M Lewis (Dir)
- ✓ Mathew Griffiths (01495) 220440
- ⏱ 9 L 1344 yds Par 28
- ♟ U SOC
- ££ On application
- ⛳ 15 miles NW of Newport via
  A467/B4251. M4 Junction 28
- ⊕ Driving range
- 🏠 Ian Goodenough

Pontnewydd
(1875)
Maesgwyn Farm, Upper Cwmbran,
Cwmbran, Torfaen, NP44 1AB
- ☎ **(01633) 482170**
- 🖥 (01633) 838598
- ✉ ctphillips@virgin.net
- 📖 422
- ♠ CT Phillips (01633) 484447
- ⏱ 11 L 5278 yds SSS 67
- ♟ WD–U WE–M SOC
- ££ £15 (£15)
- ⛳ W outskirts of Cwmbran

Pontypool
(1903)
Lasgarn Lane, Trevethin, Pontypool,
NP4 8TR
- ☎ **(01495) 763655**
- 🖥 (01495) 755564
- ✉ pontypoolgolf@btconnect.com
- 📖 444 46(L) 37(J)
- ♠ L Dodd
- ✓ K Smith (01495) 755544
- ⏱ 18 L 5712 yds SSS 69
- ♟ WD–U–SOC WE–NA–Sat
  Sun–U–SOC phone for times

Raglan Parc
(1994)
Parc Lodge, Raglan, NP5 2ER
- ☎ **(01291) 690077**
- ✉ golf@raglanparc.co.uk

The Rolls of Monmouth
(1982)
The Hendre, Monmouth, NP25 5HG
- ☎ **(01600) 715353**
- 🖥 (01600) 713115
- ✉ sandra@therollsgolfclub.co.uk
- 📖 200
- ♠ Mrs SJ Orton
- ✓ None
- ⏱ 18 L 6733 yds SSS 73
- ♟ U SOC
- ££ £41 (£45)
- ⛳ 3½ miles W of Monmouth on
  B4233
- 🖳 www.therollsgolfclub.co.uk

Shirenewton
(1995)
Shirenewton, Chepstow, NP16 6RL
- ☎ **(01291) 641642**

Tredegar & Rhymney
(1921)
Tredegar, Rhymney, NP2 5HA
- ☎ **(01685) 840743**
- ✉ tandrgc@googlemail.com
- 📖 180
- ♠ Will Price (07761) 005184
- ⏱ 18 L 5316 yds SSS 67
- ♟ U
- ££ £15 all day
- ⛳ 1½ miles W of Tredegar (B4256)
- 🖳 www.tandrgc.co.uk

Tredegar Park
(1923)
Parc-y-Brain Road, Rogerstone, Newport,
NP10 9TG
- ☎ **(01633) 895219**
- 🖥 (01633) 897152
- ✉ secretary@tredegarparkgolfclub
  .co.uk
- 📖 800
- ♠ S Salway (01633) 894433
- ✓ M Phillips (01633) 894433
- ⏱ 18 L 6564 yds SSS 72
- ♟ H SOC–WD
- ££ D–£20 (£25)
- ⛳ W of Newport, off M4 Junction 27
- 🏠 R Sandow
- 🖳 www.tredegarparkgolfclub.co.uk

Wernddu Golf Centre
(1992)
Proprietary
Old Ross Road, Abergavenny, NP7 8NG
- ☎ **(01873) 856223**
- 🖥 (01873) 852177
- ✉ info@wernddu-golf-club.co.uk
- 📖 520
- ♠ L Turvey

££ £30 (£30) WD 2–4pm £10 Sun
2–4pm £10
- ⛳ 1 mile N of Pontypool (A4042). M4
  Junction 26
- ⊕ Practice ground; indoor teaching
  academy
- 🖳 www.pontypoolgolf.co.uk

Tina Tetley
18 L 5572 yds Par 69 SSS 68
U
££ 9: £12; 18: £18
1½ miles NE of Abergavenny on B4521
Floodlit driving range; pratice area; pitch & putt
James Watkins
www.wernddu-golf-club.co.uk

West Monmouthshire (1906)
Golf Road, Pond Road, Nantyglo, Ebbw Vale, NP23 4QT
(01495) 310233
care@westmongolfclub.co.uk
300
SE Williams (01495) 310233
18 L 6118 yds SSS 69
WD/Sat–U Sun–M SOC–WD
££ £15
Nr Asda/Lakeside, off Brynmawr Bypass, towards Winchestown
20-bay driving range
Ben Sayers
www.westmongolfclub.co.uk

Woodlake Park (1993)
Proprietary
Glascoed, Usk, NP4 0TE
(01291) 673933
(01291) 673811
golf@woodlake.co.uk
500
MJ Wood
L Lancey (01291) 671135
18 L 6300 yds Par 71 SSS 72
H SOC WD WE
££ Summer–£25 (£32) Winter–£18 (£20)
3 miles W of Usk, nr Llandegfedd reservoir
www.woodlake.co.uk

Pembrokeshire

Haverfordwest (1904)
Arnolds Down, Haverfordwest, SA61 2XQ
(01437) 763565
(01437) 764143
haverfordwestgc@btconnect.com
560
M Foley (01437) 764523
A Pile (01437) 768409
18 L 6002 yds Par 70 SSS 69
U SOC
££ £22 (£22) Mondays £10
1 mile E of Haverfordwest on A40
Practice area; putting green; pro shop
www.haverfordwestgolfclub.co.uk

Milford Haven (1913)
Hubberston, Milford Haven, SA72 3RX
(01646) 697762
(01646) 697870
cerlthmhgc@aol.com
380 65(L) 90(J)
CW Pugh (01646) 697822
M Stimson (01646) 697762

18 L 6071 yds SSS 71
U SOC
££ £20 (£25)
W boundary of Milford Haven
www.mhgc.co.uk

Newport Links (1925)
Newport, SA42 0NR
(01239) 820244
(01239) 820085
newportgc@lineone.net
500
Mrs A Payne (Mgr)
Mr J Noott
18 L 6053 yds SSS 70
U SOC
2½ miles NW of Newport, towards Newport Beach
Driving range; chipping green; putting green
James Braid
www.newportlinks.co.uk

Priskilly Forest (1992)
Castle Morris, Haverfordwest, SA62 5EH
(01348) 840276
(01348) 840276
jevans@priskilly-forest.co.uk
P Evans
9 L 5874 yds Par 70 SSS 69
U SOC
££ 9: £15 18: £20 D–£24 (£22 D–£27)
2 miles off A40 at Letterston
Practice area
J Walters
www.priskilly-forest.co.uk

South Pembrokeshire (1970)
Military Road, Pembroke Dock, SA72 6SE
(01646) 621453
spgc06@tiscali.co.uk
350
M Seal (01646) 621453
18 L 6279 yds SSS 70
U before 4.30pm SOC
££ Summer: £15 all week Winter: £15 all week
Pembroke Dock, Pembrokeshire
Practice area
www.southpembsgolf.co.uk

St Davids City (1903)
Whitesands Bay, St Davids, SA62 6PT
(01437) 721751 (Clubhouse)
wjwilcox@hotmail.com

Tenby (1888)
The Burrows, Tenby, SA70 7NP
(01834) 842978
tenbygolfclub@ukk.co.uk
700
DJ Hancock (01834) 842978
R Harry (01834) 844447
18 L 6373 yds SSS 72
H SOC
££ £36 D–£54 (£45 D–£67)
Tenby, South Beach
James Braid
www.tenbygolf.co.uk

Trefloyne (1996)
Trefloyne Park, Penally, Tenby, SA70 7RG
(01834) 842165

Powys

Brecon (1902)
Newton Park, Llanfaes, Brecon, LD3 8PA
(01874) 622004
330
TJ Richards
9 L 6068 yds Par 70 SSS 70
U SOC
££ £15 (£18)
½ mile W of Brecon on A40
James Braid
www.brecongolfclub.co.uk

Builth Wells (1923)
Golf Club Road, Builth Wells, LD2 3NF
(01982) 553296
(01982) 551064
info@builthwellsgolf.co.uk
400
S Edwards (01982) 551155
S Edwards
18 L 5424 yds SSS 66
U H SOC
££ £22 D–£30 (£25 D–£32)
W of Builth Wells on Llandovery road (A483)
www.builthwellsgolf.co.uk

Cradoc (1967)
Penoyre Park, Cradoc, Brecon, LD3 9LP
(01874) 623658
(01874) 611711
secretary@cradoc.co.uk
600
Robert Southcott (01874) 623658
R Davies (01874) 625524
18 L 6188 yds Par 71 SSS 71
U SOC
££ £26 (£32)
2 miles NW of Brecon, off B4520
Driving range; chipping area; practice putting green
CK Cotton
www.cradoc.co.uk

Knighton (1906)
Ffrydd Wood, Knighton, LD7 1EF
(01547) 528646
150
DB Williams (Hon) (01547) 528046
9 L 5362 yds Par 68 SSS 66
U SOC WD–U WE–NA before 5pm
££ £10 (£15)
SW of Knighton. 20 miles NE of Llandrindod Wells
H Vardon
www.knightongolfclub.co.uk

Llandrindod Wells (1905)
The Clubhouse, Llandrindod Wells, LD1 5NY
(01597) 823873
(01597) 823873
secretary@lwgc.co.uk

☐ 300
🐟 R Southcott (01597) 823873
✓ P Davies (01597) 822247
↳ 18 L 5759 yds Par 69 SSS 69
⋔ U SOC
££ £24 (£30)
⊶ ¹/₂ mile E of Llandrindod Wells centre
⊕ Driving range, Buggies
🏠 Harry Vardon
▤ www.lwgc.co.uk

Machynlleth   (1904)
Felingerrig, Machynlleth, SY20 8UH
☎ **(01654) 702000**
✉ machgolf2@tiscali.co.uk
☐ 250
↳ 9 L 5726 yds SSS 67
⋔ U Sun–NA before 11.30am SOC
££ £18 (£18)
⊶ 1 mile E of Machynlleth, off A489

Mid-Wales Golf Centre (1992)
Maesmawr Golf Club, Caersws, Nr Newtown, SY17 5SB
☎ **(01686) 688303**
☐ (01686) 688303
🐟 Mrs Penny Dewinton Davies Mr Steve Dewinton-Davies
↳ 9 L 1277 yds Par 3
⋔ U WD–M WE–NA SOC–WD/WE
££ £6–£10 (£7–£12)
⊕ 14-bay floodlit driving range

Rhosgoch   (1984)
Proprietary
Rhosgoch, Builth Wells, LD2 3JY
☎ **(01497) 851251**
✉ rhosgochgolf@yahoo.co.uk
☐ 80
🐟 C Dance
↳ 9 L 4955 yds SSS 66
⋔ U SOC
££ £12 (£15)
⊶ 5 miles N of Hay-on-Wye
▤ www.rhosgoch-golf.co.uk

St Giles Newtown   (1895)
Pool Road, Newtown, SY16 3AJ
☎ **(01686) 625844**
✉ stgilesgolf@tiscali.co.uk
☐ 350
🐟 Wyn Evans (07739 884198)
✓ DP Owen
↳ 9 L 6012 yds SSS 70
⋔ U SOC
££ £15 (£15)
⊶ 1 mile E of Newtown (A483). 14 miles SW of Welshpool
▤ www.stgilesgolf.co.uk

St Idloes   (1920)
Club
Penrhallt, Llanidloes, SY18 6LG
☎ **(01686) 412559**
☐ 320
🐟 Mr B Downie
↳ 9 L 5510 yds SSS 66
⋔ U H Sun–restricted SOC
££ £20 (£20)
⊶ ¹/₂ mile from Llanidloes on Trefeglwys road (B4569)

⊕ Practice putting green, Driving Range, Pitch + putt (pay + play)
▤ www.stidloesgolfclub.co.uk

Welsh Border Golf Complex (1991)
Bulthy Farm, Bulthy, Middletown, SY21 8ER
☎ **(01743) 884247**
✉ jaykay@fsmail.net
☐ 200
🐟 K Farr (07966) 530042
✓ M Kendal (01686) 530042 P Seal (01743) 884247
↳ 9 L 3050 yds SSS 68
9 hole course Pay & Play Par 3
⋔ U SOC WD/WE
££ £14 18 Holes; £9 9 Holes
⊶ Between Shrewsbury and Welshpool on A458
⊕ Driving range
🏠 A Griffiths

Welshpool   (1907)
Golfa Hill, Welshpool, SY21 9AQ
☎ **(01938) 850249**
✉ welshpool.golfclub@btconnect.com
☐ 300
🐟 D Lewis
✓ None
↳ 18 L 5840 yds Par 70 SSS 70
⋔ U SOC WD WE
££ £15.50 (£15.50) winter/summer (£25.50 WE summer) £15.50 winter
⊶ 4¹/₂ miles W of Welshpool, on Dolgellau road (A458)
🏠 James Braid
▤ www.welshpoolgolfclub.co.uk

South Glamorgan

Brynhill   (1921)
Port Road, Barry, CF62 8PN
☎ **(01446) 720277**
☐ (01446) 740422
✉ postbox@brynhillgolfclub.co.uk
☐ 700
🐟 R Cook/L Thomas (01446) 720277
✓ D Prior (01446) 740004
↳ 18 L 6516 yds SSS 72
⋔ WD/Sat–H Sun–NA SOC–WD
££ £30 (£35) SOC–£20
⊶ A4050, 8 miles SW of Cardiff; M4 J33
▤ www.brynhillgolfclub.co.uk

Cardiff   (1921)
Sherborne Avenue, Cyncoed, Cardiff, CF23 6SJ
☎ **(029) 2075 3067**
☐ (029) 2068 0011
✉ cardiff.golfclub@virgin.net
☐ 850
🐟 Mrs K Newling (029) 2075 3320
✓ T Hanson (029) 2075 4772
↳ 18 L 6015 yds SSS 70
⋔ WD–H WE–H SOC–Fri
££ £50
⊶ 3 miles N of Cardiff. 2 miles W of Pentwyn exit of A48(M). M4 Jct 29
▤ www.cardiffgc.co.uk

Cottrell Park   (1996)
St Nicholas, Cardiff, CF5 6JY
☎ **(01446) 781781**
✉ admin@cottrell-park.co.uk

Dinas Powis   (1914)
Old Highwalls, Dinas Powis, CF64 4AJ
☎ **(029) 2051 2727**
☐ (029) 2051 2727
✉ dinaspowisgolfclub@yahoo.co.uk
☐ 490
🐟 Julian Rees
✓ G Bennett (029) 2051 3682
↳ 18 L 5532 yds SSS 67
⋔ H SOC
££ D–£25 (£30)
⊶ 3 miles SW of Cardiff (A4055)
▤ www.dinaspowis.golfers247.com

Glamorganshire   (1890)
Lavernock Road, Penarth, CF64 5UP
☎ **(029) 2070 1185**
☐ (029) 2070 1185
✉ glamgolf@btconnect.com
☐ 1100
🐟 BM Williams (029) 2070 1185
✓ A Kerr-Smith (029) 2070 7401
↳ 18 L 6181 yds SSS 70
⋔ WD/WE–H SOC
££ £38 (£45)
⊶ 5 miles SW of Cardiff, M4 J33
▤ www.glamorganshiregolfclub.co.uk

Llanishen   (1905)
Heol Hir, Cardiff, CF14 9UD
☎ **(029) 207 55078**
☐ (029) 207 65253
✉ secretary.llanishengc@virgin.net
☐ 850
🐟 Colin Duffield (029) 207 55078
✓ RA Jones (029) 207 55078
↳ 18 L 5301 yds SSS 67
⋔ WD–U except Wed WE–Sun pm only SOC–Thur/Fri
££ £25 D–£32
⊶ 5 miles N of Cardiff M4 Jct 32
▤ www.llanishengc.co.uk

Peterstone Lakes   (1990)
Proprietary
Peterstone, Wentloog, Cardiff, CF3 2TN
☎ **(01633) 680009**
✉ peterstone_lakes@yahoo.com

Radyr   (1902)
Drysgol Road, Radyr, Cardiff, CF15 8BS
☎ **(029) 2084 2408**
☐ (029) 2084 3914
✉ manager@radyrgolf.co.uk
☐ 935
🐟 Gareth Morgan (Mgr)
✓ S Swales (029) 2084 2476
↳ 18 L 6053 yds SSS 70
⋔ H SOC–Mon/Wed/Thurs/Fri/Sun
££ D–£40.50
⊶ 5 miles NW of Cardiff, off A470. M4 Junction 32
⊕ Large practice area; Short Game Practice Area.
🏠 Braid Colt
▤ www.radyrgolf.co.uk

RAF St Athan (1977)
Clive Road, St Athan, CF62 4JD
- ☎ **(01446) 751043**
- 📠 (01446) 751862
- ✉ rafstathan@golfclub.fsbusiness.co.uk
- 🏠 450
- 🏌 PF Woodhouse (01446) 797186
- ✓ John Hastings
- ⊳ 9 L 6452 yds SSS 72
- 👥 U exc Sun am–NA
- ££ £15 (£20)
- 🚗 2 miles E of Llantwit Major. 10 miles S of Bridgend

St Andrews Major (1993)
Proprietary
Coldbrook Road East, Cadoxton, Barry, CF6 3BB
- ☎ **(01446) 722227**
- 📠 (01446) 748953
- ✉ info@standrewsmajorgolfclub.com
- 🏠 370
- 🏌 A Edmunds
- ✓ John Hastings 07761 137265
- ⊳ 18 L 5425 yds par 71 SSS 66
- 👥 U SOC
- ££ 18: £18 (£22)
- 🚗 Barry Docks Link road. M4 Junction 33
- ⊕ 12 bay floodlit driving range; buggies and trollies for hire
- 🏠 MRM Leisure
- 🖥 www.standrewsmajorgolfclub.com

St Mellons (1937)
St Mellons, Cardiff, CF3 2XS
- ☎ **(01633) 680408**
- 📠 (01633) 681219
- ✉ stmellons@golf2003.fsnet.co.uk
- 🏠 536 89(L) 67(J)
- 🏌 M W Wake (01633) 680408
- ✓ B Thomas (01633) 680101
- ⊳ 18 L 6225 yds SSS 70
- 👥 U exc Sat WD SOC
- ££ £40
- 🚗 4 miles E of Cardiff on A48. M4 Junction 28
- 🏠 H S Colt
- 🖥 www.stmellonsgolfclub.co.uk

Vale Hotel Golf & Spa Resort (1994)
Hensol Park, Hensol, CF7 8JY
- ☎ **(01443) 665899**
- 📠 (01443) 222220
- ✉ golf@vale-hotel.com
- 🏠 1200
- 🏌 Clive Coombs
- ✓ Clive Coombs
- ⊳ Lake 18 L 6426 yds Par 72 National L 7413 yds Par 73
- 👥 H SOC WD WE
- ££ Lake £40, National £70 Ring for WE price
- 🚗 1 mile from M 4 Junction 34
- ⊕ Driving range; Golf Academy; practice bunkers & putting greens; short course practice zone
- 🏠 Terry Jones
- 🖥 www.vale-hotel.com

Wenvoe Castle (1936)
Wenvoe, Cardiff, CF5 6BE
- ☎ **(029) 205 94371**
- 📠 (029) 205 94371
- ✉ wenvoe-castlegc@virgin.net
- 🏠 600
- 🏌 N Sims (029) 2059 4371
- ✓ J Harris (029) 2059 3649
- ⊳ 18 L 6444 yds SSS 72
- 👥 WD–H SOC–WD WE–H
- ££ £30 (£40)
- 🚗 4 miles W of Cardiff, off A4050

Whitchurch (Cardiff) (1914)
Pantmawr Road, Whitchurch, Cardiff, CF14 7TD
- ☎ **(029) 2062 0985**
- 📠 (029) 2052 9860
- ✉ secretary@whitchurchcardiffgolfclub.com
- 🏠 780
- 🏌 G Perrott
- ✓ R Davies (029) 2061 4660
- ⊳ 18 L 6258 yds Par 71 SSS 71
- 👥 U H SOC–Thurs
- ££ £50 (£60)
- 🚗 3 miles NW of Cardiff on A470. M4 Junction 32
- 🏠 F Jones
- 🖥 www.whitchurchgolfclub.com

West Glamorgan

Allt-y-Graban (1993)
Allt-y-Graban Road, Pontlliw, Swansea, SA4 1DT
- ☎ **(01792) 885757**
- 🏠 154
- 🏌 P Gillis (Prop)
- ✓ P Gilly (01792) 885757
- ⊳ 9 L 2617 yds Par 67 SSS 64 14 tees
- 👥 U SOC
- ££ 9: £7 (£8); 18: £11 (£13)
- 🚗 3 miles off M4 Junction 47, on A48
- 🏠 FG Thomas

Clyne (1920)
120 Owls Lodge Lane, Mayals, Swansea, SA3 5DP
- ☎ **(01792) 401989**
- 📠 (01792) 401078
- ✉ clynegolfclub@supanet.com
- 🏠 900
- 🏌 DR Thomas (Mgr)
- ✓ J Clewett (01792) 402094
- ⊳ 18 L 6323 yds Par 70 SSS 72
- 👥 WD U H SOC WE contact Club Manager
- ££ £30 (£40)
- 🚗 3 miles SW of Swansea
- ⊕ Extensive practice area; chipping green; indoor and outdoor nets
- 🏠 Colt/Harris
- 🖥 www.clynegolfclub.com

Fairwood Park (1969)
Blackhills Lane, Fairwood, Swansea, SA2 7JN
- ☎ **(01792) 297849**
- 📠 (01792) 297849
- ✉ info@fairwoodpark.com
- 🏠 600
- 🏌 E Golbas (Mgr)
- ✓ G Hughes (01792) 299194
- ⊳ 18 L 6650 yds SSS 73
- 👥 U SOC
- ££ £22 (£27)
- 🚗 4 miles W of Swansea (A4118)
- ⊕ Driving Range, 'Explanar' Coaching available.
- 🏠 Hawtree
- 🖥 www.fairwoodpark.com

Glynneath (1931)
Penygraig, Pontneathvaughan, Glynneath, SA11 5UH
- ☎ **(01639) 720452**
- 📠 (01639) 720452
- ✉ enquiries@glynneathgc.co.uk
- 🏠 570
- 🏌 TA Roberts
- ✓ S McMenamin (01639) 720872
- ⊳ 18 L 6090 yds Par 71 SSS 70
- 👥 U SOC
- ££ £17 (£22) Mon £10
- 🚗 2 miles NW of Glynneath on Pontneathvaughan Road. 15 miles NE of Swans
- ⊕ 3 hole junior academy
- 🏠 Cotton/Pennink/Lawrie/Williams
- 🖥 www.glynneathgc.co.uk

Gower
Cefn Goleu, Three Crosses, Gowerton, Swansea SA4 3HS
- ☎ **(01792) 872480**
- ✉ adrian.richards@btconnect.com

Inco (1965)
Clydach, Swansea, SA6 5QR
- ☎ **(01792) 841257**
- 🏠 600
- 🏌 DE Jones (01792) 842929
- ⊳ 18 L 6064 yds Par 70 SSS 69
- 👥 U
- ££ £20 (£25)
- 🚗 N of Swansea (A4067)

Lakeside (1992)
Water Street, Margam, Port Talbot, SA13 2PA
- ☎ **(01639) 899959**

Langland Bay (1904)
Langland Bay Road, Langland, Swansea, SA3 4QR
- ☎ **(01792) 361721**
- 📠 (01792) 361082
- ✉ info@langlandbaygolfclub.com
- 🏠 800
- 🏌 Mrs L Coleman
- ✓ M Evans
- ⊳ 18 L 5857 yds SSS 70
- 👥 H SOC WD
- ££ D–£40 (D–£50)
- 🚗 6 miles S of Swansea (A4067). M4 Junction 45
- 🖥 www.langlandbaygolfclub.com

Morriston (1919)
160 Clasemont Road, Morriston, Swansea, SA6 6AJ

☎ (01792) 796528
✉ morristongolf@btconnect.com
📖 450
🏌 David Fellowes (01792) 796528
✓ Mark Govier (01792) 772335
🏴 18 L 5708 yds (white tees) Par 68 SSS 68
👤 U H SOC–WD, WE after 3pm
££ £25 (£35)
🚗 4 miles N of Swansea on A48. M4 Junction 46, 1 mile
⊕ Extensive practice area inc. indoor facility
🖥 www.morristongolfclub.co.uk

Neath   (1934)
Cadoxton, Neath, SA10 8AH
☎ (01639) 632759
📠 (01639) 639955
✉ neathgolf:btconnect.com
📖 750
🏌 W A Jefford
✓ RM Bennett (01639) 633693
🏴 18 L 6490 yds Par 72 SSS 72
👤 WD–U WE–U SOC
££ Apr–Sep: £25 (£30); Oct–Mar: £17; Nov–Dec: £15 Dec–Jan: £12; special rates for societies of 8 or more
🚗 2 miles NE of Neath (B4434), M4 J46 to A465
⊕ Short game practice area; 4 driving nets; 2 practice putting greens; buggies for hire
🏛 James Braid
🖥 www.neathgolfclub.co.uk

Palleg & Swansea Valley Golf Course   (1930)
Proprietary
Palleg Road, Lower Cwmtwrch, Swansea Valley, SA9 2QQ
☎ (01639) 842193
📠 (01639) 845661
✉ gc.gcgs@btinternet.com
📖 326
🏌 Graham Coombe (PGA Pro/Director)
🏴 18 L 5902 yds Par 72 SSS 70
👤 WD–U Sat/Sun/BH–phone first SOC
££ £18 D–£24 £12 with member £7 junior
🚗 12 miles NE of Swansea (A4067). M4 Junction 45
⊕ Junior Starter Centre, Buggy available, Putting Green, Practise net, Teaching Studio.
🏛 Cotten
🖥 www.palleg-golf.com

Pennard   (1896)
2 Southgate Road, Southgate, Swansea, SA3 2BT
☎ (01792) 233131

📠 (01792) 235125
✉ sec@pennardgolfclub.com
📖 775
🏌 Mrs S Crowley (01792) 235120
✓ MV Bennett (01792) 233451
🏴 18 L 6267 yds Par 71 SSS 72
👤 U H SOC–WD WE by arrangement
££ £50 (£60)
🚗 8 miles W of Swansea, by A4067 and B4436
⊕ Driving range
🏛 James Braid
🖥 www.pennardgolfclub.com

Pontardawe   (1924)
Cefn Llan, Pontardawe, Swansea, SA8 4SH
☎ (01792) 863118
📠 (01792) 830041
✉ enquiries@pontardawegolfclub .co.uk
📖 574
🏌 N Bowden (Hon), Mrs M Griffiths (Admin)
✓ Danny Evans (01792) 830977
🏴 18 L 6101 yds SSS 70
👤 H SOC–WD
££ £20; £60 for 4 ball Tue–Thur £10 Mon only
🚗 5 miles N of M4 Junction 45, off A4067
🖥 www.pontardawegolfclub.co.uk

Swansea Bay   (1892)
Jersey Marine, Neath, SA10 6JP
☎ (01792) 812198
📖 400
🏌 Mrs D Goatcher (01792) 814153
✓ M Day (01792) 816159
🏴 18 L 6103 yds Par 72 SSS 70 (Yellow)
👤 U SOC
££ £18 (£26)
🚗 5 miles E of Swansea, off A483 (B4290). M4 Junction 42

Wrexham

Chirk   (1990)
Proprietary
Chirk, Wrexham, LL14 5AD
☎ (01691) 774407
📠 (01691) 773878
✉ chirkjackbarker@btinternet.com
📖 300
🏌 Trudi Jones (Manager)
✓ C Hodges
🏴 18 L 7045 yds Par 72 SSS 73 9 hole Par 3 course
👤 U after 10am SOC
££ £14 (£18)
🚗 8 miles S of Wrexham on A483
⊕ Driving range
🖥 www.jackbarker.com

Clays Golf Centre   (1992)
Bryn Estyn Road, Wrexham, LL13 9UB
☎ (01978) 661406
📠 (01978) 661406
✉ sales@claysgolf.co.uk
📖 500
🏌 Steve Williams
✓ D Larvin
🏴 18 L 6000 yds Par 69 Par 3 short course
👤 U SOC
££ £20 (£26)
🚗 Wrexham, off A534 towards Holt
⊕ 20 bay floodlit driving range; 20 bay short game range inc 3 Huxley greens
🖥 www.claysgolf.co.uk

Moss Valley   (1990)
Moss Road, Wrexham, LL11 6HA
☎ (01978) 720518
📠 (01978) 720518
✉ info@mossvalleygolf.co.uk
📖 100
🏌 John Nolan (07917) 894151
✓ John Nolan
🏴 9 holes/18 tees 5313 yds Par 68 SSS 68
👤 No Restrictions
££ 9: MW £10, WE/BH £11 per round 18: MW £14, WE/BH £15 per round
🚗 N of Wrexham, off A541
🖥 www.mossvalleygolf.co.uk

Plassey Oaks Golf Complex   (1992)
Eyton, Wrexham, LL13 0SP
☎ (01978) 780020
📠 (01978) 781397
✉ hjones@plasseygolf.com
📖 165
🏌 OJ Jones (01978) 780020
🏴 9 L 4962 yds Par 66 SSS 64
👤 U SOC
££ 9: £10; 18: £15
🚗 2 miles SW of Wrexham, off A483
⊕ 9 hole pitch & putt course; driving range
🏛 K Williams
🖥 www.plasseygolf.com

Wrexham   (1906)
Holt Road, Wrexham, LL13 9SB
☎ (01978) 261033
📠 (01978) 362168
✉ info@wrexhamgolfclub.co.uk
📖 650
🏌 J Johnson (01978) 364268
✓ P Williams (01978) 351476
🏴 18 L 6233 yds Par 70 SSS 70
👤 H SOC–WD
££ £30 (£35)
🚗 2 miles NE of Wrexham on A534
🏛 James Braid
🖥 www.wrexhamgolfclub.co.uk

Continent of Europe – Country and Region Index

Austria

Innsbruck & Tirol

Achensee (1934)
Golf und Landclub Achensee,
6213 Pertisau/Tirol
☎ **(05243) 5377**
📠 (05243) 6202
✉ golfclub-achensee@tirol.com
▷ 18 L 6018 m Par 71
👥 U H
££ €65 (€65)
⚑ Pertisau, 50km NE of Innsbruck
🏠 Fahrenleitnner
🖥 www.golfclub-achensee.com

Innsbruck-Igls (1935)
Oberdorf 11, 6074 Rinn
☎ **(05223) 78177**
📠 (05223) 78177-77
✉ office@golfclub-innsbruck-igls.at
▷ Rinn 18 L 6055 m Par 71 CR 71.3
   SR 129
   Lans 9 L 4597 m Par 66 CR 64.8
👥 H–booking necessary
££ €60 (€60)
⚑ Rinn, 10km E of Innsbruck. Lans,
   8km from Innsbruck
🏠 G & G Hauser. Re-design D
   Fahrenleitner
🖥 www.golfclub-innsbruck-igls.at

Kaiserwinkl GC Kössen
(1988)
6345 Kössen, Mühlau 1
☎ **(05375) 2122**
📠 (05375) 2122-13
✉ club@golf-koessen.at
▷ 18 L 5645 m Par 72 CR 70.7 SR 127
👥 H
££ €63
⚑ 30km N of Kitzbühel, nr German
   border
🏠 Donald Harradine
🖥 www.golf-koessen.at

Golfclub Kitzbühel (1955)
Ried Kaps 3, 6370 Kitzbühel
☎ **(05356) 63007 Members**
   (05356) 65660891 Guests
📠 (05356) 630077
✉ gckitzbuehel@golf.at
▷ 9 hole Par 70
   White 5610 m CR 70.7 SR 131
   Yellow 5148 m CR 68.5 SR 122
   Black 4690 m CR 70.7 SR 125
   Red 4266 m CR 68.7 SR 118
👥 HCP Limit 36
££ Low Season 9: €35 18: €65 High
   Season 9: €38 18: €70
⚑ Kitzbühel
🏠 Max Graf Lamberg
🖥 www.golfclubkitzbuehel.at

Kitzbühel-Schwarzsee
(1988)
6370 Kitzbühel, Golfweg Schwarzsee 35
☎ **(05356) 71645**

Seefeld-Wildmoos (1969)
6100 Seefeld, Postfach 22
☎ **(0699) 1-606606-0**
📠 (0699) 4-606606-3
✉ info@seefeldgolf.com
▷ 18 L 5894 m CR 72 SR 130
👥 H–booking necessary
££ €54–€70
⚑ 7 km W of Seefeld. 24 km W of
   Innsbruck
🏠 Donald Harradine
🖥 www.seefeldgolf.com

Klagenfurt & South

Bad Kleinkirchheim-Reichenau (1977)
9564 Padergassen, Plass 19
☎ **(04275) 594**

Kärntner GC Dellach (1927)
Golfstrasse 3, 9082 Maria Wörth, Golfstr 3
☎ **(04273) 2515**
📠 (04273) 2515-20
✉ office@kgcdellach.at
▷ 18 L 5609 m Par 71 CR 70.5 SL
   134 (men, yellow)
👥 H
££ €75
⚑ Dellach, S side of Wörther See
   15km W of Klagenfurt
🏠 C Noskowski
🖥 www.kgcdellach.at

Golfclub Klagenfurt-Seltenheim (1996)
Seltenheimerstr. 137, A-9061 Wolfnitz
☎ **0043 463 40223**
📠 0043 463 4022320
✉ office@gcseltenheim.at
▷ 18 hole Championship Course
   9 hole Romantic Course
👥 H
££ €69
⚑ 8km Klagenfurt
🏠 Perry O'Dye
🖥 www.gcseltenheim.at

Klopeiner See-Turnersee
(1988)
9122 St Kanzian, Grabelsdorf 94
☎ **(04239) 3800-0**
📠 (04239) 3800-18
✉ office@golfklopein.at
▷ 18 L 6073 m CR 71.3 SR 122
👥 U
££ €48
⚑ 25km E of Klagenfurt
🏠 Donald Harradine
🖥 www.golfklopein.at

Golfclub Millstatter See
Am Golfplatz 1, 9872 Millstatt
☎ **+43 (0)4762 82542**
📠 +43 (0)4762 82548-10
✉ gcmillstatt@golf.at
▷ 18 Par 71
   Men: CR 70.4 SR 128
   Women: CR 71.7 SR 126

👥 H WD/WE–all day
££ €63
⚑ Seeboden near Klagenfurt
🏠 Hauser
🖥 www.golf-millstatt.at

Moosburg-Pörtschach (1986)
9062 Moosburg, Golfstr 2
☎ **(04272) 83486**
📠 (04272) 834 8620
✉ moosburg@golfktn.at
▷ 18 L 6011 m SSS 72
   9 L 2341 m SSS 35
👥 U
££ 9: D–€31; 18: €60
⚑ 3km N of Wörther See/Pörtschach
🏠 G Hauser
🖥 www.golfmoosburg.at

Wörthersee-Velden
(1988)
9231 Köstenberg, Golfweg 41
☎ **(04274) 7045**
📠 (04274) 7087-15
✉ golf-velden@golfktn.at
▷ 18 L 6081 m SSS 72
👥 H
££ €66
⚑ 30km W of Klagenfurt. 12km from
   Velden
🏠 Erhardt/Rossknecht
🖥 www.golfvelden.at

Linz & North

Amstetten-Ferschnitz (1972)
3325 Ferschnitz, Gut Edla 18
☎ **(07473) 8293**
✉ office@golfclub-amstetten.at

Böhmerwald GC Ulrichsberg (1990)
4161 Ulrichsberg, Seitelschlag 50
☎ **(07288) 8200**
✉ office@boehmerwaldgolf.at

Celtic Golf Course – Schärding (1994)
Maad 2, 4775 Taufkirchen/Pram
☎ **(0043) 7719 8110**
📠 (0043) 7719 811015
✉ office@gcschaerding.at
▷ Championship:
   Men: 18 L 6406 m CR 73.1
   SR 123
   Women: 18 L 5591 m CR 74.1
   SR 122
   6 hole Josko Academy Course Par
   18
👥 H
££ Championship: €45 (€55);
   Academy: €16, Juniors/Students
   €8
⚑ 8km S of Schärding on B137
🖥 www.gcschaerding.at

Golfresort Haugschlag
(1987)
3874 Haugschlag 160
☎ **(02865) 8441**
📞 (02865) 8441-522
📧 info@golfresort.at
🏌 18 L 6262 m CR 72.8 SL 125
   18 L 6395 m CR 72.5 SL 123
   18 hole Par 3 course
👥 H
£€ €70 (€79)
🚗 25km N of Gmund. 140km NW of
   Vienna
🏠 Max Lamberg
📧 www.golfresort.at

Herzog Tassilo   (1991)
Blankenbergerstr 30, 4540 Bad Hall
☎ **(07258) 5480**
📞 (07258) 5480-11
📧 golfherzogtassilo@golf.at
🏌 18 L 5670 m Par 71 CR 69.9
   SR 126
👥 H
£€ €50 (€60) – 2007 prices
🚗 30km SW of Linz
🏠 Peter Mayerhofer
📧 www.golfherzogtassilo.at

PGC Kremstal   (1989)
Schachen 20, 4531 Kematen/Krems
☎ **(07228) 7644-0**

Linz-St Florian   (1960)
4490 St Florian, Tillysburg 28
☎ **(07223) 828730**
📧 gclinz@golf.at

Linzer Golf Club Luftenberg
(1990)
4222 Luftenberg, Am Luftenberg 1a
☎ **(07237) 3893**
📞 (07237) 3893-40
📧 gclinz-luftenberg@golf.at
🏌 18 L 6075 m CR 70.7 SR 118
👥 U H
£€ €50 (€60); early morning
   Mon–Thur before 10.30 €35
🚗 15km NE of Linz
🏠 Keith Preston
📧 www.gclinz-luftenberg.at

Maria Theresia   (1989)
Letten 5, 4680 Haag am Hausruck
☎ **(07732) 3944**

Ottenstein   (1988)
3532 Niedergrünbach 60
☎ **(02826) 7476**
📞 (02826) 7476-4
📧 info@golfclub-ottenstein.at
🏌 18 L 6129 m CR 71.9 SR 125
👥 H
£€ €50 (€60)
🚗 90km NE of Linz. 100km NW of
   Vienna
🏠 Preston/Zinterl/Erhardt
📧 www.golfclub-ottenstein.at

St Oswald-Freistadt   (1988)
Am Golfplatz 1, 4271 St Oswald
☎ **(07945) 7938**
📞 (07945) 79384
🏌 18 L 5953 m Par 72
👥 WD–UH WE–U H restricted
£€ €45 (€60)
🚗 40km N of Linz
🏠 Mel Flanegan

St Pölten Schloss Goldegg
(1989)
3100 St Pölten Schloss Goldegg
☎ **(02741) 7360/7060**

Schloss Ernegg   (1973)
3261 Steinakirchen, Schloss Ernegg
☎ **+43 (0) 7488) 76770**
📧 info@schlossernegg.com

Traunsee Kircham
4656 Kircham, Kampesberg 38
☎ **(07619) 2576**

Weitra   (1989)
3970 Weitra, Hausschachen
☎ **(02856) 2058**
📧 gcweitra@golf.at

Wels   (1981)
4616 Weisskirchen, Golfplatzstrasse 2
☎ **(07243) 56038**
📞 (07243) 56685
📧 gcwels@golf.at
🏌 18 L 6027 m Par 72
   Yellow: CR 71.9 SR 124
   Red: CR 74.5 SR 123
👥 H
£€ €50 (€60)
🚗 5 km from Salzburg-Vienna
   highway. 8km SE of Wels
🏠 Hauser/Hunt Hastings
📧 www.golfclub-wels.at

Salzburg Region

Bad Gastein   (1960)
5640 Bad Gastein, Golfstrasse 6
☎ **(06434) 2775**
📞 (06434) 2775-4
📧 info@golfclub-gastein.com
🏌 18 L 5576 m
   Yellow Par 71 CR 69.5 SR 131
   Red Par 71 CR 71.4 SR 124
👥 H SOC WD WE U H
£€ €64 (€48 guests of partner hotel)
🚗 Bad Gastein 2 km. Salzburg 100km
🏠 B von Limburger and Keith Preston
📧 www.golfclub-gastein.com

GC Sonnberg   (1993)
5241 Höhnart, Strass 1
☎ **0043 (7743) 20066**
📞 0043 (7743) 20077
📧 golf@gcsonnberg.at
🏌 Men: 18 5112 m Par 70
   Ladies: 18 4532 m par 70
👥 H
£€ €50

🚗 50km from Salzburg. 100km from
   Linz. 150km from Munich
🏠 Heinz Schmidbauer
📧 www.gcsonnberg.at

Goldegg
5622 Goldegg, Postfach 6
☎ **(06415) 8585**
📞 (06415) 8585-4
📧 info@golfclub-goldegg.com
🏌 18 L 5429 m Par 72 CR 73.4
   SL 125 D
   CR 70.6 SL 123 H
👥 U
£€ €70
🚗 60km SW of Salzburg
🏠 Van Heel
📧 www.golfclub-goldegg.com

Gut Altentann   (1989)
Hof 54, 5302 Henndorf am Wallersee
☎ **(06214) 6026-0**
📞 (06214) 6105-81
📧 office@gutaltentann.com
🏌 18 L 6103 m CR 70 SR 125
👥 H (max 34) – booking necessary
£€ €60 (€90)
🚗 Henndorf, 16km NE of Salzburg
🏠 Jack Nicklaus
📧 www.gutaltentann.com

Gut Brandlhof G&CC
(1983)
5760 Saalfelden am Steinernen Meer,
Hohlwegen 4
☎ **(06582) 7800-555**

Lungau   (1991)
5582 St Michael, Feldnergasse 165
☎ **(06477) 7448**
📞 (06477) 7448-4
📧 gclungau@golf.at
🏌 18 L 6438 m CR 72.4 SR 121 Man
   champion
   18 L 5477 m CR 73.4 SR 128
   Women champion
   9 L 2502 m Par 56
👥 U – soft spikes only
£€ €60 (€68)
🚗 St Michael, 120km S of Salzburg
🏠 Keith Preston
📧 www.golfclub-lungau.at

Am Mondsee   (1986)
St Lorenz 1, 5310 Mondsee
☎ **(06232) 3835-0**
📞 (06232) 3835-83
📧 gcmondsee@golf.at
🏌 18 L 5.352 m Men Yellow CR 72.0
   SR 131
   18 L 6.225m Men White CR 73.2
   SR 131
   18 L 5.115 m Women Red CR 72.3
   SR 123
   18 L 5.452 m Women Black CR
   79.0 SR 128
👥 H
£€ €65: July–Aug €70 (€85 + BH)
🚗 Mondsee, 30km E of Salzburg
🏠 Max Graf Lamberg
📧 www.golfclubmondsee.at

Radstadt Tauerngolf (1991)
Römerstrasse 18, 5550 Radstadt
- ☎ (06452) 5111
- 🖶 (06452) 7336
- ✉ info@radstadtgolf.at
- ▶ 18 L 5962 m Par 71
  Men: CR 70.5 SR 127
  Women: CR 72.5 SR 127
  9 hole Par 71 course
- ᐈ U
- ££ Mon–Thur €58 (Fri–Sun €66)
- ⊕ 70km NW of Salzburg
- 🖵 www.radstadtgolf.at

Salzburg G&CC (1955)
Schloss Klessheim 21, 5071 Wals
- ☎ (0662) 850851
- 🖶 (0662) 857925
- ✉ gccsalzburg@golf.at
- ▶ 9 L 5.680 m SSS 70
  slope; yellow 126 CR 70.9
  slope; red 122 CR 70.9
- ᐈ U H–max M36 W36
- ££ €50 9 holes €30
- ⊕ 5km N of Salzburg
- ⌂ Robert Trent Jones Jr
- 🖵 www.golfclub-klessheim.com

Salzburg Romantikourse Schloss Fuschl (1865)
5322 Hof/Salzburg
- ☎ (06229) 2390
- 🖶 (06229) 2390
- ✉ fuschl@golfclub-salzburg.at
- ▶ 9 L 3384 m Par 60
  9 hole slope 98-women/101-men
- ᐈ U
- ££ 9: €25; 18: €40
- ⊕ Hof, 12km E of Salzburg
- 🖵 www.golfclub-salzburg.at

Salzkammergut (1933)
4820 Bad Ischl
- ☎ (06132) 26340
- 🖶 (06132) 26708
- ✉ office@salzkammergut-golf.at
- ▶ 18 L 5707 m Par 71
- ᐈ U
- ££ April–June, Sept–Nov, Mon–Thur
  €50 Fri–Sun €60 July–Aug W–€60
- ⊕ 6 km W of Bad Ischl, nr Strobl. 50
  km E of Salzburg
- 🖵 www.salzkammergut-golf.at

Urslautal (1991)
Schinking 81, 5760 Saalfelden
- ☎ (06584) 2000
- 🖶 (06584) 7475-10
- ✉ info@golf-urslautal.at
- ▶ 18 L 6030 m SSS 71
- ᐈ U H
- ££ €60 (€65)
- ⊕ 80km SW of Salzburg
- ⌂ Keith Preston
- 🖵 www.golf-urslautal.at

Zell am See-Kaprun (1983)
5700 Zell am See-Kaprun, Golfstr 25
- ☎ (06542) 56161
- ✉ gc.zellamsee-kaprun@telecom.at

Steiermark

Bad Gleichenberg (1984)
Am Hoffeld 3, 8344 Bad Gleichenberg
- ☎ (03159) 3717
- 🖶 (03159) 3065
- ✉ gcgleichenberg@golf.at
- ▶ 9 L 5422 m
  Men (yellow): CR 69.5 SR 129
  Women (red): CR 71.5 SR 123
- ᐈ M
- ££ €30 (€38)
- ⊕ 60km SE of Graz
- ⌂ Hauser
- 🖵 www.golf-badgleichenberg.at

Dachstein Tauern (1990)
8967 Haus/Ennstal, Oberhaus 59
- ☎ (03686) 2630
- 🖶 (03686) 2630-15
- ✉ gccschladming@golf.at
- ▶ 18 L 5910 m SSS 71
- ᐈ U
- ££ €75 (20 Juni–20 Sep €85)
- ⊕ 2km from Schladming. 100km SE of
  Salzburg
- ⌂ Bernhard Langer
- 🖵 www.schladming-golf.at

Ennstal-Weissenbach G&LC (1978)
8940 Liezen, Postfach 193
- ☎ (03612) 24821

Furstenfeld (1984)
8282 Loipersdorf, Gillersdorf 50
- ☎ (03382) 8533

Graz (1989)
8051 Graz-Thal, Windhof 137
- ☎ (0316) 572867

Gut Murstätten (1989)
8403 Lebring, Oedt 14
- ☎ (03182) 3555
- 🖶 (03182) 3688
- ✉ gcmurstaetten@golf.at
- ▶ 18 L 6395 m CR 73.1 SR 123
  9 L 6006 m CR 70.4 SR 113
- ᐈ H
- ££ €55 (€65)
- ⊕ 25km S of Graz
- ⌂ J Dudok van Heel
- 🖵 www.gcmurstaetten.at

Maria Lankowitz (1992)
Puchbacher Str 109, 8591 Maria Lankowitz
- ☎ (03144) 6970

Murhof (1963)
8130 Frohnleiten, Adriach 53
- ☎ (03126) 3010-40
- 🖶 (03126) 3000-28
- ✉ gcmurhof@golf.at
- ▶ 18 L 6326 m Par 72 CR 73.4 SR
  129
  Champions tees
- ᐈ WD–U before 1pm, M after 1pm
  (Mon–Fri) WE–M (Fri after 1pm –
  Sun)

- ££ €60 (€70)
- ⊕ Frohnleiten, 25km N of Graz.
  150km S of Vienna
- ⌂ Bernhard von Limburger
- 🖵 www.murhof.at

Murtal (1995)
Frauenbachstr 51, 8724 Spielberg
- ☎ (03512) 75213
- 🖶 (03512) 75213
- ▶ 18 L 5951 m Par 72 CR 70.6
  SR 126
- ᐈ H I
- ££ €50 (€60)
- ⊕ Knittelfeld, 80km NW of Graz, via
  Route S36
- ⌂ Jeff Howes
- 🖵 www.gcmurtal.at

Reiting G&CC (1990)
8772 Traboch, Schulweg 7
- ☎ (0663) 833308/(03847) 5008

St Lorenzen (1990)
8642 St Lorenzen, Gassing 22
- ☎ (03864) 3961
- 🖶 (03864) 3961-2
- ✉ gclorenzen@golf.at
- ▶ 9 L 5374 m Par 70 SSS 70
- ᐈ U
- ££ €33 (€40)
- ⊕ 60km N of Graz, nr Kapfenberg
- ⌂ Manfred Flasch
- 🖵 www.gclorenzen.at

Schloss Frauenthal (1988)
8530 Deutschlandsberg, Ulrichsberg 7
- ☎ (03462) 5717
- 🖶 (03462) 5717-5
- ✉ office@gcfrauenthal.at
- ▶ 18 L 5447 m SSS 70
- ᐈ U H
- ££ Mon–Thur am €50 Fri pm–Sat–Sun
  €60 Seniors half price Mon/Tue
- ⊕ 30km SW of Graz
- ⌂ Stephan Breisach
- 🖵 www.gcfrauenthal.at

Schloss Pichlarn (1972)
8952 Irdning/Ennstal, Gatschen 28
- ☎ (03682) 22841-540

Vienna & East

Adamstal (1994)
Gaupmannsgraben 21, 3172 Ramsal
- ☎ (02764) 3500
- 🖶 (02764) 3500-15
- ▶ 27 L 5915 m CR 73 SR 136
- ᐈ U
- ££ €50 Mon–Thur; €65 Fri–Sun
- ⊕ 65km SW of Vienna
- ⌂ Jeff Howes
- 🖵 www.adamstal.at

Bad Tatzmannsdorf Reiters G&CC (1991)
Am Golfplatz 2, 7431 Bad Tatzmannsdorf
- ☎ (0043) 3353 8282-0

☖ (0043) 3353 8282-1735
✉ golfclub@burgenlandresort.at
🏳 18 L 6180m Par 73 CR 72.7 SR 129
9 L 3660 m Par 60 CR 60.2 SR 103
👥 U H
££ 9: €30 (€35) 18: €45 (€55)
🚗 120km SE of Vienna
🏠 Rossknecht/Erhardt
🖃 www.reitersburgenlandresort.at

Brunn G&CC (1988)
2345 Brunn/Gebirge, Rennweg 50
☎ (02236) 33711
☖ (02236) 33863
✉ club@gccbrunn.at
🏳 18 L 5742 m Par 70 CR 70 SR 121
👥 H – soft spikes only
££ €55 (€70)
🚗 10km S of Vienna
🏠 G Hauser
🖃 www.gccbrunn.at

Colony Club Gutenhof
(1988)
2325 Himberg, Gutenhof
☎ (02235) 87055-0
✉ club@colonygolf.com

Eldorado Bucklige Welt
(1990)
Golfplatz 1, 2871 Zöbern
☎ (02642) 8451

Enzesfeld (1970)
2551 Enzesfeld
☎ (02256) 81272
☖ (02256) 81272-4
✉ office@gcenzesfeld.at
🏳 18 L 6061 m Par 72 CR 72.3 SR 129
👥 H
££ €54 (€72)
🚗 32km S of Vienna. A2 Junction 29 (Leobersdorf)
🏠 Cdr John D Harris
🖃 www.gcenzesfeld.at

Föhrenwald (1968)
2700 Wiener Neustadt, Postfach 105
☎ (02622) 29171
☖ (02622) 29171-4
✉ office@gcf.at
🏳 18 L 6317 m SSS 72
👥 H
££ €55 (€85)
🚗 5 km S of Wiener Neustadt on Route B54
🏠 Jeff Howes
🖃 www.gcf.at

Fontana (1996)
Fontana Allee 1, 2522 Oberwaltersdorf
☎ (02253) 606401
✉ gcfontana@mide.co.at

Hainburg/Donau (1977)
2410 Hainburg, Auf der Heide 762
☎ (02165) 62628
☖ (02165) 626283
✉ gchainburg@golf.at
🏳 18 L 6064 m SSS 72

👥 H
££ €50 (€70)
🚗 50km E of Vienna; 19km W of Bratislava
🏠 G Hauser
🖃 www.golfclub-hainburg.at

Lengenfeld (1995)
Am Golfplatz 1, 3552 Lengenfeld
☎ (02719) 8710

Neusiedlersee-Donnerskirchen (1988)
7082 Donnerskirchen
☎ (02683) 8171

Schloss Ebreichsdorf (1988)
2483 Ebreichsdorf, Schlossallee 1
☎ (02254)73888
☖ (02254) 73888-13
✉ office@gcebreichsdorf.at
🏳 18 L 6161 m Par 72 SSS 73
👥 WD&WE H–36 on request
££ Mon–Thur €55, Fri €60 (€80)
🚗 28km S of Vienna
🏠 Keith Preston
🖃 www.gcebreichsdorf.at

Schloss Schönborn (1987)
2013 Schönborn 4
☎ (02267) 2863/2879
✉ golfclub@gcschoenborn.com

Schönfeld (1989)
A-2291 Schönfeld, Am Golfplatz 1
☎ +43 (02213) 2063
☖ +43 (02213) 20631
✉ gcschoenfeld@golf.at
🏳 18 L 6089 m Par 72
CR 71.9 SR 123 (white)
CR 70.7 SR 121 (yellow)
CR 74.1 SR 127 (black)
CR 72.4 SR 124 (red)
9 hole Par 3 course
👥 H
££ 9: €28 (€40); 18: €45 (€70)
🚗 35km E of Vienna
🏠 G Hauser
🖃 www.golf.at /clubdetail.asp?clubnr=315

Semmering (1926)
2680 Semmering
☎ (02664) 8154

Golfclub Spillern (1993)
Wiesenerstrasse 100, A-2104 Spillern
☎ +43 (0)22 668 1211
☖ +43 (0)22 668 121120
✉ gcspillern.at
🏳 18 + 3 Par 72
White CR 70.8 SR 118
Yellow CR 68.6 SR 121
Blue CR 68.3 SR 118
Black CR 72.2 SR 118
Red CR 70.8 SR 115
Orange CR 68.2 SR 113
👥 U (member of reg club with known course)
££ €47 (€65)
🚗 20km from downtown Vienna

🏠 Haluschan
🖃 www.gcspillern.at

Thayatal Drosendorf (1994)
Autendorf 18, 2095 Drosendorf
☎ (02915) 62625

Wien (1901)
1020 Wien, Freudenau 65a
☎ (01) 728 9564 (Clubhouse)
(01) 728 9564-13 (Caddymaster)
☖ (01) 728 9564-20
✉ gcwien@golf.at
🏳 18 L 5866 m Par 70
White L 5866 m Men CR 70.3 SR 119
Yellow L 5695 m Men CR 69.3 SR 117
Ladies CR 75.3 SR 128
Blue L 5505 m Men CR 68.3 SR 115
Ladies CR 74.2 SR 125
👥 WE–NA
££ €75
🚗 10 mins SE of Vienna
🖃 www.gcwien.at

Wien-Süssenbrunn (1995)
Weingartenallee 22, 1220 Wien
☎ (01) 256 8282
☖ (01) 246 8282 -44
✉ golf@sportparkwien.at
🏳 18 L 6130 m SSS 72
👥 H
££ €50 (€72)
🚗 15km NE of Vienna City Centre
🏠 Rossknecht/Erhardt
🖃 www.sportparkwien.at

Wienerwald (1981)
1130 Wien, Altgasse 27
☎ (0222) 877 3111 (Sec)

Vorarlberg

Bludenz-Braz (1996)
Oberradin 60, 6751 Braz bei Bludenz
☎ (05552) 33503
☖ (05552) 33503-3
✉ gcbraz@golf.at
🏳 18 L 5121 m Par 68 CR 67.7 SR 119
👥 H U
££ D–€53 (€63)
🚗 5km E of Bludenz
🏠 Kurt Rossknecht
🖃 www.gc-bludenz-braz.at

Bregenzerwald (1997)
Unterlitten 3a, 6943 Riefensberg
☎ (05513) 8400
☖ (05513) 8400-4
✉ office@golf-bregenzerwald.com
🏳 18 L 5702 m Par 71
👥 U I
££ €55 (€59)
🚗 32km E of Bregenz. 150km E of Zürich
🏠 Kurt Rossknecht
🖃 www.golf-bregenzerwald.com

Montafon (1992)
6774 Tschagguns, Zelfenstrasse 110
☎ **(05556) 77011**
✉ info@golfclub-montafon.at

Belgium

Antwerp Region

Bossenstein (1989)
Moor 16, Bossenstein Kasteel, 2520 Broechem
☎ **(03) 485 64 46**
✉ bossenstein.shop@skynet.be

Cleydael G&CC (1988)
Groenenhoek 7-9, 2630 Aartselaar
☎ **(03) 870 56 80**
🖬 (03) 887 14 75
✉ info@cleydael.be
🏌 18 L 6059 m SSS 72
👥 H WE–NA before 2pm
££ €55 (€70)
⛳ 8km S of Antwerp. 40km N of Brussels
🏠 Paul Rolin
▤ www.cleydael.be

Kempense (1986)
Kiezelweg 78, 2400 Mol-Rauw
☎ 00 32 (0)14 81 46 41
(Clubhouse)
00 32 (0)14 81 62 34
(start res.)
🖬 00 32 (0)14 81 62 78
✉ kempense@pandora.be
🏌 18 L 5904 m Par 72
👥 U H–36 WD WE
££ €45 (€55)
⛳ 60km N of Antwerp
🏠 Marc de Keyser
▤ www.golf.be/kempense

Lilse G&CC (1988)
Haarlebeek 3, 2275 Lille
☎ **(014) 55 19 30**
🖬 (014) 55 19 31
✉ info@lilsegolfclub.com
🏌 9 holes Par 66
👥 U
££ €25 (€35)
⛳ Lille, 10km SW of Turnhout, nr E7. 25km E of Antwerp
▤ www.lilsegolfclub.com

Nuclea Mol (1984)
Goorstraat, 2400 Mol
☎ **+32 14 37 0915**
✉ andre.verbruggen2@telenet.be
🏌 9 L 1756 m Par 31
👥 H
££ €20 (€30)
⛳ Mol, 60km E of Antwerp
🏠 Bruno Steensels
▤ www.golf.be/nucleamol

Rinkven G&CC (1980)
Sint Jobsteenweg 120, 2970 Schilde
☎ **(03) 380 12 85**
🖬 (03) 384 29 33
✉ info@rinkven.be
🏌 36 hole course
👥 H–phone before visit
££ €65 (€85)
⛳ 17 km NE of Antwerp, off E19
🏠 Paul Rolin
▤ www.rinkven.be

Royal Antwerp (1888)
Georges Capiaulei 2, 2950 Kapellen
☎ **(03) 666 84 56**
🖬 (03) 666 44 37
✉ info@ragc.be
🏌 18 L 6200 m Par 73 CR 72.5 SR 125
9 L 2655 m Par 34 CR 68.4 SR 120
👥 WD–H (phone first)
££ €75–€90
⛳ Kapellen, 20km N of Antwerp
🏠 Willie Park/T Simpson
▤ www.ragc.be

Steenhoven (1985)
Steenhoven 89, 2400 Postel-Mol
☎ **(014) 37 36 61**
🖬 (014) 37 36 62
✉ info@steenhoven.be
🏌 18 L 5950 m SSS 71
👥 H–booking necessary
££ €55 (€65)
⛳ 30 mins W of Antwerp
🏠 Pierre de Broqueville
▤ www.steenhoven.be

Ternesse G&CC (1976)
Uilenbaan 15, 2160 Wommelgem
☎ **(03) 355 14 30**
🖬 (03) 355 14 35
✉ info@ternessegolf.be
🏌 18 L 5847 m Par 71
9 L 1981 m Par 33
👥 H–30
££ €60 (€80)
⛳ 5km E of Antwerp on E313
🏠 HJ Baker
▤ www.ternessegolf.be

Ardennes & South

Andenne (1988)
Ferme du Moulin 52, Stud, 5300 Andenne
☎ **(085) 84 34 04**

Château Royal d'Ardenne
Tour Léopold, Ardenne 6, 5560 Houyet
☎ **(082) 66 62 28**

Falnuée (1987)
Rue E Pirson 55, 5032 Mazy
☎ **(081) 63 30 90**
🖬 (081) 63 21 41
✉ info@falnuee.be
🏌 18 L 5838 m SSS 72
👥 H
££ €40 (€56)
⛳ 18km NW of Namur. Mons-Liège highway Junction 13

🏠 J Jottrand
▤ www.falnuee.be

Five Nations C C (1990)
Ferme du Grand Scley, 5372 Méan (Havelange)
☎ **(086) 32 32 32**

Mont Garni (1989)
Rue du Mont Garni 3, 7331 Saint Ghislain
☎ **(065) 62 27 19**
✉ secretariat@golfmontgarni.de

Rougemont
Chemin du Beau Vallon 45, 5170 Profondeville
☎ **(081) 41 14 18**

Royal GC du Hainaut (1933)
Rue de la Verrerie 2, 7050 Erbisoeul
☎ **(065) 22 96 10 (Clubhouse)**
(065) 22 02 00 (Sec)
🖬 (065) 22 02 09
✉ info@golfhainaut.be
🏌 Les Bruyeres 9 L 3077 m Par 36
Le Quesnoy 9 L 2897 m Par 36
Les Etangs 9 L 3158 m Par 36
👥 U H (max 36)
££ €55 (€70)
⛳ 6km NW of Mons towards Ath on N56. Paris-Brussels motorway Junction 23
🏠 Martin Hawtree
▤ www.golfhainaut.be

Brussels & Brabant

Bercuit (1965)
Les Gottes 3, 1390 Grez-Doiceau
☎ **(010) 84 15 01**
🖬 (010) 84 55 95
✉ info@golfdubercuit.be
🏌 18 L 5979 m Par 72 SR 131 Back Tee Men
👥 U H
££ €70 €85–Fri (€100)
⛳ Grez-Doiceau, 27km SE of Brussels. Brussels-Namur highway exit 8
🏠 Robert Trent Jones Sr
▤ www.golfdubercuit.be

Brabantse Golf (1982)
Steenwagenstraat 11, 1820 Melsbroek
☎ **(02) 751 82 05**
🖬 (02) 751 84 25
✉ secretariaat@brabantsegolf.be
🏌 18 L 5829 m Par 72 CR 70 SR 124
👥 H
££ €40 (€55)
⛳ 10km NE of Brussels, nr airport
🏠 Philippe Mallaerts
▤ www.brabantsegolf.be

La Bruyère (1988)
Rue Jumerée 1, 1495 Sart-Dames-Avelines
☎ **(071) 87 72 67**
✉ info@golflabruyere.be

Golf du Château de la Bawette   (1988)
Chaussée du Chateau de la Bawette 5, 1300 Wavre
☎ (010) 22 33 32
🖳 (010) 22 90 04
📧 info@labawette.com
🏌 Parc 18 L 6076 m SSS 72
Champs 9 L 2146 m SSS 63
👤 H–booking required
££ Parc €45 (€70) Champs €40 (€50)
🚗 1km N of Wavre. 15km S of Brussels. E411 Exit 5
🏠 Tom Macauley
🖥 www.labawette.com

Château de la Tournette
Chemin de Baudemont 21, 1400 Nivelles
☎ (067) 89 42 66
🖳 (067) 21 95 17
📧 info@tournette.com
🏌 US course: 18 L 6198 m Par 72
UK course: 18 L 6103 m Par 71
👤 H WE–NA after 10am SOC WD–U
££ Mon–Thur €55 (Fri–Sun €85)
🚗 29km S of Brussels (E19)
🏠 US course: Peter Alliss and Clive Clark, English course: Hawtree
🖥 www.tournette.com

L'Empereur   (1989)
Rue Emile François No.31, 1474 Ways (Genappe)
☎ (067) 77 15 71
🖳 (067) 77 18 33
📧 info@golfempereur.com
🏌 Empereur: 18 L 6201 m Par 72
La Hutte: 9 L 1650 m Par 31
👤 U H
££ 9: €28 (€39) 18: €44 (€79)
🚗 25km S of Brussels
🏠 Marcel Vercruyce
🖥 www.golfempereur.com

Hulencourt   (1989)
Bruyère d'Hulencourt 15, 1472 Vieux Genappe
☎ (067) 79 40 40
🖳 (067) 79 40 48
📧 info@golfhulencourt.be
🏌 18 L 6215 m Par 72
9 hole Par 3 course
👤 U SOC WD/WE H–max 35
££ €70 (€100)
🚗 30km SE of Brussels
🏠 JM Rossi
🖥 www.golfhulencourt.be

Kampenhout   (1989)
Wildersedreef 56, 1910 Kampenhout
☎ (016) 65 12 16
🖳 (016) 65 16 80
📧 golfclubkampenhout@skynet.be
🏌 18 L 6142 m SSS 72
👤 H
££ €40 (€55) – 2008
🚗 15km NE of Brussels (E19)
🏠 R de Vooght
🖥 www.golfclubkampenhout.be

Keerbergen   (1968)
Vlieghavelaan 50, 3140 Keerbergen
☎ (015) 22 68 78
🖳 (015) 23 57 37
📧 keerbergen.golfclub@skynet.be
🏌 18 L 5513 m SSS 70
Men: CR 69.6 SR 122
Ladies: CR 70.9 SR 125
👤 H
££ €50 (€70)
🚗 30km NE of Brussels
🏠 Frank Pennink
🖥 www.golfkeerbergen.be

Louvain-la-Neuve
Rue A Hardy 68, 1348 Louvain-la-Neuve
☎ (010) 45 05 15

Overijse   (1986)
Gemslaan 55, 3090 Overijse
☎ (02) 687 50 30
📧 ogc@golf-overijse.be

Pierpont   (1992)
1 Grand Pierpont, 6210 Frasnes-lez-Gosselies
☎ (071) 8808 30
🖳 (071) 85 15 43
📧 info@pierpont.be
🏌 18 L 6232 m Par 72
5 hole Par 3 course
👤 U
££ €38 (€65)
🚗 30km S of Brussels via N5/15km S of Waterloo
🏠 J Dudok van Heel
🖥 www.pierpont.be

Rigenée   (1981)
Rue de Châtelet 62, 1495 Villers-la-Ville
☎ (071) 87 77 65
🖳 (071) 87 77 83
📧 golf@rigenee.be
🏌 18 L 6360 m Par 73 CR 74.1 SR 128
👤 H 34 WD WE
££ €40 (€65)
🚗 35km S of Brussels towards Charleroi
🏠 Rolin/Descampe
🖥 www.rigenee.be

Royal Amicale Anderlecht   (1987)
Rue Schollestraat 1, 1070 Brussels
☎ (02) 521 16 87
📧 info@golf-anderlecht.com

Royal Golf Club de Belgique   (1906)
Château de Ravenstein, 3080 Tervuren
☎ +32 (0) 2 767 58 01
🖳 +32 (0) 2 767 28 41
📧 info@rgcb.be
🏌 18 L 6041 m SSS 72
9 L 1937 m Par 32
👤 WD–H–max 20(men) 24(ladies)–phone first. Course closed Mon WE–only in July and Aug

££ 9: €60; 18: €100
🚗 Tervuren, 10km E of Brussels
🏠 Simpson
🖥 www.rgcb.be

Royal Waterloo Golf Club   (1923)
Vieux Chemin de Wavre 50, 1380 Lasne
☎ (00) 322 633 1850
🖳 (00) 322 633 2866
📧 infos@golfwaterloo.be
🏌 La Marache: 18 L 6371 m Par 72
Le Lion: 18 L 6407 m Par 72
Le Bois-Heros: 9 L 2160 m Par 33
👤 WD–H
££ Marache €100 Lion €90
🚗 22km SE of Brussels
🏠 Hawtree
🖥 www.rwgc.be

Sept Fontaines   (1987)
1021, Chaussée d'Alsemberg, 1420 Braine L'Alleud
☎ (02) 353 02 46/353 03 46
🖳 (02) 354 68 75
📧 info@golf7fontaines.be
🏌 18 L 6000 m Par 72 SSS 72
18 L 4874 m Par 69 SSS 67
9 hole short course
👤 U H
££ Mon–Thur €55 Fri €65 (+ hols €85)
🚗 Braine L'Alleud, 15km S of Brussels. E40 exit 29 direction Huizingen
🏠 Rossi
🖥 www.golf7fontaines.be

Winge G&CC   (1988)
Leuvensesteenweg 252, 3390 Sint Joris Winge
☎ (016) 63 40 53
🖳 (016) 63 21 40
📧 winge@golf.be
🏌 18 L 6049 m Par 72 CR 72.3
👤 H
££ €50 (€70)
🚗 35km E of Brussels via Leuven
🏠 P Townsend
🖥 www.golf.be/winge

East

Avernas
Route de Grand Hallet 19A, 4280 Hannut
☎ (019) 51 30 66
🖳 (019) 51 53 43
📧 info@golfavernas.be
🏌 9 L 2674 m SSS 68
Men: CR 68.6 SR 122
Women: CR 68.3 SR 116
👤 H
££ €20 (€28)
🚗 40km W of Liège. Brussels 50km
🏠 Hawtree/Cappart
🖥 www.golfavernas.be

Durbuy   (1991)
Route d'Oppagne 34, 6940 Barvaux-su-Ourthe

☎ (086) 21 44 54
⚑ 18 L 5963 m SSS 72
9 hole Par 3 course
👥 U H
££ €50 (€60)
🚗 45km S of Liège
⌂ Martin Hawtree

Flanders Nippon Hasselt
(1988)
Vissenbroekstraat 15, 3500 Hasselt
☎ (011) 26 34 82
🖳 (011) 26 34 83
✉ flanders.nippon.golf@pandora.be
⚑ 18 L 5966 m SSS 72
9 L 1883 m SSS 33
👥 U H (for 18 only)
££ €45 (€55)
🚗 5km E of Hasselt. 85km E of
Brussels
⌂ Rolin/Wirtz
🖥 www.flandersnippongolf.be

Henri-Chapelle   (1988)
Rue du Vivier 3, B-4841 Henri-Chapelle
☎ (087) 88 19 91
✉ info@golfhenrichapelle.be

International Gomze   (1986)
Sur Counachamps 8, 4140
Gomze Andoumont
☎ (04) 360 92 07
🖳 (04) 360 92 06
✉ gomzegolf@skynet.be
⚑ 18 L 5918 m SSS 72
👥 U H
££ On application
🚗 15km S of Liège. Spa 20km
⌂ Paul Rolin

Limburg G&CC   (1966)
Golfstraat 1, 3530 Houthalen
☎ (089) 38 35 43
🖳 (089) 84 12 08
✉ limburggolf@skynet.be
⚑ 18 L 6049 m SSS 72
👥 WD WE H
££ €66 (€80)
🚗 Houthalen, 15km N of Hasselt
⌂ Hawtree
🖥 www.lgcc.lc

Royal GC du Sart Tilman
(1939)
Route du Condroz 541, 4031 Liège
☎ (041) 336 20 21
🖳 (041) 337 20 26
✉ secretariat|@rgcst.be
⚑ 18 L 6002 m SSS 72
👥 H–booking required
££ €50 (€65)
🚗 10km S of Liège on Route 620
(N35), towards Marche
⌂ T Simpson
🖥 www.rgcst.be

Royal Golf des Fagnes
(1930)
1 Ave de l'Hippodrome, 4900 Spa
☎ (087) 79 30 30

Spiegelven GC Genk   (1988)
Wiemesmeerstraat 109, 3600 Genk
☎ (0032) 893 59616
🖳 (0032) 893 64184
✉ info@spiegelven.be
⚑ Men: 18 L 6098 m SSS 72 SR 133
Women: 18 L 5293 m SSS 72
SR 128
9 hole Par 3 course
👥 H
££ €50 (€60)
🚗 Genk, 18km E of Hasselt. 20km N
of Maastricht
⌂ Ron Kirby
🖥 www.spiegelven.be

West & Oost Vlaanderen

Damme G&CC   (1987)
Doornstraat 16, 8340 Damme-Sijsele
☎ (050) 35 35 72
🖳 (050) 35 89 25
✉ info@dammegolf.be
⚑ 18 L 6046 m SSS 72
9 hole short course
👥 H 35
££ €70 (€75)
🚗 7km E of Bruges. Knokke 15km
⌂ J Dudok van Heel
🖥 www.dammegolf.be

Oudenaarde G&CC   (1975)
Kasteel Petegem, Kortrykstraat 52,
9790 Wortegem-Petegem
☎ (055) 33 41 61
🖳 (055) 31 98 49
✉ oudenaarde@golf.be
⚑ Kasteel 18 L 5910 m Par 71
Anker 18 L 6235 m Par 72
👥 H
££ €60 (€75)
🚗 4 km SW of Oudenaarde
⌂ HJ Baker
🖥 www.golfoudenaarde.be

De Palingbeek   (1991)
Eekhofstraat 14, 8902 Hollebeke-Ieper
☎ (057) 20 04 36
🖳 (057) 21 89 58
✉ golfpalingbeek@skynet.be
⚑ 18 L 6165 m Par 72
👥 H
££ €50 (€60)
🚗 5km SE of Ieper, nr Hollebeke
⌂ HJ Baker
🖥 www.golfpalingbeek.be

Royal Latem   (1909)
9830 St Martens-Latem
☎ (092) 82 54 11
🖳 (092) 82 90 19
✉ latem.golf@telnet.be
⚑ 18 L 5767 m Par 72 SR 123
👥 H
££ €60 (€70)
🚗 10 km SW of Ghent on route N43
Ghent-Deinze
🖥 www.golf.be/latem

Royal Ostend   (1903)
Koninklijke Baan 2, 8420 De Haan
☎ (059) 23 32 83

Royal Zoute   (1899)
Caddiespad 14, 8300 Knokke-le-Zoute
☎ (050) 60 16 17 (Clubhouse)
   (050) 60 37 81 (Starter)
🖳 (050) 62 30 29
✉ golf@zoute.be
⚑ No 1 18 L 6172 m Par 72
No 2 18 L 3607 m Par 64
👥 H No 1 course–max 20
WE–restricted
££ €95 Par 72; €55 Par 64
🚗 Knokke-Heist
⌂ HS Colt
🖥 www.zoute.be

Waregem   (1988)
Bergstraat 41, 8790 Waregem
☎ (056) 60 88 08
🖳 (056) 62 18 23
✉ waregem@golf.be
⚑ 18 L 6038 m SSS 72
👥 H Sun–NA before 2 p.m.
££ €50 (€60)
🚗 30km SW of Ghent (E17)
⌂ Paul Rolin
🖥 www.golf.be/waregem

Czech Republic

Karlovy Vary   (1904)
Prazska 125, PO Box 67, 360 01
Karlovy Vary
☎ (017) 333 1001-2

Lísnice   (1928)
252 10 Mnísek pod Brdy
☎ (0318) 599 151

Mariánské Lázně   (1905)
PO Box 47, 353 01 Mariánské Lázně
☎ +420 354 604300
🖳 +420 354 625195
✉ office@golfml.cz
⚑ 18 L 6195 m SSS 72
👥 H
££ WE: D–1600czk (€60) WE:
D–1800czk (€70)
🚗 2km NE of Mariánské Lázně,
opposite Parkhotel Golf
🖥 www.golfml.cz

Park GC Ostrava   (1968)
Dolni 412, 747 15 Silherovice
☎ (+420) 595 054 144
✉ office@golf-ostrava.cz

Podebrady   (1964)
Na Zalesi 530, 29080 Podebrady
☎ (0324) 610928

Semily (1970)
Bavlnarska 521, 513 01 Semily
☎ **(0431) 622443/624428**

Denmark

Bornholm Island

Bornholm (1972)
Plantagevej 3B, 3700 Rønne
☎ **56 95 68 54**
⌨ info@bornholmsgolfklub.dk

Nexø
Dueodde Golfbane, Strandmarksvejen 14, 3730 Nexø
☎ **56 48 89 87**
⌨ 56 48 89 69
⌨ ngk@dueodde-golf.dk
╠ 18 L 5470 m Par 69 CR 70.1 SR 123
👥 H
££ 250kr (250kr)
⚘ 12km S of Nexø, nr Dueodde beach
⌂ Frederik Dreyer
🖥 www.dueodde-golf.dk

Nordbornholm-Rø (1987)
Spellingevej 3, Rø, 3760 Gudhjem
☎ **56 48 40 50**
⌨ 56 48 40 52
⌨ mail@roegolfbane.dk
╠ 18 L 5369 m SSS 71 (Old Course)
18 L 6469 m SSS 72 (New Course)
👥 WD–U WE–H
££ 325kr
⚘ Rø, 8km W of Gudhjem. 22km NE of Rønne
⌂ Anders Amilon
🖥 www.roegolfbane.dk

Funen

Faaborg (1989)
Dalkildegards Allee 1, 5600 Faaborg
☎ **62 61 77 43**

Lillebaelt (1990)
O.Hougvej 130, 5500 Middelfart
☎ **64 41 80 11**
⌨ gkl@posf10.tele.dk

Odense (1927)
Hestehaven 200, 5220 Odense SØ
☎ **65 95 90 00**

Proark Golf Odense Eventyr (1993)
Falen 227, 5250 Odense SV
☎ **6565 2020**
⌨ 6562 2021
⌨ pgoe@proarkgolf.dk
╠ 18 hole course Par 72
9 hole course + 9 holes Pay & Play

👥 H
££ 370kr (390kr)
⚘ 5km SW of Odense
⌂ Michael Møller
🖥 www.proarkgolf.dk

SCT Knuds (1954)
Slipshavnsvej 16, 5800 Nyborg
☎ **65 31 12 12**
⌨ 65 30 28 04
⌨ mail@sct-knuds.dk
╠ 18 L 5792 m CR 71.1
👥 H
££ 300kr (350kr) (2D–560kr)
⚘ 3km SE of Nyborg
⌂ Cotton/Dreyer
🖥 www.sct-knuds.dk

Svendborg (1970)
Tordensgaardevej 5, Sørup, 5700 Svendborg
☎ **62 22 40 77**
⌨ 62 20 29 77
⌨ info@svendborg-golf.dk
╠ 9 L 2034 m CR 61.9 SR 106
18 L 5781 m CR 72.0 SR 138
👥 H–max 36 WE 42 WD
££ D–320kr
⚘ 4km NW of Svendborg
⌂ Frederik Dreyer/Henrick J Jacobsen
🖥 www.svendborg-golf.dk

Vestfyns (1974)
Rønnemosegård, Krengerupvej 27, 5620 Glamsbjerg
☎ **63 72 19 20**
⌨ 63 72 19 26
⌨ vestfyn@golfonline.dk
╠ 18 L 5629 m Par 72 CR 70.6
👥 H
££ 300kr (350kr)
⚘ Glamsbjerg, 25km SW of Odense
🖥 www.vestfynsgolfklub.dk

Jutland

Aalborg (1908)
Jaegersprisvej 35, Restrup Enge, 9000 Aalborg
☎ **98 34 14 76**
⌨ 98 34 15 84
⌨ mail@aalborggolfklub.dk
╠ 27 Holes (9 red/9 blue/9 yellow)
Par 71 Red/Blue 18 L 6149 m
Par 70 Blue/Yellow 18 L 5869 m
Par 71 Yellow/Red 18 L 6190 m
👥 H (max 36)
££ D–300kr
⚘ 7 km SW of Aalborg
⌂ R Harris
🖥 www.aalborgolfklub.dk

Aarhus (1931)
Ny Moesgaardvej 50, 8270 Hojbjerg
☎ **86 27 63 22**
⌨ 86 27 63 21
⌨ aarhusgolf@mail.dk
╠ 18 L 5725 m Par 72 CR 71
👥 H
££ €70 (€50)

⚘ 6km S of Aarhus, Route 451
⌂ Brian Huggett
🖥 www.aarhusgolf.dk

Blokhus Golf Klub (1993)
Hunetorpvej 115, Box 37, 9492 Blokhus
☎ **98 20 95 00**
⌨ 98 20 95 01
⌨ info@blokhusgolfklub.dk
╠ 18 L 5584 m CR 70.5
👥 U H
££ 320kr (390kr)
⚘ 35km NW of Aalborg
⌂ Frederik Dreyer
🖥 www.blokhusgolf.dk

Breinholtgård (1992)
Koksspangvej 17-19, 6710 Esbjerg V
☎ **75 11 57 00**

Brønderslev (1971)
PO Box 94, 9700 Brønderslev
☎ **98 82 32 81**

Brundtlandbanen (2000)
Brundtland Allé 1-3, 6520 Toftlund
☎ **73 83 16 00**
⌨ 73 83 16 19
⌨ info@brundtland.dk
╠ 18 L 5890 m Par 73
9 L 1255 m Par 29
👥 H (+W 9–hole course)
££ 250kr (300kr)
⚘ Toftlund, central Jutland
⌂ Henrik Jacobsen
🖥 www.brundtland.dk

Dejbjerg (1966)
Letagervej 1, Dejbjerg, 6900 Skjern
☎ **97 35 00 09**
⌨ 96 80 11 18
⌨ kontor@dejbjerggk.dk
╠ 18 L 5794 m Par 72
CR 71.1 SR 132 (men)
CR 72.2 SR 125 (women)
👥 U
££ D–300kr (D–300kr)
⚘ 6km N of Skjern. 25km from W coast on Skjern-Ringkøbing road (Route 28)
⌂ Schnack/Dreyer/Jacobsen
🖥 www.dejbjerggk.dk

Ebeltoft (1966)
Galgebakken 14, 8400 Ebeltoft
☎ **87 59 6000**
⌨ post@ebeltoft-golfclub.dk
╠ 18 L 4980 m Par 68 CR 67.5
👥 U
££ D–250kr
⚘ 1km N of Ebeltoft
⌂ Frederik Dreyer

Esbjerg (1921)
Sønderhedevej 11, Marbaek, 6710 Esbjerg
☎ **75 26 92 19**
⌨ 75 26 94 19
⌨ kontor@esbjerggolfklub.dk
╠ 18 L 6347 m Par 71 CR 74.1
18 L 5960 m Par 72 CR 72.4
👥 U H

£€ 350kr/€50 (400kr/€60)
🚗 15km N of Esbjerg
🏠 Frederik Dreyer
🖳 www.egk.dk

Fanø Golf Links   (1901)
Golfvejen 5, 6720 Fanø
☎ 76 66 00 77
🖥 76 66 00 44
📧 golf@fanoe-golf-links.dk
🏌 18 L 5080 m CR 68.7
🕴 H
£€ D–240kr (D–290kr)
🚗 W side of Fanø Island. Ferry from
     Esbjerg 15 mins; 3 km
🖳 www.fanoe-golf-links.dk

Grenaa   (1981)
Vestermarken 1, DK-8500 Grenaa
☎ +45 863 27929
🖥 +45 863 09654
📧 info@grenaagolfklub.dk
🏌 18 L 5782 m Par 70
🕴 U
£€ D–250kr (250kr)
🚗 1km W of Grenaa. 60km NE of
     Aarhus
🏠 Dreyer/Sommer
🖳 www.grenaagolfklub.dk

Gyttegård   (1974)
Billundvej 43, 7250 Hejnsvig
☎ +45 75 33 63 82
🖥 +45 75 33 68 20
📧 info@gyttegaardgolfklub.dk
🏌 18 L 5510 m Par 70 CR 69.0
     SR 122
🕴 H
£€ 250kr (300kr)
🚗 3km NE of Hejnsvig. 5km SW of
     Billund
🏠 Amilon/Bossen
🖳 www.gyttegaardgolfklub.dk

Haderslev   (1971)
Viggo Carstensvej 7, 6100 Haderslev
☎ 74 52 83 01

Han Herreds
Starkaervej 20, 9690 Fjerritslev
☎ 98 21 26 66 / 98 21 26 78

Henne   (1989)
Hennebysvej 30, 6854 Henne
☎ 75 25 56 10
🖥 75 25 56 30
📧 post@hennegolfklub.dk
🏌 18 L 5954 m Par 71 CR 71.2
     SR 121
🕴 U H
£€ 250kr
🚗 19km NW of Varde. 35km N of
     Esbjerg
🏠 Frederik Dreyer
🖳 www.hennegolfklub.dk

Herning   (1964)
Golfvej 2, 7400 Herning
☎ 97 21 00 33
📧 info@herninggolfklub.dk

Himmerland G&CC   (1979)
Centervej 1, Gatten, 9640 Farsö
☎ 96 49 61 00
📧 hgcc@himmerlandgolf.dk

Hirtshals   (1990)
Kjulvej 10, PO Box 51, 9850 Hirtshals
☎ 98 94 94 08

Hjarbaek Fjord   (1992)
Lynderup, 8832 Skals
☎ 86 69 62 88

Hjorring   (1985)
Vinstrupvej 30, 9800 Hjorring
☎ 98 91 18 28
🖥 98 90 31 00
📧 info@hjoerringgolf.dk
🏌 36 (4 x 9)
     Booking start time
     www.hjoerringgolf.dk
🕴 H
£€ 250kr (300kr)
🚗 N of Hjorring. 50km N of Aalborg
🏠 Erik Schnack and Michael Traadsdal
     Møller
🖳 www.hjoerringgolf.dk

Holmsland Klit
Klevevej 19, Søndervig, 6950 Ringkøbing
☎ 97 33 88 00

Holstebro Golf Klub   (1970)
Råsted, 7570 Vemb
☎ 97 48 51 55
🖥 97 48 51 11
📧 post@holstebro-golfklub.dk
🏌 18 L 5955 m CR 71.9 SR 131
     9 L 2549 m
🕴 H
£€ 300kr (400kr)
🚗 13km W of Holstebro (Route 16)
🏠 Erik Schnack, Robert Trent Jones Jr
     (2004)
🖳 www.holstebro-golfklub.dk

Horsens   (1972)
Silkeborgvej 44, 8700 Horsens
☎ 75 61 51 51

Hvide Klit   (1972)
Hvideklitvej 28, 9982 Aalbaek
☎ 98 48 90 21
🖥 98 48 91 12
📧 info@hvideklit.dk
🏌 18 L 5875 m SSS 72
🕴 H
£€ 300kr (350kr)
🚗 3km N of Aalbaek. 24km N of
     Frederikshavn
🏠 Anders Amilon
🖳 www.hvideklit.dk

Juelsminde   (1973)
Bobroholtvej 11a, 7130 Juelsminde
☎ 75 69 34 92
🖥 75 69 46 11
📧 golf@juelsmindegolf.dk
🏌 18 L 5680 m SSS 72
🕴 U H H'cap 41
£€ 300kr (2008/2009)

🚗 20 km S of Horsens on coast. 2km
     N of Juelsminde
🏠 Mehlsen/Jacobsen/Møller
🖳 www.juelsmindegolf.dk

Kaj Lykke   (1988)
Kirkebrovej 5, 6740 Bramming
☎ 75 10 22 46
🖥 75 10 26 68
📧 post@kaj-lykke-golfklub.dk
🏌 18 L 5975 m CR 72.3 SR 131
     Par 3 course
🕴 H U–par 3 course
£€ 300kr
🚗 18km E of Esbjerg
🏠 Bent Nielsen/Frederik Dreyer
🖳 www.kaj-lykke-golfklub.dk

Kalo   (1992)
Aarhusvej 32, 8410 Rønde
☎ 86 37 36 00
🖥 86 37 36 46
🏌 18 L 5936 m CR 72.2
     9 Par 3
🕴 H WD WE
£€ 18: 290kr (340kr) 9: 175kr (195kr)
🚗 20km E of Aarhus
🏠 Frederik Dreyer

Kolding   (1933)
Egtved Alle 10, 6000 Kolding
☎ 75 52 37 93
🖥 75 52 42 42
📧 kgc@koldinggolfclub.dk
🏌 18 L 5419 m (Yellow) CR 69.4
     SR 124
     18 L 4770 m (Red) CR 70.9 SR 128
🕴 U H
£€ 300kr (350kr)
🚗 3km N of Kolding
🏠 Line Martensea
🖳 www.koldinggolfclub.dk

Lemvig   (1986)
Søgårdevejen 6, 7620 Lemvig
☎ 97 81 09 20
📧 lemviggolfklub@lemviggolfklub.dk

Løkken   (1990)
*Vrenstedvej 226, PO Box 43, 9480
Løkken*
☎ 98 99 26 57
🖥 98 99 26 58
📧 info@loekken-golfklub.dk
🏌 18 L 5902 m CR 72.3 SR 127
     9 L 2964 m Par 29
🕴 U H
£€ 250kr (250kr) WD July 250kr
🚗 45km NW of Aalborg
🏠 Kaj Andersen
🖳 www.loekken-golfklub.dk

Nordvestjysk   (1971)
Nystrupvej 19, 7700 Thisted
☎ 97 97 41 41

Odder   (1990)
Akjaervej 200, Postbox 46, 8300 Odder
☎ 86 54 54 51
🖥 86 54 54 58
📧 oddergolf@oddergolf.dk

Red: 18 L 4639 m Par 70 CR 70
SR 118
Yellow: 18 L 5730 m Par 70 CR 70
SR 127
🏌 U H 45+
££ 250kr (300kr)
⛳ 4km SW of Odder, off Route 451
🏠 Frederik Dreyer
🖥 www.oddergolf.dk

Ornehoj Golfklub
Lundegard 70, 9260 Gistrup-
Aalborg, Denmark
☎ 98 31 43 44
✉ golfklubben@mail.dk

Randers (1958)
Himmelbovej 22, Fladbro, 8900 Randers
☎ 86 42 88 69
🖥 86 40 88 69
✉ postmaster@randersgolf.dk
⯈ 18 L 5453 m SSS 70
9 hole Par 3 course
££ 250kr (300kr)
⛳ 5km W of Randers towards Langå
🏠 Mogens Harbo
🖥 www.randersgolf.dk

Ribe (1979)
Rønnehave, Snepsgårdevej 14, 6760 Ribe
☎ 30 73 65 18

Rold Skov (1991)
Golfvej 1, 9520 Skørping
☎ 96 82 8300
🖥 96 82 8309
✉ info@roldskovgolf.dk
⯈ 18 L 5789 m Par 72 CR 71.4
SR 129
🏌 U H
££ 250kr (300kr)
⛳ 30km S of Aalborg
🏠 Henrik Jacobsen
🖥 www.roldskovgolf.dk

Royal Oak (1992)
Golfvej, Jels, 6630 Rødding
☎ 74 55 32 94
🖥 74 55 32 95
✉ golf@royal-oak.dk
⯈ 18 L 5967 m Par 72
🏌 H–booking necessary. Soft spikes
only
££ 380/400kr
⛳ 25km SW of Kolding
🏠 Per Gundtoft
🖥 www.royal-oak.dk

Silkeborg (1966)
Sensommervej 15C, 8600 Silkeborg
☎ 86 85 33 99
✉ kontor@silkeborggolf.dk

Sønderjyllands (1968)
Uge Hedegård, 6360 Tinglev
☎ 74 68 75 25
🖥 74 68 75 05
✉ sonderjylland@mail.dk
⯈ 18 L 5822 m Par 71
🏌 H
££ €41 (€48)

⛳ 9km NE of Tinglev. 9km S of
Abenraa
🏠 Erik Schnack
🖥 www.sdj-golfklub.dk

Varde (1991)
Gellerupvej 111b, 6800 Varde
☎ 75 22 49 44
🖥 75 22 48 35
✉ vardegolfklub@sport.dk
⯈ 18 L 6104 m Par 71
🏌 H Call for reservation
££ 250kr (350kr)
⛳ 20km N of Esbjerg
🏠 Erik Fauerholt
🖥 www.vardegolfklub.dk

Vejle (1970)
Faellessletgard, Ibaekvej, 7100 Vejle
☎ 75 85 81 85
✉ vejle@golfonline.dk

Viborg (1973)
Spangsbjerg Alle 50, Overlund, 8800 Viborg
☎ 86 67 30 10
✉ mail@viborggolfklub.dk

Zealand

Asserbo (1946)
Bødkergaardsvej 9, 3300
Frederiksvaerk
☎ 47 72 14 90
🖥 47 72 14 26
⯈ 18 L 5851 m Par 72
🏌 H
££ 350kr (450kr) WE + July
⛳ 2km from Frederiksvaerk towards
Liseleje
🏠 Ross/Samuelsen
🖥 www.agc.dk

Copenhagen (1898)
Dyrehaven 2, 2800 Kgs. Lyngby
☎ 39 63 04 83
🖥 39 48 40 09
✉ info@kgkgolf.dk
⯈ 18 L 5761 m SSS 71
🏌 WD–U WE after 13.00
££ 375kr (450kr)
⛳ 13 km N of Copenhagen, in deer
park (Dyrehaven)
🖥 www.kgkgolf.dk

Dragør GolfKlub (1991)
Kalvebodvej 100, 2791 Dragør
☎ 32 53 89 75
🖥 32 53 88 09
✉ post@dragor-golf.dk
⯈ 18 L 5636 m SSS 71
6 hole Par 3 course
🏌 WD–U WE–U H
££ 325kr (375kr) Booking from
07.00–17.00
⛳ 15km SE of Copenhagen centre, nr
Airport
🏠 Henning Jensen/Kierkegaard
🖥 www.dragor-golf.dk

Falster (1994)
Virketvej 44, 4863 Eskilstrup, Falster Island
☎ 54 43 81 43
🖥 54 43 81 23
✉ info@falster-golfklub.dk
⯈ 18 L 5912 m Par 72
🏌 H
££ 300kr (330kr)
⛳ 15km NE of Nykøbing (Route 271)
🏠 Anders Amilon
🖥 www.falster-golfklub.dk

Frederikssund (1974)
Egelundsgården, Skovnaesvej 9,
3630 Jaegerspris
☎ 47 31 08 77
🖥 47 31 21 77
✉ fgk@sport.dk
⯈ 18 L 5868 m SSS 71
🏌 WD–U H WE–H 30
££ 250kr (350kr)
⛳ 3km S of Frederikssund towards
Skibby (Route 53)
🏠 Dreyer/Samuelsen
🖥 www.frederikssundgolfklub.dk

Furesø (1974)
Hestkøbgård, Hestkøb Vaenge 4,
3460 Birkerød
☎ 45 81 74 44
✉ info@furesogolfklub.dk

Gilleleje (1970)
Ferlevej 52, 3250 Gilleleje
☎ 49 71 80 56
🖥 49 71 80 86
✉ info@gillelejegolfklub.dk
⯈ 18 L 6641 yds Par 72 CR 71
🏌 H–max 32
££ 1.11 – 31.03 200dkk 1.04 – 30.06
300dkk (450dkk) 1.07 – 16.08
500dkk 17.08 – 31.10 300dkk
(450dkk)
⛳ 62km N of Copenhagen
🏠 Jan Sederholm
🖥 www.gillelejegolfklub.dk

Hedeland (1980)
Staerkendevej 232A, 2640
Hedehusene
☎ 46 13 61 88/46 13 61 69

Helsingør
GL Hellebaekvej, 3000 Helsingør
☎ 49 21 29 70

Hillerød (1966)
Nysøgårdsvej 9, Ny Hammersholt,
3400 Hillerød
☎ 48 26 50 46/48 25 40 30
(Pro)
🖥 48 25 29 87
✉ klubben@hillerodgolf.dk
⯈ 18 L 5255 m CR 70
🏌 H WE–NA before noon
££ 350kr (400kr)
⛳ 3 km S of Hillerød
🏠 Sederholm/Knudsen
🖥 www.hillerodgolf.dk

Holbaek   (1964)
Dragerupvej 50, 4300 Holbaek
☎ 59 43 45 79
🖵 59 43 51 61
✉ info@holbakgolfcklub.dk
🏳 18 Par 70
    Yellow: L 5315 m
    Red: L 4607 m
    Men: CR 68.5 SR119
    Women: CR 69.8 SR 119
👫 U H(35)
££ 285Dkr (340Dkr)
⛳ Kirsebaerholmen, 2km E of
    Holbaek
🏠 Dreyer/Sederholm
🖥 www.holbakgolfklub.dk

Køge Golf Klub   (1970)
Gl.Hastrupvej12, 4600 Køge
☎ +45 56 65 10 00
🖵 +45 56 65 13 45
✉ admin@kogegolf.dk
🏳 18 L 5772 m Par 72
    9 L 3620 m Par 62
👫 WE–H max 36 WD max 36
££ 325kr (375kr)
⛳ 3km S of Køge. Copenhagen 38 km
🖥 www.kogegolf.dk

Kokkedal   (1971)
Kokkedal Alle 9, 2970 Horsholm
☎ 45 76 99 59
🖵 45 76 99 03
✉ kg@kokkedalgolf.dk
🏳 18 L 6163 m Par 72
👫 H–WD/WE All Day
££ 350kr (450kr)
⛳ Hørsholm, 30 km N of
    Copenhagen
🏠 Frank Pennink
🖥 www.kokkedalgolf.dk

Korsør   (1964)
Ornumvej 8, Postbox 53, 4220 Korsør
☎ 58 37 18 36
🖵 58 37 18 39
✉ golf@korsoergolf.dk
🏳 18 L 5763 m CR 71.1 SR 130
👫 H–NA before 9am
££ 275kr (325kr) €40 (€47)
⛳ 1km E of Korsør, on Korsør Bay
🏠 Arne Jørgensen, Morten L
    Mortensen
🖥 www.korsoergolf.dk

Mølleåens   (1970)
Stenbaekgård, Rosenlundvej 3, 3540 Lynge
☎ 48 18 86 31/48 18 86 36
    (Pro)

Odsherred   (1967)
4573 Hojby
☎ 59 30 20 76
🖵 59 30 36 76
✉ sek@odsherredgolf.dk
🏳 18 L 5549 m Par 71
    Men: CR 70.3 SR 126
    Women: CR 71.5 SR 123
    3 x 6 L 2757 m Par 57
    Men: CR 58.6 SR 97
    Women: CR 56.8 SR 84

👫 H
££ €40 (€50)
⛳ 5km SW of Nykøbing
🏠 Amilon/Dreyer/Mortensen
🖥 www.odsherredgolf.dk

Roskilde   (1973)
Gedevad, Kongemarken 34, 4000 Roskilde
☎ 46 37 01 81

Rungsted   (1937)
Vestre Stationsvej 16, 2960 Rungsted Kyst
☎ 45 86 34 44
🖵 45 86 57 70
✉ info@rungstedgolfklub.dk
🏳 18 L 5681 m Par 72 CR 71.0
    SR 128 (yellow tee–men)
👫 H–max 26 (WE–21) WE–NA
    before noon
££ 575Dkr
⛳ Rungsted, 24km N of Copenhagen
🏠 Maj CA Mackenzie
🖥 www.rungstedgolfklub.dk

Simon's   (1993)
Nybovej 5, 3490 Kvistgaard
☎ +45 49 19 14 78
🖵 +45 49 19 14 70
✉ info@simonsgolf.dk
🏳 27 L 8688 m
👫 H–max men 27.3, women 27.7
    WE–NA before 3pm
££ 500kr (650kr)
⛳ 10km S of Helsingør. 35km N of
    Copenhagen
🏠 Martin Hawtree
🖥 www.simonsgolf.dk

Skjoldenaesholm   (1992)
Skjoldenawsvej 101, 4174 Jystrup
☎ 57 53 87 00
🖵 57 53 87 15
✉ sgc@golfin.dk
🏳 36 L 5958 & 6604 m Par 71/72
👫 H–max 36
££ 310kr (395kr)
⛳ 10km N of Ringsted. 60km SW of
    Copenhagen
🏠 Otto Bojesen/Robert Trent Jones II
🖥 www.golfin.dk

Skovlunde Herlev   (1980)
Syvendehusvej 111, 2730 Herlev
☎ 44 68 90 09
🖵 44 68 90 04
✉ post@shgk.dk
🏳 18 L 5125 m CR 67.8 SR 122
    9 hole Par 3 course
👫 H WE–NA before 11am
££ 300kr (350kr)
⛳ Herlev/Ballerup, 15km NW of
    Copenhagen
🏠 Torben Starup
🖥 www.shgk.dk

Søllerød   (1972)
Brillerne 9, 2840 Holte
☎ 45 80 17 84
    45 80 18 77
🖵 45 80 70 08
✉ info@sollerodgolf.dk

🏳 18 L 5913 m SSS 72
👫 U
££ 350kr (400kr)
⛳ 19km N of Copenhagen
🖥 www.sollerodgolf.dk

Sorø   (1979)
Suserupvej 7a, 4180 Sorø
☎ 57 84 93 95

Sydsjaellands   (1974)
Borupgården, Mogenstrup, 4700 Naestved
☎ (+45) 55 76 15 55
🖵 (+45) 55 76 15 88
✉ sydsjaelland2@golfonline.dk
🏳 18 L 5663 m CR 70.5
👫 H
££ 275kr (325kr)
⛳ 10km SE of Naestved towards
    Praestø
🏠 Dreyer/Amillon
🖥 www.sydsjaellandsgolfklub.dk

Vaerlose Golfklub   (1993)
Christianshovej 22, 3500 Vaerlose
☎ (+45) 4447 2124
🖵 (+45) 4447 2128
✉ mail@vaerloese-golfklub.dk ·
🏳 18 L 5802 m Par 72 CR 71.3 SR 133
👫 H WD WE–NA before 12.00
££ 350kr (450kr)
⛳ 15km from Copenhagen
🏠 Jan Sederholm
🖥 www.vaerloese-golfklub.dk

Finland

Central

Etelä-Pohjanmaan   (1986)
P O Box 136, 60101 Seinäjoki
☎ (06) 423 4545

Karelia Golf   (1987)
Vaskiportintie, 80780 Kontioniemi
☎ (013) 732411

Kokkolan   (1957)
P O Box 164, 67101 Kokkola
☎ (06) 823 8600
✉ toimisto@kokkolangolf.fi
🏳 18 L 5776 m SSS 72
👫 U H
££ €35
⛳ 3km S of Kokkola. 500km N of
    Helsinki
🏠 KJ Indola
🖥 www.kokkolangolf.fi

Laukaan Peurunkagolf
    (1989)
Valkolantie 68, 41530 Laukaa
☎ (014) 3377 300

Tarina Golf   (1988)
Golftie 135, 71800 Siilinjärvi
☎ **(017) 462 5299**
✉ toimisto@tarinagolf.fi

Vaasan Golf   (1969)
Golfkenttätie 61, 65380 Vaasa
☎ **(06) 356 9989**
☐ (06) 356 9091
✉ toimisto@vaasangolf.fi
⚑ 27 holes
⚘ H or Green card
£€ €35
⚘ Kraklund, 6km SE of Vaasa on
   Route 724. 417km NW of Helsinki
⌂ Björn Eriksson
▤ www.golf.fi/vag

Helsinki & South

Aura Golf   (1958)
Ruissalon Puistotie 536, 20100 Turku
☎ **(02) 258 9201/9221**
☐ (02) 258 9121
✉ office@auragolf.fi
⚑ 18 L 5843 m SSS 71
⚘ H–max 30 (men) 36 (women)
£€ €50 (€55)
⚘ Ruissalo Island, 9km W of Turku
⌂ Pekka Sivula
▤ www.auragolf.fi

Espoo Ringside Golf   (1990)
Nurmikartanontie 5, 02920 Espoo
☎ **(09) 849 4940**
☐ (09) 853 7132
✉ caddie@ringsidegolf.fi
⚑ 18 L 5855 m SSS 72
⚘ H
£€ €40 D–€60 (€60)
⚘ 20km NW of Helsinki
⌂ Kosti Kuronen
▤ www.ringsidegolf.fi

Espoon Golfseura   (1982)
Mynttiläntie 1, 02780 Espoo
☎ **(09) 8190 3444**

Harjattula G&CC   (1989)
Harjattulantie 84, 20960 Turku
☎ **(02) 276 2180**

Helsingin Golfklubi   (1932)
Talin Kartano, 00350 Helsinki
☎ **+358 9 225 23710**
☐ +358 9 225 23737
✉ toimisto@helsingingolfklubi.fi
⚑ 18 L 5486 m CR 70.4 SR 131
⚘ H (max 24 men; max 30 women)
£€ €60
⚘ 7km W of Helsinki City Centre
⌂ Lauri Arkkola, Kosti Kuronen
▤ www.helsingingolfklubi.fi

Hyvinkään   (1989)
Golftie 63, 05880 Hyvinkää
☎ **(019) 456 2400**
☐ (019) 456 2410
✉ caddiemaster@hyvigolf.fi

⚑ 18 L 5457 m CR 72.1
⚘ U H
£€ €35 (€45)
⚘ 3km N of Hyvinkää. 50km N of
   Helsinki
⌂ Kosti Kuronen
▤ www.hyvigolf.fi

Keimola Golf   (1988)
Kirkantie 32, 01750 Vantaa
☎ **(09) 276 6650**

Kurk Golf   (1985)
02550 Evitskog
☎ **(09) 819 0480**
☐ (09) 819 04810
✉ kurk@kurkgolf.fi
⚑ 18 L 5848 m Par 72
   9 L 2717 m Par 36
⚘ H
£€ €45 (€55)
⚘ 40km W of Helsinki
⌂ Reijo Hillberg, Peter Fjallman
▤ www.kurkgolf.fi

Master Golf   (1988)
Bodomin kuja 7, 02940 Espoo
☎ **(09) 849 2300**
☐ (09) 849 23011
⚑ 18 L 5847 m CR 71.8 SR 129
   18 L 5553 m CR 70.7 SR 124
⚘ WD before 2pm H–max 30 (M)
   36 (L)
£€ €55 (€65)
⚘ 24km NW of Helsinki
⌂ Kuronen/Persson
▤ www.mastergolf.fi

Meri-Teijo   (1990)
Mathildedalin Kartano, 25660 Mathildedal
☎ **(02) 736 3955**

Messilä   (1988)
Messiläntie 240, 15980 Messilä
☎ **(03) 884040**

Nevas Golf   (1988)
01190 Box
☎ **(09) 272 6313**

Nordcenter G&CC   (1988)
10410 Aminnefors
☎ **(019) 2766850**

Nurmijärven   (1990)
Ratasillantie 70, 05100 Röykkä
☎ **(09) 276 6230**
☐ (09) 276 62330
✉ caddiemaster@nurmijarvi-golf.fi
⚑ 27 L 6002-6214 m SSS 73-75
⚘ H
£€ €50
⚘ 23km W of Klaukkala. 50km NW
   of Helsinki
⌂ Åke Persson
▤ www.nurmijarvi-golf.fi

Peuramaa Golf   (1991)
Peuramaantie 152, 02400 Kirkkonummi
☎ **(09) 295 588**

☐ (09) 295 58210
✉ office@peuramaagolf.com
⚑ 36 holes
⚘ H
£€ €38 (€46) – 2006
⚘ 27km W of Helsinki
⌂ Kuronen/Persson
▤ www.peuramaagolf.com

Pickala Golf   (1986)
Golfkuja 5, 02580 Siuntio
☎ **(09) 221 9080**
☐ (09) 221 90899
✉ toimisto@pickalagolf.fi
⚑ Seaside 18 L 5745 m SSS 72
   Park 18 L 5866 m SSS 72
   Forest 18 L 5775 m SSS 72
⚘ H
£€ €55 (€65)
⚘ 42km W of Helsinki, on South
   coast
⌂ Reijo Hillberg (Seaside and Park)
   Jan Sederholm (Forest)
▤ www.pickalagolf.fi

Ruukkigolf   (1986)
PL 9, 10420 Skuru
☎ **(019) 245 4485**
✉ toimisto@ruukkigolf.fi

Sarfvik   (1984)
P O Box 27, 02321 Espoo
☎ **(09) 221 9000**
✉ sarfvik@golfsarfvik.fi

Sea Golf Rönnäs   (1989)
Kabbölentie 319, 07750 Isnäs
☎ **+358 (0) 19 634 434**
☐ +358 (0) 19 634 458
✉ toimisto@seagolf.fi
⚑ 27: Old Course: White: CR 71.6
   SR 126 (men)
   Yellow: 69.6/125 (m), 75.3/128 (w)
   Red: 65.8/118 (m), 70.6/118 (w)
   New: Yelllow: 65.3/113 (m),
   70.0/122 (w)
   Red: 62.0/106 (m), 66.6/114 (w)
⚘ U
£€ €38 (€50) inc. trolleys
⚘ 27km SE of Porvoo. 80km E of
   Helsinki (1 hour)
⌂ Kosti Kuronen
▤ www.seagolf.fi

St Laurence Golf   (1989)
Kaivurinkatu 133, 08200 Lohja
☎ **+358 (0)19 357 821**
✉ caddie.master@stlaurencegolf.fi

Suur-Helsingin Golf   (1965)
Rinnekodintie 29, 02980 Espoo
☎ **+358 9 4399 7110**
☐ +358 9 437121
✉ toimisto@shg.fi
⚑ Lakisto 18 L 5455 m
   Par 72 CR 70.7 SR 129
   Luukki 18 L 5233 m
   Par 70 CR 69.3 SR 125
⚘ Luukki: Mon–U Tue–Sun–H;
   Lakisto: WD/WE–H (Fri before
   2pm H–54) otherwise H–36 or
   under

££ €35 (€45)
🚗 25km N of Helsinki
🏠 Lakisto: Ere Kokkonen; Luukki: members collaboration
🖥 www.shg.fi

Golf Talma   (1989)
Nygårdintie 115-6, 04240 Talma
☎ (09) 274 6540
🖵 (09) 274 65432
📧 golftalma@golftalma.fi
🏌 18 L 5809 m SSS 72
      18 L 5758 m SSS 72
      9 hole Par 3 course
👤 WD–H WE–H
££ €50 (€60)
🚗 35km N of Helsinki
🏠 Henrik Wartiainen
🖥 www.golftalma.fi

Tuusula   (1983)
Kirkkotie 51, 04301 Tuusula
☎ (042) 410241

Virvik Golf   (1981)
Virvik, 06100 Porvoo
☎ (915) 579292

North

Green Zone Golf   (1987)
Näräntie, 95400 Tornio
☎ (016) 431711

Katinkulta   (1990)
88610 Vuokatti
☎ (08) 669 7488
📧 golf.katinkulta@holidayclub.fi

Oulu   (1964)
Sankivaaran Golfkeskus, 90650 Oulu
☎ (08) 531 5222
🖵 (08) 531 5129
📧 caddiemaster@oulugolf.fi
🏌 Sanki: 18 holes
      Vaara: 18 holes
👤 H
££ €45–€50
🚗 Sanginsuu, 11km E of Oulu
🏠 Ronald Fream
🖥 www.oulugolf.fi

South East

Imatran Golf   (1986)
Golftie 11, 55800 Imatra
☎ (05) 473 4954

Kartano Golf   (1988)
P O Box 60, 79601 Joroinen
☎ (017) 572257
🖵 (017) 572263
🏌 18 L 5597 m Par 72 CR 71 SR 123
👤 U
££ €32 (€37)
🚗 20km S of Varkaus. 330km NE of Helsinki
🏠 Ake Persson

Kerigolf   (1990)
Kerimaantie 65, 58200 Kerimäki
☎ (015) 252600
🖵 (015) 252606
📧 clubhouse@kerigolf.fi
🏌 18 L 6218 m Par 72 SSS 75
👤 H
££ €40
🚗 15km E of Savonlinna. 350km NE of Helsinki
🏠 Ronald Fream
🖥 www.kerigolf.fi

Koski Golf   (1987)
Eerolanväylä 126, 45700 Kuusankoski
☎ +358 5 864 4600
🖵 +358 5 864 4644
📧 toimisto@koskigolf.fi
🏌 18 L 6375 m Par 73
👤 H I
££ €40 (€45)
🚗 3km E of Kuusankoski. 70km E of Lahti
🏠 Kosti Kuronen
🖥 www.koskigolf.fi

Kymen Golf   (1964)
Mussalo Golfcourse, 48310 Kotka
☎ (05) 210 3700

Lahden Golf   (1959)
Takkulantie, 15230 Lahti
☎ (03) 784 1311

Porrassalmi   (1989)
Annila, 50100 Mikkeli
☎ (015) 335518/335446
🖵 (015) 335682
🏌 18 L 5601 m CR 70.6
👤 H
££ €36–€42
🚗 5km S of Mikkeli

Vierumäen Golfseura   (1988)
Sport Institute of Finland, Vierumäki, Suomen Urheiluopisto, 19120 Vierumäki
☎ +358 3 842 4501
🖵 +358 3 842 4630
📧 caddiemaster@vierumaki.fi
🏌 18 L 5580 m CR 71.1
      Cooke: L 4732-6048 m
      Classic: L 4730-5691 m
      Coach: 9-hole Par 3
👤 U
££ Cooke €52; Classic €44; Coach €27
🚗 25km NE of Lahti
🏠 Cooke:Graham Cooke; Classic/Coach: Jan Sederholm
🖥 www.vierumakigolf.fi

South West

Porin Golfkerho   (1939)
P O Box 25, 28601 Pori
☎ (02) 630 3888
📧 toimisto@kalafornia.com

River Golf   (1988)
Taivalkunta, 37120 Nokia
☎ (03) 340 0234

Salo Golf   (1988)
Anistenkatn 1, 24100 Salo
☎ (02) 721 7300
🖵 (02) 721 7310
📧 caddiemaster@salogolf.fi
🏌 18 L 5447 m CR 69
👤 U
££ €30 (€34)
🚗 110km W of Helsinki; 50km E of Turku
🖥 www.salogolf.fi

Tammer Golf   (1965)
Toimelankatu 4, 33560 Tampere
☎ (03) 261 3316

Tawast Golf   (1987)
Tawastintie 48, 13270 Hämeenlinna
☎ (03) 630 610
🖵 (03) 630 6120
📧 tawast@tawastgolf.fi
🏌 18 L 6063 m Par 72
👤 WD/WE–H Men 36 Women 36
££ €45
🚗 5km E of Hämeenlinna
🏠 Reijo Hillberg
🖥 www.tawastgolf.fi

Vammala   (1991)
38100 Karkku
☎ (03) 513 4070

Wiurila G&CC   (1990)
Viurilantie 126, 24910 Halikko
☎ +35 8272 78100
🖵 +35 8272 78107
📧 wgcc@sannalahti.fi
🏌 18 L 5584 m CR 71.7
👤 H
££ €35 (€45) D–€50 (€60)
🚗 5km W of Salo. 115km W of Helsinki
🏠 Kurohen Kosti
🖥 www.wgcc.fi

Yyteri Golf   (1988)
Karhuluodontie 85, 28840 Pori
☎ (02) 638 0380

France

Bordeaux & South West

Albret   (1986)
Le Pusocq, 47230 Barbaste
☎ 05 53 65 53 69

Arcachon   (1955)
Golf International d'Arcachon, 35 Bd d'Arcachon, 33260 La Teste De Buch

---

☎ **05 56 54 44 00**
🖳 05 56 66 86 32
✉ golfarcachon@free.fz
⤷ 18 L 5930 m SSS 72
👥 U H
££ €29 (€52)
⛳ 60km SW of Bordeaux
🏠 CR Blandford

Arcangues (1991)

64200 Arcangues
☎ **05 59 43 10 56**
🖳 05 59 43 12 60
✉ golf.arcangues@wanadoo.fz
⤷ 18 L 6142 m Par 72
👥 U
££ Jan–Mar, Nov–Dec: 9–€34 18–€45
Apr–May, Sep–Oct: 9–€29 18–€55
Jul–Aug
⛳ 3km SE of Biarritz
🏠 Ronald Fream
📋 www.golfdarcangues.com

Biarritz (1888)

Ave Edith Cavell, 64200 Biarritz
☎ **05 59 03 71 80**
✉ info@golfbiarritz.com

Biscarrosse (1989)

Avenue du Golf, F-40600 Biscarrosse
☎ **05 58 09 84 93**
🖳 05 58 09 84 50
✉ golfdebiscarrosse@wanadoo.fr
⤷ Lake 9 L 2172 m SSS 32
Forest & Ocean 18 L 5.794 m
Par 72
👥 U (Lake) H (Forest & Ocean)
££ €30–€55
⛳ 80km SW of Bordeaux
🏠 Brizon/Veyssieres
📋 www.biscarrossegolf.com

Blue Green-Artiguelouve

(1986)
Domaine St Michel, Pau-Artiguelouve,
64230 Artiguelouve
☎ **05 59 83 09 29**

Blue Green-Seignosse

(1989)
Avenue du Belvédère, 40510 Seignosse
☎ **05 58 41 68 30**
✉ golfseignosse@wanadoo.fr

Bordeaux-Cameyrac (1972)

33450 St Sulpice-et-Cameyrac
☎ **(+33) (0)5 56 72 96 79**
🖳 (+33) (0)5 56 72 86 56
✉ contact@golf-bordeaux-cameyrac
.com
⤷ 18 L 5777 m Par 72 CR 72.3 SR 132
9 L 1188 m Par 28
👥 U
££ €35 (€45)
⛳ 15 min drive from Bordeaux and
Saint Emillion between the wine
fields
🏠 Jacques Quenot
📋 www.golf-bordeaux-cameyrac.com

Bordeaux-Lac (1976)

Public
Avenue de Pernon, 33300 Bordeaux
☎ **05 56 50 92 72**
✉ golf.bordeaux@wanadoo.fr

Bordelais (1900)

Domaine de Kater, Allee F Arago,
33200 Bordeaux-Caudéran
☎ **05 56 28 56 04**
🖳 05 56 28 59 71
✉ golfbordelais@wanadoo.fr
⤷ 18 L 4727 m Par 67 SSS 67
CR men 113, women 115
👥 H–restricted Tues
££ €35 (€45)
⛳ 3km NW of Bordeaux
🏠 Colt
📋 www.golf-bordelais.fr

Casteljaloux (1989)

Route de Mont de Marsan,
47700 Casteljaloux
☎ **05 53 93 51 60**
✉ golfdecasteljaloux@tiscali.fr

Chantaco (1928)

Route d'Ascain, 64500 St Jean-de-Luz
☎ **05 59 26 14 22/
05 59 26 19 22**
✉ pierre@golfdechantaco.com

Château des Vigiers G&CC

(1992)
24240 Monestier
☎ **05 53 61 50 33**
🖳 05 53 61 50 31
✉ golf@vigiers.com
⤷ La Vallée L 3246 m Par 36
Le Lac L 2895 m Par 35
Les Vignes L 3112 m Par 71
Vallée/Lac L 6141 m Par 71
Vallée/Vignes L 6358 m Par 72
Vignes/Lac L 6007 m Par 71
👥 H
££ Dec–Mar 9: €35 18: €55
Apr–May/Oct–Nov 9:€40 18: €65
Jun–Sep 9: €45 18: €75 Hotel
Guests
⛳ 15km SW of Bergerac. 75km E of
Bordeaux
🏠 Donald Steel
📋 www.vigiers.com

Chiberta (1926)

Boulevard des Plages, 64600 Anglet
☎ **05 59 63 83 20**

Domaine de la Marterie

(1987)
St Felix de Reillac, 24260 Le Bugue
☎ **05 53 05 61 00**

Graves et Sauternais

(1989)
St Pardon de Conques, 33210 Langon
☎ **05 56 62 25 43**
✉ golf.langon@laposte.net

Gujan (1990)

Route de Souguinet, 33470 Gujan Mestras
☎ **05 57 52 73 73**

Hossegor (1930)

333 Ave du Golf, 40150 Hossegor
☎ **05 58 43 56 99**
🖳 05 58 43 98 52
✉ golf.hossegor@wanadoo.fr
⤷ 18 L 6001 m SSS 72
👥 H–max 35
££ High season €68 Mid season €55
Low Season €50
⛳ 15km N of Bayonne, on coast
🏠 J Morrison
📋 www.golfhossegor.com

Lacanau Golf & Hotel

(1980)
Domaine de l'Ardilouse, 33680 Lacanau-
Océan
☎ **(+33) 556 039292**
✉ info@golf-hotel-lacanau.fr

Makila

Route de Cambo, 64200 Bassussarry
☎ **05 59 58 42 42**

Médoc

Chemin de Courmateau, Louens, 33290 Le
Pian Médoc
☎ **05 56 70 11 90**

Moliets (1989)

Public
Rue Mathieu Desbieys, 40660 Moliets
☎ **05 58 48 54 65**
🖳 05 58 48 54 88
✉ resa@golfmoliets.com
⤷ 18 L 6172 m SSS 73
9 hole course
👥 U H–max 30
££ €50–€63
⛳ Moliets, 40km N of Bayonne. 40km
W of Dax
🏠 Robert Trent Jones Sr
📋 www.golfmoliets.com

Pau (1856)

Rue du Golf, 64140 Billère, France
☎ **+33 (05) 5913 1856**
✉ pau.golfclub@wanadoo.fr

Pessac (1989)

Rue de la Princesse, 33600 Pessac
☎ **05 57 26 03 33**

Stade Montois (1993)

Pessourdat, 40090 Saint Avit
☎ **05 58 75 63 05**

Villeneuve sur Lot G&CC

(1987)
'La Menuisière', 47290 Castelnaud
de Gratecambe
☎ **05 53 01 60 19**
🖳 05 53 01 78 99
✉ info@vsgolf.com
⤷ 18 L 6107 m SSS 71
9 L 2184 m SSS 27

🖑 U
£€ €59.50
⊛ 10km N of Villeneuve on N21.
40km N of Agen
🏠 R Berthet
📧 www.vsgolf.com

Brittany

Ajoncs d'Or   (1976)
Kergrain Lantic, 22410 Saint-Quay Portrieux
☎ 02 96 71 90 74
📧 golfdesajoncsdor@wanadoo.fr

Baden
Kernic, 56870 Baden
☎ 02 97 57 18 96

Belle Ile en Mer   (1987)
Les Poulins, 56360 Belle-Ile-en-Mer
☎ 02 97 31 64 65

Brest Les Abers   (1990)
Kerhoaden, 29810 Plouarzel
☎ 02 98 89 68 33
📧 golf@abersgolf.com
🏳 18 L 5060 m Par 71
🖑 U
£€ €35 High Season
⊛ 15km W Of Brest (D5)
🏠 Ch Dunoyer
📧 www.abersgolf.com

Brest-Iroise   (1976)
Parc de Lann-Rohou, Saint-Urbain, 29800 Landerneau
☎ 02 98 85 16 17
📠 02 98 85 19 39
📧 golfhotel@brest-iroise.com
🏳 18 L 5672 m Par 71
9 L 3329 m Par 37
🖑 U
£€ €48 D—€60
⊛ 18km E of Brest; 3km from Landerneau
🏠 M Fenn
📧 www.brest-iroise.com

Dinard   (1890)
35800 St-Briac-sur-Mer
☎ 02 99 88 32 07

La Freslonnière   (1989)
Le Bois Briand, 35650 Le Rheu
☎ 02 99 14 84 09
📠 02 99 14 94 98
📧 lafreslo@wanadoo.fr
🏳 18 L 5657 m SSS 70.5 SR 143
🖑 U
£€ €39—€52
⊛ 4km SW of Rennes, off N24
🏠 A du Bouexic
📧 www.lafreslonniere.com

L'Odet   (1936)
Clohars-Fouesnant, 29950 Benodet
☎ 02 98 54 87 88
📧 golf.odet@wanadoo.fr

Les Ormes   (1988)
Château des Ormes, Epiniac, 35120 Dol-de-Bretagne
☎ 02 99 73 54 44

Pléneuf-Val André
Rue de la Plage des Vallées, 22370 Pléneuf-Val André
☎ 02 96 63 01 12

Ploemeur Océan Formule Golf   (1990)
Kerham Saint-Jude, 56270 Ploemeur
☎ 02 97 32 81 82

Quimper-Cornouaille   (1959)
Manoir du Mesmeur, 29940 La Forêt-Fouesnant
☎ 02 98 56 97 09

Rennes   (1957)
Le Temple du Cerisier, 35136 St-Jacques-de-la-Lande
☎ 02 99 30 18 18
📧 directeur.rennes@formulegolf.com

Rhuys-Kerver   (1988)
Public
Formule Golf, Domaine de Kerver, 56730 St-Gildas-de-Rhuys
☎ 02 97 45 30 09
📠 02 97 45 36 58
📧 golf.rhuys@formule-golf.com
🏳 18 L 5989 m Par 72 CR 72.1
SR 133 (white)
🖑 U
£€ €52
⊛ 30km S of Vannes
🏠 Olivier Brizon
📧 www.formule-golf.com

Les Rochers   (1989)
Route d'Argentré du Plessis 3, 35500 Vitré
☎ 02 99 96 52 52

Sables-d'Or-les-Pins   (1925)
22240 Fréhel
☎ 02 96 41 42 57

St Cast Pen Guen   (1926)
22380 Saint-Cast-le-Guildo
☎ 02 96 41 91 20

St Laurent   (1975)
Ploemel, 56400 Auray
☎ 02 97 56 85 18
📠 02 97 56 89 99
📧 golf.stlaurent@formule-golf.com
🏳 18 L 6128 m SSS 72
9 L 2705 m SSS 35
🖑 U
£€ 9: Low season €24, high season €30; 18: Low season €35, high season €49
⊛ Ploemel, 6km W of Auray
🏠 Fenn/Bureau
📧 www.formule-golf.com

St Malo Hotel G&CC   (1986)
Le Tronchet, 35540 Miniac-Morvan
☎ 02 99 58 96 69
📠 02 99 58 10 39
📧 saintmalogolf@st-malo.com
🏳 18 L 6014 m SSS 72
9 L 2684 m SSS 36
🖑 U
£€ D—€40—€60 20% reduction for hotel
⊛ 23km S of St Malo, off RN 137
🏠 Hubert Chesneau
📧 www.saintmalogolf.com

St Samson   (1965)
Route de Kérénoc, 22560 Pleumeur-Bodou
☎ 02 96 23 87 34

Val Queven   (1990)
Public
Kerruisseau, 56530 Queven
☎ 02 97 05 17 96

Burgundy & Auvergne

Aubazine   (1977)
Public
19190 Aubazine
☎ 03 55 27 25 66

Beaune-Levernois   (1990)
21200 Levernois
☎ 03 80 24 10 29

Chalon-sur-Saône   (1976)
Parc de Saint Nicolas, 71380 Chatenoy-en-Bresse
☎ 03 85 93 49 65
📧 contact@golfchalon.com

Chambon-sur-Lignon   (1986)
Riondet, La Pierre de la Lune, 43400 Le Chambon-sur-Lignon
☎ 04 71 59 28 10

Château d'Avoise   (1992)
9 Rue de Mâcon, 71210 Montchanin
☎ 03 85 78 19 19

Château de Chailly   (1990)
Chailly-sur-Armançon, 21320 Pouilly-en-Auxois
☎ 03 80 90 30 40
📠 03 80 90 30 05
📧 reservation@chailly.com
🏳 18 L 6146 m SSS 72
SR 130 (White), 124 (Yellow), 126 (Blue), 195 (Red)
🖑 U
£€ €55
⊛ A6 motorway, Pouilly-en-Auxois exit. 45km SW of Dijon. 40km NW of Beau
🏠 Sprecher/Watine
📧 www.chailly.com

Domaine de Roncemay
(1989)
89110 Aillant-sur-Tholon
☎ 03 86 73 50 50
🖥 03 86 73 69 46
📧 reservation@roncemay.com
🏳 18 Par 72
Men: white L 6270 m CR 73.9 SR 140
yellow L 5702 m CR 71.0 SR 128
Women: blue L CR 73.6 SR 132
red L 4864 m CR 73.8 SR 128
👥 U
££ High season: €48–€60 Low season: €40–€50
🚗 25km W of Auxerre
🏠 Jeremy Pern & Jean Garaïlde
🖳 www.roncemay.com

Jacques Laffite Dijon-Bourgogne
(1972)
Bois des Norges, 21490 Norges-la-Ville
☎ 03 80 35 71 10
🖥 03 80 35 79 27
📧 contacts@golfdijonbourgogne.com
🏳 18 L 6179 m SSS 72
👥 U
££ €43 (€54)
🚗 10km N of Dijon towards Langres
🏠 Fenn/Radcliffe
🖳 www.golfdijonbourgogne.com

Limoges-St Lazare
(1976)
Public
Avenue du Golf, 87000 Limoges
☎ 05 55 28 30 02

Mâcon La Salle
(1989)
La Salle-Mâcon Nord, 71260 La Salle
☎ 03 85 36 09 71
📧 golf.maconlasalle@wanadoo.fr

Le Nivernais
Public
Le Bardonnay, 58470 Magny Cours
☎ 03 58 18 30

La Porcelaine
Célicroux, 87350 Panazol
☎ 05 55 31 10 69
📧 golf@golf.porcelaine.com

St Junien
(1997)
Les Jouberties, 87200 Saint Junien
☎ 05 55 02 96 96
📧 info@golfdesaintjunien.com

Sporting Club de Vichy
(1907)
Allée Baugnies, 03700 Bellerive/Allier
☎ 04 70 32 39 11

Val de Cher
(1975)
03190 Nassigny
☎ 04 70 06 71 15
🖥 04 70 06 70 00
📧 golfvaldecher@free.fr
🏳 18 L 5450 m Par 70
👥 U

££ €25–€35
🚗 20km N of Montluçon on N144
🏠 Bourret/Vigand
🖳 http://golfclub.valdecher.free.fr

Les Volcans
(1984)
La Bruyère des Moines, 63870 Orcines
☎ 04 73 62 15 51
🖥 04 73 62 26 52
📧 golfdesvolcans@nat.fr
🏳 18 L 6286 m SSS 73
9 L 1377 m SSS 29
👥 U H
££ €49 (€55)
🚗 12km W of Clermont-Ferrand on RN41
🏠 Lucien Roux
🖳 www.golfdesvolcans.com

Centre

Les Aisses
(1992)
RN20 Sud, 45240 La Ferté St Aubin
☎ 02 38 64 80 87
🖥 02 38 64 80 85
📧 golfdesaisses@wanadoo.fr
🏳 27 L 6200 m Par 72
👥 U
££ 9: Low season: €25 (€30) High season: €30 (€40) 18: Low: €40 D–€60 (€50 D–€70) High: €50D–€70 (€60 D–€90)
🚗 30km S of Orléans. 140km S of Paris
🏠 Olivier Brizon
🖳 www.aissesgolf.com

Ardrée
(1988)
37360 St Antoine-du-Rocher
☎ 02 47 56 77 38
🖥 02 47 56 79 96
📧 tours.ardree@bluegreen.com
🏳 18 L 5745 m Par 71
👥 U H (green card)
££ 9: €27 (€32) 18: €37 (€54) Special rates Tues €32
🚗 10km N of Tours
🏠 Olivier Brizon
🖳 www.bluegreen.com/tours
🖳 www.golf-ardree.com

Aymerich Golf 'Les Dryades'
(1987)
36160 Pouligny-Notre-Dame
☎ 02 54 06 60 67
🖥 02 54 30 10 24
📧 aymerichgolf.lesdryades@orange.fr
🏳 18 L 6120 m SSS 72
👥 U
££ €42 (€47)
🚗 10km S of La Châtre (D940). 60km SW of Bourges
🏠 Michel Gayon

Les Bordes
(1987)
41220 Saint Laurent-Nouan
☎ 02 54 87 72 13
🖥 02 54 87 78 61
📧 golf.les.bordes@wanadoo.fr
🏳 18 L 6412 m Par 72

👥 U M H (max 36) SOC WD WE
££ €120 (€150)
🚗 30km SW of Orléans
🏠 Robert van Hagge
🖳 www.lesbordes.com

Château de Cheverny
(1989)
La Rousselière, 41700 Cheverny
☎ 02 54 79 24 70
🖥 02 54 79 25 52
📧 contact@golf-cheverny.com
🏳 18 L 6279 m Par 71
👥 U
££ High season €55 low season €37
🚗 15km S of Blois. 200km SW of Paris, via A10
🏠 O Van der Vynckt
🖳 www.golf-cheverny.com

Château de Maintenon
(1989)
Route de Gallardon, 28130 Maintenon
☎ 02 37 27 18 09

Château des Sept Tours
(1989)
Le Vivier des Landes, 37330 Courcelles de Touraine
☎ 02 47 24 69 75

Cognac
(1987)
Saint-Brice, 16100 Cognac
☎ 05 45 32 18 17

Le Connétable
(1987)
Parc Thermal, 86270 La Roche Posay
☎ 05 49 86 25 10

Domaine de Vaugouard
(1987)
Chemin des Bois, Fontenay-sur-Loing, 45210 Ferrières
☎ 02 38 89 79 00

Ganay
(1993)
Prieuré de Ganay, 41220 St Laurent-Nouan
☎ 02 54 87 26 24
📧 golfdeganay2@wanadoo.fr
🏳 Men: 18 L 6048/5672/5114/4794 m Par 72 CR 71.8/69.8/72.3/70.2 SR 120/118/119/117
Women: 18 L 6114/5646/5206/4879 m Par 72 CR 72.8/79.8/73.1/71 SR 125/121/124/119
👥 U
££ 9: €22 (€30) 18: €32 (€42)
🚗 130km S of Paris. 30km (30 min) from Orleans and Blois
🏠 Jim Shirley
🖳 www.golf-ganay.com

Haut-Poitou
(1987)
86130 Saint-Cyr
☎ 05 49 62 53 62
🖥 05 49 88 77 14
📧 contact@golfduhautpoitou.com
🏳 18 L 6590 m SSS 75
9 L 1800 m Par 31 Slope 141

ꙮ U
££ 9: €14; 18: €55 every day
⚬⚬ 20km N of Poitiers. 70km S of Tours
⌂ HG Baker
▤ www.golfduhautpoitou.com

Loudun-Roiffe   (1985)
Domaine St Hilaire, 86120 Roiffe
☎ 05 49 98 78 06

Marcilly   (1986)
Domaine de la Plaine, 45240 Marcilly-en-Villette
☎ 02 38 76 11 73
⌨ 02 38 76 18 73
✉ golf@marcilly.com
╟ 18 L 6324 m SSS 73
  9 L 1301 SSS 27
ꙮ U
££ €38 (€38)
⚬⚬ 20km SE of Orléans
⌂ Olivier Brizon
▤ www.marcilly.com

Niort
Chemin du Grand Ormeau, 79000 Niort Romagne
☎ 05 49 09 01 41

Orléans Donnery
Château de la Touche, 45450 Donnery
☎ 02 38 59 25 15

Golf du Perche   (1987)
La Vallée des Aulnes, 28400 Souancé au Perche
☎ 02 37 29 17 33
⌨ 02 37 29 12 88
✉ golfduperche@wanadoo.fr
╟ 18 L 6073 m Par 72
ꙮ U
££ €35 (€40)
⚬⚬ 60km SW of Chartres (D9). 130km SW of Paris
⌂ Laurent Heckly
▤ www.golfduperche.fr

Petit Chêne   (1987)
Le Petit Chêne, 79310 Mazières-en-Gâtine
☎ 05 49 63 20 95
⌨ 05 49 63 33 75
╟ 18 L 6060 m SSS 72
ꙮ U
££ €42
⚬⚬ 15km SW of Parthenay. 25km NE of Niort
⌂ Robert Berthet

La Picardière
Chemin de la Picardière, 18100 Vierzon
☎ 02 48 75 21 43

Poitiers
635 route de Beauvoir, 86550 Mignaloux Beauvoir
☎ 05 49 55 10 50
⌨ 05 49 62 26 70
✉ golf-poitiers@monalisahotels.com
╟ 18 L 6108 m Par 72 SSS 72.3 SR 130
ꙮ WD–U WE–H

££ Jan–Mar and Nov–Dec €32 Apr–Oct €48
⚬⚬ 6km SE of Poitiers (RN147)
⌂ Olivier Brizon

Poitou   (1991)
Domaine des Forges, 79340 Menigoute
☎ 0549 69 91 77
⌨ 0549 69 96 84
✉ info@golfdesforges.com
╟ 18 L 6400 m Par 74
  9 L 3200 m Par 37
ꙮ U SOC WD WE
££ 9: €26 (€34) 18: €37 (€42) High season
⚬⚬ 30km W of Poitiers
⌂ Bjorn Eriksson
▤ www.golfdesforges.com

La Prée-La Rochelle   (1988)
La Richardière, 17137 Marsilly
☎ 05 46 01 24 42
⌨ 05 46 01 25 84
✉ golflarochelle@wanadoo.fr
╟ 18 L 5931 m Par 72 CR 73.1
  White SR 136, Yellow SR 134, Blue SR 128, Red SR 125
ꙮ H
££ High season: €54 Low season: €42 2008 prices
⚬⚬ 8km N of La Rochelle
⌂ Olivier Brizon
▤ www.golflarochelle.com

Royan   (1977)
Maine-Gaudin, 17420 Saint-Palais
☎ 05 46 23 16 24
⌨ 05 46 23 23 38
✉ golfderoyan@wanadoo.fr
╟ 18 L 5924 m SSS 71
  6 hole short course 920 m
ꙮ U
££ €35–€58
⚬⚬ Saint-Palais, 7km W of Royan
⌂ Robert Berthet
▤ www.golfderoyan.com

Saintonge   (1953)
Fontcouverte, 17100 Saintes
☎ 05 46 74 27 61

Sancerrois   (1989)
St Thibault, 18300 Sancerre
☎ 02 48 54 11 22
⌨ 02 48 54 28 03
✉ golf.sancerre@wanadoo.fr
╟ 18 L 5820 m SSS 71
ꙮ U
££ €28–€37 (€39–€47)
⚬⚬ 45km NE of Bourges
⌂ Didier Fruchet
▤ www.sancerre.net/golf

Touraine   (1971)
Château de la Touche, 37510 Ballan-Miré
☎ 02 47 53 20 28

Val de l'Indre   (1989)
Villedieu-sur-Indre, 36320 Tregonce
☎ 02 54 26 59 44

Channel Coast & North

Abbeville   (1989)
Route du Val, 80132 Grand-Laviers
☎ 03 22 24 98 58
⌨ 03 22 24 98 58
✉ abbeville.golfclub@wanadoo.fr
╟ 18 L 5924 m Par 72
ꙮ U
££ €25–€30 (€35–€40)
⚬⚬ 3km NW of Abbeville
⌂ Didier Fruchet
▤ www.golf.abbeville.com

L'Ailette
02860 Cerny en Laonnais
☎ 03 23 24 83 99
✉ golfdelailette@wanadoo.fr

Amiens   (1925)
80115 Querrieu
☎ 03 22 93 04 26
⌨ 03 22 93 04 61
✉ golfamiens@aol.com
╟ 18 L 6114 m SSS 72
ꙮ U H
££ €33–€43 (€40–€55)
⚬⚬ 7km NE of Amiens (D929)
⌂ Ross/Pennink
▤ www.golfamiens.fr

Apremont Golf Country Club   (1992)
60300 Apremont
☎ 03 44 25 61 11
⌨ 03 44 25 11 72
✉ apremont@club-albatros.com
╟ 18 L 6395 m SSS 73 SR 134
ꙮ H
££ €42 (€78)
⚬⚬ 45km N of Paris
⌂ John Jacobs
▤ www.apremont-golf.com

Arras   (1989)
Rue Briquet Taillandier, 62223 Anzin-St-Aubin
☎ 03 21 50 24 24
⌨ 03 21 50 29 71
✉ golf@golf-arras.com
╟ 18 L 6150 m SSS 72
  9 L 1656 m SSS 31
ꙮ U
££ €30 (€55)
⚬⚬ 50km S of Lille. 110km SE of Calais
⌂ JC Cornillot
▤ www.golf-arras.com

Belle Dune
Promenade de Marquenterre, 80790 Fort-Mahon-Plage
☎ 03 22 23 45 50

Bois de Ruminghem   (1991)
1613 Rue St Antoine, 62370 Ruminghem
☎ 03 21 85 30 33

Bondues   (1968)
Château de la Vigne, 5910 Bondues
☎ 03 20 23 20 62

☎ 03 20 23 24 11
✉ contact@golfdebondues.com
⤷ 18 L 6163 m SSS 73 SR 130
18 L 6009 m SSS 72 SR 127
♟ H–max 30. Closed Tues
££ €60 (€84 July/Aug only)
🚗 10km NE of Lille
🏠 Hawtree/Trent Jones
🖥 www.golfdebondues.com

Champagne (1986)
02130 Villers-Agron
☎ 03 23 71 62 08
✉ golf.de.champagne@wanadoo.fr

Chantilly (1909)
Allée de la Ménagerie, 60500 Chantilly
☎ 03 44 57 04 43
🖥 03 44 57 26 54
✉ contact@golfdechantilly.com
⤷ Vineuil 18 L 6399 m SSS 71
Longeres 18 L 6350 m SSS 73
♟ WD
££ WD–€110
🚗 45km N of Paris
🏠 Tom Simpson
🖥 www.golfdechantilly.com

Château de Raray
4 Rue Nicolas de Lancy, 60810 Raray
☎ 03 44 54 70 61

Chaumont-en-Vexin
(1968)
Château de Bertichère, 60240 Chaumont-en-Vexin
☎ 03 44 49 00 81
✉ golfdechaumont@golf-paris.net

Club du Lys – Chantilly
(1929)
Rond-Point du Grand Cerf, 60260 Lamorlaye
☎ 03 44 21 26 00
🖥 03 44 21 35 52
✉ clubdulys@wanadoo.fr
⤷ 18 L 6022 m Par 70
18 L 4850 m Par 68
♟ M
🚗 5km S of Chantilly. 40km N of Paris
🏠 Tom Simpson

Compiègne (1896)
Avenue Royale, 60200 Compiègne
☎ 03 44 38 48 00
🖥 03 44 40 23 59
✉ directeur@golf-compiegne.com
⤷ 18 L 6015 m Par 71
♟ U
££ €33 (€28) €50 (€40)
🚗 80km NE of Paris
🏠 W Freemantel
🖥 www.golf-compiegne.com

Deauville l'Amiraute
(1992)
CD 278, Tourgéville, 14800 Deauville
☎ 02 31 14 42 00

Domaine du Tilleul (1984)
Landouzy-la-Ville, 02140 Vervins
☎ 03 23 98 48 00

Dunkerque (1991)
Public
Fort Vallières, Coudekerque-Village, 59380 Coudekerque
☎ 03 28 61 07 43
🖥 03 28 60 05 93
✉ golf@golf-dk.com
⤷ 27 3 x 9 L 6014 m Par 72
££ €50 (€60)
🚗 5km E of Dunkerque
🏠 Robert Berthet
🖥 www.golf-dk.com

Golf Dolce Chantilly
(1991)
Route d'Apremont, 60500 Vineuil St-Firmin
☎ 03 44 58 47 74
✉ golf.dolce.chantilly@wanadoo.fr

Hardelot Dunes Course
(1991)
Ave du Golf, 62152 Hardelot
☎ 03 21 83 73 10
🖥 03 21 83 24 33
✉ hardelot@opengolfclub.com
⤷ 18 L 5713 m SSS 72
♟ U H
££ High season: €68 Mon–Thur (€81 Fri–Sun) Low season: €47 Mon–Thur (€59 Fri–Sun)
🚗 15km S of Boulogne
🏠 JC Cornillot (1991), Paul Rolin
🖥 www.opengolfclub.com

Hardelot Pins Course
(1931)
Ave du Golf, 62152 Hardelot
☎ 03 21 83 73 10
🖥 03 21 83 24 33
✉ hardelot@opengolfclub.com
⤷ 18 L 5956 m SSS 73
♟ U H
££ High season: €72 Mon–Thur (€88 Fri–Sun) Low season: €50 Mon–Thur (€63 Fri–Sun)
🚗 15km S of Boulogne
🏠 Tom Simpson (1931)
🖥 www.opengolfclub.com

Morfontaine (1913)
60128 Mortefontaine
☎ 03 44 54 68 27
🖥 03 44 54 60 57
✉ morfontaine@wanadoo.fr
⤷ 18 L 5985 m Par 70 SSS 71.9 SR 135
9 L 2526 m Par 36
♟ Members' guests only
££ NA
🚗 10km S of Senlis. N of Paris
🏠 Tom Simpson/Kyle Phillips (hole 12)

Mormal (1991)
Bois St Pierre, 59144 Preux-au-Sart
☎ 03 27 63 07 00
🖥 03 27 39 93 62
✉ info@golf-mormal.com

⤷ 18 L 6022 m Par 72
♟ H
££ €40 (€50)
🚗 15km E of Valenciennes, off RN49
🏠 JC Cornillot
🖥 www.golf-mormal.com

Nampont-St-Martin (1978)
Maison Forte, 80120 Nampont-St-Martin
☎ 03 22 29 92 90/
03 22 29 89 87
🖥 03 22 29 97 54
✉ golfdenampont@wanadoo.fr
⤷ Cygnes 18 L 6051 m SSS 72
Belvédère 18 L 5275 m SSS 70
♟ U
££ Cygnes €45–€45 (€45–€50)
Belvédère €30–€35 (€35–€40)
🚗 50km S of Calais. Motorway A16 Junction 25. 12km S of Montreuil sur Mer
🏠 Thomas Chatterton
🖥 www.golfdenampont.com

Rebetz (1988)
Route de Noailles, 60240 Chaumont-en-Vexin
☎ 03 44 49 15 54

Saint-Omer
Chemin des Bois, Acquin-Westbécourt, 62380 Lumbres
☎ 03 21 38 59 90

Le Sart (1910)
5 Rue Jean-Jaurès, 59650 Villeneuve D'Ascq
☎ 03 20 72 02 51
🖥 03 20 98 73 28
✉ contact@golfdusart.com
⤷ 18 L 5721 m SSS 71
♟ H–35.4 WD from 9:00 to 18:00 WE not possible
££ €42
🚗 5km E of Lille. Motorway Lille-Gand Junction 9 (Breucq-Le Sart)
🏠 Allan Macbeth
🖥 www.golfdusart.com

Thumeries (1935)
Bois Lenglart, 59239 Thumeries
☎ 03 20 86 58 98

Le Touquet 'La Forêt'
(1904)
Ave du Golf, BP 41, 62520 Le Touquet
☎ 03 21 06 28 00
🖥 03 21 06 28 01
✉ letouquet@opengolfclub.com
⤷ 18 L 5827 m CR 71.0 SR 128
♟ U H
££ €71 (€85)
🚗 2km S of Le Touquet. 30km S of Boulogne
🏠 H Hutchinson
🖥 www.opengolfclub.com

Le Touquet 'La Mer' (1930)
Ave du Golf, BP 41, 62520 Le Touquet
☎ 03 21 06 28 00
🖥 03 21 06 28 01
✉ letouquet@opengolfclub.com

18 L 6407 m CR 75.5 SR 131
ⴲ   U H
££   €75 (€92)
⊛   As 'La Forêt'
⌂   HS Colt
🖥   www.opengolfclub.com

Le Touquet 'Le Manoir'
(1994)
Ave du Golf, BP 41, 62520 Le Touquet
☎   03 21 06 28 00
📠   03 21 06 28 01
✉   letouquet@opengolfclub.com
▷   9 L 2817 m Par 35 SR 118
ⴲ   U
££   €36 (€54)
⊛   As 'La Forêt'
⌂   HJ Baker
🖥   www.opengolfclub.com

Val Secret   (1984)
Brasles, 02400 Château Thierry
☎   03 23 83 07 25
📠   03 23 83 92 73
✉   accueil@golfvalsecret.com
▷   18 L 5703 m Par 72 SR 141
ⴲ   U
££   €31 (€46)
⊛   58km W of Reims via A4. Paris
      89km via A4
⌂   Paul Lennaerts
🖥   www.golfvalsecret.com

Vert Parc   (1991)
3 Route d'Ecuelles, 59480 Illies
☎   03 20 29 37 87
📠   03 20 49 76 39
▷   18 L 6328 m SSS 73
ⴲ   U
££   €47 (€55)
⊛   18km SW of Lille
⌂   Patrice Simon
🖥   www.golflevertparc.com

Wimereux   (1901)
Avenue F. Mitterrand, 62930 Wimereux
☎   03 21 32 43 20
📠   03 21 33 62 21
✉   accueil@golf-wimereux.com
▷   18 L 6150 m Par 72 SR 132 white
ⴲ   U
££   €37–€61
⊛   6km N of Boulogne on D940.
      30km S of Calais
⌂   Campbell/Hutchinson
🖥   www.golf-wimereux.com

Corsica

Sperone   (1990)
Domaine de Sperone, 20169 Bonifacio
☎   04 95 73 17 13
📠   04 95 73 17 85
✉   golf@sperone.com
▷   18 L 6106 m Par 72;
      Black: SR 159, White: SR 158,
      Yellow: SR 148, Blue: SR 143,
      Red: SR 137
ⴲ   H–max 28 or green card
££   €60–€95 (high season) or packages

of 4 or 7 green fees (low rate)
⊛   S point of Corsica, SE of Bonifacio.
      25km S of Figari Airport
⌂   Robert Trent Jones Sr
🖥   www.sperone.com

Ile de France

Ableiges   (1989)
95450 Ableiges
☎   01 30 27 97 00
📠   01 30 27 97 10
✉   ableigesgolf@free.fr
▷   18 L 6261 m Par 72
      9 L 2137 m Par 33
ⴲ   18 holes: U H (max 30)
££   9: €36; 18: €63
⊛   40km NW of Paris, nr Cergy
      Pontoise
⌂   Pern/Garaialde
🖥   www.ableiges-golf.com

Bellefontaine   (1987)
95270 Bellefontaine
☎   01 34 71 05 02
📠   01 34 71 90 90
✉   golf-bellefontaine@wanadoo.fr
▷   27 holes:
      6098-6306 m Par 72
ⴲ   U
££   €39 (€48)
⊛   27km N of Paris
⌂   Michel Gayon

Bussy-St-Georges   (1988)
Promenade des Golfeurs, 77600 Bussy-St-
Georges
☎   01 64 66 00 00

Cély   (1990)
Le Château, Route de Saint-Germain,
77930 Cély-en-Bière
☎   01 64 38 03 07

Cergy Pontoise   (1988)
2 Allee de l'Obstacle d'Eau, 95490 Vaureal
☎   01 34 21 03 48

Chevannes-Mennecy   (1994)
91750 Chevannes
☎   01 64 99 88 74
✉   legolfchevannes@wanadoo.fr

Clement Ader   (1990)
Domaine Château Pereire, 77220 Gretz
☎   01 64 07 34 10
✉   golfclementader@voila.fr

Coudray   (1960)
Ave du Coudray, 91830 Le Coudray-
Montceaux
☎   01 64 93 81 76
📠   01 64 93 99 95
✉   golf.du.coudray@wanadoo.fr
▷   18 L 5761 m Par 71
      9 L 1350 m Par 29
ⴲ   H (men 28, women 35) WE
      WD–NA
££   €42 (€70)

⊛   35km S of Paris on A6 (Jct 11)
⌂   CK Cotton
🖥   www.golfcoudray.org

Courson Monteloup   (1991)
91680 Bruyères-le-Chatel
☎   01 64 58 80 80

Crécy-la-Chapelle   (1987)
Domaine de la Brie, Route de Guérard, F
77580 Crécy-la-Chapelle
☎   01 64 75 34 44
✉   info@domainedelabrie.com

Disneyland Golf   (1992)
1 Allee de la Mare Houleuse,
77700 Magny-le-Hongre
☎   01 60 45 68 90
✉   dlp.nwy.golf@disney.com

Domaine de Belesbat
(1989)
Courdimanche-sur-Essonne,
91820 Boutigny-sur-Essonne
☎   01 69 23 19 10

Domont-Montmorency
Route de Montmorency, 95330 Domont
☎   01 39 91 07 50

Étiolles Colonial CC   (1990)
Vieux Chemin de Paris, 91450 Étiolles
☎   01 69 89 59 59
📠   01 69 89 59 62
✉   golf@etiollescolonial.com
▷   18 L 6239 m Par 73
      9 L 2665 m SSS 36
ⴲ   U
££   €50 (€70.50)
⊛   30km S of Paris
⌂   Michel Gayon
🖥   www.etiollescolonial.com

Fontainebleau   (1909)
Route d'Orleans, 77300 Fontainebleau
☎   01 64 22 22 95

Fontenailles   (1991)
Domaine de Bois Boudran,
77370 Fontenailles
☎   01 64 60 51 00

Forges-les-Bains   (1989)
Rue du Général Leclerc, 91470 Forges-les-
Bains
☎   01 64 91 48 18
📠   01 64 91 40 52
✉   golf.forges-les-bains@wanadoo.fr
▷   18 L 6167 m SSS 72
ⴲ   H or Green card
££   €36 (€54)
⊛   35km S of Paris, off A10
⌂   JM Rossi
🖥   www.golf-forgeslesbains.com

Greenparc   (1993)
Route de Villepech, 91280 St Pierre-du-
Perray
☎   01 60 75 40 60

L'Isle Adam (1995)
1 Chemin des Vanneaux, 95290
L'Isle Adam
☎ 01 34 08 11 11

Marivaux (1992)
Bois de Marivaux, 91640 Janvry
☎ 01 64 90 85 85
🖥 01 64 90 82 22
📧 contact@golfmarivaux.com
🏴 18 L 6158 m Par 72
SSS White 72.6 Slope 129
SSS Blue 68.2 Slope 113
👥 U
££ €41–€47 (€55–€63)
🚗 25km SW of Paris
🏠 Macauley/Quenouille
🖥 www.golfmarivaux.com

Meaux-Boutigny (1985)
Rue de Barrois, 77470 Boutigny
☎ 01 60 25 63 98

Mont Griffon (1990)
RD 909, 95270 Luzarches
☎ 01 34 68 10 10
🖥 01 34 68 04 10
📧 golf@golfmontgriffon.com
🏴 18 L 5897 m CR 70.8 SR 132
👥 U
££ €44
🚗 27km N of Paris, nr Chantilly
🏠 Nelson/Dongradi
🖥 www.golfmontgriffon.com

Montereau La Forteresse
(1989)
Domaine de la Forteresse, 77940 Thoury-Ferrottes
☎ (+33) 01 60 96 95 10
🖥 (+33) 01 60 96 01 41
📧 contact@golf-forteresse.com
🏴 18 L 5888 m Par 72
££ H or Green card
££ €34 (€55)
🚗 25km SE of Fontainebleau
🏠 Fromanger/Adam
🖥 www.golf-forteresse.com

Ormesson (1969)
Chemin du Belvédère, 94490 Ormesson-sur-Marne
☎ 01 45 76 20 71

Ozoir-la-Ferrière (1926)
Château des Agneaux, 77330 Ozoir-la-Ferrière
☎ 01 60 02 60 79

Paris International
(1991)
18 Route du Golf, 95560 Baillet-en-France
☎ 01 34 69 90 00

St Germain-les-Corbeil
6 Ave du Golf, 91250 St Germain-les-Corbeil
☎ 01 60 75 81 54

Seraincourt (1964)
Gaillonnet-Seraincourt, 95450 Vigny
☎ 01 34 75 47 28

Villarceaux (1971)
Château du Couvent, 95710 Chaussy
☎ 01 34 67 73 83
🖥 01 34 67 72 66
📧 villarceaux@wanadoo.fr
🏴 18 L 6059 m Par 72
SSS 72.4 SR 129 (men)
SSS 72.2 SR 122 (ladies)
👥 H
££ €37 (€63)
🚗 60km NW of Paris
🏠 M Backer
🖥 www.villarceaux.com

Villeray (1974)
Public
Melun-Sénart, St Pierre du Perray, 91100 Corbeil
☎ 01 60 75 17 47

Languedoc-Roussillon

Cap d'Agde (1989)
Public
4 Ave des Alizés, 34300 Cap d'Agde
☎ 04 67 26 54 40
🖥 04 67 26 97 00
📧 golf@ville-agde.fr
🏴 18 L 6286 m SSS 72
👥 U dogs and spikes forbidden; correct dress required
££ High season: €56 Low season: €46 (€56)
🚗 25km E of Béziers
🏠 Ronald Fream
🖥 www.ville-agde.fr

Carcassonne (1988)
Route de Ste-Hilaire, 11000 Carcassonne
☎ 06 13 20 85 43

Coulondres (1984)
72 Rue des Erables, 34980 Saint-Gely-du-Fesc
☎ 04 67 84 13 75

Domaine de Falgos (1992)
BP 9, 66260 St Laurent-de-Cerdans
☎ 04 68 39 51 42
🖥 04 68 39 52 30
📧 contact@falgos.com
🏴 18 L 5177 m SSS 69
👥 U
££ €35–€67
🚗 60km S of Perpignan, nr Spanish border (D115)
🏠 Alain Dehaye
🖥 www.falgos.com

Fontcaude (1991)
Route de Lodève, Domaine de Fontcaude, 34990 Juvignac
☎ 04 67 45 90 10
📧 golf@golfhotelmontpellier.com

La Grande-Motte (1987)
Clubhouse du Golf, 34280 La Grande-Motte
☎ 04 67 56 05 00

Montpellier Massane (1988)
Domaine de Massane, 34670 Baillargues
☎ 04 67 87 87 87

Nîmes Campagne (1968)
Route de Saint Gilles, 30900 Nîmes
☎ 04 66 70 17 37

Nîmes-Vacquerolles (1990)
1075 chemin du golf, 30900 Nîmes
☎ 04 66 23 33 33
🖥 04 66 23 94 94
📧 vacquerolles.opengolfclub @wanadoo.fr
🏴 18 L 6300 m SSS 72
👥 U
££ €56
🚗 W of Nîmes centre (D999)
🏠 W Baker
🖥 www.golf-nimes.com

Saint Cyprien Golf Resort
(1976)
Le Mas D'Huston, 66750 St Cyprien Plage
☎ 04 68 37 63 63
🖥 04 68 37 64 64
📧 golf@saintcyprien-golfresort.com
🏴 18 L 6480 m SSS 73
9 L 2724 m SSS 35
👥 U H
££ High Season €70 Medium Season €55 Low Season €45
🚗 15km SE of Perpignan
🏠 Wright/Tomlinson
🖥 www.saintcyprien-golfresort.com

St Thomas (1992)
Route de Bessan, 34500 Béziers
☎ 04 67 39 03 09
📧 info@golfsaintthomas.com

Loire Valley

Anjou G&CC (1990)
Route de Cheffes, 49330 Champigné
☎ 02 41 42 01 01
🖥 02 41 42 04 37
📧 info@anjougolf.com
🏴 18 L 6227 m SSS 72
6 hole short course
👥 U H
££ €36 (€45)
🚗 23km N of Angers
🏠 F Hawtree
🖥 www.anjougolf.com

Avrillé (1988)
Château de la Perrière, 49240 Avrillé
☎ 02 41 69 22 50
🖥 02 41 34 44 60
📧 avrille@bluegreen.com
🏴 18 L 6136 m SSS 71
9 hole Par 3 course
👥 U
££ €36 (€42)

🚣 5km N of Angers
🏠 Robert Berthet
🖥 www.bluegreen.com

Baugé-Pontigné   (1994)
Public
Route de Tours, 49150 Baugé
☎ 02 41 89 01 27
🖂 golf.bauge@wanadoo.fr

La Bretesche   (1967)
Domaine de la Bretesche, 44780 Missillac
☎ 02 51 76 86 86

Carquefou   (1991)
Boulevard de l'Epinay, 44470 Carquefou
☎ 02 40 52 73 74

Cholet   (1989)
Allée du Chêne Landry, 49300 Cholet
☎ 02 41 71 05 01

La Domangère
La Roche-sur-Yon, Route de la Rochelle,
85310 Nesmy
☎ 02 51 07 65 90

Fontenelles
Public
Saint-Gilles-Croix-de-Vie, 85220 Aiguillon-
sur-Vie
☎ 02 51 54 13 94

Ile d'Or   (1988)
BP 90410, 49270 La Varenne
☎ 02 40 98 58 00
🖩 02 40 98 51 62
🖂 nantesiledor@wanadoo.fr
🏳 18 L 6292 m Par 72
   9 L 1217 m Par 27
👥 U H
£€ €16–€38
🚣 25km NE of Nantes
🏠 Michel Gayon

**International Barriere-
   La Baule**   (1976)
44117 Saint-André-des Eaux
☎ 02 40 60 46 18
🖩 02 40 60 41 41
🖂 golfinterlabaule@lucienbarriere.com
🏳 18 L 6055 m Par 72 SSS 73
   18 L 6301 m Par 72 SSS 74
   9 L 2969 m Par 36
👥 U
£€ 9: €27 – €44; 18: €48 – €77
🚣 Avrillac, 3km NE of La Baule
🏠 Alliss/Thomas/Gayon
🖥 www.lucienbarriere.com

Laval-Changé   (1972)
La Chabossiere, 53000 Changé-les-Laval
☎ 02 43 53 16 03
🖩 02 43 49 35 15
🖂 golf53.laval@wanadoo.fr
🏳 18 L 6068 m Par 72 SSS 72
   9 L 3388 m
👥 U
£€ €35 (€45)
🚣 5km N of Laval. 60km E of Rennes

🏠 JP Foures
🖥 www.laval53-golf.com

Le Mansgolfier   (1990)
Rue du Golf, 72190 Sargé les Le Mans
☎ 02 43 76 25 07
🖂 lemansgolfier@wanadoo.fr

Le Mans Mulsanne   (1961)
Route de Tours, 72230 Mulsanne
☎ 02 43 42 00 36

Le Mansgolfier Golf Club
(1990)
Rue du Golf, 72190 Sarge les Le Mans
☎ 02 43 76 25 07
🖩 02 43 76 45 25
🖂 lemansgolfier@wanadoo.fr
🏳 18 L 6054 m SSS 72
👥 U
£€ €37 (€42)
🚣 6km NE of Le Mans
🏠 Antoine d'Ormesson
🖥 www.lemansgolfier.com

Nantes   (1967)
44360 Vigneux de Bretagne
☎ 02 40 63 25 82
🖩 02 40 63 64 86
🖂 golfclubnantes@aol.com
🏳 18 L 5940 m SSS 72
👥 H
£€ €45 (€56)
🚣 12km NW of Nantes
🏠 Frank Pennink
🖥 www.golfclubnantes.com

Nantes Erdre   (1990)
Chemin du Bout des Landes, 44300 Nantes
☎ 02 40 59 21 21

Les Olonnes
Gazé, 85340 Olonne-sur-Mer
☎ 02 51 33 16 16

Pornic   (1912)
49 Boulevard de l'Océan, Sainte-Marie/Mer,
44210 Pornic
☎ 02 40 82 06 69

Port Bourgenay   (1990)
Avenue de la Mine, Port Bourgenay,
85440 Talmont-St-Hilaire
☎ 02 51 23 35 45

Sablé-Solesmes   (1991)
Domaine de l'Outinière, Route de Pincé,
72300 Sablé-sur-Sarthe
☎ 02 43 95 28 78
🖩 02 43 92 39 05
🖂 golf-sable-solesmes@wanadoo.fr
🏳 27 holes SSS 72:
   Forêt 9 L 3197 m
   Rivière 9 L 2992 m
   Cascade 9 L 3069 m
👥 U
£€ 1.04–30.06/1.09–31.10 €55 (€68)
   July €62 (€62)
   1.01–31.03/1.11–31.12 €45 (€55)
   2009

🚣 40km SW of Le Mans
🏠 Michel Gayon
🖥 www.golf-sable-solesmes.com

St Jean-de-Monts   (1988)
Ave des Pays de la Loire, 85160 Saint Jean-
de-Monts
☎ 02 51 58 82 73

Savenay   (1990)
44260 Savenay
☎ 02 40 56 88 05

Normandy

Bellême-St-Martin   (1988)
Les Sablons, 61130 Bellême
☎ 02 33 73 00 07

Cabourg-Le Home   (1907)
38 Av Président Réné Coty, Le Home
Varaville, 14390 Cabourg
☎ 02 31 91 25 56
🖂 golf-cabourg-le-
   home@worldonline.fr

Caen   (1990)
Le Vallon, 14112 Bieville-Beuville
☎ 02 31 94 72 09

Champ de Bataille   (1988)
Château du Champ de Bataille, 27110
Le Neubourg
☎ 02 32 35 03 72
🖩 02 32 35 83 10
🖂 info@champdebataille.com
🏳 18 L 6575 m SSS 72
👥 U
£€ €45 (€65)
🚣 28km NW of Evreux. 45km SW of
   Rouen
🏠 Nelson/Huau
🖥 www.champdebataille.com

Clécy   (1988)
Manoir de Cantelou, 14570 Clécy
☎ 02 31 69 72 72
🖂 golf-de-clecy@golf-de-clecy.com

Coutainville   (1925)
Ave du Golf, 50230 Agon-Coutainville
☎ 02 33 47 03 31

Deauville St Gatien   (1987)
14130 St Gatien-des-Bois
☎ 02 31 65 19 99
🖩 02 31 65 11 24
🖂 contact@golfdeauville.com
🏳 18 L 6272 m Par 72
   9 L 3035 m Par 36
👥 U
£€ Low season: €31 (€46), high
   season: €46 (€58)
🚣 8km E of Deauville; 8km W of
   Honfleur
🏠 Olivier Brizon
🖥 www.golfdeauville.com

Dieppe-Pourville (1897)
51 Route de Pourville, 76200 Dieppe
- ☎ 02 35 84 25 05
- 📠 02 35 84 97 11
- ✉ golf-de-dieppe@wanadoo.fr
- ⮞ 18 L 5780 m Par 70
- 👥 U
- ££ €32 (€58)
- ⮞ 2km W of Dieppe towards Pourville
- 🏠 Willie Park Jr
- 🖥 www.golf-dieppe.com

Étretat (1908)
BP No 7, Route du Havre, 76790 Étretat
- ☎ 02 35 27 04 89

Forêt Verte
Bosc Guerard, 76710 Montville
- ☎ 02 35 33 62 94

Golf barrière de Deauville (1929)
14 Saint Arnoult, 14800 Deauville
- ☎ 02 31 14 24 24
- ✉ golfdeauville@lucienbarriere.com

Golf de Jumièges (1991)
Jumièges, 76480 Duclair
- ☎ 02 35 05 32 97
- 📠 02 35 37 99 97
- ✉ jumieges.golf@ucpa.asso.fr
- ⮞ 18 L 6003 m SSS 72
- 👥 U
- ££ €24 (€35)
- ⮞ 20km W of Rouen
- 🏠 JP Fourès

Granville (1912)
Bréville, 50290 Bréhal
- ☎ 02 33 50 23 06
- ✉ contact@golfdegranville.com

Le Havre (1933)
Hameau Saint-Supplix, 76930 Octeville-sur-Mer
- ☎ 02 35 46 36 50
- 📠 02 35 46 32 66
- ✉ golf.le-havre@wanadoo.fr
- ⮞ 18 L 5955 m SSS 72
- 👥 H
- ££ €35 (€50)
- ⮞ 10km N of Le Havre

Houlgate (1981)
Route de Gonneville, 14510 Houlgate
- ☎ 02 31 24 80 49

Omaha Beach (1986)
Ferme St Sauveur, 14520 Port-en-Bessin
- ☎ 02 31 22 12 12
- 📠 02 31 22 12 13
- ✉ omaha.beach@wanadoo.fr
- ⮞ La Mer 18 L 6216 m Par 72
  Le Nanoir 18 L 6052 m Par 71
- 👥 U H
- ££ €45–€65
- ⮞ 8km N of Bayeux
- 🏠 Yves Bureau
- 🖥 www.omahabeachgolfclub.com

Rouen-Mont St Aignan (1911)
Rue Francis Poulenc, 76130 Mont St Aignan
- ☎ 02 35 76 38 65

Golf-hotel St Saëns (1987)
Domaine du Vaudichon, 76680 St Saëns
- ☎ 02 35 34 25 24
- 📠 02 35 34 43 33
- ✉ golf@golfdesaintsaens.com
- ⮞ 18 L 6009 m Par 71
- 👥 U
- ££ €38 (€50) – 2007 rates
- ⮞ 30km NE of Rouen
- 🏠 D Robinson
- 🖥 www.golfdesaintsaens.com

Golf barrière de St Julien (1987)
St Julien-sur-Calonne, 14130 Pont-l'Évêque
- ☎ 02 31 64 30 30
- ✉ golfsaintjulien@lucienbarriere.com

Le Vaudreuil (1962)
27100 Le Vaudreuil
- ☎ 02 32 59 02 60

North East

Ammerschwihr
BP 19, Route des Trois Épis, 68770 Ammerschwihr
- ☎ 03 89 47 17 30

Bâle G&CC (1926)
Rue de Wentzwiller, 68220 Hagenthal-le-Bas
- ☎ +33 (0)3 89 68 50 91
- 📠 +33 (0)3 89 68 55 66
- ✉ info@gccbasel.ch
- ⮞ 18 L 6255 m Par 72 SSS 73
- 👥 WD–H (max 36) WE–M
- ££ €105
- ⮞ 15km SW of Bâle
- 🏠 B von Limburger
- 🖥 www.gccbasel.ch

Besançon (1968)
La Chevillote, 25620 Mamirolle
- ☎ 03 81 55 73 54

Bitche (1988)
Rue des Prés, 57230 Bitche
- ☎ 03 87 96 15 30

Château de Bournel (1990)
25680 Cubry
- ☎ 03 81 86 00 10
- ✉ info@bournel.com

Combles-en-Barrois (1948)
14 Rue Basse, 55000 Combles-en-Barrois
- ☎ 03 29 45 16 03

Épinal (1985)
Public
Rue du Merle-Blanc, 88001 Épinal
- ☎ 03 29 34 65 97

Golf de Faulquemont-Pontpierre (1993)
Avenue Jean Monnett, 57380 Faulquemont
- ☎ 03 87 81 30 52
- 📠 03 87 81 30 62
- ✉ golf.faulquemont@wanadoo.fr
- ⮞ 18 L 5985 m
  Men: SR 133 (white), 140 (yellow);
  Ladies: SR 132 (blue), 128 (red)
- 👥 U
- ££ €38 (€50) (2007 prices)
- ⮞ A14 towards Metz, exit Boulay
- 🏠 Flipo/Fourès
- 🖥 www.golf-faulquemont.com

Golf Hotel Club de la Forêt d'Orient (1990)
Route de Geraudot, 10220 Rouilly Sacey
- ☎ 03 25 43 80 80
- 📠 03 25 41 57 58
- ✉ contact@hotel-foret-orient.com
- ⮞ 18 L 6120 m Par 72
- 👥 U
- ££ €44
- ⮞ 20km E of Troyes
- 🏠 E Rossi
- 🖥 www.hotel-foret-orient.com

Gardengolf Metz
3 Rue Félix Savart, 57070 Metz
Technopole 2000
- ☎ 03 87 78 71 04
- 📠 03 87 78 68 98
- ✉ contact@gardengolfmetz.com
- ⮞ 18 L 5774 m SSS 71
  6 hole Par 3 course
- 👥 H or Green card
- ££ €34 (€44)
- ⮞ SE of Metz centre
- 🏠 Robert Berthet
- 🖥 www.gardengolfmetz.com

Grande Romanie (1988)
La Grande Romanie, 51460 Courtisols
- ☎ 06 61 50 01 00
- 📠 03 26 66 65 97
- ✉ at@par72.net
- ⮞ 18 L 6578 m SSS 76
- 👥 U
- ££ €36 (€45)
- ⮞ St Etienne-au-Temple, 6km from A4 Junction 28
- 🏠 Alain Tribout
- 🖥 wwwpar72.net

La Grange aux Ormes
La Grange aux Ormes, 57155 Marly
- ☎ 03 87 63 10 62

Kempferhof (1988)
Golf-Hôtel-Restaurant, 67115 Plobsheim
- ☎ 0033 (0) 3 88 98 72 72
- 📠 0033 (0) 3 88 98 74 76
- ✉ info@golf-kempferhof.com
- ⮞ 18 L 6024 m SSS 73 SR 145

(※) H
££ Low season: €85 High season:
€110
⛳ 15km S of Strasbourg
🏠 Bob von Hagge
🖥 www.golf-kempferhof.com

La Largue G&CC   (1988)
25 Rue du Golf, 68580 Mooslargue
☎ 03 89 07 67 67
🖳 03 89 25 62 83
📧 lalargue@golf-lalargue.com
🏴 18 L 6142 m CR 73.1 SR 138
9 Par 30
(※) U H36
££ €60 (€70)
⛳ 25km W of Basle
🏠 Jeremy Pern
🖥 www.golf-lalargue.com

Les Rousses   (1986)
*1305 Route du Noirmont, 39220
Les Rousses*
☎ 03 84 60 06 25

Metz-Cherisey   (1963)
Château de Cherisey, 57420 Cherisey
☎ 03 87 52 70 18
🖳 03 87 52 42 44
🏴 18 L 6172 m SSS 72
(※) H
££ 9: €25 (€35); 18: €40 (€46)
⛳ 15km SE of Metz
🏠 Donald Harradine

Nancy-Aingeray   (1962)
Aingeray, 54460 Liverdun
☎ 03 83 24 53 87

Nancy-Pulnoy   (1993)
10 Rue du Golf, 54425 Pulnoy
☎ 03 83 18 10 18

Reims-Champagne   (1928)
*Château des Dames de France,
51390 Gueux*
☎ 03 26 05 46 10

Rhin Mulhouse   (1969)
Ile du Rhin, F-68490 Chalampe
☎ +33 3 89 83 28 32
🖳 +33 3 89 83 28 42
📧 golfdurhin@wanadoo.fr
🏴 18 L 5977 m SSS 72
(※) WE–M
££ €55 (€65)
⛳ 20km E of Mulhouse
🏠 Donald Harradine
🖥 www.golf-rhin.com

Rougemont-le-Château
(1990)
*Route de Masevaux, 90110 Rougemont-le-
Château*
☎ 03 84 23 74 74
📧 golf.rougemont@wanadoo.fr

Strasbourg   (1934)
Route du Rhin, 67400 Illkirch
☎ 03 88 66 17 22

🖳 03 88 65 05 67
📧 golf.strasbourg@wanadoo.fr
🏴 27 holes:
6105-6138 m SSS 72-73
(※) WD–H (max 35) WE–M (H24
men, 28 women)
££ €60 (€70)
⛳ 10km S of Strasbourg
🏠 Donald Harradine
🖥 www.golf-strasbourg.com

Domaine du Val de Sorne
(1989)
*Domaine de Val de Sorne,
39570 Vernantois*
☎ 03 84 43 04 80
🖳 03 84 47 31 21
📧 info@valdesorne.com
🏴 18 L 6000 m SSS 72
(※) U
££ High season: €43–€54 Low season:
€31–€37
⛳ 5km SE of Lons-le-Saunier,
between Dijon, Lyon and Geneva
🏠 Hugues Lambert
🖥 www.valdesorne.com

La Wantzenau   (1991)
C D 302, 67610 La Wantzenau
☎ 03 88 96 37 73

Paris Region

Béthemont-Chisan CC
(1989)
*12 Rue du Parc de Béthemont,
78300 Poissy*
☎ 01 39 75 51 13

La Boulie
La Boulie, 78000 Versailles
☎ 01 39 50 59 41

Feucherolles   (1992)
78810 Feucherolles
☎ 01 30 54 94 94
🖳 01 30 54 92 37
🏴 18 L 6358 m Par 72
(※) U
££ €33–€49 (€49–€65)
⛳ 23km W of Paris
🏠 JM Poellot
🖥 www.golf-de-feucherolles.com

Fourqueux   (1963)
Rue Saint Nom 36, 78112 Fourqueux
☎ 01 34 51 41 47

Golf National   (1990)
2 Avenue du Golf, 78280 Guyancourt
☎ 01 30 43 36 00
🖳 01 30 43 85 58
📧 gn@golf-national.com
🏴 Albatros 18 L 6600 m Par 72
Aigle 18 L 5961 m Par 71
Oiselet 9 L 1955 m Par 32
(※) H max 28 on Albatros, H or Green
Card on Aigle, U on Oiselet

££ Albatros: €75 (€100) Aigle: €60
(€70) Oiselet: €30 (€30)
⛳ St Quentin-en-Yvelines, SW of
Paris (D36 or A13+A12); Paris
25km; Vers
🏠 H Chesneau
🖥 www.golf-national.com

Isabella   (1969)
RN12, Sainte-Appoline, 78370 Plaisir
☎ 01 30 54 10 62
🖳 01 30 54 67 58
📧 info@golfisabella.com
🏴 18 L 5629 m Par 71 SSS 71
(※) WD–H Sat–min 24 Sun–NA
££ €50 (€70)
⛳ 28km W of Paris (RN12)
🏠 Paul Rolin
🖥 www.golfisabella.com

Joyenval   (1992)
Chemin de la Tuilerie, 78240 Chambourcy
☎ 01 39 22 27 50
🖳 01 39 79 12 90
📧 joyenval@golfdejoyenval.com
🏴 Retz 18 L 6211 m Par 72
Marly 18 L 6249 m Par 72
(※) M
££ No visitors
⛳ 25km N of Paris, nr St Germain-en-
Laye
🏠 Robert Trent Jones Sr
🖥 www.joyenval.fr

Rochefort   (1964)
78730 Rochefort-en-Yvelines
☎ 01 30 41 31 81

St Cloud   (1911)
60 Rue du 19 Janvier, Garches 92380
☎ 01 47 01 01 85

St Germain   (1922)
Route de Poissy, 78100 St Germain-en-Laye
☎ 01 39 10 30 30
🖳 01 39 10 30 31
📧 info@golfsaintgermain.org
🏴 18 L 6117 m SSS 72
9 L 2030 m SSS 33
(※) WD–H (men 24, ladies 28) WE–M
££ €100 (€80 with French Federation
licence)
⛳ 20km W of Paris
🏠 HS Colt
🖥 www.golfsaintgermain.org

St Quentin-en-Yvelines
Public
RD 912, 78190 Trappes
☎ 01 30 50 86 40

St Nom-La-Bretêche   (1959)
*Hameau Tuilerie-Bignon, 78860 St Nom-
La-Bretèche*
☎ 01 30 80 04 40

La Vaucouleurs   (1987)
Rue de l'Eglise, 78910 Civry-la-Forêt
☎ 01 34 87 62 29
🖳 01 34 87 70 09
📧 vaucouleurs@vaucouleurs.fr

Rivière 18 L 6138 m CR 73.2
SR 138
Vallons 18 L 5553 m Par 70 CR
68.6 SR 115
🏌 H or Green card
£€ €48 (€70)
⛳ 50km W of Paris, between Mantes and Houdan
🏠 Michel Gayon
🖥 www.vaucouleurs.fr

Les Yvelines
Château de la Couharde, 78940 La-Queue-les-Yvelines
☎ 01 34 86 48 89

Provence & Côte d'Azur

Aix Marseille   (1935)
13290 Les Milles
☎ 04 42 24 40 41/
04 42 24 23 01
🖂 golfaixmarseille@aol.com

Barbaroux   (1989)
Route de Cabasse, 83170 Brignoles
☎ 04 94 69 63 63
📠 04 94 59 00 93
🖂 contact@barbaroux.com
🏴 18 L 6367 m SSS 72
🏌 H
£€ €71
⛳ Brignoles, 50km E of Aix. 40km N of Toulon
🏠 Pete Dye/PB Dye
🖥 www.barbaroux.com

Les Baux de Provence
(1989)
Domaine de Manville, 13520 Les Baux-de-Provence
☎ 04 90 54 40 20
📠 04 90 54 40 93
🖂 golfbauxdeprovence@wanadoo.fr
🏴 9 L 2812 m SSS 36
🏌 U H
£€ €36 high season €30 (€35) low season
⛳ 15km NE of Arles. 15km S of Avignon. 80km W of Marseilles
🏠 Martin Hawtree
🖥 www.golfbauxdeprovence.com

Beauvallon-Grimaud
Boulevard des Collines, 83120 Sainte-Maxime
☎ 04 94 96 16 98

Biot   (1930)
La Bastide du Roy, 06410 Biot
☎ 04 93 65 08 48

Cannes Mandelieu
(1891)
Route de Golf, 06210 Mandelieu
☎ 04 92 97 32 00

Cannes Mandelieu Riviera
(1990)
Avenue des Amazones, 06210 Mandelieu
☎ 04 92 97 49 49

Cannes Mougins   (1923)
175 Avenue du Golf, 06250 Mougins
☎ 04 93 75 79 13
📠 04 93 75 27 60
🖂 golf-cannes-mougins@wanadoo.fr
🏴 18 L 6263 m SSS 72
🏌 H–max 28
£€ €120 (€140)
⛳ 8km NE of Cannes (D35)
🏠 Alliss/Thomas (1977)
🖥 www.golf-cannes-mougins.com

Châteaublanc
Les Plans, 84310 Morières-les-Avignon
☎ 04 90 33 39 08
📠 04 90 33 43 24
🖂 info@golfchateaublanc.com
🏴 18 L 6141 m SSS 72
9 L 1267 m Par 28
£€ 9: €30 (€35), 18: €42 (€55)
Juniors: 9: €15, 18: €25
⛳ 5km SE of Avignon, nr Airport
🏠 Thierry Sprecher
🖥 www.golfchateaublanc.com

Digne-les-Bains   (1990)
Public
57 Route du Chaffaut, 0400 Digne-les-Bains
☎ 04 92 30 58 00
🖂 info@golfdigne.com

Estérel Latitudes   (1989)
Ave du Golf, 83700 St Raphaël
☎ 04 94 52 68 30

Frégate   (1992)
Dolce Frégate, RD 559, 83270 St Cyr-sur-Mer
☎ 04 94 29 38 00
📠 04 94 29 96 94
🖂 golf-fregate@wanadoo.fr
🏴 Frégate: 18 L 6210 m SSS 72
Frégalon: 9 hole short course
🏌 U
£€ Jan 1–Apr 30 and Nov 1–Dec 31 Frégate €53, Frégalon €31 May 1–Oct 31 Frégate €68, Frégalon €37
⛳ 25km W of Toulon on coast
🏠 Ronald Fream
🖥 www.fregate.dolce.com

Gap-Bayard   (1988)
Centre d'Oxygénation, 05000 Gap
☎ 04 92 50 16 83
📠 04 92 50 17 05
🖂 gap-bayard@wanadoo.fr
🏴 18 L 6023 m SSS 72
🏌 U
£€ €38 (€44.40)
⛳ 7km N of Gap. 80km S of Grenoble
🏠 Hugues Lambert
🖥 www.gap-bayard.com

Golf Claux-Amic   (1992)
1 Route des Trois Ponts, 06130 Grasse
☎ 04 93 60 55 44
🖂 info@claux-amic.com

Grand Avignon   (1989)
Les Chênes Verts, 84270 Vedene - Avignon
☎ 04 90 31 49 94
📠 04 90 31 01 21
🖂 info@golfgrandavignon.com
🏴 18 L 6046 m Par 72
🏌 U
£€ High season €60 Low season €50
⛳ Vedene, 10km NE of Avignon
🏠 Georges Roumeas
🖥 www.golfgrandavignon.com

La Grande Bastide   (1990)
Chemin des Picholines, 06740 Châteauneuf de Grasse
☎ 04 93 77 70 08

Luberon   (1986)
La Grande Gardette, 04860 Pierrevert
☎ 04 92 72 17 19
📠 04 92 72 59 12
🖂 info@golf-du-luberon.com
🏴 18 L 5623 m SSS 72
🏌 U
£€ €55
⛳ 5km SW of Manosque. 45km NE of Aix-en-Provence
🏠 Artea
🖥 www.golf-du-luberon.com

Marseille La Salette
(1988)
65 Impasse des Vaudrans, 13011 La Valentine Marseille
☎ 04 91 27 12 16
📠 04 91 27 21 33
🖂 lasalette@opengolfclub.com
🏴 18 L 5214 m Par 69 SR 135
🏌 H
£€ €45 (€55)
⛳ Nr centre of Marseilles
🏠 Michel Gayon
🖥 www.opengolfclub.com

Miramas   (1993)
Mas de Combe, 13140 Miramas
☎ 04 90 58 56 55

Monte Carlo   (1910)
Route du Mont-Agel, 06320 La Turbie
☎ 04 92 41 50 70
📠 04 93 41 09 55
🖂 monte-carlo-golf-club@wanadoo.fr
🏴 18 L 5811 m SSS 71
🏌 H
£€ €100 (€120)
⛳ Mont Agel, La Turbie, 10km N of Monte Carlo
🏠 The committee

Opio-Valbonne   (1966)
Route de Roquefort-les-Pins, 06650 Opio
☎ 04 93 12 00 08

Pont Royal   (1992)

Pont Royal, 13370 Mallemort
☎ 04 90 57 40 79

Le Roc/Golf de Roquebrune   (1989)

*Golf de Roquebrune, CD7,
83520 Roquebrune-sur-Argens*
☎ 04 94 19 60 35
🖴 04 94 82 90 22
📧 golf@le-roc.eu
🏳 9 holes – new 18 hole
   championship and 9 hole academic
   courses opened in 2008
🏌 H
££ 9 holes €24 low season, €30 high
   season 2 x 9 holes €40 low season,
   €45 high season
⛳ 35km N of Saint-Tropez. 40km SW
   of Cannes
🏠 Udo Barth
🖥 www.le-roc.eu

Royal Mougins   (1993)

424 Avenue du Roi, 06250 Mougins
☎ 04 92 92 49 69 (reception)
   04 92 92 49 79 (pro shop)
🖴 04 92 92 49 70
📧 contact@royalmougins.fr
🏳 18 L 6004 m
   Ladies CR 71.1-73.5 SR 129-137
   Men CR 70.8-72.1 SR 136-144
🏌 H
££ €175 (€225) inc. buggy
⛳ 5km N of Cannes
🏠 Robert von Hagge
🖥 www.royalmougins.fr

Saint Donat G&CC   (1993)

270 Route de Cannes, 06130 Grasse
☎ +33 493 097660
🖴 +33 493 097663
📧 mail@golfsaintdonat.com
🏳 18 L 5857 m Par 71 SR 130
   9 L 695 m Par 27
🏌 U SOC
££ High season €75 Low season €69
   week Discounts for jun/students
   (2005 rates)
⛳ Between Cannes and Grasse, exit 4
   from m/way. 30 min Nice Airport
🏠 Robert Trent Jones jun
🖥 www.golfsaintdonat.com

Les Domaines de Saint Endréol Golf & Spa Resort   (1992)

*Route de Bagnols-en-Fôret, 83 920
La Motte-en-Provence*
☎ 04 94 51 89 89
🖴 04 94 51 89 90
📧 accueil.golf@st-endreol.com
🏳 18 L 6219 m Par 72
   Men: white SR 142, yellow SR 134
   Ladies: blue SR 129, red SR 125
🏌 U H
££ €72
⛳ Situated in La Motte in the Var
   countryside between Cannes and
   St Tropez

🏠 Michel Gayon
🖥 www.st-endreol.com

Sainte Victoire   (1985)

Domaine de Château L'Arc, 13710 Fuveau
☎ 0442 298343
🖴 0442 534268
📧 saintevictoiregolfclub@wanadoo.fr
🏳 18 L 6095 m
   Black: CR 73.5 SR 131
   Yellow: CR 70.3 SR 131
   Blue: CR 73.1 SR 130
   Red: CR 70.2 SR 123
🏌 U
££ €60
⛳ 15km SE of Aix-en-Provence
🏠 Robert Trent Jones
🖥 www.saintevictoiregolfclub.com

La Sainte-Baume   (1988)

*Golf Hotel, Domaine de Châteauneuf,
83860 Nans-les-Pins*
☎ 04 94 78 60 12
🖴 04 94 78 63 52
📧 saintebaume@opengolfclub.com
🏳 18 L 6062 m Par 72 SSS 72 SR 124
🏌 U
££ High season: 9: €56; 18: €70 Low
   season: 9: €41 (€46); 18: €51
   (€67)
⛳ 30km SE of Aix-en-Provence, via
   A8 (exit Saint-Maximin)
🏠 Robert Berthet
🖥 www.opengolfclub.com

Sainte-Maxime

*Route de Débarquement, 83120 Sainte-
Maxime*
☎ 04 94 55 02 02

Servanes   (1989)

Domaine de Servanes, 13890 Mouriès
☎ 04 90 47 59 95
🖴 04 90 47 52 58
📧 servanes@opengolfclub.com
🏳 18 L 6161m Par 72 SSS 74.3
🏌 U H WD/WE
££ Low season: €48 High season: €59
⛳ 35km S of Avignon
🏠 Sprecher/Watine
🖥 www.opengolfclub.com

Taulane

*Domaine du Château de Taulane, RN 85,
83840 La Martre*
☎ 04 93 60 31 30
🖴 04 93 60 33 23
📧 resagolf@chateau-taulane.com
🏳 18 L 6250 m Par 72
🏌 H
££ April €60, May–Nov €85 (inc. meal
   at buffet)
⛳ 55km N of Cannes on N85 (Route
   Napoleon)
🏠 Gary Player
🖥 www.chateau-de-taulane.com

Valcros   (1964)

*Domaine de Valcros, 83250 La Londe-les-
Maures*
☎ 04 94 66 81 02

Valescure   (1895)

BP 451, 83704 St-Raphaël Cedex
☎ 04 94 82 40 46

Rhone-Alps

Aix-les-Bains   (1904)

Avenue du Golf, 73100 Aix-les-Bains
☎ 04 79 61 23 35
🖴 04 79 34 06 01
📧 info@golf-aixlesbains.com
🏳 18 L 5519 m Par 70 SR 124
🏌 H
££ Jan–Mar, Nov–Dec €46 (€53)
   Apr–June, Sept–Oct €57 (€63)
   July–Aug €63
⛳ 3km S of Aix
🏠 A Serond
🖥 www.golf-aixlesbains.com

Albon   (1989)

*Domaine de Senaud, Albon, 26140 St
Rambert d'Albon*
☎ 04 75 03 03 90
🖴 04 75 03 11 01
📧 golf.albon@wanadoo.fr
🏳 18 L 6087 m CR 72.5 SR 135
   9 L 1260 m Par 29
🏌 U
££ €42–€48
⛳ 60km S of Lyon, motorway exit
   Chanas
🏠 Antoine d'Ormesson/Roger Guvgui
🖥 www.golf-albon.com

Annecy   (1953)

Echarvines, 74290 Talloires
☎ (0033)4 50 60 12 89
🖴 (0033)4 50 60 08 80
📧 golflacannecy@wanadoo.fr
🏳 18 L 5017 m SSS 68
🏌 H
££ €47 (€62)
⛳ 13km E of Annecy
🏠 Cecil Blandford
🖥 www.golf-lacannecy.com

Annonay-Gourdan   (1988)

Domaine de Gourdan, 07430 Saint Clair
☎ 04 75 67 03 84

Les Arcs

B P 18, 73706 Les Arcs Cedex
☎ 04 79 07 43 95

Bossey G&CC   (1985)

Château de Crevin, 74160 Bossey
☎ 04 50 43 95 50
🖴 04 50 95 32 57
📧 accueilgolf@golfbossey.com
🏳 18 L 5954 m Par 71
🏌 WD–U WE–NA
££ €75
⛳ 6km S of Geneva
🏠 Robert Trent Jones Jr
🖥 www.golfbossey.com

La Bresse
Domaine de Mary, 01400 Condessiat
☎ 04 74 51 42 09

Chamonix (1934)
35 Route du Golf, 74400 Chamonix
☎ 04 50 53 06 28
📠 04 50 53 38 69
📧 info@golfdechamonix.com
🏌 18 L 6087 m SSS 72
👥 H
££ €34–€70 (€43–€70)
⛳ 3km N of Chamonix (RN 506). Geneva 80km
🏛 Robert Trent Jones Sr
🖥 www.golfdechamonix.com

Le Clou (1985)
01330 Villars-les-Dombes
☎ 04 74 98 19 65
📠 04 74 98 15 15
📧 golfduclou.fr@freesbee.fr
🏌 18 L 5000 m SSS 67
👥 WD–U WE–H
££ €40 (€50)
⛳ 30km NE of Lyon
🖥 www.golfduclou.fr

Divonne (1931)
Ave des Thermes, 01220 Divonne-les-Bains
☎ 04 50 40 34 11
📠 04 50 40 34 25
📧 golf@domaine-de-divonne.com
🏌 18 L 5917 m SSS 72
👥 H–max 35
££ €54 (€80)
⛳ 18km N of Geneva
🏛 Nakowski
🖥 www.domaine-de-divonne.com

Esery (1990)
Esery, 74930 Reignier
☎ 00334 50 36 58 70
📠 00334 50 36 57 62
📧 golf.esery@wanadoo.fr
🏌 18 L 6350 m SSS 73
  9 L 2024 m SSS 31
👥 WD–H WE
££ €74 High season €50 Low season
⛳ 10km S of Geneva
🏛 Michel Gayon
🖥 www.golf-club-esery.com

Evian Masters (1904)
Rive Sud du lac de Genève, 74500 Évian
☎ 04 50 26 85 00
📠 04 50 75 65 54
📧 golf@evianroyalresort.com
🏌 18 L 6054 m SSS 74.6
👥 U H
££ €50–€80 (€60–€90) Open Feb–Nov; closed Dec–Jan
⛳ 2km W of Évian. 40km NE of Geneva Airport
🏛 Cabell Robinson
🖥 www.evianroyalresort.com

Giez (1991)
Lac d'Annecy, 74210 Giez
☎ 04 50 44 48 41
📠 04 50 32 55 93

📧 as.golfdegiez@wanadoo.fr
🏌 18 L 5820 m Par 72
  9 L 2250 m Par 33
👥 H or Green card
££ €49–€64
⛳ 20km SE of Annecy
🏛 Didier Fruchet
🖥 www.golfdegiez.fr

Le Gouverneur
Château du Breuil, 01390 Monthieux
☎ 04 72 26 40 34
📧 golfgouverneur@worldonline.fr

Grenoble-Bresson (1990)
Route de Montavie, 38320 Eybens
☎ 04 76 73 65 00

Grenoble-Charmeil (1988)
38210 St Quentin-sur-Isère
☎ 04 76 93 67 28
📠 04 76 93 62 04
📧 info@golfhotelgrenoble.com
🏌 18 L 5733 m Par 73
👥 U
££ €40 (€50)
⛳ 15km NW of Grenoble, off A49
🏛 Perl/Garaialde
🖥 www.golfhotelgrenoble.com

Grenoble-Uriage (1921)
Les Alberges, 38410 Uriage
☎ 04 76 89 03 47
📠 04 76 73 15 80
📧 golfuriage@wanadoo.fr
🏌 9 L 2004 m Par 64 CR 61.3 SR 112
👥 U
££ €24 (€28)
⛳ 15km E of Grenoble
🏛 Watine/Sprecher
🖥 www.golfuriage.com

Lyon (1921)
38280 Villette-d'Anthon
☎ 04 78 31 11 33
📠 04 72 02 48 27
📧 info@golfclubdelyon.com
🏌 18 L 6229 m SSS 72
  18 L 6727 m SSS 74
👥 U H
££ €34 (€50)
⛳ 20km E of Lyon
🏛 Hawtree/Lambert
🖥 www.golfclubdelyon.com

Lyon-Verger (1977)
69360 Saint-Symphorien D'Ozon
☎ 04 78 02 84 20

Maison Blanche G&CC (1991)
01170 Echenevex
☎ 04 50 42 44 42

Méribel (1966)
BP 54, 73550 Méribel
☎ 04 79 00 52 67
📠 04 79 00 38 85
📧 info@golf-meribel.com
🏌 18 L 5538 m Par 71

👥 H
££ Early season €45 Mid–season €50 High season €65
⛳ 15km S of Moutiers. 35km S of Albertville
🏛 Sprecher/Watine/Lambat
🖥 www.golf-meribel.com

Mionnay La Dombes (1986)
Chemin de Beau-Logis, 01390 Mionnay
☎ 04 78 91 84 84

Mont-d'Arbois (1964)
74120 Megève
☎ 04 50 21 29 79

Pierre Carée (1984)
74300 Flaine
☎ 04 50 90 85 44

St Etienne (1989)
62 Rue St Simon, 42000 St Etienne
☎ 04 77 32 14 63

Salvagny (1987)
100 Rue des Granges, 69890 La Tour de Salvagny
☎ 04 78 48 83 60
📠 04 78 48 00 16
📧 accueil@golf-salvagny.com
🏌 18 L 6300 m SSS 73 Par 72
👥 U H–WE 35.4 WD–green card
££ €46 (€61)
⛳ Lyon 20km
🏛 Drancourt
🖥 www.golf-salvagny.com

La Sorelle (1991)
Domaine de Gravagnieux, 01320 Villette-sur-Ain
☎ 04 74 35 47 27

Tignes (1968)
Val Claret, 73320 Tignes
☎ 04 79 06 37 42 (Summer)
📠 04 79 06 35 64
📧 golf.tignes@compagniedesalpes.fr
🏌 18 L 5030 m SSS 68 SR 112
👥 H–max 35
££ €39
⛳ 50km E of Moutiers, off D902, nr Italian border. 90km S of Chamonix
🏛 Philippe Vallant

Valdaine (1989)
Domaine de la Valdaine, Montboucher/Jabron, 26740 Montelimar-Montboucher
☎ 04 75 00 71 33

Valence St Didier (1983)
26300 St Didier de Charpey
☎ 04 75 59 67 01

Toulouse & Pyrenees

Albi Lasbordes (1989)
Château de Lasbordes, 81000 Albi
☎ 05 63 54 98 07

☎ 05 63 54 98 06
✉ contact@golfalbi.com
╠ 18 L 6200 m SSS 72
⚐ U
££ €45 (€55) July/Aug D—€55
⛳ 70km NE of Toulouse
⌂ Garaialde/Pern
▤ www.golfalbi.com

Ariège   (1986)
Unjat, 09240 La Bastide-de-Serou
☎ 05 61 64 56 78

Auch Embats   (1970)
Route de Montesquiou, 32000 Auch
☎ 05 62 61 10 11/
  06 81 18 41 43
🖳 05 62 611057
╠ 18 L 5018 m SSS 70 Slope 132
⚐ U
££ €35 (€40)
⛳ 4km W of Auch. 80km W of
  Toulouse
⌂ André Migret
▤ www.golf-auch-embats.com

Golf County Club de
  Bigorre   (1992)
65200 Pouzac, Bagnères de Bigorre
☎ (33) (0) 5 62 91 06 20
🖳 (33) (0) 5 62 91 38 00
✉ contact@golf-bigorre.fr
╠ 18 L 5909 m SSS 72 SR 134
⚐ U
££ High Season €40 Low Season €30
⛳ Bagneres de Biforre, 20 km from
  Lourdes, nearest airport: Pau,
  Tarbes
⌂ Olivier Brizon
▤ www.golf-bigorre.fr

Étangs de Fiac   (1987)
Brazis, 81500 Fiac
☎ 05 63 70 64 70
🖳 05 63 75 32 91
✉ golf.fiac-sw@wanadoo.fr
╠ 18 L 5807 m SSS 71
  Yellow SR 128, Red SR 121
⚐ U
££ €33 (€44)
⛳ 45km NE of Toulouse
⌂ M Hawtree
▤ www.etangsdefiac.com

Florentin-Gaillac   (1990)
Le Bosc, Florentin, 81150 Marssac-sur-Tarn
☎ 05 63 55 20 50

Golf de tarbes   (1987)
1 Rue du Bois, 65310 Laloubère
☎ 05 62 45 14 50
🖳 05 62 45 11 78
✉ golf.des.tumulus@wanadoo.fr
╠ 18 L 5050 m Par 70 CR 69.2 SR 127
⚐ U
££ €29
⛳ 2km S of Tarbes, towards Bagnères
⌂ Charles de Ginestet
▤ www.perso.wanadoo.fr/tumulus

Guinlet   (1986)
32800 Eauze
☎ 05 62 09 80 84

Lannemezan   (1962)
*250 Rue uu Dr Vererschlag,
65300 Lannemezan*
☎ 0562 98 01 01
🖳 0562 98 52 32
✉ golflannemezan@wanadoo.fr
╠ 18 L 5872 m Par 70
⚐ H
££ €31 low season (Nov–Apr) €40
  high season (May–Oct)
⛳ 38km SE of Tarbes
⌂ Hirigoyen/Laserre
▤ www.golflannemezan.com

Lourdes   (1988)
Chemin du Lac, 65100 Lourdes
☎ 05 62 42 02 06
🖳 05 62 42 02 06
✉ golf.lourdes@wanadoo.fr
╠ 18 L 5482 m Par 72 CR 71.1
⚐ U
££ Low season €30–€40 High season
  €40–€50
⛳ 4km W of Lourdes, off D940
⌂ Olivier Brizon

Mazamet-La Barouge
  (1956)
81660 Pont de l'Arn
☎ 05 63 61 08 00/
  05 63 67 06 72
🖳 05 63 61 13 03
✉ golf.labarouge@wanadoo.fr
╠ 18 L 5623 m SSS 70
⚐ U
££ €42
⛳ 2km N of Mazamet. 80km E of
  Toulouse. 80km W of Béziers
⌂ Mackenzie Ross/Hawtree
▤ www.golf-mazamet.net

Toulouse   (1951)
31320 Vieille-Toulouse
☎ 05 61 73 45 48

Toulouse-Palmola   (1974)
Route d'Albi, 31660 Buzet-sur-Tarn
☎ 05 61 84 20 50
🖳 05 61 84 48 92
✉ golf.palmola@wanadoo.fr
╠ 18 L 6156 m SSS 73
⚐ H
££ €50 (€75)
⛳ 18km NE of Toulouse. A68 Jct 4
⌂ Michael Fenn

Toulouse-Teoula   (1991)
*71 Avenue des Landes, 31830 Plaisance
du Touch*
☎ 05 61 91 98 80
🖳 05 61 91 49 66
✉ contact@golftoulouseteoula.com
╠ 18 L 5500 m Par 69
⚐ H or green card
££ €34 (€53)
⛳ 15km W of Toulouse
⌂ Martin Hawtree
▤ www.golftoulouseteoula.com

Germany

Berlin & East

Balmer See   (1995)
Drewinscher Weg 1, 17429 Benz/Otbalm
☎ (038379) 28199
🖳 (038379) 28200
✉ info@golfhotel-usedom.de
╠ 2 x 18 L 5106/5442 m Par 71 SR
  126/128
⚐ U H
££ €46 (€56)
⛳ Usedom, 50km E of Greifswald
⌂ M Skeide
▤ www.golfhotel-usedom.de

Golf-und Land-Club Berlin-
  Wannsee e.V.   (1895)
Golfweg 22, 14109 Berlin
☎ (030) 806 7060
🖳 (030) 806 706-10
✉ info@glcbw.de
╠ 18 L 6088 m SR 127
  9 L 4442 m SR 102
⚐ WD–U H WE–M
££ €100, €75 with member WE with
  members only €90
⛳ Berlin (SW)
⌂ Harris Brothers (1925)
▤ www.glcbw.de

Berliner G&CC Motzener
  See   (1991)
*Am Golfplatz 5, 15749 Mittenwalde
OT Motzen*
☎ (033769) 50130
🖳 (033769) 50134
✉ info@golfclubmotzen.de
╠ 18 L5900 m Par 72
  9 L 2640 m Par 54
⚐ H U
££ €35–€70
⛳ 30km S of Berlin
⌂ Kurt Rossknecht
▤ www.golfclubmotzen.de

Elbflorenz GC Dresden
  (1992)
*Ferdinand von Schillstr 4a,
01728 Possendorf*
☎ (035206) 2430

Potsdamer GC   (1990)
Tremmener Landstrasse, 14641 Tremmen
☎ (033233) 80244
✉ potsdammer.golfclub@berlin.de

Schloss Meisdorf   (1996)
Petersberger Trift 33, 06463 Meisdorf
☎ (034743) 98450

Golfclub Schloss
  Wilkendorf   (1991)
*Am Weiher 1, 15345 Altlandsberg-
Wilkendorf*
☎ (0049) 3341 330960

☎ (0049) 3341 330961
✉ service@golfpark-schloss-wilkendorf.com
▷ Men: 18 L 6096 m
Par 72 CR 72.7 SR 132
Women: 18 L 5302 m
Par 72 CR 74.0 SR 127
۞ U H with reservation (WD 45, WE 36)
££ Mon–Wed €40, Thur €45, Fri €45, Sat–Sun €60
⚙ 5km to Strausberg. 40km to Berlin
⌂ Sandy Lyle
▤ www.golfpark-schloss-wilkendorf.com

Seddiner See (1993)
Zum Weiher 44, 14552 Wildenbruch
☎ (033205) 7320

Golfresort Semlin am See
(1992)
Ferchesarerstrasse 8b, 14712 Semlin
☎ (03385) 554410
⌨ (03385) 554400
✉ golf@golfresort-semlin.de
▷ 27 holes
Men: CR 71.7 SR 130;
CR 71.3 SR 127; CR 72.5 SR 127
Women: CR 73.9 SR 127;
CR 73.1 SR 126; CR 74.5 SR 124
9 hole public course
۞ H
££ €35 (€60) – visitors €25 (€40) – hotel guest
⚙ 75km W of Berlin (B5/B188)
⌂ Christoph Städler
▤ www.golfresort-semlin.de

Sporting Club Berlin Schwantzelsee e.V (1992)
Parkallee 3, 15526 Bad Sarrow
☎ (033631) 63300
⌨ (033631) 63310
✉ info@sporting-club-berlin.de
▷ Nick Faldo: 18 L 6095 m Par 72
Arnold Palmer:18 L 6078 m Par 72
Stan Eby: 18 L 5593 m Par 71
Jake McEwan: 9 L 1221 m
۞ U
££ See website for visitor and resident greenfees:
www.sporting–club–berlin.de/en/court/greenfees
⚙ 70km SE of Berlin
⌂ Palmer/Faldo/Eby/McEwan
▤ www.sporting-club-berlin.com

Bremen & North West

Bremer Schweiz e.v. (1991)
Wölpscherstr 4, 28779 Bremen
☎ (0421) 609 5331
⌨ (0421) 609 5333
✉ info@golfclub-bremerschweiz.de
▷ 18 L 5865 m Par 72
۞ H WD WE
££ €35 (€40)
⚙ N of Bremen
⌂ Dr Wolfgang Siegmann
▤ www.golfclub-bremerschweiz.de

Herzogstadt Celle (1985)
Beukenbusch 1, 29229 Celle
☎ (05086) 395

Küsten GC Hohe Klint
(1978)
Hohe Klint, 27478 Cuxhaven
☎ (04723) 2737

Münster-Wilkinghege
(1963)
Steinfurter Str 448, 48159 Münster
☎ (0251) 214090
⌨ (0251) 214 0940
✉ kontakt@golfclub-wilkinghege.de
▷ 18 Par 72
Yellow: L 5868 m
Red: L 5239 m
۞ WD–H WE–I
££ €40 (€60)
⚙ 2km N of Münster
⌂ W Siegmann
▤ www.golfclub-wilkinghege.de

Oldenburgischer (1964)
Gut Silberkamp, Wilhelmshavener Strasse, 26180 Rastede
☎ (04402) 7240
⌨ (04402) 70417
✉ oldenburgischer.golfclub@golf.de
▷ 18 L 6098 m SSS 72 SR 135
۞ WD–U WE–U H(36)
££ €40 (€50)
⚙ 10km N of Oldenburg, nr Rastede
⌂ Von Limburger/Schnatmeyer
▤ www.oldenburgischer.golfclub.de

Ostfriesland (1980)
Postbox 1220, 26634 Wiesmoor
☎ (04944) 6440
⌨ (04944) 6441
✉ golfclubostfriesland@golf.de
▷ 27 holes
Course A 6177 m CR 73.2 SL 131
Course B 6323 m CR 73.6 SL 130
Course C 6026 m CR 72.1 SL 128
۞ U
££ €38 (€48)
⚙ 25km SW of Wilhelmshaven
⌂ Frank Pennink/Cristoph Stadler
▤ www.golfclub-ostfriesland.de

Soltau (1982)
Hof Loh, 29614 Soltau
☎ (05191) 967 63 33
⌨ (05191) 967 63 34
✉ info@golf-soltau.de
▷ 18 L 6011 m CR 71.7 SR 128 (men)
18 L 5302 m CR 73.7 SR 122 (women)
9 L 2500 m CR 56.2 SR 86 (men)
9 L 2500 m CR 57.2 SR 82 (women)
۞ H
££ 9: €15 (€20); 18: €40 (€50)
⚙ Tetendorf, S of Soltau
⌂ Dr Wolfgang Siegmann
▤ www.golf-soltau.de

Syke (1989)
Schultenweg 1, 28857 Syke-Okel
☎ (04242) 8230

Tietlingen (1979)
29683 Fallingbostel
☎ (05162) 3889
⌨ (05162) 7564
✉ info@golfclub-tietlingen.de
▷ 18 L 6159 m Par 73 CR-Wert 72.8 SR 128
۞ H SOC
££ €35 (€45)
⚙ 65km N of Hanover, between Walsrode and Fallingbostel
⌂ Bruns/Chadwick
▤ www.golfclub-tietlingen.de

Verden (1988)
Holtumer Str 24, 27283 Verden
☎ (04230) 1470

Worpswede (1974)
Giehlermühlen, 27729 Vollersode
☎ (04763) 7313

Club Zur Vahr (1905)
Bgm-Spitta-Allee 34, 28329 Bremen
☎ Bremen (0421) 204480
Garlstedt (04795) 953316
⌨ (0421) 244 9248
✉ info@club-zur-vahr-bremen.de
▷ Garlstedt 18 L 6283 m CR 72.9 SR 134
Bremen 9 L 5777 m CR 68.5 SR 111
۞ WD–WE–M
££ Garlstedt–€45 (€55)
Bremen–€30
⚙ Garlstedt-30km N of Bremen.
Vahr-Bremen
⌂ B von Limburger
▤ www.club-zur-vahr-bremen.de

Central North

Dillenburg
Auf dem Altscheid, 35687 Dillenburg
☎ (02771) 5001
✉ info@gc-dillenburg.de

Hofgut Praforst (1992)
Dr-Detlev-Rudelsdorff-Allee 3, 36088 Hünfeld
☎ (06652) 9970
⌨ (06652) 99755
✉ info@praforst.de
▷ 27 hole course
۞ NA M H
££ €40 (€50)
⚙ Hünfeld, 16km N of Fulda, off Route 27
⌂ Deutsche Golf Consult
▤ www.praforst.de

Kassel-Wilhelmshöhe
(1958)
Ehlenerstr 21, 34131 Kassel
☎ (0561) 33509

Kurhessischer GC Oberaula
(1987)
Am Golfplatz, 36278 Oberaula
☎ **(06628) 91540**
🖳 (06628) 915424
✉ info@golfclub-oberaula.de
⊢ 18 L 6050 m SSS 72
👥 U H
££ €40 (€50)
⊙⊙ 50km S of Kassel, nr Kircheim
🏠 Deutsche Golf Consult
▤ www.golf-oberaula.de

Licher Golf Club   (1992)
35423 Lich, Golfplatz Kolnhausen
☎ **(06404) 91071**
🖳 (06404) 91072
✉ info@licher-golf-club.de
⊢ 18 L 6418 m Par 72 CR 73.9 SR 131
👥 H SOC
££ €50 (Mon/Tue until 12 €35)
        Sat/Sun €80
⊙⊙ 45km N of Frankfurt
🏠 Heinz Fehring
▤ www.licher-golf-club.de

Rhoen   (1971)
Am Golfplatz, 36145 Hofbieber
☎ **(06657) 1334**
🖳 (06657) 914809
✉ info@golfclub-fulda.de
⊢ 18 L 5521 m CR 68.6 SR 126
👥 H
££ €40 (€50)
⊙⊙ Hofbieber, 11km E of Fulda
🏠 Kurt Peters
▤ www.golfclub-fulda.de

Schloss Braunfels   (1970)
Homburger Hof, 35619 Braunfels
☎ **(06442) 4530**
✉ info@golfclub-braunfels.de

Schloss Sickendorf   (1990)
Schloss Sickendorf, 36341 Lauterbach
☎ **(06641) 96130**
✉ info@gc-lauterbach.de

Winnerod   (1999)
Parkstr 22, 35447 Reiskirchen
☎ **(06408) 9513-0**
🖳 (06408) 9513-13
✉ winnerod@golfpark.de
⊢ 18 L 6069 m Par 72
    9 hole Par 3 course
👥 U
££ €40 (€60)
⊙⊙ Hessen, 30km N of Frankfurt/Main
🏠 Michael Pinner
▤ www.golfpark.de

Zierenberg Gut Escheberg
(1995)
Gut Escheberg, 34289 Zierenberg
☎ **(05606) 2608**

Central South

Bad Kissingen   (1910)
Euerdorferstr 11, 97688 Bad Kissingen
☎ **(0971) 3608**
🖳 (0971) 60140
⊢ 18 L 5699 m SSS 70
👥 U H
££ €55 (€60)
⊙⊙ Bad Kissingen 2km. 65km N of
    Würzburg

Bad Vilbeler Golfclub Lindenhof e.V.   (1994)
61118 Bad Vilbel-Dortelweil
☎ **+49 (0)6101 5245200**
🖳 +49 (0)6101 5245202
✉ info@bvgc.de
⊢ 18 holes
👥 H membership card required
££ €40–€65 (€50–€75)
⊙⊙ 7km to Frankfurt Main
🏠 Dr Siegmann, Hannover
▤ www.bvgc.de

Golfclub Eschenrod e.V.
(1996)
Postfach 1227, Lindenstr. 46, 63679 Schotten
☎ **(06044) 8401**
🖳 (06044) 951159
✉ br.golf@t-online.de
⊢ 18 Par 70 CR 70.4 SR 123
    New 08/2008
👥 H WD/WD–U
££ €25 (€35)
⊙⊙ Hessen near Hanau & Giessen
▤ www.eschenrod.de

Frankfurter Golf Club
(1913)
Golfstrasse 41, 60528 Frankfurt/Main
☎ **(069) 666 2318**
🖳 (069) 666 7018
✉ info@fgc.de
⊢ 18 L 6769 yds CR 72.5 SR 129
👥 H–32 max
££ €80 (€100)
⊙⊙ 6km SW of Frankfurt, nr Airport
🏠 HS Colt
▤ www.fgc.de

Hanau-Wilhelmsbad   (1958)
Wilhelmsbader Allee 32, 63454 Hanau
☎ **(06181) 82071**

Hof Trages
Hofgut Trages, 63579 Freigericht
☎ **(06055) 91380**

Homburger   (1899)
Saalburgchaussee 2, 61350 Bad Homburg
☎ **(06172) 306808**

Idstein   (2001)
Am Nassen Berg, 65510 Idstein
☎ **(06126) 9322-13**

Idstein-Wörsdorf   (1989)
Gut Henriettenthal, 65510 Idstein
☎ **(06126) 9322-0**

Kitzingen   (1980)
Zufahrt über Winterleitenweg, 97318 Kitzingen
☎ **(09321) 4956**
🖳 (09321) 21936
✉ golfkitzingen@aol.com
⊢ 18 L 6093 m (men), 5373 m (ladies)
    Par 72 CR 71.4 (men), 73.2 (ladies)
👥 U H WD/WE
££ €30 (€35)
⊙⊙ 20km E of Würzburg
🏠 Greens of Scotland
▤ www.golfclub-kitzingen.de

Kronberg G&LC   (1954)
Schloss Friedrichshof, Hainstr 25, 61476 Kronberg/Taunus
☎ **(06173) 1426**

Main-Spessart   (1990)
Postfach 1204, 97821 Marktheidenfeld-Eichenfürst
☎ **(09391) 8435**
🖳 (09391) 8816
✉ info@main-spessart-golf.de
⊢ 18 holes Par 72
    6 hole short course
👥 H–max 36
££ €30 (€40)
⊙⊙ 80km E of Frankfurt/Main
🏠 Harradine
▤ www.main-spessart-golf.de

Main-Taunus   (1979)
Lange Seegewann 2, 65205 Wiesbaden
☎ **(06122) 588680 (Sec)**
✉ clubinfo@golf-club-maintaunus.de

Mannheim-Viernheim
(1930)
Alte Mannheimer Str 3, 68519 Viernheim
☎ **(06204) 607020**
🖳 (06204) 607044
✉ info@gcmv.de
⊢ 18 L 6060 m Par 72 CR72.8 SL 124
👥 WD–H WE–M H (Summer)
££ €45 (€60)
⊙⊙ 10km NE of Mannheim near the
    town of Viernheim 80km south of
    Frankfurt
🏠 Dr Von Limburger
▤ www.gcmv.de

Maria Bildhausen   (1992)
Rindhof 1, 97702 Münnerstadt
☎ **(09766) 1601**
🖳 (09766) 1602
✉ info@maria-bildhausen.de
⊢ 18 L 6284 m Par 72
    6 hole short course
👥 U H
££ €40 (€50)
⊙⊙ 70km NE of Wurzburg
🏠 Christian Habeck
▤ www.maria-bildhausen.de

Neuhof
Hofgut Neuhof, 63303 Dreieich
☎ **(06102) 327927/327010**
⌨ (06102) 327012
✉ info@golfclubneuhof.de
▷ 18 L 6177 m SSS 72
3 x 9 holes
⚭ WD–H WE–M
££ €80
⛳ Hofgut Neuhof, S of Frankfurt, off A3
🏠 Christoph Städler
▤ www.golfclubneuhof.de

Rhein Main (1977)
Steubenstrasse 9, 65189 Wiesbaden
☎ **(0611) 373014**

Rheinblick
Weisser Weg, 65201 Wiesbaden-Frauenstein
☎ **(0611) 420675**

Rheintal (1971)
An der Bundesstrr 291, 68723 Oftersheim
☎ **(06202) 56390**

St Leon-Rot Betriebsgesellschaft mbH & Co.KG (1996)
Opelstrasse 30, 68789 St Leon-Rot
☎ **+49 62 27 86 08- 312**
⌨ +49 62 27 86 08-8312
✉ manuel.funk@gc-sir.de
▷ Rot: 18 L 6047 m Par 72 SR 133
St Leon: 18 L 6178 m Par 72 SR 139
⚭ WD–U before 2pm WE–M H
££ €80 (€105)
⛳ 20km S of Heidelberg.
🏠 Hannes Schreiner (Rot),
Dave Thomas (St Leon)
▤ www.gc-slr.de

Spessart (1972)
Golfplatz Alsberg, 63628 Bad Soden-Salmünster
☎ **(06056) 91580**

Taunus Weilrod (1979)
Merzhäuser Strasse, 61276 Weilrod-Altweilnau
☎ **(06083) 95050**
✉ golfclub-taunus-weilrod.de

Wiesbadener Golf Club e.v. (1893)
Chausseehaus 17, 65199 Wiesbaden
☎ **(0611) 460238**
⌨ (0611) 463251
✉ info@wiesbadener-golfclub.de
▷ 9 L 5172 m
Par 68 CR 68.6 SR 124 (men)
Par 68 CR 70.2 SR 125 (ladies)
⚭ WD–H (max 36) WE–H (max 25)
££ €35 (€45)
⛳ 8km NW of Wiesbaden, towards Schlangenbad
🏠 Hirsch
▤ www.wiesbadener-golfclub.de

Golf- und Landclub Wiesloch (1983)
Hohenhardter Hof, 69168 Wiesloch-Baiertal
☎ **(06222) 78811-0**

Hamburg & North

Altenhof (1971)
Eckernförde, 24340 Altenhof
☎ **(04351) 41227**
(04351) 45800 (Pro)

An der Pinnau e.V. (1982)
Pinneberger strasse 81a, 25451 Quickborn-Renzel
☎ **(04106) 81800**
⌨ (04106) 82003
✉ info@pinnau.de
▷ 18 L 6023 m Par 72 SR 127
18 L 5231 m Par 72 SR 127
⚭ U H
££ €45 (€55)
⛳ 25km NW of Hamburg, nr Quickborn
🏠 David Krause
▤ www.pinnau.de

Behinderten Golf Club Deutschland e.V. (1994)
Hauptstrausse 3 c, 37434 Bodensee
☎ **+49 (0) 55079799108**
⌨ +49 (0) 5507 979144
✉ rollydrive@aol.com
▷ 18 hole course
⚭ U SOC only
££ On application
⛳ 20km NE of Hamburg
▤ www.bgc-golf.de

Brodauer Mühle (1986)
Baumallee 14, 23730 Gut Beusloe
☎ **(04561) 8140**
⌨ (04561) 407397
✉ gc-brodauermuehle@t-online.de
▷ 18 L 6113 m Par 72 SSS 72
⚭ U H–36
££ €39 (€49)
⛳ 30km N of Lübeck
🏠 Siegmann/Osterkamp
▤ www.gc-brodauermuehle.de

Buchholz-Nordheide (1982)
An der Rehm 25, 21244 Bucholz
☎ **(04181) 36200**
⌨ (04181) 97294
✉ gc-buchholz@t-online.de
▷ 18 L 6130 m SSS 72
⚭ WD–U H WE–H I before 10am
££ €45 (€60)
⛳ 30km S of Hamburg
▤ www.golfclub-buchholz.de

Buxtehude (1982)
Zum Lehmfeld 1, 21614 Buxtehude
☎ **(04161) 81333**
⌨ (04161) 87268

✉ post@golfclubbuxtehude.de
▷ 18 L 6480 m CR 73.6 SR 132
⚭ WD–H WE–H before 10am
££ €35 (€45)
⛳ 30km SW of Hamburg on Route 73 from Harburg
🏠 Wolfgang Siegmann
▤ www.golfclubbuxtehude.de

Deinster Mühle (1994)
Im Mühlenfeld 30, 21717 Deinste
☎ **(04149) 925112**
⌨ (04149) 925111
✉ golfpark@allesistgdn.de
▷ 18 L 5986 m CR 71.6 SR 129
⚭ U H
££ €39 (€49)
⛳ 50km SW of Hamburg
🏠 David Krause
▤ www.allesistgdn.de

Föhr (1925)
25938 Nieblum
☎ **(04681) 580455**
⌨ (04681) 580456
✉ info@golfclubfohr.de
▷ 18 L 5923 m CR 71.7 SR 122
⚭ H
££ €40 (€45)
⛳ 1km SW of Wyk (Island of Föhr)
🏠 Frank Pennink and Harald Harradine
▤ www.golfclubfohr.de

Gut Apeldör (1996)
Apeldör 2, 25779 Hennstedt
☎ **(04836) 9960-0**
⌨ (04836) 9960-33
✉ info@apeldoer.de
▷ 18 hole Championship course Par 72:
Men: L 5962 m CR 72.5 SR 134
Women: L 5347 m CR 75.5 SR 134
9 hole Audi Course (Par 72):
Men: L 5994 m CR 71.5 SR 123
Women: L 5046 m CR 72.7 SR 128
⚭ U
££ 9: €20 (€25) 18: €49 (€59)
⛳ 11km W of Heide. 110km N of Hamburg
🏠 David John Krause
▤ www.apeldoer.de

Gut Grambek (1981)
Schlosstr 21, 23883 Grambek
☎ **(04542) 841474**
⌨ (04542) 841476
✉ info@gcgrambek.de
▷ 18 L 5907 m SSS 71
⚭ H
££ €50 (€60)
⛳ 30km S of Lübeck. 50km E of Hamburg
🏠 Kurt Peters
▤ www.gcgrambek.de

Gut Kaden (1984)
Kadenerstrasse 9, 25486 Alveslohe
☎ **(04193) 9929-0**

Gut Uhlenhorst   (1989)
24229 D'Anischenhagen, Muhlen Str 37
- ☎ **(04349) 91700**
- 📠 (04349) 919400
- ✉ E-mail:golf@gut-uhlenhorst.de
- �️ 27 L 6195 m SSS 72
- 👥 U
- ££ €40 (€50)
- ⛳ 8km N of Kiel
- 🏠 Donald Harradine
- 🖥 www.gut-uhlenhorst.de

Gut Waldhof   (1969)
Am Waldhof, 24629 Kisdorferwohld
- ☎ **(04194) 99740**

Gut Waldshagen   (1996)
24306 Gut Waldshagen
- ☎ **(04522) 766766**
- 📠 (04522) 766767
- ✉ info@gut-golf.de
- �️ 18 L 6369 m CR 73.7 SR 131
  6 hole short course
- 👥 U
- ££ €45 (€60)
- ⛳ 35km S of Kiel. 91km NE of Hamburg
- 🖥 www.gut-golf.de

Hamburg   (1906)
In de Bargen 59, 22587 Hamburg
- ☎ **(040) 812177**

Hamburg Ahrensburg
(1964)
Am Haidschlag 39-45, 22926 Ahrensburg
- ☎ **(04102) 51309**

Hamburg Hittfeld
(1957)
Am Golfplatz 24, 21218 Seevetal
- ☎ **(04105) 2331**

Hamburg Holm   (1993)
Haverkamp 1, 25488 Holm
- ☎ **(04103) 91330**
- 📠 (04103) 913313
- ✉ info@hchh.de
- �️ 27 holes CR 72.3 SR 124
- 👥 WD–HWE M–H
- ££ D–€50 (D–€60)
- ⛳ 20km W of Hamburg
- 🏠 Harradine/Rossknecht
- 🖥 www.gchh.de

Hamburg Walddörfer
(1960)
Schevenbarg, 22949 Ammersbek
- ☎ **(040) 605 1337**
- 📠 (040) 605 4879
- ✉ info@gchw.de
- �️ 18 L 6093 m CR 72.5 SR 131
  18 hole pitch & putt course
- 👥 WD–U H WE–M H
- ££ €60 (€70)
- ⛳ 20km N of Hamburg
- 🏠 B von Limburger
- 🖥 www.gchw.de

Golfclub Hohen Wieschendorf e.V.   (1992)
Am Golfplatz 1, 23968 Hohen Wieschendorf
- ☎ **(0049) 384 28660**
- 📠 (0049) 384 286666
- ✉ info@howido.de
- �️ 18 L 5727 m Mens Par 72 CR 70.0 SR 126
  18 L 5118 m Ladies Par 72 CR 72.1 SR 12.2
- 👥 U SOC
- ££ D–€45 (€55)
- ⛳ 13km west of Wismar. 40km east of Lübeck
- 🏠 Peter Tolgreve
- 🖥 www.howido.de

Hoisdorf   (1977)
Hof Bornbek/Hoisdorf, 22952 Lütjensee
- ☎ **(04107) 7831**
- 📠 (04107) 9934
- ✉ info@gc-hoisdorf.com
- �️ 18 L 5958 m Par 71
- 👥 WD–U WE–M only
- ££ €45 (€50)
- ⛳ 25km NE of Hamburg
- 🖥 www.gc-hoisdorf.com

Jersbek   (1986)
GolfClub Jersbek e.V., Oberteicher Weg, 22941 Jersbek
- ☎ **(040) 20950**
- 📠 (040) 24779
- ✉ gcjersbek@t-online.de
- �️ 18 L 5921 m (men) 5220 (ladies) SSS 71
  CR 70.7 (men) 72.2 (ladies) SR 125
- 👥 U H36 WD WE
- ££ €50 (€60)
- ⛳ 20km N of Hamburg
- 🏠 Von Schinkel
- 🖥 www.golfclub-jersbek.de

Kieler GC Havighorst
(1988)
Havighorster Weg 20, 24211 Havighorst
- ☎ **(04302) 965980**
- ✉ golfclub.havighorst@t-online.de

Lübeck-Travemünder
(1921)
Kowitzberg 41, 23570 Lübeck-Travemünde
- ☎ **(04502) 74018**
- 📠 (04502) 72182
- ✉ info@ltgk.de
- �️ 27 L 6063 - 6152 m CR 72.7 – 74.5 SR 125 – 134
- 👥 H
- ££ Mon–Thur: D–€45 Fri–Sun + Hols: D–€60
- ⛳ 18km NE of Lübeck. 70km NE of Hamburg
- 🖥 www.ltgk.de

Mittelholsteinischer Aukrug   (1969)
Zum Glasberg 9, 24613 Aukrug-Bargfeld
- ☎ **(04873) 595**

Peiner Hof
Peiner Hag, 25497 Prisdorf
- ☎ **(04101) 73790**

Am Sachsenwald   (1985)
Am Riesenbett, 21521 Dassendorf
- ☎ **(04104) 6120**
- 📠 (04104) 6551
- ✉ gc-sachsenwald@t-online.de
- �️ 18 L 6118 m SSS 72
- 👥 WD–H WE–H
- ££ €40 (€50)
- ⛳ 20km SE of Hamburg
- 🏠 Deutsche Golf Consult
- 🖥 www.gc-sachsenwald.de

Schloss Breitenburg
25524 Breitenburg
- ☎ **(04828) 8188**
- 📠 (04828) 8100
- ✉ golfclubschlossbreitenburg @t-online.de
- �️ 27 hole course
- 👥 H
- ££ €45 (€55)
- ⛳ 50km N of Hamburg
- 🏠 Osterkamp/Krause
- 🖥 www.golfclubschlossbreitenberg.de

Schloss Lüdersburg   (1985)
Lüdersburger Strasse 21, 21379 Lüdersburg
- ☎ **(04139) 6970-0**
- 📠 (04139) 6970 70
- ✉ info@luedersburg.de
- �️ 18 L 6568 m SSS 73
  18 L 6169 m SSS 72
  4 hole par 3 and par 4 course
- 👥 WD–U WE–H (36)
- ££ From €20–€70
- ⛳ 12km E of Lüneburg. 55km SE of Hamburg
- 🏠 Wolfgang Siegmann/Nicklaus Design
- 🖥 www.luedersburg.de

St Dionys   (1972)
Widukindweg, 21357 St Dionys
- ☎ **(04133) 213311**
- 📠 (04133) 213313
- ✉ info@golfclub-st-dionys.de
- �️ 18 standard tees:
  Red: par 72 CR 72.5 SR 125
  Yellow: par 72 CR 72.1 SR 128
- 👥 By appointment only
- ££ €50 (€60)
- ⛳ 10km N of Lüneburg
- 🏠 Harold Grotenam
- 🖥 www.golfclub-st-dionys.de

GC Sylt e.V.   (1982)
Norderrung 5, 25996 Wenningstedt
- ☎ **(04651) 99598-0**
- ✉ golfclubsylt@t-online.de

Golfanlage Seeschlosschem Timmendorfer Strand
(1973)
Am Golfplatz 3, 23669 Timmendorfer Strand
- ☎ **(04503) 704400**

☎ (04503) 704400-14
✉ info@gc-timmendorf.de
► North 18 L 6323 m Par 72 CR 71.0 SR 130
South 18 L 3602 m Par 61 CR 60.2 SR 106
booking required WD–H WE–H
£€ North: Mon–Thur €46, Fri €52 (€62); South: Mon–Thur €35, Fri €42 (€46)
⊕ 15km N of Lübeck
fi B von Limburger
▤ www.gc-timmendorf.de

G&CC Treudelberg (1990)
Lemsahler Landstr 45, 22397 Hamburg
☎ (040) 608 228877
📠 (040) 608 228879
✉ golf@treudelberg.com
► 18 L 6182 m SSS 72
9 hole pitch & putt
U H–WD54/WE36
£€ €55 (+BH €75)
⊕ N of Hamburg centre
fi Donald Steel
▤ www.treudelberg.com

Wentorf-Reinbeker Golf-Club e.V. (1901)
Golfstrasse 2, 21465 Wentorf
☎ (040) 72 97 80 68
📠 (040) 72 97 80 67
✉ sekretariat@wrgc.de
► Men 18 L 5821 m CR 72.6 SR 133 Par 72
Ladies 18 L 5165 m CR 74.7 SR 130 Par 72
WD–U H WE–M
£€ €50 (€60)
⊕ 20km E of Hamburg
fi Ernst Hess
▤ www.wrgc.de

Hanover & Weserbergland

Bad Salzuflen G&LC (1956)
Schwaghof 4, 32108 Bad Salzuflen
☎ (05222) 10773

British Army Golf Club (Sennelager) (1963)
Bad Lippspringe, BFPO 16
☎ (05252) 53794
📠 (05252) 53811
✉ manager@sennelagergolfclub.de
► 18 L 5658 m SSS 72
9 L 5214 m SSS 68
H
£€ (Forces) €25 (€30) (Civilians) €35 (€45)
⊕ 9km E of Paderborn, off Route B1
▤ www.sennelagergolfclub.de

Burgdorf (1970)
Waldstr 27, 31303 Burgdorf-Ehlershausen
☎ (05085) 7628

☎ (05085) 6617
✉ info@burgdorfer-golfclub.de
► 18 L 6426 m SSS 74
H U
£€ D–€35 (D–€45)
⊕ Burgdorf-Ehlershausen, 25km NE of Hanover
▤ www.burgdorfer-golfclub.de

Gifhorn (1982)
Wilscher Weg 69, 38518 Gifhorn
☎ (05371) 16737

Gütersloh Garrison (1963)
Princess Royal Barracks, BFPO 47
☎ (05241) 236938
📠 (01241) 236838
✉ timothyholt14@hotmail.com
► 9 L 5947 yds SSS 70
Must book prior to playing
£€ €12–€20
⊕ 5km W of Gütersloh

Hamelner Golfclub e.V. (1985)
Schwöber 8, 31855 Aerzen
☎ (05154) 987 0
📠 (05154) 987 111
✉ info@hamelner-golfclub.de
► 2 x 18 holes SR 96 and SR 139
U
£€ €25–€45 (€50–€60)
⊕ 10km SW of Hameln. 60km SW of Hanover
▤ www.hamelner-golfclub.de

Hannover (1923)
Am Blauen See 120, 30823 Garbsen
☎ (05137) 73068
📠 (05137) 75851
✉ info@golfclub-hannover.de
► 18 L 5685 m Par 71 SSS 71
Men: CR 71.7 SR 136
Ladies: CR 74.0 SR 133
WD–U H 36 WE–M
£€ €60 (€70) not DGV members €45 (€55) DGV members
⊕ 15km NW of Hanover
fi Dr Bernhard von Limburger
▤ www.golfclub-hannover.de

Hardenberg (1969)
Gut Levershausen, 37154 Northeim
☎ (05551) 61915

Isernhagen (1983)
Auf Gut Lohne 22, 30916 Isernhagen
☎ (05139) 893185

Langenhagen (1989)
Hainhaus 22, D-30855 Langenhagen
☎ (0511) 736832
📠 (0511) 726 1190
✉ golf-club-langenhagen@online.de
► 27 L 6161 m Par 72
H
£€ €35 (€45)
⊕ 25km N of Hannover
fi Siegmann
▤ www.golf-club-langenhagen.de

Lippischer (1980)
Huxoll 14, 32825 Blomberg-Cappel
☎ (05236) 459
📠 (05236) 8102
✉ lippischer-golfclub@t-online.de
► 18 L 5990 m CR 71.5 SR 126
H WD WE
£€ €35 (€45) – 2006 prices
⊕ 12km E of Detmold; 9km from Blomberg
▤ www.lippischergolfclub.de

Marienfeld (1986)
Remse 27, 33428 Marienfeld
☎ (05247) 8880

Paderborner Land (1983)
Wilseder Weg 25, 33102 Paderborn
☎ (05251) 4377

Ravensberger Land
Sudstrasse 96, 32130 Enger-Pödinghausen
☎ (09224) 79751

Senne GC Gut Welschof (1992)
Augustdorferstr 72, 33758 Schloss Holte-Stukenbrock
☎ (05207) 920936
📠 (05207) 88788
✉ info@senne_golfclub.de
► 18 L 6246 m SSS 72
U H 45
£€ €40 (€50)
⊕ 20km S of Bielefeld
fi Christoph Städler
▤ www.senne_golfclub.de

Sieben-Berge Rheden (1965)
Schloss Str 1a, 31039 Rheden
☎ (05182) 52336
📠 (05182) 923350
✉ info@gc7berge.de
► 18 L 5739 m SSS 71
U H
£€ €40 (€50)
⊕ 35km S of Hanover
fi B von Limburger
▤ www.gc7berge.de

Weserbergland (1982)
Weissenfelder Mühle, 37647 Polle
☎ (05535) 8842

Westfälischer Gütersloh
Gütersloher Str 127, 33397 Rietberg
☎ (05244) 2340/10528
✉ golf-club@golf-gt.de

Widukind-Land (1985)
Auf dem Stickdorn 63, 32584 Löhne
☎ (05228) 7050

Munich & South Bavaria

Allgäuer G&LC (1984)
Hofgut Boschach, 87724 Ottobeuren
☎ (08332) 9251-0

📞 (08332) 5161
📧 info@aglc.de
🏴 18 L 6096 m CR 71.1 SR 123
6 hole short course
♟ H
££ €49 (€65)
🚗 2km S of Ottobeuren. 20km N of
Kempten
🖥 www.aglc.de

Altötting-Burghausen
(1986)
Piesing 4, 84533 Haiming
📞 (08678) 986903

Augsburg   (1959)
Engelshofer Str 2, 86399 Bobingen-
Burgwalden
📞 (08234) 5621

Bad Tölz   (1973)
83646 Wackersberg
📞 (08041) 9994

Beuerberg   (1982)
Gut Sterz, 82547 Beuerberg
📞 (08179) 671 or 782
📠 (08179) 5234
📧 beuerberg@golf.de
🏴 18 L 6250 m SL 132 CR 72.6
♟ WD–H WE–M H
££ €65 (€75)
🚗 Beuerberg, 45km SW of Munich
🏠 Donald Harradine
🖥 www.gc-beurberg.de

Chieming   (1982)
Kötzing 1, D-83339 Chieming
📞 (08669) 87330
📠 (08669) 873333
📧 info@golfchieming.de
🏴 Men: white 18 L 6250 m white
CR 72.0 SR 133,
yellow 18 L 5933 m CR 70.8
SR 134;
Women: black 18 L 5508 m
CR 74.7 SR 128,
red 5254 m CR 73.8 SR 127
9 L 1188 m Par 3
♟ H 36
££ 9: €15; 18: €50 (€65 – inc Fri after
12 noon); Students/Juniors €25
(€35)
🚗 On A8 Salzburg-Munich. 40km W
of Salzburg. Munich 100km
🏠 Thomas Himmel
🖥 www.golfchieming.de

Donauwörth   (1995)
Lederstatt 1, 86609 Donauwörth
📞 (0906) 4044

Ebersberg   (1988)
Postfach 1351, 85554 Ebersberg
📞 (08094) 8106
📧 info@gc-ebersberg.de

Erding-Grünbach   (1973)
Am Kellerberg, 85461 Grünbach
📞 (08122) 49650

Eschenried   (1983)
Kurfürstenweg 10, 85232 Eschenried
📞 (08131) 56740
📠 (08131) 567418
📧 info@golf-eschenried.de
🏴 Eschenried 18 L 5935 m Par 72
SR 129
Eschenhof 18 L 5550 m Par 70
SR 117
Gut Häusern 18 L 6710 m Par 72
SR 129
Gut Häusern 6 L 690 m Par 19
Gröbenbach 9 L 1774 m Par 32
SR 91
♟ U H; Gut Häusern H
££ Eschenried €55 (€70) Eschenhof
€45 (€55) Gut Häusern €60 (€75)
Gröbenbach €28 (€35)
🚗 8km NW of Munich
🏠 G von Mecklenburg/P Haradine
🖥 www.gc-eschenried.de

Feldafing   (1926)
Tutzinger Str 15, 82340 Feldafing
📞 (08157) 9334-0
📧 info@golfclub-Feldafing.de

Garmisch-Partenkirchen
(1928)
Gut Buchwies, 82496 Oberau
📞 (08824) 8344
📧 golfclubGAP@onlinehome.de

Gut Ludwigsberg   (1989)
Augsburgerstr 51, 86842 Turkheim
📞 (08245) 3322

Gut Rieden
Gut Rieden, 82319 Starnberg
📞 (08151) 90770

Hohenpähl   (1988)
82396 Pähl
📞 (08808) 9202-0
📠 (08808) 9202-22
📧 info@gchp.de
🏴 18 L 5971 m Par 71 CR 71.9 SR 131
♟ H36; dogs allowed WE
££ €56 (€75)
🚗 40km S of Munich on B2 (km 41)
🏠 Kurt Rossknecht
🖥 www.gchp.de

Holledau
Weihern 3, 84104 Rudelzhausen
📞 (08756) 96010

Höslwang im Chiemgau
(1975)
Kronberg 3, 83129 Höslwang
📞 (08075) 714
📠 (08075) 8134
📧 info@golfclub-hoeslwang.de
🏴 18 L 6110 m Par 72 CT 72.1 SR
126
♟ H
££ €43 (€55)
🚗 80km S of Munich
🏠 Thomas Himmel
🖥 www.golfclub-hoeslwang.de

Iffeldorf   (1989)
Gut Rettenberg, 82393 Iffeldorf
📞 0049 (8856) 92550
📠 0049 (8856) 925559
📧 sekretariat@golf-iffeldorf.de
🏴 18 L 5883 m Par 72 CR 71.7 SR
128
♟ H
££ D–€50 before 10am (except 15
July–15 Sep); D–€60 after 10am
(€80)
🚗 45km S of Munich
🏠 Peter Postel
🖥 www.golf-iffeldorf.de

Landshut   (1989)
Oberlippach 2, 84095 Furth-Landshut
📞 (08704) 8378
📠 (08704) 8379
📧 gc.landshut@t-online.de
🏴 18 L 6130 m Par 73 CR 72.5 SR 131
♟ H
££ €45 (€60)
🚗 65 km E of Munich, 16km Landshut
🏠 Kurt Rossknecht
🖥 www.golf-landshut.de

Mangfalltal G&LC
Oed 1, 83620 Feldkirchen-Westerham
📞 (08063) 6300

Margarethenhof   (1982)
Gut Steinberg,
83666 Waakirchen/Marienstein
📞 (08022) 7506-0
📠 (08022) 74818
📧 info@margarethenhof.com
🏴 18 L 5730 m Par 71
♟ WD–H WE–before 10am
££ €60 (€80)
🚗 Tegernsee, 45km S of Munich
🏠 Frank Pennink
🖥 www.margarethenhof.com

Memmingen Gut
Westerhart   (1994)
Westerhart 1b, 87740 Buxheim
📞 (08331) 71016
📠 (08331) 71018
📧 gc-memmingen@t-online.de
🏴 18 Par 72
Men (yellow): L 6077 m CR 72.3
SR 127
Women (red): L 5276 m CR 73.8
SR 126
♟ U H
££ €45 (€55)
🚗 120km W of Munich. Memmingen
5km
🖥 www.golfclub-memmingen.de

Golfclub München Nord-
Eichenried   (1989)
Münchnerstr 57, 85452 Eichenried
📞 (08123) 93080
📠 (08123) 930893
📧 info@gc-eichenried.de
🏴 27 L 6318 m Par 73/74
♟ WD–U H
££ €75 (€105)
🚗 19km NE of Munich

🏌 Kurt Rossknecht
▤ www.gc-eichenried.de

München West-Odelzhausen (1988)
Gut Todtenried, 85235 Odelzhausen
☎ (08134) 1618

München-Riedhof e.V.
(1991)
82544 Egling-Riedhof, Riedhof 16
☎ (08171) 21950
🖳 (08171) 219511
✉ info@riedhof.de
🏌 18 L 6216 m SSS 72
SR 126 CR 71.3
👥 WD–U H WE–M NA
£€ €90
🚗 25km S of Munich
🏌 Heinz Fehring
▤ www.riedhof.de

Münchener (1910)
Tölzerstrasse 95, 82064 Strasslach
☎ (08170) 450

Olching (1980)
Feursstrasse 89, 82140 Olching
☎ (08142) 48290
🖳 (08142) 482914
✉ sportbuero@golfclub-olching.de
🏌 18 L 6028 m Par 72
CR 71.6 SR 125 (men)
CR 74.2 SR 127 (ladies)
👥 H WE–NA
£€ €50 (€60)
🚗 15km W of Munich
🏌 Kurt Rossknecht
▤ www.golfclub-olching.de

Pfaffing Wasserburger
Golfclub Pfaffing München-Ost e.V, wsw
Golf AG, Köckmühle 132, 83539 Pfaffing
☎ (08076) 91650
✉ info@golfclub-pfaffing.de

Reit im Winkl-Kössen
(1986)
Postfach 1101, 83237 Reit im Winkl
☎ (08640) 798250

Rottaler G&CC (1972)
Am Fischgartl 2, 84332 Hebertsfelden
☎ (08561) 5969
🖳 (08561) 2646
✉ info@rottaler-gc.de
🏌 18 L 5960 m CR 71.8 SR 125
👥 U
£€ €40 (€45)
🚗 5km W of Pfarrkirchen on B388.
120km E of Munich
🏌 Donald Harradine
▤ www.rottaler-gc.de

Rottbach (1997)
Weiherhaus 5, 82216 Rottbach
☎ (08135) 93290
🖳 (08135) 932911
✉ info@rottbach.de
🏌 27 L 6480 m Par 72

👥 U
£€ €42 (€58)
🚗 20km NW of Munich
🏌 Thomas Himmel
▤ www.golfanlage-rottbach.de

Schloss Maxlrain
Freiung 14, 83104 Maxlrain-Tuntenhausen
☎ (08061) 1403

Sonnenalp (1976)
Hotel Sonnenalp, 87527 Ofterschwang
☎ (08321) 272181 (Sec)

Starnberg (1986)
Uneringerstr, 82319 Starnberg
☎ (08151) 12157

Tegernseer GC Bad Wiessee (1958)
Rohbognerhof, 83707 Bad Wiessee
☎ (08022) 8769
🖳 (08022) 82747
✉ info@tegernseer-golf-club.de
🏌 18 L 5466 m CR 69.5 SR 125
👥 WD–H WE–H before 9.30am
£€ €70 (€90)
🚗 Tegernsee, 50km S of Munich
🏌 D Harradine
▤ www.tegernseer-golf-club.de

Tutzing (1983)
82327 Tutzing-Deixlfurt
☎ (08158) 3600

Waldegg-Wiggensbach
(1988)
Hof Waldegg, 87487 Wiggensbach
☎ (08370) 93073
🖳 (08370) 93074
✉ info@golf-wiggensbach.com
🏌 27 holes L 5373 m 1-13 Par 70
CR 69.0 SR 133
👥 H–max 54
£€ €50 (€60)
🚗 10km W of Kempten, nr
Swiss/Austrian border
🏌 H Jersombek
▤ www.golf-wiggensbach.com

Wittelsbacher GC Rohrenfeld-Neuburg
(1988)
Rohrenfeld, 86633 Neuburg/Donau
☎ (08431) 90859-0
🖳 (08431) 90859-59
✉ info@wittelsbacher-golf.de
🏌 18 L 6700 m Par 71 SSS 73
👥 U H
£€ €60
🚗 7km E of Neuburg. 70km NW of
Munich
🏌 J Dudok van Heel
▤ www.wittelsbacher-golf.de

Wörthsee (1982)
Gut Schluifeld, 82237 Wörthsee
☎ (08153) 93477-0
🖳 (08153) 93477-40

✉ info@golfclub-woerthsee.de
🏌 18 L 5913 m CR 70.2 SR 118
👥 WD–H WE–M
£€ €70 (€85)
🚗 Wörthsee, 20km SW of Munich
🏌 Kurt Rossknecht
▤ www.golfclub-woerthsee.de

Nuremberg & North Bavaria

Abenberg (1988)
Am Golfplatz 19, 91183 Abenberg
☎ (09178) 98960

Bad Windsheim (1992)
Otmar-Schaller-Alleen, 91438
Bad Windsheim
☎ (09841) 5027
🖳 (09841) 3448
✉ gcbadwindsheim@t-online.de
🏌 18 L 6198 m Par 73 SR 126 (men)
18 L 5494 m Par 73, SR 125
(women)
👥 H
£€ €35 (€48)
🚗 60km from Nuremberg
▤ www.golf-bw.de

Bamberg (1973)
Postfach 1525, 96006 Bamberg
☎ (09547) 7109
🖳 (09547) 7817
✉ leimershof@golfclubbamberg.de
🏌 18 L 6175 m SSS 72
👥 H
£€ €40 (€50)
🚗 Gut Leimershof, 16km N of
Bamberg
🏌 Dieter Sziedat
▤ www.golfclubbamberg.de

Donau GC Passau-Rassbach
(1986)
Rassbach 8, 94136 Thyrnau-Passau
☎ (08501) 91313
🖳 (08501) 91314
✉ info@golf-passau.de
🏌 24 Par 71
👥 U
£€ €41 (€49)
🚗 10km E of Passau
🏌 Götz Mecklenburg
▤ www.golf-passau.de

Fränkische Schweiz (1974)
Kanndorf 8, 91316 Ebermannstadt
☎ (09194) 4827
▤ www.gc-fs.de

Golf Club Fürth e.V. (1951)
Am Golfplatz 10, 90768 Fürth
☎ (0911) 757522
🖳 (0911) 973 2989
✉ info@golfclub-fuerth.de
🏌 18 L 6478 yds SSS 71
👥 H tee reservations WE
£€ €35 (D–€45) 9 holes €20 WD only
🚗 10km W of Nuremburg

⌂ Dr Bernhard von Limburger (1971)
▤ www.golfclub-fuerth.de

Gäuboden (1992)
Gut Fruhstorf, 94330 Aiterhofen
☎ (09421) 72804

Hartl Golf Resort Bad Griesbach (1989)
Holzhäuser 8, 94086 Bad Griesbach
☎ (08532) 790-0
⎙ (08532) 790-45
✉ info@hartl.de
⚐ Uttlau 18 L 6115 m SSS 72
  Lederbach 18 L 5998 m SSS 71
  Brunnwies 18 L 6029 m SSS 71
  Beckenbauer 18 L 6500 m SSS 72
  Jaguar 18 L 6037 SSS 71
⚇ I H
££ €39 (€66)
⚘ 28km SW of Passau
⌂ Kurt Rossknecht
▤ www.hartl.de

Hof (1985)
Postfach 1324, 95012 Hof
☎ (09281) 470155

Lauterhofen (1987)
Ruppertslohe 18, 92283 Lauterhofen
☎ (09186) 1574

Lichtenau-Weickershof (1980)
Weickershof 1, 91586 Lichtenau
☎ (09827) 92040

Oberfranken Thurnau (1965)
Postfach 1349, 95304 Kulmbach
☎ (09228) 319

Oberpfälzer Wald G&LC (1977)
Ödengrub, 92431 Kemnath bei Fuhrn
☎ (09439) 466

Oberzwieselau (1990)
94227 Lindberg
☎ (01049) 9922/2367

Regensburg (1966)
93093 Jagdschloss Thiergarten
☎ (09403) 505
⎙ (09403) 4391
✉ gcregensburg@freenet.de
⚐ 18 L 5734 m CR 71.5 SR 138
⚇ U H
££ €45 (€60)
⚘ 14km E of Regensburg, nr Walhalla
⌂ Harradine/Himmel
▤ www.golfclub-regensburg.de

Am Reichswald (1960)
Schiestlstr 100, 90427 Nürnberg
☎ (0911) 305730
⎙ (0911) 301200
✉ info@golfclub-nuernberg.de
⚐ 18 L 6041 m CR 72.7 SR 133

⚇ U H
££ €50 (€65)
⚘ 10km N of Nuremberg
⌂ Dr Bernhard von Limburger/Thomas Himmel
▤ www.golfclub-nuernberg.de

Sagmühle (1984)
Golfplatz Sagmühle 1, 94086 Bad Griesbach
☎ (08532) 2038

Schloss Fahrenbach (1993)
95709 Tröstau
☎ (09232) 882-256

Schloss Reichmannsdorf (1991)
Schlosshof 4, 96132 Schlüsselfeld
☎ (09546) 9215-10
✉ info@golfanlage-reichmannsdorf.de

Schlossberg (1985)
Grünbach 8, 94419 Reisbach
☎ (08734) 7035

Schwanhof (1994)
Klaus Conrad Allee 1, 92706 Luhe-Wildenau
☎ (09607) 92020

Die Wutzschleife (1997)
Hillstedt 40, 92444 Rötz
☎ (09976) 18460
⎙ (09976) 18180
✉ info@golfanlage-wutzschleife.de
⚐ 18 L 4696 m Par 66
⚇ U
££ €17.50–€35 (€21–€42)
⚘ 70km N of Regensburg. 180km NE of Munich
⌂ Deutsche Golf Consult
▤ www.golfanlage-wutzschleife.de

Rhineland North

Aachen (1927)
Schurzelter Str 300, 52074 Aachen
☎ (0241) 12501
⎙ (0241) 171075
✉ info@agc-ev.de
⚐ 18 L 6063 m Par 72
⚇ H
££ €50 (€60)
⚘ Seffent, 5km NW of Aachen
⌂ Murray/Morrison/Pennink
▤ www.aachener-golfclub.de

Golf und Landclub Ahaus (1987)
Schmäinghook 36, 48683 Ahaus-Alstätte
☎ (02567) 405
⎙ (02567) 3524
✉ info@glc-ahaus.de
⚐ 27 hole course
⚇ U H
££ €50 (€70) Members €40 (€50)
⚘ 60km W of Münster

⌂ Deutsche Golf Consult
▤ www.glc-ahaus.de

Alten Fliess (1995)
Am Alten Fliess 66, 50129 Bergheim
☎ (02238) 94410

Artland (1988)
Westerholte 23, 49577 Ankum
☎ (05466) 301

Bergisch-Land
Siebeneickerst 386, 42111 Wuppertal
☎ (02053) 7177

Bochum (1982)
Im Mailand 127, 44797 Bochum
☎ (0234) 799832

Dortmund (1956)
Reichmarkstr 12, 44265 Dortmund
☎ (0231) 774133/774609

Düsseldorfer GC (1961)
Rommeljansweg 12, D-40882 Ratingen
☎ 0049 (0) 2102 81092
⎙ 0049 (0) 2102 81782
✉ info@duesseldorfer-golf-club.de
⚐ 18 holes: Medal tee: 5781 m
  Par 71 CR 70.8 SR 131
  ladies tee: L 5105 m Par 71
  CR 72.4 SR 126
⚇ WD–U WE–M HCP 36
££ €70
⚘ 11km from Düsseldorf. Take A44 in direction of Ratingen until junction Ratingen Ost then follow signs for Ratingen
⌂ FW Hawtree
▤ www.duesseldorfer-golf-club.de

Elfrather Mühle (1991)
An der Elfrather Mühle 145, 47802 Krefeld
☎ (02151) 4969-0
⎙ (02151) 477459
✉ info@gcem.de
⚐ 18 L 6125 m Par 72 SSS 72
⚇ H–max 36 M–WE+BH SOC–reservation necessary
££ €55 (+BH €75)
⚘ Krefeld 7km. Düsseldorf 25km
⌂ Ron Kirby
▤ www.gcem.de

Erftaue (1991)
Zur Mühlenerft 1, 41517 Grevenbroich
☎ (02181) 280637
⎙ (02181) 280639
✉ gc.erftaue@t-online.de
⚐ 18 L 6003 m Par 72 CR 71.2 SR 126
⚇ WD–H WE–H after 1pm
££ €40 (€50)
⚘ 25km SW of Düsseldorf
⌂ Karl Grohs
▤ www.golf-erftaue.de

Essen Haus Oefte (1959)
Laupendahler Landstr, 45219 Essen-Kettwig
☎ (02054) 83911

Euregio Bad Bentheim
(1987)
Postbox 1205, Am Hauptelick 8, 48443 Bad Bentheim
☎ (05922) 7776-0

Grevenmühle Ratingen
(1988)
Grevenmühle, 40882 Ratingen-Homberg
☎ (02102) 9595-0

Haus Bey (1992)
An Haus bey 16, 41334 Nettetal
☎ (02153) 9197-0
🖳 (02153) 919750
📧 golf@hausbey.de
🏴 18 L 5948 m CR 71.5 SR 128
👥 U H(30)
££ €50 (€60)
🚗 40km NW of Düsseldorf
🏠 Paul Krings
🖥 www.hausbey.de

Haus Kambach (1989)
Kambachstrasse 9-13, 52249 Eschweiler-Kinzweiler
☎ (02403) 50890
🖳 (02403) 21270
📧 info@golf-kambach.de
🏴 18 L 6029 m SSS 73 CR 71.4 SR 123
👥 U – please contact for tee time reservation
££ €55 (€65) 2009
🚗 20km E of Aachen
🏠 Dieter Sziedat
🖥 www.golf-kambach.de

Hubbelrath (1961)
Bergische Landstr 700, 40629 Düsseldorf
☎ (02104) 72178
🖳 (02104) 75685
📧 info@gc-hubbelrath.de
🏴 East 18 L 6282 m Par 72 CR 73.6 SR 132
West 18 L 4000 m Par 66 CR 61.8 SR 110
👥 WD–U WE–M H–max 26 East, 36 West
££ East €80 (€100) West €50 (€70)
🚗 Hubbelrath, 13km E of Düsseldorf, on Route B7
🏠 B von Limburger
🖥 www.gc-hubbelrath.de

Hummelbachaue Neuss
(1987)
Norfer Kirchstrasse, 41469 Neuss
☎ (02137) 91910

Issum-Niederrhein (1973)
Pauenweg 68, 47661 Issum 1
☎ (02835) 92310

Golf- and Land-Club Köln e.V. (1906)
Golfplatz 2, 51429 Bergisch Gladbach
☎ 0049 (0) 2204-9276-0
🖳 0049 (0) 2204-9276-15

📧 info@glckoeln.de
🏴 18 L Men 5980 m, Ladies 5286 m
Men: white Par 72 CR 72.2 SR 137 yellow Par 72 CR 71.4 SR 134
Ladies: black Par 72 CR 74.3 SR 138 red Par 72 CR 73.4 SR 136
👥 WD–H WE–M
££ €85 (WE members' guests only)
🚗 15km East from Cologne
🏠 Bernhard von Limburger
🖥 www.glckoeln.de

Kosaido International
(1989)
Am Schmidtberg 11, 40629 Düsseldorf
☎ (02104) 77060
🖳 (02104) 770611
📧 info@kosaido.de
🏴 Men: 18 L 5562 m CR 70.5 SR 135
Ladies: 18 L 5044 m CR 73.0 SR 131
👥 WD–U–H WE–MN between 11am and 1pm
££ €52 (€67) €26 (€36) after 4pm
🚗 10km NE of Düsseldorf
🏠 Hirochika Tomizawa/Rainer Preissmann
🖥 www.kosaido.de

Krefeld (1930)
Eltweg 2, 47809 Krefeld
☎ (02151) 156030
🖳 (02151) 15603 222
📧 kgc@krefelder-gc.de
🏴 18 L 6082 m SSS 72
👥 WD–U H–max 28
££ €50 (€60)
🚗 7km SE of Krefeld. Düsseldorf 16km
🏠 B von Limburger
🖥 www.krefelder-gc.de

Mühlenhof G&CC (1990)
Rheinstr., 47546 Kalkar
☎ (02824) 924092
🖳 (02824) 924093
📧 awilmsen@muehlenhof.net
🏴 18 L 6103 m Par 72 CR 72.5 SR 125 (men)
L 5301 m Par 72 CR 74.2 SR 126 (ladies)
👥 U
££ €40 (€50)
🚗 80km N of Düsseldorf (B57)
🏠 Hans Herkberger
🖥 www.muehlenhof.net

Nordkirchen (1974)
Am Golfplatz 6, 59394 Nordkirchen
☎ (02596) 9191

Op de Niep (1995)
Bergschenweg 71, 47506 Neukirchen-Vluyn
☎ (02845) 28051

Osnabrück (1955)
Am Golfplatz 3, 49143 Bissendorf
☎ (05402) 5636
🖳 (05402) 5257
📧 info@ogc.de
🏴 18 L 5731 m Par 71
👥 U

££ €40 (€60)
🚗 13km SE of Osnabrück
🏠 Frank Pennink
🖥 www.ogc.de

Rheine/Mesum (1998)
Wörstr 201, 48432 Rheine
☎ (05975) 9490
📧 info@golfclub-rheine.de

Rittergut Birkhof (1996)
Rittergut Birkhof, 41352 Korschenbroich
☎ (02131) 510660

St Barbara's Royal Dortmund (1969)
Hesslingweg, 44309 Dortmund
☎ (0231) 202551

Schloss Georghausen (1962)
Georghausen 8, 51789 Lindlar-Hommerich
☎ (02207) 4938
📧 gcschlossgeorghausengolf.de

Schloss Haag (1996)
Bartelter Weg 8, 47608 Geldern
☎ (02831) 94777

Schloss Myllendonk (1965)
Myllendonkerstr 113, 41352 Korschenbroich 1
☎ (02161) 641049
🖳 (02161) 648806
📧 info@gcsm.de
🏴 18 L 5955 m CR 72.2 SR 133
👥 H
££ €50 (€60)
🚗 1km E of Korschenbroich. 5km E of Mönchengladbach. 20km E of Düsseldorf
🏠 Donald Harradine
🖥 www.gcsm.de

Golfclub Schloss Westerholt e.V. (1993)
Schloss Strasse 1, 45701 Herten-Westerholt
☎ (0209) 165840
🖳 (0209) 1658415
📧 info@gc-westerholt.de
🏴 18 Par 72
Men: yellow L 6052 m CR 71.6 SR 126
white L 6250 m CR 72.6 SR 127
Women: red L 5365 m CR 73.7 SR 125
black L 5534 m CR 74.8 SR 128
👥 H (36) SOC–WD WE–M
££ €50 (€50)
🚗 10km Recklinghausen. 20km Essen
🏠 Christoph Städler
🖥 www.gc-westerholt.de

Golf- und Landclub Schmitzhof (1975)
Arsbeckerstr 160, 41844 Wegberg
☎ (02436) 39090
🖳 (02436) 390915
📧 info@golfclubschmitzhof.de
🏴 Men: 18 L 6.071 m CR 72.0 SR 133
Ladies: 18 L 5.229 m CR 73.2 SR 125

For list of abbreviations, key to symbols and international dialling codes see page 647

WD–H WE–M
£€ €50 (€60)
⊕ Wegberg-Merbeck, 20km SW of
     Mönchengladbach
⌂ Don Harradine
▤ www.golfclubschmitzhof.de

Siegen-Olpe   (1966)
Am Golfplatz, 57482 Wenden
☎ (02762) 9762-0
⌨ (02762) 9762-12
✉ info@gcso.de
▷ 18 L 5959 m CR 71.1 SR 127
⋔ U H–max 36
£€ €45 (€50)
⊕ 20km NW of Siegen
▤ www.gcso.de

Golfclub Siegerland e.V.
(1993)
Berghäuser Weg, 57223 Kreuztal-
Mittelhees
☎ (02732) 59470
⌨ (02732) 594724
✉ info@golfclub-siegerland.de
▷ 18 Par 72
     Men: L 5865 m CR 71.1 SR 131
     Ladies: L 5162 m CR 73 SR 125
⋔ H
£€ €45 (€50)
⊕ 15km N of Siegen
⌂ Spangemacher
▤ www.golfclub-siegerland.de

Teutoburger Wald
Postfach 1250, 33777
Halle/Westfalen, GERMANY
☎ +49 5201 6279
✉ info@gctw-halle.de

Unna-Fröndenberg   (1985)
Schwarzer Weg 1, 58730 Fröndenberg
☎ (02373) 70068
⌨ (02373) 70069
✉ golf-club-unf@t-online.de
▷ 18 White Men L 6234 m CR 73.0
     SR 133
     Yellow Men L 5977 m CR 71.7
     SR 129
     Blue Men L 5291 m CR 68.2 SR 119
     Blue Ladies CR 73.7 SR 131
     Red Men L 5069 m CR 67.0 SR 118
     Red Ladies CR 72.4 SR 128
⋔ M H (max 36)
£€ €40 (€50)
⊕ 25km W of Dortmund
⌂ Karl Grohs
▤ www.gcuf.de

Vechta-Welpe   (1989)
Welpe 2, 49377 Vechta
☎ (04441) 5539/82168
⌨ (04441) 852480
✉ info@golfclub-vechta.de
▷ 18 L 5957 m Par 72 CR 73.0 SR 139
⋔ H
£€ €40 (€50)
⊕ 50km SW of Bremen
⌂ Rainer Preissmann
▤ www.golfclub-vechta.de

Velbert – Gut Kuhlendahl
Kuhlendahler Str 283, 42553 Velbert
☎ (02053) 923290
⌨ (02053) 923291
✉ golfclub-velbert@t-online.de
▷ 18 L 5608 m CR 71.1 SR 136 (men)
     CR 72.8 SR 129 (ladies)
⋔ WD H (36), WE M H (36)
£€ €40 (€60)
⊕ Between Düsseldorf and
     Wuppertal
⌂ Grohs/Preissmann
▤ www.gcvelbert.de

Golfclub Velderhof
Velderhof, 50259 Pulheim
☎ (02238) 923940
✉ info@velderhof.de

Vestischer GC
Recklinghausen   (1974)
Bockholterstr 475, 45659 Recklinghausen
☎ (02361) 93420
✉ vest.golfclub@t-online.de

Wasserburg Anholt   (1972)
Schloss 3, 46419 Isselburg Anholt
☎ (02874) 915120
✉ sekretariat@golfclub-anholt.de

Golfclub Weselerwald
Steenbecksweg 12, 46514 Schermbeck
☎ (02856) 91370
⌨ (02856) 913715
✉ info@gcww.de
▷ 18 Par 72
     Men: L 6047 m CR 71.8 SR 127
     Women: L 5274m CR 74.1 SR 124
⋔ U H WE–M
£€ €50 (€60)
⊕ 10km Wesel. 60km Düsseldorf
⌂ Dr Siekmann
▤ www.gcww.de

West Rhine   (1956)
Javelin Barracks, BFPO 35
☎ +49 2163 974463
⌨ +49 2163 80049
✉ secretary@westrhinegc.co.uk
▷ 18 L 6522 yds SSS 71
⋔ WD–U WE–M
£€ €35 (€40)
⊕ On B230, 1km from
     Dutch/German border. 25km W of
     Mönchengladbach
▤ www.westrhinegc.co.uk

Westerwald   (1979)
Steinebacherstr, 57629 Dreifelden
☎ (02666) 8220
⌨ (02666) 8493
✉ gcwesterwald@t-online.de
▷ 18 holes SSS 72
⋔ H
£€ €40 (€50)
⊕ Hachenburg, 60km E of Bonn
▤ ww.gc-westerwald.de

Rhineland South

Bad Neuenahr G&LC
(1979)
Remagener Weg, 53474 Bad Neuenahr-
Ahrweiler
☎ (02641) 950950

Golf-Resort Bitburger Land
(1995)
Zur Weilersheck 1, 54636 Wissmannsdorf
☎ (06527) 9272-0
⌨ (06527) 9272-30
✉ info@bitgolf.de
▷ 18 L 6104 m Par 72 SR 133
⋔ H
£€ €50 (€60)
⊕ 25km NE of Trier. 40km NE of
     Luxembourg
⌂ Karl Grohs
▤ www.bitgolf.de

Bonn-Godesberg in
Wachtberg   (1960)
Landgrabenweg, 53343 Wachtberg-
Niederbachem
☎ (0228) 344003

Burg Overbach   (1984)
Postfach 1213, 53799 Much
☎ (02245) 5550
⌨ (02245) 8247
▷ 18 L 5913 m SSS 72
⋔ H
£€ €40 (€50)
⊕ Much, 45km E of Cologne, off A4
⌂ Deutsch Golf Consult
▤ www.golfclub-burg-overbach.de

Burg Zievel   (1994)
Burg Zievel, 53894 Mechernich
☎ (02256) 1651

Eifel   (1977)
Kölner Str, 54576 Hillesheim
☎ (06593) 1241

Gut Heckenhof   (1993)
53783 Eitorf
☎ (02243) 9232-0
⌨ (02243) 923299
✉ info@gut-heckenhof.de
▷ 27 L 6214 m SSS 72
⋔ H
£€ €45 (€55)
⊕ 40km SE of Cologne
⌂ William Amick
▤ www.gut-heckenhof.de

Internationaler GC Bonn
(1992)
Gut Grossenbusch, 53757 St Augustin
☎ (02241) 39880
⌨ (02241) 398888
✉ info@gcbonn.de
▷ 18 L 5927 m Par 72
⋔ U H
£€ €45 (€60)
⊕ 6km E of Bonn

⌂ Karl Grohs
▤ www.golf-course-bonn.de

Jakobsberg (1990)
Im Tal der Loreley, 56154 Boppard
☎ (06742) 808491
❑ (06742) 808493
✉ golf@jakobsberg.de
▷ 18 L 5950 m Par 72 SSS 72
♘ U
££ €45 (€60)
⛳ 80km N of Mainz
⌂ Wolfgang Jersombek
▤ www.jakobsberg.de

Kyllburger Waldeifel
Lietzenhof, 54597 Burbach, GERMANY
☎ (06553) 961039

Mittelrheinischer Bad Ems
(1938)
Denzerheide, 56130 Bad Ems
☎ (02603) 6541
❑ (02603) 13995
✉ info@mgcbadems.de
▷ 18 L 6050 m SSS 72
♘ H (36)
££ €50 (€70)
⛳ 13km E of Koblenz, nr Bad Ems
(6km)
⌂ Karl Hoffmann
▤ ww3w.mgcbadems.de

Nahetal (1971)
Drei Buchen, 55583 Bad Münster am Stein
☎ (06708) 2145
❑ (06708) 1731
▷ 18 L 5883 m Par 72 SSS 72
♘ H
££ €45 (€55)
⛳ 6 km S of Bad Kreuznach. 70km SW of Frankfurt
⌂ Armin Keller
▤ www.golfclub-nahetal.de

Stromberg-Schindeldorf
(1987)
Park Village Golfanlagen, Buchenring 6, 55442 Stromberg
☎ (06724) 93080

Trier (1977)
54340 Ensch-Birkenheck
☎ (06507) 993255
❑ (06507) 993257
✉ info@golf-club-trier-de
▷ 18 L 6069 m Par 72
♘ H–max 36
££ €50 (€60)
⛳ Trier 20km. Koblenz 80km. Highway H1, exit 'Föhren'
▤ www.golf-club-trier.de

Waldbrunnen (1983)
Brunnenstr 11, 53578 Windhagen
☎ (02645) 8041
✉ info@golfclub-waldbrunnen.de

Wiesensee (1992)
Am Wiesensee, 56459 Westerburg-Stahlhofen

☎ (02663) 991192
✉ golfclub.wiesensee@lindner.de

Saar-Pfalz

Pfalz Neustadt (1971)
Im Lochbusch, 67435 Neustadt-Geinsheim
☎ (06327) 97420
✉ gc-pfalz@t-online.de

Saarbrücken (1961)
Oberlimbergerweg, 66798 Wallerfangen-Gisingen
☎ (06837) 91800/1584
❑ (06837) 91801
▷ 18 L 5971 m CR 71.9 SR 130
♘ H
££ €45 (€55)
⛳ B406 towards Wallerfangen. 8km N of Saarlouis
⌂ Donald Harradine
▤ www.golfclub-saarbruecken.de

Websweiler Hof (1991)
Websweiler Hof, 66424 Homburg/Saar
☎ (06841) 7777-60

Westpfalz Schwarzbachtal
(1988)
66509 Rieschweiler
☎ (06336) 6442
❑ (06336) 6408
✉ egw@golf.de
▷ 18 L 5599 m Par 70 CR 69.0 SR 124
♘ H
££ €40 (€55)
⛳ 40km E of Saarbrücken
▤ www.gcwestpfalz.de

Woodlawn Golf Course
6792 Ramstein Flugplatz
☎ (06371) 476240
❑ (06371) 42158
▷ 18 L 6225 yds (Back)
5691 yds (Middle)
5089 yds (Front)
CR 67.2 SR 122 (Back)
CR 66.2 SR 119 (Middle)
CR 68.4 SR 119 (Front)
♘ M
££ $25 ($40)
⛳ Ramstein 3km. Kaiserlautern 10km
▤ www.ramsteingolf.com

Stuttgart & South West

Bad Liebenzell
Golfplatz 1-9, 75378 Bad Liebenzell
☎ (07052) 9325-0
❑ (07052) 9325-25
✉ info@gcbl.de
▷ 18 L 6113 m Par 72 SSS 72
18 L 5853 m Par 72 SSS 71
♘ H max 54
££ €50 (€70)
⛳ 35km W of Stuttgart
⌂ Elger/Mühl
▤ www.gcbl.de

Bad Rappenau (1989)
Ehrenbergstrasse 25a, 74906 Bad Rappenau
☎ (07264) 3666

Bad Salgau (1995)
Koppelweg 103, 88348 Bad Salgau
☎ (07581) 527459
✉ info@gc-bs.de

Baden Hills Golf & Curling Club e.v. (1982)
Cabot Trail G208, 77836 Rheinmünster
☎ (07229) 185100
❑ (07229) 1851011
✉ baden-hills@t-online.de
▷ 18 L 6053 m Par 72 CR 72.6 SR 129
♘ WD–U WE–H booking necessary between 9.00–15.00
££ €35 (€45)
⛳ 10km W of Baden-Baden. 50km N of Strasbourg
⌂ gds Les Furber (Canada)
▤ www.baden-hills.de

Baden-Baden (1901)
Fremersbergstr 127, 76530 Baden-Baden
☎ (07221) 23579

GC Bodensee Weissenberg eV (1986)
Lampertsweiler 51, D-88138 Weissensberg
☎ +41 (8389) 89190
❑ +41 (8389) 923907
✉ info@gcbw.de
▷ Champs: 18 L 6079 m CR 73.4 SR 143
Men: 18 L 5858 m CR 71.2 SR 141
Champs L: 18 L 5373 m CR 75.4 SR 137
Ladies: 18 L 5185 m CR 74.3 SR 137
♘ WD–H 36 WE–H 35 WD+WE teetime reservations obligatory
££ €56 (€69 + holidays)
⛳ 5km NE of Lindau, Lake Constance (Bodensee)
⌂ Robert Trent Jones Sr
▤ www.gcbw.de

Freiburg (1970)
Krüttweg 1, 79199 Kirchzarten
☎ (07661) 9847-0
❑ (07661) 984747
✉ fgc@freiburger-golfclub.de
▷ 18 L 5945 m CR 71.9 SR 131
♘ H
££ €45 (€55)
⛳ Freiburg-Kappel/Kirchzarten
⌂ B von Limburger
▤ www.freiburger-golfclub.de

Fürstlicher Golfclub Waldsee (1998)
Hopfenweiler, 88339 Bad Waldsee
☎ (07524) 4017 200

Hechingen Hohenzollern
(1955)
Postfach 1124, 72379 Hechingen

For list of abbreviations, key to symbols and international dialling codes see page 647

☎ (07471) 6478
🖳 (07471) 14776
✉ info@golfclub-hechingen.de
⛳ 18 holes SSS 72
126/124 men; 125/122 ladies
👥 U H
££ On application
🚗 Hechingen, 50km S of Stuttgart
🏠 Bernhard von Limbürger,
Götz Mecklenbürg
📧 www.golfclub-hechingen.de

Heidelberg-Lobenfeld

(1968)

Biddersbacherhof, 74931 Lobbach-Lobenfeld

☎ (06226) 952110
🖳 (06226) 952111
✉ golf@gchl.de
⛳ 18 L 5989 m SSS 72
👥 WD–H WE–M H
££ €50 (€60)
🚗 20km E of Heidelberg
🏠 Donald Harradine
📧 www.gchl.de

Heilbronn-Hohenlohe

(1964)

Hofgasse, 74639 Zweiflingen-Friedrichsruhe

☎ (07941) 920810

Hetzenhof

Hetzenhof 7, 73547 Lorch

☎ (07172) 9180-0
🖳 (07172) 9180-30
✉ info@golfclub-hetzenhof.de
⛳ 27 Holes Par 72 SR 131
6 hole short course
👥 WD–H WE–M
££ €40 (€50)
🚗 35km E of Stuttgart Airport, via B29 and B297
🏠 Thomas Himmel
📧 www.golfclub-hetzenhof.de

Hohenstaufen   (1959)

Unter den Ramsberg, 73072 Donzdorf-Reichenbach

☎ (07162) 27171
✉ gc-hohenstaufen@online.de

Kaiserhöhe   (1995)

Im Laber 4a, 74747 Ravenstein

☎ (06297) 399
🖳 (06297) 599
✉ info@gck.geoid.de
⛳ 18 L 5927 m CR 71.6 SR 126 (men)
18 L 5196 m CR 73.5 SR 125 (women)
9 hole Par 28 course
👥 U H
££ €45 (€60)
🚗 60km S of Würzburg
🏠 Kurt Rossknecht
📧 www.gc-kaiserhoehe.de

Golf-Club Konstanz e.V.

(1965)

Hofgut Kargegg 1, D-78476 Allensbach-Langenrain

☎ +49 (0) 75 33 93 03 - 0
✉ info@golfclubkonstanz.de

Lindau-Bad Schachen

(1954)

Am Schönbühl 5, 88131 Lindau

☎ (08382) 96170
🖳 (08382) 961750
✉ info@gc-lindau-bad-schachen.de
⛳ 18 L 5776 m Par 71 SSS 71
👥 H36
££ €55 (€65)
🚗 Nr Lindau, Bodensee
🏠 Kurt Rossknecht
📧 www.gc-lindau-bad-schachen.de

Markgräflerland Kandern

(1984)

Feuerbacher Str 35, 79400 Kandern

☎ (07626) 97799-0
🖳 (07626) 97799-22
✉ info@gc-mk.com
⛳ 18 L 5931 m CR 71.5 SR 131
👥 WD–H WE
🚗 Kandern, 10km N of Lörrach.
14km NW of Basle
🏠 Grohs/Benz
📧 www.golfclub-markgraeferland.com

Neckartal   (1974)

Aldinger Str. 975, 70806 Kornwestheim

☎ (07141) 871319
🖳 (07141) 81716
✉ info@gc-neckartal.de
⛳ 18 L 6159 m Par 73 CR 71.6 SR 127
👥 WD–M (only members of "Partnerclubs" can play without member) WE–M
££ €45 (€60)
🚗 5km NE of Stuttgart, nr Kornwestheim
🏠 B von Limburger
📧 www.golf.de/gcneckartal

Nippenburg   (1993)

Nippenburg 21, 71701 Schwieberdingen

☎ (07150) 39530

Obere Alp   (1989)

Am Golfplatz 1-3, 79780 Stühlingen

☎ (07703) 9203-0
🖳 (07703) 9203-18
✉ secretariat@golf-oberealp.de
⛳ 18 L 6147 m SSS 72 SR 129
9 L 3522 m SSS 60 SR 98
👥 H WD–H–SOC, sundowner rate after 4pm. WE–M–H, U after 4pm.
££ 18 hole: €60 (€90) 9 hole: €38 (€37)
🚗 40km N of Zürich, nr Swiss border
🏠 Karl Grohs
📧 www.golf-oberealp.de

Oberschwaben-Bad Waldsee   (1968)

Hopfenweiler 2d, 88339 Bad Waldsee

☎ (07524) 5900

Oeschberghof L & GC

(1976)

Golfplatz 1, 78166 Donaueschingen

☎ (0771) 84525

Land-und Golfclub Oschberghof   (1976)

Golfplatz 1, 78166 Donaueschingen

☎ (0771) 84525
🖳 (0771) 84540
✉ golf@oeschberghof.com
⛳ Standard Tees;-
18 L 5970 m (Men) CR 70.6 SL 125
18 L 5223 m (Ladies) CR 72.3 SL 125
9 L 3974 m (Men) CR 61.6 SL 101
9 L 3438 m (Ladies) CR 60.9 SL 97
Championship Tees available
👥 WD–U/H after 8pm, WE–U/H after 8pm
££ 18: €62 (€75) 9: €36 (€52)
🚗 Donaueschingen, 60km East of Freiburg.
🏠 Deutsche Golf Consult
📧 www.oeschberghof.com

Owingen-Überlingen e.V – Hofgut Lugenhof   (1989)

Alte Owinger Str 93, 88696 Owingen

☎ (07551) 83040
🖳 (07551) 830422
✉ welcome@golfclub-owingen.de
⛳ Men: 18 L 6179 m CR 73.0 SR 132
Ladies: 18 L 5550 m CR 75.7 SR 130
👥 H
££ €55 (€70)
🚗 5km N of Überlingen, nr Lake Konstanz
📧 www.golfclub-owingen.de

Pforzheim Karlshäuser Hof

(1987)

Karlshäuser Weg, 75248 Ölbronn-Dürrn

☎ (07237) 9100
🖳 (07237) 5161
✉ info@gc-pf.de
⛳ 18 hole course SSS 72
👥 H–max 36
££ Mon–Thur €45 Fri €50, Sat/Sun €60
🚗 6km N of Pforzheim. 30km E of Karlsruhe
🏠 Reinhold Weishaupt
📧 www.gc-pf.de

Reischenhof   (1987)

Industriestrasse 12, 88489 Wain

☎ (07353) 1732
🖳 (07373) 3824
⛳ 27 L 5998 m CR 71.9 SR 129
👥 H
££ €45 (€60)
🚗 30km S of Ulm
🏠 Wolfgang Jersombeck
📧 www.golf.de/gc-reischenhof

Reutlingen-Sonnenbühl

(1987)

Im Zerg, 72820 Sonnenbühl

☎ (07128) 92660

Rhein Badenweiler (1971)
79401 Badenweiler
☎ **(07632) 7970**

Rickenbach (1979)
Hennematt 20, 79736 Rickenbach
☎ **(07765) 777**
🖳 (07765) 544
📧 info@golfclub-rickenbach.de
🏳 18 L 5544 m CR 70.5 SR 133
👥 WD/Sat–U H exc Tues/Thurs am
Sun–NA before 3pm WD–U–H54
WE–H36–U when no tournament
M if tournament
££ €50 (€65)
🚗 20km N of Bad Säckingen/30 miles
from Basel
🏠 Dudok van Heel/Himmel
📧 www.golfclub-rickenbach.de

**Schloss Klingenburg-
Günzburg** (1978)
*Schloss Klingenburg, 89343 Jettingen-
Scheppach*
☎ **(08225) 3030**

Schloss Langenstein (1991)
*Schloss Langenstein, 78359 Orsingen-
Nenzingen*
☎ **(07774) 50651**
📧 golf-sekretariat@schloss-
langenstein.com

Schloss Liebenstein (1982)
Postfach 27, 74380 Neckarwestheim
☎ **(07133) 9878-0**
🖳 (07133) 9878-18
📧 info@gc-sl.de
🏳 27 L 5890-6361 m SSS 71-73
👥 U
££ €60 (€80)
🚗 35km N of Stuttgart
🏠 Donald Harradine/Deutsche Golf
Consult
📧 www.golfclubliebenstein.de

Schloss Weitenburg (1984)
Sommerhalde 11, 72181 Starzach-Sulzau
☎ **(07472) 15050**
🖳 (07472) 15051
📧 info@gcsw.de
🏳 18 L 5978 m CR 71.3 SR 123
9 hole course
👥 9: U; 18: H
££ 9: €14 (€17.50); 18: €45 (€55)
🚗 50km SW of Stuttgart in Neckar
Valley
🏠 Heinz Fehring
📧 www.gcsw.de

Sinsheim-Buchenauerhof
(1993)
Buchenauerhof 4, 74889 Sinsheim
☎ **(07265) 7258**
📧 mail@ golfclubsinsheim.de

Steisslingen (1991)
Brunnenstr 4b, 78256 Steisslingen-Wiechs
☎ **(07738) 7196**
🖳 (07738) 923297

📧 info@golfclub-steisslingen.de
🏳 18 L 6145 m Par 72
6 hole course
👥 U
££ €48 (€68)
🚗 30km N of Konstanz
🏠 Dave Thomas
📧 www.golfclub-steisslingen.de

**Stuttgarter Golf-Club
Solitude** (1927)
Schlossfeld, 71297 Mönsheim
☎ **(07044) 911 0410**
🖳 (07044) 911 0420
📧 info@golfclub-stuttgart.com
🏳 Men: 18 L 5869 m Par 72 CR 71.2
SR 125
Women: 18 L 4970 m Par 72
CR 71.7 SR 125
👥 WD–H max 26.5 WE–M
££ €70
🚗 30km W of Stuttgart
🏠 B von Limburger
📧 www.golfclub-stuttgart.com

Ulm e.V. (1963)
Wochenauer Hof 2, 89186 Illerrieden
☎ **(07306) 929500**
🖳 (07306) 9295025
📧 GolfClubUlm@t-online.de
🏳 18 L 6076 m SSS 72
👥 H–max 36
££ €48 (€65)
🚗 15km S of Ulm
🏠 Deutsche Golf Consult
📧 www.GolfClubUlm.de

Greece

Afandou (1973)
Afandou, Rhodes
☎ **(0241) 51255**

Corfu (1972)
PO Box 71, Ropa Valley, 49100 Corfu
☎ **(26610) 94220**
📧 cfugolf@hol.gr

Glyfada (1962)
PO Box 70116, 166-10 Glyfada, Athens
☎ **(01) 894 6459**

Hungary

Birdland G&CC (1991)
Thermal krt.10, 9740 Bükfürdö
☎ **(+36) 94 358060**
🖳 (+36) 94 359000
📧 info@birdland.hu
🏳 18 L 6459 m Par 72 SSS 71-75
9 hole Par 3 course
👥 U H
££ £33

🚗 120km SE of Vienna
🏠 G Hauser
📧 www.birdland.hu

Budapest G&CC
Golf u.1, 2024 Kisoroszi
☎ **(1) 36 26 392 465**

European Lakes G&CC
Kossuth u.3, 7232 Hencse
☎ **(82) 481245**
🖳 (82) 481248
📧 info@europeanlakes.com
🏳 18 L 6231 m Par 72
👥 U
££ €55 (€70) Packages from €100
🚗 20km from Kaposvar (SW
Hungary)
🏠 J Dudok van Heel
📧 www.europeanlakes.com

Old Lake
PO Box 127, 2890 Tata-Remeteségpuszta
☎ **(34) 587620**

Pannonia G&CC (1996)
Alcsútdoboz, 8087 Mariavölgy
☎ **0036 (22) 594200**
🖳 0036 (22) 594205
📧 info@golfclub.hu
🏳 18 Gold (Pro) L 6401 m Par 72 CR
74.1 SR 125
White L 6192 m (Men back) Par 72
CR 73 SR 129
Yellow L 5969 m (Men std) Par 72
CR 71.6 SR 129
Red L 5406 m (Ladies std) Par 73
CR 74.4 SR 131
Blue L 5679 m (Men snr/jnr) Par 72
CR 70.1 SR 124
Orange L 4971 m (Ladies snr)
Par 73 CR 71.3 SR 124
👥 Semi-private H (Golf Assn Card)
££ €58 (€79)
🚗 40 km Outside Budapest
🏠 H Erhardt
📧 www.golfclub.hu

St Lorence G&CC
Pellérdi ut 55, 7634 Pécs
☎ **(72) 252844/252142**

Iceland

Akureyri (1935)
PO Box 317, 602 Akureyri
☎ **(462) 2974**
📧 gagolf@simnet.is

Borgarness (1973)
Hamar, 310 Borgarnes
☎ **(345) 437 1663**
📧 hamar@gbborgarnes.net
🏳 9 L 2857 m SSS 72 SR 134 (yellow
tees)
👥 U
££ 3500 Ikr (2000 Ikr before 2pm)

4km N of Borgarnes. 83km N of
Reykjavik (tunnel) (Ringroad#1)
⌂ Torvaldur Asgeirsson & Hannes
Torsteinsson
▤ www.golf.is/gb
www.gbborgarnes.net

Eskifjardar   (1976)
735 Eskifjördur

Húsavík   (1967)
PO Box 23, Kötlum, 640 Húsavik
☎ (464) 1000
✉ palmi.palmason@tmd.is

Isafjardar   (1978)
PO Box 367, 400 Isafjördur
☎ (456) 5081
✉ gi@snerpa.is

Jökull   (1973)
Postholf 67, 355 Olafsvík
☎ (436) 1666

Keilir   (1967)
Box 148, 222 Hafnarfjördur
☎ (565) 3360
✉ keilir@ishoff.is

Kopavogs og Gardabaejar
(1994)
Postholf 214, 212 Gardabaer
☎ (+354) 565 7373
✉ gkg@gkg.is

Leynir   (1965)
PO Box 9, Akranes
☎ (00354) 431 2771
    (00354) 863 4985
▯ (00354) 431 3711
✉ leynir@simnet.is
➢ 18 L 6006 m Par 72 SR 137
♟ U
£€ 3500Ikr
➥ 2km from Akranes (SW coast)
⌂ H Thorsteinsson
▤ www.golf.is/gl   www.leynir.is

Ness-Nesklúbburinn
(1964)
PO Box 66, 172 Seltjarnarnes
☎ (561) 1930
▯ (561) 1966
✉ nk@centrum.is
➢ 9 L 5396 m Par 72 CR 71.2 SR 121
♟ U
£€ 2500 Ikr before 13.00; 3500 Ikr
    after 13.00 and WE
➥ 3km W of Reykjavík
▤ www.golf.is/nk

Oddafellowa   (1990)
Urridavatnsdölum, 210 Gardabaer
☎ (565) 9094

Olafsfjardar   (1968)
Skeggjabrekku, 625 Olafsfjördur
☎ (466) 2611

Reykjavíkur   (1934)
Grafarholt, 112 Reykjavik
☎ +354 (585) 0200/0210
✉ gr@grgolf.is

Saudárkróks   (1970)
Hlidarendi, Postholf 56, 550 Saudárkrókur
☎ (453) 5075

Sudurnesja   (1964)
PO Box 112, 232 Keflavik
☎ (421) 4100

Vestmannaeyja   (1938)
Postholf 168, 902 Vestmannaeyar
☎ (481) 2363

Italy

Como/Milan/Bergamo

Ambrosiano   (1994)
Cascina Bertacca, 20080 Bubbiano-Milan
☎ (0290) 840820
▯ (0290) 849365
✉ info@golfclubambrosiano.com
➢ 18 L 6047 m Par 72
♟ U
£€ €37 (€60)
➥ 25km SW of Milan
⌂ Cornish/Silva
▤ www.golfclubambrosiano.com

Barlassina CC   (1956)
Via Privata Golf 42, 20030 Birago di
Camnago (MI)
☎ (0362) 560621/2
▯ (0362) 560934
✉ bccgolf@libero.it
➢ 18 L 6197 m SSS 72
♟ WD–U
£€ €60 (€100)
➥ 22km N of Milan
⌂ D Harradine

Bergamo L'Albenza
(1961)
Via Longoni 12, 24030 Almenno S.
Bartolomeo (BG)
☎ (035) 640028
▯ (035) 643066
✉ secreteria@golfbeagamo.it
➢ 27 L 6.082-5431 m SSS 72.4-137/
    74.7-130
♟ U–book by mail or fax (better by
    mail) SOC WD WE – Booking
    advisable
£€ €55 Tues–Fri €77 Sat/Sun €15
    Driving Range Fee
➥ 13km NW of Bergamo. Milan 45
    km
⌂ Cotton/Sutton
▤ www.golfbeagamo.it

Bogogno   (1996)
Via Sant'Isidoro 1, 28010 Bogogno
☎ (0322) 863794
✉ info@circologolfbogogno.com

Golf Brianza Country Club
(1996)
Cascina Cazzu, 4, 20040 Usmate
Velate (Mi)
☎ (039) 682 9089/079
▯ (039) 682 9059
✉ brianzagolf@tin.it
➢ 18 L 5709 m Par 72 CR 70.2 SR 128
♟ U
£€ €45 (€60)
➥ 24km NE of Milan. Monza 6km
⌂ Marco Croze
▤ www.brianzagolf.it

Carimate   (1962)
Via Airoldi 2, 22060 Carimate (CO)
☎ (031) 790226
▯ (031) 791927
✉ golfcarimate@virgilio.it
➢ 18 L 6021 m SSS 71 SR 1290
♟ U H
£€ €50 (€70)
➥ 15km from Como. 20km from
    Milan
⌂ Piero Mancinelli
▤ www.golfcarimate.it

Castelconturbia   (1984)
Via Suno, 28010 Agrate Conturbia
☎ (0322) 832093
✉ castelconturbia@tin.it

Castello di Tolcinasco
(1993)
20090 Pieve Emanuele (MI)
☎ (02) 9042 8035
▯ (02) 9078 9051
✉ golf@golftolcinasco.it
➢ 27 L 6253-6322 m Par 72
    9 hole Par 3 course
♟ U
£€ €45 (€80)
➥ 12km S of Milan
⌂ Arnold Palmer
▤ www.golftolcinasco.it

Franciacorta   (1986)
Via Provinciale 34b, 25040 Nigoline di
Corte Franca, (Brescia)
☎ (030) 984167
▯ (030) 984393
✉ franciacortagolfclub@libero.it
➢ 18 L 5924 m Par 72 SSS 72
    9 hole Par 3 course
♟ WD–U WE–NA before 2pm
£€ €45 (€65)
➥ Nigoline, 25km E of Bergamo.
    Autostrada A4 exit Rovato
⌂ Dye/Croze

Menaggio & Cadenabbia
(1907)
Via Golf 12, 22010 Grandola E Uniti
☎ (0344) 32103
✉ segretaria@golfclubmenaggio.it

Milano   (1928)
20052 Parco di Monza (MI)
☎ **(039) 303081/2/3**

Molinetto CC   (1982)
SS Padana Superiore 11, 20063 Cernusco S/N (MI)
☎ **(02) 9210 5128/9210 5983**

Monticello   (1975)
Via Volta 63, 22070 Cassina Rizzardi (Como)
☎ **(031) 928055**
📠 (031) 880207
📧 monticello@tin.it
🏳 18 L 6413 m SSS 72
   18 L 6056 m SSS 72
👤 WD–H WE–NA
£€ €55 (€75)
🏌 10km SE of Como
🏠 Jim Fazio
🖥 www.golfmonticello.it

La Pinetina   (1971)
Via al Golf 4, 22070 Appiano Gentile (CO)
☎ **(031) 933202**
📧 info@golfpinetina.it

Le Robinie   (1992)
Via per Busto Arsizio 9, 21058 Solbiate Olona (VA)
☎ **(039) 331 329260**
📠 (039) 331 329266
📧 info@lerobinie.com
🏳 18 L 6250 m Par 72 SSS 74
👤 WD–H WE–H
£€ €51 (€77)
🏌 25km NW of Milan. Malpensa Airport 6km
🏠 Jack Nicklaus
🖥 www.lerobinie.com

La Rossera   (1970)
Via Montebello 4, 24060 Chiuduno
☎ **(035) 838600**
📠 (035) 442 7047
📧 golfrossera@libero.it
🏳 9 L 2510 m SSS 68
👤 U
£€ €30 (€45)
🏌 2km from Chiuduno. 18km SE of Bergamo

Le Rovedine   (1978)
Via Karl Marx, 20090 Noverasco di Opera (Mi)
☎ **(02) 5760 6420**
📧 info@rovedine.com

Varese   (1934)
Via Vittorio Veneto 59, 21020 Luvinate (VA)
☎ **(0332) 229302/811293**
📠 (0332) 811293
📧 info@golfclubvarese.it
🏳 18 L 5936 m SSS 72
👤 H
£€ €60 (€85)
🏌 5km NW of Varese
🏠 Gannon/Blandford
🖥 www.golfclubvarese.it

Vigevano   (1974)
Via Chitola 49, 27029 Vigevano (PV)
☎ **(0381) 346628/346077**
📠 (0381) 346091
📧 golfvigevano@yahoo.it
🏳 18 L 5678 m SSS 72
£€ €35 (€50)
🏌 25km SE of Novara. 35km SW of Milan
🏠 Luigi Rota Caremoli

Villa D'Este   (1926)
Via Cantù 13, 22030 Montorfano (CO)
☎ **(031) 200200**
📠 (031) 200786
📧 info@golfvilladeste.com
🏳 18 L 5727 m Par 69
   White CR 71.0 SR 130
   Yellow CR 70.0 SR 129
   Black CR 72.2 SR 124
   Red CR 71.3 SR 123
👤 U H
£€ €85 Italian, €100 foreign (€100 Italian, €120 foreign)
🏌 Montorfano, 7km SE of Como
🏠 Peter Gannon
🖥 www.golfvilladeste.com

Zoate
20067 Zoate di Tribiano (MI)
☎ **(02) 9063 2183/9063 1861**

Elba

Acquabona   (1971)
57037 Portoferraio, Isola di Elba (LI)
☎ **(0565) 940066**

Emilia Romagna

Adriatic GC Cervia   (1985)
Via Jelenia Gora No 6, 48016 Cervia-Milano Marittima
☎ **(0544) 992786**

Bologna   (1959)
Via Sabattini 69, 40050 Monte San Pietro (BO)
☎ **(051) 969100**

Croara Country Club   (1976)
Loc. Croara Nuova 23010 Gazzola (PC)
☎ **(0523) 977105**
📠 (0523) 977100
📧 info@croaracountryclub.com
🏳 18 L 6065 m SSS 72
👤 H
£€ €45 (€60)
🏌 16km SW of Piacenza. 84km SE of Milan
🏠 Buratti/Croze
🖥 www.croaracountryclub.com

Matilde di Canossa   (1987)
Via Casinazzo 1, 42100 San Bartolomeo, Reggio Emilia
☎ **(0522) 371295**

📠 (0522) 371204
📧 golfcanossa@libero.it
🏳 18 L 6231 m SSS 72
👤 U
£€ €35 (€45)
🏌 50km NW of Bologna
🏠 Marco Croze
🖥 www.tiscali.it/golfcanossa

Modena G&CC   (1987)
Via Castelnuovo Rangone 4, 41050 Colombaro di Formigine (MO)
☎ **(059) 553482**
📠 (059) 553696
📧 segretaria@modenagolf.it
🏳 18 L 6423 m Par 72 SSS 74
   Men: CR 73.6 SR 131 (champ.)
   72.2/128 (am)
   Ladies: CR 74.9 SR 130 (champ.)
   74.9/127 (am)
   9 hole Par 3 course
👤 H
£€ €50 (€70)
🏌 Formigine, 10km SW of Modena
🏠 Bernhard Langer and J Jim Engh
🖥 www.modenagolf.it

Golf Club Riolo   (1992)
Via Limisano 10, Riolo Terme (RA)
☎ **(0546) 74035**
📠 (0546) 74076
📧 riologolf@tele2.it
🏳 18 L 6350 m Par 72
£€ €35 (€45)
🏌 50km SW of Bologna. 15km Imola. 15km Faenza
🏠 Alberto Croze
🖥 www.riologolf.it

La Rocca   (1985)
Via Campi 8, 43038 Sala Baganza (PR)
☎ **(0521) 834037**

Gulf of Genoa

Garlenda   (1965)
Via Golf 7, 17033 Garlenda
☎ **(0182) 580012**
📠 (0182) 580561
📧 info@garlendagolf.it
🏳 18 L 6085 m Par 72 SSS 72
👤 H
£€ €58 (€78)
🏌 7km N of Alassio. Genoa 90km
🏠 John Harris
🖥 www.garlendagolf.it

Marigola   (1975)
Via Biaggini 5, 19032 Lerici (SP)
☎ **(0187) 970193**
📧 info@golfmarigola.it

Pineta di Arenzano   (1959)
Piazza del Golf 3, 16011 Arenzano (GE)
☎ **(010) 911 1817**

Rapallo   (1930)
Via Mameli 377, 16035 Rapallo (GE)
☎ **(0185) 261777**

For list of abbreviations, key to symbols and international dialling codes see page 647

Sanremo-Circolo Golf degli Ulivi (1932)
Via Campo Golf 59, 18038 Sanremo
☎ (0184) 557093
⌨ (0184) 557388
✉ info@golfsanremo.com
▷ 18 L 5203 m SSS 67
　Men: CR 68.7 SR 119
　Women: CR 71.0 SR 120
♨ U
££ €40 (€60)
⊕ 5km N of Sanremo
⌂ Peter Gannon
▤ www.golfsanremo.com

Versilia (1990)
Via Sipe 100, 55045 Pietrasanta (LU)
☎ (0584) 88 15 74

Lake Garda & Dolomites

Asiago (1967)
Via Meltar 2, 36012 Asiago (VI)
☎ (0424) 462721

Bogliaco (1912)
Via Golf 21, 25088 Toscolano-Maderno
☎ (0365) 643006
⌨ (0365) 643006
✉ golfbogliaco@tin.it
▷ 18 L 4700 m Par 67
　CR 65.0 SR 120
♨ H
££ €48 (€56)
⊕ Lake Garda, 40km NE of Brescia
▤ www.bogliaco.com

Ca' degli Ulivi (1988)
Via Ghiandare 2, 37010 Marciaga di Costermano (VR)
☎ (045) 627 9030
⌨ (045) 627 9039
✉ info@golfcadegliulivi.it
▷ 18 L 6000 m SSS 72
　9 hole course
♨ H(36) – for 18 hole course
££ 9: €25 (€35); 18: €40 (€60)
⊕ Above village of Garda on Via Ghiandare. Verona Airport 35km
⌂ Cotton, Pennick & Partners
▤ www.golfcadegliulivi.it

Campo Carlo Magno (1922)
Golf Hotel, 38084 Madonna di Campiglio (TN)
☎ (0465) 440622

Folgaria (1987)
Loc Costa di Folgaria, 38064 Folgaria (TN)
☎ (0464) 720480

Gardagolf CC (1985)
Via Angelo Omodeo 2, 25080 Soiano Del Lago (BS)
☎ (0365) 674707 (Sec)
⌨ (0365) 674788
✉ info@gardagolf.it

▷ 18 L 6505 m SSS 74
　Men: CR 75.0 SR 139
　Women: CR 77.3 SR 140
　9 L 2758 m Par 36
♨ H (min 36) U H
££ €80 (€90)
⊕ Lake Garda, 30 km NE of Brescia.
⌂ Cotton/Pennink/Steel
▤ www.gardagolf.it

Karersee-Carezza
Loc Carezza 171, 39056 Welschofen-Nova Levante
☎ (0471) 612200

Petersberg (1987)
Unterwinkel 5, 39040 Petersberg (BZ)
☎ +39 0471 615122
⌨ +39 0471 615229
✉ info@golfclubpetersberg.it
▷ 18 L 5800 m Par 71
　Men: CR 70.1 SR128
　Women: CR 72.0 SR 126
♨ U
££ €54 (€66)
⊕ 35km SE of Bolzano, nr Nova Ponente
⌂ Marco Croze
▤ www.golfclubpetersberg.it

Ponte di Legno (1980)
Corso Milano 36, 25056 Ponte di Legno (BS)
☎ (0364) 900306

Verona (1963)
Ca' del Sale 15, 37066 Sommacampagna
☎ (045) 510060
⌨ (045) 510242
✉ golfverona@libero.it
▷ 18 L 6054 m CR 71.4 SR 124
♨ H
££ €70 (€80)
⊕ 7km W of Verona
⌂ John Harris
▤ www.golfclubverona.com

Naples & South

Riva Dei Tessali (1971)
74011 Castellaneta
☎ (099) 843 9251

San Michele
Loc Bosco 8/9, 87022 Cetraro (CS)
☎ (0982) 91012
✉ sanmichele@sanmichele.it

Rome & Centre

Country Club Castelgandolfo (1987)
Via Santo Spirito 13, 00040 Castelgandolfo
☎ (06) 931 2301
⌨ (06) 931 2244
✉ info@golfclubcastelgandolfo.it
▷ 18 L 6025 m SSS 72
♨ U H Sun–restricted

££ €60 (€75)
⊕ 22km SE of Rome
⌂ Robert Trent Jones
▤ www.countryclubcastelgandolfo.it

Eucalyptus (1988)
Via Cogna 5, 04011 Aprilia (Roma)
☎ (06) 927 46252/926 8120
⌨ (06) 926 8502
✉ info@eucalyptusgolfclub.it
▷ 18 L 6310 m Par 72 SSS 73
♨ WD–U WE–U
££ €30 (€40) low season €40 (€50) high season (Easter, June–Sept)
⊕ 20km S of Rome on Aprilia-Anzio road
⌂ D'Onofrio
▤ www.eucalyptusgolfclub.it

Fioranello
CP 96, 00134 Roma (RM)
☎ (06) 713 8080 - 213
⌨ (06) 713 8212
✉ info@fioranellogolf.it
▷ 18 L 5360 m Par 70
♨ U
££ €54 (€60)
⊕ Rome
⌂ David Mezzacane
▤ www.fioranellogolf.com

Marco Simone (1989)
Via di Marco Simone, 00012 Guidonia (RM)
☎ (0774) 366469

Marediroma
Via Enna 30, 00040 Ardea (RM)
☎ (06) 913 3250
✉ info@golfmarediroma.it

Nettuno
Via della Campana 18, 00048 Nettuno (RM)
☎ (06) 981 9419

Olgiata (1961)
Largo Olgiata 15, 00123 Roma
☎ (06) 308 89141
✉ secretaria@olgiatagolfclub.it

Parco de' Medici (1989)
Viale Salvatore Rebecchini, 00148 Roma
☎ (06) 655 3477
⌨ (06) 655 3344
✉ info@sheratongolf.it
▷ 18 L 6303 m Par 71 SSS 71
　Yellow tees CR 70.7 SR 174
　9 L 2805 m Par 35
♨ U
££ €70 (€80) Special offers to Sheraton guests
⊕ 15km SW of Rome, nr Airport Mezzacane/Rebecchini
▤ www.sheraton.com/golfrome www.golfclubparcodemedici.com

Pescara (1992)
Contrado Cerreto 58, 66010 Miglianico (CH)
☎ (0871) 959566

Le Querce
San Martino, 01015 Sutri (VT)
☎ (0761) 600789
🖳 (0761) 600142
✉ info@golfclublequerce.it
🏳 18 L 6433 m SSS 72
👥 U
££ €60 (€80)
🚗 42km N of Rome
🏠 Fazio/Mezzacane
🖥 www.golfclublequerce.it

Roma   (1903)
Via Appia Nuova 716A, 00178 Roma
☎ (06) 780 3407

Tarquinia
Loc Pian di Spille, Via degli Alina 271,
01016 Marina Velca/Tarquinia (VT)
☎ (0766) 812109

Sardinia

Is Molas   (1975)
CP 49, 09010 Pula
☎ (070) 924 1013/4
🖳 (070) 924 2121
✉ ismolasgolf@ismolas.it
🏳 18 L 6383 m SSS 72
   9 L 2966 m SSS 36
👥 U
££ €90 (€100)
🚗 Pula, 32km S of Cagliari
🏠 Cotton/Pennink/Lurie
🖥 www.ismolas.it

Pevero GC Costa Smeralda
(1972)
Cala di Volpe, 07021 Porto Cervo (SS)
☎ +39 0789 958000
🖳 +39 0789 96572
✉ pevero@starwoodhotels.cpm
🏳 18 L Par 72
   White 6170 m CR 74.0 SR 136
   Yellow 5805 m CR 72.2 SR 135
   Black 5497 m CR 76.5 SR 139
   Red 5099 m CR 74.1 SR 133
👥 U–H
££ €110 High Season €90 Mid Season
   €75 Low Season
🚗 North East of the Island, 25 kn N
   of Olbia
🏠 Robert Trent Jones Snr
🖥 www.golfclubpevero.com

Sicily

Il Picciolo   (1988)
Via Picciolo 1, 95030 Castiglione di Sicilia
☎ (0942) 986252
✉ segretia@ilpicciologolf.com

Turin & Piemonte

Alpino Di Stresa   (1924)
Viale Golf Panorama 48, 28839 Vezzo (VB)

☎ (0323) 20642
🖳 (0323) 208900
✉ info@golfalpino.it
🏳 9 L 5397 m Par 69
   Men: CR 67.9 SR 131
   Women: CR 69.9 SR122
👥 WE–WE H
££ 9: €22 (€32) 18: €33 (€50)
🚗 7km W of Stresa. Milan 80km
🏠 Peter Gannon
🖥 www.golfalpino.it

Biella Le Betulle   (1958)
Valcarozza, 13887 Magnano (BI)
☎ (015) 679151
🖳 (015) 679276
✉ info@golfclubbiella.it
🏳 18 L 6427 m CR 73.1 SR 141
👥 H
££ €70 (€110)
🚗 17km SW of Biella
🏠 John Morrison
🖥 www.golfclubbiella.it

Golf Club del Cervino   (1955)
11021 Breuil- Cervinia (AO)
☎ +39 0166 949131
🖳 +39 0166 940700
✉ info@golfcervino.com
🏳 9 L 4796 m CR 65.0 SR 112
   (18 holes from 2008)
👥 U
££ €30–€50
🚗 Aosta Valley - 120 km N of Turin
🏠 Donald Harradine/Luigi Rota
   Caremoli
🖥 www.golfcervino.com

Cherasco CC   (1982)
Via Fraschetta 8, 12062 Cherasco (CN)
☎ (0172) 489772/488489
🖳 (0172) 488304
✉ info@golfcherasco.com
🏳 18 L 6050m Par 72 CR 71.4 SR 129
👥 U
££ €40 (€55)
🚗 Cherasco, 45km S of Turin
🏠 Gianmarco Croze
🖥 www.golfcherasco.com

Claviere   (1923)
Strada Nazionale 45, 10050 Claviere (TO)
☎ (0122) 878917

Courmayeur
11013 Courmayeur (AO)
☎ (0165) 89103

Cuneo   (1990)
Via degli Angeli 3, 12012 Mellana-
Bóves (CN)
☎ (0171) 387041

Le Fronde   (1973)
Via Sant-Agostino 68, 10051 Avigliana (TO)
☎ (011) 932 8053/0540

I Girasoli   (1991)
Via Pralormo 315, 10022 Carmagnola (TO)
☎ (011) 979 5088
🖳 (011) 979 5228

✉ info@girasoligolf.it
🏳 18 L 5760 m Par 71
   Men: CR 70.7 SR 132
   Ladies: CR 73.0 SR 122
   9 hole pitch & putt L 800 m
👥 H
££ €30 (€40)
🚗 25km S of Turin
🖥 www.girasoligolf.it

Iles Borromees   (1987)
Loc Motta Rossa, 28833 Brovello
Carpugnino (VB)
☎ (0323) 929285
🖳 (0323) 929190
✉ info@golfdesilesborromees.it
🏳 18 L 6445 m SSS 72
👥 U
££ €42 (€65)
🚗 5km S of Stresa. 80km NW of
   Milan
🏠 Marco Croze
🖥 www.golfdesilesborromees.it

Golf dei Laghi   (1993)
Via Trevisani 6, 21028 Travedona
Monate (VA)
☎ (0332) 978101

Margara   (1975)
Via Tenuta Margara 5, 15043 Fubine
(AL)
☎ (0131) 778555

La Margherita
Strada Pralormo 29, Carmagnola (TO)
☎ (011) 979 5113
✉ golf.lamargherita@libero.it

La Serra   (1970)
Via Astigliano 42, 15048 Valenza (AL)
☎ (0131) 954778
✉ golfclublaserra@tin.it

Sestrieres   (1932)
Piazza Agnelli 4, 10058 Sestrieres (TO)
☎ (0122) 755170/76243

Stupinigi   (1972)
Corso Unione Sovietica 506, 10135 Torino
☎ (011) 347 2640

Torino   (1924)
Via Agnelli 40, 10070 Fiano Torinese
☎ (011) 923 5440/923 5670
🖳 (011) 923 5886
✉ info@circologolftorino.it
🏳 18 L 6054 m (Blue)
   18 L 6038 m SSS 72 (Yellow)
👥 U H
££ €72 (€95)
🚗 23km NW of Turin
🏠 Morrison/Croze/Cooke
🖥 www.circologolftorino.it

Vinovo   (1986)
Via Stupinigi 182, 10048 Vinovo (TO)
☎ (011) 965 3880

Tuscany & Umbria

Casentino   (1985)
6 Via Fronzola, 52014 Poppi (Arezzo)
☎ **(0575) 529810**
✆ (0575) 520167
✉ info@golfclubcasentino.it
➤ 9 L 5550 m Par 72
Men CR 70.6 SR 123
Women CR 73.0 SR 131
♙ WD–U WE–H
££ 9: €25; 18: €35
⛳ Poppi, 50km SE of Florence. 35kn
N of Arezzo
🏠 Brami/Baracchi
🖥 www.golfclubcasentino.it

Circolo Golf Ugolino   (1933)
Strada Chiantigiana 3, 50015 Grassina
☎ **(055) 230 1009/1085**
✉ info@golfugolino.it

Conero GC Sirolo   (1987)
Via Betellico 6, 60020 Sirolo (AN)
☎ **(071) 736 0613**

Cosmopolitan G&CC   (1992)
Viale Pisorno 60, 56018 Tirrenia
☎ **(050) 33633**
✆ (050) 384707
✉ info@cosmopolitangolf.it
➤ 18 L 6291 m Par 72
Yellow (men) CR71.8 SR 129
Red (ladies) CR 73.8 SR 126
♙ U
££ €55 (€65)
⛳ 15km SW of Pisa
🏠 David Mezzacane
🖥 www.cosmopolitangolf.it

Lamborghini-Panicale
(1992)
Loc Soderi 1, 06064 Panicale (PG)
☎ **(075) 837582**
✆ (075) 837582
✉ info@lamborghini.191.it
➤ 9 L 5872 m Par 72 SSS 70
♙ U H
££ €30 (€35)
⛳ 30km W of Perugia, nr Lake
Trasimeno
🏠 Ferruccio Lamborghini
🖥 www.lamborghinionline.it

Montecatini   (1985)
*Via Dei Brogi 5, Loc Pievaccia, 51015
Monsummano Terme*
☎ **(0572) 62218**
(+39) 3291 790808 (mobile)

Le Pavoniere   (1986)
Via Traversa Il Crocifisso, 59100 Prato
☎ **(0574) 620855**

Perugia   (1959)
06074 Santa Sabina-Ellera
☎ **(075) 517 2204**
✉ segreteria@golfclubperugia.it

Poggio dei Medici   (1995)
*Via San Gavino, 27 - Loc. Cignano, I-50038
Scarperia, (Florence)*
☎ **(+39) 055 84350**
✉ info@poggiodeimedici.com

Punta Ala   (1964)
Via del Golf 1, 58040 Punta Ala (GR)
☎ **(0564) 922121/922719**

Tirrenia   (1968)
Viale San Guido, 56018 Tirrenia (PI)
☎ **(050) 37518**

Venice & North East

Albarella
Isola di Albarella, 45010 Rosolina (RO)
☎ **(0426) 330124**

Cansiglio   (1956)
CP 152, 31029 Vittorio Veneto
☎ **(0438) 585398**
✆ (0438) 585398
✉ golfcansiglio@tin.it
➤ 18 L 6077 m SSS 71 CR 69.8 SR 129
♙ WD–U WE–H
££ €42 (€55)
⛳ 21km NE of Vittorio Veneto. 80km
NE of Venice
🏠 John Harris/Croze Marco
🖥 www.golfclubcansiglio.it

Colli Berici   (1986)
*Strada Monti Comunali, 36040
Brendola (VI)*
☎ **(0444) 601780**

Frassanelle   (1990)
Via Rialto, 5/A - 35030 Rovolon (PD)
☎ **(049) 991 0722**
✆ (049) 991 0691
✉ info@golffrassanelle.it
➤ 18 L 6180 m SSS 72
♙
££ €65 (€80)
⛳ 20km S of Padova, nr Via dei Colli
🏠 Marco Croze
🖥 www.golffrassanelle.it

Lignano
*Via Bonifica 3, 33054 Lignano
Sabbiadoro (UD)*
☎ **(0431) 428025**

La Montecchia   (1989)
*Via Montecchia 12, 35030
Selvazzano (PD)*
☎ **(049) 805 5550**

Padova   (1964)
*35050 Valsanzibio di Galzignano
Terme (PD)*
☎ **(049) 913 0078**
✆ (049) 913 1193
✉ info@golfpadova.it
➤ 9 L 3001 m Par 36 (Blue)
9 L 3046 m Par 36 (Yellow)
9 L 3049 m Par 36 (Red)

♙ H WD–U WE–M
££ €54 (€62) Low season €66 (€75)
High season
⛳ Valsanzibio, 20km S of Padua
🏠 John D Harris (18), Marco Croze
(9)
🖥 www.golfpadova.it

San Floriano-Gorizia   (1987)
*Castello di San Floriano, 34070 San
Floriano del Collio (GO)*
☎ **(0481) 884252/884234**

Trieste   (1954)
Via Padriciano 80, 34012 Trieste
☎ **(040) 226159/226270**

Udine   (1971)
*Via dei Faggi 1, Località Villaverde, 33034
Fagagna (UD)*
☎ **(0432) 800418**
✆ (0432) 801312
✉ info@golfudine.com
➤ 18 L 6088 m Par 72 CR 72.1 SR 129
♙ H
££ €58 (€68)
⛳ 15km NW of Udine
🏠 Marco Croze/John D Harris
🖥 www.golfudine.com

Venezia   (1928)
Strada Vecchia 1, 30126 Alberoni (Venezia)
☎ **(041) 731333**
✆ (041) 731339
✉ info@circologolfvenezia.it
➤ 18 L 6199 m Par 72 CR 73.4 SR 139
♙ U H
££ €72 (€84)
⛳ Venice Lido
🏠 Cruickshank/Cotton/Croze
🖥 www.circologolfvenezia.it

Villa Condulmer   (1960)
*Via della Croce 3, 31020 Zerman di
Mogliano Veneto - Tv*
☎ **(041) 457062**
✆ (041) 457202
✉ golfvillacondulmer@serenacom.it
➤ 18 L 5995 m SSS 71
9 hole short course
♙ H
££ €58 (€65)
⛳ Mogliano Veneto, 17km N of
Venice
🏠 Harris/Croze
🖥 www.villacondulmer.com

Luxembourg

Christnach   (1993)
Am Lahr, 7641 Christnach
☎ **87 83 83**
✆ 87 95 64
✉ gcc@gns.lu
➤ 18 L 5311 m Par 70 CR 70.2
SR 122 + 9 hole compact course
All training facilities are floodlit

Greencard
£€ 9: €30 (€40). 18: €40 (€55) Driving
range & compact course €12 (€15)
⊙⊙ 25km E of Luxembourg city
⌂ Volker Päschel
▤ www.golfclubchristnach.lu

Clervaux (1992)
Mecherwee, 9748 Eselborn
☎ 92 93 95
⌨ 92 94 51
▨ gcclerv@pt.lu
▷ 18 L 6144 m Par 72
Men: White CR 72.0 SR 133
Yellow CR 70.3 128
Women: Blue CR 70.9 SR 128
Red CR 70.9 SR 128
⋈ H
£€ €38 (€49)
⊙⊙ 3km from Clervaux, North
Luxembourg
⌂ Green Concept
▤ www.golfclervaux.lu

Gaichel
Rue de Eischen, 8469 Gaichel
☎ 39 71 08
⌨ 39 00 75
▨ infogolf@golfgaichel.com
▷ 9 L 5155 m Par 70
⋈ U H
£€ €25 (€35)
⊙⊙ 10km W of Mersch on Belgian
border
▤ www.golfgaichel.com

Golf de Luxembourg
(1993)
Domaine de Belenhaff, L-6141 Junglinster
☎ (00252) 78 00 68-1
⌨ (00352) 78 71 28
▨ info@golfdeluxembourg.lu
▷ 18 L 6094 m Par 72 CR 73.5 SR 131
⋈ U–unrestricted (Green card)
£€ €58 (€75)
⊙⊙ 17km NE of Luxembourg City
⌂ Green Concept, Lyon, France
▤ www.golfdeluxembourg.lu

Grand-Ducal de
Luxembourg (1936)
1 Route de Trèves, 2633 Senningerberg
☎ 34 00 90-1
⌨ 34 83 91
▨ gcgd@pt.lu
▷ 18 L 5765 m SSS 71
6 L 835 m CR 70.6 SR 127
⋈ WD–U WE–NA
£€ €60
⊙⊙ 7km N of Luxembourg
⌂ Maj. Simpson and Maj. Symonds
▤ www.gcgd.lu

Kikuoka Country Club
(1991)
Scheierhaff, L-5412 Canach
☎ +352 35 61 35
⌨ +352 35 74 50
▨ playgolf@kikuoka.lu
▷ 18 L 64129 m SSS 73.4 SR 128
⋈ H 35 WD H28 WE

£€ €75 (€100)
⊙⊙ 15 km from Luxembourg Airport
⌂ Iwao Uematsu
▤ www.kikuoka.lu

Malta

Royal Malta (1888)
Aldo Moro Street, Marsa MRS 9064
☎ (356) 21 22 70 19
⌨ (356) 21 22 70 20
▨ sales@royalmaltagolfclub.com
▷ 18 L 5020 yds Men CR 67.5 SR 117
Ladies CR 68
⋈ U exc Thurs & Sat NA before
noon H
£€ €65
⊙⊙ Marsa, 3 miles from Valletta
▤ www.royalmaltagolfclub.com

Netherlands

Amsterdam & Noord Holland

Amsterdam Old Course
(1990)
Zwarte Laantje 4, 1099 CE Amsterdam
☎ (020) 663 1766
▨ info@amsterdamoldcourse.nl

Amsterdamse (1934)
Bauduinlaan 35, 1047 HK Amsterdam
☎ (020) 497 7866
⌨ (020) 497 5966
▨ agc1934@wxs.nl
▷ 18 L 6148 m CR 72.7
⋈ WD–H WE–M
£€ €55–€65
⊙⊙ 10km W of Amsterdam
⌂ Rolin/Jol
▤ www.amsterdamsegolfclub.nl

BurgGolf Purmerend (1989)
Westerweg 60, 1445 AD Purmerend
☎ (+31) 299 689160
▨ purmerend@burggolf.nl

Haarlemmermeersche Golf
Club (1986)
Spieringweg 745, 2142 ED Cruquius
☎ (023) 558 9000
⌨ (023) 558 9009
▨ info
@haarlemmermeerschegolfclub.nl
▷ 27: 18 L 5894 m Par 73, 9 L 2479
m par 34 + 9 hole short course
⋈ H
£€ €47 (€55)
⊙⊙ Haarlemmermeer, W of
Amsterdam

⌂ O'Connor Jr/Rijks
▤ www.haarlemmermeerschegolfclub
.nl

Heemskerkse (1998)
Communicatieweg 18, 1967 PR Heemskerk
☎ (0251) 250088
⌨ (0251) 241627
▨ manager@heemskerksegolfclub.nl
▷ 18 L 6138 m CR 71.9 SR 127
⋈ WD + H
£€ €50
⊙⊙ 25km NW of Amsterdam
⌂ Gerard Jol
▤ www.heemskerksegolfclub.nl

Kennemer G&CC (1910)
Kennemerweg 78, 2042 XT Zandvoort
☎ +31 (0)23 571 2836/8456
⌨ +31 (0)23 571 9520
▨ kgcc@wxs.nl
▷ 27 holes CR 71.5-73.2
Van Hengel 9 L 2951 m
Pennink 9 L 2916 m
Colt 9 L 2942 m
⋈ H WE–NA before 3pm
£€ €110
⊙⊙ Zandvoort, 6km W of Haarlem
⌂ Colt/Pennink/Van Hengel
▤ www.kennemergolf.nl

De Noordhollandse (1982)
Sluispolderweg 6, 1817 BM Alkmaar
☎ (072) 515 6807
⌨ (072) 520 9918
▨ secretariaat@dnhgc.nl
▷ 18 L 5865 m CR 70.6
⋈ H 36
£€ €47.50
⊙⊙ 2km N of Alkmaar
⌂ Ryks/Dudok van Heel
▤ www.dnhgc.nl

Olympus (1976)
*Abcouderstraatweg 46, 1105 AA
Amsterdam Zuid-Oost*
☎ (0294) 281241

Spaarnwoude (1977)
Het Hoge Land 5, 1981 LT Velsen-Zuid
☎ (023) 538 2708 (club)
(023) 538 5599 (5)
(reservations)

Waterlandse (1990)
*Buiklslotermeerdijk 141, 1027
AC Amsterdam*
☎ (020) 636 1040
▨ info@golfbaanamsterdam.nl

Zaanse (1988)
Zuiderweg 68, 1456 NH Wijdewormer
☎ (0299) 438199
⌨ (0299) 438199
▨ zaansegolfclub@planet.nl
▷ 9 L 5282 m Par 70
⋈ WD–H WE–M
£€ €35
⊙⊙ 15km NE of Amsterdam
⌂ Gerard Jol
▤ www.zaansegolfclub.com

Breda & South West

Brugse Vaart (1993)
Brugse Vaart 10, 4501 NE Oostburg
☎ (0117) 453410
✆ (0117) 455511
✉ info@golfoostburg.com
➤ 18 L 6409 m SSS 73
⚭ H
££ €52 (€62)
⊕ 15km N of Bruges, nr Knokke, Belgium
⌂ Bram de Vos/Ron Kirby
▤ www.golfoostburg.com

Domburgsche (1914)
Schelpweg 26, 4357 BP Domburg
☎ (0118) 586106
✆ (0118) 586109
✉ secretariat@domburgschegolfclub.nl
➤ 9 L 5435 m Par 70
Men: CR 69.1 SR 127
Ladies: CR 71.5 SR 127
⚭ H
££ €45–€45 (€45–€50)
⊕ 15km NW of Middelburg
⌂ Alan Rÿks
▤ www.domburgschegolfclub.nl

Efteling Golf Park (1994)
Postbus 18, 5170 AA Kaatsheuvel
☎ +31 (0)416 288389
✆ +31 (0)416 288439
✉ golfpark@efteling.com
➤ 18 L 5896 m Par 72
⚭ H
££ €48 (€59.50)
⊕ 20km NE of Breda
⌂ Donald Steel
▤ www.efteling.nl

Grevelingenhout (1988)
Oudendijk 3, 4311 NA Bruinisse
☎ (0111) 482650
✆ (0111) 481566
➤ 18 L 6151 m CR 72.0
9 hole Par 3 course
⚭ H
££ €55–€60
⊕ 55km SW of Rotterdam, 12km S of Zierikzee
⌂ Donald Harradine

Oosterhoutse (1985)
Dukaatstraat 21, 4903 RN Oosterhout
☎ (0162) 458759
✆ (0162) 433285
✉ info@ogcgolf.nl
➤ 18 L 6199 m CR 73.4 SR 137
⚭ WD–H WE–M
££ €60
⊕ 10km NE of Breda
⌂ J Dudok van Heel
▤ www.ogcgolf.nl

Princenbosch (1991)
Bavelseweg 153, 5126 PX Molenschot
☎ (0161) 431811
✆ (0161) 434254
✉ golfclub@princenbosch.net

➤ AB Men L5550 m Par 70 CR 69.3 SR 126
AB Women L4837 Par 70 CR 70.6 SR 125
BC Men L5810 Par 72 CR 70.8 SR 127
BC Women L5053 Par 72 CR 72.3 SR 125
CA Men L5890 Par 72 CR 71.3 SR 127
CA Women L5040 Par 72 CR 71.8 SR 127
⚭ WD–U–H max 36, WE–M–H max 36
££ €55 (€45)
⊕ 10km SW of Breda
⌂ Alan Rÿks
▤ www.princenbosch.net

Toxandria (1928)
Veenstraat 89, 5124 NC Molenschot
☎ (0161) 411200
✆ (0161) 411715
✉ bestuur:toxandria.bl
➤ 18 L 5834 m Par 72 CR 70.2 SR 131
⚭ WD–I Phone first H
££ €65 (€75)
⊕ 8km E of Breda
⌂ Morrison/Dudok van Heel
▤ www.toxandria.nl

De Woeste Kop (1986)
Justaasweg 4, 4571 NB Axel
☎ (0115) 564467
✉ dewoestekop@planet.nl
➤ 18 L 5473 m Par 71 SSS 71
⚭ U
££ €45 (€50)
⊕ 45km W of Antwerp
⌂ Paneels/Bosch
▤ www.dewoestekop.nl

Wouwse Plantage (1981)
Zoomvlietweg 66, 4624 RP Bergen op Zoom
☎ (0165) 377100
✆ (0165) 377101
✉ secretariaat@golfwouwseplantage.nl
➤ 18 L 5896 m CR 70.7 SR 128
⚭ H–WD WE Sat only
££ D–€70
⊕ 10km E of Bergen-op-Zoom, nr Roosendaal
⌂ Pennink/Rolin
▤ www.golfwouwseplantage.nl

East Central

Breuninkhof
Bussloselaan 6, 7383 RP Bussloo
☎ (0571) 261955
✉ carla@unigolf.ni

Edese (1978)
Papendallaan 22, 6816 VD Arnhem
☎ (026) 482 1985
✆ (026) 482 1348
✉ info@edesegolf.nl
➤ 18 L 5947 m SSS 70

⚭ H
££ €50 (€55)
⊕ National Sportcentrum Papendal. NW of Arnhem, towards Ede
⌂ Pennink/Dudok van Heel
▤ www.edesegolf.nl

De Graafschap (1987)
Sluitdijk 4, 7241 RR Lochem
☎ (0573) 254323

Hattemse G&CC (1930)
Veenwal 11, 8051 AS Hattem
☎ (038) 444 1909
✉ secretariaat@golfclub-hattemse.nl
➤ 9 L 5808 yds SSS 68
⚭ WD–H WE–M+H
££ €50
⊕ Hattem, 5km S of Zwolle
⌂ Del Court van Krimpen
▤ www.golfclub-hattem.nl

Keppelse (1926)
Oude Zutphenseweg 15, 6997 CH Hoog-Keppel
☎ (0314) 301416
✉ dekeppelse@planet.nl

De Koepel (1983)
Postbox 88, 7640 AB Wierden
☎ (0546) 576150/574070
✉ secretariaat@golfclubdekoepel.nl

Golfbaan Het Rijk van Nunspeet (1987)
Public
Plesmanlaan 30, 8072 PT Nunspeet
☎ (0341) 255255
✆ (0341) 255285
✉ info@golfbaanhetrijkvannunspeet.nl
➤ 27 L 6100 m Par 72
⚭ U
££ €52.50 (€57.50)
⊕ Nunspeet, 80km E of Amsterdam
⌂ Paul Rolin
▤ www.golfenophetrijk.nl

Rosendaelsche (1895)
Apeldoornseweg 450, 6816 SN Arnhem
☎ (026) 442 1438
✆ (026) 351 1196
✉ info@rosendaelsche.ul
➤ 18 L 6057 m CR 72.3 SR 132
⚭ WD–H WE–NA
££ €70
⊕ 5km N of Arnhem on Route N50
⌂ Frank Pennink
▤ www.rosendaelsche.ul

Sallandsche De Hoek (1934)
Golfweg 2, 7431 PR Diepenveen
☎ (0570) 593269
✆ (0570) 590102
✉ secretariaat@sallandsche.nl
➤ 18 L 5889 m SSS 71
⚭ WD–H WE–M H
££ €50
⊕ 6km N of Deventer

🏠 Pennink/Steel
✉ www.sallandsche.nl

Golfbaan Het Rijk van Sybrook (1992)
Veendijk 100, 7525 PZ Enschede
☎ **(0541) 530331**
📠 (0541) 531690
✉ info@golfbaanhetrijkvansybrook.nl
🏳 27 L 5806 m Par 72
⛳ WD–H WE–M
££ €55
🚩 10km N of Enschede
🏠 Rolin/Rijks
✉ www.golfengohetrijk.nl

Twentsche (1926)
Almelosestraat 17, 7495 TG Ambt Delden
☎ **(074) 384 1167**
📠 (074) 384 1067
✉ info@twentschegolfclub.nl
🏳 18 L 6178 m SSS 72
⛳ H
££ €50 (€60)
🚩 4km N of Delden
🏠 TJ McAuley
✉ www.twentschegolfclub.nl

Veluwse (1957)
Nr 57, 7346 AC Hoog Soeren
☎ **(055) 519 1275**
📠 (055) 519 1126
✉ secretariaat@veluwsegolfclub.nl
🏳 9 L 6264 yds SSS 70
⛳ WD–U WD–H
££ €35 (€40)
🚩 5km W of Apeldoorn
🏠 CK Cotton
✉ www.veluwsegolfclub.nl

Welderen (1994)
Grote Molenstraat 173, 6661 NH Elst
☎ **(0481) 376591**

Eindhoven & South East

Best G&CC (1988)
Golflaan 1, 5683 RZ Best
☎ **(0499) 391443**
📠 (0499) 393221
✉ vereniging@bestgolf.nl
🏳 18 L 6079 m CR 71.7 SR 131
⛳ H
££ €45 (€55)
🚩 Best, 5km NW of Eindhoven
🏠 J Dudok van Heel
✉ www.bestgolf.nl

BurgGolf Gendersteyn Veldhoven (1994)
Locht 140, 5504 RP Veldhoven
☎ **(040) 253 4444**
📠 (040) 254 9747
✉ gendersteyn@burggolf.nl
🏳 18 L 5739 m Par 71
7 L 2164 m Par 28
⛳ U
££ €47.50 (€57.50)
🚩 10km SW of Eindhoven

🏠 Alan Rijks
✉ www.burggolf.nl

Golfclub BurgGolf Wijchen (1985)
Public
Weg Door de Berendonck 40, 6603 LP Wijchen
☎ **(024) 642 0039**
✉ wijchen@burggolf.nl

Crossmoor G&CC (1986)
Laurabosweg 8, 6006 VR Weert
☎ **(0495) 518438**
✉ crossmoor@planel.nl

De Dommel (1928)
Zegenwerp 12, 5271 NC St Michielsgestel
☎ **(073) 551 9168**
📠 (073) 551 9441
✉ info@gcdedommel.nl
🏳 18 L 5679 m CR 69.3 SR 125
⛳ WD–H WE–NA
££ €50 (€50)
🚩 10km S of Hertogenbosch
🏠 Colt/Steel
✉ www.gcdedommel.nl

Eindhovensche Golf (1930)
Eindhovenseweg 300, 5553 VB Valkenswaard
☎ **(040) 201 4816**
📠 (040) 207 6177
✉ egolf@iae.nl
🏳 18 L 5923 CR 71.0 SR130/6223
CR 72.6 SR 135
⛳ H – prior reservation necessary
££ €90 (€90) – 2007
🚩 8km S of Eindhoven
🏠 HS Colt
✉ www.eindhovenschegolf.nl

Geijsteren G&CC (1974)
Het Spekt 2, 5862 AZ Geijsteren
☎ **(0478) 531809/532592**
📠 (0478) 532963
✉ gc.geijsteren@planet.nl
🏳 18 L 6090 m Par 72
⛳ U but phone first 0478 531809
££ D–€55 (€60)
🚩 Off A73 Junction 9. N270 to
Wanssum. 25km N of Venlo
🏠 Pennink/Steel
✉ www.golfclubgeijsteren.nl

Havelte (1986)
Kolonieweg 2, 7970 AA Havelte
☎ **(0521) 342200**
✉ info@golfclubhavelte.nl

Haviksoord (1976)
Maarheezerweg Nrd 11, 5595 XG Leende (NB)
☎ **(040) 206 1818**
📠 (040) 206 2761
✉ info@haviksoord.nl
🏳 18 L 6146 m CR 72.2 SR 132
⛳ H
££ €45
🚩 10km S of Eindhoven
✉ www.haviksoord.nl

Herkenbosch (1991)
Stationsweg 100, 6075 CD Herkenbosch
☎ **(0475) 529529**
📠 (0475) 533580
✉ herkenbosch@burggolf.nl
🏳 Men: 18 L 5758 m Par 72
CR 70.2 SR 136
Ladies: 18 L 4891 m par 72
CR 71.4 SR 129
⛳ U WD + WE H
££ €57.50 (€67.50)
🚩 20km S of Venlo, nr German
border
🏠 Dudok van Heel
✉ www.gccherkenbosch.nl

Het Rijk van Nijmegen (1985)
Postweg 17, 6561 KJ Groesbeek
☎ **(024) 397 6644**
📠 (024) 397 6942
✉ info@golfbaanhetrijkvannijmegen.nl
🏳 18 L 6010 m CR 70.3
18 L 5717 m CR 69.8
⛳ H
££ €52.50 (€60) – 2007
🚩 5km E of Nijmegen
🏠 Paul Rolin
✉ www.golfenophetrijk.nl

De Peelse Golf (1991)
Maasduinenweg 1, 5977 NP Evertsoord-Sevenum
☎ **(077) 467 8030**
✉ info@depeelsegolf.nl

De Schoot (1973)
Schootsedijk 18, 5491 TD Sint Oedenrode
☎ **(04134) 73011**

Tongelreep G&CC (1984)
Charles Roelslaan 15, 5644 HX Eindhoven
☎ **(040) 252 0962**
📠 (040) 293 2238
✉ gcc@golfdetongelreep.nl
🏳 9 L 5345 m CR 69.2 SR 122
⛳ WD–H WE–H by introduction
only
££ €40
🚩 Eindhoven
🏠 J van Rooy
✉ www.golfdetongelreep.nl

Welschap (1993)
Welschapsedijk 164, 5657 BB Eindhoven
☎ **(040) 251 5797**
✉ secretariaat@golfclubwelschap.nl

Limburg Province

Brunssummerheide (1985)
Rimburgerweg 50, Brunssum
☎ **(045) 527 0968**

Hoenshuis G&CC (1987)
Hoensweg 17, 6367 GN Voerendaal
☎ **(045) 575 3300**
📠 (045) 575 0900
✉ inuman@hoenshuis.nl

☞ 18 L 6074 m CR 71.2
ⓜ WE–NA 10am–2pm
££ €45 (€60)
♣ Limburg, 10km NE of Maastricht
♘ Paul Rolin
▤ www.gcchoenshuis.nl

De Zuid Limburgse G&CC
(1956)
Dalbissenweg 22, 6281 NC Gulpen-Wittem, (GPS: Landsrade 1, 6271 NZ Gulpen-Wittem)
☎ (043) 455 1397/1254
📠 (043) 455 1576
✉ zlgolf@zlgolf.nl
☞ 18 L 5902 m Par 71
ⓜ WD–H36 WE–H32
££ €48, €58 (€48, €58)
♣ Gulpen-Wittem (Mechelen), 25km SE of Maastricht
♘ Hawtree/Snelder/Rolin
▤ www.zlgolf.nl

North

BurgGolf St Nicobasga
(1990)
Legemeersterweg 16-18, 8527 DS Legemeer
☎ (0513) 499466
✉ st.nicobasga@burggolf.nl

Gelpenberg   (1970)
Gebbeveenweg 1, 7854 TD Aalden
☎ (0591) 371929
📠 (0591) 372422
✉ info@dgcdegelpenberg/nl
☞ 18 L 6031 m Par 71
ⓜ H
££ €45 (€55)
♣ 16km W of Emmen
♘ Pennink/Steel
▤ www.dgcdegelpenberg.nl

Holthuizen   (1985)
Oosteinde 7a, 9301 ZP Roden
☎ (050) 501 5103
📠 (050) 501 3685
✉ golfclub.holthuizen@planet.nl
☞ 9 L 6079 m SSS 72
ⓜ H
££ €20–€30 (€30–€45)
♣ 10km S of Groningen
♘ Rijks/Eschauzier
▤ www.gc-holthuizen.nl

Lauswolt G&CC   (1964)
Van Harinxmaweg 8A, PO Box 36, 9244 ZN Beetsterzwaag
☎ (0512) 383590
📠 (0512) 383739
✉ algemeen@golfclublauswolt.nl
☞ 18 L 6087 m CR 71.5
ⓜ H
££ €55 (€75)
♣ Beetsterzwaag, 5km S of Drachten
♘ Pennink/Steel
▤ www.golfclublauswolt.nl

Noord-Nederlandse G&CC
(1950)
Pollselaan 5, 9756 CJ Glimmen
☎ (050) 406 2004
📠 (050) 406 1922
✉ secretariaat@nngcc.nl
☞ 18 L 5709/4991 m Par 72 CR 70.4/73.6 SR 127/128
ⓜ H
££ €60 (€70)
♣ 12km S of Groningen, off A28
♘ Campbell (1950), Pennick/Steel (1987)
▤ www.nngcc.nl

De Semslanden   (1986)
Nieuwe Dijk 1, 9514 BX Gasselternijveen
☎ (0599) 564661/565531
✉ semslanden@planet.nl

Rotterdam & The Hague

Broekpolder   (1981)
Watersportweg 100, 3138 HD Vlaardingen
☎ (010) 249 5566
(010) 249 5555/249 5577
📠 (010) 249 5579
✉ secretariaat@golfclubbroekpolder.nl
☞ 18 L 6010 m CR 71.7 SR 125
ⓜ H WE–NA
££ €85 (€115)
♣ 15km W of Rotterdam, off A20
♘ Frank Pennink/Gerard Jol
▤ www.golfclubbroekpolder.nl

Golf & Country Club Capelle a/d IJssel   (1977)
Gravenweg 311, 2905 LB Capelle a/d IJssel
☎ (010) 442 2485
📠 (010) 284 0606
✉ info@golfclubcapelle.nl
☞ 18 L 5237 m CR 68.0 SR 127
ⓜ WD–U WE–M
££ €55
♣ 5km S of Rotterdam
♘ Donald Harradine
▤ www.golfclubcapelle.nl

Cromstrijen   (1989)
Veerweg 26, 3281 LX Numansdorp
☎ (0186) 654455
📠 (0186) 654681
✉ info@golfclubcromstrijen.nl
☞ 18 L 6107 m Par 72 9 L 3800 m Par 62
ⓜ H
££ €60 (€70)
♣ 30km S of Rotterdam (A29)
♘ Tom McAuley
▤ www.golfclubcromstrijen.nl

De Hooge Bergsche   (1989)
Rottebandreef 40, 2661 JK Bergschenhoek
☎ (010) 522 0052/522 0703
📠 (08) 422 32305
✉ secretariaat@hoogebergsche.nl

☞ 18 L 5336 m Par 71 SR 119
ⓜ U
££ €45 (€59.50)
♣ Bergschenhoek, 2km NE of Rotterdam
♘ Gerard Jol
▤ www.hoogebergsche.nl

Koninklijke Haagsche G&CC   (1893)
Groot Haesebroekeseweg 22, 2243 EC Wassenaar
☎ (070) 517 9607
📠 (070) 514 0171
✉ secretariaat@khgcc.nl
☞ 18 L 5674 m Par 72 SR 129
ⓜ WD–H (max 24) WE–M
££ €100
♣ 6km N of The Hague
♘ Allison/Colt
▤ www.khgcc.nl

Kralingen
Kralingseweg 200, 3062 CG Rotterdam
☎ (010) 452 2283
✉ secretaris@gckralingen.nl
☞ Men: 9 L 5327 yds CR 65.9 SR 114 Ladies: 9 L 4678 yds CR 67.4 SR 110
ⓜ H
££ €40 (€50)
♣ 5km from centre of Rotterdam
♘ Copijn/Cotton
▤ www.gckralingen.nl

Leidschendamse Leeuwenbergh   (1988)
Elzenlaan 31, 2495 AZ Den Haag
☎ (070) 395 4556
📠 (070) 399 8615
✉ secretariaat@leeuwenbergh.nl
☞ 18 L 5461 m Par 70
ⓜ H
££ €57.50
♣ E side of The Hague
♘ Bernard Jol
▤ www.leeuwenbergh.nl

De Merwelanden   (1985)
Public
Golfbaan Crayestein, Baanhoekweg 50, 3313 LP Dordrecht
☎ (078) 621 1221

Noordwijkse Golf Club
(1915)
Randweg 25, PO Box 70, 2200 AB Noordwijk
☎ (0252) 373761
📠 (0252) 370044
✉ info@noordwijksegolfclub.nl
☞ 18 L 5880 m CR 72.1 SR 135 (men) 18 L4998 m CR 72.8 SR 126 (women)
ⓜ WD–H Reservations required
££ €120
♣ 5km N of Noordwijk. 15 km NW of Leiden
♘ Frank Pennink
▤ www.noordwijksegolfclub.nl

Oude Maas   (1975)
(Rhoon Golfcenter), Veerweg 2a, 3161 EX Rhoon
☎ **(010) 501 5135**
✉ golfcluboudemaas@kebelfoon.nl

Rijswijkse   (1987)
Delftweg 58, 2289 AL Rijswijk
☎ **(070) 395 4864**
☐ (070) 399 5040
✉ secretariaat@rijswijksegolf.nl
↦ 18 L 5681 m Par 71 CR 69.6
⚑ H
£€ €50 (€65)
↝ 5km SE of The Hague
⌂ Steel/Rijks
▤ www.rijswijksegolf.nl

Wassenaarse Golfclub Rozenstein   (1984)
Dr Mansveltkade 15, 2242 TZ Wassenaar
☎ +31 (070) 511 7846
✉ info@rozenstein.nl
↦ 18 L 5783 m (Standard Tees Men)
CR 71.3 SR 117
4697 m (Forward Tees Men)
CR 65.2 SR 112
5178 m (Back Tees Ladies) CR73.3
SR 132
4875 m (Standard Tees Ladies)
CR 71.7 SR 126
3973 m (Forward Tees Ladies)
CR 65.6 SR 113
⚑ WD–U–H WE–U–H26.0
£€ €55 (€65)
↝ 14km NE of The Hague
⌂ Dudok van Heel/Jol
▤ www.rozenstein.nl

Westerpark Zoetermeer   (1985)
Heuvelweg 3, 2716 DZ Zoetermeer
☎ **(079) 351 7283**

Zeegersloot   (1984)
Kromme Aarweg 5, PO Box 190, 2400 AD Alphen a/d Rijn
☎ **(0172) 474567**
☐ (0172) 494660
✉ secretariaat@zeegersloot.nl
↦ 18 L 5793 m SSS 70
9 hole Par 3 course
⚑ U H
£€ 9: €20 (€25) 18: €42 (€60)
↝ Alphen, 15km N of Gouda. 20km S of Amsterdam
⌂ Gerard Jol
▤ www.zeegersloot.nl

Utrecht & Hilversum

Almeerderhout   (1986)
Watersnipweg 19-21, 1341 AA Almere
☎ **(036) 521 9130**

Anderstein   (1986)
Woudenbergseweg 13a, 3953 ME Maarsbergen
☎ **(0343) 431330**

☐ (0343) 432062
✉ info@golfclubanderstein.nl
↦ 27 L 6149/6345/6130 m
CR AB 72.3/BC 73.4/CA 72.4
⚑ WD–limited WE–M only
£€ €55–€65 (€60–€70)
↝ 20km E of Utrecht
⌂ Jol/Dudok van Heel/van Aalderen/Steel
▤ www.golfclubanderstein.nl

De Batouwe   (1990)
Oost Kanaalweg 1, 4011 LA Zoelen
☎ **(0344) 624370**

Flevoland   (1979)
Parlaan 2A, 8241 BG Lelystad
☎ **(0320) 230077**
☐ (0320) 230932
✉ info@golfflevo.nl
↦ 18 L 5836 m Par 71
⚑ WD–U H WE–U+H
£€ €40 Mon–Thur (€46) Fri/Sat/Sun
↝ Polder of Flevoland. 1km NW of Lelystad. 45km N of Hilversum
⌂ JS Eschauzier
▤ www.golfflevo.nl

De Haar   (1974)
PO Box 104, Parkweg 5, 3450 AC Vleuten
☎ **(030) 677 2860**

Hilversumsche   (1910)
Soestdijkerstraatweg 172, 1213 XJ Hilversum
☎ **(035) 685 7060**
☐ (035) 685 3813
↦ 18 L 5859 m Par 72 CR 71.2 SR 135
⚑ Phone booking necessary H WE–NA
£€ €100
↝ 3km E of Hilversum, nr Baarn
⌂ Burrows/Colt

De Hoge Kleij   (1985)
Appelweg 4, 3832 RK Leusden
☎ **(033) 461 6944**
☐ (033) 465 2921
✉ secretariaat@hogekleij.nl
↦ 18 L 6046 m SSS 72
⚑ WD–H
£€ €85
↝ 1km SE of Amersfoort 20km NE of Utrecht via A28
⌂ Donald Steel
▤ www.hogekleij.nl

Nieuwegeinse   (1985)
Postbus 486, 3437 AL Nieuwegein
☎ **(030) 604 2192**

Utrechtse Golf Club 'De Pan'   (1894)
Amersfoortseweg 1, 3735 LJ Bosch en Duin
☎ **(030) 696 9120**
☐ (030) 696 3769
✉ secretariaat@ugcdepan.nl
↦ 18 L 5701 m Par 72 CR 70.1 SR 124
⚑ WD–M WE–NA
£€ €100
↝ 10km E of Utrecht, off A28

⌂ HS Colt
▤ www.ugcdepan.nl

Zeewolde   (1984)
Golflaan 1, 3896 LL Zeewolde
☎ **(036) 522 2103**
☐ (036) 522 4100
✉ secretariaat@golfclub-zeewolde.nl
↦ 27 L 6259 m Par 72
9 hole course Par 58
⚑ H
£€ €55 (€65)
↝ 20km N of Hilversum. 60km NE of Amsterdam
⌂ A Rijks
▤ www.golfclub-zeewolde.nl

Norway

Arendal og Omegn   (1986)
Nes Verk, 4900 Tvedestrand
☎ **37 19 90 30**
☐ 37 16 02 11
✉ post@arendalgk.no
↦ 18 L 5528 m Par 72
9 hole P&P course
⚑ U
£€ 350kr (400kr)
↝ Nes Verk, 20km E of Arendal (E18). 95km NE of Kristiansand
▤ www.arendalgk.no

Baerum   (1972)
Hellerudveien 26, 1350 Lommedalen
☎ **67 87 67 00**
☐ 67 87 67 20
✉ bmgk@bmgk.no
↦ 18 L 5300 m Par 71
9 hole short course
⚑ U H Booking advisable
£€ 400kr (450kr)
↝ 10km W of Oslo. 10km N of Sandvika
⌂ Jeremy Turner
▤ www.bmgk.no

Bergen   (1937)
Ervikveien 120, 5106 Øvre Ervik
☎ **55 19 91 80**
☐ 55 19 91 81
✉ info@bgk.no
↦ 9 L 4461 m Par 67
⚑ U
£€ 250/300 nok
↝ 8km N of Bergen
▤ www.bgk.no

Borre   (1991)
Semb Hovedgaard, 3186 Horten
☎ **416 27000**
☐ 33 07 15 16
✉ borregb@online.no
↦ 18 L 6265 m Par 72 CR 73.7
9 L 2927 m Par 36 CR 72.1
⚑ H
£€ 9: D–300kr 18: 450kr (500kr)

In Horten, 50km S of Drammen.
100km SW of Oslo. 30kn N Torp
Airport
T Nordström
wwww.borregolf.no

Borregaard   (1927)
PO Box 348, 1702 Sarpsborg
☎ 69 12 15 00
✉ borregaardgk@golf.no

Drøbak   (1988)
Belsjøveien 50, 1440 Drøbak
☎ 64 98 96 40

Elverum   (1980)
PO Box 71, 2401 Elverum
☎ 62 41 35 88
✉ post@elverumgolf.no

Grenland   (1976)
Luksefjellvn 578, 3721 Skien
☎ 35 50 62 70
🖳 35 59 06 10
✉ post@grenlandgolf.no
⤷ 18 L 5777 m Par 72
👥 H
££ 325kr (375kr)
🚗 6km from Skien
🏠 Jan Sederholm/Tor Eia
✉ www.grenlandgolf.no

Groruddalen   (1988)
Postboks 37, Stovner, 0913 Oslo
☎ 22 79 05 60
✉ post@grorudgk.no

Hemsedal   (1994)
3560 Hemsedal
☎ 32 06 23 77

Kjekstad   (1976)
PO Box 201, 3440 Røyken
☎ 31 29 79 90

Kristiansand   (2003)
PO Box 6090 Søm, 4691 Kristiansand
☎ 38 14 85 60
🖳 38 04 34 15
✉ post@kristiansandgk.no
⤷ 9 L 2488 m SSS 72 CR 68.6 SR 133
👥 U
££ D–250Nkr (D–250 Nkr)
🚗 8 km E of Kristiansand (E18)
🏠 Nils Skøld
✉ www.kristiansandgk.no

Larvik   (1989)
Fritzøe Gård, 3267 Larvik
☎ 33 14 01 45
✉ klubben@larvikgolf.no

Narvik   (1992)
8523 Elvegard
☎ 76 95 12 01
🖳 76 95 12 06
✉ post@narvikgolf.no
⤷ 18 L 5890 m Par 72
👥 U H
££ 300kr (350kr)

🚗 30km S of Narvik
🏠 Jan Sederholm
✉ www.narvikgolf.no

Nes   (1988)
Rommen Golfpark, 2160 Vormsund
☎ 63 91 20 30
✉ bente@nesgolfklubb.no

Onsøy   (1987)
Golfveien, 1626 Manstad
☎ +47 69 33 91 50

Oppdal   (1987)
PO Box 19, 7340 Oppdal
☎ 72 42 25 10

Oppegård   (1985)
Kongeveien 198, PO Box 50,
1416 Oppegård
☎ 66 81 59 90
🖳 66 81 59 91
✉ leder@oppegardgk.no
⤷ 18 L 5280 m Par 71
👥 U H
££ 400 nok
🚗 17km S of Oslo
✉ www.oppegardgk.no

Oslo   (1924)
Bogstad, 0757 Oslo
☎ 22 51 05 60

Ostmarka   (1989)
Postboks 63, 1914 Ytre Enebakk
☎ 64 92 38 40

Oustoen CC   (1965)
PO Box 100, 1330 Fornebu
☎ 67 83 23 80/22 56 33 54
🖳 67 53 95 44/22 59 91 83
✉ occ@occ.no
⤷ 18 L 5626 m SSS 72
👥 M H
££ 500kr
🚗 Small island in Oslofjord, 10km W
    of Oslo
✉ www.occ.no

Skjeberg   (1986)
PO Box 528, 1701 Sarpsborg
☎ 69 16 63 10

Sorknes   (1990)
PB 100, 2451 Rena
☎ 45 20 86 00
✉ post@sorknesgk.no
⤷ 18 L 6150 m SSS 72
👥 U
££ 250nok (350nok)
🚗 170km N of Oslo
🏠 Juul Soegaard
✉ www.sorknesgk.no

Stavanger   (1956)
Longebakke 45, 4042 Hafrsfjord
☎ 519 39100
🖳 519 39110
✉ steinar@sgk.no
⤷ 18 L 5751 m Par 71

👥 H
££ 400kr
🚗 6km SW of Stavanger
🏠 F Smith/Niblick Golf Design
✉ www.sgk.no

Trondheim   (1950)
PO Box 169, 7401 Trondheim
☎ 73 53 18 85

Tyrifjord   (1982)
Sturoya, 3531 Krokleiva
☎ 32 16 13 60
🖳 32 16 13 40
⤷ 18 L 5747 m Par 72 SR 140
👥 H
££ 425nok (475nok)
🚗 40km NW of Oslo (E16)
🏠 Sederholm/Eia
✉ www.tyrifjord-golfklubb.no

Vestfold   (1958)
PO Box 64, 3108 Vear
☎ 33 36 25 00
🖳 33 36 25 01
✉ vgk@vestfoldgolfklubb.no
⤷ 18 L 6414 / 5979 / 4877 m SSS 72
    9 hole course Par 64
👥 H
££ 400kr (July+WE 450kr)
🚗 Tønsberg 8km
🏠 Smith/Turner
✉ www.vgk.no

Poland

Amber Baltic   (1993)
Baltycka Street 13, 72-514 Kolczewo
☎ (091) 32 65 110/120
🖳 (091) 32 65 333
✉ abgc@abgc.pol.pl
⤷ 18 L 5802 m Par 72
    9 L 1307 m Par 28
👥 U
££ €27 (€40)
🚗 80km N of Szczecin
🏠 H-G Erhardt
✉ www.abgc.pl

Portugal

Algarve

Alto Golf   (1991)
Quinta do Alto do Poço, P O Box 1, 8501
906 Alvor
☎ (00351) 282 460870
🖳 (00351) 282 460879
✉ golf@altoclub.com
⤷ 18 L 5812 m Par 70 SR 121
👥 U H
££ €52–€74

⛳ 2km W of Portimão; 4km from A22 J4
🏠 Sir Henry Cotton
📧 www.altoclub.com

Floresta Parque   (1987)
Vale do Poço, Budens, 8650 Vila do Bispo
☎ (0282) 695333

Palmares   (1975)
Apartado 74, Meia Praia, 8601 901 Lagos
☎ +351 282 790500
📠 +351 282 290509
📧 golf@palmaresgolf.com
🏌 18 L 5961 m Par 71 SSS 72
👤 U H
££ Low season: €62.50 High season: €95
⛳ Meia Praia, 5km E of Lagos
🏠 Frank Pennink
📧 www.palmaresgolf.com

Penina   (1966)
PO Box 146, Penina, 8502 Portimao
☎ (351) 282 420223
📠 (351) 282 420252
🏌 Ch'ship 18 L 6343 m SSS 73;
Resort 9 L 3987 m SSS 71;
Academy 9 L 1851 m Par 30
👤 H–max 28 (M) or 36 (L) – soft spikes only; visitors welcome according to availability of courses
££ Ch'ship €77 low season, €110 high season Resort €38, Academy €33
⛳ 5km W of Portimao. 12km E of Lagos
🏠 Sir Henry Cotton

Pestana   (1991)
Apartado 1011, 8400-908 Carvoeiro Lga
☎ (0282) 340900
📠 (0282) 340901
📧 info@pestanagolf.com
🏌 Gramacho 18 L 6107 m Par 72 SSS 71
Pinta 18 L 6127 m Par 71 SSS 72
Silves 18 L 5615 m Par 70 SSS 69
👤 U
££ Garmacho/Pinta/ Silves €95
⛳ 10km E of Portimão. 54km W of Faro Airport
🏠 Ronald Fream, Nick Price, Peter Booth, José Matias, Fausto Nascimento
📧 www.pestanagolf.com

Pine Cliffs G&CC   (1991)
Praia da Falesia, PO Box 644, 8200-909 Albufeira
☎ (+351) 289 500100
📧 sheraton.algarve@starwoodhotels.com

Pinheiros Altos   (1992)
Quinta do Lago, 8135 Almancil
☎ (0289) 359910
📧 golf@pinheirosaltos.pt

Quinta do Lago   (1974)
Quinta Do Lago, 8135-024 Almancil
☎ (+351) 289 390 700

📠 (+351) 289 394 013
📧 geral@quintadolagogolf.com
🏌 South 18 L 6488 m Par 72 CR 73.5 SR 127
North 18 L 6126 m par 72 CR 71.8 SR 131
👤 H(36)–by prior arrangement
££ 9: €75; 18: €150
⛳ 15km W of Faro. Airport 20km
🏠 Mitchell/Lee/Roquemore
📧 www.quintadolagogolf.com

Salgados
Apartado 2362, Vale do Rabelho, 8200 917 Albufeira
☎ (0289) 583030

San Lorenzo   (1988)
Quinta do Lago, 8135 Almancil
☎ (289) 396522
📠 (289) 396908
🏌 18 L 6238 m Par 72 SSS 73 SR 128
👤 H–restricted
££ €160
⛳ 16km W of Faro
🏠 Joseph Lee

Vale de Milho   (1990)
Apartado 1273, Praia do Carvoeiro, 8401-911 Carvoeiro Lga
☎ (282) 358502
📧 valedemilhogolf@mail.telepac.pt

Vale do Lobo   (1968)
Vale Do Lobo, 8135-864 Vale do Lobo-Almancil
☎ (0289) 353535

Vila Sol Spa & Golf Resort (1991)
Alto do Semino, Morgadinhos, Vilamoura, 8125-307-Quarteira
☎ (+351) 289 300505
📠 (+351) 289 316499
📧 golfreservation@vilasol.pt
🏌 27 L 6335 m Par SSS 72
👤 U H
££ Low season: €75; mid season: €100 high season: €110
⛳ 5km E of Vilamoura. Faro Airport 10km
🏠 Donald Steel
📧 www.vilasol.pt

Vilamoura Laguna   (1990)
8125-507 Vilamoura, Algarve
☎ (0289) 310180

Vilamoura Millennium (2000)
8125-507 Vilamoura, Algarve
☎ (0289) 310188

Vilamoura Old Course   (1969)
8125-507 Vilamoura, Algarve
☎ (289) 310341

Vilamoura Pinhal   (1976)
8125-507 Vilamoura, Algarve
☎ (0289) 310390

Azores

Batalha   (1996)
Rua do Bom Jesus, Aflitos, 9545-234 Fenais da Luz (Açores)
☎ +351 296 498 599/560
📠 +351 296 498 284
📧 geral@azoresgolfislands.com
🏌 27 holes:
White: L 6435 m CR 73.9 SR 144
Yellow: L 6120 m CR 72.1 SR 140
Red: L 5366 m CR 74.4 SR 132
👤 H
££ €80.50
⛳ São Miguel Island. Ponta Delgada 10km (45 min)
🏠 Cameron & Powell
📧 www.verdegolf.net

Furnas   (1939)
Achada das Furnas, 9675 Furnas
☎ (+351) 296 498559
📠 (+351) 296 498284
📧 info@azoresgolfislands.com
🏌 18 L CR 71.8 SR 121 (White)
18 L CR 70.1 SR 117 (Yellow)
18 L CR 71.6 SR 118 (Red)
👤 H U WD–U WE–U
££ €56
⛳ São Miguel Island. Furnas Villa 5km
🏠 Mackenzie Ross/Cameron & Powell
📧 www.azoresgolfislands.com

Terceira Island   (1954)
Caixa Postal 15, 9760 909 Praia da Victória (Açores)
☎ (0295) 902444

Lisbon & Central Portugal

Aroeira   (1972)
Herdade da Aroeira, 2820-567 Charneca da Caparica
☎ +351 (212) 979 110/1
📠 +351 (212) 971 238
📧 golf.reservas@aroeira.com
🏌 18 L 6044 m Par 72 SR 123
18 L 6367 m Par 72 SR 122
👤 U H
££ €50 (€80)
⛳ 20km S of Lisbon, off Setúbal/Costa da Caparica road
🏠 Frank Pennink/Donald Steel
📧 www.aroeira.com

Belas Clube de Campo (1998)
Alameda do Aqueduto, Belas Clube de Campo, 2605-193 Belas
☎ (00351) 21 962 6640
📠 (00351) 21 962 6641
📧 golfe@planbelas.pt

For list of abbreviations, key to symbols and international dialling codes see page 647

P   18 L 6200 m Par 72 CR 74.9 SR 126
👥   H
££   €76.50 (€88)
🚗   20km from Lisbon
🏠   Rocky Roquemore
📧   www.belasgolf.com

Estoril   (1945)
Avenida da República, 2765-273 Estoril
☎   (021) 466 0367
📧   reserva@golfestoril.com

Estoril-Sol Golf Academy
(1976)
Quinta do Outeira, Linhó, 2710 Sintra
☎   (01) 923 2461

Lisbon Sports Club   (1922)
Casal da Carregueira, 2605-213 Belas
☎   (21) 431 0077
📧   geral@lisbonclub.com

Marvão   (1998)
Quinta do Prado, São Salvador da
Aramenha, 7330-328 Marvão
☎   (245) 993 755

Golf do Montado   (1992)
Urbanização do Golf Montando, Lte no.1 -
Algeruz, 2950-051 Palmela
☎   (265) 708150
📧   geral@golfdomontando.com.pt

Penha Longa   (1992)
Estrada da Lagoa Azul, Linhó, 2714-
511 Sintra
☎   (021) 924 9011
📧   reservas.golf@penhalonga.com

Quinta da Beloura   (1994)
Estrada de Albarraque, 2710 692 Sintra
☎   (021) 910 6350
📱   (021) 910 6359
📧   beloura.golfe@pestana.com
P   18 L 5774 m Par 73 CR 71.2 SR 128
👥   U
££   D-€55 (D-€72.50)
🚗   Between Estoril and Sintra, off N9.
     Lisbon 34km
🏠   Rocky Roquemore
📧   www.pestanagolf.com

**Quinta da Marinha Oitavos
Golfe**   (2001)
Quinta da Marinha, Casa da Quinta No25,
2750-715 Cascais
☎   351 21 486 06 00
📧   oitavosgolfe@quinta-da-marinha.pt

Quinta do Perú
Alameda da Serra 2, 2975-666 Quinta
do Conde
☎   (021) 213 4320
📧   play@golfquintadoperu.com

**Tróia Golf Championship
Course**   (1980)
Tróia, 7570-789 Carvalhal, Portugal
☎   (+351) 265 494 112
📧   troiagolf@sonae.pt

Vimeiro
Praia do Porto Novo, Vimeiro, 2560
Torres Vedras
☎   (061) 984157

Madeira

Madeira   (1991)
Sto Antonio da Serra, 9200
Machico, Madeira
☎   (091) 552345/552356

Palheiro   (1993)
Rua do Balancal No.29, 9060-414
Funchal, Madeira
☎   (00351) 291 790 120
     (00351) 291 790 125
     (Bookings)
📱   (00351) 291 792 456
📧   reservations.golf@palheiroestate
     .com
P   18 L 6086 m Par 72 CR 71.6 SR 130
👥   May–Sept–U Oct–April–H
££   €92
🚗   5km from Funchal, off Airport road
     to Camacha
🏠   Cabell Robinson
📧   www.palheiroestate.com

North

Amarante   (1997)
Quinta da Deveza, Fregim, 4600-
593 Amarante
☎   +351 255 44 60 60
📱   +351 255 44 62 02
📧   sgagolfeamarante@oninet.pt
P   18 L 5030 m Par 68 CR 64.2 SR 114
👥   U H
££   €41 (€54)
🚗   60km from Oporto and 45km from
     Vila Real
🏠   J Santana da Silva
📧   www.amarantegolfclube.com

**Golden Eagle, Clube de
Golfe**   (1994)
E.N. 1, Km 63/64, Asseicera, 2040-481
Rio Maior
☎   +351 243 940040/
     960 148425
📱   +351 243 940049
📧   golf@goldeneagle-golfresort.com
P   18 Par 72 White L 6623 m, yellow
     L 5899 m,
     blue L 5456 m, red L 4850 m
     CR (men): white 74.2, yellow 70.7;
     (ladies): blue 73.9, red 70.5
     SR (men): white 134, yellow 127;
     (ladies): blue 128, red 119
👥   H U
££   €75 (€90)
🚗   55km from Lisbon - access via A1
     motorway
🏠   Rocky Roquemore
📧   www.goldeneagle-golfresort.com

Miramar   (1932)
Av Sacadura Cabral, Miramar, 4405-
013 Arcozelo
☎   (022) 762 2067
📱   (022) 762 7859
📧   golf.miramar@mail.telepac.pt
P   9 L 2655 m Par 70 SSS 69
👥   H WD WE
££   €50 (€70)
🚗   8km S of Oporto
🏠   Swan/Gordon
📧   www.cgm.pt

Montebelo
Farminhão, 3510 Viseu
☎   (032) 856464

Oporto Golf Club   (1890)
Sisto-Paramos, 4500 Espinho
☎   (022) 734 2008
📱   (022) 734 6895
📧   oportogolfclub@oninet.pt
P   18 L 5638 m Par 71 SSS 70 CR 70.8
     SR 122
👥   H WE–restricted
££   €60 (€75)
🚗   Espinho, 15km S of Oporto
📧   www.oportogolfclub.com

Ponte de Lima
Quinta de Pias, Fornelos, 4490 Ponte
de Lima
☎   (058) 43414

Praia d'el Rey G&CC
(1997)
Vale de Janelas, Apartado 2, 2510 Obidos
☎   (+351) 262 905005
📧   golf@praia-del-rey.com

Golfe Quinta da Barca
(1997)
Barca do Lago, 4740-476 Esposende
☎   (+351) 2539 66723
📧   lcatarino@quintabarca.com

Vidago
Parque de Vidago, Apartado 16, 5425-
307 Vidago
☎   +351 276 990 900
📧   vidago.palace@unicer.pt

Slovenia

Bled G&CC   (1937)
Public
Kidriceva 10 c, 4260 Bled
☎   +386 (0)4 537 77711
📱   +386 (0)4 537 77722
📧   info@golf.bled.si
P   18 L 6325 m SSS 73
     9 L 3092 m SSS 72
👥   H–36 max
££   €55 (€65 inc. Red Letter Days)
     Many possible discounts
🚗   3km W of Bled. 50km NW of
     Ljubljana, nr Austro-Italian border

ⓕ Donald Harradine
🖳 www.golf.bled.si

Castle Mokrice (1992)
Terme Catez, Topliska Cesta 35,
8250 Brezice
☎ (00386) 7 457 4260
🖥 (00386) 7 495 7007
📧 majda.drobnic@terme-catez.si
⊳ 18 L 5835 m Par 71 SSS 73 (men)
18 L 5235 m Par 71 SSS 73
(women)
👭 U
££ €38 (€47)
🚗 30km N of Zagreb
ⓕ Donald Harradine
🖳 www.terme-catez.si

Lipica (1989)
Lipica 5, 66210 Sezana
☎ +386 (0)5 734 6373
🖥 +386 (0)5 739 1725
📧 golf@lipica.org
⊳ 9 L 6318 m par 74 CR 71.9 SR 119
👭 H
££ 9: €23 (€28) 18: €30 (€38) 20%
discount for hotel guests
(Maestoso Klub Hotel)
🚗 11km NE of Trieste. 85km SW of
Ljubljana
ⓕ Donald Harradine
🖳 www.lipica.org

Spain

Alicante & Murcia

Alicante (1998)
Av. Locutor Vicente Hipolito 37, Playa San
Juan, 03540 Alicante
☎ (96) 515 37 94/515 20 43

Altorreal (1994)
Urb Altorreal, 30500 Molina de
Segura (Murcia)
☎ (968) 64 81 44

Bonalba (1993)
Partida de Bonalba, 03110
Mutxamiel (Alicante)
☎ (96) 595 5955
🖥 (96) 595 5985
📧 golfbonalba@golfbonalba.com
⊳ 18 L 6190m Par 72 SSS 73
👭 U
££ €65
🚗 10km N of Alicante. A7 Junction
67. Road number 340
ⓕ Ramón Espinosa
🖳 www.golfbonalba.com

Don Cayo (1974)
Apartado 341, 03599 Altea La
Vieja (Alicante)
☎ (96) 584 80 46
📧 doncayo@ctv.es

Ifach (1974)
Crta Moraira-Calpe Km 3, Apdo 28, 03720
Benisa (Alicante)
☎ (96) 649 71 14
🖥 (96) 649 9908
📧 golfifach@wanadoo.es
⊳ 9 L 3408 m SSS 60
👭 U
££ D–€28/€38
🚗 9km N of Calpe, towards Moraira
ⓕ Javier Arana

Jávea (1981)
Apartado 148, 03730 Jávea, (Alicante)
☎ (96) 579 25 84

La Manga (1971)
Los Belones, 30385 Cartagena (Murcia)
☎ (968) 175000 ext 1360
🖥 (968) 175058
📧 golf@lamangaclub.es
⊳ North 18 L 5780 m SSS 70
South 18 L 6259 m SSS 73
West 18 L 5971 m SSS 72
👭 U
🚗 30km NE of Cartagena, nr Murcia
airport
ⓕ RD Putman
🖳 www.lamangaclub.com

La Marquesa (1989)
Ciudad Quesada II, 03170
Rojales, (Alicante)
☎ (+34) 96 671 42 58
🖥 (+34) 96 671 42 67
📧 info@lamarquesagolf.es
⊳ 18 L 6111Par 72 CR 72.5 SR 132
👭 U
££ D–€59
🚗 Rojales, 14km N of Torrevieja
ⓕ Justo Quesada Samper
🖳 www.lamarquesagolf.es

Las Ramblas (1991)
Crta Alicante-Cartagena Km48, 03189 Urb
Villamartin, Orihuela (Alicante)
☎ (96) 677 4728

Real Campoamor (1989)
Crta Cartagena-Alicante Km48, Apdo 17,
03189 Orihuela-Costa (Alicante)
☎ (96) 532 13 66

La Sella Golf (1991)
Ctra La Xara-Jesús Pobre, 03749 Jesús
Pobre (Alicante)
☎ (96) 645 42 52/645 41 10
🖥 (96) 645 42 01
📧 info@lasellagolf.com
⊳ 18 Pro L 6289 m CR 73.5 SR 137
Ameteur Men L 6113 m CR 73
SR 135
Ameteur Women L 5250 m
CR 73.7 SR 126
👭 U H (35 max) SOC
££ €75
🚗 Denia 5km
ⓕ José María Olazábal
🖳 www.lasellagolfresort.com

Villamartin (1972)
Crta Alicante-Cartagena Km50, 03189 Urb
Villamartin, Orihuela (Alicante)
☎ (96) 676 51 27/676 51 60
🖥 (96) 676 51 70
📧 golfvillamartin@grupoquara.com
⊳ 18 L 6132 m SSS 72
👭 U H
££ €60
🚗 8km S of Torrevieja
ⓕ Paul Putman
🖳 www.grupoquara.com

Almería

Almerimar (1976)
Urb Almerimar, 04700 El Ejido (Almeria)
☎ (950) 48 02 34

El Cortijo Grande Golf Resort (1976)
Apdo 2, Cortijo Grande, 04639
Turre (Almería)
☎ (950) 479176
📧 golf@cortijogrande.net
⊳ 18 L 6024 m Par 72 SSS 71
👭 U
££ 9: €22; 18: €29
🚗 20km W of Turre. 85km N of
Almería, nr Mojácar
ⓕ Craig D Cooke
🖳 www.cortijogrande.net

La Envia (1993)
Apdo 51, 04720 Aguadulce (Almería)
☎ (950) 55 96 41

Playa Serena (1979)
Urb Playa Serena, 04740 Roquetas de
Mar (Almeria)
☎ (950) 33 30 55

Badajoz & West

Guadiana (1992)
Crta Madrid-Lisboa Km 393, Apdo 171,
06080 Badajoz
☎ (924) 44 81 88

Norba (1988)
Apdo 880, 10080 Cáceres
☎ (927) 23 14 41

Salamanca (1988)
Monte de Zarapicos, 37170
Zarapicos (Salamanca)
☎ (923) 32 91 00
🖥 (923) 32 91 05
📧 club@salamancagolf.com
⊳ 18 L 6265 m Par 72 SSS 72
👭 U
££ D–40€(66€)
🚗 W of Salamanca,nr Parada de
Arriba (C-517)
ⓕ Manuel Piñero
🖳 www.salamancagolf.com

Balearic Islands

Canyamel
Urb Canyamel, Crta de Cuevas, 07580
Capdepera, (Mallorca)
☎ **(971) 56 44 57**

Capdepera   (1989)
Apdo 6, 07580 Capdepera, Mallorca
☎ **(971) 56 58 75/56 58 57**

Ibiza   (1990)
Apdo 1270, 07840 Santa Eulalia, (Ibiza)
☎ **(971) 19 61 18**

Pollensa   (1986)
Ctra Palma-Pollensa Km 49, 07460
Pollensa, (Mallorca)
☎ **(971) 53 32 16**
🖥 (971) 53 32 65
✉ rec@golfpollensa.com
🏳 9 L 5304 m Par 70 SSS 70
👤 U H
£€ 9: €40; 18: €70
⛳ Pollensa, 45km N of Palma
🏠 José Gancedo
🖳 www.golfpollensa.com

Poniente   (1978)
Costa de Calvia, 07181 Calvia (Mallorca)
☎ **(971) 13 01 48**
🖥 (971) 13 01 76
✉ golf@ponientegolf.com
🏳 18 L 6430 m SSS 72
👤 U H
£€ €88 for 18 holes valid until
    31/08/09
⛳ 12km SW of Palma towards Cala
    Figuera
🏠 John Harris
🖳 www.ponientegolf.com

Pula Golf   (1995)
Ctra. Son Servera-Capdepera, E-07550
Son Servera-Mallorca
☎ **(971) 81 70 34**
🖥 (971) 81 70 35
✉ reservas@pulagolf.com
🏳 18 L 5758 m Par 72 CR 70.5 SR
    132
👤 U H
£€ 9: Oct–Feb/June–Sept €55,
    Mar–May €65; 18:
    Oct–Feb/June–Sept €100, Mar–May
    €125
⛳ 70km NE of Palma
🏠 JM Olazábal
🖳 www.pulagolf.com

Real Golf Bendinat   (1986)
C. Campoamor, 07015 Calviá, (Mallorca)
☎ **(971) 40 52 00**
🖥 (971) 70 07 86
✉ golfbendinat@terra.es
🏳 18 L 5768 m SSS 71
👤 U H
£€ €88 (2009)
⛳ 7km W of Palma
🏠 Martin Hawtree
🖳 www.realgolfbendinat.com

Santa Ponsa   (1976)
Santa Ponsa, 07180 Calvia (Mallorca)
☎ **(971) 69 02 11**
🖥 (971) 69 33 64
✉ golf1@habitatgolf.es
🏳 18 L 6520 m
    18 L 6053 m
    SR White tees 124, Yellow tees
    123
👤 No 1–U H No 2–NA
£€ €78
⛳ 18km W of Palma
🏠 Folco Nardi
🖳 www.habitatgolf.es

Son Antem   (1993)
Ctra. Llucmajor, PN 602, Km 3,4, E-
07620 Llucmajor-Mallorca
☎ **(971) 12 92 00**
✉ mhrs.pmigs.golf.reservation
    @marriott.com

Golf Son Parc Menorca
(1977)
Urb. Son Parc s/n, ES Mercadal-
Menorca, Baleares
☎ **+34 (971)-188875/359059**
🖥 +34 (971)-359591
✉ info@golfsonparc.com
🏳 18 Par 69
👤 U
£€ High season: €65; Mid season: €60
    Low season: €45 Ask about special
    offers
⛳ North side of island; 8km Mercadal.
    12km Alaior. 18km Mahon
🏠 Dave Thomas Ltd
🖳 www.golfsonparc.com

Son Servera   (1967)
Costa de Los Pinos, 07759 Son
Servera, (Mallorca)
☎ **(971) 84 00 96**

Son Vida   (1964)
Urb Son Vida, 07013 Palma (Mallorca)
☎ **(971) 79 12 10**

Vall d'Or Golf   (1985)
Apdo 23, 07660 Cala D'Or, (Mallorca)
☎ **(971) 83 70 68/83 70 01**
🖥 (971) 83 72 99
✉ valldorgolf@valldorgolf.com
🏳 18 L 5602 m SSS 71
👤 H
£€ €89 – 1/10/07–30/9/08
⛳ 60km E of Palma, between Cala
    d'Or and Porto Colóm
🏠 Benz/Bendly
🖳 www.valldorgolf.com

Barcelona & Cataluña

Aro-Mas Nou   (1990)
Apdo 429, 17250 Playa de Aro
☎ **(972) 82 69 00**
    (972) 81 67 27 (Bookings)

Bonmont Terres Noves
(1990)
Urb Terres Noves, 43300
Montroig (Tarragona)
☎ **(977) 81 81 40**

Caldes Internacional   (1992)
Apdo 200, 08140 Caldes de
Montbui (Barcelona)
☎ **(93) 865 38 28**

**Club de Golf Costa Dorada
Tarragona**   (1983)
Apartado 600, 43080 Tarragona
☎ **(977) 65 3361/(977) 65 3605**
🖥 (977) 65 3028
✉ club@golfcostadoradatarragona.com
🏳 18 L 6223 m SSS 73
👤 H Summer from 8.00 to 22.00
    Winter from 8.00 – 18.00
£€ €60 (€100)
⛳ Tarragona
🏠 José Gancedo
🖳 www.golfcostadoradatarragona.com

Costa Brava   (1962)
La Masia, 17246 Sta Cristina
d'Aro (Gerona)
☎ **(972) 83 71 50**
🖥 (972) 83 72 72
✉ info@golfcostabrava.com
🏳 18 L 5573 m SSS 70
👤 H
£€ €46–€80
⛳ Playa de Aro 5km. 30km SE of
    Gerona
🏠 J Hamilton Stutt
🖳 www.golfcostabrava.com

Empordà   (1990)
Crta Torroella de Montgri, 17257
Gualta (Gerona)
☎ **(972) 76 04 50/76 01 36**

Fontanals de Cerdanya
(1994)
Fontanals de Cerdanya, 17538
Soriguerola (Girona)
☎ **(972) 14 43 74**

Golf Girona   (1992)
Urbanització Golf Girona s/n, 17481 Sant
Julia de Ramis, (Girona)
☎ **(972) 17 16 41**
✉ golfgirona@golfgirona.com

Llavaneras   (1945)
Cami del Golf 45-51, 08392 San Andreu de
Llavaneras, (Barcelona)
☎ **(93) 792 60 50**
    (93) 792 62 27 (Bookings)
🖥 (93) 795 25 58
✉ club@golfllavaneras.com
🏳 18 Par 70 L 5028 (Yellow)
    L 4481 m (Red)
👤 U H
£€ €60 (€155)
⛳ 34km N of Barcelona (A19), C32
    Motorway Jct 105
🏠 Hawtree/Espinosa/Sardà/Viador
🖳 www.golfllavaneras.com

Masia Bach   (1990)
Ctra Martorell-Capellades, 08635 Sant
Esteve Sesrovires
☎   (93) 772 8800

Osona Montanya   (1988)
Masia L'Estanyol, 08553 El
Brull (Barcelona)
☎   (93) 884 01 70

Peralada Golf   (1993)
La Garriga, 17491 Peralada, Girona
☎   (972) 53 82 87
🖳   (972) 53 82 36
✉   casa.club@golfperalada.com
🏌   18 L 5990 m SSS 71
    9 holes Par 3
👤   H
££   €55 low season €62 mid season
    €78 high season
⛳   Costa Brava, on French border.
    40km S of Perpignan Airport, nr
    Figueres
🏠   Jorge Soler
🖥   www.golfperalada.com

Golf Platja de Pals   (1966)
Pay and play
Ctra. Golf, Num. 64, Pals - Girona 17256
☎   (+34) 972 66 77 39
🖳   (+34) 972 63 67 99
✉   recep@golfplatjadepals.com
🏌   18 Par 73 SSS 72
    White: L 6263 m CR 72.8 SR 135
    Yellow: L 5970 m CR 71.3 SR 132
    Blue: L 5419 m CR 74.1 SR 130
    Red: L 5156 m CR 72.3 SR 125
👤   H–WD/WE
££   Low season: 9: €47, 18: €60 Mid
    Season: 9: €50, 18: €65 High
    Season & WE: 9: €58, 18: €78
⛳   40km E of Gerona, 135km NE of
    Barcelona
🏠   FW Hawtree
🖥   www.golfplatjadepals.com

Reus Aigüesverds   (1989)
Crta de Cambrils, Mas Guardià, E-
43206 Reus-Tarragona
☎   (977) 75 27 25
✉   golf@aiguesverds.com

Terramar   (1922)
Apdo 6, 08870 Sitges
☎   (93) 894 05 80/894 20 43
🖳   (93) 894 70 51
✉   reservas@golfterramar.com
🏌   18 L 5878 m Par 72
👤   H
££   €75 (€115)
⛳   Sitges, 37km S of Barcelona
🏠   Hawtree/Piñero/Fazio
🖥   www.golfterramar.com

Torremirona   (1994)
Ctra N-260 Km 46, 17744 Navata (Girona)
☎   (+34) 972 55 37 37
✉   golf@torremirona.com

Burgos & North

Castillo de Gorraiz   (1993)
Urb Castillo de Gorraiz, 31620 Valle de
Egues (Navarra)
☎   (948) 33 70 73
✉   administracion@golfgorraiz.com

Izki Golf   (1992)
C/Arriba, S/N, 01119 Urturi (Alava)
☎   (945) 378262
✉   izkigolf@izkigolf.com

Larrabea   (1989)
Crta de Landa, 01170 Legutiano, (Alava)
☎   (945) 46 58 44/46 58 41

Lerma   (1991)
Ctra Madrid-Burgos Km195, 09340
Lerma (Burgos)
☎   (947) 17 12 14/17 12 16
✉   golflerma@csa.es

La Llorea   (1994)
Crta Nacional 632, Km 62, 33394
Lloreda (Gijón)
☎   (985) 18 10 30
🖳   (985) 36 47 26
✉   informaciongolf.pdm@gijon.es
🏌   18 L 5971 m Par 72
👤   H
££   €38.70 (€45.70)
⛳   10km E of Gijón
🏠   Roland Fabret
🖥   www.golflallorea.com

Real Golf Castiello   (1958)
Apdo Correos 161, 33200 Gijón
☎   (985) 36 63 13
🖳   (985) 13 18 00
✉   administracion@castiello.com
🏌   18 L 4817 m Par 70
👤   WE–restricted
££   €80
⛳   5km S of Gijón
🖥   www.castiello.com

Real Golf Pedreña   (1928)
Apartado 233, Santander
☎   (942) 50 00 01/50 02 66

Real San Sebastián   (1910)
PO Box 6, Fuenterrabia, (Guipúzcoa)
☎   (943) 61 68 45/61 68 46

Real Zarauz   (1916)
Apartado 82, Zarauz, (Guipúzcoa)
☎   (943) 83 01 45

Ulzama   (1965)
31779 Guerendiain (Navarra)
☎   (948) 30 51 62

Canary Islands

Amarilla   (1988)
Urb Amarilla Golf, San Miguel de Abona,
38630 Santa Cruz de Tenerife
☎   (922) 73 03 19

Costa Teguise   (1978)
Avenida del Golf s/n, 35508 Costa Teguise
☎   (928) 59 05 12
🖳   (928) 59 23 37
✉   info@lanzarote-
    golf.com/info@lanzarote-golf.e
🏌   18 L 6320 m SSS 72
👤   U
££   Summer €55 Winter €68
⛳   4km N of Arrecife
🏠   John Harris
🖥   www.lanzarote-golf.com

Maspalomas   (1968)
Av de Neckerman, Maspalomas, 35100
Gran Canaria
☎   (928) 76 25 81/76 73 43

Real Club de Golf de Tenerife   (1932)
Campo de Golf No.1 38350,
Tacoronte, Tenerife
☎   (922) 63 66 07
✉   director.golf@interbook.net

Real Golf Las Palmas   (1891)
PO Box 93, 35380 Santa Brigida,
Gran Canaria
☎   (928) 35 10 50/35 01 04
🖳   (928) 35 01 10
✉   rcglp@realclubdegolfdelaspalmas
    .com
🏌   18 L 5919 m SSS 71
👤   WD 8am to 12.45pm WE–M
££   €63 (summer), €83 (winter), €93
    (Christmas)
⛳   Bandama, Las Palmas 14km
🏠   Mackenzie Ross
🖥   www.realclubdegolfdelaspalmas.com

Golf del Sur   (1987)
San Miguel de Abona, 38620
Tenerife (Canarias)
☎   (922) 73 81 70
🖳   (922) 78 82 72
✉   golfdelsur@aymesichgolf.com
🏌   North 9 L 2911 m SSS 36
    Links 9 L 2853 m SSS 36
    South 9 L 2986 m SSS 36
👤   H
££   €85
⛳   Airport 3km. Playa de las Américas
    12km
🏠   Pepe Gancedo, Manuel Piñero
🖥   www.golfdelsur.es

Córdoba

Club de Campo de Córdoba
(1976)
Apartado 436, 14080 Córdoba
☎   (957) 35 02 08
✉   administracion@golfcordoba.com
🏌   18 L 5964 m Par 72 SSS 73
👤   U H36
££   €52 (€72)
⛳   9km N of Córdoba
🖥   www.golfcordoba.com

Pozoblanco   (1984)
Apdo 118, 14400 Pozoblanco, (Córdoba)
☎ (957) 33 91 71

Galicia

Aero Club de Santiago
(1976)
General Pardiñas 34, Santiago de Compostela (La Coruña)
☎ (981) 59 24 00
✉ reception@aerosantiago.es

Aero Club de Vigo   (1951)
Reconquista 7, 36201 Vigo
☎ (986) 48 66 45/48 75 09

La Toja   (1970)
Isla de La Toja, El Grove, Pontevedra
☎ (986) 73 01 58/73 08 18

Ria de Vigo   (1993)
San Lorenzo-Domaio, 36957 Moaña (Pontevedra)
☎ (986) 32 70 51
✉ info@riadevigogolf.com

Granada

Granada
Avda de los Corsarios, 18110 Las Gabias (Granada)
☎ (958) 58 44 36

Madrid Region

Barberán   (1967)
Apartado 150.239, Cuatro Vientos, 28080 Madrid
☎ (91) 509 00 59/509 11 40

La Dehesa   (1991)
Avda. de la Universidad, 10, 28691 Villanueva La Cañada
☎ (91) 815 70 22
✉ dehesa-direccion@infonegocio.com

Herreria   (1966)
PO Box 28200, San Lorenzo del Escorial, (Madrid)
☎ (91) 890 51 11
✉ lsveiro@golflaherreria.com

Jarama R.A.C.E.   (1967)
Urb Ciudalcampo, 28707 San Sebastian de los Reyes, (Madrid)
☎ (91) 657 00 11
🖶 (91) 657 04 62
✉ golf@race.es
▷ 18 L 6505 m Par 72
9 hole Par 3 course
M H
££ €85 (€120)
⛳ 28km N of Madrid on Burgos road

⌂ Javier Arana
▤ www.race.es

Lomas-Bosque   (1973)
Urb El Bosque, 28670 Villaviciosa de Odón, (Madrid)
☎ (91) 616 75 00

La Moraleja   (1976)
La Moraleja, Alcobendas (Madrid)
☎ (91) 650 07 00
✉ info@golflamoraleja.com

Olivar de la Hinojosa
(1995)
Avda de Dublin, Campo de las Naciones, 28042 Madrid
☎ (91) 721 18 89

Puerta de Hierro   (1896)
Avda de Miraflores, Ciudad Puerta de Hierro, 28035 Madrid
☎ (91) 316 1745
🖶 (91) 373 8111
✉ deportes1@realclubpuertadehierro.es
▷ High 18 L 6375 m CR 72.5 SR 124
Low 18 L 6504 m CR 73.9 SR 130
M only
££ €143 (€285)
⛳ 4km N of Madrid (Route VI)
⌂ Harris/Simpson/Trent Jones

Los Retamares   (1991)
Crta Algete-Alalpardo Km 2300, 28130 Valdeolmos (Madrid)
☎ (91) 620 25 40

Somosaguas   (1971)
Avda de la Cabaña, 28223 Pozuelo de Alarcón, (Madrid)
☎ (91) 352 16 47

Valdeláguila   (1975)
Apdo 9, Alcalá de Henares, (Madrid)
☎ (91) 885 96 59

Villa de Madrid CC   (1932)
Crta Castilla, 28040 Madrid
☎ (0034) 91 550 2010
🖶 (0034) 91 550 2023
✉ deportes@clubvillademadrid.com
▷ 27 L 5900-6321 m SSS 73-74
U H
££ €14 entry + €49.80 green fee Mon–Fri
⛳ 4km NW of Madrid, in the Casa del Campo
⌂ Javier Arana
▤ www.clubvillademadrid.com

Malaga Region

Alhaurín   (1994)
Crta 426 Km15, Alhaurin el Grande
☎ (952) 59 59 70
🖶 (952) 59 45 86
✉ reservasgolf@alhauringolf.com

▷ 18 L 6045 m Par 72
9 hole Par 3 course
U H 36hcp max
££ €38 low season €59 high season, any day
⛳ 6km from Mijas; 3km from Alhaurín el Grande; 15 km from Fuengirola; 25
⌂ Severiano Ballesteros
▤ www.alhauringolf.com

Añoreta   (1989)
Avenida del Golf, 29730 Rincón de la Victoria, (Málaga)
☎ (952) 40 40 00

La Cala Resort   (1991)
La Cala de Mijas, 29649 Mijas-Costa (Málaga)
☎ (952) 66 90 00
(952) 66 90 33
🖶 (952) 66 90 34
✉ golf@lacala.com
▷ America 18 L 6187 m Par 73
Asia 18 L 5925 m Par 72
Europa 18 L 6014 m Par 71
6 hole Par 3 course
U H
££ €70 (summer €45)
⛳ 6km from Cala de Mijas, between Fuengirola and Marbella
⌂ Cabell B Robinson
▤ www.lacala.com

Guadalhorce   (1988)
Crtra de Cártama Km7, Apartado 48, 29590 Campanillas (Málaga)
☎ (952) 17 93 78

Lauro   (1992)
Los Caracolillos, 29130 Alhaurín de la Torre, (Málaga)
☎ (95) 241 2767/296 3091
✉ info@laurogolf.com

Málaga Club de Campo
(1925)
Parador de Golf, Apdo 324, 29080 Málaga
☎ (952) 38 12 55

Mijas Golf International
(1976)
Apartado 145, Fuengirola, Málaga
☎ (952) 47 68 43
✉ info@mijasgolf.org

Miraflores   (1989)
Urb Riviera del Sol, 29647 Mijas-Costa
☎ +34 (952) 93 19 60

Torrequebrada   (1976)
Public
Apdo 120, Crta de Cadiz Km 220, 29630 Benalmadena
☎ (95) 244 27 42
🖶 (95) 256 11 29
✉ bookings@golftorrequebrada.com
▷ 18 L 5806 m Par 72 SSS 71
H (men 27, ladies 35 max)

££ 16/9/07–31/5/08 €95
1/6/08–15/9/08 €75
⛳ Benalmadena, 25km S of Málaga
Airport
🏠 Pepe Gancedo
🖥 www.golftorrequebrada.com

Marbella & Estepona

Alcaidesa Links (1992)
CN-340 Km124.6, 11315 La Linea (Cádiz)
☎ (956) 79 10 40

Aloha (1975)
Nueva Andalucía, 29660 Marbella
☎ (952) 81 37 50/90 70 85/86
(952) 81 23 88
(Caddymaster)
📧 office@clubdegolfaloha.com

Los Arqueros (1991)
Crta de Ronda Km44.5, 29679
Benahavis (Málaga)
☎ (952) 78 46 00
🖥 (952) 78 67 07
📧 caddiemaster@es.taylorwoodrow
.com
🏷 18 L 5729 m Par 71 SSS 72
🍴 H U
££ May–Sep €40, Oct–Nov €70,
Dec–Jan €55, Feb–May 08 €75
⛳ 5km N of San Pedro de Alcántara
🏠 Severiano Ballesteros

Atalaya G&CC (1968)
Crta Benahavis 7, 29688 Málaga
☎ (952) 88 28 12

Las Brisas (1968)
Apdo 147, 29660 Nueva
Andalucía, (Málaga)
☎ (952) 81 08 75/81 30 21
📧 info@lasbrisasgolf.com

La Cañada (1982)
Ctra Guadiaro Km 1, 11311
Guadiaro (Cádiz)
☎ (956) 79 41 00

Estepona (1989)
Arroyo Vaquero, Apartado 532, 29680
Estepona (Málaga)
☎ (+34) 95 293 7605
📧 information@esteponagolf.com

Guadalmina (1959)
Guadalmina Alta, San Pedro de Alcántara,
29678 Marbella (Málaga)
☎ (952) 88 65 22

Marbella (1994)
CN 340 Km 188, 29600
Marbella (Málaga)
☎ (952) 83 05 00

Monte Mayor (1989)
PO Box 962, 29679 Benahavis (Málaga)
☎ (+34) 95 293 7111
🖥 (+34) 95 293 7112

📧 reservations@montemayorgolf.com
🏷 18 L 5652 m Par 71 SSS 71
🍴 H
££ €90 high season (inc. buggy) €60
low season (inc. buggy)
⛳ Exit on N340 at km 165.5
Cancelada
🏠 Jose Gancedo
🖥 www.montemayorgolf.com

Los Naranjos (1977)
Apdo 64, 29660 Nueva
Andalucía, Marbella
☎ (952) 81 52 06/81 24 28

El Paraiso (1973)
Ctra Cádiz-Màlaga Km 167, 29680
Estepona (Málaga)
☎ (95) 288 38 35
🖥 (95) 288 58 27
📧 info@elparaisogolfclub.com
🏷 18 L 6116 m SSS 72
🍴 U H
££ €80 (summer and winter offers
available)
⛳ 14km S of Marbella
🏠 Player/Kirby
🖥 www.elparaisogolfclub.com

La Quinta G&CC (1989)
Urb. La Quinta, Nueva Andalucía
29660, (Marbella-Málaga)
☎ +34 (952) 76 23 90
🖥 +34 (952) 76 23 99
📧 reservas@laquintagolf.com
🏷 27 L 602, 5749, 5915 m
SSS 70, 71, 71
SR 125, 123, 125
🍴 U H
££ Oct–Nov & Feb–May: 9: €69; 18:
€86 Dec–Feb & May–Sept: 9: €45;
18: €55
⛳ 3km N of San Pedro de Alcántara
🏠 Piñero/García-Garrido
🖥 www.laquintagolf.com

Santa María G&CC (1991)
Urb. Elviria, Crta N340 Km 192, 29600
Marbella (Málaga)
☎ (952) 83 10 36
🖥 (952) 83 47 97
📧 info@santamariagolfclub.com
🏷 18 L 5586 m Par 70
🍴 U
££ €75
⛳ 10km E of Marbella, opp Hotel
Don Carlos
🏠 A García Garrido (1st 9 holes)
, Santa Maria's Technical Team
(2nd 9 holes)
🖥 www.santamariagolfclub.com

Sotogrande (1964)
Paseo del Parque, s/n, 11310
Sotogrande, Cádiz
☎ +34 956 785014
📧 info@golfsotogrande.com

The San Roque Club (1990)
CN 340 Km 127, San Roque, 11360 Cádiz
☎ (956) 61 30 30

🖥 (956) 61 30 12
📧 info@sanroqueclub.com
🏷 18 L 6494 m (Old) 6626 m (New)
SSS 74
🍴 U H M–Old course exc between
12.00–14.26
££ New €80–€100 Old €120–€160
⛳ 3km E of Sotogrande. 15km W of
Gibraltar
🏠 Dave Thomas (Old), Perry Dye and
Seve Ballesteros (New)
🖥 www.sanroqueclub.com

Valderrama (1985)
Avenida de los Cortjos S/N, 11310
Sotogrande (Cadiz)
☎ (956) 79 12 00

La Zagaleta (1994)
Crta San Pedro-Ronda Km 9,
29679 Benahavis
☎ (95) 285 54 53

Seville & Gulf of Cádiz

Costa Ballena (1997)
Crta Sta Maria-Chipiona, 11520 Rota
☎ (956) 84 70 70

Isla Canela (1993)
Crta de la Playa, 21400 Ayamonte (Huelva)
☎ (959) 47 72 63
📧 golf@islacanela.es

Islantilla (1993)
Urb Islantilla, Apdo 52, 21410 Isla
Cristina (Huelva)
☎ (959) 48 60 39/48 60 49

Montecastillo (1992)
Carretera de Arcos, 11406 Jérez
☎ (956) 15 12 00
📧 commercial@montecastillo.com

Montenmedio G&CC
(1996)
A-48 Km 42.5, 11150 Vejer-
Barbate (Cádiz)
☎ (956) 45 12 16
📧 commercial@montenmedio.com

Novo Sancti Petri (1990)
Urb. Novo Sancti Petri, Playa de la Barrosa,
11139 Chiclana de la Frontera
☎ 0034 (956) 49 40 05
🖥 0034 (956) 49 43 50
📧 sales@golf-novosancti.es
🏷 Course A: 18 L 6076 m Par 72
Course B: 18 L 6071 m Par 72
Course C: 18 L 5932 m Par 72
🍴 U H
££ €80
⛳ La Barrosa, 24km SE of Cádiz. Jérez
Airport 50km
🏠 Severiano Ballesteros (A+B),
Robert Trent Jones Snr (C)
🖥 www.golf-novosancti.es

For list of abbreviations, key to symbols and international dialling codes see page 647

Pineda De Sevilla   (1939)
Apartado 1049, 41080 Sevilla
☎ **(954) 61 14 00**

Real Sevilla   (1992)
Autovía Sevilla-Utrera, 41089
Montequinto (Sevilla)
☎ **(954) 12 43 01**

Vista Hermosa   (1975)
Apartado 77, Urb Vista Hermosa, 11500
Puerto de Santa María, Cádiz
☎ **(956) 87 56 05**

Zaudin
Crta Tomares-Mairena, 41940
Tomares (Sevilla)
☎ **(954) 15 41 59**
(954) 15 25 52 (reservations)

Valencia & Castellón

Escorpión   (1975)
Apartado Correos 1, Betera (Valencia)
☎ **(96) 160 12 11**

Manises   (1964)
Apartado 22.029, Manises (Valencia)
☎ **(96) 152 18 71**

Mediterraneo CC   (1978)
Urb La Coma, 12190 Borriol, (Castellón)
☎ **(964) 32 1653 (bookings)**
🖳 (964) 65 77 34
✉ club@ccmediterraneo.com
⮡ 18 L 6227 m Par 72
👥 H WD before 1pm WE–after 12
££ €50 (€60)
🚗 Borriol, 4km NW of Castellón
🏠 Ramón Espinosa
🗐 www.ccmediterraneo.com

Oliva Nova   (1995)
46780 Oliva (Valencia)
☎ **(096) 285 76 66**
✉ golf@chg.es

Panorámica   (1995)
Urb Panorámica, 12320 San
Jorge (Castellón)
☎ **(964) 49 30 72**

El Saler   (1968)
Avd. de los pinares 151, 46012 El
Saler (Valencia)
☎ **(96) 161 0384**
✉ saler.golf@parador.es

Valladolid

Entrepinos   (1990)
Avda del Golf 2, Urb Entrepinos, 47130
Simancas (Valladolid)
☎ **(983) 59 05 11/59 05 61**
🖳 (983) 59 07 65
✉ golfentrepinos@golfentrepinos.com

⮡ 18 L 5349 m Par 69 CR 68.6 SR
123
👥 U H
££ €36 (€60)
🚗 15km SW of Valladolid. N-620 exit
135 towards Simancas
🏠 Manuel Piñero
🗐 www.golfentrepinos.com

Zaragoza

La Penaza   (1973)
Apartado 3039, Zaragoza
☎ **(976) 34 28 00/34 22 48**

Sweden

East Central

Ängsö   (1979)
Box 1007, 72126 Västerås
☎ **(0171) 441012**
🖳 (0171) 441049
✉ kansli@angsogolf.org
⮡ 18 hole course Par 72 SR 130
👥 H
££ 280kr (380kr)
🚗 15km E of Västerås
🏠 Åke Hultström
🗐 www.angsogolf.org

Arboga
PO Box 263, 732 25 Arboga
☎ **(0589) 70100**
🖳 (0589) 701 90
✉ arbogagk@arbogagk.nu
⮡ 18 L 5890 m Par 72
👥 U
££ 250kr (300kr)
🚗 5km S of Arboga
🏠 Sune Linde
🗐 www.arbogagk.nu

Askersund   (1980)
Box 3002, 696 03 Ammeberg
☎ **(0583) 34943**

Burvik   (1990)
Burvik, 740 12 Knutby
☎ **(0174) 43060**
🖳 (0174) 43062
✉ info:burvik.se
⮡ 18 L 5785 m SSS 72
👥 U
££ On application
🚗 45km E of Uppsala. 70km N of
Stockholm
🏠 Bengt Lorichs
🗐 www.burvik.se

Edenhof   (1991)
740 22 Bälinge
☎ **(018) 334185**
✉ info@edenhof.se

Enköping   (1970)
Box 2006, 745 02 Enköping
☎ **(0171) 20830**
🖳 (0171) 20823
✉ info@enkopinggolf.se
⮡ 18 L 5660 m Par 71
👥 H
££ 280kr (360kr)
🚗 1km E of Enköping, off E18
🏠 Nils Skold
🗐 www.enkopinggolf.se

Eskilstuna   (1951)
Strängnäsvägen, 633 49 Eskilstuna
☎ **(016) 142629**
✉ info@eskilstunagk.se

Fagersta   (1970)
Box 2051, 737 02 Fagersta
☎ **(0223) 54060**

Frösåker Golf & Country
(1989)
Frösåker Gård, Box 17015, 720
17 Västerås
☎ **(021) 25401**
🖳 (021) 25485
✉ fgcc@telia.com
⮡ 18 L 5820 m Par 72
👥 U H
££ 400kr (550kr)
🚗 15km SE of Västerås
🏠 Sune Linde
🗐 www.fgcc.se

Fullerö   (1988)
Jotsberga, 725 91 Västerås
☎ **(021) 50132**

Gripsholm   (1991)
Box 133, 647 23 Mariefred
☎ **(0159) 350050**
🖳 (0159) 350059
⮡ 18 L 6203 m Par 73 SR 128
👥 H
££ 350kr (450kr)
🚗 Mariefred, 70km SW of Stockholm
🏠 Bengt Lorichs
🗐 www.golf.se/gripsholmsgk

Grönlund   (1989)
PO Box 38, 740 10 Almunge
☎ **(0174) 20670**
🖳 (0174) 20455
✉ info@gronlundgk.se
⮡ 18 L 5865 m SSS 71
👥 H
££ €30 (€40)
🚗 20km E of Uppsala. 25km NE of
Arlanda Airport
🏠 Åke Persson
🗐 www.gronlundgk.se

Gustavsvik   (1988)
Box 22033, 702 02 Örebro
☎ **(019) 244486**
🖳 (019) 246490
✉ info@gvgk.se
⮡ 18 holes SSS 72
👥 H

££ 280kr (350kr)
ॐ 4km S of Örebro
⌂ Turner
▤ www.gvgk.se

Katrineholm (1959)
Jättorp, 641 93 Katrineholm
☎ (0150) 39270
▯ (0150) 39011
✉ info@katrineholmsgk.golf.se
▷ 18 L 5850 m SSS 72
 9 L 2850 m
♙ U
££ 300kr (350kr)
ॐ 7km E of Katrineholm
⌂ Skjöld/Lorichs
▤ www.katrineholmsgolf.nu

Köping (1963)
Box 278, 731 26 Köping
☎ (0221) 81090
▯ (0221) 81277
✉ info@kopingsgk.golf.sc
▷ 18 L 5636 m Par 71
♙ U
££ 250kr (300kr)
ॐ 3km N of Köping (E18)
⌂ Brasier/Sederholm
▤ www.kopingsgk.nu

Kumla (1987)
Box 46, 692 21 Kumla
☎ (019) 577370

Linde (1984)
Dalkarlshyttan, 711 31 Lindesberg
☎ (0581) 87050
▯ (0581) 87059
✉ info@lindegk.com
▷ 18 L 5539 m Par 71
♙ H
££ 280kr
ॐ 42km N of Örebro on R60.
 Lindesberg 2km
⌂ Jan Sederholm
▤ www.lindegk.com

Mosjö (1989)
Mosjö Gård, 705 94 Örebrö
☎ (019) 225780

Nora (1988)
Box 108, 713 23 Nora
☎ (0587) 311660

Nyköpings (1951)
Nicolai, 611 92 Nyköping
☎ (0155) 216617
▯ (0155) 267657
✉ info@nykopingsgk.se
▷ 36 East course L5970 m
 West course L5977 m
♙ H SOC
££ 300kr (400kr)
ॐ 5km SE of Nyköping
⌂ Skjöld/Linde
▤ www.nykopingsgk.se

Örebro (1939)
Lanna, 719 93 Vintrosa
☎ (019) 164070

▯ (019) 164075
▷ 18 L 5870 m Par 71
♙ H–max 36
££ 300kr 350 high season (350kr)
ॐ 18km W of Örebro on Route E18
⌂ Sköld/Sundblom/Berglund
▤ www.golf.se/golfklubbar/orebrogk

Roslagen
Box 110, 761 22 Norrtälje
☎ (0176) 237194

Sala (1970)
Norby Fallet 100, 733 92 Sala
☎ (0224) 53077/53055/53064
▯ (0224) 53143
✉ info@salagk.nu
▷ 18 L 6025 m Par 73
 9 L 2480 m Par 34
♙ U
££ 280kr (330kr)
ॐ 9km E of Sala towards Uppsala,
 Route 67/72
⌂ Tedrup/Linde/Turner
▤ www.salagk.nu

Sigtunabygden (1961)
Box 89, 193 22 Sigtuna
☎ (08) 592 54012
▯ (08) 592 54167
✉ info@sigtunagk.com
▷ 18 + (9) holes 6151 m (3950 m)
 Par 72 (Par 68)
 18 h Men CR 70.6 SR 128
 18 h Ladies CR 71.3 SR 123
 9 h Men CR 62.6 SR 100
 9 h Ladies CR 61.4 SR 93
♙ H
££ 320kr (400kr)
ॐ Sigtuna, 50km N of Stockholm
⌂ Nils Sköld
▤ www.sigtunagk.com

Skepptuna
Skepptuna, 195 93 Märsta
☎ (08) 512 93069

Södertälje (1952)
Box 9074, 151 09 Södertälje
☎ (08) 550 91995

Strängnäs (1968)
Kilenlundavägen, 645 91 Strängnäs
☎ (0152) 14731

Torshälla (1960)
Box 128, 64422 Torshälla
☎ (016) 358722
✉ kansli@telia.com

Tortuna
Nicktuna, Tortuna, 725 96 Västerås
☎ (021) 65300
✉ kansli@tortunagk.com

Trosa (1972)
Box 80, 619 22 Trosa
☎ (0156) 22458

Upsala (1937)
Håmö Gård, Läby, 755 92 Uppsala
☎ (018) 460120
▯ (018) 461205
✉ info@upsalagk.com
▷ 18 L 5818 m SSS 72 CR 72.0 SR
 128
 9 L 2674 m SSS 70 CR 68.1 SR 112
 9 L 1673 m SSS 58 CR 58.7 SR 96
♙ H 2nd 9–hole course U
££ 300kr (350kr)
ॐ 10km W of Uppsala
⌂ Robert Kains/Greger Paulsson/
 Peter Nordwall/Nils Nyberg/
 Einar Jansson
▤ www.upsalagk.com

Vassunda (1989)
Smedby Gård, 741 91 Knivsta
☎ +46 (0) 185 72040
▯ (018) 381416
✉ info@vassundagk.se
▷ 18 L 6141 m Par 72
♙ H
££ 280kr (360kr)
ॐ 45km N of Stockholm
⌂ Sune Linde
▤ www.vassundagk.se

Västerås (1931)
Bjärby, 724 81 Västerås
☎ (021) 357543
✉ info@vasterasgk.se

Far North

Boden (1946)
Tallkronsvägen 2, 961 51 Boden
☎ (0921) 69140
▯ (0921) 72047
▷ 18 L 5495 m SSS 72
♙ H
££ 300 skr
ॐ 7km S of Boden
⌂ Björn Eriksson

Funäsdalsfjällen (1972)
Golfbanevägen 8, 840 96 Ljusnedal
☎ (0684) 668241
▯ (0684) 21142
✉ kansli@ffjgk.nu
▷ 18 L 5300 m SSS 72
♙ U
££ 275kr (290kr)
ॐ Funäsdalen, nr Norwegian border
⌂ Sköld/Linde
▤ www.ffjgk.nu

Gällivare-Malmberget
 (1973)
Box 35, 983 21 Malmberget
☎ (0970) 20770
▯ (0970) 20776
✉ gmgk@telia.com
▷ 18 L 5528 m Par 71
♙ H
££ 250kr
ॐ 4km NW of Gällivare, towards
 Malmberget

Jan Sederholm
www.gmgk.se

Haparanda (1989)
Mattila 140, 953 35 Haparanda
☎ (0922) 10660

Härnösand (1957)
Box 52, 871 22 Härnösand
☎ (0611) 67000

Kalix (1990)
Box 32, 952 21 Kalix
☎ (0923) 15945/15935

Luleå (1955)
Golfbaneväg 80, 975 96 Luleå
☎ (0920) 256300
🖬 (0920) 256362
🖂 kansli@luleagolf.se
🏳 27 L 8930 m Par 72
🚶 H
£€ 300kr
🚗 Rutvik, 12km E of Luleå
🏠 Skjöld/Tideman/Eriksson
🖥 www.luleagolf.se

Norrmjöle (1992)
905 82 Umeå
☎ (090) 81581
🖬 (090) 81565
🖂 kanslie@norrmjole-golf.se
🏳 18 L 5619 m Par 72
🚶 U
£€ 250kr (350kr); 300kr (400kr) in July
🚗 19km S of Umeå
🏠 Acke Lundgren
🖥 www.norrmjole-golf.se

Örnsköldsviks GK Puttom (1967)
Ovansjö 232, 891 95 Arnäsvall
☎ (0660) 254001
🖬 (0660) 254040
🖂 kansli@puttom.se
🏳 18 L 5795 m SSS 72
🚶 H
£€ 250kr (300kr)
🚗 15km N of Örnsköldsvik on E4
🏠 Nils Sköld
🖥 www.puttom.se

Östersund-Frösö (1947)
Kungsgården 205, 832 96 Frösön
☎ (063) 576030

Piteå (1960)
Nötöv 119, 941 41 Piteå
☎ (0911) 14990

Skellefteå (1967)
Rönnbäcken, 931 92 Skellefteå
☎ (0910) 779333
🖂 info@skelleftegolf.nu

Sollefteå (1970)
Box 213, 881 25 Sollefteå
☎ (0620) 21477/12670

Sundsvall (1952)
Golfvägen 5, 86234 Kvissleby
☎ +46 60 515175
🖂 info@sundsvallgk.golf.se

Timrå
Golfbanevägen 2, 860 32 Fagervik
☎ (060) 570153
🖂 info@timragk.golf.se

Umeå (1954)
Lövön, 913 35 Holmsund
☎ (090) 58580/58585
🖬 (090) 58589
🖂 info@umgk.se
🏳 27 - CR 71.9 SR 133, CR 71.5 SR 137, CR 69.9 SR 129
🚶 U
£€ 300/350sek – €33/€39
🚗 16km SE of Umeå
🏠 Bo Engdahl, Nils Sköld, Björn Eriksson
🖥 www.umgk.se

Gothenburg

Albatross (1973)
Lillhagsvägen, 422 50 Hisings-Backa
☎ (031) 551901/550500

Chalmers
Härrydavägen 50, 438 91 Landvetter
☎ +46 (0) 31 91 84 30
🖂 info@chgk.se

Delsjö (1962)
Kallebäck, 412 76 Göteborg
☎ (031) 406959

Forsgårdens (1982)
Gamla Forsv 1, 434 47 Kungsbacka
☎ (0300) 566350
🖬 (0300) 566351
🖂 info@forsgardensgk.golf.se
🏳 18 L 6110 m SSS 72
9 L 2915 m
🚶 WD–U WE–M before noon May–June
£€ 350kr (400kr)
🚗 1km SE of Kungsbacka. 20km S of Gothenburg
🏠 Sune Linde
🖥 www.forsgarden.se

Göteborg (1902)
Box 2056, 436 02 Hovås
☎ (031) 282444

Gullbringa G&CC (1968)
Kulperödsvägen 6, 442 95 Hålta
☎ (0303) 227161
🖬 (0303) 227778
🖂 kansli@gullbringagolf.se
🏳 27 (3 x 9):
Blue Par 35, Red Par 36, Yellow Par 34, Blue-Red Par 71, Red-Yellow Par 70, Blue-Yellow Par 69
🚶 U
£€ D–380kr/€40

🚗 14km W of Kungälv, towards Marstrand; 35km from Gothenburg
🏠 Douglas Brasier
🖥 www.gullbringagolf.se

Kungälv-Kode
Ö Knaverstad 140, 442 97 Kode
☎ (0303) 51300

Kungsbacka (1971)
Hamravägen 15, 429 44 Särö
☎ (031) 938180

Lysegården (1966)
Box 532, 442 15 Kungälv
☎ (0303) 223426
🖂 info@lysegarden.sgk.golf.se

Mölndals (1979)
Box 77, 437 21 Lindome
☎ (031) 993030
🖬 (031) 994901
🖂 molndalsgk@telia.com
🏳 18 L 5625 m SSS 73
£€ 320kr (370kr)
🚗 Lindome, 20km S of Gothenburg
🏠 Ronald Fream
🖥 www.molndalsgk.se

Öijared (1958)
Pl 1082, 448 92 Floda
☎ (0302) 37300
🖬 (0302) 37306
🖂 reception@oigc.se
🏳 18 L 5875 m Par 72
18 L 5655 m Par 71
18 L 4895 m Par 70
🚶 H WE–NA before 1pm
£€ Park Banan 300sek (350sek) Nya Banen 350sek (400sek) Gamla Banen 400sek (500sek)
🚗 35km NE of Gothenburg (E20), nr Nääs
🏠 Brasier/Amilon/chamberlaine/Fulce
🖥 www.oigk.se

Partille (1986)
Box 234, 433 24 Partille
☎ (031) 987043

Sjögärde
43963 Frillesås
☎ +46 (0) 340 657865
🖬 +46 (0) 340 657861
🖂 info@sjogarde.se
🏳 18 L 5723 m SSS 72
6 hole short course
🚶 H
£€ 350sek or €38
🚗 20km S of Kungsbacka
🏠 Lars Andreasson
🖥 www.sjogarde.se

Stenungsund (1993)
Lundby Pl 7480, 444 93 Spekeröd
☎ (0303) 778470

Stora Lundby (1983)
Valters Väg 2, 443 71 Grabo
☎ (0302) 44200

Malmö & South Coast

Abbekas (1989)
Kroppsmarksvagen, 274 56 Abbekas
- ☎ (0411) 533233
- 🖳 (0411) 533419
- ✉ info@abbekasgk.golf.se
- ▷ 18 L 5817 m Par 72
- 👥 U H
- £€ 300kr (350kr)
- 🚗 20km W of Ystad
- ♟ Tommy Nordström
- 🖥 www.abbekas.nu

Barsebäck G&CC (1969)
246 55 Löddeköpinge
- ☎ (046) 776230

Bokskogen (1963)
Torupsvägen 408-140, 230 40 Bara
- ☎ (040) 406900

Falsterbo (1909)
Fyrvägen 34, 239 40 Falsterbo
- ☎ +46 (0)40 470078/475078
- 🖳 +46 (0)40 472722
- ✉ info@falsterbogk..se
- ▷ 18 L 6577 yds Par 71 CR 73.2 SR 129
- 👥 H
- £€ €50.65 (€60.65)
- 🚗 30km SW of Malmö
- ♟ Gunnar Bauer, Peter Champerlain/Peter Nordwall
- 🖥 www.falsterbogk.com

Flommens (1935)
239 40 Falsterbo
- ☎ (040) 475016
- 🖳 (040) 473157
- ✉ info@flommensgk.se
- ▷ 18 L 5735 m SSS 72
- 👥 U H
- £€ 400kr
- 🚗 35km SW of Malmö
- ♟ Bergendorff/Kristersson
- 🖥 www.flommensgk.se

Kävlinge (1989)
Box 138, 244 22 Kävlinge
- ☎ (046) 736270
- 🖳 (046) 728486
- ✉ info@kavlingegk.golf.se
- ▷ 18 L 5800 m SSS 72
- 👥 H
- £€ 300kr
- 🚗 12km N of Lund
- ♟ Rolf Collijn
- 🖥 www.kavlingegk.com

Ljunghusen (1932)
Kinellsvag, Ljunghusen, 236 42 Höllviken
- ☎ (040) 458000
- 🖳 (040) 454265
- ✉ info@ljgk.se
- ▷ 27 holes:
  L 5455-5895 m SSS 70-73
- 👥 WD–U H WE 10 tee times for guests
- £€ €45 (€60)
- 🚗 Falsterbo Peninsula. 30km SW of Malmö

- ♟ Douglas Brasier
- 🖥 www.ljgk.se

Lunds Akademiska (1936)
Kungsmarken, 225 92 Lund
- ☎ (046) 99005
- 🖳 (046) 99146
- ✉ info@lagk.se
- ▷ 18 L 5780 m
- 👥 H
- £€ 300kr (400kr)
- 🚗 5km E of Lund
- ♟ Boström/Morrison/Fjallman
- 🖥 www.lagk.se

Malmö Burlöv (1981)
Segesvängen, 212 27 Malmö
- ☎ (040) 292535/292536
- 🖳 (040) 292228
- ✉ malmoburlovgk@telia.com
- ▷ 27 L 6008 m SSS 71 CR 72.0 SR 128
- 👥 H
- £€ 320kr/350kr
- 🚗 NE of Malmö
- ♟ Jan Sederholm and Tommy Nordstrom
- 🖥 www.malmoburlovgk.com

Örestad (1986)
Golfvägen, Habo Ljung, 234 22 Lomma
- ☎ (040) 410580
- 🖳 (040) 416320
- ✉ info@orestadsgk.com
- ▷ 18 L 6046 m Par 71
  9 L 3116 m Par 36
  18 hole Par 3 course
- 👥 H
- £€ 300kr (350kr)
- 🚗 15km N of Malmö
- ♟ Åke Persson
- 🖥 www.orestadsgk.com

Österlen (1945)
Lilla Vik, 272 95 Simrishamn
- ☎ (0414) 412550
- 🖳 (0414) 412551
- ✉ osterlengolfklubb@telia.com
- ▷ 18 L 5835 m CR 69.8
  18 L 5741 m CR 71.3
- 👥 H
- £€ 350kr (450kr)
- 🚗 Vik, 8km N of Simrishamn
- ♟ Tommy Nordström
- 🖥 www.osterlensgk.com

Romeleåsen (1969)
Kvarnbrodda, 240 14 Veberöd
- ☎ (046) 82012
- 🖳 (046) 82113
- ✉ info@ragk.se
- ▷ 18 L 5783 m Par 72
- 👥 H
- £€ 350kr
- 🚗 6km S of Veberöd. 25km E of Malmö
- ♟ Douglas Brasier
- 🖥 www.ragk.se

Söderslätts (1993)
Ellaboda, Grievievägen 260-10, 235 94 Vellinge

- ♟ Douglas Brasier
- 🖥 www.ljgk.se

- ☎ (040) 429680
- 🖳 (040) 429684
- ✉ info@soderslattsgK.golf.se
- ▷ 18 L 5800 m SSS 72
  9 hole Par 3 course
- 👥 WD–H WE–M H before noon
- £€ Jan–May and Sept–Dec 300kr; June–Aug 350kr
- 🚗 15km SE of Malmö
- ♟ Sune Linde
- 🖥 www.4.golf.se/soderslattsgk

Tegelberga (1988)
Alstad Pl 140, 231 96 Trelleborg
- ☎ (040) 485690

Tomelilla (1987)
Ullstorp, 273 94 Tomelilla
- ☎ (0417) 19430
- ✉ info@tomelillagolfklub.com

Trelleborg (1963)
Maglarp, Pl 431, 231 93 Trelleborg
- ☎ (0410) 330460
- 🖳 (0410) 330281
- ✉ kansli@trelleborgsgk.se
- ▷ 18 L 5299 m Par 70
- 👥 U H
- £€ 350kr
- 🚗 5km W of Trelleborg
- ♟ Brasier/Chamberlain
- 🖥 www.trelleborgsgk.se

Vellinge (1991)
Toftadals Gård, 235 41 Vellinge
- ☎ (040) 443255

Ystad (1930)
Långrevsvägen, 270 22 Köpingebro
- ☎ (0411) 550350
- 🖳 (0411) 550392
- ✉ info@ystadgk.com
- ▷ 18 L 5800 m Par 72
- 👥 U
- £€ 250–350kr
- 🚗 7km E of Ystad, towards Simrishamn
- ♟ Thure Bruce
- 🖥 www.ystadgk.se

North

Alvkarleby
Västanåvägen 5, 814 94 Alvkarleby
- ☎ (026) 72757
- ✉ info@alvkarlebygk.se

Avesta (1963)
Friluftsvägen 10, 774 61 Avesta
- ☎ (0226) 55913/10866/12766
- 🖳 (0226) 12578
- ✉ info@avestagk.se
- ▷ 18 L 5560 m SSS 71
- 👥 H
- £€ 250kr (300kr)
- 🚗 3km NE of Avesta
- ♟ Sune Linde
- 🖥 www.avestagk.se

Bollnäs   (1963)
Norrfly 1634, 823 91 Kilafors
☎ (0278) 650540
✉ info@bollnasgk.com

Dalsjö   (1989)
Dalsjö 3, 781 94 Borlänge
☎ (0243) 220080
✉ info@dalsjogolf.se

Falun-Borlänge   (1956)
Storgarden 10, 791 93 Falun
☎ (023) 31015

Gävle   (1949)
Bönavägen 23, 805 95 Gävle
☎ (026) 120333/120338

Hagge   (1963)
Hagge, 771 90 Ludvika
☎ (0240) 28087/28513

Hofors   (1965)
Box 117, 813 22 Hofors
☎ (0290) 85125

Högbo   (1962)
Daniel Tilas Väg 4, 811 92 Sandviken
☎ (026) 215015
🖥 (026) 215322
✉ info@hogbogk.golf.se
↦ 18 L 5760 m Par 72
    9 L 2590 m Par 35
👤 H
££ 260kr (350kr)
♣ 6km N of Sandviken (Route 272)
🏠 Sköld/Linde
🖳 www.golf.se/hogbogk/

Hudiksvall   (1964)
Tjuvskär, 824 01 Hudiksvall
☎ +46 (0) 650 542080

Leksand   (1977)
Box 25, 793 21 Leksand
☎ (0247) 14640

Ljusdal   (1973)
Svinhammarsv.2, 82735 Ljusdal
☎ (0651) 16883
    (0651) 12566 (shop)
🖥 (0651) 16883
✉ kansli@golfiljusdal.nu
↦ 18 L 5920 m Par 72
👤 U
££ 250kr
♣ 2km E of Ljusdal
🏠 Eriksson/Skjöld
🖳 www.golfiljusdal.nu

Mora   (1980)
Box 264, 792 24 Mora
☎ (0250) 592990
✉ info@moragk.se

Rättvik   (1954)
Box 29, 795 21 Rättvik
☎ (0248) 51030
🖥 (0248) 12081

↦ 18 L 5375 m SSS 70
👤 U
££ 200kr–300kr
♣ 2km N of Rättvik

Sälenfjallens   (1991)
Box 20, 780 67 Sälen
☎ (0280) 20670
✉ info@salenfjallensgk.se

Säter   (1984)
Box 89, 783 22 Säter
☎ (0225) 50030

Snöå   (1990)
Snöå Bruk, 780 51 Dala-Järna
☎ (0281) 24072

Söderhamn   (1961)
Box 117, 826 23 Söderhamn
☎ (0270) 281300

Sollerö   (1991)
Levsnäs, 79290 Sollerön
☎ (0250) 22236

Skane & South

Allerum   (1992)
Tursköpsvägen 154, 260 35 Ödåkra
☎ (042) 93051
🖥 (042) 93045
✉ info@allerumgk.nu
↦ 18 L 6201 m SSS 73
👤 U
££ 300kr
♣ 9km NE of Helsingborg
🏠 Hans Fock
🖳 www.allerumgk.nu

Ängelholm   (1973)
Box 1117, 262 22 Ängelholm
☎ (0431) 430260/431460

Araslöv
Starvägen 1, 291 75 Färlöv
☎ (044) 71600

Båstad   (1929)
Box 1037, 269 21 Båstad
☎ (0431) 78370
🖥 (0431) 73331
✉ info@ bgk.se
↦ 18 L 5632 m Par 71
    18 L 6163 m Par 72
👤 H
££ 500kr
♣ 4km W of Båstad (Route 115)
🏠 Hawtree/Taylor/Nordström
🖳 www.bgk.se

Bedinge   (1931)
Golfbanevägen, 231 76 Beddingestrand
☎ (0410) 25514

Bjäre
Salomonhög 3086, 269 93 Båstad
☎ (0431) 361053

Bosjökloster   (1974)
243 95 Höör
☎ (0413) 25858

Carlskrona   (1949)
PO Almö, 370 24 Nättraby
☎ (0457) 35123

Degeberga-Widtsköfle
Segholmsu.126, Box 71, 297 21 Degeberga
☎ (044) 355035
✉ dwgk@telia.com

Eslöv   (1966)
Box 150, 241 22 Eslöv
☎ (0413) 18610
🖥 (0413) 18613
✉ info@eslovsgk.golf.se
↦ 18 L 5610 m CR 70.7 SR 133
    Par 70
👤 H
££ 300kr (340kr)
♣ 4km S of Eslöv (Route 113)
🏠 Thure Bruce
🖳 www.eslovsgk.se

Hässleholm   (1978)
Skyrup, 282 95 Tyringe
☎ (0451) 53111

Helsingborg   (1924)
260 40 Viken
☎ (042) 236147
✉ office@helsingborgsgk.com
↦ 9 L 4578 m Par 68
👤 H SOC
££ 200kr (220kr)
♣ 15km NW of Helsingborg
🏠 W Hester
🖳 www.helsingborgsgk.com

Karlshamn   (1962)
Box 188, 374 23 Karlshamn
☎ (0454) 50085

Kristianstad GK   (1924)
Box 41, 296 21 Åhus
☎ (044) 247656
🖥 (044) 247635
✉ info@kristianstadsgk.com
↦ 18 L 5680 m SSS 72
    18 L 5866 m SSS 72
👤 H
££ 400kr
♣ 18km SE of Kristianstad. Airport
    20km
🏠 Brasier/Nordström
🖳 www.kristianstadsgk.com

Landskrona   (1960)
Erikstorp, 261 61 Landskrona
☎ (0418) 446260
🖥 (0418) 446262
✉ info@landskronagk.se
↦ Old 18 L 5700 m SSS 71
    New 18 L 4300 m SSS 64
👤 H
££ 400kr (400kr)
♣ 4km N of Landskrona, towards
    Borstahusen

🏠 Thure Bruce, Peter Chamberlain, Karl Oscar Seth, Ake Persson New Course
▤ www.landskronagk.se

Mölle (1943)
260 42 Mölle
☎ (042) 347520
🖵 (042) 347523
✉ info@mollegk.se
⌦ 18 L 5292 m Par 70
⚅ H–max 36
££ 400kr
⛳ Mölle, 35km NW of Helsingborg
🏠 Thure Bruce
▤ www.mollegk.se

Örkelljunga (1989)
Rya 472, 286 91 Örkelljunga
☎ (0435) 53690/53640
✉ info@orkelljungagk.com

Östra Göinge (1981)
Riksvägen 12, 289 21 Knislinge
☎ (044) 60060
🖵 (044) 67862
✉ info@ostragoinge.golf.se
⌦ 18 L 5906 m Par 72
⚅ H
££ 220kr (280kr)
⛳ 20km N of Kristianstad
🏠 T Nordström
▤ www.golf.se/ostragoingegk

Perstorp (1964)
Gustavsborg 501, 284 91 Perstorp
☎ (0435) 35411

Ronneby (1963)
Box 26, 372 21 Ronneby
☎ (0457) 10315

Rya (1934)
PL 5500, 255 92 Helsingborg
☎ (042) 220182
🖵 (042) 220394
✉ kansli@rya.nu
⌦ 18 L 5558 m Par 71
⚅ H
££ 400 sek – 550 sek
⛳ 10km S of Helsingborg
🏠 Petterson/Sundblom
▤ www.rya.nu

St Arild (1987)
Golfvagen 48, 260 41 Nyhamnsläge
☎ (042) 346860
🖵 (042) 346042
✉ kansliet@starild.se
⌦ 18 L 5805 m Par 72
⚅ H
££ 380kr D–500kr (380kr)
⛳ 35km N of Helsingborg
🏠 Jan Sederholm
▤ www.starild.se

Skepparslov (1984)
Sätesvägen 14, 291 92 Kristianstad
☎ (044) 229508
✉ kansli@skepparslovgk.se

Söderåsen (1966)
Box 41, 260 50 Billesholm
☎ (042) 73337
🖵 (042) 73963
✉ info@soderasensgk.golf.se
⌦ 18 L 5633 m Par 71 CR 70.8 SR 134
⚅ U H
££ 320kr (380kr)
⛳ 20km E of Helsingborg
🏠 Thure Bruce
▤ www.soderasensgk.se

Sölvesborg
Box 204, 294 25 Sölvesborg
☎ (0456) 70650
🖵 (0456) 70650
✉ info@solvesborggk.se
⌦ 18 L 5900 m Par 72
⚅ U
££ 300kr
⛳ 30km E of Kristianstad
🏠 Sune Linde
▤ www.solvesborggk.se

Svalöv (1989)
Månstorp Pl 1365, 268 90 Svalöv
☎ (0418) 662462
🖵 (0418) 663284
✉ svagk@telia.com
⌦ 18 L 5874 m SSS 73
⚅ U
££ 290kr (340kr)
⛳ 20km E of Landskrona
🏠 Tommy Nordström
▤ www.svagk.se

Torekov (1924)
Råledsv 31, 260 93 Torekov
☎ (0431) 449840
🖵 (0431) 364916
✉ info@togk.se
⌦ 18 L 5525 m Par 71
⚅ H WE–M before noon
££ 400kr (450kr)
⛳ 3km N of Torekov
🏠 Nils Sköld
▤ www.togk.se

Trummenas
373 02 Ramdala
☎ (0455) 60505

Vasatorp (1973)
Box 13035, 250 13 Helsingborg
☎ (042) 235058
🖵 (042) 235135
✉ reception@vasatorpsgk.se
⌦ 18 L 5775 m SSS 72
36 hole course
From 2008: 2x18 holes and 2x9 holes
⚅ H–max 36
££ 360kr (400kr) – 18 hole
⛳ 7km E of Helsingborg
🏠 Bruce/Persson/Fock/Sellberg/ Arthur Hills
▤ www.vasatorpsgk.se

South East

A 6 Golfklubb (1985)
Centralvägen, 553 05 Jönköping
☎ (036) 308130
✉ a6gk@a6gk.se

Älmhult (1975)
Pl 1215, 343 90 Älmhult
☎ (0476) 14135

Åtvidaberg (1954)
Västantorp, 597 41 Åtvidaberg
☎ (0120) 35425

Ekerum
387 92 Borgholm, Öland
☎ (0485) 80000
🖵 (0485) 80010
⌦ 18 L 5975 m Par 73
18 L 5862 m Par 72
⚅ U H
££ 250kr–400kr
⛳ 12km S of Borgholm. 25km N of Öland bridge
🏠 Peter Nordwall
▤ www.ekerum.com
www.ekerum.se

Eksjö (1938)
Skedhult, 575 96 Eksjö
☎ (0381) 13525
🖵 (0381) 12405
✉ kansli@eksjogk.nu
⌦ 18 L 5930 m SSS 72
⚅ WD–U WE–H
££ 300kr
⛳ 6km W of Eksjö on Nässjö road
🏠 Anders Amilon
▤ www.eksjogk.nu

Emmaboda (1976)
Kyrkogatan, 360 60 Vissefjärda
☎ (0471) 20505/20540
✉ info@emmabodagk.golf.se

Finspångs (1965)
Viberga Gård, 612 92 Finspång
☎ (0122) 13940
✉ info@finspangsgk.golf.se

Gotska (1986)
Annelund, 62141 Visby, Gotland
☎ (0498) 215545
🖵 (0498) 256332
✉ info@gotskagk.golf.se
⌦ 18 L 5202 m Par 69
9 L 5414 m Par 72
⚅ U H
££ 300sek
⛳ N outskirts of Visby
🏠 Jack Wenman
▤ www.gotskagk.se

Grönhögen (1996)
PL 1270, 380 65 Öland
☎ (0485) 665995

For list of abbreviations, key to symbols and international dialling codes see page 647

Gumbalde
Box 35, 620 13 Ståga, Gotland
☎ (0498) 482880

Hooks
560 13 Hok
☎ (0393) 21420

Isaberg   (1968)
Nissafors Bruk, 330 27 Hestra
☎ (0370) 336330

Jönköpings GK   (1936)
Kettilstorp, 556 27 Jönköping
☎ (036) 76567
⌨ (036) 76511
✉ info@jonkopingsgk.se
ᵽ 18 L 5313 m Par 70
🚶 Phone in advance H–max 36
££ 300kr (350kr)
🚗 Kettilstorp, 3km S of Jönköping
🏠 Frank Dyer
▤ www.jonkopingsgk.se

Kalmar   (1947)
Box 278, 391 23 Kalmar
☎ (0480) 472111
⌨ (0480) 472314
✉ reception@kalmar.gk.se
ᵽ Blue 18 L 5700 m SSS 72
    Red 18 L 5634 m SSS 72
🚶 H
££ 350kr (400kr)
🚗 9km N of Kalmar via E22
🏠 Brasier/Sköld/Linde
▤ www.kalmargk.se

Lagan   (1966)
Box 63, 340 14 Lagan
☎ (0372) 30450/35460

Landeryd   (1987)
Bogestad Gård, 585 93 Linköping
☎ (+46) 133 62200
⌨ (+46) 133 62208
✉ bjorngustafsson@landerydgolf.se
ᵽ North 18 L 5675 m SSS 72
    South 18 L 5085 m SSS 68
    9 hole short course
🚶 U
££ 300–350kr (400–450kr)
🚗 7km SE of Linköping
🏠 Nordström/Persson
▤ www.landerydgolf.se

Lidhems   (1988)
360 14 Väckelsång
☎ (0470) 33660

Linköping   (1945)
Box 15054, 580 15 Linköping
☎ (013) 262990
⌨ (013) 140769
✉ lggolf@telia.com
ᵽ 18 L 5659 m SSS 71
🚶 H
££ 350kr (400kr)
🚗 In the town of Linköping
🏠 Sundblom/Brasier
▤ www.linkopingsgk.se

Mjölby   (1986)
Blixberg, Miskarp, 595 92 Mjölby
☎ (0142) 12570
⌨ (0142) 16553
✉ kansli@mjolbygk.se
ᵽ 18 L 5485 m SSS 71
🚶 H
££ 280kr (350kr)
🚗 35km WSW of Linköping (E4), exit 108
🏠 Åke Persson
▤ www.mjolbygk.se

Motala   (1956)
PO Box 264, 591 23 Motala
☎ (0141) 50840
⌨ (0141) 208990
✉ info@motalagk.golf.se
ᵽ 27 L 5563 m Par 71 + L2909 Par 35
🚶 U
££ 280kr (350kr)
🚗 3km S of Motala via Route 50
🏠 Sköld/Sederholm
▤ www.motalagk.se

Nässjö   (1988)
Box 5, 571 21 Nässjö
☎ (0380) 10022

Norrköping   (1928)
Alsatersvagen 40, 605 97 Norrköping
☎ (011) 158240
⌨ (011) 158249
✉ info@ngk.nu
ᵽ 18 L 5860 m SSS 73
🚶 U H
££ 350skr (400skr)
🚗 Klinga, 9km S of Norrköping on E4
🏠 Nils Sköld
▤ www.ngk.nu

Oskarshamn   (1972)
Box 148, 572 23 Oskarshamn
☎ (0491) 94033

Skinnarebo   (1990)
Skinnarebo, 555 93 Jönköping
☎ (036) 69075
⌨ (036) 362975
✉ info@skinnarebogcc.golf.se
ᵽ 18 L 5686 m SSS 71
    9 hole Par 3 course
🚶 H
££ 180kr
🚗 14km SW of Jönköping
🏠 Björn Magnusson
▤ www.skinnarebo.se

Söderköping   (1983)
Hylinge, 605 96 Norrköping
☎ (011) 70579

Tobo   (1971)
Fredensborg 133, 598 91 Vimmerby
☎ (0492) 30346
⌨ (0492) 30871
✉ info@tobogk.com
ᵽ 18 L 5720 m Par 72
🚶 U
££ 300kr (350kr)
🚗 10km S of Vimmerby, nr Storebro. 60km SW of Västervik

🏠 Brasier/Jensen
▤ www.tobogk.com

Tranås   (1952)
Norrc byvagen 8, Norrabyvagen 8, 57343 Tranas
☎ (0140) 311661
⌨ (0140) 16161
✉ info@tranasgk.se
ᵽ 18 L 5830 m SSS 72
    + 9 pay and play
🚶 U
££ 18: 300kr (350kr) 9: 100kr
🚗 2km N of Tranås
▤ www.tranasgk.se

Vadstena   (1957)
Hagalund, Box 122, 592 23 Vadstena
☎ (0143) 12440
⌨ (0143) 12709
✉ kansli@vadstenagk.nu
ᵽ 18 L 5850 m (men) 4992 m (Ladies)
    Par 72
🚶 U
££ 280kr (350kr)
🚗 3km S of Vadstena, towards Vaderstad
🏠 Åke Persson, Svante Dahlgren, Rolf Collijn
▤ www.vadstenagk.nu

Värnamo   (1962)
Box 146, 331 21 Värnamo
☎ (0370) 23991
⌨ (0370) 23992
✉ info@varnamogk.se
ᵽ 27 L 6253 m SSS 72
🚶 U
££ 300kr (350kr)
🚗 8km E of Värnamo on Route 127
🏠 Nils Sköld, Björn Magnusson
▤ www.varnamogk.se

Västervik   (1959)
Box 62, Ekhagen, 593 22 Västervik
☎ (0490) 32420

Växjö   (1959)
Box 227, 351 05 Växjö
☎ (0470) 21515

Vetlanda   (1983)
Box 249, 574 23 Vetlanda
☎ (0383) 18310

Visby
Västergarn Kronholmen 415, 622 30 Gotlands Tofta
☎ +46 498 200930
⌨ +46 498 200932
ᵽ 18 L 5875 m Par 72
    9 L 9277 m Par 36
🚶 Jun–Aug–H
££ 300–450kr
🚗 Kronholmen, 25km S of Visby, Gotland island
🏠 Nordwall/Sköld
▤ www.visbygk.com

Vreta Kloster
Box 144, 590 70 Ljungsbro
☎ (013) 169700
✉ info@vkgk.se

South West

Alingsås (1985)
Hjälmared 4050, 441 95 Alingsås
☎ (0322) 52421

Bäckavattnet (1977)
Marbäck, 305 94 Halmstad
☎ (035) 162040

Billingens GK (1949)
St Kulhult, 540 17 Lerdala
☎ +46 511 80291
📠 +46 511 80244
✉ info@billingensgk.se
▷ 18 L 5470 m Par 71
👥 U
££ 200kr (270kr)
⚲ 20km NW of Skövde
🏠 Douglas Brasier
🖥 www.billingensgk.se

Borås (1933)
Östra Vik, Kråkered, 504 95 Borås
☎ (033) 250250

Ekarnas (1970)
Balders Väg 12, 467 31 Grästorp
☎ (0514) 12061
📠 (0514) 12062
✉ info@ekarnasgk.golf.se
▷ 18 L 5501 m SSS 71
👥 H
££ 250kr (300kr)
⚲ 25km E of Trollhätten; 35km SW of Lidköping
🏠 Jan Andersson
🖥 www.golf.se//ekarnasgk

Falkenberg (1949)
Golfvägen, 311 72 Falkenberg
☎ (0346) 50287
📠 (0346) 50997
✉ info@falkenberggk.golf.se
▷ 27 L 5575-5680 m SSS 72
👥 H
££ 360kr
⚲ 5km S of Falkenberg
🏠 Sköld-Sundblom-Sederholf-Nordström
🖥 www.falkenbergsgolfklubb.se

Falköping (1965)
Box 99, 521 02 Falköping
☎ (0515) 31270

Halmstad (1930)
302 73 Halmstad
☎ (035) 176800/176801
📠 (035) 176820
✉ info@halmstad.golf.se
▷ North: 18 L 5955 m CR 72.4
South: 18 L 5542 m CR 69.9
👥 H

££ North: 600kr South: 500kr
⚲ Tylosand, 9km W of Halmstad
🏠 Sundblom/Sköld/Pennink
🖥 www.hgk.se

Haverdals (1988)
Slingervägen 35, 31042 Haverdal
☎ (035) 144990
📠 (035) 53890
✉ info@haverdalsgk-golf.se
▷ 18 L 5840 m Par 72
👥 H
££ 380Skr
⚲ 11km NW of Halmstad
🏠 Anders Amilon/Bjorn Magnusson
🖥 www.haverdalsgk.com

Hökensås (1962)
PO Box 116, 544 22 Hjo
☎ (0503) 16059

Holms (1990)
Nannarp, 305 92 Halmstad
☎ (035) 38189
✉ info@holmsgk.golf.se

Hulta (1972)
Box 54, 517 22 Bollebygd
☎ (033) 204340

Knistad G&CC
541 92 Skövde
☎ (0500) 463170

Laholm (1964)
Vallen 15, 31298 Vaxtorp
☎ +46 430 30601
📠 +46 430 30891
✉ info@laholmgk.com
▷ 18 L 5430 m Par 70 CR 69.5 SR 128
9 L 2660 m Par 72 CR 71.0 SR 135
👥 U H
££ 300sek (320sek)
⚲ 5 miles E of Laholm on Route 24
🏠 Jan Sederholm
🖥 www.laholmgk.com

Lidköping (1967)
Box 2029, 531 02 Lidköping
☎ (0510) 546144
📠 (0510) 546495
▷ 18 L 5382 m CR 70.4 SR 128/121
👥 H
££ D–€28
⚲ 5km E of Lidköping
🏠 Douglas Brasier
🖥 www.lidkopingsgk.se

Mariestads Golf Course (1975)
Gummerstadsvägen 45, 542 94 Mariestad
☎ (0501) 47147
📠 (0501) 78117
✉ info@mariestadsgk.se
▷ 18 L 5970 m SSS 73
👥 H
££ 250kr
⚲ 4km W of Mariestad, at Lake Vänern
🖥 www.mariestadsgk.com

Marks (1962)
Brättingstorpsvägen 28, 511 58 Kinna
☎ (0320) 14220
📠 (0320) 12516
✉ info@marksgk.se
▷ 18 L 5530 m Par 70
CR 70.7 (men); 73.1 (ladies)
9 L 2675 m Par 35
👥 H
££ 300kr
⚲ Kinna, 30km S of Borås
🏠 Sköld/Sederholm
🖥 www.marksgk.se

Onsjö (1974)
Box 6331 A, 462 42 Vänersborg
☎ (0521) 68870
📠 (0521) 17106
▷ 18 L 5730 m SSS 72
👥 U
££ 280kr (300kr)
⚲ 3km S of Vänersborg. 80km N of Gothenburg
🏠 Sköld/Linde
🖥 www.onsjogk.com

Ringenäs (1987)
Strandlida, 305 91 Halmstad
☎ (035) 161590
✉ ringenas.golf@telia.com

Skogaby (1988)
312 93 Laholm
☎ (0430) 60190
✉ skogaby.gk@telia.com

Sotenas Golfklubb (1988)
Pl Onna, 450 46 Hunnebostrand
☎ (0523) 52302
📠 (0523) 52390
▷ 18 L 5695 m CR 71.1 SR 123
9 L 2735 m
👥 H–max 33
££ 330kr
⚲ 100km N of Gothenburg via E6
🏠 Jan Sederholm
🖥 www.sotenasgolf.com

Töreboda (1965)
Box 18, 545 21 Töreboda
☎ (0506) 12305

Trollhättan (1963)
Stora Ekeskogen, 466 91 Sollebrunn
☎ (0520) 441000

Ulricehamn (1947)
523 33 Ulricehamn
☎ (0321) 27950
📠 (0321) 27959
✉ info@ulricehamngk.golf.se
▷ 18 L 5509 m Par 71
👥 WD–H
££ 260kr
⚲ Lassalyckan, 2km E of Ulricehamn
🏠 Anders Amilion, Rafael Sundblom
🖥 www.golf.se/ulricehamngk

Vara-Bjertorp   (1987)
Bjertorp, 535 91 Kvänum
☎ +46 (512) 20261
☐ +46 (512) 20259
✉ info@vara-bjertorpgk.se
➻ 18 L 6335 m Par 72
⚏ H
££ 275kr (325kr)
⛳ 10km N of Vara. 110km NE of Gothenburg (E20)
⛫ Jan Sederholm
▤ www.vara-bjertorpgk.se

Varberg   (1950)
430 10 Tvååker
☎ +46 340 480380
☐ +46 340 480388
✉ info@varbergsgk.se
➻ East 18 L 5440 m Par 71 CR 71
West 18 L 6435 m Par 72 CR 76
⚏ H
££ 320kr–380kr (£25–£28)
⛳ East: 15km E of Varberg. West: 8km S of Varberg, nr E6
⛫ Sköld/Nordström
▤ www.varbergsgk.se

Vinberg   (1992)
Sannagård, 311 95 Falkenberg
☎ (0346) 19020

Stockholm

Ågesta   (1958)
123 52 Farsta
☎ (08) 447 3330

Botkyrka
Malmbro Gård, 147 91 Grödinge
☎ (08) 530 29650
✉ info@botkyrkagk.golf.se

Bro-Bålsta   (1978)
Jurstagarosvagen 2, 197 91 Bro
☎ (08) 582 41310
☐ (08) 582 40006
✉ info@bbgk@telia.com
➻ 18 L (Pro Men) White 6530 m CR 74.6 SR 138
18 L (Am Men) Yellow 5935 m CR 71.7 SR 128
18 L (Pro Women) Blue 5585 m CR 69.8 SR 127
18 L (Am Women) Red 5150 m CR 67.9 SR 120
9 L Yellow 1715 m CR 60.3 SR 102
9 L Red 1475 m CR 58.8 SR 98
⚏ WD–H (max 30) WE–NA Before Noon.
££ 500sek (500sek)
⛳ 40 km NW of Stockholm
⛫ Peter Nordwall
▤ www.brobalstagk.se

Djursholm   (1931)
Hagbardsvägen 1, 182 63 Djursholm
☎ (08) 5449 6451
☐ (08) 5449 6456
✉ info@dgk.nu

➻ 18 L 5569 m SSS 71
9 L 2135 m SSS 34
⚏ WD–U H before 5pm M after 5pm WE–M before 1pm U H after 1pm
££ 550kr (550kr)
⛳ 12km N of Stockholm
⛫ Bob Kains
▤ www.dgk.nu (Swedish only)

Fågelbro G&CC   (1991)
Fågelbro Säteri, 139 60 Värmdö
☎ +46 (08) 571 41800
☐ +46 (08) 571 40671
✉ info.fagelbro@telia.com
➻ 18 L 5522 m Par 71
⚏ WD–H WE
££ 500kr (600kr)
⛳ 35km E of Stockholm
⛫ Eriksson/Oredsson
▤ www.fagelbrogolf.se

Haninge   (1983)
Årsta Slott, 136 91 Haninge
☎ (08) 500 32850
☐ (08) 500 32851
✉ info@haninggk.golf.se
➻ 27 L 5930 m Par 73
⚏ WD–U before 1pm –M after 1pm WE–M before 1pm –U after 1pm
££ 400kr (450kr)
⛳ 30km S of Stockholm towards Nynäshamn
⛫ Jan Sederholm
▤ www.haningegk.se

Huvudstadens
Lindö Park, 186 92 Vallentuna
☎ (08) 511 70055 (Bookings)
☐ (08) 511 70613
✉ info@huvudstadensgolf.se
➻ 18 L 5800 m SSS 72
18 L 5795 m SSS 72
⚏ U H–book 3 days before play
££ 150kr–395kr (395kr–595kr)
⛳ 30km N of Stockholm
⛫ Persson/Bruce/Eriksson
▤ www.huvudstadensgolf.se

Ingarö   (1962)
Fågelviksvägen 1, 134 64 Ingarö
☎ (08) 556 50200
☐ (08) 546 50299
✉ info@igk.se
➻ Old 18 L 5024 m SSS 71
New 18 L 5203 m SSS 70
⚏ WD–U H WE–NA before 2pm
££ 400kr (400kr)
⛳ 30km E of Stockholm via Route 222
⛫ Sköld/Eriksson
▤ www.igk.se

Kungsängen   (1992)
Box 133, 196 21 Kungsängen
☎ (08) 584 50730
☐ (08) 581 71002
✉ info@kungsangengc.se
➻ Kings 18 L 6100 m Par 71
Queens 18 L 5300 m Par 69
⚏ U H
££ Kings–600kr. Queens–400kr
⛳ 25km W of Stockholm via E18 to Brunna

⛫ Anders Forsbrand
▤ www.kungsangengc.se

Lidingö   (1933)
Box 1035, 181 21 Lidingö
☎ (08) 731 7900
✉ kansli@lidingogk.se

Lindö   (1978)
186 92 Vallentuna
☎ (08) 514 30990

Nya Johannesberg G&CC   (1990)
762 95 Rimbo
☎ (08) 514 50000

Nynäshamn   (1977)
Korunda 40, 148 91 Ösmo
☎ (08) 524 30590/524 30599
☐ (08) 524 30598
✉ kansli@nynashamnsgk.se
➻ 27 L 5690 m SSS 72
9 hole par 29 course rated
⚏ H–phone first
££ 350kr (420kr)
⛳ Ösmo, 40km S of Stockholm
⛫ Sune Linde, Åke Persson, Rolf Colijn
▤ www.nynashamnsgk.a.se

Österakers
Hagby 1, 184 92 Akersberga
☎ (08) 540 85165
☐ (08) 540 66832
✉ kansli@ostgk.se
➻ 18 L 5792 m Par 72
18 L 5780 m Par 72
9 L 2740 m Par 35
⚏ U on the 9 hole course (Pay & Play); H on the 18 hole course
££ 9: 180kr (200kr) 18: 350kr–400kr (400kr–450kr)
⛳ 30km NE of Stockholm
⛫ Sederholm/Tumba
▤ www.ostgk.se   www.hagbygolf.se

Österhaninge   (1992)
Husby, 136 91 Haninge
☎ (08) 500 32285
☐ (08) 500 32293
✉ info@osterhaningegk.golf.se
➻ 18 L 5600 m Par 70
⚏ H
££ 300sek (350sek)
⛳ 20km S of Stockholm
⛫ Bengt Lorichs and Jeremy Turner
▤ www.osterhaningegk.se

Royal Drottningholm   (1958)
PO Box 183, 178 93 Drottningholm
☎ (08) 759 0085
☐ (08) 759 0851
➻ 18 L 5745 m SSS 71
⚏ WD–U H before 3pm –M after 3pm WE–M before 3pm –U H after 3pm
££ 450kr
⛳ 16km W of Stockholm

⌂ Sundblom/Sköld
▤ www.kdrgk.se

Saltsjöbaden (1929)
Box 51, 133 21 Saltsjöbaden
☎ +46 (0)8 717 0125
📠 +46 (0)8 717 9713
✉ klubb@saltsjobadengk.se
🏌 18 L 5471 m SSS 71
9 L 3756 m SSS 64
WD–U WE–M H before 2pm
££ 9: 200kr (250kr) 18: 400kr (500kr)
🚗 15km E of Stockholm city, via Route 228
▤ www.saltsjobadengk.se

Sollentuna (1967)
Skillingegården, 192 77 Sollentuna
☎ (08) 594 70995
📠 (08) 594 70999
✉ intendent@sollentunagk.se
🏌 18 L 5895 m SSS 72
U
££ 400kr
🚗 19km N of Stockholm. 1km W of E4 (Rotebro)
⌂ Nils Sköld
▤ www.sollentunagk.se

Stockholm (1904)
Kevingestrand 20, 182 57 Danderyd
☎ (08) 544 90710

Täby (1968)
Skålhamra Gård, 187 70 Täby
☎ (08) 510 23261

Ullna (1981)
Roslagsvagen 36, 184 94 Åkersberga
☎ (08) 514 41230
📠 (08) 510 26068
✉ ullna@ullnagolf.se
🏌 18 L 5825 m Par 72 SR 136
H
££ 750sek – €80
🚗 20km N of Stockholm via Route E18
⌂ Sven Tumba
▤ www.ullnagolf.se

Ulriksdal (1965)
Box 8088, 170 08 Solna
☎ (08) 855393
✉ info@ulriksdalsgk.se
🏌 18 L 3750 m SSS 63
H
££ 200sek
🚗 8km N of Stockholm
⌂ Alec Backhurst
▤ www.ulriksdalsgk.se

Vallentuna (1989)
Box 266, 186 24 Vallentuna
☎ (08) 514 30560/1

Viksjö (1969)
Fjällens Gård, 175 45 Järfälla
☎ (08) 580 31300/31310

Wäsby
Box 2017, 194 02 Upplands Väsby
☎ (08) 514 103 50

Wermdö G&CC (1966)
Torpa, 139 40 Värmdö
☎ (08) 574 60700
📠 (08) 574 60729
✉ wgcc@telia.com
🏌 18 L 5475 m Par 71
H WE–NA before 2pm
££ 600kr
🚗 25km E of Stockholm via Route 222
⌂ Nils Sköld/Robert Kains
▤ www.wgcc.se

West Central

Arvika (1974)
Box 197, 671 25 Arvika
☎ (0570) 54133

Billerud (1961)
Valnäs, 660 40 Segmon
☎ (0555) 91313
📠 (0555) 91306
✉ kansli@billerudsgk.se
🏌 18 L 5465 m SSS 71
Men: CR 69.6 SR 129
Ladies: CR 71.9 SR 127
H
££ D–260(300kr 15/6–31/8) (300kr)
🚗 Valnäs, 15km N of Säffle
⌂ Brasier/Sköld
▤ www.billerudsgk.se

Eda (1992)
Noresund, 670 40 Åmotfors
☎ (0571) 34101

Färgelanda (1987)
Box 23, Dagsholm 1, 458 21 Färgelanda
☎ (0528) 20385
📠 (0528) 20045
✉ info@fargelandagk.golf.se
🏌 18 L 6000 m SSS 71
H
££ 260kr
🚗 23km N of Uddevalla. 100km N of Gothenburg
⌂ Åke Persson
▤ www.fargelandagk.se

Fjällbacka (1965)
450 71 Fjällbacka
☎ (0525) 31150

Forsbacka (1969)
Box 137, 662 23 Åmål
☎ (0532) 61690
✉ info@forsbackagk.golf.se

Hammarö (1991)
Barrstigen 103, 663 91 Hammarö
☎ (054) 522650
📠 (054) 521863
✉ info@hammarogk.se
🏌 18 L 6075 m Par 71

H
££ 280kr (340kr)
🚗 11km S of Karlstad
⌂ Sune Linde
▤ www.hammarogk.se

Karlskoga (1975)
Bricketorp 647, 691 94 Karlskoga
☎ (0586) 728190

Karlstad (1957)
Höja 510, 655 92 Karlstad
☎ (054) 866353
📠 (054) 866478
✉ info@karlstadgk.se
🏌 18 L 5970 m Par 72
9 L 2875 m Par 36
H–36
££ 300 kr (350kr)
🚗 8km N of Karlstad (Route 63)
⌂ Sköld/Linde
▤ www.karlstadgk.se

Kristinehamn (1974)
Box 337, 681 26 Kristinehamn
☎ (0550) 82310
📠 (0550) 19535
✉ kristinehamnsgk@telia.com
🏌 18 L 5800 m SSS 72
H
££ 250kr–300kr
🚗 3km N of Kristinehamn
⌂ Nils Skeld/Sune Linde
▤ www.golf.se/golfklubbar/kristinehamnsgk

Lyckorna (1967)
Box 66, 459 22 Ljungskile
☎ (0522) 20176

Orust (1981)
Morlanda 135, 474 93 Ellös
☎ (0304) 53170
📠 (0304) 53174
✉ orustgk@telia.com
🏌 18 L 5770 m SSS 72
H
££ 250kr–380kr
🚗 Ellös, 10km from Henån. 80km N of Gothenburg
⌂ Lars Andreasson
▤ www.orustgk.se

Saxå (1964)
Saxån, 682 92 Filipstad
☎ (0590) 24070

Skaftö (1963)
Stockeviksvägen 2, 450 34 Fiskebäckskil
☎ +0046 (523) 23211
📠 +0046 (0523) 23215
✉ kansliet@skaftogk.se
🏌 18 L 4831 m SSS 69
WD–H
££ 150kr–300kr
🚗 40km W of Uddevalla, through Fiskebäckskil
⌂ Sköld/Sederholm
▤ www.skaftogk.se

Strömstad   (1967)
Golfbanevägen, 452 90 Strömstad I
☎ (0526) 61788

Sunne   (1970)
Box 108, 686 23 Sunne
☎ (0565) 14100/14210

Torreby   (1961)
Torreby Slott, 455 93 Munkedal
☎ (0524) 21365/21109

Uddeholm   (1965)
Risäter 20, 683 93 Råda
☎ (0563) 60564
🖷 (0563) 60017
✉ uddeholmsgk@telia.com
▷ 18 L 5830 m SSS 72 CR 70.4 SR 126
🛇 U H
££ D–225skr (275skr)
🏌 Lake Råda, 80km N of Karlstad, via RD62
🏠 N Sköld/J Sederholm
🖳 www.uddeholmsgk.com

Switzerland

Bern

G&CC Blumisberg   (1959)
3184 Wünnewil
☎ (026) 496 34 38
🖷 (026) 496 35 23
✉ secretariat@blumisberg.ch
▷ 18 L 6048 m Par 72
🛇 WD–U H WE–M
££ 100fr (100fr)
🏌 Wünnewil, 16km SW of Bern
🏠 B von Limburger

Les Bois   (1988)
Case Postale 26, 2336 Les Bois
☎ (032) 961 10 03

Neuchâtel   (1925)
Hameau de Voëns, 2072 Saint-Blaise
☎ (032) 753 55 50
🖷 (032) 753 29 40
✉ secretariat@golfdeneuchatel.ch
▷ 18 L 5917 m SSS 71
🛇 H
££ 90fr (110fr)
🏌 Voëns/Saint-Blaise, 5km E of Neuchâtel. 30km W of Bern
🏠 Von Limberger/Peter Herrodine
🖳 www.golfdeneuchatel.ch

Payerne   (1996)
Public
Domaine des Invuardes, 1530 Payerne
☎ (026) 662 4220
✉ golf.payerne@vtx.ch

Wallenried   (1994)
1784 Wallenried
☎ (026) 684 84 80
🖷 (026) 684 84 90
✉ info@golf-wallenried.ch
▷ 18 L 6042 m Par 72
🛇 WD–U H WE–M H
££ CHF90 (CHF110)
🏌 6km W of Fribourg
🏠 Ruzzo Reuss
🖳 www.golf-wallenried.ch

Wylihof   (1994)
4542 Luterbach
☎ (032) 682 28 28
🖷 (032 682 65 17
✉ wylihof@golfclub.ch
▷ 18 L 6580 m Par 73
   White CR 74.7 SR 138
   Yellow CR 72.1 SR 132
   Blue CR 75.1 SR 136
   Red CR 73.5 SR 136
🛇 WD–U H–max 36 WE–M H
££ 120fr
🏌 40km N of Bern. 90km W of Zürich
🏠 Ruzzo Reuss von Plauen
🖳 www.golfclub.ch

Bernese Oberland

Interlaken-Unterseen   (1964)
Postfach 110, 3800 Interlaken
☎ (033) 823 60 16
🖷 (033) 823 42 03
✉ info@interlakengolf.ch
▷ 18 L 6143 m Par 72 CR 73.2 SR 130
🛇 H max 36
££ 100fr (120fr)
🏌 Interlaken 3km
🏠 Donald Harradine; remodelled by John Chilver-Stainer
🖳 www.interlakengolf.ch

Riederalp   (1987)
3987 Riederalp
☎ (027) 927 29 32
🖷 (027) 927 29 23
✉ info@golfclub-riederalp.ch
▷ 9 L 3066 m Par 60 CR 57/8 SR 100
🛇 U
££ 9: 45fr 18: 60fr
🏌 10km NE of Brig
🏠 Donald Harradine, John Shilver-Steiner
🖳 www.golfclub-riederalp.ch

Lake Geneva & South West

Bonmont   (1983)
Château de Bonmont, 1275 Chéserex
☎ (022) 369 99 00
🖷 (022) 369 99 09
✉ golfhotel@bonmont.com

▷ 18 L 6080m CR 71.6 SR 126 (white repairs)
🛇 WD–restricted WE–M
££ WD–150chf
🏌 3km from Nyon. 30km NE of Geneva
🏠 Donald Harradine (1983), renewed by Peter Harradine (2003)
🖳 www.bonmont.com

Les Coullaux   (1989)
1846 Chessel
☎ (024) 481 22 46

Crans-sur-Sierre   (1906)
C P 112, 3963 Crans-sur-Sierre
☎ (027) 485 97 97
🖷 (027) 485 97 98
✉ info@golfcrans.ch
▷ 18 L 6341 m SSS 72
   9 L 2729 m SSS 35
   9 hole Par 3 course
🛇 H
££ On application
🏌 20km E of Sion. Geneva 2 hrs
🏠 Severiano Ballesteros
🖳 www.golfcrans.ch

Domaine Impérial   (1987)
Villa Prangins, 1196 Gland
☎ (022) 999 06 00
✉ info@golfdomaineimperial.com

Geneva   (1921)
70 Route de la Capite, 1223 Cologny
☎ (+41) 22 707 48 00
🖷 (+41) 22 707 48 20
✉ secretariat@golfgeneve.ch
▷ 18 L 6200 m Par 72CR 72.8 SR 132
🛇 WD–am only Tues–Fri WE–M MAX HCP 28
££ 150fr
🏌 4km from centre of Geneva
🏠 Robert Trent Jones Sr

Lausanne   (1921)
Route du Golf 3, 1000 Lausanne 25
☎ (021) 784 84 84
✉ info@golflausanne.ch

Montreux   (1900)
54 Route d'Evian, 1860 Aigle
☎ (024) 466 46 16
🖷 (024) 466 60 47
✉ secretariat@gcmontreux.ch
▷ 18 L 6207 m Par 72
   White CR 73.0 SR 132,
   Yellow CR 70.7 SR 130,
   Blue CR 74.1 SR 129,
   Red CR 72.1 SR 126
🛇 H
££ Visitors 130fr ASG members 110fr
🏌 Aigle, 15km S of Montreux
🏠 Ronald Fream & Dale
🖳 www.swissgolfnetwork.ch

Sion   (2002)
Rte Vissigen 150, 1950 Sion
☎ (+41) (0) 027 203 79 00
🖷 (+41) (0) 027 203 79 01

✉ info@golfclubsion.ch
☞ 18 L 5543 m Par 70 SR 120 (mens champion)
18 L 5095 m Par 70 SR 118 (men)
18 L 4859 m Par 70 SR 123 (ladies champion)
18 L 4423 m Par 70 SR 119 (ladies)
👥 H–booking necessary
££ 90 fr (100 fr)
⛳ Sion, 80km SE of Montreux
🏠 Harradine
🖥 www.golfclubsion.ch

Verbier (1970)
1936 Verbier
☎ **(027) 771 53 14**
📠 (027) 771 60 93
✉ golf.club@verbier.ch
☞ 18 L 4880 m Par 69
👥 U
££ 50fr–70fr (80fr)
⛳ Centre of Verbier
🏠 Donald Harradine
🖥 www.verbiergolf.com

Villars (1922)
CP 118, 1884 Villars
☎ **(024) 495 42 14**
📠 (024) 495 42 18
✉ info@golf-villars.ch
☞ 18 L 5288 m SSS 70
👥 U
££ 70fr (90fr)
⛳ 5km E of Villars towards Les Diablerets; 20km Montreux
🏠 Thierry Sprecher
🖥 www.golf-villars.ch

Lugano & Ticino

Lugano (1923)
6983 Magliaso
☎ **(091) 606 15 57**
📠 (091) 606 65 58
✉ info@golflugano.ch
☞ 18 L 5575 m Par 70
👥 H–max 36
££ 90fr (110fr)
⛳ 8km W of Lugano towards Ponte Tresa
🏠 Harradine/Robinson
🖥 www.golflugano.ch

Patriziale Ascona (1928)
Via al Lido 81, 6612 Ascona
☎ **(091) 785 11 77**
📠 (091) 785 11 79
✉ info@golf.ascona.ch
☞ 18 L 5933 m Par 71
👥 H–max 30
££ 130fr (150fr)
⛳ 5km W of Locarno
🏠 CK Cotton
🖥 www.golf.ascona.ch

St Moritz & Engadine

Arosa (1944)
Postfach 95, 7050 Arosa
☎ **(081) 377 42 42**

📠 (081) 377 46 77
✉ golf@arosa.ch
☞ 18 L 4340 m Par 65 CR 63.6 SR 116
👥 U
££ 75fr (85fr)
⛳ 30km S of Chur
🏠 D Harradine/P Harradine
🖥 www.arosa.ch/golf

Bad Ragaz (1957)
Hans Albrecht Strasse, 7310 Bad Ragaz
☎ **(081) 303 37 17**
✉ golfclub@resortragaz.ch

Davos (1929)
Postfach, 7260 Davos Dorf
☎ **(081) 46 56 34**

Engadin (1893)
7503 Samedan
☎ **(081) 851 04 66**
📠 (081) 851 04 67
✉ samedan@engadin-golf.ch
☞ 18 L 6217 m Par 72 SSS 73 CR 72.4 SR 134
👥 H
££ 60–100chf (80–110chf)
⛳ Samedan, 6km NE of St Moritz
🏠 M Verdieri
🖥 www.engadin-golf.ch

St Mortiz & Engadine

Lenzerheide (1950)
7078 Lenzerheide
☎ **(081) 385 13 13**
📠 (081) 385 13 19
✉ info@golf-lenzerheide.ch
☞ 18 L 5253 m CR 66.9 SR 124
👥 H 30 high season
££ CHF60–100
⛳ 20km S of Chur towards St Moritz
🏠 Donald Harradine/Kurt Rossknecht
🖥 www.golf-lenzerheide.ch

Vulpera (1923)
7552 Vulpera Spa
☎ **(081) 864 96 88**

Zürich & North

Breitenloo (1964)
8309 Oberwil b. Bassersdorf
☎ **(01) 836 40 80**

Bürgenstock (1928)
6363 Bürgenstock
☎ **(041) 610 2434**
📠 (041) 610 3761
✉ club@buergenstock-hotels.ch
☞ 9 L 2200 m Par 33
👥 WD–U WE–H
££ 70fr (90fr) Season May–October
⛳ 15km S of Lucerne
🏠 Fritz Frey
🖥 www.buergenstock-hotels.com

Dolder (1907)
Kurhausstrasse 66, 8032 Zürich
☎ **(01) 261 50 45**

Entfelden (1988)
Muhenstrasse 52, 5036 Oberentfelden
☎ **(062) 723 89 84**

Erlen (1994)
Schlossgut Eppishausen, Schlossstr 7, 8586 Erlen
☎ **(071) 648 29 30**
📠 (071) 648 29 40
✉ info@erlengolf.ch
☞ 18 L 5694 m SSS 71
👥 H–WD
££ 80fr
⛳ 30km NW of St Gallen. 60km W of Zürich
🏠 Gross J Preismann
🖥 www.erlengolf.ch

Hittnau-Zürich G&CC (1964)
8335 Hittnau
☎ **(+41) 950 24 42**
📠 (+41) 951 01 66
✉ info@gcch.ch
☞ 18 L 5519 m CR 69.4 SR 127
👥 WD–U WE–M; H
££ WD–110fr
⛳ Hittnau, 30km E of Zürich
🏠 Bernhard Limburger
🖥 www.gcch.ch

Küssnacht (1994)
Sekretariat/Grossarni, 6403 Küssnacht am Rigi
☎ **(041) 854 4020**
📠 (041) 854 4027
✉ gck@golfkuessnacht.ch
☞ 18 L 5397 m Par 68 CR 69.2 SR 121
👥 WD–U WE–M
££ 110fr (130fr)
⛳ 20km NE of Lucerne
🏠 Peter Harradine
🖥 www.golfkuessnacht.ch

Golf Kyburg (2004)
CH-8310 Kempthal, Zürich
☎ **(052) 355 06 06**
📠 (052) 355 06 16
✉ info@golf-kyburg.ch
☞ 18 L 6015 m Par 71 CR 72.4 SR 132
👥 WD–U H WE–M H
££ 110 fr
⛳ 20 km NW of Zürich
🏠 Kurt Rossknecht
🖥 www.golf-kyburg.ch

Lucerne (1903)
Dietschiberg, 6006 Luzern
☎ **(041) 420 97 87**
✉ info@golfclubluzern.ch

Ostschweizerischer Golf Club (1948)
Club
9246 Niederbüren
☎ **(071) 422 18 56**

📟 (071) 422 18 25
✉ osgc@bluewin.ch
▷ 18 L 5920 m SSS 71
👥 WD–H
££ D–110fr
🚗 Niederbüren, 25km NW of St Gallen
🏠 Donald Harradine
🖥 www.osgc.ch

Schinznach-Bad   (1929)
5116 Schinznach-Bad
📟 **(056) 443 12 26**
🖳 (056) 443 34 83
✉ golfclub.schinznach@bluewin.ch
▷ 9 L 5696 m Par 70
    Men: CR 70.2 SR 122
    Ladies: CR 72.1 SR 119
👥 WD–U–H WE–M–H
££ 140fr
🚗 6km S of Brugg. 35km W of Zürich
🏠 Donald Harradine
🖥 www.swissgolfnetwork.ch

Schönenberg G&CC   (1967)
8824 Schönenberg
📟 **(044) 788 90 40**
🖳 (044) 788 90 45
✉ gccs@swissonline.ch
▷ 18 L 6205 m CR 73.4 SR 137
👥 WD–H–by appointment WE–M H
££ 150chf
🚗 20km S of Zürich
🏠 Donald Harradine
🖥 www.swissgolfnetwork.ch

Golf Sempachersee
(1996)
CH-6024 Hildisrieden, Lucerne
📟 **(041) 462 71 71**
🖳 (041) 462 71 72

✉ info@golf-sempachersee.ch
▷ 2 x 18
    L 6687 m Par 72 CR 75.6 SR 138
    L 5591 m Par 70 CR 69.4 SR 125
👥 WD–U H WE–M H
££ Par 72: 120 fr Par 70: 190 fr
🚗 13km NW of Lucerne
🏠 Kurt Rossknecht
🖥 www.golf-sempachersee.ch

Zürich-Zumikon   (1929)
Weid 9, 8126 Zumikon
📟 **(0041) 43 288 1088**
🖳 (0041) 43 288 1078
✉ gccz.zumikon@ggaweb.ch
▷ 18 L 6389 m Par 72 CR 73.6 SR 134
👥 WD–H by appointment WE–M
££ WD–150fr
🚗 10km SE of Zürich
🏠 Donald Harradine
🖥 www.swissgolfnetwork.ch

Turkey

Gloria Golf
Acisu Mevkii PK27 Belek, Serik, Antalya
📟 **(242) 715 15 20**

Kemer G&CC
Goturk Koyu Mevkii Kemerburgaz, Eyup, Istanbul
📟 **(212) 239 70 10**

Klassis G&CC
Silivri, Istanbul
📟 **(212) 748 46 00**

National Golf Club, Antalya
(1994)
Belek Turizm Merkezi, 07500 Serik, Antalya
📟 **(242) 725 46 20**
🖳 (242) 725 46 23
▷ 18 L 6403 m Par 72 CR 75.0
    Black CR 75.0 SR 148
    White CR 72.2 SR 139
    Yellow CR 69.5 SR 130
    Red CR 72.0 SR 126
    9 L 1547 m Par 29
👥 H
££ €90 High Season €64 Low Season
🚗 Belek, 30km from Antalya
🏠 Feherty/Jones
🖥 www.nationalturkey.com

Robinson Golf Club Nobilis
(1998)
Acisu Mevkii, Belek, 07500 Serik/Antalya, Antalya
📟 **(+90) 242 7100362**
🖳 (+90) 242 7100391
✉ golf.nobilis@robinson.de
▷ Gents: 18 L 5743 m Par 71 CR 70.6 SR 121
    Ladies: 18 L 5037 m Par 71 CR 72.3 SR 124
👥 H gents 28, ladies 36
££ €78
🚗 35km E of Antalya on Mediterranean coast
🏠 Dave Thomas
🖥 www.robinson.de

Tat Golf International
Belek International Golf, Kum Tepesi Belek, 07500 Serik, Antalya
📟 **(242) 725 53 03**

Index

Harrison shoots 59 to keep his US card

American Harrison Frazer, who led the 28 players who earned their PGA Tour cards for 2009, fired a 59 at the qualifying school but it will not count on the official Tour records because it was not recorded in a Tour event.

Officially there have been only three sub-60's scores on the US Tour – Al Geiberger shot 59 at Memphis in 1977, Chip Beck equalled that at Las Vegas in 1999 and David Duval did the same at the 1999 Bob Hope Classic at Palm Springs.

Frazer failed to match Shigeki Maruyama's 58 in the US Open Qualifying in 2000 when he missed a putt on the last but that 58 is not an official record and neither is Sean Pappas 59 in an event in Kentucky in the early 90's.

Frazer's Achilles heel has been his putting. Although he was third in the Greens Hit in Regulation statistics in 2008 he was 197th in putting and finished 163rd in the money list.

Australian James Nitties, Korean YE Yang and Mathias Gronberg from Sweden, winners on the European Tour, earned their cards.

Tiger remains top earning sports star

When *Forbes Magazine* issued their end of the year Top Ten earning sports stars in 2008, Tiger Woods was still well ahead of the others. He may have played in only six events all year but his earnings were assessed at $177 million – $100 million more than second placed David Beckham.

There are three basketball players in the list, two golfers, two soccer stars and representatives from tennis, motor racing and motor cycling.

The full list was:

1 Tiger Woods (golf)	$177 million	6 Kobe Bryant (basketball)	$60 million
2 David Beckham (soccer)	$77 million	7 Le Deon James (basketball)	$60 million
3 Michael Jordan (basketball)	$71 million	8 Ronaldinho (soccer)	$56 million
4 Phil Mickelson (golf)	$70 million	9 Valentino Rossi (motor-cycling)	$55 million
5 Kimi Raikkonen (motor racing)	$68 million	10 Roger Federer (tennis)	$54 million

Thanks to all who contributed to the 2009 edition

No book of this type could ever be published without the co-operaation and help of many people behind the scenes. Once again the team worked well although saddened by the loss of Shirley Card, who had worked so tirelessly for several years on the clubs section and did proof-reading. Writer Dai Davies was also a great loss. Shirley's daughter Paula has taken over her late mother's role alongside our typographer Mick Card, whose enthusiasm matches his professionalism. Alan and Heather Elliott, whether operating in Scotland or Spain, again looked after the collation of scores and Association addresses with the same skill they showed when they were working together as teachers at Strathallan School. My thanks to all the journalistic contributors and thanks, too, to Warren Humphreys, my colleague on The Golf Channel, for his indisputable cross-checking of facts and figures. Bruno Vincent was our publisher at Macmillan and Victoria Lamb liaised with me at The R&A. Photographer Phil Sheldon's widow assisted admirably with the illustrations along with Getty Images. Now it is on to next year when we plan an exciting, more international make-over for the book, first published 110 years ago.